Collectors' Informatic

COLLECTIBLES

MARKET GUIDE & PRICE INDEX

Limited Edition: Plates • Figurines • Architecture • Bells • Graphics • Ornaments • Dolls/Plush • Steins

Sixteenth Edition

Your Complete Source for Information on Limited Edition Collectibles

Collectors' Information Bureau
Barrington, Illinois

Distributed by Krause Publications

Manufactured in the United States of America

Library of Congress Catalog Card Number: 95-71406

ISBN 0-930785-26-6 Collectors' Information Bureau

ISBN 0-87341-686-4 Krause Publications

ISSN 1068-4808

CREDITS

Printing:
Quebecor Printing – Book Division

Book Design and Graphics:
Wright Design, Grand Rapids, Michigan

Original Photography (covers and color section):
Camacho & Assoc., Dundee, Illinois

Design of Cover Artwork:
Z Graphics, Dundee, Illinois

Contributing Writers:
Susan K. Jones
Kelly Womer

Inquiries to the Collectors' Information Bureau should be mailed to:
5065 Shoreline Rd., Suite 200, Barrington, Illinois 60010
Phone: (847) 842-2200 Fax: (847) 842-2205
Website: www.collectorsinfo.com
E-mail: askcib@collectorsinfo.com

FORWARD

Dear Collector,

Welcome to the Sixteenth Edition of the COLLECTIBLES MARKET GUIDE & PRICE INDEX. Long considered the most authoritative book on collectibles in the industry, this year's edition is our most exhaustive book to date.

As our team of researchers, writers and editors pulled together all the news on the latest product introductions and all the reports about secondary market transactions, we were once again awed by the variety and quality of collectible art that exists. From tiny treasures like Akira's Little Gem Teddy Bears to a new star in the doll category, Ashton-Drake's "Gene," it's clear to see that there is no shortage of talented artists and committed manufacturers that have dedicated themselves to furthering your enjoyment of this growing hobby. We hope you find that this "encyclopedia of collectibles" helps you sift through your choices, discover the talents of new artists, and uncover a special message from the myriad of collectibles that are presented here.

We urge you to turn to the 36 pages of beautiful, full-color photos that begin on page 21. Here you'll see some of the most significant new products introduced recently. This edition also carries valuable articles on the leading manufacturers in the collectibles industry; the "ins and outs" of the secondary market and how it works; and tips on insuring and protecting your collection. You'll also get a glimpse of the personalities behind the art through the "Artists' Showcase." Clubs are covered, too, as is information about interesting tours and museums that are available. You may want to plan side-trips to some of these destinations as part of an upcoming vacation.

Our Price Index has again grown to include over 58,000 products! And, once you've found the most current prices for the pieces that have your interest, you can turn to the "CIB Directory to Secondary Market Dealers" at the end of the Price Index. This invaluable resource is at your disposal to help you connect with secondary market dealers, exchanges, brokers, locator services and retailers who can help you buy or sell a retired collectible.

We hope you enjoy the opportunity that this book offers to enhance your collecting experience. On behalf of the 88 companies who fill the roster of the Collectors' Information Bureau and our staff, I invite you to join us on the fascinating trip through the wonderful world of collectibles. We're glad you could join us!

Cordially,

Peggy Veltri

Peggy Veltri
Executive Director

A WORD OF THANKS...

A Special Thank You to the Staff of the Collectors' Information Bureau...
Joan Barcal, Sue Knappen, Patricia Rinas, Carol Van Elderen, Robin Wilkinson, Debbie Wojtysiak and Cindy Zagumny.

To the CIB Panel of Dealers...
Finally, we wish to thank the panel of over 300 limited edition retailers and secondary market experts whose knowledge and dedication have helped make our Price Index possible. We wish we could recognize each of them by name, but they have agreed that to be singled out in this manner might hinder their ability to maintain an unbiased view of the marketplace.

MEMBERSHIP ROSTER

Collectors' Information Bureau (CIB) is a not-for-profit trade association whose mission is to serve and educate collectors, members and dealers, and to provide them with credible, comprehensive and authoritative information on limited edition collectibles and their current values.

Akira Trading Co., Inc./
Little Gem Teddy Bears
The Alexander Doll Company
Anheuser-Busch, Inc.
Annalee Mobilitee Dolls, Inc.
ANRI U.S.
Armani
The Art of Glynda Turley
The Ashton-Drake Galleries
The Bradford Exchange
Brandywine Collectibles
Byers' Choice Ltd.
Cardew Design
Carlton Cards
Cast Art Industries, Inc.
Cavanagh Group International
Christian Ulbricht USA
Christopher Radko
Cottage Collectibles® by Ganz
Crystal World
Dave Grossman Creations, Inc.
David Winter Cottages
Deb Canham Artist Designs, Inc.
Department 56, Inc.
Duncan Royale
eggspressions!, inc.
Enesco Corporation
Ertl Collectibles™ Limited
FJ Designs Inc./ Cat's Meow Village™
The Fenton Art Glass Company
Fitz & Floyd Collectibles Division
Flambro Imports
Fool Moon Treasures
Forma Vitrum
The Franklin Mint
Gartlan USA, Inc.
Geo. Zoltan Lefton Co.
Georgetown Collection
GiftStar, Inc.
Goebel of North America
The Greenwich Workshop
The Hamilton Collection*
Harbour Lights
Harmony Kingdom
Hazle Ceramics
The House of Fontanini
House of Hatten, Inc.
Hudson Creek
Imperial Graphics, Ltd.
Islandia International
Jan Hagara Collectables
Kurt S. Adler, Inc.
Ladie and Friends, Inc.
Lee Middleton Original Dolls, Inc.
Lenox Collections
Lilliput Lane
Lladró
M.I. Hummel Club*
Margaret Furlong Designs
Maruri U.S.A.
Media Arts Group, Inc.
Midwest of Cannon Falls
Miss Martha Originals, Inc.
Munro Collectibles, Inc.
Original Appalachian Artworks, Inc.
Porterfield's
Possible Dreams
Precious Art, Inc.
Prizm, Inc./Pipka's Collectibles
Pulaski Furniture Corporation
Reco International Corp.*
Roman, Inc.*
Royal Copenhagen/Bing & Grondahl
Royal Doulton
Sandy Dolls
The San Francisco Music Box Co.
Sarah's Attic, Inc.
Seraphim Classics
Seymour Mann, Inc.
Shelia's Collectibles
Shenandoah Designs
International, Inc.
Sunbelt Marketing Group
Swarovski Consumer Goods, Ltd.
United Design Corporation
WACO Products Corporation
Walnut Ridge Collectibles
Walt Disney Art Classics
Willitts Designs International, Inc.
Woodland Winds from
Christopher Radko

*Charter Member

National Association of Limited Edition Dealers

Formed in 1976, NALED is a national group of retail and wholesale merchants who are in the specialized market of selling limited edition collectibles. The National Headquarters for NALED is located at 5235 Monticello Street, Dallas, Texas 75206, (214) 826-2002. To find a retailer in your area that carries your favorite collectible visit NALED's website at http://www.naled.com.

ALABAMA
Amy's Hallmark, Birmingham, AL 35206, (205) 936-4119
Collectible Cottage, Gardendale, AL 35071, (205) 631-2413
Enchanted Attic, Birmingham, AL 35216, (205) 988-3716
JD Collectibles, Vestavia Hills, AL 35243, (205) 824-1116
Margo Collectibles, Cullman, AL 35055, (205) 734-1452
Olde Post Office, Trussville, AL 35173, (205) 655-7292
Taylor's Treasures, Florence, AL 35634, (205) 764-7172
Tomorrow's Treasures, Birmingham, AL 35215, (205) 838-1887
Traditions Gift Shop, Albertville, AL 35950, (205) 891-2903

ARIZONA
Annie's Hallmark, Tucson, AZ 85711, (520) 790-7430
Barb's Christmas Etc, Tucson, AZ 85715, (520) 885-3755
Dreams & Rainbows, Kingman, AZ 86401, (520) 757-7141
Fox's Gifts & Collectables, Scottsdale, AZ 85251, (602) 947-0560
Lawton's Gifts & Collectibles, Chandler, AZ 85224, (602) 899-7977
Lemon Tree, Carefree, AZ 85377, (602) 488-3894
Marylyn's Collectibles,Tucson, AZ 85705, (520) 293-4603
Millie's Hallmark, Phoenix, AZ 85044, (602) 893-3777
Ruth's Hallmark Shop, Cottonwood, AZ 86326, (520) 634-8050
The Artisan Collectors Gallery, Mesa, AZ 85202, (602) 833-0495

ARKANSAS
Lane's Toyland & Gifts, Texarkana, AR 71854, (501) 773-2123

CALIFORNIA
Blacksmith's Corner Inc, Bellflower, CA 90706, (310) 531-7240
Carol's Gift Shop*, Artesia, CA 90701, (562) 924-6335
Collectible Corner, Brea, CA 92821, (714) 990-2955
Collectibles Unlimited, Woodland Hills, CA 91364, (818) 703-6173
Crystal Aerie, Fremont, CA 94536, (510) 791-0298
Dana Drug Store, Burbank, CA 91505, (818) 562-1177
Designers Center, San Bruno, CA 94066, (415) 873-2443 (office)
Dolls Gifts & More, Danville, CA 94526, (925) 831-8981
Dove's Secret Garden, Paradise, CA 95969, (916) 872-0551
Encore Cards & Gifts, Cypress, CA 90630, (714) 761-1266
Fran's Hallmark, Red Bluff, CA 96080, (916) 527-6789
Franco's Florist & Gift, Martinez, CA 94553, (510) 228-1525
Friends Collectibles, Canyon Country, CA 91351, (805) 298-2232
Galleria Gifts, Reedley, CA 93654, (209) 638-4060
Gallery Decor, Arcadia, CA 91007, (818) 790-0502
Gallery of Dreams, Pismo Beach, CA 93449, (805) 773-9500
Heirlooms of Tomorrow, Fullerton, CA 92832, (714) 525-1522
Kae & Rick's Hallmark, Sunland, CA 91040, (818) 353-1891
Kae & Shelly's Hallmark, Thousand Oaks, CA 91362, (805) 492-5885
Kennedy's Collectibles & Gifts, Sacramento, CA 95864-7206, (916) 973-8754
Lena's Gift Gallery*, San Mateo, CA 94401, (415) 342-8848
Louise Marie's Fine Gifts, Livermore, CA 94550, (510) 449-5757
Margie's Gifts & Collectibles, Torrance, CA 90505, (310) 378-2526
Mary Ann's Cards, Gifts & Collectibles, Yorba Linda, CA 92886, (714) 777-0999
Mc Curry's Hallmark, Sacramento, CA 95815, (916) 567-9952
Musical Moments & Collectibles, Shingle Spgs, CA 95682, (916) 677-2221
Northridge Pharmacy Gift Gallery, Northridge, CA 91324, (818) 349-7000
Nyborg Castle, Martinez, CA 94553, (925) 930-0200
Ojai Valley Hallmark Shop, Ojai, CA 93023, (805) 646-8963
Pardini's Fine Gifts & Collectibles, Stockton, CA 95207, (209) 957-2414
Peddler's Cove Gift Shop & Gallery, Loomis, CA 95650, (800) 652-4015
Rystad's Limited Editions, San Jose, CA 95125, (408) 279-1960
Seaport Unique Gifts, Manhattan Beach, CA 90266, (310) 546-4449
Sutter Street Emporium, Folsom, CA 95630, (916) 985-4647
The Allovio Gallery, Roseville, CA 95661, (916) 782-5330
The Frame Gallery, Chula Vista, CA 91910-3910, (619) 422-1700
Unique Gifts, San Bernardino, CA 92408, (909) 381-4877
Village Peddler, La Habra, CA 90631, (310) 694-6111
Wee House Fine Gifts & Collectibles, Irvine, CA 92618, (714) 552-3228
Wilson Galleries in Fig Garden Vlg, Fresno, CA 93704-2201, (209) 224-2223
Wonderland Collectibles, Fresno, CA 93711, (209) 435-1002

COLORADO
Country In The Village, Boulder, CO 80301, (303) 447-1587
Greco Collectibles, Aurora, CO 80014, (303) 755-6048
Hightower Collectibles, Colorado Springs, CO 80909, (719) 596-0267
Holiday Fantasies, Littleton, CO 80122, (303) 721-7908
Intrigue Gift Shop, Estes Park, CO 80517, (970) 586-4217
King's Gallery of Collectables, Colorado Springs, CO 80904, (719) 636-2228
Noel - Vail's Christmas Shop, Vail, CO 81657, (970) 476-6544
Plates Etc, Arvada, CO 80003, (303) 420-0752
Quality Gifts & Collectibles, Colorado Springs, CO 80918, (719) 599-0051
Silver Spur Collectibles & Fine Gifts, Lake City, CO 81235, (970) 944-2231
Simply Christmas, Estes Park, CO 80517, (970) 586-8990
Swiss Miss Shop, Cascade, CO 80809, (719) 684-9679
The Alpine Collector, Littleton, CO 80123, (303) 973-2485
The Gift House, Lakewood, CO 80226, (303) 922-7279
Tobacco Leaf Collectibles, Lakewood, CO 80226, (303) 274-8720
Village Fine Gifts & Collectibles, Greeley, CO 80634, (970) 330-3227
Village Pharmacy & Fine Gifts, Brighton, CO 80601, (303) 659-4311

CONNECTICUT
Collectibles, Danbury, CT 06810, (203) 790-1011
Denise's Hallmark Shop, Danbury, CT 06811, (203) 743-6515
Diane's Doll Shoppe, Stamford, CT 06903, (203) 968-6936
Fifth Avenue Collectibles, Groton, CT 06340, (860) 449-7100
Good Friends & Treasures, Waterbury, CT 06708, (203) 756-8001
Maurice Nasser*, New London, CT 06320, (203) 443-6523
Peter BobJohn, Newington, CT 06111, (860) 667-3603
The Gift Box, Enfield, CT 06082, (860) 745-7484
The Taylor'd Touch, Marlborough, CT 06447, (860) 295-9377
Utopia Collectables & Fine Gifts, Oxford, CT 06478, (203) 888-0233
Windsor Shoppe, North Haven, CT 06473, (203) 239-4644
Ye Olde Fashioned Christmas Shoppe, East Haddam, CT 06423, (860) 873-9352

DELAWARE
Bear Card & Gift, Wilmington, DE 19803, (302) 478-6658
Peregoy's Gift & Coll. Center, First State Plaza, Wilmington, DE 19804, (302) 999-1155
Washington Square Limited, Newark, DE 19702, (302) 453-1776

FLORIDA
Anna's Attic & Hand Made, Lakeland, FL 33803, (941) 647-9166
Ardie's Hallmark Shop, Daytona Beach, FL 32127, (904) 761-7096
Cards N' Gifts Galore, Volusia Point Shopping Center, Daytona Beach, FL 32114, (904) 255-6624
Corner Gifts, Pembroke Pines, FL 33026, (954) 432-3739
Country Memories, Ocala, FL 34471, (352) 694-1888
Fibber Magee's Kountry & Christmas Shop, Orlando, FL 32817, (407) 277-7480
Gallery of Antiques & Collectibles, Jacksonville, FL 32221, (904) 783-6787
Gifts RS, The Fashion Mall, Plantation, FL 33324, (954) 723-0481
Gifts Unlimited, Miami, FL 33176, (305) 253-0146
Heirloom Collectibles Too!, Palm Harbor, FL 34685, (813) 797-8007
Heirlooms of Tomorrow, North Miami, FL 33161, (305) 899-0920
Hollywood Ocean Gifts & Collectibles, Hollywood, FL 33019, (954) 925-3207
Hunt's Collectibles, Satellite Beach, FL 32937-2929, (407) 777-1313
Marie's Hallmark Shop, Clermont, FL 34711, (352) 394-4142
Methodist Foundation Gift Shops, Jacksonville, FL 32209, (904) 798-8210
Mitzi's Hallmark, Orlando, FL 32836, (407) 827-1075
Paper Moon Hallmark & Collectibles, West Palm Beach, FL 33415, (561) 684-2668
Rhoda's Collectibles Inc, Margate, FL 33073, (954) 984-0900
Robert's Christmas Wonderland, Clearwater, FL 33759, (813) 797-1660
Sea Breeze Collectibles, Tarpon Springs, FL 34689, (813) 943-0156
Star Gifts Inc, Fort Myers, FL 33913, (941) 768-0770

The Christmas Palace, Hialeah Gardens, FL 33016, (305) 558-5352
The Christmas Palace, Plantation, FL 33322, (305) 423-3800
The Christmas Shoppe, Tallahassee, FL 32303, (904) 422-8990
The Christmas Shoppe, Miami, FL 33176, (305) 255-5414
The Corner Emporium, Dade City, FL 33525, (352) 567-1990
The Entertainer, Regency Sq, Jacksonville, FL 32225, (904) 249-9823
Treasure Chest Collectibles & Gifts, Jensen Beach, FL 34957, (561) 692-3122
Victorian Village, Inc, Tampa, FL 33617, (813) 989-0908
Village Plate Collector*, Cocoa, FL 32922, (407) 636-6914

GEORGIA
Chamberhouse, Canton, GA 30114, (770) 479-9115
Cottage Garden, Macon, GA 31204, (912) 743-1011
Creative Gifts, Augusta, GA 30906, (706) 796-8794
Gallery II, Atlanta, GA 30093, (770) 458-5858
Glass Etc, Atlanta, GA 30084, (770) 493-7936
Gloria's Gallery, Columbus, GA 31909, (706) 596-0330
Heart of Country, Fayetteville, GA 30214, (770) 460-0337
Impressions, Brunswick, GA 31520, (912) 265-1624
Magnolia Manor, Duluth, GA 30097, (770) 814-7475
Mtn Christmas-Mtn Memories, Dahlonega, GA 30533, (706) 864-2159
Mtn Memories, Dawsonville, GA 30534, (706) 216-6210
Pam's Hallmark Shop, Fayetteville, GA 30214-7233, (770) 461-3041
Sacks Route 1, Warm Springs, GA 31830, (706) 655-9093
Swan Galleries, Stone Mountain, GA 30083, (770) 498-9696
Wesson's, Helen, GA 30545-0460, (706) 878-3544

IDAHO
Cinnamon Tree Gift & Coll. Gallery, Pocatello, ID 83201, (208) 232-6371

ILLINOIS
Bandy's Gifts Unique, Salem, IL 62881-0546, (618) 548-1500
Berry's, New Lenox, IL 60451, (815) 485-6724
Bits of Gold Jewelry & Gifts, Nashville, IL 62263, (618) 327-4261
C A Jensen, LaSalle, IL 61301, (815) 223 0377
Crown Gift Shop, Chicago, IL 60641, (773) 282-6771
Doris' Collectibles, St Peter, IL 62880, (618) 349-8780
European Imports & Gifts, Niles, IL 60714, (847) 967-5253
Ev's Cottage Collectibles, Gurnee, IL 60031, (847) 855-1015
Fine & Fancy, Aurora, IL 60504, (630) 898-1130
Giftique of Long Grove, Long Grove, IL 60047, (847) 634-9171
Grimm's Hallmark - West, St Charles, IL 60174, (708) 513-7008
Guzzardo's Hallmark, Kewanee, IL 61443, (309) 852-5621
Hall Jewelers & Gifts Ltd, Moweaqua, IL 62550, (217) 768-4990
Hawk Hollow, Galena, IL 61036, (815) 777-3616
Hummel Korner & Gifts, Wheeling, IL 60090, (847) 215-2908
JBJ the Collectors Shop, Champaign, IL 61820, (217) 352-9610
Kennedy's Kollectibles & Gifts, Plainfield, IL 60544, (815) 436-5444
Kerr's Gifts & Collectibles, Bradley, IL 60915, (815) 936-0385
Kris Kringle Haus, Geneva, IL 60134, (630) 208-0400
Lynn's & Company, Arlington Heights, IL 60005, (847) 870-1188
Oakshire Collectable Shoppe, Schaumburg, IL 60194, (847) 529-0290
Potpourri Card & Gift, Westchester, IL 60154, (708) 562-1440
Potpourri Collectibles & Gifts, Bolingbrook, IL 60440, (630) 759-8222
Royale Imports, Lisle, IL 60532, (630) 357-7002
Sandy's Dolls & Collectables Inc, Palos Heights, IL 60463, (708) 923-0730
Sav-Mor Pharmacy & Gift Shop, Fairbury, IL 61739, (815) 692-4343
Sentimental Journey, Washington, IL 61571, (309) 444-7355
Skoopers Unlimited, Richmond, IL 60071, (815) 678-4124
Something So Special, Rockford, IL 61107, (815) 226-1331
Stone's Hallmark Shops, Rockford, IL 61108, (815) 399-4481
The Depot Gallery, Sullivan, IL 61951, (217) 728-2381
Tricia's Treasures, Fairview Hgts, IL 62208, (618) 624-6334

INDIANA
Bea's Hallmark, Indianapolis, IN 46227, (317) 888-8408
Carol's Crafts, Nashville, IN 47448, (812) 988-6388
Curio Shoppe, St. Greensburg, IN 47240, (812) 663-6914
Deacon's Bench, Auburn, IN 46706, (219) 927-1904
Dearly Yours, Noblesville, IN 46060, (317) 773-2553
Diversions, Indianapolis, IN 46250, (317) 578-3336
Diversions, Greenwood, IN 46143, (317) 865-9014
Hall of Gifts, Bloomington, IN 47401, (812) 336-0878
Hilbish Drug, La Porte, IN 46350, (219) 362-2247
Louise's Hallmark, St John, IN 46373, (219) 365-3837
Mr. E's, Indianapolis, IN 46240, (317) 846-5454
Our Compliments Gift & Floral Shop, Columbia City, IN 46725, (219) 244-6120
Rose Marie's, Evansville, IN 47714, (812) 423-7557
Temptations Gifts, Valparaiso, IN 46383, (219) 462-1000
The Gift Box, Logansport, IN 46352, (219) 753-8442
Watson's*, New Carlisle, IN 46552, (219) 654-8600
Your Child Within, Pendleton, IN 46064, (765) 778-7551

IOWA
Collection Connection, Des Moines, IA 50322, (515) 276-7766
Dave & Janelle's, Mason City, IA 50401, (515) 423-6377
Davis Collectibles, Waterloo, IA 50701, (319) 232-0050
Hawk Hollow, Bellevue, IA 52031, (319) 872-5467
Jakobson Drug & Hallmark Shop, Osage, IA 50461, (515) 732-5452
S & K Collectibles, Independence, IA 50644, (319) 334-9355
Stiers Gifts & Collectibles, Coralville, IA 52241, (319) 337-5900
Stiers Gifts & Collectibles, Iowa City, IA 52240, (319) 351-0242
Toy Farmer Country Store, Dyersville, IA 52040, (701) 883-5206
Treasure Trove, Sioux City, IA 51101, (712) 258-1996
Van Den Berg's, Pella, IA 50219, (515) 628-2533

KANSAS
Carol's Decor, Salina, KS 67401, (913) 823-1739 x186
Gifts & Accents, Overland Park, KS 66212, (913) 381-8856

KENTUCKY
Ann's Hallmark, Florence, KY 41042, (606) 342-7595
Betsy's Hallmark, Benton, KY 42025, (502) 527-1848
Canter's Hallmark, Bowling Green, KY 42104, (502) 782-9582
Homefolks Gifts & Collectibles, Henderson, KY 42420, (502) 826-8888
Karen's Gifts, Louisville, KY 40222, (502) 425-3310
Respectable Collectibles, Bowling Green, KY 42104, (502) 781-9655

LOUISIANA
Ad Lib Gifts, Metairie, LA 70002, (504) 835-8755
La Tienda, Lafayette, LA 70503, (318) 984-5920
Plates and Things, Baton Rouge, LA 70817, (504) 753-2885
Plum Tree, Lake Charles, LA 70601, (318) 439-9526

MAINE
Christmas Classics & Collectibles, Rangeley, ME 04970, (207) 864-3630
Christmas Magic Inc., Wiscasset, ME 04578, (207) 882-6722
Gimbel & Sons Country Store, Boothbay Harbor, ME 04538, (207) 633-5088
Gooseberry Barn, Auburn, ME 04210, (207) 782-8964
Heritage Gifts, Oakland, ME 04963, (207) 465-3910
The Emporium, Kennebunkport, ME 04046, (207) 967-2139

MARYLAND
Between Us Collectibles, Lanham, MD 20706, (301) 459-8138
Bodzer's Collectibles, Baltimore, MD 21236, (410) 931-9222
Calico Mouse, Glen Burnie, MD 21061, (410) 760-2757
Carrolltowne Cards & Gifts, Sykesville, MD 21784, (410) 795-5400
Edwards Stores, Ocean City, MD 21842, (410) 289-7000
Hands of Time Clocks & Collectibles, Savage, MD 20763, (301) 206-3281
Keepsakes & Collectibles, Owings Mill, MD 21117, (410) 987-8755
Main Street Corner Shoppe, Laurel, MD 20707, (301) 725-3099
Penn Den, Bowie, MD 20720, (301) 262-2430
Precious Gifts, Ellicott City, MD 21043, (410) 461-6813
The Music Box, Baltimore, MD 21202, (410) 727-0444
Tiara Galleries & Gifts, Rockville, MD 20852,(301) 468-1122
Tomorrow's Treasures, Bel Air, MD 21015, (410) 893-7965
Wang's Gifts & Collectibles, White Marsh, MD 21236, (410) 931-7388
Wang's Gifts & Collectibles, Bel Air, MD 21014, (410) 838-2626

MASSACHUSETTS
Baby Me Dolls & Collectibles, Billerica, MA 01821, (978) 667-1187
Crystal Pineapple, Hyannis, MA 02601, (508) 362-1335
Cuties Bears & Stuffies, Seekonk, MA 02771, (508) 336-7868
Foster's, Weymouth, MA 02190, (781) 337-3546
Gift Gallery, Webster, MA 01570, (508) 943-4402
Honeycomb Gift Shoppe, Stoneham, MA 02180, (781) 438-1181
Kay's Hallmark, Tewksbury, MA 01876, (508) 851-7790
Linda's Originals & The Yankee Craftsmen, Brewster, MA 02631, (508) 385-4758
Savas Limited, Hanson, MA 02341, (617) 294-0177
Shropshire Curiosity Shop I, Shrewsbury, MA 01545, (508) 842-4202
Shropshire Curiosity Shop II, Shrewsbury, MA 01545, (508) 842-5001
Stacy's Gifts & Collectibles, East Walpole, MA 02032, (508) 668-4212
The Leonard Gallery, Springfield, MA 01105, (413) 733-9492
Ward's Gifts, Medford, MA 02155, (617) 395-4099
Wayside Country Store, Marlboro, MA 01752, (508) 481-3458

MICHIGAN
American Business Concepts, Inc, Center Line, MI 48015, (810) 757-5115
Block's Hallmark Shop, Saginaw, MI 48603, (517) 791-1187
Brass Town Inc., Holland, MI 49424, (616) 394-0034
Caravan Gifts & Collectibles, Fenton, MI 48430-3421, (810) 629-4212
Cindy's Hallmark, Sturgis, MI 49091, (616) 651-1424
Curio Cabinet Collectibles, Lexington, MI 48450, (810) 359-5040
Emily's Gifts, Dolls, Collectibles, St Clair Shores, MI 48081, (810) 777-5250
Eve's Hallmark, Marshall, MI 49068, (616) 789-0700
Eve's Hallmark Shop, Dearborn Heights, MI 48127, (313) 278-1060
Fritz Gifts & Collectibles, Monroe, MI 48162, (313) 241-6760
Georgia's Gift Gallery, Plymouth, MI 48170, (313) 453-7733
Harpold's, South Haven, MI 49090, (616) 637-3522
House of Cards & Gifts, Sturgis, MI 49091, (616) 651-6011
House of Collectibles, Macomb, MI 48044-3840, (810) 247-2000
Jacquelyns Gifts, Warren, MI 48093, (810) 296-9211
Keepsake Gifts, Kimball, MI 48074, (810) 985-5855
Knibloe Gift Corner, Jackson, MI 49202, (517) 782-6846
Lakeview Card & Gift Shop, Battle Creek, MI 49015, (616) 962-0650
Landmark Gifts, Fort Gratiot, MI 48059, (810) 385-5220
McCandless Hallmark, Midland, MI 48640, (517) 631-5540
Miller's Unique Gifts, Adrian, MI 49221, (517) 263-4041
Mole Hole of Holland, Holland, MI 49423, (616) 396-7467
Plate Lady, Livonia, MI 48154, (313) 261-5220
Rainbow Factory Collectibles, Clio, MI 48420, (810) 687-1351

Ray's Collectables, Clinton Twp, MI 48035, (810) 791-4349
Ray's Mart, Mt Clemens, MI 48043, (810) 979-7399
Robinette's Gift Barn, Grand Rapids, MI 49525, (616) 361-7180
Schultz Gift Gallery, Pinconning, MI 48650, (517) 879-3110
Sharon's Hallmark Shop, Rochester Hills, MI 48309, (810) 652-0090
Sobaks Gifts & Collectibles, Owosso, MI 48867, (517) 723-8221
Touch of Country, Howell, MI 48843, (517) 546-5995
Troy Stamp & Coin Exchange, Troy, MI 48083, (810) 528-1181
Village Peddler Gifts Snacks Etc, Brooklyn, MI 49230, (517) 592-8027
Whitefox Framing Gallery, Muskegon, MI 49445, (616) 744-1907

MINNESOTA

Andersen's Hallmark, Albert Lea, MN 56007, (507) 373-0996
Friendship Shop Inc, St Louis Park, MN 55416-3906, (612) 922-6332
Gartner's Hallmark, Buffalo, MN 55313, (612) 682-5061
Gustaf's, Lindstrom, MN 55045, (612) 257-6688
Helga's Hallmark, Cambridge, MN 55008, (612) 689-5000
Hunt Silver Lake Drug & Gift, Rochester, MN 55906, (507) 289-0749
Odyssey, Mankato, MN 56001, (507) 388-2006
Odyssey, Rochester, MN 55902, (507) 288-6629
Odyssey Gifts, Mankato, MN 56001, (507) 388-2004
Robin Lee's Hallmark, Brooklyn Park, MN 55443, (612) 566-5277
Seefeldt's Gallery, Roseville, MN 55113, (612) 631-1397
The Finishing Touch, Brainerd, MN 56401, (218) 828-2067

MISSOURI

Dickens Gift Shoppe, Branson, MO 65616, (417) 334-2992
Emily's Hallmark & Collectibles, Chesterfield, MO 63017, (314) 391-8755
First Capitol Trading Post, St Charles, MO 63301, (314) 946-2883
Helen's Gifts & Accessories, Rolla, MO 65401-3140, (314) 341-2300
Oak Leaf Gifts, Osage Beach, MO 65065-9702, (314) 348-0190
Sawyer's Creek, Hannibal, MO 63401, (573) 221-8221
The Fantasticks At Plaza Galleria, Cape Girardeau, MO 63703, (573) 335-4405
Tobacco Lane, Cape Girardeau, MO 63703, (573) 651-3414
Tra-Art Ltd, Jefferson City, MO 65101, (573) 635-8278
Ye Cobblestone Shoppe, Sikeston, MO 63801, (573) 471-8683

MONTANA

Traditions, Missoula, MT 59801, (406) 543-3177

NEBRASKA

Elly's Gifts - Collectibles Holiday, Hastings, NE 68901, (402) 463-1319
L & L Gifts, Fremont, NE 68025, (402) 727-7275
Marianne K Festersen*, Omaha, NE 68114, (402) 393-4454
Wood 'n Doll, North Platte, NE 69101, (308) 534-3618

NEW HAMPSHIRE

The Straw Cellar, Wolfeboro, NH 03894, (603) 569-1516

NEW JERSEY

Candles & Keepsakes, Lawrenceville, NJ 08648, (609) 716-0735
Christmas Carol, Flemington, NJ 08822, (908) 782-0700
Classic Collections, Livingston, NJ 07039, (201) 992-8605
Collectors Cellar, Pine Beach, NJ 08741, (732) 341-4107
Corbett's Collectables, Maple Shade, NJ 08052, (609) 866-9787
Crafts From the Heart, Pennsville, NJ 08070, (609) 935-4546
Diann's Gifts & Collectibles, Kenvil, NJ 07847, (201) 584-3848
Emjay Shop, Stone Harbor, NJ 08247, (609) 368-1227
Gift Gallery, Edison, NJ 08837, (908) 494-3939
Gift Gallery, Paramus, NJ 07652, (201) 845-0940
Gift World, Maple Shade, NJ 08052, (609) 321-1500
J.H. Caprice dba Caprice @Harrah's, Atlantic City, NJ 08401, (609) 345-4305
Jiana Inc, Riverdale, NJ 07457, (201) 831-0021
Joy's Hallmark Shop, Burlington, NJ 08016, (609) 386-2112
Katie's Kache, LLC, Red Bank, NJ 07701, (732) 576-1777
Little Treasures, Rutherford, NJ 07070, (201) 460-9353
Meyers Dolls-Toys-Hobbies, Edison, NJ 08817, (732) 985-2220
Notes-A-Plenty Gift Shoppe, Flemington, NJ 08822, (908) 782-0700
Prestige Collections, Short Hills, NJ 07078, (201) 376-3537
Prestige Collections, Bridgewater, NJ 08807, (908) 253-0909
Prestige Collections, Paramus, NJ 07652, (201) 291-7800
Prestige Collections, Livingston, NJ 07039, (973) 597-0111
Rhoda Turkowitz Ltd Ed Coll, E Brunswick, NJ 08816, (908) 238-3038
Someone Special, Cherry Hill, NJ 08003, (609) 424-1914
Station Gift Emporium, Whitehouse Station, NJ 08889, (908) 534-1212
Sugar Pine Workshop, Northfield, NJ 08225, (609) 641-1776
The Gift Caravan, North Arlington, NJ 07031, (201) 997-1055
The Occasion Card & Gift Shoppe Inc, Rockaway, NJ 07866, (201) 586-1818
Weston's Limited Editions, Eatontown, NJ 07724, (732) 935-0301
Weston's Limited Editions, Eatontown, NJ 07724, (732) 542-3550
Zaslow's Fine Collectibles, Middletown, NJ 07748, (908) 957-9560
Zaslow's Fine Collectibles*, Matawan, NJ 07747, (732) 583-1499

NEW MEXICO

Chezem's Inc, Albuquerque, NM 87111, (505) 292-6258
Covered Wagon Gifts & Collectibles, Ruidoso, NM 88345, (505) 257-3471
Lorrie's Collectibles, Albuquerque, NM 87112, (505) 292-0020

NEVADA

Ooh's and Ah's, Las Vegas, NV 89107, (702) 870-2078

NEW YORK

A Little Bit Country, Staten Island, NY 10314, (718) 727-4725
Andrew's Collectibles, Buffalo, NY 14219, (716) 823-4131
Andrew's Collectibles, Williamsville, NY 14221, (716) 633-1030
Ann's Hallmark Shoppe, Newburgh, NY 12550 (914) 562-3149
Ann's Hallmark Shoppe, Newburgh, NY 12550, (914) 564-5585
Canal Town Country Store, Rochester, NY 14626, (716) 225-5070
Ceramica Gift Gallery, New York, NY 10018, (212) 354-9216
Classic Gift Gallery, Centereach, NY 11720, (516) 467-4813
Clock Man Gallery, Poughkeepsie, NY 12601, (914) 473-9055
Collectibly Yours, Spring Valley, NY 10977, (914) 425-9244
Colony Collectibles & Gifts, New Hyde Park, NY 11040, (516) 354-2818
Corner Collections, Hunter, NY 12442, (518) 263-4141
Country Gallery, Poughkeepsie, NY 12601, (914) 297-1684
Cow Harbor Fine Gifts & Collectibles, Northport, NY 11768, (516) 261-7907
Ellie's Ltd Ed & Collectibles, Selden, NY 11784, (516) 698-3467
Exotic Gifts & Collectibles, Old Bethpage, NY 11804, (516) 752-0336
Fern's Creative Thimble, Huntington, NY 11743, (516) 351-1872
Forever Christmas, Hyde Park, NY 12538, (914) 229-2969
Glorious Treasures, Brooklyn, NY 11234, (718) 241-8185
Grandma's Country Corners, Albany, NY 12205, (518) 459-1209
H. N. Vantasia, E Patchogue, NY 11772, (516) 475-2149
Hand of Man, Owego, NY 13827, (607) 687-2556
Island Treasures, Staten Island, NY 10314, (718) 698-1234
Lil' Susies Keepsakes & Collectibles, Shirley, NY 11967, (516) 281-9481
Limited Collector, Corning, NY 14830, (607) 936-6195
Lyn Gift Shop, Lynbrook, NY 11563, (516) 593-6500
Malone's Hallmark, Greenburgh, NY 10607, (914) 948-8885
Maresa's Candlelight Gift Shoppe, Port Jefferson, NY 11777, (516) 331-6245
Mi-T-Fine Gifts, Massapequa Park, NY 11762, (516) 798-0123
Mrs. Van's Collectibles, Cooperstown, NY 13326, (607) 547-2138
Port of Pittsford Gifts, Pittsford, NY 14534, (716) 383-9250
Premio, Massapequa, NY 11758, (516) 795-3050
Prestige Collections, White Plains, NY 10601, (914) 686-3839
Riverfront Marketplace, Watertown, NY 13601, (315) 788-8860
Sonny's Cards N' Gifts, Miller Place, NY 11764, (516) 473-5611
TLC Collectibles Ltd., Macedon, NY 14502, (716) 872-3110
The Christmas House, Elmira, NY 14902, (607) 734-9547
The Crown Shoppe, Rockville Centre, NY 11570, (516) 536-2712
The Limited Edition*, Merrick, NY 11566, (516) 623-4400
Village Gift Shop, Tonawanda, NY 14150, (716) 695-6589

NORTH CAROLINA

Aggie's, Cary, NC 27511, (919) 467-5187
Amy's Hallmark, Washington, NC 27889, (919) 975-2403
Amy's Hallmark, Rocky Mount, NC 27804, (919) 443-2203
Aunt Edye's Collectibles, Charlotte, NC 28227, (704) 545-2658
Bear Trax, Hickory, NC 28603, (828) 328-5011
Bush Stationers & Gifts, Charlotte, NC 28207, (704) 333-4438
Olde World Christmas Shoppe, Asheville, NC 28803, (828) 274-4819
The Attic, Raleigh, NC 27612, (919) 782-4115
The Mole Hole of Asheville, Asheville, NC 28806, (704) 665-2090
Van Hoy Jewelers, Elkin, NC 28621-0026, (910) 835-3600
White Squirrel Shoppe Inc, Brevard, NC 8712, (828) 877-3530

NORTH DAKOTA

Bjornson Imports, Grand Forks, ND 58201, (701) 775-2618
Joy's Hallmark, Bismarck, ND 58501, (701) 258-9557

OHIO

Bellfair Country Stores, Beavercreek, OH 45432, (937) 426-3921
Cabbages & Kings, Grand Rapids, OH 43522, (419) 832-2709
Cellar Cache, Put-in-Bay, OH 43456, (419) 285-2738
Collection Connection, Piqua, OH 45356, (937) 778-9909
Collector's Gallery, Marion, OH 43302, (614) 387-0602
Collector's Outlet, Mentor On The Lake, OH 44060, (216) 257-1141
Collector's Passion, Heath, OH 43056, (614) 522-3133
Curio Cabinet, Worthington, OH 43085, (614) 885-1986
DeClark's Card & Gift Shop, Dayton, OH 45429, (937) 294-4741
Gift Garden, North Olmsted, OH 44070, (216) 777-0116
Hidden Treasures, Huron, OH 44839, (419) 433-2585
Historic Sauder Village, Archbold, OH 43502, (419) 446-2541
House of Tradition, Perrysburg, OH 43551, (419) 874-1151
Lake Cable Gifts & Collectibles, Canton, OH 44718, (330) 494-4173
Little Red Gift House, Birmingham, OH 44816, (216) 965-5420
Little Shop on the Portage, Woodville, OH 43469-1139, (419) 849-3742
Lola & Dale Gifts & Collectibles, Parma Heights, OH 44130, (216) 885-0444
Miller's Hallmark & Gift Gallery, Eaton, OH 45320, (937) 456-4151
Musik Box Haus, Inc., Vermilion, OH 44089, (216) 967-4744
North Hill Gift Shop, Akron, OH 44310, (330) 535-4811
Our Favorite Collectibles, Jamestown, OH 45335, (937) 675-2305

Richmond Galleries, Marblehead, OH 43440, (419) 798-5631
Rochelle's Fine Gifts, Toledo, OH 43623, (419) 472-7673
Saxony Imports, Cincinnati, OH 45202, (513) 621-7800
Schumm Collectibles & Gifts, Rockford, OH 45882, (419) 363-3630
Settler's Collections, Middlefield, OH 44062, (216) 632-1009
Story Book Kids, Cincinnati, OH 45241-3130, (513) 769-5437

OKLAHOMA
Colonial Florists, Stillwater, OK 74074, (405) 372-9166
Dody's Hallmark, Lawton, OK 73501, (405) 353-8379
Earl's Jewelers, Cushing, OK 74023-3334, (918) 225-1685
Madalan's Hallmark, Pryor, OK 74362, (918) 825-1590
North Pole City, Oklahoma City, OK 73119, (405) 685-6635
Perfect Touch, Tulsa, OK 74137, (918) 496-8118
Timeless Treasures, Ardmore, OK 73401, (580) 223-2116
W D Gifts, Okmulgee, OK 74447, (918) 756-2229

OREGON
Crown Showcase, Portland, OR 97232, (503) 280-0669
Das Haus-Am-Berg, Salem, OR 97304, (503) 363-0669
Kessel's Collectibles & Gift Shoppe, Salem, OR 97301-1814, (503) 362-5342
Mancke's Collectibles, Salem, OR 97306, (503) 371-3157
Present Peddler, Beaverton, OR 97008, (503) 641-6364
Tickled Pink Gift Shop, Portland, OR 97225, (503) 297-4102

PENNSYLVANIA
Adam's Eve of South Hills Village, Inc, Pittsburgh, PA 15241, (412) 833-8354
American Candle, Bartonsville, PA 18321, (717) 629-3388
Ashley Avery's Collectables, Willow Grove, PA 19090, (215) 784-0692
Collector's Choice, Pittsburgh, PA 15237, (412) 366-4477
Country Haus, Elizabethtown, PA 17022, (717) 367-5639
Country Kettle, East Stroudsburg, PA 18301, (717) 421-8970
Crafty Generations, Harrisburg, PA 17101, (717) 234-5051
Dutch Indoor Village, Lancaster, PA 17602, (717) 299-2348
Emporium Collectibles Gallery, Erie, PA 16506, (814) 833-2895
European Treasures, Pittsburgh, PA 15217-2903, (412) 421-8660
Gayle's Memories, Warren, PA 16365, (814) 723-6811
Gift Design Galleries, Wilkes-Barre, PA 18702, (717) 822-6704
Gift Design Galleries, N Wales, PA 19454, (215) 368-8150
Gift Design Galleries, Whitehall, PA 18052, (610) 266-1266
Gillespie Jeweler Collectors Gallery*, Northampton, PA 18067, (610) 261-0882
Goldcrafters, Springfield, PA 19064, (610) 544-9521
Irvin's Corp, Mt Pleasant Mills, PA 17853, (717) 539-8200
Jamie's Collectables, Reading, PA 19604-1808, (610) 373-4270
Lauchnor's Gifts & Collectables, Trexlertown, PA 18087, (610) 398-3008
Limited Editions, Forty Fort, PA 18704, (717) 288-0940
Limited Plates & Collectibles, Collegeville, PA 19426, (610) 489-7799
Marie's Gift Shop, Tafton, PA 18464, (717) 226-3345
Moment in Time, Philadelphia, PA 19147, (215) 551-1343
Nooks And Crannies, Pittsburgh, PA 15222, (412) 471-5099
Piccadilly Centre, Duncansville, PA 16635, (814) 695-8383
Rainbow Hallmark, Aldan, PA 19018, (610) 565-6966
Saville's Limited Editions, Pittsburgh, PA 15237, (412) 366-5458
Shaker Tree Studio, Hermitage, PA 16148, (412) 347-4141
Special Attractions, Athens, PA 18810-0256, (717) 888-2372
The Charm House, Leola, PA 17540, (717) 656-7212
The Gift Makers, Harrisburg, PA 17112, (717) 545-4438
The Personal Touch, Erie, PA 16506, (814) 838-7632
The Wishing Well, Reading, PA 19605, (610) 921-2566
Yeagle's, Lahaska, PA 18931, (215) 794-7756

RHODE ISLAND
The Golden Goose Gifts Inc., Smithfield, RI 02828, (401) 949-9940

SOUTH CAROLINA
Abrams Dolls & Collectibles, Conway, SC 29526, (803) 248-9198
Christmas Celebration, Greenville, SC 29607, (864) 242-1804
Christmas Celebration, Mauldin, SC 29662, (864) 277-7373
Duane's Hallmark Card & Gift Shop, Columbia, SC 29210, (803) 772-2624
Martha's Dollhouse & Collectibles, Denmark, SC 29042, (803) 793-4963

SOUTH DAKOTA
Akers Gifts & Collectibles, Sioux Falls, SD 57105, (605) 339-1325
Gift Gallery, Brookings, SD 57006, (605) 692-9405

TENNESSEE
Calico Butterfly, Memphis, TN 38133-5302, (901) 362-8121
Camera World, Clarksville, TN 37040, (931) 552-0542
Cox's Hallmark Shop, Maryville, TN 37801, (423) 982-0421
Gifts Unique, Lenoir City, TN 37771, (423) 986-1211
Home for the Holidays, Cordova, TN 38018, (901) 755-5554
LaWanda's Hallmark, Dayton, TN 37321, (423) 775-4869
On Display, Knoxville, TN 37922, (423) 966-2950
Orange Blossom, Martin, TN 38237, (901) 587-5091
Patty's Hallmark, Murfreesboro, TN 37129, (615) 890-8310
Something Special, Knoxville, TN 37918, (423) 922-4438
Southern Magnolia, Jackson, TN 38305, (901) 668-3858
Stage Crossing Gifts & Collectibles, Bartlett, TN 38134, (901) 372-4438
SugarDrops, Morristown, TN 37814, (423) 586-1095
The Doll & Gift Gallery, Troy, TN 38260, (901) 536-3900
The Hourglass II, Inc, Chattanooga, TN 37415, (615) 877-2328

TEXAS
Accents, Conroe, TX 77304, (409) 756-7704
Alter's Gem Jewelry, Beaumont, TX 77702, (409) 892-6631
Betty's Collectables Ltd*, Harlingen, TX 78550, (210) 423-8234
Carousel Art & Frame, The Woodlands, TX 77381, (281) 292-2269
Christmas Treasures, Baytown, TX 77521, (281) 421-1581
Collectible Heirlooms, Friendswood, TX 77546, (281) 486-5023
Collecto-Mania, Spring, TX 77373, (281) 353-9233
Earth's Treasures, Spring, TX 77373, (281) 288-1367
Eloise's Collectibles, Houston, TX 77063, (713) 783-3611
Eloise's Collectibles II, Katy, TX 77450, (281) 578-6655
Eloise's Gifts & Antiques, Rockwall, TX 75087, (972) 771-6371
Fan-Fare Gifts & Collectibles, Texarkana, TX 75503, (903) 832-8258
Gail's Gift Shop, Fort Worth, TX 76110, (817) 922-8899
Galaxy Hallmark Shop, Houston, TX 77058, (281) 335-1211
Gifts 'N' Glass, Humble, TX 77338, (281) 446-7611
Holiday House, Huntsville, TX 77340, (409) 295-7338
Lacey's Hallmark, Pasadena, TX 77504, (281) 998-7171
Loujon's Gifts, Sugar Land, TX 77478, (281) 980-1245
Monarch Collectibles, Houston, TX 77070, (281) 894-9399
Mr C Collectible Center, Carrollton, TX 75006, (972) 242-5100
RavenHome Gifts, San Antonio, TX 78232, (210) 545-5255
The Collector's Gallery, Longview, TX 75605, (903) 753-3883
The Shepherd's Shoppe, San Antonio, TX 78216, (210) 342-4811

UTAH
Riverton Drug & Gift, Riverton, UT 84065, (801) 254-3911
Wasatch Seasons, Draper, UT 84020, (801) 553-2643

VIRGINIA
Blue Ridge Bear & Gifts, Vinton, VA 24179, (540) 342-4303
Carol's Country Cupboard, Dumfries, VA 22026, (703) 221-3794
Chimney Corner, Charlottesville, VA 22903, (804) 295-1044
Collectors Cottage, Aldie, VA 20105, (703) 327-2495
Creekside Collectibles & Gifts, Winchester, VA 22601, (540) 662-0270
Gazebo Gifts, Newport News, VA 23601, (804) 591-8387
The Plate Shoppe, Lorton, VA 22079, (703) 690-0068

WASHINGTON
Classy Creations-Coll & Gift Shoppe, Sequim, WA 98382, (360) 683-1460
Crystal Cottage Gallery Inc., Seattle, WA 98133, (206) 546-4444
Fountain Galleria, Bellingham, WA 98225, (360) 733-6200
Jansen Flower & Gift Gallery, Longview, WA 98632, (360) 423-0450
Loretta's Gifts & Collectibles, Poulsbo, WA 98370, (360) 779-7171
Natalia's Collectibles, Woodinville, WA 98072, (206) 481-4575
Serendipity Gifts & Collectibles, Puyallup, WA 98373, (206) 770-1990
Tannenbaum Shoppe, Leavenworth, WA 98826, (509) 548-7014
The Chalet, Tacoma, WA 98466-5290, (206) 564-0326
Wheeler Galleries, Langley, WA 98260, (360) 221-6747

WEST VIRGINIA
Aracoma Drug Gift Gallery, Logan, WV 25601, (304) 752-3812
Fenton Gift Shop, Williamstown, WV 26187, (304) 375-7772

WISCONSIN
A Country Mouse, Milwaukee, WI 53220, (414) 281-4210
Beauchene's Coll. & Christmas Shop, Thiensville, WI 53092, (414) 242-0170
Carriage Haus, Mayville, WI 53050, (920) 387-4099
Downs', Greenfield, WI 53220, (414) 327-6109
Jan's Hallmark & Gift Gallery, Delavan, WI 53115, (414) 728-6528
Kies' Pharmacy and Gift, Racine, WI 53406, (414) 886-8160
Kristmas Kringle Shoppe, Fond Du Lac, WI 54936, (414) 922-3900
Krueger Jeweler, Fort Atkinson, WI 53538, (414) 563-3863
Lakeland Gift Shoppe, Milton, WI 53563, (608) 868-4700
Lasting Impressions-Fine Gifts, La Crosse, WI 54601-4754, (608) 784-7201
P J's Hallmark Shop, Marinette, WI 54143, (715) 735-3940
P J's Hallmark Shop, Green Bay, WI 54301, (920) 437-3443
Prism Gift Shop Inc., Hartland, WI 53029, (414) 367-2204
Spirit of Christmas, Mayville, WI 53050, (920) 387-4648
Tivoli Imports, Milwaukee, WI 53226, (414) 774-7590

AUSTRALIA
Gallery Gifts, Adelaide SA 5000, Australia, (618) 8212 5684

CANADA – ALBERTA
Durand's Ltd Editions Inc., Calgary, AB T2E 2T9, (403) 277-0008
Platefinders, Edmonton, AB T6H 1K9, (403) 435-3603

CANADA – ONTARIO
Bakerosa Collectibles & Books, London, ON N6H 3C1, (519) 472-0827
Browsers Nook, Peterborough, ON K9J 6W9, (705) 742-7985
Chornyjs' Hadke, Sault Ste Marie, ON P6A 2B4, (705) 253-0315
Over the Rainbow Collectables, Etobicoke, ON M9C 4X1, (416) 622-6835

ENGLAND
Castle China Group, Warwick, ENG, 44-1926-400513

* Charter Member

FRONT COVER

1. Anheuser-Busch's "1998 World Cup Stein"
2. "Sparkling Seduction" from the *Gene* series by The Ashton-Drake Galleries
3. "Hope - Light in the Distance" from the *Seraphim Classics Collection* by Roman, Inc.
4. Lena Liu's "Romantic Reverie" by Imperial Graphics
5. "Bluebird of Happiness" from the *Feathered Friends* series by Islandia International
6. Willitts Designs' "Forgiven" from *The MasterPeace® Collection*
7. M.I. Hummel's "Here's My Heart" from the *Century Collection* by Goebel of North America
8. Lilliput Lane's "Pastures New" from the *British Collection*
9. "Patriarch Alexis," the 1998 Special Event Piece from Kurt S. Adler's *Polonaise* collection
10. "The Capitol" from Department 56's *Heritage Village Christmas in the City* series

BACK COVER

Photo A:

1. Lee Middleton Dolls' "Loving Tribute" from the *Honey Love Series*
2. "Colonial Scroll Vase" from The Fenton Art Glass Company
3. United Design Corporation's "Spirit of Autumn"
4. "90th Anniversary Nativity" from *Fontanini Heirloom Nativities*
5. Media Arts Group's "Catalina Yacht Club" from the *Plein Air* series
6. "Celebration Reproduction Carousel" from the *American Treasures Series* by The San Francisco Music Box Company
7. "Rope Twist Console" from Pulaski Furniture
8. "Ben" from the *Georgetown* series by Jan Hagara Collectables
9. "The Owl and the Pussycat" from The Greenwich Workshop Collection
10. "Peaceful Love" from ANRI U.S.
11. "Sally" from Flambro's *Willow Hall Dolls*
12. *All Gods Children* "Marcy" from Miss Martha Originals
13. *World of Krystonia's* "Recorder" from Precious Art
14. *Pipka's Earth Angels* "The Guardian Angel" from Prizm, Inc./ Pipka's Collectibles
15. "Mighty Sioux Warrior" from The Hamilton Collection
16. "Friends" from Sarah's Attic *Colors of Life* collection
17. "Belsnickel" from Byers' Choice, Ltd.
18. Seymour Mann Inc.'s "Nicole" from *The Connoisseur Doll Collection*
19. *Melody in Motion* "Willie & Jumbo" from WACO Products Corp.
20. *Angels Triumphant* "Peaceable Kingdom Angel" from House of Hatten
21. *Cabbage Patch Kids'* "Chattahoochee Newborn" from Original Appalachian Artworks

Photo B:

1. Armani's "Lucia" the Members-Only 1998 Figurine from Miller Imports
2. Royal Doulton's "Angel of Autumn" from the *Angels of Harmony* series
3. Lladró's "Happy Anniversary"
4. "Hand in Hand" from The Art of Glynda Turley
5. GiftStar's "Engine House Number 10" from *Brian Baker's Déjà Vu Collection*
6. Margaret Furlong Designs' "Madonna of the Flowers" from the *Madonna and Child* series
7. "Simone - Nature's Own" from Roman's *Seraphim Classics Collection*
8. Enesco's *Precious Moments* "20 Years and the Vision is Still the Same"
9. Lenox Collections' "Just Like Mommy" from the *Barefoot Blessings* collection
10. The San Francisco Music Box Company's "Pie Safe" from the *Heart Tugs* series

Photo C:

1. "Highland Santa" from Possible Dreams' *Clothtique Santas*
2. Annalee Mobilitee Dolls' "Mrs. Claus and Paws"
3. "And to All a Good Bite" from Goebel of North America's *Looney Tunes Spotlight Collection*
4. Christopher Radko's "Rooftops of London"
5. Christian Ulbricht's "Toy Soldier"
6. Cavanagh Group International's "Santa's Sled"
7. "Country Fair" from *eggspressions!, inc.*
8. "Memorable Journey" from Walnut Ridge Collectibles
9. "Chickadee Pair with Holly and Berries" from Maruri USA's *Songbird Serenade* collection
10. "McKenzie Bear" from Carlton Cards
11. *Dreamsicles™* "All Aboard" (7th Edition) from Cast Art Industries
12. Eddie Walker's "1998 Holiday Rocking Horse Ornament" from Midwest of Cannon Falls

Photo D:

1. "Spirit of America" from Munro Collectibles, Inc.
2. "Winnie the Pooh" from Cardew's *Disney Character Teapot Collection*
3. *Lizzie High Dolls'*® "Winnie Valentine™" by Ladie & Friends
4. "It's Just a Small Piece of Weather" from The Bradford Exchange's *Pooh's Hunnypot Adventures*
5. Brandywine Collectibles' "Tea Room" from the *Country Lane VI* collection
6. "William Shakespurr" from Ertl Collectibles Ltd.
7. Harmony Kingdom's "Rather Large Huddle"
8. *Charming Tails* "Hear, Speak and See No Evil" from Fitz and Floyd Collectibles Division

Photo E:

1. David Winter Cottages' "Marquis Walter Manor" from Enesco
2. Cheryl Spencer Collin's "Boon Island Lighthouse, Boon Island, ME" from Dave Grossman Creations
3. Forma Vitrum's "Whispering Pines" from the *Vitreville Bed and Breakfast* series
4. Duncan Royale's "Blackbeard" from *The History of Pirates and Buccaneers* series
5. Walt Disney Classics' "Seahorse Surprise - Ariel"
6. George Z. Lefton Company's "Colonial Queen Collector's Set" from *The Colonial Village Collection*
7. Harbour Lights' "Sturgeon Bay - WI" from the *Great Lakes Region* series

Photo F:

1. "Cover Your Thirst" from Shelia's Collectibles
2. Gartlan USA's "John Lennon"
3. "The Statue of Liberty" from *The National Treasures Series* by F.J. Designs/The Makers of The Cat's Meow Village™
4. Reco International's "Salinger Mansion" from the *Rooms with a View* collection
5. Royal Copenhagen's "Dancing Around the Christmas Tree" (2 pcs.) from the *Children's Christmas Plate* series
6. Sandy Dolls' "Blue Monday" from *Sass 'n Class by Annie Lee*
7. Sunbelt Marketing's "Great Britain" from the *Coca-Cola Contour Collection*
8. "Coca-Cola Celebrates American Aviation" from The Alexander Doll Company
9. "Boyd Duce Coup Hot Rod" from The Franklin Mint

Photo G:

1. "Tucked In" from Porterfield's
2. "Tiger" from Swarovski's *Silver Crystal Endangered Species* series
3. "Once in a Blue Moon, The Magic Comes Alive" from Fool Moon Treasures
4. "Timber Wolf" from Crystal World

TABLE OF CONTENTS

Background

Features

Reference Section

Experts Offer Insights Into the Limited Edition Market

In the ever-changing collectibles market, at least one fact remains the same: Collectors are drawn to those things that hold a sentimental, nostalgic and endearing place in their hearts. Whether it's a Mickey Mouse figurine, a collector plate featuring a mother and her child, an Anheuser-Busch stein, a Coca-Cola ornament, a limited edition wildlife print or a family heirloom, collectors cherish their treasures – and seem to be adding to their collections.

"Our research indicates that more people than ever before are collecting," says Peter McEwen, president and CEO of The Greenwich Workshop. "This is an exciting time in the collectibles industry. Although collecting is not a new hobby, and some people might even think that to some extent it's a mature market, I think by its very nature the hobby is exciting. And we're now at a point where it can bring in new collectors and energize previous collectors."

As the millennium draws closer, angels and other religious-themed collectibles, such as Roman, Inc.'s "Angels To Watch Over Me" from the **Seraphim Classics®** ***collection, are expected to remain strong on the collectibles market.***

With more products and designs to choose from, today's generation of collectors is becoming more selective and more knowledgeable about their purchases. They're joining collector's clubs and clicking on the World Wide Web to find information and to interact with fellow collectors. And today's manufacturers are both meeting and fueling the demand for their products. A panel of experts from the collectibles industry offered Collectors' Information Bureau their insights on the current market and what collectors can expect in the future.

TRENDS IN SOCIETY BECOME THE COLLECTIBLES OF TODAY AND TOMORROW

Collectibles closely mirror today's trends. It's a sign of the times – and of past and coming years. With hectic lifestyles and new technology, more collectors seem to be looking back and surrounding themselves with things that reflect a simpler day and age. "Simplification is a real buzz word for people," says Jim Jelin of Our Secret, makers of *Little Lops* and the *Thread Bears* lines. "People want and need to relax by stepping back and simplifying."

As the millennium draws closer, others are looking ahead, spurring a resurgence in angels and collectibles with spiritual themes. "I think along with the overwhelming interest in angels, we will see more lines that come from the heart," says Michele Johnson of Prizm, Inc./ Pipka's Collectibles.

Nancy Fino, director of marketing for new products at Enesco Corporation, sees both the past and future coming together in collectibles. "With the millennium approaching, angels and religious-themed items remain strong and are anticipated right up until the year 2000," Fino says. "As a great deal of Americans age, they'll be looking for products that remind them of the days before voice mail, faxes and the Internet."

Carlton Cards identified several trends that are expected to impact and influence the collectible market: America's return to spirituality, interest in ethnic and multi-cultural themes, the aging population of Baby Boomers, focus on nature and preservation, and an increasing fascination with miniatures.

"With the millennium quickly approaching, collectible manufacturers have the opportunity to develop products that celebrate this milestone and products that reflect accomplishments and historical landmarks," notes Leslee Parsons Cavanaugh of Carlton Cards.

Nostalgic collectibles are becoming just as popular overseas as they are in America. "In the United Kingdom, there is a growing nostalgia for the 1950s," says Stephen W. Richardson, general manager of Hazle Ceramics. "This is mainly because the group that tends to collect are the 40-plus age group. So anything that reminds people of their youth is popular."

LICENSED COLLECTIBLES BRING BACK FAVORITE PEOPLE AND THINGS

The sense of nostalgia is creating a proliferation of licensed products and properties ranging from Elvis and Barbie to Harley-Davidson and McDonald's. "The licensing industry is experiencing a return to classic, nostalgic properties," Cavanaugh says.

Companies like Coca-Cola, Warner

In a licensing agreement with Warner Bros., Goebel launched the* Looney Tunes Spotlight Collection. *Pictured is the "Rabbit of Seville" sculpted scene highlighting two figurines, "Hare-Do," featuring Bugs Bunny, and "Bad Hare Day," which depicts poor Elmer Fudd with a fruit salad on his head.

Bros. and Disney are staples of present-day consumer culture. Goebel, for example, recently partnered with Warner Bros. to launch the *Looney Tunes Spotlight Collection* of figurines based on classic cartoon shorts. "Nostalgia is huge, but it's changed from our parent's days," says Susan Peterson, Goebel vice president of marketing. "Baby boomers and Generation Xers seek memorabilia from the world of entertainment. Anything goes – from TV shows popular during the '60s and '70s to superheroes, comic book characters, sports figures and rock stars."

It appears that these classic licensed products aren't a passing trend. "Licensed products are having a tremendous, positive impact in the industry," says Fino. "These are the products that are stirring up nostalgic feelings in the aging baby boomers. I don't believe this is a fad. We've already seen the strength in licensed items last over the past three to four years."

With the growing popularity of collectibles, it seems there are more companies and products on the market than ever before. Collectors, therefore, need to be better informed and more discerning in what they add to their collections. "Because of the proliferation of products, the collectible market has become much more competitive," Cavanaugh says. "At the same time, the consumer has become more educated and is looking for quality products that will have lasting value."

More products mean more choices for collectors and more competition for manufacturers, who are responding with new ideas and concepts. "Good products will always do well and maintain their value," says Jelin of Our Secret. "As with any market, collectible consumers are being asked to take more time and sort through what's good and what's not. In the end, the good products – the products that reach out to consumers and establish a bond – will continue to be the ones to succeed."

COLLECTORS HAVE MORE PRODUCTS TO CHOOSE FROM

Of course, quality, craftsmanship, excellence in design and customer service are also the mainstays of a successful collection. "Price is not an object, but consumers want value for their money," says Goebel's Peterson. "Quality is more important now than it ever was."

Our experts are quick to point out that it's not the manufacturer, but rather the collectors who turn products into true collectibles. "There is no limitation to define what could be a collectible," says Ru Kato of WACO Products Corporation. "Consumers make them collectible."

UP AND COMING COLLECTIBLES TO WATCH

Manufacturers pinpointed several collectible lines as leaders in the current market – and those that will continue to shine in the future. Among the favorites are Christopher Radko's hand-blown glass ornaments, the *Walt Disney Classics Collection*, The Greenwich Workshop figurines, *Cherished Teddies* figurines, Boyds Bears and Harmony Kingdom Box Figurines™. Beanie Babies plush animals by Ty also topped the list.

"Successful companies seem to be coming from markets outside the traditional collectibles industry, bringing with them fresh ideas," says Noel Wiggins, president of Harmony Kingdom. For example, Ty and Boyds came from the toy industry, The Greenwich Workshop from the publishing industry and Harmony Kingdom from the jewelry business.

Many companies are also introducing products to benefit worthy causes from children's charities to historic landmark preservation. "Our society is very conscious of their responsibility for the condition and preservation of our world," says Betty Stamatis for Geo. Z. Lefton Co. Any collectible that can "help in some way to improve the quality of life or preserve historic landmarks for future generations is going to enjoy high popularity," she adds.

A fresh idea in collectibles is Harmony Kingdom's® Box Figurines™, which combine the appeal of an English work of art with the function of a beautifully designed treasure box. "Yellow Rose" is the third issue in the popular* Harmony Garden™ *series.

With the click of the mouse, collectors can log onto the Internet to find information about their favorite collectibles. Enesco's website offers many unique features.

A WORD OF ADVICE

Above all else, experts say people should collect what they enjoy – no matter what the current trends or fads. "My best tip to collectors is: collect what pleases you," says Judith Price, consumer services manager for Department 56. "Learn more about collectibles – read, join a club or talk to your dealer."

Lynn Fenton Erb of The Fenton Art Glass Company agrees, adding that collectors should "learn as much as possible about the history of your collectible by reading publications and collector club newsletters, and, if possible, by visiting the factories where collectibles are made."

Peterson of Goebel echoes this advice, encouraging collectors to "learn everything you can about your collection. The best way to do this is by joining collector clubs and exchanging information with other members, reading books and talking to knowledgeable retailers."

COLLECTIBLES REACH INTO CYBERSPACE

If information is a key to collecting, then the Internet is the door to the latest news and products. Logging onto the Internet to search for and discover information about favorite collectibles is one of the fastest-growing trends. More and more collectible companies are creating websites, where collectors can learn about new introductions, ask questions, get answers, find helpful hints and link up with others who have similar interests. "The Internet is a low-cost resource for collectors around the world to connect with and learn from each other," says Victoria Veh, director of marketing for Swarovski.

Collectible manufacturers know that the Internet is a great way for them to keep in touch with their collectors and retailers. "Hundreds of thousands of collectors are on-line every day, trading, swapping and selling their collections," says Kevin Wixted, manager of Internet communications for Enesco. "It is the Internet-savvy collector who is driving the industry's expansion on the Net."

Manufacturers' sites are as varied as the collectibles themselves. The Enesco home page offers collectors gift suggestions for special occasions throughout the year, as well as a "Sneak Peek" of products that will be appearing on the store shelves in the near future. If collectors want to find their nearest retailer, they can type in their own address to access the location as well as a street map to guide them to stores in their area carrying Enesco products. The "OOHLALA" section allows users to rotate a product to see the collectible from every possible angle. A different piece from each line is featured in this section every month.

Department 56, Inc. answers collectors most frequently asked questions in "virtual reprints" from past issues of the company's quarterly newsletter. Department 56 also turns the tables by asking collectors questions in a quarterly trivia contest, complete with prizes. Harmony Kingdom has a chat room for collectors to exchange information, while Anheuser-Busch offers unique e-mail greeting cards. Most company sites are constantly updated, providing a new experience every time collectors visit them in cyberspace.

COLLECTORS' INFORMATION BUREAU GOES ON-LINE

The Collectors' Information Bureau web site (http://www.collectorsinfo.com) also provides a wealth of information and resources for collectors. The *CIB Collectibles Report* is recreated as an on-line newsletter. Collectors can order copies of the annual *Collectibles Market Guide & Price Index* and the *Collectibles Price Guide* through a secure credit card transaction.

CIB member companies post their latest news on a bulletin board, and there is a link to each company's own web site for easy navigation and further information. Collectors can also search a database to quickly find a secondary market dealer in their area.

For primary market dealers, collectors can visit the National Association of Limited Edition Dealers (NALED) web site at http://www.naled.com.

In the changing world of collectibles, the Internet has become a valuable tool to help collectors keep up with the trends as well as their favorite subjects and lines. "The Internet provides information and nurtures relationships," Jelin says. "It will continue to grow in popularity and cannot be ignored."

Understanding the Secondary Market

Since we were small children, many of us have traded on the secondary market, possibly without even knowing it. From the little boys who negotiate an exchange of one Ty Cobb rookie year baseball card for two Mickey Mantle cards, to the art collector who purchases an original painting at an auction, everyday life is filled with examples of secondary market trading. A secondary market transaction, in its simplest form, is merely the acquisition of something after it is no longer available through the primary market channels, most commonly the retail stores.

Within the world of limited edition collectibles, these transactions most often take place with the help of secondary market dealers, exchanges, brokers, locators and retailers who act as a conduit for the buying and selling of retired collectibles. And although most collectors don't purchase a piece with thoughts of someday trading it on the secondary market, the secondary market does have an impact on nearly every collector's life.

One of the avenues available to collectors for secondary market trading is the "Swap and Sell" often held in conjunction with The International Collectible Exposition.

After all, the secondary market is where collectors will need to turn for a replacement should a piece from their collection be lost, stolen or damaged. And if you were not in on the ground floor of collecting a particular line and want to catch up on the pieces you've missed, you'll often have to turn to the secondary market to find those earlier pieces. Since the secondary market value of individual items has an impact on the amount of insurance coverage collectors need to buy in order to adequately protect their investment, fluctuations in the secondary market values of collectibles can effect every collectors' life.

Seasoned collectors know how important it is to keep abreast of the secondary market. They know how to use it to their best advantage whether buying or selling a limited edition collectible. "Buyers and sellers are becoming better educated and understand the dynamics of the secondary market through publications like Collectors' Information Bureau's *Collectibles Market Guide & Price Index*," says Matt Rothman of Lighthouse Trading Company in Limerick, Pennsylvania. "This is making the secondary market much more efficient."

Secondary market experts like Rothman offer collectors advice and insights into buying and selling collectibles on the aftermarket. The price of a limited edition collectible on the secondary market is a function of supply and demand. "Appreciation is based on demand followed by the supply available in the marketplace," says Russ Wood of Collector's Marketplace in Montrose, Pennsylvania. "This is an indiscriminate rule of economics."

FOLLOWING THE LAW OF SUPPLY AND DEMAND

An item produced in a relatively limited supply and experiencing a great demand may appreciate in value. However, an item that is part of a lower edition size may not necessarily rise in price. People need to know about the item in order to build word of mouth and demand. Like the economic market, changes in supply and demand regularly occur. Over time, the supply of an item may diminish, particularly if the piece is fragile. Likewise, the demand for a particular piece may change as collectors' tastes and interests evolve.

With these changes, collectors should realize that prices can and do fluctuate on the secondary market – sometimes quite dramatically. "Prices are being paid that have never been seen before," Rothman says.

As prices rise, they may reach a level that collectors feel is unreasonable. As a result, demand falls. Once demand wanes, sellers may lower their price in order to make a sale. This may continue until collectors again feel that the value for the piece is reasonable and begin buying again. Then the cycle may begin anew.

GOING IT ALONE VS. USING A BROKER

"There's a lot more activity on the secondary market now than previously, probably because more and more new collectors are coming on stream trying to pick up whatever retired pieces they are missing," says Robin Yaw of The Crystal Connection in Peoria, Illinois. With this has come more secondary market dealers, which Yaw says creates more choices – and perhaps more confusion – for those venturing into the secondary market.

For this reason, secondary market experts advise collectors to do their homework in finding a qualified and knowledgeable broker to buy or sell collectibles. Some collectors think they will save money by attempting to trade on the secondary market on their own, but the services of a knowledgeable broker are often well worth the cost of his or her commission. "Secondary market dealers will charge a broker's fee, but quite often they will have a wider audience and be able to fetch a better price for the seller," says Bernice Kessler of Greco Collectibles in Aurora, Colorado.

Brokers do the work for you by placing ads, making telephone contacts, inspecting the product, ensuring that you are paid, or making sure the item you purchase is safely delivered. In most cases, the seller pays the commission, which may vary from as low as 10% to 30% or more. Shipping costs may or may not be included in these prices. Make sure you are aware about all the surcharges and costs associated with working with a broker or a buy-sell service. If in doubt with any part of the process, ask for clarification.

In addition to supply and demand, prices of a collectible vary depending on the condition of the piece. In some cases, the collectible's asking price may also rise if it bears the artist's signature. "If the artist does not get out in the public often, a signature will increase the value, but when signatures from artists are abundant, the value usually does not change," Rothman says.

The secondary market is also entering the information superhighway as collectors find they can buy and sell collectibles on the Internet as well as locate aftermarket brokers.

ASK THE EXPERTS

I'm a collector planning to buy or sell on the secondary market? What advice do you have for me?

Robin Yaw, The Crystal Connection, Peoria, Illinois

"Buyers beware. Know what you are buying. The safest way for private buyers to deal with private sellers is to meet face to face. When dealing with a business like an exchange, collectors need to check out references. Find an exchange that specializes in the particular manufacturer or product you are interested in, because they know it best. For the seller, whether you are selling an item on your own or listing your pieces with an exchange, be honest with your description of the items you are selling. Don't overstate quality. If you are listing with an exchange, make sure you know the terms of the transaction such as what your obligations are, and when you will receive payment after you send your item to them."

Blaine Garfolo, Crystal Reef, Foster City, California

"Do your homework and be realistic. When buying or selling, know the realistic price range for your collectible. Don't be shy about asking the broker for help in positioning your piece for sale. A good broker treats collectibles like stocks. They know how and when a good sale is likely. Always remember, establishing a good relationship with a broker is very important to you as a collector if you plan to use the secondary market to complete your collection and/or sell extra pieces purchased as an investment."

Terri Peters, Pictorial Treasures, Pawhuska, Oklahoma

"The most fundamental issue for a buyer is to shop around — not just for a certain collectible —but for information. Before buying, a collector needs to determine why he or she is buying. If they really like a particular piece that has special meaning to their life, or that is the perfect decorating match, then buy it. Its value to the collector is then not measured by monetary value alone."

Bernice Kessler, Greco Collectibles, Aurora, Colorado

"The single piece of advice we give to all collectors planning to buy is 'Buy what you like and what you would want to keep for your own collection.' No one can accurately predict what the market will do. We can only go by trends, and today's hot item may be tomorrow's white elephant. For those planning to sell, we would suggest that they do some research, consult CIB guides and others to get a fair idea of what the item is currently selling for."

Darlene Doyle, Linda's Originals/Yankee Craftsmen, West Brewster, Massachusetts

"Collectors need to work with a reputable dealer and understand that the price of a collectible is determined by supply and customer demand. They often want dealers to tell them what's going to go up in value. We can only advise them on what is selling well."

It seems more people are turning to the Internet for information and secondary market transactions. What impact is this having on the secondary market and what advice do you have for buying and selling via the Internet?

Blaine Garfolo, Crystal Reef, Foster City, California

"The Internet offers the collector literally tens of thousands of collectible sources from which to shop. However, just like dealing with an unknown party from a newspaper ad, it doesn't take much to start up a web site. The buyer should be especially concerned when prices and availability seem too good to be true.

On the positive side, a survey of the Internet will give a very good and realistic secondary market view of prices and availability of pieces that may not be readily available to collectors from other sources. The collector should use the Internet as just one more source of information in making a good decision about purchasing a fine collectible."

Robin Yaw, The Crystal Connection, Peoria, Illinois

"With the explosion of the Internet, we are sure there will be more and more people trying to buy and sell on the Internet. Our advice to collectors who plan to use the Internet to conduct their secondary market transactions is no different than we tell collectors who use the conventional methods. That is: 'Buyers Beware!' Know exactly what you are buying and have a clear understanding of what the guarantee or return policy is if the item is flawed or incomplete, especially when dealing with private sellers."

Bernice Kessler, Greco Collectibles, Aurora, Colorado
"The Internet is having a profound effect on the secondary market. Many companies list retailers on the Internet who deal in the resale of their product, and as a result, collectors have a wider source to draw upon. A word of caution: most advertisers are honest, but you should exercise restraint, especially when it comes to giving out credit card numbers to individuals."

Matt Rothman, Lighthouse Trading Co., Limerick, Pennsylvania
"The Internet is bringing a wider variety of collectors directly to the secondary market, giving buyers and sellers a wider selection of individuals and services to choose from when trading secondary market collectibles. Caution is the watchword. This does open up the down side of people misrepresenting what they are selling."

Some collector club pieces are the first in a line to appreciate on the secondary market. Why is this and will this trend continue?

Bernice Kessler, Greco Collectibles, Aurora, Colorado
"The reason that club pieces tend to appreciate quickly is the fact that they are only available for one year. Overall though, we find that club pieces are not necessarily any more in demand than some very specific pieces in a line."

Matt Rothman, Lighthouse Trading Co., Limerick, Pennsylvania
"The first club piece is usually the hardest to find because club membership is smaller in the beginning, making fewer pieces available to club members as the clubs increase in size."

Dee Brandt, Classic Endeavors, Greenback, Tennessee
"They are often the pieces a collector finds difficult to part with, placing fewer on the secondary market. The old 'supply and demand' rule applies here."

There are new collectibles entering the primary market every day. What impact will and does this have on the secondary market?

Blaine Garfolo, Crystal Reef, Foster City, California
"New collectibles help to strengthen the secondary market as it generates potential retirement pieces for the market in the long run. A strong, popular new line of collectibles encourages collectors to purchase them and, consequently, look for retired pieces to fill their collections. Without new, popular collectibles entering the primary market, the secondary market would slow to just a few popular lines, and the competition for those pieces would soon exhaust supply."

Bernice Kessler, Greco Collectibles, Aurora, Colorado
"Through a natural winnowing process, the number of new collectibles reaching the secondary market will vary according to collector demand. Generally speaking, the stronger, more detailed and more appealing lines will continue. Newer lines which contain items available for a limited period of time, or a relatively small limited edition, should do well."

Dee Brandt, Classic Endeavors, Greenback, Tennessee
"Competition is healthy and forces quality and excellence in a product. Collectors can be fickle. If a company isn't giving them what they feel they deserve, they will move on."

Matt Rothman, Lighthouse Trading Co., Limerick, Pennsylvania
"We are seeing more and more quality collectibles being produced. This is introducing people to collecting who may never have been involved before. For the secondary market, this is a real positive."

What changes have you seen in the secondary market in the past several years? How does this affect the collector looking to buy and sell on the secondary market?

Darlene Doyle, Linda's Originals/Yankee Craftsmen, West Brewster, Massachusetts
"I have seen the secondary market go up and down. Collectibles come and go, and the trends change. Another age of people starts collecting which also changes the secondary market, too. While some people collect what they like, a lot of people collect for the value."

Bernice Kessler, Greco Collectibles, Aurora, Colorado
"The biggest change in the secondary market has been the emergence of some totally new lines, including Harmony Kingdom and Beanie Babies. I see Harmony Kingdom as a definite strength because of the wit and substance of the collection. On the other hand, I see Beanie Babies as an overblown 'pet rock' phenomenon. Collectors who are paying astronomical prices for Beanie Babies had better sell them off quickly before the whole market folds."

Dee Brandt, Classic Endeavors, Greenback, Tennessee
"For many collectors, it has been a bull market for their investments. However, for some, expectations are too high, and what quickly rises can also quickly fall. A return to buying for enjoyment – not investment – is desirable for long-term satisfaction."

Russ Wood, Collector's Marketplace, Montrose, Pennsylvania
"We continue to see the collector becoming more sophisticated and knowledgeable. We rarely find that we have to explain what the secondary market is and how it works. If you are selling, you need to realize that if your piece is not in A+ condition, then don't expect to get the market price. We're finding collectors are getting more selective in what they will accept. The relevancy of this increases with the purpose the collector has. If the collector is buying with investment in mind, then good pieces are significant."

How to Keep Your Favorite Treasures in Top Condition

To many, collectibles are a part of the family and everyday life, holding special memories and bringing years of enjoyment. As with any treasured possession, collectibles require proper care and attention to ensure the preservation of their original beauty, detail, color and value. Here are some simple guidelines and specific tips to keep your collectibles in the best condition for many years to come.

Listen to the manufacturer's advice. "Follow the manufacturer's instructions for the care of your collection," says Stephen Richardson, general manager of Hazle Ceramics. "Your fragile pieces will probably require specific care and attention." Some manufacturers include special care instructions on the collectible's box or inserted in pamphlets. You can also find valuable information in a company's club newsletters or Internet sites.

Save the original boxes. Keeping the original box not only helps you store and properly transport your collectible, but it often enhances the marketability of your limited edition piece if you choose to sell it on the secondary market. As you add more pieces to your collection, you inevitably add more boxes, which may create a space crunch. Many boxes can be folded flat for easier storage and then placed in dry areas such as trunks, suitcases or closets.

"Save all original boxes," suggests Victoria Veh, director of marketing for Swarovski. "Keep them in a covered plastic garbage can so they will not be damaged if there is a flood."

Avoid displaying collectibles in sunlight. "It's always a good idea to keep your collectibles out of direct sunlight," recommends Nancy Fino, Enesco Corporation's director of marketing for new products. "The sun's rays are harsh and can be harmful to the coloring and detail of a collectible."

Keep your treasures safe and sound. Make sure all your displays are well constructed – whether it's a curio cabinet, adjustable shelves, plate hangers or even a Christmas tree. Avoid placing collectibles near the edge of shelves and tables. You can even take some precautions against Mother Nature. Collectors living in areas prone to earthquakes can consider products such as Quake Hold! putty or wax to securely fasten the collectibles in place.

SPECIAL CARE FOR SPECIFIC COLLECTIBLES

From plates to prints, collectibles come in all shapes, sizes and materials – each with its own requirements for protection and care. You can use the following guidelines, but check with the manufacturer for more specific information on caring for your collectibles.

Figurines, Cottages, Bells and Steins Three-dimensional works of art often need more cleaning due to the details and crevices. To clean, gently dust with a feather duster or small shaving brush. You will need to check with the manufacturer on further and more specific cleaning instructions. Enesco Corporation, for example, recommends that its porcelain bisque figurines from the *Precious Moments* collection be cleaned by wiping the object with a damp cloth. Never immerse the *Precious Moments* bisque figurine in water. Roman, Inc., maker of *Fontanini* figurines, suggests using a damp cloth dipped in clear water. No chemicals should be used on the figurines crafted of a high-density polymer, which is impossible to chip, break or nick. "Just be sure not to store or display the figures near a heat source, such as the top of a hot radiator or register," says Jennifer Wigman, Fontanini Collectors' Club coordinator. "Distortion or other damage could result."

Crystal figurines can be washed with warm water. Let your crystal dry and use a polishing cloth or chamois cloth to return the original sparkle to your piece.

Plates Most plates have their decorations fired on, allowing them to be wiped with a damp cloth or even washed gently by hand in a sink with lukewarm water and mild soap. Unglazed surfaces or hand-painted, unfired plates should never be immersed in water. Dusting is your best bet. If your plate has been hand-signed by the artist, you should also avoid using water.

Make sure that plates are firmly secured on their hangers and that the nails are firmly in place. When displaying plates in high traffic areas, consider having them framed: They'll fare better against the occasional bump or bang.

Dolls To keep your delicate porcelain dolls looking beautiful, lightly dust them, keep them away from direct sunlight, and display them in glass or wooden cases. If a doll's clothing becomes soiled, dry cleaning is the best option unless you know the fabric can be washed without damage or shrinking. Annalee Mobilitee Dolls offers this caveat: If there is any concern that the cleaning may do more harm than good, leave it as it is.

Attempts to restyle wigs can end up in disaster. Instead of brushing or combing, just use your fingers to gently smooth down any out-of-place hairs.

Ornaments Though many collectors only bring out their ornaments at Christmas, more people are displaying them all year. But if you choose to put them away, the safest bet is to store them in their original boxes.

Christopher Radko recommends wrapping ornaments in acid-free paper for the best protection. Ornaments can then be stored in boxes with divided compartments or stackable rubber tray containers lined with bubble wrap. Ornaments should never be stored in an attic or basement where water, humidity or extreme temperatures exist.

Graphics A museum-mounted, framed print is well protected, but it should still be hung out of direct sunlight to avoid fading. Other important rules in preserving your print are to minimize handling and maintain consistent temperatures in your home to prevent the build-up of moisture between the print and glass. Unframed prints should be stored within protective acetate sleeves.

RESTORING YOUR COLLECTIBLES

If the unthinkable happens — breakage or damage — restoration companies can come to the rescue. Often, collectors prefer to have the piece restored rather than accept an insurance company settlement. A qualified restorer can assist with a variety of collectibles and recover 50% to 100% of the item's original issue price. The following list of restorers has been recommended through various sources. Since we have not had the occasion to use the services of the businesses listed, CIB cannot guarantee their workmanship. You can also call a restoration expert in your area.

Even the most severely damaged collectible can be restored to its original beauty by an experienced restoration expert. This figurine was flawlessly repaired by the highly trained restorers at Pick Up the Pieces™.

China & Crystal Clinic
1808 N. Scottsdale Rd.
Tempe, AZ 85281
(800) 658-9197
Specialty: Porcelain and crystal.

T.S. Restoration
2015 N. Dobson Rd., Box 59
(mail address)
2622 N. Dobson Rd.
Chandler, AZ 85224
(602) 963-3148
Specialty: Porcelain.

Crystal World
2743 N. Campbell Ave.
Tuscon, AZ 85719
(520) 326-5990
Specialty: Crystal.

Venerable Classics
645 Fourth St., Suite 208
Santa Rosa, CA 95404
(707) 575-3626
(800) 531-2891
Specialty: Porcelain, ceramic, resin, pottery, glass, crystal, jade, ivory, marble, wood, frames, brass, bronze and pewter.

Brookes Restorations
930 S. Robertson Blvd.
Los Angeles, CA 90035
(310) 659-8253
Fax: (310) 659-8262
Specialty: Porcelain, ceramic, jade, marble, ivory, alabaster, wood, crystal, glass, paintings, soapstone, resin and china.

Geppetto's Restoration
31121 Via Colinas, Suite 1003
Westlake Village, CA 91362
(818) 889-0901
Fax: (818) 889-8922
Specialty: Porcelain, glass, crystal, ivory, jade, marble, ceramics, resin, pottery and wood.

Pick Up The Pieces
315 Newport Center Dr.
Fashion Island
Newport Beach, CA 92660
(714) 720-8183
Specialty: Porcelain, oil paintings and frames, crystal, glass, wood, jade, ivory, bronze, brass, gold, silver, pewter, resin, papier maché, iron, white metal, soapstone and china.

Herbert F. Klug Conservation and Restoration
Box 28002, #16
Denver, CO 80228
(303) 985-9261
Specialty: Porcelain, marble and ivory.

Dean's China & Glass Restoration
131 Elmwood Dr.
Cheshire, CT 06410
(203) 271-3659
(800) 669-1327
Specialty: Pottery, jade, ivory, glass, crystal, ceramic, cold cast, resin, porcelain, marble, plaster, china, bronze, silver, pewter and brass.

Beckus Studios
4511 32nd Avenue North
St. Petersburg, FL 33713
(813) 522-4288
Specialty: Wood, porcelain, metal, ceramic, pottery, ivory, jade, marble, plaster, resin, china and cold cast.

A Fine Touch
5740 Lakefield Court
Orlando, FL 32810
(407) 298-7129
Specialty: Porcelain, ceramic, pottery, clay, china, jade, marble, resin and plaster.

Bea's Ceramic Repair
3870 Capron Dr.
Rockford, IL 61109
(815) 874-8689
Speciality: Plaster, ceramic, marble, porcelain, pottery, china and ivory.

Doe Lasky
Repair and Restoration
Oak Park, IL 60302
(708) 386-1772
Specialty: Porcelain, crystal, bronze, ivory, jade, oriental screens, oil paintings, frames and wood carvings.

Rosine Green Associates, Inc.
89 School St.
Brookline, MA 02146
(617) 277-8368
Specialty: Porcelain, paintings, wood, ceramic, pottery, resin, jade, marble, lacquer, granite, alabaster, glass, soapstone, cold cast, brass, pewter and bronze.

Trefler and Sons
Antique Restoring Studio, Inc.
99 Cabot St.
Needham, MA 02194
(617) 444-2685
Specialty: Crystal, paintings, furniture, silver, resin, glass, pottery, ceramic, wood, ivory, jade and soapstone.

Imperial China
27 North Park Avenue
Rockville Center, NY 11570
(516) 764-7311
Specialty: Porcelain, ceramic, resin.

Restoration Unlimited
3009 W. Genesee St.
Syracuse, NY 13219
(315) 488-7123
Specialty: Porcelain, cold cast, resin, antique dolls, frames, pottery, china, ivory, papier maché, jade and soapstone.

Antique & Hummel Restoration by Wiebold
413 Terrace Place
Terrace Park, OH 45174
(800) 321-2541
Specialty: Porcelain, ceramic, pottery, metal art, glass, oil paintings, frames, crystal, jade, marble, soapstone, alabaster and plaster chalk.

Old World Restorations, Inc.
347 Stanley Avenue
Cincinnati, OH 45226
(513) 321-1911
Specialty: Porcelain, paintings, glass, frames, works on paper, photographs, furniture, metals and on-site architectural restoration such as murals, frescos and gold leaf.

Harry A. Eberhardt & Sons, Inc.
2010 Walnut St.
Philadelphia, PA 19103
(215) 568-4144
Specialty: Porcelain, glass, metal and crystal.

A. Ludwig Klein & Son, Inc.
P.O. Box 145
683 Sumneytown Pike
Harleysville, PA 19438
(215) 256-9004
Specialty: Glass, soapstone, ivory, jade, metal art, crystal, marble, pottery, wood, paintings and porcelain.

Sharon Lewis Restoration & Repairs
8902 Deer Haven Rd.
Austin, TX 78737
(512) 301-2294
Specialty: Porcelain, ceramic, plaster, stoneware, china, pottery, ivory, jade, marble, soapstone and wood.

McHugh's
3117 W. Clay St.
Richmond, VA 23230
(804) 353-9596
Specialty: Crystal, glass, ivory, marble, jade, pottery, soapstone and porcelain.

Artwork Restoration
30 Hillhouse Rd.
Winnipeg, MB R2V 2V9, Canada
(204) 334-7090
Specialty: Crystal, china, glass, marble, pottery, soapstone, ivory, dolls, paintings, wood frames and porcelain.

Kingsmen Antique Restoration Inc.
19 Passmore Avenue, Unit 28
Scarborough, ONT M1V 4T5, Canada
(416) 291-8939
Specialty: Porcelain, bronze, pewter, ivory, pottery, glass, crystal, jade, marble, soapstone, wood, lacquer, papier maché, brass, iron, white metal and oil paintings.

Experts Offer Ideas to Protect Your Investment

It's something most collectors shudder to think about. You're carefully packing away your collection for a move across town when one of the boxes slips out of your hands, and the figurines inside are shattered. A burglar breaks into your house and steals valuable possessions, including pieces from your collection. An earthquake rattles a curio cabinet, knocking over crystal figurines and chipping many of the pieces. A fire engulfs part of your house, causing smoke damage to your fine art prints. Your prized plate collection is neatly lined on a shelf – until your cat walks across the ledge, sending the collectibles crashing to the floor.

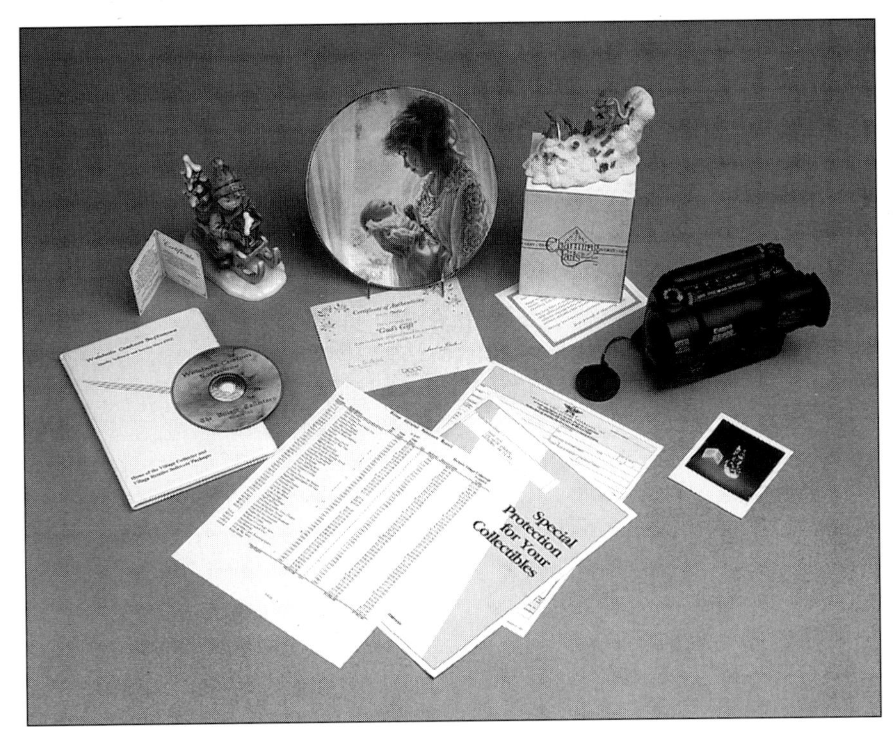

Keeping a visual and written record of your collectibles, as well as having them properly insured, will help protect your investment.

If you're like most collectors, these incidents would break your heart. After all, you have invested lots of time, money and energy into your collection. It would be difficult to put a price tag on those things that are such a highly personal reflection of your life and interests. But while a stolen or damaged collection may never be replaced, there are important steps that collectors can take to minimize their losses.

More and more collectors are finding peace of mind in protecting and insuring their treasures. "If collectors put an emotional and financial investment into acquiring their collection, why leave its security to chance?" asks Jill Bookman, director of marketing for American Collectors Insurance, Inc.

Companies such as American Collectors Insurance offer special policies to protect your collection should the unthinkable happen. With the secondary market continuing to grow in popularity and some pieces appreciating in value over time, collectors have an extra incentive to consider taking out an insurance policy.

"People are beginning to become more aware about insuring their collectibles," says Norman Carl, senior vice president of Laub Group, Inc., which provides collectibles coverage through a program with Atlantic Mutual Insurance Company. "They value their collections and want to take care of their investment."

But experts like Carl and Bookman warn that collectors often have a false sense of security in thinking their collections are adequately covered under their homeowners' insurance policy. "It's the biggest mistake that collectors make," Carl says.

Suggests Bookman: "You need to talk to your agent to find out if your collection is properly covered." Collectors may want to specifically seek a policy for their collectibles. There are basically two types of coverage: blanket and scheduled. "Blanket coverage is much easier because the insurance covers every piece and the overall value of the collection," Carl says.

For example, if a collector has 40 pieces of Swarovski crystal valued at $10,000, the blanket policy would provide protection in a lump sum amount. The items don't need to be listed separately. This coverage is sufficient unless an individual piece is valued at more than $2,000 or $2,500, depending on the policy.

Scheduled coverage is for collectibles of exceptional value that need special protection. Collectors must provide a list of the pieces in a collection and tell the insurer the value. Collectors may also choose a combination of blanket and scheduled coverages.

So what can collectors expect to pay for insuring their collectibles? Atlantic Mutual Insurance Company has a minimum annual premium of $75.00 for a $10,000 collection. Other rates through the company vary slightly by state and the value of the collection. For example, the annual premium for a $20,000 collection in Illinois costs $110, while a collection of the same value for a Florida or Missouri resident costs $96.00. There is no deductible for the policy.

American Collectors Insurance also offers a $75.00 minimum annual premium for a collection valued at $10,000. A $12,000 collection would carry a $90.00 premium. There is a $100 deductible per occurrence.

To properly insure and protect your collectibles, consider the following advice from insurance experts.

1. Keep all receipts. Collectors should make sure they get a receipt for each piece acquired, whether from a store, friend or on the secondary market. Check that the receipt accurately identifies the item purchased and the price paid.

2. Record crucial information. Whether you write it down on a piece of paper or type it into a computer document, keep crucial information on each piece and make copies of these materials, too. This documentation should include:

- Item name, number and description
- Name of manufacturer
- Year of issue
- Artist's name
- Limited edition number
- Series name or number
- Special markings
- Purchase price
- Place of purchase
- Date of purchase
- Any other relevant information

3. Make a visual record of your collection. "The single best record is to videotape the collection because you cannot only see the collectibles, but you can record a narrative, too," Carl says. He recommends updating the videotape about twice a year, or as needed, when more pieces are added to a collection. Bookman also suggests taking photographs of the pieces. If a piece is signed, a photo should also be taken of the autograph or other significant markings.

4. Keep all records off site. Make sure that all your documentation – receipts, item information, photographs, videotapes or Certificates of Authenticity – are stored safely in a location away from your collection. Experts recommend placing these records in a safety deposit box.

5. Read your policy carefully. Many collectors find out too late that their treasured belongings are uninsured or underinsured. Take the time to review your homeowners' insurance policy, and read the fine print to make sure your collectibles would be adequately covered in case of an emergency. Check if the insured items are covered for their value at the time of purchase or covered for the amount that it would take to replace them at the time you make a claim. In light of the fact that some collectibles increase in value over time, you probably want a "replacement value" policy.

6. Investigate insurance companies and coverage. "It's very important to deal with a company that is reputable and pays its claims promptly and fairly," Carl says. "If you lost some collectibles, you are going to be very upset. It will be a personal loss. The last thing you want is any hassles." Be sure you discuss all your special concerns with your insurance agent to make sure you have the coverage and sense of comfort that you need. Ask important questions such as:

- Is it an "all risk" policy – meaning earthquakes, floods and other natural disasters are covered.
- Is there a deductible? If so, what is it?
- Does the policy cover breakage and what constitutes breakage?
- Are the items covered if taken off the premises?

7. Regularly update policy information. If your collection appreciates to a higher value or you acquire new additions, it is important to update your policy. Review your policy at least once a year or whenever your collection experiences a drastic change in price. Bookman says American Collectors Insurance provides automatic 30-day coverage under an existing policy for your additional collectible purchase. "But then collectors still need to notify us to amend their policy," Bookman says.

8. Refer to the *Collectibles Market Guide & Price Index.* Whether you're determining the value of your collection for an insurance policy, assessing a loss or updating your coverage, turn to this respected reference guide published by the Collectors' Information Bureau. It is recognized by insurers as one of the most reliable and credible sources. Carl also recommends updating your personal list of collectibles each year with new secondary market prices. "Utilize the *Collectibles Market Guide & Price Index* and use the upper range of prices to insure your collections," Carl notes.

9. Care for your collection. Perhaps the easiest way to keep your collection safe and sound is to take proper care of your collectibles. Display your treasured figurines, plates, prints or other pieces in curio cabinets, firmly secured frames and hangers, enclosed cases or away from the edges of tables or shelves. Tender loving care could be your best insurance.

To learn more, contact your insurance agent or these experts who contributed to the writing of this article:

Laub Group, Inc.
Norman Carl
1701 Golf Rd., Suite 600
Rolling Meadows, IL 60008
(888) 707-4600
Fax: (847) 952-9235
URL: http://www.laubgroup.com

American Collectors Insurance, Inc.
Jill Bookman
P.O. Box 8343
498 Kings Highway North
Cherry Hill, NJ 08002
(800) 360-2277
Fax: (609) 779-7289
URL: http://www.americancollectorsins.com

Capturing life in exquisite detail...

Capturing life in exquisite, romantic detail is the specialty of a myriad of collectibles artists, including Giuseppe Armani. This breathtaking piece, titled "Artemis," is a limited edition from the *Florentine Gardens* collection. It reflects the timeless art of translating the grace and beauty of life into treasures that will endure for generations to come.

Special moments throughout our lives...

TOP ROW: "Tucked In" and "Cuddling Up" from Porterfield's; "Once in a Blue Moon" from Fool Moon Treasures' *Home Spun Goodness* series; "United States Fat Cat" from *International Fat Cats* by Islandia International; "Blue Monday" from the *Sass 'n Class* collection from Sandy Dolls.
MIDDLE ROW: The San Francisco Music Box Company's *Heart Tugs* "Pie Safe;" "Ricky" and "Cynthia," from Jan Hagara Collectables' *Georgetown* series and "Emily" from Jan Hagara Collectables' *Make-Believe* series; "75th Anniversary Wendy" from The Alexander Doll Company.
BOTTOM ROW: Islandia International's "Vietnam Veteran Memorial Plate;" "Time Out" from Porterfield's, and *Trevor's Farm Friends'* "Rollie the Rooster" from Islandia International.

...captured in collectibles that cross many media.

TOP ROW: "Snow White Collector Film Cel" from Willitts' *Disney Showcase Collection*; Jan Hagara Collectables' "Kayla" from the *Make Believe* series; Fool Moon Treasures' "Eleanor the Fairy Bearmother" from the *Oh So Wonderful* collection; and "Cinderella Collector Film Cel" from Willitts Designs.

MIDDLE ROW: *American Treasures* "Hop Toad" from The San Francisco Music Box Company; Islandia's "International Fat Cat Vase;" "U.S. Shelly," "Russia," and "Great Britain" from Sunbelt Marketing's *The Contour Collection – Folk Art Series.*

BOTTOM ROW: David Winter Cottages' "Marquis Walter;" The San Francisco Music Box Company's "Lion Family;" and David Winter Cottages' "Tickled Trout."

Colorful collectibles from many cultures...

TOP ROW: "Philadelphia Toboggan Company - Armored" from The San Francisco Music Box Company; "William" from Sandy Dolls' *Santa Collection*; and Willitts Designs' "Armored Lead Horse" from *Carousel Memories.*
BOTTOM ROW: "Santa with Long Robe," "White Buffalo" and "Angel" from Christian Ulbricht USA.

...help us share traditions that span time and miles.

TOP ROW: "Morocco" from *The Contour Collection - Folk Art Series* from Sunbelt Marketing; "The Comforter" from Willitts Designs' *Ebony Visions Collection*; and Sandy Dolls' "Little Sala" from *Sweet Spirit Baby Collection.*
BOTTOM ROW: "Cissy Barcelona" and "Coppertone Beach Set" from The Alexander Doll Company; and Sandy Dolls' "Musical Dianna" from *The Angelic Collection.*

The many faces of Santa...

The many faces of Santa grace collectibles that have become favorites enjoyed year 'round.

TOP ROW: Midwest of Cannon Falls' "1997 Santa Holding Deer" from *the Eddie Walker Collection*, Possible Dreams' "Crinkle Locomotive" and "Coal Car," Prizm's "Better Watch Out Santa" from *Pipka's Reflections of Christmas* and "Starcoat Santa" ornament from *Pipka's Stories of Christmas*.

MIDDLE ROW: Midwest of Cannon Falls' "Snow King" from the *Leo R. Smith III Folk Art Collection*, Royal Copenhagen's *1997 Annual Christmas Plate* titled "Santa in Russia," and Prizm's "Norwegian Julenisse" from *Pipka's Memories of Christmas*.

BOTTOM ROW: House of Hatten's "Ye Olde Santa Maker," Kurt S. Adler, Inc.'s "Marek, The Royal Guardsman" from the Steinbach Collector's Club, and WACO's *Melody in Motion* "1996 Santa."

...bring smiles all year 'round

Santa and friends come to town and spring to life in treasures that are destined to become the heirlooms of tomorrow.

TOP ROW: Christopher Radko's "Rooftop Mickey," "Busy Man's Pause" from Cavanagh's *Coca-Cola Heritage Collection*, ANRI U.S.' "Time to Go" from the *Christmas Eve Series*, Dave Grossman Creations' "Night Before Christmas" from *Bill Bell's Santas*, and Kurt S. Adler Inc.'s "Grandfather Frost Ornament" from the Polonaise Collector's Guild.

MIDDLE ROW: Lenox Collection's "Santa's Joy," United Design's "Wilderness Santa" from the *Legends of Santa Claus* series, and House of Hatten's "Santa's Kingdom."

BOTTOM ROW: United Design's "Bells of Christmas Morn" from the *Legends of Santa Claus* series, House of Hatten's "SnowMa'am," and Byers' Choice's "Santa Feeding Reindeer" from the *Santas* series.

Holiday favorites...

Holiday favorites need not be tucked away when the New Year rings in. Collectibles can help you revel in the Christmas spirit 365 days a year.
TOP ROW: Christopher Radko's "Sugar Hill" 3-pc. set and "The Cat in the Hat Wreath."
MIDDLE ROW: "Snowy Ride" from Walnut Ridge Collectibles, "Ride into Christmas" from M.I. Hummel Club, Lilliput Lane's "Going to Grandmother's House" from the *Christmas in America* series, Hawthorne Village's "Winter Memories" from *Thomas Kinkade's Home for the Holidays* series, and Band Creations' "Tuxedos in the Snow."
BOTTOM ROW: "Eagle Stocking Holder" from *Harley Davidson Collectibles by Cavanagh*, Walnut Ridge Collectibles' "Large Snowman," Christina's World's "Tulips on a Clear Day" from the *Garden of Eden* series, "Enchanted Tree" from the *Holiday Trees* series, and "Midnight Mardi Gras" from *Mardi Gras Masks*.

...trim your home with memories

Winter images are transformed into collectibles that warm our hearts with memories of days gone by and promises of happy memories to come.
TOP ROW: ANRI U.S.'s "Christmas Puppy" from *Sarah Kay's First Christmas*, Shelia's Inc.'s "Barnum's Animal Crackers" ornament, Lenox Collection's "Painting Stripes" from the *Finishing Touches* series, Charming Tails' "All the Trimmings," and Annalee Mobilitee Doll's "Sledding Mouse."
MIDDLE ROW: "McDonald's Restaurant" from *McDonald's Collectibles by Cavanagh*, "Roskilde Cathedral" from Royal Copenhagen's *1997 Annual Christmas Plate* series, Department 56's "The Melancholy Tavern (Revisited)" and "Chelsea Lane Shoppers" from *The Dickens' Village*.
BOTTOM ROW: Department 56's "Grand Central Railway" and "City Taxi" from *The Christmas in the City* series, and George Z. Lefton Co.'s "Montrose Manor."

Angels come in all shapes and sizes...

Angels of all shapes and sizes bring joy to collectors everywhere. From playful to spiritual, these symbols of peace are a favorite among collectors of all ages.

TOP ROW: Margaret Furlong's "Charity Angel" and "Iris Angel," "Angel" from *Cottage Collectibles* by Ganz, and Margaret Furlong's "Dogwood Angel" and "Viola Angel."

MIDDLE ROW: Cast Art Industries' "Making Memories" from the *Dreamsicles Heavenly Classics Collection*, Possible Dreams' "Blissful Ballet," and Cast Art Industries' *Dreamsicles Annual Christmas Limited Edition* "Homeward Bound."

BOTTOM ROW: United Design's *Angel Collection* "The Gift '97," Prizm's "Guardian Angel" from *Pipka's Earth Angels*, and United Design's "Spirit of Winter" from the *Angel Collection*.

...from chubby cherubs to graceful guardians

From chubby cherubs to graceful guardian angels, collectibles manufacturers have presented a wide variety of angels to watch over collectors.
TOP ROW: Cast Art Industries' *Dreamsicles* "Hear No Evil," "See No Evil" and "Speak No Evil," and Roman Inc.'s "Heaven's Treasure" from the *Seraphim Collection.*
MIDDLE ROW: Reco International's "Heavenly Hideaway" from *Sandra Kuck's Garden of Innocence*, Our Secret's "Big Bear Up There" from the *Thread Bear Collection*, and Walnut Ridge Collectibles' "Alexandra Angel."
BOTTOM ROW: Precious Art's "The Awakening" from the *Inspirations* series, Annalee Mobilitee Dolls' "'Angelica' Tree Topper" and Roman's Ariel – "Heaven's Shining Star" from the *Seraphim Collection.*

Historical sites take shape...

Historical sites take shape as architectural collectibles fashioned from a wide variety of materials. These finely detailed treasures remind us of places we've known and places we'd love to visit.

TOP ROW: Ertl Collectibles' "Round Barn" from the *American Country Barn* series, Band Creations' "Bridgeton Covered Bridge, Park City" from *America's Covered Bridges*, and Harbour Lights' "Nobska, MA."

MIDDLE ROW: Harbour Lights' "Grays Harbor, WA," Shelia's Inc.'s "Glen Auburn" from the *Historical Bed and Breakfast* series, and "Carson Mansion" from *California Mansions.*

BOTTOM ROW: Hazle Ceramics' "Corner Shop," "Chocolate Shop," "Antiques," "The Florist," and "The King's Head" from *A Nation of Shopkeepers*, and Band Creations' "Wind Beneath My Wings" from *America's Weather Vanes Collection.*

...in collectibles that illuminate our spirits

Lighthouses have stood for centuries as beacons in the night, there to guide us through rough waters and safely lead us home. Collectibles that commemorate these centuries-old sentinels bring a sense of history and security into our homes.

TOP ROW: Harbour Lights' "Navesink, NJ" and "New London Ledge, CT" from the *Great Lighthouses of the World* collection.

MIDDLE ROW: FJ Designs' "Matenicus Park Lighthouse" from *The Cat's Meow Village-Women Lightkeepers* series, Gift Star's "Chesapeake Lighthouse," and Shelia's Inc.'s "Portland Head Light" from *Panoramic Lights*.

BOTTOM ROW: Forma Vitrum's "West Quoddy Light" from the *Coastal Heritage* series, Dave Grossman Creations' "Holland Light" from the *Spencer Collin Lighthouses*, and George Z. Lefton Co.'s "Thomas Point Shoal" from the *Historic American Lighthouses* series.

From the Big Top and cozy get-aways...

From the Big Top to a cozy country cottage, architectural collectibles capture the fun and comfort we find within four walls.
TOP ROW: FJ Designs' *The Cat's Meow Village* "Big Top" from the *Circus Series* and "Burnside Bridge" from the *Civil War Collection*, Lilliput Lane's "Halcyon Days" from the *English Collection.*
MIDDLE ROW: Brandywine Woodcrafts' "Quilts & Things" and "Noah's Zoo" from the *Country Lane V* series, and "Hook and Ladder" from the *Hometown XIV* series.
BOTTOM ROW: Forma Vitrum's "Bavarian Lodge" from the *Bed and Breakfast* series, and "Klaus' Clock Shoppe" from *Vitreville.*

...to painted ladies and candy-colored cottages

Painted ladies and candy-colored cottages have dotted the landscape of our cities and countryside, creating a uniquely American tableau.
TOP ROW: Hawthorne Village's "Budzen's Roadside Stand" from *Charles Wysocki's Peppercricket Grove Collection* and "The Lace Tea Room" from *Corrine Layton's Victoriana*, Lilliput Lane's "Oh By Gosh, By Golly" from *Coca-Cola Country* and "Tailor" from *The Victorian Shops Collection*.
MIDDLE ROW: GiftStar's "Colonial Merchant," "Conch House," and "Carpenter's Gothic" from Brian Baker's *Déjà Vu Collection*.
BOTTOM ROW: Pacific Rim Import's "Somerset Cathedral" from the *Bristol Township Collection*, and "Rosita's Cantina" and "On the Road Again" from Department 56's *Original Snow Village*.

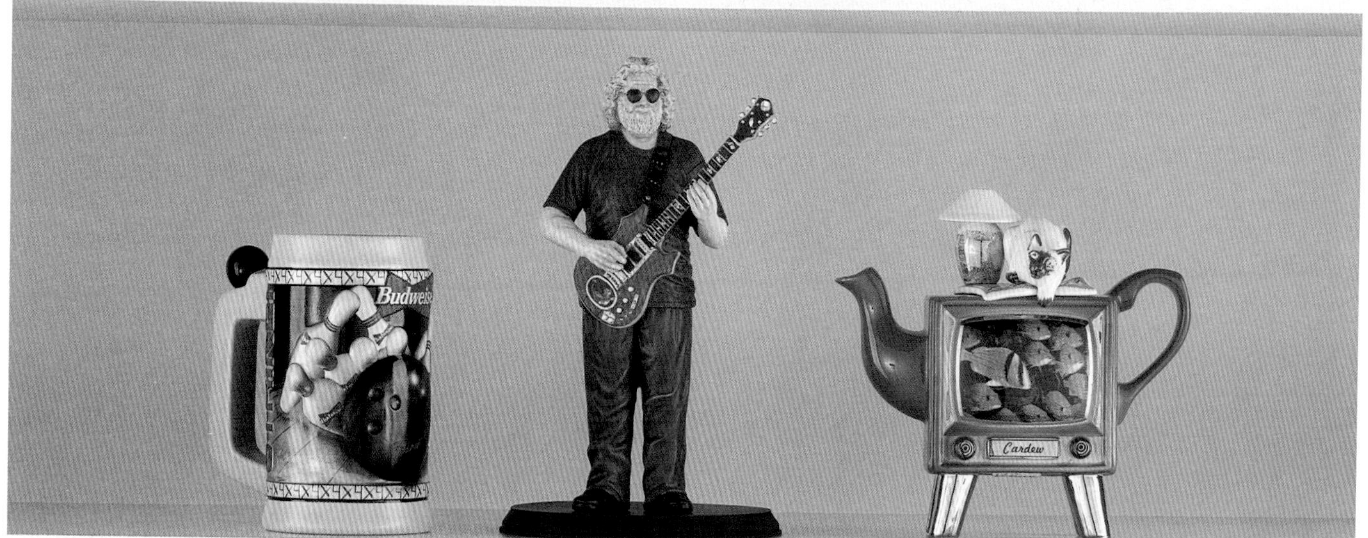

Popular culture pops up in collectibles...

Images from popular culture throughout the decades are translated into plates, figurines, steins and ornaments that keep memories of childhood close at hand.

TOP ROW: Carlton Cards' "Perfect Present" (Nancy and Sluggo), "All Set for Santa" (Lassie), "Baked with Love" (Pillsbury Doughboy), and "Come Back Here" (Tom and Jerry), and Ertl Collectibles' "Pawnee Bill Circus Wagon" from the *Circus World – Museum Collection.*

MIDDLE ROW: Anheuser-Busch's "Bud Bowling Stein," Gartlan USA's "Jerry & Tiger" from the *Jerry Garcia Collection*, and Cardew Design's "Television" from the *Two Cup* series.

BOTTOM ROW: Gartlan USA's "Kiss This!" and "Kiss Kommerative Baseball" from the *Kiss Kollection*, and "Ringo Starr" from the *All Starr Collection.*

...that remind us of silver screen favorites

Favorite characters from stage and screen find new life in collectibles that touch our hearts and tickle our funny bones.
TOP ROW: Dave Grossman Creations' "Emerald City Scene" from *The Wizard of Oz*, Arcadian Pewter's "Tractor" and "A-Express Truck" from the *Arcade Toys* collection, and Flambro Imports' "Peanuts Pen and Base Set" from the *Peanuts* collection.
MIDDLE ROW: "Charles Carmel" from *the Great American Carousel* series by George Z. Lefton Co., Dave Grossman Creations' "The Kiss" from the *Gone with the Wind* series, and Anheuser-Busch's "Play Ball!" Baseball Stein from the *Sports Action Series*.
BOTTOM ROW: Anheuser-Busch's "Bud Ice Penguin," Hudson Creek's "Simply Minnie" from the *Mickey and Company* collection, and WACO's "I Love Lucy – Vitameatavegamin" from the *Melody in Motion* series.

Colorful characters come to life...

Colorful characters come to life in exciting figurines from leaders in the collectibles field.

TOP ROW: Duncan Royale's "Anne Bonny" from the *History of Pirates & Buccaneers* collection, Chilmark's "The Cornfield" from *Antietam: The Bloodiest Day*, Arcadian Pewter's "Fire Ladder Truck" from the *Arcade Toys* collection, and Duncan Royale's "Peg Leg Pete" from the *History of Pirates & Buccaneers* collection.

BOTTOM ROW: Duncan Royale's "Black Beard" from the *History of Pirates & Buccaneers* collection, Royal Doulton's "King Arthur" and "Sir Henry," and Annalee Mobilitee Dolls' "Medicine Man (10 inch)."

...while men are depicted in their many roles

As more men join the ranks of collectors, male collectibles make a stand thanks to the growing number of pieces that portray men at work, at play, and in their many roles as father, protector and friend.

TOP ROW: KVK/Daddy's Long Legs' "Wildwood Will" from the *Old West* collection, "Tuskegee Airman II" from the *Black Heritage/Historical* series by Sarah's Attic, Character Collectibles' "Hero" from the *Red Hats of Courage* series, and Roman's "The Winning Shot" from *Declan's Finnians.*

BOTTOM ROW: Possible Dreams' "Maasai Warrior," and Duncan Royale's "Deigo" from the *History of Pirates and Buccaneers* collection.

Collectibles of color capture our hearts...

Pretty and playful girls grow up to become beautiful women and are captured in a wide variety of figurines and dolls.

TOP ROW: Miss Martha Originals' "Janae," KVK/Daddy's Long Legs' "Sugar-Convention Edition" from the *Clowns* series, and Miss Martha Originals' "Alaysha."

BOTTOM ROW: Dear Artistic Sculpture's "Lady with Dog," and Giuseppe Armani's "Whitney" from the *Via Veneto* collection.

...and mark special moments in our lives

From skipping rope and saying "I do" to sitting by the fire and sewing, the simplest and most significant moments of a woman's life are chronicled in collectibles.

TOP ROW: Pacific Rim Imports' "Jen, Bess & Ann Skip Rope" from *When Grandma Was A Girl*, and Miss Martha Originals' "Tangie" and "Robert."

BOTTOM ROW: "Willie and Tillie" print from the *Sarah's Gang* series by Sarah's Attic, and "Lovie" from KVK/Daddy's Long Legs' *Old Woman Who Lived In A Shoe* series.

Inspired by fertile imaginations...

Inspired by fertile imaginations, these colorful and clever creations take us to the magical places where dreams are made.

TOP ROW: Shenandoah Designs' "Keeper of the Cats," Mr. Sandman's "Azurine" from the *Zanandia Collection*, Hudson Creek's "Sirena" from the *SeaMyst Mermaids* collection, and Mr. Sandman's "Dragon with Egg" from the *Metallia Collection*.

BOTTOM ROW: Precious Art's "Rueggan's Workshop" and "Storyteller" from the *World of Krystonia*, Kurt S. Adler Inc.'s "The Wish Workshop" from the *Angel Heights* series, Flambro Imports' *Pocket Dragons* "Jaunty," Possible Dreams' "Bath Time," and Annalee Mobilitee Dolls' "Spellbinder (18 inch)."

From sweet to sophisticated...

From sweet to sophisticated, these charmers will steal the hearts of collectors for years to come.

TOP ROW: Ladie & Friends' "Edwina High," Flambro Imports' "Prunella" from the *Willow Hall English Collection*, Hudson Creek's *Tillie the Frog* "Tillie's New Hat," Band Creations' "Madame Sassafras" from *Coffee, Tea, My Friends & Me*, and Enesco's "Love Sealed with a Kiss" from the *Pretty As A Picture* collection.

BOTTOM ROW: The Ashton-Drake Galleries' "Gene As Sparkling Seduction," Seymour Mann's "Briana" from the *Signature* series, and "Shadow" from the *Enchantment* series.

Beautiful babies...

Beautiful babies make sweet treasures for collectors of all ages.

TOP ROW: Lee Middleton's "Honey Love – Awake" from the *Afternoon Nap-Girl* series, The Ashton-Drake Galleries' "Just Hatched" from the *Where Do Babies Come From?* series, and Lee Middleton's "First Born" from the *Wee One* series.

BOTTOM ROW: Lee Middleton's "First Born – Awake" from the *My Own Baby* series, Seymour Mann's "Sleepy Scott & Bashful Becky" from the *Signature Series*, The Ashton-Drake Galleries' "Cinderella" from *Deval's Fairy Tale Princesses*, and Lee Middleton's "Honey Love – Awake" from the *Afternoon Nap-Boy* series.

...and cuddly playmates

Cuddly playmates rekindle sweet childhood memories of favorite dolls, bears and plush animals that were our first friends.

TOP ROW: "Slugger" from *Cottage Collectibles* by Ganz, Our Secret's *Thread Bear* "Ambear Bruin," and Ertl Collectibles' "Le Mutt – Black Tie."

BOTTOM ROW: Original Appalachian Artwork's "Kasi Michelle" from the *Cabbage Patch Kids 1997 Sautee Valley Festival 'Kids* and "Hayley," the *1997 Babyland Convention Baby*, and Kurt S. Adler Inc.'s "Fremont" from the *Holly Bearies* collection.

Everything's coming up collectible...

Everything's coming up collectible in a fun-filled garden that is blossoming with all types of treasures.

TOP ROW: Character Collectibles' "Water, Water Everyhare" from *Hippity Hollow*, Harmony Kingdom's "Hyacinth" from *Lord Byron's Harmony Garden*, Ertl Collectibles' "Get One for Me" from *Lowell Davis America* series, and Character Collectibles' "Count Your Blessings" from the *Mooseberry Farms* collection.

MIDDLE ROW: Original Appalachian Artworks' "Robert London" from the *Cabbage Patch Kids Collector's Club, eggspressions! inc.'s* "Silk Treasures," Reco International's "Emma" from *Sandra Kuck's Romantic Garden, eggspressions!* "Love in Flight," and Fenton Art Glass Company's "Rubina Verde Reverse Melon Vase" from the *1997 Historic Collection.*

BOTTOM ROW: House of Hatten's "Master Gardener," Byers' Choice *Cries of London* "Milk Maid," and Our Secret's "Eujean Lopfield" from the *Little Lops Collection.*

...for special occasions throughout the year

Special occasions throughout the year provide the inspiration for a bevy of collectibles that add color to our lives and smiles to our faces.

TOP ROW: Reco International's "Angel & Alex" from *Laughables*, Pacific Rim Imports' *Bunny Toes* "The Birthday Party," and Charming Tails' "Turkey Traveller."

MIDDLE ROW: Shenandoah Designs' "Keeper of Halloween" from the *Keepers* collection, Midwest of Cannon Falls' "Drearydale Manor" from the *Creepy Hollow* collection, ANRI U.S.'s "Daddy's Big Boy," and WACO's "Side Street Circus/Balancing Dog" from the *Melody in Motion* collection.

BOTTOM ROW: Shenandoah Designs' "Zeus" from the *Limbies* collection, ANRI U.S.'s "Lily Cross" from the *Lyndon Gaither Crosses* series, Midwest of Cannon Falls' "Uncle Sam Nutcracker" from the *Erzgebirge Ore Mountain Collection*, Enesco's *Precious Moments* "You're Just Too Sweet To Be Scary," and Pacific Rim Imports' "Timothy and Tillie Give Thanks" from the *Bunny Toes* collection.

Children take center stage...

Children take center stage in collectibles that recreate the charm and carefree quality of their lives.
TOP ROW: Lladró's "Ready to Roll," Reco International's "Swing for Two" from *Sandra Kuck's Treasures*, M.I. Hummel Club's "Auf Wiedersehen," and Ladie & Friends' "Olivia High."
MIDDLE ROW: "Fond Goodbye" from the *M.I. Hummel Century Collection*, Royal Doulton's "Puppy Love" from the *Age of Innocence*, and "Bath Time" from Bing & Grondahl's *Annual Children's Day* series.
BOTTOM ROW: Ladie & Friends' "Maisie Bowman," Lladró's "Joy of Life," and Ladie & Friends' "Lottie Bowman."

...while elegant collectibles take our breath away

Elegantly detailed and exquisitely designed collectibles range from the practical to the fanciful.

TOP ROW: Fabergé Collection's "Small Gatchina Porcelain Egg," *eggspressions! inc.'s* "Silk Treasures" and "Heaven and Nature Sings," Fabergé Collection's "Pine Cone Crystal Egg" and "Rose Trellis Porcelain Egg."

MIDDLE ROW: Cardew Design's "The Globe" from *Cardew Classics, eggspressions! inc.'s* "July Treasure Box," Fabergé Collection's "Basket of Lilies Crystal Egg," and Cardew Design's "Blue Willow Tea Table" from the *Two Cup* series.

BOTTOM ROW: The Fenton Art Glass Company's "Rubina Verde Reverse Melon Vase" from the *1997 Historic Collection*, Royal Doulton's "Henley" from the *British Sporting Heritage* collection, The Fenton Art Glass Company's "Topaz Vase with Hydrangeas" from the *1997 Historic Collection* and "Opaline Vase with Floral Decorations" from the *1997 Connoisseur Collection.*

Animal attractions are hard to resist...

Animal attractions are hard to resist when they are as adorable as these charmers from leading collectibles companies.
TOP ROW: Harmony Kingdom's "Friends in High Places" from the *Treasure Jest* collection, Charming Tails' "Life's a Picnic with You," Harmony Kingdom's "Rumble Seat" from the *Treasure Jest* collection, and Charming Tails' "You Couldn't Be Sweeter."
MIDDLE ROW: Character Collectibles' "Water, Water Everyhare" from *Hippity Hollow*, Byers' Choice *Accessories*' "Dog with Lollipop," The Greenwich Workshop's "...a fool and his bunny" and "...bedtime bunnies."
BOTTOM ROW: Shenandoah Designs' "Leaper Went A-Courtin'" from the *Leapers* collection, and Enesco's "Strike Up the Band & Give 5 Cherished Teddies Years a Hand" from the *Cherished Teddies* collection.

...with collectible creatures great and small

Creatures great and small find a permanent place in collectors' hearts.
TOP ROW: The Greenwich Workshop's "Three Blind Mice – Sniffer, Fluffy, and Weevil," and Character Collectibles' "Supper for the Puppers" from the *Barkley Crossing* collection.
MIDDLE ROW: Ganz' "Splish, Splash" from *Cottage Collectibles* by Ganz, Our Secret's *Little Lops* "Lacy Lopper," and Cast Art Industries' "Trunkful of Love" from the *Dreamsicles Elephants* series.
BOTTOM ROW: Mr. Sandman's "Orca Whale – Mother & Baby" from the *Future of the Sea* series, Dear Artistic Sculpture's "Bison," and Maruri's "Robin with Blackberry" from the *Songbird Serenade* collection.

Picture-perfect collectibles...

Artwork that doubles as home décor elements make these treasures especially valued.
TOP ROW: The Art of Glynda Turley's "Wreath of Spring" and "Chrysanthemums and Apples" from the *Meaningful Harvest* series.
BOTTOM ROW: The Art of Glynda Turley's "Keeping Watch," Lladró's "Breathless," and The Fenton Art Glass Company's "Rubina Verde Reverse Melon Vase" from the *1997 Historic Collection.*

...do double duty at home

Collectibles do double duty as striking elements of a home that reflects your personal taste.
TOP ROW: The Art of Glynda Turley's "Old Mill IV" from the *Old Mill Stream* series, and Media Arts Group's "End of a Perfect Day" from *Thomas Kinkade's Inspirational Collection.*
BOTTOM ROW: The Fenton Art Glass Company's "Opaline Vase with Floral Decoration" from the *1997 Connoisseur Collection* and "Topaz Vase with Hydrangeas" from the *1997 Historic Collection*, and Media Arts Group's "Beside Still Waters" from *Thomas Kinkade's Inspirational Collection.*

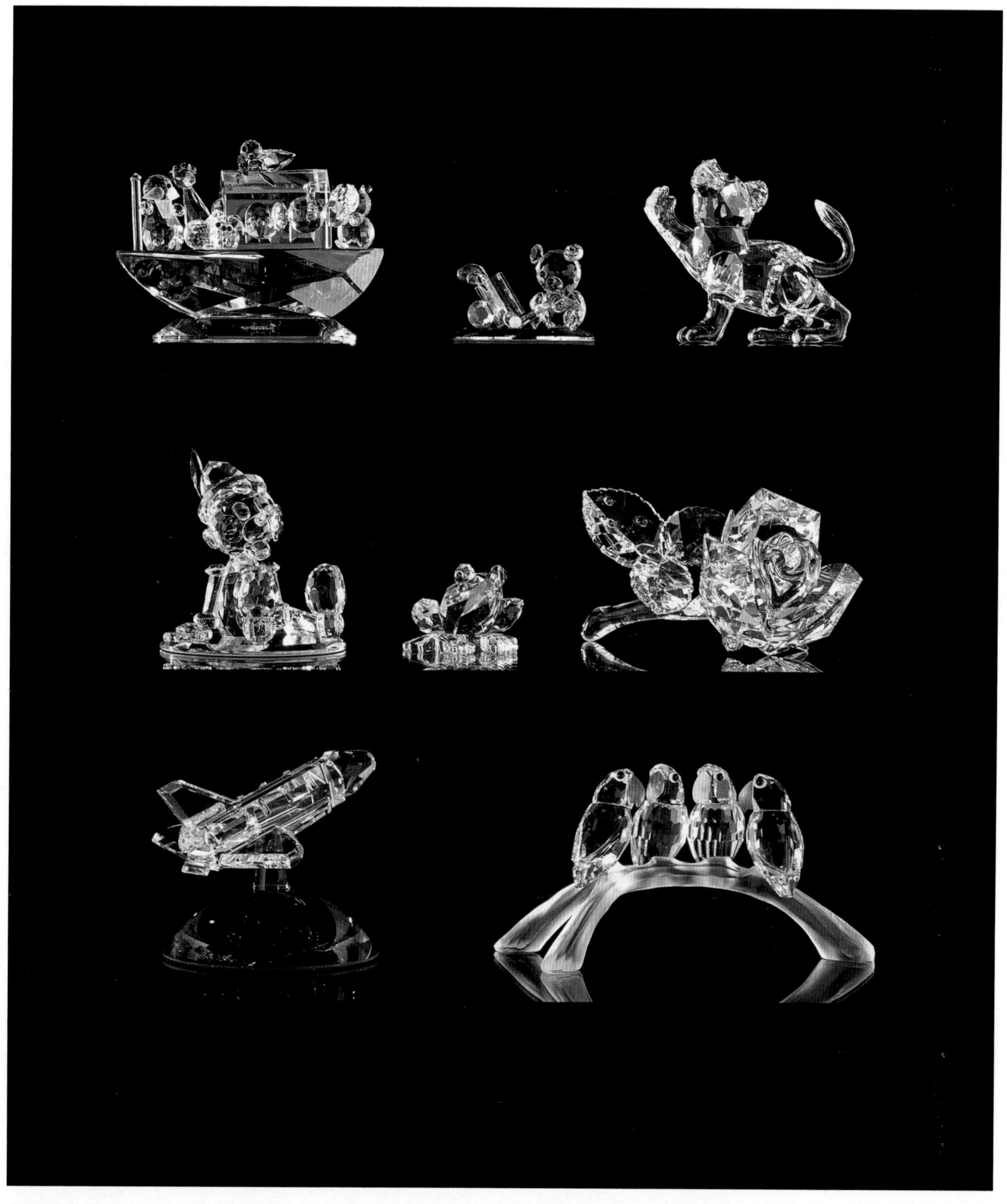

Shining examples of crystal craftsmanship...

Shining examples of craftsmanship are found in a wide assortment of crystal collectibles.
TOP ROW: Crystal World's "Noah & Friends" from the *Imagination* series and "Tee-Shot Teddy" from the *Teddy Land* collection, Swarovski's "Lion Cub" from the *African Wildlife* series.
MIDDLE ROW: Crystal World's "Pinocchio" from the *Imagination* series, and Swarovski's "Frog" from *Beauties of the Lake* and "The Rose" from the *Exquisite Accents* series.
BOTTOM ROW: Crystal World's "Orbiting Space Shuttle" from the *Bon Voyage* collection, and Swarovski's "Baby Lovebirds" from the *Feathered Friends* collection.

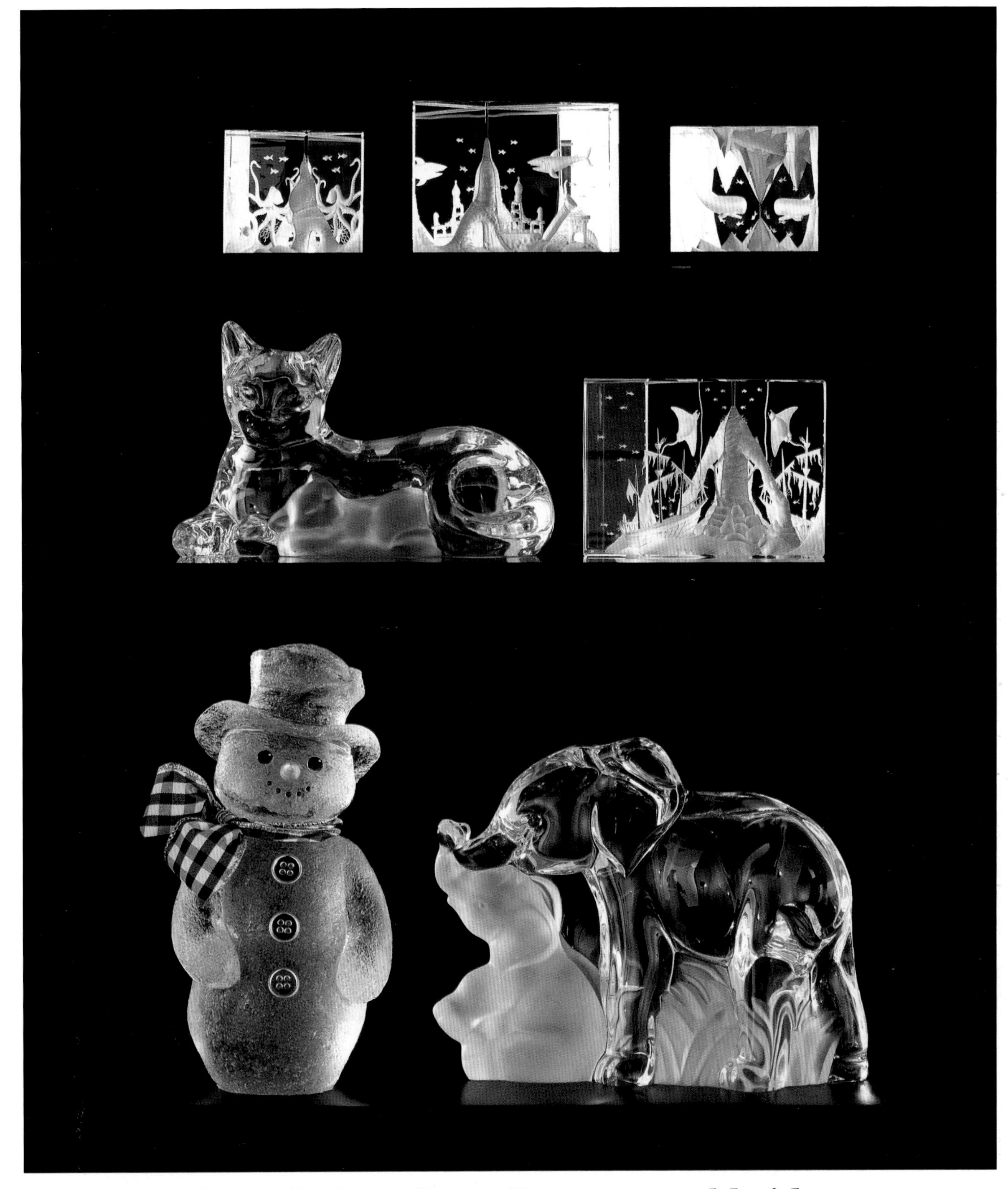

...are the clear choices for collectors worldwide

Crystal clear choices are available to collectors who choose these clearly beautiful works of art.
TOP ROW: Goebel of North America's "Octopus," "Atlantis" and "Whale" from the *Under the Sea* collection.
MIDDLE ROW: Lenox Collection's "Warm and Cozy" from the *Cats* series, and Goebel of North America's "Galleon" from the *Under the Sea* collection.
BOTTOM ROW: "Chilly" from the *Forever Ice Sculptures* by Sarah's Attic, and Lenox Collection's "Touch of Love" from the *Elephants* series.

Decorating with collectibles...

Decorating with collectibles has long been one of the added benefits of the hobby. From graphics and figurines, to plates and ornaments, years of enjoyment can be derived by surrounding yourself with some of your favorite things.

TOP ROW: "Flute Interlude" and "French Horn Melody" from Imperial Graphics' *Celestial Symphony* series.

SECOND ROW: "Potted Pansies" and "Potted Petunias" from Imperial Graphics, Ltd.

BOTTOM SHELF: Fabergé Collection's "Basket of Lilies Crystal Egg" and "Pine Cone Crystal Egg;" Lladró's "Joy of Life," Fabergé Collection's "Small Gatchina Porcelain Egg" and "Rose Trellis Porcelain Egg," and Reco International's "Emma" from *Sandra Kuck's Romantic Garden* series.

Madame Alexander's® Diamond Jubilee Anniversary

As a child, Madame Beatrice Alexander Behrman lived in an apartment over the New York City doll hospital her Russian immigrant father founded in 1895. This was the first such facility in America – where beloved dolls could be lovingly mended for their proud owners. Young Beatrice and her three sisters often played with the doll "patients," fueling her desire to create her own line of dolls.

When World War I prevented importation of dolls from Germany, Madame Alexander filled the gap by producing unbreakable cloth dolls and selling them in her father's shop. These dolls were based on characters from literary classics and poems. With the assistance of her sisters, Madame Alexander added three-dimensional features and realistic clothing.

With a $5,000 loan in 1923, Madame Alexander moved her base of operations from the family kitchen table to a small shop nearby. At this time, her husband of 11 years, Philip Behrman, joined her in her efforts. Thus began The Alexander Doll Company and its long-standing tradition of handcrafted, high-quality dolls.

Three-quarters of a century later in 1998, The Alexander Doll Company celebrated its Diamond Jubilee Anniversary as the only remaining major manufacturer in the United States creating dolls of such quality by hand. The company's operation is located in Harlem, New York City. Madame Alexander, who died in 1990, still is renowned as the First Lady of Dolls and her tradition of excellence lives on.

Madame Alexander infused a sense of excitement and wonderment in her fine quality, handcrafted dolls. She initiated a series of "firsts" in the toy industry: the first doll based on a licensed character (Scarlett from *Gone With the Wind™*), which led to the creation of dolls based on characters from popular motion pictures; the first to bring feature baby dolls to market; and the first to create dolls in honor of living people (Queen Elizabeth and the Dionne Quintuplets). Madame Alexander also was the first to introduce a full-figured fashion doll ("Cissy™") with haute couture outfits.

MADAME ALEXANDER CREATES DOLL-MAKING HISTORY

The "75th Anniversary Diamond Beauty Doll" epitomizes the elegance that is signature Madame Alexander®.

This unique legacy began with Madame Alexander's early composition dolls featuring painted features and sleep eyes. In the early 1930s, she obtained a trademark for a cloth "Alice in Wonderland" doll, introduced a cloth series of *Little Women* dolls in connection with the release of the film; and produced the *Three Little Pigs* doll series. The "Scarlett O'Hara" dolls appeared in the late 1930s, along with the successful introduction of the "Princess Elizabeth" face mold and a series of dolls based on the English princess. It was during this year that production of Walt Disney's "Snow White" doll began as well. The 1940s also saw the company begin its transition from dolls made of composition to a then-revolutionary new product called "plastic."

Based on popular Broadway performances by Mary Martin, Madame Alexander unveiled a series of "Mary Martin" dolls in short-cropped wigs in 1952. What's more, to tie in with the release of the film, the production of *Peter Pan* series dolls began. The coronation of Queen Elizabeth that same year inspired a set of coronation dolls – 36 in all – each outfitted in historically correct costumes or fashion attire designed by Madame Alexander herself.

The Madame Alexander Fan Club was started by Margaret Winson in the early 1960s, and was later re-named the Madame Alexander Doll Club and incorporated as a not-for-profit group in Illinois. By 1991, its membership had reached over 10,000 individuals. The popularity of President John F. Kennedy's family sparked the introduction of a 21" "Jacqueline" doll and 15" "Caroline" doll, during this period as well. Then in 1965, large "Sound of Music" dolls debuted as tie-ins with the release of the film.

THE DOLL CLUB ATTRACTS 10,000 MEMBERS

Based upon the popular comic strip character, the company introduced a 12" "Brenda Starr" doll in the late 1960s. Around the same time, Madame Alexander was honored on United Nations Day for her international series of dolls. The 12" "Nancy Drew" doll was introduced during this era, and The Smithsonian Institute selected two of Madame Alexander's creations for inclusion in its prestigious doll collection. Those chosen were the "Madame Doll" from the *American Revolution* series, and the "Scarlett O'Hara" doll.

In connection with the 1976 American Bicentennial, the first six dolls in Madame Alexander's *First Ladies* series were introduced. Each doll is based on one of the inaugural gowns on display at

Celebrating great periods in fashion history, "Rococo Catherine" recalls a vintage design from 1774 with rhinestone and rose embroidery and a full pannier petticoat.

the Smithsonian Museum in Washington, D.C. Soon after this, in the early 1980s, The Alexander Doll Company donated 25 *Portrait Dolls* to the Children's Home Society of California benefit auction. The dolls were dressed by the world's top couturiers and were sold for $2,900 each.

HONORS FOR MADAME ALEXANDER

In 1986, at the age of 91, Madame Alexander received *Doll Reader* magazine's first Lifetime Achievement Award. F.A.O. Schwarz honored her 65 years as the First Lady of Dolls in 1988 with its own Lifetime Achievement Award. Not long thereafter, private investors became the new primary owners of The Alexander Doll Company. Madame Alexander remained with the company as design consultant, however, until her death on October 3, 1990.

Innovations continued even after Madame Alexander's death, including the *Welcome Home* series of dolls commemorating those who served in Operation Desert Storm.

A NEW ERA FOR A CLASSIC DOLL COMPANY

Herbert E. Brown, Chairman and CEO, remarks that "This is a stellar year for The Alexander Doll Company. We celebrate our 75th Anniversary with an elegant and exciting array of dolls that exemplify the vision of Madame Alexander." With over 20 years in a variety of executive positions with Fortune 500 companies, Brown and his innovative staff have developed exciting plans for Madame Alexander® collectors all over the world.

To commemorate the Diamond Jubilee Anniversary, The Alexander Doll Company has re-introduced popular dolls including the "Dionne Quintuplets" and "Marybel Gets Well." Originally created in 1935, the "Dionne Quintuplets" were among the first dolls based on living characters. "Marybel," which originally debuted in 1959, is accompanied by a box of "get well" accessories including arm and leg casts, crutches, tape and sunglasses. In addition, every doll made during 1998 bears a special gold medallion commemorating the anniversary year.

Other Diamond Jubilee Anniversary Special Limited Edition Dolls include "Diamond Beauty," "Pearl of the Twenties" and "Rose Splendor."

A ROMANTIC JOURNEY FOR "CISSY"

Reigning as Madame Alexander's classic haute couture creation, "Cissy" recently embarked on a romantic and exciting journey, stopping at all the grand cities of Europe with a wardrobe of exotically elegant outfits.

In a fabulous mid-calf dress, "Cissy Paris" outshines the "City of Light." Her matching peplum jacket is lavished with "chinchilla." "Cissy Milan" epitomizes the elegance of one of the world's foremost fashion capitols in an organza wrap dress with leopard print lining and pleated overlay caught with a gold-and-ruby jewel. "Cissy Venice" captures all the glory of Carnivale in a strapless gown with sweeping chiffon shoulder drape and matching brocade pants lined in pink satin. She carries an elephantine mask encrusted with jewels. "Cissy Budapest" is featured in a drop-waist dress with strapless blue velvet bodice and deeply fringed skirt ablaze with rhinestones. "Cissy Barcelona," winner of the 1998 "Doll Of The Year" (DOTY) Award, is a beguiling señorita in a gown of coral charmeuse overlaid with black lace.

Originally created in 1935, The Alexander Doll Company has brought back "The Dionne Quintuplets" to help commemorate its Diamond Jubilee.

Madame Alexander's classic haute couture creation, "Cissy Barcelona," winner of the 1998 Doll Of The Year (DOTY) Award.

Over the years since her 1952 introduction, "Cissy" has led the way in the fashion doll world. Her innovative look and stylish ensembles have garnered her three Fashion Academy gold medal awards. This new collection expands on her impeccable detailing and opulent design. As Herb Brown says, "'Cissy's' couture collection represents the hottest trends in the fashion world."

Madame Alexander's *Little Women* is a timeless play doll collection based on the classic novel by Louisa May Alcott.

Girls can relive the hopes and dreams of the March sisters with* The Little Women Journals™*, a series of play dolls, accessories and books featuring new, expanded stories inspired by Louisa May Alcott's well-loved classic.

The *Little Women Journals™*, introduced in 1997, are sure to become favorites with young women of all ages. The Madame Alexander 1998 collection introduces the lovely March sisters as they don lavish costumes, sold separately, to re-enact Shakespeare's "A Midsummer Night's Dream."

LITTLE WOMEN DOLLS RECREATE "A MIDSUMMER NIGHT'S DREAM"

"Puck's" costume is a belted green velour tunic over brown stretch tights. When reversed to "Bottom," it is an ivory linen shirt and flower-bedecked fur animal hood. The "Hippolyta" costume is a sequined pink chiffon outfit with organza bows at the shoulders and fluttery sheer wings. The dress can also be reversed to pink sparkle opalescent lamé with a long overskirt.

For "Titania, Queen of the Fairies," the costume is an iridescent white lamé with petal sleeves, a rainbow braid sash and silver crown. For "Helena, Queen of the Amazons," the outfit reverses to blue lamé with a long underskirt, and the crown becomes a belt. The costume for "Oberon, King of the Fairies," is a black Lycra® hood and tights with silver reflective stars. For "Theseus," the pieces reverse to a silver tunic and tie-dyed stretch velvet hood and tights.

The 1998 collection also includes *A Midsummer Night Stage with Play Script*, enhanced by an easy-to-read forward. Painted with portraits of the sisters on the front, the theater has a blue velvet curtain that rolls up to the enchanted forest.

Today, The Alexander Doll Company enjoys fruitful relationships through licensing with a host of fine companies. In addition to some already mentioned, these include Harley-Davidson Motorcycles®, *The Wizard of Oz™*, Coca-Cola®, Coppertone®, Kellogg's® and many other show business and brand names. The firm cultivates strong ties with its valued Madame Alexander dealers, offering them three levels of exclusive products through a Dealer Recognition Program.

EXCITING LICENSING AND DEALER VENTURES

The sight of a Madame Alexander gift box has created eager anticipation in generations of doll collectors. They know the highest standards of creativity and finest craftsmanship have gone into making the doll they are about to unwrap. With 75 years of excellence as their legacy, the people of The Alexander Doll Company pledge to carry the proud tradition of Madame Alexander into the future.

CLUB

MADAME ALEXANDER DOLL CLUB
P.O. Box 330
Mundelein, IL 60060

Annual Dues: $20.00 (U.S.) – $30.00 (International)
Club Year: Annual

BENEFITS:
- Opportunity to Purchase Members-Only Dolls
- Bi-Annual Newsletter, "The Review"
- Membership Card
- Doll Club Pin
- Invitation to Annual Convention

TOUR

THE ALEXANDER DOLL CO.
FACTORY TOUR
615 W. 131st St.
New York, NY 10027
(212) 283-5900

Hours: By appointment for groups of 5 to 15. Tours must be scheduled 8 weeks in advance and are subject to change. Please contact Human Resources at the above number.
Admission Fee: None
Tours are conducted by Alexander Doll Co. personnel who guide collectors through the factory where the dolls are being made.

TO LEARN MORE:

THE ALEXANDER DOLL COMPANY
615 WEST 131ST STREET
NEW YORK, NY 10027
(212) 283-5900
FAX: (212) 283-4901
URL: http://www.alexanderdoll.com

ANHEUSER-BUSCH, INC.

Leading the Way in Stein Collecting

The popularity of collectible beer steins has grown dramatically in recent years. And it should be no surprise that Anheuser-Busch, the world leader in beer, is also the world leader in steins.

Anheuser-Busch–as a brewer and as a collectibles business – emerged from very humble beginnings. Despite a dominant position in the national and international beer markets, Anheuser-Busch started as a small and struggling brewery. And what is now a leading line of collectibles, with hundreds of thousands of loyal collectors, began as nothing more than a few promotional beer steins.

In 1860, Eberhard Anheuser purchased a floundering brewery which was ranked only 29th of 40 breweries in St. Louis. A year later, Anheuser's daughter married a young brewery supplier name Adolphus Busch, who joined the company as a salesperson, and later became a partner, and finally president of the company. As the driving force that transformed a small, struggling brewery into an industry giant, he is considered the founder of Anheuser-Busch.

THE HISTORY OF ANHEUSER-BUSCH

While it was unheard of at the time, Adolphus Busch had a dream – to brew and market the first *national* beer. To make his dream a reality, Busch pioneered the brewing application of Louis Pasteur's new pasteurization process, set up the first network of rail-side ice-houses and introduced the first fleet of refrigerated rail cars.

He then perfected his new beer – brewed with the finest ingredients, using time-consuming traditional brewing methods – which he named Budweiser. The rest, as they say, is history. The "King of Beers" was introduced in 1876 and became an overwhelming success.

The popular Budweiser Frogs continue to hop into homes with Anheuser-Busch's "Budweiser Frogs" stein, limited to an edition size of 10,000.

Today, it continues to outsell all other brands in the world.

Over the years, Anheuser-Busch has added popular beers like Michelob, Busch, Bud Light, Bud Ice and many others to its product offering. The company produced more than 90 million barrels of beer in 1996 and currently serves more than 45% of the American beer market. 1997 marked the 40th consecutive year that Anheuser-Busch has reigned as the world's largest brewer.

No discussion of the history of steins would be complete without a brief mention of the origins of beer itself, which actually dates back before recorded history! Most ancient cultures are believed to have independently discovered beer. Babylonian clay tablets more than 6,000 years old depict the brewing of beer and give detailed recipes. By the 12th century, many commercial breweries existed in Germany, with most being run by city governments or monks. Large-scale commercial brewing did not begin until the late 1800s.

THERE WOULD BE NO STEINS WITHOUT BEER

"Stein" is a shortened variation of the German word Steinzeugkrug, which translates roughly into "stoneware jug or tankard." Any beer container with both a handle and a hinged lid became known as a stein, although many collectible steins today do not have lids.

THE HISTORY OF THE STEIN

The history of the beer stein begins more than 600 years ago. During the 14th century, the bubonic plague spread throughout Europe, killing millions. Although unable to find a cure, scientists of the time determined that the plague was spread by flies carrying the disease. To protect people from these deadly flies, many towns in what is now Germany passed laws requiring that all food and beverage containers be covered.

The common beer mug was one of these containers. So to keep out the flies while still allowing the user to drink with one hand, the hinged lid and thumb lift were invented. The beer stein was born!

Before long, talented artists were employed to help create steins, which were transformed into works of art. The addition of the lid provided new artistic opportunities, as did the development of colored glazes. The personal beer stein soon became an important status symbol to virtually all Germans, from the wealthy land-owners to the common laborers.

Covered with intricate detail, from the Budweiser tie in the center to the unique pipe-shaped handle,this "Budweiser Salutes Dad" stein makes a special gift that any father will treasure.

For the next few hundred years, laws requiring lidded steins remained, even long after the need was gone. During this time, the art of stein-making grew. It wasn't until the 1800s that these laws were no longer in force. But after 300 years, the lidded stein had become an important part of German culture. And beer steins were here to stay.

Since the mid 1970s, stein collecting has enjoyed a modern renaissance, with more and more people taking up the hobby. Today, steins are appreciated by people from all walks of life, both for their artistic and investment value.

ANHEUSER-BUSCH AND THE MODERN STEIN ERA

While Anheuser-Busch commissioned its first steins in the 1950s and 1960s, it wasn't until the mid-1970s that the company began to produce a significant number of steins, becoming the first U.S. brewer to enter the consumer stein market. Many of these early steins were produced as promotional items to support the beer business, and were never intended to be "collectibles." As a result, official documentation, including edition quantities, are not available for many early items.

The mystery surrounding many of these steins, along with the small quantities which seem to be available, has caused many of them to skyrocket in value over the past 20 years. It is not uncommon for Anheuser-Busch steins from the '70s to command 10 to 20 times their original retail price on the secondary market!

GETTING SERIOUS ABOUT THE STEIN BUSINESS

By the early 1980s, it became clear to Anheuser-Busch that the stein business was here to stay. It was about this time that the company's steins began to have documented item numbers, issue years and edition limits. Also, many stein series were begun, which added to the "collectibility" of steins.

Today, there is a broad base of avid Anheuser-Busch stein collectors all across America, as well as in other countries. Many collectors have amassed more than 300 steins in their collections. When Anheuser-Busch introduced its Collectors Club in 1995, they set their first year membership goal at 20,000. By early 1996, membership had reached 40,000 – and it continues to grow.

Anheuser-Busch normally introduces 20 to 30 new steins each year and has between 50 and 60 current items available at any given time. In addition to steins, Anheuser-Busch also offers limited edition collectible figurines, plates and lithographs.

Anheuser-Busch steins are designed and illustrated by a variety of artists throughout the United States and Europe. Artists are selected based on the particular style desired for each stein. Final artwork for each stein is then turned over to the stein manufacturer, most often either Ceramarte of Brazil, or Gerz of Germany.

Anheuser-Busch has dedicated its fourth stein in the* Hunter's Companion *series to the beloved beagle.

Anheuser-Busch pays tribute to Budweiser's 100-year history of quality with the release of the "Budweiser Label" stein.

STEIN PRODUCTION

Both of these manufacturers have long-standing reputations for quality and craftsmanship, and relationships with Anheuser-Busch that date back to the 1970s. The majority of Anheuser-Busch steins are ceramic, with some being made of fine porcelain. Lids are pewter, and sometimes include a ceramic inlay, or a ceramic, resin or pewter figurine.

Over the years, Anheuser-Busch has developed a variety of stein themes, including brewery-related subjects, Clydesdales, sports, animals and many others. One of the company's very first steins, and currently one of the hottest secondary market items, is the 1975 "Bud Man" character stein. Other character steins have also been very successful, including two 1997 introductions – the "Budweiser Frog" and the "Bud Ice Penguin."

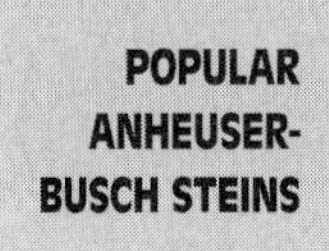

POPULAR ANHEUSER-BUSCH STEINS

Anheuser-Busch continues to produce both individual steins and stein

Budweiser is walking tall with this 8-1/4" tall "Cowboy Boot" stein.

series. A few notable series include:

***Holiday* Stein Series** - For over 15 years, the annual Anheuser-Busch "Holiday Stein" has played an important role in the growing popularity of stein collecting, as many of these steins are given as gifts, often creating new collectors. Originally introduced in 1980, the series has continued every year since. Starting in 1990, two versions of each "Holiday Stein" were produced, the open-edition, unlidded stein like those of the past, and a lidded version produced in a limited edition and personally signed by the artist.

***Endangered Species* Stein Series** - Featuring eight of the world's endangered species, this series is probably the most popular in the history of Anheuser-Busch steins. The first edition, the "Bald Eagle," has been one of the most sought after steins on the secondary market for years. The eighth and final edition, the "Mountain Gorilla," was introduced in 1996. The original artwork for a number of the steins has also been reproduced in limited edition lithographs.

***Sports Action* Stein Series** - Possibly a future classic, this on-going series debuted in January of 1997 with the "Play Ball!" Baseball Stein. Each stein in the *Sports Action* series showcases multiple illustrations which capture the action involved in the featured sport. A popular theme, excellent illustration and reproduction, and low retail cost made these steins an instant success.

***20th Century in Review* Series** - Each stein in this series highlights the major events and discoveries of a two-decade span of the 20th century. The first edition was introduced in July of 1997, and the series will continue to debut a new stein every six months, right up to the new millennium.

ANHEUSER-BUSCH COLLECTORS CLUB

Introduced in 1995, the Anheuser-Busch Collectors Club had reached approximately 43,000 members by the end of 1996. Each club member receives the annual membership stein (valued at about $60), as well as the opportunity to purchase an exclusive members-only stein.

Membership also includes a one-year subscription to *First Draft*, the full-color quarterly club magazine; a collectors club binder, filled with interesting details on the early history of Anheuser-Busch, the development of beer steins, stein production and more; and admission discounts at Anheuser-Busch Florida theme parks (Sea World-Orlando, Busch Gardens-Tampa and Adventure Island-Tampa).

Other benefits include discounts on C.I.B. publications, a personalized membership card, advance notice of new stein introductions and limited edition stein retirements, exclusive club member events and contests, a toll-free member's hotline and more. The annual club membership fee is $35.

CLUB

THE ANHEUSER-BUSCH COLLECTORS CLUB
2700 South Broadway
St. Louis, MO 63118
(800) 305-2582

Annual Dues: $35.00 - 2 Years: $65.00
Club Year: January - December

BENEFITS:
- Membership Gift: Stein
- Membership Renewal Gift
- Monthly Contest to Win "Signature Holiday Stein"
- Notification of Artist Events
- Redemption Certificate for Members-Only Stein
- Quarterly Magazine, *First Draft*
- Personalized Membership Card
- Binder with Club Logo
- Buy/Sell Matching Service

TO LEARN MORE:

ANHEUSER-BUSCH, INC.
2700 SOUTH BROADWAY
ST. LOUIS, MO 63118
(800) 325-9665
FAX: (314) 577-9656
URL: http://www.budweiser.com

The Saga of an "American Original"

The story of Annalee Thorndike is a once-upon-a-time tale of a dollmaking cottage industry that made it big. But this story is different because it's infused with the very special magic that is "uniquely Annalee."

Annalee Davis Thorndike was destined for dollmaking fame almost in spite of herself. She admits she was never much of a student and that the idea of going to college didn't appeal to her, nor did working at a non-creative job. She comes from an artistic family on both sides. Her mother was skilled in several media and was accomplished with needle and thread. Annalee loved to watch her mother sew, and together they made doll clothes. "I never played 'house' with dolls," says Annalee. "I just made clothes."

After graduating from high school in 1933, in order to "cough up some money to help out at home," Annalee Davis began making dolls. Still largely disinterested in working a 9-to-5 job, Annalee sold her dolls through the League of New Hampshire Craftsmen and circulated a clothes-making brochure. But it was the dolls the people were most interested in and, at the time, they were a lot more interested in Annalee's dolls than she was.

"My friends wouldn't leave me alone!" says Annalee. "They kept knocking on my door and saying, 'I have an idea for a doll,' or 'I know where I can get skis for your dolls!' They kept placing orders and I was always late filling them. I didn't market very heavily."

Santa himself is getting ready to decorate the house for Christmas as portrayed in "Trim Time Santa," a 7" doll from Annalee Dolls.

THE THORNDIKE DOLLMAKING FAMILY

In 1941, Annalee married Charles "Chip" Thorndike, son of a distinguished Boston surgeon. Chip attended Harvard University but, being a free-spirited individual, he preferred to go his own way as a chicken farmer. Today their original property is the site of the famous "Factory in the Woods." Back then, the first sign to grace the Thorndike Farm on Hemlock Drive in Meredith, New Hampshire read: "Eggs and Used Auto Parts."

The chicken farm failed in the early 1950s, and it was then that Annalee was forced to "really get serious" about her dollmaking business. She hired on her first employee and was now responsible for another person's paycheck. Says Annalee, "There were dolls everywhere, even in the bathroom!"

Thus, the Thorndike Farm became the "Factory in the Woods." Today, with a work force of over 350 craftspeople, Annalee's has become a Christmas and gift industry leader.

The Thorndikes believe in sharing their success and are well known for their generosity and deep commitment to the community at large. Annalee's sponsors the Annalee Scholarship Fund, dedicated to assisting Annalee employees and their families. In addition, each year the company raises tens of thousands of dollars for worthy local, state, regional and national organizations focused on the environment, conservation, homelessness and the arts.

Even now, the energetic little lady who says she didn't want a "real" job still shows up each day to lend her expertise in all areas of her company, and Chip can be found smiling behind his ever-present camera. Chip often creates charming accessories to enhance Annalee's dolls, as well. Couple this happy partnership with good health and the love of family and friends, and this once-upon-a-time success story is complete.

THE FUN OF AUCTION WEEKEND IN MEREDITH

A visit to an Annalee Doll Society Auction Weekend is enough to restore anyone's faith in good old American values. While relaxing in the sun with friends, visitors enjoy historical costumes and crazy getups, wonderful food and drink under festive tents, and the drama of skyrocketing auction prices on the rarest and most coveted of Annalee's collectible dolls, from 1950s' classics to today's one-of-a-kind "Artist's Proofs."

Annalee herself presides over the event, her ready smile a warm welcome to collectors nationwide who converge on Meredith. And as always, Chip, and sons Town and Chuck, are present to make sure all the guests are having the time of their lives.

To the uninitiated, this auction can provide a real awakening. One-of-a-kind pieces may sell for hundreds or thousands of dollars, and Annalee designs from the early years attract furious bidding. One impressive record breaker was a 10" "Halloween Girl" doll from the '50s, which brought $6,000 at the 1994 auction. In 1995, an 18" "Water Skiing Santa Claus" from the same period sold for $6,200. In 1996, the record was broken again with the sale of a circa 1955 18" Special Order Female Doll for $6,500!

Another highlight of the Summer Auction is the unveiling of the Doll Society's exclusive *Great American Eras* doll and the auction of its Artist's Proof – one of several one-of-a-kind proof dolls auctioned yearly for charitable purposes.

Prices are only part of the excitement at the auction, however. Collectors can choose from a wide range of designs and special products each year, at prices from $5.00 and up. The most recent Annalee catalog and *The Collector* magazine features limited edition pieces based on themes like sports, careers, diverse cultures and more. The rest of the line is drawn largely from seasonal and holiday themes.

All ready for Halloween is "Jack O. Lantern," popping out of his decorated pumpkin! Part of Annalee's* Itsie *Collection, and a petite 3" tall, the doll sells for $24.00.

ANNALEE AND FAMILY GREET COLLECTORS NATIONWIDE

When collectors come to Meredith, they often make a vacation of it. The Annalee Doll Museum and Town Thorndike's Antique and Classic Car Collection are within walking distance of one another, and convenient to Lake Winnipesaukee's many attractions. But for those who can't make the trek to New Hampshire, Annalee and the family provide another way to "meet the artist" – they travel throughout the country, not only visiting collectibles shows, but dropping in on Doll Society Sponsor Stores as well. A visit to one of these nearly 500 sponsors brings out crowds of Annalee admirers and collectors, eager for the chance to meet Annalee or Chuck, talk with them, and have them sign autograph cards or personal items.

Annalee's appealing "Country Bunny Boy" cradles his carrot while he shows off his checked shirt, overalls and cottontail.

THE ANNALEE DOLL SOCIETY: JOIN THE CLUB

Ever since the Annalee Doll Society was initiated in 1983 to meet the needs of Annalee collectors, it has provided fun and special opportunities for these enthusiasts. With a membership in the tens of thousands and growing, the Society offers many benefits. The Membership Kit includes a yearly 7" Logo Kid doll, annual pin and membership card, a special edition Annalee felt pin, and a subscription to *The Collector*, the full-color quarterly magazine devoted to Annalee's dolls and collectors. Each issue includes a message from Annalee herself, as well as tips on decorating and doll care, special event invitations and reports, answers to collector questions, recipes, product introductions, nostalgic memories, and much more.

Other Club benefits include admission to Doll Society events and eligibility to purchase exclusive, signed and

The 7" Logo Kid for the 1997-98 Annalee Doll Society Year is "Tea for Two?" which comes free with the Membership Kit and $29.95 annual Society membership dues.

numbered dolls available only to Society members.

While the value of the current Logo Kid alone is $50.00, the Kid and all other benefits are available to Doll Society members for only $29.95 annually. For more information or to join the Doll Society, contact any Doll Society Sponsor Store or call 1-800-43-DOLLS.

ANNALEE SPREADS JOY TO COLLECTORS

Always cheery and upbeat herself, Annalee Thorndike proclaims her goal as a simple one: she wants to "make people smile." With the happy expressions on her dolls' faces to cheer every admirer, this artist meets her goal with grace and enthusiasm. From "Eggs and Used Auto Parts" to the delightful world of Annalee Mobilitee Dolls, the Thorndikes' success story warms the hearts of all who experience the joy of Annalee, her family, and her appealing Annalee dolls.

CLUB

ANNALEE DOLL SOCIETY
P.O. Box 1137
Meredith, NH 03253-1137
(800) 433-6557

Annual Dues: $29.95
Club Year: July 1 - June 30

BENEFITS:

- Membership Gift: 7" Doll, Membership Pin and Card
- Opportunity to Purchase Members-Only Doll
- Quarterly Magazine, *The Collector*
- Annual Doll Society Gathering in Meredith, NH
- Members-Only Photo Contest
- Notification of Annalee Trunk Shows

MUSEUM

ANNALEE DOLL MUSEUM
50 Reservoir Road
Meredith, NH 03253
(800) 433-6557

Hours: Daily from 9 a.m. - 5 p.m., Memorial Day - October 31.
Closed during the Winter months.
Admission Fee: None

The Annalee Doll Museum features over 500 Annalee Doll creations, showcasing the work of Annalee Thorndike from her teen years to the present. A video of the company's history is also presented.

TO LEARN MORE:

ANNALEE MOBILITEE DOLLS, INC.
50 RESERVOIR RD.
MEREDITH, NH 03253-1137
(603) 279-3333
FAX: (603) 279-6659
URL: http://www.annalee.com

Woodcarving Traditions into Contemporary Art

Strong family traditions point the way to fine handcraftsmanship. The integrity inherent in these traditions is evident in the quality and pride of workmanship, handed down from generation to generation, not only through the family itself, but also projected by artisans descended from others associated with the company for generations.

So it is today with ANRI, a family-owned enterprise that continues to create high quality, hand-carved and hand-painted artistry sought after by connoisseurs around the world. For over 300 years, the traditions of woodcarving have thrived in the Val Gardena (Groeden Valley) of the South Tyrol.

By the turn of the 19th century, woodcarving had replaced other Valley enterprises such as cheese-making, lace and Loden cloth as the region's chief business activity. A unique method of distribution was developed through itinerant sales representatives, with Groedners traveling through Europe carrying their woodcarved wares, ultimately leading to the establishment of a major international trade. Young Luis Riffeser, at the age of 13 in 1866, was just one such representative sent abroad by his father. It was through this early start that Luis' profound devotion to the woodcarving tradition, and to his family's integrity, was nurtured.

His son Anton, born in 1887, made a great dream a reality. While in a Russian prisoner-of-war camp in Siberia during the dark days of World War I, Anton made his plans to formalize the family's business. Using the first two letters of both his names, he christened his planned company ANRI – and a new woodcarving tradition was born.

During the war years, Anton's wife, Carolina, kept the work progressing, creating a base of operations that awaited his return. After six years as a prisoner, he was finally released. Upon returning home, startled to learn that Tyrol had been ceded to Italy as part of war reparations, he went to work putting his plan into effect. In 1926, the new building, complete with workshops, warehouses, offices and living space for the family, was ready. By now, Anton Jr., a teenager, was working side by side with his parents, ultimately playing a strong role in the development of new techniques and products. In time, his own son, Ernst, took the helm, and today, Ernst's son, Thomas, is deeply involved.

A graceful addition to the Ulrich Bernardi nativity is "Shepherdess at the Well," offered in three sizes. Introduced in 1997, the sculpture lends a calming presence to the religious scene.

In 1995, ANRI embarked upon a new era in the United States. Darrell Farris, with many years of experience in collectibles, forged a partnership with ANRI as president and chief executive officer of ANRI U.S., a distribution and marketing firm spearheaded by him and based in the Dallas area. Now, strong focus was placed on the needs and interests of ANRI collectors in North America. It has led to a strengthening of awareness of the handcrafting of wood sculptures, from the early stages of carving through to the finished hand-painted piece. The association has been an influence in putting a very low limit on special editions, some as low as 250 worldwide. This concept means more exclusivity and, therefore, desirability for the discerning collector. In addition, interest in the new ANRI Collector's Society has increased significantly.

A well-directed family enterprise with focused leadership, ANRI is moving into new and exciting areas with collectors' interests in mind. The future is taking shape.

THE PERFECTION OF THE NATIVITY

Religious motifs have always carried important weight in the Groeden Valley, with many highly detailed carvings from the 17th century still surviving today in museums and churches of the region. Among the earliest religious art forms carved by the Groedners was the Nativity, the celebration of the birth of Christ. In fact, it was the Groedners who established the tradition of adding snow to the scene. Today, Nativities in a variety of styles are an important aspect of ANRI artistry.

Among the most recognizable for ANRI collectors is the gentle, tender spirit of Juan Ferrandiz, renowned for his poetry as well as his painting. His love of children and his belief in them as

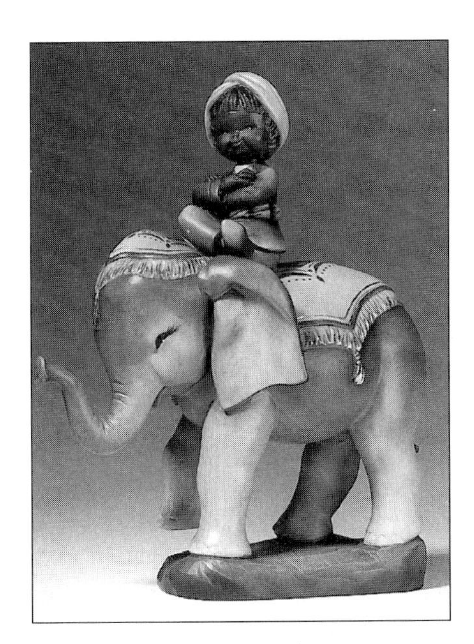

From the winsome artistry of Juan Ferrandiz comes "Elephant Rider," added to his endearing Nativity in 1997. His love of children shines through in all his work.

the future of the world shines through in the cherubic quality of his nativity.

Ulrich Bernardi, a familiar face to many American collectors through his frequent personal appearances as ANRI's most visible master carver, has been associated with ANRI for nearly four decades. Native to the Valley, his style reflects a simplicity in all his work. Among his Nativities is the "Florentiner," which was presented to His Holiness Pope John Paul II in 1986. Its gold-leaf trim, and elegance of design, make this an important addition to Bernardi's extensive work.

The *Holy Land* Nativity was developed through the study of the collection of religious art in the Biblioteca Apostolica Vaticana (Vatican Library), when ANRI artisans were honored to be invited to conduct their research. It was so highly thought of by the Vatican that it is now part of the official Vatican Library Collection.

From the stylized classic artwork of Karl Kuolt, a renowned artist who died in 1937 but whose works continue to be recreated today, comes beautiful serenity carved in wood. Much of Professor Kuolt's works can be seen in museums and private collections. In addition, monuments and statues in memorial chapels bearing his name can be found throughout Southern Germany.

Perhaps the newest star on the roster is an artist born in 1916 who has been creating beauty in wood for over 50 years for ANRI. Fini Martiner Moroder's unique Romanesque-style nativity, carved from chestnut rather than the traditional Alpine maple, giving it a still more distinctive look, now takes its place among the ANRI Nativities.

ARTISTS OF DISTINCTION CREATE FOR ANRI

A beloved artist is the Australian Sarah Kay, a teacher whose charming drawings of children, based on her own offspring, has been associated with ANRI since the early 1980s. Through the master carvings of Ulrich Bernardi, her irrepressible children come alive.

Gunther Granget, a world-renowned sculptor of horses, birds and other wildlife, is represented with distinctive carvings. The perfect blend of his astonishing artistry with that of the ANRI masters brings magnificent carvings, superbly hand-painted, to collectors' homes.

From Dallas comes Lyndon Gaither, relatively new to the ANRI family, a gifted artist whose wooden crosses intertwined with flowers have already inspired collectors. He has also created vignettes of family life, as well as a series of Christmas ornaments and figurines.

BRINGING THE WOOD TO LIFE

First comes the schooling, then the apprenticeship, followed by a supreme test to prove the success of the training. Only then may a carver be accepted by ANRI.

Four to six weeks are required for a model to be carved to the artisan's satisfaction. Generally, Alpine pine is used for a carving that will exceed 10". If the figurine will be smaller, the wood will be the harder Alpine maple. These woods grow slowly, at a high altitude on the shady mountainside; they must reach 80 to 100 years of age before they are of sufficient girth to be cut down.

After the wood is seasoned outdoors to reduce the moisture content, it is placed in a kiln for about four hours before being cut into blocks. Only about 20 per cent of the wood is ultimately used for carving; the remaining 80 per cent contain imperfections which would not meet the quality standards set by ANRI for the finished piece.

Now the work begins, as the carver takes his tools in hand to begin the formation of the figurine. The intricacies of facial expressions, graceful arms and fabric folds require great skill and time. The smooth effect of the ultimate carving is achieved by the carver and his special tools, not with sandpaper.

A coat of lacquer provides a base for the oil paints. Colors are blended as needed on each painter's palette, applied to the figurine, and then gently rubbed with a cloth. This procedure allows the grain of the wood to shine through, giving the finished piece its utterly unique look.

Each color application requires a drying period of two to three days. Finally, a finishing coat of lacquer is applied, to seal the wood and protect the paint. With quality control at ANRI demanding the highest standards, the enduring family traditions are very much in evidence.

A unique aspect of the "Lily Cross" by Lyndon Gaither is its versatility. It can rest in its own gold leaf stand, or can be removed from the stand to hang on the wall.

ANRI Collector's Society members are delighted with their exclusive offering of "Read Me A Story," introduced in 1997. This Sarah Kay figurine is representative of her deep appreciation, and understanding, of small children.

ANRI COLLECTOR'S SOCIETY

To know more and more about one's favorite collectibles lends greater meaning to the joys of ownership. It is for this reason that the ANRI Collector's Society takes great pride in its membership, and endeavors to give each member all the opportunities to enhance his or her personal pleasure in pursuit of the finest in artistry in wood.

Members can expect the latest news from ANRI, brought to them three times a year through the pages of their full-color, engaging "Newsletter." Up-to-date information on new products, as well as articles detailing artists' backgrounds, fill its pages. The "Newsletter" also discusses the history of woodcarving, the beautiful area of the South Tyrol, and much more, all designed to broaden members' knowledge of ANRI artistry.

In 1998, a trip to Val Gardena will premier; it will take members into the ANRI Workshops to meet carvers, painters and others who are responsible for this beautiful art. The full itinerary will give travelers wonderful insights into the entire region.

Society members receive a membership card, and the opportunity to purchase figurines offered exclusively to them. They also receive a full-color brochure describing current ANRI woodcarvings. For an annual fee of $35.00 ($45.00 in U.S. funds outside the continental U.S.), devotees benefit from Society research services and receive invitations to special events.

Gold Leaf Membership, a new Society-within-the-Society, brings with it ownership of one unique sculpture, in a special size and limited to only 150 pieces worldwide. Gold Leaf carvings are redesigned from retired pieces in the ANRI archives. As many as three figurines are offered each year, with the second two available for purchase through participating retailers. All other benefits of ANRI Collector's Society membership accrue to Gold Leaf members. Gold Leaf membership is $295.

CLUB

ANRI COLLECTOR'S SOCIETY
P.O. Box 380760
Duncanville, TX 75138
(800) 730-ANRI (2674)

Annual Dues: $35.00
Club Year: January-December
Collector's Year – Anniversary of Sign-Up Date

BENEFITS:

- Membership Gift
- Reservation Card to Acquire Members-Only Figurine
- Newsletter Published Three Times Yearly
- Membership Card
- Buy/Sell Matching Service through Newsletter
- Full-Color ANRI Brochure
- Authorized Retailer Listing
- Limited In-House Research Department
- In-Store ANRI Master Carver Events
- Travel Opportunities to ANRI Workshops in Italy

TOUR

ANRI WOODCARVINGS TOUR
Groden Valley
Italy

By advance reservation through ANRI Collector's Society. (See address and phone number above.)

Admission: Only for Members of ANRI Collector's Society

Society members visiting the ANRI Workshops receive a guided tour of the facility, including the painting and carving studios.

TO LEARN MORE:

ANRI U.S.
P.O. BOX 380760
1126 SOUTH CEDAR RIDGE, SUITE 122
DUNCANVILLE, TX 75138-0760
(800) 730-ANRI (2674)
FAX: (972) 283-3522
URL: http://www.anri.com
E-MAIL: anriwood@aol.com

Giuseppe Armani Creates Art for Today!

More than 500 years ago in Florence, Italy, the powerful Medici family established a great fortune in what was already a prosperous Italian town. The most dynamic of the Medici sons, Lorenzo the Magnificent (1449-92), boasted both an outstanding political savvy and an unparalleled appreciation for art. Under his leadership, Florence became the center of the Italian Renaissance. Even today, visitors marvel at the city's glorious legacy of treasures in architecture, sculpture and painting.

Florentine art history reads like a "who's who" of the Renaissance, including works by Donatello, Cellini, the Della Robbias, Fra Angelico, Fra Fillipo Lippi, Botticelli, Leonardo da Vinci, and scores more. For centuries, aspiring artists have traveled to Florence to worship at the shrine of these masters: to drink in the beauty of their works and to strive to master some of their most honored techniques.

"Bacchus and Arianna" is a recent addition to Armani's **Florentine Garden** *collection. It measures 17-1/2" in height and has been issued in a limited edition of 5,000.*

Many 15th- and 16th-century art masters made their home in or near Florence. Today, the city remains the favorite locale for Italian painters and sculptors. One such prominent artist is Giuseppe Armani — a sculptor "creating art for today" in the glorious spirit of the Florentine Renaissance.

A NATIVE OF TUSCANY EMBRACES FLORENCE'S FINE ART TRADITIONS

Giuseppe Armani has had an extraordinary life. As a young child he, like many other children, loved to draw. Unlike most children however, drawing was practically the only game he played. His drawings were uniquely colorful and fresh. Everyone was impressed with his art. His teachers, observing his obvious talent, encouraged his artistic attempts. But, had it not been for Armani's father, it is likely the boy's talent would neither have been nurtured nor developed. Dario Armani realized that his son's gifts were larger than just a simple ability to reproduce subjects.

Despite the financial hardship, Armani and his father agreed that Giuseppe would attend the Academy of Fine Arts in Florence, where the boy could more fully develop his natural talents. Most unfortunately for Giuseppe, his father became ill and died before their plans materialized. And so, Giuseppe Armani was forced to abandon his studies for more practical family needs.

The inspired young artist continued to study on his own. Solitary learning was not easy. His hometown of Calci was small, and it did not offer much material for study. There were no examples in Calci of those masterpieces for which Florence and the entire region of Tuscany are so justly famous. However, young Giuseppe persevered!

Giuseppe Armani's professional career began when he entered a classically inspired male torso in an exhibition. His work was greatly admired for its extraordinary anatomical precision. When Armani's torso was chosen for exhibition in "The Gallery" in Pisa, "The Gallery" hired him.

While working in "The Gallery," Armani sculpted in various materials such as marble, alabaster, wood and clay. Visitors from around the world came to recognize his name. It was during this tenure at "The Gallery" that Armani's reputation as an artist began.

Ever eager for artistic stimulation, Armani began traveling around Tuscany. He frequently visited Florence, where he studied Renaissance themes in both sculpture and painting. Consequently, his work evolved enormously during this time.

In the mid-1970s, Giuseppe Armani and Florence Sculture d'Arte began an inspired, exclusive and extraordinarily successful relationship. The factory of Florence Sculture d'Arte is located at the heart of Tuscany, where Florence, Siena, Volterra and San Gimignano are nestled in a surrounding of lushly verdant and rolling hills. Because the Studio of Florence Sculture d'Arte is dedicated to continuing Tuscany's glorious artistic heritage, the primary goal of the founders of the Florence factory was to create an environment in which the best Italian sculptors and painters could flourish.

THE ALLIANCE OF ARMANI WITH FLORENCE SCULTURE D'ARTE

This dramatic "Sky Watch" sculpture by Giuseppe Armani measures 21-1/4" in height and has a worldwide limited edition of 3,000.

Giuseppe Armani works in a spartan studio that is attached to his house. Armani sculpts to the same ancient rhythms that existed in the studios of Michelangelo and Leonardo da Vinci. The genius of the Renaissance inspires Armani to sculpt his modern masterpieces.

Giuseppe Armani and Florence Sculture d'Arte are currently forming a workshop in the tradition of the old renowned Renaissance workshops. Here, the world's most talented sculptors work with, and learn from, the Master-Sculptor himself.

TEAMWORK CHARACTERIZES THE FLORENCE SCULTURE D'ARTE STUDIO

Giuseppe Armani is the best-known member of the Sculture d'Arte Studio, yet he is quick to acknowledge the contributions of many members of the studio's team, as well as his American associates at Miller Import Corporation. Key "players" include Pietro Ravenni, Herb Miller, Giovanni Ottelli and Attilio Vezzosi.

Born in Florence in 1940, Attilio Vezzosi spent much of his early years visiting many of the art galleries and museums of Florence. "My father was a true Florentine," he remembers. "He loved art and loved sharing it with us." After graduating from business school in 1959, Vezzosi traveled extensively across Europe and North America, learning all he could about the different cultures. In the early 1960s, he began his career at Fratelli Alinar, one of Florence's most renowned art photo studios, and in 1972, he started his own company. A chance meeting led to his relationship with Herb Miller and Miller Import Corporation. They proceeded to search the Italian market looking for products that would be successful in America.

One day in 1974, Herb and Pat Miller discovered some figurines by Giuseppe Armani, who had just begun sculpting for Florence Sculture d'Arte. They realized that Armani's works would be enthusiastically received in America — and they were correct. Today, Attilio Vezzosi acts a dual role as Art Director for the Florence Sculture d'Arte and as the Italian Agent for Miller Import Corporation.

Pietro Ravenni is known as "the man behind the artist." Pietro Ravenni's father founded Florence Sculture d'Arte in 1973 along with Werther Tedeschi. Ravenni began working in the studio at the age of 20, specializing in the operational, as well as the creative processes, which included the decoration of figurines. Ravenni also closely supervises the apprentices who receive their art training at the factory.

Pietro Ravenni fully appreciates the genius of Armani, stating, "What symbolizes Florence Sculture d'Arte more than anything else is the art of Giuseppe Armani. In his 20-plus years with us, Giuseppe has strongly influenced every aspect of our studio. The Armani 'style,' which we all follow, is what gives our work its quality and distinction. Armani's style will continue to be our grounding for the future."

Florence Sculture d'Arte's sales manager is Giovanni Ottelli, a "citizen of the world" who speaks English, Spanish, French and Russian in addition to his native Italian. "This 'Pan-European' foundation has served me well all through my career," says Ottelli. As a life-long art lover who has visited most of the great museums of Europe, Ottelli continues, "I feel that when I sit down over a cup of coffee with Giuseppe to talk about trends in the marketplace, we communicate from a common understanding of the great history of Western art in Europe. I can also give him the perspective of someone who has spent a large part of his life living outside Italy."

RECENT RECOGNITION FOR ARMANI AND HIS WORK

In 1996, Giuseppe Armani experienced an extraordinary year. First, he presented "Madonna with Child and Young Saint John," a masterful one-of-a-kind sculpture, to Pope John Paul II. Then, in September of 1996, Armani was honored with a private two and one-half hour tour of the White House, where he presented his "Wild Hearts" sculpture to President Bill Clinton. The President will keep "Wild Hearts" prominently on view in the Oval Office.

Also that year, Armani was singularly honored by being voted "Artist of the

One of Armani's many lovely ladies poses on her elegant chair in two versions of "At Ease."

Year" by the National Association of Limited Edition Dealers (NALED). Furthermore, NALED "iced the cake" by recognizing Armani's achievements as a graphic artist. Again in 1997, he was honored as first runner-up for "Artist of the Year."

The artist's sculptural works include diverse subjects such as elegant ladies, weddings and maternities, children, social events, gardens, religious pieces, capodimonte, wildlife, home decor items, and even a special *Walt Disney Collection*. Collectors drawn to Armani's wonderfully detailed and finely crafted works include celebrities Dionne Warwick, Tony Orlando and Hershel Walker. Prices range from $35.00 to $3,500, depending on the size of the work and the number in the edition.

New works for 1997 include pieces covering most all the subjects listed above. Particularly striking is "Venetian Night," portraying a classically dressed couple aboard their own wonderfully detailed canal boat. Also on a romantic theme, "First Date" showcases a younger, more contemporary couple, riding on a swing as they happily hold hands. Angels and cherubs abound in the new collection, as do wildlife pieces. Included is a stunning soaring eagle called "Sky Watch," and a series of domesticated dog sculptures inspired by Dalmatians, Pointers, Collies, and other favorite breeds.

For American collectors of Armani's works, Miller Import Corporation began the Society of Giuseppe Armani Art in 1990. The Society helps the collector learn more about the artist, it previews the new introductions, and facilitates acquisition of Giuseppe Armani's special limited edition figurines. There are also many members-only activities and events exclusive to The Society Collectors.

THE SOCIETY OF GIUSEPPE ARMANI ART

With thousands of members, The Society recently inaugurated its own site on the World Wide Web, which allows for on-line enrollment, questions and answers, news of in-store events and color pictures of new products which can be downloaded by collectors. The Internet address is http://www.the-society.com. The Society can also be contacted via e-mail at miller_society@prodigy.com.

Giuseppe Armani is an artist on a mission. He is dedicated to his collectors, and he is impelled to bring beauty into their lives. It is for his collectors that Giuseppe Armani creates and sculpts wondrously compelling figurines out of space and air and imagination. Armani's mythic, almost mystical ability to put character and soul into his sculptures amazes and intrigues people the world over. Giuseppe Armani creates Modern Masterpieces...Giuseppe Armani Creates Art For Today!

CLUB

THE SOCIETY OF GIUSEPPE ARMANI ART
300 Mac Lane
Keasbey, NJ 08832
(800) 3-ARMANI

Annual Dues: $50.00 (U.S. $)
$70.00 (Canadian $)
Renewal: $37.50 (Canadian $)
$52.50 (Canadian $)
Club Year: January - December

BENEFITS:
- Membership Gift: Armani Figurine
- Opportunity to Purchase Members-Only Figurines
- Quarterly Magazine, *The Review*
- Framed Membership Certificate
- Magazine Holder
- Gold-Plated Pin
- Membership Card
- Special Members Events and Mailings throughout the Year

TO LEARN MORE:

THE SOCIETY OF
GIUSEPPE ARMANI ART
MILLER IMPORT CORP.
300 MAC LANE
KEASBEY, NJ 08832
(800) 3-ARMANI
FAX: (908) 417-0031
URL: http://www.the-society.com
E-MAIL: miller_society@prodigy.com

THE ART OF GLYNDA TURLEY

Sharing Romance and Nostalgia

At her home nestled in the beautiful Ozark Mountains of Arkansas, Glynda Turley finds the quiet inspiration for her exquisite oil paintings that have won her international acclaim. As president and artist of her company, The Art of Glynda Turley, she has turned her creative talents into a thriving family business that invites collectors to enjoy the simpler pleasures of life. Her artwork reflects the vibrant colors of a springtime garden, the country charm of beloved antiques or the playful afternoon pastimes of children.

"I strive to take the viewer into a time and place of beauty, peace and harmony – where time seems to stand still," Glynda says. "I suppose my style of work could be described as romantic." It is this captivating combination of romance and nostalgia that has blossomed The Art of Glynda Turley into a successful print and collectibles company. Collectors can now find Glynda's artwork adorning everything from limited edition prints to hand-painted figurines and tapestry pillows.

Glynda Turley's "Abundance III" print, part of the* Abundance *series, was nominated for an "Award of Excellence" by* Collector Editions *magazine.

"I love my work," Glynda says. "My paintings are the way I share that magical place or old-fashioned bouquet that represents the way I see things and the way I feel inside. It is a very rewarding thing to know you have helped someone to smile."

INSPIRED BEGINNINGS FOR A SELF-TAUGHT ARTIST

Glynda's artistic style has evolved since her childhood. She had no formal art training, but can't recall a time when she wasn't filling blank pieces of paper or canvases with the images in her mind and heart.

"My grandmother was probably my very first influence," she recalls. "She inspired me to be creative by her constant creativity. She was always making beautiful gifts. She never had the opportunity to paint, but I have no doubt that she could have been a great artist."

Even though this self-taught artist loved to sketch, Glynda didn't begin to paint until the mid-1970s, when as a young mother and housewife, she was introduced to oil paints. Ozark Mountain scenes and barnyard animals were among her first subjects. She sold some of her paintings at arts and crafts fairs throughout the state. During this time, she also started teaching art lessons to neighborhood children and adults in her kitchen, as well as at a local beauty shop and school gymnasium. In 1977, she opened an art supplies store in Heber Springs, Arkansas. A few years later, Glynda's first two prints were published. Soon, she was winning awards and receiving many requests for her work from galleries, gift shops and collectors.

In 1985, she founded The Art of Glynda Turley to market her prints. Since then, the number of outlets and mediums for her work has grown by leaps and bounds. Glynda's work is sold in more than 7,000 stores nationwide and in several foreign countries.

The first company-owned retail store opened in April 1996 in Branson to carry the extensive line of every Glynda Turley product, including licensed products. The complete *Glynda Turley Collection* can be found in the Glynda Turley store, including products that her company produces, such as framed prints, figurines, etc., as well as licensed products such as tapestries from Simply Country, teacups and teapots from Ebeling & Reuss, greeting cards from Lovelace Family Ltd., collector plates from The Bradford Exchange and White Oak Porcelain, and much more.

To keep up with the demand, Glynda now employs about 65 people, including 14 family members.

A STRONGER COMPANY RISES FROM TRAGIC FIRE

But the company and collectors are truly her extended family. In 1992, when a fire destroyed her manufacturing plant and 83 of her original oil paintings, her employees, suppliers, retailers and collectors came to the rescue. They gave the helping hands and encouraging words needed to rebuild the business and plant, which are located in Heber Springs, Arkansas, a picturesque resort area 80 miles north of Little Rock.

"We have a wonderful team that pulled together," Glynda says. "There's a real family bond." In recent years, Glynda has expanded the scope of her

Internationally acclaimed artist Glynda Turley captures a tranquil scene in "Old Mill Stream IV," turning a cold Winter afternoon into a nostalgically warm vision.

products through licensing agreements. Her designs appear on many different kinds of home-decor items and gifts, including soaps, candles, journals, desk calendars, pillows, throws, wallpaper borders, greeting cards, suncatchers, night lights, and more. Other items are always in the works. "Nothing is more exciting than to see one's artwork adapted to other products," she says.

Although her artwork is being translated into a variety of products, Glynda is still most renowned for her prints – especially those featuring beautiful florals. "Florals are my true love," Glynda reveals. "Flowers are so short-lived that if I can capture them on canvas, they can be enjoyed forever."

PRINTS CAPTURE EVERYTHING FROM FLORALS TO FAMILY

At her cottage-style home, Glynda enjoys working in her gardens, which grow among a backdrop of picket fences and are filled with multi-colored roses, delphiniums and foxgloves, among others. "I only have to look out my window for inspiration," she says.

But some of her ideas don't just come from her backyard. Her family also appears in many of her works. The 1996 release "Secret Garden III," for example, shows two of her grandchildren – Jordan and Crystal – sitting on the wisteria-covered arbor in her yard.

On her extensive travels, she always packs her camera and many rolls of film. In 1994, she went to England for the first time and saw Anne Hathaway's cottage and gardens. The trip inspired the 1995 print release titled "Hollyhocks III," the third in a series of Hollyhocks prints. From a visit to Victoria, British Columbia, Glynda painted a quaint Victorian house with its black iron gate and rose-covered arched walkway. The painting became "Summer In Victoria."

Glynda's 1997 release, "Keeping Watch," was inspired by a visit to the Portland Head Light in Portland, Maine, in 1995. Soon to be released is a romantic covered bridge print, also inspired by the trip to Maine. Another recent release, "Little Red River," depicts fishermen on the famous Arkansas trout stream. A portion of the sales from the limited edition print will be donated to "Friends of the Little Red River," an organization devoted to the preservation and enhancement of the stream.

Recently, five of Glynda's new print releases were a result of designs she created and painted for The Bradford Exchange. The Bradford Exchange commissioned her to paint a series of fruit and flower wreaths called *The Meaningful Harvest*, which appeared on collector plates. Besides appearing on plates and as print and canvas releases, a full collection of products bearing these plate designs is planned for the future.

"My inspiration today comes from my environment," she says. "I live in one of the most beautiful places in the world, so I only have to look around me for the inspiration to create. My head is full of ideas for paintings, many of which come from the extensive amount of traveling that I do throughout the year."

Glynda's limited edition prints include more than 100 titles, with many selling out within a matter of months. The company also offers custom framing, and some sold-out limited edition prints are available in smaller sizes in an open edition.

Glynda's artwork has also been transformed into limited edition figurines that

From her* Meaningful Harvest *plate series for The Bradford Exchange, Glynda Turley presents "Chrysanthemums and Apples."

are carefully sculpted to capture all the detail of the original paintings. The line of collectible figurines recreates some of Glynda Turley's most popular paintings, including "Secret Garden II," "Flowers For Mommy" and "Circle of Friends" — all of which feature her grandchildren or children. Also included in the collection are: "The Courtyard II," "Playing Hookie" and "Past Times."

FIGURINES ADD NEW DIMENSION TO ARTWORK

"Bringing the prints to life in the form of six figurines has been one of the most enjoyable projects we've developed, especially since three of those figurines feature members of my family," she says.

The poly-resin figurines are mounted on a wooden base with a brass-colored plaque bearing the name of the design. The figurines, which are each limited to 4,800 pieces, also come with a Certificate of Authenticity.

In the future, Glynda hopes to add more items to her range of home decor designs that will complement her prints, figurines and other collectibles. The line expanded in 1997 into greeting cards, teacups, teapots, a collector plate series, bath and bed ensembles, tile products, suncatchers, and stained glass night lights for a total of 30 licenses. "The company's goals are to keep the same quality standards and ethics that have made us successful," says Glynda

PLANS FOR EXPANDING INTO NEW MARKETS

"My personal goals as an artist are to recreate the wonderful things that I have had the privilege or opportunity to see, whether they are found in my travels, at home or in my imagination. I wish to record with my paintings some of the beauty of the past."

Today's lovely Glynda Turley prints, decorative accessories and collectibles will surely be the heirlooms of tomorrow. Whether in the Ozark Mountains or traveling around the world, Glynda is always working on new ideas and expanding her collection for more collectors to enjoy.

TO LEARN MORE:

THE ART OF GLYNDA TURLEY, INC.
P.O. BOX 1073
4354 GRETNA ROAD
BRANSON, MO 65616
(888) 4-GLYNDA
FAX: (417) 334-8722
URL: http://www.merosworld.com/glyndaturley/mainindex.html
E-MAIL: glynda@cswnet.com

One of Glynda Turley's most popular paintings is recreated in this hand-painted resin figurine, titled "Flowers For Mommy."

Defining the Collectible Doll Industry

Doll lovers have come to know The Ashton-Drake Galleries as the doll company with a difference. Since 1985, the name Ashton-Drake has been synonymous with premier-quality dolls at prices that are consistently the best in the market

Located in the Chicago suburb of Niles, Ashton-Drake began as an offshoot of the Bradford Exchange, a company deeply rooted in producing collector's plates. From its fledgling beginnings, Ashton-Drake made a mark early on the doll industry and continues to be the company where doll collectors can find dolls of irresistible value. Doll lovers still remember the dashing "Jason" and the lovely "Heather." These "first-borns" of Ashton-Drake became the cornerstone for exclusive editions that are the industry benchmark for dolls worldwide.

"Gene" steps out to "Monaco"... a fabulous bridal ensemble, much imitated in its time. This doll was retired at the end of 1997.

With dolls that appeal to every age and interest, Ashton-Drake defines the very nature of doll collecting. Whether porcelain or vinyl, all Ashton-Drake dolls have a common denominator – each creation is the epitome of personality-filled art – a goal that's at the very heart of Ashton-Drake. For this reason, many say that in just over a decade this company has literally "reinvented" the collectible doll industry...a statement few can argue.

"GENE"... SHARING THE DREAM IN STYLE

She was a small-town girl with stars in her eyes. Working in New York as an usher in a movie theatre, she gets her big break when meeting a leading Hollywood producer. Once he glimpses one of the loveliest women he's ever seen, she is whisked off to the West Coast and the legend begins.

Is this the opening scene from a classic romance movie? No, it's an early chapter from the life of "Gene™," Ashton-Drake's vinyl fashion doll that has become a runaway hit. From her introduction two years ago, "Gene" has taken the fashion doll world by storm. With her haunting good looks, based on a composite of Hollywood starlets of the 1940s and 1950s, "Gene" was the inspiration of talented, award-winning fashion illustrator Mel Odem.

"Gene's" fashion appeal is certainly based on her unique period look. But, what makes her truly special is that, along with her glamorous wardrobe and accessories, "Gene" has a "real life" as a movie star, with a story that is reminiscent of the tales found in vintage movie magazines. Her story is told little by little with every doll, costume and accessory that is introduced, so her "fans" get to know the character of "Gene" as they acquire her exciting fashions. The continuous story line keeps fans enthralled.

Since her debut, "Gene" has garnered six industry awards, including two "Doll of the Year" (DOTY) nominations, and the *Dolls* "Award of Excellence." She was recently one of only seven nominees for *Collectibles Business Trade* magazine's "Trendsetter of the Year" award for product line excellence and innovation.

"Gene" and Ashton-Drake are helping some young designers achieve stardom through the Young Designers of America contest. This annual recognition is dedicated to inspiring, recognizing and rewarding future fashion illustrators and designers in pursuit of their dreams. Two winning designs from the first competition – "Sparkling Seduction" and "The King's Daughter" – were put into the 1997 "Gene" line, with the teenage designers earning royalties that help fund their continuing education.

MORE AWARD-WINNING ARTISTS

Kathy Barry-Hippensteel. Cindy McClure. Brigitte Deval. All of these names are more than familiar to doll collectors. Each of these talented artists and others have become just as much a part of the Ashton-Drake family as the dolls they lovingly create. Doll enthusiasts have come to share in the joy, as each new member of the family is introduced, and the next arrival is anxiously anticipated.

As a sculptor of child and baby dolls, Kathy Barry-Hippensteel is another critically acclaimed, award winning artist. "Chen" was nominated for a *Dolls* magazine 1989 "Award of Excellence" and received the National Association of Limited Edition Dealers' 1990

Award-winning artist Kathy Barry Hippensteel captures a child's delight as "Jason" finds a new surprise at the park pond.

"Achievement Award." In 1992, the "Patricia, My First Tooth" doll, from the *Happiness Is...* collection, was nominated for a *Dolls* "Award of Excellence" and *Doll Reader's* "Doll of the Year." A year later, "Tickles," the first issue in the *Joys of Summer* collection, and one of her most sought-after dolls, was nominated for the same two awards. "Andrew," the first issue in the *Babies' World of Wonder* collection, has enthralled collectors with its sweet face and light-up firefly. With "Andrew," Kathy has again succeeded at her mission of bringing a smile to peoples' faces.

A perennial Ashton-Drake favorite is Cindy McClure, who continues to be a shinning star with her many "Doll of the Year" awards. "Victorian Lullaby" was nominated for the 1995 *Dolls* "Award of Excellence" and her latest creation for Ashton-Drake Galleries, "Melody," was nominated for a 1997 DOTY, as well as for a "Dolls of Excellence" award. This first issue in the *Forever Starts Today* collection is a beautiful bride wearing one of Cindy's most exquisite costume designs ever. Today, collectors eagerly seek her dolls because her originals and some of her Ashton-Drake issues have appreciated considerably on the secondary market. Most doll lovers, however, are attracted to her dolls for her ability to capture realistic emotion. Her flair for costume design perhaps has found its most natural expression to date in her *Forever Starts Today* collection.

Brigette Deval started her doll-making career very, very early. As a child, she made *stoche puppe* – dolls modeled over sticks and bottles – that were family gifts. Today, Brigette has brought her internationally acclaimed talent to Ashton-Drake, and doll collectors are lining up for the next glimpse at her wonderful dolls. Her latest offering under the Ashton-Drake name is the *Fairy Tale Princess* collection. The first issue in the series, "Cinderella," was nominated for a 1997 "Doll of the Year" award. Dressed in pale blue from head to toe, this doll has been quite a sensation with doll lovers and critics alike. This a new direction for Brigitte, who is best known for her breathtaking Madonnas in *Visions of Our Lady* and her angels in *Blessed Are the Children*.

I WANT THAT TEDDY BEAR

The ever-increasing strength of the collectible teddy bear market has led to the phenomenal acceptance of The Ashton-Drake Galleries' newest product line: *Gallery Teddy Bears*. Following the commitment to quality and value that has made them the leader in the collectible doll industry, *Gallery Teddy Bears* offers the work of today's most popular bear artists and designers, coupled with creative and animated subject matter. Each bear is fully jointed, crafted in top-quality plush, and given such important collectible touches as hand-stitched noses and mouths and beautifully tailored costumes. Every bear is hand-numbered on a pink leather heart patch sewn on the body, and a matching numbered Certificate of Authenticity is included.

Growth of this line has been rapid, starting with only two collection offerings in 1995 – *A Year with Addie* and *Nursery Rhyme Favorites* – and jumping to ten collections in the current line, for a total of 40 individual issues. Already, four *Gallery Teddy Bears* have been recognized for their outstanding artistry with nominations for the "Golden Teddy" award or the "Teddy Bear of the Year." In fact, "Little Bo Peep," by artist Joan Davis, won the 1995 "Golden Teddy" award in her category, an impressive beginning for *Gallery Teddy Bears*. Other nominations have been given to "Benjamin and His Puppy" (1996 TOBY) and "Bartholomew" (1997 TOBY), both by artists Pat Joho and Etta Foran, and the diorama, "We're All Knit Together" (1997 Gold Teddy) by Barbara Conley and Tracey Roe.

Brigitte Deval lets a young girl's fancy fly free with "Rapunzel," outfitted in a regal gown of green taffeta and a cap gleaming with "diamonds" and "pearls."

Designed by the mother-daughter team of Barbara Conley and Tracey Roe, "We All Knit Together" captures the joy that "Samantha" shares as she and "Grandma" spend an afternoon together sharing all kinds of wonderful activities.

Retirement of *Gallery Teddy Bear* issues takes place each Valentine's Day. The first bear to earn her retirement was "Little Bo Peep" on February 14, 1997. Announcement of her pending close was made in late 1996, and demand for the remaining inventory grew by dramatic proportions, forcing Ashton-Drake to remove her from catalog pages as supplies dwindled. While secondary market activity has yet to be determined, teddy bear lovers can watch the catalog each Fall for announcements about bears who will slip into a well-earned retirement.

ASHTON-DRAKE GALLERIES IN CYBERSPACE

Have you ever wanted to attend a premier doll show without leaving the comfort of your own home? Well, it's easy to do, if you log on to the Internet and visit The Ashton-Drake Galleries online at their website.

In 1996, Ashton-Drake truly became the doll company with a difference, when it turned its dolls into bits and bytes and posted them on the Internet's World Wide Web. Part of the Collectibles Today Network (www.collectibles-today.net), Ashton-Drake (www.ashtondrake.com) is the premier site for doll lovers worldwide to meet and share their experiences.

The site boasts numerous pages of content solely devoted to one interest – doll collecting. There are several chat forums for this topic alone, and one of the most frequented forums is devoted to "Gene." Freewheeling discussion abounds in these real-time chat rooms, as doll fans exchange their favorite stories, tips and rumors about the passion they all share for dolls. Other areas of the site are dedicated to doll artists, program highlights for upcoming Ashton-Drake doll segments on home shopping channels, and tips on doll care from the "doll care" professionals. There is even a game or two to test your mental mettle.

One of the most visited features of the Ashton-Drake site is the online store. Here doll lovers can purchase just about any product from the Ashton-Drake line quickly and easily. Through secure transactions, doll lovers can see a picture and read a description of the doll they want to order. With several simple mouse clicks, their order is sent for processing and the "doll of their dreams" is on its way.

TO LEARN MORE:

THE ASHTON-DRAKE GALLERIES
9200 N. MARYLAND AVENUE
NILES, IL 60714
(800) 634-5764
FAX: (847) 966-3026
URL: http://www.ashtondrake.com
E-MAIL: custsrv@ashtondrake.com

At the Heart of Plate Collecting

For more than 25 years, The Bradford Exchange has been at the heart of the limited edition plate market, playing a unique role by serving collectors interested in acquiring new releases and back issue plates

Since its birth in 1973, The Bradford Exchange, located in the Chicago suburb of Niles, has been one of the world's most successful marketers of new collector's plates. As a matter of fact, the company's legendary founder, J. Roderick MacArthur, introduced the fascinating hobby of plate collecting to the United States with the *Lafayette Legacy Collection*. Over the years The Bradford Exchange has introduced many innovative series, continually expanding the boundaries of plate collecting in the process.

The marketing of newly issued plates, or primary market plates, however is only one aspect of the remarkable services offered by The Exchange™. The company also operates an organized, orderly secondary market where collectors can buy and sell back-issue plates. To eliminate risk associated with long-distance trading, the Exchange guarantees both ends of the trade it brokers. Only Bradford-recommended plates are eligible for trading on the Exchange.

In 1997, The Bradford Exchange introduced the Collector's Choice Awards so that plate collectors could recognize their favorite artists. The "New Artist of the Year" award was presented to Chantal Poulin (left), and Lena Liu (right) received the "Artist of the Year" award.

THE COLLECTOR'S CHOICE AWARDS

In 1997, The Bradford Exchange established a series of unique awards to recognize the achievement of outstanding artists in the field of limited edition collector's plates. The criteria for choosing the winners was quite simple – allow plate collectors to vote for their favorite artists through their plate purchases.

Those chosen to receive these awards truly "embody the heart of plate collecting" which is what The Bradford Exchange strives for each and every day. Each award winning artist has brought the collector's plate medium outstanding artistic contributions, originality and insights, a high level of artistry, and most importantly, the ability to capture the hearts of plate collectors.

Chosen the Collector's Choice "New Artist of the Year," Chantal Poulin has become an overnight favorite with plate collectors. At the age of five, Chantal drew praise for her drawings and has been drawing ever since. She studied fine arts in Montreal, where she graduated from the College of Old Montreal and the Mission Renaissance School of Fine Art. Although best known for the freshness and spontaneity she brings to her paintings featuring children, it was actually landscapes that launched her career. In her heartwarming series, *Seasons of Sharing: Sisters for Life*, sisterhood is cause for celebration the whole year through. Using her talent for bringing a special knowing touch to every issue in this series, Chantal lets collectors witness a true bond that only sisters can share.

Master of the Oriental art of painting on silk, the Collector's Choice "Artist of the Year" is familiar to plate collectors. Lena Liu has become America's most beloved floral artist and a favorite among collectors. She is a past winner of NALED's "Artist of the Year" and "Plate of the Year" awards. Lena was one of the original inductees to The Bradford Exchange's Plate Artist Hall of Fame. Originally from Taiwan, where her studies in Oriental art began at an early age, Lena now resides in Maryland. She combines modern painting techniques, the gracefulness of Oriental art and traditional brushwork, in a unique style distinguished by freedom of movement, subtlety of color and a sense of tranquility.

The Collector's Choice "Canadian Artist of the Year" has always had a passion for sports and art. Glen Green has played a wide variety of sports, ranging from football to hockey to motorcycle racing. Naturally talented as an artist, Glen taught himself to draw and paint in watercolors. With a background in athletics, painting sports subjects was second nature to Glen. His enthusiasm shows most eloquently in his highly acclaimed celebrity sports portraits. In a studio behind his home, Glen has created art for the Vancouver Canucks and Montreal Canadiens, the Winnipeg Jets, B.C. Lions, the 1988 Olympic program and *TV Week* magazine. Canadian plate collectors became instant fans of the *Celebrating 25 Years of Team Canada* series. Using his

"Sisters Are Blossoms" from the* Seasons of Sharing: Sisters for Life *collection by Chantal Poulin has become an overnight favorite with plate collectors.

personal insight into hockey, Glen captured vibrant moments from Canada's greatest hockey triumphs in a well-received series of plates.

THE BRADFORD EXCHANGE PLATE ARTIST HALL OF FAME

Established in 1995 as part of its "Collectors Plates: The First 100 Years" celebration, installation in The Bradford Exchange Plate Artist Hall of Fame is an award presented to the best and brightest in the world of limited edition plate artists.

In recognition of their outstanding contribution to the fine art of collector's plates, five exceptional artists were chosen as inaugural inductees for this honor in 1995. Wildlife artist Charles Fracé; Thomas Kinkade, The Painter of Light™; romantic-realist painter Sandra Kuck; watercolor-on-silk artist Lena Liu; and the late Norman Rockwell – widely acknowledged as the "grandfather of the collector's plate artists" – earned the distinction of being named the five initial Hall of Fame inductees.

These world-class artists represent diverse and outstanding talent that has been embraced by millions of collectors the world over.

INNOVATIONS MAKE THE BRADFORD EXCHANGE UNIQUE

The Bradford Exchange is widely recognized as the industry leader in innovative plate designs, styles and enhancements. It was the first to introduce three dimensions – or sculptural artwork – on collector's plates in 1976 with "She Walks In Beauty," plate one in the *Romantic Poets* collection. Made of Incolay stone, this series featured bas-relief sculpture that captured undercut stone effects previously limited to freestanding sculptural art. This literally opened up a new dimension in collector's plates.

Since then, The Bradford Exchange's sculptural plates have grown as diverse as the collectors who choose them. Today, there's sculptural Winnie the Pooh plates for the Disney aficionado, dramatic wildlife plates with life-like eyes and majestic antlers that rise above the plate surface, the King of Rock and Roll, Elvis, on his own lit stage and Chicago's very own Michael Jordan showing off his famous "rim rocking." In short, there's something for everyone intrigued by the notion of dimension in collector's plates.

Musically inclined? With just the turn of a key, collectors can enjoy the melody of "Somewhere Over the Rainbow," the first-ever musical movie-theme collector's plate. For the sports enthusiast, listen to the first-ever "talking" plate: "Carlton Fisk: 1975 Home Run," which called a 30-second play on his famous World Series home run.

Recently, collectors were introduced to new plate shapes with the first-ever heart-shaped and angel-shaped plates. The Bradford Exchange continues to make plate market history such as it did when it brought the sights, the sounds, even the sensation of an old-fashioned carousel ride in "Swept Away," the world's first collector's plate to actually move.

THE BRADFORD EXCHANGE MUSEUM

When collectors walk into The Bradford Exchange Museum of Collector's Plates in Niles, Illinois, they have entered one of the world's largest and most prestigious exhibits of limited edition collector's plates. The museum's collection features plates from the past, as well as from contemporary painters, sculptors, illustrators and designers.

Plate enthusiasts can see the first collector's plate, a Danish blue-and-white Christmas annual titled "Behind the Frozen Window" (now valued at around $5,000 - $8,000) from Bing and Gröndahl. Visitors can also see the first collector's plates that were not blue and white, not porcelain and not issued at Christmas in the *Lalique Annual* series. These are etched crystal plates from France. Other areas of interest to the collector include Remembrances of Times Past, That's Entertainment, Stars of the Silver Screen and Playing Field, Beauty From Exotic Locations – And Your Backyard and The Home Front. Each area of the museum is designed to give the visitor a glimpse at the wide variety of collectible plates from makers around the world.

This unique and beautiful museum first opened to the public in 1978, five years after the founding of the Bradford Exchange. The display of nearly 800 plates, spanning the 100 plus years of collector's plates, beckon visitors to explore this one-of-a-kind museum. Free self-guided tours are available on Monday through Friday from 8:00 a.m. - 4:00 p.m and on weekends from

Lena Liu, Collector's Choice "Artist of the Year," captures the perfection of a delicate floral arrangement in "Remembrance."

Recently, The Bradford Exchange introduced collectors to new plate shapes, including angel-shaped plates. "Spring's Blossom," from the* Seasons of Joy *collection, is by award-winning artist Edgar Jerins.

10 a.m. - 5 p.m. The museum is closed on major holidays.

PLATE COLLECTING IN CYBERSPACE

The Bradford Exchange has a long history of firsts and the Internet is no exception. In 1996, The Bradford Exchange staked a claim in cyberspace as the first collector's plate company with a site on the Internet's World Wide Web. Part of the Collectibles Today Network (www.collectibles-today.net), The Bradford Exchange (www.bradex.com) is the premier site for plate collector's worldwide to meet and share their experiences.

The site boasts numerous pages of content solely devoted to one interest – plate collecting. There are chat forums for this topic which is one of the most frequented areas by visitors. Freewheeling discussion abounds in these real-time chat rooms as plate collectors share their favorite stories, tips and rumors about the passion they all share. Other areas of the site are dedicated to plate artists, tips on plate care from the "plate care" experts and there is even a how-to section on the secondary market.

One of the most visited features of The Bradford Exchange site is the online store. Here plate collectors can purchase just about any product from The Bradford Exchange's line quickly and easily. Through secure transactions, collectors can see a picture and read a description of the plate they want to order. With several simple mouse clicks, their order is sent for processing, and the newest edition to their collection is on its way.

MUSEUM

THE BRADFORD MUSEUM OF COLLECTOR'S PLATES
9333 Milwaukee Avenue
Niles, IL 60714
(847) 581-8654

Hours: Monday through Friday, 8 a.m. - 4 p.m.; Saturday and Sunday, 10 a.m. - 5 p.m.

Admission Fee: Free

The Bradford Museum of Collector's Plates houses almost 800 plates, spanning the 100-year history of collector's plates.

TO LEARN MORE:

THE BRADFORD EXCHANGE
9333 MILWAUKEE AVENUE
NILES, IL 60714
(800) 323-5577
URL: http://www.bradex.com
http://www.collectibles-today.net
E-MAIL: custsrv@bradex.com

Bringing Small-Town America to Life

"Gift Basket, "Corner Store" and "Pottery Barn" from **Hometown XIV**, *are shown featured on the 2"-deep, 24"-long* **Hometown** *"Picket Fence" display shelf.*

Every collector knows that a big part of the fun of collecting is being able to share their enthusiasm with others. Now, collectors of miniature buildings from Brandywine Collectibles can do just that with membership in the Brandywine Neighborhood Association.

The association was formed January 1, 1997 for Brandywine collectors and lovers of small-town Americana everywhere who want exclusive access to gifts, members-only products and detailed information about the miniature buildings that are "Capturing the Heart of America."

"The association represents a real milestone for us," says Brandywine founder and designer Marlene Whiting. "For years, we've been asking ourselves if we should start a club for our collectors, and we never could quite talk ourselves into it. Finally, we decided to listen to what our collectors and dealers have been telling us – to go ahead and take the plunge."

A BOUNTY OF BENEFITS AWAIT CLUB MEMBERS

The new-member building for the 1997 club year is Marlene's new edition of the "Moore House" in Yorktown, Virginia, where the terms of Lord Cornwallis' surrender to General Washington were drawn up in 1781, ending the Revolutionary War. (Brandywine's corporate logo also includes the "Moore House," as Yorktown is the Whiting's adopted home.) Members can select the style – *Hometown, Country Lane* or *Downtown USA* – in which they want their new-member building.

The members-only building for 1997 is "Manhasset," Marlene's family home from early childhood until she married Truman Whiting (or, as she likes to put it, "from before the invention of rope until slightly after the invention of the wheel.") Although "Manhasset" is a rather grandiose-sounding name, it refers to the street address rather than to the home itself. In reality, it was a small house of the sort popular in Pittsburgh's hilly residential neighborhoods in the 1940s and 1950s, which is still found there today.

Members also receive a catalog, storage case, Brandywine canvas book bag, the "Neighborhood News" quarterly newsletter, a building registry, shop list and free tours of Brandywine's production facility. Computer-minded collectors receive regular product updates via electronic mail.

"We're finding that collectors of all stripes are joining the association," says Marlene's daughter Donna, who administers the club's day-to-day activities. "We have some collectors with more than 100 buildings and some who joined after purchasing just a single piece. We have some who are partial to a specific Brandywine collection, and others who collect certain types of buildings regardless of what collection they're in.

"Collectors say the association is a good forum in which to learn about the history and memories behind mom's buildings, where she gets her ideas and how she translates those ideas into designs."

The fee for new members to join the Brandywine Neighborhood Association is $30.00, while the fee for renewing members in 1998 will be $25.00. Applications are available from: BNA, 4303 Manchester Rd., Portsmouth, Virginia, 23703. Fax number is: (757) 484-3961. E-mail address is: heartbwine@aol.com.

AN ANSWER TO THE DISPLAY CONUNDRUM

Another Brandywine brainstorm for 1997 is the company's collector display shelves. They make it easy for collectors who are running out of window and door frames to show off their collections. The shelves are available in several varieties.

The *Hometown* shelf is a sculpted hand-painted picket fence, complete with grass, bushes and heart-shaped wreaths on the gates. The *Downtown USA* shelf comes as a picket fence or as a brick wall, both featuring a print of an original painting by Marlene and both festooned with beautiful flowering vines, shrubs and heart-shaped wreaths.

All Brandywine shelves are available in 18" and 24" lengths and come complete with hardware so that they can be attached to virtually any type of wall. The shelves are 2" deep and are designed so that the fences do not cover the fronts of the buildings displayed on them. Marlene came up with the idea for the shelves while at a trade show in Dallas, where she was reminded that many homes, particularly in the West, are built without trim on the windows and

"Country Curtains & Furniture" is new to Brandywine's* Country Lane *collection. At approximately 6" x 6",* Country Lane *buildings are slightly larger than Brandywine's other offerings.

doors. The creation of the shelves seemed a perfect solution for these collectors.

To display on shelves and elsewhere, Brandywine has introduced a number of new buildings in recent months. For the 14th installment of the company's perennially popular *Hometown* series, Marlene designed and sculpted seven new miniature collectible buildings: the "Gift Basket," "Library," "Bakery," "Pottery Barn," "Lawyer," "Hook & Ladder" and "Corner Store."

A VARIETY OF NEW DESIGNS

Marlene introduced *Hometown* in 1990, and today the collection includes more than 70 designs recalling life in American small towns. New *Hometown* series are released twice a year and retired after two years production. Each is hand-painted, gift-boxed, hand-signed by Marlene, numbered in sequence, personalizable and eligible for a Certificate of Authenticity.

Country Lane, meanwhile, saw its fifth series released. New buildings include the "Barn Dance," "Country Curtains & Furniture," "Little League Field," "Noah's Zoo," "Uncle Joe's Farm" and "Quilts & Things." Each *Country Lane* building features a highly-detailed print of Marlene's original painting on the background with a hand-painted resin recreation of her original sculpture in the foreground. Like *Hometown*, *Country Lane* buildings are gift-boxed, numbered in sequence, personalizable and eligible for a Certificate of Authenticity.

Two new street scenes have joined the *Downtown USA* collection. "Collectors Corner" features "Coins & Stamps," "Villages & Lighthouses," "The Country Collector" and "Baseball Cards & Comics." "Hobby Hill" includes the "Pottery & Ceramics Shop," "Dance Studio," "Cross Stitch Stuff" and "Camera Shop."

Downtown USA collections are available as individual buildings or as street scenes. Collectors can buy individual buildings with standard or personalized names. Street scenes can be customized with the collector's favorite four buildings and a personalized street sign. All *Downtown USA* buildings can be ordered decorated for Christmas.

Downtown USA is taking a new twist this year by including buildings celebrating the special times in our lives, in the style of Brandywine's *Treasured Times* collection of cast resin buildings. Soon, *Downtown USA* will include buildings to celebrate "Birthdays," "Mothers Day," "Your First House," "Weddings," "Spring" and "Thanksgiving." Additionally, the "Sweethearts House" will appeal to collectors who want to acknowledge anniversaries, Valentines Day and any other day that merits a special memento.

Two new buildings have joined the *North Pole* family. The "Trim-a-Tree" shop features a big Christmas tree with colorful garland, topped with a blonde angel. (Trivia buffs take note: The "Trim-a-Tree" shop is the first Brandywine building ever with a green roof.) The "North Pole Chapel" features a snow-covered roof and stained glass windows.

Brandywine's most limited collectibles are those in its *Williamsburg* collection. The collection began in 1983, when Marlene showed her designs to a Williamsburg buyer. Soon, she and husband Tru were recreating popular and beloved buildings from the community's historic colonial district. Today, the *Williamsburg* collection includes 33 three-dimensional replicas.

THE MOST LIMITED COLLECTIBLES

For each building, the road from life-size building to miniature collectible begins with a visit to the historic district, where Marlene and Tru photograph, measure and take copious notes. Tru then recreates the original on graph paper, which he uses as a guide for cutting the real thing from Virginia poplar. At this point, Marlene takes over — hand-painting the entire building, replicating every aspect, even to such details as dogwoods and crepe myrtles.

Once the design has been accepted by the Colonial Williamsburg Foundation, Tru recreates more of the tiny buildings. Then, two of Brandywine's artisans hand-paint each, following notes from Marlene's original painting. Some of the pieces, such as "Christiana Campbell's Tavern," are so detailed that it takes eight hours just to paint one.

Marlene and Tru inspect each building and by hand add the copyright, building name, edition number and Whiting signature block to the bottoms. Each is finished with a protective

The "Carter's Grove" plantation house and "Bruton Parish Church" are part of Brandywine's exclusive* Williamsburg *collection.

The "Collectors Corner" street scene, from Brandywine's* Downtown USA *group of miniature buildings, celebrates the collector in all of us.

coating and shipped in a gift box.

Quantities of Brandywine's *Williamsburg* buildings are limited due to the painstaking design and production process. Collectors interested in these exclusive pieces can find them at the Williamsburg Inn Gift Shop.

PERSONALIZING REMAINS POPULAR

With virtually every Brandywine building, personalization continues to be an option with wide appeal. This inexpensive touch, performed in the retail shop or by Brandywine's artisans, can bring each building alive by reflecting the interests of the individual collector. Too, more and more collectors are finding that personalized buildings make cherished gifts.

For the wedding season, for example, a *Downtown USA* street scene can be personalized with the couple's last name and include four buildings with special meaning to the newlyweds.

The "Jewelry Shop" can be personalized with the name of the business at which the couple bought their rings, while the "Travel Agency" can carry the name of the company that made the couple's honeymoon arrangements. The "Brick Church" or "Clapboard Church" can be personalized with the couple's first names and wedding date, while the "Florist" can feature the name of the shop that provided the wedding floral arrangements.

Hometown collectors can get in on the fun, as well. *Hometown XI's* "Church II" and *Hometown XII's* "Travel Agency" and "Bridal/Dress Shoppe" can be personalized as appropriate.

BUILD YOUR OWN VILLAGE

Collectors have been enthusiastic about how Brandywine's buildings nicely complement other collectibles. Shopkeepers, too, note how the symbiotic relationship between various collectibles helps them with their displays and sales.

Collectors of various renditions of small cuddly animals, for instance, find that Brandywine buildings help set the perfect home display. Then too, Brandywine offers a number of accessories to complete the scene, from trees and carts to wagons and signage — and even a snowman.

ENCOURAGING CUSTOMER FEEDBACK

Whether it's about Brandywine Neighborhood Association activities, suggestions for new buildings, feedback on existing buildings, display ideas or simply requests for information about its products, Brandywine wants to continue to hear from their loyal collectors and fans. These collectors have helped the company grow from its origins on a kitchen table in 1981, to its status as one of the premier suppliers to the nation's gift and specialty industries.

"We exist solely at the pleasure of the collectors we serve," says company president Tru Whiting. "We're eager to know about their own memories of small-town America and about what we can do in our own small way to help them bring those memories alive — and to enjoy them all over again.

"We know you're out there. Let us hear from you!"

CLUB

BRANDYWINE NEIGHBORHOOD ASSOCIATION
4303 Manchester Road
Portsmouth, VA 23703
(757) 898-5031

Annual Dues: $30.00 - Renewal: $25.00
Club Year: Anniversary of Sign-Up Date

BENEFITS:

- Members-Only Piece
- Canvas Book Bag
- Quarterly Newsletter, "Neighborhood News"
- Storage Case for Newsletters
- Free Tours Available to Association Members

TOUR

BRANDYWINE COLLECTIBLES TOUR
104 Greene Drive
Yorktown, VA 23692
(757) 898-5031

Admission Fee: Free to Collector Club Members
Hours: 9 a.m. - 5 p.m.

Club members are invited to tour Brandywine's 9400 square foot manufacturing and distribution center and observe the fine craftsmanship that goes into the making of every Brandywine building.

TO LEARN MORE:

BRANDYWINE COLLECTIBLES
104 GREENE DRIVE
YORKTOWN, VA 23692-4800
(757) 898-5031
FAX: (757) 898-6895
E-MAIL: heartbwine@aol.com

Carolers Share the Christmas Spirit for All Seasons

In Bucks County, Pennsylvania, Joyce and Bob Byers celebrate Christmas all year round. There's lampposts flickering on cobblestone streets, shop windows brimming with toys, and musicians performing on one street corner and a Salvation Army band on the other. There's a postman delivering holiday cards, students walking to their school house, a children's Nativity pageant at a country church, skaters sliding across a frozen mill pond, and Santa's workshop filled ceiling high with toys.

From the beloved Charles Dickens' novel *A Christmas Carol*, there's the Cratchit family in their humble home, while Scrooge wanders throughout the village. Of course, Carolers are singing everywhere you look.

These Winter wonderland scenes greet Joyce and Bob as they go to work every day at Byers' Choice Ltd., which they built on the spirit of Christmas. For nearly two decades, the Byers have been creating a joyous choir of limited edition Caroler® figurines that re-kindle days gone by and the gentle beauty of the holiday season. From a Victorian Mrs. Claus to a man roasting chestnuts, each has its own personality and story to share.

Located in the company's Chalfont, Pennsylvania, production facility is the Byers' Choice Christmas Gallery, which opened in 1994 to display more than 400 figurines in various Winter vignettes. Collectors are invited to stop by the gallery, where they learn the history of the Carolers and see firsthand the reason why these singing characters have found a special place in the hearts of collectors around the world.

This traditional grouping of Carolers shows the Victorian beauty and harmony of the Byers' Choice Ltd. line.

CHARLES DICKENS AND CHRISTMAS INSPIRE FIRST CAROLER FIGURINES

During a trip to London in the 1960s, Joyce and Bob were browsing in an antique shop when they spotted a unique series of porcelain figures that appeared to step right from the pages of a Charles Dickens' tale. The timeless pieces captured the warm, traditional flavor of 19th century England.

When Joyce returned home, she came across a set of papier-maché choir figures that reminded her of the spirit of Christmas. While debating whether or not to purchase these as gifts, she was suddenly struck by a clever idea. She could create caroling figures that combine the feeling of 19th century England and Christmas.

An amateur artist with a degree in fashion design, Joyce began working on the project using materials she had at home: plaster, papier-maché, wire, paint and stacks of assorted fabrics. She was already adept at making crafts, which she enjoyed seeing come to life right before her eyes. Dressed in wintertime attire, each figurine opened its rounded mouth to sing favorite Christmas songs – just like carolers who go door to door during the holiday season. Joyce's first figurines reminded her of the classic characters from *A Christmas Carol*, so she simply called them "The Carolers."

BYERS' CHOICE REACHES NEW MARKETS

Family members adored The Carolers. Christmas shopping for Joyce soon became much easier, as many of the Byers' friends and relatives began asking for the figurines as gifts. A neighbor suggested taking the figurines to craft and antique shows. There, they sold out quickly, and word spread about Joyce's delightful creations. At one show, a New York display company official told Bob that his firm would be interested in buying figurines if they could be enlarged and altered according to the needs of its customers. Joyce rose to the challenge, thus sealing the fate of Byers' Choice Ltd.

Over the next years, Joyce, Bob and their two sons spent much of each autumn making figurines for friends, craft fairs, a few stores and the display company. As the demand grew, the family became busier in other seasons. After The Carolers began overtaking the Byers' dining room, they converted their garage to a workshop. In 1981, with the addition of full-time helpers, the family hobby was incorporated with Bob and Joyce officially casting their lot with The Carolers.

The holidays wouldn't be complete without the holly and poinsettias provided by "The Gardener."

A COLLECTIBLE BUSINESS THAT'S ALL IN THE FAMILY

Today, Byers' Choice Ltd. is still a family business that hires skilled handcrafters and professionally trained artists. In order to keep up with all the orders, the Byers had to make some changes in both the manufacturing process and, to a limited extent, the appearance of the figurines. While today's Carolers are very different from those produced in the early years, almost everyone agrees that the current look captures the Dickensian Christmas spirit even better.

Joyce still sculpts all of the faces and designs most of the clothing for each Caroler. Meanwhile, Bob tends to the financial and administrative side of the business. He also directs the company's extensive charitable giving to a host of local, national and international concerns. In 1987, son Robert took on the job of overseeing the figurine production process. Son Jeffrey joined the family business in 1990 as marketing manager. The company and its 150 employees moved into a larger facility in 1994. With a lot of hard work and imagination, Bob and Joyce have watched their hobby grow into a successful family business dedicated to serving the customer and, through their philanthropy, the community.

A FAMILY ALBUM OF CAROLERS

The family of Caroler figurines gets better each year and many of the older ones have become valuable collectors' items. Within the collection, there are various series and styles for everyone to enjoy. The *Traditional Carolers* portray men and women, boys and girls, and grandmothers and grandfathers dressed in wools, felts and plaids. They hold everything from scrolls and wreaths to muffs and snowballs. Each of the figurines is designed with a matching partner and is produced in an edition of 100 pieces.

The *Victorian Carolers* wear elegant satins, velvets, lace and furs. These are also produced in pairs limited to 100 of each design. *Victorian Mothers* pushing prams or helping their toddlers learn to walk have also been created.

In 1992, Joyce created the first *Salvation Army* figurine to celebrate the season of giving. A new piece is introduced annually with a portion of the proceeds benefitting the work of the Salvation Army.

In 1983, Joyce began working on a series of Caroler figurines based on *A Christmas Carol.* "Scrooge" in his nightgown was the first piece, and one or two figures were added each year for the next decade. First and second editions were produced. Now the cast of characters — from the "Fezziwigs" to "Marley's Ghost" — is complete. All but a few second edition pieces have been retired. With the close of the *Christmas Carol*, Joyce then began work on *The Nutcracker Suite* series in 1993. The figurines, which began with "Marie," are based on the German tale written by E.T.A. Hoffman that inspired Tchaikovsky to write his magical Christmas ballet.

The *Cries of London* series recreates the 19th century street vendors who often chanted catchy songs to get their customers' attention. Each year, Joyce designs a new figurine in the series, and the previous year's piece is retired.

In addition to a variety of Santas from around the world, Mrs. Claus and other holiday characters, Byers' Choice also offers specialty figurines, including Pilgrims, skaters, shoppers and various accessories.

GALLERY WELCOMES COLLECTORS TO CHRISTMAS AT BYERS' CHOICE

The Byers' Choice Christmas Gallery displays many Carolers from the past and present. Joyce and Bob always received numerous requests from collectors to tour the place where The Carolers are made, but the old facility wasn't set up to handle this activity. When the blueprints were drawn for the new Byers' Choice building, a special wing was conceived and dedicated to collectors. This visitors' center features scenes where collectors and Christmas aficionados can view The Carolers strolling among the streets of a London-like city, acting out roles in *A Christmas Carol* and much more.

Byers' Choice Ltd., home of the famous Byers' Choice Carolers, is located in Bucks County, Pennsylvania.

Visitors to the Byers' Choice Christmas Gallery can enjoy seeing the first figurines, production process and displays of more than 400 Carolers in beautiful Winter settings.

Visitors can also see Joyce's very first Carolers, retired pieces, a video of the company's history, and an observation deck overlooking the production floor. A rotating selection of 200 Carolers, as well as other Christmas-related gifts, are sold at the Emporium. As one Caroler fan said: "It is indeed Christmas 365 days a year at Byers' Choice." The Gallery is open to the public Monday through Saturday from 10 a.m. to 4 p.m. It is closed holidays. For information and directions, call (215) 822-0150.

"CAROLER CHRONICLE" KEEPS COLLECTORS UP TO DATE

From the beginning, Byers' Choice has received wonderful letters from fans telling how much the Caroler figurines mean to them. Included in the letters were an overwhelming number of questions which prompted the company to publish the "Caroler Chronicle," a color newsletter published three times a year. The "Caroler Chronicle" highlights stories behind various figurines, upcoming special events or introductions, and a chronological index of characters and the years of production.

GALLERY

BYERS' CHOICE CHRISTMAS GALLERY & EMPORIUM
4355 County Line Road
Chalfont, PA 18914
(215) 822-0150

Hours: Monday through Saturday, 10 a.m. - 4 p.m. Closed Sundays and Holidays.

Admission Fee: None

Visitors to the Byers' Choice Christmas Gallery enjoy a self-guided tour through the museum, which displays old and new Caroler® figurines. They can also see a video of the company's history and view the production floor from an observation deck. Selected gifts and caroling figures are sold at the Emporium.

TO LEARN MORE:

BYERS' CHOICE LTD.
4355 COUNTY LINE ROAD
CHALFONT, PA 18914
(215) 822-0150
FAX: (215) 822-3847
URL: http://www.byerschoice.com

Collectible Teapots Overflow with Creativity

Paul Cardew knows how to make the perfect cup of tea. It's a recipe he has been perfecting since 1991 and sharing with collectors all over the world. For Cardew, the cup floweth over. His company, Cardew Design, has brought back the fine art of teapots by adding its own sense of whimsy and style to brew one of the hottest collectibles on today's market.

There's always something growing near the "Gardener's Bench," a full-size teapot featuring watering cans, home-grown tomatoes and little helpers. The teapot is limited to 5,000 pieces.

From the company's two British pottery factories, teapots in all shapes and sizes delight collectors with their creativity. Everyday objects such as stoves, desks, toy boxes and sewing machines are transformed into teapots and embellished with miniature treasures that make each piece a fascinating vignette. Cardew Design has given this once humble item of kitchenware a new lease on life. Teapots have been elaborately designed, decorated and collected for over 300 years. Cardew Design fosters this heritage.

CARDEW BREWS A NEW BUSINESS

Paul Cardew always intended to be an architect, but the courses didn't live up to his expectations. So with his grandmother's encouragement, he entered Plymouth College for Art and Design in England. He took a ceramics class and within 10 minutes was in love. "I think it's the fact that you're working in 3-D just like architecture, only all the control and decision making is right there in your own hands," Cardew says. "This was the medium for me!"

To hone his skills, he then attended nearby Loughborough University where he met his wife, Karen, also a ceramics designer. She decided to try her hand at making brooches and earrings for a local college craft fair. For no particular reason, she made some of the jewelry in the shape of miniature teapots. They sold out, and she soon got an order for 5,000 more brooches. After a year, their newly formed company, Sunshine Ceramics, grew rapidly. More orders kept flooding in, including one from the British Tea Council. Overwhelmed with their success, they decided to focus more and more on teapots. The company successfully evolved over a number of years, including a change of name to Southwest Ceramics and additional partners. In 1991, Cardew decided to strike out on his own again with the help of Peter Kirvan. Kirvan, a close friend of Cardew, had been running his own London advertising agency but was looking for a new challenge. With Kirvan's experience in managing the creative process and Cardew's design talents, they joined forces in 1991 to form Cardew Design.

Together, they studied the fine tradition of teapots and tea drinking, which began in China more than 4,000 years ago. Tea came to Europe in the early 1600s. And, of course, with tea came teapots. Thanks to new technologies, mediums and ideas, master potters and craftsmen shared endless opportunities for teapot designs. Today, Cardew Design takes advantage of this same concept. "As a three-dimensional item, the teapot's potential for great design, and a lot of fun, is almost limitless," Cardew says.

TEAPOTS FOR ALL COLLECTOR TASTES

Teapot collectors come in all shapes and sizes, so it is only appropriate that Cardew Design's teapots should be the same. The company's goal is to make a teapot to suit every taste and show that imagination knows no bounds. The early days when they made their teapots in one standard size are long gone. Cardew and his team are creating six-, two- and one-cup teapots, along with tiny teapot ornaments.

Cardew Design initially started by making larger teapots that could hold six to eight cups. The Cardew full-size pots are all designed according to the rules of functional teapots, so that handles and spouts are in the right places and the position of the main body encloses an appropriate volume for brewing tea. These designs are also produced as a limited edition. Each piece is clearly marked in the tradition of English fine art with its own unique identity number within the run. Once the 5,000 edition limit has been reached, the designs will come out of the catalog and the production molds destroyed. Among the most recent full-size designs are a teapot resembling a farmhouse fire-

"Classical Fireplace" is prominently adorned with gold lion heads and other prized possessions, including a classical clock. The full-size teapot is limited to 5,000 pieces.

place, gardener's bench and classical fireplace.

The company began producing One-Cup Teapots in 1994 and Tiny Teapots the following year. In 1995, Cardew also developed a teapot that was practical to use for an everyday cup of tea but also collectible and fun. The result was the Brown Betty line of full-size teapots, which are dishwasher safe. The classic round teapot is fired in brownware but is a little more detailed than the traditional original. In fact, the colors of the teapot base range from dark green to bright yellow to complement the highly decorated lid, which is the only area that can carry miniature ceramic designs and decorations.

In 1997, Cardew made it easier to have an afternoon tea for two. The company developed a range of Two-Cup teapots. Artistically, they provide a marvelous platform for even more miniature detail, plus that all important extra "cuppa!" Designs include a television, jewelry box, sewing machine, Welsh dresser and birthday party table.

A range of Disney Art Classic character teapots covers all shapes, sizes and characters, including the latest introductions of "Winnie the Pooh" and "Lady and the Tramp," which are available exclusively through Disney Stores and fine collectible and gift stores throughout the U.S..

Cardew also created a licensed collection in association with Royal Doulton. The stunning collectible teapots feature the world's most popular china pattern, Royal Albert's "Old Country Roses."

CLASSIC TEAPOTS GIVE NEW LOOK TO FAMILIAR KITCHENWARE

Cardew Design has always felt it is the duty of every teapot to give pleasure and entertain. So for some time, the designers have wondered why the traditional breakfast teapot has remained so dull. That frustration has led to the launch of a range of Classic teapots that are practical yet personable.

Cardew's starting point was to create the definitive breakfast teapot shape, combining a well-balanced body (which holds six cups) with a spout and handle in perfect proportion. Taking inspiration from the forms and structures within classical Greek architecture, it took much hard work and study before Cardew was entirely satisfied with his design.

A range of classic-shaped teapots, functional and dishwasher safe for everyday use, feature a zip and flair fitting of a Cardew Design. The Classic teapots come in six- and two-cup sizes with wonderful animal skin print designs, an antique world globe and a host of other decorative features. The Cardew Classic range also doesn't stop at the six-cup pot. Cardew has crafted an elegant two-cup pot and a superb mug in the same style.

THE MAKING OF A CARDEW TEAPOT

A Cardew teapot begins life deep underground where nature has worked hard over thousands of years to make the basic ingredient – clay. The teapot also begins in the minds of Cardew and his designers, who come up with all the new concepts, handcraft all the prototypes, and create the master molds.

In deciding what ideas should be turned into three-dimensional teapots, the designers go through a standard checklist: Does the idea have magic factor X?; Can it actually function as a teapot?; Will the teapot be able to be produced with quality and at an affordable price?; and Is it something collectors will really enjoy?

From sketches and ideas, the sculptors work with the finest clay to bring the teapots to life. A master mold is created from plaster of paris. All the pots are then fired in electric kilns to carefully regulate the temperature for the best results. All Cardew teapots receive three separate firings at different temperatures. The first at 1010 degrees Centigrade turns the clay into porous biscuit. The second is hotter to turn the glazed biscuit into a glazed pot. A final gentler firing fuses the decorations, such as precious metal lustres and picture transfers, onto the pot surface.

Finally delicate miniatures, which have been separately cast and decorated, are then bonded directly to the pot surface. As the last step before shipping, each teapot is thoroughly inspected, even though every craftsperson had already checked his or her own work at every stage.

The main design studio sits on about nine acres on Woodmanton Farm, located in Devon County with its rolling green hills and meadows. The farmhouse and outbuildings have been transformed into a pottery factory.

Cardew Design combines the classic-shaped teapot with a modern flair. A tiger print design covers this six-cup pot, which is functional and dishwasher safe for everyday use.

Cardew works from the old farmhouse kitchen. The second pottery at Bovey Tracey lies near Dartmoor. Bovey, unlike Woodmanton, has the space to offer factory tours, a Mad Hatter's Tea Room, and an activity center where visitors can learn to be teapotters. During normal business hours in the week, Cardew Design invites all visitors for a free tour to see the world's most collectible teapots being made.

The growth of the Cardew Collectors' Club, which was launched in 1995, bears undeniable testimony to the magnetic attraction to teapots, especially the Cardew variety. Now American connoisseurs of Cardew collectible teapots have the opportunity to join the Cardew Collectors' Club. In 1997, the United States Club was established by Cardew's new distributor, DeVine Corporation.

CARDEW COLLECTORS' CLUB STARTS IN UNITED STATES

The 1997 members-only gift was a unique tea mug one-cup teapot with a silver spoon in its lid. Members also had the chance to acquire, through their local Cardew retailer, the special collectors' limited edition design — a one-cup tea cup teapot. It is superbly modeled after a classic English tea cup and decorated with a beautiful blue willow pattern. Limited to 5,000 pieces worldwide, each teapot comes dated, numbered and signed by Paul Cardew. Annual membership also includes a full-color catalog, subscription to "The Teapot Times" (published three times a year), and membership card. For more information on joining the U.S. Cardew Collectors' Club, please contact the customer service department at DeVine Corporation at (732) 751-0500.

CLUB

THE CARDEW COLLECTORS' CLUB
c/o DeVine Corporation
1345 Campus Parkway
Neptune, NJ 07753
(732) 751-0500
Fax: (732) 751-0550

Annual Dues: $40.00
Club Year: Anniversary of Sign-Up Date

BENEFITS:

- Tiny Teapot Membership Gift
- Opportunity to Purchase Members-Only Teapot
- Quarterly Newsletter, "Teapot Times"
- Membership Card
- The Cardew Teapot Collection Catalog

TOUR

THE CARDEW TEAPOT POTTERY TOUR
Bovey Tracey Pottery
Newton Road
Bovey Tracey TQ13 9DX England
01144 1626 832172

Hours: Tours Monday through Friday, 9:30 a.m. - 5:30 p.m.
Tea Shop and Gift Shop Open 7 days a week, 9:30 a.m. - 5:30 p.m., excluding Bank Holidays.

Admission Fee: None

Visit the Cardew Teapot Pottery and see the world's most collectible teapots actually being made.

TO LEARN MORE:

CARDEW DESIGN
C/O DEVINE CORPORATION
1345 CAMPUS PARKWAY
NEPTUNE, NJ 07753
(732) 751-0500
FAX: (732) 751-0550

CARLTON CARDS

Heirloom Collection™ Ornaments Make the Season Bright

Christmas is the number one collecting theme in the United States, and no company knows that better than Carlton Cards. For the past decade, the *Heirloom Collection* ornaments from Carlton Cards have helped celebrate the holidays and share the season's joy throughout the year. It's a Christmas collectible that continues to grow year after year.

Since its debut, the *Heirloom Collection* has become known and loved for its highly detailed, imaginative designs. Whether they mark baby's first Christmas, celebrate favorite pastimes or recognize someone special, the ornaments commemorate the true meaning of Christmas.

The *Heirloom Collection* starts new holiday traditions with a delightful selection of *Collector's Series*, licensed characters and technology ornaments featuring lights, music and motion. It just doesn't seem like the holidays without them.

"Ho-Ho-Hold On!" is the 1997 membership ornament for the Heirloom Collection Collector's Club. Santa rides in a bright green bumper car, complete with silver electroplating and charter year marking.

THE BEGINNINGS OF THE *HEIRLOOM* COLLECTION

The *Heirloom Collection* traces its history to 1988 when the Summit Corporation, an American Greetings subsidiary, introduced 41 ornaments. The ornaments were sold under the Summit logo in various stores throughout the United States and Canada. One of the most popular ornaments in the first *Heirloom Collection* was the dated "Mouse on an Ice Cube," which remains popular on the secondary market.

In 1989, Summit expanded its line to 44 ornaments. Carlton Cards, an American Greetings division, made its grand entrance into the ornament industry by offering 40 Summit-designed ornaments under the Carlton logo.

In 1990, Summit again expanded with 72 more ornaments, while Carlton offered 50 of the designs. It also marked the beginning of the popular *Collector's Series* ornaments with "Santa's Roommate," "Christmas Hello," "A Little Bit of Christmas," "Christmas Go-Round" and "Christmas Express."

Summit and Carlton were exclusively offered under the Carlton logo in 1991. The assortment included 72 ornaments, the continuation of the *Collector's Series* and the debut of Carlton's first musical, "Little Taste of Christmas," featuring the ever-popular *Honey Love Bear*. Also introduced was "Purr-fect Holidays." Although this kitten on a glass ball ornament was never intended to become a series, it was such a surprise hit with collectors that Carlton has offered the dated ornament in a new color each year since.

For 1992, Carlton expanded to 90 ornament *Heirloom Collection* designs, including three new series: *Christmas Sweets*, *North Pole Parade* and *Rodrick and Sam*. In 1993, 135 designs were introduced along with two new series: *Book of Carols* and *Tiny Toymaker*. Also introduced were Carlton's first three lighted ornaments: "Warm 'n Toasty," "Christmas Waltz" and "Up On The Housetop."

Three new ornament series started in 1994: *Big Fun*, *Snug In Their Beds* and *Santa's Toy Shop*. In 1995, the *Heirloom Collection*, which is available exclusively at Carlton retailers, debuted 135 designs with "Elvis" ranking among collectors' favorites. Carlton also debuted several new licensed ornaments, including Volkswagen™, HERSHEY'S™ and Pillsbury®.

For 1996, the *Heirloom Collection* focused on traditional themes but also used the latest technology to delight collectors with lights, motion and music. Among the *Heirloom Collection's* designs were the second in the *Elvis* series and another icon of the entertainment world, "Marilyn Monroe."

New *Collector's Series* included "Joy Is In the Air," "Merry Mischief," "O Holy Night," "Jolly Old St. Nick" and "Wonderland Express." Also premiering in 1996 were five holiday collections, each featuring three coordinating ornaments.

LICENSED ORNAMENTS ADD CHARACTER TO COLLECTION

Bigger and better than ever, the 1997 *Heirloom Collection* offered 170 different designs. From Hollywood film stars to classic cars, the *Heirloom Collection* offers six new licensed designs for 1997. The *Legend* series, begun in 1996, continues with Charlie Chaplin™ "Silent Star." With his trademark hat and cane, twitching mustache and

It's Betty Boop™, the cartoon icon and beauty of the 1930s! Now she appears in "Surprise!" – a 1997 ornament featuring her cheerful "Boop-Oop-A-Doop!" greeting.

darting eyes, Chaplin conveys many emotions without saying a word.

Betty Boop™ wiggled her way into America's heart during the 1930s. Carlton remembers everyone's favorite flapper with the ornament titled "Surprise!" The delightful ornament features her cheerful "Boop-Oop-A-Doop!" greeting.

Nancy™ & Sluggo have been winning the hearts of comic strip readers since 1938. Now Carlton introduces "Perfect Present" with the duo dressed in their authentic attire. Tom & Jerry™ "Come Back Here!" delights fans of this classic odd couple that have starred in more than 200 cartoons. In this ornament, Jerry steals all of Tom's presents.

Carlton revs up the holiday with "Classic Christmas," an exact replica of an automotive legend – the 1964 1/2 Ford Mustang™. For more than 50 years, Lassie™ has entertained audiences with courageous and heartwarming acts. Lassie comes home in the *Heirloom Collection* ornament "All Set For Santa," which lights up.

Other continuing licensed favorites are Paddington Bear™, Play-Doh®, Rocky and Bullwinkle™, Opus 'N Bill™, Campbell's® Kids and Elvis™, making his third and final appearance.

MINIATURE COLLECTION TRIMS THE SEASON

Knowing the best things often come in small packages, Carlton Cards introduced a new line of miniature ornaments. The *Little Heirloom Treasures* debuted in 1997 with 35 beautifully detailed, hand-sculpted ornament designs – each no larger than 2 1/4". Many of the ornaments are dated and accented with 14K gold plating, porcelain, glitter or fabric attachments.

Building on the *Heirloom Collection's* popular *Collector's Series*, the *Little Heirloom Treasures* includes two "first in a series" designs. "On Track For Christmas" begins a train series with Santa as the engineer. "Old Fashioned Fun" is a classic rocking horse design. Both ornaments are dated.

The collection also includes a number of nostalgic designs, including "The Nutcracker Prince," featuring the famous character; "Visit From Santa," a classic St. Nick design; and "Jennifer's Wish," a beautiful Victorian doll.

Religious designs are especially popular at Christmas. Carlton meets the collecting trend with "Heavenly Friends," an angel holding a bluebird; "Lambkin," a cute lamb with a message of love; "Mother and Child," a pastel rendition of the Madonna and child; "All Creatures Great and Small," featuring Noah's Ark; and "Christmas Messenger," a beautiful holiday angel. Whether purchased as family keepsakes, gifts or holiday decorations, the *Little Heirloom Treasures* ornaments add beauty, warmth and the spirit of Christmas that make every celebration so memorable.

In addition to the ornaments, the *Little Heirloom Treasures* lines, features a decorative miniature tree, star tree topper, mini-light string, satin tree skirt and mini-glass balls, among others. This collection is just the right size to decorate mini-trees throughout the home, thus sharing the magic of the season.

HEIRLOOM COLLECTION COLLECTOR'S CLUB WELCOMES ORNAMENT COLLECTORS

With the growing popularity of its ornaments, Carlton introduced the Heirloom Collection Collector's Club in 1997. Charter year members receive many exclusive benefits, including the membership ornament "Ho-Ho-Hold On!" featuring Santa in a bright green bumper car, complete with silver electroplating. Members also have the opportunity to purchase the 1997 members-only ornament "Heavenly Handiwork," an adorable angel stitching a gorgeous quilt. She is designed with iridescent wings, brass halo and real thread and needle. Other benefits are an annual subscription to the official club newsletter, charter year membership pin, Heirloom Collection Collector's Guide and a toll-free number to call with questions about the collection.

Like any collectible, an *Heirloom Collection* ornament begins with an idea. The collection's research and design team works throughout the year

The* Little Heirloom Treasures *features miniature ornaments with hand-sculpted details and charm. "On Track For Christmas" begins a train series with Santa as the engineer.

Charter year members of the Heirloom Collection Collector's Club have the opportunity to purchase the members-only ornament "Heavenly Handiwork." She has iridescent wings and a real needle and thread!

THE MAKING OF AN *HEIRLOOM COLLECTION* ORNAMENT

trying to find new inspirations and creative concepts for the next ornament. Sometimes ideas for the ornaments come from a popular greeting card or gift wrap. Other ideas, which may take up to three years to formulate, stem from the latest paint finish or technological advance, such as a new sound chip that could be placed inside an ornament. Designers also visit gift and toy shows searching for inspiration.

After an ornament design has been completed and approved, specifications are sent to sculptors in the Orient. They develop a prototype ornament according to the designs from the shape, size and color, right down to the sparkle in Santa's eyes. Using the prototype as a model, artisans hand-sculpt all the individual components of the ornament into a steel die. The die is then placed in a hydraulic press, and heated plastic is forced into the mold through an injection process.

After the pieces have cooled, they are carefully checked by hand for accuracy against the original line drawing and the prototype ornament. Each ornament has a specific color palette that may contain up to 56 different colors. Artisans separately hand spray each color. As the ornament moves throughout the process, more colors are added. When all the pieces are painted, each ornament is assembled by hand. Using a strong bonding agent, the workers melt each of the individual pieces together for durability. The final result is a beautiful collectible ornament that will be cherished for years to come.

CLUB

HEIRLOOM COLLECTION COLLECTOR'S CLUB
Carlton Cards
c/o Leslie Parsons Cavanaugh
One American Road
Cleveland, OH 44144
(888) 222-7898

Annual Dues: $20.00 (plus $3.75 s&h)
Club Year: July 1 - June 30

BENEFITS:

- Redemption Certificate for Members-Only Ornament
- Membership Gift
- Quarterly Newsletter, "The Collector's Chronicle"
- Heirloom Collection Collector's Guide with Binder
- Membership Pin

TO LEARN MORE:

CARLTON CARDS
A DIVISION OF AMERICAN GREETINGS
ONE AMERICAN ROAD
CLEVELAND, OHIO 44144
(888) 222-7898
FAX: (216) 252-6751

CAST ART INDUSTRIES, INC.

Offering Creative Figurines from Talented Artists

"Heaven's Gate" is the limited edition commemorating the 5th anniversary of **Dreamsicles®**. *To date, all of the retired limited editions have increased in value on the secondary market.*

Just over five years, ago, California-based Cast Art Industries took the collectible gift market by storm with the introduction of the now-famous *Dreamsicles®* collection. Since that time, the company has produced the works of additional talented artists representing a wide range of styles and subjects. The result is an exciting array of collectible figurines that are certain to please any collector.

Cast Art Industries was founded in December 1990 by Scott Sherman, Frank Colapinto and Gary Barsellotti, three friends with more than 50 years of combined experience in the gift industry. Sherman was formerly a Florida corporate president, who, despite his youth, had substantial experience in administration and marketing. Colapinto, a long time resident of California, has spent most of his career building a national sales force in the gift industry. Barsellotti, Italian-born and trained, is an expert in the manufacturing of fine quality figurines.

In record time, the company has become an important contributor to the gift and collectibles industry. Cast Art has earned a well-deserved reputation for producing fine quality handcrafted products at very affordable prices.

THE DREAMSICLES® PHENOMENON

In March 1991, Cast Art introduced *Dreamsicles*, a group of 31 adorable cherub and animal figurines designed by artist Kristin Haynes. Kristin's fresh approach to a timeless subject was an instant hit with the gift-buying public, and *Dreamsicles* rapidly became one of the most popular new lines in the world of collectibles.

Within the first year, Cast Art and *Dreamsicles* were catapulted into the forefront of the collectibles and gift industry, receiving national recognition as the Best Selling New Category at the Gift Creations Concepts (GCC) industry show in Minneapolis. In addition, *Dreamsicles* was recognized as the #1 selling general gift line, and Kristin has received numerous other industry awards.

In record time, *Dreamsicles* became recognized as one of a handful of true "collectible" product lines. This success is highly unusual, since most items of this type are not recognized as true collectibles until several years after release. Virtually all designs in the line have attained a collectible status, and many of the retired figurines have already shown substantial price increases on the secondary market.

The line now numbers over 250 designs and includes animals, holiday pieces, a nativity collection, and a gemstone series, in addition to a growing variety of cherubs. The *Dreamsicles* concept has also been successfully expanded to include related collections known as *Dreamsicles Kids™*, *Dreamsicles & Me™* and *Heavenly Classics™*.

In response to public demand, Cast Art is actively engaged in a licensing program which offers leading manufacturers of a variety of products the use of the *Dreamsicles'* designs and logo. These delightful cherubs are appearing on such items as collector plates, candles, greeting cards, watches, cross-stitch patterns, plush toys, designer checks and other products.

AN ARRAY OF CREATIVE PRODUCT LINES

The *Bumpkins* are country "folks" created by Tim and Arline Fabrizio and were first introduced to the market in 1983. Reproduced in porcelain, this line was a best-seller in the gift industry for several years.

Collectors can celebrate the true meaning of Christmas with the* Bumpkins™ *Nativity entitled, "Oh Holy Night."

By special arrangement with the Fabrizio's, Cast Art reintroduced the line in mid-1996 to include updated original pieces, along with brand new designs. The newest *Bumpkins* are involved in such themes as sports, music, motherhood, holidays, and more, to make up an extraordinary collection.

Slapstix is the name of a hilarious new line of figurines that pokes fun at folks at work and play. The collection includes a variety of side-splitting professional and sports characters. Included are a doctor, a police officer, a hairdresser, a golfer, a skier, and a hockey player, and other recognizable subjects that make the perfect gift... especially for a man. Designed by Cast Art's in-house studio team, the figurines are uniquely sculpted to capture the genuine look of fabric. *Slapstix* are proving to be show-stopping, and that's not just clownin' around.

"Downhill Thrill" from* Slapstix™*, a rib-tickling new collection that pokes fun at folks both at work and at play.

Cast Art's most recent acquisition is the innovative Victorian sculptural collection, *Ivy & Innocence*, by artist Susan Reader. This charming series of cottages, figurines and accessories is notable for Reader's highly detailed designs and her subtle use of color. Nominated for the prestigious *Collector Editions* magazine "Cottage of the Year" Award, *Ivy & Innocence* made its first appearance as a Cast Art collection in the Spring of 1997.

The collecting public got its first look at *Ivy & Innocence* during the International Collectible Exposition in Rosemont and received an overwhelmingly positive response. This new product launch included a unique opportunity for collectors to get in on the ground floor of a collectors' club. *Friends of Ivy* member kits included a special Charter Member figurine, a quarterly newspaper and a storybook album presenting the unique history of *Ivy*. Each chapter of the story describes a scene which includes characters, architecture and accessories. Yates' Antiques Shop (chapter three) is one of the seven inaugural chapters.

The *Animal Accents* collection is the creation of Cast Art's talented studio artist Leo Romero and features 12 zany animals that add a flare of fun when hung from potted plants, lamp shades, letter trays or just about anywhere. The new line was introduced in January of 1997.

THE DREAMSICLES CLUB OFFERS MANY BENEFITS

The Dreamsicles Club, formed in 1993, is one of the nation's fastest growing collector organizations. The Club offers members the opportunity to share their appreciation of the charm and beauty of Kristin Haynes' adorable cherubs and animals. Mem-

"Free Spirit" by Kristin Haynes, celebrates the fifth year of growth and fun for the Dreamsicles Club. This spirited figurine is free to Club members as the "Symbol of Membership" for 1997.

"Emily's Welcome" is the* Ivy & Innocence™ *logo piece.

bers also have the chance to purchase members-only figurines, many of which have already become highly collectible. Figurines such as "Daydream Believer" and "Makin' A List" are among the unique designs that only Club members have been able to purchase. Other benefits include a free "Symbol of Membership" figurine, a Club binder and printed photo guide to the collection, an embossed personalized membership card, and a subscription to the colorful "ClubHouse" newsletter, featuring quarterly information about new product introductions, retirements and much more. Annual membership dues are $27.50.

In the past five years, Cast Art has achieved a reputation for providing quality collectible giftware at affordable prices. The company has experienced five consecutive years of record sales and continues to introduce the works of talented artists representing a wide range of styles and subjects. The result is an exciting array of collectible figurines that touch the hearts of many, while maintaining the company's philosophy of offering competitively priced products which represent outstanding value.

PROVIDING QUALITY PRODUCTS WITH OUTSTANDING VALUES

CLUB

DREAMSICLES CLUB
1120 California Avenue
Corona, CA 91719
(800) 437-5818

Annual Dues: $27.50 - Renewal: $23.50
Club Year: Anniversary of Sign-Up Date

BENEFITS:

- Membership Gift: Cherub Figurine
- Opportunity to Purchase Members-Only Cherub Figurine
- Quarterly "ClubHouse" Newsletter
- Three Ring Binder
- Personalized, Embossed Membership Card
- Buy/Sell "Wish List" in Newsletter
- *Guide to The Dreamsicles* Photo Book
- Membership Pin
- Members-Only Contests and Special Events

TO LEARN MORE:

CAST ART INDUSTRIES, INC.
1120 CALIFORNIA AVENUE
CORONA, CA 91719
(800) 932-3020
FAX: (909) 371-0674

URL: **http://www.castart.com**
http://www.dreamsicles.com
http://www.dreamsiclesclub.com
http://www.bumpkins.com
http://www.ivy-innocence.com
http://www.slapstix.com
E-MAIL: **info@castart.com**

The innovative Victorian sculptural collection,* Ivy & Innocence, *features a charming series of cottages, figurines and accessories created by artist Susan Reader.

CAVANAGH GROUP INTERNATIONAL

The Place to Find America's Best Brand Collectibles

In 1990, Cavanagh Group International began offering refreshing collectibles that welcomed back the famous Coca-Cola Santa and other timeless images and designs that helped create America's favorite soft drink. From the classic Santa illustrations by Haddon Sundblom that appeared in *The Saturday Evening Post*, to the adorable polar bears that now appear on television commercials, Cavanagh shares the rich heritage and tradition of Coca-Cola art for everyone to enjoy.

Cavanagh added two powerful collectible brands to its already established Coca-Cola line in 1997. The company welcomed McDonald's and Harley-Davidson, making Cavanagh the place where collectors can discover – and re-discover – the most recognized and popular licensed brands in the world. With Coca-Cola, McDonald's and Harley-Davidson, Cavanagh has selected high-powered brands that have a loyal and growing collector following.

Cavanagh's 1997 collector's cookie jar combines two favorite Coca-Cola images: the famous Coca-Cola Polar Bear and the old-fashioned Coca-Cola vending machine. Limited to 25,000 pieces, this is the fourth in the* Coca-Cola Polar Bear Cookie Jar *series.

COCA-COLA MAKES A REFRESHING CHRISTMAS

It's hard to recall a time when Coca-Cola wasn't our favorite national drink! From coast to coast, the "Coke" logo fanned across billboards and magazines even before the turn-of-the-century. In 1931, Sundblom was commissioned to paint Santa Claus enjoying Coca-Cola. Sundblom's burly and fun-loving Santa soon became America's most recognized St. Nick. Since then, other illustrations and characters have endeared Coca-Cola to several generations who can now find their favorite memories in fine collectibles.

"We've been given the keys to the Coca-Cola Company archives," says John F. Cavanagh, president of Cavanagh Group International, "and we're creating a line of high-quality, authentic collectibles. It's a wonderful opportunity for collectors to discover and enjoy a wealth of Coca-Cola art and advertising images by such renowned artists as Haddon Sundblom, N.C. Wyeth and Norman Rockwell."

The company's signature line is the *Coca-Cola Christmas Collection*, which nearly doubled in size in 1997. In its eighth season of creating hand-painted Santa ornaments, Cavanagh adds one new charming subject based on Sundblom's masterpieces. The ornament, which features Santa at his desk, joins three remaining pieces. As a result of the artist's successful advertising campaign, which has continued for more than 65 holiday seasons, Cavanagh's line of Santa ornaments attracts loyal Coca-Cola collectors. To date, 20 ornaments have been retired.

Inspired by the fun-loving and popular Coca-Cola polar bears seen on television commercials, Cavanagh continues to expand its *Cola-Cola Polar Bear Collection.* Two new ornaments that are bound to become classics join four other subjects. The four ornaments issued in the premier series were retired in 1996.

A new collection of six Coca-Cola Polar Bear Cub ornaments are certain to be favorites of the next generation. The Polar Bear Cubs reflect the messages of family, friendship, as well as Christmas caring and sharing.

Two hand-painted resin ornaments were added to the highly successful *Coca-Cola North Pole Bottling Works.* The series is based on the tale that when Santa and his elves aren't busy making toys, they are bottling Coca-Cola in the North Pole! The new ornaments feature Santa riding a Coca-Cola truck and an elf polishing a Coca-Cola top.

Five more handcrafted porcelain buildings join the popular *Coca-Cola Town Square Collection*, which is authentically drawn from the archives of The Coca-Cola Company. The village welcomes "Central High," "South Station," "Mrs. Murphy's Chowder House," "Dew Drop Inn" and "Variety Store." A special deed is affixed to the bottom of each building, indicating the year of release. Since the collection's 1992 introduction, 31 buildings have been created and 23 have been retired.

The Coca-Cola mini-musical collection features three more multi-movement musicals with the Coca-Cola Polar Bear and Penguin. The musicals sway as they play famous Coca-Cola tunes including "I'd Like To Buy The World A Coke" and "Always Coca-Cola."

One of the hottest new Coca-Cola collectible categories is bean bag plush. Six whimsical little critters warm up the Christmas season with their innocence and charm. Cavanagh helps collectors round out their collection with Coca-Cola collectibles that cover the tree from top to bottom. Cavanagh introduces a plush polar bear tree topper with a Coca-Cola insignia, plus two new Coca-Cola tree skirts. Cavanagh also revives the popularity of lamp covers, gorgeous collectibles based on the late 19th century Tiffany-style lamps. The bright collection snaps over any miniature Christmas tree light.

Santa rides the "Harley Tour Glide" in this ornament that takes to the road in a line of collectibles by Cavanagh. The ornament, which replicates the motorcycle in exact 1/18th scale, retails for $20.00.

MCDONALD'S COLLECTIBLES SERVE UP FAMILY FUN

Since 1955, McDonald's has been the place where good food, fun and family come together. By focusing on kids and families, McDonald's has created an emotional experience and bond with customers all over the world. There are currently more than 14,000 restaurants worldwide with 22 million customers per day. A McDonald's restaurant opens somewhere in the world every 18 hours, and each year 96% of all adults in this country will pay a visit to McDonald's.

McDonald's is also home to Ronald McDonald, America's favorite advertising character, who has grown and developed during his 25-year history. In fact, children's recognition of Ronald McDonald is universal: 99% of all children in America know the red-headed clown. They also recognize four other popular characters: Grimace, The Hamburglar, Birdie the Early Bird and Fry Kids – all of which rank among the Top 10 of kid's favorites. The characters help serve up the entire McDonald's experience, which includes quality, service, value, image, innovation and fun – along with a great hamburger and famous french fries. These are the key ingredients that have made the fast-food restaurant into the world's largest restaurant organization and the third leading brand in the world.

So it's no surprise that Cavanagh is proud to introduce McDonald's collectibles, including a *McDonaldland Village* of lighted buildings. There's "McDonald's Restaurant," "McNugget House," "Grimace House," "Birdie's Tree House," "Hamburglar Jail House" and "McDonaldland Theater." The village, of course, is inhabited by familiar characters enjoying their favorite activities from the Fry Kids building a snowman and the Hamburglar stealing burgers to the McNuggets zooming down a slide and Grimace delivering mail.

The line also includes a Grimace cookie jar, and four different stocking holders portraying the most popular McDonald's characters – all of which are friends that children and their parents know they can trust and believe in.

McDonaldland Village ***is one of the featured products in the new line of McDonald's collectibles by Cavanagh. The ceramic buildings – from "McNugget House" to "Hamburglar Jail House" – retail for $17.99.***

HARLEY-DAVIDSON COLLECTIBLES RIDE INTO TOWN

For nearly 100 years, the Harley-Davidson brand has meant the time-honored values of freedom, defiance and self-expression which are central to the American experience. No meeting hall on the planet can hold the 300,000-member

The hottest new bean bag plush are the cool Coca-Cola Polar Bear, Penguin and Seal. Since the mid-'97 introduction, several million have already been collected and the six, original designs retired. New editions are now being introduced.

H.O.G. (Harley Owners Group), who purchase nearly $1.5 billion in motorcycles and accessories each year.

Legendary designs like the Sportster, Fat Boy, Tour Glide and Springer Softail, along with the patented V-Twin Harley engine, created an overwhelming demand that has new buyers lining up three years in advance to purchase some models. The unique culture and legacy of Harley-Davidson, with its fierce and loyal following, has raised the company to a special status among America's most treasured brands. In the simplest terms, Harley-Davidson is truly "King of the Road."

With this in mind, Cavanagh launched a new line of Harley-Davidson collectibles, including Harley ornaments, figurines, stocking holders, stockings and plush. Legendary Harley-Davidson motorcycle designs, along with the famous Harley engine, are replicated in exact 1/18th scale for the first-ever injection molded and die-cast ornaments. Among the first three ornaments is Santa riding a Harley-Davidson Electra Glide Standard while wearing a leather jacket and carrying a sack full of toys to deliver on Christmas Eve.

The Harley-Davidson brand also provides a much-needed collectible for men. According to a recent marketing report, collecting for those in the Baby Boomer generation is a personal expression of themselves, their aspirations and their values. The same is true for men. This trend is captured in Harley-Davidson collectibles.

Leila Dunbar, author of the book *Motorcycle Collectibles*, says "motorcycle stuff is really just taking off. It's a very good time to start collecting." Indeed, the Harley-Davidson brand has the power to make even the most common items instantly desirable and valuable. Harley memorabilia is hot!

So when collectors want to find the finest Coca-Cola, McDonald's and Harley-Davidson collectibles, they know they can turn to Cavanagh. "Our McDonald's and Harley-Davidson product lines will carry forward the same integrity and quality of our *Coca-Cola Christmas Collection* and continue to offer affordable prices to collectors," explains John Cavanagh.

COMMITTED TO THE BEST-LOVED BRANDS

Collectors can count on Cavanagh for spectacular and heartwarming collectibles that will become the heirlooms of tomorrow.

Saddle up for the fastest moving bean bag plush by Cavanagh. Harley-Davidson bean bag plush that is, featuring such new stars as, "Ratchet" the pig, "Motorhead" the bear, "Big Twin," "Punky" and friends.

CLUB

CAVANAGH'S COCA-COLA CHRISTMAS COLLECTORS SOCIETY
P.O. Box 768090
Roswell, GA 30076
(800) 653-1221

Annual Dues: $25.00
Club Year: January - December

Benefits:
- Membership Gift: Authentic Collectible Drawn from the Archives of the Coca-Cola Company
- Quarterly Newsletter
- Membership Certificate, Suitable for Framing
- Personalized Membership Card
- Periodic Offers on Special Items Reserved for Society Members

TO LEARN MORE:

CAVANAGH GROUP INTERNATIONAL
1000 HOLCOMB WOODS PARKWAY
#440-B
ROSWELL, GA 30076
(770) 643-1175
FAX: (770) 643-1172

The Charming Tale of *Charming Tails®*

Dean Griff, creator of the *Charming Tails®* collection, was the fourth of six children born to owners of a 500 acre farm in rural Oneida, New York. There could not have been a better setting for Dean to develop a lifelong fascination with and love for the natural world. While growing up, he took long walks through the nearby woods and observed with keen interest the animals who made their home there.

During his years at Stockbridge Valley Central School, a growing interest in drawing led Dean to study art rather than enroll in agricultural classes with his siblings. In 1983, at 23, he left the family farm to take a job as Assistant to the Curator of the Syracuse University Art Collection. Entries and awards for his wildlife paintings in university art shows followed, as did a small business in hand-painted, hanging ornaments, which Dean originally gave as gifts to his friends.

In 1989, Dean moved from New York to Florida to work as a set decorator for television programs and commercials. In 1992, Dean designed the first 12 *Charming Tails®* designs. Their success was immediate and overwhelming.

It's Fall in Squashville, and Maxine and Mackenzie have found the perfect home in an "Acorn Built for Two."

CHARMING TAILS CHARACTERS COME TO LIFE IN A MAGICAL WORLD

The woodland creatures inhabiting the magical world of this collection are often found in human situations, but can never be mistaken for cartoon animals – they appear very much as they would in their forest homes. By adding equal parts of magic, mischief and innocence, Dean succeeds in giving his collectors a lovely link back to the natural ties many of us have forgotten. Mice, bunnies, raccoons, butterflies and skunks, to name a few, have come to life to tell the charming tale.

The creations of Dean Griff have the knack of spurring memories long forgotten and evoking emotions unique to each piece. The consideration of those qualities is key to his design process. Dean feels the true essence of "collectibility" has less to do with the mechanics of availability, but much more with the feelings the items bring to their collectors. It is his wish for people to collect the things meaningful to them, and he thanks the fans of *Charming Tails* for making the group collectible!

THE EARLY YEARS OF CHARMING TAILS

The *Charming Tails* collection was introduced as a line of seasonal decorative products with a heavy emphasis on autumn and Christmas themes. Mackenzie Mouse debuted as the first named character of the group. Many of the early designs were functional. Wreaths and baskets of woven grapevine became "playgrounds" for some of the collection's adorable critters. Candleholders were also available.

Shortly thereafter, a transition to a more traditionally collectible line began. The functional accessories were discontinued, and the first dated piece appeared in 1994 with "A Mackenzie Snowball," the annual ornament for that year. Since then, a dated annual ornament has been offered each year. Annual ornaments celebrating "Our First Christmas Together" and "Baby's First Christmas" are now also available.

THE COLLECTION EVOLVES WITH EXCITING NEW INTRODUCTIONS

Already, many of the molds for these high-quality resin pieces have been retired. Care is being taken to keep the collection fresh and exciting. In 1995, the first numbered pieces were added to the collection. In 1996, the first pieces with

A clear pond provides a tranquil setting for Maxine and Mackenzie to enjoy a "Row Boat Romance."

This year, there's an airborn addition to the Squashville Parade – "The Santa Balloon."

specific production runs were introduced. These two pieces, "Mackenzie Building a Snowmouse" and "Sleigh Ride," sold out immediately. To add to all of this interest, a formalized Artist Appearance Program was successfully begun in 1996. In addition to the trade shows, Dean appears in nearly 20 retail stores for signing events annually.

Originally, the *Charming Tails* collection was divided into seasonal categories – "Easter Basket," "Spring Has Sprung," "Trick-or-Treat," "Autumn Harvest," "Deck the Halls" and "Squashville." Dimensional Greetings, originally a separate line of figurines with "greeting card" type messages and not attributed to *Charming Tails*, was introduced and sold through wider channels of distribution. The current evolution of the group has narrowed the offering to five major classifications. The *Charming Tails* group includes non-seasonal pieces and incorporates the original Dimensional Greetings line which is now distributed through the same limited channel of dealers as the rest of the collectibles. It is interesting to note that more pieces of social expression-type merchandise will be added soon, due to the many requests received. "Easter Basket" covers the Spring season. "Autumn Harvest" captures the best of Fall with Halloween, harvest and Thanksgiving themes. "Squashville" continues with figurines, as well as a lighted village group, and "Deck-The-Halls" rounds out the collection with unforgettable Christmas and Winter themes.

A BRIGHT FUTURE FOR *CHARMING TAILS*

Many things, exciting and meaningful, are planned for *Charming Tails* in the months and years to come. The news of the introduction of a Collector's Club has prompted hundreds of requests for additional information. The Leaf & Acorn Club for *Charming Tails* was launched in April 1997, at the Long Beach International Collectible Exposition and will serve as a two-way conduit for information and ideas.

New line extensions will include *Charming Tails* pins, as well as sub-groups to the classifications listed above. For instance, the *Charming Tails* group will include the new *Lazy Days of Summer* collection – one of the cutest categories ever! Over time, other small groups will follow.

The long-term direction for the distribution of *Charming Tails* pivots around the retailer as much as the

These* Charming Tails™ *"Bunny Buddies" are the best of friends.

This* Charming Tails® *figurine, titled "You Couldn't Be Sweeter," offers collectors a special way to send a message from the heart.

collector. Programs will continue to be developed and introduced to assist the retailer in anyway possible, creating a partnership of great benefit.

Work continues on expanding the advertising and marketing tool package for dealers. Dean travels extensively throughout the United States, and recently Toronto, Canada, attending signing events. These events continue to astound both retailers and collectors alike with the incredible turnout of collectors and enhanced business. The sense of occasion which accompanies them provides an intimate and friendly atmosphere for the established collector and an exciting place for a new collector to become acquainted with the world of *Charming Tails*.

Whether by walking through "Squashville," or taking a ride on the "Charming Choo Choo," or just by enjoying the many everyday moments, the *Charming Tails* family and Dean Griff want to thank collectors again for sharing in the magic!

CLUB

THE LEAF & ACORN CLUB
P.O. Box 78218
St. Louis, MO 63178-8218
(800) 486-1065

Annual Dues: $24.50
Club Year: 1st Year Charter Membership Provides Benefits through December, 1998. Subsequent Club Years run January - December

BENEFITS:
- Members-Only Figurine
- Membership Gift: Figurine
- Personalized Membership Card
- Semi-annual Newsletter, "Squashville Gazette"
- Invitations to Special Events
- Notifications of Other Members-Only Offers

TO LEARN MORE:

FITZ AND FLOYD COLLECTIBLES DIVISION
13111 N. CENTRAL EXPRESSWAY
SUITE 100
DALLAS, TX 75243
(972) 918-0098
FAX: (972) 454-1208

CHRISTOPHER RADKO

. . . AND ALL THROUGH THE HOUSE

For Christopher Radko, what appeared to be his family's loss has turned into a gain for collectors around the world. It all began in 1984 when the holiday season was unfolding according to the Radko family tradition. While Christopher was growing up in Scarsdale, New York, the highlight of his family's Christmas was decorating the tree with their astonishing collection of blown-glass ornaments. Three generations of Radkos had collected more than 2,000 of the handcrafted treasures. As a boy, Christopher loved to slide under the fresh pine tree's lowest branches, where he was mesmerized by the reflection of the bubble lights, twinkling stars and shimmering spheres.

But in 1984, as Christopher was performing his annual chore of removing sap and needles from the old tree stand, he decided that a new one was needed. After shopping around, he bought a stand guaranteed to support an 18' tree - a good 4' taller than the Radkos' own tree. With the new stand, the old traditions continued as family members trimmed the tree.

One cold December morning, however, a loud crash suddenly changed the idyllic scene. Despite its guarantee, the stand buckled and the tree fell to the floor, shattering more than half of the fragile decorations.

"I was absolutely heartbroken because those ornaments were our family's direct link to the traditions and memories of four generations of Christmas celebrations," Christopher recalls. "Even though I knew there was no way I could replace the ornaments my great-grandmother and grandmother had handed down, I thought that the least I could do was buy some substitutes so our tree wouldn't look so forlorn." He searched in the stores near his hometown and shopped the major department stores all over New York City. Sadly, he discovered that most ornaments were being made from plastic and other mysterious materials. The few glass ornaments that he found were poorly crafted, and the painted details were frightful.

Christopher Radko strongly believes in the true meaning of the holiday season. Each year he designs ornaments whose profits fund organizations that help individuals in need of support. The 1997 charity ornament, "A Caring Clown," benefits those affected by AIDS.

REVIVING A TURN-OF-THE-CENTURY TECHNIQUE

The following Spring, while Christopher was visiting relatives in Poland, a cousin introduced him to a farmer who once made blown-glass ornaments. He said he might be able to make several new ones. There was only one catch: Christopher had to supply him with detailed drawings of the kinds of ornaments he wanted. Upon seeing the designs, the glassblower said that they were just like the ornaments that his father and grandfather had made before World War II. Although the craftsman had never made such complicated pieces, he said he would be happy to try.

After Christopher returned to the United States with his newly crafted treasures, family members and friends clamored for glorious glass ornaments of their own. At that point, he realized there was an appeal to these ornaments beyond his wildest imagination.

Today, over a decade later, Christopher engages the services of 1,000 Polish, German, Czech and Italian glassblowers who masterfully create his ornaments. Ideas for his exquisite designs come from memories of his family's antique ornaments as well as his other inspirations: architecture, fabrics, films and museum collections. It takes about a week to make each ornament, which is blown, silvered, lacquered, painted and glittered entirely by hand. Designs range from the traditional Santa Claus to a pipe-smoking monkey, and from rabbits to Persian peacocks.

"My company's success has allowed me to revive Christmas crafts and techniques that were all but lost," Christopher says. "As a Christmas artist with my annual collection of new designs, I am revitalizing a tradition of designing that had its heyday at the turn-of-the-century. My glassblowers are uncovering old molds and relearning skills that their cottage industry hasn't used in over 70 years. Now, even young apprentice glassblowers are being

Christopher Radko created "Regency Santa" in 1997 as the second design in the popular* St. Nick Portraits *series. This magnificent ornament is limited to 2,500 pieces.

trained in the traditions of their great-grandfathers, ensuring that fine glass ornament making will continue into the next century. That's something to celebrate!"

CONTINUING THE TRADITION

Christopher has created over 3,000 ornament designs since he presented his first collection of 50 blown-glass Christmas ornaments in 1986. His designs have become highly collectible because half of all the ornaments in the line are retired or changed in some way each year.

Some of the designer's most revered collectibles are those ornaments within his limited edition series. Following the success of "Partridge in a Pear Tree," Christopher continues to create designs for his popular *Twelve Days of Christmas* series. "Five Gold Rings" is the fifth ornament inspired by the holiday song. Handcrafted in the Radko tradition, production is limited to 10,000 with each piece receiving a hand-numbered tag.

Introduced in 1997, "Sugar Hill" is the first ornament in the exciting *Home for the Holidays* series. The intricate three-piece set of incredibly detailed houses is limited to a production of 10,000. And a second ornament has been added to another of Christopher's successful series, *St. Nick Portraits.* Called "Regency Santa," production of this exquisite design is limited to only 2,500. Each year Christopher also makes an event ornament that is only available during Radko presentations nationwide.

Since 1993, when Christopher designed his first ornament for charity, "A Shy Rabbit's Heart," he has been producing ornaments each year to benefit organizations that help people affected by AIDS and pediatric cancer. The profits from these popular designs have provided hundreds of thousands of dollars to over 20 organizations.

Christopher also makes a soccer ball glass ornament, "Matthew's Game," to benefit The Matthew Berry Memorial Scholarship Fund in Dallas, Texas. Providing positive direction for inner city youth, this fund awards college scholarships and supports activities that teach sportsmanship and team spirit. "Watch Over Me" is the first ornament created for The Christopher Radko Foundation for Children established in 1997. Proceeds from this design will benefit the Polish Children's Home.

Committed to helping others, each year Christopher has donated fully decorated trees for auction; and he produces an ornament for ®The Make-A-Wish Foundation. Individuals who purchase this special ornament help the Foundation grant wishes of children with terminal or life-threatening illnesses.

Christopher has brought one of America's leading entertainment companies — Warner Bros. Studios — into the world of fine glass ornaments. Many of these specialty designs are limited editions. Other licensed products in the collection include the Muppets, Barbie™, The Wubbulous World of Dr. Seuss™, and Harley Davidson®. The artist's ornaments are bought year-round as gifts for birthdays, anniversaries, housewarming parties and bridal or baby showers.

EXPANDING HORIZONS

Since 1995, Christopher has reached beyond the Christmas tree to bring his fine decorative products throughout the holiday home. The talented designer also enjoys sharing creative decorating ideas that can be used during the Christmas season — or any time of year. His detailed, blown-glass ornaments, however, are the inspiration for Christopher Radko's *Home for the Holidays* collection. Decorative home products include snow globes, musical figurines, collector plates and oil paintings. All are limited editions which bring his holiday magic to every room of the house.

Christopher gathers his new line of ornaments every year to produce a magnificent collage. Called *Kaleidoscope*, this striking creation is featured on gift wrap, casual porcelain mugs and other fine decorative products. The rich, gold-burnished rim of Christopher's collector plate encircles this magnificent pattern. *Kaleidoscope* will be limited as the designer brings together his new line of hand-fashioned glass ornaments for the next year's collage.

Even though Christopher may lead his business into new dimensions, collectors can always expect the same emphasis on quality, the same attention to detail, and the same desire to bring joy to people: the everlasting hallmark of Radko designs.

All collectors seem to find something captivating and comforting

"Sugar Hill" is the first design introduced in the exciting 1997* Home for the Holidays *series. The three-ornament set of incredibly detailed houses is limited in production to 10,000.

when surrounded by Christopher's designs. Katherine Hepburn, Arnold Schwarzenegger and Maria Shriver, Barbra Streisand, Elton John and Whoopi Goldberg are numbered among the devoted Christopher Radko collectors.

Launched in 1993, The Christopher Radko Starlight Family of Collectors has encouraged family traditions through the sharing of finely crafted glass ornaments and Christmas home furnishings. The enthusiasm for Radko ornaments and home decorative accessories continues to flourish with Starlight members numbering over 26,000.

STARLIGHT CLUB WELCOMES RADKO COLLECTORS

Members receive a free gift ornament when they join or renew, and they may purchase a special members-only ornament. In addition, membership includes an exclusive subscription to *Starlight* magazine, a quarterly publication that contains the latest information on Christopher's new and special ornament designs; a list of ornaments to be retired; articles on Christmas history and holiday decorating ideas; and a sneak preview of the exciting new lines in home decorative accessories. Each Starlight member also receives a copy of the catalogue; storage folio; a Christopher Radko pin; a personalized and embossed membership card; and an ornament button. New or renewing members can receive an application savings with the introduction of the Starlight multiple year membership plan.

"I am supported by thousands of loyal collectors who recognize the care and extraordinary quality each ornament and holiday home product represents," Christopher says. And now, thanks to the Christmas mishap at his family's home years ago, any collector can trim a tree and decorate their entire home with Christopher's blown-glass, hand-painted ornaments and fine decorative holiday accessories - without going to Europe to find them.

CLUB

STARLIGHT FAMILY OF COLLECTORS
P.O. Box 533
Elmsford, NY 10523
(800) 71-RADKO

Annual Dues: $50.00 - Renewal: $37.50
Multiple-Year Membership Plan Available
Club Year: January - December

BENEFITS:

- Membership Gift: Ornament
- Opportunity to Purchase Members-Only Ornament
- Quarterly Magazine, *Starlight*
- Personalized Membership Card
- Annual Ornament Button
- Exclusive Christopher Radko Pin
- Current Collector's Catalogue

TO LEARN MORE:

THE CHRISTOPHER RADKO STARLIGHT FAMILY OF COLLECTORS
P. O. BOX 533
ELMSFORD, NY 10523
(800) 71-RADKO
URL: http://www.christopherradko.com

Christopher's* Home for the Holidays *collection features fine decorative products that can be used throughout the home. The* Decoupage on Glass *line of holiday accessories is fashioned with a technique revived from Victorian times.

COTTAGE COLLECTIBLES® BY GANZ

From Our Hearts to Yours

Ganz began in 1950 as a small, family owned and operated company that produced teddy bears. The business soon gave a new start to the Ganz family, who arrived in Canada after fleeing their native Rumania. With a $100 investment and a great deal of hard work, Ganz grew steadily and began to play a part in the U S. market, where the company became well known for its quality plush animals.

Who says they will fight like cats and dogs? "Callie" and "Snowflake" by Mary Holstad get along just fine with "Farley," "Scrubber" and "Champ" by Lorraine Chien. "Floppy Joe" and "Floppy Jill" don't need to even worry about keeping an eye on their little charges.

In 1991, company President Howard Ganz made a conscious decision to expand the product line beyond plush to include figurines, gifts and collectibles. The birth of the collectible division in that year brought the fun and whimsy of many Ganz artists to collectors all across North America. The idea to combine the well-earned reputation for quality plush characters with the growing collectible products collection had always been the dream of the family. *Cottage Collectibles*® was the perfect way to make the dream of collectors come true.

Cottage Collectibles® first came to the hearts and minds of collectors in June of 1995. *Cottage Collectibles*® is more than just teddy bears; it is the expression of love and joy each artist brings to her craft. Starting with a handful of charming characters in soft sculpture, *Cottage Collectibles*® soon offered a vast array of limited edition keepsake figurines depicting these fun little fellas in everyday, good clean fun! Not content to offer collectors just the basics, the collection now includes a complete selection of bear accessories, clothing and a few surprises along the way.

DESIGNED FROM THE HEART OF THE ARTIST

Throughout time, cottage artisans working in their homes have created their crafts with deep love and passion. They have made some of the most beautiful, charming and one-of-a-kind designs in the world. Ganz is pleased to bring a unique collection of soft sculptured characters, figurines and accessories inspired by some of these artisans to collectors all over the world. Well known and award-winning artists, such as Mary Holstad, Carol E. Kirby, Lorraine Chien, Terry Skorstad, Christy Rave and Catharine Tredger have worked together with *Cottage Collectibles*® to bring to life the dreams and hugs of their exquisite characters.

PRECIOUS PLUSH PALS

Each of these soft sculptured creations are a labor of love and comes stuffed with a little piece of each artist's heart. Not just teddy bears, but a veritable menagerie of characters, including "Floyd" and "Flora" frog, "Rita" and "Ricky" raccoon, "Camille" and "Parsley" bunny, "Callie" the calico cat and even "Jerry," the hound dog, are ready to find a good home with just the right collector. Each character is given their own name and personality profile, which are artfully presented on a parchment hangtag.

What collectible would be complete without the artist's signature? *Cottage Collectibles*® characters all feature the artist's initials on the footpads and hangtags. Handcrafted of fine fabrics, each creature has been designed by and subjected to the exacting standards of the original artist before ever coming into the Cottage for the collector.

Using special techniques, *Cottage Collectibles*® offers handcrafted, artist designed teddy bears and cuddly animals at a price to suit any collector. The attention to detail shown in fashioning realistic whiskers for cats, hand-outlined eyes, and arms sturdy enough to hug and cuddle even the biggest kid, is a challenge rewarded with the joys and smiles of collectors when they acquire their first new friend from the Cottage. These little details make the personality of each character all the more captivating.

EXCITING TIMES AT THE COTTAGE

Even though the Cottage artisans have been extremely busy making their little critters ready to go out into the world, they have taken time to find out how their creations have touched the lives of collectors. All of the artists are in touch with the hearts and minds of collectors through shows,

First in an upcoming series of "Yes-No" bears, "Dexter" is not only charming, but extremely flexible. Just move his tail up and down, and he will be the most agreeable bear yet. But, move his tail from side to side, and he will be downright stubborn in his refusal! "Honey" has not just a muff to keep her warm, but a little companion carefully holding onto her hands. Both are designed by Lorraine Chien.

magazine articles and collectors publications every chance they get. That is why they get so excited when they hear how much collectors love and cherish their creations.

In 1996, "Dempster" by Lorraine Chien was the proud winner of a "Golden Teddy" award sponsored by *Teddy Bear Review* magazine. It is a good thing "Dempster" is such a humble bear or all of the attention could have gone to his head! He is setting a good example for "Robbie" by Mary Holstad and "Patches" by Lorraine Chien, who are both nominated for 1997 TOBY℠ awards sponsored by *Teddy Bear and Friends* magazine. There was no need to explain to either of them how special they must be to be nominated, and what a great responsibility it will be to live up to those kind of expectations.

KEEPSAKE FIGURINES

While it may be true that many of the soft sculptured characters created for *Cottage Collectibles®* are at their best when lounging around and being lazy, most of these playful little friends prefer to be busy and full of spice! The *Keepsake Figurines* catch them in the midst of their many hobbies and favorite pastimes.

Reminiscent of the joys of childhood, the *Cottage Collectibles® Keepsake Figurines* depict so many of the magic moments in our lives like the first birthday, playing with our favorite toys, working in the garden or maybe even whipping up a batch of cookies. Even the most important days in the year, like Independence Day and Easter, are brought to life to rekindle so many of our fondest memories of those special days.

Each *Keepsake Figurine* is inspired by the soft sculptured characters and accurately transforms these soft and unique personalities into the highest quality figurine. The original drawing and sculpture are created with the same love and affection as the soft sculpture.

All *Keepsake Figurines* are strictly limited to 3,600 pieces of each series. Each figurine is hand-painted and is hand-numbered on the detailed and information-packed permanent understamp. To be sure they are comfortable during their long journey, figurines are placed in full-color gift boxes, each with a sturdy styrofoam bed to ensure their safety. Starting in the Fall of 1997, each figurine will also include a Certificate of Authenticity.

To be absolutely sure you have a genuine *Cottage Collectibles® Keepsake Figurine*, you will need to play a little game of hide and seek. Hidden somewhere in the world of each figurine is a little mouse. It is easy to sneak up on him and find his "hidey-hole," and once you do, he'll tell you to rest assured, you have a genuine *Keepsake Figurine*!

NOT JUST FIGURINES

It doesn't matter if you collect figurines, plates or bears: *Cottage Collectibles®* has the perfect addition to your collection with five *Limited Edition Keepsake Plates.* Strictly limited to 2,500 pieces each, the plates are gift-boxed and come with a Certificate of Authenticity and a little home of their own with a black iron display stand.

Collectors were so entranced by the artist's creations in the *Keepsake Figurines,* the company felt compelled to create ways to bring these characters to other little corners of collectors' lives. Now, you can have "Root Bear" build his little soda fountain around the treasured photograph of your family's bubbliest personality! The *Keepsake Frames* are handcrafted, gift boxed and are available to hold the

"Fore," "Tis the Life," "Bubbles 'n' Fizz" and "My American Hero" show you the wide variety of pastimes and passions of the* Cottage Collectibles® *family. Each* Keepsake Figurine *is limited to 3,600 pieces and has a hidden mouse to verify its authenticity.

Frame your family with love!* Cottage Collectibles® Keepsake Frames *depict the charming and cuddly characters you have come to know and adore. "Floyd" comes in two versatile sizes, while "Dempster" is busy finding out "The Sky's the Limit." "Annie" and "Rusty" are ready for "Bathtime." All characters are designed by Lorraine Chien.

most popular sizes of photographs.

Instead of hanging around a picture, you can have "Emily," "Buddy" or "Forest" hanging around your neck, so to speak. The *Keepsake Pin-dants* are a clever little invention that lets you pin these playful pals on your lapel or just let them hang around as a pendant. These same gleeful greeters can be found with a magnetic personality in the form of *Keepsake Magnets* for holding those important papers on the refrigerator.

It has been said that these critters will bring light to any room, but now there's a better way to say it with *Keepsake Switchplates*. The best behaved of the bunch have been put into service to be ready and waiting to help bring a little light onto any subject you choose by guarding and decorating your light switches.

FINISHING AND FURNISHING TOUCHES

Cottage Collectibles® would not be complete without their own belongings. Their wardrobe includes a variety of knit sweaters, pants, hats 'n' scarves and even spectacles! All the sweaters are designed to reflect the warmth they give the little ones when they are snuggled into them. In a variety of colors and sizes, they are sure to be the perfect accessory to luxurious living. When it comes time to lay back and relax, *Cottage Collectibles®* characters can grab a book, slip a pair of spectacles over their noses, and snuggle back into a piece of wicker furniture. Armchairs and beds will give that "home sweet home" feeling to any destination.

THE HOLIDAY COLLECTION

Cottage Collectibles® are a very festive group, and they will help collectors celebrate and decorate in style. Ten soft sculptured characters from Lorraine Chien, Carol E. Kirby and Christy Rave are complemented by 11 *Keepsake Figurines* and 12 festive *Keepsake Pin-dants*, depicting the cozy and warm sentiments of the holiday season. Rounding out the collection are 12 *Cottage Collectibles® Keepsake Ornaments* suitable for tree decorating, wreaths and package tie-ons. Of course, our selection of holiday sweaters will dress up any bear or critter for the holidays.

LOOKING TO THE FUTURE

When they think you are not looking, the *Cottage Collectibles®* collection all have their eyes firmly on the future. New companions and playmates coming in 1998 include *Cottage Collectibles® Miniature Bears*. The ideal size to tuck into the pocket of your favorite teddy, these little friends are the perfect way to hold love in the palm of your hand. Plotting and planning all through the year, *Cottage Collectibles®* artists and characters alike have lots of new ideas and surprises coming up in the future. If you need help in locating the closest Cottage to your house, just call the *Cottage Collectibles®* Service Desk toll free at 1-880-724-5902 anytime. They would love to hear from you!

TO LEARN MORE:

COTTAGE COLLECTIBLES® BY GANZ INC.
908 NIAGARA FALLS BOULEVARD
NORTH TONAWANDA, NEW YORK
14120-2060
(800) 724-5902
FAX: (905) 851-6669
URL: http://www.ganz.org
E-MAIL: headoffice@ganz.org

Where Creative Ideas Come Non-Stop

Where in the world do Crystal World artists get their amazingly diverse designs? From springtime florals to pert little pigs, from The Eiffel Tower to a luxury cruise ship, from teddy bears and Christmas trees to castles and cats – think of something wonderful, and chances are it can be found in Crystal World's collection.

"Most of our ideas begin with the world we see around us," explains Rudy Nakai, founder and leading artist of Crystal World. "We'll be walking down a street or sitting in our homes, where we'll notice a little bird on the wing, a dog playing in the yard, or a cat doing something cute the way cats always do. Before you know it, we've got an idea for a new figurine. The world is full of so many wonderful things – how can we not be inspired by it all?" Every animal in Crystal World's popular menagerie was inspired by its real counterpart as envisioned by the artist, and the idea for one of the company's most popular figurines, "Bride and Groom," came from a wedding Rudy attended some years ago.

"Just for You" (left), inspired by the beloved Disney character Mickey Mouse, and "Gee, You're the Sweetest" inspired by Minnie Mouse, are part of the **Disney Showcase Collection.** *Designed by Crystal World's founding artist Rudy Nakai, each figurine stands 4" high and is limited to an edition size of only 4,750.*

TAKING INSPIRATION ONE STEP FURTHER

Crystal World artists take this inspiration one step further, coupling it to a process they call "give and take." This means that something special is happening between the subject of the figurine and its environment. The prime example of this is probably Crystal World's "Curious Cat," the company's first selection to win a 1990 "Award of Excellence" from *Collector Editions* magazine. "Because the cat is the number one pet in the U.S.," explains designer Tom Suzuki, "we decided that we should do a very special figurine. We looked at all the books about cats and at all the calendars and pictures we could find – and also at all the other cat figurines on the market. We noticed that very few cat figures told a story, so we wanted to make a story behind ours." So the designer placed the cat looking over a fishbowl, which immediately gave the figurine a sense of action and – depending on how one looks at the situation – drama or comedy.

More recent examples of this special "give and take" include "Mozart," featuring a little dog listening to an old-time Victrola; and "CyberMouse" and "CompuBear," both of which link the computer age to collectible animals. "Jackpot Teddy," with a paw on the handle of a one-armed bandit, is in the process of winning a jackpot full of coins.

As popular as Crystal World's charming animals are, the firm's famous architectural-themed sculptures are even more unusual. In fact, this firm is known across the globe for its beautiful renditions of some of the world's most famous buildings. These pieces have proven popular not only with collectors but with visitors to the cities that are the home to these architectural wonders. Crystal World's *Wonders of the World* collection is both plentiful and dynamic. From 1997's signed and numbered limited edition titled "Capitol Hill" to India's Taj Mahal, The Eiffel Tower, and eight different versions of New York's Empire State Building, offerings in this popular series abound.

Why so many Empire State Buildings? One reason is the popularity of this famous landmark. The other is that Crystal World was founded in New York City, beginning its operation in 1983 out of a small warehouse in the borough of Queens.

THE LARGEST PRODUCER OF FACETED CRYSTAL COLLECTIBLES IN THE UNITED STATES

Today, Crystal World is located in much larger quarters in the New Jersey suburb of Lincoln Park. The years between have seen the company grow by leaps and bounds to become the largest producer of faceted crystal collectibles in the entire United States.

"Dolphin Dreams," featuring a dolphin mother and her calf, is limited to an edition size of 1,250 pieces worldwide. The sculpture is part of Crystal World's popular* Seaside Memories *series and measures 4-3/4" high.

"The reason for this," notes Nakai, "is our consistent commitment to innovation and quality. Rather than simply reproducing the kind of figurines that other companies offer, we like to pioneer new designs." It was Crystal World, after all, that copyrighted *The Original Rainbow Castle Collection®* in 1987, producing the first rainbow colored crystal castles to reach the collectibles marketplace.

One of these, "The Enchanted Castle," won another coveted "Award of Excellence" from *Collector Editions* magazine in 1993. The design of Crystal World's castles points up yet another reason for the company's popularity among collectors – extensive research coupled with extraordinary design. This research meant that designer Nakai actually traveled to Germany twice in order to see the famous Neuschwanstein Castle before designing his own version for Crystal World.

Research also figures prominently in the work of another popular Crystal World artist, Nicolo Mulargia. Mulargia is responsible for many of the pieces in Crystal World's famous *Teddyland* collection of teddy bears, the popular "Merry-Go-Round," and one of the company's most impressive pieces, "Majestic Bald Eagle," introduced to enormous acclaim in 1997. A native of Italy who has been nominated for several *Collector Editions* "Awards of Excellence," Mulargia says this eagle has a special place in his heart. "As I worked on the piece, it became a tribute to America, which has become my new homeland. The greatest challenge came in the head and the claws. Once these were correct, the rest of it fell into place." "Majestic Bald Eagle," in a signed and numbered edition limited to 1,250, comes with its own Certificate of Authenticity.

COMBINING RESEARCH WITH THE VIEW OF THE HUMAN EYE

Attention to detail is the hallmark of Crystal World's success. But this detailing must be a combination of what actually exists and what the human eye is capable of perceiving. "You must still research very carefully, taking note of all the statistics," Nakai explains. "Then you must trust your own instincts regarding design and proportion, because, no matter how correct the proportion, the finished piece must still please the eye of the collector." And the human eye, the artist insists, is very good at playing tricks. For this reason, Crystal World designers usually pay special attention to whatever feature of the building or object is most important. "Take the 'Taj Mahal,' for instance. Most people remember the large middle section of that building," notes Nakai, "so we made that section most prominent in our design."

Knock 'em dead, kid! It's the Great White Way's newest hoofer, "Broadway Ted." Standing 1-1/2" high, the figurine is part of Crystal World's* Teddyland *series.

Crystal World's attention to detail pays off with themes other than architecture. The firm's version of the U.S. Space Shuttle is of such high standards that its reproductions are sold in the Kennedy Space Center Museum Gift Shop in Florida. The company's beautifully designed ships, which have special appeal to sea lovers, are grounded in this same sense of detail and reality.

While castles and architectural wonders recall centuries past, Crystal World also offers more modern "classics" from which collectors can choose. 1995 saw the production of the firm's signed and numbered "Classic Motorcycle," which is limited to 950 worldwide and retails for a suggested $400. This unusual collectible, designed by Crystal World artist Tom Suzuki, offers an amazing array of faceted, full-lead crystal in enormous detail and also features moveable front-wheel forks and a tiny crystal kick stand. Famous movie star/body builder Arnold Schwarzenegger is the proud owner of a "Classic Motorcycle," which was given to him as a birthday gift.

CRYSTAL WORD COLLECTIBLES ARE PRICED FOR EVERYONE

Not every collector, of course, has the budget of a Schwarzenegger. So, the company has produced smaller versions of their limited editions in more affordably priced open editions. A "Small Classic Motorcycle," standing 3-1/2" tall, retails for a suggested $200. The large "Taj Mahal," limited to an edition size of 1,000, stands 6" high and retails for a suggested $2,250, but the medium and small versions of the "Taj Mahal" are priced at $750 and $200, respectively.

All Crystal World figurines are made with the finest full-lead crystal available

In "Glamour Puss," designed by Tom Suzuki, a cat discovers its reflection in the dressing table mirror. Standing just 2" high, this charming piece is part of Crystal World's* Raining Cats & Dogs *series.

today. The firm's artisans – who have many years of training in their various skills – cut, grind and polish the raw crystal and then assemble the individual figurines. Over the past few years, the firm has developed its technology to the point where it can now work with larger blocks and shapes of crystal, from which can come many more unusual and different designs. The largest of these – the company's enormous crystal Pagoda – weighs 35 pounds and retails for $50,000, while the most reasonably-priced figurines cost as little as $20.00.

Crystal World often finds itself in the forefront of trends, too. More than a year before the Academy Award-nominated film "Babe" made pig-lovers of moviegoers throughout the world, Nakai and his crew offered collectors a delightful little pig named "Wilbur." The following year, "Wilbur" appeared again, this time with a female companion in the figurine titled "Wilbur in Love."

Enthusiasts of trains, planes, fire engines and cruise ships will discover a Crystal World figurine to suit their taste, too. So will music lovers, who can find much delight in the company's new crystal clarinet, as well as its violin, guitar and amazing grand piano – available with its own tiny 3/4" piano bench!

WHAT'S NEWEST FROM CRYSTAL WORLD? DISNEY!

In 1998, Crystal World created a limited edition collection of crystal figurines inspired by beloved Disney characters. Part of the *Disney Showcase Collection*, this new series began with Mickey Mouse in a figurine titled "Just for You" and a Minnie Mouse figurine called "Gee, You're the Sweetest." Each is 4" high, limited to an edition size of 4,750 and priced at $249 suggested retail. Other new selections inspired by popular Disney classic characters include Pinocchio and Dumbo (interpreted in full-faceted crystal with sterling silver components), as well as such icons as Cinderella's Castle and Cinderella's Slipper.

The exquisite interpretation of "Cinderella's Castle" is made up of 350 individual faceted prisms and features a stunning clock tower with four sterling silver clocks – each one frozen in time at the magical hour of midnight. The 7-1/2" castle is from the* Disney Showcase Collection *and is limited to only 1,250.

Upcoming will be fully-faceted crystal interpretations of other classic Disney characters such as Donald Duck, Daisy Duck, Pluto and Goofy, and architectural figures and other icons from Walt Disney's classic animated motion pictures, including *Snow White and the Seven Dwarfs.* Disney lovers and Crystal World collectors have a lot to look forward to in the year ahead!

TO LEARN MORE:

CRYSTAL WORLD
3 BORINSKI DRIVE
LINCOLN PARK, NJ 07035
(800) 445-4251
FAX: (973) 633-0102
URL: http://www.crystalworld.com
E-MAIL: gift@crystalworld.com

Twenty-Five Years of Quality Licensed Collectibles

In 1973, Dave Grossman Creations became the first company to produce a collectible line of figurines inspired by the work of Norman Rockwell, the famed artist who painted a slice of Americana. It was the start of a new collectibles company and a long-standing commitment to bringing the best licensed figurines to collectors nationwide.

Since then, the company, which celebrated its 25th anniversary in the collectibles industry in 1998, has expanded its lines to welcome *The Original Emmett Kelly Circus Collection*, *The Gone With The Wind Collection*, *The Wizard of Oz Collection*, *Bill Bell's Happy Cats* and *Spencer Collin Lighthouses*. Most recently, three new collections have been added: *Maggie's Toybox* by artist Maggie Garvin and the *Embrace* and *Legacy* series by artist Tom Snyder. The company's longevity and creativity is a credit to founder and artist Dave Grossman's pride in the quality of his work and devotion to the collector.

Dave Grossman Creations introduces the 1998 dated ornament, "God Bless Us, Everyone!" from the* Norman Rockwell Collection, *in celebration of its 25 years of producing collectibles inspired by the artwork of Norman Rockwell.

It's a combination that continues driving the company toward even greater success. Grossman's future plans include expanding on existing licensed and limited edition collectibles while marketing new products – all with the collector in mind.

GROSSMAN LAUNCHES NEW COMPANY

An artist for more than 25 years, Dave Grossman relishes his current role as the creative and artistic force behind Dave Grossman Creations. A native of St. Louis, Grossman graduated from the University of Missouri and was commissioned to do architectural sculptures for banks, hospitals, hotels and other private and public buildings. One of his works is in New York's Lincoln Center.

He was also commissioned to create sculptures for Presidents Lyndon Baines Johnson and Richard Nixon.

Dave Grossman Creations started producing collectibles in 1973, most notably with the Norman Rockwell figurines through a licensing agreement with Curtis Publishing Company. But the company was founded a few years earlier in 1968 in St. Louis, Missouri, where the business remains. Grossman originally began the company by creating and marketing metal sculptures.

The Norman Rockwell figurines changed the company's direction. Each figurine beautifully captures Rockwell's homespun and hometown portraits that graced *The Saturday Evening Post*, among other publications. The collection features everything from "First Haircut" to "A Visit With Rockwell" – a figurine portraying the artist himself with a delivery boy. Dave Grossman Creations also offers Norman Rockwell ornaments, including a 1998 limited edition figurine ornament and a ball ornament.

MOVIE FAVORITES RECREATED IN COLLECTIBLES

Under a license through Warner Bros., Dave Grossman Creations brings two all-time favorites of the silver screen into collectors' homes. *The Gone With The Wind Collection* recreates the familiar characters in Margaret Mitchell's book and subsequent movie starring Clark Gable and Vivien Leigh. There's Rhett Butler, Scarlett, Mrs. O'Hara, Gerald O'Hara, Ashley, Suellen, Bonnie and Mammy – all portrayed in figurines, waterglobes, musicals, ornaments, wooden plaques, mugs and lithographs.

Among the most recent figurine introductions are daughter "Bonnie" holding a kitten, "Scarlett" in a striped dress, and the third introduction "Scarlett and Rhett," embracing and standing on a wooden base. The collection also features musical waterglobes recreating scenes such as "Atlanta Burning," "Tara" and "Scarlett in Green Dress." All the waterglobes play "Tara's Theme."

Sculptured architectural vignettes, including the stately plantation "Tara," the winding staircase at "Twelve Oaks" and Aunt Pittypat's house in "Atlanta," are musicals that bring back memories.

Collectors can also travel the yellow brick road to find *The Wizard of Oz™ Collection* of figurines, musicals, waterglobes, wooden plaques and framed lithographs. The figurines are each limited in the first edition to 5,000 pieces with characters including "Dorothy," "Cowardly Lion," "Tinman," "Scarecrow," "Wicked Witch," "Mayor," "Glinda Good Witch" and "Mortician." The

This musical waterglobe from* The Wizard of Oz™ Collection *features the famous "Ruby Slippers" and plays "Off to See the Wizard."

most recent figurine introductions are "Wizard," "Flying Monkey" and "Winkie Castle Guard."

Six musical figurines have also joined the collection from "Dorothy," which plays "Off To See The Wizard," to "Tinman," which plays "If I Only Had A Heart." Musical waterglobes creatively depict scenes from the movie. In "Lighted Emerald City," the waterglobe shows the towering town, while Dorothy and her friends walk along the yellow brick road at the base of the piece. The *Wizard of Oz* fans can also collect wooden plaques with photograph stills from the movie.

THE ORIGINAL EMMETT KELLY CIRCUS COLLECTION COMES TO TOWN

The beloved Emmett Kelly, the most famous circus clown of all time, continues to make people laugh in *The Original Emmett Kelly Circus Collection.* Kelly's fame was based on his clown character "Weary Willie." With his big red nose, black grease paint and a woefully sad expression, "Willie" was a down-and-out vagabond for whom nothing ever came out right. He was called "the saddest and funniest man in the world." Kelly was beloved by Ringling Bros. Barnum and Bailey Circus audiences for years!

Licensed through his estate, the collection of bisque porcelain limited edition figurines features the hobo clown performing his familiar antics, including sweeping up a spotlight, playing an organ and trying to catch a baseball. There's also the *Casino Series* and *Gallery Collection* of limited edition figurines, and collectibles produced in stiffened cloth for a more authentic look. Dated ornaments, produced since 1986, also capture Emmett Kelly at his best.

HAPPY CATS MAKE EVERYONE SMILE

Dave Grossman Creations is pleased to announce a purr-fect collection for people of all ages. *The Happy Cats* features 12 fanciful felines from the creative mind of renowned artist Bill Bell. Bell's signature style shows lots of activity mixed with nostalgia and nonsense. Known for his lighthearted, colorful style and organized clutter, Bell brings pure joy to his unique figurines that can be shared by everyone.

From "Policecat Charlie" to "Firecat Connor" and "Nursecat Clara," *Happy Cats* is one collection that shouldn't be missed! Each figurine measures 4" to 6" tall, with a suggested retail price of $15.00-$20.00.

SPENCER COLLIN LIGHTHOUSES: THE NEXT BEST THING TO BEING THERE

From sea to shining sea, Dave Grossman Creations recently welcomed *Spencer Collin Lighthouses*, a collection designed by official Coast Guard artist Cheryl Spencer Collin. After receiving a bachelor of fine arts degree in 1975 and master of fine arts degree in 1977, Spencer Collin began sculpting one-of-a-kind porcelain animal miniatures to sell in galleries. In 1984, she added a line of cottages and lighthouses. Today, her Maine barn studio is known for producing some of the finest limited edition lighthouse sculptures available. *Spencer Collin Lighthouses* is a one-artist collection that has earned a well-deserved reputation for quality and attention to detail.

***Artist Cheryl Spencer Collin's dog, Svea, and bunny, Willy, are featured on every* Spencer Collin Lighthouse.**

"San Francisco Lightship" from* Spencer Collin Lighthouses *is limited to an edition of 2,400 pieces. The first 500 pieces are personally signed by artist Cheryl Spencer Collin.

Spencer Collin believes the true beauty of a lighthouse is found in its setting. It is this "sense of place" that sets her lighthouses apart from all the others. Spencer Collin researches each site and lighthouse before she painstakingly sculpts them. Spencer Collin's joy in her work is apparent in all her sculptures — which are the next best thing to being there! In recognition for her work, Spencer Collin recently received the distinct honor of being selected an official Coast Guard artist for her many years of sculpting lighthouses and lightships.

Spencer Collin does all the sculpting herself, giving the collection unique qualities of consistent style, relative scales and detail based on actual

The new* Maggie's Toybox *line features 12 adorable animals and a toybox display by artist Maggie Garvin.

regional surroundings, flora and fauna. The observer may find sea roses, sunflowers, birch or palm trees, harbor seals or humpback whales on any given piece. Look for whimsical touches such as the keeper's dog burying a bone, a fishing pole and bait bucket, or even a New England clambake complete with lobsters, corn on the cob and fresh blueberry pie. Personal touches include Spencer Collin's pet bunny, Willy, and dog, Svea, on every piece.

Collectors can find the pets as stowaways on a life raft on the recent introduction "Nantucket Lightship," a replica of the lightship that was once stationed near Nantucket Island to guide ships with its radio beacon away from the area's dangerous shoals.

In his* Embrace *series, artist Tom Snyder portrays a happy couple on their "Wedding Day."

Spencer Collin's pets scamper at the base of "Twin Lights, N.J." – a majestic fortress-style sculpture sure to appeal to lighthouse lovers everywhere. All *Spencer Collin Lighthouses* are limited to 2,400 pieces, with the first 500 as the Gold Label Edition personally numbered and signed by Spencer Collin.

The pieces feature Spencer Collin's trademark sculpting of plants and animals native to the area.

Among recent introductions are "San Francisco Lightship;" "Boon Island, ME;" "Absecon 'Atlantic City' Lighthouse;" and "Hillsboro Inlet Light, FL," where 'gators, manatees, dolphin and the "Barefoot Mailman's" mailbag appear around the lighthouse.

COLLECTOR'S CLUB WELCOMES LIGHTHOUSE FANS

At the request of *Spencer Collin Lighthouse* enthusiasts, Dave Grossman Creations launched a collector's club. The Spencer Collin Lighthouses Collectors Club, now in its second year, lets more people discover the magic and charm of Spencer Collin's sculptures.

The $30.00 annual membership fee entitles members to an exclusive and complimentary lighthouse figurine, sculpted lighthouse pin, personalized membership card, free subscription to the quarterly newsletter, "Studio Update," current brochures and an attractive folio with a hand-signed photo of the artist. Members also have the opportunity to purchase members-only lighthouses and learn about special events and open houses where Spencer Collin's works are featured. This year's redemption piece is "Old Alcatraz Lighthouse" from Alcatraz Island in the San Francisco Bay.

CLUB

SPENCER COLLIN LIGHTHOUSES COLLECTORS CLUB
1608 N. Warson Road
St. Louis, MO 63132
(800) 325-1655

Annual Dues: $30.00 - Renewal: $25.00
Club Year: January - December

BENEFITS:
- Members-Only Club Signature Piece
- Membership Gift: Pin
- Membership Card
- Quarterly Newsletter, "Studio Update"
- Binder for Newsletter Storage
- Buy/Sell Matching Service through Newsletter
- Advance Notice of Artist Appearances

TO LEARN MORE:

DAVE GROSSMAN CREATIONS
1608 N. WARSON RD.
ST. LOUIS, MO 63132
(800) 325-1655
FAX: (314) 423-7620
E-MAIL: dgcrea@aol.com

Dave Grossman, the founder and conceptual artist of Dave Grossman Creations.

A Fascinating World of Bygone Times

A roomful of coveted awards...collectors standing in line to get his autograph and shake his hand...accolades for his meticulously sculpted cottages from admirers around the world. These are but a few of the honors David Winter has enjoyed in two decades as the creator of David Winter Cottages.

Collectors appreciate Winter's works not only for their consummate craftsmanship, but also for their ability to conjure up an earlier, less stressful way of life. There's something of the unhurried era of this bygone age about their creator, too – a tall, gently courteous man who gives the impression of having all the time in the world to meet and listen to people. He sees his sculptures as "evoking and recapturing something of the past – when communities were communities, when everyone looked out for each other, and when the pace of life was slower."

The stately "St. Christopher's Church" graces **The Churches & Chapels of Britain** *collection. It sells for $110.*

A CHILDHOOD RICH IN DISCOVERIES

When Winter was a boy, his father's army postings took the family to exotic locales like Singapore and Malaysia. Yet today, Winter loves nothing better than to live and work in a part of rural England that remains much as it was 300 years ago. His 17th-century cottage is nestled in a village on the ancient Pilgrims' Way, trodden for centuries by those who traveled from Winchester to the shrine of the martyred St. Thomas a Becket at Canterbury.

Winter was born at Catterick in Yorkshire – the son of internationally acclaimed sculptor, Faith Winter. His mother's works include the Falklands War Memorial in Port Stanley, a bust of Princess Anne and statues of Lord Dowding and Sir Arthur Harris. With such a background, it would have been surprising if young David had not thought of sculpture as a career. By his final year of school, he was headed in the direction of art college. But first he took a year out to work as his mother's assistant.

With the thorough grounding in sculpture which he received at her hands, the prospect of art college receded into the background and finally disappeared. Winter was on his way to becoming the sculptor whose work is so well-known today. It's a career that has been marked by prestigious awards, including being named 1991 "Artist of the Year" by the National Association of Limited Edition Dealers (NALED).

WINTER AND HINE FORGE A PARTNERSHIP

In 1979, at the age of 21, Winter began working with John Hine, originally making heraldic plaques which were not a commercial success. Moving away from this initial venture, Winter sculpted his first miniature cottage, "Mill House," which sold the same day that Hine persuaded a local shop to display it.

Within a week of that first sale, there were David Winter Cottages available in several shops in Winter's home territory of Surrey. From then on, the pattern has been one of steady growth, with Winter now having hundreds of titles to his credit. In the early days, he did all of the modeling and casting of the cottages in an old coal shed in his parents' garden. Today – still determinedly rural – he has a studio in the garden of his own cottage.

His models are rarely reproductions of "real" places, but his work is imaginative rather than totally imaginary. "Architecturally," he says, "they all have a basis in fact." He's a great browser among old books, and gains inspiration from prints and etchings of houses no longer in existence. What's more, his camera accompanies him wherever he goes.

ENESCO AND DAVID WINTER JOIN FORCES

In early 1997, David Winter signed an agreement with Enesco Corporation, a leading gifts and collectibles firm. Since then, Enesco has manufactured David Winter Cottages and operated the David Winter Cottages Collectors' Guild. Of the partnership, Enesco Chairman and Chief Executive

Over the past 20 years, David Winter has created some of the world's most beloved collectible cottages.

Officer Eugene Freedman says, "David Winter has an outstanding reputation for creativity and quality, and we believe the line complements our current direction of producing high quality products for the collectible cottage market."

Winter is thrilled by Enesco's support and confidence. "For me, Enesco arrived at a crucial moment in my career," he says. "Not only has Enesco shown faith in my art, but also belief in me as an individual. I am delighted with the way Enesco is producing my cottage sculptures."

As always, the cottages are completely a result of the artist's vision. Winter explains, "I stand alone in the concept of a subject. I decide how a cottage will look and I, alone, sculpt that master. As a model is manufactured, I am there too, seeing it progress through the various stages of production."

THE MAKING OF A DAVID WINTER COTTAGE

When Winter has completed an original sculpture in wax, it is taken to the studios and workshops of Enesco European Giftware Group where liquid silicon rubber is poured over it to make a master mold. This is a delicate operation, and the mold must be perfect because the original is destroyed during the process. From this mold, an exact copy of the original sculpture can be cast in tough resin. This process now can be safely repeated using the "resin master" to make further molds from which the final cottages will be cast. Next, liquid gypsum is poured into the mold. At this stage, it is important to remove any pockets of air. The mold is also tapped on the side which encourages air bubbles to the surface.

Gypsum sets rapidly, generating heat as it does so, and after approximately two hours, the cast is ready to be demolded with great care. The cottage is then "fettled," which means that tiny flashes of excess gypsum are carefully scraped away. The base of the cottage also is rubbed down at this stage until it is perfectly smooth and flat. Though the cast is now set, it is not perfectly dry, so it is left in a special temperature-controlled room for 24 hours.

Before painting, the white cast is dipped in a special sealing solution of shellac and white polish. This acts as an undercoat and stops paint from being absorbed into the gypsum. The coloration is applied by highly trained artists using strict guidelines, although some artistic license is permitted provided it adheres to high levels of quality control. Metal components and other additional items are attached at this stage and after a final, careful inspection, the painted cottage has its base covered in green felt and its identification label attached. The pieces then are boxed, each with a signed Certificate of Authenticity, before being dispatched to stores around the world.

"Thornhill Chapel from David Winter's* The Churches & Chapels of Britain *collection has an issue price of $90.00.

One of the most beloved of* The Pubs & Taverns of England *is "The Tickled Trout," beautifully rendered here by David Winter.

COLLECTORS' GUILD OFFERS MEMBERS-ONLY ITEMS

David Winter collectors enjoy the privileges of membership in the David Winter Cottages Collectors' Guild. Among the many benefits available for a $42.00 yearly membership fee are opportunities to acquire the annual Guild Symbol of Membership and two Members-Only Cottages. Additional benefits are listed at the end of this article.

As Winter explains, "Every year I sculpt three pieces exclusively for members of the Guild. I derive a great deal of satisfaction from sculpting these special cottages as they are destined for people who have shown a particular interest in, and appreciation of, my work. This in itself is a source of inspiration for me."

For 1999, the "Tile Maker's Cottage" is the Guild Symbol of Membership. It shows a wonderful old cottage where all manner of tiles have been made for generations, as well as the family's fiery kiln, which is never allowed to go out. One of the 1999 Members-Only Cottages is "The Architect's," which shows off its creator's penchant for decorative beams. Inside is an archive room with a jumble of drawings including practically every design the architect ever made. "The Joinery" is the second Members-

The Pilgrim's Way *collection features "Marquis Walter's Manor" in a limited edition of 5,000 pieces. Suggested retail price is $150.*

Only Cottage for 1999, showing a busy workshop where windows, doors and building frames are produced from local oak.

Although the pieces of Winter's collections are always referred to as "cottages," the term lends itself to a quite broad interpretation. The stately houses of worship in his *The Churches & Chapels of Britain* collection, for example, are much grander than what most of us envision when we hear the word "cottage."

THE CHURCHES & CHAPELS OF BRITAIN COLLECTION

"St. Christopher's Church" represents a wonderful building erected in honor of the patron saint of travelers. It's an appropriate name for this sculpture, for Winter is a great traveler. It also evokes his connection with the Pilgrims' Way, which attracted many a medieval traveler. This cottage was inspired by a Scottish church Winter spied from a speeding train. For him, it embodies all the aspects of a traditional village church.

"Thornhill Chapel" is based on a chapel sited at the Aldershot Military Cemetery. "I found this chapel rather enchanting for a fairly recent building, and probably quite unique in its construction," the artist says. He named the chapel after the road that leads up to it. Samuel Franklin Cody, father of Buffalo Bill Cody, is buried in the cemetery there.

Two other favorite collections by David Winter include *The Pubs & Taverns of England* and a new offering, *The Pilgrims' Way* collection. Winter discovers out-of-the-way taverns on his travels through Great Britain and often uses them as inspiration for new cottages. A recent example is "Bird Cage," a delightful little pub in a building dating back to the 15th century. "The Good Intent" features Winter's own local pub, while "The Hop Pickers," an unusually large and rambling pub, accommodates workers who pick hops each year. Finally "The Tickled Trout" serves as a favorite haunt of fishermen.

PUBS, TAVERNS AND PILGRIMS

Winter's own home village inspired *The Pilgrims' Way* collection, featuring cottages as they might have appeared in Chaucer's time. Buildings in the series include "The Alchemist's Cottage," "The Brickies," "The Dingle," "The Falconry," and four more.

Looking toward the future, Winter speaks directly to his collector friends. "Today in my art, you are seeing my depth of feeling, my own personality. Rest assured that I, and I alone, am the master of my own destiny. You have supported me through thick and thin – for which I am truly grateful. Now is the time for a new beginning, and I hope you will enjoy the real David Winter!"

CLUB

DAVID WINTER COTTAGES COLLECTORS' GUILD
P.O. Box 479
Itasca, IL 60143-0479
(800) NEAR-YOU

Annual Dues: $42.00; $80.00 for 2 years
Club Year: Anniversary of Sign-Up Date

BENEFITS:
- Membership Gift: Membership Cottage
- Opportunity to Purchase Members-Only Cottages
- Quarterly Newsletter, "Cottage Country"
- Membership Card
- Notification of National and Regional Special Events and Tour Signings
- Notification of Retirements and New Releases
- Catalog of Current Cottages

TO LEARN MORE:

DAVID WINTER COTTAGES
COLLECTORS' GUILD
P.O. BOX 479
ITASCA, IL 60143-0479
(800) NEAR-YOU
URL: http://www.enesco.com

Charming Collectors' Miniature Bears

"When I look back to see how I ended up with a collectible miniature bear company, it is almost frightening how inevitable it was," muses Deb Canham, artist for and head of Deb Canham Artist Designs, Inc. "Designing and making miniature bears has changed my life a great deal. I spent ten happy years as a police officer in London, started designing bears and discovered the world beyond the streets of London. What else could I have done that would have opened up the world and given me such a universal language – 'bears' – all from a passion for sewing with needle, thread and fabric!"

"Nutcracker Prince," "Snowflake," "Columbine" and "Moonshine Cosmic" all have garnered coveted Golden Teddy or TOBY Award nominations for Deb Canham Artist Designs, Inc.

Canham's great-grandmother was a ward of Queen Victoria who became one of the first pupils of the Royal School of Needlework in London. As Canham explains, "My grandmother was a fine seamstress who made beautiful crocheted tablecloths. My mother is an excellent seamstress as well, and she passed on her love and passion for sewing to me. Mother also shared with me her love of story telling and encouraged me to believe that each of my soft toys had its own character and personality. In fact, I never called them toys. They were my 'animals'!" Canham's father and brother are what she calls "great artists," but she herself never took to painting or sketching. With her mother's and her older sister's help, Canham eventually focused on the area where her unique talent lies: creating miniatures.

A LOVE OF "OLD THINGS" INSPIRES CANHAM

Ever since she was a child, Canham has appreciated time-worn objects and fabrics, and this love shines through in her contemporary works of art. "I really enjoyed watching the 'Antiques Road Show' as a child, and I used to think how great it was that something made years before should resurface and be so much admired, treasured and valued. Most times when the owner heard the price their item was worth, they would smile and say they would never sell it because it had sentimental value! When I see items of antique clothing, I am always fascinated by the quality and feel of the actual fabric. But the greatest thrill comes from looking at the hand stitching! In the old days, many people had beautiful handwriting and the same can be said of hand stitching. To me, behind every handcrafted item there is a story."

From 1987 to 1996, Canham worked as a "bear artist," designing and making each of her bears completely by hand and selling them as exclusive collector's pieces. She won many awards for her bear originals, wrote an in-depth *Manual on Miniature Bearmaking*, and taught workshops in England, America, Holland, Germany and Japan. Eventually, she felt constrained by the small number of bears she could personally complete, and decided she could make more impact by embracing the concept of the limited edition "artist designed bear." With that change, she also made a major geographical switch, leaving her native England for headquarters in the United States.

NEW SERIES MARK CANHAM'S U.S. DEBUT

"I moved from the United Kingdom to America in April of 1996 to start Deb Canham Artist Designs, Inc." Canham reveals. "Our first group of bears was called the *Mohair Collection*, and it consisted of seven pieces. Most of these were fairly traditional in design, but what made them so special was that they had delicate proportions. While they only measured 3" tall, they looked exactly like the big bears, made small! My very favorite was 'Sorry,' who had holes in his footpads and paw pads and that 'slouched shoulder' worn-out look. He was meant to represent an old loved bear who had been placed in the attic and forgotten. On his chest, he had a little calico heart patch. A few shops actually returned him because of the holes in his pads – but once they heard he was supposed to be like that, they found him all the more endearing!"

Also included in the *Mohair*

"Tulip" is an appealing 3" bunny character created by Deb Canham.

The 3" tall* Have a Heart Collection *features characters with many endearing traits, including being devilish, angelic, organized and shy.

Collection was a traditional English golly, a mohair rabbit called "Peter," boy and girl bears called "Flore" and "Ben," and two undressed bears named "AJ" and "BJ." Each piece in the series was limited to a worldwide edition of 3,000 and all sold out within 18 months.

At the same time, Canham released a group of four bears called the *Country Collection*, inspired by American pioneer inventiveness and attention to thrift, such as recycling everyday materials into rag dolls and other products like a quilt. As she describes, "We had 3" bears wearing dungarees and dresses carrying little animal dolls which had the same calico fabric. This was the only collection we ever did that was not mohair."

Moving up to a 5" size, Canham unveiled the *Denizens of Honey Hills* in September of 1996. "They each had a story about them which went into their box showing how they fit into the local community." There were: "Bratty Butchy," a little rascal; "Gertie the Lady of the Bag," who had a passion for food; "Simon the Curious," always getting himself into a tangle, "Poppo the Wise," who liked to nap; and finally "Willyum the Brave," a true Eagle Scout. Each bear was limited to an edition of 3,000 worldwide.

MARKING TEN YEARS WITH THE *RAINY DAY* BEARS

To honor her ten-year anniversary with miniature bears in 1997, Canham wanted to celebrate with a special new collection. While seeking inspiration, she thought back to her childhood days in England, when her mother taught her to sew. As the roaring fire warmed her hands and the rain beat against the windows, Canham would sew felt clothes for her soft toy "animals" using the simple "lazy daisy" and blanket stitches she had learned. "That's how I decided to design the *Rainy Day Collection* in which all the characters had felt accessories," she explains.

Deb Canham's* Rainy Day Collection *was created in the spirit of her reminiscences of learning to sew as a child back in her native Great Britain.

Canham feels a deep affinity for the little personalities she creates. As she notes, "When you spend time designing a collection of bears, it's impossible not to have the pieces develop into real characters. For instance, in the *Rainy Day Collection*, 'Hattie' is a little girl in a gingham dress with a felt hat and cotton drawers. The dress has a patch on it, but what she is most proud of is her new hat decorated with flowers. Her best friend is 'Hershel,' who sports a blue felt jacket decorated with patches and blanket stitch. Then there is a girl rabbit called 'Lady Ascot' who lives on the Ascot Race Course in England, where everyone wears a hat to the races – so she does, too. 'Chuckles' the monkey wears a little daisy stitched vest. 'Pilgrim,' the alley cat, came into being because I was thinking about those Pilgrims who came from Plymouth. That's where I last lived before coming to the States in 1996. It struck me that they must have had a cat aboard ship, so I named the cat 'Pilgrim.' There is also an elephant in this collection who I call 'Sticky Bun,' which is what we feed zoo elephants in England."

Also released in the 1997 anniversary year were the Martian bears "Moonshine Cosmic" and his first mate, "Gussie Galactica," who are bright green and purple respectively. "Uncle Ernie," which Canham describes as "another old worn out bear," quickly sold out in 1997, as did both Martians. Canham says, "We then released a pair of contemporary gollies, a boy and a girl named 'Spats' and 'Spangles'."

At the end of 1997, Canham debuted a *Nutcracker Collection* of seven pieces, five of which were bears, along with one cat and one panda. She comments, "It was the first collection where we used other designers. Laurie Sasaki is one of the very best miniature bear artists whose work is rarely seen except on the secondary market. We've been friends for years, and when I needed a 'Nutcracker Prince,' I knew Laurie was the person to ask. I also needed a 'Rat King' and instantly thought of another bear artist friend, Bonnie Windell, who is famous for her wonderful rats. I designed the other five pieces myself." This was the first collection the firm ever made with matching limited edition numbers available.

NEW CREATIONS FOR 1998

At the 1998 Toy Fair, Canham introduced her *Have a Heart Collection*, including "Mummy's Little Monster," "The Angel," "Peppermint," "Crispin," "Suzie," "Lilac Lil" and "Gus." From devilish to angelic, sweet and shy to efficient and organized, each of these characters has his or her own quirks and delightful personality, thanks to Canham.

Canadian bear artist Brenda Power contributed her first animals to the firm in 1998, designing two rabbits, a raccoon and a penguin.

Cloth dolls joined the line for the first time in 1998 as well, each measuring 5" in height. The first two dolls are "Molly MUSLIN" and "Mandy ORGANDIE," each presented in an edition limited to 500 each. Canham selected Jane Davies to design these dolls, saying, "What makes it all the more fun is that she is my big sister! Jane has spent 20 years developing and perfecting her artist dolls and has built a worldwide reputation both for the artistry of her work and her contribution to the promotion of dolls as an art form."

The final collection for 1998 is *Camelot*. Each of seven characters is 3" tall and they represent: "Lancelot" in appliqued tabard; distinguished "King Arthur;" pretty "Queen Guinivere;" a jolly "Jester;" "Merlin," the wizard; and both male and female dragons.

With 1997 TOBY Award nominations for "Sorry" and "Hershel," 1998 Golden Teddy nominations for "Columbine" and "Moonshine Cosmic," as well as TOBY Award nominations for Laurie Sasaki's "Nutcracker Prince" and Deb Canham's *Nutcracker* "Snowflake," Deb Canham Artist Designs, Inc. now enjoys critical acclaim and growing sales to collectors. Canham embraces this productive growth. As she says, "This company began at the kitchen table. Now it has more seats filled at the table, but we enjoy our small personal approach and always will treasure it!"

CLUB

COLLECTOR'S CLUB STARTING IN 1999.

TO LEARN MORE:

DEB CANHAM ARTIST DESIGNS, INC.
820 ALBEE ROAD, SUITE #1
NOKOMIS, FL 34275
(941) 480-1200
FAX: (941) 480-1202
E-MAIL: deb@deb-canham.acun.com
URL: www.deb-canham.acun.com

"Molly MUSLIN" and "Mandy ORGANDIE" are the first two 5" cloth dolls created by Jane Davies for Deb Canham Artist Designs, Inc.

DEPARTMENT 56, INC.

The Tradition Begins

"Department 56" may seem a curious name for a firm that designs and manufactures nostalgic, collectible villages. How the name originated is a story that intrigues the firm's many loyal collectors.

Before Department 56®, Inc. became an independent corporation, it was part of a large parent company that used a numbering system to identify each of its departments. While Department 21 was administration and Department 54 was the gift warehouse, the name assigned to wholesale gift imports was "Department 56."

Reminiscent of early times comes "Mulberrie Court" and the set of four accessory pieces, "A Christmas Carol Reading," from the* Dickens' Village *Series.

Department 56, Inc. originally began by importing fine Italian basketry. However, a new product line introduced in 1977 set the groundwork for the collectible products of today. Little did the company's staff realize that their appealing group of four lighted houses and two churches would pave the way for one of the late-20th century's most popular collectibles.

These six miniature buildings were the beginning of *The Original Snow Village®*. Each design was handcrafted of ceramic, and hand-painted to create all the charming details of an "olden day" village. To create the glow from the windows, a switched cord and bulb assembly was included with each individually boxed piece.

Collectors could see the little lighted buildings as holiday decorations under a Christmas tree or on the mantel. Glowing lights gave the impression of cozy homes and neighborhood buildings with happy, bustling townsfolk in a wintry setting. Sales were encouraging, so Department 56, Inc. decided to develop more *Snow Village* pieces to add to their 1978 line.

Word of mouth and consumer interest helped Department 56 realize that *The Original Snow Village* collection would continue. Already there were reports of collectors striving to own each new piece as it was introduced.

By 1979, the Department 56, Inc. staff made an important operational decision. In order to keep *The Original Snow Village* at a reasonable size, buildings would have to be retired from production each year to make room for new designs. Being new to the world of collectibles, they did not realize the full impact of this decision. Collectors who had not yet obtained a retired model would attempt to seek out that piece on the secondary market. This phenomenon has led to reports that early *Snow Village* pieces may be valued at considerably more than their original issue price.

Today, as in the past, the Department 56 architects continue to keep the *Village* alive by bringing collectors new techniques and new materials, all of which result in an exciting array of buildings and charming accessories.

THE HERITAGE VILLAGE COLLECTION FROM DEPARTMENT 56, INC.

Love of holiday traditions sparked the original concept of *The Heritage Village Collection®*. When decorating our homes, we are often drawn to objects reminiscent of an earlier time. Holiday memories wait, hidden in a bit of wrinkled tissue or a dusty box, until that time each year when they are rediscovered as we unpack our treasures and are magically transported to a beloved time and place.

The first *Heritage Village* grouping was *The Dickens' Village® Series* introduced in 1984. Extensive research, charming details and the fine hand-painting of the seven original porcelain shops and "Village Church" established them as favorites among collectors.

Other series followed with the introduction of *The New England Village®*, *The Alpine Village™*, *Christmas In The City®*, *The Little Town of Bethlehem™*, *The North Pole™*, and in 1994, *The Disney Parks Village Series*. Each of these collectible series has been researched for authenticity and has the same attention to detail as the original *Dickens' Village*.

"Five Part Harmony" represents the **Snowbabies** *collection of finely detailed bisque porcelain collectibles with hand-painted faces and hand-applied frosty bisque crystals.*

As each of the villages began to grow, limited edition pieces were added, along with trees, street lamps, and accessory groupings to complete the nostalgic charm of each collection. Each lighted piece is stamped in the bottom with its designated series name, title, year of introduction, and Department 56, Inc. logo to assure authenticity.

Each model is packed in its own individual styrofoam storage carton and illustrated sleeve. A special compartment in the boxing of all lighted pieces holds a UL-approved switched cord and bulb. This method not only protects the pieces during shipping, but also provides a convenient way of repacking and storing the collection for many years.

Each series within *The Heritage Village Collection* captures the holiday spirit of a bygone era. *Dickens' Village*, for instance, portrays the bustling, hearty and joyous atmosphere of the holidays in Victorian England. *New England Village* brings back memories of "over the river and through the woods," with a journey through the countryside.

The Alpine Village recreates the charm of a quaint mountain town, where glistening snow and clear lakes fed by icy streams dot the landscape. *Christmas In The City* evokes memories of busy sidewalks, street corner Santas, friendly traffic cops and bustling crowds amid cheery shops, townhouses and theaters.

In 1987, Department 56, Inc. introduced *The Little Town of Bethlehem*. The unique 12-piece set reproduces the essence of the birthplace of Jesus. This complete village scene continues to inspire and hearten those who celebrate Christmas everywhere.

In 1991, Department 56, Inc. presented *The North Pole Series*. The brightly lit *North Pole* buildings and accompanying accessories depict the wonderful Santa Claus legend with charm and details that bring childhood dreams to life for both the young and the young-at-heart.

In 1994, *The Disney Parks Village Series* became the newest addition to *The Heritage Village Collection*. Replicas of Disney theme park buildings are accompanied by Mickey and Minnie Mouse, along with other coordinated accessories. *The Disney Parks Village Series* retired in May 1996. It was the first complete series to be retired by Department 56.

CELEBRATE *SNOWBABIES™* AND OTHER DEPARTMENT 56 FAVORITES

Another popular collectible series from Department 56, Inc. is *Snowbabies™*. These adorable, whimsical figurines have bright blue eyes and creamy white snowsuits covered by flakes of new-fallen snow. They sled, make snowballs, frolic with their animal friends and are watched over by kindly Jack Frost. Since their introduction, *Snowbabies* have enchanted collectors around the country and have brightened the imagination of all of us who celebrate the gentle play of youthful innocence.

The finely detailed bisque porcelain collectibles, with hand-painted faces and hand-applied frosty bisque snow crystals, come in their own gold foil stamped storybook or green gift box.

In 1989, a line of pewter miniature *Snowbabies* was introduced, to the great delight of collectors of miniatures. These tiny treasures are made from many of the same designs as their bisque counterparts, and come packaged in little white gift boxes sprinkled with gold stars. Every year, new *Snowbaby* friends are introduced in both of these very special collections.

In addition to *Snowbabies* and the *Villages*, several other series have caught the loyal Department 56 collectors' fancy. *Winter Silhouette™* is a collection of highly detailed white porcelain figurines, many with pewter, silver, gold or red accents. *Winter Silhouette* has an elegant simplicity that brings back Christmas visions of family pleasures in a bygone era.

The year 1991 saw the beginning of another new series, *All Through The House™*. Featuring backdrops and furniture, as well as figurines, these highly detailed pieces offer warm, nostalgic memories inspired by the activities they portray. Made of cold cast porcelain and beautifully hand-painted, this charming collection celebrates family traditions *All Through The House*.

In 1992, Department 56 began producing oversized interpretations of traditional mercury glass ornaments which trace their origin to early 19th century Germany. The unique shapes and sizes, frosted and shiny colors of these *Oversized Mercury Glass* pieces can be displayed beautifully alone or as elegant additions to a Christmas tree. Along the way, mercury glass has been

"Uncle John Snaps A Christmas Photo" in this whimsical figurine from the **All Through The House** *series.*

Department 56's line of* Oversized Mercury Glass Ornaments *features the* Noel Professionals, *including (from left to right) "Mom," "Stamp Collector," "Santa Twist," "Village Collector" and "Farmer."

incorporated into other product lines including the popular *Noel Professionals*. In 1996, Department 56 began production on the *Snowbabies Mercury Glass Ornaments* and, for 1997, continued with *Great Lovers* and *Night Before Christmas Santas*.

Snowbunnies™ began in 1994 and soon became a popular Department 56 collectible. *Snowbunnies* are made of creamy bisque porcelain with delicate touches of pink on their ears and on the springtime bows tied around their necks. Their little bunny suits are covered with tiny bisque crystals, and their small cheerful faces are hand-painted with care. *Snowbunnies* are sure to hop into the springtime hearts of collectors everywhere.

COLLECTORS DISCOVER THE WIDE RANGE OF DEPARTMENT 56, INC. CREATIONS

In addition to the popular collectibles already mentioned, Department 56, Inc. continues to develop colorful and innovative giftware, as well as ongoing lines for Spring and Easter, Christmas Trim, and many beautiful Christmas ornaments.

Seldom does a firm win the attention and loyalty of collectors as quickly as Department 56, Inc. has done since its first *Original Snow Village* buildings debuted in 1977. As one enthusiast stated, "A company can't make an item collectible. People have to make it collectible, and the people have discovered Department 56."

For more information about Department 56 collectibles, subscribe to the *Quarterly* magazine. This publication is published four times a year and is available by direct mail subscription at the following address:

Department 56, Inc. Quarterly
P.O. Box 44056
Eden Prairie, MN 55344-1056

CLUB

SNOWBABIES COLLECTORS' CLUB
P.O. Box 44456
Eden Prairie, MN 55344-1456
(888) SNOWBABY

Annual Dues: $35.00
Club Year: December - November

BENEFITS:
- Welcome Gift: Special *Snowbabies* Piece
- Opportunity to Purchase Club Piece through Dealer
- Personalized Membership Card
- Membership Certificate
- Special *Snowbabies* Mechanical Drawing Signed by Kristi Pierro
- *Snowbabies* Newsletter
- *Snowbabies* Club Pin

TOUR

ONE VILLAGE PLACE SHOWROOM TOUR
6436 City West Parkway
Eden Prairie, MN 55344
(800) LIT-TOWN (548-8696)

Hours: One hour tours, every Friday during the Summer, from 9 a.m.- 4 p.m. Reservations are required.

Admission Fee: None

Collectors are greeted by staff members and are guided through historical displays of *The Original Snow Village, The Heritage Village Collection* and *Snowbabies*, plus a look at over 2,000 gift and collectible items produced by Department 56, Inc.

TO LEARN MORE:

DEPARTMENT 56, INC.
P.O. BOX 44456
EDEN PRAIRIE, MN 55344-1456
(800) 548-8696
URL: http://www.department56.com
http://www.dept56.com
http://www.d56.com

DUNCAN ROYALE

Bringing Back Memories and History Through Collectibles

Known for her innovation and creativity, as well as for enthusiasm and a warm personality, Catherine Duncan masterminded and continues to develop the Duncan Royale collections with an eye toward serious collectors everywhere. Her subjects are familiar, yet often reveal how little we actually know about a person, place or object. To the delight of collectors, Duncan Royale's unique art and sculpture tell a story and bring history to life.

A sense of character and personality is embodied in each Duncan Royale subject – whether Santa Claus, clowns, entertainers, fairies, Biblical characters, early Americans, Africa's legendary Kings and Queens, or pirates and buccaneers. What is next? Rest assured that Duncan Royale, under the leadership of Catherine Duncan, always has lofty and unique ideas in the works.

SANTA CLAUS COMES TO DUNCAN ROYALE

In 1983, Duncan Royale took the collectible gift market by storm with the introduction of the limited edition *History of Santa Claus Collection*. It wasn't simply the familiar jolly St. Nick with a flowing white beard, round belly, rosy cheeks, red coat and a team of reindeer waiting for the Christmas Eve adventure. The *History of Santa Claus Collection* retraced the origins, personalities and folklore surrounding this famous symbol of the holidays and good will.

"Santa Claus is perhaps the best loved character in the Western world and is known by almost everyone from childhood," Duncan says. "Duncan Royale was interested in a series of Santas and gift givers throughout the world."

In order to create and develop the *History of Santa Claus Collection*, the Duncan family members traveled extensively, consulting scores of experts and conducting research in libraries and museums throughout the world. Diligent efforts uncovered numerous personalities from history, literature and mythology – all of whom have influenced the present-day notions of Santa Claus. This research appears in published form, as well as a full-color volume entitled "History of Santa." The figurine collection has been expanded to include 36 different Santa personalities.

"Peg Leg & Polly" is the signature piece of the* History of Pirates and Buccaneers Collection*, which tells the tales of some of the most infamous characters of all time. Peg Leg Pete, with his trademark bottle of rum, parrot, wooden leg and eye patch, is among the best-known pirates.

COLLECTORS FIND TREASURED FIGURINES WITH PIRATES AND BUCCANEERS

Duncan Royale sailed the Seven Seas to find some of the most notorious and noteworthy swashbucklers. The *History of Pirates and Buccaneers Collection* captures these sea-faring men and women in detailed and delightfully realistic scenes. The signature piece of the collection is "Peg Leg & Polly." Peg Leg Pete, with his bottle of rum, eye patch, wooden leg and parrot, is the pirate so often seen or heard of in films, television, books and tales. For these reasons, the pirate is often looked upon with some measure of affection. However, Peg Leg's peers weren't the friendliest people, and this series tells the tale of some of the most infamous characters of all.

Pirates came from both wealthy and poor families. But they all risked the hangman's noose to escape the harshness and poverty of life on land. Many of the wealthy operated as pirates under the cloak of a privateer, including such famous historical figures as Sir Francis Drake.

The collection tells the story of pirates from all nationalities and backgrounds, including the likes of "Captain Sir Henry Morgan," "Francois L'Olonnaid," "Diego Grillo" and "Blackbeard," who was the master of intimidation and psychological warfare.

Women are also welcomed aboard the collection. "Anne Bonny," a fiery young redhead from Ireland, ran off with "Calico Jack" and took up a life of piracy. Jack was hanged in 1720 while Anne looked on, saying, "I'm sorry to see you here, but if you'd have fought like a man, you needn't hang like a dog."

Among the most recent introductions are the infamous "Mary Read," "Jean Laffite" and "Captain Kidd." English pirate Mary Read found it easier to live her life dressed as a man. She fought in the English army and navy, disguised in men's clothing.

When pirates captured her transatlantic ship, she joined them. Read's valor shamed the pirates with whom she sailed. During an attack, all but one other pirate hid. When they wouldn't

***English pirate "Mary Read" disguised herself in men's clothing to fight and sail aboard the pirate ships. This highly detailed figurine is part of the* History of Pirates and Buccaneers Collection.**

come out and "fight like men," she shot the cowards.

Each piece in the *History of Pirates and Buccaneers Collection* stands on a wooden base and is meticulously crafted to capture every detail from the parrot perched on Peg Leg's shoulder, to the jeweled necklaces plundered by Diego Grillo. The figurines are each limited to 5,000 pieces.

AFRICA'S KINGS AND QUEENS REIGN IN HISTORIC COLLECTION

History is also what Duncan Royale emphasizes in its *History of Africa's Kings and Queens Collection*, portraying some of Africa's greatest kings and queens. "We wanted to do something for African-Americans that no one had ever done before," Catherine Duncan says. "We looked back at the heritage in Africa."

Duncan and her staff turned to the library, *National Geographic* magazines and other resources to research African history and the people who built the nation. In keeping the company's commitment to research and historical accuracy, the final stories for the collection were written and authenticated by Dr. Julie Stokes, a highly regarded professor of African-American Studies at The University of California Fullerton. Prior to this, Duncan's daughter, Joan, also spearheaded the research for several months.

The *History of Africa's Kings and Queens Collection* figurines, each limited to 5,000 pieces, portray the country's different courageous kings and queens and tell their stories. Among the figurines is "Moshesh," who ruled as the King of Basutoland, provided refuge to many survivors of tribal wars and introduced his people to Christianity. "Shaka" was ruler of the Zulu Empire, organizing and unifying tribes in order to save the South African region from European domination. "Tenkamenin" ruled Ghana in the 11th century.

"The *Africa's Kings and Queens* line was partly a response to customers' requests, not for the kings and queens in particular, but for something to show the splendor of Africa," Duncan says. "We felt that bringing to people's attention some magnificent African kings and queens, unknown to the general population and not made available in general history, would be a way to give a sense of pride to African-Americans unaware that these regal and often compassionate kings and queens existed."

The stories continue with the recent introduction of "N'Zinga," a warrior queen who fought the Portuguese slave traders for more than 30 years as they encroached her territory of Ndongo, or present day Angola. She led an all-female army, winning battle after battle. After her death at age 81, Angola fell under Portuguese control, but Queen N'Zinga is forever remembered as one of the most important personalities for her resistance against European domination in Africa's interior.

Another addition is "Hannibal," who lived from 243 to 183 B.C. and took command of the Carthaginian army to become the scourge of Rome. With 21 elephants and a multi-ethnic contingent, Hannibal accomplished what is considered, even today, as the most incredible military defeat in history. His army marched across the icy and treacherous terrain of the Alps to defeat the greatest force Europe had ever thrown into a single battle.

EBONY COLLECTION CELEBRATES AFRICAN-AMERICAN CULTURE

Duncan Royale also features the *Ebony Collection* of African-American figurines, including tributes to jazz musicians, Gospel singers, traditional dancers, circus clowns and family. The *Ebony Collection* was created in honor of African-American life, accomplishments and culture.

This heritage has become one of the strongest building blocks of American society as we know it today. The musical forerunners of Soul, Gospel, Rock n' Roll, Blues and Jazz are deeply imbedded in Black American culture. The *Ebony Collection* highlights numerous compelling personalities from these diverse musical "roots." Each figurine is individually numbered with an edition limited to 5,000 pieces. These endearing characters are sure to be treasured by collectors for years to come.

Another African-American collection is *Jubilee Dancers*. The collection spotlights energetic African dancers in colorful, traditional garb. *Family and Friends* is another addition to the ongoing *Ebony Collection*.

***"Hannibal," who lived from 243 to 183 B.C., is credited with leading the most incredible military defeat in history. The figurine is part of the* History of Africa's Kings and Queens Collection.**

The* History of Africa's Kings and Queens Collection *is a tribute to African kings and queens, including "N'Zinga," who fought the Portuguese slave traders for more than 30 years and led an all-female army.

In 1987, Duncan Royale introduced the *History of Classic Clowns and Entertainers.* This 24-piece collection chronicles the evolution of clowns and entertainers during the past 4,000 years, from Greco-Roman times through the 20th century. The last character in the series is everyone's favorite, the immortal Bob Hope. Eight artists contributed their talents to painting this line.

CLOWNS AND ENTERTAINERS STAR IN POPULAR COLLECTION

"The idea originated from the same desire to inform the public of the heritage and authentic history of clowns and entertainers, and to offer a beautifully detailed figurine with a real and interesting background," Duncan says.

A beautifully illustrated, hard-cover collector's book, *History of Classic Clowns and Entertainers,* sets in prose the memorable stories of these endearing champions of comedy who made everyone laugh. Due to the popularity of the collection, Duncan Royale will be issuing these subjects in 6" figurines in 1998.

Duncan Royale collections emerge as a result of hours of painstaking research and creative production. After the theme for a collection is developed, artists sketch renderings that exemplify the theme, tradition and history of each personality.

THE MAKING OF A DUNCAN ROYALE COLLECTIBLE

Duncan meets with the artist that has been chosen to sculpt the line to discuss the information about the characters and history of the pieces, along with any illustrations and written information.

After the initial drawings are submitted, another meeting is held to make any changes. When final drawings and colors are approved, the sculptor breathes dimension and "stop-frame action" into each character, adding detail and depth as directed by Duncan.

Molds are cast from the original clay sculpture, and the porcelain figurines are produced by a cold cast process which captures minute and intricate details. The piece is scrutinized and hand-detailed in an exacting and painstaking process to ensure it reflects the quality associated with Duncan Royale.

Precision hand-painting strokes each piece with vivid, vibrant color. On some pieces, six to seven undercoatings may be used to obtain the desired colors. Each piece receives a limited edition number and its own mini book that tells a brief story about the figure. All Duncan Royale collectibles are securely packed in their own handsome gift boxes.

For those interested in learning more about these popular artists and lines, a membership in the Duncan Royale Collectors Club will answer any questions, preview upcoming introductions and provide exclusive opportunities. Members are invited to acquire special members-only pieces and to buy or sell Duncan Royale back issues on the exclusive Royale Exchange.

INVITATION TO JOIN THE DUNCAN ROYALE COLLECTORS CLUB

The "Royal Courier" is an informative and exciting newsletter that gives collectors news about product releases, company history, special offerings and more. Much-anticipated retirements are also announced in the newsletter. The club was founded in 1991 and has more than 6,000 members.

CLUB

DUNCAN ROYALE COLLECTORS CLUB
1141 S. Acacia Avenue
Fullerton, CA 92631
(714) 879-1360

Annual Dues: $30.00
Club Year: Anniversary of Sign-Up Date

BENEFITS:
- Membership Gift: Pewter Bell Ornament
- Opportunity to Purchase Members-Only Figurines
- Newsletter, "Royale Courier"
- Elegant Binder
- Membership Card
- Membership Certificate
- Catalog of Duncan Royale Limited Editions
- Free Registration of Member's Collection

TO LEARN MORE:

DUNCAN ROYALE
1141 S. ACACIA AVE.
FULLERTON, CA 92631
(714) 879-1360
FAX: (714) 879-4611
URL: http://www.duncanroyale.com

Eggceptional Collectibles Scramble Up Eggcitement

Connie Drew, founder of *eggspressions! inc*, is as distinctive as the egg designs that she and her company create for collectors around the world. "There aren't any capital letters in the name," she says with a wink. "I only capitalize God, America and the name of the bank!"

She has, however, capitalized on her love of eggs in all shapes, sizes and colors. *eggspressions!* is an "eggstension" of Connie's love affair with decorated eggs – an interest that began during her childhood as she watched her Czechoslovakian mother and grandmother decorate Easter eggs. They used a European technique of applying warm wax to an eggshell in various religious patterns and symbols.

"I think God looked down from heaven and pondered, 'What should I package life into?' And He came up with the shape of an egg," she says. "It's nature's perfect package. Eggs are wonderful and mystical. They symbolize birth and resurrection. They bring good luck."

Ever since she founded *eggspressions!* in 1992, good luck and success have been her best friends. Today, *eggspressions! inc*, located in Rapid City, South Dakota, creates a dazzling array of collectibles including hand-painted eggs, musical eggs, jewelry boxes, lamps and elaborately carved and adorned keepsakes and seasonal ornaments. All are carefully handcrafted from real eggshells ranging from tiny finch eggs, to large emu, rhea and ostrich eggs.

"We don't make anything people need," Connie adds, "so we have to concentrate on making things that people want. I'm jes' tryin' to help make this planet an 'eggstatic,' 'eggsuberent,' 'eggsquisite,' 'eggsotic,' 'eggstraordinary' place to 'eggsist.' It that so 'eggcentric?'"

Connie Drew is the "eggstraordinary" talent behind* eggspressions! inc. *The proud owner of an "eggstensive" egg collection, Connie turned her hobby into a full-time pursuit and has shared her artistry with collectors worldwide.

The eggs and collectibles have as much personality as their creator.

CONNIE DREW "EGG-SPANDS" HER TALENTS

Indeed, Connie Drew is the exclamation point in her company's name. Besides being the proud owner of a decorated egg collection, Connie fills her life with a blend of art, music, folk philosophy, glitter and whimsical delights. For a time, Connie collected owls, hoping to gain wisdom. But she stopped when she noticed they were merely keeping her up all night! Now she surrounds herself with twinkling stars, butterflies, unicorns, a Scarlett O'Hara doll "draped in the drapes," various bronze sculptures, oil paintings, Broadway musical paraphernalia, unique graphic prints and a coffee table displaying her growing collection of opulent egg-shaped Judith Leiber purses.

She has a star and a whale named after her (star-Cee and Sea-Star respectively), is an avid self-taught Macintosh computer user and paints each nail on her fingers and toes a different color. In her office, a "spe-shell" clock crows every hour. She works from "the crack of noon till pert'near midnight." And she insists that she's not "eggcentric."

"If you have a job you love, you'll never work another day in your life," Connie explains. Learning the ancient art of drop-pull egg decorating from her mother and grandmother, Connie has become an "eggspert" on ethnic and modern egg art techniques, styles, symbols, customs and folklore. Throughout history, eggs have been honored by every culture as symbols of birth and new life. Historically, decorated eggs have been exchanged to celebrate the events of life from the womb to the tomb. Because all life comes from an egg, it is believed that an egg embodies the natural energies of life, vitality and gusto! "An egg has mystical power that is said to bring good luck to its owner," Connie says.

Encouraged by craft magazines and

eggspressions! inc. ***offers limited edition eggs in all shapes, sizes and styles. Each is delicately handcrafted from real eggs, which are hollowed and then adorned with semi-precious stones, ribbons, painted designs or other embellishments.***

armed with a passion for artistic challenges, Connie began making eggs as gifts. Prior to starting her company, Connie was producing more than 1,000 eggs annually at her kitchen counter. Today, Connie's long love affair with decorated eggs has grown from her home studio to an "eggstensive" factory, or egg plant as she calls it, complete with "eggsecutive" offices and an "eggsclusive" gift shop. The facility is open all year 'round because "eggs aren't just for Easter anymore!"

The steps in creating a limited edition collectible is "eggsacting." Peter Carl Fabergé, jeweler to the last Czar of Russia, set the standard for glittering masterpieces. Now, contemporary versions of these eggs are back, thanks to Connie and her creative team.

HATCHING AN *eggspressions!* COLLECTIBLE

Ideas are formulated in the "brooder," a special room for creative thought, tucked in their 10,000 square foot purple and green offices. Supplies, materials, thoughts and energy merge to become new designs.

When the conceptual work concludes, Connie's "nesters" (her affectionate name for the artists) bring the designs to life. The production process begins in the local farms and hatcheries from which the company purchases its ostrich, duck, goose, quail, chicken and pheasant eggs. "They're all non-fertile and from non-endangered species," Connie explains.

Holes are then drilled in the top and bottom of each egg, whether it be a 10" ostrich egg or a delicate egg from a guinea hen. The yolk and albumen are removed with compressed air, and the empty shells are dried and sterilized. Broken eggs are saved and recycled into other products like cascarones™, real eggshells filled with confetti. A companion product is filled with birdseed for weddings and outdoor events.

Artisans cut delicate designs into the brittle shell or pull wax drips into dainty patterns on the shell's surface. Some eggs are embellished with semi-precious stones, while others are carved, hinged and hidden with miniature surprises.

To create its trademark hanging Christmas collectibles, the company's artisans etch a guideline onto the eggs, some of which feature intricate lattice patterns cut out of the shell. Next, the openings are carved out with a high-speed drill, and a platform is built to showcase each miniature holiday scene. Finishing touches include ribbons, crystal and sparkling icicles. For jewel boxes, goose-egg shells are painted, marked, hinged and cut. Some are even musicals.

"EGGSTRA-ORDINARY" EGGS FOR ALL SEASONS AND REASONS

Since the first *eggspressions!* line, innovative gold tags and Certificates of Authenticity were designed to distinguish the collectibles. A corporate mission to limit editions to small numbers delights collectors. Since an *eggspressions!* egg has never exceeded a limit of 500, collectors are assured "eggsclusivity." With the handcrafted designs and attention to detail, no two eggs are "eggsactly" alike. Given the growing number of egg collectors, *eggspressions!* is truly at the forefront of limited edition collectible egg art.

Collectors can find offerings for each season and occasion. *eggspressions!* has unveiled a line of jewelry boxes, ring boxes and other wedding-related items. The ring boxes are completely covered with Austrian crystals to match birthstone colors. The boxes are also hinged to reveal a ring holder and fully-lined interior to be used as a miniature treasure chest. Other wedding offerings

eggspressions! inc. ***introduces a new wedding collection featuring ring boxes, jewel boxes, cake toppers and other collectibles as special as the big day for the bride and groom.***

eggspressions! inc. ***launched the*** **Tea Pot Collection** ***with five intricate designs. The teapots are made from real eggshells and are limited to an edition of 250 each.***

include ostrich egg cake toppers and flower baskets, pheasant egg ring boxes and vases.

Music boxes created from goose eggs are also astonishing accomplishments. Cleaned egg shells are painted, marked, hinged and cut before a musical mechanism is inserted. Signature Austrian crystals, surrounded by other high quality trim and decorations, are added to produce elegant keepsakes. Similar in size and design to music boxes, *eggspressions!* keepsake jewel boxes are breathtaking. Their varied styles and embellishments charm and delight collectors of all ages.

Of course, Connie is always hatching up new ideas and ways to "eggspress" her love for eggs. Whether they're adorned with ribbons to hang or pedestals to sit, *eggspressions!* collectibles celebrate nature's beauty and bring a time-honored art to life.

TO LEARN MORE:

eggspressions! inc.
1635 DEADWOOD AVENUE
RAPID CITY, SD 57702-0353
(800) 551-9138
FAX: (605) 342-8699

A World of Collectibles for Every Collector

In the past four decades, Enesco Corporation has become one of the most respected names in the collectibles industry, setting a high standard of excellence, creativity and quality. The company's success, catapulted 20 years ago by the famous *Precious Moments* Collection, continues to grow with more collectibles that are known and loved around the world.

Today, Enesco produces more than 12,000 gifts, collectibles and home decor items, including the *Cherished Teddies, Small World of Music, Mary's Moo-Moos* and *Memories of Yesterday* collections, along with such renowned licenses as Disney, Barbie and Coca-Cola.

Enesco has come a long way from its start in 1958 as a division of N. Shure Company. Enesco was named from the phonetic spellings of the parent company's initials – N.S. Co. Now, Enesco spells success with its collectibles that have found a special place in the hearts of collectors.

"Love Grows Here" (left) and "Somebody Cares" show Enesco Corporation's dedication to the National Easter Seal Society. Proceeds from both* Precious Moments *figurines benefit the 1998 Easter Seals campaign to help children and adults with disabilities.

PRECIOUS MOMENTS COLLECTION CELEBRATES 20TH ANNIVERSARY

Under the leadership of Chairman and Chief Executive Officer Eugene Freedman, Enesco expanded its role from a gift designer to a leading collectibles producer. It all began in 1978 when Freedman discovered artist Sam Butcher's simple drawings of teardrop-eyed children.

Butcher called them "Precious Moments" because they shared messages of love, caring and sharing.

Freedman gave the drawings to Japanese Master Sculptor Yasuhei Fujioka, who transformed the illustrations into three-dimensional figurines. The first figurine was "Love One Another," followed by 16 other introductions in 1978 and four more figurines in 1979. The *Precious Moments* Collection quickly became a phenomenon in the collectibles industry. With its inspirational titles and universal appeal, the Collection is one of the nation's most popular collectibles. Each year, Enesco introduces 25 to 40 new figurines, all of which are based on Butcher's artwork and inspired by his personal experiences and collector requests.

In response to the overwhelming excitement and interest in the figurines, the Precious Moments Collectors' Club was launched in 1981 and is now the largest club of its kind. The Precious Moments Birthday Club was created in 1985 to introduce children to the joy of collecting. The Clubs have a combined membership of nearly 400,000. The Precious Moments Collectors' Club has been honored by the National Association of Limited Edition Dealers (NALED) as "Collectors' Club of the Year" five times in the past six years.

The *Precious Moments* Collection has also won prestigious awards from NALED, which honored Sam Butcher as "Artist of the Year" in 1992 and 1996. Eugene Freedman was honored with the association's "Lee Benson Award" for his contributions to the collectibles industry, including the *Precious Moments* Collection.

Throughout 1998, the Collection celebrates its 20th anniversary with special celebrations and introductions to commemorate the milestone.

COLLECTORS FALL IN LOVE WITH *CHERISHED TEDDIES*

In 1992, Enesco launched the *Cherished Teddies* Collection – an adorable line of teddy bears with tattered pawpads, individual names and Adoption Certificates for collectors to officially register them as their own. Since then, collectors have welcomed the teddy bears into their hearts and homes.

Designed by artist and children's author Priscilla Hillman, the Collection has become the world's most popular teddy bear collectible. NALED honored Hillman as the "Artist of the Year" in 1994, while the Collection has won many awards including NALED's "Collectible of the Year."

Sculpted in cold cast resin, each *Cherished Teddies* figurine has its own personality, message of friendship and love, and name – which is often based on people in Hillman's family or collectors that she meets. In 1997, the Collection celebrated its fifth anniversary with the limited edition figurine "Strike Up The Band and Give Five

The* Cherished Teddies *Collection celebrated its fifth anniversary in 1997 with the limited edition figurine "Strike Up The Band and Give Five Cherished Years a Hand."

Cherished Years a Hand." The figurine was limited to 1997 production.

In 1995, the Cherished Teddies Club was launched with more than 100,000 mem-"bears" worldwide. It has become one of Enesco's fastest growing clubs.

The success has been just as thrilling for Hillman, a self-taught artist who sketched and painted as a child but ended up studying botany at the University of Rhode Island. In the late 1980s, a serious back injury kept Hillman inactive for several months. During that time, she kept herself busy by "drawing in her mind," watching old movies and thumbing through nostalgic photos.

When she recovered, Hillman went to her drawing board and put her teddy bears on paper. In 1990, Hillman sent 36 original paintings to Enesco, which decided to turn the illustrations into figurines. Today, the Collection includes more than 600 figurines and accessories.

Collectors can also find Hillman's illustrations in other collectibles from Enesco. Hillman's artwork has been recreated in the *Calico Kittens, My Blushing Bunnies, Priscilla's Mouse Tales* and *Snow Folks* collections. *Priscilla's Mouse Tales*, a collection of mice figurines, is based on her nine "Merry Mouse" books and well-known nursery rhymes.

ENESCO WELCOMES A FAMILY OF COLLECTIBLES

The Enesco family of collectibles also features a wide variety of subjects and sentiments for everyone. Introduced in 1995, *Pretty As A Picture* has quickly become Enesco's third top-selling collectible – behind the *Precious Moments* and *Cherished Teddies* Collections. The *Pretty As A Picture* figurines are based on the well-known black-and-white portraits of children by German photographer Kim Anderson. The porcelain bisque figurines portray children imitating adults, and send messages of love and devotion.

The Enesco *Memories of Yesterday* Collection brings back memories – whether nostalgic and tender, heart-warming or humorous. The porcelain bisque collectibles recreate charming children from the beloved illustrations of the late British artist Mabel Lucie Attwell. Throughout 1997, the Collection of porcelain bisque collectibles celebrated its 10th anniversary with the limited edition figurine "Meeting Special Friends Along The Way."

In 1989, Enesco began a business relationship with Disney as a licensee for *Mickey & Co.* giftware. Since then, Enesco has also acquired the license to produce giftware based on popular Disney films including *Pocahontas* and *The Hunchback of Notre Dame.*

Enesco's *From Barbie With Love* Collection features authentically reproduced nostalgic and modern Barbie plates, musicals, figurines and accessories. The Collection includes limited edition pieces that capture the doll's glamour, beauty, style and careers over the past three decades.

Other year-round collector favorites are the Enesco *Treasury of Masterpiece Editions* and *Small World of Music* collections as well as *Mary's Moo-Moos, Mary, Mary Had A Farm, This Little Piggy* and *Mary's Hen House* based on the work of Enesco artist Mary Rhyner-Nadig.

More than three-quarters of Enesco's products are created by 60 in-house artists and designers. The company also markets licensed gifts from well-known artists, including Lucy Rigg *(Lucy & Me)*, Kathy Wise, Linda Lindquist Baldwin (*Snowsnickle & Broomsnickle* and *Belsnickle*), June Somerford (*Melly & Friends*), Ray Day and David Tate (*Lilliput Lane*).

DAVID WINTER COTTAGES JOINS ENESCO

In 1997, Enesco added to its prominence in miniature cottage collectibles by signing an agreement with David Winter. Enesco will manufacture *David Winter Cottages*, as well as operate the David Winter Cottages Collectors' Guild. The Collection joins Enesco's *Lilliput Lane*, giving the company two of the industry's best known miniature cottage collections. Enesco purchased the *Lilliput Lane* Collection in 1994.

"David Winter has an outstanding reputation for creativity and quality, and we believe the line complements our current product direction of producing high quality collectible cottages," Freedman said.

David Winter Cottages have received numerous accolades including the National Association of Limited Edition Dealers 1987 and 1988 "Collectible of the Year" award. Winter was named NALED "Artist of the Year" in 1991.

ENESCO SHARES A GIFT OF LOVE THROUGH EASTER SEALS

Enesco believes in sharing its success with others. In an effort to give back to the community, Enesco became a corporate sponsor of the National Easter Seal Society in 1987. In the past decade, Enesco employees, sales

Enesco celebrates love year 'round with the* Pretty As A Picture *Collection based on the black-and-white portraits of German photographer Kim Anderson.

"You Make My Heart Feel Glad" from the* Memories of Yesterday *Collection captures the innocence of youth. The porcelain bisque figurine is the third issue in the* Comforting Thoughts *series.

representatives, vendors, suppliers, retailers and *Precious Moments* collectors, have raised more than $28 million to help children and adults with disabilities.

The cornerstone of the company's campaign is the *Precious Moments* Collection. Each year, artist Sam Butcher designs a commemorative porcelain bisque figurine and limited edition 9" figurine to benefit Easter Seals. Retailers and Precious Moments Collectors' Club members also hold hundreds of special events ranging from bake sales to walk-a-thons.

Based on Enesco's history and prominence, more success is sure to follow as the company continues giving back to the community and giving collectors a variety of collectibles with lasting appeal.

TO LEARN MORE:

ENESCO CORPORATION
225 WINDSOR DR.
ITASCA, IL 60143
(800) 4-ENESCO
FAX: (630) 875-5464
WEBSITE: http://www.enesco.com

CLUBS

DAVID WINTER COTTAGES COLLECTORS' GUILD
P.O. Box 479
Itasca, IL 60143-0479
(800) NEAR-YOU

Annual Dues: $42.00; $80.00 for 2 Years
Club Year: Anniversary of Sign-Up Date

BENEFITS:
- Membership Gift: Membership Cottage
- Opportunity to Purchase Members-Only Cottages
- Quarterly Newsletter, "Cottage Country"
- Membership Card
- Notification of National and Regional Special Events and Tour Signings
- Notification of Retirements and New Releases
- Catalog of Current Cottages

THE CHERISHED TEDDIES CLUB
P.O. Box 99
Itasca, IL 60143-0099
(630) 875-8540

Annual Dues: $23.00; $38.00 for 2 Years
Club Year: January 1 - December 31

BENEFITS:
- Membership Gift: Symbol of Membership Figurine
- Opportunity to Purchase "Membears-Only" Figurines
- Newspaper, *The Town Tattler*
- Lapel Pin
- Membearship Ticket with Holder
- Easel Replica of "Cherished Teddies Town Depot"
- Cherished Teddies Catalog

ENESCO PRECIOUS MOMENTS BIRTHDAY CLUB
P.O. Box 689
Itasca, IL 60143-0689
(630) 875-8540

Annual Dues: $21.00; $40.00 for 2 Years
Club Year: July 1 - June 30

BENEFITS:
- Membership Gift: Symbol of Membership Figurine
- Opportunity to Purchase Members-Only Figurines
- Newsletter, "Good News Parade"
- Membership Card
- Personal Happy Birthday Card

CLUBS

ENESCO PRECIOUS MOMENTS COLLECTORS' CLUB
P.O. Box 219
Itasca, IL 60143-0219
(630) 875-8540

Annual Dues: $27.50; $53.00 for 2 Years
Club Year: January 1 - December 31

BENEFITS:
- Membership Gift: Symbol of Membership Figurine
- Opportunity to Purchase Members-Only Figurines
- Newsletter, "The GOODNEWSLETTER"
- Official Club Binder
- Membership Card
- Gift Registry Binder
- Special Mailings
- Two *Precious Moments* Table Placemats
- Invitations to Club-sponsored Events

TREASURY ORNAMENTS COLLECTORS' CLUB
P.O. Box 277
Itasca, IL 60143-0277
(630) 875-8540

Annual Dues: $22.50; $42.50 for 2 Years
Club Year: January 1 - December 31

BENEFITS:
- Membership Gift: Symbol of Membership Ornament
- Opportunity to Purchase Members-Only Ornaments
- Newsletter, "Treasured Times"
- Personalized Membership Card
- Catalog of Treasury Masterpiece Edition

MEMORIES OF YESTERDAY COLLECTORS' SOCIETY
P.O. Box 499
Itasca, IL 60143-0499
(630) 875-8540

Annual Dues: $22.50; $42.00 for 2 Years
Club Year: January 1 - December 31

BENEFITS:
- Membership Gift: Symbol of Membership Figurine
- Opportunity to Purchase Members-Only Offerings
- Quarterly Newsletter, "Sharing Memories..."
- Personalized Membership Card
- *Memories of Yesterday* Catalog
- Plush Teddy Bear

ERTL COLLECTIBLES™ LIMITED

The Art of the American Dream

"The story of The Ertl Company is really the story of the American dream," says Gary Becker, vice-president of marketing for the thriving Dyersville, Iowa manufacturer. "And now Ertl has taken that dream one giant step forward as we've launched an important new division: Ertl Collectibles Limited."

"Can't Wait" by Lowell Davis shows a farmer checking out his mail the moment it comes out of the post box. It combines a precision die cast truck with cold-cast porcelain sculpture.

Already renowned as the world's leading manufacturer of die cast collectibles, Ertl has expanded upon its solid relationships with licensors and artists to introduce a host of new limited edition lines. Ertl Collectibles Limited works in harmony with licensors of brands, as well as renowned artists and designers including Lowell Davis, Francesca Hoerlein and Joanne Callander. What's more, the new division has forged fruitful partnerships with respected organizations including the National Trust for Historic Preservation and the Circus World Museum.

The seeds for Ertl Collectibles Limited's dynamic future were sown more than 50 years ago by Fred Ertl, Sr., a journeyman molder in Dubuque, Iowa. It was right after World War II, and Ertl's job was coming to an end. With seven children to feed, he drew upon his ingenuity to develop a timely business plan. With a John Deere plant under construction on the outskirts of town, Ertl decided to create a line of toy farm equipment. With the help of his wife and children, the budding entrepreneur began crafting toy tractors from melted war-surplus aluminum in the basement of his home. Soon, The Ertl Company was producing toys bearing the trademarks of many famous farm equipment manufacturers, including John Deere, Case-International, Deutz-Allis and Massey Ferguson.

Over the past five decades, Ertl has built a sterling reputation for high quality and exceptional detail in all of its product lines, which encompass plastic model kits, basic toys and play sets, and a wide variety of licensed die cast collectibles.

AN INSPIRED ALLIANCE: LOWELL DAVIS AND ERTL

Artist Lowell Davis has rural roots perfectly suited to a joint venture with Ertl Collectibles Limited. As Davis chuckles, "My mother said I painted my first mural when I was two years old." The self-titled "Grandfather of Rural Art" continues, "She just moved my crib around the room!"

Lowell was born in a two-story farmhouse right outside Red Oak, Missouri, and he lived there until the Great Depression of the early 1930s. "My dad went to California in a *Grapes of Wrath* type of thing," he recalls with his usual wry humor. "Eventually we returned to Red Oak to the general store which my dad managed during World War II. We moved to Carthage when I was in the fifth grade. As poor as we were, my dad bought me an oil paint set that fifth grade Christmas. There was a teacher when I was in the sixth grade who saw my talent, and paid for my art school. Every Saturday for three years, an art teacher taught me to paint. That really encouraged me."

After high school, Lowell joined the Air Force and then started a small art studio in Carthage. An advertising agency hired him to move to Dallas, where he stayed for 13 years. Then after successful careers as a cartoonist and wildlife artist, Lowell met his wife Charlotte (who is affectionately known as "Charlie"), and saved up enough money to return to his roots and buy a farm.

"Then I started doing farm animals as artwork," Lowell recalls. "I wondered who would buy a pig or a chicken. But when I took sculptures to a show, there was an immediate positive response. My figurines were made in cold cast porcelain, which allowed for great detail. All the things I dreamed about in sculpting, I could do! There were no restrictions. It just went crazy!"

LOWELL DAVIS CREATES RED OAK II

With his success as a collectibles artist, Lowell set out to reconstruct his childhood town of Red Oak. For years, he and Charlie had enjoyed the hobby of photographing old buildings. "There was a sadness in seeing the old farms falling down, ones that had once been beautifully kept. It was something I couldn't handle. It was the end of an era. I just wanted to do something about it.

"My little town of Red Oak kept going

The George Washington 16-Sided Barn" is featured as part of Ertl's* American Country Barn *Signature Series of barns.

down, too. No one wanted to live in that small community any longer. So I started thinking – I was just going to get one building and then I thought that would be it – it was the Feed Store. It was my intention to put a shop in it." Lowell did not stop with one building, however – and over the past decade, he has built a wonderfully nostalgic community called Red Oak II right near his and Charlie's home, the 60-acre FoxFire Farm™.

LOWELL DAVIS SERIES HIGHLIGHTS HIS COUNTRY ROOTS

In cooperation with Ertl, Lowell Davis has created the *American Country Barn™* series to help showcase the National Trust for Historic Preservation's BARN AGAIN! program. This highly detailed line of hand-painted replicas features unique, award-winning and historically significant barns from across the country. Each year, the *American Country Signature* series will feature a "signature" edition barn that was owned by a famous historical figure. Selected for 1997 was "The George Washington 16-Sided Barn at Mount Vernon." The "George Washington" barn comes with a fully detailed booklet explaining the original barn's history and its restoration, as well as information about Lowell Davis and the Mount Vernon Ladies Association. Issue price for this first annual signature piece is $70.00.

The *Lowell Davis America™* series offers a broad selection of this award-winning artist's most cherished works, with many pieces incorporating scale die-cast vehicles and farm implements for a unique mixed-media effect. The series will also feature one individual die cast vehicle annually, the first quite naturally showcasing graphics from Davis' "Leapin Lizard" motor home.

Davis' *Farm Country Christmas™* sculptures "capture the warmth and humor of farm country life," as Gary Becker notes. "Each finely crafted piece can be displayed individually – or when collected as a series, the pieces come together in a puzzle-like form to create an entire Winter farm scene." The artist's *Sparrowsville™* holiday series offers 12 dated, whimsical birdhouse ornaments that provide rustic shelter to Davis' beloved sparrows. Shelters include a red barn house with a stone silo, an old leather shoe with a red-tile roof, and many more.

LEMUTT AND FIFI™, AND *FOREVER SISTERS™*

While Lowell Davis' art is a proud part of Ertl Collectibles Limited, the firm shows more of its fun-loving side through the romance of "LeMutt and FiFi," a pair of collectible plush canine characters that are available dressed in "high style" fashion. "LeMutt" is an appealing back-alley type, while his lady love, "FiFi," is an upper crust, high-society maiden. They say opposites attract, as collectors will learn when they share in the heart-warming story of this romantic duo. The pair are the creation of the gifted Francesca Hoerlein, who also has added niece and nephew canines, "Cher" and "Buster," to the family.

Born of Hoerlein's vivid imagination, "LeMutt" enjoyed tremendous success as a popular plush character in the 1980s. Francesca produced "LeMutt" and related characters with several partners over the years, but she is delighted now to be associated with Ertl. As she says, "Working with Ertl is just amazing. 'LeMutt' has never looked this good before!" Another Ertl Collectibles artist is Joanne Callander, whose series of limited edition dolls is titled *Forever Sisters*. The dolls are crafted in exceptionally fine Adamantine Vinyl™ with a porcelain-like appearance. Callander's hand-made porcelain dolls sell for $800 to $1,500, but thanks to her association with Ertl, a whole new world of collectors now may own her affordable creations.

Each 7" tall doll features actual glass eyes (the smallest glass eyes ever to be found in a vinyl doll), poseability, a distinctive hairstyle, and exquisite facial features. Their Victorian-inspired costumes are complemented by wonderful accessories including a hope chest, rocking chair, and wrought iron bench.

CIRCUS WORLD AND LICENSED DIE CAST PRODUCTS

In association with the Circus World Museum, Ertl presents the *Circus World Museum Collection*. This is just the first of many museum collections to be offered by Ertl. Sculpted by Ertl artisans, this series features exceptionally detailed hand-painted circus wagon replicas, complete with turning wheels and suspension detail. Crafted in cold cast porcelain and brightly hand-painted, each wagon conveys the magical splendor of the circus world. The circus wagons

Francesca Hoerlein presents the beloved plush collectible dog "LeMutt"™ in cooperation with Ertl.

presented in this dramatic collection represent some of the rarest and most spectacular examples among the 170-plus antique vehicles located at the Museum in Baraboo, Wisconsin, which served as the original Winter headquarters site for the Ringling Brothers Circus from 1884-1918.

Also capturing precious elements of American heritage are Ertl's many die cast replicas, created in the tradition of Fred Ertl, Sr. Most of these Ertl collectibles are made from die-cast molten metal, utilizing the highest quality materials available. Today, Ertl forms strategic alliances with a wide range of renowned companies, gaining licensing rights to present vehicles with a host of proud logos and traditions. These include COCA-COLA®, McDonald's®, Hershey's™, Campbell's®, Borden®, American Airlines®, Eskimo Pie®, Brink's, Chevy®, Ford®, and many more.

Joanne Callander's "Sara" represents her* Forever Sisters *series for Ertl Collectibles Limited.

Gary Becker is confident that Ertl Collectibles Limited will help bring a large group of its traditional collectors into the gift and collectibles markets. As he explains, "With Ertl's five decades of dominance in the farm toy and collectibles marketplace, literally hundreds of thousands of people know Ertl and our reputation for quality. These collectors will find immediate appeal in our new collections, and we look forward to serving them as we have the die cast collectors for more than 50 years."

TO LEARN MORE:

ERTL COLLECTIBLES
P.O. BOX 500
HWYS. 136 & 20
DYERSVILLE, IA 52040
(800) 553-4886
FAX: (319) 875-5674

America's Heritage Handcrafted in Miniature

The six-piece* War Memorial Collection *from* The Cat's Meow Village™ *includes "USMC Memorial," "Tomb of the Unknowns," "Korean War Veterans Memorial," "The Wall," "Vietnam Veterans Memorial" and "Vietnam Women's Memorial."

From an early age, Faline Fry Jones enjoyed making and selling candles, macrame hangings and other craft items. Then she came up with the idea of creating miniature architectural buildings, each handcrafted in wood and precisely painted.

So in 1982, she invested $39.00 in materials, retreated to her basement workshop and made her first house facades. Gift stores around her small hometown of Wooster, Ohio, sold the collectibles as fast as she could create them. When she entered the Columbus Gift Mart, the onslaught of orders was remarkable. By the Spring of 1994, 800 dealers were carrying her *Cat's Meow Village*, and Faline had hired 19 employees to keep up with the demand.

At first, the artist designed only fictitious buildings, but her initial attempts at creating replicas of actual places and historical landmarks generated an enthusiastic collector response. The idea, which grew from collectors' suggestions, is a trend that still shapes the company's product lines.

"We're living in an uncertain day," Faline says. "We never know what's ahead of us, but we can always grab on to what's behind us. I think the *Village* gives us something to identify with and feel good about. It really connects you with your roots."

Today, *The Cat's Meow Village* continues to grow, touching the hearts of thousands of avid collectors who find a piece of the past and the present in each architectural building. For many, Faline's creations have become just as familiar as Casper, the famous black cat that appears in silhouette on every piece along with the artist's signature — trademarks of an original *Cat's Meow Village* miniature.

BUSINESS GROWS WITH CARE AND FINE CRAFTSMANSHIP

Faline's designs were in demand from the beginning. Within a year after founding her company, Faline had to move the business from her basement to the backroom of a local woodworking shop. By 1986, it had taken over the whole building. In 1989, a new building was constructed and remains the current home of FJ (Faline Jones) Designs Inc., which she had earlier renamed from *The Cat's Meow Village*.

Also in 1989, the retirement of the first *Village* collectibles and the formation of the national Cat's Meow Collectors Club catapulted the *Village* into the national and international spotlights. Another landmark event took place on August 7, 1993: the first-ever Cat's Meow Convention was held in Wooster in celebration of the 10th anniversary. Nearly 4,000 avid fans gathered at the Wayne County Fairgrounds to view displays, see the *Village* museum, shop at the company store and chat with Faline in her autograph tent.

This sense of family and friendship has always been at the heart of Faline's unique collectibles. The company employs more than 180 people and works with several other small companies that help produce its products. Faline also prides herself in providing employment opportunities for women and offering flex-time for staff.

In giving back to the community, FJ Designs continues to contribute an annual portion of the profit from the sale of *The Cat's Meow Village* to several national charities. In addition, each year

On April 11, 1861, shots were fired at Fort Sumter in Charleston, South Carolina. The famous "Fort Sumter," now part of the* Civil War Collection, *will retire December 31, 2002.

Faline selects specific series and donates a portion of the sales to other established charitable organizations such as the American Red Cross, Salvation Army, United Negro College Fund, National Sudden Infant Death Syndrome, Children's Defense Fund, and the National Alliance of Breast Cancer Organizations (NABCO).

Even while the company grows and flourishes, Faline remains the driving force behind each design. She thrives on researching history and selects all the items in the regular product line. Her camera is a constant companion when traveling, and she continues seeking ideas from her faithful collectors.

After a design is created, the production of each *Village* piece involves a painstaking, seven-stage process. It includes hand-tracing the pattern, hand-cutting, screen printing and individual hand-finishing of sides and roof lines. Products are made from medium density hardwoods, which prove ideal both for cutting and screen printing, as well as for long-term durability in display.

HISTORY RETURNS IN *VILLAGE* INTRODUCTIONS

For 1997, Faline drew her inspiration from the past and from architectural gems from coast to coast. The *War Memorial Collection* honors national monuments that remember those who fought for freedom. They include "USMC Memorial," "Tomb of the Unknowns," "Korean War Veterans Memorial," "The Wall," "Vietnam Veterans Memorial" and "Vietnam Women's Memorial." The pieces are set to retire on December 31, 2002.

In 1997, Faline unveiled the *Civil War Collection* of eight famous buildings. From the first shots fired at Fort Sumter in 1861 to the final clashes on the road to Appomattox in 1864, the Civil War was the most violent and fateful experience in American history. *The Cat's Meow Village* captures the famous places of this time with "Shirley House," "Stone House," "Wills House," "Dunker Church," "Chatham," "McLean House," "Appomattox Manor" and "Fort Sumter," which features a new *Village* look as a perspective building. All the items are set to retire on December 31, 2002. A boxed set, which also includes "Shiloh Battle," is limited to 10,000 pieces. For the first time, Faline has also put historical information on the back of selected pieces, including the *Civil War Collection.*

The history also appears on the back of the *Women Light Keepers Series* in tribute to those who kept the country's shorelines safe. The four pieces are "Robbins Reef Rescue," "Turkey Point Light," "Matinicus Rock Light" and "Ida Lewis Rock Lighthouse." Available only with a boxed set, which is limited to 8,000, is "Ida Lewis Rescue."

The *Annual Edition Collection*, each with a special paw print mark added to the building, continued with eight introductions in 1997. Each piece is limited to one year production. Among the introductions are: "Grant Drug Store," third in *Mark Twain's Hannibal Series*; "Humpback Bridge," third in the *Covered Bridge Series*; "Big Top," third in the *Circus Series*; and "Cinderella Cottage," third in the *Martha's Vineyard Series.*

"Breast Cancer Awareness Tree" is a Special Event piece for 1997. While the front of the tree carries the pink ribbons symbolic of breast cancer, the back features the Breast Cancer Awareness stamp issued by the U.S. Postal Service.

Part of the* Annual Edition Collection, *"Humpback Bridge" is third in the* Covered Bridge Series *of four.

The retailer Special Event piece in 1997 is the "Breast Cancer Awareness Tree." The tree bears pink ribbons, and the back of the collectible features the Breast Cancer Awareness stamp issued by the U.S. Postal Service. Proceeds from this design benefit the National Alliance of Breast Cancer Organizations (NABCO).

THE CHRISTMAS SPIRIT LIVES IN THE VILLAGE

From Williamsburg to the North Pole, to Stockbridge where Norman Rockwell called home, Christmas is celebrated with tradition and joy. Faline makes the season brighter with the *Stockbridge Christmas Series* of four buildings: "Nejaime's Stockbridge Shop," "Town Offices," "Williams & Sons" and "Housatonic National Bank."

The *North Pole Collection* is only available in a boxed set, an unmatched concept in the collectibles industry. The five pieces, accented with glitter ink in the snow, are set to retire on December 31, 2002. They are: "Reindeer Barn," "Mrs. Claus Bakery," "Packing the Sleigh," "North Pole Sign" and "Santa & Mrs. Claus."

The "Reindeer Barn" is one of five pieces in the* North Pole Collection. *It can only be purchased through the* North Pole Collection *boxed set, which was introduced September 1, 1997, and will retire December 31, 2002.

Four ornaments feature buildings from historic Williamsburg, Virginia, which were taken from Faline's first *Christmas Series.* A selection of accessories add delight to any holiday.

Under a licensing agreement with Lionel Trains, *The Cat's Meow Village* created wood facade replicas of several classic Lionel sets. Lionel electric toy trains are as much a part of America's history as the real transportation giants after which they were modeled.

LIONEL TRAINS CHUG INTO *CAT'S MEOW VILLAGE*

"The General," "Pennsylvania Steam Turbine" and "Santa Fe" passenger trains are faithfully reproduced and come beautifully packaged in boxes similar to original Lionel sets. The trains are only sold as six-piece sets and are approximately 26" in length from engine to caboose. Casper appears on every train car. In addition to the three train sets, which retired on May 31, 1997, 11 train accessories were developed, from a lamp post to a crossing gate. FJ Designs introduced two new train sets and eight new accessories in August, 1997. "We're excited about adding more licensed products to the *Village* and partnering with other nationally recognized organizations," Faline says.

The Cat's Meow Collectors Club is one of the most popular clubs in the country with more than 40,000 members. Its exclusive Club pieces already have shown strong secondary market activity.

COLLECTORS CAN JOIN THE CLUB

Through the Club, new members can discover why collecting *The Cat's Meow Village* has become a passion for thousands of collectors all around the world.

Members receive a free Club Gift House, Club notebook, deed holder to keep track of a personal collection, membership card and *Cat's Meow* dealer list. They also receive a subscription to "The Village Mews" and "The Village Exchange," with secondary market information and classified advertising section where members and dealers buy, sell and trade *Cat's Meow* collectibles. Members may also purchase a collectible from the annual members-only series. A new membership is $33.00. Two-year membership is $53.00. Renewing members pay $22.00 for the same benefits. In 1998, the Club will offer a subscription-only membership at $11.00 for those collectors that simply want the newsletter and "The Village Exchange." *Cat's Meow* enthusiasts also enjoy a standing invitation to visit Club headquarters in Wooster, Ohio, and tour the production facilities for the *Village* collections. Tours take place each weekday Monday through Friday at 10 a.m. and 1 p.m.

CLUB

CAT'S MEOW COLLECTORS CLUB
2163 Great Trails Drive
Wooster, OH 44691-3738
(330) 264-1377 Ext. 225

Annual Dues: $33.00 - Renewal: $22.00
Subscription Rate: $11.00
Club Year: Anniversary of Sign-Up Date

BENEFITS:

- Membership Club House
- Opportunity to Purchase Members-Only Piece
- Quarterly Newsletter, "Mews"
- Buy/Sell Match Service in "Village Exchange" Publication
- Membership Card
- Club Binder
- Deed Holder

TOUR

FJ DESIGNS, "THE CAT'S MEOW"FACTORY TOUR
2163 Great Trails Drive
Wooster, OH 44691-3738
(330) 264-1377 Ext. 231

Hours: Monday through Friday,
10 a.m. and 1 p.m.
Closed major holidays and weekends.

Admission Fee: None

The tour of the production facilities at FJ Designs takes approximately 30 minutes. Visitors are able to watch skilled artisans produce the handcrafted *Cat's Meow Village™* collections.

TO LEARN MORE:

FJ DESIGNS, INC.
MAKERS OF THE CAT'S MEOW VILLAGE
2163 GREAT TRAILS DRIVE
WOOSTER, OH 44691-3738
(330) 264-1377
FAX: (330) 263-0219
URL: http://www.catsmeow.com
E-MAIL: cmu@fjdesign.com

A Continuing Celebration in Fine Glass

The year: 2005. The event: an extravaganza to mark the 100th anniversary of Fenton Art Glass. Today – with less than 10 years to go before this remarkable milestone – Fenton family members and artists work in a concerted effort to continue their company's rise as one of America's leading creators of collector's items.

Each year Fenton introduces new collectibles in the spirit of the company's long-standing philosophy: the production of unique glass treatments featuring the age-old techniques of hand-craftsmanship, conveyed from generation to generation.

A FAMILY OF INNOVATIVE GLASS ARTISTS

The Fenton Art Glass Company was founded in 1905 by Frank L. Fenton and his brother John, in an old glass factory building in Martins Ferry, Ohio. Here, they painted decorations on glass blanks made by other firms. The Fentons had trouble getting the glass they wanted when they wanted it, and soon decided to produce their own. The first glass from the Fenton factory in Williamstown, West Virginia, was made on January 2, 1907.

One of the first colors produced by the new company was called Chocolate Glass, and in late 1907, Fenton introduced iridescent pressed glass. (Fifty years later this glass was called Carnival Glass.) Iridescent glass was still selling in the 1920s, but it was made in delicate pastel colors with very little pattern in a treatment called "stretch glass." High quality Carnival Glass now sells for as much as $600 to $4,500 a piece. Recently, a rare piece sold for $22,500.

This lamp, five-piece epergne and vase are part of the 1997* Historic Collection *produced for a one-year period in Topaz Opalescent. This color was first produced in 1921 and is one of the few yellow glasses classified as "Vaseline Glass" by collectors. The items, hand-painted with Hydrangeas, feature the graceful drapery optic.

During the 1930s and 1940s, Fenton Art Glass struggled to survive the Depression and war shortages. Fenton included production of mixing bowls and orange juice reamers to keep people working, but did not hold back on developing beautiful new colors. Jade, Mandarin Red, Mulberry and Peach Blow from this period are eagerly sought by Fenton collectors today.

A PERFUME BOTTLE BRIGHTENS THE DEPRESSION FOR FENTON

Fenton recovered after the Depression with the help of a little hobnail perfume bottle designed at the behest of the Allen B. Wrisley Company. The bottle business made Fenton well again and also opened new business for hobnail glass and antique reproductions of Victorian glass.

FRANK AND BILL FENTON ASSUME LEADERSHIP ROLES

Between 1948 and 1949, the top three members of Fenton's original management died, and brothers Frank M. Fenton, age 33, and Bill Fenton, age 25, took over as President and Vice-President of Sales respectively. The next five years were rough ones, but then milk glass began to sell beautifully all over the country. Fenton's hob-nail milk glass became the company's bread-and-butter line.

The team of Frank and Bill Fenton led the factory through significant growth for the next 30-plus years. Together they continued to develop new designs based on the flexibility and character of handmade glass.

A THIRD GENERATION OF LEADERSHIP

In February, 1986, the leadership of Fenton Art Glass passed to the third generation when George W. Fenton became President. Bill Fenton is Chairman of the Board and Frank is retired, but both are at work every day as advisors. Today, there are 11 family members working in the management of The Fenton Art Glass Company. With 530 employees, the company is now the largest producer of handmade colored glass giftware in the United States.

While a number of hand glass companies have closed their doors over the past 15 years, Fenton has survived and grown by continuing to be flexible, and by offering a constant stream of new products to the market.

This elegant 8" "French Rose on Rosalene Vase" is the 1997 Glass Messenger Exclusive. Rosalene, made with pure gold, has attracted collectors since first introduced in 1976. Only subscribers to "The Glass Messenger" will be eligible to purchase this special piece.

AN ARRAY OF JEWEL-LIKE FENTON GLASS CREATIONS

Fenton Art Glass is renowned for creating beautiful and unique colors in glass, including exotic glass varieties in rich shades such as Cranberry, Mulberry, Opalescent and Burmese. Fenton's iridescent "Carnival" glass enjoys a history extending back to 1907, and fiery Opalescent gleams in transparent colored glass that shades to opaque white. With an appreciation of the past and an eye to the future, Fenton brings back the rare collectible treatments of bygone eras, while continually developing new and exciting colors to coordinate with current decorating trends.

At Fenton, each piece of glassware is an individual creation from a skilled hand glassworker. As seasoned collectors know, only an unfeeling machine can produce "glass armies" of unvarying detail. Much of the charm of true Fenton Art Glass comes from its stretched and fluted shapes that can only be created by hand.

Like most experts, the master glassworker makes this craft appear simple. Even so, if you watch the people making Fenton glass, you will see the hundreds of appraising glances that carefully assay each piece as it passes from hand to hand. Many of the looks say proudly, "That's mine, I created it."

Fenton has its own mould shop, which enhances the company's ability to develop and introduce new designs. Patterns and designs are chipped into the cast iron moulds by hand. Many Fenton creations are painted by hand by individual artists who proudly sign each piece.

SPECIAL FENTON OFFERINGS INTRIGUE COLLECTORS

Each year, Fenton Art Glass produces new editions for several popular series in strictly limited editions. These include the *Family Signature Series, Historical Collection, Connoisseur Collection, Collectible Eggs,* and Christmas, Valentines and Easter limited editions.

The *Family Signature Series* includes a few select pieces which represent the glass worker's and decorator's finest creations. Classic moulds from the past inspire the *Historical Collection* pieces, all made in unique colors and treatments. The *Connoisseur Collection* features a small grouping of art objects made in exotic glass treatments.

For Christmas, Fenton produces an annual limited edition collection including a plate, bell, fairy light and lamp – all entirely hand-painted. For Valentines, Fenton introduces new items each year in a Cranberry Opalescent Heart pattern, as well as one to three items in the Mary Gregory style of painting. Mouth-blown eggs and hand-pressed collectible eggs are showcased in Fenton's Easter offerings.

What's more, Fenton Showcase Dealers now may offer two exclusive Fenton special items each year.

FENTON COLLECTORS BENEFIT BY KNOWLEDGE OF GLASS MARKINGS

The Handler's Mark, Decorator's Signature, and Fenton Logo represent three markings that "savvy" Fenton collectors should know. A "Handler's Mark" – different for each craftsman – is applied to each Fenton basket by the highly skilled person who attaches the handle. The "Decorator's Signature" appears on each hand-painted piece, and the "Fenton Logo" is placed on each piece of glass to permanently mark it as authentically Fenton.

Fenton logos vary slightly depending upon when the piece was made and what type of glass it represents. These markings help collectors to authenticate their holdings and evaluate possible purchases on the secondary market.

CLUBS AND TOURS ENHANCE FENTON COLLECTING

Fenton invites collectors to subscribe to its collector publication, "The Glass Messenger." For a subscription price of $12.00, collectors will get four colorful issues of the "Glass Messenger," a decorative storage binder, and the opportunity to purchase an exclusive piece designed for subscribers only. "The Glass Messenger" will give collectors an insight into the processes of hand-made glass, new products, the history of Fenton and Fenton family and employees.

Collectors may also join one of the three national organizations formed in celebration of Fenton Art Glass. The Fenton Art Glass Collectors of America (FAGCA), the National Fenton Glass Society (NFGS) and the Pacific Northwest Fenton Association (PNWFA) all welcome members and offer newsletters, annual conventions and a great deal of sharing of knowledge of and

The "Irises on Misty Blue" Pitcher with the signature of Don Fenton is part of the* Family Signature Series. *Each year, six to eight pieces from the Fenton line are selected to be available for a limited time and to include the signature of one of the Fenton Family members.

enthusiasm for Fenton Glass.

Collectors visiting the Williamstown, West Virginia facility can take regularly scheduled tours of the glassmaking process and visit the Fenton Museum. Collectors are invited to call the Fenton Gift Shop at (304) 375-7772 for specifics on the free tours.

THE FENTON TRADITION: BORN OF A PROUD GLASSMAKING HISTORY

For three millennia, glass has delighted and served people in their homes, their industries, and their places of worship. The first industry in the American colonies was a hand glass shop started at Jamestown, Virginia, in 1608. In America, glassware reached a new zenith during the last half of the 1800s, as a newly united nation grew to its full destiny.

It is this tradition of the glassmaker's art which is painstakingly recreated in Fenton Art Glass. Now, as they approach their Centennial as a family-owned company, the Fentons take pride in the fact that Fenton glass has itself become a modern American tradition. To every beholder, Fenton handmade glass gives back a little store of the affection that went into its making. No gift seems quite as intimate in its ability to convey this care and regard. And to those who collect, display and use Fenton Art Glass pieces, this may be the greatest gift of all.

CLUBS

FENTON ART GLASS COLLECTORS OF AMERICA (FAGCA)
P.O. Box 384
Williamstown, WV 26187
(304) 375-6196

Annual Dues: $20.00
Associate Membership: $2.00
Club Year: Anniversary of Sign-Up Date

BENEFITS:
- Opportunity to Purchase Members-Only Glass Piece
- Bi-monthly Newsletter, "The Butterfly Net"
- Buy/Sell Matching Service through Newsletter
- Annual Convention
- Local Club Chapters

NATIONAL FENTON GLASS SOCIETY (NFGS)
P.O. Box 4008
Marietta, OH 45750

Annual Dues: $15.00
Associate Membership: $2.00
Club Year: Anniversary of Sign-Up Date

BENEFITS:
- Opportunity to Purchase Members-Only Glass Piece
- Bi-monthly Newsletter, "The Fenton Flyer"
- Buy/Sell Matching Service
- Annual Convention and Auctions
- Local Club Chapters

PACIFIC NORTHWEST FENTON ASSOCIATION (PNWFA)
8225 Kilchis River Road
Tillamook, OR 97141

Annual Dues: $20.00
Associate Membership: $2.00
Club Year: Anniversary of Sign-Up Date

BENEFITS:
- Members-Only Piece
- Membership Gift, Produced Exclusively for PNWFA Members
- Quarterly Newsletter, "Nor'wester"
- Special Events, including Annual Glass Show, Annual Convention and Auction

MUSEUM & TOUR

FENTON ART GLASS COMPANY MUSEUM & TOUR
420 Caroline Ave.
Williamstown, WV 26187
(304) 375-7772
Hours: Monday through Saturday, 8:30 a.m. - 4:30 p.m.
Closed on major holidays and the first two weeks in July.

Admission Fee: Free

The Fenton Art Glass Museum offers examples of Ohio Valley glass, with major emphasis on Fenton glass made from 1905 to 1955. A 30-minute movie on the making of Fenton glass is shown throughout the day.

The 40-minute factory tour allows visitors to watch highly skilled craftsmen create handmade glass from its molten state to the finished product. A gift shop is also located on the premises.

SPECIAL PUBLICATION

THE GLASS MESSENGER
700 Elizabeth Street
Williamstown, WV 26187
(800) 249-4527

Annual Subscription: $12.00

BENEFITS:
- Opportunity to Purchase Special Piece
- Decorative Storage Binder with Initial Subscription

TO LEARN MORE:

THE FENTON ART GLASS COMPANY
700 ELIZABETH STREET
WILLIAMSTOWN, WV 26187
(304) 375-6122
FAX: (304) 375-6459
URL: hhtp://wvweb.com/www/fenton_glass
E-MAIL: fentonglass@citynet.net

Emmett Kelly, Jr. and Exclusive Lines Put Flambro in the Collectibles Spotlight

At Flambro Imports, keeping collectors happy is job one. This means setting high standards, exceeding expectations and offering collectibles with enduring qualities and reasonable prices. It's a philosophy that has grown at the company since Louis and Stanley Flamm founded Flambro Imports, Inc. in 1965. The Flamm brothers launched the business with a simple plan to buy gifts from importers that they could, in turn, sell to American businesses as promotional items and give-aways to entice customers into a store.

Their venture proved to be so successful that the Flamms decided to go into the importing business themselves. Flambro continued to import inexpensive promotional items until the 1970s, when it began purchasing higher quality giftware from Taiwan. During this time, most of the less expensive ceramic factories turned to Taiwan rather than Japan, since the labor market could still support a low-cost, yet high-quality product. A new challenge for importers soon developed, as key Taiwanese employees began defecting to competitors or starting their own companies. To gain stability within the industry, Louis Flamm and one of Taiwan's top porcelain manufacturers formed a partnership to create an alliance among factories. The Taiwan Tao Tsu Ceramics Manufacturers Association was started to cooperate in purchasing raw materials, sharing technology and stopping corporate espionage. Each factory that joined the group produced a different item ranging from bisque figurines to music boxes. Flambro was named the U.S. representative to the group.

By the mid-1980s, Flambro turned to more cost-effective manufacturers in Malaysia, Indonesia, and China, where most of the company's products are made today. "Over the years, we've tried to maintain a good balance of quality, design and value," says Allan Flamm, who has been president of Flambro since 1982 when his father, Louis, retired. "We try to continually offer new products and, most important, keep our customers happy."

Each year, the **Emmett Kelly, Jr. Collection** ***introduces limited edition figurines, including the 1997 piece, "Catch of the Day." The figurine is limited to 5,000 pieces.***

The cornerstone of Flambro's success has been "America's Favorite Clown." The ever-popular *Emmett Kelly, Jr. Collection* was introduced in 1980 and has remained the company's top-selling collectible. "Emmett Kelly, Jr. is a piece of Americana – a real American classic," Flamm says. "We had been producing porcelain clown figurines before 1980, so when we had the opportunity to do Emmett Kelly, Jr., it gave us something we could base our designs on and add a little pizzazz. The products were successful from the get-go."

EMMETT KELLY, JR. MAKES COLLECTORS SMILE

Many of the early limited edition pieces in the collection have soared on the secondary market. The line now includes porcelain figurines, ornaments, waterglobes and other gift accessories. To date, Flambro has introduced about 1,500 different designs, including nearly 75 limited edition figurines.

The 1997 limited edition figurines include "25th Anniversary of White House Appearance," which illustrates Emmett Kelly, Jr.'s visit at Tricia Nixon's birthday party in 1972. It was the only such performance ever given by a clown. "Catch of the Day" shows EKJ struggling with his rod and reel while sitting above the water, realistically created using a new technique. Both figurines are each limited to 5,000 pieces.

The original *Emmett Kelly, Jr. Collection* was so popular that it spawned other series including *Real Rags*, fashioned after the tattered suits that EKJ is famous for, and *Images of Emmett*, featuring his beloved facial expressions. *Little Emmett* was created in celebration of the clown's 70th birthday in 1994. The line is a reflection of Emmett, reliving his childhood in an adorable collection of figurines and gifts that brings out the kid in collectors of all ages. *Little Emmett* includes birthday figurines for ages one to ten, musicals, bookends, a photo frame, vignette figurines, and more. New pieces are introduced annually.

In 1994, Flambro added new lines when it joined forces with Collectible World Studios Ltd. of Stoke-On-Trent, England, producer of the popular *Pocket Dragons* by Real Musgrave. Flambro is the sole U.S. distributor of the line. The *Pocket Dragons* are mischievous and clever, with a keen desire to hide away in cozy corners and collectors' pockets. The collection grew

***POCKET DRAGONS* SHARES FANTASY WORLD OF DELIGHT**

"Pretty Please" and "Daisy" join the* Pocket Dragons *collection by artist Real Musgrave, who captures the magic and mischievous side of these friendly creatures.

out of Musgrave's childhood love of dragons, which he began drawing when he was five years old. His fascination and interest in bringing the dragon's magic to life continued throughout school and his career as a professional artist. In 1974, he started a small gallery and commercial art studio where he sold his fantasy drawings, many of which featured his dragons. It was during this period that he produced a print titled "Pocket Dragon" and began to fully develop these little creatures.

Musgrave and his wife, Muff, developed and marketed limited edition etchings and prints of the *Pocket Dragons*, wizards and gargoyles. In 1978, Muff quit her job to become her husband's full-time creative partner. His artwork caught the attention of Collectible World Studios, which launched *The Whimsical World of Pocket Dragons* in 1989.

Today, Musgrave's enchanting figurines have cast a spell on collectors everywhere with their happy smiles and fun-loving personalities. In 1997, *Pocket Dragons* also became an animated children's television series. "Pocket Dragon Adventures" focuses on the antics of the Wizard and six characters, including Zoom Zoom, Scribbles and Princess Betty Bye Bell.

In addition to *Pocket Dragons*, the agreement with Collectible World Studios also allows Flambro to distribute the limited edition fantasy figurines

FLAMBRO EXCLUSIVELY DISTRIBUTES *WIZARDS AND DRAGONS*

known as *Wizards and Dragons*. Artist Hap Henriksen created the *Wizards and Dragons* sculptures, which reflect his anthropological background and love of folk and fairy tales. Over the years, Henriksen's fantasy sculptures have won numerous awards, including an "Award of Merit" in the First Annual Collection of Contemporary Fantastic Art Spectrum. Henriksen and his wife, Elizabeth, share time between studios in Texas and Kansas working on a wide selection of products.

THE *PEANUTS GANG* COMES TO FLAMBRO

In 1996, Flambro welcomed the *Peanuts Gang* collection, introduced to coincide with the 45th anniversary of the comic strip and the 75th birthday of its creator, Charles Schulz. The premiere collection included 12 colorful resin birthday figurines featuring Snoopy, Woodstock, Charlie Brown, Lucy and the whole gang of familiar characters. Future additions to the *Peanuts Gang* will include musical waterglobes, as well as limited edition figurines in porcelain and resin.

FLAMBRO SCORES WITH A WINNING LINE-UP

Flambro has also stepped onto the sports playing field. Through licensing agreements with Major League Baseball and the National Hockey League, Flambro has become a key player in the sports collectibles business. The Flambro line-up includes Major League Baseball Santa ornaments, as well as the *Cooperstown Collection* of Santa figurines, ornaments, waterglobes and musicals. The *Cooperstown Collection* recreates fond memories of a bygone baseball era. Both baseball lines have grown on a yearly basis with the addition of more teams to the lists.

In 1995, the company introduced the *Negro Leagues* collection, a tribute to the talented Black players of the early and mid-20th century. The series includes figurines, Santa ornaments, baseball ornaments, lapel pins, magnets, coffee mugs and a multi-logo collector plate. In 1996, the National Hockey League Santa figurines debuted with St. Nick ready to fight it out on the ice dressed in the uniforms of today's most popular teams, including the Philadelphia Flyers, Mighty Ducks of Anaheim, Pittsburgh Penguins and St. Louis Blues.

The *Heritage Collection* is inspired by the six remaining "founding" teams that became today's National Hockey League. The resin Santas are dressed in true-to-life uniforms from the late 1910s to 1930s. They wear real metal skates on clear resin bases that look like ice. Other introductions include goalie figurines and musical waterglobes that play the fight song "Ride of the Valkyries."

The *Sportsman Collection*, which includes figurines and mugs of young hunting dogs, is based on the limited edition prints by artist Lynn Kaatz. Recognized for his excellence in creating wildlife, landscape and seascape portraits, Kaatz travels throughout the world to research his subjects. As a dedicated conservationist and outdoorsman, Kaatz utilizes his award-winning artistic talents to preserve the natural surroundings.

COLLECTORS INVITED TO JOIN THE CLUBS

Flambro also offers collectors a way to further enjoy their favorite collectibles. Those who love the famous clown can join the Emmett Kelly, Jr. Collectors' Society. Members receive an EKJ collector's plaque, quarterly newsletter, binder, EKJ lapel pin, membership card, free registration

Flambro celebrates birthdays with the* Peanuts Gang *collection featuring the favorite comic strip characters from Charles Schulz.

Artist Hap Henriksen created the* Wizards and Dragons *sculptures, which reflect his love for the fantasy world. The collection includes (from left to right) "Solaris the Star Seeker," "Curiosity," "The Elusive Potion" and "Well of Sorrows."

of figurines, a full-color catalog, annual collector registry listing and a toll-free collectors' service hotline (1-800-EKJ-CLUB). Members also have the opportunity to purchase the exclusive members-only figurines and attend special club-sponsored events.

Collectors can also discover more adventures by joining the Pocket Dragons and Friends Collectors' Club, with many benefits including a membership figurine, quarterly newsletter, redemption coupon for the annual members-only piece and invitations to appearances by Real Musgrave.

The Wizards and Dragons Collectors' Fellowship has benefits including a quarterly newsletter, members-only redemption coupon, lapel pin, membership card and annual full-color catalog.

From Emmett Kelly, Jr. to sports collectibles, Flambro keeps collectors happy and keeps looking for new artists, designs and products to share with America.

CLUBS

EKJ COLLECTORS' SOCIETY
P.O. Box 93507
Atlanta, GA 30377-0507
(800) EKJ-CLUB

Annual Dues: $30.00
Club Year: January-December
Collectors' Year: Anniversary of Sign-Up Date

BENEFITS:
- Membership Gift: Collector's Plaque
- Redemption Coupon for Members-Only Figurine
- Quarterly Newsletter, "EKJournal"
- Binder
- Membership Card
- EKJ Catalog
- Toll Free Collectors' Hotline
- EKJ Lapel Pin
- Free Registration of Figurines
- Annual Collector Registry Listing
- Special Club-Sponsored Events

POCKET DRAGONS AND FRIENDS COLLECTORS CLUB
P.O. Box 93507
Atlanta, GA 30377-0507
(800) 355-2582

Annual Dues: $29.50; $54.00 for 2 Years

Club Year: June 1 - May 30
Collectors' Year: Anniversary of Sign-Up Date

BENEFITS:
- Membership Gift: *Pocket Dragons* Figurine
- Redemption Coupon for Members-Only Figurine
- Quarterly Magazine, *Pocket Dragons Gazette*
- Membership Card
- Catalog
- Lapel Pin
- Toll Free Collectors Hotline
- Invitations to Special Appearances by Real Musgrave
- Travel Opportunities: Pocket Dragon Collectors' Tour of Britain

CLUBS

WIZARDS AND DRAGONS COLLECTORS' FELLOWSHIP
P.O. Box 93507
Atlanta, GA 30377-0707
(800) 355-2582

Annual Dues: $10.00
Club Year: Anniversary of Sign-Up Date

BENEFITS:
- Coupon for Members-Only Redemption Piece
- Quarterly Newsletter
- Lapel Pin
- Membership Card
- Annual Full-Color Catalog

TO LEARN MORE:

FLAMBRO IMPORTS
1530 ELLSWORTH INDUSTRIAL DRIVE
ATLANTA, GA 30306
(404) 352-1381
FAX (404) 352-2150
WEBSITE: http://www.flambro.com
http://www.signaturecollections.com
E-MAIL: collsoc@flambro.com

Fourth Generation Continues Family Tradition

In 1973, Roman, Inc. became the exclusive distributor for *Fontanini® Heirloom Nativities*. Already a world famous name in Italian craftsmanship for 65 years, the much sought-after collection was prized for its life-like sculpting and meticulous hand-painting. The partnership with Roman has made *Fontanini Heirloom Nativities* the most popular in America for more than 25 years.

Heralding the 90th Anniversary of* Fontanini Heirloom Nativities *is the Fontanini Collector's Edition Nativity Set from Roman, Inc.

The family patriarch, Emanuele Fontanini, embarked on his career of figurine crafting in 1893 as a talented 13-year-old apprentice to an artist in Bagni di Lucca, Italy. Fontanini expanded his knowledge and skill in art through travels to European cities, and returned to Bagni di Lucca to launch his company in 1908. Working with the finest painters and sculptors in Tuscany, Fontanini began crafting figures and decorations of heirloom quality in a single-room shop.

In time, the House of Fontanini gained recognition for its work and Fontanini's sons, Ugo, Mario and Aldo, joined him in the business. The Fontaninis expanded into a broader selection of Nativities under Mario's leadership, who took over as head of the House of Fontanini in 1936. Later, Mario's sons, Ugo, Mariano, and Piero, became the third generation to head up the rapidly growing enterprise.

Although no longer housed in the cherished room used by Emanuele in the early 1900s, the House of Fontanini continues to operate in the village of its founding. The family's fourth generation is poised to take the House of Fontanini into the 21st century. As the namesake and great-grandson of the founder, Emanuele Fontanini acts as the liaison between the Master Sculptor and the artists who translate his work into finished pieces. Emanuele's cousins, Marco and Luca, oversee production and quality control at the House of Fontanini. Emanuele's brother, Stefano, assumes responsibility on the business side of the operation.

It was fitting that the House of Fontanini would distinguish itself as the premier designer of heirloom quality Nativities and figures. It is the custom of Italian families to sculpt figures of people from all walks of life as they pay homage to the newborn King. Fontanini focuses on this illustrious heritage and devotes both talent and skill to the production of the *Fontanini Heirloom Nativities.*

The tradition of excellence continues with one of the world's finest sculptors creating each masterpiece. Since the 1940s, Master Sculptor Elio Simonetti has created sculptures of extraordinary beauty and majesty. Breathtaking in detail and workmanship, the collection is comprised of figures ranging in seven different sizes from tiny miniatures to life-size sculptures.

Every stage of the labor-intensive process of crafting Fontanini figures is conducted under the close supervision of the Fontanini family. The following steps detail the process of bringing the figures of *Fontanini Heirloom Nativities* to life.

THE CRAFTING PROCESS

The Idea – Original ideas for new pieces are conceived by the Fontanini family and members of the Roman, Inc. creative team. As the process evolves, a sketch is developed to portray the figure. Emanuele Fontanini then meets with Master Sculptor Elio Simonetti to discuss the creation of the sculpture.

The Clay Sculpture – Slowly and meticulously Simonetti shapes and carves the image, bringing the clay to life. Emanuele works closely with Simonetti at this phase, directing any changes to the intricately detailed original sculpture while the art is at its most malleable form.

Figures are developed in the size in which they will eventually be produced. For example, Mary has been sculpted in seven different sizes, from 2.5" to 50" tall. The Holy Family, Wise Men, and certain Bethlehem villagers and animals appear in some or all of the seven different sizes.

The Wax Sculpture – Upon completion of the clay sculpture and final approval from the Fontanini family, Simonetti prepares a highly detailed model in beeswax. This is a significantly harder substance than clay, and thus the ideal medium from which to create master molds.

Mold Making – After the wax sculpture is completed, Simonetti's youngest son,

Raffaello, begins the mold-making process. He positions his father's wax model against a piece of clay which will form the base of the mold, then encases half the figure in clay applied layer by layer. He removes the model and repeats the process to create the second half of the mold. Upon completion of the clay mold, Raffaello creates a model plaster figure from his clay mold. The final molds that will produce the figures are made from either metal or rubber. Metal molds are used to produce the 2-1/2", 5", 7-1/2" and 12" figures. Rubber molds are used for the 20", 27" and 50" figures. Both processes are identical until the completion of Raffaello's first plaster figure.

From the plaster figure the foundry will create a final master mold. The master mold is then used in the test production of several figures. Simonetti's son, Giuliano, perfects the mold, utilizing tiny precision instruments to correct all defects. At the end of this procedure, the mold is ready to begin producing figures for collectors to enjoy.

"Candace, The Caregiver" tenderly cradles a little lamb as the 1998 Fontanini Collectors Club™ Symbol of Membership figure.

Casting in Polymer – The 2-1/2", 5", 7-1/2" and 12" figures are cast of durable polymer, a compound which captures every detail of the original. Injection molding allows the polymer to be shaped into figures of extraordinary beauty with fine undercuts and delicately sculpted elements. Liquid polymer is forced into the carefully crafted mold at high temperature and pressure. After an initial cooling period, the still-warm figure emerges from the mold. It is then submerged in continuously running cold water for about two hours.

The Fontanini Mark – The first Fontanini always made his mark — a spider — under each figure to identify it as a House of Fontanini exclusive. The spider represented his unique design for a popular toy, a paper maché spider. Early Fontanini figures can still be identified by this special base mark of authenticity. Today, newer creations are identified by a "fountain" mark, the modern-day Fontanini authenticator.

Hand-Painting – Artisans living in Bagni di Lucca painstakingly hand-paint Nativity figures using skills that have been passed down from generation to generation. In some cases, grandmother, mother and daughter work side by side in the family home, applying hues from the rich Tuscan palette. Generally, several pieces are painted at the same time. The face is of utmost importance to collectors. Only the best painters paint the figures' faces so that the desired expression, often one of awe and reverence, is captured.

Patina Application – After painting, the figures are again sent from the House of Fontanini for the last phase of production — the patina application. A compound of burnt oils, oil, burnt earth, lime and other ingredients, called patina, is applied to each piece with a brush, making the figures almost entirely brown. The figures are wiped with a cloth and placed in tubs containing special soaps. Finally, they are removed from the tub and carefully wiped dry. As the patina is applied to the figures, it bonds with the material and cannot be removed.

The Stories – Each figure tells his or her own story through the gifted craftsmanship of the Fontanini family and Master Sculptor Simonetti. And each 5" *Fontanini Heirloom Nativity* figure has a personal Story Card — a fictional account of the character, as they might have lived and worked in and around Bethlehem at the time of Jesus' birth.

In honor of the 90th Anniversary of the House of Fontanini in 1998, Master Sculptor Elio Simonetti created the perfect commemoration of this auspicious year, "Emanuele, The Founder."

A new dimension in the history of Fontanini premiered in 1996 with the introduction of the Lighted Nativity Village buildings. Collectors can create extensive displays of ancient Bethlehem with realistic buildings, structures, tents, walls, and accessories. The 5" village scene can be enhanced by more than 80 different figures currently available in this popular size. Fontanini also has 2-1/2" and 7-1/2" lighted Nativity Villages. In addition, Roman has introduced self-contained scenes that combine such elements as a working waterfall, back lighting and mixed media.

Since 1990, the collection has been supported by the Fontanini Collectors' Club^{SM}, a national collectors' organization with a loyal and growing following. The annual Symbol of Membership figure is among the most popular benefits of club membership. An exclusive addition to the 5" *Nativity*

FONTANINI COLLECTORS' CLUB^{SM}

Collection, each Symbol of Membership figure is created solely for the enjoyment of club members and can only be acquired through membership in the club.

A 12-month subscription to the official quarterly newsletter, a commemorative Fontanini family history booklet, an exclusive 90th Anniversary club pin and a club portfolio are just a few of the additional benefits of membership. Current members who renew their membership enjoy a Fontanini gift in addition to the other club benefits.

Members also have the opportunity to purchase an annual Members-Only Nativity Preview Figure. An exclusive addition to the 5" *Nativity Collection*, the annual Members-Only Nativity Preview Figure can only be acquired through Fontanini Guild Dealers, using a special redemption certificate, for a suggested retail price of about $15.00.

A 12-month membership in the Fontanini Collectors' Club is $22.00, with a two-year membership available for $39.00. In addition to saving $5.00, members will receive all club benefits automatically during the 24-month period.

Roman launched the Fontanini Collectors' Club eight years ago, as an extension of the successful *Fontanini Heirloom Nativities Collection* and to offer Nativity and angel enthusiasts the opportunity to learn more about the collection and share their interest with other collectors. Membership in the Club is at an all-time high, as the collection has expanded to include its lighted Nativity Village settings and other new Fontanini gifts and collectibles.

"The Greatest Story Ever Told" with Fontanini figures, buildings and accessories is recreated on this majestic 7-1/2' Christmas tree, exclusively from Roman, Inc.

CLUB

FONTANINI COLLECTORS' CLUB℠
555 Lawrence Avenue
Roselle, IL 60172
(800) 729-7662

Annual Dues: $22.00; $39.00 for 2 Years
Club Year: Anniversary of Sign-Up Date

BENEFITS

- Membership Gift: Symbol of Membership Figurine
- Opportunity to Purchase Exclusive Members-Only Nativity Preview Figure
- Quarterly Newsletter, "The Fontanini Collector"
- Portfolio with Club Logo
- Club Pin
- Personalized Membership Card
- Fontanini Registry Guide
- Advance Notice of Tour Appearances by Fontanini Family Members and Special Members-Only Events
- Contests

TOUR

HOUSE OF FONTANINI STUDIO TOUR IN ITALY
C/O THE FONTANINI COLLECTORS' CLUB
555 Lawrence Avenue
Roselle, IL 60172
(800) 729-7662

Hours: Advance Reservations through the Fontanini Collectors' Club
Admission Fee: None

For collectors planning a trip to Italy, the House of Fontanini offers tours of their facilities in Bagni di Lucca, Italy.

TO LEARN MORE:

FONTANINI HEIRLOOM NATIVITIES
ROMAN, INC.
555 LAWRENCE AVENUE
ROSELLE, IL 60172
(630) 529-3000
FAX: (630) 529-1121
URL: http://www.roman.com

FOOL MOON TREASURES

Sculpted and Produced in the U.S.A.

Collectors who appreciate the miniature art form find themselves awestruck by artist Diane Sams' intricate collectible series spanning bears, mice, fairies, elves and other creatures great and small. But it is not until they learn of Sams' determination to design and produce every piece of work completely in the United States that they appreciate this artist's true uniqueness in today's world of collectibles.

Bearly bigger than a penny, as you can see, are these* Bearly's *characters from Fool Moon Treasures. "Zeke, Mountain Music" and "Harmony, Naturalist Bear" each has a retail price of $45.00.

Many of the most popular contemporary figurines are designed by "name" artists who create images in two dimensions for sculpting and crafting by others – often in far-off countries. By contrast, Sams not only designs but also sculpts each of her intricate miniatures, then ensures that each piece is crafted, finished and packed by hand to her exacting specifications. All this becomes still more impressive considering that collectors may need a magnifying glass to effectively examine Sams' pewter and resin creations – since many of them are only one inch or less in height! Recognizing this, a magnifier is included with many of the figures.

Diane Sams has been creating one-of-a-kind sterling miniatures since 1969. However, she did not launch her company until 1991 during the economic downturn that occurred during the period surrounding the Gulf War. "How foolish can you be to start a business at a time like that?" quips Sams, thus explaining the "fool" in her company's name. Although Fool Moon Treasures initially offered fashion jewelry, keepsakes and gifts, 1998 marked the debut of the firm's collectibles division.

SMALL THINGS MEAN A LOT TO DIANE SAMS

Sams was born in Louisiana, at the Lady of the Lake Hospital (possibly explaining her fascination with the Arthurian legends). She spent many of her formative years on a Venezuelan peninsula only 40 miles wide and remote from the urban center of Caracas. She often speaks of the development of imagination and joy in small things and natural items, as there was no television to distract her from the creation of worlds and realms of play.

She studied at the Corcoran School of Art in Washington D.C., but discovered her talent for sculpting during a brief career in dental technology. Initially this talent emerged in the field of jewelry. She created small gold portrait charms of Caroline and John-John for (then) Jackie Kennedy, and her studio wall is covered with signed pictures from Judy Collins, Dolly Parton and others who own her jewelry. Moving from sculpting jewelry to sculpting figurines was a small step, though her earliest work is in sterling silver and gold.

The windows of Sams' Tallahassee, Florida studio look out onto a small hedge-encircled retreat where birds, squirrels, raccoons, opossums and other creatures are always sure of finding food and a safe haven. Sams even has pictures of her pet cat sunning himself in the yard surrounded by a flock of birds! It is in this peaceful refuge, surrounded by the glories of precious and semi-precious stones, and racks of figures in various stages of completion, that Sams works her own special magic, creating her collections of figures ranging from 3/4" in height to 8". Each figure, no matter what size, embodies what Sams refers to as a "heart smile," that automatic response to gentle humor and shared joys.

THE *BEARLY'S* REFLECTIONS OF SIMPLE PLEASURES

Diane Sams found inspiration for her charming *Bearly's* series of miniatures by recalling time spent in Gatlinburg, Tennessee, as a jewelry designer. The series reflects both the locals and the tourists she observed.

"Harmony – Naturalist Bear" wears khaki shorts with lots of zippers and pockets. He's off for a mountain trek with his walking stick and binoculars. Though he is less than 1" in height, his pockets have buttons and there are lenses in his binoculars.

Then there is "Jack – Look What I Found" mining for jewels. He thinks he's going to find garnets, sapphires and rubies in the Carolina hills. He wears faded overalls, and has a red bandanna peeking out of his pocket. He carries his slush pan used to sort out the jewels from the water and pebbles and mud. Jack reflects the joy of discovery we all feel, even if the mine is salted!

"Zeke – Mountain Music" portrays the excitement of a Saturday night out, whether at the Grand Ole Opry or the local barn dance. Sams is particularly proud of the detail on this piece.

As she describes, "You can see the grain of the wood and the nails holding the floorboards. There are strings on the banjo, and the label is still on his faded overalls. His hound dog sleeps at his feet."

The *Bearly's* got their name because being only 1" in height, they are "bearly big enough to leave home." They are each limited to an edition of 500 pieces, cast of fine pewter and hand-painted. Priced from $40.00-$45.00, they come packaged with their own magnifier so you can examine the detail. Zeke's hound dog is only 1/4" high! How else can you enjoy his sleepy expression?

HOMESPUN GOODNESS – THE WARM GLOW OF FAMILY AND FRIENDS

Homespun Goodness is a collection of seven fine pewter mice figurines with mixed media accents. Each of the figurines reflects the message that it's "the simple things in life that are important – that live in your heart." To develop this project, Sams brought a few mice home from the pet store and put them in a cozy cage next to her work table to observe their many wonderful qualities. It is fortunate that Sams likes to work in the wee hours, since mice are

From the* Homespun Goodness *series comes "Memories," in which a grandfather mouse shares his happy recollections with his grandchild.

Perched on his own shining blue moon, the premiere character from the* Homespun Goodness *series claims that "Once in a Blue Moon, the Magic Comes Alive."

nocturnal. The artist discovered that these little creatures share food, care for one another, and enjoy being together. Observing their inherent kindness, they seemed a natural choice to help extend the collectibles division.

The premiere piece was "Once in a Blue Moon, the Magic Comes Alive." Dressed in a Renaissance costume, complete with ruffled shirt and knee britches, this 2" mouse is playing a lute. He sings of the importance of little things – of simple acts – of the depth of caring – of the importance of people in our lives and the magic of friendships. This mouse sits on a "blue moon" crafted of deep aqua glass on a pewter cloud sprinkled with stars.

"Memories" continues this captivating series, featuring a grandpa mouse, dressed in shirt, vest, tie and pants, snuggling his grandchild mouse after they have just finished reading a book still clutched in the baby mouse's hand. Intricately detailed, the grandpa mouse is humorously sitting on a case of mice cakes, with a family photo album at his feet. Tucked in the case are three books, *Mice, Life* and *Night Stories.* The grandfather also is holding an Austrian crystal, representing the special glow of shared stories and the creation of special memories.

Some other mice in the collection are "We Can Patch This Up," a little tailor sitting on a real spool of thread and holding a needle; "This Will Hold It Together," a chubby little mouse presenting a real button; and a quilter mouse, proudly displaying her just finished creation, "Every Stitch of Kindness Keeps You Warm the Winter Through." These intricately crafted fine pewter figurines retail between $16.00 and $20.00, and have many little surprises in store for those who examine them closely.

CAPTURED MAGIC™, O-SO WONDERFUL AND OTHER TREASURES

Two other whimsical new collections from Diane Sams and Fool Moon Treasures are *Captured Magic* and *O-SO Wonderful.* As Sams says in the card that accompanies her *Captured Magic* fairies, "Everyone knows that you can't catch a fairy. These little magical beings want to be friends and share their magic, but they'll only share with those who try to make friends. Treat your fairy gently, share happy moments and lovely thoughts. But remember, they are fairies and like to play mischievous pranks. Listen for the bell, don't let them fly away before you've had a chance to

You can capture the magic of "Love" with this whimsical character from the* Captured Magic *series from Fool Moon Treasures.

Representing Diane Sams'* O-So Wonderful *collection are "Eleanor, the Fairy Bearmother" and "Uncle Ursa," announcing the new arrival.

TO LEARN MORE:

FOOL MOON TREASURES
P.O. BOX 10473
TALLAHASSEE, FL 32302
(850) 877-2151
FAX: (850) 877-1097

make friends." Each *Captured Magic* fairy, representing "Love," "Wishes," "Dreams" and "Success," stands approximately 2" in height and is packaged in a clear cellophane bag tied with bright ribbons. On each ribbon is a little bell that will ring if your fairy tries to escape before you've had a chance to make friends!

O-SO Wonderful is Sams' newest line of collectible bears. These playful bear children are wonderfully detailed and painted. They depict the childhood joys of growing up, led by the 2-3/4"-tall "Uncle Ursa," a bear in formal dress, announcing the latest arrival. He comes complete with cigars in his "fur" pocket. His companion is "Eleanor, the Fairy Bearmother," who is loving and giving and has a bag of birthday joy and a wand for making wishes come true. The *O-So Wonderful* collection got its name from "Oso" Spanish for bear, and they are wonderful bears. The rest of the collection consists of boy and girl bears from one to six years, each with a special activity celebrating the joys of childhood.

Also new from Fool Moon Treasures are *Flower Buddies, Desk Top Treasures* and *Dancing Delights. Flower Buddies* are fairies and elves that hold sparkling Austrian crystals and gently swing from a brass rod that can be inserted into a favorite house plant or garden border. *Desk Top Treasures* come with a pewter base and brass rod so they can "fly" over one's work space. Sams chuckles, "Who knows, they may even give warning when the boss is approaching!" *Dancing Delights* are the same creatures designed to be suncatchers and window friends.

Project and design ideas bursting forth from Sams' sketch book include 8" realistic figures of "The Peace Keepers" beginning with St. Francis of Assisi, and a return to sterling silver for a very limited series of magical designs. No matter what Sams releases, you can be assured that it will convey a feeling of joy, a sense of wonder and a delight in being.

"Davey," a light hearted kind of elf, is one of Fool Moon Treasures'* Flower Buddies. *He is attached to a brass rod that can be inserted into a favorite house plant or garden bed, and he shows off a sparkling Austrian crystal.

Artist Bill Job Brings Light into Collectors' Lives

Through the Decades, ***a licensed series based on The Coca-Cola Company artwork, includes the 1930s "Town Cinema," 1950s "Sam's Market" and 1940s "Corner Drugs."***

Raised in the Tennessee mountains, Bill Job learned to appreciate the skill of local craftsmen and soon began trying his hand at working with wood. But his artistic pursuits soon turned to another medium: glass. Bill was also inspired by the detail and precision of Louis Tiffany's pioneering techniques in stained glass art, which has delighted collectors for more than a century. Bill began making reproduction lampshades in the fine tradition of Tiffany.

Today, Bill has gone from lampshades to lighted houses and other collectible architectural works of art that have brought his handcrafted masterpieces and the timeless beauty of stained glass into homes across the country.

In 1994, his company Forma Vitrum – Latin for "beautiful glass" – launched the original stained glass collectible village with a collection of houses, churches and lighthouses. Forma Vitrum now has more than 50 innovative architectural designs, plus a wide range of accessories and home decor items.

The collections of *Vitreville, Coastal Classics, Coastal Heritage,* the retired *Woodland Village* and, the newly licensed designs, *Through the Decades*, based on The Coca-Cola Company artwork, are the evolution and evidence of Bill Job's search to create the highest quality stained glass designs for collectors everywhere to enjoy.

MASTERING STAINED GLASS ART IN CHINA

Bill Job's journey to share his love for stained glass began a decade ago when he moved his family to a small port city on the eastern coast of China. There, he learned to speak and write Mandarin. He also mastered the artistry of stained glass, which was more affordable in China. He became one of the first Americans to own a company on the mainland.

By 1989, Bill's stained glass rivaled the quality and grace of Tiffany. Initially, Tiffany reproduction lampshades were the company's mainstay, but Bill expanded his offerings to sun catchers, art panels and detailed little houses lit from within by a bulb or candle. The houses were favorites of Bill's family, who convinced him to test them in America. Always ready for new adventures, Bill packed his samples and left for a California trade show. At the Los Angeles Gift Show in 1993, Bill struck up a conversation with David MacMahan, an entrepreneur and inventor of gifts that make people laugh and cope with stress. MacMahan was curious about Bill's creations and recognized the tremendous potential of the designs.

The two quickly realized the compatibility of their business and personal outlooks. By the show's end, a handshake sealed their partnership. Bill would design and create. David would promote and market. They called their new company Forma Vitrum and divided their products into two categories. The *Vitreville* collection, a series of structures with a small town appeal, and *Woodland Village* with whimsical houses named for animals.

"Breadman's Bakery" is the first renovated design in the* Vitreville *collection. The building was suddenly retired after only 200 pieces were successfully distributed.

VITREVILLE OFFERS HOMETOWN CHARM

Vitreville, or "glass village," is modeled after the small towns that grew up across the country. Each building reflects a traditional style and quality reminiscent of houses constructed to last for generations. Often the townspeople would name each house after the profession of the resident, and the house was seen as a valuable part of the community.

Vitreville began as a small bedroom community but, as more collectors became attracted to the town, more businesses and buildings were built. From churches and lighthouses, to the post office and corner bakery, the collection keeps growing. Recent introductions include "Wildwood Chapel," a quaint and friendly church the features pressed glass and handcrafted pewter windows and doors. "Klaus' Clock Shoppe" keeps all the residents and collectors running on time with a real working clock incorporated into the tower. The shop also features Bavarian-style accents and a colorful textured glass roof. The first-ever renovated design from the *Vitreville* collection is "Breadman's Bakery" which was slightly revised from the original piece. The renovated version was suddenly retired after encountering shipping problems. Only 200 pieces were successfully distributed.

Forma Vitrum collectors can also select life-like, miniature-scaled accessories to complement their villages. Home displays are enhanced with trees, flowers, *Vitreville* residents, signs, benches, fences and lampposts.

LIGHTHOUSES SHINE IN STAINED GLASS

Since Americans have always had strong ties to their coastlines, Bill's next challenge was to design romantic lighthouses. The *Coastal Classics* collection features beautiful lighthouses, illuminated for a shimmering effect. Each incorporates anywhere from 40 to more than 100 pieces of American stained glass. Among the *Coastal Classics* subjects are "Sailor's Knoll Lighthouse," "Lookout Point Lighthouse" and "Patriot's Point," which is designed in red, white and blue glass.

In 1995, Forma Vitrum launched the *Coastal Heritage* series of replica lighthouses. This limited edition collection, developed under the guidance and sponsorship of the U.S. Lighthouse Society, comes with a history of the actual lighthouse. For each piece sold, a 50-cent donation is given to the Society to help with its preservation efforts.

The *Coastal Heritage* series is a true wonder. Using techniques developed after two years of research and experimentation, the results are amazing. No artist has ever merged so many mediums to create such exacting replicas. American glass is hand-cut and soldered with blown, slumped and fused stained glass and spin cast metals. Many of the towers are blown cylinders of glass to replicate authentic shaping and dimension. Diamond drills cut door and window openings, and fiber optics replicates a true beacon shining from each lighthouse.

Vitreville *residents can keep time with "Klaus' Clock Shoppe," which has a real working clock incorporated into its stained glass tower.*

The* Coastal Heritage *collection shines with "West Quoddy Head, Maine," which recreates the lighthouse built in 1808. The collectible is limited to 1,997 pieces worldwide.

Among the most recent introductions is "West Quoddy Head, Maine," limited to 1,997 pieces worldwide. "Lighthouses are such a fascinating part of history," Bill says. "Isn't it amazing that West Quoddy Head was built so long ago in 1808 and, according to early charts and records, had a light that could be seen for three miles?"

Other *Coastal Heritage* additions are "Cape Lookout, North Carolina" and "Jupiter Inlet, Florida," both limited to 1,997 pieces.

COCA-COLA DESIGNS COME TO FORMA VITRUM

In 1997, Job began working with The Coca-Cola Company to introduce an authentic and limited edition series of glass Coca-Cola brand collectibles. Titled *Through the Decades*, the highly anticipated collection will be expanded and enjoyed by Forma Vitrum collectors and Coca-Cola collectors for years to come. Each limited edition building reflects the architecture and particular Coca-Cola artwork for that period.

Bill Job is recognized for creating the original stained glass collectible village.

Forma Vitrum also began the *Bed & Breakfast* series of stained glass houses that offer an invitation of warmth and hospitality. Job credits "Bavarian Lodge," a recent addition to the series, as his greatest artistic accomplishment to date. "The shear complexity makes it my favorite," he says. "Hand-cutting and placing over 1,200 pieces of little glass tiles on the roof is something that I have been dreaming about for years. The effect is worth it." "Bavarian Lodge," which is limited in edition to 1,500 pieces, also comes with eight complimentary ski hill trees to further enhance the scene.

To make room for further introductions, Forma Vitrum has retired the *Woodland Village* with its animal-named subjects including "The Rabbit House" and "The Raccoon House." The collection was inspired by an imaginary community of tiny people who live peacefully in a forest, free from illness and crime. Their appreciation for nature inspires the dwelling names.

Each Bill Job design is handcrafted from American stained glass and incorporates revolutionary techniques of combining the traditional method of hand-wrapping glass in copper foil and soldering with the use of blown glass and pewter attachments. The pieces are truly works of art with their own color and cut variations.

A TRADITION OF FINE CRAFTSMANSHIP

Each collectible must pass final quality inspection before it can bear the hand-numbered Bill Job brass signature plate, which authenticates the design. All Forma Vitrum collectibles may also be registered with the company by using the form included with each design. This quality and detail is building a new tradition of stained glass designs.

For the past three years, Bill's designs have been honored by *Collector Editions* magazine for excellence in design for collectibles. He is also the recipient of two consecutive awards from The Collectors' Jubilee for "Best Lighted House" and "Best Decorative Accessory."

Bill's next challenge is to further enhance his artistic skills. "I want to get more and more detail," Bill says. "Since we can now produce some of our own glass, I want to see houses with 2,000 pieces of glass. Looking at it without the light will be impressive, but with the light – Wow!"

To stay in touch with collectors, Bill communicates regularly through a quarterly newsletter, "The Vitreville Voice." The publication features all the latest product news and information about Bill's special appearances throughout the country. Bill is one of the foremost hands-on artists, who enjoys designing and researching new subjects to share with others.

"Bavarian Lodge," part of the* Bed & Breakfast *collection, features 1,200 individually hand-cut glass pieces that are fused together.

BUILDING A BRIGHT FUTURE

So what does Bill Job want collectors to experience from his Forma Vitrum designs? "A smile," he says. "They say an artist is someone who inspires emotion. I would like people who see my pieces to be reminded of things, perhaps that only they knew, which cause them to think pleasant thoughts and to be encouraged. We learned that we are not just providing stained glass houses, but bringing light into people's lives."

TO LEARN MORE:

FORMA VITRUM
20414 N. MAIN STREET
CORNELIUS, NC 28031
(800) 596-9963
FAX: (704) 892-5438
E-MAIL: formavit@aol.com

THE FRANKLIN MINT

Bringing Collectors Exclusive Works of Art and Treasures

There is no company in the world quite like The Franklin Mint. Where else can collectors turn for a special edition of Scrabble with letters minted in gold-plated pewter, model replicas of the Harley-Davidson Heritage Softail, commemorative plates of John Wayne, and reproductions of an amethyst, emerald and diamond Fabergé ring? There's also the cast of *Gone With The Wind* recreated in porcelain figurines, an official die-cast replica of the U.S.S. Enterprise from *Star Trek* and the Battle of Waterloo chess set in solid pewter and brass.

From their headquarters in the heart of the historic Brandywine River Valley of Pennsylvania, The Franklin Mint is the world's leading creator and direct marketer of fine quality collectibles, upscale home decor, personal luxury products and works of art that can be displayed with pride today and passed on as treasured heirlooms tomorrow.

Working together with some of the world's most famous designers and the company's own skilled artisans, Franklin Mint brings works of artistic beauty and historical significance to nearly eight million collectors around the world.

In celebration on her legendary beauty and style, The Franklin Mint presents the "Diana, Princess of Wales Doll."

FORGING WORLDWIDE PARTNERSHIPS FOR THE FINEST COLLECTIBLES

At The Franklin Mint, original design and product innovation join forces to create some of the most beautiful and sought-after items in the world. At the foundation of these artworks is an in-house design studio where award-winning artists spearhead the creative effort from start to finish. They take a concept and develop it into a spectacular masterpiece. In addition, The Franklin Mint collaborates with internationally acclaimed designers such as Bill Blass, Mary McFadden, Hanae Mori, Bob Mackie and others. The company is also keenly committed to discovering and fostering new talent to the art scene.

The Franklin Mint proudly boasts long-standing partnerships with world-renowned museums, associations, companies and individuals who sponsor and authenticate its products and share its dedication to quality and excellence. Among the more than 300 organizations affiliated with The Franklin Mint are: The Vatican, the Louvre, the Victoria and Albert Museums, the National Wildlife Federation, the family of John Wayne, Turner Home Entertainment, Paramount, The House of Fratelli Coppini, The Coca-Cola Company and The Campbell Soup Company.

COMING DIRECTLY TO COLLECTORS

The Franklin Mint's major product lines include, Franklin Heirloom Dolls (porcelain collector dolls), sculpture, fashion and traditional jewelry, collector games, Franklin Mint Precision Models (scale die-cast replicas of cars, trucks and other vehicles), home decor accessories, collector plates, coins, pocket knives and historic weapon reproductions. All product is marketed and distributed directly and exclusively by The Franklin Mint through direct mail promotions, catalogs, direct response media ads and its own retail stores. In 1995, *Brandweek* ranked The Franklin Mint ahead of such companies as Pepsi, Home Depot, Coca-Cola and Nike in American print advertising.

REMEMBERING PAST TRADITIONS

The Franklin Mint has never forgotten that the traditions of the past inspire the creations of today. From the ancient civilizations of the Egyptians and Etruscans come new works to rival those buried for thousands of years. Handcarved in rich blue onyx, the Jewel of the Nile necklace features the scarab, an ancient Egyptian symbol of power. The Louvre Museum in Paris authorized the recreation of a 14K gold ring inspired by a treasure in its Egyptian collection. The ring features hieroglyphs recreated from molds crafted by artisans at the Louvre.

From the depths of Atlantis to the gods of ancient Greece and Rome come new masterpieces of sculpture to rival those found only in the world's most prestigious museums and private collections. From the Ming Dynasty to priceless works created for the Czars of Imperial Russia come porcelains of incomparable beauty and splendor. From the masters of the Renaissance to elegant reflections of the Art Deco movement come treasures that speak of power and individual achievement. The Franklin Mint introduces a precious jeweled ring from the world-famous House of Fratelli Coppini in Florence, Italy, master jewelers since the Renaissance. The pearl and ruby ring features solid 14K gold. The dazzling Art Deco legacy of Erté is captured in the House of Erté's first-ever collector plate crafted in fine porcelain and limited to only 45 firing days.

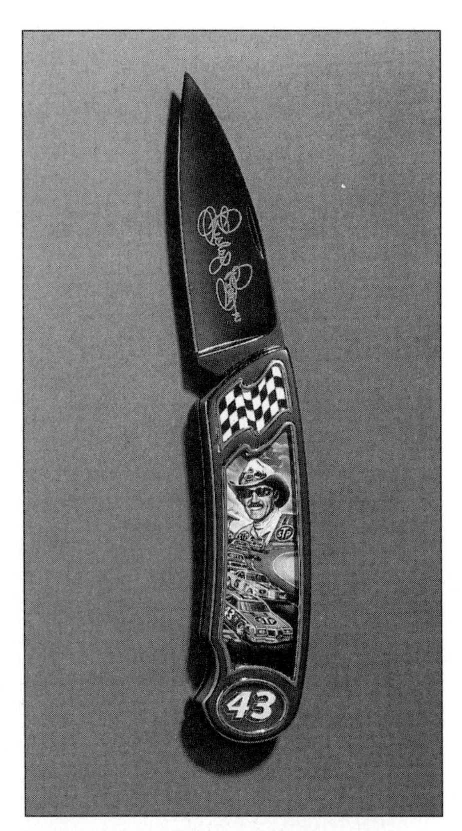

The "Richard Petty Pocket Knife" features the racing great rounding the curve in his #43 car. The knife, which is inscribed with Petty's name, has a retail value of $37.50.

From Asia's mighty warriors to America's legendary heroes come worlds of history, heritage and pride. In collaboration with the Smithsonian Institution, The Franklin Mint presents an official reproduction of Ulysses S. Grant's magnificent sword. The sword, wrought of tempered steel, is issued in a limited edition of 2,500 pieces.

HOLLYWOOD LEGENDS STAR IN THE FRANKLIN MINT

Since its founding more than 30 years ago, The Franklin Mint has brought pleasure and enjoyment to millions of collectors with works of art that recreate memorable Hollywood characters from the stage and screen. These include the legendary Scarlett O'Hara and dashing Rhett Butler from the most romantic love story of all, *Gone With The Wind*. Collectors can bring back those memories of the motion picture with hand-painted sculptures of 15 different characters, each authorized by Turner Home Entertainment.

Collectors can follow the yellow brick road with a musical golden anniversary tribute to *The Wizard of Oz*. A musical figurine, crafted in porcelain, shows Dorothy and Toto receiving instructions from the Good Witch.

The Estate of Marilyn Monroe and Franklin Heirloom Dolls present the first jointly authorized tribute of its kind. A porcelain doll captures the beauty of Marilyn Monroe, wearing a cowl-neck sweater shimmering with 80 hand-sewn faux pearls. Her cultured pearl earrings are coated with 24K gold.

John Wayne, affectionately known at "The Duke," has been honored in different collectibles through the years. The John Wayne Family has authorized The Franklin Mint to create the first collector teddy bear of its kind. Handcrafted in mohair and fully jointed, "The Duke" bear wears an authentic western outfit and has a hand-embroidered face with adorable characterized features and hand-set glass eyes. Each teddy bear is individually hand-numbered and holds a golden Mint Mark medal in his paw, noting its special status as an official Franklin Heirloom Bear.

The legend lives on in the "Frank Sinatra Singing Portrait Doll" from The Franklin Mint.

From The House of Fabergé, The Franklin Mint unveils a beautiful work of art. Fabergé "Violets in the Snow Imperial Egg" features sparkling jewels, gold accents and a "bouquet" of purple flowers. The retail value is $4,800.

PAVING A ROAD OF SUCCESS

For those driven to new heights of excitement, Franklin Mint Precision Models brings mile-a-minute thrills. These fine die-cast automotive replicas feature classics from the past, including the Rolls-Royce Silver Ghost, Mercedes Gullwing, Ford Model T, Duesenberg Twenty Grand and all-American legends like Harley-Davidson, Petty Nascar, Cadillac Eldorado, Corvette Sting Ray and Chevrolet Bel Air.

Franklin also presents Europe's elite dream machines: the fabulous Ferrari, Porsche 911, Lamborghini Countach and Bugatti Royale. Collectors also get on the fast track with a 1939 Peterbilt truck, 1912 Packard, 1924 Hispano-Suiza Tulipwood Speedster and 1937 Cord. Each is a perfect, hand-assembled replica of the original beauty from the polished brass grilles to the road wheels and steering wheels that actually turn. There's also a fully detailed recreation of the engine under the hood.

The Franklin Mint is headquartered in Franklin Center, Pennsylvania, and operates in 15 countries on four

Artist Ronald Van Ruyckevelt sculpted this majestic eagle, titled "Wings of Glory," as a symbol of pride and nature's wonders.

continents. Its 4,500 employees, including 1,500 based in Pennsylvania, are committed to quality – in product and customer service. At the heart of this commitment are co-owners Stewart and Lynda Rae Resnick, who serve as The Franklin Mint's Chairman and Vice Chairman, respectively. The Franklin Mint is a subsidiary of Roll International Corporation, a privately held, diversified network producing luxury products and services. Based in Los Angeles and co-owned by the Resnicks, Roll International ranked 123rd in *Forbes Magazines'* 1996 listing of the top 400 privately held companies in the U.S.

A HISTORY OF QUALITY AND SERVICE

The Resnicks are also community and civic leaders, lending their talents, support and expertise to institutions including The National Gallery of Art, The Metropolitan Museum of Art and The Los Angeles County Museum of Art.

The Franklin Mint Museum is located at the company's headquarters, where collectibles ranging from porcelain dolls and jewelry, to sculpture, metallic works of art and precision die-cast automobile models are on display.

THE FRANKLIN MINT MUSEUM OPEN FOR VISITORS

The Museum also houses the finest works created by the world-famous artists of The Franklin Mint, as well as original masterpieces by legendary artists Andrew Wyeth and Norman Rockwell.

On a regular basis, the Museum features changing exhibits that highlight the extraordinary personal artwork – sculpture, photography and paintings – of The Franklin Mint's in-house and affiliated artists. Many of the Mint's beautiful treasures are available at The Gallery Store, which is located within the Museum.

The Museum and Gallery Store are open Monday through Saturday, 9:30 a.m. to 4:30 p.m., and Sunday, 1 p.m. - 4:30 p.m. They are closed on major holidays. Admission and parking are free. For group tours and information, call (610) 459-6168.

MUSEUM

THE FRANKLIN MINT MUSEUM
U.S. Route 1
Media, PA 19091
(610) 459-6168

Hours: Monday through Saturday, 9:30 a.m.-4:30 p.m.; Sunday, 1 p.m.-4:30 p.m. Closed Major Holidays.
Admission Fee: None

Exhibits at The Franklin Mint Museum include sculpture, dolls, books, die-cast models, stamps and other collectibles. In one wing of the museum, a new exhibit is opened every two months. Special events are scheduled throughout the year, and exclusive Franklin Mint products are available at the Gallery Store, located within the museum.

TO LEARN MORE:

THE FRANKLIN MINT
U.S. ROUTE 1
FRANKLIN CENTER, PA 19091
(800) 843-6468 (1-800-THE-MINT)
FAX: (610) 459-6880

GARTLAN USA, INC.

Capturing Pieces of Athletic and Entertainment History

The neat thing about Gartlan USA collectors? They hold entertainment and sports history in their very hands.

Chance meetings with the world's greatest athletes or entertainment personalities are few and far between for most, but at Gartlan USA, the company provides the next best thing: limited edition, autographed collectibles featuring the biggest names in the sports and entertainment galaxies. Such collectibles include, but are not limited to: collector plates, figurines, lithographs, canvas transfers, baseballs, ceramic trading cards and much, much more.

R.H. Gartlan jokes with Ringo Starr during Beatles' historic signing session. Here Starr shares the limelight with limited edition figurine honoring the rocker.

The company was founded in May, 1985 by Robert Gartlan. A bit of Gartlan's own history yields incredible insight to the company's quality and grit in bringing the big names to us little people – no small fete in today's world of top-priced entertainment and multi-million dollar contracts. But Gartlan gets it done.

Originally from Springfield, New Jersey, Gartlan was a stand-out high school baseball player, earning All-State honors. As a catcher in his junior year, he was drafted by the Atlanta Braves. Choosing instead to attain a college degree, he graduated from Springfield's Jonathan Dayton Regional High School in 1967 and attended Belhaven College, Jackson, Mississippi, on a full baseball scholarship. Having lost interest in professional baseball and vice versa ("Actually, my knees gave out," Gartlan says), he accepted a sales position with Great Britain's Royal Doulton, a china and giftware manufacturer.

During an 11-year span with Royal Doulton, Gartlan traveled the country – learning what collectors' wanted, and as importantly, what they didn't want. He serviced Texas, California, New Jersey, back to California, and ultimately became Marketing Director out of New Jersey. Gartlan then returned to California, leaving Royal Doulton to become Vice President of Hackett American in 1982. Hackett American, a Huntington Beach ceramics company, is credited with creating the first limited edition sports collector's plate.

Gartlan says, "I proposed the idea to Reggie Jackson. His response? 'What is this, kid? A big button?'" Eventually sold on the concept, Jackson autographed the plates, and Gartlan, marketing for Hackett American, began pedaling the products. A Steve Garvey program ensued and soon a host of other athletes signed aboard. However, the programs proved precocious, and Gartlan left Hackett American for Armstrong's, a Pomona, California, supplier to the gift and collectibles industry. There, Gartlan began coordinating a ceramic baseball card program with several athletes, including Pete Rose.

BASEBALL HISTORY LAUNCHES COMPANY

Business differences stimulated Gartlan to fulfill a lifelong dream – opening his own enterprise in 1985. In anticipation of Pete Rose becoming baseball's all-time hit king, breaking Ty Cobb's career mark of 4,192 hits, Gartlan produced a series of limited edition collectibles, including a personally autographed figurine, collector's plate, the first ceramic card ever produced, signed and unsigned, and a ceramic plaque.

Contacting retail outlets familiar with Gartlan's background at Royal Doulton, he built initial sales, albeit slowly. During the course of the next two years, revenue was reinvested into subsequent programs with Roger Staubach, Reggie Jackson, George Brett, Mike Schmidt, and more.

Today, those first Pete Rose pieces trade for more than 1,600 percent above their initial retail price – a trend easily recognized among all Gartlan USA signed figurines, plates, and prints.

The business continued gaining momentum with the introduction of such superstars as Johnny Bench, Carl Yastrzemski, Kareem Abdul-Jabbar, Wayne Gretzky, John Wooden, Ted Williams, Steve Carlton, Yogi Berra, Whitey Ford, Luis Aparicio, and many more through February 1995.

It was in 1995 that the company embarked on a parallel, yet exciting new enterprise: the entertainment arena.

Gartlan USA had become premiere among all limited edition sports collectibles brands and companies. Its image was, and is, unparalleled in the sports marketing industry, having commemorated more than 40 of the greatest athletes in the world.

Now that image expands well beyond the arenas and fields of athletic endeavor. "We knew that if our concept worked in sports," Gartlan says in his trademarked understated style, "it was destined for even bigger success in the entertainment industry."

Initial entertainment introductions have included Jerry Mathers, the title

KISS guitarist Paul Stanley, sans make-up, reviews and pitches new program featuring Rock's biggest act during the past two years.

character from the 1950s and '60s hit television series, "Leave It To Beaver," and The Beatles' Ringo Starr. "Our Mathers product has enjoyed tremendous momentum at the announcement of MCA/Universal's motion picture celebrating the television series' debut 40 years ago," explains Gartlan.

"And who's bigger than the Beatles?" Gartlan quips. "Ringo's product has received tremendous response. It's the first program ever to feature autographed collectibles from the most popular and influential recording artists of our lives."

MUSIC APPRECIATION: WHO'S BIGGER THAN THE BEATLES?

The company has announced a new program for 1998 featuring the artwork of John Lennon himself captured on limited edition collectors' plates, as well as a series of figurines and collector plates featuring the late singer/songwriter/ peace activist.

Proceeds from all the Lennon products benefit John and Yoko Ono's Spirit Foundation. "The Lennon project is particularly exciting because not only do we get the chance to develop funds for worthy causes, but pewter figurines will include embedded metal from melted hand guns, which were originally confiscated from criminals or voluntarily surrendered to law enforcement officials," Gartlan says.

The company has also endeared itself to Dead Heads and recruits in the KISS Army. New projects featuring Jerry Garcia and the rock band KISS have further elevated the company throughout the entire entertainment industry.

The Jerry Garcia collection captures the essence of the Grateful Dead's leader and driving creative force. More than just an accomplished musician, however, Jerry's own artwork has developed a home among avid collectors. "Unfortunately, we did not get a chance to introduce a Jerry Garcia piece before his untimely death in 1995," Gartlan laments. "This is the first project the company has developed posthumously. It is also the first such collection Garcia's estate has ever approved."

Much of the detail and quality inherent in Gartlan USA products are a function of working closely with the family, friends, and associates of its subjects, and with the personalities themselves. Such was the case with the Garcia project. Garcia's widow, Deborah Koons Garcia, was instrumental in the art direction on the plates – a unique blend of a charcoal study and integrated water color and oil. She also wrote the backstamp copy for the collector's plate.

PERSONALITIES' INVOLVEMENT COMPRISES MORE THAN JUST AUTOGRAPHS

The same was true with the *Ringo Collection* and the KISS program.

Jerry Garcia figurine features his custom-made guitar.

Baseball's perennial star, Ken Griffey Jr., personally autographs series of collectors' plates honoring his meteoric career.

"During the plate signing for Ringo's limited series of collector's plates," Gartlan recalls, "we discussed the design for a Christmas ornament featuring his likeness.

"After discussing the intricacies of a second edition, he took a pen and sketched the concept on the table cloth where we were signing," Gartlan says. Today, that piece of cloth, and the signatures of those in attendance at the historical autograph session, hangs in Gartlan USA's New Jersey corporate offices.

In the case of KISS, guitarist Paul Stanley, himself an artist by vocation and training, took time from the band's record-setting 1996-'97 world tour to sit down with members of the Gartlan USA development team and provide insight, direction and constructive criticism that elevated the nuances of this dynamic collection.

The *KISS Kollection* includes personally hand-signed figurines and collector plates by the original members of the band – Peter Criss, Ace Frehley, Paul Stanley and Gene Simmons. And the *KISS Kollection* exemplifies why new and long-time Gartlan USA collectors' find the company's products of impeccable value. Specifically, there are incredible rewards in the company's products:

• *Actual hand autographs.* When the company touts its products as personally autographed, a collector can rest assured that, as in the KISS product,

Jerry Garcia Crystalline sculptural ornament bids his musical minions adieu – a traditional Garcia concert-ending pose.

each member of the band sat and autographed all 1,000 of the collector plates in the collection. (Which, by the way, represents the first time any plate has featured four personal autographs.)

- *Limited Editions.* Gartlan USA limits the edition to a specific number of pieces, not to a number of firing days. It declares the edition size of any item and then hand numbers the series to ensure authenticity
- *Certification.* Gartlan USA certifies its plates on the backstamps and its figurines with additional accompanying Certificates of Authenticity. But there is more behind the authenticity of Gartlan USA collections. The company's intricate licensing relationships and the painstaking review processes, which include Gartlan's own development team, the actual personality, a licensing agent, leagues (when appropriate) and other individuals, ensure the accuracy and detail in each Gartlan USA piece.

COMPANY ORCHESTRATES MORE NEW PRODUCTS

One of the fun new items in the *KISS Kollection* is the KISS Kommemorative Baseball. The pad-printed faces of the four band members and foil stamped KISS logo stand out on the black and silver panels of this unique product. "The KISS baseball is a nice hybrid of our sports past and our entertainment future," Gartlan says. "We have been amazed at how popular this item has become...almost taking on a life of its own."

The baseball notwithstanding, clearly the company's most exciting area of new product development features its personality Christmas Ornaments. "Our first ornament introduction, which was a 1996 annual featuring Ringo Starr in our Crystalline process, sold out before we even received our factory orders," Gartlan says. Gartlan anticipates the same type of performance for 1997's Jerry Garcia ornament.

GARTLAN USA'S "NEW" COLLECTORS' LEAGUE OFFERS NEW PRODUCTS, BENEFITS ALIKE

Created by the demand for its autographed items, Gartlan USA launched its "New" Collectors' League in 1989. Today the league enjoys membership worldwide; it has brought Gartlan USA collectors around the globe exclusive new pieces. Most recently, it featured the 1997 members-only figurine: a Bath Silver Ringo Starr miniature figurine.

Measuring approximately 4", the figurine is the first in a series of Bath Silver figurines, and portrays Ringo's famous Abbey Road crossing.

In addition to such special members-only pieces, every member gets a free 8-1/8" collectors plate when they join. The 1997 gift features a charcoal study of Grateful Dead's own Jerry Garcia. Crafted by noted Gartlan USA artist Michael J. Taylor, the study is offset by a blue wash background, emblematic of Garcia's musical diversity.

"Processes like cold-cast Crystalline and Bath Silver combined with such new products as Christmas Ornaments, provide collectors incredible opportunities to recall and appreciate, on a daily basis, the enjoyment athletes and musicians have provided them," Gartlan says.

And that's Robert Gartlan, and Gartlan USA for you, always thinking about the collectors...and, of course, how to make more history for collecting.

CLUB

GARTLAN USA'S "NEW" COLLECTORS' LEAGUE
575 Rt. 73 N., Suite A-6
West Berlin, NJ 08091
(609) 753-9229

Annual Dues: $30.00 - Renewal: $20.00
Club Year: Anniversary of Sign-Up Date

BENEFITS:
- Membership Gift: 8-1/8" Jerry Garcia Collectors' Plate
- Opportunity to Purchase Members-Only Products
- Quarterly Newsletter
- Membership Card
- Buy/Sell Matching Service
- Advance Notice of New Releases
- Free Gifts at Special Events

TO LEARN MORE:

GARTLAN USA, INC.
575 RT. 73 NORTH, SUITE A-6
WEST BERLIN, NJ 08091
(609) 753-9229
FAX: (609) 753-9280
URL: http://www.gartlanusa.com
E-MAIL: info@gartlanusa.com

KISS Kommemmorative Baseball mixes the Gartlan USA sports history and its entertainment future.

Welcoming Artists and Collectors as Family

It seems like only yesterday to some, but a decade has passed since Georgetown Collection proudly debuted its first collectible offering, "Hansel and Gretel," created exclusively for the company by world-renowned artist Avigail Brahms.

From that very first issue, the company's intent has never wavered. Working with some of the world's most gifted artists, Georgetown has succeeded at raising the artistic level in the world of collectible dolls.

Georgetown was the first company to recognize the benefit of working with well-known doll artists. Acknowledged for their breathtaking creations, these gifted artists add their creative genius to Georgetown's business expertise. The result has been an array of spectacular dolls that would make even the most disciplined collector swoon.

"Emerald Memories" is the newest doll in the romantic* Victorian Fantasies *collection. Created by Linda Mason, "Emerald" celebrates the tender daydreams of little girls and the innocence of a long time past.

Georgetown's president, Bob West, explains the simplicity of the company's philosophy. "Allowing our artists to do their artistic best seems to result naturally in a doll that makes an emotional connection with collectors." When you look at the awards and nominations that these artists have accumulated for their efforts, there's no question it's true.

Ask any artist involved with Georgetown and you'll hear that their relationship goes far beyond business. It's a personal relationship based on strong friendships. It's the same with collectors – Georgetown is well known for being responsive to customer needs. Ask the employees, and they'll tell you that to them, the artists and collectors are all part of the Georgetown "family."

NEW TIES MAKE GEORGETOWN'S FUTURE EVEN STRONGER!

Georgetown's second decade is off to an exciting start. Acquired by The L.L. Knickerbocker Company of California, Georgetown is the latest addition to this popular collectibles company.

In addition to successfully reviving the historic *Knickerbocker Teddy Bear* line, Knickerbocker is also well known among doll collectors.

It all started in 1990 when company president, Lou Knickerbocker, learned of Marie Osmond's love for dolls. He wondered if she might be interested in working with Knickerbocker on a project. She was thrilled and, within the next year, the Marie Osmond Fine Porcelain Collector Dolls line was launched. Since that time, Marie has appeared with her dolls countless times on QVC.

Marie enjoys working with Knickerbocker because of the freedom she's allowed in the design process. Some collectors may be surprised to learn that despite her busy schedule, Marie is involved in every aspect of a doll's creation – from concept sketches right through to the final marketing. Even so, she soon realized that she wanted even more involvement. So, she tried her hand at sculpting and, in 1995, "Olive May" was introduced – the very first porcelain doll sculpted by Marie.

Teddy bear lovers are probably quite familiar with yet another popular Knickerbocker line, the Annette Funicello Collectible Bear Company. Always a bear lover, Annette was also a big fan of the home-shopping giant QVC. She noticed that although they frequently showed collectible dolls, she was not aware of QVC offering teddy bears. When she met Lou Knickerbocker at a bear show, she discussed this with him. Her line of collectible bears was launched in 1992, and there's been no looking back.

Like Marie, Annette is deeply involved in every aspect of bear creation. Although she cannot name a favorite among her collection, Annette is particularly fond of her series of *Angel Bears*, which were inspired by all the good wishes that fans have sent to her over the years. The first *Angel Bear* was introduced on QVC in 1995. No one was surprised when the edition sold out in 20 minutes. Annette is particularly pleased to report that a portion of the proceeds from each bear sold goes to the Annette Funicello Fund for Neurological Disorders, a research fund that strives for cures to a variety of disorders including multiple sclerosis.

To the delight of bear and doll collectors, Annette and Marie have even

"Ashley," created by Pamela Phillips, is the newest edition in the highly acclaimed **Sweethearts of Summer** *collection. Just like the earlier issues, "Ashley" has the innocent charm reminiscent of a gentler time.*

put their creative talents to work together creating "I Love You Beary Much" – a delightful little girl cuddling an adorable teddy bear. It's a wonderful collaborative creation by these two devoted artists.

As Tammy Knickerbocker, Knickerbocker's vice president explains, the fit between Georgetown and Knickerbocker was a natural. "Here at Knickerbocker, the artists and celebrities are all part of the same creative team, so Georgetown's reputation for artist involvement was important to us."

GEORGETOWN ARTISTS CELEBRATE ANOTHER REWARDING YEAR!

When you review the names of artists who are involved in Georgetown Collection's *Artist's Edition* program, the list reads like a "Who's Who" of the doll world. Together, they are some of the most widely recognized and highly regarded artists in the industry. And there's no question that they are among the most acclaimed.

As this article goes to print, this year's awards nominations have been announced. Although the final decision is months away, once again the Georgetown artists have much to look forward to.

Famous among Georgetown's collectors for her beautiful little girls, Linda Mason has been nominated once again by the "Doll of the Year" Selection Committee. This year, "Emerald Memories," the newest doll in Linda's *Victorian Fantasies™* collection, has caught their attention. A favorite artist for the last two years, Pamela Phillips has received an "Award of Excellence" nomination for "Ashley" – the newest issue in the highly acclaimed *Sweethearts of Summer™* collection.

In addition, two newcomers have received nominations for works done in their premier Georgetown series. Renate Höckh, known for her moving ethnic portrayals, has received two nominations: a "Doll of the Year" for "Morning for Marisa" and an "Award of Excellence" for "Therese & Tino." Both dolls are from the *What a Beautiful World™* collection. Meanwhile, Katrina Murawska can add a nomination for a "Doll of the Year" award to her list of accolades. This nomination is for "Samantha," an adorable little girl from the *Favorite Friends™* collection.

NEW INTROS BRING FRESH FACES TO THE GEORGETOWN SCENE

In addition to Höckh and Murawska, several new artists have added their talent to the *Artist's Edition* program. "The ability to create an expressive face is the key attribute that we look for from a new artist," explains Stephanie Weaver, manager of Research & Development. "That doesn't necessarily translate to beautiful in the traditional sense of the word...but unique and life-like."

That ability is definitely what attracted them to the artistry of Lynne Randolph – one of today's most sought-after artists. Her love of dolls goes back as far as she can remember. Even in her early school days, Lynne knew she wanted to be an artist. Doll making allows her a way to combine her interest in portraiture with her love for dolls.

Lynne has a gift for portraying children in situations that are unusual, but very true to life. To the delight of her fans, she recently introduced "CeCe's Time Out" as her first issue with Georgetown. From the *Moody Cuties™* collection, "CeCe" proves to everyone that sometimes little girls are adorable even when they pout!

For Cal Massey, the freedom to carry out his artistic vision was an essential factor in his decision to work with Georgetown. Renowned throughout the world for his sensitive and realistic portrayals of African life, Massey is one of today's most highly acclaimed artists. His *Little Artists of Africa* collection is a celebration of African artistic traditions that collectors are sure to enjoy.

LONG-TIME FAVORITES REMAIN FAITHFUL TO THEIR FANS

Over the years, Linda Mason has created many of Georgetown's most famous dolls. Who could forget the elegant *Victorian Fantasies™* collection? Or "Many Stars," winner of both the "Award of Excellence" and the "Doll of the Year" titles? Today, Linda continues to thrill the collectible world with her talents.

Faithful fans will certainly be pleased to learn that Linda is working on another wonderful series of little girls. It reflects her love of Victorian sentiment and the importance of family. As you would expect, each of the little girls

"Samantha" is the playful new doll by artist Katrina Murawska. As the newest issue in the **Favorite Friends** *collection, "Samantha" celebrates the special bond between children and their most cherished playmates – their pets.*

Gifted artist Joyce Reavey has worked her magic once more with this delightful new edition to the* Songs of Innocence *collection. "Andy" is a sweet little farm boy who will surely capture your heart.

will be sumptuously dressed and beautifully accessorized. "Claire," the premier issue, will be unveiled soon!

Joyce Reavey is a favorite among collectors for her heartwarming vignettes of childhood. Always an innovator, Joyce has been busy with her first "musical" series for Georgetown. The *Songs of Innocence™* collection combines favorite childhood songs with endearing and memorable portraits. Each of the dolls includes a handcrafted accessory that houses a fine musical movement.

Joyce's most recent introduction, "Nicholas" is the premier issue in another look into the joys of childhood. From the *Caught in the Act* collection, "Nicholas" portrays one of those charming moments that a mother never forgets.

New introductions are currently in the works from Pamela Phillips, Ann Timmerman, and Renate Höckh. Collectors can also expect to meet several new and talented artists in the coming months, as well. Like the artists we know so well, each will have a talent unique unto themselves. Through their work in the *Artist's Edition* program, each of these wonderful artists share their extraordinary dolls with those who love them.

Great artists, dedicated employees and collectors who love dolls – they all come together at Georgetown Collection. This is the foundation upon which the company was built, and it's the philosophy that will carry Georgetown into the future. "We look forward to building on the close ties we've established with our artists and collectors," states Bob West. "What better way to accomplish that than to continue bringing them together with dolls whose love they share!"

CARRYING COMMITMENT FORWARD

TO LEARN MORE:

GEORGETOWN COLLECTION
P.O. BOX 9730
PORTLAND, ME 04104-5030
(800) 626-3330
FAX: (207) 775-6457

GEORGE Z. LEFTON CO.

Colonial Village Collection Builds Company into Collectibles Leader

For more than five decades, the George Z. Lefton Co. has been a driving force in the gift, collectibles and decorative accessories industry. Known as a quiet yet powerful company, Lefton is also recognized as responsive and caring about its many customers. Lefton's strong leadership and high values date back to the company's start when Mr. Lefton's goal was to "serve the customer with pride and dignity."

In 1941, Mr. George Zoltan Lefton started the company in Chicago with little more than a vision. In its early years, George Z. Lefton Co. imported fine china plates and giftware, many of which are now considered antiques. To date, the company has more than 2,000 fine quality gift items.

The* Colonial Village Collection *celebrated its 10th anniversary with a special commemorative set featuring the "Meeting House" and "Bicentennial Village Sign."

The company met the demands of a growing industry by creating collectibles, including the *Colonial Village Collection.* Introduced in 1987, the collection now boasts more than 100 illuminated buildings, as well as a variety of citizens and accessories for both seasonal and year-round enjoyment. Thanks to the *Colonial Village Collection*, Lefton has become a leader in architectural collectibles and has established a loyal following.

Lefton also produces several other collectible lines, including the *Great American Carousels, Smokey Bear* and *Historic American Lighthouse* collections.

Ten years ago, the *Colonial Village Collection* was founded as a tribute to small towns and simpler times. The village had a modest start with 12 buildings, nine of which have since been retired. Collector response, however, was anything but modest. With thoughtful planning and research, Lefton set out to create a community of buildings designed and sculpted to meet the highest standards and maintain the original charm of the collection.

COLONIAL VILLAGE GROWS INTO A PROSPEROUS COMMUNITY

Each sculpture – ranging from quaint shops, to cozy cottages and inviting inns, to Victorian mansions complete with gingerbread trim – is hand-painted and handcrafted of fine ceramic with vibrant color and detail. Each also comes with a Deed of Title that explains the history of the building and symbolizes "ownership" of that piece of real estate.

Like a trip down Main Street in any small town, you'll find churches with towering steeples and imposing public buildings. Among the most popular are the shops and stores that provide *Colonial Village* "residents" with fresh flowers, antiques, produce, toys and the other pleasures and necessities of life.

In 1991, the first limited edition sculpture, "Hillside Church," was introduced, and the 4,000 pieces were eagerly acquired by collectors who anticipated their increase in value. Each year, Lefton announces another limited edition piece, which has become much anticipated and sought after by collectors. In 1995, the first formal events program for *Colonial Village* collectors was launched. An exclusive building is available only at events held at participating retailers nationwide.

COLONIAL VILLAGE CELEBRATES 10TH ANNIVERSARY

In honor of the 10th anniversary of the *Colonial Village Collection*, a special commemorative set featuring the "Meeting House" and "Bicentennial Village Sign," was only made available through stores sponsoring exclusive *Colonial Village* anniversary party events during 1997.

The "Meeting House" is known in *Colonial Village* as the sight of numerous social and educational gatherings, including the village's recent bicentennial celebration and welcome tea for newly inaugurated Mayor Wilbur Winston. The corresponding bicentennial sign salutes the village's founding in 1697.

The events-only commemorative set includes a deed and story about the pieces, which are both crafted in ceramic and hand-painted to capture every intricate detail. In addition to the gift-boxed set, *Colonial Village* welcomes the seventh annual limited edition

"Cape Hatteras" shines as a beacon of light in this illuminated lighthouse. Each subject in the* Historic American Lighthouse *collection is carefully researched to ensure its authenticity.

building, "Sir George's Manor," of which only 5,500 pieces will be produced. The building was introduced in honor of founder George Zoltan Lefton, who recently passed away at the age of 90.

CITIZENS INHABIT *COLONIAL VILLAGE*

Just as the buildings have character, the "ceramic citizens" that populate *Colonial Village* have personalities. Many of them were named for Lefton friends, family and employees. The make-believe citizens aren't the only ones who have fallen in love with the village. Collectors have found hometown warmth and beauty among the village's quaint buildings. While the collection doesn't have a collectors' club, it does publish a quarterly newsletter, which is sent to thousands of subscribers. Readers of "Colonial Village News" receive hot-off-the-press information about what's happening around the town. They are also the first to find out about upcoming product retirements, new introductions, event locations and collectible show information.

The "News" is free with a $3 annual fee for shipping and handling of the quarterly issues. Collectors may call Lefton at (800) 628-8492 to subscribe or locate a retailer in their area. The same hotline number handles orders for replacement Deeds of Title, product brochures and catalogs, up-to-date retirement information and new product introductions.

LIGHTHOUSES SHINE WITH A BEACON OF LIGHT

The majesty and mystery of the sea comes to collectors through the *Historic American Lighthouse* collection. Introduced in 1992, the collection featured the first illuminated lighthouses on the market. These beacons of light have been carefully researched for authenticity, then hand-painted and handcrafted in porcelain to capture every original detail.

The lighthouses range in size from 7" to 11". Every full-size replica comes with a beautifully embossed hangtag, giving collectors a brief history of the lighthouse.

Today, the collection consists of more than 50 illuminated lighthouses, representing historic buildings from sea to shining sea.

With the popularity of the full-size lighthouses, Lefton introduced *Little Lighthouses*, replicas of the larger collectibles. The hand-painted porcelain miniatures, which aren't illuminated, stand 6" high. Over the past few years, Lefton has developed other successful lighthouse products, including miniatures, ornaments, magnets, illuminated musical waterballs, collector plates and clocks.

To honor and support America's great tradition of lighthouses, Lefton donates a portion of the proceeds from each subject to the United States Lighthouse Society, a non-profit organization dedicated to the preservation and restoration of these national treasures.

LEFTON TAKES COLLECTORS ON A MAJESTIC CAROUSEL RIDE

Lefton brings back childhood memories with the *Great American Carousel* collection, which debuted in 1995 with four figurines. The next year, ten more designs were introduced based on authentic designs by renowned carousel authority Tobin Fraley.

Designed exclusively for Lefton, the limited edition figurines reflect Fraley's expertise in the world of carousel art and restoration. "The *Great American Carousel* collection is made up of figures which draw from the original designs of the master carousel carvers," Fraley says. "Each horse incorporates details and decorations adapted from the most wonderful of their creations. I wanted each figure in this collection to be so authentic that it might even have appeared on the carver's original wooden carousel."

The figurines are all individually hand-numbered and feature many extra touches, including 24K gold plated limited edition plaques, up-and-down motion, traditional musical selections and careful attention to detail. The *Great American Carousel* collection also has a wide selection of sizes with figurines from 6" to 12" tall. The 10" pieces are even available with fine oak musical bases or with beautiful 24K gold plated brass stands. Both options complement the fine porcelain carousel horses, which capture one's attention and imagination with brilliant flaming manes, shining armor and sparkling jewels.

"We have always experienced success with our general carousel products," says John Lefton. "By teaming up with Tobin Fraley, we knew we could take our carousel product line

Renowned carousel authority Tobin Fraley has designed an exclusive collection of limited edition figurines for Lefton entitled the* Great American Carousel *collection.

much farther than we had. By offering beautiful and authentic figurines to the market we knew was waiting for them, we have returned collectible carousel figures to the customers who love them."

Based upon collector responses to the first figurines in the *Great American Carousel* collection, Lefton anticipates adding to the excitement with even more introductions to celebrate the golden age of the carousel.

SMOKEY BEAR SPREADS FIRE PREVENTION MESSAGE THROUGH COLLECTIBLES

"Only you can prevent forest fires." That's the message sent by Smokey the Bear, who for more than 50 years has been considered America's best-loved bear among children and parents. Now Lefton's *Smokey Bear* collection honors the favorite creature whose mission is to teach others how to prevent forest fires.

The musical figurines, which are hand-painted and handcrafted in resin, depict Smokey in ten different vignettes in which he promotes fire prevention education. A portion of Lefton's proceeds from the sale of these figurines goes to the USDA Forest Service for on-going efforts and education to prevent forest fires. Suggested retail prices start at under $20.00 to $30.00 for the figurines, which come individually gift-boxed with colorful packaging.

From Smokey the Bear to the *Colonial Village Collection*, Lefton continues its tradition of creating high-quality gifts and collectibles while always putting the customer first.

TO LEARN MORE:

GEORGE Z. LEFTON CO.
3622 S. MORGAN ST.
CHICAGO, IL 60609
(800) 628-8492

The* Smokey Bear *collection of musical figurines shares the beloved bear's fire prevention message.

Brian Baker's *Déjà Vu Collection* Brings Back Memories

"Brian Baker has tremendous potential in the collectibles field. We're delighted to have him as a featured artist, and we're putting the full resources of GiftStar behind his work," says Del W. Leutbecher, vice president of sales for GiftStar, Inc. The Napa, California-based firm recently acquired rights to Brian's popular *Déjà Vu Collection* of architectural sculptures.

Brian's creations began with a block of clay that has turned into neighborhood blocks that may look like your hometown. There's "Old White Church," "Main Street Cafe," "Country Bridge," "Dinard Mansion," "Victorian Tower House," and many other houses and buildings inspired by architecture around the world. This is also the world of Brian Baker's *Déjà Vu Collection*, where beautiful sculptures bring back warm memories and let everyone explore familiar places.

***Brian Baker's love for history, the arts and architecture inspired him to create the* Déjà Vu Collection.**

Brian was an employee of Chooch Enterprises, a Seattle-based firm serving the hobby industry, when he asked for a block of clay to make a Christmas present for a friend. Brian's sculpture of "Hotel Couronne" inspired Chooch Enterprises President Michael O'Connell to launch a new division of the firm called Michael's Limited. Now – under the ownership of GiftStar – Brian Baker's *Déjà Vu Collection* is one of the country's most exciting collectibles and decorative accessories.

BAKER TRAVELS THE WORLD FOR INSPIRATION

From Europe to Mexico and Thailand to America, Brian Baker's zest for life comes from his fascination with history and the arts. When he isn't busy creating new sculptures, Brian can be found exploring the Pacific Northwest or searching for adventure in a distant land. The culture and architecture of the world inspire him to share his experiences through the collection.

Born in 1962, Brian was raised in Seattle's Puget Sound area. In 1981, he started working for a gift company specializing in framing plaques featuring calligraphy and strips of decorative European braid. In just five years, Brian advanced quickly within the company, acquiring valuable gift industry knowledge and developing his own craft.

But Brian embarked on his most ambitious adventure in 1986 when he began a solo trip around the world. He toured throughout Asia and then parts of Europe. In Paris, Brian was enchanted by paintings that captured the character and personality of the charming buildings. This inspired him to delve into the wonderful European heritage. His keen interest quickly spread to a love for the varied styles of American architecture.

Over the years, Brian's travels have taken him to more than 40 countries from the Far East and Middle East to Europe and the South Pacific. And he has stories to tell from each destination. Brian has found beautiful architecture and friendly people throughout the world. He likes Bali for its fascinating culture and Germany for its medieval castles and lush landscapes. He often visits friends in Mexico and explores remnants of the country's ancient civilizations. In Sweden, Brian has nearly 100 distant relatives. He has visited the Scandinavian country three times.

After his travels around the world, Brian returned home to Redmond, Washington, in 1986. At this time, he began creating wall sculptures which debuted at the San Francisco Gift Show. The rest, as they say, is history.

THE BIRTH OF A *DÉJÀ VU COLLECTION* SCULPTURE

Brian crafts each new building similar to the way each is actually constructed, including additions and remodeling. He lets the building "create itself." Brian's clay sculpting talents represent the first in a series of important and often difficult steps leading to the finished work. The second step involves forming a mold for casting. All of the designs are hand cast in fine bonded stone. Brian then carefully develops a color scheme suitable for the building and its place in the overall collection. His first proof is reproduced to establish a sample for an excellent team of artisans, who faithfully follow Brian's original.

Brian's trademark in the collection is an umbrella. Although not every building has one, there is often an umbrella hidden in the shadows or quietly tucked away in a corner. Some people think the umbrellas represent the well-known rainy days in Seattle, but Brian tells a different story. "On my first building – #1000, the original "Hotel Couronne" – I wanted a hungry French cat sitting by

An 1879 cottage-style lighthouse inspired Brian Baker to create "Chesapeake Lighthouse."

the door," Brian explains. "I could not seem to design a cat that pleased me, so I left the cat's tail as the handle and made the body into an umbrella. This result became a souvenir of the rainy day when I first saw the building in Rouen."

This same detail-oriented creativity goes into every sculpture. At his sculpting table, he takes great care and pride in creating each house. Brian tries to become a resident of the building, imagining the people who would live or work there. This is just his way of bringing history to life and making one feel like déjà vu – you've been there before.

Brian Baker's travels in Louisiana and other Gulf Coast states led him to sculpt a number of wonderful tributes to the architecture of the deep South. His "French Quarter Townhouse," for example, reflects the Creole style of building: a mix of French and Spanish influence that was popular from 1790 to 1840. Brian's sculpture shows a Creole-style ground floor with Victorian details, such as the turned wooden spindles on the upper floors. These homes often had arched openings on the first level with French doors and fanlights on the facade. Two-story townhouses of this type are common along the streets of the French Quarter.

RECENT INTRODUCTIONS FROM GIFTSTAR'S *DÉJÀ VU* COLLECTION

Also a New Orleans "native" is Brian's "Bracket Cottage," a wood-framed Bracket double shotgun house. This interesting name comes from the dominant feature of the house, the large brackets beneath the gable of the hip roof overhang. The brackets are typical of the millwork of the late 1800s. "Double" refers to two side-by-side homes under a single roof, forming a single building. Finally, a shotgun house is one room wide and two or three rooms deep, placed in a row. It was said that a shot fired at the front door would pass through the house and out the back door without hitting anything!

Smaller than the "Bracket Cottage," yet significant in its own right, is the "Waterfront Property," created by Brian after he saw many similar homes while cruising through the bayous of the rural South.

This wood-framed "double shotgun" house from New Orleans is called "Bracket Cottage."

The "French Quarter Townhouse" is a Creole building with a mix of French and Spanish influence.

While Brian was in New Orleans, he took several days to explore the plantations along the banks of the Mississippi, where he made many happy discoveries. His "Riverside Plantation" is based on two mansions built there, one dating from 1829 and the other from 1840. It is Greek Revival in style, derived from the ancient Greek, but sometimes erroneously called "Southern Colonial."

On a trip to Maryland, Brian visited a cottage-style lighthouse that was built in 1879 and lighted Hooper Strait until 1954. "Chesapeake Lighthouse" was built to replace an earlier lighthouse that had been damaged by ice. After it was abandoned for 12 years, the Maritime Museum at St. Michael's adopted the lighthouse in 1966, where it was moved and reconstructed without so much as a broken window.

GiftStar's contributions to the *Déjà Vu Collection* include adding a host of excellent new benefits to the

Déjà Vu Collectors' Club, which already boasts a membership of more than 5,000. For example, there will be special, limited edition offers for members only throughout each year. A World Wide Web site is under development to offer members information on locating retailers and hard-to-find pieces, and the Club newsletter is being amplified with more on the secondary market and its own "swap meet" feature. What's more, members will be notified in advance of Brian's appearances on QVC, where special "QVC-only" pieces will be available. And a new Premiere Dealer Network will help member-collectors keep in touch with top dealers, who will host more signing opportunities and special events featuring Brian Baker in person.

MORE BENEFITS ADD EXCITEMENT TO THE DÉJÀ VU COLLECTORS' CLUB

For 1998, Club members will be invited to acquire "The Homestead House," a "members-only" piece that looks like the typical American home of the 1960s. It represents all the positive family values of "home and hearth," as well as a warm, nostalgic charm. Collectors are also invited to watch for pieces ranging from "Key West" in Florida to a "Classic Queen Anne," a "New England Farmhouse," and "Louisburg Square" – a handsome row house from Philadelphia. Leutbecher is especially excited about "The Christmas Church," with snow and wreaths and the look of stained glass windows.

As for the future, collectors can look forward to a wide range of new pieces, according to Leutbecher. "We have a strong collector base – already the average *Déjà Vu* collector owns 20 pieces," he notes. "We'll be coming out with over 40 new sculpts in 1998 alone!"

"Riverside Plantation" is offered in a limited edition of 1,200 and portrays a New Orleans landmark on the Mississippi River.

"Waterfront Property" is typical of many "shotgun houses" Brian Baker saw on his travels in the rural South.

CLUB

BRIAN BAKER'S DÉJÀ VU COLLECTORS' CLUB
GIFTSTAR, INC.
630A Airpark Road
Napa, CA 94558
(888) 893-2323

Annual Dues: $35.00
Club Year: March - February

BENEFITS:
- Membership Gift: Symbol of Membership Sculpture
- Opportunity to Purchase Members-Only Redemption Sculpture
- Quarterly Newsletter, "Brian's Backyard"
- Membership Card
- Artist Appearances

TO LEARN MORE:

GIFTSTAR, INC.
630A AIRPARK ROAD
NAPA, CA 94558
PHONE: (707) 226-2323
FAX: (707) 226-6464

An International Standard of Artistry

The year was 1871 when Franz Detleff Goebel and his son, William, realized their lifelong dream of creating their own company. Their original aim was to produce the fresh, simple and popular porcelain of Germany's Thuringia region: a goal that continues even today under the guidance of the Goebel family. Over the past 125-plus years, this dream has inspired consistent innovation in the ceramics industry, and it has touched the hearts of millions around the globe.

After five years of producing slate pencils, chalk boards and marbles to appease the ruling Duke of Coburg, the Goebel family situated their factory along the River Röden in Oeslau (now Rödental) in the heart of Germany's ceramic-producing region. With ready access to raw materials, easy transportation, capital and a family "porzelliner" tradition, father and son shipped their first high-fired porcelain tableware and decorative items in 1879. At the turn-of-the-century, the firm was one of the largest in the region with about 400 employees.

The "Little Scholar" doll is a 1997 mid-year introduction from Goebel.

Early on, William Goebel had recognized the importance of establishing an American market. To explore this possibility, he sent his son, Max Louis, to work in the United States in 1889 when the boy was just 16 years old. After studying the retail business in this country, Max Louis Goebel (1873-1929) returned to Germany. Following the death of his father in 1911, Max Louis took over the family business.

GOEBEL OVERCOMES THE TUMULT OF TWO WORLD WARS

In the years before World War I, the company flourished as Max Louis stressed innovation, variety and good value. Production was increased, and a new term came into use in mercantile circles — "Goebel-Genre," which signified moderately priced but well designed and good quality wares.

World War I and its aftermath brought upheaval to both Germany and Goebel. Max Louis, along with many of his factory workers, was called to military service. Happily, Goebel survived those difficult times when many other German firms closed their doors forever.

In 1929, two events occurred which caused another turning point in Goebel history. Max Louis died suddenly at age 57, and the American stock market crashed. Control then passed to Max Louis' son, Franz, and son-in-law, Dr. Eugen Stocke, a university-trained economist. The two made an able team, with Dr. Stocke handling financial affairs, leaving Franz Goebel free to focus on artistic matters. Like his father before him, Franz had worked in the United States as a young man and was familiar with American tastes and buying habits. He diversified the export line, and Goebel pulled through the worst years of the depression despite extensive staff cutbacks.

A BRILLIANT DISCOVERY: THE ART OF *M.I. HUMMEL*

As times gradually improved, Franz Goebel turned his attention to a search for something fresh to jump-start sales. In 1934, he discovered the work of Sister Maria Innocentia, a Franciscan nun, born Berta Hummel (1909-1946), then living in a convent at Siessen. Franz Goebel knew that a public anxious to escape from the hardships of the times would respond to the appeal of Sister M.I. Hummel's charming art. With the encouragement and cooperation of the Convent of Siessen, Sister M.I. Hummel's pictures were translated into figurines by the staff sculptors at Goebel. A special palette of warm and muted colors was developed to interpret the Sister's drawings. The figurines made their debut at the Leipzig Spring Fair in March of 1935, and were an instant hit with foreign buyers. Even today, the works of *M.I. Hummel*, crafted by Goebel, reign among the world's most cherished collectibles.

World War II caused Goebel more shortages and staff reductions. Production turned largely to military and domestic dinnerware. After the war ended in 1945, the Coburg region became part of the U.S. Zone of Occupation. Full economic and design recovery were eventually achieved

This pigtailed* M.I. Hummel *imp recalls that glorious day when children are free for the Summer. It's called "School's Out."

under the Federal Republic of Germany. During the 1950s and 1960s, Goebel expanded as never before as sales organizations were established in the United States and Canada, and new affiliations were formed with several acclaimed artists.

Franz Goebel died suddenly in 1969. Leadership of the firm passed to his son, Wilhelm, who today manages the company with his cousin, Ulrich Stocke. A highly trained ceramic engineer with much practical experience, Wilhelm also attended Berlin and Munich Universities to study industrial economics. Like his father and grandfather before him, Wilhelm continues to cultivate relationships with well-known artists to keep his company's product offerings fresh and varied. His cousin, Ulrich, also a general partner, has studied industrial economics and marketing, and has worked in Belgium, England, the Caribbean and the United States. Recently the sixth generation of Goebel family members, Christian Goebel and his cousin, Detleff Stocke, became limited partners in the firm.

Goebel has blazed many industry-wide management and marketing trails. As early as 1971, Goebel gave critical credibility to the fledgling market for ceramic plates with the issue of the first annual *M.I. Hummel* "Heavenly Angel" plate. Alliances with acclaimed artists and designers continue to yield unique and treasured new products. Anticipating "relationship" marketing, Goebel created national and international collectors clubs to stimulate awareness of and attention for important brands.

Looking to take the figurine and collectible business into the 21st century, Goebel opened the *M.I. Hummel* World Wide Web Site in March, 1997 at http://www.mihummel.com. The site features an on-line *M.I. Hummel* gallery with pictures and prices of every currently-available product, a Retailer Locator Service, and other information including a glossary, history of backstamps, and a calendar of *M.I. Hummel* events. In addition, site visitors may take advantage of global e-mail and instant enrollment in the M.I. Hummel Club.

THE LATEST GOEBEL INNOVATION: FIRM'S FIRST WEB SITE

Newly added to the Goebel Gifts line is a heartwarming new grouping of angel figurines entitled *Love From Above*. Each hand-painted porcelain angel is designed in Germany and produced of the highest quality materials. These sweet ambassadors from heaven will bring much enjoyment to those who treasure the beauty and peace symbolized by angels. The series features both "older and wiser" "guardian angels" with the children they watch over, and cherubic little "angels in training."

This lovely champagne-colored "Angel With Bell" from Goebel Gifts measures 17-3/4" in height and retails for $200.

Steinbach Crystal pieces from Goebel are, from left to right: "Lighthouse," "Three Jumping Dolphins," and "Ancient Castle Ruins."

GOEBEL ANGELS AND STEINBACH CRYSTAL

In addition to its many ceramic works of art, Goebel proudly presents a diverse collection of Steinbach crystal collectibles. The name Steinbach is synonymous with truly extraordinary crystal art. Steinbach creations are recognized among collectors of fine glass for unparalleled quality and creativity. Subjects include animals and birds, as well as famous architectural landmarks.

To create the fascinating shapes and designs of Steinbach crystal, molten glass, at temperatures exceeding 800°C, is poured into molds, cooled and then inspected. Only flawless glass is acceptable for creating these masterpieces in crystal. The artisans at the Steinbach studio painstakingly polish the crystal surface to produce its perfect finish. Once the piece is polished, it is ready for engraving at the hand of a master artist. Each design is unique in its interpretation of refractive light and geometric angles, and no two pieces are identical. It is the hand engraving and craftsmanship that makes each Steinbach crystal collectible truly one of a kind.

ARTISTS BALL, KENNEDY AND MAHONEY CREATE EXQUISITE GOEBEL DOLLS

Since the turn of the century, Goebel has been active manufacturing and distributing porcelain dolls. Today, Goebel's United States design studio is carrying on this tradition of excellence with a design staff of seven professionals. On December 31, 1997, award winning artist Bette Ball, who has been associated with Goebel products for more than 30 years, will retire and turn over the reins to her protégés, Karen Kennedy and Morgan Mahoney. Ball is best known for her line of Dolly Dingle dolls, and she and Goebel have worked with Campbell Soup, Disney, Bob Timberlake, Busch Gardens and numerous department stores to develop distinctive dolls.

Karen Kennedy joined Goebel in 1987. Today, Kennedy designs the Charlot Byj doll line and is well-known by her QVC television audience for her unique style. Designer Morgan Mahoney joined the group in 1995. She specializes in fantasy and animal dolls. The three designers produce over 125 new limited edition dolls each year for Goebel, and have been honored by having their dolls appear in over 50 museums worldwide.

THE LOONEY TUNES SPOTLIGHT COLLECTION

Warner Bros. and Goebel recently introduced 11 new figurines featuring the exploits, antics and offbeat personalities of Bugs Bunny, Daffy Duck, Elmer Fudd, the Tasmanian Devil, Sylvester, Tweety and other beloved cartoon stars. Dubbed *The Looney Tunes Spotlight Collection*, the series of fine porcelain figurines is a breakthrough in artistic collaboration between Warner Bros. and Goebel. Released in limited editions ranging from 5,098 to 15,098, the three-dimensional figurines will retail for prices starting at $70.00. Each figurine is based on an actual scene from a Warner Bros. Classic Animation Short. Also accompanying each product is a collector cel card which inspires the figurine.

According to Goebel President Ken Le Fevre, "Craftsmanship is at the heart of this collaboration. Warner Bros. are masters of animation, and we are masters of ceramics. Together we have created a spectacular collection of superbly crafted figurines that capture the spirit, subtlety and sophistication of the world's most celebrated cartoon characters."

In the last 20 years, Goebel has been a leader in maintaining the highest quality of craftsmanship and artistic integrity in highly competitive markets. With a keen sensibility for popular trends and the interests of the collecting public, Goebel's innovations and artistic excellence have defined the international standard. Today, the company concentrates on manufacturing and distributing products to over 200 markets, while nearly 2,000 employees are dedicated to continuing Franz Detleff Goebel's dream on a global scale.

"Duck Dodgers in the 24-1/2TH Century," from the* Looney Tunes Spotlight Collection, *showcases two companion figurines — "In the Name of Mars," with Marvin the Martian and "In the Name of the Earth," with Daffy Duck.

TO LEARN MORE:

GOEBEL OF NORTH AMERICA
GOEBEL PLAZA
RTE. 31 NORTH
PENNINGTON, NJ 08534-0010
(609) 737-1980
FAX: (609) 737-1545
URL: http://www.mihummel.com

THE GREENWICH WORKSHOP

Celebrating 25 Years of "The Art of the Print"

As the leading publisher of art and art-inspired products in North America, The Greenwich Workshop's mission is to brighten every room and enhance everyone's life with fine art. And there's more than one way to do just that. The art, artists, and offerings from The Greenwich Workshop, which is celebrating its Silver Anniversary this year, are as rich and varied as the people who collect them.

Limited edition prints, fine art posters, Collector's Edition™ books, art furniture, historical "docu-art," works of art in porcelain, entertaining videos created for PBS broadcast, and everything from jigsaw puzzles, cards, and calendars to 100% silk neckwear is part and parcel of The Greenwich Workshop's vision of "Art as Entertainment."

"The sudden death of my father, who co-founded the Workshop, in March was a great shock for us all," says Scott Usher, now Greenwich's Creative Director. "But, as I said at his memorial, we had never before seen Dad more excited about what the future now holds. And, as always, it was his intention to share the future with his family: you and us. So we are dedicated to carrying on his philosophy of quality, innovation, and service while exploring—as he did—the exciting new developments in the fine art world. In this, the Greenwich Workshop's 25th year, we're especially proud of our combination of the classic and the cutting edge: creating both prints which better represent the original art than ever before, and fine art entertainment that communicates the creative spark of the world's best artists."

To celebrate "The Art of the Print" in their Silver Anniversary year, the Workshop has designated the art of several artists as "Special Anniversary Selections." The first is "Crow Pipe Ceremony," a distinguished work of art by Howard Terpning, published as a Greenwich Workshop fine art textured canvas. Terpning, generally regarded as one of the world's greatest living painters, collaborated with great printing craftsmen to create a superior textured canvas which replicates the artist's original brushstrokes and can be framed without glass.

The Greenwich Workshop presents "Pay Dirt," a textured canvas by wildlife artist Luke Frazier.

THE BEST, MOST INNOVATIVE ARTISTS CONTINUE COLLABORATION

"As we near the new millenium, we are dedicated to publishing fine art in whatever format best replicates the original art," Scott Usher explains. "That includes textured canvas and cutting edge inkjet prints, as well as the classic medium of serigraphs and lithographs."

In that traditional, latter format comes the Workshop's second "Special Anniversary Selection," celebrating the phenomenon of Bev Doolittle—the best-selling artist in print. Based on the concept of romance, Doolittle's new work of art harkens back to two of her most beloved previous prints, "Let My Spirit Soar" and "The Forest Has Eyes" (both long since sold out at the publisher and much-sought on the secondary market).

"The new print is titled 'Music in the Wind,'" says the lauded, award-winning artist, "and, for me, it represents what I love the most: the freedom to respond to ideas when they come. After this particular inspiration, I met with Scott Usher, who I had been working with on my up-coming Greenwich Workshop Press book *The Earth Is My Mother*. We both agreed that to do the book justice, it would be best to create my new inspiration and give the book more time to develop."

The Earth is My Mother will be published in 1998, but the remainder of 1997 is filled with more milestones, not the least of which is the Fall publication of "Santa's Other Helpers" by James C. Christensen. As both a limited edition print and work of art in porcelain, this study celebrates "The Art of Imagination." The success of Christensen is particularly gratifying for the Workshop, since the artist's ascension marked the burgeoning popularity of fantasy fine art, yet another genre in which Greenwich provided leadership.

"We spearheaded aviation art as well," Usher remembers, "and we stuck with it while most of the industry watched and waited." The consistent success and popularity of Christensen, as well as James Gurney, whose *Dinotopia®* book was an international best-seller, has rewarded Greenwich for its patience and support. Now Christensen, too, is a popular author, with several Workshop books to his credit; *Journey of the Imagination* (50,000 in print), *Voyage of the Basset*

The watercolor original of "Dinner Guests" was created by Marjolein Bastin, one of this country's most popular greeting card and stationery artists.

(75,000 in print), and most recently, *Rhymes & Reasons.*

Though the Greenwich Workshop has a foundation of great artists who have been working with them for a decade or more, they are also constantly on the lookout for great new artists and publishing breakthroughs. Each is represented in the work of such respected greats as Marjolein Bastin and Gennady Spirin, and such "rising stars" as Braldt Bralds and Luke Frazier.

DEDICATED TO ART FOR EVERYONE

Marjolein Bastin, one of this country's most popular greeting card and stationery artists, is considered a living treasure in her native Netherlands. Her drawings and paintings have been a cherished gift for all ages since her introduction to the U.S. by Hallmark Cards, Inc.

This year, for the first time, Bastin's graceful art was made available as a collectible, limited edition fine art print. Bastin created the watercolor original of "Dinner Guests" only for her best friends as a reminder of the small miracles all around us. "I want to touch people's emotions as nature has touched me," says the artist.

Gennady Spirin, a native of Russia now living in America, has much the same goal, but comes at it from an entirely different direction. Although he and Bastin share a delicate art style, Spirin's level of complexity has been compared to the peeling of an artichoke or onion, revealing layer after layer of enchanting personality, historical delight, and charming whimsy.

Spirin came to the attention of the Workshop through their on-going program with the Society of Illustrators to introduce striking new talents to the art world. The four-time SI Gold Medal award-winner was already internationally famous for his many honored book illustrations. But he was proud and happy to create new paintings specifically to be published as Greenwich Workshop fine art inkjet prints, which are virtually identical to his watercolor originals.

Also virtually identical to the original are the Greenwich Workshop textured canvases of Luke Frazier. "I've had gallery owners react with surprise that I've sent them my original, when I actually had shown them a textured canvas of "Pay Dirt," my first Greenwich Workshop limited edition print. And not all textured canvases get that reaction. I'm proud to be working with them, because their watchwords are quality and innovation."

The Workshop is pleased to be working with Frazier as well, who the prestigious *Art of the West* magazine proclaimed "an exception to almost every rule: an extraordinary young artist whose collectors have a lot to look forward to." A consistent top 100 finalist in the Arts for the Parks competition since 1993, as well as the 1994 and 1996 National Wildlife Award-winner, his work can be seen in the permanent collection of the Wildlife Art Museum in Jackson Hole, Wyoming, and now in authorized Greenwich Workshop galleries in America, Canada, and Europe.

There, too, you can see the newest prints from the renowned Braldt Bralds, first an internationally sought-after advertising artist and now a fine art success story, courtesy of his talent and The Greenwich Workshop. Known for his unique images of animals, Bralds now concentrates on his favorite domesticated breeds—namely the look and personality of the house cat. And nearly all of his uniquely charming prints with such "punny" titles as "Bag Ladies," "Basket Cases" and "Cabinet Meeting" have sold out at the publisher.

"The Greenwich Workshop supports artists and the dreams, goals, and desires of artists," says Bralds from his new home in the American West. "And they do it with new ideas and new ways to best present the art to a discriminating audience. I think that is one of the reasons they are such a long-term success story."

Greenwich Workshop Press books are now a mainstay in almost every fine book store. They include the perennial best-sellers, *The Art of Bev Doolittle* and *An American Cele-*

THE BOOK IS THE STORY—FINE ART READING

Art and book lovers can enjoy a total reading experience, with* Drawing Closer: The Paintings and Personal Reflections of Carolyn Blish, *published by the Greenwich Workshop Press.

The Greenwich Workshop® Collection creates works of art in porcelain, portraying whimsical characters such as "Santa's Other Helpers" by James C. Christensen.

bration: The Art of Charles Wysocki, award-winners like *The Art of Howard Terpning* and *Dinotopia: The World Beneath®*, and such critically lauded works as Stephen Lyman's *Into the Wilderness* and Donna Howell-Sickles' *Cowgirl Rising*.

Their most recent releases range from the nostalgic *The Captain's Garden: A Reflective Journey Home Through the Art of Paul Landry*; to the inspiring *Drawing Closer: The Paintings and Personal Reflections of Carolyn Blish*; and the adventurous *Traildust: Cowboys, Cattle and Country—The Art of James Reynolds*.

"The Greenwich Workshop Press works very hard to combine evocative text by the finest writers with the best of the art world to create a total reading experience," says Wendy Wentworth, the Press' Director. "Scott Usher calls it a 'movie for your hands.'"

But their publications are not limited to only the famous, already established, or "rising star" artists. They have just released *The Traveler: A Magical Journey*, featuring the stunning drawings of a previously unknown West Coast architect student, Daniel Page Schallau.

FINE ART TAKES SHAPE IN PORCELAIN

Starting a whole new industry often takes as many as five years to just get going, and many more to forge a success. So it was with some pride that The Greenwich Workshop® Collection of works of art in porcelain was honored with Unity Marketing's "Trendsetter of the Year" award—voted on by the public and collectibles industry.

This acknowledgement most likely came from the Workshop's insistence on maintaining the details, colors, and character of known fine artists' work. "What really sets us apart," explains Mike Zadrovicz, the Collection's new Product Manager, "is that the fine artists collaborate in every step of the artistic process. We strive for more detail in the sculpting than almost any other company I'm aware of, and, because of the complexity and detail that is part of our artists' styles, we routinely use more molds to realize our pieces than almost anyone else."

The result is utterly charming new characters from Will Bullas' "Wonderful World of Whimsy," James C. Christensen's "Land a Little Left of Reality," and, new in 1997, Scott Gustafson's "Treasures for the Child in Each of Us." These include Christensen's "The Gift of Music," the third and final Christmas ornament following "The Angel's Gift" and "The Gift of Light"—both sold out at the publisher—and "The Sound of Christmas," the first of his new series of Christmas bells. Other holiday '97 offerings are Bullas' "frog horn" and "Rudy," a red-nosed runner duck, and Gustafson's "Brother Folio Scrivner," who has created a merry Christmas message.

These, and the other Collection offerings, are creating a growing group of enthusiastic collectors, who will be rewarded for their dedication with a Greenwich Workshop® Collection Collector's Club later in 1997.

It all adds up to a new era in fine art. "It's been a challenging, yet exciting, 25 years," concludes Scott Usher, "filled with milestones, great art, and many reasons to celebrate. Dave Usher intended the next 25 years to be just as exciting and innovative, and all the years after that as well. And, with your help, it will be."

TO LEARN MORE:

THE GREENWICH WORKSHOP
ONE GREENWICH PLACE
SHELTON, CT 06484
(203) 925-0131
FAX: (203) 925-0262
URL: http://www.greenwichworkshop.com

Celebrating 30 Years of Collecting

The year 1998 marks The Hamilton Collection's 30th anniversary as one of the world's leading direct response marketers of limited edition collectibles. And while collectors may know Hamilton best for its porcelain plates and dolls, today the firm's product base also includes a wide range of sculptures, limited edition prints, die-cast cars, apparel and figurines.

What's more, Hamilton enjoys prestigious joint ventures formed to present licensed products including STAR TREK™, *Star Wars™*, Enesco's *Precious Moments®* and *Cherished Teddies®*, *Dreamsicles®*, *I Love Lucy®*, NASCAR and others. And over the years, Hamilton has introduced many beloved and award-winning artists to the international collecting scene. Current among the firm's most promising sculptors and painters are doll artists Cindy Marschner Rolfe and Phyllis Parkins, cinematic artists Keith Birdsong and Morgan Weistling, Native America-theme artist Steve Kehrli and wildlife artist David Geenty.

While Hamilton's 30th birthday arrives in 1998, the cultural phenomenon known as STAR TREK recently celebrated its own 30th anniversary. In the three decades since visionary Gene Roddenberry first launched the "Starship Enterprise," one man's dream has become a worldwide collectors' passion.

A 30-YEAR ANNIVERSARY TRIBUTE TO STAR TREK

To commemorate 30 years of STAR TREK, The Hamilton Collection joined forces with Paramount Pictures to offer a wealth of collectibles – including the first-ever collector plate to honor all four STAR TREK television series.

Called "Captain's Tribute," and representing the *STAR TREK 30 Years* plate collection, this 8-1/4" work of art by portraitist Todd Treadway features the signatures of the actors playing captains in each of the series: William Shatner (Captain James Tiberius Kirk™), Patrick Stewart (Captain Jean-Luc Picard™), Avery Brooks (Captain Benjamin Sisko™) and Kate Mulgrew (Captain Kathryn Janeway™). Befitting its anniversary status, "Captain's Tribute" is decorated with 24K gold and platinum and is offered in an exclusive, hand-numbered edition limited to a total of 28 firing days. Each plate is accompanied by a matching Certificate of Authenticity.

"Terry Labonte Kellogg's™ Iron Man Monte Carlo®" is a precision-engineered, die-cast model of Labonte's famous Kellogg's sponsored #5 Monte Carlo®, commemorating his record-breaking 514 consecutive starts.

Thanks to their heartwarming messages of friendship and love, Enesco's *Cherished Teddies* collection reigns today among the fastest selling of all giftware lines. These huggable bears and their creator, Priscilla Hillman, earned the prestigious 1996 Miniature of the Year Award from the National Association of Limited Edition Dealers (NALED).

THE INTERNATIONAL FLAIR OF *CHERISHED TEDDIES*

Hamilton is proud to enjoy a fruitful association with Enesco Corporation, which includes the presentation of some of the most popular *Cherished Teddies* lines. Among the most recent of these launches is the delightful *Across the Seas with Cherished Teddies* figurine collection.

With these 14 appealing figurines, Hillman welcomes collectors on an exciting adventure around the world. "Bob," the American bear, acts as official tour guide as he introduces his international circle of teddie bear pals and their special homelands. Among the many bear characters in this marvelous series are "Lian" from China with her endearing panda; "Katrien" from Holland, traditionally outfitted in her tulip-bordered dress; and Fernando from Spain, perfectly suited for a fiesta! There's also "Lorna" from Scotland in her kilt and tam, carrying a lamb; and "Machiko" from Japan, wearing a cherry blossom kimono. Each original Priscilla Hillman design is highly detailed and painted by hand, and each comes with its own official Certificate of Adoption.

NASCAR racing is one of today's fastest growing sports, and Hamilton offers enthusiasts a wide range of authentic racing memorabilia. These include die-cast cars and collector plates featuring popular drivers such as Terry Labonte, 1995 Winston Cup Champion Jeff Gordon, Mark Martin, Darrell Waltrip and Dale Earnhardt. This wealth of Hamilton racing collectibles all are crafted to the highest standards – and officially authorized

A REMARKABLE REPLICA OF TERRY LABONTE'S IRON MAN MONTE CARLO®

"Laurel" won a 1996 "Doll of the Year" Award from* Doll Reader *magazine for her designer, Hildegard Günzel, and The Hamilton Collection.

by each driver.

One particularly striking issue is the "Terry Labonte Kellogg's™ Iron Man Monte Carlo®," a precision-engineered, die-cast model of Labonte's famous Kellogg's-sponsored #5 Monte Carlo® commemorating his record-breaking 514 consecutive starts. All details of this colorful car are "race-day" authentic: it features official sponsor graphics and logos, and the hood opens to reveal its impressively detailed engine compartment. A custom-designed, protective display with cover is included at no additional charge.

Hamilton also showcases "Awesome Bill from Dawsonville," Bill Elliott, on a collector plate titled "Hot & Fast," which portrays Elliott along with his #94™ Thunderbird. A collector plate series entitled *Drivers of Victory Lane* features giant of stock car racing "Rusty Wallace," as well as "Mark Martin" and his red, white and blue #6 Valvoline Ford Thunderbird. There's also a "Miller 25th Anniversary #2™ Thunderbird" portraying Rusty Wallace's famous car, and "The Rusty Wallace Plaque," featuring the Miller racing emblem.

"DOLL OF THE YEAR" WINNER "LAUREL"

When The Hamilton Collection introduced "Laurel" in 1995, this exquisite doll met with rave reviews from collectors and the doll industry. Created by German fashion designer Hildegard Günzel, "Laurel" was awarded the prestigious 1996 "Doll of the Year" Award for Manufacturer's Doll in the Under $200 category by *Doll Reader* magazine.

One look at "Laurel" is all it takes to understand how this bright-eyed blonde won the love of so many collectors. Her glowing face, framed in glistening curls, would make anyone's heart melt. Beautifully costumed and crowned with a charming laurel of budding flowers, "Laurel" delivers the message "I Love You Mom" on the wings of a pure white dove. Available exclusively from Hamilton, "Laurel" marks the firm's first partnership with the renowned Hildegard Günzel. "Laurel" is crafted of fine bisque porcelain and painted by hand, with delicately sculpted features – from her sweet expression to her graceful arms and legs.

Hamilton's growing reputation for fine doll art has grown through the introduction of more elegant dolls such as "Sally," by Cindy Marschner Rolfe and "Carol," from the artwork of Sandra Kuck. "Sally," an all-porcelain beach baby, represents Rolfe's *Summertime Beauties* doll collection. She wears an adorable blue and white bikini and a matching sun bonnet. Her smile of delight beckons everyone to join this tiny, blue-eyed blonde on the beach! "Carol" is an adorable porcelain toddler dressed in her Christmas best: a richly adorned burgundy velveteen dress. Inspired by the art of Sandra Kuck, a six-time "Artist of the Year" award winner, "Carol" is presented exclusively by Hamilton in association with Reco International.

Steve Kehrli's "Spirit of the Gray Wolf" recreates one of the most sacred Indian artifacts: the warrior's battle shield.

"African Elephant" premiers the* Protect Nature's Innocents™ *sculpture collection, an exclusive presentation of The Hamilton Collection.

STEVE KEHRLI CAPTURES THE SPIRIT OF NATIVE AMERICA

One of the strongest trends in today's world of collecting is the popularity of sculptures and figurines inspired by Native American legend and lore. The Hamilton Collection has been a strong leader in presenting collectors with a unique array of exquisitely crafted collector plates, sculptures and bell jars on American Indian subjects.

Hamilton is proud to work in association with one of today's most acclaimed creators of Native American art, Steve Kehrli, to introduce works of great power and beauty including "Spirit of the Gray Wolf." This sculpture, based on Indian warriors' battle shields, recreates one of the most sacred Indian artifacts. Every detail is faithful to the shields carried by brave warriors – from the loose-stitched folds and intricate beadwork, to the eagle feathers and image of a noble Gray Wolf. Crafted in bas-relief cold-cast porcelain, the hand-painted shield, reminiscent of authentic ceremonial stands, is ready to display on its own rustic tripod.

HAMILTON'S *PEANUT PALS™* ARE "HAVING A BALL!"

The whimsical imagination of artist Tom Newsom shines as brightly as the sun in his exclusive introduction for The Hamilton Collection: the *Peanut Pals* sculpture collection. The series premiers with "Having a Ball!," a charming miniature sculpture of a playful pachyderm enjoying a "trunk full of fun" in his very own pool. Each highly detailed, hand-painted sculpture in the collection features adorable baby elephants in playful situations.

In keeping with this celebration of the natural world, Hamilton also presents the *Protect Nature's Innocents™* sculpture collection. This series of heartwarming sculptures portrays the world's most endangered baby animals including the elephant, panda, hippo, kangaroo, and more.

THE *DREAMSICLES® NATIVITY FIGURINE COLLECTION*

When artist Kristin Haynes first created her *Dreamsicles* figurines, she had no idea what a powerful force her heavenly characters would become. Within just a few months of their initial release, they were listed among the nation's fastest-selling figurines.

Recently, The Hamilton Collection, in association with Cast Art Industries, Inc., presented *The Dreamsicles Nativity Figurine Collection*, a series of charming angelic cherubs and animals recreating the very first Christmas. The collection features 15 figurines in all, and each combines all the trademarks of Kristin's famous artistry – big blue eyes wide with wonder, cheerful expressions, and soft-pastel coloring.

Three decades after its founding, The Hamilton Collection thrives today as one of America's top direct response companies. Hamilton's staff and artistic partners remain committed to the creation and marketing of the finest, most affordable and attractive products for connoisseurs of dolls, plates, sculptures and other collectible works of art.

TO LEARN MORE:

THE HAMILTON COLLECTION
4810 EXECUTIVE PARK COURT
JACKSONVILLE, FL 32216-6069
(800) 228-2945
FAX: (904) 279-1339

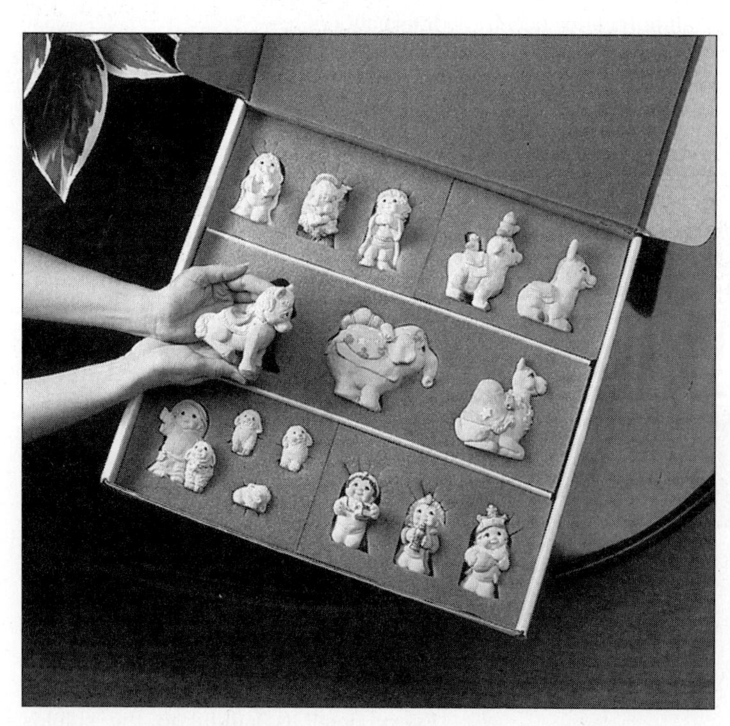

The Dreamsicles® Nativity Figurine Collection ***by Kristin Haynes features 15 delightful figurines in all.***

A Labor of Love Still Unfolding

Nothing moves the imagination like a lighthouse. – Samuel Adams Drake

On a rocky outcrop, with camera in hand, a solitary figure waits for a cloud to pass to capture just the right light. Even though his feet are wet and sore after a day of lighthouse hunting, Bill Younger's heart is filled with exhilaration. After visiting hundreds of lighthouses throughout the world, every new location is still a fresh experience for him.

In the course of his research, Bill Younger often travels to deserted locations, far off the beaten path. On some of these trips, he has to walk for several hours, sometimes through water. "When I finally arrive at the lighthouse, I forget all of the difficulties. I'm immediately taken into the past and reminded of the families that worked and played there."

As a young lad, Bill would often observe screwpile lighthouses during fishing expeditions on the Chesapeake Bay. Those memories, along with his love for architecture and history, provided fertile ground for the dream that has become Harbour Lights.

Available only to members of the Harbour Lights Collectors Society, "Sea Girt, NJ" is a remarkable replica of this historic light station known for its handsome brick Victorian keeper's cottage and red French chimney.

THE BIRTH OF HARBOUR LIGHTS

As the first sales representative for David Winter Cottages in the United States, Bill soon realized that he was not alone in his love for old buildings. In 1989, the U.S. Postal Service issued a collection of stamps in honor of our nation's lighthouses. Younger felt inspired to create a line of lighthouse sculptures that would accurately depict American architecture. At first, he approached the producers of David Winter Cottages, John Hine, Ltd. Although they were not interested in developing the line, Bill was not deterred.

Working closely with his wife and daughters, Bill's dream became a reality in the spring of 1991, when Harbour Lights was introduced to the public. The original 17 limited editions were chosen by Bill and his family from America's most famous and beloved sentinels. These included such historic lighthouses as "Cape Hatteras, NC," "Boston Lighthouse, MA" and "Sandy Hook, NJ."

HARBOUR LIGHTS: A FAMILY AFFAIR

Harbour Lights has been a family affair since its inception. Much of the original research was carried out by Bill's daughter, Kim Andrews, who serves as Managing Director for the company. Now that Bill is able to devote himself full time to Harbour Lights, he does a great deal of his own research.

Bill's wife, Nancy, serves as "Head Keeper" of the popular Harbour Lights Collectors Society, which caters to the needs of thousands of devoted collectors. Although quite busy with two little ones at home, daughter Tori Dawn fulfills a crucial role as one of the principal origination painting artists. Her husband, Harry Hine, works in the sculpting and research departments and has won several awards for his beautiful Harbour Lights booth designs.

After the overwhelming response to the first 17 releases, new items have been chosen, for the most part, based on requests from loyal collectors. Today, the collection includes more than 60 active editions, representing every coastal area in the United States, as well as Canada, Europe and Australia. Another 60 or so have been retired.

ARTISTIC DIRECTION YIELDS AUTHENTIC REPLICAS

Rather than developing a single artist, Harbour Lights decided early on to work with a small team of staff sculptors. For one thing, lighthouses were built by many different individuals, and are quite unique in their own right. Also, Bill felt that the underlying goal of Harbour Lights was to promote maritime history and architecture, rather than a particular artist. In each replica, he wants to achieve a rendering that is so accurate, it is unmistakable for the real thing.

While attention to detail and authenticity has been the hallmark of Harbour Lights' success, a sincere effort has been made not to stifle the creativity of the artists. Certain editions have revealed some wonderful expressions of artistic freedom. Retired "Cape Canaveral, FL" includes a Saturn launch vehicle, while "Middle Bay, AL" features a cow peering over the lighthouse rail! The 1998 Christmas Exclusive, "Old Field Point, NY," was sculpted with a charming keeper's cottage covered with a freshly fallen layer of snow.

Every Harbour Lights replica begins on location, usually with Bill and his camera. Extensive research is required to achieve an accurate finished product. Bill takes photographs from every angle, often including shots from the air and sea. Scores of photos are necessary to capture each nuance and detail

On the southern tip of Mount Desert Island in beautiful Acadia National Park, the light station at "Bass Harbor, ME" still casts its guiding light after 140 years.

of the sentinel.

From photographs, architectural plans and drawings, sculptors begin to work their magic.

FROM EXTENSIVE RESEARCH AND CAREFUL WORKMANSHIP TO A THING OF BEAUTY

Slowly, painstakingly, they create an authentic model. A silicon mold is then created from the finished model. Depending on the item, high-grade gypsum or cold-cast porcelain is carefully poured into the mold. Once the casting material is hardened, the sculpture is slowly pulled from the mold. Each piece is then meticulously checked for imperfections, bubbles, warping or stray bits of casting material.

One of South Florida's most famous structures, the aging brick lighthouse at "Cape Florida" stands proudly after more than 170 years.

With Bill's photos and a large reference library as a starting point, master painter Tori Dawn Hine and staff set out to create a work of art. They sometimes use shards of stone or brick from the original lighthouse to guide their work. Each paint is carefully mixed to create the proper hue, and then, with expert dexterity, the paint is carefully applied with fine brush strokes. Because these paints permanently stain the sculpture, there is no room for error. Walls are generally painted first, then roofs, towers, and finally the beacon. Gradually, from its humble beginnings as a simple cast, the sculpture is transformed into a thing of beauty, a faithful replica of the actual sentinel.

LIMITED AND OPEN EDITIONS

Much of Harbour Lights award-winning collection is devoted to limited editions, ranging from 5,500 to 10,000 pieces. These include replicas of such world-famous lighthouses as "Cape May, NJ," as well as lesser-known sentinels, such as "Faulkner's Island, CT." Each piece is beautifully gift boxed and comes complete with its own history and Certificate of Authenticity. After the edition limit is reached, molds are destroyed, often by Bill Younger himself, and the piece is officially retired.

In 1995, Harbour Lights created a wonderful new series of hand-numbered, open edition sculptures entitled *Great Lighthouses of the World*. Commemorating the world's most celebrated light stations, this remarkable series includes such favorites as "Cape Neddick, ME," "Ponce de Leon, FL," "Split Rock, MN," and "Old Point Loma, CA." When a *Great Lighthouse* is purchased, a portion of the proceeds is donated to the organization responsible for the preservation, restoration or maintenance of that particular lighthouse.

1996 marked the introduction of Harbour Lights first screwpile lighthouse, "Thomas Point, MD." Not only was this a tremendous technical achievement, but it was also Harbour Lights' fastest retirement ever. Within a few weeks of announcement, before the first piece was shipped to a store, the entire edition was purchased by dealers! Other recent editions have followed this trend.

RECENT DEVELOPMENTS

In April 1997, "Thomas Point, MD" was honored by thousands of readers of *Collector Editions* magazine as the "Best Cottage or Building under $100" of 1996.

As the line has expanded, Harbour Lights has endeavored to be a creative pioneer with its new releases. To commemorate the important role that women played in keeping our shorelines safe, the *Lady Lightkeepers* series was introduced in 1996. In January 1997, "Morris Island Then and Now" was released, representing the sentinel in its glory days, and today, with the paint worn off and erosion threatening its very survival. In April 1997, Harbour Lights released its largest sculpture to date, "Navesink, NJ." This spectacular sculpture measures 17" in length!

In addition to its regular line, Harbour Lights offers several other products for the lighthouse aficionado. These include a wonderful assortment of lighthouse Christmas ornaments, a charming series of lighthouse miniatures known as the *Spyglass Collection* and a terrific new set of accessories called *Keepers and Friends*. These miniature lighthouse keepers, families, and fishermen are scaled just right to accent any Harbour Lights collection.

In 1899, a 98-foot light tower was constructed on the Lake Michigan shoreline, illuminating the entrance to the "Sturgeon Bay" ship canal. It continues to shine brightly.

Resting in her berth at Port Huron in eastern Michigan, the Lightship "Huron" has embarked on a new adventure, educating our youth about America's maritime heritage. Commissioned in 1920, the Huron was America's last lightship to serve on the Great Lakes.

Harbour Lights released its first international edition in 1996, "Peggy's Cove, Nova Scotia."

INTERNATIONAL LIGHTHOUSES ARE HONORED

In the spring of 1997, the first pieces commemorating European lighthouses were introduced, "La Jument, France" and "Longships, England." We sometimes forget that the foundation for America's lighthouses began in Europe long before the first brick at Boston Light was laid in 1713. One recent release, "Hook Head, Ireland," honors a lighthouse established in the Twelfth Century!

Collectors are the driving force behind Harbour Lights. "When I come to

COLLECTORS SOCIETY EARNS OVERWHELMING SUPPORT

collectible expositions and see the tremendous enthusiasm and love for our line, I am truly humbled," says Managing Director Kim Andrews. Some collectors travel literally hundreds and even thousands of miles to view new releases and have their pieces signed by her dad, Bill Younger.

In 1995, the Harbour Lights Collectors Society was founded to support the growing number of collectors. The response has been overwhelming. Each member receives a number of exciting benefits, including the opportunity to purchase members-only, exclusive editions. This year's sculpture, available only through authorized dealers, is beautiful "Sea Girt, NJ." During the 1998-1999 membership period, new and renewing members will each receive a wonderful gift sculpture, "Cockspur Island, GA."

In early 1997, the Youngers announced the creation of a brand

ANCHOR BAY CAPTURES MARITIME HISTORY

new line of collectible boats and ships, ANCHOR BAY. Because of his love for maritime history and the sea, Bill Younger feels that Anchor Bay is a "natural progression" for his growing company. Each stunning sculpture is meticulously hand-painted, beautifully gift-boxed, and comes complete with a wooden base and mirrored glass case. ANCHOR BAY is a numbered, open edition collection, featuring tugboats, steamships, cutters, trawlers, schooners, skipjacks, and of course, the all-important lightship.

When Bill Younger meets collectors and shares the story of Harbour Lights,

PRESERVING OUR LEGACY

he often conveys the importance of preserving lighthouses and the memory of those who risked their lives to keep the flames lit. Lighthouses have always represented strength and hope in the face of adversity. An important symbol of the past, they remind us of a simpler time. While automation has made the need for lightkeepers all but unnecessary, their legacy is not forgotten. Harbour Lights is doing its part to keep their memory alive.

CLUB

HARBOUR LIGHTS COLLECTORS SOCIETY
1000 N. Johnson Avenue
El Cajon, CA 92020
(800) 365-1219

Annual Dues: $30.00
Club Year: May 1 - April 30

BENEFITS:
- Free Annual Membership Gift
- Redemption Letter for Members-Only Exclusive Annual Piece
- Membership Certificate Suitable for Framing
- Quarterly Newsletter, "Lighthouse Legacy"
- Binder with Society Logo
- Cloisonné Pin
- Membership Card
- Double-Matted Print of Redemption Piece Given to Renewing Members - Available for Purchase to New Members

TO LEARN MORE:

HARBOUR LIGHTS
1000 N. JOHNSON AVENUE
EL CAJON, CA 92020
(800) 365-1219
FAX: (619) 579-1911
URL: http://www.harbourlights.com

Rising from the water like a rocky fortress, "Alcatraz Island" has long been a symbol of the San Francisco Bay. In 1854, the first lighthouse on the American West Coast was illuminated here.

Hidden Treasures in Handmade Boxes

It was a chance encounter. Martin Perry, a shepherd turned designer and mold-maker, was out walking his dog when he bumped into Noel Wiggins. They both seemed to be at the right place at the right time that afternoon. Noel, an artist, entrepreneur and visionary, was traveling through Europe seeking the perfect box for his chiming silver ball that had helped him build a successful importing and manufacturing business.

One thing led to another and Martin ended up sharing his quirky carvings of animals with the stranger. Noel immediately recognized that the designer's sculptures blended perfectly with a personal philosophy that had been at the heart of many of his previous business ventures. "I love folklore," Noel says. "Most of the items I have developed tell a story. There is a built-in narrative which is universally understood."

The fateful meeting and discovery led to the creation of Harmony Kingdom, which opens up another world of beauty and adventure for collectors. With Noel's vision and Martin's artistry, Harmony Kingdom has become one of the fastest growing lines in the collectibles industry with its intriguing and ingenious Box Figurines™. The handcrafted figurines are actually treasure boxes in disguise – each one with a story to tell, secrets to reveal, masterpieces to enjoy and new nooks and crannies to explore.

Martin Perry created "White Rose" as part of the* Harmony Garden™ *series. Inside the sculpture and others in the series, you'll find Lord Byron, a distinguished lady bug, enjoying his favorite pastimes.

THE ORIGIN OF THE HARMONY KINGDOM LEGEND

Founded in 1995, Harmony Kingdom may well be seen as the latest in a series of dramatic successes spawned by a chance encounter with the company's president, Noel Wiggins. Indeed, Noel's penchant for creating, as well as recognizing trends, has given him both the experience and the confidence to develop the Harmony Kingdom collectibles.

Groomed to be a fourth generation New York artist, Noel grew up in culturally-rich places like Morocco, Panama, Sicily and Switzerland. At Brown University, he majored in semiotics, the study of how we use signs to help form our reality. It was perhaps this eclectic life experience that instilled Noel with the instinct to sense the basic human appeal in an unusual chiming ball found on a business trip to Mexico. This discovery evolved into the utterly enchanting and successful line of Harmony Ball jewelry and gift items.

In 1995, history repeated itself when he met Martin Perry, who began his artistic career at the age of 35, working for a company in England that made replicas for art museums around the world. In 1989, Martin started his own business carving figurines that had a hidden compartment for small keepsakes. Martin based his humorous sculptural concepts on his knowledge of the natural world, gained over years of working as a shepherd in North Wales. For the next several years, he perfected both his designs and the techniques to produce them.

His designs caught the attention of Noel, and together they formed Harmony Kingdom. They are united in their quest to fill collectors' homes with tiny treasures that depict nature's world with intelligence and wry wit. "I have an image in my mind of what Harmony Kingdom should look like and am steering the origination of new pieces in this direction," Martin says.

THE KINGDOM EXPANDS WITH MORE COLLECTIBLES

Since Harmony Kingdom's formal introduction at the International Collectible Exposition in Long Beach, California, in 1995, the line of Box Figurines has blossomed into a whole new category of collectibles. The original *Treasure Jests®* series is now joined by *Harmony Circus®*, a curious collection of circus characters, each with its own extraordinary legend. *Angelique™* is an intimate collection of Renaissance-inspired angels, as well as a limited edition series of hand-numbered and signed pieces.

Harmony Kingdom's family of Box Figurines also includes the *Garden Party™* series. These miniature figurines, inspired by Japanese netsuke carvings, reveal a secret compartment when the top is unscrewed. Each may be suspended from a chord and worn as a pendant, hung from the waist or displayed as a holiday ornament.

Another series, Lord Byron's *Harmony Garden™*, depicts traditional British flowers in softly colored sculptures. Each flower opens to expose the

As president of Harmony Kingdom, Noel Wiggins fuels the fire that drives an extraordinary circle of artistic talent to create the line's incredible Box Figurines™.

intriguing subterranean world of an adventurous ladybug named Lord Byron. The ladybug's story unfolds with each series introduction, creating an on-going saga which collectors eagerly anticipate.

HANDCRAFTED AUTHENTICITY REIGNS IN THE KINGDOM

In the village of Chalford in the Cotswold region of England, all Harmony Kingdom items are made in the tradition of cottage industry manufacturing. Harmony Kingdom's irresistible Box Figurines combine the appeal of handmade English collectibles with the charm and function of French Limoges boxes.

In addition to Martin Perry, several artists conjure up the creativity in Harmony Kingdom, including David Lawrence and Peter Calvesbert. David is an academically trained artist, who has turned his energies to the three-dimensional world of Harmony Kingdom. Peter began sculpting with modeling clay as a child but didn't return to that art form until 30 years later. Today, Peter's sculptures have gained a stunning reputation.

The creation of each Harmony Kingdom box begins when the original work from sculptors like Martin, David and Peter is molded using silicone rubber. This original is then used to create production molds for the casting department. Castings are created in the model using crushed marble. The casting is then fettled (cleaned up) and made ready for staining. The stain itself has been formulated by Martin and is regarded as a trade secret. The piece is then polished back to remove most of the stain prior to being sent out into the countryside for painting.

The wonderfully subtle tinting and hand-painting of all the Harmony Kingdom boxes is in the care of Martin's wife, Corinna. "The early boxes were entirely Martin's painting plan and execution," Corinna explains. "Understanding the properties and interactions of the materials he was using, he combined experience and experimentation to achieve the patina and tinting."

But when it became clear that Martin could no longer make and finish every box single-handed, Corinna left her teaching career to help him.

Martin Perry, who is the artistic director for Harmony Kingdom, went from being a shepherd to creating the amazing Box Figurines™ for which he has become known throughout the world.

In "Killing Time," part of the* Treasure Jests® *series, artist Martin Perry celebrates the Orca Whale with grace and fluidity. An intricate treasure is artfully concealed within.

Martin patiently showed his wife his technique and the reasons for the different stages in the process. "Having gained experience, I gained in confidence and dared to make suggestions for future coloring," Corinna says. "Whenever a new box arrives, we are eager to get our hands on it and start playing with the tinting."

But Martin and Corinna also needed help, so they enlisted some women friends. "We would sit around my kitchen table, children playing on the floor, as I initiated them into the secrets of tinting," she recalls. They carried on the cottage industry tradition that thrived in their region during the 19th century. "Our daily painting sessions were very satisfying and fulfilling," she says. "We felt artistic pride in our work, were earning our living, and we were able to set the world to rights in between gossip and laughter."

Corinna's kitchen was soon bulging at the seams as more painters joined them. Some of her friends volunteered to open their homes to new painters and to train them. And so the painting guild grew. "Although we have had to centralize some aspects of the business, it is still a cottage industry in the true sense of the word," Corinna says.

Created by artist Peter Calvesbert, "Something's Gotta Give" is Harmony Kingdom's Holiday Edition piece for 1997. The signature Santa is stuck in a chimney after eating too many mincemeat pies.

The artists follow a painting and quality specification, but many factors can alter the finished look: room temperature, base color, dilution of the tints or just the mood of the day. So if you find one animal is looking particularly pleased with itself, remember it is handcrafted and individual!

With the number of collectors growing daily, Harmony Kingdom formed its collectors club in 1996. The Royal Watch allows the company to communicate with collectors throughout the year, letting them know what's new and sharing with them the hidden secrets sculpted into the Harmony Kingdom Box Figurines.

THE HARMONY KINGDOM ROYAL WATCH SOCIETY

Club members receive an exclusive gift, the opportunity to purchase members-only pieces and a subscription to Harmony Kingdom's quarterly magazine, *The Queen's Courier*, which always features recent retirements, introductions and the company's artists and craftspeople. Members also receive a product folio with Harmony Kingdom's full-color brochures and a Pocket Planner listing all the introductions. As something to look forward to in the future, Harmony Kingdom is also planning a glorious fifth anniversary piece for collectors who have remained members for the first five consecutive years.

As a company built on time-honored tradition and craftsmanship, Harmony Kingdom has launched a Web site and chat room to bring up-to-the-minute, in-depth information to collectors. Harmony Kingdom's Web site, which can be found at http://www.harmonykingdom.com., has many informative sections, including an index of the entire collection. Each entry contains information and background about the artist, release date and the hidden "secrets" of each box. There's also a "virtual" bulletin board where collectors can post want ads to buy, sell or trade Harmony Kingdom boxes. Also featured on the Web site is a list of "Dealer Links" where collectors can jump to retail stores on the Web that sell Harmony Kingdom collectibles. Collectors can also listen to audio messages from Martin Perry and his band of merry carvers.

HARMONY KINGDOM GOES BACK TO THE FUTURE

The company has opened a live chat room where collectors can meet to talk and ask questions about their favorite collectibles.

In an increasingly technical and dehumanized world, the warmth and irreverent humor of Harmony Kingdom's Box Figurines serve as comforting reminders of a person's higher instincts. The boxes contain insightful references to the true nature of their subjects, cryptic inscriptions and other secrets that put Harmony Kingdom in a kingdom all its own.

CLUB

THE ROYAL WATCH SOCIETY
c/o Harmony Kingdom
232 Neilston St.
Columbus, OH 43215
(614) 469-0600

Annual Dues: $35.00
Club Year: Anniversary of Sign-Up Date

BENEFITS:
- Membership Gifts: Box Figurine and Lapel Pin
- Redemption Voucher for Members-Only Pieces
- Quarterly Newsletter, *The Queen's Courier™*
- Membership Card
- Club Sponsored Contests
- Product Folio with Catalogs
- Buy/Sell Matching Service Available on Web Site http://www.harmonykingdom.com www.harmonykingdom.com
- Special Members-Only Merchandise Available

TO LEARN MORE:

HARMONY KINGDOM
232 NEILSTON ST.
COLUMBUS, OH 43215
(614) 469-0600
FAX: (614) 469-0140
URL: http://www.harmonykingdom.com
E-MAIL: royalwatch@msn.com

A Nation of Shopkeepers Welcomes Visitors with Ceramic Collectibles

A former art and design teacher, Hazle Boyles took her love of the British High Street and transformed it into the ceramic collection, A Nation of Shopkeepers. *She still models all the pieces herself.*

Napoleon once called the English a "Nation of Shopkeepers" – a nickname that Hazle Boyles took as a compliment and quickly discovered for herself to be quite true. Walking the small town British High Streets, she admired the hodge-podge of architectural styles and bustling activity.

Bouquets of flowers adorned the florist's window. Baskets of fruits and vegetables tempted passersby to come into the green grocer. Customers waited in line outside the fish and chips restaurant. A blue-and-white striped awning covered the entrance to the butcher shop. A red bicycle rested against the gate to the bed and breakfast.

It was this clutter, color, character and charm that inspired Hazle to create her own nation of shopkeepers. A former art and design teacher, she founded Hazle Ceramics to capture the best of these British High Streets, faithfully reproducing them as low-relief miniatures. It's now an ever-expanding range of collectibles with classic representations of many periods of British history – Edwardian, Victorian, Georgian, Elizabethan and Tudor – all featuring authentic architectural detail and variety so typical of the village streets.

Individually hand-painted, glazed, signed and inspected, no two of the collectible ceramic buildings are the same – just like their real-life counterparts. Today, the company's *A Nation of Shopkeepers* collection welcomes collectors, who discover the many treasures in store for them along Hazle's British streets.

At an early age, Hazle Boyles became fascinated by shops of all shapes and sizes. When she was five, she and her family emigrated from her homeland in Northern Ireland to Canada. "In the Toronto area where I lived, we were used to shopping in big shopping malls that sold everything under one roof," she says. "So when, at the age of 16, I moved back to England with my family, that was the perspective I had on shopping."

ARTIST FINDS BEAUTY IN BRITISH SHOPS

What she found in England was a myriad of small shops. She couldn't understand why they didn't all get together in large malls. But her father explained how generations of families had built up these individual businesses and eked out a living and future for their children. Hazle kept this in mind as she studied interior design in college, and then went on to teach woodwork and art. At the same time, she was doing free-lance design work and creating low-relief clay sculptures as a hobby.

"I was fascinated by the relationship between the clay in my pictures and the brick and stone of actual buildings," she says. "So gradually my pictures moved from general landscapes to feature more and more buildings, until I got to the point where I was creating framed clay pictures of British buildings like the High Street in Woodstock."

Eventually, she decided to leave teaching to find an opportunity to use her creative talents in another way. She visited trade fairs, learned skills at ceramics manufacturers, and took the plunge in 1989 to start her own business.

With money she made from an art exhibition, she purchased a small kiln that she put in the kitchen of her two-bedroom flat in Brentwood, Essex. In her back bedroom, she made molds and cast the biscuitware. Her work day started at 9 a.m. and didn't end until 3 a.m. the next morning.

She made her ceramic buildings six days a week and then got up at 7 a.m. every Sunday morning to travel to a market where she would try to get a stand to sell her wares. She also attended other craft fairs, selling even more of her buildings. Since the product was a new concept, she decided to patent and copyright the designs. The name *A Nation of Shopkeepers* became a registered trademark.

A Nation of Shopkeepers ***lines collector's shelves with detailed ceramic buildings, each hand-painted so that no two are alike.***

FABLES FROM THE STABLES

Hazle soon outgrew the space in her home, where her cats often scampered through the studio and ceramics molds. The kiln in her kitchen also wasn't sufficient to satisfy the level of business she was generating. Around that time, Hazle's dear friend died suddenly. As part of her legacy, her friend left a sum of money to help Hazle's business. She decided to put it toward a new kiln.

She also rented a space in a barn, where she was able to fire and glaze her ceramics. In 1991, Hazle knew she had to take the next step and get her ceramics into more shops. So she tried to get into a major trade fair in Birmingham. "There was little chance of getting in as there is always a long waiting list, but then I read an advertisement that was to change everything," Hazle says. "An exhibitor at the show was looking to share his stand with someone else to offset his costs. So a quick phone call followed, and we were in."

Her ceramics were a hit! By the Summer of that year, *A Nation of Shopkeepers* won the "Best Collectible" award presented by the British Giftware Trade Association for the collection's originality and creativity. In October 1991, Hazle Ceramics moved into new workshop space on the farm and employed more painters and its first administrative assistant.

Today, the business employs 30 people and Hazle's designs are sold around the world. "It has been an exciting journey, growing this business. When I look back fondly on those days, I sometimes wonder how on earth I did it all, and how glad I am that I took that plunge in 1989," Hazle says.

THE MAKING OF A NATION OF SHOPKEEPERS

Research, care and creativity go into creating the *Nation of Shopkeepers* collectibles. Hazle studies many different buildings around England, photographing each one. When she wants to create a new shop-front, she selects one from her vast collection of photos so that she can base the pieces on actual buildings located in British towns.

Her first step is creating a scaled, technical drawing of the building. Then Hazle takes a block of plaster and begins carving the design. At various stages, she casts a "reverse" model from the plaster to create even more details. This process continues until the entire design is complete.

"The Christmas Market Hall" is based on the open Market Hall in Ross-on-Wye that was built in 1670 in a provincial classical design using the local pink sandstone.

"The Christmas Shop" celebrates the season with its window trimmed with a tree, stockings, toys and garland.

She models all the pieces herself. The model is then sent to the mold maker, who creates a master mold of high-density plaster from which some sample pieces are cast. This allows Hazle to see the finished look before it is produced for collectors.

When everything is okay, working molds are made for all the pieces to be cast in production. The casting process is similar to making a chocolate egg. The high-quality earthenware clay is poured into the mold and left for five to seven minutes. During this time, the plaster in the mold sucks the moisture out of the clay, creating a film inside the mold. After seven minutes, all the excess clay is poured out of the mold – hence the hole in the back of the plaque. When the clay left inside is dry enough, the model is lifted out of the mold. This is called "greenware," which is then fired in the kiln at 1150° Celsius. The temperature and the curing of the ceramic ensure that the pieces become a semi-porcelain plaque. This piece is called "bisque" (French for biscuit).

This bisque is what is then painted in

"The Corner Grocer" is the first piece in the* Hazle 2000 Collection, *which pays tribute to the millennium and British life in the 20th century. The forerunner of the supermarket, the grocer was open at all hours. The piece is limited to 2,000 pieces.

underglaze paints. Hazle paints all the first batches to establish color quality, and then her team of artists paints the subsequent pieces. The artists place their painter's mark (or initials) on the back of the piece. Hazle's "H" is highly sought after. After all the pieces are painted, they are cleaned and then glazed. They are put in a kiln, which is fired overnight at 1050° Celsius. This completes the process, with the exception of labeling and boxing.

COLLECTORS ENJOY SHOPPING FOR THEIR FAVORITES

Collectors await the new introductions, wondering which buildings Hazle will recreate in her detailed ceramic storefront plaques. Among recent shops are "The Chemist," based on a circa 1828 classic Georgian building, and "Harvard House," built in 1596 by a relative of Harvard University's founder.

To celebrate the millennium, Hazle is releasing special limited edition ceramics reflecting various aspects of British life in the 20th century. Each piece will be limited to 2,000 pieces, after which the molds will be destroyed. The first subject in the *Hazle 2000 Collection* is "The Corner Grocer" which typifies shopping in the 1950s, especially in the working class areas. The shop, a predecessor to the supermarket, sold everything from a tin-tack to a loaf of white bread.

Hazle has also introduced *The Miniature Teahouse Collection*, a unique combination of heritage and architecture brought together in a delightful range of functioning bone china teapots. Standing about 3-1/2" tall, the pieces depict historic buildings associated with the drinking of tea.

Hazle Ceramics also allows collectors to have their pieces personalized. Artists will paint any of the ceramic plaques to a customer's specification, whether adding someone's name, changing a window detail or putting an inscription on the back.

To keep track of retiring pieces, painter's marks, limited editions and news from the studio, Hazle Ceramics launched the "Nation of Shopkeepers" Collector's Club. Membership includes an introductory gift, signed certificate and the opportunity to purchase members-only pieces.

CLUB

"A NATION OF SHOPKEEPERS™" COLLECTOR'S CLUB
Stallion's Yard
Codham Hall, Great Warley,
Brentwood, Essex CM13 3JT
United Kingdom
01144 1277 220892

Annual Dues: $40.00 - Renewal: $16.00
Club Year: Anniversary of Sign-Up Date

BENEFITS:

- Introductory Membership Gift
- Signed Membership Certificate
- Subscription to "High Street News," Published 3 Times/Year
- Opportunity to Purchase Exclusive Members-Only Pieces

TO LEARN MORE:

HAZLE CERAMICS
STALLIONS YARD, CODHAM HALL, GREAT WARLEY
BRENTWOOD, ESSEX CM13 3JT
01144 1277 220892
FAX: 01144 1277 233768

Nutcrackers and More, with Heart

Whimsy, charm, tradition, contemporary, quality. These words sum up the delights in wood that come from Holzkunst Christian Ulbricht, the industrious firm with a heart nestled in the Erzgebirge Mountains of Saxony in eastern Germany.

The output from this family-owned company includes nutcrackers, incense burners, music boxes, ornaments, pyramids and miniature figures, each piece with its own special personality. The production techniques are based on a tradition that dates back centuries, with the Ulbricht family deeply entrenched in those traditions. Today, because of the progressive attitude of a man whose mind and heart are constantly open to new ideas and influences, the collection includes not only the traditional motifs one would expect from this region, but a totally contemporary view of the world.

Combined with legendary figures of kings, hunters and soldiers, all in many guises with differing degrees of opulence and style of dress, are newly developed limited edition figures from a variety of other influences. From literature come figures from William Shakespeare's *Romeo and Juliet*, including the two title characters and the author himself. Charles Dickens is well represented with Scrooge, Bob Cratchit and Tiny Tim and Mrs. Cratchit from *A Christmas Carol*. Dorothy and the Cowardly Lion have joined the Tin Woodsman in the *Wizard of Oz* series. And the music and ballet world are represented in Tchaikovsky's The *Nutcracker Suite* with the Prince, Clara, Dr. Drosselmeyer, the Mouse King and the Toy Soldier. And there's much more, both in limited and open editions.

Because Christian Ulbricht has been deeply influenced by American collectors and their interests, there is a series of *Great American Inventors*, with Thomas Edison, Henry Ford and Alexander Graham Bell, each limited to only 1,500. There are also colorful representations of Native Americans, with authentic costuming well researched. Santa Claus is depicted, too, in some unexpected roles as a cowboy, a tailor, a skier, and even as a canoe paddler. He also appears in more traditional poses to satisfy more conventional tastes. Bikers are included in the mix, complete with bandannas and sunglasses. This perhaps illustrates some wishful thinking on the part of Christian Ulbricht himself, since he lists biking as one of his hobbies and hopes one day to ride through the Rockies.

Christian Ulbricht Collectors' Club members are thrilled with "Snow King," the first exclusive nutcracker available to them.

Family histories can provide exciting insights into company developments and why certain life paths were taken. Christian was born in the Erzgebirge town of Seiffen, where his family can be traced back to the 17th century. Back then, the region was rich in the deposits of gold, silver and other minerals. When the unthinkable happened and the mines dried up in the 18th century, the miners turned to their long-time hobby of wood turning for their livelihood.

Christian's birth took place in 1933, around the time his father, Otto, built a new factory to house his burgeoning wood-turning facility. The business grew but, in the mid-1950s, Otto was compelled to make a drastic change, one that would uproot the family and force the start of a new life. Seiffen was part of the Eastern Bloc. It lies on the easternmost edge of Germany, right near what is now the border of the Czech Republic. Since a tenet of communism was that everything belonged to the state, not to the individual, Otto no longer controlled the family business; therefore, he decided to reestablish that business elsewhere. Late one night under cover of darkness, Otto, his wife and their four children left their beloved home and, after an arduous journey, arrived in their new surroundings.

THE EARLY YEARS

Relocated in the town of Lauingen, on the Danube near Augsburg, in Bavaria, Otto set about developing his company anew. But family traditions and the need for roots are profound. In the early 1990s, once the Berlin Wall had fallen, Christian, now the head of the family, determined that he would regain the Ulbrichts' heritage. He was able to purchase the family's holdings in Seiffen, and set about the task of rebuilding.

THE PICTURE TODAY

Today, Holzkunst Christian Ulbricht numbers 80 employees. Ulbricht family members are deeply involved in every activity, from the creation of new designs to quality control and the supervision of packing and shipping the boxes that find their way into collectors' homes. Christian's wife, Inge, is one of the major designers of the company's ornaments and some nutcrackers; she is also in charge of quality control.

Ines, their daughter, holds the distinction of being involved in many aspects of the business, including design. In addition, along with her brother, Gunther, she is a co-director of the Christian Ulbricht Collectors' Club. It debuted in 1998 and is managed out of the offices of the United States distributor, Christian Ulbricht USA in Angwin, CA. Gunther, also a designer, is an artist in his spare time as well, with portraits and landscapes among his favorite subjects.

Christian's is the leading creative voice; his designs, which begin their path to fruition when he turns the wood on the lathe, become the models used by the master craftsmen who replicate his designs for the collection.

From traditional to contemporary, the nutcrackers of Holzkunst Christian Ulbricht cover a wide range of legendary kings and the ultra modern world of computer hackers.

When they visit the United States to attend the International Collectible Expositions® in spring and summer and to make personal appearances in various retail stores across the U.S., the Ulbrichts are sought after as delightful ambassadors of their own work. Bringing the traditions of the past into contemporary life is not always easy; this family does it with charm, grace and an abundance of talent. Their expertise shines through in the nutcrackers, incense burners, music boxes, ornaments, pyramids and miniature figures that bring joy to collectors of all ages.

Christian Ulbricht works at the lathe to create his charming nutcracker designs.

HANDCRAFTING TECHNIQUES HAVEN'T CHANGED

The handcrafting of a nutcracker hasn't changed much since Ulbricht ancestors helped develop the artistry nearly 300 years ago. The choice of the woods to be used is made with great care. Some designs require a harder wood than others, and a variety may be employed in one motif. For example, the body of a nutcracker may be of linden, but the legs and arms might be beech, maple or birch. Once the wood to be used is thoroughly dried, and any not deemed satisfactory is discarded, it is cut into various sizes to fit the intricate work patterns. And now the creative process can begin.

Wood turning on the lathe is the first step. This is a painstaking procedure, one that requires significant training and experience; there are only 10 artisans at Holzkunst Christian Ulbricht who handle this exacting task, following in the footsteps of the masters of long ago. Once the wooden parts are cut, turned and stained, all the separate pieces are assembled. Then, the figure moves on to the hand-painting and decorating department, followed by costuming and the application of hair and fur, if appropriate.

Each step requires its own specialists. Of the 80 on staff, there are only ten women who paint, but four times that number in the decorating department. There are also a handful of apprentices, who study the work of the experienced artisans with an eye to learning this fascinating trade.

Of course, no completed piece leaves Holzkunst Christian Ulbricht without the close scrutiny of quality control. This ensures that what is packaged, shipped, and ultimately finds its way to its delighted owner is crafted to perfection.

Because it is clear that American collectors want to know as much as

"Lantern Child," an incense burner, represents a happy memory from Christian Ulbricht's childhood, and is the members' gift for joining the Christian Ulbricht Collectors' Club.

CHRISTIAN ULBRICHT COLLECTORS' CLUB

possible about their treasures, including how the figures are made and who is behind their designs, the Christian Ulbricht Collectors' Club has been formed to bring this information to the marketplace.

As a welcome gift upon joining, all new members in the charter year (1998-99) receive "Lantern Child," a charming incense burner whose motif is a memory from Christian Ulbricht's childhood. Tradition held that children, dressed in long cloaks, would walk from the Round Church in Seiffen down to the village center, carrying hand-made lanterns. Caroling as they walked from house to house, they would often receive small gifts in appreciation from the townspeople.

The special nutcracker that is available to charter members is the "Snow King," a cheery motif that seems to herald all good things to come. And herald it will, for 1999 will see the first club sponsored trip to Seiffen. Members will enjoy the hospitality of the Ulbricht family and will learn many things first-hand about the production process and the history of nutcrackers in the region. They will also have the great delight of traveling through the picturesque and historic countryside.

Through the pages of "The Treasure Chest," the club's bi-annual colorful and informative newsletter, members learn of the latest plans concerning the trip, read advance information on new motifs being developed, have their many questions answered, and have the opportunity to know this remarkable family in depth.

MOVING WITH STYLE AND EXPERTISE INTO THE 21ST CENTURY

Traditions may be strong in the Erzgebirge, but so is the contemporary pull of the international community. Holzkunst Christian Ulbricht is committed to keeping its expertise and capabilities in the forefront, and keeping its collectors apprised of its activities and new developments. Through its up-to-the-minute and informative web site, with E-mail and a dedicated phone line to the Christian Ulbricht Collectors' Club, collectors have so many ways to stay in touch and to learn. Holzkunst Christian Ulbricht invites you to do so!

CLUB

CHRISTIAN ULBRICHT COLLECTORS' CLUB
P.O. Box 99
Angwin, CA 94508
(888) 707-5591

Annual Dues: $45.00
Club Year: Anniversary of Sign-up Date

BENEFITS:

- Membership Gift
- Opportunity to Purchase Members-Only Nutcracker
- Bi-Annual Newsletter, "The Treasure Chest"
- Binder
- Collector's Log
- Personalized Membership Card
- Special Events
- Travel Opportunities

TO LEARN MORE:

CHRISTIAN ULBRICHT COLLECTORS' CLUB
P.O. BOX 99
ANGWIN, CA 94508
(888) 707-5591
FAX: (707) 965-4199
E-MAIL: nutcracker@culbricht.com
URL: http://www.culbricht.com

HOUSE OF HATTEN, INC.

Creating the Heirlooms of Tomorrow

House of Hatten, Inc., a recognized leader in the Christmas and giftware industry, celebrates the season throughout the year. With everything from Santa centerpieces to embroidered stockings, House of Hatten's artisans strive not for mass production but for creating one-of-a-kind heirlooms while focusing on a simple commitment to innovative designs and excellence.

Denise Calla marks her 10th anniversary with House of Hatten by introducing the* Ten Christmas *series. The "Ten Christmas Santa" centerpiece commemorates this special year while invoking enthusiasm for many more.

Founded more than two decades ago, House of Hatten established itself in the Christmas industry with the introduction of unique appliquéd stockings and tree skirts. The company was among the first to manufacture soft-sculptured Christmas decorations.

The market was impacted again when House of Hatten debuted poly-resin reproductions of original wood carvings, beginning with the introduction of artist Denise Calla's designs in 1988. With these introductions, House of Hatten became one of the pioneers in creating poly-resin reproductions of original wood carvings. To reproduce carvings using poly-resin, a mold is first formed for each carving. It is then hand-cast in poly-resin and beautifully hand-painted. These handcrafted products and fine workmanship have made House of Hatten a success, allowing collectors to enjoy the designs of some of the country's best artists.

Today, House of Hatten's products are found in fine department stores, boutiques and specialty stores across the country. Among them, House of Hatten Authorized Dealers are proud to carry House of Hatten collectibles and limited editions. Headquartered near Austin, Texas, the company has expanded by adding new designs and exploring different mediums to reflect each artist's talents. House of Hatten offers the largest line of exclusively designed Christmas products in today's high end industry. Consistently retaining the highest quality standards, House of Hatten continues to provide meticulous attention to detail.

THE MAGIC OF DENISE CALLA

A self-taught artist, Denise Calla has worked in many different mediums. In 1986, House of Hatten approached Calla to reproduce some of her Christmas wood carvings.

"From the start, our working relationship was a delight because we had the same goals," Calla says. "We wanted to celebrate our love for the traditional American Christmas. We wanted a product that was joyful, versatile, collectible and, most of all, a product that was of the highest quality so it was worth having, worth giving and worth keeping to pass on as a cherished heirloom."

The intricate detail can be seen by collectors as they delight in Calla's originality, knowledge of her subject matter and the gentle, life-like qualities of her pieces. Her artwork touches people in a special way, communicating something to their hearts and souls to transcend nationality, language or background. Calla sends each piece of her artwork into the world with the words "go and make somebody happy."

She says her inspiration comes from starting every day with a walk in the woods where she receives instructions from nature and the changing seasons. When not in her studio, she tends her family of animals – some tame, some native to the woods – and her garden. She only uses the wood of evergreen trees to carve her Santas, so she has planted acres of pine trees to give back to the earth the wood she has used for her artwork.

For the past 10 years, House of Hatten, with precision and attention to detail, has been reproducing her designs, which have been described as pure magic and have made her one of America's most highly collected artists. Her first collection was *Enchanted Forest*. From the first nine pieces, only two pieces are still available: "Santa With Teddy" and "Elf Ornament."

To commemorate her 10th anniversary with House of Hatten, Calla has created the *Ten Christmas* collectible series. The primary piece of this collection is the "Ten Christmas Santa" centerpiece featuring St. Nick carrying replicas of favorite pieces from the

The "Natureland Choir" can almost be heard singing "We Wish You A Merry Christmas" in perfect harmony in this festive introduction to the* From Out of the North *collection by Rodney Leeseberg.

artist's previous collections. These replicas represent the past 10 years and are also sold separately as ornaments. A matching tree skirt and stocking complete the *Ten Christmas* collection. Each piece is reproduced from original handcarvings and artwork designed specifically for this special anniversary.

House of Hatten also introduced its first limited edition series from Denise Calla. The *Four Seasons* collection features four very distinctive and very charming bunny figurines, each hand-painted, sequentially numbered and limited to 1,250 pieces. "Puddles" merrily splashes in the Spring, "Melons" cools off the Summer, "Cider" sweeps away the autumn leaves, and "Mistletoe" adds joy to the Winter.

LIMITED EDITION PIECES ARE PRIZED

Collectors can also find limited edition pieces from artist Susan M. Smith, who works from her studio in a small town in Alaska. Since 1995, House of Hatten has reproduced her original carvings in the *Santa's Kingdom* collection. Inspired by the wildlife that surrounds her home, Smith couples Santa with the native animals to express feelings of warmth and beauty. "I'm always making something," Smith says, "sometimes serious, sometimes silly. Creating is part of who I am." Two limited edition centerpieces will join the *Santa's Kingdom* collection in 1998.

In 1997, Smith added three whimsical, limited edition Christmas centerpieces, including Santa riding on a polar bear, whale and buffalo. These collectibles join the five limited edition pieces introduced in 1996. Each figurine is limited to 5,000 pieces. All of these exclusive *Santa's Kingdom* figurines are hand-painted and hand-cast in resin, ensuring that no two pieces are exactly alike.

FINE GIFTS FOR ALL SEASONS

Aside from these Christmas themed collectibles, House of Hatten also celebrates the other seasons and holidays of the year. The company continually adds handcrafted gift items for Spring, Easter, Independence Day, Halloween, Thanksgiving and Hanukkah.

The *Master Gardener* by Denise Calla joins his friends, the gardening elves and *Weather Fairies*, to welcome the arrival of Spring. The fairies represent weather conditions such as sunshine, rain and wind. Some elves and fairies from the *Master Gardener* series make their homes within plants. Calla's *Cupboard Keepers* pick the perfect strawberries. Artists Vaughn and Stephanie Rawson's *Garden Fairies* collection features mischievous sprites holding flower blossoms.

For Easter, bunnies are always multiplying in a variety of colors ranging from pastels to vibrant, deep tones. Also, an entire array of July 4th figurines display patriotism and pride for America.

An extensive Halloween line includes collections from several different designers. Witches are found riding on brooms, carriages, or sitting upon the moon. Pumpkins are harvested by all and are sometimes displayed "for sale." Of course, Halloween wouldn't be Halloween without its share of black cats, bats and even a ghost reading "Very Scary Ghost Stories."

Other figurines, including roosters, bunnies, cats and farm animals, can be displayed year-round. But Santas continue to be a favorite, and House of Hatten collectors delight in the diversity of Santas. As a result, House of Hatten's Santas can be found in many homes across the country. Some of the past favorite collections are *Enchanted Forest, Santas from Around the World, Santa's Kingdom, The Spirit of Gifting, Ye Olde Santa Maker* and *Heirloom Santas.*

Not only are Santas desired collectibles, but other holiday collections have proven to be just as popular: *Twelve Days of Christmas, Two By Two, Cupboard Keepers, Country Christmas, Four Seasons* and *Halloween.*

This black cat enjoys Halloween as he smiles atop the harvest moon. PJ Hornberger created this 17" centerpiece perfect for an autumn display.

Intricate detail using hand-guided machine embroidery and elaborate appliqué are what customers expect when buying from House of Hatten, Inc. This beautiful "Guardian Angel" displays such elegance and quality.

Collections new for 1997 already demonstrating their success include: *Ten Christmas, Snow Ma'am, From Out of the North, Old Fashioned Toys, Twelve Days* and *Master Gardener.*

SOFT-SCULPTURED GIFTS ADD TO HEIRLOOM TRADITIONS

House of Hatten is also one of the leading manufacturers of soft-sculptured items. Using the finest quality fabrics and materials available, House of Hatten offers a variety of tree skirts, stockings and soft-sculptured ornaments exhibiting hand-guided machine embroidery and elaborate appliqué. Many of these intricately crafted items are offered within collections that include complementery poly-resin pieces.

The company's in-house design department has created several soft-sculptured pieces. As always, the keen attention to detail is unmistakable in every appliquéd tree skirt, stocking and ornament. This standard of quality has become an industry benchmark that collectors have come to expect from House of Hatten. Some recent favorite collections include *Grandmother's Crazy Quilt, Keepsake and Patchwork Heart.*

COLLECTORS' CLUB OFFERS YEAR-ROUND EXCITEMENT

Collectors can become a part of the House of Hatten tradition of creating and passing along heirloom quality works of art. Introduced in 1996, the House of Hatten Collectors' Club allows members to enjoy exclusive benefits throughout the year, including a special membership gift from one of House of Hatten's outstanding collections. In addition, members receive a personalized membership card and subscription to House of Hatten's newsletter that provides the latest information on the company's merchandise and artists.

CLUB

HOUSE OF HATTEN COLLECTORS' CLUB
301 Inner Loop Road
Georgetown, TX 78626
(512) 819-9600

Annual Dues: $20.00
Club Year: Anniversary of Sign-Up Date

BENEFITS:

- Membership Gift from the *Cupboard Keepers™ Collection* by Denise Calla
- Membership Card
- Newsletter
- Catalog and List of Authorized House of Hatten Dealers

TO LEARN MORE:

HOUSE OF HATTEN, INC.
301 INNER LOOP ROAD
GEORGETOWN, TX 78626
(800) 5HATTEN
FAX: (512) 819-9033

A Tradition of Proud Craftsmanship

Hudson Creek is a company of New England artists and craftspeople dedicated to the production of fine gifts and collectibles. Many companies boast that their technology is state-of-the-art, and their ideas are as new as tomorrow. Hudson Creek is proud to say that their technology is people, and their craft dates back to the pewterers of colonial New England. Hudson Creek products and themes stand the test of time. Their skills are passed from generation to generation.

Although grounded in American history and culture, Hudson Creek also prides itself on innovation both in sculptural subjects and in fine art techniques. Hudson Creek is governed by four simple rules: Commission the finest original art; create the truest reproductions possible; craft only the highest quality products; charge fair prices. These simple rules, though not always easy to maintain, are followed on a day-to-day basis at Hudson Creek, whether the product is an expensive Fine Pewter sculpture or a less expensive cold-cast miniature. Hudson Creek products have the unique distinction of being proudly made in the United States. Their artisans live by a code of quality assurance brought about by learned craftsmanship and old-fashioned New England fussiness.

***"On the Horizon" is from* Where the Sun Sets *Series from Lawrence Heyda's* Chilmark American West.**

CHILMARK LIMITED EDITION SCULPTURE - A TRADITION OF QUALITY AND INNOVATION

In 1971, Chilmark sculptures revolutionized the bronze-dominated metal sculpture market with casting and finishing innovations which resulted in high quality, handcrafted pewter sculptures. Years of testing and modifying went into creating their richly patinated alloy of Fine Pewter. It's inviting – unsurpassed for its intricate detail and sharp contrast. It's a look that's 100% Chilmark, and it's easy to spot.

Although based on the craft of early English pewterers, Chilmark has plenty of new ideas. They pioneered the distinctive process of applying specially formulated translucent paints to highlight features of certain Chilmark products. Their trade secret methods allow the underlying Fine Pewter to govern the visual outcome. The process is called deNatura™ – "from nature." In 1992, Chilmark introduced MetalART™ which adds gold, silver and copper to enhance already rich art works.

THE DAYS OF CONFEDERATES AND COWBOYS

Chilmark is known as the authority on the Civil War, bringing collectors the exclusive work of Francis J. Barnum. Barnum's three-dimensional metal sculptures express his understanding and deep feelings about this incredible era in American history. Barnum brings great battles and great leaders of the Civil War to life for collectors.

Through meticulous research and attention to detail, Francis Barnum explores the ethos and drama and the most personal and emotional dynamics of ordinary people thrust into greatness as they answer their country's call to war. His great body of work for the *Chilmark Civil War Collection* includes series such as *The Leaders of Gettysburg; Antietam: The Bloodiest Day; Flags of the Civil War* and *Turning Points*, as well as many single issues such as the "C.S.S. Alabama," "The Great Beefsteak Raid," "Old Glory" and "Confederate Pride."

In 1996, Hudson Creek introduced the artistry of Lawrence Heyda to Chilmark collectors. His debut *American West Collection* is titled *Where the Sun Sets*. Heyda's well established national reputation has attracted the attention of serious collectors. While his demonstrated range is impressive, his ability to capture the essence of the person sculpted, and the era represented, is even more compelling. In *Where the Sun Sets*, Heyda undertakes a new view of the Old West. His approach calls attention to the multi-dimensional aspects of life west of the Mississippi...life populated with Plains Indians and cowboys. Through Heyda's imagination, eyes and hands, we meet judges, sheriffs, chiefs and shamans, ranchers, braves, trappers, herders, railroad men, and snake oil salesmen. Agents for good and evil, they all forged permanent marks on the American West. Heyda's first sculptures under the Chilmark banner include "Mystic Hunter," "Sprucin' Up," "On the Horizon," and "Matthew 18."

Heyda's portfolio of sculptures includes many well-known personalities, including Johnny Cash, George C. Scott, Lorne Greene, Ali McGraw and Ryan O'Neil for the Movieland Wax Museum. Other prestigious clients include Joe DiMaggio, Ted Williams, Johnny Bench, Kareem Abdul Jabar, coach John Wooden, jazz clarinetist Pete Fountain, Brett and Bobby Hull and Pope John

"Beatin' The Heat" is the first issue in Mickey & Co. Limited Editions, **Four Seasons Frolics** *series.*

Paul II. In 1990, Heyda was commissioned by the Presidential Library in Simi Valley, California, to create a life-size bust of former President Ronald Reagan. When former First Lady Nancy Reagan saw the bust, she declared that no one would ever capture the president's countenance and personality better than Heyda. The bust is now a part of Mrs. Reagan's personal collection.

THE TRADITION OF INNOVATION CONTINUES

Last year saw the introduction of another Chilmark innovation – life-sized cold cast porcelain, a process which simulates real bronze finishes so closely that experts have to look twice and touch many times to convince themselves it's not foundry-poured hot melt metal. Offered for the first time in the collection entitled *The People*, Chilmark proudly introduced both the work of sculptor Phil Coté, and their latest development in creating affordable art for discerning collectors.

Hudson Pewter presents the **Baby Ark Collection.**

HUDSON COLLECTIBLE PEWTER GIFTWARE SINCE 1968

Hudson originated the concept of collectible pewter giftware 30 years ago, and is the recognized leader in quality giftware designs. Every figurine is handcrafted to Hudson Creek's high quality and value tests for artistry and material. Collectors have made their pieces timeless treasures, given as gifts destined to become heirlooms to be passed from generation to generation. Collections include *Noah's Ark, The Villagers, After Hours on the Carousel, Fantasy* and *Americana.*

MICKEY & CO. DELIGHTS BOTH PEWTER AND DISNEYANA COLLECTORS

Hudson Creek's open edition Mickey & Co. figurines have dominated the fine pewter giftware market since their retail introduction in 1985. Collections that have been tested by time include *World of Mickey, The Birthday and Music Trains, Christmas Village,* and *Stairway to the Stars.* In addition to figurines, the open line now includes key rings and holiday ornaments featuring the Fab Five – Mickey, Minnie, Donald, Pluto and Goofy – as well as other popular Disney characters .

In 1987, the Mickey & Co. line expanded to include limited edition sculpture in Fine Pewter, MetalART™, and bronze. Pewter and Disneyana collectors alike have come to appreciate not only the quality of the Fine Pewter sculptures, but the attention to authenticity and detail that shines through in collections such as *Sweethearts Too, Highway Highjinks* and *Four Seasons Frolics.* Single issues have proved to be just as popular, especially the Annual Mickey Santas and Christmas Specials including "Jolly Old St. Mick," "Finishing Touches," "Christmas Tree Safari" and "All Wrapped Up for Christmas."

"Tillie Lighting the Dark" says "Never Give Up 'til You Croak!" This figurine is from **Tillie the Frog Collection** *by Jessica deStefano.*

HUDSON CREEK COLLECTIONS – SOMETHING FOR EVERYONE

Long respected for their museum-quality metal sculptures under the brand names of Chilmark, Hudson Pewter, and Mickey & Co., Hudson Creek also works with cold-cast porcelain, a wonderful medium that allows them to combine years of casting experience with a rainbow of colors which truly makes a sculpture come alive. These sculptures are called *Hudson Creek Collections*, a diverse array of unique collections, created, handcrafted and hand-painted in the United States of America by the artisans

"Cape Cod Light" is a **Sebastian Miniature** *by Prescott "Woody" Baston, Jr.*

***"Lewis A. Armistead" and "Winfield Scott Hancock"* Leaders of Gettysburg *is part of the series from Francis J. Barnum's* Chilmark Civil War Collection.**

of Hudson Creek.

Meet *Tillie the Frog™*. Her story is simple, but powerful. She used to live in a pond in upstate New York. Then, bulldozers filled in her home to make way for a shopping mall. Pondless and on the road, Tillie's irrepressible optimism and common sense observations teach us what it takes to survive in a sometimes indifferent world. Warm, witty and wise, Tillie has a pose and some prose for hundreds of life's tough situations like: "I never studied music, but I know the score;" "Sometimes, you just gotta move on;" and "Your dream may be a hop away, so never give up 'til you croak." *Tillie the Frog* came to life at the hands of Jessica deStefano, who has been a leader in the field of collectibles for many years.

Another of Jessica's collections, *SeaMyst Mermaids™* is also offered by *Hudson Creek Collections*. Gentle and caring, the *SeaMyst Mermaids* are ever-protective of the oceans and all creatures who seek passage in the waters they guard. Youthful and exuberant, the young *SeaMyst Mermaids* are free to frolic and explore. As the *SeaMyst Mermaids* mature, they take on the duty of preserving their world for future generations, and collectors, to enjoy.

Sebastian Miniatures, America's oldest continually produced collectible, celebrates it's 60th anniversary in 1998. First produced in 1938 in the basement of artist Prescott W. Baston's Marblehead home, *Sebastian Miniatures* have been distributed nationally since 1976 from Hudson Creek's Massachusetts factory. Even today, each figure is hand-cast and hand-painted by cottage painters — as they have been since 1938. Baston's son Prescott "Woody" Baston, Jr. has been the sole sculptor of *Sebastian Miniatures* since his father's death in 1984. His creations, like his father's before him, exhibit pure American flavor depicting themes including history, nostalgia, and "ordinary people doing ordinary things."

CLUBS

THE SEBASTIAN EXCHANGE COLLECTORS ASSOCIATION
P.O. Box 10905
Lancaster, PA 17605-0905
(717) 392-2978

Annual Dues: $32.00
Club Year: Anniversary of Sign-Up Date

BENEFITS:
- Membership Gift: Figurine
- Redemption Certificate for Members-Only Miniatures
- Newsletter, "Sebastian Exchange Collectors Association News," published 3 times per year
- Membership Card
- Tour upon Request
- Buy/Sell Matching Service
- Invitations to Special Events including Annual Sebastian Festival and Midwest Fair
- Value Register and Periodic Updates

MUSEUM

OFFICIAL SEBASTIAN MINIATURES MUSEUM
Stacy's Gifts and Collectibles
Walpole Mall - Rt. One
East Walpole, MA 02032
(800) STACYS1

Hours: Monday through Saturday, 10 a.m. - 9:30 p.m.;
Sunday, 1 p.m. - 6 p.m.
Admission Fee: None

The Official Sebastian Miniatures Museum houses the largest public display of *Sebastian Miniatures* figurines spanning "America's oldest continually produced collectible line" from 1938 to the present.

TO LEARN MORE:

HUDSON CREEK
321 CENTRAL STREET
HUDSON, MA 01749
(508) 568-1401
FAX: (508) 568-8741
E-MAIL: hudsoncrek@aol.com

Artist Lena Liu Plants a Garden of Artistic Beauty

For Lena Liu, life and art are a garden. Her award-winning artwork blooms with nature's beauty, from wisteria growing along a back window, to a bouquet of Summer flowers displayed in an ornate Oriental vase.

Her inspiration comes from within and from the comforts surrounding her own home and studio. Lena only has to look around her backyard in Maryland for many of the subjects that fill her canvases. Along her driveway, there's shade-loving plants such as lilies, Siberian irises and hostas. In the backyard, which embraces the sun, there's a white brick wall leading up to a gazebo. Both are covered with burgundy roses. Behind the gazebo is a large rose garden and a perennial garden with bearded irises, foxgloves, delphiniums and all kinds of Spring bulbs waiting for their season to blossom. "I surround myself with what I love," says Lena. "It's inspiring to me." It has also inspired collectors around the world, who have grown to love the simple pleasures of life and nature in Lena's artwork.

"Oriental Splendor" features a lavish bouquet accented with delicate vases and jacquard linen for an elegant and ethereal look. The print is limited to 5,500 signed and numbered pieces.

From its studios in Potomac, Maryland, Imperial Graphics, Ltd. introduces and distributes work by Lena Liu, an artist of unparalleled popularity in today's collectibles market. Since Lena and her husband, Bill, founded their firm in 1984, Imperial Graphics has become renowned for its versatility of subjects, highly detailed compositions, and Lena's delicate and tranquil style of painting.

LENA SHARES ORIENTAL TRADITIONS THROUGH ARTWORK

"I strive to create a sense of poetry and music in my painting like a beautiful song or poem, with that sense of romance," Lena says. "Emotion, love and nature will never change. I try to capture that in my art — in painting the human interpretation of nature, I let what touches my heart pass through my fingers. I hope you and I can keep sharing this love of nature's beauty, and continue to delight in the splendor of the world that surrounds us."

Lena was born in Tokyo of a Chinese military family, and was raised and educated in Taiwan. Her parents discovered her painting talent at a very young age and sent her to private tutors, with whom she began to learn and apply traditional Chinese brushwork. She took her first painting lessons in Taiwan under the guidance of renowned painters Professors Sun Chia-Chin and Huang Chun-Pi. Through the years, she also combined traditional Oriental brushwork with Western painting techniques, which can be seen in many of her works today.

As a young woman, Lena moved to the United States in her sophomore year in 1970 to study architecture at the State University of Buffalo. She then pursued a graduate degree at UCLA, but true love won out after her first year, as she returned to the east coast to marry Bill.

Having worked for an architectural firm for two years, Lena made the decision in 1976 to devote herself full time to art. She began selling her artwork locally, developing her own style along the way. Eventually, she was approached by a firm who began marketing her work in open editions.

It was soon discovered that Lena's artwork had broad appeal, and her popularity began to soar. So Lena and Bill launched Imperial Graphics, Ltd., with the express purpose of marketing her limited edition artwork. Subjects ranged from birds and butterflies to flowers and landscapes.

The company grew and thrived. Over the years, Lena's Chinese style evolved into her own unique blend of the past and present, where beauty and tranquility are experienced by all who collect Lena's artwork, whether as a print or canvas.

Lena is perhaps best known for her floral artistry that brings the outdoors inside the homes of many collectors. Through a soft palette of colors, she celebrates the delicate beauty of flowers and the wonder of nature. "I live with flowers all the time," Lena says. "I really love them and I study them every chance I get. I believe this separates my work from others because I paint with the spirit aspect of Oriental philosophy, yet with the precision of natural form."

SUMMER AND SPRING BLOSSOM WITH FLORAL PRINTS

Soft Summer breezes whisper delight in Lena's recent releases. The colorful pageantry of the season is revealed in window boxes overflowing with lovely flowers. Terra cotta pots filled with

"Rose Memories" contrasts a window box of Summer flowers with a weathered gray brick wall. This beautiful portrait is limited to 5,500 signed and numbered pieces.

beautiful blossoms and charming jewel-toned hummingbirds complete a fresh collection from Imperial Graphics.

"Wisteria Dreams" features a single window framed by a red brick wall. Before a backdrop of lovely lace curtains, a spectacular array of tulips, pansies and ivy spills from a window box. Vines of graceful, fragrant wisteria cascade from above to provide an ethereal framework.

The exquisite companion piece, "Rose Memories," showcases an ornate wrought iron railing as the backdrop for lush Summer flowers. Below, a window box bursts with geraniums, petunias, sweet alyssum and delicate lobelia. "Potted Pansies" and "Potted Petunias" complement the window box scenes. The natural beauty of these flowers in terra cotta pots lends a touch of class to any room.

Lena has also added to her collection of hummingbird prints. "Hummingbird With Lilac" pays tribute to Lena's favorite hummingbird, the Ruby Throat. "Hummingbirds With Fuchsia" showcases a pair of Anna's hummingbirds frolicking among the bright red blossoms.

All of the pieces are limited to 5,500 signed and numbered prints. Lena celebrates Spring with the loveliest flowers that the season has to offer. "Spring Bulbs" is a beautiful mixture of flowers, including tulips, daffodils, lilies and lilacs. They are the perfect harbingers of Spring and speak of chivalrous love, purity and humility. "Summer Bouquet" showcases the blooms of early Summer: roses, peonies and daisies. Another of Lena's classic images, "Oriental Splendor" is a richly complex work that features a lavish bouquet accented with elegant oriental vases and bowls. Each of these prints is limited to 5,500 signed and numbered pieces.

Besides her love of nature and gardens, music has also inspired Lena. Her work epitomizes the Chinese word tien-lai, which describes music so beautiful that it is considered to be from heaven.

MUSIC INSPIRES POPULAR SERIES

Each year, Imperial Graphics introduces annual additions to the *Music Room* series, which debuted in 1991 and has proven to be a favorite among collectors. Lena pays tribute to one of the most beautiful stringed instruments, the guitar, in "Music Room V - Morning Serenade." The gorgeous composition reveals a quiet corner of an elegantly decorated living room. Early morning sunlight filters through delicate lace curtains, casting its shimmering rays on a single six-string guitar resting on a Louis XV-style chair. On a nearby table, a pot of freshly brewed tea and a floral bouquet await the composer's return.

Lena also combines flowers and musical instruments in "Concerto With Violin" and "Concerto With Guitar." These decorative panels complement other *Music Room* issues. "Harmonic Duet" features a luxurious Steinway piano draped with a lacy white shawl. A shining silver flute has been placed delicately atop the piano, completing the duet. A lush floral arrangement accompanies the scene with pink, white and burgundy peonies.

"Musical Trio" showcases three popular musical instruments — a piano, cello and french horn — along with a sparkling crystal vase of peach-colored roses. Each of the music-themed prints is limited to 5,500 signed and numbered pieces.

Collectors will now be able to enjoy the beauty and soft elegance of Lena Liu's original watercolor paintings with her new Art Silk reproductions. This very unique art form gives the texture and appearance of an original silk painting. It took a year and a half to finalize this product, achieving its superior quality and unique look — a look that's unlike anything else on the market today.

NEW ART SILK REPRODUCTIONS CAPTURE THE BEAUTY OF LENA LIU'S ORIGINAL WATER-COLOR SILK PAINTINGS

Art Silks are available framed in a gold frame specially selected to enhance the beauty of the silk. Like most traditional Chinese paintings, the Art Silk is signed with the artist's red seal called a "chop." Lena feels that "since the Art Silk is my first silk reproduction, it deserves to have my personal seal on it." In addition to Lena Liu's authentic Chinese chop signature, each Art Silk comes with a Certificate of Authenticity. Art Silks can be passed down through generations, making excellent heirloom pieces for children and grandchildren. Future generations

"Music Room V - Morning Serenade" is the most recent addition to the popular **Music Room** ***series. The composition pays tribute to the guitar, which rests against a Louis XV-style chair and complements the romantic setting. This portrait is limited to 5,500 signed and numbered pieces.***

Lena Liu celebrates the arrival of Spring in a composition that combines flowers that grow from bulbs: tulips, daffodils, lilies and lilacs. "Spring Bulbs" is limited to 5,500 signed and numbered prints.

will enjoy their long-lasting beauty that never goes out of style.

The Bradford Exchange, one of the world's most successful marketers of collector plates, contacted Imperial Graphics to represent Lena in the plate field. In 1988, Lena's first plates were released in the *On Gossamer Wings* series, featuring a collection of breathtaking butterflies.

ARTWORK INSPIRES COLLECTOR PLATES AND OTHER COLLECTIBLES

The series was an instant success, with collectors eagerly anticipating each and every Lena Liu plate series.

Today, The Bradford Exchange continues marketing Lena's plates, along with other innovative products designed by this talented artist, including ornaments, music boxes and an elegant tea service collection. The Bradford Exchange honored Lena as one of the first inductees to its "Plate Hall of Fame" at the company's headquarters in Niles, Illinois. The Danbury Mint recently introduced figurines featuring Lena's exquisite Oriental maiden sculptures.

For quality, creativity and a style that has won the hearts of collectors, Imperial Graphics and the artist continue to win prestigious industry awards, including Lena's recent recognition as "Artist of the Year" in both the United States and Canada. She has also received "Plate of the Year" honors from the National Association of Limited Edition Dealers (NALED).

AWARDS RECOGNIZE ARTISTIC TALENT AND SUCCESS

Her popularity extends across the American borders. Lena was nominated in three different categories of the 1997 Canadian "Collectible of the Year" Awards, including "Artist of the Year." In addition, her plate "Garden Elegance" was nominated for "Plate of the Year" as well as "Collectible of the Year."

Lena travels to collector conventions and galleries as time permits from her hectic and demanding painting schedule. She enjoys meeting collectors and sharing her love of art with those who have come to know her and find special meaning in her portraits.

Collectors know they can also rely on Lena and Imperial Graphics for the finest artwork – both in terms of composition and material. Lena's limited editions are printed on high-quality archival acid-free paper to ensure their long-lasting beauty. Her canvases are now stamped as "Archival, Museum Quality Artwork." The stamp, which is located on the back of the stretcher bar, guarantees that collectors are receiving a museum-quality piece that is certified Ph balanced, ultraviolet ray protected, fade resistant, and meets the needs of the custom framer. These benefits assure collectors that they are making a sound investment when purchasing Lena's limited edition canvases.

TO LEARN MORE:

IMPERIAL GRAPHICS, LTD.
11516 LAKE POTOMAC DR.
POTOMAC, MD 20854
(800) 541-7696
FAX: (301) 299-4837
URL: http://www.lenaliu.com
E-MAIL: lliu@lenaliu.com

"Iris Quartet" has been reproduced on exquisite Art Silk fabric, a polyester silken fabric specially selected for its luminous qualities. The piece is personally signed and numbered by the artist, and Lena Lui's signature "chop" is hand-applied in imperial red ink.

Joseph Timmerman's Growing Gallery of Art

Not long ago it was sports, and sports alone, that dominated Joseph Timmerman's view of collectibles. But today as the President of Islandia International, Timmerman works with some of the world's most fascinating painters, offering collectible images of realistic and fanciful children and animals, as well as famous individuals. His gallery of artists includes such well-known names as Gretchen Clasby, Gale Pitt, Trevor Swanson and Sue Etém.

Timmerman is a veteran of the collectibles field with more than 20 years' experience. Beginning as a retailer, he opened his marketing firm, Sports Impressions, in 1985 to present pieces featuring facsimile autographs. "In the 1990s, however, we offered some personally autographed collectibles," Timmerman adds. "Through the association with Mickey Mantle, we went on to do famous Major League baseball players like Nolan Ryan; National Football League players like Joe Montana and Troy Aikman; National Basketball Association stars including Michael Jordan, Magic Johnson and Larry Bird; and National Hockey League players like Bobby Hull."

Timmerman realized that while some competitors were bringing men into collectibles stores with a few sports items, there was little depth to the existing lines. "We decided we would become a true gift and collectible company and make sports plaques and musicals, bells, figurines, plates, ornaments, etc. to create that needed depth. We recognized there was an interest in the marketplace."

In 1991, Enesco Corporation purchased Sports Impressions, and Timmerman stayed on as president until 1996. He notes, "I had a unique opportunity in my five years with Enesco. Although I was the President of Sports Impressions, I didn't have any everyday duties and responsibilities – Enesco did that for me. I was more or less a consultant. Whenever they needed information, I would provide that to them. I had the unique perspective of being involved with a great company, but not having the everyday responsibilities. So I was able to observe. I had an opportunity to see what was good about the industry, the challenges involved and how a successful company like Enesco went about their business. It was like getting a Ph.D. without paying tuition!"

"Remember there's a blue sky behind the blackest cloud" is the message behind this figurine based on the verse "Go Out With Joy" from Isa. 55:12. It's part of the* Sonshine Promises *collection.

THE BIRTH OF ISLANDIA

When Timmerman started Islandia International in 1996, he found that people assumed his new company would focus on sports. "Because I founded Sports Impressions, people would come up to me and would only talk to me about sports, as if that's all I knew. I was a sports fan, but certainly I wasn't a fanatic about it. I thought of different product lines where I felt there was a gap or hole in the marketplace. I really know everybody in the industry from manufacturing, to the artists, to design, to advertising people. I had done everything in the industry from sweeping floors to designing products and working with artists."

Timmerman vowed that he would only start a new company if he could do great things that would challenge him. He also looked to expand his horizons well beyond sports. "This is why I fell in love with the art of Gale Pitt," he explains. "I noticed that people who like cats, love cats. Or they hate cats. There's no in-between. And then when you combine a cat person with any ethnicity and the thing most of us like to do – eating – I thought the joining of cats, gourmet delights and ethnicity was a combination I couldn't turn down. So I decided to become involved with this project, producing Gale Pitt's *International Fat Cats* plates and figurines with great quality."

Another example of Timmerman's expanded view is his relationship with Trevor Swanson, creator of wildlife and animal art. "I have a home in Boca Raton," Timmerman says, "and one of my friends, who also owns a home there, had these gorgeous original paintings of wildlife done by Trevor. I never saw anything so beautiful in my life! It took us about four months to locate Trevor. He is what I consider an up-and-coming superstar, an unbelievable wildlife artist. He doesn't paint from photographs that he finds. He goes and photographs his own animals and his own scenes." So far Timmerman and Swanson have collaborated on four collectible series featuring both wildlife and domesticated animals.

Artist Sue Etém had been friendly with Timmerman for many years before they began their recent joint venture. "She was Plate Artist of the Year in 1982 and 1983," he remembers. "Through a series of changes in her life, she disappeared from our industry in the mid-1980s. I was speaking with a mutual

From Islandia's* International Fat Cats *series comes this feline tribute to "Mexico," complete with the garb and food of that colorful nation.

friend of ours, and I found out she was living in Alabama. We got in contact, and she joined the Islandia International team. If you look at Sue's art, you can see she really does have a special way with children. They're just cuddly kids that you would love to hug." Timmerman and Etém already have introduced three series of collector plates with more wonderful works of art to come featuring childhood subjects.

In addition to these remarkable artists, the Islandia International line-up includes several other painters of renown and talent. Wayne Anthony Still has created a dramatic *People of Africa* oval plate series capturing the pride and beauty of the continent and its inhabitants. Cliff Hayes is the painter of the *Coming Home* collection, portraying the happy moment when a member of the armed forces returns to his or her family and friends after a long separation. Hayes' newest collection of plates, ornaments and vases is called *World's Greatest*, and it features women in the workplace. Robert Tannenbaum is the artist for the *To Have and To Hold* series of wedding plates, as well as the creator of a plate series called *Celebration of Life*, featuring such memorable individuals as Mother Teresa.

Sue Etém's "Bluebird of Happiness" collector plate represents her appealing* Feathered Friends *series featuring children and birds.

"When I met Gretchen Clasby, I became enchanted with her and awe-struck by her story of survival against the odds. Her greatest success as an artist has come from painting these little blue birds with inspirational, scriptural messages," Timmerman explains.

Call it coincidence or divine intervention, but both Clasby and Timmerman felt uniquely led toward their involvement with Clasby's *Sonshine Promises* collection. At an especially low moment in her emotional and financial life, Clasby had an inspiration to draw a pair of little blue birds on a greeting card and add a scriptural message. To date, she has created 500 such uplifting images and verses, each offering a word of hope, friendship or good humor.

A DEEP AFFINITY WITH GRETCHEN CLASBY

Timmerman believes that his collaboration with Clasby is meant in some ways to fill the void left by Mickey Mantle's death a few years back. Like Mickey Mantle, Clasby was born in Oklahoma. Her favorite number is "7" – the same number Mantle wore as a New York Yankee slugger. As a girl, Clasby considered Mantle her number-one hero. Add to these coincidences the fact that Timmerman found himself deeply moved by Clasby's inspirational art, and her *Sonshine Promises* collection quickly became a high-priority line for Islandia. Speaking of Clasby's whimsical blue birds accompanied by comforting sayings and scriptural verses, Timmerman notes, "God used blue birds as his messengers. I investigated this in the Old Testament. This is not just art. It comes from the depths of Gretchen's soul."

Trevor Swanson's bold image of "The Elk" comes alive on this striking 8-1/8" collector plate from Islandia International.

Timmerman helped Clasby select the first images to appear as Islandia figurines and ornaments. They all feature one or more of the whimsical blue birds that have become a Clasby trademark. These aren't classic "blue birds," but a special type of fluffy, wide-eyed bird with webbed feet and blue feathers. As Clasby explains, "The bird became blue, because that was my favorite color. I have had people call it an owl, or a chicken or a duck. But it's just a bird, and it's blue! And the other features are rounded off – the beak is not pointed and sharp, the claws are not pointed and sharp. He's a round little fat lovable bird. The eyes are just big and expressive, because that's where you see the pain and joy and happiness in everyone."

Each image is accompanied by an

upbeat saying and a scriptural verse chosen by Clasby from the many Old and New Testament Bible passages that helped her overcome the desperation she felt when her first marriage crumbled, and she was left with a mountain of debts. Now happily remarried with a rewarding and financially successful career, Clasby considers it her mission to share her story and her words of encouragement with others.

As she explains, "If my paintings help us to remember when we embraced each moment with a new awe, then I have accomplished what I set out to impart. Our days get bombarded with the stress and demands of life, and we all need to take time to enjoy the same gifts we found around every corner in our childhood. God created a most beautiful world for us all, and His canvas is mammoth. I single out very small glimpses of His masterpiece and try to capture my own joy in his creations." As for the name of her collection, she notes, "*Sonshine Promises* is a play on the Son (standing for Jesus), who does make the sun shine! Also, they're full of life and joy and a promise that you can stand by."

A PASSION FOR GREATNESS

"So that is my stable of artists," Islandia International President Timmerman summarizes. "In a normal work week, I review about seven to ten new artists, but I don't seriously consider many. I like somebody who has a passion for the subject, be it animals, children, famous people or inspirational messages. It has to be something special that hits me, and I have to feel that this artist wants to be great!"

TO LEARN MORE:

ISLANDIA INTERNATIONAL
78 BRIDGE ROAD
ISLANDIA, NY 11722
(516) 234-9817
FAX: (516) 234-9183
E-MAIL: islandia78@aol.com
URL: http://www.islandiacoll.com

From the **Sonshine Promises** *collection comes this charming figurine, "The chorus of life brings us all together." It's inspired by Psalm 66:1 — "Make a Joyful Noise."*

The Original in Romantic Victoriana

"What I admire most about Jan," says Bill Hagara about his wife, "is that when she starts something, she puts her whole self into it, and does absolutely the best job she knows how – every time." Thanks to this devotion to excellence – and her unique ability to capture the innocence of childhood – Jan Hagara has enjoyed a nationwide reputation as an artist for over 20 years. Jan's creations include collectible prints, porcelain dolls, collector plates and figurines. Her works, all based on her original watercolor paintings, are instantly recognizable: young children in Victorian-era costumes clutching dolls, toys or flowers, while peering out at the world through wide, wistful eyes.

Adorable Brianna Rose peeps out from a lush rose flower as her friend, Baby the teddy bear, looks on in Jan Hagara's "Brianna Rose & Baby."

Jan Hagara was born in Sand Springs, Oklahoma, the second of three girls growing up in a small-town atmosphere. Her father, Rippol Brown, was an oil refinery worker who did wood carving as a hobby. For as long as she can remember, Jan has been drawing faces. "It seems like I've always had a pencil in my hand," she recalls. "I remember when I was in the fourth grade, I would draw faces on scraps of paper. I have always been fascinated with faces."

Another youthful influence was Jan's Aunt Thelma of Tulsa, a collector of antique dolls. With Aunt Thelma's help, the transition from collector to painter was easy. From the early 1960s on, Jan has painted watercolors of children – both her own and those of her neighbors – with dolls as huggable props. As she explains, "I've always thought that the years from two to five were the ideal age for children. When they are younger, they don't have as much character, and when they are older, they lose a little of the innocence. It's the age someone would want to freeze in time."

THE HAGARA PARTNERSHIP BEGINS

In 1972, Jan met Bill Hagara of Tempe, Arizona, where she was living at the time. In May of 1974, they were married in downtown Tempe. Jan's two daughters, Elaine and Karen, along with Bill's good friend, James LaBrie of Phoenix (the wedding cameraman) were in attendance.

Bill had experience as a photographer and musician and was selling stereo equipment when the Hagaras married. As time went on, these abilities would become important assets in their business. To this day, photographs are essential to Jan's work, and Bill produces them. Initially he used a simple 35mm camera, but he now relies on a massive 4x5 studio camera with a digital scanning back for brochures and ads.

During 1974, Bill and Jan displayed Jan's watercolors at local art shows, mostly in malls. In January 1975, they activated their plan to broaden their reach with Jan's paintings. They also began creating small cards and prints to add variety and a lower-cost product. In addition, Jan's signature "hash marks" were invented around this period – two small blue strokes that are in every painting, print, card and figurine to make it her own. These marks are always in the hair of the model, adding Jan's favorite color, her special blue, for variety.

At first, the Hagaras reproduced line art drawings in black and white. Then they introduced their first color print, "Trina," the portrait of a black child that Jan had painted.

The original painting of "Trina" would play an important role in the couple's move from Arizona to Texas in 1977 when cash was in short supply. The quick sale of "Trina" to a collector in Phoenix brought $500 in cash – less than their asking price of $800 – but nonetheless, cash for their trip. They put their house up for sale and loaded a U-Haul truck which Bill drove. Jan drove the Dodge van pulling their 23-foot "Prowler" travel trailer.

THE HAGARAS' ART SCOPE EXPANDS

During the period from 1976 to 1978, the Hagaras exhibited Jan's work at art shows further and further from home. They traveled to California, Texas, Colorado, Oklahoma, Kansas, Nebraska, Wisconsin and Illinois. They felt they should be more centrally

Jan Hagara's* Georgetown *series features "Miss Megan," a figurine of porcelain and metal depicting a lovely young lady with her doll and teddy bear. At 6" wide by 5" tall, it has an issue price of $69.00.

located, which is why they chose Georgetown, Texas, near Austin, as their new home base. There they bought a 1.3 acre wooded lot in late 1976 before culminating the move with the money from the sale of "Trina." Soon they began construction of their current two-story rock home. Many additions have taken place over the years, making the large, gated house several times its original size. Today, it sits on three acres, nestled among hundreds of trees.

In 1977, while at a street show in Independence, Missouri, a woman asked Jan if she had thought of putting her children on collector plates. Jan said they hadn't. The lady's name was Pat Smith, a prominent doll expert, and author of many books on the subject of antique dolls. Later that day, they all had dinner and ended up at Smith's home where they talked of dolls and plates. This "plate thing" was brand-new to both Jan and Bill. The more they thought about it, however, the more intrigued they became.

JAN HAGARA'S COLLECTOR PLATE DEBUT

At the South Bend Collectors' Show in the summer of 1978, Jan Hagara's "Lisa and the Jumeau Doll" debuted as a collector plate limited to an edition of 5,000 at an issue price of $60.00. The edition was sold out before the first dealer day had ended! A receipt book from the local stationery store held more than $150,000 in sales – all written in Bill's handwriting. To the Hagaras, it seemed as if their lives changed overnight. Jan's art had entered the "big time." She and Bill were a success!

After "Lisa and the Jumeau Doll," there were more plates done with The Carson Mint, The American Heart Association, and the Hagaras' own firm, The B&J Company. In 1982, the first seven Jan Hagara figurines debuted in association with Royal Orleans. They were an instant hit, and soon more pieces were offered along with hanging miniatures. Next came the vinyl dolls from Effanbee. Another company called Heirloom Tradition, a division of Tomy Toy, began making more expensive figurines and less expensive dolls than did Royal Orleans. All sold well. Then came the needlework, bells, plaques, tins, Christmas cards, notecards, more prints, more expensive figurines, ShelfSitters, mirrors, and in 1987, the Jan Hagara Collectors' Club. Begun at the request of many collectors, the Club offers a wealth of benefits including many products for purchase by members only, as well as complimentary pieces including bookmarks and cloisonné pins.

Sitting atop a carton of their own make-believe ice cream brand are "Butchie and Oreo," another issue from Hagara's fanciful* Make Believe *series.

A QUARTER-CENTURY OF SUCCESS

It has now been nearly 25 years since Jan Hagara entered the fields of gifts and collectibles with plates, prints, dolls and figurines. Does Jan ever get tired of doing this? She says, "Not really. There is always something new to do, or at least, a new way of doing it. Look at the changes in graphic arts. In the old days, everything was cut and paste. Today, with the magic of computers, things are faster and faster. Even I have my own computer, scanner and printer. We have a state-of-the-art graphics department with the fastest Macintosh in town and a really talented expert running it.

"Bill still does all of the photography, mostly 4"x5" transparencies and digital scans in the studio. It's exciting to see the product sitting there and in a few minutes, it's inside the computer ready for an ad or brochures of the highest quality. Bill is also knowledgeable enough to go from setting up the product, shooting it, and laying out the

Writing a pretty "thank you" with her huge make-believe paintbrush is "Mary Lou" by Jan Hagara.

page, to importing the digital art into the ad and finishing it up using Photoshop and Pagemaker software. So, he and I could still do it all if we had to."

Today, Jan's latest efforts – besides her porcelain dolls – are her stunning porcelain figurine grouping, *Georgetown* series, and her charming set of cold cast figurines, called *Make Believe.* "I feel that these are the best quality we've ever done, and the most fun to create," Jan says. "We are also very excited about Bill's new company, Country Music Greats, which features licensed, cold cast porcelain figurines of country music singers in 8" and 6" sizes. Bill has dozens of country artists signed and has a goal of producing 10 new artists a year. A 4" hanging ornament is also planned. This is Bill's love – the legendary singers he grew up with, like Hank Williams, Roy Rogers, Eddy Arnold, Tammy Wynette and Porter Wagoner. Some he met and interviewed as a country disk jockey in the 1960s. Spending the afternoon with Eddy Arnold can be pretty interesting!"

Bill adds, "Right now, I think Jan and I are happier than we've ever been. Our new Pomeranian puppy, Sony, has added a tremendous amount of pleasure to our lives." Because Jan doesn't like to fly, and because both Bill and Jan love the freedom of the road, the Hagaras travel in their own private Prevost coach. They often stop along their way to meet and spend time with the people who own Jan's lovely creations. Together, they have nine grandchildren from their five children, most of whom live nearby in Texas. Along with Sony, the Hagaras have a cat, Sarah. They enjoy family gatherings at their home in Georgetown as often as they can.

After 25 years of marriage, Bill Hagara still marvels at his wife's energy and accomplishments. "Jan has so many interests," he notes, "especially her dolls and the new series, but the stock market keeps her busy, too. She formed a women's investment club. With the club, just as with her art, she puts her whole self into it. That's why I admire her so much." For her part, Jan adds, "I'll continue to produce unique and beautiful porcelain and cold cast figurines and dolls into the new century. My goal is to bring collectors a lasting, endearing product that they are proud to show in their homes. And Bill and I are proud to be true pioneers in the collectibles industry!"

"Peppermint and Carmel" from Jan Hagara's* Make Believe *series sports a "Get Well" message. Each piece in the grouping sells for $49.00.

CLUB

JAN HAGARA COLLECTORS' CLUB
40114 Industrial Park
Georgetown, TX 78626
(512) 863-9499

Annual Dues: $44.00 – Renewal: $39.00
Club Year: July-June

BENEFITS:
- Membership Gift: Figurine and Yearly Cloisonné Pin
- Opportunity to Purchase Members-Only Figurine
- Quarterly Newsletter
- Binder with Club Logo
- Membership Card
- Buy-Sell Matching Service
- National Convention
- Special Events and Contests
- Local Club Chapters

TOUR/MUSEUM

JAN HAGARA OUTLET
40114 Industrial Park
Georgetown, TX 78926
(512) 863-3072
Hours: Monday through Friday
8 a.m. - 5 p.m.
Admission Fee: None
Collectors can tour the corporate office, and a museum featuring Jan Hagara's artwork is located in the Jan Hagara Outlet Store.

TO LEARN MORE:

JAN HAGARA COLLECTABLES
40114 INDUSTRIAL PARK
GEORGETOWN, TX 78626
(512) 869-1365
FAX: (512) 869-2093
E-MAIL: info@hagaradolls.com
URL: http://www.hagaradolls.com

KURT S. ADLER

WORLD'S LEADING RESOURCE FOR CHRISTMAS COLLECTIBLES

Christmas may only come once a year, but at Kurt S. Adler, Inc., every day feels like Christmas. In fact, for over 50-plus years, Kurt S. Adler has become almost synonymous with this great holiday, and is the leading supplier and designer of holiday decorative accessories and collectibles. Kurt S. Adler has created and designed products that have made holiday memories for millions of collectors.

A soft-spoken, charming businessman and a true gentleman in every sense of the word, Adler was gifted with an uncanny design savvy and a keen eye for style. Capturing the imagination of well-heeled, post-war consumers, he brought a European flavor and sense of fashion and integrated it with American tastes at affordable prices – bringing a whole new look to Christmas in the United States. Before long, Kurt S. Adler would become a name that consumers would come to know and trust.

When he wasn't buying and designing new products, Adler traveled all over the U.S., learning what collectors wanted. Gifted with the talent for knowing his market and a great eye for appealing designs and colors, he carried prototypes of his ideas overseas. He learned quickly that the American consumer was quality-conscious, and that his products would have to meet stringent standards to succeed in the marketplace.

"Ebenezer Scrooge" is the premier nutcracker in* A Christmas Carol *series of Steinbach nutcrackers. The nutcracker, limited to 7,500 pieces, stands 18-1/2" tall, and has been hand-turned and hand-painted in the world-famous Steinbach factory.

HISTORY-MAKING INNOVATIONS

During its history, Kurt S. Adler has been recognized for many breakthroughs and significant achievements. Ornaments have always been one of the mainstays of the line. Kurt S. Adler was the first to design, develop, import and distribute ornaments crafted of high-quality material including better woods, ceramics, stained glass, resin, fabric mache and mouth-blown glass.

Supported by one of the largest teams of first-class, exclusive designers, Kurt S. Adler was one of the first companies to go to factories in The Far East and commercially manufacture ornaments and holiday accessories. The company has maintained stringent quality control standards to meet the buying preferences of American consumers and helped to transform a cottage industry into the modern Christmas industry of today.

The firm introduced the age-old tradition of wood-turned ornaments to the Orient. In the mid-1950s and well in to the '60s, Kurt S. Adler imported the first quality made snowglobes from West Germany. These snowglobes, also called snowdomes, featured Christmas scenes with Santa and other holiday characters.

When country styles and colors became popular in home furnishings in the 1970s, Kurt S. Adler, Inc. unveiled the first ornaments with "country" motifs and colorations. From that point on, the company continued to create decorations with innovative designs, such as Victorian, contemporary, folkart and many others.

Since the early '70s, the firm utilized the unique talents of its art director and veteran designer, Marjorie Grace Rothenberg, to introduce a variety of Christmas themes – which have included ornaments and accessories that have been collected and passed-down from generation to generation. Today, the firm introduces 12 to 15 new themes and adds thousands of collectibles annually.

Kurt S. Adler retains the largest team of first-class, exclusive designers "under one roof" for collectible holiday ornaments and accessories. The firm is credited with creating the first ornaments and figurines featuring African-American Santas, Angels, etc. The company also introduced the first line of Santas designed in unique, whimsical settings from Postal Carrier, Policeman, and Fireman, to Fisherman, Golfer and Baseball Player.

Kurt S. Adler was one of the foremost companies to introduce licensed products in the Christmas industry. Today, its extensive licensed collection includes such major names as Peanuts™, Looney Tunes™, Sesame Street®, Coca-Cola™, Gear, Betty Boop™, Disney's Hercules, Raggedy Ann & Andy, It's A Wonderful Life, The Wizard of Oz, Marilyn Monroe, Gone With The Wind™, and many others.

In the 1980s, Kurt S. Adler introduced the world-renowned *Louis Nichole Heirloom Collection*, one of the most elegant ornament lines ever produced. Designed by famed designer Louis Nichole, the group featured Victorian-styled doll ornaments dressed in elaborate fabric and lace costumes

"Grand Father Frost" is the premier members-only ornament for all charter members of The Polonaise Guild. This ornament is handcrafted from mouth-blown glass in Poland and included in the membership kit.

with stunning colors. Some are included in the prestigious *White House Collection.*

In the mid-1980s, *The Smithsonian Carousel Series* was unveiled and included ornament replicas of antique carousel animal figures found on merry-go-rounds in the Smithsonian Museum Archives. Each year, Kurt S. Adler retires two figures and introduces two new figures. *The Smithsonian Collection* includes the *Milestones In Flight, Antique Toy* and *Angel* series, based on many designs found in the world-renowned museum.

LIMITED EDITION STEINBACH NUTCRACKERS

In 1991, Kurt S. Adler introduced one of the first limited edition nutcrackers, "Merlin The Magician," from the world-famous Steinbach factory. Since then, Merlin's value has soared dramatically on the secondary market. In recent years, the firm introduced popular collections depicting characters from *Camelot, Robin Hood, American Presidents, Native American Chiefs* and others.

The Steinbach Factory, the leading producer of collectible nutcrackers and smoking figures in the world, was founded in 1832 and continues to manufacture nutcrackers, smoking figures, ornaments and music boxes in the age-old tradition. Handcrafted and hand-painted from the finest northern European woods, these handicrafts are among the best examples of the medieval art of wood turning. Steinbach's "Noah and His Ark" nutcracker won an "Award of Excellence" from *Collector Editions* magazine. Collectors are invited to join the Steinbach Collector's Club, which offers members-only pieces, gifts and other items, and is gaining members every day.

AWARD-WINNING POLONAISE™ COLLECTION

The *Polonaise™ Collection,* which won the "Collector's Choice Award" for several consecutive years, has captivated collectors from around the world with its spectacular array of glass ornaments handcrafted in Poland in the age-old tradition of European master glassblowers. The hand-workmanship is very involved – from creating forms and fashioning shapes by hand-blowing glass, to silver-coating, lacquering and decorating the ornaments – which is done by Europe's most highly skilled and well-trained artisans. Collectors can join the Polonaise™ Collector's Guild to receive members-only ornaments, exciting videos and more.

HOLLY BEARIES, HOLLY DEARIES AND SNOW BEARIES

Holly Adler believes that the hand-made decorations and collectibles that she creates today are destined to become the treasured keepsakes and heirlooms of tomorrow. As both designer and collector, she hopes to create a Christmas that reflects the warm spirit of love and friendship.

One of her primary collections, *Holly Bearies,* is an assortment of resin and plush bear ornaments and figurines. Each is distinguished by its own playful character and personality and is "Looking for a Home in Your Heart." Holly also has designed *Holly Dearies,* fun little reindeer and Santas in animated poses; and *Snow Bearies,* a group of adorable bears who live and play in a winter-white wonderland.

SNOWTOWN, ANGEL HEIGHTS AND SPRINGTOWN

Michael Stoebner, a veteran sculptor, painter and illustrator, is credited with the creation of holiday designs with "a handmade look that brings a feeling of warmth and meaning back into Christmas." He created the highly acclaimed *Snowtown,* a whimsical celebration of the Christmas season. His style of integrating wood and clay originals with fabric and wire invoke the heartwarming traditions of the holidays. Look for the cleverly placed heart logo on each of his creations. *Snowtown* may be the only illuminated, wood resin Christmas village available. Inside each of these magical buildings is a special, secret story of holiday love and friendship.

Stoebner also created *Angel Heights,* a unique celestial illuminated village appealing to collectors all year round. Designed as a special place in the clouds filled with childlike wonder and a gentle reminder of all the good things in life, *Angel Heights* includes whimsical angels in Victorian-styled townhouses right out of a pastel

"Fremont" is one of the first plush figures featured in the* Holly Bearies *collection from Kurt S. Adler. Designed by veteran designer Holly Adler, "Fremont" is adorned with a red cardigan sweater and is noted by the trademark red heart on his paw.

Angel Heights *is a unique celestial village featuring whimsical angels and houses with a hand-carved look. Shown is the "Cherub Chapel" lighted building and a singing angel figure.*

glittered sugar plum fantasy. He also developed *Springtown*, a lighted, wood/resin village to be displayed for Easter and throughout the Spring season.

FLEUR-DE-LIS DOLLS EXTEND 50-YEAR TRADITION

Victoriana and Christmas doll enthusiasts in-the-know have shared a secret for years – the most exquisite modern holiday doll ornaments have been created by Kurt S. Adler. Some say that elegant Christmas dolls have been a tradition at this company. New exquisite doll ornaments have been introduced annually throughout most of its 50-year history. These exclusive porcelain doll ornaments have always appealed to the connoisseur who seeks out these dolls for their delicate, modeled facial detail, finely painted features and beautifully styled wigs.

The Fleur-de-Lis Doll Collection, created by Jocelyn Mostrom and the KSA Design Team, is the pinnacle of this design tradition. This splendid assortment includes a variety of popular themes: romantic ladies, Victorian children, heavenly angels, charming fairies and opulent Santas – each elaborately dressed in elegant fabrics with a designer touch.

PAUL BOLINGER'S SANTAS

Paul F. Bolinger, the award-winning Californian woodcarver, is a master craftsman who specializes in distinctive stylized Santas. Ever since receiving a chisel and a block of wood from a friend for Christmas, he has mastered the art of woodcarving – from relief carving, to carving in the round, to his current forms of Father Christmas. Selected twice as "America's Best Traditional Craftsman," Paul combines fine art and folkart techniques to hand-carve each of his Santas. His collection features hand-painted Santas cast in wood resin directly from the originals, many of which include traditional Gift-Givers and other characters depicted with distinctive looks and personalities. Some are inspired from old German and Celtic lore, while others are just whimsical creations.

FABRICHÉ FIGURINES

The popular *Fabriché Collection* offers many innovative designs of Santa and Mrs. Claus at work and at play. There's a Santa on computer, in his workshop, as a sailor, ice skating, and watching football on TV. *Fabriché* figurines and ornaments were created from a mixed media technique based on the traditional art of papier mache combined with modern methods and materials. *The Fabriché Collection* features the designs of Marjorie Grace Rothenberg, the KSA Design Team, and reproductions of original designs found in the Smithsonian Museum Archives.

THE VATICAN LIBRARY COLLECTION

The Vatican Library Collection offers holiday ornaments and decorative accessories inspired by the rare works of fine art housed in the world-renowned Vatican Library – all timeless treasures depicting Byzantine, Gothic and Renaissance styles from ancient European history. The collection includes *Polonaise™* glass designs, ornaments handcrafted of porcelain, metal, resin, fabric and silk prints on glass, as well as porcelain tabletop figurines.

For more than a half-a-century, Kurt S. Adler has developed a worldwide reputation as the innovator of beautiful holiday collectibles, from nutcrackers, ornaments and musicals, to figurines, snowglobes, villages, dolls, and much more. Collectors can expect more of the same, plus many new collectibles, lines and other special surprises, during the next 50 years.

CLUB

THE STEINBACH COLLECTOR'S CLUB
KURT S. ADLER, INC.
1107 Broadway
New York, NY 10010
(212) 924-0900 Ext. 281

Annual Dues: $45.00 - Renewal: $35.00
Club Year: Anniversary of Sign-Up Date

BENEFITS:
- Membership Gift: Mini Nutcracker
- Redemption Certificate for Members-Only Nutcracker
- Newsletter
- Club Portfolio
- Membership Card and Certificate
- Steinbach Pin

POLONAISE COLLECTOR'S GUILD
KURT S. ADLER, INC.
1107 Broadway
New York, NY 10010
(212) 924-0900 Ext. 214

Annual Dues: $50.00
Club Year: Anniversary of Sign-Up Date

BENEFITS:
- Members-Only Piece, Mouth-Blown Polonaise Ornament
- Membership Gift: Video Showing Artisans at Work Creating Mouth-Blown Ornaments in Poland

TO LEARN MORE:

KURT S. ADLER, INC.
1107 BROADWAY
NEW YORK, NY 10010
(212) 924-0900
FAX: (212) 807-0575

Childhood Memories Produce an Enduring Favorite

Peter and Barbara Wisber began their family business, Ladie and Friends, Inc. more than 12 years ago as an outgrowth of Barbara Wisber's crafting projects. In 1980, Barbara started decorating grapevine wreaths and selling them at markets and craft fairs in and around Bucks County, Pennsylvania. When a few talented friends joined her, a dynamic craft business began. By 1982, the business had grown, Peter had become more involved in the day-to-day operations, and a national marketing firm began to represent the creations of their growing craft company at regional trade shows. The company's growth was so impressive that the business moved to a larger location that offered both production space and an already existing store area, where the Wisbers could begin retailing both their own creations and those of others. During 1984, a dream began to take shape in Barbara's mind: how to produce a collection of wooden folk dolls that could be added to the already popular wreaths and lines of hand-painted folk art that she had developed. What she envisioned was a doll that would capture the spirit of universal delights and simpler times, when there were games to be played, friends to be made, wonderlands to be explored, adventures to be lived, and lessons learned.

"Lizzie High®" with her Goose Lily, as depicted in the First Series of figurines.

As these thoughts were swirling around in Barbara's mind, a bin of wooden balls in a hardware store set off a chain reaction that would soon have a profound effect upon the future course of Barbara's craft business. She turned over one of the balls in her hand, and pondered what could be done with it. She talked to Peter about fashioning a doll's body from a simple block of pine. The doll that soon grew from this conversation has since been copyrighted, patented and successfully defended against an army of imitators. The dimensions of the doll, the position of the arms, the rounded feet, the attire and accessories, the round head and, of course, the two dots for eyes, now constitute a "look" that has achieved prominence in the collectible world.

For many of those who have now become enthusiastic collectors of the popular *Lizzie High®* dolls, an additional part of any particular character's charm comes from the wonderful old-fashioned names Barbara continues to borrow from the Wisber family Bible and history, and the tales she creates to accompany each character. These tales are whimsical, timeless, and with the gentlest of humor, capture moments that suggest a world of wonder and adventure as seen through the shining eyes of a child.

The first nine dolls were introduced at the giftware shows in January, 1985. The collection consisted of six little girls wearing simple muslin frocks and a variety of shawls and kerchiefs in country plaids, and three young boys in painted overalls sporting checkered neckerchiefs. Since the introduction of these first dolls, Barbara has created 360 more which include 225 full-sized dolls; 90 *Little Ones™* (smaller-sized, un-named dolls that suggest universal children and richly detailed, easily recognized childhood moments); 22 full-sized and 8 smaller-sized rabbits (the *Pawtuckets™*); 11 full-sized and 2 smaller-sized bears (the *Grummels™*); 3 limited editions; 5 Lizzie High Society™ dolls; 3 *Little Ones* event pieces; 11 accessory items, and two complete sets of resin figurines that are based upon some of the most popular dolls.

LIZZIE HIGH DOLLS INTRODUCED AT GIFTWARE SHOWS

While most of the original dolls have been retired, many have been brought back in a new form. Because of the inclusion of more extensive complementary accessories such as miniature furniture, musical instruments, tiny books, animals, wagons, buttons, bows and hats, these newer editions appear to embrace a larger world than any of their predecessors, including the original "Lizzie High." Many feel that the animals, in particular, add clever moments of humor to each doll's story. Peter sculpts them in clay, then they are cast in resin that holds not only their shape, but also their character. Tiny kittens bat at each other, geese strut to some whimsical, unheard

DOLLS RETAIN THEIR HUMOR AND SIMPLE CHARM

"Lottie Bowman™" demonstrates the attention to detail and clever use of accessories that is typical of the current dolls.

tune, bunnies trip over their own ears, and they all look as though they absolutely belong with the doll that they're with. The Wisbers provide much of the reason for this unique sense of harmony between a character and its accessories. Through their art, Peter and Barbara are striving to capture moments from a simpler time, that evoke a happy or tender memory from nearly everyone who sees a particular piece. Moreover, both of them feel quite strongly that in order to succeed, their pieces – whether dolls or the more recent additions, figurines – "...must make us laugh or smile. If the buyer can't see the humor, it's not a good piece."

Today, much as she did when she turned the first ball of wood over in her hand, each new doll idea comes to Barbara as a result of playing with a wide variety of objects: a piece of fabric she likes in a store, a button, an accessory, a wooden or miniature toy. As she handles these objects, she begins to tie them all together with memories from her own childhood or from the happy childhoods of her children. A rough prototype soon appears. Somewhere along the line, she'll ask Peter, "What do you think?" and together they will shape the animals and accessories needed to complete the picture. Barbara and Peter discuss shapes, patterns, colors and poses, then names and tag lines, as well as all the other bits and pieces that form their remarkable dolls.

LIZZIE HIGH SOCIETY AND NOTEBOOK BOOST COLLECTORS' INTEREST

During the period from the late 1980s to mid-1990s the dynamic company's expansion and diversification continued. More employees were added, the company relocated to larger facilities, and a Lizzie High Doll Museum was established. By 1992, the popularity of the *Lizzie High* dolls and their increasing prominence in the collectible world led to the formation of a collector's club, the Lizzie High Society, to help satisfy the requests for literature and information from a growing number of *Lizzie High* collectors. The number of active members in this club has now reached nearly 4,000. For its members, perhaps the most prized benefits that Society membership offers are the opportunity to purchase the "Society Dolls," which are available only to members and only for one year, and a subscription to the semi-annual publication called the "Lizzie High Notebook™." The Notebook is designed like the black and white marble-patterned composition books that most of us are familiar with from our own school days. Each Notebook covers four basic "school subjects." The "Reading" section gives information about Ladie and Friends and answers questions from collectors; the "History" section sheds light on the family history that has provided the inspiration for many of the dolls, their names, and "tales;" the "Arithmetic" section tells collectors about additions and subtractions to the Ladie and Friends' collection, and provides a valuable collector's "Buy/Sell" listing; and, in a final "Art" section, the newsletter provides information about topics other than dolls that may be of interest to *Lizzie High* collectors.

During 1995, Lizzie High Society members received two additional benefits when the Wisbers announced that a series of pewter ornaments would be cast that depict each of the first nine dolls introduced in 1985. Also, a new line of "Event Dolls" would now be available at special dealer parties known as Lizzie High "Events." The ornaments, which were conceived as commemorative pieces to mark the Tenth Anniversary of the dolls, have themselves become treasured collectibles. The Event Dolls, although similar to the Society Dolls in the length of time each is available, differ from the Society Dolls in the method by which they are obtained: only those who attend an event are eligible to purchase an Event Doll.

FIGURINES CAPTURE FAVORITE DOLLS' PERSONALITIES

Perhaps the most significant of this company's most recent achievements has been its expansion into the area of figurines. These sculpted resin reproductions of various *Lizzie High* dolls stand just 4" tall and are detailed to perfection. The First Series of 12 figurines was released for sale in November 1996, followed by a Second Series of 12 figurines during the Summer of 1997, that was even more detailed and animated than the first. Each of the figurines presents a character's "tale" on the underside of the base, and is marked with a hidden trademark consisting of a blank face with two dots for eyes. The figurines come with a Certificate of Authenticity and are packaged in a distinctive burgundy and gold-trimmed collector's box. These, and subsequent series, are available for 24 months from the release date, and are then retired.

The *Lizzie High* dolls have evolved dramatically from the simple characters

"Ellie Bowman™," the 1997 Lizzie High Society™ members-only doll

"Olivia High™" is a captivating and playful representative of the second series of figurines.

MUSEUM

LIZZIE HIGH MUSEUM
A COUNTRY GIFT SHOPPE
Rt. 313, Dublin Pike
Dublin, PA 18917
(215) 249-9877

Hours: Monday through Saturday,
10 a.m. - 5 p.m.; Extended Holiday Hours
Admission Fee: None

All retired and limited/special edition *Lizzie High* Dolls are on display in the museum, as well as historical information about the company's development. Current dolls are available in the gift shop.

CLUB

THE LIZZIE HIGH SOCIETY
220 North Main Street
Sellersville, PA 18960
(800) 76-DOLLS

Annual Dues: $25.00 - Renewal: $15.00
Club Year: January - December

BENEFITS:

- Membership Gift: Pewter Lapel Pin of Lizzie High Logo
- 4" Pewter Ornament Depicting One of the First Nine Dolls from 1985
- Opportunity to Purchase Members-Only Doll
- Bi-annual Newsletter, "Lizzie High Notebook"
- Complete Color Catalog in Leather-grained Binder
- Membership Card
- Buy/Sell Matching Service

they once were. The popularity of the doll and figurine collections has grown far beyond anything Barbara and Peter could have imagined years ago. Despite the astounding growth of their business and many changes that have taken place, Barbara and Peter continue to remain 100 percent involved in the day-to-day activities of their busy company. Barbara is still the primary creator for the dolls, while Peter continues to sculpt accessories for each doll, solve technical design problems and run the business.

HARMONY + CONSISTENT VISION = ENDURING SUCCESS

Country life, parenting, a strong sense of family history and pride, cherished recollections of happy childhoods and valued friendships provide the inspiration for the Wisbers' creations. Many have come to feel that much of the secret to the Wisbers' enduring success is found in the word "harmony." The deep sense of harmony with the world and with each other that is so easily detected in the Wisbers is reflected by their company and its products. The innocence and joy that the Wisbers capture in their art have brought them into a close, consistent and harmonious partnership with collectors worldwide, who continue to be touched by the humorous and tender antics of "Lizzie High," her friends and family.

TO LEARN MORE:

LADIE AND FRIENDS, INC.
220 NORTH MAIN STREET
SELLERSVILLE, PA 18960
(800) 76-DOLLS
FAX: (215) 453-8155
URL: http://www.lizziehigh.com

LEE MIDDLETON ORIGINAL DOLLS, INC.

A Living Legacy of Innovative Artistry

"When I see a man who loves children so much, he can sit there holding and rocking one of my 'babies' with tears in his eyes, I know that man has a rare and special quality. I am happy for his wife and the children who will one day call him 'Daddy.' And I am happy that my work has been able to reach that part of him," commented Lee Middleton Urick, award-winning creator of a line of incredibly life-like baby dolls for her company, Lee Middleton Original Dolls, Inc.

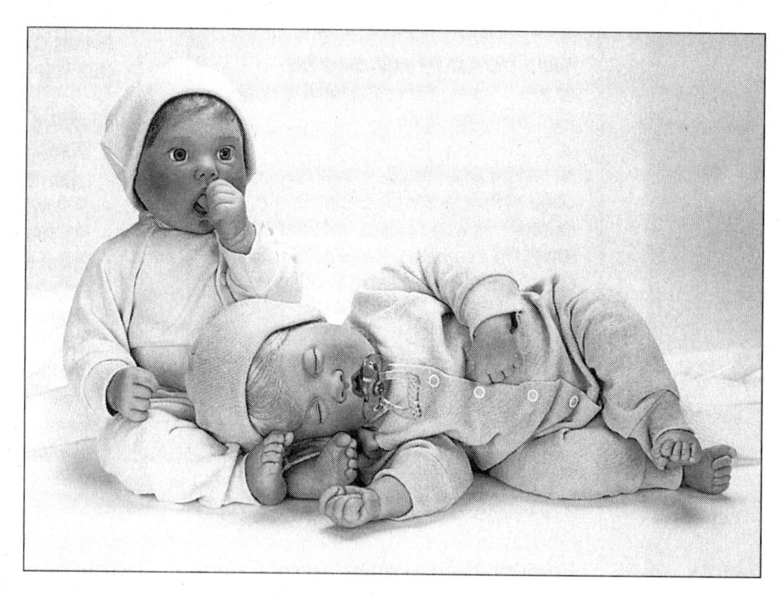

The Middleton* My Own Baby *boy and girl are the first dolls ever to be "UL Classified" for safety.

For nearly two decades, Lee's superb artistry captivated doll collectors nationwide. Her unexpected death on January 30, 1997, saddened her collectors, whose hearts were touched by each doll they held in their arms, and deeply moved by the woman who so lovingly created these precious works of art.

AN ART CAREER WAS LEE'S DESTINY

Collectors who cherish Lee's vinyl and porcelain "babies" find it hard to believe that this gifted sculptress was self-taught except for a few classes at the Scottsdale, Arizona Artist's School. To ensure the real-life quality of her work, Lee became an avid student of anatomy, fascinated by the forensic sculpture techniques of crime and police laboratories. These anatomical studies helped bring warmth and sweetness to each doll creation, as Lee drew upon her own wonderful family life as a doting mother and grandmother.

The granddaughter of an inventor, Lee was always resourceful in developing her own techniques for sculpture and doll production. She introduced the "porcelain look" in vinyl collectibles, for example, and created the first vinyl dolls to be considered truly collectible. Her "BABY SKIN"™ vinyl dolls are so life-like that it seems the dolls almost breathe. Yet she was characteristically modest about her personal creative process.

"I just start with a ball of clay, and it just kind of happens," Lee said of her sculptural method. "I refer to photos quite extensively. I specialize in babies, from birth to one year. I do some toddlers and adults. But the most challenging and rewarding work is to create newborns properly. They're hard to sculpt because the anatomy is so different. Quite often, when you start to do babies, they look too old, because you're not disciplined to work in an infant structure. It takes a lot of discipline to make the doll look younger."

FROM HOME-BASED DOLL ARTIST TO SMALL BUSINESS PERSON OF THE YEAR

When Lee founded her company in 1980, her plan was to work from home and create only as many dolls as she could produce herself. But gift and doll shop owners had other ideas. Soon they placed so many orders for Middleton dolls that Lee had to create a "cottage industry," with family members and other helpers working from their homes. Eventually, Lee spearheaded the construction of a 34,000-square-foot manufacturing facility with a beautiful pastel "gingerbread" facade that looks for all the world like a larger-than-life doll house. With the growth of her factory, Lee became a major employer in her town of Belpre, Ohio, which led to one of her proudest achievements: being named Small Business Person of the Year for the State of Ohio in 1989.

Even as her company expanded, Lee Middleton Urick remained adamant that each doll should bear the special, personal touches that set her creations apart. Every doll leaves the factory with its own tiny Bible tucked inside, which Lee considered an extension of her Christian values and "giving credit where credit is due." That credit extended even to her long list of honors including multiple "Doll of the Year" (DOTY) and "Dolls of Excellence" nominations and awards. As Lee explained, "I'm just a re-creator. There is only one Creator."

MIDDLETON'S *MY OWN BABY* WINS UNPRECEDENTED UL SAFETY CLASSIFICATION

Lee's innovative spirit is exemplified in one of her firm's most unique achievements: earning the only Underwriters Laboratory classification ever granted to a doll. For more than a century, Americans have looked to Underwriters Laboratories (UL) for recommendations on the safest and most reliable products available. Thus in this era of increasing concern about the safety of children's toys, Middleton Dolls picked UL for its safety testing of the

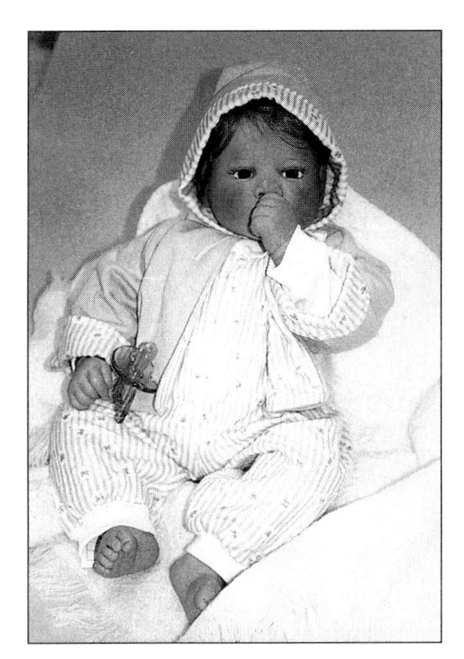

Lee Middleton's "Honey Love," is available in many different versions: awake or asleep, boy or girl, light skin or dark skin. All are adorable!

My Own Baby line.

Middleton Director of Marketing Mark Putinski explains that UL "was the best known testing laboratory. We felt that if we were going to have this doll tested, we should go for the best – the most widely recognized. Everyone recognizes UL."

It made sense for Middleton to have *My Own Baby* tested because of the dolls' very young admirers. As Putinski notes, "These are a little girl's first 'real dolls,' yet they're also an original work of art. There are several basic differences between our 'adult' collectors' dolls and the *My Own Baby* versions. These dolls are not signed and numbered, but they're the same size and have all the same top-quality components. The next major difference is the outfit. The *My Own Baby* dolls have a very simple rib-knit one-piece outfit and a simple knit cap. Our collectible line has a fancier outfit, more detail and intricacy – but these unadorned outfits are really more appropriate for 'play dolls.' All of our other dolls have real eyelashes, while this line does not. This is a positive factor, because if it is a doll for children to handle and play with, this prevents the child from pulling the eyelashes out."

UL was so convinced of the safety of *My Own Baby* that the firm pronounced it safe for all ages. Putinski says, however, that "We label our dolls for children three and up, because of the weight. A fully assembled doll weighs approximately 3-1/2 pounds. It's not that it's unsafe, but it wouldn't be practical for a child under age three to carry this doll around." The *My Own Baby* dolls are crafted of vinyl, are 19" in length, and are available at the suggested issue price of $120.

MIDDLETON COLLECTORS ENJOY CLUB AND TOUR OPPORTUNITIES

One of Lee's last projects before her death was the development of Lee's Doll Family, her own collector's club. She eagerly looked forward to introducing the club, both to her retailers and collectors nationwide. Now, in her memory, Lee Middleton Originals Dolls, Inc. has unveiled Lee's Doll Family, a living legacy honoring Lee's superb artistry and many contributions to the doll industry.

Members of this close-knit group will have the exclusive opportunity to acquire a marvelous newborn baby doll created by Lee as her debut club offering. The baby's name is "Blessed Homecoming," and she is an angelic, sleeping little girl. Her elegant layette includes a pretty pink nursery outfit and a pale pink dress, bonnet and bunting all trimmed in white eyelet lace and mint green satin bows. The baby wears a hospital wrist bracelet bearing her individual number within the edition, and she comes complete with a birth certificate so each collector can name her as their very own. In addition to the traditional Middleton Bible, "Blessed Homecoming" comes with her own Memory Book for recording those wonderful "firsts" in a baby's life.

Charter members of Lee's Doll Family will be invited to own this elegantly dressed baby doll, "Blessed Homecoming."

"Rosebud" and "Buddy" star in Middleton's* Kewpie® *collection.

Other club benefits include: a thank-you gift, the 3-1/2" praying girl figurine titled "God Bless You;" a subscription to the club's quarterly newsletter; an official binder for club materials, and an official membership card. In addition, one lucky member will win a drawing for an expense-paid trip for two to the Lee Middleton Doll House in Ohio.

THOUSANDS TOUR LEE MIDDLETON DOLL FACTORY

Thousands of people visit the Middleton facility each year to see how the dolls are made, and visit the company store. The realistic good looks of Lee's creations inspired a unique feature of the popular Middleton Doll company tours. Visitors find a nursery within the factory, just like the ones for newborns in hospitals. "Nurses" assist the visitors as they dress

Linda Henry created the first-ever* My Own Baby-Bear, *"Newborn Taylor" for Middleton Dolls.

in visiting gowns and choose their babies for "adoption." Official adoption certificates and photos of the happy occasion make a visit to the Middleton facility truly unforgettable!

NEW PRODUCTS CONTINUE THE MIDDLETON TRADITION

Sadly, Lee Middleton Urick is gone – but her spirit lives on in the creativity of the team that continues to cultivate her tradition of quality and innovation. The company will continue offering new designs of Lee's original sculptures. In addition, new artists will be hired to sculpt new faces for the growing doll line. What's more, Middleton has plans to expand its line to include selected licensed products and original creations from artists Lee herself admired and loved.

Middleton's *Kewpies®* capture the all-American charm of Rose O'Neill's original turn-of-the-century drawings for *Woman's Home Companion* magazine. Now they've debuted in the form of highly collectible, vinyl *Kewpie* character dolls called "Rosebud," "Buddy," "Almost Angelic," and "Breezy." All are crafted from the original molds so they will be identical to the *Kewpies* that people have known and loved for years.

One of Lee Middleton's closest artist friends, Linda Henry, proudly introduces "Newborn Taylor" as Middleton's first-ever *My Own Baby-Bear.* In one of Lee's last decisions before her death, she devoted a full page in the Middleton 1997 catalog to "Newborn Taylor" – shown with his teddy bear "arm" around Lee's own "First Born" (Awake Girl) doll. "Taylor" is a sweet little girl bear who can wear newborn-size clothes. At 18" in height, dressed in pink, she is weighted, jointed and poseable, just like the "human" Middleton babies.

Even today, Lee's spirit continues at Middleton Dolls. "Lee left us a legacy of beauty and quality which is unparalleled in the doll business," says Jim Armour, chief operating officer of the company. "We will use this legacy as the foundation upon which to build a living memorial to the talent, creativity and spirit of our founder, Lee Middleton Urick."

CLUB

LEE'S DOLL FAMILY
1301 Washington Boulevard
Belpre, OH 45714
(800) 238-2225

Annual Dues: $35.00
Club Year: Anniversary of Sign-Up Date

BENEFITS:
- Members-Only Exclusive Doll
- Membership Gift: 3-1/2" Sculpted Bust
- Membership Card
- Quarterly Newsletter
- Binder with Logo for Storing Newsletters

TO LEARN MORE:

LEE MIDDLETON ORIGINAL DOLLS, INC.
1301 WASHINGTON BLVD.
BELPRE, OH 45714
(614) 423-1717
FAX: (614) 423-5983

A Tradition of Fine Art in China and Collectibles

The history of Lenox Collections is the dream of Walter Scott Lenox, who devoted his life to firmly establishing an American ceramic art industry – one that would be unparalleled around the world.

Born in Trenton, New Jersey, in 1859, Lenox was only a schoolboy when the sight of the potter's wheel spurred his interest and awakened his artistic talents. He was fascinated by the transformation of dull clay into beautiful shapes that seemed to come to life. Daily he passed a little pottery on his way to and from school. The experience molded his own convictions and desire to pursue a career as a potter.

He first served as an apprentice and then became art director at a local factory. But Walter Scott Lenox saw little artistic creativity in the American ceramic products of his time. Design was crude and expression exaggerated. Lenox, dreaming of better things and yearning to satisfy his aspirations, established his own factory in 1889. No one dreamed that an American factory could turn out china of the quality of the famed manufacturers in Europe – no one except Walter Scott Lenox.

The* Barefoot Blessings *collection shares moments in a child's life that everyone can remember. "Sharing Secrets" is sculpted in ivory china with a soft bisque finish to show the girl's sweet smile.

Through ups and downs, nothing could stir him from his resolution to make the best china. In 1895, he was struck with blindness and paralysis, which only strengthened his determination and served to make him try even harder. Despite his crippled state, he went to the plant every day and attended to every part of the business.

Many early Lenox products were ornamental pieces and objects of art. But with the successful experimentation in dinnerware, a new era began. The first complete service was displayed by Tiffany and Company, and Lenox China services are now found in homes around the world. In 1917, the first American-made china service to grace The White House was composed of 1,700 pieces of Lenox. This was used continuously until 1932 when Franklin D. Roosevelt ordered a new service. This service was replaced by Harry S. Truman, and in 1981 Ronald Reagan purchased the fourth Lenox China White House service. Lenox eventually realized his dream of becoming the master potter of America and establishing the artistic prestige of this country's china industry. Today, Lenox Collections continues its founder's ideals with a relentless pursuit of excellence in quality, design and service.

TIMELESS APPEAL FOUND IN *LENOX CLASSICS*

The newest line of collectibles, known as *Lenox Classics*, utilizes the same design elements that Walter Scott Lenox used at the turn-of-the-century: the combination of ivory china with gold accents.

Using the most sought-after themes in art and nature, *Lenox Classics* includes several unique collections featuring both china and crystal figurines in open and limited edition pieces. All the ivory china pieces are special because they combine bisque and glazed finishes. The crystal figurines combine clear and frosted finishes. Discriminating collectors will find a timeless appeal and an artistry to cherish, whether their passion is cherubs, animals or simply Lenox.

In a truly unique marriage of two collecting traditions, each *Lcnox Classics* figurine comes packaged in its own decorative collectible tin. These tins are reminiscent of the decorative package tins from the Victorian age. They will also protect the *Lenox Classics* pieces for generations and enhance the collectibility of the pieces. The tins are even a collectible in their own right. Each *Lenox Classics* subject also comes with a Certificate of Authenticity.

COLLECTIONS CHARM WITH CHILD-LIKE WONDER

Lenox Classics features several collections. Cherubs are a classic artistic subject and have been represented in art forms since the Renaissance. Currently they are experiencing a resurgence in popularity, and the Lenox design team is proud to present a stunning collection of cherubs. Inspired by Victorian and angelic themes, the *Little Graces* series includes cherubs in

Angels have come down to earth in the* Little Graces *collection. "Guidance" shows the way with her candle in this figurine, which is limited to 5,000 hand-numbered pieces.

ivory china. They feature dazzling glazed togas and unglazed, painted hands, feet and faces. Their serene expressions seem to give comfort. Beautiful, airy filigree gold-plated wings make them appear to be gently floating. Each edition in the *Little Graces* series is limited to 5,000 pieces and is hand-numbered. Recent introductions include "Love," "Innocence," "Happiness," "Harmony" and "Little Surprise."

Nowhere are the qualities of innocence and purity more evident than in the faces of children. Their adorable faces mirror every precious emotion. With meticulous care, Lenox designers have created *Barefoot Blessings* – adorable children sculpted in ivory china to capture purity and beauty. With their sweet smiles and luminous eyes, *Barefoot Blessings* are humbly dressed with tiny bare feet peeking out from under their clothes. Each child features an ivory china body with bisque or unglazed hands, feet and face. This soft bisque finish preserves the intricate details of their hand-painted expressions and eyes. Each figurine reflects a moment in a child's life that every mom, dad and grandparent can remember, including "Morning Chores," "Gone Fishing," "With This Kiss" and "Just Like Mommy."

HOLIDAY COLLECTIBLES BRING JOY

For those with a passion for Christmas collectibles, *Away in a Manger* is on everyone's wish list. The collection includes Mary, Joseph, Baby Jesus, angels and wise men as an open edition Nativity scene. Their hand-painted bisque faces contemplate the miracle of the Baby Jesus. Beautiful ivory china bodies are accented in gold. *Away in a Manager* may inspire many to create their own family holiday tradition.

To further celebrate the holidays, *Lenox Classics* introduces a limited edition Santa. For 1997, "Santa's Joy" brings more than gifts to make the season bright. The ivory china Santa is accented with gold and has a little elf sitting atop his sack of toys, which is a separate ornament. "Santa's Joy" is first in a series and limited to 2,500 pieces.

A limited edition angel also starts a new tradition. "Guardian of the Stars" portrays an angel and cherub holding golden stars. The figurine, which is first in a series of angels, is also limited to 2,500 pieces and sequentially hand-numbered.

Finishing Touches is a collection of busy elves helping Santa prepare on the night before Christmas. The open edition figurines catch the elves in action from "Checking the List" to "Loading the Sleigh," and "Painting Stripes" to "Nap Time."

CRYSTAL SHINES WITH BEAUTY

A stunning crystal collection of domestic and wild animals is also included in *Lenox Classics*. These sculptures are a remarkable tribute to nature's creatures great and small. Each is formed in brilliant full-lead crystal for maximum brilliance and captures the true essence of the animals, including cats, elephants, wolves, bunnies, eagles and dolphins.

Paired groupings feature one animal in frosted crystal and the other as a clear figurine – creating a unique aspect to the collection. Many of the other pieces also feature selected frosted areas to define and add texture to the sculpture. The names of the figurines also give them individual personalities. There's the elephant pair "Peanuts and Popcorn," the cats "Preen and Serene" and the bunnies "Satin and Silk." The *Lenox Classics Crystal Collection* consists of open editions and first editions.

This little elf is "Checking the List" to make sure Santa's sleigh is ready for the Christmas adventure. This figurine from the* Finishing Touches *collection is an open edition.

"Dolphins Journey" from the* Lenox Classics Crystal Collection *captures a pair of nature's creatures in full-lead crystal. The figurine is an open edition.

THE LENOX PLEDGE OF EXCELLENCE

From the company's beginning, Walter Scott Lenox stopped at nothing to locate the most gifted craftsmen and to create the best works of art. Lenox Collections takes pride in offering works of uncompromisingly high standards of quality, crafted with care and dedication by skilled artisans. The Lenox goal, in every case, is to meet the highest expectations of artistry and fine workmanship. Satisfaction is also at the heart of the company's mission.

Walter Scott Lenox died in 1920 at the age of 60. But his dream lives on in the work of today's talented Lenox artists, designers and craftsmen. He always hoped that his company's remarkable works of art would be cherished, treasured and enjoyed by generations of collectors across America and around the world.

TO LEARN MORE:

LENOX COLLECTIONS
900 WHEELER WAY
LANGHORNE, PA 19047
(800) 63-LENOX
FAX: (215) 741-6337
URL: http://www.lenoxcollections.com

The World's Most Definitive Cottages

Authenticity, Detail, Quality, Color, Collectibility...these are the five outstanding hallmarks that characterize each work of art from David J. Tate's Lilliput Lane Limited. Tate and his family launched the firm in 1982 from a quaint old barn in Cumbria, England, as their "corporate home." The original seven team members created the first Lilliput Lane range of 14 models – a modest beginning for a staff that now has grown to more than 500 members working in studios in Penrith, Workington and Carlisle.

From left, the "Haberdashery," "Tailor" and "Apothecary" represent three of the newest additions to Lilliput Lane's **Victorian Shops** ***collection.***

An open friendliness surrounds the whole of Lilliput Lane, with managers and staff who enjoy working in an environment based on care, merit and achievement. Their inspiration comes now, as it did at the beginning more than 15 years ago, from David Tate's skills as a sculptor and master mold maker. It also springs from Tate's lifelong love of British vernacular architecture – cottages typical to a particular region.

EXPANDING MARKETS AND COVETED AWARDS

By the company's fifth anniversary in 1987, Lilliput Lane had received the "Cumbria County Export Award," and had been a finalist twice in the Confederation of British Industry (CBI) "Company of the Year" Award. In the New Year's Honors of 1988, David Tate was awarded the M.B.E., Member of the Order of the British Empire, in recognition of his achievements. He received this honor from Queen Elizabeth during a ceremony at Buckingham Palace.

By mid-1988, Lilliput Lane cottages could be bought throughout the world – in Australia, New Zealand, Canada, the United States, and many European countries. Such success brought Lilliput Lane another honor in 1988: the "Queen's Award for Export and Achievement."

From its start, Lilliput Lane has been committed to training its employees, and this was recognized in November 1989 when the firm earned, from over 1,300 nominees, the prestigious "National Training Award." In November 1993, Lilliput Group plc, the parent company of Lilliput Lane Limited, was floated on the London Stock Exchange, as a publicly quoted company. As of October 1994, Lilliput Group plc was acquired by Stanhome Inc. on behalf of its U.S. subsidiary, Enesco Corporation.

With products now widely available in over 40 countries, Lilliput Lane attributes its phenomenal growth and success to the care and attention it gives to everything it does. From the tiniest tile or leaf in a sculpture, to the detailed business plans for growth, attention to detail is the creed of Lilliput Lane. Lilliput Lane's mission is to continually improve its products and services to meet collector aspirations and customer needs. Lilliput Lane cares about its image in the giftware and collectibles market, that it meets the expectations of collectors and retailers alike, and that it shares a sense of pride in its work and achievement.

THE HALLMARKS OF LILLIPUT LANE

Lilliput Lane consistently produces what many believe to be the world's most definitive cottage sculptures. Every piece bears five outstanding hallmarks.

These are:

AUTHENTICITY – Each Lilliput Lane cottage accurately captures the essence of picturesque and vernacular architecture. This type of construction dates from the times when early house builders had to rely on whatever material was available. As a result, distinctive styles of architecture evolved, each epitomizing a region's individual character.

DETAIL – The craftspeople of Lilliput Lane are famous for producing sculptures of remarkably fine detail. Research is thorough, involving months of dedicated study. With diligent attention, each stone, cobble, and roof tile is painstakingly laid by hand. Highly skilled artists hand-paint each model to produce a magnificent work of art that preserves a piece of history.

QUALITY – Lilliput Lane is uncompromising in its search for excellence. Exhaustive research and development constantly improve techniques and materials. With quality as an essential priority, a highly trained and dedicated team ensures that only perfect sculptures ever leave the studios. Each sculpture is handcrafted in England.

COLOR – Rich, brilliant, permanent colors are hand-painted by highly skilled, trained artisans.

COLLECTIBILITY – Lilliput Lane offers a wealth of choice to the collector. Within the Lilliput Lane range, many sub-collections exist, making it possible to assemble a complete collection without the need to track down the entire range. Lilliput Lane has striven for and

Dusted with snow for holiday time, Lilliput Lane's Christmas Special "Christmas Party" (left) carries an issue price of $150, while the Christmas Ornament, "Evergreens," sells for $30.00.

maintains its position as the world's leading producer of miniature cottages.

A PAINSTAKING PROCESS FROM START TO FINISH

The most important decision in the entire creative process of developing a Lilliput Lane cottage comes as part of the research phase. A suitable region and price point are selected, and then an appropriate cottage is photographed and researched. From two-dimensional drawings, the cottage first takes its three-dimensional shape in wax. Nearly 200 sculpting tools have been devised for the intricate tasks of sculpting! Every roof tile is cut out of thin sheets of wax and placed onto the roof, one by one – with thousands of tiles needed for some pieces.

Tooling and molding come next – a process that requires up to three months and involves over 40 different processes. Next, each piece is hand-cast in amorphite, a type of gypsum rock mined in the United Kingdom. While still "green" (not completely hardened), the casts are "fettled," or made good through hand detailing, then dipped in one or more of eight different substances, representing the different stone colors throughout the United Kingdom.

After the pieces are dry, they move to the painting studio, where each cottage is painted from start to finish by one of 300 Lilliput Lane painters. Over 72 permanent, waterproof paints are used. When completed, the cottages are carefully packed to ensure that collectors all over the world receive their pieces in perfect condition.

THE LILLIPUT LANE COLLECTORS' CLUB

In response to many requests, The Lilliput Lane Collectors' Club was formed in 1986, with branches throughout the world. Benefits include an exclusive members-only Collectors' Cottage, a complimentary cottage on joining, regular issues of the Club's quarterly magazine, *Gulliver's World*, and many more advantages such as special events and exclusive studio tours. U.S. Club fees are $40.00 per year.

The 1997/98 Club Special Edition is the 4" "Hampton Manor." Dating from the 14th century, "Hampton Manor" is based upon the graceful, moated manor house at Lower Brockhampton. On this model, the lady of the house is relaxing in the garden with her book. Meanwhile, to the rear, hens are investigating some discarded barrels and pots. "Hampton Manor" is reached by a detached timbered gatehouse called "Hampton Moat," which is the 2-1/2" 1997/98 Club Symbol of Membership.

NEW ISSUES FROM DAVID TATE AND RAY DAY

Among the most intriguing new introductions from Lilliput Lane are items from David Tate's *Victorian Shops* and *Christmas collections*, and Ray Day's *American Landmarks* and *Coca Cola Country* series.

It was during the 1960s that David

"Hampton Manor" (left) is the 1997/98 Club Special Edition exclusively for members of the Lilliput Lane Collectors' Club. "Hampton Moat" is the 1997/98 Club Symbol of Membership

***Ray Day created these handsome works of art for Lilliput Lane. From left, they are: "Oh By Gosh, By Golly" from the* Coca Cola Country *collection; "Let Heaven and Nature Sing" from the* American Landmarks *collection; and "To Grandmother's House We Go," also from* American Landmarks.**

Tate first started drawing and painting the thatched cottages of the English countryside. Enjoying the creative process, Tate knew there was a chance to develop cottage sculptures full of the sunshine and beauty of England. His passion is clear when he talks of the cottages he loves and his captivation with the landscape itself.

David Tate's vision shines through in the six initial introductions for his *Victorian Shops* collection, including the "Book Shop," "Horologist," "Pawnbroker," "Apothecary," "Haberdashery," and "Tailor." Each model includes a wealth of detail, and portrays a traditional business that would have been found in many an English town a hundred years ago. Grouped together, the *Victorian Shops* look just like the real thing.

New for Christmas 1997 were Lilliput Lane's "Christmas Party" special edition cottage and the charming ornament, "Evergreens." The cottage depicts a Victorian lodge in Derbyshire, while the ornament is based on a building from the famous Shambles in York.

At the invitation of Lilliput Lane, Ray Day has been sculpting the *American Landmarks* collection since 1989. As creative director for Lilliput Lane USA, Day's years of research provided the basis for designing and creating a full range of American architectural collectibles. Each completed wax sculpture is sent to Lilliput Lane in the U.K. for molding, casting and painting. The finished miniatures, based on actual locations, are distributed in the United States through Enesco Home Gallery. Day's sculpting talent encompasses a wide range of architectural designs — from rural structures to elegant Victorian homes. His newest collection, *Coca Cola Country*, brims with exquisite detail and hometown warmth.

The success of Lilliput Lane is attributable in no small part to David Tate's determination, tenacity and sheer energy. Today, Tate is at the pinnacle of his career, overseeing and training a superb team of sculptors and artists at Lilliput Lane. With Tate's inspiration, the Lilliput Lane team continues to research and develop new systems and designs to increase the company's competitive edge in the worldwide collectible market.

CLUB

LILLIPUT LANE COLLECTORS' CLUB
P.O. Box 498
Itasca, IL 60143-0498
(630) 875-5382

Annual Dues:
$40.00; $65.00 for 2 Years (U.S)
$65.00; $112.00 for 2 Years (Canada)
Club Year: May 1 - April 30
Collector's Year — Anniversary of Sign-Up Date

BENEFITS:

- Membership Gift Cottage
- Voucher to Reserve Members-Only Redemption Piece
- Quarterly Magazine, *Gulliver's World*
- Membership Card
- Full Range Cottage Catalog
- Travel Opportunities to Tour the Lilliput Lane Studios in Penrith, England
- Painter's Demonstrations & "Paint Your Own" Cottage Events

TOUR

LILLIPUT LANE STUDIOS TOUR
Skirsgill
Penrith, Cumbria, England CA11 0DP
01144-1768-212700

Admission: Free to Club Members
Hours:
Monday - Thursday: 9:30, a.m. - 2:15 p.m.;
Friday: 9:30 a.m.- 12:30 p.m.

Visit the Club Team in the full-size actual replica of "Honeysuckle Cottage."

TO LEARN MORE:

LILLIPUT LANE/ENESCO HOME GALLERY
P.O. BOX 498
ITASCA, IL 60143-0498
(630) 875-5382
FAX: (630) 875-5348
URL: http://www.enesco.com

Look for "Little Gem" on the Paw Pad!

"If the bear does not have 'Little Gem' written on its paw pad, then it's not a Little Gem!" asserts Chu-Ming (Jamie) Wu with a smile. The Taiwanese native has made teddy bears his life – with award-winning results -- since he left his homeland in 1983 to settle in Southeast Florida. Today, Wu counts teddy bear luminaries Deb Canham, Lisa Lloyd, Carol Stewart, Bev White, Linda Spiegel and Linda Mullins among his "house designers," and he creates many a Little Gem teddy himself. Indeed, Wu now reigns over his own "teddy bear empire," selling more than 57,000 bears per year!

This miniature "Jamie Jr." bear replicates the one-of-a-kind teddy bear by Chu-Ming (Jamie) Wu that recently sold for $17,000 at auction.

Sixteen years ago, Wu fled Taiwan to try to escape the deep grief he felt after his wife's death from leukemia. Searching for solace, he thought about the kind of atmosphere he and his children would enjoy most. Sunshine and fishing were high on the list, and thus Florida became the Wu's new home.

At first, the transition was difficult. Wu spoke only a few words of English, and although he had been a Ford Motor Company sales manager in Taiwan, he considered himself lucky to acquire an American job as a landscaper at $5.00 an hour. For fun and to help feed his family, Wu pursued his favorite hobby of fishing. As luck would have it, he discovered a bait and tackle store owned by Tom and Carol Stewart. One day when Wu entered the store, he found Carol working on one of her charming miniature teddy bears.

A NATURAL TALENT FOR TEDDIES

As Patrick Lee reported in a recent issue of *Teddy Bear Review*, Stewart vividly recalls the encounter. "He seemed fascinated, insisting I teach him how," says Stewart. "My thought was, 'Yeah, right!'" She couldn't imagine that this strapping fisherman would really want to spend his time creating and clothing tiny teddy bears. "But I taught him, and he took to it like a duck to water!"

While Wu loved making teddy bears right from the start, it didn't necessarily come easily to him. It took him 27 evenings to make his first teddy bear, but when it was complete, Wu was hooked! It's hard for him to determine exactly why making bears appeals to him so much. Wu recalls many happy hours spent with his grandfather back in Taiwan, where he learned to carve miniature animals from wood as a child. His grandfather also instilled determination and drive in young Chu-Ming Wu, telling the youngster, "If you are interested in something, stay with it!"

When Wu had a small grouping of adorable bears made from upholstery cloth, Stewart christened them the "Little Gems," and the name stuck. While Wu's firm is formally known as Akira Trading Company, his creations are called Little Gem Teddy Bears.

FROM AVOCATION TO CAREER

During the 1980s, Wu perfected his talents through experimentation and hard work. At the time, he made individual miniature teddies by hand and sold them for $200 or more. Because he could make such a limited number, it was not possible for him to support his family on the teddy bear business alone. While the teddies were his true love, he sold and installed satellite dishes for extra money.

Wu realized that if he could have his original designs crafted in quantity, he could make bears that more collectors could afford – and have sufficient volume to make a living in the bargain. In 1989, he traveled to China to personally train workers in a "cottage industry" setting so that they could craft his bears according to his particular standards.

Wu's first major success occurred in 1993 when he exhibited his Little Gems at a show in England. When show attendees saw the paw pads reading, "Made with 617 loving stitches," they purchased the wonderfully detailed bears in droves. Wu was amazed when he counted the proceeds: "In two days, we sold enough bears to make $4,000!"

That English show had even more significance for Wu in that the renowned teddy bear maker Deb Canham occupied the booth next to his. Deb recalls the moment very clearly. She had been in a car accident and was "In plaster from my fingers to shoulder, and on strong pain killers. Jamie spoke hardly a word of English. We communicated in sign language. He asked me to design for him, and I sent him some of my bears but doubted he could maintain the quality. When I opened the box he sent back, I thought he had returned my own samples, instead of his copies! The quality was that high."

TWO TEDDY BEAR MASTERS MEET

Another happy meeting for Wu was his introduction to a manufacturer's representative named Tommy Thompson. Thompson remembers, "He told me he made bears, but I dismissed it. I assumed he produced big cheap bears. Some time later, I saw some wonderful miniature bears and found out they were Jamie's! I started representing him in August of 1993. I took his bears to Toy Fair in 1994, and that's when he went national."

"Jenny and Delia," designed by Deb Canham for Little Gem Teddy Bears, won a Golden Teddy Award in 1998.

in price from about $15.00 to $70.00. All dressed bears and special edition bears are numbered and signed. Wu does not plan to introduce any large editions, preferring to add new designs to his line in January and July and sell them in smaller numbers per design. Little Gem does make some exclusive editions for dealers as well, with minimum editions of 500.

Testimonials from dealers and collectors alike show how beloved the Little Gems have become in recent years. They compliment Wu on his designs, execution, variety of styles, affordability of products, creativity, customer service and much more. What's more, as collectors "downsize" to smaller homes, they find themselves drawn to miniature works like Wu's. They can still own and exhibit a variety of pieces, even in limited space.

As Debbye Jackson of Decatur, Illinois, describes, "I have over 20 Little Gems, and I display them in old cups and saucers or with a tool box. I have a smaller home, and this size suits me well. Jamie's dedication shows in the quality of his work."

The limited edition "Carrot Top" rabbit, designed by Deb Canham, features a large red heart on his chest and a hat that looks like three carrots.

Today, Wu's daughter, Jenny, manages the Akira Trading office in Miami, Florida. Originals done by Wu and his designer friends are produced in China, then distributed through a team of sales representatives to more than 1,500 stores nationwide. Wu is delighted to provide an excellent way of making a living for his "cottage industry" artists in China. As he notes, "Over 350 families in seven villages make my bears. The average age of our workers is 32, mostly mothers who want to stay home with their children. Workers in one village will make only arms and legs, in another, only heads. Another will do only assembly. I have one supervisor for every ten workers. I interview every worker myself for quality!"

A FAMILY-ORIENTED BUSINESS FLOURISHES IN MIAMI AND CHINA

When Wu makes personal appearances, he often brings a few special bears that he sells only on such occasions. They cost about $100 each, while the regular run of 1-1/2" to 3" bears range

Collectors and dealers will recognize Jamie Wu at shows because of his trademark attire – a blue vest adorned with about a dozen of his tiny bears. His

Deb Canham designed the adorable "Jingles" bear for Little Gem. His retail price is $40.00.

"Plum" is dressed in a lavender outfit trimmed with silver beads. Designed by Deb Canham, the bear is limited to an edition of 2,000.

enthusiasm for all aspects of life is apparent to his friends and collaborators. As artist Carol Stewart says, "Jamie is very energetic and rambunctious, very personable, and motivated by a genuine love for what he's doing. He's very reputable." Deb Canham agrees, noting, "He is such an honorable person, one of the world's nice guys!" Tommy Thompson chimes in admiringly, "If you could bottle Jamie's personality, you could sell it!"

WU'S PERSONALITY SHINES THROUGH

A natural competitor who earned archery championships in international competition as a youth in Taiwan, Wu is thrilled by the awards and nominations his Little Gem bears have received in recent years. These include Golden Teddy Awards in 1996, 1997 and 1998, and a TOBY nomination in 1998. He is gratified to report that a one-of-a-kind piece he made for the Disney Doll and Bear Convention in 1997 sold at auction for $17,000.

Because Wu is an archer, it may come as no surprise that his company name "Akira" means "rising star" in Chinese. As he explains, "When I was an archery sportsman, I aimed for the target. Now the Teddy Bear is my target. Before, I used an arrow. Now I use a needle!"

Collectors' Information Bureau thanks Teddy Bear Review *and Patrick Lee, author of "Shrunken Treasures" from that publication's July/August 1997 issue, for substantial contributions to this article.*

Designed by Lisa Lloyd, charming "Lester" is elaborately dressed as a jester and has a retail price of $40.00.

TO LEARN MORE:

AKIRA TRADING CO
LITTLE GEM TEDDY BEARS
6040 NW 84TH AVENUE
MIAMI, FL 33166
(305) 639-9801
FAX: (305) 639-9802

Art in Fine Porcelain

The name Lladró brings to mind an internationally renowned collection of porcelain figurines handcrafted in Spain. Few today could imagine that a porcelain company of such prestige would have such humble beginnings. However, Lladró porcelain was born from the perseverance, imagination and determination of three ambitious brothers – Juan, Jose and Vicente Lladró.

In 1951, drawing on meager resources, the Lladró brothers built their first kiln. A moruno (Moorish-style) brick structure shaped like a beehive and measuring one meter high, the kiln was built in their parents' back yard. They began experimenting with different glazing and firing techniques, and used the kiln to create their first diminutive flowers for which Lladró is still known today.

The Lladró brothers soon built a larger furnace which was able to attain high temperatures and vitrify porcelain. They quickly found that the demand for their artwork exceeded what they alone could produce. While continuing to experiment in other areas, Juan, Jose and Vicente hired and trained friends from the neighborhood to be their first workers.

As their business grew, the Lladró brothers heard of a kiln in Almacera left unfinished because of defects in construction. The enterprising young men rented the premises, renovated the kiln, and formed the foundation for what would one day come to be called Porcelain City.

Today, Lladró has become one of the leading producers of fine porcelain in the world. Together with their children, who will one day become owners and directors of Lladró, the brothers have named a Lladró Family Council. The board currently consists of Rosa Marie Lladró, daughter of Jose, Rosa Lladró, daughter of Juan, and Juan Vicente Lladró, son of Vicente. Working closely with their fathers, each of the children have contributed greatly to the recent growth of the company and are certain to carry on Lladró's tradition of excellence with capable hands.

The first in a series of four "seasonal sisters" to be introduced each year, "Spring Flirtation" embodies all of the joy and hope of the season.

After nearly 50 years, Lladró's studies in color, form and posture continue to represent a never-ending foundation of invention, a constant merging of technical expertise and supreme artistry. Lladró truly is "Art in Fine Porcelain."

The Lladró trademark color palette is one of the most instantly recognizable in the world. Soft pastel shades of blue, cream, gray, and brown form a palette of well over 5,000 colors! These delicate hues decorate the figurines that form the *Lladró Core Collection.*

The *Lladró Core Collection* is the collection for which Lladró is best known. These elegant and charming figurines are displayed and collected the world over. Many figurines in the *Core Collection* are available in a choice of finishes: glazed, or matte, which is also often called bisque. The glazed finish is the high-gloss finish found on most *Core Collection* figurines. Matte is often found as an alternative to the glazed finish and provides a softer, warmer feel to the figurine.

All Lladró figurines begin life in the same place – the drawing board. Sketches are used to study the position, movement and size of the porcelain. Once the sketch is approved, a figurine is molded in clay and carefully divided into numerous parts to produce special molds.

LLADRÓ CORE COLLECTION ATTRACTS WORLD-WIDE ATTENTION

These molds are filled with porcelain paste to create the individual pieces from which the figurine is carefully assembled. The figurines are then painstakingly hand-painted by skilled artisans. Great care must be taken to ensure that all figurines achieve the same consistency of color. However, as with any hand-made product, slight variations serve to make each figurine unique.

Before firing, the painted figurine is virtually unrecognizable as compared to the finished product. Unfired figurines are up to 20% larger than their final size, due to shrinkage during the firing process. They are also covered in a white glaze, which crystallizes and

The endearing figurine of "Gabriela" from the* Gres Collection *features warm, expressive colors with a distinctive finish.

becomes clear during firing.

Figurines are fired for hours at extremely high temperatures in scientifically-controlled kilns. After firing, the figurines are allowed to cool and are meticulously inspected for any defects. After passing these rigorous tests, the finished figurine is on its way to becoming an elegant part of a porcelain connoisseur's collection.

LLADRÓ GRES COLLECTION CELEBRATES THE VIBRANT SPIRIT OF SPAIN

In 1971, Lladró introduced a new type of porcelain to the world known as *Gres*. The *Gres Collection* from Lladró combines warm, expressive colors with a distinctive finish that complements any home decor. *Gres* possesses all the earth tones of the Spanish countryside – mellow colors from the plains of Castile and the sandstone cliffs of Aragon. Sun-drenched shades reflective of Costa del Sol and vivid contrasts of Andalucia are evident. The vibrant spirit of Spain comes to life in this rich, colorful porcelain.

Like all Lladró figurines, each *Gres* figurine is exquisitely crafted by hand. Unlike the white-based, hard paste porcelain of the *Core Collection*, *Gres* has a distinctive texture with the slightly porous quality of skin and a palette of lively colors.

The unique texture and coloration result from a secret blend of porcelain paste and enamel pigments. This special blend evolved after years of experiments directed by the Lladró brothers with the artisans and technicians in their state-of-the-art facilities at Porcelain City.

Gres gives Lladró artisans another avenue to explore in their expressive sculpting and painting. The warmth of the *Gres* palette harmonizes with Lladró's sensitive portraits of subjects renowned for their universal appeal. *Gres* also provides admirers with the popular traditional themes of Lladró in a color scheme that coordinates well with many home decors.

In fact, what is extraordinary about the *Gres Collection* is how comfortably, and graciously, it fits into any decorating style. Its warm palette enlivens the most traditional homes. Similarly, a more contemporary decor can be enriched by the classical qualities of *Gres* sculpture. Even a country casual interior can achieve a level of relaxed sophistication with the addition of Lladró *Gres*. The beauty of the *Gres Collection* is that it is at home wherever it goes.

GOYESCA COLLECTION — A NEW DEVELOPMENT IN PORCELAIN ARTISTRY

The limited edition *Goyesca Collection* created a stir of excitement and fascination from its first appearance in the Fall of 1991. The *Goyescas* represent a unique, new development in porcelain artistry. They have the appearance of a watercolor sketch miraculously realized in three dimensions.

Goyescas were born out of the restless curiosity that drives creative minds. The Lladró family's creative committee, working closely with the Lladró sculptors, began to experiment with sculpting in plasticine, instead of the traditional clay. The properties characteristic to plasticine led to an unusual quality that resembled a drawing in this ethereal airiness. The images created reminded the Lladró family of the sketches by Francisco Goya, the renowned 18th century Spanish artist. Thus, the family named the collection, *The Goyescas*.

It became the challenge of the technicians in the Lladró laboratories to devise a paste that would retain the same quality and appearance as the plasticine model. The paste, similar to that used to make Lladró porcelain flowers, provides the artists with a material that can be manipulated by hand after being removed from the mold.

Like traditional Lladró figurines, *Goyescas'* production requires an exquisite original sculpture, complex molds to recreate the original and scientific temperature control of the kiln. However, *Goyescas* demand additional, and even more individualistic, handcrafting. While the *Goyescas'* bodies are made from molds, much of the clothing and most of the accessories are individually hand-draped and formed like little pieces of fabric being nipped and tucked into shape. The extensive handcrafting is made possible by the special properties of the

***"Pensive Journey," limited to an edition size of 500 pieces, is part of Lladró's unique* Goyesca Collection.**

This charming figurine titled "Heavenly Slumber" shows the delicate hues and supreme artistry for which Lladró is known.

paste. Unlike regular porcelain paste, *Goyescas'* paste maintains a consistent malleability which will not liquify from exposure to the oils on the artist's hands, nor dry out from exposure to the air.

Liquid paints such as those that decorate the figurines in the *Core Collection* are not used in the *Goyescas.* Color pigments are mixed into the paste. The paste itself is applied with a fine point decorating brush to add on details like tiny stripes of patterns in fabrics.

Textures are achieved in a variety of ways. Frequently they are pressed in by hand or etched in. Real fabric can be pressed on the paste to create an imprint. Sometimes a design, like a polka dot, is cut out from a flat piece of porcelain of one color and is inlaid, one at a time, into a piece of another color. Special tools are used to crush, stretch, roll and cut the paste.

The *Goyescas* are fired at 1,320°C for about 12 hours and are cooled for approximately ten more, depending on their size, before emerging from the kiln as another splendid and undeniably unique creation by Lladró.

The Lladró family has built one of the most creative and exquisite houses of fine porcelain in the world. Each handcrafted figurine is a unique work of art worthy of a place of prominence in any collection. For more information on the exciting world of Lladró fine porcelain, please contact Lladró, 1 Lladró Drive, Moonachie, NJ 07074, or call toll free, (888) GIVE-LLADRO (888-448-3552).

CLUB

LLADRÓ SOCIETY
1 Lladró Drive
Moonachie, NJ 07074
(888) GIVE-LLADRO

Annual Dues: $45.00 - Renewal: $35.00
Club Year: Anniversary of Sign-Up Date

BENEFITS:

- Membership Gift
- Opportunity to Purchase Members-Only Figurine
- Quarterly Magazine, *Expressions*
- Membership Card
- Binder
- Lladró Video
- Associate Membership to the Lladró Museum in New York City
- Renewal Gift
- Figurine Research Service
- Society-sponsored Trips to Spain
- Members-Only Signing Events

MUSEUM

LLADRÓ MUSEUM AND GALLERIES
43 West 57th Street
New York, NY 10019
(212) 838-9341

Hours: Monday, Wednesday and Friday, 10 a.m.- 5:30 p.m.; Thursday, 10 a.m. - 7 p.m., and Sunday, Noon - 5 p.m.

Admission Fee: None

The Lladró Museum includes the largest collection of retired Lladró porcelains — over 1,000 pieces occupy five floors of the building.

TO LEARN MORE:

LLADRÓ USA, INC.
1 LLADRÓ DRIVE
MOONACHIE, NJ 07074
(888) 448-3552
FAX: (201) 807-1168
URL: http://www.lladro.com

Capturing the Happy Spirit of Children

For more than 125 years, the Goebel Company of Germany has reigned as one of the world's most innovative creators of figurines and other collectibles. Established in 1871 by Franz Detleff Goebel and his son, William, the company first produced slate pencils, chalk boards and marbles. Then they relocated to the heart of Germany's ceramic-producing region and began crafting figurines, dolls, vases, lamps, candy dishes and religious images.

Goebel is perhaps known best of all for its remarkable association with Sister Maria Innocentia Hummel – the gifted artist whose portraits of children have graced countless collectibles since the 1930s. Indeed, in the brief span of 12 years, Sister Maria Innocentia Hummel created a life's work of wonderful art. Then sadly, she was gone. But thanks to a remarkable and exclusive relationship between her Convent of Siessen and W. Goebel Porzellanfabrik of Germany, Sister M.I. Hummel's charming creations live on in three dimensions.

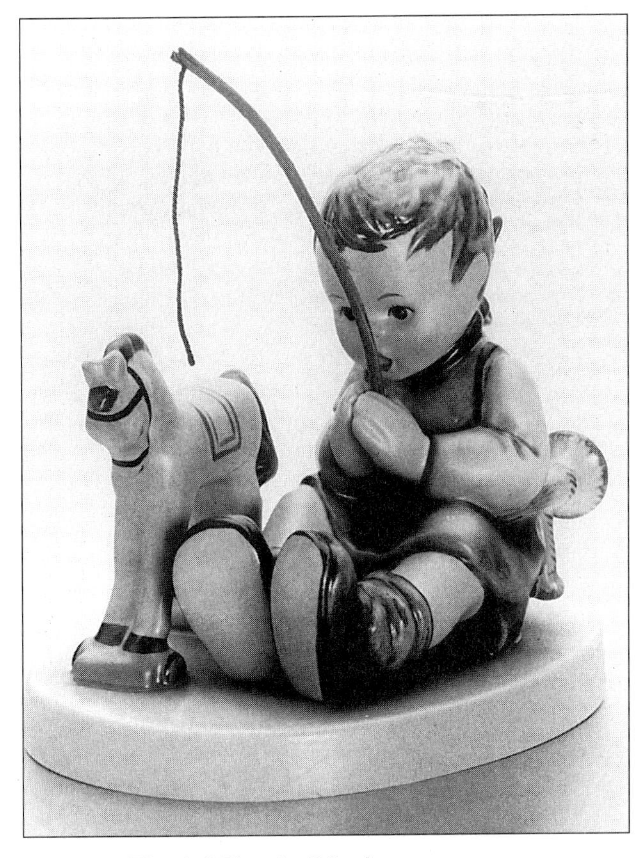

"Playful Blessing" is the M.I. Hummel Club Members' Exclusive figurine for 1997-98.

Born in Massing, Bavaria, on May 21, 1909, the future Sister Maria Innocentia, as a child, delighted in drawing and in making costumes for her dolls. During her early education at a convent school, she spent more time drawing and amusing her fellow students than studying her lessons. The sisters recognized her budding artistic talent and promoted her so that she could continue her education at the Institute of English Sisters. It was here that she was exposed for the first time to a comprehensive art department with qualified teachers who could direct and develop her talent.

At the suggestion of Sister Stephania, her mentor at the Institute, the young artist applied to and was accepted at Munich's Academy of Fine Arts. A dedicated but shy student, she was eager to learn, but reluctant to become actively involved in student life. Her friendship with two Franciscan Sisters strengthened her growing interest in pursuing a religious life. This finally outweighed the desires of many of the faculty at the Academy, who hoped that she would stay to teach after graduation.

On April 22, 1931, she entered the Siessen Convent run by the Sisters of the Third Order of Saint Francis, a teaching order. Immediately, she began teaching art to kindergarten children, often traveling by train to the many institutions served by the Convent. On August 22, 1933, she made her profession of vows. The presiding bishop named her Sister Maria Innocentia, an appropriate name for someone who was often preoccupied with the innocence and simplicity of children.

In 1933, a series of drawings done by Sister Maria Innocentia to amuse her young students gained nationwide attention at a symposium of kindergarten teachers. Publisher Ars Sacra Josef Mueller received the right to publish art card reproductions of her charming drawings.

In 1934, Franz Goebel, fourth generation owner and head of W. Goebel Porzellanfabrik, noticed her work and became interested in translating her sketches into ceramic figurines. World War I and the 1929 stock market crash had taken a toll on both Germany and Goebel, but Franz Goebel felt instinctively that Sister Maria Innocentia's enchanting works were the ideal new product introduction for the 1930s. He knew at once that a public anxious to escape from the hardships of the day would respond to the appeal of innocent young children at play, wearing quaint regional costumes.

THE WORLD DISCOVERS THE ART OF *M.I. HUMMEL*

With the encouragement and cooperation of the Convent of Siessen, Sister M.I. Hummel's pictures were translated into figurines by the staff sculptors at Goebel. They made their debut at the Leipzig Trade Fair in March of 1935 and were an instant hit. Introduced into the United States market by Marshall Field's in the Summer of 1935, *M.I. Hummel* figurines were warmly received in America, where their popularity continues to this day.

While Goebel obtained an exclusive license from Sister Maria Innocentia and the Convent to translate the motifs of her paintings into three-dimensional ceramic form, all models were sent to Sister M.I. Hummel for her approval. Even today, experts at the Convent of Siessen inspect models of all the proposed figurines, sculpted and decorated

M.I. Hummel Club members will receive "Nature's Gift" as their free renewal gift for 1997-98.

by Goebel artists, to insure that Goebel has accurately captured the unique style of the Sister's paintings.

THE HAND-CRAFTING OF *M.I. HUMMEL* FIGURINES

In a world where handcraftsmanship is disappearing, the Goebel artists continue to use a centuries-old technique of porcelain-making to create each figurine by hand. This often involves as many as 700 steps.

The first stage of figurine production begins in the sculptor's atelier, where a lump of clay is transformed by the skilled hands of the sculptor into the ultimate shape of the figurine. After the figurine is shaped, the next step is to cut the form into individual parts which will be cast and fired separately. These important cuts are designated by the sculptor whose well-trained eye can determine how many parts should be made for that particular figurine. Complicated figurines require more than 30 individual parts!

Once the figurine has been cut, the mother mold is made. After a series of positive and negative molds, the working model is ready for the liquid slip. The liquid ceramic slip is poured into the mold and allowed to settle. The excess slip is then poured off and what remains forms the outer shell of the figurine part. Assembling the parts of the figurine requires a great deal of care because the figurines are still wet. They must dry at room temperature before the first (bisque) firing. The figurine is then glazed and fired again.

Painting is one of the most captivating steps in a figurine's production. Each figurine is completely hand-painted, in many working steps, drawing from more than 2,000 colors which have been specially formulated in Goebel's laboratories. Achieving the delicate coloration is so important that the artists even make their own brushes by hand! Each figurine undergoes at least three firings, the first of which is the bisque firing at 2100°F. After it is decorated, the "decor" firing permanently fuses the paints which bring the joyous life to each figurine.

The production of each figurine is a very long and detailed process. The firings alone take many hours to complete. The production time varies according to the size and complexity of each figurine, but even a small figurine (under 6") requires several weeks of careful attention to complete.

M.I. HUMMEL CLUB CELEBRATES YEAR 21

Membership has its advantages, and members of the M.I. Hummel Club would be quick to agree. Now in its 21st year, the Club boasts 270,000 members in 50 countries. Its quarterly newsletter, *INSIGHTS*, has expanded into a handsome and entertaining magazine, full of information about *M.I. Hummel* history, handcraftsmanship and future product offerings. The Club also provides research services, drawing on its vast reference files and factory records from Germany.

The M.I. Hummel Club (formerly the Goebel Collectors' Club) was founded in the Spring of 1977 to provide information valuable to collectors of *M.I. Hummel* and other Goebel products. Since 1978 an extensive travel program has been a prime benefit to M.I. Hummel Club members. Beginning in 1985, there have been as many as ten deluxe, privately escorted trips a year to countries such as Switzerland, Italy, Austria and Holland, with the main attraction being visits to various parts of Germany. Major highlights of each trip include a behind-the-scenes tour of the Goebel factory and visits to the Convent of Siessen, home of Sister M.I. Hummel for the last 15 years of her life.

NEW PRODUCTS HERALD THE START OF THE CLUB'S THIRD DECADE

Starting in June of 1997, Club Year 21 presented a new crop of *M.I. Hummel* product introductions that only Club members may enjoy. "Nature's Gift" is the special figurine members receive free with their Club renewal. With her watering can in hand, "Nature's Gift" is set to tend her garden with love and care. Valued at $85.00, this 3-3/4" figurine will never be available to non-members at issue price.

The Club Members' Exclusive Edition for 1997-98, "Playful Blessing," is a fun-loving fellow with a mischievous streak. Ready to give his toy horse a tap with a real wooden crop and sound the alarm with a toot of his horn, this 3-1/2" charmer will add warmth to every heart and home he enters. The figurine, which has a suggested retail price of $260, bears a Club Exclusive backstamp and only Club members will ever have the

"What's That?" is the M.I. Hummel Club Preview Edition for the current two-year period.

"Forever Yours" (HUM 793) is the free gift members receive when they join the M.I. Hummel Club.

privilege of acquiring it at issue.

Goebel celebrates the irrepressible curiosity of children with "What's That?," the Preview Edition for Club Year 21. This inquisitive imp is the companion piece to last year's Preview Edition, "One, Two, Three." Together they make a delightful set, but even on her own, "What's That?" will be a fine addition to any collection. For the next two years, "What's That?" is available to members only and will bear a Club Exclusive backstamp. After that, there's a chance she could become an open edition, although there are no such plans at the moment. The figurine measures 4" and has a suggested retail price of $150.

The current M.I. Hummel Club year began on June 1, 1997 and will end on May 31, 1998. This year, membership applications and newly designed Club kits are available at all authorized *M.I. Hummel* retailers. The kits provide instant gratification because they contain everything a new member needs to belong – the "Forever Yours" figurine given as a gift to all new members, a Club binder, and a sample issue of *INSIGHTS*.

M.I. HUMMEL CLUB MEMBERSHIP PROVIDES YEAR-ROUND ENJOYMENT

M.I. Hummel Club President Ken LeFevre sums up membership this way: "The M.I. Hummel Club provides its members with the opportunity to participate in rewarding activities, gain in-depth information about the world of *M.I. Hummel* collectibles and, most of all, share the warmth, knowledge and camaraderie of fellow *M.I. Hummel* enthusiasts."

CLUB

M.I. HUMMEL CLUB
Goebel Plaza, P.O. Box 11
Pennington, NJ 08534-0011
(800) 666-CLUB (2582)

Annual Dues: $50.00 - Renewal: $37.50
Canada: $67.50 - Renewal: $50.00
Club Year: June 1 - May 31
Collector's Year: Anniversary of Sign-Up Date

BENEFITS:

- Membership Gift: *M.I. Hummel* Figurine
- Renewing Members Receive a Yearly Token of Appreciation Figurine
- Opportunity to Purchase Members-Only Figurine and Preview Editions
- Quarterly Magazine, *INSIGHTS*
- Buy/Sell Matching Service
- Research Service
- Annual Contests
- Travel Opportunities
- Local Club Chapters
- Membership Card
- Binder Includes Collector's Log, Price List, and *M.I.Hummel* History and Production Facts
- Anniversary Pins (5, 10, 15 & 20 Years)
- International Conventions

MUSEUM

THE HUMMEL MUSEUM
199 Main Plaza
New Braunfels, TX 78130
(210) 625-5636

Hours: Monday through Saturday, 10 a.m. - 5 p.m.; Sunday, Noon - 5 p.m.
Admission Fee: $5.00 Adults; $4.50 Seniors; $3.00 Students

The Hummel Museum displays the world's largest collection of Sister Maria Innocentia Hummel's original art. This one-of-a-kind museum offers guided tours, video presentations, historical vignette rooms of Sister Hummel's personal items, and an extensive display of rare *M.I. Hummel* figurines (over 1,100 on exhibit). The Museum Gift Shop offers a great variety of *Hummel* collectibles.

TO LEARN MORE:

M.I. HUMMEL CLUB
GOEBEL OF NORTH AMERICA
GOEBEL PLAZA
P.O. BOX 11, PENNINGTON, NJ 08534-0011
(800) 666-CLUB (2582)
FAX: (609) 737-1545
URL: http://www.mihummel.com

MARGARET FURLONG DESIGNS

Celebrating the Heavenly Beauty of Angels and Nature

Nearly two decades ago, Margaret Furlong Designs began in a small Midwestern studio – born out of the artist's love of nature and heart of faith. After earning her master of fine arts degree from the University of Nebraska, Margaret opened a modest art studio in Lincoln, Nebraska.

Drawing on her background in painting, pottery and sculpture, she sought to use her creative talents to celebrate God and nature's amazing beauty. For one project, she was asked to create a set of dishes adorned with a shell motif. So she studied her drawings and an array of seashells that were scattered about her studio. Moved by the incredible simplicity and beauty of this elegant and natural design, she began combining several shell forms, adding a molded face, a textured coil and a tapered trumpet. The result was her very first shell ornament, the "Trumpeter Angel," which was introduced in 1980.

Margaret then launched a series of white-on-white angel ornaments based on the shell form. She chose white bisque porcelain as the medium, allowing her to highlight the subtleties of the shell's delicate pattern and rich texture. It's a combination that has become the hallmark of her designs – each hand-cast from shells she has often found along the beach.

Today, her angels wear robes of rippled scallop shells and have formed a full choir of more than 60 different designs. The angels are also joined by a collection of other creations that blend the symbols of heaven and earth and celebrate the things Margaret values the most: God, nature, family and friendship. "Shells are such a beautiful motif used in just about every culture," she explains. "I combine them with images that represent the blessings of the world."

"Madonna of the Flowers" is the second in the* Madonna and Child *three-year series, with each design limited to 20,000 pieces. Margaret Furlong chose forget-me-nots to adorn the Madonna's gown, while the baby Jesus holds a bouquet.

STARTING A COMPANY WITH DREAMS AND FAITH

While her designs are now highly sought and admired all around the world, Margaret recalls her first year as being "rather slow and laborious." Borrowing $1,000 from her mother and $1,000 from her neighbor, she set up shop in an old stone carriage house in Nebraska and moved into the apartment above it. She began by sending letters to museum shops, earning sales of $50,000 in 1979. The following year, she got married to Jerry Alexander and moved to Seattle. In 1981, she moved to Salem, Oregon, and set up the Carriage House Studio – named after her first studio in Nebraska.

She was determined to go national with her designs and knew she couldn't do it alone. Her husband agreed to give up his job to become a full-time partner, bringing considerable fiscal and administrative skills to the company.

Through her first set of mailings, Margaret contacted the National Trust for Historic Preservation, which put her angels in its catalog – and on the White House Christmas tree in 1981. A selection of Margaret's angels adorned Ronald Reagan's personal tree. Given this remarkable exposure, it wasn't long before the media took notice. America's top publications featured Margaret's work in their holiday issues. *Victoria*, *Good Housekeeping*, *Redbook* and *Ladies' Home Journal* were among the magazines spreading the joy of Margaret's angels to millions of readers.

In 1983, Margaret produced her most distinguished work of art, daughter Caitlan Alexander. The birth of her child took Margaret's artistic spirits to new heights.

LIMITED EDITION SERIES BECOME COLLECTOR FAVORITES

Beginning in 1980, Margaret launched her first limited edition series and also introduced angels in 3", 4" and 5" sizes. For five consecutive years, Margaret's definition of the true meaning of Christmas was shared with collectors in the *Musical* series, with each 5" design limited to 3,000 pieces. In 1985, Margaret debuted her next 5" collectible series: *Gifts from God*, also limited to 3,000 of each design. The series captivated collectors with lavish touches: tiny shells, a cross, primrose, tulips, crocus, the sun and stars, and other glorious gifts of nature reflecting the

"Madonna of the Cross" is Margaret Furlong's first design in a three-year* Madonna and Child *limited edition series. The Madonna's lovely face is accented with a beautifully detailed veil and an elegant crown, and she holds the baby Jesus.

miracle of Jesus' birth.

The last decade of the century was another reason for celebration. In 1990, Margaret introduced *Joyeux Noel*, a five-year series of 5" angels limited to 10,000 of each design. Every figure has a fanciful name: "Celebration Angel," "Thanks-giving Angel," "Joyeux Noel Angel," "Star of Bethlehem Angel" and "Messiah Angel." Each design showcases Margaret's growth and relationship with God.

With the completion of *Joyeux Noel*, a new series, *Flora Angelica*, was launched in 1995. The series combines the radiance of angels with the symbolism of flowers. The series is limited to just 10,000 pieces of each annual 5" angel. The third issue in the five-year series, "Charity Angel" holds a Victorian-inspired cornucopia of garden flowers representing the spirit of giving from the infinite bounty of God.

MADONNA AND CHILD SERIES CELEBRATES GOD'S PRECIOUS GIFTS

In 1996, Margaret proudly introduced a three-part limited edition *Madonna and Child* series, inspired by Russian icons and Italian Renaissance paintings that she discovered during a trip to Europe. Her personal attraction and devotion to the theme of mother and child is influenced by her desire to protect, cherish and celebrate the precious gift of children.

The first design, "Madonna of the Cross," features an angel with her face accented with a beautifully detailed veil and elegant crown. In her arms, she is holding the baby Jesus – also wearing a crown and holding a tiny cross.

For 1997, "Madonna of the Flowers" continues the series with clusters of forget-me-nots adorning the Madonna's gown, and the baby Jesus also holding a bouquet of these dainty flowers. Each angel in the series is a limited edition of 20,000 and measures approximately 6-1/2" tall. All are individually numbered. The third and final issue will be introduced in 1998.

COLLECTION BLOOMS WITH FLOWERS AND BEAUTY

Margaret Furlong's 1997 collection celebrated the perfect joy of flowers and the beauty that they bring to everyone. "Gardening is a special part of my life," she says. "I feel a closeness to nature because it is the work of God. I believe nature reveals the character of God in its infinite creativity and beauty. As I look long and carefully at a bloom, examining the arrangement and shape of the soft petals, experiencing the luminescent color and delicate fragrance, I am in awe. In that moment of feeling and seeing the divine intricacy and beauty of one tiny blossom, time stands still and I am lost in it."

Her "From the Heart" ornament is embellished with a "shell" viola in the center, sprinkled with forget-me-nots and edged with scalloped open work. The "Love Four You" set features a quartet of the "From the Heart" ornaments.

Carrying out this same motif, a 2" angel holds a single viola – after which the piece is named. "The viola is a messenger of loving thoughts, and both this heart and the angel are sweet messengers of this sentiment," she says.

The 3" "Dogwood" heralds the coming of Spring with a dogwood blossom whose petals are embossed with a shell pattern. Her 4" "Special Edition Iris Angel" – limited to 1997 – holds an iris blossom surrounded by a fan of blade leaves. The inspiration for the piece came from seeing wild irises blooming in an Oregon field and learning the symbolism behind the three top petals of the flower: faith, wisdom and valor.

Margaret has designed a set of two

Margaret Furlong created the "Tea For Two" set of miniature angels to celebrate lasting friendship and life's simple pleasures. One angel holds a teapot and the other a tiny tea cup and saucer.

"Charity Angel" is part of the* Flora Angelica *series with each annual 5" angel limited to just 10,000 pieces.

tiny "Tea for Two" angels to celebrate that favorite afternoon pastime and the sweetness of friendship. "The flowers in my garden remind me that it is the simple and beautiful things that bring joy to the heart – especially when they are shared with good friends over a cup of tea," Margaret says. One angel holds a miniature teapot with an ivy leaf to match her ivy crown, and the other holds a shell teacup and saucer. The angels measure in at 1-1/2" – the smallest to date in the collection. These angels are the first to be sold exclusively as a set.

Other additions include sets of hearts, seashell stars and snowflakes, along with a 5" acorn and a 3" oak and acorn wreath. In the tradition of fine collectible art, retirements are also an important part of Margaret's commitment to giving collectors true limited editions. Retiring in 1997 were "Shell Fish" and "Gold Fish" – each introduced in 1994 and inspired by Margaret's daughter and her many pet goldfish. "Shell Tassel," introduced in 1994, and "Coral Tassel," introduced in 1995, were also selected for retirement.

ARTISANS CREATE INTRICATE WORKS OF ART

Today, Margaret Furlong's dreams and creations have come full circle. Each is a reflection of her personal commitment to quality, value and good design. Toward that end, Margaret uses a meticulous production process that moves her creations from prototype to first modeling, from carving to a master mold, all with methodical care. Each step of the crafting and finishing process is overseen by Margaret and her growing staff of artisans and crafters, now numbering more than 85. Her designs are also proudly made in Salem, Oregon, using the exacting techniques and standards that she pioneered back in her Nebraska studio.

With all this growth and excitement, Margaret still finds time to make herself available to collectors with tours of her studios and facility in Salem, as well as personal appearances across the country. "I think I've been successful because I've used imagery that God designed," she explains. "We can never come close to making a design as beautiful as His. I love casting shells, leaves and flowers. My work celebrates God's handiwork."

TOUR

MARGARET FURLONG DESIGNS
STUDIO TOUR
210 State Street
Salem, OR 97301
(503) 363-6004

Hours: Monday through Friday, 9 a.m.-3:15 p.m. Please phone for an appointment.
Admission Fee: None

Visitors can tour the production area at Margaret Furlong Designs Studio, where skilled craftspeople make each porcelain design by hand.

TO LEARN MORE:

MARGARET FURLONG DESIGNS
210 STATE STREET
SALEM, OR 97301
(503) 363-6004
FAX: (503) 371-0676

MARURI U.S.A.

Creating Fine Porcelain Art and Ceramics for Today's Collector

Long before America discovered the magic and beauty of porcelain, the Japanese mastered the art of ceramics. The art form flourished in the fabled ceramic capital known as Seto, located in central Japan near the exotic, old-world city of Nagoya and a region boasting the finest family workshops in the land.

It was here that one particularly successful enterprise was started by the Misuno brothers, who carefully selected the name "Maruri" for their design studio. The "ri" means "benefits." "Maru" is a time-honored symbol for a circle meaning the never-ending nature of classic, fine art.

Together, the brothers lived up to their name. The studio quickly earned a distinguished reputation for excellent bone china, delicate figurines and true-to-nature bird and animal sculptures.

A pair of wrens perch on a cactus in Maruri's **Songbird Serenade** *series of the most beloved and familiar birds in North America. The sculpture stands 7" high and retails for $80.00.*

The legacy began centuries ago and continues today. In Seto, highly skilled artisans still produce the world's most respected and treasured porcelain giftware and collectibles. More than a decade ago, Maruri entered the American market, attracting the attention of collectors from coast to coast with its highly detailed and life-like wildlife sculptures.

In a short time, Maruri has proven itself to be a powerful force in the giftware and limited edition collectibles industry. Collectors now consider Maruri a benchmark for all other wildlife sculptures on the market.

MARURI SCULPTURES CREATED WITH TIME-HONORED TECHNIQUES AND DETAIL

The art of creating exquisite porcelain sculptures requires two things above all else: talented art masters and a total commitment to quality. Throughout the world, only select studios achieve this high standard of excellence. Maruri is among the chosen few.

Maruri prides itself on upholding the "studied approach" in creating its limited edition sculptures. Each flower, eagle, bird and other animal takes many days to complete using a multi-step process that has been faithfully followed over the years.

Artisans begin by crafting multiple molds for each piece. Individual molds capture every detail with perfection. Once the molds are approved, a creamy feldspar mixture in the form of liquid slip is carefully poured. This so-called Grand Feu formula is the same one used in ancient times and continues to be the preferred ceramic material, prized for its excellent finished look and feel.

Molds are filled to a specific thickness, then allowed to dry very slowly to meet Maruri's stringent specifications. Only when a proper degree of hardness is reached are pieces carefully removed from their molds and placed together. Seam lines and points of juncture are smoothed and refined. Every step is done by hand to ensure a magnificent work of art guaranteed to delight collectors.

Sculptures are next placed in a temperature-controlled drying room, carefully braced between support molds because the hardening process continues for several days. When sufficiently dry, a sculpture is placed in a kiln and fired for 16 hours. During this critical period, temperatures in the kiln are brought to an ideal degree of heat. Then the kiln is slowly cooled to complete the firing process.

Maruri artisans carefully inspect sculptures as soon as they are removed from their kilns. As many as 40% may be eliminated as "less than perfect." Those passing inspection are sandblasted to a brilliant, strong finish. Highly trained artists then paint every sculpture by hand in subtle tones chosen by color experts. The sculpture is finally ready to be wrapped and shipped to fine stores around the world.

MARURI DESIGNS INTRICATE SCULPTURES

Maruri prides itself on the workmanship and creativity that make each sculpture a work of art. Among the most prized pieces are complex and distinguished sculptures featuring several figures placed together to create a beautiful scene from nature. "Independent Spirit," for example, portrays two American bald eagles battling for dominance amidst sturdy bronze tree branches.

The faces on the birds of prey are expressive, bold and powerful. Their

"Independent Spirit" combines the magnificent artistry of Maruri with nature's most majestic birds. The fine porcelain and bronze sculpture is limited in edition to 3,500 pieces.

wings flare out to reveal amazing detail. A palette of realistic colors stroke every inch of this porcelain masterpiece.

To create such a complex figure, the eagles' bodies, wings, tree branches and trunks all had to be sculptured independently of one another. Fusing of the individual pieces takes place as the sculpture is molded, assembled and painted. It's an arduous process, but well worth the time and effort.

Individually numbered and limited to just 3,500 pieces for worldwide distribution, "Independent Spirit" stands a remarkable 14" high. A Certificate of Authenticity accompanies the sculpture, which is displayed on a wooden base.

BIRDS FLY HIGH IN MARURI SCULPTURES

Collectors of fine aviary art know they can find their favorite birds within the Maruri collection of porcelain art. Maruri recently introduced *Songbird Serenade*, a collection of fine porcelain songbird sculptures. The nine pieces in the collection depict some of the most beloved and familiar songbird species of North America, including the goldfinch, robin, blue jay, chickadee, cardinal, wren, cedar waxwing and bluebird.

Each bird species is shown in its natural environment – perched on a branch and surrounded by colorful flowers and foliage. Every detail of these delicately crafted sculptures is hand-painted for a realistic effect. The figurines, which range in price from $65.00 to $95.00, come with a Certificate of Authenticity and wooden base.

The *Maruri Hummingbird Collection* showcases sculptures of the tiny and elusive winged creature. Maruri designed and produced "Delicate Motion," featuring three violet-crowned hummingbirds circling a bright spray of morning glories. "Delicate Motion" is sequentially numbered and limited to 3,500 pieces worldwide. This remarkable porcelain and bronze figure comes on a wooden base and includes a Certificate of Authenticity.

Other species of birds appear in *Eyes of the Night*, an exotic owl series. A fragile pair of beautiful white doves called "Wings of Love" are among the delicate sculptures in Maruri's porcelain aviary.

Maruri collectible bird sculptures are also known for their secondary market performance. Artist W.D. Gaither's "American Bald Eagle I," for example, was introduced by Maruri in 1981 for $165. The figure commanded $600 on the secondary market the following year and is now quoted at $1,750. This dramatic increase exemplifies Maruri's commitment to producing art rich in detail and value.

Maruri lets collectors catch a glimpse of elusive hummingbirds in a 16-piece collection. In this detailed porcelain sculpture, a mother feeds her young babies.

Santa's World Travels *takes collectors along for St. Nick's annual ride. In "Desert Trip," Santa rides across the Sahara on a camel and shares his water flask with an elf. The figurine is limited to 7,500 pieces.*

MARURI TRAVELS AROUND THE WORLD WITH SANTA

Even Santa Claus needs a little help from his animal friends to make his Christmas Eve deliveries around the world. Maruri introduces *Santa's World Travels*, a collection of six limited edition sculptures depicting jolly St. Nick and animals native to each region that he visits.

As he makes his rounds to different countries, the fun-loving Santa also trades in his traditional red and white costume for a colorful new wardrobe.

Maruri has captured the playful and imaginative spirit of Christmas in beautifully hand-painted, cold-cast porcelain sculptures, which are individually and sequentially numbered and come with a Certificate of Authenticity. The *Santa's World Travels* figurines range in price from $75.00 to $225.00.

In the first piece titled "Santa's Safari," St. Nick rides in style on the back of an African elephant as he totes a bag overflowing with gifts. A friendly elf perched on the elephant's trunk helps Santa by pointing the way through the

Maruri's* Polar Expedition *series introduces collectors to creatures in the Arctic region. "Baby Harp Seals" depicts the innocence and playfulness of these animals.

jungle. The sculpture is limited to 5,000 pieces, while the other pieces in the collection are limited to 7,500 pieces.

In "Desert Trip," Santa rides across the Sahara on a camel and shares his water flask with a trusty elf. Santa gets a bumpy start to the holidays in "Wild Ride," where he heads across the plains on a galloping buffalo. "Crossing the Tundra" features Santa using a dog sled and a team of loyal huskies, one of which is hiding in his sack of gifts. Aided by a gentle St. Bernard, Santa climbs the snowy Alps in "Trusted Friend." Tired from his long journey, Santa catches a nap under the watchful eye of a white Siberian tiger in "Cat Nap."

MARURI WARMS COLLECTORS' HEARTS WITH ARCTIC CREATURES

Few people have the privilege of traveling to the North Pole to see polar bears, harp seals, Arctic foxes and penguins in their natural environment on the frozen tundra. So Maruri brings these cold-weather creatures to collectors through the *Polar Expedition* collection. Each replica of its real-life counterpart is hand-painted in natural colors and so real you can almost feel the wintry air!

From the mighty "Polar Bear" to the adorable "Baby Harp Seal," and from a formally dressed "Emperor Penguin" to a sly "Arctic Fox," *Polar Expedition* introduces collectors to wonderful animals that may live in cold regions but that warm the hearts of all. Each sculpture in the *Polar Expedition* series comes with Maruri's Certificate of Authenticity, an assurance that each subject has been crafted with quality and care.

MARURI FINDS INSPIRATION IN AFRICA

Maruri artisans took their talents and vision from the icy Arctic to the scorching plains and savannas of exotic Africa. The *Gentle Giants* collection features a stunning collection of five African elephant sculptures fashioned in porcelain to capture every wrinkle and expression.

Gentle Giants collectors can choose from a single standing baby elephant, a sitting baby elephant or a playful pair of youngsters. A mother and child elephant, as well as a beautiful pair of adults, are also included in the series. A wooden base showcases these limited edition sculptures, which include a Certificate of Authenticity.

In addition to *Gentle Giants*, Maruri also developed a signature African collection by renowned artist W.D. Gaither. *African Safari* shares Gaither's firsthand experiences in Zululand, South Africa, where he sketched and photographed elephants, rhinos, buffalo, lions, leopards, kudus, impalas and other familiar beasts. Each served as an inspiration for his true-to-life *African Safari* series.

With age-old methods and award-winning sculptors, Maruri will continue spreading its wings with new introductions to delight generations of collectors. The company's time-honored traditions offer an enduring tribute to some of the world's most enchanting creatures.

TO LEARN MORE:

MARURI U.S.A.
21510 GLEDHILL ST.
CHATSWORTH, CA 91311
(818) 717-9900
FAX: (818) 717-9901

Presenting the Art of Thomas Kinkade

Thomas Kinkade is one of America's most collected living artists, a painter-communicator whose tranquil, light-infused paintings bring hope and joy to millions every year. Each painting Thomas Kinkade creates is a quiet messenger in the home, affirming the basic values of family, faith in God, and the luminous beauty of nature.

It was while growing up in the small town of Placerville, California, that these simple, yet life-guiding values were instilled in Thomas. It was also during this time that he began to explore the world around him. The young artist once spent a Summer on a sketching tour with his college friend, James Gurney (of *Dinotopia* fame), producing a best-selling instructional book, *The Artist's Guide to Sketching.* The success of the book landed the two young artists at Ralph Bakshi Studios to create background art for the animation feature, "Fire and Ice." Kinkade was able to explore light and imaginative works with abandon.

Thomas Kinkade, known as "The Painter of Light™" for his luminous style and for the life-affirming nature of the subjects he paints, is one of the most collected artists in America.

After the film, Kinkade earned his living as a painter, selling his originals in galleries throughout California. In 1982, he married his childhood sweetheart, Nanette. Two years later they began to publish his art, and in 1989, they formed Lightpost Publishing/Media Arts Group with Ken Raasch.

Since then, Kinkade has had more than 130 limited edition graphic prints published, as well as a host of works in other collectible media, such as plates and cottages.

A CELEBRATION OF SIMPLER TIMES

Kinkade has recently published *Simpler Times*, a book which shares some of his philosophy about faith and family and is illustrated with his work. In it, he encourages everyone to simplify their lives, to spend time with family and friends. The book, like his paintings, offers what the artist calls "an off ramp from the fast lane."

A recent interview with journalist Cara Denney, which appeared in the Christian publication *Release Ink* magazine, offered great insight into Kinkade's view of the world as the millennium approaches – and his efforts to reestablish a simpler way of life.

As Kinkade told Denney, "We as a generation are being fed a message in the latter part of the 20th century, which is this: Bill Gates stands up in a public setting and says electronics is the key to the future. It is the answer to the happiness of mankind. We'll all be okay if we can just get on the Internet quick enough. 'If we can just get our kids computer literate by age 6, then we'll be okay as a civilization.' That message is a lie straight from the pit. We will not be okay by intertwining our lives ever-increasingly with material things.

"We'll be okay when we return to the basic dignity of life – to moments spent in the sunshine, moments spent with each other, spending life with people one on one. What really matters is making those little choices day by day to simplify your life and to enjoy the moments that God has given us."

A FAMILY LIFE CENTERED ON FAITH

Kinkade is a devout Christian and credits the Lord for both the ability and the inspiration to create his paintings. His goal as an artist is to touch people of all faiths, to bring peace and joy into their lives through the images he creates. The letters he receives every day testify to the fact that he is achieving this goal.

A devoted husband and doting father to their four little girls, Kinkade hides the letter "N" in his paintings to pay tribute to his wife, Nanette, and the girls find their names and images in many of his paintings. The Kinkade family spends much time together, and they live a life that is nearly devoid of "consumerism" and media influence.

"Remember the old fashioned thing when people used to take a walk in the evenings? We do that almost every night," Kinkade says. "Sounds simple enough, but what a meaningful thing. Our kids are not growing up assuming that life is a rush from one mall to the next, because they've never experienced that." In addition, Kinkade has eliminated television and newspapers from his home. "Media is a peer group that will overwhelm just about anything if you allow it," he asserts. "It

Thomas Kinkade's "Bridge of Faith" combines a rustic stone bridge with lush trees and flowers, all illuminated by a glowing light that seems to emanate from a heavenly source.

will be the thing that shapes the ideas of the next generation. I don't want to be reading a newspaper when I should be talking to my children in the morning."

A TESTIMONY OF FAITH TO ART LOVERS

While his art is purchased by people from a wide range of backgrounds and religions, Kinkade sees his creations – including his new book *Simpler Times* – as a way to share his beliefs with others. As he related to Denney, "I view this book as an extension of my ministry. When I got saved in 1980, my art got saved. The Lord began to show me the value art has to influence lives. I believe the spiritual power of the painting can overwhelm just about any other tool the Lord can use; it is a universal language that can reach lives. I want my message to be very universal. We live in a culturally diverse world, but everyone can relate to a garden, to a mountain spring, flowers and trees and a little cottage you might want to go live in."

Collectors gain serenity and strength by viewing many of Kinkade's works, and he is delighted at their reactions. As he explains, "I really feel the Lord gives me ideas as I paint about how to shape that world and share it with others. People come to me and say, 'I wish I could enter the world of this painting' and my hope is I can tell them, 'You can enter that world. You may not live in a house that looks like this, but you can embody the lifestyle I try to paint. A lifestyle of peace, hope, faith in God, faith in your family, faith in one another, and return to the simpler way of living.'"

One collector even believes that she owes her life to Kinkade and his art. Deeply depressed, she had found herself with no other alternative but to submit to dangerous and radical electric shock therapy. On the day the therapy was to take place, she was in the waiting room when someone told her to "look up." She did, and saw several of Kinkade's graphics on the wall. As she examined the images, the woman felt a transformation taking place. As Kinkade recalls, "She felt strangely warm. She realized, 'The world is not an ugly place.' She had this dream that someday maybe she could have a little cottage" (like the ones in Kinkade's paintings). The woman walked out of the waiting room and felt inspired to a wonderful recovery. Today, she teaches art to children and works toward her dream of owning a "Kinkade cottage" of her own.

As empowering as such testimonies may be, Thomas Kinkade attributes any such power he may bring to bear to its source: his Christian faith. As he elaborates, "Christ was very visual. Look at the way he illustrated his teaching with strong visual pictures. We can inspire a generation through paintings that uplift. That is my goal as an artist."

KINKADE'S AWARDS AND HONORS

Kinkade has received numerous awards for his works. Most recently, he has been named by the National Association of Limited Edition Dealers (NALED) as "Graphic Artist of the Year" for the second year in a row. He is also a past "Artist of the Year" for NALED, and his works have been named "Graphic Art Print of the Year" by that group for five years in a row.

Kinkade has also won the *Collector Editions* "Award of Excellence" and was a charter inductee, along with his idol, Norman Rockwell, to The Bradford Hall of Fame for plate artists. Kinkade considers the two weeks he once spent painting in Rockwell's Vermont studio

"Cobblestone Brooke" offers a cordial welcome into a quaint, Old World town. In this work of art, Kinkade combines floral abundance with wonderful lighting and classic architecture.

"The Valley of Peace" shows a cottage in the country with beckoning lights in the window, surrounded by Fall foliage and majestic mountains in the distance.

among the most inspirational times of his life.

Kinkade reveres Rockwell because the famous illustrator's work is accessible to all – both in form and in subject matter. As the artist explained to Cara Denney, "(Rockwell's) contribution is arguably as big as anyone else (to our national identity during World War II), including Franklin Roosevelt or Churchill, because he provided a visual sense of why we were in the war. He identified the average American of that time in terms of paintings they could relate to, presented through the *Saturday Evening Post* and other vehicles. He was a humble man who served people through his art."

Kinkade is delighted that *U.S. Art* magazine has predicted that he will be inducted into its Hall of Fame for graphic artists at the earliest year of his eligibility, which is 1999. As Sara Gilbert and Rebecca Lunna of the magazine state, "...we can't imagine the Hall of Fame without him. Look for him to join the illustrious ranks when he's eligible in 1999."

Gilbert and Lunna base their assessment on Kinkade's prolific artistry, as well as his distinctive style. As they note, "Because (Kinkade's) body of work is both so large and so accessible, he has one of the most recognizable names in print today. Collectors across the country recognize his nostalgic landscapes and cozy cottages, each imbued with the luminescent glow that earned Kinkade his trademarked moniker, 'Painter of Light.'"

CLUB

THOMAS KINKADE COLLECTORS' SOCIETY
P.O. Box 90267
San Jose, CA 95109
(800) 544-4890 ext. 1543 & 1587

Annual Dues: $45.00;
$75.00 for 2 Years (US$)
Club Year: January - December
Collector's Year - Anniversary of Sign-Up Date

BENEFITS:

- Membership Gift: Full Color 10" x 10" Gift Print
- Quarterly Newsletter, "The Beacon"
- Membership Card
- Annual Lapel Pin
- Opportunity to Purchase Members-Only Items: Classic Collection Canvas, Library Print, Collectors' Cottages Portfolio
- National and Regional Special Events

TO LEARN MORE:

MEDIA ARTS GROUP, INC.
521 CHARCOT AVENUE
SAN JOSE, CA 95131
(800) 366-3733
FAX: (408) 324-2033

MIDWEST OF CANNON FALLS®

Heartland Designs...Crafted Worldwide

The lighted "Drearydale Manor" limited edition house includes a sound-activated creepy sound chip and is shown with the "Creepy Servants."

Today, Midwest of Cannon Falls, founded by Kenneth W. Althoff, ranks as one of the United States' top four designers and distributors of seasonal and year-round giftware and home decor. But it began in 1955 as a small, family-owned business specializing in importing European products.

Kenneth Althoff, a Lutheran pastor, originally opened a small store specializing in religious items. Diagnosed with multiple sclerosis, Althoff started the business after being advised to find a line of work that could accommodate what doctors predicted would be increasing physical disabilities. A lesser man might have given up after his first European shipment was lost in 1956 with the sinking of the Italian liner Andrea Doria. But Althoff proved to be a savvy strategist. After noting that other retailers were turning to him as a source of fine imports, Althoff focused his attention on importing and wholesaling full time. To ensure high quality at an affordable cost, Midwest of Cannon Falls began working with international manufacturers long before many companies even began to consider global business relationships.

The current Midwest of Cannon Falls line features more than 4,000 products including seasonal giftware, exclusive collectibles and distinctive home decor. While the company continues to import fine collectibles from the Erzgebirge region of Germany, now the majority of its line is designed exclusively by Midwest of Cannon Falls and crafted around the world. As a wholesale distributor, Midwest of Cannon Falls utilizes catalogs, gift shows and a network of independent sales representatives to sell products to more than 20,000 retailers. The company's headquarters are in Cannon Falls, Minnesota, just an hour's drive from Minneapolis/St. Paul.

Since 1985, Kathleen Brekken, daughter of Kenneth Althoff, has served as President and Chief Executive Officer of the company. She joined the firm in 1972 after graduating from the University of Minnesota. She also has attended the Owner/President Management program at Harvard University School of Business Administration.

SHAPING AND SATISFYING AMERICA'S DECORATING TASTES

Today, the Midwest of Cannon Falls product line ranges from elegant European blown-glass ornaments to limited edition folk art figurines, and from charmingly rustic home accessories to licensed reproductions of much-loved characters from books and the classics.

Christmas ornaments and decorative accessories represent about 60 percent of the company's business. Through its creations, Midwest of Cannon Falls has helped change how Americans decorate Christmas trees. In contrast to the 1960s, when every tree had the requisite tinsel and predictable glass-ball ornaments, American consumers today are opting for items that symbolize their special interests. From sports and hobby-related items to ornaments that commemorate special events, Americans increasingly are making a very personal statement with the family Christmas tree.

Midwest of Cannon Falls holds a unique niche in the giftware market, by providing products that evoke a sense of nostalgia and tradition, yet are innovative, fresh and relevant to today's tastes. The company uses a wide range of handcrafted materials, including resin, fabric, wood, metal, glass and ceramics, and techniques such as hand-painting to achieve its distinctive look.

The firm emphasizes original designs; about 90 percent of Midwest of Cannon Falls' items are created by in-house designers or are the work of exceptional artists under contract. What's more, the company relies on long-standing partnerships with a number of Asian manufacturers to meet the exacting standards Midwest of Cannon Falls' customers have come to expect.

The firm's reputation for quality has led to a number of breakthrough licensing agreements for well-known figures. Its expanding line of licensed properties include characters from Classic Pooh, Mickey & Co., The Wubbulous World of Dr. Seuss, Dilbert and many more. Midwest also custom-designs and manufactures private-label giftware for a growing number of well-known organizations, including

This limited edition lighted and musical* Cottontail Lane *carousel is crafted of porcelain and has a suggested retail price of $47.00.

Universal Studios, Disney Stores and L.L. Bean, to name just a few.

Cottontail Lane™ and *Creepy Hollow™* by Midwest of Cannon Falls were introduced in 1992 to fill collectors' desire for holiday villages other than those offered for the Christmas season.

MIDWEST PRESENTS LIGHTED HOUSES AND FIGURINES

The company coupled this with increased consumer interest in Spring seasonal products, gift-giving patterns and the trend toward "lifestyle collectibles."

Four porcelain lighted houses, resin figurines and accessories started the *Cottontail Lane* collection, making it possible for collectors to begin assembling an entire springtime village with one series. By 1997, there were 18 porcelain lighted houses and more than 40 accessories.

Collectors enjoy the precious design detail and delicate hand-painting apparent in these creations. Increased interest in animation and novelty from consumers results in adding special effect features to *Cottontail Lane*. For example, the 1997 limited edition "Musical Carousel Lighted Structure" plays "The Carousel Waltz."

The series comes alive every year by bringing collectors new and enchanting story lines. Spring 1997 saw the introduction of a Victorian-styled carnival including a limited edition "Musical Lighted Carousel," a bunny-style "Tunnel of Love," and an "Arcade" for games of chance and skill.

The *Creepy Hollow* line began with five porcelain lighted houses, resin figurines and accessories. By 1997, there were 12 porcelain lighted houses, resin figurines and accessories, and six *Creepy Hollow* lighted houses had been retired.

The *Creepy Hollow* line consists of spooky traditional houses, mansions and cottages, as well as haunting novelty castles and an opera house. The frightening characters and accessories support the story line of the scary village scene. For example, to coordinate with the 1997 limited edition "Lighted Drearydale Manor," there are creepy servants, scary sea captains and a spy witch. Haunted trees, a road of bones and street signs can be added to create a truly bewitching village scene.

Collectors enjoy the witty text that is apparent in the design of the collection. The whimsical and visual humor draws collectors into the product line along with the high quality of the sculpted details and hand-painting. Increased interest in animation and novelty from consumers results in adding these special-effect features to *Creepy Hollow*. In the future, this may include music, haunting sounds and animated movement.

THE ENDEARING FOLK ART OF EDDIE WALKER AND LEO R. SMITH III

A self-taught artist from Walla Walla, Washington, Eddie Walker has turned her love of carving into a collection of hundreds of smiling faced characters from chummy bunnies to adorable Santas — all available exclusively through Midwest of Cannon Falls. The artist and company have had an exclusive partnership since 1993, through which Midwest creates precise reproductions of Walker's original carvings.

Eddie Walker started carving in 1989 after taking one wood carving class. In just nine hours, she carved her first Santa in her backyard. In her home studio, she instinctively carves designs without ever touching a pencil to paper. Her enchanting characters celebrate every season, while creating many smiles and generating much-deserved praise across the country. Eddie Walker has created three limited editions and two limited-to-year-of-issue items. The 1995 "Noah's Ark," 1996 "Santa in Sleigh with Reindeer" and 1997 "North Pole Express" are all retired.

Now Eddie Walker has entered cyberspace with a web site dedicated to her work at www.eddiewalker.com. Her home on the World Wide Web opens with a personal greeting from the artist. Visitors on the site can learn more about her unique success as a wood carver and find pictures of her work. Collectors will be able to surf the page which highlights information about Walker's limited edition pieces, and visit several interactive areas, including a monthly drawing for free Eddie Walker products, a bulletin board for her fans, and an opportunity to send e-mail directly to Walker. The site also includes creative gift-giving and decorating tips for every season of the year, as well as dates and locations for the artist's personal appearances, and retail locations.

Leo R. Smith III finds his inspiration in the picturesque river town of

The "North Pole Express" train set by Eddie Walker is limited to 7,500 and has a suggested retail price of $200.

"Santa on White Horse" by Leo R. Smith III is available in a limited edition of 1,000 at $150 suggested retail price.

Fountain City, Wisconsin. From there, he brings legends and folk lore to life in an exclusive partnership with Midwest of Cannon Falls. His Santas, angels and other delightful characters often include the artist's own stories that help add color and dimension to his works.

NUTCRACKERS AND OTHER GERMAN COLLECTIBLES

As the largest U.S. importer of Erzgebirge nutcrackers, Midwest is pleased to present an extraordinary series called the *Ore Mountain Collection™*. These handcrafted wooden treasures come direct from the nutcracker's 17th-century birthplace. New designs are introduced each year, ranging from the classic – "Guard Nutcracker," "Drummer Nutcracker," "Prince With Red Coat Nutcracker" – to the unique – "Hippie Nutcracker," "New York Yankees, Chicago Cubs and Chicago White Sox Baseball Player Nutcrackers," and "Teddy Bear Nutcracker".

Ken Althoff's European Collection continues Althoff's 40-plus year sharing of handcrafted German treasures with American friends. This unique collection of wooden angels, animals and other wonderful pieces from the Erzgebirge and the *Wendt und Kühn Collection* brings some of the best in German craftsmanship to collectors.

Happily, Ken Althoff's disease never progressed the way doctors predicted so many years ago. Now in his 70s, he participates actively as Midwest of Cannon Falls' chairman, still helping to further the company's reputation for products designed in the heartland and crafted around the world.

TO LEARN MORE:

MIDWEST OF CANNON FALLS
32057 64TH AVENUE
CANNON FALLS, MN 55009
(800) 377-3335
FAX: (507) 263-7752
URL: http://www.eddiewalker.com

MISS MARTHA ORIGINALS

All God's Children Figurines Bring Back Childhood Memories

Like most children, Martha Root always looked forward to carefree and warm summers. She would spend her days on her grandmother's farm in the Appalachian foothills of Northeast Alabama, where there were endless adventures and places to discover. She enjoyed swimming, fishing, picking cotton and riding the old mule – not to mention raiding her grandmother's watermelon patch for a refreshing treat.

Those delightful days of long ago still rest warmly in her heart and often translate into the beautiful children that she sculpts today. Miss Martha is a self-taught artist who never stops looking for new ideas for her artwork. Collectors of the *All God's Children* line of figurines keep her supplied with photographs of their loved ones who often inspire Miss Martha's artwork, as well as the names she gives each figurine. Yet, she credits God for her artistic gifts, and it is His love for all His children that is the message behind her work.

Like all of the figurines from Miss Martha Originals, "Janae" is proudly made in the U.S.A. and sculpted by Martha Root. The little girl happily sits in a washtub waiting to be squeaky clean.

She also shows the importance of family. A native of Alabama, Miss Martha is the mother of three grown children: Lisa, Keith and Kim. She holds a degree in Mental Health Technology with professional certificates in Counseling, Bible and Christian Education. She is the proud grandmother of Garrett, Alexandria and Daylon – all of whom are represented by members-only club pieces.

THE HUMBLE BEGINNINGS OF MISS MARTHA'S DREAM

Miss Martha Originals, Inc. began in 1980 with a simple doll pattern design. In order to meet a pledge for a new roof for her Alabama church, Gadsden First Church of the Nazarene, she created a soft-sculpture doll that she sold by mail. The proceeds went to the church. It was from the children in her Sunday School class that she was given the name, Miss Martha. It stuck and seemed the perfect name for her company, since it was the needs of the church that inspired her to enter the business world.

The one doll pattern grew to a box of patterns and then enough to fill her garage. Eventually, it was necessary to move to a vacant store building, then two store buildings, and in 1985, to a brand-new facility in the Gadsden Industrial Park. The new facility soon became too small, and after continued expansion, it became apparent that a second facility was needed. In 1992, Miss Martha Originals purchased the Coca-Cola plant in Gadsden and moved all administrative offices, the showroom and the warehouse to that location, giving the original facility increased production capabilities.

It wasn't the doll patterns that spurred this tremendous growth but eight figurines that Miss Martha sculpted and introduced in 1985. The figurines started the company on its dynamic growth spurt. In search of a name for her adorable sculpted children, she simply drew from a favorite Bible verse: "See how much the Father has loved us! His love is so great that we are called God's Children." (I John 3:1) Thus the name, *All God's Children*, was given to the beautiful sculptures by Miss Martha.

At its inception, Miss Martha Originals worked with several United States companies to produce the pecan shell/resin castings from Martha Root's original sculptures. But after the first year, the quality didn't meet with the artist's high standards, so the decision was made to learn to do the entire process at the plant in Gadsden. The *All God's Children* line is not only sculpted by Miss Martha but crafted with pride in the U.S.A. at the factory in Alabama.

ANNUAL REUNION DRAWS A FAMILY OF COLLECTORS

For more than a decade, the *All God's Children* line has won the hearts of enthusiastic collectors. For some, it is the warm nostalgia of times "way back when" that Miss Martha captures in her three-dimensional portraits of African-American children. For others, it is the face of each child which seems to reflect the heart of childhood in all its innocence, tenderness and beauty. "I just love the look of the pieces and thought they were adorable in that they captured a child's innocence and reminded me of my childhood," notes one collector from Illinois.

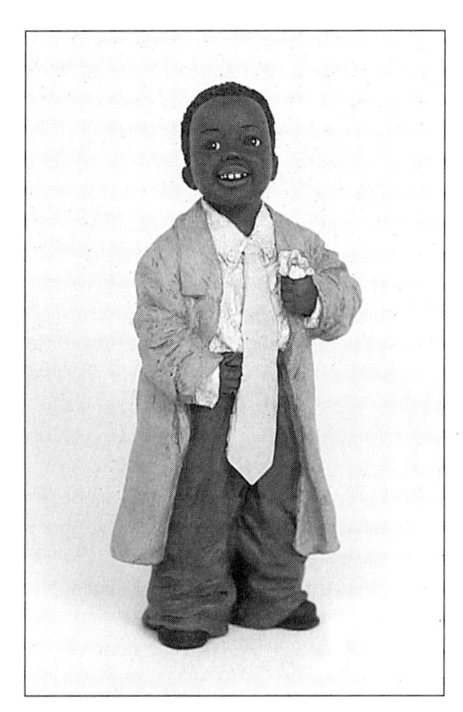

The jacket and tie may be a little too big, but "Robert" is just the right size to warm the hearts of collectors. This open edition figurine stands 5-1/4" tall and retails for $38.50.

Whatever attracts collectors, Miss Martha's sculptures become a part of the family – and make collectors themselves feel like family. Each Summer for the past seven years, collectors have traveled from far and wide to attend the annual All God's Children Family Reunion in Gadsden. The 1997 reunion was the biggest to date, drawing more than 4,000 people who came to meet Miss Martha, while enjoying a day of fellowship, fun, food, entertainment and home-spun love with other collectors and families. The reunion is a highlight for collectors across the country, as they gather to also get their pieces signed by Miss Martha and buy and trade the figurines at a swap meet.

Thousands of other collectors of Miss Martha Originals also have discovered the fun, sharing and family atmosphere that comes with membership in the All God's Children Collector's Club.

COLLECTORS INVITED TO JOIN THE CLUB

The annual fee of just $20.00 entitles members to the following benefits: a free figurine, membership card, opportunity to purchase an exclusive members-only figurine, free subscription to the quarterly magazine, *All God's Children Collector's Edition*, announcements of special appearances by Martha Root, exclusive invitations to special events such as the annual reunion, and a personal checklist to keep accurate records of the collection.

Martha Root keeps a busy schedule dividing her time between sculpting and personal appearances across the country. The Collector's Club magazine keeps collectors notified of upcoming signings, and they are among the first in line to have their collectibles autographed by the soft-spoken and gentle-mannered artist.

Miss Martha Originals and the All God's Children Collector's Club have widespread appeal because there is a little bit of child still left in each of our hearts. These delightfully sculpted children help us reach back and touch a time when our lives were filled with a sense of wonder. With open edition figurines starting as low as $24.00, these adorable sculptures certainly are a joy to own, as well as a good value.

While the nostalgic children figurines were being embraced by collectors across the country, Miss Martha also decided to focus her attention and raise awareness about an important part of African-American history.

***HISTORICAL SERIES* HONORS AFRICAN-AMERICANS**

In 1989, she launched the *Historical Series*. Miss Martha does all her own research before sculpting each original figurine in the series – a task that has enriched and challenged her own daily life. With each subject, she encounters the determination, vision and courage that men and women in Black history have unselfishly given as a legacy and gift to future generations.

Her first introduction in 1989 was "Harriet Tubman," who played an influential role in the Underground Railroad as she bravely faced all odds to secure safety for those yearning for freedom. The "Harriet Tubman" figurine retired in 1994 but is still among the most beloved and sought-after figurines.

The series proudly includes other great historical figures such as "Frederick Douglass," "Ida B. Wells," "Mary Bethune," "George Washington Carver," "Mary Mahoney," and the newest introduction "Clara Brown," a businesswoman, humanitarian and nurse who was a pioneer in the West.

One collector from New Jersey, whose first piece was "Harriet Tubman," notes: "Martha sculpts her own line, and you can feel the love she puts into each piece – somehow it just seems to come through. She puts herself into the artwork which gives a truth to it – a genuineness. There is a dignity to the line that is captivating and reflects that she views her art as a ministry."

The development of each Miss Martha Original figurine requires an intense period of research, sculpting and painstaking production.

CRAFTED WITH CARE AND PRIDE IN THE U.S.A.

The process begins when Miss Martha sculpts the original figurine using soft clay. In the mold room, silicone rubber is then poured over the original sculpture making the first master.

Next, the master prototypes are cast, and the first castings are sent back to Miss Martha for approval. Production molds are then made, and each separate mold is marked with a number which appears on each figurine crafted with that mold. Any one mold can be used only 50 to 75 times before it is destroyed to avoid loss of detail.

Figurines are cast using a special blend of resins and pecan shell flour, washed in a special solution, and then the bottoms of the figurine are sanded.

"Tangie" can't wait for her own wedding, so she puts on a white gown and veil to dream about becoming a bride. Sculpted by Martha Root, the 5-1/2" resin figurine retails for $45.00.

"Theo" is happy to be six years old! This heavenly child is among the figurines in the new* Count Your Blessings *series, which celebrates birthdays and makes them memorable for many years to come.

Mold seams are removed and each piece is inspected for quality.

Figurines are painted by skilled craftspeople, with the quality control department inspecting the painting, doing necessary touch-ups and painting facial features. Antiquing stain is applied next, followed by finishing touches such as hairbows. After a final quality control inspection, figurines are boxed for shipment.

To authenticate each figurine, the signature of Martha, the name of the piece, copyright line, the phrase "God Is Love," and the mold number are etched in. A Certificate of Authenticity is provided with each figurine at the time of purchase. Each collector is invited to establish a personal number for the *All God's Children* pieces through their retailer. As figurines retire, they are then available only on the secondary market.

Miss Martha Originals is continually introducing new figurines or launching new series. Among the most recent is the birthday series entitled *Count Your Blessings*. The first seven figurines of the ten-piece series are: "Cece," "Levi," "Anna," "Taci," "Rei," "Asia" and "Theo." The figurines stand about 2" tall.

MISS MARTHA INTRODUCES NEW BIRTHDAY SERIES

"Of all the little children created by Miss Martha, there has never been a series which reaches the very depth of your soul like *Count Your Blessings*," says Carolyn Snead, general manager for Miss Martha Originals. "Just one look and you immediately feel the warmth and happiness and a deep love for children. These figurines truly touch the heart."

For Martha Root, there is a piece of her heart in each of the figurines, and a piece of her heart that she wants to share with collectors.

CLUB

ALL GOD'S CHILDREN COLLECTOR'S CLUB
P.O. Box 5038
Glencoe, AL 35905
(205) 492-0221

Annual Dues: $20.00;
$35.00 Outside the Continental U.S.
Club Year: June 1 - May 31
Collector Year: Anniversary of Sign-Up Date

BENEFITS:
- Membership Gift: Figurine
- Opportunity to Purchase Members-Only Figurine
- Quarterly Magazine
- Membership Card
- Invitation to Annual "Family Reunion"
- Personal Checklist to Keep Accurate Records of Collection
- Local Club Chapters

SHOWROOM

MISS MARTHA ORIGINALS, INC. SHOWROOM
1119 Chastain Blvd.
Gadsden, AL 35905
(205) 492-0221

Hours: Monday through Thursday, 8 a.m. - 5 p.m.; Friday, 8 a.m. - Noon
Admission Fee: None

The showroom displays every figurine sculpted by Martha (Holcombe) Root, including *All God's Children, Miss Martha Collection, Endearing Memories Collection* and *Ragbabies*.

TO LEARN MORE:

MISS MARTHA ORIGINALS
P.O. BOX 5038
GLENCOE, AL 35905
(205) 492-0221
FAX: (205) 492-0261

MUNRO COLLECTIBLES, INC.

A Chance Taken to Create Lasting Impressions for Collectors

The year is 1977. Gas prices are high. Interest rates are beginning to soar. Corporate life is frustrating. A recent addition has just been added to the family. What a perfect time to start a new business!

So Doug and Barb Mitchell bet their life savings that they could create a business that would thrive and make them happy. Munro Enterprises (later to be changed to Munro Collectibles) was launched, and like a fine red wine, the business is now beginning to reach its peak flavor. But the vision and determination of a naturalized citizen from Scotland was required to nurture this spirit.

"Spirit of America" from the **Prestige Design** *collection represents the pursuit of the American dream.*

CHOOSING LINES AND OBTAINING DISTRIBUTION RIGHTS

Surviving the first two years of a start-up is the most crucial element to achieving a lasting enterprise. Armed with this knowledge, the Mitchells plotted the course that would take them to the American dream. Initially, Barb kept her job to provide an income to support their young family. But she also kept the books and paid the bills at Munro.

Doug committed himself to building a business full time. But what exactly would Munro do? His most recent experience was as a partner in a retail gift store. While the business was enjoyable, it did not afford him the opportunity to travel much. So he thought that with his retail experience he could seek out new gift lines and become a wholesaler. Supplying the growing number of gift stores seemed like it could be a lucrative and fun business. And he would get to travel!

Not having a product of its own, Munro would need to find lines that it could distribute. Doug's first thought was to import items from the United Kingdom. He knew that European products were considered to be high quality, and he was certain that he wanted to offer only something of which he could be proud. Having jumped into the American melting pot from Scotland, Doug was familiar with "The Potteries" in Stoke-on-Trent. There, he started his search for product only to find that as a start up business, it was difficult to convince the bigger manufacturers to take a chance on his new company.

That meant Munro would have to focus on lesser known (completely unknown in the U.S. for that matter!) companies. The task of building his company would be more difficult, but the experience led Doug to what is now a cornerstone of his business. That is: If you offer a quality product at a price just below the market leaders, you will win business. The important thing was the product had to be as good or better than the products you were selling against.

Silk screen mirrors, bone china and a line of pewter figurines were the first products secured for distribution. Knowing that he would be "on the road" traveling the gift show circuit for months, Doug threw himself into learning everything about how each product was manufactured and even packaged. He wanted to be certain that his product was well made and would arrive to stores in top condition. Understanding the details gave him the knowledge that could be passed on to store owners. That knowledge also gave him an infectious enthusiasm that his product was excellent in quality. His efforts quickly paid off, and he began successfully competing against better known companies.

A NEW MEDIUM HELPS MUNRO STAND OUT

Selling good products and making some very good friends was a great way to make a living. But with each passing year, Doug looked for a way to differentiate Munro from everyone else. During his many trips to England and countless hours spent in factories, Doug kept an eye out for something he could present to the U.S. market as an innovation. What he found was an experiment with a new medium that would change the way people viewed porcelain.

At the time, porcelain was considered to be a standard for figurines. There were many fine porcelain houses in Europe, but Munro was unable to secure distribution rights. To counter their strength, Doug decided to help pioneer the new medium he had seen being developed in England. This new medium would allow the production of a figurine with complex detail, vivid colors and subtle shading blends.

The new medium was a cold-casting process that blended porcelain with a resin mixture, hence the term cold-cast porcelain. While quite common today, the process was radically different then. Suddenly, sculptors could literally pile on detail without worrying about whether or not a mold could be made. Painters could further enhance the product with realistic detail. The result was sculptures that could mimic nature.

The first products Munro brought into the U.S. 15 years ago were a series of wildlife, bird and domesticated animal figurines. So began the company's long association with wildlife. Initially the line was met with skepticism. How could these products be of such high quality when they cost so little? Compared to the benchmark porcelain to which the market had grown accustomed, this cold-cast product was significantly less expensive.

Much education was required to convert retailers to the benefits of this new medium. Doug displayed his new products in all the market centers and for the major buying groups that were rising to prominence at the time. But it was during the annual plate and collectible show in South Bend, Indiana, that he knew for certain his product would take off. What happened? Consumers! Listening to the reaction of consumers, he realized that he was offering a product that was now affordable to a much broader market. Hence, he would be helping to bring new customers into a retailer's store. Tiny Munro Enterprises would be in the forefront of a new market!

"Bethor," from* Enchantica *fiercely depicts some of the brilliant colors found in the number-one fantasy line.

CREATING ITS OWN PRODUCTS

As cold-cast porcelain developed and other companies began working with the medium, Munro continued to look for ways to stand apart. One move was to go "up-market," and this was accomplished by securing the distribution rights from an Italian vendor. Italian sculptors had always been noted for the artistic flair with which they approached their subject. More importantly, quality was assumed with Italian product.

The cold-cast process allows for layers of detail to create realistic sculptures.

Another point of distinction would be to create product that nobody else was making and tackle subject matter that larger companies would not. Using the experience he had gained selling pewter, Doug believed there was an untapped market for fantasy figurines that were both realistic and of high quality. He also felt that such a line needed to be proprietary and based on a story so the figures could come to life. The idea was shared with a supplier in England, who in turn created what is today known as *Enchantica*. Brought to market in 1988, *Enchantica* characters are presented as relatively high-end collectibles that are sold around the world.

With a truly unique product, Munro's growth began to accelerate. But Munro did not own or control the rights to *Enchantica*. As the distributor of this and other European products, Munro's future was not in its own hands. Doug and Barb (who had long since given up her day job to handle the day-to-day operations of Munro!) decided they really needed their own products that could never be taken away from them.

Numerous attempts were made to create items to be manufactured in England that was Munro product. Successes were modest, but incomplete. Learning a little more with each attempt, Doug finally realized that it was time to look to the Orient. Other companies had already moved production to the Far East, and the quality was fast catching up to European standards. Pricing was far more advantageous, too. The market was becoming more sophisticated, though, and price was no longer king. Value had taken over.

Now, Munro is in the early stages of creating a new line that harnesses all the lessons learned during the last 20 years by a determined Scotsman. *Prestige Design* products are the combi-

"Courage" by Michael Roche demonstrates the integrity that marks each **Prestige Design** *product.*

nation of European design flair and Asian manufacturing ingenuity using cold-cast porcelain as the medium for bringing art to life. This collection of everyday product provides enthusiasts with art that truly reflects their passions, yet does not impart sticker shock. "*Prestige Design* will be coveted by collectors with rich tastes, while at the same time, it will also be affordable for most budgets," beams Doug Mitchell.

MUNRO LAUNCHES *PRESTIGE DESIGN*: BY ENTHUSIASTS, FOR ENTHUSIASTS

Sculptors and artists have been chosen to capture subject matter with which they have a first hand knowledge. For example, "noted bronze sculptor Michael Roche has produced a series of firemen that draw from his 20-plus years as a fireman. There are competitive products, but none have been crafted with the attention to true detail that Michael brings to his work," Doug said excitedly. That gives him the confidence to know that his creation has all the little features that will make it more valuable to the connoisseur. In the case of the firemen series, the equipment has been crafted to scale and even the uniforms have been painted to look dirty because a real fireman would never be seen in a clean uniform!

"I have been fortunate during my career in the gift industry to have met and learned from so many knowledgeable individuals. Listening to them has kept Munro moving forward," said Doug Mitchell. "But without a doubt, the greatest joy I have had has been the delight on the faces of numerous collectors as they have studied my products."

CLUB

ENCHANTICA COLLECTORS CLUB
1220 Waterville-Monclova Rd.
Waterville, OH 43566
(419) 878-0034

Annual Dues: $35.00; $60.00 for 2 Years
Club Year: January - December

BENEFITS:
- Membership Gift Figurine
- Opportunity to Purchase Members-Only Piece
- Full-Color Newsletter Published 3 Times per Year
- Membership Card
- Invitations to Attend Artist Events
- Opportunity to Attend Extravaganza Event Held Each May in England
- Catalog

TO LEARN MORE:

MUNRO COLLECTIBLES, INC.
1220 WATERVILLE-MONCLOVA RD
WATERVILLE, OHIO 43566
(419) 878-0034
FAX: (419) 878-2535
E-mail: robcamjac@aol.com

Enchantica *celebrates its Tenth Anniversary with "The Adventure Begins."*

ORIGINAL APPALACHIAN ARTWORKS, INC.

Cabbage Patch Kids® Find Loving Homes Around the World

In 1976, a 21-year-old art student named Xavier Roberts combined his interest in sculpture with the quilting skills passed down for generations in the Appalachian Mountains. The results were life-size cloth "babies" that looked so homely that they were adorable.

Roberts called his babies "Little People®," made them available for adoption, and began taking them to craft shows around the Southeastern United States. He dressed the babies in second-hand clothing purchased at yard sales and gave each original a single name chosen from a 1937 baby book.

By 1978, the demand to adopt these Little People was so great that Roberts and five college friends renovated an old doctor's clinic in Cleveland, Georgia, to house the babies. In that office just 70 miles north of Atlanta, BabyLand General® Hospital was officially opened to the public in July 1978, and is now one of northeast Georgia's most popular tourist attractions.

Roberts' creative company was incorporated as Original Appalachian Artworks, Inc. – the business that started a worldwide phenomenon with national publications filling their pages with feature stories on Roberts' adoptable and adorable babies.

In 1982, the babies became known as *Cabbage Patch Kids®* – a name as recognizable as the babies' smiles, personality and charm. Today, millions of people enjoy the fun and fantasy of the *Cabbage Patch Kids*, brought to life by a young artist and made possible by his dreams.

It's always a special delivery with the* Cabbage Patch Kids®*. Collectors have the opportunity to witness a birth during Mobile Patch appearances at select adoption centers across the country.

To say the world beat a path to the door of BabyLand is an understatement. Prospective "parents" and reporters from around the world flocked to see the Little People in Cleveland, Georgia. Select, privately owned gift shops, known as "Adoption Centers," made Roberts' babies available for adoption nationwide. More than 650,000 of these hand-stitched original babies from the Cabbage Patch have found happy homes around the world. In order to ensure authenticity, each baby came with a birth certificate and adoption papers, which are still recorded at BabyLand in Cleveland. Through the Oath of Adoption, the babies are assured of a caring parent.

CABBAGE PATCH KIDS GROW IN POPULARITY

The growing popularity of the hand-stitched Little People was only a hint of the fame the babies would find. In August 1982, Roberts signed his first licensing agreement to produce a smaller, mass-market version of his babies. These babies featured vinyl heads and soft, pillow-like bodies. During this period, Roberts changed the name Little People to *Cabbage Patch Kids*, a name that could be registered and protected as a trademark in all product categories.

Cabbage Patch Kids encourage a nurturing behavior in children and adults alike. Their smiling faces and outstretched arms place them among the classic favorites in the toy line. Three million *'Kids™* were delivered in 1983 and set a record as the most successful new doll in the history of the toy industry. Christmas shoppers literally could not get enough of the huggable *'Kids*. A decade later, the licensed version of *Cabbage Patch Kids* still held its position as one of the four best-selling toys of all time. Since 1983, more than 86 million licensed *Cabbage Patch Kids* have been adopted worldwide.

***With her halo, golden wings and satin robe, "Joy" is the 1989 Christmas Edition of original* Cabbage Patch Kids. *Limited to only 500 babies, "Joy" is the tenth edition in the popular* Christmas Series.**

Beginning in 1995, Mattel, the world's largest toy manufacturer, began producing and marketing licensed *Cabbage Patch Kids* through an exclusive worldwide agreement with Original Appalachian Artworks. Mattel was chosen because of its expertise in the design, manufacture and marketing of children's toys. In addition to the Mattel license, current licensing agreements for the *Cabbage Patch Kids* property in the U.S. include products in the categories of toys, gifts and collectibles.

Adoption fees for the original soft-sculpture *'Kids* range from $175 for limited editions, to $650 for extremely limited, special collectors' editions, hand-signed by Xavier Roberts. Early editions of the babies, with original adoption fees of $30.00, are now valued at $8,000 or more, according to Collectors' Information Bureau. New special editions of Xavier's soft-sculpture *'Kids* continue to be "stitched-to-birth" at the Cabbage Patch each year.

The *'Kids* from Mattel are molded in vinyl and are usually priced under $40.00. Like the original hand-made versions, the Mattel *'Kids* have soft bodies, cute little fingers, "outie" belly buttons and adorable toes.

COLLECTORS ADOPT LIMITED EDITION KIDS

Through the years, the Cabbage Patch has delivered some babies as part of special collectible series. In 1987, the *Circus Parade Series* came to town with "Baby Cakes," dressed in a traditional clown romper complete with big buttons, ruffles, bright yellow hair and green eyes. In 1989, there was "Bashful Billy," a cute *'Kid* hidden beneath a hobo disguise. "Mitzi," the smallest baby in the series at 17", was introduced in 1991. She has sweet expressions to match her pink button nose and teal eyebrows.

The fourth edition to join the highly collectible *Circus Parade Series* is "Jacqueline, the Jingling Jester." From the bells on her hat to the curled tips of her shoes, "Jacqueline" is a crowd pleaser. Her outfit is a traditional jester suit handcrafted from hot pink and chartreuse satin with a sparkling bodice of sequined royal purple trimmed in metallic silver. She is the first special edition other than the Christmas edition with white hair. Introduced in 1997, "Jacqueline" is limited to only 500 girls, the smallest edition in the series to date.

In 1993, the 15th anniversary of the original Little People and the 10th birthday of licensed *Cabbage Patch Kids*, several limited edition pieces were introduced, including "Zora Mae." This limited 10th anniversary edition was the first licensed *Cabbage Patch Kid* to have a fabric face.

Collectors of Roberts' originals welcomed the *Cabbage Patch Kids* Little People Edition. These 27" girls are reminiscent of Roberts' 1978 Helen Blue Edition of Little People. Each baby wears "recycled" clothing, has pudgy features and is hand-signed by Roberts.

In 1998, Original Appalachian Artworks celebrates the 20th anniversary of the soft-sculpture originals. To mark the milestone, collectors can look for highly collectible editions from the Cabbage Patch as well as special deliveries from the Mobile Patch at select Adoption Centers.

COLLECTORS CLUB DELIVERS EXCLUSIVES

With people all over the world who couldn't seem to get enough of their favorite *'Kids,* a collectors' club was launched in 1987. The Cabbage Patch Kids Collectors Club is devoted exclusively to enjoying these fun-loving *'Kids.* Membership includes a year's subscription to the "Limited Edition," the Club's bi-monthly newsletter packed

"Hannah," the 1997 Collectors Club Convention Baby, is full of character and charm with her red hair, denim romper and white high-tops. "Hannah," who stands 22" tall, is a limited edition of 200 signed pieces.

with the latest information on *Cabbage Patch Kids*; special Club offerings created exclusively for Club members; a membership card and pin entitling collectors to special privileges exclusive to members; and a customized binder filled with information all about the Club and *'Kids*.

For the 20th anniversary of the soft-sculpture originals in 1998, Club members can receive a VIP tour of BabyLand General Hospital by appointment only. BabyLand also is open to the public with free admission.

Since 1987, the Cabbage Patch Kids Collectors Club has held an annual convention, which draws "adoptive parents" from across the country. Collectors come to take home exclusive editions. Reminiscent of Roberts' early editions of Little People, "Hannah" and "Hayley" quickly won the hearts of attendees at the 10th annual convention in 1997. "Hannah" is the 1997 Collectors Club Convention Baby. Her little cousin, "Hayley," belongs to the 1997 BabyLand General Hospital Edition. Handstitched-to-birth by artisans in the Georgia Mountains, the *'Kids* have expressive hand-blushed faces to reflect their individuality and vulnerability.

These babies were the first to have hand-painted, three-dimensional raised eyes. Their compelling eyes also have gold flecks and swirls similar to siblings from earlier editions.

Roberts hand-signed "Hannah" and "Hayley" – each of which are limited to only 200 babies. The creative world of Xavier Roberts, Original Appalachian Artworks chief executive officer, has greatly expanded – just like his *Cabbage Patch Kids*. Always an artist, Roberts works tirelessly in a variety of mediums, including films, to bring his babies to diverse audiences. A firm believer that dreams become reality, Xavier Roberts surrounds himself with a creative environment and continues to channel his energies, bringing joy to millions of people through his creations.

CLUB

CABBAGE PATCH KIDS®
COLLECTORS CLUB
P.O. Box 714
Cleveland, GA 30528
(706) 865-2171

Annual Dues: $25.00
Club Year: Anniversary of Sign-Up Date

BENEFITS:

- Member's Only *Cabbage Patch* Baby
- Membership Card
- Subscription to Bi-monthly Newsletter, "The Limited Edition"
- Buy/Sell Matching Service through Newsletter
- Invitation to Annual Convention
- Membership Pin
- Annual Holiday Gift
- Annual Renewal Gift
- Members-Only Merchandise Available
- Binder for Storing Newsletters

TO LEARN MORE:

ORIGINAL APPALACHIAN ARTWORKS, INC.
P.O. BOX 714
CLEVELAND, GA 30528
(706) 865-2171
FAX: (706) 865-5862

Fine Art in Limited Editions

What do you get when you combine the art of one of America's most gifted painters of early childhood with the finest snow-white porcelain...add a rim of 24K gold...produce and inspect each piece to flawless precision...and sell it at a price that collectors can afford? Why, Rob Anders' stunning mini plates inspired by early childhood, of course! That's why Anders' gorgeous little "minis" for Porterfield's seem to have taken the collecting world by storm, and why Anders has been called the "fastest rising new star in the collectibles field."

More and more collectors are discovering Anders' sensitive and touching images of real children in real-life situations we can all relate to. Many assume that this phenomenal artist and marketer must be "overnight sensations" – but they're intrigued to learn that Anders' and Porterfield's success didn't come suddenly. Instead it was the ultimate result of many years' of dedication and devotion to the creation of fine art and fine collectibles.

"First Look" comes free with 1999 membership in the Rob Anders Collectors Society. The membership fee is only $19.00.

Porterfield's was established early in 1995 by Lance J. Klass. An expert in the creation of beautiful, fine-art collectibles, Klass established an ambitious vision for his new firm. Porterfield's would bring the finest new art on early childhood to collectors in strictly limited editions, with uncompromising standards of quality and service. All this would be delivered at reasonable prices to ensure that all collectors could own the works of their favorite painter of early childhood.

THE MINI PLATE AS A MAJOR COLLECTIBLE

Ten years earlier, Klass had refined and developed what has since become the standard 3-1/4" miniature plate format in response to collectors' demands for smaller, more affordable, yet beautiful collector plates on child-subject themes. So many avid collectors were running out of room on their shelves, walls and tables, and in their closets, attics and garages, that an alternative was needed. Collectors wanted a way to continue collecting and displaying beautiful art without being overwhelmed by their collections. The solution was to shrink the size and cost of limited edition plates while maintaining and even enhancing their beauty.

After extensive surveying and study, Klass devised the 3-1/4" format which he reproduced in stunning, snow-white porcelain – the finest in the world. In the years to follow, he produced a major line of over 60 fine mini plates that helped establish the "minis" as a major art form in the collectibles field. They became the standard for fine, affordable plate art, beloved by collectors and a hallmark of quality in the collectibles industry.

Few issues in plate collecting history have had such a rapid secondary market price rise as the fine miniatures on early childhood that Klass produced. It was common for the minis to double or even triple in selling price within months of having sold out, and some plates went on to post even more spectacular gains on the secondary market. Having single-handedly developed the mini plates, Klass became so identified with them in the minds of people in the industry that he became known as "Mr. Mini," even though he is over 6 feet tall!

A SUPERB "MINI CANVAS" FOR ROB ANDERS

Early in 1996, Klass moved Porterfield's to Concord, New Hampshire, where he devoted all his energies to improving upon the mini plate format. One immediate change was to begin production of his ceramic transfers at the top ceramic printing facility in the United States. That way, Klass could exercise close control over their quality and fidelity to the original art, and be assured of an excellent final product.

Each plate was decorated and fired under the close supervision of the technicians at one of the leading china decorators in North America. And each plate was now lavished with a pure 24-K gold band and hand-numbered in

"Cuddling Up" was the free mini plate that came with membership in the Rob Anders Collectors Society for 1998.

gold on the reverse. Each came in a beautiful gift box with a free easel for immediate display, a hand-numbered Certificate of Authenticity, and a story about the art written by Rob Anders himself. The overall result was an increase in the beauty and intrinsic value of each mini plate, and an assurance that fine mini plates would continue to be a part of the lives, and the homes, of collectors everywhere.

Most importantly for collectors, Klass teamed up with an old friend, the renowned American portraitist Rob Anders. Anders is a Yale-educated, award-winning artist whose major works of portraiture are on display at leading colleges and universities including Harvard, Yale, the University of Pennsylvania, Rutgers, M.I.T., and many others. His originals also hang in fine preparatory schools and educational facilities, in regional and historic landmarks, shrines and government buildings, including the Massachusetts State House and the Bunker Hill Memorial Pavilion, as well as in leading corporations and fine homes across the United States.

THE ANDERS ART LEGACY

Anders has also created over a dozen postage stamps for the U.S. Postal Service. Anders' postal issues include stamps honoring: John Harvard, for whom Harvard University was named; Red Cloud, celebrated chief of the Oglala Sioux Nation; and the famous Sioux Chief Sitting Bull. He also has created stamps honoring the military educators Alden Partridge and Sylvanus Thayer, and the physician who developed the standard evaluation system for newborns, Virginia Apgar.

For 15 years, Anders also created fine pastel portraits for Breck Shampoo print advertising and commercials on both American and Canadian network television. As spokesman for Breck, he appeared on numerous local and network television news programs and talk shows, including CNN's "Take Two" and ABC's "Entertainment Tonight."

When Lance Klass approached him, Rob Anders was at the top of his profession — nationally recognized as one of the best American portraitists with the ability to accurately and sensitively capture the essence of his subjects. Now it was time for him to strike out in a new direction and focus his enormous talents and energies into portraying the wonders and joys - and occasional ups and downs - of the first years of life.

In March, 1996, Porterfield's introduced Rob Anders' first heirloom miniature plate, "First Love," to an enthusiastic reception by collectors across America. This beautiful image of two lovely children was soon followed by many others which brought to collectors Anders' unique views of the joys, the sorrows, the wonder and magic, and the realities of early childhood in a way in which they had never before been portrayed.

Here were real-looking children in real-life settings and situations reminiscent of our own childhood, and of special moments in the early years of our children and grandchildren.

Anders' mini plates touched a deep wellspring of emotion and sentiment among collectors nationwide, so it was no wonder that when "First Love" sold out, it quickly tripled in market price. Further plates by Rob Anders have had notable success as well.

THE MAGIC OF "FIRST LOVE"

Recently *Collectors Mart* magazine named Anders' "Cookies for Daddy" Father's Day plate the "hottest" plate of 1997, and in its end-of-the-year wrap-up article, the only plates even mentioned were Anders' beautiful minis portraying early childhood.

Another charming Anders' image, "Time Out," was recently voted the "Award of Excellence" by the 130,000 readers of *Collector Editions* magazine.

Perhaps the greatest honor given Anders was when he recently won two "Best of Show" awards from Collectors' Information Bureau resulting from voting at the International Collectible Exposition®. Collectors at the show completed a survey and voted Anders "Best Plate Artist." His lovely "Tucked In" image won "Best New Plate" of the year. Responding to the awards, Klass remarked that "For a relatively new artist from a new company to win such prestigious awards is remarkable indeed."

"Tucked In" by Rob Anders debuted for Mother's Day 1998 and was voted "Best New Plate" by collectors attending a 1998 collectibles show.

Rob Anders, a leader in early childhood art.

THE ANDERS SOCIETY DEBUTS

The Rob Anders Collectors Society was introduced to collectors in early 1996 and attracted thousands of members nationwide and in Canada as well. The free members-only plate that came with Charter Membership in the Society, entitled "Short Stories," is now one of the scarcest early issues created by Rob Anders and Porterfield's. It has been valued by a leading secondary market authority at over twice its issue price.

The Society entered its second successful year in 1997 with the lovely "Cuddling Up" mini plate, which was followed by "Tucked In," a special issue for Mother's Day, 1998. "Tucked In" is a sensitive portrait of childhood at its most beautiful and most precious. It reminds us all of the miraculous gift that each new life brings into the world. An immediate sensation, "Tucked In" is such a timeless and remarkable image that it has been mentioned as a potential "Plate of the Year."

One of Anders' most compelling images of early childhood may be his "First Look" mini plate, which comes free with membership in the Rob Anders Collectors Society for 1999. "First Look" continues the tradition of beautiful, sensitive and compelling images of early childhood created by this bright new star in the collectibles field and produced in flawless porcelain and gleaming gold by Porterfield's.

A BRIGHT FUTURE FOR PORTERFIELD'S

Porterfield's has quickly risen to prominence as the leading producer of standard-sized 3-1/4" mini plates on early childhood. As the company enters its third year of active operation, the future looks bright indeed. Porterfield's is a member of the Collectibles and Platemakers Guild, an Associate Member of the National Association of Limited Edition Dealers (NALED), and a member of the Direct Marketing Association (DMA).

All Porterfield's mini plates are backed by a "Year and a Day Unconditional Guarantee of Satisfaction" which allows collectors to purchase Anders' mini plates totally risk-free. They may return their purchase for what they paid at any time within a year and a day after purchase, no questions asked. According to Klass, "We are so confident of the extremely high quality of our Anders' minis and that collectors will fall in love with each one they purchase, that we're pleased to be able to offer what may be the longest and most substantial guarantee of satisfaction in the collectibles industry." The company prides itself on its prompt shipping, excellent and friendly service and flawless quality.

Speaking about Porterfield's star artist, someone once said that "Rob Anders paints children with a smile on his face, with love in his heart and with a brush dipped in sunlight." One collector said about Anders that he "touches the heart and soul of childhood. It's a rare gift, and he uses it well." Clearly, collectors love "the Porterfield's minis," and they love Anders' art!

CLUB

ROB ANDERS COLLECTORS SOCIETY
5 Mountain Road
Concord NH 03301
(800) 660-8345

Annual Dues: $19.00
Club Year: Annual

BENEFITS:
- Membership Gift: Free Members-Only Heirloom Mini Plate
- Quarterly Newsletter, "Making Magic"
- Special Sneak Previews of Forthcoming Mini Plates and Prints
- Special Contests for Rare, Artist-Signed Prizes
- Member-Get-A-Member Program with Special Prizes
- Secondary Market Updates

TO LEARN MORE:

PORTERFIELD'S
5 MOUNTAIN ROAD
CONCORD NH 03301
(800) 660-8345
FAX: (603) 228-1888
E-MAIL: clientservices@porterfields.com
URL: http://www.porterfields.com

"A Visit to Santa," Rob Anders' first-ever Christmas mini plate, shows a beautiful little girl meeting Santa for the very first time.

Not Just Christmas Anymore

When Warren Stanley began his company, Possible Dreams®, more than 15 years ago, he was determined to create a Santa Claus line that was better than anything else on the market. His *Clothtique* Santas have evolved from just a few to over 200 different images: a collectible phenomenon treasured by diehard fans from coast to coast and around the world. Today, Stanley, together with a host of renowned artists like Tom Browning, Judith Ann Griffith, Joyce Cleveland, David Wenzel, Mary Monteiro and Judi Vaillancourt, continue to "dream up" original Santas that delight customers all year long.

"But I wanted to generate that same excitement for a few lines of non-Christmas figurines as well," Stanley recently explained from his Foxboro, Massachusetts offices. "I was fortunate enough to find five extraordinary artists who have worked closely with my own artisans to produce year-round collections that are unlike anything else on the shelves! Judge for yourself: we proudly present *African Spirit™* from Wayne Still, *Tender Treasures* from Lynn Norton Parker, *Spangler's Realm™* by Randall Spangler, *Floristine Angels™* by Barbi Sargent, and *The Thickets at Sweetbriar®* by Bronwen Ross."

Wayne Still's "Peul Woman" helps capture the heritage of the Sahel region as part of Possible Dreams'* African Spirit *collection.

Renowned artist Wayne Still has captured the heart and soul of Africa in his dramatic figurines for Possible Dreams. With the *African Spirit* collection, Still helps express his heartfelt concern with the industrialization of Africa and the resulting loss of its culture and traditions. In his works, he accurately portrays tribal members, creating a true depiction of these indigenous people including their anatomy, gestures and costumes. Presented exclusively by Possible Dreams, each cold-cast figurine is meticulously hand-painted and comes complete with a handsomely designed gift box.

WAYNE STILL HELPS COLLECTORS EMBRACE THE SPIRIT OF AFRICA

After 20 years as an artist, Still was seeking library reference material for a project when he stumbled upon a book that focused on Africa's Maasai tribe. He found the subject intriguing. As he recalls, "I began to investigate all the local libraries, as well as the surrounding suburbs and bookstores. To my surprise, the information seemed to go on and on forever. Then it hit me. Here was a flashback to my past, to my days in college when I first saw the work of the Renaissance masters. Here was the connection I had so longed for. A chance to do paintings and figurines with a feel of that glorious period. It was my renaissance."

Speaking of the rich and colorful Maasai heritage, Still explains that "the flowing robes, the brilliant colors, the beautiful jewelry, magical landscapes, and exotic animals were all there. It was a chance to present an exotic world only a very few ever see." Of his *African Spirit* works of art, Still comments, "It is my hope that this project will enlighten many to the intriguing and mysterious culture that is the people of Africa, and will help preserve a way of life that is being lost to the industrialization of a continent."

Heartwarming and beautifully detailed, the *Tender Treasures* figurines of Lynn Norton Parker introduce Possible Dreams' collectors to the artist's joyful world. Parker's artistic talents come naturally, as her father, Paul Norton, was a well-known professional watercolorist and commercial artist. As a child, Lynn was fascinated with her father's work and spent many hours sketching cuddly animals and children at play. Nurtured by her parents and older brothers, and now inspired by her husband and sons, she reflects her warm and sweet personality in her heartfelt designs.

ROMANCE AND SENTIMENTALITY COMBINE IN LYNN NORTON PARKER'S *TENDER TREASURES*

The joyful life experiences of being an elementary school teacher, falling in love, getting married, and becoming a mother are portrayed in Parker's charming works of art. Flowered accents, quilted hearts, chubby little teddy bears and cuddly bunnies often accent her nostalgic figurine designs

"Blessed Peace" by Lynn Norton Parker is among the **Tender Treasures** *this artist has created for Possible Dreams.*

for Possible Dreams. She celebrates the seasons of the year with angels and Santas, which are cold-cast and hand-painted and then packaged in special gift boxes.

RANDALL SPANGLER WELCOMES FRIENDS TO SHARE IN *SPANGLER'S REALM*

It's a fanciful world filled with mystery, intrigue and a whole lot of fun, and Randall Spangler invites us all to enter *Spangler's Realm*. It's a mystical land called Ohm, that exists just beyond the mirror's reflection. There's a secret passageway for creatures called "Draglings" to creep into our whimsical imaginations. Draglings are house dragons no bigger than kitty cats – but when the Dragling twins "Dagmar" and "Dewey" visit the old Victorian home of "Ladner," the wise old wizard, their behavior is anything but feline.

In their various guises, the Draglings indulge their taste for chocolate, strawberries and other good things to eat. They take up various sports, and occupations, such as reading and house cleaning, and generally enjoy life. The Wizard's lighted mansion, "Home is Where the Magic Is," also is available to collectors.

Artist Randall Spangler had the seeds of his fertile imagination planted early at his grandparents' farm in Missouri. There, in the wooded hills, he would engage in pretend games with gentle dragons and mysterious elves. At the Art Institute of Kansas City, he learned to translate those images using ink, watercolor, colored pencil and gouache. Now, thanks to Possible Dreams, his visions come alive in figures that are beautifully cold-cast, hand-painted, and packaged in handsome gift boxes.

THE CELESTIAL APPEAL OF BARBI SARGENT'S *FLORISTINE ANGELS*

For more than 30 years, artist Barbi Sargent's unique style and innovative images have touched the hearts of young and old around the world. Her renderings for Possible Dreams' *Floristine Angels* collection are testimony to her remarkable talent. Sargent has made her mark in the art world through four separate disciplines: fine arts, book publishing, children's literature and greeting cards. Now she shares her angelic creations in three dimensions, thanks to a partnership with Possible Dreams.

No one is more excited about Sargent's work than the Possible Dreams artisans. They consider it a rare opportunity to sculpt images this beautiful and detailed – ones that raise their own talents to a higher plane. Each cold-cast angel is true to Sargent's every graceful line, to each intricate detail. Precious faces, flowing gowns, abundant flowers and greenery all are finished with a pastel aura.

A sweet young Dragling offers "A Flour Just for You" in Randall Spangler's Possible Dreams creation for **Spangler's Realm.**

A lovely angel shares her "Lessons From Above" with a cherubic little one in Barbi Sargent's figurine from Possible Dreams' **Floristine Angels collection.**

BRONWEN ROSS CONTINUES HER POPULAR *THE THICKETS AT SWEETBRIAR* COLLECTION

For several years now, Possible Dreams has been sharing the art of Bronwen Ross with enthusiastic figurine collectors. Ross' creative fires burn brightly as she develops more and more designs for *The Thickets at Sweetbriar* collection. The artist is not content to just daydream about fanciful animals living an innocent life of leisure. She actually brings them to life on a canvas rich in delicate detailing and vivid coloration.

The Thickets at Sweetbriar is an intricately rendered neighborhood of imaginary characters that tweak the heartstrings of all who see them. Possible Dreams artists translate that cuddly emotion into cold-cast sculptures, each hand-painted in subtle pastels that capture the folds and textures of their wondrous wardrobes. Then each charming character is presented in its own gift box.

"You make me feel like singing," is the saying that accompanies Bronwen Ross' "Autumn Peppergrass," one of the many delightful characters from* The Thickets at Sweetbriar *collection for Possible Dreams.

While Possible Dreams takes pride in its diversification beyond its "roots" as a creator of Santas, the firm continues to present wonderful Santas – and to support the desires of its Santa collectors. As one of "the fastest growing Santa collector's club in the world," Possible Dreams' The Santa Claus Network (SCN) is dedicated to those who experience the magic of Christmas every day of their lives.

COLLECTORS MAY JOIN THE SANTA CLAUS NETWORK®

Each member receives a free 8" Clothtique Santa figurine entitled "A Cookie from Santa," which represents a $40.00 value. In addition, there will be an annual members-only exclusive Santa created for SCN members only. A quarterly newsletter, collector guide book, and membership card round out the benefits available for the $25.00 annual membership fee. Possible Dreams cordially invites collectors to join this club, which helps spread Santa's message of love and happiness throughout the world.

CLUB

SANTA CLAUS NETWORK®
C/O POSSIBLE DREAMS
6 Perry Drive
Foxboro, MA 02035-1051
(508) 543-6667

Annual Dues: $25.00
($30.00 Outside Continental U.S.)
Club Year: Anniversary of Sign-Up Date

BENEFITS:
- Membership Gift
- Opportunity to Purchase Members-Only Santa
- Quarterly Newsletter
- Embossed Membership Card
- Collectors Guide Book – Directory of Clothtique Santas
- Buy/Sell Matching Service through Newsletter

TO LEARN MORE:

POSSIBLE DREAMS
6 PERRY DRIVE
FOXBORO, MA 02035
(508) 543-6667
FAX: (508) 543-4255

Krystonian Fantasy...and Much More!

"I am Kephren, the Recorder of tales of the past and deeds of the present." So begins *The Chronicles of Krystonia*, a fascinating account of a fantasy world over which two moons shine. Since its inception in 1987 with 19 figurines, *The World of Krystonia* from Precious Art Inc. has delighted collectors of all ages with its magical adventures. This mystical land of expansive deserts, towering mountains and lush valleys boasts an assortment of inhabitants that come to life as hand-painted figurines. But *Krystonia* also has put a new twist on collecting. Corresponding storybooks tell the tale of this make-believe kingdom!

"Serenity" marks the third of four issues in the* Fair Maiden *series of fine English figurines for Precious Art. In this work of art, a maiden rests while her valiant protector keeps guard.

The four *Krystonia* books, as narrated by Kephren the Recorder, are filled with humorous anecdotes, colorful personalities and struggles of good versus evil. The fascinating books give collectors a way to further enjoy their figurines – and to follow the storylines of their beloved characters. It's an up-close and personal approach that sparks the imagination and has led to great success for Precious Art. What's more, the books reveal the magic found throughout the wonderful land, where the search is always on for magic krystals. Whoever controls the krystals rules all of *Krystonia!*

Among the most intriguing book characters is the evil "N'Borg," who dreams of the day when he will make *Krystonia* a bleak and barren wasteland. With his henchdragon "N'Grall," "N'Borg" plots to crush the Council of Wizards from his menacing castle "Krak N'Borg." He also has a score to settle with "Klip," who took away his beautiful "N'Leila."

The Council of Wizards looks out for the best interests of *Krystonia* by thwarting "N'Borg's" plans. A host of Wizards, each with his own spell-casting specialty, rules the day. Most agree that "Graffyn" has the toughest job of all the wizards: he negotiates the transportation contracts with the dragons' leader, "Grumblypeg Grunch." All of this and much more is ours to enjoy – thanks to the writings of "Kephren," who has delivered more scrolls to translate each day via dragon transport.

KRYSTONIA COLLECTORS CLUB ANNOUNCES EIGHTH-YEAR BENEFITS

For annual dues of $30.00 per year, Krystonia Collectors Club members stay current with *The World of Krystonia* and enjoy a fine array of benefits. These include an annual membership gift, the opportunity to purchase a yearly members-only figurine, the quarterly newsletter "Phargol-Horn," a membership card, and special invitations to store events and signings.

The newest annual membership gift is "The Glowing Mashal," and the corresponding members-only figurine for purchase is "Almost There." Each figurine stands approximately 6" tall, and they harmonize to illustrate a story. In *Krystonia* there is no electricity, but they must still light their dark paths. To do this, they place "The Glowing Mashal" along the route. "The Glowing Mashal" begins with a base of carefully bundled limbs; then a deserted bird's nest is placed on top. Inside the nest a glowing krystal is added. This will provide light until it loses its power. "Almost There" addresses the problem of a krystal losing its brightness. In this piece, "Owhey" has jumped on "Jumbly's" shoulders with the thought of replacing the diminishing krystal with a new one. He struggles, reaching for the old krystal. It seems to "Owhey" that he is losing height rather than gaining it – this is because "Jumbly's" knees are buckling!

PRECIOUS ART OFFERS *FAIR MAIDENS* AND OTHER WONDERFUL ARTWORKS

While *Krystonia* is the "leading line" for Precious Art, the firm also is proud to present a wide range of additional artworks showcasing worlds of fantasy and fun. These range from the elegance of *Expressions by Juras* and the whimsy of *Funny Galore*, to the legendary tales of the *Fair Maidens*.

According to the *Fair Maidens* legend, the animals of Teldor owe a great debt to the lovely ladies of that land. It seems that once a young dragon was ensnared by the neck during a rainstorm. When the rain subsided, the wet vines around his neck began to tighten as they dried. If a maiden had not wandered by, the

Dramatic and elegant in its fantasy style, "The Awakening" has been introduced by Precious Art as part of the* Expressions by Juras *home decor collection.

young dragon surely would have died. She cut the twine from around his neck and freed him from disaster. To this day, in a place where most creatures would disappear as they entered, the maidens are permanent in this land, and they are always protected by its inhabitants.

To honor these *Fair Maidens*, Precious Art has introduced a four-piece series of figurines in which legendary animals offer protection to lovely maids. The first three pieces in the series, "Faithful Companion," "Safe Passage" and "Serenity," were issued one per year from 1994 through 1996, with the fourth and final issue unveiled in 1997. Each figurine is finely crafted and hand-painted in England, and each sits on its own wooden base with a numbered brass plaque. Each edition is limited to 1,000 pieces, and each piece comes with a Certificate of Authenticity. Issue price for each *Fair Maidens* figurine is $350.

EXPRESSIONS BY JURAS MAKE FOR ELEGANT HOME DECOR

In answer to the demand for limited editions created especially for home decor, Precious Art has joined forces with the gifted Lithuanian artist Juras to introduce a series of beautifully sculpted, English-made figurines. Each figurine stands a dramatic 14" to 16" in height, and the collection includes *Classic Nude*, *Semi-Nude* and *Classic Fantasy* works of art.

Noted for the exceptional detail of his sculpture, Juras was born into a family of recognized artists in Kaunas, Lithuania. After art studies in his homeland, Juras worked as an instructor of sculpture, drawing and anatomy at Kaunas Art School. He came to the United States with his wife, Gabrielle, in 1991. Since then, he has divided his time among the creation of collectible figurines, sculptural and architectural restoration projects, and designing and making original furniture. His favorite materials include cold-cast metals, clay and wood. Juras prides himself on his expressive composition, great attention to detail, and figurines which convey both dynamic motion and true human emotion.

THE "FUNNY-WEIRD" CREATURES OF *FUNNY GALORE*

When artist Mary-Ann Orr and her husband moved to a small town in South Africa a few years back, they "unwound from the rat race" and saw the world in a whole new light. "We became very aware of how protected certain species were and how others had to live through man's disasters," Orr recalls. The result was a series of outlandish animals entitled the *Funny Galore* series.

Orr's original concept was that if environmental pollution left only a few animals on earth, they'd "intermingle" and form a whole new species of "funny animals." But whether they focus on her environmental message or not, collectors have adopted her *Funny Frogz* and other crazy creatures as colorful additions to their homes. Made in Staffordshire, England, the new-style animals include unique "species" that loosely resemble frogs, cats, birds and other wide-eyed, lovable animals.

***A character of mystical power and wisdom, the "Stormslayer" casts a spell to save* Krystonia.**

From left, Mary-Ann Orr's* Funny Galore *creatures include "Gidump," "Frounce" and "Jerry," hopping out of the* Funny Frogz *collection.

THE ORIGINS OF PRECIOUS ART AND *KRYSTONIA*

When Precious Art first began in 1980, the company's new line of products reflected an ancient tradition. Pictures, music boxes and other accessories captured the distinctive look of Chokin art, a beautiful 13th century Japanese technique that features engraved designs on copper, gold and silver plates. Since many of the Chokin items were musicals, Precious Art soon found a niche in this area. The firm's limited edition musicals brought Precious Art into the collectibles market and paved a path for the company's most popular

In this charming, hand-painted* Krystonia *figurine, Shadra asks Gurneyfoot the age-old question: "Where Do Dragons Come From?"

collection — *Krystonia.*

The World of Krystonia started in a tiny factory in England, where its creators tapped into the British tradition of excellence and generations of skilled artisans. Although Precious Art's original product lines were made in the Far East, company officials decided to change locations, knowing the collection needed special care in combining high-quality collectibles with enjoyable stories. *Krystonia* quickly outgrew its original studios and a modern facility was built in Chesterton, England, where all of Precious Art's English products are now produced. Using cold-cast porcelain, the hand-painted figurines are carefully monitored throughout the production process. Of course, each character must have its own sparkling krystal adornment for the finishing touch.

While *Krystonia* is made in England, the collection was born from the hearts and minds of David Lee Woodard and Pat Chandok. They spend countless hours making sure that no two characters are the same, while leading a creative team of artists who breathe life into every *Krystonia* resident. Without just the right design and color, each figurine may never make it to the stage of production and naming.

Storylines for the books come from Dave, Pat and Mark Scott. They collaborate to bring to life all the different characters and adventures. After one book is completed, they start planning the next — which is sure to be filled with pages of fantasy and fun!

And thus the excitement for collectors is just beginning, as more fanciful characters emerge in the years to come — both on the printed page and in the form of elegant figurines from *The World of Krystonia.*

CLUB

KRYSTONIA COLLECTORS CLUB
125 W. Ellsworth Road
Ann Arbor, MI 48108
(313) 663-1885

Annual Dues: $30.00
Club Year: February 1 - January 31

BENEFITS:
- Membership Gift: Figurine
- Opportunity to Purchase Members-Only Figurine
- Quarterly Newsletter, "Phargol-Horn"
- Membership Card
- Store Events/Artist Signings
- Tour of Factory in England Available by Appointment

TO LEARN MORE:

PRECIOUS ART, INC.
125 W. ELLSWORTH
ANN ARBOR, MI 48108
(313) 663-1885
FAX: (313) 663-2343

Pipka's Santas and Angels Share Folk Art Traditions

Pipka Ulviden's story begins at the end of World War II when her family emigrated from Germany to America. Her father was a doctor, but his first love was art – a talent that he shared with his children. Pipka remembers drawing since the age of five in her new home in a small North Dakota town, where she admired and learned from the Old Masters paintings found in her parents' books.

Each year, her family would return to Germany to visit relatives and maintain the customs and values of their heritage. "It was in Germany that my appreciation for primitive art blossomed," she says. While Pipka loved art, her own creative talents remained dormant until she received an unexpected gift from her mother in 1972.

While visiting Germany, her mother packed up a box filled with unpainted wood, paint brushes and books on a Bavarian folk art known as "Bauernmalerei," or peasant painting. At this point, Pipka was a divorced mother with two small children. "I used the supplies to relax and get in touch with my feelings," she says. "I loved art so much that I decided this was how I would make a living and support my family."

Since then, Pipka has been sharing her beautiful artwork of Santas, angels and florals which also weave wonderful stories of folklore, customs and traditions. Today, her work has been transformed into a line of limited edition collectibles exclusively distributed by Prizm, Inc.

According to early Christmas tradition, a little angel usually accompanies "St. Nicholas" who holds a big book listing the names of girls and boys. From **Pipka's Christmas Memories** *series, this limited edition figurine captures these customs for all to cherish.*

PRIZM BRINGS PIPKA'S TALENTS TO COLLECTORS

In 1992, a friend of Pipka's sent her drawings to Gary Meidinger and Michele Johnson, then managers for TLC, a card company owned by McCall's Pattern Company. The company's artists envisioned translating Pipka's artwork into a line of Santas featuring figurines, mugs, and other giftware items. Unfortunately, TLC closed. But Gary and Michele still wanted to pursue their dream. So in 1994, they founded Prizm, Inc. to produce collectibles and gifts featuring Pipka's talents. With Gary and Michele's experience in the gift industry and Pipka's work, they knew a unique line of limited edition Santas could be introduced to collectors. Prizm sent Pipka's artwork to China, where a talented sculptor interpreted them as three-dimensional figurines.

"Pipka, Gary and I aren't related, but we're family," says Michele. "We are dedicated to one another as life partners. We started this company with a deep devotion to each other and to Pipka's wonderful artwork. Every item we bring to the gift and collectible industry is with a tremendous amount of love and support." The founders also built the company with the collector in mind, ensuring that each product and program that bears Pipka's name will be of the highest standards and quality. Their vision is to build a collectible line that excites and warms the hearts of all. For now, Pipka is Prizm's only artist. "We see ourselves as a company devoted to one line," Gary says.

OLD WORLD SANTAS START NEW TRADITIONS

In researching every Santa that she creates, Pipka has discovered that people share many of the same Christmas traditions that have been passed down through the ages. Santa Claus, or Father Christmas, is a mythical figure that transcends all races, nationalities and countries. In that respect, Pipka sees him as being holy and spiritual – a character that brings us together in the spirit of hope.

Pipka's Christmas Memories series, originally launched in 1995, features large, limited edition Santas that bring back warm thoughts of the holiday season. For 1997, Pipka introduced six more Old World Santas – each limited to only 3,600 pieces, standing 10" to 11" tall and bearing a historical story. "Russian Santa" celebrates the customs and traditions of that country from the

"Polish Father Christmas," from* Pipka's Christmas Memories *series, carries many items used in the country's holiday traditions.

singing of the "kolyadki" Christmas carols, to trimming the trees with apples and little dolls made of dried fruit and candy.

One of the favorite Christmas gifts for Victorian era children was a rocking horse, beautifully portrayed in "Santa's Spotted Grey." "Norwegian Julenisse" is the European country's version of Santa Claus. "St. Nicholas" is the original Santa Claus born in the 14th century in Lycia, a small province of the Roman Empire. He is reputed to have been very wealthy and secretly gave away generous portions of his wealth to the poor and needy. St. Nicholas was also the patron saint of Russia. Pipka's figurine features the traditional scene of a little angel accompanying St. Nicholas, who carries a big book with the names of boys and girls.

"Polish Father Christmas" wears a heavy coat of colorful embroidery, typical of rural Polish areas. On his back, he carries many items used in Polish Christmas customs, including straw, folk pitchers and a Christmas manger decorated as a fairy tale castle. "Where's Rudolph?" shows Father Christmas standing on the edge of the forest looking for his favorite reindeer.

Four Santas will be added to the *Christmas Memories* series in 1998, followed by four more in 1999. Pipka's *Christmas Memories* sculptures have already received recognition from collectors. "Czechoslovakian Santa" and "Aussie Santa & Boomer" were nominated for *Collector Editions* "Awards of Excellence" in the Figurines $50-$100 Categories.

PIPKA CREATES SMALLER SANTAS AND COLLECTIBLE ORNAMENTS

In 1997, Prizm also launched *Pipka's Reflections of Christmas,* another series of Old World Santa figurines which are smaller versions of sold-out *Christmas Memories* figurines. Some of the pieces in the series will never be issued as larger Memories figurines. The series debuted with six cold cast figurines, each limited in edition to 9,700 pieces and standing 6" tall.

"Midnight Visitor," "Czechoslovakian Santa," "Starcoat Santa" and "Star Catcher Santa" are smaller reproductions of sold-out *Memories* figurines. Pipka also created two new designs. "Better Watch Out Santa" reminds children not to cry or pout when he comes to town. "Amish Country Santa" carries an Amish quilt and tin-punched lantern to remind everyone of the simple pleasures in life.

Perfect for trimming the tree, *Pipka's Collectible Ornaments* also premiered in 1997 with six designs. Six more ornaments will be introduced in 1998 as well as 1999.

COLLECTORS FIND HEAVENLY DELIGHTS IN *EARTH ANGELS*

Pipka believes that angels are spiritual beings that bring us messages and guidance. They are the thoughts of God. With this in mind, Pipka designed her *Earth Angels* series to represent the heavenly messengers that live among us. An angel can be found in a stranger, friend or loved one.

For 1997, Pipka's wonderful *Earth Angels* collection includes three figurines, each limited to 5,400 pieces and standing 9-1/2" tall. "Messenger Angel" features an angel wearing a sash with the translated words for: "My soul does magnify the Lord. And my spirit rejoices in God my Savior." Mary said this when the Angel of the Lord gave her the news that she would bear a child named Jesus. "I have always loved this prayer of faith and wondered about the angel who witnessed the young Virgin uttering these words," Pipka says. "Surely the angel might have been a young girl, too, with a sweet smile on her lips and a light glowing from her face."

"Angel of Roses" celebrates one of the most beautiful flowers with their soft petals, sweet scent and glorious colors. The "Guardian Angel" watches over a sleeping baby in a cradle. "It is my belief that Guardian Angels take part in our earthly activities," Pipka says. "I think they nudge us down certain paths we need to take and guide us along the way. "I've designed my Guardian Angel in an outdoor setting as it is my hope that she protects the earth as well as its children." In 1998, six figurines will be added to *Earth Angels*, followed by three in 1999.

PIPKA TEACHES OTHERS HER FOLK ART WAYS

Nestled in the heart of Sister Bay, Wisconsin, Pipka's Folk Art Studio showcases her original Santas, angels and florals in a charming Victorian house and cottage. Pipka's love of folk

"Star Catcher Santa" is a smaller version of the sold-out* Christmas Memories *series figurine. The Santa collects stars deep in the forest in this 6" piece from the new* Reflections of Christmas *series.

Pipka's* Earth Angels *series for 1997 includes (clockwise from top) "Angel of Roses," "Messenger Angel" and "Guardian Angel." Each beautifully detailed figurine is limited to only 5,400 pieces.

art has also led her to share and teach her painting techniques.

For more than 25 years, Pipka has taught classes from America to Australia, and she has also authored dozens of art instruction books. Her classes and seminars are held from May through December at the Folk Art Studio. Despite her demanding schedule and growing popularity of her designs, she still puts teaching high on her list of priorities. "I love the students," she says. "Their enthusiasm and intention to learn is so contagious. What they might not guess is that I learn as much from them as they learn from me."

With tremendous support and hundreds of requests from Pipka's fans, Prizm plans to launch a collector's club in 1998. Pipka will also travel the country for in-store artist signings during the Fall of 1998, and will also attend the two International Collectible Expositions to meet collectors and retailers.

TOUR

PIPKA'S STUDIO TOUR
334 Mill Road
Sister Bay, WI 54234
(800) 829-9235

Hours: By appointment.
Admission Fee: None

Collectors are invited to visit Pipka's Studio and Gallery and see the artist at work, as she creates her much-loved Santas.

TO LEARN MORE:

PRIZM, INC./PIPKA'S COLLECTIBLES
P.O. BOX 1106
MANHATTAN, KS 66505
(888) 427-4752
FAX: (888) 867-4752

The Collectors' Storehouse

Pulaski Furniture Corporation (PFC) is making quite a name for itself with collectors. No, the company doesn't make figurines, bells, cottages, teddy bears, or dried apple dolls. It makes the things that you put collectibles in. They're called curio cabinets. And hundreds of independent furniture stores, chains, and department stores nationwide have become authorized PFC Collectors Curio dealers. No wonder Pulaski accounts for over 60% of the curio business in America!

So how does Pulaski continue to grow if they already command the lion's share of the market? By continuing to target more collectors. By some estimates, eight out of every ten Americans collect something. Those who don't collect need a place to display their knick-knacks, family photos, or something they made at their shop class in high school. Now, Pulaski has taken its message to retail floors with banners and signage. PFC Collectors Curios are adorned with pictures of collectibles – from figurines to sports memorabilia.

At the recent International Home Furnishings Market in High Point, North Carolina, buyers were interviewed throughout the market and asked, "What Do You Collect?" Then their Polaroid pictures and their collectible choices were posted on a huge bulletin board for all to see. This theme now appears in consumer magazine advertising in publications such as *Collecting Figures, Figurines & Collectibles*, and *Teddy Bear & Friends*. Consumers can call an 800 number or respond through a Readers Service Card to locate their nearest PFC Collectors Curio dealer.

The success of Pulaski hinges on the fact that collectors want to keep their prized possessions safely and beautifully displayed for all to enjoy. With its variety of styles and finishes, featuring mirrored backs and canister lighting, Pulaski creates the ultimate showcase for most anyone's favorite things.

COLLECTIBLES DESERVE A GOOD HOME

This handsome Pulaski curio cabinet shows off a host of collectible figurines, cottages, plates and other works of art.

PFC Collectors Curios offer the perfect solution to collectors whose favorite pieces are gathering dust out in the open – often lined up on shelves that are either too high or too low to see. Worse yet, some collectors have their treasures packed away in the attic, basement or closet for lack of a proper method of display. PFC Collectors Curios give figurines a stage, dolls a house, bears a den and cottages a neighborhood, where they can be admired by friends, family and guests.

Founded in Pulaski, Virginia, in 1955, Pulaski Furniture Corporation is one of the country's largest furniture producers with domestic and export sales exceeding $175 million annually. In 1996, Pulaski repackaged its curio program under the PFC Collectors Curio umbrella. The company manufactures hundreds of design and finish combinations in its curio line, offering collectors a wide variety to choose from, and complementing any decor.

FOUR DECADES OF FINE FURNITURE TRADITION

PFC Collectors Curios advertisements promote the furniture as offering the perfect place for everything from

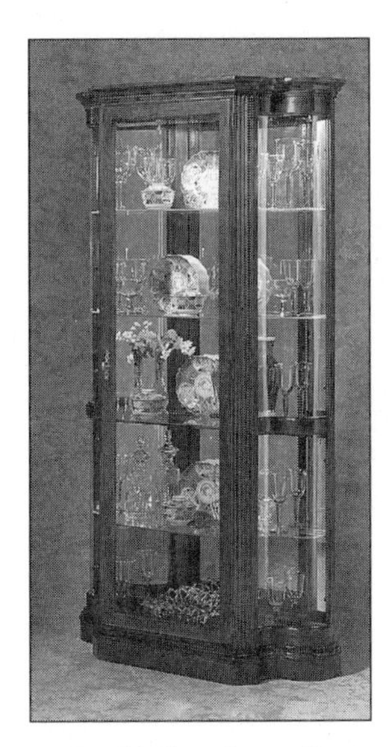

Pulaski Furniture Company creates fine furniture curio cabinets to suit every decor in traditional, transitional and contemporary styles.

Charter members of the PFC Collectors Club can receive "Curios Henry," a figurine that features a popular and adorable Jack Russell Terrier.

porcelain figurines to wooden nutcrackers. More and more collectors nationwide are educating themselves on caring for and displaying their cherished collectibles. In doing so, they are turning to Pulaski for the answers.

Thanks to its Ridgeway Curio Clocks division, Pulaski features clocks as well as cabinets. One particularly impressive design showcases an elegant grandfather clock surrounded by shelves for collectibles, making anyone's treasures even more timely.

PFC COLLECTORS CLUB WELCOMES MEMBERS

To establish stronger ties and to get to know its curio customers, Pulaski launched the PFC Collectors Club. Charter members receive the company's first limited edition figurine, "Curios Henry," an adorable and popular Jack Russell Terrier. The hand-painted polymer figurine is available free to collectors who join the Club – and can be displayed in the company's curio cabinets. An annual Club membership is $29.95.

"Curios Henry will become a very cherished collectible," predicts Randy Chrisley, Pulaski's vice president of sales. "And because of its limited distribution, we expect the series to eventually do quite well on the secondary market." More information about the Club is available by writing Pulaski Furniture Corporation, Attention: PFC Collectors Club, P.O. Box 1371, Pulaski, VA 24301.

FINE FURNITURE FROM PULASKI

Curios are part of Pulaski's accessory division, which also includes hall trees, tables and consoles. Other business segments of the corporation include Ridgeway Clocks' grandfather, wall and mantel clocks; casegoods for bedrooms, dining rooms and living rooms; Accentrics, occasional furniture with a European accent; and Accents-To-Go, a furniture line that can fold down to fit in cars.

In 1996, Pulaski launched the *HomeTrack Collection*, a line of curios, clocks, hall trees, consoles, tables and recliners that target racing fans. The collection is sold exclusively through the large furniture chain, Heilig-Meyers.

Over the years, Pulaski has been recognized for its creative furniture, most of which can be attributed to its renowned designer Leonard Eisen. Pulaski furniture, curios, clocks and accessories may be found at thousands of independent furniture stores, department stores and major furniture chains nationwide.

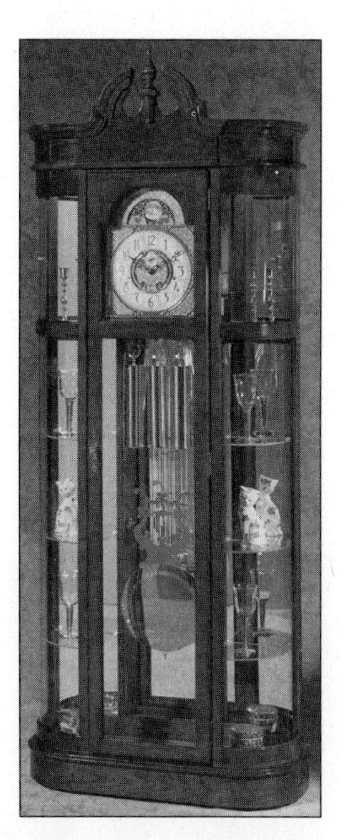

Ridgeway Clocks, a division of Pulaski Furniture Corporation, presents a line of curio clocks that make timeless keepsakes even as they display a collector's favorite treasures.

CLUB

PFC COLLECTORS CLUB
P.O. Box 1371
Pulaski, VA 24301
(540) 980-7330

Annual Dues: $29.95 - Renewal: $24.95
Club Year: Anniversary of Sign-Up Date

BENEFITS:

- Membership Kit: "Curious Henry," Limited Edition Jack Russell Terrier Figurine, and Other Special Members-Only Gifts
- Quarterly Newsletter, "The Yapper"
- Membership Card
- Special Sneak Previews and Member Incentives for Purchase of Pulaski Furniture

TO LEARN MORE:

PULASKI FURNITURE CORPORATION
ONE PULASKI SQUARE
PULASKI, VA 24301
(800) 287-4625

What's on the horizon? Pulaski is exploring licensing possibilities with well-known collectible manufacturers. These particular curios would be custom designed to best house specific products. For instance, small figurines would require more glass shelves. Plates would be safest in grooved shelves. For crystal, shelves would be made of heavier glass. Whatever the innovation, Pulaski Furniture Company is dedicated to crafting quality furniture that fits any room and budget. The company also is dedicated to providing collectors with curio cabinets that let treasures move into their own little corner of the world!

Three Decades of Quality Collectibles

When Heio Reich founded Reco International Corp. in 1967, he wanted to surround American collectors with a wide variety of world-class collectibles in an equally diverse assortment of fine art media. And he did just that. As a native of Berlin, Reich was in contact with many European art studios, allowing Reco to gain fame by introducing plates from some of Europe's most celebrated makers, including Fuerstenberg, Royale, Dredsen, Royal Germania, Crystal, King's and Moser.

Sandra Kuck combines the heavenly grace of angels with the blooming beauty of gardens in a new plate series. "Heavenly Hideaway" is the first issue in* Sandra Kuck's Gardens of Innocence *collection. Each scalloped plate is limited to 95 firing days.

Many of the plates Reco imported to the United States have risen substantially in price since their introduction in the late 1960s and early 1970s. But sensing a golden opportunity in 1977, Reich steered his business in a different and new direction. Since then, Reco International has reigned as one of the nation's top producers of limited edition plates by renowned American painters like Sandra Kuck, John McClelland and Jody Bergsma.

While some studios specialize in only one content area such as children or wildlife, Reco seeks out artists who paint in many styles and capture a variety of subjects. Kuck's Victorian children and Bergsma's fantasy visions take center stage in the current Reco line-up. Retired from the active plate market, McClelland remains an all-time collector favorite for his paintings of adorable children. Dot and Sy Barlowe have crafted vivid portraits of wildlife and nature for Reco, while Clemente Micarelli has painted homages to the ballet, religious events and weddings. Subjects as diverse as French café scenes, lighthouses and hot air balloons also may be found in the Reco archives.

While Reco's products represent a panorama of artistic styles, media and subjects, Heio Reich's company philosophy unites all creations with a shared vision of excellence. Reich's goal is for the company to create beautiful products to bring enjoyment and a life-long interest and hobby to collectors. Reco's commitment to produce only the very best art on plates and in other media will continue well into the 21st century – just as it has since 1967.

AWARDS RECOGNIZE RECO'S COMMITMENT TO QUALITY

Striving to be the best also brings well-deserved recognition. Reich and his artists have never sought personal glory or awards. Indeed, they consider their finest accolade the gleam in a happy collector's eyes. Nonetheless, Reich has received nearly every prestigious honor available to a collectibles marketer or producer. These awards include: "Vendor of the Year," "Producer of the Year," the "Lee Benson Memorial Award," the "International Collectible Achievement Award" and the "Silver Chalice Award" for selected plates.

Reich also has long been an active member and leader in the National Association of Limited Edition Dealers (NALED) and the Plate Makers Guild. He was also a charter member of the Board of Directors of Collectors' Information Bureau.

In addition to the company's leaders receiving recognition, Reco's artists have also been singled out for their work. McClelland and Kuck have been lauded at scores of conventions and collectors' gatherings with "Plate of the Year," "Artist of the Year" and many other honors. Kuck is readily acknowledged as the most honored collectibles artist of all time – including an unprecedented six consecutive "Artist of the Year" awards from NALED.

The company and its artists also enjoy a visible presence before collectors. Reich is particularly proud that Reco has exhibited at every International Collectible Exposition since the famous show began more than 20 years ago in South Bend, Indiana.

Inspired by the artistry of Sandra Kuck, "Jennifer Rose" walks down the aisle on her wedding day. From her bouquet of roses to her embroidered lace gown, no detail has been overlooked in this beautiful porcelain doll.

Although Reco's fame stems mostly from works of art in fine porcelain, the firm has marketed and manufactured pieces in many other materials and media over the years. The early King's plates, for example, featured delicate, bas-relief floral motifs, and the Royale Germania plates were crafted of gleaming crystal.

MEDIUMS FOR ALL COLLECTORS FROM PLATES TO FIGURINES

Say the name "Reco" to contemporary collectors, however, and they are likely to think of porcelain plates by Kuck, McClelland and Bergsma. Another important concentration for Reco in the porcelain plate realm is what Reich likes to call "Special Occasions" plates. The firm's early European-made series often focused on Christmas, Mother's Day, Father's Day and Easter. Kuck's Christmas series – showing children in memorable holiday scenes – has won the hearts of many collectors with the plates' holiday warmth and traditional charm. Kuck has also created original art to honor Mother's Day, christenings, weddings and other memorable occasions.

In addition to plates, Reco crafts figurines both in shimmering porcelain and cold-cast resin, a popular medium due to its ability to capture intricate details. McClelland's silky white angels helped establish Reco as an important maker of three-dimensional art. Now Bergsma enhances this well-earned reputation with the adorable animals in her *Laughables* line.

Kuck's exquisite work has been delicately recreated in a new figurine collection titled *Sandra Kuck's Treasures.* Capturing the poignant and heartwarming features of Sandra's work, and sculpted with the same incredible detail found in her paintings, these figurines represent the true treasures in our lives – the innocent and endearing memories of childhood. The line of petite figurines is approximately 3" to 4-1/2" tall and depicts lovely little children dressed in youthful, Victorian finery and lovingly engaged in favorite childhood pastimes.

Kuck's precious children also seemed destined to come alive as elegant, collectible dolls. And Reco was up to the challenge of creating heirloom-quality bisque beauties. Kuck's beautiful characters are captured in fine porcelain and painted to enhance the delicate blush of a cheek and the grace of a child's tiny fingers and hands. The dolls' costumes faithfully portray Kuck's love for Victoriana and whimsy with flowing frocks, charming accessories and marvelous trimmings in ribbon and lace. What's more, each doll tells a story. Recent additions to the doll collection designed by Kuck are a Christmas doll named "Carol" and a fabulous bride doll titled "Jennifer Rose."

Featuring artwork of its noted artists, Reco recently introduced wall wreaths and porcelain *Angel Wing* mugs from Kuck, porcelain mugs from Bergsma and a unique collection of architectural sculptings from the future by renowned science fiction artist Vincent Di Fate. Always on the alert for new ways to share the art of favorite painters, Reco has diversified its offerings to include music boxes and keepsake boxes, each enhanced by beloved artwork. Some of the boxes are handcrafted of walnut and mahogany, while others are made of shimmering porcelain.

Reco International remains a family-owned business, and the firm cultivates a warm and friendly atmosphere both in its internal operations and in its relationships with artists. Reco employees take a personal interest in the products they help create and in the artists whose work inspires each new edition.

A FAMILY OF ARTISTS MAKE COLLECTORS FEEL AT HOME

The artists are also important and beloved members of the Reco family. Although McClelland is now retired from creating plate art, many of his works are still available on the primary and secondary markets. Later series may be acquired at issue price through many dealers, while earlier McClelland favorites are available only at auctions and through secondary market exchanges. Reco continues to receive scores of letters from McClelland fans and collectors, showing the personable artist remains a favorite.

For nearly 20 years, Kuck has

Sandra Kuck's Treasures ***is the long-awaited collection of petite figurines capturing the artist's heartwarming and memorable portraits of childhood. "Teddy and Me," among the first introductions to the collection, features a little girl reading to her cuddly friend.***

These additions to the* Laughables *collection by Jody Bergsma bring smiles and joy to each special occasion that they celebrate, from Mother's Day to birthdays. The figurines are accompanied by a humorous verse to live by.

TO LEARN MORE:

RECO INTERNATIONAL CORP.
150 HAVEN AVE.
PORT WASHINGTON, NY 11050
(516) 767-2400
FAX: (516) 767-2409

charmed Reco collectors with her romantic and nostalgic portraits. Ever since her "Sunday Best" plate was introduced in 1983, Kuck has reigned as the "sweetheart" of collectors throughout North America and beyond its boundaries. She enjoys a remarkable talent for intricate, detailed work, as well as a deep love for "all things Victorian." Combine this with her ability to capture the fresh-faced innocence of little ones, and it's easy to understand why collectors are so devoted to Kuck and her artistic creations.

Bergsma has a whimsical and joyous heart – qualities which are evident in her fantasy artwork. Her unicorns and dragons combine mystery with beauty, and her "Little People" and animals mix warmth with whimsy. Bergsma expanded her repertoire beyond watercolor prints and collector plates to introduce the *Laughables* figurines – a lighthearted group of animals designed to bring a smile to everyone's face. Each comes with a humorous verse to match their laughs.

Bergsma shows her contemplative side in a plate series entitled *Totems of the West*. To create this dramatic series, she traveled extensively and researched the spiritual forces considered sacred by Native Americans.

To keep collectors updated on Kuck's artwork and newest introductions, Reco publishes a bi-annual newsletter. The publication provides an up-close and personal glimpse into the world and work of this delightful artist. It also offers Kuck collectors valuable news about upcoming products and their availability. To add your name to the mailing list and receive the Sandra Kuck Newsletter at no charge, simply send your name and address to: Sandra Kuck Newsletter, c/o Reco International Corp., P.O. Box 951, Port Washington, New York, 11050.

KUCK COLLECTORS RECEIVE FREE NEWSLETTER

ROMAN, INC.

Collectibles for Every Day and Every Occasion

Among the largest privately owned and operated firms in the industry, Roman, Inc. is a leading producer and exclusive distributor of more than 15,000 giftware items. An extraordinary blend of creativity, marketing and experience, Roman was founded 35 years ago by its president and owner Ronald T. Jedlinski. Its award-winning lines include *Fontanini® Heirloom Nativities*, the *Seraphim Classics® Collection*, *Declan's Finnians™*, *The Many Faces of Allyson Nagel™* collection, and a wide range of inspirational, special occasion and seasonal giftware items.

The story of Roman, Inc. is the story of Ron Jedlinski. He started his company with $500 and a car trunk full of inspirational products for the religious market, and now leads one of the foremost gift companies in the U.S. With a family background in giftware retailing – his father operated Roman's Art and Gift Shop – it was nearly inevitable that Jedlinski would enter some facet of the collectibles and giftware fields.

"Alexandra – Endless Dreams" is an extraordinary addition to the* Seraphim Classics® Collection, *America's number-one angel collection.

Jedlinski's eye for product development, business acumen and supplier relationships resulted in regular imports of Italy's finest offerings by the early 1970s. In 1973, Roman, Inc. became the exclusive distributor for *Fontanini Heirloom Nativities*. (See feature article on page 144.) With this splendid line, he positioned Roman as the singular North American source for the sought-after collection, prized for its life-like sculpting, meticulous hand-painting and attention to detail from a world-famous name in Italian craftsmanship.

SERAPHIM CLASSICS COLLECTION & FONTANINI HEIRLOOM NATIVITIES

In the early 1990s, Jedlinski formed Seraphim Studios, a creative umbrella of world-famous artists and sculptors. Their singular assignment was to research and develop a collection of angels that would be modern interpretations of the world's most beautiful angels. Seraphim Studios took advantage of more than 2,000 years of writings and works of art to achieve their objective. The result was introduced to the world in 1994: the *Seraphim Classics Collection*. (See feature article on page 284.) Based on the greatest artistic achievements of the Renaissance Masters, the collection immediately won the enthusiastic acceptance of both retailers and consumers. Within a single year, it was apparent that the *Seraphim Classics Collection* was destined to be a collectible.

With some of America's and Europe's finest artists creating distinctive collectibles for Roman, Jedlinski has played a major role in converting perception of figurines from "dust collectors" to "valued collectibles." He takes in stride the many changes he has weathered in the highly competitive giftware and collectibles industries with the attitude: "This is the American way, which certainly creates an exciting and dynamic marketplace."

Inspired by his passion for Ireland, its rich folklore and his particular fascination with the legend of the Blarney Stone, Declan Fearon is the creative spirit behind *Declan's Finnians™: Guardians of the Blarney Stone*.

The *Finnians* are colorful, handcrafted wee folk, each with its own clever story and a small stone from the same Irish quarry that was the source of the fabled Blarney Stone and historic Blarney Castle. Beginning with 16 *Finnians* in 1994, the collection has increased to more than 50 *Finnians* featuring bewhiskered characters ranging from a golfer and a musician, to a storyteller and a banker. The collection has grown in popularity and was honored by *Collector Editions* with a 1997 "Award of Excellence" for Best Sports Collectible.

DECLAN'S FINNIANS: GUARDIANS OF THE BLARNEY STONE

Fearon's interest in the Blarney Stone began when he visited the ruins of Blarney Castle in the Cork Village of Blarney. A standard of Irish folklore for centuries, the Blarney Stone, according to legend, is found at Blarney Castle and has the power to bestow the gifts of eloquence and good luck upon those who kiss it. Since the 14th century, people have come from all over the world to kiss the Blarney Stone. Since 1994, thanks to Declan Fearon, a journey to one of thousands of U.S. gift and

"Anthony," part of **Fontanini Heirloom Nativities** *by Roman, is the celestial guide for the Holy Family on their journey to Egypt.*

collectibles stores is all that is necessary to share in the enchantment of the fabled Blarney Stone. "Through the magic of *Declan's Finnians*," Declan promises, "the gifts of eloquence and luck will be yours when you touch the stone and release its charms."

Fearon studied at the University of Dublin and has been a successful businessman for over 30 years. A surveyor by training, Fearon found his future, not in his knowledge of the land and its boundaries, but in the knowledge of his country, its history and the personality traits that know no boundaries. Collectors often find familiar aspects of themselves, their family and their friends in the faces and stories these enchanting figures extol.

Declan's Finnians is truly a family affair. Together with his wife, Camilla, and his four children, Colin, David, Mark and Julie Anne, the family works on the concept and design. Fearon's passion for Irish lore, coupled with the family's fertile imagination, bestows personality traits upon each *Finnians* character, and each tells his tale with just a touch of blarney!

Fearon is a native of Dublin, Ireland, and continues to make his home there. His hobbies include watching rugby and playing golf. He makes regular trips to the United States to meet with enthusiastic collectors at collector shows and dealer events.

THE MANY FACES OF ALLYSON NAGEL

Allyson Nagel's experience in sculpting dolls is clearly evident in the delightful personalities of her characters which include the *Sunny Side Up Collection*, introduced in 1993 by Roman.

Nagel was a portrait artist when doll artist Faith Wick asked if she would make faces for Wick's whimsical dolls. Wick was allergic to porcelain and offered an opportunity to a number of artists to work with her and learn about porcelain doll making. When Nagel began working with Wick in 1979, she discovered that clay and dimension were more artistically stimulating for her than the two dimensional portraits she had been doing. Wick assisted Nagel in developing her skills in the special and demanding art of sculpting dolls' faces. When Wick sold her designs to companies and stopped producing dolls herself, Nagel began to develop her own lines in 1985. She created them entirely by hand and completed every step of the process herself, including researching, sculpting, painting and sewing costumes.

During her artistic career in porcelain doll making, Nagel developed the habit of filling the spaces left in her kiln with small eggs she fashioned. This egg shape became the perfect canvas for her creativity, adding extra depth to each mini-portrait she painted. Initially, Allyson simply decorated the round eggs with paint, but, she explains, "through the years, the two dimensional paintings of the eggs evolved into three dimensional characters." Her rounded canvas became whimsical sculptures with life and personality, a unique combination of doll and decorative egg. Meticulously crafted in resin to faithfully preserve the spirit of Nagel's art, each egg in her collection has a personality and "eggs-pression" all its own. That's why they're *Sunny Side Up* – happy in life and always looking to the bright side.

Additional creations from Nagel include a hauntingly charming Halloween Tea Party with delightful ghosts and witches; gingerbread ornaments and collectibles worthy of a guest appearance in any fairy tale; and whimsical winter wizards and snow-people playfully welcoming the chilly season.

VERNON G. WILSON SIGNATURE COLLECTION

Interpretations of faith in the form of pins, pendants, bracelets, plaques, wall crosses and ornaments in a variety of metals, including 14K gold, sterling silver, gold plating and/or pewter, make up the *Vernon G. Wilson Signature Collection*. Each piece of the collection is accompanied by a small card, written by Vernon's wife, Frances, which details the inspiration and symbolism of the piece. Vernon uses symbols that encourage individuals to find deeply personal meanings in the richly symbolic jewelry and ornaments. "I truly prefer to let God speak through this jewelry and hope that my interpretations don't get in His way," Vernon states. "I continue to be amazed at the different ways people interpret each piece. Often, someone will see a spiritual meaning that I never considered or incorporate their own experiences in an electrifying way. For example, a dove can be interpreted as the Holy Spirit, a sign of peace, an Old Testament sacrifice or the affirmation of God's promise to Noah. It's all in the beholder's perspective."

In "Aces High," from **Declan's Finnians™** *by Roman, Inc., the charming chap claiming the hand's victory does so with an extremely rare Five of a Kind – Aces!*

"Earl," one of three new ghosts introduced by Allyson Nagel and Roman, Inc., appears to have risen with the steam from a bubbling cauldron of witch's brew.

Wilson has won numerous local, regional and international awards for his original, handcrafted creations, including twice winning the coveted "International Pearl Design Competition" held annually in Tokyo, Japan. In addition to his numerous awards, Wilson has published design-related articles in many respected industry publications. He has also been the subject of the PBS television documentary, "The Art of Goldsmithing," and has taught graduate level courses at the University of Wisconsin.

A lifelong resident of Virginia, he owned and operated The Golden Touch, a jewelry store in Williamsburg, for 18 years. Despite the success of that business, Wilson left the venture to pursue his "calling." Now Wilson can be found at his studio in the Chesapeake Bay community of Poquoson, Virginia, where he devotes his time exclusively to making one-of-a-kind and limited edition jewelry. His work has also been commissioned by church groups, art organizations and hundreds of individuals.

With more than 15,000 giftware items in its product line, Roman, Inc. has something for every ordinary day and every special occasion. From this diversity, Roman has enchanted collectors with a wide variety of award-winning collectibles. *Fontanini Heirloom Nativities* have become a part of Christmas celebrations for generations. The *Seraphim Classics Collection* inspires many to envision themselves closer to these celestial beings. *Declan's Finnians* bring the magic of the legendary Blarney Stone to a North American audience. Allyson Nagel tickles collectors with her whimsical creations, and the *Vernon G. Wilson Signature Collection* encourages jewelry enthusiasts to join the ranks of inspired collectors. What these diverse lines have in common is Roman, Inc. and a long history of innovative, high-quality collectibles.

ROMAN: A COMPANY WITH INNOVATIVE, HIGH-QUALITY COLLECTIBLES

TO LEARN MORE:

ROMAN, INC.
555 LAWRENCE AVENUE
ROSELLE, IL 60172
(630) 529-3000
FAX: (630) 529-1121
URL: http://www.roman.com

CLUBS

FONTANINI COLLECTORS' CLUB℠
555 Lawrence Avenue
Roselle, IL 60172
(800) 729-7662

Annual Dues: $22.00; $39.00 for 2 Years
Club Year: Anniversary of Sign-Up Date

BENEFITS:
- Membership Gift: Symbol of Membership Figurine
- Opportunity to Purchase Members-Only Nativity Preview Figure
- Quarterly Newsletter, "The Fontanini Collector"
- Portfolio with Club Logo
- Club Pin
- Personalized Membership Card
- Fontanini Registry Guide
- Advance Notice of Tour Appearances by Fontanini Family Members
- Travel Opportunities
- Contests

SERAPHIM CLASSICS COLLECTORS CLUB℠
555 Lawrence Avenue
Roselle, IL 60172
(800) 729-7662

Annual Dues: $55.00 (plus $4.50 s&h)
Club Year: Anniversary of Sign-Up Date

BENEFITS:
- Membership Gift: *Seraphim Classics* Angel Figurine
- Opportunity to Purchase Exclusive Members-Only Angel
- Quarterly Newsletter, "The Seraphim Classics Herald"
- Club Pin
- Personalized Membership Card
- Catalog
- $5 of Each Charter Membership Is Donated to the Sunshine Foundation

TOUR

HOUSE OF FONTANINI STUDIO TOUR IN ITALY
C/O THE FONTANINI COLLECTORS' CLUB
555 Lawrence Avenue
Roselle, IL 60172
(800) 729-7662

Hours: Advance Reservations through the Fontanini Collectors' Club
Admission Fee: None

For collectors planning a trip to Italy, the House of Fontanini offers tours of their facilities in Bagni di Lucca, Italy.

Over 100 Years of Fine Danish Plates

"When my grandfather, the late Harald Bing, in 1895 conceived the idea of the world's first Christmas plate, he wanted not only to create a Christmas greeting or gift of particular quality and beauty, but also a series of Danish sceneries, historic buildings, etc., that would appeal to collectors all over the world, and at the same time make them interested in his beloved mother country," recalls Ebbe Simonsen, former president of Bing & Grondahl of Denmark. "My grandfather's goal was to bring the history and customs of Denmark, 'the world's oldest kingdom,' to collectors everywhere."

The work of art that started plate collecting: Bing & Grondahl's 1895 "Behind the Frozen Window."

Art lovers all over the world now marvel at the heritage of the "B&G Christmas plates," which have appeared annually since 1895 despite two World Wars and the Great Depression. They also treasure the story of Royal Copenhagen – once a rival Danish porcelain firm and now the parent company to Bing & Grondahl. Royal Copenhagen introduced its first annual Christmas plate, "Madonna and Child," in 1908, and boasts its own unbroken yearly tradition ever since.

Many collectors are surprised to learn that the "Danish plate" heritage actually had roots extending back many generations – well before Harald Bing unveiled F.A. Hallin's blue-and-white 1895 masterpiece, "Behind the Frozen Window." It seems that in centuries past, the European elite would gift their servants at Christmastime with plates of holiday delicacies – cookies, fruits, candies and other treats. Over the years, the plates themselves began to take on more significance for servants and nobles alike – as the servants began to hang their "Christmas plates" on the wall and compare the plates' quality and beauty with those of their peers.

Not to be outdone by their neighbors, wealthy landowners began to pay more attention to the plates themselves and less to the food given at Christmas. What originally were little more than crude wooden slabs gave way to gleaming metal platters, carved wooden vessels, and painted pottery. Some gift-givers even began to date each plate with the year so it would become a lasting memento for the recipient.

It was here that Harald Bing entered the picture: an entrepreneur who wondered if the holiday plate tradition could be extended throughout Danish society. Determined to test his idea during the 1895 Christmas season, Bing commissioned artist F.A. Hallin to create an original work entitled "Behind the Frozen Window." The hand-painted, limited edition plate showcased the Copenhagen skyline as seen through a frosty window pane. The year 1895 and the message "Jule Aften" (Christmas Eve) was scrolled in blue and white around the bottom of the plate.

Bing's idea was embraced by the Danish public with enthusiasm and "Behind the Frozen Window" became a legendary work of art throughout Europe, and later the world. Made in an edition size of just 400, all plates sold out in quick order, despite what was then considered a "hefty" price tag of 50¢ per plate. Today, most of the remaining plates from this small edition reside in museums and substantial private collections. On the rare chance that a "Behind the Frozen Window" becomes available at auction, it could command $5,000 to $8,000 or more, according to collectibles experts.

THE DANISH PORCELAIN TRADITION

While Bing & Grondahl was the first to present an annual blue-and-white Christmas plate, Royal Copenhagen is the older of the two prestigious Danish porcelain firms. Denmark's Queen Dowager, Juliane Marie, christened what is now Royal Copenhagen as the "Danish Porcelain Factory" in 1775. The Queen had become intrigued by the discovery of Franz Heinrich Muller, a Danish pharmacist and chemist, who happened upon the secret of true hardpaste porcelain in 1772. She was delighted that – like other royal families of Europe – she would now have her own source for treasured hardpaste porcelain.

Because of Denmark's international renown as a seafaring nation, the factory's trademark was developed as three wavy lines, symbolizing the ancient Danish waterways from the Kattegat to the Baltic: the Sound, the Great Belt and the Little Belt. Before long, the trademark and the creations of the Danish Porcelain Factory brought an emotional resurgence of national pride to the people of Denmark.

Arnold Krog, an architect, became art director of Royal Copenhagen in January 1885, and proceeded to develop a fine technique for Danish underglaze painting. This method became the basis for the Royal Copenhagen blue-and-white Christmas plate series.

Created to mark the 100th anniversary of plate collecting, Bing & Grondahl's "Centennial Platter" debuted in 1995.

As for Bing & Grondahl, the studio was founded in 1853 by artist Frederick Grondahl and the brothers Meyer and Jacob Bing. The trio shared a vision: the continuation of an art style pioneered by the legendary Danish sculptor Thorvaldsen. Hoping Thorvaldsen's style would have country-wide appeal, the three men merged their resources, energy and ideas to open a factory dedicated to crafting replicas of the sculptor's work.

Initially, Bing & Grondahl manufactured and sold figurines, but the popularity of these sculptures was so significant that Danish consumers clamored for more variety. In response, Bing & Grondahl produced elegant dinnerware and coffee services. This remarkable collection rapidly became a benchmark of tabletop fashion across Denmark.

By 1889, the company's distinguished evolution came into the spotlight at the Paris World's Fair. There, a dinner service called *Heron*, by Bing & Grondahl artistic director Pietro Krohn, was unveiled to an adoring public. Visitors from around the world admired *Heron's* bold design and the unique decorating technique used to finish each piece. That same look and finish was selected just six years later, when Harald Bing brought his idea for making a "holiday plate" in the now highly recognized cobalt glazed finish to the company. "Behind the Frozen Window" was the result.

HOW THE "DANISH BLUES" ARE MADE

Both Bing & Grondahl and Royal Copenhagen use a similar process to create their fine collector plates — a method that has remained virtually unchanged for more than 100 years! First, years of drawing, planning and subject evaluation are undertaken by the staff to pick the ideal art. Today at Royal Copenhagen, every employee in the factory is eligible to submit ideas and artwork. When everyone has agreed on the design, a master sculptor crafts a bas-relief model.

Painstakingly, a plaster of paris copy is sculpted. This will determine the all-important master mold, so it must be perfection. Finally, a cast bronze image becomes central to the production process, acting as the permanent master. From it, plaster molds are recreated and only 20 plates are made from each before the plaster is destroyed. This is a demanding production method, but one that must be followed to meet stringent quality control standards.

Plates are now ready for firing and decorating in the world-famous "underglaze technique." Colors are applied carefully by artisans receiving special training. Because exact shades of blue don't emerge until the final firing has taken place, craftsmen must know how to adjust the intensity of their colors to attain a perfect finished product.

Before the final firing, the authentication process must be completed. The date and artist's initials are placed on the backstamp, and the studio's logo is applied. Each plate is carefully dipped into glaze, then fired. In the kiln, kaolin, quartz and feldspar meld into a hard paste over a 48-hour period. The precise 2700°F temperature melts the glaze and creates an everlasting, glass-like surface of shimmering "Copenhagen Cobalt Blue."

If an issue is examined and found undesirable for a reason determined by the quality control team, the plate is destroyed. Since production of all Bing & Grondahl and Royal Copenhagen plates are strictly limited by year, this examination process is particularly critical. Of course, all molds are destroyed at the end of a year's production.

THE CENTENNIAL CELEBRATION CONTINUES

While the 100th anniversary of "Behind the Frozen Window" took place in 1995, Bing & Grondahl and Royal Copenhagen continue to celebrate a century of porcelain artistry. With the centennial of Royal Copenhagen plates coming up in 2008, there is all the more reason to honor the firms' long-standing traditions.

Bing & Grondahl marked its centennial with several landmark issues. The first, a series of five limited editions, replicate the most popular motifs from the past 100 years. Each 6" plate features a hand-applied, 24K gold rim. In 1995, this series culminated with the re-issue of a 24K gold banded "Behind the Frozen Window."

Unveiled in 1995, the magnificent "Centennial Platter" bears the image of

Continuing the tradition for 1997: the Bing & Grondahl Christmas plate, "Country Christmas."

Extending an unbroken line of annual Christmas plates that began in 1908: Royal Copenhagen's 1997 "Roskilde Cathedral."

TO LEARN MORE:

ROYAL COPENHAGEN/BING & GRONDAHL
41 MADISON AVENUE
NEW YORK, NY 10010
(800) 431-1992
FAX: (609) 719-1494

the 101st Christmas plate art. Amply sized at 13", collectors can recreate days of Christmas past in Denmark by serving sweets on this commemorative platter before putting it on display. The "Centennial Platter" features a unique, 2-1/2" border lavished with spruce twigs, pine cones and candles. Limited to just 7,500 plates, this platter marks the only time a Christmas Jubilcc Edition has been designed as anything other than a plate.

THE VERSATILITY OF B&G AND RC

While Christmas plates were the initial claims to international collectible fame for both Bing & Grondahl and Royal Copenhagen, each firm has enjoyed many other successes as well. Bing & Grondahl, for example, initiated the world's first *Mother's Day* plate series in 1969 with "Dog and Puppies." The collection continues with popular annual issues to this day. Royal Copenhagen also produced a very popular *Motherhood* plate series from 1982 to 1987.

Although Bing & Grondahl and Royal Copenhagen have exchanged technicians and artists over the years, their Christmas plates and other elegant issues have maintained their distinctive styles, which are obvious to the discerning collector. No other Christmas plates in the world have ever come close to the popularity of the Danish Christmas plates. Part of their strength is due to tradition, part to artistic brilliance. But perhaps most important of all is the fact that these are the only truly hand-decorated plates in the world of collectibles.

ROYAL DOULTON

A World-Renowned Leader in Collectibles for All Generations

In 1815, John Doulton invested his life savings in a small London pottery, which produced practical and decorative stoneware with a single kiln. By the turn of the century, the business was at the forefront of the ceramics and china industry and was authorized by His Majesty King Edward VII to use the word "Royal" to describe its products.

Today, Royal Doulton is a world-renowned leader in bone china giftware and collectibles. Five generations have treasured the fine collectibles from the famed British firm. From the familiar and beloved characters of Beatrix Potter and Winnie-the-Pooh to the timeless *Bunnykins*, Royal Doulton achieves excellence in quality and design.

Royal Doulton's* Beatrix Potter *collection marks its 50th anniversary with the first numerically limited edition figurine, "Mrs. Rabbit and the Four Bunnies."

Regarded as the world's largest manufacturer and distributor in the premium ceramic tableware and giftware market, Royal Doulton also includes the Royal Crown Derby, Minton and Royal Albert brands – each of which is internationally recognized for its innovative designs and modern production techniques. Together, these divisions total more than 1,000 years of history and tradition.

Royal Doulton continues this history. Many of the company's collectibles have or will soon become heirlooms, passed down for children and future generations to enjoy.

BEATRIX POTTER'S FAMOUS CHARACTERS COME TO LIFE

A little over 100 years ago, the fairy tale world of Beatrix Potter began with the charming stories of Peter Rabbit, Jemima Puddleduck and Benjamin Bunny. For half of those years, Beatrix Potter's animal creations have come to life for collectors and children all over the world through ceramic sculptures by Royal Doulton.

In 1947, the John Beswick Studio of Royal Doulton began reproducing the characters in ceramic. Today, they are produced under the Royal Albert name with immense care taken in designing, modelling and creating each figure as an exact representation of Potter's original illustrations right down to the last button or whisker.

In 1997, the *Beatrix Potter Collection* marked its 50th anniversary with the first numerically limited edition figurine. "Mrs. Rabbit and the Four Bunnies," including her children Flopsy, Mopsy, Cottontail and Peter, is limited to 1,997 pieces. It bears a special Beswick backstamp and comes with a Certificate of Authenticity. Other additions to the collection are a large size "Mrs. Tiggywinkle" and the double figure "Mrs. Rabbit and Peter." Nurseryware gifts feature Jemima Puddleduck and Tom Kitten.

Royal Doulton's development of the Beatrix Potter figurines is credited to Lucy Beswick, wife of the studio's chairman. In the 1940s, she was fascinated with Potter's stories and illustrations and thought the character Jemima Puddleduck would look nice in clay. The sculpture was so well received that Beswick Studios received permission to reproduce other familiar characters. By the middle of 1947, Jemima was joined by friends Peter Rabbit, Tom Kitten, Timmy Tiptoes, Squirrel Nutkin, Mrs. Tittlemouse, Samuel Whiskers and Little Pig Robinson, among several others.

Many of Potter's stories are told through the figurines, which are portrayed in characteristic settings. Today, millions of collectors eagerly await the newest introductions.

BUNNYKINS CELEBRATES FAMILY AND CHILDHOOD DELIGHTS

For more than 60 years, Royal Doulton's *Bunnykins* has been found in nurseries and homes around the world. The whimsical characters that comprise the *Bunnykins* family have delighted generations.

The world of *Bunnykins* was originally created in 1934 by Barbara Vernon, a young nun who taught history at an English convent school. In her spare time, she illustrated the simple antics of a family of bunnies. Her sketches caught the attention of her father, the general manager of Royal Doulton's Burslem Pottery Studio, who had them turned into a range of products. By 1937, there was a new world of *Bunnykins* in earthenware and bone china. *Bunnykins* has stood the test of time, proving itself with an enduring appeal of childhood imagination and innocent pleasures.

In 1996, the *Bunnykins of the Year* series was launched featuring various family members enjoying a Summer holiday. The 1997 addition was "Sailor Bunnykins," limited to the year of issue. Another recent figurine is "Mother and Baby," an ideal sentiment

"Sailor Bunnykins" joins the **Bunnykins of the Year** *series which features members of the adorable family enjoying a Summer holiday.*

for a birth or christening.

Royal Doulton has also introduced a new line of resin *Bunnykins* figurines based on scenes from "Happy Birthday Bunnykins," an animated film shown on the Disney Channel. The film introduces new characters in the *Bunnykins* family and events in the imaginary town of Little Twitching. Future films are in production, with the next focusing on a Christmas theme. Royal Doulton has also begun licensing the *Bunnykins* artwork to other companies that will produce wallpaper, dinnerware sets, juvenile rugs, soft toy dolls and other child-related items.

BRAMBLY HEDGE TAKES COLLECTORS TO AN IMAGINARY WORLD

The enchanting and charming world of *Brambly Hedge* and its family of mice has become part of the imaginative life of young and old alike. Royal Doulton, along with millions of readers, was captivated by Jill Barklem's illustrations and books about the self-sufficient mice community. "Brambly Hedge is on the other side of the stream, across the field," Barklem writes. "If you can find it, and you look hard amongst the tangled roots and stems, you may even see a wisp of smoke from a small chimney, or through an open door, a steep flight of stairs deep within the trunk of a tree – for this is the home of the mice of *Brambly Hedge*."

For more than a decade, Royal Doulton has beautifully translated Barklem's words and artwork into a classic collection of china tableware and figurines, each hand-cast and lovingly painted with all the gentle attributes bestowed on them by their creator.

Royal Doulton works closely with Barklem in developing the entire collection. The company's designers even accompanied Barklem to places such as England's Epping Forest, where the artist had been inspired to create her enchanting characters.

Barklem's first four books, *Spring, Summer, Autumn* and *Winter*, were used as the basis for launching the series. The success of the *Four Seasons* plates led to other products and images from subsequent books.

The line is collected mostly by adults, who find something special in the little make-believe town. A series of annual teacups, saucers and 8" plates was launched in 1996. The 1997 introductions feature scenes from the "Summer Story."

The original ideas for the *Brambly Hedge* books came from sketches and notes Barklem made while travelling to attend St. Martin's College of Art in London. She took her notebook to a London publisher, and the *Four Seasons* books were printed in 1980. Since then, Barklem has seen sales of *Brambly Hedge* books exceed three million copies. They have been sold in more than 15 countries.

WINNIE-THE-POOH COMES TO ROYAL DOULTON

Deep in the Hundred Acre Woods, Winnie-the-Pooh and his friends – Christopher Robin, Piglet, Tigger and Eeyore – enjoy their favorite games and pastimes. Now Royal Doulton has introduced a line of fine china gifts and nurseryware featuring the lovable bear. Designs for the nurseryware – including a three-piece children's plate and mug set, two-piece baby set and a one-and two-handled mug – include a picnic with Christopher Robin, Pooh and Piglet; Pooh and Tigger sharing a pot of honey; and Pooh stocking his shelves. A wall clock, photo frame and book bank show Pooh and his friends playing games. The designs are faithfully reproduced from the beloved books by A.A. Milne and illustrations by E.H. Shephard.

INTERNATIONAL CLUB LINKS COLLECTORS

The tremendous enthusiasm for Royal Doulton gifts and collectibles prompted the company to form the Royal Doulton International Collectors Club in 1980. Today, it has many thousands of members worldwide, all of whom receive information to further their awareness and understanding of Royal Doulton. Members also have the opportunity to add to their collections as the Club commissions exclusive Royal Doulton pieces every year. Among the other benefits are a quarterly magazine, free tours of the Royal Doulton factories in England, and a historical inquiry service helping members identify and date unusual items.

Club headquarters is established in England with branches in Australia, Canada, Europe, New Zealand and America, ensuring that all members are kept up-to-date with what is happening in their part of the Royal Doulton world.

Jill Barklem's **Brambly Hedge** *characters from her "Summer Story" are recreated in this addition to a series of annual teacups, saucers and 8" plates.*

Royal Doulton has introduced a line of fine china gifts and nurseryware featuring Winnie-the-Pooh with his familiar friends from the Hundred Acre Woods.

Royal Doulton has its own in-house design team, combining artistic talent and technical expertise. Giftware ranges have also increasingly been designed to incorporate new working practices and decorating techniques, such as spray painting, the use of color clay, and the use of lithographic transfers for fine detail. These changes have resulted in greater consistency in quality, greater productivity, and the reduction of various decorating costs. Of course, a high level of hand work will always be maintained.

ATTENTION TO DETAIL AND TRADITION

CLUBS

ROYAL DOULTON INTERNATIONAL COLLECTORS CLUB
701 Cottontail Lane
Somerset, NJ 08873
(800) 747-3045

Annual Dues: $55.00
Club Year: Anniversary of Sign-Up Date

BENEFITS:
- Membership Gift: Figurine
- Opportunity to Purchase Members-Only Figurines and Jugs
- Quarterly *Gallery* Magazine
- Annual Convention
- Local Club Chapters
- Binder Available for Purchase
- Free Admission to Museums & Tours in England
- Buy/Sell Matching Service through Magazine
- Historical Enquiry Service
- Advance Information on Introductions

ROYAL CROWN DERBY COLLECTORS GUILD
701 Cottontail Lane
Somerset, NJ 08873
(800) 747-3045

Annual Dues: $50.00
Club Year: Anniversary of Sign-Up Date

BENEFITS:
- Members-Only Pieces: 2 to 3 Paperweights per Year
- Membership Gift: Paperweight
- Membership Card
- Quarterly *Gallery* Magazine
- Free Admission to Museums/Tours in England
- Buy/Sell Matching Service through Listings in Magazine
- Historical Enquiry Service
- Special Events throughout the Year

MUSEUMS/TOURS

ROYAL DOULTON MUSEUM AND FACTORY TOURS
Nile Street
Burslem Stoke-on-Trent Staffs ST6 2AJ
England
01144 1782 292292

Museum Hours: Open 9 a.m. - 4 p.m. Daily
Tour Hours: 10:30 a.m. - 2 p.m., Monday through Friday

Admission Fee: Nominal charge. For safety reasons, the tour is not available for babies or children under ten years of age.

The Royal Doulton Factory Tour takes you behind the scenes at the world's leading fine china company. The tour also includes the Sir Henry Doulton Gallery, displaying examples of Royal Doulton products spanning over 170 years, and a factory gift shop.

ROYAL CROWN DERBY MUSEUM
184 Osmaston Road, Derby
England
01144 1782 292292

Admission Fee: None
Hours: 9 a.m. - 4 p.m., Monday through Friday

A wide variety of pieces from the archives of the Royal Crown Derby and Minton dinnerware and giftware lines are on display for collectors to admire and learn about.

TO LEARN MORE:

ROYAL DOULTON
701 COTTONTAIL LANE
SOMERSET, NJ 08873
(800) 68-CHINA
FAX: (732) 356-9467
URL: http://www.royal-doulton.com

Capturing the Proud Spirit of Ethnic Dolls

For years, Robert N. Nocera dreamed of presenting historically researched and authentically attired Native American dolls to the collectibles market. So when Sandy Corporation of Manila, the Philippines, approached him in the fall of 1993, Nocera was excited and intrigued. The Philippine firm wanted Nocera to form an American-based company which would exclusively design, manufacture and wholesale ethnic dolls!

Nocera moved quickly in response to Sandy Corporation's request. Just months later, in April of 1994, the Sandy Dolls *Native American* series and *The Warrior & Princess* series made their debuts in the U.S. market. Since then, Sandy Dolls has expanded its presence as a creator of Native American dolls — and developed licenses and new product lines for a host of other wonderful ethnic and angel designs.

Today, there are 26 dolls in the *Native American* series of 13" open-edition dolls, and three others have been retired. Currently *The Warrior & Princess* series features 18 dolls — all of which are 12" in height and have editions limited to 5,000 of each. Three dolls in this series already have seen their limited editions sell out. What's more, to fill the niche for larger Native American dolls, Sandy Dolls unveiled the *Traditions* series of 16" and 17" characters in limited editions of 3,500 each.

Draped around the right shoulder of "Little Sala — Kenyan Girl," from the* Sweet Spirit Baby *series, is a traditional "kiondo" basket that accents her colorful layered cotton dress.

ANGELS WATCH OVER SANDY DOLLS

Near the end of its first year in business, Sandy Dolls presented a line of angels done with the same exquisite vinyl sculpting as its dolls. The angels are robed in gowns of sumptuous satins and velvets. *The Angelic Collection* met with instant acceptance and has now developed, along with *The Santa Collection*, into a full line of holiday designs including coordinating ornaments. Both Caucasian and African-American characters grace the *Santa* series, which includes five richly attired 14" characters to date.

Realizing that ethnic art interests extended far beyond Native American designs, Sandy Dolls began developing holiday designs for the African-American market in 1995. The very first such angel, "Asha," was such a success that even on Christmas Eve, retailers were still trying to order her! The African-American *Angelic Collection* now includes four designs, each available in four sizes. After "Asha," each design was created from the input of both consumers and retailers. In this manner, each subject has been what the market most wanted, resulting in tremendous success. Indeed, this has been the philosophy of Sandy Dolls since its first day in business: to provide high-quality ethnic products which are designed with respect and dignity according to the needs and wishes of the market.

The success of the Native American doll lines and the African-American holiday line quickly led to the development of new products in those market segments. The *Sweet Spirit Baby* series of toddler dolls — authentically attired and presented in a seated position — debuted in 1995. These delightful dolls are the work of acclaimed artist Ruben M. Tejada, whose 20 years' experience as an ethnic doll designer shines through in these marvelous vinyl-and-cloth creations.

SWEET SPIRIT BABY AND SARAH'S GANG

Of the five *Sweet Spirit Baby* dolls that have been released through 1998, the first three have already sold out. Each doll carries a handcrafted and authentic accessory which can be detached. For example, "Little Blossom" carries a dreamcatcher made by Native American craftsmen. It can be removed from her hand and used over the bed, cradle, or crib of a baby or small child. Two to three dolls will continue to be released annually in this series. Future dreams for *Sweet Spirit Baby* include expanding into a multicultural presence.

Sarah's Gang from Sarah's Attic became a license for Sandy Dolls in 1995. The firm is licensed to do dolls based on the *Sarah's Gang* resin figurines created from the heart of Sarah Schultz. This particular line has been well received in the educational market because of its multicultural focus

"Jumping the Broom" represents the* Sass 'N Class by Annie Lee *collection, which reflects the satire, humor and realism of everyday life shown through the eyes of this renowned artist.

centered around the understanding and encouragement of values. The elementary school systems of Beaumont, Texas, and Saginaw, Michigan, already are using *Sarah's Gang* dolls within their curriculums. There are eight dolls to date, with the following themes: "Willie," focuses on respect; "Tillie" and "Buddy," teach about manners; "Katie," stresses responsibility; "Maria," celebrates thankfulness; "Miguel," espouses patience; "Shina," offers forgiveness; and "Sammy," recommends honesty.

Each 11" sculpted vinyl doll comes with an eight-page booklet proclaiming a specific value and written as if that doll were speaking to other children to encourage their usage and understanding of that social value. Overall, the "gang" represents Love, Respect and Dignity, as presented by their creator, Sarah Schultz. She considers her affiliation with Sandy Dolls "the culmination of a dream come true." Speaking to collectors and dealers, Schultz adds, "I hope you will find these dolls, and the values they share, to be as important to you...as they are to me personally. Our world needs this 'Good Gang'!"

The presentation of Sandy Dolls' angels on the BET Home-Shopping Show offered a whole new direction for the firm in the summer of 1996. The art of Annie Lee also was shown on that network. BET's buyer put Sandy Dolls and Annie Lee in touch with each other, and as the cliché goes, the rest is history. Lee's paintings of African-American family life are sold throughout the United States and Europe. Her works are currently shown on episodes of the hit shows "ER" and "Hanging With Mr. Cooper," and previously have been seen on Bill Cosby's spin-off show "A Different World," Marla Gibbs' "227," Sherman Helmsley's "Amen" and in Eddie Murphy's movies "Coming to America" and "Boomerang." Indeed, Lee's art has been internationally acclaimed and warmly received not only by the African-American culture, but also by art lovers everywhere.

A FRUITFUL AFFILIATION WITH ANNIE LEE

Sandy Dolls is now the exclusive licensee of *Sass 'N Class by Annie Lee.* This series is currently composed of resin figurines recreated from the canvas artwork of Lee. The collection, which has captured the satire, humor, and real-life emotions of Annie Lee's paintings, has been a huge success since the very first pieces were unveiled in October of 1997. By the end of 1998, 15 pieces had been introduced. Future plans for this series include dolls and seasonal products, as well as the formation of a collectors' club.

SOULMATES® SHARE WARM WISHES

During the same period, Sandy Dolls aspired to expand its angel lines to include resin figurines. The result was *SoulMates* by Sandra Bedard. Each adorable little 4" angel is costumed in holiday or special occasion outfits with animated and innocent expressions. This exclusive license for Sandy Dolls has proven to be a true delight.

Bedard receives the inspiration for these darling little cherubs in her dreams and then sculpts her inspirations! Each wide-eyed African-American angel is created with an expression that melts its viewers' hearts. Four special occasions are represented by these brightly costumed little angel children: "Happy Birthday," "Get Well," "Missing You" and "To a Special Friend." In addition, other *SoulMates* issues celebrate the seven major holidays of the year, with two designs each for Valentine's Day, Easter, Mother's Day, Halloween and Thanksgiving; three designs for Christmas; and one design for the Fourth of July.

THE LATEST FROM SANDY DOLLS

In the summer of 1998, two completely new product lines were introduced: *The Angelic Maillé Collection* and the *Gentle Dreams Baby* series. *The Angelic Maillé Collection* is comprised of angels exquisitely crafted of wire mesh. Each angel appears to be floating – as only an angel could do – and is simultaneously delicate, elegant and strong. A truly unique type of angel in gold or silver mesh, these works of art are available in Caucasian and African-American designs.

***"Deandra" is a captivating 14" angel from Sandy Dolls' line of stunning wire mesh angels designed by artist Gigi Dy for* The Angelic Maillé Collection.**

Also released was the *Gentle Dreams Baby* series of Native American dolls in seated positions – only 7" in height. Each little doll comes clutching a woven blanket. This series was developed to answer the many requests for a smaller version of the *Sweet Spirit Baby* series which sits 11" tall. They are not only adorable, but their authentic attire makes them true to our nation's roots.

To enhance Sandy Dolls' angels in holiday display, the firm also has introduced a series of handcrafted ball ornaments made of high quality velvets, velours and satins. Their exquisite trims include faux pearl, gold braid, decorative braid and colored bead. All have been specifically designed to coordinate with the firm's angel themes. Of course, they also may be purchased independent of the angels they enhance.

Because of Sandy Dolls' exclusive relationship to its parent company, Sandy Corporation, the firm has been able to respond immediately to the needs and wants of customers – presenting designs to the marketplace within four to six months of origination. Since research is required for all of the authentically designed products, this is an ongoing process which has been both educational and inspirational. Sandy Dolls never releases a product until its leaders are completely pleased with its authenticity. What's more, with the firm's seasonal designs, Sandy Corporation helps ensure that all fabrics and adornments are of the ultimate high quality. Dolls and seasonal lines are crafted in Manila; resin figurines are made both in Manila and in Guangzhou, China.

AUTHENTICITY IS PARAMOUNT AT SANDY DOLLS

Sandy Dolls pledges always to grow and diversify according to the demands of its collectibles markets. The firm's leaders personally derive a great deal of satisfaction from the loyalty of its collectors and the joy their collections bring them. Five years after Sandy Dolls' founding, Nocera and his staff confirm that they are proud to be part of this great industry!

From the new* Gentle Dream Baby *series of Native American dolls is "Gentle Dewdrop – Sioux Girl," clutching her tribal blanket.

TO LEARN MORE:

SANDY DOLLS, INC.
P.O. BOX 3222
SPRINGFIELD, MO 65808
(800) 607-2639
(417) 831-0111
FAX: (417) 831-4477

Home to Over 1,500 Musical Collectibles

When San Francisco's bustling Pier 39 opened in 1978, The San Francisco Music Box Company was one of the original stores at the internationally famous shopping site. Just a stone's throw from the famed Fisherman's Wharf, that first store opened its doors on October 4, 1978 with only 500 square feet of space. Within weeks, it was clear that this would become one of the most popular establishments on the Pier.

Buoyed by their success, store founders and marriage partners Marcia and John Lenser exercised their entrepreneurial flair with great optimism, soon opening a second location in a traditional suburban mall. When the mall store also proved successful, the Lensers expanded their scope again and again. By 1991, when the Venator Group (formerly Woolworth Corporation) bought the thriving chain, there were already 100 locations nationwide. In its 20th-anniversary year of 1998, the Company boasted 180 stores in 36 states (plus 200 more stores for the holiday season only) – as well as a nationally distributed catalog reaching over 10,000,000 households annually!

This magnificent 12-animal version of the* American Treasures *Reproduction Carousel includes replicas of some of the nation's most historic carousel animals.

The San Francisco Music Box Company carries over 1,500 musical gifts and collectibles including musically exclusive collections from Boyds, *Dreamsicles*, *Snowbabies*, Christopher Radko and Lynn Haney. The firm also holds licenses for *Phantom of the Opera*, Betty Boop, Hershey®, Classic Muppets and Raggedy Ann and Andy.

A COLORFUL AND MELODIC PRODUCT RANGE

In addition, the Company is proud to carry a line of exclusive, musical artworks from Victoria Dammann of Egg Fantasy. They are immensely pleased to present for 1998 her magnificent musical creation, "The Princess Coach Egg," in a limited edition of 700 pieces. The egg is precision cut with double doors, trimmed in Austrian crystals and gold braid, decoupaged with glittering roses on the inside, and a large window covered with a gold screen in the rear. Mother of pearl cabochons in 24K gold-plated settings decorate the coach from top to bottom, and the finished work sits on a gold-plated undercarriage. Inside, exquisite pink bisque porcelain roses and drop-faceted crystals accent a crystal and faux pearl tiara on a silk pillow.

The San Francisco Music Box Company is the largest purveyor of hand-carved wood-inlay music boxes from Sorrento, Italy, offered with 18-note, 36-note and 72-note musical movements. These jewel boxes are created from the Renaissance art of intarsia, a traditional craft of wood inlay practiced only in 56 tiny workshops in the region.

The San Francisco Music Box Company hosts a team of 12 outstanding freelance artists who work in combination with its own Product Development staff to create proprietary lines of musical gifts and collectibles. Over 60% of the items offered in their stores and the catalog have been created by these in-house artists and cannot be found elsewhere. The proprietary lines include a grouping of collectible dolls and an extensive selection of figurines.

The company's own collectible figurine lines include the popular *Heart Tugs™*, designed by Matt and Mathew Danko. The *Heart Tugs* collection is designed around a rag doll with sentimental messages about story time, tea time, family and friends. In spring 1998, the company introduced a new line of collectibles from the Dankos called *Teddy Hugs™*. "Love is Sharing" from this line was nominated by *Collector Editions* magazine for its "Awards of Excellence" in the musical category.

A DOZEN MASTER ARTISTS AT WORK

Matt Danko's Studios, The Boyds Collection, Ltd., *Seraphim Classics®* by Roman, *Dreamsicles* by Cast Art and Victoria Dammann of Egg Fantasy have created commemorative collectibles to celebrate The San Francisco Music Box Company's 20th anniversary.

MANY WAYS TO MARK THE 20TH ANNIVERSARY

Designed around a rag doll with a sentimental message, Matt and Mathew Danko's* Heart Tugs *collection is a favorite with many collectors.

"Old Friendships" by Matt Danko is being released in a limited edition of 2,500 pieces. Boyds has created a special edition musical figurine just for the company called "Born to Shop," with Grace and Jonathan overloaded with packages as they leave their local San Francisco Music Box store. In a limited edition of only 300 pieces, Victoria Dammann has designed her "Celebration Egg." Handcrafted from a real goose egg, this work of art is adorned with ruby red Austrian crystals and golden filigree musical notes. "Monica, Under Love's Wing," a *Seraphim Classics® Event Angel*, has been made musically exclusive for the company in honor of their two decades of offering the finest in musical collectibles from artists around the world.

The company's signature product has always been beautiful carousels of heirloom quality, designed exclusively for its stores and catalogs alone. The firm considers itself without peer when it comes to creating the four-horse, six-horse, and 12-animal merry-go-round. During its 20-year history, the firm has developed over 200 exclusive carousel subjects. What's more, they produce an annual, limited edition four-horse carousel.

CAROUSELS + MUSIC = A DELIGHTFUL COMBINATION

In 1992, The San Francisco Music Box Company introduced its first collections of 12-animal and six-horse carousel reproductions. These one-of-a-kind collectibles are based on authentic reproductions from the Golden Age of Carousels. Each is released as a limited edition and reflects a particular time in carousel history. In 1998, the company introduced a magnificent 12-animal version of the *American Treasures* Reproduction Carousel that includes Hershell-Spillman's "Hop Toad" Frog c. 1915 and Dentzell/Cernigliaro Lion and Giraffe and a Dentzell Tiger. These pieces are also available in limited edition single animal figurines standing an average of 10" tall. The complete carousels stand, on average, 15" to 20" in height. All pieces are musical with independent movement and rotation. Meticulously sculpted, the animals are mounted on 24K gold-plated brass poles which move up and down with the music. They stand on a mahogany-finished hardwood base which rotates and carries a 24K gold-plated coin minted with its edition number.

The year 1998 marked the company's most ambitious period to date for carousel collectibles. Altogether it released eight collections, three of which have full merry-go-rounds in their groupings. These carousels include the stunning jade porcelain "Jewels of the Empire," "Four Seasons" six-horse and "Royal Crest" six-horse, all in limited editions of 5,000. "Sultan's Dream" by Maureen Drdak is a 1998 fall release – a six-horse carousel with jewels. For 1999, the company is developing a four-horse carousel designed in elegant cloisonné.

Crafted of jade porcelain, this "Jewels of the Empire" carousel is part of an edition limited to 5,000.

"The Bald Eagle" was designed by Michael Adams for The San Francisco Music Box Company's wildlife reproduction series in collaboration with the National Geographic Society.

THE NATIONAL GEOGRAPHIC SOCIETY CONNECTION

The San Francisco Music Box Company has formed a very exciting partnership with the National Geographic Society. In the fall of 1997, they introduced their first line of wildlife reproductions with an 11-figurine assortment. In 1998, they presented a 35-piece assortment. These exceptional sculptures have the 110-year history of the Society's knowledge, education and exploration behind them.

Featured in the series are the "African Lion" family, "Scarlet Macaw," "Red-eyed Tree Frog," "Gray Wolves," "Mayan Jaguar" and "The Bald Eagle." Each is authentically portrayed in its natural habitat. And, as with all merchandise developed under the

Victoria Dammann of Egg Fantasy created this stunning "The Princess Coach Egg" in a limited edition of 700 pieces.

National Geographic brand, these pieces are designed to educate and enlighten the consumer, just as the National Geographic magazine and television shows do. All of the featured pieces will be released in editions of 7,500. In 1999, the company will be introducing a complete line of baby animals under the society's banner.

The National Geographic Society is dedicated to its 110-year-old mission: "To increase and diffuse geographic knowledge," and it has been at the leading edge of scientific exploration since its inception. Together with the Society, the Company has designed these musical limited editions to support the National Geographic's worthy efforts. Under their guidelines, which impose a standard of accuracy and graphic excellence, each exclusive figurine is reproduced in anatomically correct and realistic detail.

THE MUSICAL *SERAPHIM* ANGELS

The San Francisco Music Box Company is also proud to announce the release of its new and musically exclusive *Seraphim Classics*, the premier collection of angel figurines. This introduction includes an assortment of six 7" figurines, a 13" limited edition figurine, a 12" exclusive limited edition and the first exclusive 120mm waterglobe. The large "Rosalie" waterglobe has been created for the company by Roman, Inc. and will not be available elsewhere.

The company also is delighted to be presenting a musical version of "Hope - Light in the Distance," which is Roman's masterpiece created to support the Susan G. Koman Foundation for breast cancer research and education. "Avalon Angel," a limited edition for 1998 only, is a highly powerful design retailing at $150 and is available while quantities last. "Annabella," retailing for $75.00, is a celebration to music. "Simone," seated on a magnificent white horse as she ascends into the clouds, typifies the feeling of motion and excitement so beautifully expressed by this collection. "Noelle" is the very first of a new Christmas series from *Seraphim Classics* that will be produced only once a year with a different seraph each year. All of the *Musical Seraphim Angels* have Certificates of Authenticity.

VISIT A STORE OR CALL FOR A CATALOG

Janet Thompson, Vice President of Catalog for The San Francisco Music Box Company, says, "It would be hard to find another resource for the rare and exceptional treasures we offer. Like the city we call home, we are an original. We invite you to discover this for yourself by visiting us on the World Wide Web at www.sfmusicbox.com. We also publish a catalog ten times per year, with item prices ranging from $10.00 to $1,500. Call 1-800-227-2190 to order a catalog or speak with one of our Customer Service Associates."

The company prides itself on its very generous Lifetime Guarantee, which states: "We guarantee your satisfaction with every wind-up music box you purchase from us for life. If you are ever dissatisfied with your purchase for whatever reason — at any time — we'll replace it at no cost to you or reimburse you 100%. If you ordered through the catalog, we will arrange to pick up the item for you and also refund your shipping charges."

Thompson concludes, "For the past 20 years, we have been creating or finding unique items that become even more memorable with the addition of music. We pride ourselves in presenting our customers with gifts that will never be forgotten by their recipient."

CLUB

SAN FRANCISCO MUSIC BOX COMPANY COLLECTOR'S CLUB
P.O. Box 7465
San Francisco, CA 94120
(800) 635-9064

Annual Dues: Free Club Enrollment
Club Year: Anniversary of Sign-Up Date

BENEFITS:
- Opportunity to Purchase Members-only Collectible Items
- $10.00 Collector's Certificate Awarded Every Time a Customer Accumulates $100 in Purchases
- Newsletter
- Membership Card
- Advance Notice of Sales
- Private Sales for Collector's Club Members

TO LEARN MORE:

THE SAN FRANCISCO MUSIC BOX COMPANY
390 NORTH WIGET LANE, SUITE 200
WALNUT CREEK, CA 94598
(925) 939-4800
FAX: (925) 927-2999
E-MAIL: sfmbsn@aol.com
URL: http://www.sfmusicbox.com

Collectibles "From the Heart"

In 1983, Sarah Schultz was working in her husband's pharmacy, where she managed the gift department. The best-selling products were her own creations – stenciled slates, boards, pictures and dolls which included the multicultural *Sarah's Gang*. But she also traveled to gift shows throughout the country looking for other unique items to sell at the pharmacy.

Artist Sarah Schultz captures the innocence and beauty of childhood and angels in this adorable resin figurine. "Jovae Angel" wears a blue dress, fanciful hat and wings, of course!

While at a Charlotte, North Carolina gift show, a sales representative complimented Sarah on her handmade, stenciled tote bag, noting that she had a special talent and suggesting she market the items. At first Sarah declined. Later that evening, however, her thoughts drifted home to her five children. She really needed a new couch, and her oldest son would be starting college that Fall. Perhaps she should start a small business venture.

The same sales representative approached her again about selling her stenciled items. This time, she agreed. She decided to call the business "Granny's Attic" only to find out the name was already taken. So she came up with "Sarah's Attic – From the Heart" and founded her company on three simple principles – Love, Respect and Dignity. She painted a heart on each piece to symbolize her belief in these ideals and that all mankind is created equal. It became her trademark of quality and originality. Today, Sarah's Attic follows these same three important words to live by with collectibles that are truly from the heart.

SARAH'S ATTIC GROWS TO MEET COLLECTOR DEMAND

Sarah's business rapidly expanded from her dining room table to a 5' by 20' room in the back of her husband's pharmacy located in Chesaning, Michigan. In 1984, no longer able to fit everything and everyone in that space, Sarah moved the business from the back room to the "Attic," consisting of 1,200 square feet above the pharmacy. In the Spring of 1986, the business expanded to include resin figurines, replacing the stenciled rulers and slates as the company's top sellers. It was the beginning of the *Sarah's Gang* collection of figurines with children including "Tillie," "Willie," "Cupcake," "Twinkie," "Katie," "Whimpy" and baby "Rachel." The figurines became best sellers. Even though their poses and settings have changed over the years, they are still a mainstay of Sarah's Attic.

Through all this growth and change, one thing remained the same: Sarah's devotion to quality. By the Spring of 1989, Sarah's Attic had expanded to 5,000 square feet which covered nearly a city block. In the Fall of 1991, with space running out and delivery people carrying boxes up a flight of 22 stairs, Sarah's Attic was on the move once again. Sarah purchased and remodeled a former grocery store with 10,000 square feet of work area. The art room, mail room and business office remain in the "Attic." The production facility overlooks the same river where Sarah and her father once fished together. Her figurines are nationally known and available in the United States and Canada.

Sarah's goal that began with the need for a new couch has helped four of her five children through college. Her youngest son is currently enrolled at Michigan State University. Now there are other goals and dreams, including a Sarah's Attic theme park and shelters for the homeless – both promoting Love, Respect and Dignity.

CAPTURING MEMORIES FOR ALL TO TREASURE

Each of the collections created by Sarah and Sarah's Attic reflect a personal experience from the present or from her childhood. As a young girl, Sarah was quite a tomboy. She rode her bike around Chesaning as the town's first paper girl. When she was growing up, an African-American family lived in a nearby apartment. While delivering the paper to them, a loving friendship developed. She never forgot the kindness and warmth that they shared.

When Sarah's Attic expanded in 1986 to include resin figurines, she was among the first to create African-American figurines portrayed with respect and dignity. Remembering the African-American neighbors from her

Sarah's Attic, the only company in America licensed to produce Martin Luther King, Jr. and his family as figurines, introduces "I Have A Dream." The figurine, which is limited to 10,000 pieces, portrays Dr. King's famous speech.
***Licensed by the Estate of Martin Luther King, Jr., 1994.**

childhood and seeing that African-Americans were seemingly being ignored by the collectibles industry, Sarah was inspired to create the *Black Heritage Collection.* The series of figurines pays tribute to influential and pioneering African-Americans. Other collections of memories include *Labor of Love* (mementos of pleasant pastimes), *Daisy Petals* (depicting Sarah's children), *Tender Moments-From Our Heart To Yours* (promoting cherished memories) and *Angels in the Attic* (inspired by a collection of angels given to Sarah by her dad).

HONORING MARTIN LUTHER KING, JR. AND ROSA PARKS

Sarah's Attic is honored to produce two exclusive series in tribute to two African-American legends: Martin Luther King, Jr.* and Rosa Parks**. Sarah's Attic is the only company in America licensed to produce a likeness of Martin Luther King, Jr. and his family as figurines. The first five pieces from the collection were originally set to retire on December 31, 1996. However, due to the contract being extended by the Estate of Dr. Martin Luther King, Jr., Sarah's Attic is now producing second editions with a "2E" on the bottom of those premiere pieces: "Martin Luther King, Jr.," "Coretta Scott King," "Martin Luther King, Jr., Sign," "Letter From Birmingham Jail" and "Wedding Day."

Other first edition pieces are "I Have A Dream" which captures the famous speech that Dr. King made for marchers who walked from the Washington Monument to the Lincoln Memorial. The figurine won the 1997 "Award of Excellence" from *Collector Editions.* "Racial Harmony" depicts the moment when Dr. King and other civil rights leaders met with President Kennedy at The White House immediately following the "I Have A Dream" speech.

"Triumphant March" features Dr. King resting with two children after the five day, 54-mile march from Selma to Montgomery, Alabama. "Nobel Peace Prize" (Dr. King) and "Nobel Peace Prize" (Coretta) show the moment in October 1964 when Dr. King won this coveted award. He donated the $54,000 prize to the Freedom Movement.

In June 1995, Sarah's Attic was given permission to produce a likeness of Rosa Parks as a resin figurine. The first figurine in the *Rosa Parks Legacy* collection features Mrs. Parks sitting on a bus seat, representing her refusal to surrender her seat to a white man in Montgomery, Alabama, on December 1, 1955. The second figurine, "Dear Mrs. Parks," was introduced in June 1996 in conjunction with a book that published letters which have been sent to her from thousands of children seeking her wisdom, guidance and direction. Both pieces were retired as of June 1, 1997. Additional pieces will be added to the collection.

LOVE AND CARE MAKE EACH DESIGN SPECIAL

Each design is guided by Sarah's artistic philosophy. First, the designs must come "from the heart." Second, she believes art is an expression of what you feel inside, and it reflects your values for all the world to see. Finally, Sarah says everyone is an artist in one form or another.

With this as a foundation, the products begin as an idea in Sarah's head. Then she works with her design staff to make the idea come to life in clay form. The clay is cast in resin before Sarah painstakingly chooses colors for the figurines.

The products fit into any decor from country to contemporary. Sarah's Attic is also trying various manufacturing processes to offer collectors a wide range of products and styles and has also started working with different artists.

Sarah's Attic has launched a new line of limited edition figurines called *Colors of Life,* with the first six pieces designed by artist Norman Hughes. Each delicate figurine portrays a poignant scene and important aspect of one's life: Embrace, Shelter, Rites, Peace, Ancestors and Friends. A story relates the touching sentiments behind the figurines, which are each limited to 5,797 pieces. Additional *Colors of Life* pieces, introduced by other artists, will soon be available.

Colors of Life ***is a beautiful new collection from Sarah's Attic. "Ancestors," designed by Norman Hughes, stands 14" and is limited to 5,797 pieces. It shows the importance of one's heritage and family.***

**Licensed by the Estate of Dr. Martin Luther King, Jr., 1994*
***Licensed by Rosa Parks, 1995*

From the* Forever Ice Sculptures *collection, this teddy bear is "clearly" irresistible. The resin figurine titled "Burley Country" is beautifully sculpted and adorned with a plaid ribbon and a button.

CLUB

SARAH'S ATTIC FOREVER FRIENDS COLLECTORS' CLUB
P.O. Box 448
Chesaning, MI 48616
(800) 4-FRIEND

Annual Dues: $32.50
Club Year: January - December

BENEFITS:
- Complimentary Figurine
- Opportunity to Purchase Members-Only Figurines
- Quarterly Newsletter
- Folder with Logo
- Membership Card
- Special Events
- Local Club Chapters

TO LEARN MORE:

SARAH'S ATTIC
126-1/2 WEST BROAD
P.O. BOX 448
CHESANING, MI 48616
(800) 4-FRIEND (1-800-437-4363)
FAX: (517) 845-3477
E-MAIL: sarahattic@aol.com

To bring collectors together and to further share her company's philosophy, Sarah launched the Forever Friends Collectors' Club. Members receive their choice of a complimentary figurine, and they have the opportunity to purchase members-only figurines. They also receive a personalized membership card, Forever Friends Club folder, product catalog and Sarah's Attic literature, including newsletters and a store listing.

FOREVER FRIENDS COLLECTORS' CLUB

For the 1997 Club year, members can choose from the complimentary figurines "Basket of Treasures" or "Basket of Memories." The members-only redemption pieces are "Treasured Moments" and "Sharing Memories." The membership fee is $32.50. For an additional $25.00, both pieces can be purchased.

Regardless of the collectible, Sarah Attic's items are created genuinely from the heart. Sarah's major concern is to create figurines portraying Love, Respect and Dignity. She knows everyone will reach this goal only by respecting the differences in each other. Togetherness, leading to peace in the world, is Sarah's fervent prayer.

The Most Angels This Side of Heaven...

For more than three decades, Roman, Inc., has been a recognized leader in inspirational gifts and collectibles. Founder and CEO Ron Jedlinski made his company renowned for its range of angels – the most angels this side of heaven. So when the national trend turned once again toward angels in a wide scope of roles and interpretations, Roman was already positioned as the industry source for the most majestic of winged heralds.

It was in the early 1990s that Jedlinski moved to form Seraphim Studios, a creative umbrella of world-famous artists and sculptors. Their singular assignment was to research and develop a collection that would be modern interpretations of the world's most beautiful angels. Seraphim Studios took advantage of more than 2,000 years of writings and works of art to achieve their objective. The result was introduced to the world in 1994: the *Seraphim Classics® Collection.*

Based on the greatest artistic achievements of the Renaissance Masters, the collection immediately won the enthusiastic acceptance of both retailers and consumers. Within a single year, it was apparent that the collection was destined to be a collectible. Awards followed, specifically:

1994 *Collector Editions* "Award of Excellence," Plates: $50 and over "Rosalyn – Rarest of Heaven"
1994 NALED Achievement Award, Musical of the Year "Francesca – Loving Guardian"
1995 *Collector Editions* "Award of Excellence," Figurines under $50 "Seraphina – Heaven's Helper"
1995 *Collector Editions* "Award of Excellence," Plates: $50 and over "Helena – Heaven's Herald"
1995 NALED Achievement Award, Figurine of the Year "Alyssa – Nature's Angel"
1996 *Collector Editions* "Award of Excellence," Plates: $50 and over "Flora – Flower of Heaven"
1996 NALED Achievement Award, Figurine of the Year "Vanessa – Heavenly Maiden"

***"Noelle – Giving Spirit" debuts in 1998 as the first issue in the* Annual Christmas Angel Series *from the* Seraphim Classics Collection.**

1997 *Collector Editions* "Award of Excellence," Ornaments "Emily – Heaven's Treasure"
1997 *Collector Editions* "Award of Excellence," Figurines $50-$100 "Harmony – Love's Guardian"
1997 *Collector Editions* "Award of Excellence," Figurines $101-$250 "Ariel – Heaven's Shining Star"

These prestigious awards confirmed collector enthusiasm, as authorized dealers found it difficult to keep up with demand for the highly detailed, flowing sculptures with their pale, pastel wings.

Creating the world's most beautiful angels is a complicated and time-intensive undertaking. Following are the details of the process used in creating America's Number One Angel Collection.

CREATING *SERAPHIM CLASSICS*

Design – Angel design begins with sketches and may spring from a variety of sources including artists, collectors and store owners. Sketches are revised over and over until approved by the Seraphim Studios team.

Sculpting – Gaylord Ho, Master Sculptor for Seraphim Studios, transforms the sketch into a three-dimensional clay model. One of the world's greatest artisans, Ho instills a sense of motion into every angel, from the rich folds of flowing fabric to the intricate detail of each feather in the sheltering wings. Like the initial sketch, the first sculpture is reviewed and revised until every detail meets the extremely high standards that are the signature of the collection. Once completed and approved, the process of making a mold begins.

Mold Making – Seraphim Studios creates a "mother mold" using thin layers of silicone painted over the clay model. Additional layers of silicone are added to thicken the mold. The silicone mother mold is peeled from the clay. The original sculpt is completely destroyed in the making of the mother mold. Upon completion, a perfect negative of the sculpt is created.

After the mother mold is cleaned and all remnants of clay are removed, a sample figurine is cast. Only 4 or 5 of these samples can be cast in the mother mold before the intricate details begin to deteriorate.

Once the sample is approved, a "master mold" is cast in the mother mold. The master mold is a positive image of the original sculpt, and is made from epoxy. Epoxy is an extremely hard material that can handle repeated use without damage. Generally two epoxies are cast so that there is a back-up master mold.

One master mold is used to make production molds from which the *Seraphim Classics* angels are cast.

Casting – The *Seraphim Classics* figurines are formulated of resin, porcelain powder and marble dust which yields a mixture with the consistency of pancake batter. It is poured into the production molds and left to harden for approximately five minutes. The hardened figure – with all of the details on the original sculpt – is removed from the mold.

Trimming – Upon removal from the mold, the figure is cleaned in a gentle soda wash to remove the oily film left from the molding process. After washing, the figure is trimmed to eliminate any mold lines.

Polishing – Polishing is a step that is unique to the *Seraphim Classics Collection*, and involves hours of painstaking hand labor. The figure's face, hands, arms and legs are gently polished with a slightly abrasive cloth until the skin is completely smooth like finely sanded wood. It is this step that creates the translucence that gives the figures their life-like glow.

Decorating – Each figurine is meticulously hand-painted using a special pastel palette. Talented and well-trained artists paint the features of each *Seraphim Classics* angel. The most talented painters paint the faces, and the best painters from that select group paint the eyes. It takes a sharp eye and a very steady hand to paint the delicate details to meet the exacting standards of the collection. The painting process is completed when a mist of pink coloration is airbrushed on the angels' cheeks, tops of feet and backs of hands.

Understamping – A gold understamp provides an assurance of authenticity on the base of each *Seraphim Classics* angel. Using an ink with real gold imprinted on a base sanded to a smooth, flawless finish, the understamp provides the name of the collection, the name of the angel, the item number and copyright information. Since 1996, the understamp has also included a year of production mark: a harp for 1996, a dove for 1997 and a heart for 1998.

Packing – At each step of the production process, quality inspections are done before a figure moves to the next phase. At the packing table, a final inspection assures that every *Seraphim Classics* angel shipped is as perfect as humanly possible. Each angel is then wrapped, packed and shipped to Roman for distribution to *Seraphim Classics* dealers, and ultimately to *Seraphim Classics* collectors.

"Rebecca – Beautiful Dreamer" is the first event angel to be limited to the calendar year, and will be part of the year-long 1999 celebration of the* Seraphim Classics Collection's *Fifth Anniversary.

As one of Nature's Caregivers, "Simone" celebrates the infinite bounty and splendid beauty of creation.

COLLECTION HIGHLIGHTED BY SPECIAL EVENTS PROGRAM

Although the collection is relatively small – necessitated both by the intricacy of production and the limited time the collection has been offered – it is nonetheless well-established in the collectibles industry. In 1996, the first figures were retired; in 1997, three more attained this status; and in 1998 an additional four were heralded with this honor. Annual limited editions and special editions are offered, already gaining in value on the secondary market as they are withdrawn from production. Major philanthropic programs have also been undertaken – one in support of The Sunshine Foundation, an organization that grants the wishes of critically and terminally ill children and their families, and a second in support of the Susan G. Komen Breast Cancer Foundation.

The collection is supported by an extensive special event program, launched in 1996. The program consists of annual Limited Edition Event Angels featured at authorized Seraphim Classics Dealers' Open Houses and Personal Appearances. The annual Limited Edition Event Angel is available exclusively at special events and can only be purchased on event days. The program began with "Dawn – Sunshine's Guardian Angel" as the first Limited Edition Event Angel. Dawn was available beginning September 1, 1996 through May 31, 1997. Dawn was followed by "Monica – Under Love's Wing," which was available from September 1, 1997 through May 31, 1998. Unlike predecessors Dawn and Monica that were available at both fall and spring open houses, the 1998 Limited Edition Event Angel "Alexandra – Endless Dreams" is available only during fall 1998 open houses between September 1 and December 31, 1998.

In 1997, personal appearances by The Seraphim Classics Angel and Rosemary, the Seraphim Classics Messenger were added to the special event program. The majestically winged Seraphim Classics Angel is available for free keepsake photographs with collectors and is authorized to mark angels purchased

The special limited edition ornament, "Hope – Light in the Distance," benefits the Susan B. Komen Breast Cancer Foundation.

during the event with an "Angel's Touch." Wearing a pastel gown symbolic of the pastel-winged angels in the collection, Rosemary is the official spokesperson for the *Seraphim Classics Collection* and is authorized to sign angels purchased during the event.

The angelic emissaries of America's number-one angel collectible were warmly received by collectors as they participated in a variety of activities, including presentation of Angel on Earth Awards to local citizens. These awards, presented by the dealer and Roman, recognize individuals and their selfless acts and deeds that exemplify the qualities associated with angels.

For three years, *Seraphim Classics* special event program has been dedicated to the good works and caring spirit of The Sunshine Foundation®, a not-for-profit organization that grants wishes to critically and terminally ill children. Recognized as "The Original Dream Makers®," The Sunshine Foundation was founded more than 30 years ago by Bill Sample, who remains at the helm of the organization. As a result of the *Seraphim Classics* event program, Roman has donated more than $50,000 to the Foundation.

THE SERAPHIM CLASSICS COLLECTORS CLUB℠

The popularity and collectibility of the collection was validated when Roman, Inc. announced formation of The Seraphim Classics Collectors Club℠...A Club For People Who Care. The club focuses on the premise that helping others is the highest calling for its members. Members receive an exclusive Symbol of Membership angel figure; a specially designed club pin; a personalized membership card; a 12-month subscription to the official club newsletter, "The Seraphim Classics Herald," mailed quarterly; a 1998 *Seraphim Classics* catalog; and the opportunity to purchase the exclusive Members-Only Angel. In 1998 dues are $55.00, plus $4.50 shipping and handling, with $5.00 of each charter membership donated to The Sunshine Foundation.

CLUB

SERAPHIM CLASSICS COLLECTORS CLUB℠
555 Lawrence Avenue
Roselle, IL 60172
(800) 729-7662

Annual Dues: $55.00 (plus $4.50 s&h)
Club Year: Anniversary of Sign-Up Date

BENEFITS:

- Membership Gift: *Seraphim Classics* Angel Figurine
- Opportunity to Purchase Exclusive Members-Only Angel
- Quarterly Newsletter, "The Seraphim Classics Herald"
- Club Pin
- Personalized Membership Card
- Catalog
- $5 of Each Charter Membership Is Donated to the Sunshine Foundation

TO LEARN MORE:

ROMAN, INC.
555 LAWRENCE AVENUE
ROSELLE, IL 60172
(630) 529-3000
FAX: (630) 529-1121
URL: http://www.roman.com

50 Years with a Tradition of Excellence

Seymour Mann and Seymour Mann, Inc. are celebrating their 50th anniversary in the gift, tabletop and porcelain collectibles industry. In the late 1940s Seymour Mann began to produce collectible animals such as mice with cheese and dogs on chains. The company also produced a very popular series of Salt and Pepper Scotties. In the 1960s, a collection of Italian porcelain collectibles called *The Lovables* were created. In the next decade, Seymour Mann, Inc. designed and produced figurines, ornaments, musicals and dolls for the collectibles industry. Recently, the company has undertaken the largest expansion to date by introducing more collectible dolls. Several new doll artists have signed on, bringing the total to over 15.

Seymour Mann, Inc. recently enlarged its New York showroom by moving up to the fifth floor of 225 Fifth Avenue. A new doll gallery has been created to showcase the new product introductions. In addition, the company has redesigned their permanent showrooms in Atlanta, Los Angeles, Chicago and High Point, North Carolina.

"Pia," by Edna Dali, is 17-1/2" tall. The porcelain doll is a limited edition of only 1,200 pieces.

The doll artist, the individual artist with a distinctive style, is still the heart of the company, according to Gideon S. Oberweger, CEO. The stable of artists has evolved into the Studios of Seymour Mann, Inc. and the creation of the *Connoisseur Collection*.

THE ARTISTS ARE THE HEART OF THE COMPANY

Some of the doll artists include such notables as Pat Kolesar, a doll artist since 1979, who has won over 40 awards for her designs. Among some of her designs are "Clair Mann," "Enid," "Sparkle," and the kissing series of "Kyle, Kelly and Casey."

Edna Dali, a resident of Ra'Anna, Israel, took up sculpture and doll making after graduating from Ben Gurion University in her native land. Her one-of-a-kind dolls and limited editions are sought after the world over. Some of her recent creations include "Patricia," "Stacy," and "Cara."

Hanna Kahl Hyland started as a sculptor and then began carving all-wood dolls. Her first porcelain doll for Seymour Mann, "Reilly," was an instant hit, as have been all of her dolls. In 1997, she appeared for Seymour Mann, Inc. at the Disney Doll and Teddy Bear Show.

Eda Mann has been painting for years before she painted her first doll portrait. Her work is included in the Metropolitan Museum of Art's permanent collection.

The list goes on with Valerie Pike, a resident of Australia, who started as a portrait painter. That led to hand-painted clothing and soft-sculpture dolls. Until joining the Studios of Seymour Mann, her dolls were usually limited to editions of only 25. Since Toy Fair '96, her dolls are now available to a much larger audience.

Another Australian artist, Gwen McNeill, is the creator of "Chelsea" and "Lady Windemere."

Pamela Phillips created her first doll for Seymour Mann in 1993. Since that time, her dolls have garnered several awards and nominations.

New to the Seymour Mann family is B.K. Lee, designer of "Kirsten," a proud recipient of nominations for "Doll of the Year" and "Dolls of Excellence" awards. B. K. is an unusually talented artist who sculpted "Kirsten" with a porcelain head, large blue eyes, and a gorgeous open mouth. "Kirsten" is a masterpiece with a full porcelain chest and legs. Her exquisite costume is made from organza and trimmed with turquoise cotton, and she is limited to an edition of 5,000 pieces worldwide.

In addition, the pool of artists at Seymour Mann, Inc. has grown to include Margie Costa, Janet Sauerbrey, Mitzie Hargrave, Joanna Cayot, Heloise, Catherine Wang, Jill Neveroni, Joan Pushie, Bruny and Tomas Francieck.

"Kirsten," designed by B.K. Lee, is the proud recipient of nominations for "Doll of the Year" and "Dolls of Excellence" 1997 awards.

AWARD-WINNING DOLLS

Gideon Oberweger works closely with the artists, selecting all the overseas factories and overseeing the manufacturing process. His goal is to reproduce, as accurately as possible, the original creation. "It's critical to our overall success to supervise the manufacturing and guarantee the transformation of the artist's work to a first-rate collectible," states Oberweger. Some adjustments have to be made to accommodate cost and production objectives, but these decisions are always made with the full participation of the doll artist.

When asked to name a doll that the company is particularly proud of, all the family members look immediately to Eda Mann, who answers without missing a beat: "Hope." This doll is actually four dolls in one. Oberweger tells us that Eda, who is several times a grandmother, was so distressed by the effect of world events on children, that she created the guardian angel "Hope" holding three children: one Black, one Caucasian and one Asian. "Eda doesn't see the doll as politicizing art, but she wanted to create an emotional plea to save children, because they are the only hope for the future." "Hope" has also been deeded to the Museum of the City of New York with three other Seymour Mann collectible dolls for their permanent collection.

Over the years, Seymour Mann, Inc. has won numerous awards for its dolls and collectibles. 1997 was no exception, for the company was honored with a total of ten major nominations. "Winning these nominations" says Oberweger, "simply means that our team has done a great job. We have an obligation to our artists, and ultimately our collectors, to reproduce faithfully from the original. Securing a nomination confirms it."

For years, the company has been proud of its involvement with charities and hospitals. Many Seymour Mann dolls have been donated to causes aiding children less fortunate than others. Some of the recipients have been Cancer Care, Cystic Fibrosis Foundation, Heart Share, Mount Sinai Medical Center, as well as many schools. These philanthropic commitments are dedicated to all in need, and especially children. As expressed by the Hope Collection theme, "The Hope of the Future is With Our Children."

"Beauty" designed by Tomas Francieck, stands 18" tall and retails for $150.

Fashion Ceramic Hats from the **Milano Collection** *are designed by Sandra for the Studios of Seymour Mann, Inc.*

THE DOLL CLUB

Another anniversary took place in 1997 for Seymour Mann, Inc.; the Connoisseur Collectors Doll Club celebrated its tenth year. Originally created for a small group of collectors, the Connoisseur Collectors Club has grown to over 100,000 members. These members are offered special promotions, newsletters and collectible items not available to the general public. The club has been a huge success and illustrates the involvement of the collector.

MUCH MORE THAN JUST DOLLS

In addition to the doll business, the Studios of Seymour Mann, Inc., have created collectible musicals, plates, bells, figurines and clocks as part of the *Bernini Series*. The nature theme of beautiful flowers and birds has highlighted many of the new designs which include, Magnolias, Lilies, Hummingbirds, Monarch Butterflies, Cardinals and Turtle Doves. The limited edition pieces have been retired when their original run has sold out. Many of these collectibles have been award winners, as well.

The "Monarch Butterfly" series features bells, clocks, plates, musicals, sculptures and desk accessories.

CLUB

SEYMOUR MANN, INC. DOLL CLUB
230 Fifth Avenue, Suite 1500
New York, NY 10001
(212) 683-7262

Annual Dues: $17.50
Club Year: January - December

BENEFITS:
- Membership Gift: Poster
- Newsletter
- Membership Card
- Buy/Sell Matching Service
- Special Members-Only Dolls

TO LEARN MORE:

SEYMOUR MANN, INC.
225 FIFTH AVENUE
NEW YORK, NY 10010
(212) 683-7262
FAX: (212) 213-4920

Also in the introductory stage are fashion hats from Italy. Known as "Milano," these porcelain hats are all original designs from the Studios of Seymour Mann. Available in many color groups including white, blue, yellow and pink, with coordinating baskets, "Milano" is perfect for beautiful home wall decorating in the bedroom, hallway or powder room. The hats and baskets are quite large pieces and will command a retail price tag of over $100 each.

In tabletop and gifts, a new collection of *China Blue* porcelains was introduced in 1996. *China Blue* is a collection of traditional English and Chinese accessories featuring floral and natural motifs. The collection has expanded to over 85 items and is still growing. Some of the latest introductions include vases, umbrella jars, pitchers and mugs, as well as several oversized urns.

"A commitment to quality, obviously is essential to success" says Gideon Oberweger. So is keeping costs down, always a key factor in manufacturing, which ensures an affordable product. The company plans on holding the line on prices so that Seymour Mann, Inc. dolls and collectibles will remain within the reach of the average consumer. "Creating collectible dolls is a wonderful, rewarding business," insists Oberweger. "I don't think a week goes by that we don't get letters and pictures from collectors who want to share the joy our dolls have brought into their lives. Really, who could ask for anything more?"

History Repeats Itself — in Miniature Buildings

As a young girl growing up in the South in the 1940s and 1950s, Shelia Thompson was raised in true Southern fashion – young women were not expected to further their education beyond high school, let alone aspire to own their own companies! Like most Southern women, Shelia's own grandmother believed that a woman's role as a good mother and good wife was the best that life could offer – a true measure of success. It was in this atmosphere that Shelia Thompson, who always excelled artistically, was never encouraged to pursue her talents, except as they related to being a wife and mother.

Shelia's "Charleston Houses, South of Broad" ooze Southern charm and hospitality.

So how did Shelia's Collectibles get its start and continue to expand to its present success? How did Shelia Thompson become known as the "woman who makes history every day?" And how is it that Shelia Thompson, both wife and mother, presents seminars to women's groups today about the secret of success as a self-taught artist: "Don't impose limitations! Are credentials important? They may open doors faster, but it is your drive, determination and desire, and being in the right place at the right time, that makes all the difference in the world."

CHILDHOOD LOVE OF ART PLANTS SEEDS FOR SUCCESS

During her childhood, Shelia Thompson loved anything related to art. "As a child, you assume that if you can do it, everyone else can too," explains Shelia. "It wasn't until later that I discovered my artistic talent was a gift, a part of me that couldn't be denied. At four or five, I used to carefully remove the family portraits from the wall and trace the outline of my ancestors' faces and try to draw their eyes and lips. I would then take these masterpieces to my grandmother, but I never did tell her how I composed my pictures!"

Thompson's artistic endeavors continued in high school. Anytime there was an art project in high school, she headed the committee, whether it was making posters or creating backdrops for the school plays. Years later, Thompson's love of art turned into a hobby, as she cared for her two young daughters and experimented with various materials and media.

Many collectible companies were started by women who sought innovative ways to add income to meet their families' needs, and Shelia is no exception. This talented artist was looking for a way to raise some extra cash for the holidays in 1978 and decided to make wall-mounted Mallard ducks to sell at the famed Charleston Market. These ducks were a hit, Shelia caught the entrepreneurial bug, and Shelia's Collectibles was launched!

With the Charleston Market at her fingertips, Shelia observed thousands of tourists passing through this historic market looking for something to take home as a remembrance. Shelia's love for old houses, combined with numerous requests from customers asking for historic buildings, made it a natural for her to begin creating miniature wooden replicas of historic houses and public buildings. Shelia began this venture by creating the *Charleston* series, and today, Shelia's Collectibles' series span the nation.

Shelia has always taken great pride in developing concepts that are uniquely and distinctively hers. With this goal in mind, she researched the market and thus created an interpretation with an exciting new look: the layered facade house. "I wanted each miniature replica to look as if you could actually walk into the building," explains Shelia. Instead of creating designs on both sides of the structures, Shelia felt collectors would appreciate learning some of the history of the locales; therefore, the backs of all pieces contain pertinent facts about the residences, the people who built them and other fascinating information. For example, "Ivy Green," Helen Keller's birthplace, featured a message in braille on the back of this Collector Society piece, and members received the written transcription in their Society notebooks.

CREATING A MINIATURE REPLICA

Today, the Shelia's Collectibles manufacturing facility hums with activity, as each house designed by Shelia begins as a block of wood, which is first sanded. The wood is then cut to design specifications and sprayed with its base color of paint. The house begins to take shape, as artisans print the designated design on each wood form. Roofs are hand-painted, in addition to the beautiful bushes, flowers and trees which grace each structure: a trademark of Shelia's attractive houses. The layers of the houses are then assembled, forming complete pieces. "We're always improving our quality," explains Shelia.

Boasting all the hallmarks of a true Queen Anne, "Harvard House" is a traditional blue-and-white Victorian home from Shelia's* Victorian Springtime IV *series.

"We experiment with raw materials such as wood and paint. We try different color combinations and locate different ways to create sharper details, such as our laser cutting methods."

BACKED BY HISTORY

Shelia's deep appreciation of history is apparent upon examining the company's product line. "What started out as my love of old houses and customers' requests for historic buildings, has evolved into our mission of acting as ambassadors to help people appreciate the history of the United States," relates Shelia. "Our country is so diversified, whether you're studying the South and the effects of the Civil War on the beautiful plantations, or the North, where you can appreciate the significance of our forefathers responsible for signing the Declaration of Independence and what they contributed to history – the buildings they built, the homes in which they lived and the meetings that took place there. Of course, we can't forget the western expansion to California, the famous Gold Rush and the architectural styles unique to this region.

"Now that I have grandchildren, I understand the importance of preserving the past. We hope to encourage people to appreciate their heritage by saving it for their grandchildren and, in turn, their grandchildren."

How does an artist go about selecting her subject matter? For Shelia Thompson, the ideas came naturally. Once she introduced the *Charleston* series and observed collectors' enthusiasm for historic areas, Shelia proceeded to research and select sites around the country to launch other historic series. Although Shelia and her husband and business partner, Jim, travel extensively to locate buildings for their historical miniature house series, they rely on recommendations from collectors and retailers, who send postcards, photographs and news clippings to share their recommendations. Most of Shelia's series are ongoing, as she selects historic cities that, according to the artist, "include so many wonderful buildings that I could add to them my entire lifetime and never run out of sites!" Some of these ongoing series include *Savannah, Williamsburg, Martha's Vineyard, Key West, Lighthouses, American Barns, Charleston, Amish Village, Atlanta* and *Victorian Springtime.*

INNOVATIONS SHAPE SHELIA'S

Although Shelia creates miniature homes in various architectural styles, she is best known for her lovely Victorian homes, which collectors admire for their intricate gingerbread motifs, expansive entrances, turrets, and lace curtains at the windows. The *Victorian Springtime* series features a Victorian home from every state, complete with springtime flowers in bloom to commemorate this lovely season. On the back of each piece is the history of the house, along with the state bird, tree, flower, motto and nickname. Five homes will be added to this series each year until all 50 states are represented.

One of Shelia's favorite annual introductions is what the company calls the *Artist's Choice* series. Shelia describes this strictly limited edition series as "the freedom to have the ability to explore those things no one is asking for and to offer them as part of my line!" Prior releases have included such innovations as the "Mail-Order Victorians," four striking Victorian homes from George F. Barber's catalog of home plans dating back to the 1800s.

Always interested in experimenting with various techniques, Shelia achieved a glow-in-the-dark look in her *Ghost Houses* series. Collectors beware, because this series includes all real, documented ghost houses, with folklore included on the back of each piece! Stemming from a fascination with ghosts, Shelia also studied the various moon phases and introduced two houses per year featuring a moon phase, which glows in the dark.

Another 'first' for Shelia's Collectibles is their venture into licensing, and the firm began in grand style with the introduction of everyone's favorite, *Gone With The Wind.* "Collectors' enthusiasm for memorabilia and items related to this epic novel and movie were so overwhelming," reminisces Shelia, "that we obtained a license through Turner Entertainment to create favorite landmarks such as 'Tara,' and 'Twelve Oaks.'" The designs were all approved by the licensing firm, and each piece bears the Turner trademark and licensing information.

With the intent of sharing their love of history with collectors, another licensing agreement has come about – a joint venture between Shelias' and the National Trust for Historic Preservation.

"Drayton Hall" was created through Shelia's joint venture with the National Trust for Historic Preservation.

Shelia's innovative trading cards premier a brand-new way to collect historic homes. There are 46 colorful 2-1/2" x 3-1/2" limited edition cards featuring Shelia's current and retired pieces.

Shelia will develop products, and the National Trust's stamp of approval will appear on all of the artwork associated with this project. Shelia's will proudly donate a dollar from each Trust collectible sold back to the National Trust for Historic Preservation for use in the preservation of the actual historic homes they have replicated. "We see this project as an educational tool – a way to provide the public with information about periods of history, architectural styles and a wide variety of cultures," says Shelia. "In our eyes, we're creating more than a house."

The houses created by Shelia's for the joint venture with the National Trust will be available wherever Shelia's Collectibles are sold. The first three issues are "Drayton Hall-Charleston, South Carolina," "Montepelier-Orange County, Virginia" and "Cliveden-Philadelphia, Pennsylvania."

Just when Shelia thought her miniature replicas couldn't get any smaller, a large firm known for their metalwork ornaments, contacted the artist regarding the creation of painted metal ornaments. Prototypes were created, and much to Shelia's delight, they were historically accurate, right down to the coloration of each original structure. Nine ornaments debuted the collection, carefully selected by Shelia from her existing series. Lighthouses, Victorian homes and a cottage from the *Martha's Vineyard* series were painstakingly created, and each includes a 'romance card' featuring historical facts.

Shelia's Collectibles is certainly a company on the move, as the firm is constantly seeking other exciting projects to parlay into wonderful collector series. Plans include more licensing opportunities like the *Gone With The Wind* series, in addition to locating ways to use Shelia's images on other materials, as they did with the Christmas ornaments. Collectors can keep current on news about the company through membership in the Collectors Society, with benefits including the chance to obtain exclusive Society pieces, and information about Shelia and her latest introductions and travels. Collectors will be particularly interested in hearing that Shelia's Collectibles has ventured into television, with appearances on "Start to Finish" on the Discovery Channel and "The Contemporary Collectibles Show," the first industry-wide television show for collectors.

LOOKING TO THE FUTURE

Shelia Thompson is a Southern woman, proud of her heritage, who followed her dreams like other artists, to create artwork for collectors' enjoyment. "I strive for quality and a sense of color and design. When I create a piece of artwork, I'm saying something about myself and the way I interpret life. Anytime you buy an artist's work, you're truly buying a piece of that artist who has put his or her heart and soul into the project. But above all, what makes my job so rewarding is the collectors that I meet while traveling and the letters I receive. It's a real honor to recreate historical buildings and to put them on the real estate market, an honor I will enjoy for many years to come!"

CLUB

SHELIA'S COLLECTORS SOCIETY
1856 Belgrade Avenue
Charleston, SC 29407
(800) 695-8686

Annual Dues: $32.50
Club Year: January - December
Collector's Year: Anniversary of Sign-Up Date

Benefits:
- Special Society Gifts
- Opportunity to Purchase Members-Only House
- Quarterly Magazine
- Personalized Membership Card Issued Annually
- Members-Only Tour of Shelia's Collectibles Factory
- Travel Case

TOUR

SHELIA'S COLLECTORS SOCIETY TOUR
1856 Belgrade Avenue
Charleston, SC 29407
(800) 695-8686

Hours: By Appointment
Society Members Only

Members of Shelia's Collectors Society are welcome to tour the art studio and manufacturing facility of Shelia's Collectibles by appointment only.

TO LEARN MORE:

SHELIA'S COLLECTIBLES
P.O. BOX 31028
CHARLESTON, SC 29417
(800) 695-8686
FAX: (803) 556-0040
URL: http://www.shelias.com
E-MAIL: shelias@charleston.net

SHENANDOAH DESIGNS INTERNATIONAL, INC.

Creators of Outstanding Collectibles

"Do you know how many Virginians it takes to change a light bulb?" asks Shenandoah Designs President Jack B. Weaver with a twinkle in his eyes. "Three! One to install the new light bulb, and two to reminisce about how great the old one was." That slow-paced, down-home spirit characterizes Weaver's company – and the business philosophy he shares with partners Anne R. Suit and Carole Forrest Hart. But while Shenandoah's design team always takes time for a cozy chat and a friendly joke, their success results from much hard work and a sharp eye for trends in the collectibles marketplace.

Located in tiny Rural Retreat, Virginia, Shenandoah Designs represents a successful change of lifestyle for Weaver, Suit and Hart. Not so long ago, Weaver ran a private label firm in North Carolina, casting figurines and other products in resin. "The creativity wasn't there anymore," Weaver recalls. "As we grew larger, it seemed like all I had time to do was address personnel problems. I wanted to get out of the rat race." He and Suit – a writer and marketing expert – decided to place their new firm, Shenandoah, in Weaver's hometown of Rural Retreat. They invited Hart to join them because she was the most impressive artist whose work ever was cast at the North Carolina facility. "Carole does the best faces I've ever seen," Weaver notes with admiration. Hart was intrigued by the opportunity to specialize in her art without having to worry about the business aspects of the field.

Thus, the harmonious trio began their new business together. "We have the most talented team I know of," Weaver notes proudly. "We have age and experience on our side. I'm good at spotting the trends, Carole does the sculpting, and Anne puts the package together. We joke that in total, we make one really great person!"

Like all of Shenandoah's* Keepers, *this bright-eyed character features red hair and mustache.

SHENANDOAH'S FIRST HIT: IT'S A *KEEPER*™

He's a red-headed chap with dancing eyes and a mustache, and he's anxious to share his inspiring spirit and kind words. He's a *Keeper* produced by Shenandoah Designs, and his mission is to be a constant, positive companion for collectors everywhere.

The first *Keepers* made their debut in 1993, and since then, a new generation of these jolly friends has been introduced annually by Shenandoah. Each *Keeper* reigns over a place, a profession or a special aspect of life, and his dress and demeanor display his devotion to his subject. Carole Forrest Hart sculpts and selects colors for each *Keeper*, while Anne R. Suit writes a poem to enhance every character's meaning. All *Keepers* "sit," and each comes with a velcro spot to secure him to the collector's chosen spot. This enables creative placement: *Keepers* can be "perched" on bedposts, headboards, picture frames, windowsills, bookshelves or stacks of books, edges of tables, mantels or hearths, on grandfather clocks, in wreaths, or wherever the collector's imagination places them. What's more, some *Keepers* have parts that hang or dangle – giving movement and life to their being.

The *Keeper* poems are always written to be uplifting, supportive and nurturing. The poem allows the *Keeper* to communicate with its owner and his or her friends and family. It gives the *Keeper* a "voice" that enables him to tell you his reason for being. Many collectors even frame the poems in a standard miniature frame.

Some *Keepers* reign over professions such as a cowboy, railway man, firefighter, seaman, clergyman, policeman or teacher. Other *Keepers* celebrate favorite pastimes and hobbies including music, fishing, golfing, gardening, photography, auto racing and many more. Still others watch over certain rooms of the home: the bath, bedchamber, kitchen, laundry, entry, hearth, nursery, home office, sunroom or library. Additional *Keepers* focus on emotional ties – notably the *Keepers* of mothers and fathers, of love, of secrets and of friendship. There are also holiday *Keepers* for Christmas, Thanksgiving and Halloween.

KEEPERS SHELVES™ ENLIVEN HOME DECOR

Shenandoah Designs offers a delightful range of shelves sized to hold and display a *Keeper* or any number of other special items like candlesticks or figurines. Some of the shelves are classical: depicting antique scrolls,

This handsome "King Frog"* Keeper Shelf *can hold one of Shenandoah's Keepers, or any decorative item.

books, angels, and other elegant designs. Some feature "flora and fauna" including a frog prince, grapes, squashes, pumpkins, bird nest, morning glory, and even a "Chef Pig."

Anne Suit offers collectors a host of ideas on how to use their *Keeper Shelves*. As she says, "There are so many places just waiting for a *Keeper Shelf*. What about beside your bed...just over your bedside table...or use two shelves like sconces on either side of a picture or mirror. *Keeper Shelves* are great for that 'little spot' in the bath or kitchen entry or hallway. Or buy many of your favorite ones and line them up like a chair rail around a room to form a spectacular ledge!"

THE KEEPER KLUB: FOR "KEEPING IN TOUCH"

Collectors of *Keepers* now may join a special Keepers Klub sponsored by Shenandoah. One unique aspect of this organization is the shoulder satchel: a handsome carry-all available to members only. For a $37.50 annual membership fee, participants also receive: a *Keeper* key chain, special "Yours for Keepers" stationery, letter and brochure, a premier set of *Keeper* Kards, a membership Kard, and a "surprise" gift. In addition, there's a Klub members-only *Keeper Shelf* provided as an exclusive with each membership, as well as a redemption certificate for the first Klub piece, "The Keeper of Collectors."

Members will receive the quarterly newsletter, "Keeping In Touch," which includes news from Keeper Klub Director Dana Pike, information on new and retiring *Keepers*, comments from the Shenandoah Design team, and profiles of fellow collectors.

SHENANDOAH DESIGNS PRESENTS *LIMBIES™*

"Everybody knows the light of the moon brings out the lunacy and fun in all of us," say Weaver, Suit and Hart of one of their newest col lections, whimsical *Limbies* teddy bear figurines. The word *Limbies* combines the terms "limerick" and "bears" – just as the resulting hand-painted figurines do – with delightful results. Each bear character boasts his or her own distinct personality, look, costume and accessories – in keeping with the heartwarming limerick that inspired the figurine's creation. As a unifying element, each *Limbies* features a small lantern (for the light of the moon).

The most unique aspect of *Limbies* is the fact that each bear figurine has a corresponding limerick which brings it to life right before your eyes. The first six *Limbies* include: "Zeus," complete with his rhyming friend the goose; "Queen," the country bear; polar bear "Bruno;" a "Guitarist" bear playing by the light of the moon; "First Bear," depicting part of the story of Adam and Eve; and a little old lady bear named "Grace." "Zeus" recently was nominated for a coveted TOBY™ award from *Teddy Bear and Friends* magazine, and he sells for $49.95. The other five *Limbies* are $39.95 each. Each piece is being introduced in an edition limited to 6,000 individually numbered pieces.

SHENANDOAH EXPANDS BY *LEAPERS™* AND BOUNDS

At a time when frogs are much in demand by collectors, Shenandoah Designs breaks new ground with a whimsical new series of frogs called the *Leapers*. Based upon artwork by noted author and illustrator Rex Schneider, the *Leapers* are sculpted by Carole Hart. Each *Leaper* is approximately 11" in height, and each is presented atop a fine mahogany oval base. Because dragonflies symbolize the privilege of seizing life's beautiful moments, each *Leaper* is accompanied by his own dragonfly "touchmark."

The first six *Leapers* include: "To Leap or Not to Leap," a Hamlet-type frog; "Learn and Leap," a studious frog with books called *Pond Tails* and *Fly Fishing* and long, striped socks; "To Leap – To Dream," a take-off on Shakespeare's "to sleep perchance to dream;" "Leaper Went A-Courtin'," complete with top hat; "Leap of Faith," whereby a frog with rolled tongue tries his best to catch his dragonfly; and "Kiss A Leaper," a frog prince who has just been kissed by a princess.

THE *SIGNATURE SANTA* COLLECTION

Artist D. Morgan enjoys widespread fame for her wonderfully detailed, limited edition Santa prints. For some time, she dreamed of seeing her Santa characters transformed into three dimensions. Then Morgan's husband discovered Shenandoah's *Keepers* and began to collect them. When Morgan saw the personality and intricacy Carole Hart captured in her *Keepers*, she knew that this was the ideal sculptor for her *Signature Santas*.

"St. Nicholas," from a 1989 painting by D. Morgan, shows Santa with a handsome dark red, fleece-trimmed costume, holly crown, and walking stick. "Father Christmas," from a 1991 painting by Morgan, wears a long white robe and carries a sprig of snow-dusted evergreen in one hand. "The Magic Never Ends,"

"Zeus" from Shenandoah's* Limbies *collection recently was nominated for a TOBY™ award from* Teddy Bear and Friends *magazine.

"Leaper Went A-Courtin" is one of the first six issues in Shenandoah's **Leapers** *series.*

sculpted from a 1994 painting, shows Santa checking his map for the big Christmas Eve trip around the world. A special accessory group, designed to go with "The Magic Never Ends," also is available in an edition limited to 2,000 worldwide. Each Santa measures 11" tall, is numbered in an edition of 6,000 for worldwide distribution, and comes with a frameable card featuring D. Morgan's original artwork. In all, there will be nine issues in the *Signature Santa* collection.

A firm as innovative as Shenandoah Designs has much to share with collectors on a frequent basis – and that's why the studio has launched its own site on the World Wide Web. Check http://www.shenandoahdesigns.com for new product news, updates on current series, and much more. Or visit Weaver, Suit and Hart in Rural Retreat, Virginia – population 500. But don't expect to stop at a red light. "We did have a stoplight for awhile, but we had to take it out. It just confused people!" confesses the happy, small-town collectibles "trend setter," Jack Weaver.

CHECK THE SHENANDOAH WEB SITE FOR NEWS

CLUB

KEEPER™ KLUB
C/O SHENANDOAH DESIGNS
INTERNATIONAL, INC.
P.O. Box 911
Rural Retreat, VA 24368
(800) 338-7644

Annual Dues: $37.50
Club Year: Anniversary of Sign-Up Date

BENEFITS:

- Shoulder Satchel
- Keeper™ Key Chain
- "Yours for Keepers™" Stationary
- Membership Certificate
- Redemption Certificate for Klub Piece
- Exclusive Members-Only *Keeper™ Shelf*
- Premier Set of Keeper™ Kards
- Membership Kard
- Surprise Gift
- Quarterly Newsletter, "Keeping In Touch"

TO LEARN MORE:

SHENANDOAH DESIGNS
INTERNATIONAL, INC.
204 W. RAIL ROAD
RURAL RETREAT, VA 24368
(540) 686-6188
FAX: (540) 686-4921
URL: http://www.shenandoahdesigns.com
E-MAIL: shenandoah@nays.com

SUNBELT MARKETING GROUP

Official Licensee of The Cola-Cola Company

Presenting The *Coca-Cola Contour Collection™*

For generations, Coca-Cola® drinkers have recognized "The Real Thing" not only by its sweet taste, rich brown color and tongue-tickling fizz...but also by its wonderfully unique bottle. That world-renowned contoured container dates all the way back to 1915 – when Coca-Cola executives asked The Root Company of Terre Haute, Indiana, to design a peerless vessel for its beloved beverage. Coca-Cola declared that the bottle had to be so distinctive that it could be recognized by feel, even in the dark!

Since its much-heralded introduction, The Root Company's curvy creation has become a worldwide symbol of packaging excellence. It was the subject of a trademark registration in the United States in 1960 – one of the first containers ever to attain such recognition.

As befits its historic significance, the world's most famous bottle has become one of today's most fascinating collectibles. *The Coca-Cola Contour Bottle Collection* was inspired by The Olympic Salute to Folk Art exhibited by The Coca-Cola Company during the 1996 Centennial Olympic Games. Artists from 54 countries produced works, all starting with the same inspirational "canvas" – a three-dimensional Coca-Cola bottle. They applied their folk art traditions and indigenous materials to make each bottle their own.

A handful of countries commissioned well-known artists to create submissions; others held competitions, some open to the public, some involving students at a variety of schools. Many of the bottles are now being featured in a European touring exhibit, signifying the strong impact The Coca-Cola Company and the contour bottle have had internationally. The remaining originals, some of which are too fragile to travel, are displayed in the United States at the World of Coca-Cola in Atlanta and Las Vegas. What's more, new bottles from Norway and Poland already have joined the touring collection.

Today, many of the loveliest of these artistic bottles also are available in reproduction form as part of strictly limited editions presented by Sunbelt Marketing Group. This international collection, known as *The Salute to Folk Art* bottles, has been lovingly created in the finest materials, including hand-carved stone and porcelain, and features interior bottle painting and cloisonné enamel techniques. What's more, Sunbelt Marketing has introduced other series of collectible bottles as well — all enhancing different aspects of Coca-Cola's universal appeal.

The "Floral Splendor" bottle from the* Decorative *series is adorned with cloisonné in an elegant filigree design.

A WORLDWIDE SALUTE TO COCA-COLA BOTTLES

When Bill Combs, former president of The Coca-Cola Collectors Club, first saw Sunbelt Marketing's remarkable works of bottle art in late 1997, he declared, "*The Contour Collection* is a hit!" The first five bottles in the series represent the United States, Morocco, Great Britain, Singapore and Russia. Each of these magnificently crafted bottles is limited to 2,500 for worldwide distribution, hand-numbered, and accompanied by a Certificate of Authenticity.

Inspired by the original *Folk Art* bottle produced for The Coca-Cola Company and exhibited during the 1996 Olympics, the "United States Shelley" bottle stands 7-3/4" tall and 2-1/2" wide. Each bottle is molded in polystone and meticulously hand-painted to capture every detail of Mary M. Shelley's award-winning design. The artist's name appears in a ribbon-like adornment below the bottle's main image, which shows a soda fountain scene with youngsters and grown-ups alike enjoying "The Pause That Refreshes™."

The bottle honoring "Morocco" also made its debut during the 1996 Olympics. Sunbelt Marketing's exact replica stands 7-1/4" tall and 2-1/4" wide and was reproduced by Hutschenreuther of Germany, one of Europe's oldest and finest porcelain companies. Richly decorated with touches of gold, the "Morocco" bottle combines jewel-toned colors of ruby red, sapphire blue, emerald green and yellow-gold in an exotic floral motif on pure white porcelain.

The "Great Britain" bottle takes on an historical aspect with its recreation of a portion of England's ancient Stonehenge monument. Standing 7" tall and 6" wide, this collectible consists of three separate bottles, each carved in marble to resemble part of Stonehenge. All three bottles are unattached, yet they are designed to fit perfectly together atop their base.

An actual Coca-Cola bottle serves as the basis for each "Singapore" piece within the limited edition. Standing 7-1/4" tall by 2-1/4" wide, each bottle has been richly adorned by hand using a unique Chinese art technique called "inside painting." Employing a method handed down for many generations, the artist uses bent brushes made of single and multistrand hairs to create incredibly detailed scenes on the inside of the glass form. All this is done through the narrow bottle opening.

In keeping with the beloved tradition of "dolls within a doll" or "matrioshka," the "Russia" *Folk Art* bottle represents this traditional toy which is present in old fairy tales. Each doll – from the tallest to the shortest – is molded in polystone and meticulously hand-painted. The largest doll measures 7-1/2" tall by 3-1/4" wide.

TWO NEW BOTTLES JOIN THE *FOLK ART* SERIES

For 1998, the *Folk Art* series boasts two more bottles to bring the total to seven. New bottles represent the Asian nations of "Vietnam" and "China." Both bottles again are inspired by the originals presented during the 1996 Olympic Games.

The "Vietnam" bottle showcases that nation's traditional folk art of bamboo and rattan weaving and features the well-known Vietnamese conical hat. The bamboo and rattan weaving covers an actual Coca-Cola glass bottle. This limited edition bottle stands 9-1/4" tall and 2-2/5" wide. The bamboo is from the Sichuan Province in Southwest China. This bottle is limited to only 1,000 pieces worldwide.

The second new introduction for 1998 is the "China" bottle. The title of this piece is "Peking Opera Facial Makeup." The distinctive colors that distinguish the opera's five archetypal characters are reproduced in polystone and are hand-painted. This bottle also is limited to 1,000 pieces worldwide.

Mary M. Shelley designed this "United States Shelley" bottle, which has been molded in polystone and meticulously hand-painted.

This "Great Britain"* Folk Art *bottle replica is meticulously hand-carved in marble to resemble the ancient monument of Stonehenge. The set of three bottles fits perfectly together.

ELEGANCE MARKS THE *DECORATIVE* SERIES

Sunbelt Marketing Group has crafted two exquisite new bottles using classic cloisonné techniques of adornment to premier its *Decorative* series as part of *The Coca-Cola Contour Collection*. "Floral Splendor" is presented in textured filigree cloisonné, while "Twilight's Garden" shows off a much smoother cloisonné finish.

"Floral Splendor" continues the traditional enamelware technique known in China as "Blue of Jintai," with a history of over 500 years. It was so called because blue was the typical color used for enameling, and "Jintai" was the title of the seventh Emperor's reign in the Ming Dynasty. The "Floral Splendor" bottle stands 7-1/4" tall by 2-1/2" wide and is limited to 1,000 pieces worldwide.

"Twilight's Garden" has been designated as the 1997 Charter Dealer Bottle by Sunbelt Marketing Group. Each year a new Charter Dealer Bottle will be offered to all authorized dealers as of December 31 of the prior year.

"Twilight's Garden," issued in an edition of 1,000 pieces worldwide, stands 7-1/4" tall by 2-1/4" wide. The making of this cloisonné bottle with its rich metallic touches requires elaborate and complicated processes: base hammering, copper-strip inlay, soldering, enamel-filling, polishing and gilding.

THE SIX-STEP CLOISONNÉ PROCESS

To create a bottle as stunning as "Twilight's Garden," an artist begins by base-hammering the copper body of the bottle. This step requires the coppersmith to have sound judgment in the shaping of the bottle. Step two is filigree soldering and requires great care and a high level of creativity. The artisan adheres copper strips onto the body of the bottle. The strips of filigree make up a complicated but complete pattern.

The third step is to apply colors through a process called "enamel-filling." The color or enamel is like the glaze on ceramics: it is called "Falang." The colors are ground into fine powder and then hand-applied by the artists. The fourth step is enamel-firing. During the firing process, the enamel shrinks into the filigree compartments. Colors are applied again. This process continues until the compartments are filled with enamel colors.

The fifth step is polishing. The first polishing is done with an emery cloth to level the enamel surface. After a second firing, the bottle is polished with whetstone and lastly with hard carbon to obtain a high gloss finish. The sixth step is gilding. This is done by placing the bottle in liquid gold or silver charged with an electric current. The bottle will undergo electroplating which gives it a slight polish. The result? A magnificent, jewel-toned bottle with shimmering accents of precious metal.

"Twilight's Garden" was designated as the 1997 Charter Dealer Bottle.

In addition to the *Folk Art* series, Sunbelt introduced the *Christmas* series in 1997. This collection was inspired by artist Haddon Sundblom and his vision of Santa Claus. The premier bottle in the *Christmas* series is the first rendering Sundblom produced in 1931 titled "My Hat's Off to The Pause That Refreshes." This *Christmas* series issue is limited to 3,500 bottles worldwide and each is hand-numbered. All subsequent bottles in this series, however, will be much more limited: to just 1,000 bottles worldwide.

THE *CHRISTMAS* COLLECTION DEBUTS

The 1998 *Christmas* issue, "1932 Santa," again salutes Haddon Sundblom by depicting another of the gifted artist's Coca-Cola illustrations. We see Santa reading a note from young Jimmy, who invites St. Nick to "Please Pause Here." Produced by Hutschenreuther, the new bottle made its debut in July of 1998.

THE ART OF COCA-COLA CONTINUES

With many more international *Folk Art* bottles to reproduce, an extensive archive of Haddon Sundblom's beloved illustrations, and the energy and imagination of its staff, Sunbelt Marketing Group foresees many upcoming introductions for *The Contour Collection.* Their pledge is that every bottle will be individually produced to exacting standards to insure lasting integrity, incredible beauty, and superior quality. The rich combination of history, artistry and international appeal makes each bottle in *The Coca-Cola Contour Collection* a rare and cherished collectible.

TO LEARN MORE:

SUNBELT MARKETING GROUP
4275 ARCO LANE, SUITE L
NORTH CHARLESTON, SC 29418
(800) 794-6194
FAX: (843) 554-5946

Over 100 Years of Crystal Perfection

In October of 1895, Daniel Swarovski I left his Bohemian homeland with his wife and three sons in pursuit of a dream. His destination was Wattens in the Austrian Tyrol, where he planned to set up a factory for the industrial production of cut crystal jewelry stones. At that time, he could hardly have foreseen that he was laying the foundations of a corporation which, less than a century later, would be the world's leading manufacturer of cut crystal jewelry stones. Today, Swarovski produces 20 billion stones annually, as well as decorative objects, jewelry, accessories, chandelier parts, grinding and abrasive tools, optical instruments, and glass reflecting elements for road and rail safety.

Daniel Swarovski, his wife, Marie, and three sons, Whilhelm, Friedrich and Alfred.

HISTORY OF SWAROVSKI

The first of four children, Daniel Swarovski was born in Georgenthal, a small village located in the Iser mountains of northern Bohemia. Daniel's father was a glass cutter and, like countless other skilled artisans in Bohemia, had a workshop at home. As a young man, Daniel Swarovski completed a two-year apprenticeship in gem engraving with his father and produced small hand-cut stones which were fitted with copper studs and used to decorate pins, combs, hat pins, and other accessories. Even then, he realized that the days of manual cutting were numbered, and he had already started experimenting with ways of automating the process.

In 1883, he visited the International Electric Exhibition in Vienna and saw machines invented by the early giants of technology such as Edison, Schuckert and Siemens. Swarovski realized the world stood on the threshold of a major technological revolution.

Nine year later in 1892, Daniel applied for a patent on his first invention, a machine which cut crystal jewelry stones with unmatched speed and precision. It also gave him a significant edge over the local competition, an advantage which he was reluctant to lose.

He began to scout around for a site that would enable him to develop his idea. Eventually, he found an old factory in Wattens, a small village of 7,444 inhabitants outside of Innsbruck in the Tyrolean Inn valley. The Alpine setting was idyllic – the mountain stream running through the village supplied water power in abundance, while local trains provided a direct link to the West and Paris, which was to be a major market for Swarovski crystal. By the end of the century, his Tyrolean cut stones had established a reputation for such quality and precision that they were in demand not only in jewelry making centers in England, France and Germany, but also on the other side of the Atlantic in America.

By 1908, he and his three sons, Whilhelm, Friedrich and Alfred, were carrying out experiments in the manufacture of glass. Within three years, they had designed furnaces and perfected a method of producing and refining crystal to a state of flawless brilliance.

HOW IS SWAROVSKI CRYSTAL MADE?

The basic material used in the production of Swarovski crystal is a unique man-made product produced for a combination of natural minerals, including quartz sand, potash and sodium carbonate. When these materials are fused together at a very high temperature (2,732°F), they attain a clarity and brilliance far surpassing natural rock or quartz crystal. Each solid crystal mass in then precisely cut, polished and faceted. A facet is a small angular cut plane or slanted edge, designed to give optimum color refraction to a stone. The precise edges on each facet are the hallmark of Swarovski crystal stones and give the product the famous "Swarovski sparkle."

People often wonder how Swarovski achieves the frosted effect featured in pieces link the "Unicorn," "Sea Horse" and "Butterfly on Leaf." A crystal piece is finished according to design specifications and placed into a cylindrical cone with draining holes. The cone, filled with the secured crystal pieces, is then dipped in specially formulated liquid acid solution. The acid wears away the surface area, creating the smooth, fine, frosted surface. These frosted pieces are made with the same careful attention to detail as any other Swarovski stone. Swarovski uses the frosted effect on certain design elements in a piece to create a wonderful contrast between it and the sharp, crystal clear focal stones.

The entrance to Swarovski Crystal Worlds, located in Wattens, Austria, features this impressive sculpture of a giant's head with two huge crystal eyes and a mouth of flowing water pouring into a manmade pool.

Each Swarovski object is designed by an artist, and each component stone is cut specifically for that design. These component pieces are not available to any other company. However, other crystal giftware manufacturers do purchase standard Swarovski chandelier stones and assemble them into decorative objects. Swarovski's continuing technological advances in stone cutting are resulting in more complex and realistic designs to delight collectors.

A VISIT TO SWAROVSKI CRYSTAL WORLDS

Swarovski enjoyed its 100th Anniversary in 1995, and a celebration of this special anniversary culminated in the opening of the remarkable Swarovski Kristallwelten, also known as Swarovski Crystal Worlds, in Wattens.

Designed to astonish and amuse, Crystal Worlds is an awe-inspiring experience for the senses and a mecca for collectors of Swarovski crystal objects all over the world and anyone captivated by the subject of crystal. For the first time in its history, Swarovski ceased to be merely a manufacturer of industrial products and international brand name articles – it is now recreating itself as a source of inspiration to the worlds of art and culture.

The brainchild of André Heller, a renowned Austrian multimedia artist, the Kristallwelten is an extraordinary combination of the arts, industry and entertainment which places the fascinating material of crystal on center stage, enabling it to be experienced firsthand. A spectacular subterranean journey leads through a labyrinth of encounters inviting amazement and wonder, while drawing one into a crystalline dream world of fantasy and surrealism.

Crystal Worlds is nestled unobtrusively on five acres nestled at the foot of the Tyrolean Alps in picturesque Wattens, Austria. The building reaches 36' above ground and dips down 12' into the earth. In keeping with its natural environment, the structure is covered with grass and a network of footpaths lined with alpine plants. And nearly invisible, except from the entrance, is the head of a giant with two huge crystal eyes and a mouth of flowing water pouring into a manmade pond.

Visitors to Swarovski Crystal Worlds enter through the main hall, where they begin to see a unique crystal wall measuring 36' high and 138' long. Visitors are instantly captivated by the magic and mystery of crystal, as crystal stones of all colors, shapes and sizes sparkle behind the glass wall. The links that have long existed between crystal and the arts are dramatically displayed in an exhibition of works by Salvador Dalí, Nicki de St. Phalle and Keith Haring.

Visitors then embark on a truly amazing journey through six different "chambers of wonders." One chamber entitled "Crystal Meditation" was designed by Brian Eno, one of the most creative and fascinating composers on the music scene today. This exhilarating presentation of sights and sound is Eno's first permanent installation.

Swarovski Crystal Worlds also offers shopping, dining, and a special club room dedicated to the over 280,000 members of the Swarovski Collectors Society worldwide. Members of the Society can enjoy this private room, where they can seek personal advice about their crystal collections.

THE SPARKLING TREASURES OF SWAROVSKI SILVER CRYSTAL

During the Fall of 1976, four chandelier parts were glued together to create the first member of Swarovski's crystal menagerie – a tiny, stylized, full-cut crystal mouse.

This "Baby Carriage" is a brilliant example of the sparkling beauty of Swarovski Silver Crystal.

Since then Swarovski Silver Crystal has been captivating the imagination and emotions of crystal lovers the world over.

Swarovski Silver Crystal was not named so because the crystal contains traces of silver, but because if you hold up a piece of crystal to the light, its spectral brilliance creates a "silvery" glow.

Today, this line of cut crystal, hand-assembled giftware and collectibles features over 140 artist-designed figurines and decorative objects in 20 theme groups. New introductions are made four times a year, and each year, a selection of items is retired from the line.

Theme groups include delightful collections such as *Our Woodland Friends, Among Flowers and Foliage*, and *Pets' Corner. The Beauties of the Lake* series includes swans, the corporate symbol of Swarovski, ducks, and a frog. The *Barnyard Friends* features a myriad of farm animals including pigs, chicks, and geese.

In recent years, Swarovski's continued technological innovation has allowed Swarovski Silver Crystal designers to create more complex, true-to-life and intricate designs, making these sparkling treasures even more appealing to those with a love for crystal.

SWAROVSKI COLLECTORS SOCIETY CELEBRATES 10TH ANNIVERSARY

For many owners of Swarovski Silver Crystal, their figurines are more than just decorative objects – they are a passion.

In 1987, the Swarovski Collectors Society (SCS) was formed to

The 1997 Annual Edition from the Swarovski Collectors Society is "Fabulous Creatures" — The Dragon, which explores the theme of myth and legend.

bring together serious collectors of Swarovski Silver Crystal and to add a completely new dimension to collecting pleasure. Through publications, events and trips, members meet other collectors and obtain information about their pieces, Swarovski products, and the company. Membership also provides collectors with the exclusive opportunity to purchase the SCS Annual Edition.

Launched initially in the major English-speaking markets — U.S., U.K., Canada — where collecting was a well-established tradition, widespread interest made it clear that membership would have to be extended to include the European and Asian markets as well. Although Swarovski management had been optimistic about the Society, no one anticipated the large number of membership applications that flooded in. Since then, the number of SCS members has skyrocketed, and today there are over 280,000 members worldwide and more than 90,000 in the U.S.

Annual editions are presented as part of a themed three-pieces series. The first annual edition series was named "Togetherness" and included the Lovebirds, Woodpeckers, and Turtledoves. Next came "Mother and Child" which included the Dolphins, Seals, and Whales. The year 1993 introduced the "Inspiration Africa" series which was comprised of the Elephant, Kudu, and Lion. And most recently, the "Fabulous Creatures" trilogy was introduced in 1996 with the Unicorn, followed by the Dragon, which explores the theme of myth and legend.

The year 1997 marked the 10th Anniversary of the Swarovski Collectors Society. And to commemorate this milestone, Swarovski created "The Squirrel," one of the greatest collectors in the animal kingdom. Accurate to the tiniest detail and enchanting in its interpretation, it is a brilliant symbol that collectors from all over the world will easily identify. Like annual editions, this special edition Squirrel is only available to SCS members during its year of issue.

Given the spirited excitement and enthusiasm of its members around the world, the Swarovski Collectors Society can look forward to years of continued growth and success.

CLUB

SWAROVSKI COLLECTORS SOCIETY
2 Slater Road
Cranston, RI 02920
(800) 426-3088

Annual Dues: $35.00 - Renewal: $30.00
Club Year: January - December

BENEFITS:
- Opportunity to Purchase SCS Annual Edition Figurine
- Membership Card
- Membership Gift and Renewal Gift
- Quarterly Magazine
- Magazine Box Available for Purchase
- Travel Opportunities
- Special Events

TOURS

SWAROVSKI COLLECTORS SOCIETY
EUROPEAN TOURS
C/O SWAROVSKI AMERICA LIMITED
2 Slater Road
Cranston, RI 02920
(800) 426-3088

Details: Each year, a variety of tours is offered to SCS members and a guest. Participants are escorted through the picturesque countryside of Europe, stopping at local points of interest. Tour length averages between 10 and 13 days.

TO LEARN MORE:

SWAROVSKI AMERICA LIMITED
2 SLATER ROAD
CRANSTON, RI 02920
(800) 426-3088
FAX: (401) 463-8459
URL: http://www.swarovski.com

Creativity, Quality and Hands-On Craftsmanship

Anyone visiting the stunning, 200,000 square foot plant and office complex in Noble, Oklahoma, will find it difficult to believe that Gary and Jeanie Clinton's first art studio was housed in their backyard chicken coop. The Clintons have come a long way since then, but their devotion to creativity, quality, and "hands on" craftsmanship has set United Design™ and its multitude of appealing products apart.

Today, United Design is a zoo of creations. A backyard hobby has been transformed into a thriving multi-national company that currently offers 15 product catalogs featuring everything from miniature animal and angel figures, to imaginative and intricate limited edition Santa and Angel designs, to near life-sized animal sculptures.

"Wilderness Santa" is the second in a genre of Santa exploring our country's wooded backtrails and uncharted rivers. Santa's indomitable spirit is skillfully captured by sculptor, Larry Miller.

The charming animals produced for *Animal Classics®*, *Stone Critters®*, *Animal Magnetism®*, and *Itty Bitty World™* find a home indoors; while those featured in the *Stone Garden®* catalog are comfortable gracing the porch, patio, or garden. The charm of nature's collectible creatures can also be seen in United Design's home decor accessory lines — *Candlelights™* candle holders, *Frame•ology™* photo frames, *StoneGlow™* oil lamps, and *Children's Garden of Critters™* banks, bookends and lamps. If you collect animals or need a gift for giving, chances are United Design has one for every occasion or setting.

United Design's goal is "put a twinkle in the eye of every beholder," and the award winning sculptors and design staff play a major role in achieving that goal with their input for each initial creation. Picking up the task where they leave off are over 600 artisans and support personnel dedicated to giving the consumer a product that is truly inspired by the joy and wonder of the world around us. Oklahoma-based United Design is joined in its mission by a sister facility in Norwich, Ontario, which produces some of the product lines, and a European sales and distribution company headquartered in Nottingham, England.

United Design started with the dreams, ideas, and a lot of hard work by the company's founders, Gary and Jeanie Clinton. Today, those dreams, ideas, and everyone's efforts together account for the fact that United Design's fine collectibles and gift lines are sold in 40 countries around the world.

LIMITED EDITION SANTAS AND ANGELS DELIGHT COLLECTORS

To honor the legendary figure of Santa Claus and provide cherished Christmas memories for collectors, the artists at United Design™ have created a series of richly detailed, limited edition figurines called *The Legend of Santa Claus™*. Handmade and hand-painted, some *Legend of Santa* figurines depict Santa as he appears in various cultures and situations, while others provide a unique glimpse of Santa going about his typical yearly routine of delivering toys.

Artist Larry Miller is credited with the creation of *The Legend of Santa Claus*. In 1986, he sculpted a remembrance of his grandfather, who just happened to look a lot like Santa. From that moment on, the collectibility and popularity of this collection has continued to grow. Larry's best work yet has to be the "High Country Santa" and "Wilderness Santa" designs created respectively for the 1996 and 1997 introductions.

Artist Larry Miller died March 14, 1997. His friendship and talent will be greatly missed. His contributions will continue to be a vital element of United Design's collectible presentation.

Ken Memoli adds his many talents as well. Sculpting for *The Legend of Santa Claus* collection, Ken's most notable depictions of Santa are "The Story of Christmas" and "Into The Wind." These Santas, like many others in the collection, are offered in two color versions — traditional red and greens and Victorian pastels. Miniaturist Penni Jo Jonas-Pendergast also designed the tiny toys that would fill Santa's bag in a 1990 Santa sculpted by Ken.

Every limited edition Santa is accompanied by a Certificate of Authenticity and collector's booklet. Santas introduced in 1996 and 1997 include Story Cards that recount the inspiration behind the figurine from the sculptor's point of view.

Since 1991, the *Angels Collection* has been pleasing collectors around the world. The mainstay of the collection is the annual "The Gift" design,

"Spirit of Winter" is the first in a series of Angels designed to represent each of the four seasons. They will be sculpted by the popular artist, G.G. Santiago.

representing an Angel giving a star to a young child. The star is a symbol of wishes granted. This Angel has grown from an edition limit of 2,000 in 1991 to an edition limit of 7,500 for 1997.

Other cxtremely popular Angels are "Angel, Roses & Bluebirds," "A Little Closer to Heaven," and the retired "Angel, Lion & Lamb."

Sculptors for the limited edition *Angels Collection* are Ken Memoli and Dianna Newburn, but for 1997, Penni Jo Jonas-Pendergast joins this talented duo as the sculptor for "The Gift '97." Renowned sculptor and winner of the *Collector Editions* "Award of Excellence" for 1994, G.G. Santiago, also contributed to the collection for 1997.

FOLLOWING IN SANTA'S FOOTSTEPS

The Legend of Santa Claus™ Unlimited Edition follows a winning tradition of quality and detail established by *The Legend of Santa Claus™*, but the footprints are smaller. This new line for 1997 takes its cue from its larger predecessors and captures one of the best loved holiday characters in a variety of scenes and situations. The collection includes all the sculptural and storytelling charm of their larger, limited edition cousins.

The unlimited collection is the work of Larry Miller and Ken Memoli, who are well recognized for their imagination and originality in *The Legend of Santa Claus* limited edition figurines.

ANIMALS FROM A TO Z

Stone Critters® was United Design's first collectible line offered. It features more than 800 different designs from marine mammals to feathered fowl, and domesticated animals to natural wildlife. This variety has made the *Stone Critters Animal Collection* America's most popular collectible animal figurine.

Every phase of a *Stone Critters* creation – from heartwarming poses and expressions, to the sculptured detail, to the hand-painting and finishing – combines to achieve a natural look. Realistic eyes are added, which seem to magically bring each *Stone Critter* to life. Whether a collector is just beginning or looking for a special piece, the *Stone Critters* line is a great place to start and end.

Stone Critters come in a wide range of sizes from the small *Stone Critters® Littles™*, which top the rule at less than 2" tall; to the regular *Stone Critters*, which measure about 4" tall. *Stone Critters® Babies™* average about 3" in height and feature some of the cutest animal offspring around.

If you're looking for larger animal designs, look no farther that the *Animal Classics* collection. It features many of the same animal designs found in *Stone Critters*, but in sizes from 1' to 2' high.

BRINGING THE DESIGNS TO LIFE

While many United Design™ "fans" have long been familiar with the company's collectible giftware items such as *Stone Critters®* and *Itty Bitty Critters®*, collectors are intrigued with both the charm and the exceptional detail also found in its limited edition collectibles. *The Legend of Santa Claus™* and *Angels Collection* are prime examples of the fine craftsmanship visible in United Design's many products. A process known as cold-casting allows the intricate detail of expression and pose to come through in each finished work.

The talents of many dedicated artisans and craftspeople are required for each figurine at all stages from start to completion. The first step in the process is the creation of the original sculpture by one of United Design's master artists. These include Larry Miller, Donna Kennicutt, Ken Memoli, Penni Jo Jonas-Pendergast, Dianna Newburn, Midge Ramsey and Terri Russell. Using a variety of tools and a lot of imagination, the sculptor creates an original from clay, shaping and modeling the intricate detail to be molded into the finished piece.

Upon completion of the original clay sculpture, it is carefully delivered to the mold room. There, a master mold is made by applying latex or silicone over the original, layer by layer. The first hard cast model from the mold is called a "master." The master is then returned to the sculptor to be reworked for exact detail. Next, production molds are created. Two separate raw materials are used for casting the majority of United Design's figurines: bonded porcelain and Hydrostone. Both allow for retention of the remarkable surface detail. The mineral Hydrostone is mined locally in Oklahoma.

Casting is actually done by hand, with

The Stone Critters® Animal Collection *offers collectors a "sea of animals." With over 800 animal designs – it's enough to fill an ark.*

The Legend of Santa Claus™ Unlimited Edition ***debuts six smaller Santas whose appeal and attention to detail are just as great as that of their limited edition cousins. Ken Memoli's unlimited talents are obvious in "North Country Carols."***

the caster mixing the material and then filling the molds. When set, he "pulls" the mold – something like removing a glove from your hand. The result is a near-perfect replica of the original sculpture.

Each piece then makes its way to a "fettling" area. Here, precision drills are used to carefully remove any extra or unwanted material from the cast piece. This operation prepares each figurine for the painting process.

Painting is done by hand, but depending on the effect desired, sometimes both regular brush and air brush techniques are used. Because of this hand-painting process, no two pieces are ever exactly alike. Every one is an original!

Supplementing the artisans painting at United Design's on-site facility is a "cottage industry," or a group who paint from home. The pieces are checked out for painting and returned when completed. The cottage industry has been an exciting part of the growth at United Design.

Near the end of the production cycle, United Design adds those trademark eyes that seem to truly "bring the design to life."

A final inspection is given to make sure everything looks just right before the figurine is carefully boxed. Most United Design products are packaged in decorative giftboxes – ready for collecting or giving.

UNITED DESIGN COMMUNICATES WITH COLLECTORS

Collectors of the limited edition Santas and Angels have the opportunity to receive the annual *The Legend of Santa Claus™* and *Angels Collection* newsletters. They keep collectors informed about new releases and retirements, and provide a checklist of all pieces offered in the collection. Sometimes they even provide collectors with a peek at designs the sculptors are working on for the next introduction.

WELCOME TO UNITED DESIGN

Collectors are invited to visit and experience the fascinating processes involved in creating a United Design collectible. A tour guide explains the procedure and points out interesting details as visitors watch the moldmaking, pouring and pulling, painting, and finishing techniques first-hand. On finishing the tour, collectors are also invited to visit the on-site Showroom where thousands of the company's figurines are displayed.

GIFT SHOP/TOUR

UNITED DESIGN GIFT SHOP
& FACTORY TOUR
1600 N. Main
Noble, OK 73068
(800) 527-4883

Hours:
Tours - Monday through Friday;
Call for Times.
Gift Shop - Monday through Friday,
9 a.m. - 5 p.m.; Saturdays, from Thanksgiving through Christmas, 10 a.m. - 4 p.m. Open First Saturday of the Month during the Rest of the Year, 10 a.m. - 4 p.m.
Admission Fee: None

The tour of the United Design factory, which lasts about 25 minutes, shows visitors how figurines are made, beginning with a clay sculpture, through molding, casting, hand-painting and finishing.

TO LEARN MORE:

UNITED DESIGN CORPORATION
1600 N. MAIN
NOBLE, OK 73068
(800) 727-4883
FAX: (405) 360-4442
URL: http://www.united-design.com

Melody In Motion — A Special Experience

Since its inception in 1985, WACO Products Corporation has delighted collectors worldwide with their unique line of *Melody In Motion* musical figurines. Handcrafted and hand-painted, these figurines are prized for their fine finish, as well as their studio-recorded music and life-like movements. But their universal appeal goes much deeper: there is a special experience that accompanies each figurine, and it is this experience that sustains *Melody In Motion's* popularity.

The real value of art is the impact it has on its owner. With *Melody In Motion*, that value is so high it is impossible to calculate. The tremendous satisfaction each owner obtains from the viewing, listening, sharing, and displaying of a *Melody In Motion* figurine is truly amazing.

According to Ru Kato, WACO Products president and *Melody In Motion* creative director, "Many collectors regularly write to us and speak strongly of the different ways Willie and the other figurines add enjoyment and pleasure to their lifestyles. They always tell me they entertain their guests or children and grandchildren with *Melody In Motion* figurines."

Created exclusively for the Collectors Society, this special piece, "Willie On Parade/Drum," plays "God Bless America."

A HISTORICAL PERSPECTIVE

To appreciate *Melody In Motion's* attraction, it's helpful to understand the history of this type of art. Although *Melody In Motion* figurines are truly unique, the concept of a moving figure as an artistic tableau is very old. In fact, mankind's fascination with "automata" can be traced back for literally hundreds of years.

As early as the 3rd century B.C., during the Han dynasty in China, a mechanical orchestra was handcrafted for the Emperor. In those days, these entertaining devices were powered by water movement or air pressure. By the mid-15th century, wind-up spring mechanisms were introduced, and they became a portable power source for automata. By the end of the 1700s, very intricate automatons in human form were created by master artisans who were only able to produce a few pieces in their lifetime. All were made for wealthy persons, and only a handful of those works survived. Today, these pieces can be found in museums or private collections.

Eventually, a lack of skilled artisans and the introduction of the electric motor eliminated almost all the automata production by the 1900s. At the same time, the use of automata shifted from home entertainment to include commercial applications. Department store windows became popular places for automatons. And in these developments were the roots of the high-tech animated figures in today's entertainment parks like Disneyland and Universal Studios.

THE ENDLESS FASCINATION

What the automata manufacturers had discovered was that humans were endlessly fascinated by reproductions of themselves, particularly in settings that captured essential truths about the human condition. And if these reproductions moved and had sound, the appreciation of them was limitless.

WACO believes that *Melody In Motion* figurines are today's automatons. By combining exquisite craftsmanship with precision technology for both sound and motion, *Melody In Motion* pieces tell a story about the human condition and provide hours of entertainment.

Consider how *Melody In Motion* owners talk about their experiences. They never speak in commercial terms. They talk about how the figurines add a pleasurable aspect to their life. They talk of how the figurines bring back warm memories. "For this reason alone," says Kato, "every piece we produce must be capable of bringing a smile to each viewer's face when the figurine moves and the music plays."

SEE ME MOVE, HEAR MY MELODY

All *Melody In Motion* figurines begin with Kato himself, who, thanks to a family heritage that includes writers, movie directors and painters, has artistry in his blood. A multi-faceted individual, Kato often wears many hats, as he directs the artistic development and production of the *Melody In Motion* figurines. Preferring a hands-on approach, he creates the original concept and selects the music and movements appropriate to the storyline. The concept passes on to a designer who creates a drawing; a musical director who writes an arrangement; and a sculptor who makes the clay models for the basic figurine and its separate moving parts; and, finally, onto an engineer who designs the internal mechanism.

Each figurine is carefully hand-assembled, adjusted and fitted with a

The 1997 Santa continues a tradition that began in 1986: The production of a limited edition Santa that uniquely celebrates the Yuletide season.

state-of-the-art electronic motor which drives a tape player that plays the music and sets in motion a series of cams and levers that produce the realistic movements in each figurine. All parts are custom-made for that particular style of figurine, with each mechanism designed and engineered to achieve the specific movement. Each part is hand-painted and fitted with the precision mechanical and electronic devices. All tolled, there are over 150 individual pieces that combine to bring the creative tableau to life.

THE STAR OF *MELODY IN MOTION*

Twelve years ago, WACO created the "star" of *Melody In Motion* – Willie, a lovable whistling hobo with a free spirit. Designed by master sculptor Seiji Nakane (now retired), Willie provides unlimited creative opportunities. As a hobo, Willie can go anywhere, be anything, and with the help of concept artists, Willie's dreams continue to come to life. Each year new introductions chronicle his adventures and present storylines that spark the imagination and evoke a sense of fun.

As WACO enters its 12th year of production, Willie is off on a host of new dream-world adventures. Appearing in 1997, "Willie On Parade," is a beautifully detailed four-piece series that pays special tribute to marching music. Playing tunes from famous composers of marching band music, our star, resplendent in his band uniform, is featured individually playing a Trombone; a Sousaphone; a Trumpet; and a bass Drum. While the entire series includes four figurines, one piece, "Willie On Parade/Drum," is reserved for members only.

Other recent pieces showcase Willie as a Photographer (complete with a useable frame); an Organ Grinder (joined by a playful monkey); an auto Racer (accompanied by his dog riding shotgun); and a world class soccer Champion (gold trophy in hand)! As always, each figurine features professionally recorded music and life-like movements unique to the piece.

A 25 YEAR MEMORY COMES ALIVE WITH MUSIC THAT LASTS FOREVER!

Some collectors may recall, or even own, the very first WACO figurine, the 1972 "Whistling Hobo." This piece simulated a hand-carved wooden Black Forest German hobo figurine – a folk art piece that captured the imagination of Kato. In fact, for over 25 years, Kato has dreamed of creating a *MIM* series based on the soft texture and fine hand-painted finish of this wooden figurine. That dream became a reality with a new five-piece series introduced in 1997, the *Side Street Circus*.

At first glance, collectors will notice that each clown truly has a warm, hand-carved look. There's an extraordinary amount of detail in the jackets, pants and facial expressions, and there's a wonderful soft texture that is captured by the subtle, vivid color variations. These figurines are smaller than their porcelain cousins. WACO has created a new internal chassis and designed a new method for amplifying the music from the speaker. And speaking of music, it will last forever! Co-developed with Oki Electric in Japan, the *Circus* figurines feature a sound device that gives the *MIM* music the lasting life of a CD.

Introduced in 1995, this is the 4th piece in the Coke® line of licensed figurines. Always a popular character, the Coke bear plays the music from the Always Coca-Cola advertising campaign.

Over the years, WACO has introduced new Willies as well as other characters with broad appeal. Of particular interest to collectors are the showpiece carousels. Complete with moving horses, popular carousel music, masterful scroll work and exquisite detail, the four WACO carousels are magnificent sculp-

Side Street Circus ***is a unique, five piece series with full sound and motion, inspired by a folk art figurine that captured the imagination of Ru Kato 25 years ago!***

Lucy's at it again...spooning her way to health. And collectors will love the actual Lucy dialogue WACO has combined with the original TV show theme music.

tures. The ultimate in porcelain art, "The Grand Carousel" was recently retired with a market value exceeding $3,000! Another collection features handcrafted and hand-painted figurines with built-in clocks. Depending on the specific piece, the clock can be switched on manually or set to play every hour on the hour. Or, the clock can be set as an alarm. Of course, each piece includes music and movement, and most feature Willie.

SHARE THE MAGIC WITH THE COMPLETE CAST OF CHARACTERS

Each year since 1986, WACO has introduced an annual Santa. And each year, these appealing limited editions have sold out and retired.

In 1993, WACO secured an agreement with The Coca-Cola Co. to create licensed products. To date, four Coke® brand musical figurines have been created: two 6,000-piece limited edition Santas inspired by the illustrator Haddon Sundblom; "Gone Fishin'," a piece based on a Coca-Cola commissioned original Norman Rockwell painting, and a 6,000-piece limited edition based on the popular advertising character, the Coca-Cola Polar Bear.

WACO has a second licensing agreement with CBS Entertainment/Desilu too, that has inspired two pieces based on classic episodes from the I Love Lucy TV comedy series. The first Lucy figurine, "The Candy Factory - I Love Lucy®," captures the hilarity of the famous job-switching episode in which Lucy tries frantically to keep up with a conveyor belt of freshly made chocolates. "Vitameatavegamin," released in 1997, portrays Lucy's intoxicating encounter with an alcohol laced pep tonic as she "spoons her way to health." Both Lucy pieces showcase the theme music from the original television show, while "Vitameatavegamin" includes actual dialogue from the original television episode.

According to Kato, "Our licensed products have helped us reach new and different types of consumers, and different age groups." He adds, "Believe it or not, a lot of our new customers have come from the younger generation who know 'I Love Lucy' from watching reruns on Nick at Night."

While Kato is unsure if new licensing agreements will be pursued in the future, he is certain that the *Melody In Motion* family will expand and continue to bring enjoyment and entertainment to a wide range of collectors.

Gaining in popularity are the *Melody In Motion* signing events. Held throughout the country at various Collectors Centers, these events give collectors the opportunity to share common experiences and exchange views about their collections. Collectors can also meet Ru Kato. To mark these special events, collectors have the opportunity to purchase a full-sized Willie created for, and only available at, a special signing event.

SHARE A SPECIAL EXPERIENCE

The success of the Melody In Motion Collectors Society is additional proof that Willie and his friends are part of a way of life and not just another consumer product. To support the collection of fine musicals, WACO invites collectors to join the Melody In Motion Collectors Society. Dues are $27.50 for the first year, or $50.00 for a two-year membership. Collectors are also invited to purchase gift memberships for family and friends.

THE COLLECTORS SOCIETY

As an enrollment bonus, members receive a distinctive hand-made and hand-painted figurine that cannot be purchased anywhere else. In addition, the complimentary newsletter, "Melody Notes," provides all the latest news and collecting opportunities such as new issues, soon-to-be retired pieces, and exclusive, limited edition introductions. Members also receive the latest *Melody In Motion* catalog, a $10.00 member coupon which can be applied to the purchase of any figurines except the members-only issue, and a Redemption Certificate entitling members to purchase a Collectors Society figurine created exclusively for members.

Whether a collection is being started, or added to, membership in the Melody In Motion Collectors Society is an informative and rewarding investment.

CLUB

MELODY IN MOTION COLLECTORS CLUB
WACO PRODUCTS CORPORATION
P.O. Box 898
Pine Brook, NJ 07058-0898
(973) 882-1820

Annual Dues: $27.50
Club Year: Anniversary of Sign-Up Date

BENEFITS:
- Membership Gift: Porcelain Bisque Figurine
- Redemption Certificate for Members-Only Figurine
- Newsletter, "Melody Notes"
- Membership Card & Certificate
- Members "Savings" Coupon
- *Melody in Motion* Catalog
- Personal Purchasing Record
- Retired Edition Summary
- List of Collectors' Centers
- Signing Events

TO LEARN MORE:

WACO PRODUCTS CORP.
I-80 & NEW MAPLE AVENUE
P.O. BOX 898
PINE BROOK, NJ 07058-0898
(973) 882-1820
FAX: (973) 882-3661
URL: http://www.wacoproducts.com
http://www.melodyinmotion.com
E-MAIL: waco_mim@compuserve.com

Artistry from Antique Chocolate Molds

"From the time I was a small girl, I always had a love for antiques and history," reveals Kathi Lorance Bejma, president and artist for Walnut Ridge Collectibles. "As I seriously began to collect antiques, I became more and more attracted to chalkware. My penchant for early Father Christmases inspired me to use some of my antique chocolate molds and cast my own chalkware – thus, Walnut Ridge Collectibles was born."

Today, Bejma is acknowledged as one of the world's most serious and successful collectors of antique molds. She owns nearly 4,000 chocolate and ice cream molds – some of them 100 years old or more. Indeed, the tradition of molding chocolate dates back to the mid-1800s in France and Germany, where many small family firms crafted intricate molds for chocolate, ice cream, biscuits and other candies.

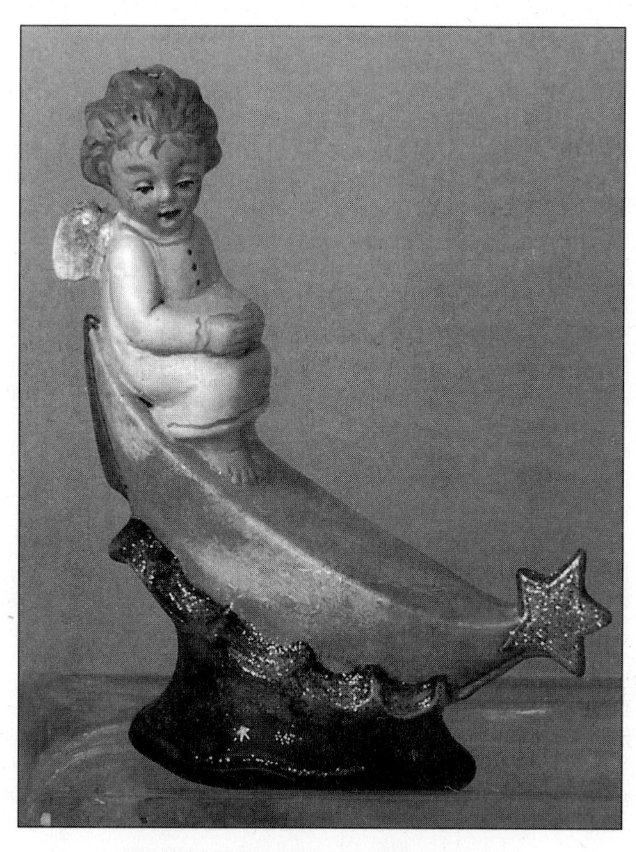

"Glimmer of Hope II" is the second Annual Angel Charity Ornament from Walnut Ridge Collectibles.

SANTAS TO SNOW CHILDREN... AND MORE!

Bejma's first chalkware pieces were created almost as a lark: while packing her favorite Father Christmas figures after the holidays, it occurred to her that she might be able to create a piece of chalkware in his image. After a number of experiments, she came up with a chalkware formula that was both strong and ideal for detail work and hand-painting. The first Father Christmas design was an immediate hit with collectors, and Bejma was off and running!

In addition to hand-painting in Old World colors, she developed a unique way of adding sparkle to many of her pieces: a process she calls "diamond dusting." The "diamond dust" not only makes the figurines shimmer in the light, but also captures a look that was quite popular in Victorian times.

Before long, Bejma began experimenting with other chocolate molds and ice cream molds from her impressive collection. The results included marvelous lines of snowmen, angels, snow children and even rabbits – many of which are "diamond dusted," as well as richly detailed and hand-painted. Not only are her pieces available in figurine form, but Bejma also has branched out into other art and decorative media in both chalkware and porcelain. These include Christmas ornaments, centerpieces, figural lamps, seasonal pieces for Halloween and Thanksgiving, and creche scenes.

A CONTINUING COMMITMENT TO CHARITY

"I feel very fortunate with my life, and where I'm at, and wish to give something back," says Kathi Bejma of her ongoing project with Communities in Schools (CIS). "With my Annual Angel Charity Ornaments, I want to help bring a 'glimmer of hope' to many needy youngsters and their families."

Bejma's second charity ornament, the 1997 "Glimmer of Hope II," portrays a whimsical, hand-painted porcelain angel. As she describes, "It's a little angel sitting on a moon-shaped boat. There are little waves lapping at the bottom, but there are stars in the waves. So it could be either the sky or waves – or it could be a reflection from the sky in the waves!" Richly adorned with golden accents, "Glimmer of Hope II" has an issue price of $46.00 and measures 4-1/2" in height.

The selection of an angel subject was no accident. As Bejma explains, "Angels represent a quality that we're missing. We often experience a 'hustle-bustle' lifestyle, so we don't take time to think about what we are doing and where we are going." She believes that angels help collectors re-connect with their spiritual selves and all the best life has to offer.

Walnut Ridge's first charity angel ornament, the 1996 "Glimmer of Hope," raised about $10,000 for CIS, the nation's largest stay-in-school network. For 20 years, the Alexandria, Virginia organization has coordinated local teams of counselors, social workers, nurses and tutors to serve needy students in communities across the country. All CIS efforts provide four basics for the children who are served: a personal relationship with a caring adult; a safe place to learn and grow; a marketable skill to use upon graduation; and a chance to give back to peers and the community.

Kathi Bejma's classic* Topiaries *make exceptional decor items for home display all year 'round.

TOPIARIES PROVIDE EVERYDAY PLEASURE

While many of her creations are somewhat seasonal in nature, Kathi Bejma tries to make each piece something a collector would feel good about displaying all year long. In an effort to enhance her collectors' daily lives, she has turned considerable attention recently to the creation of what she calls her *Walnut Ridge Everyday Collection* – pieces to use as part of a charming and welcoming home decor. To help launch the *Everyday Collection*, Bejma introduces a trio of ornate classic *Topiaries*.

Traditionally, topiaries are found in formal English gardens – indeed, the word "topiary" means a trimmed hedge or shrub. But instead of opting for an all-green foliage creation, Bejma reveals, "We wanted to do something that was a bit more classical – a little bit more dressy looking and decorative."

Kathi Lorance Bejma's *Topiaries* capture the elegant shape of some of the classic garden topiaries, but like the chalkware pieces that inspired them, they feature an abundance of fruits and other good things to eat. With the collector's home decor in mind, Bejma notes, "The *Topiaries* have a formal appearance, so they would look wonderful on a sideboard or a dining room table, or perhaps in pairs at either end of a traditional fireplace mantel. In the Fall, they would be ideal as Thanksgiving decor – but I know many of my collectors will want to display them all year. To that end, I've carefully blended all the natural colors of the fruits and vegetables so that they will harmonize with most any color scheme." Issue prices for the *Topiaries* range from $80.00 to $170.

COLLECTORS REQUEST BABY ORNAMENTS

"I never thought about creating 'Baby Ornaments' until my collectors started asking for them," relates Kathi Bejma about one of her newest ornament lines. "I listened to my customers. They meant what they said! Our very first 'Baby Ornament,' a precious little infant in a basket, was Walnut Ridge's top selling item in both dollars and units for 1996!"

The appeal of this very popular porcelain ornament is clear in both its universality and its utter sweetness. The dear little baby – which could be a girl or boy as the collector prefers to imagine – rests cozily in a basket of wonderful detail. "You can actually see the weaving in the basket!" Bejma points out with pride, "and I've placed a lace-like edging around the top." The eyes of the gently blushing baby are closed in restful sleep, while a bonnet cradles its tiny head.

"This baby has a little blanket, which I've adorned with delicately painted holly and berries, although the holiday touches are subtle enough that the ornament is ideal for year-round display," Bejma continues. "On the side, I've vined some graceful ivy, with a ribbon running though that says 'Baby's First.' The ornament also is available without the wording, and some of our dealers are personalizing these ornaments as special and memorable gifts!" Issue price for this 3-3/4" ornament, which is still available, is $36.00.

New for 1997 was another heartwarming "Baby Ornament," this time featuring a cherub with wings, resting on a curved moon and gathering bright, shining stars. The cuddly charmer appears to be tossing some of the stars back into the night sky, while clutching other stars tightly. Attached to the moon is a bag filled with more stars, tied with a copper-colored ribbon.

While the first "Baby Ornament" featured an infant, this new work of art portrays a toddler. The little one's eyes are tightly closed, and her brunette hair peeks out from the hood of her jumpsuit. For a special touch, this work of art is "diamond dusted" with wonderful, sparkling accents. What's more, the golden moon seems aglow with star dust! Also selling for $36.00, this ornament measures 3-1/2" in height.

SANTA AND RABBITS HIGHLIGHT 1997 NEW EDITIONS

As the latest addition to her annual *Limited Edition Christmas Series*, Kathi Bejma has created a handsome new Santa called "Glad Tidings." This elegant St. Nick has been cast from a German antique chocolate mold dating back to the late 1800s. The "Glad Tidings" Old World Santa sports a long white coat trimmed in gray fur, with accents of pewter and silver. His pewter-colored hood features bright silver dots, and he wears high white boots to protect against the cold. Santa stands on a

"Glad Tidings" marks the 1997 edition in Kathi Bejma's* Limited Edition Christmas *series.

Shimmering "diamond dust" accents capture the Victorian look of "Venetian Dew" in these* Rabbits *from Walnut Ridge.

TO LEARN MORE:

WALNUT RIDGE COLLECTIBLES
39048 WEBB DR.
WESTLAND, MI 48185
(800) 275-1765
FAX: (313) 728-5950

snow-covered base with holly delicately painted around the edge. His vibrant red bag has a pine tree motif and a flag peeking out that bears the year, "1997." This "diamond dusted" Santa measures 7-1/2" in height and has an issue price of $60.00.

Bejma's many antique books inspired her new collection of three elegant *Rabbits*, named "Harry," "Robert" and "Harriet." A Victorian technique called "Venetian Dew" was beautifully reproduced using her own "diamond dusting," and the rabbits' textured fur was captured using some of Bejma's own classic rabbit molds. Beautifully hand-painted with expressive eyes, the *Rabbits* can be accessorized to celebrate any season of the year.

Everyone at Walnut Ridge Collectibles is delighted that their chalkware and porcelain pieces alike are tagged "Made in the U.S.A." "We're very proud to let everyone know that our products are totally handmade right here in the U.S.," Bejma notes. She concludes, "From the original prototype to the complete work of art, I strive for a quality product, fine in detail at an affordable price. Each piece from Walnut Ridge Collectibles is individually hand-cast, hand-painted and detailed, signed and dated. Every step involved in producing our chalkware and porcelain is painstakingly executed by our fine staff – from the casting of each piece to the final shipment of the product. My hope is that my love for 'treasures of old' will enlighten our collectors' lives as it has mine."

MADE WITH PRIDE IN THE U.S.A.

A New Dimension in Animation Art

"Disney characters touch us, take hold of our hearts, and linger in our imaginations," says Roy E. Disney of The Walt Disney Studios. "They speak to that part in all of us that will always believe in the whimsy of a silly old bear and the power of a young girl's dreams. The characters seem so real, they become beloved friends. We sigh when Tramp and Lady first kiss. We laugh aloud at Donald's antics. And we share a breathtaking moment of courage with Pocahontas as she dares to follow her own path.

"The *Walt Disney Classics Collection* uses the principles of Disney animated film-making to capture the essence of Disney characters and the settings in which they come to life. Transformed into three dimensions, each sculpture seems to stop time so we can relive the emotion and beauty that touched us on the screen."

***Minnie Mouse enjoys skating "On Ice" in this new introduction from the* Walt Disney Classics Collection.**
©Disney

For the past five years, the *Walt Disney Classics Collection*, produced by Walt Disney Art Classics, has been capturing in sculpture the unforgettable characters and settings that are the magic of Disney animated films. From the spark of innocence in Pinocchio's step, to the majesty of the Beast's Castle, to the playful charm of a cake-covered Mickey, the "illusion of life" that is central to Walt Disney's vision endures through the detailed work of Disney's gifted artists.

AN INNOVATION FOR DISNEY

The *Walt Disney Classics Collection* is the first major line of fine animation sculptures introduced by Disney to capture memorable moments from Disney animated films and short cartoons. The Collection is created at The Walt Disney Studios in Burbank, California, by artists utilizing original Disney animation sketches and color palettes. It represents the first time Disney's unique animation principles have been applied to a three-dimensional art program.

Sculptures and groupings "tell a story," recreating special moments from films such as *Bambi*, *Peter Pan* and *Fantasia*, as well as short cartoons starring Mickey Mouse, Donald Duck, and other beloved Disney characters. Additional films, characters and scenes will be introduced regularly. The Collection offers special hand-numbered limited editions, time-limited editions, and anniversary commemoratives in addition to the open editions.

The Collection also represents the first time many Disney scenes and characters have been portrayed in three dimensions.

THE DISNEY CREATIVE PROCESS

An entire team of Disney animators, sculptors and artisans work in concert to faithfully translate every nuance of a two-dimensional character or setting into a three-dimensional work of art. Each sculpture is meticulously handcrafted out of fine porcelain to capture the character's look and personality, hand-painted, and often "plussed" with materials such as blown glass, crystal, or platinum to further the Disney "illusion of life."

The *Enchanted Places* where magic happens are recreated in vivid detail out of resin and alabaster. Hand-painting for all pieces is done strictly according to the film's original palette, and enhanced with finishing treatments to mirror looks and textures as diverse as a ball gown shimmering in the moonlight, to a cascading waterfall sparkling in the sun. Whether it's humorous, tender or a little frightening, each piece is filled with a bit of Disney magic.

As an enduring tribute to everyone who has ever been touched by this Disney magic, the *Walt Disney Classics Collection* offers three categories of film recreations. *Cartoon Classics* includes non-feature films such as *The Delivery Boy* (1931) and *Canine Caddy* (1941). *Timeless Treasures* represents the early feature films whose production was overseen by Walt himself, from *Snow White* (1937) through *The Jungle Book* (1967). And of course, *Modern Masterpieces* captures the wonder of today's Disney features like *Beauty and the Beast* (1991) and *Hercules* (1997).

Each *Walt Disney Classics Collection* sculpture bears a backstamp with Walt Disney's signature. An incised production year mark symbolizes a major chronological milestone in Disney histo-

Miniature versions of three favorite* Enchanted Places *pieces are now available in ornament form. They are, from left, "Cinderella's Coach," "Hook's Ship" and "Cruella's Car."

ry and represents the year in which a particular sculpture was made. The 1997 production year mark is a music stand, honoring *The Band Concert* (1935), Mickey Mouse's first color cartoon. Each *Enchanted Places* sculpture produced in 1997 will also bear the 1997 production year mark. In addition, each piece features a hand-engraved serial number and comes with a registration card redeemable for a deed "signed" by the setting's original "owner."

THE MARK OF AUTHENTICITY

All sculptures from all categories come with a Certificate of Authenticity signed by Roy E. Disney, symbolizing the care that has gone into making each piece a tribute to Disney animation magic and a beautiful work of art.

THE EVOLUTION OF A COLLECTION

In 1992, when the *Walt Disney Classics Collection* first made its debut, Disney introduced a very special piece from one of Walt Disney's personal favorites, *Bambi.* This sculpture didn't capture the main character, or even a defining moment in the film. In fact, the little guy didn't even have a name, but he did represent the beauty of nature that was so brilliantly depicted in *Bambi.*

The "Field Mouse" from *Bambi* was one of the Collection's first limited editions. Based on demand for the piece, which was issued in an edition of 7,500, it was clear that collectors recognized its unique quality. Today, the "Field Mouse" remains one of the most sought-after pieces in the entire collection!

Another "signature" piece has a similar story. This time it was from the animated masterpiece, *Cinderella.* The sculpture didn't portray the lovely heroine, or even the evil villain, but it was a moment that symbolized hope. It captured the mice and birds making Cinderella's wonderful dress for the ball.

Yet another example of an important milestone in the Collection's history to date was the introduction of a truly classic scene, Mickey and Minnie from *The Delivery Boy.* This film conveyed the early flavor of Disney animation. It was a black and white film with music and sound. The characters were drawn in a particular style known as "rubber hose animation" because of the rubber hose look of the characters' arms and legs. Drawing these characters on paper was one thing, but translating them into porcelain took more than a year of trial and error and an entirely new production facility. Finally, Disney artists accomplished the look by combining metal arms and legs with a porcelain body.

Disney presents "Hades' Chariot" from* Hercules, *along with miniature sculptures of the evil henchmen Pain and Panic.

THE WALT DISNEY COLLECTORS SOCIETY

In 1993, Disney launched the Walt Disney Collectors Society, the first Disney-sponsored club for collectors and enthusiasts. To help establish the Society's own identity, Jiminy Cricket was selected as its official mascot. Jiminy is one of the most lovable Disney characters ever created. He stands for honor, loyalty and a belief in our hopes and dreams.

Beauty and the Beast *characters Mrs. Potts, Chip, Cogsworth and Lumiere join Belle and Beast as figurine favorites.*

Membership in the Society carries a number of privileges, including the opportunity to own the many popular sculptures created just for Society members. Each year, members receive a special gift sculpture as a special thank-you for joining or renewing. They also receive the opportunity to acquire other members-only pieces.

The *Animators' Choice* series is a definite favorite among the members-only selections. Each year, the Society teams up with a group of animators from Disney Feature Animation to select a "high point" in a character's career. Animators review hours of film footage and other reference materials to determine a "breakthrough" in a character's development in terms of personality, fluidity of movement or design. They select the specific film and pose, and that moment is captured in the annual *Animators' Choice* sculpture.

Ariel and her under sea friends from* The Little Mermaid *star in this* Enchanted Places *piece, timed to coincide with the theatrical re-release of the movie.

CLUB

WALT DISNEY COLLECTORS SOCIETY
500 S. Buena Vista St.
Burbank, CA 91521-8028
(800) 932-5749

Annual Dues: $49.00; $95.00 for 2 Years
Club Year: Anniversary of Sign-Up Date

BENEFITS:
- Membership Gift: Disney Sculpture
- Redemption Certificates for Members-Only Figurines
- Quarterly Magazine, *Sketches*
- Personalized Membership Card
- Cloisonné Membership Pin
- Quarterly Newsletter, "NewsFlash"

TO LEARN MORE:

THE WALT DISNEY COMPANY
500 SOUTH BUENA VISTA STREET
BURBANK, CA 91521-6876
(800) WD-CLSIX
URL: http://www.disneyartclassics.com

Over the years, several stars have enjoyed the *Animators' Choice* spotlight, from Mickey as the "Brave Little Tailor," to one of Disney's most flamboyant villains, Cruella DeVil, to the lovable klutz, Goofy.

Each year, Society members may also purchase a festive ornament, created in the likeness of that year's free gift sculpture. For 1997, the subject for both the free gift sculpture and ornament was "On With The Show," starring Mickey Mouse himself.

Beginning in 1997, the Society has announced a brand-new members-only offer, the *Disney Villains Series.* Walt Disney believed that the strength of the story depended on the strength of the villain, because their dastardly deeds are what make you care about and root for the heroes. There have been many evildoers throughout Disney history, motivated by a myriad of selfish reasons. But only one was driven by an all-encompassing hatred for *all* things good...the dark and sinister Maleficent from *Sleeping Beauty.* Thus, she stars in her own members-only premier sculpture, "The Mistress of All Evil."

Another favorite membership benefit is a free subscription to the Society magazine, *Sketches.* Issued four times a year, the entertaining magazine is created by Disney artists and writers. It's filled with fascinating articles about Disney and preview information on all *Walt Disney Classics Collection* releases and events.

Members also receive *NewsFlash*, a quarterly newsletter that keeps them up-to-date on Society activities; a beautiful cloisonné pin designed to match the gift sculpture; a personalized membership card that extends the Society's special benefits; and a Member Services Hotline. All of this is available for a membership fee of $49.00. Prospective members may join by calling 1-800-932-5749.

The first five years of the *Walt Disney Classics Collection* have yielded a number of impressive honors for Disney, including many of the top figurine awards in the collectibles field. More important to Disney has been the positive response of avid collectors, who delight in surrounding themselves with objects of art that convey that special Disney magic. As Roy Disney says, "I hope (collectors) enjoy seeing familiar faces and settings. And that each sculpture recalls a memory of laughter, excitement or joy shared 'once upon a time' ... and in years to come."

WILLITTS DESIGNS INTERNATIONAL, INC.

Celebrating Classics and Entertainment

"The emergence of this small gift company as a trendsetter has been a roller coaster journey – and in many ways it mirrors the development of the industry as a whole," says Joseph Walsmith, President and CEO of Willitts Designs International, Inc. Founded as Willitts Imports in 1961 by the late William Willitts, Sr., the company first moved into the field of collectibles in the 1980s under the direction of Bill Willitts, Jr.

Walsmith, who with his management team purchased Willitts from Hallmark Cards in the early 1990s, focused the firm's creative energies solely on the field of collectibles. As he says, "With the exciting success of our Classic Collectibles Division, and the promise of our Entertainment Division, the company is poised for exceptional growth as we move into the 21st century."

Today, Willitts Designs creates, manufactures and markets high quality, innovative, limited edition collectibles within two divisions. The Classic Collectibles Division utilizes a cadre of uniquely talented artists to develop, under exclusive contract, proprietary limited edition collectibles based on distinct cultural and artistic themes. Positioned as affordable art, these products have both an educational value and an emotional appeal created around the innocence, beauty and romance of our American culture. Based upon original sculptures, these three-dimensional statements illustrate diverse backgrounds that make up the broad mosaic of our cultural history. Through the success of the Classic Collectibles Division, Willitts is fast becoming a leader in limited edition, collectible figurines with issue prices ranging from $75.00 to $2,000.

Through its Entertainment Division, Willitts Designs has created a whole new category of limited edition collectibles based upon one-of-a-kind film cels, and lenticular motion cels utilizing a unique depth imaging technology. Though in its infancy, the collectible film cel category is positioned to expand dramatically as new licensed properties are introduced and consumer awareness expands.

Thomas Blackshear's "Night in Day" was seen on the front cover of Toni Morrison's best seller,* Song of Solomon. *The 14-1/2" tall hand-painted figurine now debuts at $225.

THOMAS BLACKSHEAR PRESENTS *EBONY VISIONS*

Already renowned as a world-class illustrator and the creator of award-winning limited edition prints and collector plates, Thomas Blackshear now exhibits his extraordinary versatility with limited edition sculptures created exclusively for Willitts Designs' Classic Collectibles Division. His *Ebony Visions* collection emphasizes the beauty of the human form and symbolizes the universal aspirations and ideals of humankind depicted through images that reflect the unique characteristics of the black race. Blackshear's style, influenced by both Art Nouveau and African culture, is appropriately termed Afro Nouveau.

As the artist explains, "*Ebony Visions* reflects not only my own visions as a black man, but also unique visions of black people. The designs reflect visions we all share, regardless of the color of our skin. Emotions like hope, love, tenderness, faith, and serenity know no boundaries."

Ebony Visions depicts this full range of emotions in ways that are both powerful and, at the same time, subtle. Blackshear deliberately portrays the figures in a timeless setting in order to transcend a specific time, place or culture. Response to *Ebony Visions* was so overwhelming in its first year of introduction that the National Association of Limited Edition Dealers (NALED) awarded Blackshear its "Rising Star Award" for 1996. Blackshear also was named "Fine Arts Artist of the Year" with the 1996 PRAME Award. When asked where his inspiration comes from, Blackshear's response is, "through prayer and intervention from the Creator."

Blackshear entered the Art Institute of Chicago on a scholarship and later attended the American Academy of Art in Chicago studying commercial art. As an artist, Blackshear's dream has always been to create paintings and sculptures that have a lasting quality. His hope is to elevate the black experience by focusing on the beauty, grace and spirituality of the black culture in his art. He is proud to have received four recent nominations for "Awards of Excellence" from *Collector Editions* magazine for his *Ebony Visions* figurines.

Blackshear and his wife, Ami, who met years ago in art school, are the proud parents of Elisha Thomas Blackshear, born February 18, 1998.

Thomas Blackshear and Willitts Designs proudly invite collectors to join

"Forgiven" by Thomas Blackshear is inspired by the Bible verse, "I will give you a new heart and put a new spirit within you" (Ezekiel 36:26). The 12" figurine with cherry wood base issued at $200 in an edition of 3,500.

The Ebony Visions Circle collectors club during its inaugural period which ends on December 31, 1998. Membership in the club provides collectors with exclusive benefits, including the opportunity to purchase the charter members-only sculpture, "A Child Shall Lead Them," through 1998. A new members-only piece will be offered each subsequent year.

THE EBONY VISIONS CIRCLE COLLECTORS CLUB

Additional benefits to members include: a 22K gold-plated medallion with chain, for use as a pendant or pin ($45.00 value); "The Circle" quarterly newsletter; advance notice and invitations for special events; and a member services toll-free number. The cost of membership is $40.00 per year.

Ann Dezendorf, creator of Willitts' popular *Amish Heritage* collection, has won several impressive honors for that series through the Parkwest Publications Awards. Now she has expanded her horizons to create *Carousel Memories™* for the firm. A seasoned artist with credits including Hallmark Cards, Avon Products and Dakin, Inc., Dezendorf appreciates the opportunity to create diverse product lines for Willitts.

THE HISTORICAL ART OF ANN DEZENDORF

As she said in a recent interview for *Collector Editions* magazine, "Willitts was flexible with my family commitments, allowing me to bring my third baby with me while I researched and developed the *Amish Heritage* collection. Willitts and I have a great relationship, and they know I love design projects with educational and historical value. That's why my latest project, *Carousel Memories*, is a perfect fit."

Each *Carousel Memories* figure pays homage to the artistry and imagination of the great American carvers of the golden era of carousels. These include Marcus C. Illions, Charles I.D. Looff, Stein & Goldstein, Charles Carmel, Gustav A. Dentzel, Daniel Carl Muller, and the artists of the Philadelphia Toboggan Company and the Herschell-Spillman Company.

The finial atop the real brass pole for each *Carousel Memories* horse is unique to its design and is an exclusive Willitts feature. Each horse is limited to a hand-numbered edition of 9,500. The base design is inspired by carousel rounding boards. Each 10-1/2" horse is adorned with elaborate detail, "jeweled," and hand-painted.

Carousel Memories *by Ann Dezendorf features this "German Musical Karussell" with handsome Dresden parade mirror horse. The 9-1/2" tall carousel plays the tune "Hanschen Klein Geht Allein" and sells for $100 in an edition of 9,500.*

This high heeled stunner is called "The Pave" (The Rhinestone Shoe) and it was all the rage circa 1950. It's one of the elegant additions to Willitts'* Just the Right Shoe *collection.

Dezendorf's *International Musical* collection is part of Willitts' *Carousel Memories*, and it pays tribute to the carousel traditions of various lands. "The German Karussell," "The American Carousel," "The English Galloper" and "The French Carousel" all are beautifully replicated in keeping with their designer's extensive research. Each carousel plays an appropriate tune and features both a carousel horse and a backdrop in harmony with its theme.

In addition to the dramatic works of Thomas Blackshear and Ann Dezendorf, Willitts Designs boasts a full complement of other handsome lines as part of its Collectible Classics Division. These include: *Just the Right Shoe™*, the *MasterPeace®* collection, and Ami Blackshear's *Rainbow Babies™*.

WILLITTS OFFERS A WIDE RANGE OF COLLECTIBLE CLASSICS

Just the Right Shoe showcases 18 miniature (4" heel to toe) right shoe sculptures of hand-painted, cold-cast porcelain. Created to provide a historical perspective of women's shoes inspired by famous designers, the collection features shoes from circa 1780 to circa 1990.

The *MasterPeace* collection is a group of inspirational figurines based on

Willitts Designs features film cels from classic Disney animated films. Pictured is the "Snow White" lithograph with lighted film cels.

the original paintings of well-known, contemporary Christian artists. Such eminently skilled painters as Thomas Blackshear, Michael Dudash and Morgan Weistling have brought their talents to this striking collection of limited and open edition lithographs. Each painting combines great visual beauty with powerful life-changing imagery and compelling spiritual content.

Ami Blackshear's *Rainbow Babies* figurines were inspired by the artist's beautiful watercolor illustrations. They reflect Ami's faith in God and her love for babies and nature. The idea of rainbow-colored, butterfly-winged babies in a beautiful garden came to her while visiting the Garden of the Gods in Manitou Springs, Colorado. She feels the babies represent a unity and purity of spirit alive in the souls of all children. Ami, her husband Thomas Blackshear, their baby son and Ami's parrot, Rainbow, currently reside in Colorado Springs, Colorado.

WILLITTS' ENTERTAINMENT DIVISION FOCUSES ON FILM CELS

When Willitts Designs introduced its first series of limited edition collectible cels in late 1995, a whole new collecting category was born. That initial series consisted of 12 editions featuring characters from Lucasfilm's original *Star Wars* movie. Each film cel collectible is encased in a diamond-cut, acrylic mint keeper featuring a full-color, wide screen scene reproduction and a one-of-a-kind film frame from the movie. A serial-numbered identification code and tamper-proof holographic seals help ensure authenticity and avoid fraudulent duplication.

Building upon the success of these *Star Wars* film cels, Willitts introduced new film cel collectibles under license from 20th Century Fox, and Major League Baseball and Cooperstown Hall of Fame in 1997. Baseball stars featured in these collectibles include Babe Ruth, Lou Gehrig, Ted Williams, Hank Aaron and Jackie Robinson.

In 1998, the Entertainment Division moved collectible film cels to a new level with the addition of a Disney license featuring limited edition collector film cels, limited edition lithographs with lighted film cels and collector motion cels from the classic films *Cinderella* and *Snow White and the Seven Dwarfs*.

Another new introduction is limited edition collectible film cels taken from James Cameron's epic, *Titanic*. Each limited edition piece features one 70mm film cel cut from the blockbuster feature film.

The popular "X-Files" television show is commemorated in Willitts' film cels as well, with cels taken from the original TV series pilot and three popular first-season episodes already available. As Willitts Designs Vice President Daryn Reif says, "For $25.00, you can own a piece of the hottest show on TV!"

A COMPANY "ON THE MOVE"

As a company "on the move," Willitts Designs keeps abreast of the evolving collectibles market and stands ready to serve the changing wants and needs of collectors. Indeed, one of the company's slogan states, "The customer is the boss at Willitts Designs." President Joseph Walsmith comments, "As we look to the future of the collectibles market, there are clear signals of a continued steady growth pattern with figurines maintaining their position as the number-one collectible. Trends fueling this growth market are the baby boomer generation's entry into the collectible market, a growing ethnic population with increased consumer spending power, a changing consumer buying pattern, and the expanded role of licensing in collectibles. Those who understand the changing market and offer high quality and innovative programs to the new consumer will continue to grow within the collectibles industry."

CLUB

THE EBONY VISIONS CIRCLE
P.O. Box 750009
Petaluma, CA 94975
(888) 701-2373

Annual Dues: $40.00
Club Year: January-December

BENEFITS:
- Membership Gift: 22K Gold-plated Medallion Designed by Thomas Blackshear
- Opportunity to Purchase Members-Only Piece
- Quarterly Newsletter, "The Circle"
- Membership Card
- Invitations to Special Club Events

TO LEARN MORE:

WILLITTS DESIGNS INTERNATIONAL, INC.
1129 INDUSTRIAL AVENUE
PETALUMA, CA 94952
(707) 778-7211
FAX: (707) 769-0304
E-MAIL: info@willitts.com
URL: http://www.willitts.com

WOODLAND WINDS FROM CHRISTOPHER RADKO

A Collection of Enchanting Friends

With his new assortment of collectibles and decorative accessories known as *Woodland Winds*, Christopher Radko for the first time offers a single, delightful collection crafted from a variety of materials. In addition to Christopher's celebrated mouth-blown, hand-painted glass ornaments, *Woodland Winds: A Collection of Enchanting Friends* includes figurines and ornaments of cold cast porcelain, musicals and snowglobes.

"*Woodland Winds* is my first offering of collectible designs that collectors can look forward to expanding year after year, as the adventures of its cast of characters continue to unfold," says Christopher. "This is more than a village: It's a magical world inhabited by lovable, endearing woodland creatures in the form of musical pieces, snowglobes, character figurines and ornaments. In its conception, as well as in the different media used in its production, *Woodland Winds* really broadens the range of what I have for collectors."

Breathtaking beauty and irresistible charm are found in a **Frosty Leaf** ***grouping of snowglobe, musical figurine, glass ornament, cold cast porcelain ornament and cold cast figurine from Christopher Radko's*** **Woodland Winds** ***collection.***

MORE THAN GLASS ALONE

When asked why he chose to work with a variety of media to create the collection, Christopher explains, "The spirit of these designs transcends the Christmas tree, and the conception of the characters calls for more than glass alone. I wanted to introduce them as figurines for collectors, not just as hanging ornaments. That led me to cold cast porcelain, where an incredible level of detail is possible in both sculpting and hand-painting. That was crucial, because the characters in *Woodland Winds* were developed with distinct personalities and expressions."

The renowned designer of glass ornaments smiles at the suggestion that he has taken an entirely new direction with *Woodland Winds*. "Whether it's cold cast porcelain or mouth-blown glass," says Christopher, "I think every piece is made with the same precious ingredient that has always been my standard: magic!"

A COLLABORATION BETWEEN FRIENDS

Yet, there is an important difference about *Woodland Winds*: "It marks my first-ever collaboration with another artist," says Christopher. "A wonderful friend of mine, who is also an artist, happens to have a very great love of nature, in much the same way that I have a great love of Christmas. As we began to work together, these two influences came together in really enchanting ways—one of the reasons we called the results '*A Collection of Enchanting Friends*.' The animal characters of *Woodland Winds* all live harmoniously in nature, and the introduction of Christmas themes to the collection with StarDust Santa and Frosty Leaf Santa heightens this harmony, because the holidays are a time of love and unity."

Woodland Winds' debut offering of 70 pieces depicts a delightful cast of forest creatures in two related lines, *Frosty Leaf* and *Deer Friends*. The lines may be shown separately or together in displays at home; the styling and scale of the pieces are complementary throughout *Woodland Winds*. Each piece in the collection has been sculpted and hand-painted with the care and attention to detail that are the Christopher Radko signature.

FROSTY LEAF AND DEER FRIENDS

With a bold crimson leaf motif that appears throughout the line, *Frosty Leaf* recalls the late days of autumn. The central character to this line is Frosty Leaf Santa, who helps bring in the fall season and protects all the little animals in the Northern Forest. Frosty Leaf Santa is surrounded by a delightful troop of bunnies, bears and other woodland friends including the jolly Carlton the Snowman, created from the season's first snowfall. *Frosty Leaf* includes two musicals, two figurines of cold cast porcelain, one limited edition table top figurine (5,000 pieces), two additional tabletop figurines, three snowglobes

This 14"-tall tabletop figurine of "Frosty Leaf Santa" is a limited edition of 5,000 pieces. This character is beloved by all the animals in the* Frosty Leaf *line for the warmth and security he represents.

(limited editions of 7,500 each), eight glass ornaments and 12 ornaments of cold cast porcelain.

The second line in *Woodland Winds* is *Deer Friends.* Its cast of characters includes a speckled fawn named Madison, the little rabbits known as the Twins, their visiting relative Cuz and the beautiful cardinals Twinkle and Star. Visitors from another land are Blizzard and Flurry, two well-dressed rabbits who encourage the *Deer Friends* to decorate their Christmas Tree and prepare for a visit from StarDust Santa, a magical character who rides in on the North Winds. His appearance in musicals, a snowglobe and a figurine extends *Deer Friends* – and the entire cast of *Woodland Winds* – into the holiday season. *Deer Friends* includes one snowglobe, two cold cast porcelain votives, five musicals, eight figurines of cold cast porcelain, 12 ornaments of cold cast porcelain and 12 glass ornaments.

The antics and adventures that elaborate upon and enhance the characters of *Woodland Winds* are being collected into lovingly illustrated storybooks soon to be available to collectors. They really help bring the characters to life! Here's a condensed version of the first story, *Frosty Leaf Santa and Carlton Save the Day.*

STORIES ACCOMPANY THE COLLECTION

It's a windy day in late autumn. Leaves of red and gold mix with the gentle snow that's begun to fall. All the animals, big and small, are gathering and storing food to prepare for winter. The sun sets early now, so the animals work swiftly. They gather round a grand oak to look at the piles of food they have harvested. A large hollow in the tree will keep their food dry and warm. One of the rabbits will live there during the winter to keep an eye on the food supply. The guardian rabbit takes his position in the food tree. The animals settle in for a good night's sleep.

As morning arrives, fluffy clouds sail across the brilliant blue sky. On the ground, snow is everywhere. The animals gather and begin to roll around in the snow, having a little fun before their hard work continues. Slowly but surely, they roll the snow into the most wonderful snowman ever. A new friend is born, tenderly created by the animals' own paws and wings. As the wind blows, causing snow and leaves to fly around, the animals take refuge in the safety of their snowman.

"StarDust Santa with Scepter" from the* Deer Friends *line is a musical figurine that plays "Winter Wonderland." Standing 8-1/2" high, the piece is available in an open edition at the suggested retail price of $50.00.

Frosty Leaf Santa and Carlton the Snowman are central characters in one of several forthcoming children's storybooks inspired by Christopher Radko's* Woodland Winds: A Collection of Enchanting Friends. *Standing beside the limited-edition "Frosty Leaf Santa" tabletop figurine is the 8" "Carved Carlton," which has a suggested retail price of $40.00.

The guardian rabbit goes back to the stash of food and finds some missing. He runs back to his friends to tell them food has been taken. Upset, the animals look to their snowman for help. As if the snowman could talk, the animals communicate with their new friend, then each animal goes off to look for the culprit.

The animals can find no trace of their food. The birds decide to go to Frosty Leaf Santa's home for help, as the other animals go to the snowman for comfort. Again, the spirit of the snowman calms them. Frosty Leaf Santa will arrive soon, and Frosty Leaf Santa will figure everything out!

The brilliance of day gives way to the stillness of night. The animals huddle near their snowman for protection. The birds haven't returned with Frosty Leaf Santa, and the animals take shifts watching the oak tree and their food. As morning arrives, Frosty Leaf Santa

"Snow Tunes" from* Deer Friends *depicts Blizzard and Flurry as Bunny Carolers. With a suggested retail of $35.00, this 6" musical figurine plays "Jingle Bells."

stands studying mysterious tracks that lead away from their food. The animals run to Frosty Leaf Santa, jumping in his pockets and on his hat. He follows the tracks back into the deep forest. The animals come with him. Frosty Leaf Santa senses their desperation and says, "Don't worry, we'll find your food! I promise."

FROSTY LEAF SANTA FOLLOWS THE TRACKS

Frosty Leaf Santa spots a group of acorns protected by a giant leaf. Just as he tells the animals they may have to turn back, Frosty Leaf Santa sees something curious next to a fallen tree. Lo and behold, it's a fox putting on a disguise. Quietly, Frosty Leaf Santa and the animals watch the fox walk from around the fallen tree. As Frosty Leaf Santa and the other animals move toward him, the fox tries to run away. Frosty Leaf Santa gently lowers his walking stick to prevent the fox from leaving.

Frosty Leaf Santa asks why the fox is taking the food. The fox responds that he meant no harm. He had watched the animals putting food in the oak tree, then saw the guardian rabbit fall asleep. He thought he could protect the food better himself. He meant to help, but he didn't think he would be allowed into this part of the forest because he had no friends there. He was going to "save the day" by finding their food. Then the animals would have to welcome him, he was sure!

Frosty Leaf Santa and the animals go to the fox's hiding place a few steps away. There it was: all the food the animals had gathered, neatly piled at the base of a large tree, out of the rain and cold. There was room for more food and for several animals to stay over the winter months. The little fox really wanted new friends and had meant no harm.

Frosty Leaf Santa asks the animals to welcome the little fox into the family. With a resounding yes, they take the fox to meet their snowman, whom Frosty Leaf Santa decides to call Carlton. Frosty Leaf Santa takes a scarf of his own and places it around Carlton's neck for the winter.

THE MYSTERY IS SOLVED

Frosty Leaf Santa says good-bye and promises to come back to see his little friends. All the animals bid him farewell. Carlton's new scarf waves in the breeze, as if to say "So long" to Frosty Leaf Santa.

The animals give hugs and pecks to Carlton, then gather together around the fox's tree for the night. The moon is full, shining on Carlton. The animals drift off to sleep. Tomorrow is another day for gathering, and they have a new friend to help them.

CLUB

STARLIGHT FAMILY OF COLLECTORS
P.O. Box 533
Elmsford, NY 10523
(800) 71-RADKO

Annual Dues: $50.00 – Renewal: $37.50
Multiple-Year Membership Plan Available
Club Year: January-December

BENEFITS:
- Membership Gift: Ornament
- Opportunity to Purchase Members-Only Ornament
- Quarterly Magazine, *Starlight*
- Personalized Membership Card
- Annual Ornament Button
- Exclusive Christopher Radko Pin
- Current Collector's Catalogue

TO LEARN MORE:

CHRISTOPHER RADKO
P.O. BOX 533
ELMSFORD, NY 10523
(800) 71-RADKO
URL: http://www.christopherradko.com

Biographies of Today's Most Popular and Talented Artists in the Field of Limited Edition Collectibles

HOLLY ADLER

Delight and anticipation await collectors as they seek out the works of famed artist Holly Adler. Holly believes that the hand-made decorations and collectibles that she creates today are destined to become the treasured keepsakes and heirlooms of tomorrow. As both designer and collector, she hopes to create a Christmas that reflects the warm spirit of love and friendship.

Holly's artistic skills were inherited from her father, who was a prize-winning photographer. He taught Holly how to draw and gave her a sense of color and style that would help begin her career in design.

Holly, who is not related to the family that owns Kurt S. Adler, Inc., is a sculptor, painter and illustrator. For the past decade, Holly has served as a veteran and accomplished designer for Kurt S. Adler, Inc. In 1995, she introduced the famous *Holly Bearies* collection. Her two new collections are *Holly Dearies* and *Snow Bearies.*

MARTYN ALCOCK

Martyn Alcock became a modeller for Royal Doulton at the John Beswick Studio in 1986. Through the years, he has worked on several figurines for the *Bunnykins* collection. Martyn has contributed several studies of *Beatrix Potter* characters to the Royal Albert figure collection, including "Peter and the Red Handkerchief" and "Christmas Stocking." He also recreated several of the most popular *Beatrix Potter* subjects in a large size.

Like all the modellers in the Beswick Studio, Martyn has been encouraged to show his versatility, and more recently has turned his hand to Character Jugs. His first Character Jug, "Captain Hook," was selected to be Royal Doulton's "Character Jug of the Year" for 1994. He also modelled the charming miniature "Snowman" Character Jug.

Away from the studio, Martyn spends time with his family and still finds time to be the goalkeeper for Royal Doulton's Nile Street soccer team. As Martyn says, "To know that people enjoy and appreciate my work is the most rewarding part of my job."

ROB ANDERS

Recently voted by collectors as America's "Best Plate Artist," Rob Anders has become one of the "fastest-rising stars" in the collectibles field for his sensitive and realistic portrayals of the wonder and joy – and occasional ups and downs – of the early years of life.

Anders studied art at Yale and at the Museum School of the Boston Museum of Fine Arts. His major works of portraiture are on display in prestigious universities and educational institutions, among them Harvard, Yale, M.I.T., the University of Pennsylvania, Phillips Exeter Academy, Loomis-Chaffee, Boston College, Brandeis University and many others.

Other works hang in government and historical sites, including the Bunker Hill Pavilion, the Boston Public Library, as well as in private and corporate collections throughout America. He is said to be the first painter since the famed Gilbert Stuart to have two portraits hanging at once in the Hall of Governors in the Massachusetts State House.

Recently, Rob has been creating realistic images of early childhood that speak to the child in all of us, and remind us of the days when our children and grandchildren were little. His award-winning mini plates carry on the tradition of excellence at Porterfield's and are beloved by collectors everywhere.

GIUSEPPE ARMANI

Giuseppe Armani has had quite an extraordinary life. As a young child, he loved to draw. His teachers encouraged his artistic attempts, as did his father, who agreed that Giuseppe should attend the Academy of Fine Arts in Florence. Unfortunately when his father died, Giuseppe was forced to abandon his studies, but he continued to study on his own.

Giuseppe's professional career began in a gallery in Pisa where he sculpted in various materials. Often visiting Florence, he studied Renaissance themes in both sculpture and painting. In 1975, Giuseppe Armani and Florence Sculture d'Arte began an inspired, exclusive and extraordinarily successful relationship.

In a spartan studio attached to his house, Giuseppe Armani sculpts to the same ancient rhythms that existed in the studios of Michelangelo and Leonardo da Vinci. The genius of the Renaissance inspires Armani to sculpt his modern masterpieces. His mythic, almost mystical ability to put character and soul into his sculptures amazes and intrigues people the world over. Giuseppe Armani "Creates Art For Today."

BRIAN BAKER

Brian Baker's fascination for history, architecture, and the arts led him to visit more than 40 countries. His experiences inspired him to delve into the wonderful heritage of European and American architecture and to share those discoveries with others through the creation of the *Déjà Vu Collection.*

Brian's trademark in his *Déjà Vu Collection* is an umbrella. On many of his sculptures, one is hidden in the shadows or tucked away in a corner. Brian explains, "On my first building, I wanted a hungry French cat sitting by the door. I couldn't seem to design a cat that pleased me, so I left the cat's tail as the handle and made the body into an umbrella."

That same creativity shines through in every sculpture by Brian. He takes great care and pride in creating each and every building himself. He tries to become part of the house, imagining the people who would live or work there. It is his way of bringing history to life and making one feel the "Déjà Vu."

DOT AND SY BARLOWE

Collaborating as fellow artists at New York's Museum of Natural History in the 1940s, Dot and Sy Barlowe have been illustrating since then – together and separately – and earning national recognition for their historic and naturalist art.

The Barlowes have illustrated nature books for some of the largest publishing houses in America. Additionally, they have contributed illustrations to Audubon Society guides and to *The Audubon Society Encyclopedia of North American Birds.* They also teach nature illustration and botany at the Parsons School of Design in New York. Their works have been honored with numerous awards and exhibitions at the Society of Illustrators in New York and Expo '67 in Montreal.

Past collections from Reco International include the *Vanishing Animal Kingdoms*, *Town and Country Dogs* and *Our Cherished Seas* by Sy, and *Gardens of Beauty* by Dot. Recent introductions from Sy are *Land of the Free* and *Out of the Wild*, premiering with "The Pride."

FRANCIS J. BARNUM

Francis J. Barnum, master sculptor of *The Civil War Collection* for Hudson Creek's Chilmark brand, came to Chilmark in the midst of a long and varied career as a designer, model maker and sculptor. Early in his professional career, Barnum worked as a freelance model maker for toy companies. His early designs include toys that many of us remember from our childhood – Fort Apache, Ben Hur, the Six Million Dollar Man and figures from the sci-fi favorite, *Star Wars.*

Barnum went from designing toys to creating limited edition pewter sculpture for Chilmark in 1987. The move gave him a chance to incorporate two of his greatest passions, sculpting and American history, into a successful career as a prominent Civil War artist.

Barnum does meticulous research for each scene and figure he sculpts. His figures are technically and historically accurate, but each sculpture tells a unique story and vividly captures the emotions of the personalities portrayed in each scene.

KATHY BARRY-HIPPENSTEEL

Kathy Barry-Hippensteel has received widespread acclaim for the life-like quality of her child and baby dolls and has been bestowed with many awards.

"Chen" was nominated for *Dolls* magazine's 1989 "Award of Excellence" and received the National Association of Limited Edition Dealers' 1990 "Achievement Award." "Patricia, My First Tooth" was also nominated for an "Award of Excellence," plus *Doll Reader's* DOTY award. In 1993, "Tickles," one of her most sought-after dolls, was nominated for the same two awards.

In 1994, the International Doll Exposition (IDEX) recognized Kathy, giving her international acclaim. She displays her dolls in Canada and the U.S, and both "Tickles" and "Elizabeth's Homecoming" have received the prestigious "Canadian Collectibles of the Year Award" from *Collectibles Canada.*

Most recently, "Andrew," the first issue in the *Babies' World of Wonder* collection, has entranced collectors with his sweet face and light-up firefly. With "Andrew," Kathy has again succeeded at her mission of bringing "a smile to people's faces."

PRESCOTT "WOODY" BASTON, JR.

In 1938, Prescott Baston was asked by a friend to sculpt a pair of figures to sell at her restaurant. From this modest beginning came *Sebastian Miniatures.* Over a 46 year period, Baston sculpted more than 1,200 designs and variations, many of which are highly collectible today.

Baston's son, Prescott, Jr. or Woody, worked in the Sebastian Studio throughout his youth, and later went on to earn a bachelor's degree in sculpture from Boston University. Under his father's tutelage, Woody designed his first miniature, "First Kite," in 1981. Since Baston, Sr.'s death in 1984, Woody has been the sole creative force behind *Sebastian Miniatures*, America's oldest continually produced collectible line.

Woody has sculpted over 300 miniatures including figures in both cold cast porcelain and pewter. He has also created a line of Christmas ornaments. Currently offered series include *Holiday Traditions*, *The Civil War* and *Main Street America.*

SANDRA BEDARD

Ever since she can remember, Sandra Bedard has loved to draw and create. Growing up in the Northeast, art was Sandra's favorite subject all through school. School officials took notice of her artistic talent and commissioned her to paint a mural for them. Sandra proudly recalls that she paid one year of her school tuition with the money she received from that commission.

Before she could begin a career in commercial art, Sandra fell in love and became a Mom. Every night after the children were settled in their beds and the household was quiet, Sandra would enter her own little world and draw angels which came into her imagination. She thought of them as her *SoulMates*.

Until recently, all of Sandra's angels were just drawings. Then, explains Sandra, "I found sculpting, or it found me!" Sculpting is where her heart is because it allows her to create adorable little *SoulMates* from Sandy Dolls to share with everyone.

Now that her family is grown, Sandra's dream is to make everyone happy through these adorable little angel babies – her *SoulMates*.

KATHI BEJMA

From the time she was a young girl, Kathi Lorance Bejma was fascinated by both antiques and history. As an adult, she began collecting Father Christmases and exhibiting at craft shows, where she sold items made of clay, wood and soft sculpture.

At about the time her *Father Christmas* collection numbered 400, Bejma discovered an antique chocolate mold to add to her collection. She experimented with the mold, creating a piece of chalkware. This design was so popular with her customers that she began collecting these fascinating antique molds, which now number nearly 4,000, and founded a thriving business. Through her company, Walnut Ridge Collectibles, Bejma creates numerous chalkware and porcelain designs for both the giftware and limited edition collectibles industries. Subjects include Santas, angels, snowmen, rabbits, cats, trees, and many others.

Bejma oversees the entire operation at Walnut Ridge Collectibles, where all products are tagged "Made in the USA."

YOLANDA BELLO

As a child in Venezuela, Yolanda Bello "restyled" her dolls into new and exciting characters. At age 14, Bello moved to Chicago, Illinois, where she worked as a figurine sculptor and pursued doll design and sculpture. In 1981, Bello created a pair of porcelain Spanish dolls, which turned her doll making into a full-time profession.

Bello has earned more than 60 awards, including a "Doll of the Year" (DOTY) award in 1985 for one of her studio dolls, and in 1993 for her Ashton-Drake doll, "Meagan Rose."

Bello's designs range from dolls portraying characters in the opera to her most sought-after limited edition dolls, such as *Picture Perfect Babies®*. In 1996, Ashton-Drake introduced Yolanda's *Miracle of Life* collection which features porcelain dolls portraying milestones in the first year of a child's life. Also introduced by Ashton-Drake is "Ginny," the first issue in the *Spice of Life* collection.

JODY BERGSMA

Attending a small college in Vancouver, Canada, Jody Bergsma was influenced by the Canadian impressionists called the "Group of Seven." In 1978, she traveled to Europe and painted in southern France, Venice and Florence, ending her studies in Athens and the Greek Islands. Returning home, Bergsma withdrew from her engineering studies and became a serious, full-time artist.

Jody has released over 300 different "Little People" prints through the Jody Bergsma Gallery. She teamed up with Reco International to produce her first plate series, *Guardians of the Kingdom*. Since then, they have produced a Mother's Day series, two Christmas series, *The Castles and Dreams* series and her newest, *Magic Companions*. Her trip to the Queen Charlotte Islands inspired the plate series entitled *Totems of the West*.

Jody designed the *Laughables*, a line of 25 figurines which brings a joyful chuckle to all. The collection now includes special occasions pieces to celebrate a birthday, anniversary, Mother's day, wedding, new baby and graduation.

ULRICH BERNARDI

Born in the Groden Valley of Northern Italy's Dolomite Mountains, Ulrich Bernardi dreamed of becoming a woodcarver. There, woodcarving has been passed from generation to generation for more than 300 years.

Bernardi's grandfather, an altar builder, and his grandmother, an ornamental wood sculptress, inspired him and shared their knowledge and skills with him. During World War II, Bernardi, a deeply religious man, applied those skills by carving madonnas and crucifixes which he gave as symbols of hope to soldiers heading to the battlefields.

Bernardi earned a master of art degree at the Academy of Art in St. Ulrich and served a four-year apprenticeship with a master woodcarver. At age 30, his sculpture of a madonna earned him the rank of master woodcarver.

Working with the House of ANRI for more than 35 years, Bernardi's religious woodcarvings, including the Florentine Nativity presented to Pope John Paul II, and his woodcarvings of the works of Australian artist Sarah Kay, have earned him a worldwide reputation for finely detailed, inspirational art.

DAVID BIGGS

David Biggs was born in Church Stretton, Shropshire, England. He attended Shrewsbury Art College, where he successfully attained his National Diploma in Design and Pottery.

David began his career as a tableware modeller for Royal Doulton in 1958 under the guiding hand of Max Henk. He then proceeded to begin his successful range of Character Jug pieces in 1960 with "The Town Crier." His keenness for Character Jugs has not waned, and he has continued to create exciting pieces such as "Alfred Hitchcock," "Cyrano de Bergerac" and "Mr. Macawber." His "Dracula" jug was the 1996 Royal Doulton "Character Jug of the Year."

David is due to retire in 1998, after a fruitful and rewarding career spanning 40 years.

ANDREW BILL

English artist Andrew Bill is the creator and driving force behind *Enchantica*, the world's foremost collection of fantasy figures, presented by Munro Collectibles.

In July 1988, Andrew sculpted the first of many figures that was to become the standard of excellence in fantasy products. Ten years, four novels and tens of thousands of collectors later, Andrew is still happily designing and sculpting limited edition wizards, dragons, and various other creatures that inhabit the world of *Enchantica*.

Born in Shropshire, England, and growing up in neighboring Staffordshire, Andrew had a keen interest in nature and wildlife, which continues to have a strong influence on his work. Even the mythical fantastic creatures of Andrew's imagination are based closely on nature to give them the look and vitality of real creatures.

After studying ceramic design at college, Andrew worked for a division of Wedgwood, sculpting animals and cottages. He joined Holland Studiocraft in 1987 as their principal sculptor, where he originally sculpted a range of wildlife and farm animals. The following year, he created what is now the *Enchantica* fantasy collection. As a companion and guide to this fantastical world, Andrew has also written four *Enchantica* novels. The development of this long-running epic saga has shaped and inspired the collection of enchanted characters for the past ten years.

AMI BLACKSHEAR

Ami Blackshear's *Rainbow Babies™* from Willitts Designs were inspired by her beautiful watercolor illustrations. They reflect her faith in God and love for babies and nature. The idea of rainbow-colored, butterfly-winged babies in a beautiful garden came to her while visiting the Garden of the Gods in Manitou Springs, Colorado. She feels the babies represent a unity and purity of spirit alive in the souls of all children.

Ami Blackshear graduated in 1978 from the American Academy of Art in Chicago. She began her career as an illustrator for several leading Midwest advertising agencies before marrying the multi-talented artist, Thomas Blackshear, in 1986.

The Blackshears relocated to Novato, California, and Ami began her freelance career illustrating children's books. Her delicate watercolor illustrations appear in *Diamonds & Toads* and *A Child's Book of Angels*. Her work has been published by Bantam Books, Chariot Books, Current Inc., DaySpring, MacMillan-McGraw-Hill, and many other publishers. Ami, her husband and their son, Elisha Thomas, currently reside in Colorado Springs, Colorado.

THOMAS BLACKSHEAR

In 1995, Thomas Blackshear introduced *Ebony Visions*, a collection of three-dimensional figurines that capture the beauty, elegance and emotions of the African-American culture. In his own words, "*Ebony Visions* reflects not only my own visions as a black man but also unique visions of black people. The designs reflect visions we all share, regardless of the color of our skin."

As an artist, it has always been his dream to create paintings and sculptures that have a lasting quality to them. When asked where his inspiration comes from, Thomas' response was "through prayer and intervention from the Creator."

Blackshear entered the Art Institute of Chicago on a scholarship and later attended and graduated from the American Academy of Art in Chicago. In 1982, after working for Hallmark Cards and an advertising agency, he became a free-lance illustrator.

His fascination with the movie industry led Thomas to Marin County in California where he earned the assignment for George Lucas' "Tucker" video cover. Blackshear's entry into the collectibles arena came when the art director at Lucas Studios invited him to paint a series of eight limited edition *Star Wars* collectible plates. He followed that up with a series of *Wizard of Oz* plates.

Blackshear's illustrations from the book, *I Have A Dream*, were on exhibit at the Smithsonian Institution, and his art has also graced a collection of black heritage stamps created for the U.S. Postal Service.

PAUL BOLINGER

A master craftsman who specializes in distinctive stylized Santas, Paul Bolinger is an award-winning artist and professional woodcarver who creates highly sought-after figurines for Kurt S. Adler, Inc.

Ever since receiving a chisel and a block of wood from a

friend for Christmas, he has mastered the art of woodcarving – from relief carving, to carving in the round, to his current forms of Father Christmas. He is a self-taught woodcarver who creates holiday legends from his "Three Bears Cottage" studio in the Santa Cruz Mountains in California.

Selected twice as "America's Best Traditional Craftsman" by *Early American Homes* magazine, Paul has been featured in a multitude of national magazines and has also published two books.

His collection features hand-painted Santas cast in wood resin directly from his originals. Many are inspired from old German and Celtic lore and include traditional Gift Givers and other characters with distinctive looks and personalities.

HAZLE BOYLES

After studying interior design in college, Hazle Boyles taught art classes, worked in a graphic design studio, and as a hobby, created low-relief clay miniature buildings of British High Street shops. Her art has been exhibited at the Royal Academy, the Mall Galleries in London, and at the Oxfordshire County Museum, where some of her work forms part of a permanent exhibition.

What started as a hobby soon grew into a thriving business, as people snapped up her exquisite, hand-painted wall plaques at craft fairs. In 1990, Hazle set up Hazle Ceramics, registering "A Nation of Shopkeepers" as the trademark for her ceramics; operating, complete with kiln, from the spare room and kitchen in her small flat.

Now based in workshops in converted farm buildings in Essex, Hazle Ceramics is well established as one of the leaders in the field of quality British collectibles. Hazle still carves all the original designs, the majority of which are faithful replicas of real buildings.

BRALDT BRALDS

Braldt Bralds combines "domestic whimsy" with a bright, unique art style, developed through years of commercial artwork in his homeland of the Netherlands. His first job in the U.S. was illustrating a cover for *Time* magazine. This led to illustrations in *Newsweek, Omni, TV Guide, Rolling Stone*, and *National Geographic*, among many others. His awards include three gold medals, three silver medals, and the "Hamilton King Award" from the Society of Illustrators.

Bralds is proud of his contribution to education. He has taught at New Yorks' School of Visual Arts and was an independent student counselor for their masters program. He now serves on the International Advisory Board of Art Institutes International, which established a Braldt Bralds Illustration Scholarship in 1993. He joined The Greenwich Workshop in 1995 and embarked on a string of sold-out limited editions.

ADRIENNE BROWN

Adrienne Brown descended from two generations of accomplished artists, and was raised in a home where the love of dolls was encouraged. After earning a degree in fine art from the Philadelphia College of Art, Brown designed and sculpted porcelain dolls professionally, earning several prestigious awards for her work. She lived and worked in London, designing baby dolls that earned wide recognition in the European market. Today, she lives and works in the U.S., creating her own doll designs for discriminating customers.

Working with Ashton-Drake for the past three years, Adrienne Brown has created two very popular collections that were inspired by her three sons. *Just Caught Napping* portrays four toddlers who have fallen asleep while playing, and the *Boys and Bears* collection features little boys with their cuddly teddy bear companions.

DENNIS BROWN

Dennis Brown is a self-taught artist who has been designing and sculpting for over 25 years. Brown is the creator of Enesco Corporation's "The Bethlehem Experience," a nativity scene that recreates the birth of Christ. Brown also created the *Reasons to Believe* collection of whimsical resin figurines, which includes *A Jester For All Times, Just Believe*, and the *Historically Speaking* series of whimsical figurines.

Brown's inspiration for his collections comes from his love of watching smiles come to people's faces. He hopes that when people view his work, it will rekindle a spirit of joy from within.

Brown has won numerous state fair awards, including 12 first-place ribbons for 12 consecutive years at the Southern California Expo. At the 1995 Washington State Fair, Brown was crowned the "Grand Champion of Show" and was awarded Best of Show, Best Category, Best Craftsmanship, as well as four first place ribbons.

Brown resides with his wife, Linda, in Kirkland, Washington.

RICK BROWN

With a combined passion for drawing, painting and football, Rick Brown, a native of Omaha, Nebraska, knew he could be happy with only one career – as a professional freelance sports artist.

After graduating from the University of Nebraska-Omaha, Brown moved to California, where he studied at the Art Center College of Design in Pasadena and Long Beach State. He then

landed a position with a major California studio working with noted illustrators. In 1984, Brown began freelancing with an impressive client list that includes Disney, Universal Studios, Milton Bradley, Pro-Line and Pro-Set trading cards and NFL Properties.

Brown's extraordinary skills and stunning success in combining acrylics, airbrush and brush painting brought him to the attention of plate collectors through *The Great Super Bowl Quarterbacks* series available from The Bradford Exchange. Brown's latest series are *The Brett Favre Collection* and *The NFL Quarterback Club.*

TOM BROWNING

Tom Browning found that art was an important part of his childhood, and what he wanted to do with his life. Today, he is one of America's leading artists. His work is displayed at galleries throughout the West and Northwest, including Settlers West in Tucson and Wadles Gallery in Santa Fe. He is a member of the Northwest Rendezvous Group (NWR) in Helena, Montana.

In addition to painting full time, Browning and his wife, Joyce, own and operate Arbor Green Publishers, where they publish and distribute the popular *Santa's Time Off™* greeting cards and prints.

Tom Browning's work is also featured in the *American Artist Collection®* and the *Santa's Time Off™* porcelain collection from Possible Dreams.

Browning describes himself as a quiet, sensitive person who produces "a picture that is simple and straightforward."

WILL BULLAS

Will Bullas makes fine art fun with his "watercolor one-liners." Born in Ohio and raised in the Southwest, Bullas was studying at Arizona State University when he was drafted. His first professional pieces were pencil portraits of fellow soldiers in Vietnam, which were sent to loved ones back home. Returning from that grim beginning, Bullas decided to combine his burgeoning artistic skill with humor. Since then he has been honored with the "Strathmore Award," the "William G. Morrison Award," and the "First Place Award of the National Watercolor Society."

Bullas joined The Greenwich Workshop in 1992, and his art now graces greeting cards, coffee mugs, high-fashion limited edition prints, and works of art in porcelain. His first Greenwich Workshop Press book, *a fool and his bunny...the art of Will Bullas* (complete with foreword by Bullas fan Clint Eastwood), is now in its third printing.

FRANCES BURTON

Frances Elaine Montgomery Burton has always loved art. After completing the Famous Artist Course, she began her training as a Fenton decorator in 1973. For the next ten years, she balanced work with raising her children. Later returning to Fenton full-time, she quickly progressed from decorator to trainer, designer, head designer and finally department supervisor.

In her spare time, Frances likes walking, sewing and growing the beautiful flowers she later brings to life on glass. Her delicate floral Vining Garden enhanced the beauty of Fenton's Transparent Seamist Green glass and started a new direction for Fenton hand-painted glass.

Romance novels and old movies also capture her interest. She is content when curled by the fire with a good book, her three cats, and Nikki, the dog. Frances and Lanny, her husband of 25 years, love to escape to Vermillion on Lake Erie where they fish, share the quiet beauty and their dream of residing there someday.

SAM BUTCHER

Sam Butcher is the artist and creator behind the Enesco *Precious Moments Collection*, one of the most popular collectibles in the world. The collection depicts Butcher's teardrop-eyed children through porcelain bisque figurines with inspirational messages.

Butcher creates all art work for the collection and coordinates with Enesco and the Precious Moments Design Studio in Japan to create dozens of new subjects each year, all inspired by personal events and collector requests.

Butcher has been honored with a multitude of awards within the collectibles industry including NALED's 1988 "Special Recognition Award" and "Artist of the Year" in 1992 and 1996. His artwork has won the 1992 "Collectible of the Year" and 1994 "Figurine and Ornament of the Year," also from NALED.

Butcher's devotion to his faith and art has led to the construction of the Precious Moments Chapel located in Carthage, Missouri. It houses a myriad of hand-painted murals, statues, stained glass windows and a painted ceiling, all featuring *Precious Moments* children.

Sam Butcher has seven children and 13 grandchildren.

JOYCE F. BYERS

Joyce Fritz Byers' artistic curiosity began at age 12 and expanded from sewing doll costumes to sculpting and oil painting.

After graduating from Drexel University, Joyce married Bob Byers, had two sons, and settled in Bucks County, Pennsylvania. Joyce began making caroling Christmas figures, first for herself, and then as gifts for her family and friends. For about ten years, Joyce perfected the construction methods and

refined her sculpting skills.

In the late 1970s, the demand for the Carolers® became so great that with Bob's assistance, they turned a hobby into a business. Joyce sculpts each original face style in clay and designs the costumes. She teaches artisans the skills necessary for quantity production of the hand-made Byers' Choice figurines. This handwork imparts each figurine with the delightful personality sought by nearly 180,000 collectors.

The incredible success of Byers' Choice figurines has enabled Bob and Joyce to share the joy of giving in Christmas' true spirit. Each year, they give a substantial amount of their company's profits to charities.

DENISE CALLA

The self-taught authenticity that Denise Calla brings to her artwork has been described as pure magic and has made her one of America's most highly collected artists. Denise's inspiration stems from taking daily walks within majestic woods. She says that she lives her life being led through the course of a year by the instructions coming from nature and the changing seasons.

Denise only uses the wood of evergreen trees to carve her Santas, so she has planted acres of pine trees to give back to the earth the wood she has used for her artwork. Not only is she a superb woodcarver and accomplished painter, but she also designs and makes furniture with her husband.

In order to meet the overwhelming demand for her creations while continuing to meet high-quality standards, Denise joined House of Hatten, Inc., who introduced her first designs, *Enchanted Forest*, in 1988. Now 17 of her collections make up a significant portion of House of Hatten's Christmas and gift lines.

JOANNE CALLANDER

Joanne Callander pursued her artwork as a childhood pastime for the pure enjoyment of it. She took art classes in high school and community college, and in her mid-thirties, took a class in mold making.

In 1984, Joanne started making dolls, but it wasn't until 1990 that she introduced her first two porcelain dolls. At her first Toy Fair in 1991, Joanne sold out of her limited edition dolls within the first few hours.

Now for Ertl Collectibles Limited, Joanne has created the nostalgic and beautifully dressed *Forever Sisters™* dolls. The collection premiered with outdoorsy "Kaitlin," whimsical "Julie" and caring "Sara." Each doll comes complete with a stunning, Victorian-style outfit and a "place of repose" such as a hope chest, rocking chair or wood and wrought iron bench.

In her spare time, Joanne enjoys watching vintage movies and gardening. She also incorporates her doll-making business into another hobby: attending art and rummage sales, where she locates antique trims and fabrics for her creations.

PETER CALVESBERT

In 1963, as a three-year-old in Hereford, England, Peter Calvesbert picked up a piece of modeling clay and made his first sculpted figure. It would take 30 years for him to return to this mode of expression.

After completing his schooling, Peter began traveling and dabbling in various occupations including brick laying, plumbing, cartooning and journalism. One day as he watched a friend sculpting, Peter remembered his childhood clay model. "I can do that," he said.

Today, Peter's sculptures for Harmony Kingdom have gained a stunning reputation, and he has built a fanatic following on both sides of the Atlantic. He now lives and works in England's West Country, spending time with his wife, sculpting, and perching in trees, where he is able to contemplate the spirit and magic of the animal kingdom.

DEB CANHAM

Disbelief and enchantment strike the beholder when they place a Deb Canham miniature bear or other animal creation in the palm of their hand. These tiny, jointed fabric collectibles may be small but their personality is "big."

Deb has created over 75 designs for the Little Gem Teddy Bear Company, since she became their first guest designer in 1993. Many of the old favorites like the *Friends Collection*, *Fancy Dress Collection* and *Jack & Jenny* designs are her creations. Deb still designs for the company today, as well as for the Teddy Hermann Original Company in Germany.

In 1996, Deb moved to America and started her own company, Deb Canham Artist Designs, Inc. She specializes in creating her "artist designed" miniature bears and other animals in mohair, much to the delight of collectors everywhere.

PAUL CARDEW

Design phenomenon Paul Cardew is the award-winning artist acknowledged worldwide as the most talented and prolific creator of collectible teapots.

An honors graduate of Loughborough Art College, later to become head of his department at Exeter Art College, Cardew was the first designer to concentrate on collectible teapots. His innovative work over the past 20 years has won wide recognition in exhibitions and from museums such as the Victoria & Albert, as well as from collectors around the world.

Together with long-time friend and partner, Peter Kirvan, Cardew established Cardew Design in 1991. Since then, the company has produced more than 45,000 highly collectible, whimsical and functional teapots which are sold in 20 countries. Cardew Design employs over 200 full-time craftsmen who handcraft unique designs using exactly the same production techniques used by Josiah Wedgwood over 300 years ago. Their product range includes full-size (6-cup) limited edition teapots, 2-cups, 1-cups and also tiny teapot ornaments. Cardew teapots are imported and distributed in the United States by DeVine Corporation.

PAT CHANDOK

A native of Bombay, India, Pat Chandok came to the U.S. in 1971 after marrying Dr. Sam Chandok. Coming from a business family, Pat was exposed at an early age to the dedication it takes to achieve success.

With her business expertise and her love of fine items, Pat found that the gift industry was a natural fit. Following her dream, she opened a gift shop and later developed and imported giftware. Influenced by her Asian and American backgrounds, Pat has created many exciting new gift lines. Her drive for innovation sets her apart from others in the industry.

After opening a manufacturing plant in England, Pat introduced collectors to the *World of Krystonia*, a whimsical make-believe kingdom. The success of this line has been one of her greatest pleasures, but with new ideas on the horizon, she is hard at work creating her latest innovative designs.

LORRAINE CHIEN

Lorraine Chien brings life and love to her menagerie of soft creatures, designed for *Cottage Collectibles* by Ganz. Her much sought-after collectible plush personalities have captivating faces and a spirit that captures the heart.

As a child in her native China, Lorraine Chien did not have many plush toys to play with. Instead, she enjoyed reading story books and creating her own toys from bits of scraps. Thus began her life-long love of toy making. After settling in Pickering, Ontario, Canada, Lorraine's creativity continued as she made plush toys for her now grown children.

Lorraine Chien is the artist behind the "Golden Teddy" award-winning design, "Dempster," from *Cottage Collectibles.*

JAMES C. CHRISTENSEN

James Christensen's "land a little left of reality" is now enjoyed in paintings, limited edition prints, fine art posters, books, works of art in porcelain, sculptures, yearly calendars,

and even best-selling jigsaw puzzles. He had only recently embarked on his fine arts career when he joined The Greenwich Workshop in 1985, after years of what he called "anything for a buck."

Since that time, he has had one-man shows across the country, and his work is prized in collections throughout the U.S. and Europe. Recent awards include the "Association of Science Fiction" and "Fantasy Artists' Chesley Award," and the World Science Fiction Convention's "Best in Show" award. His first book, *A Journey of the Imagination: The Art of James Christensen* (1994) has 40,000 copies in print. His second, the adventure fantasy, *Voyage of the Basset*, (1996) has over 70,000 copies in print. His newest book is titled *Rhymes & Reasons.*

GRETCHEN CLASBY

A full-time artist for over 25 years, Gretchen Clasby's watercolor and acrylic paintings of children and small wildlife cause the viewer to become involved in the "wonder of life." Gretchen's love of the joy in life gives her paintings an endearing and warm quality that tugs at the heart of the child in every collector.

"If my paintings help us to remember when we embraced each moment with new awe, then I have accomplished what I set out to impart," says Gretchen. "Our days get bombarded with the stress and demands of life; we all need to take time to enjoy the same gifts we found around every corner in our childhood."

It is this background and experience that has led Gretchen to create a line of art featuring "little blue birds" called "Sonshine Promises." Inspired by the art of Gretchen Clasby, Islandia International has developed the *Sonshine Promises Collection*, a cold cast resin line of bluebird figurines, each with a message that will transcend boundaries and beliefs, and touch the hearts of all with inspiration. The messages are encouraging and uplifting, the style is humorous and whimsical. The initial collection, all gift-oriented in concept and design, will consist of 18 figurines plus one limited edition grouping, as well as eight ornament figurines.

CHERYL SPENCER COLLIN

Cheryl Spencer Collin began her career sculpting one-of-a-kind porcelain animal miniatures to sell in galleries. In 1984, she added a line of cottages and lighthouses. Her meticulously detailed Spencer Collin Lighthouses have received a well-deserved reputation for quality, and are considered some of the finest lighthouse sculptures available.

Recently, Cheryl received the distinct honor of being selected as Official Coast Guard Artist for her years of work sculpting lighthouses and lightships.

Cheryl believes the true beauty of a lighthouse is found in its setting. It is this "sense of place" that sets her lighthouses apart from all the others. Cheryl researches and painstakingly sculpts each site, as well as the lighthouse itself, giving the collection unique qualities of consistent style, relative scale, and detail based on actual regional surroundings. The observer may find sea roses, sunflowers, birch or palm trees, harbor seals, or humpback whales on any given piece. Adding a personal touch, Cheryl's pet bunny, Willy, and dog, Svea, can be found on every piece.

PHIL COTÉ

Phil Coté's attraction to native people began at a very early age, and throughout his childhood, he identified strongly with Native American images. Even though he grew up in New England, the native people he learned about were the Western Plains Indians. As an adult, however, his research revealed an entirely different native culture and history in his own backyard: The Eastern Woodlands Indians – The Mohawk, the Pequot, the Wampanoag and the Mohegan.

Phil did his formal art training at the Worcester Art Museum and The Massachusetts College of Art. His bronzes are much sought after worldwide and proudly displayed in galleries throughout New England and New York. Phil's work was chosen for participation in the 1996 Charles M. Russell Auction, a prestigious recognition bestowed on only 30 sculptors.

His scholarship regarding Eastern Woodland Indians has gained him an enthusiastic audience for his latest series, *The People*, for the *Chilmark Collection* produced by Hudson Creek.

EDNA DALI

A graduate of Ben-Gurion University in Israel, Edna Dali immigrated to Nottingham, England, in 1977, where she studied painting and sculpting. She and her family later moved to the United States. She continued her art studies in Massachusetts, where she first became interested in doll sculpture. This interest has won her a "Public's Favorite Award" at IDEX and two "Awards of Excellence" from *Dolls* magazine.

Edna creates a few one-of-a-kind dolls, much prized by high-end collectors, as well as limited edition dolls that are more accessible to the amateur collector. She makes her home in Ra'Anna, Israel, with her husband, Avi, and their three children, Tamir, Assaf and Ma'ayan. Her creations for the Seymour Mann Gallery include "Patricia," "Stacy" and "Cara."

MATT AND MATHEW DANKO

For several years, the amazing talents of the father-son creative team of Matt and Mathew Danko have graced the stores and catalog of The San Francisco Music Box Company with their *Heart Tugs* line of musical figurines.

Drawing from the inspiration of their rural Ohio experiences, the Dankos create touching works of art that literally tug

at the heart. They are noted for their meticulous design details and their remarkably expressive and endearing sentiments about both the human and animal worlds.

The team's creative process begins with research and storytelling. They scour through countless books on dolls, teddy bears, antiques, toys and country decor found in their rather extensive library. The two then sit for hours going through the storytelling process. "Our primary goal is to continue to find new ways to tell the story of life through our creations," says Matt. "With so many emotions encountered in our everyday lives with family and friends, we have an endless flow of ideas." Their commitment and passion for their art is reflected in each figurine, bringing to life emotions with a universal appeal.

JANE DAVIES

At an early age, Jane Davies was fascinated by all types of arts and crafts and wanted to be a potter. However, she followed another career path which included fashioning gold and silver jewelry, china restoration and doll repair. From there, it was just a short step to making her own all-porcelain miniature dolls.

Jane specializes in creating small dolls. Her current work in porcelain includes one-of-a-kind artist figures that are 12" tall, limited editions of 6" and smaller sized dolls, and one-twelfth scale dollhouse dolls. Recently, Jane began creating cloth dolls. Her designs for Deb Canham Artist Designs, Inc. include a 5" fully jointed cloth doll available in a numbered limited edition.

Jane has been involved in the doll industry for 20 years and has been active in the Global Doll Society as an exhibitor, judge and lecturer. In 1991, she was selected as an artist member of the National Institute of American Doll Artists and has served as its first vice-president since 1995.

LOWELL DAVIS

Born in Red Oak, Missouri, Lowell Davis' life-long artistic interest in animals and rural settings was nurtured by the family and friends that gathered at the general store to tell stories and whittle. After spending 13 years as an art director in a Dallas advertising agency, Davis realized that he greatly missed the freedom of his hometown, so he headed back to Missouri to pursue art and the open skies.

Now, Lowell Davis has paired his talents with Ertl Collectibles™, a leading manufacturer of die cast replicas, to create several collectible series – *The American Country Barn Series™* featuring historically significant barns; the *Lowell Davis America™* collection of rural-life scenes; the

Sparrowsville™ series of whimsical birdhouse ornaments; and the dazzling *Farm Country Christmas™* Winter farm scene.

Through the years, Lowell has virtually reconstructed his old hometown, buying homes and businesses and restoring them to their original grandeur. Now known as Red Oak II™, Lowell considers it and his 60-acre FoxFire Farm™ as living works-of-art.

RAY DAY

At the invitation of Lilliput Lane, Ray Day has been sculpting the *American Landmarks* collection since 1989.

As Creative Director for Lilliput Lane USA, Ray's years of research provided the basis for designing and creating a full range of American architectural collectibles. Each completed wax sculpture is sent to Lilliput Lane in the U.K. for molding, casting and painting. The finished miniatures, based on actual locations, are distributed in the United States through Enesco.

Ray's sculpting talent encompasses a wide range of architectural designs, from rural structures to elegant Victorian homes. He created a special Disneyland 40th Anniversary limited edition piece, "Fire Station 105," for the 1995 Disneyana Collectors Convention and "The Hall of Presidents" for the 1996 Convention. His newest collection, *The Allegiance Collection*, expresses the nostalgia, emotion and patriotism felt by flying the American flag.

Since 1973, Ray and his wife, Eileen, have published limited editions of his watercolor originals. Porcelain plates followed in 1986.

JESSICA DESTEFANO

Hudson Creek artist Jessica deStefano's natural artistic abilities emerged at an early age, and by the time she was a senior in high school, she had earned a reputation as a talented sketch artist. After entering Edinboro State College to study art education, she began to work in clay, sculpting, firing and painting intricate faces on tiny beads which she strung into necklaces.

In the 1970s, Jessica studied under several well-known members of the National Sculpture Society. Since then, her gallery and museum pieces, which range from Greek mythological figures to handcrafted chess sets, have won several prestigious awards. Her lifework has been featured in *National Sculpture Review*.

Jessica's recent collections, *SeaMyst Mermaids™* and *Tillie the Frog™* are available from Hudson Creek of Hudson, Massachusetts. These series are part of *Hudson Creek Collections*, and each quality cold-cast porcelain sculpture is handcrafted and hand-painted in the USA by the artisans of Hudson Creek.

BRIGITTE DEVAL

Brigitte Deval has been creating dolls since her childhood days in Munich, Germany. Her first dolls were *stoche puppe* – dolls modeled over sticks and bottles – that she made as family gifts. In 1968, she began creating one-of-a-kind dolls in wax over ceramic, which won her international acclaim.

Her latest offering under the Ashton-Drake name is the *Fairy Tale Princess* collection. The first issue in the series, "Cinderella," was nominated for the 1997 "Doll of the Year" (DOTY) Award. Dressed in pale blue from head to toe, she's been a sensation with collectors and critics. This is a new direction for Brigitte, who is probably best known for her breathtaking madonnas for *Visions of Our Lady* and her angels for *Blessed Are the Children*.

ANN DEZENDORF

Her love of children and strong traditional values have always led Ann Dezendorf to create lines that touch the hearts of people – at any age. Her *Carousel Collection* is no exception.

Collectors all over the world have been in awe of the majestic carousels. Ann has taken the horse/menagerie animal designs from the master carvers of the late 1800s to a new level. Each carousel base is inspired from the rounding boards of the great carousels and decorated with a cabochon stone. Ann has added her own special touch by creating a finial (Willitts Designs exclusive) that is unique in design to match each horse.

Ann attended the Ringling College of Art in Florida and graduated from the Paier College of Art in Connecticut. Immediately upon graduating, Ann went to work for Hallmark Cards, Inc. as a product and package designer. After a successful career there, she moved to New York to embark on a career with Avon Products in the International Gift and Collectible Design Division. In 1986, Dakin, Inc. recruited her as the director of product design.

Ann and her husband moved to California, where she was able to follow her dream of becoming a plush designer. In 1991, she joined Willitts Designs as an art director in charge of numerous projects. Ann, her husband and three children enjoy spending time together researching new projects. She says it has led them on some fun and historical adventures.

BEV DOOLITTLE

One of the most popular and innovative concept artists in print, Bev Doolittle creates artwork that has been called visual poetry, and even magical. After studying at the Art Center College of Design in Los Angeles, Doolittle embarked on a fine arts career, anxious to share her message of conservation and to give something back to nature.

After developing her own water-color technique and joining

The Greenwich Workshop in 1979, Doolittle's artwork was so unique that a category was named for it – Camouflage Art. It gave her collectors a new way of appreciating art, which was beyond the obvious. Doolittle continues to explore the wonders of nature and the unlimited opportunities of art. Her newest work is the book titled *The Earth is My Mother.*

MAUREEN DRDAK

As a young girl, Maureen Drdak was so crazy about horses that she would tie a rope around the handle bars of her bike, pretending they were reins, and simulate jumping, as if her bike was the horse she always dreamed of owning. So, it seemed a natural progression for Maureen to later design beautiful horses.

After completing her studies and receiving a bachelor of fine arts degree, Drdak served as the head of the design studio for Fabergé and was also a principal designer for The Franklin Mint. Most recently, The San Francisco Music Box Company licensed her to design a line of Carousel Horses.

Drdak works out of her home studio in Ardmore, Pennsylvania, which she shares with her husband and daughter, and a menagerie of pets. Inspiration for her designs comes from reading a variety of magazines, visiting antique shops and even channel surfing on the TV to keep up on the latest trends. She enjoys gardening and loves to read and travel.

CONNIE DREW

Connie Drew, *eggspressions! inc.* founder, is as distinctive as the egg designs she and her company create for a worldwide market. Besides being the proud owner of an "*eggstensive*" decorated egg collection, her life is a blend of art, music, folk philosophy, glitter and whimsical delights. She surrounds herself with twinkling stars, butterflies, unicorns, Scarlett O'Hara dolls, bronze sculptures, Broadway musical paraphernalia, and an "*eggceptional*" collection of opulent egg-shaped Judith Leiber purses.

Learning the art of drop-pull egg decorating from her mother and grandmother, Connie has become an "*eggspert*" on ethnic and modern egg art techniques, styles, symbols, customs and folklore. Today, Connie's long love affair with decorated eggs has grown from her home studio to an "*eggstensive*" factory complete with "*eggsecutive*" offices and an "*eggsclusive*" gift shop. Located in Rapid City, South Dakota, *eggspressions! inc.* is open all year because, as Drew says, "eggs aren't just for Easter anymore!"

MICHAEL DUDASH

Michael Dudash has been a professional artist/illustrator for the past 21 years. Since his education at the Minneapolis College of Art and Design, and the Macalaster College in St. Paul, Minnesota, Dudash has earned a national reputation. His paintings have won him numerous awards from the Society of Illustrators, the Society of Publication Designers and several magazines.

Dudash has completed over 900 paintings and assignments including corporate and advertising art, movie posters, book illustrations and covers, limited edition prints, magazine art and covers, collectibles, sculpture design, gallery paintings and several commemorative stamps for the U.S. Postal Service and the United Nations. He has been a guest lecturer at colleges and various art industry associations, and has conducted several painting and illustration workshops.

A Christian who happens to be an artist, Dudash uses his abilities and talent to spread the Gospel of Jesus Christ through his art. His paintings are a thing of beauty and inspiration, but more importantly, instill something greater in the viewer. To this end, he has created several art prints and sculptures for the *MasterPeace® Collection* from Willitts Designs International, Inc.

Dudash currently resides in Vermont with his wife and three children.

SUE ETÉM

From the tender age of three, Sue Etém has been perfecting her art. In high school, she won many awards while studying various art techniques. Traveling throughout Europe in the '60s and '70s, Sue studied the works of master painters in the museums she visited. During this time, she explored multiple painting styles while raising three sons.

By the late 1970s, Etém had developed a personal style, painting boats, portraits and children at play. She would later become well known for her very successful artistic creations of toddlers and children. In 1980, she entered the collectibles market with her first plate, "Renee," which was awarded the prestigious title of "Plate of the Year - 1981," as well as increasing in value more than any other plate of its time. Etém was an "instant" success, and every plate and lithograph produced was a sell-out through 1983. In 1982 and 1983, she was voted "Artist of the Year" by the plate collectors of the United States and Canada.

More recently, private commissions for her artwork and sculpting, and spending time with her grandchildren have kept Etém busy, but her heart has longed to return to the collectibles field. In 1997, a past friendship with the President of Islandia International, Joe Timmerman, was rekindled, and Etém has proudly joined forces with this fast-growing company. She has already developed many new masterpieces for her exclusive fine art collection at Islandia International.

ARLINE FABRIZIO AND TIM FABRIZIO

Arline Fabrizio has enjoyed a diverse career in commercial art, including designing advertisements, greeting cards, and kitchen and bath fabrics. When her son, Tim, graduated from art school, they formed a partnership to design and produce their own kitchen textiles. They also sold designs to various West Coast giftware companies. It was during this time that they developed the whimsical *Bumpkins™* collection, a series of cute characters from a mythical place called Bumpkinville.

Cast Art Industries has signed an exclusive agreement with Arline and Tim Fabrizio to re-introduce the *Bumpkins*. Some of the original pieces have been updated, and new versions have been created for Cast Art. With heart-tugging designs and soft pastel colorations, the fun-filled *Bumpkins* are sure to delight collectors young and old.

DECLAN FEARON

Inspired by his passion for Ireland, its folklore and his fascination with the legend of the Blarney Stone, Declan Fearon is the creative spirit behind *Declan's Finnians™: Guardians of the Blarney Stone* from Roman, Inc.

Finnians are handcrafted wee folk, each with its own clever story and a small stone from the same Irish quarry that was the source of the fabled Blarney Stone. Since the 14th century, people have come from all over the world to kiss the Blarney Stone and release its gifts of eloquence and luck. Declan introduced the collection to U.S. collectors through Roman in 1995. The collection has grown in popularity and was honored by *Collector Editions* magazine with a 1997 "Award of Excellence" for Best Sports Collectible.

Declan is a native of Dublin, Ireland, and continues to make his home there. He makes regular trips to the United States to meet with enthusiastic collectors at collector shows and dealer events.

JUAN FERRANDIZ

Born in Barcelona, Juan Ferrandiz Castells was a poet, a painter, an author and an illustrator of children's books. In the United States, his widest acclaim came from his charming ANRI wood carvings. Ferrandiz first studied in Barcelona at the Bellas Artes School. He continued to refine his artistic style through classes in private art schools and self-teaching.

He was a widely cultivated man, responsive to the social and political events of our time. Ferrandiz's works are known around the world. He lived simply, yet beautifully, and was considered the quintessential cultured European, a man for all seasons.

Ferrandiz believed that children are the hope for the salvation of mankind. His ANRI figurines have a cherubic quality that reflect the innocent spirit and eternal hope of youth. He often included small animals, cats, dogs, squirrels, and birds with his figures to express the tenderness, harmony and communion found in childhood and nature.

Sadly, this beloved man, known to ARNI collectors for more than 30 years, died in Barcelona after a long illness in the fall of 1997.

HELMUT FISCHER

Born in Coburg, Germany, in 1950, Helmut Fischer comes from a family of skilled craftsmen who recognized his talent and encouraged his development. At the age of 14, Fischer enrolled in the Goebel apprenticeship program as a sculptor. After joining Goebel, he utilized his talent and skills to create numerous models in porcelain, fine earthenware and glass.

In the 1980s, Helmut created several series including *Serengeti, The DeGrazia Collection*, and Goebel's line of Walt Disney figurines. Since 1988, Fischer has been entrusted with the development and sculpting responsibilities of *M.I. Hummel* figurines. With his unique artistic talents and over 20 years of experience with the company, he has assumed the position of M. I. Hummel Master Sculptor at W. Goebel Porzellanfabrik.

Fischer lives in Neustadt, Germany, and enjoys drawing, photographing nature, kayaking and riding his mountain bike.

CHARLES FRACÉ

As a five-year-old, Charles Fracé began sketching the sights around his home in East Mauch Chunk, Pennsylvania. Decades later, honors such as his one-man exhibits at the National Museum of Natural History of the Smithsonian Institute in Washington, D.C., confirmed exactly what he had become – one of the most important wildlife artists of our time.

Fracé is a dedicated conservationist, tireless researcher and, clearly, an amazingly talented artist. He has created a body of work that will forever preserve many of the most incredible sights in our natural world – the soaring birds of prey, the rare and majestic big cats, and the young animals of countless species that are the hope for the future.

His latest series from The Bradford Exchange is *Charles Fracé: Soul of the Wild*. Other of his paintings have been reproduced on eight plate series, also from The Bradford Exchange, including the *World's Most Magnificent Cats* and *Kingdom of Great Cats: the Gold Signature Collection*.

TOBIN FRALEY

Renowned carousel designer, restorer and author Tobin Fraley has designed an exclusive collection of colorful carousel figures for the George Z. Lefton Company.

Fraley, whose fascination with carousels dates back to childhood experiences at his grandfather's amusement park, has been involved with carousal restoration and design for more than three decades.

Under his own publishing company, Zephyr Press, Fraley published more than 100 wall calendars and a coffee table book, *The Carousel Animal*, which traces the rich history of the carousel from its beginning to the early 20th century. Formerly a gift designer for Hallmark Galleries and Willitts Designs, he has created original carousel collections and ornaments.

"I am thrilled to be associated with such a distinguished member of the giftware industry," Fraley says of his association with Lefton. "I believe carousels are an artistic category that will never die. The carousel is something that everyone has experienced – it has universal appeal."

MARGARET FURLONG

Drawing on her pottery and painting background, Margaret Furlong established a modest art studio in 1979 and began experimenting with the design of things found in nature. Working on a shell motif, the artist began combining several shell forms; she added a molded face, a textured coil and a tapered trumpet, forming her first "shell angel" ornament.

Margaret then launched a heavenly series of all-white angel ornaments fashioned after sea shells. She wanted the ornaments to exemplify the real meaning of Christmas – "sort of a celebration of God and nature."

Furlong is the sole designer for her company. She gets her inspiration from God, nature, family and friends. Each of her limited edition angels carries a theme and comes with a scriptural quote.

Margaret's deep-seated Christian beliefs are at the heart of her artwork. She hopes that when people look at her designs, they will sense her love and celebration of God and His beautiful creations.

LYNDON GAITHER

Texan Lyndon Gaither has gained international acclaim as a graphic designer, illustrator and painter. In collaboration with the master carvers of ANRI, Gaither has designed a series of figures and Christmas ornaments that evoke poignant tales by capturing fleeting moments in exquisitely carved wood. Gaither has also created a series of magnificent wooden crosses entwined with delicately carved flowers.

Lyndon seizes revealing moments and then weaves the most subtle nuances of the moments into his final compositions to give them vitality and charm. "I begin my illustrations by researching the subject. Then I produce several sketches before creating my final concept. My finished illustration is then rendered in black and white with color added to complete my design," says Lyndon.

Lyndon is considered one of ANRI's most promising artists. With his attention to detail, his timeless creations transcend the medium to tell a story that expresses more about each figure than words can possibly say.

DEE GANN

There's a noted workshop in the North Pole where Santa and his elves toil away making toys to put a smile on someone's face come Christmas Day. But there's another, lesser-known workshop, tucked away in a small town in Illinois. It is there that Dee Gann toils away for the same purpose; to put a smile on someone's face.

Spending her childhood within her father's "curiosity shop" among Tiffany lamps and ancient trunks, Dee gained a love and appreciation for "old things." Now, as a designer, she embellishes her exceptional Santas with findings from her expeditions to antique stores and rummage sales.

Dee, who holds the meaning of Christmas very dear, feels that Christmas is enhanced by the magic of Santa figures. "I don't want to get off the track of the true meaning of Christmas, but Santas are gift givers who convey feelings of love and sharing, and I think our Saviour would approve of that." Her *Ye Olde Santa Maker* line was introduced by House of Hatten, Inc. in 1993.

NATE GIORGIO

Nate Giorgio has already made a name for himself in the fine-arts arena. He has created commissioned artwork for some of today's most famous celebrities, including Michael Jackson, Quincy Jones, Elizabeth Taylor, Madonna, the artist formerly known as Prince, Johnny Cash, the Beatles and Elvis.

Working in a variety of media, including oils and watercolor, Giorgio explores and celebrates the spirit of the entertainer – his favorite subject. His world-tour program cover and 1989 calendar for Michael Jackson was enthusiastically received, and led him to create posters for the movie industry, logos for entertainment companies and numerous pieces for private collectors throughout the United States and England.

Plate collectors will remember several of his series from The Bradford Exchange, including *The Beatles Collection*, *Elvis Presley Hit Parade*, *Superstars of Country Music* and *Remembering the King*. His latest series making a hit with collectors is *Solid Gold Elvis*.

CHRISTIAN GOEBEL

Christian Goebel represents the sixth generation of the family-owned firm of W. Goebel Porzellanfabrik, manufacturer of the world renowned *M.I. Hummel* collectibles.

Presently training with the international operations of the Goebel group, Christian Goebel's apprenticeship duties included the development of new marketing opportunities worldwide. This on-the-job training continues the father-to-son management tradition established back in 1871, and the company's commitment to the pursuit of excellence.

Christian Goebel majored in industrial engineering at the University Fridericina in Karlsruhe and is presently completing his doctorate.

An avid runner, Christian has participated in many major European events and, in 1991, competed in the New York City marathon.

DEAN GRIFF

As the fourth of six children, Dean Griff grew up on a 500-acre farm in rural Oneida, New York. After completing his chores, Dean would escape to the nearby woods with his sketch pad to draw animals.

Dean's creative interests eventually led him to an artistic career, rather than the agricultural one his siblings pursued. In 1983, at the age of 23, Dean left the family farm for a job as an assistant to the curator of the Syracuse University Art Collection. He began hand-painting hanging ornaments which, originally created as gifts for friends, soon developed into a small business. Meanwhile, his wildlife paintings were winning awards in art shows at the University.

In 1989, Dean relocated to Florida, where he resides today designing *Charming Tails™* figurines and hanging ornaments. The prolific nature of his work promises to continue delighting collectors for many years to come with the mischievous and fun-loving antics of the adorable characters of Squashville.

JAMES GRIFFIN

A native of Ontario, Canada, James Griffin has a bachelor's degree in fine arts from the prestigious Pratt Institute. Griffin's work has been admired at numerous exhibits from New York City and the Midwest to South America.

As an illustrator, his creations have appeared in numerous publications, ranging from *Parents* and *Good Housekeeping* magazines, to *The Wall Street Journal*. He has also served as an illustrator for such publishing and media giants as Harcourt Brace Jovanovitch, Random House, Doubleday, NBC and Warner Communications.

A seasoned world-traveler who enjoys drawing on foreign cultures for artistic inspiration, Griffin has toured France, Italy, Japan, Mexico and Turkey. He has lived in England, Peru and Brazil. He currently resides in the Hudson Valley of New York.

Plate collectors may recall Griffin's first plate series from The Bradford Exchange, an exciting recreation in fine china of the film masterpiece, *Casablanca*. His other series include *World War II: A Remembrance* and *Battles of the American Civil War*.

JUDITH ANN GRIFFITH

Growing up in rural Pennsylvania, it was natural for Judith Ann Griffith to start drawing pictures of birds and animals at an early age. Later she attended an art college in Philadelphia and, after graduation, worked for a large greeting card company. There, her artistic style continued to grow.

Today, Judith lives in the Ozark Mountains of Arkansas, a wooded setting she discovered while on a vacation. She finds inspiration surrounded by this vast natural area.

Judith's artwork celebrates a deep reverence for life, and for the beauty and peace which truly exist on earth. She hopes that her art is an inspiration for others to work in love and harmony for the well-being of life on this planet.

Judith Ann Griffith has designed figurines for the *American Artist Collection®* from Possible Dreams.

DAVE GROSSMAN

An artist for more than 25 years, Dave Grossman relishes his current role as the creative and artistic force behind Dave Grossman Creations. A native of St. Louis, he graduated from the University of Missouri. Later, Grossman was commissioned to do architectural sculptures for banks, hospitals, hotels, and public and private buildings. He was also commissioned to create sculptures for Presidents Johnson and Nixon.

In 1973, Dave Grossman Creations began producing limited edition collectibles that were inspired by the works of Norman Rockwell. The company has since expanded to include many other licensed collectibles including *The Wizard of Oz*, *The Original Emmett Kelly Circus Collection*, *Gone with the Wind*, and *Bill Bell's Happy Cats*.

Grossman's plans include expanding the existing licensed and limited edition collectible lines and marketing new collectibles. He takes great pride in the quality of his work and his devotion to the collector.

SCOTT GUSTAFSON

Scott Gustafson combined his opulent artistry with his energetic imagination to create "treasures for the child in each

of us" for The Greenwich Workshop, starting in 1993. His popular work is found in limited edition prints, on collector's plates and music boxes, and in books. Born and raised in Illinois, Gustafson pursued art and animation at the Chicago Academy of Fine Arts and Columbia College.

His work soon started to appear in the *Saturday Evening Post* and *Playboy*, among others. He illustrated anew such children's classics as *The Night Before Christmas*, *The Nutcracker*, and *Peter Pan*, while writing and illustrating his own books, including *Alphabet Soup* and the *Animal Orchestra* for The Greenwich Workshop Press.

Gustafson's limited edition fine art prints from *The Greenwich Workshop Classics™ Collection* continue to delight collectors. His work will soon appear in fine art porcelain from The Greenwich Workshop® Collection.

STEVE AND GIGI HACKETT

Steve and Gigi Hackett are a husband and wife team playing a crucial role in Cast Art's in-house design studio. Their unique team approach has added to the Cast Art family of collectibles with the creation of the traditional angels in the popular figurine series, *Dreamsicles Heavenly Classics™*.

These wonderful works are available as collectible figurines. Like all Cast Art products, the reproductions are painstakingly handcast and hand-painted, and are available in fine gift and collectible stores.

In addition, Steve and Gigi have designed and sculpted a vast array of delightful teddy bears and other figurines, two of which have been nominated for TOBY (Teddy Bear of the Year) awards.

Recently, Steve and Gigi brought enchantment to collectors with some wonderful new expressions for the *Dreamsicles Heavenly Classics* line, including themes depicting marriage, motherhood and other miracles.

JAN HAGARA

Jan Hagara was born in Sand Springs, Oklahoma, the second of three girls growing up in a small-town atmosphere. For as long as she can remember, Jan has been drawing faces. "It seems like I've always had a pencil in my hand," says the popular artist. "I remember when I was in the fourth grade, I would draw faces on scraps of paper. I have always been fascinated with faces."

She still is, and today, Jan Hagara's unique ability to capture the innocence of childhood has earned her a world-wide reputation as an artist and as a creator of collectible prints and porcelain dolls, collectible plates and figurines. Her works, all based on her original watercolor paintings, are instantly recognizable: young children in Victorian-era costumes clutching dolls, toys, or flowers while looking out through wide, wistful eyes.

Jan Hagara paints – not just with her brush but with her whole personality. She describes her painting style as "Romantic Victoriana," and she could well describe her life the same way.

HANS HENRIK HANSEN

Born in 1952, Hans Henrik Hansen graduated from the Academy of Applied Art in Copenhagen with an emphasis on graphic design.

For 12 years, he was the principal decorator at the retail store for the Royal Copenhagen Porcelain Manufactory, where his window decorations were the rage of fashionable Copenhagen. Since 1987, Hansen has been devoted almost exclusively to creating designs and illustrations for the porcelain manufactory. His first Christmas series, *Jingle Bells*, was very successful.

With the introduction of the *Santa Claus* collection in 1989, Hansen became the first artist since 1895 to create a colorful Christmas plate for Bing & Grondahl.

For the first time since 1908, Royal Copenhagen issued a series of six colorful annual Christmas plates and coordinating ornaments titled *Christmas in Denmark*. The original art for this epoch-making series was created by Hans Henrik Hansen.

KRISTIN HAYNES

From her farmhouse studio in Idaho, Kristin Haynes creates her endearing cherub and animal sculptures, each with a distinctive warmth and charm. Under her direction, her sculptures are reproduced by the talented artisans of Cast Art Industries. Individual casting, finishing and painting by hand, with natural floral decorations and subtle finishing touches, assures that no two *Dreamsicles* are ever exactly alike.

Kristin began sculpting in college, and later designed a variety of characters which she sold at weekend craft shows. Kristin's now famous cherub designs became so popular that she could not keep up with demand. She met with Cast Art, a giftware manufacturer, who developed methods for handcrafting reproductions. Introduced in 1991, the *Dreamsicles* collection became an overnight phenomenon.

Since the introduction of Kristin's *Dreamsicles*, the line has successfully expanded to include *Dreamsicles Kids™*, a collection of adorable children with angelic faces and cute expressions; the *Dreamsicles Heavenly Classics™*, a combination of cherubs with traditional angels; and the *Dreamsicles and Me™* collection, Kristin's interpretation of the guardian angel theme.

ELKE HELAND

In 1984, Elke Heland, a talented young artist, was selected by W. Goebel Porzellanfabrik to participate in the company's prestigious training program for ceramic painters. After completing the program, she was assigned a series of positions in Goebel's painting departments to further develop and enhance her talents.

Four years ago, Elke was chosen to join the Goebel team of promotion painters. Since that time, she has traveled in Germany and abroad, demonstrating the remarkable artistry that gives *M.I. Hummel* figurines their unique charm and appeal.

In her spare time, Elke enjoys reading, painting and traveling.

HAP HENRIKSEN

Hap Henriksen holds a pre-eminent position in the world of fantastic art. After studying anthropology in college, he began a successful career sculpting Western art. By 1983, he was working on an exhibition of fantastic art to celebrate the 25th anniversary of NASA. Since then, he has put together several museum exhibits, and his fantasy sculptures have won numerous awards.

Hap and his wife, Elizabeth, have worked with Collectible World Studios in the U.K. since 1989, creating several successful product ranges including *Wizards and Dragons*, reflecting his anthropological background and love for folk and fairy tales. Very much a team, Hap and Elizabeth share time between studios in Texas and Kansas, working on a wide selection of products which are distributed in the U.S. by Flambro Imports.

LINDA HENRY

Linda Henry, a freelance commercial artist, began her doll sculpting career over 15 years ago. In 1987, she and her husband, Mike, began designing their own original teddy bears which have won numerous awards.

Teaming with Lee Middleton Original Dolls, Linda Henry presented an exciting new bear collection in the image of Lee Middleton's *My Own Baby* series. The *My Own Baby-Bear* series debuted with "Newborn Taylor," a wonderfully expressive bear, complete with pacifier, baby clothing and matching headband.

Linda has designed dolls and bears for several leading manufacturers. Recently she has exhibited her creations in The Netherlands, Belgium and Germany. Her "Tobey" bear was featured on Japan's Home Shopping Show, where it rapidly sold-out. Linda is also a featured artist in numerous doll and teddy bear books and magazines, and is a freelance writer for several publications.

PEGGY HERRICK

Nestled in a small town within California's old gold rush territory, Peggy Herrick carves the designs her witty perspective narrates. Since childhood, she has expressed her artistic ability through drawing and painting. However, Peggy's carving talent remained unknown to her until 17 years ago. In order to spend more time with her husband, an avid woodworker, she agreed to be introduced to the workshop he loved. Amazing herself, she discovered her carving ability which finally allowed her personality to be truly expressed. Remarking on the results, Peggy says that "in no time my hobby became my profession, and my poor husband was doomed to share his shop forever."

Peggy portrays an extremely unique style uninfluenced by others. Conveying her love for both animals and antique toys, Peggy has created the collection entitled *Old Fashioned Toys*. Demonstrating only superb quality, House of Hatten, Inc. is proud to reproduce this collection in resin.

LAWRENCE HEYDA

Lawrence Heyda was born in Chicago, Illinois. He attended the University of Illinois and graduated with degrees in rhetoric and painting.

After college, Larry worked for a company producing animated figures and multimedia displays and perfected a technique for creating realistic human figures by computer. He has done full-figure sculptures for the Movieland Wax Museum, including Johnny Cash and George C. Scott. Larry also sculpted busts and figures of famous sports figures, and, in 1990, sculpted a bronze bust of Ronald Reagan, as well as a miniature of Reagan on his famous horse "El Alamain."

In 1986, Larry set up his own bronze foundry to produce wildlife sculptures. His sculptures are displayed in many California galleries and have been featured in *Southwest Art* magazine. In 1997, Larry joined the Chilmark Gallery of artists for Hudson Creek. His premier collection of American West pewter sculptures, entitled *Where the Sun Sets*, include "Sprucin' Up" and "On The Horizon."

PRISCILLA HILLMAN

Although art was always a central part of Priscilla Hillman's life, she decided to study botany at the University of Rhode Island, where she took only one art course. After graduating, she worked for the U.S. Oceanographic Office but continued pursing her artistic interests.

After illustrating and writing two children's books, Priscilla illustrated and wrote nine *Merry Mouse* books for Doubleday. In 1995, Enesco Corporation transformed her drawings of

Merry Mouse into a three-dimensional resin collection of figurines titled *Mouse Tails.*

In 1990, Priscilla sent sketches of teddy bears to Enesco Corporation President and CEO Eugene Freedman, who decided her drawing's should be reproduced as a giftware collection. The *Cherished Teddies® Collection* was introduced in 1992 and has since been honored with dozens of prestigious awards, including "Collectible of the Year" and "Figurine of the Year" by the National Association of Limited Edition Dealers. Priscilla was also recognized in 1994 as "Artist of the Year."

Priscilla has proceeded to expand her artistry and creativity by designing another award-winning collection, *Calico Kittens™*. She also is the creator of *My Blushing Bunnies, Priscilla's Mouse Tales* and *Snow Folks.*

TORI DAWN YOUNGER HINE

As a child, Tori Dawn Hine exhibited natural artistic talent. At eight years old, she was submitting drawings to national publications. At nine, she undertook formal training in the use of oils, acrylics and pastels.

In 1985, Tori Dawn's father, Bill Younger, introduced David Winter Cottages in the United States. The following year, Tori Dawn traveled to England to study cottage painting and became the first American painting artist for John Hine Studios. She spent much of the next three years painting, traveling and promoting David Winter Cottages. Collectors responded enthusiastically to this talented young woman and were thrilled when she began painting lighthouse sculptures for Harbour Lights.

During a later visit to England, Tori Dawn met Harry Hine, whom she married in 1990. They currently live in the San Diego area where Tori Dawn keeps busy with her painting and caring for their two sons.

ANTON HIRZINGER

Anton Hirzinger was born in 1955 in Kramsach, Tyrol, home of the famous technical school for glass craft and design. "Even as a child, I was fascinated by glass production, and knew at a very early age that when I grew up, I wanted to make it my career," says Anton, who studied at his "hometown school." He initially worked as a hollow glass craftsman at a small company.

Now, Anton has been working for Swarovski for more than ten years. He initially started work in the Swarovski Crystal Shop in Wattens, providing countless visitors from all over the world a closer insight to glass and crystal craftsmanship. Transferring to the Design Center in 1991, Anton created the Swarovski Silver Crystal "Pelican" and "Owlet." His greatest achievements so far are the "Centenary Swan" design, a commemorative edition for the company's 100th anniversary in 1995, and the Swarovski Collectors Society 10th Anniversary Edition, "The Squirrel."

RENATE HÖCKH

If there was an artist with a soft spot in her heart for children, it's Renate Höckh. Through her remarkable doll artistry, Renate has found a way to bring the children of the world to life for all of us to know.

Renate is known for the realism of her ethnic portrayals. She is passionate about her commitment to helping children of developing countries. Within these children, she finds an inner peace and soulful beauty that inspire her.

For the Georgetown Collection, Renate recently created her first limited editions available to the general public. Each one is remarkable on its own merit, but together they make a truly extraordinary family group – "Marisa," "Mora" and "Therese & Tino" – three sisters and a baby brother from the *What a Beautiful World™* collection. These works have won instant acclaim and award nominations. "Marisa" was nominated for a "Doll of the Year" (DOTY) award and "Therese & Tino" for an "Award of Excellence."

FRANCESCA HOERLEIN

Francesca Hoerlein has always felt compelled to express herself through art. Francesca was diagnosed with dyslexia, which unfortunately intruded upon her formal education, and she left high school after just one year. During the early years on her own, she worked for a photographer, did some runway modeling, and worked for a puppet maker.

Francesca produced "LeMutt" and related characters with several partners over the years, but she is delighted to now be associated with Ertl Collectibles Limited. She has won awards for her work, and "LeMutt," "FiFi La Femme" and company are considered contemporary classics.

In 1994, she was one of 25 individuals selected for a puppet-making class sponsored by the Muppet Foundation. Currently, Francesca has 17 puppets built for her own show, centered around "LeMutt" and "FiFi La Femme," his elegant lady friend.

Francesca finds time for meditation, writing, and her family. Her husband, Bob, is an artist, and they have two children, Aleya and Anya.

JOSEPH HOFFMAN

Joseph Hoffman, originally from Harrisburg, Pennsylvania, has always loved sculpting. An accomplished art student, he studied various media, and by age 14, the three dimensions of sculpting overshadowed his exceptional academic inclinations. His sculptures were featured in exhibitions at several galleries.

At 18, he was commissioned to create a portrait of Pennsylvania's governor.

In 1980, Joseph and his wife, Sheryl, launched Hoffman Dolls and Designs, originally creating portrait dolls. Soon, they were designing dolls for such companies as Hershey Foods, recreating many images from Hershey's vintage advertising.

Beyond his own unique and popular creations, Hoffman also contributed to the continuing Gartlan USA legacy with one of the company's most popular figurines – Ringo Starr. He sculpted images of the Beatles' drummer at his drum set during the Fab Four's 1964 "Ed Sullivan Show" appearance, as well as a strolling pose from the Abbey Road album fame.

Hoffman's most recent work features John Lennon – a moving commemorative featuring one of the world's greatest musicians, artists and peace activists.

MARY HOLSTAD

Mary Holstad spent her childhood playtime drawing paper dolls and sewing doll clothes with her older sister. Trying many arts and crafts, Mary realized she loved the three dimensional art form best. In the early 1980s, Mary bought a book on how to make teddy bears, and she has been hooked ever since.

Over the years, Mary has been honored with numerous awards and nominations including the "Golden Teddy" and "T.O.B.Y" awards. Although she is very proud of these achievements, she considers the best part of her work to be the many friendships she has made with people from all over the world.

Mary is best known for her bear and pet sets, which capture a bear holding its own pet with the pride and innocence of a child. Mary's unique and widely loved designs are produced for *Cottage Collectibles* by Ganz.

AMANDA HUGHES-LUBECK

Amanda Hughes-Lubeck was one of the first students at the Sir Henry Doulton School of Sculpture. Over the two-year course, she developed her skills in drawing and sculpture through human and animal studies. Upon completion of the course, she began her career as a modeller in the Beswick Studio at Royal Doulton.

After five years as a sculptor, Amanda was promoted to "Head of Studio," where her role was broadened to encompass administrative and project management duties.

Her favorite subject matter is horses, and she has modelled a number of breeds including Red Rum. Amanda has exhibited her work alongside Dame Elizabeth Frink at Keele University, and at Shugborough Hall. She continues her creativity at home, sketching and modelling both figurative and animal studies.

In her spare time, Amanda enjoys golfing and keeping fit.

SISTER MARIA INNOCENTIA HUMMEL

Sister Maria Innocentia Hummel created hundreds of colorful and charming sketches, drawings and paintings of children. Her work is the basis for scores of appealing, hand-painted fine earthenware figurines, as well as limited edition plates and bells, created and offered exclusively by W. Goebel Porzellanfabrik of Germany.

Born Berta Hummel in Bavaria in 1909, she had inclinations toward art from an early age. She graduated from the Munich Academy of Applied Art, meanwhile devoting much of her energy toward her religion.

After graduation, Berta entered a convent, taking the name Sister Maria Innocentia. Because the convent of Siessen, a teaching order, was quite poor, she sold some of her artwork in the form of postcards to raise money. In 1934, Franz Goebel, the fourth-generation head of the porcelain-producing firm, discovered her art.

The first *M.I. Hummel* figurines debuted at the Leipzig Fair in 1935, and since then have been popular with collectors around the world. Sadly, Sister M.I. Hummel died in 1946 at the age of 37, not yet aware of her full triumph as an artist.

CLIFF JACKSON

Cliff Jackson started his career as an artist while a youngster in Georgia, filling sketchbooks with the faces and places of his neighborhood.

Later, he won a scholarship to the prestigious School of Visual Arts in New York City. It was here that the young artist honed his talents for illustration and design, graduating with a degree in fine arts.

Plate collectors may remember Jackson's stunning bas-relief sculptures for the Bradford Exchange titled *Egypt: Splendors of an Ancient World*, and his sculptural interpretations of artist Lynn Kaatz's hunting-dogs-to-be in the *Field Pup Follies* series. Disney lovers are sure to remember his charming sculptural work from the *Winnie the Pooh* plate collection.

BILL JOB

Raised in the Tennessee mountains, Bill Job appreciated the skill of the local craftsmen. Ten years ago, he moved his family to a port city on the eastern coast of China. There he learned Mandarin and mastered the artistry of stained glass. Focusing on his love of the native people, and applying western management styles, he built a workshop to create the highest quality stained glass treasures.

Bill is recognized for creating the original stained glass collectible village. *Vitreville*, *Coastal Classics*, *Coastal Heritage*, and the retired *Woodland Village* are handcrafted from

American stained glass. Two new series were added in 1997: *Through the Decades*, licensed and based on The Coca-Cola Company artwork; and the *Disney Lighted Village*, featuring Snow White's Cottage. Because each piece is hand-made, it is truly a work of art with its own color and cut variation.

For the past three years, Bill's designs have been honored by *Collector Editions* for excellence in design for collectibles. He is also a consecutive two-year recipient of awards from the Collectors' Jubilee for "Best Lighted House" and "Best Decorative Accessory."

PENNI JO JONAS-PENDERGAST

Penni Jo Jonas-Pendergast is known as a "master miniaturist." Along with sculpting many of United Design's™ small and miniature figurines, she is spreading her talents to the large and limited edition *Angels Collection*. One very special angel is "The Gift '97."

Penni Jo began her career sculpting tiny figurines in her kitchen, which she sold at craft shows. Using colored clays, a food processor, and a toaster oven, Penny Jo created miniature teddy bears that propelled her into the national spotlight among collectible figurine artists.

Today, Penni Jo still uses the toaster oven, along with many other innovative tools, to create designs for several figurine collections. Many of the lively animals featured in the *Stone Critters®*, and *Itty Bitty Critters®* series are a reflection of Penni Jo's creativity. Penni Jo says, "We can learn noble qualities from animals - like self-reliance and loyalty." This point is echoed in her charming collection of teddy bear angels called *Teddy Angels™*.

FALINE FRY JONES

Faline Fry Jones developed her concept of architectural reproductions of America's past in the basement of her home in 1982. She patterned her designs after actual buildings and historic landmarks and named these pieces *The Cat's Meow Village™*. By 1989, a new facility was built to house the company's 175 employees, and the name of the firm was changed to FJ Designs Inc. Today, Faline runs a highly successful multi-million dollar international collectibles company.

Faline Jones has won several awards for her business and artistic efforts including: Small Business of the Year (1989), Entrepreneur of the Year (1993), Business of the Year (1994), and Finalist in *Inc* magazine's Entrepreneur of the Year (1995).

In addition to FJ Designs and motherhood, Faline is active in several local and national organizations and sits on the board of directors at Junior Achievement and the Wooster Area Chamber of Commerce.

LYNN R. KAATZ

Lynn Kaatz has established an international reputation as a result of his artistic talent and versatile skills. He paints from knowledge and experience. His formal art training, combined with extensive field research, gives Kaatz' paintings a realistic, true-to-life feel.

Kaatz, a native of the Great Lakes region of northern Ohio, is a demanding and dedicated artist who excels in painting scenes of nature – whether it be landscapes, wildlife, or seascapes. He spends hours observing his subjects, so his paintings feature accurate details, quality and realism.

When one of his paintings conveys not only a scene, but his emotions as well, then Kaatz and the viewer have a special relationship. And that relationship is the greatest tribute any artist can achieve.

RU KATO

For Ru Kato, WACO President and Artistic Director of *Melody In Motion*, entertainment is every bit as important as the complex manufacturing process that brings the *MIM* figurines to life.

Born in Kamakura, an ancient, historical city in eastern Japan, Ru Kato grew up in an artistic environment. His father, a scenario writer for a Japanese movie company, and his uncle, the Academy award-winning director, Akira Kurosawa, provided real-life confirmation of the importance of imagination and its ability to transport us away from the mundane and commonplace.

All *MIM* figurines begin with Kato. He writes a story line describing the concept and movement, and selects the music, thus beginning a process that unites 150 pieces in a typical figurine. To date, there are more than 125 *MIM* characters, including eight licensed Coca-Cola products and two "I Love Lucy"® figurines, licensed through CBS Entertainment/ Desilu too.

GARRI KATZ

As a child in the Soviet Union, Garri Katz drew and painted to calm his fears during World War II. After the war, Katz studied at the Odessa Institute of Fine Arts, before launching his career as a painter and illustrator.

In 1973, having immigrated to Israel, Katz painted religious and historic subjects and his celebrations of everyday life in Israel, which he displayed in many one-man shows in Israel. Then in 1984, Katz began a series of shows in the U.S. sponsored by patrons who discovered his genius on trips to Israel. Today, art connoisseurs from all over the world purchase Katz' paintings and watercolors for as high as $12,000 each. His works are on display in Israel, Belgium, Germany, Canada and the U.S. Katz resides in Florida.

Katz' first limited edition collector plate series, *Great Stories from the Bible* was commissioned by Reco International Corp. and features eight plates which portray a memorable moment from a beloved Bible story.

SARAH KAY

The Sarah Kay story began only a few years ago when an unassuming school teacher from a quiet suburb of Sydney sold a few drawings of her children and their pets to a greeting card publisher.

ANRI first recognized the elements which link Sarah Kay's works with the evocative expressions common to interpretative art over the centuries. They transformed her renderings into three dimensional figures that express the wonder, simplicity, and joy of childhood. By coupling her drawings with the traditional vision of master woodcarver Ulrich Bernardi, ANRI produced a series of carved figurines, dolls and music boxes, which combine the ageless quality of this medium with a charm and spirit that makes them seem to come alive.

Sarah Kay continues to be one of the most sought after names in the wood carvings of ANRI. And ANRI continues to produce new and exciting creations of Sarah Kay's precious artwork.

KAREN KENNEDY

Like Mozart, Karen Kennedy, one of Goebel's award-winning doll designers, was a child prodigy. At age five, Karen's grandmother taught her to sew, and by the time she turned 11, the precocious youngster won her first competition with a handmade doll she entered in Philadelphia's prestigious Nutcracker Doll Contest.

Karen studied fashion design at Drexel University and earned a bachelor's degree from the Philadelphia College of Textiles and Science. While still an undergraduate, her design work was displayed at the Nesbitt Gallery in Philadelphia.

In 1987, Kennedy began working at Goebel with world-famous doll designer Bette Ball. Kennedy looks to fabrics, family and even pets for her design inspirations. In 1993, she translated Charlot Byj's popular drawings of children into limited edition porcelain dolls.

The birth of Karen's daughter, Veronica, brought about a brand new doll, "Veronica." According to Kennedy, the newborn baby doll is intended to bring its new owner as much joy and love as Karen's own baby has given to her and her husband.

DONNA KENNICUTT

Primarily self-taught, Donna Kennicutt says she loved art during her high school years but never pursued it as a career until her children were grown. Even then, her painting and sculpting began as a hobby. Her talents, however, have won her wide recognition as one of Oklahoma's outstanding women artists.

Early on, Donna's subjects for her cast bronze pieces were primarily animals, which gave her an ideal background for creating the originals for the animal figurines produced by United Design™. Donna says she never tires of working with animals because they are so fascinating. "Doing my hobby and getting paid for it is the best part of working at United Design," comments Donna.

One of the most popular collectible editions Donna has created and sculpted since coming to United Design is the *Easter Bunny Family™* collection. She is also responsible for *Children's Garden of Critters™* and many of the *Stone Critters®* and *Animal Magnetism®* designs.

THOMAS KINKADE

Thomas Kinkade is one of America's most collected living artists, a painter-communicator whose tranquil, light-infused paintings affirm the basic values of family and home, faith in God and the luminous beauty of nature.

Kinkade is a devout Christian and credits the Lord for both the ability and the inspiration to create his paintings. His goal as an artist is to touch people of all faiths, to bring peace and joy into their lives through the images he creates.

A devoted husband and doting father to their four little girls, Kinkade hides the letter "N" in his paintings to pay tribute to his wife, Nanette, and the girls find their names and images in many of his paintings.

Kinkade has received numerous awards for his works. Most recently, he has been named by the National Association of Limited Edition Dealers as "Graphic Artist of the Year" for the second year in a row. He has also been named "Artist of the Year," and his works have been named "Graphic Art Print of the Year" for five years in a row. Kinkade has also won *Collector Editions'* "Award of Excellence" and was a charter inductee to The Bradford Hall of Fame for plate artists.

CAROL E. KIRBY

Taught to sew by her mother when she was a little girl, Carol Kirby carries this creative talent wherever she goes.

Never owning a teddy bear throughout her childhood, Carol began collecting them as an adult. By 1991, she had designed her own line of mohair artist bears. Now, with a following of many collectors across the

United States, Carol travels to several teddy bear shows each year, where she exhibits her creations.

Carol believes teddy bears are the universal symbol for love and friendship. These qualities are evident in her carefully designed and high quality bears she designs for *Cottage Collectibles* by Ganz.

PAT KOLESAR

As an avid doll collector, Pat Kolesar complained that all dolls look the same, and in 1979, she decided to take matters into her own hands. Today, she is well known for dolls whose faces reveal the varied and unpredictable moods of children. Her realistic dolls show on the outside what people feel on the inside.

Pat has won more than 40 blue ribbons at regional and national UFDC conventions. She has also received eight "Dolls of Excellence" nominations from *Dolls* magazine, including one each for "Enoc the Eskimo Boy," "Baby Cakes" and "Baby Cake Crumbs," all for the Seymour Mann Gallery. In addition, she has designed several of Seymour Mann's most popular dolls, including "Clair Mann," "Enid," "Sparkle," "Kissing Kyle," "Kissing Kelly" and "Kissing Casey."

Pat is an accomplished painter and sculptor. Among her commissions are a portrait doll of former Treasury Secretary William Simon. Several of her dolls are on display in museums across the country.

MICHAEL KORTAN

Michael Kortan is one of the most talented emerging woodcarvers in America. At the age of five, he worked with cardboard and masking tape, and a rapid progression of skill and talent led to the use of knives, chisels, and mallets.

He is a master woodcarver, and his main interests lie in folk art, historical figures, folk heroes and legends. The fascination with this style of art led Michael to carve a Santa figure nearly 14 years ago at the age of 13. Since that time, collector interest grew to the point where Michael was hand-carving and painting 500 individual reproductions of his Annual Santas.

The 27-year-old Ohio native was only 18 when chosen to help carve 17 armored carousel horses for the EuroDisney theme park in France.

Since 1997, Michael has been working with Hudson Creek to reproduce his line of Santa carvings as limited edition sculptures.

SANDRA KUCK

In 1979, Heio Reich, President of Reco International Corp., discovered Sandra Kuck's paintings of children in a Long Island gallery. Sandra's career skyrocketed with the creation of the

plate "Sunday Best" in 1983. Since then, NALED honored her with many awards, including an unprecedented six-time honor as "Artist of the Year."

Sandra's list of awards and accomplishments in the collectible field are far too lengthy to list. Her most recent works include the *Friends for Keeps* and *Everlasting Friends* plate series and the new *Gardens of Innocence* series. "Welcome Home" is the newest addition to the *Mother's Day* series, and "Wrapped with Love" is the latest in the *Victorian Christmas* series. Her newest doll releases include the bride doll, "Jennifer Rose," and a miniature angel doll named "Gabriella."

Adding another successful category, Reco International released *Sandra Kuck's Treasures* in 1997. This exquisite line of figurines captures the poignant and heartwarming features and incredible detail of Sandra's artistry.

PROFESSOR KARL KUOLT

In the annals of European wood carving, no artist is held in higher esteem than Professor Karl Kuolt. Born in Spaichingen, Germany, on April 3, 1878, he was a pupil of the Munich School of Art. He also attended the Munich Academy and later became a professor at this prestigious Academy. Besides a large number of well-known monuments and memorial chapels throughout southern Germany, he created countless smaller works which are now possessed by museums and private collectors.

The master craftsmen of ANRI have kept his art alive by faithfully reproducing Professor Kuolt's finest creations. ANRI's world-famous nativity figurines, that bear his name, are an example of his art that has endured for decades. Although Professor Kuolt died 60 years ago, each piece produced by ANRI is hand-carved and decorated with the same love and care as the original.

PAUL LANDRY

Paul Landry's bright, airy, lushly colored art can brighten a room. One of the most popular nostalgia artists in North America, Landry was born on the coast of Canada, in Halifax, Nova Scotia. He worked his way through the Nova Scotia College of Art as a photoengraver, sports coach, and sports racer, and also attended the Art Students League in New York City.

Landry eventually settled in Connecticut, where he taught for many years at Westport's prestigious Famous Artists School, and wrote the respected textbook titled *On Drawing and Painting*. He joined The Greenwich Workshop in 1984, where his prints have a loyal and growing audience.

Today, he is the proud author of the *Captain's Garden: A Reflective Journey Home Through the Art of Paul Landry*, and is one of the world's most successful and imitated artists of flower-filled seaside gardens, cozy cottages and ocean shores.

DAVID LAWRENCE

Born in Kent, England, David Lawrence received a degree in scientific illustration and worked in various disciplines, including medical illustration, children's illustration, and packaging. David also worked for the advertising trade creating " masterpieces" such as sausages painted in the style of Rembrandt and margarine in the style of Monet. "It may have been painting, but it was not art," says Lawrence.

David eventually fled the clamor of London and the advertising world for the obscure sanctuary of rural Somerset. Here, his thoughts turned to creating something that people might actually want to own – something that they could treasure for years. He began thumbing through old notebooks looking for new ideas and new directions.

When he met Martin Perry, chief designer of Harmony Kingdom, Martin suggested that he turn his focus to the three dimensional world of objects. Suddenly, David had a new direction for his energies. Sketches, sculptures and writing have been pouring forth ever since.

ANNIE LEE

Annie Lee began painting at the ripe old age of ten, winning her first competition during that year. Her accomplishments continued throughout her teens, culminating in an offer of a four-year scholarship to Northwestern University. Though declining that scholarship, Annie Lee later returned to northern Illinois to study art at Mundelein College and the American Academy of Art. She also earned a master of education degree from Loyola University.

Annie Lee's art reflects her remarkable ability to observe and draw life as she sees it, combining the elements of humor, satire and realism to relay those observations to the viewer. As a result, her work has been internationally acclaimed and warmly received by not only African-Americans, but by art lovers everywhere.

The *Sass 'N Class by Annie Lee* exclusive license from Sandy Dolls recreates the artwork of Annie Lee from the canvas into resin figurines, each full of life, satire and humor. The *Sass 'N Class by Annie Lee* series contains both open and limited edition pieces.

RODNEY LEESEBERG

1997 was a landmark year for Rodney Leeseberg. Not only was he named one of the top traditional craftsmen by *Early American Home* magazine, but his designs have also become a part of the Christmas line at House of Hatten, Inc. Notable accomplishments like these were not just luck for Rodney. The fourth grade teacher from northern Minnesota was persistent in making his long-time dream of gaining national exposure come true.

Rodney carved his first Santa in 1988. After selling a few of his first creations, he decided that he had found his forté. He has experimented with painting, stained glass and hand pottery, but enjoys whittling the most because it allows him to attain a three-dimensional shape. Years of practice reveal Rodney's own personal style which shines through each of his uniquely crafted carvings.

NEAL LINDBLADE

In 1982, Neal Lindblade, founder of Arcadian Pewter, Inc., started his first company, a custom spin casting business, in his garage. Several years later, Neal wanted a unique 20th wedding anniversary gift for his wife. Combining his long-time interest in antique toys with his casting experience, he crafted a pewter replica of a toy farm wagon and filled it with tiny straw flowers. His wife loved it, and so did everyone else who saw it, prompting Neal to produce other cast-iron toys in pewter.

At auctions and other secondary markets, Neal sought out more antique toys originally made by the Arcade Manufacturing Co. over 50 years ago. By 1994, he acquired a large enough assortment to produce the first *Arcade Toys Fine Pewter Replica Collection.*

In 1998, the production and marketing of the Arcade product line was licensed by Shenandoah Designs International, Inc. due to its vast worldwide marketing and the availability of expanded overseas production. Both companies are excited about this alliance and its impact on the next generation of Arcade products.

LENA LIU

Lena Liu is an artist of unparalleled popularity in today's collectibles market. Her beautiful birds, tranquil landscapes, and breathtaking floral and musical still lifes are enjoyed in various media, including limited edition prints, porcelain collector's plates, music boxes, cards and calendars.

Lena had her first painting lesson as a child in Taiwan. In 1970, she studied architecture at the State University of Buffalo, and later did graduate work at the School of Architecture at U.C.L.A. However, her true passion for painting never left her, and in 1977 she began to paint full-time.

Lena has achieved recognition at national shows and exhibits. In 1993, she was honored as the "Artist of the Year," and her collector plate was awarded "Plate of the Year" by the National Association of Limited Edition Dealers. She was also named the "Canadian Artist of the Year" at the Canadian Collectible of the Year Awards. Lena was recently inducted into The Bradford Hall of Fame for plate artists.

Lena and her husband, Bill, live in Maryland in the home she designed to accommodate their joint love of art, music and nature.

JOSE LLADRÓ

Nearly 50 years ago, Jose Lladró joined his brothers in founding what would become one of the most famous houses of porcelain in the world.

As Jose was decorating ceramics with his brothers at their Valencia home, the increasing demands of their business turned the young artists into businessmen and entrepreneurs. A born organizer, Jose has been credited with possessing the imagination and foresight necessary to bring to fruition the dreams of a family porcelain dynasty.

On a private note, he enjoys playing squash and has been instrumental in developing the Lladró sports facilities and fostering a basketball team for the handicapped. Jose, along with his brothers, has also been granted the "Medal of Civic Merit" by the Spanish Ministry of Foreign Affairs for their activities abroad and their contribution to the export of Spanish products.

JUAN LLADRÓ

Juan Lladró is the eldest of the three brothers who founded Lladró, one of the world's most respected houses of porcelain. A connoisseur and collector of fine art, Juan Lladró possesses an intense curiosity about nature, people and landscapes that constantly fuels his imagination.

With a small kiln in their backyard in Valencia, Spain, Juan and his brothers began their experiments in porcelain in 1951. Using the skills they obtained at Valencia's San Carlos School of Arts and Crafts, he began decorating lamps with delicate porcelain flowers that have become the Lladró signature.

Juan Lladró has been described as possessing an "ever-critical spirit that demands accuracy and elaborate delicacy." And these standards are applied to all of the products made by Lladró. As an artist, he is constantly looking for new discoveries in line, color and shadow. As an art expert, Juan is always searching for new interpretations of subjects and themes.

VICENTE LLADRÓ

The youngest of the three Lladró brothers, Vicente Lladró pooled his sculpting talents with his older brothers' and established what would become the internationally renowned porcelain house that bears their name.

As the brothers worked at their backyard kiln in Valencia, each brother continued to develop his talents. Vicente began specializing in sculpting and supervising the firing process, while his brothers decorated the ceramics.

Today, when not in his office, Vicente Lladró is often found in various departments of the factory, sharing with fervor his ideas and enthusiasm. When he is not contributing his time and expertise to the Lladró enterprise in Valencia, he travels extensively, attending trade shows and other related events around the world.

LISA LLOYD

Lisa Lloyd has been making miniature bears since 1988. In 1997, she began designing bears for Little Gem Teddy Bears, including some delightful jester bears. Lisa also creates her own artist bears, which are hand-sewn and made entirely by her.

Many of Lisa's bears have been nominated for national awards and have been featured in numerous magazines and books. She was invited to be an artist at five Walt Disney World Teddy Bear & Doll Conventions. She has also traveled throughout the world attending shows, teaching workshops and meeting many wonderful collectors and fellow artists.

MORGAN MAHONEY

When she joined Goebel's Doll Design Studio, Morgan Mahoney saw the opportunity to bring together two of her favorite interests – costume design and theater. Morgan graduated from Philadelphia College of Textile & Science, where she studied television production and fashion design. With both degrees in hand, she set her sights on a career in costuming for television and movies.

Those plans changed slightly, when Morgan met Bette Ball and Karen Kennedy at the Goebel Studio. Seeing the beautiful porcelain dolls that filled the Studio, she knew that she had to be involved in designing dolls. Morgan has since designed a variety of dolls introduced by Goebel, including *Fairy Dolls*, animal dolls and baby dolls. One of her *Fairy Dolls*, "Gaelic," was inspired by Morgan's rich Irish upbringing.

The attention to detail and the exceptional fabric choices she makes are two of the reasons that Bette Ball and Karen Kennedy selected Morgan to work with them. Goebel Design Studio is proud to welcome her into their family.

ALAN MASLANKOWSKI

Alan Maslankowski was born in 1952 in Stoke-on-Trent, England. His mother was a semi-skilled pottery worker, and his father a coal miner from Gdansk in Northern Poland. He had an interest in modelling from an early age, and after leaving school, was offered an apprenticeship at Royal Doulton.

Among his early successful works were a "Cat and Owl"

made in Flambe and "The Wizard." More recent works include: *The Sentiment Collection*, *The Elegance Collection*, *The Charleston Collection*, and two very prestigious pieces, "The Charge of the Light Brigade" and "Henry V at Agincourt." He has also modelled various animal studies for John Beswick which reflect his love for animals.

LINDA MASON

Almost a decade has passed since Linda Mason introduced her first doll. In that time, she has consistently created some of the most beautiful dolls found anywhere in the world. Her creations are timeless, with a classic beauty and feminine charm that collectors find irresistible.

Linda continues her reign as one of the doll world's most celebrated artists. Among her accolades, she counts seven "Awards of Excellence" in addition to one "Doll of the Year" (DOTY) award.

Despite her superstar status, Linda is still warm and friendly. The only noticeable change is that success has forced her to move her studio out of her home. Now as before, she works diligently on new dolls for Georgetown Collection while keeping up with the demands of her own limited editions. Her more recent introductions include "Emerald Memories," the newest doll in the popular *Victorian Fantasies™* collection offered exclusively through Georgetown Collection.

CHRISTINE MCALLISTER

Christine McAllister originally trained in fashion drawing at South London Polytechnical College. She did freelance work for many years before joining Hazle Ceramics in 1992.

Christine's artistic talent was quickly noticed, and she is now Hazle Boyles' "right hand" painter. She is responsible for developing many of the recent window designs for "A Nation of Shopkeepers" buildings and for most of the "personalized" ceramics created for Hazle Ceramics' avid collectors. Having learned the skills of preparing and glazing ceramics, Christine also holds the title of assistant ceramicist.

In her spare time, Christine plays tennis and often hops across the English Channel to France, to visit her daughter and new grandson.

JOHN MCCLELLAND

Some years back, John McClelland created a life-sized portrait of his daughter Susan. The portrait was used for an ad in a trade magazine, and Miles Kimball, the mail order company, spotted it and asked McClelland to do a Christmas cover for their catalog. That was the beginning of an association which continues today.

In the mid-1970s, Reco International arranged for McClelland to create limited edition plates. Today, he is one of the field's most celebrated artists with numerous "Plate of the Year" and "Artist of the Year" awards. He also has designed several figurine series and a number of limited edition lithographs.

McClelland is a portraitist and has taught both intermediate and advanced classes in portrait painting. Scores of his illustrations have appeared in magazines, and he has written two "how to" books for artists.

Among his works for Reco are *The Treasured Songs of Childhood*, *The Wonder of Christmas* and *A Children's Garden* plate series, as well as *The Children's Circus Doll Collection*, based upon the popular Reco plate series.

CINDY MCCLURE

Cindy McClure is one of a few artists in the world to win the prestigious "Doll of the Year" (DOTY) award from the International Doll Academy in 1986 and 1987. "Victorian Lullaby" was nominated for the 1995 *Dolls* "Award of Excellence." Her latest creation for the Ashton-Drake Galleries, "Melody," was recently nominated for the 1997 DOTY, as well as for a "Dolls of Excellence Award." This first issue in the *Forever Starts Today* collection is a beautiful bride wearing one of Cindy's most exquisite costume designs. In all, she has captured more than 20 awards.

Today, Cindy's dolls are eagerly sought by collectors because her originals and some of her Ashton-Drake issues have appreciated considerably on the secondary market.

Most collectors, however, are attracted to Cindy's dolls for her ability to capture realistic emotion. Her flair for costume design, perhaps, has found its most natural expression to date in her *Forever Starts Today* collection.

GWEN MCNEILL

In a career only 12 years old, Gwen McNeill has become one of the leading doll artists in Australia. She began by making reproduction porcelain dolls but felt limited by the painting and finishing techniques. After perfecting her own methods, she began to design and sell her own dolls. In addition to creating dolls, she now teaches painting and sculpture in Australia and serves as an expert judge in doll competitions around the world.

Gwen first came to the New York Toy Fair in 1993. Since then she has become a leading doll artist among U.S. collectors. While Gwen's specialty is modern dolls, she is equally at home working with period costumes.

Her fanciful "Lady Windemere" for Seymour Mann received a nomination for an "Award of Excellence" from *Dolls* magazine. Another McNeill favorite for Seymour Mann is "Chelsea."

KEN MEMOLI

Ken Memoli grew up surrounded by art. His grandfather was one of the sculptors of Mount Rushmore and the General Lee

monument in Stone Mountain, Georgia. "That influence," Kens says, "and a lot of good art in the house inspired my interest in nature and the arts."

Ken studied sculpture at the University of Hartford Art School. His talent in sculpting animals brought him to the attention of United Design™ in 1988, where he now works sculpting many of United Design's large life-like *Animal Classics®* figurines and outdoor statuary for the *Stone Garden®* line.

In addition to the intricately detailed wildlife and domestic animals Ken creates, he also sculpts figurines for the company's limited edition collections: *The Legend of Santa Claus™* figurines and *Angels Collection.*

"My goal is not to be an artist, but to live a creative life," states Ken. "That means leaving more than what was here when you came."

Ken works in his studio daily and enjoys photography and playing the guitar.

CLEMENTE MICARELLI

Clemente Micarelli studied art at both the Pratt Institute and The Art Students League in New York and the Rhode Island School of Design.

His paintings have been exhibited in numerous shows and have won many awards. Represented nationally by Portraits, Inc. and C.C. Price Gallery in New York, Micarelli has painted the portraits of prominent personalities throughout the United States and Europe.

Micarelli has done fashion illustrations for many leading department stores and has taught at the Rhode Island School of Design, the Art Institute of Boston and the Scituate Arts Association and South Shore Art Center.

For Reco International, Micarelli has created *The Nutcracker Ballet* plate series, a *Wedding Series* of plates and bells, and *The Glory of Christ Collection*, a plate series depicting revered events in the life of Jesus Christ.

LARRY MILLER

Larry Miller described sculpture as "more than just capturing an animal portrait in clay – it's revealing the creature's essence, giving it personality, and telling a story."

When he sculpted for United Design's™ collection of large and exceptionally life-like *Animal Classics®*, Larry said, "I do research, go to the zoo, watch how the animal moves and reacts – that's where my inspiration comes from."

After working in graphic arts, Larry went to United Design in 1981 seeking the opportunity to work in three dimensional art. He had always loved the feel and texture of sculpture, so working independently, he developed his technique by sculpting western bronzes. Larry's love for the work he did is evident in the charming humor and rich detail he sculpted into all his designs.

Larry Miller is also credited with creating many of *The Legend of Santa Claus™* limited edition figurines and many designs in the *Stone Garden®* line of outdoor animals and statuary.

Larry Miller, artist and friend, died on March 14, 1997. His life and his talent will be truly missed.

FINI MARTINER MORODER

Born in Ortisei in 1916, Fini Martiner Moroder is truly a daughter of the Groden Valley. She studied as an apprentice wood sculptor at the Ortisei Academy of Arts for three years before launching her career. During the 1930s and 1940s, she created many models for ANRI.

A deeply religious woman, Moroder had an inspired vision to create a new nativity. She formed the figures exactly as it was shown to her through divine enlightenment, with their dark eyes, expressionless faces and simplistic robes. They evoke the dramatic awe-inspired emotions of that wondrous night.

Having participated in many expositions and competitions, Moroder is considered to be one of the most famous artists in the Tyrolean region. Her personal creative style makes the beauty of her distinctively Romanesque carved nativity one which transcends generations.

JOCELYN MOSTROM

Jocelyn Mostrom, a nationally recognized doll artist, has captured the Age of Innocence with her nostalgic doll collection. An exclusive designer for Kurt S. Adler, Inc. for most of this decade, Jocelyn and her dolls and doll ornaments have been featured in numerous national magazines and books.

Jocelyn creates life-like dolls by first selecting a favorite historical period and then immersing herself in research of the people, their times and lifestyles. She uses her imagination to capture those images and transform them into exquisite doll designs.

Jocelyn's designs are known for their modeled facial detail, hand-painted features, delicately sculpted porcelain heads, beautifully styled wigs, detailed costumes and accessories. Creating dolls with unique personalities, she depicts them with open-mouths, outstretched arms and bodies poised for clearly defined activities.

Jocelyn has played a key role in Kurt S. Adler's *Fleur-de-Lis* doll collection which includes romantic ladies, Victorian children, heavenly angels, charming fairies and opulent Santas.

NICOLO MULARGIA

A native of Sardinia, a beautiful island in the Mediterranean Sea, Nicolo Mulargia brings a special warmth and vitality to Crystal World. Nicolo's love of life and family are reflected in

each captivating design.

His whimsical *Teddyland* collection has warmed the hearts of collectors and teddy bear lovers everywhere. "Teddies at Eight" and "Beach Teddies" remain two of the most popular crystal teddies ever produced by Crystal World.

Two of his recent figures, "Merry-go-Round" and "Jukebox," have been nominated for national awards. Recently, his fertile imagination brought collectors "Up and Away" and the limited edition "Majestic Bald Eagle."

LINDA MULLINS

Linda Mullins' collection of more than 2,000 bears began when her husband gave her an antique teddy bear as a gift. That hobby escalated into a full-time profession, and today, Linda's expertise and knowledge about teddy bears are in demand throughout the United States, Europe and the Pacific Rim.

In addition to collecting, speaking, educating and traveling, Linda has written 14 books and countless articles on the past, present and future of teddy bears. She also produces Linda's San Diego Teddy Bear, Doll & Antique Toy Show and Sale, a popular two-day event that has drawn international attention for its excellent antique, collectible and artist teddy bears, dolls and toys.

After coordinating an auction of international artist's bears to raise funds for the earthquake victims of Kobe, Japan, Linda became instrumental in shaping Huis Ten Bosch's Teddy Bear Kingdom. She is a supervisor and honorary director of the museum.

Linda is currently working with Little Gem Teddy Bears to reproduce some of her rare, early bears. It is her lifelong goal to continue her mission to make the teddy bear an ambassador of world love and peace.

KATRINA MURAWSKA

When Katrina Murawska has something to say, she reaches for her sculpting tools. She's driven by the need to communicate. And doll collectors around the world are paying close attention!

A talented painter and sculptor, Katrina finds inspiration in the simple joys experienced by children. In fact, it was the birth of her daughter that inspired her to try creating a doll. Before she knew it, that doll was in New York, displayed in the prestigious booth of Thomas Boland & Co. at Toy Fair.

Today, Katrina divides her time between creating dolls for Georgetown Collection's *Artist's Edition®* program and her own line of limited editions. Each doll she creates carries a message direct from her heart. With an IDEX Award for "Best Ethnic Doll," the prestigious European "Magic Wand," and over six additional nominations for top awards, it's clear that collectors appreciate what she has to say!

REAL MUSGRAVE

Real Musgrave carefully sculpts every piece in *The Whimsical World of Pocket Dragons*, infusing the characters with their wonderful personality and charm. Using the events in his own household, he brings each *Pocket Dragon* to life with a clever sense of humor. Real's whimsical style and obvious talent attracted the attention of Bill Dodd, President of Collectible World Studios in Staffordshire, England. Shortly thereafter, the *Whimsical World of Pocket Dragons* was launched exclusively in the U.S. by Flambro Imports.

In the Fall of 1997, *Pocket Dragons* debuted in a televised animated series, "Pocket Dragon Adventures," produced by Bohbot Enterprises. Also on Real's drawing board are illustrations for a wonderful new line of Golden Books featuring his whimsical *Pocket Dragons*. Who knows where these little characters may take him next!

ALLYSON NAGEL

Allyson Nagel was a portrait artist, when doll artist Faith Wick asked if she would make faces for Wick's whimsical dolls. Allyson discovered that clay and dimension were more artistically stimulating for her than the two dimensional portraits she had been creating.

Allyson developed the habit of filling the spaces left in her kiln with small eggs she fashioned. Initially, she simply decorated the round eggs with paint but, she explains, "through the years, the two dimensional paintings on the eggs evolved into three dimensional characters." Her rounded canvas became whimsical sculptures with life and personality, a unique combination of doll and decorative egg.

These "eggspressive" personalities developed into the *Sunny Side Up™ Collection*, introduced by Roman, Inc. in 1993. Meticulously crafted in resin to faithfully preserve the spirit of Allyson's art, each egg in her collection has a personality and "egg-pression" all its own.

RUDY NAKAI

One of the pioneering crystal figurine artists in the United States, Rudy Nakai founded Crystal World in 1983. Since then, this award-winning designer has continued to delight collectors with his yearly introductions. Originator of the popular *Rainbow Castle Collection®*, he was also the creator of the inspiring limited edition "Empire State Building."

His love of the ocean prompted him to sculpt the beautiful "Tall Ship" in 1996 for the *Seaside Memories* collection. In 1997, this tradition continued with the release of "Coastal Lighthouse." For Crystal World's wildlife collectors, Nakai has designed a wonderful new elephant set, "Mama and Junior."

DIANNA NEWBURN

"I married early, had my children young, and now this is my time," declares Dianna Newburn. These days, her time and energies are directed toward her life-long interest in art.

When Dianna's children were small, she taught decorative painting, but her true talent and love of sculpture was discovered when she began experimenting with making miniature clay dolls.

In 1990, Dianna's work had become so popular that she was exhausted from trying to keep up with demand. It was then that she agreed to join the staff of artists at United Design™, where she continues to create figurines for the company's many different figurine lines.

Currently, Dianna is sculpting figurines for several collections. In the *Angels Collection*, she has created several designs of limited edition and small angels. Dianna is also kept busy working on *Itty Bitty Critters®*, *Stone Critters® Littles™* and *Tiny Wings™* cherub miniatures.

RUTH NINNEMAN

Juggling a career, a husband and four children may be demanding, yet artist Ruth Ninneman wouldn't have it any other way. "My husband, Scott, and the kids are all very supportive of what I do," says Ruth. Working out of her in-home studio, she has designed several whimsical country and folk art Christmas pieces for The San Francisco Music Box Company.

Although Ruth had no formal education in art, creating art as a young girl with her Mother, attending several art classes and coming from a long line of "hobby artists" has helped her develop and refine her techniques. By paying close attention to details and putting emotion into her drawings, Ruth is a master at giving life to her figurines.

"When I turn a thought or an idea into something that works, it feels like magic!," explains the artist. Ruth also derives a great deal of satisfaction from just "doing the artwork and knowing that it is going to evolve into something that will bring pleasure to someone."

LYNN NORTON PARKER

Lynn Norton Parker's artistic talents come naturally. Her father, Paul Norton, was a well-known professional watercolorist and commercial artist.

As a child, Lynn was fascinated with her father's artwork and spent hours sketching cuddly animals and children at play. Her creativity and warm personality, which was nurtured by both

parents, is reflected in all her designs.

The joyful life experiences of being an elementary school teacher, falling in love, getting married, and becoming a mother are reflected in Lynn's *Tender Treasures* offerings. A tribute to home-spun romance and sentimentality, this delightful series has been faithfully captured in cold cast by the talented artisans at Possible Dreams.

MICHAEL V. PASCUCCI

More than just a talented sculptor, Michael Pascucci's range of knowledge and experiences in figural production span the scope of figurine development. Sculpting, molding, casting and final production in porcelain, bronze, plastic and a multitude of other media have made Pascucci a valued member of the Gartlan USA team. He created original art for the company's *KISS* figurine collection.

With more than 20 years of related experience, Pascucci earned a master's degree in sculpture and foundry from Southern Illinois University, Carbondale, in 1983. His bachelor's in fine art was earned at Pennsylvania State University in 1976. Since then, Pascucci has been featured in national media campaigns, has managed world-renowned foundries, and built his own flourishing sculpting business.

When he is not crafting figural designs or building budding businesses, Pascucci, an Army veteran, spends his time actively involved in his children's interests, including coaching basketball and soccer teams, and volunteering with the Boy Scouts. He resides in Yardley, Pennsylvania, with his wife, Beth, and their three children.

DONNA PEMBERTON

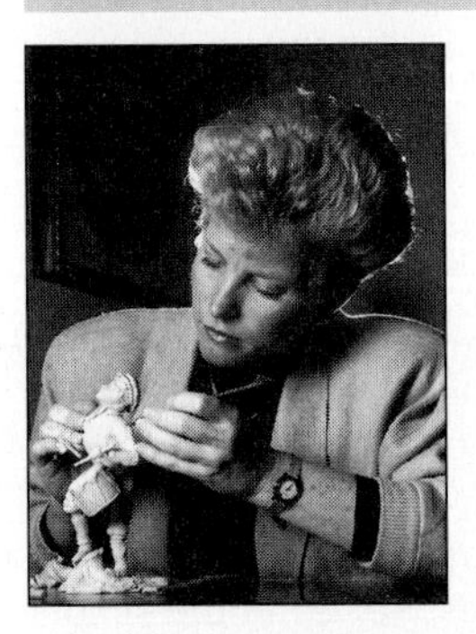

Artist Donna Pemberton showed a remarkable talent for drawing at the early age of four. Her art progressed from finger painting to ceramics, sculpting, and graphic arts. Donna received her formal training at U.C.L.B., where she was one of the few students elected for the coveted ceramic program. Since graduating at the top of her class, Donna has worked with some of the world's best known and highly qualified artists in various disciplines.

Donna's original works, which she creates in her own studio in Orange County, California, have been commissioned and purchased by such well-known art collectors as John Dupont, Dick Clark and Herb Albert, to name a few.

At Duncan Royale, Donna has a wide range of responsibilities overseeing all in-house art work.

"My life is art," explains Donna. "I am forever excited by it."

MARTIN PERRY

For over a decade, Martin Perry worked as a shepherd on 5,000 of the bleakest, wettest, and most windswept acres in the mountains of Snowdownia in North Wales. When an injury forced him to retire from shepherding, Martin worked for a company which manufactured replicas for art museums. He discovered a dormant talent for artistic creation that would eventually lead to the creation of the amazing Box Figurines for which he has become known.

In 1995, Perry met Noel Wiggins and Lisa Yashon, owners of the Harmony Ball Company. In them, he found the missing keystone to the extraordinary circle of talent which is now known as Harmony Kingdom. Martin, Noel and Lisa have become best friends in their quest to fill collectors' homes with tiny treasures that depict nature's world with intelligence and wry wit.

PAMELA PHILLIPS

A doll by Pamela Phillips is a feast for any collector's eyes. Although still considered a newcomer to the doll world, she has certainly made a lasting mark.

In addition to producing her limited edition designs, Pamela has created two extremely popular series with the Georgetown Collection. In fact, she received the "Doll of the Year" (DOTY) award in 1995 for "Caroline" and again in 1996 for "Madeleine & Harry," both from the *Sweethearts of Summer™* collection. "Ashley," the newest issue in the collection, has been nominated for an "Award of Excellence." She received another "Doll of the Year" (DOTY) award in 1995 for "Mary Elizabeth" and the "Award of Excellence" in 1996 for "Sophie," both from the *Yesterday's Dreams™* collection.

Creating dolls offers Pamela an opportunity to portray her love of children and her great appreciation for the beauty of nature. She loves her work, so you can be sure that this newcomer is here to stay!

Pamela has also created award-winning dolls for the Seymour Mann Gallery including "Alyssa," "Nizhoni" and "Guinevere."

VALERIE PIKE

A resident of Australia's Gold Coast, Valerie Pike's first artistic efforts were in oil portraits. Later, she turned to hand-painted clothing and soft sculpture, which she regards as a natural progression toward doll sculpting. The people she sees around her inspire her life-like creations, which have won many enthusiasts in the South Pacific.

Valerie sculpts her dolls from a water-based clay, from which she makes a mold for the porcelain head, shoulder plate, hands and feet. She designs her own body patterns and often makes her own wigs from mohair.

Until recently, Valerie's dolls were produced only in limited editions of ten to 25. By joining the Seymour Mann Studios, she now makes her works available in editions of 5,000 each.

PIPKA

Born in Germany, folk artist Pipka came to America with her parents and brother after World War II, settling in North Dakota.

Pipka's interest in folk art began when her mother sent her a package filled with art supplies, wooden boxes, and instruction books on Bauermalerei, Bavarian peasant painting. When she picked up the brush, she never put it down again.

Pipka designed her first "Father Christmas" image, a Russian Santa for her mother. Since that time, she has studied, researched and has become enamored with the stories, myths, and traditions surrounding Father Christmas, or Santa Claus.

While painting her Santas, Pipka was also inspired to research and design Angels. Her Angels have become a part of her spiritual journey, and they reflect the warm, giving spirit that is found in Pipka.

Through her Santas and Angels, Pipka celebrates Christmas and life. She shares her passion for folk art by teaching her painting techniques and sharing the stories and traditions of Santa Claus with students and Christmas enthusiasts around the world.

GALE PITT

A multi-faceted talent, Gale Pitt mixes her love of art with her personal interests in travel, gourmet food and felines. Gale resides in London and graduated with an honors degree in English language and literature from the University of London in 1977. She has had solo exhibitions of her paintings in Oxford, Stamford, Birmingham and Ilford, England, as well as others too numerous to mention. Her extensive travel around the world to places as varied as the United States, Russia, Egypt, Tunisia, and Pakistan, and a solo trip around the world to draw and paint, has armed her with the visual and intellectual information needed to master her detailed and visually stimulating form of artwork.

Gale Pitt's artistic capabilities allow her to paint with equal ability in pastel, oil, and water color. She has been commissioned by British Telecom to paint three telephone book covers, has illustrated four children's books, and been involved in various independent painting projects.

In 1997, Islandia International added Gale Pitt's adorable *International Fat Cat* art to its growing arsenal of exclusive fine art collections. This extraordinary art features cats dressed in the native costume of various countries around the world. Each cat is surrounded by the famous sights and gourmet food delicacies best known for each respective country. Gail's fascination with travel, food and cats have all merged in a wonderful display for all to enjoy!

WARREN PLATT

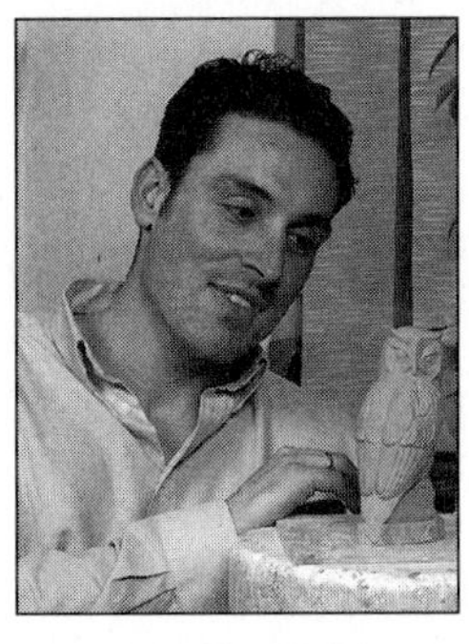

Warren Platt joined the John Beswick modelling team in 1985 on a Youth Training Program. In 1986, he became a full-time modeller and continued his art education by attending Stafford Art College. All modellers at Beswick must be adaptable and versatile, and Warren has demonstrated this through his excellent work.

His works are featured in the *Beatrix Potter*, *Snowman* and *Bunnykins* collections, including "Ice Cream and Brownie Bunnykins." He also designed "Bulldog" and "Jack Russell," horse models for the *Spirit Horse* collection, and the small size "Desert Orchid" and "Mr. Frisk." Warren feels that horses are his favorite subject to model and enjoys visiting them and getting to know their character. He likes the challenge of developing an idea into a three dimensional model.

Warren's leisure activities include cycling and sketching.

KIM PLAUCHÉ

Sometimes a person identifies so completely with their occupation that it becomes difficult to separate what they do from who they are. That is the case with Kim Plauché.

Kim identifies herself as an artist and a Pisces. From her first design submitted to the Society of Ceramic and Glass Decorators, to her most recent designs for Fenton Art Glass Co. which include the Lighthouse and Sandcarved Favrene with Dolphins Collectible Eggs, Kim is drawn to scenes which include water.

Kim Plauché is also drawn to people. She began working at Fenton in 1979 and moved up through many different departments, getting to know handmade glass and the employees at Fenton. She now holds a position as decorating designer of handmade glass. "Most of my art education has been on-the-job experience here at Fenton," she says. "I believe in staying busy with my rewarding job and my hobby of collecting Elvis and Marilyn Monroe memorabilia, as well as spending time with my husband and five children."

BRENDA POWER

Brenda Power has had a life-long involvement in art. She started making full-size dolls and soft toys over 20 years ago, which she sold at local craft shows. She then began to paint scenes on Christmas ornaments made of eggshells and did portrait paintings of children. However, when she discovered the joys of designing miniature bears, she states, "I came full circle."

Drawing on her considerable talents as an artist and her previous experience with soft toys, Brenda has been able to design and create tiny realistic, three-dimensional animals using mohair. In 1997, she was invited to design some pieces for Deb Canham Artist Designs, Inc. The *Brenda Power Collection* features a push-a-long penguin, a raccoon, a standing rabbit and a rabbit on wheels. More designs are planned for 1999 including a duck, goose and two realistic cats.

CHRISTOPHER RADKO

When Christopher Radko began designing his collection of fine glass Christmas ornaments 12 years ago, there were only 50 styles in the collection. Today, there are over 750 styles which encompass a wide variety of themes and include many limited editions, as well as sensational licensed properties. In 1997, he also expanded his artistry to every room of the home with new products from snowglobes and nutcrackers, to holiday placemats and candles.

In an effort to replace his family's lost ornament collection – caused by their Christmas tree falling over – Christopher started designing and creating ornaments "with the quality of the old days." Growing up with diverse traditions handed down from relatives in Poland, Austria and France, Christopher's desire to create exquisitely blown and intricately decorated ornaments has led him to select only expert craftsmen in Italy, the Czech Republic, Germany and Poland. Through his designs, Christopher has put both quality and magic back into Christmas.

RAINE

Putting her best foot forward, artist Raine offers a delightful commentary on art, culture and taste with her collection, *Just The Right Shoe* from Willitts Designs.

A successful illustrator and sculptor with strong formal training in composition and form, Raine's forté is a rich combination of realism, symbolism and fantasy, making use of historical references, contemporary culture, and artistic license to stretch the viewer's interpretation of the world around us.

Raine first got her foot in the door of the art world with an apprenticeship at age 15, followed by a full scholarship for her bachelor of fine arts degree. Her career is on excellent footing with an impressive list of publications, gallery exhibits, public and private commissions and collections, television appearances and awards.

MIDGE RAMSEY

Midge Ramsey's interest in art began as soon as she could open her first box of crayons. As a child, her early inspirations were Dr. Seuss and Disney. She remembers wanting to make cartoons when she grew up. She began to take art seriously in high school with a progressive program in London. Later, she received her bachelor of fine arts in printmaking from the

University of Oklahoma.

In 1988, Midge began designing a line of sculpted jewelry with aquatic themes, called FINZ, that was sold at arts and crafts festivals and specialty shops.

Midge went to work at United Design™ in 1989, where she was employed as a Paint Design Manager. During that time, she made several contributions in sealife sculptures to the *Animal Magnetism®* and *Fancy Frames®* lines. Today, she is a full time artist for the company and is still sculpting marine life for the *Animal Classics®* and *Stone Critters®* collections.

Midge says, "Every figure I sculpt is a challenge in its own way."

LYNNE RANDOLPH

An avid sketch artist and painter since childhood, Lynne Randolph turned to calligraphy after the birth of her second child. From there she progressed to sculpting, a phase she describes as "a classic plaster-all-over-the-kitchen-floor story." While on vacation in 1990, she visited a doll shop in Maine, where she admired some porcelain baby dolls. "I was instantly fascinated," she remembers, "and I said to my husband 'I have to learn to do this.'" Soon afterwards she created her first original doll, "Rachel Beth," using her own daughter as a model.

Her many awards include a DOTY nomination from *Doll Reader*. Her favorite dolls for the Seymour Mann Gallery include "Tiffany," "Meredith" and "Ginnie." Speaking of her dolls, she says, "They are a gentle reminder that children are ours to protect, nurture and love."

CHRISTY RAVE

Christy Rave was born on Christmas Day and raised on Long Island. She completed her college education and later taught elementary school. While awaiting the birth of her son, Teddy, Carol began designing her line of *Benevolent Bears*.

Along with her mother, Christie exhibits her original handmade creations throughout the north eastern part of the United States. Christy Rave's characters, created for *Cottage Collectibles* by Ganz, are specially designed bears that show the unique style and fun typical of Christy's original designs.

VAUGHN AND STEPHANIE RAWSON

The whimsical theme of the carved basswood figures created by husband and wife team Vaughn and Stephanie Rawson evoke childhood memories and the magic of Christmas past. Their distinctively styled folk art is the epitome of a creative collaboration.

Full-time artists since 1992, the Rawsons design each project together and are never at a loss for new ideas. Vaughn, using traditional knives and chisels, approaches each new project with "the personal goal of it resulting in the best carving I've done." Stephanie completes each newly carved figure by using painting and finishing techniques that capture a timeless, old-world patina of warm color.

The Rawsons' carvings have been selected several times for inclusion in *Early American Life's* annual directory of the "200 Best Crafts Persons." House of Hatten, Inc. is pleased that the Rawsons have provided them with exclusive carving designs for reproduction. Highly detailed hand-painting creates the original look that they designed, proving to be a pure delight for all who anxiously anticipate the joy and magic of Christmas.

JOYCE REAVEY

Joyce Reavey is recognized throughout the doll world as a designer with a broad range. One minute, she dazzles collectors with brilliant fashion statements like "Catherine the Victorian Bride Doll." In the next, she melts collectors' hearts with children that are filled with life, portrayed in touching childhood vignettes.

Recently, Joyce treated us to the *Songs of Innocence™* — a wonderful collection of dolls in moments that pull at the heart strings. Created for the Georgetown Collection, each doll includes an accessory that is fitted with a musical movement which plays a favorite childhood song.

Winner of the "Award of Excellence," Joyce's work is influenced by her love of fashion design and a great appreciation for the lavish details of Victorian styles. But as the mother of three active children, she's surrounded by the best inspiration of all — the joyful, everyday experiences of her family.

MARTHA REYNOLDS

Vibrant — a wonderful word that describes both Martha Reynolds and her art.

A Fenton designer for over seven years, Martha constantly experiments with new materials and styles, creating designs that range from simple and contemporary, to the ornate and richly embellished look of Victorian glass.

Martha has frequently been honored with design awards since graduating cum laude from Shepherd College. Her "Best of Show" awards cover a variety of media including sculpture, water-color and woodcuts. In 1993, the Society for Glass and Ceramic Decorators honored her with their prestigious Vandenoever Award.

Few artists choose to paint on glass because it is difficult to adjust to the different background colors, shapes and the non-absorbent slick surfaces. Martha welcomes these challenges, and her ringing laughter lifts everyone's spirits when deadlines are short.

Martha's glass painting is featured in several collections from Fenton Art Glass.

MARY RHYNER-NADIG

Whether a heartwarming reindeer, whimsical cow or chocolate bunny, Enesco's Senior Product Designer Mary Rhyner-Nadig brings to life colorful animal figurines through her creative artwork.

Nadig made her mark in the giftware and collectibles industry with *Mary's Moo Moos*, a whimsical collection of cows with "punny" titles. Now entering its third year, the collection is ranked as the leading collectible in the cow-theme category, according to *Giftbeat*, an industry research organization. Nadig's most recent Enesco hit, *Christmas Cards*, a holiday cardinal collection, joins her other farmyard and domestic animal lines.

Since joining Enesco in 1990, Nadig has received many awards including "Division Designer of the Year" and "Enesco Associate of the Month." She was also recognized by Stanhome, Enesco's parent company, when she received the Stanhome Achievement Award.

Nadig received her degree from the American Academy of Art, located in Chicago, and resides in the area with her family.

SHANE RIDGE

Shane Ridge entered the pottery industry in 1978 as a moldmaker. Four years later, he began a new career as a tableware and low-relief modeller. In 1987, Shane joined Royal Doulton as their tableware modeller.

Since then, Shane has worked on various projects, ranging from standard tableware items to more elaborate semi-sculptural pieces. For *The Minton Archive Teapot Collection*, he modelled the "Monkey/Cockerel Teapot" and "Flat Iron Teapot."

In 1994, Shane was invited to spend six months in the John Beswick Studio, where he was able to develop his skills on wholly sculptural projects including *Bunnykins* and a large size horse, "The Lipizzaner."

Having shown great potential as a sculptural modeller, Shane was offered a permanent position in the John Beswick Studio, and to date, Shane's modelling projects have covered the entire Beswick product range.

In his spare time, Shane likes spending time with his family. He also enjoys playing football and video games.

XAVIER ROBERTS

Xavier Roberts drew upon Georgia Mountain folklore, the art of needle molding, and his own creativity to build the foundation for the internationally famous *Cabbage Patch Kids*®.

After dressing his soft-sculpture creations in clothes found at yard sales, the college art student put the "babies" up for adoption. By 1977, the "Little People," now called *Cabbage Patch Kids*, gained recognition as award-winning works of art.

In 1978, the artist formed Original Appalachian Artworks Inc., and transformed a country doctor's clinic in Cleveland, Georgia, into BabyLand General® Hospital, staffed with "doctors" and "nurses" to deliver the *'Kids*. The tradition, which started almost 20 years ago, continues with the highly collectible, soft-sculpture *'Kids™* still hand-stitched to birth.

Based on his belief that no dream is ever too big, Xavier continues to throw himself into his creations with an enthusiasm that matches the excitement of those who enjoy them.

MARTHA ROOT

Martha Root has affectionately been called Miss Martha since it was first bestowed upon her by her Sunday School class many years ago. To friends and collectors alike, the name seems to fit perfectly, as it reflects her gentle nature and warm, ready smile.

Her own childhood is sculpted into each piece of art she creates. She draws upon the multitude of memories that rest gently in her heart, memories that are part and parcel of the summers spent on her grandmother's farm. It was there that childhood came alive in the cotton fields, the watermelon patch, and the ol' swimming hole.

Martha's deep personal faith and precious childhood memories give birth to her sculptures, whose expressions and situations reflect the tenderness, innocence and love of childhood. The name of the line, *All God's Children*, fittingly carries the message of her life and her work.

Each piece sculpted by Martha is handcrafted in the USA at the Miss Martha Originals factory located in Gadsden, Alabama.

TERRI RUSSELL

Terri Russell's exceptional eye for detail and the expression seen in her animal characters are what brought her to the attention of United Design™. Terri's animal characters take on a life of their own – they definitely have something to say.

Terri's talent was encouraged by her grandmother, an oil painter, and her father, a graphic designer. At a very early age, she worked in several media including pencil, pastels, and oils. Later, a high school art instructor saw her potential and introduced her to sculpture. Terri recalls, when introduced to the medium of clay, "It was love at first touch."

Terri maintained an independent studio for several years and exhibited throughout the U.S. In 1994, she received a fine arts degree from Friends University in Wichita, Kansas.

For United Design, Terri has created and developed many of the figures in the *100 Bunnies Collection* of *Stone Critters®*. She also sculpts animal designs for the *Animal Classics®* and *Stone Garden®* collections.

KEVIN RYAN

A native of San Diego, Kevin Ryan has always been interested in art since his childhood. This interest, combined with a strong influence from his grandmother and a little formal training, laid the foundation for what was later to become a rare opportunity to help preserve the historical monuments of maritime folklore.

Kevin also credits his grandmother with introducing him to his fascination with lighthouses. In 1969, he first visited San Diego's Cabrillo Monument for the grand tour of Old Point Loma. A year ago, his love of art and lighthouses collided, when he came to work for Harbour Lights.

"When I'm helping to recreate something as important to our past as these lighthouses, I not only feel a historical connection and a sense of artistic accomplishment," Ryan says, "but quite honestly, I'm often taken back to my childhood. And can't we all use a little of that?"

DIANE SAMS

Diane Sams has been creating one-of-a-kind sterling miniatures since 1969. In 1991, her company, Fool Moon Treasures, was launched. Although the company initially offered fashion jewelry, keepsakes and gifts, the firm recently debuted several intricate collectible series featuring bears, mice, fairies, elves, and other creatures great and small.

Sams was born in Louisiana, but spent many years in Venezuela. Today, she works and resides in Tallahassee, Florida. She studied at the Corcoran School of Art in Washington, D.C., but discovered her interest in and talent for sculpting during a brief career in dental technology. Besides sculpting, Sams remains active in the jewelry business, collecting precious and semi-precious gemstones from all over the world. As a testament to her work, autographed photos hang on her studio wall from Dolly Parton and Judy Collins, two of the celebrities for whom Sams has designed jewelry.

"Lagniappe" (pronounced lan-yap) is a Louisiana French word which means 'a little something extra.' Diane Sams and Fool Moon Treasures pledge to provide collectors unique designs to touch their hearts – with a little "lagniappe" thrown in for good measure!

BARBI SARGENT

Barbi Sargent is a multi-talented artist who has made her mark in the art world through four separate disciplines: fine arts, book publishing, children's literature and greeting cards.

For more than 30 years, her unique style and innovative images have touched the hearts of young and old around the world. Her renderings for Possible Dreams' *Floristine Angels™* are testimony to her amazing talent and are an inspiration for the craftsmen at Possible Dreams to sculpt heavenly embodiments which are precious to behold.

The sacred majesty of Barbi Sargent's *Floristine Angels* brings joy to collectors everywhere.

MARJORIE SARNAT

For the past ten years, Marjorie Sarnat's designs for The San Francisco Music Box Company have captured consumer's hearts. Her *Folk Art Figurines, Nine Lives Cat Collection, Mythological Crystal Visions* pieces, and *Valentine* and *Angel Teddy Bears* are perennial favorites.

Sarnat attended the Chicago Art Institute and the Boston Museum of Fine Arts, earning a bachelor's degree in fine arts. She now lives with her husband and toddler son in Granada Hills, California, where her home studio is located.

Sarnat's greatest satisfaction comes from "seeing her art come to life." Inspired by her desire to communicate emotions through her work, her designs frequently take their cues from art history or pop culture. "In my work, I like to create the comfort of tradition with the surprise of originality," says the artist.

SARAH SCHULTZ

In 1983, Sarah Schultz of Chesaning, Michigan, (pop. 2,500) began an odyssey that today has resulted in her philosophy of Love, Respect and Dignity becoming easily recognized all over the country. Sarah's Attic, Inc. had its beginnings on the dining room floor of the Schultz family home. Each year has brought progress and growth, but Sarah's' philosophy is still the backbone of Sarah's Attic. The company has grown from a regional phenomenon to an international force in the world of fine collectibles and gifts. However, those small town, tight-knit family ideals are still evident in each figurine created.

Every creation from Sarah's Attic is influenced by Sarah's love for her children, her family and her country. Sarah is dedicated to Americana and to promoting the values on which this country was founded.

Each figurine created by Sarah's Attic must meet the test of these simple but powerful words that are easily said but are not always practiced. Love, Respect and Dignity are Always in Style at Sarah's Attic.

MARK SHERMAN

Mark Sherman's creations in pastels, oils and watercolors reveal his wide range of interests and talents. A Brooklyn-born artist, who studied at the Art Student's League in New York, and in California with Rex Brandt and Joseph Mugnaini, Mark's paintings have appeared in juried exhibitions and are included in many private and corporate collections. Currently a professor in San Diego, Mark instructs a studio art class as part of his school's humanities program.

Mark enjoys traveling with his family, and many of his transparent watercolors are inspired by North American and European landscape and architecture. He has long admired our nation's lighthouses, and so it came as no surprise that he chose Old Point Loma, located just a few miles from his home, as the subject of his first lighthouse watercolor.

Harbour Lights takes great pleasure in introducing Mark Sherman to their family of lighthouse enthusiasts and collectors, and eagerly anticipates his future contributions.

ELIO SIMONETTI

Creating the life-sized *Fontanini® Heirloom Nativities* by Roman, Inc. is the crowning achievement of Elio Simonetti's distinguished artistic career. Receiving the Fontanini family gift of a 50" nativity, Pope John Paul II expressed his admiration of Simonetti's work with the statement, "I hope God grants him a long life to continue his fantastic sculpting." The Pontiff's prayer has been answered, and Simonetti's talent spans more than five decades of sculpting with the House of Fontanini.

Born in Lucca in 1924, Simonetti studied at the Liceo of Arts in Lucca before leaving school to help support his large family. From the very beginning, Simonetti was lauded for his magical ability to infuse sculptures with life-like qualities. This mastery has led to a collection of hundreds of *Fontanini Nativity* pieces in seven different sizes – from 2-1/2" miniatures to near life-size scenes.

TERRY SKORSTAD

Inspired by the birth of her first child, Terry Skorstad's first design was an expectant plush bear named "Bear-to-be." Soon, friends started asking to buy some of her "Terry Bears." More orders came in, and Terry's fledgling business was off and running.

An avid seamstress since childhood, Terry combines her passion for sewing and artistic talents in her bears. Now living in Vermont, her child-like bears, created for *Cottage Collectibles* by Ganz, express all the love that Terry puts into them.

Her creations include "Root Beer Bear," "Little Salty Bear" and "Justine Bear," to name a few.

GERHARD SKROBEK

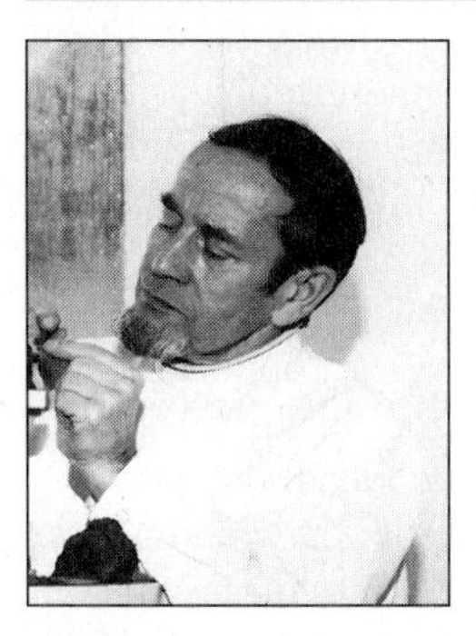

Gerhard Skrobek, a master sculptor of the Goebel company, was born in Silesia, the northernmost part of Germany, and subsequently moved with his family to Berlin. There, surrounded by museum art treasures and encouraged by his artist mother, Skrobek became immersed in the artistic tradition. From early childhood, he was fascinated with sculpture and its many artistic forms. He studied at the Reimannschule in Berlin, a renowned private academy of arts, and continued his studies in Coburg. Through a professor, he was introduced to porcelain sculpture at W. Goebel Porzellanfabrik.

Skrobek joined Goebel in 1951, becoming one of its leading sculptors and eventually the predominant interpreter of Sister Maria Innocentia Hummel's drawings into three-dimensional form.

With the publication of his revealing new book entitled, *Hummels and Me: Life Stories*, Skrobek breaks his 50-year silence to discuss the impact of Hitler and World War II on art in Germany, the simple aesthetics that have motivated him, and the appeal of *M.I. Hummel* figurines.

LEO R. SMITH III

Inspired by the picturesque river town of Fountain City, Wisconsin, Leo R. Smith III brings legends and folklore to life.

In an exclusive partnership with this nationally-recognized wood carver, Midwest of Cannon Falls creates limited edition reproductions of his original designs.

After being precisely hand-cast in resin, every piece is hand-painted, based on color schemes developed by Leo and his wife, Marilyn. It is then numbered to ensure its authenticity. As the perfect finishing touch, the limited edition collectible is accompanied by the legend or personal vision that inspired the artist.

Midwest of Cannon Falls is proud to be in partnership with Leo R. Smith III and to share his legendary folk art.

SUSAN M. SMITH

In a small Alaskan town, situated between breathtaking snow-tipped mountains and thick wilderness, one finds a cozy workshop where Susan M. Smith carves her next creation.

Always interested in art and expression, Susan prefers working with wood due to its limitless capabilities and flexibility. When Susan first began to carve, she concentrated on depicting real life, with all its details and intricacies. She soon realized she was only expressing what she saw instead of what she felt. Wanting to convey her own feelings of warmth and contentment, Susan relaxed her style and began to have more fun with her designs. Carving now for 22 years, her style has evolved into creating whimsical designs.

Because of her location, it was difficult for Susan to enter contests and gain national exposure. So, she was elated when House of Hatten, Inc. began to reproduce her designs in 1995 with the introduction of her *Santa's Kingdom* collection, which includes limited edition centerpieces.

RANDALL SPANGLER

Randall Spangler creates fanciful worlds filled with mystery, intrigue and a whole lot of fun. The seeds of his fertile imagination were planted early at his grandparent's farm in Missouri. There, in the wooded hills, he would engage in pretend games with gentle dragons and mischievous elves.

At the Art Institute of Kansas City, he learned to translate those images using ink, watercolor, colored pencil and gouache.

Once the artists at Possible Dreams discovered *Spangler's Realm™*, they worked night and day to perfect these three-dimensional cold cast Draglings, and a delightful collection was born. Invite *Spangler's Realm* into your home and let them cast their spell!

ROBIN SPINDLER

While visiting the Fenton Gift Shop, Robin Spindler and her mother admired the hand-painted glass. "You can paint like that," exclaimed Robin's mother. That thought stayed with Robin, and in 1979, she decided to try her hand at glass painting. Developing a personal style which is reflected in her work, Robin became a Fenton designer in 1994.

Robin, who was born and grew up in Morgantown, West Virginia, loves the outdoors, and animals are her favorite subjects. "I want to capture the spirit in their eyes," she says. Just recently she began creating "Animal Rocks" for her friends.

When you find a piece signed J.K. Spindler (Judith Kay) then you've found Robin. She truly believes there is "power in the brushes. It's where emotions shine through." "Meadow Beauty," "Folk Art Animals" and "Tranquility" are some of her creations.

GABRIELE STAMEY

Born in the small Tyrolean town of Worgl, Gabriele Stamey began her professional career designing hand-blown stemware after studying at the world-famous technical school of glassmaking and design in Kramsach, Tyrol.

In 1986, Gabriele accepted a full-time design position with Swarovski Silver Crystal. Her professional skills and lively imagination were immediately evident in her first designs comprising a whimsical "Miniature-Rooster," a "Miniature-Hen" and three "Miniature-Chicks" in fine cut crystal.

She created the first designs in the theme group, "When We Were Young," which brings back childhood memories. Her designs in this series include a cut crystal train complete with "Locomotive," "Tender" and three "Wagons," and the "Airplane," dedicated to man's fascination with flight and travel. Another piece, the "Santa Maria," is the flagship which Gabriele designed especially for the "Columbus Quincentennial."

Gabriele is the designer of the Swarovski Collectors Society 1997 Annual Edition, "Fabulous Creatures" - The Dragon. This is her first design for the Society.

MICHAEL STAMEY

Michael Stamey was born in Munich, West Germany, in 1951. He developed his handcrafting skills through a thorough four-year education at the world-famous technical school of glass craft and design at Kramsach in the Austrian Tyrol.

In 1977, Michael started work for Swarovski Silver Crystal. Among his designs are such popular items as the "Rose," "Orchid" and "Cheetah." Many years of snorkeling gave him the inspiration for his designs in the *South Seas* series, including the "Dolphin," "Miniature-Crab," "Shell with Pearl" and "Maritime Trio."

Stamey also created the Swarovski Collectors Society Annual Editions, "Lead Me" - The Dolphins, "Save Me" - The Seals, and "Care For Me" - The Whales for the *Mother and Child* trilogy, and the "Kudu" in the *Inspiration Africa* trilogy.

The most important influence in his artistic work is nature. "If you just look at something beautiful or complex long enough, parallels to nature become obvious," says Stamey. Through the brilliant crystal objects he creates for Swarovski, this philosophy becomes clearly visible.

HERR CHRISTIAN & KARLA STEINBACH

Herr Christian and Karla Steinbach are the current President and Vice President of the Steinbach factory in Germany, the leading producer of collectible nutcrackers and smoking figures in the world. Together they oversee product development and manufacturing of limited edition nutcrackers and smoking figures for Kurt S. Adler, Inc.

Founded in 1832, the Steinbach company continues to manufacture nutcrackers, smoking figures, ornaments and music boxes in the age-old tradition. Kurt S. Adler, Inc. introduced the first limited edition design from the Steinbach factory in 1991. Each year, new designs appear in such sought-after groups as the *Biblical Series*, *Christmas Legends*, *A Christmas Carol*, *Tales of Sherwood Forest* and *Camelot Series*. Not just limited to larger nutcrackers ranging from 16" to 19" tall, Kurt S. Adler also offers 6" and 7" mini nutcrackers.

The Steinbach Collector's Club, which began in 1996, is gaining members every day and continues to grow.

CAROL STEWART

Well known for her exquisitely designed teddy bears, Carol Stewart also creates miniature wood carvings, miniature room boxes and custom reproduction work in miniature. Often starting with a larger prototype, she works her way down to the smallest size possible, which will still have all of the details of the design. "For me," states Carol, "the most fun is the design work. I love the challenge of taking an idea and working out the problems to get it exactly as it should be – only in miniature."

Carol started making miniature teddy bears in 1982 and has been designing for Little Gem Teddy Bears since 1996. Her bears have received numerous Toby Award nominations, and she has won two Golden Teddy Awards; the latest in 1997 for "Ashley," which was designed for Little Gem Teddy Bears.

Carol has been invited several times as a guest artist to the Walt Disney World Teddy Bear Convention. She was also honored to be only one of three American teddy bear artists asked to specially design and make a bear for Princess Nobuko of the Japanese Royal Family.

WAYNE STILL

Wayne Still has worked for nearly 25 years as an accomplished illustrator and designer for many prestigious companies and institutions.

His heartfelt concern with the industrialization of Africa and the resulting loss of its culture and traditions is the motivation for *The African Spirit™* collection. This accurate portrayal of tribal members is a true depiction of those indigenous people.

Their anatomy, gestures, and authentic wardrobes are brought to vivid life as the gifted artisans at Possible Dreams interpret Wayne's masterful talent into the stunning *African Spirit* cold cast collection.

ADI STOCKER

Born in St. Johann in Tyrol, Austria, Adi Stocker studied at the world-famous technical school for glass craft and design in Kramsach, Tyrol. After graduating in 1977, he worked in a glass studio in New Hampshire for four years. Then he traveled around the world for a year, visiting Japan, China, Thailand, Nepal and India. Upon his return, he began working for Swarovski.

From his home in St. Ulrich am Pillersee, he creates his newest figures, but maintains contact with his colleagues in Wattens.

His Swarovski Silver Crystal designs include the limited edition "Eagle" and "Polar Bear." His creation, the "Lion," rounded off the *Inspiration Africa* trilogy for the Swarvoski Collectors Society as the 1995 Annual Edition. Designer objects, such as jewelry boxes and pen holders designed for Swarovski Selection, testify to Adi's highly diversified talent.

MICHAEL STOEBNER

From his Minnesota home, Michael Stoebner has been busy cooking up a new holiday look for Kurt S. Adler, Inc., the world's leading resource of holiday decorative accessories.

Michael, a veteran sculptor, painter and illustrator, is credited with creating holiday designs with "a handmade look that brings back a feeling of warmth and meaning back into Christmas."

Michael joined Kurt S. Adler in 1995 and began creating the whimsical *Snowtown*, an illuminated, wood resin holiday village. His style of integrating wood and clay originals with fabric and wire invoke the heartwarming traditions of the holidays. He also created *Spring Town*, a lighted, wood resin village consisting of cute cottages with Easter bunny figurines and accessories. Another of his creations is *Angel Heights*, a unique celestial illuminated village which includes delightful angels in Victorian-styled houses.

KANDY SUMNER

Kandy Sumner employs many mediums to give life to her incredible array of Santas, cats, whimsical creatures and other folk-art designs, made exclusively for Kurt S. Adler Inc.

Kandy is a whirlwind of energy and emits a tremendous sense of excitement in each project she develops. "We never are sure what she will think of next, as her inspiration can be sparked by a scrap of material, the flash of a mental image, or a piece of oddly shaped wood," explained one of the

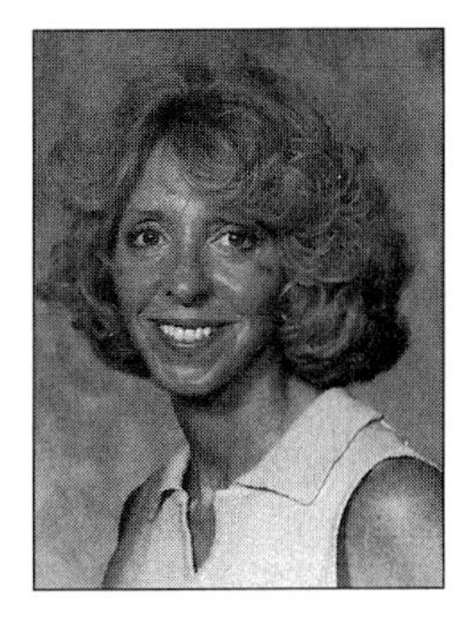

company's product mangers. "We do know that each work reflects the best of American country art."

Kandy created a broad variety of collections including: the new country look of the *Spirit of Christmas* series, adorable cats in *Kitty Whiskers*, charming mice at work and play in the *Hole-in-the-Wall Gang*, highly sought-after *Folk Art* designs, and the elegant *Florentine* collection of holiday ornaments and figurines.

TOM SUZUKI

Without a doubt Tom Suzuki is one of the most skillful crystal artists in the world. Suzuki has an amazing sense for detail, proportion and stylistic beauty.

From his smaller and more imaginative objects d'art, like the award-winning "Curious Cat," to impressive masterpieces such as "Taj Mahal," Tom shows an enormous range of talent. He was recently nominated for an "Award of Excellence" by *Collector Editions* magazine for his handsome "Small Classic Motorcycle."

Never content to rest on past accomplishments, Tom has recently created the magnificent "Capitol Hill," along with the playful "Tee-shot Teddy" for Crystal World.

TREVOR SWANSON

Trevor Swanson, the son of world-renowned wildlife artist Gary R. Swanson, is a brilliant example of an artistic inheritance passing from one generation to another. Each of his canvases is an expression of the influence created by the artistic environment in which he grew up.

Trevor began painting professionally in 1989 and has worked hard to develop his skills to achieve a high level of realism in his paintings. Trevor's art shows an appreciation for detail and the complexities of the value systems essential to any fine artwork. He has also mastered the patience needed to make each of his paintings something very special. Invitations to shows and winning the Foundation for North American Wild Sheep Artist of the Year Award has helped to further his outstanding career. Throughout his life, Trevor has spent much time outdoors, and has traveled throughout the United States, as well as Canada, Africa and Spain. Time in the field gives him his keen insight into the precise details of the animals and their environments, which he paints with attention to the fundamentals of artistic realism.

Islandia International has transformed Trevor Swanson's art into beautiful true-to-life wildlife treasures in the form of figurines, collector plates, ornaments and vases that are as inspiring as his original art.

ROBERT TABBENOR

Robert Tabbenor joined the Royal Doulton sculpture studio in 1973. Although he had always enjoyed drawing and painting, he had no experience in clay modelling before joining Royal Doulton. He quickly realized what a rewarding challenge it was to be able to form a lump of clay into any shape he desired.

Robert's first few production models were character figures. Now his work is represented in most of Royal Doulton's lines, including the *Pretty Ladies*, *Vanity Fair*, *Images* and *Reflections* series, as well as International Collector Club commissions, *Character Jugs* and Royal Crown Derby paperweights. Recently, he has modelled limited edition pieces including "Robert E. Lee," "General Ulysses S. Grant" and "Field Marshall Montgomery."

He combines his sculptural duties with that of Studio Head, acting as the liaison for the company production staff, to help alleviate any problems that may arise during the manufacturing process.

DAVID JOHN TATE, MBE

David Tate founded Lilliput Lane in 1982, and he has been an integral part of its growth and success ever since.

During the 1960s, David started drawing and painting the thatched cottages of the English countryside. He portrayed the thatched roofs, their styles and colors, thus starting his lifelong romance with the vernacular. Enjoying the creative process, David knew there was a chance to develop cottage sculptures full of the sunshine and beauty of the English countryside. His passion is clear when he talks of the cottages he loves and the captivation with the landscape itself. The success of Lilliput Lane is attributable in no small part to his determination, tenacity and sheer energy.

Today, David is at the pinnacle of his career. He oversees and trains a superb team of sculptors and artists at Lilliput Lane, who continue to research and develop new systems and designs to increase the company's competitive edge in the worldwide collectibles market.

MICHAEL J. TAYLOR

Influenced by an artistic correspondence course during his collegiate days, Gartlan USA artist Michael J. Taylor has spent more than a dozen years doing commercial and advertising illustrations.

In his spare time, Taylor created drawings and paintings for local art shows in his native state of Michigan. With a passion for sports, his moonlighting efforts featured many local heroes, and he was often asked by parents to draw a portrait of their son or daughter athletes.

In 1984, Taylor began creating original portraits of renowned athletes and worked to get them autographed. Taylor's enthusiasm for sports and artistic talent attracted the critical eye of Gartlan USA, a leader in limited edition sports and entertainment collectibles. Subsequently, Taylor has created original art for Gartlan USA featuring Kareem Abdul-Jabar, Joe Montana, John Wooden, Yogi Berra, Whitey Ford, Kristi Yamaguchi, Sam Snead, Bob Cousy, Rod Carew, and Brett and Bobby Hull.

Taylor also produced the original artwork featured on the *KISS Kollection*, *Leave It To Beaver* and *Ringo Starr* series of collectors' plates for Gartlan USA. His recent pencil study featured on the *Jerry Garcia* collectors' plate series was a collaborative effort, directed by Garcia's widow, Deborah Koons Garcia.

RUBEN M. TEJADA

Artist Ruben M. Tejada, a fine arts graduate, brings over 20 years of designing experience to his doll creations. Specializing in Native American designs which he carefully researches for authenticity in costume design and sculpting, Tejada's efforts have indeed resulted in awards and recognition.

The *Sweet Spirit Baby* series and the new *Gentle Dreams Baby* series of infant dolls proudly carry on that great tradition! Each doll is created to be hugged, with outstretched hands and adorable expressions. Sandy Dolls is proud to exclusively represent the great artistry of Ruben M. Tejada.

SIGRID THEN

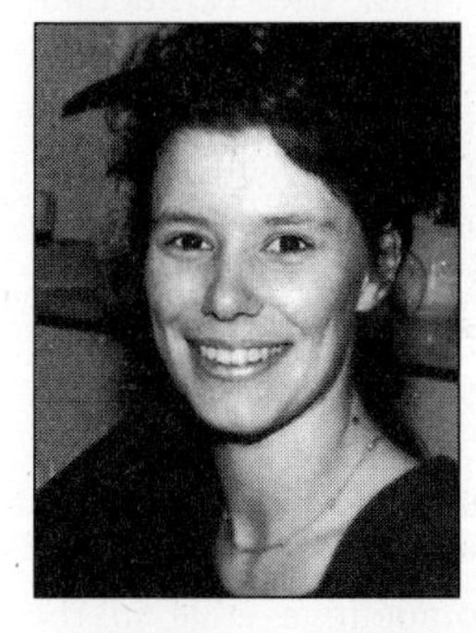

A gifted young artist, Sigrid Then was admitted to the W. Goebel Porzellanfabrik three-year apprenticeship program in 1989. After successfully completing the program, and passing the required test with top honors, she was assigned a series of retail promotional tours in Germany and Europe. Sigrid, who speaks English fluently, has also made several visits to the United States on behalf of Goebel.

When not traveling for Goebel, Sigrid works in the company's painting department where she continues to perfect her ceramic painting skills for *M.I. Hummel* figurines. Everyone who sees her lively painting demonstrations will agree that she is not only a talented artist, but she also loves her work.

Sigrid lives in Wargolshausen, Germany, near the Goebel factory. She devotes her spare time to a variety of pursuits including drawing, needlework, dancing and reading.

ALLAN THERKELSEN

Artist Allan Jochum Therkelsen has created all six motifs in Bing & Grondahl's popular *Annual Figurine Collection*. He is also credited with the creation of three new and very successful underglaze figurine collections – *Swans*, *Cats* and

Pandas – for Royal Copenhagen, one of Europe's oldest porcelain manufacturers.

Recognized as a sculptor, Therkelsen's work is a part of many permanent museum collections, including the McHenry Library at the University of California in Santa Cruz. In addition to a successful career in sculpting, Therkelsen has taught art at the University of California in Santa Cruz, the Skolen for Biddedkunst in Copenhagen and Grundtvig Hojskolen in Denmark.

Allan Therkelsen, representing the next generation of Royal Copenhagen sculptors, currently resides in Copenhagen.

SHELIA THOMPSON

As a young girl growing up in the South, Shelia Thompson showed an aptitude for art by removing the family portraits off the wall to study and then hone her talents. In high school, Shelia headed up numerous committees, creating posters and play backdrops.

Shelia's Collectibles was founded in 1978 when this self-taught artist discovered a creative way to increase her family's income by making wooden replicas of historic houses to sell at the Charleston City Market.

Shelia's work can be best recognized by the layered facade interpretation she gives each building, with colorful foliage and a fascinating history on the back. She is best known for, but not limited to, her creations of Victorian-style houses.

Shelia is highly creative and imaginative, as shown by her designs, including the *Ghost House* series which glows in the dark; her first licensed series, *Gone With The Wind*; and a category of painted metal ornaments. Shelia's Collectibles was honored with "The Blue Chip Enterprise Initiative Program Award" for their effective use of resources to overcome adversity and create business opportunities.

ANNALEE THORNDIKE

Annalee Davis Thorndike was destined for doll-making fame almost in spite of herself. Coming from an artistic family, Annalee loved to watch her mother sew, and they made doll clothes together. "I never played 'house' with dolls," says Annalee, "I just made clothes."

After graduating from high school, in order to "cough up some money to help at home," Annalee began making dolls, selling them through the League of New Hampshire Craftsmen.

In 1941, Annalee married Charles "Chip" Thorndike, son of a distinguished Boston surgeon. Chip, a free-spirited individual, preferred poultry farming. When the poultry business in New Hampshire went South, their farm became the "Factory in the

Woods" for Annalee's doll hobby turned business. By the 1960s, an entire work force was involved in meeting the demand for Annalee dolls. With a work force of 350, Annalee's has become a leader in the Christmas and gift industry.

CHUCK THORNDIKE

Chuck Thorndike has inherited the family's artistic talents, and has long been identified with Annalee Dolls.

Born March 17, 1945, Chuck attended Meredith schools, was a student at Paul Smith College, the University of New Hampshire, and is a Vietnam veteran. His wife, Karen, established the Annalee Gift Shop, which opened over 20 years ago. She and Chuck are the parents of two sons and a daughter. Chuck is also an inventor, having designed and patented a material handling device for lifting logs and stones, as well as having made many improvements to tools and the assembly processes of doll making.

Chuck's hobbies have centered around seasonal sports activities found in the lakes and mountains of New Hampshire, which are the source for many of the ideas that appear in each line of dolls.

Chuck recalls growing up in a household where, at one time, Rhode Island Red hens roamed the premises when his parents ran the Thorndike poultry farm. The tables and beds were piled high with Annalee Dolls, and a squadron of doll makers worked around the dining room table. "It was an enchanted childhood," he says.

ANN TIMMERMAN

From the very beginning, it was clear to all that Ann Timmerman was going to be a star in the doll world. Early creations, like "Peaches & Cream" from the *Portraits of Perfection* collection, left collectors breathless with anticipation for more.

Innovative designs are Ann's trademark. Convinced that an angel should appear to fly, she designed a unique pose and display stand for each of her angels in the *Little Bit of Heaven™* collection.

With a successful limited edition business, as well as a great following for her Georgetown *Artist's Editions*, Ann continues to create exciting new dolls. An eye for detail and a remarkable ability to capture the most subtle nuance of an expression give her dolls a unique, life-like quality.

Included in recent introductions is "Cherry Pie," the premier doll in the *Portraits of a Perfect World* collection. With each new introduction, Ann's star continues to rise – to the delight of all!

TITUS TOMESCU

Titus Tomescu is one of the leading names in the doll collecting world. His dolls have been praised for their realism and intricate detailing. The breadth of his images range from

the gentle innocence of babies, to the towering spiritual strength of Jesus.

Among his most recent achievements is *Flurry of Activity*, a follow-up collection to his first Ashton-Drake *SnowBabies* series. Also new from Tomescu is a collection of babies, each one offering a cleaver answer to the question, *Where Do Babies Come From?* A collection that introduces collectors to favorite storybook characters as babies is called *Tales From the Nursery*. And an all-porcelain collection, called the *Twinkle Toes' Recital*, features toddler ballerinas in interactive dancing poses.

Tomescu's work has received many nominations for prestigious awards, and "Cute As a Button" was the 1994 dual winner of a DOTY® Award from *Doll Reader* magazine and the "Award of Excellence" from *Dolls* magazine.

CATHARINE TREDGER

Born in Toronto, Ontario, Canada, Catharine Tredger first attended art college and then designed jewelry, corporate logos, graphics and illustrations. Desiring a more gratifying outlet for her creativity that included her fondness for animals, Catharine began designing her exciting plush creations.

It is through the love of her canine creations, now available from *Cottage Collectibles* by Ganz, that Catharine can reach out and touch the hearts of collectors.

Catharine and her family make their home in a resort community in Ontario, commonly known as "Cottage Country."

GLYNDA TURLEY

At her home nestled in the beautiful Ozark Mountains of Arkansas, Glynda Turley finds the quiet inspiration for her exquisite oil paintings that have won her international acclaim.

As president and artist of her company, The Art of Glynda Turley, she has turned her creative talents into a thriving family business that invites collectors to enjoy the simpler pleasures of life.

Collectors can find Glynda's artwork adorning everything from limited edition prints and hand-painted figurines to tapestry pillows. "I love my work," Glynda says. "My paintings are the way I see things and the way I feel inside. It is a very rewarding thing to know you helped someone to smile."

Whether in the Ozark Mountains or traveling around the world, Glynda is always working on new ideas and expanding her collection for more collectors to enjoy. Her prints, decorative accessories, and collectibles will surely be the heirlooms of tomorrow.

CHRISTIAN ULBRICHT

Christian Ulbricht, founder of Holzkunst Christian Ulbricht, has truly earned the title of master wood carver, a family tradition begun by his father more than 65 years ago. Ulbricht carries on the centuries-old tradition of wood turning on the lathe, letting his natural warmth and humor shine through. These are the attributes that distinguish his intriguingly hand-carved wooden creations and bring delight to those who collect his nutcrackers, ornaments, music boxes, incense burners, and more.

Christian and his family take great pride in continuing the legendary handcraftsmanship that has existed for generations. It is easy to see why the nutcrackers that carry the Ulbricht family name are so popular. Not only do they bring to life the folklore of the beautiful German region that is their home; they also depict up-to-date life everywhere in the world today. Included among the more traditional motifs one expects to see, such as kings, soldiers and hunters, are bikers, Santa Claus, literary figures, American heroes, and even a computer hacker!

Holzkunst Christian Ulbricht is truly a family affair. Working along with Christian, and the trained artisans who carry out the master designs, are his wife, Inge, and their son and daughter, Gunther and Ines. Together, they have developed their studio into a creative, well-knit, productive organization dedicated to bringing high quality craftsmanship to collectors.

LEE MIDDLETON URICK

Lee Middleton Urick's unexpected death on January 30, 1997 saddened her collectors, whose hearts were touched by each doll this artist so lovingly created.

Lee founded her home-based company in 1980, and planned to create only as many dolls as she could produce. But gift and doll shop owners placed so many orders, that Lee had to create a "cottage industry" with family members and other helpers. Eventually, she spearheaded the construction of a 34,000 square foot manufacturing facility. Even as her company expanded, Lee remained adamant that each doll bear the special, personal touches that set her creations apart, such as having every doll leave the factory with its own tiny Bible.

Lee's inspirational spirit continues through Lee's Doll Family, her collectors club, which debuted shortly after her death. Lee left a legacy of beauty and quality which is unparalleled in the doll business. Lee Middleton Original Dolls, Inc. is a living memorial to the talent, creativity and spirit of its founder, Lee Middleton Urick.

SVEN VESTERGAARD

Sven Vestergaard became an apprentice at the Royal Copenhagen Porcelain Manufactory at the age of 16. Four years later, he was given the highest award – the Silver Medal – and

remained at the factory as an overglaze painter until 1959.

He then worked as a designer at Denmark's oldest newspaper, Berlinske Tidenade, as well as at various advertising agencies. In 1965, he returned to the factory as a draftsman and became the head of Royal Copenhagen's drawing office in 1976.

Vestergaard has become well known and respected throughout the world for his designs for Royal Copenhagen's *Christmas, Olympic, Hans Christian Andersen, National Parks of America* and *Mother's Day* plates and *Children's Day* series.

Vestergaard lives 30 miles south of Copenhagen on an estate originally owned by nobility, where he creates the many themes for Royal Copenhagen plates and his oil paintings of peaceful Danish landscapes, animals and nature.

EDDIE WALKER

A unique talent, combined with the ability to create whimsical images that make people feel good, has led to success for Eddie Walker, a wood carver whose designs are carried exclusively by Midwest of Cannon Falls®.

Since her venture into carving just seven years ago, Eddie's homespun style has earned her a national following, with her smiling decorative figures brightening millions of American homes.

Walker, a mother, wife, and former school secretary in Walla Walla, Washington, began carving in 1989 after a neighbor convinced her to take a two-hour carving class from a local gift shop.

Her designs run the gamut from whimsical Easter bunnies to merry cats and pink-cheeked Santas. Each figure has a distinctive Eddie Walker smile. Since 1995, Midwest of Cannon Falls has been reproducing and distributing Walker's designs, ranging from figurines and candlesticks, to picture frames and Christmas tree ornaments.

JACK WEAVER

Jack Weaver, president and designer of Shenandoah Designs International, Inc., has 35 years of history and experience in the gift industry as a designer, consultant and corporate manager.

Jack has designed and marketed decorative lamps and other furniture accessories, as well as several figurine collectible lines. The collectible *Annie and Jack Bears*, now retired, are a Jack Weaver Design, as are the charming *Appalachian Forest Folks* series of the 1970s.

For Shenandoah's *Keeper™* line, Jack personally goes over every piece the sculptor creates with an opti magnifier to make sure every detail is clear and refined.

"Collectors of Shenandoah designed collectibles can be assured of high quality, interesting, and exclusively unique collectibles which will not be poured into the market place in tonage quantities," says Weaver.

Jack also personally handles contracts with all of Shenandoah's overseas manufacturers, and personally inspects products to insure quality reproductions of all Shenandoah Designs.

MARLENE WHITING

Miniature village collectors know Marlene Whiting of Yorktown, Virginia, for her ability to capture with a brush the spirit, charm and timelessness that defines small-town America.

The founder of Brandywine Woodcrafts Inc. grew up in Pittsburgh, Pennsylvania, fascinated by the color and diversity of the small shops, businesses and homes of the city's ethnic neighborhoods. Since Brandywine's beginning in 1981, she has incorporated these memories, along with her love of architecture, literature and gardening, into her collections of nostalgic, historic and whimsical buildings.

Though Brandywine has grown since its beginnings on a kitchen table, Marlene has insisted that the company never lose sight of its American heritage and family orientation. She still designs and hand-paints the original of every creation, and each Brandywine building is made in the USA. Her husband, Tru, serves as company president, while daughter, Donna, manages the company's collector club, the Brandywine Neighborhood Association.

VERNON WILSON

Inspired by his favorite Scriptures, award-winning jewelry designer Vernon Wilson creates inspirational jewelry and gifts. With the ability to transform lifeless metals into exquisite art, Vernon expresses his personal beliefs through the *Vernon G. Wilson Signature Collection*, by Roman, Inc.

Interpretations of faith in the form of pins, pendants, bracelets, plaques, wall crosses and ornaments in a variety of metals, including 14K gold and sterling silver, make up the collection. Each piece is inspired by a favorite Bible verse and uses symbols that encourage individuals to find deeply personal meanings in each piece. All of the elements of the *Vernon G. Wilson Signature Collection* are crafted with a wealth of intricate features, such as tiny moving mountains and a door that opens.

Vernon annually tours the U.S. meeting enthusiastic collectors, sharing the creative process behind his designs, and signing the keepsake cards that detail the inspiration of each piece.

DAVID WINTER

English sculptor David Winter is regarded as one of the foremost creators of miniature architectural structures. A gifted sculptor, Winter has gained worldwide acclaim for his unique miniature cottages. With their remarkable detail and whimsical touches, his sculptures convey a nostalgic view of how people lived and worked in days gone by.

Born in Caterick, Yorkshire, David is the son of an army colonel and the famed British sculptor Faith Winter. Inspired by his mother, David created his first miniature cottage in 1979. Since then, David has received many awards, among them the coveted "Collectible of the Year Award" in 1987 and 1988, and "Artist of the Year" in 1991.

David works from a studio in the garden of his home in a small English village near Guildford, 30 miles west of London. Always traveling with a camera, David also researches buildings from old photographs and etchings. Although he does not exactly replicate buildings, he finds a feature he likes and uses that as a starting point, with his imagination filling out the rest. Somehow, he makes you feel as though you can step back into history!

BARBARA AND PETER WISBER

The Wisbers began their family business, Ladie & Friends, Inc., as an outgrowth of Barbara's crafting projects and Peter's skill in woodworking and cabinetry. During 1984, an idea emerged for a collection of wooden folk dolls, leading to the introduction of the first nine *Lizzie High®* dolls in 1985. With natural talent and an abundance of love, Barbara and Peter found a way to translate the joys of their partnership into a highly successful line of carefully crafted dolls and, more recently, resin figurines that are based upon their beloved characters.

Barbara and Peter were married in 1971. Over the years, country life, the joys of raising two children, a strong sense of family history and pride, treasured childhood memories, and valued friendships have provided the inspiration for the Wisbers' best-known creations.

Barbara is still the primary creator of the dolls. Peter continues to actively manage the day-to-day operations of the business, sculpt accessories for each doll, and solve technical design problems.

IWONA WISZNIEWSKA

Born in Bialystok, Poland, Iwona Wiszniewska came to the United States in 1992. She is an accomplished artist, educated in home decor, fashion accessories, interior design and crafts. She joined the staff at Kurt S. Adler, Inc. and was trained at the Komozja factory where the *Polonaise™ Collection* of hand-blown glass ornaments is created.

At the factory in Poland, Iwona became familiar with the intricacies of creating hand-blown ornaments and was assigned to the Prototype Room, where the painting process begins. She is especially excited about her new "Bible" ornament, as she wanted to "create something that would be totally unique in glass and which would have meaning."

Iwona has toured the United States on behalf of Kurt S. Adler, Inc. and the *Polonaise™ Collection*. "I've done a lot of traveling over the past year and met a lot of nice and good-hearted people," says Iwona. "I cannot wait to get back on the road to meet my old friends and hopefully make some new ones."

DAVID LEE WOODARD

David Lee Woodard believes that creativity and marketing are prime ingredients to making successful products. Many wonderful ideas of great potential are left hanging on the vine as they wait to be discovered.

Woodard specializes in taking an innovation and bringing it to life. Working in the collectibles industry for 20 years, he waits to see a collector's first reaction to a new figurine. Although creating a product brings him great joy, success is only achieved once an item is accepted by its future owner.

While a figurine can be beautiful, Dave feels that it must also tell a story. He has always enjoyed story telling, and fondly remembers getting together with neighborhood kids to make up tall tales.

Along with Pat Chandok, Dave has developed music boxes, carousels, and the award-winning *World of Krystonia* line. He currently is developing three new gift lines.

CHU-MING "JAMIE" WU

A chance meeting in 1983 with an artist who made miniature bears led Chu-Ming "Jamie" Wu to become a top teddy bear designer and successful entrepreneur. Jamie had just immigrated to the United States, spoke little English, and was a day laborer when he met Carol Stewart. Under her guidance, Jamie made his first bear, working diligently for 27 nights! Fifteen years later, his company, Akira Trading Company, sells thousands of Little Gem Teddy Bears that are made by cottage workers in China.

Chu-Ming Wu, known to his English speaking friends as "Jamie," was born in 1947 in Taiwan. At an early age, his grandfather taught him to carve small animals and encouraged him to follow his interests. A delightful, down-to-earth and honorable man, Jamie is motivated by a genuine love for what he is doing. Renowned for his work, he has been invited as a guest artist to the Walt Disney World Teddy Bear & Doll Convention both in 1997 and 1998. His unique designs, combined with fine craftsmanship and an affordable price, make his teddy bears truly "Little Gems."

BILL YOUNGER

If Bill Younger could have his way, all lighthouses would be open to the public. As a lad, he would often observe lighthouses during trips to the Chesapeake Bay. Those memories, and his love for history, old buildings, and architecture, set the stage for Harbour Lights.

Bill feels that the true purpose of Harbour Lights is to promote history and maritime tradition. In each replica, he hopes to achieve a rendering that is artistically pleasing, and so accurate, that it is unmistakable from the real thing.

In the Spring of 1997, Bill Younger embarked on an exciting new adventure with the release of *Anchor Bay*, a brand new line of collectible boats and ships. Bill has longed to create a collection of sculptures devoted to watercraft and ocean-going vessels. Featuring hand-painted replicas of tugboats, steamships, cutters, trawlers, schooners, skipjacks, and the all-important lightship, *Anchor Bay* commemorates nautical history, recent, as well as past.

MARTIN ZENDRON

Born in the medieval town of Hall in Tyrol, Austria, Martin Zendron now lives and works only a few miles away in Wattens, the home of Swarovski.

In his late teens, Martin attended the world famous technical school for glass craft and design in Kramsach in Tyrol. Here he studied glass design with a special course in cutting and engraving. After graduation, he worked for a well-known Tyrolean retailer specializing in glass objects. There his work came to Swarovski's attention, where he became a designer in 1988.

His first creations for Swarovski Silver Crystal were the "Harp" and the "Lute," followed by the "Grand Piano," which all reveal a rare artistic talent and craftsmanship. He also created the first piece in the *Inspiration Africa* series, the "Elephant," and the "Unicorn" in the *Fabulous Creatures* series for the Swarovski Collectors Society.

Although Martin spends much of his spare time in the mountains, his real passion is deep-sea diving. For him, it is a wonderful way of relaxing from the precision and concentration required for his work with Swarovski.

PUBLICATIONS AND SHOWS

The following publications and show listings are designed to keep you current on the latest news about limited edition collectibles. In addition, many manufacturers and collectors' clubs publish newsletters that will help you enjoy your hobby to the fullest. See the club listing beginning on page 362 for information.

— BOOKS —

AMERICAN TEDDY BEAR ENCYCLOPEDIA
by Linda Mullins.
Hobby House Press.

THE CHILMARK COLLECTION
by Glenn S. Johnson and James E. Secky.
Commonwealth Press, Worcester, Massachusetts.

CHRISTMAS THROUGH THE DECADES
by Robert Brenner.
Schiffer Publishing.

CHRISTOPHER RADKO – THE FIRST DECADE (1986-1995)
by Christopher Radko for Starad, Inc.

DECK THE HALLS
by Robert Merck.
Abbeville Press.

DECORATING WITH COLLECTIBLES
by Annette R. Lough
Krause Publications

FENTON GLASS, THE FIRST TWENTY-FIVE YEARS (1905-1930)
by William Heacock.
Richardson Printing.

FENTON GLASS, THE SECOND TWENTY-FIVE YEARS (1931-1955)
by William Heacock.
Richardson Printing.

FENTON GLASS, THE THIRD TWENTY-FIVE YEARS (1956-1980)
by William Heacock.
Richardson Printing.

LLADRÓ – THE MAGIC WORLD OF PORCELAIN
by Several. Salvat.

MORE PRECIOUS THAN GOLD (A CHEESERVILLE TALE)
by Christine Thammavongsa.
GANZ.

NUMBER ONE PRICE GUIDE TO M.I. HUMMEL FIGURINES, PLATES, MINIATURES AND MORE
by Robert Miller.
Portfolio Press.

THE OFFICIAL LLADRÓ COLLECTION IDENTIFICATION CATALOG AND PRICE GUIDE
by Glenn S. Johnson.
Lladró Collectors Society.

THE OFFICIAL MSA IDENTIFICATION AND PRICE GUIDE TO THE CHILMARK COLLECTION
by Glenn S. Johnson and Ann Hagenstein. Grafacon, Hudson, Massachusetts.

THE SEBASTIAN MINIATURE COLLECTION
by Glenn S. Johnson.
Commonwealth Press, Worcester, Massachusetts.

THE STRACYL OF UNITY
by Allan Frost.
AJF Desk Top Publishing.

SWAROVSKI: THE MAGIC OF CRYSTAL
by Vivienne Becker.
Abrams, New York.

VALUE REGISTER HANDBOOK FOR SEBASTIAN MINIATURES
by Paul J. Sebastian.
The Sebastian Exchange, Lancaster, Pennsylvania.

— SHOWS —

INTERNATIONAL COLLECTIBLE EXPOSITION
c/o Krause Publications
700 E. State Street, Iola, WI 54990 (715) 445-2214

— MAGAZINES/NEWSLETTERS —

AMERICAN ARTIST
1515 Broadway
New York, NY 10036
(212) 536-5178

ANTIQUES & COLLECTING
1006 S. Michigan Avenue
Chicago, IL 60605
(312) 939-4767

THE ANTIQUE TRADER
P.O. Box 1050
Dubuque, IA 52004
(800) 334-7165

CIB COLLECTIBLES REPORT
5065 Shoreline Road, Suite 200
Barrington, IL 60010
(847) 842-2200

COLLECTOR EDITIONS
170 Fifth Avenue, 12th Floor
New York, NY 10010
(800) 728-2729

COLLECTOR'S MART
700 E. State Street
Iola, WI 54990
(715) 445-2214

COLLECTORS NEWS
P.O. Box 156
Grundy Center, IA 50638
(319) 824-6981

CONTEMPORARY DOLL COLLECTOR
30595 8 Mile
Livonia, MI 48152-1798
(248) 477-6650

DOLLS MAGAZINE
170 Fifth Avenue, 12th Floor
New York, NY 10010
(800) 728-2729

THE DOLL READER
6405 Flank Drive
Harrisburg, PA 17112
(717) 657-9555

FIGURINES & COLLECTIBLES
6405 Flank Drive
Harrisburg, PA 17112
(717) 657-9555

JOY OF COLLECTING
1333 Grandview Parkway
Sturtevant, WI 53177
(414) 884-3665

KOVELS ON ANTIQUES & COLLECTIBLES
P.O. Box 420347
Palm Coast, FL 32142-0347
(800) 829-9158

MINIATURE COLLECTOR
30595 8 Mile Rd.
Livonia, MI 48152-1798
(248) 477-6650

SOUTHWEST ART
P.O. Box 460535
Houston, TX 77056
(713) 850-0990

TEDDY BEAR AND FRIENDS
6405 Flank Drive
Harrisburg, PA 17112
(717) 657-9555

TEDDY BEAR REVIEW
170 Fifth Avenue, 12th Floor
New York, NY 10010
(800) 728-2729

U.S. ART
220 S. 6th Street, Suite 500
Minneapolis, MN 55402
(612) 339-7571

VILLAGE CHRONICLE
757 Park Ave.
Cranston, RI 02910
(401) 467-9343

WILDLIFE ART
4725 Highway 7
St. Louis Park, MN 55416
(612) 927-9056

NATIONAL COLLECTORS' CLUBS

Club	Annual Dues/Renewals	Club Year	Membership Gift	Members-Only Piece	Club Publication	Binder	Membership Card	Buy-Sell Matching Service	Local Chapters	Tours/Special Events	Other Benefits
"A Nation of Shopkeepers™" Collectors Club* **Hazle Ceramics** Stallion's Yard Codham Hall, Great Warley Brentwood, Essex CMI3 3JT United Kingdom 01144 1277 220892	$40./16.	Anniv. of Sign-Up Date	●	●	3/yr.						Membership Certificate
All God's Children Collector's Club* **Miss Martha Originals** P.O. Box 5038 Glencoe, AL 35905 (205) 492-0221	20.	June 1-May 31	●	●	4/yr.		●		●	●	Personal Checklist
The Anheuser-Busch Collectors Club* 2700 South Broadway St. Louis, MO 63118 (800) 305-2582	35.-1yr. 65.-2yrs.	Jan.-Dec.	●	●	4/yr.	●	●	●			Monthly Contests, Notification of Artist Events
Annalee Doll Society* P.O. Box 1137 Meredith, NH 03253-1137 (800) 433-6557	29.95	July 1-June 30	●	●	4/yr.		●			●	Membership Pin
ANRI Collector's Society* P.O. Box 380760 Duncanville, TX 75138 (800) 730-ANRI (2674)	35.	Jan.-Dec.	●	●	3/yr.		●	●		●	Full-Color Brochure, Research Dept., Authorized Retailer Listing
The Belleek Collectors International Society 9893 Georgetown Pike, Suite 525 Great Falls, VA 22066 (800)-BELLEEK	38.50/ 28.50	Anniv. of Sign-Up Date	●	●	3/yr.	●	●	●	●	●	Membership Certificate, Full Color Catalog, Annual Renewal Gift
Boehm Porcelain Society 25 Fairfacts Street Trenton, NJ 08638 (800) 257-9410	15.	Jan.-Dec.		●	1/yr.			●		●	Catalogs
Brandywine Neighborhood Association* 4303 Manchester Rd. Portsmouth, VA 23703 (757) 898-5031	30./25.	Anniv. of Sign-Up Date	●	●	4/yr.					●	Canvas Book Bag, Storage Case for Newsletters
Brian Baker's Déjà Vu Collectors' Club* **GiftStar, Inc.** 630A Airpark Rd. Napa, CA 94558 (888) 893-2323	35.	Mar.-Feb.	●	●	4/yr.		●			●	
Cabbage Patch Kids® Collectors Club* **Original Appalachian Artworks** P.O. Box 714 Cleveland, GA 30528 (706) 865-2171	25.	Anniv. of Sign-Up Date	●	●	6/yr.	●	●	●		●	Pin, Members-Only Merchandise Available
Caithness Glass Paperweight Collectors' Club 141 Lanza Ave., Bldg. 12 Garfield, NJ 07026 (201) 340-3330	40.-1yr. 70.-2yrs.	Anniv. of Sign-Up Date	●	●	4/yr.	●	●	●		●	Catalogs
The Cardew Collectors' Club* c/o DeVine Corporation 1345 Campus Parkway Neptune, NJ 07753 (732) 751-0500	40.	Anniv. of Sign-Up Date	●	●	4/yr.		●			●	Cardew Teapot Collection Catalog
Cat's Meow Collectors Club* **FJ Designs** 2163 Great Trails Dr. Wooster, OH 44691-3738 (330) 264-1377 Ext. 225	$33./22.	Anniv. of Sign-Up Date	●	●	4/yr.	●	●	●		●	Deed Holder

* For more information, see company feature articles (pp. 57-319).

NATIONAL COLLECTORS' CLUBS

Club	Annual Dues/Renewals	Club Year	Membership Gift	Members-Only Piece	Club Publication	Binder	Membership Card	Buy-Sell Matching Service	Local Chapters	Tours/Special Events	Other Benefits
Cavanagh's Coca-Cola Christmas Collectors Society* P.O. Box 768090 Roswell, GA 30076 (800) 653-1221	$ 25.	Jan.-Dec.	●		4/yr.		●				Membership Certificate, Special Items Offer
The Cherished Teddies Club* **Enesco Corporation** P.O. Box 99 Itasca, IL 60143-0099 (630) 875-8540	23.-1yr./ 38.-2yrs.	Jan. 1-Dec. 31	●	●	●						Lapel Pin, Easel Replica, Catalog, Membership Ticket with Holder
Christian Ulbricht Collectors' Club* P.O. Box 99 Angwin, CA 94508 (888) 707-5591	45.	Anniv. of Sign-Up Date	●	●	2/yr.	●	●			●	Collector's Log
Daddy's Long Legs Collectors Club 300 Bank St. Southlake, TX 76092 (888) 2-DADDYS	25.	Anniv. of Sign-Up Date	●	●	4/yr.		●	●		●	Advance Notice of Retirements and New Releases, Contests
David Winter Cottages Collectors' Guild* **Enesco Corporation** P.O. Box 479 Itasca, IL 60143-0479 (800) NEAR-YOU	42./80.	Anniv. of Sign-Up Date	●	●	4/yr.		●			●	Notification of Retirements and New Releases, Catalog,
Dreamsicles Collectors' Club* **Cast Art Industries** 1120 California Avenue Corona, CA 91719 (800) 437-5818	27.50/ 23.50	Anniv. of Sign-Up Date	●	●	4/yr.	●	●	●		●	Pin, Photo Book
Duncan Royale Collectors Club* 1141 S. Acacia Ave. Fullerton, CA 92631 (714) 879-1360	30.	Anniv. of Sign-Up Date	●	●	●	●	●				Certificate, Catalog, Free Figurine Registration
EKJ Collectors' Society* **Flambro Imports** P.O. Box 93507 Atlanta, GA 30377-0507 (800) EKJ-CLUB	30.	Jan.-Dec.	●	●	4/yr.	●	●			●	Toll Free Hotline, EKJ Pin, Catalog, Free Figurine Registration, Collector Registry Listing
The Ebony Visions Circle* **Willitts Designs International** P.O. Box 750009 Petaluma, CA 94975 (888) 701-2373	40.	Jan.-Dec.	●	●	4/yr.		●			●	
Edna Hibel Society P.O. Box 9721 Coral Springs, FL 33075 (561) 848-9663	20.-1yr./ 35.-2yrs.	Anniv. of Sign-Up Date	●	●	2/yr.		●			●	Previews of Hibel Artworks, 4 Types of Membership
Enchantica Collectors Club* **Munro Collectibles, Inc.** 1220 Waterville-Monclova Rd. Waterville, OH 43566 (419) 878-0034	35.-1yr. 60.-2yrs.	Jan.-Dec.	●	●	3/yr.		●			●	Catalog
Fenton Art Glass Collectors of America (FAGCA)* P.O. Box 384 Williamstown, WV 26187 (304) 375-6196	20.	Anniv. of Sign-Up Date		●	6/yr.			●	●	●	
Fontanini Collectors' Club* **Roman, Inc.** 555 Lawrence Avenue Roselle, IL 60172 (800) 729-7662	22.-1yr./ 39.-2yrs.	Anniv. of Sign-Up Date	●	●	4/yr.		●			●	Registry Guide, Pin, Portfolio, Contests
Gartlan USA's "New" Collectors' League* 575 Rt. 73 N., Ste. A-6 West Berlin, NJ 08091 (609) 753-9229	30./20.	Anniv. of Sign-Up Date	●	●	4/yr.		●	●		●	Advance Notice of New Releases, Free Gifts at Special Events

* For more information, see company feature articles (pp. 57-319).

NATIONAL COLLECTORS' CLUBS

Club	Annual Dues/Renewals	Club Year	Membership Gift	Members-Only Piece	Club Publication	Binder	Membership Card	Buy-Sell Matching Service	Local Chapters	Tours/Special Events	Other Benefits
The Great American Collectors' Club P.O. Box 428 Aberdeen, NC 28315 (910) 944-7447	None	Jan.-Dec.		●	3/yr.			●		●	Membership Free with Purchase of Club Piece, Early Preview of New Releases
Hallmark Keepsake Ornament Collector's Club P.O. Box 419824 Kansas City, MO 64141-6824 (800) 523-5839	$22.50	Jan.-Dec.	●	●	4/yr.		●	●	●	●	Early Mailing of *Dreambook* and Events
Harbour Lights Collectors Society* 1000 N. Johnson Ave. El Cajon, CA 92020 (800) 365-1219	30.	May 1-Apr. 30	●	●	4/yr.	●	●				Cloissoné Pin, Membership Certificate, Print of Redemption Piece Free to Renewing Members
Heirloom Collection Collector's Club* **Carlton Cards** One American Rd. Cleveland, OH 44144 (888) 222-7898	20.	July 1-June 30	●	●	4/yr.	●					Pin, Collector's Guide
House of Hatten Collectors' Club* 301 Inner Loop Rd. Georgetown, TX 78626 (512) 819-9600	20.	Anniv. of Sign-Up Date	●		●		●				Catalog, List of Authorized Dealers
Jan Hagara Collectors' Club* 40114 Industrial Park Georgetown, TX 78626 (512) 863-9499	44./39.	July 1-June 30	●	●	4/yr.	●	●	●	●	●	Cloisonné Pin, Contests, National Convention, Drawings, Savings on Products
Keeper™ Klub* **Shenandoah Designs International, Inc.** P.O. Box 911 Rural Retreat, VA 24368 (800) 338-7644	37.50	Anniv. of Sign-Up Date	●	●	4/yr.		●				Satchel, Key Chain, Stationery, Certificate, Keeper™ Shelf, Keeper™ Kards
Krystonia Collectors Club* **Precious Art** 125 W. Ellsworth Rd. Ann Arbor, MI 48108 (313) 663-1885	30.	Feb. 1-Jan. 31	●	●	4/yr.		●			●	
The Leaf & Acorn Club* **Charming Tails/** **Fitz & Floyd Collectibles Division** P.O. Box 78218 St. Louis, MO 63178-8218 (800) 486-1065	24.50	Jan.-Dec.	●	●	●		●			●	Members-Only Offers
Lee's Doll Family* **Lee Middleton Original Dolls** 1301 Washington Blvd. Belpre, OH 45714 (800) 238-2225	35.	Anniv. of Sign-Up Date	●	●	4/yr.	●	●				
Lilliput Lane Collectors' Club* P.O. Box 498 Itasca, IL 60143-0498 (630) 875-5382	40.-1yr. 65.-2yrs.	May 1-Apr. 30	●	●	4/yr.		●			●	Catalog
The Lizzie High Society* **Ladie and Friends** 220 North Main Street Sellersville, PA 18960 (800) 76-DOLLS	25./15.	Jan.-Dec.	●	●	2/yr.	●	●	●		●	Catalog, Pewter Ornament
Lladró Society* 1 Lladró Drive Moonachie, NJ 07074 (888) GIVE-LLADRO	$45./35.	Anniv. of Sign-Up Date	●	●	4/yr.	●	●			●	Video, Research Service Associate Membership to Lladró Museum
M.I. Hummel Club* Goebel Plaza, P.O. Box 11 Pennington, NJ 08534-0011 (800) 666-CLUB (2582)	50./37.50	June 1-May 31	●	●	4/yr.	●	●	●	●	●	Research Service, Annual Contests, Anniversary Pins

* For more information, see company feature articles (pp. 57-319).

NATIONAL COLLECTORS' CLUBS

	Annual Dues/Renewals	Club Year	Membership Gift	Members-Only Piece	Club Publication	Binder	Membership Card	Buy-Sell Matching Service	Local Chapters	Tours/Special Events	Other Benefits
Madame Alexander Doll Club* P.O. Box 330 Mundelein, IL 60060	$20.(US) 30.(International)	Annual	●	●	2/yr.		●	●		●	
Mark Hopkins Bronze Guild 21 Shorter Industrial Blvd. Rome, GA 30165-1838 (800) 678-6564	None				2/yr.			●		●	
Melody In Motion Collectors Club* **WACO Products Corporation** P.O. Box 898 Pine Brook, NJ 07058-0898 (973) 882-1820	27.50	Anniv. of Sign-Up Date	●	●	●		●			●	Catalog, "Savings" Coupon, Personal Purchasing Record, Retired Edition Summary, List of Collectors' Centers
Memories of Yesterday Collectors' Society* **Enesco Corporation** P.O. Box 499 Itasca, IL 60143-0499 (630) 875-8540	22.50-1yr. 42.-2yrs.	Jan. 1-Dec. 31	●	●	4/yr.		●				Catalog, Plush Teddy Bear
Myth and Magic Collectors' Club The Tudor Mint 2601 South Park Rd. Pembroke Park, FL 33009 (800) 455-8715	37.50	July 1-June 30	●		2/yr.		●			●	Catalog and Updates
National Fenton Glass Society (NFGS)* P.O. Box 4008 Marietta, OH 45750	15.	Anniv. of Sign-Up Date		●	6/yr.			●	●	●	
Old World Christmas Collectors' Club P.O. Box 8000 Department C Spokane, WA 99203 (800) 962-7669	30.-1yr. 57.-2yrs. 83.-3yrs.	Anniv. of Sign-Up Date	●	●	4/yr.		●	●			Collectors' Guide, Local Retailer Listings, Video
PFC Collectors Club* **Pulaski Furniture Corporation** P.O. Box 1371 Pulaski, VA 24301 (540) 980-7330	29.95/ 24.95	Anniv. of Sign-Up Date	●		4/yr.		●				Sneak Previews, Member Incentives for Purchase of Pulaski Furniture
Pacific Northwest Fenton Association (PNWFA)* 8225 Kilchis River Rd. Tillamook, OR 97141	20.	Anniv. of Sign-Up Date	●	●	4/yr.					●	
PenDelfin Family Circle Miller Import Corp. 230 Spring Street N.W. Atlanta Gift Mart, Suite 1238 Atlanta, GA 30303 (404) 523-3380 or (800) 872-4876	30.	Jan.-Dec.	●	●	4/yr.		●	●		●	Membership Certificate
Pennibears Collectors Club 1413 N.E. Lincoln Avenue Moore, OK 73160 (405) 799-0006	5.	Anniv. of Sign-Up Date		●	1/yr.		●				
Pipka's Memories of Christmas Collectors' Club* P.O. Box 1106 Manhattan, KS 66505 (888) 427-4752	40.	Anniv. of Sign-Up Date	●	●	●	●					Membership Certificate Suitable for Framing, Autographed Photo of Pipka, Pin
Pocket Dragons and Friends Collectors Club* **Flambro Imports** P.O. Box 93507 Atlanta, GA 30377-0507 (800) 355-2582	29.50-1yr. 54.-2yrs.	June 1-May 30	●	●	4/yr.		●			●	Pin, Catalog, Toll Free Hotline
Polonaise Collector's Guild* **Kurt S. Adler, Inc.** 1107 Broadway New York, NY 10010 (212) 924-0900 Ext. 214	50.	Anniv. of Sign-Up Date	●	●							

* For more information, see company feature articles (pp. 57-319).

NATIONAL COLLECTORS' CLUBS

Club	Annual Dues/Renewals	Club Year	Membership Gift	Members-Only Piece	Club Publication	Binder	Membership Card	Buy-Sell Matching Service	Local Chapters	Tours/Special Events	Other Benefits
Precious Moments Birthday Club* P.O. Box 689 Itasca, IL 60143-0689 (630) 875-8540	$ 21.-1yr. 40.-2yrs.	July 1- June 30	●	●	●		●				Personal, Happy Birthday Card
Precious Moments Collectors' Club* P.O. Box 219 Itasca, IL 60143-0219 (630) 875-8540	27.50-1yr. 53.-2yrs	Jan. 1- Dec. 31	●	●	●	●	●			●	2 Table Placemats, Special Mailings
Red Mill Collectors Society One Hunters Ridge Summersville, WV 26651 (304) 872-5237	15.	Mar. 31 and Sept. 30		●	3/yr.		●	●			
Rob Anders Collectors Society* Porterfield's 5 Mountain Rd. Concord, NH 03301 (800) 660-8345	19.	Annual	●		4/yr.						Sneak Previews, Special Contests for Prizes, Secondary Market Updates
Ron Lee's Collectors Club 330 Carousel Parkway Henderson, NV 89014 (800) 829-3928	30.	Anniv. of Sign-Up Date	●	●	4/yr.					●	New Product Brochures
Royal Crown Derby Collectors Guild* Royal Doulton 701 Cottontail Lane Somerset, NJ 08873 (800) 747-3045	50.	Anniv. of Sign-Up Date	●	●	4/yr.		●	●		●	Free Admission to Royal Crown Derby Museum and Factory Tours, Historical Enquiry Service
Royal Doulton International Collectors Club* 701 Cottontail Lane Somerset, NJ 08873 (800) 747-3045	50.	Anniv. of Sign-Up Date	●	●	4/yr.	●		●	●	●	Free Admission to Royal Doulton Museum and Factory Tours, Historical Enquiry Services, Advance Mailings
The Royal Watch™ Society* Harmony Kingdom 232 Neilston St. Columbus, OH 43215 (614) 469-0600	35.	Anniv. of Sign-Up Date	●	●	4/yr.		●	●			Product Folio with Catalogs, Contests, Members-Only Merchandise Available
Sandicast Collectors Guild P.O. Box 910079 San Diego, CA 92191 (800) 722-3316	25.-1yr. 48.-2yrs.	Anniv. of Sign-Up Date	●		2/yr.		●	●		●	Catalog Reference Guide
San Francisco Music Box Company Collector's Club* P.O. Box 7465 San Fransisco, CA 94120 (800) 635-9064	Free with Purchase	Anniv. of Sign-Up Date			●		●			●	$10 Collector's Certificate Awarded Every Time Customer Accumulates $100 in Purchases, Advance Notice of Sales, Private Club Sales
Santa Claus Network* Possible Dreams 6 Perry Drive Foxboro, MA 02035-1051 (508) 543-6667	25.	Anniv. of Sign-Up Date	●	●	4/yr.		●	●			Collectors Guide Book — Directory of Clothtique Santas
Sarah's Attic Forever Friends Collectors' Club* P.O. Box 448 Chesaning, MI 48616 (800) 4-FRIEND	32.50	Jan.- Dec.	●	●	4/yr.		●		●	●	Folder with Logo
The Sebastian Exchange Collectors Association* Hudson Creek P.O. Box 10905 Lancaster, PA 17605-0905 (717) 392-2978	32.	Anniv. of Sign-Up Date	●	●	3/yr.		●	●		●	Annual Value Register and Updates

* For more information, see company feature articles (pp. 57-319).

NATIONAL COLLECTORS' CLUBS

	Annual Dues/Renewals	Club Year	Membership Gift	Members-Only Piece	Club Publication	Binder	Membership Card	Buy-Sell Matching Service	Local Chapters	Tours/Special Events	Other Benefits
Seraphim Classics Collectors Club[SM]* Roman, Inc. 555 Lawrence Ave. Roselle, IL 60172 (800) 729-7662	$55. (plus $4.50 s&h)	Anniv. of Sign-Up Date	●	●	4/yr.		●				Catalog, Pin
Seymour Mann, Inc. Doll Club* 230 Fifth Ave., Suite 1500 New York, NY 10001 (212) 683-7262	17.50	Jan.-Dec.	●	●	●		●	●			
Shelia's Collectors Society* 1856 Belgrade Avenue Charleston, SC 29407 (800) 695-8686	32.50	Anniv. of Sign-Up Date	●	●	4/yr.		●			●	Travel Case
Snowbabies Collectors' Club* Department 56, Inc. P.O. Box 44456 Eden Prairie, MN 55344-1456 (888) SNOWBABY	35.	Dec.-Nov.	●	●	●		●			●	Certificate, Snowbabies Mechanical Drawing, Pin
The Society of Giuseppe Armani Art* 300 Mac Lane Keasbey, NJ 08832 (800) 3-ARMANI	50./37.50	Jan.-Dec.	●	●	4/yr.		●			●	Framed Membership Certificate, Magazine Holder, Pin
Spencer Collin Lighthouses Collectors Club* Dave Grossman Creations 1608 N. Warson Rd. St. Louis, MO 63132 (800) 325-1655	30./25.	Jan.-Dec.	●	●	●	●	●	●		●	
Starlight Family of Collectors* Christopher Radko P.O. Box 533 Elmsford, NY 10523 (800) 71-RADKO	50./37.50	Jan.-Dec.	●	●	4/yr.		●				Ornament Button, Pin, Catalog, Multiple Year Membership Plan Available
The Steinbach Collectors' Club* Kurt S. Adler, Inc. 1107 Broadway New York, NY 10010 (212) 924-0900 Ext. 281	45./35.	Anniv. of Sign-Up Date	●	●	●		●				Portfolio, Pin, Membership Certificate
Swarovski Collectors Society* 2 Slater Road Cranston, RI 02920 (800) 426-3088	35./30.	Jan.-Dec.	●	●	4/yr.		●			●	Magazine Box Available for Purchase
Thomas Kinkade Collectors' Society* Media Arts Group Inc. P.O. Box 90267 San Jose, CA 95109 (800) 544-4890 Ext. 1543 and 1587	45.-1yr. 75.-2yrs.	Jan.-Dec.	●	●	4/yr.		●			●	Lapel Pin
Treasury Ornaments Collectors' Club* Enesco Corporation P.O. Box 277 Itasca, IL 60143-0277 (630) 875-8540	22.50-1yr. 42.50-2yrs.	Jan. 1-Dec. 31	●	●	●		●				Catalog
Walt Disney Collectors Society* 500 S. Buena Vista St. Burbank, CA 91521-8028 (800) 932-5749	49.-1yr. 95.-2yrs.	Anniv. of Sign-Up Date	●	●	4/yr.		●			●	Cloissoné Pin
Wizards and Dragons Collectors' Fellowship* Flambro Imports P.O. Box 93507 Atlanta, GA 30377-0707 (800) 355-2582	10.	Anniv. of Sign-Up Date		●	4/yr.		●				Pin, Catalog

* For more information, see company feature articles (pp. 57-319).

DIRECTORY OF COLLECTIBLES MANUFACTURERS

"Who's Who" in Limited Edition Collectibles

This directory provides information about many companies actively involved in the field of limited edition collectibles. Collectors will find this listing helpful when inquiring about a firm's products and services.

Ace Product Management Group
9053 N. Deerbrook Trail
Brown Deer, WI 53223
(414) 365-5400
Fax: (414) 365-5410
Specialty: Figurines.

Akira Trading Co., Inc./
Little Gem Teddy Bears
6040 N.W. 84th Ave.
Miami, FL 33166
(305) 639-9801
Fax: (305) 639-9802
Specialty: See article on page 219.

Alexander Doll Company, Inc.
615 West 131st St.
New York, NY 10027
(212) 283-5900
Fax: (212) 283-4901
URL: http://www.alexanderdoll.com
Specialty: See article on page 57.

American Artist Portfolio, Inc.
9625 Tetley Drive
Somerset, VA 22972
(540) 672-0400
Fax: (540) 672-0286
Specialty: Graphics.

American Artists
66 Poppasquash Road
Bristol, RI 02809
(401) 254-1191
Fax: (401) 254-8881
Specialty: Lithos and plates.

Andrew D. Darvas Inc.
2165 Dwight Way
Berkeley, CA 94704
(510) 843-7838
Fax: (510) 843-1815
Specialty: Wall plaques.

Angela Trotta Thomas
1107 E. Longwood Drive
Clarks Summit, PA 18411
(717) 586-0774
Fax: (717) 586-0774
Specialty: Graphics.

Anheuser-Busch, Inc.
2700 South Broadway
St. Louis, MO 63118
(800) 325-9665
Fax: (314) 577-9656
URL: http://www.budweiser.com
Specialty: See article on page 60.

Annalee Mobilitee Dolls, Inc.
50 Resevoir Road
Meredith, NH 03253-1137
(603) 279-3333
Fax: (603) 279-6659
URL: http://www.annalee.com
Specialty: See article on page 63.

Anna-Perenna Inc.
35 River Street
New Rochelle, NY 10801
(914) 633-3777
Fax: (914) 633-8727
Specialty: Figurines, ornaments and plates.

ANRI U.S.
P.O. Box 380760
1126 So. Cedar Ridge, Ste. 122
Duncanville, TX 75138-0760
(800) 730-ANRI (2674)
Fax: (972) 283-3522
E-mail: anriwood@aol.com
URL: http://www.anri.com
Specialty: See article on page 66.

The Society of
Giuseppe Armani Art
Miller Import Corp.
300 Mac Lane
Keasbey, NJ 08832
(800) 3-ARMANI
Fax: (732) 417-0031
E-mail: miller_society @prodigy.com
URL: http://www.the-society.com
Specialty: See article on page 69.

The Art of Glynda Turley
P.O. Box 1073
4354 Gretna Road
Branson, MO 65616
(888) 4-GLYNDA
Fax: (417) 334-8722
E-mail: glynda@cswnet.com
URL: http://www.nerosworld.com/glyndaturley/mainindex.html
Specialty: See article on page 72.

Artists of the World
2915 N. 67th Place
Scottsdale, AZ 85251
(602) 946-6361
Fax: (602) 941-8918
Specialty: DeGrazia plates and figurines.

The Ashton-Drake Galleries
9200 N. Maryland Avenue
Niles, IL 60714
(800) 634-5164
Fax: (847) 966-3026
E-mail: custsrv@ashtondrake.com
URL: http://www.ashtondrake.com
Specialty: See article on page 75.

The B & J Company
P.O. Box 67
Georgetown, TX 78626
(512) 863-8318
Fax: (512) 863-0833
Specialty: Dolls, figurines, miniatures, plates and prints.

Belleek Collectors' International Society
9893 Georgetown Pike
Great Falls, VA 22066
(800) - BELLEEK
Fax: (703) 847-6201
Specialty: Belleek china and plates.

Bill Vernon Studios
4248 Burning Town Road
Franklin, NC 28734
(800) 327-6923
Fax: (704) 349-3253
Specialty: Figurines.

Boehm Porcelain Studio
25 Fairfacts Street
Trenton, NJ 08638
(800) 257-9410
Fax: (609) 392-1437
Specialty: Dolls, figurines and plates.

BORSE, Inc.
P.O. Box 455
Blooming Prairie, MN 55917
(800) 339-6329
Fax: (507) 583-2860
Specialty: Figurines.

The Boyds Collection Ltd.
Somethin' Ta Say Dept.
Gettysburg, PA 17325-4385
Specialty: Figurines.

The Bradford Exchange
9333 Milwaukee Avenue
Niles, IL 60714
(800) 323-5577
E-mail: custsrv@bradex.com
URL: http://www.bradex.com
http://www.collectibles-today.net
Specialty: See article on page 78.

Bradley Doll
1400 N. Spring Street
Los Angeles, CA 90012
(213) 221-4162
Fax: (213) 221-8272
Specialty: Dolls.

Brandywine Collectibles
104 Greene Dr.
Yorktown, VA 23692-4800
(757) 898-5031
Fax: (757) 898-6895
E-mail: heartbwine@aol.com
URL: http://www.brandywinecollectibles.com
Specialty: See article on page 81.

Briant & Sons
5250 SW Tomahawk
Redmond, OR 97756
(541) 923-1473
Fax: (541) 923-7403
Specialty: Plate hangers, accessories and ornament stands.

Buccellati Silver Ltd.
P.O. Box 360
East Longmeadow, MA 01028
(413) 525-4800
Fax: (413) 525-8877
Specialty: Ornaments.

Byers' Choice Ltd.
4355 County Line Road
Chalfont, PA 18914
(215) 822-0150
Fax: (215) 822-3847
URL: http://www.byerschoice.com
Specialty: See article on page 84.

Cairn Studio
P.O. Box 400
Davidson, NC 28036
(704) 892-3581
Specialty: Figurines.

Caithness Glass Inc.
141 Lanza Avenue, Bldg. 12
Garfield, NJ 07026
(973) 340-3330
Fax: (973) 340-9415
Specialty: Glass paperweights.

Cameo Guild Studios
5217 Verdugo Way, Suite D
Camarillo, CA 93012
(805) 388-1223
Specialty: California missions, miniatures and plates.

Cardew Design
c/o Devine Corp.
1345 Campus Parkway
Neptune, NJ 07753
(732) 751-0500
Fax: (732) 751-0550
Specialty: See article on page 87.

Carlton Cards
One American Road
Cleveland, OH 44114
(888) 222-7898
Fax: (216) 252-6751
Specialty: See article on page 90.

Cast Art Industries, Inc.
1120 California Avenue
Corona, CA 91719
(800) 932-3020
Fax: (909) 371-0674
E-mail: info@castart.com
URL: http://www.castart.com
http://www.dreamsicles.com
http://www.dreamsiclesclub.com
http://www.bumpkins.com
http://www.ivy-innocence.com
http://www.slapstix.com
Specialty: See article on page 93.

Cavanagh Group International
1000 Holcomb Woods Pkwy. #440-B
Roswell, GA 30076
(770) 643-1175
Fax: (770) 643-1172
Specialty: See article on page 96.

Cazenovia Abroad
67 Albany Street
Cazenovia, NY 13035
(315) 655-3433
Fax: (315) 655-4249
Specialty: Sterling silver figurines and ornaments.

Character Collectibles
10861 Business Drive
Fontana, CA 92337
(909) 822-9999
Fax: (909) 823-6666
E-mail: characoll@aol.com
Specialty: Figurines.

Christian Ulbricht USA
P.O. Box 99
Angwin, CA 94508
(888) 707-5591
Fax: (707) 965-4199
E-mail: nutcracker@culbricht.com
URL: http://www.culbricht.com
Specialty: See article on page 186.

Christina's World
27 Woodcreek Court
Deer Park, NY 11729
(516) 242-9664
Fax: (516) 586-1918
E-mail: buytrim@aol.com
Specialty: Ornaments.

Christopher Radko
P.O. Box 533
Elmsford, NY 10523
(800) 71-RADKO
URL: http://www.christopher radko.com
Specialty: See article on page 102.

Clay Art
239 Utah Avenue
So. San Francisco, CA 94080
(415) 244-4970
Fax: (415) 244-4979
Specialty: Masks.

The Constance Collection
11700 Rogues Rd.
Midland, VA 22728
(540) 788-4500
Fax: (540) 788-3150
Specialty: Figurines.

Cottage Collectibles by Ganz, Inc.
908 Niagara Falls Blvd.
North Tonawanda, NY 14120-2060
(800) 724-5902
Fax: (905) 851-6669
URL: http://www.ganz.org
E-mail: headoffice@ganz.org
Specialty: See article on page 105.

Country Artists US
9305 Gerwig Lane, Ste. P
Columbia, MD 21046
(410) 290-8990
Fax: (410) 290-5480
Specialty: Figurines.

Coyne's & Company
7400 Boone Avenue North
Minneapolis, MN 55428
(612) 425-8666
Fax: (612) 425-1653
Specialty: Figurines, ornaments and dolls.

Cross Gallery, Inc.
180 N. Center
(Mail: P.O. Box 4181)
Jackson Hole, WY 83001
(307) 733-2200
Fax: (307) 733-1414
Specialty: Graphics, ornaments and plates.

Crystal World
3 Borinski Drive
Lincoln Park, NJ 07035
(800) 445-4251
Fax: (973) 633-0102
E-mail: gift@crystalworld.com
URL: http://www.crystal world.com
Specialty: See article on page 108.

Cybis
65 Norman Avenue
Trenton, NJ 08618
(609) 392-6074
Specialty: Figurines and ornaments.

Dave Grossman Creations, Inc.
1608 N. Warson Road
St. Louis, MO 63132
(800) 325-1655
Fax: (314) 423-7620
E-mail: dgcrea@aol.com
Specialty: See article on page 111.

David Winter Cottages
c/o Enesco Corporation
P.O. Box 479
Itasca, IL 60143-0479
(800) NEAR-YOU
URL: http://www.enesco.com
Specialty: See article on page 114.

Dear Artistic Sculpture, Inc.
P.O. Box 860
Oaks, PA 19456-0860
(610) 666-1650
Fax: (610) 666-1379
E-mail: napusa@aol.com
Specialty: Figurines.

Deb Canham Artist Designs, Inc.
820 Albee Rd., Suite 1
Nokomis, FL 34275
(941) 480-1200
Fax: (941) 480-1202
E-mail: deb@deb-canham.acun.com
URL: http://www.deb-canham. acun.com
Specialty: See article on page 117.

Department 56, Inc.
P.O. Box 44456
Eden Prairie, MN 55344-1456
(800) 548-8696
URL: http://www.department56.com
http://www.dept56.com
http://www.d56.com
Specialty: See article on page 120.

Donald Zolan Studio
29 Cambridge Drive
Hershey, PA 17033-2173
(717) 534-2446
Specialty: Plates and prints.

Donjo Studios Inc.
31149 Via Colinas, Suite 503
Westlake Village, CA 91362
(818) 865-2390
Fax: (818) 865-0990
Specialty: Crystal figurines and miniatures.

Dram Tree/C.U.I.
1502 N. 23rd Street
Wilmington, NC 28405
(910) 251-1110
Specialty: Steins.

Duncan Royale
1141 S. Acacia St.
Fullerton, CA 92631
(714) 879-1360
Fax: (714) 879-4611
URL: http://www.duncan royale.com
Specialty: See article on page 123.

Ebeling & Reuss Co.
P.O. Box 1289
Allentown, PA 18105-1289
(610) 366-8304
Fax: (610) 366-8307
Specialty: Figurines and teacups.

Edna Hibel Studio
P.O. Box 9967
Riviera Beach, FL 33419
(561) 848-9633
Fax: (561) 848-9640
Specialty: Bells, crystal, dolls, figurines, graphics (original lithographs and serigraphs, limited edition reproductions), ornaments and plates.

Egg Fantasy
4040 Schiff Drive
Las Vegas, NV 89103
(702) 368-7747
Specialty: Egg creations.

eggspressions! inc.
1635 Deadwood Avenue
Rapid City, SD 57702
(800) 551-9138
Fax: (605) 342-8699
Specialty: See article on page 126.

Eklund's Ltd.
1701 W. St. Germain
St. Cloud, MN 56301
(320) 252-1318
Fax: (320) 252-9397
Specialty: Plates and mugs.

Enesco Corporation
225 Windsor Drive
Itasca, IL 60143
(800) 4-ENESCO
Fax: (630) 875-5464
URL: http://www.enesco.com
Specialty: See article on page 129.

Ertl Collectibles™ Limited
P.O. Box 500
Highways 136 & 20
Dyersville, IA 52040
(800) 553-4886
Fax: (319) 875-5674
Specialty: See article on page 132.

FJ Designs, Inc.
Makers of Cat's Meow Village
2163 Great Trails Drive
Wooster, OH 44691-3738
(330) 264-1377
Fax: (330) 263-0219
E-mail: cmu@fjdesign.com
URL: http://www.catsmeow.com
Specialty: See article on page 135.

The Fabergé Collection
35 Danbury Road
Wilton, CT 06897
(203) 761-8882
Fax: (203) 834-2178
Specialty: Egg art.

Federica Doll Company
4501 W. Highland Road
Milford, MI 48380
(810) 887-9575
Fax: (810) 887-9575
Specialty: Dolls.

The Fenton Art Glass Company
700 Elizabeth Street
Williamstown, WV 26187
(304) 375-6122
Fax: (304) 375-6459
E-mail: fentonglass@citynet.net
URL: http://www.fenton-glass.com
Specialty: See article on page 138.

Figaro Import Corporation
325 South Flores Street
San Antonio, TX 78204-1178
(210) 225-1167
Specialty: Figurines.

Figi Graphics
3636 Gateway Center
San Diego, CA 92102
(619) 262-8811
Fax: (619) 264-7781
Specialty: Figurines.

Fitz and Floyd Collectibles Division
501 Corporate Dr.
Lewisville, TX 75057
(800) 527-9550
Fax: (800) 276-2605
Specialty: See article on page 99.

Flambro Imports
1530 Ellsworth Industrial Dr.
Atlanta, GA 30306
(404) 352-1381
Fax: (404) 352-2150
E-mail: collsoc@flambro.com
URL: http://www.flambro.com
http://www.signature collections.com
Specialty: See article on page 141.

Fontanini Heirloom Nativities
c/o Roman, Inc.
555 Lawrence Ave.
Roselle, IL 60172-1599
(630) 529-3000
Fax: (630) 529-1121
URL: http://www.roman.com
Specialty: See article on page 144.

Fool Moon Treasures
P.O. Box 10473
Tallahasee, FL 32302
(850) 877-2151
Fax: (850) 877-1097
Specialty: See article on page 147.

Forest Lamps & Gifts, Inc.
728 61st Street
Brooklyn, NY 11220-4298
(718) 492-0200
Fax: (718) 439-7719
Specialty: Figurines.

Forma Vitrum
20414 N. Main Street
Cornelius, NC 28031
(800) 596-9963
Fax: (704) 892-5438
E-mail: formavit@aol.com
Specialty: See article on page 150.

Fort, Inc.
54 Taylor Drive
E. Providence, RI 02916
(800) 678-3678
Fax: (401) 434-6956
Specialty: Pewter figurines.

The Franklin Mint
U.S. Route 1
Franklin Center, PA 19091
(800) 843-6468
Fax: (610) 459-6880
Specialty: See article on page 153.

Fraser International
5990 N. Belt East, Unit 606
Humble, TX 77396
(800) 878-5448
Fax: (281) 441-7707
Specialty: Miniature historical buildings.

Gartlan USA, Inc.
575 Rt. 73 North, Suite A-6
West Berlin, NJ 08091
(609) 753-9229
Fax: (609) 753-9280
E-mail: info@gartlanusa.com
URL: http://www.gartlanusa.com
Specialty: See article on page 156.

Georgetown Collection
P.O. Box 9730
Portland, ME 04104-5030
(800) 626-3330
Fax: (207) 775-6457
Specialty: See article on page 159.

George Z. Lefton Co.
3622 S. Morgan St.
Chicago, IL 60609
(800) 628-8492
Specialty: See article on page 162.

Giftstar, Inc.
630A Airpark Road
Napa, CA 94558
(707) 226-2323
Fax: (707) 226-6464
Specialty: See article on page 165.

Goebel of North America
Goebel Plaza
Rte. 31 North
Pennington, NJ 08534-0010
(609) 737-1980
Fax: (609) 737-1545
URL: http://www.mihummel.com
Specialty: See article on page 168.

Good-Krüger Dolls
1842 William Penn Way, Ste.A
Lancaster, PA 17601
(717) 399-3602
Specialty: Dolls.

Great American Doll Co.
1050 N. Batavia, Bldg. B
Orange, CA 92867
(800) VIP-DOLL
Specialty: Dolls.

Great American Taylor
Collectilbles Corp.
110 Sandhills Blvd.
P.O. Box 428
Aberdeen, NC 28315
(910) 944-7447
Fax: (910) 944-7449
Specialty: Figurines.

The Greenwich Workshop
One Greenwich Place
Shelton, CT 06484
(203) 925-0131
Fax: (203) 925-0262
URL: http://www.greenwich
workshop.com
Specialty: See article on page 171.

Gund Inc.
1 Runyons Lane, P.O. Box H
Edison, NJ 08818
(908) 248-1500
Specialty: Bears, stuffed toys.

H & G Studios Inc.
5660 Corporate Way
West Palm Beach, FL 33407
(561) 615-9900
Fax: (407) 615-8400
Specialty: Figurines, music
boxes, graphics and plates.

Hadley House
11001 Hampshire Avenue S.
Bloomington, MN 55438
(800) 927-0880
Fax: (612) 943-8098
Specialty: Cottages, graphics,
ornaments, plates, steins.

Hallmark Cards, Inc.
Keepsake Ornament Collectors
Club #161
P.O. Box 412734
Kansas City, MO 64141-2734
Specialty: Ornaments and
figurines.

The Hamilton Collection
4810 Executive Park Court
Jacksonville, FL 32216-6069
(800) 228-2945
Fax: (904) 279-1339
Specialty: See article on page 174.

Hand & Hammer Silversmiths
2610 Morse Lane
Woodbridge, VA 22192
(800) SILVERY
Fax: (703) 491-2031
Specialty: Ornaments.

Harbour Lights
1000 N. Johnson Ave.
El Cajon, CA 92020
(800) 365-1219
Fax: (619) 579-1911
URL: http://www.harbour
lights.com
Specialty: See article on page 177.

Harmony Kingdom
232 Neilston St.
Columbus, OH 43215
(614) 469-0600
Fax: (614) 469-0140
E-mail: royalwatch@msn.com
URL: http://www.harmony
kingdom.com
Specialty: See article on page 180.

Harold Rigsby Graphics
4108 Scottsville Rd.
Glasgow, KY 42141
(800) 892-4984
Specialty: Graphics.

Hawthorne Village
9210 N. Maryland Street
Niles, IL 60714-1322
(800) 772-4277
E-mail: custsrv@hawthorne.com
URL: http://hawthorne.com
Specialty: Miniature buildings.

Hazle Ceramics
Stallion's Yard, Codham Hall
Great Warley
Brentwood, Essex,
United Kingdom CM13 3JT
(011) 441-277-220892
Fax: (011) 441-277-233768
Specialty: See article on page 183.

Heirloom Editions Ltd.
25100-B So. Normandie Ave.
Harbor City, CA 90710
(800) 433-4785
Fax: (310) 539-8891
Specialty: Bells, Staffordshire
dogs & teapots, thimbles and
figurines.

Heirloom Ltd.
4330 Margaret Circle
Mound, MN 55364
(612) 474-2402
Specialty: Dolls and lithos.

Helen Sabatte Designs, Inc.
6041 Acacia Avenue
Oakland, CA 94618
(510) 653-4616
Fax: (510) 547-5806
Specialty: Figurines.

Heritage Artists
560 Sauve West
Montreal, Quebec
Canada H3L 2A3
(514) 385-7000
Fax: (514) 385-0026
Specialty: Wildlife figurines.

The Heritage Collections, Ltd.
6647 Kerns Road
Falls Church, VA 22042-4231
(703) 533-7800
Fax: (703) 533-7801
Specialty: Music boxes, ornaments, paperweights and wall
plaques.

House of Hatten, Inc.
301 Inner Loop Road
Georgetown, TX 78626
(800) 5HATTEN
Fax: (512) 819-9033
Specialty: See article on page 189.

Hudson Creek
321 Central Street
Hudson, MA 01749
(978) 568-1401
Fax: (978) 568-8741
E-mail: hudsoncrek@aol.com
Specialty: See article on page 192.

Imperial Graphics, Ltd.
11516 Lake Potomac Dr.
Potomac, MD 20854
(800) 541-7696
Fax: (301) 299-4837
E-mail: lliu@erols.com
URL: http://www.lenaliu.com
Specialty: See article on page 195.

Incolay Studios Inc.
520 Library Street
San Fernando, CA 91340-2599
(818) 365-2521
Specialty: Plates.

Iris Arc Crystal
114 East Haley Street
Santa Barbara, CA 93101
(888) IRIS-ARC
Fax: (805) 965-2458
Specialty: Crystal and
figurines.

Islandia International
78 Bridge Rd.
Islandia, NY 11722
(516) 234-9817
Fax: (516) 234-9183
E-mail: islandia78@aol.com
URL: http://www.islandiacoll.com
Specialty: See article on page 198.

Jack Terry Fine Art Publishing
25251 Freedom Trail
Kerrville, TX 78028
(210) 367-4242
Fax: (210) 367-4243
Specialty: Limited edition prints
and sculptures.

Jan Hagara Collectables, Inc.
40114 Industrial Park
Georgetown, TX 78626
(512) 869-1365
Fax: (512) 869-2093
E-mail: info@hagaradolls.com
URL: http://www.hagaradolls.com
Specialty: See article on page 201.

Janco Studio
P.O. Box 30012
Lincoln, NE 68503
(800) 490-1430
Fax: (402) 435-1430
Specialty: Figurines, miniatures,
ornaments and pins.

Jody Bergsma Galleries
1344 King Street
Bellingham, WA 98226
(800) BERGSMA
Fax: (360) 647-2758
Specialty: Graphics and plates.

Johannes Zook Originals
P.O. Box 256
Midland, MI 48640
(517) 835-9388
Specialty: Dolls.

June McKenna Collectibles, Inc.
P.O. Box 846
Ashland, VA 23005
(804) 798-2024
Fax: (804) 798-2618
Specialty: Figurines.

KVK Inc./Daddy's Long Legs
300 Bank Street
Southlake, TX 76092
(817) 481-4800
Fax: (817) 488-8876
Specialty: Dolls.

Kaiser Porcelain (US)
RR #3
Shelburne, Ontario
Canada L0N 1S7
(800) 287-0077
Fax: (705) 466-3542
Specialty: Figurines and plates.

Kurt S. Adler, Inc.
1107 Broadway
New York, NY 10010
(212) 924-0900
Fax: (212) 807-0575
Specialty: See article on page 204.

L.M. Cape Craftsmen, Inc.
210A Old Dairy Road
Wilmington, NC 28405
(800) 262-5447
Fax: (910) 452-7721
Specialty: Figurines.

Ladie and Friends, Inc.
220 North Main Street
Sellersville, PA 18960
(800) 76-DOLLS
Fax: (215) 453-8155
URL: http://www.lizziehigh.com
Specialty: See article on page 207.

Lalique
400 Veterans Blvd.
Carlstadt, NJ 07072
(800) CRISTAL
Specialty: Crystal.

Lang & Wise Ltd.
514 Wells Street
Delafield, WI 53018
(414) 646-5499
Fax: (414) 646-4427
Specialty: Ornaments and
figurines.

The Lawton Doll Company
548 North First Street
Turlock, CA 95380
(209) 632-3655
Fax: (209) 632-6788
Specialty: Dolls.

Lee Middleton Original Dolls, Inc.
1301 Washington Blvd.
Belpre, OH 45714
(740) 423-1717
Fax: (740) 423-5983
URL: http://www.leemiddleton.com
Specialty: See article on page 210.

Legacy Works
4020 Will Rogers Parkway,
Suite 700
Oklahoma City, OK 73108
(405) 948-8555
Fax: (405) 948-1784
Specialty: Figurines.

Lemax, Inc.
25 Pequot Way
Canton, MA 02021
(617) 821-4555
Fax: (617) 821-4455
Specialty: Christmas village
collectibles and accessories.

Lenox Collections
900 Wheeler Way
Langhorne, PA 19047
(800) 63-LENOX
Fax: (215) 741-6337
URL: http://www.lenox
collections.com
Specialty: See article on page 213.

Lilliput Lane/
Enesco Home Gallery
P.O. Box 498
Itasca, IL 60143-0498
(630) 875-5382
Fax: (630) 875-5348
URL: http://www.enesco.com
Specialty: See article on page 216.

Living Stone
P.O. Box 5476
Chula Vista, CA 91912
(800) 621-3647
Specialty: Figurines.

Lladró USA, Inc.
1 Lladró Drive
Moonachie, NJ 07074
(888) GIVE-LLADRO
Fax: (201) 807-1168
URL: http://www.lladro.com
Specialty: See article on page 222.

Lynette Decor Products
4225 Prado Road, Unit 106
Corona, CA 91720
(800) 223-8623
Fax: (909) 279-1337
Specialty: Collectible displays and accessories.

M C K Gifts Inc.
P.O. Box 621848
Littleton, CO 80162-1814
(303) 948-1382
Fax: (303) 979-6838
Specialty: Figurines.

M. Cornell Importers, Inc.
1462-18th St. N.W.
St. Paul, MN 55112
(612) 633-8690
Fax: (612) 636-3568
Specialty: Steins and teapots.

M.I. Hummel Club
Goebel of North America
Goebel Plaza
P.O. Box 11
Pennington, NJ 08534-0011
(800) 666-2582
Fax: (609) 737-1545
URL: http://www.mihummel.com
Specialty: See article on page 225.

Magus Fine Arts &
Collectibles, Inc.
9437 Kilimanjaro Rd.
Columbia, MD 21045
Specialty: Dolls.

Margaret Furlong Designs
210 State Street
Salem, OR 97301
(503) 363-6004
Fax: (503) 371-0676
Specialty: See article on page 228.

Mark Hopkins Sculptures
21 Shorter Industrial Blvd.
Rome, GA 30165-1838
(800) 678-6564
Fax: (706) 235-2814
Specialty: Sculptures.

Mark Klaus, Ltd.
P.O. Box 470758
Broadview Heights, OH
44147-0758
(216) 582-5003
Specialty: Figurines and ornaments.

Marty Bell Fine Art
9550 Owens Mouth Ave.
Chatsworth, CA 91311
(800) 637-4537
Fax: (818) 709-7668
Specialty: Graphics.

Marty Sculpture, Inc.
P.O. Box 15067
Wilmington, NC 28408
(800) 654-0478
Specialty: Figurines.

Maruri, U.S.A.
21510 Gledhill St.
Chatsworth, CA 91311
(818) 717-9900
Fax: (818) 717-9901
Specialty: See article on page 231.

Media Arts Group, Inc.
521 Charcot Avenue
San Jose, CA 95131
(800) 366-3733
Fax: (408) 324-2033
Specialty: See article on page 234.

Michael Boyett Studio
411 Esther Blvd.
Nacogdoches, TX 75964
(409) 560-4477
Specialty: Figurines and graphics.

Michael Garman
Productions, Inc.
2418 W. Colorado Avenue
Colorado Springs, CO 80904
(800) 874-7144
Fax: (719) 471-3659
Specialty: Figurines.

Midwest of Cannon Falls
32057 64th Avenue
Cannon Falls, MN 55009
(800) 377-3335
Fax: (507) 263-7752
URL: http://www.eddie
walker.com
Specialty: See article on page 237.

Miss Martha Originals, Inc.
P.O. Box 5038
Glencoe, AL 35905
(205) 492-0221
Fax. (205) 492-0261
Specialty: See article on page 240.

The Moss Portfolio
1 Poplar Grove Lane
Mathews, VA 23109
(804) 725-7378
Specialty: Graphics.

Munro Collectibles, Inc.
1220 Waterville-Monclova Road
Waterville, OH 43566
(419) 878-0034
Fax: (419) 878-2535
Specialty: See article on page 243.

Napoleon
P.O. Box 860
Oakes, PA 19456
(610) 666-1650
Fax: (610) 666-1379
Specialty: Capidimonte figurines .

New Masters Publishing Co., Inc.
2301 14th Street, Ste. 105
Gulfport, MS 39501
(800) 647-9578
Fax: (601) 863-5145
Specialty: Bronzes and graphics.

North American Bear Co.
401 North Wabash, Suite 500
Chicago, IL 60611
(312) 329-0020
Fax: (312) 329-1417
Specialty: Teddy bears.

Oldenburg Originals
N2646 Pheasant Valley Court
Waldo, WI 53093
(920) 528-7127
Fax: (920) 528-7127
Specialty: Limited edition and porcelain original dolls.

Old World Christmas
P.O. Box 8000
Spokane, WA 99203
(509) 534-9000
Fax: (509) 534-9098
Specialty: Figurines and ornaments.

Olszewski Studios
355 N. Lantana, Suite 500
Camarillo, CA 93010
(805) 374-9990
Fax: (805) 484-4993
Specialty: Miniature figurines.

Original Appalachian Artworks, Inc.
73 W. Underwood Street
P.O. Box 714
Cleveland, GA 30528
(706) 865-2171
Fax: (706) 865-5862
Specialty: See article on page 246.

Orrefors of Sweden
140 Bradford Drive
Berlin, NJ 08009
(609) 768-5400
Fax: (609) 768-9726
Specialty: Figurines and ornaments.

Pacific Rim Import Corp.
5930 4th Avenue South
Seattle, WA 98108
(206) 767-5000
Fax: (206) 767-5316
Specialty: Figurines.

Past Impressions
P.O. Box 188
Belvedere, CA 94920
(800) 732-7332
Fax: (415) 358-8676
Specialty: Graphics.

PenDelfin Studios
c/o Miller Import Corp.
300 Mac Lane
Keasbey, NJ 08832
(800) 547-2006
Fax: (908) 417-0031
Specialty: Figurines.

Penni Jo's Originals Ltd.
1413 N.E. Lincoln Ave.
Moore, OK 73160
(405) 799-0006
Specialty: Figurines.

Pickard Inc.
782 Pickard Ave.
Antioch, IL 60002
(847) 395-3800
Specialty: China.

Polland Studios
P.O. Box 2468
Prescott, AZ 86301-1146
(520) 778-1900
Fax: (520) 778-4034
Specialty: Pewter and porcelain figurines.

Porsgrunds Porselaensfabrik
A/S grunds PorselaeN-3907
Porsgrunn/Norway
+4735550040
Fax: +4735559110
Specialty: Christmas plates .

Porterfield's
5 Mountain Road
Concord, NH 03301-5479
(800) 660-8345
Fax: (603) 228-1888
E-mail: clientservices@
porterfields.com
URL: http://www.porterfields.com
Specialty: See article on page 249.

Possible Dreams
6 Perry Drive
Foxboro, MA 02035
(508) 543-6667
Fax: (508) 543-4255
Specialty: See article on page 252.

Precious Art, Inc.
738 Airport Blvd. #5
Ann Arbor, MI 48108
(734) 663-2155
Fax: (734) 663-2343
Specialty: See article on page 255.

Prizm, Inc./Pipka's Collectibles
P.O. Box 1106
Manhattan, KS 66505
(888) 427-4752
Fax: (785) 776-6550
URL: http://www.pipka.com
Specialty: See article on page 258.

Pulaski Furniture Corporation
One Pulaski Square
Pulaski, VA 24301
(800) 287-4625
Specialty: See article on page 261.

R. John Wright Dolls, Inc.
15 West Main Street
Cambridge, NY 12816
(518) 677-8567
Fax: (518) 677-5202
Specialty: Dolls.

R.R. Creations
P.O. Box 8707
Pratt, KS 67124
(800) 779-3610
Fax: (316) 672-5850
Specialty: Architecture.

Raikes Collectables
P.O. Box 8428
Tucson, AZ 85738
(520) 825-5788
Fax: (520) 825-5789
Specialty: Traditional wood sculptures.

Rawcliffe Corporation
155 Public Street
Providence, RI 02903
(800) 343-1811
Fax: (401) 751-8545
Specialty: Figurines.

Reco International Corp.
150 Haven Avenue
Port Washington, NY 11050
(516) 767-2400
Fax: (516) 767-2409
Specialty: See article on page 263.

Red Mill Mfg., Inc.
1023 Arbuckle Road
Summersville, WV 26651
(304) 872-5231
Fax: (304) 872-5234
Specialty: Character and wildlife figurines.

Rhyn-Rivet
395 Hwy. MM
Brooklyn, WI 53521
(608) 835-7886
Specialty: Ornaments.

Rick Cain Studios
3500 N.E. Waldo Road
Gainesville, FL 32609
(800) 535-3949
Fax: (352) 377-7038
Specialty: Wildlife sculptures.

Roman, Inc.
555 Lawrence Avenue
Roselle, IL 60172-1599
(630) 529-3000
Fax: (630) 529-1121
URL: http://www.roman.com
Specialty: See article on page 266.

Ron Lee's World of Clowns, Inc.
330 Carousel Pkwy.
Henderson, NV 89014
(702) 434-1700
Fax: (702) 434-4310
Specialty: Figurines.

**Royal Copenhagen/
Bing & Grondahl**
41 Madison Avenue
New York, NY 10010
(800) 431-1992
Fax: (609) 719-1494
Specialty: See artictle on page 269.

Royal Doulton
701 Cottontail Lane
Somerset, NJ 08873
(800) 682-4462
Fax: (732) 356-9467
URL: http://www.royal-
doulton.com
Specialty: See article on page 272.

Royal Worcester
Severn Street
Worcester, England
(01905) 23221
Fax: (01905) 23601
Specialty: Figurines, ornaments and plates.

Saint-Alexis Santons
P.O. Box 307
Searsport, ME 04974
(800) 829-0243
Fax: (207) 548-0244
Specialty: Figurines and villages.

Salvino, Inc.
1379 Pico Street, Ste. 103
Corona, CA 91719
(909) 273-7850
Fax: (909) 279-3409
Specialty: Sports figurines.

Sandicast, Inc.
8480 Miralani Drive
San Diego, CA 92126
(800) 722-3316
Fax: (619) 695-0015
Specialty: Cast stone animal figurines.

Sandy Clough Studio
25 Trail Road
Marietta, GA 30064-1535
(770) 428-9406
Specialty: Limited edition prints.

Sandy Dolls
P.O. Box 3222
Springfield, MO 65808
(800) 607-2639
Fax: (417) 831-4477
Specialty: See article on page 275.

The San Francisco Music Box Company
390 North Wiget Lane, Suite 200
Walnut Creek, CA 94598
(925) 939-4800
Fax: (925) 927-2999
E-mail: sfmbsn@aol.com
URL: http://www.sfmusicbox.com
Specialty: See article on page 278.

Sarah's Attic, Inc.
126-1/2 West Broad
P.O. Box 448
Chesaning, MI 48616
(800) 437-4363
Fax: (517) 845-3477
E-mail: sarahattic@aol.com
Specialty: See article on page 281.

Sculpture Workshop Designs
510 School Rd. P.O. Box 420
Blue Bell, PA 19422
(215) 643-7447
Fax: (215) 643-7447
Specialty: Sterling silver ornaments.

Second Nature Design
110 S. Southgate Bldg. C-4, #2
Chandler, AZ 85226
(602) 961-3963
Specialty: Figurines.

Seraphim Classics
c/o Roman, Inc.
555 Lawrence Ave.
Roselle, IL 60172-1599
(630) 529-3000
Fax: (630) 529-1121
URL: http://www.roman.com
Specialty: See article on page 284.

Seymour Mann, Inc.
225 Fifth Avenue
Showroom #102
New York, NY 10010
(212) 683-7262
Fax: (212) 213-4920
Specialty: See article on page 287.

Shade Tree Creations
4248 Burning Town Road
Franklin, NC 28734
(800) 327-6923
Fax: (704) 349-3253
Specialty: Figurines.

Shelia's Collectibles
P.O. Box 31028
Charleston, SC 29417
(800) 695-8686
Fax: (803) 556-0040
E-mail: shelias@charleston.net
URL: http://www.shelias.com
Specialty: See article on page 290.

Shenandoah Designs International, Inc.
204 W. Rail Road
Rural Retreat, VA 24368
(540) 686-6188
Fax: (540) 686-4921
E-mail: shenandoah@nays.com
URL: http://www.shenandoah designs.com
Specialty: See article on page 293.

Silver Deer Ltd.
963 Transport Way
Petaluma, CA 94954
(800) 729-3337
Fax: (707) 765-0770
Specialty: Figurines.

Spencer Collin Lighthouses
2 Government Street
Kittery, ME 03904
(207) 439-6016
Fax: (204) 439-5787
Specialty: Lighthouses.

Steiff USA
31 E. 28th Street, 9th Floor
New York, NY 10016
(212) 675-2727
Fax: (800) 791-2215
Specialty: Plush bears.

Studio Collection
32 Jonathan-Bourne Drive
Pocasset, MA 02559
(800) 314-7748
Fax: (508) 563-3663
Specialty: Figurines and ornaments.

Sunbelt Marketing Group
4275 Arco Lane, Suite L
North Charleston, SC 29418
(800) 794-6194
Fax: (843) 554-5946
Specialty: See article on page 296.

Susan Rios Co.
P.O. Box 129
Verdugo, CA 91046
(818) 500-1705
Specialty: Graphics.

The Susan Wakeen Doll Company
425 Bantam Road
P.O. Box 1321
Litchfield, CT 06759
(860) 567-0007
Fax: (860) 567-4636
Specialty: Dolls.

Swarovski Consumer Goods Ltd.
2 Slater Road
Cranston, RI 02920
(800) 426-3088
Fax: (401) 463-8459
URL: http://www.swarovski.com
Specialty: See article on page 299.

Talsco of Florida
5427 Crafts Street
New Port Richey, FL 34652
(813) 847-6370
Fax: (813) 847-6786
Specialty: Collectible accessories, glass displays and plate frames.

Texas Stamps
P.O. Box 42388
Houston, TX 77242-2388
(800) 779-4100
Fax: (713) 541-1988
Specialty: Stamps.

Timeless Creations
333 Continental Blvd.
El Segundo, CA 90245-5012
(252) 524-2000
Specialty: Dolls.

Towle Silversmiths
144 Addison Street
Boston, MA 02128
(617) 568-1300
Fax: (617) 568-9185
Specialty: Bells and ornaments.

The Tudor Mint
2601 South Park Road
Pembroke, FL 33009
(800) 455-8715
Specialty: Figurines.

United Design Corporation
1600 N. Main Street
Noble, OK 73068
(800) 727-4883
Fax: (405) 360-4442
URL: http://www.united-design.com
Specialty: See article on page 302.

VF Fine Arts
1737 Stebbins #240
Houston, TX 77043
(713) 461-1944
Specialty: Graphics.

Vaillancourt Folk Art
145 Armsby Road
Sutton, MA 01590
(508) 865-9183
Fax: (508) 865-4140
Specialty: Figurines.

Viletta China Company
100137 Greenridge Street
Stafford, TX 77477
(281) 261-5451
Fax: (281) 261-7686
Specialty: Plates.

Vivi
31 Collegeview Avenue
Poughkeepsie, NY 12603
(888) 819-8484
Specialty: Figurines.

W.T. Wilson Limited Editions
185 York Avenue
Pawtucket, RI 02860
(800) 722-0485
Specialty: Bells and figurines.

WACO Products Corporation
I-80 & New Maple Avenue
P.O. Box 898
Pine Brook, NJ 07058-0898
(973) 882-1820
Fax: (973) 882-3661
E-mail: waco_mim@com-puserve.com
URL: http://www.waco products.com
http://www.melodyinmotion.com
Specialty: See article on page 305.

Wade Ceramics Ltd.
3330 Cobb Parkway, Suite 17-333
Acworth, GA 30101
(770) 529-9908
Specialty: Figurines.

Wallace Silversmiths
175 McClellan Highway
E. Boston, MA 02128-9114
(617) 561-2200
Fax: (617) 568-9185
Specialty: Bells and ornaments.

Walnut Ridge Collectibles
39048 Webb Dr.
Westland, MI 48185
(800) 275-1765
Fax: (734) 728-5950
Specialty: See article on page 308.

The Walt Disney Company
500 South Buena Vista Street
Burbank, CA 91521-6876
(800) WD-CLSIX
URL: http://www.disneyart classics.com
Specialty: See article on page 311.

Waterford Crystal
1330 Campus Parkway
Wall, NJ 07719
(908) 938-5800
Specialty: Crystal.

Wedgwood
1330 Campus Parkway
Wall, NJ 07719
(908) 938-5800
Specialty: Ornaments and plates.

Wild Wings
2101South Highway 61
Lake City, MN 55041-0451
(651) 345-2981
Fax: (651) 345-2981
Specialty: Wildlife graphics and figurines.

Willitts Designs International, Inc.
1129 Industrial Avenue
Petaluma, CA 94952
(707) 778-7211
Fax: (707) 769-0304
E-mail: info@willitts.com
URL: http://www.willitts.com
Specialty: See article on page 314.

The Wimbledon Collection
P.O. Box 21948
Lexington, KY 40522
(606) 277-8531
Fax: (606) 277-9231
Specialty: Dolls.

Windstone Editions
13012 Saticoy Street #3
North Hollywood, CA 91605
(800) 982-4464
Fax: (818) 982-4674
Specialty: Figurines.

Winston Roland Ltd.
1909 Oxford Street E.
Unit 17
London, Ont. CAN N5V 2Z7
(519) 659-6601
Fax: (519) 659-2923
Specialty: Graphics and plates.

Woodland Winds from Christopher Radko
P.O. Box 533
Elmsford, NY 10523
(800) 71-RADKO
URL: http://www.christopher radko.com
Specialty: See article on page 317.

Some Terms Commonly Used by Collectors, Dealers and Manufacturers to Describe Limited Edition Collectibles

Acid-free. A description of paper and materials treated to remove the acids that cause deterioration.

Alabaster. A fine-textured gypsum which is usually white and translucent. Some collectors' plates are made of a material called ivory alabaster which is not translucent, but has the look and patina of old ivory.

Allotment. The number within a limited edition which a manufacturer allows to a given dealer, direct marketer or collector.

Annual. The term is used to describe a plate or other limited edition which is issued yearly. Many annual plates commemorate holidays or anniversaries, and they are commonly named by that special date, i.e. the Annual Bing & Grondahl Christmas plate.

Artist/gallery/publishers' proofs. Originally, the first few prints in an edition of lithographs were used to test colors and then given to the artist. They were not numbered but were signed. Artist's proofs are not considered part of the edition. Gallery and publishers' proofs are used as a means of increasing the number of prints in an edition.

Baby doll. A doll with the proportions of a baby; with a short-limbed body and lips parted to take a nipple.

Back issue. An issue in a series other than the issue that is currently being produced. It can be either open or closed and may or may not be available.

Backstamp. The information on the back of a plate or other limited edition which documents it as part of a limited edition. This information may be hand-painted onto the plate, or it may be incised, or applied as a transfer (decal). Information which typically appears on the backstamp includes the name of the series, name of the item, year of issue, some information about the subject, the artist's name and/or signature, the edition limit, the item's number within that edition, initials of the firing master or production supervisor, etc.

Band. Also known as a rim, as in "24K gold banded, or rimmed." A popular finishing technique is to band plates and bells with gold, platinum or silver which is then adhered to the plate through the firing process. Details from the primary artwork may also be adapted to form a decorative rim.

Bas-relief. A technique in which the collectible has a raised design. This design may be achieved by pouring liquid material into a mold before firing, or by applying a three-dimensional design element to the flat surface of a plate, figurine or other "blank" piece.

Bavaria. A section of Germany that is one of the world's richest sources of kaolin clay, an essential component of fine porcelain. The region is home to a number of renowned porcelain factories.

Bisque or biscuit. A fired ware which has neither a glaze nor enamel applied to it. Bisque may be white or colored. The name comes from its biscuit-like, matte texture.

Body. The basic form of a plate, figurine, bell or other collectible, or its component materials.

Bone ash. Fire is used to reduce animal bones to calcium phosphate, a powder which is an ingredient of bone china or porcelain.

Bone china/bone porcelain. Bone porcelain is similar to hard porcelain in its ingredients, except that bone ash is the main component of the mix and is the primary contributor to the vitrification and translucency. Bone clay allows for extreme thinness and translucency without sacrificing strength or durability.

Bottomstamp. The same as a backstamp, but usually refers to documentation material found on the bottom of a figurine or the inside of a bell.

Bye-lo-baby. Grace Storey Putman copyrighted this life-sized baby doll (three days old) in 1922. This style of baby doll is a favorite among limited edition collectors.

Cameo. Relief decoration with a flat surface around it, similar to the look of a jeweler's cameo. A technique used by Wedgwood, Incolay, Avondale and others.

Cancelled plate. A plate that was planned as part of a series, but never produced because of technical problems or lack of interest in early issues.

Canvas transfer process. A lithograph is treated with a latex emulsion. The paper is removed and the image on the latex emulsion is placed on a cotton duck canvas. It is then topcoated, retouched and highlighted by hand before being hand-numbered.

Capodimonte. Originally a fine porcelain produced at a "castle on the mountain" overlooking Naples. The term currently describes a highly ornate style rather than an actual product. Frequently features flowers, fruits and courtly or native figures.

Cast. The process of creating a copy of an original model by pouring liquid clay or slip into a mold.

Ceramic. The generic term for a piece which is made of some form of clay and finished by firing at high temperatures.

Certificate/Certificate of Authenticity. A document which accompanies a limited edition item to establish its place within the edition. Certificates may include information such as the series name, item title, artist's name and/or signature, brief description of the item and its subject, signatures of sponsoring and marketing organizations' representatives, and other documentation material, along with the item's individual number or a statement of the edition limit.

Character dolls. These dolls are often created to resemble actors or celebrities. Character dolls also include fairytale images, folk heroes and cartoon characters.

Chasing. A sculpting process in which tiny hammers and punches are used to create decorative details on ornaments.

China. Originally "china" referred to all wares which came from China. Now the term means products which are fired at a high temperature. China usually consists of varying percentages of kaolin clay, feldspar and quartz. Also see "porcelain."

Cinnabar. A red mineral found in volcanic regions, and an ingredient in mercury. It is used to create collectors' items.

Cire perdue. See lost wax.

Clay. A general term for materials used to make ceramic items. Pliable when moist, clay becomes hard and strong when fired. It may be composed of any number of earthen materials.

Cloissoné. An enameling process in which thin metal strips are soldered on the base of a piece to create a pattern. Then, various enamels are poured in to provide the color.

Closed edition. A limited edition that is no longer being issued because it has reached the designated limit, or no longer has market appeal.

Closed end edition. A series with a predetermined, and usually pre-announced, number of issues.

Cobalt blue. Also known as Copenhagen blue, this rich color was an early favorite because it was the only color that could withstand high firing temperatures needed for glazing. Cobalt oxide is a black powder when applied, but fires to a deep blue.

Cold cast. A relatively new process which combines polyester resins and a variety of materials (metal powders, ground porcelain, wood shavings and other natural materials). The combination is forced into a mold or die under high pressure and a forging process occurs. Allows for exceptional detailing which can be easily hand-painted.

Collector plate. A limited edition plate which is created to be collected for its decorative appearance.

Commemorative. An item created to mark a special date, holiday or event.

Dealer. An individual or store where collectors can purchase collectibles at retail prices.

Decal. Also known as a transfer, this is a lithographic or silkscreen rendering of a piece of artwork, which is applied to ceramic or other materials and then fired on to fuse it to the surface.

Delftware. Heavy earthenware coated with an opaque white glaze that contains tin oxide. First developed in Delft, Holland, in the 16th century.

Drafting. Process for shaping metal into hollowware.

Earthenware. A non-vitrified ceramic made of ball clay, kaolin and pegmatite. Remains porous until glazed and fired at a low temperature.

Edition. A term referring to the number of items created with the same name and decorations.

Embossing. A process of producing an image in relief by using dies or punches on a surface.

Engraving. An intaglio process in which an image is cut into the surface. Term also used to describe a print made by an engraving process.

Etched design. Decoration produced by cutting into a surface with acid. An acid-resistant paint or wax is applied and the design is inscribed through this coating. When immersed in acid, the acid etches the surface to form the design.

Faience. Named after an Italian town, Faenza, faience is similar to Delftware and Majolica because it is earthenware coated with a glaze that contains tin oxide.

Feldspar. When decomposed, this mineral becomes kaolin, which is the essential ingredient in china and porcelain. Left in its undercomposed form, feldspar adds hardness to a ware.

Fire. To heat, and thus harden, a ceramic ware in a kiln.

Firing period. A time period – usually 10 to 75 days, which serves to limit an edition, usually of plates. The number of items is limited to the capacity of the manufacturer over that 10 to 75 days.

First issue. The premiere item in a series, whether closed-ended or open-ended.

French bronze. Also known as "spelter," this is zinc refined to 99.97% purity. It has been used as an alternative to bronze for casting for more than a century.

Glaze. The liquid material which is applied to a ware for various purposes. Cosmetically, it provides shine and decorative value. It also makes the item more durable. Decorations may be applied before or after glaze is applied.

Graphic. A print produced by one of the "original" print processes such as etching, engraving, woodblocks, lithographs and serigraphs. This term is frequently used interchangeably with "print."

Greenware. Undecorated ceramic before it is fired.

Hallmark. The mark or logo of the manufacturer of an item.

Hard paste porcelain. The hardest porcelain made, this material uses feldspar to enhance vitrification and translucency, and is fired at about 2642 degrees Fahrenheit.

Hydrostone. The hardest form of gypsum cement from which many limited edition collectibles are produced. A registered trademark of the United States Gypsum Co.

Incised. Writing or design which is etched or inscribed into a piece to provide a backstamp or decorative design.

Incolay stone. A man-made material combining minerals including carnelian and crystal quartz. Used by Incolay Studios to make cameo-style collectibles.

Inlay. To fill an etched or incised design with another material such as enamel, metal or jewels.

In stock. A term used to refer to an item of a given edition still available from the producers' inventory.

Issue. As a verb, to introduce. As a noun, the term means an item within a series.

Issue Price. The price established by the manufacturer or principal marketer when a collectible is introduced.

Jasper ware. Josiah Wedgwood's unglazed stoneware material, first introduced in the 1770s. Although jasper is white in its original form, it can be stained a medium blue called "Wedgwood Blue," or a darker blue, black, green, lilac, yellow, brown and gray. Colored Wedgwood "bodies" are often decorated with white bas-relief, or vice/versa.

Kaolin. The essential ingredient in china and porcelain, this special clay is found in several spots throughout the world. Many famous porcelain factories are located near these deposits.

Lead crystal. Lead oxide is added to glass to give it weight, brilliance and a clear ring. Lead crystal has a lead oxide content of 24%, while "full" lead crystal contains more than 30%.

Limited edition. An item produced only in a certain quantity or only during a certain time period. Collectible editions are limited by: specific numbers, years, specific time periods or firing periods.

Limoges. A town in France with rich deposits of kaolin clay and other essential ingredients for making china and porcelain. Home of a number of famed porcelain manufacturers.

Lost wax. An ancient method used by sculptors to create a detailed wax "positive" which is then used to form a ceramic "negative" shell. This shell becomes the original mold used in the creation of finely carved three-dimensional pieces.

Majolica. Similar to Delftware and Faience, this glazed earthenware was first produced on the Spanish island, Majorca.

Market. The organized buy-sell medium for collectibles.

Marks or markings. The logo or insignia which certifies that an item was made by a particular firm.

Miniatures. Collectibles, including figurines, plates, graphics, dolls, ornaments and bells, which are very small originals or smaller versions of larger pieces. Usually finely detailed, many figurine miniatures are created using the lost wax process.

Mint condition. The term originated in coin collecting. In limited edition collectibles, it means that an item is still in its original, like-new condition, with all accompanying documents.

Mold. The form that supplies the shape of a plate, bell, figurine or other items.

Open edition. A reproduction of an original with no limit on time of production or the number of pieces produced, and no announcement of edition size.

Open-ended series. A collection of plates or other limited editions which appear at intervals, usually annually, with no limit as to the number of years it will be produced.

Overglaze. A decoration which is applied to an item after its original glazing and firing.

Paste. The raw material of porcelain before shaping and firing. See "slip."

Pewter. An alloy containing at least 85% tin.

Polyester resin. A bonding compound mixed with powdered, ground or chipped materials (pulverized porcelain, wood, shells and other materials) to form cold-cast products. Cold-cast porcelain is made by mixing resin with porcelain dust; cold-cast bronze is made by blending resin with ground bronze.

Porcelain. Made of kaolin, quartz and feldspar, porcelain is fired at up to 1450 degrees centigrade. Porcelain is noted for its translucency and its true ring. Also called "china".

Pottery. Ceramic ware, more specifically that which is earthenware or non-vitrified. Also a term for manufacturing plants where such objects are made and fired.

Primary market. The first buy-sell market used by manufacturers to reach collectors. Sold at issue price, collectibles are offered to the public through retailers, direct mail and home shopping networks.

Print. A photomechanical reproduction process such as offset, lithography, collotypes and letterpress.

Printed remarque. A hand drawn image by the artist that is photomechanically reproduced in the margin of a print.

Queen's ware. Cream-colored earthenware developed by Josiah Wedgwood; now used as a generic term for similar materials.

Quote. The average selling price of a collectible at any given time. It may be the issue price, or above or below.

Release price. The price for which each print in the edition is sold until the edition is sold out and a secondary market is established.

Relief. A raised design in various levels above a background.

Remarque. A hand-drawn original image by the artist, either in pencil, pen and ink, watercolor or oil, that is sketched in the margin of a limited edition print.

Resin. See polyester resin.

Retired. No longer available from the producer, and none of the pieces will ever be produced again.

Sculpted crystal. A general term for products made by assembling faceted Austrian crystal prisms with a 32% lead content

Second. An item which is not first quality and should not be included in the limited edition. Normally, such items are destroyed or at least marked on the backstamp or bottomstamp to indicate they are not first quality.

Secondary market. Once the original edition has been sold out, the buying and selling among collectors, through dealers or exchanges, takes place on the "secondary" market.

Secondary market price. The price a customer is willing to sell or buy an item for once it is no longer available on the primary market. These prices will vary from one part of the country to another, depending on the supply and demand for the collectible.

Serigraphy. A direct printing process used by artists to design, make and print their own stencils. A serigraph differs from other prints in that its images are created with paint films instead of printing inks.

Signed and numbered. Each print is signed and consecutively numbered by the artist, in pencil, either in the image area or in the margin. Edition size is limited.

Signed in the plate. The only signature on the artwork is reproduced from the artist's original signature. Not necessarily limited in edition size.

Signed only. Usually refers to a print that is signed without consecutive numbers. May not be limited in edition size.

Silver crystal. Faceted Austrian crystal prisms with a 32% lead content used to produce sculpted crystal. The name is registered by Swarovski.

Silverplate. A process of manufacturing ornaments in which pure silver is electroplated onto a base metal, usually brass or pewter.

Slip. A creamy material used to fill the molds in making greenware. Formulas for slip are closely guarded secrets.

Soft paste. A mixture of clay and ground glass first used in Europe to produce china. The vitrification point of soft paste is too low to produce the hardness required for true porcelain.

Sold out. The classification given to an edition which has been 100% sold out by the producer.

Spin casting. A process of casting multiple ornaments from rubber molds; commonly used for low-temperature metals such as pewter.

Sterling silver. An alloy of 92-1/2% pure silver and 7-1/2% copper.

Stoneware. A vitrified ceramic material, usually a silicate clay that is very hard, heavy and impervious to liquids and most stains.

Suspended. Not currently available from the producer – production has ceased but may be resumed at a later date.

Terra cotta. A reddish earthenware or a general term for any fired clay.

Tin glaze. The glaze on Delftware, Faience or Majolica. This material results in a heavy white and opaque surface after firing.

Transfer. See decal.

Translucency. Allowing light to shine through a nontransparent object. A positive quality of fine china or porcelain.

Triptych. A three-panel art piece, often of religious significance.

Underglaze. A decoration which is applied before the final glazing and firing of an item. Most often, such decorations are painted by hand.

Vinyl. A relatively new synthetic material developed with the special properties of color, durability and skin-like texture which is molded into collectible dolls.

Vitrification. The process by which ceramic artwork becomes vitrified or totally nonporous at high temperatures.

COLLECTIBLE INVENTORY RECORD

Item Name:

Manufacturer's Name: Artist's Name:

Series Name/Number:

Special Markings:

Year of Issue: Edition Limit:

Purchase Price: Date of Purchase:

Purchased From:

Address: Phone:

Secondary Market Price:

Additional Information:

Item Name:

Manufacturer's Name: Artist's Name:

Series Name/Number:

Special Markings:

Year of Issue: Edition Limit:

Purchase Price: Date of Purchase:

Purchased From:

Address: Phone:

Secondary Market Price:

Additional Information:

Item Name:

Manufacturer's Name: Artist's Name:

Series Name/Number:

Special Markings:

Year of Issue: Edition Limit:

Purchase Price: Date of Purchase:

Purchased From:

Address: Phone:

Secondary Market Price:

Additional Information:

Collectors' Information Bureau

PRICE INDEX

Limited Edition

Figurines • Architecture • Plates • Dolls/Plush • Ornaments • Graphics • Steins • Bells

This index includes over 58,000 of the most widely traded limited editions in today's collectibles market. It is based on surveys and interviews with several hundred of the most experienced and informed limited edition dealers in the United States, as well as many independent market advisors.

HOW TO USE THIS INDEX

Listings are set up using the following format:

Harbour Lights ❶

Western Region ❷ **— Harbour Lights** ❸

❹	❺	❻	❼	❽	❾
1991	Coquille River OR-111	1138	1993	60.00	2400-3200

❶ Harbour Lights = Company Name

❷ Western Region = Series Name

❸ Harbour Lights = Artist's Name. In this case, the presence of the company name indicates that Harbour Lights staff artists created the piece. In some cases, a single artist's name may appear here. The word "Various" may also appear, meaning that several artists have created pieces within the series. The artist's name then appears after the title of the collectible. In some cases, the artist's name will be indicated after the series name "with exceptions noted." If no artist name is listed, company staff artists have created the piece.

❹ 1991 = Year of Issue

❺ Coquille River OR-111 = Title of the collectible. Many titles also include the model number for further identification purposes.

❻ 1138 = Edition Limit. This indicates that this collectible was produced in an edition limited to 1,138 pieces. The edition limit category generally refers to the number of items created with the same name and decoration. Edition limits may indicate a specific number (i.e. 10,000) or the number of firing days for plates (i.e. 100-day, the capacity of the manufacturer to produce collectibles during a given firing period). You may also see a term like "Retrd.," "Open," "Suspd.," "Annual," and "Yr. Iss." Refer to "Terms and Abbreviations" below for their meanings.

❼ 1993 = Year of Retirement. May also indicate the year the manufacturer ceased production of the collectible. If N/A appears in this column, it indicates the information is not available at this time, but research is continuing.
Note: In the plate section, the year of retirement may not be indicated because many plates are limited to firing days and not years.

❽ 60.00 = Original Issue Price in U.S. Dollars

❾ 2400-3200 = Current Quote Price listed may show a price or price range. Quotes are based on interviews with retailers across the country, who provide their actual sales transactions. Quotes have been rounded up to the nearest dollar. Quote may also reflect a price increase for pieces that are not retired or closed.

A Special Note to Beanie Babies, Beatrix Potter, Boyds Bears, Cherished Teddies, Disney Classics, Goebel Miniatures, M.I. Hummel and Precious Moments Collectors: *These collectibles carry special marks which change according to production and/or year. The secondary market value for each piece may vary because of these distinctive markings. Our pricing reflects a range for all marks.*
A Special Note to Hallmark Keepsake Ornament Collectors: *All quotes in this section are for ornaments in mint condition in their original box.*
A Special Note to Department 56 Collectors: *Year of Introduction indicates the year in which the piece was designed, sculpted and copyrighted. It is possible these pieces may not be available to collectors until the following calendar year.*
A Special Note to Annalee Doll Collectors: *Previous editions of this book have only reflected prices paid at Annalee auctions. Beginning with this edition, secondary market dealer prices are also reported. As a rule, auction prices are higher than secondary market dealer prices.*
A Special Note to Cardew Design and Hazle Ceramics Collectors: *Prices may include U.S. and international pricing.*

TERMS AND ABBREVIATIONS

Annual = Issued once a year.
A/P = Artist Proof.
Closed = An item or series no longer in production.
G/P = Gallery Proof.
N/A = Not available at this time.
Open = Not limited by number or time, available until manufacturer stops production, "retires" or "closes" the item or series.
Numbrd. = Numbered series.
P/P = Publisher's Proof.
Retrd. = Retired.
R/E = Rennaissance Proof.
S/N = Signed and Numbered.
S/O = Sold Out.
S/P = Studio Proof.
Set = Refers to two or more items issued together for a single price.
Suspd. = Suspended (not currently being produced: may be produced in the future).
Unkn. = Unknown.
Yr. Iss. = Year of issue (limited to a calendar year).
28-day, 10-day, etc. = Limited to this number of production (or firing) days, usually not consecutive.

Finding Your Way Through CIB's Price Index Is As Easy As 1, 2, 3!

1. Determine the category that your collectible falls into. CIB's Price Index is divided into 8 general categories that are organized alphabetically. They include: Architecture, Bells, Dolls/Plush, Figurines, Graphics, Ornaments, Plates and Steins. Hint: Figurines is by far our most extensive category. If the product you're looking for doesn't fit neatly into one of the other categories, chances are you'll find it in the Figurines section.
2. Locate your manufacturer. Manufacturers are listed alphabetically within each category.
3. Once you turn to the pages that contain information about the manufacturer you're looking for, you'll find that products are listed by line, and by series within each line, if applicable.

ARCHITECTURE

Brandywine Collectibles

The Brandywine Neighborhood Association - M. Whiting

YEAR ISSUE	EDITION LIMIT	YEAR RETD.	ISSUE PRICE	*QUOTE U.S.$
1997 Moore House	Yr.Iss.	1997	Gift	N/A
1997 Manhassett House-Hometown	Yr.Iss.	1997	32.00	32
1997 Manhassett House-Country Lane	Yr.Iss.	1997	32.00	32
1998 Moore House	Yr.Iss.		Gift	N/A
1998 Brandywine Shop-Hometown	Yr.Iss.		32.00	32
1998 Brandywine Shop-Country Lane	Yr.Iss.		32.00	32

Accessories - M. Whiting

YEAR ISSUE	EDITION LIMIT	YEAR RETD.	ISSUE PRICE	*QUOTE U.S.$
1998 Apple Tree	Open		22.00	22
1992 Apple Tree/Tire Swing	Closed	1998	10.00	12
1998 Autumn Sassafras Tree	Open		22.00	22
1991 Baggage Cart	Closed	1998	10.50	11
1990 Bandstand	Closed	1992	10.50	11
1997 Bunny & Stone Wall	Open		16.00	16
1994 Elm Tree with Benches	Open		16.00	17
1998 Flag	Open		22.00	22
1988 Flag	Closed	1998	10.00	11
1990 Flower Cart	Closed	1998	13.00	14
1990 Gate & Arbor	Closed	1992	9.00	9
1998 Gazebo	Open		24.00	24
1990 Gooseneck Lamp	Closed	1998	7.50	9
1989 Horse & Carriage	Closed	1998	13.00	14
1994 Lamp with Barber Pole	Closed	1998	10.50	11
1988 Lampost, Wall & Tree	Closed	1998	11.00	12
1989 Mailbox, Tree & Fence	Closed	1998	10.00	12
1997 Maple Tree & Stoplight	Open		24.00	24
1997 Pickett Fence Display Shelf, 18"	Open		30.00	36
1997 Pickett Fence Display Shelf, 24"	Open		40.00	48
1997 Pickett Fence, 6"	Open		12.00	12
1998 Pumpkin Wagon	Open		16.00	16
1989 Pumpkin Wagon	Closed	1998	11.50	12
1998 Spring Cherry Tree	Open		20.00	20
1997 Stone Wall & Bunny	Open		16.00	16
1998 Street Sign	Open		16.00	16
1991 Street Sign	Closed	1998	8.00	9
1987 Summer Tree with Fence	Closed	1998	7.00	7
1991 Town Clock	Closed	1998	7.50	9
1998 Town Clock	Open		16.00	16
1992 Tree with Birdhouse	Closed	1998	10.00	11
1989 Victorian Gas Light	Closed	1998	6.50	7
1990 Wishing Well	Closed	1998	10.00	11

Barnsville Collection - M. Whiting

YEAR ISSUE	EDITION LIMIT	YEAR RETD.	ISSUE PRICE	*QUOTE U.S.$
1991 B & O Station	Open		28.00	32
1996 Barnesville High School	Open		50.00	50
1992 Barnesville Presbyterian Church	Open		44.00	45
1997 Bradfield Bank Bldg	Open		44.00	44
1991 Bradfield House	Closed	1996	32.00	32
1990 Candace Bruce House	Closed	1996	30.00	30
1998 City Building	Open		44.00	44
1990 Gay 90's Mansion	Closed	1996	32.00	32
1992 Plumtree Bed & Breakfast	Open		44.00	60
1997 Smith House	Open		32.00	32
1990 Thompson House	Closed	1996	32.00	32
1990 Treat-Smith House	Closed	1996	32.00	32
1991 Whiteley House	Closed	1996	32.00	32

Country Lane - M. Whiting

YEAR ISSUE	EDITION LIMIT	YEAR RETD.	ISSUE PRICE	*QUOTE U.S.$
1995 Berry Farm	Closed	1998	30.00	35
1995 Country School	Closed	1998	30.00	35
1995 Dairy Farm	Closed	1998	30.00	35
1995 Farm House	Closed	1998	30.00	35
1995 The General Store	Closed	1998	30.00	35

Country Lane II - M. Whiting

YEAR ISSUE	EDITION LIMIT	YEAR RETD.	ISSUE PRICE	*QUOTE U.S.$
1995 Antiques & Crafts	Open		30.00	35
1995 Basketmaker	Open		30.00	35
1995 Country Church	Open		30.00	35
1995 Fishing Lodge	Open		30.00	35
1995 Herb Farm	Open		30.00	35
1995 Olde Mill	Open		30.00	35
1995 Spinners & Weavers	Open		30.00	35

Country Lane III - M. Whiting

YEAR ISSUE	EDITION LIMIT	YEAR RETD.	ISSUE PRICE	*QUOTE U.S.$
1996 Airport	Open		30.00	35
1996 Country Club	Open		30.00	35
1996 Country Fair	Open		30.00	35
1996 Firehouse	Open		30.00	35
1996 Old Orchard	Open		30.00	35
1996 Post Office	Open		30.00	35

Country Lane IV - M. Whiting

YEAR ISSUE	EDITION LIMIT	YEAR RETD.	ISSUE PRICE	*QUOTE U.S.$
1996 Candles & Country	Open		30.00	35
1996 Country Inn	Open		30.00	35
1996 Farmer's Market	Open		30.00	35
1996 Lighthouse	Open		30.00	35
1996 Train Station	Open		30.00	35
1996 Valley Stables	Open		30.00	35

Country Lane V - M. Whiting

YEAR ISSUE	EDITION LIMIT	YEAR RETD.	ISSUE PRICE	*QUOTE U.S.$
1997 Barn Dance	Open		31.00	35
1997 Country Curtains & Furniture	Open		31.00	35
1997 Little League Field	Open		31.00	35
1997 Noah's Zoo	Open		31.00	35
1997 Quilts & Things	Open		31.00	35
1997 Uncle Joe's Farm	Open		31.00	35

Country Lane VI - M. Whiting

YEAR ISSUE	EDITION LIMIT	YEAR RETD.	ISSUE PRICE	*QUOTE U.S.$
1998 '98 School	Open		34.00	34
1998 Coffee & Tea Emporium	Open		34.00	34
1998 Country Kids Daycare	Open		34.00	34
1998 Garden & Nursery Center	Open		34.00	34
1998 Seaport	Open		34.00	34

Custom Collection - M. Whiting

YEAR ISSUE	EDITION LIMIT	YEAR RETD.	ISSUE PRICE	*QUOTE U.S.$
1988 Burgess Museum	Open		15.50	16
1992 Cumberland County Courthouse	Open		15.00	15
1990 Doylestown Public School	Open		32.00	33
1991 Jamestown Tower	Closed	1991	9.00	9
1990 Jared Coffin House	Open		32.00	33
1989 Lorain Lighthouse	Closed	1992	11.00	11
1992 Loudon County Courthouse	Open		15.00	15
1988 Princetown Monument	Closed	1989	9.70	10
1991 Smithfield VA. Courthouse	Closed	1992	12.00	12
1989 Yankee Candle Co.	Open		13.50	14

Hilton Village - M. Whiting

YEAR ISSUE	EDITION LIMIT	YEAR RETD.	ISSUE PRICE	*QUOTE U.S.$
1987 Dutch House	Closed	1991	8.50	9
1987 English House	Closed	1991	8.50	9
1987 Georgian House	Closed	1991	8.50	9
1987 Gwen's House	Closed	1991	8.50	9
1987 Hilton Firehouse	Closed	1991	8.50	9

Hometown I - M. Whiting

YEAR ISSUE	EDITION LIMIT	YEAR RETD.	ISSUE PRICE	*QUOTE U.S.$
1990 Barber Shop	Closed	1992	14.00	14
1990 General Store	Closed	1992	14.00	14
1990 School	Closed	1992	14.00	14
1990 Toy Store	Closed	1992	14.00	14

Hometown II - M. Whiting

YEAR ISSUE	EDITION LIMIT	YEAR RETD.	ISSUE PRICE	*QUOTE U.S.$
1991 Church	Closed	1993	14.00	14
1991 Dentist	Closed	1993	14.00	14
1991 Ice Cream Shop	Closed	1993	14.00	14
1991 Stitch-N-Sew	Closed	1993	14.00	14

Hometown III - M. Whiting

YEAR ISSUE	EDITION LIMIT	YEAR RETD.	ISSUE PRICE	*QUOTE U.S.$
1991 Basket Shop	Closed	1993	15.50	16
1991 Dairy	Closed	1993	15.50	16
1991 Firehouse	Closed	1993	15.50	16
1991 Library	Closed	1993	15.50	16

Hometown IV - M. Whiting

YEAR ISSUE	EDITION LIMIT	YEAR RETD.	ISSUE PRICE	*QUOTE U.S.$
1992 Bakery	Closed	1994	21.00	21
1992 Country Inn	Closed	1994	21.50	22
1992 Courtnhouse	Closed	1994	21.50	22
1992 Gas Station	Closed	1994	21.00	21

Hometown V - M. Whiting

YEAR ISSUE	EDITION LIMIT	YEAR RETD.	ISSUE PRICE	*QUOTE U.S.$
1992 Antiques Shop	Closed	1995	22.00	22-45
1992 Gift Shop	Closed	1995	22.00	22-45
1992 Pharmacy	Closed	1995	22.00	22-45
1992 Sporting Goods	Closed	1995	22.00	22-45
1992 Tea Room	Closed	1995	22.00	22-45

Hometown VI - M. Whiting

YEAR ISSUE	EDITION LIMIT	YEAR RETD.	ISSUE PRICE	*QUOTE U.S.$
1993 Church	Closed	1995	24.00	24-45
1993 Diner	Closed	1995	24.00	24-45
1993 General Store	Closed	1995	24.00	24-45
1993 School	Closed	1995	24.00	24-45
1993 Train Station	Closed	1995	24.00	24-45

Hometown VII - M. Whiting

YEAR ISSUE	EDITION LIMIT	YEAR RETD.	ISSUE PRICE	*QUOTE U.S.$
1993 Candy Shop	Closed	1996	24.00	24
1993 Dress Shop	Closed	1996	24.00	24
1993 Flower Shop	Closed	1996	24.00	24
1993 Pet Shop	Closed	1996	24.00	24
1993 Post Office	Closed	1996	24.00	24-45
1993 Quilt Shop	Closed	1996	24.00	24

Hometown VIII - M. Whiting

YEAR ISSUE	EDITION LIMIT	YEAR RETD.	ISSUE PRICE	*QUOTE U.S.$
1994 Barber Shop	Closed	1996	28.00	28
1994 Country Store	Closed	1996	28.00	28
1994 Fire Company	Closed	1996	28.00	28-45
1994 Professional Building	Closed	1996	28.00	28-45
1994 Sewing Shop	Closed	1996	26.00	26

Hometown IX - M. Whiting

YEAR ISSUE	EDITION LIMIT	YEAR RETD.	ISSUE PRICE	*QUOTE U.S.$
1994 Bed & Breakfast	Closed	1997	29.00	30-45
1994 Cafe/Deli	Closed	1997	29.00	30
1994 Hometown Bank	Closed	1997	29.00	30
1994 Hometown Gazette	Closed	1997	29.00	30-45
1994 Teddys & Toys	Closed	1997	29.00	30-45

Hometown X - M. Whiting

YEAR ISSUE	EDITION LIMIT	YEAR RETD.	ISSUE PRICE	*QUOTE U.S.$
1995 Brick Church	Closed	1997	29.00	30
1995 The Doll Shoppe	Closed	1997	29.00	30
1995 General Hospital	Closed	1997	29.00	30-45
1995 The Gift Box	Closed	1997	29.00	30
1995 Police Station	Closed	1997	29.00	30

Hometown XI - M. Whiting

YEAR ISSUE	EDITION LIMIT	YEAR RETD.	ISSUE PRICE	*QUOTE U.S.$
1995 Antiques	Closed	1998	29.00	36
1995 Church II	Closed	1998	29.00	36
1995 Grocer	Closed	1998	29.00	36
1995 Pharmacy	Closed	1998	29.00	36
1995 School II	Closed	1998	29.00	36

Hometown XII - M. Whiting

YEAR ISSUE	EDITION LIMIT	YEAR RETD.	ISSUE PRICE	*QUOTE U.S.$
1996 Bridal & Dress Shoppe	Closed	1998	29.00	36
1996 Five & Dime	Closed	1998	29.00	36
1996 Hometown Theater	Closed	1998	29.00	36
1996 Post Office	Closed	1998	29.00	36
1996 Travel Agency	Closed	1998	29.00	36

Hometown XIII - M. Whiting

YEAR ISSUE	EDITION LIMIT	YEAR RETD.	ISSUE PRICE	*QUOTE U.S.$
1996 Baby Shoppe	Open		29.00	36
1996 Beauty Shoppe	Open		29.00	36
1996 Gem Shoppe	Open		29.00	36
1996 House of Flowers	Open		29.00	36
1996 Robins & Roses	Open		29.00	36

Hometown XIV - M. Whiting

YEAR ISSUE	EDITION LIMIT	YEAR RETD.	ISSUE PRICE	*QUOTE U.S.$
1997 Bakery	Open		30.00	36
1997 The Corner Store	Open		30.00	36
1997 The Gift Basket	Open		30.00	36
1997 Hook & Ladder	Open		30.00	36
1997 Lawyer	Open		30.00	36
1997 Library	Open		30.00	36
1997 Pottery Barn	Closed	1997	30.00	36

Hometown XV - M. Whiting

YEAR ISSUE	EDITION LIMIT	YEAR RETD.	ISSUE PRICE	*QUOTE U.S.$
1997 Bed & Breakfast II	2-Yr.		31.00	36
1997 Classic Cars	2-Yr.		30.00	36
1997 Country Court	2-Yr.		30.00	36
1997 Dog & Burger	2-Yr.		30.00	36
1997 The Pottery	2-Yr.		30.00	36

Hometown XVI - M. Whiting

YEAR ISSUE	EDITION LIMIT	YEAR RETD.	ISSUE PRICE	*QUOTE U.S.$
1998 Spring Home	2-Yr.		36.00	36
1998 Summer Home	2-Yr.		36.00	36
1998 Fall Home	2-Yr.		36.00	36
1998 Winter Home	2-Yr.		36.00	36
1998 Ivy-Covered Church	2-Yr.		36.00	36
1998 School	2-Yr.		36.00	36
1998 Spring Sign	2-Yr.		20.00	20
1998 Summer Sign	2-Yr.		20.00	20
1998 Fall Sign	2-Yr.		20.00	20
1998 Winter Sign	2-Yr.		20.00	20
1998 Spring Shelf, 12"	2-Yr.		24.00	24
1998 Summer Shelf, 12"	2-Yr.		24.00	24
1998 Fall Shelf, 12"	2-Yr.		24.00	24
1998 Winter Shelf, 12"	2-Yr.		24.00	24

North Pole Collection - M. Whiting, unless otherwise noted

YEAR ISSUE	EDITION LIMIT	YEAR RETD.	ISSUE PRICE	*QUOTE U.S.$
1992 3 Winter Trees - D. Whiting	Closed	1998	10.50	12
1993 Candy Cane Factory	Closed	1998	24.00	30
1991 Claus House	Closed	1998	24.00	30
1993 Elf Club	Closed	1998	24.00	30
1992 Elves Workshop	Closed	1996	24.00	30
1991 Gingerbread House	Closed	1998	24.00	30
1995 New Reindeer Barn	Closed	1998	24.00	30
1996 North Pole Chapel	Open		25.50	30
1997 North Pole Train Station	Open		30.00	36
1994 Post Office	Closed	1998	25.00	30
1991 Reindeer Barn	Closed	1996	24.00	30
1992 Snowflake Lodge	Closed	1998	24.00	30
1992 Snowman with St. Sign	Closed	1998	11.50	13
1995 Stocking Shop	Closed	1998	24.00	30
1992 Sugarplum Bakery	Closed	1998	24.00	30
1993 Teddybear Factory	Closed	1998	24.00	30
1993 Town Christmas Tree	Closed	1998	20.00	24
1994 Town Hall	Closed	1998	25.00	30
1996 Trim-a-Tree Shop	Open		25.50	30

Old Salem Collection - M. Whiting

YEAR ISSUE	EDITION LIMIT	YEAR RETD.	ISSUE PRICE	*QUOTE U.S.$
1987 Boys School	Closed	1997	18.50	19
1987 First House	Closed	1997	12.80	13
1987 Home Moravian Church	Closed	1997	18.50	19
1987 Miksch Tobacco Shop	Closed	1993	12.00	12
1987 Salem Tavern	Closed	1997	20.50	21
1987 Schultz Shoemaker	Closed	1997	10.50	11
1987 Vogler House	Closed	1997	20.50	21
1987 Winkler Bakery	Closed	1997	20.50	21

Patriots Collection - M. Whiting

YEAR ISSUE	EDITION LIMIT	YEAR RETD.	ISSUE PRICE	*QUOTE U.S.$
1992 Betsy Ross House	Closed	1997	17.50	26
1992 Washingtons Headquarters	Closed	1997	24.00	36

Seymour Collection - M. Whiting

YEAR ISSUE	EDITION LIMIT	YEAR RETD.	ISSUE PRICE	*QUOTE U.S.$
1991 Anderson House	Closed	1997	20.00	21
1991 Blish Home	Closed	1997	20.00	21
1992 Majestic Theater	Closed	1997	22.00	23
1991 Seymour Church	Closed	1997	19.00	20
1991 Seymour Library	Closed	1997	20.00	21

Treasured Times - M. Whiting

YEAR ISSUE	EDITION LIMIT	YEAR RETD.	ISSUE PRICE	*QUOTE U.S.$
1994 Birthday House	750	1997	32.00	33
1994 Halloween House	750	1997	32.00	33
1994 Mother's Day House	750	1997	32.00	33
1994 New Baby Boy House	750	1997	32.00	33
1994 New Baby Girl House	750	1997	32.00	33
1994 Valentine House	750	1997	32.00	33

Victorian Collection - M. Whiting

YEAR ISSUE	EDITION LIMIT	YEAR RETD.	ISSUE PRICE	*QUOTE U.S.$
1989 Broadway House	Closed	1994	22.00	22
1989 Elm House	Closed	1994	25.00	25
1989 Fairplay Church	Closed	1994	19.50	20
1989 Hearts Ease Cottage	Closed	1994	15.30	16
1989 Old Star Hook & Ladder	Closed	1994	23.00	23
1989 Peachtree House	Closed	1994	22.50	23
1989 Seabreeze Cottage	Closed	1994	15.30	16
1989 Serenity Cottage	Closed	1994	15.30	16
1989 Skippack School	Closed	1994	22.50	23

Williamsburg Collection - M. Whiting

YEAR ISSUE	EDITION LIMIT	YEAR RETD.	ISSUE PRICE	*QUOTE U.S.$
1993 Campbell's Tavern	Open		28.00	29

*Quotes have been rounded up to nearest dollar

YEAR ISSUE	EDITION LIMIT	YEAR RETD.	ISSUE PRICE	*QUOTE U.S.$
1988 Colonial Capitol	Open		43.50	45
1988 Court House of 1770	Open		26.50	28
1988 Governor's Palace	Open		37.50	39
1993 Kings Arms Tavern	Open		25.00	26
1988 The Magazine	Open		23.50	25
1988 Wythe House	Open		25.00	26

Yorktown Collection - M. Whiting

YEAR ISSUE	EDITION LIMIT	YEAR RETD.	ISSUE PRICE	*QUOTE U.S.$
1987 Custom House	Open		17.50	22
1993 Digges House	Open		22.00	30
1987 Grace Church	Open		19.00	30
1987 Medical Shop	Open		13.00	27
1987 Moore House	Open		22.00	30
1987 Nelson House	Open		22.00	30
1987 Pate House	Open		19.00	27
1987 Swan Tavern	Open		22.00	30

The Cat's Meow

Collector Club Gift - Houses - F. Jones

YEAR ISSUE	EDITION LIMIT	YEAR RETD.	ISSUE PRICE	*QUOTE U.S.$
1989 Betsy Ross House	Retrd.	1989	Gift	200
1990 Amelia Earhart	Retrd.	1990	Gift	100
1991 Limberlost Cabin	Retrd.	1991	Gift	50
1992 Abigail Adams Birthplace	Retrd.	1992	Gift	50
1993 Pearl S. Buck House	Retrd.	1993	Gift	50
1994 Lillian Gish	Retrd.	1994	Gift	7-30
1995 Eleanor Roosevelt	Retrd.	1995	Gift	25
1996 Mother's Day Church	Retrd.	1996	Gift	25
1997 Barbara Fritchie House	Retrd.	1997	Gift	N/A
1997 Playhouse	Retrd.	1997	Gift	N/A
1998 The Elizabeth Cady Stanton House	12/98		Gift	N/A

Collector Club - Famous Authors - F. Jones

YEAR ISSUE	EDITION LIMIT	YEAR RETD.	ISSUE PRICE	*QUOTE U.S.$
1989 Harriet Beecher Stowe	Retrd.	1989	8.75	N/A
1989 Orchard House	Retrd.	1989	8.75	N/A
1989 Longfellow House	Retrd.	1989	8.75	N/A
1989 Herman Melville's Arrowhead	Retrd.	1989	8.75	800
1989 Set	Retrd.	1989	35.00	800

Collector Club - Great Inventors - F. Jones

YEAR ISSUE	EDITION LIMIT	YEAR RETD.	ISSUE PRICE	*QUOTE U.S.$
1990 Thomas Edison	Retrd.	1990	9.25	N/A
1990 Ford Motor Co.	Retrd.	1990	9.25	N/A
1990 Seth Thomas Clock Co.	Retrd.	1990	9.25	75
1990 Wright Cycle Co.	Retrd.	1990	9.25	50
1990 Set	Retrd.	1990	37.00	350-500

Collector Club - American Songwriters - F. Jones

YEAR ISSUE	EDITION LIMIT	YEAR RETD.	ISSUE PRICE	*QUOTE U.S.$
1991 Benjamin R. Hanby House	Retrd.	1991	9.25	N/A
1991 Anna Warner House	Retrd.	1991	9.25	N/A
1991 Stephen Foster Home	Retrd.	1991	9.25	22
1991 Oscar Hammerstein House	Retrd.	1991	9.25	22
1991 Set	Retrd.	1991	37.00	200

Collector Club - Signers of the Declaration - F. Jones

YEAR ISSUE	EDITION LIMIT	YEAR RETD.	ISSUE PRICE	*QUOTE U.S.$
1992 Josiah Bartlett Home	Retrd.	1992	9.75	N/A
1992 George Clymer Home	Retrd.	1992	9.75	N/A
1992 Stephen Hopkins Home	Retrd.	1992	9.75	N/A
1992 John Witherspoon Home	Retrd.	1992	9.75	N/A
1992 Set	Retrd.	1992	39.00	150-163

Collector Club -19th Century Master Builders - F. Jones

YEAR ISSUE	EDITION LIMIT	YEAR RETD.	ISSUE PRICE	*QUOTE U.S.$
1993 Henry Hobson Richardson	Retrd.	1993	10.25	25
1993 Samuel Sloan	Retrd.	1993	10.25	25
1993 Alexander Jackson Davis	Retrd.	1993	10.25	25
1993 Andrew Jackson Downing	Retrd.	1993	10.25	25
1993 Set	Retrd.	1993	41.00	75-100

Collector Club - Williamsburg Merchants - F. Jones

YEAR ISSUE	EDITION LIMIT	YEAR RETD.	ISSUE PRICE	*QUOTE U.S.$
1994 East Carlton Wigmaker	Retrd.	1994	11.15	12
1994 J. Geddy Silversmith	Retrd.	1994	11.15	12
1994 Craig Jeweler	Retrd.	1994	11.15	12
1994 M. Hunter Millinery	Retrd.	1994	11.15	12
1994 Set	Retrd.	1994	44.60	75-150

Collector Club - Mt. Rushmore Presidential Series - F. Jones

YEAR ISSUE	EDITION LIMIT	YEAR RETD.	ISSUE PRICE	*QUOTE U.S.$
1995 George Washington Birthplace	Retrd.	1995	12.00	12
1995 Metamora Courthouse	Retrd.	1995	12.00	12
1995 Theodore Roosevelt Birthplace	Retrd.	1995	12.00	12
1995 Tuckahoe Plantation	Retrd.	1995	12.00	12
1995 Set	Retrd.	1995	48.00	60-75

Collector Club - American Holiday Series - F. Jones

YEAR ISSUE	EDITION LIMIT	YEAR RETD.	ISSUE PRICE	*QUOTE U.S.$
1996 And to all a Goodnight	Retrd.	1996	11.00	12
1996 Boo to You	Retrd.	1996	11.00	12
1996 Easter's On Its Way	Retrd.	1996	11.00	12
1996 Let Freedom Ring	Retrd.	1996	11.00	45-85
1996 Set	Retrd.	1996	44.00	50-70

Collector Club - The Civil War Generals - F. Jones

YEAR ISSUE	EDITION LIMIT	YEAR RETD.	ISSUE PRICE	*QUOTE U.S.$
1997 Sherman Home	Retrd.	1997	12.00	12
1997 Jackson Home	Retrd.	1997	12.00	12
1997 Lee Memorial Chapel	Retrd.	1997	12.00	12
1997 Grant House	Retrd.	1997	12.00	12

Collector Club - F. Jones

YEAR ISSUE	EDITION LIMIT	YEAR RETD.	ISSUE PRICE	*QUOTE U.S.$
1998 Boots Motel (available 3/98)	Retrd.	1998	14.00	14
1998 3 Ghosts of Christmas (set/3) (available 7/98)	Retrd.	1998	20.00	20
1998 The Ingalls Family (available 11/98)	12/98		7.00	7

Accessories - F. Jones

YEAR ISSUE	EDITION LIMIT	YEAR RETD.	ISSUE PRICE	*QUOTE U.S.$
1990 1909 Franklin Limousine	Retrd.	1995	4.00	7
1990 1913 Peerless Touring Car	Retrd.	1995	4.00	7
1990 1914 Fire Pumper	Retrd.	1995	4.00	7
1983 5" Hedge	Retrd.	1988	3.00	20-35
1983 5" Iron Fence	Retrd.	1988	3.00	15-30
1987 5" Picket Fence	Retrd.	1992	3.00	20-30
1990 5" Wrought Iron Fence	Retrd.	1995	3.00	7
1983 8" Hedge	Retrd.	1988	3.25	40
1983 8" Iron Fence	Retrd.	1988	3.25	35-40
1983 8" Picket Fence	Retrd.	1988	3.25	40
1989 Ada Belle	Retrd.	1994	4.00	6
1990 Amish Buggy	Retrd.	1995	4.00	8
1991 Amish Garden	Retrd.	1996	4.00	7
1987 Band Stand	Retrd.	1992	6.50	20
1991 Barnyard	Retrd.	1996	4.00	7
1990 Blue Spruce	Retrd.	1995	4.00	8
1990 Bus Stop	Retrd.	1995	4.00	7
1987 Butch & T.J.	Retrd.	1992	4.00	10-14
1986 Cable Car	Retrd.	1991	4.00	9-25
1993 Cannonball Express Train	Retrd.	1998	14.00	14
1986 Carolers	Retrd.	1991	4.00	7-25
1987 Charlie & Co.	Retrd.	1992	4.00	10-14
1985 Cherry Tree	Retrd.	1990	4.00	35-85
1991 Chessie Hopper Car	Retrd.	1996	4.00	7
1986 Chickens	Retrd.	1991	3.25	10-25
1993 Chippewa Lake Billboard	Retrd.	1998	14.00	14
1990 Christmas Tree Lot	Retrd.	1995	4.00	7-10
1989 Clothesline	Retrd.	1994	4.00	7-9
1988 Colonial Bread Wagon	Retrd.	1993	4.00	7-10
1991 Concert in the Park	Retrd.	1996	4.00	7
1986 Cows	Retrd.	1991	4.00	15
1986 Dairy Wagon	Retrd.	1991	4.00	15-25
1986 Ducks	Retrd.	1991	3.25	13
1990 Eugene	Retrd.	1995	4.00	7
1985 Fall Tree	Retrd.	1990	4.00	20-35
1987 FJ Express	Retrd.	1992	4.00	12-15
1986 FJ Real Estate Sign	Retrd.	1991	3.00	10-24
1988 Flower Pots	Retrd.	1993	4.00	9-11
1993 Garden House (one side X-mas)	Retrd.	1998	14.00	14
1988 Gas Light	Retrd.	1993	4.00	7-11
1990 Gerstenslager Buggy	Retrd.	1995	4.00	7
1993 Getting Directions (Policeman)	Retrd.	1998	14.00	14
1993 Grape Arbor	Retrd.	1998	14.00	14
1989 Harry's Hotdogs	Retrd.	1994	4.00	7-10
1986 Horse & Carriage	Retrd.	1991	4.00	15-25
1987 Horse & Sleigh	Retrd.	1992	4.00	13
1986 Ice Wagon	Retrd.	1991	4.00	11-25
1983 Iron Gate	Retrd.	1988	3.00	30-50
1991 Jack The Postman	Retrd.	1996	3.25	7
1993 Jennie & George's Wedding	Retrd.	1998	14.00	14
1993 Johnny Appleseed Statue	Retrd.	1998	14.00	14
1986 Liberty St. Sign	Retrd.	1991	3.25	7-13
1983 Lilac Bushes	Retrd.	1988	3.00	200-400
1993 Little Marine (Children)	Retrd.	1998	14.00	14
1990 Little Red Caboose	Retrd.	1995	4.00	9
1988 Mail Wagon	Retrd.	1993	4.00	8-10
1988 Main St. Sign	Retrd.	1993	3.25	10
1991 Marble Game	Retrd.	1996	4.00	7
1986 Market St. Sign	Retrd.	1991	3.25	10-25
1993 Market Wagon	Retrd.	1998	14.00	14
1991 Martin House	Retrd.	1996	3.25	7
1987 Nanny	Retrd.	1992	4.00	10-14
1993 Nativity Trio Set	Retrd.	1998	21.00	21
1993 Nativity Visitors Trio Set	Retrd.	1998	21.00	21
1991 On Vacation	Retrd.	1996	4.00	7
1989 Passenger Train Car	Retrd.	1994	4.00	9
1985 Pine Tree	Retrd.	1990	4.00	30-40
1988 Pony Express Rider	Retrd.	1993	4.00	11-15
1991 Popcorn Wagon	Retrd.	1996	4.00	7
1985 Poplar Tree	Retrd.	1990	4.00	25-40
1989 Pumpkin Wagon	Retrd.	1994	3.25	9
1989 Quaker Oats Train Car	Retrd.	1994	4.00	9
1987 Railroad Sign	Retrd.	1992	3.00	6-13
1990 Red Maple Tree	Retrd.	1995	4.00	7
1989 Rose Trellis	Retrd.	1994	3.25	9-15
1993 Rubbermaid Train Car	Retrd.	1998	14.00	14
1989 Rudy & Aldine	Retrd.	1994	4.00	8
1993 Rustic Fence (one side X-mas)	Retrd.	1998	14.00	14
1990 Santa & Reindeer	Retrd.	1995	4.00	7-10
1991 Scarey Harry (Scarecrow)	Retrd.	1996	4.00	8
1991 School Bus	Retrd.	1996	4.00	8
1991 Ski Party	Retrd.	1996	4.00	7
1988 Skipjack	Retrd.	1993	6.50	15-18
1996 Smucker Train Car	Retrd.	1996	5.00	20-95
1989 Snowmen	Retrd.	1994	4.00	9
1993 Stock (Train) Car	Retrd.	1998	14.00	14
1988 Street Clock	Retrd.	1993	4.00	10
1985 Summer Tree	Retrd.	1990	4.00	35-90
1989 Tad & Toni	Retrd.	1994	4.00	9
1988 Telephone Booth	Retrd.	1993	4.00	10
1986 Touring Car	Retrd.	1991	4.00	9
1990 Tulip Tree	Retrd.	1995	4.00	7
1988 U.S. Flag	Retrd.	1993	4.00	7-11
1991 USMC War Memorial	Retrd.	1996	6.50	7-15
1990 Veterinary Wagon	Retrd.	1995	4.00	7-13
1990 Victorian Outhouse	Retrd.	1995	4.00	7
1991 Village Entrance Sign	Retrd.	1996	6.50	7-10
1990 Watkins Wagon	Retrd.	1995	4.00	7
1986 Wells, Fargo Wagon	Retrd.	1991	4.00	15-25
1987 Windmill	Retrd.	1992	3.25	10
1986 Wishing Well	Retrd.	1991	3.25	8-25
1987 Wooden Gate (two-sided)	Retrd.	1992	3.00	15
1985 Xmas Pine Tree	Retrd.	1990	4.00	26
1985 Xmas Pine Tree w/Red Bows	Retrd.	1990	3.00	125-200
1990 Xmas Spruce	Retrd.	1995	4.00	7-10

Black Heritage Series - F. Jones

YEAR ISSUE	EDITION LIMIT	YEAR RETD.	ISSUE PRICE	*QUOTE U.S.$
1994 Martin Luther King Birthplace	Retrd.	1994	8.00	15-50

Chippewa Lake Series - F. Jones

YEAR ISSUE	EDITION LIMIT	YEAR RETD.	ISSUE PRICE	*QUOTE U.S.$
1993 Ballroom	Retrd.	1998	11.00	11
1993 Bath House	Retrd.	1998	11.00	11
1993 Midway	Retrd.	1998	11.00	11
1993 Pavilion	Retrd.	1998	11.00	11

Christmas '83-Williamsburg - F. Jones

YEAR ISSUE	EDITION LIMIT	YEAR RETD.	ISSUE PRICE	*QUOTE U.S.$
1983 Christmas Church	Retrd.	1983	6.00	N/A
1983 Federal House	Retrd.	1983	6.00	N/A
1983 Garrison House	Retrd.	1983	6.00	N/A
1983 Georgian House	Retrd.	1983	6.00	450
1983 Set	Retrd.	1983	24.00	3500-4000

Christmas '84-Nantucket - F. Jones

YEAR ISSUE	EDITION LIMIT	YEAR RETD.	ISSUE PRICE	*QUOTE U.S.$
1984 Christmas Shop	Retrd.	1984	6.50	N/A
1984 Powell House	Retrd.	1984	6.50	350
1984 Shaw House	Retrd.	1984	6.50	350
1984 Wintrop House	Retrd.	1984	6.50	250
1984 Set	Retrd.	1984	26.00	1600-1800

Christmas '85-Ohio Western Reserve - F. Jones

YEAR ISSUE	EDITION LIMIT	YEAR RETD.	ISSUE PRICE	*QUOTE U.S.$
1985 Bellevue House	Retrd.	1985	7.00	175
1985 Gates Mills Church	Retrd.	1985	7.00	200
1985 Olmstead House	Retrd.	1985	7.00	175
1985 Western Reserve Academy	Retrd.	1985	7.00	175
1985 Set	Retrd.	1985	27.00	600-1500

Christmas '86-Savannah - F. Jones

YEAR ISSUE	EDITION LIMIT	YEAR RETD.	ISSUE PRICE	*QUOTE U.S.$
1986 J.J. Dale Row House	Retrd.	1986	7.25	150
1986 Lafayette Square House	Retrd.	1986	7.25	140-150
1986 Liberty Inn	Retrd.	1986	7.25	200
1986 Simon Mirault Cottage	Retrd.	1986	7.25	200
1986 Set	Retrd.	1986	29.00	500-925

Christmas '87-Maine - F. Jones

YEAR ISSUE	EDITION LIMIT	YEAR RETD.	ISSUE PRICE	*QUOTE U.S.$
1987 Cappy's Chowder House	Retrd.	1987	7.75	250
1987 Captain's House	Retrd.	1987	7.75	250
1987 Damariscotta Church	Retrd.	1987	7.75	250
1987 Portland Head Lighthouse	Retrd.	1987	7.75	250
1987 Set	Retrd.	1987	31.00	800-1050

Christmas '88-Philadelphia - F. Jones

YEAR ISSUE	EDITION LIMIT	YEAR RETD.	ISSUE PRICE	*QUOTE U.S.$
1988 Elfreth's Alley	Retrd.	1988	7.75	150-200
1988 Graff House	Retrd.	1988	7.75	150-200
1988 The Head House	Retrd.	1988	7.75	150-200
1988 Hill-Physick-Keith House	Retrd.	1988	7.75	150-200
1988 Set	Retrd.	1988	31.00	125-520

Christmas '89-In New England - F. Jones

YEAR ISSUE	EDITION LIMIT	YEAR RETD.	ISSUE PRICE	*QUOTE U.S.$
1989 Hunter House	Retrd.	1989	8.00	50-70
1989 The Old South Meeting House	Retrd.	1989	8.00	21-80
1989 Sheldon's Tavern	Retrd.	1989	8.00	125
1989 The Vermont Country Store	Retrd.	1989	8.00	80-125
1989 Set	Retrd.	1989	32.00	250-350

Christmas '90-Colonial Virginia - F. Jones

YEAR ISSUE	EDITION LIMIT	YEAR RETD.	ISSUE PRICE	*QUOTE U.S.$
1990 Dulany House	Retrd.	1990	8.00	15-50
1990 Rising Sun Tavern	Retrd.	1990	8.00	17-70
1990 Shirley Plantation	Retrd.	1990	8.00	50-75
1990 St. John's Church	Retrd.	1990	8.00	100
1990 St. John's Church (blue)	Retrd.	1990	8.00	150-200
1990 Set	Retrd.	1990	32.00	400-775

Christmas '91-Rocky Mountain - F. Jones

YEAR ISSUE	EDITION LIMIT	YEAR RETD.	ISSUE PRICE	*QUOTE U.S.$
1991 First Presbyterian Church	Retrd.	1991	8.20	30
1991 Tabor House	Retrd.	1991	8.20	55-75
1991 Western Hotel	Retrd.	1991	8.20	25-55
1991 Wheller-Stallard House	Retrd.	1991	8.20	25-55
1991 Set	Retrd.	1991	32.80	150-260

Christmas '92-Hometown - F. Jones

YEAR ISSUE	EDITION LIMIT	YEAR RETD.	ISSUE PRICE	*QUOTE U.S.$
1992 August Imgard House	Retrd.	1992	8.50	25-50
1992 Howey House	Retrd.	1992	8.50	16-50
1992 Overholt House	Retrd.	1992	8.50	30-50
1992 Wayne Co. Courthouse	Retrd.	1992	8.50	25-40
1992 Set	Retrd.	1992	34.00	25-80

Christmas '93-St. Charles - F. Jones

YEAR ISSUE	EDITION LIMIT	YEAR RETD.	ISSUE PRICE	*QUOTE U.S.$
1993 Lewis & Clark Center	Retrd.	1993	9.00	15-20
1993 Newbill-McElhiney House	Retrd.	1993	9.00	15-20
1993 St. Peter's Catholic Church	Retrd.	1993	9.00	15-20
1993 Stone Row	Retrd.	1993	9.00	15-20
1993 Set	Retrd.	1993	36.00	60-80

Christmas '94-New Orleans Series - F. Jones

YEAR ISSUE	EDITION LIMIT	YEAR RETD.	ISSUE PRICE	*QUOTE U.S.$
1994 Beauregard-Keyes House	Retrd.	1994	10.00	14-24
1994 Gallier House	Retrd.	1994	10.00	15-24
1994 Hermann-Grima House	Retrd.	1994	10.00	14-20
1994 St. Patrick's Church	Retrd.	1994	10.00	20-50
1994 Set	Retrd.	1994	40.00	65-70

Christmas '95-New York Series - F. Jones

YEAR ISSUE	EDITION LIMIT	YEAR RETD.	ISSUE PRICE	*QUOTE U.S.$
1995 Clement C. Moore House	Retrd.	1995	10.00	15
1995 Fraunces Taver	Retrd.	1995	10.00	15
1995 Fulton Market	Retrd.	1995	10.00	15
1995 St. Marks-In-the-Bowery	Retrd.	1995	10.00	15
1995 Set	Retrd.	1995	40.00	55-65

Christmas '96-Atlanta Series - F. Jones

YEAR ISSUE	EDITION LIMIT	YEAR RETD.	ISSUE PRICE	*QUOTE U.S.$
1996 Callanwolde	Retrd.	1996	11.00	14
1996 First Baptist Church	Retrd.	1996	11.00	14
1996 Fox Theatre	Retrd.	1996	11.00	14

*Quotes have been rounded up to nearest dollar

YEAR ISSUE	EDITION LIMIT	YEAR RETD.	ISSUE PRICE	*QUOTE U.S.$
1996 Swan House	Retrd.	1996	11.00	14
1996 Set	Retrd.	1996	44.00	52-60

Christmas '97-Stockbridge - F. Jones

YEAR ISSUE	EDITION LIMIT	YEAR RETD.	ISSUE PRICE	*QUOTE U.S.$
1997 Housatonic National Bank	Retrd.	1997	12.00	13-15
1997 Nejaimie's Stockbridge Shop	Retrd.	1997	12.00	13-15
1997 Town Offices	Retrd.	1997	12.00	13-15
1997 William's & Sons	Retrd.	1997	12.00	13-15

Christmas '98-Dickens Christmas Carol Series - F. Jones

YEAR ISSUE	EDITION LIMIT	YEAR RETD.	ISSUE PRICE	*QUOTE U.S.$
1998 The Crachit's House	Retrd.	1998	12.00	12
1998 Fezziwig's Warehouse	Retrd.	1998	12.00	12
1998 Scrooge & Marley	Retrd.	1998	12.00	12
1998 Scrooge's Flat	Retrd.	1998	12.00	12

Circus Series - F. Jones

YEAR ISSUE	EDITION LIMIT	YEAR RETD.	ISSUE PRICE	*QUOTE U.S.$
1997 Big Top	Retrd.	1997	10.50	11-13
1998 Clowns	Retrd.	1998	11.00	12-14
1996 Ferris Wheel	Retrd.	1996	10.00	12-15
1995 Sideshow	Retrd.	1995	10.00	12-16

Covered Bridge Series - F. Jones

YEAR ISSUE	EDITION LIMIT	YEAR RETD.	ISSUE PRICE	*QUOTE U.S.$
1998 Cornish/Windsor Bridge	Retrd.	1998	11.00	11-13
1995 Creamery Bridge	Retrd.	1995	10.00	14-20
1997 Humpback Bridge	Retrd.	1997	10.50	15-17
1996 Kennedy Bridge	Retrd.	1996	10.00	16-19

Fall - F. Jones

YEAR ISSUE	EDITION LIMIT	YEAR RETD.	ISSUE PRICE	*QUOTE U.S.$
1986 Golden Lamb Buttery	Retrd.	1991	8.00	18
1986 Grimm's Farmhouse	Retrd.	1991	8.00	30-40
1986 Mail Pouch Barn	Retrd.	1991	8.00	15
1986 Vollant Mills	Retrd.	1991	8.00	30-60
1986 Set	Retrd.	1991	32.00	150-175

General Store Series - F. Jones

YEAR ISSUE	EDITION LIMIT	YEAR RETD.	ISSUE PRICE	*QUOTE U.S.$
1994 Calef's Country Store	Retrd.	1998	11.00	11-13
1994 Davoll's General Store	Retrd.	1998	11.00	11
1994 Peltier's Market	Retrd.	1998	11.00	11
1994 South Woodstock Country Store	Retrd.	1998	11.00	11

Great Americans Series - F. Jones

YEAR ISSUE	EDITION LIMIT	YEAR RETD.	ISSUE PRICE	*QUOTE U.S.$
1996 Daniel Boone Home	Retrd.	1996	10.00	12-15
1998 Father Flanagan's Home	Retrd.	1998	11.00	11-13
1997 Ivy Green	Retrd.	1997	10.50	12-14

Green Gables Series - F. Jones

YEAR ISSUE	EDITION LIMIT	YEAR RETD.	ISSUE PRICE	*QUOTE U.S.$
1997 Bright River Station	Retrd.	1997	10.50	12-14
1996 Green Gables House	Retrd.	1996	10.00	15-17
1998 Silver Bush	Retrd.	1998	11.00	11-13

Hagerstown - F. Jones

YEAR ISSUE	EDITION LIMIT	YEAR RETD.	ISSUE PRICE	*QUOTE U.S.$
1988 J Hager House	Retrd.	1993	8.00	10-15
1988 Miller House	Retrd.	1993	8.00	10-17
1988 Woman's Club	Retrd.	1993	8.00	10-17
1988 The Yule Cupboard	Retrd.	1993	8.00	10-15
1988 Set	Retrd.	1993	32.00	60-75

Liberty St. - F. Jones

YEAR ISSUE	EDITION LIMIT	YEAR RETD.	ISSUE PRICE	*QUOTE U.S.$
1988 County Courthouse	Retrd.	1993	8.00	10-14
1988 Graf Printing Co.	Retrd.	1993	8.00	10-14
1988 Wilton Railway Depot	Retrd.	1993	8.00	10-14
1988 Z. Jones Basketmaker	Retrd.	1993	8.00	10-17
1988 Set	Retrd.	1993	32.00	32-52

Lighthouse - F. Jones

YEAR ISSUE	EDITION LIMIT	YEAR RETD.	ISSUE PRICE	*QUOTE U.S.$
1990 Admiralty Head	Retrd.	1995	8.00	12-22
1990 Cape Hatteras Lighthouse	Retrd.	1995	8.00	12-22
1990 Sandy Hook Lighthouse	Retrd.	1995	8.00	12-22
1990 Split Rock Lighthouse	Retrd.	1995	8.00	12-22

Limited Edition Promotional Items - F. Jones

YEAR ISSUE	EDITION LIMIT	YEAR RETD.	ISSUE PRICE	*QUOTE U.S.$
1998 Black Cat Alley	Retrd.	1998	12.00	12
1993 Convention Museum	Retrd.	1993	12.95	13
1993 FJ Factory	Open		12.95	13
1994 FJ Factory/5 Yr. Banner	Retrd.	1994	10.00	18
1993 FJ Factory/Gold Cat Edition	Retrd.	1993	12.95	490
1994 FJ Factory/Home Banner	Retrd.	1994	10.00	10
1990 Frycrest Farm Homestead	Retrd.	1991	10.00	125
1992 Glen Pine	Retrd.	1993	10.00	15-25
1998 Goblins & Giggles	Retrd.	1998	12.00	12
1993 Nativity Cat on the Fence	Retrd.	1993	19.95	30
1998 Two Brothers Statue	Retrd.	1998	9.00	9

Main St. - F. Jones

YEAR ISSUE	EDITION LIMIT	YEAR RETD.	ISSUE PRICE	*QUOTE U.S.$
1987 Franklin Library	Retrd.	1992	8.00	18-30
1987 Garden Theatre	Retrd.	1992	8.00	45
1987 Historical Museum	Retrd.	1992	8.00	13-18
1987 Telegraph/Post Office	Retrd.	1992	8.00	18
1987 Set	Retrd.	1992	32.00	100

Mark Twain's Hannibal Series - F. Jones

YEAR ISSUE	EDITION LIMIT	YEAR RETD.	ISSUE PRICE	*QUOTE U.S.$
1995 Becky Thatcher House	Retrd.	1995	10.00	14-16
1997 Grant Drug Store	Retrd.	1997	10.50	11-15
1996 Hickory Stick	Retrd.	1996	10.00	15
1998 Mark Twain Boyhood Home	Retrd.	1998	11.00	11-13

Market St. - F. Jones

YEAR ISSUE	EDITION LIMIT	YEAR RETD.	ISSUE PRICE	*QUOTE U.S.$
1989 Schumacher Mills	Retrd.	1993	8.00	15
1989 Seville Hardware Store	Retrd.	1993	8.00	15
1989 West India Goods Store	Retrd.	1993	8.00	15
1989 Yankee Candle Company	Retrd.	1993	8.00	15
1989 Set	Retrd.	1993	32.00	32

Martha's Vineyard Series - F. Jones

YEAR ISSUE	EDITION LIMIT	YEAR RETD.	ISSUE PRICE	*QUOTE U.S.$
1998 Black Dog Tavern	Retrd.	1998	11.00	11-13
1997 Cinderella Cottage	Retrd.	1997	10.50	12-15
1995 John Coffin House	Retrd.	1995	10.00	16-20
1996 West Chop Lighthouse	Retrd.	1996	10.00	14-17

Miscellaneous - F. Jones

YEAR ISSUE	EDITION LIMIT	YEAR RETD.	ISSUE PRICE	*QUOTE U.S.$
1985 Pencil Holder	Retrd.	1988	3.95	210-500
1985 Recipe Holder	Retrd.	1988	3.95	250-350
1986 School Desk-blue	Retrd.	1988	12.00	250
1986 School Desk-red	Retrd.	1988	12.00	175-250

Nantucket - F. Jones

YEAR ISSUE	EDITION LIMIT	YEAR RETD.	ISSUE PRICE	*QUOTE U.S.$
1987 Jared Coffin House	Retrd.	1992	8.00	15
1987 Maria Mitchell House	Retrd.	1992	8.00	15
1987 Nantucket Atheneum	Retrd.	1992	8.00	20-40
1987 Unitarian Church	Retrd.	1992	8.00	20
1987 Set	Retrd.	1992	32.00	100

Nautical - F. Jones

YEAR ISSUE	EDITION LIMIT	YEAR RETD.	ISSUE PRICE	*QUOTE U.S.$
1987 H & E Ships Chandlery	Retrd.	1992	8.00	18
1987 Lorain Lighthouse	Retrd.	1992	8.00	18-25
1987 Monhegan Boat Landing	Retrd.	1992	8.00	18
1987 Yacht Club	Retrd.	1992	8.00	18
1987 Set	Retrd.	1992	32.00	75

Neighborhood Event Series - F. Jones

YEAR ISSUE	EDITION LIMIT	YEAR RETD.	ISSUE PRICE	*QUOTE U.S.$
1995 Peter Seitz Tavern & Stagecoach	Retrd.	1995	12.95	15
1995 Birely Place	Retrd.	1995	12.95	15-18
1996 Sea-Chimes	Retrd.	1996	12.95	15-17
1996 Bailey-Gombert House	Retrd.	1996	12.95	15-17

Ohio Amish - F. Jones

YEAR ISSUE	EDITION LIMIT	YEAR RETD.	ISSUE PRICE	*QUOTE U.S.$
1991 Ada Mae's Quilt Barn	Retrd.	1996	8.00	13-15
1991 Brown School	Retrd.	1996	8.00	13-15
1991 Eli's Harness Shop	Retrd.	1996	8.00	13-15
1991 Jonas Troyer Home	Retrd.	1996	8.00	13-15
1991 Set	Retrd.	1996	32.00	32

Painted Ladies - F. Jones

YEAR ISSUE	EDITION LIMIT	YEAR RETD.	ISSUE PRICE	*QUOTE U.S.$
1988 Andrews Hotel	Retrd.	1993	8.00	14-32
1988 Lady Amanda	Retrd.	1993	8.00	15
1988 Lady Elizabeth	Retrd.	1993	8.00	15
1988 Lady Iris	Retrd.	1993	8.00	7-15
1988 Set	Retrd.	1993	32.00	70

Postage Stamp Lighthouse Series - F. Jones

YEAR ISSUE	EDITION LIMIT	YEAR RETD.	ISSUE PRICE	*QUOTE U.S.$
1996 The Great Lakes Postage Stamp Lighthouse, set/5	6,000	1996	75.00	75-150

Roscoe Village - F. Jones

YEAR ISSUE	EDITION LIMIT	YEAR RETD.	ISSUE PRICE	*QUOTE U.S.$
1986 Canal Company	Retrd.	1991	8.00	35-65
1986 Jackson Twp. Hall	Retrd.	1991	8.00	25-45
1986 Old Warehouse Rest.	Retrd.	1991	8.00	30-45
1986 Roscoe General Store	Retrd.	1991	8.00	18-35
1986 Set	Retrd.	1991	32.00	125-150

Series I - F. Jones

YEAR ISSUE	EDITION LIMIT	YEAR RETD.	ISSUE PRICE	*QUOTE U.S.$
1983 Antique Shop	Retrd.	1988	8.00	58-125
1983 Apothecary	Retrd.	1988	8.00	67
1983 Barbershop	Retrd.	1988	8.00	60-70
1983 Book Store	Retrd.	1988	8.00	50-125
1983 Cherry Tree Inn	Retrd.	1988	8.00	N/A
1983 Federal House	Retrd.	1988	8.00	89
1983 Florist Shop	Retrd.	1988	8.00	60-125
1983 Garrison House	Retrd.	1988	8.00	40
1983 Red Whale Inn	Retrd.	1988	8.00	N/A
1983 School	Retrd.	1988	8.00	68
1983 Sweetshop	Retrd.	1988	8.00	68
1983 Toy Shoppe	Retrd.	1988	8.00	63-70
1983 Victorian House	Retrd.	1988	8.00	70
1983 Wayside Inn	Retrd.	1988	8.00	N/A
1983 Set of 12 w/ 1 Inn	Retrd.	1988	96.00	450-1300
1983 Set of 14 w/ 3 Inns	Retrd.	1988	112.00	2000-3000

Series II - F. Jones

YEAR ISSUE	EDITION LIMIT	YEAR RETD.	ISSUE PRICE	*QUOTE U.S.$
1984 Attorney/Bank	Retrd.	1989	8.00	95
1984 Brocke House	Retrd.	1989	8.00	40-65
1984 Church	Retrd.	1989	8.00	45-60
1984 Eaton House	Retrd.	1989	8.00	20-35
1984 Grandinere House	Retrd.	1989	8.00	25-75
1984 Millinery/Quilt	Retrd.	1989	8.00	100-150
1984 Music Shop	Retrd.	1989	8.00	65-100
1984 S&T Clothiers	Retrd.	1989	8.00	100-150
1984 Tobacconist/Shoemaker	Retrd.	1989	8.00	75-100
1984 Town Hall	Retrd.	1989	8.00	50-120
1984 Set	Retrd.	1989	96.00	500-750

Series III - F. Jones

YEAR ISSUE	EDITION LIMIT	YEAR RETD.	ISSUE PRICE	*QUOTE U.S.$
1985 Allen-Coe House	Retrd.	1990	8.00	50-60
1985 Connecticut Ave. FireHouse	Retrd.	1990	8.00	40-75
1985 Dry Goods Store	Retrd.	1990	8.00	50-75
1985 Edinburgh Times	Retrd.	1990	8.00	16-40
1985 Fine Jewelers	Retrd.	1990	8.00	40-50
1985 Hobart-Harley House	Retrd.	1990	8.00	30-40
1985 Kalorama Guest House	Retrd.	1990	8.00	20-35
1985 Main St. Carriage Shop	Retrd.	1990	8.00	30-50
1985 Opera House	Retrd.	1990	8.00	5-27
1985 Ristorante	Retrd.	1990	8.00	50-75
1985 Set	Retrd.	1990	80.00	150-250

Series IV - F. Jones

YEAR ISSUE	EDITION LIMIT	YEAR RETD.	ISSUE PRICE	*QUOTE U.S.$
1986 Bennington-Hull House	Retrd.	1991	8.00	38-50
1986 Chagrin Falls Popcorn Shop	Retrd.	1991	8.00	38-50
1986 Chepachet Union Church	Retrd.	1991	8.00	38-50
1986 John Belville House	Retrd.	1991	8.00	38-50
1986 Jones Bros. Tea Co.	Retrd.	1991	8.00	38-50
1986 The Little House Giftables	Retrd.	1991	8.00	38-50
1986 O'Malley's Livery Stable	Retrd.	1991	8.00	38-50
1986 Vandenberg House	Retrd.	1991	8.00	38-50
1986 Village Clock Shop	Retrd.	1991	8.00	38-50
1986 Westbrook House	Retrd.	1991	8.00	38-50
1986 Set	Retrd.	1991	80.00	320-350

Series V - F. Jones

YEAR ISSUE	EDITION LIMIT	YEAR RETD.	ISSUE PRICE	*QUOTE U.S.$
1987 Amish Oak/Dixie Shoe	Retrd.	1992	8.00	18
1987 Architect/Tailor	Retrd.	1992	8.00	18-35
1987 Congruity Tavern	Retrd.	1992	8.00	18-22
1987 Creole House	Retrd.	1992	8.00	18-22
1987 Dentist/Physician	Retrd.	1992	8.00	18
1987 M. Washington House	Retrd.	1992	8.00	18
1987 Markethouse	Retrd.	1992	8.00	18
1987 Murray Hotel	Retrd.	1992	8.00	18
1987 Police Department	Retrd.	1992	8.00	18
1987 Southport Bank	Retrd.	1992	8.00	18-25
1987 Set	Retrd.	1992	80.00	200-250

Series VI - F. Jones

YEAR ISSUE	EDITION LIMIT	YEAR RETD.	ISSUE PRICE	*QUOTE U.S.$
1988 Burton Lancaster House	Retrd.	1993	8.00	16
1988 City Hospital	Retrd.	1993	8.00	16
1988 First Baptist Church	Retrd.	1993	8.00	16-25
1988 Fish/Meat Market	Retrd.	1993	8.00	16
1988 Lincoln School	Retrd.	1993	8.00	16
1988 New Masters Gallery	Retrd.	1993	8.00	16
1988 Ohliger House	Retrd.	1993	8.00	10-16
1988 Pruyn House	Retrd.	1993	8.00	16
1988 Stiffenbody Funeral Home	Retrd.	1993	8.00	16-20
1988 Williams & Sons	Retrd.	1993	8.00	16
1988 Set	Retrd.	1993	80.00	150-200

Series VII - F. Jones

YEAR ISSUE	EDITION LIMIT	YEAR RETD.	ISSUE PRICE	*QUOTE U.S.$
1989 Black Cat Antiques	Retrd.	1994	8.00	15
1989 Hairdressing Parlor	Retrd.	1994	8.00	17
1989 Handcrafted Toys	Retrd.	1994	8.00	15
1989 Justice of the Peace	Retrd.	1994	8.00	15
1989 Octagonal School	Retrd.	1994	8.00	15
1989 Old Franklin Book Shop	Retrd.	1994	8.00	15
1989 Thorpe House Bed & Breakfast	Retrd.	1994	8.00	15-25
1989 Village Tinsmith	Retrd.	1994	8.00	15
1989 Williams Apothecary	Retrd.	1994	8.00	15
1989 Winkler Bakery	Retrd.	1994	8.00	15-25
1989 Set	Retrd.	1994	80.00	120-200

Series VIII - F. Jones

YEAR ISSUE	EDITION LIMIT	YEAR RETD.	ISSUE PRICE	*QUOTE U.S.$
1990 FJ Realty Company	Retrd.	1995	8.00	15
1990 Globe Corner Bookstore	Retrd.	1995	8.00	15
1990 Haberdashers	Retrd.	1995	8.00	15
1990 Medina Fire Department	Retrd.	1995	8.00	12-25
1990 Nell's Stems & Stitches	Retrd.	1995	8.00	15
1990 Noah's Ark Veterinary	Retrd.	1995	8.00	9-15
1990 Piccadilli Pipe & Tobacco	Retrd.	1995	8.00	11-15
1990 Puritan House	Retrd.	1995	8.00	15-20
1990 Victoria's Parlour	Retrd.	1995	8.00	9-15
1990 Walldorff Furniture	Retrd.	1995	8.00	12-15
1990 Set	Retrd.	1995	80.00	100-200

Series IX - F. Jones

YEAR ISSUE	EDITION LIMIT	YEAR RETD.	ISSUE PRICE	*QUOTE U.S.$
1991 All Saints Chapel	Retrd.	1996	8.00	15
1991 American Red Cross	Retrd.	1996	8.00	15
1991 Central City Opera House	Retrd.	1996	8.00	15
1991 City Hall	Retrd.	1996	8.00	15
1991 CPA/Law Office	Retrd.	1996	8.00	15
1991 Gov. Snyder Mansion	Retrd.	1996	8.00	15
1991 Jeweler/Optometrist	Retrd.	1996	8.00	15
1991 Osbahr's Upholstery	Retrd.	1996	8.00	15
1991 Spanky's Hardware Co.	Retrd.	1996	8.00	15
1991 The Treble Clef	Retrd.	1996	8.00	15-18
1991 Set	Retrd.	1996	80.00	80

Series X - F. Jones

YEAR ISSUE	EDITION LIMIT	YEAR RETD.	ISSUE PRICE	*QUOTE U.S.$
1992 Cape May Fudge Kitchen	Retrd.	1997	10.40	11-15
1992 City News	Retrd.	1997	10.40	11-15
1992 Grand Haven	Retrd.	1997	10.40	11-15
1992 Henyan's Athletic Shop	Retrd.	1997	10.40	11-15
1992 Leppert's 5 & 10	Retrd.	1997	10.40	15-20
1992 Madelines	Retrd.	1997	10.40	11-15
1992 The Owl & the Pussycat	Retrd.	1997	10.40	11-15
1992 Pickles Pub	Retrd.	1997	10.40	11-15
1992 Pure Gas Station	Retrd.	1997	10.40	11-15
1992 United Church of Acworth	Retrd.	1997	10.40	11-15

Series XI - F. Jones

YEAR ISSUE	EDITION LIMIT	YEAR RETD.	ISSUE PRICE	*QUOTE U.S.$
1993 Barber Shop/Gallery	Retrd.	1998	11.00	11
1993 Haddonfield Bank	Retrd.	1998	11.00	11
1993 Immanuel Church	Retrd.	1998	11.00	11
1993 Johann Singer Boots & Shoes	Retrd.	1998	11.00	11
1993 Pet Shop//Gift Shop	Retrd.	1998	11.00	11
1993 Police - Troop C	Retrd.	1998	11.00	11
1993 Shrimplin & Jones Produce	Retrd.	1998	11.00	11
1993 Stones Restaurant	Retrd.	1998	11.00	11
1993 U.S. Armed Forces	Retrd.	1998	11.00	11
1993 U.S. Post Office	Retrd.	1998	11.00	11

Southern Belles Series - F. Jones

YEAR ISSUE	EDITION LIMIT	YEAR RETD.	ISSUE PRICE	*QUOTE U.S.$
1996 Auburn	Retrd.	1996	10.00	13-17
1997 Hay House	Retrd.	1997	10.50	11-15
1998 Oak Alley Plantation	Retrd.	1998	11.00	11

Special Item - F. Jones

YEAR ISSUE	EDITION LIMIT	YEAR RETD.	ISSUE PRICE	*QUOTE U.S.$
1997 Breast Cancer Awareness Tree	Retrd.	1997	13.00	15-25
1996 Discus Thrower	Retrd.	1996	10.00	10-15
1997 Eerie Estates	Retrd.	1997	12.00	12-25

*Quotes have been rounded up to nearest dollar

YEAR ISSUE	EDITION LIMIT	YEAR RETD.	ISSUE PRICE	*QUOTE U.S.$
1997 Helping Children Learn	8/98		12.00	12
1997 Mystery Manor	Retrd.	1997	12.00	12
1995 Pocahontas	Retrd.	1995	9.00	15-25
1996 Smithsonian Castle/Stamp Edition	Retrd.	1996	15.00	12-20
1995 Smokey Bear	Retrd.	1995	8.95	13-15
1994 Smokey Bear w/ 50th stamp	Retrd.	1994	8.95	13-20

Tradesman - F. Jones

YEAR ISSUE	EDITION LIMIT	YEAR RETD.	ISSUE PRICE	*QUOTE U.S.$
1988 Buckeye Candy & Tobacco	Retrd.	1993	8.00	15
1988 C.O. Wheel Company	Retrd.	1993	8.00	15
1988 Hermannhof Winery	Retrd.	1993	8.00	15-20
1988 Jenney Grist Mill	Retrd.	1993	8.00	15-31
1988 Set	Retrd.	1993	32.00	60

Washington - F. Jones

YEAR ISSUE	EDITION LIMIT	YEAR RETD.	ISSUE PRICE	*QUOTE U.S.$
1991 National Archives	Retrd.	1996	8.00	13-15
1991 U.S. Capitol	Retrd.	1996	8.00	13-15
1991 U.S. Supreme Court	Retrd.	1996	8.00	13-15
1991 White House	Retrd.	1996	8.00	15-20

Wild West - F. Jones

YEAR ISSUE	EDITION LIMIT	YEAR RETD.	ISSUE PRICE	*QUOTE U.S.$
1989 Drink 'em up Saloon	Retrd.	1993	8.00	15
1989 F.C. Zimmermann's Gun Shop	Retrd.	1993	8.00	15
1989 Marshal's Office	Retrd.	1993	8.00	15-40
1989 Wells, Fargo & Co.	Retrd.	1993	8.00	15
1989 Wells, Fargo & Co.	Retrd.	1993	32.00	75

Williamsburg Series - F. Jones

YEAR ISSUE	EDITION LIMIT	YEAR RETD.	ISSUE PRICE	*QUOTE U.S.$
1993 Bruton Parish Church	Retrd.	1998	11.00	11-13
1993 Governor's Palace	Retrd.	1998	11.00	11-13
1993 Grissel Hay Lodging House	Retrd.	1998	11.00	11-13
1993 Raleigh Tavern	Retrd.	1998	11.00	11-13

Wine Country Series - F. Jones

YEAR ISSUE	EDITION LIMIT	YEAR RETD.	ISSUE PRICE	*QUOTE U.S.$
1997 Beringer Vineyards	Retrd.	1997	10.50	12-14
1996 Charles Krug Winery	Retrd.	1996	10.00	15-17
1998 Chateau Montelena	Retrd.	1998	11.00	11-13

Cavanagh Group Intl.

Coca-Cola Brand North Pole Bottling Works - CGI

YEAR ISSUE	EDITION LIMIT	YEAR RETD.	ISSUE PRICE	*QUOTE U.S.$
1995 All in a Day's Work	Closed	1997	25.00	25
1996 Art Department	Closed	1997	50.00	50
1996 An Artist's Touch	Closed	1997	25.00	25
1996 Big Ambitions	Closed	1997	25.00	25
1995 Checking His List	Closed	1997	30.00	30
1996 Delivery for Mrs. Claus	Closed	1997	25.00	25
1996 Elf in Training	Closed	1997	25.00	25
1995 An Elf's Favorite Chore	Closed	1997	30.00	30
1995 Filling Operations	Closed	1997	45.00	45
1995 Front Office	Closed	1997	50.00	50
1995 The Kitchen Corner	Closed	1997	55.00	55
1995 Maintenance Mischief	Closed	1997	25.00	20-25
1995 Making the Secret Syrup	Closed	1997	30.00	30
1996 Oops!	Closed	1997	25.00	25
1996 Order Department	Closed	1997	55.00	55
1996 Precious Cargo	Closed	1997	25.00	25
1995 Quality Control	Closed	1997	25.00	25-30
1996 Shipping Department	Closed	1997	55.00	55
1996 Special Delivery	Closed	1997	25.00	25
1996 A Stroke of Genius	Closed	1997	25.00	25
1995 Top Secret	Closed	1997	30.00	30

Coca-Cola Brand Town Square Collection - CGI

YEAR ISSUE	EDITION LIMIT	YEAR RETD.	ISSUE PRICE	*QUOTE U.S.$
1992 Candler's Drugs	Closed	1993	40.00	100-130
1996 Carlson's General Store	Closed	1997	40.00	65-70
1997 Central High	Closed	1997	40.00	40-50
1996 Chandler's Ski Resort	Closed	1997	40.00	40-55
1993 City Hall	Closed	1994	40.00	135-165
1996 Clara's Christmas Shop	Closed	1996	40.00	100-150
1995 Coca-Cola Bottling Works	Closed	1995	40.00	32-50
1996 Cooper's Tree Farm	Closed	1997	20.00	25
1992 Dee's Boarding House	Closed	1993	40.00	600-650
1997 Dew Drop Inn	Open		40.00	40
1996 Diamond Service Station	Closed	1996	40.00	100
1992 Dick's Luncheonette	Closed	1993	40.00	100-180
1994 Flying "A" Service Station	Closed	1996	40.00	60-65
1992 Gilbert's Grocery	Closed	1993	40.00	165
1995 Grist Mill	Closed	1995	40.00	40-50
1992 Howard Oil	Closed	1993	40.00	100-165
1993 Jacob's Pharmacy	5,000	1993	25.00	850
1995 Jenny's Sweet Shoppe	Closed	1995	40.00	42-50
1998 Joe's Diner	Open		40.00	40
1995 Lighthouse Point Snack Bar	Closed	1996	40.00	40
1994 McMahon's General Store	Closed	1995	40.00	50-60
1998 Moe's Café & Grill	Open		40.00	40
1993 Mooney's Antique Barn	Closed	1994	40.00	165
1997 Mrs. Murphy's Chowder House	Open		40.00	40
1994 Plaza Drugs	Closed	1995	20.00	70
1993 Route 93 Covered Bridge	Closed	1995	20.00	35-50
1996 Scooter's Drive In	Closed	1997	40.00	50
1997 South Station	Open		40.00	40
1998 Speedy Burger	Open		40.00	40
1998 Star Drive-In	Open		40.00	40
1998 State Theater	Open		40.00	40
1994 Station #14 Firehouse	Closed	1996	40.00	50-70
1994 Strand Theatre	Closed	1996	40.00	50-60
1993 T. Taylor's Emporium	Closed	1994	40.00	70-90
1993 The Tick Tock Diner	Closed	1995	40.00	50-60
1998 Tommy's Service Station	Open		40.00	40
1996 Town Barber Shop	Closed	1997	40.00	40
1994 Town Gazebo	Closed	1995	20.00	25-50
1992 Train Depot	Closed	1993	40.00	300-325
1997 Variety Store	Closed	1997	40.00	40-80
1996 Walton's 5 & 10	Closed	1997	40.00	40-70
1997 Wiley's Hardware	Closed	1997	40.00	40-60

Coca-Cola Brand Town Square Collection Accessories - CGI

YEAR ISSUE	EDITION LIMIT	YEAR RETD.	ISSUE PRICE	*QUOTE U.S.$
1992 Ad Car "Coca-Cola"	Closed	1993	9.00	25
1992 After Skating	Closed	1993	8.00	11-14
1998 Airplane Ads (motion)	Open		36.50	37
1997 Angela	Closed	1997	8.00	8-11
1998 Bandstand	Open		30.00	30
1996 Billboard (large)	Closed	1997	15.00	17
1995 Boys with Snowballs	Closed	1996	11.00	14
1992 Bringing It Home	Closed	1993	8.00	17
1997 Charity Santa	Open		9.00	9
1994 Checker Players	Closed	1995	15.00	15-20
1997 Conductor	Open		8.00	8
1995 Couple on Bench	Closed	1997	11.00	11
1998 Couple with Vending Machine	Open		14.00	14
1996 Covertible	Closed	1996	9.00	9-12
1994 Crowley Cab Co.	Closed	1995	11.00	25-40
1992 Delivery Man	Closed	1993	8.00	23
1992 Delivery Truck "Coca-Cola"	Closed	1993	15.00	36
1996 Drive-In Girl	Closed	1997	7.00	8
1997 Elderly Couple on Bench	Closed	1997	15.00	15
1993 Extra! Extra!	Closed	1994	7.00	20
1997 Father/Son Cutting Tree	Open		15.00	15
1998 Fence Strips with Banner	Open		16.00	16
1998 Fence with Banner	Open		16.00	16
1998 Gas Station Attendent	Open		12.00	12
1992 Gil the Grocer	Closed	1993	8.00	23
1993 Gone Fishing	Closed	1994	11.00	13-18
1994 Homeward Bound	Closed	1995	8.00	12-15
1992 Horse-Drawn Wagon	Closed	1993	12.00	60
1997 Kids on Cooler	Closed	1997	15.00	16
1998 Kids Toasting Marshmellows	Open		12.00	12
1997 Last Minute Shoppers	Closed	1997	11.00	11
1998 Lighted Café Sign	Open		14.00	14
1998 Lighted Diner Sign	Open		14.00	14
1995 Lunch Wagon	Closed	1995	15.00	18
1996 Mailbox	Closed	1996	7.00	7
1996 Mailman	Closed	1996	7.00	7-10
1998 Man with Shovel	Open		11.50	12
1993 Officer Pat	Closed	1995	7.00	13
1993 Old Number Seven	Closed	1995	15.00	25
1997 Pizza Delivery Man	Closed	1997	16.00	16-20
1997 Pizza Delivery Truck	Closed	1997	16.00	16
1996 Proprietor	Closed	1997	7.00	8
1997 Red Delivery Truck	Open		16.00	16
1995 Skiers From Ad	Closed	1995	8.00	8
1994 Sledders	Closed	1995	11.00	14
1994 Sleigh Ride	Closed	1995	15.00	18
1997 Snow Day Fun	Closed	1997	8.00	8
1993 Soda Jerk	Closed	1995	7.00	10-20
1993 Street Vendor	Closed	1994	11.00	11-23
1996 Telephone Booth	Closed	1996	15.00	15-25
1996 Thermometer	Open		12.00	12
1992 Thirsty the Snowman	Closed	1993	9.00	25
1998 Toboggan Sledders	Open		12.00	12
1998 Town Clock Tower with Clock	Open		29.00	29
1998 Waitress on Roller Skates	Open		7.00	7
1997 Yellow Delivery Truck	Closed	1997	16.00	16
1998 Young Boy Vendor	Open		7.00	7

Jerry Berta's Neon America Collection - J. Berta

YEAR ISSUE	EDITION LIMIT	YEAR RETD.	ISSUE PRICE	*QUOTE U.S.$
1998 Blue Diner	5,000		175.00	175
1998 The Diner	5,000		200.00	200
1998 Rosie's Diner	3,000		250.00	250
1998 Star Theater	5,000		175.00	175
1998 Teapot Diner	5,000		200.00	200

Cherished Teddies/Enesco Corporation

Our Cherished Neighbearhood - P. Hillman

YEAR ISSUE	EDITION LIMIT	YEAR RETD.	ISSUE PRICE	*QUOTE U.S.$
1998 Christmas Decorated House 352667	Open		20.00	20
1998 Winter Church 352659	Open		20.00	20
1998 Winter Post Office 352675	Open		20.00	20
1998 Winter Train Depot 352683	Open		20.00	20

Dave Grossman Creations

Spencer Collin Lighthouses Collector Club - C. Spencer Collin

YEAR ISSUE	EDITION LIMIT	YEAR RETD.	ISSUE PRICE	*QUOTE U.S.$
1997 Portsmouth Harbor, NH	Yr.Iss.	1997	40.00	40
1997 Membership Lighthouse	Yr.Iss.	1997	Gift	N/A
1998 Willy & Svea Charting a New Course CSC-CP2	Yr.Iss.		Gift	N/A
1998 Old Alcatraz Lighthouse	Yr.Iss.		40.00	40

Spencer Collin-Admiral's Flag Quarters Series - C. Spencer Collin

YEAR ISSUE	EDITION LIMIT	YEAR RETD.	ISSUE PRICE	*QUOTE U.S.$
1996 Alki Point Light, VA 748G	5,000		74.00	74
1994 Alki Point Light, VA 748M	3,000	1996	74.00	74
1996 Diamond Head Light, CT 749G	5,000		130.00	130
1994 Diamond Head Light, CT 749M	3,000	1996	130.00	130
1996 Hospital Point Light, MA 750G	5,000		71.00	71
1994 Hospital Point Light, MA 750M	3,000	1996	71.00	71
1996 Yerba Buena Light, CA 747G	5,000		101.00	101
1994 Yerba Buena Light, CA 747M	3,000	1996	101.00	101

Spencer Collin-Commemorative Series - C. Spencer Collin

YEAR ISSUE	EDITION LIMIT	YEAR RETD.	ISSUE PRICE	*QUOTE U.S.$
1996 Admirality Head, WA 720G	2,400	1997	118.00	118
1990 Admirality Head, WA 720M	1,500	1996	98.00	110
1996 American Shoals, FL 722G	2,400	1997	97.00	97
1990 American Shoals, FL 722M	1,500	1996	90.00	97
1990 Cape Hatteras, NC 718M	1,500	1994	70.00	70-95
1996 Sandy Hook Light, NJ 721G	2,400		95.00	95
1990 Sandy Hook Light, NJ 721M	1,500	1996	84.00	95-120
1996 West Quoddy Light, ME 719G	2,400		107.00	107
1990 West Quoddy Light, ME 719M	1,500	1996	95.00	98-107

Spencer Collin-Gold Label Signature Series - C. Spencer Collin

YEAR ISSUE	EDITION LIMIT	YEAR RETD.	ISSUE PRICE	*QUOTE U.S.$
1998 Absecon, NJ (signed/gold label) 776	500		90.00	90
1998 Absecon, NJ 776	1,900		90.00	90
1998 Boon Island, ME (signed/gold label) 775	500		85.00	85
1998 Boon Island, ME 775	1,900		85.00	85
1998 Hillsboro Inlet, FL (signed/gold label) 774	500		80.00	80
1998 Hillsboro Inlet, FL 774	1,900		80.00	80
1997 Holland Light, MI (signed/gold label) 766	500	1998	70.00	70
1997 Holland Light, MI 766	1,900		70.00	70
1997 Lightship Nantucket (signed/gold label) 767	500	1997	120.00	120
1997 Lightship Nantucket 767	1,900		120.00	120
1997 Mukiteo, WA 772	1,900		55.00	55
1997 Mukiteo, WA (signed/gold label) 772	500		55.00	55
1997 New Dungeness, WA (signed/gold label) 765	500	1998	70.00	70
1997 New Dungeness, WA 765	1,900		70.00	70
1997 Piedras Blancas, CA (signed/gold label) 770	500		75.00	75
1997 Piedras Blancas, CA 770	1,900		75.00	75
1998 S.F. Lightship (signed/gold label) 773	500		120.00	120
1998 S.F. Lightship 773	1,900		120.00	120
1997 San Luis Obispo, CA (signed/gold label) 771	500		90.00	90
1997 San Luis Obispo, CA 771	1,900		90.00	90
1997 Twin Lights, NJ (signed/gold label) 769	500		120.00	120
1997 Twin Lights, NJ 769	1,900		120.00	120

Spencer Collin-Lighthouses - C. Spencer Collin

YEAR ISSUE	EDITION LIMIT	YEAR RETD.	ISSUE PRICE	*QUOTE U.S.$
1996 10th Year Anniversary 751G	2,400		100.00	100
1994 10th Year Anniversary 751M	Retrd.	1994	100.00	100
1996 Annisquam Harbor Light, MA 742G	2,400		50.00	50
1993 Annisquam Harbor Light, MA 742M	2,000	1996	45.00	50
1996 Assateague Light, VA 727G	2,400		76.00	76
1991 Assateague Light, VA 727M	Retrd.	1996	69.00	76
1996 Barnegat Light, NJ 723G	2,400	1998	71.00	71
1990 Barnegat Light, NJ 723M	Retrd.	1996	71.00	71
1996 Bass Harbor Light, ME 715G	2,400		103.00	103
1989 Bass Harbor Light, ME 715M	Retrd.	1996	95.00	103
1996 Boston Harbor Light, MA 710G	2,400		61.00	61
1987 Boston Harbor Light, MA 710M	Retrd.	1996	45.00	61
1985 Brant Point Lighthouse, MA 703M	Retrd.	1996	75.00	75
1996 Cape Hatteras Lighthouse, NC 802G	2,400	1998	118.00	118
1995 Cape Hatteras Lighthouse, NC 802M	Retrd.	1996	118.00	118-250
1996 Cape May Light, NJ 738G	2,400		88.00	88
1992 Cape May Light, NJ 738M	Retrd.	1996	79.00	88-100
1996 Cape Neddick "Nubble" Light, ME 709G	2,400	1998	95.00	95
1987 Cape Neddick "Nubble" Light, ME 709M	Retrd.	1996	80.00	95
1996 Castle Hill Light, RI 716G	2,400		32.00	32
1990 Castle Hill Light, RI 716M	Retrd.	1996	22.00	32
1985 Chatham Light, MA 706M	Retrd.	1996	68.00	80
1996 Christmas Eve Light 760G	2,400	1997	86.00	86
1995 Christmas Eve Light 760M	Retrd.	1996	86.00	86
1996 Concord Point Light, MD 761G	2,400		60.00	60
1995 Concord Point Light, MD 761M	2,000	1996	60.00	60
1996 Curtis Island Light, ME 734G	2,400		44.00	44
1992 Curtis Island Light, ME 734M	Retrd.	1996	40.00	44
1996 Edgartown Light, MA 801G	2,400		48.00	48
1994 Edgartown Light, MA 801M	Retrd.	1996	48.00	48
1985 Edgartown, MA (1st ed.) 705M	Retrd.	1996	24.00	24
1996 Eggrock Light, ME 731G	2,400	1997	99.00	99
1992 Eggrock Light, ME 731M	Retrd.	1996	91.00	99
1996 Fire Island Light, NY 732G	2,400		122.00	122
1992 Fire Island Light, NY 732M	Retrd.	1996	114.00	122
1996 Fort Gratiot Light, MI 746G	2,400		57.00	57
1994 Fort Gratiot Light, MI 746M	2,000	1996	54.00	54-57
1996 Goat Island Light, ME 763G	2,400		50.00	50
1995 Goat Island Light, ME 763M	2,000	1996	50.00	50
1990 Great Point Light, MA 717M	Retrd.	1996	36.00	40
1996 Heceta Head Light, OR 753G	2,400		155.00	155
1994 Heceta Head Light, OR 753M	2,000	1996	155.00	155
1996 Highland "Cape Cod" Light, MA 733G	2,400	1997	101.00	101
1992 Highland "Cape Cod" Light, MA 733M	Retrd.	1996	94.00	101
1996 Jeffrey's Hook Light, NY 735G	2,400		50.00	50
1992 Jeffrey's Hook Light, NY 735M	Retrd.	1996	45.00	50
1996 Jupiter Inlet Light, FL 743G	2,400		88.00	88
1993 Jupiter Inlet Light, FL 743M	2,000	1996	82.00	84-88
1986 Kennebec River Light, ME 707M	Retrd.	1995	23.00	27
1995 Logo Light w/Flashing Beacon 755M	Retrd.	1995	116.00	116
1996 Logo Mini-Plaque 757G	Open		53.00	53
1995 Logo Mini-Plaque 757M	Retrd.	1996	53.00	53
1996 Marblehead Light, OH 724G	2,400		46.00	46
1990 Marblehead Light, OH 724M	Retrd.	1996	36.00	46
1996 Marshall Point Light, ME 741G	2,400		50.00	50
1993 Marshall Point Light, ME 741M	2,000	1996	45.00	50
1996 Minots Ledge Light, MA 714G	2,400		59.00	59
1989 Minots Ledge Light, MA 714M	Retrd.	1996	50.50	59

*Quotes have been rounded up to nearest dollar

YEAR ISSUE	EDITION LIMIT	YEAR RETD.	ISSUE PRICE	*QUOTE U.S.$
1996 Monhegan Island Light, ME 730G	2,400		50.00	50
1991 Monhegan Island Light, ME 730M	Retrd.	1996	44.00	50
1996 Montauk Point Light, NY 711G	2,400		88.00	88
1988 Montauk Point Light, NY 711M	Retrd.	1996	80.00	84
1996 Mystic Seaport Light, CT 728G	2,400		32.00	32
1991 Mystic Seaport Light, CT 728M	Retrd.	1996	29.00	32
1986 Nauset Beach Light, MA 708M	Retrd.	1995	32.00	40
1996 New London Ledge Light, CT 745G	2,400	1998	126.00	126
1993 New London Ledge Light, CT 745M	2,000	1996	124.00	126
1996 Nobska Light, MA 729G	5,000		40.00	40
1991 Nobska Light, MA 729M	Retrd.	1996	35.00	40
1996 Old Point Loma Light, CA 726G	2,400		86.00	86
1991 Old Point Loma Light, CA 726M	Retrd.	1996	80.00	86
1996 Peggy's Point Light, Nova Scotia 739G	2,400		44.00	44
1993 Peggy's Point Light, Nova Scotia 739M	Retrd.	1996	38.00	44
1996 Pemaquid Bell House, ME 704G	2,400		29.00	29
1984 Pemaquid Bell House, ME 704M	Retrd.	1996	16.00	29
1996 Personalized Lighthouse 712G	2,400		34.00	34
1988 Personalized Lighthouse 712M	Retrd.	1996	24.00	34
1996 Point Isabel, TX 752G	2,400		55.00	55
1994 Point Isabel, TX 752M	2,000	1996	55.00	55
1997 Polar Light	2,400		60.00	60
1996 Ponce Inlet Light, FL 744G	2,400		90.00	90
1993 Ponce Inlet Light, FL 744M	2,000	1996	83.00	90
1996 Portland Head Light, ME 701G	2,400	1997	82.00	82
1984 Portland Head Light, ME 701M	Retrd.	1996	75.00	75
1984 Portsmouth Light, NH 702M	Retrd.	1994	16.00	16
1996 Rock of Ages Light, OH 725G	2,400	1997	63.00	63
1991 Rock of Ages Light, OH 725M	Retrd.	1996	58.00	63
1996 Round Island Light, MI 758G	2,400		120.00	120
1995 Round Island Light, MI 758M	2,000	1996	120.00	120
1996 Rudolph's Light 759G	2,400	1997	68.00	68
1995 Rudolph's Light 759M	Retrd.	1996	68.00	68
1996 Sand Island Light, AL 740G	2,400		71.00	71
1993 Sand Island Light, AL 740M	Retrd.	1996	65.00	71
1996 Split Rock Lighthouse, MI 737G	2,400		118.00	118
1992 Split Rock Lighthouse, MI 737M	Retrd.	1996	99.00	118
1996 St. Joseph's Pier Lights, MI 762G	2,400		114.00	114
1995 St. Joseph's Pier Lights, MI 762M	2,000	1996	114.00	114
1996 St. Simons Island Light, GA 736G	2,400		124.00	124
1992 St. Simons Island Light, GA 736M	Retrd.	1996	116.00	124
1996 Thomas Point Light, MD 754G	2,400		109.00	109
1995 Thomas Point Light, MD 754M	2,000	1996	109.00	109
1996 Whaleback Light, NH 713G	2,400		38.00	38
1989 Whaleback Light, NH 713M	Retrd.	1996	30.00	38
1995 Willie & Svea's Light 756M	Retrd.	1995	N/A	N/A

Spencer Collin-New England Collection - C. Spencer Collin

YEAR ISSUE	EDITION LIMIT	YEAR RETD.	ISSUE PRICE	*QUOTE U.S.$
1984 Historical Homes, set/10	Retrd.	1990	N/A	N/A
1984 Home Town, set/10	Retrd.	1990	200.00	200
1984 New England Cottages, set/10 w/base	Retrd.	1990	195.00	195
1984 New England Village, set/12 w/base	Retrd.	1990	227.00	227

David Winter Cottages/Enesco Corporation

David Winter Collectors Guild Exclusives - D. Winter

YEAR ISSUE	EDITION LIMIT	YEAR RETD.	ISSUE PRICE	*QUOTE U.S.$
1987 Robin Hood's Hideaway	Closed	1987	54.00	328-450
1987 Queen Elizabeth Slept Here	Closed	1987	183.00	223-377
1988 Black Bess Inn	Closed	1988	60.00	70-261
1988 The Pavillion	Closed	1988	52.00	205-298
1988 Street Scene	Closed	1988	Gift	135-149
1989 Home Guard	Closed	1989	105.00	205-298
1989 Coal Shed	Closed	1989	112.00	205-298
1990 The Plucked Ducks	Closed	1990	Gift	65-149
1990 The Cobblers Cottage	Closed	1990	40.00	40-75
1990 The Pottery	Closed	1990	40.00	40-142
1991 Pershore Mill	Closed	1991	Gift	68-149
1991 Tomfool's Cottage	Closed	1991	100.00	50-180
1991 Will-O' The Wisp	Closed	1991	120.00	132-156
1992 Irish Water Mill	Closed	1992	Gift	40-89
1992 Patrick's Water Mill	Closed	1992	Gift	80-105
1992 Candlemaker's	Closed	1992	65.00	70-134
1992 Beekeeper's	Closed	1992	65.00	70-111
1993 On The River Bank	Closed	1993	Gift	32-119
1993 Thameside	Closed	1993	79.00	70-126
1993 Swan Upping Cottage	Closed	1993	69.00	70-105
1993 Plum Cottage (U.K. only/Guild Membership incentive piece)	Closed	1993	N/A	121-150
1994 15 Lawnside Road	Closed	1994	Gift	40-60
1994 While Away Cottage	Closed	1994	70.00	65-82
1994 Ashe Cottage	Closed	1994	62.00	64-70
1995 Buttercup Cottage	Closed	1995	60.00	65-82
1995 The Flowershop	Closed	1995	150.00	120-201
1995 Gardener's Cottage	Closed	1995	Gift	40-75
1996 Punch Stables	Closed	1996	150.00	150
1996 Plough Farmstead	Closed	1996	125.00	125
1996 Model Dairy	Closed	1996	Gift	40-64
1997 Abbots	Closed	1997	75.00	75
1997 Gameskeeper	Closed	1997	85.00	85
1997 Sextons	Closed	1997	Gift	N/A
1998 The Charcoal Burner's	Closed	1998	85.00	85
1998 The Coppicer's Cottage	Closed	1998	90.00	90
1998 Mistletoe Cottage	Closed	1998	Gift	40

Painting Event Pieces - D. Winter

YEAR ISSUE	EDITION LIMIT	YEAR RETD.	ISSUE PRICE	*QUOTE U.S.$
1992 Birthstone Wishing Well	Closed	1992	40.00	68-80
1993 Birthday Cottage (Arches Thwonce)	Closed	1994	55.00	60
1994 Wishing Falls Cottage	Closed	1995	65.00	80-127
1995 Whisper Cottage	Closed	1995	65.00	80-97
1996 Primrose Cottage	Closed	1996	65.00	60

Appearance Piece - D. Winter

YEAR ISSUE	EDITION LIMIT	YEAR RETD.	ISSUE PRICE	*QUOTE U.S.$
1993 Arches Thrice	Closed	1993	150.00	200-410
1994 Winter Arch	Closed	1995	N/A	17-45
1995 Grumbleweed's Potting Shed	Closed	1995	99.00	130-149
1995 Grumbleweed's Potting Shed Colorway	Closed	1995	99.00	100
1996 The Derby Arms	Closed	1996	65.00	65-97
1997 Suffolk Gardens	Yr.Iss.	1997	60.00	60-119
1998 The Truffleman's	Yr.Iss.	1998	75.00	75

At The Centre of the Village Collection - D. Winter

YEAR ISSUE	EDITION LIMIT	YEAR RETD.	ISSUE PRICE	*QUOTE U.S.$
1983 The Bakehouse	Closed	1996	31.40	40-78
1984 The Chapel	Closed	1992	48.80	80-94
1985 The Cooper Cottage	Closed	1993	57.90	75-80
1983 The Green Dragon Pub/ Inn	Closed	1996	31.40	33-97
1980 Ivy Cottage	Closed	1992	22.00	33-89
1980 Little Market	Closed	1993	28.90	55-60
1980 Market Street	Closed	1996	48.80	65-90
1984 Parsonage	Closed	1996	390.00	330-447
1980 Rose Cottage	Closed	1996	28.90	45-51
1984 Spinner's Cottage	Closed	1991	28.90	59-126
1982 The Village Shop	Closed	1996	22.00	20-52
1980 The Wine Merchant	Closed	1993	28.90	39-80

British Traditions - D. Winter

YEAR ISSUE	EDITION LIMIT	YEAR RETD.	ISSUE PRICE	*QUOTE U.S.$
1990 Blossom Cottage	Closed	1995	59.00	50-65
1990 The Boat House	Closed	1995	37.50	60-104
1990 Bull & Bush	Closed	1995	37.50	30-50
1990 Burns' Reading Room	Closed	1995	31.00	28-70
1990 Grouse Moor Lodge	Closed	1995	48.00	35-52
1990 Guy Fawkes	Closed	1995	31.00	30-50
1990 Harvest Barn	Closed	1995	31.00	30-50
1990 Knight's Castle	Closed	1995	59.00	75-85
1991 The Printers and The Bookbinders	Closed	1994	120.00	150-171
1990 Pudding Cottage	Closed	1995	78.00	39-60
1990 St. Anne's Well	Closed	1995	48.00	50-59
1990 Staffordshire Vicarage	Closed	1995	48.00	52-65
1990 Stonecutters Cottage	Closed	1995	48.00	50-112

Cameos - D. Winter

YEAR ISSUE	EDITION LIMIT	YEAR RETD.	ISSUE PRICE	*QUOTE U.S.$
1992 Barley Malt Kilns	Closed	1996	12.50	10-25
1992 Brooklet Bridge	Closed	1996	12.50	10-25
1992 Diorama-Bright	Closed	1996	50.00	50-80
1992 Diorama-Light	Closed	1992	30.00	30-50
1992 Greenwood Wagon	Closed	1996	12.50	13-25
1992 Lych Gate	Closed	1996	12.50	10-25
1992 Market Day	Closed	1996	12.50	13-25
1992 One Man Jail	Closed	1996	12.50	13-25
1992 Penny Wishing Well	Closed	1996	12.50	18-25
1992 The Potting Shed	Closed	1996	12.50	10-25
1992 Poultry Ark	Closed	1996	12.50	25-31
1992 The Privy	Closed	1996	12.50	10-25
1992 Saddle Steps	Closed	1996	12.50	13-25
1992 Welsh Pig Pen	Closed	1996	12.50	11-13

Carnival Premier Castles-England - D. Winter

YEAR ISSUE	EDITION LIMIT	YEAR RETD.	ISSUE PRICE	*QUOTE U.S.$
1993 Castle Cottage of Warwick	Closed	1993	160.00	424-525
1994 Kingmaker's Castle	Closed	1994	240.00	375-424
1995 Castle Tower of Windsor	Closed	1995	280.00	375-395
1996 Rochester Castle	Closed	1996	312.00	365-425
1997 Richard III Castle	Closed	1997	184.00	372-395

Castle Collection - D. Winter

YEAR ISSUE	EDITION LIMIT	YEAR RETD.	ISSUE PRICE	*QUOTE U.S.$
1995 Bishopsgate	Closed	1996	175.00	149-175
1995 Bishopsgate Premier	Closed	1996	225.00	201-225
1994 Castle Wall	Closed	1996	65.00	65-90
1996 Christmas Castle	Closed	1996	160.00	160
1996 Guinevere's Castle	Closed	1996	299.00	248-299
1996 Guinevere's Castle Premier	Closed	1996	350.00	550-559
1994 Kingmaker's Castle (w/Ivy)	Closed	N/A	N/A	375-390
1996 Rochester Castle (without snow)	Closed	1996	312.00	160-325

Celebration Cottages - D. Winter

YEAR ISSUE	EDITION LIMIT	YEAR RETD.	ISSUE PRICE	*QUOTE U.S.$
1994 Celebration Chapel	Closed	1996	75.00	68-75
1994 Celebration Chapel Premier	Closed	1996	150.00	134-150
1995 Mother's Cottage	Closed	1996	65.00	65
1995 Mother's Cottage Premier	Closed	1996	89.50	82-90
1994 Spring Hollow	Closed	1996	65.00	59-65
1994 Spring Hollow Premier	Closed	1996	125.00	112-125
1995 Stork Cottage Boy	Closed	1996	65.00	52-65
1995 Stork Cottage Girl	Closed	1996	65.00	52-65
1994 Sweetheart Haven	Closed	1996	60.00	54-60
1994 Sweetheart Haven Premier	Closed	1996	115.00	104-115

Chapels & Churches Collection - D. Winter

YEAR ISSUE	EDITION LIMIT	YEAR RETD.	ISSUE PRICE	*QUOTE U.S.$
1998 St. Christopher's Church	Open		110.00	110
1998 Thornhill Chapel	Open		90.00	90

Charitable Models - D. Winter

YEAR ISSUE	EDITION LIMIT	YEAR RETD.	ISSUE PRICE	*QUOTE U.S.$
1988 Jim'll Fixit-Wintershill	Closed	1988	350.00	2500-3000
1990 Cartwright's Cottage	Closed	1990	45.00	40-104

Dicken's Christmas - D. Winter

YEAR ISSUE	EDITION LIMIT	YEAR RETD.	ISSUE PRICE	*QUOTE U.S.$
1987 Ebenezer Scrooge's Counting House	Closed	1988	96.90	208-275
1988 Christmas in Scotland & Hogmanay	Closed	1988	100.00	150-199
1989 A Christmas Carol	Closed	1989	135.00	75-250
1990 Mr. Fezziwig's Emporium	Closed	1990	135.00	150-223
1991 Fred's Home: "A Merry Christmas, Uncle Ebenezer saids Scrooge's Nephew Fred, and a Happy New Year.	Closed	1991	145.00	99-130
1992 Scrooge's School	Closed	1992	160.00	132-149
1993 Old Joe's Beetling Shop, A Veritable Den of Iniquity!	Closed	1993	175.00	149-250
1994 Scrooge's Family Home	Closed	1994	175.00	132-149
1994 Scrooge's Family Home Premier	Closed	1994	230.00	186-230
1994 Scrooge's Family Home, Plaque	3,500	1994	125.00	33-80
1995 Miss Belle's Cottage	Closed	1995	185.00	99-130
1995 Miss Belle's Cottage Premier	2,200	1995	235.00	235-298
1995 Miss Belle's Christmas Plaque	4,000	1995	120.00	33-112
1996 Tiny Tim	Closed	1996	150.00	150-250
1996 Tiny Tim Premier	2,200	1996	180.00	180-298
1996 Tiny Tim Christmas Plaque	4,000	1996	110.00	104-150

English Village - D. Winter

YEAR ISSUE	EDITION LIMIT	YEAR RETD.	ISSUE PRICE	*QUOTE U.S.$
1994 Cat & Pipe Inn	Closed	1997	53.00	55
1994 Chandlery	Closed	1997	53.00	55
1994 Church & Vestry	Closed	1997	57.00	44-55
1994 Constabulary	Closed	1997	60.00	38-55
1994 Crystal Cottage	Closed	1997	53.00	44-55
1995 Engine House (brown door)	Closed	1997	55.00	50-55
1994 Engine House (Disney/red door)	Closed	1997	55.00	55
1994 Glebe Cottage	Closed	1997	53.00	38-55
1994 Guardian Castle	8,490	1994	275.00	281-420
1994 Guardian Castle Premier	1,500	1994	350.00	495-625
1994 The Hall	Closed	1997	55.00	50-55
1994 One Acre Cottage	Closed	1997	55.00	42-55
1994 The Post Office	Closed	1997	53.00	47-55
1994 The Quack's Cottage	Closed	1997	57.00	38-55
1994 The Rectory	Closed	1997	55.00	55
1994 The Seminary	Closed	1997	57.00	38-55
1994 The Smithy	Closed	1997	50.00	38-55
1994 The Tannery	Closed	1997	50.00	27-55

Forest of Dean Collection - D. Winter

YEAR ISSUE	EDITION LIMIT	YEAR RETD.	ISSUE PRICE	*QUOTE U.S.$
1996 Abbey Ruins	Open		55.00	55
1997 The Artist's Studio	Open		55.00	55
1996 The Citadel	Open		55.00	55
1996 Forest of DEAN MINE	Open		55.00	55
1997 The Observatory	Open		55.00	55
1997 The Sawmill	Open		55.00	55

Garden Cottages of England - D. Winter

YEAR ISSUE	EDITION LIMIT	YEAR RETD.	ISSUE PRICE	*QUOTE U.S.$
1996 The Park	Closed	1996	275.00	275
1996 The Park, Premier	Closed	1996	299.50	300-475
1995 Spencer Hall Gardens	Closed	1996	395.00	275-372
1995 Spencer Hall Gardens, Premier	Closed	1996	495.00	484-495
1995 Willow Gardens	Closed	1995	225.00	201-297
1995 Willow Gardens, Premier	Closed	1995	299.00	268-299

The Haunted House Collection - D. Winter

YEAR ISSUE	EDITION LIMIT	YEAR RETD.	ISSUE PRICE	*QUOTE U.S.$
1998 The House of Usher	Yr.Iss.		175.00	175

Heart of England Series - D. Winter

YEAR ISSUE	EDITION LIMIT	YEAR RETD.	ISSUE PRICE	*QUOTE U.S.$
1985 The Apothecary Shop	Closed	1995	24.10	35-51
1985 Blackfriars Grange	Closed	1994	24.10	30-38
1985 Craftsmen's Cottage	Closed	1995	24.10	29-43
1985 The Hogs Head Tavern/Beer House	Closed	1995	24.10	35-60
1985 Meadowbank Cottages	Closed	1995	24.10	28-51
1985 The Schoolhouse	Closed	1995	24.10	46-52
1985 Shirehall	Closed	1995	24.10	35-51
1985 St. George's Church	Closed	1995	24.10	35-51
1985 The Vicarage	Closed	1995	24.10	51-117
1985 The Windmill	Closed	1995	37.50	75-99
1985 Yeoman's Farmhouse	Closed	1995	24.10	35-51

In The Country Collection - D. Winter

YEAR ISSUE	EDITION LIMIT	YEAR RETD.	ISSUE PRICE	*QUOTE U.S.$
1983 The Bothy	Closed	1996	31.40	40-67
1982 Brookside Hamlet	Closed	1991	74.80	75-83
1981 Drover's Cottage	Closed	1996	22.00	25-37
1983 Fisherman's Wharf	Closed	1996	31.40	30-97
1994 Guardian Gate	Closed	1996	150.00	129-134
1994 Guardian Gate Premier	Closed	1996	199.00	248-429
1987 John Benbow's Farmhouse	Closed	1993	78.00	35-80
1996 Lover's Tryst	Closed	1996	125.00	125-238
1983 Pilgrim's Rest	Closed	1993	48.80	65-94
1984 Snow Cottage	Closed	1992	24.80	83-149
1986 There was a Crooked House	Closed	1996	96.90	100-186
1996 There was a Narrow House	Closed	1996	115.00	115
1984 Tollkeeper's Cottage	Closed	1992	87.00	140-149

Irish Collection - D. Winter

YEAR ISSUE	EDITION LIMIT	YEAR RETD.	ISSUE PRICE	*QUOTE U.S.$
1992 Fogartys	Closed	1994	75.00	70-104
1992 Irish Round Tower	Closed	1996	65.00	70-79
1992 Murphys	Closed	1996	100.00	82-110
1992 O'Donovan's Castle	Closed	1996	145.00	170
1991 Only A Span Apart	Closed	1993	80.00	70-90
1991 Secret Shebeen	Closed	1993	70.00	70-127

Landowners - D. Winter

YEAR ISSUE	EDITION LIMIT	YEAR RETD.	ISSUE PRICE	*QUOTE U.S.$
1984 Castle Gate	Closed	1992	155.00	176-270
1982 The Dower House	Closed	1993	22.00	29-37
1988 The Grange	Closed	1989	120.00	1200-1450
1985 Squire Hall	Closed	1990	92.30	125-149
1981 Tudor Manor House	Closed	1992	48.80	99-127

Main Collection - D. Winter

YEAR ISSUE	EDITION LIMIT	YEAR RETD.	ISSUE PRICE	*QUOTE U.S.$
1983 The Alms Houses	Closed	1987	59.90	248-510
1992 Audrey's Tea Room	Closed	1992	90.00	72-80
1992 Audrey's Tea Shop	Closed	1992	90.00	165-510
1982 Blacksmith's Cottage	Closed	1986	22.00	200-473
1991 Castle in the Air	Closed	1996	675.00	710-750
1982 Castle Keep	Closed	1982	30.00	1200-1400
1981 Chichester Cross	Closed	1981	50.00	3000-3200
1980 The Coaching Inn	Closed	1983	165.00	3600
1981 Cornish Cottage	Closed	1986	30.00	700
1983 Cornish Tin Mine	Closed	1989	22.00	80-127

*Quotes have been rounded up to nearest dollar

YEAR ISSUE	EDITION LIMIT	YEAR RETD.	ISSUE PRICE	*QUOTE U.S.$
1983 Cotton Mill	Closed	1989	41.30	484
1981 Double Oast	Closed	1982	60.00	3300
1980 Dove Cottage	Closed	1983	60.00	825-900
1982 Fairytale Castle	Closed	1989	115.00	195-300
1986 Falstaff's Manor	10,000	1990	242.00	160-500
1980 The Forge	Closed	1983	60.00	825-900
1996 Golf Clubhouse	Closed	1996	160.00	160
1996 Haunted House	4,900	1996	325.00	350-596
1983 The Haybarn	Closed	1987	22.00	182-341
1997 Hereward the Wake's Castle	3,500	1997	175.00	175
1985 Hermit's Humble Home	Closed	1988	87.00	248-300
1993 Horatio Persnickety's Amorous Intent	9,900	1993	375.00	249-298
1984 House of the Master Mason	Closed	1988	74.80	165-200
1982 House on Top	Closed	1988	92.30	249-261
1991 Inglenook Cottage	Closed	1996	60.00	75
1980 Little Forge	Closed	1983	40.00	495-1200
1980 Little Mill	Closed	1980	40.00	750-950
1980 Little Mill-remodeled	Closed	1983	Unkn.	825-999
1992 Mad Baron Fourthrite's Folly	Closed	1992	275.00	165-264
1997 Milestone Cottage	Open		130.00	130
1980 Mill House	Closed	1980	50.00	2500
1980 Mill House-remodeled	Closed	1983	50.00	999-1250
1982 Miner's Cottage	Closed	1987	22.00	199-237
1991 Moonlight Haven	Closed	1996	120.00	104-155
1982 Moorland Cottage	Closed	1987	22.00	270
1995 Newtown Millhouse	Closed	1996	195.00	195
1981 The Old Curiosity Shop	Closed	1983	40.00	799-1300
1980 Provencal One (French Market Only)	Closed	N/A	N/A	N/A
1980 Provencal Two (French Market Only)	Closed	N/A	N/A	N/A
1980 Quayside	Closed	1985	60.00	799-1100
1994 Quindene Manor	3,000	1994	695.00	605-650
1994 Quindene Manor Premier	1,500	1994	850.00	782-1080
1982 Sabrina's Cottage	Closed	1982	30.00	1250-2000
1996 St. George & The Dragon	Closed	1996	150.00	127-150
1997 St. George & The Dragon (modified)	Open		150.00	150
1981 St. Paul's Cathedral	Closed	1982	40.00	825-999
1985 Suffolk House	Closed	1989	48.80	50-66
1980 Three Duck Inn	Closed	1983	60.00	699-1500
1998 Tom's Yard	5,000		130.00	130
1981 Tythe Barn	Closed	1986	39.30	900-1452
1981 The Village	Closed	1996	362.00	495-580
1986 The Village-remodeled	Closed	N/A	580.00	580
1991 The Weaver's Lodgings	Closed	1996	65.00	54-75
1995 Welcome Home Cottage	Closed	1995	99.00	99-150
1995 Welcome Home Cottage Military	Closed	1995	99.00	99
1982 William Shakespeare's Birthplace (large)	Closed	1984	60.00	900-1573
1983 Woodcutter's Cottage	Closed	1988	87.00	179-248

Midlands Collection - D. Winter

YEAR ISSUE	EDITION LIMIT	YEAR RETD.	ISSUE PRICE	*QUOTE U.S.$
1988 Bottle Kilns	Closed	1991	78.00	80-99
1988 Coal Miner's Row	Closed	1996	90.00	51-90
1988 Derbyshire Cotton Mill	Closed	1994	65.00	99-149
1988 The Gunsmiths	Closed	1996	78.00	65-104
1988 Lacemaker's Cottage	Closed	1996	120.00	80-119
1988 Lock-keepers Cottage	Closed	1996	65.00	75-80

The Mystical Castles of Britain - D. Winter

YEAR ISSUE	EDITION LIMIT	YEAR RETD.	ISSUE PRICE	*QUOTE U.S.$
1998 Halidon Hill	Open		130.00	130
1998 Hotspur's Keep	Open		110.00	110
1998 Myton Tower	Open		130.00	130
1998 Witch's Castle	4,250		175.00	175

The Oliver Twist Christmas Collection - D. Winter

YEAR ISSUE	EDITION LIMIT	YEAR RETD.	ISSUE PRICE	*QUOTE U.S.$
1997 Mr. Bumble's	Closed	1997	110.00	110
1998 Mr. Fang The Magistrate's House	Open		110.00	110

The Pilgrim's Way Collection - D. Winter

YEAR ISSUE	EDITION LIMIT	YEAR RETD.	ISSUE PRICE	*QUOTE U.S.$
1997 The Alchemist's Cottage	Open		50.00	50
1997 The Brickies	Open		50.00	50
1997 The Dingle	Open		50.00	50
1997 The Falconry	Open		50.00	50
1998 Griselda's Cottage	Open		90.00	90
1998 Marquis Walter's Manor	5,000		150.00	150
1997 The Serf's Cottage	Open		50.00	50
1997 St. Joseph's Cottage	Open		50.00	50

Porridge Pot Alley - D. Winter

YEAR ISSUE	EDITION LIMIT	YEAR RETD.	ISSUE PRICE	*QUOTE U.S.$
1995 Cob's Bakery	Closed	1996	125.00	125
1995 Cob's Bakery Premier	Closed	1996	165.00	165
1995 Porridge Pot Arch	Closed	1996	50.00	50
1995 Sweet Dreams	Closed	1996	79.00	80
1995 Sweet Dreams Premier	Closed	1996	99.00	99
1995 Tartan Teahouse	Closed	1996	99.00	99
1995 Tartan Teahouse Premier	Closed	1996	129.00	129

The Pubs & Taverns of England - D. Winter

YEAR ISSUE	EDITION LIMIT	YEAR RETD.	ISSUE PRICE	*QUOTE U.S.$
1998 The Bird Cage	Open		100.00	100
1998 The Good Intent	Open		100.00	100
1998 The Hop Pickers	Open		130.00	130
1998 The Tickled Trout	4,500		150.00	150

Regions Collection - D. Winter

YEAR ISSUE	EDITION LIMIT	YEAR RETD.	ISSUE PRICE	*QUOTE U.S.$
1981 Cotswold Cottage	Closed	1996	22.00	37
1982 Cotswold Village	Closed	1990	59.90	77-80
1983 Hertford Court	Closed	1992	87.00	125-149
1985 Kent Cottage	Closed	1996	48.80	80
1981 Single Oast	Closed	1993	22.00	50-74
1981 Stratford House	Closed	1996	47.80	80-130
1981 Sussex Cottage	Closed	1996	22.00	29-46
1981 Triple Oast (old version)	Closed	1994	59.90	163-328

Scottish Collection - D. Winter

YEAR ISSUE	EDITION LIMIT	YEAR RETD.	ISSUE PRICE	*QUOTE U.S.$
1986 Crofter's Cottage	Closed	1989	51.00	52-128
1989 Gatekeeper's Cottage	Closed	1996	65.00	85
1990 Gillie's Cottage	Closed	1996	65.00	50-85
1989 The House on the Loch	Closed	1994	65.00	90-95
1989 MacBeth's Castle	Closed	1996	200.00	201-260
1982 Old Distillery	Closed	1993	312.00	462
1992 Scottish Crofter's	Closed	1996	42.00	65

Seaside Boardwalk - D. Winter

YEAR ISSUE	EDITION LIMIT	YEAR RETD.	ISSUE PRICE	*QUOTE U.S.$
1995 The Barnacle Theatre	4,500	1996	175.00	175-249
1995 Dock Accessory	Closed	1998	N/A	N/A
1995 The Fisherman's Shanty	Closed	1998	110.00	110
1995 Harbour Master's Watch-House	Closed	1998	125.00	125
1995 Jolly Roger Tavern	Closed	1998	199.00	199
1995 Lodgings and Sea Bathing	Closed	1998	165.00	180
1995 Trinity Lighthouse	Closed	1998	135.00	150
1995 Waterfront Market	Closed	1998	125.00	125

Sherwood Forest Collection - D. Winter

YEAR ISSUE	EDITION LIMIT	YEAR RETD.	ISSUE PRICE	*QUOTE U.S.$
1998 Alan-a-Dale	Retrd.	1998	55.00	55
1995 Friar Tuck's Sanctum	Closed	1998	45.00	50
1995 King Richard's Bower	Closed	1998	45.00	50
1995 Little John's Riverloft	Closed	1998	45.00	50
1995 Loxley Castle	Closed	1998	150.00	150
1995 Maid Marian's Retreat	Closed	1998	49.50	50
1995 Much's Mill	Closed	1998	45.00	50
1995 Sherwood Forest Diorama	Closed	1998	100.00	40-100
1995 Will Scarlett's Den	Closed	1998	49.50	50

Shires Collection - D. Winter

YEAR ISSUE	EDITION LIMIT	YEAR RETD.	ISSUE PRICE	*QUOTE U.S.$
1993 Berkshire Milking Byre	Closed	1995	38.00	30-40
1993 Buckinghamshire Bull Pen	Closed	1994	38.00	25-30
1993 Cheshire Kennels	Closed	1995	36.00	25-30
1993 Derbyshire Dovecote	Closed	1995	36.00	25-30
1993 Gloucestershire Greenhouse	Closed	1995	40.00	25-30
1993 Hampshire Hutches	Closed	1995	34.00	25-30
1993 Lancashire Donkey Shed	Closed	1995	38.00	30-40
1993 Oxfordshire Goat Yard	Closed	1994	32.00	25-30
1993 Shropshire Pig Shelter	Closed	1995	32.00	30-40
1993 Staffordshire Stable	Closed	1995	36.00	30-40
1993 Wiltshire Waterwheel	Closed	1995	34.00	30-40
1993 Yorkshire Sheep Fold	Closed	1995	38.00	25-30

South Downs - D. Winter

YEAR ISSUE	EDITION LIMIT	YEAR RETD.	ISSUE PRICE	*QUOTE U.S.$
1996 Elfin Cottage (10th Anniversary of the Collectors' Guild)	Closed	1996	65.00	65-119
1996 The Parish School House	Closed	1997	55.00	55
1997 Sunday School	Closed	1997	55.00	55

Special Pieces - D. Winter

YEAR ISSUE	EDITION LIMIT	YEAR RETD.	ISSUE PRICE	*QUOTE U.S.$
1987 The Village Scene, 1988 Street Scene - Bas Relief Plaque	Closed	1987	Gift	231
1997 Thank You	Yr.Iss.	1997	Gift	N/A

Tiny Series - D. Winter

YEAR ISSUE	EDITION LIMIT	YEAR RETD.	ISSUE PRICE	*QUOTE U.S.$
1980 Anne Hathaway's Cottage	Closed	1982	Unkn.	325-500
1980 Cotswold Farmhouse	Closed	1982	Unkn.	450-525
1980 Crown Inn	Closed	1982	Unkn.	525
1981 Provencal A (French Market Only)	Closed	N/A	N/A	N/A
1981 Provencal B (French Market Only)	Closed	N/A	N/A	N/A
1980 St. Nicholas' Church	Closed	1982	Unkn.	525
1980 Sulgrave Manor	Closed	1982	Unkn.	325-1050
1980 William Shakespeare's Birthplace	Closed	1982	Unkn.	325-550

Welsh Collection - D. Winter

YEAR ISSUE	EDITION LIMIT	YEAR RETD.	ISSUE PRICE	*QUOTE U.S.$
1993 A Bit of Nonsense	Closed	1996	50.00	50-97
1993 Pen-y-Craig	Closed	1996	88.00	90-97
1993 Tyddyn Siriol	Closed	1994	88.00	70-89
1993 Y' Ddraig Goch	Closed	1994	88.00	59-112

West Country Collection - D. Winter

YEAR ISSUE	EDITION LIMIT	YEAR RETD.	ISSUE PRICE	*QUOTE U.S.$
1988 Cornish Engine House	Closed	1996	120.00	80-155
1988 Cornish Harbour	Closed	1996	120.00	65-119
1986 Devon Combe	Closed	1994	73.00	80-110
1987 Devon Creamery	Closed	1996	62.90	80-110
1986 Orchard Cottage	Closed	1991	91.30	55-99
1987 Smuggler's Creek	Closed	1996	390.00	424-447
1987 Tamar Cottage	Closed	1996	45.30	75-80
1996 Wreckers Cottages	Closed	1996	225.00	179-225
1996 Wreckers Cottages Premier	Closed	1996	275.00	275

Winterville Collection - D. Winter

YEAR ISSUE	EDITION LIMIT	YEAR RETD.	ISSUE PRICE	*QUOTE U.S.$
1996 At Home with Comfort & Joy	Closed	1996	110.00	104-125
1996 At Home with Comfort & Joy Premier	Closed	1996	145.00	142
1994 The Christmastime Clockhouse	Closed	1996	165.00	83-115
1994 The Christmastime Clockhouse Premier	3,500	1994	215.00	179-215
1995 St. Stephen's	Closed	1996	150.00	83-99
1995 St. Stephen's Premier	1,750	1995	195.00	171-195
1994 Toymaker	Closed	1996	135.00	83-99
1994 Toymaker Premier	3,500	1994	175.00	164-175
1995 Winterville Square	Closed	1996	75.00	75
1995 Ye Merry Gentlemen's Lodgings	Closed	1996	125.00	83-99
1995 Ye Merry Gentlemen's Lodgings Premier	1,750	1995	170.00	156-170

Disneyana Convention - John Hine Studio

YEAR ISSUE	EDITION LIMIT	YEAR RETD.	ISSUE PRICE	*QUOTE U.S.$
1992 Cinderella Castle	500	1992	250.00	1210-1593
1993 Sleeping Beauty Castle	500	1993	250.00	402-975
1994 Euro Disney Castle	500	1994	250.00	242-400

David Winter Scenes - Cameo Guild, unless otherwise noted

YEAR ISSUE	EDITION LIMIT	YEAR RETD.	ISSUE PRICE	*QUOTE U.S.$
1992 At Rose Cottage Vignette - D. Winter	Closed	1996	39.00	39
1992 Daughter - D. Winter	Closed	1996	30.00	30
1992 Father	Closed	1996	45.00	45
1992 Mother	Closed	1996	50.00	50
1992 Son	Closed	1996	30.00	30
1992 At The Bake House Vignette - D. Winter	Closed	1996	35.00	35
1992 Girl Selling Eggs	Closed	1996	30.00	30
1992 Hot Cross Bun Seller	Closed	1996	60.00	60
1992 Lady Customer	Closed	1996	45.00	45
1992 Small Boy And Dog	Closed	1996	45.00	45
1992 Woman At Pump	Closed	1996	45.00	45
1992 At The Bothy Vignette Base - D. Winter	Closed	1996	39.00	39
1992 Farm Hand And Spade	Closed	1996	40.00	40
1992 Farmer And Plough	Closed	1996	60.00	60
1992 Farmer's Wife	Closed	1996	45.00	45
1992 Goose Girl	Closed	1996	45.00	45
1993 Christmas Snow Vignette - D. Winter	Closed	1996	50.00	50
1993 Bob Cratchit And Tiny Tim	Closed	1996	50.00	50
1993 Ebenezer Scrooge	Closed	1996	45.00	45
1993 Fred	Closed	1996	35.00	35
1993 Miss Belle	Closed	1996	35.00	35
1993 Mrs. Fezziwig	Closed	1996	35.00	35
1993 Tom The Street Shoveler	Closed	1996	60.00	60

Department 56

Alpine Village Series - Department 56

YEAR ISSUE	EDITION LIMIT	YEAR RETD.	ISSUE PRICE	*QUOTE U.S.$
1987 Alpine Church 6541-2	Closed	1991	32.00	113-175
1987 Alpine Church (white) 6541-2	Closed	N/A	32.00	285-357
1992 Alpine Shops 5618-9, set/2	Open		75.00	75
1992 • Kukuck Uhren 56191	Open		37.50	38
1992 • Metterniche Wurst 56190	Closed	1997	37.50	30-45
1986 Alpine Village 6540-4, set/5	Closed	1997	150.00	150-185
1986 • Apotheke 65407	Closed	1997	39.00	25-40
1986 • Besson Bierkeller 65405	Closed	1996	30.00	30-50
1986 • Gasthof Eisl 65406	Closed	1996	30.00	28-45
1986 • Milch-Kase 65409	Closed	1996	30.00	30-45
1986 • E. Staubr Backer 65408	Closed	1997	39.00	28-46
1990 Bahnhof 5615-4	Closed	1993	42.00	50-75
1994 Bakery & Chocolate Shop 5614-6	Open		37.50	38
1997 Bernhardiner Hundchen 56174	Open		50.00	50
1998 Federbetten Und Steppdecken 56176	Open		48.00	48
1988 Grist Mill 5953-6	Closed	1997	42.00	27-55
1987 Josef Engel Farmhouse 5952-8	Closed	1989	33.00	805-985
1995 Kamm Haus 5617-1	Open		42.00	42
1998 Spielzeug Laden 56192	Open		65.00	65
1993 Sport Laden 5612-0	Open		50.00	50
1991 St. Nikolaus Kirche 5617-0	Open		37.50	38

Christmas In the City Series - Department 56

YEAR ISSUE	EDITION LIMIT	YEAR RETD.	ISSUE PRICE	*QUOTE U.S.$
1989 5607 Park Avenue Townhouse 5977-3	Closed	1992	48.00	66-125
1989 5609 Park Avenue Townhouse 5978-1	Closed	1992	48.00	48-100
1991 All Saints Corner Church 5542-5	Open		96.00	110
1991 Arts Academy 5543-3	Closed	1993	45.00	50-125
1995 Brighton School 5887-6	Open		52.00	52
1994 Brokerage House 5881-5	Closed	1997	48.00	40-60
1995 Brownstones on the Square 5887-7, set/2 (Beekman House, Pickford Place)	Open		90.00	90
1998 The Capitol 58887	Open		110.00	110
1987 The Cathedral 5962-5	Closed	1990	60.00	200-355
1992 Cathedral Church of St. Mark 5549-2	3,024	1993	120.00	1218-1900
1988 Chocolate Shoppe 5968-4	Closed	1991	40.00	85-160
1987 Christmas In The City 6512-9, set/3	Closed	1990	112.00	563-660
1987 • Bakery 6512-9	Closed	1990	37.50	95-155
1987 • Tower Restaurant 6512-9	Closed	1990	37.50	241-297
1987 • Toy Shop and Pet Store 6512-9	Closed	1990	37.50	233-275
1997 The City Globe 58883	Open		65.00	65
1988 City Hall (small) 5969-2	Closed	1991	65.00	168-190
1988 City Hall (standard) 5969-2	Closed	1991	65.00	140-195
1991 The Doctor's Office 5544-1	Closed	1994	60.00	60-95
1989 Dorothy's Dress Shop 5974-9	12,500	1991	70.00	230-375
1994 First Metropolitan Bank 5882-3	Closed	1997	60.00	44-88
1998 The Grand Movie Theater 58870	Open		50.00	50
1988 Hank's Market 5970-6	Closed	1992	40.00	80-115
1994 Heritage Museum of Art 5883-1	Open		96.00	96
1997 Hi-De-Ho Nightclub 58884	Open		52.00	52
1991 Hollydale's Department Store 5534-4	Closed	1997	75.00	60-100
1995 Holy Name Church 5887-5	Open		96.00	96
1995 Ivy Terrace Apartments 5887-4	Closed	1997	60.00	45-87
1998 Johnson's Grocery & Deli 58886	Open		60.00	60
1991 Little Italy Ristorante 5538-7	Closed	1995	50.00	65-85
1987 Palace Theatre 5963-3	Closed	1989	45.00	750-895
1990 Red Brick Fire Station 5536-0	Closed	1995	55.00	60-85
1989 Ritz Hotel 5973-0	Closed	1994	55.00	52-85
1998 Riverside Row Shops 58888	Open		52.00	52
1987 Sutton Place Brownstones 5961-7	Closed	1989	80.00	625-850
1992 Uptown Shoppes 5531-0, set/3	Closed	1996	150.00	150-185
1992 • Haberdashery 55311	Closed	1996	30.00	30-60
1992 • City Clockworks 55313	Closed	1996	30.00	42-73
1992 • Music Emporium 55312	Closed	1996	30.00	40-75
1988 Variety Store 5972-2	Closed	1990	45.00	150-180
1996 Washington Street Post Office 58880	Open		52.00	52
1993 West Village Shops 5880-7, set/2	Closed	1996	90.00	90-120
1993 • Potters' Tea Seller 58808	Closed	1996	45.00	34-75
1993 • Spring St. Coffee House 58809	Closed	1996	45.00	34-75
1990 Wong's In Chinatown 5537-9	Closed	1994	55.00	60-110

*Quotes have been rounded up to nearest dollar

Dickens' Village Series - Department 56

YEAR ISSUE	EDITION LIMIT	YEAR RETD.	ISSUE PRICE	*QUOTE U.S.$
1991 Ashbury Inn 5555-7	Closed	1995	55.00	38-95
1998 Ashwick Lane Hose & Ladder 58305	Open		54.00	54
1987 Barley Bree 5900-5, set/2 (Farmhouse, Barn)	Closed	1989	60.00	225-415
1997 Barmby Moor Cottage 58324	Open		48.00	48
1990 Bishops Oast House 5567-0	Closed	1992	45.00	49-125
1995 Blenham Street Bank 5833-0	Open		60.00	60
1986 Blythe Pond Mill House 6508-0	Closed	1990	37.00	157-315
1986 By The Pond Mill House 6508-0	Closed	1990	37.00	69-140
1994 Boarding & Lodging School 5810-6	Open		48.00	48
1993 Boarding and Lodging School 5809-2 (Christmas Carol Commemorative Piece)	Yr.Iss.	1993	48.00	95-200
1987 Brick Abbey 6549-8	Closed	1989	33.00	194-495
1996 Butter Tub Barn 58338	Open		48.00	48
1996 Butter Tub Farmhouse 58337	Open		40.00	40
1988 C. Fletcher Public House 5904-8	12,500	1989	35.00	444-575
1986 Chadbury Station and Train 6528-5	Closed	1989	65.00	250-375
1987 Chesterton Manor House 6568-4	7,500	1988	45.00	1250-1695
1986 Christmas Carol Cottages 6500-5, set/3	Closed	1995	75.00	92-135
1986 • The Cottage of Bob Cratchit & Tiny Tim 6500-5	Closed	1995	25.00	30-65
1986 • Fezziwig's Warehouse 6500-5	Closed	1995	25.00	18-45
1986 • Scrooge and Marley Counting House 6500-5	Closed	1995	25.00	30-60
1996 The Christmas Carol Cottages (revisited) 58339	Open		60.00	60
1988 Cobblestone Shops 5924-2, set/3	Closed	1990	95.00	265-350
1988 • Booter and Cobbler 5924-2	Closed	1990	32.00	88-120
1988 • T. Wells Fruit & Spice Shop 5924-2	Closed	1990	32.00	65-100
1988 • The Wool Shop 5924-2	Closed	1990	32.00	143-165
1989 Cobles Police Station 5583-2	Closed	1991	37.50	115-150
1988 Counting House & Silas Thimbleton Barrister 5902-1	Closed	1990	32.00	50-95
1998 Crooked Fence Cottage 58304	Open		60.00	60
1992 Crown & Cricket Inn (Charles Dickens' Signature Series), 5750-9	Yr.Iss.	1992	100.00	120-170
1989 David Copperfield 5550-6, set/3	Closed	1992	125.00	137-245
1989 • Betsy Trotwood's Cottage 5550-6	Closed	1992	42.50	35-70
1989 • Peggotty's Seaside Cottage 5550-6 (green boat)	Closed	1992	42.50	31-115
1989 • Peggotty's Seaside Cottage 5550-6 (tan boat)	Closed	1992	42.50	89-175
1989 • Mr. Wickfield Solicitor 5550-6	Closed	1992	42.50	65-95
1989 David Copperfield 5550-6, set/3 with tan boat	Closed	1992	125.00	195-250
1994 Dedlock Arms 5752-5 (Charles Dickens' Signature Series)	Yr.Iss.	1994	100.00	82-165
1985 Dickens' Cottages 6518-8 set/3	Closed	1988	75.00	795-895
1985 • Stone Cottage 6518-8	Closed	1988	25.00	280-495
1985 • Thatched Cottage 6518-8	Closed	1988	25.00	105-200
1985 • Tudor Cottage 6518-8	Closed	1988	25.00	280-415
1986 Dickens' Lane Shops 6507-2, set/3	Closed	1989	80.00	450-522
1986 • Cottage Toy Shop 6507-2	Closed	1989	27.00	149-220
1986 • Thomas Kersey Coffee House 6507-2	Closed	1989	27.00	138-225
1986 • Tuttle's Pub 6507-2	Closed	1989	27.00	150-220
1984 Dickens' Village Church (lt. cream) 6516-1	Closed	1989	35.00	198-462
1984 Dickens' Village Church (cream-yellow) 6516-1	Closed	1989	35.00	209-215
1985 Dickens' Village Church (dark) 6516-1	Closed	1989	35.00	110-165
1985 Dickens' Village Church (green) 6516-1	Closed	1989	35.00	226-495
1985 Dickens' Village Church (tan) 6516-1	Closed	1989	35.00	162-215
1985 Dickens' Village Mill 6519-6	2,500	1986	35.00	3200-4950
1995 Dudden Cross Church 5834-3	Closed	1997	45.00	45-50
1995 Dursley Manor, 5832-9	Open		50.00	55
1998 East Indies Trading Co. 58302	Open		65.00	65
1991 Fagin's Hide-A-Way 5552-2	Closed	1995	68.00	43-92
1989 The Flat of Ebenezer Scrooge 5587-5	Open		37.50	38
1997 Gad's Hill Place (Charles Dickens' Signature Series), 57535	Yr.Iss.	1997	98.00	82-98
1994 Giggelswick Mutton & Ham, 5822-0	Closed	1997	48.00	33-67
1996 The Grapes Inn, 57534 (Charles Dickens' Signature Series)	Yr.Iss.	1996	120.00	65-160
1993 Great Denton Mill 5812-2	Closed	1997	50.00	33-75
1989 Green Gate Cottage 5586-7	22,500	1990	65.00	188-295
1994 Hather Harness 5823-8	Closed	1997	48.00	33-55
1992 Hembleton Pewterer, 5800-9	Closed	1995	72.00	38-90
1988 Ivy Glen Church 5927-7	Closed	1991	35.00	44-90
1995 J.D. Nichols Toy Shop 5832-8	Open		48.00	50
1997 J. Lytes Coal Merchant 58323	Open		50.00	50
1987 Kenilworth Castle 5916-1	Closed	1988	70.00	535-675
1992 King's Road Post Office 5801-7	Open		45.00	45
1993 Kingford's Brewhouse 5811-4	Closed	1996	45.00	28-75
1990 Kings Road 5568-9, set/2	Closed	1996	72.00	60-110
1990 • Tutbury Printer 55690	Closed	1996	36.00	23-52
1990 • C.H. Watt Physician 55691	Closed	1996	36.00	30-52
1998 Leacock Poulterer (Revisted) 58303	Open		48.00	48
1989 Knottinghill Church 5582-4	Closed	1995	50.00	24-75
1995 The Maltings 5833-5	Open		50.00	50
1998 Manchester Square 58301, set/25 (G. Choir's Weights & Scales, Frogmore Chemist, Custom House, Lydby Trunk & Satchel Shop, Manchester Square Accessories, set/7, 12 trees, road, snow)	Open		250.00	250
1996 The Melancholy Tavern (Revisited) 58347	Open		45.00	45
1988 Merchant Shops 5926-9, set/5	Closed	1993	150.00	195-230
1988 • Geo. Weeton Watchmaker 5926-9	Closed	1993	30.00	28-65
1988 • The Mermaid Fish Shoppe 5926-9	Closed	1993	30.00	44-85
1988 • Poulterer 5926-9	Closed	1993	30.00	40-75
1988 • Walpole Tailors 5926-9	Closed	1993	30.00	28-75
1988 • White Horse Bakery 5926-9	Closed	1993	30.00	36-95
1996 Mulberrie Court 58345	Open		90.00	90
1991 Nephew Fred's Flat 5557-3	Closed	1994	35.00	61-95
1996 Nettie Quinn Puppets & Marionettes 58344	Open		50.00	50
1988 Nicholas Nickleby 5925-0, set/2	Closed	1991	72.00	107-170
1988 • Nicholas Nickleby Cottage 5925-0	Closed	1991	36.00	51-95
1988 • Wackford Squeers Boarding School 5925-0	Closed	1991	36.00	50-85
1988 Nickolas Nickleby Cottage 5925-0-misspelled	Closed	1991	36.00	95-135
1988 Nickolas Nickleby set/2, 5925-0-misspelled	Closed	1991	36.00	190-205
1986 Norman Church 6502-1	3,500	1987	40.00	2250-3800
1987 The Old Curiosity Shop 5905-6	Open		32.00	42
1998 The Old Globe Theatre, set/4 (Historical Landmark Series™)	Yr.Iss.		175.00	175
1992 Old Michaelchurch, 5562-0	Closed	1996	42.00	42-66
1996 The Olde Camden Town Church (Revisited) 58346	Open		55.00	55
1991 Oliver Twist 5553-0, set/2	Closed	1993	75.00	70-130
1991 • Brownlow House 5553-0	Closed	1993	38.00	47-75
1991 • Maylie Cottage 5553-0	Closed	1993	38.00	32-75
1984 The Original Shops of Dickens' Village 6515-3, set of 7	Closed	1988	175.00	1095-1295
1984 • Abel Beesley Butcher 6515-3	Closed	1988	25.00	88-150
1984 • Bean And Son Smithy Shop 6515-3	Closed	1988	25.00	164-195
1984 • Candle Shop 6515-3	Closed	1988	25.00	145-215
1984 • Crowntree Inn 6515-3	Closed	1988	25.00	210-295
1984 • Golden Swan Baker 6515-3	Closed	1988	25.00	125-170
1984 • Green Grocer 6515-3	Closed	1988	25.00	94-180
1984 • Jones & Co. Brush & Basket Shop 6515-3	Closed	1988	25.00	258-295
1993 The Pied Bull Inn (Charles Dickens' Signature Series), 5751-7	Closed	1993	100.00	95-165
1994 Portobello Road Thatched Cottages 5824-6, set/3	Closed	1997	120.00	120-150
1994 • Browning Cottage 58249	Closed	1997	40.00	28-40
1994 • Cobb Cottage 58248	Closed	1997	40.00	33-50
1994 • Mr. & Mrs. Pickle 58247	Closed	1997	40.00	33-50
1993 Pump Lane Shoppes 5808-4, set/3	Closed	1996	112.00	110-115
1993 • Bumpstead Nye Cloaks & Canes 58085	Closed	1996	37.35	22-49
1993 • Lomas Ltd. Molasses 58086	Closed	1996	37.35	22-49
1993 • W.M. Wheat Cakes & Puddings 58087	Closed	1996	37.35	35-54
1996 Ramsford Palace 58336, set/17 (Ramsford Palace, Palace Guards, set/2 Accessory, Palace Gate Accessory, Palace Fountain Accessory, Wall Hedge, set/8 Accessory, Corner Wall Topiaries, set/4 Accessory)	27,500	1996	175.00	250-550
1989 Ruth Marion Scotch Woolens 5585-9	17,500	1990	65.00	313-395
1995 Sir John Falstaff Inn 5753-3 (Charles Dickens' Signature Series)	Closed	1995	100.00	66-150
1995 Start A Tradition Set 5832-7, set/13 (The Town Square Carolers Accessory, set/3, 6 Sisal Trees, Bag of Real Plastic Snow, Cobblestone Road)	Closed	1996	85.00	80-110
1995 • Faversham Lamps & Oil	Closed	1996	N/A	N/A
1995 • Morston Steak and Kidney Pie	Closed	1996	N/A	43
1997 Start A Tradition Set 58322, set/13 (Sudbury Church, Old East Rectory, The Spirit of Giving Accessory, set/3, 6 Sisal Trees, Bag of Real Plastic Snow, Cobblestone Road)	Open		75.00	100
1989 Theatre Royal 5584-0	Closed	1992	45.00	50-80
1998 Thomas Mudge Timepieces 58307	Open		60.00	60
1997 Tower of London 58500, set/5 (Historical Landmark Series™)	Closed	1997	165.00	165-375
1989 Victoria Station 5574-3	Open		100.00	112
1994 Whittlesbourne Church, 5821-1	Open		85.00	85
1995 Wrenbury Shops 5833-1, set/3 (T. Puddlewick Spectacle Shop)	Open		100.00	100
1995 • The Chop Shop 58333	Closed	1997	35.00	28-40
1995 • Wrenbury Baker 58332	Closed	1997	35.00	29-45
1995 • T. Puddlewick Spectacle Shop 58334	Open		35.00	35

Disney Parks Village Series - Department 56

YEAR ISSUE	EDITION LIMIT	YEAR RETD.	ISSUE PRICE	*QUOTE U.S.$
1994 Fire Station No. 105 5352-0 Disneyland, CA	Closed	1996	45.00	20-54
1994 Fire Station No. 105 744-7 (theme park backstamp) Disneyland, CA	Closed	1996	45.00	86-88
1994 Mickey's Christmas Shop 5350-3, set/2 Disney World, FL	Closed	1996	144.00	60-265
1994 Mickey's Christmas Shop 742-0 (theme park backstamp), set/2 Disney World, FL	Closed	1996	144.00	109-540
1994 Olde World Antiques 5351-1, set/2 Disney World, FL	Closed	1996	90.00	45-108
1994 Olde World Antiques 743-9 (theme park backstamp), set/2 Disney World, FL	Closed	1996	90.00	70-240
1995 Silversmith 5352-1 Disney World, FL	Closed	1996	50.00	175-360
1995 Silversmith 744-8 (theme park backstamp) Disney World, FL	Closed	1996	50.00	265-450
1995 Tinker Bell's Treasures 5352-2 Disney World, FL	Closed	1996	60.00	200-275
1995 Tinker Bell's Treasures 744-9 (theme park backstamp) Disney World, FL	Closed	1996	60.00	275-450

Disney Parks Village Series Accessories - Department 56

YEAR ISSUE	EDITION LIMIT	YEAR RETD.	ISSUE PRICE	*QUOTE U.S.$
1995 The Balloon Seller 5353-9, set/2	Closed	1996	25.00	20-55
1994 Disney Parks Family, set/3 5354-6	Closed	1996	32.50	15-38
1994 Mickey and Minnie 5353-8, set/2	Closed	1996	22.50	17-40
1994 Olde World Antiques Gate 5355-4	Closed	1996	15.00	7-20

Event Piece - Heritage Village Collection Accessory - Department 56

YEAR ISSUE	EDITION LIMIT	YEAR RETD.	ISSUE PRICE	*QUOTE U.S.$
1992 Gate House 5530-1	Closed	1992	22.50	19-60
1996 Christmas Bells 98711	Closed	1996	35.00	35-45
1997 The Holly & The Ivy, set/2 56100	Yr.Iss.	1997	17.50	18-21

Homes For The Holidays - Department 56

YEAR ISSUE	EDITION LIMIT	YEAR RETD.	ISSUE PRICE	*QUOTE U.S.$
1997 Ronald McDonald House ® (Fund Raiser Piece) 8960	Yr.Iss.	1997	N/A	219-475
1998 Snowy Pines Inn Gift Set 54934, set/9	Yr.Iss.		65.00	65
1998 Seton, Morris Spice Merchant Gift Set 58308, set/10	Yr.Iss.		65.00	65
1998 Scottie's Toy Shop Gift Set 58871, set/10	Yr.Iss.		65.00	65
1998 The House That Love Built™ 1998 2210	Yr.Iss.		N/A	N/A
1998 Kensington Palace	Yr.Iss.		195.00	195

Little Town of Bethlehem Series - Department 56

YEAR ISSUE	EDITION LIMIT	YEAR RETD.	ISSUE PRICE	*QUOTE U.S.$
1987 Little Town of Bethlehem 5975-7, set/12	Open		150.00	150

New England Village Series - Department 56

YEAR ISSUE	EDITION LIMIT	YEAR RETD.	ISSUE PRICE	*QUOTE U.S.$
1993 A. Bieler Farm 5648-0, set/2	Closed	1996	92.00	75-115
1993 • Pennsylvania Dutch Farmhouse 56481	Closed	1996	46.00	42-62
1993 • Pennsylvania Dutch Barn 56482	Closed	1996	46.00	44-75
1988 Ada's Bed and Boarding House (lemon yellow) 5940-4	Closed	1991	36.00	240-315
1988 Ada's Bed and Boarding House (pale yellow) 5940-4	Closed	1991	36.00	88-125
1996 Apple Valley School 56172	Open		35.00	35
1994 Arlington Falls Church 5651-0	Closed	1997	40.00	30-60
1989 Berkshire House (medium blue) 5942-0	Closed	1991	40.00	121-160
1989 Berkshire House (teal) 5942-0	Closed	1991	40.00	70-125
1993 Blue Star Ice Co. 5647-2	Closed	1997	45.00	39-54
1992 Bluebird Seed and Bulb 5642-1	Closed	1996	48.00	33-63
1996 Bobwhite Cottage 56576	Open		50.00	50
1995 Brewster Bay Cottage 5657-0, set/2	Closed	1997	90.00	80-90
1995 • Jeremiah Brewster House 56568	Closed	1997	45.00	40-55
1995 • Thomas T. Julian House 56569	Closed	1997	45.00	40-50
1994 Cape Keag Cannery 5652-9	Open		48.00	48
1990 Captain's Cottage 5947-1	Closed	1996	40.00	25-57
1988 Cherry Lane Shops 5939-0, set/3	Closed	1990	80.00	285-307
1988 • Anne Shaw Toys 5939-0	Closed	1990	27.00	124-170
1988 • Ben's Barbershop 5939-0	Closed	1990	27.00	85-125
1988 • Otis Hayes Butcher Shop 5939-0	Closed	1990	27.00	70-95
1987 Craggy Cove Lighthouse 5930-7	Closed	1994	35.00	41-88
1995 Chowder House 5657-1	Open		40.00	40
1998 East Willet Pottery 56578	Open		45.00	45
1998 The Emily Louise 56581, set/2	Open		70.00	70
1996 J. Hudson Stoveworks 56574	Open		60.00	60
1986 Jacob Adams Farmhouse and Barn 6538-2	Closed	1989	65.00	157-550
1989 Jannes Mullet Amish Barn 5944-7	Closed	1992	48.00	62-160
1989 Jannes Mullet Amish Farm House 5943-9	Closed	1992	32.00	75-115
1991 McGrebe-Cutters & Sleighs 5640-5	Closed	1995	45.00	33-65
1986 New England Village 6530-7, set/7	Closed	1989	170.00	995-1095
1986 • Apothecary Shop 6530-7	Closed	1989	25.00	95-115
1986 • Brick Town Hall 6530-7	Closed	1989	25.00	132-225
1986 • General Store 6530-7	Closed	1989	25.00	275-325
1986 • Livery Stable & Boot Shop 6530-7	Closed	1989	25.00	109-165
1986 • Nathaniel Bingham Fabrics 6530-7	Closed	1989	25.00	130-175
1986 • Red Schoolhouse 6530-7	Closed	1989	25.00	219-265
1986 • Steeple Church (Original) 6530-7	Closed	1989	25.00	125-185
1988 Old North Church 5932-3	Open		40.00	48
1995 Pierce Boat Works 5657-3	Open		55.00	55
1994 Pigeonhead Lighthouse 5653-7	Open		50.00	50
1998 Semple's Smokehouse 56580	Open		45.00	45
1990 Shingle Creek House 5946-3	Closed	1994	37.50	28-60
1990 Sleepy Hollow 5954-4, set/3	Closed	1993	96.00	140-180
1990 • Ichabod Crane's Cottage 5954-4	Closed	1993	32.00	24-75
1990 • Sleepy Hollow School 5954-4	Closed	1993	32.00	63-94
1990 • Van Tassel Manor 5954-4	Closed	1993	32.00	32-75
1990 Sleepy Hollow Church 5955-2	Closed	1993	36.00	40-65
1987 Smythe Woolen Mill 6543-9	7,500	1988	42.00	850-1095
1998 Steen's Maple House (Smoking House) 56579	Open		60.00	60
1986 Steeple Church (Second Version) 6539-0	Closed	1990	30.00	68-125
1992 Stoney Brook Town Hall 5644-8	Closed	1995	42.00	28-60
1987 Timber Knoll Log Cabin 6544-7	Closed	1990	28.00	125-185
1997 Van Guilder's Ornamental Ironworks 56577	Open		50.00	50
1987 Weston Train Station 5931-5	Closed	1989	42.00	234-295
1995 Woodbridge Post Office 5657-2	Open		40.00	40
1992 Yankee Jud Bell Casting 5643-0	Closed	1995	44.00	28-75

North Pole Series - Department 56

YEAR ISSUE	EDITION LIMIT	YEAR RETD.	ISSUE PRICE	*QUOTE U.S.$
1994 Beard Barber Shop 5634-0	Closed	1997	27.50	23-35
1992 Elfie's Sleds & Skates 5625-1	Closed	1996	48.00	40-69
1995 Elfin Forge & Assembly Shop 5638-4	Open		65.00	65
1994 Elfin Snow Cone Works 5633-2	Closed	1997	40.00	28-60

*Quotes have been rounded up to nearest dollar

YEAR ISSUE	EDITION LIMIT	YEAR RETD.	ISSUE PRICE	*QUOTE U.S.$
1998 Elsie's Gingerbread (Smoking House) 56398	Yr.Iss.		65.00	65
1995 Elves' Trade School 5638-7	Open		50.00	50
1993 Express Depot 5627-8	Open		48.00	48
1997 The Glacier Gazette 56394	Open		48.00	48
1998 Glass Ornament Works 56396	Open		60.00	60
1996 Hall of Records 56392	Open		50.00	50
1998 Mrs. Claus' Greenhouse 56395	Open		68.00	68
1991 Neenee's Dolls & Toys 5620-0	Closed	1995	37.50	30-66
1990 North Pole 5601-4, set/2	Open		70.00	80
1990 • Elf Bunkhouse 56016	Closed	1996	35.00	22-50
1990 • Reindeer Barn 56015	Open		35.00	40
1993 North Pole Chapel 5626-0	Open		45.00	45
1994 North Pole Dolls & Santa's Bear Works 5635-9, set/3 (North Pole Dolls, Santa's Bear Works, Entrance)	Closed	1997	96.00	83-135
1992 North Pole Post Office 5623-5	Open		45.00	50
1991 North Pole Shops 5621-9, set/2	Closed	1995	75.00	78-128
1991 • Orly's Bell & Harness Supply	Closed	1995	37.50	33-77
1991 • Rimpy's Bakery	Closed	1995	37.50	34-85
1992 Obbie's Books & Letrinka's Candy 5624-3	Closed	1996	70.00	58-99
1996 Popcorn & Cranberry House 56388	Closed	1997	45.00	45-85
1996 Route 1, North Pole, Home of Mr. & Mrs. Claus 56391	Open		110.00	110
1996 Santa's Bell Repair 56389	Open		45.00	45
1998 Santa's Light Shop 56397	Open		52.00	52
1993 Santa's Lookout Tower 5629-4	Open		45.00	48
1995 Santa's Rooming House 5638-6	Open		50.00	50
1993 Santa's Woodworks 5628-6	Closed	1996	42.00	40-60
1990 Santa's Workshop 5600-6	Closed	1993	72.00	255-425
1996 Start a Tradition Set 56390, set/12 (Candy Cane Elves, set/2 Accessory)	Closed	1996	85.00	45-115
1996 • Candy Cane & Peppermint Shop	Closed	1996	N/A	120
1996 • Gift Wrap & Ribbons	Closed	1996	N/A	N/A
1991 Tassy's Mittens & Hassel's Woolies 5622-7	Closed	1995	50.00	42-91
1995 Tin Soldier Shop 5638-3	Closed	1997	42.00	42-75
1995 Weather & Time Observatory 5638-5	Open		50.00	50

The Original Snow Village Collection - Department 56

YEAR ISSUE	EDITION LIMIT	YEAR RETD.	ISSUE PRICE	*QUOTE U.S.$
1986 2101 Maple 5043-1	Closed	1986	32.00	250-345
1990 56 Flavors Ice Cream Parlor 5151-9	Closed	1992	42.00	125-198
1979 Adobe House 5066-6	Closed	1980	18.00	1992-2700
1992 Airport 5439-9	Closed	1996	60.00	60-90
1992 Al's TV Shop 5423-2	Closed	1995	40.00	35-65
1986 All Saints Church 5070-9	Closed	1997	38.00	38-45
1986 Apothecary 5076-8	Closed	1990	34.00	88
1981 Bakery 5077-6	Closed	1983	30.00	196-265
1986 Bakery 5077-6	Closed	1991	35.00	57-90
1982 Bank 5024-5	Closed	1983	32.00	470-550
1981 Barn 5074-1	Closed	1984	32.00	275-314
1984 Bayport 5015-6	Closed	1986	30.00	184-217
1986 Beacon Hill House 5065-2	Closed	1988	31.00	140-165
1995 Beacon Hill Victorian 5485-7	Open		60.00	60
1996 Birch Run Ski Chalet 54882	Open		60.00	60
1979 Brownstone 5056-7	Closed	1981	36.00	408-594
1996 Boulder Springs House 54873	Closed	1997	60.00	60-68
1995 Bowling Alley 5485-8	Open		42.00	42
1998 The Brandon Bungalow 54918	Open		55.00	55
1978 Cape Cod 5013-8	Closed	1980	20.00	262-440
1994 Carmel Cottage 5466-6	Closed	1997	48.00	35-57
1998 The Carnival Carousel (musical) 54933	Open		150.00	150
1982 Carriage House 5021-0	Closed	1984	28.00	254-259
1986 Carriage House 5071-7	Closed	1988	29.00	90-125
1987 Cathedral Church 5019-9	Closed	1990	50.00	75-100
1980 Cathedral Church 5067-4	Closed	1981	36.00	1728-3000
1982 Centennial House 5020-2	Closed	1984	32.00	271-338
1983 Chateau 5084-9	Closed	1984	35.00	380-385
1998 Christmas Barn Dance 54910	Open		65.00	65
1995 Christmas Cove Lighthouse 5483-6	Open		60.00	60
1996 Christmas Lake High School 54881	Open		52.00	52
1991 The Christmas Shop 5097-0	Closed	1996	37.50	50-70
1985 Church of the Open Door 5048-2	Closed	1988	34.00	104-110
1988 Cobblestone Antique Shop 5123-3	Closed	1992	36.00	64-84
1994 Coca-Cola® Brand Bottling Plant 5469-0	Closed	1997	65.00	65-100
1995 Coca-Cola® Brand Corner Drugstore 5484-4	Open		55.00	55
1989 Colonial Church 5119-5	Closed	1992	60.00	52-85
1980 Colonial Farm House 5070-9	Closed	1982	30.00	252-325
1984 Congregational Church 5034-2	Closed	1985	28.00	551-600
1988 Corner Cafe 5124-1	Closed	1991	37.00	77-100
1981 Corner Store 5076-8	Closed	1983	30.00	178-225
1976 Country Church 5004-7	Closed	1979	18.00	330-369
1979 Countryside Church 5051-8 Meadowland Series	Closed	1980	25.00	264-700
1979 Countryside Church 5058-3	Closed	1984	27.50	192-275
1989 Courthouse 5144-6	Closed	1993	65.00	160-215
1992 Craftsman Cottage (American Architecture Series), 5437-2	Closed	1995	55.00	55-75
1987 Cumberland House 5024-5	Closed	1995	42.00	44-75
1993 Dairy Barn 5446-1	Closed	1997	55.00	55-85
1984 Delta House 5012-1	Closed	1986	32.00	187-228
1985 Depot and Train w/2 Train Cars 5051-2	Closed	1988	65.00	89-115
1993 Dinah's Drive-In 5447-0	Closed	1996	45.00	60-148
1989 Doctor's House 5143-8	Closed	1992	56.00	50-107
1991 Double Bungalow 5407-0	Closed	1994	45.00	33-90
1985 Duplex 5050-4	Closed	1987	35.00	114-165
1995 Dutch Colonial 5485-6 (American Architecture Series)	Closed	1996	45.00	55-85
1981 English Church 5078-4	Closed	1982	30.00	322-358
1981 English Cottage 5073-3	Closed	1982	25.00	248-295
1983 English Tudor 5033-4	Closed	1985	30.00	185-209
1987 Farm House 5089-0	Closed	1992	40.00	55-84
1998 Farm House 54912	Open		50.00	50
1994 Federal House (American Architecture Series) 5465-8	Closed	1997	50.00	50-60
1991 Finklea's Finery: Costume Shop 5405-4	Closed	1993	45.00	51-65
1983 Fire Station 5032-6	Closed	1984	32.00	544-550
1987 Fire Station No. 2 5091-1	Closed	1989	40.00	120-200
1994 Fisherman's Nook Cabins 5461-5, set/2, (Fisherman's Nook Bass Cabin, Fisherman's Nook Trout Cabin)	Open		50.00	50
1994 Fisherman's Nook Resort 5460-7	Open		75.00	75
1982 Flower Shop 5082-2	Closed	1983	25.00	468-487
1976 Gabled Cottage 5002-1	Closed	1979	20.00	289
1982 Gabled House 5081-4	Closed	1983	30.00	329-440
1984 Galena House 5009-1	Closed	1985	32.00	250-375
1978 General Store (tan) 5012-0	Closed	1980	25.00	610-770
1978 General Store (white) 5012-0	Closed	1980	25.00	409-419
1979 Giant Trees 5065-8	Closed	1982	20.00	174-240
1996 Treetop Tree House 54890	Open		35.00	35
1983 Gingerbread House Bank (Non-lighted) 5025-3	Closed	1984	24.00	310
1983 Gingerbread House Bank (lighted) 5025-3	Closed	1984	24.00	296-303
1994 Glenhaven House 5468-2	Closed	1997	45.00	34-50
1992 Good Shepherd Chapel & Church School 5424-0, set/2	Closed	1996	72.00	67-85
1983 Gothic Church 5028-8	Closed	1986	36.00	228-270
1991 Gothic Farmhouse (American Architecture Series), 5404-6	Closed	1997	48.00	48-85
1983 Governor's Mansion 5003-2	Closed	1985	32.00	201-225
1998 Gracie's Dry Goods & General Store 54915, set/2	Open		70.00	70
1992 Grandma's Cottage 5420-8	Closed	1996	42.00	42-68
1983 Grocery 5001-6	Closed	1985	35.00	321-363
1996 Harley-Davidson Motorcycle Shop 54886	Open		65.00	65
1992 Hartford House 5426-7	Closed	1995	55.00	68-78
1998 Haunted House 54935	Open		110.00	110
1984 Haversham House 5008-3	Closed	1987	37.00	175-280
1998 Hershey's® Chocolate Shop 54913	Open		55.00	55
1986 Highland Park House 5063-6	Closed	1988	35.00	104-155
1995 Holly Brothers Garage 5485-4	Open		48.00	48
1988 Home Sweet Home/House & Windmill 5126-8	Closed	1991	60.00	99-110
1978 Homestead 5011-2	Closed	1984	30.00	169-176
1991 Honeymooner Motel 5401-1	Closed	1993	42.00	75-82
1993 Hunting Lodge 5445-3	Closed	1996	50.00	50-195
1976 The Inn 5003-9	Closed	1979	20.00	297-300
1998 Italianate Villa (American Architecture Series), 54911	Open		55.00	55
1989 J. Young's Granary 5149-7	Closed	1992	45.00	65-87
1991 Jack's Corner Barber Shop 5406-2	Closed	1994	42.00	60-143
1987 Jefferson School 5082-2	Closed	1991	36.00	137-175
1989 Jingle Belle Houseboat 5114-4	Closed	1991	42.00	100-185
1988 Kenwood House 5054-7	Closed	1990	50.00	109-160
1979 Knob Hill (gold) 5055-9	Closed	1981	30.00	260-280
1979 Knob Hill 5055-9	Closed	1981	30.00	212-303
1981 Large Single Tree 5080-6	Closed	1989	17.00	28-42
1987 Lighthouse 5030-0	Closed	1988	36.00	313-395
1986 Lincoln Park Duplex 5060-1	Closed	1988	33.00	110-135
1998 Linden Hills Country Club 54917, set/2	Open		60.00	60
1979 Log Cabin 5057-5	Closed	1981	22.00	378-589
1984 Main Street House 5005-9	Closed	1986	27.00	185-187
1990 Mainstreet Hardware Store 5153-5	Closed	1993	42.00	42-110
1977 Mansion 5008-8	Closed	1979	30.00	369-625
1988 Maple Ridge Inn 5121-7	Closed	1990	55.00	47-65
1994 Marvel's Beauty Salon 5470-4	Closed	1997	37.50	28-45
1998 McDonald's® 54914	Open		65.00	65
1986 Mickey's Diner 5078-4	Closed	1987	22.00	574-595
1979 Mission Church 5062-5	Closed	1980	30.00	1063-1068
1979 Mobile Home 5063-3	Closed	1980	18.00	1380-1990
1990 Morningside House 5152-7	Closed	1992	45.00	48-60
1993 Mount Olivet Church 5442-9	Closed	1996	65.00	59-95
1976 Mountain Lodge 5001-3	Closed	1979	20.00	341-440
1978 Nantucket 5014-6	Closed	1986	25.00	187-275
1993 Nantucket Renovation 5441-0	Closed	1993	55.00	32-100
1997 New Hope Church 54904	Open		60.00	60
1984 New School House 5037-7	Closed	1986	35.00	175-215
1982 New Stone Church 5083-0	Closed	1984	32.00	289-327
1996 Nick's Tree Farm 54871, set/10 (Nick's Tree Farm, Nick The Tree Farmer Accessory)	Open		40.00	40
1989 North Creek Cottage 5120-9	Closed	1992	45.00	45-60
1991 Oak Grove Tudor 5400-3	Closed	1994	42.00	41-85
1997 Old Chelsea Mansion 54903	Open		85.00	85
1994 The Original Snow Village Starter Set 5462-3 (Sunday School Serenade Accessory, 3 asst. Sisal Trees, 1.5 oz. bag of real plastic snow)	Closed	1996	50.00	33-65
1994 • Shady Oak Church	Closed	1996	N/A	N/A
1986 Pacific Heights House 5066-0	Closed	1988	33.00	79-95
1988 Palos Verdes 5141-1	Closed	1990	37.50	60-85
1989 Paramount Theater 5142-0	Closed	1993	42.00	150-189
1984 Parish Church 5039-3	Closed	1986	32.00	236-250
1983 Parsonage 5029-6	Closed	1985	35.00	346-358
1995 Peppermint Porch Day Care 5485-2	Closed	1997	45.00	44-70
1989 Pinewood Log Cabin 5150-0	Closed	1995	37.50	38-78
1982 Pioneer Church 5022-9	Closed	1984	30.00	262-272
1995 Pisa Pizza 5485-1	Open		35.00	35
1985 Plantation House 5047-4	Closed	1987	37.00	71-105
1992 Post Office 5422-4	Closed	1995	35.00	58-77
1990 Prairie House (American Architecture Series), 5156-0	Closed	1993	42.00	48-85
1992 Print Shop & Village News 5425-9	Closed	1994	37.50	60-75
1990 Queen Anne Victorian (American Architecture Series), 5157-8	Closed	1996	48.00	48-85
1986 Ramsey Hill House 5067-9	Closed	1989	36.00	75-125
1987 Red Barn 5081-4	Closed	1992	38.00	75-94
1988 Redeemer Church 5127-6	Closed	1992	42.00	44-90
1996 Reindeer Bus Depot 54874	Closed	1997	42.00	32-55
1985 Ridgewood 5052-0	Closed	1987	35.00	124-173
1984 River Road House 5010-5	Closed	1987	36.00	154-259
1996 Rockabilly Records 54880	Open		45.00	45
1998 Rock Creek Mill 54932	Open		64.00	64
1998 Rollerama Roller Rink 54916	Open		56.00	56
1996 Rosita's Cantina 54883	Open		50.00	50
1995 Ryman Auditorium 5485-5	Closed	1997	75.00	75-100
1986 Saint James Church 5068-7	Closed	1988	37.00	130-160
1979 School House 5060-9	Closed	1982	30.00	313-316
1996 The Secret Garden Florist 54885	Open		50.00	50
1988 Service Station 5128-4	Closed	1991	37.50	188-265
1996 Shingle Victorian (American Architecture Series), 54884	Open		55.00	55
1988 Single Car Garage 5125-0	Closed	1990	22.00	42-55
1994 Skate & Ski Shop 5467-4	Open		50.00	50
1982 Skating Pond 5017-2	Closed	1984	25.00	294-315
1978 Skating Rink, Duck Pond (set) 5015-3	Closed	1979	16.00	442-1265
1976 Small Chalet 5006-2	Closed	1979	15.00	443-563
1978 Small Double Trees w/ blue birds 5016-1	Closed	1989	13.50	176-219
1978 Small Double Trees w/ red birds 5016-1	Closed	1989	13.50	20-40
1996 Smokey Mountain Retreat 54872	Open		65.00	65
1995 Snow Carnival Ice Palace 5485-0	Open		95.00	95
1987 Snow Village Factory 5013-0	Closed	1989	45.00	107-125
1987 Snow Village Resort Lodge 5092-0	Closed	1989	55.00	105-125
1993 Snowy Hills Hospital 5448-8	Closed	1996	48.00	48-110
1986 Sonoma House 5062-8	Closed	1988	33.00	107-175
1991 Southern Colonial (American Architecture Series), 5403-8	Closed	1994	48.00	50-95
1990 Spanish Mission Church 5155-1	Closed	1992	42.00	61-85
1987 Springfield House 5027-0	Closed	1990	40.00	40-57
1985 Spruce Place 5049-0	Closed	1987	33.00	208-225
1987 St. Anthony Hotel & Post Office 5006-7	Closed	1989	40.00	91-110
1992 St. Luke's Church 5421-6	Closed	1994	45.00	43-60
1995 Starbucks Coffee 5485-9	Open		48.00	48
1997 Start A Tradition Set 54902, set/8 (Kringle's Toy Shop, Hot Chocolate Stand, Saturday Morning Downtown Accessory, set/4, Bag of Real Plastic Snow, Cobblestone Road)	Open		75.00	100
1976 Steepled Church 5005-4	Closed	1979	25.00	458-550
1977 Stone Church (10") 5009-6	Closed	1979	35.00	508-557
1979 Stone Church (8") 5059-1	Closed	1980	32.00	712-930
1980 Stone Mill House 5068-2	Closed	1982	30.00	395-495
1988 Stonehurst House 5140-3	Closed	1994	37.50	32-90
1984 Stratford House 5007-5	Closed	1986	28.00	145-175
1982 Street Car 5019-9	Closed	1984	16.00	235-375
1985 Stucco Bungalow 5045-8	Closed	1986	30.00	278-298
1984 Summit House 5036-9	Closed	1985	28.00	293-314
1982 Swiss Chalet 5023-7	Closed	1984	28.00	359-388
1979 Thatched Cottage 5050-0 Meadowland Series	Closed	1980	30.00	600-660
1980 Town Church 5071-7	Closed	1982	33.00	208-374
1983 Town Hall 5000-8	Closed	1984	32.00	277-307
1986 Toy Shop 5073-3	Closed	1990	36.00	75-91
1980 Train Station w/ 3 Train Cars 5085-6	Closed	1985	100.00	360-563
1996 Treetop Tree House 54890	Open		35.00	35
1984 Trinity Church 5035-0	Closed	1986	32.00	200-245
1979 Tudor House 5061-7	Closed	1981	25.00	207-238
1983 Turn of the Century 5004-0	Closed	1986	36.00	183-215
1986 Twin Peaks 5042-3	Closed	1986	32.00	250-361
1979 Victorian 5054-2	Closed	1982	30.00	266-275
1983 Victorian Cottage 5002-4	Closed	1984	35.00	278-286
1977 Victorian House 5007-0	Closed	1979	30.00	299-350
1983 Village Church 5026-1	Closed	1984	30.00	347-380
1991 Village Greenhouse 5402-0	Closed	1995	35.00	35-75
1988 Village Market 5044-0	Closed	1991	39.00	55-91
1995 Village Police Station 5485-3	Open		48.00	48
1993 Village Public Library 5443-7	Closed	1997	55.00	55-82
1990 Village Realty 5154-3	Closed	1993	42.00	50-85
1992 Village Station 5438-0	Closed	1997	65.00	58-72
1988 Village Station and Train 5122-5	Closed	1992	65.00	76-125
1992 Village Vet and Pet Shop 5427-5	Closed	1995	32.00	55-78
1989 Village Warming House 5145-4	Closed	1992	42.00	55-70
1986 Waverly Place 5041-5	Closed	1986	35.00	272-305
1994 Wedding Chapel 5464-0	Open		55.00	55
1985 Williamsburg House 5046-6	Closed	1988	37.00	133-165
1993 Woodbury House 5444-5	Closed	1996	45.00	45-63
1983 Wooden Church 5031-8	Closed	1985	30.00	250-308
1981 Wooden Clapboard 5072-5	Closed	1984	32.00	157-167

The Original Snow Village Collection Accessories Retired - Department 56

YEAR ISSUE	EDITION LIMIT	YEAR RETD.	ISSUE PRICE	*QUOTE U.S.$
1987 3 Nuns With Songbooks 5102-0	Closed	1988	6.00	111-130
1988 Apple Girl/Newspaper Boy 5129-2, set/2	Closed	1990	11.00	11-22
1979 Aspen Trees 5052-6, Meadowland Series	Closed	1980	16.00	450-495
1989 Bringing Home The Tree 5169-1	Closed	1992	15.00	19-27
1989 Calling All Cars 5174-8, set/2	Closed	1991	15.00	64-75
1979 Carolers 5064-1	Closed	1986	12.00	75-115

*Quotes have been rounded up to nearest dollar

YEAR ISSUE		EDITION LIMIT	YEAR RETD.	ISSUE PRICE	*QUOTE U.S.$
1987	Caroling Family 5105-5, set/3	Closed	1990	20.00	17-30
1980	Ceramic Car 5069-0	Closed	1986	5.00	40-59
1981	Ceramic Sleigh 5079-2	Closed	1986	5.00	38-44
1993	Check It Out Bookmobile 5451-8, set/3	Closed	1995	25.00	20-45
1987	Children In Band 5104-7	Closed	1989	15.00	15-35
1989	Choir Kids 5147-0	Closed	1992	15.00	15-28
1993	Christmas at the Farm 5450-0, set/2	Closed	1996	16.00	11-33
1991	Christmas Cadillac 5413-5	Closed	1994	9.00	10-20
1987	Christmas Children 5107-1, set/4	Closed	1990	20.00	20-30
1992	Christmas Puppies 5432-1, set/2	Closed	1996	27.50	16-42
1994	Coca-Cola® brand Billboard 5481-0	Closed	1997	18.00	10-25
1991	Cold Weather Sports 5410-0, set/4	Closed	1994	27.50	20-50
1991	Come Join The Parade 5411-9	Closed	1992	13.00	12-18
1991	Country Harvest 5415-1	Closed	1993	13.00	18-20
1989	Crack the Whip 5171-3, set/3	Closed	1996	25.00	18-33
1988	Doghouse/Cat In Garbage Can 5131-4, set/2	Closed	1992	15.00	20-27
1990	Down the Chimney He Goes 5158-6	Closed	1993	6.50	8
1992	Early Morning Delivery 5431-3, set/3	Closed	1995	27.50	15-40
1985	Family Mom/Kids, Goose/Girl 5057-1	Closed	1988	11.00	23-40
1994	Feeding The Birds 5473-9, set/3	Closed	1997	25.00	25-29
1987	For Sale Sign 5108-0	Closed	1989	3.50	5-8
1990	Fresh Frozen Fish 5163-2, set/2	Closed	1993	20.00	29-35
1995	Frosty Playtime 54860, set/3	Closed	1997	30.00	27-38
1986	Girl/Snowman, Boy 5095-4	Closed	1987	11.00	63-83
1995	Grand Ole Opry Carolers 54867	Closed	1997	25.00	21-28
1988	Hayride 5117-9	Closed	1990	30.00	45-60
1993	A Herd Of Holiday Heifers 5455-0, set/3	Closed	1997	18.00	13-28
1990	Here We Come A Caroling 5161-6, set/3	Closed	1992	18.00	15-20
1990	Home Delivery 5162-4, set/2	Closed	1992	16.00	18-29
1990	A Home For the Holidays 5165-9	Closed	1996	7.00	7-14
1986	Kids Around The Tree (large) 5094-6	Closed	1990	15.00	38-46
1986	Kids Around The Tree (small) 5094-6	Closed	1990	15.00	31-37
1990	Kids Decorating the Village Sign 5134-9	Closed	1993	13.00	15-25
1989	Kids Tree House 5168-3	Closed	1991	25.00	46-65
1988	Man On Ladder Hanging Garland 5116-0	Closed	1992	7.50	10-17
1984	Monks-A-Caroling (brown) 5040-7	Closed	1988	6.00	28-35
1983	Monks-A-Caroling (butterscotch) 6459-9	Closed	1984	6.00	57-60
1994	Mush! 5474-7, set/2	Closed	1997	20.00	17-22
1992	Nanny and the Preschoolers 5430-5, set/2	Closed	1994	27.50	17-40
1987	Park Bench (green) 5109-8	Closed	1993	3.00	4-8
1993	Pint-Size Pony Rides 5453-4, set/3	Closed	1996	37.50	19-50
1987	Praying Monks 5103-9	Closed	1988	6.00	35-50
1996	A Ride On The Reindeer Lines 54875, set/3	Closed	1997	35.00	35-44
1992	Round & Round We Go! 5433-0, set/2	Closed	1995	18.00	18-24
1993	Safety Patrol 5449-6, set/4	Closed	1997	27.50	20-28
1985	Santa/Mailbox 5059-8	Closed	1988	11.00	48-53
1994	Santa Comes To Town, 1995 5477-1	Closed	1995	30.00	11-48
1995	Santa Comes To Town, 1996 54862	Closed	1996	32.50	24-45
1996	Santa Comes To Town, 1997 54899	Closed	1997	35.00	35-40
1988	School Bus, Snow Plow 5137-3, set/2	Closed	1991	16.00	44-60
1988	School Children 5118-7, set/3	Closed	1990	15.00	13-25
1984	Scottie With Tree 5038-5	Closed	1985	3.00	176-180
1979	Sheep, 9 White, 3 Black 5053-4 Meadowland Series	Closed	1980	12.00	400
1986	Shopping Girls w/Packages (large) 5096-2	Closed	1988	11.00	32-35
1986	Shopping Girls w/Packages (small) 5096-2	Closed	1988	11.00	28
1985	Singing Nuns 5053-9	Closed	1987	6.00	110-140
1988	Sisal Tree Lot 8183-3	Closed	1991	45.00	66-75
1989	Skate Faster Mom 5170-5	Closed	1991	13.00	17-28
1990	Sleighride 5160-8	Closed	1992	30.00	40-44
1990	Sno-Jet Snowmobile 5159-4	Closed	1993	15.00	12-21
1987	Snow Kids 5113-6, set/4	Closed	1990	20.00	44-50
1985	Snow Kids Sled, Skis 5056-3	Closed	1987	11.00	45
1991	Snowball Fort 5414-3, set/3	Closed	1993	28.00	30-35
1982	Snowman With Broom 5018-0	Closed	1990	3.00	8-10
1992	Spirit of Snow Village Airplane 5440-2	Closed	1996	32.50	20-45
1992	Spirit of Snow Village Airplane 5458-5, 2 assorted	Closed	1996	12.50	17-40
1989	Statue of Mark Twain 5173-0	Closed	1991	15.00	28-40
1989	Street Sign, set/6 5167-5	Closed	1992	7.50	8-20
1990	SV Special Delivery 5197-7, set/2	Closed	1992	16.00	22-65
1993	Tour The Village 5452-6	Closed	1997	12.50	8-14
1989	Through the Woods 5172-1, set/2	Closed	1991	18.00	17-25
1990	A Tree For Me 5164-0, set/2	Closed	1995	8.00	8-13
1989	US Mailbox 5179-9	Closed	1990	3.50	12-15
1989	US Special Delivery 51489, (red, white, blue) set/2	Closed	1990	16.00	40-45
1990	US Special Delivery 51977, (red, green) set/2	Closed	1992	16.00	16-20
1989	Village Birds 5180-2, set/6	Closed	1994	3.50	8-17
1989	Village Gazebo 5146-2	Closed	1995	30.00	23-52
1991	Village Greetings 5418-6, set/3	Closed	1994	5.00	5-7
1993	Village News Delivery 5459-3, set/2	Closed	1996	15.00	17-34
1991	Village Marching Band 5412-7, set/3	Closed	1992	30.00	40-60
1992	Village Used Car Lot 5428-3, set/5	Closed	1997	45.00	45
1988	Water Tower 5133-0	Closed	1991	20.00	62-85
1989	Water Tower-John Deer 568-0	Closed	1991	20.00	618
1992	We're Going to a Christmas Pageant 5435-6	Closed	1994	15.00	15-24
1991	Winter Fountain 5409-7	Closed	1993	25.00	40-59
1992	Winter Playground 5436-4	Closed	1995	20.00	20-38
1988	Woodsman and Boy 5130-6, set/2	Closed	1991	13.00	23-25
1988	Woody Station Wagon 5136-5	Closed	1990	6.50	25-28
1991	Wreaths For Sale 5408-9,set/4	Closed	1994	27.50	22-40

Profile Series - Department 56

YEAR ISSUE		EDITION LIMIT	YEAR RETD.	ISSUE PRICE	*QUOTE U.S.$
1996	Heinz House	Closed	1996	N/A	60-95
1997	State Farm Insurance 75th Anniversary 56000	Closed	1997	N/A	80-95

Retired Heritage Village Collection Accessories - Department 56

YEAR ISSUE		EDITION LIMIT	YEAR RETD.	ISSUE PRICE	*QUOTE U.S.$
1991	All Around the Town 5545-0, set/2	Closed	1993	18.00	17-40
1987	Alpine Village Sign 6571-4	Closed	1993	6.00	10-20
1986	Alpine Villagers 6542-0, set/3	Closed	1992	13.00	24-40
1990	Amish Buggy 5949-8	Closed	1992	22.00	44-68
1990	Amish Family 5948-0, set/3	Closed	1992	20.00	20-45
1990	Amish Family, w/Moustache 5948-0, set/3	Closed	1992	20.00	40-60
1987	Automobiles 5964-1, set/3	Closed	1996	22.00	13-32
1995	Bachman's Squash Cart 753-6	Closed	1996	50.00	77-125
1997	Bachman's Wilcox Truck 880-8	Closed	1997	29.95	55-61
1991	Baker Elves 5603-0, set/3	Closed	1995	27.50	20-40
1992	The Bird Seller 5803-3, set/3	Closed	1995	25.00	17-32
1987	Blacksmith 5934-0, set/3	Closed	1990	20.00	60-75
1993	Blue Star Ice Harvesters 5650-2, set/2	Closed	1997	27.50	17-42
1989	Boulevard 5916-6, set/14	Closed	1993	25.00	40-55
1990	Busy Sidewalks 5535-2, set/4	Closed	1992	28.00	37-50
1992	Buying Bakers Bread 5619-7, set/2	Closed	1995	20.00	15-31
1993	C. Bradford, Wheelwright & Son 5818-1, set/2	Closed	1996	24.00	15-32
1990	Carolers on the Doorstep 5570-0, set/4	Closed	1993	25.00	20-40
1984	Carolers, w/ Lamppost (bl) 6526-9, set/3	Closed	1990	10.00	19-40
1984	Carolers, w/ Lamppost (wh) 6526-9, set/3	Closed	1990	10.00	65-95
1995	Charting Santa's Course 56364, set/2	Closed	1997	25.00	17-38
1993	Chelsea Market Fish Monger & Cart 5814-9, set/2	Closed	1997	25.00	17-32
1993	Chelsea Market Fruit Monger & Cart 5813-0, set/2	Closed	1997	25.00	20-32
1988	Childe Pond and Skaters 5903-0, set/4	Closed	1991	30.00	40-80
1986	Christmas Carol Figures 6501-3, set/3	Closed	1990	12.50	55-85
1996	A Christmas Carol Reading by Charles Dickens 58404, set/8 (Charles Dickens' Signature Series)	42,500	1997	75.00	75-168
1994	Christmas Carol Revisited Holiday Trimming Set 5831-9, set/21	Closed	1997	65.00	33-65
1987	Christmas in the City Sign 5960-9	Closed	1993	6.00	7-20
1992	Churchyard Fence Extensions 5807-6, set/4	Closed	1997	16.00	16
1992	Churchyard Gate & Fence 5806-8, set/3	Closed	1997	15.00	10-25
1992	Churchyard Gate and Fence 5563-8, set/3	Closed	1992	15.00	45-83
1988	City Bus & Milk Truck 5983-8, set/2	Closed	1991	15.00	20-40
1988	City Newsstand 5971-4, set/4	Closed	1991	25.00	48-75
1987	City People 5965-0, set/5	Closed	1990	27.50	40-68
1987	City Workers 5967-6, set/4	Closed	1988	15.00	24-50
1995	Cobbler & Clock Peddler 58394, set/2	Closed	1997	25.00	17-32
1991	Come into the Inn, 5560-3	Closed	1994	22.00	18-30
1989	Constables 5579-4, set/3	Closed	1991	17.50	58-75
1986	Covered Wooden Bridge 6531-5	Closed	1990	10.00	25-48
1989	David Copperfield Characters 5551-4, set/5	Closed	1992	32.50	22-42
1987	Dickens' Village Sign 6569-2	Closed	1993	6.00	8-18
1992	Don't Drop The Presents! 5532-8, set/2	Closed	1995	25.00	22-38
1987	Dover Coach 6590-0	Closed	1990	18.00	40-83
1987	Dover Coach w/o Mustache 6590-0	Closed	1990	18.00	44-85
1989	Farm Animals 5945-5, set/4	Closed	1991	15.00	25-45
1987	Farm People And Animals 5901-3, set/5	Closed	1989	24.00	62-90
1988	Fezziwig and Friends 5928-5, set/3	Closed	1990	12.50	32-60
1991	The Fire Brigade 5546-8, set/2	Closed	1995	20.00	18-40
1991	Fire Truck, "City Fire Dept." 5547-6, set/2	Closed	1995	18.00	20-33
1992	Harvest Seed Cart 5645-6, set/3	Closed	1995	27.50	25-32
1989	Heritage Village Sign 9953-8	Closed	1989	10.00	10-20
1994	Hot Dog Vendor 5886-6, set/3	Closed	1997	27.50	17-32
1993	Knife Grinder 5649-9, set/2	Closed	1996	22.50	17-30
1992	Letters for Santa 5604-9, set/3	Closed	1994	30.00	35-65
1986	Lighted Tree With Children & Ladder 6510-2	Closed	1989	35.00	165-295
1992	Lionhead Bridge 5864-5	Closed	1997	22.00	14-22
1987	Maple Sugaring Shed 6589-7, set/3	Closed	1989	19.00	200-245
1991	Market Day 5641-3, set/3	Closed	1993	35.00	22-45
1987	New England Village Sign 6570-6	Closed	1993	6.00	8-20
1986	New England Winter set 6532-3, set/5	Closed	1990	18.00	19-50
1988	Nicholas Nickleby Characters 5929-3, set/4	Closed	1991	20.00	19-45
1992	The Old Puppeteer 5802-5, set/3	Closed	1995	32.00	23-42
1991	Oliver Twist Characters 5554-9, set/3	Closed	1993	35.00	24-58
1988	One Horse Open Sleigh 5982-0	Closed	1993	20.00	20-45
1989	Organ Grinder 5957-9, set/3	Closed	1991	21.00	18-40
1987	Ox Sled (blue pants) 5951-0	Closed	1989	20.00	58-150
1987	Ox Sled (tan pants) 5951-0	Closed	1989	20.00	167-275
1993	Pine Cone Trees 522-13, set/2	Closed	1995	15.00	10-15
1993	Playing in the Snow 5556-5, set/3	Closed	1996	25.00	21-35
1989	Popcorn Vendor 5958-7, set/3	Closed	1992	22.00	22-40
1986	Porcelain Trees 6537-4, set/2	Closed	1992	14.00	23-40
1994	Postern 9871-0, (Dickens' Village Ten Year Accessory Anniversary Piece)	Closed	1994	17.50	9-25
1991	Poultry Market 5559-0, set/3	Closed	1995	32.00	22-40
1988	Red Covered Bridge 5987-0	Closed	1994	17.00	10-30
1989	River Street Ice House Cart 5959-5	Closed	1991	20.00	37-56
1989	Royal Coach 5578-6	Closed	1992	55.00	57-85
1988	Salvation Army Band 5985-4, set/6	Closed	1991	24.00	74-90
1990	Santa's Little Helpers 5610-3, set/3	Closed	1993	28.00	33-65
1987	Shopkeepers 5966-8, set/4	Closed	1988	15.00	23-40
1987	Silo And Hay Shed 5950-1	Closed	1989	18.00	107-158
1993	Sing a Song For Santa, set/3 5631-6	Closed	1993	28.00	46-70
1987	Skating Pond 6545-5	Closed	1990	24.00	44-75
1990	Sleepy Hollow Characters 5956-0, set/3	Closed	1992	27.50	30-45
1986	Sleighride 6511-0	Closed	1990	19.50	25-60
1988	Snow Children 5938-2	Closed	1994	17.00	12-25
1994	Snow Cone Elves 5637-5, set/4	Closed	1997	30.00	22-35
1987	Stone Bridge 6546-3	Closed	1990	12.00	43-75
1993	Street Musicians 5564-6, set/3	Closed	1997	25.00	17-33
1994	Thatchers 5829-7, set/3	Closed	1997	35.00	22-44
1990	Tis the Season 5539-5	Closed	1994	12.95	9-17
1992	Town Tinker 5646-4, set/2	Closed	1995	24.00	13-30
1991	Toymaker Elves 5602-2, set/3	Closed	1995	27.50	20-38
1990	Trimming the North Pole 5608-1	Closed	1993	10.00	22-45
1994	Two Rivers Bridge 5656-1	Closed	1997	35.00	22-40
1989	U.S. Mail Box and Fire Hydrant 5517-4	Closed	1990	5.00	12-20
1987	Village Express Train (electric, black),5997-8	Closed	1988	89.95	191-295
1988	Village Express Train 5980-3, set/22	Closed	1996	100.00	84-149
1993	Village Express Van (black), 9951-1	Closed	1993	25.00	55-125
1993	Village Express Van (gold), 9977-5 (promotional)	Closed	1993	N/A	490-900
1992	Village Express Van (green) 5865-3	Closed	1996	25.00	14-27
1994	Village Express Van-Bachman's 729-3	Closed	1994	22.50	40-50
1994	Village Express Van-Bronner's 737-4	Closed	1994	22.50	34-40
1995	Village Express Van-Canadian 2163-7	Closed	1995	N/A	22-67
1994	Village Express Van-Christmas Dove 730-7	Closed	1994	25.00	30-33
1994	Village Express Van-European Imports 739-0	Closed	1994	22.50	28-50
1994	Village Express Van-Fortunoff's 735-8	Closed	1994	22.50	69-77
1994	Village Express Van-Limited Edition 733-1	Closed	1994	25.00	61-72
1994	Village Express Van-Lock, Stock & Barrel 731-5	Closed	1994	22.50	85-140
1994	Village Express Van-North Pole City 736-6	Closed	1994	25.00	30-33
1995	Village Express Van-Park West 0755-2	Closed	1995	N/A	413-460
1994	Village Express Van-Robert's Christmas Wonderland 734-0	Closed	1994	22.50	25-31
1995	Village Express Van-St. Nicks 756-0	Closed	1995	25.00	40-55
1994	Village Express Van-Stat's 741-2	Closed	1994	22.50	19-40
1994	Village Express Van-The Incredible Christmas (Pigeon Forge) 732-3	Closed	1994	24.98	30-85
1994	Village Express Van-The Lemon Tree 721-8	Closed	1994	30.00	30-40
1994	Village Express Van-William Glen 738-2	Closed	1994	22.50	30-45
1994	Village Express Van-Windsor Shoppe 740-4	Closed	1994	25.00	27-30
1988	Village Harvest People 5941-2, set/4	Closed	1991	27.50	25-49
1994	Village Porcelain Pine Trees 5251-5, set/2	Closed	1997	15.00	15-19
1992	Village Porcelain Pine, large 5218-3	Closed	1997	12.50	13-15
1992	Village Porcelain Pine, small 5219-1	Closed	1997	10.00	10-13
1989	Village Sign with Snowman 5572-7	Closed	1994	10.00	6-9
1992	Village Street Peddlers 5804-1, set/2	Closed	1994	16.00	11-29
1985	Village Train Brighton 6527-7, set/3	Closed	1986	12.00	326-425
1988	Village Train Trestle 5981-1	Closed	1990	17.00	33-48
1987	Village Well And Holy Cross 6547-1, set/2	Closed	1989	13.00	105-160
1989	Violet Vendor/Carolers/Chestnut Vendor 5580-8, set/3	Closed	1992	23.00	24-45
1993	Vision of a Christmas Past 5817-3, set/3	Closed	1996	27.50	20-48
1992	Welcome Home 5533-6, set/3	Closed	1995	27.50	18-37
1988	Woodcutter And Son 5986-2, set/2	Closed	1990	10.00	25-45
1993	Woodsmen Elves 5630-8, set/3	Closed	1995	27.50	42-50
1996	Yeomen of the Guard 58397, set/5	Closed	1997	30.00	30-70

Village CCP Miniatures - Department 56

YEAR ISSUE		EDITION LIMIT	YEAR RETD.	ISSUE PRICE	*QUOTE U.S.$
1987	Christmas Carol Cottages 6561-7, set/3	Closed	1989	30.00	84-150
1987	• The Cottage of Bob Cratchit & Tiny Tim 6561-7	Closed	1989	10.00	38-55
1987	• Fezziwig's Warehouse 6561-7	Closed	1989	10.00	35
1987	• Scrooge/ Marley Countinghouse 6561-7	Closed	1989	10.00	35-48
1987	Dickens' Chadbury Station & Train 6592-7	Closed	1989	27.50	50-70
1987	Dickens' Cottages 6559-5, set/3	Closed	1989	30.00	345
1987	• Stone Cottage 6559-5	Closed	1989	10.00	125-155
1987	• Thatched Cottage 6559-5	Closed	1989	10.00	100-135
1987	• Tudor Cottage 6559-5	Closed	1989	10.00	125-187
1988	Dickens' Kenilworth Castle 6565-0	Closed	1989	30.00	130-175
1987	Dickens' Lane Shops 6591-9, set/3	Closed	1989	30.00	140-150

*Quotes have been rounded up to nearest dollar

YEAR ISSUE	EDITION LIMIT	YEAR RETD.	ISSUE PRICE	*QUOTE U.S.$
1987 • Cottage Toy Shop 6591-9	Closed	1989	10.00	28-45
1987 • Thomas Kersey Coffee House 6591-9	Closed	1989	10.00	35-45
1987 • Tuttle's Pub 6591-9	Closed	1989	10.00	50
1987 Dickens' Village Assorted 6560-9, set/3	Closed	1989	48.00	140
1987 • Blythe Pond Mill House 6560-9	Closed	1989	16.00	46-50
1987 • Dickens Village Church 6560-9	Closed	1989	16.00	40-49
1987 • Norman Church 6560-9	Closed	1989	16.00	120-150
1987 Dickens' Village Assorted 6562-5, set/4	Closed	1989	60.00	300
1987 • Barley Bree Farmhouse 6562-5	Closed	1989	15.00	60-68
1987 • Brick Abbey 6562-5	Closed	1989	15.00	118-125
1987 • Chesterton Manor House 6562-5	Closed	1989	15.00	125-140
1987 • The Old Curiosity Shop 6562-5	Closed	1989	15.00	60-84
1987 Dickens' Village Original 6558-7, set/7	Closed	1989	72.00	240
1987 • Abel Beesley Butcher 6558-7	Closed	1989	12.00	28-40
1987 • Bean and Son Smithy Shop 6558-7	Closed	1989	12.00	38-42
1987 • Candle Shop 6558-7	Closed	1989	12.00	36-38
1987 • Crowntree Inn 6558-7	Closed	1989	12.00	32-38
1987 • Golden Swan Baker 6558-7	Closed	1989	12.00	21-30
1987 • Green Grocer 6558-7	Closed	1989	12.00	40-45
1987 • Jones & Co Brush & Basket Shop 6558-7	Closed	1989	12.00	55-60
1987 Little Town of Bethlehem 5976-5, set/12	Closed	1989	85.00	175-220
1988 New England Village Assorted 5937-4, set/6	Closed	1989	85.00	400-500
1988 • Craggy Cove Lighthouse 5937-4	Closed	1989	14.50	82-85
1988 • Jacob Adams Barn 5937-4	Closed	1989	14.50	50-66
1988 • Jacob Adams Farmhouse 5937-4	Closed	1989	14.50	44-50
1988 • Maple Sugaring Shed 5937-4	Closed	1989	14.50	41-50
1988 • Smythe Wollen Mill 5937-4	Closed	1989	14.50	125-165
1988 • Timber Knoll Log Cabin 5937-4	Closed	1989	14.50	58-85
1988 New England Village Original 5935-8, set/7	Closed	1989	72.00	680
1988 • Apothecary Shop 5935-8	Closed	1989	10.50	44-48
1988 • Brick Town Hall 5935-8	Closed	1989	10.50	55-64
1988 • General Store 5935-8	Closed	1989	10.50	66-76
1988 • Livery Stable & Boot Shop 5935-8	Closed	1989	10.50	67
1988 • Nathaniel Bingham Fabrics 5935-8	Closed	1989	10.50	67
1988 • Red Schoolhouse 5935-8	Closed	1989	10.50	78-99
1988 • Village Steeple Church 5935-8	Closed	1989	10.50	220-260
1986 Victorian Miniatures, set/2 6564-1	Closed	1987	45.00	275
1986 • Church 6564-1	Closed	1987	22.50	93
1986 • Estate 6564-1	Closed	1987	22.50	88
1986 Victorian Miniatures 6563-3, set/5	Closed	1987	65.00	275
1986 Williamsburg Snowhouse Series, set/6	Closed	1987	60.00	625
1986 • Williamsburg Church, White 6566-8	Closed	1987	10.00	62-120
1986 • Williamsburg House Brown Brick 6566-8	Closed	1987	10.00	50-75
1986 • Williamsburg House, Blue 6566-8	Closed	1987	10.00	50-75
1986 • Williamsburg House, Brown Clapboard	Closed	1987	10.00	50-75
1986 • Williamsburg House, Red 6566-8	Closed	1987	10.00	50-80
1986 • Williamsburg House, White 6566-8	Closed	1987	10.00	62-100

Ertl Collectibles

American Country Barn Series - L. Davis

YEAR ISSUE	EDITION LIMIT	YEAR RETD.	ISSUE PRICE	*QUOTE U.S.$
1997 Arch Roofed Stone Barn 2483	12/98		50.00	55
1998 Cross-Gambrel Roofed Barn 2486	Yr.Iss.		55.00	55
1996 Gambrel Roofed Bank Barn F910	Retrd.	1997	50.00	50
1998 Glacial Rock Barn 2489	Yr.Iss.		55.00	55
1998 Italianate Barn 2487	Yr.Iss.		55.00	55
1998 Octagon Barn 2071	Yr.Iss.		55.00	55
1997 Round Barn H093	Retrd.	1998	50.00	50
1998 Shaker Round Stone Barn 2488	Yr.Iss.		55.00	55
1996 Victorian Barn F909	Retrd.	1997	50.00	50
1996 Western Log Barn F904	Retrd.	1997	50.00	50
1997 Western Prairie Barn 2484	12/98		50.00	55

Farm Country Christmas - L. Davis

YEAR ISSUE	EDITION LIMIT	YEAR RETD.	ISSUE PRICE	*QUOTE U.S.$
1996 Barn H045	Open		90.00	95
1996 Cat & Bird House H053	Open		25.00	25
1997 Chicken House H050	Open		60.00	60
1996 Dinner Bell H091	Open		25.00	25
1996 Farm House H046	Open		85.00	85
1997 Garage H057	Open		65.00	65
1997 Geese H047	Open		35.00	35
1996 Mailbox H056	Open		25.00	25
1996 Silo H052	Open		65.00	65
1996 Smokehouse H054	Open		70.00	70

Signature Edition Barns - L. Davis

YEAR ISSUE	EDITION LIMIT	YEAR RETD.	ISSUE PRICE	*QUOTE U.S.$
1998 Frank Lloyd Wright's Midway Barn 2492	Open		75.00	75
1997 George Washington's Barn at Mount Vernon H273	Open		70.00	70

Fitz & Floyd

Charming Tails Squashville Lighted Village - D. Griff

YEAR ISSUE	EDITION LIMIT	YEAR RETD.	ISSUE PRICE	*QUOTE U.S.$
1994 Acorn Street Lamp 87/948	Suspd.		5.00	5-12
1995 Butternut Squash Dairy 87/562	7,500	1996	45.00	60-150
1996 Candy Apple Candy Store 87/611	9,000	1997	45.00	65-150
1996 Cantaloupe Cathedral 87/597	Suspd.		45.00	45-48
1995 Carrot Post Office 87/583	Closed	1996	45.00	59-100
1994 Chestnut Chapel 87/521	Closed	1996	45.00	45-150
1995 Great Oak Town Hall 87/584	Suspd.		45.00	45-150
1994 Leaf Fence 87/947	Suspd.		6.00	6-12
1995 Mail Box, Bench 87/560	Suspd.		11.00	12
1995 Mushroom Depot 87/563	Suspd.		45.00	45-48
1994 Old Cob Mill 87/524	7,500	1997	45.00	45-150
1994 Pumpkin Inn 87/522	Suspd.		45.00	45-48
1995 Street Light/Sign 87/561	Suspd.		11.00	12
1994 Village Sign 87/533	Suspd.		30.00	31

Forma Vitrum

Annual Christmas - B. Job

YEAR ISSUE	EDITION LIMIT	YEAR RETD.	ISSUE PRICE	*QUOTE U.S.$
1995 Confectioner's Cottage 41101	2,500	1995	100.00	125-190
1996 Lollipop Shoppe 41102	2,500	1996	110.00	125-200
1997 Peppermint Place 41103	2,500	1997	100.00	125-200
1998 Holly Day Chapel 41104	1,500		120.00	120
1998 Holly Day Home 41105	1,500		120.00	120

Bed & Breakfast - B. Job

YEAR ISSUE	EDITION LIMIT	YEAR RETD.	ISSUE PRICE	*QUOTE U.S.$
1997 Bavarian Lodge 11306	1,500		225.00	225
1995 Brookview Bed & Breakfast 11303	1,250	1995	295.00	580-700
1996 Edgewater Inn 11305	1,500	1996	310.00	350-375
1997 Whispering Pines 11308	1,250		250.00	250
1998 White Oak Inn 11309	1,250		275.00	275

Coastal Classics - B. Job

YEAR ISSUE	EDITION LIMIT	YEAR RETD.	ISSUE PRICE	*QUOTE U.S.$
1995 Bayside Beacon Lighthouse 21013	Open		65.00	65
1996 Cape Hope Lighthouse 21014	Open		100.00	100
1993 Carolina Lighthouse 21003	Open		65.00	65
1996 Cozy Cottage 21500	Open		70.00	70
1994 Lookout Point Lighthouse 21012	Open		60.00	60
1993 Maine Lighthouse 21002	Open		50.00	50
1993 Michigan Lighthouse 21001	Open		50.00	50
1996 Patriot's Point 29010	Open		70.00	70
1994 Sailor's Knoll Lighthouse 21011	Open		65.00	65

Coastal Heritage - B. Job

YEAR ISSUE	EDITION LIMIT	YEAR RETD.	ISSUE PRICE	*QUOTE U.S.$
1996 Barnegat (NJ) 25006	2,996		85.00	85
1996 Cape Hatteras (NC) 25102	3,867		120.00	120
1997 Cape Lookout (NC) 25105	1,997		80.00	80
1995 Cape Neddick (ME) 25002	1,995	1995	140.00	168-185
1996 Fire Island (NY) 25005	2,996		150.00	150
1998 Harbor Towne @ Hilton Head (SC) 25106	2,998		65.00	65
1996 Holland Harbor (MI) 25203	1,996		125.00	125
1997 Jupiter (FL) 25104	1,997		80.00	80
1995 Marble Head (OH) 25201	1,995	1996	75.00	90-108
1997 Montauk Point (NY) 25008	997		145.00	145
1996 New London (CT) 25004	2,996		145.00	145
1995 North Head (WA) 25302	1,995		100.00	120
1995 Old Point Loma (CA) 25301	1,995		100.00	120
1996 Peggy's Cove (NS) 25501	2,500		75.00	75
1996 Pigeon Point (CA) 25303	2,996		125.00	125
1995 Portland Head (ME) 25003	1,995	1997	140.00	140-185
1995 Sandy Hook (NJ) 25001	3,759		140.00	156
1998 SE Block Island (RI) 25009	998		160.00	160
1996 Split Rock (MN) 25202	2,996		130.00	130
1996 St. Augustine (FL) 25103	2,996		130.00	130
1995 St. Simon's (GA) 25101	1,995	1997	120.00	120-130
1997 West Quoddy (ME) 25007	1,997		140.00	140

Disney Light Village - B. Job

YEAR ISSUE	EDITION LIMIT	YEAR RETD.	ISSUE PRICE	*QUOTE U.S.$
1998 Belle's Cottage 11703	1,991		225.00	225
1997 Dwarf's Cottage from Snow White 11701	1,937		215.00	215
1998 Geppetto's Toy Shop 11702	1,940		215.00	215

Event Piece - B. Job

YEAR ISSUE	EDITION LIMIT	YEAR RETD.	ISSUE PRICE	*QUOTE U.S.$
1997 Gifts and Collectibles ART01	Open		60.00	60

Special Production - B. Job

YEAR ISSUE	EDITION LIMIT	YEAR RETD.	ISSUE PRICE	*QUOTE U.S.$
1993 The Bavarian Church 11503	2,712	1994	90.00	110-175
1994 Gingerbread House 19111	1,020	1994	100.00	232-350
1995 Miller's Mill (Musical) 11304	Open		115.00	115
1993 Pillars of Faith 11504	2,448	1994	90.00	110-165

Through The Decades "Coca Cola" - B. Job

YEAR ISSUE	EDITION LIMIT	YEAR RETD.	ISSUE PRICE	*QUOTE U.S.$
1997 Corner Drug 11903	5,000		145.00	145
1998 Grady's Barber Shop 11906	5,000		70.00	70
1998 Gus' Gas Station 11905	5,000		90.00	90
1998 Murray's Mercantile Company 11904	5,000		85.00	85
1997 Sam's Grocery 11901	5,000		85.00	85
1998 Sandy Shoal Lighthouse 11907	5,000		85.00	85
1997 Town Cinema 11902	5,000		145.00	145

Vitreville ™ - B. Job

YEAR ISSUE	EDITION LIMIT	YEAR RETD.	ISSUE PRICE	*QUOTE U.S.$
1997 Breadman's Bakery (Renovation) 11301R	200	1997	85.00	210-425
1993 Breadman's Bakery 11301	5,933	1996	70.00	85-88
1993 Candlemaker's Delight 11801	4,997	1996	60.00	65-80
1993 Candymaker's Cottage 11102	8,368	1996	65.00	100-160
1994 Community Chapel 19510	Open		95.00	95
1993 Country Church 11502	12,500	1995	100.00	125-175
1993 Doctor's Domain 11201	Open		70.00	74
1998 Farah's Flower Shop 11311	Open		80.00	80
1995 Fire Station 11403	Open		100.00	100
1996 First Bank & Trust 11405	Open		110.00	110
1998 Jessie's Barber Shop 11310	Open		75.00	75
1997 Klaus Clock Shop 11307	Open		75.00	75
1996 Kramer Building 11404	Open		100.00	100
1994 Maplewood Elementary School 11401	Open		100.00	100
1995 Mayor's Manor 11205	Open		85.00	85
1993 Painter's Place 11202	Open		70.00	74
1993 Pastor's Place 11101	Open		65.00	70
1993 Roofer's Roost 11203	7,250	1995	70.00	90-108
1993 Tailor's Townhouse 11204	5,215	1995	70.00	94-155
1994 Thompson's Drug 11302	5,000	1996	140.00	150-350
1993 Tiny Town Church 11501	Open		95.00	100
1994 Trinity Church 11511	7,000		130.00	130
1994 Vitreville Post Office 11402	3,908	1997	90.00	90-180
1998 Whitestone Chapel 11506	1,250		85.00	85
1997 Wildwood Chapel 11505	Retrd.	1998	60.00	60

Woodland Village™ - B. Job

YEAR ISSUE	EDITION LIMIT	YEAR RETD.	ISSUE PRICE	*QUOTE U.S.$
1993 Badger House 31003	1,056	1996	80.00	85-108
1993 Chipmunk House 31005	1,080	1996	80.00	85-102
1993 Owl House 31004	991	1996	80.00	85-102
1993 Rabbit House 31001	926	1996	90.00	85-115
1993 Racoon House 31002	1,154	1996	80.00	85-102

Geo. Zoltan Lefton Company

Accessories - Lefton

YEAR ISSUE	EDITION LIMIT	YEAR RETD.	ISSUE PRICE	*QUOTE U.S.$
1990 Abe Smith 07483	Suspd.		5.00	14
1988 Allison Davis 06547	Suspd.		5.00	20
1991 Annette & Rebecca 07827	Suspd.		10.00	10
1988 Billy O'Malley 06740	Suspd.		7.00	16-21
1990 Bonnie Charles & Spot 07824	Suspd.		10.00	19-21
1987 Cab 06459	Suspd.		13.00	32
1988 CV Express 05826	Suspd.		27.00	27-124
1991 Da Vinci Bros. 00269	Suspd.		12.00	12
1990 Dashing Through Snow 07322	Suspd.		16.00	16
1988 Dick's Delivery 06548	Suspd.		8.00	23-25
1987 Doc Olsens' Wagon 06457	Suspd.		14.00	28
1987 Eberhardt's (4pc./set) 05910	Suspd.		20.00	15-20
1987 Fire Engine Co. NO. 5 06458	Suspd.		14.00	26-31
1991 Frank Pendergast 07776	Suspd.		5.50	6
1991 The Griffiths 00661	Suspd.		13.00	13
1987 Ivan the Lamplighter 06741	Suspd.		7.00	7
1991 Jeffrey Sawyer 00659	Suspd.		8.00	8
1988 Kalenko Family Choir 06887	Suspd.		13.00	25-47
1988 Lisa & Selena 06549	Suspd.		7.00	20
1991 Major & Mrs. 00214	Suspd.		12.00	12
1990 Mary & Jack Cobb 07825	Suspd.		10.00	19
1987 Matt's Milk Wagon 06461	Suspd.		13.00	18-25
1988 Merrymaker Ed 06739	Suspd.		7.00	23
1988 Mr. Watts 06742	Suspd.		7.00	19-21
1988 Nina & Fillipe 06737	Suspd.		9.00	25
1987 One Horse Open Sleigh 06460	Suspd.		13.00	29
1991 The Parkers 00218	Suspd.		13.00	13
1988 Steven & Stacey 06744	Suspd.		9.00	22
1988 Stone Church Carolers 06554	Suspd.		12.00	44-50
1990 Sylvester The Sweep 07778	Suspd.		5.00	16-21
1992 Tim & Lucy Morgan 00662	Suspd.		9.00	9

Colonial Village - Lefton

YEAR ISSUE	EDITION LIMIT	YEAR RETD.	ISSUE PRICE	*QUOTE U.S.$
1993 Antiques & Curiosities 00723	Closed	1998	50.00	50
1995 Applegate-CVRA Exclusive 01327	Closed	1995	50.00	100-125
1990 The Ardmore House 07338	Closed	1995	45.00	50-91
1997 Ashton House-CVRA Exclusive 10829	Open		50.00	50
1993 Baldwin's Fine Jewelry 00722	Closed	1997	50.00	49-59
1991 Belle-Union Saloon 07482	Closed	1994	45.00	60-91
1998 Berkely House-CVRA Exclusive 11262	Open		50.00	50
1989 Bijou Theatre 06897	Closed	1990	40.00	446-563
1994 Black Sheep Tavern 01003	Open		50.00	50
1993 Blacksmith 00720	Suspd.		47.00	47
1998 Blue Bell Flour 11263	Open		50.00	50
1992 Brenner's Apothecary 07961	Open		45.00	50
1996 The Brookfield 11996	5,500		75.00	105-120
1994 Brown's Book Shop 01001	Open		50.00	50
1993 Burnside 00717	Open		50.00	50
1989 Capper's Millinery 06904	Suspd.		40.00	60-62
1988 City Hall 06340	Suspd.		40.00	100-325
1989 Cobb's Bootery 06903	Suspd.		40.00	66-98
1990 Coffee & Tea Shoppe 07342	Suspd.		45.00	72-132
1996 Collectors Set 10740	Closed	1998	100.00	100
1989 Cole's Barn 06750	Closed	1994	40.00	55-85
1995 Colonial Queen Showboat (Collectors' Set - musical) 11266	Open		100.00	100
1995 Colonial Savings and Loan 01321	Open		50.00	50
1995 Colonial Village News 01002	Open		50.00	50
1998 Cooper's Shop 11259	Open		50.00	50
1990 Country Post Office 07341	Closed	1994	45.00	50-78
1992 County Courthouse 00233	Open		45.00	50
1991 Daisy's Flower Shop 07478	Closed	1996	45.00	47-59
1993 Dentist's Office 00724	Open		50.00	50
1993 Doctor's Office 00721	Open		50.00	50
1992 Elegant Lady Dress Shop 00232	Suspd.		45.00	50
1988 Engine Co. No. 5 Firehouse 06342	Open		40.00	50
1996 Fairbanks House 10397	Open		50.00	50
1988 Faith Church 06333	Closed	1991	40.00	196-282
1989 Fellowship Church 07334	Suspd.		45.00	50
1990 The First Church 07333	Open		45.00	50
1988 First Post Office 06343	Open		40.00	50
1996 Franklin College 10393	Open		50.00	50
1988 Friendship Chapel 06334	Closed	1994	40.00	51-91
1993 Green's Grocery 00725	Open		50.00	50
1988 Greystone House 06339	Closed	1995	40.00	51-91
1989 Gull's Nest Lighthouse 06747	Open		40.00	50
1990 Hampshire House 07336	Closed	1996	45.00	45-50
1996 The Hermitage 10394	Closed	1998	55.00	50-55
1990 Hillside Church 11991	Closed	1991	60.00	435-500
1995 Historical Society Museum 01328	Open		50.00	50
1998 Holmer's Bait Shop, set/3 11534	Open		60.00	60
1988 House of Blue Gables 06337	Closed	1995	40.00	50-91
1988 Johnson's Antiques 06346	Closed	1993	40.00	50-85
1993 Joseph House 00718	Open		50.00	50
1993 Kirby House-CVRA Exclusive 00716	Closed	1994	50.00	103-121
1992 Lakehurst House 11992	Closed	1992	55.00	341-382
1996 Lattimore House-CVRA Exclusive 10391	Closed	1997	50.00	50-72

YEAR ISSUE	EDITION LIMIT	YEAR RETD.	ISSUE PRICE	*QUOTE U.S.$
1997 Law Office 10825	Open		50.00	50
1992 Main St. Church 00230	Open		45.00	50
1989 The Major's Manor 06902	Closed	1998	40.00	46-78
1989 Maple St. Church 06748	Closed	1993	40.00	50-85
1993 Mark Hall 00719	Open		50.00	50
1989 Miller Bros. Silversmiths 06905	Suspd.		40.00	60-157
1998 M.S. Miller-Painter 11261	Open		50.00	50
1997 Montrose Manor 10828	Open		50.00	50
1994 Mt. Zion Church 11994	Closed	1994	70.00	73-195
1994 Mt. Zion Church (Hillside Church-error) 11994	Closed	1994	70.00	475
1990 Mulberry Station 07344	Open		50.00	65
1995 Mundt Manor 01008	Open		50.00	50
1988 New Hope Church (musical) 06470	Suspd.		40.00	883-1117
1990 The Nob Hill 07337	Closed	1995	45.00	49-91
1992 Northpoint School 07960	Open		45.00	50
1994 Notfel Cabin 01320	Open		50.00	50
1995 O'Doul's Ice House 01324	Open		50.00	50
1988 Old Stone Church (musical) 06471	Suspd.		25.00	60
1988 Old Time Station 06335	Closed	1997	40.00	48-54
1998 Opera House 11260	Open		50.00	50
1986 Original Set of 6 05818	Unkn.		210.00	N/A
1986 • Charity Chapel 05818 (05895)	Closed	1989	35.00	886
1986 • King's Cottage 05818 (05890)	Closed	1997	35.00	49-54
1986 • McCauley House 05818 (05892)	Closed	1988	35.00	422
1986 • Nelson House 05818 (05891)	Closed	1989	35.00	422-460
1986 • Old Stone Church 05818 (05825)	Open		35.00	50
1986 • The Welcome Home 05818 (05824)	Closed	1997	35.00	50
1986 Original Set of 6 05819	Unkn.		210.00	N/A
1986 • Church of the Golden Rule 05819 (05820)	Open		35.00	50
1986 • General Store 05819 (05823)	Closed	1988	35.00	792
1986 • Lil Red School House 05819 (05821)	Open		35.00	50
1986 • Penny House 05819 (05893)	Closed	1988	35.00	565
1986 • Ritter House 05819 (05894)	Closed	1989	35.00	565
1986 • Train Station 05819 (05822)	Closed	1989	35.00	157-498
1997 Park Vista-Convention Piece 11141	Closed	1997	50.00	481-625
1995 Patriot Bridge 01325	Open		50.00	50
1997 Photography Studio 10872	Open		50.00	50
1990 Pierpont-Smithe's Curios 07343	Closed	1993	45.00	50-111
1997 Potter House 10826	Open		50.00	50
1995 Queensgate 01329	Open		50.00	50
1989 Quincy's Clock Shop 06899	Suspd.		40.00	60-117
1995 Rainy Days Barn 01323	Open		50.00	50
1994 Real Estate Office -CVRA Exclusive 01006	Open		50.00	50
1988 The Ritz Hotel 06341	Closed	1997	40.00	155-423
1994 Rosamond 00988	Open		50.00	50
1990 Ryman Auditorium-Special Edition 08010	Suspd.		50.00	55-111
1992 San Sebastian Mission 00231	Closed	1995	45.00	62-91
1991 Sanderson's Mill 07927	Open		45.00	50
1997 Sawyer's Creek 11030	Open		55.00	55
1990 Ship's Chandler's Shop 07339	Suspd.		45.00	50-94
1997 Sir George's Manor 11997	5,500	1997	75.00	75
1994 Smith and Jones Drug Store 01007	Open		50.00	50
1991 Smith's Smithy 07476	Closed	1991	45.00	449-532
1994 Springfield 00989	Open		50.00	50
1993 St. James Cathedral 11993	Closed	1993	75.00	125-325
1996 St. Paul's Church 10735	Open		50.00	55
1993 St. Peter's Church w/Speaker 00715	Open		60.00	60
1996 Stable 10395	Open		33.00	33
1988 The State Bank 06345	Closed	1997	40.00	49-59
1992 Stearn's Stable 00228	Open		45.00	50
1988 The Stone House 06338	Closed	1998	40.00	50
1991 Sweet Shop 07481	Open		45.00	50
1989 Sweetheart's Bridge 06751	Suspd.		40.00	50
1991 The Toy Maker's Shop 07477	Open		45.00	50
1988 Trader Tom's Gen'l Store 06336	Open		40.00	50
1996 Trading Post 10732	Open		50.00	50
1996 Treviso House 10392	Open		50.00	50
1998 Trinity Church 11998	5,500		75.00	75
1992 Vanderspeck's Mill 00229	Closed	1996	45.00	84-86
1997 Variety Store 10827	Open		50.00	50
1990 The Victoria House 07335	Closed	1993	45.00	50-98
1989 Victorian Apothecary 06900	Closed	1991	40.00	288
1991 Victorian Gazebo 07925	Open		45.00	50
1989 The Village Bakery 06898	Open		40.00	50
1989 Village Barber Shop 06901	Open		40.00	50
1986 Village Express 05826	Closed	N/A	27.00	125-157
1992 Village Green Gazebo 00227	Open		22.00	22
1990 Village Hardware 07340	Closed	1996	45.00	50-78
1994 Village Hospital 01004	Open		50.00	50
1992 The Village Inn 07962	Closed	1998	45.00	45-50
1989 Village Library 06752	Suspd.		40.00	47-50
1988 Village Police Station 06344	Open		40.00	50
1989 Village School 06749	Closed	1991	40.00	198-390
1991 Watt's Candle Shop 07479	Closed	1994	45.00	58-78
1987 Welcome Home 05824	Closed	1997	45.00	49-54
1994 White's Butcher Shop 01005	Open		50.00	50
1998 Wright's Emporium 11264	Open		50.00	50
1991 Wig Shop 07480	Suspd.		45.00	51-104
1995 Wycoff Manor 11995	5,500		75.00	92-195
1995 Zachary Peters Cabinet Maker 01322	Open		50.00	50

Colonial Village Special Event - Lefton

YEAR ISSUE	EDITION LIMIT	YEAR RETD.	ISSUE PRICE	*QUOTE U.S.$
1995 Bayside Inn 01326	Yr.Iss.	1995	50.00	82-88
1996 Town Hall 10390	Yr.Iss.	1996	50.00	78
1997 Meeting House 10830	Yr.Iss.	1997	65.00	65
1998 Good Neighbor's Haven 11505	Yr.Iss.		55.00	55

Historic American Lighthouse Collection - Lefton

YEAR ISSUE	EDITION LIMIT	YEAR RETD.	ISSUE PRICE	*QUOTE U.S.$
1995 1716 Boston Lighthouse 08607	7,500	1995	50.00	150-250
1994 Admirality Head, WA 01126	Open		40.00	43
1997 Alcatraz Island-1854 08649	9,000	1997	55.00	55-65
1998 Alcatraz, CA 11526	Open		65.00	65
1992 Assateaque, VA 00137	Open		40.00	43
1995 Barneget, NJ 01333	Open		40.00	43
1993 Big Sable Point, MI 00885	Open		40.00	43
1998 Biloxi Lighthouse, MS 11522	Open		40.00	43
1996 Block Island, RI 10105	Open		50.00	50
1994 Bodie Island, NC 01118	Open		40.00	43
1993 Boston Harbor, MA 00881	Open		40.00	43
1996 Buffalo, NY 10076	Open		40.00	43
1994 Cana Island, WI 01117	Open		40.00	43
1993 Cape Cod, MA 00882	Open		40.00	43
1994 Cape Florida, FL 01125	Open		40.00	43
1992 Cape Hatteras, NC 00133	Closed	1998	40.00	40-49
1997 Cape Henlopen, DE	9,000	1997	55.00	55-60
1992 Cape Henry, VA 00135	Open		40.00	43
1992 Cape Lookout, NC 00134	Open		40.00	43
1994 Cape May, NJ 01013	Closed	1995	40.00	115-288
1995 Cape May, NJ 01013R	Open		40.00	43
1996 Cape Neddick, ME 10106	Open		47.00	47
1994 Chicago Harbor, IL 01010	Open		40.00	43
1997 Currituck Beach, NC 10834	Open		40.00	43
1996 Destruction Island, WA 10108	Open		40.00	43
1995 Fire Island, NY 01334	Open		40.00	43
1997 Fort Niagra, NY 10965	Open		40.00	43
1994 Ft. Gratiot, MI 01123	Open		40.00	43
1993 Gray's Harbor, WA 00880	Open		40.00	43
1994 Heceta Head, OR 01122	Open		40.00	43
1996 Holland Harbor, MI 10104	Open		45.00	45
1995 Jupiter Inlet, FL 01336	Open		40.00	43
1996 Key West, FL 10075	Open		40.00	43
1996 Los Angeles Harbor, CA 10109	Open		45.00	45
1993 Marblehead, OH 00879	Open		40.00	43
1993 Montauk, NY 00884	Open		40.00	43
1998 Morris Island, SC 08657	9,000	1998	50.00	50-55
1998 New London Harbor, CT 11524	Open		40.00	43
1994 New London Ledge, CT 01119	Open		40.00	43
1998 New Presque Isle, MI 11523	Open		40.00	43
1994 Ocracoke, NC 01124	Open		40.00	43
1996 Old Cape Henry, VA 08619	7,500	1996	47.00	99-105
1994 Old Point Loma, CA 01011	Open		40.00	43
1998 Pemaquid Point, ME 11525	Open		42.00	42
1995 Pigeon Point, CA 01289	Open		40.00	43
1997 Point Arena, CA 10968	Open		40.00	43
1995 Point Betsie, MI 01335	Open		47.00	47
1997 Point Bolivar, TX 10967	Open		40.00	43
1995 Point Cabrillo, CA 01330	Open		47.00	47
1993 Point Wilson, WA 00883	Open		40.00	43
1995 Ponce De Leon, FL 01332	Open		40.00	43
1994 Portland Head, ME 01121	Open		40.00	43
1996 Pt. Isabel, TX 10074	Open		40.00	43
1997 Round Island, MI 10969	Open		47.00	47
1992 Sandy Hook, NJ 00132	Open		40.00	43
1994 Split Rock, MN 01009	Open		40.00	43
1994 St. Augustine, FL 01015	Open		40.00	43
1994 St. Simons, GA 01012	Open		40.00	43
1996 Thomas Point, MO 10107	Open		45.00	45
1995 Toledo Harbor, OH 01331	Open		47.00	47
1994 Tybee Island, GA 01014	Open		40.00	43
1992 West Quoddy Head, ME 00136	Open		40.00	43
1993 White Shoal, MI 00878	Open		40.00	43
1997 Wind Point, WI 10966	Open		40.00	43
1994 Yerba Buena, CA 01120	Open		40.00	43

Historic Williamsburg Collection - Lefton

YEAR ISSUE	EDITION LIMIT	YEAR RETD.	ISSUE PRICE	*QUOTE U.S.$
1997 Bruton Parish Church 11051	Open		55.00	55
1997 The Capitol 11054	Open		75.00	75
1997 George Wythe House 11053	Open		50.00	50
1997 The Govenor's Palace 11052	Open		75.00	75
1997 King Arms Taverns 11050	Open		50.00	50

GiftStar

Collectors' Corner - B. Baker

YEAR ISSUE	EDITION LIMIT	YEAR RETD.	ISSUE PRICE	*QUOTE U.S.$
1993 City Cottage (Membership Sculpture)-rose/grn.1682	Retrd.	1994	35.00	125-135
1993 Brian's First House (Redemption Sculpture) red1496	Retrd.	1994	71.00	150-175
1994 Gothic Cottage (Membership Sculpture) 1571	Retrd.	1995	35.00	75-95
1994 Duke of Gloucester Street (Redemption Sculpture) 1459	Retrd.	1995	108.00	150-165
1995 Marie's Cottage-grey (Membership Sculpture) 1942	Retrd.	1996	35.00	75-95
1995 Welcome Home-brick (Redemption Sculpture) 1599	Retrd.	1996	65.00	95
1996 Queen Ann Cottage-rose/blue (Membership Sculpture) 1676	Retrd.	1997	39.00	39
1996 Oak Street-brick/brown (Redemption Sculpture) 1685	Retrd.	1997	65.00	65
1997 Michael's House-blue (Membership Sculpture) 1719	Retrd.	1998	40.00	40
1997 Michael's Garage (Redemption Sculpture) 1720	Retrd.	1998	34.50	35
1998 Empire Tower House (Membership Sculpture) 16510	Yr.Iss.		40.00	40
1998 Main Street Café Ornament (Redemption Sculpture) 18000	Yr.Iss.		17.00	17

Signing Piece - B. Baker

YEAR ISSUE	EDITION LIMIT	YEAR RETD.	ISSUE PRICE	*QUOTE U.S.$
1995 Joe's Newstand 1348	Yr.Iss.	1995	27.00	27
1996 Yellow Rose Cottage 1444	Yr.Iss.	1996	62.00	62
1997 Umbrella Shop 1179	Yr.Iss.	1997	29.50	30
1998 The Coffee House 11780	Yr.Iss.		34.00	34

Brian Baker's Déjà Vu Collection - B. Baker

YEAR ISSUE	EDITION LIMIT	YEAR RETD.	ISSUE PRICE	*QUOTE U.S.$
1988 Adam Colonial Cottage-blue/white 1515	Retrd.	1992	53.00	53
1993 Admiralty Head Lighthouse-white 1532	Retrd.	1995	62.00	62
1998 Alameda Avenue 16280	Open		49.50	50
1998 All Aboard 11700	Open		46.00	46
1998 Alpine Chalet 14990	Open		31.50	32
1992 Alpine Ski Lodge-brown/white 1012	Retrd.	1993	62.00	92
1988 Andulusian Village-white 1060	Retrd.	1993	53.00	63
1996 Angel of the Sea II-blue/white 1592	Retrd.	1997	69.00	69
1996 Angel of the Sea II-mauve/white 1591	Open		69.00	69
1992 Angel of the Sea-blue/white 1587	Retrd.	1997	67.00	67
1992 Angel of the Sea-mauve/white 1586	Open		67.00	67
1989 Antebellum Mansion-blue/rose 1505	Retrd.	1993	53.00	73
1988 Antebellum Mansion-blue/white 1519	Retrd.	1988	49.00	49
1989 Antebellum Mansion-peach 1506	Retrd.	1991	49.00	56
1988 Antebellum Mansion-peach 1517	Retrd.	1988	49.00	49
1988 Antebellum Mansion-white/green 1518	Retrd.	1988	49.00	49
1998 Autumn Harvest 13010	Open		21.50	22
1998 Back Bay Rowhouse 17450	Open		31.50	32
1994 Barber Shop 1164	Retrd.	1996	53.00	53
1987 Bavarian Church-white 1021	Retrd.	1988	38.00	38
1987 Bavarian Church-yellow 1020	Retrd.	1988	38.00	38
1987 The Bernese Guesthouse-golden brown 1010	Retrd.	1990	49.00	49
1998 Bless Our House 19540	Open		30.00	30
1989 Blumen Shop-white/brown 1023	Retrd.	1993	53.00	73
1997 Bourbon Street Cottage 1718	Open		41.00	41
1997 Bracket Cottage-blue 1714	Open		37.00	37
1997 Bracket Cottage-cream 1715	Open		37.00	37
1996 Brick & Brackets-brick 1933	Open		65.00	65
1998 The Brownstone 17460	Open		32.00	32
1994 Cabbagetown 1704	Retrd.	1997	65.00	65
1996 Cape Cottage-grey/white 1442	Open		63.00	63
1998 Cape Hatteras Lighthouse 15970	Open		46.00	46
1998 Cape May Classic 16010	Open		49.50	50
1997 Cape May Gingerbread-cream 1594	Open		48.00	48
1997 Cape May Gingerbread-rose 1593	Open		48.00	48
1997 Carpenter's Gothic-blue 1575	Open		40.00	40
1997 Carpenter's Gothic-rose 1576	Open		40.00	40
1988 Casa Chiquita-natural 1400	Retrd.	1992	53.00	60
1998 Casablanca 17430	Open		36.00	36
1994 Castle in the Clouds 1090	Retrd.	1995	75.00	85
1998 Central Market 117300	Open		46.00	46
1998 Charleston 16940	Open		43.00	43
1993 Charleston Single House -blue/white 1583	Retrd.	1997	60.00	60
1993 Charleston Single House -peach/white 1584	Retrd.	1997	60.00	60
1996 Chateau in the Woods-stone 1683	Yr.Iss.	1996	79.00	79
1997 Chesapeake Lighthouse 1595	Open		43.00	43
1994 Christmas at Church 1223	Retrd.	1996	63.00	63
1998 Christmas Church 14230	Open		51.00	51
1988 Christmas House-blue 1225	Retrd.	1992	51.00	51
1998 City Living 17480	Open		31.50	32
1998 Classic Queen Anne 16520	Open		50.00	50
1998 Classic Queen Anne 16530	Open		50.00	50
1990 Classic Victorian-blue/white 1555	Retrd.	1994	60.00	80
1990 Classic Victorian-peach 1557	Retrd.	1994	60.00	80
1990 Classic Victorian-rose/blue 1556	Retrd.	1994	60.00	80
1991 Colonial Color-brown 1508	Retrd.	1993	62.00	82
1991 Colonial Cottage-white/bue 1509	Retrd.	1994	59.00	80
1987 Colonial House-blue 1510	Retrd.	1988	49.00	70
1987 Colonial House-wine 1511	Retrd.	1987	40.00	60
1997 Colonial Merchant 1452	Open		37.00	37
1987 Colonial Store-brick 1512	Retrd.	1993	53.00	73
1997 Conch House-blue 1670	Open		48.00	48
1997 Conch House-cream 1671	Open		48.00	48
1993 Corner Grocery-brick 1141	Open		67.00	67
1987 The Cottage House-blue 1531	Retrd.	1988	42.00	42
1987 The Cottage House-white 1530	Retrd.	1993	47.00	67
1989 Country Barn-blue 1528	Retrd.	1991	49.00	70
1989 Country Barn-red 1527	Retrd.	1993	53.00	73
1994 Country Bridge 1513	Retrd.	1997	69.00	69
1996 Country Christmas-red 1219	Retrd.	1997	68.00	68
1988 Country Church-white/blue 1522	Retrd.	1994	49.00	50-70
1992 Country Station-blue/rust 1156	Retrd.	1997	64.00	64
1994 Country Store 1122	Retrd.	1996	61.00	61
1994 Craftsman Cottage-cream 1478	Retrd.	1997	56.00	56
1994 Craftsman Cottage-grey 1477	Retrd.	1997	56.00	56
1989 Deja Vu Sign-ivory/brown 1600	Retrd.	1991	21.00	24-29
1992 Deja Vu Sign-ivory/brown 1999	Retrd.	1996	21.00	21
1998 Desert Garden 17340	Open		29.50	30
1993 Dinard Mansion-beige/brick 1005	Retrd.	1996	67.00	67
1996 Dixie Landing-white 1740	Open		68.00	68
1998 Drayton Place 16930	Open		56.50	57
1997 Eaton Street Gingerbread-blue 1672	Open		48.00	48
1997 Eaton Street Gingerbread-white 1673	Open		48.00	48
1998 Elegant Lady 16450	Open		49.50	50
1994 Ellis Island 1250	Retrd.	1996	62.00	62
1993 Enchanted Cottage-natural 1205	Retrd.	1995	63.00	68
1998 Engine House No. 10 11720	Open		57.00	57
1988 Fairy Tale Cottage-white/brown 1200	Retrd.	1992	46.00	46
1997 Farm Country-red 1494	Open		43.00	43
1997 Farm Country-white 1495	Open		43.00	43

*Quotes have been rounded up to nearest dollar

YEAR ISSUE	EDITION LIMIT	YEAR RETD.	ISSUE PRICE	*QUOTE U.S.$
1987 The Farm House-beige/blue 1525	Retrd.	1991	49.00	49
1987 The Farm House-spiced tan 1526	Retrd.	1991	49.00	49
1992 Firehouse-brick 1140	Retrd.	1997	60.00	60
1992 Flower Store-tan/green 1145	Open		67.00	67
1988 French Colonial Cottage-beige 1516	Retrd.	1990	42.00	65
1997 French Quarter Townhouse-cream/teal 1717	Open		40.00	40
1997 French Quarter Townhouse -rose/blue 1716	Open		40.00	40
1988 Georgian Colonial House -white/blue 1514	Retrd.	1992	53.00	53
1990 Gothic Victorian-blue/mauve 1534	Retrd.	1991	47.00	52-54
1988 Gothic Victorian-peach 1536	Retrd.	1992	51.00	60
1988 Gothic Victorian-sea green 1537	Retrd.	1990	47.00	47
1993 Grandpa's Barn-brown 1498	Retrd.	1997	63.00	63
1988 Hampshire House-brick 1040	Retrd.	1988	49.00	60
1989 Hampshire House-brick 1041	Retrd.	1990	49.00	56
1996 Harbor Sentry-white 1590	Open		59.00	59
1989 Henry VIII Pub-white/brown 1043	Retrd.	1993	56.00	76
1998 Home Sweet Home 14020	Open		30.00	30
1998 The Homestead 14690	Open		50.00	50
1993 Homestead Christmas-red 1224	Retrd.	1995	57.00	57
1987 Hotel Couronne (original)wh./br. 1000	Retrd.	1988	49.00	49
1989 Hotel Couronne-white/brown 1003	Retrd.	1992	55.00	55
1987 Italianate Victorian-brown 1543	Retrd.	1990	52.00	52
1987 Italianate Victorian-lavendar 1550	Retrd.	1988	45.00	45
1987 Italianate Victorian-mauve/blue 1545	Retrd.	1991	49.00	49
1989 Italianate Victorian-peach/teal 1552	Retrd.	1991	51.00	62
1989 Italianate Victorian-rose/blue 1551	Retrd.	1991	51.00	55-58
1987 Italianate Victorian-rust/blue 1544	Retrd.	1988	49.00	49
1987 Japanese House-white/brown 1100	Retrd.	1988	47.00	47
1996 Japanese Tea House-brown/white 1101	Retrd.	1997	59.00	59
1998 Key Cottage 16680	Open		27.00	27
1998 Key Cottage 16690	Open		27.00	27
1987 The Lighthouse-white 1535	Retrd.	1992	53.00	60
1991 Log Cabin-brown 1501	Retrd.	1994	55.00	75
1992 Looks Like Nantucket-grey 1451	Retrd.	1997	59.00	59
1998 Louisburg Square 17490	Open		34.00	34
1995 Main Street Cafe-blue 1142	Open		61.00	61
1997 Main Street Church 1163	Open		49.00	49
1993 Mansard Lady-blue/rose 1606	Open		64.00	64
1993 Mansard Lady-tan/green 1607	Open		64.00	64
1995 Maple Lane-blue/white 1904	Open		72.00	72
1995 Maple Lane-desert/white 1905	Retrd.	1997	72.00	72
1991 Mayor's Mansion-blue/peach 1585	Retrd.	1994	57.00	77
1996 Mediteranean Ave-cream/tile 1741	Retrd.	1997	65.00	65
1995 Mesa Manor 1733	Retrd.	1997	75.00	75
1994 Mission Dolores (no umbrella) 1435	Retrd.	N/A	47.00	75
1994 Mission Dolores 1435	Retrd.	1997	47.00	47
1993 Monday's Wash-cream/blue 1450	Retrd.	1996	62.00	62
1993 Monday's Wash-white/blue 1449	Retrd.	1996	62.00	62
1995 Mountain Homestead-brown 1401	Retrd.	1997	78.00	78
1997 Mountain Meadows-brown 1497	Open		52.00	52
1998 Mountain Mill 14040	Open		36.00	36
1994 Mukilteo Lighthouse 1569	Retrd.	1997	55.00	55
1998 New England Farmhouse 14750	Open		39.00	39
1998 Northside Rowhouse 17470	Open		32.00	32
1989 Norwegian House-brown 1051	Retrd.	1990	51.00	58
1997 Oak Bluff-brown 1573	Open		42.00	42
1997 Oak Bluff-grey 1572	Open		42.00	42
1990 Old Country Cottage-blue 1502	Retrd.	1992	51.00	58
1992 Old Country Cottage-peach 1504	Retrd.	1991	47.00	65
1990 Old Country Cottage-red 1503	Retrd.	1992	51.00	65
1996 Old Glory-brick 1567	Retrd.	1997	59.00	59
1994 The Old School House 1439	Retrd.	1997	61.00	61
1987 Old West General Store-white/grey 1520	Retrd.	1991	50.00	68
1987 Old West General Store -yellow/white 1521	Retrd.	1988	50.00	50
1993 Old West Hotel-cream 1120	Retrd.	1996	62.00	62
1995 Old West Sheriff-red 1125	Retrd.	1997	56.00	56
1995 Old White Church-white 1424	Retrd.	1997	65.00	65
1988 One Room School House-red 1524	Retrd.	1993	53.00	73
1994 Orleans Cottage-white/blue 1447	Retrd.	1996	63.00	63
1994 Orleans Cottage-white/red 1448	Retrd.	1996	63.00	63
1990 Palm Villa-desert/green 1421	Retrd.	1995	54.00	61
1990 Palm Villa-white/blue 1420	Retrd.	1995	54.00	61
1994 Paris by the Bay 1004	Retrd.	1996	55.00	55
1989 Parisian Apartment-beige/blue 1002	Retrd.	1993	53.00	73
1987 Parisian Apartment-golden brown 1001	Retrd.	1993	53.00	73
1995 Peggy's Cove Light-white 1533	Open		56.00	56
1996 Pennridge-white/stone 1429	Open		70.00	70
1997 Point Fermin Lighthouse 1568	Yr.Iss.		54.00	54
1994 Police Station-stone 1147	Retrd.	1997	55.00	55
1993 Post Office-light green 1146	Retrd.	1997	60.00	60
1987 Queen Ann Victorian-peach/green 1540	Retrd.	1993	53.00	73
1987 Queen Ann Victorian-rose 1541	Retrd.	1993	53.00	73
1987 Queen Ann Victorian-rust/green 1542	Retrd.	1988	49.00	49
1995 Quiet Neighborhood-cream/blue 1623	Retrd.	1997	71.00	71
1995 Quiet Neighborhood-rose/blue 1622	Retrd.	1997	71.00	71
1995 River Belle Steamer-white 1092	Retrd.	1997	70.00	70
1994 Riverside Mill 1507	Retrd.	1997	65.00	65
1988 Roeder Gate, Rothenburg-brown 1022	Retrd.	1990	49.00	49
1992 Rose Cottage-grey 1443	Open		59.00	59
1996 Ruby's Watch-blue/white 1630	Open		56.00	56
1996 Ruby's Watch-cream/white 1631	Retrd.	1997	56.00	56
1998 San Francisco Cottage 16360	Open		45.00	45
1998 San Francisco Lady 16340	Open		49.50	50
1994 San Francisco Stick-brick/teal 1625	Retrd.	1996	61.00	61
1994 San Francisco Stick-cream/blue 1624	Retrd.	1996	61.00	61
1998 Santa Fe 17350	Open		45.00	45
1995 Scenic Route 100-red/green 1426	Retrd.	1997	71.00	71
1995 Scenic Route 100-red/yellow 1425	Retrd.	1997	71.00	71
1996 Seaside Cottage-blue/white1691	Open		64.00	64
1996 Seaside Cottage-rose/white 1690	Open		64.00	64
1988 Second Empire House -sea grn./desert 1539	Retrd.	1991	50.00	50
1988 Second Empire House-white/blue 1538	Retrd.	1993	54.00	74
1993 Smuggler's Cove-grey/brown 1529	Retrd.	1997	72.00	72
1987 Snow Cabin-brown/white 1500	Retrd.	1994	51.00	70
1995 Southern Exposure-cream/rose 1582	Retrd.	1997	62.00	62
1995 Southern Exposure-tan/green 1581	Retrd.	1997	62.00	62
1995 Southern Mansion-brick 1744	Yr.Iss.	1995	79.00	79
1995 St. Nicholas Church-white/blue 1409	Retrd.	1997	56.00	56
1993 Steiner Street-peach/green 1674	Retrd.	1997	63.00	63
1993 Steiner Street-rose/blue 1675	Retrd.	1997	63.00	63
1993 The Stone House-stone/blue 1453	Open		63.00	63
1988 Stone Victorians-browns 1554	Retrd.	1994	56.00	76
1993 Sunday Afternoon-brick 1523	Retrd.	1995	62.00	62
1989 Swedish Home-Swed.red 1050	Retrd.	1990	51.00	58
1998 Taking The Back Road 14050	Open		41.00	32
1991 Teddy's Place-teal/rose 1570	Retrd.	1997	61.00	61
1994 Towered Lady-blue/rose 1688	Retrd.	1997	65.00	65
1994 Towered Lady-rose 1689	Retrd.	1997	65.00	65
1992 Tropical Fantasy-blue/coral 1410	Retrd.	1997	67.00	67
1992 Tropical Fantasy-rose/blue 1411	Retrd.	1997	67.00	67
1992 Tropical Fantasy-yellow/teal 1412	Retrd.	1997	67.00	67
1996 Tropical Paradise-white/brown 1115	Retrd.	1997	65.00	65
1995 Tudor Christmas-red brick 1221	Open		67.00	67
1995 Tudor Home-tan brick 1222	Open		67.00	67
1987 Turreted Victorian-beige/blue 1546	Retrd.	1992	55.00	55
1987 Turreted Victorian-peach 1547	Retrd.	1992	55.00	57
1987 Ultimate Victorian-lt. blue/rose 1549	Retrd.	1993	60.00	80
1987 Ultimate Victorian-maroon/slate 1548	Retrd.	1993	60.00	80
1989 Ultimate Victorian-peach/green 1553	Retrd.	1993	60.00	65
1992 Victorian Bay View-cream/teal 1564	Retrd.	1997	63.00	63
1992 Victorian Bay View-rose/blue 1563	Retrd.	1997	63.00	63
1992 Victorian Charm-cream 1588	Retrd.	1996	61.00	61
1992 Victorian Charm-mauve 1589	Retrd.	1996	61.00	61
1990 Victorian Country Estate-desert/br. 1560	Retrd.	1994	62.00	82
1990 Victorian Country Estate -peach/blue 1562	Retrd.	1994	62.00	82
1990 Victorian Country Estate-rose/blue 1561	Retrd.	1994	62.00	82
1991 Victorian Farmhouse-goldenbrown 1565	Retrd.	1994	59.00	90
1995 Victorian Living-clay/white 1927	Retrd.	1997	70.00	70
1995 Victorian Living-teal/tan 1926	Open		70.00	70
1992 Victorian Tower House-blue/maroon 1558	Open		63.00	63
1992 Victorian Tower House-peach/blue 1559	Retrd.	1997	63.00	63
1996 Village Pharmacy-brick 1157	Open		65.00	65
1998 Waiting For The Bell 14060	Open		30.00	30
1997 Waterfront Property-brown 1737	Open		37.00	37
1996 Willow Road-brick 1713	Open		68.00	68
1998 Wimbledon Court 16480	Open		44.00	44
1991 Wind and Roses-brick 1470	Retrd.	1997	63.00	63
1989 Windmill on the Dike-beige/green 1034	Retrd.	1994	60.00	90

Brian Baker's Déjà Vu Collection Accessories - B. Baker

YEAR ISSUE	EDITION LIMIT	YEAR RETD.	ISSUE PRICE	*QUOTE U.S.$
1995 Apple Tree 1317	Retrd.	1997	36.00	36
1996 Autumn Birch 1323	Retrd.	1997	26.00	26
1996 Autumn Flame 1328	Retrd.	1997	29.00	29
1996 Banana Tree 1318	Retrd.	1997	36.00	36
1997 Beach Umbrella 1362	Open		28.00	28
1997 Beauford's Friends-red 1337	Open		32.00	32
1997 Beauford's Friends-white 1336	Open		32.00	32
1997 Bird Bath 1302	Open		18.00	18
1996 Blue Spruce 1352	Retrd.	1998	24.00	24
1995 Cactus Garden 1334	Retrd.	1997	27.50	28
1995 Coconut Palms 1319	Retrd.	1997	25.00	25
1997 Courtyard Garden 1303	Open		18.00	18
1995 Date Palm 1320	Retrd.	1997	24.00	24
1995 Doghouse 1306	Open		23.00	23
1997 End of Harvest 1316	Open		21.00	21
1996 Farm Truck 1357	Retrd.	1997	47.00	47
1998 Flower Cart 13460	Open		16.00	16
1996 Forest Fir 1358	Retrd.	1997	24.00	24
1996 Forest Giant 1333	Retrd.	1997	36.00	36
1996 Garden Trellis 1308	Retrd.	1998	24.00	24
1996 Hemlock 1344	Retrd.	1997	24.00	24
1995 House For Sale 1307	Open		24.00	24
1996 Huckleberry's Cat 1343	Retrd.	1997	20.00	20
1995 In The Park 1340	Retrd.	1998	30.00	30
1996 Japanese Bridge 1330	Retrd.	1997	34.00	34
1996 Japanese Pine 1331	Retrd.	1997	36.00	36
1996 Large Blue Spruce 1361	Retrd.	1997	24.00	24
1998 Lemonade Stand 13390	Open		18.00	18
1995 Long Picket Fence 1309	Open		23.00	23
1995 Members Only 1312	Retrd.	1997	46.00	46
1998 New England Carriage House 14760	Open		29.00	29
1998 On The Beach 13640	Open		20.00	20
1995 Outhouse 1305	Retrd.	1997	26.00	26
1998 Picnic in the Shade 13410	Open		20.00	20
1995 Rope Swing 1311	Retrd.	1997	36.00	36
1995 Route 1 1313	Retrd.	1997	28.00	28
1997 Shade Tree 1355	Open		21.00	21
1995 Short Picket Fence 1310	Retrd.	1997	20.00	20
1997 Spanish Moss 1314	Open		21.00	21
1996 Summer Birch 1322	Retrd.	1997	26.00	26
1996 Summer Shade 1327	Retrd.	1997	29.00	29
1997 Swamp Cypress 1349	Open		21.00	21
1996 Tom's Fence 1342	Retrd.	1997	20.00	20
1998 Victorian Lamppost 13290	Open		16.00	16
1997 Wall Flowers 1304	Open		14.00	14
1995 Weeping Willow 1326	Retrd.	1997	39.00	39
1995 Windy Day 1321	Retrd.	1997	35.00	35
1996 Winter Green 1360	Retrd.	1997	24.00	24
1996 Winter Mantel 1351	Retrd.	1997	24.00	24

Limited Editions From Brian Baker - B. Baker

YEAR ISSUE	EDITION LIMIT	YEAR RETD.	ISSUE PRICE	*QUOTE U.S.$
1993 American Classic-rose 1566	500	1993	99.00	450-550
1987 Amsterdam Canal-brown, S/N 1030	1,000	1993	79.00	225
1998 Get Hooked 14080	750		68.00	68
1998 Haight Ashbury 16320	2,500		67.50	68
1994 Hill Top Mansion 1598	1,200	1995	97.00	125-150
1993 James River Plantation-brick 1454	Retrd.	1994	108.00	300-400
1996 London 1045	1,200	1997	119.00	119-135
1994 Painted Ladies 1190	1,200	1996	125.00	125
1995 Philadelphia-brick 1441	1,500	1997	110.00	110-125
1997 Riverside Plantation 1739	1,200		60.00	60
1994 White Point 1596	700	1996	100.00	165

Goebel/M.I. Hummel

M.I. Hummel Bavarian Village Collection - M.I. Hummel

YEAR ISSUE	EDITION LIMIT	YEAR RETD.	ISSUE PRICE	*QUOTE U.S.$
1996 All Aboard	Open		60.00	60
1995 Angel's Duet	Open		50.00	60
1995 The Bench and Tree Set (accessory)	Open		25.00	30
1995 Christmas Mail	Open		50.00	60
1995 Company's Coming	Open		50.00	60
1997 Evergreen Tree Set	Open		30.00	30
1998 Heavenly Harmony Church	Open		60.00	60
1996 Holiday Fountain (accessory)	Open		35.00	35
1997 Holiday Lights (accessory)	Open		30.00	20
1996 Horse With Sled (accessory)	Open		35.00	35
1997 The Mailbox (accessory)	Open		30.00	20
1996 Off for the Holidays	Open		60.00	60
1998 Practice Makes Perfect	Open		65.00	65
1998 Scholarly Thoughts	Open		65.00	65
1996 Shoe Maker Shop	Open		60.00	60
1995 The Sled and Pine Tree Set (accessory)	Open		25.00	30
1995 The Village Bakery	Open		50.00	60
1995 The Village Bridge (accessory)	Open		25.00	30
1998 Warm Winter Wishes	Open		65.00	65
1995 Winter's Comfort	Open		50.00	60
1995 The Wishing Well (accessory)	Open		25.00	30

Hamilton Collection

Dreamsicles Heavenly Village - K. Haynes

YEAR ISSUE	EDITION LIMIT	YEAR RETD.	ISSUE PRICE	*QUOTE U.S.$
1996 Flight School	Open		49.95	50
1997 Wreath Makers	Open		49.95	50
1997 Cherub Concerto	Open		49.95	50
1996 Star Factory	Open		49.95	50

Harbour Lights

Harbour Lights Collector's Society - Harbour Lights

YEAR ISSUE	EDITION LIMIT	YEAR RETD.	ISSUE PRICE	*QUOTE U.S.$
1995 Point Fermin CA 501 (Charter Member Piece)	Retrd.	1996	80.00	185-375
1995 Framed Point Fermin CA Print (numbrd.)	Retrd.	1996	Gift	20-30
1996 Stonington Harbor CT 502	Retrd.	1997	70.00	70-210
1996 Spyglass Collection 503	Retrd.	1997	Gift	75
1996 Point Fermin CA (Ornament)	Retrd.	1997	15.00	15-45
1997 Port Sanilac MI 506	Retrd.	1998	80.00	80-150
1997 Amelia Island FL	Retrd.	1998	Gift	50
1997 Stonington Harbor CT (Ornament)	Retrd.	1998	15.00	15
1998 Sea Girt NJ	Yr.Iss.		80.00	80
1998 Cockspur GA	Yr.Iss.		Gift	N/A
1998 Port Sanilac MI (Ornament)	Yr.Iss.		15.00	15

Event Piece - Harbour Lights

YEAR ISSUE	EDITION LIMIT	YEAR RETD.	ISSUE PRICE	*QUOTE U.S.$
1996 Sunken Rock NY 602	Yr.Iss.	1996	25.00	48-125
1997 New Point Loma 604 (1997 Collector's Reunion)	950	1997	70.00	750-1600
1997 New Point Loma-mini 605 (1997 Collector's Reunion)	480	1997	Gift	300-900
1997 Edgartown MA 603	Yr.Iss.	1997	35.00	70-125
1998 Roosevelt Island NY 612	Yr.Iss.		25.00	25

Chesapeake Series - Harbour Lights

YEAR ISSUE	EDITION LIMIT	YEAR RETD.	ISSUE PRICE	*QUOTE U.S.$
1996 Concord MD 186	9,500		66.00	66
1997 Drum Point MD 180	9,500	1997	99.00	99-250
1996 Sandy Point MD 167	9,500		70.00	70
1996 Sharps Island MD 185	9,500	1997	70.00	70
1996 Thomas Point MD 181	9,500	1996	99.00	132-204

Christmas - Harbour Lights

YEAR ISSUE	EDITION LIMIT	YEAR RETD.	ISSUE PRICE	*QUOTE U.S.$
1995 Christmas 1995 - Big Bay Point MI 700	5,000	1995	75.00	175-360
1996 Christmas 1996 - Colchester VT 701	8,200	1996	75.00	90-300
1997 Christmas 1997 - White Shoal MI 704	8,000	1997	80.00	80-150
1998 Christmas 1998 - Old Field Point NY 707	10,000		80.00	80

From Glow to Limited - Harbour Lights

YEAR ISSUE	EDITION LIMIT	YEAR RETD.	ISSUE PRICE	*QUOTE U.S.$
1996 Alcatraz CA 407 to 177	Closed	1996	77.00	125-250
1996 Cape Lookout 405 to 175	Closed	1996	64.00	64-150
1996 Fire Island NY 406 to 176	Closed	1996	70.00	70-150

*Quotes have been rounded up to nearest dollar

ARCHITECTURE

YEAR ISSUE	EDITION LIMIT	YEAR RETD.	ISSUE PRICE	*QUOTE U.S.$
1996 Mukilteo WA 417 to 178	Closed	1996	55.00	55
1996 Spectacle Reef MI 410 to 182	Closed	1996	60.00	60-150
1996 St. Joseph MI 411 to 183	Closed	1996	60.00	85-150
1996 Thirty Mile Point NY 414 to 184	Closed	1996	62.00	62-150

Great Lakes Region - Harbour Lights

YEAR ISSUE	EDITION LIMIT	YEAR RETD.	ISSUE PRICE	*QUOTE U.S.$
1992 Buffalo NY 122	5,500	1996	60.00	96-200
1992 Cana Island WI 119	5,500	1995	60.00	90-200
1996 Charlotte-Genesee NY 165	9,500		77.00	77
1998 Chicago Harbor IL 208	10,000		73.00	73
1991 Fort Niagara NY 113	5,500	1995	60.00	115-250
1998 Grand Haven MI 212	10,000		90.00	90
1997 Grand Traverse MI 191	9,500		80.00	80
1992 Grosse Point IL 120	5,500	1996	60.00	92-250
1994 Holland (Big Red) MI 142	5,500	1995	60.00	150-300
1998 Lorain OH 207	10,000		75.00	75
1992 Marblehead OH 121	5,500	1995	50.00	90-200
1992 Michigan City IN 123	5,500	1996	60.00	80-160
1992 Old Mackinac Point MI 118	5,500	1995	65.00	139-310
1998 Point Betsie MI 218	10,000		75.00	75
1997 Presque Isle PA 201	9,500		75.00	75
1995 Round Island MI 153	9,500		85.00	85
1991 Sand Island WI 112	5,500	1996	60.00	64-85
1995 Selkirk NY 157	9,500		75.00	75
1992 Split Rock MI 124 (incorrect state)	Closed	1992	60.00	1740-2000
1992 Split Rock MN 124	5,500	1995	60.00	78-110
1998 Sturgeon Bay WI 217	10,000		90.00	90
1995 Tawas Pt. MI 152	5,500	1996	75.00	75-120
1996 Toledo OH 179	9,500		85.00	85
1995 Wind Point WI 154	9,500		78.00	78

Great Lighthouses of the World - Harbour Lights

YEAR ISSUE	EDITION LIMIT	YEAR RETD.	ISSUE PRICE	*QUOTE U.S.$
1998 Alcatraz CA 417	Open		70.00	70
1997 Barnegat NJ (blue water) 414	Closed	1997	45.00	45-138
1997 Barnegat NJ (green water) 414	Closed	1997	45.00	45-90
1998 Barnegat NJ 414R	Open		50.00	50
1998 Bolivar TX 422	Open		65.00	65
1996 Boston Harbor MA 402	Open		50.00	50
1998 Cape Canaveral FL 420	Open		50.00	50
1994 Cape Hatteras NC 401	Open		50.00	50
1997 Cape Neddick ME 410	Open		50.00	50
1998 Holland MI 407	Open		50.00	50
1997 Montauk NY 405	Open		55.00	55
1997 New London Ledge CT 406	Ooen		55.00	55
1998 Old Mackinac MI 419	Open		65.00	65
1997 Point Loma CA 409	Open		50.00	50
1997 Ponce De Leon FL 408	Open		55.00	55
1995 Portland Head ME 404	Open		50.00	50
1996 Sandy Hook NJ 418	Open		50.00	50
1997 Sea Pines (Hilton Head) SC 415	Open		50.00	50
1995 Southeast Block Island RI 403	Open		50.00	50
1997 St. Augustine FL 411	Open		45.00	45
1997 St. Simons GA 416	Open		50.00	50
1998 Thomas Point MD 421	Open		90.00	90

Gulf Coast Region - Harbour Lights

YEAR ISSUE	EDITION LIMIT	YEAR RETD.	ISSUE PRICE	*QUOTE U.S.$
1995 Biloxi MS 149	5,500	1997	60.00	84-150
1995 Bolivar TX 146	5,500	1997	70.00	70-150
1997 Middle Bay AL 187	9,500	1997	99.00	99-250
1995 New Canal LA 148	5,500	1996	65.00	94-97
1995 Pensacola FL 150	9,000	1997	80.00	120-200
1995 Port Isabel TX 147	5,500	1997	65.00	90-150

International Series - Harbour Lights

YEAR ISSUE	EDITION LIMIT	YEAR RETD.	ISSUE PRICE	*QUOTE U.S.$
1997 Hook Head Ireland 198	9,500		71.00	71
1997 La Jument France 192	9,500	1998	68.00	68-85
1997 Longship UK 193	9,500		68.00	68
1997 Macquarie Australia 197	9,500		68.00	68
1996 Peggy's Cove Canada 169	9,500		68.00	68

Lady Lightkeepers - Harbour Lights

YEAR ISSUE	EDITION LIMIT	YEAR RETD.	ISSUE PRICE	*QUOTE U.S.$
1996 Chatham MA 172	9,500		70.00	70
1996 Ida Lewis RI 174	9,500		70.00	70
1996 Matinicus ME 173	9,500		77.00	77
1996 Point Piños CA 170	9,500		70.00	70
1996 Saugerties NY 171	9,500		75.00	75

Northeast Region - Harbour Lights

YEAR ISSUE	EDITION LIMIT	YEAR RETD.	ISSUE PRICE	*QUOTE U.S.$
1994 Barnegat NJ (blue water)139	5,500	1995	60.00	200-486
1994 Barnegat NJ (green water) 139	5,500	1995	60.00	360-406
1998 Bass Harbour ME 214	10,000		75.00	75
1997 Beavertail RI (gray) 188	6,500		80.00	80
1997 Beavertail RI (tan) 188	3,000		80.00	80
1991 Boston Harbor MA 117	5,500	1995	60.00	150-360
1995 Brant Point MA 162	9,500		66.00	66
1998 Cape Elizabeth ME 215	10,000		75.00	75
1997 Cape Henry VA 196	9,500	1997	82.00	80-150
1996 Cape May NJ 168	9,500	1997	75.00	68-75
1994 Cape Neddick (Nubble) ME 141	5,500	1995	66.00	150-360
1991 Castle Hill RI 116	5,500	1996	60.00	85-101
1998 Dunkirk NY 221	10,000		70.00	70
1998 Execution Rock NY 210	10,000		78.00	78
1998 Faulkner's Island CT 216	10,000		70.00	70
1998 Fenwick DE 213	10,000		82.00	82
1996 Fire Island NY 176	9,500	1998	70.00	70-160
1998 Gay Head MA 219	10,000		75.00	75
1998 Goat Island ME 222	10,000		75.00	75
1991 Gt. Captain Island CT 114	5,500	1996	60.00	92-150
1995 Highland MA (w/o "s") 161	3,500	1998	75.00	75
1995 Highlands MA (w/ "s") 161	6,000	1998	75.00	75
1998 Horton Point NY 205	10,000		75.00	75
1997 Jeffrey's Hook NY 195	9,500		66.00	66
1992 Minot's Ledge MA (blue water) 131	5,500	1996	60.00	125-350
1992 Minot's Ledge MA (green water) 131	5,500	1996	60.00	191-240
1994 Montauk NY 143	5,500	1995	85.00	180-300
1992 Nauset MA 126	5,500	1995	66.00	158-350
1992 New London Ledge CT (blue water) 129	5,500	1995	66.00	135-300
1992 New London Ledge CT (green water) 129	5,500	1995	66.00	260-275
1997 Nobska MA 203	9,500	1998	75.00	75
1998 Old Saybrook CT 206	10,000		69.00	69
1996 Pemaquid ME 164	9,500	1998	90.00	90-108
1998 Point Judith RI 223	10,000		82.00	82
1992 Portland Breakwater ME 130	5,500	1996	60.00	108-140
1992 Portland Head ME 125	5,500	1994	66.00	585-932
1991 Sandy Hook NJ 104	5,500	1994	60.00	240-750
1996 Scituate MA 166	9,500	1998	77.00	77
1992 Southeast Block Island RI 128	5,500	1994	71.00	360-550
1991 West Quoddy Head ME 103	5,500	1995	60.00	124-162
1992 Whaleback NH 127	5,500	1996	60.00	90-120

Signature Series - Harbour Lights

YEAR ISSUE	EDITION LIMIT	YEAR RETD.	ISSUE PRICE	*QUOTE U.S.$
1998 Thomas Point MD 421, S/N	Open		90.00	90
1998 Tybee GA 423, S/N	Open		65.00	65

Southeast Region - Harbour Lights

YEAR ISSUE	EDITION LIMIT	YEAR RETD.	ISSUE PRICE	*QUOTE U.S.$
1994 Assateague VA 145-mold one	988	1994	69.00	274-475
1994 Assateague VA 145-mold two	4,512	1995	69.00	137-192
1996 Bald Head NC 155	9,500	1998	75.00	75-150
1996 Cape Canaveral FL 163	9,500	1996	80.00	105-400
1998 Cape Florida FL 209	10,000		78.00	78
1991 Cape Hatteras NC 102 (with house)	Retrd.	1991	60.00	3852-4120
1992 Cape Hatteras NC 102R	5,500	1993	60.00	600-722
1993 Hilton Head SC 136	5,500	1994	60.00	399-750
1998 Hunting Island SC 211	10,000		75.00	75
1995 Jupiter FL 151	9,500	1996	77.00	108-175
1993 Key West FL 134	5,500	1995	60.00	270-375
1993 Ocracoke NC 135	5,500	1995	60.00	181-400
1993 Ponce de Leon FL 132	5,500	1994	60.00	300-750
1997 Sanibel FL 194	9,500	1997	120.00	120-350
1993 St. Augustine FL 138	5,500	1994	71.00	438-750
1993 St. Simons GA 137	5,500	1995	66.00	365-600
1993 Tybee GA 133	5,500	1995	60.00	272-500

Special Editions - Harbour Lights

YEAR ISSUE	EDITION LIMIT	YEAR RETD.	ISSUE PRICE	*QUOTE U.S.$
1997 Keepers & Friends 606	Open		55.00	55
1995 Legacy Light (blue) 601	Retrd.	1996	65.00	85-97
1995 Legacy Light (red) 600	Retrd.	1996	65.00	110-150
1997 Navesink NJ 200	9,500		245.00	245
1997 Spyglass Collection 607	Open		83.00	83
1998 Spyglass Collection-Southern Belles, set/7 613	Open		83.00	83

Stamp Series - Harbour Lights

YEAR ISSUE	EDITION LIMIT	YEAR RETD.	ISSUE PRICE	*QUOTE U.S.$
1995 Marblehead OH 413	Open		50.00	50
1995 Spectacle Reef MI 182	9,500	1996	60.00	60-90
1995 Split Rock MN 412	Open		60.00	60
1995 St. Joseph MI 183	9,500	1996	60.00	60-90
1995 Thirty Mile Point NY 184	9,500	1996	62.00	62-150
1995 Five Piece Matched Numbered Set 400	5,300	1995	275.00	250-325

Tall Towers - Harbour Lights

YEAR ISSUE	EDITION LIMIT	YEAR RETD.	ISSUE PRICE	*QUOTE U.S.$
1996 Bodie NC 159	9,500	1998	77.00	77-150
1996 Cape Lookout NC 175	9,500	1997	64.00	64-150
1995 Currituck NC 158	9,500	1997	80.00	80-150
1997 Morris Island - Now, SC 190	9,500	1997	65.00	65-75
1997 Morris Island - Then, SC 189	9,500	1997	85.00	85-95
1997 Morris Island - Now & Then, set SC 189	9,500	1997	170.00	170-210

Western Region - Harbour Lights

YEAR ISSUE	EDITION LIMIT	YEAR RETD.	ISSUE PRICE	*QUOTE U.S.$
1991 Admiralty Head WA 101(misspelled)	Closed	1994	60.00	113-168
1991 Admiralty Head WA 101	Retrd.	1994	60.00	120-199
1996 Alcatraz CA 177	9,500	1996	77.00	125-200
1991 Burrows Island OR 108 (incorrect state)	Closed	1991	60.00	622-1080
1991 Burrows Island WA 108	2,563	1994	60.00	285-550
1991 Cape Blanco OR 109	5,500	1997	60.00	60-93
1996 Cape Meares OR 160	9,500		68.00	68
1991 Coquille River OR 111	1,138	1993	60.00	2400-3200
1994 Diamond Head HI 140	5,500	1995	60.00	150-234
1997 Gray's Harbor WA 202	9,500		75.00	75
1994 Heceta Head OR 144	5,500	1996	65.00	90-119
1996 Mukilteo WA 178	9,500		55.00	55
1991 North Head WA 106	5,500	1996	60.00	60-110
1991 Old Point Loma CA 105	5,500	1995	60.00	95-195
1997 Pigeon Point CA 199	9,500		68.00	68
1995 Pt. Arena CA 156	5,428	1996	80.00	130-360
1991 St. George's Reef CA 115	5,500	1996	60.00	60-90
1998 Tillamook OR 224	10,000		75.00	75
1991 Umpqua River OR 107	5,500	1996	60.00	60-119
1997 Yaquina Bay OR 204	9,500		77.00	77
1991 Yaquina Head WA 110	5,500	1996	60.00	81-150

Hawthorne Village

Baseball Stadiums - Hawthorne

YEAR ISSUE	EDITION LIMIT	YEAR RETD.	ISSUE PRICE	*QUOTE U.S.$
1997 Comiskey Park	Open		50.95	51
1997 Fenway Park	Open		49.95	50
1996 Wrigley Field-D. Kessinger	Closed	1996	49.95	50
1995 Wrigley Field-Ernie Banks	Open		99.95	100
1996 Wrigley Field-Ernie signature/cert.	Open		49.95	50
1996 Wrigley Field-R. Huntley	Closed	1996	49.95	50
1996 Wrigley Field-R. Rushell	Closed	1996	49.95	50
1996 Wrigley Field-R. Santo	Closed	1996	49.95	50
1996 Yankee Stadium	Closed	1997	49.95	50
1996 Yankee Stadium-signed Joe DiMaggio	Open		299.95	300

Beacons of Freedom - Unknown

YEAR ISSUE	EDITION LIMIT	YEAR RETD.	ISSUE PRICE	*QUOTE U.S.$
1995 Portland Head Lighthouse	Closed	1996	39.90	40
1996 Sandy Hook Lighthouse	Closed	1996	39.90	40
1995 West Quoddy Head Lighthouse	Open		39.90	40

Bearly Angels (Illuminated) - G. Gilchrist

YEAR ISSUE	EDITION LIMIT	YEAR RETD.	ISSUE PRICE	*QUOTE U.S.$
1995 Bearsmith Halo Shop	Closed	1995	39.90	40
1995 Heavenly Pastry Shop	Closed	1996	39.90	40
1995 Wishhouse	Closed	1997	39.90	40

Chestnut Hill Station - K.&H. LeVan

YEAR ISSUE	EDITION LIMIT	YEAR RETD.	ISSUE PRICE	*QUOTE U.S.$
1994 Bicycle Shop	Closed	1995	29.90	30
1993 Chestnut Hill Depot	Closed	1994	29.90	30
1993 Parkside Cafe	Closed	1995	29.90	30
1993 Wishing Well Cottage	Closed	1994	29.90	30

Concord: The Hometown of American Literature - K.&H. LeVan

YEAR ISSUE	EDITION LIMIT	YEAR RETD.	ISSUE PRICE	*QUOTE U.S.$
1993 Alcott's Orchard House	Closed	1995	39.90	40
1992 Emerson's Old Manse	Closed	1995	39.90	40
1991 Hawthorne's Wayside Retreat	Closed	1995	39.90	40

Gone With the Wind (Illuminated) - Hawthorne

YEAR ISSUE	EDITION LIMIT	YEAR RETD.	ISSUE PRICE	*QUOTE U.S.$
1994 Atlanta Church	Closed	1996	39.90	40
1995 Butler's Mansion	Closed	1996	39.90	40
1994 Kennedy Store	Closed	1997	39.90	40
1994 Red Horse Saloon	Closed	1997	39.90	40
1993 Tara	Closed	1996	39.90	40
1994 Twelve Oaks	Closed	1996	39.90	40

Gone With the Wind Collection - K.&H. LeVan

YEAR ISSUE	EDITION LIMIT	YEAR RETD.	ISSUE PRICE	*QUOTE U.S.$
1993 Against Her Will	Closed	1996	42.90	43-125
1994 Alone	Closed	1996	45.90	46-110
1995 Ashley's Safe	Closed	1996	45.90	46
1995 Dignity & Respect	Closed	1995	45.90	46-150
1994 Hope for a New Tomorrow	Closed	1994	42.90	43-110
1994 I Have Done Enough	Closed	1996	45.90	46-110
1993 A Message for Captain Butler	Closed	1996	42.90	43-125
1995 Revenge on Shantytown	Open		45.90	46
1993 Rhett's Return	Closed	1996	39.90	40-105
1996 Surrendered at Last	Closed	1996	47.90	50
1994 Swept Away	Closed	1996	45.90	46-125
1994 Take Me to Tara	Closed	1995	45.90	46-125
1992 Tara . . .Scarlett's Pride	Closed	1995	39.90	40-125
1992 Twelve Oaks: The Romance Begins	Closed	1995	39.90	40-110

Hometown America - Rockwell Inspired

YEAR ISSUE	EDITION LIMIT	YEAR RETD.	ISSUE PRICE	*QUOTE U.S.$
1994 Evergreen General Store	Closed	1996	39.95	40
1994 Evergreen Valley Church	Closed	1996	37.95	38
1993 Evergreen Valley School	Closed	1996	34.95	35
1995 Happy Holidays	Closed	1996	39.95	40
1993 The Village Bakery	Closed	1994	37.95	38
1994 Waiting For Santa	Closed	1995	39.95	40
1994 Woodcutter's Rest	Closed	1996	37.95	38

Kinkade's St. Nicholas Square (Illuminated) - Kinkade-Inspired

YEAR ISSUE	EDITION LIMIT	YEAR RETD.	ISSUE PRICE	*QUOTE U.S.$
1994 Evergreen Apothecary	Closed	1995	39.90	40
1994 The Firehouse	Closed	1995	39.90	40
1994 Holly House Inn	Closed	1995	39.90	40
1994 Kringle Brothers	Closed	1995	39.90	40
1994 Mrs. C. Bakery	Closed	1995	39.90	40
1994 Noel Chapel (free sign in box)	Closed	1996	39.90	40
1994 S.C. Toy Maker	Closed	1996	39.90	40
1993 Town Hall	Closed	1996	39.90	40

Lost Victorians of Old San Francisco - Hawthorne

YEAR ISSUE	EDITION LIMIT	YEAR RETD.	ISSUE PRICE	*QUOTE U.S.$
1992 Empress of Russian Hill	Closed	1993	34.90	35
1991 Grande Dame of Nob Hill	Closed	1994	34.90	35
1993 Princess of Pacific Heights	Closed	1993	34.90	35

Main Street Memories - Unknown

YEAR ISSUE	EDITION LIMIT	YEAR RETD.	ISSUE PRICE	*QUOTE U.S.$
1996 Dairy Queen	Open		39.95	40
1996 Mobilgas	Open		39.95	45

Main Street Memories Accessories - Unknown

YEAR ISSUE	EDITION LIMIT	YEAR RETD.	ISSUE PRICE	*QUOTE U.S.$
1996 Mobilgas Sign & Pumps	Open		19.00	20

McDonald's Accessories - Hawthorne

YEAR ISSUE	EDITION LIMIT	YEAR RETD.	ISSUE PRICE	*QUOTE U.S.$
1997 Burger Truck & Ronald	Open		21.95	24
1997 McDuties	Open		21.95	23
1997 Thumbs Up - Billboard Sign	Open		24.95	30

McMemories - Hawthorne

YEAR ISSUE	EDITION LIMIT	YEAR RETD.	ISSUE PRICE	*QUOTE U.S.$
1996 Look For the Golden Arches	Open		39.95	50
1997 McDonald's Golden Classic (domed)	Open		69.95	70
1995 McDonald's Restaurant	Open		39.95	50

Rockwell's Home for the Holidays - Rockwell-Inspired

YEAR ISSUE	EDITION LIMIT	YEAR RETD.	ISSUE PRICE	*QUOTE U.S.$
1992 Bringing Home the Christmas Tree	Closed	1994	34.90	35
1992 Carolers In The Church Yard	Closed	1996	37.90	38
1992 Christmas Eve at the Studio	Closed	1994	34.90	35
1994 A Golden Memory	Closed	1995	41.90	42
1994 Late for the Dance	Closed	1996	41.90	42
1993 Letters to Santa	Closed	1996	39.90	40
1993 Over the River	Closed	1995	37.90	38
1995 Ready & Waiting	Closed	1995	41.90	42
1993 A Room at the Inn	Closed	1996	39.90	40
1993 School's Out	Closed	1994	39.90	40
1993 Three-Day Pass	Closed	1996	37.90	38
1994 A White Christmas	Closed	1995	41.90	42

Rockwell's Hometown Collection - Rockwell-Inspired

YEAR ISSUE	EDITION LIMIT	YEAR RETD.	ISSUE PRICE	*QUOTE U.S.$
1991 The Bell Tower	Closed	1995	36.95	37

*Quotes have been rounded up to nearest dollar

YEAR ISSUE	EDITION LIMIT	YEAR RETD.	ISSUE PRICE	*QUOTE U.S.$
1992 Berkshire Playhouse	Closed	1993	42.95	43
1991 The Church on the Glen	Closed	1995	39.95	40
1992 Citizen's Hall	Closed	1994	42.95	43
1991 The Fire House	Closed	1995	36.95	37
1991 Grey Stone Church	Closed	1995	34.95	35
1992 The Mission House	Closed	1995	42.95	43
1992 The Old Corner House	Closed	1995	42.95	43
1994 Old Rectory	Closed	1994	42.95	43
1993 Parsonage Cottage	Closed	1995	42.95	43
1993 Plain School	Closed	1995	42.95	43
1990 Rockwell's Residence	Closed	1995	34.95	35
1992 Towne Hall	Closed	1993	39.95	40
1993 Train Station	Closed	1995	42.95	43

Rockwell's Main Street - Rockwell-Inspired

YEAR ISSUE	EDITION LIMIT	YEAR RETD.	ISSUE PRICE	*QUOTE U.S.$
1992 Bringing Home the Tree	Closed	1994	34.90	35
1992 Carolers in the Churchyard	Closed	1994	37.90	38
1992 Christmas Eve at the Studio	Closed	1993	34.90	35
1995 A Golden Memory	Closed	1995	41.90	42
1994 Late for the Dance	Open		41.90	42
1992 Letters to Santa	Open		39.90	40
1993 Over the River	Closed	1995	37.90	38
1995 Ready & Waiting	Closed	1995	41.90	42
1993 A Room at the Inn	Open		39.90	40
1993 School's Out	Closed	1994	37.90	38
1993 Three-Day Pass	Open		37.90	38
1994 A White Christmas	Closed	1995	41.90	42

Stonefield Valley - K.&H. LeVan

YEAR ISSUE	EDITION LIMIT	YEAR RETD.	ISSUE PRICE	*QUOTE U.S.$
1992 Church in the Glen	Closed	1994	37.90	38
1993 Ferryman's Cottage	Closed	1994	39.90	40
1993 Hillside Country Store	Closed	1994	39.90	40
1992 Meadowbrook School	Closed	1994	34.90	35
1993 Parson's Cottage	Closed	1994	37.90	38
1992 Springbridge Cottage	Closed	1994	34.90	35
1993 Valley View Farm	Closed	1994	39.90	40
1992 Weaver's Cottage	Closed	1994	37.90	38

Strolling Through Colonial America - K.&H. LeVan

YEAR ISSUE	EDITION LIMIT	YEAR RETD.	ISSUE PRICE	*QUOTE U.S.$
1992 Captain Lee's Grammar School	Closed	1995	39.90	40
1992 Court House on the Green	Closed	1995	37.90	38
1992 Eastbrook Church	Closed	1995	37.90	38
1993 Everett's Joiner Shop	Closed	1993	39.90	40
1992 Higgins' Grist Mill	Closed	1995	37.90	38
1991 Jefferson's Ordinarie	Closed	1995	34.90	35
1992 Millrace Store	Closed	1995	34.90	35
1992 The Village Smithy	Closed	1993	39.90	40

Tara: The Only Thing Worth Fighting For Plantation - K.&H. LeVan

YEAR ISSUE	EDITION LIMIT	YEAR RETD.	ISSUE PRICE	*QUOTE U.S.$
1994 Carriage House	Closed	1996	29.90	30
1993 A Dream Remembered	Closed	1996	29.90	30
1994 Kitchen & Gateway	Closed	1995	29.90	30
1994 The Mill	Closed	1996	29.90	30
1994 Spring House & Hideaway	Closed	1995	29.90	30
1995 The Stable	Closed	1996	29.90	30

Thatcher's Crossing - R. Dowding

YEAR ISSUE	EDITION LIMIT	YEAR RETD.	ISSUE PRICE	*QUOTE U.S.$
1993 Chapel Crossing	Closed	1995	29.90	30
1993 Midsummer's Cottage	Closed	1995	29.90	30
1993 Rose Arbour Cottage	Closed	1994	29.90	30
1994 Woodcutter's Cottage	Closed	1995	29.90	30

Victorian Grove Collection - K.&H. LeVan

YEAR ISSUE	EDITION LIMIT	YEAR RETD.	ISSUE PRICE	*QUOTE U.S.$
1993 Cherry Blossom	Closed	1994	34.90	35
1992 Lilac Cottage	Closed	1995	34.90	35
1992 Rose Haven	Closed	1994	34.90	35

Hazle Ceramics

A Nation of Shopkeepers Collectors' Club - H. Boyles

YEAR ISSUE	EDITION LIMIT	YEAR RETD.	ISSUE PRICE	*QUOTE U.S.$
1995 Anne Frank's "The Hiding Place"	Retrd.	1998	76.00	76
1996 Jewellers	200	1997	68.00	68-116
1996 County Bank	200	1998	76.00	76-145
1998 Street Scenes - The Telephone Box Queue	Yr.Iss.		Gift	N/A

Hazle 2000 - H. Boyles

YEAR ISSUE	EDITION LIMIT	YEAR RETD.	ISSUE PRICE	*QUOTE U.S.$
1997 Corner Grocers	2,000	1998	90.00	90
1998 Sainsbury's	2,000		90.00	90
1997 Thos. Cook & Son	2,000		120.00	120

The Miniature Teahouse Collection - H. Boyles

YEAR ISSUE	EDITION LIMIT	YEAR RETD.	ISSUE PRICE	*QUOTE U.S.$
1996 Corner Teahouse	Open		30.00	30
1996 Farrer's	Open		30.00	30
1996 God Begot House	Open		30.00	30
1996 Nell Gwynn's House	Open		30.00	30
1996 Sally Lunn's House	Open		30.00	30
1998 Sherlock Holmes	Open		25.00	25
1996 Stonegate House	Open		30.00	30

A Nation of Shopkeepers - H. Boyles

YEAR ISSUE	EDITION LIMIT	YEAR RETD.	ISSUE PRICE	*QUOTE U.S.$
1997 "Collect It!"	500		90.00	90
1997 Accountant	Open		72.00	72
1995 Antique Shop	Open		72.00	76
1993 Attorney at Law	Open		72.00	76
1997 Baby Shop	Open		74.00	74
1993 Bagel Bakery	Retrd.	1997	63.00	63
1995 Bakery/Coffee Shop	Retrd.	1998	72.00	76
1998 Bakery/Tearoom	Open		76.00	76
1991 Barber	Retrd.	1997	64.00	75-80
1998 Batchelor's Saddlemaker	200		120.00	120
1992 Bed & Breakfast	Open		72.00	76
1993 Bookshop	Retrd.	1998	72.00	76
1993 Bookshop & Postbox	Retrd.	1998	76.00	76
1996 Bridal Shop	Open		72.00	76
1997 Bridal Shop (Spring)	Open		76.00	76
1997 Bright Ideas	50		76.00	76
1998 Butcher	Open		76.00	76
1991 Butcher Shop	Retrd.	1997	64.00	115-145
1991 Chemist	Open		72.00	76
1991 Chocolate Shop	Open		72.00	76
1994 Christmas Ironmonger-red	300	1996	84.00	651
1996 Christmas Market Hall	Open		86.00	86
1995 Christmas Shop	Open		84.00	84
1990 Clock Shop	Retrd.	1992	54.00	54
1991 Corner Shop	Retrd.	1998	62.00	64
1996 Dentist	Open		72.00	76
1996 Doctor	Open		72.00	76
1995 East End Deli (London)	Retrd.	1998	75.00	75
1996 East Side Deli (NY)	Retrd.	1998	75.00	80
1995 Farrers	500		72.00	76
1994 Fine Art Saleroom	Retrd.	1998	124.00	124
1990 Fish & Chips	Open		58.00	70
1990 Fish & Chips (no line up)	Retrd.	1993	58.00	215
1991 Fishmonger	Retrd.	1997	68.00	95-116
1990 Florist	Open		58.00	70
1995 Forever Flowers	50	1997	70.00	70
1990 Gents Hats	Retrd.	1992	54.00	54
1993 Gift Shop	Retrd.	1997	72.00	76
1991 Greengrocer	Retrd.	1995	62.00	62
1995 Greengrocer (Revised)	Open		64.00	70
1995 Green Fingers	50	1997	70.00	70
1991 Hairdresser	Retrd.	1997	64.00	64-116
1994 Hardware/Ironmonger-green	1,200	1996	84.00	205-362
1991 Harvard House	Retrd.	1997	58.00	58
1996 Hat & Shoe Shop	Open		76.00	76
1992 Indian Restaurant	Retrd.	1997	72.00	72
1995 Irish Linen	Open		64.00	70
1990 Ladies Hat Shop	Retrd.	1992	54.00	54
1997 The London Trading Co.	200		80.00	80
1997 Moore's China Shop	200		80.00	80
1997 Mrs. Thomas' China Shop	Open		72.00	72
1993 Needlewoman	300	1995	72.00	72-362
1993 Nell Gwynn's House	250	1996	90.00	90-362
1998 The Optician	Retrd.	1998	70.00	116
1998 Painswick Post Office	Open		76.00	76
1991 The Pawnbroker	Retrd.	1994	72.00	120-165
1997 A Pet Is For Life....	800		120.00	120
1994 Saddlery	Retrd.	1997	76.00	76
1996 Sally Lunn's	Open		76.00	76
1995 Sewing Room	500	1996	76.00	200-254
1990 Shoe Shop	Retrd.	1992	54.00	54
1990 Small Post Office	Retrd.	1992	54.00	205-290
1993 Smiths of Bermuda	200	1996	70.00	95
1998 Sweet Shop	Open		76.00	76
1991 Teashop & Roses	Open		72.00	76
1991 Teashop with Telephone Box	Open		76.00	76
1994 Tom Morris Golf Shop	Retrd.	1997	76.00	76-145
1995 Tudor Pub-Fox & Hounds	Retrd.	1997	72.00	72-145
1992 Tudor Pub-Royal Oak	Open		72.00	76
1994 Turret Pub	Retrd.	1998	78.00	78
1995 Turret Pub-King's Head (USA only)	Open		78.00	78
1996 Victorian Police Station	Retrd.	1997	75.00	145
1993 Victorian Post Office	Retrd.	1997	78.00	106-145
1995 Victorian Pub-Irish	Open		74.00	76
1997 Victorian Pub-Red Lion	Open		74.00	76
1997 Victorian Pub-Victoria & Albert	Retrd.	1997	74.00	76
1998 Village Pet Shop	Open		76.00	76

Pastille Burners - H. Boyles

YEAR ISSUE	EDITION LIMIT	YEAR RETD.	ISSUE PRICE	*QUOTE U.S.$
1997 Anne Hathaway's Cottage	Open		90.00	90
1996 The Cricketers	Open		90.00	90
1996 Marygreen Manor	Open		90.00	90
1997 Shakespeare's Birthplace	Open		90.00	90

Lilliput Lane Ltd./Enesco Corporation

Collectors Club Specials - Various

YEAR ISSUE	EDITION LIMIT	YEAR RETD.	ISSUE PRICE	*QUOTE U.S.$
1986 Packhorse Bridge - D. Tate	Retrd.	1987	Gift	350-675
1986 Packhorse Bridge (dealer) - D. Tate	Retrd.	1987	Gift	450-750
1986 Crendon Manor - D. Tate	Retrd.	1989	285.00	850
1986 Gulliver - Unknown	Retrd.	1986	65.00	325-369
1987 Little Lost Dog - D. Tate	Retrd.	1988	Gift	225-450
1987 Yew Tree Farm - D. Tate	Retrd.	1988	160.00	132-300
1988 Wishing Well - D. Tate	Retrd.	1989	Gift	82-100
1989 Dovecot - D. Tate	Retrd.	1990	Gift	44-75
1989 Wenlock Rise - D. Tate	Retrd.	1989	175.00	125-185
1990 Cosy Corner - D. Tate	Retrd.	1991	Gift	32-44
1990 Lavender Cottage - D. Tate	Retrd.	1991	50.00	75-90
1990 Bridle Way - D. Tate	Retrd.	1991	100.00	94-200
1991 Puddlebrook - D. Tate	Retrd.	1992	Gift	25-70
1991 Gardeners Cottage - D. Tate	Retrd.	1992	120.00	75-175
1991 Wren Cottage - D. Tate	Retrd.	1993	13.95	57-63
1992 Pussy Willow - D. Tate	Retrd.	1993	Gift	29-40
1992 Forget-Me-Not - D. Tate	Retrd.	1993	130.00	94-200
1993 The Spinney - Lilliput Lane	Retrd.	1994	Gift	24-30
1993 Heaven Lea Cottage - Lilliput Lane	Retrd.	1994	150.00	175-245
1993 Curlew Cottage - Lilliput Lane	Retrd.	1995	18.95	54-69
1994 Petticoat Cottage - Lilliput Lane	Retrd.	1995	Gift	19-32
1994 Woodman's Retreat - Lilliput Lane	Retrd.	1995	135.00	150-200
1995 Thimble Cottage - Lilliput Lane	Retrd.	1996	Gift	75
1995 Porlock Down - Lilliput Lane	Retrd.	1996	135.00	150-175
1996 Wash Day - Lilliput Lane	Retrd.	1997	Gift	N/A
1996 Meadowsweet Cottage - Lilliput Lane	Retrd.	1997	110.00	94-110
1996 Nursery Cottage - Lilliput Lane	Retrd.	1997	Gift	85
1996 Winnows - Lilliput Lane	Open		22.50	23
1997 Hampton Moat - Lilliput Lane	Retrd.	1998	Gift	N/A
1997 Hampton Manor - Lilliput Lane	Retrd.	1998	100.00	100
1997 Cider Apple Cottage - Lilliput Lane	Retrd.	1998	Gift	85
1998 The Pottery - Lilliput Lane	4/99		170.00	170
1998 Kiln Cottage - Lilliput Lane	4/99		Gift	N/A

Anniversary Collection - Lilliput Lane

YEAR ISSUE	EDITION LIMIT	YEAR RETD.	ISSUE PRICE	*QUOTE U.S.$
1992 Honeysuckle Cottage	Yr.Iss.	1992	195.00	180-250
1993 Cotman Cottage	Yr.Iss.	1993	220.00	132-250
1994 Watermeadows	Yr.Iss.	1994	189.00	113-200
1995 Gertrude's Garden	Yr.Iss.	1995	192.00	250
1996 Cruck End	Yr.Iss.	1996	130.00	130
1997 Summer Days	Yr.Iss.	1997	165.00	165
1998 Shades of Summer	Yr.Iss.		170.00	170

South Bend Dinner Collection - Various

YEAR ISSUE	EDITION LIMIT	YEAR RETD.	ISSUE PRICE	*QUOTE U.S.$
1989 Commemorative Medallion - D. Tate	Retrd.	1989	N/A	130-200
1990 Rowan Lodge - D. Tate	Retrd.	1990	N/A	200-400
1991 Gamekeepers Cottage - D. Tate	Retrd.	1991	N/A	188-250
1992 Ashberry Cottage - D. Tate	Retrd.	1992	N/A	138-400
1993 Magnifying Glass - Lilliput Lane	Retrd.	1993	N/A	N/A

Special Event Collection - Lilliput Lane

YEAR ISSUE	EDITION LIMIT	YEAR RETD.	ISSUE PRICE	*QUOTE U.S.$
1990 Rowan Lodge	Retrd.	1990	50.00	120
1991 Gamekeepers Cottage	Retrd.	1991	75.00	200
1992 Ploughman's Cottage	Retrd.	1992	75.00	44-60
1993 Aberford Gate	Retrd.	1993	95.00	150
1994 Leagrave Cottage	Retrd.	1994	75.00	75
1995 Vanbrugh Lodge	Retrd.	1995	60.00	75
1996 Amberly Rose	Retrd.	1996	45.00	45
1997 Dormouse Cottage	Retrd.	1997	60.00	60
1998 Comfort Cottage	Yr.Iss.		50.00	50

American Collection - D. Tate

YEAR ISSUE	EDITION LIMIT	YEAR RETD.	ISSUE PRICE	*QUOTE U.S.$
1984 Adobe Church	Retrd.	1985	22.50	700-1100
1984 Adobe Village	Retrd.	1985	60.00	900-1500
1984 Cape Cod	Retrd.	1985	22.50	570-910
1984 Country Church	Retrd.	1985	22.50	500-800
1984 Covered Bridge	Retrd.	1985	22.50	1000-2000
1984 Forge Barn	Retrd.	1985	22.50	550-660
1984 General Store	Retrd.	1985	22.50	600-800
1984 Grist Mill	Retrd.	1985	22.50	102-500
1984 Light House	Retrd.	1985	22.50	650-800
1984 Log Cabin	Retrd.	1985	22.50	625-1000
1984 Midwest Barn	Retrd.	1985	22.50	189-345
1984 San Francisco House	Retrd.	1985	22.50	850
1984 Wallace Station	Retrd.	1985	22.50	400

The Bed & Breakfast Collection - Lilliput Lane, unless otherwise noted

YEAR ISSUE	EDITION LIMIT	YEAR RETD.	ISSUE PRICE	*QUOTE U.S.$
1998 Seaview	Open		80.00	80
1998 Tarnside	Open		85.00	85
1998 Walker's Rest	Open		85.00	85
1998 York Gate	Open		85.00	85

Blaise Hamlet Classics - Lilliput Lane

YEAR ISSUE	EDITION LIMIT	YEAR RETD.	ISSUE PRICE	*QUOTE U.S.$
1993 Circular Cottage	Retrd.	1995	95.00	53-88
1993 Dial Cottage	Retrd.	1995	95.00	53-95
1993 Diamond Cottage	Retrd.	1995	95.00	40-95
1993 Double Cottage	Retrd.	1995	95.00	95-150
1993 Jasmine Cottage	Retrd.	1995	95.00	40-90
1993 Oak Cottage	Retrd.	1995	95.00	95-110
1993 Rose Cottage	Retrd.	1995	95.00	75-95
1993 Sweet Briar Cottage	Retrd.	1995	95.00	95-150
1993 Vine Cottage	Retrd.	1995	95.00	95-135

Blaise Hamlet Collection - D. Tate

YEAR ISSUE	EDITION LIMIT	YEAR RETD.	ISSUE PRICE	*QUOTE U.S.$
1989 Circular Cottage	Retrd.	1993	110.00	150-175
1990 Dial Cottage	Retrd.	1995	110.00	150-175
1989 Diamond Cottage	Retrd.	1993	110.00	100-150
1991 Double Cottage	Retrd.	1996	200.00	150
1991 Jasmine Cottage	Retrd.	1996	140.00	110-150
1989 Oak Cottage	Retrd.	1993	110.00	125-150
1991 Rose Cottage	Retrd.	1997	140.00	110-150
1990 Sweetbriar Cottage	Retrd.	1995	110.00	108-150
1990 Vine Cottage	Retrd.	1995	110.00	135-150

Christmas Collection - Various

YEAR ISSUE	EDITION LIMIT	YEAR RETD.	ISSUE PRICE	*QUOTE U.S.$
1992 Chestnut Cottage	Retrd.	1996	46.50	35-50
1992 Cranberry Cottage	Retrd.	1996	46.50	35-50
1988 Deer Park Hall - D. Tate	Retrd.	1989	120.00	190-250
1993 The Gingerbread Shop	Retrd.	1997	50.00	35-50
1992 Hollytree House	Retrd.	1996	46.50	35-50
1991 The Old Vicarage at Christmas - D. Tate	Retrd.	1992	180.00	150-180
1993 Partridge Cottage	Retrd.	1997	50.00	35-50
1994 Ring O' Bells	Retrd.	1997	50.00	35-50
1993 St. Joseph's Church	Retrd.	1997	70.00	50-70
1994 St. Joseph's School	Retrd.	1997	50.00	35-50
1989 St. Nicholas Church - D. Tate	Retrd.	1990	130.00	113-150
1994 The Vicarage	Retrd.	1997	50.00	50-150
1990 Yuletide Inn - D. Tate	Retrd.	1991	145.00	75-150

Christmas Lodge Collection - Lilliput Lane

YEAR ISSUE	EDITION LIMIT	YEAR RETD.	ISSUE PRICE	*QUOTE U.S.$
1993 Eamont Lodge	Retrd.	1993	185.00	125-300
1992 Highland Lodge	Retrd.	1992	180.00	100-138
1995 Kerry Lodge	Retrd.	1995	160.00	60-120
1994 Snowdon Lodge	Retrd.	1994	175.00	175

Christmas Special - Lilliput Lane

YEAR ISSUE	EDITION LIMIT	YEAR RETD.	ISSUE PRICE	*QUOTE U.S.$
1996 St. Stephen's Church	Yr.Iss.	1996	100.00	100-149
1997 Christmas Party	Yr.Iss.	1997	150.00	150
1998 Frosty Morning	Yr.Iss.		150.00	150

*Quotes have been rounded up to nearest dollar

Countryside Scene Plaques - D. Simpson

YEAR ISSUE	EDITION LIMIT	YEAR RETD.	ISSUE PRICE	*QUOTE U.S.$
1989 Bottle Kiln	Retrd.	1991	49.50	50
1989 Cornish Tin Mine	Retrd.	1991	49.50	50
1989 Country Inn	Retrd.	1991	49.50	50
1989 Cumbrian Farmhouse	Retrd.	1991	49.50	50
1989 Lighthouse	Retrd.	1991	49.50	50
1989 Norfolk Windmill	Retrd.	1991	49.50	50
1989 Oasthouse	Retrd.	1991	49.50	50
1989 Old Smithy	Retrd.	1991	49.50	50
1989 Parish Church	Retrd.	1991	49.50	50
1989 Post Office	Retrd.	1991	49.50	50
1989 Village School	Retrd.	1991	49.50	50
1989 Watermill	Retrd.	1991	49.50	50

Disneyana Convention - R. Day

YEAR ISSUE	EDITION LIMIT	YEAR RETD.	ISSUE PRICE	*QUOTE U.S.$
1995 Fire Station 105	501	1995	195.00	440-695
1996 The Hall of Presidents	500	1996	225.00	336-715
1997 The Haunted Mansion	500	1997	250.00	425-494
1998 Walt Disney World Train Station	500	1998	275.00	275

Dutch Collection - D. Tate

YEAR ISSUE	EDITION LIMIT	YEAR RETD.	ISSUE PRICE	*QUOTE U.S.$
1991 Aan de Amstel	Retrd.	1998	79.00	80-85
1991 Begijnhof	Retrd.	1998	55.00	60-80
1991 Bloemenmarkt	Retrd.	1998	79.00	80-85
1991 De Branderij	Retrd.	1998	72.50	55-80
1991 De Diamantair	Retrd.	1998	79.00	85-160
1991 De Pepermolen	Retrd.	1998	55.00	60-80
1991 De Wolhandelaar	Retrd.	1998	72.50	55-80
1991 De Zijdewever	Retrd.	1998	79.00	85-160
1991 Rembrant van Rijn	Retrd.	1998	120.00	80-85
1991 Rozengracht	Retrd.	1998	72.50	80-160

English Cottages - Lilliput Lane, unless otherwise noted

YEAR ISSUE	EDITION LIMIT	YEAR RETD.	ISSUE PRICE	*QUOTE U.S.$
1982 Acorn Cottage-Mold 1 - D. Tate	Retrd.	1983	30.00	250-350
1983 Acorn Cottage-Mold 2 - D. Tate	Retrd.	1987	30.00	60
1996 The Anchor	Open		85.00	85
1982 Anne Hathaway's-Mold 1 - D. Tate	Retrd.	1983	40.00	2148
1983 Anne Hathaway's-Mold 2 - D. Tate	Retrd.	1984	40.00	430
1984 Anne Hathaway's-Mold 3 - D. Tate	Retrd.	1988	40.00	375
1989 Anne Hathaway's-Mold 4 - D. Tate	Retrd.	1997	130.00	150
1991 Anne of Cleves - D. Tate	Retrd.	1996	360.00	250-395
1997 Appleby East	Open		70.00	70
1994 Applejack Cottage	Open		45.00	35-45
1982 April Cottage-Mold 1 - D. Tate	Retrd.	1984	Unkn.	350-500
1982 April Cottage-Mold 2 - D. Tate	Retrd.	1989	Unkn.	100
1991 Armada House - D. Tate	Retrd.	1997	175.00	83-88
1989 Ash Nook - D. Tate	Retrd.	1995	47.50	60
1986 Bay View - D. Tate	Retrd.	1988	39.50	40-90
1987 Beacon Heights	Retrd.	1992	125.00	140
1989 Beehive Cottage - D. Tate	Retrd.	1995	72.50	95
1997 Best Friends	Open		25.00	25
1996 Birchwood Cottage	Retrd.	1998	55.00	44-55
1993 Birdlip Bottom	Retrd.	1998	80.00	50-80
1996 Blue Boar	Open		85.00	85
1996 Bluebell Farm	Retrd.	1998	250.00	170-250
1998 The Bobbins	Open		85.00	85
1998 Bobby Blue	Open		120.00	120
1992 Bow Cottage - D. Tate	Retrd.	1995	128.00	135
1998 Bowbeams	Open		180.00	180
1996 Boxwood Cottage	Open		30.00	30
1990 Bramble Cottage - D. Tate	Retrd.	1995	55.00	70-100
1988 Bredon House - D. Tate	Retrd.	1990	145.00	175
1989 The Briary - D. Tate	Retrd.	1995	47.50	60-68
1982 Bridge House-Mold 1 - D. Tate	Retrd.	N/A	15.95	450
1982 Bridge House-Mold 2 - D. Tate	Retrd.	1990	15.95	175
1991 Bridge House-Mold 3 - D. Tate	Retrd.	1998	25.00	20-30
1988 Brockbank - D. Tate	Retrd.	1993	58.00	90
1985 Bronte Parsonage - D. Tate	Retrd.	1987	72.00	80-88
1998 Buckle My Shoe	Open		85.00	85
1997 Bumble Bee Cottage	Open		35.00	35
1982 Burnside - D. Tate	Retrd.	1985	30.00	600
1990 Buttercup Cottage - D. Tate	Retrd.	1992	40.00	65
1997 Buttermilk Farm	Open		120.00	120
1989 Butterwick - D. Tate	Retrd.	1996	52.50	65
1995 Button Down	Retrd.	1998	37.50	30-38
1996 Calendar Cottage	Open		55.00	55
1994 Camomile Lawn	Retrd.	1997	125.00	90-125
1998 Campden Cot	Open		35.00	35
1997 Canterbury Bells	Open		170.00	170
1982 Castle Street - D. Tate	Retrd.	1986	130.00	240-275
1993 Cat's Coombe Cottage	Retrd.	1995	95.00	95
1997 Catkin Cottage	Open		70.00	70
1996 Chalk Down	Open		35.00	35
1998 Chatsworth Blooms	Open		120.00	120
1991 Chatsworth View - D. Tate	Retrd.	1996	250.00	170-275
1995 Cherry Blossom Cottage	Retrd.	1997	128.00	76-95
1990 Cherry Cottage - D. Tate	Retrd.	1995	33.50	45
1989 Chiltern Mill - D. Tate	Retrd.	1995	87.50	120
1989 Chine Cot-Mold 1 - D. Tate	Retrd.	1989	36.00	N/A
1989 Chine Cot-Mold 2 - D. Tate	Retrd.	1996	35.00	50
1995 Chipping Combe	3,000	1998	525.00	420-525
1992 The Chocolate House	Retrd.	1998	130.00	61-90
1985 Clare Cottage - D. Tate	Retrd.	1993	30.00	32
1993 Cley-next-the-sea	2,500	1995	725.00	625-725
1987 Clover Cottage - D. Tate	Retrd.	1994	27.50	60
1997 The Coach & Horses	Open		90.00	90
1982 Coach House - D. Tate	Retrd.	1985	100.00	1100-1895
1986 Cobblers Cottage - D. Hall	Retrd.	1994	42.00	40-96
1997 Cockleshells	Open		25.00	25
1998 Coniston Crag	3,000		650.00	650
1990 Convent in The Woods - D. Tate	Retrd.	1996	175.00	150-210
1983 Coopers - D. Tate	Retrd.	1986	15.00	440-825
1998 Country Living	Open		275.00	275
1998 Cowslip Cottage	Open		120.00	120
1996 Cradle Cottage	Open		100.00	100
1997 Crathie Church, Balmoral	Open		60.00	60
1994 Creel Cottage	Retrd.	1997	40.00	35-40
1996 Crispin Cottage	Open		50.00	50
1988 Crown Inn - D. Tate	Retrd.	1992	120.00	40-120
1996 The Cuddy	Open		30.00	30
1991 Daisy Cottage - D. Tate	Retrd.	1997	37.50	17-30
1982 Dale Farm-Mold 1 - D. Tate	Retrd.	1986	30.00	1300
1982 Dale Farm-Mold 2 - D. Tate	Retrd.	1986	30.00	875
1986 Dale Head - D. Tate	Retrd.	1988	75.00	90-150
1982 Dale House - D. Tate	Retrd.	1986	25.00	840
1996 The Dalesman	Retrd.	1998	95.00	95
1992 Derwent-le-Dale	Retrd.	1998	75.00	55-80
1997 Devon Leigh	Open		90.00	90
1983 Dove Cottage-Mold 1 - D. Tate	Retrd.	1984	35.00	725-1800
1984 Dove Cottage-Mold 2 - D. Tate	Retrd.	1988	35.00	63-95
1991 Dovetails - D. Tate	Retrd.	1996	90.00	100
1982 Drapers-Mold 1 - D. Tate	Retrd.	1983	15.95	5000
1982 Drapers-Mold 2 - D. Tate	Retrd.	1983	15.95	4025
1995 Duckdown Cottage	Retrd.	1997	95.00	70-95
1994 Elm Cottage	Retrd.	1997	65.00	50-65
1985 Farriers - D. Tate	Retrd.	1990	40.00	80
1991 Farthing Lodge - D. Tate	Retrd.	1996	37.50	40
1996 Fiddlers Folly	Open		35.00	35
1992 Finchingfields	Retrd.	1995	82.50	57-95
1997 First Snow at Bluebell	3,500	1998	250.00	250
1985 Fisherman's Cottage - D. Tate	Retrd.	1989	30.00	55-70
1989 Fiveways - D. Tate	Retrd.	1995	42.50	60
1991 The Flower Sellers - D. Tate	Retrd.	1996	110.00	110
1996 Flowerpots	Open		55.00	55
1987 Four Seasons - M. Adkinson	Retrd.	1991	70.00	44-125
1993 Foxglove Fields	Retrd.	1997	130.00	85-130
1998 Free Range	Open		35.00	35
1996 Fry Days	Open		70.00	70
1996 Fuchsia Cottage	Open		30.00	30
1987 The Gables	Retrd.	1992	145.00	113-300
1997 The George Inn	Open		225.00	225
1998 Golden Memories	Open		90.00	90
1997 Golden Years	Open		25.00	25
1996 Gossip Gate	Open		170.00	170
1992 Granny Smiths - D. Tate	Retrd.	1996	60.00	36-45
1997 Granny's Bonnet	Open		25.00	25
1992 Grantchester Meadows	Retrd.	1996	275.00	195-275
1997 Green Gables	Open		225.00	225
1989 Greensted Church - D. Tate	Retrd.	1995	72.50	95
1994 Gulliver's Gate	Retrd.	1997	45.00	35-45
1998 Gulls Cry	Open		35.00	35
1997 Halcyon Days	Open		150.00	150
1998 Harebell Cottage	Open		35.00	35
1996 Harriet's Cottage	Open		85.00	85
1997 Harvest Home	4,950	1998	250.00	180-250
1989 Helmere Cottage - D. Tate	Retrd.	1995	65.00	90
1997 Hestercombe Garden	3,950	1998	350.00	350-400
1998 The Hideaway	Open		120.00	120
1992 High Ghyll Farm	Retrd.	1998	360.00	250-395
1982 Holly Cottage - D. Tate	Retrd.	1988	42.50	85
1987 Holme Dyke - D. Tate	Retrd.	1990	50.00	47-70
1996 Honey Pot Cottage	Open		60.00	60
1982 Honeysuckle Cottage - D. Tate	Retrd.	1987	45.00	190
1991 Hopcroft Cottage - D. Tate	Retrd.	1995	120.00	117-130
1998 Hubble Bubble	Open		35.00	35
1987 Inglewood - D. Tate	Retrd.	1994	27.50	24-40
1987 Izaak Waltons Cottage - D. Tate	Retrd.	1989	75.00	115
1991 John Barleycorn Cottage - D. Tate	Retrd.	1995	130.00	56-140
1993 Junk and Disorderly	Retrd.	1998	150.00	110-150
1987 Keepers Lodge - D. Tate	Retrd.	1988	75.00	90-110
1985 Kentish Oast - D. Tate	Retrd.	1990	55.00	75-110
1990 The King's Arms - D. Tate	Retrd.	1995	450.00	400-550
1991 Lace Lane - D. Tate	Retrd.	1997	90.00	52-70
1995 Ladybird Cottage	Retrd.	1998	40.00	28-35
1982 Lakeside House-Mold 1 - D. Tate	Retrd.	1983	40.00	1500
1982 Lakeside House-Mold 2 - D. Tate	Retrd.	1986	40.00	810-940
1991 Lapworth Lock - D. Tate	Retrd.	1993	82.50	85-100
1995 Larkrise	Retrd.	1998	50.00	45-50
1995 Lazy Days	Retrd.	1998	60.00	60
1994 Lenora's Secret	2,500	1995	350.00	375-400
1997 Lilac Lodge	Open		60.00	60
1998 The Lion House	Open		70.00	70
1995 Little Hay	Retrd.	1998	55.00	50-55
1996 Little Lupins	Open		40.00	40
1995 Little Smithy	Retrd.	1998	65.00	48-60
1998 Loch Ness Lodge	Open		170.00	170
1996 Loxdale Cottage	Open		35.00	35
1987 Magpie Cottage - D. Tate	Retrd.	1990	70.00	115-165
1997 Mangerton Mill	Open		185.00	185
1993 Marigold Meadow	Retrd.	1998	120.00	80-120
1998 Medway Manor	Open		120.00	120
1991 Micklegate Antiques - D. Tate	Retrd.	1997	90.00	80-95
1995 Milestone Cottage	Retrd.	1998	40.00	35-40
1983 Millers - D. Tate	Retrd.	1986	15.00	120-150
1983 Miners-Mold 1 - D. Tate	Retrd.	1985	15.00	590
1983 Miners-Mold 2 - D. Tate	Retrd.	1985	15.00	400-500
1991 Moonlight Cove - D. Tate	Retrd.	1996	82.50	60-85
1985 Moreton Manor - D. Tate	Retrd.	1989	55.00	85-125
1998 Mosswood	Open		85.00	85
1990 Mrs. Pinkerton's Post Office - D. Tate	Retrd.	1997	72.50	75
1998 Nest Egg	Retrd.	1998	25.00	25
1998 Nightingale Cottage	Open		25.00	25
1992 The Nutshell	Retrd.	1995	75.00	80
1982 Oak Lodge-Mold 1 - D. Tate	Retrd.	N/A	40.00	1000
1982 Oak Lodge-Mold 2 - D. Tate	Retrd.	1987	40.00	50-75
1992 Oakwood Smithy - D. Tate	Retrd.	1998	450.00	204-300
1985 Old Curiosity Shop - D. Tate	Retrd.	1989	62.50	90-100
1998 The Old Forge	Open		55.00	55
1982 Old Mine - D. Tate	Retrd.	1983	15.95	6500
1993 Old Mother Hubbard's	Retrd.	1998	185.00	96-120
1982 The Old Post Office - D. Tate	Retrd.	1986	35.00	500
1984 Old School House - D. Tate	Retrd.	1985	25.00	1000-1400
1991 Old Shop at Bignor - D. Tate	Retrd.	1995	215.00	119-220
1989 Olde York Toll - D. Tate	Retrd.	1991	82.50	69-130
1994 Orchard Farm Cottage	Retrd.	1998	145.00	110-145
1985 Ostlers Keep - D. Tate	Retrd.	1991	55.00	32-75
1990 Otter Reach - D. Tate	Retrd.	1996	33.50	18-40
1997 Out of the Storm	3,000	1998	1250.00	925-1250
1991 Paradise Lodge - D. Tate	Retrd.	1996	130.00	112
1988 Pargetters Retreat - D. Tate	Retrd.	1990	75.00	125
1998 Parson's Retreat	Open		90.00	90
1998 Pastures New	Open		350.00	350
1991 Pear Tree House - D. Tate	Retrd.	1995	82.50	40-85
1995 Penny's Post	Retrd.	1998	55.00	40-50
1990 Periwinkle Cottage - D. Tate	Retrd.	1996	165.00	175
1995 Pipit Toll	Retrd.	1998	64.00	50-64
1992 Pixie House - D. Tate	Retrd.	1995	55.00	33-60
1997 The Poppies	Open		50.00	50
1996 Potter's Beck	Retrd.	1998	35.00	35
1991 The Priest's House - D. Tate	Retrd.	1995	180.00	195
1991 Primrose Hill - D. Tate	Retrd.	1996	46.50	35-50
1998 Puddle Duck	Open		80.00	80
1992 Puffin Row - D. Tate	Retrd.	1997	128.00	95-135
1993 Purbeck Stores	Retrd.	1997	55.00	21-35
1996 Railway Cottage	Open		60.00	60
1983 Red Lion Inn - D. Tate	Retrd.	1987	125.00	250-400
1996 Reflections of Jade	3,950	1998	350.00	350-450
1988 Rising Sun - D. Tate	Retrd.	1992	58.00	64-90
1987 Riverview - D. Tate	Retrd.	1994	27.50	40
1990 Robin's Gate - D. Tate	Retrd.	1996	33.50	50
1997 Rose Bouquet	Open		25.00	25
1996 Rosemary Cottage	Open		70.00	70
1988 Royal Oak - D. Tate	Retrd.	1991	145.00	175-271
1990 Runswick House - D. Tate	Retrd.	1998	62.50	55-80
1992 Rustic Root House - D. Tate	Retrd.	1997	110.00	80-120
1995 The Rustlings	Retrd.	1998	128.00	95-128
1987 Rydal View - D. Tate	Retrd.	1989	220.00	200-275
1987 Saddlers Inn - M. Adkinson	Retrd.	1989	50.00	72-80
1994 Saffron House	Retrd.	1997	220.00	136-170
1985 Sawrey Gill - D. Tate	Retrd.	1992	30.00	125
1991 Saxham St. Edmunds - D. Tate	Retrd.	1994	1550.00	1850
1988 Saxon Cottage - D. Tate	Retrd.	1989	245.00	200-400
1997 Scotney Castle Garden	4,500	1998	300.00	204-300
1986 Scroll on the Wall - D. Tate	Retrd.	1987	55.00	119-125
1987 Secret Garden - M. Adkinson	Retrd.	1994	145.00	140-150
1988 Ship Inn	Retrd.	1992	210.00	230-345
1997 Silver Bells	Open		25.00	25
1988 Smallest Inn - D. Tate	Retrd.	1991	42.50	95-125
1996 Sore Paws	Open		70.00	70
1996 The Spindles	Retrd.	1998	85.00	65-85
1986 Spring Bank - D. Tate	Retrd.	1991	42.00	60-69
1994 Spring Gate Cottage	Retrd.	1997	130.00	95-130
1996 St. John the Baptist	Retrd.	1998	75.00	60-75
1989 St. Lawrence Church - D. Tate	Retrd.	1998	110.00	90
1988 St. Marks - D. Tate	Retrd.	1991	75.00	88-200
1985 St. Mary's Church - D. Tate	Retrd.	1988	40.00	98
1989 St. Peter's Cove - D. Tate	Retrd.	1991	1375.00	938-1000
1993 Stocklebeck Mill	Retrd.	1998	325.00	156-195
1982 Stone Cottage-Mold 1 - D. Tate	Retrd.	1983	40.00	195-354
1982 Stone Cottage-Mold 2 - D. Tate	Retrd.	1986	40.00	185
1986 Stone Cottage-Mold 3 - D. Tate	Retrd.	1986	40.00	200
1998 The Stonemason	Open		120.00	120
1987 Stoneybeck - D. Tate	Retrd.	1992	45.00	65
1993 Stradling Priory	Retrd.	1997	130.00	68-85
1990 Strawberry Cottage - D. Tate	Retrd.	1998	36.00	35-45
1987 Street Scene No. 1 - Unknown	Retrd.	1987	40.00	120
1987 Street Scene No. 2 - Unknown	Retrd.	1987	45.00	120
1987 Street Scene No. 3 - Unknown	Retrd.	1987	45.00	120
1987 Street Scene No. 4 - Unknown	Retrd.	1987	45.00	120
1987 Street Scene No. 5 - Unknown	Retrd.	1987	40.00	120
1987 Street Scene No. 6 - Unknown	Retrd.	1987	40.00	120
1987 Street Scene No. 7 - Unknown	Retrd.	1987	40.00	120
1987 Street Scene No. 8 - Unknown	Retrd.	1987	40.00	120
1987 Street Scene No. 9 - Unknown	Retrd.	1987	45.00	120
1987 Street Scene No. 10 - Unknown	Retrd.	1987	45.00	120
1987 Street Scene Set - Unknown	Retrd.	1987	425.00	800-1000
1990 Sulgrave Manor - D. Tate	Retrd.	1992	120.00	88-175
1987 Summer Haze - D. Tate	Retrd.	1993	90.00	50-57
1994 Sunnyside	Retrd.	1997	40.00	35-40
1982 Sussex Mill - D. Tate	Retrd.	1986	25.00	325-450
1988 Swan Inn - D. Tate	Retrd.	1992	120.00	175-225
1994 Sweet Pea Cottage	Retrd.	1997	40.00	28-35
1997 Sweet William	Retrd.	1998	25.00	25
1988 Swift Hollow - D. Tate	Retrd.	1990	75.00	95
1989 Tanglewood Lodge - D. Tate	Retrd.	1992	97.00	155-165
1987 Tanners Cottage - D. Tate	Retrd.	1992	27.50	29-45
1994 Teacaddy Cottage	Retrd.	1998	79.00	41-60
1983 Thatcher's Rest - D. Tate	Retrd.	1988	185.00	254
1986 Three Feathers - D. Tate	Retrd.	1989	115.00	158-250
1991 Tillers Green - D. Tate	Retrd.	1995	60.00	65
1984 Tintagel - D. Tate	Retrd.	1988	39.50	110-170
1994 Tired Timbers	Retrd.	1997	80.00	60-80
1989 Titmouse Cottage - D. Tate	Retrd.	1995	92.50	120
1993 Titwillow Cottage	Retrd.	1997	70.00	45-70
1983 Toll House - D. Tate	Retrd.	1987	15.00	75-165
1995 Tranquillity - D. Tate	2,500	1995	425.00	425

*Quotes have been rounded up to nearest dollar

YEAR ISSUE	EDITION LIMIT	YEAR RETD.	ISSUE PRICE	*QUOTE U.S.$
1983 Troutbeck Farm - D. Tate	Retrd.	1987	125.00	230-300
1983 Tuck Shop - D. Tate	Retrd.	1986	35.00	650-900
1986 Tudor Court	Retrd.	1992	260.00	345-375
1998 Tuppeny Bun	Open		35.00	35
1994 Two Hoots	Retrd.	1997	75.00	33-55
1989 Victoria Cottage - D. Tate	Retrd.	1993	52.50	40-80
1991 Village School - D. Tate	Retrd.	1996	120.00	85-130
1998 Wagtails	Open		35.00	35
1997 Walton Lodge	Open		65.00	65
1983 Warwick Hall-Mold 1 - D. Tate	Retrd.	1983	185.00	3000-4000
1983 Warwick Hall-Mold 2 - D. Tate	Retrd.	1985	185.00	1300-1800
1985 Watermill - D. Tate	Retrd.	1993	40.00	55-70
1998 Waters Edge	Open		170.00	170
1994 Waterside Mill	Open		65.00	50-65
1987 Wealden House - D. Tate	Retrd.	1990	125.00	140
1992 Wedding Bells	Open		75.00	50-80
1991 Wellington Lodge - D. Tate	Retrd.	1995	55.00	60
1992 Wheyside Cottage	Retrd.	1998	46.50	35-50
1989 Wight Cottage - D. Tate	Retrd.	1994	52.50	65
1982 William Shakespeare-Mold 1 - D. Tate	Retrd.	1983	55.00	1500-3000
1983 William Shakespeare-Mold 2 - D. Tate	Retrd.	1986	55.00	240
1986 William Shakespeare-Mold 3 - D. Tate	Retrd.	1989	55.00	200
1989 William Shakespeare-Mold 4 - D. Tate	Retrd.	1992	130.00	150
1996 Windy Ridge	Retrd.	1998	50.00	40-50
1991 Witham Delph - D. Tate	Retrd.	1994	110.00	120
1983 Woodcutters - D. Tate	Retrd.	1987	15.00	140-300
1997 Yorkvale Cottage	Open		50.00	50

English Tea Room Collection - Lilliput Lane

YEAR ISSUE	EDITION LIMIT	YEAR RETD.	ISSUE PRICE	*QUOTE U.S.$
1995 Bargate Cottage Tea Room	Open		160.00	120-160
1995 Bo-Peep Tea Rooms	Retrd.	1997	120.00	58-85
1995 Grandma Batty's Tea Room	Retrd.	1998	120.00	90-120
1995 Kendal Tea House	Open		120.00	85-120
1995 New Forest Teas	Open		160.00	120-160
1998 Strawberry Teas	Open		100.00	100
1996 Swalesdale Teas	Open		85.00	85

Founders Collection - Lilliput Lane

YEAR ISSUE	EDITION LIMIT	YEAR RETD.	ISSUE PRICE	*QUOTE U.S.$
1996 The Almonry	Yr.Iss.	1996	275.00	275

Framed English Plaques - D. Tate

YEAR ISSUE	EDITION LIMIT	YEAR RETD.	ISSUE PRICE	*QUOTE U.S.$
1990 Ashdown Hall	Retrd.	1991	59.50	70
1990 Battleview	Retrd.	1991	59.50	70
1990 Cat Slide Cottage	Retrd.	1991	59.50	70
1990 Coombe Cot	Retrd.	1991	59.50	70
1990 Fell View	Retrd.	1991	59.50	70
1990 Flint Fields	Retrd.	1991	59.50	70
1990 Huntingdon House	Retrd.	1991	59.50	70
1990 Jubilee Lodge	Retrd.	1991	59.50	70
1990 Stowside	Retrd.	1991	59.50	70
1990 Trevan Cove	Retrd.	1991	59.50	70

Framed Irish Plaques - D. Tate

YEAR ISSUE	EDITION LIMIT	YEAR RETD.	ISSUE PRICE	*QUOTE U.S.$
1990 Ballyteag House	Retrd.	1991	59.50	70
1990 Crockuna Croft	Retrd.	1991	59.50	70
1990 Pearses Cottages	Retrd.	1991	59.50	70
1990 Shannons Bank	Retrd.	1991	59.50	70

Framed Scottish Plaques - D. Tate

YEAR ISSUE	EDITION LIMIT	YEAR RETD.	ISSUE PRICE	*QUOTE U.S.$
1990 Barra Black House	Retrd.	1991	59.50	70
1990 Fife Ness	Retrd.	1991	59.50	70
1990 Kyle Point	Retrd.	1991	59.50	70
1990 Preston Oat Mill	Retrd.	1991	59.50	70

French Collection - D. Tate

YEAR ISSUE	EDITION LIMIT	YEAR RETD.	ISSUE PRICE	*QUOTE U.S.$
1991 L' Auberge d'Armorique	Retrd.	1997	220.00	200-250
1991 La Bergerie du Perigord	Retrd.	1997	230.00	200-250
1991 La Cabane du Gardian	Retrd.	1997	55.00	50-60
1991 La Chaumiere du Verger	Retrd.	1997	120.00	100-130
1991 La Maselle de Nadaillac	Retrd.	1997	130.00	100-140
1991 La Porte Schoenenberg	Retrd.	1997	75.00	80-85
1991 Le Manoir de Champfleuri	Retrd.	1997	265.00	123-225
1991 Le Mas du Vigneron	Retrd.	1997	120.00	100-130
1991 Le Petite Montmartre	Retrd.	1997	130.00	100-140
1991 Locmaria	Retrd.	1997	65.00	50-90

German Collection - D. Tate

YEAR ISSUE	EDITION LIMIT	YEAR RETD.	ISSUE PRICE	*QUOTE U.S.$
1992 Alte Schmiede	Retrd.	1998	175.00	120-185
1987 Das Gebirgskirchlein	Retrd.	1998	120.00	120-140
1988 Das Rathaus	Retrd.	1998	140.00	140-160
1992 Der Bücherwurm	Retrd.	1998	140.00	100-160
1988 Der Familienschrein	Retrd.	1991	52.50	100
1988 Die Kleine Backerei	Retrd.	1994	68.00	80
1987 Haus Im Rheinland	Retrd.	1998	220.00	215-250
1987 Jaghutte	Retrd.	1998	82.50	83-95
1987 Meersburger Weinstube	Retrd.	1998	82.50	70-95
1987 Moselhaus	Retrd.	1998	140.00	140-160
1987 Nurnberger Burgerhaus	Retrd.	1998	140.00	140-160
1992 Rosengartenhaus	Retrd.	1998	120.00	90-130
1987 Schwarzwaldhaus	Retrd.	1998	140.00	120-160
1992 Strandvogthaus	Retrd.	1998	120.00	90-130

Historic Castles of England - Lilliput Lane

YEAR ISSUE	EDITION LIMIT	YEAR RETD.	ISSUE PRICE	*QUOTE U.S.$
1994 Bodiam Castle	Retrd.	1997	129.00	76-95
1994 Castell Coch	Retrd.	1998	149.00	82-120
1995 Penkill Castles	Retrd.	1998	130.00	92-115
1994 Stokesay Castle	Retrd.	1998	99.00	58-85

Irish Cottages - D. Tate

YEAR ISSUE	EDITION LIMIT	YEAR RETD.	ISSUE PRICE	*QUOTE U.S.$
1989 Ballykerne Croft	Retrd.	1996	75.00	80
1987 Donegal Cottage	Retrd.	1992	29.00	65-72
1989 Hegarty's Home	Retrd.	1992	68.00	63-75
1989 Kennedy Homestead	Retrd.	1996	33.50	30-45
1989 Kilmore Quay	Retrd.	1992	68.00	100

YEAR ISSUE	EDITION LIMIT	YEAR RETD.	ISSUE PRICE	*QUOTE U.S.$
1989 Limerick House	Retrd.	1992	110.00	88-160
1989 Magilligan's	Retrd.	1996	33.50	30-45
1989 O'Lacey's Store	Retrd.	1996	68.00	60-85
1989 Pat Cohan's Bar	Retrd.	1996	110.00	125-140
1989 Quiet Cottage	Retrd.	1992	72.50	120
1989 St. Columba's School	Retrd.	1996	47.50	32-40
1989 St. Kevin's Church	Retrd.	1996	55.00	48-57
1989 St. Patrick's Church	Retrd.	1993	185.00	185
1989 Thoor Ballylee	Retrd.	1992	105.00	125-165

Lakeland Bridge Plaques - D. Simpson

YEAR ISSUE	EDITION LIMIT	YEAR RETD.	ISSUE PRICE	*QUOTE U.S.$
1989 Aira Force	Retrd.	1991	35.00	35
1989 Ashness Bridge	Retrd.	1991	35.00	35
1989 Birks Bridge	Retrd.	1991	35.00	35
1989 Bridge House	Retrd.	1991	35.00	105-120
1989 Hartsop Packhorse	Retrd.	1991	35.00	35
1989 Stockley Bridge	Retrd.	1991	35.00	35

Lakeland Christmas - Lilliput Lane

YEAR ISSUE	EDITION LIMIT	YEAR RETD.	ISSUE PRICE	*QUOTE U.S.$
1995 Langdale Cottage	Retrd.	1998	48.00	35-48
1995 Patterdale Cottage	Retrd.	1998	48.00	35-48
1995 Rydal Cottage	Retrd.	1998	44.75	35-45
1996 All Saints Watermillock	Open		50.00	50
1996 Borrowdale School	Open		35.00	35
1996 Millbeck Cottage	Open		35.00	35

London Plaques - D. Simpson

YEAR ISSUE	EDITION LIMIT	YEAR RETD.	ISSUE PRICE	*QUOTE U.S.$
1989 Big Ben	Retrd.	1991	39.50	40
1989 Buckingham Palace	Retrd.	1991	39.50	40
1989 Piccadilly Circus	Retrd.	1991	39.50	40
1989 Tower Bridge	Retrd.	1991	39.50	40
1989 Tower of London	Retrd.	1991	39.50	40
1989 Trafalgar Square	Retrd.	1991	39.50	40

Ray Day/Allegiance Collection - R. Day

YEAR ISSUE	EDITION LIMIT	YEAR RETD.	ISSUE PRICE	*QUOTE U.S.$
1998 By Dawn's Early Light	Open		70.00	70
1998 Fourth of July	1,776		70.00	70
1997 Home of the Brave	Open		75.00	80
1997 I Pledge Allegiance	Open		75.00	80
1998 I'll Be Home For Christmas	Open		75.00	75
1997 In Remembrance	Open		75.00	80
1997 One Nation Under God	Open		75.00	80
1998 Stars & Stripes Forever	Open		75.00	75

Ray Day/America's Favorites - R. Day

YEAR ISSUE	EDITION LIMIT	YEAR RETD.	ISSUE PRICE	*QUOTE U.S.$
1998 Budweiser Tavern	Open		37.50	38
1998 Chevy Dealership	Open		37.50	38
1998 Coca-Cola Café	Open		37.50	38
1998 John Deere Barn	Open		37.50	38
1998 Texaco Filling Station	Open		37.50	38

Ray Day/American Landmark Series - R. Day

YEAR ISSUE	EDITION LIMIT	YEAR RETD.	ISSUE PRICE	*QUOTE U.S.$
1992 16.9 Cents Per Gallon	Open		150.00	95-150
1995 Afternoon Tea	1,995		495.00	520
1994 Birdsong	Retrd.	1997	120.00	51-100
1990 Country Church	Retrd.	1992	82.50	30-150
1989 Countryside Barn	Retrd.	1992	75.00	125-150
1990 Covered Memories	Retrd.	1993	110.00	125-200
1989 Falls Mill	Retrd.	1992	130.00	112-150
1991 Fire House 1	Retrd.	1997	87.50	72-85
1994 Fresh Bread	Open		150.00	95-150
1992 Gold Miners' Claim	Retrd.	1997	110.00	95-120
1992 Gold Miners' Claim (no snow)	Retrd.	N/A	95.00	500-750
1990 Great Point Light	Open		39.50	45-55
1994 Harvest Mill	3,500		395.00	400
1994 Holy Night	Open		225.00	116-170
1992 Home Sweet Home	Retrd.	1998	120.00	95-130
1990 Hometown Depot	Retrd.	1993	68.00	40-90
1998 Lobster at the Pier	Open		90.00	90
1989 Mail Pouch Barn	Retrd.	1993	75.00	120-130
1990 Pepsi Cola Barn	Retrd.	1991	87.00	62-185
1990 Pioneer Barn	Retrd.	1991	30.00	50
1991 Rambling Rose	Retrd.	1995	60.00	100
1990 Riverside Chapel	Retrd.	1993	82.50	40-99
1990 Roadside Coolers	Retrd.	1994	75.00	110-145
1991 School Days	Retrd.	1997	60.00	60-80
1993 See Rock City	Retrd.	1997	60.00	23-35
1998 Seek and Find	Open		80.00	80
1993 Shave and A Haircut	Retrd.	1997	160.00	95-160
1990 Sign Of The Times	Retrd.	1996	27.50	35
1993 Simply Amish	Retrd.	1998	160.00	110-160
1992 Small Town Library	Retrd.	1995	130.00	140
1994 Spring Victorian	Retrd.	1998	250.00	170-250
1991 Victoriana	Retrd.	1992	295.00	340-700
1992 Winnie's Place	Retrd.	1993	395.00	313-550

Ray Day/An American Journey - R. Day

YEAR ISSUE	EDITION LIMIT	YEAR RETD.	ISSUE PRICE	*QUOTE U.S.$
1998 Day Dreams	Open		75.00	75
1998 Dog Days of Summer	Open		55.00	55
1998 Lace House	Open		85.00	85
1998 Morning Has Broken	Open		85.00	85
1998 Safe Harbor	1,783		75.00	75
1998 Victorian Elegance	Open		130.00	130

Ray Day/Christmas in America - R. Day

YEAR ISSUE	EDITION LIMIT	YEAR RETD.	ISSUE PRICE	*QUOTE U.S.$
1996 Home For the Holidays	2,596		495.00	495
1997 Let Heaven & Nature Sing	Yr.Iss.	1997	158.00	158
1997 To Grandmother's House We Go	Yr.Iss.	1997	158.00	108-158

Ray Day/Coca Cola Country - R. Day

YEAR ISSUE	EDITION LIMIT	YEAR RETD.	ISSUE PRICE	*QUOTE U.S.$
1996 A Cherry Coke...Just the Prescription	Open		95.00	100
1997 Country Canvas	Open		15.00	16
1996 Country Fresh Pickins	Open		150.00	160
1996 Fill'er Up & Check the Oil	Open		125.00	130

YEAR ISSUE	EDITION LIMIT	YEAR RETD.	ISSUE PRICE	*QUOTE U.S.$
1996 Hazards of the Road	Open		50.00	55
1996 Hook, Line & Sinker	Open		95.00	100
1997 The Lunch Line	Open		40.00	43
1998 Milk For Mom & A Coke For Me	Open		95.00	95
1997 Mmmmm...Just Like Home	Open		125.00	130
1997 Oh By Gosh, By Golly	Yr.Iss.	1997	85.00	90-170
1997 Saturday Night Jive	Open		95.00	100
1998 They Don't Make 'em Like They Used To	Open		70.00	70
1996 We've Got it or They Don't Make it	Open		95.00	100
1997 Wet Your Whistle	Open		40.00	43

Scottish Collection - D. Tate, unless otherwise noted

YEAR ISSUE	EDITION LIMIT	YEAR RETD.	ISSUE PRICE	*QUOTE U.S.$
1985 7 St. Andrews Square - A. Yarrington	Retrd.	1986	15.95	85-120
1995 Amisfield Tower - Lilliput Lane	Retrd.	1998	55.00	50-55
1989 Blair Atholl	Retrd.	1992	275.00	200-370
1985 Burns Cottage	Retrd.	1988	35.00	100
1989 Carrick House	Retrd.	1998	47.50	35-60
1990 Cawdor Castle	3,000	1992	295.00	330-438
1989 Claypotts Castle	Retrd.	1997	72.50	70-80
1989 Craigievar Castle	Retrd.	1991	185.00	300-525
1984 The Croft (renovated)	Retrd.	1991	36.00	65-100
1982 The Croft (without sheep)	Retrd.	1984	29.00	800-1250
1989 Culloden Cottage	Retrd.	1998	36.00	35-45
1992 Culross House	Retrd.	1997	90.00	70-95
1992 Duart Castle	3,000	1997	450.00	475
1987 East Neuk	Retrd.	1991	29.00	60-75
1993 Edzell Summer House - Lilliput Lane	Retrd.	1997	110.00	70-110
1990 Eilean Donan	Retrd.	1998	145.00	145-185
1992 Eriskay Croft	Retrd.	1998	50.00	40-55
1990 Fishermans Bothy	Retrd.	1998	36.00	18-35
1990 Glenlochie Lodge	Retrd.	1993	110.00	88-120
1990 Hebridean Hame	Retrd.	1992	55.00	82-145
1989 Inverlochie Hame	Retrd.	1998	47.50	40-60
1989 John Knox House	Retrd.	1992	68.00	75-200
1989 Kenmore Cottage	Retrd.	1993	87.00	110
1990 Kinlochness	Retrd.	1993	79.00	85-125
1990 Kirkbrae Cottage	Retrd.	1993	55.00	70-95
1998 Lady Jane's Cottage	Open		35.00	35
1994 Ladybank Lodge - Lilliput Lane	Retrd.	1998	80.00	60-80
1992 Mair Haven	Retrd.	1998	46.50	28-35
1998 The Pineapple House	Open		60.00	60
1985 Preston Mill-Mold 1	Retrd.	1986	45.00	125
1986 Preston Mill-Mold 2	Retrd.	1992	62.50	78
1998 Scotch Mist	Open		70.00	70
1989 Stockwell Tenement	Retrd.	1996	62.50	63-80

Specials - Various

YEAR ISSUE	EDITION LIMIT	YEAR RETD.	ISSUE PRICE	*QUOTE U.S.$
1997 Arbury Lodge - Lilliput Lane	Retrd.	1997	N/A	N/A
1985 Bermuda Cottage (3 Colors) - D. Tate	Retrd.	1991	29.00	40-50
1985 Bermuda Cottage (3 Colors)-set - D. Tate	Retrd.	1991	87.00	345-450
1983 Bridge House Dealer Sign - D. Tate	Retrd.	1984	N/A	375
1988 Chantry Chapel - D. Tate	Retrd.	1991	N/A	200-250
1983 Cliburn School - D. Tate	Retrd.	1984	Gift	6000-7000
1987 Clockmaker's Cottage - D. Tate	Retrd.	1990	40.00	200-270
1996 Cornflower Cottage	Retrd.	1996	N/A	100
1993 Counting House Corner (mounted) - Lilliput Lane	Retrd.	1993	N/A	N/A
1993 Counting House Corner - Lilliput Lane	3,093	1993	N/A	N/A
1987 Guildhall - D. Tate	Retrd.	1989	N/A	145-174
1998 Hadleigh Cottage - Lilliput Lane	5,000	1998	N/A	N/A
1998 Honeysuckle III - Lilliput Lane	Open		N/A	N/A
1996 Honeysuckle Plaque (with doves) - Lilliput Lane	Retrd.	1996	N/A	90
1996 Honeysuckle Plaque (without doves) - Lilliput Lane	Retrd.	1996	N/A	N/A
1989 Mayflower House - D. Tate	Retrd.	1990	79.50	150-213
1991 Rose Cottage Skirsgill-Mold 1 - Lilliput Lane	200	1991	N/A	700
1991 Rose Cottage Skirsgill-Mold 2 - Lilliput Lane	Retrd.	1991	N/A	93-250
1994 Rose Cottage Skirsgill-Mold 3 - Lilliput Lane	Open		N/A	N/A
1991 Settler's Surprise - Lilliput Lane	Open		135.00	135
1986 Seven Dwarf's Cottage - D. Tate	Retrd.	1986	146.80	450-500
1998 Thornery - Lilliput Lane	Retrd.	1998	N/A	150
1994 Wycombe Toll House - Lilliput Lane	Retrd.	1994	33.00	150-240

Studley Royal Collection - Lilliput Lane

YEAR ISSUE	EDITION LIMIT	YEAR RETD.	ISSUE PRICE	*QUOTE U.S.$
1994 Banqueting House	5,000	1998	65.00	18-65
1995 Fountains Abbey	3,500	1998	395.00	276-395
1994 Octagon Tower	5,000	1998	85.00	61-85
1994 St. Mary's Church	5,000	1998	115.00	49-115
1994 Temple of Piety	5,000	1998	95.00	27-95

Unframed Plaques - D. Tate

YEAR ISSUE	EDITION LIMIT	YEAR RETD.	ISSUE PRICE	*QUOTE U.S.$
1989 Large Lower Brockhampton	Retrd.	1991	120.00	120
1989 Large Somerset Springtime	Retrd.	1991	130.00	130
1989 Medium Cobble Combe Cottage	Retrd.	1991	68.00	68
1989 Medium Wishing Well	Retrd.	1991	75.00	75
1989 Small Stoney Wall Lea	Retrd.	1991	47.50	48
1989 Small Woodside Farm	Retrd.	1991	47.50	48

Victorian Shops - Lilliput Lane

YEAR ISSUE	EDITION LIMIT	YEAR RETD.	ISSUE PRICE	*QUOTE U.S.$
1997 Apothecary	Open		90.00	90
1997 Book Shop	Open		75.00	75
1997 Haberdashery	Open		90.00	90
1997 Horologist	Open		75.00	75
1997 The Jeweller's	Open		75.00	75
1997 Pawnbroker	Open		75.00	75
1997 Tailor	Open		90.00	90

*Quotes have been rounded up to nearest dollar

YEAR ISSUE	EDITION LIMIT	YEAR RETD.	ISSUE PRICE	*QUOTE U.S.$

Village Shop Collection - Various

YEAR ISSUE	EDITION LIMIT	YEAR RETD.	ISSUE PRICE	*QUOTE U.S.$
1995 The Baker's Shop	Open		120.00	85-120
1995 The Chine Shop	Open		120.00	85-120
1992 The Greengrocers - D. Tate	Retrd.	1998	120.00	80-130
1993 Jones The Butcher	Retrd.	1998	120.00	80-120
1992 Penny Sweets	Retrd.	1998	130.00	80-130
1993 Toy Shop	Open		120.00	80-120

Welsh Collection - Various

YEAR ISSUE	EDITION LIMIT	YEAR RETD.	ISSUE PRICE	*QUOTE U.S.$
1986 Brecon Bach - D. Tate	Retrd.	1993	42.00	40-56
1991 Bro Dawel - D. Tate	Retrd.	1998	37.50	30-40
1998 Bythyn Bach Gwyn	Open		35.00	35
1985 Hermitage - D. Tate	Retrd.	1986	30.00	175-300
1987 Hermitage Renovated - D. Tate	Retrd.	1990	42.50	50-70
1992 St. Govan's Chapel	Open		75.00	50-80
1991 Tudor Merchant - D. Tate	Retrd.	1997	90.00	70-95
1991 Ugly House - D. Tate	Retrd.	1998	55.00	50-60

A Year In An English Garden - Lilliput Lane

YEAR ISSUE	EDITION LIMIT	YEAR RETD.	ISSUE PRICE	*QUOTE U.S.$
1994 Autumn Hues	Retrd.	1997	120.00	85-120
1995 Spring Glory	Retrd.	1997	120.00	85-120
1995 Summer Impressions	Retrd.	1997	120.00	85-120
1994 Winter's Wonder	Retrd.	1997	120.00	85-120

Lowell Davis Farm Club

Davis Farm Set - L. Davis

YEAR ISSUE	EDITION LIMIT	YEAR RETD.	ISSUE PRICE	*QUOTE U.S.$
1985 Barn 25352	Closed	1987	47.50	425
1985 Chicken House 25358	Closed	1987	19.00	50
1985 Corn Crib and Sheep Pen 25354	Closed	1987	25.00	65
1985 Garden and Wood Shed 25359	Closed	1987	25.00	65
1985 Goat Yard and Studio 25353	Closed	1987	32.50	85
1985 Hen House 25356	Closed	1987	32.50	80
1985 Hog House 25355	Closed	1987	27.50	85
1985 Main House 25351	Closed	1987	42.50	100
1985 Privy 25348	Closed	1987	12.50	35
1985 Remus' Cabin 25350	Closed	1987	42.50	95
1985 Smoke House 25357	Closed	1987	12.50	65
1985 Windmill 25349	Closed	1987	25.00	45

Midwest of Cannon Falls

Cottontail Lane Figurines and Accessories - Midwest

YEAR ISSUE	EDITION LIMIT	YEAR RETD.	ISSUE PRICE	*QUOTE U.S.$
1993 Arbor w/ Fence Set 02188-0	Retrd.	1998	14.00	15
1993 Birdbath, Bench & Mailbox, 02184-2	Retrd.	1993	4.00	4-25
1994 Birdhouse, Sundial & Bunny Fountain, 3 asst. 00371-8	Retrd.	1998	4.50	12
1993 Bridge & Gazebo, 2 asst. 02182-9	Retrd.	1996	11.50	19-25
1998 Bunnies Around Maypole 23657-4	Retrd.	1997	11.00	11
1998 Bunnies at Fence 23656-7	Retrd.	1998	7.00	7
1997 Bunnies on an Afternoon Stroll 18656-5	Retrd.	1998	5.00	5
1998 Bunnies on Bench 23655-0	Retrd.	1997	7.50	8
1996 Bunnies Sitting in Gazebo 15801-2	Retrd.	1998	10.00	10
1998 Bunnies Under Tree 23658-1	Retrd.	1997	7.50	8
1998 Bunnies with Wagon 23659-8	Retrd.	1998	6.50	7
1996 Bunny Band Quartet, set/4 15799-2	Retrd.	1997	16.00	16
1995 Bunny Chef, 2 asst. 12433-8	Retrd.	1998	4.50	5
1993 Bunny Child Collecting Eggs, 2 asst. 02880-3	Retrd.	1993	4.20	20
1996 Bunny Children Working in Garden, 2 asst. 15796-1	Retrd.	1998	3.50	4
1997 Bunny Clown, 2 asst. 18659-6	Retrd.	1998	4.00	4
1995 Bunny Couple at Cafe Table 12444-4	Retrd.	1998	7.00	7
1993 Bunny Couple on Bicycle 02978-7	Retrd.	1993	5.30	6
1997 Bunny Flower Girl & Ring Bearer, 2 asst. 18651-0	Retrd.	1998	3.50	4
1995 Bunny Kids at Carrot Juice Stand 12437-6	Retrd.	1998	5.30	6-19
1997 Bunny Kissing Booth 18660-2	Retrd.	1998	9.00	9
1994 Bunny Marching Band, 6 asst. 00355-8	Retrd.	1998	4.20	5
1995 Bunny Minister, Soloist, 2 asst. 12434-8	Retrd.	1998	5.00	5
1996 Bunny Picnicking, set/4 15798-5	Retrd.	1998	15.00	15
1995 Bunny Playing Piano 12439-0	Retrd.	1998	5.30	6
1995 Bunny Playing, 2 asst. 12442-0	Retrd.	1998	6.50	7
1995 Bunny Popcorn, Balloon Vendor, 2 asst. 12443-7	Retrd.	1998	6.70	7
1994 Bunny Preparing for Easter, 3 asst. 02971-8	Retrd.	1996	4.20	10
1994 Bunny Shopping Couple, 2 asst. 10362-3	Retrd.	1998	4.20	5
1997 Bunny Throwing Pie 18657-2	Retrd.	1998	3.00	3
1997 Bunny Vendor 18658-9	Retrd.	1998	4.00	4
1998 Bunny with Toys 23660-4	Retrd.	1998	3.50	4
1997 Carrot Fence 19625-0	Retrd.	1997	10.00	10
1994 Cobblestone Road 10072-1	Retrd.	1996	9.00	9
1994 Cone-Shaped Tree Set 10369-2	Retrd.	1996	7.50	8
1997 Cotton Candy Vendor Bunny 18661-9	Retrd.	1998	5.00	5
1994 Cottontail Lane Sign 10063-9	Retrd.	1998	5.00	5-13
1994 Easter Bunny Figure, 2 asst. 00356-5	Retrd.	1998	4.20	5
1994 Egg Stand & Flower Cart, 2 asst. 10354-8	Retrd.	1998	6.00	6
1995 Electric Street Lamppost, set/4 12461-1	Retrd.	1996	25.00	25
1996 Garden Shopkeeper, set/2 15800-5	Retrd.	1998	10.00	10
1996 Garden Table with Potted Plants and Flowers 15802-9	Retrd.	1998	9.00	9
1996 Garden with Waterfall and Pond 15797-8	Retrd.	1996	15.00	15
1997 Just Married Getaway Car 18650-3	Retrd.	1998	10.00	10
1993 Lamppost, Birdhouse & Mailbox, 3 asst. 02187-3	Retrd.	1993	4.50	5
1995 Mayor Bunny and Bunny with Flag Pole, 2 asst. 12441-3	Retrd.	1998	5.50	6
1995 Outdoor Bunny, 3 asst. 12435-2	Retrd.	1998	5.00	5
1994 Policeman, Conductor Bunny, 2 asst. 00367-1	Retrd.	1998	4.20	5
1995 Professional Bunny, 3 asst. 12438-3	Retrd.	1998	5.00	5
1995 Street Sign, 3 asst. 12433-8	Retrd.	1998	4.50	5
1993 Strolling Bunny, 2 asst. 02976-3	Retrd.	1993	4.20	5
1995 Strolling Bunny, 2 asst. 12440-6	Retrd.	1998	5.50	6
1994 Sweeper & Flower Peddler Bunny Couple, 2 asst. 00359-6	Retrd.	1998	4.20	5
1997 Ticket Vendor 18654-1	Retrd.	1998	10.00	10
1994 Topiary Trees, 3 asst. 00346-6	Retrd.	1994	2.50	3
1994 Train Station Couple, 2 asst. 00357-2	Retrd.	1998	4.20	5
1994 Tree & Shrub, 2 asst. 00382-4	Retrd.	1997	5.00	5
1996 Tree with Painted Flowers, set/3 15924-8	Retrd.	1998	20.00	20
1993 Trees, 3 asst. 02194-1	Retrd.	1994	6.20	7-25
1997 Wedding Bunny Couple 18652-7	Retrd.	1998	5.00	5
1994 Wedding Bunny Couple, 2 asst. 00347-3	Retrd.	1998	4.20	5
1993 Wishing Well, Vegetable Stand, 2 asst. 02185-5	Retrd.	1993	6.50	N/A
1993 • Wishing Well 02185-5	Retrd.	1993	N/A	15
1993 • Vegetable Stand 02185-5	Retrd.	1993	N/A	15

Cottontail Lane Houses - Midwest

YEAR ISSUE	EDITION LIMIT	YEAR RETD.	ISSUE PRICE	*QUOTE U.S.$
1997 Arcade Booth (lighted) 18655-8	Retrd.	1998	33.00	33
1993 Bakery (lighted) 01396-0	Retrd.	1996	43.00	60
1996 Bandshell (lighted) 15753-4	Retrd.	1997	50.00	50
1994 Bed & Breakfast House (lighted) 00337-4	Retrd.	1997	43.00	45
1995 Boutique and Beauty Shop (lighted) 12301-0	Retrd.	1997	45.00	45
1996 Bungalow (lighted) 15752-7	Retrd.	1997	45.00	45
1997 Bunny Chapel (lighted) 18653-4	Retrd.	1998	40.00	40
1995 Cafe (lighted) 12303-4	Retrd.	1997	45.00	45
1997 Carousel (lighted & musical) 18649-7	5,000	1998	47.00	47
1995 Cathedral (lighted) 12302-7	Retrd.	1997	47.00	47
1994 Chapel (lighted) 00331-2	3,000	1993	43.00	219-232
1993 Church (lighted) 01385-4	3,000	1993	42.00	188-219
1992 Confectionary Shop (lighted) 06335-5	Retrd.	1994	43.00	50-68
1998 Cottage (lighted) 23667-3	Retrd.	1998	43.00	43
1993 Cottontail Inn (lighted) 01394-6	Retrd.	1996	43.00	45
1996 Fire Station w/Figures, set/6 (lighted) 15830-2	5,000	1997	90.00	90
1992 Flower Shop (lighted) 06333-9	Retrd.	1994	43.00	50-75
1994 General Store (lighted) 00340-4	Retrd.	1998	43.00	45
1998 Library (lighted) 23671-0	Retrd.	1998	43.00	43
1998 Mansion (lighted) 23672-7	2,500	1998	47.00	47
1993 Painting Studio (lighted) 01395-5	Retrd.	1994	43.00	50-90
1993 Rose Cottage (lighted) 01386-1	Retrd.	1994	43.00	75-94
1995 Rosebud Manor (lighted) 12304-1	3,500	1994	45.00	85-92
1998 Row House (lighted) 23670-3	Retrd.	1998	45.00	45
1993 Schoolhouse (lighted) 01378-6	Retrd.	1997	43.00	45
1992 Springtime Cottage (lighted) 06329-8	Retrd.	1994	43.00	94-100
1996 Town Garden Shoppe (lighted) 15751-0	Retrd.	1997	45.00	45
1995 Town Hall (lighted) 12300-3	Retrd.	1997	45.00	45
1998 Toy Store (lighted) 23668-0	Retrd.	1998	37.00	37
1994 Train Station (lighted) 00330-5	Retrd.	1997	43.00	45
1997 Tunnel of Love w/Swan (lighted)18648-0	Retrd.	1998	40.00	40
1992 Victorian House (lighted) 06332-1	Retrd.	1997	43.00	45

Creepy Hollow Figurines and Accessories - Midwest

YEAR ISSUE	EDITION LIMIT	YEAR RETD.	ISSUE PRICE	*QUOTE U.S.$
1994 Black Picket Fence 10685-3	Retrd.	1996	3.50	25-30
1996 Bone Fence 16961-2	Open		9.50	10
1993 Bride of Frankenstein 06663-8	Retrd.	1993	5.00	60-90
1995 Cemetery Gate 13366-8	Retrd.	1997	16.00	19-32
1996 Covered Bridge 16664-2	Retrd.	1997	22.00	22
1994 Creepy Hollow Sign 10647-1	Open		5.50	6
1992 Dracula (standing) 06707-9	Retrd.	1994	7.30	60-125
1996 Dragon 16936-0	Retrd.	1998	8.50	9
1995 Flying Witch, Ghost, 2 asst. 13362-0	Retrd.	1996	11.00	25-33
1992 Frankenstein 06704-8	Retrd.	1994	6.00	37-60
1997 Garden Statue, 2 asst. 19827-8	Open		7.50	8
1994 Ghost, 3 asst. 10652-5	Retrd.	1997	6.00	7-50
1996 Ghostly King 16659-8	Retrd.	1997	8.00	13
1995 Ghoul Usher 13515-0	Open		6.50	7
1995 Ghoulish Organist Playing Organ 13363-7	Retrd.	1997	13.00	13
1995 Grave Digger, 2 asst. 13360-6	Retrd.	1997	10.00	13-20
1996 Gypsy 16656-7	Retrd.	1997	8.00	10
1996 Gypsy Witch 16655-0	Open		8.00	8
1992 Halloween Sign, 2 asst. 06709-3	Retrd.	1995	6.00	25-50
1992 • Keep Out 06709-3	Retrd.	1995	N/A	14-24
1992 • Ghost Town 06709-3	Retrd.	1995	N/A	14-24
1997 Haunted Lighted Trees, 2 asst. 21458-9	Open		24.00	24
1993 Haunted Tree, 2 asst. 05892-3	Retrd.	1997	7.00	7-19
1996 Headless Horseman 16658-1	Retrd.	1997	11.00	13
1995 Hearse with Monsters 13364-4	Retrd.	1997	15.00	16
1993 Hinged Dracula's Coffin 08545-5	Retrd.	1995	11.00	47-49
1995 Hinged Tomb 13516-7	Retrd.	1995	15.00	45-80
1995 Hunchback 13359-0	Retrd.	1997	9.00	10-18
1996 Inn Keeper 16660-4	Open		7.00	7
1994 Mad Scientist 10646-4	Retrd.	1997	6.00	8
1998 Mailbox 24374-9	Open		7.00	7
1993 Mummy 06705-5	Retrd.	1994	6.00	32-60
1997 Mummy Box 19846-9	Open		16.00	16
1994 Outhouse 10648-8	Retrd.	1997	7.00	15-30
1994 Phantom of the Opera 10645-7	Retrd.	1997	6.00	12-32
1997 Potted Plant, 3 asst. 19826-1	Retrd.	1998	7.00	7
1993 Pumpkin Head Ghost 06661-4	Retrd.	1993	5.50	60
1993 Pumpkin Patch Sign, 2 asst. 05898-5	Retrd.	1995	6.50	44-60
1993 • Dead End 05898-5	Retrd.	1995	N/A	15-25
1993 • Pumpkin Patch (Cat Crossing) 05898-5	Retrd.	1995	N/A	25
1995 Pumpkin Street Lamp, set/4 13365-1	Retrd.	1996	25.00	25-60
1998 Railroad Conductor, Railroad Crossing Sign, Traveler, 3 asst. 24370-1	Open		7.00	7
1993 Resin Skeleton 06651-5	Retrd.	1994	5.50	60-85
1995 Road of Bones 13371-2	Retrd.	1997	9.00	9
1996 School Teacher 16657-4	Open		8.00	8
1997 Sea Captains, 2 asst. 19823-0	Open		7.50	8
1997 Servant, 2 asst. 19825-4	Open		7.50	8
1998 Sign, 3 asst. 24372-5	Open		6.00	6
1997 Siren on Rock, 3 asst. 19824-7	Open		7.50	8
1996 Skeleton Butler 16661-1	Open		7.00	7
1997 Skeleton in Dinghy 19821-6	Open		12.00	12
1995 Spooky Black Tree 13752-9	Open		4.50	5
1994 Street Sign, 2 asst. 10644-0	Retrd.	1996	5.70	15-35
1995 Street Sign, 3 asst. 13357-6	Retrd.	1996	5.50	33
1995 Theatre Goer, set/2 13358-3	Retrd.	1997	9.00	20-44
1995 Ticket Seller 13361-3	Retrd.	1997	10.00	11-25
1993 Tombstone 06712-3	Retrd.	1993	6.00	30-57
1994 Tombstone Sign, 3 asst. 10642-6	Retrd.	1997	3.50	18-32
1998 Train with Engineer (sound activated) 24373-2	Open		18.00	18
1993 Trick or Treater, 3 asst. 08591-2	Retrd.	1995	5.50	32-60
1998 Trick or Treaters, 3 asst. 24371-8	Open		6.00	6
1994 Werewolf 10643-4	Retrd.	1997	6.00	9-19
1992 Witch 06706-2	Retrd.	1996	6.00	23-55
1997 Witch with Telescope 19822-3	Open		7.50	8

Creepy Hollow Lighted Houses - Midwest

YEAR ISSUE	EDITION LIMIT	YEAR RETD.	ISSUE PRICE	*QUOTE U.S.$
1995 Bewitching Belfry 13355-2	Retrd.	1997	50.00	50-75
1993 Blood Bank 08548-6	Retrd.	1996	40.00	70-90
1998 Candy, Costume and Barbershop 23274-3	Open		48.00	48
1997 Cape Odd Lighthouse 19569-7	Retrd.	1998	45.00	45
1996 Castle 16959-9	5,000	1997	50.00	50-95
1994 Cauldron Cafe 10649-5	Retrd.	1996	40.00	60-75
1998 Cozy Coffin Motel 23276-7	Open		35.00	35
1992 Dr. Frankenstein's House 01621-3	Retrd.	1995	40.00	125-150
1992 Dracula's Castle 01627-5	Retrd.	1995	40.00	163-190
1997 Drearydale Manor House (sound activated) 19568-0	5,000		50.00	50
1997 Eerie Eatery House 19571-0	Retrd.	1998	45.00	45
1995 Funeral Parlor 13356-9	Retrd.	1997	50.00	60-75
1998 Gasp N Go Gas Station 23275-0	Open		35.00	35
1998 Ghost Post Office 23273-6	Open		30.00	30
1996 Gypsy Wagon 16663-5	Open		45.00	45
1993 Haunted Hotel 08549-3	Retrd.	1996	40.00	90-95
1996 Jack-O' Lant-Inn 16665-9	Retrd.	1997	45.00	60-65
1994 Medical Ghoul School 10651-8	Retrd.	1997	40.00	50-65
1992 Mummy's Mortuary 01641-1	Retrd.	1995	40.00	190-219
1997 Norman's Bait & Tackle House 19572-7	Retrd.	1998	36.00	36
1994 Phantom's Opera 10650-1	Retrd.	1996	40.00	90-120
1996 School House 16662-8	Retrd.	1997	45.00	51-55
1997 Shipwreck House 19570-3	Retrd.	1998	45.00	45
1993 Shoppe of Horrors 08550-9	Retrd.	1995	40.00	90-113
1995 Skeleton Cinema 13354-5	5,000	1995	50.00	95-150
1998 Train Depot 23272-9	3,500		45.00	45
1992 Witches Cove 01665-7	Retrd.	1995	40.00	125-138

Possible Dreams

Crinkle Village - Staff

YEAR ISSUE	EDITION LIMIT	YEAR RETD.	ISSUE PRICE	*QUOTE U.S.$
1997 Crinkle Barn 659654	Open		43.30	44
1997 Crinkle Candy Store (lighted) 659661	Open		62.00	62
1996 Crinkle Castle (lighted) 659652	Open		70.00	70
1996 Crinkle Church (lighted) 659651	Open		70.00	70
1997 Crinkle Claus Village Display 965006	Open		10.00	10
1996 Crinkle Cottage (lighted) 659653	Open		70.00	70
1997 Crinkle Farmhouse 659657	Open		43.30	44
1998 Crinkle Fire Station (lighted) 659660	Open		62.00	62
1997 Crinkle Grist Mill 659656	Open		43.30	44
1997 Crinkle Inn 659655	Open		43.30	44
1998 Crinkle Police Station (lighted) 659662	Open		62.00	62
1998 Crinkle Post Office (lighted) 659659	Open		62.00	62
1998 Crinkle Toy Shop (lighted) 659658	Open		62.00	62
1996 Crinkle Workshop (lighted) 659650	Open		70.00	70
1996 Santa Castle 659019	Open		15.00	15
1996 Santa Christmas House 659017	Open		15.00	15
1996 Santa Church 659020	Open		15.00	15
1996 Santa Farm House 659018	Open		15.00	15
1996 Santa Palace 659016	Open		15.00	15
1996 Santa Windmill 659021	Open		15.00	15

Reco International

The Age of Exploration - V. Di Fate

YEAR ISSUE	EDITION LIMIT	YEAR RETD.	ISSUE PRICE	*QUOTE U.S.$
1997 Crystal Enclave	Open		40.00	40
1997 Lunar Base One	Open		30.00	30
1997 The Moon Castle	Open		100.00	100
1997 Outpost on Argaeus	Open		35.00	35

Rooms With A View - Various

YEAR ISSUE	EDITION LIMIT	YEAR RETD.	ISSUE PRICE	*QUOTE U.S.$
1998 Archway - J. O'Brien	Open		40.00	40

*Quotes have been rounded up to nearest dollar

YEAR ISSUE	EDITION LIMIT	YEAR RETD.	ISSUE PRICE	*QUOTE U.S.$
1998 Gourmet Delight - B. Terney	Open		40.00	40
1998 In The Garden - J. O'Brien	Open		40.00	40
1998 Nantucket - F. Ledan	Open		40.00	40
1998 New York Nights - F. Ledan	Open		40.00	40
1998 Remembering - J. O'Brien	Open		40.00	40
1998 Rustic Repose - E. Dentner	Open		40.00	40
1998 Salinger Mansion - F. Ledan	Open		40.00	40
1998 Salon Sur La Cite - F. Ledan	Open		40.00	40
1998 Terrasse-Sur-Riviera - F. Ledan	Open		40.00	40
1998 Top of the Morning - E. Dentner	Open		40.00	40
1998 Yellow Roses, Red Poppies - F. Ledan	Open		40.00	40

Roman, Inc.

Fontanini Nativity Village 2.5" - E. Simonetti

YEAR ISSUE	EDITION LIMIT	YEAR RETD.	ISSUE PRICE	*QUOTE U.S.$
1998 Carpenter's Shop	Open		32.50	33
1998 Corral (For Animals)	Open		32.50	33
1997 Gold King's Tent	Open		22.50	23
1998 Lighted Stable (revised design)	Open		32.50	33
1997 Marketplace	Open		32.50	33
1997 Pottery Shop	Open		32.50	33
1998 Poultry Shop	Open		32.50	33
1997 Purple King's Tent	Open		22.50	23
1997 Town Gate	Open		32.50	33
1996 Blue King's Tent	Open		17.50	18
1996 Inn	Open		29.50	30
1996 Shepherd's Camp	Open		29.50	30
1996 Stable	Open		29.50	30
1996 Town Building	Open		25.00	25
1996 Town Store	Open		25.00	25
1996 6 pc. set w/ lighted base	Open		270.00	270

Fontanini Nativity Village 5" - E. Simonetti

YEAR ISSUE	EDITION LIMIT	YEAR RETD.	ISSUE PRICE	*QUOTE U.S.$
1996 Bakery	Open		80.00	80
1996 Blue King's Tent	Open		50.00	50
1998 Carpenter's Shop	Open		90.00	90
1998 Corral (For Animals)	Open		90.00	90
1997 Gold King's Tent	Open		65.00	65
1996 Inn	Open		85.00	85
1997 Marketplace	Open		90.00	90
1997 Pottery Shop	Open		90.00	90
1998 Poultry Shop	Open		90.00	90
1997 Purple King's Tent	Open		65.00	65
1996 Shepherd's Camp	Open		80.00	80
1996 Stable	Open		75.00	75
1997 Town Gate	Open		90.00	90

Fontanini Nativity Village 7.5" - E. Simonetti

YEAR ISSUE	EDITION LIMIT	YEAR RETD.	ISSUE PRICE	*QUOTE U.S.$
1997 Blue King's Tent	Open		99.50	100
1998 Fish Market	Open		120.00	120
1998 Gold King's Tent	Open		110.00	110
1997 Inn	Open		55.00	55
1998 Lighted Stable	Open		125.00	125
1997 Lighted Stable	Open		75.00	75
1997 Marketplace	Open		65.00	65
1998 Purple King's Tent	Open		95.00	95
1997 Town Building	Open		65.00	65
1997 Town Gate	Open		40.00	40

Shelia's Collectibles

Shelia's Collectors' Society - S. Thompson

YEAR ISSUE	EDITION LIMIT	YEAR RETD.	ISSUE PRICE	*QUOTE U.S.$
1993 Anne Peacock House SOC01	Retrd.	1994	16.00	115-125
1993 Susan B. Anthony CGA93	Retrd.	1994	Gift	104-115
1993 Anne Peacock House SOC01 & Susan B. Anthony CGA93, set/2	Retrd.	1994	16.00	300
1993 Anne Peacock House Print	Retrd.	1994	Gift	75
1994 Seaview Cottage SOC02	Retrd.	1995	17.00	75-125
1994 Helen Keller's Birthplace-Ivy Green CGA94	Retrd.	1995	Gift	56-86
1994 Seaview Cottage SOC02 & Helen Keller's Birthplace-Ivy Green CGA94, set/2	Retrd.	1995	17.00	200
1994 Collector's Society T-Shirt	Retrd.	1995	Gift	N/A
1995 Pink Lady SOC03	Retrd.	1996	20.00	24-40
1995 Red Cross CGA95	Retrd.	1996	Gift	30-42
1995 Pink Lady SOC03 & Red Cross CGA95, set/2	Retrd.	1996	20.00	50-200
1995 Collector's Society T-Shirt & Collector's Society Pin	Retrd.	1996	Gift	45-115
1996 Tinker Toy House SOC04	Retrd.	1997	20.00	47-63
1996 Tatman House CGA96	Retrd.	1997	Gift	40-50
1996 Tinker Toy House SOC04 & Tatman House CGA96, set/2	Retrd.	1997	20.00	200
1996 Tinker Toy House Ornament	Retrd.	1997	Gift	45
1997 25 Meeting St. SOC97	Retrd.	1998	26.00	26-60
1997 23 Meeting Street CGA97	Retrd.	1998	Gift	45
1997 23 Meeting St. SOC97 & 23 Meeting Street CGA97, set/2	Retrd.	1998	26.00	150
1997 25 Meeting Street Ornament OCS02	Retrd.	1998	Gift	N/A
1998 Old North Church II CGA98	12/98		Gift	N/A
1998 Paul Revere's Ride CGA98	12/98		Gift	N/A
1998 Munroe Tavern SOC98	12/99		26.00	26

Signing & Event Pieces - S. Thompson

YEAR ISSUE	EDITION LIMIT	YEAR RETD.	ISSUE PRICE	*QUOTE U.S.$
1994 Star Barn SOP01	Retrd.	1994	24.00	47-60
1995 Shelia's Real Estate Office SOP02	Retrd.	1995	20.00	40-75
1996 Thompson's Mercantile SOP03	Retrd.	1996	24.00	25-35
1997 27 Meeting St. SOP97	Retrd.	1997	26.00	34-63
1998 The Old Manse SOP98	12/98		26.00	26

Accessories - S. Thompson

YEAR ISSUE	EDITION LIMIT	YEAR RETD.	ISSUE PRICE	*QUOTE U.S.$
1994 Amish Quilt Line COL12	Retrd.	1994	18.00	35-37
1993 Apple Tree COL09	Retrd.	1996	12.00	15-22
1996 Autumn Tree ACC09	Open		14.00	15
1996 Barber Gazebo ACC05	Open		13.00	14
1997 Crepe Myrtle ACC13	Open		15.00	15
1993 Dogwood Tree COL08	Retrd.	1996	12.00	22-50
1992 Fence 5" COL04	Retrd.	1993	9.00	17-25
1992 Fence 7" COL05	Retrd.	1995	10.00	19-30
1995 Flower Garden ACC02	Retrd.	1998	13.00	13
1994 Formal Garden COL13	Retrd.	1994	18.00	30-50
1992 Gazebo With Victorian Lady COL02	Retrd.	1995	11.00	21-50
1996 Grazing Cows ACC04	Open		12.00	12
1992 Lake With Swan COL06	Retrd.	1993	11.00	14-35
1997 Magnolia Tree ACC11	Open		15.00	15
1992 Oak Bower COL03	Retrd.	1993	11.00	19-38
1996 Palm Tree ACC07	Open		14.00	15
1995 Real Estate Sign ACC03	Retrd.	1998	12.00	12
1997 Sabal Palm ACC12	Open		14.00	14
1996 Sailboat ACC06	Open		12.00	13
1996 Spring Tree ACC10	Open		14.00	15
1996 Summertime Picket Fence ACC08	Open		12.00	13
1994 Sunrise At 80 Meeting COL10	Retrd.	1994	18.00	30-50
1992 Tree With Bush COL07	Retrd.	1996	10.00	12-20
1994 Victorian Arbor COL11	Retrd.	1994	18.00	35-50
1997 White Dogwood ACC14	Open		15.00	15
1995 Wisteria Arbor ACC01	Retrd.	1998	12.00	12-14
1992 Wrought Iron Gate With Magnolias COL01	Retrd.	1993	11.00	21-25

American Barns - S. Thompson

YEAR ISSUE	EDITION LIMIT	YEAR RETD.	ISSUE PRICE	*QUOTE U.S.$
1995 Casey Barn AP BAR04	Retrd.	1997	18.00	26-60
1995 Casey Barn BAR04	Retrd.	1997	18.00	18-30
1995 Mail Pouch Barn AP BAR03	Retrd.	1996	18.00	26-47
1995 Mail Pouch Barn BAR03	Open		18.00	21
1996 Mr. Peanut Barn BAR05	Open		19.00	21
1996 Mr. Peanut Barn, AP BAR05	97	1996	24.00	28-60
1995 Pennsylvania Dutch Barn AP BAR02	Retrd.	1995	20.00	90
1995 Pennsylvania Dutch Barn BAR02	Retrd.	1996	18.00	30-35
1994 Rock City Barn AP BAR01	Retrd.	1994	20.00	29-48
1994 Rock City Barn BAR01	Open		18.00	21

American Heritage - S. Thompson

YEAR ISSUE	EDITION LIMIT	YEAR RETD.	ISSUE PRICE	*QUOTE U.S.$
1998 Faneuil Hall II AHC02	Open		20.00	20
1998 Faneuil Hall II, AP AHC02	275		24.00	24
1998 Old South Meeting House AHC03	Open		22.00	22
1998 Old South Meeting House, AP AHC03	250		26.00	26
1998 Old State House AHC01	Open		22.00	22
1998 Old State House, AP AHC01	250		26.00	26
1998 Paul Revere's House II AHC04	Open		18.00	18
1998 Paul Revere's House II, AP AHC04	250		22.00	22

Amish Village - S. Thompson

YEAR ISSUE	EDITION LIMIT	YEAR RETD.	ISSUE PRICE	*QUOTE U.S.$
1994 Amish Barn (renovated) AMS04II	Retrd.	1997	17.00	33-35
1993 Amish Barn AMS04	Retrd.	1997	17.00	25-30
1993 Amish Barn, AP AMS04	Retrd.	1993	20.00	60
1997 Amish Barnraising AMS09	Open		22.00	22
1994 Amish Buggy (renovated) AMS05II	Retrd.	1997	12.00	35
1993 Amish Buggy AMS05	Retrd.	1997	12.00	11-35
1993 Amish Buggy, AP AMS05	Retrd.	1993	16.00	35
1997 Amish Corn Cribs AMS07	Retrd.	1997	18.00	18
1997 Amish Farmhouse AMS08	Open		22.00	22
1994 Amish Home (renovated) AMS01II	Retrd.	1997	17.00	33-35
1993 Amish Home AMS01	Retrd.	1997	17.00	28-30
1993 Amish Home, AP AMS01	Retrd.	1993	20.00	35
1994 Amish School (renovated) AMS02II	Retrd.	1997	15.00	15-20
1993 Amish School AMS02	Retrd.	1997	15.00	28-30
1993 Amish School, AP AMS02	Retrd.	1993	20.00	60
1997 Amish Schoolhouse AMS10	Open		18.00	18
1994 Covered Bridge (renovated) AMS03II	Retrd.	1997	16.00	23-30
1993 Covered Bridge AMS03	Retrd.	1997	16.00	26-30
1993 Covered Bridge, AP AMS03	Retrd.	1993	20.00	60
1995 Roadside Stand AMS06	Open		17.00	18
1995 Roadside Stand, AP AMS06	Retrd.	1995	24.00	42-60

Arkansas Ladies - S. Thompson

YEAR ISSUE	EDITION LIMIT	YEAR RETD.	ISSUE PRICE	*QUOTE U.S.$
1996 Handford Terry House ARK02	Open		19.00	22
1996 Handford Terry House, AP ARK02	50	1996	24.00	46
1996 Pillow-Thompson House ARK04	Open		19.00	22
1996 Pillow-Thompson House, AP ARK04	101	1996	24.00	46
1996 Rosalie House ARK01	Open		19.00	22
1996 Rosalie House, AP ARK01	102	1996	24.00	46
1996 Wings ARK03	Open		19.00	22
1996 Wings, AP ARK03	103	1996	24.00	46

Art Deco - S. Thompson

YEAR ISSUE	EDITION LIMIT	YEAR RETD.	ISSUE PRICE	*QUOTE U.S.$
1996 Berkeley Shore DEC03	Open		19.00	21
1996 Berkeley Shore, AP DEC03	95	1996	24.00	46
1996 The Carlyle DEC02	Open		19.00	21
1996 The Carlyle, AP DEC02	97	1996	24.00	46
1996 Hotel Webster DEC01	Open		19.00	21
1996 Hotel Webster, AP DEC01	99	1996	24.00	46
1996 Marlin DEC04	Open		19.00	21
1996 Marlin, AP DEC04	89	1996	24.00	46

Artist Choice-American Gothic - S. Thompson

YEAR ISSUE	EDITION LIMIT	YEAR RETD.	ISSUE PRICE	*QUOTE U.S.$
1993 Gothic Revival Cottage ACL01	Retrd.	1993	20.00	65
1993 Mele House ACL04	Retrd.	1993	20.00	45-65
1993 Perkins House ACL02	Retrd.	1993	20.00	22-40
1993 Rose Arbor ACL05	Retrd.	1993	14.00	27-65
1993 Roseland Cottage ACL03	Retrd.	1993	20.00	22-50
1993 Set of 5	Retrd.	1993	94.00	173

Artist Choice-Barber Houses - S. Thompson

YEAR ISSUE	EDITION LIMIT	YEAR RETD.	ISSUE PRICE	*QUOTE U.S.$
1995 Banta House ACL12	4,000	1995	24.00	45-85
1995 Greenman House ACL11	4,000	1995	24.00	30-50
1995 Riley-Cutler House ACL10	4,000	1995	24.00	26-45
1995 Weller House ACL13	4,000	1995	24.00	25-45
1995 Set of 4	4,000	1995	96.00	132-138

Artist Choice-Mail-Order Victorians (Barber Houses) - S. Thompson

YEAR ISSUE	EDITION LIMIT	YEAR RETD.	ISSUE PRICE	*QUOTE U.S.$
1994 Brehaut House ACL09	3,300	1994	24.00	31-40
1994 Goeller House ACL08	3,300	1994	24.00	45-47
1994 Henderson House ACL07	3,300	1994	24.00	58-60
1994 Titman House ACL06	3,300	1994	24.00	60-75
1994 Set of 4	3,300	1994	96.00	136-144

Artist Choice-My Favorite Places - S. Thompson

YEAR ISSUE	EDITION LIMIT	YEAR RETD.	ISSUE PRICE	*QUOTE U.S.$
1997 Garden Bench ACL18	5,000	1997	24.00	24
1997 Reflecting Pond ACL19	5,000	1997	24.00	24
1997 Sunflower Field ACL21	5,000	1997	21.00	21-24
1997 Tranquil Arbor ACL20	5,000	1997	22.00	22-24

Artist Choice-Winter White Collection - S. Thompson

YEAR ISSUE	EDITION LIMIT	YEAR RETD.	ISSUE PRICE	*QUOTE U.S.$
1996 Drain House ACL16	4,500	1996	25.00	37-45
1996 Moses Bulkeley House ACL14	4,500	1996	25.00	25-45
1996 Paul House ACL17	4,500	1996	25.00	25-45
1996 Penn House ACL15	4,500	1996	25.00	25-75

Atlanta - S. Thompson

YEAR ISSUE	EDITION LIMIT	YEAR RETD.	ISSUE PRICE	*QUOTE U.S.$
1995 Fox Theatre ATL06	Retrd.	1998	19.00	20-27
1995 Hammond's House ATL05	Retrd.	1997	18.00	20-30
1996 Margaret Mitchell House ATL07	Open		19.00	21
1996 Margaret Mitchell House, AP ATL07	89	1996	24.00	33-46
1995 Swan House ATL03	Retrd.	1998	18.00	20-26
1995 Tullie Smith House ATL01	Retrd.	1997	17.00	26-35
1995 Victorian Playhouse ATL02	Retrd.	1997	17.00	22-35
1995 Wren's Nest ATL04	Retrd.	1998	19.00	19-35

California Mansions - S. Thompson

YEAR ISSUE	EDITION LIMIT	YEAR RETD.	ISSUE PRICE	*QUOTE U.S.$
1997 Carson Mansion CAM04	Open		22.00	22
1997 Carson Mansion, AP CAM04	260		28.00	28
1997 Edwards Mansion CAM01	Open		22.00	22
1997 Edwards Mansion, AP CAM01	250		28.00	28
1997 Long-Waterman Mansion CAM05	Open		22.00	22
1997 Long-Waterman Mansion, AP CAM05	255		28.00	28
1997 Morey Mansion CAM02	Open		22.00	22
1997 Morey Mansion, AP CAM02	260		28.00	28
1997 Tuttle Mansion CAM03	Open		22.00	22
1997 Tuttle Mansion, AP CAM03	260		28.00	28

Charleston - S. Thompson

YEAR ISSUE	EDITION LIMIT	YEAR RETD.	ISSUE PRICE	*QUOTE U.S.$
1994 #2 Meeting Street (renovated) CHS06II	Retrd.	1997	16.00	25-45
1991 #2 Meeting Street CHS06	Retrd.	1997	15.00	22-45
1990 90 Church St. CHS17	Retrd.	1993	12.00	40-80
1994 Ashe House (renovated) CHS51II	Retrd.	1997	16.00	45
1993 Ashe House CHS51	Retrd.	1997	16.00	22-45
1991 Beth Elohim Temple CHS20	Retrd.	1993	15.00	22-30
1994 The Citadel (renovated) CHS22II	Retrd.	1997	16.00	40-45
1993 The Citadel CHS22	Retrd.	1997	16.00	30-50
1993 City Hall (No banner) CHS21	Retrd.	1993	15.00	200-400
1993 City Hall (without Spuleto colors) CHS21	Retrd.	1993	15.00	275
1993 City Hall CHS21	Retrd.	1993	15.00	81-94
1991 City Market (closed gates) CHS07	Retrd.	1991	15.00	100
1991 City Market (open gates) CHS07	Retrd.	1994	15.00	20-22
1994 City Market (renovated) CHS07II	Retrd.	1998	15.00	22
1994 College of Charleston (renovated) CHS40II	Retrd.	1996	16.00	45-75
1993 College of Charleston CHS40	Retrd.	1996	16.00	31-60
1993 College of Charleston, AP CHS40	Retrd.	1993	20.00	85
1992 Dock Street Theater (chimney) CHS08	Retrd.	1993	15.00	37-85
1991 Dock Street Theater (no chimney) CHS08	Retrd.	1992	15.00	60-75
1994 Edmonston-Alston (renovated) CHS04II	Retrd.	1995	16.00	30-85
1991 Edmonston-Alston CHS04	Retrd.	1995	15.00	24-45
1990 Exchange Building CHS15	Retrd.	1994	15.00	24-30
1990 Heyward-Washington House CHS02	Retrd.	1993	15.00	24-45
1994 John Rutledge House Inn (renovated) CHS50II	Retrd.	1997	16.00	30-45
1993 John Rutledge House Inn CHS50	Retrd.	1997	16.00	30-45
1991 Magnolia Plantation House (beige curtains) CHS03	Retrd.	1996	16.00	24-65
1994 Magnolia Plantation House (renovated) CHS03II	Retrd.	1996	16.00	24-65
1991 Magnolia Plantation House (white curtains) CHS03	Retrd.	1996	16.00	24-65
1990 Manigault House CHS01	Retrd.	1993	15.00	25-45
1990 Middleton Plantation CHS19	Retrd.	1991	9.00	250-288
1990 Pink House CHS18	Retrd.	1993	12.00	19-30
1990 Powder Magazine CHS16	Retrd.	1991	9.00	207-230
1994 Single Side Porch (renovated) CHS30II	Retrd.	1997	16.00	35-45
1993 Single Side Porch CHS30	Retrd.	1997	16.00	16-27
1993 Single Side Porch, AP CHS30	Retrd.	1993	20.00	60
1990 St. Michael's Church CHS14	Retrd.	1994	15.00	34-40
1994 St. Philip's Church (renovated) CHS05II	Retrd.	1996	15.00	55-60
1991 St. Philip's Church CHS05	Retrd.	1996	15.00	32-40
1991 St. Phillip's Church (misspelling Phillips) CHS05	Retrd.	1996	15.00	90

Charleston Battery - S. Thompson

YEAR ISSUE	EDITION LIMIT	YEAR RETD.	ISSUE PRICE	*QUOTE U.S.$
1996 22 South Battery CHB01	Open		19.00	21
1996 22 South Battery, AP CHB01	109	1996	24.00	28-46
1996 24 South Battery CHB02	Open		19.00	21
1996 24 South Battery, AP CHB02	99	1996	24.00	28-46

*Quotes have been rounded up to nearest dollar

YEAR ISSUE	EDITION LIMIT	YEAR RETD.	ISSUE PRICE	*QUOTE U.S.$
1996 26 South Battery CHB03	Open		19.00	21
1996 26 South Battery, AP CHB03	74	1996	24.00	28-46
1996 28 South Battery CHB04	Open		19.00	21
1996 28 South Battery, AP CHB04	74	1996	24.00	28-46
1998 30 South Battery CHB05	Open		21.00	21
1998 30 South Battery, AP CHB05	275		25.00	25

Charleston Gold Seal - S. Thompson

YEAR ISSUE	EDITION LIMIT	YEAR RETD.	ISSUE PRICE	*QUOTE U.S.$
1988 90 Church St. CHS17	Retrd.	1990	9.00	40
1988 CHS31 Rainbow Row-rust	Retrd.	1990	9.00	30
1988 CHS32 Rainbow Row-tan	Retrd.	1990	9.00	30
1988 CHS33 Rainbow Row-cream	Retrd.	1990	9.00	30
1988 CHS34 Rainbow Row-green	Retrd.	1990	9.00	30
1988 CHS35 Rainbow Row-lavender	Retrd.	1990	9.00	30
1988 CHS36 Rainbow Row-pink	Retrd.	1990	9.00	30
1988 CHS37 Rainbow Row-blue	Retrd.	1990	9.00	30
1988 CHS38 Rainbow Row-lt. yellow	Retrd.	1990	9.00	30
1988 CHS39 Rainbow Row-lt. pink	Retrd.	1990	9.00	30
1988 Exchange Building CHS15	Retrd.	1990	9.00	N/A
1988 Middleton Plantation CHS19	Retrd.	1990	9.00	222
1988 Pink House CHS18	Retrd.	1990	9.00	35
1988 Powder Magazine CHS16	Retrd.	1990	9.00	250
1988 St. Michael's Church CHS14	Retrd.	1990	9.00	N/A

Charleston II - S. Thompson

YEAR ISSUE	EDITION LIMIT	YEAR RETD.	ISSUE PRICE	*QUOTE U.S.$
1995 Boone Hall Plantation CHS56	Open		18.00	21
1995 Boone Hall Plantation, AP CHS56	Retrd.	1995	24.00	46-60
1998 Dr. Vincent LeSigneur House CHS68	Open		22.00	22
1994 Drayton House CHS52	Open		18.00	21
1994 Drayton House, AP CHS52	Retrd.	1994	24.00	46-75
1996 Huguenot Church CHS58	Open		19.00	21
1996 Huguenot Church, AP CHS58	95	1996	24.00	28-46
1996 Magnolia Garden CHS57	Open		19.00	21
1998 Middleton Plantation II CHS67	Open		24.00	24
1995 O'Donnell's Folly CHS55	Open		18.00	21
1995 O'Donnell's Folly, AP CHS55	Retrd.	1995	24.00	46-50
1996 Sotille CHS59	Open		19.00	21
1996 Sotille, AP CHS59	98	1996	24.00	28-46

Charleston III - S. Thompson

YEAR ISSUE	EDITION LIMIT	YEAR RETD.	ISSUE PRICE	*QUOTE U.S.$
1997 South of Broad, Cream CHS65	Open		18.00	18
1997 South of Broad, Cream, AP CHS65	197		24.00	46
1997 South of Broad, Dark Pink CHS64	Open		18.00	18
1997 South of Broad, Dark Pink, AP CHS64	214		24.00	46
1997 South of Broad, Lavender CHS63	Open		18.00	18
1997 South of Broad, Lavender, AP CHS63	205		24.00	46
1997 South of Broad, Light Pink CHS66	Open		18.00	18
1997 South of Broad, Light Pink, AP CHS66	207		24.00	46
1997 South of Broad, Tan CHS62	Open		18.00	18
1997 South of Broad, Tan, AP CHS62	198		24.00	46

Charleston Public Buildings - S. Thompson

YEAR ISSUE	EDITION LIMIT	YEAR RETD.	ISSUE PRICE	*QUOTE U.S.$
1997 Bethel United Methodist Church CHS61	Open		21.00	21
1997 Summerall Chapel CHS60	Open		21.00	21

Charleston Rainbow Row '97 - S. Thompson

YEAR ISSUE	EDITION LIMIT	YEAR RETD.	ISSUE PRICE	*QUOTE U.S.$
1997 89 East Bay CRR05	Open		18.00	18
1997 91 East Bay CRR06	Open		18.00	18
1997 93 East Bay CRR07	Open		18.00	18
1997 95 East Bay CRR08	Open		18.00	18
1997 97 East Bay CRR09	Open		18.00	18
1997 99-101 East Bay CRR10	Open		18.00	18
1997 103 East Bay CRR11	Open		18.00	18
1997 105 East Bay CRR12	Open		18.00	18
1997 107 East Bay CRR13	Open		18.00	18

Charleston Rainbow Row - S. Thompson

YEAR ISSUE	EDITION LIMIT	YEAR RETD.	ISSUE PRICE	*QUOTE U.S.$
1990 CHS31 Rainbow Row-rust	Retrd.	1993	9.00	19-55
1990 CHS32 Rainbow Row-cream	Retrd.	1993	9.00	17-25
1990 CHS33 Rainbow Row-tan	Retrd.	1993	9.00	20-22
1990 CHS34 Rainbow Row-green	Retrd.	1993	9.00	20-25
1990 CHS35 Rainbow Row-lavender	Retrd.	1993	9.00	17-20
1990 CHS36 Rainbow Row-pink	Retrd.	1993	9.00	25-69
1990 CHS37 Rainbow Row-blue	Retrd.	1993	9.00	32-44
1990 CHS38 Rainbow Row-lt. yellow	Retrd.	1993	9.00	25-44
1990 CHS39 Rainbow Row-lt. pink	Retrd.	1993	9.00	25-55
1993 CHS41 Rainbow Row-aurora	Retrd.	1997	13.00	15-28
1994 CHS41II Rainbow Row-aurora (renovated)	Retrd.	1997	13.00	17-22
1993 CHS42 Rainbow Row-off-white	Retrd.	1997	13.00	22-28
1994 CHS42II Rainbow Row-off-white (renovated)	Retrd.	1997	13.00	17-22
1993 CHS43 Rainbow Row-cream	Retrd.	1997	13.00	21-28
1994 CHS43II Rainbow Row-cream (renovated)	Retrd.	1997	13.00	17-22
1993 CHS44 Rainbow Row-green	Retrd.	1997	13.00	15-28
1994 CHS44II Rainbow Row-green (renovated)	Retrd.	1997	13.00	17-22
1993 CHS45 Rainbow Row-lavender	Retrd.	1997	13.00	21-25
1994 CHS45II Rainbow Row-lavender (renovated)	Retrd.	1997	13.00	17-22
1993 CHS46 Rainbow Row-pink	Retrd.	1997	13.00	21-26
1994 CHS46II Rainbow Row-pink (renovated)	Retrd.	1997	13.00	17-22
1993 CHS47 Rainbow Row-blue	Retrd.	1997	13.00	15-28
1994 CHS47II Rainbow Row-blue (renovated)	Retrd.	1997	13.00	17-22
1993 CHS48 Rainbow Row-yellow	Retrd.	1997	13.00	15-28
1994 CHS48 Rainbow Row-yellow (renovated)	Retrd.	1997	13.00	17-22
1993 CHS49 Rainbow Row-gray	Retrd.	1997	13.00	15-28
1994 CHS49II Rainbow Row-gray (renovated)	Retrd.	1997	13.00	17-22

YEAR ISSUE	EDITION LIMIT	YEAR RETD.	ISSUE PRICE	*QUOTE U.S.$
1993 Rainbow Row Sign	Retrd.	N/A	12.50	25-40

Coca-Cola "The Real Thing" - S. Thompson

YEAR ISSUE	EDITION LIMIT	YEAR RETD.	ISSUE PRICE	*QUOTE U.S.$
1998 Barnyard Refreshment COK06	Open		26.00	26
1998 Barnyard Refreshment, AP COK06	275		30.00	30
1998 Cover Your Thirst COK05	Open		26.00	26
1998 Cover Your Thirst, AP COK05	275		30.00	30
1998 Down Home Flavor COK03	Open		26.00	26
1998 Down Home Flavor, AP COK03	275		30.00	30
1998 Refreshing Delivery COK02	Open		17.00	17
1998 Refreshing Delivery, AP COK02	275		21.00	21
1998 Sign of Good Taste COK04	Open		20.00	20
1998 Sign of Good Taste, AP COK04	275		24.00	24
1998 Soda Pop Stop COK01	Open		26.00	26
1998 Soda Pop Stop, AP COK01	275		30.00	30

Colored Metal Accessories - S. Thompson

YEAR ISSUE	EDITION LIMIT	YEAR RETD.	ISSUE PRICE	*QUOTE U.S.$
1997 Burma Shave Sign: Past... Schoolhouse, set/6 CMA01	Retrd.	1997	17.00	17
1997 Burma Shave Sign: Don't Lose Your Head, set/6 CMA02	Retrd.	1997	17.00	17
1997 Daimler 1910 Car CMA03	Retrd.	1997	18.00	18

Custom Designs - S. Thompson

YEAR ISSUE	EDITION LIMIT	YEAR RETD.	ISSUE PRICE	*QUOTE U.S.$
1996 7 Meeting Street, SC C0027 (Andy's Hallmark)	Open		26.00	26
1996 Angel of the Sea, NJ C0014 (Gifts Galore)	Open		26.00	26
1997 Annabell's Bed and Breakfast, MD C0033 (The Courtesy Shop)	Open		28.00	28
1997 Ballard School House, CA C0036 (Home Connection)	Open		28.00	28
1998 Barnegat Lighthouse, NJ C0079 (The Bywatyr Shop)	Open		28.00	28
1996 Bayard House Row I, MD C0018 (Back Creek General Store)	Open		26.00	26
1997 Bayard House Row II, MD C0062 (Back Creek General Store)	Open		26.00	26
1996 Best Friend of Charleston, SC C0028 (Broughton Christmas)	Open		22.00	22
1997 Bonaventure's Art, GA C0051 (Sander's Country Store)	Open		28.00	28
1996 Bouevalt House, LA C0026 (French Market Gift Shop)	Open		26.00	26
1997 Calhoun Mansion, SC C0057 (Broughton Christmas)	Open		26.00	26
1998 Callahan's Calabash Nautical Gifts, NC C0087 (Callahan's Calabash Nautical Gifts)	Open		28.00	28
1997 Cape Canaveral Light, FL C0045 (Fibber MaGee's Kountry & Christmas Shoppe)	Open		26.00	26
1998 Cape May Pink House, NJ C0077 (Swede Things in America)	Open		28.00	28
1995 Cape May Point Lighthouse, NJ C0001 (Gifts Galore)	Open		22.00	22
1998 Captain Mey's Bed & Breakfast, NJ C0083 (Gifts Galore)	Open		28.00	28
1995 The Carolina Opry, SC C0010 (Gifts For All)	Open		26.00	26
1997 Cass Scenic Railroad, WV C0052 (Adam's Fine Gifts)	Open		26.00	26
1997 Central Station, SC C0035 (Charleston Market)	Open		26.00	26
1995 Christ Church, GA C0011 (Lauren's)	Open		26.00	26
1997 Christiana Campbell's Tavern, VA C0066 (The Christmas Shop)	Open		26.00	26
1995 Christmas Tree Hill In The Mansion, PA C0004 (Christmas Tree Hill)	Open		26.00	26
1996 Danish Capitol of America, CA C0029 (Home Connection)	Open		26.00	26
1996 Deer Park Tavern, DE C0023 (Washington Square)	Open		26.00	26
1997 Dunleith, MS C0044 (Southern Arts & Gardens)	Open		28.00	28
1997 Ellis Island, NY C0061 (Merry Go-Round)	Open		26.00	26
1995 F.F. Beattie Home, SC C0009 (Christmas Celebration)	Open		26.00	26
1996 Fenwick Island Lighthouse, DE C0013 (Courtesy Shop)	Open		26.00	26
1997 Gallaher House, OH C0050 (Debbie's Cards and Collectibles)	Open		26.00	26
1996 Gamble House, OH C0020 (Debbie's Collectibles)	Open		26.00	26
1997 George Allen House, NJ C0063 (Swede Things in America)	Open		26.00	26
1996 George Wythe House, VA C0025 (Christmas Shop)	Open		22.00	22
1995 Glade Creek Grist Mill, WV C0008 (Adam's Fine Gifts)	Open		26.00	26
1997 Grand Victorian, MI C0055 (Mason's)	Open		26.00	26
1995 Green Meldrim, GA C0002 (Nellie's Nook)	Open		26.00	26
1996 Hamilton Turner Mansion, GA C0016 (Sanders Country Store)	Open		26.00	26
1997 Hartville Kitchen, OH C0048 (Hartville Collectibles)	Open		26.00	26
1998 Henry S. Willink Cottage, GA C0076 (Nellie's Nook)	Open		28.00	28
1995 Hershey's Chocolate Factory, PA C0005 (Community Creations)	Open		26.00	26
1997 Inn at 22 Jackson, NJ C0037 (Gifts Galore)	Open		28.00	28
1995 Inn at the Canal, MD C0006 (Back Creek General Store)	Open		26.00	26
1998 Isle of Hope United Methodist Church, GA C0071 (Sarah's Hallmark)	Open		28.00	28
1998 Jingle Bells Church, GA C0074 (Sander's Country Store)	Open		28.00	28
1996 John Lowe Jr. Home, FL C0015 (Tropicals Shells & Gifts)	Open		26.00	26
1997 The Kehoe House, GA C0041 (Nellie's Nook)	Open		28.00	28
1997 Key West Custom House, FL C0064 (Tropical Shells & Gifts)	Open		28.00	28
1998 Laughlin Mill, PA C0072 (Village of Colonial Peddlers)	Open		28.00	28
1995 Mainstay Inn, NJ C0007 (Swede Things In America)	Open		26.00	26
1996 Merry Go Round, NJ C0022 (Merry Go Round)	Open		26.00	26
1998 Montauk Point Lighthouse, NY C0075 (Victoria's Treasrues)	Open		28.00	28
1996 Mud River Covered Bridge, WV C0032 (Adam's Fine Gifts)	Open		26.00	26
1997 Music Pier, NJ C0043 (Drift In and Sea)	Open		26.00	26
1997 The Myrtle Beach Pavillion, SC C0049 (Christy's Christmas)	Open		28.00	28
1997 New York State Capitol, NY C0058 (Grandma's Country Corner)	Open		26.00	26
1996 Ocean City Life Saving Station, MD C0012 (Donald's Duck Shoppe)	Open		26.00	26
1998 Ohio State University Stadium, OH C0082 (Pamela's)	Open		28.00	28
1997 Old Mill, TN C0038 (Christmas Shoppe)	Open		28.00	28
1995 Old Savannah Cotton Exchange, GA C0003 (Sarah's Hallmark)	Open		26.00	26
1998 Open Air City Market, SC C0078 (Decker's Hallmark)	Open		28.00	28
1998 The Palace Theater, NC C0089 (Christy's Christmas)	Open		28.00	28
1997 Pat O'Brien's, LA C0059 (French Market Gift Shop)	Open		26.00	26
1998 Phillip's Crab House, MD C0081 (Donald Duck's Shoppe)	Open		28.00	28
1997 The Pink House, SC C0039 (Lynn's Hallmark)	Open		26.00	26
1996 Pirate's House II, GA C0030 (Sarah's Hallmark)	Open		26.00	26
1996 Plough Tavern & Gates House, PA C0017 (Christmas Tree Hill)	Open		26.00	26
1996 Queen Victoria, NJ C0024 (Swede Things In America)	Open		26.00	26
1996 Record Building, SC C0031 (Christmas Celebration)	Open		26.00	26
1998 Rex-Laurel Fire Station, PA C0080 (Christmas Tree Hill)	Open		28.00	28
1996 Savannah City Hall, GA C0019 (Nellie's Nook)	Open		26.00	26
1996 Savannah's Waving Girl, GA C0021 (Lauren's Hallmark)	Open		22.00	22
1997 The Secret Garden, MA C0046 (The Secret Garden)	Open		28.00	28
1997 Springer's Homemade Ice Cream, NJ C0053 (Coventry Crossing)	Open		26.00	26
1997 St. Andrew's Parish Church, SC C0047 (Andy's Hallmark)	Open		26.00	26
1997 St. Vincent's Academy, GA C0067 (Lauren's Hallmark)	Open		26.00	26
1998 Stanton Hall, MS C0069 (Southern Arts and Gardens)	Open		28.00	28
1997 Strand-Capitol Performing Arts Center, PA C0065 (Christmas Tree Hill)	Open		26.00	26
1997 Swiss German Plaza, GA C0054 (Kaiser Bill's II)	Open		26.00	26
1998 Tabernacle, MA C0068 (The Secret Garden)	Open		28.00	28
1997 Tawas Point Light, MI C0034 (The Blue Cottage)	Open		28.00	28
1998 Thomas Point Lighthouse, MD C0073 (The Courtesy Shop)	Open		28.00	28
1997 Trinity Episcopal Cathedral, SC C0056 (Country Junction)	Open		28.00	28
1998 Tyler Davidson Fountain, OH C0070 (Debbie's Cards and Collectibles)	Open		28.00	28
1997 Warren House, FL C0060 (Tropical Shell & Gifts)	Open		26.00	26
1997 Wesley Monumental UMC, GA C0040 (Sarah's Hallmark)	Open		26.00	26

Dicken's Village - S. Thompson

YEAR ISSUE	EDITION LIMIT	YEAR RETD.	ISSUE PRICE	*QUOTE U.S.$
1991 Butcher Shop XMS03	Retrd.	1993	15.00	22-25
1991 Evergreen Tree XMS08	Retrd.	1993	11.00	30-35
1991 Gazebo & Carolers XMS06	Retrd.	1993	12.00	20-40
1991 Scrooge & Marley's Shop XMS01	Retrd.	1993	15.00	29-45
1991 Scrooge's Home XMS05	Retrd.	1993	15.00	20-30
1991 Toy Shoppe XMS04	Retrd.	1993	15.00	29-65
1991 Victorian Apartment Building XMS02	Retrd.	1993	15.00	30
1992 Victorian Church XMS09	Retrd.	1993	15.00	65-69
1991 Victorian Skaters XMS07	Retrd.	1993	12.00	19-30
1992 Set of 9	Retrd.	1993	125.00	200-325

Famous Homes of America - S. Thompson

YEAR ISSUE	EDITION LIMIT	YEAR RETD.	ISSUE PRICE	*QUOTE U.S.$
1998 Biltmore FHA03	Open		27.00	27
1998 Monticello FHA01	Open		24.00	24
1998 Orchard House FHA02	Open		20.00	20

*Quotes have been rounded up to nearest dollar

Galveston - S. Thompson

YEAR ISSUE	EDITION LIMIT	YEAR RETD.	ISSUE PRICE	*QUOTE U.S.$
1995 Beissner House GLV04	Retrd.	1998	18.00	18-22
1995 Dancing Pavillion GLV03	Retrd.	1998	18.00	21-28
1995 Frenkel House GLV01	Retrd.	1998	18.00	18-21
1995 Reymershoffer House GLV02	Retrd.	1998	18.00	20-22

George Barber - S. Thompson

YEAR ISSUE	EDITION LIMIT	YEAR RETD.	ISSUE PRICE	*QUOTE U.S.$
1996 Newton House GFB03	Open		19.00	22
1996 Newton House, AP GFB03	71		24.00	24
1997 Nunan House GFB05	Open		22.00	22
1996 Phillippi House GFB02	Open		19.00	22
1996 Phillippi House, AP GFB02	46		24.00	24
1996 Pine Crest GFB04	Open		19.00	22
1996 Pine Crest, AP GFB04	95		24.00	24
1996 Renaissance GFB01	Open		19.00	22
1996 Renaissance, AP GFB01	67		24.00	24

Georgia Peaches - S. Thompson

YEAR ISSUE	EDITION LIMIT	YEAR RETD.	ISSUE PRICE	*QUOTE U.S.$
1998 Hunter House GAP01	Open		22.00	22
1998 Hunter House, AP GAP01	275		26.00	26
1998 Jekyll Island Club (dark green on trees) GAP03	1,000		22.00	22
1998 Jekyll Island Club (dark green on trees), AP GAP03	275		26.00	26
1998 Jekyll Island Club GAP03	Open		22.00	22
1998 Moss House GAP02	Open		22.00	22
1998 Moss House, AP GAP02	275		26.00	26

Ghost House Series - S. Thompson

YEAR ISSUE	EDITION LIMIT	YEAR RETD.	ISSUE PRICE	*QUOTE U.S.$
1996 31 Legare St. GHO06	Open		19.00	22
1997 Catfish Plantation GHO07	Open		22.00	22
1995 Gaffos House GHO04	Retrd.	1998	19.00	20-25
1997 Hampton Lillbridge Home GHO08	Open		22.00	22
1994 Inside-Outside House GHO01	Retrd.	1996	18.00	25-27
1994 Inside-Outside House, AP GHO01	Retrd.	1994	20.00	40-50
1996 Kings Tavern GHO05	Open		19.00	22
1996 Kings Tavern, AP GHO05	102	1996	24.00	28-46
1994 Pirates' House GHO02	Retrd.	1996	18.00	40-56
1994 Pirates' House, AP GHO02	Retrd.	1994	20.00	150
1995 Red Castle GHO03	Retrd.	1998	19.00	20-22

Gone with the Wind - S. Thompson

YEAR ISSUE	EDITION LIMIT	YEAR RETD.	ISSUE PRICE	*QUOTE U.S.$
1995 Aunt Pittypat's GWW03	Retrd.	1996	24.00	24-38
1995 Aunt Pittypat's, AP GWW03	Retrd.	1995	30.00	58-75
1998 Butler's Atlanta Mansion GWW09	Open		27.00	27
1995 General Store GWW04	Retrd.	1996	24.00	26-38
1998 Home of Ashley Wilkes GWW08	Open		29.00	29
1998 Honeymoon Embrace Poster GWW10	Open		20.00	20
1995 General Store, AP GWW04	Retrd.	1995	30.00	50-58
1995 Loew's Grand GWW05	Retrd.	1995	24.00	35-125
1998 Scarlett's Passion, Tara GWW07	Open		29.00	29
1995 Loew's Grand, AP GWW05	Retrd.	1995	30.00	65-150
1996 Silhouette GWW06	Retrd.	1996	16.00	20-28
1995 Tara GWW01	Retrd.	1996	24.00	24-50
1995 Tara, AP GWW01	Retrd.	1995	30.00	50-60
1995 Twelve Oaks GWW02	Retrd.	1996	24.00	35-38
1995 Twelve Oaks, AP GWW02	Retrd.	1995	30.00	40 55
1995 Set of 5, AP	Retrd.	1995	150.00	288

Historic Bed & Breakfast - S. Thompson

YEAR ISSUE	EDITION LIMIT	YEAR RETD.	ISSUE PRICE	*QUOTE U.S.$
1998 Ann Starrett Mansion HBB05	Open		22.00	22
1998 Combellack-Blair House HBB04	Open		22.00	22
1997 Glen Auburn HBB02	Open		21.00	21
1997 Grand Anne HBB03	Open		21.00	21
1997 Grand Anne, AP HBB03	260		27.00	27
1997 Green Gables Inn HBB01	Open		21.00	21
1997 Green Gables Inn, AP HBB01	200		27.00	27

Inventor Series - S. Thompson

YEAR ISSUE	EDITION LIMIT	YEAR RETD.	ISSUE PRICE	*QUOTE U.S.$
1993 Ford Motor Company (green) INV01	Retrd.	1993	17.00	35-50
1993 Ford Motor Company (grey) INV01	Retrd.	1994	17.00	25-29
1993 Ford Motor Company, AP INV01	Retrd.	1993	20.00	45-70
1993 Menlo Park Laboratory (cream) INV02	Retrd.	1993	16.00	30-50
1993 Menlo Park Laboratory (grey) INV02	Retrd.	1994	16.00	40
1993 Menlo Park Laboratory, AP INV02	Retrd.	1993	20.00	35-70
1993 Noah Webster House INV03	Retrd.	1994	15.00	30-50
1993 Noah Webster House, AP INV03	Retrd.	1993	20.00	40-70
1993 Wright Cycle Shop INV04	Retrd.	1994	17.00	25-30
1993 Wright Cycle Shop, AP INV04	Retrd.	1993	20.00	40-70

Jazzy New Orleans Series - S. Thompson

YEAR ISSUE	EDITION LIMIT	YEAR RETD.	ISSUE PRICE	*QUOTE U.S.$
1994 Beauregard-Keys House JNO04	Retrd.	1996	18.00	22-26
1994 Beauregard-Keys House, AP JNO04	Retrd.	1994	20.00	45-65
1994 Gallier House JNO02	Retrd.	1998	18.00	22-29
1994 Gallier House, AP JNO02	Retrd.	1994	20.00	22-50
1994 La Branche Building JNO01	Retrd.	1998	18.00	22-27
1994 La Branche Building, AP JNO01	Retrd.	1994	20.00	22-50
1994 LePretre House JNO03	Retrd.	1998	18.00	18-28
1994 LePretre House, AP JNO03	Retrd.	1994	20.00	50

Key West - S. Thompson

YEAR ISSUE	EDITION LIMIT	YEAR RETD.	ISSUE PRICE	*QUOTE U.S.$
1995 Artist House KEY06	Open		19.00	21
1995 Artist House, AP KEY06	Retrd.	1995	24.00	46
1995 Eyebrow House KEY01	Retrd.	1998	18.00	21
1995 Eyebrow House, AP KEY01	Retrd.	1995	24.00	46
1995 Hemingway House KEY07	Open		19.00	21
1995 Hemingway House, AP KEY07	Retrd.	1995	24.00	46
1995 Illingsworth Gingerbread House KEY05	Open		19.00	21
1995 Illingsworth Gingerbread House, AP KEY05	Retrd.	1995	24.00	46
1995 Shotgun House KEY03	Retrd.	1997	17.00	28-75
1995 Shotgun House, AP KEY03	Retrd.	1995	24.00	75
1995 Shotgun Sister KEY04	Retrd.	1997	17.00	24-27
1995 Shotgun Sister, AP KEY04	Retrd.	1995	24.00	75
1995 Southernmost House KEY02	Open		19.00	21
1995 Southernmost House, AP KEY02	Retrd.	1995	24.00	46
1996 Southernmost Point KEY08	Open		12.00	12

Ladies By The Sea - S. Thompson

YEAR ISSUE	EDITION LIMIT	YEAR RETD.	ISSUE PRICE	*QUOTE U.S.$
1996 Abbey II LBS01	Open		19.00	22
1996 Abbey II, AP LBS01	93	1996	24.00	28-75
1998 Cape S Cape LBS06	Open		22.00	22
1998 Cape S Cape, AP LBS06	250		26.00	26
1996 Centennial Cottage LBS02	Open		19.00	22
1996 Centennial Cottage, AP LBS02	94	1996	24.00	28-50
1996 Hall Cottage LBS04	Open		19.00	22
1996 Hall Cottage, AP LBS04	108	1996	24.00	28-50
1996 Heart Blossom LBS03	Open		19.00	22
1996 Heart Blossom, AP LBS03	107	1996	24.00	28-50
1998 Ocean Pathway Princess LBS05	Open		22.00	22
1998 Ocean Pathway Princess, AP LBS05	275		26.00	26

Lighthouse Series - S. Thompson

YEAR ISSUE	EDITION LIMIT	YEAR RETD.	ISSUE PRICE	*QUOTE U.S.$
1991 Anastasia Lighthouse (burgundy) FL103	Retrd.	1991	15.00	20-30
1991 Anastasia Lighthouse (red) FL103	Retrd.	1994	15.00	55-150
1993 Assateague Island Light LTS07	Retrd.	1997	17.00	29-32
1994 Assateague Island Light, AP LTS07	Retrd.	1994	20.00	60
1995 Cape Hatteras Light LTS09	Retrd.	1997	17.00	26-30
1995 Cape Hatteras Light, AP LTS09	Retrd.	1995	24.00	60
1991 Cape Hatteras Lighthouse NC103	Retrd.	1994	15.00	29-60
1994 Charleston Light (renovated) LTS01	Retrd.	1995	15.00	60
1993 Charleston Light LTS01	Retrd.	1995	15.00	22-30
1993 New London Ledge Light LTS08	Retrd.	1996	17.00	22-30
1994 New London Ledge Light, AP LTS08	Retrd.	1994	20.00	55
1993 Round Island Light LTS06	Retrd.	1997	17.00	22-30
1994 Round Island Light, AP LTS06	Retrd.	1994	20.00	65
1990 Stage Harbor Lighthouse NEW06	Retrd.	1993	15.00	166-190
1993 Thomas Point Light LTS05	Retrd.	1997	17.00	22-29
1994 Thomas Point Light, AP LTS05	Retrd.	1994	20.00	55-65
1990 Tybee Lighthouse SAV07	Retrd.	1994	15.00	38-127

Limited Pieces - S. Thompson

YEAR ISSUE	EDITION LIMIT	YEAR RETD.	ISSUE PRICE	*QUOTE U.S.$
1991 Bridgetown Library NJ102	Retrd.	N/A	16.00	75-85
1993 Comley-Rich House (misspelling) XXX01	Retrd.	N/A	12.00	25-77
1993 Comly-Rich House XXX01	Retrd.	N/A	12.00	25-77
1991 Delphos City Hall OH101	Retrd.	N/A	15.00	85-265
1991 Historic Burlington County Clubhouse NJ101	Retrd.	N/A	16.00	65-75
1991 Mark Twain Boyhood Home MO101	Retrd.	N/A	15.00	N/A
1990 Newton County Court House GA101	Retrd.	N/A	16.00	65-100

Lone Star State - S. Thompson

YEAR ISSUE	EDITION LIMIT	YEAR RETD.	ISSUE PRICE	*QUOTE U.S.$
1998 Ashton Villa LSS02	Open		22.00	22
1998 Ashton Villa, AP LSS02	250		26.00	26
1998 Blue Bonnets LSS03	Open		13.00	13
1998 Redington House LSS01	Open		22.00	22
1998 Redington House, AP LSS01	250		26.00	26

Louisiana - S. Thompson

YEAR ISSUE	EDITION LIMIT	YEAR RETD.	ISSUE PRICE	*QUOTE U.S.$
1998 Commander's Palace LOU02	Open		22.00	22
1998 Commander's Palace, AP LOU02	275		26.00	26
1998 Jackson Square LOU01	Open		22.00	22
1998 Jackson Square, AP LOU01	275		26.00	26

Mackinac - S. Thompson

YEAR ISSUE	EDITION LIMIT	YEAR RETD.	ISSUE PRICE	*QUOTE U.S.$
1996 Amberg Cottage MAK01	Open		19.00	22
1996 Amberg Cottage, AP MAK01	102	1996	24.00	28-46
1996 Anne Cottage MAK02	Open		19.00	22
1996 Anne Cottage, AP MAK02	95	1996	24.00	28-46
1996 Grand Hotel (3 pc. set) MAK05	Retrd.	1998	57.00	60-65
1996 Grand Hotel (3 pc. set), AP MAK05	95		72.00	72
1996 Rearick Cottage MAK03	Open		19.00	22
1996 Rearick Cottage, AP MAK03	103	1996	24.00	28-46
1996 Windermere Hotel MAK04	Open		19.00	22
1996 Windermere Hotel, AP MAK04	105	1996	24.00	28-46

Martha's Vineyard - S. Thompson

YEAR ISSUE	EDITION LIMIT	YEAR RETD.	ISSUE PRICE	*QUOTE U.S.$
1994 Alice's Wonderland (renovated) MAR08II	Retrd.	1998	16.00	18-20
1993 Alice's Wonderland MAR08	Retrd.	1994	16.00	20
1993 Alice's Wonderland, AP MAR08	Retrd.	1993	20.00	30
1995 Blue Cottage MAR13	Open		17.00	20
1995 Blue Cottage, AP MAR13	Retrd.	1995	24.00	45
1997 Butterfly Cottage MAR14	Open		20.00	20
1994 Campground Cottage (renovated) MAR07II	Retrd.	1995	16.00	25-45
1993 Campground Cottage MAR07	Retrd.	1995	16.00	27-40
1993 Campground Cottage, AP MAR07	Retrd.	1993	20.00	41-50
1994 Gingerbread Cottage-grey (renovated) MAR09II	Retrd.	1996	16.00	25-35
1993 Gingerbread Cottage-grey AP MAR09	Retrd.	1993	20.00	41-50
1993 Gingerbread Cottage-grey MAR09	Retrd.	1996	16.00	35-50
1998 Summer Love MAR16	Open		21.00	21
1998 Summer Love, AP MAR16	275		25.00	25
1995 Trails End MAR11	Retrd.	1998	17.00	17-25
1995 Trails End, AP MAR11	Retrd.	1995	24.00	46
1998 Tranquility MAR15	Open		21.00	21
1998 Tranquility, AP MAR15	275		25.00	25
1995 White Cottage MAR12	Open		17.00	20
1995 White Cottage, AP MAR12	Retrd.	1995	24.00	46
1994 Wood Valentine (renovated) MAR10II	Retrd.	1998	16.00	20
1993 Wood Valentine MAR10	Retrd.	1994	16.00	20
1993 Wood Valentine, AP MAR10	Retrd.	1993	20.00	46

Nantucket - S. Thompson

YEAR ISSUE	EDITION LIMIT	YEAR RETD.	ISSUE PRICE	*QUOTE U.S.$
1998 Brant Point Lighthouse NTK01	Open		22.00	22
1998 Brant Point Lighthouse, AP NTK01	265		26.00	26
1998 Pedal Shop NTK03	Open		13.00	13
1998 Swain Cottage NTK02	Open		22.00	22
1998 Swain Cottage, AP NTK02	265		26.00	26

National Park Treasures - S. Thompson

YEAR ISSUE	EDITION LIMIT	YEAR RETD.	ISSUE PRICE	*QUOTE U.S.$
1998 Independence Hall NPT04	Open		21.00	21
1998 Liberty Bell NPT05	Open		15.00	15
1998 Mount Rushmore National Memorial NPT03	Open		20.00	20
1998 Statue of Liberty NPT02	Open		20.00	20
1998 White House NPT01	Open		26.00	26

National Trust Houses - S. Thompson

YEAR ISSUE	EDITION LIMIT	YEAR RETD.	ISSUE PRICE	*QUOTE U.S.$
1997 Cliveden NHP03	Open		24.00	24
1997 Cliveden, AP NHP03	240	1997	30.00	30-65
1998 Decatur House NHP04	Open		24.00	24
1998 Decatur House, AP NHP04	130		44.00	44
1997 Drayton Hall NHP01	Open		24.00	24
1997 Drayton Hall, AP NHP01	266	1997	30.00	30-65
1997 Montpelier NHP02	Open		24.00	24
1997 Montpelier, AP NHP02	200	1997	30.00	30-65
1998 Oatlands NHP07	Open		24.00	24
1998 Oatlands, AP NHP07	130		44.00	44
1998 Woodlawn Plantation NHP05	Open		24.00	24
1998 Woodlawn Plantation, AP NHP05	130		44.00	44
1998 Woodrow Wilson House NHP06	Open		24.00	24
1998 Woodrow Wilson House, AP NHP06	130		44.00	44

New England - S. Thompson

YEAR ISSUE	EDITION LIMIT	YEAR RETD.	ISSUE PRICE	*QUOTE U.S.$
1991 Faneuil Hall NEW09	Retrd.	1993	15.00	37-45
1990 Longfellow's House NEW01	Retrd.	1993	15.00	24-28
1990 Malden Mass. Victorian Inn NEW05	Retrd.	1992	10.00	36-63
1990 Martha's Vineyard Cottage -blue/mauve MAR06	Retrd.	1993	15.00	42-48
1990 Martha's Vineyard Cottage -blue/orange MAR05	Retrd.	1993	15.00	17-50
1990 Motif #1 Boathouse NEW02	Retrd.	1993	15.00	47-50
1990 Old North Church NEW04	Retrd.	1993	15.00	37-42
1990 Paul Revere's Home NEW03	Retrd.	1993	15.00	31-90
1991 President Bush's Home NEW07	Retrd.	1993	15.00	58-69
1991 Wedding Cake House NEW08	Retrd.	1993	15.00	37-40
1991 Set of 10	Retrd.	1993	145.00	374

North Carolina - S. Thompson

YEAR ISSUE	EDITION LIMIT	YEAR RETD.	ISSUE PRICE	*QUOTE U.S.$
1990 Josephus Hall House NC101	Retrd.	1993	15.00	45-60
1990 Presbyterian Bell Tower NC102	Retrd.	1993	15.00	17-22
1991 The Tryon Palace NC104	Retrd.	1993	15.00	23-50

Old-Fashioned Christmas - S. Thompson

YEAR ISSUE	EDITION LIMIT	YEAR RETD.	ISSUE PRICE	*QUOTE U.S.$
1994 Conway Scenic Railroad Station OFC04	Retrd.	1997	18.00	23-25
1994 Conway Scenic Railroad Station, AP OFC04	Retrd.	1994	20.00	50
1994 Dwight House OFC02	Retrd.	1996	18.00	22-35
1994 Dwight House, AP OFC02	Retrd.	1994	20.00	60
1994 General Merchandise OFC03	Retrd.	1997	18.00	22-35
1994 General Merchandise, AP OFC03	Retrd.	1994	20.00	60
1994 Old First Church OFC01	Retrd.	1997	18.00	25-35
1994 Old First Church, AP OFC01	Retrd.	1994	20.00	60
1994 Set of 4 1994 AP	Retrd.	1994	80.00	199
1995 Christmas Inn OFC05	Retrd.	1997	18.00	35-38
1995 Town Square Tree OFC06	Retrd.	1997	18.00	26-30

Painted Ladies I - S. Thompson

YEAR ISSUE	EDITION LIMIT	YEAR RETD.	ISSUE PRICE	*QUOTE U.S.$
1990 The Abbey LAD08	Retrd.	1992	10.00	86-175
1990 Atlanta Queen Anne LAD07	Retrd.	1992	10.00	86-200
1990 Cincinnati Gothic LAD05	Retrd.	1992	10.00	58-100
1990 Colorado Queen Anne LAD04	Retrd.	1992	10.00	52-100
1990 Illinois Queen Anne LAD06	Retrd.	1991	10.00	450-625
1990 San Francisco Italianate-yellow LAD03	Retrd.	1992	10.00	54-200
1990 San Francisco Stick House-blue LAD02	Retrd.	1991	10.00	70-84
1990 San Francisco Stick House-yellow LAD01	Retrd.	1991	10.00	63-150
1990 Painted Ladies I Sign	Retrd.	N/A	12.50	30

Painted Ladies II - S. Thompson

YEAR ISSUE	EDITION LIMIT	YEAR RETD.	ISSUE PRICE	*QUOTE U.S.$
1994 Cape May Gothic (renovated) LAD13II	Retrd.	1995	16.00	31-35
1992 Cape May Gothic LAD13	Retrd.	1995	15.00	28-45
1994 Cape May Victorian Pink House (renovated) LAD16II	Retrd.	1996	16.00	28-30
1992 Cape May Victorian Pink House LAD16	Retrd.	1996	15.00	30-35
1994 The Gingerbread Mansion (renovated) LAD09II	Retrd.	1994	16.00	25-37
1992 The Gingerbread Mansion LAD09	Retrd.	1993	15.00	20-45
1994 Morningstar Inn (renovated) LAD15II	Retrd.	1994	16.00	24-32
1992 Morningstar Inn LAD15	Retrd.	1994	15.00	25
1994 Pitkin House (renovated) LAD10II	Retrd.	1996	16.00	30-35
1992 Pitkin House LAD10	Retrd.	1996	15.00	48
1994 Queen Anne Townhouse (renovated) LAD12II	Retrd.	1994	16.00	30-35
1992 Queen Anne Townhouse LAD12	Retrd.	1994	15.00	35
1994 The Victorian Blue Rose (renovated) LAD14II	Retrd.	1996	16.00	35-60
1992 The Victorian Blue Rose LAD14	Retrd.	1996	15.00	17-25
1994 The Young-Larson House (renovated) LAD11II	Retrd.	1996	16.00	35-45
1992 The Young-Larson House LAD11	Retrd.	1996	15.00	25-45

Painted Ladies III - S. Thompson

YEAR ISSUE	EDITION LIMIT	YEAR RETD.	ISSUE PRICE	*QUOTE U.S.$
1994 Cape May Green Stockton Row (renovated) LAD20II	Retrd.	1995	16.00	25-35
1993 Cape May Green Stockton Row LAD20	Retrd.	1995	16.00	30-45
1994 Cape May Linda Lee (renovated) LAD17II	Retrd.	1996	16.00	25-30
1993 Cape May Linda Lee LAD17	Retrd.	1996	16.00	23-45
1994 Cape May Pink Stockton Row (renovated)LAD19II	Retrd.	1998	16.00	21
1993 Cape May Pink Stockton Row LAD19	Retrd.	1998	16.00	21
1994 Cape May Tan Stockton Row (renovated)LAD18II	Retrd.	1998	16.00	16-21
1993 Cape May Tan Stockton Row LAD18	Retrd.	1998	16.00	21
1996 Cream Stockton LAD22	Retrd.	1998	19.00	19-21
1996 Cream Stockton, AP LAD22	101	1996	24.00	28-48
1995 Steiner Cottage LAD21	Retrd.	1998	17.00	18-21
1995 Steiner Cottage, AP LAD21	Retrd.	1995	24.00	48

Panoramic Lights - S. Thompson

YEAR ISSUE	EDITION LIMIT	YEAR RETD.	ISSUE PRICE	*QUOTE U.S.$
1996 Jeffrys Hook Light PLH02	Open		19.00	21
1996 Jeffrys Hook Light, AP PLH02	97	1996	24.00	28-48
1996 New Canal Light PLH03	Open		19.00	21
1996 New Canal Light, AP PLH03	104	1996	24.00	28-48
1997 Portland Head Light PLH05	Open		21.00	21
1996 Quoddy Head Light PLH04	Open		19.00	21
1996 Quoddy Head Light, AP PLH04	102	1996	24.00	28-48
1996 Split Rock Light PLH01	Open		19.00	21
1996 Split Rock Light, AP PLH01	105	1996	24.00	38-48

Panoramic Lights II - S. Thompson

YEAR ISSUE	EDITION LIMIT	YEAR RETD.	ISSUE PRICE	*QUOTE U.S.$
1998 Cape Hatterous Lighthouse PLH06	Open		22.00	22
1998 Middle Bay Lighthouse PLH09	Open		22.00	22
1998 Pensacola Lighthouse PLH07	Open		22.00	22
1998 Sanibel Lighthouse PLH08	Open		22.00	22

Philadelphia - S. Thompson

YEAR ISSUE	EDITION LIMIT	YEAR RETD.	ISSUE PRICE	*QUOTE U.S.$
1990 "Besty" Ross House (misspelling) PHI03	Retrd.	1990	15.00	20-45
1990 Betsy Ross House PHI03	Retrd.	1993	15.00	58-75
1990 Carpenter's Hall PHI01	Retrd.	1993	15.00	47-50
1990 Elphreth's Alley PHI05	Retrd.	1993	15.00	35-40
1990 Graff House PHI07	Retrd.	1993	15.00	37-41
1990 Independence Hall PHI04	Retrd.	1993	15.00	75-86
1990 Market St. Post Office PHI02	Retrd.	1993	15.00	24-45
1990 Old City Hall PHI08	Retrd.	1993	15.00	24-45
1990 Old Tavern PHI06	Retrd.	1993	15.00	27-45
1990 Set of 8	Retrd.	1993	120.00	230

Plantations - S. Thompson

YEAR ISSUE	EDITION LIMIT	YEAR RETD.	ISSUE PRICE	*QUOTE U.S.$
1996 Dickey House PLA05	Retrd.	1998	19.00	18-21
1995 Farley PLA04	Retrd.	1996	18.00	29
1995 Farley, AP PLA04	Retrd.	1995	24.00	25-70
1995 Longwood PLA02	Retrd.	1998	19.00	19-21
1995 Longwood, AP PLA02	Retrd.	1995	24.00	48
1995 Merry Sherwood PLA03	Retrd.	1998	18.00	18-21
1995 Merry Sherwood, AP PLA03	Retrd.	1995	24.00	48
1995 San Francisco PLA01	Retrd.		19.00	19-21
1995 San Francisco, AP PLA01	Retrd.	1995	24.00	29-65

San Francisco - S. Thompson

YEAR ISSUE	EDITION LIMIT	YEAR RETD.	ISSUE PRICE	*QUOTE U.S.$
1995 Brandywine SF101	Retrd.	1998	18.00	19-21
1995 Brandywine, AP SF101	Retrd.	1995	24.00	48
1995 Eclectic Blue SF103	Retrd.	1998	19.00	19-21
1995 Eclectic Blue, AP SF103	Retrd.	1995	24.00	48
1995 Edwardian Green SF104	Retrd.	1998	18.00	18-21
1995 Edwardian Green, AP SF104	Retrd.	1995	24.00	48
1995 Queen Rose SF102	Retrd.	1998	19.00	19-27
1995 Queen Rose, AP SF102	Retrd.	1995	24.00	27-48

San Francisco II/ Postcard Row - S. Thompson

YEAR ISSUE	EDITION LIMIT	YEAR RETD.	ISSUE PRICE	*QUOTE U.S.$
1998 716 Steiner Street SF108	Open		21.00	21
1998 716 Steiner Street, AP SF108	275		25.00	25
1998 718 Steiner Street SF107	Open		21.00	21
1998 718 Steiner Street, AP SF107	275		25.00	25
1998 720 Steiner Street SF106	Open		21.00	21
1998 720 Steiner Street, AP SF106	275		25.00	25
1998 722 Steiner Street SF105	Open		21.00	21
1998 722 Steiner Street, AP SF105	275		25.00	25

Savannah - S. Thompson

YEAR ISSUE	EDITION LIMIT	YEAR RETD.	ISSUE PRICE	*QUOTE U.S.$
1990 Andrew Low Mansion SAV02	Retrd.	1994	15.00	41-45
1996 Asendorf House SAV13	Open		19.00	22
1996 Asendorf House, AP SAV13	100	1996	24.00	75-80
1994 Cathedral of St. John (renovated) SAV09II	Retrd.	1995	16.00	110-150
1992 Cathedral of St. John SAV09	Retrd.	1995	16.00	70-200
1994 Chestnutt House SAV11	Open		18.00	22
1994 Chestnutt House, AP SAV11	Retrd.	1994	24.00	50
1990 Davenport House SAV03	Retrd.	1994	15.00	37-225
1990 Herb House SAV05	Retrd.	1993	15.00	40-109
1994 Juliette Low House (renovated) SAV04II	Retrd.	1998	15.00	21
1990 Juliette Low House (w/logo) SAV04	Retrd.	1994	15.00	21
1990 Juliette Low House (w/o logo) SAV04	Retrd.	1990	15.00	100-130
1998 King Tisdale SAV14	Open		22.00	22
1995 Mercer House SAV12	Retrd.	1998	18.00	20-58
1995 Mercer House, AP SAV12	Retrd.	1995	24.00	42-225
1990 Mikve Israel Temple SAV06	Retrd.	1994	15.00	65-275
1994 Olde Pink House (renovated) SAV01II	Retrd.	1996	15.00	40-195
1990 Olde Pink House SAV01	Retrd.	1996	15.00	27-52
1994 Owens Thomas House (renovated) SAV10II	Retrd.	1996	16.00	55-80
1993 Owens Thomas House SAV10	Retrd.	1996	16.00	29-40
1993 Owens Thomas House, AP SAV10	Retrd.	1993	20.00	27-140
1990 Savannah Gingerbread House I SAV08	Retrd.	1990	15.00	145-210
1990 Savannah Gingerbread House II SAV08	Retrd.	1992	15.00	450
1998 Tybee Island Light Station II SAV15	Open		23.00	23

Shadow Play Silhouettes - S. Thompson

YEAR ISSUE	EDITION LIMIT	YEAR RETD.	ISSUE PRICE	*QUOTE U.S.$
1996 Girl w/Hoop & Boy w/Dog SPO03	Open		12.00	15
1996 Horse and Carriage SPO01	Open		15.00	20
1996 Victorian Couple & Bicycle SPO02	Open		15.00	20

Shadow Play Silhouettes Accessories - S. Thompson

YEAR ISSUE	EDITION LIMIT	YEAR RETD.	ISSUE PRICE	*QUOTE U.S.$
1997 Lamp Post, set/2 SPO07	Retrd.	1997	12.00	12

Shadow Play Silhouettes II - S. Thompson

YEAR ISSUE	EDITION LIMIT	YEAR RETD.	ISSUE PRICE	*QUOTE U.S.$
1996 Amish Buggy SPO04	Open		19.50	20
1996 Amish Clothesline SPO05	Open		19.50	20
1996 Amish Couple and Amish Boy SPO06	Open		15.00	15

Show Pieces - S. Thompson

YEAR ISSUE	EDITION LIMIT	YEAR RETD.	ISSUE PRICE	*QUOTE U.S.$
1995 Baldwin House SHW01	Retrd.	1995	20.00	29-34
1996 The Winnie Watson House SHW02	Retrd.	1996	20.00	22-24

Sights to See - S. Thompson

YEAR ISSUE	EDITION LIMIT	YEAR RETD.	ISSUE PRICE	*QUOTE U.S.$
1998 Belle of Louisville SEE07	Open		19.00	19
1998 Coffee Pot SEE05	Open		19.00	19
1998 Coffee Pot, AP SEE05	130		39.00	39
1997 Cypress Garden Gazebo SEE01	Open		19.00	19
1998 Elephant Hotel SEE04	Open		18.00	18
1998 Elephant Hotel, AP SEE04	130		38.00	38
1997 Sorensen Windmill SEE02	Open		18.00	18
1998 Space Needle SEE06	Open		24.00	24
1998 Space Needle, AP SEE06	130		44.00	44
1997 Swan Boat SEE03	Open		16.00	16

South Carolina - S. Thompson

YEAR ISSUE	EDITION LIMIT	YEAR RETD.	ISSUE PRICE	*QUOTE U.S.$
1991 All Saints' Church SC105	Retrd.	1993	15.00	26-42
1990 The Governer's Mansion (misspelling) SC102	Retrd.	1990	15.00	30-100
1994 The Governor's Mansion (renovated) SC102II	Retrd.	1995	15.00	30-50
1990 The Governor's Mansion SC102	Retrd.	1995	15.00	22-30
1994 The Hermitage (renovated) SC101II	Retrd.	1995	15.00	45-50
1990 The Hermitage SC101	Retrd.	1995	15.00	55
1994 The Lace House (renovated) SC103II	Retrd.	1995	15.00	15-75
1990 The Lace House SC103	Retrd.	1995	15.00	35-40
1994 The State Capitol (renovated) SC104II	Retrd.	1994	15.00	22-115
1991 The State Capitol SC104	Retrd.	1994	15.00	30

South Carolina Ladies - S. Thompson

YEAR ISSUE	EDITION LIMIT	YEAR RETD.	ISSUE PRICE	*QUOTE U.S.$
1996 Cinnamon Hill SCL04	Open		19.00	22
1996 Cinnamon Hill, AP SCL04	93	1996	24.00	28-48
1996 Davis-Johnsey House SCL02	Open		19.00	22
1996 Davis-Johnsey House, AP SCL02	104	1996	24.00	28-48
1996 Inman House SCL01	Open		19.00	22
1996 Inman House, AP SCL01	107	1996	24.00	28-48
1996 Montgomery House SCL03	Open		19.00	22
1996 Montgomery House, AP SCL03	105	1996	24.00	24-48

St. Augustine - S. Thompson

YEAR ISSUE	EDITION LIMIT	YEAR RETD.	ISSUE PRICE	*QUOTE U.S.$
1991 Anastasia Lighthousekeeper's House FL104	Retrd.	1993	15.00	40-55
1991 Mission Nombre deDios FL105	Retrd.	1993	15.00	45-50
1991 Old City Gates FL102	Retrd.	1993	15.00	25-30
1991 The "Oldest House" FL101	Retrd.	1993	15.00	30-55
1991 Set	Retrd.	1993	60.00	115

Texas - S. Thompson

YEAR ISSUE	EDITION LIMIT	YEAR RETD.	ISSUE PRICE	*QUOTE U.S.$
1990 The Alamo TEX01	Retrd.	1993	15.00	157-350
1990 Mission Concepcion TEX04	Retrd.	1993	15.00	47-94
1990 Mission San Francisco TEX03	Retrd.	1993	15.00	63-94
1990 Mission San Jose' TEX02	Retrd.	1993	15.00	47-94
1990 Texas Sign	Retrd.	N/A	12.50	20

Town Square Nativity Series - S. Thompson

YEAR ISSUE	EDITION LIMIT	YEAR RETD.	ISSUE PRICE	*QUOTE U.S.$
1998 Borrowed Elf TSN04	Open		15.00	15
1998 Heartsville Gazebo TSN01	Open		26.00	26
1998 Heartsville's Lil Angels TSN03	Open		19.00	19
1998 Michael Keeping Watch TSN02	Open		19.00	19
1998 Town Square Church TSN05	Open		22.00	22
1998 Town Square Nativity OFC07L	11,997	1998	27.00	27-30

Victorian Springtime - S. Thompson

YEAR ISSUE	EDITION LIMIT	YEAR RETD.	ISSUE PRICE	*QUOTE U.S.$
1993 Heffron House VST03	Retrd.	1996	17.00	25-50
1993 Heffron House, AP VST03	Retrd.	1993	20.00	60
1993 Jacobsen House VST04	Retrd.	1996	17.00	25-45
1993 Jacobsen House, AP VST04	Retrd.	1993	20.00	60
1993 Ralston House VST01	Retrd.	1996	17.00	25-40
1993 Ralston House, AP VST01	Retrd.	1993	20.00	100
1993 Sessions House VST02	Retrd.	1996	17.00	25-40
1993 Sessions House, AP VST02	Retrd.	1993	20.00	70
1993 Set of 4, AP	Retrd.	1993	100.00	180

Victorian Springtime II - S. Thompson

YEAR ISSUE	EDITION LIMIT	YEAR RETD.	ISSUE PRICE	*QUOTE U.S.$
1995 Dragon House VST07	Retrd.	1997	18.00	22-25
1995 Dragon House, AP VST07	Retrd.	1995	24.00	60
1995 E.B. Hall House VST08	Retrd.	1997	19.00	21-25
1995 E.B. Hall House, AP VST08	Retrd.	1995	24.00	60
1995 Gibney Home VST09	Retrd.	1997	18.00	25-35
1995 Gibney Home, AP VST09	Retrd.	1995	24.00	60
1995 Ray Home VST05	Retrd.	1997	18.00	25-29
1995 Ray Home, AP VST05	Retrd.	1995	24.00	60
1995 Victoria VST06	Retrd.	1997	18.00	25-35
1995 Victoria, AP VST06	Retrd.	1995	24.00	25-60

Victorian Springtime III - S. Thompson

YEAR ISSUE	EDITION LIMIT	YEAR RETD.	ISSUE PRICE	*QUOTE U.S.$
1996 Clark House VST14	Open		19.00	22
1996 Clark House, AP VST14	96	1996	24.00	28-50
1996 Goodwill House VST13	Open		19.00	22
1996 Goodwill House, AP VST13	88	1996	24.00	25-50
1996 Queen-Anne Mansion VST12	Open		19.00	22
1996 Queen-Anne Mansion, AP VST12	103	1996	24.00	28-50
1996 Sheppard House VST11	Open		19.00	22
1996 Sheppard House, AP VST11	98	1996	24.00	28-50
1996 Urfer House VST10	Open		19.00	22
1996 Urfer House, AP VST10	71	1996	24.00	25-50

Victorian Springtime IV - S. Thompson

YEAR ISSUE	EDITION LIMIT	YEAR RETD.	ISSUE PRICE	*QUOTE U.S.$
1997 Allyn Mansion VST19	Open		22.00	22
1997 Allyn Mansion, AP VST19	200		28.00	28
1997 Halstead House VST16	Open		22.00	22
1997 Halstead House, AP VST16	217		28.00	28
1997 Harvard House VST15	Open		22.00	22
1997 Harvard House, AP VST15	234		28.00	28
1997 Rosewood VST18	Open		22.00	22
1997 Rosewood, AP VST18	244		28.00	28
1997 Zabriskie House VST17	Open		22.00	22
1997 Zabriskie House, AP VST17	230		28.00	28

Victorian Springtime V - S. Thompson

YEAR ISSUE	EDITION LIMIT	YEAR RETD.	ISSUE PRICE	*QUOTE U.S.$
1997 Angel Sister VST24	Open		22.00	22
1997 Angel Sister, AP VST24	270		28.00	28
1997 Frank Hastings House VST21	Open		22.00	22
1997 Frank Hastings House, AP VST21	265		28.00	28
1997 George Little House VST20	Open		22.00	22
1997 George Little House, AP VST20	250		28.00	28
1997 George Roberts VST25	Open		22.00	22
1997 George Roberts, AP VST25	255		28.00	28
1997 Kirby House VST22	Open		22.00	22
1997 Kirby House, AP VST22	240		28.00	28
1997 Southdown VST23	Open		22.00	22
1997 Southdown, AP VST23	250		28.00	28

Victorian Springtime VI - S. Thompson

YEAR ISSUE	EDITION LIMIT	YEAR RETD.	ISSUE PRICE	*QUOTE U.S.$
1998 Anderson House VST28	Open		23.00	23
1998 Barnes Penn House VST29	Open		23.00	23
1998 Gladus Pyle Home VST26	Open		23.00	23
1998 Parrot Camp Soucy House VST27	Open		23.00	23

Washington D.C. - S. Thompson

YEAR ISSUE	EDITION LIMIT	YEAR RETD.	ISSUE PRICE	*QUOTE U.S.$
1992 Cherry Trees DC005	Retrd.	1993	12.00	34-37
1992 Library of Congress DC002	Retrd.	1993	16.00	37-86
1991 National Archives DC001	Retrd.	1993	16.00	37-42
1991 Washington Monument DC004	Retrd.	1993	16.00	37-47
1992 White House DC003	Retrd.	1993	16.00	157-161
1992 Set of 5	Retrd.	1993	76.00	190-750

West Coast Lighthouse Series - S. Thompson

YEAR ISSUE	EDITION LIMIT	YEAR RETD.	ISSUE PRICE	*QUOTE U.S.$
1995 East Brother Light WCL01	Retrd.	1998	19.00	21
1995 East Brother Light, AP WCL01	Retrd.	1995	24.00	48
1995 Mukilteo Light WCL02	Retrd.	1998	18.00	21
1995 Mukilteo Light, AP WCL02	Retrd.	1995	24.00	48
1995 Point Fermin Light WCL04	Retrd.	1998	18.00	21
1995 Point Fermin Light, AP WCL04	Retrd.	1995	24.00	48
1995 Yaquina Bay Light WCL03	Retrd.	1998	18.00	21
1995 Yaquina Bay Light, AP WCL03	Retrd.	1995	24.00	48

Williamsburg - S. Thompson

YEAR ISSUE	EDITION LIMIT	YEAR RETD.	ISSUE PRICE	*QUOTE U.S.$
1990 Apothecary WIL09	Retrd.	1994	12.00	22-35
1994 Bruton Parish Church (renovated) WIL13II	Retrd.	1997	15.00	28-30
1992 Bruton Parish Church WIL13	Retrd.	1997	15.00	25-50
1995 Capitol WIL15	Open		18.00	21
1995 Capitol, AP WIL15	Retrd.	1995	24.00	50
1994 Courthouse (renovated) WIL11II	Retrd.	1995	15.00	25-40
1990 Courthouse WIL11	Retrd.	1995	15.00	24-30
1990 The Golden Ball Jeweler WIL07	Retrd.	1994	12.00	21-24
1997 Govenor's Palace Formal Entrance WIL17	Open		22.00	22
1997 Govenor's Palace Formal Entrance, AP WIL17	265		28.00	28
1994 Governor's Palace (renovated) WIL04II	Retrd.	1997	15.00	22-30
1990 Governor's Palace WIL04	Retrd.	1997	15.00	17-40
1994 Homesite (renovated) WIL12II	Retrd.	1996	15.00	17-35
1990 Homesite WIL12	Retrd.	1996	15.00	17-35
1994 King's Arm Tavern (renovated) WIL10II	Retrd.	1995	15.00	32-50
1990 King's Arm Tavern WIL10	Retrd.	1995	15.00	27-45
1990 Milliner WIL06	Retrd.	1994	12.00	29-51
1990 Nicolson Shop WIL08	Retrd.	1994	12.00	20-25
1990 The Printing Offices WIL05	Retrd.	1993	12.00	23-30
1995 Raleigh Tavern WIL14	Open		18.00	21
1995 Raleigh Tavern, AP WIL14	Retrd.	1995	24.00	45
1997 Taylor House WIL16	Open		21.00	21
1997 Taylor House, AP WIL16	235		27.00	27

BELLS

Artists of the World

DeGrazia Bells - T. DeGrazia

YEAR ISSUE	EDITION LIMIT	YEAR RETD.	ISSUE PRICE	*QUOTE U.S.$
1980 Festival of Lights	5,000	N/A	40.00	39-75
1980 Los Ninos	7,500	N/A	40.00	46-80
1980 Los Ninos (signed)	500	N/A	80.00	250

Belleek

Belleek Bells - Belleek

YEAR ISSUE	EDITION LIMIT	YEAR RETD.	ISSUE PRICE	*QUOTE U.S.$
1988 Bell, 1st Ed.	Yr.Iss.	1988	38.00	38
1989 Tower, 2nd Ed.	Yr.Iss.	1989	35.00	35
1990 Leprechaun, 3rd Ed.	Yr.Iss.	1990	30.00	30
1991 Church, 4th Ed.	Yr.Iss.	1991	32.00	32
1992 Cottage, 5th Ed.	Yr.Iss.	1992	30.00	30
1993 Pub, 6th Ed.	Yr.Iss.	1993	30.00	30
1994 Castle, 7th Ed.	Yr.Iss.	1994	30.00	30
1995 Georgian House, 8th Ed.	Yr.Iss.	1995	30.00	30
1996 Cathedral, 9th Ed.	Yr.Iss.	1996	30.00	30
1997 Hazlewood House	Yr.Iss.	1997	30.00	30
1998 Ballylist Mill	Yr.Iss.		30.00	30

Twelve Days of Christmas - Belleek

YEAR ISSUE	EDITION LIMIT	YEAR RETD.	ISSUE PRICE	*QUOTE U.S.$
1991 A Partridge in a Pear Tree	Yr.Iss.	1991	30.00	30
1992 Two Turtle Doves	Yr.Iss.	1992	30.00	30
1993 Three French Hens	Yr.Iss.	1993	30.00	30
1994 Four Calling Birds	Yr.Iss.	1994	30.00	30

Cherished Teddies/Enesco Corporation

Cherished Teddies Bell - P. Hillman

YEAR ISSUE	EDITION LIMIT	YEAR RETD.	ISSUE PRICE	*QUOTE U.S.$
1992 Angel Bell 906530	Suspd.		20.00	88-120

Dave Grossman Creations

Norman Rockwell Collection - Rockwell-Inspired

YEAR ISSUE	EDITION LIMIT	YEAR RETD.	ISSUE PRICE	*QUOTE U.S.$
1975 Faces of Christmas NRB-75	Retrd.	N/A	12.50	35
1976 Drum for Tommy NRB-76	Retrd.	N/A	12.00	30
1976 Ben Franklin (Bicentennial)	Retrd.	N/A	12.50	25
1980 Leapfrog NRB-80	Retrd.	N/A	50.00	60

Fenton Art Glass Company

1996 Designer Bell - Various

YEAR ISSUE	EDITION LIMIT	YEAR RETD.	ISSUE PRICE	*QUOTE U.S.$
1996 Floral Medallion, 6" - M. Reynolds	2,500	1996	50.00	50-60
1996 Gardenia, 7" - R. Spindler	2,500	1996	55.00	55-60
1996 Gilded Berry, 6 1/2" - F. Burton	2,500	1996	60.00	55-60
1996 Wild Rose, 5 1/2" - K. Plauché	2,500	1996	60.00	50-60

1997 Designer Bell - Various

YEAR ISSUE	EDITION LIMIT	YEAR RETD.	ISSUE PRICE	*QUOTE U.S.$
1997 Butterflies, 6" - M. Reynolds	2,500	1997	59.00	59
1997 Feathers, 6 3/4" - R. Spindler	2,500	1997	59.00	59
1997 Forest Cottage, 7" - F. Burton	2,500	1997	59.00	59
1997 Roses on Ribbons, 6 1/2" - K. Plauché	2,500	1997	59.00	59

1998 Designer Bell - Various

YEAR ISSUE	EDITION LIMIT	YEAR RETD.	ISSUE PRICE	*QUOTE U.S.$
1998 Bleeding Hearts, 7" - R. Spindler	2,500	1998	59.00	59
1998 Fairy Roses, 6" - K. Plauché	2,500	1998	59.00	59
1998 Hibiscus, 6 1/2" - F. Burton	2,500	1998	59.00	59
1998 Topaz Swirl, 7" - M. Reynolds	2,500	1998	59.00	59

Christmas - Various

YEAR ISSUE	EDITION LIMIT	YEAR RETD.	ISSUE PRICE	*QUOTE U.S.$
1978 Christmas Morn - M. Dickinson	Yr.Iss.	1978	25.00	25-45
1979 Nature's Christmas - K. Cunningham	Yr.Iss.	1979	30.00	30-45
1980 Going Home - D. Johnson	Yr.Iss.	1980	32.50	35-45
1981 All Is Calm - D. Johnson	Yr.Iss.	1981	35.00	35-45
1982 Country Christmas - R. Spindler	Yr.Iss.	1982	35.00	35
1983 Anticipation - D. Johnson	7,500	1983	35.00	35-48
1984 Expectation - D. Johnson	7,500	1984	37.50	38-45
1985 Heart's Desire - D. Johnson	7,500	1986	37.50	38-45
1987 Sharing The Spirit - L. Everson	Yr.Iss.	1987	37.50	38-45
1987 Cardinal in the Churchyard - D. Johnson	4,500	1987	29.50	30-45
1988 A Chickadee Ballet - D. Johnson	4,500	1988	29.50	30-45
1989 Downy Pecker - Chisled Song - D. Johnson	4,500	1989	29.50	30-45
1990 A Blue Bird in Snowfall - D. Johnson	4,500	1990	29.50	30-45
1990 Sleigh Ride - F. Burton	3,500	1990	39.00	39-50
1991 Christmas Eve - F. Burton	3,500	1991	35.00	35-50
1992 Family Tradition - F. Burton	3,500	1992	39.00	39-50
1993 Family Holiday - F. Burton	3,500	1993	39.50	40-50
1994 Silent Night - F. Burton	2,500	1994	45.00	45-60
1995 Our Home Is Blessed - F. Burton	2,500	1995	45.00	45-50
1996 Star of Wonder - F. Burton	2,500	1996	48.00	48-65
1997 The Way Home - F. Burton	2,500	1997	65.00	65
1998 The Arrival - F. Burton	2,500		55.00	55

Connoisseur Bell - Various

YEAR ISSUE	EDITION LIMIT	YEAR RETD.	ISSUE PRICE	*QUOTE U.S.$
1983 Bell, Burmese Handpainted - L. Everson	2,000	1983	50.00	125
1983 Craftsman Bell, White Satin Carnival - Fenton	3,500	1983	25.00	50
1984 Bell, Famous Women's Ruby Satin Irid. - Fenton	3,500	1984	25.00	50-65
1985 Bell, 6 1/2" Burmese, Hndpt. - L. Everson	2,500	1985	55.00	125
1986 Bell, Burmese-Shells, Hndpt. - D. Barbour	2,500	1986	60.00	125
1988 Bell, 7" Wisteria, Hndpt. - L. Everson	4,000	1988	45.00	85-125
1989 Bell, 7" Handpainted Rosalene Satin - L. Everson	3,500	1989	50.00	85
1991 Bell, 7" Roses on Rosalene, Hndpt. - M. Reynolds	2,000	1991	50.00	85

Mary Gregory - M. Reynolds

YEAR ISSUE	EDITION LIMIT	YEAR RETD.	ISSUE PRICE	*QUOTE U.S.$
1993 Bell, 6" Ruby	Closed	1993	49.00	75
1994 Bell, 6" Ruby - Loves Me, Loves Me Not	Closed	1994	49.00	75
1995 Bell, 6 1/2"	Closed	1995	49.00	75

Goebel/M.I. Hummel

M.I. Hummel Collectibles Annual Bells - M. I. Hummel

YEAR ISSUE	EDITION LIMIT	YEAR RETD.	ISSUE PRICE	*QUOTE U.S.$
1978 Let's Sing 700	Closed	N/A	50.00	22-195
1979 Farewell 701	Closed	N/A	70.00	18-70
1980 Thoughtful 702	Closed	N/A	85.00	19-95
1981 In Tune 703	Closed	N/A	85.00	22-115
1982 She Loves Me, She Loves Me Not 704	Closed	N/A	90.00	49-156
1983 Knit One 705	Closed	N/A	90.00	44-170
1984 Mountaineer 706	Closed	N/A	90.00	54-145
1985 Sweet Song 707	Closed	N/A	90.00	37-145
1986 Sing Along 708	Closed	N/A	100.00	52-295
1987 With Loving Greetings 709	Closed	N/A	110.00	124-325
1988 Busy Student 710	Closed	N/A	120.00	80-225
1989 Latest News 711	Closed	N/A	135.00	82-240
1990 What's New? 712	Closed	N/A	140.00	105-265
1991 Favorite Pet 713	Closed	N/A	150.00	119-325
1992 Whistler's Duet 714	Closed	N/A	160.00	69-275

Gorham

Currier & Ives - Mini Bells - Currier & Ives

YEAR ISSUE	EDITION LIMIT	YEAR RETD.	ISSUE PRICE	*QUOTE U.S.$
1976 Christmas Sleigh Ride	Annual	1976	9.95	35
1977 American Homestead	Annual	1977	9.95	25
1978 Yule Logs	Annual	1978	12.95	20
1979 Sleigh Ride	Annual	1979	14.95	20
1980 Christmas in the Country	Annual	1980	14.95	20
1981 Christmas Tree	Annual	1981	14.95	18
1982 Christmas Visitation	Annual	1982	16.50	18
1983 Winter Wonderland	Annual	1983	16.50	18
1984 Hitching Up	Annual	1984	16.50	18
1985 Skaters Holiday	Annual	1985	17.50	18
1986 Central Park in Winter	Annual	1986	17.50	18
1987 Early Winter	Annual	1987	19.00	19

Mini Bells - N. Rockwell

YEAR ISSUE	EDITION LIMIT	YEAR RETD.	ISSUE PRICE	*QUOTE U.S.$
1981 Tiny Tim	Annual	1981	19.75	20
1982 Planning Christmas Visit	Annual	1982	20.00	20

Various - N. Rockwell

YEAR ISSUE	EDITION LIMIT	YEAR RETD.	ISSUE PRICE	*QUOTE U.S.$
1975 Sweet Song So Young	Annual	1975	19.50	50
1975 Santa's Helpers	Annual	1975	19.50	50
1975 Tavern Sign Painter	Annual	1975	19.50	30
1976 Flowers in Tender Bloom	Annual	1976	19.50	40
1976 Snow Sculpture	Annual	1976	19.50	45
1977 Fondly Do We Remember	Annual	1977	19.50	55
1977 Chilling Chore (Christmas)	Annual	1977	19.50	35
1978 Gaily Sharing Vintage Times	Annual	1978	22.50	23
1978 Gay Blades (Christmas)	Annual	1978	22.50	45
1979 Beguiling Buttercup	Annual	1979	24.50	45
1979 A Boy Meets His Dog (Christmas)	Annual	1979	24.50	50
1980 Flying High	Annual	1980	27.50	45
1980 Chilly Reception (Christmas)	Annual	1980	27.50	28
1981 Sweet Serenade	Annual	1981	27.50	45
1981 Ski Skills (Christmas)	Annual	1981	27.50	45
1982 Young Mans Fancy	Annual	1982	29.50	30
1982 Coal Season's Coming	Annual	1982	29.50	30
1983 Christmas Medley	Annual	1983	29.50	30
1983 The Milkmaid	Annual	1983	29.50	30
1984 Tiny Tim	Annual	1984	29.50	45
1984 Young Love	Annual	1984	29.50	45
1984 Marriage License	Annual	1984	32.50	45
1984 Yarn Spinner	5,000	1984	32.50	33
1985 Yuletide Reflections	5,000	1985	32.50	50
1986 Home For The Holidays	5,000	1986	32.50	45
1986 On Top of the World	5,000	1986	32.50	45
1987 Merry Christmas Grandma	5,000	1987	32.50	33
1987 The Artist	5,000	1987	32.50	33
1988 The Homecoming	15,000	1988	37.50	38

Greenwich Workshop

The Greenwich Workshop Collection - J. Christensen

YEAR ISSUE	EDITION LIMIT	YEAR RETD.	ISSUE PRICE	*QUOTE U.S.$
1997 The Sound of Christmas	4,896		59.00	59
1997 Christmas Bell	5,000		59.00	59
1998 '98 Mrs. Claus Bell	Open		59.00	59

Jan Hagara Collectables

Figural Bells - J. Hagara

YEAR ISSUE	EDITION LIMIT	YEAR RETD.	ISSUE PRICE	*QUOTE U.S.$
1986 Jenny Bell	2-Yr.	1988	25.00	25-35
1986 Jody Bell	2-Yr.	1988	25.00	25-35
1986 Lisa Bell	2-Yr.	1988	25.00	25-35
1986 Carol Bell	2-Yr.	1988	25.00	25
1986 Chris Bell	2-Yr.	1988	25.00	25
1986 Noel Bell	2-Yr.	1988	25.00	25
1986 Lydia Bell	2-Yr.	1988	25.00	25-35
1986 Betsy Bell	2-Yr.	1988	25.00	25-35
1986 Jimmy Bell	2-Yr.	1988	35.00	25-35
1986 Jill Bell	2-Yr.	1988	35.00	35-75
1987 Holly Bell	Yr.Iss.	1988	35.00	35
1988 Marie Bell	Yr.Iss.	1989	35.00	35

Kirk Stieff

Bell - Kirk Stieff

YEAR ISSUE	EDITION LIMIT	YEAR RETD.	ISSUE PRICE	*QUOTE U.S.$
1992 Santa's Workshop	3,000		40.00	40
1993 Santa's Reindeer	Closed	N/A	30.00	30

Musical Bells - Kirk Stieff

YEAR ISSUE	EDITION LIMIT	YEAR RETD.	ISSUE PRICE	*QUOTE U.S.$
1977 Annual Bell 1977	Closed	N/A	17.95	40-125
1978 Annual Bell 1978	Closed	N/A	17.95	21-100
1979 Annual Bell 1979	Closed	N/A	17.95	21-60
1980 Annual Bell 1980	Closed	N/A	19.95	21-55
1981 Annual Bell 1981	Closed	N/A	19.95	21-30
1982 Annual Bell 1982	Closed	N/A	19.95	21-30
1983 Annual Bell 1983	Closed	N/A	19.95	21-30
1984 Annual Bell 1984	Closed	N/A	19.95	21-30
1985 Annual Bell 1985	Closed	N/A	19.95	21-30
1986 Annual Bell 1986	Closed	N/A	19.95	21-30
1987 Annual Bell 1987	Closed	N/A	19.95	21-30
1988 Annual Bell 1988	Closed	N/A	22.50	21-30
1989 Annual Bell 1989	Closed	N/A	25.00	21-30
1990 Annual Bell 1990	Closed	N/A	27.00	21-30
1991 Annual Bell 1991	Closed	N/A	28.00	21-30
1992 Annual Bell 1992	Closed	N/A	30.00	21-30
1993 Annual Bell 1993	Closed	N/A	30.00	21-30
1994 Annual Bell 1994	Open	N/A	30.00	21-30

Lenox China

Songs of Christmas - Unknown

YEAR ISSUE	EDITION LIMIT	YEAR RETD.	ISSUE PRICE	*QUOTE U.S.$
1991 We Wish You a Merry Christmas	Yr.Iss.	1992	49.00	49
1992 Deck the Halls	Yr.Iss.	1993	53.00	53
1993 Jingle Bells	Yr.Iss.	1994	57.00	57
1994 Silver Bells	Yr.Iss.	1995	62.00	62
1995 Hark The Herald Angels Sing	Yr.Iss.	1996	62.50	63

Lenox Crystal

Annual Bell Series - Lenox

YEAR ISSUE	EDITION LIMIT	YEAR RETD.	ISSUE PRICE	*QUOTE U.S.$
1987 Partridge Bell	Yr.Iss.	1990	45.00	45
1988 Angel Bell	Open	1991	45.00	45
1989 St. Nicholas Bell	Open	1991	45.00	45
1990 Christmas Tree Bell	Open	1993	49.00	49
1991 Teddy Bear Bell	Yr.Iss.	1992	49.00	49
1992 Snowman Bell	Yr.Iss.	1993	49.00	49
1993 Nutcracker Bell	Yr.Iss.	1994	49.00	49
1994 Candle Bell	Yr.Iss.	1995	49.00	49
1995 Bell	Yr.Iss.	1996	49.50	50
1996 Bell	Yr.Iss.		49.50	50

Lladró

Lladró Bell - Lladró

YEAR ISSUE	EDITION LIMIT	YEAR RETD.	ISSUE PRICE	*QUOTE U.S.$
XX Crystal Wedding Bell L4500	Closed	1985	35.00	195

Lladró Christmas Bell - Lladró

YEAR ISSUE	EDITION LIMIT	YEAR RETD.	ISSUE PRICE	*QUOTE U.S.$
1987 Christmas Bell - L5458M	Annual	1987	29.50	52-80
1988 Christmas Bell - L5525M	Annual	1988	32.50	39-59
1989 Christmas Bell - L5616M	Annual	1989	32.50	125-293
1990 Christmas Bell - L5641M	Annual	1990	35.00	60-104
1991 Christmas Bell - L5803M	Annual	1991	37.50	32-45
1992 Christmas Bell - L5913M	Annual	1992	37.50	38-59
1993 Christmas Bell - L6010M	Annual	1993	39.50	40-51
1994 Christmas Bell - L6139M	Annual	1994	39.50	50-163
1995 Christmas Bell - L6206M	Annual	1995	39.50	55-228
1996 Christmas Bell - L6297M	Annual	1996	39.50	40-98
1997 Christmas Bell - L6441M	Annual	1997	40.00	34-45
1998 Christmas Bell - 16560	Annual		40.00	40

Lladró Limited Edition Bell - Lladró

YEAR ISSUE	EDITION LIMIT	YEAR RETD.	ISSUE PRICE	*QUOTE U.S.$
1994 Eternal Love 7542M	Annual	1994	95.00	67-95

Lowell Davis Farm Club

RFD Bell - L. Davis

YEAR ISSUE	EDITION LIMIT	YEAR RETD.	ISSUE PRICE	*QUOTE U.S.$
1979 Blossom	Closed	1983	65.00	400
1979 Kate	Closed	1983	65.00	375-400
1979 Willy	Closed	1983	65.00	375
1979 Caruso	Closed	1983	65.00	275
1979 Wilbur	Closed	1983	65.00	375-400
1979 Old Blue Lead	Closed	1983	65.00	275
1993 Cow Bell "Blossom"	Closed	1994	65.00	75
1993 Mule Bell "Kate"	Closed	1994	65.00	75
1993 Goat Bell "Willy"	Closed	1994	65.00	75
1993 Rooster Bell "Caruso"	Closed	1994	65.00	75
1993 Pig Bell "Wilbur"	Closed	1994	65.00	75
1993 Dog Bell "Old Blue and Lead"	Closed	1994	65.00	75

Memories of Yesterday/Enesco Corporation

Annual Bells - M. Attwell

YEAR ISSUE	EDITION LIMIT	YEAR RETD.	ISSUE PRICE	*QUOTE U.S.$
1990 Here Comes the Bride-God Bless Her 523100	Suspd.		25.00	25
1994 Time For Bed 525243	Open		25.00	25

Precious Moments/Enesco Corporation

Annual Bells - S. Butcher

YEAR ISSUE	EDITION LIMIT	YEAR RETD.	ISSUE PRICE	*QUOTE U.S.$
1981 Let the Heavens Rejoice E-5622	Yr.Iss.	1981	17.00	225-250
1982 I'll Play My Drum for Him E-2358	Yr.Iss.	1982	17.00	65-82
1983 Surrounded With Joy E-0522	Yr.Iss.	1983	18.00	45-75
1984 Wishing You a Merry Christmas E-5393	Yr.Iss.	1984	19.00	45-50
1985 God Sent His Love 15873	Yr.Iss.	1985	19.00	35-45
1986 Wishing You a Cozy Christmas 102318	Yr.Iss.	1986	20.00	40-44
1987 Love is the Best Gift of All 109835	Yr.Iss.	1987	22.50	35
1988 Time To Wish You a Merry Christmas 115304	Yr.Iss.	1988	25.00	40
1989 Oh Holy Night 522821	Yr.Iss.	1989	25.00	35-38
1990 Once Upon A Holy Night 523828	Yr.Iss.	1990	25.00	35

*Quotes have been rounded up to nearest dollar

YEAR ISSUE	EDITION LIMIT	YEAR RETD.	ISSUE PRICE	*QUOTE U.S.$
1991 May Your Christmas Be Merry 524182	Yr.Iss.	1991	25.00	35
1992 But The Greatest Of These Is Love 527726	Yr.Iss.	1992	25.00	40
1993 Wishing You The Sweetest Christmas 530174	Yr.Iss.	1993	25.00	35-40
1994 Your're As Pretty as a Christmas Tree 604216	Yr.Iss.	1994	27.50	28-35

Various Bells - S. Butcher

YEAR ISSUE	EDITION LIMIT	YEAR RETD.	ISSUE PRICE	*QUOTE U.S.$
1981 Jesus Loves Me (B) E-5208	Suspd.		15.00	48-58
1981 Jesus Loves Me (G) E-5209	Suspd.		15.00	50
1981 Prayer Changes Things E-5210	Suspd.		15.00	55-60
1981 God Understands E-5211	Retrd.	1984	15.00	45-60
1981 We Have Seen His Star E-5620	Suspd.		15.00	50-60
1981 Jesus Is Born E-5623	Suspd.		15.00	50-60
1982 The Lord Bless You and Keep You E-7175	Suspd.		17.00	35-65
1982 The Lord Bless You and Keep You E-7176	Suspd.		17.00	55-65
1982 The Lord Bless You and Keep You E-7179	Suspd.		22.50	50-65
1982 Mother Sew Dear E-7181	Suspd.		17.00	45
1982 The Purr-fect Grandma E-7183	Suspd.		17.00	48-62

Reed & Barton

Noel Musical Bells - Reed & Barton

YEAR ISSUE	EDITION LIMIT	YEAR RETD.	ISSUE PRICE	*QUOTE U.S.$
1980 Bell 1980	Closed	1980	20.00	60-80
1981 Bell 1981	Closed	1981	22.50	30-60
1982 Bell 1982	Closed	1982	22.50	25-50
1983 Bell 1983	Closed	1983	22.50	25-60
1984 Bell 1984	Closed	1984	22.50	25-60
1985 Bell 1985	Closed	1985	25.00	25-55
1986 Bell 1986	Closed	1986	25.00	25-60
1987 Bell 1987	Closed	1987	25.00	25-60
1988 Bell 1988	Closed	1988	25.00	25-60
1989 Bell 1989	Closed	1989	25.00	25-60
1990 Bell 1990	Closed	1990	27.50	30
1991 Bell 1991	Closed	1991	30.00	30
1992 Bell 1992	Closed	1992	30.00	30-45
1993 Bell 1993	Yr.Iss.	1993	30.00	30-40
1994 Bell 1994	Yr.Iss.	1994	30.00	30-45
1995 Bell 1995	Yr.Iss.	1995	30.00	30
1996 Bell 1996	Yr.Iss.	1996	35.00	35
1997 Bell 1997	Yr.Iss.	1997	35.00	35
1998 Noel Bell 1998	Yr.Iss.		35.00	35

Yuletide Bell - Reed & Barton

YEAR ISSUE	EDITION LIMIT	YEAR RETD.	ISSUE PRICE	*QUOTE U.S.$
1981 Yuletide Holiday	Closed	1981	14.00	25
1982 Little Shepherd	Closed	1982	14.00	25
1983 Perfect Angel	Closed	1983	15.00	25
1984 Drummer Boy	Closed	1984	15.00	25
1985 Caroler	Closed	1985	16.50	25
1986 Night Before Christmas	Closed	1986	16.50	25
1987 Jolly St. Nick	Closed	1987	16.50	25
1988 Christmas Morning	Closed	1988	16.50	25
1989 The Bell Ringer	Closed	1989	16.50	25
1990 The Wreath Bearer	Closed	1990	18.50	20
1991 A Special Gift	Closed	1991	22.50	25
1992 My Special Friend	Closed	1992	22.50	25
1993 My Christmas Present	Yr.Iss.	1993	22.50	25
1994 Holiday Wishes	Yr.Iss.	1994	22.50	25
1995 Christmas Puppy	Yr.Iss.	1995	20.00	20
1996 Yuletide Bell	Yr.Iss.	1996	22.50	23
1997 Angel Bell	Yr.Iss.	1997	20.00	20
1998 Angel Bell	Yr.Iss.		20.00	20

River Shore

Norman Rockwell Single Issues - N. Rockwell

YEAR ISSUE	EDITION LIMIT	YEAR RETD.	ISSUE PRICE	*QUOTE U.S.$
1981 Grandpa's Guardian	7,000	N/A	45.00	45-75
1981 Looking Out to Sea	7,000	N/A	45.00	95-125
1981 Spring Flowers	347	N/A	175.00	150-175

Rockwell Children Series I - N. Rockwell

YEAR ISSUE	EDITION LIMIT	YEAR RETD.	ISSUE PRICE	*QUOTE U.S.$
1977 First Day of School	7,500	N/A	30.00	50-75
1977 Flowers for Mother	7,500	N/A	30.00	50-60
1977 Football Hero	7,500	N/A	30.00	50-75
1977 School Play	7,500	N/A	30.00	50-75

Rockwell Children Series II - N. Rockwell

YEAR ISSUE	EDITION LIMIT	YEAR RETD.	ISSUE PRICE	*QUOTE U.S.$
1978 Dressing Up	15,000	N/A	35.00	50
1978 Five Cents A Glass	15,000	N/A	35.00	40-50
1978 Future All American	15,000	N/A	35.00	50
1978 Garden Girl	15,000	N/A	35.00	40-50

Roman, Inc.

Annual Nativity Bell - I. Spencer

YEAR ISSUE	EDITION LIMIT	YEAR RETD.	ISSUE PRICE	*QUOTE U.S.$
1990 Nativity	Closed	N/A	15.00	15
1991 Flight Into Egypt	Closed	N/A	15.00	15
1992 Gloria in Excelsis Deo	Closed	N/A	15.00	15
1993 Three Kings of Orient	Closed	N/A	15.00	15

F. Hook Bells - F. Hook

YEAR ISSUE	EDITION LIMIT	YEAR RETD.	ISSUE PRICE	*QUOTE U.S.$
1985 Beach Buddies	15,000	N/A	25.00	28
1986 Sounds of the Sea	15,000	N/A	25.00	28
1987 Bear Hug	15,000	N/A	25.00	28

The Masterpiece Collection - Various

YEAR ISSUE	EDITION LIMIT	YEAR RETD.	ISSUE PRICE	*QUOTE U.S.$
1979 Adoration - F. Lippe	Closed	N/A	20.00	20
1980 Madonna with Grapes - P. Mignard	Closed	N/A	25.00	25
1981 The Holy Family - G. Notti	Closed	N/A	25.00	25
1982 Madonna of the Streets - R. Ferruzzi	Closed	N/A	25.00	25

Seymour Mann, Inc.

Connoisseur Christmas Collection™ - Bernini™

YEAR ISSUE	EDITION LIMIT	YEAR RETD.	ISSUE PRICE	*QUOTE U.S.$
1996 Cardinal CLT-312	Open		15.00	15
1996 Chickadee CLT-302	Open		15.00	15
1996 Dove CLT-307	Open		15.00	15

Connoisseur Collection™ - Bernini™

YEAR ISSUE	EDITION LIMIT	YEAR RETD.	ISSUE PRICE	*QUOTE U.S.$
1995 Bluebird CLT-15	Closed	1996	15.00	15
1995 Canary CLT-12	Closed	1997	15.00	15
1995 Cardinal CLT-9	Closed	1997	15.00	15
1995 Dove CLT-3	Closed	1997	15.00	15
1995 Hummingbird CLT-6	Closed	1997	15.00	15
1995 Pink Rose CLT-72	Open		15.00	15
1995 Robin CLT-18	Closed	1997	15.00	15
1995 Swan CLT-52	Open		15.00	15
1996 Butterfly/Lily CLT-332	Open		15.00	15
1996 Hummingbirds, Morning Glory, blue CLT-322B	Open		15.00	15
1996 Hummingbirds, Morning Glory, pink CLT-322	Open		15.00	15
1996 Magnolia CLT-78	Open		15.00	15
1996 Roses/Forget-Me-Not CLT-342	Open		15.00	15
1997 Bluebird/Lily CLT-392	Open		15.00	15
1997 Cardinal/Dogwood CLT-407	Open		15.00	15
1997 Dove/Magnolia CLT-352	Open		15.00	15
1997 Love Doves/Roses	Open		15.00	15
1997 Star Gazer Lily	Open		15.00	15
1997 Anna's Hummingbird	Open		15.00	15
1997 Violet Crowned Hummingbird	Open		15.00	15
1997 Blue Butterfly	Open		15.00	15
1998 Ruby Hummingbird Chicks CLT-462	Open		12.00	12
1998 Costa's Hummingbird CLT-472	Open		12.00	12

DOLLS/PLUSH

Alexander Doll Company

Madame Alexander Doll Club (M.A.D.C.)-Convention Dolls - Madame Alexander Design Staff

YEAR ISSUE	EDITION LIMIT	YEAR RETD.	ISSUE PRICE	*QUOTE U.S.$
1984 Ballerina 8" - Schumburg, IL	360	1984	N/A	N/A
1985 Happy Birthday 8" - Miami, FL	450	1985	N/A	N/A
1986 Scarlett 8" - Atlanta, GA	625	1986	N/A	N/A
1987 Cowboy 8" - San Antonio, TX	720	1987	N/A	N/A
1988 Flapper 10" - Chicago, IL	720	1988	N/A	N/A
1989 Briar Rose 8" - Los Angelos, CA	804	1989	N/A	N/A
1990 Riverboat Queen (Lena) 8" - New Orleans, LA	925	1990	N/A	N/A
1991 Queen Charlotte 10" - Charlotte, NC	900	1991	N/A	N/A
1992 Prom Queen (Memories) 8" - Chicago, IL	1,100	1992	N/A	N/A
1993 Diamond Lil (Days Gone By) 10" - Kansas City, MO	876	1993	N/A	N/A
1994 Navajo Women 8" - Phoenix, AZ	835	1994	N/A	N/A
1995 Frances Folsom 10" - Washington DC	N/A	1995	N/A	175
1996 Showgirl 10" - Las Vegas, NV	N/A	1996	N/A	N/A
1997 A Little Bit of Country 8" - Nashville, TN	N/A	1997	N/A	N/A

Madame Alexander Annual Member's Only - Madame Alexander Design Staff

YEAR ISSUE	EDITION LIMIT	YEAR RETD.	ISSUE PRICE	*QUOTE U.S.$
1989 Wendy 8"	4,878	1989	49.95	N/A
1990 Polly Pigtails 8"	4,896	1990	49.95	N/A
1991 Miss Liberty 10"	Retrd.	1992	69.95	N/A
1992 Little Miss Godey 8"	Retrd.	1993	79.95	N/A
1994 Wendy's Best Friend Maggie 8"	Retrd.	1994	74.95	N/A
1995 Wendy Joins M.A.D.C. 8"	Retrd.	1995	49.95	N/A
1996 Wendy Honors Margaret Winson 8"	Retrd.	1996	69.95	N/A
1997 From The Madame's Sketchbook 8"	Retrd.	1997	69.95	N/A

Alice in Wonderland - Madame Alexander Design Staff

YEAR ISSUE	EDITION LIMIT	YEAR RETD.	ISSUE PRICE	*QUOTE U.S.$
1996 Alice in Wonderland 13001	Open		69.95	70
1996 Cheshire Cat 13070	Open		54.95	60
1998 Dormouse 13090	Open		89.95	90
1996 Humpty Dumpty 13060	12/99		64.95	70
1996 Knave 13040	Open		69.95	75
1996 Red Queen 13010	Open		109.95	115
1997 Red Queen and White King, set 13030	Open		199.95	200
1998 Tweedledee 13120	Open		79.95	80
1998 Tweedledum 13110	Open		79.95	80
1998 Tweedledum and Tweedledee 13080, set	Open		159.95	160
1996 White King 13020	Open		89.95	95
1997 White Rabbit 13050	Retrd.	1997	59.95	60

Cinderella - Madame Alexander Design Staff

YEAR ISSUE	EDITION LIMIT	YEAR RETD.	ISSUE PRICE	*QUOTE U.S.$
1997 Cinderella's Prince, 8" 13420	Retrd.	1997	64.95	65
1997 Cinderella, 8" 13400	Open		64.95	70
1997 Fairy Godmother, 8" 13430	Open		69.95	75
1997 Poor Cinderella, 8" 13410	Open		69.95	75
1997 Really Ugly Stepsister, 8" 13450	Open		79.95	85
1997 Ugly Stepsister, 10" 13440	Open		79.95	85

Cissette - Madame Alexander Design Staff

YEAR ISSUE	EDITION LIMIT	YEAR RETD.	ISSUE PRICE	*QUOTE U.S.$
1997 Cissette Houndstooth (African American) 22193	1/99		119.95	120
1997 Cissette Houndstooth 22190	1/99		119.95	120
1997 Cissette Onyx 22170	1/99		119.95	120
1997 Cissette Café Rose (African American) 22203	1/99		119.95	120
1997 Cissette Café Rose 22200	1/99		119.95	120
1997 Cissette Leopard w/ Shopping Bag (African American) 22183	1/99		119.95	120
1997 Cissette Leopard w/ Shopping Bag 22180	1/99		119.95	120
1997 Cissette Onyx (African American) 22173	1/99		119.95	120

Cissy - Madame Alexander Design Staff

YEAR ISSUE	EDITION LIMIT	YEAR RETD.	ISSUE PRICE	*QUOTE U.S.$
1998 Cissy Barcelona (African American) 22333	1,500		589.95	590
1998 Cissy Barcelona 22330	1,500		589.95	590
1998 Cissy Budapest 22340	1,500		589.95	590
1998 Cissy Milan 22320	1,500		589.95	590
1998 Cissy Paris 22300	1,500		589.95	590
1998 Cissy Venice 22310	1,500		589.95	590

The Dionne Quintuplets - Madame Alexander Design Staff

YEAR ISSUE	EDITION LIMIT	YEAR RETD.	ISSUE PRICE	*QUOTE U.S.$
1998 Annette (yellow) 12250	1/99		84.95	85
1998 Cécile (green) 12270	1/99		84.95	85
1998 Emilie (lilac) 12280	1/99		84.95	85
1998 Marie (blue) 12260	1/99		84.95	85
1998 Yvonne (pink) 12240	1/99		84.95	85

Disneyana Convention - Madame Alexander Design Staff

YEAR ISSUE	EDITION LIMIT	YEAR RETD.	ISSUE PRICE	*QUOTE U.S.$
1993 Annette	1,000	1993	395.00	484-780

Gone With The Wind™ - Madame Alexander Design Staff

YEAR ISSUE	EDITION LIMIT	YEAR RETD.	ISSUE PRICE	*QUOTE U.S.$
1997 Mammy 15010	Open		89.95	95
1998 Poor Scarlett 14970	Open		94.95	95
1997 Rhett 15050	Retrd.	1997	89.95	90
1997 Scarlett 15040	Retrd.	1997	109.95	110
1996 Scarlett Hoop-Petti 15000	Open		99.95	100
1996 Scarlett Hoop-Petti Mammy & Flower Dress 15020	Open		219.95	230
1997 Scarlett Rose Picnic Dress 15070	Retrd.	1997	349.95	350
1997 Shadow Scarlett Rose Picnic 15030	12/99		74.95	80

Harley Davidson® - Madame Alexander Design Staff

YEAR ISSUE	EDITION LIMIT	YEAR RETD.	ISSUE PRICE	*QUOTE U.S.$
1997 Billy 17410	Retrd.	1997	99.95	100
1998 Cissette 17390	Open		149.95	150
1997 Cissette 17440	Retrd.	1997	120.00	120
1997 David 17430	Retrd.	1997	120.00	120
1997 Wendy 17420	Retrd.	1997	99.95	100

Sleeping Beauty - Madame Alexander Design Staff

YEAR ISSUE	EDITION LIMIT	YEAR RETD.	ISSUE PRICE	*QUOTE U.S.$
1997 Evil Sorceress, 8" 13610	Retrd.	1997	69.95	75
1997 Fairy of Beauty (pink), 8" 13620	Open		69.95	75
1997 Fairy of Song (green), 8" 13630	Open		69.95	75
1997 Fairy of Virtue (blue), 8" 13640	Open		69.95	75
1997 Sleeping Beauty, 8" 13600	Open		69.95	70

The Sound of Music™ - Madame Alexander Design Staff

YEAR ISSUE	EDITION LIMIT	YEAR RETD.	ISSUE PRICE	*QUOTE U.S.$
1998 Brigitta Von Trapp 14040	Open		99.95	100
1998 Captain Von Trapp 14030	Open		124.95	125
1998 Friedrick Von Trapp, 9" 14020	Open		99.95	100
1998 Gretl Von Trapp 14060	Open		99.95	100
1998 Kurt Von Trapp, 10" 14090	Open		99.95	100
1998 Liesl Von Trapp, 10" 14170	Open		99.95	100
1998 Louisa Von Trapp, 10" 14160	Open		99.95	100
1997 Maria at the Abbey 13890	Open		124.95	125
1997 Maria Travel Ensemble 13880	Open		124.95	125
1998 Marta Von Trapp 14050	Open		99.95	100
1997 Mother Superior 13870	Open		114.95	115

The Wizard of Oz™ - Madame Alexander Design Staff

YEAR ISSUE	EDITION LIMIT	YEAR RETD.	ISSUE PRICE	*QUOTE U.S.$
1993 The Cowardly Lion™ 13220	Open		64.95	70
1991 Dorothy™ with Toto™ 13200	Open		46.95	60
1997 Glinda the Good Witch™ 13250	Open		109.95	115
1997 Miss Gulch™ with Bicycle and Toto™ 13240	Open		119.95	120
1993 The Scarecrow™ 13230	Open		59.95	65
1993 The Tin Man™ 13210	Open		64.95	70
1997 The Wicked Witchn of the West™ 13270	Open		99.95	100
1998 The Wizard of Oz™ 13281	Open		94.95	95
1998 The Wizard™ with State Fair Balloon 13280	Open		139.95	140

All God's Children/Miss Martha Originals

Anika Series - M. Root

YEAR ISSUE	EDITION LIMIT	YEAR RETD.	ISSUE PRICE	*QUOTE U.S.$
1996 Anika - 2600	5,000	1996	175.00	175-395
1997 Skating Anika - 2601	7,500	1998	125.00	125-250
1998 Anika III - 2602	5,000		135.00	135

Annalee Mobilitee Dolls, Inc.

Doll Society-Animals - A. Thorndike

YEAR ISSUE	EDITION LIMIT	YEAR RETD.	ISSUE PRICE	*QUOTE U.S.$
1985 10" Penguin and Chick	3,000	N/A	29.95	85
1985 10" Penguin and Chick w/ dome	3,000	N/A	29.95	100
1986 10" Unicorn	3,000	N/A	36.95	110
1987 7" Kangaroo 9624	3,000	N/A	37.45	100
1988 5" Owl 9630	3,000	N/A	37.45	100
1989 7" Polar Bear Cub 9636	3,000	N/A	37.50	100
1990 7" Thorndike Chicken 9642	3,000	N/A	37.50	90

Doll Society-Folk Heroes - A. Thorndike

YEAR ISSUE	EDITION LIMIT	YEAR RETD.	ISSUE PRICE	*QUOTE U.S.$
1984 10" Johnny Appleseed w/ dome	1,500	N/A	80.00	575
1984 10" Robin Hood w/ dome	1,500	N/A	90.00	550
1985 10" Annie Oakley w/ dome	1,500	N/A	95.00	450
1986 10" Mark Twain w/ dome	2,500	N/A	117.50	350
1987 10" Ben Franklin w/ dome 9622	2,500	N/A	119.50	325

*Quotes have been rounded up to nearest dollar

YEAR ISSUE	EDITION LIMIT	YEAR RETD.	ISSUE PRICE	*QUOTE U.S.$
1988 10" Sherlock Holmes w/ dome 9628	2,500	N/A	119.50	300
1989 10" Abraham Lincoln w/ dome 9634	2,500	N/A	119.50	275
1990 10" Betsy Ross w/ dome 9644	2,500	N/A	119.50	275
1991 10" Christopher Columbus w/ dome 9649	2,500	N/A	119.50	275
1992 10" Uncle Sam 9652	2,500	N/A	87.50	275
1993 10" Pony Express Rider 9654	2,500	N/A	97.50	275
1994 10" Bean Nose Santa w/dome 9657	2,500	N/A	119.50	275
1995 10" Pocahontas w/dome 9659	1,300	N/A	87.50	275

Doll Society-Great American Era - A. Thorndike

YEAR ISSUE	EDITION LIMIT	YEAR RETD.	ISSUE PRICE	*QUOTE U.S.$
1996 10" Fabulous 50's Couple w/ dome 9961	1,500	1997	150.00	225-275
1997 10" Roaring Twenties 9663	Yr.Iss.	1997	160.00	160-225
1998 10" Gay Nineties	Yr.Iss.		175.00	175

Doll Society-Logo Kids - A. Thorndike

YEAR ISSUE	EDITION LIMIT	YEAR RETD.	ISSUE PRICE	*QUOTE U.S.$
1985 7" Kid w/Milk & Cookies w/ pin	3,562	1986	10.00	375
1986 7" Sweetheart Kid w/ pin	6,271	1987	18.00	190
1987 7" Naughty Kid w /pin	11,100	1988	18.00	130
1988 7" Raincoat Kid w/ pin	13,646	1989	20.00	110
1989 7" Christmas Morning Kid w/ pin	16,641	1990	20.00	100
1990 7" Clown Kid w/ pin	20,049	1991	20.00	100
1991 7" Reading Kid w/ pin	26,516	1992	20.00	80
1992 7" Schoolgirl Kid w/ pin	17,524	1993	25.00	60
1993 7" Ice Cream Logo w/ pin 9653	Yr.Iss.	1994	28.00	60
1994 7" Dress Up Santa Logo 9656	Yr.Iss	1995	28.00	50
1995 7" Goin' Fishin' Logo 9658	Yr.Iss	1995	30.00	40
1996 7" Little Mae Flower Logo 9660	Yr.Iss	1997	30.00	40-50
1997 7" Tea For Two 9662	Yr.Iss	1997	30.00	30
1998 7" 15th Anniversary	Yr.Iss		37.95	38

Doll Society-Around The World Couples - A. Thorndike

YEAR ISSUE	EDITION LIMIT	YEAR RETD.	ISSUE PRICE	*QUOTE U.S.$
1997 India Couple	N/A	1998	90.00	90-150
1998 Japan Couple	N/A		95.00	95

Event Pieces - A. Thorndike

YEAR ISSUE	EDITION LIMIT	YEAR RETD.	ISSUE PRICE	*QUOTE U.S.$
1994 10" Redcoat w/Cannon, signed by Annalee	Yr.Iss	1994	84.00	195
1995 10" Tennessee Fiddler, signed by Annalee	Yr.Iss	1995	80.00	275
1995 3" C'mas Morn Itsie Vignette, signed by Chuck	Yr.Iss	1995	68.00	250
1996 3" Dreams of Gold Vignette (w/ dome)	Yr.Iss	1996	85.00	175
1996 10" Candlemaker Women (Fall Auction) 9703	Yr.Iss	1996	90.00	275
1997 10" Summer School Elf (June Auction) 9706	Yr.Iss	1997	23.00	65-90
1997 7" Ringmaster Mouse, signed by Chuck 9705	Yr.Iss	1997	50.00	50
1998 10" Fabulous Floozy Frogs (trunk show) 970998	Yr.Iss		50.00	50
1998 3" Hugs and Kisses (National Open House) 988798	Yr.Iss		25.00	25

Limited Editions - A. Thorndike

YEAR ISSUE	EDITION LIMIT	YEAR RETD.	ISSUE PRICE	*QUOTE U.S.$
1997 5" Don't Open Til Christmas I (Parkwest) 9903	500	1997	27.50	75-95
1997 5" Don't Open Til Christmas II (Parkwest) 9889	625	1997	30.00	60
1997 5" Sleigh Ride Couple 4539	2,500	1997	100.00	100-150
1997 7" Bathtime For Buddy 2336	3,500	1997	55.00	55-85
1997 7" Fortunoff 75th Anniversary 9919	750	1997	29.00	65
1997 10" Crystal Angel (QVC Exclusive) 9917	1,000	1997	55.00	125-175
1997 10" Little Lord Taylor (green) 9904	375	1997	65.00	150-250
1997 10" Little Lord Taylor (red) 9934	1,000	1997	65.00	95-165
1997 10" Merry Christmas To All 9705	750	1997	85.00	150
1997 18" Tis The Night Before Christmas 5611	3,500	1997	95.00	125

Museum Collection - A. Thorndike

YEAR ISSUE	EDITION LIMIT	YEAR RETD.	ISSUE PRICE	*QUOTE U.S.$
1997 12" 1956 Ski Doll 9752-97	3,500		95.00	95
1997 14" Rogers Clothing Store Man & Woman 9750-97	3,500		225.00	225
1997 15" Woman with Red Felt Coat 9751-97	3,500		65.00	65

Disney Pieces - A. Thorndike

YEAR ISSUE	EDITION LIMIT	YEAR RETD.	ISSUE PRICE	*QUOTE U.S.$
1991 7" Fun in the Sun w/pin, signed	300	1991	65.00	300
1992 7" Nick w/pin, signed	300	1992	95.00	300
1993 7" Eric & Shane w/pin, signed	100	1993	110.00	375
1994 10" Piper Bear w/pin, signed	200	1994	130.00	275
1995 10" Chip Bear in Boat w/pin, signed	200	1995	125.00	300
1996 10" Indian Chief Bear w/pin, signed	200	1996	130.00	275

Angels - A. Thorndike

YEAR ISSUE	EDITION LIMIT	YEAR RETD.	ISSUE PRICE	*QUOTE U.S.$
1995 5" Angel w/ 18" Christmas Moon (yellow) 7173	Closed	1995	55.00	45-95
1993 7" Angel (Blonde Hair) 7108	Closed	1996	25.00	40
1976 7" Angel on Cloud 7105	Closed	1976	13.00	30
1992 7" Angel on Moon (white) 7171	Yr.Iss.	1992	40.00	100
1990 7" Angel on Sled w/ Cloud 7168	Closed	1991	30.00	65
1995 7" Angel Playing Harp 7111	Closed	1996	27.00	45
1982 7" Angel w/ Instrument 7110	Closed	1996	22.00	30
1976 7" Angel w/ Mistletoe 7140	Closed	1993	19.00	30
1950 7" Baby Angel w/ Feather Hair & Wreath on Head	Closed	N/A	3.00	300
1994 7" Flying Angel 7113	Closed	1996	26.00	26-45
1968 7" Flying Star Angel	Closed	1969	3.00	225
1981 7" Naughty Angel 7115	Closed	1986	18.00	28-50
1956 10" Baby Angel (feather hair)	Closed	1957	N/A	550
1991 10" Nativity Angel w/ placque 5430	Yr.Iss.	1991	60.00	110
1976 12" Angel on Cloud N-125	Closed	1983	11.00	85
1987 12" Flying Angel w/ Instrument 7162	Closed	1987	37.00	85
1984 12" Naughty Angel 7160	Closed	1986	37.00	85
1984 12" Tree Top Angel (holds gold star) 7165	Closed	1985	37.00	75
1991 12" Tree Top Angel (white outfit w/ red bow) 7165	Closed	1991	43.00	65
1990 18" Angel w/ Instrument 7170	Closed	1991	56.00	110
1990 30" Angel 7172	Closed	1990	76.00	150

Assorted Animals & Birds - A. Thorndike

YEAR ISSUE	EDITION LIMIT	YEAR RETD.	ISSUE PRICE	*QUOTE U.S.$
1979 4" Boy Pig (white body) N-571	Closed	1979	N/A	65
1979 4" Girl Pig (white body) N-570	Closed	1979	N/A	65
1996 4" Puppy Present 7421	Closed	1997	21.00	19-35
1989 5" Baby Swan 7408	Closed	1991	14.00	30
1993 5" Christmas Lamb (black) 7425	Closed	1996	18.00	30
1992 5" Christmas Lamb (white) 7424	Closed	1996	18.00	18-30
1988 5" Duck in Egg 1532	Closed	1990	21.00	45
1986 5" Duck on Sled 8070	Closed	1994	27.00	27-45
1986 5" Duck w/ Raincoat & Umbrella 1565	Closed	1986	20.00	60
1983 5" Duckling in Hat 7955	Closed	1984	13.00	50
1985 5" E.P. Boy & Girl Duckling 1510	Closed	1985	28.00	22-55
1991 5" Fawn (spotted) 6426	Closed	N/A	17.00	15-17
1991 5" Fluffy Yellow Chick 1728	Closed	1992	18.00	25
1989 5" Lamb 5424	Closed	1991	17.00	35
1984 5" Pilot Duckling 1515	Closed	1985	16.00	60
1992 5" Raincoat Duck 1560	Closed	1994	28.00	28-50
1995 5" Sailor Duck 1724	Closed	1996	28.00	45
1989 5" Sailor Duck 1724	Closed	1991	22.00	28-35
1991 5" Spring Lamb 1726	Closed	1992	18.00	10-35
1981 7" Boy Monkey w/ Banana Trapeze R-572	Closed	1981	10.00	175
1993 7" Christmas Chicken 7428	Closed	1993	35.00	35-70
1993 7" Christmas Dove 7426	Closed	1995	28.00	28-55
1981 7" Lady & Escort Fox (Designer Series) R630	Closed	1981	26.00	350
1976 7" Rooster A-352	Closed	1977	6.00	225
1981 7" Santa Fox w/ Bag R-173	Closed	1982	13.00	195
1981 7" Santa Monkey R-181	Closed	1981	10.00	155
1992 7" Santa Skunk 7422	Closed	1993	28.00	50
1993 7" Spring Boy Rooster 1596	Closed	1993	35.00	70
1992 7" Spring Girl Chicken 1595	Closed	1993	35.00	60
1992 7" Spring Skunk 1590	Closed	1993	23.00	24-50
1981 8" Ballerina Pig w/ Umbrella G-575	Closed	1982	13.00	145
1980 8" Boy Barbecue Pig (frying pan or spatula) G-570	Closed	1982	22.00	115
1976 8" Elephant A-310	Closed	1976	N/A	225
1968 8" Elephant C-47	Closed	1968	4.00	275
1972 8" Elephant R-3	Closed	1972	4.00	250
1980 8" Girl Barbecue Pig R-542	Closed	1981	11.00	130
1989 10" Barbecue Pig 2410	Yr.Iss.	1989	28.00	70
1991 10" Black Cat 2984	Closed	1992	26.00	80
1987 10" Bride and Groom Cats 2904	Closed	1987	72.00	275-350
1987 10" Christmas Goose 7402	Closed	1989	31.00	60
1989 10" Country Boy & Girl Pig 1544	Yr.Iss.	1989	52.00	125
1989 10" Country Boy & Girl Goose 1574	Closed	1989	64.00	135
1988 10" E.P. Boy & Girl Pig 1542	Yr.Iss.	1988	50.00	125
1987 10" Easter Parade Goose 1566	Closed	1988	30.00	65
1968 10" Honkey Donkey C-45	Closed	1968	4.00	275
1991 10" Huskie w/ 5" Puppy in Dog Sled 8057	Closed	1991	55.00	125
1987 10" Kitten on Sled 8062	Closed	1991	36.00	65
1987 10" Kitten w/ Knit Mittens 8064	Closed	1992	34.00	55
1993 10" Kitten w/ Ornament 7427	Closed	1995	36.00	36-65
1986 10" Kitten w/ Yarn & Basket 2900	Closed	1987	30.00	95
1970 10" Reindeer C-144	Closed	1974	N/A	75
1965 10" Reindeer w/ 10" Elf	Closed	1965	8.00	625
1987 10" Reindeer w/ Santa Hat & Bell 6434	Closed	1995	25.00	25
1970 10" Reindeer w/ Santa Hat C-141	Closed	1974	6.00	75
1975 10" Reindeer w/ Santa Hat R-100	Closed	1982	18.00	75
1990 10" Santa Pig 7414	Closed	1991	32.00	65
1987 10" Stork w/ 3" Baby in Basket 1958	Closed	1988	50.00	150
1976 10" Vote 76 Donkey A-313	Closed	1976	6.00	200
1981 12" Boy & Girl Skunk G-655, G-650	Closed	1982	56.00	300
1981 12" Boy Monkey w/ Banana Trapeze R-573	Closed	1981	24.00	275
1982 12" Boy Skunk G-655	Closed	1982	28.00	150
1996 12" Brown Horse 2885	Closed	1996	36.00	75-80
1967 12" Cat Sneaky	Closed	1969	7.00	325
1997 12" Champagne the Carousel Horse (last in series) 2842	Closed	1997	68.00	68-90
1991 12" Christmas Swan 7403	Closed	1991	64.00	120
1985 12" Duck w/ Raincoat & Umbrella 1560	Closed	1986	40.00	28-90
1983 12" E.P. Duck w/ Basket 1555	Closed	1986	29.00	90
1990 12" Easter Duck w/ Watering Can 1552	2,891	1991	50.00	65
1995 12" Empress the Carousel Horse (1st in series) 2840	Closed	1996	62.00	62-100
1982 12" Girl Skunk G-650	Closed	1982	28.00	150
1996 12" Mother Duck 1550	Closed	1996	50.00	75
1997 12" Mr & Mrs Quack Quack 1551	Closed	1997	120.00	60-145
1990 12" Santa Duck 7416	Closed	1991	54.00	54-225
1981 12" Santa Monkey R-181	Closed	1981	24.00	250
1981 12" Skunk w/ Snowball S-659	Closed	1982	29.00	225
1979 14" Mother & Father Pig N-572, N-573	Closed	1979	38.00	295
1979 14" Mother Pig N-572	Closed	1979	19.00	150
1986 15" Hobo Cat 3040	Closed	1988	36.00	95
1985 15" Jazz Cat w/Trumpet 7585	Closed	1985	32.00	160
1976 15" Rooster A-353	Closed	1977	14.00	375
1981 18" Cat w/ Mouse 7590	Closed	1988	47.00	160
1975 18" Horse A-354	Closed	1976	17.00	250
1981 18" Lady & Escort Fox (Designer Series) R-639	Closed	1981	58.00	625-650
1994 18" Old World Reindeer w/ Bells 6650	Closed	1995	62.00	62-75
1986 18" Reindeer w/ Saddlebags 6600	Closed	1994	60.00	53-70
1981 18" Santa Fox w/Bag R-173	Closed	1982	30.00	295
1981 22" Giraffe w/ 10" Elf R-280	Closed	1982	37.00	375
1987 24" Christmas Goose w/ Basket 7404	Closed	1989	58.00	150
1989 24" Christmas Swan 7406	Closed	1990	63.00	150
1987 24" Easter Parade Goose 1568	Closed	1988	53.00	150
1983 24" Flying Stork w/ Baby 1700	Closed	1983	37.00	150
1989 24" Spring Swan 1575	Closed	1990	63.00	125

Bears - A. Thorndike

YEAR ISSUE	EDITION LIMIT	YEAR RETD.	ISSUE PRICE	*QUOTE U.S.$
1973 7" Christmas Panda C-310	Yr.Iss.	1973	9.00	295-350
1993 10" Angel Bear 8053	Closed	1994	36.00	65
1986 10" Baby Bear w/ Bee 2800	Closed	1986	20.00	90
1987 10" Bear in Nightshirt w/Candle 8056	Closed	1993	34.00	60
1987 10" Bear in Velour Santa Suit 8054	Closed	1992	33.00	75
1986 10" Bear w/ Sled 8060	Closed	1989	29.00	60
1987 10" Bear w/ Snowball, Knit Hat & Scarf 8052	Closed	1992	30.00	60
1991 10" Bride & Groom Bear 2324	Closed	1991	80.00	165
1985 10" Christmas Panda w/Toy Bag 7595	Closed	1986	19.00	85
1993 10" Doctor Bear 2829	Yr.Iss.	1993	36.00	90
1988 10" Eskimo Bear 8058	Closed	1990	36.00	90
1986 10" Fishing Bear 2830	Yr.Iss.	1986	20.00	175
1986 10" Girl Bear 2835	Closed	1987	21.00	85
1992 10" Mrs Nightshirt Bear 8059	Closed	1993	39.00	70
1993 10" Santa's Helper Bear 8051	Closed	1993	33.00	34-70
1985 18" Ballerina Bear 2820	918	1985	40.00	225
1984 18" Bear w/ Brush 2810	Yr.Iss.	1984	40.00	195
1973 18" Bear w/ Butterfly S-201	Yr.Iss.	1973	11.00	400
1985 18" Bear w/ Honey Pot & Bee 2815	2,032	1986	42.00	175
1984 18" Christmas Panda w/Toy Bag 7595	Closed	1986	46.00	125-150

Bunnies - A. Thorndike

YEAR ISSUE	EDITION LIMIT	YEAR RETD.	ISSUE PRICE	*QUOTE U.S.$
1984 5" E.P. Boy & Girl Bunny 0520	Yr.Iss.	1984	24.00	195
1991 7" Artist Bunny 0622	Closed	1995	23.00	40
1994 7" Baby Bunny w/ Bottle 0930	Closed	1995	21.00	45
1992 7" Bride & Groom Bunny2915	Closed	1993	46.00	100
1970 7" Bunny (yellow)	Closed	1970	N/A	150
1993 7" Country Boy & Girl Bunny 0625, 0617	Closed	1993	42.00	21-60
1988 7" Country Boy Bunny w/ Hoe 0625	Closed	1988	16.00	25-35
1984 7" E.P. Boy Bunny 0615	Closed	1984	13.00	32-35
1993 7" E.P. Girl Bunny w/ 14" Wreath 0616	Closed	1994	35.00	50
1981 7" I'm Late Bunny (special order)	100	1981	N/A	300
1989 10" Bunnies (2) on Flexible Flyer Sled 8058	4,104	1989	53.00	125
1989 10" Bunnies (3) on Revolving Maypole 0646	647	1989	190.00	300
1987 10" Carrot Balloon w/ 7" Bunny 1572	Closed	1987	50.00	50-150
1989 10" Country Boy Bunny w/ Basket & Girl w/ Flowers 0652, 0650	Closed	1989	90.00	85
1997 10" Strolling Bunny w/ 7" Baby 0665	Closed	1997	70.00	145-150
1988 18" Artist Bunny 0739	Closed	1989	52.00	110
1978 18" Boy Bunny w/ Basket S-41	Closed	1978	14.00	150
1988 18" Country Boy & Girl Bunny 0725, 0720	Closed	1988	90.00	68-135
1988 18" Country Mother Bunny w/ 10" Baby Bunny 0738	Closed	1989	69.00	125
1996 18" E.P. Boy & Girl Bunny 0715, 0710	Closed	1996	135.00	70-145
1977 18" E.P. Boy & Girl Bunny S-45, S-44	Closed	1977	28.00	250
1990 18" E.P. Boy Bunny 0715	Closed	1990	70.00	68-95
1982 29" E.P. Girl Bunny D-52	Closed	1982	66.00	225
1979 29" Pop Bunny B-56	Closed	1979	43.00	225
1986 30" E.P. Boy & Girl Bunny 0815, 0810	Closed	1986	190.00	425-500

Clowns - A. Thorndike

YEAR ISSUE	EDITION LIMIT	YEAR RETD.	ISSUE PRICE	*QUOTE U.S.$
1987 10" Clown 1956	Closed	1987	18.00	80
1984 10" Clown 2950	Closed	1984	14.00	55-85
1985 10" Clown 2950	Closed	1986	15.00	75
1978 10" Clown A-340	Closed	1978	7.00	40-75
1976 10" Clown A-340	Closed	1976	11.00	115-125
1980 10" Clown R-620	Closed	1980	10.00	80
1981 10" Clown R-620	Closed	1981	10.00	85
1990 10" Clown w/ stand 2966	Closed	1990	28.00	50
1994 10" Hobo Clown 2974	Closed	1994	31.00	45
1990 10" Hobo Clown 2974	Closed	1991	26.00	55-60
1991 15" Hobo Clown 2975	Closed	1991	48.00	125
1980 18" Clown	Closed	1980	N/A	225
1978 18" Clown	Closed	1978	14.00	225
1981 18" Clown	Closed	1981	N/A	200-225
1976 18" Clown A-341	Closed	1976	14.00	295
1985 18" Clown w/ Balloon 2955	Closed	1986	56.00	150-165
1981 48" Clown	Closed	1981	N/A	620
1985 Hot Air Balloon w/ 10" Clown 2925	Closed	1986	50.00	150

Elves/Fairies/Gnomes - A. Thorndike

YEAR ISSUE	EDITION LIMIT	YEAR RETD.	ISSUE PRICE	*QUOTE U.S.$
1991 7" Christmas Gnome 7367	Closed	1993	19.00	19-45
1970 10" Casualty Ski Elf w/ Arm in Sling	Closed	1972	N/A	275
1970 10" Casualty Ski Elf w/ Crutch & Leg in Cast C-170	Closed	1972	5.00	300
1980 10" Christmas (green) 7358	Closed	1996	17.00	100
1960 10" Christmas Elf (white)	Closed	N/A	N/A	175
1980 10" Christmas Elf (white)	Closed	1995	17.00	75
1950 10" Christmas Elf w/ Instrument	Closed	N/A	N/A	250
1978 10" Elf w/ Planter	Yr.Iss.	1978	7.00	195
1987 10" Elves (two) w/ Tree, Sled & Axe 7360	Closed	1988	44.00	125
1987 10" Fall Elf 3300	Closed	1989	15.00	45

YEAR ISSUE	EDITION LIMIT	YEAR RETD.	ISSUE PRICE	*QUOTE U.S.$
1974 10" Fur Trimmed Elf w/ Candy Basket C-150	Closed	1974	6.00	125
1982 10" Jack Frost Elf w/ 10" Snowflake R-820	Closed	1982	14.00	135
1981 10" Jack Frost Elf w/ 5" Snowflake R-200	Closed	1981	12.50	125
1964 10" Robin Hood Elf	Closed	1965	N/A	225
1985 10" Ski Elf 8180	Closed	1986	18.00	85
1987 10" Ski Elf w/ Sweater 8180	Closed	1987	20.00	125
1960 10" Spring Elf (pink)	Closed	N/A	N/A	225
1987 10" Spring Elf 2962	Closed	1991	16.00	45
1960 10" Woodsprite w/ Broom	Closed	1960	N/A	475
1981 10" Workshop Elf 7350	Closed	1983	12.00	65
1978 12" Gnome C-151	Closed	1978	10.00	150
1969 12" Gnome w/ Candy Basket	Closed	1972	7.00	225
1991 12" Santa's Helper Painting Boat 7646	Closed	1992	39.00	75
1991 12" Santa's Postman w/ Cardholder Mailbag 7674	Closed	1993	41.00	75
1981 18" Butterfly w/ 10" Elf G-610	Closed	1982	28.00	195
1979 18" Gnome R-111	Closed	1980	20.00	225
1970 18" Gnome w/ Apron - Santa's Helper X-43	Closed	1970	8.00	325
1971 18" Gnome w/ Pajama Suit & Buttons	Closed	1972	9.00	300
1973 18" Santa's Helper C-151	Closed	1973	10.00	275
1976 18" Snow Gnome C-155	Closed	1976	14.00	275
1990 20" Spring Elf (pink) 1585	Yr.Iss.	1990	35.00	100
1990 20" Spring Elf (yellow) 1585	Yr.Iss.	1990	35.00	100
1974 22" Workshop Elf w/ Apron (red) C-152	Closed	1974	N/A	175
1997 30" Autumn Jester 3301	Yr.Iss.	1997	100.00	100-200
1991 Tinsel the "Elf" 7365	Closed	1992	21.00	45

Frogs - A. Thorndike

YEAR ISSUE	EDITION LIMIT	YEAR RETD.	ISSUE PRICE	*QUOTE U.S.$
1991 10" Avaitor Frog 9937	Closed	1991	20.00	60
1979 10" Boy Frog R-503	Closed	1981	10.00	75
1980 10" Bride and Groom Frog R507, R508	Closed	1981	30.00	250
1988 10" Frog 2406	Closed	1988	16.00	40
1987 10" Frog in Top Hat w/ Tails and Brass Instrument 2400	Closed	1988	24.00	24-75
1979 10" Girl Frog R-502	Closed	1980	10.00	75
1981 10" Girl Frog R-502	Closed	1981	10.00	95
1987 10" Leap Frogs 2402	Closed	1987	32.00	95
1987 10" Santa Frog w/ Toy Bag & Stand 8080	Closed	1987	20.00	65
1980 10" Santa Frog w/ Toy Bag R-163	Closed	1980	10.00	90
1980 18" Boy & Girl Frog R-505, R-504	Closed	1980	46.00	350
XX 18" Frog (all yellow) RARE	Closed	N/A	N/A	675
1980 18" Santa Frog w/ Toy Bag R-164	2,126	1980	25.00	250-275

Halloween - A. Thorndike

YEAR ISSUE	EDITION LIMIT	YEAR RETD.	ISSUE PRICE	*QUOTE U.S.$
1995 2" Pumpkin 9028	Closed	1996	7.00	18
1987 3" Baby Witch w/Diaper 3004	Yr.Iss.	1987	14.00	125
1992 7" Ballerina Kid 3052	Closed	1993	28.00	28-55
1996 7" Banana Kid 3065	Closed	1996	28.00	28-55
1988 7" Bunny Trick or Treat Kid 3032	Closed	1991	26.00	55
1993 7" Butterfly Kid 3061	Closed	1994	29.00	55
1992 7" Devil Kid 3043	Closed	1993	24.00	55
1992 7" Dracula Kid 3054	Closed	1994	27.00	27-55
1989 7" Dragon Kid 3033	Closed	1991	32.00	32-55
1989 7" Duck Kid 1675	Closed	1989	26.00	50
1993 7" Flower Kid (yellow)	Closed	1994	29.00	55
1987 7" Ghost Kid w/ Pumpkin 3002	Closed	1991	26.00	55
1993 7" Ghost Mouse 3060	Closed	1995	28.00	28-55
1995 7" Gypsy Girl 3035	Closed	1996	32.00	55
1992 7" Ladybug Kid 3056	Closed	1993	30.00	55
1995 7" Mouse Kid 3037	Closed	1996	26.00	23-55
1992 7" Pirate Kid 3038	Closed	1994	25.00	55
1989 7" Pumpkin Kid 3031	Closed	1992	28.00	55
1992 7" Scarecrow Kid 3058	Closed	1993	28.00	34-55
1988 7" Skeleton Kid 3034	Closed	1991	25.00	22-55
1996 7" Spider Kid 3064	Yr.Iss.	1996	28.00	55
1997 7" Tatters & Tags 3051, 3053	Closed	1997	84.00	130
1977 7" Trick or Treat Mouse 3005	Closed	1989	17.00	17-45
1988 7" Witch Kid w/ Nose 3036	Closed	1992	28.00	55
1993 7" Witch Mouse 3009	Closed	1996	28.00	40
1980 7" Witch Mouse on Broom 3010	Closed	1986	20.00	17-55
1981 7" Witch Mouse on Broom w/ Moon 3015	Closed	1985	34.00	140
1993 7" Wizard Mouse 3007	Closed	1995	30.00	40
1991 10" Bat 2980	Closed	1992	32.00	80
1987 10" Pumpkin (medium) 3027	Yr.Iss.	1987	35.00	165
1991 10" Spider 2982	Closed	1992	39.00	80
1994 12" Cat Kid 3063	Closed	1995	37.00	37-75
1993 12" Devil Kid 3062	Closed	1994	40.00	40-85
1986 12" Trick or Treat Halloween Mouse 3045	Closed	1990	43.00	85
1980 12" Witch Mouse on Broom 3030	Closed	1984	36.00	95
1986 14" Pumpkin (solid) 3025	Closed	1992	49.00	125
1986 14" Pumpkin Balloon w/ 7" Witch Mouse 3020	Closed	1987	60.00	300
1993 14" Pumpkin w/ Removable Lid 3028	Closed	1995	50.00	150
1996 15" Haunted Tree 3024	Closed	1996	45.00	45-75
1990 18" Dragon Kid 3012	Closed	1990	70.00	160
1990 18" Pumpkin Kid 3014	Closed	1991	76.00	150
1997 18" Spellbinder 3021	Closed	1997	90.00	90-150
1989 18" Thorny the Ghost 3006	Closed	1991	52.00	125
1990 18" Trick or Treat Bunny Kid 3016	Closed	1991	50.00	150
1989 18" Witch (flying) 3008	Closed	1992	64.00	100
1992 18" Witch w/ Stand 3011	Closed	1995	70.00	100
1996 30" Skeleton Kid 3019	Closed	1996	85.00	195-250

YEAR ISSUE	EDITION LIMIT	YEAR RETD.	ISSUE PRICE	*QUOTE U.S.$
1993 30" Witch Kid 3013	Closed	1995	150.00	275
1995 Bewitching Moon Mobile 3003	Closed	1996	45.00	75

Mice - A. Thorndike

YEAR ISSUE	EDITION LIMIT	YEAR RETD.	ISSUE PRICE	*QUOTE U.S.$
1991 7" Baker Mouse 2013	Yr.Iss.	1991	26.00	45
1992 7" Caroller Mouse w/ Hat & Tree 7754	Closed	1995	22.00	35
1997 7" Cleaning Day Mouse (holds mop & bucket) 2135	Closed	1997	27.00	26-45
1975 7" Colonial Boy & Girl Mouse M-493, M-492	Closed	1976	12.00	225
1975 7" Colonial Boy mouse M-493	Closed	1976	18.00	75
1968 7" Country Cousin Boy Mouse	Closed	1968	N/A	225
1968 7" Country Cousin Girl Mouse	Closed	1968	N/A	225
1996 7" Country Girl Mouse 2233	Closed	1997	26.00	40
1991 7" Desert Storm Mouse 9931	Closed	1991	30.00	50
1991 7" Desert Storm Nurse Mouse 9932	Closed	1991	30.00	45
1982 7" Equestrienne Mouse 2185	Closed	1983	13.00	125
1990 7" Friar Tuck Mouse 2010	Yr.Iss.	1990	27.00	50
1992 7" Green Thumb Mouse 2045	Yr.Iss.	1992	26.00	45
1993 7" Habitat Mouse 9954	Closed	1995	31.00	55
1985 7" Hiker Mouse w/Backpack 2305	Closed	1985	15.00	55
1970 7" Housewife Mouse	Closed	N/A	12.00	60
1996 7" Laundry Day Mouse (clothes basket) 2135	Closed	1996	26.00	50
1993 7" Mouse (white) on Toboggan 7726	Closed	1995	32.00	31-50
1992 7" Mouse on Cheese 7756	Closed	1993	27.00	27-45
1991 7" Mouse w/ Mailbag and Letters 7752	Closed	1993	26.00	26-45
1993 7" Mouse w/ Present (white) 7721	Closed	1994	23.00	45
1984 7" Mouse w/Presents 7735	Closed	1992	18.00	18-45
1991 7" Mr & Mrs Tuckered Mice 7747, 7749	Closed	1993	40.00	23-65
1998 7" Star Spangled Mouse 283198	Closed	1998	24.50	45

Miscellaneous - A. Thorndike

YEAR ISSUE	EDITION LIMIT	YEAR RETD.	ISSUE PRICE	*QUOTE U.S.$
1995 2" Tomatoes (3) , 8 " Ear Corn w/ faces, set 9024, 9025	Closed	1996	N/A	120
1990 5" Christmas Dragon 7420	Closed	1992	24.00	50
1987 5" Leprechaun 1706	Closed	1992	22.00	30
1993 5" Leprechaun w/ Pot O' Gold 1706	Closed	1996	22.00	35
1991 7" Snowman "Ritz" 7507	Closed	1995	29.00	45
1983 7" Snowman (holding broom) 7505	Yr.Iss.	1983	13.00	85
1993 7" Snowman on Toboggan (carrot nose) 7508	Closed	1995	31.00	55
1984 7" Snowman w/ Pipe 7505	Closed	1992	24.00	35
1993 7" Snowwoman 7506	Closed	1995	27.00	40
1991 10" Gingerbread Boy 7295	Closed	1994	24.00	45
1984 10" Gingerbread Boy 7295	Closed	1984	16.00	24-55
1978 10" Leprechaun (lime green body) N-501	Closed	1979	7.00	75
1992 10" Leprechaun w/ Pot O' Gold 1710	Yr.Iss.	1992	21.00	60
1974 10" Leprechaun w/ Sack S-202	Closed	1974	6.00	125
1978 10" Scarecrow (blue/maroon patchwork, red vest) A-345	Closed	1978	7.00	140
1983 10" Scarecrow (blue/wh ticking, red vest) 3105	Closed	1984	16.00	100
1976 10" Scarecrow (denim patchwork) A-345	Closed	1976	6.00	125
1977 10" Scarecrow (multicolored patchwork, burlap hat) A-345	Closed	1977	6.00	175
1978 10" Snowman N-160	Closed	1979	6.95	55
1988 10" Toy Soldier 7560	Closed	1990	33.00	75
1994 12" Girl Scarecrow (blue stone washed dress) 3073	Closed	1995	50.00	90
1989 12" Scarecrow (blue stone washed, red shirt) 3047	Closed	1993	42.00	90
1992 12" Snowman 7510	Closed	1993	42.00	70
1980 14" Dragon w/7" Bushbeater R-555	Closed	1982	33.00	300
1990 15" Christmas Dragon 7418	Closed	1990	50.00	100
1983 18" Gingerbread Boy 7300	Closed	1984	29.00	135
1991 18" Gingerbread Boy 7300	Closed	1992	51.00	100-135
1978 18" Scarecrow (blue/maroon patchwork, red vest) A-346	Closed	1978	N/A	295
1983 18" Scarecrow (blue/wh ticking, red vest) (no stand) 3150	Closed	1984	33.00	200
1976 18" Scarecrow (denim patchwork) (no stand) A-346	Closed	1976	13.50	275
1996 18" Snowman " Puttin on the Ritz" 7527	Yr.Iss.	1996	65.00	100
1978 18" Snowman (holding bird) N-161	Closed	1979	16.00	165
1983 18" Snowman w/ Broom 7525	Closed	1996	55.00	60
1996 18" Sunflower 1841	Closed	1996	24.00	24-50
1988 18" Toy Soldier 7562	Closed	1990	55.00	110-125
1981 22" Sun Mobile 1850	Closed	1985	37.00	225
1996 24" Country Cattail 1843	Closed	1996	30.00	29-50
1996 25" Sunflower 1842	Closed	1996	26.00	60
1978 29" Snowman N-162	Closed	1979	43.00	250
1994 30" Snowman w/ broom 7536	Closed	1995	120.00	225
1989 30" Toy Soldier 7558	Closed	1989	100.00	300
1987 48" Carrot 1570	Yr.Iss.	1987	40.00	175
1976 48" Scarecrow A-348	Closed	1978	58.00	875
1995 5' & 12" Cactus Set 9027	Closed	1996	24.00	24-50

Picks/Pins - A. Thorndike

YEAR ISSUE	EDITION LIMIT	YEAR RETD.	ISSUE PRICE	*QUOTE U.S.$
1982 3" Butterfly Pin 1816	Closed	1982	N/A	150
1996 3" Ladypick Pick 1818	Closed	1997	N/A	25
1982 Bunny (boy) Head Pick G-692	Closed	1982	5.50	45
1982 Bunny (girl) Head Pick G-690	Closed	1982	6.00	45
1976 Colonial Boy & Girl Heads Pin, set A-357, A-356	Closed	1976	2.00	200
1991 Desert Storm Mouse Head Pin 9935	Closed	1991	8.00	9-30
1991 Desert Storm Nurse Mouse Head Pin 9936	Closed	1991	8.00	30
1972 Donkey Head Pin	Closed	1972	N/A	100
1976 Elephant Head Pin A-361	Closed	1976	N/A	110
1995 Frog Head Pin	Closed	1995	N/A	100
1997 Graduate Girl Head Pin 9707	Closed	1997	N/A	95
1995 Nashville Santa Head Pin	Closed	1995	N/A	150
1996 Poodle Head Pin	Closed	1996	N/A	95

Santas - A. Thorndike

YEAR ISSUE	EDITION LIMIT	YEAR RETD.	ISSUE PRICE	*QUOTE U.S.$
1983 5" Mr & Mrs Tuckered 4600	Closed	1983	23.00	175
1984 5" Mrs Santa 4505	Closed	1985	12.00	50
1982 5" Mrs Santa w/ Gift Box 4525	Closed	1984	12.00	50
1994 5" Old World Santa w/ 9" Wreath 4550	Closed	1996	33.00	60
1982 5" Santa w/ 5" Deer & Sleigh 4540	Closed	1984	60.00	250
1981 5" Santa w/ 5" Deer 4535	Closed	1984	23.00	80
1982 5" Santa w/ Bag 4510	Closed	1985	12.00	55
1982 5" Santa w/ Stove 4530	Closed	1984	14.00	60
1982 5" Santa with Gift Box & Card 4520	Closed	1985	13.00	45
1992 7" Chef Santa 5045	Closed	1996	30.00	45
1979 7" Cross Country Santa w/ Skis & Poles R-4	Closed	1981	11.00	70
1960 7" Mr & Mrs Santa	Closed	N/A	N/A	150
1993 7" Mr & Mrs Victorian Santa 6810, 6815	Closed	1993	60.00	95
1986 7" Mr & Mrs Victorian Santa 6810, 6815	Closed	1988	N/A	90
1984 7" Mrs Santa 5010	Closed	1984	N/A	40
1977 7" Mrs Santa C-4	Closed	1977	N/A	40
1991 7" Mrs Santa Hanging Merry Christmas Sign 5236	Closed	1993	28.00	40
1992 7" Santa & Mrs Santa w/ Candle Holder 5042, 5040	Closed	1993	52.00	80
1976 7" Santa & Toy Sack in Sleigh C-21	Closed	1978	8.00	45
1983 7" Santa at North Pole 5030	Closed	1987	18.00	30
1991 7" Santa Bringing Home Christmas Tree 5232	Closed	1993	28.00	50
1982 7" Santa in Sleigh 5025	Closed	1986	20.00	40
1975 7" Santa on Bike C-14	Closed	1978	7.00	65
1970 7" Santa w/ 10" Deer C-143	Closed	N/A	35.00	125
1970 7" Santa w/ 10" Deer on Christmas Mushroom C-253	Closed	1970	11.00	275
1976 7" Santa w/ Firewood C-12	Closed	1977	6.00	55
1975 7" Santa w/ Fur Trim	Closed	1982	N/A	30
1985 7" Santa w/ Gift List & Toy Bag 5225	Closed	1992	24.00	25
1991 7" Santa w/ Mailbag & Letters 5234	Closed	1993	28.00	50
1976 7" Santa w/ Pot Belly Stove R-10	Closed	1982	N/A	50
1975 7" Santa w/ Skis & Poles C-8	Closed	1977	N/A	85
1987 7" Santa w/ Sleigh & One Reindeer 5110	Closed	1990	66.00	120
1994 7" Santa w/ Snowshoe & Tree 5243	Closed	1995	29.00	30-55
1994 7" Santa w/ Tree & Sled 5244	Closed	1994	29.00	55
1983 7" Santa w/ White Felt Moon 5200	Closed	1984	25.00	100
1993 7" Skiing Santa 5242	Closed	1996	30.00	45
1977 7" Tennis Santa N-5	Closed	1979	8.00	50
1986 7" Victorian Santa w/ Sleigh & Deer 6820	Closed	1988	52.00	100
1994 10" Mrs Santa Last Minute Mend w/ plaque 5399	Yr.Iss.	1994	48.00	100
1993 10" Skating Mr & Mrs Santa w/ plaque 5409, 5411	Yr.Iss.	1993	100.00	190
1988 10" St. Nicholas w/ plaque 5410	Yr.Iss.	1990	70.00	50-100
1997 10" True Blue Santa w/ Certificate 5390	Closed	1997	63.00	125
1991 12" Tuckered Couple 5487	Closed	1994	90.00	63-125
1988 18" Chef Santa (animated) (bowl) 5632	Closed	1989	120.00	300
1987 18" Chef Santa (Gingerbread) 5632	Closed	1996	61.00	75
1990 18" Day-After-Christmas Santa 5514	Closed	1991	80.00	140
1987 18" Mr & Mrs Santa in Rocking Chair 5610,5627	Closed	1988	125.00	275
1981 18" Santa w/ 18" Reindeer R-103	Closed	1981	52.00	100
1991 18" Santa w/ Cardholder Mail Bag 5640	Yr.Iss.	1992	60.00	125
1985 18" Velour Mr & Mrs Santa 5615, 5620	Closed	1990	122.00	110
1986 18" Victorian (Velour) Mr & Mrs Santa 6850, 6855	Closed	1987	115.00	250
1987 18" Victorian Santa w/ Stocking 6860	Closed	1987	62.50	145
1981 18" Workshop Santa 5625	Closed	1990	44.00	65

Thanksgiving - A. Thorndike

YEAR ISSUE	EDITION LIMIT	YEAR RETD.	ISSUE PRICE	*QUOTE U.S.$
1993 7" Girl Eating Turkey 3081	Yr.Iss.	1993	39.00	80
1993 7" Harvest Basket (Pilgrim) Mice 3074	Closed	1996	48.00	47-65
1987 7" Indian Boy & Indian Girl 3154, 3152	Closed	1996	62.00	30-95
1980 7" Indian Boy 3154	Closed	N/A	N/A	30-40
1987 7" Indian Girl 3152	Closed	1996	N/A	40
1993 7" Pilgrim Boy w/ Fawn & Girl w/Pie 3159, 3157	Closed	1995	71.00	42-90
1994 7" Pilgrim Girl w/Pie (blue) 3157	Closed	1994	N/A	28-45
1987 7" Pilgrim Kids w/ Basket 3156	Closed	1992	54.00	75
1984 7" Pilgrim Mice Set w/ Basket 3050	Closed	1992	44.00	75
1994 7" Thanksgiving Boy 3200	Yr.Iss.	1994	40.00	40-75
1988 8" Boy Turkey (tan/brown body) 3160, 3161	Closed	1995	35.00	50
1993 8" Girl Turkey 3163	Closed	1995	37.00	36-75
1991 10" Indian Chief & Maiden 3167, 3170	Closed	1991	86.00	115
1995 10" Indian Chief & Maiden 3168, 3170	Closed	1996	86.00	140
1997 10" Medicine Man 3169	Closed	1997	48.00	48-100
1978 10" Pilgrim Boy & Girl A358, A357	Closed	1978	N/A	225
1991 10" Pilgrim Man w/ Basket & Woman w/ Turkey, set 3166, 3164	Closed	1992	90.00	45-140

*Quotes have been rounded up to nearest dollar

YEAR ISSUE	EDITION LIMIT	YEAR RETD.	ISSUE PRICE	*QUOTE U.S.$
1993 12" Indian Boy 3155	Closed	1993	36.00	80
1985 12" Indian Boy and Girl Mice 3095, 3100	Closed	1987	72.00	160
1991 12" Pilgrim Boy & Girl Mouse 3080, 3075	Closed	1991	86.00	140
1981 12" Pilgrim Boy & Girl Mice 3080, 3075	Closed	1989	74.00	175
1993 12" Pilgrim Boy w/Basket & Girl w/Pie 3083, 3084	Closed	1995	95.00	125
1996 12" Tommy Turkey 3162	Closed	1996	76.00	125
1988 12" Turkey (large) 3162	Closed	1992	58.00	125
1994 17" Tee Pee 9026	Closed	1996	38.00	55
1994 24" Turkey 3167	Yr.Iss.	1994	100.00	350

Valentine - A. Thorndike

YEAR ISSUE	EDITION LIMIT	YEAR RETD.	ISSUE PRICE	*QUOTE U.S.$
1987 3" Cupid in Heart Balloon 0302	Closed	1987	39.00	150
1990 5" Valentine Dragon 1990	Closed	1990	26.00	65
1984 7" Cupid Kid 0325	Closed	1985	16.00	50
1984 7" Cupid Kid in Hanging Heart 0330	Closed	1985	33.00	135
1986 7" Cupid Kid in Hot Air Balloon 0315	Closed	1986	55.00	200
1986 7" Cupid Mobile 0320	Closed	1987	17.00	60
1996 7" Sweetheart Boy & Girl Mouse 0341, 0340	Closed	1996	43.00	24-43
1993 7" Sweetheart Boy & Girl Mouse 2001, 2014	Closed	1993	40.00	43
1996 7" Sweetheart Boy 0391	Closed	1996	33.00	75
1991 7" Sweetheart Boy Mouse 2014	Closed	1991	24.00	25
1994 7" Sweetheart Girl 0390	Closed	1996	28.00	55
1984 7" Valentine Bunny 0335	Closed	1985	14.00	80
1998 10" I'm All Heart Elf 037098	Yr.Iss.	1998	33.50	34-55
1998 10" Sweetheart Boy Elf 36698	Closed	1998	20.50	35-45
1998 10" Sweetheart Girl Elf 36598	Closed	1998	20.50	35-45
1997 10" Valentine Angel 1930	Closed	1997	45.00	45-70
1986 10" Valentine Panda 0350	Yr.Iss.	1986	20.00	150-200
1985 18" Valentine Cat w/ Heart 0380	Closed	1986	35.00	195

Various People - A. Thorndike

YEAR ISSUE	EDITION LIMIT	YEAR RETD.	ISSUE PRICE	*QUOTE U.S.$
1987 3" Baby in Basket 1960	Closed	1987	16.00	100
1987 3" Boy w/ Snowball 8040	Closed	1988	14.00	45
1987 3" Bride and Groom 0306	Closed	1987	39.00	40-200
1983 3" PJ Kid 7600	Closed	1983	11.00	175
1986 3" Skier 8025	Closed	1988	14.00	45
1991 3" Water Baby in Pond Lily 1677	Closed	1991	15.00	15-55
1995 3" Winken, Blynken & Nod 1919	Closed	1996	68.00	95
1987 5" Christmas Morning Kid w/ 3" Bear in Box 8018	Closed	1989	32.00	65
1992 5" Equestrian Kid on 10" Horse 9943	Closed	1992	75.00	75-130
1987 5" Monk 2500	Closed	1987	14.00	85
1994 5" Old World Caroller Boy & Girl 7251, 7252	Closed	1995	46.00	65
1995 5" Pixie Piccolo Player 1920	Closed	1996	30.00	45
1993 7" Arab Boy w/ Lamb 2349	Yr.Iss.	1993	36.00	60
1968 7" Baby "I'm Reading"	Closed	1968	N/A	275
1992 7" Baby New Year 8200	Closed	1993	27.00	30-55
1987 7" Baby w/ Blanket & Knit Sweater 1962	Closed	1989	22.00	50
1971 7" Baby w/ Wreath on Head	Closed	1971	N/A	175
1996 7" Baker Kid 2331	Yr.Iss.	1996	31.00	31-45
1993 7" Ballerina on Music Box 2345	Yr.Iss.	1993	42.00	100
1993 7" Bar Mitzuah Boy 2348	Yr.Iss.	1993	26.50	55
1993 7" Basketball Boy (black) 2352	Yr.Iss.	1993	26.00	50
1987 7" Boy on Victorian Sled 7258	Closed	1989	23.00	65
1984 7" Boy w/ Firecracker 1650	Yr.Iss.	1984	20.00	125-150
1984 7" Boy w/ Snowball 8005	Closed	1988	19.00	45
1988 7" Bunny Kid 1672	Closed	1990	24.00	55
1994 7" Cheerleader Girl 2354	Yr.Iss.	1994	27.00	50
1993 7" Choir Boy & Girl 7249, 7248	Closed	1995	56.00	75
1993 7" Choir Boy 7249	Closed	1995	28.00	40
1994 7" Choir Boy w/ Black Eye 7247	Closed	1995	28.00	28-45
1994 7" Christa McAuliffe Skateboard Kid 9955	Closed	1994	N/A	75
1984 7" Christmas Morning Kid 8015	Closed	1986	22.00	45
1985 7" Dress-Up Boy & Girl 1670, 1665	Closed	1985	40.00	160
1989 7" Dress-Up Boy & Girl 1673, 1674	Closed	1990	56.00	80
1989 7" Dress-Up Boy 1673	Closed	1990	N/A	27-35
1996 7" Drummer Boy 7200	Closed	1996	29.00	29-40
1993 7" Drummer Boy 7200	Closed	1995	29.00	40
1985 7" Drummer Boy 7225	Closed	1992	29.00	40
1995 7" Easter Bunny Kid 1672	Closed	1996	25.00	45
1988 7" Eskimo Boy 8022	Closed	1989	24.00	65
1994 7" Girl Building Snowman (pink) 7231	Closed	1995	25.00	75
1984 7" Girl on Sled 8010	Closed	1986	19.00	50
1987 7" Graduate Girl 1662	Closed	1987	20.00	80
1994 7" Hershey Kid 9951	Closed	1996	40.00	65
1995 7" Hockey Kid 2361	Yr.Iss.	1995	31.00	50
1994 7" Hot Shot Business Girl 2355	Yr.Iss.	1994	37.00	55
1993 7" Hot Shot Businessman Kid 2351	Yr.Iss.	1993	36.00	55
1982 7" I'm a Ten G-555	Yr.Iss.	1982	13.00	75
1995 7" Joseph, Mary & Shepherd Child w/ Lamb 7070, 7071, 7072	Closed	1995	98.00	150
1993 7" Jump Rope Girl 2346	Closed	1993	26.00	27-50
1997 7" Karate Kid 2344	Closed	1997	27.00	45
1993 7" Kid Building Snowman (blue) 7230	Closed	1993	22.00	75
1994 7" Marbles Kid 9956	Closed	1994	N/A	75
1993 7" Pink Flower Kid 1597	Yr.Iss.	1993	26.00	26-55
1996 7" Powder Puff Baby 2332	Yr.Iss.	1996	21.00	21-45
1994 7" Scottish Lad 2356	Yr.Iss.	1994	30.00	55
1992 7" Skateboard Kid 2330	Yr.Iss.	1992	30.00	45
1985 7" Skiing Kid 8020	Closed	1987	19.00	90
1996 7" Snowball Fight Kid 7233	Closed	1996	31.00	31-50
1996 7" St. Patricks Day Boy 1713	Closed	1997	32.00	45-55
1997 7" St. Patricks Day Girl 1714	Closed	1997	32.00	32-60
1982 08" Caroller Girl 7250	Closed	1986	20.00	40
1983 8" Monk w/ Jug 7915	Closed	1984	18.00	80
1984 10" Aerobic Girl 1950	Closed	1985	19.00	50
1989 10" Americana Couple w/ plaque 2445	Closed	1990	110.00	150
1990 10" Annalee Collector Doll w/ dome 2448	Closed	1991	150.00	350
1992 10" Baseball Batter 9941	Closed	1993	30.00	75
1994 10" Baseball Catcher 9946	Closed	1994	39.00	75
1993 10" Baseball Pitcher 9944	Closed	1993	36.00	75
1989 10" Bob Cratchet & 5" Tiny Tim w/ plaque 5462	Closed	1990	100.00	160
1984 10" Bride & Groom 2705, 2710	Closed	1985	63.00	50-300
1995 10" Bruins Hockey Player (signed by Chuck & S. Leech) 2610	Closed	1995	N/A	150
1995 10" Bruins Hockey Player 2610	Closed	1995	48.00	95
1994 10" Canadian Mountie on Horse (brass plaque) 9959	Closed	1995	130.00	275
1994 10" Canadian Mountie on Horse 9959	Closed	1995	130.00	250
1984 10" Caroller Boy 7255	Closed	1986	20.00	45
1975 10" Caroller Boy C-210	Closed	1976	N/A	125
1976 10" Caroller Girl C-209	Closed	1976	6.00	125
1967 10" Choir Boy	Closed	1969	N/A	225
1970 10" Choir Boy C-210	Closed	1973	N/A	150
1970 10" Choir Girl (red hair) C-209	Closed	1974	N/A	165
1994 10" Christa McAuliffe Ski Doll 9947	Yr.Iss.	1994	N/A	100
1992 10" Christmas Eve Bob Cratchet / plaque 5470	Yr.Iss.	1992	70.00	225
1992 10" Christmas Eve Scrooge w/ plaque 5468	Yr.Iss.	1992	60.00	225
1976 10" Colonial Drummer Boy A-304	Closed	1976	6.00	125
1975 10" Drummer Boy C-225	Closed	1975	6.00	175
1992 10" Father Time 8202	Closed	1993	55.00	100
1963 10" Friar (brown)	Closed	1965	3.00	375
1996 10" Ghost of Christmas Future 5457	Closed	1996	30.00	100
1996 10" Ghost of Christmas Past 5455	Closed	1996	40.00	100
1996 10" Ghost of Christmas Present 5456	Closed	1996	56.00	125
1996 10" Golfer Woman 2881	Closed	1996	44.00	75
1993 10" Headless Horseman w/ Horse 3070	Closed	1994	57.00	130
1987 10" Huck Finn w/ Dome 2550	Closed	1988	103.00	250
1990 10" Jacob Marley w/ plaque 5464	Closed	1992	90.00	175-200
1991 10" Man & Woman Skaters 7267, 7269	Closed	1992	92.00	46-165
1991 10" Martha Cratchet w/ plaque 5466	Closed	1992	60.00	150
1989 10" Merlin the Magician w/ brass plaque 3042	Closed	1990	70.00	150
1960 10" Monk	Closed	N/A	3.00	225
1996 10" Mr. Farmer 2883	Closed	1996	35.00	75
1996 10" Mr. Scrooge 5467	Closed	1996	38.00	38-100
1990 10" N. H. Music Festival Conductor Doll w/ dome 9915	Closed	1991	110.00	450
1987 10" Nativity Set w/ dome & plaque 5420	Closed	1990	150.00	300
1994 10" Old World Caroller Man & Woman 7251, 7252	Closed	1995	58.00	30-100
1988 10" Scrooge w/ plaque 5460	Closed	1990	90.00	125
1988 10" Shepherd Boy & Lamb w/ plaque 5422	Closed	1990	90.00	90-175
1984 10" Skier (cross country) 8160	Closed	1986	36.00	125
1984 10" Skier (downhill) 8150	Closed	1988	35.00	95
1992 10" Snow Queen 7008	Yr.Iss.	1992	40.00	80
1990 10" Spirit of 76 w/ dome 9646	Closed	1991	195.00	450
1987 10" State Trooper w/ dome	Closed	1987	134.00	395-425
1990 10" Wiseman w/ Camel w/ plaque 5428	Closed	1991	110.00	250
1989 10" Wisemen (2) w/ plaque 5426	Closed	1990	110.00	240
1992 12" Drummer Boy 7225	Closed	1995	40.00	55
1985 12" Drummer Boy 7225	Closed	1992	50.00	55
1985 12" Kid w/ Sled 8050	Closed	1986	33.00	100
1992 12" P.J. Boy 7635	Closed	1993	30.00	60
1992 12" P.J. Girl 7630	Closed	1993	30.00	60
1991 12" P.J. Kid (blonde hair) 7644	Closed	1992	30.00	60
1991 12" P.J. Kid (red hair) 7642	Closed	1991	30.00	60
1991 12" P.J. Kid (brown hair) 7640	Closed	1992	30.00	60
1982 16" Caroller Girl 7275	Closed	1984	30.00	95
1983 16" Monk w/ Jug 7915	Closed	1984	35.00	140
1988 18" Americana Couple w/ plaque 2552	Closed	1988	170.00	325
1987 18" Bottle Cover Monk 2502	Closed	1987	30.00	150
1990 18" Bunny Kid w/ Slippers 1671	Closed	1992	50.00	100
1976 18" Caroller Girl C-211	Closed	1976	13.00	150
1990 18" Choir Girl 5708	Closed	1991	58.00	90
1990 18" Christmas Morning Kid w/ Train 5702	Closed	1990	66.00	110
1983 18" Girl & Boy w/ Sleigh 7670	Closed	1983	80.00	195
1990 18" Girl on Sled 5706	Closed	1990	56.00	125
1990 18" Naughty Kid 2976	Closed	1991	75.00	140
1987 18" P.J. Kid 7650	Closed	1987	40.00	85
1989 18" P.J. Kid Hanging Stocking 7672	Closed	1991	47.00	95
1987 18" P.J. Kid w/ 2' Christmas Stocking 7658	Closed	1995	60.00	62-110
1983 18" Sledding Boy 7665	Closed	1984	30.00	100
1983 18" Sledding Girl 7660	Closed	1984	30.00	100
1975 18" Yankee Doodle Dandy on 18" Horse A-306	Closed	1976	58.00	425

Annette Himstedt

Annette Himstedt Club - A. Himstedt

YEAR ISSUE	EDITION LIMIT	YEAR RETD.	ISSUE PRICE	*QUOTE U.S.$
1996 Morgana	Retrd.	1997	N/A	N/A
1996 Virpi	Retrd.	1997	N/A	N/A
1996 Copper Box w/Morgana & Virpi on top	Retrd.	1997	Gift	N/A
1997 Freeke w/Bibi	Retrd.	1998	N/A	N/A
1997 Keshia & Orjo	Retrd.	1998	N/A	N/A
1997 Klara & Paulinchen	Retrd.	1998	N/A	N/A
1997 Freeke w/Bibi Pendant	Retrd.	1998	Gift	N/A
1997 Sita Bust	Retrd.	1998	Gift	N/A
1998 Baby Lieschen	3/99		698.00	698
1998 Baby Lieschen Miniature	3/99		Gift	N/A

Puppen Kinder - A. Himstedt

YEAR ISSUE	EDITION LIMIT	YEAR RETD.	ISSUE PRICE	*QUOTE U.S.$
1989 Adrienne-France	2-Yr.	1991	560.00	800-900
1994 Alke-Norway	2-Yr.	1996	618.00	618
1997 AnMei-China	1-Yr.		680.00	680
1998 Anna I-Germany	2-Yr.		605.00	605
1998 Anna II-Germany	2-Yr.		605.00	605
1990 Ännchen-Germay	2-Yr.	1992	560.00	700
1996 Aura-Spain	1,013	1997	1020.00	1020-1350
1989 Ayoka-Africa	2-Yr.	1991	560.00	1000-1050
1987 Bastian-Germany	2-Yr.	1989	329.00	725
1987 Beckus-Nepal	2-Yr.	1989	329.00	1200-1500
1998 Catalina-Italy (Bolzano)	1-Yr.		725.00	725
1996 Charly-Chicago	1-Yr.	1997	685.00	685
1987 Ellen-Germany	2-Yr.	1989	329.00	825
1992 Enzo-Italy	2-Yr.	1994	582.00	500-599
1997 Esme-Scotland	1-Yr.		725.00	725
1987 Fatou (Cornroll)-Senegal	2-Yr.	1989	329.00	1200-1500
1987 Fatou-Senegal	2-Yr.	1989	329.00	950-1050
1990 Fiene-Belgium	2-Yr.	1992	560.00	800
1997 Freeke & Bibi-Netherlands	1-Yr.		860.00	860
1988 Friederike-Alsace	2-Yr.	1990	525.00	1600-2200
1997 Irmi-Austria	1-Yr.		690.00	690
1989 Janka-Hungry	2-Yr.	1991	560.00	800-900
1992 Jule-Sweden	2-Yr.	1994	582.00	650-700
1989 Kai-Germany	2-Yr.	1991	560.00	700-900
1988 Kasimir-Germany	2-Yr.	1990	525.00	1700-1900
1987 Käthe-Germany	2-Yr.	1989	329.00	825
1998 Keri-Africa	1-Yr.		690.00	690
1993 Kima-Greenland	2-Yr.	1995	582.00	625-675
1991 Liliane-Netherlands	2-Yr.	1993	569.00	695-725
1996 Lina-Germany	1-Yr.	1997	680.00	680
1987 Lisa-Germany	2-Yr.	1989	329.00	825-875
1993 Lona-California	2-Yr.	1995	601.00	550-599
1998 Lonneke-Denmark	1-Yr.		690.00	690
1995 Madino-Russia	2-Yr.	1997	640.00	640
1988 Makimura-Japan	2-Yr.	1990	525.00	1000-1200
1988 Malin-Sweden	2-Yr.	1990	525.00	1500-1650
1996 Marlie-Germany	1-Yr.	1997	685.00	685
1994 Melvin-Ireland	2-Yr.	1996	618.00	550-618
1988 Michiko-Japan	2-Yr.	1990	525.00	1100-1450
1995 Minou-Corsica	2-Yr.	1997	650.00	650
1990 Mo-USA	2-Yr.	1992	560.00	625-700
1996 Morgana-Tuskani	1-Yr.	1997	685.00	700
1991 Neblina-Switzerland	2-Yr.	1993	569.00	595-725
1998 Oscar-Ireland	1-Yr.		1250.00	1250
1994 Panchita-Mexico	2-Yr.	1996	618.00	550-618
1994 Pancho-Mexico	2-Yr.	1996	618.00	550-618
1987 Paula-Germany	2-Yr.	1989	329.00	825
1992 Pemba-USA	2-Yr.	1994	569.00	500-599
1992 Sanga-USA	2-Yr.	1994	569.00	500-599
1991 Shireem-Bali	2-Yr.	1993	569.00	595-650
1990 Taki-Japan	2-Yr.	1992	560.00	800-1100
1995 Takuma-Cheyenne Indian Boy	2-Yr.	1997	640.00	640
1995 Takumi-Cheyenne Indian Girl	2-Yr.	1997	650.00	650
1993 Tara-Germany	2-Yr.	1995	582.00	599
1988 Timi-Germany	2-Yr.	1990	329.00	400-500
1997 Tinka-Friesland	1,013		1250.00	1250
1988 Toni-Germany	2-Yr.	1990	329.00	400-500

ANRI

Disney Dolls - Disney Studios

YEAR ISSUE	EDITION LIMIT	YEAR RETD.	ISSUE PRICE	*QUOTE U.S.$
1990 Daisy Duck, 14"	2,500	1991	895.00	1250
1990 Donald Duck, 14"	2,500	1991	895.00	1250
1989 Mickey Mouse, 14"	2,500	1991	850.00	1000
1989 Minnie Mouse, 14"	2,500	1991	850.00	1000
1989 Pinocchio, 14"	2,500	1991	850.00	895

Ferrandiz Dolls - J. Ferrandiz

YEAR ISSUE	EDITION LIMIT	YEAR RETD.	ISSUE PRICE	*QUOTE U.S.$
1991 Carmen, 14"	1,000	1992	730.00	730
1991 Fernando, 14"	1,000	1992	730.00	730
1989 Gabriel, 14"	1,000	1991	550.00	575
1991 Juanita, 7"	1,500	1992	300.00	300
1990 Margarite, 14"	1,000	1992	575.00	730
1989 Maria, 14"	1,000	1991	550.00	575
1991 Miguel, 7"	1,500	1992	300.00	300
1990 Philipe, 14"	1,000	1992	575.00	680

Sarah Kay Dolls - S. Kay

YEAR ISSUE	EDITION LIMIT	YEAR RETD.	ISSUE PRICE	*QUOTE U.S.$
1991 Annie, 7"	1,500	1993	300.00	300
1989 Bride to Love And To Cherish	750	1992	750.00	790
1989 Charlotte (Blue)	1,000	1991	550.00	575
1990 Christina, 14"	1,000	1993	575.00	730
1989 Eleanor (Floral)	1,000	1991	550.00	575
1989 Elizabeth (Patchwork)	1,000	1991	550.00	575
1988 Emily, 14"	Closed	1989	500.00	500
1990 Faith, 14"	1,000	1993	575.00	685
1989 Groom With This Ring Doll, 14"	750	1992	550.00	730
1989 Helen (Brown), 14"	1,000	1991	550.00	575
1989 Henry, 14"	1,000	1991	550.00	575
1991 Janine, 14"	1,000	1993	750.00	750
1988 Jennifer, 14"	Closed	1989	500.00	500
1991 Jessica, 7"	1,500	1993	300.00	300
1991 Julie, 7"	1,500	1993	300.00	300
1988 Katherine, 14"	Closed	1989	500.00	250-500

*Quotes have been rounded up to nearest dollar

YEAR ISSUE	EDITION LIMIT	YEAR RETD.	ISSUE PRICE	*QUOTE U.S.$
1988 Martha, 14"	Closed	1989	500.00	500
1989 Mary (Red)	1,000	1991	550.00	575
1991 Michelle, 7"	1,500	1993	300.00	300
1991 Patricia, 14"	1,000	1993	730.00	730
1991 Peggy, 7"	1,500	1993	300.00	300
1990 Polly, 14"	1,000	1993	575.00	680
1988 Rachael, 14"	Closed	1989	500.00	500
1988 Rebecca, 14"	Closed	1989	500.00	250-500
1988 Sarah, 14"	Closed	1989	500.00	500
1990 Sophie, 14"	1,000	1993	575.00	660
1991 Susan, 7"	1,500	1993	300.00	300
1988 Victoria, 14"	Closed	1989	500.00	500

Ashton-Drake Galleries

All I Wish For You - J. Good-Krüger

YEAR ISSUE	EDITION LIMIT	YEAR RETD.	ISSUE PRICE	*QUOTE U.S.$
1994 I Wish You Love	Closed	1995	49.95	50
1995 I Wish You Faith	Closed	1998	49.95	50
1995 I Wish You Happiness	Closed	1998	49.95	50
1995 I Wish You Wisdom	Closed	1998	49.95	50
1996 I Wish You Charity	12/99		49.95	50
1996 I Wish You Luck	12/99		49.95	50

All Precious in His Sight - J. Ibarolle

YEAR ISSUE	EDITION LIMIT	YEAR RETD.	ISSUE PRICE	*QUOTE U.S.$
1998 Naomi	12/00		72.99	73
1998 Kristina	12/01		72.99	73
1998 Rosa	12/01		72.99	73
1998 Su-Lee	12/01		72.99	73

Amish Blessings - J. Good-Krüger

YEAR ISSUE	EDITION LIMIT	YEAR RETD.	ISSUE PRICE	*QUOTE U.S.$
1990 Rebeccah	Closed	1993	68.00	95-100
1991 Rachel	Closed	1993	69.00	125
1991 Adam	Closed	1993	75.00	125-150
1992 Ruth	Closed	1993	75.00	90-110
1992 Eli	Closed	1993	79.95	95-125
1993 Sarah	Closed	1994	79.95	125

Anne of Green Gables - J. Kovacik

YEAR ISSUE	EDITION LIMIT	YEAR RETD.	ISSUE PRICE	*QUOTE U.S.$
1995 Anne	Closed	1998	69.95	70
1996 Diana Barry	12/99		69.95	70
1996 Gilbert Blythe	12/00		69.95	70
1996 Josie Pye	12/00		69.95	70

As Cute As Can Be - D. Effner

YEAR ISSUE	EDITION LIMIT	YEAR RETD.	ISSUE PRICE	*QUOTE U.S.$
1993 Sugar Plum	Closed	1994	49.95	75-95
1994 Puppy Love	Closed	1995	49.95	75-95
1994 Angel Face	Closed	1995	49.95	50-75
1995 Patty Cake	Closed	1998	49.95	50

Babies World of Wonder - K. Barry-Hippensteel

YEAR ISSUE	EDITION LIMIT	YEAR RETD.	ISSUE PRICE	*QUOTE U.S.$
1996 Andrew	12/99		59.95	60
1996 Sarah	12/00		59.95	60
1997 Jason	12/01		59.95	60
1997 Kristen	12/01		69.95	70
1998 Alex	12/01		69.95	70

Baby Book Treasures - K. Barry-Hippensteel

YEAR ISSUE	EDITION LIMIT	YEAR RETD.	ISSUE PRICE	*QUOTE U.S.$
1990 Elizabeth's Homecoming	Closed	1993	58.00	58
1991 Catherine's Christening	Closed	1994	58.00	58
1991 Christopher's First Smile	Closed	1992	63.00	58-63

Baby Talk - J. Good-Krüger

YEAR ISSUE	EDITION LIMIT	YEAR RETD.	ISSUE PRICE	*QUOTE U.S.$
1994 All Gone	Closed	1995	49.95	75
1994 Bye-Bye	Closed	1995	49.95	50-75
1994 Night, Night	Closed	1995	49.95	50-75

Ballet Recital - P. Bomar

YEAR ISSUE	EDITION LIMIT	YEAR RETD.	ISSUE PRICE	*QUOTE U.S.$
1996 Chloe	12/00		69.95	70
1996 Kylie	12/00		69.95	70
1996 Heidi	12/00		69.95	70

Barely Yours - T. Tomescu

YEAR ISSUE	EDITION LIMIT	YEAR RETD.	ISSUE PRICE	*QUOTE U.S.$
1994 Cute as a Button	Closed	1994	69.95	95-125
1994 Snug as a Bug in a Rug	Closed	1995	75.00	75-125
1995 Clean as a Whistle	Closed	1996	75.00	75-125
1995 Pretty as a Picture	Closed	1996	75.00	75-125
1995 Good as Gold	Closed	1996	75.00	75-125
1996 Cool As A Cucumber	12/99		75.00	75

Beach Babies - C. Jackson

YEAR ISSUE	EDITION LIMIT	YEAR RETD.	ISSUE PRICE	*QUOTE U.S.$
1996 Carly	12/00		79.95	80
1996 Kyle	12/00		79.95	80
1997 Kellie	12/00		79.95	80

Bears of Memories/Plush - B. Ferrier

YEAR ISSUE	EDITION LIMIT	YEAR RETD.	ISSUE PRICE	*QUOTE U.S.$
1997 Cinnamon Bear	Open		79.99	80

Beautiful Dreamers - G. Rademann

YEAR ISSUE	EDITION LIMIT	YEAR RETD.	ISSUE PRICE	*QUOTE U.S.$
1992 Katrina	Closed	1993	89.00	125-150
1992 Nicolette	Closed	1994	89.95	95-100
1993 Brigitte	Closed	1994	94.00	94
1993 Isabella	Closed	1994	94.00	94
1993 Gabrielle	Closed	1994	94.00	94-105

Beauty And Grace - B. Hanson

YEAR ISSUE	EDITION LIMIT	YEAR RETD.	ISSUE PRICE	*QUOTE U.S.$
1997 Isabella	12/01		99.95	100
1997 Patrice	12/01		99.95	100
1998 Collette	12/01		99.95	100
1998 Lara	12/01		99.95	100

Bedtime for Bears/Plush - J. Davis

YEAR ISSUE	EDITION LIMIT	YEAR RETD.	ISSUE PRICE	*QUOTE U.S.$
1998 Eliza	Open		42.99	43
1998 Genie	Open		42.99	43
1998 Jilly	Open		42.99	43
1997 Sarah	Open		42.99	43

Birthstone Bears/Plush - P. Blair

YEAR ISSUE	EDITION LIMIT	YEAR RETD.	ISSUE PRICE	*QUOTE U.S.$
1997 January Garnet	Open		39.95	40
1997 February Amethyst	Open		39.95	40
1997 March Aquamarine	Open		39.95	40
1997 April Diamond	Open		39.95	40
1997 May Emerald	Open		39.95	40
1997 June Pearl	Open		39.95	40
1997 July Ruby	Open		39.95	40
1997 August Peridot	Open		39.95	40
1997 September Sapphire	Open		39.95	40
1997 October Opal	Open		39.95	40
1997 November Topaz	Open		39.95	40
1997 December Turquoise	Open		39.95	40

Blessed Are The Children - B. Deval

YEAR ISSUE	EDITION LIMIT	YEAR RETD.	ISSUE PRICE	*QUOTE U.S.$
1996 Blessed Are The Peacemakers	12/99		69.95	70
1996 Blessed Are The Pure of Heart	12/00		69.95	70
1997 Blessed Are The Meek	12/01		79.95	80
1997 Blessed Are The Merciful	12/01		79.95	80

Blossoming Belles - S. Freeman

YEAR ISSUE	EDITION LIMIT	YEAR RETD.	ISSUE PRICE	*QUOTE U.S.$
1997 Yellow Rose	12/00		82.99	83
1998 Peach Blossom	12/01		82.99	83
1998 Honeysuckle Rose	12/01		82.99	83
1998 Magnolia Blossom	12/01		82.99	83

Born To Be Famous - K. Barry-Hippensteel

YEAR ISSUE	EDITION LIMIT	YEAR RETD.	ISSUE PRICE	*QUOTE U.S.$
1989 Little Sherlock	Closed	1991	87.00	90
1990 Little Florence Nightingale	Closed	1991	87.00	87-95
1991 Little Davey Crockett	Closed	1994	92.00	92
1992 Little Christopher Columbus	Closed	1993	95.00	95

Boys & Bears - A. Brown

YEAR ISSUE	EDITION LIMIT	YEAR RETD.	ISSUE PRICE	*QUOTE U.S.$
1996 Cody and Cuddle Bear	12/00		62.99	63
1997 Bobby and Buddy Bear	12/01		62.99	63
1997 Nicky and Naptime Bear	12/01		62.99	63
1998 Sammy and Sharing Bear	12/02		62.99	63

Boys Will Be Bears/Plush - P. Joho & E. Foran

YEAR ISSUE	EDITION LIMIT	YEAR RETD.	ISSUE PRICE	*QUOTE U.S.$
1997 Charlie	Open		49.95	50
1998 Davey	Open		49.95	50
1998 Frankie	Open		49.95	50
1998 Jimmy	Open		49.95	50

Calendar Babies - Ashton-Drake

YEAR ISSUE	EDITION LIMIT	YEAR RETD.	ISSUE PRICE	*QUOTE U.S.$
1995 New Year	Open		24.95	25
1995 Cupid	Open		24.95	25
1995 Leprechaun	Open		24.95	25
1995 April Showers	Open		24.95	25
1995 May Flowers	Open		24.95	25
1995 June Bride	Open		24.95	25
1995 Uncle Sam	Open		24.95	25
1995 Sun & Fun	Open		24.95	25
1995 Back to School	Open		24.95	25
1995 Happy Haunting	Open		24.95	25
1995 Thanksgiving Turkey	Open		24.95	25
1995 Jolly Santa	Open		24.95	25

Caught In The Act - M. Tretter

YEAR ISSUE	EDITION LIMIT	YEAR RETD.	ISSUE PRICE	*QUOTE U.S.$
1992 Stevie, Catch Me If You Can	Closed	1994	49.95	125-145
1993 Kelly, Don't I Look Pretty?	Closed	1994	49.95	60-95
1994 Mikey (Look It Floats)	Closed	1994	55.00	55
1994 Nickie (Cookie Jar)	Closed	1995	59.95	60
1994 Becky (Kleenex Box)	Closed	1995	59.95	60

Caught In The Act/Plush - M. Tretter

YEAR ISSUE	EDITION LIMIT	YEAR RETD.	ISSUE PRICE	*QUOTE U.S.$
1994 Sandy	Closed	1995	59.95	60

Caught In The Act/Plush - S. Schutt

YEAR ISSUE	EDITION LIMIT	YEAR RETD.	ISSUE PRICE	*QUOTE U.S.$
1995 Bailey	Open		39.95	40
1995 Bonnie	Open		39.95	40
1995 Katie	Open		39.95	40
1995 Nathaniel	Open		39.95	40

Century of Beautiful Brides - S. Bilotto

YEAR ISSUE	EDITION LIMIT	YEAR RETD.	ISSUE PRICE	*QUOTE U.S.$
1997 Katherine	12/01		62.99	63
1997 Grace	12/01		62.99	63
1998 Donna	12/01		62.99	63
1998 Heather	12/01		62.99	63
1999 Joanna	12/02		62.99	63

Charming Discoveries - S. Freeman

YEAR ISSUE	EDITION LIMIT	YEAR RETD.	ISSUE PRICE	*QUOTE U.S.$
1996 Celeste	12/00		89.95	90
1996 Marie	12/00		89.95	90
1997 Cynthia	12/01		89.95	90

Cherished Teddies Friends/Plush - Ashton-Drake

YEAR ISSUE	EDITION LIMIT	YEAR RETD.	ISSUE PRICE	*QUOTE U.S.$
1998 January	Open		19.95	20
1998 February	Open		19.95	20
1998 March	Open		19.95	20
1998 April	Open		19.95	20
1998 May	Open		19.95	20
1998 June	Open		19.95	20
1998 July	Open		19.95	20
1998 August	Open		19.95	20
1998 September	Open		19.95	20
1998 October	Open		19.95	20
1998 November	Open		19.95	20
1998 December	Open		19.95	20

Cherished Teddies Nursery Rhyme/Plush - Ashton-Drake

YEAR ISSUE	EDITION LIMIT	YEAR RETD.	ISSUE PRICE	*QUOTE U.S.$
1998 Bo Peep	Open		29.95	30
1998 Jack and Jill	Open		29.95	30
1998 Jack Horner	Open		29.95	30
1998 Mary, Mary	Open		29.95	30
1998 Miss Muffet	Open		29.95	30
1998 Tom Tom	Open		29.95	30

Cherished Teddies/Plush - Ashton-Drake

YEAR ISSUE	EDITION LIMIT	YEAR RETD.	ISSUE PRICE	*QUOTE U.S.$
1998 Bazza/Australia	Open		29.99	30
1998 Carlos/Mexico	Open		29.99	30
1998 Claudette/France	Open		29.99	30
1998 Fernando/Spain	Open		29.99	30
1998 Franz/Germany	Open		29.99	30
1998 Katrien/Dutch	Open		29.99	30
1998 Kerstin/Sweden	Open		29.99	30
1998 Lian/China	Open		29.99	30
1998 Lorna/Scotland	Open		29.99	30
1998 Machiko/Japan	Open		29.99	30
1998 Nadia/Russia	Open		29.99	30
1998 Preston/Canada	Open		29.99	30
1998 Rajul/India	Open		29.99	30
1998 Sophia/Italy	Open		29.99	30
1998 USA Bob	Open		29.99	30
1998 William/England	Open		29.99	30

Children of Christmas - M. Sirko

YEAR ISSUE	EDITION LIMIT	YEAR RETD.	ISSUE PRICE	*QUOTE U.S.$
1994 The Little Drummer Boy	Closed	1995	79.95	125-150
1994 The Littlest Angel	Closed	1995	79.95	80
1995 O Christmas Tree	Closed	1998	79.95	80
1995 Sugar Plum Fairy	Closed	1998	79.95	80

Children of Mother Goose - Y. Bello

YEAR ISSUE	EDITION LIMIT	YEAR RETD.	ISSUE PRICE	*QUOTE U.S.$
1987 Little Bo Peep	Closed	1988	58.00	95-110
1987 Mary Had a Little Lamb	Closed	1989	58.00	110-175
1988 Little Jack Horner	Closed	1989	63.00	63
1989 Miss Muffet	Closed	1991	63.00	63-150

A Children's Circus - J. McClelland

YEAR ISSUE	EDITION LIMIT	YEAR RETD.	ISSUE PRICE	*QUOTE U.S.$
1990 Tommy The Clown	Closed	1993	78.00	70-125
1991 Katie The Tightrope Walker	Closed	1993	78.00	70-125
1991 Johnnie The Strongman	Closed	1994	83.00	83-125
1992 Maggie The Animal Trainer	Closed	1994	83.00	83-150

Classic Brides of The Century - E. Williams

YEAR ISSUE	EDITION LIMIT	YEAR RETD.	ISSUE PRICE	*QUOTE U.S.$
1990 Flora, The 1900s Bride	Closed	1993	145.00	195-300
1991 Jennifer, The 1980s Bride	Closed	1992	149.00	225-300
1993 Kathleen, The 1930s Bride	Closed	1993	149.95	150

Classic Collection - D. Effner

YEAR ISSUE	EDITION LIMIT	YEAR RETD.	ISSUE PRICE	*QUOTE U.S.$
1996 Hillary	12/00		79.95	80
1996 Willow	12/00		79.95	80
1996 Emily	12/00		79.95	80
1997 Jenny	12/01		79.95	80
1997 Schoolgirl Jenny	12/01		79.95	80

Country Sweethearts - M. Tretter

YEAR ISSUE	EDITION LIMIT	YEAR RETD.	ISSUE PRICE	*QUOTE U.S.$
1996 Millie	12/00		62.99	63

Cuddle Chums - K. Barry-Hippensteel

YEAR ISSUE	EDITION LIMIT	YEAR RETD.	ISSUE PRICE	*QUOTE U.S.$
1995 Heather	Closed	1998	59.95	60
1995 Jeffrey	Closed	1998	59.95	60

Day in the Life of Emily Ann - A. Tsalikhan

YEAR ISSUE	EDITION LIMIT	YEAR RETD.	ISSUE PRICE	*QUOTE U.S.$
1996 Breaktime	12/00		82.99	83

Decorating The Tree - M. Tretter

YEAR ISSUE	EDITION LIMIT	YEAR RETD.	ISSUE PRICE	*QUOTE U.S.$
1996 Trisha	12/00		59.95	60
1996 Patrick	12/00		59.95	60
1996 Ryan	12/00		59.95	60
1996 Melissa	12/00		59.95	60

Deval's Fairytale Princesses - B. Deval

YEAR ISSUE	EDITION LIMIT	YEAR RETD.	ISSUE PRICE	*QUOTE U.S.$
1996 Cinderella	12/00		92.99	93
1996 Rapunzel	12/00		92.99	93
1997 The Snow Queen	12/01		94.99	95
1997 Sleeping Beauty	12/01		94.99	95
1997 Princess and the Frog	12/01		94.99	95

Diana the People's Princess - T. Tomescu

YEAR ISSUE	EDITION LIMIT	YEAR RETD.	ISSUE PRICE	*QUOTE U.S.$
1998 Princess Diana	12/10		132.99	133

Dianna Effner's Classic Collection - D. Effner

YEAR ISSUE	EDITION LIMIT	YEAR RETD.	ISSUE PRICE	*QUOTE U.S.$
1995 Hilary	Closed	1998	79.95	80
1996 Willow	12/99		79.95	80
1996 Emily	12/00		79.95	80

Dianna Effner's Mother Goose - D. Effner

YEAR ISSUE	EDITION LIMIT	YEAR RETD.	ISSUE PRICE	*QUOTE U.S.$
1990 Mary, Mary, Quite Contrary	Closed	1992	78.00	175-200
1991 The Little Girl With The Curl (Horrid)	Closed	1992	79.00	150-250
1991 The Little Girl With The Curl (Good)	Closed	1993	79.00	125-200
1992 Little Boy Blue	Closed	1993	85.00	75-85
1993 Snips & Snails	Closed	1994	85.00	125-150
1993 Sugar & Spice	Closed	1994	89.95	110-125
1993 Curly Locks	Closed	1995	89.95	90-100

Down on the Beanbag Farm - R. Clark

YEAR ISSUE	EDITION LIMIT	YEAR RETD.	ISSUE PRICE	*QUOTE U.S.$
1997 Janie	12/00		62.99	63
1998 Emma	12/01		62.99	63

Emily Anne's Busy Day - A. Tsalikhan

YEAR ISSUE	EDITION LIMIT	YEAR RETD.	ISSUE PRICE	*QUOTE U.S.$
1996 Emily Anne	12/00		69.95	70
1997 Emily Anne Playing Mommy	12/01		69.95	70
1997 Emily Anne Calling Grandma	12/01		69.95	70
1997 Naptime for Emily Anne	12/00		82.99	83
1997 Calling Grandma	12/00		82.99	83
1997 Snacktime	12/00		82.99	83

Eternal Love - T. Tomescu

YEAR ISSUE	EDITION LIMIT	YEAR RETD.	ISSUE PRICE	*QUOTE U.S.$
1997 Eternal Love	12/00		92.99	93

*Quotes have been rounded up to nearest dollar

European Fairytales - G. Rademann

YEAR ISSUE	EDITION LIMIT	YEAR RETD.	ISSUE PRICE	*QUOTE U.S.$
1994 Little Red Riding Hood	Closed	1995	79.95	80
1995 Snow White	Closed	1996	79.95	80

Family Ties - M. Tretter

YEAR ISSUE	EDITION LIMIT	YEAR RETD.	ISSUE PRICE	*QUOTE U.S.$
1994 Welcome Home Baby Brother	Closed	1995	79.95	80
1995 Kiss and Make it Better	Closed	1996	89.95	80-90
1995 Happily Ever Better	Closed	1996	89.95	80-90

Flurry of Activity - T. Tomescu

YEAR ISSUE	EDITION LIMIT	YEAR RETD.	ISSUE PRICE	*QUOTE U.S.$
1996 Making Snowflakes	12/00		72.99	73
1997 Making Icicles	12/01		72.99	73
1997 Making Sunshine	12/00		72.99	73

Forever Starts Today - C. McClure

YEAR ISSUE	EDITION LIMIT	YEAR RETD.	ISSUE PRICE	*QUOTE U.S.$
1996 Melody	12/99		199.95	200
1997 Angelica	12/00		199.95	200
1997 Caroline	12/01		199.95	200

From This Day Forward - P. Tumminio

YEAR ISSUE	EDITION LIMIT	YEAR RETD.	ISSUE PRICE	*QUOTE U.S.$
1994 Elizabeth	Closed	1995	89.95	90-150
1995 Betty	Closed	1996	89.95	90-150
1995 Beth	Closed	1996	89.95	90-175
1995 Lisa	Closed	1996	89.95	90

Garden of Innocence - D. Richardson

YEAR ISSUE	EDITION LIMIT	YEAR RETD.	ISSUE PRICE	*QUOTE U.S.$
1996 Hope	12/00		92.99	93
1996 Serenity	12/00		92.99	93
1997 Charity	12/01		92.99	93
1997 Grace	12/01		92.99	93
1997 Kindness	12/01		92.99	93

Garden of Inspirations - B. Hanson

YEAR ISSUE	EDITION LIMIT	YEAR RETD.	ISSUE PRICE	*QUOTE U.S.$
1994 Gathering Violets	Closed	1995	69.95	75
1994 Daisy Chain	Closed	1995	69.95	70
1995 Heart's Bouquet	Closed	1996	74.95	75
1995 Garden Prayer	Closed	1996	74.95	75

Gentle Joys - J. Good-Krüger

YEAR ISSUE	EDITION LIMIT	YEAR RETD.	ISSUE PRICE	*QUOTE U.S.$
1997 A Day Filled With Hugs & Kisses	12/01		49.99	50

Gibson Girl in Fashion - S. Bilotto

YEAR ISSUE	EDITION LIMIT	YEAR RETD.	ISSUE PRICE	*QUOTE U.S.$
1998 Garden Walk	12/01		132.99	133
1998 Evening at the Opera	12/01		132.99	133
1998 Derby Day	12/01		132.99	133
1998 The Masquerade Ball	12/01		132.99	133

Gifts For Mommy - M. Girard-Kassis

YEAR ISSUE	EDITION LIMIT	YEAR RETD.	ISSUE PRICE	*QUOTE U.S.$
1997 Mother's Day	12/01		62.99	63
1997 Christmas	12/01		62.99	63
1998 Be My Valentine	12/01		62.99	63
1998 Happy Birthday	12/01		62.99	63

Gingham & Bows - S. Freeman

YEAR ISSUE	EDITION LIMIT	YEAR RETD.	ISSUE PRICE	*QUOTE U.S.$
1995 Gwendolyn	Closed	1998	69.95	70
1996 Mallory	12/99		69.95	70
1996 Ashleigh	12/00		69.95	70
1996 Bridget	12/00		69.95	70

God Hears the Children - B. Conner

YEAR ISSUE	EDITION LIMIT	YEAR RETD.	ISSUE PRICE	*QUOTE U.S.$
1995 Now I Lay Me Down	Closed	1998	79.95	80
1996 God Is Great, God Is Good	12/99		79.95	80
1996 We Give Thanks For Things We Have	12/99		79.95	80
1996 All Creatures Great & Small	12/00		79.95	80

Growing Up Like Wildflowers - B. Madeja

YEAR ISSUE	EDITION LIMIT	YEAR RETD.	ISSUE PRICE	*QUOTE U.S.$
1996 Annie	12/99		49.95	50
1996 Bonnie	12/00		49.95	50

Happily Ever After - G. Rademann

YEAR ISSUE	EDITION LIMIT	YEAR RETD.	ISSUE PRICE	*QUOTE U.S.$
1998 Cinderella Bride	12/01		82.99	83
1998 Snow White Bride	12/01		82.99	83

Happiness Is Homemade - J. Good-Krüger

YEAR ISSUE	EDITION LIMIT	YEAR RETD.	ISSUE PRICE	*QUOTE U.S.$
1997 Hugs Made By Hand	12/01		72.99	73

Happiness Is... - K. Barry-Hippensteel

YEAR ISSUE	EDITION LIMIT	YEAR RETD.	ISSUE PRICE	*QUOTE U.S.$
1991 Patricia (My First Tooth)	Closed	1993	69.00	125
1992 Crystal (Feeding Myself)	Closed	1994	69.95	100
1993 Brittany (Blowing Kisses)	Closed	1993	69.95	100
1993 Joy (My First Christmas)	Closed	1993	69.95	70-85
1994 Candy Cane (Holly)	Closed	1994	69.95	70
1994 Patrick (My First Playmate)	Closed	1994	69.95	70-85

Happy Meals World of Play - Y. Bello

YEAR ISSUE	EDITION LIMIT	YEAR RETD.	ISSUE PRICE	*QUOTE U.S.$
1997 McDonald's Express	12/01		59.95	60
1997 McDonald's Old West	12/02		64.99	65

Hats Off To The Seasons - L. Dunsmore

YEAR ISSUE	EDITION LIMIT	YEAR RETD.	ISSUE PRICE	*QUOTE U.S.$
1997 Christmas Carol	12/00		72.99	73
1997 Springtime Robin	12/00		82.99	83
1998 Mary Sunshine	12/01		82.99	83
1998 Autumn Joy	12/01		82.99	83

Heavenly Inspirations - C. McClure

YEAR ISSUE	EDITION LIMIT	YEAR RETD.	ISSUE PRICE	*QUOTE U.S.$
1992 Every Cloud Has a Silver Lining	Closed	1994	59.95	48-75
1993 Wish Upon A Star	Closed	1994	59.95	60-65
1994 Sweet Dreams	Closed	1994	65.00	65
1994 Luck at the End of Rainbow	Closed	1994	65.00	65
1994 Sunshine	Closed	1994	69.95	65-70
1994 Pennies From Heaven	Closed	1995	69.95	65-70

Heritage of American Quilting - J. Lundy

YEAR ISSUE	EDITION LIMIT	YEAR RETD.	ISSUE PRICE	*QUOTE U.S.$
1994 Eleanor	Closed	1995	79.95	80
1995 Abigail	Closed	1996	79.95	80
1995 Louisa	Closed	1996	84.95	85
1995 Ruth Anne	Closed	1996	84.95	85

Heroines from the Fairy Tale Forests - D. Effner

YEAR ISSUE	EDITION LIMIT	YEAR RETD.	ISSUE PRICE	*QUOTE U.S.$
1988 Little Red Riding Hood	Closed	1990	68.00	195-250
1989 Goldilocks	Closed	1991	68.00	68-150
1990 Snow White	Closed	1992	73.00	175
1991 Rapunzel	Closed	1993	79.00	175-250
1992 Cinderella	Closed	1993	79.00	175-295
1993 Cinderella (Ballgown)	Closed	1994	79.95	175-250

I Want Mommy - K. Barry-Hippensteel

YEAR ISSUE	EDITION LIMIT	YEAR RETD.	ISSUE PRICE	*QUOTE U.S.$
1993 Timmy (Mommy I'm Sleepy)	Closed	1994	59.95	145-150
1993 Tommy (Mommy I'm Sorry)	Closed	1994	59.95	125
1994 Up Mommy (Tammy)	Closed	1994	65.00	65

I'd Rather Be Fishin' - M. Tretter

YEAR ISSUE	EDITION LIMIT	YEAR RETD.	ISSUE PRICE	*QUOTE U.S.$
1996 What A Catch	12/00		72.99	73
1997 Fishin' Buddies	12/01		72.99	73
1997 Hooked on Fishin'	12/01		72.99	73
1997 Fish Story	12/01		72.99	73

I'm Just Little - K. Barry-Hippensteel

YEAR ISSUE	EDITION LIMIT	YEAR RETD.	ISSUE PRICE	*QUOTE U.S.$
1995 I'm a Little Angel	Closed	1996	49.95	50
1995 I'm a Little Devil	Closed	1996	49.95	50
1996 I'm a Little Cutie	12/99		49.95	50

Imagine Where He'll Go - R. Miller

YEAR ISSUE	EDITION LIMIT	YEAR RETD.	ISSUE PRICE	*QUOTE U.S.$
1997 Adam	12/00		62.99	63
1998 David	12/01		62.99	63

International Festival of Toys and Tots - K. Barry-Hippensteel

YEAR ISSUE	EDITION LIMIT	YEAR RETD.	ISSUE PRICE	*QUOTE U.S.$
1989 Chen, a Little Boy of China	Closed	1990	78.00	78-150
1989 Natasha	Closed	1992	78.00	78-150
1990 Molly	Closed	1993	83.00	75-83
1991 Hans	Closed	1993	88.00	88
1992 Miki, Eskimo	Closed	1994	88.00	88

It's So Much Friendlier With Pooh - C. McClure

YEAR ISSUE	EDITION LIMIT	YEAR RETD.	ISSUE PRICE	*QUOTE U.S.$
1998 You Need a Hug Pooh	12/01		72.99	73
1998 You Look Sleepy Pooh	12/01		72.99	73

Joy Forever - C. McClure

YEAR ISSUE	EDITION LIMIT	YEAR RETD.	ISSUE PRICE	*QUOTE U.S.$
1996 Victorian Serenity	12/00		129.95	130
1997 Victorian Bliss	12/01		129.95	130
1997 Victorian Harmony	12/01		129.95	130
1997 Victorian Peace	12/01		129.95	130

Joys of Summer - K. Barry-Hippensteel

YEAR ISSUE	EDITION LIMIT	YEAR RETD.	ISSUE PRICE	*QUOTE U.S.$
1993 Tickles	Closed	1994	49.95	110-120
1993 Little Squirt	Closed	1994	49.95	65
1994 Yummy	Closed	1994	55.00	65
1994 Havin' A Ball	Closed	1994	55.00	65
1994 Lil' Scoop	Closed	1994	55.00	65

Just Caught Napping - A. Brown

YEAR ISSUE	EDITION LIMIT	YEAR RETD.	ISSUE PRICE	*QUOTE U.S.$
1996 Asleep in the Saddle	12/99		69.95	70
1996 Oatmeal Dreams	12/00		69.95	70
1997 Dog Tired	12/01		69.95	70

The King & I - P. Ryan Brooks

YEAR ISSUE	EDITION LIMIT	YEAR RETD.	ISSUE PRICE	*QUOTE U.S.$
1991 Shall We Dance	Closed	1992	175.00	395

Lawton's Nursery Rhymes - W. Lawton

YEAR ISSUE	EDITION LIMIT	YEAR RETD.	ISSUE PRICE	*QUOTE U.S.$
1994 Little Bo Peep	Closed	1995	79.95	80-95
1994 Little Miss Muffet	Closed	1995	79.95	80
1994 Mary, Mary	Closed	1995	85.00	80-85
1994 Mary/Lamb	Closed	1995	85.00	80-85

The Legends of Baseball - Various

YEAR ISSUE	EDITION LIMIT	YEAR RETD.	ISSUE PRICE	*QUOTE U.S.$
1994 Babe Ruth - T. Tomescu	Closed	1995	79.95	110-140
1994 Lou Gehrig - T. Tomescu	Closed	1995	79.95	80
1995 Ty Cobb - E. Shelton	Closed	1996	79.95	80

Let's Play Mother Goose - K. Barry-Hippensteel

YEAR ISSUE	EDITION LIMIT	YEAR RETD.	ISSUE PRICE	*QUOTE U.S.$
1994 Cow Jumped Over the Moon	Closed	1995	69.95	70
1994 Hickory, Dickory, Dock	Closed	1995	69.95	95

Life's Little Blessings - R. Mattingly

YEAR ISSUE	EDITION LIMIT	YEAR RETD.	ISSUE PRICE	*QUOTE U.S.$
1997 Charity Is A Blessing	12/01		82.99	83
1997 Kindness Is A Blessing	12/00		72.99	73
1998 Patience Is A Blessing	12/01		72.99	73
1998 Laughter Is A Blessing	12/01		72.99	73

Little Girls of Classic Literature - W. Lawton

YEAR ISSUE	EDITION LIMIT	YEAR RETD.	ISSUE PRICE	*QUOTE U.S.$
1995 Pollyanna	Closed	1998	79.95	80
1996 Laura Ingalls	12/99		79.95	80
1996 Rebecca of Sunnybrook Farm	12/99		79.95	80

Little Gymnast - K. Barry-Hippensteel

YEAR ISSUE	EDITION LIMIT	YEAR RETD.	ISSUE PRICE	*QUOTE U.S.$
1996 Little Gymnast	12/99		59.95	60

Little House On The Prairie - J. Ibarolle

YEAR ISSUE	EDITION LIMIT	YEAR RETD.	ISSUE PRICE	*QUOTE U.S.$
1992 Laura	Closed	1993	79.95	95
1993 Mary Ingalls	Closed	1993	79.95	300-395
1993 Nellie Olson	Closed	1994	85.00	145-150
1993 Almanzo	Closed	1994	85.00	95
1994 Carrie	Closed	1994	85.00	95-100
1994 Ma Ingalls	Closed	1995	85.00	85
1994 Pa Ingalls	Closed	1995	85.00	85
1995 Baby Grace	Closed	1996	69.95	75

Little Lacy Sleepyheads - J. Wolf

YEAR ISSUE	EDITION LIMIT	YEAR RETD.	ISSUE PRICE	*QUOTE U.S.$
1996 Jacqueline	12/00		99.99	100

The Little Performers - C. McClure

YEAR ISSUE	EDITION LIMIT	YEAR RETD.	ISSUE PRICE	*QUOTE U.S.$
1997 Joelle	12/01		94.99	95
1997 Lauren	12/01		94.99	95
1998 Nicole	12/02		94.99	95
1998 Alyssa	12/02		94.99	95

Little Women - W. Lawton

YEAR ISSUE	EDITION LIMIT	YEAR RETD.	ISSUE PRICE	*QUOTE U.S.$
1994 Jo	Closed	1995	59.95	60-75
1994 Meg	Closed	1995	59.95	60-125
1994 Beth	Closed	1996	59.95	75-125
1994 Amy	Closed	1996	59.95	150-175
1995 Marmie	Closed	1996	59.95	60-75

Lots Of Love - T. Menzenbach

YEAR ISSUE	EDITION LIMIT	YEAR RETD.	ISSUE PRICE	*QUOTE U.S.$
1993 Hannah Needs A Hug	Closed	1994	49.95	100
1993 Kaitlyn	Closed	1994	49.95	95
1994 Nicole	Closed	1995	55.00	55
1995 Felicia	Closed	1998	55.00	55

Love, Marriage, Baby Carriage/Plush - Various

YEAR ISSUE	EDITION LIMIT	YEAR RETD.	ISSUE PRICE	*QUOTE U.S.$
1996 Sam - B. Dewey	Open		49.95	50
1996 Katherine - M. Sibol	Open		49.95	50
1997 Carrie - D. Ortega	Open		49.95	50

Lucky Charmers - C. McClure

YEAR ISSUE	EDITION LIMIT	YEAR RETD.	ISSUE PRICE	*QUOTE U.S.$
1995 Lucky Star	Closed	1998	69.95	70
1996 Bit O' Luck	12/00		69.95	70

Madonna & Child - B. Deval

YEAR ISSUE	EDITION LIMIT	YEAR RETD.	ISSUE PRICE	*QUOTE U.S.$
1996 Madonna & Child	12/99		99.95	100

Magic Moments - K. Barry-Hippensteel

YEAR ISSUE	EDITION LIMIT	YEAR RETD.	ISSUE PRICE	*QUOTE U.S.$
1996 Birthday Boy	12/99		69.95	70

Magical Moments of Summer - Y. Bello

YEAR ISSUE	EDITION LIMIT	YEAR RETD.	ISSUE PRICE	*QUOTE U.S.$
1995 Whitney	Closed	1998	59.95	48-60
1996 Zoe	12/99		59.95	60

McDonald's And Me - D. Effner

YEAR ISSUE	EDITION LIMIT	YEAR RETD.	ISSUE PRICE	*QUOTE U.S.$
1996 You Deserve a Break Today	12/00		59.95	60
1997 Sharing a Good Time	12/01		59.95	60

McDonald's Future All Stars - B. Madeja

YEAR ISSUE	EDITION LIMIT	YEAR RETD.	ISSUE PRICE	*QUOTE U.S.$
1997 Joey	12/01		62.99	63

McDonald's Happy Times - K. Barry-Hippensteel

YEAR ISSUE	EDITION LIMIT	YEAR RETD.	ISSUE PRICE	*QUOTE U.S.$
1997 Ritchie	12/01		62.99	63

McDonald's Learning is Fun - T. Tomescu

YEAR ISSUE	EDITION LIMIT	YEAR RETD.	ISSUE PRICE	*QUOTE U.S.$
1996 Katie	12/99		79.95	80

McDonald's Pillow Talk - B. Madeja

YEAR ISSUE	EDITION LIMIT	YEAR RETD.	ISSUE PRICE	*QUOTE U.S.$
1997 Sweet Dreams Ronald	12/00		62.99	63

McDonald's Treats For Tots - Y. Bello

YEAR ISSUE	EDITION LIMIT	YEAR RETD.	ISSUE PRICE	*QUOTE U.S.$
1996 Erik's First French Fry	12/00		59.95	60
1997 Nathan Picks a Pickle	12/01		59.95	60
1998 Krissy's Ice Cream Cone	12/01		59.95	60

Memories of Victorian Childhood - M. Girard-Kassis

YEAR ISSUE	EDITION LIMIT	YEAR RETD.	ISSUE PRICE	*QUOTE U.S.$
1998 Lydia	12/01		82.99	83
1998 Paige	12/01		82.99	83
1998 Olivia	12/01		82.99	83
1998 Estelle	12/01		82.99	83

Messages of Hope - T. Tomescu

YEAR ISSUE	EDITION LIMIT	YEAR RETD.	ISSUE PRICE	*QUOTE U.S.$
1994 Let the Little Children Come to Me	Closed	1995	129.95	130-175
1995 Good Shepherd	Closed	1996	129.95	130
1995 I Stand at the Door	Closed	1996	129.95	130
1996 Our Father	12/99		129.95	130

Miracle of Life - Y. Bello

YEAR ISSUE	EDITION LIMIT	YEAR RETD.	ISSUE PRICE	*QUOTE U.S.$
1996 Beautiful Newborn	12/99		49.95	50
1996 Her Very First Smile	12/00		49.95	50
1996 She's Sitting Pretty	12/00		49.95	50
1996 Watch Her Crawl	12/00		49.95	50

Miracles of Christ - T. Tomescu

YEAR ISSUE	EDITION LIMIT	YEAR RETD.	ISSUE PRICE	*QUOTE U.S.$
1996 Water Into Wine	12/00		99.95	100
1996 Multiplying the Loaves	12/00		99.95	100
1997 Walking on Water	12/01		99.95	100
1998 Ascension Into Heaven	12/02		99.95	100

Moments To Remember - Y. Bello

YEAR ISSUE	EDITION LIMIT	YEAR RETD.	ISSUE PRICE	*QUOTE U.S.$
1991 Justin	Closed	1994	75.00	75-85
1992 Jill	Closed	1993	75.00	75-85
1993 Brandon (Ring Bearer)	Closed	1994	79.95	80-90
1993 Suzanne (Flower Girl)	Closed	1994	79.95	80-90

Mommy Can I Keep It?/Plush - P. Joho & E. Foran

YEAR ISSUE	EDITION LIMIT	YEAR RETD.	ISSUE PRICE	*QUOTE U.S.$
1995 Bartholomew & His Goldfish	Open		49.95	50
1995 Becky & Her Bunny	Open		49.95	50
1995 Belinda & Her Kitty	Open		49.95	50
1995 Benjamin & His Puppy	Retrd.	1997	49.95	50

Mommy Can You Fix It?/Plush - A. Cranshaw

YEAR ISSUE	EDITION LIMIT	YEAR RETD.	ISSUE PRICE	*QUOTE U.S.$
1997 Edgar	Open		49.95	50
1998 Edith	Open		49.95	50
1997 Emma	Open		49.95	50
1996 Emmett	Open		49.95	50

Morning Glories - B. Bambina

YEAR ISSUE	EDITION LIMIT	YEAR RETD.	ISSUE PRICE	*QUOTE U.S.$
1996 Rosebud	12/00		49.95	50
1996 Dew Drop	12/00		49.95	50

A Mother's Work Is Never Done - T. Menzenbach

YEAR ISSUE	EDITION LIMIT	YEAR RETD.	ISSUE PRICE	*QUOTE U.S.$
1995 Don't Forget To Wash Behind Your Ears	Closed	1998	59.95	60
1996 A Kiss Will Make It Better	12/99		59.95	60
1996 Who Made This Mess	12/99		59.95	60

*Quotes have been rounded up to nearest dollar

DOLLS/PLUSH

YEAR ISSUE	EDITION LIMIT	YEAR RETD.	ISSUE PRICE	*QUOTE U.S.$
My Closest Friend - J. Goodyear				
1991 Boo Bear 'N Me	Closed	1992	78.00	125-225
1991 Me and My Blankie	Closed	1993	79.00	95
1992 My Secret Pal (Robbie)	Closed	1993	85.00	85
1992 My Beary Softest Blanket	Closed	1993	79.95	85
My Fair Lady - P. Ryan Brooks				
1991 Eliza at Ascot	Closed	1992	125.00	395-450
My Little Ballerina - K. Barry-Hippensteel				
1994 My Little Ballerina	Closed	1995	59.95	60-75
Naturally Playful - S. Housely				
1997 Peek-A-Boo Bunny	12/01		72.99	73
Nostalgic Toys - C. McClure				
1996 Amelia	12/00		79.95	80
1996 Charlotte	12/00		79.95	80
1997 Tess	12/01		79.95	80
Nursery Newborns - J. Wolf				
1994 It's A Boy	Closed	1995	79.95	80
1994 It's A Girl	Closed	1995	79.95	80
Nursery Rhyme Favorites/Plush - J. Davis				
1995 Little Bo Peep	Closed	1997	39.95	40
1995 Little Miss Muffet	Open		39.95	40
1995 Mary, Mary	Open		39.95	40
1995 Little Lucy Locket	Open		39.95	40
Oh Holy Night - J. Good-Krüger				
1994 The Holy Family (Jesus, Mary, Joseph)	Closed	1995	129.95	130
1995 The Kneeling King	Closed	1995	59.95	60
1995 The Purple King	Closed	1995	59.95	60
1995 The Blue King	Closed	1995	59.95	60
1995 Shepherd with Pipes	Closed	1995	59.95	60
1995 Shepherd with Lamb	Closed	1995	59.95	60
1995 Angel	Closed	1995	59.95	60
Only At Grandma and Grandpa's - Y. Bello				
1996 I'll Finish The Story	12/99		89.95	90
Our Own Ballet Recital - P. Bomar				
1996 Chloe	12/99		69.95	70
Passports to Friendship - J. Ibarolle				
1995 Serena	Closed	1998	79.95	80
1996 Kali	12/99		79.95	80
1996 Asha	12/99		79.95	80
1996 Liliana	12/00		79.95	80
Patchwork of Love - J. Good-Krüger				
1995 Warmth of the Heart	Closed	1998	59.95	60
1996 Love One Another	12/99		59.95	60
1996 Family Price	12/99		59.95	60
1996 Simplicity Is Best	12/99		59.95	60
1996 Fondest Memory	12/99		59.95	60
1996 Hard Work Pays	12/99		59.95	60
Perfect Companions/Plush - Various				
1998 Big Ears - B. Dewey	Open		59.99	60
1998 Big Hugs - A. Cranshaw	Open		59.99	60
Perfect Pairs - B. Bambina				
1995 Amber	Closed	1996	59.95	60
1995 Tiffany	Closed	1996	59.95	60
1995 Carmen	Closed	1996	59.95	60
1996 Susie	12/99		59.95	60
Petting Zoo - Y. Bello				
1995 Andy	Closed	1996	59.95	60
1995 Kendra	Closed	1996	59.95	60
1995 Cory	Closed	1996	59.95	60
1995 Maddie	Closed	1996	59.95	60
Please Come To Tea - R. Miller				
1998 Abby	12/00		62.99	63
1998 Clarissa	12/00		62.99	63
Precious Memories of Motherhood - S. Kuck				
1989 Loving Steps	Closed	1991	125.00	125-225
1990 Lullaby	Closed	1993	125.00	130-200
1991 Expectant Moments	Closed	1993	149.00	130-250
1992 Bedtime	Closed	1993	150.00	150-200
Precious Papooses - S. Housely				
1995 Sleeping Bear	Closed	1998	79.95	80
1996 Bright Feather	12/99		79.95	80
1996 Cloud Chaser	12/00		79.95	80
1996 Swift Fox	12/00		79.95	80
Rainbow of Love - Y. Bello				
1994 Blue Sky	Closed	1995	59.95	60
1994 Yellow Sunshine	Closed	1995	59.95	60
1994 Green Earth	Closed	1995	59.95	60
1994 Pink Flower	Closed	1996	59.95	60
1994 Purple Mountain	Closed	1996	59.95	60
1994 Orange Sunset	Closed	1996	59.95	60
Ruffle & Ribbons, Buttons & Bows - B. Madeja				
1998 Ruffles For Rebecca	12/01		62.99	63
Seasonal Carousel/Plush - B. Conley				
1998 Daisy	Open		74.99	75
1998 Holly	Open		74.99	75
1998 Punkin	Open		74.99	75
1997 Rosie	Open		74.99	75
Seasons of Joy - J. Ibarolle				
1997 Nicholas	12/01		74.99	75
1997 Kimberly	12/01		74.99	75
1998 Molly	12/01		74.99	75
1998 Brandon	12/01		74.99	75
Secret Garden - J. Kovacik				
1994 Mary	Closed	1995	69.95	70
1995 Colin	Closed	1996	69.95	70
1995 Martha	Closed	1996	69.95	70
1995 Dickon	Closed	1996	69.95	70
A Sense of Discovery - K. Barry-Hippensteel				
1993 Sweetie (Sense of Discovery)	Closed	1994	59.95	60
Sense of Security - G. Rademann				
1996 Amy	12/00		62.99	63
She Walks In Beauty - S. Bilotto				
1996 Winter Romance	12/00		92.99	93
1997 Spring Promise	12/01		92.99	93
1997 Summer Dream	12/01		92.99	93
1998 Autumn Reflection	12/01		92.99	93
Siblings Through Time - C. McClure				
1995 Alexandra	Closed	1996	69.95	70
1995 Gracie	Closed	1996	59.95	60
Simple Gifts - J. Good-Krüger				
1996 Roly Poly Harvest	12/00		49.95	50
1997 Sweet Sensation	12/01		49.95	50
1997 Papa's Helper	12/01		49.95	50
1997 Naptime at Noon	12/01		49.95	50
1997 Cuddly Companions	12/01		49.95	50
Simple Pleasures, Special Days - J. Lundy				
1996 Gretchen	12/99		79.95	80
1996 Molly	12/99		79.95	80
1996 Adeline	12/00		79.95	80
1996 Eliza	12/00		79.95	80
Smile For the Camera/Plush - S. Howey				
1995 Josh	Open		39.95	40
1995 Josh	Open		39.95	40
Snow Babies - T. Tomescu				
1995 Beneath the Mistletoe	Closed	1995	69.95	70
1995 Follow the Leader	Closed	1996	75.00	75
1995 Snow Baby Express	Closed	1996	75.00	75
1996 Slip Slidn'	12/00		75.00	75
1996 Learning To Fly	12/00		75.00	75
1996 Catch of the Day	12/00		75.00	75
Someone to Watch Over Me - K. Barry-Hippensteel				
1994 Sweet Dreams	Closed	1995	69.95	70
1995 Night-Night Angel	Closed	1995	24.95	25
1995 Lullaby Angel	Closed	1995	24.95	25
1995 Sleepyhead Angel	Closed	1996	24.95	25
1995 Stardust Angel	Closed	1996	24.95	25
1995 Tuck-Me-In Angel	Closed	1996	24.95	25
Special Edition Tour 1993 - Y. Bello				
1993 Miguel	Closed	1993	69.95	70-150
1993 Rosa	Closed	1993	69.95	70-150
Spending Time With Grandparents/Plush - B. Conley & T. Roe				
1996 Grandma and Sam	Open		49.95	50
Spice of Life - Y. Bello				
1997 Ginny	12/01		49.95	46
1997 Megan	12/01		49.95	46
1997 Cindy	12/01		49.95	46
Sunday's Best - C. Jackson				
1997 Brianne	12/00		72.99	73
1998 Jacob	12/01		72.99	73
1998 Tmara	12/01		72.99	73
Tales From the Nursery - T. Tomescu				
1997 Baby Bo Peep	12/00		82.99	83
1998 Baby Red Riding Hood	12/01		82.99	83
1998 Baby Goldilocks	12/01		82.99	83
1998 Baby Miss Muffet	12/01		82.99	83
They Are All Precious In His Sight - J. Ibarolle				
1997 Naomi	12/01		72.99	73
Together Forever - S. Krey				
1994 Kirsten	Closed	1995	59.95	60
1994 Courtney	Closed	1995	59.95	60
1994 Kim	Closed	1995	59.95	60
Too Cute to Resist - M. Girard-Kassis				
1997 Ally	12/00		49.99	50
1997 Kayla	12/00		49.99	50
1998 Jennifer	12/01		49.99	50
Toy Chest Treasures/Plush - P. Joho & E. Foran				
1996 Tad	Open		49.95	50
1997 Theo	Open		49.95	50
Treasured Togetherness - M. Tretter				
1994 Tender Touch	Closed	1995	99.95	100
1994 Touch of Love	Closed	1995	99.95	100
Tumbling Tots - K. Barry-Hippensteel				
1993 Roly Poly Polly	Closed	1994	69.95	70
1994 Handstand Harry	Closed	1995	69.95	70
Twinkle Toes Recital - T. Tomescu				
1997 Little Carnation	12/00		72.99	73
1998 Little Daffodil	12/01		72.99	73
1998 Little Violet	12/01		72.99	73
Two Much To Handle - K. Barry-Hippensteel				
1993 Julie (Flowers For Mommy)	Closed	1994	59.95	60
1993 Kevin (Clean Hands)	Closed	1995	59.95	145
Under Her Wings - P. Bomar				
1995 Guardian Angel	Closed	1998	79.95	80
Victorian Childhood - M. Girard-Kassis				
1997 Lydia	12/01		82.99	83
1997 Paige	12/01		82.99	83
1997 Olivia	12/01		82.99	83
1998 Estelle	12/01		82.99	83
Victorian Dreamers - K. Barry-Hippensteel				
1995 Rock-A-Bye/Good Night	Closed	1996	49.95	55
1995 Victorian Storytime	Closed	1996	49.95	50
Victorian Lace - C. Layton				
1993 Alicia	Closed	1994	79.95	125
1994 Colleen	Closed	1995	79.95	85
1994 Olivia	Closed	1995	79.95	80
Victorian Nursery Heirloom - C. McClure				
1994 Victorian Lullaby	Closed	1995	129.95	130-150
1995 Victorian Highchair	Closed	1996	129.95	130-150
1995 Victorian Playtime	Closed	1996	139.95	140
1995 Victorian Bunny Buggy	Closed	1996	139.95	140
Visions Of Our Lady - B. Deval				
1996 Our Lady of Grace	12/99		99.95	100
1996 Our Lady of Lourdes	12/00		99.95	100
1997 Our Lady of Fatima	12/01		99.95	100
1997 Our Lady of Medjugorje	12/01		99.95	100
Warner Brothers Baby - A. Tsalikhan				
1998 Tweet Dreams	12/01		74.99	75
What Little Girls Are Made Of - D. Effner				
1994 Peaches and Cream	Closed	1995	69.95	125
1995 Lavender & Lace	Closed	1998	69.95	70
1995 Sunshine & Lollipops	Closed	1998	69.95	70
Where Do Babies Come From - T. Tomescu				
1996 Special Delivery	12/99		79.95	80
1996 Fresh From The Patch	12/00		79.95	80
1996 Just Hatched	12/00		79.95	80
1997 Handle With Care	12/01		79.95	80
The Wonderful Wizard of Oz - M. Tretter				
1994 Dorothy	Closed	1995	79.95	80-125
1994 Scarecrow	Closed	1995	79.95	80
1994 Tin Man	Closed	1995	79.95	80
1994 The Cowardly Lion	Closed	1996	79.95	80
Wreathed in Beauty - G. Rademann				
1996 Winter Elegance	12/00		89.95	90
1997 Spring Promise	12/00		99.99	100
1997 Summer Sweetness	12/00		99.99	100
1997 Autumn Harmony	12/00		99.99	100
A Year With Addie/Plush - B. Conley & T. Roe				
1995 January Ice Skating	Open		39.95	40
1995 February Valentine	Open		39.95	40
1995 March Kite Flying	Open		39.95	40
1995 April Easter Fun	Open		39.95	40
1995 May Gardening Time	Open		39.95	40
1995 June Dress Up	Open		39.95	40
1995 July Summer Fun	Open		39.95	40
1995 August Autumn Adventure	Open		39.95	40
1995 September Back to School	Open		39.95	40
1995 October Masquerade	Open		39.95	40
1995 November Give Thanks	Open		39.95	40
1995 December Trim a Tree	Open		39.95	40
Yolanda's Heaven Scent Babies - Y. Bello				
1993 Meagan Rose	Closed	1994	49.95	75-125
1993 Daisy Anne	Closed	1994	49.95	50
1993 Morning Glory	Closed	1995	49.95	50
1993 Sweet Carnation	Closed	1995	54.95	55
1993 Lily	Closed	1995	54.95	55
1993 Cherry Blossom	Closed	1995	54.95	55
Yolanda's Lullaby Babies - Y. Bello				
1991 Christy (Rock-a-Bye)	Closed	1993	69.00	75-105
1992 Joey (Twinkle, Twinkle)	Closed	1994	69.00	75
1993 Amy (Brahms Lullaby)	Closed	1994	75.00	75
1993 Eddie (Teddy Bear Lullaby)	Closed	1994	75.00	75
1993 Jacob (Silent Night)	Closed	1994	75.00	75
1994 Bonnie (You Are My Sunshine)	Closed	1994	80.00	80
Yolanda's Picture - Perfect Babies - Y. Bello				
1985 Jason	Closed	1988	48.00	650-695
1986 Heather	Closed	1988	48.00	225-250
1987 Jennifer	Closed	1989	58.00	200-225
1987 Matthew	Closed	1990	58.00	195-200

*Quotes have been rounded up to nearest dollar

YEAR ISSUE	EDITION LIMIT	YEAR RETD.	ISSUE PRICE	*QUOTE U.S.$
1987 Sarah	Closed	1990	58.00	95-175
1988 Amanda	Closed	1990	63.00	125-150
1989 Jessica	Closed	1993	63.00	95-175
1990 Michael	Closed	1992	63.00	115-125
1990 Lisa	Closed	1992	63.00	100-150
1991 Emily	Closed	1992	63.00	110-150
1991 Danielle	Closed	1993	69.00	125-250

Yolanda's Playtime Babies - Y. Bello

YEAR ISSUE	EDITION LIMIT	YEAR RETD.	ISSUE PRICE	*QUOTE U.S.$
1993 Todd	Closed	1994	59.95	60
1993 Lindsey	Closed	1994	59.95	65
1993 Shawna	Closed	1994	59.95	60

Yolanda's Precious Playmates - Y. Bello

YEAR ISSUE	EDITION LIMIT	YEAR RETD.	ISSUE PRICE	*QUOTE U.S.$
1992 David	Closed	1994	69.95	125-250
1993 Paul	Closed	1994	69.95	125
1994 Johnny	Closed	1994	69.95	70

Attic Babies

Attic Babies' Collector Club - M. Maschino-Walker

YEAR ISSUE	EDITION LIMIT	YEAR RETD.	ISSUE PRICE	*QUOTE U.S.$
1992 Burtie Buzbee, SNL	Retrd.	1992	40.00	40
1993 Izzie B. Ruebottom, SNL	277	1993	35.00	35
1994 Sunflower Flossie, SNL	Retrd.	1994	42.00	80
1995 Tricia Kay Yum-Yum, SNL	Retrd.	1995	40.00	50
1996 Baby Savannah, SNL	Retrd.	1996	39.95	50
1997 Fertile Mertle	Retrd.	1997	64.95	65
1997 Optional Bookend Stand	Retrd.	1997	14.95	15
1998 Little Red Riding Hood	Yr.Iss.		42.95	43

Retired Dolls - M. Maschino-Walker

YEAR ISSUE	EDITION LIMIT	YEAR RETD.	ISSUE PRICE	*QUOTE U.S.$
1994 Abner Abernathy	Retrd.	1995	55.95	85
1994 Addie Abernathy	Retrd.	1995	61.95	75-95
1991 Alma Alley Cat	Retrd.	1997	59.95	60
1992 Americana Raggedy Santa (1st ed.), SNL	Retrd.	1992	85.95	150
1992 Americana Raggedy Santa (2nd ed.), SNL	Retrd.	1992	89.95	150
1989 Annie Fannie	Retrd.	1992	43.95	70-110
1987 Annie Lee	Retrd.	1996	50.00	55
1990 Anniversary Couple	Retrd.	1996	138.00	138
1992 Artilma Hunnicut	Retrd.	1995	73.95	74
1992 Augie Whippermeyer	Retrd.	1996	66.00	66
1991 Ba Ba Shnookems	Retrd.	1997	53.95	54
1991 Baggie Bear	Retrd.	1994	11.95	12
1991 Baggie Girl	Retrd.	1994	19.95	20
1991 Baggie Rabbit	Retrd.	1994	19.95	20
1991 Baggie Santa	Retrd.	1994	19.95	20
1996 Basket Case Beulah, SNL	Retrd.	1997	64.95	90
1990 Beary Bashful Bonnie Bear	Retrd.	1997	87.95	88
1990 Beary Harriette Bear	Retrd.	1995	87.95	88
1990 Beary Harry Bear	Retrd.	1995	87.95	88
1990 Beary Merry Raggady Santa	Retrd.	1995	113.95	114
1987 Bessie Jo	Retrd.	1989	31.95	98
1987 Beth Sue	Retrd.	1991	27.95	75
1994 Boliver Pluckingbush	Retrd.	1997	45.95	46
1994 Boo Bonoggins	Retrd.	1997	67.95	68
1988 Bootsie Wootsie Angel	Retrd.	1996	44.00	44-69
1989 Bouncing Baby Roy	Retrd.	1995	49.95	65
1991 Buffy Muffy	Retrd.	1996	60.00	60
1988 Bunnifer	Retrd.	1990	39.95	100-160
1988 Buttons	Retrd.	1991	27.95	28
1992 Candy Applebee	Retrd.	1994	15.95	18
1992 Christopher Columbus, SNL	Retrd.	1992	79.95	200-250
1989 Cloddy Clyde	Retrd.	1995	69.95	70-140
1989 Cotton Pickin' Ninny	Retrd.	1992	47.95	100-140
1987 Country Clyde	Retrd.	1988	27.95	28
1992 Daddy's Lil Punkin Patty, SNL	Retrd.	1993	79.95	175
1989 Dandy Randy	Retrd.	1997	55.95	56
1992 Darcie Duckworth	Retrd.	1995	59.95	60
1987 Dirty Harry	Retrd.	1991	27.95	55-100
1990 Doctor Doodles	Retrd.	1997	73.95	74
1994 Dollie Boots (1st ed.)	100	1994	79.95	300-395
1995 Dollie Boots (2nd ed.)	2,000	1995	84.95	85
1992 Dotin' Dodie	Retrd.	1996	66.00	66-91
1990 Duckie Dinkle	Retrd.	1991	95.95	96
1992 Durwin Duckworth	Retrd.	1995	59.95	60
1996 Eggbert Yolkum	Retrd.	1997	49.95	50
1995 Elmira Truelove	Retrd.	1997	79.95	80
1995 Eppie Moneyworth	Retrd.	1997	93.95	94
1988 Fatty Matty	Retrd.	1996	50.00	50
1988 Fertile Mertle	Retrd.	1996	50.00	50-75
1988 Fester Chester	Retrd.	1994	39.95	75-100
1989 Flakey Jakey	Retrd.	1995	59.95	76
1989 Flopsy Mopsy	Retrd.	1996	70.00	70
1994 Florella Pluckingbush	Retrd.	1997	57.95	58
1990 Frannie Farkle	Retrd.	1991	129.95	130
1990 Frizzy Lizzy	Retrd.	1992	95.95	250
1995 Fuzzy Sweezy (1st ed.)	2,000	1995	77.95	78
1990 Gabbie Abbie	Retrd.	1995	109.95	110
1988 Goosey Lucy	Retrd.	1997	55.95	56
1988 Grandpappy Burtie	Retrd.	1996	50.00	75-100
1988 Granny Grunt	Retrd.	1996	50.00	50
1988 Grungy Greta	Retrd.	1997	49.95	50
1992 Hadden Hobnobber	Retrd.	1996	66.00	66
1988 Hannah Lou	Retrd.	1994	39.95	50-100
1990 Happy Huck	Retrd.	1992	47.95	102
1993 Happy Pappy Claus SNL	805	1994	73.95	100-135
1987 Harold	Retrd.	1990	27.95	80
1989 Harvey Hog	Retrd.	1996	60.00	60
1995 Hazel Lynora Grimsley	2,000	1995	68.95	69
1989 Heavenly Heather	Retrd.	1992	59.95	100
1988 Heffy Cheffy	Retrd.	1994	75.95	125-160
1992 Hillary Hobnobber	Retrd.	1996	66.00	66
1990 Holly Ho	Retrd.	1997	109.95	110
1990 Homer Hare	Retrd.	1995	147.95	225
1990 Hunnie Bunnie	Retrd.	1995	147.95	148
1991 Iggy Piggy Dumplin	Retrd.	1997	51.95	52
1994 Ima Emmie Mudge	Retrd.	1997	77.95	78
1989 Itsy Bitsy Mitzy	Retrd.	1995	49.95	50
1993 Itty Bitty Santa	Retrd.	1993	5.95	6
1990 Ivan Ivie	Retrd.	1991	129.95	230
1987 Jacob	Retrd.	1988	27.95	100
1993 Jammy Mammy Claus SNL	653	1994	67.95	85
1987 Jenny Lou	Retrd.	1992	35.95	36
1992 Jessabell	Retrd.	1996	40.00	43
1989 Jingle Jangle Jo	Retrd.	1995	69.95	86
1990 Johnathan Poo Bear	Retrd.	1996	148.00	148
1989 Jolly Jim	Retrd.	1992	31.95	130
1990 Josie Posie Poo Bear	Retrd.	1996	148.00	148
1990 Jumpin Pumkin Jill	Retrd.	1994	55.95	56
1988 Katy	Retrd.	1995	59.95	60
1992 Keribell	Retrd.	1997	39.95	40
1990 Lampsie Divie Ivie	Retrd.	1991	129.95	285
1995 Lani Frumpet (1st ed.)	2,000	1995	56.95	57
1988 Lazy Daisy	Retrd.	1992	39.95	60
1988 Lazy Liza Jane	Retrd.	1991	47.95	48
1995 Lily Lumpbucket	2,000	1995	61.95	62
1996 Linus Griswold	Retrd.	1997	69.95	70
1988 Little Dove	Retrd.	1988	39.95	40
1994 Lollie Ann	Retrd.	1994	39.95	75
1989 Luscious Lulu	Retrd.	1997	69.95	70
1987 Maggie Mae	Retrd.	1991	25.95	250
1991 Maizie Mae	Retrd.	1994	51.95	52
1995 Mama Lou	Retrd.	1997	73.95	74
1991 Mandi Mae	Retrd.	1994	51.95	52
1991 Memsie Mae	Retrd.	1994	51.95	52
1993 Merry Beary Raggady Santy	1,000	1995	113.95	150-164
1994 Merry Ole Farley Fagan Dooberry, SNL	Retrd.	1994	131.95	200
1987 Messy Tessy	Retrd.	1995	43.95	44
1993 Millie Wilset	2,000	1994	39.95	40
1987 Miss Pitty Pat	Retrd.	1988	27.95	100
1988 Molly Bea	Retrd.	1990	39.95	45-80
1995 Monty Thumpet	2,000	1995	56.95	57
1988 Moosey Matilda	Retrd.	1990	39.95	150-300
1989 Mr. Gardner	Retrd.	1995	109.95	110
1993 Mr. Kno Mo Sno, SNL	1,800	1994	51.95	68
1991 Mr. Raggedy Claus, SNL	Retrd.	1992	69.95	85
1989 Mrs. Gardner	Retrd.	1995	109.95	110
1991 Mrs. Raggedy Claus, SNL	Retrd.	1992	69.95	85-140
1989 Ms. Waddles	Retrd.	1990	47.95	48
1987 Muslin Bunny	Retrd.	1993	7.95	8
1987 Muslin Teddy	Retrd.	1993	7.95	8
1987 Nasty Cathy	Retrd.	1996	50.00	50-65
1988 Nathan	Retrd.	1995	59.95	60
1994 Natty Fae Tucker	Retrd.	1994	N/A	N/A
1988 Naughty Nellie	Retrd.	1990	31.95	85
1990 Nerdie Nelda	Retrd.	1995	69.95	140
1988 Ninny Nanny	Retrd.	1996	56.00	56
1992 Norville Newton	Retrd.	1996	66.00	66
1990 Nurse Noodles	Retrd.	1997	73.95	74
1994 Old Raggady Noah	2,500	1995	73.95	150
1996 Old Riley Nicolas Canterbury	Retrd.	1996	79.95	80
1993 Old St. Knickerbocker, SNL	Retrd.	1993	79.95	80
1992 Old St. Nick, SNL	Retrd.	1993	95.95	130
1989 Old Tyme Santy	Retrd.	1989	79.95	80
1992 Party Marty	Retrd.	1997	53.95	54
1995 Pea Pod Sweezy (1st ed.)	2,000	1995	74.95	75
1990 Pearly Rose	Retrd.	1996	110.00	110-135
1996 Peony Paige	Retrd.	1997	63.95	64
1994 Petunia Kay Alvertie	Retrd.	1997	53.95	54
1990 Phylbert Farkle	Retrd.	1991	129.95	225
1991 Pippy Pat	Retrd.	1994	47.95	52
1996 Polly Patches	Retrd.	1996	49.95	50
1990 Pranky Spanky	Retrd.	1997	109.95	110
1988 Prissy Missy	Retrd.	1990	31.95	32
1987 Rachel	Retrd.	1988	29.95	85
1995 Raggady Cornell G. Hockenberry w/Workbench, set	Retrd.	1996	104.00	135
1995 Raggady Cornell G. Hockenberry Workbench	Retrd.	1996	38.00	38
1995 Raggady Cornell G. Hockenberry, SNL	Retrd.	1996	66.00	66
1987 Raggady Kitty	Retrd.	1988	29.95	30
1995 Raggady Old Wooly Tackitt	2,000	1995	46.95	47
1990 Raggady Ole Chris Cringle (1st ed.)	Retrd.	1990	189.95	262
1990 Raggady Ole Chris Cringle (2nd ed.)	Retrd.	1991	189.95	190
1994 Raggady P. Shagnasty	Retrd.	1995	139.95	195
1996 Raggady Pippin Peabody, SNL	Retrd.	1997	59.95	85
1988 Raggady Sam (1st ed.)	Retrd.	1991	55.95	115
1991 Raggady Sam (2nd ed.)	500	1995	399.95	500
1987 Raggady Santy (1st ed.)	Retrd.	1988	75.95	250
1990 Raggady Santy (2nd ed.)	Retrd.	1991	89.95	90
1987 Raggady Teddy	Retrd.	1995	9.95	10
1989 Rammy Sammy	Retrd.	1990	43.95	44
1987 Rose Ann	Retrd.	1991	39.95	75
1988 Rotten Wilber	Retrd.	1990	35.95	140
1988 Rufus	Retrd.	1992	35.95	70-80
1989 Sadie Sow	Retrd.	1996	60.00	60-85
1987 Sally Francis	Retrd.	1993	35.95	36
1987 Sara (muslin)	Retrd.	1992	39.95	180
1987 Sara (satin)	Retrd.	1992	39.95	86
1989 Sassy Cassy	Retrd.	1997	55.95	56
1992 Scary Larry Scarecrow, SNL	Retrd.	1994	79.95	80
1989 Shotgun Pappy	Retrd.	1996	60.00	60
1990 Shy Shannon Bunny	Retrd.	1997	69.95	70
1988 Silly Willie	Retrd.	1990	39.95	76
1992 Sissy Whippermeyer	Retrd.	1996	66.00	66
1989 Skinny Minnie	Retrd.	1997	59.95	60
1989 Skitty Kitty	Retrd.	1991	43.95	140
1991 Sleazy Sneezles	Retrd.	1997	59.95	60
1990 Sollie Ollie Otis	Retrd.	1991	129.95	130
1995 Spirit of Christmas Santy	Retrd.	1995	87.95	113-130
1988 Spring Santy	Retrd.	1989	47.95	48
1991 Stressie Bessie	Retrd.	1997	69.95	70
1990 Sweet Emmaline	Retrd.	1997	147.95	148
1988 Sweet William	Retrd.	1989	35.95	152
1992 Teeny Weenie Christmas Angel	Retrd.	1994	9.95	15
1992 Teeny Weenie Country Angel	Retrd.	1994	9.95	20
1987 Toddy Sue	Retrd.	1990	27.95	87
1995 Tootie Twinkles (1st ed.)	5,000	1995	59.95	60
1994 Treddie Pinrose	Retrd.	1997	67.95	68
1989 Tricky Ricky	Retrd.	1996	46.00	46
1988 Tubby Timbo	Retrd.	1996	50.00	50
1990 Verlie Mae	Retrd.	1995	49.95	50
1989 Virtuous Virgie	Retrd.	1996	70.00	70
1988 Wacky Jackie	Retrd.	1990	39.95	40
1989 Wild Wilma	Retrd.	1996	44.00	44
1995 Willa Thumpet	2,000	1995	73.95	74
1991 Winkie Binkie	Retrd.	1993	53.95	54
1992 Witchy Wanda, SNL	Retrd.	1994	79.95	80
1989 Wood Doll, black-large	Retrd.	1991	36.00	36
1989 Wood Doll, white-large	Retrd.	1991	36.00	36
1989 Wood Doll-medium	Retrd.	1991	31.95	32
1989 Wood Doll-small	Retrd.	1991	23.95	24
1990 Yankee Doodle Debbie	Retrd.	1993	95.95	325-350
1990 Zitty Zelda, SNL	Retrd.	1993	89.95	180

Beanie Babies/Ty, Inc.

Beanie Babies - Ty

YEAR ISSUE	EDITION LIMIT	YEAR RETD.	ISSUE PRICE	*QUOTE U.S.$
1996 Ally the Alligator 4032	Retrd.	1997	5.00	13-50
1998 Ants the Anteater	Retrd.	1998	5.00	13-25
1997 Baldy the Eagle (76ers) 4074	Retrd.	1998	5.00	137
1997 Baldy the Eagle 4074	Retrd.	1998	5.00	10-45
1996 Batty the Bat	Open		5.00	5-12
1998 Batty the Bat (Brewers)	Retrd.	1998	5.00	105
1998 Batty the Bat (Mets)	Retrd.	1998	5.00	77
1996 Batty the Bat (pink)	Retrd.	1996	5.00	5-35
1997 Bernie the St. Bernard 4109	Open		5.00	5-17
1995 Bessie the Brown Cow 4009	Retrd.	1997	5.00	23-63
1995 Blackie the Black Bear 4011	Open		5.00	5-22
1998 Blizzard the White Tiger (White Sox) 4163	Retrd.	1998	5.00	105
1997 Blizzard the White Tiger 4163	Open		5.00	5-25
1998 Bones the Dog (Yankees) 4001	Retrd.	1998	5.00	137
1994 Bones the Dog 4001	Open		5.00	5-22
1998 Bongo the Monkey (Cavaliers) 4067	Retrd.	1998	5.00	122
1995 Bongo the Monkey (dark tail) 4067	Open		5.00	5-75
1995 Bongo the Monkey (light tail) 4067	Open		5.00	5-25
1998 Britannia	Retrd.	1998	5.00	295
1995 Bronty the Brontosaurus 4085	Retrd.	1996	5.00	735-800
1993 Brownie the Brown Bear	Retrd.	1997	5.00	2500-2748
1997 Bruno the Terrier	Open		5.00	5-16
1995 Bubbles the Fish (yellow & black) 4078	Retrd.	1997	5.00	63-199
1996 Bucky the Beaver 4016	Retrd.	1997	5.00	10-38
1995 Bumble the Bee 4045	Retrd.	1996	5.00	450-795
1997 Bunny, set/3 (lilac, mint, pink)	Open		15.00	15-60
1995 Caw the Crow 4071	Retrd.	1996	5.00	450-630
1995 Chilly the Polar Bear 4012	Retrd.	1996	5.00	1400-1453
1997 Chip the Calico Cat 4121	Open		5.00	5-20
1998 Chocolate the Moose (Nuggets) 4015	Retrd.	1998	5.00	119
1994 Chocolate the Moose 4015	Open		5.00	5-19
1996 Chops the Lamb 4019	Retrd.	1997	5.00	169-250
1997 Claude the Crab 4083	Open		5.00	5-16
1996 Conga the Gorilla 4160	Open		5.00	5-16
1995 Coral the Fish (tie-dyed) 4079	Retrd.	1997	5.00	94-200
1997 Crunch the Shark 4130	Open		5.00	5-16
1998 Cubbie the Brown Bear (Cubs 5/18/97) 4010	Retrd.	1998	5.00	168
1998 Cubbie the Brown Bear "Cubs 9/6/97) 4010	Retrd.	1998	5.00	140
1994 Cubbie the Brown Bear 4010	Retrd.	1997	5.00	15-40
1998 Curly the Bear (Spurs) 4052	Retrd.	1998	5.00	158
1996 Curly the Bear 4052	Retrd.	1998	5.00	5-32
1998 Daisy the Black & White Cow (Cubs-Harry Caray) 4006	Retrd.	1998	5.00	333
1994 Daisy the Black & White Cow 4006	Open		5.00	5-17
1995 Derby the Horse (No Star) 4008	Retrd.	1997	5.00	10
1995 Derby the Horse w/Star 4008	Open		5.00	5-27
1994 Digger the Crab (orange) 4027	Retrd.	1995	5.00	395-648
1995 Digger the Crab (red) 4027	Retrd.	1997	5.00	75-175
1997 Doby the Doberman 4110	Open		5.00	5-17
1997 Doodle the Rooster 4171	Retrd.	1997	5.00	19-57
1997 Dotty the Dalmatian 4100	Open		5.00	5-17
1998 Early the Robin	Open		5.00	5-10
1996 Ears the Rabbit 4018	Retrd.	1998	5.00	5-25
1997 Echo the Dolphin 4180	Retrd.	1998	5.00	5-19
1997 Erin the Bear	Retrd.	1997	5.00	40-313
1997 Fetch the Golden Retriever	Retrd.	1998	5.00	14
1994 Flash the Dolphin 4021	Retrd.	1997	5.00	50-145
1997 Fleece the Lamb 4125	Open		5.00	5-17
1996 Flip the White Cat 4012	Retrd.	1997	5.00	19-50
1997 Floppity the Lilac Bunny 4118	Retrd.	1998	5.00	5-20
1995 Flutter the Butterfly 4043	Retrd.	1996	5.00	600-872
1997 Fortune the Panda	Retrd.	1998	5.00	43
1996 Freckles the Leopard 4066	Open		5.00	5-20

*Quotes have been rounded up to nearest dollar

YEAR ISSUE	EDITION LIMIT	YEAR RETD.	ISSUE PRICE	*QUOTE U.S.$
1996 Garcia the Bear 4051	Retrd.	1997	5.00	80-188
1997 Gigi the Poodle	Retrd.	1998	5.00	15
1998 Glory the Bear	Retrd.	1998	5.00	83
1998 Glory the Bear (98 All Star)	Retrd.	1998	5.00	322
1996 Gobbles the Turkey	Open		5.00	5-27
1995 Goldie the Goldfish 4023	Retrd.	1997	5.00	25-138
1997 Gracie the Swan 4126	Retrd.	1998	5.00	5-20
1996 Grunt the Razorback 4096	Retrd.	1997	5.00	147-250
1995 Happy the Hippo (gray) 4061	Retrd.	1995	5.00	450-507
1994 Happy the Hippo (lavender) 4061	Retrd.	1998	5.00	5-27
1997 Hippity the Mint Bunny 4119	Retrd.	1998	5.00	5-22
1997 Hissy the Snake	Open		5.00	5-20
1998 Hissy the Snake (Razorbacks)	Retrd.	1998	5.00	98
1996 Hoot the Owl 4073	Retrd.	1997	5.00	13-50
1997 Hoppity the Pink Bunny 4117	Retrd.	1998	5.00	5-22
1994 Humphrey the Camel 4060	Retrd.	1996	5.00	1200-1680
1997 Iggy the Iguana	Retrd.	1998	5.00	5-20
1996 Inch the Worm (felt antennas) 4044	Retrd.	1996	5.00	150-200
1996 Inch the Worm 4044	Retrd.	1998	5.00	5-25
1995 Inky the Octopus (pink) 4028	Retrd.	1998	5.00	5-27
1995 Inky the Octopus (tan w/mouth) 4028	Retrd.	1995	5.00	350-489
1994 Inky the Octopus (tan w/o mouth) 4028	Retrd.	1994	5.00	313-400
1997 Jabber the Parrot	Retrd.	1998	5.00	16
1997 Jake the Mallard Duck	Retrd.	1998	5.00	15
1997 Jolly the Walrus 4082	Retrd.	1998	5.00	5-25
1995 Kiwi the Toucan 4070	Retrd.	1997	5.00	94-275
1997 Kuku the Cockatoo	Retrd.	1998	5.00	14
1996 Lefty the Donkey (w/American flag) 4085	Retrd.	1997	5.00	125-420
1996 Lefty the Donkey (w/o American flag) 4085	Retrd.	1997	5.00	300-400
1994 Legs the Frog 4020	Retrd.	1997	5.00	14-25
1996 Libearty the Bear w/American Flag 4057	Retrd.	1997	5.00	300-480
1996 Lizzy the Lizard (blue/black) 4033	Retrd.	1997	5.00	15-40
1995 Lizzy the Lizard (tie-dyed) 4033	Retrd.	1995	5.00	600-788
1996 Lucky the Ladybug (11 dots) 4040	Open		5.00	5-22
1996 Lucky the Ladybug (21 dots) 4040	Retrd.	1996	5.00	450
1994 Lucky the Ladybug (seven glued on spots) 4040	Retrd.	1996	5.00	150-295
1995 Magic the Dragon (hot pink lines) 4088	Retrd.	1997	5.00	200
1995 Magic the Dragon (light pink lines) 4088	Retrd.	1997	5.00	10-75
1996 Manny the Manatee 4081	Retrd.	1997	5.00	107-275
1997 Maple/Maple the Canadian Exclusive Bear 4600	Open		5.00	5-300
1997 Maple/Pride the Canadian Exclusive Bear 4600	Retrd.	1997	5.00	245-525
1997 Mel the Koala Bear 4162	Open		5.00	5-20
1996 Mystic the Unicorn (coarse mane/iridescent horn) 4007	Open		5.00	5-35
1996 Mystic the Unicorn (coarse mane/tan horn) 4007	Retrd.	1997	5.00	23
1994 Mystic the Unicorn (fine mane) 4007	Retrd.	1995	5.00	195-200
1998 Nana the Monkey	Retrd.	1998	5.00	1960
1997 Nanook the Husky 4104	Open		5.00	5-19
1995 Nip the Cat (all gold) 4003	Retrd.	1995	5.00	450-480
1996 Nip the Cat (gold cat/white paws) 4003	Retrd.	1997	5.00	13-25
1995 Nip the Cat (white belly) 4003	Retrd.	1995	5.00	250-300
1997 Nuts the Squirrel 4114	Open		5.00	5-17
1996 Patti the Platypus (fuchsia) 4025	Open		5.00	5-22
1995 Patti the Platypus (magenta) 4025	Retrd.	1995	5.00	450
1994 Patti the Platypus (raspberry) 4025	Retrd.	1994	5.00	450
1997 Peace the tie-dyed Bear (embroidered) 4053	Retrd.	1997	5.00	5-94
1996 Peanut the Elephant (light blue) 4062	Retrd.	1998	5.00	5-22
1995 Peanut the Elephant (royal blue) 4062	Retrd.	1995	5.00	3500-3800
1994 Peking the Panda Bear 4013	Retrd.	1996	5.00	1063-1680
1994 Pinchers the Lobster (red) 4026	Retrd.	1998	5.00	5-20
1998 Pinky the Flamingo (Spurs) 4072	Retrd.	1998	5.00	140
1995 Pinky the Flamingo 4072	Open		5.00	5-20
1997 Pouch the Kangaroo 4161	Open		5.00	5-17
1997 Pounce the Cat	Open		5.00	5-15
1997 Prance the Cat	Open		5.00	5-15
1997 Princess the Bear (Princess Diana) (Non-Charity)	Retrd.	1997	5.00	25-100
1997 Princess the Bear (Princess Diana) (PE Pellets)	Retrd.	1997	5.00	25-115
1997 Princess the Bear (Princess Diana) (purple) (PVC Pellets)	Retrd.	1997	5.00	93-275
1997 Puffer the Puffin	Open		5.00	5-10
1997 Pugsly the Pug Dog 4106	Open		5.00	5-17
1994 Punchers the Lobster (misprint)	Retrd.	1994	5.00	800-1020
1994 Quackers the Duck (w/o wings) 4024	Retrd.	1995	5.00	1350-1500
1995 Quackers the Duck (w/wings) 4024	Retrd.	1995	5.00	10-20
1996 Radar the Bat 4091	Retrd.	1997	5.00	80-200
1997 Rainbow the Chameleon	Open		5.00	5-20
1995 Rex the Tyrannosaurus 4086	Retrd.	1996	5.00	714-900
1996 Righty the Elephant 4086	Retrd.	1997	5.00	188-420
1996 Ringo the Racoon 4014	Open		5.00	5-17
1997 Roary the Lion (Royals) 4069	Retrd.	1998	5.00	88
1997 Roary the Lion 4069	Open		5.00	5-17
1998 Rocket the Blue Jay	Retrd.	1998	5.00	15
1996 Rover the Red Dog 4101	Retrd.	1998	5.00	5-22
1996 Scoop the Pelican 4107	Open		5.00	5-20
1996 Scottie the Black Terrier 4102	Open		5.00	5-24
1994 Seamore the White Seal 4029	Retrd.	1997	5.00	55-180
1996 Seaweed the Otter 4080	Open		5.00	5-32
1994 Slither the Snake 4031	Retrd.	1996	5.00	1000-1190
1996 Sly the Fox (brown belly) 4115	Retrd.	1996	5.00	100-125
1996 Sly the Fox (white belly) 4115	Open		5.00	5-10
1997 Smoochy the Frog	Open		5.00	5-20
1997 Snip the Siamese Cat 4120	Open		5.00	5-22
1997 Snort the Bull 4002	Open		5.00	5-20
1996 Snowball the Snowman	Retrd.	1997	5.00	18-50
1996 Sparky the Dalmatian 4100	Retrd.	1997	5.00	63-175
1994 Speedy the Turtle 4030	Retrd.	1997	5.00	15-27
1996 Spike the Rhinoceros 4060	Open		5.00	5-20
1997 Spinner the Spider	Open		5.00	5-10
1994 Splash the Orca Whale 4022	Retrd.	1997	5.00	86-145
1996 Spook the Ghost 4090	Retrd.	1997	5.00	207
1996 Spooky the Ghost 4090	Retrd.	1997	5.00	13-50
1994 Spot the Black & White Dog (black spot) 4000	Retrd.	1997	5.00	19-69
1994 Spot the Black & White Dog (no spot) 4000	Retrd.	1994	5.00	1371-1680
1997 Spunky the Cocker Spaniel	Open		5.00	5-20
1994 Squealer the Pig 4005	Retrd.	1998	5.00	5-27
1995 Steg the Stegosaurus 4087	Retrd.	1996	5.00	625-840
1995 Sting the Manta Ray 4077	Retrd.	1996	5.00	125-250
1997 Stinger the Scorpion	Retrd.	1998	5.00	14
1995 Stinky the Skunk 4017	Open		5.00	5-17
1997 Stretch the Ostrich	Open		5.00	5-25
1998 Stretch the Ostrich (Cardinals)	Retrd.	1998	5.00	122
1996 Stripes the Tiger (black/tan) 4065	Retrd.	1998	5.00	5-22
1998 Stripes the Tiger (Detroit) 4065	Retrd.	1998	5.00	122
1995 Stripes the Tiger (orange/black) 4065	Retrd.	1996	5.00	175-325
1997 Strut the Rooster	Open		5.00	5-38
1998 Strut the Rooster (Pacers)	Retrd.	1998	5.00	147
1995 Tabasco the Bull 4002	Retrd.	1997	5.00	157-250
1996 Tank the Armadillo (7 rib lines) 4031	Retrd.	1996	5.00	150-193
1996 Tank the Armadillo (7-9 rib lines w/shell) 4031	Retrd.	1997	5.00	67-100
1996 Tank the Armadillo (9 rib lines) 4031	Retrd.	1996	5.00	193-350
1997 Teddy the Brown Teddy Bear (Holiday 97) 4050	Retrd.	1997	5.00	35
1995 Teddy the Brown Teddy Bear (new face) 4050	Retrd.	1997	5.00	27-94
1994 Teddy the Brown Teddy Bear (old face) 4050	Retrd.	1994	5.00	1440-1880
1995 Teddy the Colored Teddies-Cranberry (new face) 4052	Retrd.	1996	5.00	1020-1540
1994 Teddy the Colored Teddies-Cranberry (old face) 4052	Retrd.	1994	5.00	1200-1470
1995 Teddy the Colored Teddies-Jade (new face) 4057	Retrd.	1996	5.00	1020-1540
1994 Teddy the Colored Teddies-Jade (old face) 4057	Retrd.	1994	5.00	900-1470
1995 Teddy the Colored Teddies-Magenta (new face) 4056	Retrd.	1996	5.00	1400-1540
1994 Teddy the Colored Teddies-Magenta (old face) 4056	Retrd.	1994	5.00	1100-1470
1995 Teddy the Colored Teddies-Teal (new face) 4051	Retrd.	1996	5.00	1540-1600
1994 Teddy the Colored Teddies-Teal (old face) 4051	Retrd.	1994	5.00	700-1470
1995 Teddy the Colored Teddies-Violet (new face) 4055	Retrd.	1996	5.00	1400-1540
1994 Teddy the Colored Teddies-Violet (old face) 4055	Retrd.	1994	5.00	1300-1470
1997 Tracker the Basset Hound	Retrd.	1998	5.00	15
1994 Trap the Mouse 4042	Retrd.	1996	5.00	900-1383
1995 Tuck the Walrus (misprint)	Retrd.	1996	5.00	100-125
1997 Tuffy the Brown Terrier 4108	Open		5.00	5-17
1995 Tusk the Walrus 4076	Retrd.	1997	5.00	82-160
1996 Twigs the Giraffe 4068	Retrd.	1998	5.00	5-25
1996 Valentino the Bear (Toys For Tots) 4058	Retrd.	1997	5.00	227
1996 Valentino the Bear (Yankees) 4058	Retrd.	1997	5.00	168
1995 Valentino the Bear 4058	Retrd.	1997	5.00	5-27
1995 Velvet the Panther 4064	Retrd.	1997	5.00	5-35
1995 Waddle the Penguin 4075	Retrd.	1998	5.00	5-25
1997 Waves the Orca Whale 4084	Retrd.	1998	5.00	5-12
1994 Web the Spider 4041	Retrd.	1996	5.00	900-1173
1996 Weenie the Dog 4013	Retrd.	1998	5.00	5-35
1997 Whisper the Deer	Retrd.	1998	5.00	15
1997 Wise the Owl	Retrd.	1998	5.00	25
1996 Wrinkles the Bulldog 4103	Open		5.00	5-17
1995 Ziggy the Zebra 4063	Retrd.	1998	5.00	5-32
1994 Zip the Black Cat (all black) 4004	Retrd.	1995	5.00	1200-1750
1994 Zip the Black Cat (white face & belly) 4004	Retrd.	1995	5.00	400-625
1994 Zip the Black Cat (white paws) 4004	Retrd.	1998	5.00	5-75

McDonald Teenie Beanies - Ty

YEAR ISSUE	EDITION LIMIT	YEAR RETD.	ISSUE PRICE	*QUOTE U.S.$
1997 Chocolate Moose	Retrd.	1997	N/A	5-44
1997 Chops the Lamb	Retrd.	1997	N/A	15-35
1997 Goldie the Goldfish	Retrd.	1997	N/A	14-22
1997 Lizz the Lizard	Retrd.	1997	N/A	8-22
1997 Patti the Platypus	Retrd.	1997	N/A	15-35
1997 Pinky the Flamingo	Retrd.	1997	N/A	15-35
1997 Quacks the Duck	Retrd.	1997	N/A	7-22
1997 Seamore the Seal	Retrd.	1997	N/A	8-35
1997 Snort the Bull	Retrd.	1997	N/A	10-25
1997 Speedy the Turtle	Retrd.	1997	N/A	14-33
1997 Set of 10	Retrd.	1997	N/A	75-250
1998 Bones the Dog	Open		N/A	N/A
1998 Bongo the Monkey	Open		N/A	N/A
1998 Doby the Doberman	Open		N/A	N/A
1998 Happy the Hippo	Open		N/A	N/A
1998 Inch the Worm	Open		N/A	N/A
1998 Mel the Koala	Open		N/A	N/A
1998 Pinchers the Lobster	Open		N/A	N/A
1998 Scoop the Pelican	Open		N/A	N/A
1998 Twigs the Giraffe	Open		N/A	N/A
1998 Waddles the Penguin	Open		N/A	N/A
1998 Zip the Cat	Open		N/A	N/A
1998 Peanut the Elephant	Open		N/A	N/A

Cavanagh Group Intl.

Coca-Cola Brand Bean Bag - CGI

YEAR ISSUE	EDITION LIMIT	YEAR RETD.	ISSUE PRICE	*QUOTE U.S.$
1997 SCO101 Seal with Holiday Scarf	Yr.Iss.	1997	5.00	15
1997 SCO102 Seal with Long Snowflake Cap	Yr.Iss.	1997	5.00	15
1997 SCO103 Penguin with Snowflake Cap	Yr.Iss.	1997	5.00	15
1997 SCO104 Polar Bear with Snowflake Cap	Yr.Iss.	1997	5.00	20
1997 SCO105 Polar Bear with Plaid Bow Tie	Yr.Iss.	1997	5.00	15
1997 SCO106 Polar Bear with Red Bow	Yr.Iss.	1997	5.00	15
1997 SCO107 Seal with Baseball Cap	Yr.Iss.	1997	5.00	15
1997 SCO108 Penguin with Delivery Cap	Yr.Iss.	1997	5.00	15
1997 SCO109 Polar Bear with Coke Bottle	Yr.Iss.	1997	5.00	15
1997 SCO110 Polar Bear with Pink Bow	Yr.Iss.	1997	5.00	15
1997 SCO111 Polar Bear with Baseball Cap	Yr.Iss.	1997	5.00	20
1997 SCO112 Polar Bear with Tee Shirt	Yr.Iss.	1997	5.00	20
1997 SCO113 Polar Bear with Long Snowflake Cap (Musicland Exclusive)	Yr.Iss.	1997	5.00	15
1998 SCO114 Seal with Red & Green Ski Cap	Yr.Iss.		6.00	5
1998 SCO116 Polar Bear with a Red & Green Sweater	Yr.Iss.		6.00	6
1998 SCO118 Polar Bear with Snowflake Hat	Yr.Iss.		5.00	5
1998 SCO120 Polar Bear with Long Red Scarf	Yr.Iss.		5.00	5
1998 SCO123 Seal with Long Green Scarf	Yr.Iss.		5.00	5
1998 SCO124 Walrus with a Snowflake Scarf	Yr.Iss.		6.00	6
1998 SCO127 Penguin with Chef's Hat	Yr.Iss.		5.00	5
1998 SCO131 Polar Bear in Argyle Shirt	Yr.Iss.		5.00	5
1998 SCO132 Coca-Cola Can Topped by a Cap & Sunglasses	Yr.Iss.		6.00	6
1998 SCO133 Reindeer in a Coca-Cola Tee Shirt	Yr.Iss.		6.00	6
1998 SCO135 Walrus	Yr.Iss.		5.00	5
1998 SCO136 Husky	Yr.Iss.		5.00	5
1998 SCO137 Whale	Yr.Iss.		5.00	5
1998 SCO140 Polar Bear with a Green Delivery Cap	Yr.Iss.		6.00	6
1998 SCO141 Walrus with Snowflake Hat	Yr.Iss.		5.00	5
1998 SCO142 Reindeer with Snowflake Scarf	Yr.Iss.		5.00	5
1997 SCO144 Polar Bear with Green Bow (Blockbuster Exclusive)	Yr.Iss.	1997	N/A	N/A
1997 SCO145 Seal with Green Striped Scarf (Blockbuster Exclusive)	Yr.Iss.	1997	N/A	N/A
1997 SCO146 Polar Bear in Driver's Cap (Blockbuster Exclusive)	Yr.Iss.	1997	N/A	N/A
1997 SCO147 Seal with Long Snowflake Cap (Blockbuster Exclusive)	Yr.Iss.	1997	N/A	N/A
1997 SCO148 Penguin with Snowflake Cap (Blockbuster Exclusive)	Yr.Iss.	1997	N/A	N/A
1997 SCO149 Polar Bear with Red Vest and Black Bow Tie (Blockbuster Exclusive)	Yr.Iss.	1997	N/A	N/A
1998 SCO152 Reindeer	Yr.Iss.		5.00	5
1997 SCO153 & 154 Kissing Bears (White's Guide to Collecting Figures Magazine Exclusive)	15,000	1997	15.00	15-30
1998 SCO155 Penguin with Snowflake Scarf	Yr.Iss.		5.00	5
1998 SCO158 Seal with White Tee Shirt (Coca-Cola Exclusive)	Yr.Iss.		6.00	6
1998 SCO159 Polar Bear with Long Coca-Cola scarf (Coca-Cola Exclusive)	Yr.Iss.		6.00	6
1998 McDonald's Boy with Vest & Girl with Bow, set/2	Yr.Iss.		Gift	N/A

Coca-Cola Brand Heritage Collection (Sundblom) - P. Hamel

YEAR ISSUE	EDITION LIMIT	YEAR RETD.	ISSUE PRICE	*QUOTE U.S.$
1997 Hospitality	3,000		200.00	200

Coca-Cola Brand Heritage Soda Fountain Bears - CGI

YEAR ISSUE	EDITION LIMIT	YEAR RETD.	ISSUE PRICE	*QUOTE U.S.$
1998 Bearry Bearresford	5,000		50.00	50
1998 Cubby Bearringer	5,000		50.00	50
1998 Dr. Pembearton	5,000		60.00	60
1998 Lillian Bearica	5,000		70.00	70
1998 Tessie Bear Bearringer	5,000		50.00	50

Harley-Davidson Bean Bag - CGI

YEAR ISSUE	EDITION LIMIT	YEAR RETD.	ISSUE PRICE	*QUOTE U.S.$
1998 Baby Blue & Studs	Open		8.00	8
1998 Chopper	Open		8.00	8
1998 Clutch Carbo	Open		8.00	8
1997 Enforcer	Open		8.00	8
1998 Evo	Open		8.00	8
1998 Fat Bob	Open		8.00	8
1998 Kickstart	Open		8.00	8
1998 Manifold Max	Open		8.00	8
1997 Motorhead	Open		8.00	8
1997 Punky	Open		8.00	8
1997 Racer	Open		8.00	8

*Quotes have been rounded up to nearest dollar

YEAR ISSUE	EDITION LIMIT	YEAR RETD.	ISSUE PRICE	*QUOTE U.S.$
1997 Rachet	Open		8.00	8
1997 Roamer	Open		8.00	8
1998 Spike	Open		8.00	8

Harley-Davidson Plush - B. Yaney

YEAR ISSUE	EDITION LIMIT	YEAR RETD.	ISSUE PRICE	*QUOTE U.S.$
1998 Clutch Carbo	Open		50.00	50
1997 Cruiser	Open		50.00	50
1998 Curt Chrome	Open		50.00	50
1997 Panhead Pete	Open		50.00	50
1997 Sissy Bar	Open		50.00	50
1997 V-Twin	Open		50.00	50

Humbug Beannie Bugs - T. Fraley

YEAR ISSUE	EDITION LIMIT	YEAR RETD.	ISSUE PRICE	*QUOTE U.S.$
1998 Humbug	Open		8.00	8
1998 Santa Bug	Open		8.00	8
1998 Scroogy Bug	Open		8.00	8
1998 Sleepy Bug	Open		8.00	8

Save The Children Bean Bag Collection - Save The Children

YEAR ISSUE	EDITION LIMIT	YEAR RETD.	ISSUE PRICE	*QUOTE U.S.$
1998 Haruko	Open		8.00	8
1998 Juji	Open		8.00	8
1998 Mackenzie	Open		8.00	8
1998 Patrick	Open		8.00	8
1998 Paz	Open		8.00	8
1998 Sila	Open		8.00	8

Daddy's Long Legs/KVK, Inc.

Daddy's Long Legs/Collectors Club Members Only - K. Germany

YEAR ISSUE	EDITION LIMIT	YEAR RETD.	ISSUE PRICE	*QUOTE U.S.$
1993 Faith	2,290	1993	65.00	250-260
1994 Bubby, w/Heart blanket	580	1994	65.00	295-325
1994 Bubby, w/Star blanket	1,537	1994	65.00	175-225
1994 Sissy	1,963	1995	65.00	225-295
1995 Bull Bishop	1,529	1995	65.00	140-175
1995 Cherry	1,010	1995	65.00	140-175
1995 Joy (Angel)	Closed	1995	Gift	100
1996 Jack	1,574	1996	65.00	100-125
1996 Jill	1,578	1996	65.00	100-125
1996 Carrie (Angel)	Closed	1996	Gift	50
1997 Joseph	Closed	1997	65.00	65-95
1997 Mary	Closed	1997	65.00	65-95
1997 Baby Jesus	Closed	1997	Gift	N/A
1998 Jeffy	Yr.Iss.		65.00	65
1998 Jenni	Yr.Iss.		65.00	65
1998 Boo	Yr.Iss.		Gift	N/A

Daddy's Long Legs/Advertising - K. Germany

YEAR ISSUE	EDITION LIMIT	YEAR RETD.	ISSUE PRICE	*QUOTE U.S.$
1997 Boots	1,204	1997	90.00	125-180
1996 Gigi	931	1996	90.00	125-150
1995 Gretchen	982	1995	80.00	125-150
1998 Jodi	Closed	1998	90.00	90
1995 Pistol	1,352	1995	80.00	150-285
1993 Priscilla	501	1993	70.00	285-375
1997 Skipper	Closed	1997	90.00	90-110
1994 Ticker	1,714	1994	76.00	185-210
1994 Wendy	1,609	1994	80.00	150-175

Daddy's Long Legs/Angels - K. Germany

YEAR ISSUE	EDITION LIMIT	YEAR RETD.	ISSUE PRICE	*QUOTE U.S.$
1995 Demetria	1	1995	2500.00	N/A
1994 Glory	692	1994	118.00	225-265
1994 Hope	345	1994	118.00	225-275
1994 Kara	424	1994	76.00	150-225
1996 Monica	Closed	1998	150.00	150-185
1994 Precious	824	1994	76.00	150-215

Daddy's Long Legs/Animals - K. Germany

YEAR ISSUE	EDITION LIMIT	YEAR RETD.	ISSUE PRICE	*QUOTE U.S.$
1990 Abigail the Cow, blue	3,498	1995	62.00	200-275
1990 Abigail the Cow, red	1,063	1995	68.00	225-300
1990 Cat in Jump Suit	66	1990	60.00	600-700
1990 Goat-boy	109	1991	62.00	650-750
1990 Goat-girl	154	1991	62.00	650-750
1990 Hugh Hoofner	1,453	1994	68.00	225-300
1991 Kitty Kat	527	1992	78.00	525-575
1991 Mamie the Pig, blue	425	1992	84.00	550-600
1990 Mamie the Pig, green	425	1992	68.00	550-600
1990 Pig-boy	124	1990	58.00	650-700
1990 Raccoon	123	1990	66.00	750-850
1990 Rachael Rabbit	377	1992	15.00	175-200
1990 Robby Rabbit	529	1992	44.00	575-600
1990 Rose Rabbit	684	1992	54.00	800-900
1990 Roxanne Rabbit	351	1992	52.00	575-600
1990 Rudy Rabbit	547	1992	54.00	800-900
1990 Wedding Rabbits	3	1990	240.00	3200-3400

Daddy's Long Legs/Arts & Theater - K. Germany

YEAR ISSUE	EDITION LIMIT	YEAR RETD.	ISSUE PRICE	*QUOTE U.S.$
1994 Margo	2,349	1996	126.00	175-200
1990 Mime	57	1990	58.00	1200-1575
1990 Witch Hazel	1,971	1995	86.00	275-300

Daddy's Long Legs/Babies & Toddlers - K. Germany

YEAR ISSUE	EDITION LIMIT	YEAR RETD.	ISSUE PRICE	*QUOTE U.S.$
1995 Annie Lee w/blanket	450	1995	150.00	275-320
1995 Annie Lee w/o blanket	100	1995	150.00	225-275
1996 Bunny	682	1996	80.00	150-175

Daddy's Long Legs/Clowns - K. Germany

YEAR ISSUE	EDITION LIMIT	YEAR RETD.	ISSUE PRICE	*QUOTE U.S.$
1996 Buttons	2,030	1996	80.00	165-175
1997 Dr. Tickles (convention ed.)	659	1997	125.00	250-325
1995 Sugar (convention ed.)	475	1995	120.00	475-550

Daddy's Long Legs/Family - K. Germany

YEAR ISSUE	EDITION LIMIT	YEAR RETD.	ISSUE PRICE	*QUOTE U.S.$
1993 Abe	2,483	1995	94.00	175-195
1994 Aunt Fannie	1,475	1996	90.00	150-180
1992 Bessie	4,926	1996	94.00	150-175
1993 Billye	1,863	1995	98.00	185-225
1995 Camille	2,000	1997	184.00	184-275
1994 Charles Louis	1,184	1996	90.00	150-180
1992 Doc Moses	2,494	1993	98.00	250-350
1996 Earl	693	1996	98.00	350-375
1996 Ella	693	1996	98.00	350-375
1993 Esther	3,000	1993	158.00	350-395
1992 Gracie	3,133	1996	94.00	150-175
1993 Jackie	2,425	1995	98.00	200-210
1992 Jasmine	3,977	1994	90.00	235-275
1993 Judge	1,866	1995	98.00	225-250
1994 Maxine	1,538	1996	90.00	150-180
1992 Nurse Garnet	1,415	1993	90.00	225-350
1993 Sam	1,813	1995	94.00	175-195
1993 Slats	2,323	1995	98.00	225-250
1990 Sofie	5,548	1992	44.00	425-450
1994 Uncle Leon	1,547	1996	90.00	150-180

Daddy's Long Legs/Old West - K. Germany

YEAR ISSUE	EDITION LIMIT	YEAR RETD.	ISSUE PRICE	*QUOTE U.S.$
1990 Cowboy Buck	1,824	1994	78.00	350-425
1990 Indian, 1st ed.	304	1990	78.00	800-950
1992 Lucky the Gambler	939	1992	90.00	600-650
1990 Miss Lilly	1,664	1994	78.00	350-450
1991 Still River (Indian, 2nd ed.)	1,452	1995	98.00	325-350
1996 Sweet Savannah	2,000	1997	260.00	260-325
1996 Wildwood Will	1,000	1996	290.00	525-650

Daddy's Long Legs/Patriotic - K. Germany

YEAR ISSUE	EDITION LIMIT	YEAR RETD.	ISSUE PRICE	*QUOTE U.S.$
1992 Jeremiah	3,219	1994	90.00	235-275
1995 Uncle Sam, black	1,510	1997	120.00	240-275
1991 Uncle Sam, white	729	1991	150.00	1250-1500

Daddy's Long Legs/Santa Claus - K. Germany

YEAR ISSUE	EDITION LIMIT	YEAR RETD.	ISSUE PRICE	*QUOTE U.S.$
1990 Santa-1990, white	48	1990	64.00	1700-1900
1990 Santa-Red Velvet	25	1990	180.00	1800-2000
1990 Santa-Tapestry	25	1990	180.00	1800-2000
1991 Santa-1991, black	1,101	1991	98.00	325-450
1991 Santa-1991, white	311	1991	98.00	350-450
1992 Santa-1992, black	511	1993	158.00	375-475
1992 Santa-1992, special ed.	213	1993	158.00	400-500
1992 Santa-1992, white	166	1993	158.00	400-500
1993 Santa-1993, black	1,112	1994	178.00	325-375
1994 Santa-1994, Tubbin' Santa	1,859	1995	150.00	200-375
1994 Odessa Claus, 1st ed.	778	1995	144.00	225-275
1995 Santa-1995, black	1,010	1996	160.00	200-300
1995 Santa-1995, white	565	1996	160.00	200-300
1995 Odessa Claus, 2nd ed.	Closed	1998	144.00	144-175
1996 Santa-1996, black	985	1997	200.00	200-275
1997 Santa-1997, black	Closed	1998	250.00	250
1998 Santa-1998, black	6/99		250.00	250

Daddy's Long Legs/Schoolhouse Days - K. Germany

YEAR ISSUE	EDITION LIMIT	YEAR RETD.	ISSUE PRICE	*QUOTE U.S.$
1992 Choo-Choo	3,618	1993	56.00	115-135
1991 Daphne	1,060	1992	72.00	250-275
1993 Emily	1,278	1993	80.00	175-215
1991 Iric, Teacher	997	1992	90.00	350-375
1994 Jane	3,768	1994	70.00	95-150
1992 Josie	4,132	1993	56.00	115-135
1992 Katy	5,533	1996	64.00	100-125
1993 Lucy	1,946	1995	64.00	140-150
1995 Marcus	1,511	1995	76.00	125-150
1992 Micah	4,789	1996	64.00	100-150
1995 Molly	1,498	1995	76.00	125-150
1993 Phoebe	2,789	1995	64.00	140-150
1993 Priscilla	501	1993	70.00	285-375
1993 Timothy	750	1993	76.00	275-400

Daddy's Long Legs/Storybook - K. Germany

YEAR ISSUE	EDITION LIMIT	YEAR RETD.	ISSUE PRICE	*QUOTE U.S.$
1996 Little Miss Muffet	1,117	1996	90.00	110-175
1994 Little Red Riding Hood	1,824	1994	80.00	200-295
1995 Mary and her Lamb	1,627	1995	80.00	165-185

Daddy's Long Legs/Sunday School & Church - K. Germany

YEAR ISSUE	EDITION LIMIT	YEAR RETD.	ISSUE PRICE	*QUOTE U.S.$
1993 Cassie	1,521	1993	70.00	100-150
1993 Polly	1,523	1995	70.00	100-150
1993 Sister Carter	1,719	1995	94.00	150-200
1992 Sister Mary Kathleen	1,844	1994	98.00	200-300

Daddy's Long Legs/Wedding Party - K. Germany

YEAR ISSUE	EDITION LIMIT	YEAR RETD.	ISSUE PRICE	*QUOTE U.S.$
1992 James, Groom (originally sold as set/2)	1,295	1992	125.00	300-350
1992 Olivia, Bride (originally sold as set/2)	1,295	1992	125.00	300-350
1992 James, Groom & Olivia, Bride, set	Closed	1992	250.00	600-725
1996 Joshua, Ringbearer	2,500	1997	98.00	110-125
1994 Maggie, Flower Girl	2,500	1996	98.00	140-175
1996 Maurice, Groom	2,500	1997	118.00	118-175
1994 Victoria, Bride	2,500	1995	178.00	250-300

Deb Canham Artist Designs Inc.

Brenda Power Collection - B. Power

YEAR ISSUE	EDITION LIMIT	YEAR RETD.	ISSUE PRICE	*QUOTE U.S.$
1998 Penguin	2,000		54.00	54
1998 Rabbit on Wheels	2,000		54.00	54
1998 Racoon	2,000		56.00	56
1998 Standing Rabbit	2,000		54.00	54

Camelot Collection - D. Canham, unless otherwise noted

YEAR ISSUE	EDITION LIMIT	YEAR RETD.	ISSUE PRICE	*QUOTE U.S.$
1998 Guinivere	2,500		54.00	54
1998 Jester	2,500		54.00	54
1998 King Arthur	2,500		54.00	54
1998 Merlin - L. Sasaki	2,500		54.00	54
1998 Sir Dennis	2,500		54.00	54
1998 Sir Lancelot	2,500		54.00	54
1998 Slap-a-Roo	2,500		54.00	54

Cloth Dolls - J. Davis

YEAR ISSUE	EDITION LIMIT	YEAR RETD.	ISSUE PRICE	*QUOTE U.S.$
1998 Mandy Organdie	500		99.50	100
1998 Mollie Muslin	500		99.50	100

Country Collection - D. Canham

YEAR ISSUE	EDITION LIMIT	YEAR RETD.	ISSUE PRICE	*QUOTE U.S.$
1996 Annalee and Miss Goosey	3,000		40.00	45
1996 Missi and Miss Moo	3,000		40.00	45
1996 Tom and Mr. P	3,000		40.00	45
1996 Zack and Mr. H	3,000		40.00	45

Denizens of Honey Hills - D. Canham

YEAR ISSUE	EDITION LIMIT	YEAR RETD.	ISSUE PRICE	*QUOTE U.S.$
1996 Bratty Butchy	3,000		60.00	60
1996 Gertie Lady of the Bag	3,000		60.00	60
1996 Poppo the Wise	3,000		60.00	60
1996 Simon the Curious	3,000		60.00	60
1996 Willyum the Brave	3,000		60.00	60

Gollies - D. Canham

YEAR ISSUE	EDITION LIMIT	YEAR RETD.	ISSUE PRICE	*QUOTE U.S.$
1997 Spangles	2,000		52.00	52
1997 Spats	2,000		52.00	52

Have a Heart Collection - D. Canham

YEAR ISSUE	EDITION LIMIT	YEAR RETD.	ISSUE PRICE	*QUOTE U.S.$
1998 Angel	2,500		52.00	52
1998 Crispin	2,500		52.00	52
1998 Gus	2,500		52.00	52
1998 Lilac Lil	2,500		52.00	52
1998 Mummy's Little Monster	2,500		52.00	52
1998 Peppermint	2,500		52.00	52
1998 Susie	2,500		52.00	52

Martians - D. Canham

YEAR ISSUE	EDITION LIMIT	YEAR RETD.	ISSUE PRICE	*QUOTE U.S.$
1997 Gussie Galactica	1,000	1998	54.00	54
1997 Moonshine Cosmic	1,000	1998	54.00	54

Mohair Collection - D. Canham

YEAR ISSUE	EDITION LIMIT	YEAR RETD.	ISSUE PRICE	*QUOTE U.S.$
1996 A.J.	5,000	1998	40.00	45
1996 B.J.	5,000	1998	40.00	45
1996 Benjamin	3,000	1997	40.00	45
1996 Flore	3,000	1997	40.00	45
1996 Golly Gosh	3,000	1997	40.00	45
1996 Panda	5,000		40.00	45
1996 Peter	3,000	1997	40.00	45
1996 Sorry	5,000	1997	40.00	45

Nutcracker Suite - D. Canham, unless otherwise noted

YEAR ISSUE	EDITION LIMIT	YEAR RETD.	ISSUE PRICE	*QUOTE U.S.$
1997 Columbine	2,000		52.00	52
1997 Harlequin	2,000		52.00	52
1997 Magician	2,000		52.00	52
1997 Nutcracker Prince - L. Sasaki	2,000		52.00	52
1997 Rat King - B. Windell	2,000		52.00	52
1997 Snowflake	2,000		52.00	52
1997 Sugar Plum	2,000		52.00	52

Rainy Days Collection - D. Canham

YEAR ISSUE	EDITION LIMIT	YEAR RETD.	ISSUE PRICE	*QUOTE U.S.$
1997 Chuckles	2,000		48.00	48
1997 Hattie	2,000	1998	48.00	48
1997 Herschel	2,000	1997	48.00	48
1997 Lady Ascot	2,000		48.00	48
1997 Pilgrim	2,000	1998	48.00	48
1997 Sticky Bun	2,000		48.00	48

Specials - D. Canham

YEAR ISSUE	EDITION LIMIT	YEAR RETD.	ISSUE PRICE	*QUOTE U.S.$
1998 Button Jester	200	1998	60.00	60
1998 Tulip	400	1998	54.00	54
1997 Uncle Ernie	700	1997	48.00	48

Department 56

Heritage Village Doll Collection - Department 56

YEAR ISSUE	EDITION LIMIT	YEAR RETD.	ISSUE PRICE	*QUOTE U.S.$
1987 Christmas Carol Dolls 1000-6 set/4 (Tiny Tim, Bob Crachet, Mrs. Crachet, Scrooge)	250	1988	1500.00	900-1100
1987 Christmas Carol Dolls 5907-2 set/4 (Tiny Tim, Bob Crachet, Mrs. Crachet, Scrooge)	Closed	1993	250.00	192-242
1988 Christmas Carol Dolls 1001-4 set/4 (Tiny Tim, Bob Crachet, Mrs. Crachet, Scrooge)	350	1989	1600.00	1600
1988 Mr. & Mrs. Fezziwig 5594-8 set/2	Closed	1995	172.00	140-180

Snowbabies Dolls - Department 56

YEAR ISSUE	EDITION LIMIT	YEAR RETD.	ISSUE PRICE	*QUOTE U.S.$
1988 Allison & Duncan-Set of 2, 7730-5	Closed	1989	200.00	660-995

Dolls by Jerri

Dolls by Jerri - J. McCloud

YEAR ISSUE	EDITION LIMIT	YEAR RETD.	ISSUE PRICE	*QUOTE U.S.$
1986 Alfalfa	1,000		350.00	350
1986 Allison	1,000		350.00	450
1986 Amber	1,000		350.00	900
1986 Annabelle	300		600.00	585
1986 Ashley	1,000		350.00	500
1986 Audrey	300		550.00	550
1982 Baby David	538		290.00	2000
XX Boy	1,000		350.00	425
1985 Bride	1,000		350.00	400
1986 Bridgette	300		500.00	500
1985 Candy	1,000		340.00	2000
1986 Cane	1,000		350.00	1200
1986 Charlotte	1,000		330.00	450
1984 Clara	1,000		320.00	1200-1500
1986 Clown-David 3 Yrs. Old	1,000		340.00	450
1986 Danielle	1,000		350.00	500
1986 David-2 Years Old	1,000		330.00	550
1986 David-Magician	1,000		350.00	450
XX Denise	1,000		380.00	550

*Quotes have been rounded up to nearest dollar

YEAR ISSUE	EDITION LIMIT	YEAR RETD.	ISSUE PRICE	*QUOTE U.S.$
1986 Elizabeth	1,000		340.00	350
1984 Emily	1,000		330.00	2500
1986 The Fool	1,000		350.00	850
XX Gina	1,000		350.00	475
XX Goldilocks	1,000		370.00	700-800
1989 Goose Girl, Guild	Closed		300.00	700
1986 Helenjean	1,000		350.00	500-675
1988 Holly	1,000		370.00	825
1986 Jacqueline	300		500.00	500
XX Jamie	800		380.00	450
1986 Joy	1,000		350.00	350
XX Laura	1,000		350.00	500
1989 Laura Lee	1,000		370.00	575
XX Little Bo Peep	1,000		340.00	450
XX Little Miss Muffet	1,000		340.00	450
1986 Lucianna	300		500.00	500
1986 Mary Beth	1,000		350.00	350
XX Megan	750		420.00	550
XX Meredith	750		430.00	600
1985 Miss Nanny	1,000		160.00	275
1986 Nobody	1,000		350.00	650-800
1986 Princess and the Unicorn	1,000		370.00	400
1986 Samantha	1,000		350.00	550
1985 Scotty	1,000		340.00	1800
1986 Somebody	1,000		350.00	750-850
1986 Tammy	1,000		350.00	900
1985 Uncle Joe	1,000		160.00	250-300
XX Uncle Remus	500		290.00	450
1986 Yvonne	300		500.00	500

Elke's Originals, Ltd.

Elke Hutchens - E. Hutchens

YEAR ISSUE	EDITION LIMIT	YEAR RETD.	ISSUE PRICE	*QUOTE U.S.$
1991 Alicia	250		595.00	700-995
1989 Annabelle	250		575.00	1400-1500
1990 Aubra	250		575.00	900-1050
1990 Aurora	250		595.00	900-1050
1991 Bellinda	400		595.00	800-895
1992 Bethany	400		595.00	700-895
1991 Braelyn	400		595.00	1400-1600
1991 Brianna	400		595.00	1000-1200
1992 Cecilia	435		635.00	800-900
1992 Charles	435		635.00	600-900
1992 Cherie	435		635.00	900
1992 Clarissa	435		635.00	800-900
1993 Daphne	435		675.00	700-850
1993 Deidre	435		675.00	795
1993 Desirée	435		675.00	700-900
1990 Kricket	500		575.00	400
1992 Laurakaye	435		550.00	550
1990 Little Liebchen	250		475.00	1000
1990 Victoria	500		645.00	645

Ganz

Cottage Collectibles® Collection - L. Chien, unless otherwise noted

YEAR ISSUE	EDITION LIMIT	YEAR RETD.	ISSUE PRICE	*QUOTE U.S.$
1998 Abby-Bear - S. Coe	Open		20.00	20
1998 Alex-Bear - S. Coe	Open		44.00	44
1995 Alfalfa-Bunny	Open		9.00	9
1997 Andrew-Bear - C. Kirby	Open		18.00	18
1997 Angel-Bear - C. Rave	Open		14.00	14
1995 Annie-Bear - C. Kirby	Retrd.	1998	20.00	20
1995 Anthony-Bear	10,524	1997	8.00	8
1998 Arthur Twiggins III-Bear	Open		20.00	20
1998 Ashley-Bear - S. Coe	Open		18.00	18
1995 Bailey-Bear - C. Kirby	Open		25.00	25
1996 Barkley-Dog	Retrd.	1998	25.00	25
1997 Basil-Bear - M. Holstad	Open		70.00	70
1998 Becca-Bear - C. Kirby	Open		44.00	44
1997 Becky-Bear	Open		20.00	20
1998 Becky-Bear - S. Coe	Open		27.00	27
1997 Benny-Dog - M. Holstad	Open		17.00	17
1998 Bentley-Bear - S. Coe	Open		46.00	46
1995 Bernard-Dog	Open		17.00	17
1998 Bernie (Christmas)-Bear - M. Holstad	Open		36.00	36
1996 Bernie-Bear - M. Holstad	Open		26.00	26
1995 Betsy-Bear - C. Kirby	9,856	1997	19.00	19
1996 Bianca-Bunny	Retrd.	1998	25.00	25
1995 Bilzi-Bear - C. Rave	6,600	1997	17.00	17
1998 Bingo-Bear - C. Rave	Open		10.00	10
1995 Bluebeary-Bear	Open		6.00	6
1998 Bo Jingles-Bear - C. Tredger	Open		17.00	17
1998 Bongo-Bear - C. Rave	Open		10.00	10
1998 Bosco-Bear - C. Tredger	Open		20.00	20
1998 Boz-Bear - C. Rave	Open		10.00	10
1995 Brad-Bear	Retrd.	1998	8.00	8
1998 Brandon-Bear - S. Coe	Open		21.00	21
1998 Brewster-Dog - C. Kirby	Open		14.00	14
1995 Buckley-Bear - C. Rave	Open		30.00	30
1998 Bud-Bear	Open		15.00	15
1995 Buddy-Bear	Retrd.	1998	18.00	18
1995 Buffy-Bear - C. Kirby	Retrd.	1998	20.00	20
1996 Bumbershoot-Bunny	Retrd.	1998	25.00	25
1997 Buster Brown-Bear	Open		33.00	33
1995 Buttercup-Bear - C. Kirby	Retrd.	1998	8.00	8
1995 Buttercup-Bunny	Open		20.00	20
1997 Callie-Cat - M. Holstad	Open		25.00	25
1997 Camille-Bunny - M. Holstad	Open		48.00	48
1997 Candice-Bear - M. Holstad	Open		26.00	26
1997 Casey-Puppy - M. Holstad	Open		6.00	6
1998 Celeste-Bear - C. Kirby	Open		68.00	68
1997 Champ-Dog	Open		20.00	20
1997 Checkers-Bear - C. Kirby	Retrd.	1998	30.00	30
1998 Christine-Bear - S. Coe	Open		20.00	20
1998 Chuckles	Open		40.00	40
1998 Clair-Bear - S. Coe	Open		35.00	35
1995 Clancey-Bear	Retrd.	1998	18.00	18
1997 Clover Bunny - M. Holstad	Open		8.00	8
1997 Coco-Bear	Open		12.00	12
1997 Connor-Dog - C. Tredger	Open		31.00	31
1996 Copper-Bear - T. Skorstad	Open		10.00	10
1995 Cranbeary-Bear	Open		6.00	6
1998 Daisy-Bear - C. Kirby	Open		70.00	70
1997 Dakota-Bear - C. Kirby	Open		17.00	17
1995 Dandy-Lion	2,400	1996	18.00	18
1997 Daniel-Bear - M. Holstad	Open		20.00	20
1998 Danny-Bear - C. Kirby	Open		64.00	64
1997 Daphne-Bear - M. Holstad	Open		20.00	20
1996 Dempster-Bear	Open		35.00	35
1998 Dennis-Bear - C. Tredger	Open		18.00	18
1995 Dewbeary-Bear	Open		6.00	6
1997 Dexter-Yes/No Bear	Open		48.00	48
1995 Dickey-Bear - C. Rave	Retrd.	1998	12.00	12
1995 Dieter-Bear	Retrd.	1998	30.00	30
1997 Dimples-Bear - C. Kirby	Retrd.	1998	19.00	19
1997 Dixie-Bear	Open		48.00	48
1998 Dorothy-Bear - C. Tredger	Open		18.00	18
1995 Dudley-Bear	7,200	1997	18.00	18
1995 Dumpling-Bear	Retrd.	1998	35.00	35
1997 Duncan-Bear	Open		34.00	34
1997 Eddie-Rabbit - C. Kirby	Open		14.50	15
1997 Edmund-Bear - C. Rave	Open		37.00	37
1997 Edward-Bear - C. Kirby	Open		96.00	96
1995 Ellie-Elephant	Retrd.	1996	17.00	17
1997 Elmer-Bear	Open		13.00	13
1997 Emily Lou-Bear - C. Rave	Open		48.00	48
1996 Emily-Bear - T. Skorstad	Retrd.	1998	26.00	26
1997 Emmet-Bear - C. Rave	Open		48.00	48
1998 Ethel Elderberry-Bear	Open		23.00	23
1997 Farley-Dog	Open		15.00	15
1998 Fifi-Dog	Open		17.00	17
1997 Floppy Jill-Bear	Open		16.50	17
1997 Floppy Joe-Bear	Open		13.00	13
1997 Flora-Frog	Open		32.00	32
1996 Floyd-Frog	Open		32.00	32
1995 Forest-Bear	Retrd.	1998	18.00	18
1995 Fran-Fox	Retrd.	1998	17.00	17
1995 Freddie-Fox	Retrd.	1998	17.00	17
1997 Freddy-Bear - M. Holstad	Open		17.00	17
1995 Frizzy-Bear	8,400	1997	20.00	20
1997 Gabearella-Bear	Open		29.00	29
1998 Gingersnap-Bear - C. Kirby	Open		20.00	20
1998 Good Golly-Doll	Open		20.00	20
1997 Gus-Bear - C. Kirby	Open		44.00	44
1998 Hallie-Bunny - C. Rave	Open		30.00	30
1995 Harvey-Bunny	Retrd.	1998	9.00	9
1998 Hattie-Bunny - C. Rave	Open		30.00	30
1995 Higgins-Bear	Open		25.00	25
1998 Higi-Bear - C. Rave	Open		17.00	17
1997 Holly Beary-Bear - C. Rave	Open		8.00	8
1998 Holly-Bear - T. Skorstad	Open		25.00	25
1997 Honey-Bear	Open		50.00	50
1997 Hopper-Frog	Open		8.00	8
1998 Hucklebeary-Bear	Open		12.00	12
1998 Jackson-Bunny	Open		50.00	50
1995 Jacob-Bear	Retrd.	1998	18.00	18
1995 Jake-Bear - C. Kirby	Open		20.00	20
1998 Jasper-Bear - C. Tredger	Open		14.00	14
1998 Jefferson-Bear - C. Tredger	Open		30.00	30
1997 Jerry Hound-Dog - C. Tredger	Open		30.00	30
1997 Jigsaw-Bear C. Kirby	Open		24.00	24
1996 Jordan-Bear - T. Skorstad	Retrd.	1998	25.00	25
1997 Jumper-Bear - C. Kirby	Open		23.00	23
1996 Justine-Bear - T. Skorstad	Retrd.	1998	25.00	25
1998 Kathy (Christmas)-Bear - M. Holstad	Open		52.00	52
1996 Kathy-Bear - M. Holstad	Open		52.00	52
1995 Katrina-Cat	Open		20.00	20
1997 Kitty-Cat	Open		12.00	12
1997 Kringle-Bear	Open		11.00	11
1997 Kringle-Bear - C. Rave	Open		19.00	19
1998 Kristen-Bear - C. Kirby	Open		38.00	38
1997 Kurtis-Dog - C. Tredger	Open		31.00	31
1997 Lacey-Dog - M. Holstad	Open		28.00	28
1996 Li'l Annie-Bear	Open		25.00	25
1995 Li'l Dieter-Bear	Retrd.	1998	15.00	15
1995 Li'l Lucas-Bear	Open		15.00	15
1995 Li'l Mulberry-Bear	Open		8.00	8
1997 Li'l Panda-Bear	Open		11.00	11
1995 Li'l Pandee-Bear - C. Kirby	Open		12.00	12
1995 Li'l Taylor-Bear	3,598	1996	16.00	16
1995 Li'l Theodore-Bear	3,756	1996	17.00	17
1997 Li'l Wriggles-Bear	Open		9.00	9
1995 Lilac-Bunny	Retrd.	1998	20.00	20
1997 Little Salty-Bear - T. Skorstad	Open		25.00	25
1995 Lucas-Bear	Retrd.	1998	30.00	30
1997 Lynda-Bear - C. Kirby	Open		31.00	31
1997 MacPherson-Puppy - M. Holstad	Open		13.00	13
1998 Mango-Monkey	Open		48.00	48
1998 Marble-Cat - M. Holstad	Open		23.00	23
1997 Margo-Bear - M. Holstad	Open		40.00	40
1995 Marvin-Monkey	Open		13.00	13
1998 Mary Lou-Bear - M. Holstad	Open		28.00	28
1995 Matthew-Bear	Retrd.	1998	13.00	13
1996 Mattie-Bear	Open		25.00	25
1996 Maxwell-Bear - C. Kirby	Open		32.00	32
1997 McKenzie-Dog - C. Tredger	Open		31.00	31
1998 Meatball-Mouse	Open		12.00	12
1996 Meredith-Bear - C. Kirby	Open		32.00	32
1997 Mikey-Bear - M. Holstad	Open		29.00	29
1997 Milo-Bear - M. Holstad	Open		25.00	25
1998 Milton-Bear - C. Tredger	Open		21.00	21
1998 Mischief-Cat - M. Holstad	Open		13.00	13
1997 Mistletoe-Bear - C. Rave	Open		8.00	8
1998 Misty-Bear - M. Holstad	Open		70.00	70
1997 Monterey Jack-Bear	Open		12.00	12
1998 Morris-Mouse - C. Tredger	Open		13.00	13
1997 Motley-Bear	Retrd.	1998	27.00	27
1997 Mozzarella-Mouse	Open		12.00	12
1998 Mr. Hopkins-Bunny	Open		32.00	32
1998 Mrs. Hopkins-Bunny	Open		32.00	32
1995 Muffin-Bear	Open		6.00	6
1995 Mulberry-Bear	Retrd.	1998	15.00	15
1997 Murphy-Dog - M. Holstad	Open		12.00	12
1996 Natasha-Bunny - C. Kirby	Retrd.	1998	18.00	18
1997 Nathan-Bear	Retrd.	1998	40.00	40
1995 Ned-Bear	Retrd.	1998	20.00	20
1997 Nicki-Bear	Open		40.00	40
1995 Nilla-Bear - T. Skorstad	Retrd.	1998	25.00	25
1998 Noah-Bear	Open		37.00	37
1995 Noel-Bear - C. Kirby	Retrd.	1998	30.00	30
1996 Noodles-Bear - C. Kirby	Retrd.	1998	18.00	18
1998 Nutasha-Squirrel	Open		15.00	15
1998 Nutcracker-Squirrel	Open		15.00	15
1998 Ol' Chum-Bear	Open		60.00	60
1997 Ol' Wabbit-Bunny	Open		27.00	27
1995 Oliver-Bear	Retrd.	1998	19.00	19
1998 Olivia-Bear - C. Rave	Open		18.00	18
1997 Owen-Bear - C. Kirby	Open		31.00	31
1997 P.J.-Bear - C. Kirby	Open		37.00	37
1995 Paddy-Bear	Open		15.00	15
1998 Pamper-Cat - M. Holstad	Open		23.00	23
1997 Papa "D"-Bear - C. Kirby	Open		29.00	29
1997 Parsley-Bunny - M. Holstad	Open		25.00	25
1997 Patches-Bear	Open		27.00	27
1995 Penelope-Bear	Open		34.00	34
1996 Pipkin-Bunny	Open		7.00	7
1997 Pippin-Bear - C. Rave	Open		12.00	12
1997 Polly-Bear - C. Kirby	Open		80.00	80
1998 Potluck-Panda Bear	Open		48.00	48
1998 Pudding- Bear	Open		37.00	37
1997 Puddy-Kitten - M. Holstad	Open		12.00	12
1998 Punkin (Christmas)-Kitten - M. Holstad	Open		8.00	8
1998 Punkin-Kitten - M. Holstad	Open		8.00	8
1998 Rachel-Bear - M. Holstad	Open		13.00	13
1996 Rafferty-Bunny	Retrd.	1998	25.00	25
1998 Ramona (Christmas)-Bear - M. Holstad	Open		24.00	24
1998 Ramona-Bear - M. Holstad	Open		24.00	24
1995 Raymond-Bear	Open		16.00	16
1996 Reba-Bunny	Open		15.00	15
1997 Reggie-Bear - C. Rave	Open		16.00	16
1997 Rhonda-Raccoon	Open		12.00	12
1995 Ricky-Raccoon	Retrd.	1998	18.00	18
1995 Rita-Raccoon	Retrd.	1998	18.00	18
1996 Robbie-Bear - M. Holstad	Open		22.00	22
1997 Rocky-Raccoon	Open		12.00	12
1997 Root Beer-Bear - T. Skorstad	Open		35.00	35
1995 Rosebud-Bear	Retrd.	1998	13.00	13
1995 Rosey-Bear	3,370	1996	28.00	28
1995 Ross-Bear - C. Kirby	6,480	1997	14.00	14
1996 Rover-Bear - M. Holstad	Open		7.00	7
1995 Ruff-Dog	Open		15.00	15
1996 Rusty-Bear	Open		10.00	10
1997 Sadie-Bear - C. Kirby	Open		12.50	13
1997 Sam-Bear - C. Kirby	Open		12.50	13
1998 Sammy-Siamese Cat	Open		27.00	27
1995 Schneider-Dog	Open		7.00	7
1997 Scrooge-Bear	Open		23.00	23
1997 Scrubber-Dog	Open		20.00	20
1998 Shannon-Bear - S. Coe	Open		27.00	27
1995 Simi-Bear - C. Rave	Retrd.	1998	13.00	13
1997 Slugger-Bear	Open		34.00	34
1997 Smitty-Bear	Open		26.00	26
1997 Smokey-Cat	Open		12.00	12
1995 Sneakers-Cat	Open		25.00	25
1998 Snowbear - S. Coe	Open		40.00	40
1998 Snowflake-Bear - C. Tredger	Open		20.00	20
1997 Snowflake-Cat - M. Holstad	Open		17.00	17
1997 Sparky Puppy - M. Holstad	Open		6.00	6
1997 Stu-Bear	Open		38.00	38
1997 Sue-Bear	Open		38.00	38
1997 Sugar-Kitty - M. Holstad	Open		6.00	6
1995 Tad-Bear	9,984	1997	18.00	18
1998 Taffy-Dog - M. Holstad	Open		8.00	8
1995 Taylor-Bear	6,864	1996	30.00	30
1997 Teddy Rousseau-Bear	Open		70.00	70
1998 Tedrick-Bear	Open		70.00	70
1995 Theodore-Bear	2,820	1996	28.00	28
1998 Tillie-Bear - C. Kirby	Open		13.00	13
1997 Toby & Tad-Bear - C. Rave	Open		22.00	22
1998 Tota-Bear - C. Kirby	Open		13.00	13
1996 Tracy & Binky-Bear - M. Holstad	Open		14.00	14
1998 Travis-Bear - S. Coe	Open		27.00	27
1995 Trisbit-Bear	7,200	1997	13.00	13

*Quotes have been rounded up to nearest dollar

YEAR ISSUE	EDITION LIMIT	YEAR RETD.	ISSUE PRICE	*QUOTE U.S.$
1998 Trixie-Siamese Cat	Open		27.00	27
1998 Tupper-Bear - C. Rave	Open		10.00	10
1995 Tyler-Bear	6,000	1997	18.00	18
1995 Victoria-Bear	4,128	1996	17.00	17
1998 Wally (Christmas)-Bear - M. Holstad	Open		12.00	12
1996 Wally-Bear - M. Holstad	Open		12.00	12
1997 Webb-Bear - C. Rave	Open		30.00	30
1995 Wilbur-Pig	3,000	1996	10.00	10
1995 Wooster-Bear	Retrd.	1998	25.00	25
1997 Yvonne-Bear - M. Holstad	Open		44.00	44

Cottage Collectibles® Miniatures Collection - L. Kunz, unless otherwise noted

YEAR ISSUE	EDITION LIMIT	YEAR RETD.	ISSUE PRICE	*QUOTE U.S.$
1998 Arnold-Bear	Open		12.00	12
1998 Becky-Bear	Open		12.00	12
1998 Bellhop-Bear - L. Chien	Open		11.00	11
1998 Betty-Bunny	Open		11.00	11
1998 Billy-Bear	Open		12.00	12
1998 Bruno-Bear - L. Chien	Open		11.00	11
1998 Bunnykin & Benny-Bunnies - L. Chien	Open		19.00	19
1998 Charles-Bear	Open		12.00	12
1998 Charlet-Cat	Open		11.00	11
1998 Claira-Bear	Open		13.00	13
1998 Faith Angel-Bear	Open		16.00	16
1998 Flopsie-Bear - M. Holstad	Open		11.50	12
1998 Franklin-Bear	Open		11.00	11
1998 Greg-Bear	Open		11.00	11
1998 Janet-Bear	Open		12.00	12
1998 Joey-Bear	Open		12.00	12
1998 Joey-Bear - M. Holstad	Open		11.00	11
1998 Joker-Bear - L. Chien	Open		11.00	11
1998 Kathy-Bear	Open		15.00	15
1998 Kelly-Bear - M. Holstad	Open		13.00	13
1998 Kyle-Bear	Open		14.00	14
1998 Lady Bug-Bear - M. Holstad	Open		11.50	12
1998 Maxie-Mouse - M. Holstad	Open		13.00	13
1998 Meow-Cat - L. Chien	Open		11.00	11
1998 Miguel-Bear	Open		11.00	11
1998 Mittens-Cat	Open		11.00	11
1998 Panda Bear - M. Holstad	Open		12.00	12
1998 Ribbit-Bear - L. Chien	Open		11.00	11
1998 Ross-Bear - L. Chien	Open		12.00	12
1998 Rusty-Bear	Open		11.00	11
1998 Samson-Bear	Open		11.00	11
1998 Santa-Bear	Open		13.00	13
1998 Steve-Bear	Open		12.00	12
1998 Stitches-Bear - L. Chien	Open		12.00	12
1998 Sue-Bear	Open		12.00	12
1998 Tammie-Bear	Open		12.00	12
1998 Terry-Bear	Open		12.00	12
1998 Tutu-Cat - M. Holstad	Open		12.00	12
1998 Tyler-Bear - M. Holstad	Open		12.00	12
1998 Whiskers-Cat - L. Chien	Open		11.00	11

Cottage Collectibles® Porcelain Dolls Collection - Various

YEAR ISSUE	EDITION LIMIT	YEAR RETD.	ISSUE PRICE	*QUOTE U.S.$
1998 Ali - L. Steele	3,000		90.00	90
1998 Annie - P. Hamel	3,000		74.00	74
1998 Brenda - P. Dey	3,000		130.00	130
1998 Ellen - P. Hamel	3,000		74.00	74
1998 Faith - P. Dey	3,000		130.00	130
1998 Faith - P. Hamel	3,000		74.00	74
1998 Gillian - P. Hamel	3,000		74.00	74
1998 Heidi - P. Dey	3,000		120.00	120
1998 Jan - P. Hamel	3,000		74.00	74
1998 Jenny Shea - P. Hamel	3,000		74.00	74
1998 Kammie - L. Steele	3,000		120.00	120
1998 Kate - P. Dey	3,000		120.00	120
1998 Kendra - L. Steele	3,000		90.00	90
1998 Ling Lee - P. Hamel	3,000		74.00	74
1998 Lisa - P. Dey	3,000		120.00	120
1998 Lizbeth - P. Hamel	3,000		74.00	74
1998 Megan - P. Hamel	3,000		74.00	74
1998 Neunya - L. Steele	3,000		90.00	90
1998 Nicole - P. Hamel	3,000		74.00	74
1998 Penny - P. Dey	3,000		120.00	120
1998 Penny - P. Hamel	3,000		74.00	74
1998 Pippi - L. Steele	3,000		90.00	90
1998 Scooter - L. Steele	3,000		120.00	120
1998 Shayhler - L. Steele	3,000		90.00	90
1998 Su Mae - P. Hamel	3,000		74.00	74
1998 T.J. - L. Steele	3,000		90.00	90

Gene/Ashton-Drake Galleries

Accessories - J. Greene, unless otherwise noted

YEAR ISSUE	EDITION LIMIT	YEAR RETD.	ISSUE PRICE	*QUOTE U.S.$
1996 Dress Form 94390	Open		19.95	20
1996 Gene's Trunk 96504	Open		69.95	70
1997 Hot Day in Hollywood 93548	Open		34.95	35
1997 Out For a Stroll 93547 - E. Foran	Open		29.95	30
1997 White Christmas 94398	Open		44.95	45

Costumed Gene Dolls- M.Odom

YEAR ISSUE	EDITION LIMIT	YEAR RETD.	ISSUE PRICE	*QUOTE U.S.$
1997 Bird of Paradise 94397	Open		79.95	80
1996 Blue Goddess 93503	Open		69.95	70
1998 Champagne Supper 94662	Open		79.95	80
1998 Covent Garden (Parkwest/NALED Exclusive) 94664	Open		99.95	100
1998 Crème de Cassis 94685	Open		79.95	80
1998 Daughter of the Nile 94667	Open		79.95	80
1998 Destiny (YDA Winner) 94656	Yr.Iss		89.95	90
1998 Hello Hollywood, Hello 94657	Open		79.95	80
1997 Iced Coffee 94396	Open		79.95	80
1998 Incognito 94659	Open		79.95	80
1997 The King's Daughter (YDA Winner) 93525	5,000	1997	99.95	325-750
1998 Midnight Gamble (Retailer's Exclusive) 94666	9,500		99.95	100
1997 Midnight Romance (Parkwest/NALED Exclusive) 93550	Closed	1997	89.95	150-195
1995 Monaco 96403	Retrd.	1997	69.95	100-150
1997 My Favorite Witch (Convention Exclusive) 93549	350	1997	N/A	500-995
1997 A Night At Versailles (FAO Schwarz Exclusive) 93551	5,000	1997	90.00	232-295
1998 On The Avenue (FAO Schwarz Spring Exclusive) 94668	5,000	1998	90.00	160-295
1996 Pin-Up 93507	Open		69.95	70
1995 Premiere 96401	Retrd.	1996	69.95	650-795
1995 Red Venus 96402	Open		69.95	70
1997 Sparkling Seduction (YDA Winner) 94394	Open		79.95	80
1998 Warmest Wishes (FOA Schwarz Fall Exclusive) 94663	Open		110.00	110
1997 White Hyacinth 94395	Retrd.	1998	79.95	80

Costumes - Various

YEAR ISSUE	EDITION LIMIT	YEAR RETD.	ISSUE PRICE	*QUOTE U.S.$
1996 Afternoon Off 93508 - D. James	Retrd.	1998	29.95	30
1996 Atlantic City Beauty (Convention Exclusive) 94393 - P. James	250	1996	N/A	795-995
1995 Blonde Lace 96404 - T. Kennedy	Retrd.	1998	29.95	30
1997 Blossoms in the Snow (Retailer's Exclusive) 93544 - T. Kennedy	5,000	1997	44.95	100-125
1995 Blue Evening 96409 - T. Alberts	Open		29.95	30
1998 Cameo (YDA Winner) 94655 - K. Johnson	Open		29.95	30
1996 Crescendo 96505 - D. James	Open		39.95	40
1995 Crimson Sun 93502 - D. James	Open		29.95	30
1996 El Morocco 93506 - T. Alberts	Open		29.95	30
1998 Embassy Luncheon 94652 - L. Meisner	Open		39.95	40
1998 Forget Me Not 94653 - T. Alberts	Open		39.95	40
1998 Gold Sensation 94686 - T. Kennedy	Open		39.95	40
1995 Goodbye New York 93501 - D. James	Open		34.95	35
1998 Hi Fi 94669 - D. James	Open		34.95	35
1996 Holiday Magic 94392 - T. Kennedy	2,000	1996	44.95	275-550
1995 The Kiss 96410 - T. Kennedy	Open		29.95	30
1998 Love After Hours 94658 - T. Kennedy	Open		34.95	35
1995 Love's Ghost 96406 - D. James	Open		29.95	30
1997 Mandarin Mood 93543 - T. Kennedy	Open		34.95	35
1998 Midnight Angel (YDA Winner) 94674 - N. Burke	Open		39.95	40
1997 Personal Secretary 93542 - T. Kennedy	Open		34.95	35
1995 Pink Lightening 96405 - T. Kennedy	Retrd.	1998	29.95	30
1997 Promenade 93541 - T. Kennedy	Retrd.	1998	29.95	30
1998 Rain Song 94675 - D. James	Open		29.95	30
1998 Ransom in Red (Retailer's Exclusive) 94676 - T. Kennedy	7,500		44.95	45
1998 Safari 94673 - T. Alberts	Open		39.95	40
1997 Sea Spree 93546 - T. Kennedy	Open		34.95	35
1998 Smart Set 94687 - D. James	Open		39.95	40
1995 Striking Gold 96407 - T. Albert	Retrd.	1998	29.95	30
1997 Tango 93545 - T. Kennedy	Open		39.95	40
1995 Uherette 96408 - T. Kennedy	Open		29.95	30

Georgetown Collection, Inc.

Age of Romance - J. Reavey

YEAR ISSUE	EDITION LIMIT	YEAR RETD.	ISSUE PRICE	*QUOTE U.S.$
1994 Catherine	Closed	1998	150.00	150

American Diary Dolls - L. Mason

YEAR ISSUE	EDITION LIMIT	YEAR RETD.	ISSUE PRICE	*QUOTE U.S.$
1991 Bridget Quinn	Closed	1996	129.25	130
1991 Christina Merovina	Closed	1996	129.25	130
1990 Jennie Cooper	Closed	1996	129.25	130-155
1994 Lian Ying	Closed	1996	130.00	130
1991 Many Stars	Closed	1997	129.25	130
1992 Rachel Williams	Closed	1996	129.25	130
1993 Sarah Turner	Closed	1996	130.00	130
1992 Tulu	100-day		129.25	130

Baby Kisses - T. DeHetre

YEAR ISSUE	EDITION LIMIT	YEAR RETD.	ISSUE PRICE	*QUOTE U.S.$
1992 Michelle	Closed	1996	118.60	119

Blessed Are The Children - J. Reavey

YEAR ISSUE	EDITION LIMIT	YEAR RETD.	ISSUE PRICE	*QUOTE U.S.$
1994 Faith	100-day		83.00	83

Boys Will Be Boys - J. Reavey

YEAR ISSUE	EDITION LIMIT	YEAR RETD.	ISSUE PRICE	*QUOTE U.S.$
1996 Just Like Dad	100-day		96.00	96
1994 Mr. Mischief	100-day		96.00	96
1997 Tyler	100-day		96.80	97

Caught in the Act - J. Reavey

YEAR ISSUE	EDITION LIMIT	YEAR RETD.	ISSUE PRICE	*QUOTE U.S.$
1997 Nicholas	Closed	1998	115.00	121

Children of Main St. - G. Braun

YEAR ISSUE	EDITION LIMIT	YEAR RETD.	ISSUE PRICE	*QUOTE U.S.$
1996 Alice	100-day		130.00	130
1997 Sara	100-day		131.00	131

Children of the Great Spirit - C. Theroux

YEAR ISSUE	EDITION LIMIT	YEAR RETD.	ISSUE PRICE	*QUOTE U.S.$
1993 Buffalo Child	100-day		140.00	140
1994 Golden Flower	100-day		130.00	130
1994 Little Fawn	Closed	1997	114.00	114
1993 Winter Baby	Closed	1997	160.00	160

The Christening Day - J. Reavey

YEAR ISSUE	EDITION LIMIT	YEAR RETD.	ISSUE PRICE	*QUOTE U.S.$
1998 Jasmine	100-day		131.00	131

Class Portraits - J. Kissling

YEAR ISSUE	EDITION LIMIT	YEAR RETD.	ISSUE PRICE	*QUOTE U.S.$
1995 Anna	Closed	1997	140.00	140

The Cottage Garden - P. Phillips

YEAR ISSUE	EDITION LIMIT	YEAR RETD.	ISSUE PRICE	*QUOTE U.S.$
1996 Emily	100-day		131.00	131

Counting Our Blessings - N/A

YEAR ISSUE	EDITION LIMIT	YEAR RETD.	ISSUE PRICE	*QUOTE U.S.$
1998 Tama	100-day		121.00	121

Country Quilt Babies - B. Prusseit

YEAR ISSUE	EDITION LIMIT	YEAR RETD.	ISSUE PRICE	*QUOTE U.S.$
1996 Hannah	Closed	1998	104.00	104

Cultures of the World - M. Aldred

YEAR ISSUE	EDITION LIMIT	YEAR RETD.	ISSUE PRICE	*QUOTE U.S.$
1998 Maya	100-day		131.00	131

Dreams Come True - M. Sirko

YEAR ISSUE	EDITION LIMIT	YEAR RETD.	ISSUE PRICE	*QUOTE U.S.$
1995 Amanda	Closed	1996	120.00	120

Enchanted Garden - S. Blythe

YEAR ISSUE	EDITION LIMIT	YEAR RETD.	ISSUE PRICE	*QUOTE U.S.$
1998 Floral Whimsies	100-day		94.50	95

Enchanted Nursery - S. Lekven

YEAR ISSUE	EDITION LIMIT	YEAR RETD.	ISSUE PRICE	*QUOTE U.S.$
1998 Aria	100-day		131.00	131

Faerie Princess - B. Deval

YEAR ISSUE	EDITION LIMIT	YEAR RETD.	ISSUE PRICE	*QUOTE U.S.$
1989 Faerie Princess	Closed	1996	248.00	248

Fanciful Dreamers - A. Timmerman

YEAR ISSUE	EDITION LIMIT	YEAR RETD.	ISSUE PRICE	*QUOTE U.S.$
1995 Sweetdreams & Moonbeams	Closed	1997	130.00	130

Faraway Friends - S. Skille

YEAR ISSUE	EDITION LIMIT	YEAR RETD.	ISSUE PRICE	*QUOTE U.S.$
1994 Dara	100-day		140.00	140
1993 Kristin	Closed	1996	140.00	140
1994 Mariama	100-day		140.00	140

Favorite Friends - K. Murawska

YEAR ISSUE	EDITION LIMIT	YEAR RETD.	ISSUE PRICE	*QUOTE U.S.$
1997 Brittany	100-day		131.00	131
1995 Christina	100-day		130.00	130
1996 Samantha	100-day		130.00	130

Friendships of the Heart - P. Erff

YEAR ISSUE	EDITION LIMIT	YEAR RETD.	ISSUE PRICE	*QUOTE U.S.$
1998 Kari & Danielle	100-day		156.00	156

Fuzzy Friends - A. DiMartino

YEAR ISSUE	EDITION LIMIT	YEAR RETD.	ISSUE PRICE	*QUOTE U.S.$
1996 Sandy & Sam	100-day		130.00	130

Georgetown Collection - Various

YEAR ISSUE	EDITION LIMIT	YEAR RETD.	ISSUE PRICE	*QUOTE U.S.$
1995 Buffalo Boy - C. Theroux	Closed	1997	130.00	130
1993 Quick Fox - L. Mason	Closed	1996	138.95	139
1994 Silver Moon - L. Mason	100-day		140.00	140

Gifts From Heaven - B. Prusseit

YEAR ISSUE	EDITION LIMIT	YEAR RETD.	ISSUE PRICE	*QUOTE U.S.$
1994 Good as Gold	Closed	1998	88.00	88
1995 Sweet Pea	100-day		88.00	88

Gifts of Endearment - J. Reavey

YEAR ISSUE	EDITION LIMIT	YEAR RETD.	ISSUE PRICE	*QUOTE U.S.$
1997 Katie	100-day		115.00	115

Hearts in Song - J. Galperin

YEAR ISSUE	EDITION LIMIT	YEAR RETD.	ISSUE PRICE	*QUOTE U.S.$
1994 Angelique	100-day		150.00	150
1992 Grace	100-day		149.60	150
1993 Michael	100-day		150.00	150

Heavenly Messages - M. Sirko

YEAR ISSUE	EDITION LIMIT	YEAR RETD.	ISSUE PRICE	*QUOTE U.S.$
1996 David	100-day		104.00	104
1995 Gabrielle	Closed	1997	104.00	104

Hidden Realms - S. Lekven

YEAR ISSUE	EDITION LIMIT	YEAR RETD.	ISSUE PRICE	*QUOTE U.S.$
1998 Brianna	100-day		153.50	154

A House Just For Me - G. Braun

YEAR ISSUE	EDITION LIMIT	YEAR RETD.	ISSUE PRICE	*QUOTE U.S.$
1998 Anne	100-day		156.00	156

I Love It - K. Murawska

YEAR ISSUE	EDITION LIMIT	YEAR RETD.	ISSUE PRICE	*QUOTE U.S.$
1998 Jamila	100-day		131.00	131

Irish Traditions - L. Mason

YEAR ISSUE	EDITION LIMIT	YEAR RETD.	ISSUE PRICE	*QUOTE U.S.$
1998 Kathleen	100-day		151.00	151

Kindergarten Kids - V. Walker

YEAR ISSUE	EDITION LIMIT	YEAR RETD.	ISSUE PRICE	*QUOTE U.S.$
1992 Nikki	Closed	1996	129.60	130

Let There Be Light - K. Murawska

YEAR ISSUE	EDITION LIMIT	YEAR RETD.	ISSUE PRICE	*QUOTE U.S.$
1997 Charlotte	100-day		130.00	130

Let's Play - T. DeHetre

YEAR ISSUE	EDITION LIMIT	YEAR RETD.	ISSUE PRICE	*QUOTE U.S.$
1992 Eentsy Weentsy Willie	Closed	1996	118.60	119
1992 Peek-A-Boo Beckie	Closed	1996	118.60	119

Linda's Little Ladies - L. Mason

YEAR ISSUE	EDITION LIMIT	YEAR RETD.	ISSUE PRICE	*QUOTE U.S.$
1993 Shannon's Holiday	Closed	1997	169.95	170

Little Artists of Africa - C. Massey

YEAR ISSUE	EDITION LIMIT	YEAR RETD.	ISSUE PRICE	*QUOTE U.S.$
1997 Little Ashanti Weaver	100-day		125.00	125
1996 Oluwa Fumike	100-day		131.00	131

Little Bit of Heaven - A. Timmerman

YEAR ISSUE	EDITION LIMIT	YEAR RETD.	ISSUE PRICE	*QUOTE U.S.$
1996 Adriana	100-day		135.00	135
1994 Arielle	Closed	1997	130.00	131
1995 Cupid	100-day		135.00	135
1995 Noelle	100-day		130.00	130

Little Bloomers - J. Reavey

YEAR ISSUE	EDITION LIMIT	YEAR RETD.	ISSUE PRICE	*QUOTE U.S.$
1995 Darling Daisy	Closed	1997	99.00	99

Little Dreamers - A. DiMartino

YEAR ISSUE	EDITION LIMIT	YEAR RETD.	ISSUE PRICE	*QUOTE U.S.$
1994 Beautiful Buttercup	100-day		130.00	130
1995 Julie	Closed	1997	130.00	130
1996 Nicole	100-day		130.00	130

*Quotes have been rounded up to nearest dollar

Little Loves - B. Deval

YEAR ISSUE	EDITION LIMIT	YEAR RETD.	ISSUE PRICE	*QUOTE U.S.$
1988 Emma	Closed	1996	139.20	140
1989 Katie	Closed	1996	139.20	140
1990 Laura	Closed	1996	139.20	140
1989 Megan	Closed	1996	138.00	160

Little Performers - M. Sirko

YEAR ISSUE	EDITION LIMIT	YEAR RETD.	ISSUE PRICE	*QUOTE U.S.$
1996 Tickled Pink	Closed	1997	100.00	100

Little Sweethearts - J. Reavey

YEAR ISSUE	EDITION LIMIT	YEAR RETD.	ISSUE PRICE	*QUOTE U.S.$
1997 Melanie & Michael	100-day		152.50	153

Loving Moments - J. Reavey

YEAR ISSUE	EDITION LIMIT	YEAR RETD.	ISSUE PRICE	*QUOTE U.S.$
1998 A Hug Just Because	100-day		181.00	181

Maud Humphrey's Little Victorians - M. Humphrey

YEAR ISSUE	EDITION LIMIT	YEAR RETD.	ISSUE PRICE	*QUOTE U.S.$
1996 Papa's Little Sailor	100-day		130.00	130

Messengers of the Great Spirit - Various

YEAR ISSUE	EDITION LIMIT	YEAR RETD.	ISSUE PRICE	*QUOTE U.S.$
1994 Noatak - L. Mason	100-day		150.00	150
1994 Prayer for the Buffalo - C. Theroux	100-day		120.00	120

Miss Ashley - P. Thompson

YEAR ISSUE	EDITION LIMIT	YEAR RETD.	ISSUE PRICE	*QUOTE U.S.$
1989 Miss Ashley	Closed	1996	228.00	228

Mommy's World - A. Hollis

YEAR ISSUE	EDITION LIMIT	YEAR RETD.	ISSUE PRICE	*QUOTE U.S.$
1996 Julia	100-day		136.00	136

Moody Cuties - L. Randolph

YEAR ISSUE	EDITION LIMIT	YEAR RETD.	ISSUE PRICE	*QUOTE U.S.$
1997 Cece	100-day		130.00	130
1998 Tasha	100-day		136.00	136

My Hero - C. Joniak

YEAR ISSUE	EDITION LIMIT	YEAR RETD.	ISSUE PRICE	*QUOTE U.S.$
1998 Matthew	100-day		105.00	105

Naturally Curious Kids - A. Hollis

YEAR ISSUE	EDITION LIMIT	YEAR RETD.	ISSUE PRICE	*QUOTE U.S.$
1996 Jennifer	Closed	1997	100.00	100

Nursery Babies - T. DeHetre

YEAR ISSUE	EDITION LIMIT	YEAR RETD.	ISSUE PRICE	*QUOTE U.S.$
1990 Baby Bunting	Closed	1996	118.20	150
1991 Diddle, Diddle	Closed	1996	118.20	119
1991 Little Girl	Closed	1996	118.20	119
1990 Patty Cake	Closed	1996	118.20	119
1991 Rock-A-Bye Baby	Closed	1996	118.20	119
1991 This Little Piggy	Closed	1996	118.20	119

Nutcracker Sweethearts - S. Skille

YEAR ISSUE	EDITION LIMIT	YEAR RETD.	ISSUE PRICE	*QUOTE U.S.$
1995 Sugar Plum	100-day		130.00	130

The Old Country - L. Mason

YEAR ISSUE	EDITION LIMIT	YEAR RETD.	ISSUE PRICE	*QUOTE U.S.$
1998 Elsa	100-day		136.00	136

Pictures of Innocence - J. Reavey

YEAR ISSUE	EDITION LIMIT	YEAR RETD.	ISSUE PRICE	*QUOTE U.S.$
1994 Clarissa	Closed	1997	135.00	135

Portraits From the Bible - T. Francirek

YEAR ISSUE	EDITION LIMIT	YEAR RETD.	ISSUE PRICE	*QUOTE U.S.$
1998 Madonna & Child	100-day		156.00	156

Portraits of a Perfect World - A. Timmerman

YEAR ISSUE	EDITION LIMIT	YEAR RETD.	ISSUE PRICE	*QUOTE U.S.$
1997 Cherry Pie	100-day		136.00	136
1998 Lemon Drop	100-day		136.00	136
1997 Orange Blossom	100-day		136.00	136

Portraits of Enchantment - A. Timmerman

YEAR ISSUE	EDITION LIMIT	YEAR RETD.	ISSUE PRICE	*QUOTE U.S.$
1996 Sleeping Beauty	100-day		150.00	150

Portraits of Perfection - A. Timmerman

YEAR ISSUE	EDITION LIMIT	YEAR RETD.	ISSUE PRICE	*QUOTE U.S.$
1993 Apple Dumpling	100-day		149.60	150
1994 Blackberry Blossom	100-day		149.60	150
1993 Peaches & Cream	Closed	1997	149.60	150
1993 Sweet Strawberry	100-day		149.60	150

Prayers From The Heart - S. Skille

YEAR ISSUE	EDITION LIMIT	YEAR RETD.	ISSUE PRICE	*QUOTE U.S.$
1995 Hope	Closed	1997	115.00	115

Proud Moments - P. Erff

YEAR ISSUE	EDITION LIMIT	YEAR RETD.	ISSUE PRICE	*QUOTE U.S.$
1996 Chelsea	100-day		126.00	126

Reflections of Childhood - L. Mason

YEAR ISSUE	EDITION LIMIT	YEAR RETD.	ISSUE PRICE	*QUOTE U.S.$
1996 Courtney	Closed	1997	152.50	153

Russian Fairy Tales Dolls - B. Deval

YEAR ISSUE	EDITION LIMIT	YEAR RETD.	ISSUE PRICE	*QUOTE U.S.$
1993 Vasilisa	Closed	N/A	190.00	190

Small Wonders - B. Deval

YEAR ISSUE	EDITION LIMIT	YEAR RETD.	ISSUE PRICE	*QUOTE U.S.$
1991 Abbey	Closed	1996	97.60	98
1990 Corey	Closed	1996	97.60	98
1992 Sarah	Closed	1996	97.60	98

A Song in My Heart - J. Reavey

YEAR ISSUE	EDITION LIMIT	YEAR RETD.	ISSUE PRICE	*QUOTE U.S.$
1998 Caitlyn	100-day		121.00	121

Songs of Innocence - J. Reavey

YEAR ISSUE	EDITION LIMIT	YEAR RETD.	ISSUE PRICE	*QUOTE U.S.$
1997 Andy	100-day		99.00	99
1996 Eric	100-day		105.00	105
1995 Kelsey	100-day		104.00	104
1996 Meagan	100-day		104.00	104

Sugar & Spice - L. Mason

YEAR ISSUE	EDITION LIMIT	YEAR RETD.	ISSUE PRICE	*QUOTE U.S.$
1992 Little Sunshine	Closed	1996	141.10	142
1991 Little Sweetheart	Closed	1996	118.25	119
1991 Red Hot Pepper	Closed	1996	118.25	119

Sweethearts of Summer - P. Phillips

YEAR ISSUE	EDITION LIMIT	YEAR RETD.	ISSUE PRICE	*QUOTE U.S.$
1997 Ashley	100-day		135.00	135
1994 Caroline	100-day		140.00	140
1995 Jessica	100-day		140.00	140
1995 Madeleine & Harry	100-day		140.00	140

Sweets For the Sweet - V. Ohms

YEAR ISSUE	EDITION LIMIT	YEAR RETD.	ISSUE PRICE	*QUOTE U.S.$
1996 Elise	100-day		130.00	130

Tansie - P. Coffer

YEAR ISSUE	EDITION LIMIT	YEAR RETD.	ISSUE PRICE	*QUOTE U.S.$
1988 Tansie	Closed	1996	81.00	81

Victorian Fantasies - L. Mason

YEAR ISSUE	EDITION LIMIT	YEAR RETD.	ISSUE PRICE	*QUOTE U.S.$
1995 Amber Afternoon	100-day		150.00	150
1997 Emerald Memories	100-day		145.00	145
1995 Lavender Dreams	100-day		150.00	150
1996 Reflections of Rose	100-day		150.00	150

Victorian Innocence - L. Mason

YEAR ISSUE	EDITION LIMIT	YEAR RETD.	ISSUE PRICE	*QUOTE U.S.$
1994 Annabelle	Closed	N/A	130.00	130

Victorian Splendor - J. Reavey

YEAR ISSUE	EDITION LIMIT	YEAR RETD.	ISSUE PRICE	*QUOTE U.S.$
1994 Emily	Closed	1997	130.00	130

Warm Hearts in Winter - L. Mason

YEAR ISSUE	EDITION LIMIT	YEAR RETD.	ISSUE PRICE	*QUOTE U.S.$
1997 Claire	100-day		145.00	145

Warm World - A. Hollis

YEAR ISSUE	EDITION LIMIT	YEAR RETD.	ISSUE PRICE	*QUOTE U.S.$
1997 Alison & Angus	100-day		140.00	140

The Wedding Day - S. Sauer

YEAR ISSUE	EDITION LIMIT	YEAR RETD.	ISSUE PRICE	*QUOTE U.S.$
1997 Elizabeth	100-day		121.00	121

What a Beautiful World - R. Hockh

YEAR ISSUE	EDITION LIMIT	YEAR RETD.	ISSUE PRICE	*QUOTE U.S.$
1996 Marisa	100-day		130.00	130
1996 Mora	100-day		126.00	126
1996 Therese & Tino	100-day		155.00	155

Wings of Love - L. Randolph

YEAR ISSUE	EDITION LIMIT	YEAR RETD.	ISSUE PRICE	*QUOTE U.S.$
1998 Angel Dreams	100-day		105.00	105
1998 Angel Hugs	100-day		105.00	105
1997 Angel Kisses	100-day		125.00	125

Yesterday's Dreams - P. Phillips

YEAR ISSUE	EDITION LIMIT	YEAR RETD.	ISSUE PRICE	*QUOTE U.S.$
1994 Mary Elizabeth	100-day		130.00	130
1996 Sophie	100-day		130.00	130

Goebel of North America

Bob Timberlake Dolls - B. Ball

YEAR ISSUE	EDITION LIMIT	YEAR RETD.	ISSUE PRICE	*QUOTE U.S.$
1996 Abby Liz 911350	2,000	1997	195.00	195
1996 Ann 911352	2,000	1997	195.00	195
1996 Carter 911351	2,000	1997	195.00	195
1996 Kate 911353	2,000	1997	195.00	195

Cindy Guyer Romance Dolls - B. Ball

YEAR ISSUE	EDITION LIMIT	YEAR RETD.	ISSUE PRICE	*QUOTE U.S.$
1996 Cordelia 911824	1,000	1997	225.00	225
1996 Cynthia 911830	1,000	1997	225.00	225
1996 Mackenzie 911825	1,000	1997	225.00	225

Dolly Dingle - B. Ball

YEAR ISSUE	EDITION LIMIT	YEAR RETD.	ISSUE PRICE	*QUOTE U.S.$
1995 Melvis Bumps 911617	1,000	1997	99.00	99

Goebel Dolls - B. Ball

YEAR ISSUE	EDITION LIMIT	YEAR RETD.	ISSUE PRICE	*QUOTE U.S.$
1995 Brother Murphy 911100	2,000	1997	125.00	125

Hummel Dolls - B. Ball

YEAR ISSUE	EDITION LIMIT	YEAR RETD.	ISSUE PRICE	*QUOTE U.S.$
1998 Apple Tree Boy 911213	N/A		250.00	250
1998 Apple Tree Girl 911214	N/A		250.00	250
1998 Kiss Me 911216	N/A		200.00	200
1996 Little Scholar, 14" 911211	N/A		200.00	200
1997 School Girl, 14" 911212	N/A		200.00	200

United States Historical Society - B. Ball

YEAR ISSUE	EDITION LIMIT	YEAR RETD.	ISSUE PRICE	*QUOTE U.S.$
1995 Mary-911155	1,500	1997	195.00	195

Victoria Ashlea® Birthstone Dolls - K. Kennedy

YEAR ISSUE	EDITION LIMIT	YEAR RETD.	ISSUE PRICE	*QUOTE U.S.$
1995 January-Garnet-912471	2,500	1996	29.50	30
1995 February-Amethyst-912472	2,500	1996	29.50	30
1995 March-Aquamarine-912473	2,500	1996	29.50	30
1995 April-Diamond-912474	2,500	1996	29.50	30
1995 May-Emerald-912475	2,500	1996	29.50	30
1995 June -Lt. Amethyst-912476	2,500	1996	29.50	30
1995 July-Ruby-912477	2,500	1996	29.50	30
1995 August-Peridot-912478	2,500	1996	29.50	30
1995 September-Sapphire-912479	2,500	1996	29.50	30
1995 October-Rosestone-912480	2,500	1996	29.50	30
1995 November-Topaz-912481	2,500	1996	29.50	30
1995 December-Zircon-912482	2,500	1996	29.50	30

Victoria Ashlea® Originals - B. Ball, unless otherwise noted

YEAR ISSUE	EDITION LIMIT	YEAR RETD.	ISSUE PRICE	*QUOTE U.S.$
1985 Adele-901172	Closed	1989	145.00	275
1989 Alexa-912214	Closed	1991	195.00	195
1989 Alexandria-912273	Closed	1991	275.00	275
1987 Alice-901212	Closed	1991	95.00	135
1990 Alice-912296 - K. Kennedy	Closed	1992	65.00	65
1992 Alicia-912388	500	1994	135.00	135
1992 Allison-912358	Closed	1993	160.00	165
1987 Amanda Pouty-901209	Closed	1991	150.00	215
1988 Amanda-912246	Closed	1991	180.00	180
1993 Amanda-912409	2,000	1995	40.00	40
1984 Amelia-933006	Closed	1988	100.00	100
1990 Amie-912313 - K. Kennedy	Closed	1991	150.00	150
1990 Amy-901262	Closed	1993	110.00	110
1990 Angela-912324 - K. Kennedy	Closed	1994	130.00	135
1988 Angelica-912204	Closed	1991	150.00	150
1992 Angelica-912339	1,000	1995	145.00	145
1990 Annabelle-912278	Closed	1992	200.00	200
1988 Anne-912213	Closed	1991	130.00	150
1990 Annette-912333 - K. Kennedy	Closed	1993	85.00	85
1988 April-901239	Closed	1992	225.00	225
1989 Ashlea-901250	Closed	1992	550.00	550
1988 Ashley-901235	Closed	1991	110.00	110
1992 Ashley-911004	Closed	1994	99.00	105
1986 Ashley-912147	Closed	1989	125.00	125
1986 Baby Brook Beige Dress-912103	Closed	1989	60.00	60
1986 Baby Courtney-912124	Closed	1990	120.00	120
1988 Baby Daryl-912200	Closed	1991	85.00	85
1987 Baby Doll-912184	Closed	1990	75.00	75
1988 Baby Jennifer-912210	Closed	1992	75.00	75
1988 Baby Katie-912222	Closed	1993	70.00	70
1986 Baby Lauren Pink-912086	Closed	1991	120.00	120
1987 Baby Lindsay-912190	Closed	1990	80.00	80
1984 Barbara-901108	Closed	1987	57.00	110
1990 Baryshnicat-912298 - K. Kennedy	Closed	1991	25.00	25
1988 Bernice-901245	Closed	1991	90.00	90
1993 Beth-912430 - K. Kennedy	2,000	1996	45.00	45
1992 Betsy-912390	500	1994	150.00	150
1990 Bettina-912310	Closed	1993	100.00	105
1988 Betty Doll-912220	Closed	1993	90.00	90
1987 Bonnie Pouty-901207	Closed	1992	100.00	100
1988 Brandon-901234	Closed	1992	90.00	90
1990 Brandy-912304 - K. Kennedy	Closed	1992	150.00	150
1987 Bride Allison-901218	Closed	1993	180.00	180
1988 Brittany-912207	Closed	1990	130.00	145
1992 Brittany-912365 - K. Kennedy	Closed	1993	140.00	145
1987 Caitlin-901228	Closed	1991	260.00	260
1988 Campbell Kid-Boy-758701	Closed	1988	13.80	14
1988 Campbell Kid-Girl-758700	Closed	1988	13.80	14
1989 Candace-912288 - K. Kennedy	Closed	1992	70.00	70
1992 Carol-912387 - K. Kennedy	1,000	1996	140.00	140
1987 Caroline-912191	Closed	1990	80.00	80
1990 Carolyn-901261 - K. Kennedy	Closed	1993	200.00	200
1992 Cassandra-912355 - K. Kennedy	1,000	1996	165.00	165
1988 Cat Maude-901247	Closed	1993	85.00	85
1986 Cat/Kitty Cheerful Gr Dr-901179	Closed	1990	60.00	60
1987 Catanova-901227	Closed	1991	75.00	75
1988 Catherine-901242	Closed	1992	240.00	240
XX Charity-912244	Closed	1990	70.00	70
1982 Charleen-912094	Closed	1986	65.00	65
1985 Chauncey-912085	Closed	1988	75.00	110
1988 Christina-901229	Closed	1991	350.00	400
1987 Christine-912168	Closed	1989	75.00	75
1992 Cindy-912384	1,000	1994	185.00	190
1985 Claire-901158	Closed	1988	115.00	160
1984 Claude-901032	Closed	1987	110.00	225
1984 Claudette-901033	Closed	1987	110.00	225
1989 Claudia-901257 - K. Kennedy	Closed	1993	225.00	225
1987 Clementine-901226	Closed	1991	75.00	75
1986 Clown Calypso-912104	Closed	1990	70.00	70
1985 Clown Casey-912078	Closed	1988	40.00	40
1986 Clown Cat Cadwalader-912132	Closed	1988	55.00	55
1987 Clown Champagne-912180	Closed	1989	95.00	95
1986 Clown Christabel-912095	Closed	1988	100.00	150
1985 Clown Christie-912084	Closed	1988	60.00	90
1986 Clown Clarabella-912096	Closed	1989	80.00	80
1986 Clown Clarissa-912123	Closed	1990	75.00	110
1988 Clown Cotton Candy-912199	Closed	1990	67.00	67
1986 Clown Cyd-912093	Closed	1988	70.00	70
1985 Clown Jody-912079	Closed	1988	100.00	150
1982 Clown Jolly-912181	Closed	1991	70.00	70
1986 Clown Kitten-Cleo-912133	Closed	1989	50.00	50
1986 Clown Lollipop-912127	Closed	1989	125.00	225
1984 Clown-901136	Closed	1988	90.00	120
1988 Crystal-912226	Closed	1992	75.00	75
1983 Deborah-901107	Closed	1987	220.00	400
1990 Debra-912319 - K. Kennedy	Closed	1992	120.00	120
1992 Denise-912362 - K. Kennedy	1,000	1994	145.00	175-225
1989 Diana Bride-912277	Closed	1992	180.00	180
1984 Diana-901119	Closed	1987	55.00	135
1988 Diana-912218	Closed	1992	270.00	270
1987 Dominique-901219	Closed	1991	170.00	225
1987 Doreen-912198	Closed	1990	75.00	75
1985 Dorothy-901157	Closed	1988	130.00	275
1992 Dottie-912393 - K. Kennedy	1,000	1996	160.00	160
1988 Elizabeth-901214	Closed	1991	90.00	90
1988 Ellen-901246	Closed	1991	100.00	100
1990 Emily-912303	Closed	1992	150.00	150
1988 Erin-901241	Closed	1991	170.00	170
1990 Fluffer-912293	Closed	1994	135.00	150-225
1985 Garnet-901183	Closed	1988	160.00	295
1990 Gigi-912306 - K. Kennedy	Closed	1994	150.00	150
1986 Gina-901176	Closed	1989	300.00	300
1989 Ginny-912287 - K. Kennedy	Closed	1993	140.00	140
1986 Girl Frog Freda-912105	Closed	1989	20.00	20
1988 Goldilocks-912234 - K. Kennedy	Closed	1992	65.00	65
1986 Googley German Astrid-912109	Closed	1989	60.00	60
1988 Heather-912247	Closed	1990	135.00	150
1990 Heather-912322	Closed	1992	150.00	150
1990 Heidi-901266	2,000	1995	150.00	150
1990 Helene-901249 - K. Kennedy	Closed	1991	160.00	160
1990 Helga-912337	Closed	1994	325.00	325
1984 Henri-901035	Closed	1986	100.00	200
1984 Henrietta-901036	Closed	1986	100.00	200
1992 Hilary-912353	Closed	1993	130.00	135
1992 Holly Belle-912380	500	1994	125.00	125
1982 Holly-901233	Closed	1985	160.00	200
1989 Holly-901254	Closed	1992	180.00	180
1989 Hope Baby w/ Pillow-912292	Closed	1992	110.00	110
1992 Iris-912389 - K. Kennedy	500	1995	165.00	165
1987 Jacqueline-912192	Closed	1990	80.00	80
1990 Jacqueline-912329 - K. Kennedy	Closed	1993	136.00	150-225
1984 Jamie-912061	Closed	1987	65.00	100

*Quotes have been rounded up to nearest dollar

YEAR ISSUE	EDITION LIMIT	YEAR RETD.	ISSUE PRICE	*QUOTE U.S.$
1984 Jeannie-901062	Closed	1987	200.00	550
1988 Jennifer-901248	Closed	1991	150.00	150
1988 Jennifer-912221	Closed	1990	80.00	80
1992 Jenny-912374 - K. Kennedy	Closed	1993	150.00	150
1988 Jesse-912231	Closed	1994	110.00	115
1987 Jessica-912195	Closed	1990	120.00	135
1993 Jessica-912410	2,000	1994	40.00	40
1990 Jillian-912323	Closed	1993	150.00	150
1989 Jimmy Baby w/ Pillow-912291 - K. Kennedy	Closed	1992	165.00	165
1989 Jingles-912271	Closed	1991	60.00	60
1990 Joanne-912307 - K. Kennedy	Closed	1991	165.00	165
1987 Joy-912155	Closed	1989	50.00	50
1989 Joy-912289 - K. Kennedy	Closed	1992	110.00	110
1987 Julia-912174	Closed	1989	80.00	80
1990 Julia-912334 - K. Kennedy	Closed	1993	85.00	85
1993 Julie-912435 - K. Kennedy	2,000	1995	45.00	45
1990 Justine-901256	Closed	1992	200.00	200
1988 Karen-912205	Closed	1991	200.00	250
1993 Katie-912412	2,000	1996	40.00	40
1993 Kaylee-912433 - K. Kennedy	2,000	1996	45.00	45
1992 Kelli-912361	1,000	1995	160.00	165
1990 Kelly-912331	Closed	1991	95.00	95
1990 Kimberly-912341	1,000	1996	140.00	145
1987 Kittle Cat-912167	Closed	1989	55.00	55
1987 Kitty Cuddles-901201	Closed	1990	65.00	65
1992 Kris-912345 - K. Kennedy	Closed	1992	160.00	160
1989 Kristin-912285 - K. Kennedy	Closed	1994	90.00	95
1984 Laura-901106	Closed	1987	300.00	575
1988 Laura-912225	Closed	1991	135.00	135
1988 Lauren-912212	Closed	1991	110.00	110
1992 Lauren-912363 - K. Kennedy	1,000	1996	190.00	195
1993 Lauren-912413	2,000	1996	40.00	40
1993 Leslie-912432 - K. Kennedy	2,000	1996	45.00	45
1989 Licorice-912290	Closed	1991	75.00	75
1987 Lillian-901199	Closed	1990	85.00	100
1989 Lindsey-901263	Closed	1991	100.00	100
1989 Lisa-912275	Closed	1991	160.00	160
1989 Loni-912276	Closed	1993	125.00	150-185
1985 Lynn-912144	Closed	1988	90.00	135
1992 Margaret-912354 - K. Kennedy	1,000	1994	150.00	150
1989 Margot-912269	Closed	1991	110.00	110
1989 Maria-912265	Closed	1990	90.00	90
1982 Marie-901231	Closed	1985	95.00	95
1989 Marissa-901252 - K. Kennedy	Closed	1993	225.00	225
1988 Maritta Spanish-912224	Closed	1990	140.00	140
1992 Marjorie-912357	Closed	1993	135.00	135
1990 Marshmallow-912294 - K. Kennedy	Closed	1992	75.00	75
1985 Mary-912126	Closed	1988	60.00	90
1990 Matthew-901251	Closed	1993	100.00	100
1989 Megan-901260	Closed	1993	120.00	120
1987 Megan-912148	Closed	1989	70.00	70
1989 Melanie-912284 - K. Kennedy	Closed	1992	135.00	135
1990 Melinda-912309 - K. Kennedy	Closed	1991	70.00	70
1988 Melissa-901230	Closed	1991	110.00	110
1988 Melissa-912208	Closed	1990	125.00	125
1989 Merry-912249	Closed	1990	200.00	200
1987 Michelle-901222	Closed	1991	90.00	90
1985 Michelle-912066	Closed	1989	100.00	225
1992 Michelle-912381 - K. Kennedy	Closed	1992	175.00	175
1985 Millie-912135	Closed	1988	70.00	125
1989 Missy-912283	Closed	1993	110.00	115
1988 Molly-912211 - K. Kennedy	Closed	1992	75.00	75
1990 Monica-912336 - K. Kennedy	Closed	1993	100.00	105
1990 Monique-912335 - K. Kennedy	Closed	1993	85.00	85
1988 Morgan-912239 - K. Kennedy	Closed	1992	75.00	75
1990 Mrs. Katz-912301	Closed	1993	140.00	145
1993 Nadine-912431 - K. Kennedy	2,000	1995	45.00	45
1989 Nancy-912266	Closed	1990	110.00	110
1987 Nicole-901225	Closed	1991	575.00	575
1993 Nicole-912411	2,000	1996	40.00	40
1987 Noel-912170	Closed	1989	125.00	125
1992 Noelle-912360 - K. Kennedy	1,000	1994	165.00	170
1990 Pamela-912302	Closed	1991	95.00	95
1986 Patty Artic Flower Print-901185	Closed	1990	140.00	140
1990 Paula-912316	Closed	1992	100.00	100
1988 Paulette-901244	Closed	1991	90.00	90
1990 Penny-912325 - K. Kennedy	Closed	1993	130.00	150-225
1986 Pepper Rust Dr/Appr-901184	Closed	1990	125.00	200
1985 Phyllis-912067	Closed	1989	60.00	60
1989 Pinky Clown-912268 - K. Kennedy	Closed	1993	70.00	75
1988 Polly-912206	Closed	1990	100.00	125
1990 Priscilla-912300	Closed	1993	185.00	190
1990 Rebecca-901258	Closed	1992	250.00	250
1988 Renae-912245	Closed	1990	120.00	120
1990 Robin-912321	Closed	1993	160.00	165
1985 Rosalind-912087	Closed	1988	145.00	225
1985 Roxanne-901174	Closed	1988	155.00	275
1984 Sabina-901155	Closed	1988	75.00	N/A
1990 Samantha-912314	Closed	1993	185.00	190
1988 Sandy-901240 - K. Kennedy	Closed	1993	115.00	115
1989 Sara-912279	Closed	1991	175.00	175
1988 Sarah w/Pillow-912219	Closed	1991	105.00	105
1987 Sarah-901220	Closed	1992	350.00	350
1993 Sarah-912408	2,000	1996	40.00	40
1993 Shannon-912434 - K. Kennedy	2,000	1996	45.00	45
1990 Sheena-912338	Closed	1992	115.00	115
1984 Sheila-912060	Closed	1988	75.00	135
1990 Sheri-912305 - K. Kennedy	Closed	1992	115.00	115
1992 Sherise-912383 - K. Kennedy	Closed	1992	145.00	145
1989 Sigrid-912282	Closed	1992	145.00	145
1988 Snow White-912235 - K. Kennedy	Closed	1992	65.00	65
1987 Sophia-912173	Closed	1989	40.00	40
1988 Stephanie-912238	Closed	1992	200.00	200
1990 Stephanie-912312	Closed	1993	150.00	150
1984 Stephanie-933012	Closed	1988	115.00	115
1988 Susan-901243	Closed	1991	100.00	100
1990 Susie-912328	Closed	1993	115.00	120
1987 Suzanne-901200	Closed	1990	85.00	100
1989 Suzanne-912286	Closed	1992	120.00	120
1989 Suzy-912295	Closed	1991	110.00	110
1992 Tamika-912382	500	1994	185.00	185
1989 Tammy-912264	Closed	1990	110.00	110
1987 Tasha-901221	Closed	1990	115.00	130
1990 Tasha-912299 - K. Kennedy	Closed	1992	25.00	25
1989 Terry-912281	Closed	1994	125.00	130
1987 Tiffany Pouty-901211	Closed	1991	120.00	160
1990 Tiffany-912326 - K. Kennedy	Closed	1992	180.00	180
1984 Tobie-912023	Closed	1987	30.00	30
1992 Toni-912367 - K. Kennedy	Closed	1993	120.00	120
1990 Tracie-912315	Closed	1993	125.00	125
1992 Trudie-912391	500	1996	135.00	135
1982 Trudy-901232	Closed	1985	100.00	100
1992 Tulip-912385 - K. Kennedy	500	1994	145.00	145
1989 Valerie-901255	Closed	1994	175.00	175
1989 Vanessa-912272	Closed	1991	110.00	110
1984 Victoria-901068	Closed	1987	200.00	1500
1992 Wendy-912330 - K. Kennedy	1,000	1995	125.00	130
1988 Whitney Blk-912232	Closed	1994	62.50	65

Victoria Ashlea® Originals-Birthday Babies - K. Kennedy

YEAR ISSUE	EDITION LIMIT	YEAR RETD.	ISSUE PRICE	*QUOTE U.S.$
1996 January-913017	2,500		30.00	30
1996 February-913018	2,500		30.00	30
1996 March-913019	2,500		30.00	30
1996 April-913020	2,500		30.00	30
1996 May-913021	2,500		30.00	30
1996 June-913022	2,500		30.00	30
1996 July-913023	2,500		30.00	30
1996 August-913024	2,500		30.00	30
1996 September-913025	2,500		30.00	30
1996 October-913026	2,500		30.00	30
1996 November-913027	2,500		30.00	30
1996 December-913028	2,500		30.00	30

Victoria Ashlea® Originals-Collectible Cats - K. Kennedy

YEAR ISSUE	EDITION LIMIT	YEAR RETD.	ISSUE PRICE	*QUOTE U.S.$
1996 Charmer-913005	2,000		39.50	40
1996 Copper-913006	2,000		39.50	40
1996 Cuddles-913007	2,000		39.50	40
1996 Fluffy-913008	2,000		39.50	40
1996 Lollipop-913009	2,000		39.50	40
1996 Mittens-913010	2,000		39.50	40
1996 Patches-913011	2,000		39.50	40
1996 Pebbles-913012	2,000		39.50	40
1996 Pepper-913013	2,000		39.50	40
1996 Ruffles-913014	2,000		39.50	40
1996 Tumbles-913015	2,000		39.50	40
1996 Whiskers-913016	2,000		39.50	40

Victoria Ashlea® Originals-Holiday Babies - K. Kennedy

YEAR ISSUE	EDITION LIMIT	YEAR RETD.	ISSUE PRICE	*QUOTE U.S.$
1996 Boo!-913001	1,000		30.00	30
1996 Happy Easter-913002	1,000		30.00	30
1996 Happy Holidays-913003	1,000		30.00	30
1996 I Love You-913004	1,000		30.00	30

Victoria Ashlea® Originals-Tiny Tot Clowns - K. Kennedy

YEAR ISSUE	EDITION LIMIT	YEAR RETD.	ISSUE PRICE	*QUOTE U.S.$
1994 Danielle-912461	2,000	1996	45.00	45
1994 Lindsey-912463	2,000	1996	45.00	45
1994 Lisa-912458	2,000	1996	45.00	45
1994 Marie-912462	2,000	1996	45.00	45
1994 Megan-912460	2,000	1996	45.00	45
1994 Stacy-912459	2,000	1996	45.00	45

Victoria Ashlea® Originals-Tiny Tot School Girls - K. Kennedy

YEAR ISSUE	EDITION LIMIT	YEAR RETD.	ISSUE PRICE	*QUOTE U.S.$
1994 Andrea- 912456	2,000	1996	47.50	48
1994 Christine- 912450	2,000	1996	47.50	48
1994 Monique- 912455	2,000	1996	47.50	48
1994 Patricia- 912453	2,000	1996	47.50	48
1994 Shawna- 912449	2,000	1996	47.50	48
1994 Susan- 912457	2,000	1996	47.50	48

Goebel/M.I. Hummel

M. I. Hummel Collectible Dolls - M. I. Hummel

YEAR ISSUE	EDITION LIMIT	YEAR RETD.	ISSUE PRICE	*QUOTE U.S.$
1964 Chimney Sweep 1908	Closed	N/A	55.00	200
1964 For Father 1917	Closed	N/A	55.00	100-150
1964 Goose Girl 1914	Closed	N/A	55.00	150-390
1964 Gretel 1901	Closed	N/A	55.00	200
1964 Hansel 1902	Closed	N/A	55.00	200
1964 Little Knitter 1905	Closed	N/A	55.00	200
1964 Lost Stocking 1926	Closed	N/A	55.00	200
1964 Merry Wanderer 1906	Closed	N/A	55.00	200-390
1964 Merry Wanderer 1925	Closed	N/A	55.00	200-390
1964 On Secret Path 1928	Closed	N/A	55.00	200
1964 Rosa-Blue Baby 1904/B	Closed	N/A	45.00	150
1964 Rosa-Pink Baby 1904/P	Closed	N/A	45.00	150
1964 School Boy 1910	Closed	N/A	55.00	200
1964 School Girl 1909	Closed	N/A	55.00	200
1964 Visiting and Invalid 1927	Closed	N/A	55.00	200

M. I. Hummel Porcelain Dolls - M. I. Hummel

YEAR ISSUE	EDITION LIMIT	YEAR RETD.	ISSUE PRICE	*QUOTE U.S.$
1984 Birthday Serenade/Boy	Closed	N/A	225.00	300
1984 Birthday Serenade/Girl	Closed	N/A	225.00	300-325
1985 Carnival	Closed	N/A	225.00	300
1985 Easter Greetings	Closed	N/A	225.00	299-325
1998 Kiss Me 805	Open		200.00	200
1996 Little Scholar 522	Open		200.00	200
1985 Lost Sheep	Closed	N/A	225.00	300
1984 On Holiday	Closed	N/A	225.00	299-390
1984 Postman	Closed	N/A	225.00	390-520
1996 School Girl 521	Open		200.00	200
1985 Signs of Spring	Closed	N/A	225.00	300

Good-Krüger

Limited Edition - J. Good-Krüger

YEAR ISSUE	EDITION LIMIT	YEAR RETD.	ISSUE PRICE	*QUOTE U.S.$
1990 Alice	Retrd.	1991	250.00	250
1992 Anne with an E	Retrd.	1992	240.00	400
1990 Annie-Rose	Retrd.	1990	219.00	425
1994 Christmas Carols	1,000	1995	240.00	240
1990 Christmas Cookie	Retrd.	1993	199.00	225
1995 Circus Trainer	500	1995	250.00	250
1990 Cozy	Retrd.	1992	179.00	275-375
1990 Daydream	Retrd.	1990	199.00	350
1993 Good Friends	1,000	1993	179.00	179
1994 Heidi	1,000	1994	250.00	250
1992 Jeepers Creepers (Porcelain)	Retrd.	1992	725.00	800
1992 Jody	500	1992	240.00	240
1991 Johnny-Lynn	Retrd.	1991	240.00	650-800
1992 Karen	500	1992	240.00	240
1995 Letter to Santa	1,000	1995	250.00	250
1995 Little Princess	1,500	1995	250.00	250
1991 Moppett	Retrd.	1991	179.00	275
1994 Mother's Love	1,000	1994	275.00	275
1992 Snuggle Ebony	750	1992	240.00	240
1994 Stuffed Animal Zoo	1,000	1994	189.00	189
1990 Sue-Lynn	Retrd.	1990	240.00	300
1991 Teachers Pet	Retrd.	1991	199.00	250
1995 Tiny Newborns	500	1995	225.00	225
1991 Victorian Christmas	Retrd.	1992	219.00	275

Gorham

Beverly Port Designer Collection - B. Port

YEAR ISSUE	EDITION LIMIT	YEAR RETD.	ISSUE PRICE	*QUOTE U.S.$
1988 The Amazing Calliope Merriweather 17"	Closed	1990	275.00	1000
1988 Baery Mab 9-1/2"	Closed	1990	110.00	250
1987 Christopher Paul Bearkin 10"	Closed	1990	95.00	400
1988 Hollybeary Kringle 15"	Closed	1990	350.00	450
1987 Kristobear Kringle 17"	Closed	1990	200.00	450
1988 Miss Emily 18"	Closed	1990	350.00	1400
1987 Molly Melinda Bearkin 10"	Closed	1990	95.00	300
1987 Silver Bell 17"	Closed	1990	175.00	400
1988 T.R. 28-1/2"	Closed	1990	400.00	700
1987 Tedward Jonathan Bearkin 10"	Closed	1990	95.00	350
1987 Tedwina Kimelina Bearkin 10"	Closed	1990	95.00	350
1988 Theodore B. Bear 14"	Closed	1990	175.00	550

Bonnets & Bows - B. Gerardi

YEAR ISSUE	EDITION LIMIT	YEAR RETD.	ISSUE PRICE	*QUOTE U.S.$
1988 Belinda	Closed	1990	195.00	450
1988 Annemarie	Closed	1990	195.00	450
1988 Allessandra	Closed	1990	195.00	350
1988 Lisette	Closed	1990	285.00	495
1988 Bettina	Closed	1994	285.00	495
1988 Ellie	Closed	1994	285.00	495
1988 Alicia	Closed	1994	385.00	700
1988 Bethany	Closed	1994	385.00	1350
1988 Jesse	Closed	1994	525.00	675
1988 Francie	Closed	1994	625.00	800

Celebrations Of Childhood - L. Di Leo

YEAR ISSUE	EDITION LIMIT	YEAR RETD.	ISSUE PRICE	*QUOTE U.S.$
1992 Happy Birthday Amy	Closed	1994	160.00	225

Children Of Christmas - S. Stone Aiken

YEAR ISSUE	EDITION LIMIT	YEAR RETD.	ISSUE PRICE	*QUOTE U.S.$
1989 Clara, 16"	Closed	1994	325.00	650
1990 Natalie, 16"	1,500	1994	350.00	500
1991 Emily	1,500	1994	375.00	400
1992 Virginia	1,500	1994	375.00	400

Dollie And Me - J. Pilallis

YEAR ISSUE	EDITION LIMIT	YEAR RETD.	ISSUE PRICE	*QUOTE U.S.$
1991 Dollie's First Steps	Closed	1994	160.00	225

Gifts of the Garden - S. Stone Aiken

YEAR ISSUE	EDITION LIMIT	YEAR RETD.	ISSUE PRICE	*QUOTE U.S.$
1991 Alisa	Closed	1994	125.00	250
1991 Deborah	Closed	1994	125.00	250
1991 Holly (Christmas)	Closed	1994	150.00	250
1991 Irene	Closed	1994	125.00	250
1991 Joelle (Christmas)	Closed	1994	150.00	250
1991 Lauren	Closed	1994	125.00	250
1991 Maria	Closed	1994	125.00	250
1991 Priscilla	Closed	1994	125.00	250
1991 Valerie	Closed	1994	125.00	250

Gorham Baby Doll Collection - Aiken/Matthews

YEAR ISSUE	EDITION LIMIT	YEAR RETD.	ISSUE PRICE	*QUOTE U.S.$
1987 Christening Day	Closed	1990	245.00	350
1987 Leslie	Closed	1990	245.00	350
1987 Matthew	Closed	1990	245.00	350

Gorham Dolls - S. Stone Aiken, unless otherwise noted

YEAR ISSUE	EDITION LIMIT	YEAR RETD.	ISSUE PRICE	*QUOTE U.S.$
1985 Alexander, 19"	Closed	1990	275.00	400
1981 Alexandria, 18"	Closed	1990	250.00	500
1986 Alissa	Closed	1990	245.00	300
1985 Amelia, 19"	Closed	1990	275.00	325
1982 Baby in Apricot Dress, 16"	Closed	1990	175.00	375
1982 Baby in Blue Dress, 12"	Closed	1990	150.00	300
1982 Baby in White Dress, 18" - Gorham	Closed	1990	250.00	350
1982 Benjamin, 18"	Closed	1990	200.00	600
1981 Cecile, 16"	Closed	1990	200.00	800
1981 Christina, 16"	Closed	1990	200.00	425

*Quotes have been rounded up to nearest dollar

YEAR ISSUE	EDITION LIMIT	YEAR RETD.	ISSUE PRICE	*QUOTE U.S.$
1981 Christopher, 19"	Closed	1990	250.00	500
1982 Corrine, 21"	Closed	1990	250.00	500
1981 Danielle, 14"	Closed	1990	150.00	300
1981 Elena, 14"	Closed	1990	150.00	650
1982 Ellice, 18"	Closed	1990	200.00	400
1986 Emily, 14"	Closed	1990	175.00	395
1986 Fleur, 19"	Closed	1990	300.00	450
1985 Gabrielle, 19"	Closed	1990	225.00	350
1983 Jennifer, 19" Bridal Doll	Closed	1990	325.00	750
1982 Jeremy, 23"	Closed	1990	300.00	700
1986 Jessica	Closed	1990	195.00	275
1981 Jillian, 16"	Closed	1990	200.00	400
1986 Julia, 16"	Closed	1990	225.00	350
1987 Juliet	Closed	1990	325.00	400
1982 Kristin, 23"	Closed	1990	300.00	575
1986 Lauren, 14"	Closed	1990	175.00	350
1985 Linda, 19"	Closed	1990	275.00	600
1982 M. Anton, 12" - Unknown	Closed	1990	125.00	175
1982 Melanie, 23"	Closed	1990	300.00	600
1981 Melinda, 14"	Closed	1990	150.00	300
1986 Meredith	Closed	1990	295.00	350
1982 Mlle. Jeanette, 12"	Closed	1990	125.00	175
1982 Mlle. Lucille, 12"	Closed	1990	125.00	375
1982 Mlle. Marsella, 12" - Unknown	Closed	1990	125.00	275
1982 Mlle. Monique, 12"	Closed	1990	125.00	275
1982 Mlle. Yvonne, 12" - Unknown	Closed	1990	125.00	375
1985 Nanette, 19"	Closed	1990	275.00	325
1985 Odette, 19"	Closed	1990	250.00	450
1981 Rosemond, 18"	Closed	1990	250.00	750
1981 Stephanie, 18"	Closed	1990	250.00	2000

Gorham Holly Hobbie Childhood Memories - Holly Hobbie

YEAR ISSUE	EDITION LIMIT	YEAR RETD.	ISSUE PRICE	*QUOTE U.S.$
1985 Mother's Helper	Closed	1990	45.00	175
1985 Best Friends	Closed	1994	45.00	175
1985 First Day of School	Closed	1994	45.00	175
1985 Christmas Wishes	Closed	1994	45.00	175

Gorham Holly Hobbie For All Seasons - Holly Hobbie

YEAR ISSUE	EDITION LIMIT	YEAR RETD.	ISSUE PRICE	*QUOTE U.S.$
1984 Summer Holly 12"	Closed	1994	42.50	195
1984 Fall Holly 12"	Closed	1994	42.50	195
1984 Winter Holly 12"	Closed	1994	42.50	195
1984 Spring Holly 12"	Closed	1994	42.50	195
1984 Set of 4	Closed	1994	170.00	750

Holly Hobbie - Holly Hobbie

YEAR ISSUE	EDITION LIMIT	YEAR RETD.	ISSUE PRICE	*QUOTE U.S.$
1983 Blue Girl, 14"	Closed	1994	80.00	245
1983 Blue Girl, 18"	Closed	1994	115.00	295
1983 Christmas Morning, 14"	Closed	1994	80.00	245
1983 Heather, 14"	Closed	1994	80.00	275
1983 Little Amy, 14"	Closed	1994	80.00	245
1983 Robbie, 14"	Closed	1994	80.00	275
1983 Sunday Best, 18"	Closed	1994	115.00	295
1983 Sweet Valentine, 16"	Closed	1994	100.00	295
1983 Yesterday's Memories, 18"	Closed	1994	125.00	375

Joyful Years - B. Gerardi

YEAR ISSUE	EDITION LIMIT	YEAR RETD.	ISSUE PRICE	*QUOTE U.S.$
1989 Katrina	Closed	1994	295.00	375
1989 William	Closed	1994	295.00	375

Kezi Doll For All Seasons - Kezi

YEAR ISSUE	EDITION LIMIT	YEAR RETD.	ISSUE PRICE	*QUOTE U.S.$
1985 Ariel 16"	Closed	1994	135.00	500
1985 Aubrey 16"	Closed	1994	135.00	500
1985 Amber 16"	Closed	1994	135.00	500
1985 Adrienne 16"	Closed	1994	135.00	500
1985 Set of 4	Closed	1994	540.00	1900

Kezi Golden Gifts - Kezi

YEAR ISSUE	EDITION LIMIT	YEAR RETD.	ISSUE PRICE	*QUOTE U.S.$
1984 Charity 16"	Closed	1990	85.00	175
1984 Faith 18"	Closed	1990	95.00	195
1984 Felicity 18"	Closed	1990	95.00	195
1984 Grace 16"	Closed	1990	85.00	175
1984 Hope 16"	Closed	1990	85.00	175
1984 Merrie 16"	Closed	1990	85.00	175
1984 Patience 18"	Closed	1990	95.00	195
1984 Prudence 18"	Closed	1990	85.00	195

Les Belles Bebes Collection - S. Stone Aiken

YEAR ISSUE	EDITION LIMIT	YEAR RETD.	ISSUE PRICE	*QUOTE U.S.$
1993 Camille	1,500	1994	375.00	395
1991 Cherie	Closed	1994	375.00	475
1991 Desiree	1,500	1994	375.00	395

Limited Edition Dolls - S. Stone Aiken

YEAR ISSUE	EDITION LIMIT	YEAR RETD.	ISSUE PRICE	*QUOTE U.S.$
1982 Allison, 19"	Closed	1990	300.00	4500
1983 Ashley, 19"	Closed	1990	350.00	1000
1984 Nicole, 19"	Closed	1990	350.00	875
1984 Holly (Christmas), 19"	Closed	1990	300.00	850
1985 Lydia,19"	Closed	1990	550.00	1800
1985 Joy (Christmas), 19"	Closed	1990	350.00	695
1986 Noel (Christmas), 19"	Closed	1990	400.00	750
1987 Jacqueline, 19"	Closed	1994	500.00	700
1987 Merrie (Christmas), 19"	Closed	1994	500.00	750
1988 Andrew, 19"	Closed	1994	475.00	750
1988 Christa (Christmas), 19"	Closed	1994	550.00	1500
1990 Amey (10th Anniversary Edition)	Closed	1994	650.00	1100

Limited Edition Sister Set - S. Stone Aiken

YEAR ISSUE	EDITION LIMIT	YEAR RETD.	ISSUE PRICE	*QUOTE U.S.$
1988 Kathleen	Closed	1994	550.00	750
1988 Katelin	Set	1994	Set	Set

Little Women - S. Stone Aiken

YEAR ISSUE	EDITION LIMIT	YEAR RETD.	ISSUE PRICE	*QUOTE U.S.$
1983 Amy, 16"	Closed	1994	225.00	500
1983 Beth, 16"	Closed	1994	225.00	500
1983 Jo, 19"	Closed	1994	275.00	575
1983 Meg, 19"	Closed	1994	275.00	650

Precious as Pearls - S. Stone Aiken

YEAR ISSUE	EDITION LIMIT	YEAR RETD.	ISSUE PRICE	*QUOTE U.S.$
1986 Colette	Closed	1994	400.00	1500
1987 Charlotte	Closed	1994	425.00	750
1988 Chloe	Closed	1994	525.00	850
1989 Cassandra	Closed	1994	525.00	1250
XX Set	Closed	1994	1875.00	4000

Southern Belles - S. Stone Aiken

YEAR ISSUE	EDITION LIMIT	YEAR RETD.	ISSUE PRICE	*QUOTE U.S.$
1985 Amanda, 19"	Closed	1990	300.00	1400
1986 Veronica, 19"	Closed	1990	325.00	750
1987 Rachel, 19"	Closed	1990	375.00	800
1988 Cassie, 19"	Closed	1990	500.00	875

Special Moments - E. Worrell

YEAR ISSUE	EDITION LIMIT	YEAR RETD.	ISSUE PRICE	*QUOTE U.S.$
1991 Baby's First Christmas	Closed	1994	135.00	235
1992 Baby's First Steps	Closed	1994	135.00	135

Sporting Kids - R. Schrubbe

YEAR ISSUE	EDITION LIMIT	YEAR RETD.	ISSUE PRICE	*QUOTE U.S.$
1993 Up At Bat	Closed	1994	49.50	80

Times To Treasure - L. Di Leo

YEAR ISSUE	EDITION LIMIT	YEAR RETD.	ISSUE PRICE	*QUOTE U.S.$
1991 Bedtime	Closed	1994	195.00	250
1993 Playtime	Closed	1994	195.00	250
1990 Storytime	Closed	1994	195.00	250

Valentine Ladies - P. Valentine

YEAR ISSUE	EDITION LIMIT	YEAR RETD.	ISSUE PRICE	*QUOTE U.S.$
1987 Anabella	Closed	1994	145.00	395
1987 Elizabeth	Closed	1994	145.00	450
1988 Felicia	Closed	1994	225.00	325
1987 Jane	Closed	1994	145.00	350
1988 Judith Anne	Closed	1994	195.00	325
1989 Julianna	Closed	1994	225.00	275
1987 Lee Ann	Closed	1994	145.00	325
1988 Maria Theresa	Closed	1994	225.00	350
1987 Marianna	Closed	1994	160.00	425
1987 Patrice	Closed	1994	145.00	325
1988 Priscilla	Closed	1994	195.00	325
1987 Rebecca	Closed	1994	145.00	325
1987 Rosanne	Closed	1994	145.00	325
1989 Rose	Closed	1994	225.00	275
1987 Sylvia	Closed	1994	160.00	350

Victorian Cameo Collection - B. Gerardi

YEAR ISSUE	EDITION LIMIT	YEAR RETD.	ISSUE PRICE	*QUOTE U.S.$
1990 Victoria	1,500	1994	375.00	425
1991 Alexandra	Closed	1994	375.00	425

Victorian Children - S. Stone Aiken

YEAR ISSUE	EDITION LIMIT	YEAR RETD.	ISSUE PRICE	*QUOTE U.S.$
1992 Sara's Tea Time	1,000	1994	495.00	750
1993 Catching Butterflies	1,000	1994	495.00	495

The Victorian Collection - E. Woodhouse

YEAR ISSUE	EDITION LIMIT	YEAR RETD.	ISSUE PRICE	*QUOTE U.S.$
1992 Victoria's Jubilee	Yr.Iss.	1994	295.00	350

Hallmark

Holiday Homecoming Collection

YEAR ISSUE	EDITION LIMIT	YEAR RETD.	ISSUE PRICE	*QUOTE U.S.$
1997 Holiday Traditions Barbie	Yr.Iss.	1997	50.00	50
1998 Holiday Voyage Barbie	Yr.Iss.		50.00	50

Special Edition Hallmark Barbie Dolls

YEAR ISSUE	EDITION LIMIT	YEAR RETD.	ISSUE PRICE	*QUOTE U.S.$
1994 Victorian Elegance Barbie	Yr.Iss.	1994	40.00	110-150
1995 Holiday Memories Barbie	Yr.Iss.	1995	45.00	45
1996 The Yuletide Romance Barbie	Yr.Iss.	1996	45.00	45

Hamilton Collection

Abbie Williams Doll Collection - A. Williams

YEAR ISSUE	EDITION LIMIT	YEAR RETD.	ISSUE PRICE	*QUOTE U.S.$
1992 Molly	Closed	N/A	155.00	200

American Country Doll Collection - T. Tucker

YEAR ISSUE	EDITION LIMIT	YEAR RETD.	ISSUE PRICE	*QUOTE U.S.$
1995 Carson	Open		95.00	95
1995 Bonnie	Open		195.00	195
1996 Patsy	Open		95.00	95
1996 Delaney	Open		95.00	95
1996 Arizona	Open		95.00	95
1996 Kendra	Open		195.00	195

Annual Connossieur Doll - N/A

YEAR ISSUE	EDITION LIMIT	YEAR RETD.	ISSUE PRICE	*QUOTE U.S.$
1992 Lara	7,450		295.00	295

The Antique Doll Collection - Unknown

YEAR ISSUE	EDITION LIMIT	YEAR RETD.	ISSUE PRICE	*QUOTE U.S.$
1989 Nicole	Closed	N/A	195.00	195-300
1990 Colette	Closed	1996	195.00	195
1991 Lisette	Closed	1996	195.00	225
1991 Katrina	Closed	1996	195.00	195

Baby Portrait Dolls - B. Parker

YEAR ISSUE	EDITION LIMIT	YEAR RETD.	ISSUE PRICE	*QUOTE U.S.$
1991 Melissa	Closed	1993	135.00	175-200
1992 Jenna	Closed	N/A	135.00	135-200
1992 Bethany	Closed	1996	135.00	150
1993 Mindy	Closed	1996	135.00	150-160

Bed Time Angels - M. Snyder

YEAR ISSUE	EDITION LIMIT	YEAR RETD.	ISSUE PRICE	*QUOTE U.S.$
1997 Now I Lay Me Down To Sleep	Open		49.95	50
1998 I Pray The Lord My Soul To Keep	Open		49.95	50
1998 Keep Me Safe All Through The Night	Open		49.95	50
1998 Wake Me Up At Morning Light	Open		49.95	50

Belles of the Countryside - C. Heath Orange

YEAR ISSUE	EDITION LIMIT	YEAR RETD.	ISSUE PRICE	*QUOTE U.S.$
1992 Erin	Closed	1997	135.00	150
1992 Rose	Open		135.00	135
1993 Lorna	Closed	1997	135.00	150
1994 Gwyn	Open		135.00	135

The Bessie Pease Gutmann Doll Collection - B.P. Gutmann

YEAR ISSUE	EDITION LIMIT	YEAR RETD.	ISSUE PRICE	*QUOTE U.S.$
1989 Love is Blind	Closed	N/A	135.00	220
1989 He Won't Bite	Closed	N/A	135.00	135
1991 Virginia	Closed	1996	135.00	135
1991 First Dancing Lesson	Closed	1996	135.00	135
1991 Good Morning	Closed	1996	135.00	135
1991 Love At First Sight	Closed	1996	135.00	135

Best Buddies - C.M. Rolfe

YEAR ISSUE	EDITION LIMIT	YEAR RETD.	ISSUE PRICE	*QUOTE U.S.$
1994 Jodie	Closed	1997	69.00	69-90
1994 Brandy	Closed	1997	69.00	69
1995 Joey	Open		69.00	69-100
1996 Stacey	Open		69.00	69

Boehm Christening - Boehm Studio

YEAR ISSUE	EDITION LIMIT	YEAR RETD.	ISSUE PRICE	*QUOTE U.S.$
1994 Elena's First Portrait	Closed	1996	155.00	180-250
1994 Elena	Closed	1996	155.00	180-250

Bridal Elegance - Boehm

YEAR ISSUE	EDITION LIMIT	YEAR RETD.	ISSUE PRICE	*QUOTE U.S.$
1994 Camille	Closed	1996	195.00	225

Bride Dolls - Unknown

YEAR ISSUE	EDITION LIMIT	YEAR RETD.	ISSUE PRICE	*QUOTE U.S.$
1991 Portrait of Innocence	Closed	1996	195.00	210
1992 Portrait of Loveliness	Closed	1996	195.00	250

Brooker Tickler - Harris/Brooker

YEAR ISSUE	EDITION LIMIT	YEAR RETD.	ISSUE PRICE	*QUOTE U.S.$
1995 Nellie	Open		95.00	95
1996 Callie	Open		95.00	95

Brooks Wooden Dolls - P. Ryan Brooks

YEAR ISSUE	EDITION LIMIT	YEAR RETD.	ISSUE PRICE	*QUOTE U.S.$
1993 Waiting For Santa	15,000	1994	135.00	200-250
1993 Are You the Easter Bunny?	15,000		135.00	135
1994 Be My Valentine	Open		135.00	135
1995 Shh! I Only Wanna Peek	Open		135.00	135

Byi Praying Dolls - C. Byi

YEAR ISSUE	EDITION LIMIT	YEAR RETD.	ISSUE PRICE	*QUOTE U.S.$
1996 Mark & Mary	Open		89.95	90

Catherine Mather Dolls - C. Mather

YEAR ISSUE	EDITION LIMIT	YEAR RETD.	ISSUE PRICE	*QUOTE U.S.$
1993 Justine	15,000		155.00	155-200

Central Park Skaters - Unknown

YEAR ISSUE	EDITION LIMIT	YEAR RETD.	ISSUE PRICE	*QUOTE U.S.$
1991 Central Park Skaters	Closed	1996	245.00	245

A Child's Menagerie - B. Van Boxel

YEAR ISSUE	EDITION LIMIT	YEAR RETD.	ISSUE PRICE	*QUOTE U.S.$
1993 Becky	Closed	1996	69.00	69-100
1993 Carrie	Closed	1996	69.00	69
1994 Mandy	Closed	1996	69.00	69
1994 Terry	Closed	1996	69.00	69

Children To Cherish - Cybis

YEAR ISSUE	EDITION LIMIT	YEAR RETD.	ISSUE PRICE	*QUOTE U.S.$
1991 A Gift of Innocence	Yr.Iss.	1991	135.00	135
1991 A Gift of Beauty	Closed	1996	135.00	135

Ciambra - M. Ciambra

YEAR ISSUE	EDITION LIMIT	YEAR RETD.	ISSUE PRICE	*QUOTE U.S.$
1995 Chloe	Closed	1997	155.00	135-180
1996 Lydia	Open		155.00	155

Cindy Marschner Rolfe Dolls - C.M. Rolfe

YEAR ISSUE	EDITION LIMIT	YEAR RETD.	ISSUE PRICE	*QUOTE U.S.$
1993 Shannon	Closed	1996	95.00	95
1993 Julie	Open		95.00	95
1993 Kayla	Open		95.00	95
1994 Janey	Open		95.00	95

Cindy Marschner Rolfe Twins - C.M. Rolfe

YEAR ISSUE	EDITION LIMIT	YEAR RETD.	ISSUE PRICE	*QUOTE U.S.$
1995 Shelby & Sydney	Closed	1996	190.00	190-210

Connie Walser Derek Baby Dolls - C.W. Derek

YEAR ISSUE	EDITION LIMIT	YEAR RETD.	ISSUE PRICE	*QUOTE U.S.$
1990 Jessica	Closed	1993	155.00	350-500
1991 Sara	Closed	1995	155.00	180-200
1991 Andrew	Closed	1996	155.00	155-180
1991 Amanda	Closed	1996	155.00	155-180
1992 Samantha	Closed	1996	155.00	155-180

Connie Walser Derek Baby Dolls II - C.W. Derek

YEAR ISSUE	EDITION LIMIT	YEAR RETD.	ISSUE PRICE	*QUOTE U.S.$
1992 Stephanie	Closed	1996	95.00	200
1992 Beth	Closed	1996	95.00	160

Connie Walser Derek Baby Dolls III - C.W. Derek

YEAR ISSUE	EDITION LIMIT	YEAR RETD.	ISSUE PRICE	*QUOTE U.S.$
1994 Chelsea	Open		79.00	79
1995 Tina	Open		79.00	79
1995 Tabitha	Open		79.00	79
1995 Ginger	Open		79.00	79

Connie Walser Derek Dolls - C.W. Derek

YEAR ISSUE	EDITION LIMIT	YEAR RETD.	ISSUE PRICE	*QUOTE U.S.$
1992 Baby Jessica	Closed	1996	75.00	75
1993 Baby Sara	Closed	1996	75.00	75

Connie Walser Derek Toddlers - C.W. Derek

YEAR ISSUE	EDITION LIMIT	YEAR RETD.	ISSUE PRICE	*QUOTE U.S.$
1994 Jessie	Closed	1996	79.00	120
1994 Casey	Closed	1996	79.00	120
1995 Angie	Closed	1996	79.00	120
1995 Tori	Open		79.00	79

Daddy's Little Girls - M. Snyder

YEAR ISSUE	EDITION LIMIT	YEAR RETD.	ISSUE PRICE	*QUOTE U.S.$
1992 Lindsay	Closed	1996	95.00	95
1993 Cassie	Closed	1996	95.00	95
1993 Dana	Closed	1996	95.00	120
1994 Tara	Closed	1996	95.00	95

Dey Recital Dolls - P. Dey

YEAR ISSUE	EDITION LIMIT	YEAR RETD.	ISSUE PRICE	*QUOTE U.S.$
1996 Mallory	9,500		195.00	195

Dolls by Autumn Berwick - A. Berwick

YEAR ISSUE	EDITION LIMIT	YEAR RETD.	ISSUE PRICE	*QUOTE U.S.$
1993 Laura	Closed	1995	135.00	135-150

*Quotes have been rounded up to nearest dollar

YEAR ISSUE	EDITION LIMIT	YEAR RETD.	ISSUE PRICE	*QUOTE U.S.$
Dolls By Kay McKee - K. McKee				
1992 Shy Violet	Closed	1993	135.00	200-300
1992 Robin	Closed	1995	135.00	135
1993 Katie Did It!	Closed	1995	135.00	135-150
1993 Ryan	Open		135.00	135-180
Dolls of America's Colonial Heritage - A. Elekfy				
1986 Katrina	Closed	1994	55.00	55
1986 Nicole	Closed	1994	55.00	55
1987 Maria	Closed	1994	55.00	55
1987 Priscilla	Closed	1994	55.00	55
1987 Colleen	Closed	1994	55.00	55
1988 Gretchen	Closed	1994	55.00	55
Dreamsicle Dolls - K. Haynes				
1997 Sweet Dreams Teddy	Open		49.95	50
1998 Story Time With Bunny	Open		49.95	50
Elaine Campbell Dolls - E. Campbell				
1994 Emma	Closed	1994	95.00	95-120
1995 Abby	Open		95.00	95
1995 Jana	Open		95.00	95
1995 Molly	Open		95.00	95
Eternal Friends Doll Collection - Precious Moments				
1996 Love One Another	Open		135.00	135
1997 Friendship Hits The Spot	Open		135.00	135
First Recital - N/A				
1993 Hillary	Closed	1998	135.00	135
1994 Olivia	Closed	1998	135.00	135
Grobben Ethnic Babies - J. Grobben				
1994 Jasmine	Closed	1996	135.00	180
1995 Taiya	Closed	1996	135.00	160
Grothedde Dolls - N. Grothedde				
1994 Cindy	Closed	1996	69.00	100
1995 Holly	Closed	1997	69.00	69
Hargrave Dolls - M. Hargrave				
1994 Angela	Open		79.00	79-110
1995 April	Open		79.00	79-100
Heath Babies - C. Heath Orange				
1995 Hayley	Open		95.00	95
1996 Ellie	Open		95.00	95
Heavenly Clowns Doll Collection - K. McKee				
1996 Blue Moon	Open		95.00	95
Helen Carr Dolls - H. Carr				
1994 Claudia	Open		135.00	135-175
1995 Jillian	Open		135.00	135
1996 Abigail	Open		135.00	135-160
1996 Rosalee	Open		135.00	135
Helen Kish II Dolls - H. Kish				
1992 Vanessa	Open		135.00	135
1994 Jordan	Open		95.00	95
Holiday Carollers - U. Lepp				
1992 Joy	Closed	1996	155.00	155
1993 Noel	Closed	1996	155.00	155
Honkytonk Gals Doll Collection - C. Johnston				
1996 Kendall	Open		95.00	76-95
1997 Logan	Open		95.00	95
Huckleberry Hill Kids - B. Parker				
1994 Gabrielle	Open		95.00	95-125
1994 Alexandra	Open		95.00	95
1995 Jeremiah	Open		95.00	95
1996 Sarah	Open		95.00	95
I Love Lucy (Porcelain) - Unknown				
1990 Lucy	Closed	N/A	95.00	240-300
1991 Ricky	Closed	N/A	95.00	350
1992 Queen of the Gypsies	Closed	N/A	95.00	245
1992 Vitameatavegamin	Closed	N/A	95.00	200-300
I Love Lucy (Vinyl) - Unknown				
1988 Ethel	Closed	N/A	40.00	100
1988 Fred	Closed	N/A	40.00	100
1990 Lucy	Closed	N/A	40.00	100
1991 Ricky	Closed	N/A	40.00	150
1992 Queen of the Gypsies	Open		40.00	40
1992 Vitameatavegamin	Open		40.00	40
I'm So Proud Doll Collection - L. Cobabe				
1992 Christina	Closed	1996	95.00	95-125
1993 Jill	Closed	1996	95.00	120
1994 Tammy	Closed	1996	95.00	95-110
1994 Shelly	Closed	1996	95.00	115
Inga Manders - I. Manders				
1995 Miss Priss	Open		79.00	79
1995 Miss Hollywood	Open		79.00	79
1995 Miss Glamour	Open		79.00	79
1996 Miss Sweetheart	Open		79.00	79
International Children - C. Woodie				
1991 Miko	Closed	N/A	49.50	80
1991 Anastasia	Closed	1996	49.50	50
1991 Angelina	Closed	1996	49.50	50
1992 Lian	Closed	1996	49.50	50
1992 Monique	Closed	1996	49.50	50
1992 Lisa	Closed	1996	49.50	50
Jane Zidjunas Party Dolls - J. Zidjunas				
1991 Kelly	Closed	1994	135.00	135-150
1992 Katie	Closed	1994	135.00	135
1993 Meredith	Closed	1994	135.00	135
Jane Zidjunas Sleeping Dolls - J. Zidjunas				
1995 Annie	Open		79.00	79-110
1995 Jamie	Open		79.00	79-120
Jane Zidjunas Toddler Dolls - J. Zidjunas				
1991 Jennifer	Closed	1995	135.00	135
1991 Megan	Closed	1995	135.00	160
1992 Kimberly	Closed	1995	135.00	135
1992 Amy	Closed	1995	135.00	135-150
Jane Zidjunas Victorian - J. Zidjunas				
1996 Constance	9,500		195.00	195-210
Jeanne Wilson Dolls - J. Wilson				
1994 Priscilla	Open		155.00	155
Johnston Cowgirls - C. Johnston				
1994 Savannah	Closed	1998	79.00	79
1994 Skyler	Open		79.00	79
1995 Cheyene	Open		79.00	79
1995 Austin	Open		79.00	79
Join The Parade - N/A				
1992 Betsy	Closed	1996	49.50	50
1994 Peggy	Closed	1996	49.50	50
1994 Sandy	Closed	1996	49.50	50
1995 Brian	Closed	1996	49.50	50
Joke Grobben Dolls - J. Grobben				
1992 Heather	Closed	1995	69.00	69
1993 Kathleen	Closed	1995	69.00	69
1993 Brianna	Closed	1995	69.00	69
1994 Bridget	Closed	1995	69.00	69-90
Joke Grobben Tall Dolls - J. Grobben				
1995 Jade	Open		135.00	135
1996 Raven	Open		135.00	135
Just Like Mom - H. Kish				
1991 Ashley	Closed	1993	135.00	250-300
1992 Elizabeth	Closed	1994	135.00	160
1992 Hannah	Closed	1994	135.00	135
1993 Margaret	Closed	1994	135.00	135
Kay McKee Downsized Dolls - K. McKee				
1995 Kyle	Open		79.00	79
1996 Cody	Open		79.00	79
Kay McKee Klowns - K. McKee				
1993 The Dreamer	15,000	1995	155.00	155
1994 The Entertainer	15,000	1996	155.00	180
Kuck Fairy - S. Kuck				
1994 Tooth Fairy	Closed	1996	135.00	135
Laura Cobabe Dolls - L. Cobabe				
1992 Amber	Closed	1994	195.00	225
1992 Brooke	Closed	1994	195.00	195
Laura Cobabe Dolls II - L. Cobabe				
1993 Kristen	Closed	1994	75.00	75
Laura Cobabe Ethnic - L. Cobabe				
1995 Nica	Open		95.00	95
1996 Kenu	Open		95.00	95
Laura Cobabe Indians - L. Cobabe				
1994 Snowbird	Open		135.00	135
1995 Little Eagle	Open		135.00	135
1995 Desert Bloom	Open		135.00	135
1996 Call of the Coyote	Open		135.00	135
Laura Cobabe Tall Dolls - L. Cobabe				
1994 Cassandra	Closed	1997	195.00	250
1994 Taylor	Closed	1997	195.00	250
Laura Cobabe's Costume Kids - L. Cobabe				
1994 Lil' Punkin	Closed	1996	79.00	110
1994 Little Ladybug	Open		79.00	79
1995 Miss Dinomite	Open		79.00	79
1995 Miss Flutterby	Open		79.00	79
Little Gardners - J. Galperin				
1996 Daisy	Open		95.00	95
Little Rascals™ - S./J. Hoffman				
1992 Spanky	Open		75.00	75
1993 Alfalfa	Open		75.00	75
1994 Darla	Open		75.00	75
1994 Buckwheat	Open		75.00	75
1994 Stymie	Open		75.00	75
1995 Pete The Pup	Open		75.00	75
Littlest Members of the Wedding - J. Esteban				
1993 Matthew & Melanie	Closed	1995	195.00	195
Lucy Dolls - Unknown				
1996 Lucy	Open		95.00	95
Maud Humphrey Bogart Dolls - Unknown				
1992 Playing Bridesmaid	Closed	N/A	195.00	225
Maud Humphrey Bogart Doll Collection - M.H. Bogart				
1989 Playing Bride	Closed	N/A	135.00	225
1990 First Party	Closed	N/A	135.00	150
1990 The First Lesson	Closed	N/A	135.00	149
1991 Seamstress	Closed	N/A	135.00	149
1991 Little Captive	Closed	1996	135.00	135
1992 Kitty's Bath	Closed	1996	135.00	135
Mavis Snyder Dolls - M. Snyder				
1994 Tara	Closed	1995	95.00	95
Parker Carousel - B. Parker				
1996 Annelise's Musical Ride	4,500		295.00	295
Parker Fairy Tale - B. Parker				
1995 Claire	Open		155.00	155
1996 Marissa	Open		155.00	155
Parker Levi Toddlers - B. Parker				
1992 Courtney	Closed	1994	135.00	200
1992 Melody	Closed	1994	135.00	135
Parkins Baby - P. Parkins				
1995 Baby Alyssa	Open		225.00	225
Parkins Connisseur - P. Parkins				
1993 Faith	Closed	1995	135.00	180
Parkins Portraits - P. Parkins				
1993 Lauren	Closed	1995	79.00	79-110
1993 Kelsey	Closed	1997	79.00	79-110
1994 Morgan	Open		79.00	79
1994 Cassidy	Closed	1996	79.00	100
Parkins Toddler Angels - P. Parkins				
1995 Celeste	Open		135.00	135
1996 Charity	Open		135.00	108-135
1996 Charisse	Open		135.00	135
1996 Chantelle	Open		135.00	135
Parkins Treasures - P. Parkins				
1992 Tiffany	Closed	1994	55.00	120
1992 Dorothy	Closed	1995	55.00	80
1993 Charlotte	Closed	1995	55.00	80
1993 Cynthia	Closed	1995	55.00	80
Phyllis Parkins Dolls - P. Parkins				
1992 Swan Princess	9,850	1995	195.00	220-250
Phyllis Parkins II Dolls - P. Parkins				
1995 Dakota	Open		135.00	135
1996 Kerrie	Open		135.00	135
1996 Ginny	Open		135.00	135
1996 Dixie	Open		135.00	135
Phyllis Parkins Musical Dolls - P. Parkins				
1995 Nite, Nite Pony	Open		95.00	95
1996 Twice As Nice	Open		95.00	95
1996 Sleep Tight, Sweetheart	Open		95.00	95
1996 Cradled in Love	Open		95.00	95
Picnic In The Park - J. Esteban				
1991 Rebecca	Closed	1995	155.00	155-180
1992 Emily	Closed	1995	155.00	155
1992 Victoria	Closed	1995	155.00	155
1993 Benjamin	Closed	1995	155.00	155-180
Pitter Patter Doll Collection - C. W. Derek				
1996 Bobbie Jo	Open		79.00	79
1997 Mary Anne	Open		79.00	79
A Pocket Full of Love Doll Collection - S. Kuck				
1997 Gabriella	Open		29.95	30
1998 Tanya	Open		39.95	40
Precious Moments - S. Butcher				
1994 Tell Me the Story of Jesus	Open		79.00	79
1995 God Loveth a Cheerful Giver	Open		79.00	79
1995 Mother Sew Dear	Open		79.00	79
1996 You Are the Type I Love	Open		79.00	79
Precious Moments Christening - S. Butcher				
1996 Anna	Open		95.00	95
1996 Elise	Open		95.00	95
Proud Indian Nation - R. Swanson				
1992 Navajo Little One	Closed	1993	95.00	200
1993 Dressed Up For The Pow Wow	Closed	1996	95.00	150
1993 Autumn Treat	Closed	1997	95.00	115
1994 Out with Mama's Flock	Closed	1998	95.00	95
Rachel Cold Toddlers - R. Cold				
1995 Jenny	Open		95.00	95
1996 Trudy	Open		95.00	95
The Royal Beauty Dolls - Unknown				
1991 Chen Mai	Closed	1994	195.00	195-225
Russian Czarra Dolls - Unknown				
1991 Alexandra	Closed	N/A	295.00	350
Sandra Kuck Dolls - S. Kuck				
1993 A Kiss Goodnight	Closed	N/A	79.00	79-95
1994 Teaching Teddy	Open		79.00	79
1995 Reading With Teddy	Open		79.00	79
1996 Picnic With Teddy	Closed	N/A	79.00	79-95

*Quotes have been rounded up to nearest dollar

Santa's Little Helpers - C.W. Derek

YEAR ISSUE	EDITION LIMIT	YEAR RETD.	ISSUE PRICE	*QUOTE U.S.$
1992 Nicholas	Closed	1996	155.00	155-250
1993 Hope	Closed	1996	155.00	155-225

Schmidt Babies - J. Schmidt

YEAR ISSUE	EDITION LIMIT	YEAR RETD.	ISSUE PRICE	*QUOTE U.S.$
1995 Baby	Open		79.00	79
1996 Snookums	Open		79.00	79

Schmidt Dolls - J. Schmidt

YEAR ISSUE	EDITION LIMIT	YEAR RETD.	ISSUE PRICE	*QUOTE U.S.$
1994 Kaitlyn	Closed	1995	79.00	120
1995 Kara	Closed	1995	79.00	79
1995 Kathy	Open		79.00	79
1996 Karla	Open		79.00	79

Schrubbe Santa Dolls - R. Schrubbe

YEAR ISSUE	EDITION LIMIT	YEAR RETD.	ISSUE PRICE	*QUOTE U.S.$
1994 Jolly Old St. Nick	Closed	1995	135.00	135-150

Sentiments From the Garden - M. Severino

YEAR ISSUE	EDITION LIMIT	YEAR RETD.	ISSUE PRICE	*QUOTE U.S.$
1996 Fairy of Innocence	Open		59.00	59
1997 Fairy of Loveliness	Open		59.00	59

Shelton II Doll - V. Shelton

YEAR ISSUE	EDITION LIMIT	YEAR RETD.	ISSUE PRICE	*QUOTE U.S.$
1996 Josie	Open		79.00	79

Shelton Indians - V. Shelton

YEAR ISSUE	EDITION LIMIT	YEAR RETD.	ISSUE PRICE	*QUOTE U.S.$
1995 Little Cloud	Open		95.00	95-120
1996 Little Basketweaver	Open		95.00	95
1996 Little Warrior	Open		95.00	95
1996 Little Skywatcher	Open		95.00	95

Simon Indians - S. Simon

YEAR ISSUE	EDITION LIMIT	YEAR RETD.	ISSUE PRICE	*QUOTE U.S.$
1994 Meadowlark	Open		95.00	95
1995 Tashee	Open		95.00	95
1996 Star Dreamer	Open		95.00	95
1996 Sewanka	Open		95.00	95

Songs of the Seasons Hakata Doll Collection - T. Murakami

YEAR ISSUE	EDITION LIMIT	YEAR RETD.	ISSUE PRICE	*QUOTE U.S.$
1985 Winter Song Maiden	9,800	1991	75.00	75
1985 Spring Song Maiden	9,800	1991	75.00	75
1985 Summer Song Maiden	9,800	1991	75.00	75
1985 Autumn Song Maiden	9,800	1991	75.00	75

Star Trek Doll Collection - E. Daub

YEAR ISSUE	EDITION LIMIT	YEAR RETD.	ISSUE PRICE	*QUOTE U.S.$
1988 Mr. Spock	Closed	N/A	75.00	150
1988 Captain Kirk	Closed	N/A	75.00	120
1989 Dr. Mc Coy	Closed	N/A	75.00	120
1989 Scotty	Closed	N/A	75.00	120
1990 Sulu	Closed	N/A	75.00	120
1990 Chekov	Closed	N/A	75.00	120
1991 Uhura	Closed	N/A	75.00	120

Storybook Dolls - L. Di Leo

YEAR ISSUE	EDITION LIMIT	YEAR RETD.	ISSUE PRICE	*QUOTE U.S.$
1991 Alice in Wonderland	Closed	1996	75.00	75

Summertime Beauties - C. Marschner

YEAR ISSUE	EDITION LIMIT	YEAR RETD.	ISSUE PRICE	*QUOTE U.S.$
1995 Sally	Open		95.00	95
1996 Lacey	Open		95.00	95
1997 Cassie	Open		95.00	95
1997 Marcie	Open		95.00	95

Through The Eyes of Virginia Turner - V. Turner

YEAR ISSUE	EDITION LIMIT	YEAR RETD.	ISSUE PRICE	*QUOTE U.S.$
1992 Michelle	Closed	1993	95.00	150-180
1992 Danielle	Closed	1997	95.00	113
1993 Wendy	Closed	1995	95.00	125
1994 Dawn	Closed	1996	95.00	95

Toddler Days Doll Collection - D. Schurig

YEAR ISSUE	EDITION LIMIT	YEAR RETD.	ISSUE PRICE	*QUOTE U.S.$
1992 Erica	Closed	1995	95.00	125
1993 Darlene	Closed	1995	95.00	95
1994 Karen	Closed	1995	95.00	95
1995 Penny	Closed	1995	95.00	95

Treasured Toddlers - V. Turner

YEAR ISSUE	EDITION LIMIT	YEAR RETD.	ISSUE PRICE	*QUOTE U.S.$
1992 Whitney	Closed	1996	95.00	200
1993 Natalie	Closed	1996	95.00	150

Vickie Walker 1st's - V. Walker

YEAR ISSUE	EDITION LIMIT	YEAR RETD.	ISSUE PRICE	*QUOTE U.S.$
1995 Leah	Closed	1998	79.00	79
1995 Leslie	Open		79.00	79
1995 Lily	Open		79.00	79
1995 Leanna	Open		79.00	79

Victorian Treasures - C.W. Derek

YEAR ISSUE	EDITION LIMIT	YEAR RETD.	ISSUE PRICE	*QUOTE U.S.$
1992 Katherine	Closed	1996	155.00	155
1993 Madeline	Closed	1996	155.00	155

Virginia Turner Dolls - V. Turner

YEAR ISSUE	EDITION LIMIT	YEAR RETD.	ISSUE PRICE	*QUOTE U.S.$
1995 Amelia	Open		95.00	95
1995 Mckenzie	Open		95.00	95
1996 Grace	Open		95.00	95
1996 Alexis	Open		95.00	95
1997 Felicia	Open		95.00	95
1997 Courtney	Open		95.00	95
1998 Miranda	Open		95.00	95

Virginia Turner Little Sisters - V. Turner

YEAR ISSUE	EDITION LIMIT	YEAR RETD.	ISSUE PRICE	*QUOTE U.S.$
1996 Allie	Open		95.00	95

Wooden Dolls - N/A

YEAR ISSUE	EDITION LIMIT	YEAR RETD.	ISSUE PRICE	*QUOTE U.S.$
1991 Gretchen	9,850	1995	225.00	280
1991 Heidi	9,850	1995	225.00	250

Wright Indian Dolls - D. Wright

YEAR ISSUE	EDITION LIMIT	YEAR RETD.	ISSUE PRICE	*QUOTE U.S.$
1994 Sacajawea	Open		135.00	135
1994 Minnehaha	Open		135.00	135
1995 Pine Leaf	Open		135.00	135
1995 Lozen	Open		135.00	135
1997 White Rose	Open		135.00	135
1997 Falling Star	Open		135.00	135

Year Round Fun - D. Schurig

YEAR ISSUE	EDITION LIMIT	YEAR RETD.	ISSUE PRICE	*QUOTE U.S.$
1992 Allison	Closed	1995	95.00	95
1993 Christy	Closed	1995	95.00	95
1993 Paula	Closed	1995	95.00	95
1994 Kaylie	Closed	1995	95.00	125

Zolan Dolls - D. Zolan

YEAR ISSUE	EDITION LIMIT	YEAR RETD.	ISSUE PRICE	*QUOTE U.S.$
1991 A Christmas Prayer	Closed	1993	95.00	250-280
1992 Winter Angel	Closed	1996	95.00	95
1992 Rainy Day Pals	Closed	1996	95.00	125
1992 Quiet Time	Closed	1996	95.00	125
1993 For You	Closed	1996	95.00	125
1993 The Thinker	Closed	1996	95.00	180

Zolan Double Dolls - D. Zolan

YEAR ISSUE	EDITION LIMIT	YEAR RETD.	ISSUE PRICE	*QUOTE U.S.$
1993 First Kiss	Closed	1995	155.00	155-180
1994 New Shoes	Closed	1995	155.00	155

Jan Hagara Collectables

Jan Hagara Collector's Club - J. Hagara

YEAR ISSUE	EDITION LIMIT	YEAR RETD.	ISSUE PRICE	*QUOTE U.S.$
1987 Jan at Age 4 Plaque (Charter Member)	Closed	1988	Gift	100
1987 Jan at Age 4 Pin (Charter Member)	Closed	1988	Gift	25
1987 Mattie Print	Closed	1988	55.00	55-150
1988 Cloud Pin	Closed	1989	Gift	N/A
1988 Bonnie Print	Closed	1989	45.00	45-85
1988 Mattie Figurine	Closed	1989	47.50	48-100
1989 Mattie Doll	Closed	1990	550.00	550
1989 Cloud Figurine	Closed	1990	30.00	30-45
1989 Jan at Age 4 Miniature	Closed	1990	22.00	22-35
1989 Brandon Print	Closed	1990	45.00	45-65
1989 Bonnie Pin	Closed	1990	Gift	N/A
1990 Bonnie Figurine	Closed	1991	40.00	40-65
1990 Cloud Miniature	Closed	1991	20.00	20-30
1990 Brandon Pin	Closed	1991	Gift	N/A
1990 Tiffany Print	Closed	1991	55.00	55
1991 Tiffany Pin	Closed	1992	Gift	N/A
1991 Brandon Figurine	Closed	1992	40.00	40-65
1991 Bonnie Doll	Closed	1992	395.00	395
1991 Mattie Miniature	Closed	1992	22.50	23
1991 Cherished (Bonnie's Bear) Miniature	Closed	1992	Gift	15
1991 Peggy Sue Print	Closed	1992	Gift	48
1991 Peggy Sue Figurine (Charter Member)	Closed	1992	27.50	28-55
1991 Peggy Sue Pin (Charter Member)	Closed	1992	Gift	20
1991 Larka Print	Closed	1992	75.00	75
1992 Enya Print	Closed	1992	Gift	55
1992 Larka Pin	Closed	1993	Gift	N/A
1992 Tiffany Figurine	Closed	1993	50.00	50-65
1993 Audrey Print	Closed	1993	Gift	35
1993 Brandon Doll	Closed	1994	360.00	360
1993 Audrey Pin	Closed	1994	Gift	N/A
1993 Audrey Figurine	Closed	1994	55.00	55
1994 Tara Pin	Closed	1995	Gift	N/A
1994 Tara Print	Closed	1995	55.00	55
1994 Courtney Print	Closed	1994	Gift	20
1994 Larka Figurine	Closed	1996	115.00	115-135
1995 Daniet Print	Closed	1995	Gift	25
1995 Daniel Pin	Closed	1996	Gift	N/A
1995 Tara Figurine	Closed	1996	Gift	65
1995 Tara Figurine	Closed	1996	60.00	60-65
1995 Star's Buggy II	Closed	1996	27.00	27-35
1996 Sean Print (matted)	Closed	1997	40.00	40
1996 Sean Print (fr. canvas)	Closed	1997	165.00	165
1996 Sean Print (gallery-w/o frame)	Closed	1997	250.00	250
1996 Sean Print (gallery-w/frame)	Closed	1997	338.00	338
1996 Peggy Sue Doll	Closed	1997	395.00	395
1996 Courtney Figurine	Closed	1997	Gift	39
1996 Barbara Print (fr. canvas)	Closed	1997	144.00	144
1996 Barbara Print (unfr. canvas)	Closed	1997	99.00	99
1996 Barbara Print (matted)	Closed	1997	25.00	25
1996 Sean Figurine (Charter)	6/99		47.50	48
1996 Sean Figurine	6/99		52.00	52
1996 Larka's Toys	Closed	1997	27.00	27
1997 Barbara Figurine	Closed	1998	Gift	39
1997 Inya Figurine	6/99		55.00	55
1997 Peppermint Print (gallery-w/o frame)	Closed	1998	85.00	85
1997 Peppermint Print (gallery-w/frame)	Closed	1998	143.00	143
1997 Peppermint Print	Closed	1998	Gift	N/A
1996 Star's Buggy Pin	Closed	1997	Gift	N/A
1997 Peppermint Figurine	Closed	1998	49.00	49
1997 Peppermint Pin	Closed	1998	Gift	N/A
1998 Debbie Pin	6/99		Gift	N/A

B&J Co. - J. Hagara

YEAR ISSUE	EDITION LIMIT	YEAR RETD.	ISSUE PRICE	*QUOTE U.S.$
1995 Addie w/Princess 23"	85	1997	2000.00	2000
1988 Adrianne 14"	2-Yr.	1990	125.00	125-250
1987 Allegra 12"	250	1988	800.00	800-1000
1988 Amy 13"	2-Yr.	1990	160.00	160-250
1992 Ann Marie 14"	500	1993	425.00	425-495
1988 Ashley 13"	2-Yr.	1990	160.00	160-200
1992 Brianna 7 1/2"	300	1993	300.00	300
1990 Clara 18"	120	1990	375.00	375-795
1992 Dacy 18"	700	1995	495.00	495-595
1995 Debra 15"	250	1997	425.00	425
1993 Jackie 18"	300	1996	495.00	495
1993 Jamie 14"	350	1995	395.00	395-450
1990 Jessica 18"	350	1991	700.00	700
1995 Joseph 12" (blue)	150	1997	250.00	250-300
1995 Joseph 12" (pink)	150	1997	250.00	250-300
1995 June 12"	300	1997	250.00	250
1995 Kelton 7"	300	1997	250.00	250
1988 Lee 8"	100	1988	300.00	300
1995 May 12"	300	1997	250.00	250
1987 Meg 15"	2-Yr.	1989	250.00	250
1987 Michael 12"	250	1989	650.00	850
1986 Paige 12"	430	1988	195.00	195-800
1995 Princess 12"	100	1997	270.00	270-350
1994 Renny 18"	300	1996	495.00	495
1991 Renny 23"	50	1994	2500.00	2500
1993 Rosie 18"	300	1994	495.00	495
1992 Sheldon 18"	500	1995	495.00	495
1990 Shelley 18"	1,200	1992	550.00	550-595
1994 Star 18"	100	1994	800.00	800-1000
1992 Tina 14"	500	1994	425.00	425
1994 Tiny Lee 6"	900	1997	52.50	55
1994 Todd 14"	75	1995	425.00	425
1986 Tracy 12"	2-Yr.	1988	125.00	125-200
1994 Wendy 25"	60	1996	2500.00	2500

Danbury Mint - J. Hagara

YEAR ISSUE	EDITION LIMIT	YEAR RETD.	ISSUE PRICE	*QUOTE U.S.$
1991 Adell 19"	Yr.Iss.	1992	195.00	195
1990 Brook 19"	Yr.Iss.	1991	195.00	195
1990 Goldie 19"	Yr.Iss.	1991	195.00	195
1989 Sophie 19"	Yr.Iss.	1990	195.00	195

Effanbee Vinyl Dolls - J. Hagara

YEAR ISSUE	EDITION LIMIT	YEAR RETD.	ISSUE PRICE	*QUOTE U.S.$
1984 Belinda	2-Yr.	1986	55.00	55-100
1984 Beth	2-Yr.	1986	55.00	55-125
1984 Bobby	2-Yr.	1986	55.00	55-125

Heirloom Dolls - J. Hagara

YEAR ISSUE	EDITION LIMIT	YEAR RETD.	ISSUE PRICE	*QUOTE U.S.$
1985 Amanda 12"	2-Yr.	1987	125.00	125-300
1985 Carol 12"	2-Yr.	1987	85.00	165-300
1985 Jimmy 12"	2-Yr.	1987	125.00	125-250
1985 Lisa 12"	2-Yr.	1987	125.00	125-250
1985 Sharice 12"	2-Yr.	1987	125.00	125-250

Royal Orleans Porcelain Dolls - J. Hagara

YEAR ISSUE	EDITION LIMIT	YEAR RETD.	ISSUE PRICE	*QUOTE U.S.$
1984 Jenny & the Bye Lo 17"	2-Yr.	1986	375.00	375-750
1985 Jody & the Toy Horse 17"	2-Yr.	1987	375.00	375

Vinyl Dolls - J. Hagara

YEAR ISSUE	EDITION LIMIT	YEAR RETD.	ISSUE PRICE	*QUOTE U.S.$
1983 Cristina #1	2-Yr.	1985	65.00	65-100
1984 Larry #3	2-Yr.	1986	65.00	65-100
1984 Laurel #2	2-Yr.	1986	65.00	65-100
1984 Lesley #3	2-Yr.	1986	65.00	65-100
1985 Mary Ann #4	2-Yr.	1987	70.00	70-150
1985 Molly #4	2-Yr.	1987	50.00	50-100

Jan McLean Originals

Flowers of the Heart Collection - J. McLean

YEAR ISSUE	EDITION LIMIT	YEAR RETD.	ISSUE PRICE	*QUOTE U.S.$
1991 Marigold	100	N/A	2400.00	2900-3200
1990 Pansy	100	N/A	2200.00	2800-2900
1990 Pansy (bobbed blonde)	Retrd.	N/A	2200.00	2800-3000
1990 Pansy, A/P	Retrd.	N/A	4300	4800
1990 Poppy	100	N/A	2200.00	2700
1991 Primrose	100	N/A	2500.00	2500-2600

Jan McLean Originals - J. McLean

YEAR ISSUE	EDITION LIMIT	YEAR RETD.	ISSUE PRICE	*QUOTE U.S.$
1991 Lucrezia	15		6000.00	6000
1990 Phoebe I	25	N/A	2700.00	3300-3600

Kurt S. Adler, Inc.

Fleur-dis-Lis Enchanted Garden - J. Mostrom

YEAR ISSUE	EDITION LIMIT	YEAR RETD.	ISSUE PRICE	*QUOTE U.S.$
1997 Alexandra in Plum W3340	Open		20.00	20
1998 Bethany with Flowers W3461	Open		21.00	21
1997 Bonnie in Ribbons W3343	Open		21.00	21
1997 Celeste the Garden Angel W3344	Retrd.	1997	45.00	45
1998 Jennifer Ballerina W3462	Open		18.00	18
1997 Jenny Lind W3336	Open		28.00	28
1997 Lilac Fairy W3342	Open		22.00	22
1997 Lily Fairy W3342	Open		22.00	22
1997 Marissa In Mauve W3340	Open		20.00	20
1997 Melissa in Lace W3343	Open		21.00	21
1998 Michael with Dog W3463	Open		22.00	22
1998 Monica Ballerina W3462	Open		18.00	18
1998 Natalie with Doll W3461	Open		21.00	21
1998 Pauline with Cat W3463	Open		22.00	22
1997 Rose Fairy W3342	Open		22.00	22
1998 Sarah with Present W3461	Open		21.00	21

Fleur-dis-Lis Victorian Manor - J. Mostrom

YEAR ISSUE	EDITION LIMIT	YEAR RETD.	ISSUE PRICE	*QUOTE U.S.$
1997 Barbara With Muff W3348	Retrd.	1997	30.00	30
1997 Caroling Jane with Book W3338	Retrd.	1997	22.00	22
1997 Jonathan with Horn W3338	Retrd.	1997	22.00	22
1997 Kathryn with Cape W3338	Retrd.	1997	22.00	22
1997 Rebecca Burgundy Skater Lady W3337	Open		32.00	32

Fleur-dis-Lis Winter Dreams - J. Mostrom

YEAR ISSUE	EDITION LIMIT	YEAR RETD.	ISSUE PRICE	*QUOTE U.S.$
1997 Charlotte with Hat & Cape W3345	Retrd.	1997	22.00	22
1997 George with Box W3345	Retrd.	1997	22.00	22
1998 Jack Frost W3483	Open		21.00	21
1998 Joshua with Sled W3485	Open		25.00	25
1998 Kristen with Muff W3485	Open		25.00	25
1998 Patricia with Snowflake W3485	Open		25.00	25
1997 Sandra with Box W3345	Retrd.	1997	22.00	22
1998 Snow Fairy W3483	Open		21.00	21
1998 Snowflake Babies W3482	Open		18.00	18

*Quotes have been rounded up to nearest dollar

Holly Bearies - H. Adler

YEAR ISSUE	EDITION LIMIT	YEAR RETD.	ISSUE PRICE	*QUOTE U.S.$
1998 Ashton, 10" K2032	Open		40.00	40
1997 Charlie, 6 1/2" H6006	Open		11.00	11
1997 Freemont, 15" K2027	Open		80.00	80
1998 Holden, 18" K2031	Open		50.00	50
1998 Merry, Merry Holly Bearie, 12" K2030	Open		35.00	35
1997 Toby, 8" K2025	Open		18.00	18
1998 Zoe, 10" K2033	Open		28.00	28

Royal Heritage Collection - J. Mostrom

YEAR ISSUE	EDITION LIMIT	YEAR RETD.	ISSUE PRICE	*QUOTE U.S.$
1993 Anastasia J5746	3,000	1996	125.00	125
1993 Good King Wenceslas W2928	2,000	1996	130.00	130
1993 Medieval King of Christmas W2981	2,000	1994	390.00	390
1994 Nicholas on Skates J5750	3,000	1996	120.00	120
1994 Sasha on Skates J5749	3,000	1996	130.00	130

Small Wonders - J. Mostrom

YEAR ISSUE	EDITION LIMIT	YEAR RETD.	ISSUE PRICE	*QUOTE U.S.$
1995 America-Hollie Blue W3162	Open		30.00	30
1995 America-Texas Tyler W3162	Open		30.00	30
1995 Ireland-Cathleen W3082	Retrd.	1997	28.00	28
1995 Ireland-Michael W3082	Retrd.	1997	28.00	28
1995 Kwanza-Mufaro W3161	Retrd.	1996	28.00	28
1995 Kwanza-Shani W3161	Retrd.	1996	28.00	28

When I Grow Up - J. Mostrom

YEAR ISSUE	EDITION LIMIT	YEAR RETD.	ISSUE PRICE	*QUOTE U.S.$
1995 Dr. Brown W3079	Retrd.	1996	27.00	27
1995 Freddy the Fireman W3163	Open		28.00	28
1995 Melissa the Teacher W3081	Retrd.	1996	28.00	28
1995 Nurse Nancy W3079	Retrd.	1996	27.00	27
1995 Scott the Golfer W3080	Open	1996	28.00	28

Ladie and Friends

Lizzie High Society™ Members-Only Dolls - B.&P. Wisber

YEAR ISSUE	EDITION LIMIT	YEAR RETD.	ISSUE PRICE	*QUOTE U.S.$
1993 Audrey High -1301	Closed	1992	59.00	450-525
1993 Becky High -1330	Closed	1994	96.00	400-500
1994 Chloe Valentine -1351	Closed	1995	79.00	175-200
1996 Dottie Bowman -1371	Closed	1996	78.00	100-110
1997 Ellie Bowman -1396	Closed	1997	62.00	74-100
1998 Fiona High -1415	12/98		67.00	67

The Christmas Concert - B.&P. Wisber

YEAR ISSUE	EDITION LIMIT	YEAR RETD.	ISSUE PRICE	*QUOTE U.S.$
1990 Claire Valentine -1262	Closed	1997	56.00	68
1993 James Valentine -1310	Closed	1997	60.00	72
1992 Judith High -1292	Closed	1997	70.00	88
1993 Stephanie Bowman -1309	Closed	1998	74.00	77-96

The Christmas Pageant™ - B.&P. Wisber

YEAR ISSUE	EDITION LIMIT	YEAR RETD.	ISSUE PRICE	*QUOTE U.S.$
1985 "Earth" Angel -1122	Closed	1989	30.00	110
1985 "Noel" Angel (1st ed.) -1126	Closed	1989	30.00	110
1989 "Noel" Angel (2nd ed.) -1126	Open		48.00	52
1985 "On" Angel -1121	Closed	1989	30.00	110
1985 "Peace" Angel (1st ed.) -1120	Closed	1989	30.00	110
1989 "Peace" Angel (2nd ed.) -1120	Open		48.00	52
1985 Christmas Wooly Lamb -1133	Closed	1991	11.00	35
1985 Joseph and Donkey -1119	Open		30.00	39
1985 Mary and Baby Jesus -1118	Open		30.00	39
1996 Meredith High -1383	Open		79.50	80
1996 Phillip Valentine -1384	Open		79.50	80
1986 Shepherd -1193	Open		32.00	39
1985 Wiseman #1 -1123	Closed	1996	30.00	47
1985 Wiseman #2 -1124	Closed	1996	30.00	47
1985 Wiseman #3 -1125	Closed	1996	30.00	47
1985 Wooden Creche -1132	Open		28.00	33

The Grummels of Log Hollow™ - B.&P. Wisber

YEAR ISSUE	EDITION LIMIT	YEAR RETD.	ISSUE PRICE	*QUOTE U.S.$
1986 Aunt Gertie Grummel™ -1171	Closed	1988	34.00	115
1986 Aunt Hilda Grummel™ -1174	Closed	1988	34.00	115
1986 Aunt Polly Grummel™ -1169	Closed	1988	34.00	115
1986 Cousin Lottie Grummel™ -1170	Closed	1988	36.00	115
1986 Cousin Miranda Grummel™ -1165	Closed	1988	47.00	115
1986 Grandma Grummel™ -1173	Closed	1988	45.00	115
1986 Grandpa Grummel™ -1176	Closed	1988	36.00	180
1986 The Little Ones -Grummels™ (boy/girl) -1196	Closed	1988	15.00	40
1986 Ma Grummel™ -1167	Closed	1988	36.00	115
1986 Pa Grummel™ -1172	Closed	1988	34.00	115
1986 Sister Nora Grummel™ -1177	Closed	1988	34.00	115
1986 Teddy Bear Bed -1168	Closed	1988	15.00	115
1986 Uncle Hollis Grummel™ -1166	Closed	1988	34.00	115
1986 Washline -1175	Closed	1988	15.00	70-100

The Little Ones at Christmas-Nativity™ - B.&P. Wisber

YEAR ISSUE	EDITION LIMIT	YEAR RETD.	ISSUE PRICE	*QUOTE U.S.$
1995 Donkey -1362	Open		17.00	18
1995 Little Angel -1359	Open		36.00	37
1995 Little Joseph -1358	Open		31.00	32
1995 Little Mary w/Baby in Manger -1357	Open		33.00	34
1995 Little Ones' Creche -1361	Open		24.00	25
1995 Little Shepherd w/Lamb -1360	Open		45.00	46

The Little Ones at Christmas™ - B.&P. Wisber

YEAR ISSUE	EDITION LIMIT	YEAR RETD.	ISSUE PRICE	*QUOTE U.S.$
1990 Girl (black) w/Basket of Greens -1263	Closed	1996	22.00	32
1990 Girl (white) w/Cookie -1264	Closed	1997	22.00	32
1990 Girl (white) w/Gift -1266	Closed	1997	22.00	32
1990 Girl (white) w/Tree Garland -1265	Closed	1997	22.00	32
1991 Boy (black) w/Santa Photo -1273A	Closed	1996	24.00	34
1991 Boy (white) w/Santa Photo -1273	Closed	1996	24.00	34
1991 Girl (black) w/Santa Photo -1272A	Closed	1996	24.00	34
1991 Girl (white) w/Santa Photo -1272	Closed	1996	24.00	34
1993 Boy Peeking (Alone) -1314	Closed	1997	22.00	28
1993 Boy Peeking w/Tree -1313	Closed	1997	60.00	68
1993 Girl w/Baking Table -1317	Open		38.00	40
1993 Girl w/Note for Santa -1318	Open		36.00	38
1993 Girl Peeking (Alone) -1316	Closed	1997	22.00	30
1993 Girl Peeking w/Tree -1315	Closed	1997	60.00	68
1992 Girl w/Christmas Lights -1287	Closed	1998	34.00	37-44
1994 Girl w/Greens on Table -1337	Open		46.00	48
1996 Boy Tangled in Lights -1390	Open		31.00	31
1996 Girl Tangled in Lights -1389	Open		35.00	35
1996 Boy with Ornament -1388	Closed	1997	26.00	30
1996 Girl with Ornament -1387	Closed	1997	30.00	36
1995 Little Santa -1364	Open		50.00	51
1998 Santa -1438	Open		29.95	30

The Little Ones™ - B.&P. Wisber

YEAR ISSUE	EDITION LIMIT	YEAR RETD.	ISSUE PRICE	*QUOTE U.S.$
1985 Boy (black) (1st ed.) -1130	Closed	1989	15.00	45-65
1989 Boy (black) (2nd ed.) -1130I	Closed	1994	20.00	26
1985 Boy (white) (1st ed.) -1130	Closed	1989	15.00	45-65
1989 Boy (white) (2nd ed.) -1130H	Closed	1994	20.00	26
1985 Girl (black) (1st ed.) -1130	Closed	1989	15.00	45-65
1989 Girl (black) -country color (2nd ed.) -1130G	Closed	1994	20.00	26
1989 Girl (black) -pastels (2nd ed.) -1130E	Closed	1994	20.00	26
1985 Girl (white) (1st ed.) -1130	Closed	1989	15.00	45-65
1989 Girl (white) -country color (2nd ed.) -1130F	Closed	1994	20.00	26
1989 Girl (white) -pastels (2nd ed.) -1130H	Closed	1994	20.00	26
1993 4th of July Boy -1307	Open		28.00	30
1993 4th of July Girl -1298	Open		30.00	32
1993 Ballerina -1321	Open		40.00	42
1996 Baseball (boy) -1399	Open		44.00	44
1996 Baseball (girl) -1398	Open		44.00	44
1995 Basketweaver -1363	Open		48.00	49
1997 Blowing Bubbles -1430	Open		41.50	42
1994 Bonnie Valentine -1323	Closed	1998	35.00	37-44
1994 Boy Dyeing Eggs -1327	Open		30.00	32
1993 Boy w/Easter Flowers -1306	Open		30.00	32
1994 Boy w/Pumpkin -1341	Open		29.00	31
1992 Boy w/Sled -1289	Open		30.00	33
1996 Bride -1374	Open		41.50	42
1993 Bunny -1297	Open		36.00	38
1992 Clown -1290	Open		32.00	35
1986 Ghost Petey -1197	Closed	1996	15.00	24
1998 Ghost Petey (2nd ed.) -1197	Open		23.50	24
1994 Girl Dyeing Eggs -1326	Open		30.00	32
1996 Girl Hopscotching -1385	Open		45.00	45
1997 Girl Ironing -1411	Open		48.00	48
1996 Girl in Chair Eating Ice Cream 1400	Open		52.50	53
1993 Girl Picnicking w/ Teddy Bear -1320	Open		34.00	36
1992 Girl Reading -1286	Closed	1997	36.00	39
1996 Girl Rollerskating (black) -1377	Open		40.00	40
1996 Girl Rollerskating (white) -1376	Open		40.00	40
1992 Girl w/Apples -1277	Open		26.00	29
1992 Girl w/Beach Bucket -1275	Open		26.00	29
1992 Girl w/Birthday Gift -1279	Open		26.00	29
1997 Girl w/Dried Flowers & Herbs -1412	Open		32.50	33
1992 Girl w/Easter Eggs -1276	Closed	1997	26.00	29
1993 Girl w/Easter Flowers -1296	Open		34.00	36
1992 Girl w/Kitten and Milk -1280	Closed	1997	32.00	35
1992 Girl w/Kitten and Yarn -1278	Closed	1997	34.00	37
1994 Girl w/Laundry Basket -1338	Open		38.00	40
1993 Girl w/Mop -1300	Open		36.00	38
1994 Girl w/Pumpkin Wagon -1340	Open		42.00	44
1994 Girl w/Puppy in Tub -1339	Open		43.00	45
1997 Girl w/Sheep -1410	Open		44.00	44
1992 Girl w/Snowman -1288	Open		36.00	39
1992 Girl w/Spinning Wheel -1299	Open		36.00	38
1996 Girl w/Sunflower -1373	Open		37.00	37
1992 Girl w/Valentine -1291	Closed	1998	30.00	33-38
1993 Girl w/Violin -1319	Open		28.00	30
1996 Groom -1375	Open		23.50	24
1997 Graduation Boy -1429	Open		29.95	30
1997 Graduation Girl -1428	Open		29.95	30
1994 Jamie Bowman -1324	Closed	1998	35.00	37-44
1995 June Fete (boy) -1350	Closed	1997	33.00	40
1995 June Fete (girl) -1349	Closed	1997	33.00	40
1994 Nurse -1328	Open		40.00	42
1996 Pumpkin Girl -1386	Open		34.00	34
1994 Teacher -1329	Open		38.00	40

Lizzie High® Dolls - B.&P. Wisber

YEAR ISSUE	EDITION LIMIT	YEAR RETD.	ISSUE PRICE	*QUOTE U.S.$
1987 Abigail Bowman (1st ed.) -1199	Closed	1994	40.00	92-100
1997 Abigail Bowman (2nd ed.) -1199	Open		68.50	69
1996 Adam Valentine -1380	Open		69.50	70
1987 Addie High -1202	Closed	1996	37.00	58
1990 Albert Valentine -1260	Closed	1995	42.00	65-85
1986 Alice Valentine (1st ed.) -1148	Closed	1987	32.00	100
1995 Alice Valentine (2nd ed.) -1148	Closed	1998	56.00	58-74
1988 Allison Bowman -1229	Closed	1996	56.00	74-105
1985 Amanda High (1st ed.) -1111	Closed	1988	30.00	116
1990 Amanda High (2nd ed.) -1111	Closed	1995	54.00	65-85
1989 Amelia High -1248	Open		45.00	50
1987 Amy Bowman -1201	Closed	1994	37.00	82
1986 Andrew Brown -1157	Closed	1988	45.00	125
1991 Annabelle Bowman -1267	Closed	1997	68.00	72
1986 Annie Bowman (1st ed.) -1150	Closed	1989	32.00	100
1993 Annie Bowman (2nd ed.) -1150	Closed	1997	68.00	71
1993 Ashley Bowman -1304	Closed	1997	48.00	50
1992 Barbara Helen -1274	Closed	1996	58.00	74
1997 Beatrice High (alone) -1405A	Open		59.50	60
1997 Beatrice High (w/platform) -1405	Open		72.00	72
1985 Benjamin Bowman (Santa) -1134	Closed	1996	34.00	42-50
1985 Benjamin Bowman -1129	Closed	1987	30.00	100
1988 Bess High (2nd ed.) -1241	Open		72.95.	73
1988 Bess High -1241	Closed	1996	45.00	60-100
1996 Beth Bowman (2nd ed.) -1149A	Open		28.50	29
1988 Betsy Valentine -1245	Closed	1996	42.00	56-84
1996 Beverly Ann Bowman -1379	Open		69.50	70
1987 Bridget Bowman (1st ed.) -1222	Closed	1994	40.00	95
1996 Bridget Bowman (2nd ed.) -1222	Open		76.00	76
1997 Caitlin Valentine 1414	Open		79.50	80
1992 Carol Anne Bowman -1282	Closed	1994	70.00	142
1986 Carrie High (1st ed.) -1190	Closed	1989	45.00	100
1989 Carrie High (2nd ed.) -1190	Closed	1997	46.00	50
1986 Cassie Yocum (1st ed.) -1179	Closed	1988	36.00	150
1993 Cassie Yocum (2nd ed.) -1179	Closed	1998	80.00	83-105
1987 Cat on Chair -1217	Closed	1991	16.00	45
1996 Cecelia Brown (alone) -1366A	Closed	1998	27.50	32
1996 Cecelia Brown (w/Mother) -1366	Closed	1998	101.00	118
1987 Charles Bowman (1st ed.) -1221	Closed	1990	34.00	100
1992 Charles Bowman (2nd ed.) -1221	Closed	1995	46.00	58
1996 Charlotte High -1370	Open		73.50	74
1998 Chelsea Bowman -1436	Open		69.95	70
1985 Christian Bowman -1110	Closed	1987	30.00	100
1994 Christine Bowman -1332	Open		62.00	65
1993 Christmas Tree w/Cats -1293A	Open		42.00	44
1986 Christopher High -1182	Closed	1992	34.00	80-100
1997 Clarrisa Bowman -1422	Open		51.95	52
1997 Colleen Bowman -1427	Open		73.50	74
1985 Cora High -1115	Closed	1987	30.00	115
1991 Cynthia High -1127A	Closed	1995	60.00	75
1997 Daisy Bowman -1424	Open		53.95	54
1996 Daniel Brown (alone) -1367A	Closed	1998	27.50	32
1996 Daniel Brown (w/Mother) -1367	Closed	1998	101.00	118
1997 Danielle Valentine -1403	Open		53.50	54
1988 Daphne Bowman -1235	Closed	1994	38.00	76
1996 Darla High -1394	Open		59.50	60
1996 Darlene Bowman -1368	Closed	1997	77.50	78
1986 David Yocum -1195	Closed	1995	33.00	66-85
1986 Delia Valentine (1st ed.) -1153	Closed	1988	32.00	100
1996 Delia Valentine (2nd ed.) -1153	Open		65.50	66
1991 The Department Store Santa -1270	Closed	1996	76.00	100
1986 Dora Valentine (1st ed.) -1152	Closed	1989	30.00	100
1992 Dora Valentine (2nd ed.) -1152	Open		48.00	51
1986 Edward Bowman (1st ed.) -1158	Closed	1988	45.00	125
1994 Edward Bowman (2nd ed.) -1158	Closed	1998	76.00	79-92
1992 Edwin Bowman -1281	Closed	1994	70.00	90
1995 Edwina High -1343	Open		56.00	58
1985 Elizabeth Sweetland (1st ed.) -1109	Closed	1987	30.00	115
1991 Elizabeth Sweetland (2nd ed.) -1109	Closed	1996	56.00	72-85
1998 Elliot Bowman -1435	Open		68.95	69
1994 Elsie Bowman -1325	Open		64.00	67
1986 Emily Bowman (1st ed.) -1185	Closed	1990	34.00	115
1990 Emily Bowman (2nd ed.) -1185	Closed	1996	48.00	58-85
1985 Emma High (1st ed.) -1103	Closed	1988	30.00	100
1996 Emma High (2nd ed.) -1103	Closed	1997	69.50	70
1989 Emmy Lou Valentine -1251	Closed	1997	45.00	59-75
1985 Esther Dunn (1st ed.) -1127	Closed	1987	45.00	125
1991 Esther Dunn (2nd ed.) -1127	Closed	1995	60.00	75-95
1988 Eunice High -1240	Closed	1994	56.00	115-125
1997 Father Christmas -1409	2-Yr.		84.00	84
1985 Flossie High (1st ed.) -1128	Closed	1988	45.00	125
1989 Flossie High (2nd ed.) -1128	Closed	1997	54.00	59-72
1987 The Flower Girl -1204	Closed	1995	17.00	50
1996 Francine Bowman -1381	Open		60.00	60
1993 Francis Bowman -1305	Closed	1997	48.00	50-60
1994 Gilbert High -1335	Open		65.00	68
1996 Glenda Brown -1382	Open		60.00	60
1986 Grace Valentine (1st ed.) -1146	Closed	1989	32.00	100
1991 Grace Valentine (2nd ed.) -1146	Open		48.00	51
1987 Gretchen High -1216	Closed	1994	40.00	88
1994 Gwendolyn High -1342	Open		56.00	59
1997 Haley Valentine - 1418	Open		81.95	82
1985 Hannah Brown -1131	Closed	1988	45.00	125
1997 Harriet Bowman -1417	Open		51.95	52
1988 Hattie Bowman -1239	Closed	1996	40.00	88
1985 Ida Valentine -1116	Closed	1988	30.00	100
1987 Imogene Bowman -1206	Closed	1994	37.00	90
1988 Jacob High -1230	Closed	1994	44.00	88-102
1988 Janie Valentine -1231	Closed	1996	37.00	52
1997 Jared Valentine 1418A	Open		81.95	82
1989 Jason High (alone) -1254A	Closed	1996	20.00	30-50
1989 Jason High (with Mother) -1254	Closed	1996	58.00	75-85
1986 Jenny Valentine (1st ed.) -1181	Closed	1989	34.00	110
1997 Jenny Valentine (2nd ed.) -1181	Open		52.00	52
1986 Jeremy Bowman -1192	Closed	1991	36.00	80
1989 Jessica High (alone) -1253A	Closed	1996	20.00	30-50
1989 Jessica High (with Mother) -1253	Closed	1996	58.00	75-85
1986 Jillian Bowman (1st ed.) -1180	Closed	1990	34.00	110
1995 Jillian Bowman (2nd ed.) -1180	Closed	1998	90.00	92-108
1992 Joanie Valentine -1295	Closed	1998	48.00	51-60
1989 Johann Bowman -1250	Closed	1997	40.00	44-52
1987 Johanna Valentine -1198	Closed	1988	37.00	100
1992 Joseph Valentine -1283	Closed	1995	62.00	75
1994 Josie Valentine -1322	Closed	1998	76.00	79-92
1986 Juliet Valentine (1st ed.) -1147	Closed	1988	32.00	100
1990 Juliet Valentine (2nd ed.) -1147	Closed	1996	48.00	62
1993 Justine Valentine -1302	Closed	1997	84.00	87
1986 Karl Valentine (1st ed.) -1161	Closed	1988	30.00	100
1994 Karl Valentine (2nd ed.) -1161	Open		54.00	57
1987 Katie and Barney (1st Costume)-1219	Closed	1996	38.00	43
1987 Katie and Barney (2nd Costume)-1219	Closed	1996	38.00	43-85
1986 Katie Bowman -1178	Closed	1994	36.00	96
1985 Katrina Valentine -1135	Closed	1989	30.00	125
1997 Kelsey Bowman -1420	Open		64.95	65
1988 Kinch Bowman -1237	Closed	1996	47.00	62
1987 Laura Valentine -1223	Closed	1994	36.00	86-95

*Quotes have been rounded up to nearest dollar

YEAR ISSUE	EDITION LIMIT	YEAR RETD.	ISSUE PRICE	*QUOTE U.S.$
1995 Leona High -1355	Open		68.00	70
1998 Lindsey Valentine -1434	Open		74.95	75
1987 Little Witch -1225	Closed	1996	17.00	28
1998 The Littlest Angel (Christmas Tree Topper) -1437	Open		49.50	50
1985 Lizzie High® (1st ed.) -1100	Closed	1995	30.00	100-115
1996 Lizzie High® (2nd ed.) -1100	Open		92.00	92
1996 Lottie Bowman -1395	Open		96.50	97
1985 Louella Valentine -1112	Closed	1991	30.00	100
1996 Louis Bowman -1149B	Open		28.50	29
1989 Lucy Bowman -1255	Closed	1997	45.00	49-59
1985 Luther Bowman (1st ed.) -1108	Closed	1987	30.00	100
1993 Luther Bowman (2nd ed.) -1108	Open		60.00	63
1995 Lydia Bowman -1347	Closed	1997	54.00	55-66
1986 Madaleine Valentine (1st ed.) -1187	Closed	1989	34.00	90
1989 Madaleine Valentine (2nd ed.) -1187	Closed	1997	37.00	50-60
1986 Maggie High -1160	Closed	1988	30.00	100
1996 Maisie Bowman -1392	Open		57.50	58
1987 Margaret Bowman -1213	Closed	1996	35.00	53-70
1986 Marie Valentine (1st ed.) -1184	Closed	1990	47.00	125
1992 Marie Valentine (2nd ed.) -1184	Closed	1996	68.00	86-95
1986 Marisa Valentine (alone) (1st ed.) -1194A	Closed	1996	33.00	66
1998 Marisa Valentine (alone) (2nd ed.) -1194A	Open		57.50	58
1986 Marisa Valentine (w/ Brother Petey) (1st ed.) -1194	Closed	1996	45.00	88
1998 Marisa Valentine (w/ Brother Petey) (2nd ed.) -1194	Open		79.95	80
1994 Marisa Valentine -1333	Open		58.00	61
1986 Marland Valentine -1183	Closed	1990	33.00	100-150
1990 Marlene Valentine -1259	Closed	1995	48.00	75-85
1986 Martha High -1151	Closed	1989	32.00	100
1985 Martin Bowman (1st ed.) -1117	Closed	1992	30.00	85-100
1996 Martin Bowman (2nd ed.) -1117	Open		64.00	64
1988 Mary Ellen Valentine -1236	Closed	1996	40.00	54
1985 Mary Valentine -1105	Closed	1988	30.00	100
1996 Matilda High -1393	Open		59.50	60
1986 Matthew Yocum -1186	Closed	1988	33.00	100
1995 Mattie Dunn -1344	Open		56.00	58
1998 Maureen Valentine -1433	Open		55.95	56
1988 Megan Valentine -1227	Closed	1994	44.00	94
1987 Melanie Bowman (1st ed.) -1220	Closed	1990	36.00	125
1992 Melanie Bowman (2nd ed.) -1220	Closed	1995	46.00	48-58
1996 Melody Valentine -1401	Open		66.50	67
1991 Michael Bowman -1268	Closed	1997	52.00	55-66
1997 Millicent High -1407	Open		59.00	59
1994 Minnie Valentine -1336	Open		64.00	67
1997 Miranda High - 1426	Open		57.50	58
1989 Miriam High -1256	Closed	1997	46.00	50-60
1986 Molly Yocum (1st ed.) -1189	Closed	1989	34.00	80-100
1989 Molly Yocum (2nd ed.) -1189	Closed	1997	39.00	43-52
1993 Mommy -1312	Closed	1998	48.00	49-59
1989 Mrs. Claus -1258	Closed	1997	42.00	46-54
1990 Nancy Bowman -1261	Closed	1997	48.00	52-62
1987 Naomi Valentine -1200	Closed	1993	40.00	88
1992 Natalie Valentine -1284	Closed	1995	62.00	75-90
1995 Nathan Bowman -1354	Open		70.00	72
1985 Nettie Brown (1st ed.) -1102	Closed	1987	30.00	100
1988 Nettie Brown (2nd ed.) -1102	Closed	1995	36.00	72-85
1985 Nettie Brown (Christmas) (1st ed.) -1114	Closed	1987	30.00	100
1996 Nettie Brown (Christmas) (2nd ed.) -1114	Open		66.00	66
1996 Nicholas Valentine (alone) -1365A	Closed	1998	27.50	32
1996 Nicholas Valentine (w/Mother) -1365	Closed	1998	101.00	118
1997 Nicole Bowman -1421	Open		66.95	67
1987 Olivia High -1205	Closed	1997	37.00	43-52
1998 Ophelia High -1432	Open		97.50	98
1987 Patsy Bowman -1214	Closed	1995	50.00	110-115
1988 Pauline Bowman -1228	Closed	1996	44.00	58-75
1993 Pearl Bowman -1303	Closed	1998	56.00	59-68
1989 Peggy Bowman -1252	Closed	1995	58.00	90-100
1987 Penelope High -1208	Closed	1991	40.00	100
1993 Penny Valentine -1308	Open		60.00	63
1985 Peter Valentine (1st ed.) -1113	Closed	1991	30.00	75
1995 Peter Valentine (2nd ed.) -1113	Open		55.00	57
1988 Phoebe High (1st ed.) -1246	Closed	1992	48.00	90
1997 Phoebe High (2nd ed.) -1246	Open		65.50	66
1997 Polly Bowman -1404	Open		65.00	65
1987 Priscilla High -1226	Closed	1995	56.00	130-135
1986 Rachel Bowman (1st ed.) -1188	Closed	1989	34.00	100
1989 Rachel Bowman (2nd ed.) -1188	Closed	1997	34.00	60
1987 Ramona Brown -1215	Closed	1989	40.00	66
1985 Rebecca Bowman (1st ed.) -1104	Closed	1988	30.00	100
1989 Rebecca Bowman (2nd ed.) -1104	Closed	1997	56.00	62-74
1987 Rebecca's Mother (2nd ed.) -1207	Closed	1995	75.95	76
1987 Rebecca's Mother -1207	Closed	1995	37.00	86-100
1995 Regina Bowman -1353	Open		70.00	72
1995 Robert Bowman -1348	Closed	1997	64.00	66-80
1985 Russell Dunn -1107	Closed	1987	30.00	110
1988 Ruth Anne Bowman -1232	Closed	1994	44.00	92-100
1985 Sabina Valentine (1st ed.) -1101	Closed	1987	30.00	110
1988 Sabina Valentine (2nd ed.) -1101	Closed	1996	40.00	53-80
1986 Sadie Valentine -1163	Closed	1996	45.00	72-105
1986 Sally Bowman (1st ed.) -1155	Closed	1991	32.00	110
1996 Sally Bowman (2nd ed.) -1155	Open		75.50	76
1988 Samantha Bowman -1238	Closed	1996	47.00	61-85
1989 Santa (with Tub) -1257	Closed	1997	58.00	64-78
1987 Santa Claus (sitting) -1224	Closed	1991	50.00	75-125
1993 Santa Claus -1311	Closed	1998	48.00	50-59
1991 Santa's Helper -1271	Closed	1996	52.00	62-75
1986 Sara Valentine -1154	Closed	1994	32.00	90
1997 Sean Fitzpatrick - 1419	Open		59.50	60
1996 Shannon Fitzpatrick -1391	Open		59.00	59
1994 Shirley Bowman -1334	Open		63.00	66
1986 Sophie Valentine (1st ed.) -1164	Closed	1991	45.00	125
1996 Sophie Valentine (alone) -1164A	Closed	1998	27.50	32
1996 Sophie Valentine (w/Mother) (2nd ed.) -1164	Closed	1998	101.00	118
1995 St. Nicholas -1356	Open		98.00	100
1986 Susanna Bowman (1st ed.) -1149	Closed	1988	45.00	125
1996 Susanna Bowman (2nd ed.) -1149	Open		49.50	50
1997 Theodore Bowman -1408	Open		59.00	59
1997 Theresa Valentine -1406	Open		53.00	53
1986 Thomas Bowman (1st ed.) -1159	Closed	1987	30.00	100
1996 Thomas Bowman (2nd ed.) -1159	Open		59.50	60
1986 Tillie Brown -1156	Closed	1988	32.00	100
1992 Timothy Bowman -1294	Open		56.00	60
1997 Travis Bowman -1402	Open		53.50	54
1991 Trudy Valentine -1269	Closed	1997	64.00	68-82
1996 Tucker Bowman -1369	Closed	1997	77.50	78
1989 Vanessa High -1247	Closed	1996	45.00	60
1989 Victoria Bowman -1249	Closed	1997	40.00	44-52
1997 Webster Bowman -1425	Open		68.50	69
1987 The Wedding (Bride) -1203	Closed	1995	37.00	100
1987 The Wedding (Groom) -1203A	Closed	1995	34.00	75
1985 Wendel Bowman (1st ed.) -1106	Closed	1987	30.00	100
1992 Wendel Bowman (2nd ed.) -1106	Closed	1996	60.00	75
1992 Wendy Bowman -1293	Open		78.00	82
1986 William Valentine -1191	Closed	1992	36.00	80
1986 Willie Bowman -1162	Closed	1992	30.00	72
1997 Winnie Valentine - 1423	Open		82.95	83

The Pawtuckets of Sweet Briar Lane™ - B.&P. Wisber

YEAR ISSUE	EDITION LIMIT	YEAR RETD.	ISSUE PRICE	*QUOTE U.S.$
1986 Aunt Lillian Pawtucket™ (1st ed.) -1141	Closed	1989	32.00	125
1994 Aunt Lillian Pawtucket™ (2nd ed.) -1141	Closed	1998	58.00	61-70
1987 Aunt Mabel Pawtucket™ -212	Closed	1989	45.00	140
1986 Aunt Minnie Pawtucket™ (w/Flossie) (1st ed.) -1136	Closed	1989	45.00	115
1994 Aunt Minnie Pawtucket™ (2nd ed.) -1136	Closed	1998	72.00	75-88
1986 Brother Noah Pawtucket™ -1140	Closed	1989	32.00	115
1987 Bunny Bed -1218	Closed	1989	16.00	115
1987 Cousin Alberta Pawtucket™ -1210	Closed	1989	36.00	115
1986 Cousin Clara Pawtucket™ (1st ed.) -1144	Closed	1989	32.00	115
1996 Cousin Clara Pawtucket™ (2nd ed.) -1144	Closed	1998	84.00	84-100
1987 Cousin Isabel Pawtucket™ -1209	Closed	1989	36.00	115
1988 Cousin Jed Pawtucket™ -1234	Closed	1990	34.00	115
1988 Cousin Winnie Pawtucket™ -1233	Closed	1990	49.00	115
1994 Flossie Pawtucket™ (2nd ed.) -1136A	Closed	1998	33.00	35-40
1986 Grammy Pawtucket™ (1st ed.) -1137	Closed	1989	32.00	115-150
1994 Grammy Pawtucket™ (2nd ed.) -1137	Closed	1998	68.00	71-82
1995 The Little One Bunnies (1995) -female w/ laundry basket -1211A	Closed	1998	33.00	34-40
1986 The Little One Bunnies -boy (1st ed.) -1145	Closed	1989	15.00	50
1994 The Little One Bunnies -boy (2nd ed.) -1145A	Closed	1998	33.00	35-40
1986 The Little One Bunnies -girl (1st ed.) -1145	Closed	1989	15.00	40-50
1994 The Little One Bunnies -girl (2nd ed.) -1145	Closed	1998	33.00	35
1986 Mama Pawtucket™ (1st ed.) -1142	Closed	1989	34.00	115
1994 Mama Pawtucket™ (2nd ed.) -1142	Closed	1998	86.00	89-106
1986 Pappy Pawtucket™ (1st ed.) -1143	Closed	1989	32.00	115
1995 Pappy Pawtucket™ (2nd ed.) -1143	Closed	1998	56.00	58-68
1994 Pawtucket™ Bunny Hutch -1141A	Closed	1998	38.00	40-47
1995 Pawtucket™ Wash Line -1211B	Closed	1998	20.00	21-24
1987 Sister Clemmie Pawtucket™ (1st ed.) -1211	Closed	1989	34.00	115
1995 Sister Clemmie Pawtucket™ (2nd ed.) -1211	Closed	1998	60.00	62-72
1986 Sister Flora Pawtucket™ (1st ed.) -1139	Closed	1989	32.00	115
1996 Sister Flora Pawtucket™ (2nd ed.) -1139	Closed	1998	63.50	64-75
1986 Uncle Harley Pawtucket™ (1st ed.) -1138	Closed	1989	32.00	115
1994 Uncle Harley Pawtucket™ (2nd ed.) -1138	Closed	1998	74.00	77-90

Special Editions - B.&P. Wisber

YEAR ISSUE	EDITION LIMIT	YEAR RETD.	ISSUE PRICE	*QUOTE U.S.$
1992 Kathryn Bowman™ -1992 -1285	3,000	1992	140.00	800
1994 Prudence Valentine™ -1994 -1331	4,000	1994	180.00	350-400
1995 Little Lizzie High® -Anniversary Special Event Edition	Yr.Iss.	1995	40.00	60-100
1995 Lizzie High® -10th Anniversary Signature Edition -1100A	Yr.Iss.	1995	90.00	120-200
1996 Little Rebecca Bowman™ -1996 Special Event Edition -1372	Yr.Iss.	1996	37.00	57-80
1996 Lizzie & The Pawtuckets™ -1378	3,000	1996	180.00	180-250
1997 Libby Bowman - One-of-a-Kind Auction Doll & Teddy Bear Expo West	1	1997	N/A	1500
1997 Michelle Valentine -1997 Doll & Teddy Bear Expo Show Special (East & West)	150	1997	59.00	120-275
1997 Little Amanda High -1997 Special Event Edition -1397	Closed	1997	36.00	36-42
1998 Caroline Rebecca High - Golden Goose Store Exclusive	750	1998	79.95	80
1998 Courtney Valentine -1431	3,000	1998	158.00	158
1998 Little Sally Bowman -1998 Special Event Edition -1416	Closed	1998	36.95	37

The Thanksgiving Play - B.&P. Wisber

YEAR ISSUE	EDITION LIMIT	YEAR RETD.	ISSUE PRICE	*QUOTE U.S.$
1998 Father Pilgrim (2nd ed.) -1242	Open		55.95	56
1988 Indian Squaw -1244	Closed	1995	36.00	62-90
1998 Mother Pilgrim (2nd ed.) -1243	Open		65.95	66
1988 Pilgrim Boy -1242	Closed	1995	40.00	52-90
1998 Pilgrim Boy -1242A	Open		29.95	30
1988 Pilgrim Girl -1243	Closed	1995	48.00	60-90
1998 Pilgrim Girl -1243A	Open		32.95	33

Lawtons

Guild Dolls - W. Lawton

YEAR ISSUE	EDITION LIMIT	YEAR RETD.	ISSUE PRICE	*QUOTE U.S.$
1989 Baa Baa Black Sheep	1,003	1989	395.00	650-700
1990 Lavender Blue	781	1990	395.00	400
1991 To Market, To Market	683	1991	495.00	600
1992 Little Boy Blue	510	1992	395.00	395
1993 Lawton Logo Doll	575	1993	350.00	500
1994 Wee Handful	540	1994	250.00	295
1995 Uniquely Yours	500	1995	395.00	395
1996 Teddy And Me	601	1996	450.00	450
1997 The Lawton Travel Doll	485	1997	695.00	695
1998 Baby Boutique Blue	Yr.Iss.		495.00	495
1998 Baby Boutique Pink	Yr.Iss.		495.00	495

Cherished Customs - W. Lawton

YEAR ISSUE	EDITION LIMIT	YEAR RETD.	ISSUE PRICE	*QUOTE U.S.$
1990 The Blessing/Mexico	500	1990	395.00	1000-1200
1992 Carnival/Brazil	750	1992	425.00	495
1992 Cradleboard/Navajo	750	1993	425.00	495
1991 Frolic/Amish	500	1991	395.00	395
1990 Girl's Day/Japan	500	1990	395.00	450
1990 High Tea/Great Britain	500	1990	395.00	500-550
1994 Kwanzaa/Africa	500	1994	425.00	495
1990 Midsommar/Sweden	500	1990	395.00	450
1993 Nalauqataq-Eskimo	500	1993	395.00	450
1991 Ndeko/Zaire	500	1991	395.00	550
1992 Pascha/Ukraine	750	1992	495.00	495
1995 Piping the Haggis	350	1995	495.00	550
1993 Topeng Klana-Java	250	1993	495.00	495

Childhood Classics® - W. Lawton

YEAR ISSUE	EDITION LIMIT	YEAR RETD.	ISSUE PRICE	*QUOTE U.S.$
1983 Alice In Wonderland	100	1983	225.00	2000
1986 Anne Of Green Gables	250	1986	325.00	1600-2400
1991 The Bobbsey Twins: Flossie	350	1991	364.50	500
1991 The Bobbsey Twins: Freddie	350	1991	364.50	500
1985 Hans Brinker	250	1985	325.00	1800
1984 Heidi	250	1984	325.00	650
1991 Hiawatha	500	1991	395.00	500
1989 Honey Bunch	250	1989	350.00	550
1987 Just David	250	1987	325.00	700
1986 Laura Ingalls	250	1986	325.00	500
1991 Little Black Sambo	500	1991	395.00	695
1988 Little Eva	250	1988	350.00	700-900
1989 Little Princess	250	1989	395.00	600
1990 Mary Frances	350	1990	350.00	350
1987 Mary Lennox	250	1987	325.00	550-600
1987 Polly Pepper	250	1987	325.00	450
1986 Pollyanna	250	1986	325.00	1600
1990 Poor Little Match Girl	350	1990	350.00	550
1988 Rebecca	250	1988	350.00	450
1988 Topsy	250	1988	350.00	750

The Children's Hour - W. Lawton

YEAR ISSUE	EDITION LIMIT	YEAR RETD.	ISSUE PRICE	*QUOTE U.S.$
1991 Edith With Golden Hair	500	1991	395.00	475
1991 Grave Alice	500	1991	395.00	475
1991 Laughing Allegra	500	1991	395.00	475

Christmas Dolls - W. Lawton

YEAR ISSUE	EDITION LIMIT	YEAR RETD.	ISSUE PRICE	*QUOTE U.S.$
1988 Christmas Joy	500	1988	325.00	800
1989 Noel	500	1989	325.00	450
1990 Christmas Angel	500	1990	325.00	450
1991 Yuletide Carole	500	1991	395.00	450
1996 The Bird's Christmas Carol	500	1996	450.00	450

Newcomer Collection - W. Lawton

YEAR ISSUE	EDITION LIMIT	YEAR RETD.	ISSUE PRICE	*QUOTE U.S.$
1987 Ellin Elizabeth, Eyes Closed	49	1987	335.00	750-1000
1987 Ellin Elizabeth, Eyes Open	19	1987	335.00	900-1200

Playthings Past - W. Lawton

YEAR ISSUE	EDITION LIMIT	YEAR RETD.	ISSUE PRICE	*QUOTE U.S.$
1989 Edward And Dobbin	500	1989	395.00	495-600
1989 Elizabeth And Baby	500	1989	395.00	495-650
1989 Victoria And Teddy	500	1989	395.00	395

Special Edition - W. Lawton

YEAR ISSUE	EDITION LIMIT	YEAR RETD.	ISSUE PRICE	*QUOTE U.S.$
1993 Flora McFlimsey	250	1993	895.00	1000
1988 Marcella And Raggedy Ann	2,500	1988	395.00	800-950
1994 Mary Chilton	350	1994	395.00	395
1995 Through The Looking Glass	180	1995	N/A	1700

Special Occasion - W. Lawton

YEAR ISSUE	EDITION LIMIT	YEAR RETD.	ISSUE PRICE	*QUOTE U.S.$
1990 First Birthday	500	1990	295.00	350
1989 First Day Of School	500	1989	325.00	525
1988 Nanthy	500	1988	325.00	525

Sugar 'n' Spice - W. Lawton

YEAR ISSUE	EDITION LIMIT	YEAR RETD.	ISSUE PRICE	*QUOTE U.S.$
1987 Ginger	454	1987	275.00	395-550
1986 Jason	27	1986	250.00	800-1700
1986 Jessica	30	1986	250.00	800-1700
1986 Kersten	103	1986	250.00	550-800
1986 Kimberly	87	1986	250.00	550-800

*Quotes have been rounded up to nearest dollar

YEAR ISSUE	EDITION LIMIT	YEAR RETD.	ISSUE PRICE	*QUOTE U.S.$
1987 Marie	208	1987	275.00	450

Timeless Ballads® - W. Lawton

YEAR ISSUE	EDITION LIMIT	YEAR RETD.	ISSUE PRICE	*QUOTE U.S.$
1987 Annabel Lee	250	1987	550.00	600-695
1987 Highland Mary	250	1987	550.00	700-900
1988 She Walks In Beauty	250	1988	550.00	700-800
1987 Young Charlotte	250	1987	550.00	900-950

Wee Bits - W. Lawton

YEAR ISSUE	EDITION LIMIT	YEAR RETD.	ISSUE PRICE	*QUOTE U.S.$
1989 Wee Bit O'Bliss	250	1989	295.00	350
1988 Wee Bit O'Heaven	250	1988	295.00	350
1988 Wee Bit O'Sunshine	250	1988	295.00	350
1988 Wee Bit O'Woe	250	1988	295.00	350
1989 Wee Bit O'Wonder	250	1989	295.00	350

Lee Middleton Original Dolls

Lee's Doll Family - Lee Middleton

YEAR ISSUE	EDITION LIMIT	YEAR RETD.	ISSUE PRICE	*QUOTE U.S.$
1997 Bye Baby Blessed Homecoming	Retrd.	1998	175.00	175
1998 Bye Baby To Grandmother's House We Go	3/99		175.00	175

Birthday Babies - Lee Middleton

YEAR ISSUE	EDITION LIMIT	YEAR RETD.	ISSUE PRICE	*QUOTE U.S.$
1992 Winter	Retrd.	1994	180.00	180
1992 Fall	Retrd.	1994	170.00	170
1992 Summer	Retrd.	1994	160.00	160
1992 Spring	3,000	1994	170.00	170

Christmas Angel Collection - Lee Middleton

YEAR ISSUE	EDITION LIMIT	YEAR RETD.	ISSUE PRICE	*QUOTE U.S.$
1987 Christmas Angel 1987	4,174	1987	130.00	500-600
1988 Christmas Angel 1988	8,969	1988	130.00	250-300
1989 Christmas Angel 1989	7,500	1991	150.00	225
1990 Christmas Angel 1990	5,000	1991	150.00	200
1991 Christmas Angel 1991	5,000	1992	180.00	225
1992 Christmas Angel 1992	5,000	1995	190.00	200
1993 Christmas Angel 1993-Girl	3,144	1995	190.00	200
1993 Christmas Angel 1993 (set)	1,000	1993	390.00	500
1994 Christmas Angel 1994	5,000	1996	190.00	190
1995 Christmas Angel 1995 (wh. or blk.)	3,000	1996	190.00	225
1996 Christmas Angel 1996 (Shall I Play For You)	2,000		250.00	250

Fifties Series - Lee Middleton

YEAR ISSUE	EDITION LIMIT	YEAR RETD.	ISSUE PRICE	*QUOTE U.S.$
1996 Angel Kisses Earth Angel	1,500	1997	130.00	130
1996 Angel Kisses Splish Splash	1,500	1997	130.00	130
1996 Little Angel Leader of the Pack	1,500	1997	130.00	130
1996 Polly Esther Car Hop	1,500	1997	130.00	130
1996 Polly Esther Peggy Sue	1,500	1997	130.00	130

First Collectibles - Lee Middleton

YEAR ISSUE	EDITION LIMIT	YEAR RETD.	ISSUE PRICE	*QUOTE U.S.$
1990 Sweetest Little Dreamer (Asleep)	Retrd.	1993	40.00	59
1990 Day Dreamer (Awake)	Retrd.	1993	42.00	59
1991 Day Dreamer Sunshine	Retrd.	1993	49.00	49
1991 Teenie	Retrd.	1993	59.00	59

First Moments Series - Lee Middleton

YEAR ISSUE	EDITION LIMIT	YEAR RETD.	ISSUE PRICE	*QUOTE U.S.$
1984 First Moments (Sleeping)	40,861	1990	69.00	300
1992 First Moments Awake in Blue	1,230	1994	170.00	170
1992 First Moments Awake in Pink	856	1994	170.00	170
1986 First Moments Blue Eyes	14,494	1990	120.00	150
1987 First Moments Boy	6,075	1989	130.00	160
1986 First Moments Brown Eyes	5,324	1989	120.00	150
1987 First Moments Christening (Asleep)	9,377	1992	160.00	250
1987 First Moments Christening (Awake)	16,384	1992	160.00	180
1993 First Moments Heirloom	1,372	1995	190.00	190
1991 First Moments Sweetness	6,323	1995	180.00	180
1990 First Moments Twin Boy	2,971	1991	180.00	180
1990 First Moments Twin Girl	2,544	1991	180.00	180
1994 Sweetness-Newborn	Retrd.	1995	190.00	190

Home Shopping Network Series - Lee Middleton

YEAR ISSUE	EDITION LIMIT	YEAR RETD.	ISSUE PRICE	*QUOTE U.S.$
1996 Bye Baby Bundle of Joy	2,000	1996	129.00	129
1996 Cherish Ribbons and Bows	2,000	1996	129.00	129
1997 Cherish Sleeping Angels	2,000	1997	129.00	129
1996 First Born Dark Precious Baby Girl	1,000	1996	129.00	129
1997 First Born Dark Snug As A Bug	1,000	1997	129.00	129
1996 First Born Gingham and Lace	2,000	1996	129.00	129
1996 First Born Katie	2,000	1996	129.00	129
1997 First Born Mother's Dream	2,000	1997	129.00	129
1997 First Born Open Eye Bed of Roses	2,000	1997	129.00	129
1997 First Born Open Eye Dark Snug As A Bug	1,000	1997	129.00	129
1997 First Born Open Eye Precious Traditions	2,000	1997	129.00	129
1996 First Moments Open Eye Baseball Boy	2,000	1996	129.00	129
1997 Honey Love Answered Prayer Boy	2,000	1997	129.00	129
1997 Honey Love Answered Prayer Girl	2,000	1997	129.00	129
1997 Honey Love Dark Baby's Sleeping	1,000	1997	129.00	129
1997 Honey Love Open Eye Little Peep	2,000	1997	129.00	129
1996 Little Blessing Awake Grandma's Little Boy	2,000	1997	129.00	129
1997 Little Blessing Open Eye Bundle Up Boy	2,000	1997	129.00	129
1997 Little Blessing Open Eye Bundle Up Girl	2,000	1997	129.00	129
1997 Little Blessing Open Eye Mother's Little Sweetheart (blue)	2,000	1997	129.00	129
1997 Little Blessing Open Eye Mother's Little Sweetheart (pink)	2,000	1997	129.00	129
1997 Little Love Baby Brother	2,000	1997	129.00	129
1997 Little Love Baby Sister	2,000	1997	129.00	129
1996 Little Love Baby's First Book	2,000	1996	129.00	129
1997 Little Love Bunny Surprise	2,000	1997	129.00	129
1996 Little Love Sleepy Time	2,000	1996	129.00	129

Kewpie Series - R. O'Neill

YEAR ISSUE	EDITION LIMIT	YEAR RETD.	ISSUE PRICE	*QUOTE U.S.$
1997 Almost Angelic	Open		42.00	42
1997 Breezy	Open		42.00	42
1997 Buddy	Open		52.00	52
1997 Rosebud	Open		52.00	52

Limited Edition Vinyl - Lee Middleton

YEAR ISSUE	EDITION LIMIT	YEAR RETD.	ISSUE PRICE	*QUOTE U.S.$
1998 All Dolled Up	5,000		180.00	180
1993 Amanda Springtime	612	1994	180.00	225
1989 Angel Fancy	5,310	1992	120.00	195
1995 Angel Kisses-Belly Dancer	1,000	1995	139.00	139
1990 Angel Locks	8,140	1992	140.00	150
1991 Baby Grace	4,862	1991	190.00	250
1994 Beloved-Happy Birthday (Blue)	1,000	1995	220.00	250
1994 Beloved-Happy Birthday (Pink)	1,000	1995	220.00	250
1992 Beth	1,414	1994	160.00	160
1995 Beth-Flapper	1,000	1995	119.00	119
1995 Bethie Bows	1,000	1996	150.00	150
1995 Bethie Buttons	1,000	1996	150.00	150
1998 Bo Peep	2,000		170.00	170
1995 The Bride	1,000	1995	250.00	250
1991 Bubba Batboy	3,925	1994	190.00	190
1997 Bunny Love	5,000		180.00	180
1998 Cat Nap	2,000		170.00	170
1997 Christmas Surprise Asleep Red Stocking	Open		180.00	180
1997 Christmas Surprise Asleep White Stocking	Open		180.00	180
1997 Christmas Surprise Awake Red Stocking	Open		180.00	180
1997 Christmas Surprise Awake White Stocking	Open		180.00	180
1992 Cottontop Cherish	3,525	1994	180.00	180
1998 Country Cozy	2,500		170.00	170
1991 Dear One-Sunday Best	1,371	1994	140.00	140
1991 Devan Delightful	4,520	1994	170.00	160-295
1997 Feelin' Froggy	2,000	1998	160.00	160
1990 Forever Cherish	5,000	1991	170.00	200
1995 Gordon-Growing Up	1,000	1995	220.00	220
1995 Grace-Growing Up	1,000	1995	220.00	220
1992 Gracie Mae (Blond Hair)	3,660	1995	250.00	250
1992 Gracie Mae (Brown Hair)	2,551	1994	250.00	250
1993 Gracie Mae (Red Velvet)	100	1993	250.00	250
1997 Heaven Sent Asleep	7,500		180.00	180
1997 Heaven Sent Awake	7,500		180.00	180
1994 Joey-Newborn	1,000	1995	180.00	180
1991 Johanna	1,388	1994	190.00	250
1994 Johanna-Newborn	2,000	1994	180.00	180
1995 Little Angel-Ballerina	1,000	1995	119.00	119
1985 Little Angel-King-2 (Hand Painted)	Retrd.	1985	40.00	200
1981 Little Angel-Kingdom (Hand Painted)	Retrd.	1981	40.00	300
1995 Little Blessings Awake Boy	1,000	1995	180.00	180
1995 Little Blessings Awake Girl	1,000	1995	180.00	180
1995 Little Blessings Blessed Event	1,500	1995	190.00	190
1995 Little Blessings Sleeping Boy	1,000	1995	180.00	180
1995 Little Blessings Sleeping Girl	1,000	1995	180.00	180
1998 Little Boy Blue	2,000		170.00	170
1998 Little Patty Cake	2,800		170.00	170
1998 Little Playmate	2,000		170.00	170
1998 Loving Tribute	Yr.Iss.		220.00	220
1997 Lullaby Baby Boy	5,000	1998	180.00	180
1997 Lullaby Baby Girl	5,000	1997	180.00	180
1998 Mary Mary	2,000		170.00	170
1991 Missy- Buttercup	4,748	1994	160.00	200
1992 Molly Rose	2,981	1994	196.00	196
1991 My Lee Candy Cane	2,240	1994	170.00	295
1993 Patty	4,000	1995	49.00	49
1998 Patty Cake	2,000		170.00	170
1997 Picture Perfect	7,500		190.00	190
1998 Proud Heritage/Boy	2,000		164.00	164
1998 Proud Heritage/Girl	2,000		164.00	164
1998 Quiet As A Mouse	Yr.Iss.		180.00	180
1998 Santa's Little Helper/Boy	Yr.Iss.		180.00	180
1998 Santa's Little Helper/Girl	Yr.Iss.		180.00	180
1992 Serenity Berries & Bows	458	1993	250.00	250
1992 Sincerity Petals & Plums	414	1993	250.00	250
1991 Sincerity-Apples n' Spice	1,608	1993	250.00	250
1991 Sincerity-Apricots n' Cream	1,789	1993	250.00	250
1998 Slumber Kisses	1,000		170.00	170
1998 Softly Sleeping	2,000		164.00	164
1998 Starry Night	2,500		170.00	170
1997 Summerfun - Asleep Boy	5,000		170.00	170
1997 Summerfun - Asleep Dark Boy	2,000		170.00	170
1997 Summerfun - Asleep Dark Girl	2,000		170.00	170
1997 Summerfun - Asleep Girl	5,000		170.00	170
1997 Summerfun - Awake Boy	5,000		170.00	170
1997 Summerfun - Awake Dark Boy	2,000		170.00	170
1997 Summerfun - Awake Dark Girl	2,000		170.00	170
1997 Summerfun - Awake Girl	5,000		170.00	170
1995 Sweetness-Newborn	Retrd.	1995	190.00	190
1998 Tough Guy	1,000		170.00	170
1997 Treasured Traditions	5,000		170.00	170
1998 Wee Willie Winkie	2,000		170.00	170

My Own Baby Series - Lee Middleton, unless otherwise noted

YEAR ISSUE	EDITION LIMIT	YEAR RETD.	ISSUE PRICE	*QUOTE U.S.$
1997 First Born Awake My Own Baby Boy	Open		120.00	120
1997 First Born Awake My Own Baby Girl	Open		120.00	120
1996 First Born Dark My Own Baby Boy	Open		120.00	120
1996 First Born Dark My Own Baby Girl	Open		120.00	120
1996 First Born My Own Baby Boy	Open		120.00	120
1996 First Born My Own Baby Girl	Open		120.00	120
1997 First Moments Awake My Own Baby Boy	Retrd.	1997	120.00	120
1997 First Moments Awake My Own Baby Girl	Retrd.	1997	120.00	120
1997 First Moments My Own Baby Boy	Retrd.	1997	120.00	120
1997 First Moments My Own Baby Girl	Retrd.	1997	120.00	120
1998 Honey Love Asleep Boy Dark Skin My Own Baby	Open		120.00	120
1998 Honey Love Asleep Girl My Own Baby	Open		120.00	120
1998 Honey Love Awake Boy Dark Skin My Own Baby	Open		120.00	120
1998 Honey Love Awake Girl My Own Baby	Open		120.00	120
1996 Little Blessings My Own Baby Awake Boy	Open		120.00	120
1996 Little Blessings My Own Baby Awake Girl	Open		120.00	120
1996 Little Blessings My Own Baby Boy	Open		120.00	120
1996 Little Blessings My Own Baby Girl	Open		120.00	120
1996 Little Love My Own Baby Boy	Open		120.00	120
1996 Little Love My Own Baby Girl	Open		120.00	120
1997 Newborn Taylor Bear - L. Henry	Open		120.00	120

Porcelain Bears & Bunny - Lee Middleton

YEAR ISSUE	EDITION LIMIT	YEAR RETD.	ISSUE PRICE	*QUOTE U.S.$
1993 Buster Bear	Retrd.	1994	250.00	250
1993 Baby Buster	Retrd.	1994	230.00	230
1993 Bye Baby Bunting	Retrd.	1994	270.00	270

Porcelain Collector Series - Lee Middleton

YEAR ISSUE	EDITION LIMIT	YEAR RETD.	ISSUE PRICE	*QUOTE U.S.$
1992 Beloved & Bé Bé	362	1994	590.00	590
1993 Cherish - Lilac & Lace	141	1994	500.00	500
1992 Sencerity II - Country Fair	253	1994	500.00	500

Porcelain Limited Edition Series - Lee Middleton

YEAR ISSUE	EDITION LIMIT	YEAR RETD.	ISSUE PRICE	*QUOTE U.S.$
1990 Baby Grace	500	1990	500.00	650-800
1994 Blossom	86	1995	500.00	500
1994 Bride	200	1994	1390.00	1500
1988 Cherish -1st Edition	750	1988	350.00	550
1986 Dear One	750	1988	450.00	450
1989 Devan	543	1991	500.00	500-650
1995 Elise - 1860's Civil War	200	1996	1790.00	1800
1991 Johanna	381	1992	500.00	500
1991 Molly Rose	500	1991	500.00	850
1989 My Lee	655	1991	500.00	650
1988 Sincerity -1st Edition -Nettie/Simplicity	750	1988	330.00	350-600
1995 Tenderness - Baby Clown	250	1996	590.00	590
1994 Tenderness-Petite Pierrot	250	1995	500.00	500

Reva Schick Vinyl Series - R. Schick

YEAR ISSUE	EDITION LIMIT	YEAR RETD.	ISSUE PRICE	*QUOTE U.S.$
1998 Angel Love	2,000		180.00	180
1998 Baby Mine	2,000		164.00	164
1998 Bear Hug/Boy	1,000		180.00	180
1998 Bear Hug/Girl	1,000		180.00	180
1998 Bunny Dreams	2,000		180.00	180
1998 Cherry Blossom	2,000		180.00	180
1998 Cuddle Cub	2,500		190.00	190
1998 Fine & Frilly	2,000		174.00	174
1998 Forever Friend/Boy	1,500		170.00	170
1998 Forever Friend/Girl	2,500		170.00	170
1998 Gimme a Hug	2,000	1998	180.00	180
1998 Grandmother's Dream	2,500		198.00	198
1998 Hearts & Flowers	2,000		170.00	170
1998 Hunny Bunny	2,500		190.00	190
1998 In The Pink	2,000		180.00	180
1998 Little Chickadee	2,000		180.00	180
1998 Little Scottie/Boy	1,000		180.00	180
1998 Little Scottie/Girl	1,000		180.00	180
1998 Oops A Daisy	2,000		174.00	174
1998 Puppy Love	2,500		190.00	190
1998 Snoozy Bear	2,500		190.00	190
1998 Snow Baby	1,000		170.00	170
1998 Soft & Innocent	2,500		180.00	180
1998 Star Struck	2,000		170.00	170
1998 Sugar Plum	2,000		170.00	170
1998 Surprise	2,500		180.00	180
1998 Too Cute/Boy	2,500		180.00	180
1998 Too Cute/Girl	2,500		180.00	180
1998 Yesterday's Dream/ Boy	1,500		184.00	184
1998 Yesterday's Dream/ Girl	2,500		184.00	184

Romper Series - Lee Middleton

YEAR ISSUE	EDITION LIMIT	YEAR RETD.	ISSUE PRICE	*QUOTE U.S.$
1996 First Born Dark Romper Boy	2,000		160.00	160
1996 First Born Dark Romper Girl	2,000	1997	160.00	160
1996 First Born Romper Boy	2,000	1996	160.00	160
1996 First Born Romper Girl	2,000	1996	160.00	160
1996 Little Love Twin Boy	2,000	1996	160.00	160
1996 Little Love Twin Girl	2,000	1996	160.00	160

Scootles - R. O'Neill

YEAR ISSUE	EDITION LIMIT	YEAR RETD.	ISSUE PRICE	*QUOTE U.S.$
1997 Scootles	Open		50.00	50

Vinyl Collectors Series - Lee Middleton

YEAR ISSUE	EDITION LIMIT	YEAR RETD.	ISSUE PRICE	*QUOTE U.S.$
1987 Amanda - 1st Edition	3,778	1989	140.00	295
1985 Angel Face	20,200	1989	90.00	150
1994 Angel Kisses Boy	Retrd.	1997	98.00	98
1994 Angel Kisses Girl	Retrd.	1997	98.00	98
1996 Beloved Bedtime Story	1,500	1997	170.00	170
1996 Beloved Good Friends	1,500	1997	180.00	180
1997 Beloved Sunbeams and Flowers	2,500		170.00	170
1996 Bitsy Sister	1,500	1997	130.00	130
1995 The Bride (Ruby Slipper Edition)	1,000	1995	250.00	250
1986 Bubba Chubbs	5,550	1988	100.00	275-350
1996 Bubba Chubbs Bubba The Kid	1,000	1997	196.00	220

*Quotes have been rounded up to nearest dollar

YEAR ISSUE	EDITION LIMIT	YEAR RETD.	ISSUE PRICE	*QUOTE U.S.$
1988 Bubba Chubbs Railroader	7,925	1994	140.00	170
1988 Cherish	14,790	1992	160.00	250
1996 Cherish - Hug A Bug	5,000		170.00	170
1997 Cherish Little Guy	2,500		170.00	170
1994 Country Boy	Retrd.	1996	118.00	118
1994 Country Boy (Dark Flesh)	Retrd.	1996	118.00	118
1994 Country Girl	Retrd.	1996	118.00	118
1994 Country Girl (Dark Flesh)	Retrd.	1996	118.00	118
1986 Dear One - 1st Edition	4,935	1988	90.00	250
1989 Devan	8,336	1991	170.00	200
1997 Devan Happy Birthday	2,500		170.00	170
1993 Echo	Retrd.	1995	180.00	180
1996 Echo All Dressed Up	500	1996	180.00	180
1995 Echo Little Eagle	500	1997	180.00	180
1997 First Born - Awake Beauty	2,500	1997	180.00	180
1997 First Born - Awake Berry Sweet	2,500	1997	170.00	170
1997 First Born - Berry Sweet	2,500		170.00	170
1995 First Born - My Baby Boy	1,500	1995	160.00	160
1995 First Born - Newborn Twin Boy	2,000	1996	160.00	160
1995 First Born - Newborn Twin Girl	2,000	1996	160.00	160
1996 First Born - So Snuggly	1,000	1996	170.00	190
1996 First Born - Wee One	5,000		170.00	170
1996 First Moments - Battenburg Christening	1,000	1997	238.00	238
1995 First Moments - Lullaby Time	1,000	1996	180.00	180
1996 First Moments - Toot Sweet	5,000		170.00	170
1996 Grace Fresh As A Daisy	300	1996	176.00	176
1996 Hershey's Baker Girl	Retrd.	1997	130.00	130
1996 Hershey's Cake Kids Set (2)	Retrd.	1997	220.00	220
1996 Hershey's Chocolate Soldier	Retrd.	1997	130.00	130
1995 Hershey's Kisses - Gold	Retrd.	1996	99.50	130
1996 Hershey's Kisses - Green	Retrd.	1996	199.00	200
1996 Hershey's Kisses - Red	Retrd.	1996	199.00	200
1994 Hershey's Kisses - Silver	Retrd.	1997	99.50	140
1997 Honey Love - Awake Boy	5,000		170.00	170
1997 Honey Love - Awake Dark Boy	2,000		170.00	170
1997 Honey Love - Awake Dark Girl	2,000	1997	170.00	170
1997 Honey Love - Awake Girl	5,000	1997	170.00	170
1997 Honey Love - Dark Sleeping Boy	2,000		170.00	170
1997 Honey Love - Dark Sleeping Girl	2,000		170.00	170
1997 Honey Love - Sleeping Boy	5,000		170.00	170
1997 Honey Love - Sleeping Girl	5,000		170.00	170
1996 Joey Go Bye Bye	1,000		190.00	190
1986 Little Angel - 3rd Edition	15,158	1992	90.00	110
1992 Little Angel Boy	Retrd.	1997	130.00	150
1992 Little Angel Girl	Retrd.	1997	130.00	150
1997 Little Angel Wish Finders Star Bright	Retrd.	1997	120.00	120
1997 Little Angel Wish Finders Twinkle Twinkle	Retrd.	1997	120.00	120
1996 Little Blessings Cuddle Up	1,000	1997	180.00	180
1996 Little Blessings Newborn Twins Awake Boy	1,500	1996	180.00	180
1996 Little Blessings Newborn Twins Awake Girl	1,500	1996	180.00	180
1996 Little Blessings Newborn Twins Sleeping Boy	1,000	1996	180.00	180
1996 Little Blessings Newborn Twins Sleeping Girl	1,000	1996	180.00	180
1995 Little Blessings Pretty in Pink	1,500	1997	190.00	190
1997 Little Blessings Ships Ahoy	2,500		170.00	170
1996 Little Love - Cuddle Bumps	5,000		170.00	170
1997 Little Love - Peek A Boo Boy	2,500		170.00	170
1997 Little Love - Peek A Boo Girl	2,500		170.00	170
1996 Little Love - Such A Good Boy	1,000	1996	160.00	190
1995 Little Love - Violets	1,500	1995	160.00	160
1987 Missy	11,855	1991	100.00	120
1996 Molly Rose Good Friends	1,500	1997	180.00	180
1996 My Darling Boy	2,000		170.00	170
1996 My Darling Girl	2,000		170.00	170
1989 My Lee	3,794	1991	170.00	275
1992 Polly Esther	2,137	1994	160.00	160
1995 Polly Esther "Sock Hop"	1,000	1995	119.00	119
1996 Polly Esther - Hershey's Country Girl	Retrd.	1997	130.00	150
1996 Pretty Baby Sister	1,500	1997	170.00	170
1988 Sincerity - Limited 1st Ed. - Nettie/Simplicity	3,711	1989	160.00	200-250
1989 Sincerity-Schoolgirl	6,622	1992	180.00	295
1982 Sweet Dreams	Retrd.	1994	39.00	39
1995 Tenderness French BeBe	1,500	1997	220.00	220
1996 Tenderness So Brave	1,500	1997	170.00	170
1994 Town Boy	Retrd.	1995	118.00	118
1994 Town Boy (Dark Flesh)	Retrd.	1995	118.00	118
1994 Town Girl	Retrd.	1995	118.00	118
1994 Town Girl (Dark Flesh)	Retrd.	1995	118.00	118
1996 Young Lady Bride in White Satin	1,000	1997	250.00	250

Wise Penny Collection - Lee Middleton

YEAR ISSUE	EDITION LIMIT	YEAR RETD.	ISSUE PRICE	*QUOTE U.S.$
1993 Jennifer (Peach Dress)	Retrd.	1995	140.00	140
1993 Jennifer (Print Dress)	Retrd.	1995	140.00	140
1993 Molly Jo	Retrd.	1995	140.00	140
1993 Gordon	Retrd.	1995	140.00	140
1993 Ashley (Brown Hair)	Retrd.	1995	120.00	120
1993 Merry	Retrd.	1995	140.00	140
1993 Grace	Retrd.	1995	140.00	200
1993 Ashley (Blond Hair)	Retrd.	1995	120.00	120
1993 Baby Devan	Retrd.	1995	140.00	140

Little Gem/Akira Trading Co.

Little Gem - D. Canham, unless otherwise noted

YEAR ISSUE	EDITION LIMIT	YEAR RETD.	ISSUE PRICE	*QUOTE U.S.$
1995 Alex	3,000	1997	40.00	40
1995 Amelia Baby Blue	3,000	1997	40.00	40-60
1993 Annie	3,000	1995	40.00	40
1995 Banana & Chip	3,000	1997	40.00	40-80
1993 Bonnie	3,000	1995	40.00	40-50
1995 Bosworth & Chichi	3,000	1997	40.00	40-65
1996 Bumble Bee	3,000	1998	40.00	40
1993 Cameo - Chu-Ming Wu	3,000	1996	40.00	40
1994 Caramel- Chu-Ming Wu	3,000	1996	40.00	40
1994 Chico	3,000	1996	40.00	40-62
1994 Chilly	3,000	1998	40.00	40-45
1994 Chocolate - Chu-Ming Wu	500	1997	40.00	40-45
1994 Chu-Ming - S. Dotson	3,000	1995	40.00	40-60
1993 Connie - Chu-Ming Wu	3,000	1995	40.00	40-60
1994 Cupid	3,000	1995	40.00	40-70
1994 Darcy - Chu-Ming Wu	3,000	1997	40.00	40
1996 Dizzy	3,000	1998	40.00	40
1994 Jester Blue	3,000	1995	40.00	40-45
1994 Jester Grey	3,000	1995	40.00	40-50
1994 Jester Pink	3,000	1995	40.00	40-50
1994 Juliet (pin)	3,000	1998	40.00	40
1995 Kiki	3,000	1998	40.00	40
1996 Lady Bug	3,000	1998	40.00	40
1996 Latte - Chu-Ming Wu	3,000	1998	40.00	40
1994 Li-Ling - Chu-Ming Wu	3,000	1996	40.00	40
1994 Lopsy Blue	3,000	1995	40.00	40-50
1994 Lopsy Plum	3,000	1995	40.00	40-50
1994 Marcy - Chu-Ming Wu	3,000	1997	40.00	40
1994 Max (Ceylon) - Chu-Ming Wu	3,000	1996	40.00	40
1994 Mei-Mei - Chu-Ming Wu	3,000	1995	40.00	40-50
1995 Milly & Quackers	3,000	1997	40.00	40-50
1994 Mopsy - Chu-Ming Wu	3,000	1998	40.00	40
1995 Nicholas	3,000	1998	40.00	40
1996 No-No (Amber)	3,000	1998	40.00	40-50
1993 Onyx	3,000	1995	40.00	40
1993 Pearl	3,000	1995	40.00	40
1996 Perfume Bottle - Chu-Ming Wu	3,000	1998	40.00	40-50
1994 Perky	3,000	1996	40.00	40-60
1995 Rags - Chu-Ming Wu	3,000	1998	40.00	40
1994 Razz	3,000	1997	40.00	40-50
1993 Rex - Chu-Ming Wu	3,000	1997	40.00	40
1995 Rhonda - Chu-Ming Wu	3,000	1997	40.00	40
1994 Romeo (pin)	3,000	1998	40.00	40
1995 Rosie - Chu-Ming Wu	3,000	1996	40.00	40
1994 Rudolph - Chu-Ming Wu	3,000	1997	40.00	40
1995 Samantha - S. Dotson	3,000	1997	40.00	40-80
1994 Santa	3,000	1998	40.00	40
1995 Saphire (honey) - Chu-Ming Wu	3,000	1996	40.00	40
1994 Scottie	3,000	1998	40.00	40
1995 Sharon	3,000	1997	40.00	40
1995 Sophie	3,000	1998	40.00	40
1994 Strawberry (Alpaca) - Chu-Ming Wu	500	1995	40.00	40-75
1996 Tabatha	3,000	1998	40.00	40
1996 Teddy's Bear - L. Mullin	3,000	1998	49.00	49
1995 Thai - Chu-Ming Wu	3,000	1996	40.00	40
1994 Vanilla - Chu-Ming Wu	500	1995	40.00	40
1996 Winter Sprite	3,000	1998	40.00	40-60
1994 Zack - S. Dotson	3,000	1997	40.00	40-50
1994 Zev - Chu-Ming Wu	3,000	1998	40.00	40

Mattel

Members Choice-Official Barbie Collectors Club - Mattel

YEAR ISSUE	EDITION LIMIT	YEAR RETD.	ISSUE PRICE	*QUOTE U.S.$
1997 Grand Premier	Retrd.	1997	59.00	120
1998 Café Society	Yr.Iss.		59.00	60

35th Anniversary Dolls by Mattel - Mattel

YEAR ISSUE	EDITION LIMIT	YEAR RETD.	ISSUE PRICE	*QUOTE U.S.$
1994 Gift Set	Retrd.	1994	79.97	75-125
1994 Golden Jubilee	Retrd.	1994	299.00	300-700

Annual Holiday (white) Barbie Dolls - Mattel

YEAR ISSUE	EDITION LIMIT	YEAR RETD.	ISSUE PRICE	*QUOTE U.S.$
1988 Holiday Barbie	Retrd.	1990	24.95	795-1000
1989 Holiday Barbie	Retrd.	1991	N/A	275-350
1990 Holiday Barbie	Retrd.	1991	N/A	195-250
1991 Holiday Barbie	Retrd.	1993	N/A	175-195
1992 Holiday Barbie	Retrd.	1992	N/A	145-195
1993 Holiday Barbie	Retrd.	1993	N/A	100-130
1994 Holiday Barbie	Retrd.	1994	44.95	195-225
1995 Holiday Barbie	Retrd.	1995	44.95	75-120
1996 Holiday Barbie	Retrd.	1996	34.95	49-65
1997 Holiday Barbie	Retrd.	1997	34.95	40-49
1998 Holiday Barbie	Yr.Iss.		34.95	35

Bob Mackie Barbie Dolls - B. Mackie

YEAR ISSUE	EDITION LIMIT	YEAR RETD.	ISSUE PRICE	*QUOTE U.S.$
1992 Empress Bride Barbie 4247	Retrd.	1992	232.00	875-1000
1995 Goddess of the Sun	Retrd.	1995	198.00	195-230
1990 Gold Barbie 5405	Retrd.	1990	120.00	795-900
1997 Madame Du Barbie	Retrd.	1997	259.00	259-275
1993 Masquerade	Retrd.	1993	175.00	395-495
1996 Moon Goddess	Retrd.	1996	198.00	210-230
1992 Neptune Fantasy Barbie 4248	Retrd.	1993	160.00	850-995
1991 Platinum Barbie 2703	Retrd.	1991	153.00	700-725
1994 Queen of Hearts	Retrd.	1994	175.00	225-295
1991 Starlight Splendor Barbie 2704	Retrd.	1991	135.00	600-795

Classique Collection - Mattel

YEAR ISSUE	EDITION LIMIT	YEAR RETD.	ISSUE PRICE	*QUOTE U.S.$
1992 Benefit Ball	Retrd.	1994	59.95	120-175
1993 City Style	Retrd.	1994	59.95	105
1993 Evening Extravaganza	Retrd.	1995	59.95	80-90
1998 Evening Sophisticate	Yr.Iss.		59.95	60
1995 Midnight Gala	Retrd.	1996	59.95	75-80
1993 Opening Night	Retrd.	1994	59.95	60-150
1997 Romantic Interlude	Retrd.	1997	59.95	60-70
1996 Starlight Dance	Retrd.	1996	59.95	60-65
1993 Uptown Chic	Retrd.	1995	53.95	75-80

Designer - Mattel

YEAR ISSUE	EDITION LIMIT	YEAR RETD.	ISSUE PRICE	*QUOTE U.S.$
1996 Christian Dior 50th Anniversary	Retrd.	1996	499.00	200-500

Great Eras - Mattel

YEAR ISSUE	EDITION LIMIT	YEAR RETD.	ISSUE PRICE	*QUOTE U.S.$
1993 Egyptian Queen	Retrd.	1993	53.99	145-190
1994 Elizabethan Queen	Retrd.	1995	53.99	49-60
1993 Flapper	Retrd.	1995	53.99	150-250
1993 Gibson Girl	Retrd.	1995	53.99	100-175
1994 Medieval Lady	Retrd.	1994	53.99	49-69
1993 Southern Belle	Retrd.	1993	53.99	120-175

Nostalgic Porcelain Barbie Dolls - Mattel

YEAR ISSUE	EDITION LIMIT	YEAR RETD.	ISSUE PRICE	*QUOTE U.S.$
1988 Benefit Performance	Retrd.	1988	N/A	290-350
1986 Blue Rhapsody	Retrd.	1986	N/A	200-350
1987 Enchanted Evening	Retrd.	1987	N/A	200-275
1991 Gay Parisienne	Retrd.	1991	N/A	200-325
1991 Plantation Belle	Retrd.	1991	N/A	200-225
1992 Silken Flame	Retrd.	1992	N/A	200
1990 Solo in the Spotlight 7613	Retrd.	1990	198.00	200-295
1990 Sophisticated Lady 5313	Retrd.	1990	198.00	200-295
1989 Wedding Day Barbie 2641	Retrd.	1989	198.00	300-550

Ultra Limited - Mattel

YEAR ISSUE	EDITION LIMIT	YEAR RETD.	ISSUE PRICE	*QUOTE U.S.$
1997 Billions of Dreams	Retrd.	1997	299.00	299-320
1996 Pink Splendor	Retrd.	1996	900.00	500-900

The Winter Princess Collection - Mattel

YEAR ISSUE	EDITION LIMIT	YEAR RETD.	ISSUE PRICE	*QUOTE U.S.$
1994 Evergreen Princess	Retrd.	1994	59.95	105-175
1994 Evergreen Princess (Red Head)	Retrd.	1994	59.95	250-375
1995 Peppermint Princess	Retrd.	1995	59.95	50-75
1993 Winter Princess	Retrd.	1993	59.95	525-550

Original Appalachian Artworks

Collectors Club Editions - X. Roberts

YEAR ISSUE	EDITION LIMIT	YEAR RETD.	ISSUE PRICE	*QUOTE U.S.$
1987 Baby Otis	1,275	1987	250.00	275-500
1989 Anna Ruby	693	1990	250.00	300-650
1990 Lee Ann	468	1991	250.00	300-500
1991 Richard Russell	490	1991	250.00	300-650
1992 Baby Dodd & 'Ittle Bitty	354	1993	250.00	300-500
1993 Patti w/ Cabbage Bud Boutonnier	358	1994	280.00	300-350
1994 Mother Cabbage	245	1995	150.00	150
1995 Rosie	322	1996	275.00	275
1996 Gabriella (Angel)	Closed	1997	265.00	265
1997 Robert London	Closed	1997	275.00	275
1998 Dexter (Anniversary)	Yr.Iss.		395.00	395

BabyLand Career - X. Roberts

YEAR ISSUE	EDITION LIMIT	YEAR RETD.	ISSUE PRICE	*QUOTE U.S.$
1992 BabyLand (Engineer -Career Kid)	Closed	1992	220.00	250-300
1993 BabyLand (Miss BLGH Career 'Kid)	240	1993	220.00	220-300
1994 BabyLand (Child Star Career 'Kid)	241	1994	220.00	220-250
1995 BabyLand (Career Nurse)	83	1995	210.00	220-275
1997 BabyLand (Ballerina)	Closed	1997	210.00	210

BabyLand General Hospital Convention Baby - X. Roberts

YEAR ISSUE	EDITION LIMIT	YEAR RETD.	ISSUE PRICE	*QUOTE U.S.$
1990 Charlie (Amber)	200	1990	175.00	350-375
1991 Nurse Payne (Garnet)	160	1991	210.00	350-400
1992 Princess Nacoochee (BabyLand)	160	1992	210.00	250-275
1993 Baby BeBop (BabyLand)	199	1993	210.00	300-325
1994 Norma Jean (BabyLand)	250	1994	225.00	350-475
1995 Delta (BabyLand)	200	1995	230.00	230
1996 Marlene (BabyLand)	200	1996	230.00	230
1997 Hayley (BabyLand)	200	1997	220.00	220
1998 Marisa (BabyLand)	200	1998	250.00	250

BunnyBees - X. Roberts

YEAR ISSUE	EDITION LIMIT	YEAR RETD.	ISSUE PRICE	*QUOTE U.S.$
1986 Girl	Closed	N/A	13.00	20-50
1986 Boy	Closed	N/A	13.00	20-50
1994 Girl w/Squeaker	Closed	N/A	18.00	18
1994 Boy w/Squeaker	Closed	N/A	18.00	18

Cabbage Patch Kids (10 Character Kids) - X. Roberts

YEAR ISSUE	EDITION LIMIT	YEAR RETD.	ISSUE PRICE	*QUOTE U.S.$
1982 Amy L.	206	1982	125.00	500-700
1982 Bobbie J.	314	1982	125.00	450-600
1982 Billy B.	201	1982	125.00	450-600
1982 Dorothy J.	126	1982	125.00	550-700
1982 Gilda R.	105	1982	125.00	700-2500
1982 Marilyn S.	275	1982	125.00	595-800
1982 Otis L.	308	1982	125.00	700
1982 Rebecca R.	301	1982	125.00	500-700
1982 Sybil S.	502	1982	125.00	450-700
1982 Tyler B.	94	1982	125.00	2000-3000

Cabbage Patch Kids - X. Roberts

YEAR ISSUE	EDITION LIMIT	YEAR RETD.	ISSUE PRICE	*QUOTE U.S.$
1989 Amber (Reg. & Halloween)	1,356	1990	195.00	150-225
1989 Amber (Halloween, Asian)	654	1989	175.00	150-225
1989 Amber (Toddler)	272	1989	150.00	100-225
1986 Amethyst	9,250	1986	135.00	100-200
1988 Aquamarine	5,000	1988	150.00	100-225
1994 BabyLand (Bald)	Closed	1994	210.00	200-250
1994 BabyLand (Preemie)	Closed	1994	175.00	175-250
1995 BabyLand (Preemie)	Closed	1995	175.00	175-225
1997 BabyLand (Preemie)	Closed	1997	175.00	175
1991 BabyLand (Reg.)	969	1991	190.00	190-240
1992 BabyLand (Reg.)	770	1992	190.00	190-240
1994 BabyLand (Reg.)	Closed	1994	210.00	210-260
1995 BabyLand (Reg.)	Closed	1994	210.00	210-260
1994 BabyLand (Sweet Sixteen "Casey Ann")	191	1994	260.00	295-500
1993 Blackberry Preemie	438	1993	175.00	175
1992 Brass	321	1992	190.00	190
1992 Brass (Flower Girl Toddler)	Closed	1992	175.00	175-225
1992 Brass (Garden Party Girl)	Closed	1992	190.00	190-240

*Quotes have been rounded up to nearest dollar

YEAR ISSUE	EDITION LIMIT	YEAR RETD.	ISSUE PRICE	*QUOTE U.S.$
1992 Brass (Hispanic Girl Toddler)	Closed	1992	175.00	175-225
1992 Brass (Ring Bearer Boy Toddler)	Closed	1992	175.00	175-225
1992 Brass (Toddler)	424	1992	175.00	175-225
1995 Bucky (California Collectors Club)	105	1995	220.00	220
1983 Champagne (Andre)	1,000	1983	250.00	500
1983 Champagne (Madeira)	1,000	1983	250.00	500
1998 Chattahoochee Kid	Open		255.00	255
1998 Chattahoochee (Newborn)	Open		195.00	195
1998 Chattahoochee (Preemie)	Open		185.00	185
1983 Cleveland "Green"	2,000	1983	125.00	250-450
1991 Copper	241	1991	190.00	190
1991 Copper (Halloween)	273	1991	190.00	240-252
1991 Copper (Toddler)	241	1991	175.00	175-225
1986 Corporate 'Kid	2,000	1986	400.00	400
1991 Crystal	176	1991	190.00	190
1991 Crystal (Easter Fashions)	302	1991	190.00	210-240
1991 Crystal (Toddler)	41	1991	175.00	175-225
1991 Crystal (Valentine Fashions)	256	1991	190.00	190-240
1991 Crystal (Valentine Toddler Fashions)	189	1991	175.00	175-225
1984 Daddy's Darlins' (Kitten)	500	1984	300.00	400-500
1984 Daddy's Darlins' (Princess)	500	1984	300.00	400-750
1984 Daddy's Darlins' (Pun'kin)	500	1983	300.00	400-500
1984 Daddy's Darlins' (Tootsie)	500	1984	300.00	400-500
1984 Daddy's Darlins', set/4	2,000	1984	1200.00	1200-2000
1992 Diamond	360	1993	210.00	210
1992 Diamond (Choir Christmas)	54	1992	210.00	210-260
1992 Diamond (Thanksgiving Indian)	123	1992	210.00	210-260
1992 Diamond (Thanksgiving Toddler Indian)	55	1992	195.00	195-245
1992 Diamond (Toddler)	51	1993	195.00	195-245
1985 Emerald	35,000	1985	135.00	100-135
1985 Four Seasons (Autumn)	2,000	1985	160.00	160
1985 Four Seasons (Crystal)	2,000	1985	160.00	160
1985 Four Seasons (Morton)	2,000	1985	160.00	160
1985 Four Seasons (Sunny)	2,000	1985	160.00	160
1991 Garnet	376	1991	190.00	190
1991 Garnet (Father's Day Toddler)	85	1991	175	175-275
1991 Garnet (Father's Day)	173	1991	190.00	190-290
1991 Garnet (Mother's Day Girl)	259	1991	190.00	190-290
1991 Garnet (Mother's Day Toddler Girl)	364	1991	175.00	175-275
1991 Garnet (Toddler)	49	1991	175.00	175
1993 Georgia Power (Special Stork Delivery)	288	1993	230.00	250-350
1985 Gold	50,000	1985	135.00	100-185
1995 Graceland Elvis	500	1995	300.00	300
1993 Happily Ever After (Bride)	343	1993	230.00	230-275
1993 Happily Ever After (Groom)	343	1993	230.00	230-275
1994 House of Tyrol (Christina Marie)	1,000	1994	200.00	200
1994 House of Tyrol (Markus Michael)	1,000	1994	200.00	200
1987 Iddy Buds	750	1987	650.00	375-650
1986 Identical Twins, set/2	5,000	1987	150.00	150-250
1985 Ivory	45,000	1985	135.00	135
1989 Jade	Closed	1989	150.00	150
1989 Jade (4th of July Fashions)	Closed	1989	150.00	150-200
1989 Jade (Mother's Day Fashions)	338	1989	150.00	150-200
1989 Jade (Toddler)	Closed	1989	150.00	150-200
1992 JC Penney 1992 Catalog Exclusive (Cocoa-Girl)	245	1992	200.00	200
1992 JC Penney 1992 Catalog Exclusive (Lemon Girl)	248	1992	200.00	200
1983 KP Darker Green	2,000	1983	125.00	250-400
1983 KPB Burgundy	10,000	1983	130.00	200-250
1984 KPF Turquoise	30,000	1984	130.00	130
1984 KPG Bronze	30,000	1984	130.00	130
1984 KPG Coral	35,000	1984	130.00	130
1984 KPP Purple	20,000	1984	130.00	130
1983 KPR Red	2,000	1983	125.00	200-400
1989 Lapis (Swimsuit Fashions)	645	1989	150.00	150-240
1989 Lapis (Swimsuit Fashions-Toddler)	836	1989	150.00	150-225
1993 Little People 27" (Girl)	300	1993	325.00	700-1000
1994 Little People 27" (Boy)	300	1994	325.00	450-500
1996 Little People Girls 27"	300	1996	375.00	375
1997 Little People 27" (Boy)	300	1997	395.00	395
1994 Mt. Laurel (African Inspired Toddler)	Closed	1994	195.00	195
1994 Mt. Laurel (African Inspired) (Reg.)	Closed	1994	210.00	210
1994 Mt. Laurel (Mrs. Pauls)	Closed	1994	198.00	198
1994 Mt. Laurel (Mysterious Barry)	Closed	1994	225.00	225
1994 Mt. Laurel (Northern)	Closed	1995	210.00	210
1994 Mt. Laurel (Twins Baby Sidney & Baby Lanier)	100	1994	390.00	390
1994 Mt. Laurel (Western)	Closed	1994	210.00	210
1994 Mt. Laurel St. Patrick Boys	100	1994	210.00	210
1994 Mt. Laurel St. Patrick Girls	200	1994	210.00	210
1995 Mt. Yonah (Easter)	Closed	1995	215.00	215
1995 Mt. Yonah (Valentine)	Closed	1995	200.00	200
1996 Nacoochee Valley (Easter)	Closed	1996	215.00	215
1996 Nacoochee Valley (Halloween)	Closed	1996	210.00	210
1991 Newborn (BLGH)	909	1991	195.00	195
1992 Newborn (BLGH)	869	1992	195.00	195
1993 Newborn (BLGH)	1,136	1993	195.00	195
1994 Newborn (BLGH)	1,107	1994	195.00	195
1995 Newborn (BLGH)	1,042	1995	195.00	195
1996 Newborn (BLGH)	1,710	1996	195.00	195
1997 Newborn (BLGH)	Closed	1997	195.00	195
1998 Newborn (BLGH)	Yr.Iss.		195.00	195
1991 Onyx (Thanksgiving Pilgrim)	349	1991	190.00	220-240
1991 Onyx (Toddler)	297	1991	175.00	175-225
1991 Onyx 22"	297	1991	190.00	190
1990 Opal (Easter Toddler Fashions)	751	1989	175.00	175-225
1990 Opal (Garden Fashions)	Closed	1989	175.00	175-225
1990 Opal (Toddler)	Closed	1990	175.00	175
1990 Pearl	542	1990	190.00	190-240
1990 Pearl (Toddler)	226	1990	175.00	175-225
1990 Peridot	680	1990	190.00	175-225
1990 Peridot (Halloween Toddler Fashions)	588	1990	175.00	210
1990 Peridot (Toddler)	794	1990	175.00	220-320
1992 Platinum	Closed	1992	210.00	220-320
1992 Platinum (Best Man)	Closed	1992	220.00	320
1992 Platinum (Maid of Honor)	Closed	1992	220.00	320
1992 Platinum (Summertime 'Kids-Watermelon)	Closed	1992	210.00	210
1992 Platinum (Toddler)	19	1992	195.00	195
1985 Preemie (boy)	3,750	1985	150.00	110-125
1985 Preemie (girl)	11,250	1985	150.00	110-125
1985 Preemie Twins, set/2	1,500	1985	600.00	375-600
1990 Quartz (Toddler)	347	1989	175.00	175
1990 Quartz (Valentine Toddler Fashions)	708	1989	175.00	175-225
1992 QVC Exclusive (Janeen Sybil)	200	1992	275.00	275
1992 QVC Exclusive (Preemie) (Celeste Diane)	500	1992	250.00	250
1992 QVC Exclusive (Toddler) (Abigail Sydney)	1,000	1992	225.00	225
1993 QVC Exclusive (Newborn)	187	1993	N/A	200
1985 Rose	40,000	1985	135.00	135
1989 Ruby	1,325	1989	150.00	150
1985 Sapphire	35,000	1985	135.00	135
1997 Sautee Valley	Closed	1997	210.00	210
1997 Sautee Valley (Festival Kid)	Closed	1997	220.00	220
1992 Silver	73	1992	190.00	190
1992 Silver (Asian Toddler)	219	1992	175.00	175-225
1992 Silver (Toddler)	59	1992	175.00	175
1992 Silver (Valentine Toddler)	283	1992	190.00	190-240
1995 Skitts Mountain	192	1995	210.00	210
1986 Southern Belle "Georgiana"	4,000	1990	160.00	160
1984 Sweetheart (Beau)	750	1984	150.00	300-400
1984 Sweetheart (Candi)	750	1984	150.00	300-400
1988 Tiger's Eye	3,653	1989	150.00	150
1988 Tiger's Eye (Easter)	788	1989	150.00	150-190
1989 Tiger's Eye (Mother's Day)	231	1989	150.00	200-300
1988 Tiger's Eye (Valentine's Day)	328	1989	150.00	150-300
1987 Topaz	5,000	1987	135.00	135
1993 Unicoi	Closed	1993	210.00	210
1993 Unicoi (Ballerina Toddler)	Closed	1993	195.00	195-260
1993 Unicoi (Spring Toddler)	Closed	1993	195.00	195-260
1993 Unicoi (Spring)	Closed	1993	210.00	210-260
1993 Unicoi (Summer Dinosaur)	Closed	1993	210.00	210-260
1993 Unicoi (Summer Toddler Dinosaur)	Closed	1993	210.00	210-260
1993 Unicoi (Toddler)	Closed	1993	210.00	210
1993 White Christmas - Regular Kids (only)	223	1993	210.00	260
1984 World Class	2,500	1984	150.00	400

Cabbage Patch Kids Anniversary - X. Roberts

YEAR ISSUE	EDITION LIMIT	YEAR RETD.	ISSUE PRICE	*QUOTE U.S.$
1998 Spring Sass	300		395.00	395
1998 Summer Mischief	300		395.00	395
1998 Autumn Scholar	300		395.00	395
1998 Winter Snuggles	300		395.00	395

Cabbage Patch Kids Baby Character - X. Roberts

YEAR ISSUE	EDITION LIMIT	YEAR RETD.	ISSUE PRICE	*QUOTE U.S.$
1990 Baby Amy Loretta Nursery	509	1990	200.00	225-250
1991 Baby Billy Badd Nursery	306	1991	200.00	225-250
1991 Baby Bobbie Jo Nursery	393	1991	200.00	225-250
1988 Baby Dorothy Jane Nursery	2,000	1992	165.00	225-250
1992 Baby Gilda Roxanne Nursery	351	1992	200.00	225-250
1988 Baby Marilyn Suzanne Nursery	2,000	1992	165.00	225-250
1992 Baby Rebecca Ruby Nursery	373	1992	200.00	225-250
1988 Baby Sybil Sadie Nursery	2,000	1992	165.00	225-250
1988 Baby Tyler Bo Nursery	2,000	1993	165.00	225-250

Cabbage Patch Kids Circus Parade - X. Roberts

YEAR ISSUE	EDITION LIMIT	YEAR RETD.	ISSUE PRICE	*QUOTE U.S.$
1987 Big Top Clown-Baby Cakes	2,000	1987	180.00	350-400
1991 Big Top Tot-Mitzi	1,000	1993	220.00	320-400
1989 Happy Hobo-Bashful Billy	1,000	1989	180.00	300-350
1997 Jingling Jester-Jacqueline	500	1997	275.00	275

Cabbage Patch Kids International - X. Roberts

YEAR ISSUE	EDITION LIMIT	YEAR RETD.	ISSUE PRICE	*QUOTE U.S.$
1983 American Indian/Pair	500	1983	300.00	800-1200
1984 Bavarian/Pair	500	1984	300.00	450-800
1983 Hispanic/Pair	500	1983	300.00	400-500
1983 Irish/Pair	2,000	1985	320.00	320
1983 Oriental/Pair	500	1983	300.00	500-1000
1987 Polynesian (Lokelina)	1,000	1987	180.00	180
1987 Polynesian (Ohana)	1,000	1987	180.00	180

Cabbage Patch Kids OlympiKids™ - X. Roberts

YEAR ISSUE	EDITION LIMIT	YEAR RETD.	ISSUE PRICE	*QUOTE U.S.$
1996 Baseball Boy	159	1996	275.00	275-280
1996 Basketball Boy & Girl	199	1996	275.00	275
1996 Basketball Girl	302	1996	275.00	275
1996 Cyclist Boy	126	1996	275.00	275
1996 Equestrian Girl	350	1996	275.00	275-350
1996 Gymnastics Boy	241	1996	275.00	275
1995 Rowing Girl	205	1996	275.00	275
1995 Soccer Boy	162	1996	275.00	275
1995 Soccer Girl	262	1996	275.00	275
1996 Softball Girl	140	1996	275.00	275
1995 Track & Field Girl	422	1996	275.00	275
1995 Weight Lifting Boy	158	1996	275.00	275

Cabbage Patch Kids Porcelain - X. Roberts

YEAR ISSUE	EDITION LIMIT	YEAR RETD.	ISSUE PRICE	*QUOTE U.S.$
1994 Porcelain Angel (Angelica)	208	1994	160.00	160
1994 Porcelain Friends (Karen Lee)	59	1994	150.00	150
1994 Porcelain Friends (Kassie Lou)	58	1994	150.00	150
1994 Porcelain Friends (Katie Lyn)	61	1994	150.00	150
1995 Porcelain Peirrot (Sharri Starr)	198	1995	160.00	160

Cabbage Patch Kids Storybook - X. Roberts

YEAR ISSUE	EDITION LIMIT	YEAR RETD.	ISSUE PRICE	*QUOTE U.S.$
1986 Mark Twain (Becky Thatcher)	2,500	1986	160.00	200-250
1986 Mark Twain (Huck Finn)	2,500	1986	160.00	160-220
1986 Mark Twain (Tom Sawyer)	2,500	1986	160.00	160-200
1987 Sleeping Beauty (Prince Charming)	1,250	1991	180.00	180
1987 Sleeping Beauty (Sleeping Beauty)	1,250	1991	180.00	180

Christmas Collection - X. Roberts

YEAR ISSUE	EDITION LIMIT	YEAR RETD.	ISSUE PRICE	*QUOTE U.S.$
1979 X Christmas	1,000	1979	150.00	3000-5500
1980 Christmas-Nicholas/Noel	500	1980	400.00	1000-1200
1982 Christmas-Baby Rudy/Christy Nicole	500	1982	400.00	1000-1600
1983 Christmas-Holly/Berry	1,000	1983	400.00	800
1984 Christmas-Carole/Chris	1,000	1984	400.00	600
1985 Christmas-Baby Sandy/Claude	2,500	1990	400.00	400
1986 Christmas-Hilliary/Nigel	2,000	1990	400.00	400-425
1987 Christmas-Katrina/Misha	2,000	1990	500.00	500
1988 Christmas-Kelly/Kane	2,000	1993	500.00	500-600
1989 Christmas-Joy	500	1989	250.00	300-400
1990 Christmas-Krystina	596	1991	250.00	260-300
1991 Christmas-Nick	700	1991	275.00	275
1992 Christmas-Christy Claus	700	1993	285.00	285
1993 Christmas-Rudolph	500	1993	275.00	275
1994 Christmas-Natalie	500	1994	275.00	275
1995 Christmas-Treena	500	1995	275.00	275
1996 Christmas-Sammy The Snowman	500	1996	275.00	275
1997 Christmas-Melody	300	1997	295.00	295-400
1998 Christmas-Ginger	300		315.00	315

Convention Baby - X. Roberts

YEAR ISSUE	EDITION LIMIT	YEAR RETD.	ISSUE PRICE	*QUOTE U.S.$
1989 Ashley (Jade)	200	1989	250.00	500-800
1990 Bradley (Opal)	200	1990	175.00	300-600
1991 Caroline (Garnet)	200	1991	200.00	300
1992 Duke (Brass)	200	1992	225.00	375-400
1993 Ellen (Unicoi)	200	1993	225.00	300-400
1994 Justin (Mt. Laurel)	200	1994	225.00	300-400
1995 Fifi (Mt. Yonah)	200	1995	250.00	450-700
1996 Gina (Nacoochee Valley)	200	1996	275.00	275
1997 Hannah (Sautee Valley)	200	1997	275.00	275-500
1998 Ian (Chattahoochee)	200	1998	310.00	310

Furskins - X. Roberts

YEAR ISSUE	EDITION LIMIT	YEAR RETD.	ISSUE PRICE	*QUOTE U.S.$
1983 Humphrey Furskin	2,500	1993	75.00	150-200
1985 Boone (no letter)	25,000	1985	55.00	50-125
1985 Farrell (no letter)	25,000	1985	55.00	50-125
1985 Dudley (no letter)	25,000	1985	55.00	50-125
1985 Hattie (no letter)	25,000	1985	55.00	50-125
1985 Boone (A)	25,000	1985	55.00	55
1985 Farrell (A)	25,000	1985	55.00	55
1985 Dudley (A)	25,000	1985	55.00	55
1985 Hattie (A)	25,000	1985	55.00	55
1985 Boone (B)	75,000	1985	55.00	55
1985 Farrell (B)	75,000	1985	55.00	55
1985 Dudley (B)	75,000	1985	55.00	55
1985 Hattie (B)	75,000	1985	55.00	55
1985 Boone (C)	100,000	1985	55.00	55
1985 Farrell (C)	100,000	1985	55.00	55
1985 Dudley (C)	100,000	1985	55.00	55
1985 Hattie (C)	100,000	1985	55.00	55
1985 Boone (D)	125,000	1985	55.00	55
1985 Farrell (D)	125,000	1985	55.00	55
1985 Dudley (D)	125,000	1985	55.00	55
1985 Hattie (D)	125,000	1985	55.00	55
1986 Orville T. (no letter)	5,000	1986	55.00	75-125
1986 Jedgar (no letter)	5,000	1986	55.00	75-125
1986 Selma Jean (no letter)	5,000	1986	55.00	75-125
1986 Fannie Fay (no letter)	5,000	1986	55.00	75-125
1986 Orville T. (A)	5,000	1986	55.00	55-100
1986 Jedgar A)	5,000	1986	55.00	55
1986 Selma Jean (A)	5,000	1986	55.00	55
1986 Fannie Fay (A)	5,000	1986	55.00	55
1986 Bubba (licensed)	Closed	1986	30.00	40-45
1986 Cecelia ("CeCe") (licensed)	Closed	1986	30.00	40-45
1986 Hank "Spitball" (licensed)	Closed	1986	30.00	40-45
1986 J. Livingston Clayton ("Scout") (licensed)	Closed	1986	30.00	40-45
1986 Junie Mae (licensed)	Closed	1986	30.00	40-45
1986 Lila Claire (licensed)	Closed	1986	30.00	40-45
1986 Persimmon (licensed)	Closed	1986	30.00	40-45
1986 Thistle (licensed)	Closed	1986	30.00	30-75

Little People - X. Roberts

YEAR ISSUE	EDITION LIMIT	YEAR RETD.	ISSUE PRICE	*QUOTE U.S.$
1978 "A" Blue	1,000	1978	45.00	7000-8500
1978 "B" Red	1,000	1978	80.00	3500-6000
1979 "C" Burgundy	5,000	1979	80.00	1200-2000
1979 "D" Purple	10,000	1979	80.00	1000-1500
1979 "E" Bronze	15,000	1980	80.00	495-500
1982 "PE" New 'Ears Preemie	5,000	1982	140.00	300-450
1981 "PR II" Preemie	10,000	1981	130.00	200-450
1980 "SP" Preemie	5,000	1980	100.00	400-500
1982 "U" Unsigned	21,000	1982	125.00	300-450
1980 "U" Unsigned (& 1980)	73,000	1981	125.00	300-450
1980 Celebrity	5,000	1980	200.00	400-500
1980 Grand Edition	1,000	1988	1000.00	600-1000
1978 Helen Blue	Closed	1978	30.00	6500-10000
1981 Little People Pals 12"	10,000	N/A	75.00	250-450
1981 New 'Ears	15,000	1981	125.00	250-450
1981 Standing Edition	5,000	1988	300.00	300-500

Mobile Patch Babies - X. Roberts

YEAR ISSUE	EDITION LIMIT	YEAR RETD.	ISSUE PRICE	*QUOTE U.S.$
1992 Garden Party Sprout (Babyland "Miss Eula")	140	1992	250.00	350-500
1992 Garden Party Sprout (Chris' Corner Clown-Daisy)	110	1992	250.00	350-500

*Quotes have been rounded up to nearest dollar

YEAR ISSUE	EDITION LIMIT	YEAR RETD.	ISSUE PRICE	*QUOTE U.S.$
1992 Garden Party Sprout (Cottage of Memories Indian Girl)	80	1992	250.00	350-500
1992 Garden Party Sprout (Doll House Sweet Dreams)	82	1992	250.00	350-500
1992 Garden Party Sprout (Hobby City "Tinkerbell")	160	1992	250.00	350-500
1992 Garden Party Sprout (Wee Heather Victorian-Heather)	62	1992	250.00	350-500
1997 Sautee Valley (Mama's Babies & Bears)	Closed	1997	195.00	195
1997 Sautee Valley (Doll & Teddy Bear Expo)	Closed	1997	195.00	195
1997 Sautee Valley (Rainbow's End)	Closed	1997	195.00	195
1997 Sautee Valley (Roxanne's Doll Shoppe)	Closed	1997	195.00	195
1997 Sautee Valley (S.W. Randall Toys & Gifts)	Closed	1997	195.00	195
1997 Sautee Valley (Rainbow Connection)	Closed	1997	195.00	195
1997 Sautee Valley (Heirlooms of Tomorrow)	Closed	1997	195.00	195
1998 Chattahoochee Newborn (Rainbow Connection)	Closed	1998	225.00	225
1998 Chattahoochee Newborn (Hobby City)	Closed	1998	225.00	225
1998 Chattahoochee Newborn (West Coast Expo)	Closed	1998	225.00	225
1998 Chattahoochee Newborn (Cape Art Mart)	Closed	1998	225.00	225
1998 Chattahoochee Newborn (Rainbow's End)	Closed	1998	225.00	225
1998 Chattahoochee Newborn (Black Gold Dolls)	Closed	1998	225.00	225
1998 Chattahoochee Newborn (Int'l Collector Expo)	Closed	1998	225.00	225
1998 Chattahoochee Newborn (East Coast Expo)	Closed	1998	225.00	225
1998 Chattahoochee Newborn (Mama's Babies & Bears)	Closed	1998	225.00	225
1998 Chattahoochee Newborn (Puppenkinder)	Closed	1998	225.00	225
1998 Chattahoochee Newborn (Doll House)	Closed	1998	225.00	225
1998 Chattahoochee Newborn (Dolls, Bears & Collectibles)	Closed	1998	225.00	225
1998 Chattahoochee Newborn (Merry Christmas Shoppe)	Closed	1998	225.00	225
1998 Chattahoochee Newborn (Contemporary Dolls)	Closed	1998	225.00	225
1998 Chattahoochee Newborn (Roxanne's Doll Shoppe)	Closed	1998	225.00	225
1998 Chattahoochee Newborn (SW Randall)	Closed	1998	225.00	225
1998 Chattahoochee Newborn (Heirlooms of Tomorrow)	Closed	1998	225.00	225

Show Specials - X. Roberts

YEAR ISSUE	EDITION LIMIT	YEAR RETD.	ISSUE PRICE	*QUOTE U.S.$
1986 Amethyst (Rusty)	250	1986	135.00	300-450
1986 Amethyst (Tiffy)	500	1986	135.00	400-450
1987 Topaz (Iris)	1,500	1985	135.00	450-600
1998 Chattahoochee Preemie (Aimee)	20	1998	225.00	450-600
1998 Chattahoochee Preemie (Abigail)	20	1998	225.00	225

Precious Moments/Enesco Corporation

Jack-In-The-Boxes - S. Butcher

YEAR ISSUE	EDITION LIMIT	YEAR RETD.	ISSUE PRICE	*QUOTE U.S.$
1991 You Have Touched So Many Hearts 422282	2-Yr.	1993	175.00	175
1991 May You Have An Old Fashioned Christmas 417777	2-Yr.	1993	200.00	200
1990 The Voice of Spring 408735	2-Yr.	1992	200.00	200
1990 Summer's Joy 408743	2-Yr.	1992	200.00	200
1990 Autumn's Praise 408751	2-Yr.	1992	200.00	200
1990 Winter's Song 408778	2-Yr.	1992	200.00	200

Precious Moments Dolls - S. Butcher

YEAR ISSUE	EDITION LIMIT	YEAR RETD.	ISSUE PRICE	*QUOTE U.S.$
1981 Mikey, 18" E-6214B	Suspd.		150.00	235-250
1981 Debbie, 18" E-6214G	Suspd.		150.00	250-375
1982 Cubby, 18" E-7267B	5,000		200.00	350-450
1982 Tammy, 18" E-7267G	5,000		300.00	450-500
1983 Katie Lynne, 16" E-0539	Suspd.		165.00	175-185
1984 Mother Sew Dear, 18" E-2850	Retrd.	1985	350.00	350-369
1984 Kristy, 12" E-2851	Suspd.		150.00	170-175
1984 Timmy, 12" E-5397	Suspd.		125.00	120-150
1985 Aaron, 12" 12424	Suspd.		135.00	160
1985 Bethany, 12" 12432	Suspd.		135.00	160
1985 P.D., 7" 12475	Suspd.		50.00	70-85
1985 Trish, 7" 12483	Suspd.		50.00	95-100
1986 Bong Bong, 13" 100455	12,000		150.00	225-265
1986 Candy, 13" 100463	12,000		150.00	280-300
1986 Connie, 12" 102253	7,500		160.00	240-250
1987 Angie, The Angel of Mercy 12491	12,500		160.00	275-300
1990 The Voice of Spring 408786	2-Yr.	1992	150.00	150
1990 Summer's Joy 408794	2-Yr.	1992	150.00	150
1990 Autumn's Praise 408808	2-Yr.	1992	150.00	150
1990 Winter's Song 408816	2-Yr.	1992	150.00	170
1991 You Have Touched So Many Hearts 427527	2-Yr.	1993	90.00	90
1991 May You Have An Old Fashioned Christmas 417785	2-Yr.	1993	150.00	175
1991 The Eyes Of The Lord Are Upon You (Boy Action Musical) 429570	Suspd.		65.00	65-70
1991 The Eyes Of The Lord Are Upon You (Girl Action Musical) 429589	Suspd.		65.00	65

Reco International

Childhood Doll Collection - S. Kuck

YEAR ISSUE	EDITION LIMIT	YEAR RETD.	ISSUE PRICE	*QUOTE U.S.$
1994 A Kiss Goodnight	Retrd.	1995	79.00	79-125
1995 Reading With Teddy	Retrd.	1995	79.00	79-125
1994 Teaching Teddy His Prayers	Retrd.	1997	79.00	79-125
1996 Teddy's Picnic	Retrd.	1997	79.00	79-125

Children's Circus Doll Collection - J. McClelland

YEAR ISSUE	EDITION LIMIT	YEAR RETD.	ISSUE PRICE	*QUOTE U.S.$
1991 Johnny The Strongman	Retrd.	1998	83.00	83
1991 Katie The Tightrope Walker	Retrd.	1998	78.00	78
1992 Maggie The Animal Trainer	Retrd.	1998	83.00	83
1991 Tommy The Clown	Retrd.	1998	78.00	78

Christmas Doll Collection - S. Kuck

YEAR ISSUE	EDITION LIMIT	YEAR RETD.	ISSUE PRICE	*QUOTE U.S.$
1996 Carol	Open		135.00	135
1997 Kristen	Open		135.00	135

Little Valentina - S. Kuck

YEAR ISSUE	EDITION LIMIT	YEAR RETD.	ISSUE PRICE	*QUOTE U.S.$
1998 Little Valentina	Open		N/A	N/A

Pocket Full of Love - S. Kuck

YEAR ISSUE	EDITION LIMIT	YEAR RETD.	ISSUE PRICE	*QUOTE U.S.$
1997 Gabriella	Open		30.00	30
1998 Tanya	Open		30.00	30

Precious Memories of Motherhood - S. Kuck

YEAR ISSUE	EDITION LIMIT	YEAR RETD.	ISSUE PRICE	*QUOTE U.S.$
1993 Bedtime	Retrd.	1994	149.00	149
1992 Expectant Moments	Retrd.	1993	149.00	149
1990 Loving Steps	Retrd.	1992	125.00	150-195
1991 Lullaby	Retrd.	1995	125.00	125-150

Wedding Doll - S. Kuck

YEAR ISSUE	EDITION LIMIT	YEAR RETD.	ISSUE PRICE	*QUOTE U.S.$
1997 Jennifer Rose	Open		195.00	195
1998 Audrey & Lindsey	Open		195.00	195

Roman, Inc.

Abbie Williams Collection - E. Williams

YEAR ISSUE	EDITION LIMIT	YEAR RETD.	ISSUE PRICE	*QUOTE U.S.$
1991 Molly	5,000	N/A	155.00	155

A Christmas Dream - E. Williams

YEAR ISSUE	EDITION LIMIT	YEAR RETD.	ISSUE PRICE	*QUOTE U.S.$
1990 Carole	5,000	N/A	125.00	125
1990 Chelsea	5,000	N/A	125.00	125

Classic Brides of the Century - E. Williams

YEAR ISSUE	EDITION LIMIT	YEAR RETD.	ISSUE PRICE	*QUOTE U.S.$
1991 Flora-The 1900's Bride	Yr.Iss.	1991	145.00	145
1992 Jennifer-The 1980's Bride	Yr.Iss.	1992	149.00	149
1993 Kathleen-The 1930's Bride	Yr.Iss.	1993	149.00	149

Ellen Williams Doll - E. Williams

YEAR ISSUE	EDITION LIMIT	YEAR RETD.	ISSUE PRICE	*QUOTE U.S.$
1989 Noelle	5,000	N/A	125.00	125
1989 Rebecca 999	7,500	N/A	195.00	195

San Francisco Music Box Company

Boyds Bears Musicals - G. M. Lowenthal

YEAR ISSUE	EDITION LIMIT	YEAR RETD.	ISSUE PRICE	*QUOTE U.S.$
1997 Allison Babbit Hare	Open		24.95	25
1997 Ariel with Heart Ornament	Open		9.95	10
1997 Ashley Hare	Closed	1998	24.95	25
1997 Benjamin Honey Bear with Sweater	Open		24.95	25
1998 Braxton B. Bear	Open		25.00	25
1998 Clarissa Bear	Open		57.00	57
1997 Cleo P. Pussytoes	Open		39.95	40
1997 Eugenia Bear	Closed	1998	49.95	50
1998 Fidelity B. Morgan IV Bear	Open		35.00	35
1997 Guinevere Bear	Open		24.95	25
1998 Heranamous	Open		35.00	35
1998 Momma McBear	Open		30.00	30
1997 Rosalind Bear	Closed	1998	39.95	40
1998 Rosalind II Bear	Open		40.00	40
1998 Rosie O'Pigg	Open		18.00	18
1997 Smith Witter II	Open		34.95	35

Musical Porcelain Dolls - San Francisco Music Box Company

YEAR ISSUE	EDITION LIMIT	YEAR RETD.	ISSUE PRICE	*QUOTE U.S.$
1997 Angelica Angel	600		200.00	200
1999 Ballerina	2,500		100.00	100
1999 Bride	2,500		200.00	200
1997 Christina Ballroom	1,500	1998	200.00	200
1998 Elizabeth Victorian	1,200		200.00	200
1999 Fairy	2,500		200.00	200
1997 Julia Bride	1,600	1998	200.00	200
1998 Michelle with Baby	1,200		200.00	200
1999 Mom & Toddler	2,500		200.00	200
1997 Priscilla Bride	600		200.00	200
1999 Rapunzel	2,500		100.00	100
1997 Therese Victorian	600	1998	200.00	200
1997 Tiffany Victorian	1,800	1998	200.00	200

Sandy Dolls Inc.

Angelic Maillé - G. Dy

YEAR ISSUE	EDITION LIMIT	YEAR RETD.	ISSUE PRICE	*QUOTE U.S.$
1998 Darielle	Open		75.00	75
1998 Deandra	Open		75.00	75
1998 Maribel	Open		75.00	75
1998 Moriah	Open		75.00	75

Gentle Dreams Baby - R. Tejada

YEAR ISSUE	EDITION LIMIT	YEAR RETD.	ISSUE PRICE	*QUOTE U.S.$
1998 Gentle Blossom - Cherokee	Open		35.00	35
1998 Gentle Dewdrop - Sioux	Open		35.00	35
1998 Gentle Fawn - Cheyenne	Open		35.00	35
1998 Gentle Flower - Hopi	Open		35.00	35
1998 Gentle Night - Blackfoot	Open		35.00	35
1998 Gentle Wind - Apache	Open		35.00	35

Sarah's Gang - S. Schultz

YEAR ISSUE	EDITION LIMIT	YEAR RETD.	ISSUE PRICE	*QUOTE U.S.$
1996 Buddy	Open		25.00	25
1996 Katie	Open		25.00	25
1997 Maria	Open		25.00	25
1997 Miguel	Open		25.00	25
1997 Sammy	Open		25.00	25
1997 Shina	Open		25.00	25
1996 Tillie	Open		25.00	25
1996 Willie	Open		25.00	25

Sweet Spirit Baby - R. Tejada

YEAR ISSUE	EDITION LIMIT	YEAR RETD.	ISSUE PRICE	*QUOTE U.S.$
1996 Little Blossom	1,500	1996	65.00	65
1997 Little Moonbeam	2,500	1997	85.00	85
1997 Little Raindrop	2,500	1998	85.00	85
1998 Little Bear's Track	2,500		85.00	85
1998 Little Sala	2,500		85.00	85

Traditions - R. Tejada

YEAR ISSUE	EDITION LIMIT	YEAR RETD.	ISSUE PRICE	*QUOTE U.S.$
1996 Angeni - Spirit Angel	500	1998	175.00	175

Warrior & Princess - R. Tejada

YEAR ISSUE	EDITION LIMIT	YEAR RETD.	ISSUE PRICE	*QUOTE U.S.$
1995 Bear's Track - Fox	5,000		37.50	38
1997 Evening Star - Ute	5,000		37.50	38
1997 Flying Falcon - Assiniboine	5,000		37.50	38
1997 Graceful Song - Cherokee	5,000		37.50	38
1996 Growling Bear - Mohegan	5,000		37.50	38
1995 Howling Dog - Cheyenne	5,000		37.50	38
1995 Laughing Brook - Comanche	5,000		37.50	38
1996 Leaping Water - Apache	5,000		37.50	38
1995 Little Otter - Hupa	5,000		37.50	38
1995 Pocahontas - Powhatan	5,000	1996	37.50	38
1996 Radiant Dove - Sioux	5,000		37.50	38
1994 Shining Cloud - Cheyenne	5,000	1997	37.50	38
1994 Soaring Hawk - Comanche	5,000	1997	37.50	38
1995 Swaying Reed - Chippewa	5,000		37.50	38
1997 White Stone - Cherokee	5,000		37.50	38
1996 Wind Rider with Horse - Nez Perce	5,000		60.00	60
1996 Wise Buffalo - Sioux	5,000		37.50	38

Sarah's Attic, Inc.

Heirlooms from the Attic - Sarah's Attic

YEAR ISSUE	EDITION LIMIT	YEAR RETD.	ISSUE PRICE	*QUOTE U.S.$
1991 Adora 1823	500	1991	90.00	200
1991 All Cloth Muffin blk. Doll 1820	Closed	1991	90.00	200
1991 All Cloth Puffin blk. Doll 1821	Closed	1991	90.00	200
1997 Burley Bear w/Sweater 5030	Closed	1998	130.00	130
1997 Country Patty 5034	Closed	1998	170.00	170
1997 Country Sassy 5033	Closed	1998	170.00	170
1991 Enos 1822	500	1991	90.00	200
1993 Granny Quilting Lady Doll 3576	Closed	1993	130.00	150
1989 Harmony-Victorian Clown 1464	500	1992	120.00	250
1992 Harpster w/Banjo 3591	Closed	1992	250.00	350
1997 Hazel Doll w/Bible 5032	Closed	1998	280.00	280
1990 Hickory-Americana 1771	Closed	1993	150.00	170
1990 Hickory-Beachtime 1769	2,000	1993	140.00	150-175
1991 Hickory-Christmas 1810	2,000	1993	150.00	150-175
1990 Hickory-Playtime 1768	2,000	1993	140.00	175
1990 Hickory-School Days 1766	2,000	1993	140.00	200
1991 Hickory-Springtime 1814	2,000	1993	150.00	195
1990 Hickory-Sunday's Best 1770	2,000	1993	150.00	225
1990 Hickory-Sweet Dreams 1767	2,000	1993	140.00	175
1992 Hilary-Victorian 1831	500	1993	200.00	250
1986 Holly Black Angel 0410	Closed	1986	34.00	34
1986 Holly blk. Angel 0410	Retrd.	1986	34.00	200
1992 Kiah Guardian Angel 3570	2,000	1993	170.00	200
1993 Lilla Quilting Lady Doll 3581	Closed	1993	130.00	200
1986 Maggie Cloth Doll 0012	Closed	1989	70.00	120
1986 Matt Cloth Doll 0011	Closed	1989	70.00	120
1993 Millie Quilting Lady Doll 3586	Closed	1993	130.00	150
1992 Peace on Earth Santa 3564	200	1992	175.00	500
1986 Priscilla Doll 0030	Closed	1989	140.00	300
1990 Sassafras-Americana 1685	2,000	1993	150.00	175
1990 Sassafras-Beachtime 1683	2,000	1993	140.00	175
1991 Sassafras-Christmas 1809	2,000	1993	150.00	150-175
1990 Sassafras-Playtime 1682	2,000	1993	140.00	200
1989 Sassafras-School Days 1680	2,000	1993	140.00	175
1991 Sassafras-Springtime 1813	2,000	1993	150.00	195
1990 Sassafras-Sunday's Best 1684	2,000	1993	150.00	225
1990 Sassafras-Sweet Dreams 1681	2,000	1993	140.00	195
1988 Smiley Clown Doll 3050	Closed	1988	126.00	126
1996 Snowman Doll 5047	Closed	1998	120.00	120
1990 Teddy Bear-Americana 1775	Closed	1992	160.00	160
1990 Teddy Bear-School Days 1774	Closed	1992	160.00	160
1997 Timmery 5031	Closed	1998	350.00	350
1986 Twinkie Doll 0039A	Closed	1986	32.00	32
1986 Whimpy Doll 0039E	Closed	1986	32.00	32
1992 Whoopie 3597	Closed	1992	200.00	200
1992 Wooster 3602	Closed	1992	160.00	160

Tattered n' Torn Collection - Sarah's Attic

YEAR ISSUE	EDITION LIMIT	YEAR RETD.	ISSUE PRICE	*QUOTE U.S.$
1994 Belle-Girl Rag Doll 4180	2,500	1996	30.00	30
1994 Britches-Boy Rag Doll 4181	2,500	1996	30.00	30

Seymour Mann, Inc.

Connossieur Doll Collection - E. Mann, unless otherwise noted

YEAR ISSUE	EDITION LIMIT	YEAR RETD.	ISSUE PRICE	*QUOTE U.S.$
1991 Abby 16" Pink Dress-C3145	Closed	1993	100.00	100
1995 Abby C-3229	2,500	1996	30.00	30
1994 Abby YK-4533	3,500	1995	135.00	135
1991 Abigail EP-3	Closed	1993	100.00	100

*Quotes have been rounded up to nearest dollar

YEAR ISSUE	EDITION LIMIT	YEAR RETD.	ISSUE PRICE	*QUOTE U.S.$
1991 Abigal WB-72WM	Closed	1993	75.00	75
1994 Adak PS-412	2,500	1995	150.00	150
1993 Adrienne C-3162	Closed	1994	135.00	135
1995 Aggie PS-435	2,500	1996	80.00	80
1991 Alexis 24" Beige Lace-EP32	Closed	1993	220.00	220
1994 Alice GU-32	2,500	1995	150.00	150
1994 Alice IND-508	2,500	1995	115.00	115
1992 Alice JNC-4013	Closed	1993	90.00	90
1998 Alicia AWL-522 - S. Mann	2,500		175.00	175
1995 Alicia C-3235	2,500	1996	65.00	65
1991 Alicia YK-4215	Closed	1993	90.00	90
1995 Allison CD-18183	2,500		35.00	35
1995 Allison TR-92	2,500	1996	125.00	125
1994 Ally FH-556	2,500	1995	115.00	115
1994 Alyssa C-3201	2,500	1995	110.00	110
1994 Alyssa PP-1	2,500	1996	275.00	300
1991 Amanda Toast-OM-182	Closed	1993	260.00	260
1995 Amanda TR-96	2,500	1996	135.00	135
1989 Amber DOM-281A	Closed	1993	85.00	85
1991 Amelia-TR-47	Closed	1993	105.00	105
1991 Amy C-3147	Closed	1993	135.00	135
1995 Amy GU-300A	2,500	1995	30.00	30
1994 Amy OC-43M	2,500	1996	115.00	115
1992 Amy OM-06	2,500	1993	150.00	200
1990 Anabelle C-3080	Closed	1992	85.00	85
1990 Angel DOM-335	Closed	1992	105.00	105
1995 Angel FH-291DP	2,500		70.00	70
1994 Angel LL-956	2,500	1996	90.00	90
1994 Angel SP-460	2,500	1996	140.00	140
1998 Angela AWL-518 - S. Mann	7,500		75.00	75
1990 Angela C-3084	Closed	1992	105.00	105
1990 Angela C-3084M	Closed	1992	115.00	115
1995 Angela Doll 556	2,500	1996	35.00	35
1995 Angela FH-511	2,500		85.00	85
1995 Angela OM-87	2,500		150.00	150
1995 Angelica FH-291B	2,500		70.00	70
1994 Angelica FH-291E	2,500		85.00	85
1995 Angelica FH-511B	2,500		85.00	85
1994 Angelina FH-291S	2,500		85.00	85
1995 Angelina FH-291S	2,500		70.00	70
1995 Angeline FH-291WG	2,500		75.00	75
1994 Angeline FH-291WG	2,500		85.00	85
1995 Angeline OM-84	2,500		100.00	100
1994 Angelita FH-291G	2,500		85.00	85
1994 Angelo OC-57	2,500		135.00	135
1990 Anita FH-277G	Closed	1992	65.00	65
1991 Ann TR-52	Closed	1993	135.00	135
1995 Annette FH-635	2,500		110.00	110
1991 Annette TR-59	Closed	1993	130.00	130
1996 Annie PS-462	2,500	1998	100.00	100
1991 Antoinette FH-452	Closed	1993	100.00	100
1993 Antonia OM-227	2,500	1993	350.00	350
1994 Antonia OM-42	2,500	1996	150.00	150
1997 Antonio FH-820	7,500	1998	150.00	150
1995 April CD-2212B	2,500		50.00	50
1991 Arabella C-3163	Closed	1993	135.00	135
1991 Ariel 34" Blue/White-EP-33	Closed	1993	175.00	175
1995 Ariel OM-81	2,500		185.00	240
1994 Arilene LL-940	2,500	1994	90.00	90
1993 Arlene SP-421	Closed	1993	100.00	100
1988 Ashley C-278	Closed	1990	80.00	80
1989 Ashley C-278	Closed	1993	80.00	80
1990 Ashley FH-325	Closed	1993	75.00	75
1995 Ashley OC-76	2,500		40.00	40
1995 Ashley PS-433	2,500		110.00	110
1994 Atanak PS-414	2,500	1994	150.00	150
1991 Audrey FH-455	2,500	1993	125.00	125
1990 Audrey YK-4089	Closed	1992	125.00	125
1987 Audrina YK-200	Closed	1986	85.00	140
1991 Aurora Gold 22"-OM-181	2,500	1993	260.00	260
1991 Azure AM-15	2,500	1993	175.00	175
1994 Baby Belle C-3193	2,500	1994	150.00	150
1991 Baby Beth DOLL-406P	2,500	1993	27.50	28
1995 Baby Betsy Doll 336	2,500		75.00	75
1990 Baby Betty YK-4087	Closed	1991	125.00	125
1991 Baby Bonnie SP-341	Closed	1993	55.00	55
1990 Baby Bonnie SP-341	Closed	1991	55.00	55
1991 Baby Brent EP-15	Closed	1993	85.00	110
1991 Baby Carrie DOLL-402P	2,500	1993	27.50	28
1990 Baby Ecru WB-17	Closed	1991	65.00	65
1991 Baby Ellie Ecru Musical DOLL-402E	2,500	1993	27.50	28
1991 Baby Gloria Black Baby PS-289	Closed	1993	75.00	75
1991 Baby John PS-498	Closed	1993	85.00	85
1989 Baby John PS-49B	Closed	1991	85.00	85
1990 Baby Kate WB-19	Closed	1991	85.00	85
1991 Baby Linda DOLL-406E	2,500	1993	27.50	28
1990 Baby Nelly PS-163	Closed	1991	95.00	95
1994 Baby Scarlet C-3194	2,500	1994	115.00	115
1991 Baby Sue DOLL-402B	2,500	1993	27.50	28
1990 Baby Sue DOLL-402B	Closed	1992	27.50	28
1990 Baby Sunshine C-3055	Closed	1992	90.00	90
1995 Barbara PS-439	2,500		65.00	65
1991 Belinda C-3164	Closed	1993	150.00	150
1991 Bernetta EP-40	Closed	1993	115.00	115
1995 Beth OC-74	2,500		40.00	40
1992 Beth OM-05	Closed	1993	135.00	135
1990 Beth YK-4099A/B	Closed	1992	125.00	125
1991 Betsy AM-6	Closed	1993	105.00	105
1997 Betsy AWL-506 - S. Mann	2,500		50.00	50
1995 Betsy C-3224	2,500		45.00	45
1995 Betsy OM-89B	2,500		125.00	175
1995 Betsy RDK-230	2,500		35.00	35
1992 Bette OM-01	2,500	1993	115.00	115
1990 Bettina TR-4	Closed	1991	125.00	125
1991 Bettina YK-4144	Closed	1993	105.00	105
1995 Betty LL-996	2,500	1996	115.00	115
1989 Betty PS27G	Closed	1993	65.00	125
1995 Bianca CD-1450C	2,500		35.00	35
1990 Billie YK-4056V	Closed	1992	65.00	65
1993 Blaine C-3167	Closed	1993	100.00	100
1994 Blair YK-4532	3,500	1994	150.00	150
1991 Blythe CH-15V	Closed	1993	135.00	135
1991 Bo-Peep w/Lamb C-3128	Closed	1993	105.00	105
1994 Bobbi NM-30	2,500	1994	135.00	135
1994 Brandy YK-4537	3,500	1995	165.00	165
1995 Brenda Doll 551	2,500		60.00	60
1989 Brett PS27B	Closed	1992	65.00	125
1997 Briana OM-164 - C. Wang	5,000		150.00	200
1995 Brianna GU-300B	2,500		30.00	30
1997 Bride VL-159 - S. Mann	2,500		200.00	200
1991 Bridget SP-379	2,500	1993	105.00	105
1995 Brie C-3230	2,500		30.00	30
1995 Brie CD-16310C	2,500		30.00	30
1995 Brie OM-89W	2,500		125.00	125
1995 Britt OC-77	2,500		40.00	40
1995 Brittany Doll 558	2,500		35.00	35
1989 Brittany TK-4	Closed	1990	150.00	150
1997 Brooke Ashley VL -154 - S. Mann	2,500		135.00	135
1991 Brooke FH-461	2,500	1993	115.00	115
1994 Browyn IND-517	2,500	1994	140.00	140
1991 Bryna AM-100B	2,500	1993	70.00	70
1995 Bryna DOLL-555	2,500		35.00	35
1995 Bunny TR-97	2,500		85.00	85
1995 Burgundy Angel FH-291D	2,500		75.00	75
1994 Cactus Flower Indian LL-944	2,500	1994	105.00	105
1990 Caillin DOLL-11PH	Closed	1992	60.00	60
1995 Caitlin LL-997	2,500		115.00	115
1990 Caitlin YK-4051V	Closed	1992	90.00	90
1994 Callie TR-76	2,500	1994	140.00	140
1994 Calypso LL-942	2,500	1994	150.00	150
1991 Camellia FH-457	2,500	1993	100.00	100
1986 Camelot Fairy C-84	Closed	1988	75.00	225
1993 Camille OM-230	2,500	1994	250.00	250
1995 Candice TR-94	2,500	1995	135.00	135
1995 Carmel TR-93	2,500		125.00	125
1994 Carmen PS-408	2,500	1994	150.00	150
1990 Carole YK-4085W	Closed	1992	125.00	125
1991 Caroline LL-838	2,500	1993	110.00	110
1991 Caroline LL-905	2,500	1993	110.00	110
1997 Caroline RDK-838B - S. Mann	2,500		80.00	125
1995 Carolotta OM-80	2,500		175.00	200
1995 Carrie C-3231	2,500		30.00	30
1994 Casey C-3197	2,500	1995	140.00	140
1995 Catherine RDK-231	2,500		30.00	30
1994 Cathy GU-41	2,500	1994	140.00	140
1995 Cecily Doll 552	2,500		60.00	60
1995 Celene FH-618	2,500		120.00	120
1995 Celestine LL-982	2,500	1996	100.00	100
1997 Charity & Joshua TEC-564B/G - S. Mann	2,500		85.00	85
1990 Charlene YK-4112	Closed	1992	90.00	90
1992 Charlotte FH-484	2,500	1993	115.00	115
1995 Chelsea DOLL-560	2,500		35.00	35
1992 Chelsea IND-397	Closed	1993	85.00	85
1995 Cherry FH-616	2,500	1994	100.00	100
1991 Cheryl TR-49	2,500	1993	120.00	120
1991 Chin Chin YK-4211	Closed	1993	85.00	85
1990 Chin Fa C-3061	Closed	1992	95.00	95
1990 Chinook WB-24	Closed	1992	85.00	85
1994 Chris FH-561	2,500	1994	85.00	85
1994 Chrissie FH-562	2,500	1994	85.00	85
1990 Chrissie WB-2	Closed	1992	75.00	75
1991 Christina PS-261	Closed	1993	115.00	115
1985 Christmas Cheer 125	Closed	1988	40.00	100
1995 Christmas Kitten IND-530	2,500		100.00	140
1991 Cindy Lou FH-464	2,500	1993	85.00	85
1994 Cindy OC-58	2,500	1994	140.00	140
1993 Cinnamon JNC-4014	Closed	1993	90.00	90
1988 Cissie DOM263	Closed	1990	65.00	135
1991 Cissy EP-56	2,500	1993	95.00	95
1995 Clancy GU-54	2,500	1995	80.00	80
1994 Clara IND-518	2,500	1994	140.00	140
1994 Clara IND-524	2,500	1994	150.00	150
1991 Clare DOLL-465	Open	1993	100.00	100
1993 Clare FH-497	2,500	1993	100.00	100
1994 Claudette TR-81	2,500	1995	150.00	150
1991 Claudine C-3146	Closed	1993	95.00	95
1993 Clothilde FH-469	2,500	1993	125.00	125
1995 Cody FH-629	2,500	1995	120.00	120
1991 Colette WB-7	Closed	1993	65.00	65
1991 Colleen YK-4163	Closed	1993	120.00	120
1991 Cookie GU-6	2,500	1993	110.00	110
1994 Copper YK-4546C	3,500		150.00	150
1994 Cora FH-565	2,500		140.00	140
1992 Cordelia OM-09	2,500	1993	250.00	250
1991 Courtney LL-859	2,500	1993	150.00	150
1991 Creole AM-17	2,500	1993	160.00	200
1989 Crying Courtney PS-75	Closed	1992	115.00	115
1991 Crystal YK-4237	3,500	1993	125.00	125
1997 Cute Kathy TEC-591	7,500	1998	30.00	30
1987 Cynthia DOM-211	Closed	1986	85.00	85
1995 Cynthia GU-300C	2,500		30.00	30
1998 Cynthia TR-4240 - S. Mann	7,500		105.00	105
1990 Daisy EP-6	Closed	1992	90.00	90
1994 Dallas PS-403	2,500	1994	150.00	150
1991 Danielle AM-5	Closed	1993	125.00	175
1995 Danielle MER-808	2,500	1996	65.00	65
1995 Danielle PS-432	2,500		100.00	100
1989 Daphne Ecru/Mint Green C3025	Closed	1992	85.00	85
1991 Darcy EP-47	Closed	1993	110.00	110
1991 Darcy FH-451	2,500	1993	105.00	105
1995 Darcy FH-636	2,500	1996	80.00	80
1995 Darcy LL-986	2,500		110.00	110
1991 Daria C-3122	Closed	1993	110.00	110
1995 Darla LL-988	2,500	1996	100.00	100
1991 Darlene DOLL-444	2,500	1993	75.00	75
1994 Daryl LL-947	2,500	1994	150.00	150
1991 Dawn C-3135	Closed	1993	130.00	130
1987 Dawn C185	Closed	1986	75.00	175
1992 Debbie JNC-4006	Open	1993	90.00	90
1994 Dee LL-948	2,500	1994	110.00	110
1992 Deidre FH-473	2,500	1993	115.00	115
1992 Deidre YK-4083	Closed	1993	95.00	95
1994 Delilah C-3195	2,500	1994	150.00	150
1991 Delphine SP-308	Closed	1993	135.00	135
1991 Denise LL-852	2,500	1993	105.00	105
1995 Denise LL-994	2,500	1996	105.00	105
1991 Desiree LL-898	2,500	1993	120.00	120
1995 Diana RDK-221A	2,500		35.00	35
1990 Diane FH-275	Closed	1992	90.00	90
1995 Diane PS-444	2,500		110.00	110
1990 Dianna TK-31	Closed	1992	175.00	175
1995 Dinah OC-79	2,500		40.00	40
1988 Doll Oliver FH392	Closed	1990	100.00	100
1990 Domino C-3050	Closed	1992	145.00	200
1992 Dona FH-494	2,500	1993	100.00	100
1993 Donna DOLL-447	2,500	1993	85.00	85
1990 Dorothy TR-10	Closed	1992	135.00	150
1991 Duanane SP-366	Closed	1993	85.00	85
1995 Dulcie FH-622	2,500		110.00	110
1991 Dulcie YK-4131V	Closed	1993	100.00	100
1991 Edie YK-4177	Closed	1993	115.00	115
1998 Edwina NY-134 - S. Mann	2,500		85.00	85
1990 Eileen FH-367	Closed	1992	100.00	100
1995 Elaine CD-02210	2,500		50.00	50
1995 Eleanor C16669	2,500		35.00	35
1991 Elisabeth and Lisa C-3095	2,500	1993	195.00	195
1989 Elisabeth OM-32	Closed	1990	120.00	120
1991 Elise PS-259	Closed	1993	105.00	105
1997 Elizabeth & Child VL-151 - S. Mann	2,500		200.00	200
1991 Elizabeth AM-32	2,500	1993	105.00	105
1989 Elizabeth C-246P	Closed	1990	150.00	200
1995 Elizabeth DOLL-553	2,500		35.00	40
1997 Elizabeth VL-151 - S. Mann	2,500		200.00	200
1993 Ellen YK-4223	3,500	1994	150.00	150
1995 Ellie FH-621	2,500	1996	125.00	125
1998 Elvira NY-133 - S. Mann	2,500		85.00	85
1996 Emily DOLL-718E	7,500	1998	40.00	40
1989 Emily PS-48	Closed	1990	110.00	110
1988 Emily YK-243V	Closed	1990	70.00	70
1995 Emma DOLL-559	2,500		35.00	35
1995 Emma GU-300E	2,500		30.00	30
1991 Emmaline Beige/Lilac OM-197	Closed	1993	300.00	300
1991 Emmaline OM-191	2,500	1993	300.00	300
1991 Emmy C-3099	Closed	1993	125.00	125
1991 Erin DOLL-4PH	Closed	1993	60.00	60
1995 Erin RDK-223	2,500		30.00	30
1992 Eugenie OM-225	2,500	1993	300.00	300
1991 Evalina C-3124	Closed	1993	135.00	135
1994 Faith IND-522	2,500	1994	135.00	135
1994 Faith OC-60	2,500	1994	115.00	115
1995 Fawn C-3228	2,500		55.00	55
1995 Felicia GU-300F	2,500		30.00	30
1990 Felicia TR-9	Closed	1992	115.00	115
1991 Fifi AM-100F	Closed	1993	70.00	70
1995 Fleur C-16415	2,500		30.00	30
1991 Fleurette PS-286	2,500	1993	75.00	75
1994 Flora FH-583	2,500	1994	115.00	115
1991 Flora TR-46	Closed	1993	125.00	125
1994 Florette IND-519	2,500	1994	140.00	140
1998 Flower Fairie TEC-566 - S. Mann	5,000		45.00	45
1988 Frances C-233	Closed	1990	80.00	125
1991 Francesca AM-14	2,500	1993	175.00	175
1990 Francesca C-3021	Closed	1992	100.00	175
1994 Gardiner PS-405	2,500		150.00	150
1993 Gena OM-229	Closed	1994	250.00	250
1997 Gena VL-156 - S. Mann	2,500		125.00	125
1998 Gene TR-4184 - S. Mann	2,500		105.00	105
1994 Georgia IND-510	2,500	1995	220.00	220
1995 Georgia IND-528	2,500		125.00	125
1994 Georgia SP-456	2,500		115.00	115
1991 Georgia YK-4131	Closed	1993	100.00	100
1991 Georgia YK-4143	Closed	1993	150.00	150
1990 Gerri Beige YK4094	Closed	1992	95.00	140
1991 Gigi C-3107	Closed	1993	135.00	135
1991 Ginger LL-907	Closed	1993	115.00	115
1995 Ginnie FH-619	2,500		110.00	125
1990 Ginny YK-4119	Closed	1995	100.00	100
1992 Giselle OM-02	Closed	1993	90.00	90
1988 Giselle on Goose FH176	Closed	1990	105.00	225
1991 Gloria AM-100G	2,500	1993	70.00	70
1991 Gloria YK-4166	Closed	1993	105.00	105
1995 Gold Angel FH-511G	2,500		85.00	85
1995 Green Angel FH-511C	2,500		85.00	85
1991 Gretchen DOLL-446	Open	1993	45.00	45
1995 Gretchen FH-620	2,500	1995	120.00	120

*Quotes have been rounded up to nearest dollar

YEAR ISSUE	EDITION LIMIT	YEAR RETD.	ISSUE PRICE	*QUOTE U.S.$
1991 Gretel DOLL-434	Closed	1993	60.00	60
1995 Guardian Angel OM-91	2,500		150.00	150
1995 Guardian Angel TR-98	2,500		85.00	85
1996 Hali MC-11	2,500	1998	100.00	100
1991 Hansel and Gretel DOLL-448V	Closed	1993	60.00	60
1989 Happy Birthday C3012	Closed	1990	80.00	125
1993 Happy FH-479	2,500	1994	105.00	105
1995 Happy RDK-238	2,500		25.00	25
1994 Hatty/Matty IND-514	2,500		165.00	165
1995 Heather LL-991	2,500		115.00	115
1995 Heather PS-436	2,500		115.00	115
1994 Heather YK-4531	3,500		165.00	165
1993 Hedy FH-449	Closed	1994	95.00	95
1989 Heidi 260	Closed	1990	50.00	95
1991 Helene AM-29	2,500	1993	150.00	150
1995 Holly CD-16526	2,500		30.00	30
1991 Holly CH-6	Closed	1993	100.00	100
1991 Honey Bunny WB-9	Closed	1993	70.00	70
1991 Honey FH-401	Closed	1993	100.00	100
1994 Honey LL-945	2,500	1996	150.00	150
1991 Hope FH-434	2,500	1993	90.00	90
1996 Hope FH-800G	2,500	1998	75.00	75
1990 Hope YK-4118	Closed	1992	90.00	90
1995 Hyacinth C-3227	2,500		130.00	130
1990 Hyacinth DOLL-15PH	Closed	1992	85.00	85
1994 Hyacinth LL-941	2,500	1995	90.00	90
1990 Indian Doll FH-295	Closed	1992	60.00	60
1994 Indian IND-520	2,500		115.00	115
1991 Indira AM-4	2,500	1993	125.00	125
1995 Irene GU-56	2,500		85.00	85
1995 Irina RDK-237	2,500		35.00	35
1993 Iris FH-483	2,500	1994	95.00	95
1991 Iris TR-58	Closed	1993	120.00	120
1995 Ivana RDK-233	2,500		35.00	35
1994 Ivy C-3203	2,500	1996	85.00	85
1991 Ivy PS-307	Closed	1993	75.00	75
1994 Jacqueline C-3202	2,500		150.00	150
1995 Jamaica LL-989	2,500		75.00	75
1993 Jan Dress-Up OM-12	2,500	1994	135.00	175
1994 Jan FH-584R	2,500		115.00	115
1992 Jan OM-012	9,200	1993	135.00	135
1991 Jane PS-243L	Closed	1993	115.00	115
1992 Janet FH-496	2,500	1993	120.00	120
1990 Janette DOLL-385	Closed	1992	85.00	85
1991 Janice OM-194	2,500	1993	300.00	300
1994 Janis FH-584B	2,500		115.00	115
1989 Jaqueline DOLL-254M	Closed	1990	85.00	85
1998 Jasmine SJ-512 - S. Mann	7,500		30.00	30
1995 Jennifer PS-446	2,500		145.00	145
1998 Jennifer TR-4197 - S. Mann	2,500		105.00	105
1995 Jenny CD-16673B	2,500		35.00	50
1994 Jenny OC-36M	2,500		115.00	115
1995 Jerri PS-434	2,500		100.00	100
1988 Jessica DOM-267	Closed	1990	90.00	90
1991 Jessica FH-423	2,500	1993	95.00	95
1995 Jessica RDK-225	2,500		30.00	30
1992 Jet FH-478	2,500	1993	115.00	150
1995 Jewel TR-100	2,500		110.00	110
1994 Jillian C-3196	2,500		150.00	150
1990 Jillian DOLL-41PH	Closed	1992	90.00	90
1993 Jillian SP-428	Closed	1994	165.00	165
1994 Jo YK-4539	3,500	1995	150.00	150
1988 Joanne Cry Baby PS-50	Closed	1990	100.00	100
1990 Joanne TR-12	Closed	1992	175.00	175
1992 Jodie FH-495	2,500	1993	115.00	115
1995 Joella CD-16779	2,500	1996	35.00	35
1988 Jolie C231	Closed	1990	65.00	150
1994 Jordan SP-455	2,500		150.00	150
1995 Joy CD-1450A	2,500		35.00	35
1991 Joy EP-23V	Closed	1993	130.00	130
1995 Joy TR-99	2,500		85.00	135
1991 Joyce AM-100J	2,500	1993	35.00	35
1991 Julia C-3102	Closed	1993	135.00	135
1995 Julia C-3234	2,500		100.00	100
1995 Julia RDK-222	2,500		35.00	35
1997 Juliana PS-481 - S. Mann	2,500		90.00	90
1988 Julie C245A	Closed	1990	65.00	160
1990 Julie WB-35	Closed	1992	70.00	70
1988 Juliette Bride Musical C246LTM	Closed	1990	150.00	200
1992 Juliette OM-08	2,500	1993	175.00	175
1991 Juliette OM-192	2,500	1993	300.00	300
1993 Juliette OM-8	2,500	1994	175.00	175
1995 June CD-2212	2,500		50.00	50
1991 Karen EP-24	Closed	1993	115.00	115
1990 Karen PS-198	Closed	1992	150.00	150
1991 Karmela EP-57	2,500	1993	120.00	120
1995 Karyn RDK-224	2,500		35.00	35
1990 Kate C-3060	Closed	1992	95.00	95
1994 Kate OC-55	2,500		150.00	150
1997 Katherine VL-158 - S. Mann	2,500		200.00	200
1990 Kathy w/Bear-TE1	Closed	1992	70.00	70
1994 Katie IND-511	2,500		110.00	110
1989 Kayoko PS-24	Closed	1991	75.00	175
1991 Kelly AM-8	Closed	1993	125.00	125
1997 Kelly AWL-500 - S. Mann	2,500		75.00	75
1994 Kelly YK-4536	3,500		150.00	150
1995 Kelsey Doll 561	2,500		35.00	35
1993 Kendra FH-481	2,500	1994	115.00	115
1991 Kerry FH-396	Closed	1993	100.00	100
1994 Kevin MS-25	2,500		150.00	150
1994 Kevin YK-4543	3,500		140.00	140
1990 Kiku EP-4	Closed	1992	100.00	100

YEAR ISSUE	EDITION LIMIT	YEAR RETD.	ISSUE PRICE	*QUOTE U.S.$
1991 Kim AM-100K	2,500	1993	70.00	70
1995 Kimmie CD-15816	2,500		30.00	30
1991 Kinesha SP-402	2,500	1993	110.00	110
1989 Kirsten PS-40G	Closed	1991	70.00	70
1993 Kit SP-426	Closed	1994	55.00	55
1994 Kit YK-4547	3,500		115.00	115
1994 Kitten IND-512	2,500	1996	110.00	110
1995 Kitty IND-527	2,500	1996	40.00	40
1991 Kristi FH-402	Closed	1993	100.00	100
1991 Kyla YK-4137	Closed	1993	95.00	150
1994 Lady Caroline LL-830	2,500		120.00	120
1994 Lady Caroline LL-939	2,500		120.00	120
1994 Laughing Waters PS-410	2,500		150.00	150
1990 Laura DOLL-25PH	Closed	1992	55.00	55
1992 Laura OM-010	2,500	1993	250.00	250
1991 Laura WB-110P	Closed	1993	85.00	85
1990 Lauren SP-300	Closed	1992	85.00	85
1994 Lauren SP-458	2,500		125.00	125
1992 Laurie JNC-4004	Open	1993	90.00	90
1990 Lavender Blue YK-4024	Closed	1992	95.00	135
1991 Leigh DOLL-457	2,500	1993	95.00	95
1991 Leila AM-2	Closed	1993	125.00	125
1995 Lenore FH-617	2,500		120.00	120
1991 Lenore LL-911	2,500	1993	105.00	105
1995 Lenore RDK-229	2,500		50.00	50
1991 Lenore YK-4218	3,500	1995	135.00	135
1995 Leslie LL-983	2,500		105.00	105
1995 Leslie MER-809	2,500		65.00	65
1991 Libby EP-18	Closed	1993	85.00	85
1990 Lien Wha YK-4092	Closed	1992	100.00	150
1991 Lila AM-10	2,500	1993	125.00	125
1991 Lila FH-404	2,500	1993	100.00	125
1995 Lila GU-55	2,500		55.00	55
1995 Lili CD-16888	2,500		30.00	30
1995 Lily FH-630	2,500	1996	120.00	175
1995 Lily in pink stripe IND-533	2,500	1995	85.00	85
1987 Linda C190	Closed	1986	60.00	120
1993 Linda SP-435	Closed	1994	95.00	95
1995 Lindsay PS-442	2,500		175.00	175
1994 Lindsay SP-462	2,500		150.00	150
1991 Lindsey C-3127	Closed	1993	135.00	175
1991 Linetta C-3166	Closed	1993	135.00	135
1990 Ling-Ling DOLL	Closed	1992	50.00	50
1989 Ling-Ling PS-87G	Closed	1991	90.00	90
1988 Lionel FH206B	Closed	1990	50.00	120
1991 Lisa AM-100L	2,500	1993	70.00	70
1990Lisa Beige Accordian Pleat YK4093	Closed	1992	125.00	125
1990 Lisa FH-379	Closed	1992	100.00	100
1995 Lisette LL-993	2,500		105.00	105
1995 Little Bobby RDK-235	2,500		25.00	25
1991 Little Boy Blue C-3159	Closed	1993	100.00	100
1995 Little Lisa OM-86	2,500		125.00	125
1995 Little Lori RDK-228	2,500		20.00	20
1995 Little Lou RDK-227	2,500		20.00	20
1995 Little Mary RDK-234	2,500		25.00	25
1995 Little Patty PS-429	2,500		50.00	50
1994 Little Red Riding Hood FH-557	2,500		140.00	140
1991 Liz C-3150	2,500	1993	100.00	100
1989 Liz YK-269	Closed	1991	70.00	100
1990 Liza C-3053	Closed	1992	100.00	100
1991 Liza YK-4226	3,500	1993	35.00	35
1991 Lola SP-363	2,500	1993	90.00	90
1990 Lola SP-79	Closed	1992	105.00	105
1991 Loni FH-448	2,500	1993	100.00	100
1990 Loretta FH-321	Closed	1992	90.00	90
1994 Loretta SP-457	2,500		140.00	140
1991 Lori EP-52	2,500	1993	95.00	95
1990 Lori WB-72BM	Closed	1992	75.00	75
1991 Louise LL-908	2,500	1993	105.00	105
1995 Lucie MER-607	2,500		65.00	65
1988 Lucinda DOM-293	Closed	1990	90.00	90
1989 Lucinda DOM-293	Closed	1990	90.00	90
1994 Lucinda PS-406	2,500		150.00	150
1991 Lucy LL-853	Closed	1993	80.00	80
1992 Lydia OM-226	2,500	1993	250.00	250
1993 Lynn FH-498	2,500	1994	120.00	120
1995 Lynn LL-995	2,500	1996	105.00	105
1990 Madame De Pompadour C-3088	Closed	1992	250.00	250
1991 Madeleine C-3106	Closed	1993	95.00	95
1995 Mae PS-431	2,500		70.00	70
1992 Maggie FH-505	Closed	1993	125.00	125
1995 Maggie IND-532	2,500		80.00	80
1990 Maggie PS-151P	Closed	1992	90.00	90
1990 Maggie WB-51	Closed	1992	105.00	105
1994 Magnolia FH-558	2,500		150.00	150
1989 Mai-Ling PS-79	2,500	1991	100.00	100
1994 Maiden PS-409	2,500	1995	150.00	150
1994 Mandy YK-4548	3,500		115.00	115
1989 Marcey YK-4005	3,500	1995	90.00	90
1991 Marcy TR-55	Closed	1993	135.00	135
1987 Marcy YK122	Closed	1986	55.00	100
1989 Margaret 245	Closed	1991	100.00	150
1994 Margaret C-3204	2,500		150.00	150
1994 Maria GU-35	2,500		115.00	115
1997 Maria VL-160 - S. Mann	2,500		175.00	175
1990 Maria YK-4116	Closed	1992	85.00	85
1993 Mariah LL-909	Closed	1993	135.00	135
1991 Mariel 18" Ivory-C-3119	Closed	1993	125.00	125
1995 Marielle PS-443	2,500		175.00	175
1998 Marilyn AWL-515 - S. Mann	7,500		90.00	90
1995 Marla PS-437	2,500		125.00	125
1995 Martina RDK-232	2,500		35.00	50

YEAR ISSUE	EDITION LIMIT	YEAR RETD.	ISSUE PRICE	*QUOTE U.S.$
1995 Mary Ann FH-633	2,500	1996	110.00	110
1994 Mary Ann TR-79	2,500		125.00	125
1995 Mary Elizabeth OC-51	2,500	1996	50.00	50
1994 Mary Jo FH-552	2,500		150.00	150
1994 Mary Lou FH-565	2,500		135.00	135
1994 Mary OC-56	2,500		135.00	135
1991 Maude AM-100M	2,500	1993	70.00	70
1989 Maureen PS-84	Closed	1990	90.00	90
1995 Maxine C-3225	2,500		125.00	125
1995 Mc Kenzie LL-987	2,500		100.00	100
1994 Megan C-3192	2,500		150.00	150
1995 Megan RDK-220	2,500		30.00	30
1989 Meimei PS22	Closed	1990	75.00	225
1990 Melanie YK-4115	Closed	1992	80.00	80
1991 Melissa AM-9	Closed	1993	120.00	120
1991 Melissa CH-3	Closed	1993	110.00	110
1990 Melissa DOLL-390	Closed	1992	75.00	75
1989 Melissa LL-794	Closed	1990	95.00	95
1991 Melissa LL-901	Closed	1993	135.00	135
1992 Melissa OM-03	2,500	1993	135.00	135
1997 Mercedes AWL-501 - S. Mann	2,500		75.00	75
1991 Meredith FH-391-P	Closed	1993	95.00	95
1995 Meredith MER-806	2,500	1996	65.00	65
1995 Merri MER-810	2,500	1996	65.00	65
1990 Merry Widow 20" C-3040M	Closed	1992	140.00	140
1991 Meryl FH-463	2,500	1993	95.00	95
1991 Michael w/School Books FH-439B	2,500	1993	95.00	95
1988 Michelle & Marcel YK176	Closed	1990	70.00	150
1991 Michelle Lilac/Green EP36	Closed	1993	95.00	95
1991 Michelle w/School Books FH-439G	Closed	1993	95.00	95
1995 Mindi PS-441	2,500	1995	125.00	125
1995 Mindy LL-990	2,500		75.00	75
1995 Miranda C16456B	2,500		30.00	30
1991 Miranda DOLL-9PH	Closed	1993	75.00	75
1995 Miranda TR-91	2,500		135.00	135
1984 Miss Debutante Debi	Closed	1987	75.00	180
1994 Miss Elizabeth SP-459	2,500		150.00	150
1989 Miss Kim PS-25	Closed	1990	75.00	175
1991 Missy DOLL-464	Closed	1993	70.00	70
1994 Missy FH-567	2,500	1996	140.00	140
1991 Missy PS-258	Closed	1993	90.00	90
1991 Mon Yun w/Parasol TR33	2,500	1993	115.00	150
1995 Monica TR-95	2,500		135.00	135
1994 Morning Dew Indian PS-404	2,500		150.00	150
1998 Musical Cathy TEC-591 - S. Mann	7,500		30.00	30
1994 Musical Doll OC-45M	2,500		140.00	140
1991 Nancy 21" Pink w/Rabbit EP-31	Closed	1993	165.00	165
1997 Nancy AWL-502 - S. Mann	2,500		60.00	60
1995 Nancy FH-615	2,500		100.00	100
1992 Nancy JNC-4001	Open	1993	90.00	90
1991 Nancy WB-73	2,500	1993	65.00	65
1990 Nanook WB-23	Closed	1992	75.00	75
1994 Natalie PP-2	2,500		275.00	275
1990 Natasha PS-102	Closed	1992	100.00	100
1995 Natasha TR-90	2,500		125.00	125
1991 Nellie EP-1B	Closed	1993	75.00	75
1996 Nicki MCC-501	2,500	1998	105.00	105
1991 Nicole AM-12	Closed	1993	135.00	135
1994 Nikki PS-401	2,500	1995	150.00	150
1994 Nikki SP-461	2,500		150.00	150
1993 Nina YK-4232	3,500	1993	135.00	135
1987 Nirmala YK-210	Closed	1995	50.00	50
1994 Noel MS-27	2,500		150.00	150
1994 Noelle C-3199	2,500		195.00	195
1994 Noelle MS-28	2,500		150.00	150
1991 Noelle PS-239V	Closed	1993	95.00	95
1995 Norma C-3226	2,500		135.00	135
1990 Odessa FH-362	Closed	1992	65.00	65
1994 Odetta IND-521	2,500	1995	140.00	140
1993 Oona TR-57	Closed	1993	135.00	135
1994 Oriana IND-515	2,500		140.00	140
1998 Orlando VL131 - S. Mann	2,500		250.00	250
1995 Our First Skates RDK-226/BG	2,500		50.00	50
1994 Paige GU-33	2,500		150.00	150
1995 Paige IND-529	2,500		80.00	80
1994 Pamela LL-949	2,500		115.00	115
1995 Pan Pan GU-52	2,500		60.00	60
1994 Panama OM-43	2,500		195.00	195
1989 Patricia/Patrick 215GBB	Closed	1990	105.00	135
1997 Patsy OM-134	2,500		95.00	95
1991 Patti DOLL-440	2,500	1993	65.00	65
1995 Patty C-3220	2,500		60.00	60
1994 Patty GU-34	2,500		115.00	115
1991 Patty YK-4221	3,500	1993	125.00	125
1989 Paula PS-56	Closed	1990	75.00	75
1995 Paulette PS-430	2,500		80.00	80
1989 Pauline Bonaparte OM68	Closed	1990	120.00	120
1995 Pauline PS-440	2,500		65.00	65
1988 Pauline YK-230	Closed	1990	90.00	90
1996 Pavlovia Ballerina TEC-560	7,500	1998	55.00	55
1994 Payson YK-4541	3,500		135.00	135
1994 Payton PS-407	2,500	1995	150.00	150
1995 Peaches IND-531	2,500		80.00	80
1994 Pearl IND-523	2,500	1996	275.00	275
1994 Pegeen C-3205	2,500	1996	150.00	150
1994 Peggy TR-75	2,500		185.00	185
1991 Pepper PS-277	Closed	1993	130.00	150
1994 Petula C-3191	2,500		140.00	140
1991 Pia-PS 246L	Closed	1993	115.00	115
1990 Ping-LingDOLL-363RV	Closed	1992	50.00	50
1990 Polly DOLL-22PH	Closed	1992	90.00	90
1996 Praying Pennie TEC-549	7,500	1998	50.00	50

*Quotes have been rounded up to nearest dollar

YEAR ISSUE	EDITION LIMIT	YEAR RETD.	ISSUE PRICE	*QUOTE U.S.$
1990 Princess Fair Skies FH-268B	Closed	1992	75.00	75
1994 Princess Foxfire PS-411	2,500		150.00	150
1994 Princess Moonrise YK-4542	3,500		140.00	140
1990 Princess Red Feather PS-189	Closed	1992	90.00	90
1994 Princess Snow Flower PS-402	2,500	1995	150.00	150
1991 Princess Summer Winds FH-427	2,500	1993	120.00	120
1990 Priscilla WB-50	Closed	1992	105.00	105
1994 Priscilla YK-4538	3,500		135.00	135
1991 Prissy White/Blue C-3140	Closed	1993	100.00	100
1995 Rainie LL-984	2,500	1996	125.00	125
1989 Ramona PS-31B	Closed	1992	80.00	80
1991 Rapunzel C-3157	2,500	1993	150.00	150
1987 Rapunzel C158	Closed	1986	95.00	165
1998 Rapunzel C3-276	2,500		134.00	134
1993 Rebecca C-3177	2,500	1993	135.00	135
1989 Rebecca PS-34V	Closed	1992	45.00	45
1998 Rebecca TR-4186 - S. Mann	2,500		105.00	105
1991 Red Wing AM-30	2,500	1993	165.00	165
1994 Regina OM-41	2,500		150.00	150
1994 Rita FH-553	2,500	1996	115.00	115
1994 Robby NM-29	2,500		135.00	135
1991 Robin AM-22	Closed	1993	120.00	120
1995 Robin C-3236	2,500		60.00	60
1991 Rosalind C-3090	Closed	1992	150.00	150
1989 Rosie 290M	Closed	1992	55.00	85
1995 Rusty CD-1450B	2,500		35.00	35
1987 Sabrina C208	Closed	1986	65.00	95
1990 Sabrina C3050	Closed	1992	105.00	105
1987 Sailorette DOM217	Closed	1986	70.00	150
1992 Sally FH-492	2,500	1993	105.00	105
1990 Sally WB-20	Closed	1992	95.00	95
1991 Samantha GU-3	Closed	1992	100.00	100
1995 San San GU-53	2,500		60.00	60
1991 Sandra DOLL-6-PHE	2,500	1992	65.00	65
1992 Sapphires OM-223	2,500	1993	250.00	250
1992 Sara Ann FH-474	2,500	1993	115.00	115
1995 Sarah C-3214	2,500		110.00	110
1993 Saretta SP-423	2,500	1993	100.00	100
1995 Sasha GU-57	2,500		75.00	75
1991 Scarlett FH-399	2,500	1992	100.00	100
1991 Scarlett FH-436	2,500	1992	135.00	135
1992 Scarlett FH-471	2,500	1993	120.00	120
1991 Shaka SP-401	2,500	1992	110.00	110
1994 Shaka TR-45	2,500		100.00	100
1993 Shaka TR-45	2,500	1993	100.00	100
1991 Sharon 21" Blue EP-34	Closed	1992	120.00	120
1995 Sharon C-3237	2,500		95.00	95
1991 Shau Chen GU-2	2,500	1992	85.00	85
1991 Shelley CH-1	2,500	1992	110.00	110
1995 Shimmering Caroline LL-992	2,500		115.00	115
1990 Shirley WB-37	Closed	1992	65.00	65
1988 Sister Agnes 14" C250	Closed	1990	75.00	75
1988 Sister Ignatius Notre Dame FH184	Closed	1990	75.00	75
1989 Sister Mary C-249	Closed	1992	75.00	125
1990 Sister Mary WB-15	Closed	1992	70.00	70
1994 Sister Suzie IND-509	2,500	1995	95.00	95
1988 Sister Teresa FH187	Closed	1990	80.00	80
1995 Sleeping Beauty OM-88	2,500		115.00	115
1992 Sonja FH-486	2,500	1994	125.00	125
1995 Sophia PS-445	2,500		125.00	125
1990 Sophie OM-1	Closed	1992	65.00	65
1991 Sophie TR-53	2,500	1992	135.00	135
1995 Southern Belle Bride FH-637	2,500		160.00	185
1994 Southern Belle FH-570	2,500		140.00	140
1994 Sparkle OM-40	2,500	1996	150.00	150
1991 Stacy DOLL-6PH	Closed	1992	65.00	65
1995 Stacy FH-634	2,500		110.00	110
1995 Stacy OC-75	2,500		40.00	40
1990 Stacy TR-5	Closed	1992	105.00	105
1991 Stephanie AM-11	Closed	1992	105.00	105
1991 Stephanie FH-467	Closed	1992	95.00	95
1991 Stephanie Pink & White OM-196	Closed	1992	300.00	300
1994 Stephie OC-41M	2,500		115.00	115
1990 Sue Chuen C-3061G	Closed	1992	95.00	95
1992 Sue JNC-4003	Closed	1994	90.00	90
1994 Sue Kwei TR-73	2,500		110.00	110
1994 Sugar Plum Fairy OM-39	2,500	1996	150.00	150
1991 Summer AM-33	Closed	1992	200.00	200
1990 Sunny FH-331	Closed	1992	70.00	70
1989 Sunny PS-59V	Closed	1992	71.00	71
1990 Susan DOLL-364MC	Closed	1992	75.00	75
1997 Susannah OM-133	2,500		95.00	95
1995 Suzanna Doll 554	2,500		35.00	35
1994 Suzanne LL-943	2,500		105.00	105
1994 Suzie GU-38	2,500		135.00	135
1995 Suzie OC-80	2,500		50.00	50
1989 Suzie PS-32	Closed	1992	80.00	80
1993 Suzie SP-422	2,500	1993	164.00	164
1995 Sweet Pea LL-981	2,500	1996	90.00	90
1991 Sybil 20" Beige C-3131	Closed	1992	135.00	135
1991 Sybil Pink DOLL-12PHMC	2,500	1992	75.00	75
1995 Sylvie CD-16634B	2,500		35.00	35
1995 Tabitha C-3233	2,500		50.00	50
1994 Taffey TR-80	2,500		150.00	150
1994 Tallulah OM-44	2,500		275.00	275
1991 Tamara OM-187	Closed	1992	135.00	135
1990 Tania DOLL-376P	Closed	1992	65.00	65
1989 Tatiana Pink Ballerina M-60	Closed	1991	120.00	175
1998 Taylor NY-132 - S. Mann	2,500		75.00	75
1994 Teresa C-3198	2,500	1995	110.00	110
1995 Terri OM-78	2,500		150.00	150
1989 Terri PS-104	Closed	1991	85.00	85
1991 Terri TR-62	Closed	1992	75.00	75
1991 Tessa AM-19	Closed	1992	135.00	135
1998 Tiffanny TR-4253 - S. Mann	2,500		105.00	105
1998 Tiffany & Friends JAY-104	2,500		135.00	135
1994 Tiffany OC-44M	2,500	1996	140.00	140
1992 Tiffany OM-014	2,500	1994	150.00	150
1991 Tina AM-16	Closed	1992	130.00	130
1990 Tina DOLL-371	Closed	1992	85.00	85
1995 Tina OM-79	2,500		150.00	150
1990 Tina WB-32	Closed	1992	65.00	65
1994 Tippy LL-946	2,500	1995	110.00	110
1995 Tobey C-3232	2,500		50.00	50
1994 Todd YK-4540	3,500		45.00	45
1990 Tommy-C-3064	Closed	1992	75.00	75
1994 Topaz TR-74	2,500	1995	195.00	195
1998 Tracy AWL-519 - S. Mann	2,500		100.00	100
1988 Tracy C-3006	Closed	1990	95.00	150
1992 Trina OM-011	Closed	1994	165.00	165
1994 Trixie TR-77	2,500		110.00	110
1991 Vanessa AM-34	Closed	1992	90.00	90
1991 Vicki C-3101	Closed	1992	200.00	200
1991 Violet EP-41	Closed	1992	135.00	135
1991 Violet OM-186	2,500	1992	270.00	270
1992 Violette FH-503	2,500	1994	120.00	120
1991 Virginia SP-359	Closed	1992	120.00	120
1994 Virginia TR-78	2,500		195.00	195
1987 Vivian C-201P	Closed	1986	80.00	80
1991 Wah-Ching Watching Oriental Toddler YK-4175	Closed	1992	110.00	110
1995 Wei Lin GU-44	2,500		70.00	70
1994 Wendy MS-26	2,500		150.00	150
1989 Wendy PS-51	Closed	1991	105.00	105
1990 Wendy TE-3	Closed	1992	75.00	75
1985 Wendy-C120	Closed	1987	45.00	150
1990 Wilma PS-174	Closed	1992	75.00	75
1995 Windy in Rose Print FH-626	2,500	1995	200.00	200
1995 Winnie LL-985	2,500	1996	75.00	75
1995 Winter Wonderland RDK-301	2,500		35.00	35
1995 Woodland Sprite OM-90	2,500		100.00	100
1995 Yelena RDK-236	2,500		35.00	35
1990 Yen Yen YK-4091	Closed	1992	95.00	95
1992 Yvette OM-015	2,500	1994	150.00	150

Signature Doll Series - Various

YEAR ISSUE	EDITION LIMIT	YEAR RETD.	ISSUE PRICE	*QUOTE U.S.$
1997 Abigail MCOM-106 - C. Wang	5,000		200.00	200
1992 Abigail MS-11 - M. Severino	5,000	1994	125.00	125
1995 Adak PPA-21 - P. Phillips	5,000	1996	110.00	110
1998 Addy OM-174 - B.K. Lee	2,500		175.00	175
1998 Agnesy VP-20 - V. Pike	1,200		174.00	174
1997 Ahna HHVL-200 - M. Hargrave	5,000		175.00	175
1998 Akia OM-208 - B.K. Lee	1,200		149.00	149
1997 Alexandria MS-70 - M. Severino	5,000		75.00	125
1992 Alexandria PAC-19 - P. Aprile	5,000	1995	300.00	300
1997 Alice MCC-510 - M. Costa	5,000		65.00	65
1991 Alice MS-7 - M. Severino	5,000	1996	120.00	120
1995 Amanda KSFA-1 - K. Fitzpatrick	5,000		175.00	175
1991 Amber MS-1 - M. Severino	Closed	1994	95.00	95
1995 Amelia PAC-28 - P. Aprile	5,000		130.00	130
1995 Amy Rose HKHF-200 - H.K. Hyland	5,000		125.00	150
1997 Anna MHVL-200 - M. Hargrave	5,000		175.00	175
1997 Anna TF-9 - T. Francirek	1,200		150.00	150
1998 Antonia FH-820 - C.I. Lee	5,000		150.00	150
1998 April MCOM-104 - M. Costa	5,000		174.00	174
1998 Ashley DEA-205 - Heléne	5,000		135.00	135
1997 Audrey OM-197 - B.K. Lee	2,500		150.00	150
1996 Aurora HKHO - H.K. Hyland	5,000		250.00	250
1992 Baby Cakes Crumbs PK-CRUMBS - P. Kolesar	5,000		17.50	35
1992 Baby Cakes Crumbs/Black PK-CRUMBS/B - P. Kolesar	5,000		17.50	35
1998 Baby Sunshine NU-015 - S. Bilotto	5,000		95.00	95
1997 The Bear Collector FH-853 - J. Sauerbrey	5,000		250.00	250
1997 Beauty TF-6 - T. Francirek	1,200		150.00	150
1997 Bebe TF-8- T. Franciek	5,000		150.00	150
1991 Becky MS-2 - M. Severino	5,000	1994	95.00	95
1997 Bette DALI-030 - E. Dali	1,200		150.00	150
1997 Birth of Hope OM-140 - C. Wang	5,000		175.00	175
1993 Bonnett Baby MS-17W - M. Severino	5,000	1996	175.00	175
1995 Brad HKH-15 - H.K. Hyland	5,000		85.00	100
1998 Brett JS-3 - J. Sauerbrey	1,200		150.00	150
1998 Briana OM-199 - B.K. Lee	5,000		195.00	195
1997 Briana OM164 - C. Wang	2,500		135.00	135
1992 Bride & Flower Girl PAC-6 - P. Aprile	5,000	1996	600.00	600
1998 Camilla DEA-223 - Heléne	2,500		175.00	175
1995 Cara DALI-1 - E. Dali	5,000		400.00	400
1995 Casey PPA-23 - P. Phillips	5,000		85.00	85
1992 Cassandra PAC-8 - P. Aprile	Closed	1994	450.00	450
1998 Cassidy MCOM-100 - M. Costa	5,000		175.00	175
1992 Cassie Flower Girl PAC-9 - P. Aprile	Closed	1994	175.00	175
1997 Cathy Ann MCOM-105 - M. Costa	5,000		200.00	200
1998 Cathy TF-20 - T. Francirek	1,200		175.00	175
1998 Celene DH-3 - D. Hardwick	1,200		175.00	175
1992 Celine PAC-11 - P. Aprile	5,000	1995	165.00	165
1998 Cheyenne OM-128 - B.K. Lee	2,500		195.00	195
1998 Chloe Sofia GMN-205 - G. Mc Neil	1,200		174.00	174
1995 Christmas Alyssa - P. Phillips	5,000	1995	100.00	175
1997 Christmas Ashley - J. Sauerbrey	10,000	1997	96.00	150
1998 Christopher Daniel MHF-501 - M Hargrave	5,000		149.00	149
1991 Clair-Ann PK-252 - P. Kolesar	5,000		100.00	100
1998 Claire CK-102 - C. Koch	1,200		350.00	350
1998 Claire, Princess Bride FH-864 - C.I. Lee	2,500		175.00	175
1992 Clarissa PAC-3 - P. Aprile	5,000	1996	165.00	165
1998 Colette MC-1 - M. Costa	5,000		350.00	350
1997 Consuelo CK-101 - C. Koch	11,200		400.00	400
1997 Courtney MC-15 - M. Costa	1,200		149.00	149
1997 Courtney MCA-100 - M. Costa	5,000		250.00	250
1991 Daddy's Little Darling MS-8 - M. Severino	5,000		165.00	185
1992 Darla HP-204 - H. Payne	5,000	1996	250.00	250
1998 Delja MSF-500 - M. Severino	1,200		160.00	160
1998 Delores DALI-034 - E. Dali	1,200		150.00	150
1998 Delphine OM-183 - B.K. Lee	2,500		250.00	250
1998 Desiree DH-1 - D. Hardwick	1,200		150.00	150
1998 Diana TF-16 - T. Francirek	1,200		175.00	175
1992 Dulcie HP-200 - H. Payne	Closed	1993	250.00	250
1998 Ella DEA-226 - Heléne	2,500		175.00	175
1997 Emmy Lou CK-3 - C. Koch	5,000		250.00	250
1997 Engrid OM-173 - B.K. Lee	2,500		175.00	175
1991 Enoc PK-100 - P. Kolesar	5,000		100.00	135
1992 Eugenie Bride PAC-1 - P. Aprile	5,000	1996	165.00	165
1998 Fall Bride TFH-102 - T. Francirek	1,200		250.00	250
1998 Fiona DEA-230 - Heléne	2,500		175.00	175
1997 Frenchie CK-100 - C. Koch	5,000		300.00	300
1997 Gabriella OM-165 - C. Wang	5,000		250.00	250
1997 Galena DALI-015 - E. Dali	1,200		150.00	150
1998 Geoffrey AND-1 - A. Oliv	2,500		175.00	175
1997 Gigi MCC-508 - M. Costa	5,000		65.00	65
1997 Ginger DALI-036 - E. Dali	1,200		150.00	150
1995 Ginny LR-2 - L. Randolph	5,000		360.00	360
1993 Grace HKH-2 - H. Kahl-Hyland	5,000	1996	250.00	250
1995 Guardian Angel of Marriage OM-112 - K. Wang	1,500	1996	150.00	150
1997 Hailey MCC-511 - M. Costa	5,000		65.00	65
1997 Haley MC-11 - M. Costa	5,000		100.00	100
1997 Hanna's Enchanted Garden HKHT-10 - H. Hyland	5,000		95.00	95
1997 Heidi MCC-503 - M. Costa	5,000		65.00	65
1993 Helene HKH-1 - H. Kahl-Hyland	5,000	1996	250.00	250
1997 India GMNO-8 - G. McNeil	5,000		250.00	250
1997 Irene OM-170 - C. Wang	5,000		150.00	150
1998 Irina OM-220 - B.K. Lee	2,500		200.00	200
1997 Isabelle & Baby OM-132 - C. Wang	5,000		175.00	175
1997 Jacqueline OM-137 - C. Wang	5,000		300.00	300
1998 Jason JAY-103 - J. Lee	1,200		50.00	50
1997 Jean DALI-037 - E. Dali	1,200		150.00	150
1998 Jennifer JS-5 - J. Sauerbrey	5,000		135.00	135
1997 Jillian JPOM-250 - J. Pushee	1,200		149.00	149
1998 Jing Jing MCX-1 - M. Costa	2,500		55.00	55
1997 Juliet HKRO-307 - H. Hyland	5,000		175.00	175
1998 Katherine DEA-228 - Heléne	2,500		175.00	175
1998 Katy JS-21 - J. Sauerbrey	5,000		175.00	175
1997 Kelsey OM-135 - C. Wang	5,000		135.00	135
1997 Kirsten OM-172 - B.K. Lee	5,000		175.00	175
1997 Kit MCC-500 - M. Costa	5,000		65.00	65
1997 Kyla MC-9 - M. Costa	5,000		100.00	100
1998 Laraline CK-10 - C. Koch	1,200		300.00	300
1997 Latisha MS-97 - M. Severino	5,000		40.00	40
1995 Latisha PPA-25 - P. Phillips	5,000	1996	110.00	110
1995 Laurel HKH-17R - H.K. Hyland	5,000		110.00	110
1995 Lauren HKH-202 - H.K. Hyland	5,000	1996	150.00	150
1997 Liliac Fairie OM-201 - B.K. Lee	2,500		175.00	175
1992 Little Match Girl HP-205 - H. Payne	Closed	1994	150.00	150
1998 Louisa DEA-227 - Heléne	2,500		175.00	175
1995 Lucy HKH-14 - H.K. Hyland	2,500	1996	105.00	105
1997 Lyndsey MCA-101 - M. Costa	5,000		200.00	200
1997 Madame Charpentier TF-5 - T. Francirek	1,200		150.00	150
1997 Maisie JC-2 - J. Cayot	5,000		120.00	120
1997 Margo OM-136 - C. Wang	5,000		150.00	150
1998 Maritza OM-209 - C. Wang	5,000		135.00	135
1997 Marlene DALI-031 - E. Dali	1,200		150.00	150
1997 Mary Ann JS-8 - J. Sauerbrey	5,000		150.00	150
1997 Maureen DALI-26B - E. Dali	1,200		100.00	100
1992 Megan MS-12 - M. Severino	5,000	1995	125.00	125
1997 Megan PP-112 - P. Phillips	5,000		150.00	150
1997 Melissa Ann VP-10 - V. Pike	5,000		325.00	325
1997 Memina MSA-10 - M. Severino	5,000		165.00	165
1995 Meredith LR-3 - L. Randolph	5,000		375.00	375
1997 Mickey & Hanna BRU-600/3 - Bruny	5,000		50.00	50
1991 Mikey MS-3 - M. Severino	5,000	1994	95.00	95
1997 Milou MAV-303 - M. Synder	5,000		175.00	175
1997 Missy MS-117 - M. Severino	5,000		55.00	55
1997 Mme. De Champs TF-2 - T. Francirek	1,200		150.00	150
1997 Mme. De Falaise TF-17 - T. Francirek	1,200		150.00	150
1997 Mme. Fourtot TF-3 - T. Francirek	1,200		150.00	150
1991 Mommy's Rays of Sunshine MS-9 - M. Severino	5,000		165.00	185
1997 Monique OM-167 - C. Wang	5,000	1997	150.00	150
1997 Morgan MHVL-202 - M. Hargrave	5,000		175.00	175
1997 Myrna DALI-033 - E. Dali	1,200		150.00	150
1995 Natasha HKH-17P - H.K. Hyland	5,000		110.00	110
1997 Nichole PPA-39 - P. Phillips	5,000		175.00	175
1998 Nicole DEA-204 - Heléne	2,500		135.00	135
1997 Night & Day DALI-02/3 - E. Dali	1,200		300.00	300
1998 Odette OM-210 - C. Wang	1,200		135.00	135
1997 Odile (The Black Swan) OM-168 - C. Wang	5,000		135.00	135

*Quotes have been rounded up to nearest dollar

YEAR ISSUE	EDITION LIMIT	YEAR RETD.	ISSUE PRICE	*QUOTE U.S.$
1997 Odile OM-168 - C. Wang	1,200		135.00	135
1997 Orchid CK-5 - C. Koch	1,200		350.00	350
1995 Patricia DALI-3 - E. Dali	5,000		280.00	280
1991 Paulette PAC-2 - P. Aprile	5,000		250.00	300
1991 Paulette PAC-4 - P. Aprile	5,000		250.00	300
1998 Pauline DH-2 - D. Hardwick	1,200		150.00	150
1992 Pavlova PAC-17 - P. Aprile	5,000	1994	145.00	145
1998 Peekaboo Sue JAY-105 - J. Lee	1,200		125.00	125
1998 Penny CK-4 - C. Koch	5,000		149.00	149
1998 Penny Sue JAY-101 - J. Lee	1,200		85.00	85
1997 Pete & Sally BRU-602/4 - Bruny	5,000		50.00	50
1998 Pia DALI-07 - E. Dali	1,200		150.00	150
1992 Polly HP-206 - H. Payne	5,000		120.00	120
1991 Precious Baby SB-100 - S. Bilotto	5,000	1996	250.00	250
1991 Precious Pary Time SB-102 - S. Bilotto	5,000		250.00	275
1998 Rapunzel's Wedding FH-866 - P. Phillips	5,000		149.00	149
1992 Rebecca Beige Bonnet MS-17B - M. Severino	5,000	1995	175.00	175
1993 Reilly HKH-3 - H. Kahl-Hyland	5,000		260.00	260
1997 Rosey GMNO-3 - G. McNeil	5,000		250.00	300
1992 Ruby MS-18 - M. Severino	5,000		135.00	135
1996 Sabrina and Child - C.I. Lee	7,500	1996	126.00	200
1997 Sabrina MCC-507 - M. Costa	5,000		65.00	65
1998 Sapphire TF-18 - T. Francirek	1,200		200.00	200
1998 Sarah (w/rug/bear/stool JAY-100 - J. Lee	1,200		135.00	135
1998 Sarah OM-190 - B.K. Lee	2,500		175.00	175
1997 Scott & Becky BRU-601/5 - Bruny	5,000		50.00	50
1998 Serena DH-4 - D. Hardwick	1,200		150.00	150
1998 Shadow DALI-01 - E. Dali	1,200		150.00	150
1995 Shao Ling PPA-22 - P. Phillips	5,000		110.00	110
1997 Shelia MC-10 - M. Costa	5,000		100.00	100
1998 Simonetta TF-19 - T. Francirek	1,200		200.00	200
1998 Sitting Pretty (Penny w/chair) JS-14 - J. Sauerbrey	5,000		200.00	200
1997 Snow Flake MS-90 - M. Severino	5,000		55.00	55
1991 Sparkle PK-250 - P. Kolesar	5,000	1996	100.00	100
1998 Spring Bride TFH-100 - T. Francirek	1,200		250.00	250
1995 Stacy DALI-2 - E. Dali	5,000		360.00	360
1998 Stacy MHVL-203 - M. Hargrave	5,000		175.00	175
1992 Stacy MS-24 - M. Severino	Closed	1993	110.00	110
1997 Starr MSA-14 - M. Severino	5,000		175.00	175
1991 Stephie MS-6 - M. Severino	Closed	1994	125.00	125
1991 Su Lin MS-5 - M. Severino	5,000	1994	105.00	105
1998 Summer Bride TFH-101 - T. Francirek	1,200		250.00	250
1997 Suryah MS-88 - M. Severino	5,000		40.00	40
1995 Suzie HKH-16 - H.K. Hyland	5,000		100.00	100
1991 Sweet Pea PK-251 - P. Kolesar	Closed		100.00	100
1997 Tam MSA-15 - M. Severino	5,000		150.00	150
1998 Tara DEA-203 - Heléne	2,500		95.00	95
1998 Taylor JAY-106 - J. Lee	1,200		120.00	120
1998 Teacher's Pet MS-114 - M. Severino	5,000		75.00	75
1998 Tiffany & Friends JAY-104 - J. Lee	2,500		135.00	135
1994 Tracy JAG-111 - J. Grammer	5,000	1996	150.00	150
1994 Trevor JAG-112 - J. Grammer	5,000	1996	115.00	115
1998 Venus CK-103 - C. Koch	1,200		300.00	300
1997 Vicki FH-815 - C.I. Lee	5,000		150.00	150
1992 Violetta PAC-16 - P. Aprile	5,000	1994	165.00	165
1997 Willow DALI-05 - E. Dali	1,200		150.00	150
1998 Winter Bride TFH-103 - T. Francirek	1,200		250.00	250
1998 Woodland Fairie OM-200 - B.K. Lee	2,500		175.00	175
1997 Xena DALI-05 - E. Dali	1,200		150.00	150
1991 Yawning Kate MS-4 - M. Severino	Closed	1994	105.00	105
1997 Zoe OM-138 - C. Wang	5,000		300.00	300

Susan Wakeen Doll Co. Inc.

The Littlest Ballet Company - S. Wakeen

YEAR ISSUE	EDITION LIMIT	YEAR RETD.	ISSUE PRICE	*QUOTE U.S.$
1985 Cynthia	375		198.00	350
1987 Elizabeth	250		425.00	1000
1985 Jeanne	375		198.00	800
1985 Jennifer	250		750.00	750
1987 Marie Ann	50		1000.00	1000
1985 Patty	375		198.00	400-500

FIGURINES

All God's Children/Miss Martha Originals

Collectors' Club - M. Root

YEAR ISSUE	EDITION LIMIT	YEAR RETD.	ISSUE PRICE	*QUOTE U.S.$
1989 Molly -1524	Retrd.	1990	38.00	325-690
1990 Joey -1539	Retrd.	1991	32.00	325-555
1991 Mandy -1540	Retrd.	1992	36.00	215-370
1992 Olivia -1562	Retrd.	1993	36.00	225-300
1993 Garrett -1567	Retrd.	1994	36.00	275-315
1993 Peek-a-Boo	Retrd.	1994	Gift	95-115
1994 Alexandria -1575	Retrd.	1995	36.00	70-163
1994 Lindy	Retrd.	1995	Gift	25-97
1995 Zamika -1581	Retrd.	1996	36.00	100-124
1995 Zizi	Retrd.	1996	Gift	50-64
1996 Donnie -1585	Retrd.	1997	36.00	75-90
1996 Dinky	Retrd.	1997	Gift	40-50
1997 Daylon - 1586	Retrd.	1998	36.00	36-72
1997 Snuffles	Retrd.	1998	Gift	40
1998 Rebekka - 1600	5/99		38.00	38
1998 Kat	5/99		Gift	N/A

Event Piece - M. Root

YEAR ISSUE	EDITION LIMIT	YEAR RETD.	ISSUE PRICE	*QUOTE U.S.$
1994 Uriel - 2000	Yr.Iss.	1994	45.00	160-200
1995 Jane - 2001 (ten year Anniversary)	Yr.Iss.	1995	45.00	140-165
1996 Patti - 2002-Spring (rose colored dress for girl, green colored dress for doll)	Yr.Iss.	1996	45.00	90-105
1996 Patti - 2002-Fall (dark blue dress for girl, peach colored dress for doll)	Yr.Iss.	1996	45.00	90-105
1997 Shalisa - 2003	Yr.Iss.	1997	45.00	90

All God's Children - M. Root

YEAR ISSUE	EDITION LIMIT	YEAR RETD.	ISSUE PRICE	*QUOTE U.S.$
1985 Abe - 1357	Retrd.	1988	25.00	1450-1560
1989 Adam - 1526	Open		36.00	44
1997 Alaysha (clock) - 2800	6,000	1997	59.50	85-125
1987 Amy - 1405W	Retrd.	1996	22.00	70-100
1987 Angel - 1401W	Retrd.	1995	20.00	35-88
1986 Annie Mae 6" -1311	Retrd.	1989	19.00	187-205
1986 Annie Mae 8 1/2" - 1310	Retrd.	1989	27.00	275-300
1987 Aunt Sarah - blue - 1440	Retrd.	1989	45.00	300-320
1987 Aunt Sarah - red - 1440	Retrd.	1989	45.00	400-435
1992 Barney - 1557	Retrd.	1995	32.00	55-120
1988 Bean (Clear Water) - 1521	Retrd.	1992	36.00	345-350
1992 Bean (Painted Water) - 1521	Retrd.	1993	36.00	145-160
1987 Becky - 1402W	Retrd.	1995	22.00	35-95
1987 Becky with Patch - 1402W	Retrd.	N/A	19.00	245-264
1987 Ben - 1504	Retrd.	1988	22.00	390-480
1991 Bessie & Corkie - 1547	Open		70.00	75
1998 Bessie Coleman, 9 1/4"	Open		71.50	74
1992 Beth - 1558	Retrd.	1995	32.00	50-95
1988 Betsy (Clear Water) - 1513	Retrd.	1992	36.00	335-350
1992 Betsy (Painted Water) - 1513	Retrd.	1993	36.00	140-160
1989 Beverly (small) - 1525	Retrd.	1990	50.00	670-710
1991 Billy (lg. stars raised) - 1545	Retrd.	1993	36.00	125-178
1991 Billy (stars imprinted) - 1545	Retrd.	1993	36.00	155-184
1987 Blossom (blue) - 1500	Retrd.	1989	60.00	150-475
1987 Blossom (red) - 1500	Retrd.	1989	60.00	830-875
1989 Bo - 1530	Retrd.	1994	22.00	28-108
1987 Bonnie & Buttons - 150	Retrd.	1992	24.00	175-200
1985 Booker T - 1320	Retrd.	1988	19.00	1495-1525
1987 Boone - 1510	Retrd.	1989	16.00	193-200
1989 Bootsie - 1529	Retrd.	1994	22.00	90-108
1992 Caitlin - 1554	Retrd.	1994	36.00	50-145
1985 Callie 2 1/4" - 1362	Retrd.	1988	12.00	300-330
1985 Callie 4 1/2" - 1361	Retrd.	1988	19.00	540-556
1988 Calvin - 777	Retrd.	1988	200.00	2195-2240
1987 Cassie - 1503	Retrd.	1989	22.00	152-220
1994 Chantel - 1573	Suspd.		39.00	40-85
1987 Charity - 1408	Retrd.	1994	28.00	120-140
1996 Charles - 1588	Open		36.00	40
1994 Cheri - 1574	Open		38.00	42
1989 David - 1528	Open		28.00	35
1996 Debi - 1584	Open		36.00	42
1998 Denise - 1596	Open		39.00	41
1991 Dori (green dress) - 1544	Retrd.	N/A	30.00	400-430
1991 Dori (peach dress) - 1544	Open		28.00	36
1987 Eli - 1403W	Open		26.00	34
1985 Emma - 1322	Retrd.	1988	27.00	2045-2110
1987 Faith - 1555	Retrd.	1993	32.00	89-145
1995 Gina - 1579	Open		38.00	45
1987 Ginnie - 1508	Retrd.	1988	22.00	450-464
1986 Grandma - 1323	Retrd.	1987	30.00	3725-3765
1988 Hannah - 1515	Open		36.00	44
1988 Hope - 1519	Retrd.	1998	36.00	40-80
1987 Jacob - 1407W	Retrd.	1996	26.00	80-90
1998 James - 1599	Open		41.50	42
1989 Jeremy - 1523	800	1993	195.00	750-1000
1989 Jerome - 1532	Open		30.00	38
1989 Jessica - 1522	800	1993	195.00	700-1000
1989 Jessica and Jeremy -1522-1523	Retrd.	1993	390.00	2000-2150
1987 Jessie (no base) -1501W	Retrd.	1989	19.00	400-461
1989 Jessie - 1501	Open		30.00	39
1988 John - 1514	Retrd.	1990	30.00	265-295
1989 Joseph - 1537	Open		30.00	35
1991 Joy - 1548	Open		30.00	36
1994 Justin - 1576	Open		37.00	43
1989 Kacie - 1533	Open		38.00	39
1988 Kezia - 1518	Retrd.	1997	36.00	76-90
1998 Krishna - 1593	Open		40.00	44
1998 Leroy - 1597	Open		40.00	44
1986 Lil' Emmie 3 1/2" - 1345	Retrd.	1989	14.00	105-200
1986 Lil' Emmie 4 1/2" - 1344	Retrd.	1989	18.00	115-220
1988 Lisa - 1512	Retrd.	1991	36.00	275-295
1997 Martin (nativity) - 1595	Open		38.00	40
1989 Mary - 1536	Open		30.00	35
1988 Maya - 1520	Retrd.	1993	36.00	75-165
1987 Meg (beige dress) - 1505	Retrd.	1988	21.00	1240
1988 Meg (blue dress, long hair) - 1505	Retrd.	1988	21.00	400-450
1988 Meg (blue dress, short hair) - 1505	Retrd.	1988	21.00	900-950
1992 Melissa - 1556	Retrd.	1995	32.00	32-55
1992 Merci - 1559	Open		36.00	42
1986 Michael & Kim - 1517	Open		36.00	45
1988 Moe & Pokey - 1552	Retrd.	1993	16.00	40-110
1987 Moses - 1506	Retrd.	1992	30.00	90-195
1993 Nathaniel - 11569	Open		36.00	40
1991 Nellie - 1546	Retrd.	1993	36.00	85-180
1994 Niambi - 1577	Open		34.00	37
1987 Paddy Paw & Lucy - 1553	Suspd.		24.00	60-105
1987 Paddy Paw & Luke - 1551	Suspd.		24.00	60-105
1988 Peanut -1509	Retrd.	1990	16.00	150-200
1989 Preshus - 1538	Open		24.00	29
1987 Primas Jones (w/base) - 1377	Retrd.	1988	40.00	800-860
1987 Primas Jones - 1377	Retrd.	1988	40.00	600-850
1986 Prissy (Bear) - 1348	Retrd.	1997	18.00	30-55
1986 Prissy (Moon Pie) - 1347	Open		20.00	39
1986 Prissy with Basket - 1346	Retrd.	1989	16.00	150-180
1986 Prissy with Yarn Hair (6 strands) - 1343	Retrd.	1989	19.00	250-330
1986 Prissy with Yarn Hair (9 strands) - 1343	Retrd.	1989	19.00	450-550
1987 Pud - 1550	Retrd.	1988	11.00	1300-1386
1987 Rachel - 1404W	Retrd.	1998	20.00	30
1992 Rakiya - 1561	Open		36.00	40
1992 Rakiya - 1561 (w/white tassel)	Retrd.	N/A	36.00	500
1997 Robert - 1591	Open		38.50	41
1988 Sally -1507	Retrd.	1989	19.00	115-225
1991 Samantha - 1542	Retrd.	1994	38.00	40-50
1991 Samuel - 1541	Retrd.	1994	32.00	45-145
1989 Sasha - 1531	Open		30.00	39
1986 Selina Jane (6 strands) - 1338	Retrd.	1989	21.95	295-325
1986 Selina Jane (9 strands) - 1338	Retrd.	1989	21.95	525-625
1995 Shani - 1583	Open		33.00	39
1996 Shari - 1586	Open		38.00	46
1998 Sharon - 1604	Open		45.00	45
1986 St. Nicholas-B - 1316	Retrd.	1990	30.00	125-175
1986 St. Nicholas-W - 1315	Retrd.	1990	30.00	75-175
1992 Stephen (Nativity Shepherd) - 1563	Open		36.00	40
1988 Sunshine - 1535	Retrd.	1997	38.00	59-78
1993 Sylvia - 1564	Open		36.00	42
1997 Tangie - 1590	Open		45.00	47
1988 Tansi & Tedi (green socks, collar, cuffs) - 1516	Retrd.	N/A	30.00	338
1988 Tansy & Tedi - 1516	Retrd.	1998	N/A	38
1989 Tara - 1527	Open		36.00	44
1987 Tess - 1534	Retrd.	1998	30.00	40
1990 Thaliyah - 778	Retrd.	1990	200.00	1900
1991 Thomas - 1549	Retrd.	1998	30.00	38
1987 Tiffany - 1511	Open		32.00	40
1994 Tish - 1572	Open		38.00	41
1986 Toby 3 1/2" - 1332	Retrd.	1989	13.00	180-200
1986 Toby 4 1/2" - 1331	Retrd.	1989	16.00	225-231
1985 Tom - 1353	Retrd.	1988	16.00	475-485
1986 Uncle Bud 6"- 1304	Retrd.	1991	19.00	225-235
1986 Uncle Bud 8 1/2"- 1303	Retrd.	1991	27.00	425-440
1992 Valerie - 1560	Open		36.00	41
1995 William - 1580	Open		38.00	41
1987 Willie - 1406W	Retrd.	1996	22.00	77-90
1987 Willie - 1406W (no base)	Retrd.	1987	22.00	450-480
1993 Zack - 1566	Open		34.00	38

All God's Children Ragbabies - M. Root

YEAR ISSUE	EDITION LIMIT	YEAR RETD.	ISSUE PRICE	*QUOTE U.S.$
1995 Honey - 4005	Retrd.	1998	33.00	35
1995 Issie - 4004	Open		33.00	35
1995 Ivy - 4008	Open		33.00	35
1995 Josie - 4003	Retrd.	1997	33.00	34-80
1995 Mitzi - 4000	Open		33.00	35
1995 Muffin - 4001	Open		33.00	35
1995 Puddin - 4006	Open		33.00	35
1995 Punkin - 4007	Open		33.00	35
1995 Sweetie - 4002	Retrd.	1997	33.00	34-80

Angelic Messengers - M. Root

YEAR ISSUE	EDITION LIMIT	YEAR RETD.	ISSUE PRICE	*QUOTE U.S.$
1994 Cieara - 2500	Open		38.00	40
1996 Demetrious - 2503	Open		38.00	40
1994 Mariah - 2501	Open		38.00	40
1994 Mariah - 2501 (scratched in letters)	Retrd.	N/A	38.00	100-120
1995 Sabrina - 2502	Open		38.00	40

Christmas - M. Root

YEAR ISSUE	EDITION LIMIT	YEAR RETD.	ISSUE PRICE	*QUOTE U.S.$
1987 1987 Father Christmas-W - 1750	Retrd.	N/A	145.00	745-775
1987 1987 Father Christmas-B - 1751	Retrd.	N/A	145.00	745-775
1988 1988 Father Christmas-W - 1757	Retrd.	N/A	195.00	640-660
1988 1988 Father Christmas-B - 1758	Retrd.	N/A	195.00	640-660
1988 Santa Claus-W - 1767	Retrd.	N/A	185.00	665-670
1988 Santa Claus-B - 1768	Retrd.	N/A	185.00	665-670
1989 1989 Father Christmas-W - 1769	Retrd.	N/A	195.00	700-750
1989 1989 Father Christmas-B - 1770	Retrd.	N/A	195.00	700-750
1990 1990-91 Father Christmas-W - 1771	Retrd.	N/A	195.00	650-730
1990 1990-91 Father Christmas-B - 1772	Retrd.	N/A	195.00	650-730
1991 1991-92 Father Christmas-W - 1773	Retrd.	N/A	195.00	500-525
1991 1991-92 Father Christmas-B - 1774	Retrd.	N/A	195.00	500-730
1992 Father Christmas Bust-W - 1775	Retrd.	N/A	145.00	380-400
1992 Father Christmas Bust-B - 1776	Retrd.	N/A	145.00	380-400

Count Your Blessings - M. Root

YEAR ISSUE	EDITION LIMIT	YEAR RETD.	ISSUE PRICE	*QUOTE U.S.$
1997 Anna - 2703	Open		24.50	26
1997 Asia - 2705	Open		24.50	26
1997 Baby Rei - 2700	Open		24.50	26
1997 Cece - 2701	Open		24.50	26
1997 Levi - 2702	Open		24.50	26
1997 Taci - 2704	Open		24.50	26
1997 Theo - 2706	Open		24.50	26

Historical Series - M. Root

YEAR ISSUE	EDITION LIMIT	YEAR RETD.	ISSUE PRICE	*QUOTE U.S.$
1994 Augustus Walley (Buffalo Soldier) - 1908	Retrd.	1995	95.00	198-265
1994 Bessie Smith - 1909	Open		70.00	74
1997 Clara Brown - 1912	Open		71.00	74
1992 Dr. Daniel Williams - 1903	Retrd.	1995	70.00	85-225
1992 Frances Harper - 1905	Retrd.	1998	70.00	74
1991 Frederick Douglass - 1902	Open		70.00	74
1992 George Washington Carver - 1907	Open		70.00	74
1989 Harriet Tubman - 1900	Retrd.	1994	65.00	150-350
1992 Ida B. Wells - 1906	Retrd.	1996	70.00	175-225
1992 Mary Bethune (misspelled) - 1904	Retrd.	1992	70.00	290-332

*Quotes have been rounded up to nearest dollar

YEAR ISSUE	EDITION LIMIT	YEAR RETD.	ISSUE PRICE	*QUOTE U.S.$
1992 Mary Bethune - 1904	Open		70.00	74
1995 Mary Mahoney - 1911	Open		65.00	74
1995 Richard Allen - 1910	Open		70.00	74
1990 Sojourner Truth - 1901	Retrd.	1997	65.00	132-180

International Series - M. Root

YEAR ISSUE	EDITION LIMIT	YEAR RETD.	ISSUE PRICE	*QUOTE U.S.$
1987 Juan - 1807	Retrd.	1993	26.00	165-175
1987 Kameko - 1802	Open.		26.00	32
1987 Karl - 1808	Retrd.	1996	26.00	70-85
1987 Katrina - 1803	Retrd.	1993	26.00	170-191
1987 Kelli - 1805	Open		30.00	36
1987 Little Chief - 1804	Open		32.00	40
1993 Minnie - 1568	Open		36.00	40
1987 Pike - 1806	Retrd.	1997	30.00	33-68
1987 Tat - 1801	Retrd.	1996	30.00	83-92

Little Missionary Series - M. Root

YEAR ISSUE	EDITION LIMIT	YEAR RETD.	ISSUE PRICE	*QUOTE U.S.$
1994 Nakia - 3500	Retrd.	1995	40.00	120-125
1994 Nakia - 3500 (Mat.)	Retrd.	1995	40.00	110-125

Sugar And Spice - M. Root

YEAR ISSUE	EDITION LIMIT	YEAR RETD.	ISSUE PRICE	*QUOTE U.S.$
1987 Blessed are the Peacemakers (Eli) -1403	Retrd.	1988	22.00	550
1987 Friend Show Love (Becky) -1402	Retrd.	1988	22.00	550
1987 Friendship Warms the Heart (Jacob) -1407	Retrd.	1988	22.00	550
1987 God is Love (Angel) -1401	Retrd.	1988	22.00	550
1987 Jesus Loves Me (Amy) -1405	Retrd.	1989	22.00	550
1987 Old Friends are Best (Rachel) - 1404	Retrd.	1988	22.00	550
1987 Sharing with Friends (Willie) - 1406	Retrd.	1988	22.00	550

Through His Eyes - M. Root

YEAR ISSUE	EDITION LIMIT	YEAR RETD.	ISSUE PRICE	*QUOTE U.S.$
1993 Simon & Andrew - 1565	Open		45.00	51
1995 Jewel & Judy - 1582	Open		45.00	50

Amaranth Productions

Father Christmas - L. West

YEAR ISSUE	EDITION LIMIT	YEAR RETD.	ISSUE PRICE	*QUOTE U.S.$
1994 Anniversary Father Christmas 4330	300	1995	750.00	750
1992 Christmas Glory 4310	350	1993	750.00	750
1989 Christmas Majesty 2300	250	1988	750.00	750
1993 Christmas Majesty Special Ed. 4270	100	1993	1590.00	2500
1994 Christmas Peace 4275	100	1995	1450.00	2950
1993 Father Christmas with Staff 4250	200	1994	1300.00	2100
1991 Father Nikolai 4305	500	1993	750.00	750
1989 Grand Father Christmas 3520	300	1991	750.00	750
1993 Special Delivery 4320	350	1993	750.00	750
1994 Victorian Saint Nicholas 4255	150	1995	1300.00	1800-2600
1990 Winter Majesty 4300	350	1992	750.00	950

Old Time Santa Series - L. West

YEAR ISSUE	EDITION LIMIT	YEAR RETD.	ISSUE PRICE	*QUOTE U.S.$
1992 Old Time Santa-1st in Series 3540	300	1993	530.00	750
1993 Still Fits-2nd in Series 3545	300	1993	700.00	900
1994 Old Time Santa and Tree-3rd in Series 3546	250	1995	650.00	925

Santas - L. West

YEAR ISSUE	EDITION LIMIT	YEAR RETD.	ISSUE PRICE	*QUOTE U.S.$
1992 Classic Santa With Chair 2451	200	1993	1450.00	1850
1988 Kris Kringle Special Edition 1115	50	1988	2000.00	2000
1990 Large Santa 4400	250	1993	700.00	700
1991 Last Minute Details w/ Beard 6005BRD	950	1992	550.00	700
1991 Last Minute Details-M.B. 6005	950	1992	430.00	430
1991 Saint Nick 6000	950	1991	370.00	370
1989 Santa At The North Pole 3535	300	1991	450.00	450
1988 Spencer 2301	150	1991	850.00	850
1994 Standing Santa with Toypack 9002	Retrd.	1994	450.00	450

American Artists

Fred Stone Figurines - F. Stone

YEAR ISSUE	EDITION LIMIT	YEAR RETD.	ISSUE PRICE	*QUOTE U.S.$
1986 Arab Mare & Foal	2,500		150.00	225
1985 The Black Stallion, (bronze)	1,500		150.00	175
1985 The Black Stallion, (porcelain)	2,500		125.00	260
1987 Rearing Black Stallion, (bronze)	1,250		175.00	195
1987 Rearing Black Stallion, (porcelain)	3,500		150.00	175
1986 Tranquility	2,500		175.00	275

Anchor Bay

Great Ships of the World - Staff

YEAR ISSUE	EDITION LIMIT	YEAR RETD.	ISSUE PRICE	*QUOTE U.S.$
1997 Lightship "Chesapeake"	Open		155.00	155
1997 Lightship "Chesapeake" (special ed.)	4,000	1997	170.00	170
1998 Lightship "Columbia"	Open		154.00	154
1997 Lightship "Huron"	Open		155.00	155
1997 Lightship "Huron" (special ed.)	4,000		170.00	170
1998 Lightship "Portsmouth"	Open		170.00	170
1997 Motor Yacht "Kim"	Open		139.00	139
1997 Motor Yacht "Kim" (special ed.)	4,000		154.00	154
1998 Purse Seiner "The Tori Dawn"	Open		154.00	154
1997 Sardine "Lori"	Open		159.00	159
1997 Sardine "Lori" (special ed.)	4,000		174.00	174
1997 Skipjack "Nancy"	Open		151.00	151
1997 Skipjack "Nancy" (special ed.)	4,000		166.00	166
1997 Tugboat "Toledo"	Open		131.00	131
1997 Tugboat "Toledo" (special ed.)	4,000		146.00	146

Anheuser-Busch, Inc.

Anheuser-Busch Collectible Figurines - A. Busch, Inc., unless otherwise noted

YEAR ISSUE	EDITION LIMIT	YEAR RETD.	ISSUE PRICE	*QUOTE U.S.$
1994 Buddies N4575 - M. Urdahl	7,500	1997	65.00	52-65
1995 Horseplay F1 - P. Radtke	7,500		65.00	65
1996 "Bud-weis-er Frogs" F4	Open		30.00	30
1996 Something Brewing F-3	7,500		65.00	65
1997 "Gone Fishing" Beagle Puppies F5	7,500		65.00	65
1997 "Boy Meets Girl" Budweiser Frogs F7	Open		30.00	30
1998 "Free Ride" Budweiser Frogs F8	Open		35.00	35
1998 "Louie and Frank" Budweiser Lizards F9	Open		35.00	35

The Clydesdale Collection - A. Busch, Inc.

YEAR ISSUE	EDITION LIMIT	YEAR RETD.	ISSUE PRICE	*QUOTE U.S.$
1998 An Apple For King CLYD5	Open		60.00	60
1998 Clydesdale Football CLYD3	10,000		85.00	85
1998 Full Parade Dress CLYD1	Open		50.00	50
1998 Mare & Foal CLYD4	Open		70.00	70
1998 Pals CLYD2	Open		65.00	65

ANRI

Club ANRI - Various

YEAR ISSUE	EDITION LIMIT	YEAR RETD.	ISSUE PRICE	*QUOTE U.S.$
1983 Welcome, 4" - J. Ferrandiz	Yr.Iss.	1984	110.00	350-400
1984 My Friend, 4" - J. Ferrandiz	Yr.Iss.	1985	110.00	350-400
1984 Apple of My Eye, 4 1/2" - S. Kay	Yr.Iss.	1985	135.00	425
1985 Harvest Time, 4" - J. Ferrandiz	Yr.Iss.	1986	125.00	400
1985 Dad's Helper, 4 1/2" - S. Kay	Yr.Iss.	1986	135.00	400
1986 Harvest's Helper, 4" - J. Ferrandiz	Yr.Iss.	1987	135.00	400
1986 Romantic Notions, 4" - S. Kay	Yr.Iss.	1987	135.00	310-400
1986 Celebration March, 5" - J. Ferrandiz	Yr.Iss.	1987	165.00	290-350
1987 Will You Be Mine, 4" - J. Ferrandiz	Yr.Iss.	1988	135.00	310-350
1987 Make A Wish, 4" - S. Kay	Yr.Iss.	1988	165.00	400-445
1987 A Young Man's Fancy, 4" - S. Kay	Yr.Iss.	1988	135.00	260-350
1988 Forever Yours, 4" - J. Ferrandiz	Yr.Iss.	1989	170.00	250-300
1988 I've Got a Secret, 4" - S. Kay	Yr.Iss.	1989	170.00	205-300
1988 Maestro Mickey, 4 1/2" - Disney Studio	Yr.Iss.	1989	170.00	175-300
1989 Diva Minnie, 4 1/2" - Disney Studio	Yr.Iss.	1990	190.00	190-300
1989 I'll Never Tell, 4" - S. Kay	Yr.Iss.	1990	190.00	190-250
1989 Twenty Years of Love, 4" - J. Ferrandiz	Yr.Iss.	1990	190.00	190-250
1990 You Are My Sunshine, 4" - J. Ferrandiz	Yr.Iss.	1991	220.00	220-275
1990 A Little Bashful, 4" - S. Kay	Yr.Iss.	1991	220.00	220-275
1990 Dapper Donald, 4" - Disney Studio	Yr.Iss.	1991	199.00	199-275
1991 With All My Heart, 4" - J. Ferrandiz	Yr.Iss.	1992	250.00	250-300
1991 Kiss Me, 4" - S. Kay	Yr.Iss.	1992	250.00	250-300
1991 Daisy Duck, 4 1/2" - Disney Studio	Yr.Iss.	1992	250.00	250-300

ANRI Club - Various

YEAR ISSUE	EDITION LIMIT	YEAR RETD.	ISSUE PRICE	*QUOTE U.S.$
1992 You Are My All, 4" - J. Ferrandiz	Yr.Iss.	1993	260.00	260
1992 My Present For You, 4" - S. Kay	Yr.Iss.	1993	270.00	270
1992 Gift of Love - S. Kay	Yr.Iss.	1993	Gift	65
1993 Truly Yours, 4" - J. Ferrandiz	Yr.Iss.	1994	290.00	290
1993 Sweet Thoughts, 4" - S. Kay	Yr.Iss.	1994	300.00	300
1993 Just For You - S. Kay	Yr.Iss.	1994	Gift	65
1994 Sweet 'N Shy, 4" - J. Ferrandiz	Yr.Iss.	1994	250.00	250
1994 Snuggle Up, 4" - S. Kay	Yr.Iss.	1994	300.00	300
1994 Dapper 'N Dear, 4" - J. Ferrandiz	Yr.Iss.	1994	250.00	250

ANRI Collectors' Society - Various

YEAR ISSUE	EDITION LIMIT	YEAR RETD.	ISSUE PRICE	*QUOTE U.S.$
1995 On My Own, 4" - S. Kay	Yr.Iss.	1996	175.00	175
1995 Sealed With A Kiss - J. Ferrandiz	Yr.Iss.	1997	275.00	275
1995 ANRI Artists' Tree House - ANRI	Yr.Iss.	1997	695.00	695
1996 On Cloud Nine - J. Ferrandiz	Yr.Iss.	1997	275.00	275
1996 Sweet Tooth - S. Kay	Yr.Iss.	1997	199.50	200
1997 Read Me A Story - S. Kay	Yr.Iss.	1998	395.00	395
1998 Little Leaguer - S. Kay	Yr.Iss.		295.00	295

ANRI Collectors' Society Gold Leaf Level - Various

YEAR ISSUE	EDITION LIMIT	YEAR RETD.	ISSUE PRICE	*QUOTE U.S.$
1996 Helping Mother, 6" - S. Kay	150		595.00	595
1996 Little Gardner, 6" - J. Ferrandiz	150		595.00	595
1997 La Moderna, 10" - Flavio	150		815.00	815
1997 Talking To The Animals, 6" - J. Ferrandiz	150		595.00	595
1997 Ballerina, 6" - S. Kay	150		595.00	595
1998 Chimney Sweep Girl - S. Kay	150		675.00	675
1998 The Artist - J. Ferrandiz	150		595.00	595
1998 "Reflective Moment" Clown Blanc - M. Fujita	150		595.00	595

Bernardi Reflections - U. Bernardi

YEAR ISSUE	EDITION LIMIT	YEAR RETD.	ISSUE PRICE	*QUOTE U.S.$
1996 Learning the Skills, 4"	500		275.00	285
1996 Learning the Skills, 6"	250		550.00	670
1994 Master Carver, 4"	500		350.00	375
1994 Master Carver, 6"	250	1995	600.00	670
1995 Planning the Tour, 4"	500		250.00	250
1995 Planning the Tour, 6"	250		300.00	475

Christmas Eve Series - L. Gaither

YEAR ISSUE	EDITION LIMIT	YEAR RETD.	ISSUE PRICE	*QUOTE U.S.$
1998 First Gift of Christmas, Mr. Santa	500		325.00	325
1998 First Gift of Christmas, Mrs. Santa	500		325.00	325

Disney Studios Mickey Mouse Thru The Ages - Disney Studios

YEAR ISSUE	EDITION LIMIT	YEAR RETD.	ISSUE PRICE	*QUOTE U.S.$
1991 The Mad Dog, 4"	1,000	1991	500.00	500-600
1990 Steam Boat Willie, 4"	1,000	1990	295.00	450-600

Disney Woodcarving - Disney Studio

YEAR ISSUE	EDITION LIMIT	YEAR RETD.	ISSUE PRICE	*QUOTE U.S.$
1991 Bell Boy Donald, 4" 656029	Closed	1991	250.00	250
1991 Bell Boy Donald, 6" 656110	500	1991	400.00	450-600
1990 Chef Goofy, 2 1/2" 656222	Closed	1991	125.00	150-185
1990 Chef Goofy, 5" 656227	Closed	1991	265.00	275-300
1989 Daisy, 4" 656021	Closed	1991	190.00	250-300
1990 Donald & Daisy, 6" 656108	500	1991	700.00	750-800
1988 Donald Duck, 1 3/4" 656209	Closed	1990	80.00	150
1988 Donald Duck, 2" 656204	Closed	1990	85.00	125-165
1987 Donald Duck, 4" 656004	Closed	1989	150.00	225-300
1988 Donald Duck, 4" 656014	Closed	1990	180.00	225-300
1988 Donald Duck, 6" 656102	500	1988	350.00	525
1989 Donald, 4" 656020	Closed	1991	190.00	250-300
1988 Goofy, 1 3/4" 656210	Closed	1990	80.00	125-175
1988 Goofy, 2" 656205	Closed	1990	85.00	125-175
1987 Goofy, 4" 656005	Closed	1989	150.00	200-300
1988 Goofy, 4" 656015	Closed	1990	180.00	205-300
1989 Goofy, 4" 656022	Closed	1991	190.00	200-300
1988 Goofy, 6" 656103	500	1988	380.00	550-600
1989 Mickey & Minnie Set, 6" 656106	500	1991	700.00	800-950
1989 Mickey & Minnie, 20" matched set	50	1991	7000.00	7000
1987 Mickey & Minnie, 6" 656101	500	1987	625.00	900-1000
1988 Mickey Mouse, 1 3/4" 656206	Closed	1990	80.00	200-300
1988 Mickey Mouse, 2" 656201	Closed	1990	85.00	175
1990 Mickey Mouse, 2" 656220	Closed	1991	100.00	225-350
1987 Mickey Mouse, 4" 656001	Closed	1989	150.00	200-225
1988 Mickey Mouse, 4" 656011	Closed	1990	180.00	205-225
1990 Mickey Mouse, 4" 656025	Closed	1991	199.00	250-325
1991 Mickey Skating, 2" 656224	Closed	1991	120.00	300-375
1991 Mickey Skating, 4" 656030	Closed	1991	250.00	250-300
1988 Mickey Sorcerer's Apprentice, 2" 656211	Closed	1991	80.00	300-400
1988 Mickey Sorcerer's Apprentice, 4" 656016	Closed	1991	180.00	180-250
1988 Mickey Sorcerer's Apprentice, 6" 656105	500	1991	350.00	600-700
1989 Mickey, 10" 656800	250	1991	700.00	850-950
1989 Mickey, 20" 656850	50	1991	3500.00	3500
1989 Mickey, 4" 656018	Closed	1991	190.00	180-300
1988 Mini Donald, 1 3/4" 656204	Closed	1991	85.00	150-200
1989 Mini Donald, 2" 656215	Closed	1991	85.00	150-200
1988 Mini Goofy, 1 3/4" 656205	Closed	1991	85.00	175-200
1989 Mini Goofy, 2" 656217	Closed	1991	85.00	175-200
1988 Mini Mickey, 1 3/4" 656201	Closed	1991	85.00	200
1989 Mini Mickey, 2" 656213	Closed	1991	85.00	200
1988 Mini Minnie, 1 3/4" 656202	Closed	1991	85.00	200
1989 Mini Minnie, 2" 656214	Closed	1991	85.00	200
1989 Mini Pluto, 2" 656218	Closed	1991	85.00	100-150
1989 Minnie Daisy, 2" 656216	Closed	1991	85.00	100-150
1988 Minnie Mouse, 2" 656202	Closed	1990	85.00	100-150
1990 Minnie Mouse, 2" 656221	Closed	1991	100.00	150
1987 Minnie Mouse, 4" 656002	Closed	1989	150.00	200-250
1990 Minnie Mouse, 4" 656026	Closed	1991	199.00	250
1988 Minnie Pinocchio, 1 3/4" 656203	Closed	1991	85.00	250-350
1991 Minnie Skating, 2" 656225	Closed	1991	120.00	150
1991 Minnie Skating, 4" 656031	Closed	1991	250.00	250-350
1989 Minnie, 10" 656801	250	1991	700.00	900
1989 Minnie, 20" 656851	50	1991	3500.00	3500
1989 Minnie, 4" 656019	Closed	1991	190.00	205-300
1988 Pinocchio, 1 3/4" 656208	Closed	1990	80.00	200-300
1989 Pinocchio, 10" 656802	250	1991	700.00	1000
1988 Pinocchio, 2" 656203	Closed	1990	85.00	85
1989 Pinocchio, 2" 656219	Closed	1991	85.00	100
1989 Pinocchio, 20" 656851	50	1991	3500.00	3500
1987 Pinocchio, 4" 656003 (apple)	Closed	1989	150.00	200-400
1988 Pinocchio, 4" 656013	Closed	1990	180.00	199-205
1989 Pinocchio, 4" 656024	Closed	1991	190.00	199
1989 Pinocchio, 6" 656107	500	1991	350.00	400-500
1988 Pluto, 1 3/4" 656207	Closed	1990	80.00	100-125
1988 Pluto, 4" 656012	Closed	1990	180.00	250-300
1989 Pluto, 4" 656023	Closed	1991	190.00	205-250
1988 Pluto, 6" 656104	500	1991	350.00	475
1990 Sorcerer's Apprentice w/ crystal, 2" 656223	Closed	1991	125.00	500-750
1990 Sorcerer's Apprentice w/ crystal, 4" 656028	Closed	1991	265.00	400-500
1990 Sorcerer's Apprentice w/ crystal, 6" 656109	1,000	1991	475.00	475-650
1990 Sorcerer's Apprentice w/ crystal, 8" 656803	350	1991	790.00	800-900
1990 Sorcerer's Apprentice w/ crystal,16" 656853	100	1991	3500.00	3500

Ferrandiz Boy and Girl - J. Ferrandiz

YEAR ISSUE	EDITION LIMIT	YEAR RETD.	ISSUE PRICE	*QUOTE U.S.$
1983 Admiration, 6"	2,250	1983	220.00	295
1990 Alpine Friend, 3"	1,500	1990	225.00	365
1990 Alpine Friend, 6"	1,500	1990	450.00	610
1990 Alpine Music, 3"	1,500	1990	225.00	225
1990 Alpine Music, 6"	1,500	1990	450.00	580
1989 Baker Boy, 3"	1,500	1989	170.00	170
1989 Baker Boy, 6"	1,500	1989	340.00	340
1978 Basket of Joy, 6"	1,500	1978	140.00	220-350
1983 Bewildered, 6"	2,250	1983	196.00	295
1991 Catalonian Boy, 3"	1,500	1993	227.50	228
1991 Catalonian Boy, 6"	1,500	1993	500.00	500
1991 Catalonian Girl, 3"	1,500	1993	227.50	228
1991 Catalonian Girl, 6"	1,500	1993	500.00	500
1976 Cowboy, 6"	1,500	1976	75.00	500-600
1987 Dear Sweetheart, 3"	2,250	1989	130.00	130
1987 Dear Sweetheart, 6"	2,250	1989	250.00	250
1988 Extra, Extra!, 3"	1,500	1988	145.00	145
1988 Extra, Extra!, 6"	1,500	1988	320.00	320
1979 First Blossom, 6"	2,250	1979	135.00	200-345
1987 For My Sweetheart, 3"	2,250	1989	130.00	130
1987 For My Sweetheart, 6"	2,250	1989	250.00	250
1984 Friendly Faces, 3"	2,250	1984	93.00	110
1984 Friendly Faces, 6"	2,250	1984	210.00	225-295
1980 Friends, 6"	2,250	1980	200.00	300-350
1986 Golden Sheaves, 3"	2,250	1986	125.00	125
1986 Golden Sheaves, 6"	2,250	1986	245.00	245
1982 Guiding Light, 6"	2,250	1982	225.00	275-350
1979 Happy Strummer, 6"	2,250	1979	160.00	395
1976 Harvest Girl, 6"	1,500	1976	75.00	400-800

*Quotes have been rounded up to nearest dollar

FIGURINES

YEAR ISSUE	EDITION LIMIT	YEAR RETD.	ISSUE PRICE	*QUOTE U.S.$
1977 Leading the Way, 6"	1,500	1977	100.00	300-375
1992 May I, Too?, 3"	1,000	1993	230.00	230
1992 May I, Too?, 6"	1,000	1993	440.00	440
1980 Melody for Two, 6"	2,250	1980	200.00	350
1981 Merry Melody, 6"	2,250	1981	210.00	300-350
1989 Pastry Girl, 3"	1,500	1989	170.00	170
1989 Pastry Girl, 6"	1,500	1989	340.00	340
1978 Peace Pipe, 6"	1,500	1978	140.00	325-450
1985 Peaceful Friends, 3"	2,250	1985	120.00	120
1985 Peaceful Friends, 6"	2,250	1985	250.00	295
1986 Season's Bounty, 3"	2,250	1986	125.00	125
1986 Season's Bounty, 6"	2,250	1986	245.00	245
1988 Sunny Skies, 3"	1,500	1988	145.00	145
1988 Sunny Skies, 6"	1,500	1988	320.00	320
1985 Tender Love, 3"	2,250	1985	100.00	125
1985 Tender Love, 6"	2,250	1985	225.00	250
1981 Tiny Sounds, 6"	2,250	1981	210.00	300-350
1982 To Market, 6"	1,500	1982	220.00	295
1977 Tracker, 6"	1,500	1977	100.00	400
1984 Wanderer's Return, 3"	2,250	1984	93.00	135
1984 Wanderer's Return, 6"	2,250	1984	196.00	250
1992 Waste Not, Want Not, 3"	1,000	1993	190.00	200
1992 Waste Not, Want Not, 6"	1,000	1993	430.00	430

Ferrandiz Children of the World - J. Ferrandiz

YEAR ISSUE	EDITION LIMIT	YEAR RETD.	ISSUE PRICE	*QUOTE U.S.$
1998 Kareem	Open		285.00	285
1998 Keisha	Open		285.00	285
1997 Maria, 4"	Open		285.00	285
1997 Miguel, 4"	Open		285.00	285

Ferrandiz Circus - J. Ferrandiz

YEAR ISSUE	EDITION LIMIT	YEAR RETD.	ISSUE PRICE	*QUOTE U.S.$
1986 Balancing Ballerina, 2 1/2"	Closed	1988	100.00	100
1986 Balancing Ballerina, 5"	3,000	1988	150.00	150
1986 Ballerina on Horse, 2 1/2"	Closed	1988	125.00	125
1986 Ballerina on Horse, 5"	3,000	1988	200.00	200
1986 Cat on Stool, 2 1/2"	Closed	1988	50.00	50
1986 Cat on Stool, 5"	3,000	1988	110.00	110
1986 Clown on Elephant, 2 1/2"	Closed	1988	125.00	125
1986 Clown on Elephant, 5"	3,000	1988	200.00	200
1986 Clown on Unicycle, 2 1/2"	Closed	1988	80.00	80
1986 Clown on Unicycle, 5"	3,000	1988	175.00	175
1987 Clown w/Bunny, 2 1/2"	Closed	1988	80.00	80
1987 Clown w/Bunny, 5"	3,000	1988	175.00	175
1986 Clown w/Sax, 2 1/2"	Closed	1988	80.00	80
1986 Clown w/Sax, 5"	3,000	1988	175.00	175
1987 Clown w/Umbrella, 2 1/2"	Closed	1988	80.00	80
1987 Clown w/Umbrella, 5"	3,000	1988	175.00	175
1986 Lion Tamer, 2 1/2"	Closed	1988	80.00	80
1986 Lion Tamer, 5"	3,000	1988	175.00	175
1986 Ring Master, 2 1/2"	Closed	1988	80.00	80
1986 Ring Master, 5"	3,000	1988	175.00	175

Ferrandiz Memorial - J. Ferrandiz

YEAR ISSUE	EDITION LIMIT	YEAR RETD.	ISSUE PRICE	*QUOTE U.S.$
1998 Peaceful Love, 3"	Open		225.00	225
1998 Peaceful Love, 6"	Open		450.00	450
1998 Peaceful Love, 10"	Open		950.00	950
1998 Peaceful Love, 20"	250		4500.00	4500
1998 Peaceful Love, 40"	12		11500.00	11500

Ferrandiz Message Collection - J. Ferrandiz

YEAR ISSUE	EDITION LIMIT	YEAR RETD.	ISSUE PRICE	*QUOTE U.S.$
1990 Christmas Carillon, 4 1/2"	2,500	1992	299.00	299
1990 Count Your Blessings, 4 1/2"	5,000	1992	300.00	300
1990 God's Creation, 4 1/2"	5,000	1992	300.00	300
1989 God's Miracle, 4 1/2"	5,000	1991	300.00	300
1989 God's Precious Gift, 4 1/2"	5,000	1991	300.00	300
1989 He Guides Us, 4 1/2"	5,000	1991	300.00	300
1989 He is the Light, 4 1/2"	5,000	1991	300.00	300
1989 He is the Light, 9"	5,000	1991	600.00	600
1989 Heaven Sent, 4 1/2"	5,000	1991	300.00	300
1989 Light From Within, 4 1/2"	5,000	1991	300.00	300
1989 Love Knows No Bounds, 4 1/2"	5,000	1991	300.00	300
1989 Love So Powerful, 4 1/2"	5,000	1991	300.00	300

Ferrandiz Mini Nativity Set - J. Ferrandiz

YEAR ISSUE	EDITION LIMIT	YEAR RETD.	ISSUE PRICE	*QUOTE U.S.$
1985 Baby Camel, 1 1/2"	Closed	1993	45.00	53
1985 Camel Guide, 1 1/2"	Closed	1993	45.00	53
1985 Camel, 1 1/2"	Closed	1993	45.00	53
1988 Devotion, 1 1/2"	Closed	1993	53.00	53
1985 Harmony, 1 1/2"	Closed	1993	45.00	53
1984 Infant, 1 1/2"	Closed	1993	Set	Set
1988 Jolly Gift, 1 1/2"	Closed	1992	53.00	53
1984 Joseph, 1 1/2"	Closed	1993	Set	Set
1984 Leading the Way, 1 1/2"	Closed	1993	Set	Set
1988 Long Journey, 1 1/2"	Closed	1993	53.00	53
1984 Mary, 1 1/2"	Closed	1993	300.00	540
1986 Mini Angel, 1 1/2"	Closed	1993	45.00	53
1986 Mini Balthasar, 1 1/2"	Closed	1993	45.00	53
1986 Mini Caspar, 1 1/2"	Closed	1993	45.00	53
1986 Mini Free Ride, plus Mini Lamb, 1 1/2"	Closed	1993	45.00	53
1986 Mini Melchoir, 1 1/2"	Closed	1993	45.00	53
1986 Mini Star Struck, 1 1/2"	Closed	1993	45.00	53
1986 Mini The Hiker, 1 1/2"	Closed	1993	45.00	53
1986 Mini The Stray, 1 1/2"	Closed	1993	45.00	53
1986 Mini Weary Traveller, 1 1/2"	Closed	1993	45.00	53
1984 Ox Donkey, 1 1/2"	Closed	1993	Set	Set
1985 Rest, 1 1/2"	Closed	1993	45.00	53
1985 Reverence, 1 1/2"	Closed	1993	45.00	53
1984 Sheep Kneeling, 1 1/2"	Closed	1993	Set	Set
1984 Sheep Standing, 1 1/2"	Closed	1993	Set	Set
1985 Small Talk, 1 1/2"	Closed	1993	45.00	53
1988 Sweet Dreams, 1 1/2"	Closed	1993	53.00	53
1988 Sweet Inspiration, 1 1/2"	Closed	1992	53.00	53
1985 Thanksgiving, 1 1/2"	Closed	1993	45.00	53

Ferrandiz Shepherds of the Year - J. Ferrandiz

YEAR ISSUE	EDITION LIMIT	YEAR RETD.	ISSUE PRICE	*QUOTE U.S.$
1982 Companions, 6"	2,250	1982	220.00	275-300
1984 Devotion, 3"	2,250	1984	82.50	125
1984 Devotion, 6"	2,250	1984	180.00	200-250
1979 Drummer Boy, 3"	Yr.Iss.	1979	80.00	250
1979 Drummer Boy, 6"	Yr.Iss.	1979	220.00	400-425
1980 Freedom Bound, 3"	Yr.Iss.	1980	90.00	225
1980 Freedom Bound, 6"	Yr.Iss.	1980	225.00	400
1977 Friendship, 3"	Yr.Iss.	1977	53.50	330
1977 Friendship, 6"	Yr.Iss.	1977	110.00	500-675
1983 Good Samaritan, 6"	2,250	1983	220.00	300-320
1981 Jolly Piper, 6"	2,250	1981	225.00	375
1978 Spreading the Word, 3"	Yr.Iss.	1978	115.00	250-275
1978 Spreading the Word, 6"	Yr.Iss.	1978	270.50	500

Ferrandiz Woodcarvings - J. Ferrandiz

YEAR ISSUE	EDITION LIMIT	YEAR RETD.	ISSUE PRICE	*QUOTE U.S.$
1988 Abracadabra, 3"	1,500	1991	145.00	165
1988 Abracadabra, 6"	1,500	1991	315.00	345
1976 Adoration, 12"	Closed	1987	350.00	350
1981 Adoration, 20"	250	1987	3200.00	3200
1976 Adoration, 3"	Closed	1987	45.00	45
1976 Adoration, 6"	Closed	1987	100.00	100
1987 Among Friends, 3"	3,000	1990	125.00	151
1987 Among Friends, 6"	3,000	1990	245.00	291
1969 Angel Sugar Heart, 6"	Closed	1973	25.00	2500
1974 Artist, 3"	Closed	1981	30.00	195
1970 Artist, 6"	Closed	1981	25.00	350
1982 Bagpipe, 3"	Closed	1983	80.00	95
1982 Bagpipe, 6"	Closed	1983	175.00	190
1978 Basket of Joy, 3"	Closed	1984	65.00	120
1984 Bird's Eye View, 3"	Closed	1989	88.00	129
1984 Bird's Eye View, 6"	Closed	1989	216.00	700
1987 Black Forest Boy, 3"	3,000	1990	125.00	151
1987 Black Forest Boy, 6"	3,000	1990	250.00	301
1987 Black Forest Girl, 3"	3,000	1990	125.00	151
1987 Black Forest Girl, 6"	3,000	1990	250.00	300-350
1977 The Blessing, 3"	Closed	1982	45.00	150
1977 The Blessing, 6"	Closed	1982	125.00	250
1988 Bon Appetit, 3"	500	1991	175.00	195
1988 Bon Appetit, 6"	500	1991	395.00	440
1974 The Bouquet, 3"	Closed	1981	35.00	175
1974 The Bouquet, 6"	Closed	1981	75.00	325
1982 Bundle of Joy, 3"	Closed	1990	100.00	300
1982 Bundle of Joy, 6"	Closed	1990	225.00	323
1985 Butterfly Boy, 3"	Closed	1990	95.00	140
1985 Butterfly Boy, 6"	Closed	1990	220.00	322
1976 Catch a Falling Star, 3"	Closed	1983	35.00	150
1976 Catch a Falling Star, 6"	Closed	1983	75.00	250
1986 Celebration March, 11"	750	1987	495.00	495
1986 Celebration March, 20"	200	1987	2700.00	2700
1982 The Champion, 3"	Closed	1985	98.00	110
1982 The Champion, 6"	Closed	1985	225.00	250
1975 Cherub, 2"	Open		32.00	90
1975 Cherub, 4"	Open		32.00	275
1993 Christmas Time, 5"	750		360.00	420
1982 Circus Serenade, 3"	Closed	1988	100.00	160
1982 Circus Serenade, 6"	Closed	1988	220.00	220
1982 Clarinet, 3"	Closed	1983	80.00	100
1982 Clarinet, 6"	Closed	1983	175.00	200
1982 Companions, 3"	Closed	1984	95.00	115
1975 Courting, 3"	Closed	1982	70.00	235
1975 Courting, 6"	Closed	1982	150.00	450
1984 Cowboy, 10"	Closed	1989	370.00	500
1983 Cowboy, 20"	250	1989	2100.00	2100
1976 Cowboy, 3"	Closed	1989	35.00	140-160
1994 Donkey Driver, 3"	Open		160.00	160
1994 Donkey Driver, 6"	Open		360.00	360
1994 Donkey, 3"	Open		200.00	200
1994 Donkey, 6"	Open		450.00	450
1980 Drummer Boy, 3"	Closed	1988	130.00	200
1980 Drummer Boy, 6"	Closed	1988	300.00	400
1970 Duet, 3"	Closed	1991	36.00	165
1970 Duet, 6"	Closed	1991	Unkn.	355
1986 Edelweiss, 10"	Open		500.00	1080
1986 Edelweiss, 20"	250		3300.00	5420
1983 Edelweiss, 3"	Open		95.00	245
1983 Edelweiss, 6"	Open		220.00	575
1982 Encore, 3"	Closed	1984	100.00	115
1982 Encore, 6"	Closed	1984	225.00	235
1979 First Blossom, 3"	Closed	1985	70.00	78-110
1974 Flight Into Egypt, 3"	Closed	1986	35.00	125
1974 Flight Into Egypt, 6"	Closed	1986	70.00	500
1976 Flower Girl, 3"	Closed	1988	40.00	40
1976 Flower Girl, 6"	Closed	1988	90.00	310
1982 Flute, 3"	Closed	1983	80.00	95
1982 Flute, 6"	Closed	1983	175.00	190-225
1976 Gardener, 3"	Closed	1984	32.00	195
1976 Gardener, 6"	Closed	1985	65.00	275-350
1975 The Gift, 3"	Closed	1982	40.00	195
1975 The Gift, 6"	Closed	1982	70.00	295
1973 Girl in the Egg, 3"	Closed	1988	30.00	127
1973 Girl in the Egg, 6"	Closed	1988	60.00	272
1973 Girl with Dove, 3"	Closed	1984	30.00	110
1973 Girl with Dove, 6"	Closed	1984	50.00	175-200
1976 Girl with Rooster, 3"	Closed	1982	32.50	175
1976 Girl with Rooster, 6"	Closed	1982	60.00	275
1986 God's Little Helper, 2"	3,500	1991	170.00	255
1986 God's Little Helper, 4"	2,000	1991	425.00	550
1975 Going Home, 3"	Closed	1988	40.00	175
1975 Going Home, 6"	Closed	1988	70.00	325
1986 Golden Blossom, 10"	Open		500.00	1060
1986 Golden Blossom, 20"	250		3300.00	5420
1983 Golden Blossom, 3"	Open		95.00	250
1986 Golden Blossom, 40"	50	1994	8300.00	12950
1983 Golden Blossom, 6"	Open		220.00	550
1982 The Good Life, 3"	Closed	1984	100.00	200
1982 The Good Life, 6"	Closed	1984	225.00	295
1969 The Good Shepherd, 3"	Closed	1988	12.50	121
1971 The Good Shepherd, 10"	Closed	1988	90.00	90
1969 The Good Shepherd, 6"	Closed	1988	25.00	237
1974 Greetings, 3"	Closed	1976	30.00	300
1974 Greetings, 6"	Closed	1976	55.00	475
1982 Guiding Light, 3"	Closed	1984	100.00	115-140
1982 Guitar, 3"	Closed	1983	80.00	95
1982 Guitar, 6"	Closed	1983	175.00	190
1979 Happy Strummer, 3"	Closed	1986	75.00	110
1973 Happy Wanderer, 10"	Closed	1985	120.00	500
1974 Happy Wanderer, 3"	Closed	1986	40.00	105
1974 Happy Wanderer, 6"	Closed	1986	70.00	200
1982 Harmonica, 3"	Closed	1983	80.00	95
1982 Harmonica, 3"	Closed	1983	80.00	95
1982 Harmonica, 6"	Closed	1983	175.00	190
1978 Harvest Girl, 3"	Closed	1986	75.00	110-140
1975 Have You Heard, 3"	Closed	1987	50.00	112
1979 He's My Brother, 3"	Closed	1984	70.00	130
1979 He's My Brother, 6"	Closed	1984	155.00	240
1987 Heavenly Concert, 2"	3,000	1991	200.00	200
1987 Heavenly Concert, 4"	2,000	1991	450.00	550
1969 Heavenly Gardener, 6"	Closed	1973	25.00	2000
1969 Heavenly Quintet, 6"	Closed	1973	25.00	2000
1969 The Helper, 3"	Closed	1987	12.50	13
1969 The Helper, 5"	Closed	1987	25.00	25
1974 Helping Hands, 3"	Closed	1976	30.00	350
1974 Helping Hands, 6"	Closed	1976	55.00	700
1984 High Hopes, 3"	Closed	1986	81.00	81-100
1984 High Hopes, 6"	Closed	1986	170.00	255
1979 High Riding, 3"	Closed	1984	145.00	200
1979 High Riding, 6"	Closed	1984	340.00	475
1974 The Hiker, 3"	Closed	1993	36.00	36
1974 The Hiker, 6"	Closed	1993	80.00	80
1982 Hitchhiker, 3"	Closed	1986	98.00	85-110
1982 Hitchhiker, 6"	Closed	1986	125.00	230
1993 Holiday Greetings, 3"	1,000	1993	200.00	200
1993 Holiday Greetings, 6"	1,000	1993	450.00	450
1975 Holy Family, 3"	Closed	1988	75.00	250
1975 Holy Family, 6"	Closed	1988	200.00	670
1996 Homeward Bound, 3"	Open		155.00	155
1996 Homeward Bound, 6"	Open		410.00	410
1977 Hurdy Gurdy, 3"	Closed	1988	53.00	150
1977 Hurdy Gurdy, 6"	Closed	1988	112.00	390
1975 Inspector, 3"	Closed	1981	40.00	250
1975 Inspector, 6"	Closed	1981	80.00	395
1988 Jolly Gift, 3"	Closed	1991	129.00	129
1988 Jolly Gift, 6"	Closed	1991	296.00	296
1981 Jolly Piper, 3"	Closed	1984	100.00	120
1977 Journey, 3"	Closed	1983	67.50	175
1977 Journey, 6"	Closed	1983	120.00	400
1977 Leading the Way, 3"	Closed	1984	62.50	120
1976 The Letter, 3"	Closed	1988	40.00	40
1976 The Letter, 6"	Closed	1988	90.00	600
1982 Lighting the Way, 3"	Closed	1984	105.00	150
1982 Lighting the Way, 6"	Closed	1984	225.00	295
1974 Little Mother, 3"	Closed	1981	136.00	290
1974 Little Mother, 6"	Closed	1981	85.00	285
1989 Little Sheep Found, 3"	Open		120.00	180
1989 Little Sheep Found, 6"	Open		275.00	335
1993 Lots of Gifts, 3"	1,000	1993	200.00	200
1993 Lots of Gifts, 6"	1,000	1993	450.00	450
1975 Love Gift, 3"	Closed	1982	40.00	175
1975 Love Gift, 6"	Closed	1982	70.00	295
1969 Love Letter, 3"	Closed	1982	12.50	150
1969 Love Letter, 6"	Closed	1982	25.00	176-250
1983 Love Message, 3"	Closed	1990	105.00	151
1983 Love Message, 6"	Closed	1990	240.00	366
1969 Love's Messenger, 6"	Closed	1973	25.00	2000
1992 Madonna With Child, 3"	1,000	1994	190.00	190
1992 Madonna With Child, 6"	1,000	1994	370.00	370
1981 Merry Melody, 3"	Closed	1984	90.00	115
1989 Mexican Boy, 3"	1,500	1993	170.00	175
1989 Mexican Boy, 6"	1,500	1993	340.00	350
1989 Mexican Girl, 3"	1,500	1993	170.00	175
1989 Mexican Girl, 6"	1,500	1993	340.00	350
1975 Mother and Child, 3"	Closed	1983	45.00	150
1975 Mother and Child, 6"	Closed	1983	90.00	295
1981 Musical Basket, 3"	Closed	1984	90.00	115
1981 Musical Basket, 6"	Closed	1984	200.00	225
1986 A Musical Ride, 4"	Closed	1990	165.00	237
1986 A Musical Ride, 8"	Closed	1990	395.00	559
1973 Nature Girl, 3"	Closed	1988	30.00	30
1973 Nature Girl, 6"	Closed	1988	60.00	272
1987 Nature's Wonder, 3"	3,000	1990	125.00	151
1987 Nature's Wonder, 6"	3,000	1990	245.00	291
1974 New Friends, 3"	Closed	1976	30.00	275
1974 New Friends, 6"	Closed	1976	55.00	550
1977 Night Night, 3"	Closed	1983	45.00	120
1977 Night Night, 6"	Closed	1983	67.50	250-315
1992 Pascal Lamb, 3"	1,000	1993	210.00	210
1992 Pascal Lamb, 6"	1,000	1993	460.00	460
1988 Peace Maker, 3"	1,500	1991	180.00	200
1988 Peace Maker, 6"	1,500	1991	360.00	395
1983 Peace Pipe, 10"	Closed	1986	460.00	495
1984 Peace Pipe, 20"	250	1986	2200.00	3500
1979 Peace Pipe, 3"	Closed	1986	85.00	120
1988 Picnic for Two, 3"	500	1991	190.00	210

*Quotes have been rounded up to nearest dollar

YEAR ISSUE	EDITION LIMIT	YEAR RETD.	ISSUE PRICE	*QUOTE U.S.$
1988 Picnic for Two, 6"	500	1991	425.00	465
1982 Play It Again, 3"	Closed	1984	100.00	120
1982 Play It Again, 6"	Closed	1984	250.00	255
1977 Poor Boy, 3"	Closed	1986	50.00	110
1977 Poor Boy, 6"	Closed	1986	125.00	215
1977 Proud Mother, 3"	Closed	1988	52.50	150
1977 Proud Mother, 6"	Closed	1988	130.00	350
1971 The Quintet, 10"	Closed	1990	100.00	750
1971 The Quintet, 20"	Closed	1990	Unkn.	4750
1969 The Quintet, 3"	Closed	1990	12.50	175
1969 The Quintet, 6"	Closed	1990	25.00	395
1970 Reverance, 3"	Closed	1991	30.00	30
1970 Reverance, 6"	Closed	1991	56.00	56
1977 Riding Thru the Rain, 10"	Open		400.00	1190
1985 Riding Thru the Rain, 20"	100	1988	3950.00	3950
1977 Riding Thru the Rain, 5"	Open		145.00	470
1976 Rock A Bye, 3"	Closed	1987	60.00	60
1976 Rock A Bye, 6"	Closed	1987	125.00	125
1974 Romeo, 3"	Closed	1981	50.00	250
1974 Romeo, 6"	Closed	1981	85.00	275-395
1993 Santa and Teddy, 5"	750		360.00	380
1994 Santa Resting on Bag, 5"	750		400.00	400
1987 Serenity, 3"	3,000	1989	125.00	151
1987 Serenity, 6"	3,000	1989	245.00	291
1976 Sharing, 3"	Closed	1983	32.50	130
1976 Sharing, 6"	Closed	1983	32.50	225-275
1984 Shipmates, 3"	Closed	1989	81.00	119
1984 Shipmates, 6"	Closed	1989	170.00	248
1975 Small Talk, 3"	Closed	1987	35.00	90
1978 Spreading the Word, 3"	Closed	1989	115.00	194
1978 Spreading the Word, 6"	Closed	1989	270.00	495
1980 Spring Arrivals, 10"	Open		435.00	770
1980 Spring Arrivals, 20"	250		2000.00	3360
1973 Spring Arrivals, 3"	Open		30.00	160
1973 Spring Arrivals, 6"	Open		50.00	350
1978 Spring Dance, 12"	Closed	1984	950.00	1750
1978 Spring Dance, 24"	Closed	1984	4750.00	6200
1974 Spring Outing, 3"	Closed	1976	30.00	625
1974 Spring Outing, 6"	Closed	1976	55.00	900
1982 Star Bright, 3"	Closed	1984	110.00	125
1982 Star Bright, 6"	Closed	1984	250.00	295
1982 Star Struck, 10"	Closed	1987	490.00	490
1982 Star Struck, 20"	250	1987	2400.00	2400
1974 Star Struck, 3"	Closed	1987	97.50	98
1974 Star Struck, 6"	Closed	1987	210.00	210
1981 Stepping Out, 3"	Closed	1984	95.00	110-145
1981 Stepping Out, 6"	Closed	1984	220.00	275
1979 Stitch in Time, 3"	Closed	1984	75.00	125
1979 Stitch in Time, 6"	Closed	1984	150.00	235
1975 Stolen Kiss, 3"	Closed	1987	80.00	80
1975 Stolen Kiss, 6"	Closed	1987	150.00	150-400
1969 Sugar Heart, 3"	Closed	1973	12.50	450
1969 Sugar Heart, 6"	Closed	1973	25.00	525
1975 Summertime, 3"	Closed	1989	35.00	35
1975 Summertime, 6"	Closed	1989	70.00	258
1982 Surprise, 3"	Closed	1988	100.00	150
1982 Surprise, 6"	Closed	1988	225.00	325
1973 Sweeper, 3"	Closed	1981	35.00	130
1973 Sweeper, 6"	Closed	1981	75.00	250-425
1981 Sweet Arrival Blue, 3"	Closed	1985	105.00	110
1981 Sweet Arrival Blue, 6"	Closed	1985	225.00	255
1981 Sweet Arrival Pink, 3"	Closed	1985	105.00	110
1981 Sweet Arrival Pink, 6"	Closed	1985	225.00	225
1981 Sweet Dreams, 3"	Closed	1990	100.00	140
1982 Sweet Dreams, 6"	Closed	1990	225.00	330
1989 Sweet Inspiration, 3"	Closed	1991	129.00	129
1989 Sweet Inspiration, 6"	Closed	1991	296.00	296
1982 Sweet Melody, 3"	Closed	1985	80.00	90
1982 Sweet Melody, 6"	Closed	1985	198.00	210
1989 Swiss Boy, 3"	Closed	1993	180.00	180
1986 Swiss Boy, 3"	Closed	1993	122.00	162
1989 Swiss Boy, 6"	Closed	1993	380.00	380
1986 Swiss Boy, 6"	Closed	1993	245.00	324
1986 Swiss Girl, 3"	Closed	1993	122.00	122
1989 Swiss Girl, 3"	Closed	1993	200.00	200
1989 Swiss Girl, 6"	Closed	1993	470.00	470
1986 Swiss Girl, 6"	Closed	1993	245.00	304
1971 Talking to Animals, 20"	Closed	1989	Unkn.	3000
1971 Talking to the Animals, 10"	Closed	1989	90.00	600
1969 Talking to the Animals, 3"	Closed	1989	12.50	155
1969 Talking to the Animals, 6"	Closed	1989	45.00	385
1995 Tender Care, 3" 55710/52	Open		125.00	150
1995 Tender Care, 6" 55700/52	Open		275.00	396
1974 Tender Moments, 3"	Closed	1976	30.00	375
1974 Tender Moments, 6"	Closed	1976	55.00	575
1981 Tiny Sounds, 3"	Closed	1984	90.00	105
1982 To Market, 3"	Closed	1984	95.00	115
1977 Tracker, 3"	Closed	1984	70.00	120-200
1982 Treasure Chest w/6 mini figurines	10,000	1984	300.00	300
1980 Trumpeter, 10"	Closed	1986	500.00	500
1984 Trumpeter, 20"	250	1986	2350.00	3050
1973 Trumpeter, 3"	Closed	1986	69.00	115
1973 Trumpeter, 6"	Closed	1986	120.00	240
1980 Umpapa, 4"	Closed	1984	125.00	140
1982 Violin, 3"	Closed	1983	80.00	95
1982 Violin, 6"	Closed	1983	175.00	195
1976 Wanderlust, 3"	Closed	1983	32.50	125
1975 Wanderlust, 6"	Closed	1983	70.00	450
1972 The Weary Traveler, 3"	Closed	1989	24.00	24
1972 The Weary Traveler, 6"	Closed	1989	48.00	48
1988 Winter Memories, 3"	1,500	1991	180.00	195
1988 Winter Memories, 6"	1,500	1991	398.00	440

Gunther Granget Animals - G. Granget

YEAR ISSUE	EDITION LIMIT	YEAR RETD.	ISSUE PRICE	*QUOTE U.S.$
1980 Barn Owl, 6 1/2"	Closed	1984	240.00	240
1974 Barn Owl, 10"	2,500	1984	800.00	800
1974 Barn Owl, 12 1/2"	1,500	1984	1050.00	1050
1974 Barn Owl, 20"	250	1984	3350.00	3350
1980 Black Grouse, 3 3/4"	Closed	1984	265.00	265
1972 Black Grouse, 6"	1,000		1150.00	3510
1972 Black Grouse, 11"	200		5600.00	16660
1998 Dolphin w/ Young	Open		450.00	450
1972 Female Fox w/Young	1,000	1984	1100.00	1100
1972 Female Fox w/Young	200	1984	4300.00	4300
1980 Fox, 3 3/4"	Closed	1984	180.00	180
1980 Golden Eagle, 5 3/4"	Closed	1985	265.00	265
1972 Golden Eagle, 8"	1,000		800.00	2390
1972 Golden Eagle, 15"	250		3600.00	10500
1974 Great Horned Owl Family (plaque)	Closed	1976	550.00	550
1974 Great Horned Owl Family (plaque)	Closed	1976	800.00	800
1974 Great Horned Owl Family (plaque)	Closed	1976	2500.00	2500
1976 The Green Woodpecker	1,500	1980	393.00	393
1976 The Green Woodpecker	750	1980	1132.00	1132
1976 The Jay	1,500	1980	393.00	393
1976 The Jay	750	1980	1132.00	1132
1998 Lioness	Open		595.00	595
1980 Lynx, 3 3/4"	Closed	1984	240.00	240
1972 Lynx	1,000	1980	600.00	600
1972 Lynx	250	1980	2900.00	2900
1974 Mallard Family (plaque)	Closed	1976	550.00	550
1974 Mallard Family (plaque)	Closed	1976	800.00	800
1974 Mallard Family (plaque)	Closed	1976	2500.00	2500
1980 Mallard, 4"	Closed	1985	265.00	265
1972 Mallard, 5"	1,000		700.00	2200
1972 Mallard, 10"	250		3600.00	10800
1980 Partridge, 4 1/4"	Closed	1984	195.00	195
1972 Partridges, 6"	1,000		800.00	2680
1972 Partridges, 13"	200		4200.00	13100
1980 Peregrine Falcon, 6"	Closed	1984	240.00	240
1974 Peregrine Falcon, 10"	2,500	1984	700.00	700
1974 Peregrine Falcon, 12 1/2"	1,500	1984	1000.00	1000
1974 Peregrine Falcon, 20"	250	1984	3350.00	3350
1980 Pheasant (Ringed neck), 6 1/2"	Closed	1985	280.00	280
1972 Pheasant (Ringed neck), 9"	1,000		800.00	2620
1972 Pheasant (Ringed neck), 17"	250		3700.00	10930
1980 Roadrunner, 6"	Closed	1984	300.00	300
1980 Roadrunner	1,000	1980	1750.00	1750
1980 Roadrunner	250	1980	6500.00	6500
1980 Rooster, 7"	Closed	1984	300.00	300
1974 Rooster, 11"	1,000		805.00	2800
1974 Rooster, 22"	250		3800.00	10500
1980 Shoveler, 4"	Closed	1984	240.00	240
1980 Shoveler	1,000	1980	1600.00	1600
1980 Shoveler	200	1980	8000.00	8000
1972 Wild Sow w/Young	1,000	1984	950.00	950
1972 Wild Sow w/Young	200	1984	4000.00	4000

Limited Edition Couples - J. Ferrandiz

YEAR ISSUE	EDITION LIMIT	YEAR RETD.	ISSUE PRICE	*QUOTE U.S.$
1985 First Kiss, 8"	750	1985	590.00	950
1987 Heart to Heart, 8"	750	1991	590.00	850
1988 A Loving Hand, 8"	750	1991	795.00	850
1986 My Heart Is Yours, 8"	750	1991	590.00	850
1985 Springtime Stroll, 8"	750	1990	590.00	950
1986 A Tender Touch, 8"	750	1990	590.00	850

Lyndon Gaither Christmas Eve Series - L. Gaither

YEAR ISSUE	EDITION LIMIT	YEAR RETD.	ISSUE PRICE	*QUOTE U.S.$
1995 Hitching Prancer, 3 1/2" figurine & ornament	500		499.00	525
1996 Getting Ready, 3 1/2" figurine & ornament	500		499.00	525
1997 Time To go, 5" figurine & ornament	500		595.00	595

Lyndon Gaither Religious - L. Gaither

YEAR ISSUE	EDITION LIMIT	YEAR RETD.	ISSUE PRICE	*QUOTE U.S.$
1998 Holy Family Plaque	Open		995.00	995
1998 Moses And The Ten Commandments	Open		995.00	995

Sarah Kay Figurines - S. Kay

YEAR ISSUE	EDITION LIMIT	YEAR RETD.	ISSUE PRICE	*QUOTE U.S.$
1985 Afternoon Tea, 11"	750	1993	650.00	770
1985 Afternoon Tea, 20"	100	1993	3100.00	3500
1985 Afternoon Tea, 4"	4,000	1990	95.00	185
1985 Afternoon Tea, 6"	4,000	1990	195.00	325-365
1987 All Aboard, 1 1/2"	7,500	1990	50.00	90
1987 All Aboard, 4"	4,000	1990	130.00	185
1987 All Aboard, 6"	2,000	1990	265.00	355
1987 All Mine, 1 1/2"	7,500	1988	49.50	95
1987 All Mine, 4"	4,000	1988	130.00	225
1987 All Mine, 6"	4,000	1988	245.00	465
1986 Always By My Side, 1 1/2"	7,500	1988	45.00	95
1986 Always By My Side, 4"	4,000	1988	95.00	195
1986 Always By My Side, 6"	4,000	1988	195.00	375
1990 Batter Up, 1 1/2"	3,750	1991	90.00	95
1990 Batter Up, 4"	2,000		220.00	280
1990 Batter Up, 6"	2,000		440.00	540
1983 Bedtime, 1 1/2"	7,500	1984	45.00	110
1983 Bedtime, 4"	Closed	1987	95.00	230
1983 Bedtime, 6"	4,000	1987	195.00	435
1994 Bubbles & Bows, 4"	1,000		300.00	310
1994 Bubbles & Bows, 6"	1,000		600.00	620
1986 Bunny Hug, 1 1/2"	7,500	1989	45.00	85
1986 Bunny Hug, 4"	4,000	1989	95.00	172
1986 Bunny Hug, 6"	2,000	1989	210.00	395
1989 Cherish, 1 1/2"	Closed	1991	80.00	95
1989 Cherish, 4"	2,000	1994	199.00	290
1989 Cherish, 6"	2,000	1994	398.00	560
1993 Christmas Basket, 4"	1,000		310.00	298
1993 Christmas Basket, 6"	1,000		600.00	590
1994 Christmas Wonder, 4"	1,000		370.00	420
1994 Christmas Wonder, 6"	1,000		700.00	770
1994 Clowning Around, 4"	1,000		300.00	300
1994 Clowning Around, 6"	1,000		550.00	600
1998 Coffee Break, 4"	2,000		295.00	295
1998 Coffee Break, 6"	1,000		575.00	575
1987 Cuddles, 1 1/2"	7,500	1988	49.50	95
1987 Cuddles, 4"	4,000	1988	130.00	225
1987 Cuddles, 6"	4,000	1988	245.00	465
1984 Daydreaming, 1 1/2"	7,500	1984	45.00	125
1984 Daydreaming, 4"	4,000	1988	95.00	235
1984 Daydreaming, 6"	4,000	1988	195.00	445
1991 Dress Up, 1 1/2"	3,750	1991	110.00	110
1991 Dress Up, 4"	2,000	1993	270.00	270
1991 Dress Up, 6"	2,000	1993	550.00	570
1983 Feeding the Chickens, 1 1/2"	7,500	1984	45.00	110
1983 Feeding the Chickens, 4"	Closed	1987	95.00	250
1983 Feeding the Chickens, 6"	4,000	1987	195.00	450
1991 Figure Eight, 1 1/2"	3,750	1991	110.00	110
1991 Figure Eight, 4"	2,000		270.00	375
1991 Figure Eight, 6"	2,000		550.00	740
1984 Finding Our Way, 1 1/2"	7,500	1984	45.00	135
1984 Finding Our Way, 4"	4,000	1988	95.00	245
1984 Finding Our Way, 6"	2,000	1984	210.00	495
1986 Finishing Touch, 1 1/2"	7,500	1989	45.00	85
1986 Finishing Touch, 4"	4,000	1989	95.00	172
1986 Finishing Touch, 6"	4,000	1989	195.00	312
1989 First School Day, 1 1/2"	Closed	1991	85.00	95
1989 First School Day, 4"	2,000	1993	290.00	350
1989 First School Day, 6"	2,000	1993	550.00	650
1989 Fisherboy, 1 1/2"	Closed	1991	85.00	95
1989 Fisherboy, 4"	2,000	1994	220.00	250
1989 Fisherboy, 6"	1,000	1994	440.00	475
1984 Flowers for You, 1 1/2"	7,500	1984	45.00	125
1984 Flowers for You, 4"	4,000	1988	95.00	250
1984 Flowers for You, 6"	4,000	1988	195.00	450
1991 Fore!!, 1 1/2"	3,750	1991	110.00	115
1991 Fore!!, 4"	2,000		270.00	325
1991 Fore!!, 6"	2,000		550.00	590
1992 Free Skating, 4"	1,000		310.00	325
1992 Free Skating, 6"	1,000		590.00	620
1983 From the Garden, 1 1/2"	7,500	1984	45.00	110
1983 From the Garden, 4"	Closed	1987	95.00	235
1983 From the Garden, 6"	4,000	1987	195.00	450
1989 Garden Party, 1 1/2"	Closed	1991	85.00	95
1989 Garden Party, 4"	2,000	1993	220.00	240
1989 Garden Party, 6"	2,000	1993	440.00	475
1985 Giddyap!, 4"	4,000	1990	95.00	250
1985 Giddyap!, 6"	4,000	1990	195.00	325
1988 Ginger Snap, 1 1/2"	Closed	1990	70.00	90
1988 Ginger Snap, 4"	2,000	1990	150.00	185
1988 Ginger Snap, 6"	1,000	1990	300.00	355
1986 Good As New, 1 1/2"	7,500	1991	45.00	90
1986 Good As New, 4"	4,000	1994	95.00	290
1986 Good As New, 6"	4,000	1994	195.00	500
1998 Having Fun, 4"	2,000		295.00	295
1998 Having Fun, 6"	1,000		575.00	575
1983 Helping Mother, 1 1/2"	7,500	1983	45.00	110
1983 Helping Mother, 4"	Closed	1983	95.00	300
1983 Helping Mother, 6"	2,000	1983	210.00	495
1988 Hidden Treasures, 1 1/2"	Closed	1990	70.00	90
1988 Hidden Treasures, 4"	2,000	1990	150.00	185
1988 Hidden Treasures, 6"	1,000	1990	300.00	355
1990 Holiday Cheer, 1 1/2"	3,750	1991	90.00	95
1990 Holiday Cheer, 4"	2,000		225.00	365
1990 Holiday Cheer, 6"	1,000		450.00	720
1989 House Call, 1 1/2"	Closed	1991	85.00	95
1989 House Call, 4"	2,000	1991	190.00	195
1989 House Call, 6"	2,000	1991	390.00	390
1993 Innocence, 4"	1,000		345.00	315
1993 Innocence, 6"	1,000		630.00	630
1994 Jolly Pair, 4"	1,000		350.00	350
1994 Jolly Pair, 6"	1,000		650.00	670
1993 Joy to the World, 4"	1,000		310.00	310
1993 Joy to the World, 6"	1,000		600.00	610
1987 Let's Play, 1 1/2"	7,500	1990	49.50	90
1987 Let's Play, 4"	4,000	1990	130.00	185
1987 Let's Play, 6"	2,000	1990	265.00	355
1994 Little Chimney Sweep, 4"	1,000		300.00	350
1994 Little Chimney Sweep, 6"	1,000		600.00	680
1987 Little Nanny, 1 1/2"	7,500	1990	49.50	90
1987 Little Nanny, 4"	4,000	1990	150.00	200
1987 Little Nanny, 6"	4,000	1990	295.00	400
1987 A Loving Spoonful, 1 1/2"	7,500	1991	49.50	90
1987 A Loving Spoonful, 4"	4,000	1994	150.00	290
1987 A Loving Spoonful, 6"	4,000	1994	295.00	550
1992 Merry Christmas, 1 1/2"	3,750	1994	110.00	115
1992 Merry Christmas, 4"	1,000	1994	350.00	350
1992 Merry Christmas, 6"	1,000	1994	580.00	580
1983 Morning Chores, 1 1/2"	7,500	1983	45.00	110
1983 Morning Chores, 4"	Closed	1983	95.00	300
1983 Morning Chores, 6"	2,000	1983	210.00	550
1993 Mr. Santa, 4"	750		375.00	390
1993 Mr. Santa, 6"	750		695.00	745
1993 Mrs. Santa, 4"	750		375.00	390
1993 Mrs. Santa, 6"	750		695.00	745
1993 My Favorite Doll, 4"	1,000		315.00	354
1993 My Favorite Doll, 6"	1,000		600.00	670
1988 My Little Brother, 1 1/2"	Closed	1991	70.00	90
1988 My Little Brother, 4"	2,000	1991	195.00	225
1988 My Little Brother, 6"	2,000	1991	375.00	450
1988 New Home, 1 1/2"	Closed	1991	70.00	90

*Quotes have been rounded up to nearest dollar

YEAR ISSUE	EDITION LIMIT	YEAR RETD.	ISSUE PRICE	*QUOTE U.S.$
1988 New Home, 4"	2,000	1991	185.00	240
1988 New Home, 6"	2,000	1991	365.00	500
1985 Nightie Night, 4"	4,000	1990	95.00	185
1985 Nightie Night, 6"	4,000	1990	195.00	325
1984 Off to School, 1 1/2"	7,500	1984	45.00	125
1984 Off to School, 11"	750		590.00	960
1984 Off to School, 20"	100		2900.00	4200
1984 Off to School, 4"	4,000		95.00	270
1984 Off to School, 6"	4,000		195.00	510
1986 Our Puppy, 1 1/2"	7,500	1990	45.00	90
1986 Our Puppy, 4"	4,000	1990	95.00	185
1986 Our Puppy, 6"	2,000	1990	210.00	355
1988 Penny for Your Thoughts, 1 1/2"	Closed	1991	70.00	90
1988 Penny for Your Thoughts, 4"	2,000		185.00	315
1988 Penny for Your Thoughts, 6"	2,000		365.00	635
1983 Playtime, 1 1/2"	7,500	1984	45.00	110
1983 Playtime, 4"	Closed	1987	95.00	250
1983 Playtime, 6"	4,000	1987	195.00	495
1988 Purrfect Day, 4"	2,000	1991	184.00	215
1988 Purrfect Day, 1 1/2"	Closed	1991	70.00	90
1988 Purrfect Day, 6"	2,000	1991	265.00	455
1992 Raindrops, 1 1/2"	3,750	1994	110.00	110
1992 Raindrops, 4"	1,000	1994	350.00	350
1992 Raindrops, 6"	1,000	1994	640.00	640
1988 School Marm, 6"	500	1988	398.00	398
1991 Season's Joy, 1 1/2"	3,750	1991	110.00	115
1991 Season's Joy, 4"	2,000		270.00	410
1991 Season's Joy, 6"	1,000		550.00	784
1990 Seasons Greetings, 1 1/2"	3,750	1991	90.00	95
1990 Seasons Greetings, 4"	2,000		225.00	335
1990 Seasons Greetings, 6"	1,000		450.00	650
1990 Shootin' Hoops, 4"	2,000	1993	220.00	250
1990 Shootin' Hoops, 6"	2,000	1993	440.00	450
1990 Shootin' Hoops,1 1/2"	3,750	1991	90.00	95
1985 A Special Day, 4"	4,000	1990	95.00	195
1985 A Special Day, 6"	4,000	1990	195.00	325
1984 Special Delivery, 1 1/2"	7,500	1984	45.00	125
1984 Special Delivery, 4"	4,000	1989	95.00	187
1984 Special Delivery, 6"	4,000	1989	195.00	312-350
1990 Spring Fever, 1 1/2"	3,750	1991	90.00	95
1990 Spring Fever, 4"	2,000		225.00	365
1990 Spring Fever, 6"	2,000		450.00	735
1983 Sweeping, 1 1/2"	7,500	1984	45.00	110
1983 Sweeping, 4"	Closed	1987	95.00	230
1983 Sweeping, 6"	4,000	1987	195.00	435
1986 Sweet Treat, 1 1/2"	7,500	1989	45.00	85
1986 Sweet Treat, 4"	4,000	1989	95.00	172
1986 Sweet Treat, 6"	4,000	1989	195.00	312
1984 Tag Along, 1 1/2"	7,500	1984	45.00	130
1984 Tag Along, 4"	4,000	1988	95.00	225
1984 Tag Along, 6"	4,000	1988	195.00	290
1989 Take Me Along, 1 1/2"	Closed	1991	85.00	95
1992 Take Me Along, 11"	400		950.00	1050
1992 Take Me Along, 20"	100		4550.00	4780
1989 Take Me Along, 4"	2,000		220.00	315
1989 Take Me Along, 6"	1,000		440.00	640
1993 Ten Roses For You, 4"	1,000		290.00	295
1993 Ten Roses For You, 6"	1,000		525.00	590
1990 Tender Loving Care, 1 1/2"	3,750	1991	90.00	95
1990 Tender Loving Care, 4"	2,000	1993	220.00	240
1990 Tender Loving Care, 6"	2,000	1993	440.00	475
1985 Tis the Season, 4"	4,000	1993	95.00	250
1985 Tis the Season, 6"	2,000	1985	210.00	425
1986 To Love And To Cherish, 1 1/2"	7,500	1989	45.00	85
1986 To Love and To Cherish, 11"	1,000	1989	Unkn.	350-667
1986 To Love and To Cherish, 20"	200	1989	Unkn.	3600
1986 To Love And To Cherish, 4"	4,000	1989	95.00	172
1986 To Love And To Cherish, 6"	4,000	1989	195.00	312
1991 Touch Down, 1 1/2"	3,750	1994	110.00	110
1991 Touch Down, 4"	2,000	1994	270.00	310
1991 Touch Down, 6"	2,000	1994	550.00	550
1992 Tulips For Mother, 4"	1,000		310.00	325
1992 Tulips For Mother, 6"	1,000		590.00	620
1983 Waiting for Mother, 1 1/2"	7,500	1984	45.00	110
1983 Waiting for Mother, 11"	750	1987	495.00	795
1983 Waiting for Mother, 4"	Closed	1987	95.00	230
1983 Waiting for Mother, 6"	4,000	1987	195.00	445
1984 Wake Up Kiss, 1 1/2"	7,500	1984	45.00	550
1984 Wake Up Kiss, 4"	4,000	1993	95.00	195
1983 Wake Up Kiss, 6"	2,000	1984	210.00	550
1984 Watchful Eye, 4"	4,000	1988	95.00	235
1984 Watchful Eye, 6"	4,000	1988	195.00	445
1984 Watchful Eye,1 1/2"	7,500	1984	45.00	125
1992 Winter Cheer, 4"	2,000	1993	300.00	300
1992 Winter Cheer, 6"	1,000	1993	580.00	580
1991 Winter Surprise, 1 1/2"	3,750	1994	110.00	110
1991 Winter Surprise, 4"	2,000	1994	270.00	290
1991 Winter Surprise, 6"	1,000	1994	550.00	570
1986 With This Ring, 1 1/2"	7,500	1989	45.00	85
1986 With This Ring, 11"	1,000	1989	Unkn.	330-668
1986 With This Ring, 20"	200	1989	Unkn.	3600
1986 With This Ring, 4"	4,000	1989	95.00	172
1986 With This Ring, 6"	4,000	1989	195.00	312
1989 Yearly Check-Up, 1 1/2"	Closed	1991	85.00	95
1989 Yearly Check-Up, 4"	2,000	1991	190.00	195
1989 Yearly Check-Up, 6"	2,000	1991	390.00	390
1985 Yuletide Cheer, 4"	4,000	1993	95.00	250
1985 Yuletide Cheer, 6"	Closed	1985	210.00	435

Sarah Kay Koalas - S. Kay

YEAR ISSUE	EDITION LIMIT	YEAR RETD.	ISSUE PRICE	*QUOTE U.S.$
1986 Green Thumb, 3"	3,500	1986	81.00	81
1985 Green Thumb, 5"	2,000	1986	165.00	165
1985 Honey Bunch, 3"	3,500	1986	75.00	75
1985 Honey Bunch, 5"	2,000	1986	165.00	165
1985 A Little Bird Told Me, 3"	3,500	1986	75.00	75
1985 A Little Bird Told Me, 5"	2,000	1986	165.00	165
1985 Party Time, 3"	3,500	1986	75.00	75
1985 Party Time, 5"	2,000	1986	165.00	165
1986 Scout About, 3"	3,500	1986	81.00	81
1986 Scout About, 5"	2,000	1986	178.00	178
1986 A Stitch with Love, 3"	3,500	1986	81.00	81
1986 A Stitch with Love, 5"	2,000	1986	178.00	178

Sarah Kay Mini Santas - S. Kay

YEAR ISSUE	EDITION LIMIT	YEAR RETD.	ISSUE PRICE	*QUOTE U.S.$
1992 Father Christmas, 1 1/2"	2,500	1993	110.00	110
1992 A Friend to All, 1 1/2"	2,500	1993	110.00	110
1991 Jolly Santa, 1 1/2"	2,500	1993	110.00	110
1991 Jolly St. Nick, 1 1/2"	2,500	1993	110.00	110
1991 Kris Kringle, 1 1/2"	2,500	1993	110.00	110
1991 Sarah Kay Santa, 1 1/2"	2,500	1993	110.00	110

Sarah Kay Santas - S. Kay

YEAR ISSUE	EDITION LIMIT	YEAR RETD.	ISSUE PRICE	*QUOTE U.S.$
1995 Checking It Twice, 4" 57709	500		250.00	305
1995 Checking It Twice, 6" 57710	250		395.00	580
1992 Father Christmas, 4"	750	1994	350.00	350
1992 Father Christmas, 6"	750	1994	590.00	590
1991 A Friend To All, 4"	750	1994	300.00	300
1991 A Friend To All, 6"	750	1994	590.00	590
1989 Jolly Santa, 12"	150	1990	1300.00	1300
1988 Jolly Santa, 4"	750	1989	235.00	300-350
1988 Jolly Santa, 6"	750	1989	480.00	600
1988 Jolly St. Nick, 4"	750	1989	199.00	300-550
1988 Jolly St. Nick, 6"	750	1989	398.00	850
1990 Kris Kringle Santa, 4"	750	1990	275.00	350
1990 Kris Kringle Santa, 6"	750	1990	550.00	550
1997 Santa's Helper, 4"	500		350.00	350
1997 Santa's Helper, 6"	250		630.00	630
1989 Santa, 4"	750	1990	235.00	350
1989 Santa, 6"	750	1990	480.00	480
1998 Uo on the Rooftop, 4"	500		295.00	295
1998 Uo on the Rooftop, 6"	250		695.00	695
1996 Workshop Santa, 4"	500		295.00	320
1996 Workshop Santa, 6"	250		495.00	610

Sarah Kay School Days - S. Kay

YEAR ISSUE	EDITION LIMIT	YEAR RETD.	ISSUE PRICE	*QUOTE U.S.$
1996 Head of the Class, 4"	500		295.00	360
1996 Head of the Class, 6"	250		495.00	610
1997 Homework, 4"	500		315.00	315
1997 Homework, 6"	250		520.00	520
1995 I Know, I Know, 4" 57701	500		250.00	310
1995 I Know, I Know, 6" 57702	250		395.00	565
1998 Straight A's, 4"	500		375.00	375
1998 Straight A's, 6"	250		650.00	650

Sarah Kay Tribute To Mother - S. Kay

YEAR ISSUE	EDITION LIMIT	YEAR RETD.	ISSUE PRICE	*QUOTE U.S.$
1998 Don't Forget, 7"	250		650.00	650
1995 Mom's Joy, 5" 57902	250	1995	297.00	325
1997 Storytime, 5 1/2"	250		650.00	650
1996 Sweets for My Sweet, 6"	250		399.00	520

Sarah Kay's First Christmas - S. Kay

YEAR ISSUE	EDITION LIMIT	YEAR RETD.	ISSUE PRICE	*QUOTE U.S.$
1994 Sarah Kay's First Christmas, 4"	500		350.00	440
1994 Sarah Kay's First Christmas, 6"	250	1995	600.00	804
1995 First Christmas Stocking, 4" 57553	500		250.00	335
1995 First Christmas Stocking, 6" 57554	250		395.00	450
1996 All I Want For Christmas, 4" 57555	500		325.00	360
1996 All I Want For Christmas, 6" 57556	250		550.00	700
1997 Christmas Puppy, 4"	500		375.00	375
1997 Christmas Puppy, 6"	250		625.00	630

Armani

G. Armani Society Members Only Figurine - G. Armani

YEAR ISSUE	EDITION LIMIT	YEAR RETD.	ISSUE PRICE	*QUOTE U.S.$
1990 My Fine Feathered Friends (Bonus)122S	Closed	1990	175.00	500
1990 Awakening 591C	Closed	1991	137.50	1040-1800
1991 Peace & Harmony (Bonus) 824C	7,500	1991	300.00	403-720
1991 Ruffles 745E	Closed	1991	139.00	280-585
1992 Ascent 866C	Closed	1992	195.00	495-650
1992 Julie (Bonus) 293P	Closed	1992	90.00	240-260
1992 Juliette (Bonus) 294P	Closed	1992	90.00	240-265
1993 Venus 881E	Closed	1993	225.00	403-550
1993 Lady Rose (Bonus) 197C	Closed	1993	125.00	395-455
1994 Harlequin 1994 Fifth Anniversary 490C	Closed	1994	300.00	390-625
1994 Flora 212C	Closed	1994	225.00	450-488
1994 Aquarius (Bonus) 248C	Closed	1994	125.00	225-450
1995 Melody 656C	Closed	1995	250.00	325-390
1995 Scarlette (Bonus) 698C	Closed	1995	200.00	450-520
1996 Allegra 345C	Closed	1996	250.00	350-520
1996 Arianna (Bonus) 400C	Closed	1996	125.00	125-160
1997 It's Mine (Bonus) 136C	Closed	1997	200.00	200
1997 Sabrina 110C	Closed	1997	275.00	275-350
1998 Beth (Bonus) 519C	Yr.Iss.		115.00	115
1998 Lucia 755C	Yr.Iss.		325.00	325

G. Armani Society Member Gift - G. Armani

YEAR ISSUE	EDITION LIMIT	YEAR RETD.	ISSUE PRICE	*QUOTE U.S.$
1993 Petite Maternity 939F	Closed	1993	Gift	75-100
1994 Lady w/Dogs 245F	Closed	1994	Gift	65-125
1995 Lady w/Doves mini 546F	Closed	1995	Gift	55-125
1996 Perfect Match 358F	Closed	1996	Gift	100
1997 Quiet Please 446F	Closed	1997	Gift	50-60
1998 Puppy Love 114F	Yr.Iss.		Gift	60

G. Armani Society Sponsored Event - G. Armani

YEAR ISSUE	EDITION LIMIT	YEAR RETD.	ISSUE PRICE	*QUOTE U.S.$
1990 Pals (Boy w/ Dog) '90 & '91 409S	Closed	1991	200.00	450
1992 Springtime 961C	Closed	1992	250.00	358-450
1993 Loving Arms 880E	Closed	1993	250.00	295-423
1994 Daisy 202E	Closed	1994	250.00	325-390
1995 Iris 628E	Closed	1995	250.00	390-423
1996 Rose 678C	Closed	1997	250.00	350-520
1997 Marianne 135C	Closed	1997	275.00	275-520
1998 Victoria 525C	Yr.Iss.		275.00	275

Ashley Avery Collection - Armani

YEAR ISSUE	EDITION LIMIT	YEAR RETD.	ISSUE PRICE	*QUOTE U.S.$
1998 Aurora 884M	125		375.00	375
1997 Giselle 681M	100		425.00	425
1997 Juliette 682M	100		425.00	425
1998 Lilacs and Roses 882M	125		375.00	375

Capodimonte - G. Armani

YEAR ISSUE	EDITION LIMIT	YEAR RETD.	ISSUE PRICE	*QUOTE U.S.$
1985 Boy Reading w/Dog 685C	Suspd.		110.00	300
1976 Country Girl (Little Shepherdess) 3153	Closed	1991	47.50	150
1997 Gallant Approach 146C	750		1250.00	1250
1985 Girl Reading w/Cat 686C	Suspd.		100.00	300
1976 Lawyer 414	Retrd.	1986	60.00	60
1985 Little Vagabond 328C	Suspd.		55.00	55
1998 Morning Ride 147C	5,000		770.00	770
1977 Napoleon (5464) 464C	Closed	1991	250.00	500
1980 Old Drunk (Richard's Night Out) 3243	Closed	1988	130.00	240
1978 Organ Grinder 3323	Closed	1989	140.00	350
1985 Peasant Group Clock 1115E	Retrd.	1990	320.00	320
1976 The Picture 441B	Retrd.	1983	N/A	N/A
1976 Shepherd 439	Retrd.	1988	N/A	N/A
1976 Shepherdess 440	Retrd.	1988	N/A	N/A
1977 Swing MIC#7471	Retrd.	1989	275.00	275
1980 The Tender Clown 217C	Suspd.		75.00	75
1997 Venetian Night 125C	975		2000.00	2000
1995 Young Hearts 679C	1,500		900.00	1000

Clown Series - G. Armani

YEAR ISSUE	EDITION LIMIT	YEAR RETD.	ISSUE PRICE	*QUOTE U.S.$
1991 Bust of Clown (The Fiddler Clown) 725E	5,000		500.00	500
1984 Clown with Dog 653E	Closed	1991	135.00	100

Commemorative - G. Armani

YEAR ISSUE	EDITION LIMIT	YEAR RETD.	ISSUE PRICE	*QUOTE U.S.$
1992 Discovery of America - Columbus Plaque 867C	2,500	1994	400.00	425
1993 Mother's Day Plaque 899C	Closed	1993	100.00	104
1994 Mother's Day Plaque-The Swing 254C	Closed	1994	100.00	120
1995 Mother's Day Plaque-Love/Peace 538C	Closed	1995	125.00	125
1996 Mother's Day Plaque-Mother's Rosebud 341C	Closed	1996	150.00	150
1997 Mother's Day Figurine-Mother's Angel 155C	Closed	1997	175.00	175
1998 Mother's Day Figurine-Mother's Bouquet 799C	Yr.Iss.		175.00	175

Disneyana - G. Armani

YEAR ISSUE	EDITION LIMIT	YEAR RETD.	ISSUE PRICE	*QUOTE U.S.$
1992 Cinderella '92 783C	500	1992	500.00	3250-4235
1993 Snow White '93 199C	2,000	1993	750.00	1029-1080
1994 Ariel (Little Mermaid) '94 505C	1,500	1994	750.00	1320-1531
1995 Beauty and the Beast '95 543C	2,000	1995	975.00	1320-1593
1996 Jasmine & Rajah '96 410C	1,200	1996	800.00	1029-1600
1997 Cinderella & Prince 107C	1,000	1997	825.00	990-1200
1998 Geppetto & Pinocchio 490C	1,075		775.00	775

Etrusca - G. Armani

YEAR ISSUE	EDITION LIMIT	YEAR RETD.	ISSUE PRICE	*QUOTE U.S.$
1993 Lady with Bag 2149E	Retrd.	1996	350.00	375

Figurine of the Year - G. Armani

YEAR ISSUE	EDITION LIMIT	YEAR RETD.	ISSUE PRICE	*QUOTE U.S.$
1996 Lady Jane 390C	Yr.Iss.	1996	200.00	375-390
1997 April 121C	Yr.Iss.	1997	250.00	250
1998 Violet 756C	Yr.Iss.		250.00	250

Florence/Disney - G. Armani

YEAR ISSUE	EDITION LIMIT	YEAR RETD.	ISSUE PRICE	*QUOTE U.S.$
1995 Jiminy Cricket "Special Backstamp" 379C	1,200	1995	300.00	650-850
1996 Jiminy Cricket 379C	Open		300.00	375
1996 Sleeping Beauty (Briar Rose) 106C	Open		650.00	675
1996 Pinocchio & Figaro 464C	Open		500.00	550
1995 Bashful 916C	Open		150.00	155
1995 Doc 326C	Open		150.00	155
1993 Dopey 200C	Open		105.00	155
1997 Fauna 609C	Open		200.00	200
1997 Flora 608C	Open		200.00	200
1995 Grumpy 917C	Open		145.00	155
1995 Happy 327C	Open		150.00	155
1997 Merryweather 607C	Open		200.00	200
1995 Sleepy 915C	Open		125.00	155
1995 Sneezy 914C	Open		125.00	155
1993 Snow White 209C	Open		400.00	450
1997 Tinkerbell 108C	Open		425.00	425

Florentine Gardens - G. Armani

YEAR ISSUE	EDITION LIMIT	YEAR RETD.	ISSUE PRICE	*QUOTE U.S.$
1992 Abundance 870C	10,000	1996	600.00	675-775
1994 Ambrosia 482C	5,000		435.00	550
1994 Angelica 484C	5,000		575.00	715
1998 Aprhodite 230C	3,000		1350.00	1350
1995 Aquarius 426C	5,000		600.00	650
1997 Artemis 126C	5,000		1750.00	1750
1993 Aurora-Lady With Doves 884C	7,500		370.00	400
1997 Bacchus & Arianna 419C	5,000		1500.00	1500
1998 Capricorn 699C	5,000		650.00	650
1992 Dawn 874C	10,000	1996	500.00	700-1170
1995 Ebony 372C	5,000		550.00	600
1994 The Embrace 480C	3,000	1996	1450.00	3200-3835

YEAR ISSUE	EDITION LIMIT	YEAR RETD.	ISSUE PRICE	*QUOTE U.S.$
1998 Flora 173C	5,000		600.00	600
1993 Freedom-Man And Horse 906C	3,000	1996	850.00	875-1235
1995 Gemini 426C	5,000		600.00	650
1998 Golden Nectar 212C	1,500		2000.00	2000
1997 Leo 149C	5,000		650.00	650
1993 Liberty-Girl On Horse 903C	5,000	1996	750.00	1040-1800
1993 Lilac & Roses-Girl w/Flowers 882C	7,500		410.00	440
1993 Lovers 191C	3,000	1996	450.00	780-950
1997 Pisces 171C	5,000		650.00	650
1998 Pomona 174C	5,000		550.00	550
1998 Sagittarius 698C	5,000		650.00	650
1994 Summertime-Lady on Swing 485C	5,000		650.00	775
1997 Taurus 170C	5,000		650.00	650
1992 Twilight 872C	10,000	1996	560.00	700-975
1992 Vanity 871C	10,000	1996	585.00	1073-1170
1995 Virgo 425C	5,000		600.00	650
1993 Wind Song-Girl With Sail 904C	5,000		520.00	575

Four Seasons - G. Armani

YEAR ISSUE	EDITION LIMIT	YEAR RETD.	ISSUE PRICE	*QUOTE U.S.$
1990 Skating-Winter 542P	Suspd.		355.00	355-435

Galleria Collection - G. Armani

YEAR ISSUE	EDITION LIMIT	YEAR RETD.	ISSUE PRICE	*QUOTE U.S.$
1995 Eros 406T	1,500		750.00	775
1994 Grace 1029T	1,000		465.00	485
1994 Joy 1028T	1,000		465.00	485
1995 Pearl 1019T	1,000		550.00	600
1993 Leda & The Swan 1012T	1,500	1996	550.00	1300-2495
1993 The Sea Wave 1006T	1,500	1996	500.00	633
1993 The Sea Wave, signed 1006T	Retrd.	1996	500.00	715-1008
1993 Spring Herald 1009T	1,500	1996	500.00	715-845
1993 Spring Herald, signed 1009T	Retrd.	1996	500.00	600
1993 Spring Water 1007T	1,500	1996	500.00	715-1300
1993 Zephyr 1010T	1,500	1996	500.00	585-715
1993 Set (Sea Wave, Spring Water, Spring Herald, Leda & Swan, Zephyr)	Retrd.	1996	2550.00	3000-3500

Golden Age - G. Armani

YEAR ISSUE	EDITION LIMIT	YEAR RETD.	ISSUE PRICE	*QUOTE U.S.$
1995 Fragrance 340C	3,000		500.00	560
1998 Lacey 655C	3,000		700.00	700
1997 Morning Ride 147C	5,000		770.00	770
1995 Promenade 339C	3,000		600.00	650
1998 Reverie 646C	3,000		600.00	600
1995 Soiree 338C	3,000		600.00	630
1995 Spring Morning 337C	3,000	1998	600.00	650-895

Gulliver's World - G. Armani

YEAR ISSUE	EDITION LIMIT	YEAR RETD.	ISSUE PRICE	*QUOTE U.S.$
1994 The Barrel 659T	1,000		225.00	255
1981 Boy with Fish 185C	Retrd.	1985	45.00	45
1981 Boy with Pistol 191T (original "Cowboy")	Retrd.	1988	45.00	50
1981 Children in Shoe 309C	Retrd.	1983	300.00	300
1994 Cowboy 657T	1,000	1996	125.00	125
1981 Dice Game 305C	Retrd.	1985	265.00	265
1994 Getting Clean 661T	1,000	1998	130.00	150
1981 Indian Girl w/Dog 262C	Retrd.	1985	60.00	60
1994 Ray of Moon 658T	1,000	1998	100.00	100
1994 Serenade 660T	1,000	1998	200.00	235
1981 Serenade on Barrel 306C	Retrd.	1987	190.00	190
1976 Stealing Puppies 432C	Retrd.	1989	55.00	55
1981 Wine Curriers 199T	Retrd.	1983	130.00	130

Impressions - G. Armani

YEAR ISSUE	EDITION LIMIT	YEAR RETD.	ISSUE PRICE	*QUOTE U.S.$
1990 Bittersweet 528C	Retrd.	1993	400.00	1300
1990 Bittersweet 528P	Retrd.	1993	275.00	595
1990 Masquerade 527C	Retrd.	1993	400.00	430
1990 Masquerade 527P	Retrd.	1993	300.00	595
1990 Mystery 523C	Retrd.	1993	370.00	370
1990 Temptation 522C	Retrd.	1993	400.00	400

Masterworks - G. Armani

YEAR ISSUE	EDITION LIMIT	YEAR RETD.	ISSUE PRICE	*QUOTE U.S.$
1995 Aurora 680C	1,500	1996	3500.00	3500-4940
1998 Circle of Joy 760C	1,500		2750.00	2750

Moonlight Masquerade - G. Armani

YEAR ISSUE	EDITION LIMIT	YEAR RETD.	ISSUE PRICE	*QUOTE U.S.$
1991 Lady Clown 742C	7,500	1995	390.00	465-520
1991 Lady Clown with Puppet 743C	7,500	1995	410.00	410-435
1991 Lady Harlequin 740C	7,500	1995	450.00	450-465
1991 Lady Pierrot 741C	7,500	1995	390.00	495-595
1991 Queen of Hearts 744C	7,500	1995	450.00	595
1991 Set	Retrd.	1995	2090.00	2090

My Fair Ladies™ - G. Armani

YEAR ISSUE	EDITION LIMIT	YEAR RETD.	ISSUE PRICE	*QUOTE U.S.$
1994 At Ease 634C	5,000		650.00	715
1998 Brief Encounter 167C	5,000		350.00	350
1990 Can-Can Dancer 589P	Retrd.	1991	460.00	566-910
1989 Can-Can Dancers 516C	Retrd.	1993	880.00	900
1998 Charm 197C	3,000		850.00	850
1993 Elegance 195C	5,000		525.00	660
1993 Fascination 192C	5,000		500.00	633
1987 Flamenco Dancer 389C	5,000		400.00	600
1997 Garden Delight 157C	3,000		1000.00	1000
1995 Georgia 414C	5,000		550.00	625
1996 Grace 383C	5,000		475.00	515
1995 In Love 382C	5,000		450.00	500
1998 In The Mood 164C	5,000		425.00	425
1994 Isadora 633C	3,000		920.00	1050
1987 Lady with Book 384C	5,000		300.00	475
1987 Lady with Fan 387C	5,000		300.00	450
1988 Lady with Great Dane 429C	5,000	1996	385.00	595-800
1987 Lady with Mirror (Compact) 386C	5,000	1993	300.00	700-1040
1987 Lady with Muff 388C	5,000		250.00	375
1990 Lady with Parrot 616C	5,000	1995	460.00	1040-1395
1987 Lady with Peacock 385C	5,000	1992	380.00	2600-3025
1987 Lady with Peacock 385F	Retrd.	1996	230.00	1800
1987 Lady with Peacock 385P	Retrd.	1996	300.00	1073
1993 Lady with Umbrella-Nellie 196C	5,000		370.00	450
1995 Lara 415C	5,000		450.00	500
1993 Mahogany 194C	5,000	1995	500.00	1235-2500
1998 Moonlight 151C	1,500		1250.00	1250
1993 Morning Rose 193C	5,000		450.00	515
1998 Mystical Fountain 159C	3,000		900.00	900
1998 Opal 758C	5,000		450.00	450
1998 Starlight 150C	1,500		1250.00	1250
1997 Swans Lake 158C	3,000		900.00	900
1988 The Tango 431F	Retrd.	1983	330.00	330
1988 The Tango 441P	Retrd.	1993	550.00	910
1989 Two Can-Can Dancers 516C	Retrd.	1993	880.00	1100-2000

Pearls Of The Orient - G. Armani

YEAR ISSUE	EDITION LIMIT	YEAR RETD.	ISSUE PRICE	*QUOTE U.S.$
1990 Chu Chu San 612C	10,000	1994	550.00	715-910
1990 Lotus Blossom 613C	10,000	1994	475.00	475
1990 Madame Butterfly 610C	10,000	1994	500.00	715-910
1990 Turnadot 611C	10,000	1994	500.00	550
1990 Set	Retrd.	1994	2025.00	2025

Premiere Ballerinas - G. Armani

YEAR ISSUE	EDITION LIMIT	YEAR RETD.	ISSUE PRICE	*QUOTE U.S.$
1989 Ballerina 508C	10,000	1994	470.00	1658
1989 Ballerina Group in Flight 518C	7,500	1994	780.00	1200-1755
1989 Ballerina with Drape 504C	10,000	1994	500.00	624-910
1991 Dancer with Peacock 727C	Retrd.	1993	460.00	530
1989 Flying Ballerina 503C	10,000	1994	440.00	500
1989 Kneeling Ballerina 517C	10,000	1994	340.00	429-1300
1989 Two Ballerinas 515C	7,500	1994	670.00	775

Religious - G. Armani

YEAR ISSUE	EDITION LIMIT	YEAR RETD.	ISSUE PRICE	*QUOTE U.S.$
1994 The Assumption 697C	5,000		650.00	725
1983 Choir Boys 900	5,000	1996	400.00	787
1994 Christ Child (Nativity) 1020C	1,000		175.00	195
1987 Crucifix 1158C	10,000	1990	155.00	650-950
1993 Crucifix 786C	7,500		285.00	315
1987 Crucifix 790C	15,000		160.00	250
1991 Crucifix Plaque 711C	15,000	1996	265.00	285
1995 The Crucifixion 780C	5,000		500.00	550
1994 Donkey (Nativity) 1027C	1,000		185.00	210
1995 The Holy Family 788C	5,000		1000.00	1100
1994 La Pieta 802C	5,000		950.00	1100
1994 Madonna (Nativity) 1022C	1,000		365.00	430
1994 Magi King Gold (Nativity) 1023C	1,000		600.00	650
1994 Magi King Incense (Nativity) 1024C	1,000		600.00	650
1994 Magi King Myrrh (Nativity) 1025C	1,000		450.00	500
1995 Moses 606C	2,500		365.00	400
1994 Ox (Nativity) 1026C	1,000		300.00	350
1994 Renaissance Crucifix 1017T	5,000		265.00	275
1994 St. Joseph (Nativity) 1021C	1,000		500.00	550

Siena Collection - G. Armani

YEAR ISSUE	EDITION LIMIT	YEAR RETD.	ISSUE PRICE	*QUOTE U.S.$
1993 Back From The Fields 1002T	1,000	1995	400.00	512-748
1994 Country Boy w/Mushrooms 1014T	2,500		135.00	155
1993 Encountering 1003T	1,000	1995	350.00	600-780
1993 Fresh Fruit 1001T	2,500	1995	155.00	332-450
1993 The Happy Fiddler 1005T	1,000	1997	225.00	299-390
1993 Mother's Hand 1008T	2,500	1998	250.00	285-371
1993 Soft Kiss 1000T	2,500	1995	155.00	331-390
1993 Sound The Trumpet! 1004T	1,000	1995	225.00	350-390
1993 Set of 8	N/A		1895.00	1895

Special Events in a Life - G. Armani

YEAR ISSUE	EDITION LIMIT	YEAR RETD.	ISSUE PRICE	*QUOTE U.S.$
1994 Black Maternity 502C	3,000		535.00	650
1984 Bride & Groom 641C	Retrd.	1994	125.00	1238
1993 Carriage Wedding 902C	2,500		1000.00	1100
1986 Enfance 694C	Retrd.	1992	380.00	380
1991 Just Married 827C	5,000		1000.00	1100
1988 Maternity 405C	5,000	1998	415.00	570
1994 Perfect Love 652C	3,000		1200.00	1250
1995 Tenderness 418C	5,000		950.00	1000
1995 Tomorrow's Dream 336C	5,000		700.00	730
1991 Wedding Couple At Threshold 813C	7,500		400.00	475
1991 Wedding Couple Kissing 815C	7,500		500.00	575
1991 Wedding Couple With Bicycle 814C	7,500		600.00	665
1994 Wedding Waltz (black) 501C	3,000		750.00	800
1994 Wedding Waltz (white) 493C	3,000		750.00	875

Special Releases - G. Armani

YEAR ISSUE	EDITION LIMIT	YEAR RETD.	ISSUE PRICE	*QUOTE U.S.$
1989 Bust of Eve 590T	1,000	1991	250.00	423-585
1993 Doctor in Car 848C	2,000	1996	800.00	825-1229
1992 Girl in Car 861C	3,000	1995	900.00	925
1992 Lady with Dove (Dove Dancer) 858E	1,000	1994	320.00	450-845
1992 Old Couple in Car (Two Hearts Remember) 862C	5,000		1000.00	1000

Valentine - G. Armani

YEAR ISSUE	EDITION LIMIT	YEAR RETD.	ISSUE PRICE	*QUOTE U.S.$
1983 Hoopla 107E	Retrd.	1996	190.00	200
1983 Little Nativity 115C	Retrd.	1991	270.00	270
1983 Soccer Boy 109C	Retrd.	1994	80.00	80

Vanity Fair - G. Armani

YEAR ISSUE	EDITION LIMIT	YEAR RETD.	ISSUE PRICE	*QUOTE U.S.$
1992 Beauty at the Mirror 850P	Retrd.	1996	300.00	350
1992 Beauty w/Perfume 853P	Retrd.	1996	330.00	370-450

Via Veneto - G. Armani

YEAR ISSUE	EDITION LIMIT	YEAR RETD.	ISSUE PRICE	*QUOTE U.S.$
1994 Alessandra 648C	5,000		355.00	400
1997 Black Orchid 444C	5,000		1100.00	1100
1998 Cuddle Up 322C	3,000		475.00	475
1998 Free Spirit 321C	3,000		825.00	825
1994 Marina 649C	5,000		450.00	530
1994 Nicole 651C	5,000		500.00	600
1998 Poetry 231C	5,000		600.00	600
1998 Roman Holiday 271C	3,000		1500.00	1500
1997 Summer Stroll 431C	5,000		650.00	650
1997 Tiger Lily 244C	5,000		1200.00	1200
1994 Valentina 647C	5,000		400.00	440
1997 Whitney 432C	5,000		750.00	750

Wildlife - G. Armani

YEAR ISSUE	EDITION LIMIT	YEAR RETD.	ISSUE PRICE	*QUOTE U.S.$
1997 Alert (Irish Setters) 550S	975		900.00	900
1998 Back To The Barn 591S	3,000		400.00	400
1989 Bird of Paradise 454S	5,000		475.00	550
1991 Bird of Paradise 718S	5,000	1996	500.00	550
1998 Bonding 744S	3,000		3000.00	3000
1998 Brilliance 586S	1,500		850.00	850
1982 Cardinal 546C	Retrd.	1989	100.00	100
1997 Collie 304S	975		500.00	500
1995 Companions (Two Collies) 302S	3,000		900.00	950
1998 Crystal Morning 597S	1,500		900.00	900
1997 Dalmation 552S	975		600.00	600
1998 Descent 604S	3,000		500.00	500
1998 Early Arrivals 593S	1,500		600.00	600
1997 Early Days (Deer) 557S	975		1200.00	1200
1994 Elegance in Nature (Herons) 226S	3,000		1000.00	1200
1998 Ever Watchful 602S	3,000		450.00	450
1994 The Falconer 224S	3,000		1000.00	1200
1995 Feed Us! (Mother/Baby Owls) 305S	1,500	1998	950.00	1000
1997 First Days (Mare & Foal) 564S	1,500		800.00	800
1991 Flamingo 713S	5,000		430.00	465
1991 Flying Duck 839S	3,000		470.00	530
1993 Galloping Horse 905S	7,500		465.00	500
1998 Garden Delight 734S	1,500		500.00	500
1991 Great Argus Pheasant 717S	3,000	1996	625.00	650
1991 Hummingbird 719S	Retrd.	1996	300.00	370
1995 The Hunt (Falcon) 290S	3,000		850.00	880
1991 Large Owl 842S	5,000		520.00	570
1995 Lone Wolf 285S	3,000		550.00	575
1995 Midnight 284S	3,000		600.00	630
1997 Monarch (Stag) 555S	1,500		1200.00	1200
1998 Moon Flight 603S	3,000		600.00	600
1998 Morning Call 742S	3,000		465.00	465
1998 Morning Mist 737S	3,000		335.00	335
1997 Mother's Touch (Elephants) 579S	3,000		700.00	700
1997 Nature's Colors (Pheasant) 582S	1,500		1350.00	1350
1997 Nature's Dance (Herons) 576S	750		1750.00	1750
1995 Night Vigil (Owl) 306S	3,000		650.00	675
1995 Nocturne 976S	1,500		1000.00	1100
1998 On Guard 605S	3,000		475.00	475
1998 On Watch 589S	3,000		400.00	400
1989 Peacock 455S	5,000		620.00	700
1989 Peacock 458S	5,000		650.00	730
1998 Peacock's Pride 733S	1,500		400.00	400
1997 Please Play (Cocker Spaniels) 312S	975		600.00	600
1997 Pointer 554S	975		700.00	700
1995 Proud Watch (Lion) 278S	1,500		700.00	750
1993 Rampant Horse 907S	7,500		550.00	585
1997 Royal Couple (Afghan Hounds) 310S	975		850.00	850
1994 Running Free (Greyhounds) 972S	3,000		850.00	930
1993 Running Horse 909S	7,500		515.00	550
1997 Shepherd (Dog) 307S	975		450.00	450
1998 Silent Flight 592S	3,000		450.00	450
1995 Silent Watch (Mtn. Lion) 291S	1,500		700.00	750
1997 Sky Watch (Flying Eagle) 559S	3,000		1200.00	1200
1990 Soaring Eagle 970S	5,000	1996	620.00	750
1998 Spring Orchestra 584S	975		1250.00	1250
1998 Stallions 572S	1,500		1100.00	1100
1997 Standing Tall (Heron) 577S	1,500		800.00	800
1998 Summer Song 585S	1,500		750.00	750
1991 Swan 714S	5,000		550.00	600
1990 Three Doves 996S	5,000		690.00	750
1998 Tropical Gossip 726S	3,000		450.00	450
1998 Tropical Splendor 288S	1,500		1750.00	1750
1997 Trumpeting (Elephant) 578S	3,000		850.00	850
1995 Vantage Point (Eagle) 270S	3,000		600.00	650
1993 Vase with Doves 204S	3,000	1996	375.00	484-650
1993 Vase with Parrot 736S	3,000	1996	460.00	475-748
1993 Vase with Peacock 735S	3,000		450.00	500
1998 Wild Colors 727S	3,000		450.00	450
1995 Wild Hearts (Horses) 282S	3,000		2000.00	2100
1998 Winter's End 583S	1,500		900.00	900
1995 Wisdom (Owl) 281S	3,000		1250.00	1300

Armstrong's

Armstrong's/Ron Lee - R. Skelton

YEAR ISSUE	EDITION LIMIT	YEAR RETD.	ISSUE PRICE	*QUOTE U.S.$
1984 Captain Freddie	7,500	N/A	85.00	350-450
1984 Freddie the Torchbearer	7,500	N/A	110.00	400-450

Happy Art - W. Lantz

YEAR ISSUE	EDITION LIMIT	YEAR RETD.	ISSUE PRICE	*QUOTE U.S.$
1982 Woody's Triple Self-Portrait	5,000	N/A	95.00	350

Pro Autographed Ceramic Baseball Card Plaque - Unknown

YEAR ISSUE	EDITION LIMIT	YEAR RETD.	ISSUE PRICE	*QUOTE U.S.$
1985 Brett, Garvey, Jackson, Rose, Seaver, auto, 3-1/4X5	1,000	N/A	150.00	150-250

The Red Skelton Collection - R. Skelton

YEAR ISSUE	EDITION LIMIT	YEAR RETD.	ISSUE PRICE	*QUOTE U.S.$
1981 Clem Kadiddlehopper	Retrd.	N/A	75.00	165-175
1981 Freddie in the Bathtub	5,000	N/A	80.00	95-100
1981 Freddie on the Green	5,000	1997	80.00	125-135
1981 Freddie the Freeloader	Retrd.	N/A	70.00	150-195
1981 Jr., The Mean Widdle Kid	Retrd.	N/A	75.00	160-175
1981 San Fernando Red	Retrd.	N/A	75.00	150-160
1981 Sheriff Deadeye	Retrd.	N/A	75.00	150-160

*Quotes have been rounded up to nearest dollar

The Red Skelton Porcelain Plaque - R. Skelton

YEAR ISSUE	EDITION LIMIT	YEAR RETD.	ISSUE PRICE	*QUOTE U.S.$
1991 All American	1,500	1993	495.00	1000-1500
1994 Another Day	1,994	N/A	675.00	750-1000
1992 Independance Day?	1,500	1997	525.00	575-685
1993 Red & Freddie Both Turned 80	1,993	1993	595.00	1000-1500

Artaffects

Members Only Limited Edition Redemption Offerings - G. Perillo

YEAR ISSUE	EDITION LIMIT	YEAR RETD.	ISSUE PRICE	*QUOTE U.S.$
1983 Apache Brave (Bust)	Closed	N/A	50.00	150-195
1986 Painted Pony	Closed	N/A	125.00	175
1991 Chief Crazy Horse	Closed	N/A	195.00	250-300

Limited Edition Free Gifts to Members - G. Perillo

YEAR ISSUE	EDITION LIMIT	YEAR RETD.	ISSUE PRICE	*QUOTE U.S.$
1986 Dolls	Closed	N/A	Gift	35
1991 Sunbeam	Closed	N/A	Gift	35-49
1992 Little Shadow	Closed	N/A	Gift	35-49

The Chieftains - G. Perillo

YEAR ISSUE	EDITION LIMIT	YEAR RETD.	ISSUE PRICE	*QUOTE U.S.$
1983 Cochise	5,000	N/A	65.00	275
1983 Crazy Horse	5,000	N/A	65.00	200-250
1983 Geronimo	5,000	N/A	65.00	250-300
1983 Joseph	5,000	N/A	65.00	285-300
1983 Red Cloud	5,000	N/A	65.00	275-300
1983 Sitting Bull	5,000	N/A	65.00	200-300

Pride of America's Indians - G. Perillo

YEAR ISSUE	EDITION LIMIT	YEAR RETD.	ISSUE PRICE	*QUOTE U.S.$
1988 Brave and Free	10-day	N/A	50.00	150
1989 Dark Eyed Friends	10-day	N/A	45.00	75
1989 Kindred Spirits	10-day	N/A	45.00	50
1989 Loyal Alliance	10-day	N/A	45.00	75
1989 Noble Companions	10-day	N/A	45.00	50
1989 Peaceful Comrades	10-day	N/A	45.00	50
1989 Small & Wise	10-day	N/A	45.00	50
1989 Winter Scouts	10-day	N/A	45.00	50

Special Issue - G. Perillo

YEAR ISSUE	EDITION LIMIT	YEAR RETD.	ISSUE PRICE	*QUOTE U.S.$
1984 Apache Boy Bust	Closed	N/A	40.00	75-150
1984 Apache Girl Bust	Closed	N/A	40.00	75
1985 Lovers	Closed	N/A	70.00	125
1984 Papoose	325	N/A	500.00	500
1982 The Peaceable Kingdom	950	N/A	750.00	750

The Storybook Collection - G. Perillo

YEAR ISSUE	EDITION LIMIT	YEAR RETD.	ISSUE PRICE	*QUOTE U.S.$
1981 Cinderella	10,000	N/A	65.00	95
1982 Goldilocks & 3 Bears	10,000	N/A	80.00	110
1982 Hansel and Gretel	10,000	N/A	80.00	110
1980 Little Red Ridinghood	10,000	N/A	65.00	95

The Tribal Ponies - G. Perillo

YEAR ISSUE	EDITION LIMIT	YEAR RETD.	ISSUE PRICE	*QUOTE U.S.$
1984 Arapaho	1,500	N/A	65.00	175-200
1984 Comanche	1,500	N/A	65.00	175-200
1984 Crow	1,500	N/A	65.00	175-200

The War Pony - G. Perillo

YEAR ISSUE	EDITION LIMIT	YEAR RETD.	ISSUE PRICE	*QUOTE U.S.$
1983 Apache War Pony	495	N/A	150.00	175-200
1983 Nez Perce War Pony	495	N/A	150.00	175-200
1983 Sioux War Pony	495	N/A	150.00	175-200

Artists of the World

DeGrazia Annual Christmas Collection - T. DeGrazia

YEAR ISSUE	EDITION LIMIT	YEAR RETD.	ISSUE PRICE	*QUOTE U.S.$
1992 Feliz Navidad	1,992		195.00	200
1993 Fiesta Angels	1,993	1995	295.00	450-485
1994 Littlest Angel	1,994		165.00	150
1995 Bethlehem Bound	1,995	1996	195.00	200
1996 Christmas Serenade	1,996		145.00	145
1997 Christmas Bride	1,997		125.00	125
1998 Christmas Angel of Light	1,998		145.00	145

DeGrazia Figurine - T. DeGrazia

YEAR ISSUE	EDITION LIMIT	YEAR RETD.	ISSUE PRICE	*QUOTE U.S.$
1990 Alone	S/O	1994	395.00	585-800
1995 Apache Mother	3,500	1996	165.00	195-225
1988 Beautiful Burden	Closed	1990	175.00	200-390
1990 Biggest Drum	Closed	1992	110.00	150-300
1996 Blessed Madonna	2,500	1997	195.00	200-225
1986 The Blue Boy	Suspd.		70.00	100-163
1992 Coming Home	3,500	1995	165.00	200-228
1990 Crucifixion	S/O	1995	295.00	300-500
1990 Desert Harvest	S/O	1993	135.00	150-300
1986 Festival Lights	Suspd.		75.00	100-175
1994 Festive Flowers	Closed	1996	145.00	150-300
1984 Flower Boy	Closed	1992	65.00	130-225
1988 Flower Boy Plaque	Closed	1990	80.00	100-175
1984 Flower Girl	Suspd.		65.00	98-200
1984 Flower Girl Plaque	Closed	1985	45.00	85-150
1996 Homeward Bound	2,500	1997	195.00	195-200
1985 Little Madonna	Closed	1993	80.00	124-250
1993 Little Medicine Man	Closed	1997	175.00	180-190
1988 Los Ninos	S/O	1989	595.00	1170-1500
1989 Los Ninos (Artist's Edition)	S/O	N/A	695.00	2000-3500
1987 Love Me	Closed	1992	95.00	250
1988 Merrily, Merrily, Merrily	Closed	1991	95.00	189-200
1986 Merry Little Indian	12,500	1989	175.00	250-358
1996 Mother's Warmth	950	1997	295.00	295-300
1989 My Beautiful Rocking Horse	Suspd.		225.00	250-350
1989 My First Arrow	Closed	1992	95.00	130-250
1984 My First Horse	Closed	1990	65.00	156-300
1990 Navajo Boy	Closed	1992	110.00	200-275
1992 Navajo Madonna	Closed	1993	135.00	250-275
1991 Navajo Mother	3,500	1995	295.00	300-423
1985 Pima Drummer Boy	Closed	1991	65.00	100-200
1993 Saddle Up	5,000	1995	195.00	200-280
1984 Sunflower Boy	Closed	1985	65.00	195-300
1990 Sunflower Girl	Closed	1993	95.00	300-325
1987 Wee Three	Closed	1990	180.00	195-300
1984 White Dove	Closed	1992	45.00	125
1984 Wondering	Closed	1987	85.00	156-250

DeGrazia Nativity Collection - T. DeGrazia

YEAR ISSUE	EDITION LIMIT	YEAR RETD.	ISSUE PRICE	*QUOTE U.S.$
1993 Balthasar	Closed	N/A	135.00	125-135
1988 Christmas Prayer Angel (red)	Closed	1991	70.00	150-293
1990 El Burrito	Closed	N/A	60.00	95-100
1993 El Toro	Closed	N/A	95.00	98
1993 Gaspar	Closed	N/A	135.00	125-135
1985 Jesus	Closed	N/A	35.00	65
1985 Joseph	Closed	N/A	50.00	110-125
1990 Little Prayer Angel (white)	Closed	1992	85.00	200-215
1985 Mary	Closed	N/A	40.00	125
1993 Melchoir	Closed	N/A	135.00	125
1996 Music For Baby Jesus	Closed	N/A	145.00	145
1985 Nativity Set-3 pc. (Mary, Joseph, Jesus)	Closed	N/A	275.00	275-300
1995 Pima Indian Drummer Boy	Closed	N/A	135.00	135
1991 Shepherd's Boy	Closed	N/A	95.00	100-135
1989 Two Little Lambs	Closed	1992	70.00	200-293

DeGrazia Pendants - R. Olszewski

YEAR ISSUE	EDITION LIMIT	YEAR RETD.	ISSUE PRICE	*QUOTE U.S.$
1987 Festival of Lights 562-P	Suspd.		90.00	200-300
1985 Flower Girl Pendant 561-P	Suspd.		125.00	291-350

DeGrazia Village Collection - T. DeGrazia

YEAR ISSUE	EDITION LIMIT	YEAR RETD.	ISSUE PRICE	*QUOTE U.S.$
1992 The Listener	Closed	1992	48.00	75-90
1992 Little Feather	Closed	1995	53.00	100-175
1992 Medicine Man	Closed	1995	75.00	100-150
1992 Standing Tall	Closed	1996	65.00	100-150
1992 Telling Tales	Closed	1992	48.00	75-90
1992 Tiny Treasure	Closed	1995	53.00	100-200
1993 Water Wagon	Closed	1995	295.00	295

DeGrazia: Goebel Miniatures - R. Olszewski

YEAR ISSUE	EDITION LIMIT	YEAR RETD.	ISSUE PRICE	*QUOTE U.S.$
1988 Adobe Display 948D	Suspd.		45.00	100-200
1990 Adobe Hacienda (large) Display 958-D	Suspd.		85.00	90-125
1989 Beautiful Burden 554-P	Suspd.		110.00	90-150
1990 Chapel Display 971-D	Suspd.		95.00	90-150
1986 Festival of Lights 507-P	Suspd.		85.00	250-350
1985 Flower Boy 502-P	Suspd.		85.00	100-150
1985 Flower Girl 501-P	Suspd.		85.00	175-225
1986 Little Madonna 552-P	Suspd.		93.00	125-150
1989 Merry Little Indian 508-P (new style)	Suspd.		110.00	150-200
1987 Merry Little Indian 508-P (old style)	Closed	N/A	95.00	200-250
1991 My Beautiful Rocking Horse 555-P	Suspd.		110.00	175-200
1985 My First Horse 503-P	Suspd.		85.00	90-150
1986 Pima Drummer Boy 506-P	Suspd.		85.00	200-300
1985 Sunflower Boy 551- P	Suspd.		93.00	175-200
1985 White Dove 504-P	Suspd.		80.00	80-150
1985 Wondering 505-P	Suspd.		93.00	90-150

Barbie/Enesco Corporation

Happy Holidays Musicals - Enesco

YEAR ISSUE	EDITION LIMIT	YEAR RETD.	ISSUE PRICE	*QUOTE U.S.$
1995 Happy Holidays Barbie, 1988 154199	Yr.Iss.	1995	100.00	100
1996 Holiday, 1989 188832	Yr.Iss.	1996	100.00	100
1997 Happy Holidays Barbie, 1990 274313	Yr.Iss.	1997	100.00	100
1996 Happy Holidays Barbie, 1996 274321	Yr.Iss.	1997	100.00	100
1998 Happy Holidays Barbie, 1991 362794	Yr.Iss.		100.00	100
1998 Happy Holidays Barbie, 1997 362786	Yr.Iss.		100.00	100

Bing & Grondahl

Centennial Anniversary Commemoratives - F.A. Hallin

YEAR ISSUE	EDITION LIMIT	YEAR RETD.	ISSUE PRICE	*QUOTE U.S.$
1995 Centennial Vase: Behind the Frozen Window	1,250	1995	295.00	295

Boyds Collection Ltd.

The Loyal Order of Friends of Boyds ("F.o.B.s" for Short) - G.M. Lowenthal

YEAR ISSUE	EDITION LIMIT	YEAR RETD.	ISSUE PRICE	*QUOTE U.S.$
1996 Raeburn (6" plush bear)	Retrd.	1997	Gift	N/A
1996 Uncle Elliot Pin	Retrd.	1997	Gift	N/A
1996 Uncle Elliot...The Head Bean Wants You	Retrd.	1997	Gift	23
1996 Velma Q. Berriweather...The Cookie Queen (11" plush)	Retrd.	1997	29.00	28-32
1996 Velma Q. Berriweather...The Cookie Queen (figurine)	Retrd.	1997	19.00	19
1998 Eleanor (6" plush bear)	12/98		Gift	N/A
1998 Lady Libearty Patriotic Pin	12/98		Gift	N/A
1998 Zelma G. Berriweather (11" plush bear)	12/98		32.00	32
1998 Zelma G. Berriweather's Cottage (figurine)	12/98		21.00	21

Special Event - G.M. Lowenthal

YEAR ISSUE	EDITION LIMIT	YEAR RETD.	ISSUE PRICE	*QUOTE U.S.$
1997 Prince Hamalot	Retrd.	1997	30.00	30
1998 Elizabeth...I am the Queen	12/98		34.00	34

The Bearstone Collection ™ - G.M. Lowenthal

YEAR ISSUE	EDITION LIMIT	YEAR RETD.	ISSUE PRICE	*QUOTE U.S.$
1994 Agatha & Shelly-'Scardy Cat' 2246	Open		16.25	17-75
1995 Amelia's Enterprise 'Carrot Juice' 2258	12/98		16.25	17-80
1995 Angelica...'the Guardian' 2266	Open		17.95	18-57
1995 Angelica...the Guardian Angel (waterglobe) 2702	Open		37.50	38-69
1993 Arthur...with Red Scarf 2003-03	Retrd.	1994	10.50	115-137
1994 Bailey & Emily...'Forever Friends' 2018	Retrd.	1996	34.00	81-107
1994 Bailey & Wixie 'To Have and To Hold' 2017	Open		15.75	16-325
1994 Bailey at the Beach 2020-09	Retrd.	1995	15.75	65-169
1993 Bailey Bear with Suitcase (old version) 2000	Retrd.	1993	14.20	325-331
1993 Bailey Bear with Suitcase (revised version) 2000	Open		14.20	15-485
1994 Bailey's Birthday 2014	Open		15.95	16-188
1995 Bailey...'The Baker with Sweetie Pie' 2254	Open		12.50	13-104
1995 Bailey...'The Baker with Sweetie Pie' 2254CL	3,600	1995	15.00	220-250
1995 Bailey...'the Cheerleader' 2268	Open		15.95	16-51
1995 Bailey...'The Honeybear' 2260	Open		15.75	16-75
1996 Bailey...Heart's Desire 2272	Open		15.00	15-90
1993 Bailey...in the Orchard 2006	Retrd.	1996	14.20	52-219
1997 Bailey..Poor Old Bear 227704	Retrd.	1997	14.00	14-75
1997 Bailey..The Graduate 227701-10	Open		16.50	17-50
1998 Beatrice...We are always the Same Age Inside 227802	Yr.Iss.		62.00	62
1994 Bessie the Santa Cow 2239	Retrd.	1996	15.75	49-75
1993 Byron & Chedda w/Catmint 2010	Retrd.	1994	14.20	44-144
1994 Celeste...'The Angel Rabbit' 2230	Retrd.	1997	16.25	17-270
1994 Charlotte & Bebe...'The Gardeners' 2229	Retrd.	1995	15.75	37-88
1993 Christian by the Sea 2012	12/98		14.20	15-108
1994 Christmas Big Pig, Little Pig BC2256	Retrd.	N/A	N/A	58-171
1994 Clara...'The Nurse' 2231	Open		16.25	17-485
1994 Clarence Angel Bear (rust) 2029-11	Retrd.	1995	12.60	31-119
1998 The Collector 227707	Open		21.00	21
1995 Cookie Catberg...'Knittin' Kitten' 2250	Retrd.	1997	18.75	19-75
1994 Cookie the Santa Cat 2237	Retrd.	1995	15.25	27-195
1995 Daphne and Eloise...'Women's Work' 2251	Open		18.00	18-75
1993 Daphne Hare & Maisey Ewe 2011	Retrd.	1995	14.20	63-138
1994 Daphne...The Reader Hare 2226	12/98		14.20	15-119
1994 Edmond & Bailey...'Gathering Holly' 2240	Open		24.25	25-250
1997 Edmond..The Graduate 227701-07	Open		16.50	17-50
1994 Elgin the Elf Bear 2236	Retrd.	1997	14.20	63-75
1994 Elliot & Snowbeary 2242	Open		15.25	16-92
1994 Elliot & The Tree 2241	Open		16.25	17-219
1995 Elliot & the Tree Water Globe 2704	Retrd.	1997	35.00	52-69
1996 Elliot...the Hero 2280	Open		16.75	17-52
1998 Elvira & Chauncey Fitzbruin...Shipmates 227708	Open		19.00	19
1996 Emma & Bailey...Afternoon Tea 2277	Open		18.00	18-63
1995 Emma...'the Witchy Bear' 2269	Open		16.75	17-57
1996 Ewell/Walton Manitoba Moosemen BC2228	12,000		24.99	25-56
1993 Father Chrisbear and Son 2008	Retrd.	1993	15.00	332-500
1998 Feldman D. Finklebearg & Dooley..."Painless" & The Patient 227710	Open		20.00	20
1994 The Flying Lesson (waterglobe) 270601	Retrd.	1997	62.00	119-165
1994 The Flying Lesson 227801	Yr.Iss.	1994	62.00	62-97
1994 Grenville & Beatrice...'Best Friends' 2016	Open		26.25	27-560
1996 Grenville & Beatrice...True Love 2274	Open		36.00	36-75
1995 Grenville & Knute...Football Buddies 2255	Open		19.95	20-63
1993 Grenville & Neville...'The Sign' (prototype) 2099	Retrd.	1993	15.75	50-95
1993 Grenville & Neville...'The Sign' 2099	Open		15.75	16-55
1994 Grenville the Santabear 2030	Retrd.	1996	14.20	300-560
1994 Grenville the Santabear Musical Waterball 2700	Retrd.	1996	35.75	58-75
1996 Grenville with Matthew & Bailey...Sunday Afternoon 2281	Open		34.50	35-58
1994 Grenville...'The Graduate' 2233	Retrd.	1996	16.25	50-90
1995 Grenville...'The Storyteller' 2265	Retrd.	1995	50.00	50-125
1993 Grenville...with Green Scarf 2003-04	Retrd.	1994	10.50	558-675
1993 Grenville...with Red Scarf 2003-08	Retrd.	1995	10.50	100-163
1998 The Head Bean & Co....Work is Love Made Visible 227803	18,000	1998	61.00	61
1994 Homer on the Plate 2225	Open		15.75	16-98
1994 Homer on the Plate BC2210	Open		24.99	25-75
1995 Hop-a-Long...'The Deputy' 2247	Open		14.00	14-60
1994 Juliette Angel Bear (ivory) 2029-10	Retrd.	1995	12.60	50-138
1994 Justina & M. Harrison...'Sweetie Pie' 2015	Open		26.25	27-86
1996 Justina...The Message "Bearer" 2273	Open		16.00	16-50
1994 Knute & The Gridiron 2245	Retrd.	1997	16.25	20-86
1994 Kringle & Bailey with List 2235	Open		14.20	15-80
1996 Kringle And Company 2283	Open		17.45	18-50
1995 Lefty...'On the Mound' 2253	Open		15.00	15-75
1995 Lefty...'On the Mound' BC2056	Open		24.99	25-86
1994 Lucy Big Pig, Little Pig BC2250	Retrd.	1996	24.99	125-150
1996 M. Harrison's Birthday 2275	Open		17.00	17-40
1994 Manheim the 'Eco-Moose' 2243	Open		15.25	16-60
1998 Margot...The Ballerina 227709	Open		18.00	18
1994 Maynard the Santa Moose 2238	Retrd.	1997	15.25	52-75

*Quotes have been rounded up to nearest dollar

YEAR ISSUE	EDITION LIMIT	YEAR RETD.	ISSUE PRICE	*QUOTE U.S.$
1995 Miss Bruin & Bailey 'The Lesson' 2259	Open		18.45	19-90
1998 Momma Mcbear & Caledonia...Quiet Time 227711	Open		20.00	20
1996 Momma Mcbear...Anticipation 2282	Open		14.95	15-58
1993 Moriarty-'The Bear in the Cat Suit' 2005	Retrd.	1995	13.75	54-138
1996 Ms. Griz...Monday Morning 2276	Open		34.00	34-100
1996 Ms. Griz...Saturday Night GCC 2284	Open		15.00	15-75
1993 Neville...The 'Bedtime Bear' 2002	Retrd.	1996	14.20	52-111
1997 Neville...compubear 227702	Open		15.50	16-44
1996 Noah & Co...Ark Builders 2278	Retrd.	1996	61.00	63-125
1996 Noah & Company (waterglobe) 2706	6,000	1996	50.95	196-250
1995 Otis...'Taxtime' 2262	Retrd.	1997	18.75	37-95
1995 Otis...'The Fisherman' 2249-06	12/98		15.75	16-75
1994 Sebastian's Prayer 2227	Retrd.	1996	16.25	26-90
1997 The Secret 227705	Open		18.00	18-47
1994 Sherlock & Watson-In Disguise 2019	Retrd.	1996	15.75	115-175
1995 Simone & Bailey...'Helping Hands' 2267	Open		25.95	26-69
1996 Simone and Bailey...Helping Hands 2705	Open		34.80	35-55
1993 Simone De Bearvoire and Her Mom 2001	Retrd.	1996	14.20	30-69
1996 Sir Edmund... Persistence 2279	Open		20.75	21-75
1994 Ted & Teddy 2223	Retrd.	1997	15.75	53-100
1995 Union Jack...'Love Letters' 2263	12/98		18.95	19-63
1993 Victoria...'The Lady' 2004	Open		18.40	19-219
1994 Wilson at the Beach 2020-06	Retrd.	1997	15.75	65-138
1994 Wilson the "Perfesser" 2222	Retrd.	1997	16.25	52-94
1993 Wilson with Love Sonnets 2007	Retrd.	1997	12.60	160-587
1995 Wilson...'the Wonderful Wizard of Wuz' 2261	Open		15.95	16-75
1994 Xmas Bear Elf with List BC2051	1,865	1994	24.99	700-1020
1997 Zoe...Angel of Life (GCC Exclusive) 2286	Retrd.	1997	15.00	38

The Bearstone Collection Nativity™ - G.M. Lowenthal

YEAR ISSUE	EDITION LIMIT	YEAR RETD.	ISSUE PRICE	*QUOTE U.S.$
1997 Ariel & Clarence Angels 2411	12/99		14.00	14-35
1995 Baldwin...as the Child 2403	12/99		14.95	15-56
1997 Bruce...as the Shepherd 2410	12/99		15.00	15
1998 Caledonia...as the Narrator 2412	12/99		16.00	16
1997 Essex...as the Donkey 2408	12/99		15.00	15
1996 Heath as Casper 2405	12/99		14.00	14-42
1998 Matthew...as the Drummer 2415	12/99		16.00	16
1998 Mrs. Bruin...as the Teacher 2414	12/99		16.00	16
1995 Neville...as Joseph 2401	12/99		14.95	15-32
1996 Raleigh as Balthasar 2406	12/99		14.00	14-42
1998 Serendipity...as the Guardian 2416	12/99		16.00	16
1995 The Stage...the School Pagent 2425	12/99		34.50	35-120
1996 Thatcher & Eden as the Camel 2407	12/99		17.00	17-38
1995 Theresa...as Mary 2402	12/99		14.95	15-40
1996 Wilson as Melchior 2404	12/99		14.00	14-37
1996 Wink & Dink as the Lambs 2409	12/99		11.00	11-38

The Dollstone Collection ™ - G.M. Lowenthal

YEAR ISSUE	EDITION LIMIT	YEAR RETD.	ISSUE PRICE	*QUOTE U.S.$
1996 Betsey and Edmund with Union Jack BC35031	Open		24.99	25-75
1995 Betsey & Edmund 3503PE	Retrd.	1995	19.50	49-125
1995 Katherine, Amanda & Edmund 3505PE	Retrd.	1995	19.50	80-100
1995 Meagan 3504PE	Retrd.	1995	19.50	85-400
1995 Victoria with Samantha 3502PE	Retrd.	1995	19.50	80-100
1995 Set of 4 PE	Retrd.	1995	78.00	440-575
1997 The Amazing Bailey...'Magic Show' 3518	Yr.Iss.	1997	60.00	60-75
1998 Amy and Edmund...Momma's Clothes 3529	Open		29.50	30
1996 Anne...the Masterpiece 3599	Open		24.25	25-75
1996 Ashley with Chrissie...Dress Up 3506	12/98		20.50	21-50
1997 Benjamin with Mattew...The Speed Trap 3524	Open		30.00	30
1996 Betsey with Edmond...The Patriots 3503	Open		20.00	20-63
1997 Caitlin with Emma & Edmund...Diapering Baby 3525	12/98		20.00	20
1996 Candice with Matthew...Gathering Apples 3514	12/98		18.95	19-98
1996 Christy w/Nicole...Mother's Presence GCC 3516	Open		26.00	26-75
1996 Courtney with Phoebe...over the River and Thru the Woods (waterglobe) 3512	Retrd.	1997	24.25	35-57
1996 Emily with Kathleen & Otis...The Future 3508	Open		30.00	30-75
1998 Jamie and Thomasina...the Last One 3530	Open		20.00	20
1996 Jean with Elliot & Debbie...The Bakers 3510	Open		19.50	20-45
1996 Jennifer with Priscilla...The Doll in the Attic 3500	Retrd.	1997	20.50	35-48
1997 Julia with Emmy Lou...Garden Friends 3520	Open		19.00	19-55
1998 Jessica & Timmy...Animal Hospital	72,000		40.00	40
1996 Karen & Wilson..Skater's Waltz GCC 3515	Open		26.00	26-69
1997 Karen with Wilson and Eloise...Mother's Present 3515-01	12/98		20.00	20
1996 Katherine with Amanda & Edmond...Kind Hearts 3505	Open		20.00	20-75
1997 Kristi with Nicole...Skater's Waltz 3516	Open		22.00	22
1997 Laura with Jane...First Day of School 3522	Open		23.00	23
1996 Mallory w/Patsy & J.B....Trick or Treat 3517	Retrd.	1996	27.00	130-150
1998 Mary and Paul...The Prayer 3531-01	Open		16.00	16
1996 Megan with Elliot & Annie...Christmas Carol 3504	Retrd.	1997	19.50	57-130
1996 Megan with Elliot...Christmas Carol (waterglobe) 2720	Open		39.45	40-69
1996 Michelle with Daisy...Reading is Fun 3511	Open		17.95	18-50
1997 Natalie & Joy 3519	Open		22.00	22-63
1996 Patricia with Molly...Attic Treasures 3501	12/98		14.00	14-55
1996 Rebecca with Elliot...Birthday 3509	Open		20.50	21-50
1996 Sara & Heather with Elliot & Amelia...Tea for Four 3507	Retrd.	1997	46.00	69-138
1998 Shelby...Asleep in Teddy's Arms 3527	Open		15.00	15
1998 Teresa and John...The Prayer 3531	Open		14.00	14
1996 Victoria with Samantha...Victorian Ladies 3502	Open		20.00	20-120
1997 Wendy...Wash Day 3521	12/98		22.00	22-50
1997 Whitney & Wilson...Tea Party 3523	Open		19.00	19-63

The Folkstone Collection ™ - G.M. Lowenthal

YEAR ISSUE	EDITION LIMIT	YEAR RETD.	ISSUE PRICE	*QUOTE U.S.$
1995 Abigail...Peaceable Kingdom 2829	Open		18.95	19-48
1996 Alvin T. Mac Barker...Dogface 2872	Retrd.	1997	19.00	50
1994 Angel of Freedom 2820	Retrd.	1996	16.75	52-88
1994 Angel of Love 2821	Retrd.	1996	16.75	63-94
1994 Angel of Peace 2822	Retrd.	1996	16.75	52-88
1997 Astrid Isinglass...Snow Angel 28206-06	Yr.Iss.	1997	23.50	62
1996 Athena...The Wedding Angel 28202	Open		19.00	19-50
1998 Auntie Cocoa M. Maximus...Chocolate Angel (NQGA) 28242	Open		20.00	20
1997 Bearly Nick & Buddies 28001	Open		19.50	20
1994 Beatrice-Birthday Angel 2825	Open		20.00	20-63
1995 Beatrice...the Giftgiver 2836	Open		17.95	18-48
1996 Bernie... I Got Wat I wanted St. Bernard Santa 2873	Open		17.75	18-48
1996 Betty Cocker 2870	Open		19.00	19-60
1998 Birdie Holeinone...NQGA of Golfers 28245	Open		20.00	20
1995 Boowinkle Vonhindenmoose ...2831	Open		17.95	18-69
1996 Buster Goes A' Courtin' 2844	Retrd.	1998	19.00	19-38
1994 Chilly & Son with Dove 2811	Retrd.	1997	17.75	45-75
1997 Constance & Felicity 28205	14,000		37.50	38-88
1996 Cosmos...The Gardening Angel 28201	Open		19.00	19-42
1994 December 26th 3003	Retrd.	1997	32.00	32-57
1996 Egon...the Skier 2837	Open		17.75	18-48
1994 Elmer-Cow on Haystacks 2851	12/98		19.00	19-28
1996 Elmo "Tex" Beefcake...On the Range 2853	Retrd.	1997	19.00	19-38
1995 Ernest Hemmingmoose...the Hunter 2835	Open		17.95	18-57
1995 Esmeralda...the Wonderful Witch 2860	Open		17.95	18-57
1996 Fixit...Santa's Faerie 3600	Open		17.45	18-40
1996 Flora & Amelia...The Gardeners 2843	Open		19.00	19-69
1996 Flora, Amelia & Eloise...The Tea Party 2846	Open		19.00	19-50
1994 Florence-Kitchen Angel 2824	Retrd.	1996	20.00	42-50
1998 Francoise & Suzanne...the Spree 2875	Open		20.00	20
1996 G.M.'s Choice, Etheral...Angel of Light 28203-06	7,200	1996	18.25	88-115
1997 Gabrielle "Gabby" Faeriejabber 36003	12/98		18.50	19
1997 Helga with Ingrid & Anna ...Be Warm 2818	Open		19.00	19
1995 Icabod Mooselman...the Pilgrim 2833	Retrd.	1997	17.95	50-69
1994 Ida & Bessie-The Gardeners 2852	Retrd.	1998	19.00	44-50
1996 Illumina...Angel of Light 28203	Open		18.45	19-57
1997 Infiniti Faerielove...the Wedding Faerie 36101	12/98		16.00	16
1996 Jean Claude & Jacque...the Skiers (waterglobe) 2710	Open		37.50	38-75
1995 Jean Claude & Jacques...the Skiers 2815	Open		16.95	17-69
1994 Jill-Language of Love 2842	Retrd.	1997	19.00	47-82
1994 Jingle Moose 2830	Retrd.	1996	17.75	70-100
1994 Jingles & Son with Wreath 2812	Retrd.	1996	17.75	28-138
1997 Krystal Isinglass...Snow Angel 28206	Open		19.00	19
1998 Liddy Pearl...How Does Your Garden Grow 2881	12,000	1998	40.00	40
1994 Lizzie Shopping Angel 2827	12/98		20.00	20-60
1996 Loretta Moostein..."Yer Cheatin' Heart" 2854	Open		19.00	19-45
1997 Madge...The Magician/Beautician (NQGA) 28243	Open		19.00	19
1997 Mercy...Angel of Nurses (NQGA) 28240	Open		19.00	19
1994 Minerva-Baseball Angel 2826	Retrd.	1997	20.00	20-45
1998 Miss Prudence P. Carrotjuice...Multiplication 2848	Open		18.50	19
1997 Montague Von Hindenmoose...Surprise! 2839	Open		19.00	19
1997 Ms. Patience...Angel of Teachers (NQGA) 28241	Open		19.00	19
1994 Myrtle-Believe 2840	12/98		20.00	20-60
1995 Na-Nick of the North 2804	Open		17.95	18-50
1998 Nana Mchare...and the Love Gardeners 2849	Open		20.00	20
1996 Nanick & Siegfried the Plan 2807	10,000	1996	32.50	80-109
1996 Nanny...the Snowmom 2817	Open		17.95	18-38
1994 Nicholai with Tree 2800	Retrd.	1997	17.75	50-63
1994 Nicholas with Book 2802	Retrd.	1996	17.75	27-57
1994 Nick on Ice (1st ed. GCC) 3001	3,600	1995	49.95	32-85
1994 Nick on Ice 3001	Retrd.	1997	32.95	50-75
1996 Nick, Siegfried 2807	Yr.Iss.	1996	35.00	100
1996 Nicknoak...Santa with Ark 2806	Open		17.95	18-44
1994 Nikki with Candle 2801	Retrd.	1997	17.75	18-47
1996 No-No Nick...Bad Boy Santa 2805	Open		17.95	18-44
1995 Northbound Wille 2814	Retrd.	1997	16.95	17-44
1994 Oceana-Ocean Angel 2823	Open		16.75	17-94
1994 Oceania...Ocean Angel 2838	12/98		16.00	16-42
1997 Olaf...Mogul Meister 2819	Open		16.50	17
1994 Peter-The Whopper 2841	Retrd.	1997	19.00	37-50
1997 Polaris & The North Star...on Ice 2880	Open		19.00	19
1997 Prudence & Daffodils 2847	Open		18.00	18-47
1995 Prudence Mooselmaid...the Pilgrim 2834	Retrd.	1997	17.95	50-63
1998 Purrscilla G. Pussenboots...Mitten Knitters 2865	Open		20.50	21
1996 Robin...the Snowbird Lover 2816	Open		17.95	18-38
1994 Rufus-Hoedown 2850	12/98		19.00	19-38
1994 Santa's Challenge (1st ed. GCC) 3002	3,600	1995	49.95	69-75
1994 Santa's Challenge 3002	Retrd.	1997	32.95	33-45
1994 Santa's Flight Plan (1st ed. GCC) 3000	3,600	1995	49.95	81-88
1995 Santa's Flight Plan (waterglobe) 2703	Retrd.	1996	37.00	37-75
1994 Santa's Flight Plan 3000	Retrd.	1997	32.95	33
1996 Santa's Hobby 3004	Retrd.	1997	36.00	36-65
1995 Seraphina with Jacob & Rachael...the Choir Angels 2828	Retrd.	1997	19.95	20-35
1996 Serenity...the Mother's Angel 28204	Open		18.25	19-44
1997 Sgt. Rex & Matt...The Runaway 2874	Open		19.50	20
1995 Siegfried and Egon...the Sign 2899	Open		18.95	19-50
1995 Sliknick the Chimney Sweep 2803	Open		17.95	18-58
1996 Sparky McPlug 2871	Open		19.00	19-38
1997 St. Nick...the Quest 2808	Open		19.00	19-63
1996 Too Loose Lapin...The Arteest 2845	12/98		19.00	19-27
1994 Windy with Book 2810	Retrd.	1996	17.75	95-119
1997 Yukon, Kodiak & Nanuk...Nome Sweet Home (waterglobe) 271001	Open		38.50	39
1997 Ziggy...The Duffer 2838	Open		39.50	40

Byers' Choice Ltd.

Accessories - J. Byers

YEAR ISSUE	EDITION LIMIT	YEAR RETD.	ISSUE PRICE	*QUOTE U.S.$
1995 Cat in Hat	Closed	1995	10.00	18
1997 Cat with Milk	Closed	1997	18.50	19-25
1996 Dog with Hat	Closed	1996	18.50	19
1997 Dog with Lollipop	Closed	1997	18.50	19
1995 Dog with Sausages	Closed	1995	18.00	30-50
1998 Door	Open		52.00	52
1986 Singing Cats	Open		13.50	17
1986 Singing Dogs	Open		13.00	17
1992 Snowman	Open		19.00	20
1996 Street Clock	Closed	1997	85.00	85-95

Carolers - J. Byers

YEAR ISSUE	EDITION LIMIT	YEAR RETD.	ISSUE PRICE	*QUOTE U.S.$
1978 Hilltown Traditional Lady	Closed	N/A	N/A	600
1996 Teenagers (Traditional)	Open		46.00	46
1996 Teenagers (Victorian)	Open		49.00	49
1976 Traditional Adult (1976-80)	Closed	1980	N/A	475
1981 Traditional Adult (1981-current)	Open		45.00	45-300
XX Traditional Adult (undated)	Closed	N/A	N/A	400-700
1978 Traditional Colonial Lady (w/ hands)	Closed	1978	N/A	1500
1986 Traditional Grandparents	Open		35.00	46
1982 Victorian Adult (1st ed.)	Closed	1982	32.00	400
1982 Victorian Adult (2nd ed./dressed alike)	Closed	1983	46.00	300-400
1983 Victorian Adult (assorted) (2nd ed.)	Open		35.00	49
1982 Victorian Child (1st ed. w/floppy hats)	Closed	1982	32.00	300-375
1983 Victorian Child (2nd ed./sailor suit)	Closed	1983	33.00	300-400
1983 Victorian Child (assorted) (2nd. ed.)	Open		33.00	49
1988 Victorian Grandparent	Open		40.00	49

Children of The World - J. Byers

YEAR ISSUE	EDITION LIMIT	YEAR RETD.	ISSUE PRICE	*QUOTE U.S.$
1993 Bavarian Boy	Closed	1993	50.00	175-290
1992 Dutch Boy	Closed	1992	50.00	260-300
1992 Dutch Girl	Closed	1992	50.00	260-300
1994 Irish Girl	Closed	1994	50.00	100-250
1997 Mexican Children	Closed	1997	50.00	50-75
1996 Saint Lucia	Open		52.00	52

Colonial Williamsburg - J. Byers

YEAR ISSUE	EDITION LIMIT	YEAR RETD.	ISSUE PRICE	*QUOTE U.S.$
1998 Colonial Boy w/Recorder	Open		50.00	50
1998 Colonial Girl w/Hoop	Open		50.00	50
1998 Colonial Man w/Music Book	Open		50.00	50
1998 Colonial Woman w/Music Book	Open		50.00	50

Cries Of London - J. Byers

YEAR ISSUE	EDITION LIMIT	YEAR RETD.	ISSUE PRICE	*QUOTE U.S.$
1991 Apple Lady (red stockings)	Closed	1991	80.00	950-1200
1991 Apple Lady (red/wh stockings)	Closed	1991	80.00	1180-1200

*Quotes have been rounded up to nearest dollar

FIGURINES

YEAR ISSUE	EDITION LIMIT	YEAR RETD.	ISSUE PRICE	*QUOTE U.S.$
1992 Baker	Closed	1992	62.00	175-350
1998 Candlestick Maker	Yr.Iss.		72.00	72
1993 Chestnut Roaster	Closed	1993	64.00	219-395
1996 Children Buying Gingerbread	Closed	1996	46.00	80-110
1998 Children Holding Candles	Open		48.00	48
1995 Dollmaker	Closed	1995	64.00	95-150
1994 Flower Vendor	Closed	1994	64.00	110-250
1996 Gingerbread Vendor	Closed	1996	75.00	80-150
1995 Girl Holding Doll	Closed	1995	48.00	125-150
1997 Milk Maid	Closed	1997	67.00	75-150

Dickens Series - J. Byers

YEAR ISSUE	EDITION LIMIT	YEAR RETD.	ISSUE PRICE	*QUOTE U.S.$
1990 Bob Cratchit & Tiny Tim (1st ed.)	Closed	1990	84.00	250-365
1991 Bob Cratchit & Tiny Tim (2nd ed.)	Open		86.00	90
1991 Happy Scrooge (1st ed.)	Closed	1991	50.00	350-365
1992 Happy Scrooge (2nd ed.)	Closed	1992	50.00	148-350
1986 Marley's Ghost (1st ed.)	Closed	1986	40.00	225-450
1987 Marley's Ghost (2nd ed.)	Closed	1992	42.00	175-365
1985 Mr. Fezziwig (1st ed.)	Closed	1985	43.00	450-500
1986 Mr. Fezziwig (2nd ed.)	Closed	1990	43.00	400-438
1984 Mrs. Cratchit (1st ed.)	Closed	1984	38.00	500-900
1985 Mrs. Cratchit (2nd ed.)	Open		39.00	50
1985 Mrs. Fezziwig (1st ed.)	Closed	1985	43.00	450-600
1986 Mrs. Fezziwig (2nd ed.)	Closed	1990	43.00	350-400
1983 Scrooge (1st ed.)	Closed	1983	36.00	975-1450
1984 Scrooge (2nd ed.)	Open		38.00	50
1989 Spirit of Christmas Future (1st ed.)	Closed	1989	46.00	280-365
1990 Spirit of Christmas Future (2nd ed.)	Closed	1991	48.00	250-345
1987 Spirit of Christmas Past (1st ed.)	Closed	1987	42.00	365-400
1988 Spirit of Christmas Past (2nd ed.)	Closed	1991	46.00	313-345
1988 Spirit of Christmas Present (1st ed.)	Closed	1988	44.00	350-365
1989 Spirit of Christmas Present (2nd ed.)	Closed	1991	48.00	282-345

Display Figures - J. Byers

YEAR ISSUE	EDITION LIMIT	YEAR RETD.	ISSUE PRICE	*QUOTE U.S.$
1998 20th Anniversary Santa in Sleigh	1,000		750.00	750
1986 Display Adults	Closed	1987	170.00	500-600
1983 Display Carolers	Closed	1983	200.00	500
1985 Display Children (Boy & Girl)	Closed	1987	140.00	1200-1500
1982 Display Drummer Boy-1st	Closed	1983	96.00	800-1200
1985 Display Drummer Boy-2nd	Closed	1986	160.00	400-600
1981 Display Lady	Closed	1981	N/A	2000
1981 Display Man	Closed	1981	N/A	2000
1985 Display Old World Santa	Closed	1985	260.00	500-600
1982 Display Santa	Closed	1983	96.00	450-600
1990 Display Santa-bayberry	Closed	1990	250.00	450-600
1990 Display Santa-red	Closed	1990	250.00	600-650
1984 Display Working Santa	Closed	1985	260.00	500
1987 Mechanical Boy with Drum	Closed	1987	N/A	700-850
1987 Mechanical Girl with Bell	Closed	1987	N/A	450-800

Lil' Dickens/Toddlers - J. Byers

YEAR ISSUE	EDITION LIMIT	YEAR RETD.	ISSUE PRICE	*QUOTE U.S.$
1998 Assorted Toddler Groups	Open		20.00	20
1996 Book - "Night Before Christmas"	Open		20.00	20
1996 Doll - "Night Before Christmas"	Open		20.00	20
1993 Gingerbread Boy	Closed	1994	18.50	27
1993 Package	Closed	1993	18.50	35
1992 Shovel	Closed	1993	17.00	35-50
1994 Skis (snowsuit)	Closed	1996	19.00	20
1994 Sled (black toddler)	Closed	1994	19.00	19
1992 Sled (white toddler)	Closed	1993	17.00	20
1995 Sled (white toddler-2nd ed.)	Closed	1995	19.00	20
1991 Sled with Dog/toddler	Closed	1991	30.00	110-125
1992 Snowball	Closed	1994	17.00	35
1994 Snowflake	Closed	1994	18.00	18
1993 Teddy Bear	Closed	1993	18.50	35
1997 Toddler Holding Merry Christmas Banner	Closed	1997	20.00	20
1997 Toddler in Sleigh	Open		27.50	28
1997 Toddler on Rocking Horse	Open		27.50	28
1998 Toddler with Cat	Open		36.00	36
1998 Toddler with Dog	Open		36.00	36
1997 Toddler with Skis (sweater)	Closed	1997	21.50	25
1997 Toddler with Tricycle (sweater)	Closed	1997	21.50	25
1994 Tree	Closed	1996	18.00	20
1996 Tricycle (snowsuit)	Closed	1996	20.00	20-25
1995 Victorian Boy Toddler	Closed	1995	19.50	20
1995 Victorian Girl Toddler	Closed	1995	19.50	20
1995 Wagon	Closed	1996	19.50	20

Musicians - J. Byers

YEAR ISSUE	EDITION LIMIT	YEAR RETD.	ISSUE PRICE	*QUOTE U.S.$
1991 Boy with Mandolin	Closed	1991	48.00	195-350
1985 Horn Player	Closed	1985	38.00	550-750
1985 Horn Player, chubby face	Closed	1985	37.00	500-900
1991 Musician with Accordian	Closed	1991	48.00	275-563
1989 Musician with Clarinet	Closed	1989	44.00	450-650
1992 Musician with French Horn	Closed	1992	52.00	125-150
1990 Musician with Mandolin	Closed	1990	46.00	225-320
1986 Victorian Girl with Violin	Closed	1986	39.00	330-345
1983 Violin Player Man (1st ed.)	Closed	1983	38.00	1500
1984 Violin Player Man (2nd ed.)	Closed	1984	38.00	1500

Nativity - J. Byers

YEAR ISSUE	EDITION LIMIT	YEAR RETD.	ISSUE PRICE	*QUOTE U.S.$
1989 Angel Gabriel	Closed	1991	37.00	178-210
1987 Angel-Great Star (Blonde)	Closed	1991	40.00	210-250
1987 Angel-Great Star (Brunette)	Closed	1991	40.00	250
1987 Angel-Great Star (Red Head)	Closed	1991	40.00	175-250
1987 Black Angel	Closed	1987	36.00	200-250
1990 Holy Family with stable	Closed	1991	119.00	300-350
1989 King Balthasar	Closed	1991	40.00	95-150
1989 King Gaspar	Closed	1991	40.00	95-150
1989 King Melchior	Closed	1991	40.00	95-150
1988 Shepherds	Closed	1991	37.00	95-165

The Nutcracker - J. Byers, unless otherwise noted

YEAR ISSUE	EDITION LIMIT	YEAR RETD.	ISSUE PRICE	*QUOTE U.S.$
1996 Drosselmeier w/Music Box (1st ed.)	Closed	1996	83.00	63-150
1997 Drosselmeier w/Music Box (2nd ed.)	Open		83.00	83
1994 Fritz (1st ed.)	Closed	1994	56.00	75-150
1995 Fritz (2nd ed.)	Closed	1997	57.00	65-85
1995 Louise Playing Piano (1st ed.)	Closed	1995	82.00	150
1996 Louise Playing Piano (2nd ed.)	Closed	1996	83.00	83-150
1993 Marie (1st ed.)	Closed	1993	52.00	85-250
1994 Marie (2nd ed.)	Open		53.00	55
1997 Mouse King (1st ed.) - Jeff Byers	Closed	1997	70.00	70-100
1998 Mouse King (2nd ed.) - Jeff Byers	Open		70.00	70
1998 Prince (1st ed.)	Open		68.00	68

Salvation Army Band - J. Byers

YEAR ISSUE	EDITION LIMIT	YEAR RETD.	ISSUE PRICE	*QUOTE U.S.$
1994 Black Woman w/Tambourine	Closed	1994	58.00	400
1997 Boy with Flag	Open		57.00	57
1995 Girl with War Cry	Open		55.00	56
1996 Man with Bass Drum	Open		60.00	60
1993 Man with Cornet	Closed	1997	54.00	57-150
1998 Salvation Army Man w/Tuba	Open		58.00	58
1992 Woman with Kettle	Open		64.00	150-175
1992 Woman with Kettle (1st ed.)	Closed	1992	64.00	175
1993 Woman with Tambourine	Closed	1995	58.00	100-150

Santas - J. Byers

YEAR ISSUE	EDITION LIMIT	YEAR RETD.	ISSUE PRICE	*QUOTE U.S.$
1994 Befana	Open		53.00	55
1998 Belsnickel	Open		64.00	64
1991 Father Christmas	Closed	1992	48.00	119-125
1988 Knecht Ruprecht (Black Peter)	Closed	1989	38.00	125-150
1996 Knickerbocker Santa	Open		58.00	58
1984 Mrs. Claus	Closed	1991	38.00	100-275
1992 Mrs. Claus (2nd ed.)	Closed	1993	50.00	150
1986 Mrs. Claus on Rocker	Closed	1986	73.00	600
1995 Mrs. Claus' Needlework	Closed	1995	70.00	110-200
1978 Old World Santa	Closed	1986	33.00	375-395
1989 Russian Santa	Closed	1989	85.00	475-650
1988 Saint Nicholas	Closed	1992	44.00	125-160
1997 Santa Feeding Reindeer	Closed	1997	64.50	85
1982 Santa in a Sleigh (1st ed.)	Closed	1983	46.00	800
1998 Santa in Gold Sleigh	400		95.00	95
1984 Santa in Sleigh (2nd ed.)	Closed	1985	70.00	750
1996 Santa in Sleigh (in select stores)	Closed	1996	70.00	250
1998 Seated Santa with Toddler	Open		90.00	90
1997 Shopping Mrs. Claus	Closed	1997	59.50	65-150
1993 Skating Santa	Closed	1993	60.00	100-125
1987 Velvet Mrs. Claus	Open		44.00	54
1978 Velvet Santa	Closed	1993	Unkn.	300
1994 Velvet Santa with Stocking (2nd ed.)	Open		47.00	52
1986 Victorian Santa	Closed	1989	39.00	310
1990 Weihnachtsmann (German Santa)	Closed	1990	56.00	162-180
1992 Working Santa	Closed	1996	52.00	55-60
1983 Working Santa (1st yr. issue)	Closed	1991	38.00	250-275
1992 Working Santa (1st yr. issue)	Closed	1992	52.00	150-250

Shoppers - J. Byers

YEAR ISSUE	EDITION LIMIT	YEAR RETD.	ISSUE PRICE	*QUOTE U.S.$
1995 Shopper-Man	Closed	1995	56.00	75-95
1995 Shopper-Woman	Closed	1995	56.00	75-95
1996 Shoppers - Grandparents	Open		56.00	56
1997 Traditional Adult Shoppers	Open		58.00	58
1995 Traditional Adult Shoppers (1st ed.)	Closed	1995	56.00	75-95
1996 Traditional Grandparent Shoppers	Open		56.00	58
1997 Victorian Adult Shoppers	Open		61.00	61

Skaters - J. Byers

YEAR ISSUE	EDITION LIMIT	YEAR RETD.	ISSUE PRICE	*QUOTE U.S.$
1991 Adult Skaters	Closed	1994	50.00	125-150
1991 Adult Skaters (1991 ed.)	Closed	1991	50.00	130-150
1993 Boy Skater on Log	Closed	1993	55.00	80-150
1988 Children Holding Skates	Open		40.00	50
1992 Children Skaters	Open		50.00	53
1992 Children Skaters (1992 ed.)	Closed	1992	50.00	150
1993 Grandparent Skaters	Closed	1993	50.00	65-100
1993 Grandparent Skaters (1993 ed.)	Closed	1993	50.00	145-153
1995 Man Holding Skates	Open		52.00	53
1995 Woman Holding Skates	Open		52.00	53

Special Characters - J. Byers

YEAR ISSUE	EDITION LIMIT	YEAR RETD.	ISSUE PRICE	*QUOTE U.S.$
1996 Actress	Closed	1996	52.00	65-100
1979 Adult Male "Icabod"	Closed	1979	32.00	2400-2600
1988 Angel Tree Top	100	1988	Unkn.	275-375
1994 Baby in Basket	Closed	1994	7.50	30
1989 Black Boy w/skates	Closed	N/A	N/A	400-450
1989 Black Drummer Boy	Closed	N/A	N/A	500
1989 Black Girl w/skates	Closed	N/A	N/A	400-450
1989 Black Mother w/Baby	Closed	1989	45.00	400
1983 Boy on Rocking Horse	300	1983	85.00	2400-2600
1987 Boy on Sled	Closed	1987	50.00	300-375
1991 Boy with Apple	Closed	1991	41.00	150-275
1994 Boy with Goose	Closed	1995	49.50	125-150
1996 Boy with Lamb	Open		52.00	52
1995 Boy with Skis	Open		49.50	50
1991 Boy with Tree	Closed	1994	49.00	125-150
1995 Butcher	Closed	1995	54.00	100-150
1987 Caroler with Lamp	Closed	1987	40.00	125-200
1998 Children with Toys	Open		57.00	57
1997 Children with Treats	Open		58.00	58
1984 Chimney Sweep-Adult	Closed	1984	36.00	1200-1500
1991 Chimney Sweep-Child	Closed	1994	50.00	125-150
1982 Choir Children, boy and girl set	Closed	1986	32.00	600-625
1993 Choir Director, lady/music stand	Closed	1995	56.00	100-125
1982 Conductor	Closed	1992	32.00	99-125
1994 Constable	Closed	1996	53.00	78-85
1995 Couple in Sleigh	Closed	1995	110.00	125-175
1997 Crabtree & Evelyn Man & Woman	Closed	1997	113.00	113
1996 Crabtree & Evelyn Man & Woman	Closed	1996	113.00	175-250
1982 Drummer Boy	Closed	1992	34.00	157-175
1982 Easter Boy	Closed	1983	32.00	550-1000
1982 Easter Girl	Closed	1983	32.00	550-1000
1997 Gardener	Open		69.50	70
1996 Girl Holding Holly Basket	Closed	1997	52.00	55
1991 Girl with Apple	Closed	1991	41.00	125-200
1991 Girl with Apple/coin purse	Closed	1991	41.00	335-350
1989 Girl with Hoop	Closed	1990	44.00	150-165
1995 Girl with Skis	Open		49.50	50
1982 Icabod	Closed	1982	32.00	1150-1500
1998 Indian Children	Open		53.50	54
1993 Lamplighter	Closed	1996	48.00	65-125
1993 Lamplighter (1st yr. issue)	Closed	1993	48.00	110
1982 Leprechauns	Closed	1982	34.00	1200-2000
1997 Man Feeding Birds on Bench	Closed	1997	83.00	85
1998 Man with Bicycle	Open		82.00	82
1988 Mother Holding Baby	Closed	1993	40.00	125-200
1987 Mother's Day	225	1987	125.00	250-400
1988 Mother's Day (Daughter)	Closed	1988	125.00	450
1993 Mother's Day (green)	Closed	1993	N/A	125
1988 Mother's Day (Son)	Closed	1988	125.00	450
1989 Mother's Day (with Carriage)	3,000	1989	75.00	465-485
1994 Nanny	Closed	1997	66.00	70-180
1989 Newsboy with Bike	Closed	1992	78.00	125-200
1998 Nurse	Open		60.00	60
1997 One Man Band	Open		69.50	70
1985 Pajama Children (painted flannel)	Closed	1989	35.00	245-275
1985 Pajama Children (red flannel)	Closed	1989	35.00	275-338
1990 Parson	Closed	1993	44.00	125-180
1998 Peddler	Open		120.00	120
1998 Photographer	Open		70.00	70
1996 Pilgrim Adults	Open		53.00	54
1997 Pilgrim Children	Open		53.50	54
1990 Postman	Closed	1993	45.00	125-250
1996 Puppeteer	Open		54.00	54
1994 Sandwich Board Man (red board)	Closed	1994	52.00	135-150
1994 Sandwich Board Man (white board)	Closed	1996	52.00	75-125
1993 School Kids	Closed	1994	48.00	85-250
1992 Schoolteacher	Closed	1994	48.00	112-125
1998 Seated Victorian Woman w/ Baby	Open		70.00	70
1981 Thanksgiving Lady (Clay Hands)	Closed	1981	Unkn.	2000
1981 Thanksgiving Man (Clay Hands)	Closed	1981	Unkn.	2000
1994 Treetop Angel	Closed	1996	50.00	50
1982 Valentine Boy	Closed	1983	32.00	550-940
1982 Valentine Girl	Closed	1983	32.00	550-940
1990 Victorian Girl On Rocking Horse (blonde)	Closed	1991	70.00	180
1990 Victorian Girl On Rocking Horse (brunette)	Closed	1991	70.00	200-210
1992 Victorian Mother with Toddler (Fall/Win-green)	Closed	1993	60.00	150-200
1993 Victorian Mother with Toddler (Spr/Sum-blue)	Closed	1993	61.00	150
1992 Victorian Mother with Toddler (Spr/Sum-white)	Closed	1993	60.00	100-125
1998 Woman Selling Candles	Open		66.00	66
1997 Woman Selling Wreath	Open		68.00	68
1997 Woman w/ Gingerbread House	Open		60.00	60

Store Exclusives-Christmas Dove - J. Byers

YEAR ISSUE	EDITION LIMIT	YEAR RETD.	ISSUE PRICE	*QUOTE U.S.$
1995 Dove Children (pr)	Closed	1996	96.00	350-360

Store Exclusives-Christmas Loft - J. Byers

YEAR ISSUE	EDITION LIMIT	YEAR RETD.	ISSUE PRICE	*QUOTE U.S.$
1991 Russian Santa	40	1991	100.00	600-650

Store Exclusives-Country Christmas - J. Byers

YEAR ISSUE	EDITION LIMIT	YEAR RETD.	ISSUE PRICE	*QUOTE U.S.$
1988 Toymaker	600	1988	59.00	850-1000

Store Exclusives-Foster's Exclusives - J. Byers

YEAR ISSUE	EDITION LIMIT	YEAR RETD.	ISSUE PRICE	*QUOTE U.S.$
1995 American Boy	100	1995	50.00	500

Store Exclusives-Long's Jewelers - J. Byers

YEAR ISSUE	EDITION LIMIT	YEAR RETD.	ISSUE PRICE	*QUOTE U.S.$
1981 Leprechaun (with bucket)	Closed	N/A	N/A	2000

Store Exclusives-Nuance - J. Byers

YEAR ISSUE	EDITION LIMIT	YEAR RETD.	ISSUE PRICE	*QUOTE U.S.$
1995 Kids w/Mittens (pr)	Closed	1995	94.00	94

Store Exclusives-Port-O-Call - J. Byers

YEAR ISSUE	EDITION LIMIT	YEAR RETD.	ISSUE PRICE	*QUOTE U.S.$
1986 Cherub Angel-blue	Closed	1987	N/A	275-400
1986 Cherub Angel-cream	Closed	1987	N/A	400
1986 Cherub Angel-pink	Closed	1987	N/A	275-400
1987 Cherub Angel-rose	Closed	1987	N/A	275-400

Store Exclusives-Snow Goose - J. Byers

YEAR ISSUE	EDITION LIMIT	YEAR RETD.	ISSUE PRICE	*QUOTE U.S.$
1988 Man with Goose	600	1988	60.00	400-650

Store Exclusives-Stacy's Gifts & Collectibles - J. Byers

YEAR ISSUE	EDITION LIMIT	YEAR RETD.	ISSUE PRICE	*QUOTE U.S.$
1987 Santa in Rocking Chair with Boy	100	1987	130.00	1000
1987 Santa in Rocking Chair with Girl	100	1987	130.00	1000

Store Exclusives-Talbots - J. Byers

YEAR ISSUE	EDITION LIMIT	YEAR RETD.	ISSUE PRICE	*QUOTE U.S.$
1990 Victorian Family of Four	Closed	N/A	N/A	375-450
1993 Skating Girl/Boy	Retrd.	N/A	N/A	280-400
1994 Man w/Log Carrier	Closed	N/A	N/A	130-150
1994 Family of Four/Sweaters	Retrd.	N/A	N/A	550
1995 Santa in Sleigh	1,625	1995	88.00	125-200
1995 Boy & Girl Skaters	Closed	1995	110.00	250

Store Exclusives-Truffles - J. Byers

YEAR ISSUE	EDITION LIMIT	YEAR RETD.	ISSUE PRICE	*QUOTE U.S.$
1997 Peddler	Closed	1997	110.00	110

Store Exclusives-Tudor Cottage Exclusives - J. Byers

YEAR ISSUE	EDITION LIMIT	YEAR RETD.	ISSUE PRICE	*QUOTE U.S.$
1993 Penny Children (boy/girl)	Closed	1993	42.00	500

*Quotes have been rounded up to nearest dollar

Store Exclusives-Wayside Country Store Exclusives - J. Byers

YEAR ISSUE	EDITION LIMIT	YEAR RETD.	ISSUE PRICE	*QUOTE U.S.$
1988 Colonial Lady s/n	600	1988	49.00	500-600
1986 Colonial Lamplighter s/n	600	1986	46.00	750
1987 Colonial Watchman s/n	600	1987	49.00	750
1995 Sunday School Boy	150	1995	55.00	200-250
1995 Sunday School Girl	150	1995	55.00	200-250
1996 Victorian Lady Centerpiece	50	1996	N/A	200-250
1995 Victorian Lady Centerpiece	50	1995	N/A	200-250

Store Exclusives-Wooden Soldier - J. Byers

YEAR ISSUE	EDITION LIMIT	YEAR RETD.	ISSUE PRICE	*QUOTE U.S.$
XX Victorian Lamp Lighter	Closed	N/A	N/A	175-200

Store Exclusives-Woodstock Inn - J. Byers

YEAR ISSUE	EDITION LIMIT	YEAR RETD.	ISSUE PRICE	*QUOTE U.S.$
1987 Skier Boy	200	1987	40.00	250-350
1987 Skier Girl	200	1987	40.00	250-350
1991 Sugarin Kids (Woodstock)	Closed	1991	41.00	300-350
1988 Woodstock Lady	Closed	1988	41.00	350
1988 Woodstock Man	Closed	1988	41.00	350
1988 Woodstock Man & Woman Set	Closed	1988	82.00	563

Tour Pieces - J. Byers

YEAR ISSUE	EDITION LIMIT	YEAR RETD.	ISSUE PRICE	*QUOTE U.S.$
1996 Amish Boy (blue or purple)	Closed	1996	54.00	200-263
1997 Amish Girl (blue or purple)	Closed	1997	54.00	54
1998 Best of Times Lady	Yr.Iss.		49.00	49
1998 20th Anniversary Newsboy	Yr.Iss.		48.00	48

Calico Kittens/Enesco Corporation

Calico Kittens - P. Hillman

YEAR ISSUE	EDITION LIMIT	YEAR RETD.	ISSUE PRICE	*QUOTE U.S.$
1995 Always Thinking Of You 112437	Retrd.	1998	14.50	15
1996 April Showers 155500	Retrd.	1998	17.50	18
1995 Buttoned Up with Love 104094	Retrd.	1996	13.50	14
1993 Dressed In Our Holiday Best 628190	Retrd.	1996	15.50	16
1994 Extra Special 624624	Retrd.	1996	15.00	15
1995 Fishing For A Friend 112453	Retrd.	1998	14.50	15
1993 Friends Are Cuddles Of Love 627976	Retrd.	1996	20.00	20
1996 Friendship Grows When Shared 129321	Retrd.	1998	15.00	15
1995 Good As New 113301	Retrd.	1998	14.50	15
1993 A Good Friend Warms The Heart 627984	Retrd.	1996	15.00	15
1995 Grandma's Are Sew Full Of Love 104108	Retrd.	1996	13.50	14
1994 Hand Knitted With Love 626023	Retrd.	1996	13.50	27
1994 Home Sweet Home 624705	Retrd.	1996	15.00	15
1993 I'm All Fur You 627968	Retrd.	1996	15.00	15
1995 I'm Lost Without You 112488	Retrd.	1998	14.50	15
1994 Joy To The World "Joy" 625264	Retrd.	1997	22.50	23
1996 Kite Tails 155497	Retrd.	1998	17.50	18
1994 Love 624721	Retrd.	1996	15.00	15
1995 Love Pours From My Heart 102210	Retrd.	1998	22.50	23
1994 A Loving Gift "Love" 625272	Retrd.	1997	22.50	25
1995 My Favorite Companion 112410	Retrd.	1998	14.50	15
1995 Nothing Is Sweeter Than Mom 104086	Retrd.	1996	13.50	14
1993 Our Friendship Blossomed From The Heart 627887	Retrd.	1996	15.00	15
1994 Our Friendship Is A Quilt Of Love 626015	Retrd.	1996	13.50	14
1994 Peace On Earth "Peace" 625256	Retrd.	1997	22.50	23
1995 A Playful Afternoon 112429	Retrd.	1998	14.50	15
1994 Purr-fect Friends 624691	Retrd.	1996	15.00	15
1995 A Purr-fect Pair 112445	Retrd.	1998	14.50	15
1994 Sew Happy It's Your Birthday 625965	Retrd.	1996	13.50	14
1995 Sweet Dreams 112461	Retrd.	1998	14.50	15
1994 Tea And You Hit The Spot 625981	Retrd.	1996	13.50	14
1994 Thinking Of You 624713	Retrd.	1996	15.00	15
1994 True Love (musical) 622702	Retrd.	1996	60.00	60
1995 An Unexpected Treat 112321	Retrd.	1998	14.50	15
1993 Waiting For A Friend Like You 627895	Retrd.	1996	30.00	30
1993 We Wish You a Merry Christmas (musical) 627526	Retrd.	1997	50.00	50
1993 We're A Purr-fect Pair 627925	Retrd.	1996	25.00	25
1993 Wrapped In The Warmth Of Friendship 628174	Retrd.	1996	17.50	18
1994 You Always Top Off My Days 626007	Retrd.	1996	13.50	14
1994 You And Me 624748	Retrd.	1996	15.00	15
1993 You're A Friend Fur-ever 628018	Retrd.	1996	20.00	28-34
1994 You're A Special Aunt 651117	Retrd.	1997	12.00	12
1994 You're A Special Friend 651117	Retrd.	1997	12.00	12
1994 You're A Special Grandma 651117	Retrd.	1997	12.00	12
1994 You're A Special Mom 651117	Retrd.	1997	12.00	12
1994 You're A Special Niece 651117	Retrd.	1997	12.00	12
1994 You're A Special Sister 651117	Retrd.	1997	12.00	12
1994 Your Friendship Is My Silver Lining 625973	Retrd.	1996	13.50	14

Calico Kittens-Nativity - P. Hillman

YEAR ISSUE	EDITION LIMIT	YEAR RETD.	ISSUE PRICE	*QUOTE U.S.$
1994 Friends Come From Afar 625248	Retrd.	1997	17.50	18
1993 I'll Bring A Special Gift For You, Friendship Is The Best Gift Of All, Sharing The Gift Of Friendship, set/3 628476	Retrd.	1997	55.00	55
1993 A Purr-fect Angel From Above 628468	Retrd.	1997	15.00	15
1993 Sharing A Special Gift Of Love, Always Watching Over You, set/2 628484	Retrd.	1997	35.00	35

Calico Kittens-Springtime Friends - P. Hillman

YEAR ISSUE	EDITION LIMIT	YEAR RETD.	ISSUE PRICE	*QUOTE U.S.$
1993 A Bundle Of Love 628433	Retrd.	1997	13.50	14-17
1995 Friendship Is The Best Blessing 102679	Retrd.	1997	20.00	20
1995 Furry And Feathered Friends 102636	Retrd.	1997	20.00	20
1995 Hats Off To A Perfect Friendship 129437	Retrd.	1997	20.00	20
1993 Just Thinking About You 627917	Retrd.	1997	20.00	20
1995 Love Blooms Fur-Ever 102644	Retrd.	1997	17.50	18
1993 Loves Special Delivery 628425	Retrd.	1997	13.50	14
1994 A Purr-fect Love Knot 626031	Retrd.	1997	50.00	50
1995 You Make Life Colorful 102601	Retrd.	1997	25.00	25
1993 You'll Always Be Close To My Heart 627909	Retrd.	1997	20.00	20
1993 You're Always There When I Need You 627992	Retrd.	1997	25.00	25
1995 Your Patchwork Charm Shows Through 129453	Retrd.	1997	17.50	18

Cardew Design

"English Bettys" - P. Cardew

YEAR ISSUE	EDITION LIMIT	YEAR RETD.	ISSUE PRICE	*QUOTE U.S.$
1995 Cat Got the Cream-Brown Betty	Retrd.	1998	50.00	58
1996 Chess-Black Betty	Retrd.	1998	50.00	55
1996 Gardening-Green Betty	Open		50.00	60
1996 Golf-White Betty	Retrd.	1998	50.00	55
1995 Harvest Pies-Brown Betty	Retrd.	1998	50.00	60
1996 London Touring-Black Betty	Retrd.	1998	50.00	55
1996 Magician-Black Betty	Retrd.	1996	50.00	55
1995 Ploughman's Lunch-Brown Betty	Retrd.	1996	50.00	55
1995 Rise & "Shoe" Shine-Brown Betty	Retrd.	1996	50.00	55
1995 Summer Picnic-Brown Betty	Retrd.	1996	50.00	55
1995 Tea Table-Brown Betty	Open		50.00	60
1996 Teddy Bear's Picnic-Yellow Betty	Open		50.00	65

Cardew Collectors' Club - P. Cardew

YEAR ISSUE	EDITION LIMIT	YEAR RETD.	ISSUE PRICE	*QUOTE U.S.$
1995 Moving Day	5,000	1997	175.00	200
1995 Tiny Tea Chest	Retrd.	1997	Gift	N/A
1997 Willow Pattern Tea Cup Teapot	Yr.Iss.	1997	45.00	45
1997 Mug One-Cup	Yr.Iss.	1997	Gift	N/A
1998 Collectors Tea For Two/Victorian Tea Table	Yr.Iss.		Gift	N/A
1998 Sewing Machine	5,000		185.00	185

Disney Full Sized Teapots - P. Cardew

YEAR ISSUE	EDITION LIMIT	YEAR RETD.	ISSUE PRICE	*QUOTE U.S.$
1996 Donald in Mangle	5,000		140.00	170
1997 Goofy - Baking Day	5,000		225.00	225
1997 Mickey - Stove	5,000		225.00	225
1997 Minnie - Dressing Table	5,000		225.00	225
1998 Minnie/Mickey Piano - 70th Anniversary	5,000		250.00	250
1998 Winnie The Pooh	5,000		250.00	250

Disney One-Cup Teapots - P. Cardew

YEAR ISSUE	EDITION LIMIT	YEAR RETD.	ISSUE PRICE	*QUOTE U.S.$
1998 Donald Santa	5,000		75.00	75
1998 Goofy Santa	5,000		75.00	75

Disney Tiny Teapots - P. Cardew

YEAR ISSUE	EDITION LIMIT	YEAR RETD.	ISSUE PRICE	*QUOTE U.S.$
1998 Donald	10,000		20.00	20
1998 Goofy	10,000		20.00	20
1998 Mickey	10,000		20.00	20
1996 Mickey Santa	5,000	1996	75.00	75

Disney Two-Cup Teapots - P. Cardew

YEAR ISSUE	EDITION LIMIT	YEAR RETD.	ISSUE PRICE	*QUOTE U.S.$
1996 101 Dalmatians	5,000		110.00	110
1996 Beauty & The Beast	5,000		80.00	80
1996 Cinderella's Dress	10,000	1998	80.00	110
1998 Jungle Book	5,000		110.00	110
1997 Lady & Tramp	5,000		95.00	95
1996 Madhatters Tea Party	5,000	1998	80.00	80
1998 Mickey Automobile	5,000		225.00	225
1998 Mickey Aviator	5,000		225.00	225
1997 Pooh Bear	5,000	1998	95.00	95
1998 Winnie The Pooh Hutch	5,000		120.00	120

Event Piece - P. Cardew

YEAR ISSUE	EDITION LIMIT	YEAR RETD.	ISSUE PRICE	*QUOTE U.S.$
1996 "Travellers Return"	5,000	1996	45.00	75

Limited Edition Full Sized Teapots - P. Cardew

YEAR ISSUE	EDITION LIMIT	YEAR RETD.	ISSUE PRICE	*QUOTE U.S.$
1990 Allsorts of Liquorice	Retrd.	1993	60.00	405-450
1998 Blue Willow Tea Table	5,000		185.00	185
1970 Cactus	Retrd.	1978	60.00	1080-1260
1997 Charles Atlas Stand	5,000		250.00	375
1997 Classical Fireplace	5,000		175.00	180
1998 Do-It-Yourself	5,000		185.00	185
1997 Farmhouse Dresser	5,000		175.00	188
1997 Farmhouse Fireplace	5,000		175.00	180
1997 Gardener's Bench	5,000		175.00	188
1996 Heart	Retrd.	N/A	N/A	315
1998 Kirvan's Tea Merchant	5,000		225.00	229
1998 Kirvan's Tea Van	5,000		225.00	229
1995 Kitchen Sink	5,000		175.00	188
1995 Ladies Dressing Table	5,000	1998	175.00	175
1996 Lilliput Lane Market Stall	Retrd.	1996	250.00	250
1993 Punctualitea	Retrd.	1995	N/A	180
1995 Refrigerator	5,000		175.00	180
1997 Rington's Tea Merchant	5,000	1997	250.00	250
1998 Sewing Machine II	5,000		185.00	185
1995 Snowman	Retrd.	N/A	N/A	360-405
1995 Teapot Market Stall	5,000	1996	199.00	199
1996 Teapot Market Stall Mark II	5,000		199.00	265
1996 Teddy Bear's Picnic	5,000		175.00	229
1995 Washing Machine	5,000	1998	175.00	180
1996 Welsh Dresser	5,000	1996	175.00	175

Market Stall Series - P. Cardew

YEAR ISSUE	EDITION LIMIT	YEAR RETD.	ISSUE PRICE	*QUOTE U.S.$
1993 Antiques Market Stall	Retrd.	1996	160.00	160
1993 China Market Stall	Retrd.	1997	160.00	175
1993 Hardware Market Stall	5,000	1997	160.00	175
1995 Shoe Market Stall	5,000	1998	160.00	188

One-Cup Teapot Collection - P. Cardew

YEAR ISSUE	EDITION LIMIT	YEAR RETD.	ISSUE PRICE	*QUOTE U.S.$
1995 50's Stove	Retrd.	1996	45.00	45
1990 Allsorts of Liquorice	Retrd.	1995	N/A	85
1994 Baking Day	Retrd.	1995	45.00	45
1996 Bloomingdales	Retrd.	1997	45.00	45
1995 China Stall	Retrd.	1998	45.00	64
1995 Christmas Presents	Retrd.	1998	45.00	45
1996 Christmas Tree	Retrd.	1998	45.00	64
1994 Crimewriter's Desk	Retrd.	1996	45.00	45
1996 Egg Cup	Open		45.00	48
1996 Gardening	Open		45.00	70
1996 Golf Bag	Open		45.00	48
1996 Grandfather Clock	Open		45.00	48
1997 Hiker's Rest	Retrd.	1998	60.00	64
1995 Kitchen Sink	Retrd.	1996	45.00	45
1995 Lady's Dressing Table	Retrd.	1998	45.00	48
1995 Moving Day	Retrd.	1998	45.00	70
1995 Refrigerator	Retrd.	1998	45.00	64
1996 Romance/Heart/Valentine	Retrd.	1998	45.00	48
1996 Santa Claus	Retrd.	1998	45.00	64
1995 Sewing Machine	Open		45.00	64
1995 Snowman	Retrd.	1998	N/A	65
1995 Tea Scoop	Retrd.	1996	45.00	45
1995 Tea Shop Counter	Retrd.	1996	45.00	45
1995 Teddy Bear's Picnic	Open		45.00	70
1995 Toy Box	Retrd.	1996	45.00	45
1997 Victorian Fireplace	Open		45.00	64
1995 Victorian Tea Table	Retrd.	1996	45.00	45
1997 Victorian Washstand	Retrd.	1998	45.00	64
1995 Washing Machine	Retrd.	1998	45.00	64
1995 Washing Mangle	Retrd.	1996	45.00	45
1995 Welsh Dresser	Retrd.	1998	45.00	64

Standard Teapots - P. Cardew

YEAR ISSUE	EDITION LIMIT	YEAR RETD.	ISSUE PRICE	*QUOTE U.S.$
1991 50's Stove	Retrd.	1996	140.00	140
1992 Baking Day	Retrd.	1998	140.00	180
1992 Crime Writer's Desk	Open		140.00	180
1991 Cupid's Cloud & Pedestal	Retrd.	1994	125.00	1080-1440
1991 Mechanics Bench	Retrd.	1994	100.00	450-540
1991 Safe	Retrd.	1994	100.00	270
1992 Sewing Machine	Retrd.	1997	140.00	140
1993 Tea Shop Counter	Retrd.	1995	140.00	140
1991 Toy Box	Retrd.	1996	140.00	217-315
1992 Victorian Tea Table	Retrd.	1997	140.00	145
1993 Victorian Washstand	Retrd.	1995	140.00	140
1992 Washing Mangle	Retrd.	1996	140.00	140

Tiny Teapots - P. Cardew

YEAR ISSUE	EDITION LIMIT	YEAR RETD.	ISSUE PRICE	*QUOTE U.S.$
1995 50's Stove	Retrd.	1997	10.00	10
1995 Baking Day	Retrd.	1996	10.00	10
1996 Bedside Table	Retrd.	1996	10.00	10
1995 Crime Writer's Desk	Retrd.	1996	10.00	12
1995 Kitchen Sink	Retrd.	1997	10.00	10
1995 Refrigerator	Retrd.	1996	10.00	10
1995 Sewing Machine	Retrd.	1997	10.00	10
1995 Tea Shop Counter	Retrd.	1996	10.00	12
1995 Teddy Bear's Picnic	Retrd.	1996	10.00	10
1995 Toy Box	Retrd.	1996	10.00	10
1995 Victorian Wash Stand	Retrd.	1996	10.00	10
1995 Washing Machine	Retrd.	1996	10.00	10
1995 Washing Mangle	Retrd.	1997	10.00	10
1996 Golf Trolley	Retrd.	1997	10.00	10
1996 Petrol Pump	Retrd.	1996	10.00	10
1996 Heart	Retrd.	1996	10.00	10
1996 Radio	Retrd.	1997	10.00	10
1996 Safe	Retrd.	1996	10.00	10
1996 50's TV	Retrd.	1997	10.00	10
1996 Fireplace	Retrd.	1997	10.00	10
1996 Grandfather's Clock	Retrd.	1997	10.00	10
1996 Lady's Dressing Table	Retrd.	1996	10.00	10
1996 Victorian Tea Table	Retrd.	1996	10.00	10
1996 Welsh Dresser	Retrd.	1997	10.00	10

Two-Cup Teapot Collection - P. Cardew

YEAR ISSUE	EDITION LIMIT	YEAR RETD.	ISSUE PRICE	*QUOTE U.S.$
1997 Anniversary Teatable	Retrd.	1998	75.00	75
1997 Birthday Teatable	Retrd.	1998	75.00	80
1997 Cats on Dresser/Colour Box Welsh Dresser	Retrd.	1998	75.00	75
1997 Christening Teatable	Retrd.	1998	75.00	80
1997 Jewelery Box	Open		75.00	87
1997 Safe	Retrd.	1998	75.00	87
1997 Sewing Machine	Open		75.00	80
1997 Tea Service Tea Table	Retrd.	1998	75.00	87
1997 Television	Retrd.	1998	75.00	80
1997 Welsh Dresser	Open		75.00	75
1997 Willow Pattern Teatable	Open		75.00	87

Cast Art Industries

Bumpkins - A. & T. Fabrizio

YEAR ISSUE	EDITION LIMIT	YEAR RETD.	ISSUE PRICE	*QUOTE U.S.$
1996 Angel Baby 01031	Closed	1998	13.00	13
1996 Angel of Mercy 01009	Closed	1998	13.00	13
1997 Angel Wings (bell) 01060	Closed	1998	15.00	15
1996 Anxious Groom 01011	Closed	1998	13.00	13
1996 Baby Boomer (heart box) 01043	Closed	1998	20.00	20
1996 Baby Makes Three 01006	Closed	1998	12.00	12
1997 Ballet Beauty (ballerina box) 01054	Closed	1998	20.00	20

*Quotes have been rounded up to nearest dollar

FIGURINES

YEAR ISSUE	EDITION LIMIT	YEAR RETD.	ISSUE PRICE	*QUOTE U.S.$
1996 Bare Facts 01003	Closed	1998	13.00	13
1997 Be Mine 01056	Closed	1998	14.00	14
1997 Beau Bean Bag 01066	Closed	1998	5.00	5
1996 Best Friends 01018	Closed	1998	25.00	25
1996 Blushing Bride 01012	Closed	1998	13.00	13
1996 Born to Shop 01017	Closed	1998	16.00	16
1996 Bottoms Up 01002	Closed	1998	13.00	13
1996 Bumpkinville Choo Choo, set/3 01037	Closed	1998	150.00	150
1996 Bumpkinville Gothic Lady 01014	Closed	1998	13.00	13
1996 Bumpkinville Gothic Man 01015	Closed	1998	13.00	13
1996 Bumpkinville's Finest 01020	Closed	1998	16.00	16
1996 Busy, Busy, Busy 01035	Closed	1998	14.00	14
1997 Button Bean Bag 01067	Closed	1998	5.00	5
1996 Catch of the Day 01033	Closed	1998	25.00	25
1996 Cheers To You 01036	Closed	1998	13.00	13
1996 Do-Si-Do 01038	Closed	1998	14.00	14
1996 The Doctor Is In 01010	Closed	1998	14.00	14
1996 Dreamin' of You 01008	Closed	1998	13.00	13
1996 Everything Nice 01046	Closed	1998	6.00	6
1997 First Love 01055	Closed	1998	25.00	25
1996 Forever Friends 01013	Closed	1998	25.00	25
1996 Free Kick 01041	Closed	1998	13.00	13
1997 Free Throw 01087	Closed	1998	13.00	13
1996 Golden Years 01029	Closed	1998	30.00	30
1997 Happy Face 01057	Closed	1998	14.00	14
1997 Heel & Toe 01086	Closed	1998	13.00	13
1996 Here's My Heart (heart box) 01023	Closed	1998	20.00	20
1996 Honey Bee Mine (heart box) 01032	Closed	1998	20.00	20
1996 Hot Shot 01019	Closed	1998	14.00	14
1996 It's a Boy 01004	Closed	1998	12.00	12
1996 It's a Gril 01005	Closed	1998	12.00	12
1997 Just Ducky 01064	Closed	1998	14.00	14
1997 Just Hatched 01065	Closed	1998	12.00	12
1996 Lil' Slugger 01007	Closed	1998	13.00	13
1997 Match Point 01088	Closed	1998	13.00	13
1997 Pencils 'N Stuff 01061	Closed	1998	16.00	16
1996 A Penny For Your Thoughts (bank) 01025	Closed	1998	25.00	25
1996 A Penny Saved (bank) 01024	Closed	1998	25.00	25
1996 Ride 'em Cowboy 01021	Closed	1998	16.00	16
1996 Ride 'em Cowgirl 01022	Closed	1998	16.00	16
1996 Saturday Hero 01016	Closed	1998	13.00	13
1997 School's Out 01059	Closed	1998	13.00	13
1997 Secretary Stuff 01063	Closed	1998	16.00	16
1996 Shooting Star 01042	Closed	1998	13.00	13
1996 Sleighmates 01030	Closed	1998	25.00	25
1996 Spice 01045	Closed	1998	6.00	6
1996 Standing Room Only 01034	Closed	1998	18.00	18
1996 Sugar 01044	Closed	1998	6.00	60
1997 Teacher Stuff 01062	Closed	1998	16.00	16
1997 Tooth Fairy Box 01058	Closed	1998	19.00	19
1996 Two Step 01040	Closed	1998	14.00	14
1996 Unplugged 01039	Closed	1998	14.00	14
1996 Welcome To Bumpkinville (logo) 01001	Closed	1998	25.00	25

Bumpkins Nativity - A. & T. Fabrizio

YEAR ISSUE	EDITION LIMIT	YEAR RETD.	ISSUE PRICE	*QUOTE U.S.$
1997 Oh Holy Night Nativity Assortment, set/10	Closed	1998	130.00	130
1997 Baby Jesus 01072	Closed	1998	set	set
1997 Mary 01073	Closed	1998	set	set
1997 Joseph 01074	Closed	1998	set	set
1997 Wise Man w/Teddy 01075	Closed	1998	set	set
1997 Wise Man w/Gift 01076	Closed	1998	set	set
1997 Wise Man w/Goose 01077	Closed	1998	set	set
1997 Shepherd 01078	Closed	1998	set	set
1997 Standing Lamb 01079	Closed	1998	set	set
1997 Resting Lamb 01080	Closed	1998	set	set
1997 Manger in Collector Box 01082	Closed	1998	set	set

Dreamsicles - K. Haynes

YEAR ISSUE	EDITION LIMIT	YEAR RETD.	ISSUE PRICE	*QUOTE U.S.$
1997 Anticipation - ICE Commemorative Figurine-SP002	Open		29.95	30
1992 Baby Love-DC147	Retrd.	1995	7.00	10
1995 Best Buddies-DC159	12/98		14.00	14
1991 Best Pals-DC103	Retrd.	1994	15.00	35-45
1992 Bluebird On My Shoulder-DC115	Retrd.	1995	19.00	25-30
1994 Born This Day-DC230	Retrd.	1998	16.00	16
1995 Brotherhood-DC307	12/98		20.00	20
1996 Bubble Bath-DC416	12/98		22.00	22
1992 Bundle of Joy-DC142	Retrd.	1995	7.00	145-295
1993 By the Silvery Moon-DC253	10,000	1994	100.00	125-150
1992 Caroler - Center Scroll-DC216	Retrd.	1995	19.00	25
1992 Caroler - Left Scroll-DC218	Retrd.	1995	19.00	25
1992 Caroler - Right Scroll-DC217	Retrd.	1995	19.00	25
1996 Carousel Ride-DS283	12/98		150.00	150
1994 Carousel-DC174	Suspd.		35.00	45-50
1993 Catch a Falling Star-DC166	Retrd.	1997	12.00	12
1991 Cherub and Child-DC100	Retrd.	1995	15.00	100
1992 Cherub For All Seasons-DC114	Retrd.	1995	23.00	75-95
1992 Cherub-DC111	10,000	1992	50.00	100
1992 Cherub-DC112	10,000	1993	50.00	225-250
1996 A Child Is Born-DC256	10,000	1996	95.00	95
1992 A Child's Prayer-DC145	Retrd.	1995	7.00	7
1996 Corona Centennial	Retrd.	1996	Gift	N/A
1996 Crossing Guardian-DC422	12/98		40.00	40
1994 Cuddle Blanket-DC153	Retrd.	1995	6.50	7
1997 Cutie Pie-10241	12,500		42.00	42
1996 Daffodil Days DC343 (American Cancer Society Figurine)	Retrd.	1998	15.00	15-35
1992 Dance Ballerina Dance-DC140	Retrd.	1995	37.00	42
1991 Dimples DA-100	Retrd.	1991	5.50	6
1992 Dream A Little Dream-DC144	Retrd.	1995	7.00	10
1997 Dreamboat-10060 (special edition)	Retrd.	1998	90.00	90
1994 Eager to Please-DC154	Retrd.	1995	6.50	10
1992 Flying Lesson-DC251	10,000	1993	80.00	950-1500
1997 Follow Me-10050	12/98		28.00	28
1991 Forever Friends-DC102	Retrd.	1994	15.00	45-50
1993 Forever Yours-DC110	Retrd.	1995	44.00	75
1996 Free Kittens-DK038	12/98		18.00	18
1996 Free Puppies-DK039	12/98		18.00	18
1995 Get Well Soon-DC244	Retrd.	1997	11.00	11
1997 Handmade With Love-10324	10,000		78.00	78
1997 Happy Landings-10156	5,000	1997	88.00	88
1997 Hear No Evil-10040	Open		18.00	18
1996 Heaven's Gate-DC257 (5th Anniversary piece)	15,000		129.00	129
1991 Heavenly Dreamer-DC106	Retrd.	1996	11.50	12
1994 Here's Looking at You-DC172	Retrd.	1995	25.00	35
1995 Hugabye Baby-DC701	Retrd.	1997	12.50	13
1991 Hunny Buns DA-101	Retrd.	1995	5.50	6
1994 I Can Read-DC151	Retrd.	1995	6.50	10
1994 International Collectible Exposition Commemorative Figurine	Retrd.	1995	34.95	116-150
1997 It's Your Day-10220	12/98		30.00	30
1992 Life Is Good-DC119	Retrd.	1996	10.00	15
1992 Little Darlin'-DC146	Retrd.	1995	7.00	10
1993 Little Dickens-DC127	Retrd.	1995	24.00	25
1992 Littlest Angel-DC143	Retrd.	1995	7.00	10
1993 Long Fellow-DC126	Retrd.	1995	24.00	25-32
1995 Love Me Do-DC194	12/98		15.00	15
1993 Love My Kitty-DC130	Retrd.	1997	14.50	15-18
1993 Love My Puppy-DC131	Retrd.	1997	12.50	13-18
1993 Love My Teddy-DC132	Retrd.	1997	14.50	15-18
1997 Lyrical Lute-10169	12/98		29.00	29
1993 Me And My Shadow-DC116	Retrd.	1996	19.00	19-22
1997 Mellow Cello-10170	12/98		39.00	39
1991 Mischief Maker-DC105	Retrd.	1996	10.00	10
1993 Miss Morningstar-DC141	Retrd.	1996	25.00	35
1994 Moon Dance-DC210	Retrd.	1997	29.00	29-38
1994 Moon Dance-DC210	Retrd.	1997	29.00	29-38
1991 Musician w/Cymbals-5154	Suspd.		22.00	22
1991 Musician w/Drums-5152	Suspd.		22.00	22
1991 Musician w/Flute-5153	Suspd.		22.00	22-75
1991 Musician w/Trumpet-5151	Suspd.		22.00	22
1992 My Funny Valentine-DC201	Suspd.		17.00	28
1995 Nursery Rhyme-DC229	Suspd.		42.00	50
1995 One World-DC306	12/98		24.00	24
1993 P.S. I Love You-DC203	Retrd.	1997	7.50	8
1995 Picture Perfect-DC255	10,000	1995	100.00	125
1993 Poetry In Motion-DC113 (spec. ed.)	Retrd.	1997	80.00	80-90
1996 Pull Toy-DK027	12/98		18.00	18
1995 Range Rider-DC305	12/98		15.00	15
1994 The Recital-DC254	10,000	1994	135.00	165-225
1997 See No Evil-10041	Open		18.00	18
1994 Side By Side-DC169	Retrd.	1995	31.50	32-50
1991 Sitting Pretty-DC101	Retrd.	1996	9.50	12
1994 Snowflake-DC117	Suspd.		10.00	14
1997 Speak No Evil-10042	Open		18.00	18
1997 String Serenade-10168	12/98		30.00	30
1994 Sucking My Thumb-DC156	Retrd.	1995	6.50	7-10
1994 Sugarfoot-DC167	Retrd.	1998	25.00	25
1994 Surprise Gift-DC152	Retrd.	1995	6.50	10
1993 Sweet Dreams-DC125	Retrd.	1995	29.00	35-45
1996 Swimming For Hope-DC016	Retrd.	1996	75.00	75
1997 Taking Aim-DC432	12/98		33.00	33
1996 Tea Party-DC015 (GCC event)	Retrd.	1996	19.00	20-40
1993 Teacher's Pet-DC124	Retrd.	1997	11.00	11
1993 Teeter Tots-DC252	10,000	1993	100.00	150-175
1993 Thinking of You-DC129	Retrd.	1997	42.00	44
1993 Tiny Dancer-DC165	Retrd.	1998	14.00	14
1995 Twinkle, Twinkle-DC700	Retrd.	1997	14.50	15
1994 Up All Night-DC155	Retrd.	1995	6.50	10
1998 We Are Winning-10380 (American Cancer Society)	Open		17.00	17
1991 Wild Flower-DC107	Retrd.	1996	10.00	10
1993 Wishin' On A Star-DC120	12/98		10.00	10
1996 Wishing Well-DC423	12/98		35.00	35
1995 Wistful Thinking-DC707	Retrd.	1998	7.00	7

Dreamsicles Club - K. Haynes

YEAR ISSUE	EDITION LIMIT	YEAR RETD.	ISSUE PRICE	*QUOTE U.S.$
1993 A Star is Born-CD001	Retrd.	1993	Gift	75-85
1994 Daydream Believer-CD100	Retrd.	1994	29.95	50-75
1994 Join The Fun-CD002	Retrd.	1994	Gift	40-50
1994 Makin' A List-CD101	Retrd.	1994	47.95	65-75
1995 Three Cheers-CD003	Retrd.	1995	Gift	50-60
1995 Town Crier-CD102	Retrd.	1995	24.95	25
1995 Snowbound-CD103	Retrd.	1996	24.95	25-30
1996 Star Shower-CD004	Retrd.	1996	Gift	35
1996 Heavenly Flowers-CD104	Retrd.	1997	24.95	25
1996 Bee-Friended-CD105	Open		24.95	25
1997 Free Spirit-CD005	Retrd.	1997	Gift	N/A
1997 Peaceable Kingdom-CD106	Open		14.75	15
1997 First Blush-CD109	12,000		49.95	50
1997 Sweet Tooth (w/cookbook)-CD110	Open		19.95	20
1997 Editor's Choice (Newsletter Participation)-CD107	N/A		Gift	N/A
1997 Golden Halo ("Good Samaritan" award)-CD108	N/A		Gift	N/A
1998 Let's Get Together-CD006	Yr.Iss.		Gift	N/A
1998 Summertime Serenade-CD111	Open		14.75	15

Dreamsicles Animals - K. Haynes

YEAR ISSUE	EDITION LIMIT	YEAR RETD.	ISSUE PRICE	*QUOTE U.S.$
1991 Armadillo -5176	Suspd.		13.50	14
1992 Fat Cat-DA555	Retrd.	1994	27.00	27
1991 Hambone-DA344	Retrd.	1996	10.75	20-25
1991 Hamlet-DA342	Retrd.	1996	10.75	11-20
1991 King Rabbit-DA124	Retrd.	1994	73.00	73-115
1991 Mr. Bunny-DA107	Retrd.	1994	28.00	28
1996 Naptime-DA556	Suspd.		18.00	18
1992 Papa Pelican-DA602	Retrd.	1994	22.50	23-30
1991 Pigmalion-DA340	Retrd.	1995	6.25	15-20
1991 Pigtails-DA341	Retrd.	1995	6.25	7-15
1991 Ricky Raccoon -5170	Suspd.		28.00	28
1992 Sir Hareold-DA123	Retrd.	1996	41.50	42
1991 Socrates The Sheep -5029	Suspd.		19.00	19
1991 Wooley Bully-DA327	Retrd.	1994	7.75	8

Dreamsicles Calendar Collection - K. Haynes

YEAR ISSUE	EDITION LIMIT	YEAR RETD.	ISSUE PRICE	*QUOTE U.S.$
1994 Winter Wonderland (January)-DC180	Retrd.	1995	24.00	30
1994 Special Delivery (February)-DC181	Retrd.	1995	24.00	30
1994 Ride Like The Wind (March) -DC182	Retrd.	1995	24.00	30
1994 Springtime Frolic (April)-DC183	Retrd.	1995	24.00	30
1994 Love In Bloom (May)-DC184	Retrd.	1995	24.00	30
1994 Among Friends (June)-DC185	Retrd.	1995	24.00	30-35
1994 Pool Pals (July)-DC186	Retrd.	1995	24.00	30
1994 Nature's Bounty (August)-DC187	Retrd.	1995	24.00	30
1994 School Days (September)-DC188	Retrd.	1995	24.00	30
1994 Autumn Leaves (October)-DC189	Retrd.	1995	24.00	30-35
1994 Now Give Thanks (November)-DC190	Retrd.	1995	24.00	30
1994 Holiday Magic (December)-DC191	Retrd.	1995	24.00	30

Dreamsicles Christmas - K. Haynes

YEAR ISSUE	EDITION LIMIT	YEAR RETD.	ISSUE PRICE	*QUOTE U.S.$
1998 All Aboard!-10364 (7th Ed.)	Yr.Iss.		78.00	78
1992 Baby Love-DX147	Retrd.	1995	7.00	30
1992 Bluebird On My Shoulder-DX115	Retrd.	1995	19.00	19-25
1992 Bundle of Joy-DX142	Retrd.	1995	7.00	7
1992 Caroler - Center Scroll-DX216	Retrd.	1995	19.00	25
1992 Caroler - Left Scroll-DX218	Retrd.	1995	19.00	25
1992 Caroler - Right Scroll-DX217	Retrd.	1995	19.00	25
1996 Carousel Ride-DX283	12/98		150.00	150
1991 Cherub and Child-DX100	Retrd.	1995	14.00	30
1992 A Child's Prayer-DX145	Retrd.	1995	7.00	7
1998 Christmas Eve-10420	5,000		78.00	78
1992 Dream A Little Dream-DX144	Retrd.	1995	7.00	7
1993 Father Christmas-DX246	Suspd.		42.00	42
1993 The Finishing Touches-DX248 (2nd Ed.)	Retrd.	1994	85.00	95-120
1991 Forever Yours-DX110	Retrd.	1995	44.00	44
1991 Heavenly Dreamer-DX106	Retrd.	1996	11.00	11
1994 Here's Looking at You-DX172	Retrd.	1995	25.00	35-37
1994 Holiday on Ice-DX249 (3rd Ed.)	Retrd.	1995	85.00	130-175
1996 Homeward Bound-DX251 (5th Ed.)	Retrd.	1997	80.00	80
1995 Hugabye Baby-DX701	Retrd.	1997	12.50	13
1992 Life Is Good-DX119	Retrd.	1996	10.50	12
1992 Little Darlin'-DX146	Retrd.	1995	7.00	10
1993 Little Dickens-DX127	Retrd.	1995	24.00	25
1992 Littlest Angel-DX143	Retrd.	1995	7.00	7
1993 Long Fellow-DX126	Retrd.	1995	24.00	25
1996 Mall Santa-DX258	12/98		35.00	35
1993 Me And My Shadow-DX116	Retrd.	1996	19.50	20
1991 Mischief Maker-DX105	Retrd.	1996	10.50	11
1993 Miss Morningstar-DX141	Retrd.	1996	25.50	28-40
1995 Poetry In Motion-DX113 (Sp. Ed.)	Retrd.	1996	80.00	100
1991 Santa Bunny-DX203	Retrd.	1994	32.00	32
1992 Santa In Dreamsicle Land-DX247 (1st Ed.)	Retrd.	1993	85.00	250-300
1991 Santa's Elf-DX240	Retrd.	1996	19.00	22
1995 Santa's Kingdom-DX250 (4th Ed.)	Retrd.	1995	80.00	100
1991 Santa's Little Helper-DX109	Retrd.	1998	9.50	10
1994 Side By Side-DX169	Retrd.	1995	31.50	45-50
1991 Sitting Pretty-DX101	Retrd.	1996	10.00	10-15
1997 Sleigh Bells Ring-10187	2,500	1997	48.00	48-95
1994 Stolen Kiss-DX162	Suspd.		12.50	14
1993 Sweet Dreams-DX125	Retrd.	1995	29.00	29
1993 Sweet Dreams-DX125	Retrd.	1995	29.00	29
1993 Sweet Dreams-DX125	Retrd.	1995	29.00	29
1997 Time To Dash-10184 (6th Ed.)	Retrd.	1998	78.00	78
1998 Tis Better to Give-10421	5,000		38.00	38
1995 Twinkle Twinkle-DX700	Retrd.	1997	14.50	15
1991 Wildflower-DX107	Retrd.	1996	10.50	15

Dreamsicles Day Event - K. Haynes

YEAR ISSUE	EDITION LIMIT	YEAR RETD.	ISSUE PRICE	*QUOTE U.S.$
1995 1995 Dreamsicles Event Figurine-DC075	Retrd.	1995	20.00	35-65
1996 Glad Tidings-DD100	Retrd.	1996	15.95	27
1996 Time to Retire-DD103	Retrd.	1996	15.95	16
1997 The Golden Rule-E9701	Retrd.	1997	19.95	20
1998 A Day of Fun-E9801	Yr.Iss.		18.00	18

Dreamsicles Heavenly Classics - K. Haynes & S. Hackett

YEAR ISSUE	EDITION LIMIT	YEAR RETD.	ISSUE PRICE	*QUOTE U.S.$
1996 Bundles of Love-HC370	327	1996	80.00	625-750
1995 The Dedication-DC351	10,000	1996	118.00	150-165
1997 Making Memories-10096 (spec. ed.)	Suspd.		100.00	100

Cavanagh Group Intl.

Coca-Cola Christmas Collectors Society Members' Only - Sundblom, unless otherwise noted

YEAR ISSUE	EDITION LIMIT	YEAR RETD.	ISSUE PRICE	*QUOTE U.S.$
1993 Ho Ho Ho (ornament)	Closed	1993	Gift	25-50
1994 Fishing Bear (ornament) - CGI	Closed	1994	Gift	28-35
1995 Hospitality (ornament)	Closed	1995	Gift	25
1996 Sprite (ornament)	Closed	1996	Gift	N/A
1996 Hollywood - CGI	Closed	1996	35.00	35
1997 Carousel Capers (ornament) - CGI	Closed	1997	Gift	N/A

*Quotes have been rounded up to nearest dollar

YEAR ISSUE	EDITION LIMIT	YEAR RETD.	ISSUE PRICE	*QUOTE U.S.$
1997 Always Friends - CGI	Closed	1997	35.00	35
1998 Passing The Day In A Special Way	12/98		Gift	N/A
1998 I Belong - CGI	12/98		35.00	35
1998 Polar Bear Bean Bag CSO151	25,000		Gift	N/A

Coca-Cola Brand Heritage Collection - Various

YEAR ISSUE	EDITION LIMIT	YEAR RETD.	ISSUE PRICE	*QUOTE U.S.$
1995 Always - CGI	Closed	1996	30.00	30
1995 Always-Musical - CGI	Closed	1996	50.00	50
1998 And Now the Gift For Thirst-Snowglobe - Sundblom	Open		40.00	40
1995 Boy at Well - N. Rockwell	5,000	1997	60.00	60-65
1995 Boy Fishing - N. Rockwell	5,000	1997	60.00	60
1996 Busy Man's Pause - Sundblom	Closed	1997	80.00	80
1998 C Is For Coca-Cola - CGI	10,000		45.00	45
1994 Calendar Girl 1916-Music Box - CGI	500	1996	60.00	60-100
1996 Coca-Cola Stand - CGI	Open		45.00	45
1996 Cool Break - CGI	Open		40.00	45
1994 Dear Santa, Please Pause Here - Sundblom	2,500	1995	80.00	85
1994 Dear Santa, Please Pause Here-Musical - Sundblom	2,500	1995	100.00	100
1996 Decorating The Tree - CGI	Closed	1996	45.00	45
1997 Downhill Derby-CGI	10,000		22.50	23
1994 Eight Polar Bears on Wood - CGI	15,000	1998	100.00	140
1994 Eight Polar Bears on Wood-Musical - CGI	15,000	1998	150.00	150
1995 Elaine - CGI	2,500	1996	100.00	100
1994 Extra Bright Refreshment -Snowglobe - Sundblom	2,500	1996	50.00	50
1996 For Me - Sundblom	Open		40.00	40
1997 For Me-Snowglobe - Sundblom	Open		25.00	25
1998 Friends Make the Job Easier - CGI	10,000		40.00	40
1995 Girl on Swing - CGI	2,500	1996	100.00	100
1996 Gone Fishing - CGI	Closed	1997	60.00	60
1994 Good Boys and Girl - Sundblom	2,500	1995	80.00	80
1994 Good Boys and Girls-Musical - Sundblom	2,500	1995	100.00	100
1994 Good Boys and Girls-Snowglobe - Sundblom	2,000	1995	45.00	45
1994 Hilda Clark 1901-Music Box - CGI	500	1996	60.00	60-85
1994 Hilda Clark 1903-Music Box - CGI	500	1996	60.00	60
1996 Hollywood-Snowglobe - CGI	Closed	1997	50.00	50
1995 The Homecoming - S. Stearman	2,500	1995	125.00	125
1995 Hospitality - Sundblom	5,000	1997	35.00	35
1998 It Will Refresh You Too - Sundblom	10,000		40.00	40
1998 It Will Refresh You Too-Musical - Sundblom	Open		60.00	60
1997 A Job Well Done Deserves a Coke - CGI	10,000		22.50	23
1997 Mama Look! Is He a Bear Too? - CGI	10,000	1998	22.50	23
1998 On The Road to Adventure - CGI	10,000		45.00	45
1995 Playing with Dad - CGI	Closed	1996	40.00	40
1996 A Refreshing Break - N. Rockwell	Closed	1997	60.00	60
1996 Refreshing Treat - CGI	Closed	1996	45.00	45
1998 Rub-A-Dub-Dub - CGI	10,000		45.00	45
1994 Santa at His Desk - Sundblom	5,000	1996	80.00	80
1994 Santa at His Desk-Musical - Sundblom	5,000	1996	100.00	100
1994 Santa at His Desk-Snowglobe - Sundblom	Closed	1996	45.00	45
1994 Santa at the Fireplace - Sundblom	5,000	1996	80.00	80
1994 Santa at the Fireplace-Musical - Sundblom	5,000	1996	100.00	100
1994 Santa at the Lamppost-Snowglobe - Sundblom	Closed	1996	50.00	50
1995 Santa with Polar Bear-Snowglobe - CGI	Closed	1997	50.00	50
1996 Say Uncle-Snowglobe - CGI	Closed	1997	50.00	50
1994 Single Polar Bear on Ice-Snowglobe - CGI	Closed	1996	40.00	50
1996 Sshh!-Musical - Sundblom	Closed	1997	55.00	55
1995 They Remember Me-Musical - Sundblom	5,000	1997	50.00	50
1997 A Time to Share-Musical - Sundblom	5,000		100.00	100
1997 Times With Dad are Special - CGI	10,000	1998	22.50	23
1998 Travel Refreshed-Snowglobe - Sundblom	Open		45.00	45
1994 Two Polar Bears on Ice - CGI	Open		25.00	25
1994 Two Polar Bears on Ice-Musical -CGI	Closed	1996	45.00	50

Coca-Cola Brand Heritage Collection Polar Bear Cubs - CGI

YEAR ISSUE	EDITION LIMIT	YEAR RETD.	ISSUE PRICE	*QUOTE U.S.$
1996 Balancing Act	Open		16.00	16
1996 The Bear Cub Club	Open		20.00	20
1996 Bearing Gifts of Love and Friendship	10,000		30.00	30
1996 The Big Catch	Open		16.00	16
1997 Caring Is A Special Gift	Open		16.00	16
1996 A Christmas Wish	Open		10.00	10
1997 Dad Showed Me How-Musical	Open		35.00	35
1997 Everybody Needs A Friend	Open		12.00	12
1997 Fire Chief	Open		16.00	16
1996 Friends Are Forever	Open		16.00	16
1997 Friends Double the Joy	Open		30.00	30
1997 Friends Make the Holiday Special	10,000		30.00	30
1997 Friendship is A Hiddlen Treaure	Open		20.00	20
1997 Friendship is the Best Gift	Open		16.00	16
1997 Friendship is the Perfect Medicine	Open		20.00	20
1997 Friendship Makes Life Bearable	Open		16.00	16
1996 Giving Is Better Than Receiving	Open		12.00	12
1997 Graduation Day	Closed	1997	12.00	12
1997 Happy Birthday	Open		12.00	12
1996 A Helping Hand	Open		20.00	20
1997 I Can Do Anything with You By My Side-Snowglobe	Open		45.00	45
1997 I Can't Bear To See You Sick	Open		20.00	20
1998 I Carved This Just for You	Open		16.00	16
1997 I Get A Kick Out of You	Open		16.00	16
1998 I'd Follow You Anywhere-Snowglobe	Open		40.00	40
1996 I'm Not Sleepy...Really	Open		10.00	10
1996 It's My Turn to Hide	Open		12.00	12
1997 Just For You	Open		16.00	16
1997 Just Like My Dad	Open		16.00	16
1997 Little Boys are Best	Open		16.00	16
1997 Little Girls are Special	Open		16.00	16
1996 Look What I Can Do	Open		12.00	12
1998 Look What I Do-Snowglobe	Open		40.00	40
1997 Love Bears All Things	Open		12.00	12
1997 Lucky O'Bear and McPuffin	Open		16.00	16
1997 On The Road to Adventure-Musical - CGI	Open		15.00	15
1998 Peek A Boo-Mini Musical	Open		30.00	30
1998 A Perfect Time for a Refreshing Treat-Snowglobe	Open		40.00	40
1997 Polar Bear Cub Sign	Open		16.00	16
1996 Ride 'em Cowboy	Open		20.00	20
1997 Seeds of Friendship Grow with Caring	Open		16.00	16
1996 Skating Rink Romance	Open		16.00	16
1997 Sled Racing-Snowglobe	Open		35.00	35
1996 Snowday Adventure	Open		12.00	12
1996 Sweet Dreams	Open		12.00	12
1997 Thanks For All You Taught Me	Open		16.00	16
1998 There's No Place Like Home-Mini Musical	Open		30.00	30
1996 To Grandmother's House We Go	Open		12.00	12
1997 Visits with You are Special	Open		20.00	20
1997 We Did It	Closed	1997	20.00	20
1996 Who Says Girls Can't Throw	Open		16.00	16
1997 With All My Heart	Open		16.00	16
1997 You're the Greatest	Open		20.00	20

Coca-Cola Brand Mercury Glass - CGI, unless otherwise noted

YEAR ISSUE	EDITION LIMIT	YEAR RETD.	ISSUE PRICE	*QUOTE U.S.$
1998 Hollywood	Open		29.50	30
1998 Polar Bear at Vending Machine	Open		29.50	30
1998 Santa - Sundblom	Open		29.50	30
1998 Vending Machine	Open		29.50	30

Coca-Cola Brand Musical - Various

YEAR ISSUE	EDITION LIMIT	YEAR RETD.	ISSUE PRICE	*QUOTE U.S.$
1993 Dear Santa, Please Pause Here - Sundblom	Closed	1996	50.00	50
1994 Santa's Soda Shop - CGI	Closed	1996	50.00	50

Coca-Cola Brand Santa Animations - Sundblom

YEAR ISSUE	EDITION LIMIT	YEAR RETD.	ISSUE PRICE	*QUOTE U.S.$
1991 Ssshh! (1st Ed.)	Closed	1992	99.99	365
1992 Santa's Pause for Refreshment (2nd Ed.)	Closed	1993	99.99	265-295
1993 Trimming the Tree (3rd Ed.)	Closed	1994	99.99	235-265
1995 Santa at the Lamppost (4th Ed.)	Closed	1996	110.00	115-225

Harley-Davidson - CGI

YEAR ISSUE	EDITION LIMIT	YEAR RETD.	ISSUE PRICE	*QUOTE U.S.$
1997 The Age Old Urge to Run Away	10,000		40.00	40
1997 Born to Ride	10,000		50.00	50
1997 Harley Eagle	2,500		50.00	50
1997 Santa's Sled	10,000		50.00	50
1998 Santa's Sled-Musical	10,000		50.00	50

Harley-Davidson Little Cruisers - CGI

YEAR ISSUE	EDITION LIMIT	YEAR RETD.	ISSUE PRICE	*QUOTE U.S.$
1997 Daddy's Little Helper	Open		16.00	16
1997 Following in Mom's Footsteps	Open		16.00	16
1997 Harley Club House	Open		25.00	25
1997 Here's Looking at You	Open		16.00	16
1997 I Wrapped It Myself	Open		16.00	16
1997 Just Like My Dad	Open		16.00	16
1997 Mr. Fix-It	Open		16.00	16
1997 On the Road to Adventure	Open		16.00	16
1997 Varoom	Open		16.00	16
1997 With You I Will Go Anywhere	Open		20.00	20
1998 Can I Have A Harley	Open		25.00	25
1998 Hide & Seek	Open		16.00	16
1998 The Mechanics	Open		20.00	20
1998 On the Open Road	Open		16.00	16
1998 Santa Bear Rides Again	Open		20.00	20

Humbug - T. Fraley

YEAR ISSUE	EDITION LIMIT	YEAR RETD.	ISSUE PRICE	*QUOTE U.S.$
1998 Holding Down the Fort	Open		20.00	20
1998 Let Me Call You Sweetheart	Open		20.00	20
1998 Let Me Call You Sweetheat-Musical	Open		35.00	35
1998 Making Faces	Open		20.00	20
1998 A Nutty Humbug-Musical	Open		35.00	35
1998 That's More Like It-Snowglobe	Open		35.00	35
1998 This "Was" For Santa	Open		20.00	20
1998 Where to Next?-Snowglobe	Open		35.00	35

Cherished Teddies/Enesco Corporation

Cherished Teddies Club - P. Hillman

YEAR ISSUE	EDITION LIMIT	YEAR RETD.	ISSUE PRICE	*QUOTE U.S.$
1995 Cub E. Bear CT001	Yr.Iss.	1995	Gift	44-88
1995 Mayor Wilson T. Beary CT951	Yr.Iss.	1995	20.00	50-145
1995 Hilary Hugabear CT952	Yr.Iss.	1995	17.50	50-140
1996 R. Harrison Hartford-New Membear (red pencil) CT002	Yr.Iss.	1996	Gift	25-40
1996 R. Harrison Hartford-Charter Membear (yellow pencil) CT102	Yr.Iss.	1996	Gift	35-75
1996 Emily E. Claire CT962	Yr.Iss.	1996	17.50	35-50
1996 Kurtis D. Claw CT961	Yr.Iss.	1996	17.50	35-50
1996 Town Tattler Building CT953	Yr.Iss.	1996	50.00	45-50
1996 Club Flag 901350	Yr.Iss.	1996	20.00	20-50
1997 Lloyd, CT Town Railway Conductor-Membearship (red suitcase) CT003	Yr.Iss.	1997	Gift	20-43
1997 Lloyd, CT Town Railway Conductor-Charter Membear (green suitcase) CT103	Yr.Iss.	1997	Gift	20-37
1997 Bernard and Bernice CT972	Yr.Iss.	1997	17.50	18-33
1997 Eleanor P. Beary CT971	Yr.Iss.	1997	17.50	18-33
1997 Mary Jane "My Favorite Things" 277002 (Cherished Rewards)	Yr.Iss.	1997	Gift	50
1997 Amelia "You Make Me Smile" 273554 (Cherished Rewards)	Yr.Iss.	1997	Gift	50-63
1997 Benny "Let's Ride Through Life Together" 273198 (Cherished Rewards)	Yr.Iss.	1997	Gift	20-63
1997 Blaire Beary (mini figurine) 297550	Yr.Iss.	1997	Gift	38
1997 Cherished Teddies Playing Cards CRT458	Yr.Iss.	1997	Gift	N/A
1998 Cherished Teddies Town Accessory Set CT983	Yr.Iss.		17.50	18
1998 Lela Nightingale CT981	Yr.Iss.		15.00	15
1998 Wade Weathersbee CT982	Yr.Iss.		13.50	14
1998 Cherished Teddies First Aid Kit CRT541	Yr.Iss.		Gift	N/A
1998 Cherished Teddies Lithograph 128058 (Cherished Rewards)	Yr.Iss.		Gift	N/A
1998 Bubble Waterton (mini figurine) 466808	Yr.Iss.		Gift	N/A

Cherished Teddies - P. Hillman

YEAR ISSUE	EDITION LIMIT	YEAR RETD.	ISSUE PRICE	*QUOTE U.S.$
1993 Abigail "Inside We're All The Same" 900362	Suspd.		16.00	32-110
1993 Alice "Cozy Warm Wishes Coming Your Way" (9") 903620	Suspd.		100.00	210-250
1993 Alice "Cozy Warm Wishes Coming Your Way" Dated 1993 912875	Yr.Iss.	1993	17.50	145-233
1995 Allison & Alexandria "Two Friends Mean Twice The Love" 127981	Open		25.00	25
1995 Amanda "Here's Some Cheer to Last The Year" 141186	Yr.Iss.	1995	17.50	24-50
1993 Amy "Hearts Quilted With Love" 910732	Open		13.50	15
1996 Andy "You Have A Special Place In My Heart" 176265	Open		18.50	19
1992 Anna "Hooray For You" 950459	Retrd.	1997	22.50	27-55
1997 Annie, Brittany, Colby, Danny, Ernie "Strike Up The Band And Give Five Cherished Years A Hand" (5th Anniversary) 205354	Yr.Iss.		75.00	65-99
1994 Baby Boy Jointed (musical-"Schubert's Lullaby") 699314	Open		60.00	60
1994 Baby Girl Jointed (musical) 699322	Open		60.00	60
1993 Baby in Cradle (musical-"Brahms' Lullaby") 914320	Open		60.00	60
1998 Ballerina in Jewelry Box (musical-"Music Box Dancer") 331473	Open		40.00	40
1997 Barry "I'm Batty Over You" 270016	Open		17.50	18
1995 Bea "Bee My Friend" 141348	Open		12.50	14
1994 Bear as Bunny Jointed (musical) 625302	Retrd.	1996	60.00	115-125
1998 Bear by Tree (musical gift box) 967688	Closed	N/A	25.00	30
1995 Bear Cupid Girl "Love" "Be Mine" 2 Asst 103640	Suspd.		15.00	27-30
1994 Bear Holding Harp (musical-"Love Makes The World Go Round") 916323	Retrd.	1997	40.00	50-70
1996 Bear In Bunny Outfit Resin Egg Dated 1996 156507	Yr.Iss.	1996	8.50	20-83
1998 Bear in Crib "Tucked in Teddie" (musical-"Brahm's Lullaby") 335797	Open		75.00	75
1992 Bear on Rocking Reindeer (musical-"Jingle Bells") 950815	Suspd.		60.00	120-150
1998 Bear on Swing in Tree "Picnic in the Park" (musical-"That's What Friends Are For") 335827	Open		50.00	50
1993 Bear Playing w/Train (musical-"Santa Claus is Coming to Town") 912964	Open		40.00	40
1994 Bear w/Goose (musical-"Wind Beneath My Wings") 627445	Retrd.	1997	45.00	45-109
1994 Bear w/Horse (musical-"My Favorite Things") 628565	Retrd.	1996	150.00	100-195
1994 Bear w/Rocking Reindeer (musical-"Jingle Bells") 629618	Open		165.00	165
1994 Bear w/Toy Chest (musical-"My Favorite Things") 627453	Open		60.00	60
1995 Beary Scary Halloween House 152382	Open		20.00	20
1994 Becky "Springtime Happiness" 916331	Suspd.		20.00	36-45
1992 Benji "Life Is Sweet, Enjoy" 950548	Retrd.	1995	13.50	42-110
1994 Bessie "Some Bunny Loves You" 916404	Suspd.		15.00	160-205
1995 The Best Is Yet To Come 127949	Open		12.50	14
1995 The Best Is Yet To Come 127957	Open		12.50	14
1992 Beth & Blossom "Friends Are Never Far Apart" 950564	Retrd.	1997	50.00	58-95
1992 Beth & Blossom "Friends Are Never Far Apart" w/butterfly 950564	Closed	1992	50.00	138-218
1992 Beth "Bear Hugs" 950637	Retrd.	1995	17.50	40-96
1992 Beth "Happy Holidays, Deer Friend" 950807	Suspd.		22.50	35-90

YEAR ISSUE		EDITION LIMIT	YEAR RETD.	ISSUE PRICE	*QUOTE U.S.$
1994	Betty "Bubblin' Over With Love" 626066	Open		18.50	20
1994	Billy "Everyone Needs A Cuddle", Betsey "First Step To Love" Bobbie "A Little Friendship To Share" 624896	Open		12.50	13
1994	Billie (spelling error) "Everyone Needs A Cuddle", Betsey "First Step To Love" Bobbie "A Little Friendship To Share" 624896	Closed	N/A	12.50	43
1998	Bonnie & Harold "Ring in the Holidays with Me" 466301	Open		25.00	25
1995	Boy Bear Cupid "Sent With Love" 103551	Suspd.		17.50	28-35
1995	Boy Bear Flying Cupid "Sending You My Heart" 103608	Suspd.		13.00	13-27
1998	Boy in Train Car (musical-"Toyland") 331465	Open		40.00	50
1993	Boy Praying (musical-"Jesus Loves Me") 914304	Retrd.	1997	37.50	77
1994	Boy/Girl in Laundry Basket (musical-"Love Will Keep Us Together") 624926	Open		60.00	60
1994	Boy/Girl in Sled (musical-"Oh, What a Merry Christmas Day") 651435	Open		100.00	100
1998	Brandon "Friendship Is My Goal" 354252	Open		20.00	20
1994	Breanna "Pumpkin Patch Pals" 617180	Open		15.00	15
1994	Bride/Groom (musical-"Mendelssohn Wedding March") 699349	Open		50.00	50
1998	Brooke "Arriving With Love And Care" 302686	Open		25.00	25
1993	Buckey & Brenda "How I Love Being Friends With You" 912816	Retrd.	1995	15.00	45-87
1993	• Brenda "How I Love Being Friends With You" 912816	Retrd.	1995	N/A	37-65
1993	• Buckey "How I Love Being Friends With You" 912816	Retrd.	1995	N/A	25-60
1995	Bunny "Just In Time For Spring" 103802	Retrd.	1998	13.50	14
1996	Butch "Can I Be Your Football Hero?" 156388	Open		15.00	15
1992	Camille "I'd Be Lost Without You" 950424	Retrd.	1996	20.00	27-45
1997	Can't Bear To See You Under The Weather 215856	Open		15.00	15
1998	Carol "Angels Snow How To Fly" 352969	Open		17.50	18
1993	Carolyn "Wishing You All Good Things" 912921	Retrd.	1996	22.50	42-57
1995	Carrie "The Future 'Beareth' All Things" 141321	Open		18.50	19
1997	Cathy "An Autumn Breeze Blows Blessings To Please" 269980	Open		25.00	25
1993	Charity "I Found A Friend In Ewe" 910678	Retrd.	1996	20.00	187-260
1992	Charlie "The Spirit of Friendship Warms The Heart" 950742	Retrd.	1996	22.50	39-93
1993	Chelsea "Good Friends Are A Blessing" 910694	Retrd.	1995	15.00	249-400
1996	Cheryl & Carl "Wishing You A Cozy Christmas" 141216	Open		25.00	25
1995	Christian "My Prayer Is For You" 103837	Open		18.50	19
1995	Christine "My Prayer Is For You" 103845	Open		18.50	19
1992	Christopher "Old Friends Are The Best Friends" 950483	Open		50.00	50
1998	Clown on Ball (musical-"You Are My Sunshine") 336459	Open		40.00	40
1993	Connie "You're A Sweet Treat" 912794	Retrd.	1996	15.00	30-72
1992	Couple in Basket/Umbrella (musical-"Let Me Be Your Teddy Bear") 950645	Retrd.	1997	60.00	60-120
1994	Courtney "Springtime Is A Blessing From Above" 916390	Retrd.	1996	15.00	93-150
1995	Cupid Baby on Pillow "Little Bundle of Joy", 2 Asst. 103659	Suspd.		13.50	14-30
1995	Cupid Boy Sitting "From My Heart", "Sealed With Love", 2 Asst. 869074	Suspd.		13.50	25
1995	Cupid Boy/Girl Double "Aiming For Your Heart" 103594	Suspd.		25.00	37-50
1995	Cupid Boy/Girl Double "Heart to Heart", "My Love", 2 Asst. 869082	Suspd.		18.50	25-37
1993	Daisy "Friendship Blossoms With Love" 910651	Retrd.	1996	15.00	688-1100
1996	Daniel "You're My Little Pumpkin" 176214	Open		22.50	23
1997	Danielle, Sabrina, & Tiffany "We're Three Of A Kind" 1997 Adoption Center Only 265780	Yr.Iss.	1997	35.00	35-90
1996	Debbie "Let's Hear It For Friendship!" 156361	Open		15.00	15
1995	Donald "Friends Are Egg-ceptional Blessings" 103799	Retrd.	1998	20.00	20
1992	Douglas "Let's Be Friends" 950661	Retrd.	1995	20.00	47-90
1995	Earl "Warm Hearted Friends" 131873	Open		17.50	18
1994	Elizabeth & Ashley "My Beary Best Friend" 916277	Retrd.	1996	25.00	50-90
1994	Eric "Bear Tidings Of Joy" 622796	Open		22.50	25
1996	Erica "Friends Are Always Pulling For You" 176028	Open		22.50	23
1998	Erin "My Irish Eyes Smile When You're Near" 203068	Open		15.00	15
1998	Evan "May Your Christmas Be Trimmed In Happiness" (Naled Catalog Exclusive) 484822	Open		27.50	28
1994	Faith "There's No Bunny Like You" 916412	Suspd.		20.00	50-88
1998	Frank & Helen "Snow One Like You" 352950	Open		22.50	23
1993	Freda & Tina "Our Friendship Is A Perfect Blend" 911747	Open		35.00	35
1995	Gail "Catching the First Blooms of Friendship" 103772	Retrd.	1998	20.00	20
1993	Gary "True Friendships Are Scarce" 912786	Suspd.		18.50	24-32
1995	Girl Bear Cupid "Be My Bow" 103586	Suspd.		15.00	30-48
1995	Girl Bear Flying Cupid "Sending You My Heart" 103616	Suspd.		13.00	26-29
1995	Girl Bear on Ottoman (musical-"Au Clair De La Lune") 128058	Open		55.00	55
1998	Girl in Teacup with Saucer (musical-"My Favorite Things") 331457	Open		40.00	45
1993	Girl Praying (musical-"Jesus Loves Me") 914312	Retrd.	1997	37.50	75
1993	Gretel "We Make Magic, Me And You" 912778	Open		18.50	20
1998	Growing Better Each Year 302651	Open		22.50	23
1993	Hans "Friends In Toyland" 912956	Retrd.	1995	20.00	89-144
1993	Heidi & David "Special Friends" 910708	Suspd.		25.00	30-65
1993	Henrietta "A Basketful of Wishes" 910686	Suspd.		22.50	157-180
1994	Henry "Celebrating Spring With You" 916420	Suspd.		20.00	30-80
1995	Hope "Our Love Is Ever-Blooming" 103764	Retrd.	1998	20.00	20-26
1998	Humphrey "Just the Bear Facts, Ma'am" 1998 Regional Event Piece 352977	Yr.Iss.		15.00	35-58
1998	Hunter "Me Cavebear, You Friend" 354104	Open		15.00	15
1994	Ingrid "Bundled-Up With Warm Wishes" Dated 1994 617237	Yr.Iss.	1994	20.00	34-105
1992	Jacob "Wishing For Love" 950734	Suspd		22.50	28-40
1996	Jamie & Ashley "I'm All Wrapped Up In Your Love" 141224	Open		25.00	25
1998	Janet "You're Sweet As A Rose" (Avon Exclusive) 336521	Open		9.00	9
1992	Jasmine "You Have Touched My Heart" 950475	Suspd.		22.50	25-60
1997	Jean "Cup Full Of Peace" 269859	Open		25.00	25
1994	Jedediah "Giving Thanks For Friends" 617091	Retrd.	1997	17.50	24-35
1996	Jeffrey "Striking Up Another Year" Dated 1996 176044	Yr.Iss.	1996	17.50	18-20
1995	Jennifer "Gathering The Blooms of Friendship" 103810	Retrd.	1998	22.50	23-31
1992	Jeremy "Friends Like You Are Precious And Few" 950521	Retrd.	1995	15.00	21-72
1997	Jessica "A Mother's Heart Is Full of Love" 155438	Retrd.	1997	25.00	55-75
1996	Jessica "A Mother's Heart Is Full of Love" GCC Early Introduction 155438A	Retrd.	1996	25.00	82-200
1997	Joann "Cup Full Of Love" 269840	Open		25.00	25
1993	Jointed Bear Christmas (musical-"Jingle Bells") 903337	Suspd.		60.00	70-120
1997	Jordan "Cup Full Of Joy" 269832	Open		25.00	25
1998	Joseph "Everyone Has Their 'Old' Friends to Hug" (Palmer Catalog Exclusive) 476471A	Open		25.00	25
1992	Joshua "Love Repairs All" 950556	Retrd.	1997	20.00	20-44
1997	Kara "You're A Honey Of A Friend" Adoption Center 1997 National Event 265799	Yr.Iss.		15.00	15-27
1994	Kathleen "Luck Found Me A Friend In You" 916447	Open		12.50	13
1992	Katie "A Friend Always Knows When You Need A Hug" 950440	Retrd.	1997	20.00	25-97
1998	Keith & Deborah "The Holidays Are Twice As "Ice"" 354244	Open		30.00	30
1994	Kelly "You're My One And Only" 916307	Suspd.		15.00	49-55
1995	Kevin "Good Luck To You" 103896	Retrd.	1996	12.50	23-63
1995	Kiss The Hurt And Make It Well 127965	Open		15.00	15
1996	Kittie "You Make Wishes Come True" 1996 Adoption Center Event 131865	Yr.Iss.	1996	17.50	23-60
1995	Kristen "Hugs of Love And Friendship" 141194	Open		20.00	20
1998	Lance "Come Fly With Me" 1998 National Event Piece 337463	Yr.Iss.		20.00	20
1997	Larry "You're My Shooting Star" 203440	Open		17.50	18
1996	Laura "Friendship Makes It All Better" 156396	Open		15.00	15
1997	Lee "You're A Bear's Best Friend" 272167	Yr.Iss.	1997	20.00	20-40
1998	Libby "My Country Tis Of Thee" 305979	Retrd.	1998	20.00	20
1997	Lily "Lilies Bloom With Petals of Hope" (Spring Catalog Exclusive) 202959A	Open		15.00	30-83
1996	Linda "ABC And 1-2-3, You're A Friend To Me!" 156426	Open		15.00	15
1996	Lindsey & Lyndon "Walking In A Winter Wonderland" Fall Catalog Exclusive 141178A	Yr.Iss.	1996	30.00	30-60
1995	Lisa "My Best Is Always You" 103780	Retrd.	1998	20.00	20
1998	Lou "Take Me Out To The Ball Game" 203432	Open		15.00	15
1997	Lynn "A Handmade Holiday Wish" (Fall Catalog Exclusive) 310735A	Yr.Iss.		25.00	25-83
1998	Lynn "A Handmade Holiday Wish" 310735	Open		25.00	25
1995	Madeline "A Cup Full of Friendship" 135593	Open		20.00	20
1992	Mandy "I Love You Just The Way You Are" 950572	Retrd.	1995	15.00	26-75
1995	Margaret "A Cup Full of Love" 103667	Open		20.00	20
1993	Marie "Friendship Is A Special Treat" 910767	Open		20.00	20
1995	Marilyn "A Cup Full of Cheer" 135682	Open		20.00	20
1993	Mary "A Special Friend Warms The Season" 912840	Open		25.00	25
1995	Maureen "Lucky Friend" 135690	Retrd.	1996	12.50	19-30
1995	Melissa "Every Bunny Needs A Friend" 103829	Retrd.	1998	20.00	20-26
1993	Michael & Michelle "Friendship Is A Cozy Feeling" 910775	Suspd.		30.00	50-109
1998	Mike "I'm Sweet On You" 1998 Adoption Center Only 356255	Yr.Iss.		15.00	15
1993	Miles "I'm Thankful For A Friend Like You" 912751	Open		17.00	18
1995	Millie, Christy, Dorothy "A. Love Me Tender, B. Take Me To Your Heart, C. Love Me True" 128023	Retrd.	1996	37.50	34-77
1995	• Dorothy "A. Love Me Tender, B. Take Me To Your Heart, C. Love Me True" 128023	Retrd.	1996	N/A	18-25
1995	• Millie, "A. Love Me Tender, B. Take Me To Your Heart, C. Love Me True" 128023	Retrd.	1996	N/A	25
1995	• Christy, "A. Love Me Tender, B. Take Me To Your Heart, C. Love Me True" 128023	Retrd.	1996	N/A	20
1996	Mindy "Friendship Keeps Me On My Toes" 156418	Open		15.00	15
1993	Molly "Friendship Softens A Bumpy Ride" 910759	Retrd.	1996	30.00	38-65
1998	Mother Goose and Friends "Friends of a Feather Flock Together" 154016	Open		50.00	50
1994	Nancy "Your Friendship Makes My Heart Sing" 916315	Retrd.	1996	15.00	83-120
1998	Nathan "Leave Your Worries Behind" 176222	Open		17.50	18
1992	Nathaniel & Nellie "It's Twice As Nice With You" 950513	Retrd.	1996	30.00	50-114
1997	Newton "Ringing In The New Year With Cheer" 272361	Open		15.00	15
1994	Nils "Near And Deer For Christmas" 617245	Retrd.	1997	22.50	35-65
1997	Nina "Beary Happy Wishes" 1997 National Event Piece 215864	Yr.Iss.	1997	17.50	35-83
1996	Olga "Feel The Peace...Hold The Joy...Share The Love" 182966	Yr.Iss.	1996	50.00	58-100
1994	Oliver & Olivia "Will You Be Mine?" 916641	Suspd.		25.00	45-70
1996	Park Bench w/Bears "Heart to Heart" 1996 National Event Piece CRT240	Yr.Iss.	1996	12.50	35-45
1995	Pat "Falling For You" 141313	Open		22.50	23
1994	Patience "Happiness Is Homemade" 617105	Retrd.	1997	17.50	23-40
1993	Patrice "Thank You For The Sky So Blue" 911429	Open		18.50	20
1993	Patrick "Thank You For A Friend That's True" 911410	Open		18.50	20
1998	Penny, Chandler, Boots "We're Inseparable" 1998 Adoption Center Exclusive 337579	Yr.Iss.		25.00	25
1995	Peter "You're Some Bunny Special" 104973	Retrd.	1998	17.50	20-40
1994	Phoebe "A Little Friendship Is A Big Blessing" 617113	Retrd.	1995	13.50	25-80
1993	Priscilla "Love Surrounds Our Friendship" 910724	Retrd.	1997	15.00	24-72
1995	Priscilla & Greta "Our Hearts Belong to You" 128031	19,950		50.00	86-138
1993	Prudence "A Friend To Be Thankful For" 912808	Open		17.00	18
1996	Pumpkins/Corn Stalk/Scarecrow Mini 3 Asst. 176206	Open		15.00	15
1997	Rex "Our Friendship Will Never Be Extinct" 269999	Open		17.50	18
1998	Rich "Always Paws For Holiday Treats" 352721	Yr.Iss.		22.50	23
1993	Robbie & Rachel "Love Bears All Things" 911402	Open		27.50	30
1996	Robert "Love Keeps Me Afloat" 156272	Open		13.50	14
1998	Roy "I'm Your Country Cowboy" (Special Limited Edition) 466298	Closed	1998	17.50	18
1997	Ryan "I'm Green With Envy For You" 203041	Open		20.00	20
1998	Sam "I Want You...To Be My Friend" 302619	Retrd.	1998	17.50	18
1992	Sara "LoveYa" Jacki Hugs & Kisses", Karen "Best Buddy" 950432	Open		10.00	10
1995	Sculpted Irish Plaque "A Cherished Irish Blessing" 110981	Open		13.50	14
1994	Sean "Luck Found Me A Friend In You" 916439	Open		12.50	13

*Quotes have been rounded up to nearest dollar

YEAR ISSUE	EDITION LIMIT	YEAR RETD.	ISSUE PRICE	*QUOTE U.S.$
1998 Segrid, Justaf, Ingmar "The Spirit of Christmas Grows In Our Hearts" 352799	Yr.Iss.		45.00	45
1995 Seth & Sarabeth "We're Beary Good Pals" 128015	Open		25.00	25
1998 Shannon "A Figure 8, Our Friendship Is Great!" 354260	Open		20.00	20
1998 Sierra "You're My Partner" (Special Limited Edition) 466271	Closed	1998	17.50	18
1992 Signage Plaque (Hamilton) 951005	Closed	N/A	15.00	24-44
1992 Signage Plaque 951005	Open		15.00	15
1998 Sixteen Candles and Many More Wishes 302643	Open		22.50	23
1994 Sonja "Holiday Cuddles" 622818	Open		20.00	20
1994 Stacie "You Lift My Spirit" 617148	Open		18.50	20
1992 Steven "A Season Filled With Sweetness" 951129	Retrd.	1995	20.00	46-97
1997 Sven & Liv "All Paths Lead To Kindness & Friendship" 272159	Yr.Iss.	1997	55.00	55-66
1997 Sylvia "A Picture Perfect Friendship" Regional Event Piece 265810	Yr.Iss.	1997	15.00	44-115
1996 Tabitha "You're The Cat's Meow" 176257	Open		15.00	15
1996 Tasha "In Grandmother's Attic" 1996 Adoption Center Exclusive 156353	19,960	1996	50.00	138-220
1994 Taylor "Sail The Seas With Me" 617156	Suspd.		15.00	22-55
1994 Thanksgiving Quilt 617075	Open		12.00	12
1992 Theadore, Samantha & Tyler "Friends Come In All Sizes" 950505	Open		20.00	20
1993 Theadore, Samantha & Tyler "Friendship Weathers All Storms" (9") 912883	Suspd.		160.00	160
1993 Theadore, Samantha & Tyler "Friendship Weathers All Storms" (musical-"Jingle Bells") 904546	Suspd.		170.00	170-250
1992 Theadore, Samantha & Tyler "Friendship Weathers All Storms" 950769	Retrd.	1997	20.00	25-40
1992 Theadore, Samantha & Tyler (9") "Friends Come In All Sizes" 951196	Open		130.00	130
1997 This Calls For A Celebration 215910	Open		15.00	15
1993 Thomas "Chuggin' Along", Jonathan "Sail With Me", Harrison "We're Going Places" 911739	Retrd.	1997	15.00	25-45
1993 • Thomas "Chuggin' Along" 911739	Retrd.	1997	N/A	N/A
1993 • Jonathan "Sail With Me" 911739	Retrd.	1997	N/A	30
1993 • Harrison "We're Going Places" 911739	Retrd.	1997	N/A	33
1993 Timothy "A Friend Is Forever" 910740	Retrd.	1996	15.00	32-85
1995 Town Tattler Sign 1995 National Event Piece CRT109	Yr.Iss.	1995	6.00	25-69
1998 Toy Cabinet "My Cherished Treasures" (musical-"My Favorite Things") 335681	Open		100.00	100
1993 Tracie & Nicole "Side By Side With Friends" 911372	Open		35.00	35
1998 Trevor "You Bring Out The Devil In Me" 354112	Open		17.50	18
1995 Tucker & Travis "We're in This Together" 127973	Open		25.00	25
1996 Two Boys By Lamp Post (musical-"The First Noel") 141089	Open		50.00	50
1995 UK Bears, Bertie "Friends Forever Near or Far" (International Exclusive) 163457	Retrd.	1996	17.50	27-50
1995 UK Bears, Duncan "Your Friendship Is Music To My Ears" (International Exclusive) 163473	Retrd.	1996	17.50	26-50
1995 UK Bears, Gordon "Keepin' A Watchful Eye on You" (International Exclusive) 163465	Retrd.	1996	17.50	26-40
1995 UK Bears, Sherlock "Good Friends Are Hard To Find" (International Exclusive) 163481	Retrd.	1996	17.50	18-26
1995 UK Bears, set/4 (Bertie, Gordon, Duncan, Sherlock)	Retrd.	1996	70.00	115-140
1998 Veronica "You Make Happiness Bloom" (Spring Catalog Exclusive) 366854	Open		15.00	15
1994 Victoria "From My Heart To Yours" 916293	Suspd.		16.50	60-138
1996 Violet "Blessings Bloom When You Are Near" 156280	Open		15.00	15
1998 Whitney "We Make A Winning Team" 302678	Open		15.00	15
1994 Willie "Bears Of A Feather Stay Together" 617164	Retrd.	1997	15.00	25-50
1994 Winona "Little Fair Feather Friend" 617172	Retrd.	1997	15.00	22-50
1994 Wyatt "I'm Called Little Running Bear" 629707	Open		15.00	15
1994 Wylie "I'm Called Little Friend" 617121	Open		15.00	15
1998 You're The Frosting on the Birthday Cake 306398	Open		22.50	23
1992 Zachary "Yesterday's Memories Are Today's Treasures" 950491	Retrd.	1997	30.00	40-50

Special Limited Edition - P. Hillman

YEAR ISSUE	EDITION LIMIT	YEAR RETD.	ISSUE PRICE	*QUOTE U.S.$
1993 Holding On To Someone Special-Collector Appreciation Fig. 916285	Yr.Iss.	1993	20.00	215-465
1994 Priscilla Ann "There's No One Like Hue" Collectible Exposition Exclusive available only at Secaucus and South Bend in 1994 and at Long Beach in 1995 CRT025	Yr.Iss.	1994	24.00	212-285
1993 Teddy & Roosevelt "The Book of Teddies 1903-1993" (90th Anniversary Commemorative) 624918	Yr.Iss.	1993	20.00	125-250

Across The Seas - P. Hillman

YEAR ISSUE	EDITION LIMIT	YEAR RETD.	ISSUE PRICE	*QUOTE U.S.$
1997 Bazza "I'm Lost Down Under Without You" 276995	Open		17.50	18
1996 Bob with Passport "Our Friendship Is From Sea To Shining Sea" 202444P	Open		17.50	18
1996 Carlos "I Found An Amigo In You" 202339	Open		17.50	18
1996 Claudette "Our Friendship Is Bon Appetit!" 197254	Open		17.50	18
1998 Colleen "The Luck Of The Irish To You" 373966	Open		17.50	18
1996 Fernando "You Make Everday A Fiesta" 202355	Open		17.50	18
1996 Franz "Our Friendship Knows No Boundaries" 202436	Open		17.50	18
1996 Katrien "Tulips Blossom With Friendship" 202401	Open		17.50	18
1996 Kerstin "You're The Swedish of Them All" 197289	Open		17.50	18
1998 Leilani "Tahiti - Sending Warm And Friendly Island Breezes" 302627	Retrd.	1998	17.50	18
1996 Lian "Our Friendship Spans Many Miles" 202347	Retrd.	1998	17.50	18
1996 Lorna "Our Love Is In The Highlands" 202452	Open		17.50	18
1996 Machiko "Love Fans A Beautiful Friendship" 202312	Retrd.	1998	17.50	18
1996 Nadia "From Russia, With Love" 202320	Open		17.50	18
1996 Preston "Riding Across The Great White North" 216739	Retrd.	1998	17.50	18
1996 Rajul "You're The Jewel Of My Heart" 202398	Open		17.50	18
1997 Sophia "Like Grapes On The Vine, Our Friendship Is Divine" 276987	Open		17.50	18
1996 William "You're a Jolly Ol' Chap" 202878	Open		17.50	18

The Angel Series - P. Hillman

YEAR ISSUE	EDITION LIMIT	YEAR RETD.	ISSUE PRICE	*QUOTE U.S.$
1998 Angela "Peace On Earth And Mercy Mild" 175986	Yr.Iss.		20.00	20
1997 Grace "Glory To The Newborn King" (Angel) 175994	Yr.Iss.	1997	20.00	20-32
1996 Stormi "Hark The Herald Angels Sing" 176001	Yr.Iss.	1996	20.00	25-45

Anniversary Figurines - P. Hillman

YEAR ISSUE	EDITION LIMIT	YEAR RETD.	ISSUE PRICE	*QUOTE U.S.$
1997 You Grow More Dear With Each Passing Year 215880	Open		25.00	25
1998 A Decade of Teddy Bear Love 302694 (10 Yr. Anniversary)	Open		30.00	30
1998 25 Years To Treasure Together 302708 (25 Yr. Anniversary)	Open		30.00	30
1998 Forever Yours, Forever True 302716 (40 or 50 Yr. Anniversary)	Open		30.00	30

Beta Is For Bear - P. Hillman

YEAR ISSUE	EDITION LIMIT	YEAR RETD.	ISSUE PRICE	*QUOTE U.S.$
1998 Alpha 305995	Open		7.50	8
1998 Beta 306002	Open		7.50	8
1998 Gamma 306010	Open		7.50	8
1998 Delta 306037	Open		7.50	8
1998 Epsilon 306045	Open		7.50	8
1998 Zeta 306053	Open		7.50	8
1998 Eta 306088	Open		7.50	8
1998 Theta 306096	Open		7.50	8
1998 Iota 306118	Open		7.50	8
1998 Kappa 306126	Open		7.50	8
1998 Lambda 306134	Open		7.50	8
1998 Mu 306142	Open		7.50	8
1998 Nu 306150	Open		7.50	8
1998 Xi 306185	Open		7.50	8
1998 Omicron 306193	Open		7.50	8
1998 Pi 306207	Open		7.50	8
1998 Rho 306215	Open		7.50	8
1998 Sigma 306223	Open		7.50	8
1998 Tau 306231	Open		7.50	8
1998 Upsilon 306258	Open		7.50	8
1998 Phi 306266	Open		7.50	8
1998 Chi 306274	Open		7.50	8
1998 Psi 306282	Open		7.50	8
1998 Omega 306290	Open		7.50	8

Blossoms of Friendship - P. Hillman

YEAR ISSUE	EDITION LIMIT	YEAR RETD.	ISSUE PRICE	*QUOTE U.S.$
1997 Dahlia "You're The Best Pick of the Bunch" 202932	Open		15.00	15
1997 Iris "You're The Iris of My Eye" 202908	Open		15.00	15
1998 Lily "Lilies Bloom With Petals Of Hope" 202959	Open		15.00	15
1997 Rose "Everything's Coming Up Roses" 202886	Open		15.00	15
1997 Susan "Love Stems From Our Friendship" 202894	Open		15.00	15

By The Sea, By The Sea - P. Hillman

YEAR ISSUE	EDITION LIMIT	YEAR RETD.	ISSUE PRICE	*QUOTE U.S.$
1997 Gregg "Everything Pails in Comparison To Friends" 203505	Open		20.00	20
1997 Jerry "Ready To Make a Splash" 203475	Open		17.50	18
1997 Jim and Joey "Underneath It All We're Forever Friends" 203513	Open		25.00	25
1997 Judy "I'm Your Bathing Beauty" 203491	Open		35.00	35
1997 Sandy "There's Room In My Sand Castle For You" 203467	Open		20.00	20

The Cherished Seasons - P. Hillman

YEAR ISSUE	EDITION LIMIT	YEAR RETD.	ISSUE PRICE	*QUOTE U.S.$
1997 Megan "Spring Brings A Season Of Beauty" 203300	Open		20.00	20
1997 Kimberly "Summer Brings A Season Of Warmth" 203335	Open		22.50	23
1997 Hannah "Autumn Brings A Season Of Thanksgiving" 203343	Open		20.00	20
1997 Gretchen "Winter Brings A Season Of Joy" 203351	Open		25.00	25

A Christmas Carol - P. Hillman

YEAR ISSUE	EDITION LIMIT	YEAR RETD.	ISSUE PRICE	*QUOTE U.S.$
1994 Bear Cratchit "And A Very Merry Christmas To You Mr. Scrooge" 617326	Suspd.		17.50	24-42
1994 Counting House (Nite-Lite) 622788	Suspd.		75.00	75-90
1994 Cratchit's House (Nite-Lite) 651362	Suspd.		75.00	75-90
1994 Ebearnezer Scrooge "Bah Humbug!" 617296	Suspd.		17.50	30-38
1994 Gloria "I am the Ghost of Christmas Past", Garland "I am the Ghost Of Christmas Present", Gabriel "I am the Ghost of Christmas Yet To Come" 614807	Suspd.		55.00	55
1994 Jacob Bearly "You Will Be Haunted By Three Spirits" 614785	Suspd.		17.50	18-30
1994 Mrs. Cratchit "A Beary Christmas And Happy New Year!" 617318	Suspd.		18.50	19-30
1994 Tiny Ted-Bear "God Bless Us Every One" 614777	Suspd.		10.00	10-20

Circus Tent - P. Hillman

YEAR ISSUE	EDITION LIMIT	YEAR RETD.	ISSUE PRICE	*QUOTE U.S.$
1996 Bruno "Step Right Up And Smile" 103713	Open		17.50	18
1996 Claudia "You Take Center Ring With Me" 103721	Open		17.50	18
1996 Clown on Ball (musical-"Put on a Happy Face") 111430	Open		40.00	40
1997 Dudley "Just Clowning Around" 103748	Open		17.50	18
1996 Elephant-Trunk Full of Bear Hugs 103977	Open		22.50	23
1997 Lion-"You're My Mane Attraction" 203548	Open		12.50	13
1997 Logan "Love Is A Bear Necessity" 103756	Open		17.50	18
1996 Seal "Seal of Friendship" 137596	Open		10.00	10
1997 Shelby "Friendship Keeps You Popping" 203572	Open		17.50	18
1997 Tonya "Friends Are Bear Essentials" 103942	Open		20.00	20
1996 Wally "You're The Tops With Me" 103934	Open		17.50	18

Count on Me - P. Hillman

YEAR ISSUE	EDITION LIMIT	YEAR RETD.	ISSUE PRICE	*QUOTE U.S.$
1998 Bear w/number 0 302945	Open		5.00	5
1998 Bear w/number 1 302821	Open		5.00	5
1998 Bear w/number 2 302848	Open		5.00	5
1998 Bear w/number 3 302856	Open		5.00	5
1998 Bear w/number 4 302864	Open		5.00	5
1998 Bear w/number 5 302872	Open		5.00	5
1998 Bear w/number 6 302899	Open		5.00	5
1998 Bear w/number 7 302902	Open		5.00	5
1998 Bear w/number 8 302910	Open		5.00	5
1998 Bear w/number 9 302929	Open		5.00	5

Down Strawberry Lane - P. Hillman

YEAR ISSUE	EDITION LIMIT	YEAR RETD.	ISSUE PRICE	*QUOTE U.S.$
1997 Diane "I Picked The Beary Best For You" 202991	Yr.Iss.	1997	25.00	25
1996 Ella "Love Grows in My Heart" 156329	Open		15.00	15
1996 Jenna "You're Berry Special To Me" 156337	Open		15.00	15
1996 Matthew "A Dash of Love Sweetens Any Day!" 156299	Open		15.00	15
1996 Tara "You're My Berry Best Friend!" 156310	Open		15.00	15
1996 Thelma "Cozy Tea For Two" 156302	Open		22.50	23
1996 Sign/Bunny/Basket of Strawberries Mini 3 Asst. 900931	Open		3.50	4

Follow The Rainbow - P. Hillman

YEAR ISSUE	EDITION LIMIT	YEAR RETD.	ISSUE PRICE	*QUOTE U.S.$
1998 Carter & Elsie "We're Friends Rain Or Shine" 302791	Open		35.00	35
1998 Ellen "You Color My Rainbow" 302775	Open		20.00	20
1998 Joyce "Plant A Rainbow And Watch It Grow" 302767	Open		25.00	25

Happily Ever After - P. Hillman

YEAR ISSUE	EDITION LIMIT	YEAR RETD.	ISSUE PRICE	*QUOTE U.S.$
1998 Alicia "Through The Looking Glass, I See You!" 302465	Open		22.50	23
1998 Brett "Come To Neverland With Me" 302457	Open		22.50	23
1998 Christina "I Found My Prince In You" 302473	Open		22.50	23
1998 Harvey & Gigi "Finding The Path To Your Heart" 302481	Open		30.00	30
1998 Kelsie "Be The Apple Of My Eye" 302570	Open		20.00	20
1998 Lois "To Grandmother's House We Go" 302511	Open		22.50	23

*Quotes have been rounded up to nearest dollar

Holiday Dangling - P. Hillman

YEAR ISSUE		EDITION LIMIT	YEAR RETD.	ISSUE PRICE	*QUOTE U.S.$
1996	Holden "Catchin' The Holiday Spirit" 176095	Suspd.		15.00	15
1996	Jolene "Dropping You A Holiday Greeting" 176133	Suspd.		20.00	20
1996	Joy "You Always Bring Joy" 176087	Suspd.		15.00	15
1996	Noel "An Old-Fashioned Noel To You" 176109	Suspd.		15.00	15
1996	Nolan "A String Of Good Tidings" 176141	Suspd.		20.00	20
1996	Santa Bear 2 asst. "Joy" "Ho Ho" 176168	Open		12.50	13

Just Between Friends - P. Hillman

YEAR ISSUE		EDITION LIMIT	YEAR RETD.	ISSUE PRICE	*QUOTE U.S.$
1998	Forgive Me 303100	Open		7.50	8
1998	Good Luck 303143	Open		7.50	8
1998	Having A Good Day/Having A Bad Day 303119	Open		7.50	8
1998	I Miss You 303127	Open		7.50	8
1998	I'm Sorry 303097	Open		7.50	8
1998	Please Smile 303135	Open		7.50	8

Little Sparkles - P. Hillman

YEAR ISSUE		EDITION LIMIT	YEAR RETD.	ISSUE PRICE	*QUOTE U.S.$
1997	Bear w/January Birthstone Mini Figurine 239720	Open		7.50	8
1997	Bear w/February Birthstone Mini Figurine 239747	Open		7.50	8
1997	Bear w/March Birthstone Mini Figurine 239763	Open		7.50	8
1997	Bear w/April Birthstone Mini Figurine 239771	Open		7.50	8
1997	Bear w/May Birthstone Mini Figurine 239798	Open		7.50	8
1997	Bear w/June Birthstone Mini Figurine 239801	Open		7.50	8
1997	Bear w/July Birthstone Mini Figurine 239828	Open		7.50	8
1997	Bear w/August Birthstone Mini Figurine 239836	Open		7.50	8
1997	Bear w/September Birthstone Mini Figurine 239844	Open		7.50	8
1997	Bear w/October Birthstone Mini Figurine 239852	Open		7.50	8
1997	Bear w/November Birthstone Mini Figurine 239860	Open		7.50	8
1997	Bear w/December Birthstone Mini Figurine 239933	Open		7.50	8

Love Letters From Teddie Mini - P. Hillman

YEAR ISSUE		EDITION LIMIT	YEAR RETD.	ISSUE PRICE	*QUOTE U.S.$
1997	Bear w/ "I Love Bears" Blocks 902950	Open		7.50	8
1997	Bear w/ "I Love Hugs" Blocks 902969	Open		7.50	8
1997	Bear w/"I Love You" Blocks 156515	Open		7.50	8
1997	Bear w/Heart Dangling Blocks 203084	Open		7.50	8
1997	Bears w/ "Love" Double 203076	Open		13.50	14

Monthly Friends to Cherish - P. Hillman

YEAR ISSUE		EDITION LIMIT	YEAR RETD.	ISSUE PRICE	*QUOTE U.S.$
1993	Jack January Monthly "A New Year With Old Friends" 914754 (Also available through Hamilton Collection)	Open		15.00	15
1993	Phoebe February Monthly "Be Mine" 914762 (Also available through Hamilton Collection)	Open		15.00	15
1993	Mark March Monthly "Friendship Is In The Air" 914770 (Also available through Hamilton Collection)	Open		15.00	15
1993	Alan April Monthly "Showers of Friendship" 914789 (Also available through Hamilton Collection)	Open		15.00	15
1993	May May Monthly "Friendship Is In Bloom" 914797 (Also available through Hamilton Collection)	Open		15.00	15
1993	June June Monthly "Planting The Seed of Friendship" 914800 (Also available through Hamilton Collection)	Open		15.00	15
1993	Julie July Monthly "A Day in The Park" 914819 (Also available through Hamilton Collection)	Open		15.00	15
1993	Arthur August Monthly "Smooth Sailing" 914827 (Also available through Hamilton Collection)	Open		15.00	15
1993	Seth September Monthly "School Days" 914835 (Also available through Hamilton Collection)	Open		15.00	15
1993	Oscar October Monthly "Sweet Treats" 914843 (Also available through Hamilton Collection)	Open		15.00	15
1993	Nicole November Monthly "Thanks For Friends" 914851 (Also available through Hamilton Collection)	Open		15.00	15
1993	Denise December Monthly "Happy Holidays, Friend" 914878 (Also available through Hamilton Collection)	Open		15.00	15

Nativity - P. Hillman

YEAR ISSUE		EDITION LIMIT	YEAR RETD.	ISSUE PRICE	*QUOTE U.S.$
1993	"Friendship Pulls Us Through" & "Ewe Make Being Friends Special" 912867	Open		13.50	14
1992	Angie "I Brought The Star" 951137	Open		15.00	15
1995	Celeste "An Angel To Watch Over You" 141267	Open		20.00	20
1992	Creche & Quilt 951218	Open		50.00	50
1992	Maria, Baby & Josh "A Baby Is God's Gift of Love" "Everyone Needs a Daddy"- 950688	Open		35.00	35
1993	Nativity "Cherish The King" (musical-"O Little Town of Bethlehem") 912859	Suspd.		60.00	120-175
1993	Nativity Camel "Friends Like You Are Precious And True" 904309	Retrd.	1997	30.00	35-55
1994	Nativity Cow "That's What Friends Are For" 651095	Retrd.	1997	22.50	40-45
1993	Nativity Figurine Gift Set w/Creche 916684	Open		100.00	100
1996	Nativity Prayer Plaque "The Cherished One" 176362	Open		13.50	14
1993	Nativity w/ Creche (musical-"Silent Night") 903485	Suspd.		85.00	390
1994	Ronnie "I'll Play My Drum For You" 912905	Open		13.50	14-18
1992	Sammy "Little Lambs Are In My Care" 950726	Open		17.50	18
1992	Three Kings-Richard "My Gift Is Loving", Edward "My Gift Is Caring", Wilbur "My Gift Is Sharing" 950718	Open		55.00	55

Nursery Rhyme - P. Hillman

YEAR ISSUE		EDITION LIMIT	YEAR RETD.	ISSUE PRICE	*QUOTE U.S.$
1994	Jack & Jill "Our Friendship Will Never Tumble" 624772	Retrd.	1998	30.00	20-30
1994	Little Bo Peep "Looking For A Friend Like You" 624802	Retrd.	1998	22.50	23
1994	Little Jack Horner "I'm Plum Happy You're My Friend" 624780	Retrd.	1998	22.50	23-37
1994	Little Miss Muffet "I'm Never Afraid With You At My Side" 624799	Retrd.	1998	20.00	20
1994	Mary, Mary Quite Contrary "Friendship Blooms With Loving Care" 626074	Retrd.	1998	22.50	23-75
1994	Tom, Tom The Piper's Son "Wherever You Go I'll Follow" 624810	Retrd.	1998	20.00	20

Nutcracker Suite - P. Hillman

YEAR ISSUE		EDITION LIMIT	YEAR RETD.	ISSUE PRICE	*QUOTE U.S.$
1997	Collector's Set: Mouse King, Herr Drosselmeyer, Clara, & Boy Prince 272388	Yr.Iss.	1997	70.00	75
1997	Nutcracker Suite Tree (musical-"Dance of the Sugar-Plum Fairy") 292494	Open		45.00	45

Our Cherished Family - P. Hillman

YEAR ISSUE		EDITION LIMIT	YEAR RETD.	ISSUE PRICE	*QUOTE U.S.$
1994	Father "A Father Is The Bearer Of Strength" 624888	Open		13.50	14
1998	A Gift To Behold (boy) 127922	Open		7.50	8
1998	A Gift To Behold (girl) 599352	Open		7.50	8
1998	Grandma Is God's Special Gift 127914	Open		17.50	18
1998	Grandpa Is God's Special Gift 127906	Open		17.50	18
1994	Mother "A Mother's Love Bears All Things" 624861	Open		20.00	20
1994	Older Daughter "Child Of Love" 624845	Open		10.00	10
1994	Older Son "Child Of Pride" 624829	Open		10.00	10
1994	Young Daughter "Child Of Kindness" 624853	Open		9.00	9
1994	Young Son "Child of Hope" 624837	Open		9.00	9

Santa - P. Hillman

YEAR ISSUE		EDITION LIMIT	YEAR RETD.	ISSUE PRICE	*QUOTE U.S.$
1995	Nickolas "You're At The Top Of My List" 141100	Yr.Iss.	1995	20.00	30-70
1996	Klaus "Bearer of Good Tidings" 176036	Yr.Iss.	1996	20.00	20-40
1997	Kris "Up On The Rooftop" 272140	Yr.Iss.		22.50	23
1998	Santa "A Little Holiday R & R" 352713	Yr.Iss.		22.50	23

Santa Express - P. Hillman

YEAR ISSUE		EDITION LIMIT	YEAR RETD.	ISSUE PRICE	*QUOTE U.S.$
1996	Car of Toys "Riding Along With Friends and Smiles" 219096	Open		17.50	18
1996	Casey "Friendship Is The Perfect End To The Holidays" 219525	Open		22.50	23
1997	Cindy "This Train Is Bound For Holiday Surprises!" 219177	Open		17.50	18
1996	Colin "He Knows If You've Been Bad or Good" 219088	Open		17.50	18
1997	Kirby "Heading Into The Holidays With Deer Friends" 219118	Open		17.50	18
1996	Lionel "All Aboard the Santa Express" 219061	Open		22.50	23
1997	Nick "Ho, Ho, Ho — To The Holidays We Go!" 219312	Open		17.50	18
1997	Snow Bear 269905	Open		12.50	13
1997	Street Lamp and Bear 269913	Open		15.00	15
1996	Tony "A First Class Delivery For You!" 219487	Open		17.50	18

Santa's Workshop - P. Hillman

YEAR ISSUE		EDITION LIMIT	YEAR RETD.	ISSUE PRICE	*QUOTE U.S.$
1995	Ginger "Painting Your Holidays With Love" 141127	Open		22.50	23
1995	Holly "A Cup of Homemade Love" 141119	Open		18.50	19
1995	Meri "Handsewn Holidays" 141135	Open		20.00	20
1996	Ornaments/Mailsack/North Pole Sign Mini 3 Asst. 176079	Open		15.00	15
1995	Santa's Workshop Nightlight 141925	Open		75.00	75
1995	Yule "Building a Sturdy Friendship" 141143	Open		22.50	23

Sugar & Spice - P. Hillman

YEAR ISSUE		EDITION LIMIT	YEAR RETD.	ISSUE PRICE	*QUOTE U.S.$
1998	Missy, Cookie, Riley "A Special Recipe For Our Friendship" 352586	Open		35.00	35
1998	Pamela & Grayson "A Dash of Love to Warm Your Heart" 352616	Open		22.50	23
1998	Sharon "Sweetness Pours From My Heart" 352594	Open		20.00	20
1998	Wayne "Spoonfuls of Sweetness" 352608	Open		20.00	20

Sweet Heart Ball - P. Hillman

YEAR ISSUE		EDITION LIMIT	YEAR RETD.	ISSUE PRICE	*QUOTE U.S.$
1996	Craig & Cheri "Sweethearts Forever" 156485	Open		25.00	25
1996	Darla "My Heart Wishes For You" 156469	Open		20.00	20
1996	Darrel "Love Unveils A Happy Heart" 156450	Open		17.50	18
1997	Harry/Katherine "You're The Queen/King Of My Heart" 302732	Yr.Iss.	1997	65.00	65
1996	Jilly "Won't You Be My Sweetheart?" 156477	Open		17.50	18
1996	Marian "You're The Hero Of My Heart" 156442	Open		20.00	20
1996	Robin "You Steal My Heart Away" 156434	Open		17.50	18
1997	Sweetheart Collector Set/3, (Balcony displayer, Romeo "There's No Sweeter Rose Than You" & Juliet "Wherefore Art Thou Romeo?" 203114	Yr.Iss.	1997	60.00	60-83

T Is For Teddies - P. Hillman

YEAR ISSUE		EDITION LIMIT	YEAR RETD.	ISSUE PRICE	*QUOTE U.S.$
1995	Bear w/"A" Block 158488A	Open		5.00	5
1995	Bear w/"B" Block 158488B	Open		5.00	5
1995	Bear w/"C" Block 158488C	Open		5.00	5
1995	Bear w/"D" Block 158488D	Open		5.00	5
1995	Bear w/"E" Block 158488E	Open		5.00	5
1995	Bear w/"F" Block 158488F	Open		5.00	5
1995	Bear w/"G" Block 158488G	Open		5.00	5
1995	Bear w/"H" Block 158488H	Open		5.00	5
1995	Bear w/"I" Block 158488I	Open		5.00	5
1995	Bear w/"J" Block 158488J	Open		5.00	5
1995	Bear w/"K" Block 158488K	Open		5.00	5
1995	Bear w/"L" Block 158488L	Open		5.00	5
1995	Bear w/"M" Block 158488M	Open		5.00	5
1995	Bear w/"N" Block 158488N	Open		5.00	5
1995	Bear w/"O" Block 158488O	Open		5.00	5
1995	Bear w/"P" Block 158488P	Open		5.00	5
1995	Bear w/"Q" Block 158488Q	Open		5.00	5
1995	Bear w/"R" Block 158488R	Open		5.00	5
1995	Bear w/"S" Block 158488S	Open		5.00	5
1995	Bear w/"T" Block 158488T	Open		5.00	5
1995	Bear w/"U" Block 158488U	Open		5.00	5
1995	Bear w/"V" Block 158488V	Open		5.00	5
1995	Bear w/"W" Block 158488W	Open		5.00	5
1995	Bear w/"X" Block 158488X	Open		5.00	5
1995	Bear w/"Y" Block 158488Y	Open		5.00	5
1995	Bear w/"Z" Block 158488Z	Open		5.00	5

Through The Years - P. Hillman

YEAR ISSUE		EDITION LIMIT	YEAR RETD.	ISSUE PRICE	*QUOTE U.S.$
1993	"Cradled With Love" Baby 911356	Open		16.50	17
1993	"Beary Special One" Age 1 911348	Open		13.50	14
1993	"Two Sweet Two Bear" Age 2 911321	Open		13.50	14
1993	"Three Cheers For You" Age 3 911313	Open		15.00	15
1993	"Unfolding Happy Wishes Four You" Age 4 911305	Open		15.00	15
1993	"Color Me Five" Age 5 911291	Open		15.00	15
1993	"Chalking Up Six Wishes" Age 6 911283	Open		16.50	17
1998	"Seven Is As Sweet As Honey" Age 7 466239	Open		16.50	17
1998	"Being Eight Is Really Great!" Age 8 466247	Open		16.50	17
1998	"Being Nine Is Really Fine!" Age 9 466255	Open		16.50	17
1998	"Count To Ten...& Celebrate!" Age 10 466263	Open		16.50	17

Toybox Teddies - P. Hillman

YEAR ISSUE		EDITION LIMIT	YEAR RETD.	ISSUE PRICE	*QUOTE U.S.$
1998	Andie "A,B,C Spell With Me" 354139	Open		5.00	5
1998	Corey "Learn About Colors With Corey The Color Bear" 354147	Open		5.00	5
1998	Frankie "What Says Moo?...How About You!" 354163	Open		5.00	5
1998	Nicki "1,2,3 Count With Me" 354120	Open		5.00	5
1998	Shelley "Circles, Squares, Teddie Bears With Shelley The Shape Bear" 354155	Open		5.00	5
1998	Tellie "Tick, Tock Look At The Clock" 354171	Open		5.00	5

Up In The Attic - P. Hillman

YEAR ISSUE		EDITION LIMIT	YEAR RETD.	ISSUE PRICE	*QUOTE U.S.$
1998	Kaitlyn "Old Treasures, New Memories" 302600	Yr.Iss.		50.00	50

We Bear Thanks - P. Hillman

YEAR ISSUE		EDITION LIMIT	YEAR RETD.	ISSUE PRICE	*QUOTE U.S.$
1996	Barbara "Giving Thanks For Our Family" 141305	Retrd.	1997	12.50	26
1996	Dina "Bear In Mind, You're Special" 141275	Retrd.	1997	15.00	30
1996	John "Bear In Mind, You're Special" 141283	Retrd.	1997	15.00	30
1996	Rick "Suited Up For The Holidays" 141291	Retrd.	1997	12.50	25
1996	Table With Food / Dog " We Bear Thanks" 141542	Retrd.	1997	30.00	30

*Quotes have been rounded up to nearest dollar

Winter Bear Festival - P. Hillman

YEAR ISSUE	EDITION LIMIT	YEAR RETD.	ISSUE PRICE	*QUOTE U.S.$
1997 Adam "It's A Holiday On Ice" 269751	Open		20.00	20
1997 Boy Waterball (musical-"White Christmas") 292575	Open		45.00	45
1997 Candace "Skating On Holiday Joy" 269778	Open		20.00	20
1997 Girl Waterball (musical-"Let It Snow") 272884	Open		45.00	45
1997 James "Going My Way For The Holidays" 269786	Open		25.00	25
1997 Lindsey & Lyndon "Walking In A Winter Wonderland" 141178	Open		30.00	30
1997 Mitch "Friendship Never Melts Away" 269735	Open		30.00	30
1997 Spencer "I'm Head Over Skis For You" 269743	Open		20.00	20
1997 Ted "Snow Fun When You're Not Around" 269727	Open		18.50	19

Christian Ulbricht USA

Christian Ulbricht Collectors' Club - C. Ulbricht

YEAR ISSUE	EDITION LIMIT	YEAR RETD.	ISSUE PRICE	*QUOTE U.S.$
1998 The Lantern Child	4/99		Gift	N/A
1998 SnowKing 000501	4/99		154.00	154

Christian Ulbricht Event - C. Ulbricht

YEAR ISSUE	EDITION LIMIT	YEAR RETD.	ISSUE PRICE	*QUOTE U.S.$
1997 Woodpecker 32-450	2,500	1997	49.95	65-100
1998 Penguin 32-451	Yr.Iss.	1998	49.95	50

American Folk Hero/Midwest© - C. Ulbircht

YEAR ISSUE	EDITION LIMIT	YEAR RETD.	ISSUE PRICE	*QUOTE U.S.$
1994 Davy Crockett 12960-9	1,500	1996	160.00	170-179
1994 Johnny Appleseed 12959-3	1,500	1996	160.00	170-220
1995 Paul Bunyan 12800-8	1,500	1996	170.00	170-179
1996 Sacajawea 17018-2	1,000	1996	200.00	180-200
1996 Wyatt Earp 17019-9	1,000	1996	200.00	200

A Christmas Carol - C. Ulbircht

YEAR ISSUE	EDITION LIMIT	YEAR RETD.	ISSUE PRICE	*QUOTE U.S.$
1997 Bob Cratchit & Tiny Tim 000145	5,000		236.00	236
1994 Bob Cratchit and Tiny Tim/Midwest© 09577-5	2,500	1996	210.00	219-245
1996 Ghost of Christmas Past/Midwest© 18299-4	1,500	1996	200.00	225-300
1992 Ghost of Christmas Present/Midwest© 12041-5	1,500	1996	170.00	179-300
1996 Ghost of Christmas Yet to Come/Midwest© 17021-2	1,500	1996	190.00	199-300
1998 Mrs. Cratchit 000149	5,000		230.00	230
1996 Scrooge 000123	5,000		228.00	228
1993 Scrooge/Midwest© 09584-3	2,500	1996	200.00	200-219

Great American Inventors - C. Ulbircht

YEAR ISSUE	EDITION LIMIT	YEAR RETD.	ISSUE PRICE	*QUOTE U.S.$
1998 Alexander Graham Bell 000148	1,500		250.00	250
1997 Henry Ford 000146	1,500		260.00	260
1996 Thomas Edison 000129	1,500		270.00	270

Limited Edition Nutcrackers - C. Ulbircht

YEAR ISSUE	EDITION LIMIT	YEAR RETD.	ISSUE PRICE	*QUOTE U.S.$
1998 Angel 000147	2,500		230.00	230
1997 Biker Lady 000124	5,000		198.00	198
1997 Doc Holiday 000137	3,000		222.00	222
1997 Eagle Dancer 000144	3,000		240.00	240
1996 Elf on Reindeer 000128	5,000		180.00	180
1997 Frosty 000143	3,000		117.00	117
1997 Jack the Hacker 000135	3,000		240.00	240
1998 Lawyer 000149	2,500		222.00	222
1996 Lone Wolf 000107	5,000		209.00	209
1996 Moon & Star Santa 000112	5,000		219.00	219
1994 Mr. Santa Claus/Midwest© 9588-1	2,500	1996	160.00	165-169
1998 Mr. Snowman 000154	2,500		154.00	154
1994 Mrs. Santa Claus/Midwest© 9587-4	2,500	1996	160.00	165-198
1998 Mrs. Snowman 000155	2,500		154.00	154
1997 Nic Taylor 000134	3,000		240.00	240
1998 Santa in Canoe 000163	2,500		230.00	230
1996 Santa in Chimney 000131	5,000		219.00	219
1997 Santa MacNic 000133	3,000		230.00	230
1997 Santa O'Claus 000132	3,000		230.00	230
1996 Santa on Reindeer 000127	5,000		180.00	180
1998 Santa w/ Long Robe 000161	2,500		222.00	222
1998 Santa w/ Short Robe 000152	2,500		222.00	222
1997 Santa Winterwonderland 000140	3,000		230.00	230
1997 Santa's Ark 000139	3,000		230.00	230
1997 Stars & Stripes Forever 000138	3,000		222.00	222
1998 Summer Wonderland 000153	3,000		230.00	230
1996 Teddybear Santa 000111	5,000	1998	200.00	200-230
1998 White Buffalo 000157	3,000		240.00	240
1996 White Feather 000108	5,000		209.00	209

Nutcracker Ballet - C. Ulbircht

YEAR ISSUE	EDITION LIMIT	YEAR RETD.	ISSUE PRICE	*QUOTE U.S.$
1996 Clara 000121	5,000		219.00	219
1996 Herr Drosselmeyer 000119	5,000		228.00	228
1996 Mouse King 000120	5,000		228.00	228
1996 Prince 000122	5,000		219.00	219
1998 Toy Soldier 000165	5,000		238.00	238

Nutcracker Ballet/Midwest© - C. Ulbircht

YEAR ISSUE	EDITION LIMIT	YEAR RETD.	ISSUE PRICE	*QUOTE U.S.$
1991 Clara 03657-0	Retrd.	1996	124.00	137-200
1991 Herr Drosselmeyer 03656-3	Retrd.	1996	160.00	160
1991 Mouse King 04510-7	Retrd.	1996	160.00	160
1991 Prince 03665-5	Retrd.	1996	154.00	154
1991 Toy Soldier 03666-2	Retrd.	1996	154.00	154

Plays of Shakespeare - C. Ulbircht

YEAR ISSUE	EDITION LIMIT	YEAR RETD.	ISSUE PRICE	*QUOTE U.S.$
1997 Juliet 000136	5,000		230.00	230
1998 Romeo 000156	5,000		236.00	236
1997 Shakespeare 000142	5,000		236.00	236

Santa Claus/Midwest© - C. Ulbircht

YEAR ISSUE	EDITION LIMIT	YEAR RETD.	ISSUE PRICE	*QUOTE U.S.$
1992 Father Christmas (1st) 07094-9	Retrd.	N/A	210.00	350
1993 Toymaker (2nd) 09531-7	2,500	1996	210.00	210
1994 Victorian Santa (3rd) 2961-6	2,500	1996	210.00	210-275
1995 King of Christmas (4th) 13665-2	2,500	1996	210.00	210-750

Three Musketeers - C. Ulbircht

YEAR ISSUE	EDITION LIMIT	YEAR RETD.	ISSUE PRICE	*QUOTE U.S.$
1996 Portos 000114	5,000		200.00	200

Three Wisemen - C. Ulbircht

YEAR ISSUE	EDITION LIMIT	YEAR RETD.	ISSUE PRICE	*QUOTE U.S.$
1996 Caspar 000115	5,000		209.00	209

Wizard of Oz - C. Ulbircht

YEAR ISSUE	EDITION LIMIT	YEAR RETD.	ISSUE PRICE	*QUOTE U.S.$
1998 Cowardly Lion 000151	5,000		240.00	240
1998 Dorothy 000150	5,000		230.00	230
1997 Tin Woodsman 000141	5,000		230.00	230

Christopher Radko

Nutcrackers - C. Radko

YEAR ISSUE	EDITION LIMIT	YEAR RETD.	ISSUE PRICE	*QUOTE U.S.$
1997 The Bishop 97-K01-00	5,000		485.00	485
1997 Candy Stripe 97-K03-00	5,000		445.00	445
1997 Snow Gent 97-K04-00	5,000		445.00	445
1997 Winter Dream 97-K02-00	5,000		485.00	485

Crystal World

All God's Creatures - R. Nakai, unless otherwise noted

YEAR ISSUE	EDITION LIMIT	YEAR RETD.	ISSUE PRICE	*QUOTE U.S.$
1997 Allie Gator - T. Suzuki	Open		100.00	100
1983 Alligator	Closed	N/A	46.00	46
1996 Baby Bird Bath	Open		45.00	45
1990 Baby Dinosaur - T. Suzuki	Closed	N/A	50.00	50
1990 Barney Dog - T. Suzuki	Closed	N/A	32.00	32
1984 Beaver	Closed	N/A	30.00	30
1990 Betsy Bunny - T. Suzuki	Closed	N/A	32.00	32
1997 Buffalo - Team	Open		350.00	350
1984 Butterfly	Closed	N/A	36.00	36
1986 Butterfly, mini - N. Mulargia	Closed	N/A	15.00	15
1987 Circus Puppy, lg.	Closed	N/A	50.00	50
1987 Circus Puppy, sm.	Closed	N/A	28.00	28
1990 Clara Cow - T. Suzuki	Closed	N/A	32.00	32
1998 Cottontail - T. Suzuki	Open		70.00	70
1984 Dachshund	Closed	N/A	28.00	28
1986 Dachshund, mini - N. Mulargia	Closed	N/A	15.00	15
1984 Dog	Closed	N/A	28.00	28
1984 Donkey	Closed	N/A	40.00	40
1984 Duck	Closed	N/A	30.00	30
1990 Duck Family	Closed	N/A	70.00	70
1987 Duckling - T. Suzuki	Closed	N/A	60.00	60
1983 Elephant	Closed	N/A	40.00	40
1985 Elephant, large	Closed	N/A	54.00	54
1996 Freddy Frog	Open		30.00	30
1996 Frieda Frog	Open		37.00	37
1984 Frog & Mushroom	Closed	N/A	46.00	46
1986 Frog Mushroom, mini - N. Mulargia	Closed	N/A	15.00	15
1983 Frog, lg.	Closed	N/A	30.00	30
1983 Frog, mini	Closed	N/A	14.00	14
1983 Frog, sm.	Closed	N/A	26.00	26
1990 Georgie Giraffe - T. Suzuki	Closed	N/A	32.00	32
1990 Henry Hippo - T. Suzuki	Closed	N/A	32.00	32
1984 Hippo, lg.	Closed	N/A	50.00	50
1984 Hippo, sm.	Closed	N/A	30.00	30
1990 Jumbo Elephant - T. Suzuki	Open		32.00	32
1997 Junior (Elephant)	Open		110.00	110
1984 Kangaroo, lg.	Closed	N/A	50.00	50
1984 Kangaroo, sm.	Closed	N/A	34.00	34
1984 Koala Bear	Closed	N/A	50.00	50
1986 Koala, mini - N. Mulargia	Closed	N/A	15.00	15
1984 Koala, sm.	Closed	N/A	28.00	28
1995 Ling Ling - T. Suzuki	Closed	1997	53.00	53
1985 Lion, lg.	Closed	N/A	60.00	60
1985 Lion, sm.	Closed	N/A	36.00	36
1998 Little Owl - T. Suzuki	Open		100.00	100
1997 Mama Elephant	Open		250.00	250
1990 Mikey Monkey - T. Suzuki	Closed	N/A	32.00	32
1987 Mother Koala and Cub	Closed	N/A	55.00	55
1983 Mouse Standing	Closed	N/A	34.00	34
1983 Mouse, lg.	Closed	N/A	36.00	36
1983 Mouse, med.	Closed	N/A	28.00	28
1986 Mouse, mini - N. Mulargia	Closed	N/A	15.00	15
1983 Mouse, sm.	Closed	N/A	20.00	20
1994 Owls - N. Mulargia	Open		53.00	53
1987 Panda, lg.	Closed	1995	45.00	46
1987 Panda, sm.	Closed	N/A	30.00	30
1984 Peacock	Closed	N/A	50.00	50
1984 Penguin	Closed	N/A	34.00	34
1987 Penguin On Cube	Closed	1996	30.00	31
1991 Penguin On Cube	Closed	1996	40.00	41
1996 Penguin On Cube	Open		48.00	48
1995 Percy Piglet - T. Suzuki	Closed	1997	19.00	19
1993 Pig - N. Mulargia	Closed	1995	50.00	51
1983 Pig, lg.	Closed	N/A	50.00	50
1983 Pig, med.	Closed	N/A	32.00	32
1983 Pig, sm.	Closed	N/A	22.00	22
1993 Playful Seal - T. Suzuki	Closed	1997	42.00	42
1991 Polar Bear Paperweight	Open		98.00	98
1984 Poodle	Closed	N/A	30.00	30
1987 Poodle, lg.	Closed	N/A	64.00	64
1987 Poodle, sm.	Closed	1994	35.00	35
1984 Porcupine	Closed	N/A	42.00	42
1987 Posing Penguin	Closed	N/A	85.00	85
1997 Proud Peacock - R. Nakai	Open		150.00	150
1990 Puppy Love - T. Suzuki	Closed	N/A	45.00	45
1987 Rabbit with Carrot, lg.	Closed	N/A	55.00	55
1987 Rabbit with Carrot, sm.	Closed	N/A	32.00	32
1983 Rabbit, lg.	Closed	N/A	50.00	50
1986 Rabbit, mini - N. Mulargia	Closed	N/A	15.00	15
1983 Rabbit, sm.	Closed	N/A	28.00	28
1985 Racoon	Closed	N/A	50.00	50
1984 Racoon, lg.	Closed	N/A	44.00	44
1987 Racoon, sm.	Closed	N/A	30.00	30
1984 Racoon, sm.	Closed	N/A	30.00	30
1989 Rainbow Dog, mini	Closed	N/A	25.00	25
1989 Rainbow Owl, mini	Closed	N/A	25.00	25
1989 Rainbow Penguin, mini	Closed	N/A	25.00	25
1989 Rainbow Squirrel, mini	Closed	N/A	25.00	25
1987 Rhinoceros	Closed	N/A	55.00	55
1994 Seal	Closed	1996	46.00	47
1987 Snowbunny, lg.	Closed	N/A	45.00	45
1987 Snowbunny, sm.	Closed	N/A	25.00	25
1991 Spike	Closed	N/A	50.00	50
1991 Spot	Closed	N/A	50.00	50
1985 Squirrel	Closed	1994	30.00	32
1986 Swan - N. Mulargia, mini	Open		15.00	28
1998 Timber Wolf	1,250		175.00	175
1992 Trumpeting Elephant - T. Suzuki	Closed	1996	50.00	51
1993 Turtle	Closed	1996	65.00	67
1983 Turtle, lg.	Closed	N/A	56.00	56
1983 Turtle, med.	Closed	N/A	38.00	38
1984 Turtle, mini	Closed	N/A	18.00	18
1983 Turtle, sm.	Closed	N/A	28.00	28
1986 Unicorn	Closed	1994	110.00	114
1987 Walrus	Closed	N/A	70.00	70
1987 Walrus, sm. - T. Suzuki	Closed	N/A	60.00	60
1995 Wilbur in Love - N. Mulargia	Closed	1997	90.00	90
1994 Wilbur the Pig - T. Suzuki	Open		48.00	48

Bird Collection - R. Nakai, unless otherwise noted

YEAR ISSUE	EDITION LIMIT	YEAR RETD.	ISSUE PRICE	*QUOTE U.S.$
1986 Bird Bath - N. Mulargia	Closed	1989	54.00	77
1984 Bird Family	Closed	1990	22.00	36
1984 Love Bird	Closed	1988	44.00	69
1986 Love Birds	Closed	1992	54.00	78
1990 Ollie Owl - T. Suzuki	Closed	1993	32.00	40
1983 Owl Standing	Closed	1987	40.00	72
1983 Owl, lg.	Closed	1987	44.00	75
1983 Owl, sm.	Closed	1987	22.00	36
1991 Parrot Couple	Closed	1992	90.00	100
1985 Parrot, extra lg.	Closed	1988	300.00	450
1987 Parrot, lg.	Closed	1993	130.00	170
1987 Parrot, sm.	Closed	1989	30.00	45
1985 Parrot, sm.	Closed	1989	100.00	110
1990 Tree Top Owls - T. Suzuki	Closed	1993	96.00	98
1990 Wise Owl - T. Suzuki	Closed	1993	55.00	65
1990 Wise Owl, sm. - T. Suzuki	Closed	1993	40.00	65

Bon Voyage Collection - Various

YEAR ISSUE	EDITION LIMIT	YEAR RETD.	ISSUE PRICE	*QUOTE U.S.$
1990 Airplane, sm. - T. Suzuki	Closed	1993	200.00	200
1995 Amish Buggy - R. Nakai	Closed	1997	160.00	160
1995 Amish Buggy w/Wood Base - R. Nakai	Closed	1997	190.00	190
1994 Bermuda Rig Sailboat - R. Nakai	Open		105.00	105
1998 Bi-Plane - Team	Open		75.00	75
1992 Bi-Plane, mini - T. Suzuki	Open		65.00	65
1992 Cable Car, mini - T. Suzuki	Closed	1996	40.00	43
1991 Cable Car, sm. - T. Suzuki	Closed	1997	70.00	70
1984 Classic Car - T. Suzuki	Closed	N/A	160.00	160
1991 Cruise Ship -T. Suzuki	1,000		2000.00	2000
1997 Cruise Ship, med. - R. Nakai	Open		550.00	550
1995 Cruise Ship, mini - N. Mulargia	Open		105.00	105
1994 Cruise Ship, sm. - T. Suzuki	Open		575.00	575
1993 Express Train - N. Mulargia	Closed	1993	95.00	100
1998 Float Plane - Team	Open		75.00	75
1997 Grand Cable Car - T. Suzuki	Closed	1997	157.50	158
1991 Large Cable Car, large - T. Suzuki	Open		130.00	130
1984 Limousine - R. Nakai	Closed	N/A	46.00	46
1994 Mainsail Sailboat - R. Nakai	Open		230.00	230
1990 Orbiting Space Shuttle - T. Suzuki	Open		300.00	300
1991 Orbiting Space Shuttle, sm. - T. Suzuki	Closed	1997	90.00	90
1984 Pickup Track - R. Nakai	Closed	N/A	38.00	38
1991 The Rainbow Express - N. Mulargia	Closed	1993	125.00	130
1993 Riverboat - N. Mulargia	350		570.00	600
1994 Riverboat, sm. - N. Mulargia	Open		210.00	210
1993 Sailboat - R. Nakai	Open		100.00	115
1992 Sailing Ship - N. Mulargia	Closed	1997	38.00	38
1993 San Francisco Cable Car, lg. - R. Nakai	Open		59.00	59
1993 San Francisco Cable Car, sm. - R. Nakai	Open		40.00	40
1991 Schooner - N. Mulargia	Closed	1995	95.00	98
1997 Schooner - R. Nakai	Open		60.00	60
1990 Space Shuttle Launch, sm. - T. Suzuki	Closed	1996	265.00	270
1994 Spinnaker Sailboat - R. Nakai	Open		265.00	265
1984 Sports Car - T. Suzuki	Closed	N/A	140.00	140
1990 Square Rigger - R. Nakai	Open		250.00	250
1995 Tall Ship - R. Nakai	Open		395.00	395
1984 Touring Car - T. Suzuki	Closed	N/A	140.00	140
1984 Tractor Trailer - R. Nakai	Closed	N/A	40.00	40
1990 Train Set, lg. - T. Suzuki	Closed	N/A	480.00	480
1990 Train Set, sm. - T. Suzuki	Open		100.00	100
1997 Truckin' -T. Suzuki	Open		260.00	260
1997 Up and Away - N. Mulargia	Open		39.50	40

*Quotes have been rounded up to nearest dollar

Castles and Legends - R. Nakai, unless otherwise noted

YEAR ISSUE	EDITION LIMIT	YEAR RETD.	ISSUE PRICE	*QUOTE U.S.$
1991 Castle In The Sky	Closed	1994	150.00	165
1994 Castle Rainbow Rainbow Mtn. Bs.	Open		1575.00	1575
1994 Castle Royale/Clear Mountain Bs	Open		1300.00	1300
1989 Dragon Baby	Closed	1994	80.00	85
1996 Emerald Castle	Open		105.00	105
1993 Enchanted Castle	750		800.00	895
1993 Fantasy Castle, lg.	Open		230.00	245
1993 Fantasy Castle, med.	Open		130.00	142
1992 Fantasy Castle, mini - N. Mulargia	Open		40.00	40
1992 Fantasy Castle, sm.	Open		85.00	95
1995 Fantasy Coach, lg. - N. Mulargia	Open		368.00	368
1995 Fantasy Coach, med. - N. Mulargia	Open		158.00	158
1995 Fantasy Coach, sm. - N. Mulargia	Open		100.00	100
1990 I Love You Unicorn - N. Mulargia	Closed	N/A	58.00	58
1987 Ice Castle	Closed	N/A	150.00	150
1988 Imperial Castle	Open		320.00	345
1988 Imperial Ice Castle	Closed	N/A	320.00	320
1989 Magic Fairy	Closed	N/A	40.00	40
1991 Majestic Castle - A. Kato	Open		390.00	390
1995 Mouse Coach, mini - N. Mulargia	Open		52.00	52
1995 Mouse Coach, sm. - N. Mulargia	Open		95.00	95
1988 Mystic Castle	Open		90.00	90
1988 Mystic Ice Castle	Closed	N/A	90.00	90
1990 Pegasus - N. Mulargia	Closed	N/A	50.00	50
1987 Rainbow Castle	Open		150.00	184
1989 Rainbow Castle, mini	Open		60.00	62
1989 Star Fairy	Closed	N/A	65.00	65
1989 Starlight Castle	Closed	1994	155.00	165
1989 Unicorn & Friend	Closed	N/A	100.00	100
1990 Unicorn - N. Mulargia	Closed	1994	38.00	40

Celebration of Life - Various

YEAR ISSUE	EDITION LIMIT	YEAR RETD.	ISSUE PRICE	*QUOTE U.S.$
1998 Baby Booties - Team	Open		35.00	35
1997 Baby Boy Carriage - T. Suzuki	Open		52.50	53
1997 Baby Girl Carriage - T. Suzuki	Open		52.50	53
1995 Happy Birthday Cake - R. Nakai	Open		63.00	63
1998 Wedding Bells - R. Nakai	Open		125.00	125
1989 Wedding Couple - N. Mulargia	Open		75.00	75
1985 Wedding Couple - R. Nakai	Closed	N/A	38.00	38
1995 Wedding Couple, med. - N. Mulargia	Open		63.00	63
1992 Wedding Couple, mini - N. Mulargia	Closed	1997	30.00	30

Clown Collection - R. Nakai, unless otherwise noted

YEAR ISSUE	EDITION LIMIT	YEAR RETD.	ISSUE PRICE	*QUOTE U.S.$
1985 Acrobatic Clown	Closed	N/A	50.00	50
1992 Baby Clown - N. Mulargia	Closed	N/A	30.00	30
1985 Baseball Clown	Closed	N/A	54.00	54
1984 Clown	Closed	N/A	42.00	42
1985 Clown On Unicycle	Closed	N/A	54.00	54
1985 Clown, sm.	Closed	N/A	30.00	30
1992 Flower Clown - N. Mulargia	Closed	N/A	70.00	70
1985 Golf Clown	Closed	N/A	54.00	54
1985 Jack In The Box, sm.	Closed	N/A	24.00	24
1985 Juggler	Closed	N/A	54.00	54
1985 Large Clown	Closed	N/A	42.00	42
1985 Large Jack In The Box	Closed	N/A	64.00	64
1985 Tennis Clown	Closed	N/A	54.00	54

Crystal Concerto - Various

YEAR ISSUE	EDITION LIMIT	YEAR RETD.	ISSUE PRICE	*QUOTE U.S.$
1997 Clarinet - J. Makoto	Open		235.00	235
1998 Grand Piano with Bench - Team	Open		125.00	125

Crystal Village - Various

YEAR ISSUE	EDITION LIMIT	YEAR RETD.	ISSUE PRICE	*QUOTE U.S.$
1994 Country Church - R. Nakai	Closed	1997	53.00	53
1994 Country Church w/Rainbow Base - R. Nakai	Open		63.00	63
1993 Country Gristmill -T. Suzuki	1,250		320.00	340
1992 Waterfront Village - N. Mulargia	Closed	1997	190.00	190

Disney Showcase Collection - Various

YEAR ISSUE	EDITION LIMIT	YEAR RETD.	ISSUE PRICE	*QUOTE U.S.$
1998 Cinderella's Castle - T. Suzuki	1,250		1495.00	1495
1998 Cinderella's Slipper - R. Nakai	9,750		49.50	50
1998 Dumbo & Timothy - T. Suzuki	2,750		279.00	279
1998 Gee, You're the Sweetest (Minnie) - R. Nakai	4,750		249.00	249
1998 Just For You (Mickey) - R. Nakai	4,750		249.00	249
1998 Pinocchio & Jiminy Cricket - T. Suzuki	2,750		299.00	299

Fruit Collection - R. Nakai

YEAR ISSUE	EDITION LIMIT	YEAR RETD.	ISSUE PRICE	*QUOTE U.S.$
1985 Pear	Closed	N/A	30.00	30
1991 Pear, lg.	Closed	N/A	42.00	42
1996 Pineapple	Open		53.00	53
1991 Pineapple, med.	Closed	N/A	27.00	27
1991 Pineapple, sm.	Closed	N/A	16.00	16
1985 Strawberries	Closed	N/A	28.00	28

Games of Chance - R. Nakai, unless otherwise noted

YEAR ISSUE	EDITION LIMIT	YEAR RETD.	ISSUE PRICE	*QUOTE U.S.$
1991 Dice, sm.	Closed	1997	27.00	27
1991 Lucky 7	Closed	N/A	50.00	50
1997 Lucky Dice	Open		68.25	69
1994 Lucky Roll	Open		95.00	95
1996 One Arm Bandit	Open		70.00	70
1991 Rolling Dice - T. Suzuki	Closed	N/A	110.00	110
1993 Rolling Dice, lg.	Closed	1997	60.00	60
1993 Rolling Dice, med.	Open		48.00	48
1992 Rolling Dice, mini	Open		32.00	32
1993 Rolling Dice, sm.	Closed	1996	40.00	43
1993 Slot Machine, lg. - T. Suzuki	Open		83.00	83
1991 Slot Machine, mini	Open		30.00	30
1991 Slot Machine, sm. - T. Suzuki	Open		58.00	58
1994 Super Slot	Open		295.00	295

Holiday Treasures - R. Nakai, unless otherwise noted

YEAR ISSUE	EDITION LIMIT	YEAR RETD.	ISSUE PRICE	*QUOTE U.S.$
1984 Angel	Closed	N/A	28.00	28
1997 Angel with Heart - T. Suzuki	Open		30.00	30
1985 Angel, lg.	Closed	N/A	30.00	30
1995 Angel, lg.	Open		53.00	53
1985 Angel, mini	Closed	1996	16.00	16
1995 Baby Bear's Christmas - T. Suzuki	Open		48.00	48
1994 Cathedral w/Rainbow Base	Open		104.00	104
1994 Christmas Tree, Extra lg.	Open		315.00	315
1985 Christmas Tree, lg.	Open		126.00	126
1985 Christmas Tree, mini	Closed	N/A	10.00	10
1985 Christmas Tree, sm.	Open		50.00	68
1996 Frosty	Open		41.00	41
1991 Holy Angel Blowing A Trumpet - T. Suzuki	Closed	1997	38.00	38
1991 Holy Angel Holding A Candle - T. Suzuki	Open		38.00	38
1991 Holy Angel Playing A Harp - T. Suzuki	Closed	1997	38.00	38
1991 Merry Christmas Teddy - T. Suzuki	Open		55.00	55
1986 Nativity - N. Mulargia	Open		150.00	179
1991 Nativity, sm. - T. Suzuki	Open		85.00	90
1987 Rainbow Christmas Tree, lg.	Closed	1995	40.00	40
1987 Rainbow Christmas Tree, sm.	Closed	1993	25.00	28
1991 Santa Bear Christmas - T. Suzuki	Closed	1997	70.00	70
1991 Santa Bear Sleighride - T. Suzuki	Closed	1997	70.00	70
1984 Snowman	Closed	N/A	38.00	38
1987 Teddy Bear Christmas	Open		100.00	100
1990 Trumpeting Angel	Closed	N/A	60.00	60

Imagination - Various

YEAR ISSUE	EDITION LIMIT	YEAR RETD.	ISSUE PRICE	*QUOTE U.S.$
1996 Bo-Bo The Clown - N. Mulargia	Open		53.00	53
1998 Carousel Horse - R. Nakai	Open		125.00	125
1992 Fire Engine - T. Suzuki	Open		100.00	100
1997 Frog Prince - R. Nakai	Open		55.00	55
1998 Glass Slipper - Team	Open		29.00	29
1996 Merry-Go-Round - N. Mulargia	750		280.00	280
1996 Merry-Go-Round, sm. - N. Mulargia	Open		150.00	150
1996 Noah and Friends - N. Mulargia	Open		150.00	150
1996 Pinocchio - T. Suzuki	Open		150.00	150
1990 Rainbow Unicorn - N. Mulargia	Open		50.00	58
1995 Treasure Chest - R. Nakai	Open		63.00	63
1998 Wishin' and a Hoppin' - T. Suzuki	Open		95.00	95

It's Raining Cats and Dogs - R. Nakai, unless otherwise noted

YEAR ISSUE	EDITION LIMIT	YEAR RETD.	ISSUE PRICE	*QUOTE U.S.$
1998 Coffee Break - T. Suzuki	Open		50.00	50
1998 Glamour Puss - T. Suzuki	Open		70.00	70

Limited Edition Collection Series - Various

YEAR ISSUE	EDITION LIMIT	YEAR RETD.	ISSUE PRICE	*QUOTE U.S.$
1986 Airplane -T. Suzuki	Closed	1992	400.00	500
1986 Crucifix - N. Mulargia	Closed	1992	300.00	400
1989 Dream Castle - R. Nakai	500		9000.00	10000
1991 Ellis Island - R. Nakai	Closed	1992	450.00	500
1996 The Empire State Bldg. - R. Nakai	475		1315.00	1315
1985 Empire State Bldg., extra lg. - R. Nakai	Closed	1992	1000.00	1300
1987 Empire State Bldg., lg. - R. Nakai	2000		650.00	700
1989 Grand Castle - R. Nakai	Closed	1996	2500.00	2500
1987 Manhattanscape - G. Veith	Closed	1992	1000.00	1100
1992 Santa Maria - N. Mulargia	Closed	1993	1000.00	1050
1989 Space Shuttle Launch -T. Suzuki	Closed	1992	900.00	1000
1998 Titanic -T. Suzuki	1,912		175.00	175
1990 Tower Bridge -T. Suzuki	Closed	1992	600.00	650
1987 US Capitol Bldg., lg. -T. Suzuki	Closed	1992	1000.00	1100
1993 Victorian House - N. Mulargia	Closed	1996	190.00	190
1992 The White House - R. Nakai	200	1993	3000.00	3000

New York Collection - R. Nakai, unless otherwise noted

YEAR ISSUE	EDITION LIMIT	YEAR RETD.	ISSUE PRICE	*QUOTE U.S.$
1993 Apple with Red Heart, med.	Open		37.00	39
1993 Apple with Red Heart, sm.	Closed	1997	21.00	22
1985 Apple, lg.	Open		44.00	68
1985 Apple, med.	Open		30.00	39
1987 Apple, mini	Open		15.00	16
1985 Apple, sm.	Open		15.00	15
1995 Chrysler Building	Open		275.00	275
1992 Contemp. Empire State Bldg., lg. - A. Kato	Closed	1996	475.00	475
1992 Contemp. Empire State Bldg., med.	Open		170.00	170
1992 Contemp. Empire State Bldg., sm.	Closed	1996	95.00	95
1992 Contemp. Empire State Bldg., sm. MV	Open		95.00	95
1992 Empire State Bldg. w/Windows, mini	Open		74.00	74
1987 Empire State Bldg., med.	Open		250.00	250
1991 Empire State Bldg., mini	Open		60.00	60
1987 Empire State Bldg., sm.	Open		120.00	120
1993 Holiday Empire State building - N. Mulargia	Open		205.00	205
1989 Liberty Island - N. Mulargia	Open		75.00	75
1990 Manhattan Island	Open		240.00	240
1993 Manhattan Island, sm. - N. Mulargia	Open		105.00	105
1993 Rainbow Contemp. Empire, sm.	Open		95.00	95
1985 The Statue of Liberty	Open		250.00	250
1987 Statue of Liberty, med.	Open		120.00	120
1992 Statue Of Liberty, mini	Open		50.00	50
1987 Statue of Liberty, sm. - N. Mulargia	Open		50.00	50
1992 Twin Towers, sm.	Open		130.00	130
1991 World Trade Center Bldg.	Open		170.00	170

Nostalgia Collection - Various

YEAR ISSUE	EDITION LIMIT	YEAR RETD.	ISSUE PRICE	*QUOTE U.S.$
1995 Classic Motorcycle -T. Suzuki	950		420.00	420
1996 Classic Motorcycle, sm. - T. Suzuki	Open		210.00	210
1996 Fabulous Fifties Jukebox - N. Mulargia	Open		79.00	79

Raining Cats and Dogs - T. Suzuki, unless otherwise noted

YEAR ISSUE	EDITION LIMIT	YEAR RETD.	ISSUE PRICE	*QUOTE U.S.$
1991 Calamity Kitty	Open		60.00	60
1984 Cat - R. Nakai	Closed	N/A	36.00	36
1990 Cat N Mouse	Closed	1996	45.00	45
1987 Cat with Ball, lg. - R. Nakai	Closed	N/A	70.00	70
1994 Cheese Mouse - R. Nakai	Open		53.00	53
1992 Country Cat	Open		60.00	62
1990 The Curious Cat	Open		62.00	62
1991 Curious Cat, lg.	Open		90.00	90
1997 CyberMouse - N. Mulargia	Closed	1997	52.50	53
1995 Fido the Dog	Closed	1997	27.00	27
1995 Frisky Fido	Closed	1996	27.00	27
1991 Hello Birdie	Open		65.00	68
1992 Kitten in Basket - C. Kido	Closed	1997	35.00	40
1993 Kitty Kare	Closed	1995	70.00	70
1991 Kitty with Butterfly	Closed	N/A	60.00	60
1991 Kitty with Heart	Closed	1997	27.00	29
1990 Moonlight Cat - R. Nakai	Closed	1993	100.00	110
1995 Moonlight Kitties	Closed	1997	83.00	83
1994 Mozart	Open		48.00	48
1991 Peek-A-Boo Kitties	Open		65.00	65
1993 Pinky	Closed	1996	50.00	50
1992 Playful Kitty	Open		32.00	32
1993 Playful Kitty, lg.	Closed	1996	50.00	50
1994 Playful Pup - T. Suzuki	Open		53.00	53
1987 Playful Pup, lg.	Closed	N/A	85.00	85
1987 Playful Pup, sm.	Closed	1995	32.00	32
1993 Puppy-Gram	Open		58.00	58
1989 Rainbow Mini Cat - R. Nakai	Closed	N/A	25.00	25
1991 Rock-A-Bye Kitty - R. Nakai	Open		80.00	83
1992 See Saw Pals - A. Kato	Open		40.00	41
1987 Small Cat with Ball - R. Nakai	Closed	1993	32.00	35
1997 Sparkie	Open		50.00	50
1991 Strolling Kitties	Closed	1993	65.00	70
1994 Sweetie	Open		28.00	28
1995 Tea Time - R. Nakai	Open		50.00	50
1996 Wanna Play?	Open		65.00	65

Religious Moment Collection - N. Mulargia, unless otherwise noted

YEAR ISSUE	EDITION LIMIT	YEAR RETD.	ISSUE PRICE	*QUOTE U.S.$
1987 Church - T. Suzuki	Closed	N/A	40.00	40
1987 Cross On Mountain	Closed	N/A	30.00	30
1987 Cross On Mountain, lg.	Closed	N/A	85.00	85
1992 Cross with Rose	Closed	N/A	30.00	30
1987 Cross, small	Closed	1993	40.00	45
1987 Crucifix	Closed	N/A	50.00	50
1987 Crucifix On Mountain	Closed	N/A	40.00	40
1987 Face Of Christ - R. Nakai	Closed	N/A	35.00	35
1992 Peace On Earth - I. Nakamura	Closed	1995	95.00	98
1987 Star Of David - R. Nakai	Closed	1993	40.00	45

Seaside Memories - R. Nakai, unless otherwise noted

YEAR ISSUE	EDITION LIMIT	YEAR RETD.	ISSUE PRICE	*QUOTE U.S.$
1992 Baby Seal - T. Suzuki	Open		21.00	21
1991 Beaver	Closed	1996	47.00	50
1997 Coastal Lighthouse	Open		85.00	85
1983 Crab, lg.	Closed	N/A	20.00	20
1983 Crab, sm.	Closed	N/A	28.00	28
1996 Crabbie le Crab	Closed	1997	38.00	38
1992 Cute Crab - T. Suzuki	Closed	1997	27.00	32
1988 Dancing Dolphin	Closed	N/A	130.00	130
1998 Dolphin Dreams	1,250		220.00	220
1988 Dolphin, sm.	Closed	N/A	55.00	55
1993 Extra Large Oyster with Pearl	Closed	1996	75.00	78
1984 Fish	Closed	N/A	36.00	36
1993 Harbor Lighthouse - N. Mulargia	Open		75.00	79
1988 Hatching Sea Turtle - T. Suzuki	Open		45.00	47
1988 Island Paradise, lg.	Closed	N/A	90.00	90
1988 Island Paradise, sm.	Closed	N/A	50.00	50
1988 Lighthouse, lg.	Closed	1994	150.00	160
1988 Lighthouse, sm.	Closed	1997	80.00	80
1998 Lobster - T. Suzuki	Open		125.00	125
1993 Manatee Paperweight	Open		125.00	130
1994 Oscar Otter - T. Suzuki	Closed	1997	53.00	53
1983 Oyster, lg.	Closed	1994	30.00	33
1983 Oyster, mini	Closed	N/A	12.00	12
1983 Oyster, sm.	Closed	1994	18.00	20
1987 Palm Tree	Closed	N/A	160.00	160
1996 Pelican	Open		65.00	65
1996 Playful Dolphin	Open		125.00	125
1996 Playful Dolphin, sm.	Open		75.00	75
1992 Playful Dolphins - T. Suzuki	Closed	1996	60.00	60
1993 Playful Seal - T. Suzuki	Closed	1997	45.00	45
1998 Sea Turtle at Play - T. Suzuki	Open		85.00	85
1994 Seal	Closed	1996	47.00	50
1992 Seaside Pelican - T. Suzuki	Closed	1995	55.00	55
1998 Splash	Open		80.00	80
1992 Tropical Fish	Closed	1995	95.00	95
1992 Tuxedo Penguin	Closed	1995	75.00	75
1992 The Whales - T. Suzuki	Closed	1994	60.00	65

Spring Parade - Various

YEAR ISSUE	EDITION LIMIT	YEAR RETD.	ISSUE PRICE	*QUOTE U.S.$
1990 African Violet - I. Nakamura	Open		32.00	32
1996 American Beauty Rose - N. Mulargia	Closed	1997	53.00	53
1992 Barrel Cactus - I. Nakamura	Closed	1995	45.00	48
1991 Blossom Bunny - T. Suzuki	Open		42.00	42
1991 Bunnies On Ice - T. Suzuki	Closed	1996	58.00	60
1991 Bunny Buddy with Carrot - T. Suzuki	Open		32.00	32
1985 Butterfly Caterpillar - R. Nakai	Closed	N/A	40.00	40
1985 Butterfly on Daisy - R. Nakai	Closed	N/A	30.00	30

*Quotes have been rounded up to nearest dollar

YEAR ISSUE	EDITION LIMIT	YEAR RETD.	ISSUE PRICE	*QUOTE U.S.$
1992 Candleholder - N. Mulargia	Closed	1995	125.00	130
1991 Cheep Cheep - T. Suzuki	Open		35.00	35
1998 Cottontail - T. Suzuki	Open		70.00	70
1990 Crocus - R. Nakai	Closed	N/A	45.00	45
1992 Cute Bunny - T. Suzuki	Closed	1995	38.00	40
1995 Desert Cactus - N. Mulargia	Closed	1997	48.00	50
1994 The Enchanted Rose - R. Nakai	Open		126.00	126
1985 Flower Basket - R. Nakai	Closed	1995	36.00	38
1987 Flower Basket, sm. - R. Nakai	Closed	N/A	40.00	40
1992 Flowering Cactus - I. Nakamura	Closed	1996	58.00	60
1992 Half Dozen Flower Arrangement - N. Mulargia	Closed	1996	20.00	22
1992 Happy Heart - N. Mulargia	Closed	1996	25.00	25
1992 Hummingbird - T. Suzuki	Open		58.00	58
1992 Hummingbird, mini - T. Suzuki	Open		29.00	29
1990 Hyacinth - I. Nakamura	Closed	1997	50.00	50
1987 King Swan - R. Nakai	Closed	N/A	110.00	110
1989 Large Windmill - R. Nakai	Closed	1991	160.00	170
1992 Long Stem Rose - N. Mulargia	Open		35.00	35
1994 Long Stem Rose in Vase - R. Nakai	Open		82.00	82
1986 Love Swan - N. Mulargia	Closed	N/A	70.00	70
1995 Love Swans - N. Mulargia	Open		83.00	83
1996 Love Swans, lg. - N. Mulargia	Open		252.00	252
1992 Loving Hearts - N. Mulargia	Open		35.00	35
1995 Pink Rose - R. Nakai	Closed	1997	53.00	53
1995 Pink Rose in Vase - R. Nakai	Open		41.00	41
1991 Rainbow Butterfly, mini - R. Nakai	Closed	1997	27.00	27
1994 Rainbow Rose - N. Mulargia	Open		82.00	82
1987 Red Rose - R. Nakai	Open		35.00	35
1992 Rose Bouquet - I. Nakamura	Closed	N/A	100.00	100
1996 Rose Bouquet, sm. - R. Nakai	Open		45.00	45
1993 Songbirds - I. Nakamura	Open		90.00	90
1997 Spring Blossoms - S. Yamada	Open		90.00	90
1995 Spring Butterfly - R. Nakai	Open		62.00	62
1989 Spring Chick - R. Nakai	Open		50.00	53
1992 Spring Flowers - T. Suzuki	Closed	1997	40.00	40
1990 Swan Family - T. Suzuki	Closed	N/A	70.00	70
1987 Swan, lg. - R. Nakai	Closed	1996	70.00	70
1985 Swan, lg. - R. Nakai	Closed	N/A	70.00	70
1983 Swan, lg. - R. Nakai	Closed	N/A	44.00	44
1987 Swan, med. - R. Nakai	Open		45.00	63
1985 Swan, med. - R. Nakai	Closed	N/A	54.00	54
1985 Swan, mini - R. Nakai	Open		28.00	29
1987 Swan, sm. - R. Nakai	Open		32.00	47
1983 Swan, sm. - R. Nakai	Closed	N/A	28.00	28
1985 Swan, sm. - R. Nakai	Closed	N/A	44.00	44
1996 Water Lily, Medium, AB - R. Nakai	Open		210.00	210
1997 Water Lily, small AB- R. Nakai	Open		105.00	105
1987 White Rose - R. Nakai	Closed	N/A	35.00	35
1989 Windmill, small - R. Nakai	Closed	1993	90.00	95

Teddyland Collection - Various

YEAR ISSUE	EDITION LIMIT	YEAR RETD.	ISSUE PRICE	*QUOTE U.S.$
1990 Baron Von Teddy - T. Suzuki	Closed	1993	60.00	65
1997 Batter's Up -T. Suzuki	Open		60.00	60
1987 Beach Teddies - N. Mulargia	Open		60.00	60
1992 Beach Teddies, sm. - N. Mulargia	Open		55.00	55
1992 Billard Buddies - T. Suzuki	Open		70.00	70
1993 Black Jack Teddies - N. Mulargia	Open		97.00	97
1988 Bouquet Teddy, lg. - N. Mulargia	Closed	N/A	50.00	50
1988 Bouquet Teddy, sm. - N. Mulargia	Open		35.00	35
1998 Broadway Ted - T. Suzuki	Open		45.00	45
1990 Choo Choo Teddy - T. Suzuki	Closed	1993	100.00	110
1991 Christmas Wreath Teddy - T. Suzuki	Closed	1993	70.00	75
1995 CompuBear - N. Mulargia	Open		63.00	63
1996 Cuddly Bear - R. Nakai	Open		48.00	48
1993 Flower Teddy - T. Suzuki	Closed	1997	50.00	50
1995 Fly A Kite Teddy - T. Suzuki	Closed	1997	41.00	41
1995 Get Well Teddy - R. Nakai	Closed	1996	48.00	50
1989 Golfing Teddies - R. Nakai	Open		100.00	100
1991 Gumball Teddy - T. Suzuki	Closed	1996	63.00	63
1989 Happy Birthday Teddy - R. Nakai	Open		50.00	50
1991 Heart Bear - T. Suzuki	Open		27.00	27
1991 High Chair Teddy - T. Suzuki	Closed	1993	75.00	78
1988 I Love You Teddy - N. Mulargia	Open		50.00	50
1994 I Love You Teddy Couple - N. Mulargia	Open		95.00	95
1995 I Love You Teddy w/lg. Heart - R. Nakai	Open		48.00	48
1992 Ice Cream Teddies - N. Mulargia	Open		55.00	55
1997 Jackpot Teddy - T. Suzuki	Open		62.50	63
1987 Loving Teddies - N. Mulargia	Open		75.00	75
1990 Loving Teddies, sm. - N. Mulargia	Open		60.00	60
1991 Luck Of The Irish - R. Nakai	Closed	1993	60.00	69
1985 Mother and Cub - R. Nakai	Closed	N/A	64.00	64
1990 Mountaineer Teddy - N. Mulargia	Closed	N/A	80.00	80
1991 My Favorite Picture - T. Suzuki	Open		45.00	45
1998 Mystic Teddy - T. Suzuki	Open		70.00	70
1992 Patriotic Teddy - N. Mulargia	Open		30.00	30
1991 Play It Again Ted - T. Suzuki	Open		65.00	65
1991 Playground Teddy - R. Kido	Closed	N/A	90.00	90
1989 Rainbow Bear, mini - R. Nakai	Closed	N/A	25.00	25
1990 Rainbow Teddies - N. Mulargia	Closed	1993	95.00	97
1990 Rocking Horse Teddy - N. Mulargia	Closed	N/A	80.00	80
1987 Sailing Teddies - N. Mulargia	Open		100.00	100
1991 School Bears - H. Serino	Closed	1993	75.00	78
1991 Scuba Bear - T. Suzuki	Closed	1993	65.00	67
1989 Shipwreck Teddies - N. Mulargia	Closed	1993	100.00	105
1992 Singing Baby Bear - T. Suzuki	Open		55.00	55
1987 Skateboard Teddy - R. Nakai	Closed	1993	30.00	32
1987 Skiing Teddy - R. Nakai	Closed	1997	50.00	50
1989 Speedboat Teddies - R. Nakai	Open		90.00	90
1990 Storytime Teddies - T. Suzuki	Open		70.00	70
1987 Surfing Teddy - R. Nakai	Closed	1993	45.00	48
1988 Surfing Teddy, large - R. Nakai	Closed	N/A	80.00	80
1991 Swinging Teddies - N. Mulargia	Open		100.00	100
1988 Teddies At Eight - N. Mulargia	Open		100.00	100
1988 Teddies with Heart - R. Nakai	Open		45.00	45
1989 Teddy Balloon - R. Nakai	Closed	1993	70.00	75
1994 Teddy Bear - R. Nakai	Closed	1997	63.00	63
1994 Teddy Bear with Rainbow Base - R. Nakai	Open		75.00	75
1983 Teddy Bear, lg. - R. Nakai	Closed	N/A	68.00	68
1983 Teddy Bear, med. - R. Nakai	Closed	N/A	44.00	44
1983 Teddy Bear, sm. - R. Nakai	Closed	N/A	28.00	28
1988 Teddy Family - N. Mulargia	Closed	1993	50.00	53
1995 Teddy's Self Portrait - T. Suzuki	Closed	1997	53.00	53
1986 Teddy, mini - N. Mulargia	Closed	N/A	15.00	15
1997 Tee-Shot Teddy - T. Suzuki	Open		22.50	23
1987 Teeter Totter Teddies - N. Mulargia	Closed	1993	65.00	70
1988 Touring Teddies - N. Mulargia	Open		90.00	90
1990 Tricycle Teddy - T. Suzuki	Closed	1993	40.00	42
1991 Trim A Tree Teddy - R. Nakai	Closed	1996	50.00	50
1989 Vanity Teddy - R. Nakai	Closed	1993	100.00	105
1989 Windsurf Teddy - R. Nakai	Closed	1993	85.00	87
1988 Winter Teddies - N. Mulargia	Closed	N/A	90.00	90

The Well Dressed Desk (Paperweights) - Various

YEAR ISSUE	EDITION LIMIT	YEAR RETD.	ISSUE PRICE	*QUOTE U.S.$
1993 100 mm Diamond - R. Nakai	Open		525.00	525
1996 40 mm Diamond - R. Nakai	Open		48.00	48
1993 50 mm Diamond - R. Nakai	Open		70.00	70
1993 75 mm Diamond - R. Nakai	Open		285.00	285
1997 Around the World - Team	Open		85.00	85
1990 Baseball - I. Nakamura	Closed	N/A	170.00	170
1995 Boston "Cityscape" Paperweight - R. Nakai	Open		105.00	105
1995 Boston Skyline Paperweight, med. - R. Nakai	Open		80.00	80
1989 Chicago - I. Nakamura	Open		150.00	150
1995 Chicago Skyline Clock Paperweight, med. - R. Nakai	Closed	1996	158.00	158
1996 Crystal Egg and Stand - R. Nakai	Open		83.00	83
1991 Dallas Skyline - I. Nakamura	Open		180.00	180
1988 Empire State - G. Veith	Closed	N/A	120.00	120
1990 Fishing - I. Nakamura	Closed	N/A	170.00	170
1990 Golfing - I. Nakamura	Closed	N/A	170.00	170
1992 Heart Clock - R. Nakai	Closed	N/A	100.00	100
1992 Manhattan Reflections - R. Nakai	Open		95.00	95
1997 Moravian Star - J. Makoto	Open		85.00	85
1988 N.Y. Skyline - G. Veith	Open		100.00	100
1988 Nativity - R. Nakai	Closed	1994	100.00	100
1994 NY "Cityscape" Pwght. - G. Veith	Open		105.00	105
1994 NY Dome Paperweight - G. Veith	Closed	1995	75.00	75
1994 NY Skyline Clock Pwght. - R. Nakai	Closed	1996	158.00	158
1994 NY Skyline Pwght., med. - G. Veith	Open		80.00	80
1992 NY, sm. - G. Veith	Open		45.00	45
1995 Philadelphia "Cityscape" Pwght. - R. Nakai	Open		105.00	105
1995 Philadelphia Skyline Pwght., med. - R. Nakai	Open		80.00	80
1994 S.F. Skyline Clock Pwght. - R. Nakai	Closed	1996	158.00	158
1994 San Francisco "Cityscape" Pwght. - G. Veith	Open		105.00	105
1989 San Francisco - I. Nakamura	Open		150.00	150
1994 San Francisco Dome Pwght. - G. Veith	Closed	1995	75.00	75
1995 San Francisco Skyline Clock Pwght. - R. Nakai	Closed	1996	158.00	158
1994 San Francisco Skyline Pwght., med. - G. Veith	Open		80.00	80
1993 San Francisco Skyline, sm.	Open		45.00	45
1990 Tennis - I. Nakamura	Closed	N/A	170.00	170
1994 Wash. DC "Cityscape" Pwght. - R. Nakai	Open		105.00	105
1994 Wash. DC Skyline Clock Pwght. - R. Nakai	Closed	1996	158.00	158
1994 Wash. DC Skyline Pwght., med. - G. Veith	Open		80.00	80
1989 Washington - I. Nakamura	Open		150.00	150
1994 Washington DC Dome Pwght. - G. Veith	Closed	1995	75.00	75
1994 Washington Vietnam Memorial Pwght.. - R. Nakai	Closed	1996	105.00	105

Wonders of the World Collection - R. Nakai, unless otherwise noted

YEAR ISSUE	EDITION LIMIT	YEAR RETD.	ISSUE PRICE	*QUOTE U.S.$
1993 Capitol Building, small - N. Mulargia	Open		100.00	100
1997 Capitol Hill -T. Suzuki	350		1350.00	1350
1991 Chicago Water Tower w/Base -T. Suzuki	Closed	1997	300.00	300
1991 Chicago Water Tower w/o Base -T. Suzuki	Closed	1996	280.00	280
1986 The Eiffel Tower -T. Suzuki	2000		1000.00	1300
1988 Eiffel Tower, sm. -T. Suzuki	2000		500.00	600
1995 Independence Hall	750		370.00	370
1990 Le Petit Eiffel -T. Suzuki	Open		240.00	240
1995 The Liberty Bell	Open		160.00	160
1992 Niagara Falls Pwght.	Open		85.00	85
1993 Sears Tower	Closed	1997	150.00	150
1986 Space Needle, lg.	Closed	N/A	160.00	160
1986 Space Needle, sm. - N. Mulargia	Closed	N/A	50.00	50
1986 Taj Mahal	Open		1050.00	1050
1987 Taj Mahal -T. Suzuki	1,000		2000.00	2100
1995 Taj Mahal, med.	Open		790.00	790
1995 Taj Mahal, sm.	Open		215.00	215
1987 U.S. Capitol Building	Open		250.00	250
1994 White House w/Oct. Mirror, sm. - N. Mulargia	Open		185.00	185

Dave Grossman Creations

Emmett Kelly Casino Series - Inspired by Emmett Kelly

YEAR ISSUE	EDITION LIMIT	YEAR RETD.	ISSUE PRICE	*QUOTE U.S.$
1995 Black Jack	10,000		65.00	65
1995 Dice Table	10,000		80.00	80
1995 Jack Pot	10,000		70.00	70

Emmett Kelly Sr. "The Original Emmett Kelly Circus Collection - B. Leighton-Jones

YEAR ISSUE	EDITION LIMIT	YEAR RETD.	ISSUE PRICE	*QUOTE U.S.$
1986 "Fore"	10,000		36.00	36
1998 100th Birthday!	10,000		50.00	50
1986 All Washed Up	10,000	1987	48.00	48
1987 Cabbage Routine	10,000	1988	30.00	30
1986 The Cheaters	10,000	1987	70.00	70
1986 Christmas Carol	10,000	1988	35.00	35
1996 The Christmas Tree	10,000		50.00	50
1992 Christmas Tunes	10,000	1998	40.00	40
1989 Cotton Candy	10,000	1995	55.00	55
1993 Dear Emmett	10,000		45.00	45
1990 A Dog's Life	10,000		52.00	52
1988 Dressing Room	10,000		64.00	64
1992 Emmett At The Organ	10,000		50.00	50
1992 Emmett The Caddy	10,000		45.00	45
1991 Emmett The Snowman	10,000		45.00	45
1988 Feather Act	10,000	1998	40.00	40
1986 Feels Like Rain	10,000	1987	34.00	34
1996 Fire Fighter	10,000		45.00	45
1987 Fisherman	10,000		44.00	44
1993 Hard Times	10,000		45.00	45
1995 Holiday Skater	10,000		55.00	55
1986 I Love You	10,000		36.00	36
1994 I've Got It	10,000		45.00	45
1986 Kelly Plaque	10,000		30.00	30
1993 The Lion Tamer	10,000		55.00	55
1992 Look At The Birdie	10,000		40.00	40
1995 Looking Out	10,000		45.00	45
1997 Missed	10,000		50.00	50
1989 Missing Parents	10,000	1998	38.00	38
1997 Mystery Spotlight	10,000		40.00	40
1997 Off To the Races	10,000		85.00	85
1994 Parenthood	10,000		55.00	55
1995 Pierrot & Emmett	10,000		50.00	50
1990 The Proposal	10,000	1993	65.00	65
1992 Self Portrait	2,400		150.00	150
1987 Self-Portrait	10,000		60.00	60
1994 Stuck on Bowling	10,000		45.00	45
1993 Sunday Driver	10,000		55.00	55
1986 The Thinker	10,000		37.00	37
1986 Till Death Do Us Part	10,000	1987	48.00	48
1986 The Titanic	10,000	1987	50.00	50
1987 Wagon Wheel	10,000	1988	40.00	40
1986 Wallstreet	10,000		40.00	40
1986 Where Did I Go Wrong	10,000	1987	80.00	80
1990 With This Ring	10,000	1993	65.00	65

Gone With The Wind Series - Inspired by Film

YEAR ISSUE	EDITION LIMIT	YEAR RETD.	ISSUE PRICE	*QUOTE U.S.$
1987 Ashley GWW-2	Retrd.	1989	65.00	195
1993 Belle Waiting GWW-10	Retrd.	N/A	70.00	95
1997 Bonnie GWW-21	Open		50.00	50
1994 Gerald O'Hara GWW-15	Retrd.	N/A	70.00	85
1988 Mammy GWW-6	Retrd.		70.00	70
1995 Mrs. O'Hara GWW-16	Retrd.	1997	70.00	75
1991 Prissy GWW-8	Open		50.00	50
1993 Rhett & Bonnie GWW-11	Retrd.	N/A	80.00	80
1987 Rhett GWW-4	Retrd.	1989	65.00	249-270
1996 Rhett in Tuxedo GWW-19	Open		70.00	70
1993 Rhett in White Suit GWW-12	Retrd.	N/A	70.00	149-195
1998 Scarlett & Rhett GWW-22	Open		90.00	90
1990 Scarlett & Rhett on Stairs GWW-50	Retrd.	1992	130.00	130-249
1990 Scarlett (red dress) GWW-7	Retrd.	1992	70.00	149-195
1987 Scarlett GWW-1	Retrd.	1989	65.00	300
1997 Scarlett in Atlanta Dress GWW-20	Open		70.00	70
1994 Scarlett in Bar B Que Dress GWW-14	Retrd.	N/A	70.00	125-195
1996 Scarlett in Blue Dress GWW-18	Open		70.00	70
1992 Scarlett in Green Dress GWW-9	Open		70.00	70
1995 Suellen GWW-17	Retrd.	1997	70.00	95
1987 Tara GWW-5	Retrd.	N/A	70.00	90

Gone With The Wind Series 6" - Inspired by Film

YEAR ISSUE	EDITION LIMIT	YEAR RETD.	ISSUE PRICE	*QUOTE U.S.$
1994 Ashley GWW-102	Open		40.00	40
1995 Mammy GWW-106	Open		40.00	40
1994 Rhett GW-104	Open		40.00	40
1996 Scarlett (B-B-Q Dress) GWW-114	Open		40.00	40
1994 Scarlett GWW-101	Open		40.00	40
1995 Suellen GWW-105	Open		40.00	40

Gone With The Wind-Scarlett & Her Beaus - Inspired by Film

YEAR ISSUE	EDITION LIMIT	YEAR RETD.	ISSUE PRICE	*QUOTE U.S.$
1995 The Kiss GWWL-200	750	1995	150.00	300
1995 The Kiss GWWL-200AP	75	1995	180.00	180
1997 Scarlett & Ashley GWWL-202	750		150.00	150
1997 Scarlett & Ashley GWWL-202AP	75		180.00	180
1996 The Wedding GWWL-201	750	1996	150.00	150
1996 The Wedding GWWL-201AP	75	1996	180.00	180

Lladró-Norman Rockwell Collection Series - Rockwell-Inspired

YEAR ISSUE	EDITION LIMIT	YEAR RETD.	ISSUE PRICE	*QUOTE U.S.$
1982 Court Jester RL-405G	5,000	N/A	600.00	1050-1200
1982 Daydreamer RL-404G	5,000	N/A	450.00	1400-1500
1982 Lladró Love Letter RL-400G	5,000	N/A	650.00	725-1200
1982 Practice Makes Perfect RL-402G	5,000	N/A	725.00	600-800
1982 Springtime RL-406G	5,000	N/A	450.00	1200-1450
1982 Summer Stock RL-401G	5,000	N/A	750.00	650-900
1982 Young Love RL-403G	5,000	N/A	450.00	900-1350

*Quotes have been rounded up to nearest dollar

Norman Rockwell America Collection - Rockwell-Inspired

YEAR ISSUE	EDITION LIMIT	YEAR RETD.	ISSUE PRICE	*QUOTE U.S.$
1989 Bottom of the Sixth NRC-607	Retrd.	N/A	140.00	140
1981 Breaking Home Ties NRV-300	Retrd.	N/A	2000.00	2300
1989 Doctor and Doll NRP-600	Retrd.	N/A	90.00	60
1989 First Day Home NRC-606	Retrd.	N/A	80.00	80
1989 First Haircut NRC-604	Retrd.	N/A	75.00	100
1989 First Visit NRC-605	Retrd.	N/A	110.00	110
1982 Lincoln NRV-301	Retrd.	N/A	300.00	375
1989 Locomotive NRC-603	Retrd.	N/A	110.00	125
1989 Runaway NRP-610	Retrd.	N/A	140.00	190
1982 Thanksgiving NRV-302	Retrd.	N/A	2500.00	2650
1989 Weigh-In NRP-611	Retrd.	N/A	120.00	140

Norman Rockwell America Collection-Lg. Ltd. Edition - Rockwell-Inspired

YEAR ISSUE	EDITION LIMIT	YEAR RETD.	ISSUE PRICE	*QUOTE U.S.$
1975 Baseball NR-102	Retrd.	N/A	125.00	450
1989 Bottom of the Sixth NRP-307	Retrd.	N/A	190.00	190
1982 Circus NR-106	Retrd.	N/A	500.00	500
1974 Doctor and Doll NR-100	Retrd.	N/A	300.00	1400
1989 Doctor and Doll NRP-300	Retrd.	N/A	150.00	150
1981 Dreams of Long Ago NR-105	Retrd.	N/A	500.00	750
1979 Leapfrog NR-104	Retrd.	N/A	440.00	750
1984 Marble Players NR-107	Retrd.	N/A	500.00	750
1975 No Swimming NR-101	Retrd.	N/A	150.00	550-600
1989 Runaway NRP-310	Retrd.	N/A	190.00	190
1974 See America First NR-103	Retrd.	N/A	100.00	500-550
1989 Weigh-In NRP-311	Retrd.	N/A	160.00	125-175

Norman Rockwell Collection - Rockwell-Inspired

YEAR ISSUE	EDITION LIMIT	YEAR RETD.	ISSUE PRICE	*QUOTE U.S.$
1982 American Mother NRG-42	Retrd.	N/A	100.00	125
1978 At the Doctor NR-29	Retrd.	N/A	108.00	165-275
1979 Back From Camp NR-33	Retrd.	N/A	96.00	145
1973 Back To School NR-02	Retrd.	N/A	20.00	75
1975 Barbershop Quartet NR-23	Retrd.	N/A	100.00	650-1300
1974 Baseball NR-16	Retrd.	N/A	45.00	160-175
1975 Big Moment NR-21	Retrd.	N/A	60.00	130-150
1973 Caroller NR-03	Retrd.	N/A	22.50	75
1975 Circus NR-22	Retrd.	N/A	55.00	145
1983 Country Critic NR-43	Retrd.	N/A	75.00	125
1982 Croquet NR-41	Retrd.	N/A	100.00	150
1973 Daydreamer NR-04	Retrd.	N/A	22.50	60-75
1975 Discovery NR-20	Retrd.	N/A	55.00	130-175
1973 Doctor & Doll NR-12	Retrd.	N/A	65.00	130-285
1979 Dreams of Long Ago NR-31	Retrd.	N/A	100.00	125-156
1976 Drum For Tommy NRC-24	Retrd.	N/A	40.00	98-104
1980 Exasperated Nanny NR-35	Retrd.	N/A	96.00	100-160
1978 First Day of School NR-27	Retrd.	N/A	100.00	150
1974 Friends In Need NR-13	Retrd.	N/A	45.00	100-111
1983 Graduate NR-44	Retrd.	N/A	30.00	85
1979 Grandpa's Ballerina NR-32	Retrd.	N/A	100.00	110-130
1980 Hankerchief NR-36	Retrd.	N/A	110.00	100-125
1973 Lazybones NR-08	Retrd.	N/A	30.00	250-455
1973 Leapfrog NR-09	Retrd.	N/A	50.00	600-1040
1973 Love Letter NR-06	Retrd.	N/A	25.00	60-75
1973 Lovers NR-07	Retrd.	N/A	45.00	70-110
1978 Magic Potion NR-28	Retrd.	N/A	84.00	150-235
1973 Marble Players NR-11	Retrd.	N/A	60.00	390-425
1973 No Swimming NR-05	Retrd.	N/A	25.00	65-145
1977 Pals NR-25	Retrd.	N/A	60.00	120-150
1986 Red Cross NR-47	Retrd.	N/A	67.00	100
1973 Redhead NR-01	Retrd.	N/A	20.00	210
1980 Santa's Good Boys NR-37	Retrd.	N/A	90.00	100
1973 Schoolmaster NR-10	Retrd.	N/A	55.00	225
1984 Scotty's Home Plate NR-46	Retrd.	N/A	30.00	60
1983 Scotty's Surprise NRS-20	Retrd.	N/A	25.00	60-175
1974 See America First NR-17	Retrd.	N/A	50.00	150-163
1981 Spirit of Education NR-38	Retrd.	N/A	96.00	125
1974 Springtime '33 NR-14	Retrd.	N/A	30.00	60-75
1977 Springtime '35 NR-19	Retrd.	N/A	50.00	60-65
1974 Summertime '33 NR-15	Retrd.	N/A	45.00	65-78
1974 Take Your Medicine NR-18	Retrd.	N/A	50.00	150-175
1979 Teacher's Pet NRA-30	Retrd.	N/A	35.00	65-100
1980 The Toss NR-34	Retrd.	N/A	110.00	225-250
1982 A Visit With Rockwell NR-40	Retrd.	N/A	120.00	100-120
1988 Wedding March NR-49	Retrd.	N/A	110.00	175
1978 Young Doctor NRD-26	Retrd.	N/A	100.00	120-195
1987 Young Love NR-48	Retrd.	N/A	70.00	120

Norman Rockwell Collection-Boy Scout Series - Rockwell-Inspired

YEAR ISSUE	EDITION LIMIT	YEAR RETD.	ISSUE PRICE	*QUOTE U.S.$
1981 Can't Wait BSA-01	Retrd.	N/A	30.00	130
1981 Good Friends BSA-04	Retrd.	N/A	58.00	65-130
1981 Good Turn BSA-05	Retrd.	N/A	65.00	125-130
1982 Guiding Hand BSA-07	Retrd.	N/A	58.00	150
1981 Physically Strong BSA-03	Retrd.	N/A	56.00	150
1981 Scout Is Helpful BSA-02	Retrd.	N/A	38.00	150
1981 Scout Memories BSA-06	Retrd.	N/A	65.00	100
1983 Tomorrow's Leader BSA-08	Retrd.	N/A	45.00	55

Norman Rockwell Collection-Country Gentlemen Series - Rockwell-Inspired

YEAR ISSUE	EDITION LIMIT	YEAR RETD.	ISSUE PRICE	*QUOTE U.S.$
1982 Bringing Home the Tree CG-02	Retrd.	N/A	60.00	110
1982 The Catch CG-04	Retrd.	N/A	50.00	100
1982 On the Ice CG-05	Retrd.	N/A	50.00	60-75
1982 Pals CG-03	Retrd.	N/A	36.00	95
1982 Thin Ice CG-06	Retrd.	N/A	50.00	60
1982 Turkey Dinner CG-01	Retrd.	N/A	85.00	110

Norman Rockwell Collection-Huck Finn Series - Rockwell-Inspired

YEAR ISSUE	EDITION LIMIT	YEAR RETD.	ISSUE PRICE	*QUOTE U.S.$
1980 Listening HF-02	Retrd.	N/A	110.00	135
1980 No Kings HF-03	Retrd.	N/A	110.00	150-175
1979 The Secret HF-01	Retrd.	N/A	110.00	130
1980 Snake Escapes HF-04	Retrd.	N/A	110.00	135-195

Norman Rockwell Collection-Miniatures - Rockwell-Inspired

YEAR ISSUE	EDITION LIMIT	YEAR RETD.	ISSUE PRICE	*QUOTE U.S.$
1984 At the Doctor's NR-229	Retrd.	N/A	35.00	35
1979 Back To School NR-202	Retrd.	N/A	18.00	50
1982 Barbershop Quartet NR-223	Retrd.	N/A	40.00	50
1980 Baseball NR-216	Retrd.	N/A	40.00	50
1982 Big Moment NR-221	Retrd.	N/A	36.00	40
1979 Caroller NR-203	Retrd.	N/A	20.00	50
1982 Circus NR-222	Retrd.	N/A	35.00	40
1979 Daydreamer NR-204	Retrd.	N/A	20.00	30-50
1982 Discovery NR-220	Retrd.	N/A	35.00	45
1979 Doctor and Doll NR-212	Retrd.	N/A	40.00	75
1984 Dreams of Long Ago NR-231	Retrd.	N/A	30.00	30
1982 Drum For Tommy NRC-224	Retrd.	N/A	25.00	30
1989 First Day Home MRC-906	Retrd.	N/A	45.00	45
1984 First Day of School NR-227	Retrd.	N/A	35.00	35
1989 First Haircut MRC-904	Retrd.	N/A	45.00	45
1980 Friends In Need NR-213	Retrd.	N/A	30.00	40
1979 Lazybones NR-208	Retrd.	N/A	22.00	50
1979 Leapfrog NR-209	Retrd.	N/A	32.00	60-90
1979 Love Letter NR-206	Retrd.	N/A	26.00	50-65
1979 Lovers NR-207	Retrd.	N/A	28.00	30-60
1984 Magic Potion NR-228	Retrd.	N/A	30.00	40
1979 Marble Players NR-211	Retrd.	N/A	36.00	75
1979 No Swimming NR-205	Retrd.	N/A	22.00	30-60
1984 Pals NR-225	Retrd.	N/A	25.00	25
1979 Redhead NR-201	Retrd.	N/A	18.00	50
1983 Santa On the Train NR-245	Retrd.	N/A	35.00	55
1979 Schoolmaster NR-210	Retrd.	N/A	34.00	45
1980 See America First NR-217	Retrd.	N/A	28.00	50
1980 Springtime '33 NR-214	Retrd.	N/A	24.00	80
1982 Springtime '35 NR-219	Retrd.	N/A	24.00	30
1980 Summertime '33 NR-215	Retrd.	N/A	22.00	50
1980 Take Your Medicine NR-218	Retrd.	N/A	36.00	40
1984 Young Doctor NRD-226	Retrd.	N/A	30.00	50

Norman Rockwell Collection-Pewter Figurines - Rockwell-Inspired

YEAR ISSUE	EDITION LIMIT	YEAR RETD.	ISSUE PRICE	*QUOTE U.S.$
1980 Back to School FP-02	Retrd.	N/A	25.00	25
1980 Barbershop Quartet FP-23	Retrd.	N/A	25.00	25
1980 Big Moment FP-21	Retrd.	N/A	25.00	25
1980 Caroller FP-03	Retrd.	N/A	25.00	25
1980 Circus FP-22	Retrd.	N/A	25.00	25
1980 Doctor and Doll FP-12	Retrd.	N/A	25.00	25
1980 Figurine Display Rack FDR-01	Retrd.	N/A	60.00	60
1980 Grandpa's Ballerina FP-32	Retrd.	N/A	25.00	25
1980 Lovers FP-07	Retrd.	N/A	25.00	25
1980 Magic Potion FP-28	Retrd.	N/A	25.00	25
1980 No Swimming FP-05	Retrd.	N/A	25.00	25
1980 See America First FP-17	Retrd.	N/A	25.00	25
1980 Take Your Medicine FP-18	Retrd.	N/A	25.00	25

Norman Rockwell Collection-Rockwell Club Series - Rockwell-Inspired

YEAR ISSUE	EDITION LIMIT	YEAR RETD.	ISSUE PRICE	*QUOTE U.S.$
1982 Diary RCC-02	Retrd.	N/A	35.00	75
1984 Gone Fishing RCC-04	Retrd.	N/A	30.00	55
1983 Runaway Pants RCC-03	Retrd.	N/A	65.00	75
1981 Young Artist RCC-01	Retrd.	N/A	96.00	179

Norman Rockwell Collection-Select Collection, Ltd. - Rockwell-Inspired

YEAR ISSUE	EDITION LIMIT	YEAR RETD.	ISSUE PRICE	*QUOTE U.S.$
1982 Boy & Mother With Puppies SC-1001	Retrd.	N/A	27.50	28
1982 Father With Child SC-1005	Retrd.	N/A	22.00	22
1982 Football Player SC-1004	Retrd.	N/A	22.00	22
1982 Girl Bathing Dog SC-1006	Retrd.	N/A	26.50	27
1982 Girl With Dolls In Crib SC-1002	Retrd.	N/A	26.50	27
1982 Helping Hand SC-1007	Retrd.	N/A	32.00	32
1982 Lemonade Stand SC-1008	Retrd.	N/A	32.00	32
1982 Save Me SC-1010	Retrd.	N/A	35.00	35
1982 Shaving Lesson SC-1009	Retrd.	N/A	30.00	30
1982 Young Couple SC-1003	Retrd.	N/A	27.50	28

Norman Rockwell Collection-Tom Sawyer Miniatures - Rockwell-Inspired

YEAR ISSUE	EDITION LIMIT	YEAR RETD.	ISSUE PRICE	*QUOTE U.S.$
1983 First Smoke TSM-02	Retrd.	N/A	40.00	75
1983 Lost In Cave TSM-05	Retrd.	N/A	40.00	75
1983 Take Your Medicine TSM-04	Retrd.	N/A	40.00	75
1983 Whitewashing the Fence TSM-01	Retrd.	N/A	40.00	75

Norman Rockwell Collection-Tom Sawyer Series - Rockwell-Inspired

YEAR ISSUE	EDITION LIMIT	YEAR RETD.	ISSUE PRICE	*QUOTE U.S.$
1976 First Smoke TS-02	Retrd.	N/A	60.00	235
1978 Lost In Cave TS-04	Retrd.	N/A	70.00	175
1977 Take Your Medicine TS-03	Retrd.	N/A	63.00	235
1975 Whitewashing the Fence TS-01	Retrd.	N/A	60.00	235

Norman Rockwell Saturday Evening Post - Rockwell-Inspired

YEAR ISSUE	EDITION LIMIT	YEAR RETD.	ISSUE PRICE	*QUOTE U.S.$
1992 After the Prom NRP-916	Retrd.	1997	75.00	75
1994 Almost Grown Up NRC-609	Open		75.00	75
1993 Baby's First Step NRC-604	Open		100.00	100
1993 Bed Time NRC-606	Retrd.	1997	100.00	100
1990 Bedside Manner NRP-904	Retrd.	1997	65.00	85
1990 Big Moment NRP-906	Retrd.	N/A	100.00	100-135
1990 Bottom of the Sixth NRP-908	Retrd.	1997	165.00	165
1993 Bride & Groom NRC-605	Open		100.00	100
1991 Catching The Big One NRP-909	Retrd.	1997	75.00	75-125
1992 Choosin Up NRP-912	Retrd.	N/A	110.00	130-150
1990 Daydreamer NRP-902	Retrd.	1997	55.00	55
1990 Doctor and Doll NRP-907	Retrd.	N/A	110.00	150
1995 First Down NRC-614	Open		130.00	130
1995 First Haircut NRC-610	Open		85.00	85
1994 For A Good Boy NRC-608	Open		100.00	100
1992 Gone Fishing NRP-915	Open		65.00	65
1991 Gramps NRP-910	Open		85.00	85
1994 Little Mother NRC-607	Open		75.00	75
1998 Marriage License NRP-917	Open		65.00	65
1997 Missed NRP-914	Open		110.00	110
1995 New Arrival NRC-612	Open		90.00	90
1990 No Swimming NRP-901	Retrd.	N/A	50.00	85
1991 The Pharmacist NRP-911	Retrd.	1997	70.00	70
1990 Prom Dress NRP-903	Retrd.	N/A	60.00	60
1990 Runaway NRP-905	Retrd.	1997	130.00	165
1995 Sweet Dreams NRC-611	Open		85.00	85
1994 A Visit with Rockwell (100th Anniversary)-NRP-100	1,994		100.00	100

Norman Rockwell Saturday Evening Post-Miniatures - Rockwell-Inspired

YEAR ISSUE	EDITION LIMIT	YEAR RETD.	ISSUE PRICE	*QUOTE U.S.$
1991 A Boy Meets His Dog BMR-01	Retrd.	N/A	35.00	40
1991 Downhill Daring BMR-02	Retrd.	N/A	40.00	40
1991 Flowers in Tender Bloom BMR-03	Retrd.	N/A	32.00	40
1991 Fondly Do We Remember BMR-04	Retrd.	N/A	30.00	30
1991 In His Spirit BMR-05	Retrd.	N/A	30.00	30
1991 Pride of Parenthood BMR-06	Retrd.	N/A	35.00	40
1991 Sweet Serenade BMR-07	Retrd.	N/A	32.00	40
1991 Sweet Song So Young BMR-08	Retrd.	N/A	30.00	40

Department 56

All Through The House - Department 56

YEAR ISSUE	EDITION LIMIT	YEAR RETD.	ISSUE PRICE	*QUOTE U.S.$
1993 All Snug in Their Bed 9322-0	Closed	1997	48.00	72-96
1992 Aunt Martha With Turkey 9317-3	Closed	1995	27.50	66-90
1993 Away To The Window 9321-1	Closed	1997	42.00	50-84
1995 Carrie Feeds The Cardinals 93339	Closed	1997	18.00	29-36
1994 Children With New Tree 9330-2-0, set/4	Closed	1997	85.00	105-155
1991 Christmas Tree 9302-5	Closed	1997	25.00	38-75
1992 Christopher Tasting Cookies, Caroline Stringing Cranberries 9310-6, (2 assorted)	Closed	1997	15.00	18-30
1992 Christopher Tasting Cookies 9310-6	Closed	1997	15.00	15
1992 Caroline Stringing Cranberries 9310-6	Closed	1997	15.00	15
1992 Dinner Table 9313-0	Closed	1995	65.00	85-145
1991 Down the Chimney & Sugar Plum Chair 9300-9, set/2	Closed	1997	96.00	132-192
1993 Elizabeth Spies Santa, Emily Spies Santa 9325-4, (2 assorted)	Closed	1997	16.00	25-32
1993 Elizabeth Spies Santa 9325-4	Closed	1997	16.00	24
1993 Emily Spies Santa 9325-4	Closed	1997	16.00	16
1994 Fletcher Playing Flute, Kenneth & Katie Singing Carols 9327-0, (3 assorted)	Closed	1997	16.00	32-66
1992 Grandma & Kitchen Table 9308-4, set/2	Closed	1997	55.00	75-110
1994 I Saw Mama Kissing Santa Claus 9332-7, set/2	Closed	1997	45.00	66-135
1993 Johnny Riding His Pony, Judith and Her Jack-In-The-Box 9319-0, (2 assorted)	Closed	1997	15.00	24-30
1993 Johnny Riding His Pony 9319-0	Closed	1997	15.00	15
1993 Judith and Her Jack-In-The-Box 9319-0	Closed	1997	15.00	30
1991 Jolly Old Elf 9303-3	Closed	1997	25.00	38-50
1992 Kitchen 9307-6	Closed	1997	75.00	113-150
1995 Let's Sing "Here Comes Santa Claus" 93336, set/3	Closed	1997	96.00	96-121
1992 Madeline Making Cookies 9309-2	Closed	1997	24.00	29-48
1991 Mama in Her Kerchief, Papa in His Cap 9304-1	Closed	1997	30.00	33-45
1991 Mary Jo, Billy 9306-8 (2 assorted)	Closed	1997	15.00	32-46
1996 Michael Makes a Snowman 93340	Closed	1997	32.50	33-75
1992 Mr. & Mrs. Bell at Dinner 9314-9, set/2	Closed	1995	40.00	66-80
1992 Nicholas Hanging Coat 9311-4	Closed	1997	22.50	30-45
1992 Nicholas, Natalie, & Spot The Dog 9315-7, set/3	Closed	1995	45.00	72-90
1993 Not A Creature Was Stirring, Not Even a Mouse 9318-1	Closed	1997	37.50	50-75
1993 Pamela & Peter's Pillow Fight 9324-6, (2 assorted)	Closed	1997	16.00	24-32
1993 Pamela's Pillow Fight 9324-6	Closed	1997	16.00	16
1993 Peter's Pillow Fight 9324-6	Closed	1997	16.00	16
1993 Ruthan & Baby Patrick, Bradley Builds With Blocks 9320-3, (2 assorted)	Closed	1997	16.00	24-32
1991 Sarah Kate & Andy, Sue Ellen 9305-0 (2 assorted)	Closed	1997	27.50	30-55
1991 Sarah Kate & Andy 9305-0	Closed	1997	27.50	24-45
1991 Sue Ellen 9305-0	Closed	1997	27.50	24-45
1992 Sideboard 9316-5	Closed	1995	45.00	80-135
1994 Sleigh Full of Toys and St. Nicholas Too 9328-9	Closed	1997	75.00	99-150
1995 Sliding Down The Bannister 9333-5	Closed	1997	70.00	99-140
1994 Snowman with Plexi Sign 9874-4	Closed	1996	25.00	44-50
1991 Staircase 9301-7	Closed	1997	48.00	48-72
1995 Steven Skis on New-Fallen Snow 93338	Closed	1997	15.00	24-30
1995 Suzy and Spencer Making Snowballs 93337, set/2	Closed	1997	30.00	39-60
1992 Theodore Adjusting Time on Grandfather Clock 9312-2, set/2	Closed	1997	32.50	48-65
1994 To His Team Gave a Whistle 9329-7, (2 assorted)	Closed	1997	20.00	28-40

*Quotes have been rounded up to nearest dollar

YEAR ISSUE	EDITION LIMIT	YEAR RETD.	ISSUE PRICE	*QUOTE U.S.$
1996 Uncle John Takes a Family Portrait 93348, set/2	Closed	1997	72.00	90-144
1994 Under The Mistletoe 9331-9	Closed	1997	35.00	48-70
1994 Up On The Rooftop 9326-2	Closed	1997	85.00	90-170
1993 Visions of Sugarplums Danced in His Head 9323-8	Closed	1997	24.00	36-48

Dickens' Hinged Boxes - Department 56

YEAR ISSUE	EDITION LIMIT	YEAR RETD.	ISSUE PRICE	*QUOTE U.S.$
1998 Bah, Humbug! 58430	Open		15.00	15
1998 God Bless Us, Every One! 58432	Open		15.00	15
1998 The Spirit of Christmas 58431	Open		15.00	15

Easter Collectibles - Department 56

YEAR ISSUE	EDITION LIMIT	YEAR RETD.	ISSUE PRICE	*QUOTE U.S.$
1995 Bisque Chick, Large 2464-3	Closed	1996	8.50	14-15
1995 Bisque Chick, Small 2465-1	Closed	1996	6.50	11-13
1993 Bisque Duckling, set	Closed	1993	15.00	18-36
1993 Bisque Duckling, Large 3.5" 7282-6	Closed	1993	8.50	10-21
1993 Bisque Duckling, Small 2.75" 7281-8	Closed	1993	6.50	10-46
1994 Bisque Fledgling in Nest, Large 2.75" 2400-7	Closed	1994	6.00	8-21
1994 Bisque Fledgling in Nest, Small 2.5" 2401-5	Closed	1994	5.00	6-52
1991 Bisque Lamb, set	Closed	1991	12.50	60-78
1991 Bisque Lamb, Large 4" 7392-0	Closed	1991	7.50	21-59
1991 Bisque Lamb, Small 2.5" 7393-8	Closed	1991	5.00	20-23
1992 Bisque Rabbit, set	Closed	1992	14.00	40-48
1992 Bisque Rabbit, Large 5" 7498-5	Closed	1992	8.00	15-25
1992 Bisque Rabbit, Small 4" 7499-3	Closed	1992	6.00	15-17
1996 Bisque Rabbit, Large 2765-0	Closed	1996	8.50	9-13
1996 Bisque Rabbit, Small 2764-2	Closed	1996	7.50	8-11

Merry Makers - Department 56

YEAR ISSUE	EDITION LIMIT	YEAR RETD.	ISSUE PRICE	*QUOTE U.S.$
1995 Barnaby The Breadman 9361-0	Closed	1996	20.00	20-40
1992 Bartholomew The Baker w/Cart 9366-1	Closed	1996	35.00	35
1994 Bremwell The Bell-A-Ringer 9387-4	Closed	1996	22.00	22-44
1995 Brewster The Bird Feeder 93976	Closed	1996	25.00	25-72
1994 Calvin The Candycane Striper	Closed	1996	22.00	22-36
1991 Charles The Cellist 9355-6	Closed	1995	19.00	22-57
1995 Chester The Tester & His Kettle 93972	Closed	1996	27.50	70-74
1993 Clarence the Concertinist (waterglobe/music box) 9377-7	Closed	1996	25.00	25-42
1991 Clarence The Concertinist 9353-0	Closed	1995	19.00	30-57
1991 Frederick The Flutist 9352-1	Closed	1995	19.00	29-57
1993 Garrison The Guzzler 9379-3	Closed	1996	20.00	20-44
1993 Godfrey The Gatherer 9380-7	Closed	1996	20.00	20-40
1995 Halsey The Stocking Hanger 93974	Closed	1996	32.50	22-33
1993 Heavenly Bakery Entrance 9371-8	Closed	1996	20.00	30-60
1991 Horatio The Hornblower 9351-3	Closed	1995	19.00	24-57
1994 Leo The Lamp-A-Lighter 9386-6	Closed	1996	22.00	22-44
1994 Leopold The Lollipopman 9390-4	Closed	1996	22.00	22-44
1994 Lollipop Shop Entrance 9389-0	Closed	1996	35.00	37
1993 Martin The Mandolinist (waterglobe/music box) 9377-7	Closed	1996	25.00	25-60
1991 Martin The Mandolinist 9350-5	Closed	1995	19.00	19-51
1993 Maxwell The Mixer at his Table, set/8 9372-6	Closed	1996	50.00	50-72
1994 Merrily We Roll Carolers & Gabriel The Goat 9382-3	Closed	1996	144.00	144-288
1992 Merry Makers Papier-Mache Church 9356-9	Closed	1995	95.00	95-99
1993 Merry Mountain Chapel, lighted 9370-0	Closed	1996	60.00	60-120
1995 Ollie The Optimist 93973	Closed	1996	25.00	25-29
1993 Otto The Ovenman at his Table, set/2 9373-4	Closed	1996	45.00	45-55
1994 The Peppermint Tree 9394-7	Closed	1996	18.00	18-36
1993 Percival The Puddingman (waterglobe/music box) 9362-9	Closed	1996	25.00	26-30
1992 Percival The Puddingman 9362-9	Closed	1996	20.00	20-40
1994 Percy The Pudding-A-Bringer 9388-2	Closed	1996	22.00	22-44
1994 Peter The Peppermint Maker 9393-9	Closed	1996	22.00	22-44
1993 Porter The Presser & His Press, set/2	Closed	1996	65.00	65-132
1993 Samuel the Sampler & Cider Barrel, set/3 9381-5	Closed	1996	27.50	28-55
1992 Sebastian The Snowball Maker 9367-0	Closed	1996	20.00	20-40
1993 Seigfried & The Snowman (waterglobe/music box) 9374-2	Closed	1996	30.00	30-38
1992 Seymore, Seigfried & The Snowman9365-3	Closed	1996	45.00	45
1995 Sheridan Thinks Santa, set/2 93975	Closed	1996	27.50	28
1991 Sidney The Singer 9354-8	Closed	1995	19.00	28-36
1992 Sigmund The Snowshoer 9358-0	Closed	1996	20.00	20-40
1993 Simon The Pieman (waterglobe/music box) 9376-9	Closed	1996	25.00	30-60
1992 Simon The Pieman 9363-7	Closed	1996	20.00	20-40
1993 Solomon The Sledder (waterglobe/music box) 9385-8	Closed	1996	37.50	38
1992 Solomon The Sledder 9356-4	Closed	1996	24.00	24-48
1992 Sweet Treats Tree 9364-5	Closed	1996	18.00	18-36
1992 Thaddeus The Tobogganist (waterglobe/music box) 9375-0	Closed	1996	30.00	30-44
1993 Thaddeus The Tobogganist 9357-2	Closed	1996	24.00	24-48
1994 Timothy The Taffy Twister 9392-0	Closed	1996	22.00	22

Snowbabies Collectors' Club - Department 56

YEAR ISSUE	EDITION LIMIT	YEAR RETD.	ISSUE PRICE	*QUOTE U.S.$
1997 You Better Watch Out	Open		Gift	N/A
1998 Together We Can Make The Season Bright 68852	Open		75.00	75

Snowbabies - Department 56

YEAR ISSUE	EDITION LIMIT	YEAR RETD.	ISSUE PRICE	*QUOTE U.S.$
1989 All Fall Down 7984-7, set/4	Closed	1991	36.00	50-85
1998 All We Need Is Love (1998 Mother's Day Event Piece) 68860	Open		32.50	33
1988 Are All These Mine? 7977-4	Open		10.00	13
1995 Are You On My List? 6875-6	Open		25.00	25
1986 Best Friends 7958-8	Closed	1989	12.00	95-185
1997 Best Little Star 68842	Open		16.00	16
1994 Bringing Starry Pines 6862-4	Closed	1997	35.00	28-35
1992 Can I Help, Too? 6806-3	18,500	1992	48.00	45-111
1993 Can I Open it Now? 6838-1 (Event Piece)	Closed	1993	15.00	15-52
1997 Bisque Friendship Pin (Event Piece) 68849	Closed	1997	5.00	5
1998 Candle Light...Season Bright (tree topper) 68863	Open		20.00	20
1998 Candlelight Trees, set/3 68861	Open		25.00	25
1997 Celebrating A Snowbabies Journey, 1987-1997..."Let's Go See Jack Frost" 68850 (Event Piece)	Closed	1997	60.00	60
1996 Climb Every Mountain 68816	22,500	1996	75.00	85-145
1986 Climbing on Snowball, Bisque Votive w/Candle 7965-0	Closed	1989	15.00	90-165
1987 Climbing On Tree 7971-5, set/2	Closed	1989	25.00	782-950
1993 Crossing Starry Skies 6834-9	Closed	1997	35.00	28-42
1991 Dancing To a Tune 6808-0, set/3	Closed	1995	30.00	24-46
1987 Don't Fall Off 7968-5	Closed	1990	12.50	91-195
1987 Down The Hill We Go 7960-0	Open		20.00	23
1989 Finding Fallen Stars 7985-5	6,000	1989	32.50	132-195
1991 Fishing For Dreams 6809-8	Closed	1994	28.00	33-49
1996 Five-Part Harmony 68824	Open		32.50	45
1986 Forest Accessory "Frosty Forest" 7963-4, set/2	Open		15.00	20
1988 Frosty Frolic 7981-2	4,800	1989	35.00	895-1050
1989 Frosty Fun 7983-9	Closed	1991	27.50	39-65
1995 Frosty Pines 76687, set/3	Open		12.50	13
1986 Give Me A Push 7955-3	Closed	1990	12.00	55-85
1998 Heigh-Ho, Heigh-Ho, To Frolic Land We Go! 68853	Open		48.00	48
1986 Hanging Pair (votive) 7966-9	Closed	1989	15.00	141-195
1992 Help Me, I'm Stuck 6817-9	Closed	1994	32.50	33-52
1989 Helpful Friends 7982-0	Closed	1993	30.00	29-65
1986 Hold On Tight 7956-1	Open		12.00	14
1998 Hold On Tight 68884 (hinged box)	Open		15.00	15
1998 How Many Days 'Til Christmas? 68882	Open		36.00	36
1995 I Can't Find Him 68800	Open		37.50	38
1995 I Found The Biggest Star of All! 6874-8	Open		16.00	16
1993 I Found Your Mittens 6836-5, set/2	Closed	1996	30.00	32-55
1998 I Love You, (hinged box) (Mother's Day Event Piece) 68867	Open		15.00	15
1991 I Made This Just For You 6802-0	Open		15.00	15
1992 I Need A Hug 6813-6	Open		20.00	20
1995 I See You! 6878-0, set/2	Open		27.50	28
1995 I'll Play A Christmas Tune 68801	Open		16.00	16
1991 I'll Put Up The Tree 6800-4	Closed	1995	24.00	23-45
1993 I'll Teach You A Trick 6835-7	Closed	1996	24.00	23-40
1993 I'm Making an Ice Sculpture 6842-0	Closed	1996	30.00	30-46
1986 I'm Making Snowballs 7962-6	Closed	1992	12.00	24-46
1994 I'm Right Behind You! 6852-7	Closed	1997	60.00	48-60
1996 I'm So Sleepy 68810	Open		16.00	16
1998 I'm The Star Atop Your Tree! (tree topper) 68862	Open		20.00	20
1996 It's A Grand Old Flag 68822	Open		25.00	25
1996 It's Snowing! 68821	Open		16.50	17
1989 Icy Igloo 7987-1	Open		37.50	38
1991 Is That For Me 6803-9, set/2	Closed	1993	32.50	27-59
1996 Jack Frost...A Sleighride Through the Stars 68811, set/3	Open		110.00	110
1994 Jack Frost...A Touch of Winter's Magic 6854-3	Open		90.00	95
1998 Jingle Bell 68855	Open		16.00	16
1992 Join The Parade 6824-1	Closed	1994	37.50	40-78
1998 A Journey For Two By Caribou! 68881	Open		50.00	50
1992 Just One Little Candle 6823-3	Open		15.00	15
1993 Let's All Chime In! 6845-4, set/2	Closed	1995	37.50	42-59
1994 Let's Go Skating 6860-8	Open		16.50	17
1992 Let's Go Skiing 6815-2	Open		15.00	15
1994 Lift Me Higher, I Can't Reach 6863-2	Open		75.00	75
1996 A Little Night Light 68823	Open		32.50	33
1992 Look What I Can Do! 6819-5	Closed	1996	16.50	19-34
1993 Look What I Found 6833-0	Closed	1997	45.00	36-45
1994 Mickey's New Friend 714-5 (Disney Exclusive)	Retrd.	1995	60.00	500-650
1995 Mush 68805	Open		48.00	48
1993 Now I Lay Me Down to Sleep 6839-0	Open		13.50	14
1996 Once Upon A Time... 68815	Open		25.00	25
1998 Once Upon A Time... 68883 (hinged box)	Open		15.00	15
1998 One For You, One For Me 68858	Open		27.50	28
1992 Over the Milky Way 6828-4	Closed	1995	32.00	32-59
1995 Parade of Penguins 68804, set/6	Open		15.00	15
1989 Penguin Parade 7986-3	Closed	1992	25.00	32-60
1994 Pennies From Heaven 6864-0	Open		17.50	18
1990 Playing Games Is Fun 7947-2	Closed	1993	30.00	30-59
1988 Polar Express 7978-2	Closed	1992	22.00	70-115
1998 Polar Express (hinged box) 68869	Open		15.00	15
1990 Read Me a Story 7945-6	Open		25.00	25
1995 Ring The Bells...It's Christmas! 6876-4	Open		40.00	40
1997 Rock-A-Bye Baby (Event Piece) 68848	Closed	1997	15.00	15-20
1992 Shall I Play For You? 6820-9	Open		16.50	17
1998 Ship O' Dreams 68859, set/2	Open		135.00	135
1996 Sliding Through The Milky Way 6883-3	Open		37.50	38
1995 Snowbabies Animated Skating Pond 7668-6, set/14	Open		60.00	60
1993 Snowbabies Picture Frame, Baby's First Smile 6846-2	Open		30.00	30
1996 Snowbaby Display Shelf 6883-8	Open		45.00	45
1986 Snowbaby Holding Picture Frame 7970-7, set/2	Closed	1987	15.00	510-650
1986 Snowbaby Nite-Lite 7959-6	Closed	1989	15.00	274-338
1991 Snowbaby Polar Sign 6804-7	Closed	1996	20.00	20-34
1998 Snowbaby Shelf Unit 68874	Open		20.00	20
1993 So Much Work To Do 6837-3	Open		18.00	18
1993 Somewhere in Dreamland 6840-3	Closed	1997	85.00	75-85
1994 Somewhere in Dreamland (1 snowflake) 6840-3	Closed	1994	85.00	98-145
1995 Somewhere in Dreamland (2 snowflake) 6840-3	Closed	1995	85.00	65-85
1996 Somewhere in Dreamland (3 snowflake) 6840-3	Closed	1996	85.00	65-85
1997 Somewhere in Dreamland (4 snowflake) 6840-3	Closed	1997	85.00	65-85
1990 A Special Delivery 7948-0	Closed	1994	15.00	18-39
1995 Star Gazing 7800 (Starter Set)	Open		40.00	40
1995 A Star in the Box (GCC exclusive) 68803	Closed	1996	18.00	25-45
1996 Stargazing 68817, set/9	Open		40.00	40
1998 Starlight Seranade 68856	Open		25.00	25
1992 Starry Pines 6829-2, set/2	Open		17.50	18
1992 Stars-In-A-Row, Tic-Tac-Toe 6822-5	Closed	1995	32.50	28-45
1994 Stringing Fallen Stars 6861-6	Open		25.00	25
1998 Sweet Dreams (hinged box) 68868	Open		15.00	15
1998 Thank You 68857	Open		32.50	33
1994 There's Another One!, 6853-5	Open		24.00	24
1996 There's No Place Like Home 68820	Open		16.50	17
1991 This Is Where We Live 6805-5	Closed	1994	60.00	49-98
1992 This Will Cheer You Up 6816-0	Closed	1994	30.00	22-52
1998 Three Tiny Trumpeters 68888, set/2 (1998 Winter Celebration Event Piece)	Open		50.00	50
1988 Tiny Trio 7979-0, set/3	Closed	1990	20.00	145-225
1987 Tumbling In the Snow 7957-0, set/5	Closed	1993	35.00	55-104
1990 Twinkle Little Stars 7942-1, set/2	Closed	1993	37.50	28-46
1997 Two Little Babies On The Go! 68840	Open		32.50	33
1992 Wait For Me 6812-8	Closed	1994	48.00	35-85
1991 Waiting For Christmas 6807-1	Closed	1993	27.50	25-52
1993 We Make a Great Pair 6843-8	Open		30.00	30
1990 We Will Make it Shine 7946-4	Closed	1992	45.00	50-104
1994 We'll Plant the Starry Pines 6865-9, set/2	Closed	1997	37.50	38
1995 We're Building An Icy Igloo 68802	Open		70.00	70
1995 What Shall We Do Today? 6877-2	Closed	1997	32.50	33-65
1996 When the Bough Breaks 68819	Open		30.00	30
1993 Where Did He Go? 6841-1	Open		35.00	35
1994 Where Did You Come From? 6856-0	Closed	1997	40.00	40
1996 Which Way's Up 68812	Closed	1997	30.00	30
1998 Whistle While You Work 68854	Open		32.50	33
1990 Who Are You? 7949-9	12,500	1991	32.50	117-145
1991 Why Don't You Talk To Me 6801-2	Open		24.00	24
1993 Will it Snow Today? 6844-6	Closed	1995	45.00	45-72
1992 Winken, Blinken, and Nod 6814-4	Open		60.00	65
1998 Winter Play On A Snowy Day 68880, set/4	Open		48.00	48
1987 Winter Surprise 7974-0	Closed	1992	15.00	30-59
1997 Wish Upon a Falling Star 68839	Open		75.00	75
1990 Wishing on a Star 7943-0	Closed	1994	22.00	27-52
1997 Wishing You A Merry Christmas 68843	Open		40.00	40
1996 With Hugs & Kisses 68813, set/2	Open		32.50	33
1996 You Are My Lucky Star 68814, set/2	Open		35.00	35
1992 You Can't Find Me! 6818-7	Closed	1996	45.00	36-65
1992 You Didn't Forget Me 6821-7	Open		32.50	33
1996 You Need Wings Too! 68818	Open		25.00	25
1996 You're My Snowbaby 6883-4	Open		15.00	15

Snowbabies Pewter Miniatures - Department 56

YEAR ISSUE	EDITION LIMIT	YEAR RETD.	ISSUE PRICE	*QUOTE U.S.$
1989 All Fall Down 7617-1, set/4	Closed	1993	25.00	37-52
1989 Are All These Mine? 7605-8	Closed	1992	7.00	10-15
1995 Are You On My List? 7669-1, set/2	Closed	1997	9.00	9-15
1989 Best Friends 7604-0	Closed	1994	10.00	15-21
1998 Best Little Star 76718	Open		6.50	7
1994 Bringing Starry Pines 7666-0, set/2	Closed	1997	18.00	18-22
1991 Dancing to a Tune 7630-9, set/3	Closed	1993	18.00	23-39
1989 Don't Fall Off! 7603-1	Closed	1994	7.00	17-25
1989 Finding Fallen Stars 7618-0, set/2	Closed	1992	12.50	24-46
1989 Frosty Frolic 7613-9, set/4	Closed	1993	24.00	24-39
1989 Frosty Fun 7611-2, set/2	Closed	1997	13.50	13-30
1989 Give Me a Push! 7601-5	Closed	1994	7.00	16-20
1998 Heigh-Ho, Heigh-Ho, To Frolic Land We Go! 76711	Open		22.50	23
1992 Help Me, I'm Stuck 7638-4, set/2	Closed	1997	15.00	15-19
1989 Helpful Friends 7608-2, set/4	Closed	1992	13.50	19-39
1991 I Made This Just for You! 7628-7	Closed	1994	7.00	13-18
1992 I Need A Hug 7640-6	Closed	1997	10.00	10-13
1991 I'll Put Up The Tree 7627-9	Closed	1996	9.00	11-12
1994 I'm Right Behind You 7662-7, set/5	Closed	1997	27.50	22-32
1989 Icy Igloo, w/tree 7610-4, set/2	Closed	1992	7.50	16-21

*Quotes have been rounded up to nearest dollar

YEAR ISSUE	EDITION LIMIT	YEAR RETD.	ISSUE PRICE	*QUOTE U.S.$
1991 Is That For Me? 7631-7, set/2	Closed	1993	12.50	20-26
1998 Jack Frost...A Touch of Winter's Magic 76716, set/3	Open		27.50	28
1998 Jingle Bell 76713	Open		7.00	7
1992 Join the Parade 7645-7, set/4	Closed	1995	22.50	26-35
1994 Lift Me Highter, I Can't Reach! 7667-8, set/5	Closed	1997	25.00	20-25
1989 Penguin Parade 7616-3, set/4	Closed	1993	12.50	26-33
1990 Playing Games is Fun! 7623-6, set/2	Closed	1993	13.50	22-38
1989 Polar Express 7609-0, set/2	Closed	1992	13.50	26-49
1990 Read Me a Story 7622-8	Closed	1997	11.00	9-12
1993 Somewhere in Dreamland 7656-2, set/5	Closed	1997	30.00	24-33
1990 A Special Delivery 7624-4	Closed	1993	7.00	16-21
1998 Starlight Serenade 76714	Open		12.00	12
1998 Thank You 76715, set/3	Open		20.00	20
1994 There's Another One 7661-9	Closed	1997	10.00	8-11
1992 This Will Cheer You Up 7639-2	Closed	1995	13.75	14-20
1989 Tiny Trio 7615-5, set/3	Closed	1993	18.00	22-40
1989 Tumbling in the Snow! 7614-7, set/5	Closed	1992	30.00	47-85
1990 Twinkle Little Stars 7621-0, set/2	Closed	1993	15.00	23-30
1992 Wait For Me! 7641-4, set/4	Closed	1995	22.50	23-30
1991 Waiting for Christmas 7629-5	Closed	1993	13.00	21-30
1993 We Make a Great Pair 7652-0	Closed	1997	13.50	11-14
1994 We'll Plant The Starry Trees 7663-5, set/4	Closed	1997	22.00	22
1998 Whistle While You Work 76712	Open		18.00	18
1989 Winter Surprise! 7607-4	Closed	1994	13.50	10-23
1998 Wish Upon A Falling Star 76717, set/4	Open		25.00	25
1991 Wishing on a Star 7626-0	Closed	1995	10.00	15-34
1992 You Can't Find Me! 7637-6, set/4	Closed	1996	22.50	18-28
1992 You Didn't Forget Me! 7643-0, set/3	Closed	1995	17.50	17-34

Snowbabies-Bisque Porcelain Boxes - Department 56

YEAR ISSUE	EDITION LIMIT	YEAR RETD.	ISSUE PRICE	*QUOTE U.S.$
1997 Celebrate 68847	Open		15.00	15
1997 Surprise 68846	Open		15.00	15

Snowbabies-Music Boxes - Department 56

YEAR ISSUE	EDITION LIMIT	YEAR RETD.	ISSUE PRICE	*QUOTE U.S.$
1993 Can I Open it Now?, mini 7648-1	Closed	1994	20.00	23-46
1994 Catch a Falling Star 6871-3	Closed	1997	37.50	39-48
1986 Catch a Falling Star 7950-2	Closed	1987	27.50	578-995
1987 Don't Fall Off 7972-3	Closed	1993	30.00	46-55
1998 Did He See You? 68870	Open		37.50	38
1991 Frosty Frolic 7634-1	Closed	1993	110.00	120-141
1993 Frosty Fun, mini 7650-3	Closed	1994	20.00	26-46
1993 I'm So Sleepy 6851-9	Open		37.50	38
1993 Let It Snow 6857-8	Closed	1995	100.00	110-125
1996 Once Upon a Time 68832	Open		30.00	30
1991 Penguin Parade 7633-3	Closed	1994	72.00	77-83
1993 Penquin Parade, mini 7646-5	Closed	1994	20.00	28-52
1995 Play Me a Tune 68809	Open		37.50	38
1993 Play Me a Tune, mini 7651-1	Closed	1994	20.00	27-52
1991 Playing Games Is Fun 7632-5	Closed	1993	72.00	98-110
1993 Reading a Story, mini 7649-0	Closed	1994	20.00	25-48
1991 We Wish You a Merry Christmas (Advent Tree) 7635-0	Closed	1994	135.00	160-225
1992 What Will I Catch? 6826-8	Open		48.00	48
1993 Wishing on a Star 7647-3	Closed	1994	20.00	22-52

Snowbabies-Waterglobes - Department 56

YEAR ISSUE	EDITION LIMIT	YEAR RETD.	ISSUE PRICE	*QUOTE U.S.$
1990 All Tired Out 7937-5	Closed	1992	55.00	42-75
1995 Are You On My List? 6879-7	Closed	1997	32.50	33
1986 Catch a Falling Star 7967-7	Closed	1987	18.00	528-770
1992 Fishing For Dreams 6832-2	Closed	1994	32.50	33-54
1998 Heigh-Ho 68872	Open		32.50	33
1995 I'll Hug You Goodnight 68798	Open		32.50	33
1998 Jingle Bell 68871	Open		32.50	33
1989 Let It Snow 7992-8	Closed	1993	25.00	33-65
1994 Look What I Found 6872-1	Closed	1997	32.50	33
1998 Moon Beams 68873	Open		32.50	33
1996 Now I Lay Me Down To Sleep 6883-1	Open		32.50	33
1991 Peek-A-Boo 7938-3	Closed	1993	50.00	60-98
1994 Planting Starry Pines 6870-5	Closed	1996	32.50	33-40
1991 Play Me a Tune 7936-7	Closed	1993	50.00	43-79
1996 Practice Makes Perfect 6883-0	Open		32.50	33
1992 Read Me a Story 6831-4	Closed	1996	32.50	26-33
1995 Skate With Me 68799	Open		32.50	33
1987 Winter Wonderland 7975-8	Closed	1988	40.00	707-990
1986 Snowbaby Standing 7964-2	Closed	1987	7.50	313-440
1987 Snowbaby with Wings 7973-1	Closed	1988	20.00	416-550
1993 So Much Work To Do 6849-7	Closed	1995	32.50	24-39
1993 You Didn't Forget Me 6850-0	Closed	1997	32.50	26-33
1990 What Are You Doing? 7935-9	Closed	1990	55.00	55

Snowbunnies - Department 56

YEAR ISSUE	EDITION LIMIT	YEAR RETD.	ISSUE PRICE	*QUOTE U.S.$
1997 Abracadabra (porcelain hinged box) 26298	Open		15.00	15
1997 And 'B' Is For Bunny, (music box) 26290	Open		30.00	30
1997 Are You My Momma? 26289	Open		18.00	18
1997 Be My Bunny Bee, (music box) 26294	Open		32.50	33
1997 Bunny Express 26287	Open		22.50	23
1996 Counting The Days 'Til Easter 26282	Yr.Iss.	1996	22.50	23-34
1995 Don't Get Lost! 26166	Closed	1998	32.50	33
1997 Double Yolk 26293	Yr.Iss.	1997	20.00	20
1994 Easter Delivery 26085	Closed	1997	27.50	22-28
1996 Easy Does It, set/2 26274	Closed	1998	30.00	30
1995 Goosey, Goosey, & Gander, set/2 26174	Closed	1997	30.00	30-41
1996 Happy Birthday To You, set/2 26273	Open		30.00	30
1994 Help Me Hide The Eggs 26077	Closed	1996	25.00	25-45
1995 I'll Color The Easter Egg 26212	Yr.Iss.	1995	20.00	17-21
1995 I'll Love You Forever 26158	Open		16.00	16
1994 I'll Paint The Top... 26034	Closed	1996	30.00	30-37
1995 I'm Tweeter, You're Totter 26204	Closed	1998	30.00	30
1996 I've Got A Brand New Pair of Roller Skates 26272	Closed	1998	25.00	25
1994 I've Got A Surprise 26000	Closed	1997	15.00	15-18
1997 Is There Room For Me? (waterglobe, music box) 26295	Open		25.00	25
1996 Is There Room For Me? 26275	Open		18.00	18
1995 It's Working...We're Going Faster! 26190	Open		35.00	35
1996 Just A Little Off The Top, set/3 26278	Closed	1998	25.00	25
1996 Let's All Sing Like The Birdies Sing, set/2 26276	Open		37.50	38
1994 Let's Do The Bunny Hop! 26096	Open		32.50	33
1995 Let's Play In The Meadow (waterglove, music box) 26271	Closed	1998	25.00	25
1997 Little Birdies Go Tweet, set/2 26288	Open		28.00	28
1995 Look What I've Got! (waterglobe, music box) 26263	Closed	1997	25.00	20-25
1995 My Woodland Wagon, At Dragonfly Hollow 26255	Closed	1997	32.50	33
1995 My Woodland Wagon, By Turtle Creek 26239	Closed	1996	32.50	33-40
1995 My Woodland Wagon, Parked In Robins Nest Thicket 26247	Open		35.00	35
1996 On A Trycle Built For Two 26283	17,500	1998	32.50	33
1994 Oops! I Dropped One! 26018	Closed	1998	16.00	16
1997 Piggyback? (porcelain hinged box) 26299	Open		15.00	15
1997 Rain, Rain, Go Away 26291	Open		45.00	45
1996 Rock-A-Bye Bunny, (waterglobe, music box) 26285	Open		25.00	25
1995 Rub-A-Dub-Dub, 3 Bunnies in a Tub 26115	Closed	1997	32.50	26-33
1995 Shrubs-In-A-Tub, single, set/4 26123	Closed	1997	12.50	10-13
1995 Shrubs-In-A-Tub, tall, set/2 26140	Closed	1997	9.00	9
1995 Shrubs-In-A-Tub, triple 26131	Closed	1997	10.00	8-10
1996 Slow-Moving Vehicle 26280	Open		45.00	45
1994 Surprise! It's Me! 26042	Closed	1998	25.00	25
1994 A Tisket, A Tasket (waterglobe) 26107	Closed	1998	12.50	13
1994 A Tisket, A Tasket 26026	Closed	1996	15.00	15-18
1997 A Tisket, A Tasket Basket 26286	Open		45.00	45
1996 To Market, To Market, Delivering Eggs! 26281	Open		65.00	65
1994 Tra-La-La 26069	Closed	1997	37.50	38-42
1997 Tweet, Tweet, Tweet (porcelain hinged box) 26297	Open		15.00	15
1996 Welcome To The Neighborhood 26277	Open		25.00	25
1995 Wishing You A Happy Easter 26182	Closed	1997	32.50	33-35
1995 You Better Watch Out Or I'll Catch You! 26220	Open		17.00	17
1996 You Make Be Laugh, (music box) 26284	Open		32.50	33
1997 You're Cute As A Bug's Ear 26292	Open		16.50	17

Winter Silhouette - Department 56

YEAR ISSUE	EDITION LIMIT	YEAR RETD.	ISSUE PRICE	*QUOTE U.S.$
1991 Angel Candle Holder 7794-1	Closed	1997	95.00	140-190
1990 Angel Candle Holder w/Candle 6767-9	Closed	1992	32.50	38-66
1991 Bedtime Stories 7792-5	Closed	1997	42.00	50-84
1992 Bedtime Stories Waterglobe 7838-7	Closed	1995	30.00	55-60
1993 A Bright Star on Christmas Eve 7843-3, set/2	Closed	1997	48.00	48-96
1989 Bringing Home The Tree 7790-9, set/4	Closed	1993	75.00	94-150
1989 Camel w/glass Votive 6766-0	Closed	1993	25.00	50
1987 Carolers 7774-7, set/4	Closed	1993	120.00	150-240
1991 Caroling Bells 7798-4, set/3	Closed	1997	60.00	60-120
1995 Cat Nap Santa & Finishing Touches Santa Bookends/Stocking Hangers 78560, (2 assorted)	Closed	1997	16.50	17-33
1994 Cat Nap Santa 7855-7	Closed	1997	37.50	38-75
1991 Chimney Sweep 7799-2	Closed	1993	37.50	60-75
1993 A Christmas Kiss 7845-0, set/2	Closed	1997	32.50	33-65
1992 Christmas Presents 7805-0, set/2	Closed	1997	35.00	35-70
1989 Father Christmas 7788-7	Closed	1993	50.00	88-100
1995 Finishing Touches Santa 78559	Closed	1997	37.50	38-75
1991 Grandfather Clock 7797-6	Closed	1995	27.50	55-65
1991 Hanging The Ornaments 7793-3, set/3	Closed	1997	30.00	30-60
1988 Joy To The World 5595-6	Closed	1990	42.00	84-120
1995 Kneeling Angel With Mandolin 78585	Closed	1997	48.00	48-96
1994 Mantelpiece Santa 7854-9	Closed	1997	55.00	55-110
1992 The Marionette Performance 7807-7, set/3	Closed	1997	75.00	75-150
1995 Naughty Or Nice? Santa waterglobe/music box 7859-0	Closed	1997	30.00	30-60
1989 Putting Up the Tree 7789-5, set/3	Closed	1997	90.00	150-195
1993 Santa Lucia 7844-1	Closed	1997	27.50	28-55
1991 Santa's Reindeer 7796-8, (2 assorted)	Closed	1997	14.00	14-28
1988 Silver Bells Music Box 8271-6	Closed	1990	75.00	140-150
1988 Skating Children 7773-9, set/2	Closed	1997	33.00	33-66
1988 Skating Couple 7772-0	Closed	1995	35.00	55-70
1987 Snow Doves 8215-5, set/2	Closed	1992	60.00	72-120
1992 Snowy White Deer 7837-9, set/2	Closed	1995	55.00	110
1995 Standing Angel With Horn 78584	Closed	1997	48.00	48-96
1989 Three Kings Candle Holder 6765-2, set/3	Closed	1992	85.00	149-170
1991 Town Crier 7800-0	Closed	1994	37.50	60-75

Disneyana

Disneyana Conventions - Various

YEAR ISSUE	EDITION LIMIT	YEAR RETD.	ISSUE PRICE	*QUOTE U.S.$
1992 1947 Mickey Mouse Plush J20967 - Gund	1,000	1992	50.00	303-350
1992 Big Thunder Mountain A26648 - R. Lee	100	1992	1650.00	2360-2800
1992 Carousel Horse 022482 - PJ's	250	1992	125.00	424-455
1992 Cinderella 022076 - Armani	500	1992	500.00	3250-4235
1992 Cinderella Castle 022077 - John Hine Studios	500	1992	250.00	1210-1593
1992 Cruella DeVil Doll-porcelain 22554 - J. Wolf	25	1992	3000.00	3000-3500
1992 Disneyana Logo Charger - B. White	25	1992	600.00	2800
1992 Medallion	N/A	1992	Gift	165-182
1992 Nifty-Nineties Mickey & Minnie 022503 - House of Laurenz	250	1992	650.00	605-700
1992 Pinocchio - R. Wright	100	1992	750.00	1000-2000
1992 Steamboat Willie-Resin - M. Delle	500	1992	125.00	1452-1650
1992 Tinker Bell 022075 - Lladró	1,500	1992	350.00	2200-3380
1992 Two Merry Wanderers 022074 - Goebel/M.I. Hummel	1,500	1992	250.00	950-1250
1992 Walt's Convertible (Cel) - Disney Art Ed.	500	1992	950.00	2300
1993 1947 Minnie Mouse Plush - Gund	1,000	1993	50.00	110-130
1993 Alice in Wonderland - Malvern	10	1993	8000.00	N/A
1993 Annette Doll - Alexander Doll	1,000	1993	395.00	484-780
1993 The Band Concert "Maestro Mickey" - Disney Art Ed.	275	1993	2950.00	N/A
1993 The Band Concert-Bronze - B. Toma	25	1993	650.00	815-2600
1993 Bandleader (pewter)	N/A	1993	Gift	100-110
1993 Bandleader-Resin - M. Delle	1,500	1993	125.00	241-303
1993 Family Dinner Figurine - C. Boyer	1,000	1993	600.00	1089-1625
1993 Jumper from King Arthur Carousel - PJ's	250	1993	125.00	303-488
1993 Mickey & Pluto Charger - White/Rhodes	25	1993	850.00	2750-3300
1993 Mickey Mouse, the Bandleader - Arribas Bros.	25	1993	700.00	1870-2600
1993 Mickey's Dreams - R. Lee	250	1993	400.00	699-715
1993 Peter Pan - Lladró	2,000	1993	400.00	750-1200
1993 Sleeping Beauty Castle - John Hine Studios	500	1993	250.00	365-567
1993 Snow White - Armani	2,000	1993	750.00	1029-1080
1993 Two Little Drummers - Goebel/M.I. Hummel	1,500	1993	325.00	424-507
1993 Walt's Train Celebration - Disney Art Ed.	950	1993	950.00	1800
1994 Ariel - Armani	1,500	1994	750.00	1320-1531
1994 Cinderella/Godmother - Lladró	2,500	1994	875.00	605-1170
1994 Cinderella's Slipper - Waterford	1,200	1994	250.00	336-624
1994 Euro Disney Castle - John Hine Studios	750	1994	250.00	242-400
1994 Jessica & Roger Charger - White/Rhodes	25	1994	2000.00	3146
1994 Mickey Triple Self Portrait - Goebel Miniatures	500	1994	295.00	847-1235
1994 Minnie Be Patient - Goebel/M.I. Hummel	1,500	1994	395.00	396-650
1994 MM/MN w/House Kinetic - F. Prescott	10	1994	4000.00	N/A
1994 MM/MN/Goofy Limo (Stepin' Out) - Ron Lee	500	1994	500.00	500-1073
1994 Neat & Pretty Music Box	N/A	1994	Gift	100-110
1994 Scrooge in Money Bin/Bronze - Carl Barks	100	1994	1800.00	5445-6050
1994 Sleeping Beauty - Malvern	10	1994	5500.00	N/A
1994 Sorcerer Mickey (bronze) - B. Toma	100	1994	1000.00	1815-2400
1994 Sorcerer Mickey (crystal) - Arribas Bros.	50	1994	1700.00	2035-2239
1994 Sorcerer Mickey (pewter)	N/A	1994	Gift	110-455
1994 Sorcerer Mickey (resin) - M. Delle	2,000	1994	125.00	182-423
1995 Ah, Venice - M. Pierson	100	1995	2600.00	2600
1995 Ariel's Dolphin Ride - Wyland	250	1995	2500.00	2500
1995 Barbershop Quartet - Goebel Miniatures	750	1995	300.00	275-650
1995 Beauty and the Beast - Armani	2,000	1995	975.00	1320-1593
1995 Brave Little Tailor Charger - White/Rhodes	15	1995	2000.00	3146
1995 Celebrating-Resin - M. Delle	1,500	1995	125.00	182-228
1995 Donald Duck Gong	N/A	1995	Gift	105-110
1995 Donald Duck Mini-Charger - White/Rhodes	1,000	1995	75.00	75
1995 Ear Force One - R. Lee	500	1995	600.00	787-1300
1995 Engine No. One - R. Lee	500	1995	650.00	726-765
1995 Fire Station #105 - Lilliput Lane	501	1995	195.00	440-695
1995 For Father - Goebel/M.I. Hummel	1,500	1995	450.00	462-485
1995 Grandpa's Boys - Goebel/M.I. Hummel	1,500	1995	340.00	385-413
1995 Mad Minnie Charger - White/Rhodes	10	1995	2000.00	4000
1995 Memories - B. Toma	200	1995	1200.00	968-1029
1995 Neat & Pretty Mickey (crystal) - Arribas Bros.	50	1995	1700.00	1760-2420
1995 Neat & Pretty Mickey (resin) - M. Delle	2,000	1995	135.00	165-182
1995 Plane Crazy - Arribas	50	1995	1750.00	1936-1997
1995 The Prince's Kiss - P Gordon	25	1995	250.00	1980-2178
1995 "Proud Pocahontas" Lithograph - D. Struzan	500	1995	195.00	413

*Quotes have been rounded up to nearest dollar

YEAR ISSUE	EDITION LIMIT	YEAR RETD.	ISSUE PRICE	*QUOTE U.S.$
1995 Sheriff of Bullet Valley - Barks/Vought	200	1995	1800.00	1936-2200
1995 Showtime - B. Toma	200	1995	1400.00	1694-1788
1995 Simba - Bolae	200	1995	1500.00	1500
1995 Sleeping Beauty Castle Mirror - P. Gordon	250	1995	1200.00	1200
1995 Sleeping Beauty Dance - Lladró	1,000	1995	1280.00	1271-2340
1995 Sleeping Beauty's Tiara - Waterford	1,500	1995	250.00	285-305
1995 Snow White's Apple - Waterford	1,500	1995	225.00	270-423
1995 "Snow White & Friends" Brooch/Pendant - R. Viramontes	25	1995	1500.00	1500
1995 Thru the Mirror - Barks/Vought	200	1995	2600.00	1760-1980
1995 "Uncle Scrooge" Tile - Barks/Vought	50	1995	900.00	1595-1650
1996 Brave Little Taylor - Arribas Bros.	50	1996	1700.00	2200-2420
1996 Brave Little Taylor (resin) - M. Delle	1,500	1996	125.00	242-325
1996 Brave Little Taylor Inlaid Leather Box - P. Gordon	25	1996	300.00	300
1996 Breakfast of Tycoons-Scrooge (litho) - C. Barks	295	1996	295.00	385-473
1996 Cinderella's Castle (bronze) - B. Toma	100	1996	1400.00	1815-2178
1996 Flying Dumbo (bronze) - Wolf's Head	N/A	1996	2000.00	2000
1996 Hall of Presidents - Lilliput Lane	500	1996	225.00	336-715
1996 Heigh Ho - R. Lee	350	1996	500.00	726-900
1996 Jasmine & Rajah - Armani	N/A	1996	800.00	1029-1600
1996 Mickey - Armani	N/A	1996	Gift	242-350
1996 Jasmine & Rajah w/Mickey - Armani	N/A	1996	800.00	900-1205
1996 Minnie for Mother - Goebel/M.I. Hummel	1,200	1996	470.00	470
1996 Proud Pongo (w/backstamp) - Walt Disney Classics	1,200	1996	175.00	325-520
1996 Puppy Love - Goebel Miniatures	750	1996	325.00	325-650
1996 Self Control-Donald Duck (bronze) - C. Barks	150	1996	1800.00	2514-2600
1996 Sorcerer - Waterford	1,200	1996	275.00	352-585
1996 Uncle Scrooge Charger Plate - B. White	25	1996	2500.00	2662-2904
1997 Chernabog Charger - B. White	15	1997	2000.00	3025-3328
1997 Chernabog - Walt Disney Classics	1,500	1997	750.00	1331-1800
1997 Cinderella & Prince - Armani	1,000	1997	825.00	990-1200
1997 Peg Leg Pete - M. Delle	1,000	1997	125.00	220
1997 Crocodile Clock	N/A	1997	Gift	100-110
1997 Cruella Car Box - P. Gordon	30	1997	500.00	1265-1392
1997 Disneyland's 40th (pewter)	N/A	1997	Gift	100-110
1997 Disney Villain Ornament set/6 - Walt Disney Classics	12,000	1997	40.00	100-110
1997 Dragon (Malificent) (pewter)	N/A	1997	Gift	110-228
1997 Grandma's Girl - Goebel/M.I. Hummel	1,000		350.00	350
1997 Hands Off My Playthings (bronze) - C. Banks	176	1997	1950.00	2662-3025
1997 Haunted Mansion - Lilliput Lane	500	1997	250.00	425-494
1997 Lonesome Ghost - Arribas Bros.	50	1997	1700.00	1815-1925
1997 Magical Scrooge Serigraph - C. Banks	295	1997	395.00	555-589
1997 Mistletoe Mickey & Minnie - C. Radko	1,500	1997	250.00	292-450
1997 Mickey's 70th (bronze) - B. Toma	100	1997	1400.00	1650-1815
1997 Mickey's 70th Sericel - Disney Art Ed.	1,500	1997	295.00	415
1997 Peg Leg Pete - Lynn Yi	1,000	1997	125.00	220-245
1997 Tinkerbell - Waterford Crystal	750	1997	250.00	402-450
1997 The Perfect Disguise - Goebel Miniatures	500	1997	300.00	380-525
1997 Walt's Railroad "Lilliebel" - Visions in Scale	75	1997	1600.00	1600
1998 Ariel (Crystal) - Waterford Crystal	750		250.00	250
1998 Bella Note - Goebel Miniatures	500		300.00	300
1998 Best Friends - C. Radko	1,000		70.00	70
1998 Casting Call Ornament set/6 - Disney Merchandise	1,500		45.00	45
1998 Decades of Reel Memories - P. Gordon	50		750.00	750
1998 Fond Memories w/Mickey & Friends Sericel - Disney Art Classics	N/A		N/A	N/A
1998 A Friendly Day Poster - R. Souders	1,000		25.00	25
1998 Friends Forever - Goebel/M.I. Hummel	N/A		N/A	N/A
1998 Heat Wave Serigraph - C. Banks	195		295.00	295
1998 Mickey & Pluto (resin) - M. Delle	1,500		125.00	125
1998 Snow White & Prince - Walt Disney Classics	1,650		750.00	750
1998 Tinkerbell Tile - M. Davis	75		495.00	495
1998 Tribute to Walt Disney Paperweight - Swarovski Crystal	25		495.00	495
1998 Walt Disney World Railroad Train Station - Lilliput Lane	500		275.00	275
1998 Who's Out There (bronze) - C. Banks	176		1950.00	1950

Duncan Royale

Collector Club - Duncan Royale

YEAR ISSUE	EDITION LIMIT	YEAR RETD.	ISSUE PRICE	*QUOTE U.S.$
1991 Today's Nast	Retrd.	1993	80.00	150
1994 Winter Santa	Retrd.	1994	125.00	150
1995 Santa's Gift	Retrd.	1995	100.00	150
1996 Santa's Choir	Retrd.	1996	90.00	90
1996 Magi Pewter Bell	1,000	1996	Gift	30
1997 Angel Pewter Bell	1,000	1997	Gift	35
1998 Anniversary Santa	Yr.Iss.		N/A	N/A

Special Event Piece - Duncan Royale

YEAR ISSUE	EDITION LIMIT	YEAR RETD.	ISSUE PRICE	*QUOTE U.S.$
1991 Nast & Music	Retrd.	1993	79.95	95-124

Conquerors - R. Lamb

YEAR ISSUE	EDITION LIMIT	YEAR RETD.	ISSUE PRICE	*QUOTE U.S.$
1998 Genghis Khan	5,000		150.00	150

Duncan Royale Figurines - Duncan Royale

YEAR ISSUE	EDITION LIMIT	YEAR RETD.	ISSUE PRICE	*QUOTE U.S.$
1996 Guardian Angel	2,500	1996	150.00	150
1996 Peace & Harmony	2,500	1998	200.00	200

Ebony Collection - Duncan Royale

YEAR ISSUE	EDITION LIMIT	YEAR RETD.	ISSUE PRICE	*QUOTE U.S.$
1990 Banjo Man	5,000	1997	80.00	80
1993 Ebony Angel	5,000	1997	170.00	170
1991 Female Gospel Singer	5,000	1997	90.00	90
1990 The Fiddler	5,000	1997	90.00	90
1990 Harmonica Man	5,000	1997	80.00	80
1991 Jug Man	5,000	1997	90.00	90
1992 Jug Tooter	5,000	1997	90.00	90
1992 A Little Magic	5,000	1997	80.00	80
1991 Male Gospel Singer	5,000	1997	90.00	90
1996 O' Happy Day (Youth Gospel)	5,000	1997	70.00	71
1996 Pigskin (Youth Football)	5,000	1997	70.00	71
1991 Preacher	5,000	1997	90.00	90
1991 Spoons	5,000	1996	90.00	90

Ebony Collection- Heroes of Black History - R. Lamb

YEAR ISSUE	EDITION LIMIT	YEAR RETD.	ISSUE PRICE	*QUOTE U.S.$
1998 Frederick Douglass	5,000		120.00	120
1998 Harriet Tubman	5,000		120.00	120

Ebony Collection- History of Africa's Kings & Queens - Duncan Royale/Nigel

YEAR ISSUE	EDITION LIMIT	YEAR RETD.	ISSUE PRICE	*QUOTE U.S.$
1996 Gbadebo	5,000		300.00	300
1998 Hannibal	5,000		150.00	150
1996 Moshesh	5,000		150.00	150
1996 Nandi	5,000		150.00	150
1998 Nzinga	5,000		150.00	150
1996 Shaka	5,000		150.00	150
1996 Sunni Ali Bear	5,000		150.00	150
1996 Tenkamenin	5,000		150.00	150

Ebony Collection-Buckwheat - Duncan Royale

YEAR ISSUE	EDITION LIMIT	YEAR RETD.	ISSUE PRICE	*QUOTE U.S.$
1992 O'Tay	5,000	1997	70.00	90
1992 Painter	5,000	1997	80.00	90
1992 Petee & Friend	5,000	1997	90.00	90
1992 Smile For The Camera	5,000	1996	80.00	90

Ebony Collection-Friends & Family - Duncan Royale

YEAR ISSUE	EDITION LIMIT	YEAR RETD.	ISSUE PRICE	*QUOTE U.S.$
1994 Agnes	5,000		100.00	120
1994 Daddy	5,000	1997	120.00	125
1994 Lunchtime	5,000	1997	100.00	100
1994 Millie	5,000		100.00	100
1994 Mommie & Me	5,000		125.00	125

Ebony Collection-Jazzman - Duncan Royale

YEAR ISSUE	EDITION LIMIT	YEAR RETD.	ISSUE PRICE	*QUOTE U.S.$
1992 Bass	5,000	1997	90.00	110
1992 Bongo	5,000	1997	90.00	100
1992 Piano	5,000	1997	130.00	140
1992 Sax	5,000	1997	90.00	100
1992 Trumpet	5,000	1997	90.00	100

Ebony Collection-Jubilee Dancers - Duncan Royale

YEAR ISSUE	EDITION LIMIT	YEAR RETD.	ISSUE PRICE	*QUOTE U.S.$
1993 Bliss	5,000	1997	200.00	200
1993 Fallana	5,000	1997	100.00	100
1993 Keshia	5,000	1997	100.00	100
1993 Lamar	5,000	1997	100.00	100
1993 Lottie	5,000	1997	125.00	125
1993 Wilfred	5,000	1997	100.00	100

Ebony Collection-Special Releases - Duncan Royale

YEAR ISSUE	EDITION LIMIT	YEAR RETD.	ISSUE PRICE	*QUOTE U.S.$
1991 Signature Piece	Retrd.	1997	50.00	75

Heart and Soul - A. Fennell

YEAR ISSUE	EDITION LIMIT	YEAR RETD.	ISSUE PRICE	*QUOTE U.S.$
1998 Cultural Rhythm	5,000		195.00	195
1998 Heart and Soul	5,000		150.00	150
1998 Sun Goddess	5,000		150.00	150

Heroes of Modern Literature - S. Joyce

YEAR ISSUE	EDITION LIMIT	YEAR RETD.	ISSUE PRICE	*QUOTE U.S.$
1998 Don Quixote	5,000		150.00	150
1998 Rob Roy	5,000		150.00	150
1998 Robin Hood	5,000		150.00	150

History of Classic Entertainers - P. Apsit

YEAR ISSUE	EDITION LIMIT	YEAR RETD.	ISSUE PRICE	*QUOTE U.S.$
1987 American	Retrd.	1995	160.00	350
1987 Auguste	Retrd.	1995	220.00	350
1987 Greco-Roman	Retrd.	1995	180.00	350
1987 Grotesque	Retrd.	1995	230.00	350
1987 Harlequin	Retrd.	1995	250.00	350
1987 Jester	Retrd.	1995	410.00	800-1170
1987 Pantalone	Retrd.	1995	270.00	234-300
1987 Pierrot	Retrd.	1995	180.00	225
1987 Pulcinella	Retrd.	1995	220.00	350
1987 Russian	Retrd.	1995	190.00	350
1987 Slapstick	Retrd.	1995	250.00	300
1987 Uncle Sam	Retrd.	1995	160.00	325-350

History of Classic Entertainers II - P. Apsit

YEAR ISSUE	EDITION LIMIT	YEAR RETD.	ISSUE PRICE	*QUOTE U.S.$
1988 Bob Hope	Retrd.	1995	250.00	250-295
1988 Feste	Retrd.	1995	250.00	250
1988 Goliard	Retrd.	1995	200.00	300
1988 Mime	Retrd.	1995	200.00	300
1988 Mountebank	Retrd.	1995	270.00	300
1988 Pedrolino	Retrd.	1995	200.00	300
1988 Tartaglia	Retrd.	1995	200.00	250
1988 Thomassi	Retrd.	1995	200.00	300
1988 Touchstone	Retrd.	1995	200.00	300
1988 Tramp	Retrd.	1995	200.00	300
1988 White Face	Retrd.	1995	250.00	300
1988 Zanni	Retrd.	1995	200.00	300

History of Classic Entertainers-Special Releases - Duncan Royale

YEAR ISSUE	EDITION LIMIT	YEAR RETD.	ISSUE PRICE	*QUOTE U.S.$
1990 Bob Hope-18"	Retrd.	1995	1500.00	1700
1990 Bob Hope-6" porcelain	Retrd.	1995	130.00	130
1990 Mime-18"	Retrd.	1995	1500.00	1500
1988 Signature Piece	Retrd.	1995	50.00	50

History of Pirates and Buccaneers - Duncan Royale

YEAR ISSUE	EDITION LIMIT	YEAR RETD.	ISSUE PRICE	*QUOTE U.S.$
1997 Anne Bonny	5,000		150.00	150
1997 Blackbeard	5,000		150.00	150
1997 Calico Jack	5,000		150.00	150
1997 Captain Morgan	5,000		150.00	150
1997 Diego Grillo	5,000		150.00	150
1998 Jean Laffite	5,000		150.00	150
1997 L' Olonnais	5,000		150.00	150
1998 Mary Read	5,000		150.00	150
1997 Peg Leg	5,000		150.00	150

History of Santa Claus I (12") - P. Apsit

YEAR ISSUE	EDITION LIMIT	YEAR RETD.	ISSUE PRICE	*QUOTE U.S.$
1983 Black Peter	Retrd.	1991	145.00	225-424
1983 Civil War	Retrd.	1991	145.00	221-545
1983 Dedt Moroz	Retrd.	1989	145.00	410-650
1983 Kris Kringle	Retrd.	1988	165.00	1008-1320
1983 Medieval	Retrd.	1988	220.00	1430-1800
1983 Nast	Retrd.	1987	90.00	2145-2904
1983 Pioneer	Retrd.	1989	145.00	254-605
1983 Russian	Retrd.	1989	145.00	338-605
1983 Soda Pop	Retrd.	1988	145.00	1005-1600
1983 St. Nicholas	Retrd.	1989	175.00	429-1210
1983 Victorian	Retrd.	1990	120.00	156-280
1983 Wassail	Retrd.	1991	90.00	300-545

History of Santa Claus II (12") - P. Apsit

YEAR ISSUE	EDITION LIMIT	YEAR RETD.	ISSUE PRICE	*QUOTE U.S.$
1986 Alsace Angel	Retrd.	1997	250.00	250-400
1986 Babouska	Retrd.	1997	170.00	200
1986 Bavarian	Retrd.	1997	250.00	260-400
1986 Befana	Retrd.	1997	200.00	250
1986 Frau Holda	Retrd.	1997	160.00	180
1986 Lord of Misrule	Retrd.	1997	160.00	200
1986 The Magi	Retrd.	1997	350.00	273-500
1986 Mongolian/Asian	Retrd.	1997	240.00	350-500
1986 Odin	Retrd.	1996	200.00	300
1986 The Pixie	Retrd.	1997	140.00	124-175
1986 Sir Christmas	Retrd.	1997	150.00	175
1986 St. Lucia	Retrd.	1997	180.00	300

History of Santa Claus III - Duncan Royale

YEAR ISSUE	EDITION LIMIT	YEAR RETD.	ISSUE PRICE	*QUOTE U.S.$
1990 Druid	Retrd.	1996	250.00	250
1991 Grandfather Frost & Snow Maiden	Retrd.	1997	400.00	500
1991 Hoteisho	Retrd.	1997	200.00	200
1991 Judah Maccabee	Retrd.	1997	300.00	300
1990 Julenisse	Retrd.	1997	200.00	200
1991 King Wenceslas	Retrd.	1997	300.00	300
1991 Knickerbocker	Retrd.	1997	300.00	300
1991 Samichlaus	Retrd.	1997	350.00	500
1991 Saturnalia King	Retrd.	1996	200.00	200
1990 St. Basil	Retrd.	1997	300.00	300
1990 Star Man	Retrd.	1997	300.00	350
1990 Ukko	Retrd.	1996	250.00	250

History of Santa Claus I (6") - Duncan Royale

YEAR ISSUE	EDITION LIMIT	YEAR RETD.	ISSUE PRICE	*QUOTE U.S.$
1988 Black Peter-6" porcelain	6,000/yr	1997	80.00	80
1988 Civil War-6" porcelain	6,000/yr	1997	80.00	80-104
1988 Dedt Moroz -6" porcelain	6,000/yr	1997	80.00	80
1988 Kris Kringle-6" porcelain	6,000/yr	1998	80.00	80
1988 Medieval-6" porcelain	6,000/yr	1998	80.00	80
1988 Nast-6" porcelain	6,000/yr	1998	80.00	80-104
1988 Pioneer-6" porcelain	6,000/yr	1997	80.00	80
1988 Russian-6" porcelain	6,000/yr	1997	80.00	80
1988 Soda Pop-6" porcelain	6,000/yr	1998	80.00	80-85
1988 St. Nicholas-6" porcelain	6,000/yr	1998	80.00	80
1988 Victorian-6" porcelain	6,000/yr	1997	80.00	80-85
1988 Wassail-6" porcelain	6,000/yr	1997	80.00	80

History of Santa Claus II (6") - Duncan Royale

YEAR ISSUE	EDITION LIMIT	YEAR RETD.	ISSUE PRICE	*QUOTE U.S.$
1988 Alsace Angel-6" porcelain	6,000/yr	1997	80.00	90
1988 Babouska-6" porcelain	6,000/yr	1998	80.00	80
1988 Bavarian-6" porcelain	6,000/yr	1998	90.00	100
1988 Befana-6" porcelain	6,000/yr	1997	80.00	80
1988 Frau Holda-6" porcelain	6,000/yr	1997	80.00	80
1988 Lord of Misrule-6" porcelain	6,000/yr	1997	80.00	80-91
1988 Magi-6" porcelain	6,000/yr	1997	130.00	150
1988 Mongolian/Asian-6" porcelain	6,000/yr	1998	80.00	90
1988 Odin-6" porcelain	6,000/yr	1997	80.00	90
1988 Pixie-6" porcelain	6,000/yr	1998	80.00	80-85
1988 Sir Christmas-6" porcelain	6,000/yr	1998	80.00	80
1988 St. Lucia-6" porcelain	6,000/yr	1998	80.00	80

History of Santa Claus (18") - Duncan Royale

YEAR ISSUE	EDITION LIMIT	YEAR RETD.	ISSUE PRICE	*QUOTE U.S.$
1989 Kris Kringle-18"	1,000	1995	1500.00	1500
1989 Medieval-18"	1,000	1995	1500.00	1500
1989 Nast-18"	1,000	1995	1500.00	1500
1989 Russian-18"	1,000	1995	1500.00	1500
1989 Soda Pop-18"	1,000	1995	1500.00	1500
1989 St. Nicholas-18"	1,000	1995	1500.00	1500

History of Santa Claus I -Wood - Dolfi

YEAR ISSUE	EDITION LIMIT	YEAR RETD.	ISSUE PRICE	*QUOTE U.S.$
1987 Black Peter-8" wood	500	1993	450.00	450-700
1987 Civil War-8" wood	500	1993	450.00	450-700
1987 Dedt Moroz-8" wood	500	1993	450.00	450-750
1987 Kris Kringle-8" wood	500	1993	450.00	450-550
1987 Medieval-8" wood	500	1993	450.00	1200
1987 Nast-8" wood	500	1993	450.00	1500
1987 Pioneer-8" wood	500	1993	450.00	450-700
1987 Russian-8" wood	500	1993	450.00	450-700
1987 Soda Pop-8" wood	500	1993	450.00	850
1987 St. Nicholas-8" wood	500	1993	450.00	700
1987 Victorian-8" wood	500	1993	450.00	450

*Quotes have been rounded up to nearest dollar

YEAR ISSUE	EDITION LIMIT	YEAR RETD.	ISSUE PRICE	*QUOTE U.S.$
1987 Wassail-8" wood	500	1993	450.00	450-600

History Of Santa Claus-Special Releases - Duncan Royale

YEAR ISSUE	EDITION LIMIT	YEAR RETD.	ISSUE PRICE	*QUOTE U.S.$
1991 Signature Piece	Retrd.	1996	50.00	50-100
1992 Nast & Sleigh	5,000	1996	500.00	650
1997 The Silver Nast	1,000	1996	500.00	500

Painted Pewter Miniatures-Santa 1st Series - Duncan Royale

YEAR ISSUE	EDITION LIMIT	YEAR RETD.	ISSUE PRICE	*QUOTE U.S.$
1986 Black Peter	500	1993	30.00	30-39
1986 Civil War	500	1993	30.00	30
1986 Dedt Moroz	500	1993	30.00	30
1986 Kris Kringle	500	1993	30.00	30
1986 Medieval	500	1993	30.00	30
1986 Nast	500	1993	30.00	30
1986 Pioneer	500	1993	30.00	30-39
1986 Russian	500	1993	30.00	30
1986 Soda Pop	500	1993	30.00	30
1986 St. Nicholas	500	1993	30.00	30
1986 Victorian	500	1993	30.00	30
1986 Wassail	500	1993	30.00	30-39
1986 Set of 12	500	1993	360.00	500

Painted Pewter Miniatures-Santa 2nd Series - Duncan Royale

YEAR ISSUE	EDITION LIMIT	YEAR RETD.	ISSUE PRICE	*QUOTE U.S.$
1988 Alsace Angel	500	1993	30.00	30
1988 Babouska	500	1993	30.00	30
1988 Bavarian	500	1993	30.00	30
1988 Befana	500	1993	30.00	30
1988 Frau Holda	500	1993	30.00	30
1988 Lord of Misrule	500	1993	30.00	30
1988 Magi	500	1993	30.00	30
1988 Mongolian	500	1993	30.00	30
1988 Odin	500	1993	30.00	30
1988 Pixie	500	1993	30.00	30
1988 Sir Christmas	500	1993	30.00	30
1988 St. Lucia	500	1993	30.00	30
1988 Set of 12	500	1993	360.00	500

Santa Collection - J. Jones

YEAR ISSUE	EDITION LIMIT	YEAR RETD.	ISSUE PRICE	*QUOTE U.S.$
1998 Santa '98	2,000		180.00	180

eggspressions! inc.

Angel Collection - Various

YEAR ISSUE	EDITION LIMIT	YEAR RETD.	ISSUE PRICE	*QUOTE U.S.$
1995 Angel Bunny 30016 (musical) - L. Pollard	250		220.00	230
1995 Angel Divine 69120 - B. Gabrielli	250	1996	120.00	120
1996 Angel of Glory 69124 - D. Husokowski	Closed	1998	145.00	145
1994 Angel of Hope 69094 - L. Pollard	250	1998	130.00	130
1994 Angel of Love - B. Gabrielli	250	1995	110.00	110
1996 Courtney (musical) 30055 - C. Johnson	250		110.00	110
1996 For Heaven's Sake 69123 - D. Husokowski	250	1998	115.00	115
1996 Guilding Hands 30001 (muscial) - B. Gabrielli	250	1998	160.00	160
1995 Heavenly 006-EG1-099 - B. Gabrielli	250	1996	120.00	120
1996 Little Angel 20078 - S. Arnett	250	1998	145.00	145
1996 Music From Above 67026 - D. Botts	250	1998	80.00	80
1996 Music in the Clouds 67025 - D. Botts	Closed	1998	130.00	130
1996 Sara 69130 - B. Gabrielli	250	1998	140.00	140
1996 Whisper of Love 69030 - S. Arnett	500	1998	160.00	160

Birthstone-Jeweled Treasure Boxes - eggspresions

YEAR ISSUE	EDITION LIMIT	YEAR RETD.	ISSUE PRICE	*QUOTE U.S.$
1997 Siam-January 50019	Open		78.00	78
1997 Amethyst-February 50020	Open		78.00	78
1997 Aqua-Blue-March 50021	Open		78.00	78
1997 Crystal-April 50022	Open		78.00	78
1997 Emerald-May 50023	Open		78.00	78
1997 Light Amethyst-June 50024	Open		78.00	78
1997 Light Siam-July 50025	Open		78.00	78
1997 Peridot-August 50026	Open		78.00	78
1997 Rose-October 50027	Open		78.00	78
1997 Sapphire-September 50028	Open		78.00	78
1997 Topaz-November 50029	Open		78.00	78
1997 Zircon-December 50030	Open		78.00	78

Childhood Collection - Various

YEAR ISSUE	EDITION LIMIT	YEAR RETD.	ISSUE PRICE	*QUOTE U.S.$
1997 Brandon's Birds 69148 - C. Vermillion	250	1998	114.00	114
1997 Brittany's Love 69150 - C. Johnson	250	1998	130.00	130
1996 Busting Out 20077 - B. Gabrielli	250		100.00	100
1997 Charisma 69137 - B. Gabrielli	250		120.00	120
1996 Danielle 20000 - D. Botts	250	1998	120.00	120
1997 Erin 69151 - C. Johnson	250	1998	100.00	100
1996 Hailey 69125 - B. Gabrielli	Closed	1998	115.00	115
1995 Harvest Fairy 69013 - eggspressions	Closed	1998	95.00	95
1997 Humpty 20091 - D. Budd	250	1998	150.00	150
1997 Innocence 67152 - eggspressions	Open		50.00	50
1997 Jess 69147 - L. Pollard	250	1998	150.00	150
1997 Lovelee 69149 - L. Pollard	250	1998	170.00	170
1994 Playing Grown-Up - eggspressions	Retrd.	1997	84.00	84
1994 Pre-School Play 20064 - eggspressions	Closed	1998	108.00	120
1994 Purr-fect Hug - C. Johnson	250	1994	150.00	150
1997 Reading With Dad 20090 - L. Pollard	250	1998	160.00	160
1997 Rosie Day 20084 - D. Botts	250	1998	170.00	170
1997 Sitting Pretty 69139 - C. Johnson	250	1998	98.00	98
1994 Skip A Long - B. Gabrielli	Closed	1998	118.00	135
1996 Snow Much Fun 69131 - eggspressions	Closed	1998	120.00	120
1994 Sweet Dreams 69061 - eggspressions	Closed	1998	99.00	115
1997 Thru The Looking Glass 20092 - D. Budd	250	1998	220.00	220
1997 Venessa 20088 - L. Pollard	250	1998	160.00	160

Christmas Collection (hanging) - Various

YEAR ISSUE	EDITION LIMIT	YEAR RETD.	ISSUE PRICE	*QUOTE U.S.$
1992 Candyland 69020 - eggspressions	Closed	1998	94.00	115
1994 Caroling Mice - B. Gabrielli	Closed	1998	120.00	140
1992 Choo Choo Christmas 69004 - eggspressions	Open		124.00	130
1992 Christmas Curiosity - eggspressions	Closed	1998	104.00	110
1994 Christmas Joy 69095 - L. Pollard	250	1998	104.00	120
1992 Drummer Bear - eggspressions	Closed	1998	97.00	115
1995 Father Christmas 69102 - B. Gabrielli	250	1998	135.00	135
1996 Heav'n and Nature sing 69148 - D. Leffler	250	1998	72.00	72
1992 In Tune 69012 - eggspressions	Closed	1998	120.00	145
1996 Kitty's First Christmas 67147 - D. Husokowski	250		80.00	80
1995 Santa's Here 67021 - S. Fiddament	250	1998	130.00	130
1994 Santa's Little Elves - B. Gabrielli	Closed	1998	130.00	145
1994 Santa's Little Sweetheart - B. Gabrielli	100	1997	98.00	100
1992 Santa's Workshop 69019 - D. Husokowski	125	1998	145.00	145
1995 Shining Star - D. Leffler	250	1997	72.00	72
1992 Tiny Treasures 67001 - eggspressions	Closed	1998	100.00	125
1996 Traditions 69129 - S. Arnett	250	1998	160.00	160
1992 Waiting - S. Arnett	Closed	1997	92.00	110
1992 Winter Wonderland (musical) - eggspressions	Closed	1998	98.00	105

Christmas Collection (on bases) - Various

YEAR ISSUE	EDITION LIMIT	YEAR RETD.	ISSUE PRICE	*QUOTE U.S.$
1994 Holiday Memories (musical) - C. Johnson	250	1995	190.00	190
1994 Making Spirits Bright (musical) - B. Gabrielle	25	1995	300.00	300
1996 Meeting Santa (musical) 30059 - D. Leffler	250	1998	230.00	230
1994 O' Holy Night (musical) - B. Gabrielli	250	1997	160.00	185
1995 Reflections on Ice (musical) - D. Leffler	250	1997	230.00	230
1996 Yuletide 30057 - B. Gabrielli	250	1998	160.00	160

Clown Collection - eggspressions, unless otherwise noted

YEAR ISSUE	EDITION LIMIT	YEAR RETD.	ISSUE PRICE	*QUOTE U.S.$
1997 Balancing Act 69144 - D. Budd	250		130.00	130
1997 Cathy's Clown 69143 - C. Johnson	250	1998	94.00	94
1996 Dreams 69024 - B. Gabrielli	250	1998	190.00	190
1994 Happy Thoughts	Closed	1998	78.00	78
1994 Spring Frolic	Closed	1998	64.00	64

Easter Egg Collection - eggspressions, unless otherwise noted

YEAR ISSUE	EDITION LIMIT	YEAR RETD.	ISSUE PRICE	*QUOTE U.S.$
1994 Chicks & Bunnies 69064	Closed	1998	88.00	100
1994 Dinner for Six	Closed	1997	98.00	98
1997 Easter Egger - C. Johnson	250	1998	160.00	160
1994 Easter Preparation	Closed	1998	84.00	84
1994 Grandma's Goodies 69062	Closed	1998	99.00	105
1994 Grandpa's Tricks	Closed	1998	90.00	90
1994 Home Sweet Home	Closed	1998	120.00	120
1995 Tara - D. Leffler	250	1998	80.00	85

Florals - eggspressions, unless otherwise noted

YEAR ISSUE	EDITION LIMIT	YEAR RETD.	ISSUE PRICE	*QUOTE U.S.$
1992 Apple Blossom Bouquet 67008	Retrd.	1997	62.00	75
1997 Birdhouse Blossoms 20080 - J. Melanson	250		70.00	70
1997 Blue Buttercups 69134	Open		90.00	90
1997 Glass Flowers 20079 - S. Fox	250	1998	98.00	98
1997 Pansy Blossoms 69135	Open		90.00	90
1997 Pink Perfection 69133	Open		90.00	90
1992 Violet Medley 69136	Open		62.00	90

Hand Carved Collection - eggspressions

YEAR ISSUE	EDITION LIMIT	YEAR RETD.	ISSUE PRICE	*QUOTE U.S.$
1992 Angelica (angel)	Closed	1998	50.00	50
1992 Bells (wedding)	Closed	1998	55.00	55
1992 Birthday - January	Closed	1998	40.00	40
1992 Birthday - February	Closed	1998	40.00	40
1992 Birthday - March	Closed	1998	40.00	40
1992 Birthday - April	Closed	1998	40.00	40
1992 Birthday - May	Closed	1998	40.00	40
1992 Birthday - June	Closed	1998	40.00	40
1992 Birthday - July	Closed	1998	40.00	40
1992 Birthday - August	Closed	1998	40.00	40
1992 Birthday - September	Closed	1998	40.00	40
1992 Birthday - October	Closed	1998	40.00	40
1992 Birthday - November	Closed	1998	40.00	40
1992 Birthday - December	Closed	1998	40.00	40
1992 Butterfly Wings	Closed	1996	50.00	50
1992 Dogwood	Closed	1998	50.00	50
1992 Fantasia	Closed	1998	45.00	45
1992 Gabriela (angel)	Closed	1998	45.00	45
1992 Misty Rose	Closed	1998	45.00	45
1992 Poinsettia	Closed	1998	60.00	60
1992 Snowflake	Closed	1998	50.00	50
1992 Summer Rose	Closed	1998	45.00	45
1992 Tabitha (angel)	Closed	1998	40.00	40
1992 Tannenbaum	Closed	1998	55.00	55
1992 Welcome Candle	Closed	1998	63.00	63

Hand Painted - eggspressions, unless otherwise noted

YEAR ISSUE	EDITION LIMIT	YEAR RETD.	ISSUE PRICE	*QUOTE U.S.$
1992 America's Pride	Closed	1995	139.00	140
1992 Brrr Rabbit	Closed	1997	139.00	140
1992 Buttercup	Closed	1998	85.00	85
1994 Frosty's Cheer - K. Steuckrath	Closed	1998	64.00	70
1992 Lobo	Closed	1997	85.00	85
1994 Old St. Nicholas - K. Steuckrath	Closed	1998	64.00	70
1992 Serena	Closed	1998	139.00	140
1992 Slumbering Steggy	Closed	1998	85.00	85
1992 Star Prancer	Closed	1997	139.00	140
1992 Tryke	Closed	1998	90.00	90
1992 Warrior's Pride	Closed	1998	85.00	85

Humor Collection - Various

YEAR ISSUE	EDITION LIMIT	YEAR RETD.	ISSUE PRICE	*QUOTE U.S.$
1997 C'Mon Burro 20089 - L. Pollard	250	1998	190.00	190
1996 Chill Out 69127 - A. Downs	250	1998	175.00	175
1997 Early Rise 69140 - C. Johnson	250	1998	130.00	130
1996 Help Wanted 69128 - D. Husokowski	250	1998	145.00	145
1997 Rex 20085 - C. Bailey	250	1998	170.00	170

Jeweled Baskets - eggspressions

YEAR ISSUE	EDITION LIMIT	YEAR RETD.	ISSUE PRICE	*QUOTE U.S.$
1994 Absolutely Amethyst	Closed	1998	98.00	100
1994 Black Tie	Closed	1998	178.00	178
1994 Jaded Jealousy	Closed	1997	158.00	158
1994 Pastel & Pearls 90019	Closed	1998	110.00	110
1994 Pristine Pearls 90020	Closed	1998	110.00	110
1994 Rose Marie 90021	Closed	1998	110.00	110

Jeweled Ornaments - eggspressions, unless otherwise noted

YEAR ISSUE	EDITION LIMIT	YEAR RETD.	ISSUE PRICE	*QUOTE U.S.$
1996 Bedazzled 69126- A. Downs	250		150.00	150
1995 Dawn 67142	250	1998	200.00	200
1992 Golden Crystal	Closed	1998	170.00	170
1996 Hidden Treasure (musical-clock) 70004 - C. Johnson	250		120.00	120
1992 Romantique 67006	Retrd.	1998	66.00	75

Keepsake Treasure Chest - eggspressions, unless otherwise noted

YEAR ISSUE	EDITION LIMIT	YEAR RETD.	ISSUE PRICE	*QUOTE U.S.$
1995 Amber's Treasure	250	1997	120.00	120
1996 As Time Goes By 70003 (musical-clock) - C. Johnson	250	1998	200.00	200
1992 Blush	Closed	1998	105.00	105
1997 Catrina 50015	Open		105.00	130
1995 Dynasty - C. Johnson	25	1996	700.00	700
1992 Ebony	Closed	1998	105.00	105
1997 Eggsquisite Crystals (musical) 50018	Open		360.00	360
1992 Elegant Choice 50001	Open		110.00	110
1997 Empress 50013	Open		100.00	100
1994 Eternity 90052 - C. Johnson	250	1998	180.00	180
1996 Fall Harvest 90058 - L. Pollard	50		550.00	550
1995 First Love (musical) 30047 - C. Johnson	250	1998	190.00	190
1997 Golden Flutterbye 50012	Open		105.00	105
1994 Golden Harmony - B. Gabrielli	Closed	1998	160.00	160
1997 Grace 90060 - L. Pollard	100		550.00	550
1997 Heart's Desire	Closed	1998	100.00	100
1996 Infinity 90059 - D. Leffler	50		700.00	700
1992 Lara (musical)	Closed	1998	115.00	115
1997 Love's Treasures 50090 (musical)	Closed	1998	120.00	120
1992 Maria (musical)	Closed	1997	115.00	115
1992 Midas	Closed	1997	105.00	105
1992 Mint Julep	Closed	1998	100.00	100
1994 Passion - D. Leffler	25	1995	500.00	500
1992 Pearl	Closed	1996	100.00	100
1997 Precious Mementos (blue) 50011	Open		100.00	100
1997 Precious Mementos (pink) 50010	Open		100.00	100
1995 Princess 90055 - D. Leffler	250	1998	100.00	100
1997 Royal Charms (musical) 50017	Open		110.00	110
1995 Royalty (musical) - T. Long	Closed	1998	170.00	170
1992 Secret Garden 50002	Open		80.00	80
1997 Silk Treasures 90061	Closed	1998	95.00	95
1992 Silver Jewels	Closed	1998	105.00	105
1992 Skye	Closed	1997	100.00	100
1996 Somewhere in Time (musical-clock) 70002 - C. Johnson	250	1998	220.00	220
1995 Sophia 90056 - D. Leffler	250		110.00	110
1995 Summertime Fantasy - L. Pollard	25	1996	450.00	450
1992 Velvet Princess 50000	Closed	1998	100.00	100
1997 Wings of a Dove (musical)	Open		105.00	105
1992 Yellow Rose	Closed	1997	105.00	105

Love & Romance - Various

YEAR ISSUE	EDITION LIMIT	YEAR RETD.	ISSUE PRICE	*QUOTE U.S.$
1992 Bill & Coo 67003 - eggspressions	Closed	1998	53.00	70
1995 Coo 69007 - D. Husokowski	250	1997	115.00	120
1996 Grace in the Garden - B. Gabrielli	Closed	1998	120.00	120
1994 Lavender Love - B. Gabrielli	Closed	1998	130.00	150
1996 Lifetime Together 67027 - D. Botts	250		120.00	120
1994 Love Birds - B. Gabrielli	250	1998	118.00	140
1997 Love Bunnies 69142 - C. Johnson	250		150.00	150
1992 Love Duet 69011 - eggspressions	Open		125.00	130
1992 Love in Flight 69000 - eggspressions	Closed	1998	95.00	115
1996 Nestle In 67034 - B. Gabrielli	125	1997	90.00	90
1994 Serenade - B. Gabrielli	Closed	1998	120.00	140
1994 Serenity - B. Gabrielli	Closed	1998	114.00	115
1994 Wedding in White - B. Gabrielli	250	1998	160.00	180

Nature's Collection - Various

YEAR ISSUE	EDITION LIMIT	YEAR RETD.	ISSUE PRICE	*QUOTE U.S.$
1996 Birdhouse Buddies 67149 - A. Kolb	250	1998	90.00	90
1992 Bluebirds of Happiness 67014 - eggspressions	Closed	1998	79.00	79
1995 Cabbage Patch 20074 - B. Gabrielli	250		105.00	110
1992 Cardinals 67015 - eggspressions	Closed	1998	58.00	70
1996 First Light 67033 - B. Gabrielli	125	1997	90.00	90
1995 Left Behind 67145 - D. Botts	250		80.00	80
1992 McGregor's Garden 67009 - eggspressions	Closed	1998	98.00	115

*Quotes have been rounded up to nearest dollar

YEAR ISSUE	EDITION LIMIT	YEAR RETD.	ISSUE PRICE	*QUOTE U.S.$
1995 Peekin' Out - B. Gabrielli	Closed	1998	55.00	55
1996 Play Bunnies 67035 - B. Gabrielli	250		100.00	100
1994 Spring Melody - B. Gabrielli	250	1998	130.00	145
1992 Winter Colt (hanging) - eggspressions	Closed	1998	104.00	105
1992 Winter Colt (stand) - eggspressions	Closed	1997	104.00	105
1992 Winter Song - eggspressions	Closed	1998	99.00	135
1997 Yellowbirds 67150 - B. Gabrielli	250	1998	80.00	80

Southwesten Collection - eggspressions

YEAR ISSUE	EDITION LIMIT	YEAR RETD.	ISSUE PRICE	*QUOTE U.S.$
1992 Kachina	Closed	1998	112.00	130
1992 Storyteller	Closed	1995	112.00	130

Springtime Collection - Various

YEAR ISSUE	EDITION LIMIT	YEAR RETD.	ISSUE PRICE	*QUOTE U.S.$
1997 Cat & The Hat 67151 - B. Gabrielli	250		110.00	110
1996 Fairy Dance 69029 - D. Botts	250	1998	95.00	95
1996 Hummingbird Melody 67028 - D. Botts	250		120.00	120
1997 In The Meadow (musical) 30063 - D. Leffler	250		230.00	230
1992 Isadora 69010 - eggspressions	Closed	1998	145.00	145
1994 Jessica - L. Pollard	Closed	1998	270.00	270
1996 Little Girls Fancy - D. Mac Dougal	Closed	1998	230.00	230
1996 Magical Garden 67032 - D. Leffler	250	1998	110.00	110
1997 Pot O' Gold 20086 - J. Beemer	250	1998	110.00	110
1997 Pretty in Pink 69145 - L. Pollard	250	1998	170.00	170
1997 Rainy Day Kitty 69132 - D. Husokowski	250	1998	150.00	150
1997 Spring Lamb - D. Botts	250	1998	90.00	90

Teapot Collection - Various

YEAR ISSUE	EDITION LIMIT	YEAR RETD.	ISSUE PRICE	*QUOTE U.S.$
1997 Mail Mouse (spring) 20081 - S. Fox	250		144.00	144
1996 Mouse Chief (Christmas) 20075 - S. Fox	250	1998	175.00	175
1997 Oriental Rose 20082 - S. Fox	250	1998	170.00	170
1996 Snow Busters (children) 20076 - D. Botts	100		270.00	270
1996 Tina & Teddy (children) 20001 - D. Botts	100		270.00	270

Teddy Bears & Dolls - Various

YEAR ISSUE	EDITION LIMIT	YEAR RETD.	ISSUE PRICE	*QUOTE U.S.$
1995 Andrea - D. Leffler	250	1998	85.00	85
1997 Ann's Rainbow 69146 - L. Pollard	250		170.00	170
1994 Beary Blue Christmas 69097 - B. Gabrielli	250	1998	110.00	110
1994 Beary Pink Christmas - B. Gabrielli	250	1998	110.00	110
1997 Hot Bear Balloon - B. Gabrielli	250	1998	200.00	200
1995 Jamie - D. Leffler	250	1998	80.00	85
1992 Kewpie Doll 69016 - eggspressions	Closed	1998	99.00	130
1994 Teddy Bear Sing Along - D. Husokowski	Closed	1998	114.00	130
1997 Teddy's Turn (musical) 69138 - B. Gabrielli	250		150.00	150

Wedding Heirlooms - eggspressions

YEAR ISSUE	EDITION LIMIT	YEAR RETD.	ISSUE PRICE	*QUOTE U.S.$
1997 "I Do" Caketop (personalized) 80001	Open		170.00	170
1997 "I Do" Caketop 80000	Open		160.00	160
1997 Destiny Ring Box 50033	Closed	1998	66.00	66
1997 Flower Basket 80007	Open		120.00	120
1997 Flowers & Lace Caketop (personalized) 80003	Open		170.00	170
1997 Flowers & Lace Caketop 80002	Open		160.00	160
1997 Hearts Afire Ring Box 50031	Closed	1998	66.00	66
1997 Marry Me? Ring Box 50032	Closed	1998	66.00	66
1997 Mememto Vase (personalized) 80004	Closed	1998	160.00	160
1997 Ostrich Vase 80008	Closed	1998	80.00	80

Whimsicals - eggspressions

YEAR ISSUE	EDITION LIMIT	YEAR RETD.	ISSUE PRICE	*QUOTE U.S.$
1992 Colours	Closed	1996	45.00	55
1992 Kris Kringle	Closed	1997	38.00	45
1992 Marcella	Closed	1995	38.00	45
1992 Miss Ellie	Closed	1998	38.00	45
1992 Peter	Closed	1998	38.00	45
1992 Petunia	Closed	1998	38.00	45

Wilderness Collection - eggspressions, unless otherwise noted

YEAR ISSUE	EDITION LIMIT	YEAR RETD.	ISSUE PRICE	*QUOTE U.S.$
1992 Daytime Den	Closed	1997	124.00	125
1992 Dear One	Closed	1998	98.00	100
1992 Family Outing	Closed	1997	98.00	100
1994 Mother's Pride - B. Gabrielli	Closed	1998	120.00	140
1992 Oh, Nuts	Closed	1998	98.00	100
1992 Togetherness 67002	Open		84.00	84
1995 Winter Bunny 67143 - B. Gabrielli	250	1998	90.00	90
1992 Winter Haven	Closed	1996	98.00	105
1995 Woodland Bunnies 69100 - B. Gabrielli	250	1998	120.00	120

Enchantica

Enchantica Collectors Club - Various

YEAR ISSUE	EDITION LIMIT	YEAR RETD.	ISSUE PRICE	*QUOTE U.S.$
1991 Snappa on Mushroom-2101 - A. Hull	Retrd.	1991	Gift	200-285
1991 Rattajack with Snail-2102 - A. Bill	Retrd.	1991	60.00	300
1992 Jonquil-2103 - A. Hull	Retrd.	1992	Gift	165-200
1992 Ice Demon-2104 - K. Fallon	Retrd.	1992	85.00	290-400
1992 Sea Dragon-2106 - A. Bill	Retrd.	1993	99.00	300-825
1993 White Dragon-2107 - A. Bill	Retrd.	1993	Gift	128-165
1993 Jonquil's Flight-2108 - A. Bill	Retrd.	1993	140.00	200-370
1994 Verratus-2111 - A. Bill	Retrd.	1994	Gift	50-125
1994 Mimmer-Spring Fairy-2112 - A. Bill	Retrd.	1994	100.00	100-325
1994 Gorgoyle Cameo piece-2113 - K. Fallon	Retrd.	1994	Gift	25-50
1995 Destroyer-2116 - A. Hull	Retrd.	1995	100.00	100-150
1995 Cloudbreaker-2115 - J. Oliver	Retrd.	1995	Gift	50-80
1996 Sheylag's Trophy-2119	Retrd.	1996	125.00	80-125
1996 Jacarand-2118 - A. Hull	Retrd.	1996	Gift	40-50
1997 Dragonskeep-2126 - D. Mayer	Retrd.	1997	129.00	80-129
1997 Silverflame-2125 - A. Bill	Retrd.	1997	Gift	28-50
1998 Zemorga-2129 - A. Bill	Yr.Iss.		115.00	115
1998 Addax-2128 - A. Bill	Yr.Iss.		Gift	N/A

Retired Enchantica Collection - Various

YEAR ISSUE	EDITION LIMIT	YEAR RETD.	ISSUE PRICE	*QUOTE U.S.$
1994 Anaxorg-Six Leg Dragon-2094 - A. Hull	Retrd.	1996	83.00	110-120
1989 Arangast-Summer Dragon-2026 - A. Bill	7,500	1992	165.00	358-600
1995 Avenger-2154 - A. Bill	450	1996	2700.00	3000-3200
1991 Bledderag, Goblin Twin-2048 - K. Fallon	8,532	1993	115.00	140-225
1988 Blick Scoops Crystals-2015 - A. Bill	Retrd.	1991	47.00	70-125
1992 Breen-Carrier Dragon-2053 - K. Fallon	12,374	1993	156.00	175-199
1992 Cave Dragon-2065 - A. Bill	6,246	1995	200.00	200-285
1989 Cellandia-Summer Fairy-2029 - A. Bill	Retrd.	1992	115.00	150-225
1996 Changeling-2121 - A. Bill	1,250	1996	120.00	120-125
1997 Charlock-2201E - A. Bill	Retrd.	1997	150.00	150
1988 Chuckwalla-2021 - A. Bill	Retrd.	1994	43.00	60-80
1994 Coracob-Cobra Dragon-2093 - A. Hull	Retrd.	1996	83.00	87
1994 Daggerback-2114 - K. Fallon	Retrd.	1995	95.00	95-100
1992 Desert Dragon-2064 - A. Bill	4,786	1995	175.00	175-200
1997 Dragonbrood-2174 - K. Fallon	2,950	1998	359.00	359
1995 Dragongorge Logo-2169 - J. Oliver	Retrd.	1998	50.00	35-40
1994 Dromelaid, Tunnel Serpent-2097 - A. Bill	Retrd.	1997	83.00	108-150
1994 Escape (5th Anniversary)-2110 - A. Bill	Retrd.	1994	250.00	250-358
1988 Fantazar- Spring Wizard-2016 - A. Bill	7,500	1991	132.50	325-400
1991 Flight to Danger-2044 - A. Bill	450	1991	3000.00	5000-6500
1989 Fossfex - Autumn Fairy-2030 - A. Bill	Retrd.	1992	115.00	150-410
1991 Furza - Carrier Dragon-2050 - K. Fallon	10,024	1993	137.50	165-199
1996 Glostomorg-2122 - A. Bill	Retrd.	1996	250.00	165-275
1988 Gorgoyle - Spring Dragon-2017 - A. Bill	7,500	1991	132.50	410-450
1991 Grawlfang '91 Winter Dragon-2046 - A. Bill	14,800	1995	295.00	330-350
1988 Grawlfang - Winter Dragon-2019 - A. Bill	7,500	1991	132.50	450-750
1994 Grogoda, She Troll-2150 - A. Bill	2,950	1997	220.00	220-240
1988 Hepna Pushes Truck-2014 - A. Bill	Retrd.	1994	47.00	57-125
1988 Hest Checks Crystals-2013 - A. Bill	Retrd.	1994	47.00	57-125
1988 Hobba, Hellbenders Twin Son-2023 - A. Bill	Retrd.	1992	69.00	105-205
1996 Hoolock-2177 - A. Bill	2,950	1997	250.00	170-270
1993 Ice Dragon-2109 - A. Bill	Retrd.	1994	95.00	95-225
1995 Infernos-2165 - A. Hull	3,950	1997	145.00	115-168
1996 JáQuara-2170 - K. Fallon	2,950	1998	240.00	240
1993 Jonquil and Snappa-2055 - A. Hull	Retrd.	1996	83.00	83-99
1988 Jonquil- Dragons Footprint-2004 - A. Bill	Retrd.	1991	55.00	67-124
1995 Kirrock of Dragon Duel-2159 - A. Bill	1,950	1996	400.00	435-550
1997 Leviathan-2123	Retrd.	1997	285.00	285
1995 Mal'terith-2164 - K. Fallon	2,950	1997	250.00	190-297
1992 Manu Manu-Peeper-2105 - A. Bill	Retrd.	1993	40.00	110-400
1994 Mezereon "Grand Corrupter"-2091 - A. Bill	5,100	1996	175.00	180-187
1996 Mezereon-2176 - A. Bill	2,950	1997	250.00	250-270
1994 Necranon-Raptor Dragon-2095 - A. Bill	Retrd.	1996	105.00	75-120
1996 Nosfertus-2173 - J. Woodward	2,950	1998	290.00	290-297
1990 Ogrod-Ice Troll-2032 - A. Bill	Retrd.	1995	235.00	220-375
1990 Okra, Goblin Princess-2031 - A. Bill	Retrd.	1994	105.00	124-165
1988 Old Yargle-2020 - A. Bill	Retrd.	1993	55.00	115-450
1990 Olm & Sylphen, Mer-King & Queen-2059 - A. Bill	4,251	1994	350.00	350-410
1989 Orolan-Summer Wizard-2025 - A. Bill	7,500	1992	165.00	300-350
1992 Peeper "Burra Burra"-2057 - A. Hull	Retrd.	1997	50.00	40-58
1993 Peeper "Pia Pia"-2079 - A. Bill	Retrd.	1998	47.00	40-60
1993 Peeper "Rio Rio"-2080 - A. Bill	Retrd.	1998	53.00	40-68
1992 Peeper "Sollo Sollo"-2058 - A. Bill	Retrd.	1997	50.00	40-59
1995 Piasharn-2162 - K. Fallon	2,950	1996	250.00	270-297
1991 Quillion-Autumn Witch-2045 - A. Bill	13,891	1995	205.00	220-325
1993 Rattajack "All Alone"-2089 - A. Bill	Retrd.	1996	48.00	52
1991 Rattajack "Bowled Over"-2037 - A. Hull	Retrd.	1997	65.00	66-80
1993 Rattajack "Gone Fishing"-2090 - A. Bill	Retrd.	1996	70.00	77
1993 Rattajack "Lazybones"-2087 - A. Bill	Retrd.	1997	49.00	60
1993 Rattajack "Soft Landing"-2088 - A. Bill	Retrd.	1996	49.00	46-65
1993 Rattajack & Snappa-2056 - A. Hull	Retrd.	1996	70.00	73-99
1988 Rattajack - Circles-2003 - A. Bill	Retrd.	1993	40.00	66-125
1988 Rattajack - My Ball-2001 - A. Bill	Retrd.	1993	40.00	58-70
1988 Rattajack - Please-2000 - A. Bill	Retrd.	1993	40.00	65-87
1988 Rattajack - Terragon Dreams-2002 - A. Bill	Retrd.	1993	40.00	60-80
1991 Rattajack - Up & Under-2038 - A. Hull	Retrd.	1995	65.00	50-75
1995 Saberath-2117 - K. Fallon	Retrd.	1996	100.00	100
1991 Samphire-Carrier Dragon-2049 - A. Bill	11,800	1995	137.50	165-199
1991 Snappa Caught Napping-2039 - A. Hull	Retrd.	1995	39.50	30-60
1988 Snappa Climbs High-2008 - A. Bill	Retrd.	1993	25.00	38-80
1988 Snappa Dozing -2011 - A. Bill	Retrd.	1993	25.00	35-120
1988 Snappa Finds a Collar-2009 - A. Bill	Retrd.	1991	25.00	35-99
1993 Snappa Flapping-2082 - A. Bill	Retrd.	1996	29.50	30-33
1988 Snappa Hatches Out-2006 - A. Bill	Retrd.	1991	25.00	60-125
1993 Snappa If The Cap Fits-2084 - A. Bill	Retrd.	1996	32.50	35
1991 Snappa in Pool "Splash"-2035 - A. Hull	Retrd.	1997	39.50	30-48
1993 Snappa Nature Watch-2086 - J. Oliver	Retrd.	1996	26.00	28
1991 Snappa Nods Off-2043 - A. Hull	Retrd.	1995	30.00	40-50
1988 Snappa Plays Ball-2010 - A. Bill	Retrd.	1993	25.00	36-80
1991 Snappa Posing-2042 - A. Hull	Retrd.	1995	30.00	50
1993 Snappa Rollaball-2081 - A. Bill	Retrd.	1996	32.50	35
1991 Snappa Snowdrift-2041 - A. Hull	Retrd.	1995	30.00	30-40
1991 Snappa Tickled Pink-2036 - A. Hull	Retrd.	1997	39.50	30-48
1991 Snappa Tumbles-2047 - A. Hull	Retrd.	1995	30.00	27-40
1993 Snappa w/Enchantica Rose-2083 - A. Bill	Retrd.	1996	24.50	30
1993 Snappa What Ball-2085 - J. Oliver	Retrd.	1996	30.00	30-33
1988 Snappa's First Feast-2007 - A. Bill	Retrd.	1993	25.00	36-80
1990 Snarlgard - Autumn Dragon-2034 - A. Bill	7,500	1993	337.00	400-550
1993 Snow Dragon-2066 - A. Bill	7,500	1996	150.00	80-175
1995 Snowhawk of Dragon Duel-2160 - A. Bill	1,950	1996	400.00	435-550
1992 Snowthorn & Wargren-2062 - A. Bill	7,500	1997	570.00	570-650
1992 Sorren & Gart-2054 - K. Fallon	3,978	1994	220.00	265-300
1991 Spring Wizard and Yim-2060 - A. Bill	4,554	1993	410.00	410-450
1989 The Swamp Demon-2028 - A. Bill	Retrd.	1992	69.00	85-205
1988 Tarbet with Sack-2012 - A. Bill	Retrd.	1991	47.00	57-125
1992 Thrace-Gladiator-2061 - K. Fallon	3,751	1993	280.00	300-500
1992 The Throne Citadel-2063 - J. Woodward	539	1995	2000.00	2000
1997 Tuatara-2215 - A. Bill	2,950	1998	240.00	155-240
1989 Tuatara-Evil Witch-2027 - A. Bill	6,977	1995	174.00	185-325
1995 Valkaria-2161 - K. Fallon	2,950	1997	250.00	165-270
1996 Vladdigor-2171 - A. Bill	2,950	1996	290.00	290-400
1989 Vrorst - The Ice Sorcerer-2018 - A. Bill	7,500	1991	155.00	500-700
1990 Vrorst-Ice Sorcerer on Throne-2040 - A. Bill	11,111	1996	500.00	500-745
1994 Vyzauga-Twin Headed Dragon-2092 - A. Bill	Retrd.	1996	83.00	87-105
1990 Waxifrade - Autumn Wizard-2033 - A. Bill	7,500	1993	265.00	265-325
1995 Wolfarlis-2163 - K. Fallon	2,950	1996	250.00	297-400
1996 Woodwidger-2120 - A. Bill	Retrd.	1997	100.00	100-132
1994 Zadragul, Tunnel Serpent-2151 - A. Bill	Retrd.	1997	83.00	96-150
1995 Zadratus-2168 - J. Oliver	3,950	1998	156.00	156-173
1994 Zorganoid-Crab Dragon-2096 - K. Fallon	Retrd.	1996	93.00	75-120

Ertl Collectibles

Cat Hall of Fame - T. Epstein/J. Epstein Gage

YEAR ISSUE	EDITION LIMIT	YEAR RETD.	ISSUE PRICE	*QUOTE U.S.$
1998 Albert Felinestein 257	Open		20.00	20
1998 Cats Domino 247	5,000		57.00	57
1998 Cats Fifth Avenue 241	Open		20.00	20
1998 Catsablanca 240	5,000		59.50	60
1998 George S. Catton 242	Open		20.00	20
1998 Liza Mewnelli 253	Open		20.00	20
1998 Lucy & Ricky Ricatto 237	5,000		57.00	57
1998 Marie Catoinette 254	Open		20.00	20
1998 Miss Americat 256	Open		20.00	20
1998 Sitting Cat 252	Open		20.00	20
1998 William Shakespurr 255	Open		20.00	20

Circus World/Museum Collection - Ertl

YEAR ISSUE	EDITION LIMIT	YEAR RETD.	ISSUE PRICE	*QUOTE U.S.$
1997 Bostock & Wombwell's Menagerie 2481	3,500		75.00	75
1997 Lion And Mirror Bandwagon 2479	3,500		90.00	90
1997 Pawnee Bill 2478	3,500		90.00	90
1997 Twin Lions 2480	3,500		90.00	90

Harley Davidson America - S. Hodges

YEAR ISSUE	EDITION LIMIT	YEAR RETD.	ISSUE PRICE	*QUOTE U.S.$
1998 Eagle Lookout 66	Open		80.00	80
1998 Fishin' 65	Open		80.00	80
1998 Last Chance Café 67	Open		100.00	100
1998 Loyal Friends 64	Open		80.00	80

Harley Davidson Memories - Ertl

YEAR ISSUE	EDITION LIMIT	YEAR RETD.	ISSUE PRICE	*QUOTE U.S.$
1998 Anticipation 80	Open		80.00	80
1998 Tender Loving Care 68	Open		80.00	80

Lowell Davis America - L. Davis

YEAR ISSUE	EDITION LIMIT	YEAR RETD.	ISSUE PRICE	*QUOTE U.S.$
1997 "A Friend In Need" 2525	4,500		70.00	70
1997 "Can't Wait" 1217	3,500		150.00	150
1998 "Country Doctor" 2498	3,500		280.00	290
1998 "Dog Days" 2522	Open		90.00	90
1997 "Get One For Me" 2523	4,500		75.00	75
1997 "Last of the Litter" 2497	5,500		60.00	60
1997 "Next" 2496	4,500		70.00	70
1997 "Nine Lives?" 2534	3,500		120.00	120
1997 "Oh! She'll Be Driving Six White Horses..." 2494	3,500		250.00	250
1997 "Sooie" 2521	3,500		160.00	160
1998 Red Oak II 1923 Chevy Panel Truck	Open		25.00	25
1996 Red Oak II 1923 Chevy Panel Truck	Open		25.00	25

*Quotes have been rounded up to nearest dollar

Fenton Art Glass Company

Fenton Art Glass Collectors - Fenton

YEAR ISSUE	EDITION LIMIT	YEAR RETD.	ISSUE PRICE	*QUOTE U.S.$
1978 Cranberry Opalescent Baskets w/variety of spot moulds	Yr.Iss.	1978	20.00	100-125
1979 Vasa Murrhina Vases (Variety of colors)	Yr.Iss.	1979	25.00	60-115
1980 Velva Rose Bubble Optic "Melon" Vases	Yr.Iss.	1980	30.00	60-115
1981 Amethyst w/White Hanging Hearts Vases	Yr.Iss.	1981	37.50	150-175
1982 Overlay Baskets in pastel shades (Swirl Optic)	Yr.Iss.	1982	40.00	75-115
1983 Cranberry Opalescent 1 pc. Fairy Lights	Yr.Iss.	1983	40.00	150-295
1984 Blue Burmese w/peloton Treatment Vases	Yr.Iss.	1984	25.00	75-125
1985 Overlay Vases in Dusty Rose w/Mica Flecks	Yr.Iss.	1985	25.00	95-100
1986 Ruby Iridized Art Glass Vase	Yr.Iss.	1986	30.00	100-200
1987 Dusty Rose Overlay/Peach Blow Interior w/dark blue Crest Vase	Yr.Iss.	1987	38.00	75-110
1988 Teal Green and Milk marble Basket	Yr.Iss.	1988	30.00	100-110
1989 Mulberry Opalescent Basket w/Coin Dot Optic	Yr.Iss.	1989	37.50	100-175
1990 Sea Mist Green Opalescent Fern Optic Basket	Yr.Iss.	1990	40.00	50-75
1991 Rosalene Leaf Basket and Peacock & Dahlia Basket	Yr.Iss.	1991	65.00	95
1992 Blue Bubble Optic Vases	Yr.Iss.	1992	35.00	50-75
1993 Cranberry Opalescent "Jonquil" Basket	Yr.Iss.	1993	35.00	70-110
1994 Cranberry Opalescent Jacqueline Pitcher	Yr.Iss.	1994	55.00	85-125
1994 Rosalene Tulip Vase-1994 Convention Pc.	Yr.Iss.	1994	45.00	125-150
1995 Fairy Light-Blue Burmese-1995 Convention Pc.	Yr.Iss.	1995	45.00	185-195
1996 Temple Jar, Burmese-1996 Convention Pc.	Yr.Iss.	1996	65.00	75-150
1997 Mouthblown Egg, Topaz Opal Irid. Hndpt.	Yr.Iss.	1997	65.00	65

Collector's Club-Glass Messenger Subscribers Only - M. Reynolds, unless otherwise noted

YEAR ISSUE	EDITION LIMIT	YEAR RETD.	ISSUE PRICE	*QUOTE U.S.$
1996 Basket, Roselle on Cranberry	Yr.Iss.	1996	89.00	100-125
1997 Vase, French Rose on Rosalene	Yr.Iss.	1997	95.00	95
1998 Vase, Morning Glory on Burmese - F. Burton	Yr.Iss.		95.00	95

1983 Connoisseur Collection - Fenton

YEAR ISSUE	EDITION LIMIT	YEAR RETD.	ISSUE PRICE	*QUOTE U.S.$
1983 Basket, 9" Vasa Murrhina	1,000	1983	75.00	125
1983 Craftsman Stein, White Satin Carnival	1,500	1983	35.00	50
1983 Cruet/Stopper Vasa Murrhina	1,000	1983	75.00	195
1983 Epergne Set, 5 pc. Burmese	500	1983	200.00	550-895
1983 Vase, 4 1/2" Sculptured Rose Quartz	2,000	1983	32.50	95-125
1983 Vase, 7" Sculptured Rose Quartz	1,500	1983	50.00	110-120
1983 Vase, 9" Sculptured Rose Quartz	850	1983	75.00	175-220

1984 Connoisseur Collection - Fenton, unless otherwise noted

YEAR ISSUE	EDITION LIMIT	YEAR RETD.	ISSUE PRICE	*QUOTE U.S.$
1984 Basket, 10" Plated Amberina Velvet	1,250	1984	85.00	175-195
1984 Candy Box w/cover, 3 pc. Blue Burmese	1,250	1984	75.00	150-250
1984 Cane, 18" Plated Amberina Velvet	Yr.Iss.	1984	35.00	195-225
1984 Top Hat, 8" Plated Amberina Velvet	1,500	1984	65.00	175-195
1984 Vase, 9" Rose Velvet Hndpt. Floral - L. Everson	750	1984	75.00	150-195
1984 Vase, 9" Rose Velvet-Mother/Child	750	1984	125.00	150-250
1984 Vase, Swan, 8" Gold Azure	1,500	1984	65.00	195-295

1985 Connoisseur Collection - Fenton, unless otherwise noted

YEAR ISSUE	EDITION LIMIT	YEAR RETD.	ISSUE PRICE	*QUOTE U.S.$
1985 Basket, 8 1/2" Buremese, Hndpt. - L. Everson	1,250	1985	95.00	150-250
1985 Epergne Set, 4 pc. Diamond Lace Green Opal.	1,000	1985	95.00	150-250
1985 Lamp, 22" Burmese-Butterfly, Hndpt. - L. Everson	350	1985	300.00	500-795
1985 Punch Set, 14 pc. Green Opalescent	500	1985	250.00	325-350
1985 Vase, 12" Gabrielle Scul. French Opal.	800	1985	150.00	225-250
1985 Vase, 7 1/2" Burmese-Shell - D. Barbour	950	1985	135.00	275-300
1985 Vase, 7 1/2" Chrysanthemums/Circlet, Hndpt. - L. Everson	1,000	1985	125.00	150

1986 Connoisseur Collection - Fenton, unless otherwise noted

YEAR ISSUE	EDITION LIMIT	YEAR RETD.	ISSUE PRICE	*QUOTE U.S.$
1986 Basket, Top hat Wild Rose/Teal Overlay	1,500	1986	49.00	75-110
1986 Boudoir Lamp, Cranberry Pearl	750	1986	145.00	250-295
1986 Cruet/Stopper, Cranberry Pearl	1,000	1986	75.00	250-295
1986 Handled Urn, 13" Cranberry Satin	1,000	1986	185.00	450-550
1986 Handled Vase, 7" French Royale	1,000	1986	100.00	175-195
1986 Lamp, 20" Burmese Shells Hndpt. - D. Barbour	500	1986	350.00	500-795
1986 Vanity Set, 4 pc. Blue Ridge	1,000	1986	125.00	225-395
1986 Vase 10 1/2" Danielle Sandcarved - R. Delaney	1,000	1986	95.00	195
1986 Vase, 10 1/2" Misty Morn, Hndpt. - L. Everson	1,000	1986	95.00	195

1987 Connoisseur Collection - Various

YEAR ISSUE	EDITION LIMIT	YEAR RETD.	ISSUE PRICE	*QUOTE U.S.$
1987 Pitcher, 8" Enameled Azure Hndpt. - L. Everson	950	1987	85.00	125
1987 Vase, 7 1/4" Blossom/Bows on Cranberry Hndpt.- D. Barbour	950	1987	95.00	125-195

1988 Connoisseur Collection - Fenton, unless otherwise noted

YEAR ISSUE	EDITION LIMIT	YEAR RETD.	ISSUE PRICE	*QUOTE U.S.$
1988 Basket, Irid. Teal Cased Vasa Murrhina	2,500	1988	65.00	125-150
1988 Candy, Wave Crest, CranberryHndpt. - L. Everson	2,000	1988	95.00	150-195
1988 Pitcher, Cased Cranberry/ Opal Teal Ring	3,500	1988	60.00	125-175
1988 Vase, 6" Cased Cranberry/Opal Teal/Irid.	3,500	1988	50.00	100-125

1989 Connoisseur Collection - Fenton, unless otherwise noted

YEAR ISSUE	EDITION LIMIT	YEAR RETD.	ISSUE PRICE	*QUOTE U.S.$
1989 Basket, 7" Cranberry w/Crystal Ring Hndpt.- L. Everson	2,500	1989	85.00	100-175
1989 Candy Box, w/cover, Cranberry, Hndpt. - L. Everson	2,500	1989	85.00	125-195
1989 Epergne Set 5 pc., Rosalene	2,000	1989	250.00	400-595
1989 Lamp, 21" Rosalene Satin Hndpt. - L. Everson	1,000	1989	250.00	300-450
1989 Pitcher, Diamond Optic, Rosalene	2,500	1989	55.00	100-110
1989 Vase, Basketweave, Rosalene	2,500	1989	45.00	85-95
1989 Vase, Pinch, 8" Vasa Murrhina	2,000	1989	65.00	100-110

1990-85th Anniversary Collection - Various

YEAR ISSUE	EDITION LIMIT	YEAR RETD.	ISSUE PRICE	*QUOTE U.S.$
1990 Basket, 5 1/2" Trees on Burmese, Hndpt. - Piper/F. Burton	Closed	1990	57.50	125
1990 Basket, 7" Raspberry on Burmese, Hndpt. - L. Everson	Closed	1990	75.00	150-195
1990 Cruet/Stopper Petite Floral on Burmese, Hndpt. - L. Everson	Closed	1990	85.00	150-195
1990 Epergne Set, 2 pc. Pt. Floral on Burmese, Hndpt. - L. Everson	Closed	1990	125.00	175-295
1990 Lamp, 20" Rose Burmese, Hndpt. - Piper/D. Barbour	Closed	1990	250.00	350-495
1990 Lamp, 21" Raspberry on Burmese, Hndpt. - L. Everson	Closed	1990	295.00	450-595
1990 Vase, 6 1/2" Rose Burmese, Hndpt. - Piper/F. Burton	Closed	1990	45.00	100-110
1990 Vase, 9" Trees on Burmese, Hndpt. - Piper/F. Burton	Closed	1990	75.00	175-220
1990 Vase, Fan 6" Rose Burmese, Hndpt. - Piper/D. Barbour	Closed	1990	49.50	95-110
1990 Water Set, 7 pc. Raspberry on Burmese, Hndpt. - L. Everson	Closed	1990	275.00	500-695

1991 Connoisseur Collection - Various

YEAR ISSUE	EDITION LIMIT	YEAR RETD.	ISSUE PRICE	*QUOTE U.S.$
1991 Basket, Floral on Rosalene, Hndpt. - M. Reynolds	1,500	1991	64.00	110-130
1991 Candy Box, 3 pc. Favrene - Fenton	1,000	1991	90.00	225-250
1991 Fish, Paperweight, Rosalene - Fenton	2,000	1991	30.00	60-75
1991 Lamp, 20" Roses on Burmese, Hndpt. - Piper/F. Burton	500	1991	275.00	450-495
1991 Vase, 7 1/2" Raspberry on Burmese, Hndpt. - L. Everson	1,500	1991	65.00	100-110
1991 Vase, Floral on Favrene, Hndpt. - M. Reynolds	850	1991	125.00	350
1991 Vase, Fruit on Favrene, Hndpt. - F. Burton	850	1991	125.00	350-395

1992 Connoisseur Collection - Various

YEAR ISSUE	EDITION LIMIT	YEAR RETD.	ISSUE PRICE	*QUOTE U.S.$
1992 Covered Box, Poppy/Daisy, Hndpt. - F. Burton	1,250	1992	95.00	200-225
1992 Pitcher, 4 1/2" Berries on Burmese, Hndpt. - M. Reynolds	1,500	1992	65.00	120-150
1992 Pitcher, 9" Empire on Cranberry, Hndpt. - M. Reynolds	950	1992	110.00	200-225
1992 Vase, 6 1/2" Raspberry on Burmese, Hndpt. - L. Everson	1,500	1992	45.00	95-110
1992 Vase, 8" Seascape, Hndpt. - F. Burton	750	1992	150.00	175-225
1992 Vase, Twining Floral Rosalene Satin, Hndpt. - M. Reynolds	950	1992	110.00	175-195

1993 Connoisseur Collection - Various

YEAR ISSUE	EDITION LIMIT	YEAR RETD.	ISSUE PRICE	*QUOTE U.S.$
1993 Amphora w/Stand, Favrene, Hndpt. - M. Reynolds	850	1993	285.00	350-395
1993 Bowl, Ruby Stretch w/Gold Scrolls, Hndpt. - M. Reynolds	1,250	1993	95.00	100-150
1993 Lamp, Spring Woods Reverse Hndpt. - F. Burton	500	1993	595.00	595-795
1993 Owl Figurine, 6" Favrene - Fenton	1,500	1993	95.00	125
1993 Perfume/Stopper, Rose Trellis Rosalene, Hndpt. - F. Burton	1,250	1993	95.00	125
1993 Vase, 9" Gold Leaves Sandcarved on Plum Irid., - M. Reynolds	950	1993	175.00	225-250
1993 Vase, Victorian Roses Persian Blue Opal., Hndpt. - M. Reynolds	950	1993	125.00	150-195

1993 Family Signature Collection - Various

YEAR ISSUE	EDITION LIMIT	YEAR RETD.	ISSUE PRICE	*QUOTE U.S.$
1993 Basket, 8 1/2" Lilacs - Bill Fenton	Closed	1993	65.00	90-95
1993 Vase, 9" Alpine Thistle/Ruby Carnival - Frank M. Fenton	Closed	1993	105.00	175-195
1993 Vase, 9" Cottage Scene - Shelley Fenton	Closed	1993	90.00	150-195
1993 Vase, 10" Vintage on Plum - Don Fenton	Closed	1993	80.00	100-150
1993 Vase, 11" Cranberry Dec. - George Fenton	Closed	1993	110.00	110-140

1994 Connoisseur Collection - Various

YEAR ISSUE	EDITION LIMIT	YEAR RETD.	ISSUE PRICE	*QUOTE U.S.$
1994 Bowl, 14" Cranberry Cameo Sandcarved - Reynolds/Delaney	500	1994	390.00	390-450
1994 Clock, 4 1/2" Favrene, Hndpt. - F. Burton	850	1994	150.00	175-225
1994 Lamp, Hummingbird Reverse, Hndpt. - F. Burton	300	1994	590.00	600-750
1994 Pitcher, 10" Lattice on Burmese, Hndpt. - F. Burton	750	1994	165.00	225-295
1994 Vase, 7" Favrene, Hndpt. - M. Reynolds	850	1994	185.00	200-225
1994 Vase, 8" Plum Opalescent, Hndpt. - M. Reynolds	750	1994	165.00	175-225
1994 Vase, 11" Gold Amberina, Hndpt. - M. Reynolds	750	1994	175.00	225-295

1994 Family Signature Collection - Various

YEAR ISSUE	EDITION LIMIT	YEAR RETD.	ISSUE PRICE	*QUOTE U.S.$
1994 Basket, 7 1/2" Lilacs - Shelley Fenton	Closed	1994	65.00	95
1994 Basket, 8" Stiegel Green - Bill Fenton	Closed	1994	60.00	95
1994 Basket, 8 1/2" Ruby Carnival - Tom Fenton	Closed	1994	60.00	95-110
1994 Basket, 11" Autumn Gold Opal - Frank Fenton	Closed	1994	70.00	90-95
1994 Candy w/cover, 9 1/2" Autumn Leaves - Don Fenton	Closed	1994	60.00	75-95
1994 Pitcher, 6 1/2" Cranberry - Frank M. Fenton	Closed	1994	85.00	125-150
1994 Vase, 9 1/2" Pansies on Cranberry - Bill Fenton	Closed	1994	95.00	125
1994 Vase, 10" Fuchsia - George Fenton	Closed	1994	95.00	125-150

1995 Burmese Historic Collection - Various

YEAR ISSUE	EDITION LIMIT	YEAR RETD.	ISSUE PRICE	*QUOTE U.S.$
1995 Basket, 8" "Butterflies" - M Reynolds	790	1995	135.00	195-200
1995 Bowl, 10 1/4" Rolled Rim "Vintage" - M. Reynolds	790	1995	150.00	200-225
1995 Lamp, 33" "Daybreak" - F. Burton	300	1995	495.00	650-795
1995 Pitcher, 10" "Cherry Blossoms & Butterfly" - M. Reynolds	790	1995	175.00	250-295
1995 Vase, 9" "Hummingbird", 11 Family Signatures - M. Reynolds	790	1995	150.00	195-200

1995 Connoisseur Collection - M. Reynolds, unless otherwise noted

YEAR ISSUE	EDITION LIMIT	YEAR RETD.	ISSUE PRICE	*QUOTE U.S.$
1995 Amphora w/stand, 10 1/4" Royal Purple, Hndpt.	890	1995	195.00	250-300
1995 Ginger Jar, 3 Pc. 8 1/2" Favrene, Hndpt.	790	1995	275.00	400
1995 Lamp, 21" Butterfly/Floral Reverse, Hndpt. - F. Burton	300	1995	595.00	700-850
1995 Pitcher, 9 1/2" Victorian Art Glass, Hndpt.	490	1995	250.00	250-295
1995 Vase, 7" Aurora Wild Rose, Hndpt.	890	1995	125.00	175-195

1995 Family Signature Collection - Various

YEAR ISSUE	EDITION LIMIT	YEAR RETD.	ISSUE PRICE	*QUOTE U.S.$
1995 Basket, 8 1/2" Trellis - Lynn Fenton	Closed	1995	85.00	85-95
1995 Basket, 9 1/2" Coralene Floral - Frank M./Bill Fenton	Closed	1995	75.00	75-95
1995 Candy w/cover, 9" Red Carnival - Mike Fenton	Closed	1995	65.00	65-85
1995 Pitcher, 9 1/2" Thistle - Don Fenton	Closed	1995	125.00	125-150
1995 Vase, 7" Gold Pansies on Cranberry - George Fenton	Closed	1995	75.00	75-95
1995 Vase, 9" Summer Garden on Spruce - Don Fenton	Closed	1995	85.00	85
1995 Vase, 9 1/2" Golden Flax on Cobalt - Shelley Fenton	Closed	1995	95.00	95

1996 Connoisseur Collection - Various

YEAR ISSUE	EDITION LIMIT	YEAR RETD.	ISSUE PRICE	*QUOTE U.S.$
1996 Covered Box, 7" Mandarin Red, Hndpt. - K. Plauche	1,250	1996	150.00	150-195
1996 Lamp, 33" Reverse Painted Poppies, Hndpt. - F. Burton	400	1996	750.00	750-895
1996 Pitcher, 8" Dragonfly on Burmese, Hndpt. - F. Burton	1,450	1996	165.00	165-195
1996 Vase, 11" Berries on Wildrose, Hndpt. - M. Reynolds	1,250	1996	195.00	195-295
1996 Vase, 11" Queen's Bird on Burmese, Hndpt. - M. Reynolds	1,350	1996	250.00	250-295
1996 Vase, 7 1/2" Favrene Cut-Back Sandcarved - M. Reynolds	1,250	1996	195.00	195-250
1996 Vase, 8" Trout on Burmese, Hndpt. - R. Spindler	1,450	1996	135.00	135-195

1996 Family Signature Collection - Various

YEAR ISSUE	EDITION LIMIT	YEAR RETD.	ISSUE PRICE	*QUOTE U.S.$
1996 Basket, 7 1/2" Starflower on Cran. Pearl - M. Fenton	Closed	1996	75.00	75-95
1996 Basket, 8" Mountain Berry - Don Fenton	Closed	1996	85.00	85
1996 Candy Box w/cover Pansies - Shelley Fenton	Closed	1996	65.00	65-75
1996 Pitcher, 6 1/2" Asters - Lynn Fenton	Closed	1996	70.00	70-95
1996 Vase, 10" Magnolia & Berry on Spruce - Tom Fenton	Closed	1996	85.00	80-85
1996 Vase, 11" Meadow Beauty - Nancy Fenton	Closed	1996	95.00	95
1996 Vase, 8 1/2" Blush Rose on Opaline - George Fenton	Closed	1996	75.00	75-95

1996 Mulberry Historic Collection - Various

YEAR ISSUE	EDITION LIMIT	YEAR RETD.	ISSUE PRICE	*QUOTE U.S.$
1996 Basket, 8" "Hummingbird & Wildrose" - M. Reynolds	1,250	1996	95.00	95-150
1996 Lamp, 21" "Evening Blossom w/ Ladybug" - R. Spindler	500	1996	495.00	495-695
1996 Pitcher, 7 1/2" "Evening Blossom w/ Ladybug" - R. Spindler	1,250	1996	95.00	95-195

*Quotes have been rounded up to nearest dollar

YEAR ISSUE	EDITION LIMIT	YEAR RETD.	ISSUE PRICE	*QUOTE U.S.$
1996 Vase, 8" Melon Herringbone "Hummingbird" - M. Reynolds	1,250	1996	85.00	85-150
1996 Vase, 9 1/2" "Hummingbird & Wildrose" - M. Reynolds	1,250	1996	95.00	95-150

1997 Connoisseur Collection - Various

YEAR ISSUE	EDITION LIMIT	YEAR RETD.	ISSUE PRICE	*QUOTE U.S.$
1997 Basket, 11 1/2" Burmes Fenced Garden - R. Spindler	1,750	1997	160.00	160
1997 Lamp, 24 1/2" Reverse painted Scenic Floral - F. Burton	550	1997	750.00	750
1997 Pitcher, 6 1/2" Wildrose - K. Plauché	1,350	1997	175.00	175
1997 Vase, 8" French Opal, "Tranquility" - R. Spindler	1,500	1997	135.00	135
1997 Vase, 9" Faverne Daisy w/Lid - M. Reynolds	1,350	1997	295.00	295
1997 Vase, 9" Opaline Floral - M. Reynolds	1,500	1997	95.00	95
1997 Vase, 9 1/2" Trillium - R. Spindler	1,750	1997	195.00	195-225

1997 Family Signature Collection - Various

YEAR ISSUE	EDITION LIMIT	YEAR RETD.	ISSUE PRICE	*QUOTE U.S.$
1997 Basket, 9" Sweetbriar on Plum Overlay - L. Fenton	Closed	1997	85.00	85
1997 Fairy Light, 7 1/2" Hydrangeas on Topaz - F. Fenton	Closed	1997	125.00	125-250
1997 Pitcher, 7 1/2" Irisies on Misty Blue - D. Fenton	Closed	1997	85.00	85
1997 Urn, 13" Magnolia & Berry - G. Fenton	Closed	1997	84.00	84
1997 Vase, 6" Field Flowers on Champ. Satin - S. Fenton	Closed	1997	55.00	55
1997 Vase, 8" Hydrangeas on Topaz - T. Fenton	Closed	1997	70.00	70
1997 Vase, 8" Medallion Collect. Floral on Black - M. Fenton	Closed	1997	75.00	75

1997 Rubina Verde Historic Collection - M. Reynolds

YEAR ISSUE	EDITION LIMIT	YEAR RETD.	ISSUE PRICE	*QUOTE U.S.$
1997 Basket, 7 1/2" Melon	1,750	1997	99.00	99
1997 Box, 5 1/4" Melon	1,750	1997	135.00	135
1997 Lamp, 24"	650	1997	495.00	495
1997 Pitcher, 6"	1,750	1997	95.00	95
1997 Vase, 11" Melon	1,750	1997	135.00	135
1997 Vase, 8" Reverse Melon	1,750	1997	95.00	95

1998 Connoisseur Collection - Various

YEAR ISSUE	EDITION LIMIT	YEAR RETD.	ISSUE PRICE	*QUOTE U.S.$
1998 Basket, 7 1/2" Bouquet - K. Plauché	2,250		135.00	135
1998 Lamp, 20" Trysting Place - F. Burton	750		650.00	650
1998 Lamp, 23 1/2" Jacobean Floral - M. Reynolds	750		495.00	495
1998 Pitcher, 7" Bountiful Harvest - R. Spindler	2,250		155.00	155
1998 Vase, 10" Papillon - K. Plauché	2,250		165.00	165
1998 Vase, 6" Alhambra - M. Reynolds	4,604		145.00	145
1998 Vase, 9 1/2" Fields of Gold, Showcase Only - M. Reynolds	1,350		150.00	150
1998 Vase, 9" Leaves & Vines - D. Fetty	950		245.00	245
1998 Vase, 9" Seasons - M. Reynolds	1,350		250.00	250

1998 Family Signature Collection - Various

YEAR ISSUE	EDITION LIMIT	YEAR RETD.	ISSUE PRICE	*QUOTE U.S.$
1998 Basket, 10 1/2" Topaz - S. Fenton	Closed	1998	135.00	125-135
1998 Basket, Hat 9" - T. Fenton	Closed	1998	95.00	95
1998 Bell, 6 1/2" Royal Purple - D. Fenton	Closed	1998	99.00	99
1998 Clock, 4 1/2" Misty Blue - L. Fenton	Closed	1998	95.00	95
1998 Sleigh, 7 1/2" Twining Berries - M. Fenton	Closed	1998	67.50	68
1998 Tulip Vase, Sea Green Satin - N. & G. Fenton	Closed	1998	99.00	99
1998 Vase, 8" After The Rain - R. Spindler	2,250		185.00	185

1998 Royal Purple Historic Collection - F. Burton, unless otherwise noted

YEAR ISSUE	EDITION LIMIT	YEAR RETD.	ISSUE PRICE	*QUOTE U.S.$
1998 Basket, 8" "Colonial Scroll"	2,250		115.00	115
1998 Blown Bell, 6 1/2" "Colonial Scroll" - D. Fenton	Closed	1998	99.00	99
1998 Fairy Light, 7 1/2" "Colonial Scroll"	2,250		175.00	175
1998 Lamp, 20" "Colonial Scroll"	750		350.00	350
1998 Perfume 6 1/2" "Colonial Scroll"	2,250		125.00	125
1998 Pitcher, 6 1/2" "Colonial Scroll"	2,250		129.00	129
1998 Vase, 6 1/2" "Colonial Scroll"	2,950		145.00	145
1998 Vase, 9 1/2" "Colonial Scroll"	2,250		125.00	125

American Classic Series - M. Dickinson

YEAR ISSUE	EDITION LIMIT	YEAR RETD.	ISSUE PRICE	*QUOTE U.S.$
1986 Jupiter Train on Opal Satin, Lamp, 23"	1,000	1986	295.00	395-400
1986 Studebaker-Garford Car on Opal Satin, Lamp, 16"	1,000	1986	235.00	300-375

Christmas - Various

YEAR ISSUE	EDITION LIMIT	YEAR RETD.	ISSUE PRICE	*QUOTE U.S.$
1978 Christmas Morn, Lamp, 16" - M. Dickinson	Yr.Iss.	1978	125.00	200-250
1978 Christmas Morn, Fairy Light - M. Dickinson	Yr.Iss.	1978	25.00	50-95
1979 Nature's Christmas, Lamp, 16" - K. Cunningham	Yr.Iss.	1979	150.00	200-250
1979 Nature's Christmas, Fairy Light - K. Cunningham	Yr.Iss.	1979	30.00	50-95
1980 Going Home, Lamp, 16" - D. Johnson	Yr.Iss.	1980	165.00	200-250
1980 Going Home, Fairy Light - D. Johnson	Yr.Iss.	1980	32.50	50-95
1981 All Is Calm, Lamp, 16" - D. Johnson	Yr.Iss.	1981	175.00	200-295
1981 All Is Calm, Lamp, 20" - D. Johnson	Yr.Iss.	1981	225.00	250-295
1981 All Is Calm, Fairy Light - D. Johnson	Yr.Iss.	1981	35.00	50-95
1982 Country Christmas, Lamp, 16" - R. Spindler	Yr.Iss.	1982	175.00	250-295
1982 Country Christmas, Lamp, 21" - R. Spindler	Yr.Iss.	1982	225.00	250-350
1982 Country Christmas, Fairy Light - R. Spindler	Yr.Iss.	1982	35.00	50-95
1983 Anticipation, Fairy Light - D. Johnson	7,500	1983	35.00	50-95
1984 Expectation, Lamp, 10 1/2" - D. Johnson	7,500	1984	75.00	200-275
1984 Expectation, Fairy Light - D. Johnson	7,500	1984	37.50	50-95
1985 Heart's Desire, Fairy Light - D. Johnson	7,500	1986	37.50	50-95
1987 Sharing The Spirit, Fairy Light - L. Everson	Yr.Iss.	1987	37.50	50-95
1987 Cardinal in the Churchyard, Lamp, 18 1/2" - D. Johnson	500	1987	250.00	295
1987 Cardinal in the Churchyard, Fairy Light - D. Johnson	4,500	1987	29.50	75-95
1988 A Chickadee Ballet, Lamp, 21" - D. Johnson	500	1988	274.00	295
1988 A Chickadee Ballet, Fairy Light - D. Johnson	4,500	1988	29.50	75-95
1989 Downy Pecker, Lamp, 16" - Chisled Song - D. Johnson	500	1989	250.00	295
1989 Downy Pecker, Fairy Light - Chisled Song - D. Johnson	4,500	1989	29.50	75-95
1990 A Blue Bird in Snowfall, Lamp, 21" - D. Johnson	500	1990	250.00	295
1990 A Blue Bird in Snowfall, Fairy Light - D. Johnson	4,500	1990	29.50	75-95
1990 Sleigh Ride, Lamp, 16" - F. Burton	1,000	1990	250.00	295
1990 Sleigh Ride, Fairy Light - F. Burton	3,500	1990	39.00	75-95
1991 Christmas Eve, Lamp, 16" - F. Burton	1,000	1991	250.00	295
1991 Christmas Eve, Fairy Light - F. Burton	3,500	1991	39.00	95
1992 Family Tradition, Lamp, 20" - F. Burton	1,000	1992	250.00	295
1992 Family Tradition, Fairy Light - F. Burton	3,500	1992	39.00	75
1993 Family Holiday, Lamp, 16" - F. Burton	1,000	1993	265.00	295
1993 Family Holiday, Fairy Light - F. Burton	3,500	1993	39.00	75
1994 Silent Night, Lamp, 16" - F. Burton	500	1994	275.00	325-350
1994 Silent Night, Fairy Light - F. Burton	1,500	1994	45.00	75-95
1994 Silent Night, Egg on Stand - F. Burton	1,500	1994	45.00	65-95
1995 Our Home Is Blessed, Lamp, 21" - F. Burton	500	1995	275.00	275-295
1995 Our Home Is Blessed, Egg - F. Burton	1,500	1995	45.00	45-85
1995 Our Home Is Blessed, Fairy Light - F. Burton	1,500	1995	45.00	45-95
1996 Star of Wonder, Lamp, 16" - F. Burton	750	1996	175.00	175-250
1996 Star of Wonder, Egg - F. Burton	1,750	1996	45.00	45-65
1996 Star of Wonder, Fairy Light - F. Burton	1,750	1996	48.00	48-65
1997 The Way Home, Lamp, 20" - F. Burton	750	1997	299.00	299
1997 The Way Home, Egg - F. Burton	1,750	1997	59.00	59
1997 The Way Home, Fairy Light - F. Burton	1,750	1997	65.00	65
1997 Holy Family Nativity, set/3 (1st ed.) - J. Saffell	Closed	1997	125.00	125
1997 Olde World Santa - M. Reynolds	3,750	1997	75.00	75-79
1998 Wise Men, set/3 (Melchoir, Gaspar, Belthazar) (1st ed.) - J. Saffell	Closed	1998	155.00	155
1998 Santa, 8 1/2" Patriotic - M. Reynolds	4,750		79.00	79
1998 Santa, 8" Northern Lights - R. Spindler	Closed	1998	75.00	75
1998 Angel Girl, 5 3/4" - K. Plauché	Closed	1998	47.50	48
1998 Radiant Angel, 7 1/2" - K. Plauché	Closed	1998	67.50	68
1998 The Arrival, Egg - F. Burton	2,500		49.00	49
1998 The Arrival, Fairy Light - F. Burton	2,500		55.00	55
1998 The Arrival, Lamp - F. Burton	850		285.00	285

Designer Series - Various

YEAR ISSUE	EDITION LIMIT	YEAR RETD.	ISSUE PRICE	*QUOTE U.S.$
1983 Lighthouse Point, Lamp, 23 1/2", - M. Dickinson	150	1983	350.00	450-550
1983 Lighthouse Point, Lamp, 25 1/2", - M. Dickinson	150	1983	350.00	575-695
1983 Down Home, Lamp, 21" - G. Finn	300	1983	300.00	450-495
1984 Smoke 'N Cinders, Lamp, 16" - M. Dickinson	250	1984	195.00	325-375
1984 Smoke 'N Cinders, Lamp, 23" - M. Dickinson	250	1984	350.00	450-595
1984 Majestic Flight, Lamp, 16" - B. Cumberledge	250	1984	195.00	295-395
1984 Majestic Flight, Lamp, 23 1/2" - B. Cumberledge	250	1984	350.00	450-495
1985 In Season, Lamp, 16" - M. Dickinson	250	1985	225.00	325-450
1985 In Season, Lamp, 23" - M. Dickinson	250	1985	295.00	395-495
1985 Nature's Grace, Lamp, 16" - B. Cumberland	250	1985	225.00	325-450
1985 Nature's Grace, Lamp, 23" - B. Cumberland	295	1985	295.00	400-495

Easter Series - M. Reynolds

YEAR ISSUE	EDITION LIMIT	YEAR RETD.	ISSUE PRICE	*QUOTE U.S.$
1995 Fairy Light	Closed	1995	49.00	55-95

Mary Gregory - M. Reynolds

YEAR ISSUE	EDITION LIMIT	YEAR RETD.	ISSUE PRICE	*QUOTE U.S.$
1994 Basket, 7 1/2" Oval	Closed	1994	59.00	75-95
1995 Basket, 7 1/2" Oval	Closed	1995	65.00	75-110
1995 Egg on stand, 4" - Butterfly Delight	Closed	1995	37.50	45-95
1996 Hat Basket on Cranberry, 6 1/2"	2,000	1996	95.00	95
1996 Vase on Cranberry, 9"	1,500	1996	135.00	135-150
1997 Guest Set, 7" Cranberry	1,500		189.00	189
1997 Fairy Light, 5" Cranberry	1,500		79.00	79
1997 Basket, 8" Cranberry	1,500		115.00	115
1998 Basket, Hex 11 1/2" Cranberry	1,950		150.00	150
1998 Pitcher, 6 1/2" Cranberry	1,950		125.00	125
1998 Perfume, 5 1/2" Cranberry	1,950		115.00	115

Miniatures - Fenton

YEAR ISSUE	EDITION LIMIT	YEAR RETD.	ISSUE PRICE	*QUOTE U.S.$
1998 Epergne, 4 1/2" Champagne	Closed	1998	65.00	65
1996 Epergne, 4 1/2" Opaline	Closed	1996	35.00	35
1996 Punch Bowl Set, 3 3/4" Dusty Rose	Closed	1996	59.00	59
1997 Punch Bowl Set, 3 3/4" Seamist Green	Closed	1997	59.00	59
1998 Punch Set, 3 3/4" Champagne	Closed	1998	75.00	75
1998 Water Set, 4 1/2" Champagne	Closed	1998	85.00	85

Valentine's Day Series - Fenton, unless otherwise noted

YEAR ISSUE	EDITION LIMIT	YEAR RETD.	ISSUE PRICE	*QUOTE U.S.$
1992 Basket, 6" Cranberry Opal/Heart Optic	Closed	1992	50.00	75-110
1992 Vase, 4" Cranberry Opal/Heart Optic	Closed	1992	35.00	60-95
1992 Perfume, w/oval stopper Cranberry Opal/Heart Optic	Closed	1992	60.00	125-150
1993 Basket, 7" Caprice Cranberry Opal/Heart Optic	Closed	1993	59.00	85-110
1993 Trinket Box, 5" Cranberry Opal/Heart Optic	Closed	1993	79.00	95-120
1993 Vase, 5 1/2" Melon Cranberry Opal/Heart Optic	Closed	1993	45.00	70-95
1993 Southern Girl, 8", Hndpt. Opal Satin - M. Reynolds	Closed	1993	49.00	75-95
1993 Southern Girl, 8", Rose Pearl Irid.	Closed	1993	45.00	75-95
1994 Basket, 7" Cranberry Opal/Heart Optic	Closed	1994	65.00	95-120
1994 Vase, 5 1/2" Ribbed Cranberry Opal/Heart Optic	Closed	1994	47.50	60-75
1994 Perfume, w/ stopper, 5" Cranberry Opal/Heart Optic	Closed	1994	75.00	125-150
1995 Basket, 8" Melon Cranberry Opal/Heart Optic	Closed	1995	69.00	95-110
1995 Pitcher, 5 1/2" Melon Cranberry Opal/Heart Optic	Closed	1995	69.00	75-110
1995 Perfume, w/ heart stopper, Kristen's Floral Hndpt. - M. Reynolds	2,500	1995	49.00	60-95
1995 Doll, 7", Kristen's Floral Hndpt. Ivory Satin - M. Reynolds	2,500	1995	49.00	60-95
1996 Basket, 8" Melon Cranberry Opalescent	Closed	1996	75.00	75-110
1996 Perfume, 5" Melon Cranberry Opalescent	Closed	1996	95.00	95-125
1996 Fairy Light, 3 pc. Cranberry Opalescent	Closed	1996	135.00	135-150
1996 Vanity Set, 4 pc. Tea Rose - M. Reynolds	1,500	1996	250.00	250-295
1996 Doll, w/Musical Base Tea Rose - M. Reynolds	2,500	1996	55.00	55-95
1997 Pitcher, 6 1/2" Cranberry Opal/Heart Optic	Closed	1997	89.00	89
1997 Puff Box, 4" Cranberry Opal/Heart Optic	Closed	1997	79.00	79
1997 Hat Basket, 7" Cranberry Opal/Heart Optic	Closed	1997	79.00	79
1997 Vanity Set, 7" Burmese Floral & Butterfly Hndpt. - R. Spindler	2,000	1997	225.00	225
1997 Girl Figurine, 8" Burmese Floral Hndpt. - R. Spindler	2,000	1997	75.00	75
1997 Pendant & Trinket Box, Champagne Satin	2,500	1997	65.00	65
1998 Fairy Light, 5", Cranberry Opal/Heart Optic	Closed	1998	65.00	65
1998 Vase, 5", Cranberry Opal/Heart Optic	Closed	1998	39.50	40
1998 Covered Box, 4 1/2", Cranberry Opal/Heart Optic	Closed	1998	125.00	125
1998 "Natalie" Ballerina, 6 1/2", Rosalene - R. Spindler	Closed	1998	85.00	85
1998 Vase, 6", Rosebuds on Rosalene - R. Spindler	Closed	1998	69.50	70
1998 Perfume, 6 1/2", Rosebuds on Rosalene - R. Spindler	Closed	1998	85.00	85
1998 Puffbox, 4 1/2", Rosebuds on Rosalene - R. Spindler	Closed	1998	99.50	100
1998 Pendant & Earrings Box, Amethyst	Closed	1998	95.00	95

Fitz & Floyd

The Leaf & Acorn Club - D. Griff

YEAR ISSUE	EDITION LIMIT	YEAR RETD.	ISSUE PRICE	*QUOTE U.S.$
1997 Thank You	12/98		Gift	N/A
1997 Maxine's Leaf Collection 98/701	12/98		15.00	15
1999 This One Is For You	Yr.Iss.		Gift	N/A
1999 Ring Around The Rosie	Yr.Iss.		N/A	N/A

Charming Tails Autumn Harvest Figurines - D. Griff

YEAR ISSUE	EDITION LIMIT	YEAR RETD.	ISSUE PRICE	*QUOTE U.S.$
1993 Acorn Built For Two 85/403	Open		10.00	12
1996 Bag of Tricks...Or Treats 87/436	Open		15.50	17
1996 Binkey's Acorn Costume 87/429	Open		11.50	13
1998 Boooo! 85/417	Open		18.00	18
1995 Candy Apples 85/611	Closed	1998	16.00	17
1995 Candy Corn Vampire 85/607	Closed	1996	18.00	35-75
1993 Caps Off to You 85/402	Closed	1996	10.00	20-27
1996 Chauncey's Pear Costume 87/431	Closed	1998	12.00	13
1993 Cornfield Feast 85/399	Closed	1994	15.00	75-125
1993 Fall Frolicking 85/401	Closed	1996	13.00	41-95
1994 Frosting Pumpkins 85/511	Closed	1996	16.00	36-47
1995 Garden Naptime 85/615	Closed	1996	18.00	32-35
1997 Ghost Stories 85/703	Open		18.50	19
1995 Giving Thanks 85/608	Open		16.00	17
1997 The Good Witch 85/704	Open		18.50	19
1993 Gourd Slide 85/398	Closed	1996	16.00	40-44
1994 Harvest Fruit 85/507	Closed	1995	16.00	32-50
1995 Horn of Plenty 85/610	Closed	1996	20.00	20-35
1996 Indian Impostor 87/446	Open		14.00	15
1998 Jack O'Lantern Jalopy 85/410	Open		18.00	18
1994 Jumpin' Jack O' Lanterns 85/512	Closed	1996	16.00	17-35
1995 Let's Get Crackin' 85/776	Closed	1997	20.00	20-40

YEAR ISSUE	EDITION LIMIT	YEAR RETD.	ISSUE PRICE	*QUOTE U.S.$
1996 Look! No Hands 87/428	Open		15.50	17
1996 Maxine's Pumpkin Costume 87/430	Open		12.00	13
1993 Mouse Candleholder 85/400	Closed	1995	13.00	100-250
1994 Mouse on Leaf Candleholder 87/503	Closed	1995	17.00	66-95
1996 Oops, I Missed 87/443	Closed	1998	16.00	17
1994 Open Pumpkin 85/508	Closed	1994	15.00	55-75
1994 Painting Leaves 85/514	Closed	1996	16.00	25-37
1994 Pear Candleholder 85/509	Closed	1995	14.00	45-72
1996 Pickin' Time 87/438	Closed	1997	16.00	17-25
1996 Pilgrim's Progress 87/445	Open		13.50	15
1995 Pumpkin Pie 85/606	Closed	1996	16.00	35-75
1994 Pumpkin Slide 85/513	Closed	1995	16.00	32-49
1994 Pumpkin Votive 85/510	Closed	1995	13.50	25-50
1998 Pumpkin's First Pumpkin 85/411	Open		17.00	17
1997 Reginald's Gourd Costume 85/701	Open		12.50	13
1995 Reginald's Hideaway 85/777	Closed	1996	14.00	20-32
1998 Stack O'Lanterns 85/416	Open		18.00	18
1997 Stewart's Apple Costume 85/700	Open		12.50	13
1994 Stump Candleholders 85/516	Closed	1995	20.00	125-250
1997 Turkey Traveller 85/702	Open		18.50	19
1998 Turkey With Dressing 85/412	Open		18.00	18
1996 You're Not Scary 87/440	Closed	1998	14.00	15
1996 You're Nutty 87/451	Closed	1998	12.00	13

Charming Tails Easter Basket Figurines - D. Griff

YEAR ISSUE	EDITION LIMIT	YEAR RETD.	ISSUE PRICE	*QUOTE U.S.$
1995 After the Hunt 87/372	Open		18.00	19
1993 Animals in Eggs 89/313	Closed	1996	11.00	44-100
1995 Binkey's Bouncing Bundle 87/422	7,500	1995	18.00	37-44
1994 Bunny Imposter 89/609	Closed	1998	12.00	28
1995 Bunny Love 87/424	Open		18.00	19
1998 Chickie Back Ride 88/700	Open		15.00	15
1993 Duckling in Egg with Mouse 89/316	Closed	1994	15.00	158-250
1995 Gathering Treats 87/377	Closed	1998	12.00	28
1994 Jelly Bean Feast 89/559	Closed	1996	14.00	20-35
1995 Look Out Below 87/373	Closed	1997	20.00	20-32
1996 No Thanks, I'm Stuffed 88/603	Open		15.00	16
1998 Paint By Paws 88/701	Open		16.00	16
1994 Wanna Play? 89/561	2,500	1994	15.00	88-140
1995 Want a Bite? 87/379	Closed	1997	18.00	22-45
1996 What's Hatchin' 88/600	Open		16.00	17

Charming Tails Event Piece - D. Griff

YEAR ISSUE	EDITION LIMIT	YEAR RETD.	ISSUE PRICE	*QUOTE U.S.$
1996 Take Me Home 87/691	Closed	1996	17.00	40-65

Charming Tails Everyday Figurines - D. Griff

YEAR ISSUE	EDITION LIMIT	YEAR RETD.	ISSUE PRICE	*QUOTE U.S.$
1996 Ach-Choo, Get Well Soon 89/624	Open		12.00	13
1994 After Lunch Snooze 89/558	Closed	1997	15.00	16-23
1996 The Berry Best 87/391	Open		16.00	17
1994 Binkey Growing Carrots 89/605	Closed	1995	15.00	44-60
1993 Binkey in a Lily 89/305	Closed	1996	16.00	25-40
1995 Binkey's First Cake 98/349	Closed	1997	16.00	17-40
1994 Binkey's New Pal 89/586	Closed	1996	14.00	32-35
1996 Bunny Buddies 89/619	Open		20.00	21
1994 Bunny w/Carrot Candleholder 89/317	Closed	1995	12.00	55-90
1994 Butterfly Smelling Zinnia 89/606	Closed	1995	15.00	63-75
1994 Can I Keep Him? 89/600	2,500	1994	13.00	238-300
1995 Catchin' Butterflies 87/423	Closed	1998	16.00	17
1996 Cattail Catapult 87/448	Closed	1998	16.00	17
1996 Charming Tails Display Sign 87/690	Open		20.00	20
1996 The Chase is On 87/386	Closed	1998	16.00	17
1994 Chauncey Growing Tomatoes 89/607	Closed	1995	15.00	50-63
1998 A Collection of Friends (Convention Piece) 98/206	7,500	1998	23.00	23-63
1994 Duckling Votive 89/315	Closed	1994	12.00	100-175
1998 Even The Ups And Downs Are Fun 89/705	Open		16.50	17
1995 Feeding Time 98/417	Closed	1996	16.00	41-48
1996 Flower Friends 89/608	Closed	1998	15.00	16
1996 Fragile...Handle with Care (no numbers on bottom)	Closed	1997	18.00	130
1996 Fragile...Handle with Care 89/601	15,000	1997	18.00	19-35
1996 Fragile...Handle with Love (mismarked) 89/601	Closed	1997	18.00	122
1995 Gardening Break 87/364	Open		16.00	17
1994 Get Well Soon 97/719	Closed	1997	15.00	16-27
1994 Good Luck 97/716	Open		15.00	16
1997 Guess What? 89/714	Open		16.50	17
1996 Hangin' Around 89/623	Open		18.00	19
1994 Happy Birthday 97/715	Open		15.00	16
1998 Hear, Speak and See No Evil 89/717	Open		17.50	18
1995 Hello, Sweet Pea 87/367	Closed	1997	12.00	23-35
1993 Hide and Seek 89/307	Closed	1994	13.50	113-120
1994 Hope You're Feeling Better 97/723	Closed	1997	15.00	18-27
1996 Hoppity Hop 87/425	Closed	1998	16.00	15
1994 How Do You Measure Love 98/461	Closed	1996	15.00	35-50
1998 How Many Candles? 89/713	Open		16.50	17
1996 I Have a Question for You 89/603	Open		16.00	17
1994 I Love You 97/724	Open		15.00	16
1997 I Love You a Whole Bunch 89/715	Open		17.00	17
1997 I Picked This Just for You (Artist Event) 98/197	Yr.Iss.	1997	18.00	94
1996 I See Things Clearly Now 89/626	Open		14.00	15
1998 I'm A Winner 89/719	Open		16.00	16
1998 I'm Here For You 89/706	Open		17.50	18
1994 I'm So Sorry 97/720	Closed	1998	15.00	17
1997 I'm Thinking of You 89/701	Open		15.00	15
1994 It's Not the Same Without You 97/721	Closed	1997	15.00	16-23
1998 It's Your Move 89/704	Open		17.00	17
1996 Just "Plane" Friends 89/627	Open		18.00	19
1997 Keeping Our Love Alive 89/710	Open		19.50	20
1993 King of the Mushroom 89/318	Closed	1996	16.00	19-41
1998 A Little Bird Told Me	Open		17.00	17
1996 Love Blooms (GCC Spring Exclusive) 87/862	Closed	1996	16.00	32-60
1993 Love Mice 89/314	Closed	1994	15.00	63-100
1994 Mackenzie Growing Beans 89/604	Closed	1995	15.00	30-60
1997 Maxine Goes On-Line 89/702	Open		17.00	17
1994 Mender of Broken Hearts 98/460	Closed	1996	15.00	30-41
1996 Mid-day Snooze 89/617	Open		18.00	19
1993 Mouse on a Grasshopper 89/321	Closed	1994	15.00	140-250
1994 New Arrival 97/717	Open		15.00	17
1995 One for Me... 87/360	Closed	1996	16.00	20-41
1995 One for You... 87/361	Closed	1997	16.00	20-32
1998 Picture Perfect 89/722	Open		18.50	19
1993 Rabbit/Daffodil Candleholder 89/312	Closed	1995	13.50	115-250
1994 Reach for the Stars 97/718	Open		15.00	17
1994 Slumber Party 89/560	Closed	1996	16.00	32-58
1993 Spring Flowers 89/310	Closed	1996	16.00	30-63
1998 Steady Wins The Race 89/716	Yr.Iss.		20.00	20
1995 Surrounded By Friends 87/353	Closed	1996	16.00	17-32
1996 Taggin' Along 87/399	Closed	1998	14.00	15
1996 Take Time To Reflect 87/396	Closed	1997	16.00	17-22
1997 Teacher's Pets 89/700	Open		19.50	20
1994 Thanks for Being There 89/754	Closed	1996	15.00	15-20
1998 There's No "US" Without "U" 89/703	Open		19.50	20
1995 This Is Hot! 87/366	Closed	1996	15.00	16-23
1996 Training Wings 87/398	Closed	1997	16.00	17
1995 Tuggin' Twosome 87/362	10,000	1997	18.00	40-44
1993 Two Peas in a Pod 89/306	Closed	1996	14.00	32-50
1996 The Waterslide 87/384	Open		20.00	21
1994 We'll Weather the Storm Together 97/722	Open		15.00	17
1995 Why, Hello There! 87/357	Closed	1996	14.00	15-20
1995 You Are Not Alone 98/929	Closed	1996	20.00	35-60
1996 You Couldn't Be Sweeter 89/625	Open		16.00	17
1996 You Love me-You Love Me Not 87/395	Open		16.00	17

Charming Tails Everyday Lazy Days of Summer Figurines - D. Griff

YEAR ISSUE	EDITION LIMIT	YEAR RETD.	ISSUE PRICE	*QUOTE U.S.$
1997 The Blossom Bounce 83/704	Open		20.00	20
1997 Building Castles 83/802	Open		17.00	17
1998 Camping Out 83/703	Open		18.50	19
1998 Come On In -The Water's Fine! 83/804	Open		18.00	18
1998 A Day At The Lake 83/803	Open		18.50	19
1997 Gone Fishin' 83/702	Open		16.00	16
1997 Life's a Picnic With You 83/701	Open		18.00	18
1997 Row Boat Romance 83/801	Open		15.50	16
1998 Stewart's Day In The Sun 83/805	Open		17.00	17
1998 Toasting Marshmellows 83/700	Open		20.00	20

Charming Tails Musicals and Waterglobes - D. Griff

YEAR ISSUE	EDITION LIMIT	YEAR RETD.	ISSUE PRICE	*QUOTE U.S.$
1994 Jawbreakers Musical 87/542	Closed	1995	40.00	60-107
1994 Letter to Santa Waterglobe 87/518	Closed	1994	45.00	69-95
1995 Me Next! Musical 89/555	Closed	1995	45.00	110-198
1994 Mini Surprise Waterglobe 87/956	Closed	1994	22.00	44-62
1994 Mouse on Cheese, Waterglobe 92/224	Closed	1995	44.00	44
1994 Mouse on Rubber Duck, Waterglobe 92/225	Closed	1995	44.00	117-150
1994 My Hero! Waterglobe 89/557	Closed	1995	45.00	70-100
1995 Pumpkin Playtime Musical 85/778	Closed	1995	35.00	72-102
1993 Rocking Mice Musical 86/790	Closed	1994	65.00	135-240
1994 Sailing Away Waterglobe 87/200	Closed	1994	50.00	90-120
1994 Sharing the Warmth Waterglobe 87/517	Closed	1994	40.00	77-108
1993 Skating Mice Musical 87/511	Closed	1994	25.00	48-125
1994 Sweet Dreams Waterglobe 87/534	Closed	1994	40.00	40-48
1994 Together at Christmas, Mini Waterglobe 87/532	Closed	1995	30.00	45-54
1994 Trimming the Tree Waterglobe 87/516	Closed	1994	45.00	80-150
1994 Underwater Explorer Waterglobe 89/556	Closed	1995	45.00	99-120
1994 Up, Up and Away Musical 89/602	Closed	1995	70.00	175-282

Charming Tails Squashville Figurines - D. Griff

YEAR ISSUE	EDITION LIMIT	YEAR RETD.	ISSUE PRICE	*QUOTE U.S.$
1996 Airmail 87/698	Closed	1997	16.00	16-23
1996 All I Can Give You is Me 87/498	Closed	1996	15.00	16-33
1996 All Snug in Their Beds Waterglobe 87/476	Closed	1996	30.00	50-60
1997 All The Trimmings 87/703	Yr.Iss.	1997	15.00	15-20
1996 Angel of Light 87/481	Open		12.00	13
1997 Baby's 1st Christmas 1997 Annual 87/705	Yr.Iss.	1997	18.50	19
1996 Baby's 1st Christmas Waterglobe 87/475	Closed	1996	28.00	28-50
1997 Bearing Gifts 87/600	Open		16.00	16
1996 Binkey in a Bed of Flowers 87/426	Closed	1996	15.00	30-39
1996 Binkey Snow Shoeing 87/580	Open		14.00	15
1995 Binkey's 1995 Ice Sculpture 87/572	Yr.Iss.	1995	20.00	32-40
1996 Building a Snowbunny 87/692	Open		16.00	17
1998 Building Blocks Christmas 87/619	Open		17.00	17
1995 Charming Choo-Choo and Cabbose 87/579	Open		35.00	36
1997 Chauncey's Choo Choo Ride 87/707	Open		19.00	19
1996 Chauncey's Noisemakers 87/554	Open		12.00	13
1995 Christmas Pageant Stage 87/546	Open		30.00	31
1996 Christmas Stroll 87/575	Open		16.00	17
1997 Christmas Trio 87/713	Open		15.50	16
1998 Dashing Through The Snow 87/624	Open		16.50	17
1997 Decorating Binkey 87/714	Open		16.00	16
1996 The Drum Major 87/556	Open		12.00	13
1996 Extra! Extra! 87/590	Closed	1997	14.00	15-23
1996 Farmer Mackenzie 87/695	Open		16.00	17
1996 The Float Driver 87/587	Open		12.00	13
1995 Flying Leaf Saucer 87/305	Open		16.00	17
1996 Follow in my Footsteps 87/473	Open		12.00	13
1996 Holiday Trumpeteer 87/555	Open		12.00	13
1995 Holy Family Players 87/547	Open		20.00	21
1994 Hot Doggin' 87/993	Closed	1995	20.00	35-80
1996 Jingle Bells 87/513	Closed	1997	15.00	16-23
1994 Lady Bug Express 87/188	Closed	1994	18.00	126-195
1994 Leaf Vine Ornament Hanger 87/519	Closed	1995	25.00	25-50
1996 Lil' Drummer Mouse 87/480	Open		12.00	13
1996 Little Drummer Boy 87/557	Open		12.00	13
1994 Mackenzie and Maxine Caroling 87/925	Closed	1995	18.00	41-75
1994 Mackenzie Building a Snowmouse 87/203	7,500	1994	18.00	80-160
1996 Mackenzie Claus on Parade 87/576	Open		22.00	23
1995 Mail Mouse 87/573	Closed	1996	12.00	17-32
1996 Manger Animals 87/482	Open		20.00	21
1994 Maxine Makin Snow Angels 87/510	Open		20.00	21
1997 Maxine the Snowman 98/196	Retrd.	1998	17.00	17
1997 Maxine's Snowmobile Ride 87/612	Open		17.00	17
1998 Merry Christmas From Our House To Yours 87/622	Open		23.00	23
1994 Mice on Vine Basket 87/506	Closed	1995	55.00	55-66
1994 Mouse Candle Climber 87/189	Closed	1995	8.00	41
1994 Mouse Card Holder 87/501	Closed	1995	13.00	25-41
1994 Mouse in Tree Hole Candleholder 87/502	Closed	1995	17.00	63-85
1994 Mouse on Basket 87/529	Closed	1995	50.00	60-85
1994 Mouse on Vine Candleholder 87/504	Closed	1995	55.00	66-85
1994 Mouse on Vine Wreath 87/505	Closed	1995	55.00	66-125
1993 Mouse Star Treetop 87/958	Closed	1995	14.00	45-50
1996 My New Toy 87/500	Closed	1997	14.00	18-35
1997 Not a Creature Was Stirring 87/704	Open		17.00	17
1996 Oops! Did I Do That? 87/469	Closed	1997	14.00	15-25
1996 Parade Banner 87/543	Open		16.00	17
1995 Pear Taxi 87/565	Closed	1996	16.00	25-36
1996 Peeking at Presents 87/527	Closed	1997	13.00	14-18
1998 Please, Just One More... 87/625	Open		16.50	17
1994 Pyramid with Mice Candleholder 87/509	Closed	1995	40.00	42-48
1998 Reginald's Choo-Choo Ride 87/620	Open		19.00	19
1996 Reginald's Newstand 87/591	Closed	1997	20.00	20-25
1997 The Santa Balloon 87/708	Open		25.00	25
1997 Shepherd's set 87/710	Open		12.50	13
1995 Sleigh Ride 87/569	7,500	1995	16.00	50-95
1996 Snack for the Reindeer 87/512	Closed	1996	13.00	15-36
1995 Snow Plow 87/566	Open		16.00	17
1996 The Snowball Fight 87/570	Open		18.00	17
1998 Snowman Float 87/628	Open		25.00	25
1995 Stewart's Choo Choo Ride 87/694	Open		17.50	19
1998 Team Igloo 87/623	Yr.Iss.		23.00	23
1995 Teamwork Helps 87/571	Open		16.00	17
1996 Testing the Lights 87/514	Closed	1997	14.00	17-25
1995 Three Wise Mice 87/548	Open		20.00	21
1996 Town Crier 87/696	Open		14.00	15
1997 Trimming A Tree 87/702	Open		27.50	28
1996 Waiting For Christmas 87/496	14,000	1997	16.00	25-36
1998 Who Put That Tree There? 87/621	Open		16.50	17
1997 You Melted My Heart 87/472	Open		20.00	21

Charming Tails Wedding Figurines - D. Griff

YEAR ISSUE	EDITION LIMIT	YEAR RETD.	ISSUE PRICE	*QUOTE U.S.$
1998 The Altar of Love 82/108	Open		24.00	24
1998 The Best...Bunny 82/103	Open		16.00	16
1998 The Get-Away Car 82/107	Open		22.00	22
1998 Here Comes The Bride 82/100	Open		17.00	17
1998 Maid of Honor 82/102	Open		16.00	16
1998 My Heart's All A-Flutter (Groom) 82/101	Open		17.00	17
1998 The Ring Bearer 82/104	Open		16.00	16
1998 Together Forever 82/109	Open		25.00	25
1998 Wedding Day Blossoms 82/105	Open		16.00	16

Teeny Tiny Tails Squashville Country Fair Booths - D. Griff

YEAR ISSUE	EDITION LIMIT	YEAR RETD.	ISSUE PRICE	*QUOTE U.S.$
1998 Berry Toss 80/7	Open		14.00	14
1998 The Big Winner 80/10	Open		12.00	12
1998 Candy Apples 80/3	Open		12.00	12
1998 Off to the Fair 80/1	Open		16.00	16
1998 Test Your Strength 80/5	Open		14.00	14
1998 Ticket Seller Booth 80/2	Open		16.00	16

Teeny Tiny Tails Squashville Country Fair Musical Rides - D. Griff

YEAR ISSUE	EDITION LIMIT	YEAR RETD.	ISSUE PRICE	*QUOTE U.S.$
1998 Daffodil Twirl 80/4	Open		49.50	50
1998 Mushroom Carousel 80/6	Open		49.50	50
1998 Tulip Ferris Wheel 80/8	Open		49.50	50

Flambro Imports

Emmett Kelly Jr. Members Only Figurine - Undisclosed

YEAR ISSUE	EDITION LIMIT	YEAR RETD.	ISSUE PRICE	*QUOTE U.S.$
1990 Merry-Go-Round	Closed	1990	125.00	375-550
1991 10 Years Of Collecting	Closed	1991	100.00	202-250
1992 All Aboard	Closed	1992	75.00	143-300
1993 Ringmaster	Closed	1993	125.00	175-234
1994 Birthday Mail	Closed	1994	100.00	200-300

*Quotes have been rounded up to nearest dollar

YEAR ISSUE	EDITION LIMIT	YEAR RETD.	ISSUE PRICE	*QUOTE U.S.$
1995 Salute To Our Vets	Closed	1995	75.00	195-200
1996 I Love You	Closed	1996	95.00	250-300
1997 Filet of Sole	Closed	1997	130.00	130
1998 Autographs	Yr.Iss.		100.00	100
1999 Birthday Bath	Yr.Iss.		100.00	100

Emmett Kelly Jr. Annual Figurine - Undisclosed

YEAR ISSUE	EDITION LIMIT	YEAR RETD.	ISSUE PRICE	*QUOTE U.S.$
1996 EKJ For President	Retrd.	1996	60.00	125-150
1997 Send in the Clowns	Retrd.	1997	70.00	70
1998 Smile and the World Smiles with You	12/98		50.00	50
1999 Our National Treasure	Yr.Iss.		N/A	N/A

EKJ Professionals - Undisclosed

YEAR ISSUE	EDITION LIMIT	YEAR RETD.	ISSUE PRICE	*QUOTE U.S.$
1987 Accountant	Retrd.	1994	50.00	105-125
1991 Barber	Retrd.	1995	50.00	80-100
1988 Bowler	Retrd.	1994	50.00	105-115
1996 Bowler	Open		55.00	55
1991 Carpenter	Retrd.	1996	50.00	65-110
1991 The Chef	Retrd.	1994	50.00	60-145
1995 Coach	Open		55.00	55
1990 Computer Whiz	Open		50.00	50
1997 Computer Whiz (w/garbage can)	Open		55.00	55
1987 Dentist	Retrd.	1995	50.00	85-110
1996 Dentist	Open		55.00	55
1999 Doctor	Open		50.00	50
1987 Doctor	Retrd.	1995	50.00	85-150
1995 Doctor	Open		55.00	55
1987 Engineer	Retrd.	1995	50.00	100-110
1987 Executive	Open		50.00	50
1997 Executive (talking on phone)	Open		55.00	55
1996 Farmer	Open		55.00	55
1988 Fireman	Retrd.	1994	50.00	60-125
1995 Fireman	Open		55.00	55
1999 Fireman	Open		50.00	50
1990 Fisherman	Open		50.00	50
1997 Fisherman (w/fish & dog)	Open		55.00	55
1997 Fitness (runaway weight loss)	Open		55.00	55
1997 Gardener (w/rake)	Open		55.00	55
1995 Golfer	Open		55.00	55
1988 Golfer	Retrd.	1996	50.00	140-195
1999 Golfer	Open		50.00	50
1998 Graduate	Open		60.00	60
1990 Hunter	Open		50.00	50
1997 Hunter (w/orange camouflauge)	Open		55.00	55
1999 Lawyer	Open		50.00	50
1987 Lawyer	Retrd.	1995	50.00	80-135
1995 Lawyer	Open		55.00	55
1988 Mailman	Retrd.	1996	50.00	95-115
1996 Mailman	Open		55.00	55
1993 On Maneuvers	Open		50.00	50
1991 Painter	Open		50.00	50
1991 Pharmacist	Open		50.00	50
1990 Photographer	Open		50.00	50
1993 Pilot	Open		50.00	50
1991 Plumber	Retrd.	1994	50.00	100-110
1995 Policeman	Open		55.00	55
1988 Policeman	Retrd.	1994	50.00	100-125
1999 Policeman	Open		50.00	50
1990 The Putt	Open		50.00	50
1998 Race Fan	Open		60.00	60
1993 Realtor	Open		50.00	50
1998 Retirement	Open		65.00	65
1998 Salesman	Open		60.00	60
1988 Skier	Retrd.	1995	50.00	95-135
1996 Skier	Open		55.00	55
1987 Stockbrocker	Retrd.	1997	50.00	50-125
1999 Teacher	Open		50.00	50
1987 Teacher	Retrd.	1995	50.00	75-125
1993 Veterinarian	Retrd.	1997	50.00	115-125

Emmett Kelly Jr. - Undisclosed, unless otherwise noted

YEAR ISSUE	EDITION LIMIT	YEAR RETD.	ISSUE PRICE	*QUOTE U.S.$
1995 20th Anniversary of All Star Circus	5,000	1995	240.00	240-350
1997 25th Anniversary of White House Appearance	5,000		240.00	240
1995 35 Years of Clowning	5,000	1995	240.00	240-300
1989 65th Birthday Commemorative	1,989	1989	300.00	780-2000
1993 After The Parade	7,500		190.00	190
1988 Amen	12,000	1991	120.00	390-400
1996 American Circus Extravaganza	5,000		240.00	240
1991 Artist At Work	7,500	1997	285.00	260-325
1992 Autumn - D. Rust	Retrd.	1996	60.00	175
1983 The Balancing Act	10,000	1985	75.00	900-975
1983 Balloons For Sale	10,000	1985	75.00	650-750
1990 Balloons for Sale II	7,500		250.00	250
1986 Bedtime	12,000	1991	98.00	228-325
1984 Big Business	9,500	1987	110.00	900
1998 Block Set (Economy Class)	1,500		275.00	275
1998 Block Set (Our Perennial Favorite)	1,500		275.00	275
1997 Catch of the Day	5,000		240.00	240
1990 Convention-Bound	7,500		225.00	230
1986 Cotton Candy	12,000	1987	98.00	225-400
1996 Daredevil Thrill Motor Show	5,000		240.00	240
1988 Dining Out	12,000	1991	120.00	325-350
1984 Eating Cabbage	12,000	1986	75.00	475-500
1985 Emmett's Fan	12,000	1986	80.00	475-495
1986 The Entertainers	12,000	1991	120.00	156-300
1986 Fair Game	2,500	1987	450.00	1800-2000
1991 Finishing Touch	7,500		230.00	230
1991 Follow The Leader	7,500		200.00	200
1994 Forest Friends	7,500	1997	190.00	190-325
1983 Hole In The Sole	10,000	1986	75.00	455-650
1989 Hurdy-Gurdy Man	9,500	1991	150.00	260-350
1985 In The Spotlight	12,000	1989	103.00	400-450
1993 Kittens For Sale	7,500		190.00	190
1994 Let Him Eat Cake	3,500	1995	300.00	300-455
1994 The Lion Tamer	7,500	1997	190.00	190-295
1981 Looking Out To See	12,000	1982	75.00	1500-3000
1986 Making New Friends	9,500	1988	140.00	350-390
1989 Making Up	7,500	1995	200.00	286-475
1985 Man's Best Friend	9,500	1989	98.00	618-650
1990 Misfortune?	3,500	1989	350.00	520-780
1987 My Favorite Things	9,500	1988	109.00	600-700
1989 No Loitering	7,500	1994	200.00	250-500
1985 No Strings Attached	9,500	1991	98.00	300-350
1992 No Use Crying	7,500		200.00	200
1987 On The Road Again	9,500	1991	109.00	450
1988 Over a Barrel	9,500	1991	130.00	293-450
1992 Peanut Butter?	7,500		200.00	200
1984 Piano Player	9,500	1988	160.00	695-800
1992 Ready-Set-Go	7,500		200.00	200
1987 Saturday Night	7,500	1988	153.00	625-650
1983 Spirit of Christmas I	3,500	1984	125.00	2178-2600
1984 Spirit of Christmas II	3,500	1985	270.00	390-650
1985 Spirit of Christmas III	3,500	1989	220.00	525-780
1986 Spirit of Christmas IV	3,500	1989	150.00	300-550
1987 Spirit of Christmas V	2,400	1989	170.00	358-550
1988 Spirit of Christmas VI	2,400	1989	194.00	244-600
1990 Spirit of Christmas VII	3,500	1990	275.00	425-450
1991 Spirit of Christmas VIII	3,500	1992	250.00	350-375
1993 Spirit of Christmas IX	3,500		200.00	200
1993 Spirit of Christmas X	3,500		200.00	200
1994 Spirit of Christmas XI	3,500	1995	200.00	260-325
1995 Spirit of Christmas XII	3,500	1997	200.00	295-300
1996 Spirit of Christmas XIII	3,500		200.00	200
1997 Spirit of Christmas XIV	3,500		200.00	200
1998 Spirit of Christmas XV	1,500		250.00	250
1992 Spring - D. Rust	Retrd.	1996	60.00	65-150
1992 Summer - D. Rust	Retrd.	1996	60.00	200-250
1981 Sweeping Up	12,000	1982	75.00	750-1500
1982 The Thinker	15,000	1986	60.00	1100-1300
1987 Toothache	12,000	1995	98.00	200-295
1990 Watch the Birdie	9,500		200.00	225
1982 Wet Paint	15,000	1983	80.00	560-850
1988 Wheeler Dealer	7,500	1990	160.00	350-650
1982 Why Me?	15,000	1984	65.00	377-475
1992 Winter - D. Rust	Retrd.	1996	60.00	65-125
1983 Wishful Thinking	10,000	1985	65.00	325-700
1993 World Traveler	7,500	1997	190.00	190-225

Emmett Kelly Jr. A Day At The Fair - Undisclosed

YEAR ISSUE	EDITION LIMIT	YEAR RETD.	ISSUE PRICE	*QUOTE U.S.$
1990 75 Please	Retrd.	1994	65.00	150-175
1991 Coin Toss	Retrd.	1994	65.00	125-175
1990 Look At You	Retrd.	1994	65.00	125-175
1991 Popcorn!	Retrd.	1994	65.00	125-175
1990 Ride The Wild Mouse	Retrd.	1994	65.00	95-175
1990 Step Right Up	Retrd.	1994	65.00	165-175
1990 The Stilt Man	Retrd.	1994	65.00	125-175
1990 Thanks Emmett	Retrd.	1994	65.00	125-175
1990 Three For A Dime	Retrd.	1994	65.00	125-175
1991 The Trouble With Hot Dogs	Retrd.	1994	65.00	175
1990 You Can Do It, Emmett	Retrd.	1994	65.00	125-175
1990 You Go First, Emmett	Retrd.	1994	65.00	175

Emmett Kelly Jr. Appearance Figurine - Undisclosed

YEAR ISSUE	EDITION LIMIT	YEAR RETD.	ISSUE PRICE	*QUOTE U.S.$
1992 Now Appearing	Open		100.00	100
1993 The Vigilante	Open		75.00	75
1996 Going My Way	Open		90.00	90

Emmett Kelly Jr. Diamond Jubilee Birthday Series - Undisclosed

YEAR ISSUE	EDITION LIMIT	YEAR RETD.	ISSUE PRICE	*QUOTE U.S.$
1999 Big Cake	1,999		100.00	100
1998 Birthday Cleanup	1,999		125.00	125
1998 Birthday Parade	1,999		150.00	150
1999 Block Set (Jazz)	1,500		N/A	N/A
1999 Block Set (Oops! Another Birthday)	1,500		N/A	N/A
1999 Surprise	1,999		125.00	125

Emmett Kelly Jr. Diamond Jubilee Celebration (Birthday Miniatures) - Undisclosed

YEAR ISSUE	EDITION LIMIT	YEAR RETD.	ISSUE PRICE	*QUOTE U.S.$
1999 Cabbage?	Open		60.00	60
1999 Cake For 2	Open		65.00	65
1999 The Ultimate Gift	Open		60.00	60

Emmett Kelly Jr. Images of Emmett - Undisclosed

YEAR ISSUE	EDITION LIMIT	YEAR RETD.	ISSUE PRICE	*QUOTE U.S.$
1994 Baby's First Christmas	Retrd.	1997	80.00	80
1994 Best of Friends	Retrd.	1997	55.00	55-110
1994 Healing Heart	Retrd.	1997	90.00	90-150
1994 Holding The Future	Retrd.	1996	65.00	125-135
1994 Learning Together	Retrd.	1997	85.00	85-100
1994 Tightrope	Retrd.	1997	70.00	70-115
1994 Why Me, Again?	Retrd.	1997	60.00	60-100

Emmett Kelly Jr. Miniatures - Undisclosed

YEAR ISSUE	EDITION LIMIT	YEAR RETD.	ISSUE PRICE	*QUOTE U.S.$
1994 65th Birthday	Retrd.	1994	70.00	150-175
1998 All Aboard	Open		30.00	30
1996 Amen	Open		35.00	35
1998 Artist at Work	Open		55.00	55
1986 Balancing Act	Retrd.	1992	25.00	165-200
1986 Balloons for Sale	Retrd.	1993	25.00	100-130
1997 Balloons for Sale II	Open		55.00	55
1995 Bedtime	Open		35.00	35
1997 Big Boss	Open		55.00	55
1988 Big Business	Retrd.	1995	35.00	130-150
1997 Convention Bound	Open		55.00	55
1989 Cotton Candy	Retrd.	1991	30.00	125-135
1995 Dining Out	Open		35.00	35
1987 Eating Cabbage	Retrd.	1990	30.00	90-135
1987 Emmett's Fan	Retrd.	1994	30.00	100-130
1995 The Entertainers	Open		45.00	45
1994 Fair Game	Open		75.00	75
1997 Forest Friends	Open		55.00	55
1986 Hole in the Sole	Retrd.	1989	25.00	140-150
1995 Hurdy Gurdy Man	Open		40.00	40
1991 In The Spotlight	Retrd.	1996	35.00	85-90
1999 Let Him Eat Cake	Open		65.00	65
1999 Lion Tamer	Open		60.00	60
1986 Looking Out To See	Retrd.	1987	25.00	200-225
1992 Making New Friends	Retrd.	1996	40.00	50-135
1996 Making Up	Open		55.00	55
1989 Man's Best Friend?	Retrd.	1994	35.00	120-130
1997 Merry Go Round	Open		65.00	65
1996 Misfortune	Open		60.00	60
1990 My Favorite Things	Retrd.	1995	45.00	125-130
1995 No Loitering	Open		50.00	50
1991 No Strings Attached	Retrd.	1996	35.00	50-135
1992 On the Road Again	Numbrd.		35.00	35
1994 Over a Barrel	Open		30.00	30
1992 Piano Player	Numbrd.		50.00	50
1999 Ringmaster	Open		60.00	60
1990 Saturday Night	Retrd.	1995	50.00	135-150
1988 Spirit of Christmas I	Retrd.	1990	40.00	50-175
1992 Spirit of Christmas II	Retrd.	1995	50.00	125-150
1990 Spirit Of Christmas III	Retrd.	1993	50.00	75-155
1993 Spirit of Christmas IV	Retrd.	1997	40.00	40-135
1994 Spirit of Christmas V	Retrd.	1996	50.00	50-100
1996 Spirit of Christmas VI	Open		55.00	55
1997 Spirit of Christmas VII	Open		50.00	50
1998 Spirit of Christmas IX	Open		55.00	55
1986 Sweeping Up	Retrd.	1987	25.00	200-225
1998 Take Good Care of Her	Open		50.00	50
1986 The Thinker	Retrd.	1991	25.00	150-163
1996 The Toothache	Open		35.00	35
1997 Watch the Birdie	Open		55.00	55
1986 Wet Paint	Retrd.	1993	25.00	125-170
1996 Wheeler Dealer	Open		65.00	65
1986 Why Me?	Retrd.	1989	25.00	125-140
1986 Wishful Thinking	Retrd.	1988	25.00	120-130
1998 World Traveler	Open		55.00	55

Emmett Kelly Jr. Real Rags Collection - Undisclosed

YEAR ISSUE	EDITION LIMIT	YEAR RETD.	ISSUE PRICE	*QUOTE U.S.$
1993 Big Business II	Retrd.	1996	140.00	165-275
1993 Checking His List	Closed	N/A	100.00	115-200
1994 Eating Cabbage II	3,000		100.00	100
1994 A Good Likeness	3,000		120.00	120
1993 Looking Out To See II	3,000	1996	100.00	115-165
1994 On in Two	3,000	1996	100.00	135-150
1994 Rudolph Has A Red Nose, Too	3,000	1996	135.00	135-350
1993 Sweeping Up II	3,000	1996	100.00	125-135
1993 Thinker II	3,000	1996	120.00	150-275

Little Emmetts - M. Wu

YEAR ISSUE	EDITION LIMIT	YEAR RETD.	ISSUE PRICE	*QUOTE U.S.$
1998 #1 Teacher	Open		10.00	10
1996 Balancing Act	Open		25.00	25
1996 Balloons for Sale	Open		25.00	25
1994 Birthday Haul	Open		30.00	30
1995 Dance Lessons	Open		50.00	50
1998 Get Well Soon	Open		10.00	10
1998 Happy Birthday	Open		10.00	10
1998 I Love You	Open		10.00	10
1994 Little Artist Picture Frame	Retrd.	1997	22.00	22
1994 Little Emmett Fishing	Open		35.00	35
1995 Little Emmett Noel, Noel	Open		40.00	40
1994 Little Emmett Shadow Show	Retrd.	1997	40.00	40
1995 Little Emmett Someday	Open		50.00	50
1994 Little Emmett w/Blackboard	Retrd.	1997	30.00	30
1994 Little Emmett, Counting Lession (Musical)	Open		30.00	30
1994 Little Emmett, Country Road (Musical)	Open		35.00	35
1994 Little Emmett, Raindrops (Musical)	Open		35.00	35
1994 Little Emmett, You've Got a Friend (Musical)	Open		33.00	33
1996 Long Distance	Open		50.00	50
1996 Looking Back Musical Waterglobe	Open		75.00	75
1995 Looking Forward Musical Waterglobe	Open		75.00	75
1996 Looking Out To See	Open		25.00	25
1998 Miss You	Open		10.00	10
1994 Playful Bookends	Open		40.00	40
1998 Sorry	Open		10.00	10
1996 Sweeping Up	Open		25.00	25
1996 Thinker	Open		25.00	25
1996 Wet Paint	Open		40.00	40
1994 EKJ, Age 1	Open		9.00	9
1994 EKJ, Age2	Open		9.50	10
1994 EKJ, Age 3	Open		12.00	12
1994 EKJ, Age 4	Open		12.00	12
1994 EKJ, Age 5	Open		15.00	15
1994 EKJ, Age 6	Open		15.00	15
1994 EKJ, Age 7	Open		17.00	17
1994 EKJ, Age 8	Open		21.00	21
1994 EKJ, Age 9	Open		22.00	22
1994 EKJ, Age 10	Open		25.00	25
1996 January-New Years	Open		35.00	35
1996 February-Valentine's Day	Open		35.00	35
1996 March-St. Patrick's Day	Open		35.00	35
1996 April-April Showers	Open		35.00	35
1996 May-May Flowers	Open		35.00	35
1996 June-School Is Out	Open		35.00	35
1996 July-Independence Day	Open		35.00	35
1996 August-Summer Picnic	Open		35.00	35

*Quotes have been rounded up to nearest dollar

YEAR ISSUE	EDITION LIMIT	YEAR RETD.	ISSUE PRICE	*QUOTE U.S.$
1996 September-School Is In	Open		35.00	35
1996 October-Pumpkins for Fall & Halloween	Open		35.00	35
1996 November-Thanksgiving	Open		35.00	35
1996 December-Snow Sledding w/Friends	Open		35.00	35

Pocket Dragon Land of Legends Collector Club - T. Raine

YEAR ISSUE	EDITION LIMIT	YEAR RETD.	ISSUE PRICE	*QUOTE U.S.$
1988 Sword in the Stone	Retrd.	1989	Gift	225-258

Pocket Dragon Collector Club - R. Musgrave

YEAR ISSUE	EDITION LIMIT	YEAR RETD.	ISSUE PRICE	*QUOTE U.S.$
1989 Take a Chance	Retrd.	1990	Gift	260-300
1991 Collecting Butterflies	Retrd.	1992	Gift	150-195
1992 The Key to My Heart	Retrd.	1993	Gift	150-195
1993 Want A Bite?	Retrd.	1994	Gift	104-125
1993 Bitsy	Retrd.	1994	Gift	N/A
1994 Friendship Pin	Open		Gift	85
1994 Blue Ribbon Dragon	Retrd.	1995	Gift	50-80
1995 Making Time For You	Retrd.	1996	Gift	75-80
1996 Good News	Retrd.	1997	Gift	55-60
1997 Lollipop	5/98		Gift	55

Pocket Dragon Land of Legends Members Only Pieces -Various

YEAR ISSUE	EDITION LIMIT	YEAR RETD.	ISSUE PRICE	*QUOTE U.S.$
1988 Hubble Bubble (LOL) - T. Raine	Retrd.	1989	95.00	275-455
1989 Self Taught (LOL) - H. Henriksen	Retrd.	1990	100.00	300-325
1989 Best Friends (LOL) - H. Henriksen	Retrd.	1990	95.00	170-205

Pocket DragonMembers Only Pieces - R. Musgrave

YEAR ISSUE	EDITION LIMIT	YEAR RETD.	ISSUE PRICE	*QUOTE U.S.$
1991 A Spot of Tea Won't You Join Us (set)	Retrd.	1992	75.00	300-361
1991 Wizard's House Print	Retrd.	1993	39.95	80-98
1992 Book Nook	Retrd.	1993	140.00	232-250
1993 Pen Pals	Retrd.	1994	90.00	150-165
1994 The Best Seat in the House	Retrd.	1995	75.00	115-150
1995 Party Time	Retrd.	1996	75.00	100-110
1996 Looking For The Right Words	Retrd.	1997	80.00	80-105
1997 Sticking Together	Retrd.	1998	75.00	75

Pocket Dragon Annual Figurines - R. Musgrave

YEAR ISSUE	EDITION LIMIT	YEAR RETD.	ISSUE PRICE	*QUOTE U.S.$
1993 A Big Hug	Retrd.	1994	35.00	65-105
1994 Packed and Ready	Retrd.	1995	47.00	70
1995 Attention to Detail	Retrd.	1996	24.00	55-65
1996 On The Road Again	Retrd.	1997	30.00	40-60
1997 Jaunty	Open		31.00	31
1998 Rise & Shine	12/98		20.00	20

Pocket Dragon Christmas Editions - R. Musgrave

YEAR ISSUE	EDITION LIMIT	YEAR RETD.	ISSUE PRICE	*QUOTE U.S.$
1992 A Pocket-Sized Tree	Retrd.	1992	18.95	108-170
1993 Christmas Angel	Retrd.	1993	45.00	78-120
1991 I've Been Very Good	Retrd.	1991	37.50	200-300
1989 Putting Me on the Tree	Retrd.	1994	52.50	155-163
1994 Dear Santa	Retrd.	1995	50.00	65-140
1995 Chasing Snowflakes	Retrd.	1995	35.00	85-120
1996 Christmas Skates	Retrd.	1996	36.00	50-80
1997 Deck The Halls	Retrd.	1997	39.00	39-50
1998 The Littlest Reindeer	Yr.Iss.		40.00	40

Pocket Dragons - R. Musgrave

YEAR ISSUE	EDITION LIMIT	YEAR RETD.	ISSUE PRICE	*QUOTE U.S.$
1998 And I Won't Be Any Trouble	Open		20.00	20
1990 The Apprentice	Retrd.	1994	22.50	70-95
1989 Attack	Retrd.	1992	45.00	175-195
1989 Baby Brother	Retrd.	1992	19.50	85-90
1993 Bath Time	Retrd.	1995	90.00	120-125
1997 Bathing the Gargoyle	3,500		250.00	250
1997 Big Heart	Open		21.50	22
1993 The Book End	Retrd.	1996	90.00	110-140
1994 A Book My Size	Retrd.	1998	30.00	30
1992 Bubbles	Retrd.	1996	55.00	80-95
1995 But I am Too Little!	Open		14.50	15
1994 Butterfly Kissess	Open		29.50	30
1994 Candy Cane	Retrd.	1998	22.50	23
1997 A Choice of Ties	Open		38.00	38
1995 Classical Dragon	Retrd.	1998	80.00	80
1997 Clean Hands	Open		28.50	29
1994 Coffee Please	Open		24.00	24
1996 D-Pressing	Open		28.00	28
1997 Daisy	Open		17.00	17
1994 Dance Partner	Retrd.	1998	23.00	23
1992 A Different Drummer	Retrd.	1994	32.50	60-85
1989 Do I Have To?	Retrd.	1996	45.00	45-85
1997 Doodles	Open		26.50	27
1991 Dragons in the Attic	Retrd.	1995	120.00	124-200
1997 The Driver	Open		27.50	28
1989 Drowsy Dragon	Retrd.	1996	27.50	30-55
1995 Elementary My Dear	Open		35.00	35
1989 Flowers For You	Retrd.	1992	42.50	50-145
1993 Friends	Retrd.	1997	55.00	55
1991 Fuzzy Ears	Retrd.	1997	16.50	17
1989 The Gallant Defender	Retrd.	1992	36.50	150-175
1989 Gargoyle Hoping For Raspberry Teacakes	Retrd.	1990	139.50	1800-2500
1994 Gargoyles Just Wanna Have Fun	Retrd.	1997	30.00	30
1989 A Good Egg	Retrd.	1991	36.50	201-225
1998 Grr I'm A Monster	Open		30.00	30
1998 Happy Birthday	Open		30.00	30
1996 He Ain't Heavy...He's My Puffin	Open		34.00	34
1995 Hedgehog's Joke	Open		27.00	27
1996 Hopalong Gargoyle	Open		42.00	42
1993 I Ate the Whole Thing	Retrd.	1996	32.50	33-45
1991 I Didn't Mean To	Open		32.50	33
1991 I'm A Kitty	Retrd.	1993	37.50	55-75
1996 I'm So Pretty	Open		22.50	23
1997 I've Had a Hard Day	Open		23.50	24
1994 In Trouble Again	Open		35.00	35
1995 It's a Present	Open		21.00	21
1994 It's Dark Out There	Retrd.	1998	45.00	45
1994 It's Magic	Retrd.	1998	31.00	31
1997 It's Me	Open		21.50	22
1994 Jingles	Retrd.	1998	22.50	23
1991 A Joyful Noise	Retrd.	1996	16.50	17-27
1992 The Juggler	Retrd.	1997	32.50	33
1993 Let's Make Cookies	Retrd.	1996	90.00	93-105
1992 The Library Cat	Retrd.	1994	38.50	75-80
1993 Little Bit (lapel pin)	Retrd.	1996	16.50	22-35
1993 Little Jewel (brooch)	Retrd.	1994	19.50	25-35
1994 A Little Security	Open		20.00	20
1989 Look at Me	Retrd.	1990	42.50	250-275
1992 Mitten Toes	Retrd.	1996	16.50	17-30
1994 My Big Cookie	Retrd.	1998	35.00	35
1992 Nap Time	Open		15.00	15
1997 The Navigator	Open		30.00	30
1989 New Bunny Shoes	Retrd.	1992	28.50	75-85
1989 No Ugly Monsters Allowed	Retrd.	1992	47.50	108-145
1993 Oh Goody!	Retrd.	1997	16.50	17
1996 Oh Happy Day	Open		22.00	22
1990 One-Size-Fits-All	Retrd.	1993	16.50	25-65
1992 Oops!	Retrd.	1996	16.50	17-30
1989 Opera Gargoyle	Retrd.	1991	85.00	300-395
1992 Percy	Retrd.	1994	70.00	100-165
1998 Perfect Fit	Open		17.50	18
1991 Pick Me Up	Retrd.	1995	16.50	17-30
1996 Pillow Fight	3,500	1997	157.00	157-225
1989 Pink 'n' Pretty	Retrd.	1992	23.90	60-77
1994 Playing Dress Up	Retrd.	1997	30.00	30
1991 Playing Footsie	Retrd.	1994	16.50	25-40
1998 Playtime	Open		15.00	15
1997 Pocket Cruise	Open		38.00	38
1989 Pocket Dragon Countersign	Retrd.	1991	50.00	360-395
1989 The Pocket Minstrel	Retrd.	1991	36.50	195
1996 Pocket Piper	Open		37.00	37
1992 Pocket Posey	Retrd.	1995	16.50	20-30
1993 Pocket Rider (brooch)	Retrd.	1995	19.50	30-35
1991 Practice Makes Perfect	Retrd.	1993	32.50	65-80
1997 Pretty Please	Open		17.00	17
1991 Putt Putt	Retrd.	1993	37.50	91-115
1996 Quartet	Open		80.00	80
1994 Raiding the Cookie Jar	3,500	1995	200.00	250-325
1993 Reading the Good Parts	Retrd.	1997	70.00	70-80
1996 Red Ribbon	Open		16.50	17
1997 Rub My Tummy?	Open		17.00	17
1991 Scales of Injustice	Retrd.	1997	45.00	45-52
1998 The Scholar	Open		50.00	50
1989 Scribbles	Retrd.	1994	32.50	42-65
1989 Sea Dragon	Retrd.	1991	45.00	232-285
1995 Sees All, Knows All	Open		35.00	35
1989 Sir Nigel Smythebe-Smoke	Retrd.	1993	120.00	258-300
1991 Sleepy Head	Retrd.	1995	37.50	40-50
1994 Snuggles	Retrd.	1998	35.00	35
1997 Spilt Milk	Open		31.50	32
1989 Stalking the Cookie Jar	Retrd.	1997	27.50	28-38
1997 Stars!	Open		85.00	85
1989 Storytime at Wizard's House	Retrd.	1993	375.00	600-800
1996 Sweetie Pie	Open		28.00	28
1990 Tag-A-Long	Retrd.	1993	15.00	55-65
1998 Take Your Medicine	Open		15.00	15
1997 The Teacher	Open		39.00	39
1989 Teddy Magic	Retrd.	1991	85.00	150-170
1995 Telling Secrets	Retrd.	1998	48.00	48
1991 Thimble Foot	Retrd.	1994	38.50	50-75
1991 Tickle	Retrd.	1996	27.50	30-40
1996 Tiny Bit Tired	Open		16.00	16
1989 Toady Goldtrayler	Retrd.	1993	55.00	129-150
1993 Treasure	Retrd.	1997	90.00	90
1995 Tumbly	Open		21.00	21
1991 Twinkle Toes	Retrd.	1995	16.50	17-30
1992 Under the Bed	2,500	1995	450.00	575-813
1997 Varoom	Open		38.00	38
1996 The Volunteer	2,500	1996	350.00	395-475
1989 Walkies	Retrd.	1992	65.00	119-250
1996 Watcha Doin	Open		22.50	23
1995 Watson	Open		22.50	23
1993 We're Very Brave	Retrd.	1996	37.50	65-85
1989 What Cookie?	Retrd.	1997	38.50	39-48
1989 Wizardry for Fun and Profit	Retrd.	1992	375.00	575-700
1993 You Can't Make Me	Open		15.00	15
1989 Your Paint is Stirred	Retrd.	1991	42.50	125-200
1992 Zoom Zoom	Open		37.50	38

Wizards & Dragons - H. Henriksen

YEAR ISSUE	EDITION LIMIT	YEAR RETD.	ISSUE PRICE	*QUOTE U.S.$
1995 Alkmyne	2,500		135.00	135
1996 Apothes	1,500		195.00	195
1996 Archimedes	1,500		195.00	195
1995 Atnanticus	Retrd.	1996	150.00	175-330
1996 The Awakening	Retrd.	1997	150.00	150
1995 Confrontation	1,500		295.00	295
1996 Conversation	1,500		175.00	175
1997 The Crystal Gazer	1,500		150.00	150
1997 Curiosity	1,500		190.00	190
1997 The Dragon Lord	1,500		195.00	195
1997 The Elusive Potion	1,500		270.00	270
1997 The Hatchling	1,500		100.00	100
1997 Histra Rex	999		295.00	295
1996 Laidley Worm	1,500		150.00	150
1997 The Magic Sword	1,500		150.00	150
1995 Pelryn	2,500		175.00	175
1995 Rammis	2,500		150.00	150
1997 Seeking Council	999		450.00	450
1997 Solaris The Star Seeker	1,500		190.00	190
1996 Storm Bringer	1,500		150.00	150
1997 Tallonous Wyvrenous	1,500		150.00	150
1996 Tholief	1,500		250.00	250
1994 The Travellers	1,500	1996	295.00	295-300
1997 Well of Sorrows	1,500		270.00	270

Fool Moon Treasures

The Bearly's - D. Sams

YEAR ISSUE	EDITION LIMIT	YEAR RETD.	ISSUE PRICE	*QUOTE U.S.$
1998 Bo: Here Comes A Hug	500		20.00	20
1998 Buster: Stories & Friends	500		35.00	35
1998 David: Read This One	500		35.00	35
1998 Franklin: Didn't Get Away	500		45.00	45
1998 Harmony: Naturalist Bear	500		45.00	45
1998 Jack: Look What I Found	500		40.00	40
1998 Miss Ida Mae: Story Time	500		40.00	40
1998 Patrick: My Heart Sings To You	500		40.00	40
1998 Randall: Please Say Yes	500		40.00	40
1998 Rudy: You're So Special	500		40.00	40
1998 Victor: Stories Last Forever	500		35.00	35
1998 Zeke: Mountain Music	500		45.00	45

Fool Moon Treasures - D. Sams

YEAR ISSUE	EDITION LIMIT	YEAR RETD.	ISSUE PRICE	*QUOTE U.S.$
1992 Autumn	Open		15.00	15
1992 Best Buddies	Open		15.00	15
1992 Earth Guardian	Open		15.00	15
1992 Jest - a - Cat	Open		15.00	15
1992 Sandman	Open		15.00	15
1992 Sea Guardian	Open		15.00	15
1992 Spring	Open		15.00	15
1992 Summer	Open		15.00	15
1992 Tooth Fairy	Open		15.00	15
1992 Winter	Open		15.00	15

Homespun Goodness - D. Sams

YEAR ISSUE	EDITION LIMIT	YEAR RETD.	ISSUE PRICE	*QUOTE U.S.$
1998 Angels Everywhere	Open		15.00	15
1998 Every Stitch of Kindness	Open		15.00	15
1998 Hold It Together	Open		15.00	15
1998 Made With Love	Open		16.00	16
1998 Once In a Blue Moon	Open		20.00	20
1998 This is for You	Open		16.00	16
1998 We Can Patch This Up	Open		16.00	16

O-So Wonderful - D. Sams

YEAR ISSUE	EDITION LIMIT	YEAR RETD.	ISSUE PRICE	*QUOTE U.S.$
1998 Eleanor: Fairy BearMother	Open		20.00	20
1998 Uncle Ursa: New Arrival	Open		22.00	22
1998 Becky Ann: Year One	Open		15.00	15
1998 Denny: Year One	Open		15.00	15
1998 Susan: Year Two	Open		15.00	15
1998 Jon: Year Two	Open		15.00	15
1998 Cookie: Year Three	Open		15.00	15
1998 Jeffrey: Year Three	Open		15.00	15
1998 Dorothy: Year Four	Open		16.00	16
1998 Oscar: Year Four	Open		16.00	16
1998 Flossie: Year Five	Open		16.00	16
1998 Pilot Bob: Year Five	Open		16.00	16
1998 Jeanne: Year Six	Open		16.00	16
1998 Jess: Year Six	Open		16.00	16

Franklin Mint

Joys of Childhood - N. Rockwell

YEAR ISSUE	EDITION LIMIT	YEAR RETD.	ISSUE PRICE	*QUOTE U.S.$
1976 Coasting Along	3,700		120.00	175
1976 Dressing Up	3,700		120.00	175
1976 The Fishing Hole	3,700		120.00	175
1976 Hopscotch	3,700		120.00	175
1976 The Marble Champ	3,700		120.00	175
1976 The Nurse	3,700		120.00	175
1976 Ride 'Em Cowboy	3,700		120.00	175
1976 The Stilt Walker	3,700		120.00	175
1976 Time Out	3,700		120.00	175
1976 Trick or Treat	3,700		120.00	175

Ganz

Cottage Collectibles® Christmas Collection - Ganz

YEAR ISSUE	EDITION LIMIT	YEAR RETD.	ISSUE PRICE	*QUOTE U.S.$
1996 Finishing Touch	10,800		25.00	25
1997 Happy Holidays	10,800		17.00	17
1997 Love	10,800		17.00	17
1997 Noel	10,800		17.00	17
1996 Our Tree	10,800		28.00	28
1997 Peace	10,800		17.00	17
1996 Snowy Days	10,800		28.00	28
1997 T'was The Night Before Christmas	10,800		30.00	30
1997 Tis The Season	10,800		27.00	27
1996 Touch of Heaven	10,800		20.00	20

Cottage Collectibles® Collection - Ganz, unless otherwise noted

YEAR ISSUE	EDITION LIMIT	YEAR RETD.	ISSUE PRICE	*QUOTE U.S.$
1996 All Aboard	Retrd.	1998	20.00	20
1997 The Aviators	10,800		28.00	28
1998 Back To School - L. Chien	Open		17.00	17
1995 Bath Time	Retrd.	1996	17.00	17
1995 Best Friends	Retrd.	1996	16.00	16
1997 Birthday Wishes	10,800		14.00	14
1996 Blowing the Blues	10,800		17.00	17
1996 Boy's will be Boys	10,800		20.00	20
1997 Bubbles 'N' Fizz	Retrd.	1998	19.00	19
1995 Circus Parade	Retrd.	1996	23.00	23
1996 Derby Day	10,800		28.00	28

*Quotes have been rounded up to nearest dollar

YEAR ISSUE	EDITION LIMIT	YEAR RETD.	ISSUE PRICE	*QUOTE U.S.$
1997 Downstream	10,800		25.00	25
1996 Everyone Needs A Hug	Retrd.	1998	16.00	16
1996 Extra, Extra	10,800		16.00	16
1997 Fall Harvest	10,800		28.00	28
1996 Family Portrait	10,800		28.00	28
1995 First Love	Retrd.	1996	20.00	20
1996 First Steps	Retrd.	1998	20.00	20
1996 Fish is Fryin'	Retrd.	1998	23.00	23
1997 Fore	10,800		16.00	16
1997 The Gardener	10,800		20.00	20
1998 Goin' Down Smooth - T. Skorstad	Open		40.00	40
1995 Goin' Fishin'	Retrd.	1996	16.00	16
1996 Good Ole Summertime	Open		25.00	25
1996 Good Ole Time	Open		21.00	21
1995 Grandma's Treasures	Retrd.	1996	25.00	25
1997 Happy Birthday	10,800		19.00	19
1997 The Happy Li'l Hikers	10,800		22.00	22
1997 I Got It!	10,800		17.00	17
1995 A Job Well Done...	Retrd.	1998	25.00	25
1997 Lending A Hand	10,800		21.00	21
1997 Mama's Little Helper	10,800		31.00	31
1996 Maxwell's ABC's	10,800		16.00	16
1997 My American Hero	10,800		16.00	16
1995 My Favorite Things	Retrd.	1996	16.00	16
1996 My Girl	10,800		25.00	25
1996 My Horsey	Retrd.	1998	16.00	16
1996 My Toys	10,800		19.00	19
1995 Naptime	Retrd.	1996	23.00	23
1995 Play Time	Retrd.	1996	23.00	23
1996 Round 'Em Up	10,800		20.00	20
1995 School Days	Retrd.	1996	16.00	16
1996 Sharing	10,800		16.00	16
1996 The Sky's the Limit	Retrd.	1998	17.00	17
1998 Sleuthing For Clues - C. Tredger	Open		19.00	19
1998 Soapboxin' Summer - C. Tredger	Open		24.00	24
1997 Something Fishy	10,800		22.00	22
1997 Splish Splash	Retrd.	1998	28.00	28
1996 A Stroll in the Park	10,800		28.00	28
1997 Sunken Treasures	10,800		21.00	21
1997 Sweet Dreams	10,800		24.00	24
1995 Tea Time	Retrd.	1996	23.00	23
1997 Tis The Life	Retrd.	1998	25.00	25
1996 True Friends	10,800		20.00	20
1996 Uh oh	10,800		16.00	16
1996 Yvonne's Treasures	10,800		16.00	16

Cottage Collectibles® Easter Collection - Ganz

YEAR ISSUE	EDITION LIMIT	YEAR RETD.	ISSUE PRICE	*QUOTE U.S.$
1996 Artist at Work	10,800		16.00	16
1996 Carrots for Sale	10,800		20.00	20
1996 Sweet Spring	10,800		16.00	16

Cottage Collectibles® Valentine Collection - Ganz

YEAR ISSUE	EDITION LIMIT	YEAR RETD.	ISSUE PRICE	*QUOTE U.S.$
1996 Be Mine	10,800		16.00	16
1996 Can Anyone Spare A Kiss	10,800		21.00	21
1996 Lovestruck	10,800		16.00	16
1996 Valentines For Me	10,800		21.00	21

Perfect Little Place Collection - C.Thammavongsa, unless otherwise noted

YEAR ISSUE	EDITION LIMIT	YEAR RETD.	ISSUE PRICE	*QUOTE U.S.$
1995 All Star Angel	Retrd.	1996	14.00	14
1995 Angel Face	Retrd.	1997	15.00	15
1995 Angel's Food	Retrd.	1996	15.00	15
1997 Anniversary Bliss - L. Sunarth	Open		20.50	21
1996 Bless This Marriage	Retrd.	1997	20.00	20
1995 Divine Intervention	Retrd.	1997	15.00	15
1997 Friendship Blossoms - L. Sunarth	Open		20.50	21
1997 Green Thumb Angel - L. Sunarth	Open		15.50	16
1997 Happy Birthday - L. Sunarth	Open		17.00	17
1997 Hear My Prayer - L. Sunarth	Open		14.50	15
1995 Heaven & Nature	Retrd.	1997	14.00	14
1996 Heaven Makes All Things New	Retrd.	1997	18.00	18
1995 Heavenly Grace	Retrd.	1997	14.00	14
1995 Match Made in Heaven	Retrd.	1996	18.00	18
1997 New Companions - L. Sunarth	Open		17.00	17
1995 Paradise	Retrd.	1996	13.00	13
1995 Perfect Little Place	Open		16.00	16
1995 Pray the Lord My Soul to Keep	Retrd.	1996	13.00	13
1995 Ride Like The Wind	Retrd.	1996	15.00	15
1996 Showered With Love	Retrd.	1996	16.00	16
1997 Spring Melody - L. Sunarth	Open		15.50	16
1995 Sweet Sleep, Angel Mild	Open		13.50	14
1997 Wrapped in Joy- L. Sunarth	Open		17.00	17

Perfect Little Place/Christmas Collection - C.Thammavongsa, unless otherwise noted

YEAR ISSUE	EDITION LIMIT	YEAR RETD.	ISSUE PRICE	*QUOTE U.S.$
1995 Angel of Light - L. Sunarth	Retrd.	1997	12.00	12
1996 Angels in the Snow	Retrd.	1997	15.00	15
1995 Bearer of Blessings	Retrd.	1997	17.00	17
1996 Celestial Wonders	Retrd.	1997	17.00	17
1995 A Child is Born	Retrd.	1997	21.00	21
1996 Songs of Praise	Retrd.	1997	17.00	17

Perfect Little Place/Cultures of the World Collection - C.Thammavongsa

YEAR ISSUE	EDITION LIMIT	YEAR RETD.	ISSUE PRICE	*QUOTE U.S.$
1996 Dream Homes	Retrd.	1997	16.00	16
1996 Healing Touch	Retrd.	1997	16.00	16
1996 Praise the Lord	Retrd.	1997	17.00	17
1996 Smooth Sailing	Retrd.	1997	18.00	18
1996 Teacher's Pet	Retrd.	1997	17.00	17
1996 The Three R's	Retrd.	1997	17.50	18

Perfect Little Place/Valentine Collection - C.Thammavongsa, unless otherwise noted

YEAR ISSUE	EDITION LIMIT	YEAR RETD.	ISSUE PRICE	*QUOTE U.S.$
1995 Be My Angel	Retrd.	1997	16.00	16
1996 First Love	Retrd.	1996	22.50	23
1996 He Loves me...he loves me not - L. Sunarth	Retrd.	1996	15.50	16
1996 The Proposal	Retrd.	1996	15.50	16
1995 Sweet Innocence	Retrd.	1997	16.00	16
1995 Whispers of Love	Retrd.	1997	21.00	21

Gartlan USA

Members Only Figurine

YEAR ISSUE	EDITION LIMIT	YEAR RETD.	ISSUE PRICE	*QUOTE U.S.$
1990 Wayne Gretzky-Home Uniform - L. Heyda	Closed	1991	75.00	295-550
1991 Joe Montana-Road Uniform - F. Barnum	Closed	1992	75.00	200-489
1991 Kareem Abdul-Jabbar - L. Heyda	Closed	1993	75.00	175-395
1992 Mike Schmidt - J. Slockbower	Closed	1993	79.00	100-495
1993 Hank Aaron - J. Slockbower	Closed	1994	79.00	100-195
1994 Shaquille O'Neal - L. Cella	Closed	1995	39.95	275-350
1997 Ringo Starr (bath silver) - J. Hoffman	1,000	1997	80.00	80
1998 John Lennon (bath silver), (4 1/2") A/P - J. Hoffman	1,000		195.00	195

Brandon Lee-The Crow - W. Merklein

YEAR ISSUE	EDITION LIMIT	YEAR RETD.	ISSUE PRICE	*QUOTE U.S.$
1996 Brandon Lee-The Crow, (9")	5,700		225.00	275

Jerry Garcia - S. Sun

YEAR ISSUE	EDITION LIMIT	YEAR RETD.	ISSUE PRICE	*QUOTE U.S.$
1997 Jerry Garcia, (4")	10,000		50.00	50
1997 Jerry Garcia, (9")	1,995		195.00	195
1997 Jerry Garcia, A/P (9")	300		295.00	295
1997 Jerry Garcia, marquee (6")	5,000		125.00	125

John Lennon - J. Hoffman

YEAR ISSUE	EDITION LIMIT	YEAR RETD.	ISSUE PRICE	*QUOTE U.S.$
1998 John Lennon, pewter (9")	2,000		495.00	495
1998 John Lennon, pewter (honed in silver), (9") A/P	250		895.00	895
1998 John Lennon, pewter, (4 1/2")	5,000		125.00	125

Kareem Abdul-Jabbar Sky-Hook Collection - L. Heyda

YEAR ISSUE	EDITION LIMIT	YEAR RETD.	ISSUE PRICE	*QUOTE U.S.$
1989 Kareem Abdul-Jabbar "The Captain", signed	1,989	1990	175.00	320-450
1989 Kareem Abdul-Jabbar, A/P	100	1990	200.00	500
1989 Kareem Abdul-Jabbar, Commemorative	33	1990	275.00	3700-4000

Kiss - M. Paseurri

YEAR ISSUE	EDITION LIMIT	YEAR RETD.	ISSUE PRICE	*QUOTE U.S.$
1997 Kiss A/P, (10")	250		595.00	595
1997 Kiss, (10"), signed	1,000		395.00	395
1997 Kiss, (5")	10,000		89.00	89

Leave It To Beaver - Noble Studio

YEAR ISSUE	EDITION LIMIT	YEAR RETD.	ISSUE PRICE	*QUOTE U.S.$
1995 Jerry Mathers, (5")	5,000		49.95	50
1995 Jerry Mathers, (7 1/2"), signed	1,963		195.00	195

Magic Johnson Collection - R. Sun

YEAR ISSUE	EDITION LIMIT	YEAR RETD.	ISSUE PRICE	*QUOTE U.S.$
1988 Magic Johnson -"Magic in Motion"	1,737	1989	125.00	195-275
1988 Magic Johnson A/P "Magic in Motion", signed	250	1989	175.00	2000-2300
1988 Magic Johnson Commemorative, signed	32	1989	275.00	5000-7500

Mike Schmidt "500th" Home Run Edition - R. Sun

YEAR ISSUE	EDITION LIMIT	YEAR RETD.	ISSUE PRICE	*QUOTE U.S.$
1987 Mike Schmidt "500th" Home Run, A/P signed	20	1988	275.00	1200-1395
1987 Mike Schmidt "500th" Home Run, signed	1,987	1988	150.00	625-650

Neil Diamond - J. Hoffman

YEAR ISSUE	EDITION LIMIT	YEAR RETD.	ISSUE PRICE	*QUOTE U.S.$
1998 Neil Diamond, (4")	5,000		30.00	30
1998 Neil Diamond, (4") Marquee™	5,000		30.00	30
1998 Neil Diamond, (9") A/P signed	250		395.00	400
1998 Neil Diamond, (9") signed	1,000		295.00	300

Plaques - Various

YEAR ISSUE	EDITION LIMIT	YEAR RETD.	ISSUE PRICE	*QUOTE U.S.$
1986 George Brett-"Royalty in Motion", signed - J. Martin	2,000	1987	75.00	250-300
1987 Mike Schmidt-"Only Perfect", A/P - Paluso	20	1988	200.00	450-550
1987 Mike Schmidt-"Only Perfect", signed - Paluso	500	1988	150.00	350-400
1985 Pete Rose-"Desire to Win", signed - T. Sizemore	4,192	1986	75.00	325-350
1986 Reggie Jackson A/P-The Roundtripper, signed - J. Martin	44	1987	175.00	475-550
1986 Reggie Jackson-"The Roundtripper" signed - J. Martin	500	1987	150.00	350-400
1987 Roger Staubach, signed - C. Soileau	1,979	1988	85.00	325-350

Ringo Starr - J. Hoffman

YEAR ISSUE	EDITION LIMIT	YEAR RETD.	ISSUE PRICE	*QUOTE U.S.$
1996 Ringo Starr with drums, (6")	5,000		150.00	150
1996 Ringo Starr, (4")	10,000		49.95	50
1996 Ringo Starr, (8 1/2") A/P signed	250		600.00	600
1996 Ringo Starr, (8 1/2") signed	1,000		350.00	350

Signed Figurines - Various

YEAR ISSUE	EDITION LIMIT	YEAR RETD.	ISSUE PRICE	*QUOTE U.S.$
1991 Al Barlick - V. Bova	1,989	1995	195.00	250-295
1993 Bob Cousy - L. Heyda	950	1995	150.00	100-195
1991 Bobby Hull - The Golden Jet - L. Heyda	1,983	1995	250.00	150-225
1992 Bobby Hull, A/P - L. Heyda	300	1994	350.00	350-500
1991 Brett Hull - The Golden Brett - L. Heyda	1,986	1995	250.00	150-250
1992 Brett Hull, A/P - L. Heyda	300	1994	350.00	400-600
1989 Carl Yastrzemski-"Yaz" - L. Heyda	1,989	1990	150.00	300-375
1989 Carl Yastrzemski-"Yaz", A/P - L. Heyda	250	1990	150.00	400-700
1992 Carlton Fisk - J. Slockbower	1,972	1995	225.00	225-275
1990 Darryl Strawberry - L. Heyda	2,500	1995	225.00	150-350
1994 Eddie Matthews - R. Sun	1,978	1995	195.00	100-200
1994 Frank Thomas - D. Carroll	500	1995	225.00	350-390
1990 George Brett - F. Barnum	2,250	1995	225.00	175-275
1992 Gordie Howe - L. Heyda	2,358	1994	225.00	250-350
1990 Gordie Howe, signed A/P - L. Heyda	250	1994	395.00	395
1992 Hank Aaron - F. Barnum	1,982	1994	225.00	200-400
1992 Hank Aaron Commemorative w/displ. case - F. Barnum	755	1994	275.00	275-350
1991 Hull Matched Figurines - L. Heyda	950	1993	500.00	500
1989 Joe DiMaggio - L. Heyda	2,214	1990	275.00	875-1100
1990 Joe DiMaggio- Pinstripe Yankee Clipper - L. Heyda	325	1990	695.00	1750-2300
1990 Joe DiMaggio- Pinstripe Yankee Clipper, A/P - L. Heyda	12	1990	1500.00	4000-8000
1991 Joe Montana - F. Barnum	2,250	1991	325.00	500-795
1991 Joe Montana, A/P - F. Barnum	250	1991	500.00	700-1100
1989 John Wooden-Coaching Classics - L. Heyda	1,975	1995	175.00	175
1989 John Wooden-Coaching Classics, A/P - L. Heyda	250	1995	350.00	350
1989 Johnny Bench - L. Heyda	1,989	1990	150.00	250-260
1989 Johnny Bench, A/P - L. Heyda	250	1990	150.00	400-500
1994 Ken Griffey Jr., - J. Slockbower	1,989	1995	225.00	300-400
1993 Kristi Yamaguchi - K. Ling Sun	950	1995	195.00	260-275
1990 Luis Aparicio - J. Slockbower	1,984	1995	225.00	150-295
1991 Monte Irvin - V. Bova	1,973	1995	195.00	195
1991 Negro League, Set/3	950	1995	500.00	650-750
1985 Pete Rose-"For the Record", signed - H. Reed	4,192	1987	125.00	775-950
1992 Ralph Kiner - J. Slockbower	1,975	1995	225.00	225
1991 Rod Carew - Hitting Splendor - J. Slockbower	1,991	1995	225.00	225-250
1994 Sam Snead - L. Cella	950	1995	225.00	100-250
1994 Shaquille O'Neal - R. Sun	500	1995	225.00	500-795
1992 Stan Musial - J. Slockbower	1,969	1995	325.00	195-350
1992 Stan Musial, A/P - J. Slockbower	300	1995	425.00	250-425
1989 Steve Carlton - L. Heyda	3,290	1992	175.00	125-375
1989 Steve Carlton, A/P - L. Heyda	300	1992	350.00	400-500
1989 Ted Williams - L. Heyda	2,654	1990	295.00	475-495
1989 Ted Williams, A/P - L. Heyda	250	1990	650.00	595-700
1992 Tom Seaver - J. Slockbower	1,992	1995	225.00	325-400
1994 Troy Aikman - V. Davila	500	1995	225.00	350-500
1991 Warren Spahn - J. Slockbower	1,973	1995	225.00	250-275
1989 Wayne Gretzky - L. Heyda	1,851	1989	225.00	500-1000
1989 Wayne Gretzky, A/P - L. Heyda	300	1989	695.00	1000-1200
1990 Whitey Ford - S. Barnum	2,360	1995	225.00	100-350
1990 Whitey Ford, A/P - S. Barnum	250	1995	350.00	350
1989 Yogi Berra - F. Barnum	2,150	1994	225.00	250-350
1989 Yogi Berra, A/P - F. Barnum	250	1994	350.00	350

Geo. Zoltan Lefton Company

Child Within - M. Garvin

YEAR ISSUE	EDITION LIMIT	YEAR RETD.	ISSUE PRICE	*QUOTE U.S.$
1998 Apples 11650	Open		15.00	15
1998 Bee 11641	Open		13.00	13
1998 Butterfly 11640	Open		15.00	15
1998 Chick 11638	Open		15.00	15
1998 Christmas Tree 11630	Open		15.00	15
1998 Cow 11635	Open		13.00	13
1998 Elephant 11633	Open		13.00	13
1998 Frog 11637	Open		13.00	13
1998 Grape 11631	Open		15.00	15
1998 Polar Bear 11636	Open		13.00	13
1998 Rabbit 11639	Open		13.00	13
1998 Reindeer 11634	Open		15.00	15
1998 Rose 11629	Open		15.00	15
1998 Snowman 11628	Open		15.00	15
1998 Strawberries 11651	Open		15.00	15
1998 Sunflower 11632	Open		15.00	15
1998 Watermelons 11649	Open		15.00	15

Gary Paterson Collections - G. Paterson

YEAR ISSUE	EDITION LIMIT	YEAR RETD.	ISSUE PRICE	*QUOTE U.S.$
1998 #1 Dad 11756	Open		25.00	25
1998 Art of Casting 11758	Open		40.00	40
1998 Fully Equiped 11760	Open		25.00	25
1998 Golf Lover 11759	Open		25.00	25
1998 It's Only A Game 11763	Open		40.00	40
1998 Mr. Fix It 11762	Open		40.00	40
1998 Now What 11752	Open		25.00	25
1998 Sports Fan 11751	Open		40.00	40
1998 Super Fan 11764	Open		25.00	25
1998 Super Mom 11757	Open		25.00	25
1998 Thrill of Victory 11753	Open		40.00	40
1998 Tips Up 11755	Open		25.00	25
1998 Up The Creek 11754	Open		40.00	40
1998 World's Greatest Golfer 11765	Open		25.00	25

Tobin Fraley Collector Society (Willitts) - T. Fraley

YEAR ISSUE	EDITION LIMIT	YEAR RETD.	ISSUE PRICE	*QUOTE U.S.$
1992 TF-Collector's Society Horse	Closed	1992	35.00	100

Tobin Fraley Collection (Willitts) - T. Fraley

YEAR ISSUE	EDITION LIMIT	YEAR RETD.	ISSUE PRICE	*QUOTE U.S.$
1986 C.W. Parker - C. 1915 5050	Closed	1986	70.00	200-250
1986 Charles Carmel - C. 1914 5039	Closed	1986	75.00	125-200
1986 Charles Carmel - C. 1914 5043	Closed	1986	35.00	70
1986 Charles Looff - C. 1915 5040	Closed	1986	75.00	125-200
1986 Charles Looff - C. 1917 5038	Closed	1986	75.00	125-200
1986 Charles Looff - C. 1917 5044	Closed	1986	35.00	70
1986 Charles Looff/Ram - C. 1915 5234	Closed	1986	35.00	70
1986 D.C. Muller & Brother - C. 1911 5049	Closed	1986	35.00	70
1986 D.C. Muller & Brother - C. 1911 5233	Closed	1986	25.00	60
1986 Four Horse Musical Carousel 5213	Closed	1986	400.00	800-1000

*Quotes have been rounded up to nearest dollar

YEAR ISSUE	EDITION LIMIT	YEAR RETD.	ISSUE PRICE	*QUOTE U.S.$
1986 Gustav Dentzel Co. - C. 1905 5036	Closed	1986	75.00	200-275
1986 Gustav Dentzel Co./Cat - C. 1905 5235	Closed	1986	35.00	100-175
1986 Herschell-Spillman Co. - C. 1915 5046	Closed	1986	35.00	70
1986 Herschell-Spillman Co. - C. 1915 5230	Closed	1986	25.00	50
1986 Ptc - C. 1925 5047	Closed	1986	35.00	70
1986 Ptc - C. 1925 5231	Closed	1986	25.00	50
1986 Spillman Engineering - C. 1922 5041	Closed	1986	75.00	200-250
1986 Spillman Engineering - C. 1922 5042	Closed	1986	35.00	70
1986 Stein & Goldstein - C. 1914 5037	Closed	1986	75.00	125-200
1986 Stein & Goldstein - C. 1914 5045	Closed	1986	35.00	70
1986 Wm. Dentzel Co. - C. 1910 5048	Closed	1986	35.00	70
1986 Wm. Dentzel Co. - C. 1910 5051	Closed	1986	70.00	200-400
1986 Wm. Dentzel Co. - C. 1910 5232	Closed	1986	25.00	50

Tobin Fraley-American Carousel Collection (Willitts) - T. Fraley

YEAR ISSUE	EDITION LIMIT	YEAR RETD.	ISSUE PRICE	*QUOTE U.S.$
1987 Charles Carmel - C. 1915 5968	Closed	1987	70.00	125
1987 Charles Carmel - C. 1915 5986	Closed	1987	35.00	70
1987 Charles Looff - C. 1905 5980	Closed	1987	100.00	700-800
1987 Charles Looff - C. 1905 7127	Closed	1987	500.00	800-1000
1987 Charles Looff - C. 1905 7132	Closed	1987	125.00	125
1987 Charles Looff - C. 1909 5966	Closed	1987	70.00	95
1987 Charles Looff - C. 1909 5967	Closed	1987	70.00	95
1987 Charles Looff - C. 1909 5979	Closed	1987	100.00	600-700
1987 Charles Looff - C. 1909 5984	Closed	1987	35.00	70
1987 Charles Looff - C. 1909 5985	Closed	1987	35.00	70
1987 Charles Looff - C. 1909 7126	Closed	1987	500.00	700-900
1987 Charles Looff - C. 1909 7131	Closed	1987	125.00	500-950
1987 Charles Looff - C. 1909 / Rocker 5983	Closed	1987	70.00	175
1987 Charles Looff - C. 1914 5978	Closed	1987	100.00	200
1987 Charles Looff - C. 1914 7125	Closed	1987	500.00	700
1987 Charles Looff - C. 1914 7130	Closed	1987	125.00	250
1987 Daniel Muller - C. 1912 / Rocker 5982	Closed	1987	70.00	130-150
1987 Looff 5972	Closed	1987	400.00	700-900
1987 M.C. Illions - C. 1910 5971	Closed	1987	70.00	125-135
1987 M.C. Illions - C. 1910 5989	Closed	1987	35.00	70
1987 M.C. Illions - C. 1912 5970	Closed	1987	70.00	95
1987 M.C. Illions - C. 1912 5988	Closed	1987	35.00	70
1987 M.C. Illions - C. 1923 5973	Closed	1987	500.00	700-1100
1987 M.C. Illions - C. 1923 6390	Closed	1987	500.00	500
1987 M.C. Illions - C. 1923 7128	Closed	1987	100.00	190-250
1987 M.C. Illions - C. 1923 7129	Closed	1987	125.00	190-250
1987 Ptc - C. 1922 5969	Closed	1987	70.00	125
1987 Ptc - C. 1922 5987	Closed	1987	35.00	100
1987 Ptc - C. 1922 / Rocker 5981	Closed	1987	70.00	140

Tobin Fraley-American Carousel Collection II (Willitts) - T. Fraley

YEAR ISSUE	EDITION LIMIT	YEAR RETD.	ISSUE PRICE	*QUOTE U.S.$
1988 C.W. Parker - C. 1914 8322	Closed	1988	250.00	250
1988 C.W. Parker - C. 1914 8323	Closed	1988	135.00	250-350
1988 C.W. Parker - C. 1914 8468	Closed	1988	165.00	300
1988 Charles Looff - C. 1914 8213	Closed	1988	65.00	200
1988 Charles Looff - C. 1914 8214	Closed	1988	95.00	200
1988 Charles Looff - C. 1914/Snowglobe 8216	Closed	1988	80.00	80
1988 Charles Looff - C. 1917 8320	Closed	1988	250.00	250
1988 Charles Looff - C. 1917 8321	Closed	1988	135.00	250
1988 Charles Looff - C. 1917 8467	Closed	1988	165.00	250
1988 Daniel Muller - C. 1910 8317	Closed	1988	55.00	95
1988 Daniel Muller - C. 1910 8318	Closed	1988	85.00	125
1988 Dentzel - C. 1905 8329	Closed	1988	150.00	500-750
1988 Dentzel - C. 1905 8474	Closed	1988	235.00	235
1988 Dentzel - C. 1905 8475	Closed	1988	135.00	500
1988 Herschell-Spillman Co. - C. 1909 8331	Closed	1988	150.00	500
1988 Herschell-Spillman Co. - C. 1909 8470	Closed	1988	235.00	235
1988 Herschell-Spillman Co. - C. 1909 8471	Closed	1988	135.00	500
1988 Herschell-Spillman Co. - C. 1912 8330	Closed	1988	150.00	400-500
1988 Herschell-Spillman Co. - C. 1912 8472	Closed	1988	235.00	235
1988 Herschell-Spillman Co. - C. 1912 8473	Closed	1988	135.00	500
1988 M.C. Illions - C. 1912-25 8319	Closed	1988	500.00	750-900
1988 M.C. Illions - C. 1919 8324	Closed	1988	235.00	235
1988 M.C. Illions - C. 1919 8325	Closed	1988	235.00	300-400
1988 M.C. Illions - C. 1919 8340	Closed	1988	550.00	600-700
1988 M.C. Illions - C. 1919 8469	Closed	1988	150.00	275
1988 Ptc - C. 1912 8218	Closed	1988	65.00	100-200
1988 Ptc - C. 1912 8219	Closed	1988	95.00	100-200
1988 Ptc - C. 1912/Snowglobe 8221	Closed	1988	80.00	80
1988 Ptc - C. 1918 8222	Closed	1988	65.00	95
1988 Ptc - C. 1918 8223	Closed	1988	95.00	120
1988 Ptc - C. 1918 8224	Closed	1988	65.00	120
1988 Ptc - C. 1918 8225	Closed	1988	95.00	120
1988 Ptc - C. 1918 8315	Closed	1988	55.00	100
1988 Ptc - C. 1918 8316	Closed	1988	85.00	100

Tobin Fraley-American Carousel Collection III (Willitts) - T. Fraley

YEAR ISSUE	EDITION LIMIT	YEAR RETD.	ISSUE PRICE	*QUOTE U.S.$
1989 C.W. Parker - C. 1900-25 9024	Closed	1989	32.50	75
1989 C.W. Parker - C. 1900-25 9025	Closed	1989	32.50	75
1989 C.W. Parker - C. 1900-25 9032	Closed	1989	57.50	100-140
1989 C.W. Parker - C. 1900-25 9033	Closed	1989	57.50	100-140
1989 C.W. Parker - C. 1900-25 9034	Closed	1989	57.50	100-140
1989 C.W. Parker - C. 1900-25 9035	Closed	1989	57.50	100-140
1989 C.W. Parker - C. 1900-25 9071	Closed	1989	52.50	100-140
1989 C.W. Parker - C. 1900-25 9072	Closed	1989	52.50	100-140
1989 C.W. Parker - C. 1900-25 9073	Closed	1989	52.50	100-140
1989 C.W. Parker - C. 1900-25 9074	Closed	1989	52.50	100-140
1989 C.W. Parker - C. 1900-25 9075	Closed	1989	37.50	90
1989 C.W. Parker - C. 1900-25 9076	Closed	1989	37.50	90
1989 C.W. Parker - C. 1900-25 9077	Closed	1989	37.50	90
1989 C.W. Parker - C. 1900-25 9078	Closed	1989	37.50	90
1989 C.W. Parker - C. 1900-25 9079	Closed	1989	32.50	75
1989 C.W. Parker - C. 1900-25 9080	Closed	1989	32.50	75
1989 Charles Carmel - C. 1910 9910	Closed	1989	165.00	300-400
1989 Charles Carmel - C. 1915 9018	Closed	1989	80.00	150
1989 Charles Carmel - C. 1915 9019	Closed	1989	80.00	150
1989 Charles Carmel - C. 1915 9070	Closed	1989	165.00	300
1989 Charles Carmel - C. 1915 9088	Closed	1989	57.50	100-140
1989 Charles Carmel - C. 1915 9089	Closed	1989	57.50	58
1989 Charles Carmel - C. 1915 9094	Closed	1989	95.00	120-160
1989 Charles Carmel - C. 1915 9095	Closed	1989	95.00	120-160
1989 Charles Looff - C. 1909 9020	Closed	1989	80.00	125
1989 Charles Looff - C. 1909 9090	Closed	1989	57.50	140
1989 Charles Looff - C. 1909 9096	Closed	1989	95.00	125-160
1989 Charles Looff - C. 1917 9023	Closed	1989	80.00	120
1989 Charles Looff - C. 1917 9093	Closed	1989	57.50	100
1989 Charles Looff - C. 1917 9373	Closed	1989	95.00	125-150
1989 Daniel Muller - C. 1912 9021	Closed	1989	80.00	120
1989 Daniel Muller - C. 1912 9091	Closed	1989	57.50	75
1989 Daniel Muller - C. 1912 9097	Closed	1989	95.00	125-160
1989 M.C. Illions - C. 1922 9911	Closed	1989	165.00	600-850
1989 Ptc - C. 1922 9022	Closed	1989	80.00	95
1989 Ptc - C. 1922 9092	Closed	1989	57.50	75
1989 Ptc - C. 1922 9372	Closed	1989	95.00	160

Tobin Fraley-American Carousel Collection IV (Willitts) - T. Fraley

YEAR ISSUE	EDITION LIMIT	YEAR RETD.	ISSUE PRICE	*QUOTE U.S.$
1990 C.W. Parker - C. 1900-25 4020	Closed	1990	57.50	95
1990 C.W. Parker - C. 1900-25 4021	Closed	1990	57.50	95
1990 C.W. Parker - C. 1900-25 4022	Closed	1990	57.50	95
1990 C.W. Parker - C. 1900-25 4023	Closed	1990	57.50	95
1990 C.W. Parker - C. 1900-25 4024	Closed	1990	57.50	95
1990 C.W. Parker - C. 1900-25 4025	Closed	1990	57.50	95
1990 C.W. Parker - C. 1900-25 4027	Closed	1990	57.50	95
1990 C.W. Parker - C. 1900-25 4028	Closed	1990	37.50	75
1990 C.W. Parker - C. 1900-25 4029	Closed	1990	37.50	75
1990 C.W. Parker - C. 1900-25 4030	Closed	1990	37.50	75
1990 C.W. Parker - C. 1900-25 4031	Closed	1990	37.50	75
1990 C.W. Parker - C. 1900-25 4032	Closed	1990	37.50	75
1990 C.W. Parker - C. 1900-25 4033	Closed	1990	37.50	75
1990 C.W. Parker - C. 1900-25 4034	Closed	1990	37.50	75
1990 C.W. Parker - C. 1900-25 4056	Closed	1990	37.50	75
1990 Charles Carmel - C. 1915 4035	Closed	1990	95.00	95
1990 Charles Carmel - C. 1915 4036	Closed	1990	95.00	95
1990 Charles Carmel - C. 1915 4037	Closed	1990	85.00	85
1990 Charles Carmel - C. 1915 4038	Closed	1990	85.00	85
1990 Charles Carmel - C. 1915 / Complete 40290	Closed	1990	925.00	925
1990 Charles Looff 4053	Closed	1990	85.00	125
1990 Charles Looff 4054	Closed	1990	110.00	150
1990 Charles Looff 4055	Closed	1990	57.50	58
1990 Charles Looff - C. 1917 4003	Closed	1990	85.00	125-175
1990 Charles Looff - C. 1917 4005	Closed	1990	110.00	200
1990 Charles Looff - C. 1917 4007	Closed	1990	57.50	100-125
1990 The Four Seasons 4058	Closed	1990	500.00	800-1000
1990 The Four Seasons - Autumn 4010	Closed	1990	85.00	125
1990 The Four Seasons - Autumn 4014	Closed	1990	57.50	58
1990 The Four Seasons - Autumn 4018	Closed	1990	110.00	150
1990 The Four Seasons - Spring 4008	Closed	1990	85.00	120
1990 The Four Seasons - Spring 4012	Closed	1990	57.50	58
1990 The Four Seasons - Spring 4016	Closed	1990	110.00	150
1990 The Four Seasons - Summer 4009	Closed	1990	85.00	120
1990 The Four Seasons - Summer 4013	Closed	1990	57.50	58
1990 The Four Seasons - Summer 4017	Closed	1990	110.00	150
1990 The Four Seasons - Winter 4011	Closed	1990	85.00	120
1990 The Four Seasons - Winter 4015	Closed	1990	57.50	58
1990 The Four Seasons - Winter 4019	Closed	1990	110.00	300-400
1990 Herschell-Spillman Co. - C. 1912 4002	Closed	1990	85.00	85
1990 Herschell-Spillman Co. - C. 1912 4004	Closed	1990	110.00	110
1990 Herschell-Spillman Co. - C. 1912 4006	Closed	1990	57.50	58
1990 Inspired By Charles Looff 4047	Closed	1990	175.00	175
1990 Inspired By Charles Looff 4049	Closed	1990	185.00	225
1990 Inspired By Ptc 4048	Closed	1990	185.00	185
1990 Inspired By Ptc 4057	Closed	1990	175.00	220
1990 Ornament / Charles Carmel - C. 1915 4050	Closed	1990	25.00	25
1990 Tribute To Barney Illions 4001	Closed	1990	110.00	200

Tobin Fraley-American Carousel Collection V (Willitts) - T. Fraley

YEAR ISSUE	EDITION LIMIT	YEAR RETD.	ISSUE PRICE	*QUOTE U.S.$
1991 Carmel's Carousel Band Organ 4039	Closed	1990	60.00	60
1990 Carmel's Carousel Horses 4035	Closed	1990	90.00	90
1990 Carmel's Carousel Horses 4036	Closed	1990	90.00	90
1990 Carmel's Carousel Horses 4037	Closed	1990	90.00	90
1991 Carmel's Carousel Horses 4038	Closed	1990	90.00	90
1991 Charles Looff - C. 1908 4082	Closed	1991	70.00	125
1991 Charles Looff - C. 1908 4088	Closed	1991	50.00	125
1991 Charles Looff - C. 1908 4094	Closed	1991	90.00	150
1991 Charles Looff - C. 1911 4083	Closed	1991	70.00	70
1991 Charles Looff - C. 1911 4089	Closed	1991	50.00	50
1991 Charles Looff - C. 1911 4095	Closed	1991	90.00	90
1991 Charles Looff - C. 1912 4084	Closed	1991	70.00	70
1991 Charles Looff - C. 1912 4090	Closed	1991	50.00	50
1991 Charles Looff - C. 1914 4081	Closed	1991	70.00	125
1991 Charles Looff - C. 1914 4086	Closed	1991	70.00	150
1991 Charles Looff - C. 1914 4087	Closed	1991	50.00	75-125
1991 Charles Looff - C. 1914 4092	Closed	1991	50.00	95
1991 Charles Looff - C. 1914/Snowglobe 4107	Closed	1991	40.00	40
1991 Charles Looff - C. 1915 4085	Closed	1991	70.00	100-125
1991 Charles Looff - C. 1915 4091	Closed	1991	50.00	100
1991 Charles Looff/John Zalar - C. 1908-14 4080	Closed	1991	500.00	800-1000
1991 Charles Looff/John Zalar - C. 1908-14 4105	Closed	1991	200.00	300-450
1991 The Four Seasons - Autumn 4078	Closed	1991	140.00	170
1991 The Four Seasons - Spring 4076	Closed	1991	140.00	500-600
1991 The Four Seasons - Spring/50 Note Mus. 4104	Closed	1991	450.00	250
1991 The Four Seasons - Summer 4077	Closed	1991	140.00	300-400
1991 The Four Seasons - Winter 4075	Closed	1991	140.00	300-400
1991 Herschel-Spillman Co. - C. 1908-24 4059	Closed	1991	50.00	50
1991 Herschel-Spillman Co. - C. 1908-24 4062	Closed	1991	50.00	50
1991 Herschell-Spillman Co. - C. 1908-24 4065	Closed	1991	50.00	50
1991 Herschell-Spillman Co. - C. 1908-24 4068	Closed	1991	30.00	30
1991 Herschel-Spillman Co. - C. 1908-24 4072	Closed	1991	30.00	30
1991 Herschell-Spillman Co. - C. 1908-24 4060	Closed	1991	50.00	50
1991 Herschell-Spillman Co. - C. 1908-24 4061	Closed	1991	50.00	50
1991 Herschell-Spillman Co. - C. 1908-24 4063	Closed	1991	50.00	50
1991 Herschell-Spillman Co. - C. 1908-24 4064	Closed	1991	50.00	50
1991 Herschell-Spillman Co. - C. 1908-24 4066	Closed	1991	50.00	50
1991 Herschell-Spillman Co. - C. 1908-24 4067	Closed	1991	50.00	30
1991 Herschell-Spillman Co. - C. 1908-24 4069	Closed	1991	30.00	30
1991 Herschell-Spillman Co. - C. 1908-24 4070	Closed	1991	30.00	30
1991 Herschell-Spillman Co. - C. 1908-24 4071	Closed	1991	30.00	30
1991 Herschell-Spillman Co. - C. 1908-24 4073	Closed	1991	30.00	30
1991 Herschell-Spillman company - C. 1908-24 4074	Closed	1991	30.00	30

Tobin Fraley-American Carousel Collection VI (Willitts) - T. Fraley

YEAR ISSUE	EDITION LIMIT	YEAR RETD.	ISSUE PRICE	*QUOTE U.S.$
1992 Dentzel - C. 1895 4112	Closed	1992	70.00	70
1992 Dentzel - C. 1895 4116	Closed	1992	50.00	50
1992 Dentzel - C. 1905 4111	Closed	1992	70.00	70
1992 Dentzel - C. 1905 4115	Closed	1992	50.00	50
1992 The Four Elements - 4 Horse Carousel 4118	Closed	1992	500.00	500
1992 The Four Elements - Air 4117	Closed	1992	165.00	200
1992 The Four Elements - Earth 4121	Closed	1992	165.00	185
1992 The Four Elements - Fire 4119	Closed	1992	165.00	250-300
1992 The Four Elements - Water 4120	Closed	1992	165.00	200-300
1992 Ptc - C. 1918 4109	Closed	1992	70.00	70
1992 Ptc - C. 1918 4110	Closed	1992	70.00	70
1992 Ptc - C. 1918 4113	Closed	1992	50.00	50
1992 Ptc - C. 1918 4114	Closed	1992	50.00	50

Tobin Fraley-American Carousel Collection VII (Willitts) - T. Fraley

YEAR ISSUE	EDITION LIMIT	YEAR RETD.	ISSUE PRICE	*QUOTE U.S.$
1993 Am Apirit/Four Horse Carousel 4139	Closed	1993	250.00	250
1993 Am Spirit/Freedom 4136	Closed	1993	175.00	200-400
1993 Am Spirit/Mardi Gras 4135	Closed	1993	175.00	350-450
1993 Am Spirit/Mardi Gras-Snowglobe 4141	Closed	1993	55.00	100-125
1993 Am Spirit/Pathfinder 4138	Closed	1993	175.00	200-400
1993 Am Spirit/Wind Racer 4137	Closed	1993	175.00	300-400
1993 Carousels: The Myth	Closed	1993	25.00	25

Tobin Fraley-Great American Carousel Collection - T. Fraley

YEAR ISSUE	EDITION LIMIT	YEAR RETD.	ISSUE PRICE	*QUOTE U.S.$
1995 Am Spirit/Heartland 8620	4,500		115.00	115
1995 Am Spirit/Heartland 8624	4,500		125.00	125
1995 Am Spirit/Liberty-Lincoln 8621	4,500		115.00	115
1995 Am Spirit/Liberty/Lincoln 8625	4,500		125.00	125
1995 Am Spirit/Sage 8623	4,500		115.00	115
1995 Am Spirit/Sage 8627	4,500		125.00	125
1995 Am Spirit/Southern Bell 8622	4,500		115.00	115
1995 Am Spirit/Southern Bell 8626	4,500		125.00	125
1998 Birthday Carousel-Age1 11451	Open		39.00	39
1998 Birthday Carousel-Age2 11452	Open		39.00	39
1998 Birthday Carousel-Age3 11453	Open		39.00	39
1998 Birthday Carousel-Age4 11454	Open		39.00	39
1998 Birthday Carousel-Age5 11455	Open		39.00	39
1998 Birthday Carousel-Age6 11456	Open		39.00	39
1998 Birthday Carousel-Age7 11457	Open		39.00	39
1998 Birthday Carousel-Age8 11458	Open		39.00	39
1996 C.W. Parker - C. 1915 08646	4,500	1997	57.00	57
1996 Charles Carmel - C. 1912 08644	4,500		75.00	75
1996 Charles Carmel - C. 1915 08643	4,500		75.00	75
1996 Charles Looff - C. 1908 08638	2,500		140.00	140
1998 Horse 4" on Antimony base, set/4 11460	Open		60.00	60

*Quotes have been rounded up to nearest dollar

YEAR ISSUE	EDITION LIMIT	YEAR RETD.	ISSUE PRICE	*QUOTE U.S.$
1996 M.C. Illions - C. 1911 08642	4,500		110.00	110
1996 M.C. Illions - C. 1911 18641	4,500		115.00	115
1996 M.C. Illions - C. 1912 08647	4,500		57.00	57
1998 Musical 4", oval base set/3 11442	Open		111.00	111
1998 Musical 4", round base set/3 11445	Open		87.00	87
1996 Philadelphia Toboggan Co. - C. 1912 08637	2,500		140.00	140
1996 Philadelphia Toboggan Co. - C. 1914 08648	4,500	1997	57.00	57
1996 Philadelphia Toboggan Co. - C. 1919 08645	4,500		75.00	75
1998 Rocking Horse 4", set/4 11465	Open		72.00	72
1996 Stein & Goldstein - C. 1910 08639	4,500		115.00	115
1996 Stein & Goldstein - C. 1910 08640	4,500		110.00	110

Tobin Fraley-Hallmark Galleries - T. Fraley

YEAR ISSUE	EDITION LIMIT	YEAR RETD.	ISSUE PRICE	*QUOTE U.S.$
1991 C.W. Parker - C. 1922 QHG0005	Closed	1991	30.00	60
1991 C.W. Parker - C. 1922 QHG0013	Closed	1991	40.00	40
1991 Charles Carmel - C. 1914 QHG0008	Closed	1991	30.00	60
1991 Charles Carmel - C. 1914 QHG0016	Closed	1991	40.00	40
1991 Charles Looff - C. 1915 QHG0001	Closed	1991	50.00	50
1991 Charles Looff - C. 1915 QHG0006	Closed	1991	30.00	60
1991 Charles Looff - C. 1915 QHG0009	Closed	1991	60.00	60
1991 Charles Looff - C. 1915 QHG0014	Closed	1991	40.00	40
1992 Daniel Müller - C1910 QHG0021	1,200	1992	275.00	450
1991 Display Stand For 4 - 3.5 " Horses QHG0019	Closed	1991	40.00	80
1991 M.C. Illions & Sons - C. 1910 QHG0003	Closed	1991	50.00	50
1991 M.C. Illions & Sons - C. 1910 QHG0011	Closed	1991	60.00	60
1991 Medallion QHG0020	Closed	1991	45.00	45
1991 Philadelphia Toboggan Co. - C. 1910 QHG0007	Closed	1991	30.00	50
1991 Philadelphia Toboggan Co. - C. 1910 QHG0015	Closed	1991	40.00	40
1993 Philadelphia Toboggan Co. - C. 1914 QHG0028	Closed	1993	60.00	100
1993 Philadelphia Toboggan Co. - C. 1919 QHG0027	Closed	1993	60.00	80
1993 Philadelphia Toboggan Co. - C. 1924 QHG0025	Closed	1993	60.00	80
1993 Philadelphia Toboggan Co. - C. 1925 QHG0026	Closed	1993	60.00	80
1991 Philadelphia Toboggan Co. - C. 1928 QHG0002	Closed	1991	50.00	100
1991 Philadelphia Toboggan Co. - C. 1928 QHG0010	Closed	1991	60.00	150
1991 Playland Carousel/4 Horses QHG0017	Closed	1991	195.00	300
1991 Stein & Goldstein 1914 QHG0004	Closed	1991	50.00	50
1991 Stein & Goldstein 1914 QHG0012	Closed	1991	60.00	60

Glynda Turley Prints

Turley - G. Turley

YEAR ISSUE	EDITION LIMIT	YEAR RETD.	ISSUE PRICE	*QUOTE U.S.$
1995 Circle of Friends	4,800	1997	67.00	67
1995 The Courtyard II	4,800	1997	99.00	99
1995 Flowers For Mommy	4,800	1997	85.00	85
1994 Old Mill Stream	4,800	1997	64.00	64
1995 Past Times	4,800	1997	78.00	78
1995 Playing Hookie Again	4,800	1997	83.00	83
1995 Secret Garden II	4,800	1997	95.00	95

Goebel of North America

Charlot Byj Blondes - C. Byj

YEAR ISSUE	EDITION LIMIT	YEAR RETD.	ISSUE PRICE	*QUOTE U.S.$
1968 Bless Us All	Closed	1987	6.00	50-60
1968 A Child's Prayer	Closed	1987	6.00	36-60
1968 Evening Prayer	Closed	1986	8.00	65-90
1969 Her Shining Hour	Closed	1988	14.00	165-185
1969 Little Prayers Are Best	Closed	1987	12.00	70-90
1972 Love Bugs	Closed	1986	38.00	127-200
XX Love Bugs (music box)	Closed	1986	80.00	300-325
1968 Madonna of the Doves	Closed	1993	25.00	88-240
1968 Mother Embracing Child	Closed	N/A	12.00	50-190
1968 Rock-A-Bye-Baby	Closed	N/A	7.50	50-115
XX Rock-A-Bye-Baby (music box)	Closed	1985	50.00	250-275
1968 Sitting Pretty	Closed	1983	9.00	90-110
1968 Sleepy Head	Closed	1986	9.00	35-90
1968 Tender Shepherd	Closed	1974	8.00	350-500
1968 The Way To Pray	Closed	1988	8.50	75-90

Charlot Byj Redheads - C. Byj

YEAR ISSUE	EDITION LIMIT	YEAR RETD.	ISSUE PRICE	*QUOTE U.S.$
1982 1-2 Ski-Doo	Closed	1986	75.00	140-150
1985 All Gone	Closed	1988	42.00	75-80
1987 Almost There	Closed	1988	45.00	95
1987 Always Fit	Closed	1988	45.00	100-150
1968 Atta Boy	Closed	1984	6.50	45-125
1972 Baby Sitter	Closed	1983	28.00	55-175
1972 Bachelor Degree	Closed	1986	18.00	65-85
1975 Barbeque	Closed	1983	55.00	150-175
1985 Bedtime Boy	Closed	1987	26.00	90-100
1985 Bedtime Girl	Closed	1987	26.00	90-100
1975 Bird Watcher	Closed	1983	48.00	130-150
1971 Bongo Beat	Closed	1980	18.50	150-200
1975 Camera Shy	Closed	1983	48.00	150
1984 Captive Audience	Closed	1988	55.00	110-125
1968 Cheer Up	Closed	1988	8.00	85-95
1987 Come Along	Closed	1988	47.50	85-100
1970 Copper Topper	Closed	1986	10.00	62-95
1968 Daisies Won't Tell	Closed	1986	6.00	36-90
1983 A Damper on the Camper	Closed	1986	75.00	135-150
1983 Dating and Skating	Closed	N/A	60.00	126-163
1983 Dear Sirs	Closed	1988	40.00	125-135
1968 Dropping In	Closed	1988	6.00	75-95
1968 E-e-eek	Closed	1986	8.00	110-125
1985 Farm Friends	Closed	1988	46.00	75-120
1987 Figurine Collector	Closed	1988	64.00	200-250
1972 First Degree	Closed	1986	18.00	90-98
1968 Forbidden Fruit	Closed	1978	7.00	125
1975 Fore	Closed	1983	48.00	83-150
1983 Four Letter Word For Ouch	Closed	1988	40.00	75-110
1983 A Funny Face From Outer Space	Closed	1987	65.00	177-200
1968 Gangway	Closed	1986	8.50	51-104
1968 Good News	Closed	1988	6.00	31-85
1988 Greetings	Closed	1988	55.00	125-198
1968 Guess Who	Closed	1979	8.50	90-120
1983 Heads or Tails	Closed	1986	60.00	100-135
1968 The Kibitzer	Closed	1983	7.50	95-150
1975 Lazy Day	Closed	1986	55.00	160-200
1969 Let It Rain	Closed	1988	26.00	160-175
1968 Little Miss Coy	Closed	1988	6.00	37-85
1968 Little Prayers Are Best	Closed	1969	13.00	50-65
1969 Little Shopper	Closed	1978	13.00	96-150
1968 Lucky Day	Closed	1986	5.50	38-85
1984 Not Yet a Vet	Closed	1988	65.00	75-150
1983 Nothing Beats a Pizza	Closed	1988	55.00	100-175
1971 The Nurse	Closed	1988	13.00	75-175
1968 O'Hair For President	Closed	1983	6.00	75-85
1968 Off Key	Closed	1986	7.50	89-110
1984 Once Upon a Time	Closed	1988	55.00	85-135
1984 One Puff's Enough (Yech)	Closed	1988	55.00	90-125
1968 Oops	Closed	1988	8.00	120-125
1987 Please Wait	Closed	1988	47.50	75-90
1968 Plenty of Nothing	Closed	1986	5.50	33-90
1987 The Practice	Closed	1988	64.00	150-250
1968 Putting on the Dog	Closed	1986	9.00	80-125
1968 The Roving Eye	Closed	1986	6.00	41-90
1972 Say A-a-a-aah	Closed	1986	19.00	125-150
1982 Sea Breeze	Closed	1986	65.00	135-195
1988 Shall We Dance?	Closed	1988	72.50	75-125
1985 Sharing Secrets	Closed	1988	44.00	125
1968 Shear Nonsense	Closed	1986	10.00	85-135
1970 Skater's Waltz	Closed	1986	15.00	150
XX Skater's Waltz (Musical)	Closed	1986	70.00	250
1983 Something Tells Me	Closed	1987	40.00	75-100
1988 A Special Friend (Black Angel)	Closed	1988	55.00	75-100
1968 Spellbound	Closed	1986	12.00	135-150
1968 Spring Time	Closed	1983	7.50	98-125
1968 The Stolen Kiss	Closed	1978	13.00	75-150
1968 Strike	Closed	1986	6.00	36-85
1968 Super Service	Closed	1979	9.00	117-150
1985 Sweet Snack	Closed	1988	40.00	90-100
1971 Swinger	Closed	1983	15.00	85-150
1969 Trim Lass	Closed	1978	14.00	75-175
1971 Trouble Shooter (This Won't Hurt)	Closed	1986	13.00	46-95
1975 Wash Day	Closed	1986	55.00	125-200
1984 Yeah Team	Closed	1987	65.00	200-229
1968 A Young Man's Fancy	Closed	1988	10.00	90-150

Co-Boy - G. Skrobek

YEAR ISSUE	EDITION LIMIT	YEAR RETD.	ISSUE PRICE	*QUOTE U.S.$
1981 Al the Trumpet Player	Closed	N/A	45.00	90-120
1987 Bank-Pete the Pirate	Closed	N/A	80.00	125-150
1987 Bank-Utz the Money Bank	Closed	N/A	80.00	125-150
1981 Ben the Blacksmith	Closed	N/A	45.00	80-90
XX Bert the Soccer Player	Closed	N/A	Unkn.	90-120
1971 Bit the Bachelor	Closed	N/A	16.00	90-120
1972 Bob the Bookworm	Closed	N/A	20.00	90-100
1984 Brad the Clockmaker	Closed	N/A	75.00	250-275
1972 Brum the Lawyer	Closed	N/A	20.00	100-125
XX Candy the Baker's Delight	Closed	N/A	Unkn.	115-125
1980 Carl the Chef	Closed	N/A	49.00	85-90
1984 Chris the Shoemaker	Closed	N/A	45.00	100-120
1987 Chuck on His Pig	Closed	N/A	75.00	200-250
1984 Chuck the Chimney Sweep	Closed	N/A	45.00	125-150
1987 Clock-Conny the Watchman	Closed	N/A	125.00	300-350
1987 Clock-Sepp and the Beer Keg	Closed	N/A	125.00	200-250
1972 Co-Boy Plaque (English)	Closed	N/A	20.00	120-125
1972 Co-Boy Plaque (German)	Closed	N/A	N/A	250-400
XX Conny the Night Watchman	Closed	N/A	Unkn.	100-125
1980 Doc the Doctor	Closed	N/A	49.00	125-130
XX Ed the Wine Cellar Steward	Closed	N/A	Unkn.	100-120
1984 Felix the Baker	Closed	N/A	45.00	90-100
1971 Fips the Foxy Fisherman	Closed	N/A	16.00	90-100
1971 Fritz the Happy Boozer	Closed	N/A	16.00	120-125
1981 George the Gourmand	Closed	N/A	45.00	95-125
1980 Gerd the Diver	Closed	N/A	49.00	125
1978 Gil the Goalie	Closed	N/A	34.00	90-120
1981 Greg the Gourmet	Closed	N/A	45.00	90-100
1981 Greta the Happy Housewife	Closed	N/A	45.00	80-125
1980 Herb the Horseman	Closed	N/A	49.00	95-150
1984 Herman the Butcher	Closed	N/A	45.00	90-95
1984 Homer the Driver	Closed	N/A	45.00	120-140
XX Jack the Village Pharmacist	Closed	N/A	Unkn.	120-125
XX Jim the Bowler	Closed	N/A	Unkn.	95-120
XX John the Hawkeye Hunter	Closed	N/A	Unkn.	90-95
1972 Kuni the Painter	Closed	N/A	20.00	100-120
XX Mark-Safety First	Closed	N/A	Unkn.	90-100
1984 Marthe the Nurse	Closed	N/A	45.00	80-150
XX Max the Boxing Champ	Closed	N/A	Unkn.	90-120
1971 Mike the Jam Maker	Closed	N/A	16.00	90-125
1980 Monty the Mountain Climber	Closed	N/A	49.00	90-120
1981 Nick the Nightclub Singer	Closed	N/A	45.00	95-120
1981 Niels the Strummer	Closed	N/A	45.00	100-120
1978 Pat the Pitcher	Closed	N/A	34.00	90-120
1984 Paul the Dentist	Closed	N/A	45.00	125-150
1981 Peter the Accordionist	Closed	N/A	45.00	95-120
XX Petri the Village Angler	Closed	N/A	Unkn.	95-100
1971 Plum the Pastry Chef	Closed	N/A	16.00	120-125
1972 Porz the Mushroom Muncher	Closed	N/A	20.00	80-100
1984 Rick the Fireman	Closed	N/A	45.00	150-175
1971 Robby the Vegetarian	Closed	N/A	16.00	90-95
1984 Rudy the World Traveler	Closed	N/A	45.00	90-125
1971 Sam the Gourmet	Closed	N/A	16.00	110-120
1972 Sepp the Beer Buddy	Closed	N/A	20.00	85-90
1984 Sid the Vintner	Closed	N/A	45.00	100-120
1980 Ted the Tennis Player	Closed	N/A	49.00	90-95
1971 Tom the Honey Lover	Closed	N/A	16.00	90-100
1978 Tommy Touchdown	Closed	N/A	34.00	90-120
XX Toni the Skier	Closed	N/A	Unkn.	100-125
1972 Utz the Banker	Closed	N/A	20.00	115-120
1981 Walter the Jogger	Closed	N/A	45.00	85-90
1971 Wim the Court Supplier	Closed	N/A	16.00	90-120

Co-Boys-Culinary - Welling/Skrobek

YEAR ISSUE	EDITION LIMIT	YEAR RETD.	ISSUE PRICE	*QUOTE U.S.$
1994 Mike the Jam Maker 301050	Closed	N/A	25.00	30
1994 Plum the Sweets Maker 301052	Closed	N/A	25.00	30
1994 Robby the Vegetarian 301054	Closed	N/A	25.00	30
1994 Sepp the Drunkard 301051	Closed	N/A	25.00	30
1994 Tom the Sweet Tooth 301053	Closed	N/A	25.00	30

Co-Boys-Professionals - Welling/Skrobek

YEAR ISSUE	EDITION LIMIT	YEAR RETD.	ISSUE PRICE	*QUOTE U.S.$
1994 Brum the Lawyer 301060	Closed	N/A	25.00	30
1994 Conny the Nightwatchman 301062	Closed	N/A	25.00	30
1994 Doc the Doctor 301064	Closed	N/A	25.00	30
1994 John the Hunter 301063	Closed	N/A	25.00	30
1994 Utz the Banker 301061	Closed	N/A	25.00	30

Co-Boys-Sports - Welling/Skrobek

YEAR ISSUE	EDITION LIMIT	YEAR RETD.	ISSUE PRICE	*QUOTE U.S.$
1994 Bert the Soccer Player 301059	Closed	N/A	25.00	30
1994 Jim the Bowler 301057	Closed	N/A	25.00	30
1994 Petri the Fisherman 301055	Closed	N/A	25.00	30
1994 Ted the Tennis Player 301058	Closed	N/A	25.00	30
1994 Toni the Skier 301056	Closed	N/A	25.00	30

Goebel Figurines - N. Rockwell

YEAR ISSUE	EDITION LIMIT	YEAR RETD.	ISSUE PRICE	*QUOTE U.S.$
1963 Advertising Plaque 218	Closed	N/A	Unkn.	750-1000
1963 Boyhood Dreams (Adventurers between Adventures) 202	Closed	N/A	12.00	350-400
1963 Buttercup Test (Beguiling Buttercup) 214	Closed	N/A	10.00	350-400
1963 First Love (A Scholarly Pace) 215	Closed	N/A	30.00	350-400
1963 His First Smoke 208	Closed	N/A	9.00	350-400
1963 Home Cure 211	Closed	N/A	16.00	350-400
1963 Little Veterinarian (Mysterious Malady) 201	Closed	N/A	15.00	350-400
1963 Mother's Helper (Pride of Parenthood) 203	Closed	N/A	15.00	350-400
1963 My New Pal (A Boy Meets His Dog) 204	Closed	N/A	12.00	350-400
1963 Patient Anglers (Fisherman's Paradise) 217	Closed	N/A	18.00	350-400
1963 She Loves Me (Day Dreamer) 213	Closed	N/A	8.00	350-400
1963 Timely Assistance (Love Aid) 212	Closed	N/A	16.00	350-400

Looney Tunes Spotlight Collection - Goebel

YEAR ISSUE	EDITION LIMIT	YEAR RETD.	ISSUE PRICE	*QUOTE U.S.$
1998 Accelleratti Incredibus	7,598		175.00	175
1997 And to All a Good Bite	15,098		75.00	75
1997 Bad Hare Day	10,098		110.00	110
1997 Bad Ol' Puddy Tat	5,098		400.00	400
1998 Carnivorous Vulgaris	7,598		175.00	175
1998 Dis Guy's a Pushover	10,098		175.00	175
1997 Duck Dodgers in the 24 1/2 TH Century ("Planet X")	10,098		80.00	80
1997 Gift Wrapped ("Christmas Morning")	10,098		80.00	80
1997 Hare-Do	10,098		80.00	80
1997 In the Name of Mars	10,098		110.00	110
1997 In the Name of the Earth	10,098		110.00	110
1997 Isn't She Wovewe	10,098		185.00	185
1997 Kiss the Little Birdie	10,098		100.00	100
1997 Looney Tunes Latest News-M.I. Hummel	7,598		320.00	320
1998 Michigan Rag	10,098		160.00	160
1997 Mine, Mine, Mine	7,598		245.00	245
1998 Monster Manicure	10,098		190.00	190
1997 Rabbit of Seville ("The Barbershop")	10,098		85.00	85
1998 Snowbird (Premier Edition)	Open		48.00	48
1998 That's All Folks!™ (75th Anniversary)	Open		48.00	48
1997 What a Present!	10,098		70.00	70
1997 Zie Broken Heart of Love	10,098		150.00	150

Miniatures-Americana Series - R. Olszewski

YEAR ISSUE	EDITION LIMIT	YEAR RETD.	ISSUE PRICE	*QUOTE U.S.$
1982 American Bald Eagle 661-B	Closed	1989	45.00	175-285
1986 Americana Display 951-D	Closed	1995	80.00	80-105
1989 Blacksmith 667-P	Closed	1989	55.00	95-150
1986 Carrousel Ride 665-B	Closed	1995	45.00	59-150
1985 Central Park Sunday 664-B	Closed	1995	45.00	95-125
1984 Eyes on the Horizon 663-B	Closed	1995	45.00	125-130
1981 The Plainsman 660-B	Closed	1989	45.00	175-295
1983 She Sounds the Deep 662-B	Closed	1995	45.00	125-150
1987 To The Bandstand 666-B	Closed	1995	45.00	75-125

Miniatures-Bob Timberlake Signature Series - B. Timberlake

YEAR ISSUE	EDITION LIMIT	YEAR RETD.	ISSUE PRICE	*QUOTE U.S.$
1996 Autumn Afternoons Vignette 818061	500		490.00	490

Miniatures-Children's Series - R. Olszewski

YEAR ISSUE	EDITION LIMIT	YEAR RETD.	ISSUE PRICE	*QUOTE U.S.$
1983 Backyard Frolic 633-P	Closed	1995	65.00	100-250

*Quotes have been rounded up to nearest dollar

YEAR ISSUE	EDITION LIMIT	YEAR RETD.	ISSUE PRICE	*QUOTE U.S.$
1980 Blumenkinder-Courting 630-P	Closed	1989	55.00	200-400
1990 Building Blocks Castle (lg.) 968-D	Closed	1995	75.00	100
1987 Carrousel Days (plain base) 637-P	Closed	1989	85.00	815-995
1987 Carrousel Days 637-P	Closed	1989	85.00	250-295
1988 Children's Display (small)	Closed	1995	45.00	60-65
1989 Clowning Around 636-P (new style)	Closed	1995	85.00	175-195
1986 Clowning Around 636-P (old style)	Closed	N/A	85.00	200-250
1984 Grandpa 634-P	Closed	1995	75.00	100-125
1988 Little Ballerina 638-P	Closed	1995	85.00	125-175
1982 Out and About 632-P	Closed	1989	85.00	375-385
1985 Snow Holiday 635-P	Closed	1995	75.00	100-245
1981 Summer Days 631-P	Closed	1989	65.00	225-375

Miniatures-Classic Clocks - Larsen

YEAR ISSUE	EDITION LIMIT	YEAR RETD.	ISSUE PRICE	*QUOTE U.S.$
1995 Alexis 818040	2,500		200.00	200
1995 Blinking Admiral 818042	2,500		200.00	200
1995 Play 818041	2,500		250.00	250

Miniatures-DeGrazia - R. Olszewski

YEAR ISSUE	EDITION LIMIT	YEAR RETD.	ISSUE PRICE	*QUOTE U.S.$
1988 Adobe Display 948D	Closed	N/A	45.00	60-90
1990 Adobe Hacienda (large) Display 958-D	Closed	N/A	85.00	95-150
1989 Beautiful Burden 554-P	Closed	N/A	110.00	130-200
1990 Chapel Display 971-D	Closed	N/A	95.00	100-120
1986 Festival of Lights 507-P	Closed	N/A	85.00	225-300
1985 Flower Boy 502-P	Closed	N/A	85.00	110-200
1985 Flower Girl 501-P	Closed	N/A	85.00	110-200
1986 Little Madonna 552-P	Closed	N/A	93.00	150-225
1989 Merry Little Indian 508-P (new style)	Closed	N/A	110.00	100-300
1987 Merry Little Indian 508-P (old style)	Closed	N/A	95.00	175-200
1991 My Beautiful Rocking Horse 555-P	Closed	N/A	110.00	150-175
1985 My First Horse 503-P	Closed	N/A	85.00	110-150
1986 Pima Drummer Boy 506-P	Closed	N/A	85.00	250-300
1985 Sunflower Boy 551- P	Closed	N/A	93.00	135-195
1985 White Dove 504-P	Closed	N/A	80.00	110-125
1985 Wondering 505-P	Closed	N/A	93.00	125-175

Miniatures-Disney-Cinderella - Disney

YEAR ISSUE	EDITION LIMIT	YEAR RETD.	ISSUE PRICE	*QUOTE U.S.$
1991 Anastasia 172-P	Suspd.		85.00	100-175
1991 Cinderella 176-P	Suspd.		85.00	125-195
1991 Cinderella's Coach Display 978-D	Suspd.		95.00	115-180
1991 Cinderella's Dream Castle 976-D	Suspd.		95.00	120-200
1991 Drizella 174-P	Suspd.		85.00	100-175
1991 Fairy Godmother 180-P	Suspd.		85.00	100-175
1991 Footman 181-P	Suspd.		85.00	100-175
1991 Gus 177-P	Suspd.		80.00	90-150
1991 Jaq 173-P	Suspd.		80.00	90-145
1991 Lucifer 175-P	Suspd.		80.00	90-165
1991 Prince Charming 179-P	Suspd.		85.00	100-200
1991 Stepmother 178-P	Suspd.		85.00	100-165

Miniatures-Disney-Peter Pan - Disney

YEAR ISSUE	EDITION LIMIT	YEAR RETD.	ISSUE PRICE	*QUOTE U.S.$
1994 Captain Hook 188-P	Suspd.		160.00	160-225
1992 John 186-P	Suspd.		90.00	110-180
1994 Lost Boy-Fox 191-P	Suspd.		130.00	130-225
1994 Lost Boy-Rabbit 192-P	Suspd.		130.00	130-225
1992 Michael 187-P	Suspd.		90.00	110-165
1992 Nana 189-P	Suspd.		95.00	110-165
1994 Neverland Display 997-D	Suspd.		150.00	150-215
1992 Peter Pan 184-P	Suspd.		90.00	125-215
1992 Peter Pan's London 986-D	Suspd.		125.00	135-215
1994 Smee 190-P	Suspd.		140.00	140-195
1992 Wendy 185-P	Suspd.		90.00	110-195

Miniatures-Disney-Pinocchio - Disney

YEAR ISSUE	EDITION LIMIT	YEAR RETD.	ISSUE PRICE	*QUOTE U.S.$
1991 Blue Fairy 693-P	Suspd.		95.00	110-120
1990 Geppetto's Toy Shop Display 965-D	Suspd.		95.00	120-200
1990 Geppetto/Figaro 682-P	Suspd.		90.00	110-180
1990 Gideon 683-P	Suspd.		75.00	100-165
1990 J. Worthington Foulfellow 684-P	Suspd.		95.00	115-195
1990 Jiminy Cricket 685-P	Suspd.		75.00	118-185
1991 Little Street Lamp Display 964-D	Suspd.		65.00	80-180
1992 Monstro The Whale 985-D	Suspd.		120.00	135-270
1990 Pinocchio 686-P	Suspd.		75.00	110-205
1991 Stromboli 694-P	Suspd.		95.00	120-185
1991 Stromboli's Street Wagon 979-D	Suspd.		105.00	125-210

Miniatures-Disney-Snow White - Disney

YEAR ISSUE	EDITION LIMIT	YEAR RETD.	ISSUE PRICE	*QUOTE U.S.$
1987 Bashful 165-P	Suspd.		60.00	95-116
1991 Castle Courtyard Display 981-D	Suspd.		105.00	125-155
1987 Cozy Cottage Display 941-D	Suspd.		35.00	138-300
1987 Doc 162-P	Suspd.		60.00	95-116
1987 Dopey 167-P	Suspd.		60.00	95-110
1987 Grumpy 166-P	Suspd.		60.00	95-100
1987 Happy 164-P	Suspd.		60.00	95-110
1988 House In The Woods Display 944-D	Suspd.		60.00	110-125
1992 Path In The Woods 996-D	Suspd.		140.00	150-225
1987 Sleepy 163-P	Suspd.		60.00	95-110
1987 Sneezy 161-P	Suspd.		60.00	95-100
1987 Snow White 168-P	Suspd.		60.00	120-154
1990 Snow White's Prince 170-P	Suspd.		80.00	115-130
1992 Snow White's Queen 182-P	Suspd.		100.00	115-125
1992 Snow White's Witch 183-P	Suspd.		100.00	115-175
1990 The Wishing Well Display 969-D	Suspd.		65.00	85-100

Miniatures-Disneyana Convention - P. Larsen

YEAR ISSUE	EDITION LIMIT	YEAR RETD.	ISSUE PRICE	*QUOTE U.S.$
1994 Mickey Self Portrait	500	1994	295.00	847-1235
1995 Barbershop Quartet	750	1995	325.00	275-650
1996 Puppy Love	750	1996	325.00	325-650
1997 The Perfect Disguise	500	1997	415.00	380-525

Miniatures-Historical Series - R. Olszewski

YEAR ISSUE	EDITION LIMIT	YEAR RETD.	ISSUE PRICE	*QUOTE U.S.$
1985 Capodimonte 600-P (new style)	Closed	N/A	90.00	200-425
1980 Capodimonte 600-P (old style)	Closed	1987	90.00	325-355
1983 The Cherry Pickers 602-P	Closed	N/A	85.00	145-295
1990 English Country Garden 970-D	Closed	N/A	85.00	110
1989 Farmer w/Doves 607-P	Closed	N/A	85.00	115-125
1985 Floral Bouquet Pompadour 604-P	Closed	N/A	85.00	125-150
1990 Gentleman Fox Hunt 616-P	Closed	N/A	145.00	200-225
1988 Historical Display 943-D	Closed	1996	45.00	60-65
1981 Masquerade-St. Petersburg 601-P	Closed	1989	65.00	295-350
1987 Meissen Parrot 605-P	Closed	1996	85.00	125-150
1988 Minton Rooster 606-P	7,500		85.00	100
1984 Moor With Spanish Horse 603-P	Closed	1996	85.00	150-300
1992 Poultry Seller 608-G	1,500		200.00	200

Miniatures-Jack & The Beanstalk - R. Olszewski

YEAR ISSUE	EDITION LIMIT	YEAR RETD.	ISSUE PRICE	*QUOTE U.S.$
1994 Beanseller 742-P	5,000	N/A	200.00	200-225
1994 Jack & The Beanstalk Display 999-D	5,000	N/A	225.00	225-260
1994 Jack and the Cow 743-P	5,000	N/A	180.00	180-225
1994 Jack's Mom 741-P	5,000	N/A	145.00	145-180
1994 Set of 4	5,000	N/A	750.00	975

Miniatures-Mickey Mouse - Disney

YEAR ISSUE	EDITION LIMIT	YEAR RETD.	ISSUE PRICE	*QUOTE U.S.$
1990 Fantasia Living Brooms 972-D	Suspd.		85.00	125-325
1990 The Sorcerer's Apprentice 171-P	Suspd.		80.00	175-295
1990 Set	Suspd.		165.00	500-620

Miniatures-Nativity Collection - R. Olszewski

YEAR ISSUE	EDITION LIMIT	YEAR RETD.	ISSUE PRICE	*QUOTE U.S.$
1992 3 Kings Display 987-D	Closed	1996	85.00	105-125
1992 Balthazar 405-P	Closed	1996	135.00	200
1994 Camel & Tender 819292	Closed	1996	380.00	375-395
1992 Caspar 406-P	Closed	1996	135.00	150-200
1994 Final Nativity Display 991-D	Closed	1996	260.00	275
1994 Guardian Angel 407-P	Closed	1996	200.00	225-295
1991 Holy Family Display 982-D	Closed	1996	85.00	95-100
1991 Joseph 401-P	Closed	1996	95.00	130-150
1991 Joyful Cherubs 403-P	Closed	1996	130.00	165-185
1992 Melchoir 404-P	Closed	1996	135.00	200
1991 Mother/Child 440-P	Closed	1996	120.00	155-165
1994 Sheep & Shepherd 819290	Closed	1996	230.00	240-295
1991 The Stable Donkey 402-P	Closed	1996	95.00	125-150

Miniatures-Night Before Christmas (1st Edition) - R. Olszewski

YEAR ISSUE	EDITION LIMIT	YEAR RETD.	ISSUE PRICE	*QUOTE U.S.$
1990 Eight Tiny Reindeer 691-P	5,000	N/A	110.00	110-135
1990 Mama & Papa 692-P	5,000	N/A	110.00	110-140
1990 St. Nicholas 690-P	5,000	N/A	95.00	95-125
1990 Sugar Plum Boy 687-P	5,000	N/A	70.00	70-100
1990 Sugar Plum Girl 689-P	5,000	N/A	70.00	70-100
1991 Up To The Housetop 966-D	5,000	N/A	95.00	110-115
1990 Yule Tree 688-P	5,000	N/A	90.00	110-160

Miniatures-Oriental Series - R. Olszewski

YEAR ISSUE	EDITION LIMIT	YEAR RETD.	ISSUE PRICE	*QUOTE U.S.$
1986 The Blind Men and the Elephant 643-P	Closed	N/A	70.00	150-195
1990 Chinese Temple Lion 646-P	Suspd.		90.00	135-150
1987 Chinese Water Dragon 644-P	Closed	N/A	70.00	150-195
1990 Empress' Garden Display 967-D	Suspd.		95.00	130-135
1982 The Geisha 641-P	Closed	N/A	65.00	125-225
1984 Kuan Yin 640-W (new style)	Closed	N/A	45.00	125-275
1980 Kuan Yin 640-W (old style)	Closed	1992	40.00	155-295
1987 Oriental Display (small) 945-D	Closed	N/A	45.00	70
1985 Tang Horse 642-P	Closed	N/A	65.00	95-175
1989 Tiger Hunt 645-P	Closed	N/A	85.00	105-125

Miniatures-Pendants - R. Olszewski

YEAR ISSUE	EDITION LIMIT	YEAR RETD.	ISSUE PRICE	*QUOTE U.S.$
1986 Camper Bialosky 151-P	Closed	1988	95.00	235-375
1991 Chrysanthemum Pendant 222-P	Closed	1996	135.00	155
1991 Daffodil Pendant 221-P	Closed	1996	135.00	155
1990 Hummingbird 697-P	Closed	1996	125.00	155-175
1988 Mickey Mouse 169-P	5,000	1989	92.00	265-300
1991 Poinsettia Pendant 223-P	Closed	1996	135.00	155
1991 Rose Pendant 220-P	Closed	1996	135.00	155

Miniatures-Portrait of America/Saturday Evening Post - N. Rockwell

YEAR ISSUE	EDITION LIMIT	YEAR RETD.	ISSUE PRICE	*QUOTE U.S.$
1989 Bottom Drawer 366-P	7,500	1995	85.00	85-95
1988 Bottom of the Sixth 365-P	Closed	1996	85.00	85-195
1988 Check-Up 363-P	Closed	1996	85.00	85-125
1988 The Doctor and the Doll 361-P	Closed	1996	85.00	100-200
1991 Home Coming Vignette-Soldier/Mother 990-D	2,000	1995	190.00	200-300
1988 Marbles Champion (Pewter) 362-P	Closed	1995	85.00	85-125
1988 No Swimming (Pewter) 360-P	Closed	1995	85.00	85-125
1988 Rockwell Display (Pewter) 952-D	Closed	1995	80.00	100-140
1988 Triple Self-Portrait (Pewter) 364-P	Closed	1996	85.00	175-275

Miniatures-Precious Moments Series I - Goebel

YEAR ISSUE	EDITION LIMIT	YEAR RETD.	ISSUE PRICE	*QUOTE U.S.$
1995 Fields of Friendship-Diorama (display)	Open		135.00	135
1995 God Loveth a Cheerful Giver	Open		70.00	70
1995 His Burden is Light	Open		70.00	70
1995 I'm Sending You a White Christmas	5,000		100.00	100
1995 Love Is Kind	Open		70.00	70
1995 Love One Another	Open		70.00	70
1995 Make a Joyful Noise	Open		70.00	70
1995 Praise the Lord Anyhow	Open		70.00	70
1995 Prayer Changes Things	Open		70.00	70

Miniatures-Precious Moments Series II - Goebel

YEAR ISSUE	EDITION LIMIT	YEAR RETD.	ISSUE PRICE	*QUOTE U.S.$
1996 Heart & Home-Diorama (display)	Open		150.00	150
1996 Jesus is the Answer	Open		70.00	70
1996 Jesus is the Light	Open		70.00	70
1996 Jesus Loves Me (boy)	Open		70.00	70
1996 Jesus Loves Me (girl)	Open		70.00	70
1996 Merry Christmas Deer	5,000		100.00	100
1996 O, How I Love Jesus	Open		70.00	70
1996 Smile, God Loves You	Open		70.00	70
1996 Unto Us A Child is born	Open		70.00	70

Miniatures-Precious Moments Series III - Goebel

YEAR ISSUE	EDITION LIMIT	YEAR RETD.	ISSUE PRICE	*QUOTE U.S.$
1997 Come Let Us Adore Him Cameo	Open		70.00	70
1997 God Understands Cameo	Open		70.00	70
1997 He Careth For You Cameo	Open		70.00	70
1997 He Leadeth Me Cameo	Open		70.00	70
1997 Jesus is Born Cameo	Open		70.00	70
1997 Love Lifted Me Cameo	Open		70.00	70
1997 Prayers of Peace Diorama	Open		150.00	150
1997 Process Stick: God Loveth A Cheerful Giver	Open		200.00	200
1997 Tell Me The Story of Jesus	5,000		100.00	100
1997 We Have Seen His Star Cameo	Open		70.00	70

Miniatures-Special Release-Alice in Wonderland - R. Olszewski

YEAR ISSUE	EDITION LIMIT	YEAR RETD.	ISSUE PRICE	*QUOTE U.S.$
1982 Alice In the Garden 670-P	Closed	1982	60.00	625-835
1984 The Cheshire Cat 672-P	Closed	1984	75.00	395-550
1983 Down the Rabbit Hole 671-P	Closed	1983	75.00	405-540

Miniatures-Special Release-Wizard of Oz - R. Olszewski

YEAR ISSUE	EDITION LIMIT	YEAR RETD.	ISSUE PRICE	*QUOTE U.S.$
1986 The Cowardly Lion 675-P	Closed	1987	85.00	285-344
1992 Dorothy/Glinda 695-P	Closed	1995	135.00	150
1992 Good-Bye to Oz Display 980-D	Closed	1996	110.00	175-315
1988 The Munchkins 677-P	Closed	1995	85.00	125-140
1987 Oz Display 942-D	Closed	1994	45.00	500-650
1984 Scarecrow 673-P	Closed	1985	75.00	313-455
1985 Tinman 674-P	Closed	1986	80.00	250-355
1987 The Wicked Witch 676-P	Closed	1995	85.00	88-175

Miniatures-Special Releases - R. Olszewski

YEAR ISSUE	EDITION LIMIT	YEAR RETD.	ISSUE PRICE	*QUOTE U.S.$
1994 Dresden Timepiece 450-P	750	N/A	1250.00	1250-1300
1991 Portrait Of The Artist (convention) 658-P	Closed	1991	195.00	525-600
1991 Portrait Of The Artist (promotion) 658-P	Closed	N/A	195.00	210-225
1992 Summer Days Collector Plaque 659-P	Closed	N/A	130.00	160-165

Miniatures-The American Frontier Collection - Various

YEAR ISSUE	EDITION LIMIT	YEAR RETD.	ISSUE PRICE	*QUOTE U.S.$
1987 American Frontier Museum Display 947-D - R. Olszewski	Closed	N/A	80.00	100-115
1987 The Bronco Buster 350-B - Remington	Closed	N/A	80.00	110-150
1987 Eight Count 310-B - Pounder	Closed	N/A	75.00	75-100
1987 The End of the Trail 340-B - Frazier	Closed	N/A	80.00	75-125
1987 The First Ride 330-B - Rogers	Closed	N/A	85.00	75-125
1987 Grizzly's Last Stand 320-B - Jonas	Closed	N/A	65.00	75-100
1987 Indian Scout and Buffalo 300-B - Bonheur	Closed	N/A	95.00	100-200

Miniatures-Three Little Pigs - R. Olszewski

YEAR ISSUE	EDITION LIMIT	YEAR RETD.	ISSUE PRICE	*QUOTE U.S.$
1991 The Hungry Wolf 681-P	7,500	N/A	80.00	80-110
1991 Little Bricks Pig 680-P	7,500	N/A	75.00	80-110
1989 Little Sticks Pig 678-P	7,500	N/A	75.00	80-110
1990 Little Straw Pig 679-P	7,500	N/A	75.00	80-110
1991 Three Little Pigs House 956-D	7,500	N/A	50.00	75-130

Miniatures-Wildlife Series - R. Olszewski

YEAR ISSUE	EDITION LIMIT	YEAR RETD.	ISSUE PRICE	*QUOTE U.S.$
1985 American Goldfinch 625-P	Closed	N/A	65.00	120-125
1986 Autumn Blue Jay 626-P	Closed	N/A	65.00	135-200
1992 Autumn Blue Jay 626-P (Archive release)	Closed	N/A	125.00	125-140
1980 Chipping Sparrow 620-P	Closed	N/A	55.00	175-450
1987 Country Display (small) 940-D	Closed	N/A	45.00	70
1990 Country Landscape (large) 957-D	Closed	N/A	85.00	115
1989 Hooded Oriole 629-P	Closed	N/A	80.00	125-175
1990 Hummingbird 696-P	Closed	N/A	85.00	175-200
1987 Mallard Duck 627-P	Closed	N/A	75.00	150-185
1981 Owl-Daylight Encounter 621-P	Closed	N/A	65.00	185-325
1983 Red-Winged Blackbird 623-P	Closed	N/A	65.00	150-175
1988 Spring Robin 628-P	Closed	N/A	75.00	125-195
1982 Western Bluebird 622-P	Closed	N/A	65.00	125-195
1984 Winter Cardinal 624-P	Closed	N/A	65.00	150-295

Miniatures-Winter Lights - Norrgard

YEAR ISSUE	EDITION LIMIT	YEAR RETD.	ISSUE PRICE	*QUOTE U.S.$
1995 Once Upon a Winter Day	Closed	1996	275.00	275

Miniatures-Women's Series - R. Olszewski

YEAR ISSUE	EDITION LIMIT	YEAR RETD.	ISSUE PRICE	*QUOTE U.S.$
1980 Dresden Dancer 610-P	Closed	1989	55.00	425-550
1985 The Hunt With Hounds (new style) 611-P	Closed	N/A	75.00	130-225
1981 The Hunt With Hounds (old style) 611-P	Closed	1984	75.00	275-425
1986 I Do 615-P	Closed	N/A	85.00	250-300
1983 On The Avenue 613-P	Closed	1995	65.00	175-195
1982 Precious Years 612-P	Closed	N/A	65.00	170-320
1984 Roses 614-P	Closed	1995	65.00	80-150
1989 Women's Display (small) 950-D	Closed	1995	40.00	65-115

Goebel/M.I. Hummel

M.I. Hummel Collectors Club Exclusives - M.I. Hummel, unless otherwise noted

YEAR ISSUE	EDITION LIMIT	YEAR RETD.	ISSUE PRICE	*QUOTE U.S.$
1977 Valentine Gift 387	Closed	N/A	45.00	325-462
1978 Smiling Through Plaque 690	Closed	N/A	50.00	81-225
1979 Bust of Sister-M.I.Hummel HU-3 - G. Skrobek	Closed	N/A	75.00	149-350
1980 Valentine Joy 399	Closed	N/A	95.00	149-425
1981 Daisies Don't Tell 380	Closed	N/A	80.00	130-425
1982 It's Cold 421	Closed	N/A	80.00	149-425
1983 What Now? 422	Closed	N/A	90.00	140-425

*Quotes have been rounded up to nearest dollar

YEAR ISSUE	EDITION LIMIT	YEAR RETD.	ISSUE PRICE	*QUOTE U.S.$
1983 Valentine Gift Mini Pendant 248-P - R. Olszewski	Closed	N/A	85.00	176-275
1984 Coffee Break 409	Closed	N/A	90.00	125-300
1985 Smiling Through 408/0	Closed	N/A	125.00	190-375
1986 Birthday Candle 440	Closed	N/A	95.00	139-350
1986 What Now? Mini Pendant 249-P - R. Olszewski	Closed	N/A	125.00	156-350
1987 Morning Concert 447	Closed	N/A	98.00	137-325
1987 Little Cocopah Indian Girl - T. DeGrazia	Closed	N/A	140.00	350-620
1988 The Surprise 431	Closed	N/A	125.00	137-350
1989 Mickey and Minnie - H. Fischer	Closed	N/A	275.00	500-950
1989 Hello World 429	Closed	N/A	130.00	157-275
1990 I Wonder 486	Closed	N/A	140.00	143-300
1991 Gift From A Friend 485	Closed	N/A	160.00	125-175
1991 Miniature Morning Concert w/ Display 269-P - R. Olszewski	Closed	N/A	175.00	150-325
1992 My Wish Is Small 463/0	Closed	N/A	170.00	163-295
1992 Cheeky Fellow 554	Closed	N/A	120.00	104-150
1993 I Didn't Do It 626	Closed	1995	175.00	141-234
1993 Sweet As Can Be 541	Closed	1995	125.00	113-150
1994 Little Visitor 563/0	Closed	1996	180.00	142-215
1994 Little Troubadour 558	Closed	1996	130.00	98-160
1994 At Grandpa's 621	10,000	1996	1300.00	1300
1994 Miniature Honey Lover Pendant 247-P	Closed	1996	165.00	195-250
1995 Country Suitor 760	Closed	1997	195.00	156-195
1995 Strum Along 557	Closed	1997	135.00	110-135
1995 A Story From Grandma 620	10,000	1996	1300.00	1200-1300
1996 Valentine Gift Plaque 717	Closed	1996	250.00	250
1996 What's New 418	Closed	1997	310.00	300-310
1996 Celebrate with Song 790	Closed	1998	295.00	250-295
1996 One, Two, Three 555	Closed	1998	145.00	116-145
1997 What's That? 488	5/99		150.00	150
1997 Playful Blessing 658	5/99		260.00	260

Special Edition Anniversary Figurines For 5/10/15/20 Year Membership - M.I. Hummel

YEAR ISSUE	EDITION LIMIT	YEAR RETD.	ISSUE PRICE	*QUOTE U.S.$
1990 Flower Girl 548 (5 year)	Open		105.00	140
1990 The Little Pair 449 (10 year)	Open		170.00	225
1991 Honey Lover 312 (15 year)	Open		190.00	235
1996 Behave 339 (20 year)	Open		350.00	350

M.I. Hummel 60th Anniversary Figurines - M.I. Hummel

YEAR ISSUE	EDITION LIMIT	YEAR RETD.	ISSUE PRICE	*QUOTE U.S.$
1998 Heavenly Protection	Open		495.00	495
1998 Angel Serenade w/Lamb	Open		245.00	245
1998 Brother	Open		230.00	230
1998 For Father	Open		240.00	240
1998 Happiness	Open		150.00	150
1998 Little Cellist	Open		240.00	240
1998 School Boy	Open		225.00	225
1998 School Girl	Open		225.00	225
1998 Sister	Open		160.00	160
1998 Worship	Open		180.00	180

M.I. Hummel Candleholders - M.I. Hummel

YEAR ISSUE	EDITION LIMIT	YEAR RETD.	ISSUE PRICE	*QUOTE U.S.$
XX Angel Duet 193	Open		245.00	245
XX Angel w/Accordian 1/39/0	Open		60.00	60
XX Angel w/Lute 1/38/0	Open		60.00	60
XX Angel w/Trumpet 1/40/0	Open		60.00	60
XX Boy w/Horse 117	Open		60.00	60
XX Candlelight 192	Open		255.00	265
XX Girl w/Fir Tree 116	Open		60.00	60
XX Girl w/Nosegay 115	Open		60.00	60
XX Lullaby 241/I	Open		210.00	210
XX Silent Night 54	Open		360.00	360

M.I. Hummel Collectibles Century Collection - M.I. Hummel

YEAR ISSUE	EDITION LIMIT	YEAR RETD.	ISSUE PRICE	*QUOTE U.S.$
1986 Chapel Time 442	Closed	N/A	500.00	1050-2500
1987 Pleasant Journey 406	Closed	N/A	500.00	1398-2800
1988 Call to Worship 441	Closed	N/A	600.00	675-1200
1989 Harmony in Four Parts 471	Closed	N/A	850.00	1350-2200
1990 Let's Tell the World 487	Closed	N/A	875.00	650-1500
1991 We Wish You The Best 600	Closed	N/A	1300.00	900-1750
1992 On Our Way 472	Closed	N/A	950.00	950-1250
1993 Welcome Spring 635	Closed	N/A	1085.00	1000-1500
1994 Rock-A-Bye 574	Closed	N/A	1150.00	860-1350
1995 Strike Up the Band 668	Closed	N/A	1200.00	750-1200
1996 Love's Bounty 751	Yr.Iss.	1996	1200.00	1200
1997 Fond Goodbye 660	Yr.Iss.	1997	1450.00	1450
1998 Here's My Heart 766	Yr.Iss.		1375.00	1375

M.I. Hummel Collectibles Christmas Angels - M.I. Hummel

YEAR ISSUE	EDITION LIMIT	YEAR RETD.	ISSUE PRICE	*QUOTE U.S.$
1993 Angel in Cloud 585	Open		25.00	35
1993 Angel with Lute 580	Open		25.00	35
1993 Angel with Trumpet 586	Open		25.00	35
1993 Celestial Musician 578	Open		25.00	35
1993 Festival Harmony with Flute 577	Open		25.00	35
1993 Festival Harmony with Mandolin 576	Open		25.00	35
1993 Gentle Song 582	Open		25.00	35
1993 Heavenly Angel 575	Open		25.00	35
1993 Prayer of Thanks 581	Open		25.00	35
1993 Song of Praise 579	Open		25.00	35

M.I. Hummel Collectibles Figurines - M.I. Hummel

YEAR ISSUE	EDITION LIMIT	YEAR RETD.	ISSUE PRICE	*QUOTE U.S.$
1988 The Accompanist 453	Open		Unkn.	86-115
XX Adoration 23/I	Open		Unkn.	210-285
XX Adoration 23/III	Open		Unkn.	506-555
XX Adventure Bound 347	Open		Unkn.	2100-2985
1997 All Smiles (Special Event)	25,000		175.00	175
XX Angel Duet 261	Open		Unkn.	184-245
XX Angel Serenade 214/D/I	Open		Unkn.	75-130
XX Angel Serenade with Lamb 83	Open		Unkn.	245-319
XX Angel with Accordion 238/B	Open		Unkn.	54-60
XX Angel with Lute 238/A	Open		Unkn.	50-54
XX Angel With Trumpet 238/C	Open		Unkn.	45-60
XX Angelic Song 144	Open		Unkn.	124-180
1995 The Angler 566	Open		Unkn.	263-350
1989 An Apple A Day 403	Open		Unkn.	233-310
XX Apple Tree Boy 142/3/0	Open		Unkn.	120-160
XX Apple Tree Boy 142/I	Open		Unkn.	310-444
XX Apple Tree Boy 142/V	Open		Unkn.	1350
XX Apple Tree Boy 142/X	Open		Unkn.	24000
XX Apple Tree Girl 141/3/0	Open		Unkn.	110-221
XX Apple Tree Girl 141/I	Open		Unkn.	210-310
XX Apple Tree Girl 141/V	Open		Unkn.	1013-1350
XX Apple Tree Girl 141/X	Open		Unkn.	24000
1991 Art Critic 318	Open		Unkn.	236-315
XX Artist, The 304	Open		Unkn.	150-275
XX Auf Wiedersehen 153/0	Open		Unkn.	175-270
XX Auf Wiedersehen 153/I	Open		Unkn.	180-330
XX Autumn Harvest 355	Open		Unkn.	125-191
XX Baker 128	Open		Unkn.	150-225
XX Baking Day 330	Open		Unkn.	165-310
XX Band Leader 129	Open		Unkn.	175-293
XX Barnyard Hero 195/2/0	Open		Unkn.	132-241
XX Barnyard Hero 195/I	Open		Unkn.	298-350
XX Bashful 377	Open		Unkn.	169-225
1990 Bath Time 412	Open		Unkn.	364-485
XX Be Patient 197/2/0	Open		Unkn.	115-293
XX Begging His Share 9	Open		Unkn.	175-238
1997 Best Wishes (personalized) 540	Open		180.00	180
1997 Best Wishes (Special Event) 540	Open		180.00	180
XX Big Housecleaning 363	Open		Unkn.	170-268
XX Bird Duet 169	Open		Unkn.	120-160
XX Bird Duet (personalized)169	Open		Unkn.	160
XX Bird Watcher 300	Open		Unkn.	125-240
1989 Birthday Cake 338	Open		Unkn.	85-160
1994 Birthday Present 341/3/0	Open		140.00	131-160
XX Birthday Serenade 218/2/0	Open		Unkn.	190
XX Birthday Serenade 218/0	Open		Unkn.	248-349
XX Blessed Event 333	Open		Unkn.	210-350
1996 Blossom Time 608	Open		155.00	116-155
XX Bookworm 8	Open		Unkn.	184-245
XX Bookworm 3/I	Open		Unkn.	251-335
XX Boots 143/0	12/98		Unkn.	225-600
XX Boots 143/I	12/98		Unkn.	360
XX The Botanist 351	Open		Unkn.	150-200
1998 The Botanist w/Vase Sampler 151271	Open		210.00	210
XX Boy with Accordion 390	Open		Unkn.	75-100
XX Boy with Horse 239/C	Open		Unkn.	45-60
XX Boy with Toothache 217	Open		Unkn.	120-299
XX Brother 95	Open		Unkn.	145-299
XX The Builder 305	Open		Unkn.	150-248
XX Busy Student 367	Open		Unkn.	95-180
XX Call to Glory 739/I	Open		250.00	206-275
1996 Carefree 490	Open		120.00	90-120
XX Carnival 328	Open		Unkn.	180-240
1993 Celestial Musician 188/4/0	Open		Unkn.	86-115
XX Celestial Musician 188/0	Open		Unkn.	184-245
XX Celestial Musician 188/I	Open		255.00	295
XX Chick Girl 57/2/0	Open		Unkn.	124-165
XX Chick Girl 57/0	Open		Unkn.	120-241
XX Chick Girl 57/I	Open		Unkn.	233-403
XX Chicken-Licken 385	Open		Unkn.	233-918
XX Chimney Sweep 12/2/0	Open		Unkn.	98-169
XX Chimney Sweep 12/I	Open		Unkn.	165-319
XX Christ Child 18	Open		Unkn.	120-208
1989 Christmas Angel 301	Open		Unkn.	210-280
1998 Christmas Delivery 2014/I	Open		485.00	485
1996 Christmas Song 343/4/0	Open		110.00	86-115
XX Christmas Song 343	Open		Unkn.	125-245
XX Cinderella 337	Open		Unkn.	236-315
XX Close Harmony 336	Open		Unkn.	195-320
1995 Come Back Soon 545	Open		Unkn.	120-160
XX Confidentially 314	Open		Unkn.	244-276
XX Congratulations 17	Open		Unkn.	130-293
XX Coquettes 179	Open		Unkn.	276-423
1990 Crossroads (Commemorative) 331	20,000	N/A	360.00	550-710
XX Crossroads (Original) 331	Open		Unkn.	245-383
XX Culprits 56/A	Open		Unkn.	250-423
1989 Daddy's Girls 371	Open		Unkn.	188-250
1996 Delicious 435/3/0	Open		155.00	116-155
XX Doctor 127	Open		Unkn.	128-280
XX Doll Bath 319	Open		Unkn.	185-315
XX Doll Mother 67	Open		Unkn.	125-299
XX Easter Greetings 378	Open		Unkn.	150-225
XX Easter Time 384	Open		Unkn.	150-275
1998 Echoes of Joy	Open		180.00	180
1998 Echoes of Joy 642/4/0	Open		120.000	90-120
1998 Echoes of Joy 642/0	Open		180.00	135-180
1992 Evening Prayer 495	Open		Unkn.	90-120
XX Eventide 99	Open		Unkn.	270-468
XX A Fair Measure 345	Open		Unkn.	244-450
XX Farm Boy 66	Open		Unkn.	140-260
1996 Fascination 649/0 (Special Event)	25,000	1996	190.00	190-240
XX Favorite Pet 361	Open		Unkn.	185-284
XX Feathered Friends 344	Open		Unkn.	170-310
XX Feeding Time 199/0	Open		Unkn.	225-293
XX Feeding Time 199/I	Open		Unkn.	185-315
1994 Festival Harmony w/Mandolin 172/4/0	Open		95.00	110-125
XX Festival Harmony, with Mandolin 172/0	Open		Unkn.	263-350
XX Festival Harmony, with Flute 173/4/0	Open		Unkn.	200-350
XX Festival Harmony, with Flute 173/0	Open		Unkn.	170-380
XX Flower Vendor 381	Open		Unkn.	234-275
XX Follow the Leader 369	Open		Unkn.	700-1122
1998 For Father (personalized) 87	Open		240.00	240
XX For Father 87	Open		Unkn.	160-240
XX For Mother 257/2/0	Open		Unkn.	130-150
XX For Mother 257	Open		Unkn.	169-225
XX Forest Shrine 183	Open		Unkn.	446-595
1993 A Free Flight 569	Open		Unkn.	150-200
1997 A Free Flight (O Canada edition) 469	1,997	1997	210.00	210
1996 Free Spirit 564	Open		120.00	90-120
1991 Friend Or Foe 434	Open		Unkn.	184-245
XX Friends 136/I	Open		Unkn.	160-299
XX Friends 136/V	Open		Unkn.	1148-1350
1993 Friends Together 662/0 (Commemorative)	Open		260.00	300-310
1993 Friends Together 662/I (Limited)	25,000		475.00	413-550
1997 From My Garden 795/0	Open		180.00	180
1996 From The Heart 761	Open		120.00	90-120
XX Gay Adventure 356	Open		Unkn.	165-220
1995 Gentle Fellowship (Limited) 628	25,000		550.00	413-550
XX A Gentle Glow 439	Open		Unkn.	173-230
XX Girl with Doll 239/B	Open		Unkn.	60
XX Girl with Nosegay 239/A	Open		Unkn.	45-60
XX Girl with Sheet Music 389	Open		Unkn.	80-100
XX Girl with Trumpet 391	Open		Unkn.	85-100
XX Going Home 383	Open		Unkn.	263-350
XX Going to Grandma's 52/0	Open		Unkn.	145-275
XX Good Friends 182	Open		Unkn.	191-293
XX Good Hunting 307	Open		Unkn.	230-270
1997 Good News (personalized) 539	Open		180.00	180
XX Good Shepherd 42	Open		Unkn.	210-364
XX Goose Girl 47/3/0	Open		Unkn.	150-185
XX Goose Girl 47/0	Open		Unkn.	195-338
1997 Goose Girl Sampler 47/3/0	Open		200.00	185-200
XX Grandma's Girl 561	Open		Unkn.	120-160
XX Grandpa's Boy 562	Open		Unkn.	120-160
1991 The Guardian 455	Open		Unkn.	135-180
1991 The Guardian (personalized) 455	Open		Unkn.	180
1998 The Guardian Gift Set 156017	Open		180.00	135-180
XX Guiding Angel 357	Open		Unkn.	55-100
XX Happiness 86	Open		Unkn.	113-150
XX Happy Birthday 176/0	Open		Unkn.	180-312
XX Happy Birthday 176/I	Open		Unkn.	248-330
XX Happy Days 150/2/0	Open		Unkn.	143-190
XX Happy Days 150/0	Open		Unkn.	248-330
XX Happy Days 150/I	Open		Unkn.	375-425
XX Happy Traveller 109/0	Open		Unkn.	140-215
XX Hear Ye! Hear Ye! 15/2/0	Open		Unkn.	170-190
1997 Hear Ye! Hear Ye! (Gift Set) 15/2/0	Open		170.00	170
XX Hear Ye! Hear Ye! 15/0	Open		Unkn.	169-293
XX Hear Ye! Hear Ye! 15/I	Open		Unkn.	210-364
1996 Heart and Soul 559	Open		120.00	90-120
1998 Traveling Trio 787	20,000		490.00	490
1998 Heart's Delight (w/wooden chair) 698	Open		220.00	165-220
XX Heavenly Angel 21/0	Open		Unkn.	95-182
XX Heavenly Angel 21/0/1/2	Open		Unkn.	184-208
XX Heavenly Angel 21/I	Open		Unkn.	251-295
XX Heavenly Lullaby 262	Open		Unkn.	210
XX Heavenly Protection 88/I	Open		Unkn.	325-495
XX Heavenly Protection 88/II	Open		Unkn.	800
1995 Hello (Perpetual Calendar) 788A	Open		295.00	295
XX Hello 124/0	Open		Unkn.	184-249
1997 Holy Child 472	Open		280.00	280
XX Home from Market 198/2/0	Open		Unkn.	145-221
XX Home from Market 198/I	Open		Unkn.	180-312
XX Homeward Bound 334	Open		Unkn.	326-360
1990 Horse Trainer 423	Open		Unkn.	184-245
1989 Hosanna 480	Open		Unkn.	90-120
1989 I'll Protect Him 483	Open		Unkn.	100
1994 I'm Carefree 633	Open		365.00	400-487
1989 I'm Here 478	Open		Unkn.	90-120
1989 In D Major 430	Open		Unkn.	169-225
XX In The Meadow 459	Open		Unkn.	169-225
XX In Tune 414	Open		Unkn.	233-310
XX Is It Raining? 420	Open		Unkn.	225-300
XX Joyful 53	Open		Unkn.	119-182
XX Joyous News 27/III	Open		Unkn.	184-245
1995 Just Dozing 451	Open		Unkn.	180-240
XX Just Fishing 373	Open		Unkn.	188-250
XX Just Resting 112/3/0	Open		Unkn.	105-165
XX Just Resting 112/I	Open		Unkn.	320-473
XX The Kindergartner 467	Open		Unkn.	169-225
XX Kiss Me 311	Open		Unkn.	185-650
XX Knit One, Purl One 432	Open		Unkn.	70-101
XX Knitting Lesson 256	Open		Unkn.	473-525
1991 Land in Sight 530	30,000		1600.00	1050-1600
XX Latest News 184	Open		Unkn.	205-364
XX Latest News (personalized) 184	Open		Unkn.	320
1997 Latest News ("Green Bay Wins") - Mader's Exclusive	Closed	1997	650.00	650
1998 Latest News ("Denver Wins")	45-day	1998	320.00	320
XX Let's Sing 110/0	Open		Unkn.	140-182
XX Let's Sing 110/I	Open		Unkn.	167-185
XX Letter to Santa Claus 340	Open		Unkn.	270-360
1993 The Little Architect 410/I	Open		Unkn.	248-330
XX Little Bookkeeper 306	Open		Unkn.	185-315
XX Little Cellist 89/I	Open		Unkn.	160-380
XX Little Drummer 240	Open		Unkn.	90-215
XX Little Fiddler 4	Open		Unkn.	160-293
XX Little Fiddler 2/0	Open		Unkn.	184-319
XX Little Gabriel 32	Open		Unkn.	124-165

*Quotes have been rounded up to nearest dollar

YEAR ISSUE		EDITION LIMIT	YEAR RETD.	ISSUE PRICE	*QUOTE U.S.$
XX	Little Gardener 74	Open		Unkn.	111-169
XX	Little Goat Herder 200/0	Open		Unkn.	169-293
XX	Little Goat Herder 200/I	Open		Unkn.	195-338
XX	Little Guardian 145	Open		Unkn.	124-165
XX	Little Helper 73	Open		Unkn.	98-169
XX	Little Hiker 16/2/0	Open		Unkn.	130-140
XX	Little Nurse 376	Open		Unkn.	203-270
XX	Little Pharmacist 322/E	Open		Unkn.	148-270
XX	Little Scholar 80	Open		Unkn.	180-312
XX	Little Shopper 96	Open		Unkn.	120-208
1988	Little Sweeper 171/0	Open		Unkn.	115-125
XX	Little Tailor 308	Open		Unkn.	234-275
XX	Little Thrifty 118	Open		Unkn.	170-299
XX	Lost Stocking 374	Open		Unkn.	124-140
1998	Love In Bloom (w/wooden wagon) 699	Open		220.00	220
1995	Lucky Boy (Special Event) 335	25,000	1995	190.00	204-250
XX	The Mail is Here 226	Open		Unkn.	310-595
1996	Making New Friends 2002	Open		595.00	446-595
XX	March Winds 43	Open		Unkn.	128-170
XX	Max and Moritz 123	Open		Unkn.	208-245
XX	Meditation 13/2/0	Open		Unkn.	120-144
XX	Meditation 13/0	Open		Unkn.	184-325
XX	Merry Wanderer 11/2/0	Open		Unkn.	110-237
XX	Merry Wanderer 11/0	Open		Unkn.	150-293
XX	Merry Wanderer 7/0	Open		Unkn.	264-310
XX	Merry Wanderer 7/X	Open		Unkn.	N/A
XX	Mischief Maker 342	Open		Unkn.	210-264
1994	Morning Stroll 375/3/0	Open		170.00	146-195
XX	Mother's Helper 133	Open		Unkn.	168-225
XX	Mountaineer 315	Open		Unkn.	130-240
1991	A Nap 534	Open		Unkn.	98-130
1996	Nimble Fingers w/wooden bench 758	Open		225.00	173-230
1996	No Thank You 535	Open		120.00	90-120
XX	Not For You 317	Open		Unkn.	188-375
XX	On Holiday 350	Open		Unkn.	128-170
XX	On Secret Path 386	Open		Unkn.	206-234
1989	One For You, One For Me 482	Open		Unkn.	90-120
1993	One Plus One 556	Open		Unkn.	94-145
XX	Ooh My Tooth 533	Open		Unkn.	101-130
XX	Out of Danger 56/B	Open		Unkn.	244-423
1993	Parade Of Lights 616	Open		Unkn.	206-275
XX	The Photographer 178	Open		Unkn.	250-315
1995	Pixie 768	Open		Unkn.	90-120
XX	Playmates 58/2/0	Open		Unkn.	124-165
XX	Playmates 58/0	Open		Unkn.	139-241
1994	The Poet 397/I	Open		220.00	200-250
1989	Postman 119/2/0	Open		Unkn.	120-160
XX	Postman Sampler 119/2/0	Open		Unkn.	120-160
XX	Postman 119	Open		Unkn.	150-225
1997	Practice Makes Perfect (w/wooden rocker) 771	Open		250.00	188-250
XX	Prayer Before Battle 20	Open		Unkn.	139-241
1996	Pretty Please 489	Open		120.00	90-120
1992	The Professor 320	Open		Unkn.	169-225
1995	Puppy Love Display Plaque 767	Closed	1995	Unkn.	159-199
1997	Rainy Day (Gift Set) 71/2/0	Open		305.00	305
XX	Retreat to Safety 201/2/0	Open		Unkn.	135-180
XX	Retreat to Safety 201/I	Open		Unkn.	263-350
XX	Ride into Christmas 396/2/0	Open		Unkn.	140-260
XX	Ride into Christmas 396/I	Open		Unkn.	485
XX	Ring Around the Rosie 348	Open		Unkn.	1430-2002
1998	Roses Are Red 762	Open		120.00	90-120
XX	The Run-A-Way 327	Open		Unkn.	238-280
1997	Ruprecht 475	20,000		450.00	450
1992	Scamp 553	Open		Unkn.	90-120
XX	School Boy 82/2/0	Open		Unkn.	111-208
XX	School Boy 82/0	Open		Unkn.	169-293
XX	School Boy 82/II	Open		Unkn.	375-500
XX	School Boys 170/I	Open		Unkn.	1122-1320
XX	School Girl 81/2/0	Open		Unkn.	188-208
XX	School Girl 81/0	Open		Unkn.	191-234
XX	School Girls 177/I	Open		Unkn.	725-1188
1997	School's Out 538	Open		170.00	128-170
XX	Sensitive Hunter 6/2/0	Open		Unkn.	165-275
XX	Sensitive Hunter 6/0	Open		Unkn.	200-293
XX	Sensitive Hunter 6/I	Open		Unkn.	210-238
XX	Serenade 85/0	Open		Unkn.	98-195
XX	Serenade 85/II	Open		Unkn.	375-500
XX	She Loves Me, She Loves Me Not 174	Open		Unkn.	145-220
1996	Shepherd Boy 395/0	Open		295.00	221-295
XX	Shepherd's Boy 64	Open		Unkn.	195-338
XX	Shining Light 358	Open		Unkn.	85-100
XX	Sing Along 433	Open		Unkn.	300-350
XX	Sing With Me 405	Open		Unkn.	263-350
XX	Singing Lesson 63	Open		Unkn.	101-176
1995	Sister (Perpetual Calendar) 788B	Open		295.00	295
XX	Sister 98/2/0	Open		Unkn.	120-144
XX	Sister 98/0	Open		Unkn.	173-230
XX	Skier 59	Open		Unkn.	169-460
1990	Sleep Tight 424	Open		Unkn.	184-245
XX	Smart Little Sister 346	Open		Unkn.	165-275
XX	Soldier Boy 332	Open		Unkn.	130-216
XX	Soloist 135	Open		Unkn.	113-150
1988	Song of Praise 454	Open		Unkn.	86-115
1988	Sound the Trumpet 457	Open		Unkn.	90-120
1988	Sounds of the Mandolin 438	Open		Unkn.	105-140
XX	Spring Dance 353/0	Open		Unkn.	190-263
XX	St. George 55	Open		Unkn.	263-350
1997	St. Nicholas' Day 2012	20,000		650.00	650-825
XX	Star Gazer 132	Open		Unkn.	125-230
XX	A Stitch in Time 255/I	Open		Unkn.	180-293
XX	Stormy Weather 71/2/0	Open		Unkn.	170-248
XX	Stormy Weather 71/I	Open		Unkn.	371-495
1992	Storybook Time 458	Open		Unkn.	220-440
XX	Street Singer 131	Open		Unkn.	165-286
1998	Summertime Surprise 428/3/0	Open		220.00	140-170
1997	Sunshower 634/2/0	10,000		360.00	270-360
XX	Surprise 94/3/0	Open		Unkn.	169-221
XX	Surprise 94/I	Open		Unkn.	244-325
1998	Sweet As Can Be Birthday Sampler 156021	Open		150.00	150
XX	Sweet Greetings 352	Open		Unkn.	150-200
XX	Sweet Music 186	Open		Unkn.	150-293
XX	Telling Her Secret 196/0	Open		Unkn.	281-429
1997	Thanksgiving Prayer 641/4/0	Open		120.00	86-120
1997	Thanksgiving Prayer 641/0	Open		180.00	135-180
XX	Thoughtful 415	Open		Unkn.	184-245
XX	Timid Little Sister 394	Open		Unkn.	250-364
1995	To Keep You Warm w/ Wooden Chair 759	Open		Unkn.	173-230
XX	To Market 49/3/0	Open		Unkn.	131-228
XX	To Market 49/0	Open		Unkn.	244-423
1998	Traveling Trio 787	20,000		490.00	368-490
1997	Trio of Wishes 721	20,000		475.00	356-475
1989	Tuba Player 437	Open		Unkn.	225-330
XX	Tuneful Angel 359	Open		Unkn.	85-100
1996	A Tuneful Trio	20,000		450.00	356-475
XX	Umbrella Boy 152/A/0	Open		Unkn.	488-585
XX	Umbrella Boy 152/A/II	Open		Unkn.	1200-1690
XX	Umbrella Girl 152/B/0	Open		Unkn.	350-488
XX	Umbrella Girl 152/B/II	Open		Unkn.	1440-1800
XX	Village Boy 51/3/0	Open		Unkn.	98-169
XX	Village Boy 51/2/0	Open		Unkn.	124-149
XX	Village Boy 51/0	Open		Unkn.	210-280
XX	Visiting an Invalid 382	Open		Unkn.	169-191
XX	Volunteers 50/2/0	Open		Unkn.	184-319
XX	Volunteers 50/0	Open		Unkn.	170-248
XX	Waiter 154/0	Open		Unkn.	180-240
XX	Waiter 154/I	Open		Unkn.	244-423
XX	Wash Day 321/I	Open		Unkn.	170-276
XX	Watchful Angel 194	Open		Unkn.	325-442
XX	Wayside Devotion 28/II	Open		Unkn.	338-450
XX	Wayside Devotion 28/III	Open		Unkn.	600-854
XX	Wayside Harmony 111/3/0	Open		Unkn.	165-218
XX	Wayside Harmony 111/I	Open		Unkn.	233-480
1993	We Come In Peace (Commemorative) 754	Open		385.00	385
XX	We Congratulate 214/E/I	Open		Unkn.	135-261
XX	We Congratulate 220	Open		Unkn.	122-221
1997	We Congratulate (Gift Set) 220	Open		170.00	128-170
1990	What's New? 418	Open		Unkn.	223-310
XX	Which Hand? 258	Open		Unkn.	169-225
1992	Whistler's Duet 413	Open		Unkn.	233-310
XX	Whitsuntide 163	Open		Unkn.	330
1988	A Winter Song 476	Open		Unkn.	94-125
XX	With Loving Greetings 309	Open		Unkn.	125-165
XX	Worship 84/0	Open		Unkn.	153-234

M.I. Hummel Collectibles Figurines Retired - M.I. Hummel

YEAR ISSUE		EDITION LIMIT	YEAR RETD.	ISSUE PRICE	*QUOTE U.S.$
1947	Accordion Boy 185	Closed	1994	Unkn.	161-550
1939	Duet 130	Closed	1995	Unkn.	275-600
1937	Farewell 65 TMK1-5	Closed	1993	Unkn.	225-550
1937	Globe Trotter 79 TMK1-7	Closed	1991	Unkn.	150-350
XX	Happy Pastime 69	Closed	1996	Unkn.	131-475
1937	Lost Sheep 68/0 TMK1-7	Closed	1992	Unkn.	166-250
1955	Lost Sheep 68/2/0 TMK2-7	Closed	1992	7.50	132-372
XX	Mother's Darling 175	Closed	1997	Unkn.	191-328
1935	Puppy Love I TMK1-6	Closed	1988	125.00	225-550
1948	Signs Of Spring 203/2/0 TMK2-6	Closed	1990	120.00	169-400
1948	Signs Of Spring 203/I TMK2-6	Closed	1990	155.00	206-450
1935	Strolling Along 5 TMK1-6	Closed	1989	115.00	265-400

M.I. Hummel Collectibles Madonna Figurines - M.I. Hummel

YEAR ISSUE		EDITION LIMIT	YEAR RETD.	ISSUE PRICE	*QUOTE U.S.$
XX	Flower Madonna, color 10/I/II	Open		Unkn.	253-490
1996	Flower Madonna, white 10 (Commemorative)	Closed	1996	225.00	180-225
XX	Madonna with Halo, color 45/I/6	Open		Unkn.	140-182

M.I. Hummel Collectibles Nativity Components - M.I. Hummel, unless otherwise noted

YEAR ISSUE		EDITION LIMIT	YEAR RETD.	ISSUE PRICE	*QUOTE U.S.$
XX	12-Pc. Set Figs. only, Color, 214/A/M/I, B/I, A/K/I, F/I G/I J/I K/I, L/I, M/I, N/I, O/I, 366/I	Open		Unkn.	1680
XX	Angel Serenade 214/D/I	Open		Unkn.	100-150
XX	Camel Kneeling - Goebel	Open		Unkn.	165-206
XX	Camel Lying - Goebel	Open		Unkn.	206-275
XX	Camel Standing - Goebel	Open		Unkn.	206-275
XX	Donkey 214/J/0	Open		Unkn.	41-55
XX	Donkey 214/J/I	Open		Unkn.	56-75
XX	Flying Angel/color 366/I	Open		Unkn.	140
XX	Good Night 214/C/I	Open		Unkn.	100
XX	Holy Family, 3 Pcs., Color 214/A/M/0, B/0, A/K/0	Open		Unkn.	200-335
XX	Holy Family, 3 Pcs., Color 214/A/M/I, B/I, A/K/I	Open		Unkn.	460
1997	Holy Family, 3 Pcs., White 214	Open		200.00	200
XX	Infant Jesus 214/A/K/0	Open		Unkn.	34-45
XX	Infant Jesus 214/A/K/I	Open		Unkn.	70-90
XX	King, Kneeling 214/M/I	Open		Unkn.	176-195
XX	King, Kneeling 214M/0	Open		Unkn.	116-155
XX	King, Kneeling w/ Box 214/N/0	Open		Unkn.	113-150
XX	King, Kneeling w/Box 214/N/I	Open		Unkn.	131-175
XX	King, Moorish 214/L/0	Open		Unkn.	124-165
XX	King, Moorish 214/L/I	Open		Unkn.	150-200
XX	Lamb 214/O/0	Open		Unkn.	17-22
XX	Lamb 214/O/I	Open		Unkn.	22-42
XX	Little Tooter 214/H/I	Open		Unkn.	135-150
XX	Little Tooter 214/H/O	Open		Unkn.	110
XX	Madonna 214/A/M/0	Open		Unkn.	109-145
XX	Madonna 214/A/M/I	Open		Unkn.	176-195
XX	Ox 214/K/0	Open		Unkn.	41-55
XX	Ox 214/K/I	Open		Unkn.	68-75
XX	Shepherd Boy 214/G/I	Open		Unkn.	109-145
XX	Shepherd Kneeling 214/G/0	Open		Unkn.	130
XX	Shepherd Standing 214/F/0	Open		Unkn.	165-185
XX	Shepherd with Sheep-1 piece 214/F/I	Open		Unkn.	195-228
XX	Small Camel Kneeling - Goebel	Open		Unkn.	220
XX	Small Camel Lying - Goebel	Open		Unkn.	220
XX	Small Camel Standing - Goebel	Open		Unkn.	220
XX	St. Joseph 214/B/0	Open		Unkn.	109-145
XX	St. Joseph color 214/B/I	Open		Unkn.	176-195
XX	Stable only fits12 or 16-pc. HUM214/II Set	Open		Unkn.	50-83
XX	Stable only, fits 16-piece HUM260 Set	Open		Unkn.	440
XX	Stable only, fits 3-pc. HUM214 Set	Open		Unkn.	50
XX	We Congratulate 214/E/I	Open		Unkn.	180

M.I. Hummel Disneyana Figurines - M.I. Hummel

YEAR ISSUE		EDITION LIMIT	YEAR RETD.	ISSUE PRICE	*QUOTE U.S.$
1992	Two Merry Wanderers 022074	1,500	1992	250.00	950-1250
1993	Two Little Drummers	1,500	1993	325.00	424-507
1994	Minnie Be Patient	1,500	1994	395.00	396-650
1995	For Father	1,500	1995	450.00	462-485
1995	Grandpa's Boys	1,500	1995	340.00	385-413
1996	Minnie For Mother	1,200	1996	470.00	470
1997	Grandma's Girl	1,000	1998	350.00	350
1998	Friends Forever	N/A		N/A	N/A

M.I. Hummel First Edition Miniatures - M.I. Hummel

YEAR ISSUE		EDITION LIMIT	YEAR RETD.	ISSUE PRICE	*QUOTE U.S.$
1991	Accordion Boy -37225	Suspd.		105.00	105-125
1989	Apple Tree Boy -37219	Suspd.		115.00	130-210
1990	Baker -37222	Suspd.		100.00	130-300
1992	Bavarian Church (Display) -37370	Closed	N/A	60.00	70-75
1988	Bavarian Cottage (Display) -37355	Closed	N/A	60.00	64-95
1990	Bavarian Marketsquare Bridge (Display) -37358	Closed	N/A	110.00	125-130
1988	Bavarian Village (Display) -37356	Closed	N/A	100.00	105-125
1991	Busy Student -37226	Suspd.		105.00	105-120
1990	Cinderella -37223	Suspd.		115.00	125-195
1991	Countryside School (Display) -37365	Closed	N/A	100.00	100-125
1989	Doll Bath -37214	Suspd.		95.00	105-185
1992	Goose Girl -37238	Suspd.		130.00	180-300
1989	Little Fiddler -37211	Suspd.		90.00	115-250
1989	Little Sweeper -37212	Suspd.		90.00	115-300
1990	Marketsquare Flower Stand (Display) -37360	Closed	N/A	35.00	50-80
1990	Marketsquare Hotel (Display)-37359	Closed	N/A	70.00	90-125
1989	Merry Wanderer -37213	Suspd.		95.00	250-300
1991	Merry Wanderer Dealer Plaque -37229	Closed	N/A	130.00	160-300
1989	Postman -37217	Suspd.		95.00	120-195
1991	Roadside Shrine (Display)-37366	Closed	N/A	60.00	60-85
1992	School Boy -37236	Suspd.		120.00	180-300
1991	Serenade -37228	Suspd.		105.00	120-275
1992	Snow-Covered Mountain (Display)-37371	Closed	N/A	100.00	100-125
1989	Stormy Weather -37215	Suspd.		115.00	130-150
1992	Trees (Display)-37369	Closed	N/A	40.00	50-55
1989	Visiting an Invalid -37218	Suspd.		105.00	130-175
1990	Waiter -37221	Suspd.		100.00	115-195
1992	Wayside Harmony -37237	Suspd.		140.00	180-300
1991	We Congratulate -37227	Suspd.		130.00	150-300

M.I. Hummel Fonts - M.I. Hummel

YEAR ISSUE		EDITION LIMIT	YEAR RETD.	ISSUE PRICE	*QUOTE U.S.$
XX	Angel Cloud 205	Open		55.00	41-55
XX	Angel Duet 146	Open		55.00	41-60
XX	Angel Facing Left 91/A	Open		45.00	34-45
XX	Angel Facing Right 91/B	Open		45.00	34-45
XX	Angel Shrine 147	Open		55.00	41-55
XX	Angel Sitting 22/0	Open		45.00	45
XX	Angel w/Bird 167	Open		55.00	41-55
XX	Child Jesus 26/0	Open		45.00	34-45
XX	Child w/Flowers 36/0	Open		45.00	38-45
XX	Good Shepherd 35/0	Open		45.00	34-45
XX	Guardian Angel 248/0	Open		55.00	41-55
XX	Heavenly Angel 207	Open		55.00	41-55
XX	Holy Family 246	Open		55.00	41-55
XX	Madonna & Child 243	Open		55.00	47-55
XX	White Angel 75	Open		45.00	34-45
XX	Worship 164	Open		55.00	41-55

M.I. Hummel Hummel Scapes - M.I. Hummel

YEAR ISSUE		EDITION LIMIT	YEAR RETD.	ISSUE PRICE	*QUOTE U.S.$
1997	Around The Town	Open		75.00	56-75
1997	Castle On A Hill	Open		75.00	56-75
1997	Going To Church	Open		75.00	75
1996	Heavenly Harmonies	Open		100.00	100
1996	Home Sweet Home	Closed	1997	130.00	130
1996	Little Music Makers	Closed	1997	130.00	98-130
1997	Strolling Through The Park	Open		75.00	56-75

M.I. Hummel Pen Pals - M.I. Hummel

YEAR ISSUE		EDITION LIMIT	YEAR RETD.	ISSUE PRICE	*QUOTE U.S.$
1995	For Mother 257/5/0	Open		55.00	55
1995	March Winds 43/5/0	Open		55.00	55
1995	One For You, One For Me 482/5/0	Open		55.00	55
1995	Sister 98/5/0	Open		55.00	55

*Quotes have been rounded up to nearest dollar

YEAR ISSUE		EDITION LIMIT	YEAR RETD.	ISSUE PRICE	*QUOTE U.S.$
1995	Soloist 135/5/0	Open		55.00	55
1995	Village Boy 151/5/0	Open		55.00	55

M.I. Hummel Tree Toppers - M.I. Hummel

YEAR ISSUE		EDITION LIMIT	YEAR RETD.	ISSUE PRICE	*QUOTE U.S.$
1994	Heavenly Angel 755	Open		450.00	371-495

M.I. Hummel Vignettes w/Solitary Domes - M.I. Hummel

YEAR ISSUE		EDITION LIMIT	YEAR RETD.	ISSUE PRICE	*QUOTE U.S.$
1992	Bakery Day w/Baker & Waiter 37726	3,000		225.00	225-230
1992	The Flower Market w/Cinderella 37729	3,000		135.00	135
1993	The Mail Is Here Clock Tower 826504	Open		495.00	575
1995	Ring Around the Rosie Musical 826101	10,000		675.00	675
1992	Winterfest w/Ride Into Christmas 37728	5,000		195.00	195

M.I. Hummel's Temporarily Out of Production (including trademarks) - M.I. Hummel

YEAR ISSUE		EDITION LIMIT	YEAR RETD.	ISSUE PRICE	*QUOTE U.S.$
XX	16-Pc. Set Figs. only, Color, 214/A/M/I, B/I, A/K/I, C/I, D/I, E/I, F/I, G/I, H/I, J/I, K/I, L/I, M/I, N/I, O/I, 366/I	Suspd.		Unkn.	1990
XX	17-Pc. Set Large Color 16 Figs.& Wooden Stable 260 A-R	Suspd.		Unkn.	4540
XX	Angel Serenade 260/E	Suspd.		Unkn.	445-450
XX	Apple Tree Boy 142/X	Suspd.		Unkn.	17000-24000
XX	Apple Tree Girl 141/X	Suspd.		Unkn.	17000-24000
XX	Band Leader 129/4/0	Suspd.		Unkn.	115
XX	Be Patient 197/I	Suspd.		Unkn.	281-330
XX	Blessed Child 78/I/83	Suspd.		Unkn.	35-40
XX	Blessed Child 78/II/83	Suspd.		Unkn.	50-60
XX	Blessed Child 78/III/83	Suspd.		Unkn.	60-75
XX	Bookworm 3/II	Suspd.		Unkn.	935-1350
XX	Bookworm 3/III	Suspd.		Unkn.	2100-2860
1988	A Budding Maestro 477	Suspd.		Unkn.	90-120
XX	Celestial Musician 188/I	Suspd.		Unkn.	251-475
XX	Chicken-Licken 385/4/0	Suspd.		Unkn.	115
XX	Christ Child 18	Suspd.		Unkn.	208-325
XX	Donkey 260/L	Suspd.		Unkn.	135
XX	Festival Harmony, with Flute 173/II	Suspd.		Unkn.	1000-1200
XX	Festival Harmony, with Mandolin 172/II	Suspd.		Unkn.	1000-1200
XX	Flower Madonna, color 10/III/II	Suspd.		Unkn.	225-420
XX	Flower Madonna, white 10/I/W	Suspd.		Unkn.	420-450
XX	Flower Madonna, white 10/III/W	Suspd.		Unkn.	470-750
XX	Going to Grandma's 52/I	Suspd.		Unkn.	336-900
XX	Good Night 260/D	Suspd.		Unkn.	145-150
XX	Goose Girl 47/II	Suspd.		Unkn.	357-410
XX	Happy Traveler 109/II	Suspd.		Unkn.	975-1050
XX	Hear Ye! Hear Ye! 15/II	Suspd.		Unkn.	383-1500
XX	Heavenly Angel 21/II	Suspd.		Unkn.	361-1025
XX	Heavenly Protection 88/II	Suspd.		Unkn.	900-975
XX	Hello 124/I	Suspd.		Unkn.	230-385
XX	Holy Child 70	Suspd.		Unkn.	210-400
XX	Hummel Display Plaque 187	Suspd.		Unkn.	125-175
XX	Infant Jesus 260/C	Suspd.		Unkn.	120
1985	Jubilee 416 TMK6	Suspd.		200.00	263-380
XX	King, Kneeling 260/P	Suspd.		Unkn.	480
XX	King, Moorish 260/N	Suspd.		Unkn.	430-500
XX	King, Standing 260/O	Suspd.		Unkn.	300-500
XX	Little Band 392	Suspd.		Unkn.	196-350
XX	Little Cellist 89/II	Suspd.		Unkn.	340-880
XX	Little Fiddler 2/4/0	Suspd.		Unkn.	86-115
XX	Little Fiddler 2/I	Suspd.		Unkn.	300-400
XX	Little Fiddler 2/II	Suspd.		Unkn.	750-935
XX	Little Fiddler 2/III	Suspd.		Unkn.	900-1800
XX	Little Hiker 16/I	Suspd.		Unkn.	184-319
XX	Little Sweeper 171/4/0	Suspd.		Unkn.	86-115
XX	Little Tooter 260/K	Suspd.		Unkn.	170-195
XX	Lullaby 24/III	Suspd.		Unkn.	1800-1900
XX	Madonna 260/A	Suspd.		Unkn.	590
XX	Madonna Holding Child, color 151/II	Suspd.		Unkn.	115-135
XX	Madonna Holding Child, white 151/W	Suspd.		Unkn.	320-350
XX	Madonna Praying, color 46/III/6	Suspd.		Unkn.	400-425
XX	Madonna Praying, white 46/0/W	Suspd.		Unkn.	195-225
XX	Madonna Praying, white 46/I/W	Suspd.		Unkn.	175-185
XX	Madonna w/o Halo, color 46/I/6	Suspd.		Unkn.	300-315
XX	Madonna w/o Halo, white 45/I/W	Suspd.		Unkn.	175-185
XX	Madonna w/o Halo, white 46/I/W	Suspd.		Unkn.	175-185
1989	Make A Wish 475	Suspd.		Unkn.	150-225
XX	Meditation 13/V	Suspd.		Unkn.	720-1600
XX	Meditation, color 13/II	Suspd.		Unkn.	450-4000
XX	Merry Wanderer 7/II	Suspd.		Unkn.	900-2350
XX	Merry Wanderer 7/III	Suspd.		Unkn.	1300-1400
XX	Merry Wanderer 7/X	Suspd.		Unkn.	20000-24000
XX	Merry Wanderer Stepbase 7/I	Suspd.		Unkn.	960-1075
1995	Ooh My Tooth (Special Event) 533	Suspd.		Unkn.	125-175
XX	Ox 260/M	Suspd.		Unkn.	135
XX	Playmates 58/I	Suspd.		Unkn.	310
XX	School Boys 170/III	Suspd.		Unkn.	2000-3255
XX	School Girls 177/III	Suspd.		Unkn.	1440-3255
XX	Sensitive Hunter 6/II	Suspd.		Unkn.	375-1150
XX	Serenade 85/4/0	Suspd.		Unkn.	86-115
XX	Sheep (Lying) 260/R	Suspd.		Unkn.	100
XX	Sheep (Standing) w/ Lamb 260/H	Suspd.		Unkn.	110
XX	Shepherd Boy, Kneeling 260/J	Suspd.		Unkn.	300
XX	Shepherd, Standing 260/G	Suspd.		Unkn.	525
XX	Soloist 135/4/0	Suspd.		Unkn.	86-115
XX	Spring Cheer 72	Suspd.		Unkn.	135-319
XX	Spring Dance 353/I	Suspd.		Unkn.	385-516
XX	St. Joseph 260/B	Suspd.		Unkn.	520
XX	A Stitch in Time 255/4/0	Suspd.		Unkn.	115
1984	Supreme Protection 364 TMK6	Suspd.		150.00	268-455
XX	Telling Her Secret 196/I	Suspd.		Unkn.	800-900
XX	To Market 49/I	Suspd.		Unkn.	361-850
XX	Trumpet Boy 97	Suspd.		Unkn.	128-195
XX	Village Boy 51/I	Suspd.		Unkn.	255-650
XX	Volunteers 50/I	Suspd.		Unkn.	550-1400
1989	Wash Day 321/4/0	Suspd.		Unkn.	86-115
XX	We Congratulate 260/F	Suspd.		Unkn.	400-555
XX	Weary Wanderer 204	Suspd.		Unkn.	210-364
XX	Worship 84/V	Suspd.		Unkn.	1100-2800

Gorham

(Four Seasons) A Boy And His Dog - N. Rockwell

YEAR ISSUE		EDITION LIMIT	YEAR RETD.	ISSUE PRICE	*QUOTE U.S.$
1972	A Boy Meets His Dog	2,500	1980	200.00	1300-1575
1972	Adventurers Between Adventures	2,500	1980	Set	Set
1972	The Mysterious Malady	2,500	1980	Set	Set
1972	Pride of Parenthood	2,500	1980	Set	Set

(Four Seasons) A Helping Hand - N. Rockwell

YEAR ISSUE		EDITION LIMIT	YEAR RETD.	ISSUE PRICE	*QUOTE U.S.$
1980	Year End Court	2,500	1980	650.00	700-1100
1980	Closed For Business	2,500	1980	Set	Set
1980	Swatter's Right	2,500	1980	Set	Set
1980	Coal Seasons Coming	2,500	1980	Set	Set

(Four Seasons) Dad's Boy - N. Rockwell

YEAR ISSUE		EDITION LIMIT	YEAR RETD.	ISSUE PRICE	*QUOTE U.S.$
1981	Ski Skills	2,500	1990	750.00	800-1200
1981	In His Spirit	2,500	1990	Set	Set
1981	Trout Dinner	2,500	1990	Set	Set
1981	Careful Aim	2,500	1990	Set	Set

(Four Seasons) Four Ages of Love - N. Rockwell

YEAR ISSUE		EDITION LIMIT	YEAR RETD.	ISSUE PRICE	*QUOTE U.S.$
1974	Gaily Sharing Vintage Times	2,500	1980	300.00	600-1250
1974	Sweet Song So Young	2,500	1980	Set	Set
1974	Flowers In Tender Bloom	2,500	1980	Set	Set
1974	Fondly Do We Remember	2,500	1980	Set	Set

(Four Seasons) Going On Sixteen - N. Rockwell

YEAR ISSUE		EDITION LIMIT	YEAR RETD.	ISSUE PRICE	*QUOTE U.S.$
1978	Chilling Chore	2,500	1980	400.00	650-675
1978	Sweet Serenade	2,500	1980	Set	Set
1978	Shear Agony	2,500	1980	Set	Set
1978	Pilgrimage	2,500	1980	Set	Set

(Four Seasons) Grand Pals - N. Rockwell

YEAR ISSUE		EDITION LIMIT	YEAR RETD.	ISSUE PRICE	*QUOTE U.S.$
1977	Snow Sculpturing	2,500	1980	350.00	1000-1200
1977	Soaring Spirits	2,500	1980	Set	Set
1977	Fish Finders	2,500	1980	Set	Set
1977	Ghostly Gourds	2,500	1980	Set	Set

(Four Seasons) Grandpa and Me - N. Rockwell

YEAR ISSUE		EDITION LIMIT	YEAR RETD.	ISSUE PRICE	*QUOTE U.S.$
1975	Gay Blades	2,500	1980	300.00	800-1000
1975	Day Dreamers	2,500	1980	Set	Set
1975	Goin' Fishing	2,500	1980	Set	Set
1975	Pensive Pals	2,500	1980	Set	Set

(Four Seasons) Life With Father - N. Rockwell

YEAR ISSUE		EDITION LIMIT	YEAR RETD.	ISSUE PRICE	*QUOTE U.S.$
1983	Big Decision	2,500	1990	250.00	250
1983	Blasting Out	2,500	1990	Set	Set
1983	Cheering The Champs	2,500	1990	Set	Set
1983	A Tough One	2,500	1990	Set	Set

(Four Seasons) Me and My Pal - N. Rockwell

YEAR ISSUE		EDITION LIMIT	YEAR RETD.	ISSUE PRICE	*QUOTE U.S.$
1976	A Licking Good Bath	2,500	1980	300.00	1200-1400
1976	Young Man's Fancy	2,500	1980	Set	Set
1976	Fisherman's Paradise	2,500	1980	Set	Set
1976	Disastrous Daring	2,500	1980	Set	Set

(Four Seasons) Old Buddies - N. Rockwell

YEAR ISSUE		EDITION LIMIT	YEAR RETD.	ISSUE PRICE	*QUOTE U.S.$
1984	Shared Success	2,500	1990	250.00	250
1984	Hasty Retreat	2,500	1990	Set	Set
1984	Final Speech	2,500	1990	Set	Set
1984	Endless Debate	2,500	1990	Set	Set

(Four Seasons) Old Timers - N. Rockwell

YEAR ISSUE		EDITION LIMIT	YEAR RETD.	ISSUE PRICE	*QUOTE U.S.$
1982	Canine Solo	2,500	1990	250.00	250
1982	Sweet Surprise	2,500	1990	Set	Set
1982	Lazy Days	2,500	1990	Set	Set
1982	Fancy Footwork	2,500	1990	Set	Set

(Four Seasons) Tender Years - N. Rockwell

YEAR ISSUE		EDITION LIMIT	YEAR RETD.	ISSUE PRICE	*QUOTE U.S.$
1979	New Year Look	2,500	1979	500.00	1200-1400
1979	Spring Tonic	2,500	1979	Set	Set
1979	Cool Aid	2,500	1979	Set	Set
1979	Chilly Reception	2,500	1979	Set	Set

(Four Seasons) Traveling Salesman - N. Rockwell

YEAR ISSUE		EDITION LIMIT	YEAR RETD.	ISSUE PRICE	*QUOTE U.S.$
1985	Horse Trader	2,500	1985	275.00	250-275
1985	Expert Salesman	2,500	1985	Set	Set
1985	Traveling Salesman	2,500	1985	Set	Set
1985	Country Pedlar	2,500	1985	Set	Set

(Four Seasons) Young Love - N. Rockwell

YEAR ISSUE		EDITION LIMIT	YEAR RETD.	ISSUE PRICE	*QUOTE U.S.$
1973	Downhill Daring	2,500	1973	250.00	1100
1973	Beguiling Buttercup	2,500	1973	Set	Set
1973	Flying High	2,500	1973	Set	Set
1973	A Scholarly Pace	2,500	1973	Set	Set

Miniature Christmas Figurines - Various

YEAR ISSUE		EDITION LIMIT	YEAR RETD.	ISSUE PRICE	*QUOTE U.S.$
1979	Tiny Tim - N. Rockwell	Yr.Iss.	1979	15.00	20
1980	Santa Plans His Trip - N. Rockwell	Yr.Iss.	1980	15.00	15
1981	Yuletide Reckoning - N. Rockwell	Yr.Iss.	1981	20.00	20
1982	Checking Good Deeds - N. Rockwell	Yr.Iss.	1982	20.00	20
1983	Santa's Friend - N. Rockwell	Yr.Iss.	1983	20.00	20
1984	Downhill Daring - N. Rockwell	Yr.Iss.	1984	20.00	20
1985	Christmas Santa - T. Nast	Yr.Iss.	1985	20.00	20
1986	Christmas Santa - T. Nast	Yr.Iss.	1986	25.00	25
1987	Annual Thomas Nast Santa - T. Nast	Yr.Iss.	1987	25.00	25

Miniatures - N. Rockwell

YEAR ISSUE		EDITION LIMIT	YEAR RETD.	ISSUE PRICE	*QUOTE U.S.$
1982	The Annual Visit	Closed	1990	50.00	75
1981	At the Vets	Closed	1990	27.50	40-50
1987	Babysitter	15,000	1990	75.00	75
1981	Beguiling Buttercup	Closed	1990	45.00	45
1985	Best Friends	Closed	1990	27.50	28
1987	Between The Acts	15,000	1990	60.00	60
1981	Boy Meets His Dog	Closed	1990	37.50	38-60
1984	Careful Aims	Closed	1990	55.00	55
1987	Cinderella	15,000	1990	70.00	75
1981	Downhill Daring	Closed	1990	45.00	75
1985	Engineer	Closed	1990	55.00	55
1981	Flowers in Tender Bloom	Closed	1990	60.00	60
1986	Football Season	Closed	1990	60.00	60
1981	Gay Blades	Closed	1990	45.00	75
1984	Ghostly Gourds	Closed	1990	60.00	60
1984	Goin Fishing	Closed	1990	60.00	60
1986	The Graduate	Closed	1990	30.00	40
1984	In His Spirit	Closed	1990	60.00	60
1984	Independence	Closed	1990	60.00	80
1986	Lemonade Stand	Closed	1990	60.00	60
1986	Little Angel	Closed	1990	50.00	60
1985	Little Red Truck	Closed	1990	25.00	25
1982	Marriage License	Closed	1990	60.00	75
1987	The Milkmaid	15,000	1990	80.00	85
1986	Morning Walk	Closed	1990	60.00	60
1985	Muscle Bound	Closed	1990	30.00	30
1985	New Arrival	Closed	1990	32.50	35
1984	The Oculist	Closed	1990	60.00	80
1986	The Old Sign Painter	Closed	1990	70.00	80
1984	Pride of Parenthood	Closed	1990	50.00	50
1987	The Prom Dress	15,000	1990	75.00	75
1982	The Runaway	Closed	1990	50.00	50
1984	Shear Agony	Closed	1990	60.00	60
1986	Shoulder Ride	Closed	1990	50.00	65
1981	Snow Sculpture	Closed	1990	45.00	70
1985	Spring Checkup	Closed	1990	60.00	60
1987	Springtime	15,000	1990	65.00	75
1987	Starstruck	15,000	1990	75.00	80
1981	Sweet Serenade	Closed	1990	45.00	45
1981	Sweet Song So Young	Closed	1990	55.00	55
1985	To Love & Cherish	Closed	1990	32.50	35
1982	Triple Self Portrait	Closed	1990	60.00	90-175
1983	Trout Dinner	15,000	1990	60.00	60
1982	Vintage Times	Closed	1990	50.00	50
1986	Welcome Mat	Closed	1990	70.00	75
1984	Years End Court	Closed	1990	60.00	60
1981	Young Man's Fancy	Closed	1990	55.00	55

Parasol Lady - Unknown

YEAR ISSUE		EDITION LIMIT	YEAR RETD.	ISSUE PRICE	*QUOTE U.S.$
1991	On the Boardwalk	Closed	1993	95.00	95
1994	Sunday Promenade	Closed	1993	95.00	95
1994	At The Fair	Closed	1993	95.00	95

Rockwell - N. Rockwell

YEAR ISSUE		EDITION LIMIT	YEAR RETD.	ISSUE PRICE	*QUOTE U.S.$
1983	Antique Dealer RW48	7,500	1990	130.00	200
1982	April Fool's (At The Curiosity Shop) RW39	Closed	1990	55.00	100-110
1974	At The Vets RW4	Closed	1990	25.00	125
1974	Batter Up RW6	Closed	1990	40.00	150-200
1977	Beguiling Buttercup RW-19	Closed	1990	85.00	150
1978	Big Decision RW-25	Closed	1990	55.00	55
1975	Boy And His Dog RW9	Closed	1990	38.00	150
1974	Captain RW8	Closed	1990	45.00	95
1984	Card Tricks	7,500	1990	110.00	180
1978	Choosing Up RW24	Closed	1990	85.00	275
1981	Christmas Dancers RW37	7,500	1990	130.00	250-275
1988	Confrontation	15,000	1990	75.00	75
1988	Cramming	15,000	1990	80.00	80
1981	Day in the Life Boy II RW34	Closed	1990	75.00	95
1982	A Day in the Life Boy III RW40	Closed	1990	85.00	95
1982	A Day in the Life Girl III RW41	Closed	1990	85.00	150
1988	The Diary	15,000	1990	80.00	80
1988	Dolores & Eddie NRM59	15,000	1990	75.00	80
1986	Drum For Tommy RW53	Annual	1986	90.00	N/A
1983	Facts of Life RW45	7,500	1990	110.00	180
1974	Fishing RW5	Closed	1990	50.00	175
1977	Gaily Sharing Vintage Time RW-20	Closed	1990	60.00	165
1988	Gary Cooper in Hollywood	15,000	1990	90.00	90
1977	Gay Blades RW-21	Closed	1990	50.00	50
1976	God Rest Ye Merry Gentlemen RW13	Closed	1990	50.00	1000-1500
1988	Home for the Holidays	7,500	1990	100.00	100
1976	Independence RW15	Closed	1990	40.00	150
1980	Jolly Coachman RW33	7,500	1990	75.00	175-200
1982	Marriage License (10 3/4") RW38	5,000	1990	110.00	400-600
1976	Marriage License (6 1/4") RW16	Closed	1990	50.00	195-325
1982	Merrie Christmas RW43	7,500	1990	75.00	150
1978	Missed RW23	Closed	1990	85.00	275
1974	Missing Tooth RW2	Closed	1990	30.00	150
1975	No Swimming RW18	Closed	1990	35.00	175
1976	The Oculist RW17	Closed	1990	50.00	175
1978	Oh Yeah RW22	Closed	1990	85.00	275
1975	Old Mill Pond RW11	Closed	1990	45.00	145
1985	The Old Sign Painter	7,500	1990	130.00	210
1977	Pride of Parenthood RW18	Closed	1990	50.00	125
1985	Puppet Maker	7,500	1990	130.00	130-200
1987	Santa Planning His Annual Visit	7,500	1990	95.00	95
1984	Santa's Friend	7,500	1990	75.00	160
1976	Saying Grace (5 1/2") RW12	5,000	1990	75.00	275
1982	Saying Grace (8") RW42	Closed	1990	110.00	500-600
1984	Serenade	7,500	1990	95.00	165
1974	Skating RW7	Closed	1990	37.50	140

*Quotes have been rounded up to nearest dollar

YEAR ISSUE	EDITION LIMIT	YEAR RETD.	ISSUE PRICE	*QUOTE U.S.$
1976 Tackled (Ad Stand)	Closed	1990	35.00	125-150
1982 Tackled (Rockwell Name Signed) RW8662	Closed	1990	45.00	100
1974 Tiny Tim RW3	Closed	1990	30.00	125
1980 Triple Self Portrait (10 1/2") RW32	5,000	1990	300.00	600
1979 Triple Self Portrait (7 1/2") RW27	Closed	1990	125.00	425
1974 Weighing In RW1	Closed	1990	40.00	150
1981 Wet Sport RW36	Closed	1990	85.00	100

Great American Taylor Collectibles

Great American Collectors' Club - L. Smith

YEAR ISSUE	EDITION LIMIT	YEAR RETD.	ISSUE PRICE	*QUOTE U.S.$
1993 William Claus-USA 700s	1,392	1994	35.00	125-300
1994 Winston-England 716	836	1995	35.00	60
1995 Timothy Claus-Ireland 717	946	1996	35.00	50-60
1996 Palmer-USA 723	689	1997	50.00	50
1997 Bowline-USA 734	12/98		50.00	50
1998 Reinhart-USA 748	12/99		50.00	50

Jim Clement Collectors' Club - L. Smith

YEAR ISSUE	EDITION LIMIT	YEAR RETD.	ISSUE PRICE	*QUOTE U.S.$
1995 Kris Jingle 817	280	1996	70.00	80
1996 Big Catch 830	236	1997	60.00	60
1997 Mogul Master 839	12/98		60.00	60
1998 Star Wish 845	12/99		70.00	70

Jim Clement Collection - J. Clement

YEAR ISSUE	EDITION LIMIT	YEAR RETD.	ISSUE PRICE	*QUOTE U.S.$
1994 Americana Patriotic Santa 807	329	1994	20.00	20-30
1994 Bearded Shorty Santa 812	533	1994	13.50	16-30
1994 Mrs. Clement's Santa 808	259	1994	17.00	17-30
1994 Santa High Hat 815	290	1994	30.00	35
1996 Santa w/Tree 804	425	1994	15.00	18-30
1994 Day After Christmas 809	494	1995	16.50	17
1994 Down the Chimney Santa 814	426	1995	28.00	30
1994 Golfer Santa 806	684	1995	28.00	33
1994 Mr. Egg Santa 802	397	1995	19.50	22
1994 Sm. Hobby Horse Santa 803	468	1995	28.00	33
1994 Big Santa w/Toys 813	510	1996	70.00	75-100
1994 Night After Christmas 810	776	1996	16.50	17
1994 Noah Santa 805	788	1996	28.00	30
1994 Santa w/Rover 811	537	1996	20.00	20
1994 Tennis Santa 816	656	1996	28.00	29
1995 Doe a Deer 818	456	1997	29.00	30
1995 Ho! Ho! Ho! 819	522	1997	11.50	12
1995 Mountain Dream 821	441	1997	27.00	30
1995 Silent Night 820	967	1997	29.00	32
1995 Visions of Sugar Plums 822	513	1997	23.00	25

Old World Santas - L. Smith

YEAR ISSUE	EDITION LIMIT	YEAR RETD.	ISSUE PRICE	*QUOTE U.S.$
1988 Jangle Claus-Ireland 335s	664	1990	20.00	160-180
1988 Hans Von Claus-Germany 337s	560	1990	20.00	160-180
1988 Ching Chang Claus-China 338s	570	1990	20.00	180
1988 Kris Kringle Claus-Switzerland 339s	607	1990	20.00	150-180
1988 Jingle Claus-England 336s	571	1990	20.00	150-180
1989 Rudy Claus-Austria 410s	709	1991	20.00	150
1989 Noel Claus-Belguim 412s	676	1991	20.00	150
1989 Pierre Claus-France 414s	702	1991	20.00	150
1989 Nicholai Claus-Russia 413s	768	1991	20.00	150
1989 Yule Claus-Germany 411s	565	1991	20.00	150
1990 Matts Claus-Sweden 430s	1,243	1992	20.00	95-130
1990 Vander Claus-Holland 433s	1,136	1992	20.00	95-130
1990 Sven Claus-Norway 432s	1,639	1992	20.00	95-130
1990 Cedric Claus-England 434s	1,087	1992	20.00	95-130
1990 Mario Claus-Italy 431s	887	1992	20.00	95-130
1991 Mitch Claus-England 437s	1,962	1993	25.00	80-110
1991 Samuel Claus-USA 436s	2,656	1993	25.00	80-110
1991 Duncan Claus-Scotland 439s	2,754	1993	25.00	80-110
1991 Benjamin Claus-Israel 438s	2,358	1993	25.00	80-110
1991 Boris Claus-Russia 435s	2,588	1993	25.00	80-110
1992 Mickey Claus-Ireland 701s	3,722	1994	25.00	75-95
1992 Jacques Claus-France 702s	2,792	1994	25.00	85-100
1992 Terry Claus-Denmark 703s	3,094	1994	25.00	75-85
1992 José Claus-Spain 704s	2,797	1994	25.00	65-75
1992 Stu Claus-Poland 705s	3,243	1994	25.00	75-85
1993 Otto Claus-Germany 707s	2,712	1995	27.50	75
1993 Franz Claus-Switzerland 706s	2,708	1995	27.50	75
1993 Bjorn Claus-Sweden 709s	2,749	1995	27.50	75-90
1993 Ryan Claus-Canada 710s	2,868	1995	27.50	75-85
1993 Vito Claus-Italy 708s	2,784	1995	27.50	75-85
1994 Angus Claus-Scotland 713s	4,981	1996	27.50	40-50
1994 Ivan Claus-Russia 712s	3,256	1996	27.50	40-45
1994 Desmond Claus-England 715s	3,275	1996	27.50	40-45
1994 Gord Claus-Canada 714s	3,743	1996	27.50	40-50
1994 Wilhelm-Holland 711s	3,318	1996	27.50	40-45
1995 Tomba Claus-South Africa 718s	3,127	1997	29.00	32-40
1995 Butch Claus-United States 719s	2,894	1997	29.00	32-40
1995 Lars Claus-Norway 720s	3,503	1997	29.00	32-40
1995 Stach Claus-Poland 721s	2,974	1997	29.00	32-40
1995 Raymond Claus-Galapagos Islands 722s	2,209	1997	29.00	32-40

Greenwich Workshop

Bronze - Various

YEAR ISSUE	EDITION LIMIT	YEAR RETD.	ISSUE PRICE	*QUOTE U.S.$
1994 Bird Hunters (Bronze) - J. Christensen	50	N/A	4500.00	4500
1990 The Candleman, AP (Bronze) - J. Christensen	100	N/A	2250.00	4500
1991 Comanche Raider - K. McCarthy	100	N/A	812.50	813
1989 The Fish Walker (Bronze) - J. Christensen	100	N/A	3200.00	4500
1991 Pony Express - K. McCarthy	10	N/A	934.00	934
1994 Thunder of Hooves - K. McCarthy	10	N/A	875.00	875

The Greenwich Workshop Collection - Various

YEAR ISSUE	EDITION LIMIT	YEAR RETD.	ISSUE PRICE	*QUOTE U.S.$
1998 The Ancient Angel - J. Christensen	1,750		195.00	195
1997 And The Wolf - S. Gustafson	945		350.00	350
1996 And They...Crooked House - J. Christensen	Retrd.	1998	295.00	295
1996 Another Fish Act - J. Christensen	2,500		350.00	350
1998 The Artist - W. Bullas	622		95.00	95
1998 Baby Bear - S. Gustafson	1,950		50.00	50
1998 Back Quackers - W. Bullas	1,200		125.00	125
1997 Bassoonist - J. Christensen	1,500		395.00	395
1996 Bed Time Buddies - W. Bullas	Open		75.00	75
1998 Brother Avery - S. Gustafson	2,500		95.00	95
1997 Brother Folio Scrivner - S. Gustafson	2,364		95.00	95
1998 California Stylin - W. Bullas	Open		125.00	125
1996 Candleman - J. Christensen	2,500		295.00	295
1996 Christmas Angel - W. Bullas	1,996	1996	75.00	200
1996 Christmas Elf - W. Bullas	1,996	1996	75.00	200
1997 Consultant - W. Bullas	Open		95.00	95
1997 Crooked Cat, Crooked Mouse - J. Christensen	1,724	1998	60.00	60-90
1996 The Dare Devil - W. Bullas	Retrd.	1998	75.00	75
1998 Dressed for the Holidays - W. Bullas	1,500		95.00	95
1997 Duck Tape - W. Bullas	600		95.00	95
1996 Ductor - W. Bullas	Open		75.00	75
1997 Dust Bunnies - W. Bullas	500		75.00	75
1997 Fish Walker - J. Christensen	571		350.00	350
1996 Fool and His Bunny - W. Bullas	Open		75.00	75
1998 Fool Moon - W. Bullas	1,750		125.00	125
1997 Forest Fish Rider - J. Christensen	2,500		175.00	175
1998 Fowl Ball - W. Bullas	828		95.00	95
1997 Frog Horn - W. Bullas	2,028		85.00	85
1998 Froggy Goes A-Wooing - S. Gustafson	2,500		125.00	125
1998 Goldilocks - S. Gustafson	1,950		130.00	130
1998 The Hare - S. Gustafson	1,950		95.00	95
1996 He Bought a Crooked Cat - J. Christensen	Retrd.	1998	60.00	60
1996 Head of the Class - W. Bullas	Retrd.	1998	75.00	75
1997 Hocus Pocus - W. Bullas	547		125.00	125
1997 How Many Angels Can Fit on Head - J. Christensen	536		215.00	215
1997 Humpty Dumpty - S. Gustafson	600		250.00	250
1996 Jack Be Nimble - J. Christensen	Open		295.00	295
1998 Jack Sprat Could Eat No Fat - J. Christensen	1,500		175.00	175
1998 Jack's Wife Could Eat No Lean - J. Christensen	1,500		185.00	185
1996 Jailbirds - W. Bullas	Open		75.00	75
1996 Lawrence Pretended Not to Notice... - J. Christensen	2,500		350.00	350
1996 Levi Levitates a Stone Fish - J. Christensen	2,500		295.00	295
1997 Little Red Riding Hood - S. Gustafson	974		150.00	150
1998 The Lute Player - J. Christensen	1,500		450.00	450
1998 Mama Bear - S. Gustafson	1,950		175.00	175
1996 Man Who Minds the Moon - J. Christensen	2,500		295.00	295
1998 The Miniature Artist - J. Christensen	1,500		95.00	95
1996 Mother Goose - J. Christensen	Open		275.00	275
1998 Mrs. Claus - J. Christensen	2,500		295.00	295
1998 The Nurse - W. Bullas	2,500		95.00	95
1995 Olde World Santa - J. Christensen	950	1995	295.00	600
1996 The Oldest Angel - J. Christensen	2,500		295.00	295
1998 Ottist - S. Gustafson	1,500		95.00	95
1998 The Owl and the Pussycat - S. Gustafson	2,500		250.00	250
1998 Papa Bear - S. Gustafson	1,950		180.00	180
1997 Puppy Glove - W. Bullas	Open		95.00	95
1998 Puss in Boots - S. Gustafson	2,500		165.00	165
1998 Responsible Man - J. Christensen	1,950		450.00	450
1996 The Responsible Woman - J. Christensen	2,500		595.00	595
1997 Rudy - W. Bullas	2,553		125.00	125
1998 Sandtrap Pro - W. Bullas	828		95.00	95
1998 Santa's Hopper - W. Bullas	1,250		85.00	85
1997 Santa's Other Helpers - J. Christensen	2,500		295.00	295
1997 The Scholar - J. Christensen	1,700		375.00	375
1998 Snow Buddies - W. Bullas	1,250		125.00	125
1998 Sock Hop - W. Bullas	Open		125.00	125
1998 Space Cadet - W. Bullas	2,500		95.00	95
1998 Supermom - W. Bullas	1,228		95.00	95
1996 There Was a Crooked Man... - J. Christensen	Retrd.	1998	225.00	225
1996 Three Blind Mice: Fluffy - J. Christensen	Retrd.	1998	75.00	75
1996 Three Blind Mice: Sniffer - J. Christensen	Retrd.	1998	75.00	75
1996 Three Blind Mice: Weevil - J. Christensen	Retrd.	1998	75.00	75
1997 Tommy Tucker - J. Christensen	1,250		295.00	295
1998 The Tortoise - S. Gustafson	1,950		125.00	125
1997 The Traveling Fish Salesman - J. Christensen	546		150.00	150
1996 Trick or Treat - W. Bullas	Retrd.	1998	75.00	75
1996 The Trick Rider - W. Bullas	Open		75.00	75
1996 Tweedle Dee - J. Christensen	1,250		295.00	295
1996 Tweedle Dum - J. Christensen	1,250		295.00	295
1998 Wetland Bird Hunter - J. Christensen	1,950		250.00	250
1996 Zippo...the Fire Eater - W. Bullas	Open		75.00	75

Hallmark Galleries

Kiddie Car Classics - E. Weirick

YEAR ISSUE	EDITION LIMIT	YEAR RETD.	ISSUE PRICE	*QUOTE U.S.$
1998 1929 Steelcraft Roadster by Murray® QHG9040	Open		70.00	70
1998 1930 Custom Biplane QHG7104	Open		55.00	55
1998 1930 Spirit of Christmas Custom Biplane QHG7105	Open		60.00	60
1996 1935 Steelcraft Airplane by Murray® QHG9032	Retrd.	1997	50.00	95-113
1996 1935 Steelcraft by Murray® (Luxury Edition) QHG9029	24,500	1996	65.00	132-144
1994 1936 Steelcraft Lincoln Zephyr by Murray® QHG9015	19,500	1996	50.00	125-138
1997 1937 GARTON® Ford QHG9035	Retrd.	1997	65.00	93-104
1995 1937 Steelcraft Auburn Luxury Ed. QHG9021	24,500	1996	65.00	160-175
1995 1937 Steelcraft Chrysler Airflow by Murray® QHG9024	24,500	1996	65.00	104-119
1997 1938 GARTON® Lincoln Zephyr Luxury Edition QHX9038	Retrd.	1997	65.00	65-138
1997 1939 GARTON® Ford Station Wagon QHX9034	Open		55.00	55
1998 1940 Custom Roadster with Trailer QHG7106	39,500		75.00	75
1997 1940 Gendron "Red Hot" Roadster, (2nd in Winner's Circle Series) QHX9037	Open		55.00	55
1992 1941 Murray® Airplane QHG9003	14,500	1993	50.00	412-420
1997 1941 Murray® Junior Service Truck QHG9031	Open		55.00	55
1998 1941 Steelcraft by Murray® Fire Truck QHG9042	Open		60.00	60
1997 1941 Steelcraft Oldsmobile by Murray® QHG9036	Open		55.00	55
1994 1941 Steelcraft Spitfire Airplane QHG9009	19,500	1996	50.00	150-200
1998 1941Steelcraft Chrysler by Murray® QHG9044	Open		55.00	55
1995 1948 Murray® Pontiac QHG9026	Retrd.	1998	50.00	50-80
1995 1950 Murray® Torpedo QHG9020	Retrd.	1996	50.00	140-154
1992 1953 Murray® Dump Truck QHG9012	14,500	1993	48.00	219-260
1998 1955 Custom Chevy® QHG7103	Open		50.00	50
1992 1955 Murray® Champion QHG9008	14,500	1993	45.00	360-375
1994 1955 Murray® Dump Truck QHG9011	19,500	1996	48.00	104-110
1993 1955 Murray® Fire Chief QHG9006	19,500	1996	45.00	105-130
1992 1955 Murray® Fire Truck QHG9001	14,500	1993	50.00	420-450
1994 1955 Murray® Fire Truck QHG9010	19,500	1996	50.00	275-300
1994 1955 Murray® Ranch Wagon QHG9007	24,500	1996	48.00	90-125
1994 1955 Murray® Red Champion QHG9002	19,500	1996	45.00	99-119
1995 1955 Murray® Royal Deluxe QHG9025	29,500		55.00	55
1992 1955 Murray® Tractor and Trailer QHG9004	14,500	1993	55.00	300-350
1994 1956 GARTON® Dragnet Police Car QHG9016	24,500	1997	50.00	90-125
1996 1956 GARTON® Hot Rod Racer (1st in Winner's Circle Series) QHG9028	Open		55.00	55
1994 1956 GARTON® Kidillac (Sp. Ed.) QHX9094	Retrd.	1994	50.00	42-85
1994 1956 GARTON® Mark V QHG9022	24,500	1997	45.00	60-95
1997 1956 Murray® Golden Eagle QHG9033	Retrd.	1997	50.00	50-95
1994 1958 Murray® Atomic Missile QHG9018	24,500	1997	55.00	100-125
1998 1958 Murray® Champion QHG9041	Open		55.00	55
1995 1959 GARTON® Deluxe Kidillac QHG9017	Retrd.	1996	55.00	80-88
1998 1960 Eight Ball Racer QHG9039	Open		55.00	55
1995 1961 GARTON® Casey Jones Locomotive QHG9019	Retrd.	1996	55.00	94-120
1994 1961 Murray® Circus Car QHG9014	24,500	1997	48.00	48-75
1994 1961 Murray® Speedway Pace Car 4500QHG9013	24,500	1997	45.00	90-95
1996 1961 Murray® Super Deluxe Tractor w/Trailer QHG9027	Open		55.00	55
1995 1962 Murray® Super Deluxe Fire Truck QHG9095	Retrd.	1997	55.00	55
1996 1964 1/2 Ford Mustang QHG9030	Open		55.00	55
1995 1964 GARTON® Tin Lizzie QHG9023	Retrd.	1997	50.00	50-75
1993 1968 Murray® Boat Jolly Roger QHG9005	19,500	1996	50.00	115-119

Tender Touches - E. Seale

YEAR ISSUE	EDITION LIMIT	YEAR RETD.	ISSUE PRICE	*QUOTE U.S.$
1990 Baby Bear in Backpack QEC9863	Retrd.	1991	16.00	60
1988 Baby Raccoon QHG7031	Retrd.	1992	20.00	40
1991 Baby's 1st Riding Rocking Bear QEC9349	Retrd.	1991	16.00	45
1989 Bear Decorating Tree QHG7050	Retrd.	1995	18.00	40
1992 Bear Family Christmas QHG7002	9,500	1995	45.00	42-55
1990 Bear Graduate QHG7043	Retrd.	1995	15.00	10-15
1988 Bear w/ Umbrella QHG7029	Retrd.	1994	16.00	35
1990 Bear's Easter Parade QHG7040	Retrd.	1995	23.00	23
1990 Bears Playing Baseball QHG7039	Retrd.	1994	20.00	20
1990 Bears w/ Gift QEC9461	Retrd.	1991	18.00	50-65
1992 Beaver Growth Chart QHG7007	19,500	1995	20.00	20

YEAR ISSUE	EDITION LIMIT	YEAR RETD.	ISSUE PRICE	*QUOTE U.S.$
1992 Beaver w/ Double Bass QHG7058	Retrd.	1995	18.00	15-18
1990 Beavers w/Tree QHG7052	Retrd.	1994	23.00	23
1989 Birthday Mouse QHG7010	Retrd.	1993	16.00	45
1992 Breakfast in Bed QHG7059	Retrd.	1995	18.00	18
1989 Bride & Groom QHG7009	Retrd.	1994	20.00	40
1992 Building a Pumpkin Man QHG7061	Retrd.	1995	18.00	18
1990 Bunnies Eating Ice Cream QHG7038	Retrd.	1995	20.00	20
1990 Bunnies w/ Slide QHG7016	Retrd.	1994	20.00	15-20
1990 Bunny Cheerleader QHG7018	Retrd.	1994	16.00	45
1992 Bunny Clarinet QHG7063	Retrd.	1994	16.00	45
1990 Bunny Hiding Valentine QHG7035	Retrd.	1995	16.00	16
1990 Bunny in Boat QHG7021	Retrd.	1994	18.00	40
1989 Bunny in Flowers QHG7012	Retrd.	1992	16.00	30
1991 Bunny in High Chair QHG7054	Retrd.	1995	16.00	30
1990 Bunny Pulling Wagon QHG7008	Retrd.	1994	23.00	15-23
1990 Bunny w/ Ice Cream QHG7020	Retrd.	1993	15.00	15
1992 Bunny w/ Kite QHG7006	19,500	1995	19.00	12-19
1991 Bunny w/ Large Eggs QHG7056	Retrd.	1995	16.00	85
1990 Bunny w/ Stocking QEC9416	Retrd.	1990	15.00	35
1992 Chatting Mice QHG7003	19,500	1995	23.00	45
1989 Chipmunk Praying QEC9431	Retrd.	1991	18.00	35
1989 Chipmunk w/Roses QHG7023	Retrd.	1992	16.00	35
1992 Chipmunks w/Album QHG7057	Retrd.	1995	23.00	35
1991 Christmas Bunny Skiing QHG7046	Retrd.	1995	18.00	15-18
1990 Dad and Son Bears QHG7015	Retrd.	1992	23.00	33
1992 Delightful Fright QHG7067	19,500	1995	23.00	50-75
1993 Downhill Dash QHG7080	Retrd.	1995	23.00	20-23
1990 Easter Egg Hunt QEC9866	Retrd.	1991	18.00	275
1993 Easter Stroll QHG7084	Retrd.	1995	21.00	15-21
1993 Ensemble Chipmunk Kettledrum QHG7087	Retrd.	1994	18.00	15-18
1991 Father Bear Barbequing QHG7041	Retrd.	1995	23.00	15-23
1994 Fireman QHG7090	Retrd.	1995	23.00	23
1991 First Christmas Mice @ Piano QEC9357	Retrd.	1991	23.00	23
1992 Fitting Gift QHG7065	Retrd.	1995	23.00	15-23
1991 Foxes in Rowboat QHG7053	Retrd.	1995	23.00	23
1992 From Your Valentine QHG7071	Retrd.	1995	20.00	20
1993 Garden Capers QHG7078	Retrd.	1995	20.00	15-20
1994 Golfing QHG7091	Retrd.	1995	23.00	23
1994 Halloween QHG7093	Retrd.	1995	23.00	40
1989 Halloween Trio QEC9714	Retrd.	1990	18.00	85-125
1993 Handling a Big Thirst QHG7076	Retrd.	1995	21.00	21
1994 Happy Campers QHG7092	Retrd.	1995	25.00	15-25
1994 Jesus, Mary, Joseph QHG7094	Retrd.	1995	23.00	40
1993 Love at First Sight QHG7085	Retrd.	1995	23.00	23
1991 Love-American Gothic-Farmer Raccoons QHG7047	Retrd.	1995	20.00	15-20
1993 Making A Splash QHG7088	Retrd.	1995	20.00	20
1988 Mice at Tea Party QHG7028	Retrd.	1993	23.00	23
1991 Mice Couple Slow Waltzing QEC9437	Retrd.	1991	20.00	500
1990 Mice in Red Car QEC9886	Retrd.	1991	20.00	65-75
1988 Mice in Rocking Chair QHG7030	Retrd.	1994	18.00	20
1990 Mice w/Mistletoe QEC9423	Retrd.	1990	20.00	30
1990 Mice w/Quilt QHG7017	Retrd.	1994	20.00	25
1992 Mom's Easter Bonnet QHG7072	Retrd.	1995	18.00	18
1991 Mother Raccoon Reading Bible Stories QHG7042	Retrd.	1994	20.00	20
1989 Mouse at Desk QEC9434	Retrd.	1990	18.00	15-25
1991 Mouse Couple Sharing Soda QHG7055	Retrd.	1995	23.00	23
1990 Mouse in Pumpkin QEC9473	Retrd.	1991	18.00	135-150
1992 Mouse Matinee QHG7073	Retrd.	1995	22.00	22
1990 Mouse Nurse QHG7037	Retrd.	1995	15.00	15
1988 Mouse w/Heart QHG7024	Retrd.	1993	18.00	18
1989 Mouse w/Violin QHG7049	Retrd.	1992	16.00	30-50
1993 Mr. Repair Bear QHG7075	Retrd.	1995	18.00	18
1992 New World, Ahoy! QHG7068	Retrd.	1995	25.00	22-30
1992 Newsboy Bear QHG7060	Retrd.	1995	16.00	16
1993 The Old Swimming Hole QHG7086	9,500	1995	45.00	55-95
1990 Pilgrim Bear Praying QEC9466	Retrd.	1991	18.00	29-65
1989 Pilgrim Mouse QEC9721	Retrd.	1990	16.00	50
1993 Playground Go-Round QHG7089	Retrd.	1995	23.00	15-23
1989 Rabbit Painting Egg QHG7022	Retrd.	1994	18.00	30
1988 Rabbit w/Ribbon QHG7027	Retrd.	1994	15.00	15
1988 Rabbits at Juice Stand QHG7033	Retrd.	1994	23.00	18-23
1989 Rabbits Ice Skating QEC9391	Retrd.	1991	18.00	28
1988 Rabbits w/Cake QHG7025	Retrd.	1992	20.00	40
1992 Raccoon in Bath QHG7069	Retrd.	1993	18.00	35
1990 Raccoon Mail Carrier QHG7013	Retrd.	1995	16.00	16
1988 Raccoon w/Cake QEC9724	Retrd.	1991	18.00	45
1990 Raccoon Watering Roses QHG7036	Retrd.	1994	20.00	20
1991 Raccoon Witch QHG7045	Retrd.	1994	16.00	20
1988 Raccoons Fishing QHG7034	Retrd.	1994	18.00	18
1992 Raccoons on Bridge QHG7004	19,500	1995	25.00	25
1988 Raccoons Playing Ball QEC9771	Retrd.	1991	18.00	40
1990 Raccoons w/Flag QHG7044	Retrd.	1994	23.00	45
1990 Raccoons w/Wagon QHG7014	Retrd.	1993	23.00	15-30
1990 Romeo & Juliet Mice QEC9903	Retrd.	1991	25.00	500
1990 Santa in Chimney QHG7051	Retrd.	1994	18.00	15-18
1989 Santa Mouse in Chair QEC9394	Retrd.	1990	20.00	135-150
1993 Sculpting Santa QHG7083	Retrd.	1995	20.00	20
1992 Soapbox Racer QHG7005	19,500	1995	23.00	23
1988 Squirrels w/Bandage QHG7032	Retrd.	1993	18.00	18
1992 Stealing a Kiss QHG7066	19,500	1995	23.00	15-23
1992 Sweet Sharing QHG7062	Retrd.	1995	20.00	15-20
1992 Swingtime Love QHG7070	Retrd.	1993	21.00	100
1990 Teacher & Student Chipmunks QHG7019	Retrd.	1992	20.00	30
1988 Teacher w/Student QHG7026	Retrd.	1995	18.00	18
1993 Teeter For Two QHG7077	Retrd.	1995	23.00	15-23
1992 Tender Touches Tree House QHG7001	9,500	1995	55.00	35-55
1992 Thanksgiving Family Around Table QHG7048	Retrd.	1995	25.00	25
1990 Tucking Baby in Bed QHG7011	Retrd.	1993	18.00	18
1992 Waiting for Santa QHG7064	Retrd.	1995	20.00	20
1993 Woodland Americana-Liberty Mouse QHG7081	Retrd.	1995	21.00	30
1993 Woodland Americana-Patriot George QHG7082	Retrd.	1995	25.00	40
1993 Woodland Americana-Stitching the Stars and Stripes QHG7079	Retrd.	1995	21.00	35
1992 Younger Than Springtime QHG7074	19,500	1995	35.00	25-50

Hamilton Collection

American Garden Flowers - D. Fryer

YEAR ISSUE	EDITION LIMIT	YEAR RETD.	ISSUE PRICE	*QUOTE U.S.$
1987 Azalea	15,000		75.00	75
1988 Calla Lilly	15,000		75.00	75
1987 Camelia	9,800		55.00	75
1988 Day Lily	15,000		75.00	75
1987 Gardenia	15,000		75.00	75
1989 Pansy	15,000		75.00	75
1988 Petunia	15,000		75.00	75
1987 Rose	15,000		75.00	75

American Wildlife Bronze Collection - H./N. Deaton

YEAR ISSUE	EDITION LIMIT	YEAR RETD.	ISSUE PRICE	*QUOTE U.S.$
1980 Beaver	7,500		60.00	65
1979 Bobcat	7,500		60.00	75
1979 Cougar	7,500		60.00	125
1980 Polar Bear	7,500		60.00	65
1980 Sea Otter	7,500		60.00	65
1979 White-Tailed Deer	7,500		60.00	105

Arrowhead Spirits - M. Richter

YEAR ISSUE	EDITION LIMIT	YEAR RETD.	ISSUE PRICE	*QUOTE U.S.$
1996 Path of the Wolf	28-day		29.95	30
1996 Piercing The Night	28-day		29.95	30
1996 Soul of the Hunter	28-day		29.95	30

Camelot Frogs - S. Kehrli

YEAR ISSUE	EDITION LIMIT	YEAR RETD.	ISSUE PRICE	*QUOTE U.S.$
1997 Jumping Jester	Open		19.95	20
1996 King Ribbit	Open		19.95	20
1997 Knight of The Lily Pad	Open		19.95	20
1996 Lady of The Lily Pad	Open		19.95	20
1997 Queen Ribbit	Open		19.95	20
1996 Royal Ribbiteer	Open		19.95	20
1996 Sir Hop A Lot	Open		19.95	20
1996 Wizard of Camelot	Open		19.95	20

A Celebration of Roses - N/A

YEAR ISSUE	EDITION LIMIT	YEAR RETD.	ISSUE PRICE	*QUOTE U.S.$
1989 Brandy	Open		55.00	55
1989 Color Magic	Open		55.00	55
1989 Honor	Open		55.00	55
1989 Miss All-American Beauty	Open		55.00	55
1991 Ole'	Open		55.00	55
1990 Oregold	Open		55.00	55
1991 Paradise	Open		55.00	55
1989 Tiffany	Open		55.00	55

Cherished Teddies Village - P. Hillman

YEAR ISSUE	EDITION LIMIT	YEAR RETD.	ISSUE PRICE	*QUOTE U.S.$
1997 Appletree Schoolhouse	Open		45.00	45
1997 Camille's Quilt Shop	Open		45.00	45
1995 A Picnic For Two	Open		45.00	45
1996 Sweet Treats For Teddie	Open		45.00	45
1996 Teddie's Boat Shop	Open		45.00	45
1997 Teddies Nursery	Open		45.00	45
1996 Toys For Teddies	Open		45.00	45
1996 The Wedding Gazebo	Open		45.00	45

Cleaver Birds w/Water - B. Cleaver

YEAR ISSUE	EDITION LIMIT	YEAR RETD.	ISSUE PRICE	*QUOTE U.S.$
1998 Splashin' Around	N/A		17.95	18
1998 Chill'n Good Time	N/A		17.95	18

Coral Reef Beauties - Everhart

YEAR ISSUE	EDITION LIMIT	YEAR RETD.	ISSUE PRICE	*QUOTE U.S.$
1996 Coral Paradise	Open		39.95	40
1996 Ocean's Bounty	Open		39.95	40
1996 Sentinel of the Sea	Open		39.95	40

Dreamsicles Animal Pals - K. Haynes

YEAR ISSUE	EDITION LIMIT	YEAR RETD.	ISSUE PRICE	*QUOTE U.S.$
1998 African Pals	Open		19.90	20
1998 Frontier Friends	Open		19.90	20
1998 Outback Chums	Open		19.90	20
1998 Striped Companions	Open		19.90	20
1998 Underwater Buddies	Open		19.90	20
1998 Woodland Playmates	Open		19.90	20

Dreamsicles Anniversary Carousel Clock - K. Haynes

YEAR ISSUE	EDITION LIMIT	YEAR RETD.	ISSUE PRICE	*QUOTE U.S.$
1997 Dreamsicles Anniversary Carousel Clock	Open		95.00	95

Dreamsicles International Friends Collection - K. Haynes

YEAR ISSUE	EDITION LIMIT	YEAR RETD.	ISSUE PRICE	*QUOTE U.S.$
1998 I'll Always Be Your Amigo	Open		14.95	15
1998 Your Friendship Is Wünderbar	Open		14.95	15
1998 Friendship Spans All Distances	Open		14.95	15
1998 Your Friendship Is A Home Run	Open		14.95	15

Dreamsicles Special Friends Music Box - K. Haynes

YEAR ISSUE	EDITION LIMIT	YEAR RETD.	ISSUE PRICE	*QUOTE U.S.$
1997 The Best Gift of All	Open		29.95	30
1997 Bless Us All	Open		29.95	30
1997 Heaven's Little Helper	Open		29.95	30
1997 A Heavenly Hoorah!	Open		29.95	30
1997 A Hug From The Heart	Open		29.95	30
1997 A Love Like No Other	Open		29.95	30

Early Discoveries - Adams-Hart

YEAR ISSUE	EDITION LIMIT	YEAR RETD.	ISSUE PRICE	*QUOTE U.S.$
1997 Curious Encounters	Open		19.95	20
1997 Ducky Discoveries	Open		19.95	20
1996 First Recital	Open		19.95	20
1997 Friendly Encounters	Open		19.95	20
1997 Friendly Foes	Open		19.95	20
1997 Nature's Scent	Open		19.95	20
1997 New Explorers	Open		19.95	20
1996 New Friends	Open		19.95	20
1997 Peaceful Pals	Open		19.95	20
1997 Springtime Melodies	Open		19.95	20
1997 Strolling Along	Open		19.95	20
1996 Sweet Nature	Open		19.95	20

Elephant Tales - M. Adams

YEAR ISSUE	EDITION LIMIT	YEAR RETD.	ISSUE PRICE	*QUOTE U.S.$
1998 Cinderella	Open		17.95	18
1998 The Frog & Princess	Open		17.95	18
1998 The Princess & Swans	Open		17.95	18
1998 Princess & The Pea	Open		17.95	18
1998 Rapunzel	Open		17.95	18
1998 Rumpelstilskin	Open		17.95	18
1998 Sleeping Beauty	Open		17.95	18
1998 Snow White	Open		17.95	18

First on Race Day Figurine Collection - N/A

YEAR ISSUE	EDITION LIMIT	YEAR RETD.	ISSUE PRICE	*QUOTE U.S.$
1996 Bill Elliott	Open		45.00	45
1996 Jeff Gordon	Open		45.00	45

Freshwater Challenge - M. Wald

YEAR ISSUE	EDITION LIMIT	YEAR RETD.	ISSUE PRICE	*QUOTE U.S.$
1992 Prized Catch	Open		75.00	75
1991 Rainbow Lure	Open		75.00	75
1991 The Strike	Open		75.00	75
1991 Sun Catcher	Open		75.00	75

Garden Romances Are Forever - B. Cleaver

YEAR ISSUE	EDITION LIMIT	YEAR RETD.	ISSUE PRICE	*QUOTE U.S.$
1997 Bundles of Love	Open		14.95	15
1997 Endless Love Songs	Open		14.95	15
1997 Falling In Love	Open		14.95	15
1997 Flowered With Love	Open		14.95	15
1997 Fragrant Love	Open		14.95	15
1997 Fruits of Love	Open		14.95	15
1997 Heartfelt Love	Open		14.95	15
1997 Humming With Love	Open		14.95	15
1997 Love Buds	Open		14.95	15
1997 Love Has Its Ups and Downs	Open		14.95	15
1996 Love Is In The Air	Open		14.95	15
1997 Love Pecks	Open		14.95	15

Gifts of the Ancient Spirits - S. Kehrli

YEAR ISSUE	EDITION LIMIT	YEAR RETD.	ISSUE PRICE	*QUOTE U.S.$
1996 Talisman of Courage	Open		79.00	79
1996 Talisman of the Buffalo	Open		79.00	79
1996 Talisman of Strength	Open		79.00	79

Gone With The Wind-Porcelain Trading Cards - N/A

YEAR ISSUE	EDITION LIMIT	YEAR RETD.	ISSUE PRICE	*QUOTE U.S.$
1995 Fire and Passion	28-day		14.95	15
1995 Scarlett and Her Suitors	28-day		14.95	15
1996 Portrait of Scarlett	28-day		14.95	15
1996 Portrait of Rhett	28-day		14.95	15
1996 The Proposal	28-day		14.95	15
1996 Scarlett and Mammy	28-day		14.95	15
1996 Rhett at Twelve Oaks	28-day		14.95	15
1996 The Bold Entrance	28-day		14.95	15
1996 Sunset Embrace	28-day		14.95	15
1996 The Jail Scene	28-day		14.95	15
1996 The Exodus	28-day		14.95	15
1996 Anger Turns to Passion	28-day		14.95	15
1996 The Reunion	28-day		14.95	15
1997 Belle & Rhett	28-day		14.95	15
1997 Portrait of Ashley	28-day		14.95	15
1997 Rhett & Bonnie	28-day		14.95	15
1997 Scarlett & Ashley	28-day		14.95	15

Happy Owlidays - W. Henry

YEAR ISSUE	EDITION LIMIT	YEAR RETD.	ISSUE PRICE	*QUOTE U.S.$
1998 Back to Schoo-owl	Open		17.95	18
1998 Easter Owlebration	Open		17.95	18
1998 Giving Owl Thanks	Open		17.95	18
1998 Happy Owloween	Open		17.95	18
1998 Luck of the Owlrish	Open		17.95	18
1998 Owl Be Home For Christmas	Open		17.95	18
1998 Owl Be Your Valentine	Open		17.95	18
1998 Owl Dependence Day	Open		17.95	18
1998 Owl Lang Syne	Open		17.95	18
1998 Owl What a Beautiful Day	Open		17.95	18
1998 Splashin-Owl Around	Open		17.95	18
1998 Suma Dependence Day	Open		17.95	18

Heroes of Baseball-Porcelain Baseball Cards - N/A

YEAR ISSUE	EDITION LIMIT	YEAR RETD.	ISSUE PRICE	*QUOTE U.S.$
1990 Brooks Robinson	Open		19.50	20
1991 Casey Stengel	Open		19.50	20
1990 Duke Snider	Open		19.50	20
1991 Ernie Banks	Open		19.50	20
1991 Gil Hodges	Open		19.50	20
1991 Jackie Robinson	Open		19.50	20
1991 Mickey Mantle	Open		19.50	20
1990 Roberto Clemente	Open		19.50	20
1991 Satchel Page	Open		19.50	20
1991 Whitey Ford	Open		19.50	20
1990 Willie Mays	Open		19.50	20
1991 Yogi Berra	Open		19.50	20

International Santa - N/A

YEAR ISSUE	EDITION LIMIT	YEAR RETD.	ISSUE PRICE	*QUOTE U.S.$
1995 Alpine Santa	Open		55.00	55
1993 Belsnickel	Open		55.00	55
1995 Dedushka Moroz	Open		55.00	55

*Quotes have been rounded up to nearest dollar

FIGURINES

YEAR ISSUE	EDITION LIMIT	YEAR RETD.	ISSUE PRICE	*QUOTE U.S.$
1992 Father Christmas	Open		55.00	55
1992 Grandfather Frost	Open		55.00	55
1993 Jolly Old St. Nick	Open		55.00	55
1993 Kris Kringle	Open		55.00	55
1994 Pére Nöel	Open		55.00	55
1992 Santa Claus	Open		55.00	55
1994 Yuletide Santa	Open		55.00	55

Jeweled Carousel - M. Griffin

YEAR ISSUE	EDITION LIMIT	YEAR RETD.	ISSUE PRICE	*QUOTE U.S.$
1996 Amethyst Jumper	Open		55.00	55
1996 Diamond Dancer	Open		55.00	55
1996 Emerald Stander	Open		55.00	55
1996 Ruby Prancer	Open		55.00	55
1995 Sapphire Jumper	Open		55.00	55
1997 Topaz Trotter	Open		55.00	55

Little Friends of the Arctic - M. Adams

YEAR ISSUE	EDITION LIMIT	YEAR RETD.	ISSUE PRICE	*QUOTE U.S.$
1995 The Young Prince	Open		37.50	38
1995 Princely Fishing	Open		37.50	38
1996 Playful Prince	Open		37.50	38
1996 Snoozing Prince	Open		37.50	38
1996 Princely Disguise	Open		37.50	38
1996 Slippery Prince	Open		37.50	38
1996 Prince Charming	Open		37.50	38
1996 Prince of the Mountain	Open		37.50	38
1996 Frisky Prince	Open		37.50	38
1996 Dreamy Prince	Open		37.50	38

Little Messengers - P. Parkins

YEAR ISSUE	EDITION LIMIT	YEAR RETD.	ISSUE PRICE	*QUOTE U.S.$
1997 Cleanliness Is Next To Godliness	Open		29.95	30
1997 Let Your Light Shine Before All	Open		29.95	30
1997 Love Is Contagious	Open		29.95	30
1996 Love Is Happiness	Open		29.95	30
1997 Love Is Harmony	Open		29.95	30
1996 Love Is Kind	Open		29.95	30
1997 Love Is Sharing	Open		29.95	30
1997 Love Knows No Bounds	Open		29.95	30
1996 Practice Makes Perfect	Open		29.95	30
1996 Pretty Is As Pretty Does	Open		29.95	30
1997 Seek And You Shall Find	Open		29.95	30
1996 Love Is Patient	Open		29.95	30

Little Messengers Heavenly Gardeners -N/A

YEAR ISSUE	EDITION LIMIT	YEAR RETD.	ISSUE PRICE	*QUOTE U.S.$
1998 Enjoy The Fruits of Your Labors	Open		19.95	20
1997 He Showers Us With Blessings	Open		19.95	20
1998 Plant the Seeds of Love	Open		19.95	20
1998 Sweet Rewards	Open		19.95	20
1998 We Reap What We Sow	Open		19.95	20

Little Night Owls - D.T. Lyttleton

YEAR ISSUE	EDITION LIMIT	YEAR RETD.	ISSUE PRICE	*QUOTE U.S.$
1990 Barn Owl	Open		45.00	45
1991 Barred Owl	Open		45.00	45
1991 Great Grey Owl	Open		45.00	45
1991 Great Horned Owl	Open		45.00	45
1991 Short-Eared Owl	Open		45.00	45
1990 Snowy Owl	Open		45.00	45
1990 Tawny Owl	Open		45.00	45
1991 White-Faced Owl	Open		45.00	45

Masters of the Evening Wilderness - N/A

YEAR ISSUE	EDITION LIMIT	YEAR RETD.	ISSUE PRICE	*QUOTE U.S.$
1994 The Great Snowy Owl	Open		37.50	38
1995 Autumn Barn Owls	Open		37.50	38
1995 Great Grey Owl	Open		37.50	38
1995 Great Horned Owl	Open		37.50	38
1996 Barred Owl	Open		37.50	38
1996 Screech Owl	Open		37.50	38
1996 Burrowing Owl	Open		37.50	38
1996 Eagle Owl	Open		37.50	38

Mickey Mantle Collector's Edition-Porcelain Baseball Cards - N/A

YEAR ISSUE	EDITION LIMIT	YEAR RETD.	ISSUE PRICE	*QUOTE U.S.$
1995 1952 Card #311/1969 Card #500	Open		39.90	40
1996 1956 Card #135/1965 Card #350	Open		39.90	40
1996 1953 Card #82/1964 Card #50	Open		39.90	40
1996 1957 Card #95/1959 Card #10	Open		39.90	40
1996 1958 Card #150/1962 Card #318	Open		39.90	40
1996 1959 Card #564/1961 Card #300	Open		39.90	40

Mickey Mantle Figurine Collection - N/A

YEAR ISSUE	EDITION LIMIT	YEAR RETD.	ISSUE PRICE	*QUOTE U.S.$
1995 Mickey Swings Home	Open		45.00	45
1996 The Switch Hitter Connects	Open		45.00	45
1996 The Ultimate Switch Hitter	Open		45.00	45
1996 On Deck	Open		45.00	45
1996 Bunting From the Left	Open		45.00	45

Mickey Mantle Sculpture - N/A

YEAR ISSUE	EDITION LIMIT	YEAR RETD.	ISSUE PRICE	*QUOTE U.S.$
1996 Tribute to a Yankee Legend	Open		195.00	195

Mother's Instinct - W. Henry

YEAR ISSUE	EDITION LIMIT	YEAR RETD.	ISSUE PRICE	*QUOTE U.S.$
1997 Mother's First Born	Open		17.95	18
1998 Mother's Guidance	Open		17.95	18
1997 Mother's Inspiration	Open		17.95	18
1998 Mother's Love	Open		17.95	18
1997 Mother's Warmth	Open		17.95	18
1997 Nourishing Mother	Open		17.95	18
1997 Picked Just For Mother	Open		17.95	18
1997 A Song For Mother	Open		17.95	18

Mystic Spirits - S. Douglas

YEAR ISSUE	EDITION LIMIT	YEAR RETD.	ISSUE PRICE	*QUOTE U.S.$
1995 Spirit of the Wolf	Open		55.00	55
1995 Spirit of the Buffalo	Open		55.00	55
1995 Spirit of the Golden Eagle	Open		55.00	55
1996 Spirit of the Bear	Open		55.00	55
1996 Spirit of the Mountain Lion	Open		55.00	55
1996 Hawk Dancer	Open		55.00	55

YEAR ISSUE	EDITION LIMIT	YEAR RETD.	ISSUE PRICE	*QUOTE U.S.$
1996 Wolf Scout	Open		55.00	55
1996 Spirit of the Deer	Open		55.00	55

Nature's Beautiful Bonds - R. Roberts

YEAR ISSUE	EDITION LIMIT	YEAR RETD.	ISSUE PRICE	*QUOTE U.S.$
1996 A Mother's Vigil	Open		29.95	30
1996 A Moment's Peace	Open		29.95	30
1996 A Warm Embrace	Open		29.95	30
1996 Safe By Mother's Side	Open		29.95	30
1996 Curious Cub	Open		29.95	30
1996 Under Mother's Watchful Eye	Open		29.95	30
1996 Time To Rest	Open		29.95	30
1996 Sheltered From Harm	Open		29.95	30

Nature's Little Cherubs - J. Smith

YEAR ISSUE	EDITION LIMIT	YEAR RETD.	ISSUE PRICE	*QUOTE U.S.$
1997 Cherub of the Birds	Open		17.95	18
1997 Cherub of the Creatures	Open		17.95	18
1997 Cherub of the Flowers	Open		17.95	18
1997 Cherub of the Forest	Open		17.95	18
1997 Cherub of the Night	Open		17.95	18
1997 Cherub of the Stars	Open		17.95	18
1997 Cherub of the Sun	Open		17.95	18
1997 Cherub of the Waters	Open		17.95	18

Nature's Majestic Cats - D. Geenty

YEAR ISSUE	EDITION LIMIT	YEAR RETD.	ISSUE PRICE	*QUOTE U.S.$
1995 Tigress and Cubs	Open		55.00	55
1995 Himalayan Snow Leopard	Open		55.00	55
1996 Cougar and Cubs	Open		55.00	55
1996 Pride of the Lioness	Open		55.00	55

Nature's Spiritual Realm - S. Kehrli

YEAR ISSUE	EDITION LIMIT	YEAR RETD.	ISSUE PRICE	*QUOTE U.S.$
1998 Spirit of the Earth	Open		69.00	69
1998 Spirit of the Fire	Open		69.00	69
1998 Spirit of the Water	Open		69.00	69
1997 Spirit of the Wind	Open		69.00	69

Nesting Instincts - R. Willis

YEAR ISSUE	EDITION LIMIT	YEAR RETD.	ISSUE PRICE	*QUOTE U.S.$
1995 By Mother's Side	Open		19.50	20
1995 Learning to Fly	Open		19.50	20
1995 Like Mother, Like Son	Open		19.50	20
1995 A Mother's Pride	Open		19.50	20
1997 Out on a Limb	Open		19.50	20
1995 Peaceful Perch	Open		19.50	20
1995 Safe and Sound	Open		19.50	20
1997 Two of a Kind	Open		19.50	20
1995 Under Mother's Wings	Open		19.50	20
1995 A Watchful Eye	Open		19.50	20

Noah's Endearing Mates - E. Harris

YEAR ISSUE	EDITION LIMIT	YEAR RETD.	ISSUE PRICE	*QUOTE U.S.$
1997 Cow Mates	Open		19.90	20
1997 Elephant Mates	Open		set	set
1997 Giraffe Mates	Open		set	set
1997 Lion Mates	Open		set	set
1997 Panda Mates	Open		set	set
1997 Pig Mates	Open		set	set
1997 Polar Bear Mates	Open		set	set
1997 Tiger Mates	Open		set	set
1997 Wolf Mates	Open		set	set
1997 Zebra Mates	Open		set	set

Noble American Indian Women - N/A

YEAR ISSUE	EDITION LIMIT	YEAR RETD.	ISSUE PRICE	*QUOTE U.S.$
1994 Falling Star	Open		55.00	55
1995 Lily of the Mohawks	Open		55.00	55
1995 Lozen	Open		55.00	55
1994 Minnehaha	Open		55.00	55
1994 Pine Leaf	Open		55.00	55
1995 Pocahontas	Open		55.00	55
1993 Sacajawea	Open		55.00	55
1993 White Rose	Open		55.00	55

The Noble Swan - G. Granget

YEAR ISSUE	EDITION LIMIT	YEAR RETD.	ISSUE PRICE	*QUOTE U.S.$
1985 The Noble Swan	5,000		295.00	295

Noble Warriors - N/A

YEAR ISSUE	EDITION LIMIT	YEAR RETD.	ISSUE PRICE	*QUOTE U.S.$
1993 Deliverance	Open		135.00	135
1994 Spirit of the Plains	Open		135.00	135
1995 Top Gun	Open		135.00	135
1995 Windrider	Open		135.00	135

The Nolan Ryan Collectors Edition-Porcelain Baseball Cards - N/A

YEAR ISSUE	EDITION LIMIT	YEAR RETD.	ISSUE PRICE	*QUOTE U.S.$
1993 Angels 1972-C #595	Open		19.50	20
1993 Astros 1985-C #7	Open		19.50	20
1993 Mets 1968-C #177	Open		19.50	20
1993 Mets 1969-C #533	Open		19.50	20
1993 Rangers 1990-C #1	Open		19.50	20
1993 Rangers 1992-C #1	Open		19.50	20

North Pole Bears - T. Newsom

YEAR ISSUE	EDITION LIMIT	YEAR RETD.	ISSUE PRICE	*QUOTE U.S.$
1996 All I Want For Christmas	Open		29.95	30
1996 Beary Best Snowman	Open		29.95	30
1996 Beary Started	Open		29.95	30
1996 Papa's Cozy Chair	Open		29.95	30

Ocean Odyssey - W. Youngstrom

YEAR ISSUE	EDITION LIMIT	YEAR RETD.	ISSUE PRICE	*QUOTE U.S.$
1995 Breaching the Waters	Open		55.00	55
1995 Return to Paradise	Open		55.00	55
1995 Riding the Waves	Open		55.00	55
1996 Baja Bliss	Open		55.00	55
1996 Arctic Blue	Open		55.00	55
1996 Splashdown	Open		55.00	55
1996 Free Spirit	Open		55.00	55
1996 Beluga Belles	Open		55.00	55

Pals of the Month - M. Adams

YEAR ISSUE	EDITION LIMIT	YEAR RETD.	ISSUE PRICE	*QUOTE U.S.$
1997 Back to School	Open		14.95	15
1997 Batter Up	Open		14.95	15
1997 Be Mine, Sweet Valentine	Open		14.95	15
1997 Bringing in the New Year	Open		14.95	15
1997 Have Yourself a Merry Xmas	Open		14.95	15
1997 July on Parade	Open		14.95	15
1997 Let's Give Thanks	Open		14.95	15
1997 Making the Grade	Open		14.95	15
1997 Singing in the Rain	Open		14.95	15
1997 Spring is Sprung	Open		14.95	15
1997 Trick or Treat	Open		14.95	15
1997 You're My Lucky Charm	Open		14.95	15

Peanut Pals - T. Newsom

YEAR ISSUE	EDITION LIMIT	YEAR RETD.	ISSUE PRICE	*QUOTE U.S.$
1996 All Aboard!	Open		19.95	20
1997 Feline Frolic	Open		19.95	20
1996 Having a Ball	Open		19.95	20
1997 The One That Got Away	Open		19.95	20
1997 Over The Bunny Slopes	Open		19.95	20
1997 Saturday Night	Open		19.95	20
1996 Shall I Pour?	Open		19.95	20
1997 Sidewalk Speedster	Open		19.95	20
1997 Sidewalk Surfin'	Open		19.95	20
1997 A Slice of Fun	Open		19.95	20
1996 Teeter Totter Fun!	Open		19.95	20

Polar Playmates - M. Adams

YEAR ISSUE	EDITION LIMIT	YEAR RETD.	ISSUE PRICE	*QUOTE U.S.$
1997 Belly Floppin'	Open		14.95	15
1997 Dreamin' Away	Open		14.95	15
1996 Goin' Fishin'	Open		14.95	15
1997 Hide'n & A Seek'n	Open		14.95	15
1997 Kickin' Back	Open		14.95	15
1996 Look Who's Nappin'	Open		14.95	15
1997 Lookin' Out	Open		14.95	15
1997 Reachin' for the Stars	Open		14.95	15
1996 Slip'n & Slide'n	Open		14.95	15
1997 Star Gazen'	Open		14.95	15
1997 Strollin' Along	Open		14.95	15
1997 Touchin' Toes	Open		14.95	15

Polar Playmates Playroom - N/A

YEAR ISSUE	EDITION LIMIT	YEAR RETD.	ISSUE PRICE	*QUOTE U.S.$
1998 Let's Have a Ball	N/A		17.95	18
1998 Time Out With Teddy	N/A		17.95	18
1998 Up, Up and Away	N/A		17.95	18

Portraits of Christ - Inspired by the Art of Warner Saltman

YEAR ISSUE	EDITION LIMIT	YEAR RETD.	ISSUE PRICE	*QUOTE U.S.$
1997 Christ At Dawn	Open		49.95	50
1996 His Presence	Open		49.95	50
1997 Jesus, The Children's Friend	Open		49.95	50
1997 Jesus, The Light of the World	Open		49.95	50
1997 The Lord Is My Shepherd	Open		49.95	50
1997 The Lord's Supper	Open		49.95	50

Prayer of the Warrior - N/A

YEAR ISSUE	EDITION LIMIT	YEAR RETD.	ISSUE PRICE	*QUOTE U.S.$
1998 Buffalo Prayer	Open		75.00	75
1997 Protector of Dreams	Open		75.00	75
1997 Proud Dreamer	Open		55.00	55
1997 Shield of Courage	Open		75.00	75
1998 Victory of Prayer	Open		75.00	75

Princess of the Plains - N/A

YEAR ISSUE	EDITION LIMIT	YEAR RETD.	ISSUE PRICE	*QUOTE U.S.$
1995 Mountain Princess	Open		55.00	55
1995 Nature's Guardian	Open		55.00	55
1995 Noble Beauty	Open		55.00	55
1994 Noble Guardian	Open		55.00	55
1995 Proud Dreamer	Open		55.00	55
1994 Snow Princess	Open		55.00	55
1994 Wild Flower	Open		55.00	55
1995 Winter's Rose	Open		55.00	55

Protect Nature's Innocents - R. Manning

YEAR ISSUE	EDITION LIMIT	YEAR RETD.	ISSUE PRICE	*QUOTE U.S.$
1995 African Elephant	Open		14.95	15
1995 Giant Panda	Open		14.95	15
1995 Snow Leopard	Open		14.95	15
1995 Rhinoceros	Open		14.95	15
1996 Orangutan	Open		14.95	15
1996 Key Deer	Open		14.95	15
1996 Bengal Tiger	Open		14.95	15
1996 Pygmy Hippo	Open		14.95	15
1996 Gray Wolf	Open		14.95	15
1996 Fur Seal	Open		14.95	15
1996 Gray Kangaroo	Open		14.95	15
1996 Sea Otter	Open		14.95	15

Puppy Playtime Sculpture Collection - J. Lamb

YEAR ISSUE	EDITION LIMIT	YEAR RETD.	ISSUE PRICE	*QUOTE U.S.$
1991 Cabin Fever	Open		29.50	30
1991 Catch of the Day	Open		29.50	30
1990 Double Take	Open		29.50	30
1991 Fun and Games	Open		29.50	30
1991 Getting Acquainted	Open		29.50	30
1991 Hanging Out	Open		29.50	30
1991 A New Leash on Life	Open		29.50	30
1991 Weekend Gardner	Open		29.50	30

Rainbow Dreams Unicorn - T. Fabrizio

YEAR ISSUE	EDITION LIMIT	YEAR RETD.	ISSUE PRICE	*QUOTE U.S.$
1998 Butterflies and Rainbow Skies	Open		14.95	15

Ringling Bros. Circus Animals - P. Cozzolino

YEAR ISSUE	EDITION LIMIT	YEAR RETD.	ISSUE PRICE	*QUOTE U.S.$
1983 Acrobatic Seal	9,800		49.50	50
1983 Baby Elephant	9,800		49.50	55
1983 Miniature Show Horse	9,800		49.50	68
1983 Mr. Chimpanzee	9,800		49.50	50
1984 Parade Camel	9,800		49.50	50
1983 Performing Poodles	9,800		49.50	50
1984 Roaring Lion	9,800		49.50	50

*Quotes have been rounded up to nearest dollar

YEAR ISSUE	EDITION LIMIT	YEAR RETD.	ISSUE PRICE	*QUOTE U.S.$
1983 Skating Bear	9,800		49.50	50

Santa Clothtique - Possible Dreams

YEAR ISSUE	EDITION LIMIT	YEAR RETD.	ISSUE PRICE	*QUOTE U.S.$
1992 Checking His List	Open		95.00	95
1993 Last Minute Details	Open		95.00	95
1993 Twas the Nap Before Christmas	Open		95.00	95
1994 Upon the Rooftop	Open		95.00	95
1994 O Tannenbaum!	Open		95.00	95
1995 Baking Christmas Cheer	Open		95.00	95
1995 Santa to the Rescue	Open		95.00	95
1996 Toyshop Tally	Open		95.00	95

Seeing Spots - J. Smith

YEAR ISSUE	EDITION LIMIT	YEAR RETD.	ISSUE PRICE	*QUOTE U.S.$
1997 Spot Finds a Snowman	Open		19.95	20
1997 Spot Gets A Boo-Boo	Open		19.95	20
1997 Spot Gets Caught	Open		19.95	20
1997 Spot Goes Camping	Open		19.95	20
1997 Spot Goes On A Picnic	Open		19.95	20
1997 Spot Goes Sledding	Open		19.95	20
1997 Spot Plays With Fire Truck	Open		19.95	20
1997 Spot Sees A Crab	Open		19.95	20
1996 Spot Takes A Bath	Open		19.95	20
1997 Spot Takes A Nap	Open		19.95	20
1996 Spot Takes A Ride	Open		19.95	20
1997 Spot Visits Friends	Open		19.95	20

Shield of the Mighty Warrior - S. Kehrli

YEAR ISSUE	EDITION LIMIT	YEAR RETD.	ISSUE PRICE	*QUOTE U.S.$
1995 Spirit of the Grey Wolf	Open		45.00	45
1996 Spirit of the Bear	Open		45.00	45
1996 Protection of the Cougar	Open		45.00	45
1996 Protection of the Buffalo	Open		45.00	45
1996 Protection of the Bobcat	Open		45.00	45

Spirit of the Eagle - T. Sullivan

YEAR ISSUE	EDITION LIMIT	YEAR RETD.	ISSUE PRICE	*QUOTE U.S.$
1994 Spirit of Independence	Open		55.00	55
1995 Blazing Majestic Skies	Open		55.00	55
1995 Noble and Free	Open		55.00	55
1995 Proud Symbol of Freedom	Open		55.00	55
1996 Legacy of Freedom	Open		55.00	55
1996 Protector of Liberty	Open		55.00	55

STAR TREK® : Captain James T. Kirk Autographed Wall Plaque - N/A

YEAR ISSUE	EDITION LIMIT	YEAR RETD.	ISSUE PRICE	*QUOTE U.S.$
1995 Captain James T. Kirk	5,000		195.00	195

STAR TREK® : Captain Jean-Luc Picard Autographed Wall Plaque - N/A

YEAR ISSUE	EDITION LIMIT	YEAR RETD.	ISSUE PRICE	*QUOTE U.S.$
1994 Captain Jean-Luc Picard	5,000		195.00	175-200

STAR TREK® : First Officer Spock® Autographed Wall Plaque - N/A

YEAR ISSUE	EDITION LIMIT	YEAR RETD.	ISSUE PRICE	*QUOTE U.S.$
1994 First Officer Spock®	2,500		195.00	195

STAR TREK® : The Spock® Commemorative Wall Plaque - N/A

YEAR ISSUE	EDITION LIMIT	YEAR RETD.	ISSUE PRICE	*QUOTE U.S.$
1993 Spock®/STAR TREK VI The Undiscovered Country	2,500		195.00	195

STAR TREK®: The Next Generation-Porcelain Cards - S. Hillios

YEAR ISSUE	EDITION LIMIT	YEAR RETD.	ISSUE PRICE	*QUOTE U.S.$
1996 Deanna Troi & Data	28-day		39.90	40
1997 Inner Light & All Good Things	28-day		39.90	40
1996 Jean-Luc Picard & Q	28-day		39.90	40
1996 Ship In a Bottle & Best of Both Worlds	28-day		39.90	40
1996 USS Enterprise NCC-1701-D & William T. Riker	28-day		39.90	40
1997 Worf & Klingon Bird-of-Prey	28-day		39.90	40

STAR TREK®: The Voyagers-Porcelain Cards - K. Birdsong

YEAR ISSUE	EDITION LIMIT	YEAR RETD.	ISSUE PRICE	*QUOTE U.S.$
1996 Klingon Bird-of-Prey & Cardassian Galor Warship	28-day		39.90	40
1996 Triple Nacelled USS Enterprise & USS Excelsior	28-day		39.90	40
1996 USS Enterprise NCC-1701 & Klingon Battlecruiser	28-day		39.90	40
1996 USS Enterprise NCC-1701-A & Ferengi Marauder	28-day		39.90	40
1996 USS Enterprise NCC-1701-D & Romulan Warbird	28-day		39.90	40
1996 USS Voyager NCC-74656 & USS Defiant NX-74205	28-day		39.90	40

Star Wars: A New Hope-Porcelain Cards - N/A

YEAR ISSUE	EDITION LIMIT	YEAR RETD.	ISSUE PRICE	*QUOTE U.S.$
1996 Good Versus Evil & Leia's Rescue	28-day		39.90	40
1996 Hiding the Plans & Viewing the Hologram	28-day		39.90	40
1996 In A Tight Spot & Millennium Falcon	28-day		39.90	40
1996 Leia in Detention & Luke Skywalker	28-day		39.90	40
1996 Millennium Falcon Cockpit & Capture of Leia's Ship	28-day		39.90	40
1996 Obi Wan & Luke & A Daring Escape	28-day		39.90	40
1996 Obi-wan Kenobi & C-3PO and R2-D2	28-day		39.90	40
1996 Stormtroopers & X-Wing Attack	28-day		39.90	40

A Touch of Heaven - S. Kuck

YEAR ISSUE	EDITION LIMIT	YEAR RETD.	ISSUE PRICE	*QUOTE U.S.$
1997 Alexandra	Open		17.95	18
1998 Amanda	Open		17.95	18
1998 Brianna	Open		17.95	18
1998 Katherine	Open		17.95	18
1998 Miranda	Open		17.95	18
1997 Victoria	Open		17.95	18

Tropical Treasures - M. Wald

YEAR ISSUE	EDITION LIMIT	YEAR RETD.	ISSUE PRICE	*QUOTE U.S.$
1990 Beaked Coral Butterfly Fish	Open		37.50	38
1990 Blue Girdled Angel Fish	Open		37.50	38
1989 Flag-tail Surgeonfish	Open		37.50	38
1989 Pennant Butterfly Fish	Open		37.50	38
1989 Sail-finned Surgeonfish	Open		37.50	38
1989 Sea Horse	Open		37.50	38
1990 Spotted Angel Fish	Open		37.50	38
1990 Zebra Turkey Fish	Open		37.50	38

Unbridled Spirits - C. DeHaan

YEAR ISSUE	EDITION LIMIT	YEAR RETD.	ISSUE PRICE	*QUOTE U.S.$
1994 Wild Fury	Open		135.00	135

Under The Sea Crystal Shell - R. Koni

YEAR ISSUE	EDITION LIMIT	YEAR RETD.	ISSUE PRICE	*QUOTE U.S.$
1997 Dolphin Dance	Open		29.95	30
1997 Fluid Grace	Open		29.95	30
1997 Manatee Minuet	Open		29.95	30
1997 Orca Ballet	Open		29.95	30
1997 Seahorse Samba	Open		29.95	30
1997 Slow Dance	Open		29.95	30
1997 Soft Serenade	Open		29.95	30
1997 Tropical Twist	Open		29.95	30

Visions of Christmas - M. Griffin

YEAR ISSUE	EDITION LIMIT	YEAR RETD.	ISSUE PRICE	*QUOTE U.S.$
1995 Gifts From St. Nick	Open		135.00	135
1994 Mrs. Claus' Kitchen	Open		135.00	135
1993 Santa's Delivery	Open		135.00	135
1993 Toys in Progress	Open		135.00	135

Warrior's Quest - S. Kehrli

YEAR ISSUE	EDITION LIMIT	YEAR RETD.	ISSUE PRICE	*QUOTE U.S.$
1996 Cry of the Eagle	Open		95.00	95
1996 Strength of the Wolf	Open		95.00	95

Waterful Ways & Elephant Days - N/A

YEAR ISSUE	EDITION LIMIT	YEAR RETD.	ISSUE PRICE	*QUOTE U.S.$
1997 Back Splash	Open		17.95	18
1997 The Big Splash!	Open		19.95	20
1997 Catch of the Day	Open		19.95	20
1996 Clean Fun	Open		14.95	15
1997 How Does Your Garden Grow	Open		19.95	20
1997 Just Splashin' Ducky	Open		14.95	15
1997 Lazy Days	Open		19.95	20
1997 Merrily, Merrily	Open		19.95	20
1997 Rainy Day Splash	Open		19.95	20
1997 Sudsy Fun	Open		19.95	20
1997 Surfer Dude	Open		19.95	20
1997 Water Bathing Beauty	Open		17.95	18

The Way of the Warrior - J. Pyre

YEAR ISSUE	EDITION LIMIT	YEAR RETD.	ISSUE PRICE	*QUOTE U.S.$
1995 One With the Eagle	Open		45.00	45
1996 Star Shooter	Open		45.00	45
1996 Bear Warrior	Open		45.00	45
1996 Beckoning Back the Buffalo	Open		45.00	45
1996 Great Feather Warrior	Open		45.00	45
1996 Calling His Guardian	Open		45.00	45

Wild and Free - C. De Haan

YEAR ISSUE	EDITION LIMIT	YEAR RETD.	ISSUE PRICE	*QUOTE U.S.$
1996 Wild and Free	Open		195.00	195

The Wildlife Nursery - N/A

YEAR ISSUE	EDITION LIMIT	YEAR RETD.	ISSUE PRICE	*QUOTE U.S.$
1997 Go For A Ride, Mommy?	Open		14.95	15
1997 I Love My Doll, Mommy!	Open		14.95	15
1997 I'll Spell, Mommy!	Open		14.95	15
1997 I'm So Pretty, Mommy!	Open		14.95	15
1997 Mommy's Little Shaker	Open		14.95	15
1997 Mommy, Baby Go Boom	Open		14.95	15
1997 More Milk, Mommy	Open		14.95	15
1997 More Please, Mommy!	Open		14.95	15
1997 My Duck, Mommy!	Open		14.95	15
1997 Naptime, Mommy?	Open		14.95	15
1997 Pacify Me, Mommy!	Open		14.95	15
1997 Quiet Time, Mommy	Open		14.95	15

Wolves of the Wilderness - D. Geenty

YEAR ISSUE	EDITION LIMIT	YEAR RETD.	ISSUE PRICE	*QUOTE U.S.$
1995 A Wolf's Pride	Open		55.00	55
1995 Mother's Watch	Open		55.00	55
1996 Time For Play	Open		55.00	55
1996 Morning Romp	Open		55.00	55
1996 First Adventure	Open		55.00	55
1996 Tumbling Twosome	Open		55.00	55

Harmony Kingdom

Royal Watch™ Collector's Club - Various

YEAR ISSUE	EDITION LIMIT	YEAR RETD.	ISSUE PRICE	*QUOTE U.S.$
1996 Big Blue - P. Calvesbert	Retrd.	1997	75.00	200-450
1996 The Big Day - P. Calvesbert	Retrd.	1996	Gift	120-249
1996 Purrfect Fit - D. Lawrence	Retrd.	1996	Gift	230-450
1996 Complete Charter Member Kit	Retrd.	1996	N/A	350-360
1997 Paper Anniversary - P. Calvesbert	Retrd.	1997	20.00	100-160
1997 Toad Pin - P. Calvesbert	Retrd.	1997	Gift	70
1997 Sweet as a Summer's Kiss - D. Lawrence	Retrd.	1997	Gift	N/A
1997 Big Blue 1997 - P. Calvesbert	Retrd.	1997	75.00	100-199
1997 The Sunflower - M. Perry	Retrd.	1997	70.00	100-175
1998 Cat Pin - P. Calvesbert	Open		Gift	N/A
1998 Mutton Chops - P. Calvesbert	Open		Gift	N/A
1998 Behold The King - D. Lawrence	Open		100.00	100
1998 The Mushroom - M. Perry	Open		120.00	120
1998 April's Fool Pen - D. Lawrence	Open		45.00	45

Event Pieces - P. Calvesbert

YEAR ISSUE	EDITION LIMIT	YEAR RETD.	ISSUE PRICE	*QUOTE U.S.$
1997 Oktobearfest	Retrd.	1997	38.50	39-72
1997 Octobearfest (misprint on label)	Retrd.	1997	38.50	75-100

Show Pieces - P. Calvesbert

YEAR ISSUE	EDITION LIMIT	YEAR RETD.	ISSUE PRICE	*QUOTE U.S.$
1996 Secaucus Frog Pendent	210	1996	Gift	300-750
1996 Rosemont Frog Pendent	403	1996	Gift	200-600
1997 Long Beach Rose Pendent	552	1997	Gift	200-350
1997 Rosemont Rose Pendent	857	1997	Gift	150-350
1997 Puffin Pin	120	1997	Gift	300-575
1998 Edison Pendant	Retrd.	1998	Gift	100-200
1998 Rosemont Pendant	Retrd.	1998	Gift	100-150

I.C.E. Piece - P. Calvesbert

YEAR ISSUE	EDITION LIMIT	YEAR RETD.	ISSUE PRICE	*QUOTE U.S.$
1998 Sneak Preview	5,000	1998	65.00	125-250

GCC Exclusive - P. Calvesbert

YEAR ISSUE	EDITION LIMIT	YEAR RETD.	ISSUE PRICE	*QUOTE U.S.$
1998 Queen's Council	11/98		45.00	45

Angelique - D. Lawrence

YEAR ISSUE	EDITION LIMIT	YEAR RETD.	ISSUE PRICE	*QUOTE U.S.$
1996 Bon Chance	Open		35.00	35
1996 Fleur-de-lis	Open		35.00	35
1996 Gentil Homme	Open		35.00	35
1996 Ingenue	Open		35.00	35
1996 Joie De Vivre	Retrd.	1998	35.00	400

Biblical Series - P. Calvesbert

YEAR ISSUE	EDITION LIMIT	YEAR RETD.	ISSUE PRICE	*QUOTE U.S.$
1998 SinCity	5,000		600.00	600

Disney Gallery

YEAR ISSUE	EDITION LIMIT	YEAR RETD.	ISSUE PRICE	*QUOTE U.S.$
1998 Fab 5	Open		95.00	95
1997 Pooh and Friends	Open		60.00	75

Garden Party - Various

YEAR ISSUE	EDITION LIMIT	YEAR RETD.	ISSUE PRICE	*QUOTE U.S.$
1996 Baroness Trotter - P. Calvesbert	Open		17.50	18
1997 Count Belfry - D. Lawrence	Open		17.50	18
1996 Courtiers At Rest - P. Calvesbert	Open		17.50	18
1997 Duc de Lyon - D. Lawrence	Open		17.50	18
1997 Earl of Oswald - D. Lawrence	Open		17.50	18
1996 Garden Prince - P. Calvesbert	Open		17.50	18
1996 Ladies In Waiting - P. Calvesbert	Open		17.50	18
1997 Lord Busby - D. Lawrence	Open		17.50	18
1997 Major Parker - D. Lawrence	Open		17.50	18
1997 Marquis de Blanc - D. Lawrence	Open		17.50	18
1996 Royal Flotilla - P. Calvesbert	Open		17.50	18
1996 Yeoman Of The Guard - P. Calvesbert	Open		17.50	18

Harmony Circus - D. Lawrence

YEAR ISSUE	EDITION LIMIT	YEAR RETD.	ISSUE PRICE	*QUOTE U.S.$
1996 The Audience	Open		150.00	150
1996 Ball Brothers	Open		35.00	35
1996 Beppo And Barney The Clowns	Open		35.00	35
1996 Circus Ring	Open		100.00	100
1996 Clever Constantine	Open		35.00	35
1996 Great Escapo	Open		35.00	35
1996 Harmony Circus Arch	Open		80.00	80
1996 Henry The Human Cannonball	Open		35.00	35
1996 Il Bendi	Open		35.00	35
1996 Lionel Loveless	Open		35.00	35
1996 Mr. Sediments	Open		35.00	35
1996 Olde Time Carousel	Open		35.00	35
1996 Pavareata The Little Big Girl	Open		35.00	35
1996 The Ringmaster	Open		35.00	35
1996 Road Dogs	Open		35.00	35
1996 Suave St. John	Open		35.00	35
1996 Top Hat	Open		35.00	35
1996 Vlad The Impaler	Open		35.00	35
1996 Winston The Lion Tamer	Open		35.00	35
1996 Matched Number Harmony Circus Set	1,000		890.00	890
1998 Bozini the Clown	10,000	1998	29.50	30-35
1998 Madeline of the High Wire	10,000	1998	29.50	30-35

Hi-Jinx - P. Calvesbert

YEAR ISSUE	EDITION LIMIT	YEAR RETD.	ISSUE PRICE	*QUOTE U.S.$
1994 Antarctic Antics	Open		100.00	100
1994 Hold That Line	Open		100.00	100
1994 Mad Dogs and Englishmen	Open		100.00	100
1995 Open Mike	Open		100.00	100

Holiday Edition - D. Lawrence, unless otherwise noted

YEAR ISSUE	EDITION LIMIT	YEAR RETD.	ISSUE PRICE	*QUOTE U.S.$
1995 Chatelaine	Retrd.	1995	35.00	350-375
1996 Bon Enfant	Retrd.	1996	35.00	130-250
1996 Bon Enfant (1st ed.)	Retrd.	1996	35.00	400-750
1996 Nick Of Time - P. Calvesbert	Retrd.	1996	35.00	100-250
1997 Celeste	Retrd.	1997	45.00	45-75
1997 Something's Gotta Give - P. Calvesbert	Retrd.	1997	35.00	40-121

Large Treasure Jest® - P. Calvesbert, unless otherwise noted

YEAR ISSUE	EDITION LIMIT	YEAR RETD.	ISSUE PRICE	*QUOTE U.S.$
1991 Awaiting A Kiss	Open		55.00	55
1990 Drake's Fancy	Open		55.00	55
1995 Holding Court	Open		55.00	55
1991 Horn A' Plenty	Retrd.	1997	55.00	55-110
1991 Journey Home	Open		55.00	55
1990 Keeping Current	Open		55.00	55
1992 On A Roll	Open		55.00	55
1994 One Step Ahead	Open		55.00	55
1991 Pen Pals	Open		55.00	55
1990 Pondering	Retrd.	1997	55.00	125-225
1993 Pride And Joy	Open		55.00	55
1990 Quiet Waters	Open		55.00	55
1993 Standing Guard	Retrd.	1997	55.00	75-150
1993 Step Aside	Open		55.00	55
1991 Straight From The Hip	Open		55.00	55
1991 Sunnyside Up	Open		55.00	55
1991 Tea For Two	Open		55.00	55
1997 Terra Incognita - D. Lawrence	Open		75.00	75

Limited Editions - P. Calvesbert, unless otherwise noted

YEAR ISSUE	EDITION LIMIT	YEAR RETD.	ISSUE PRICE	*QUOTE U.S.$
1998 Family Reunion - D. Lawrence	7,200	1998	120.00	120
1998 Have a Heart	3,600	1998	55.00	138-295
1998 Ivory Tower - D. Lawrence	7,200	1998	120.00	120
1997 Killing Time (black sand) - D. Lawrence	3,600	1997	100.00	150-295
1997 Killing Time (gold sand) - D. Lawrence	3,600	1997	100.00	275-299

*Quotes have been rounded up to nearest dollar

YEAR ISSUE	EDITION LIMIT	YEAR RETD.	ISSUE PRICE	*QUOTE U.S.$
1995 Noah's Lark	5,000	1998	400.00	400-425
1997 Original Kin	2,500	1998	250.00	250-360
1998 Pieces of Eight (orange) - D. Lawrence	5,000	1998	120.00	650-1200
1998 Pieces of Eight (pink) - D. Lawrence	5,000	1998	120.00	275-650
1998 Pieces of Eight (red) - D. Lawrence	5,000	1998	120.00	120-275
1998 Play Ball - D. Lawrence	7,200	1998	120.00	120
1998 SinCity	5,000		600.00	600
1995 Unbearables	2,500	1998	400.00	400-425

Lord Byron's Harmony Garden™ - M. Perry

YEAR ISSUE	EDITION LIMIT	YEAR RETD.	ISSUE PRICE	*QUOTE U.S.$
1998 Begonia	Open		45.00	45
1998 Cactus	Open		45.00	45
1997 Chrysanthemum	Open		38.50	39
1997 Cranberry	Open		38.50	39
1997 Daisy	Open		38.50	39
1998 Double Rose (red)	5,000	1998	55.00	55-130
1998 Double Rose (pink)	5,000	1998	55.00	55
1998 Double Rose (violet)	5,000	1998	55.00	55
1998 Double Rose (yellow)	5,000	1998	55.00	55
1997 English Chrysanthemum	Retrd.	1997	38.50	80-90
1997 English Cranberry	Retrd.	1997	38.50	80-85
1997 English Daisy	Retrd.	1997	38.50	80-85
1997 English Hyacinth	Retrd.	1997	38.50	80-85
1997 English Hydrangea	Retrd.	1997	38.50	80-85
1997 English Marsh Marigold	Retrd.	1997	38.50	80-85
1997 English Morning Glory	Retrd.	1997	38.50	80-85
1997 English Peace Lily	Retrd.	1997	38.50	80-85
1997 English Rhododendron	Retrd.	1997	38.50	80-85
1997 English Snow Drop	Retrd.	1997	38.50	70-85
1997 English Roses, set/10	Retrd.	1997	385.00	750
1998 Forget Me Not	Open		45.00	45
1998 Gardenia	Open		45.00	45
1997 Hyacinth	Open		38.50	39
1997 Hydrangea	Open		38.50	39
1998 Iris	Open		45.00	45
1997 Marsh Marigold	Open		38.50	39
1997 Morning Glory	Open		38.50	39
1997 Peace Lily	Open		38.50	39
1997 Peach Rose	3,600	1997	38.50	100-125
1998 Peony	Open		45.00	45
1997 Pink Rose	3,600	1997	38.50	100-125
1997 Red Rose	3,600	1997	38.50	200-395
1997 Rhododendron	Open		38.50	39
1997 Rose Basket	3,600	1997	65.00	125-250
1998 Rose Bud	Open		45.00	45
1998 Rose Party	5,000	1998	100.00	100-160
1998 Snapdragon	Open		45.00	45
1998 Silver Rose	1,000	1998	400.00	400-525
1997 Snow Drop	Open		38.50	39
1998 Sunflower	Open		45.00	45
1997 Violet Rose	3,600	1997	38.50	100-157
1997 White Rose	3,600	1997	38.50	100-200
1997 Yellow Rose	3,600	1997	38.50	100-188

Naled Special Editions - D. Lawrence

YEAR ISSUE	EDITION LIMIT	YEAR RETD.	ISSUE PRICE	*QUOTE U.S.$
1997 Cat's Cradle	1,000	1997	38.50	270-390
1997 Cat's Cradle Too	1,000	1997	38.50	250-325
1998 Kitty's Kippers	5,600	1998	45.00	45
1998 Peace Offering	4,200	1998	45.00	135-175

Paradoxicals - P. Calvesbert

YEAR ISSUE	EDITION LIMIT	YEAR RETD.	ISSUE PRICE	*QUOTE U.S.$
1995 Paradise Found	Retrd.	1997	35.00	35-70
1995 Paradise Lost	Open		35.00	35

Rather Large Series - P. Calvesbert

YEAR ISSUE	EDITION LIMIT	YEAR RETD.	ISSUE PRICE	*QUOTE U.S.$
1996 Rather Large Friends	Open		65.00	65
1996 Rather Large Hop	Open		65.00	65
1996 Rather Large Huddle	Open		65.00	65
1996 Rather Large Safari	Open		65.00	65

Romance Annual - D. Lawrence

YEAR ISSUE	EDITION LIMIT	YEAR RETD.	ISSUE PRICE	*QUOTE U.S.$
1997 Pillow Talk	Retrd.	1998	120.00	120

Small Treasure Jest® - P. Calvesbert

YEAR ISSUE	EDITION LIMIT	YEAR RETD.	ISSUE PRICE	*QUOTE U.S.$
1998 Algenon (1st Ed.)	3,000	1998	45.00	45-99
1998 Algenon (2nd Ed.)	Open		45.00	45
1994 All Angles Covered	Open		35.00	35
1993 All Ears	Retrd.	1996	35.00	100-250
1993 All Tied Up	Retrd.	1996	35.00	100-250
1998 Antipasto	Open		45.00	45
1998 Aria Amorosa	Open		45.00	45
1993 At Arm's Length	Retrd.	1996	35.00	300-600
1995 At The Hop	Open		35.00	35
1998 Baby Boomer (1st Ed.)	3,000	1998	45.00	45-99
1998 Baby Boomer (2nd Ed.)	Open		45.00	45
1993 Baby on Board	Retrd.	1997	35.00	35-94
1993 Back Scratch	Retrd.	1995	35.00	2000-3500
1997 Bamboozled	Open		45.00	45
1995 Beak To Beak	Retrd.	1997	35.00	35-94
1996 Brean Sands	Open		35.00	35
1996 Changing of the Guard	Open		35.00	35
1996 Close Shave	Open		35.00	35
1998 Croc Pot (1st Ed.)	3,000	1998	45.00	45-80
1998 Croc Pot (1st Ed.-w/McD)	Retrd.	1998	45.00	45-99
1998 Croc Pot (2nd Ed.)	Open		45.00	45
1995 Damnable Plot	Open		35.00	35
1993 Day Dreamer	Retrd.	1996	35.00	250-395
1995 Den Mothers	Retrd.	1996	35.00	100-280
1994 Dog Days	Open		35.00	35
1997 Down Under	Open		35.00	35
1997 Driver's Seat	Open		45.00	45
1995 Ed's Safari	Open		35.00	35
1994 Family Tree	Open		35.00	35
1997 Faux Paw	Open		45.00	45
1992 Forty Winks	Retrd.	1996	35.00	100-210
1997 Friends in High Places	Open		45.00	45
1995 Fur Ball	Open		35.00	35
1994 Group Therapy	Retrd.	1996	35.00	125-325
1993 Hammin' It Up	Retrd.	1996	35.00	75-100
1996 Hog Heaven	Open		35.00	35
1995 Horse Play	Retrd.	1996	35.00	225-495
1997 In Fine Feather	Open		45.00	45
1994 Inside Joke	Open		35.00	35
1993 It's A Fine Day	Retrd.	1996	35.00	250-495
1995 Jersey Belles	Open		35.00	35
1993 Jonah's Hideaway	Retrd.	1996	35.00	250-395
1994 Let's Do Lunch	Retrd.	1995	35.00	360-500
1996 Liberty and Justice	Open		45.00	45
1995 Life's a Picnic	Open		35.00	35
1994 Love Seat	Retrd.	1997	35.00	45-55
1995 Major's Mousers	Retrd.	1997	45.00	45-115
1995 Mud Bath	Retrd.	1997	35.00	45-110
1997 Murphy's Last Stand	Retrd.	1997	35.00	45-85
1994 Neighborhood Watch	Retrd.	1997	35.00	55-195
1993 Of The Same Stripe	Open		35.00	35
1991 Panda	100	1995	35.00	650-1500
1997 Photo Finish	Open		45.00	45
1996 Pink Paradise	Open		35.00	35
1996 Pink Paradise (black beaks)	Retrd.	1996	35.00	150
1994 Play School	Open		35.00	35
1992 Princely Thoughts	Retrd.	1996	35.00	115-235
1995 Puddle Huddle	Open		35.00	35
1994 Purrfect Friends	Open		35.00	35
1991 Ram	100	1995	35.00	1000-1200
1993 Reminiscence	Retrd.	1996	35.00	115-250
1998 Rocky's Raiders	Open		45.00	45
1997 Rooster	300	1997	35.00	350-980
1996 Rumble Seat	Open		45.00	45
1993 School's Out	Open		35.00	35
1997 Shaggy Dog (Sheep Dog)	300	1997	35.00	400-980
1991 Shark	100	1995	35.00	1025-2000
1993 Shell Game	Open		35.00	35
1997 Shoe Bill	300	1997	35.00	400-980
1993 Side Steppin'	Retrd.	1996	35.00	75-150
1997 Sleepy Hollow	Open		35.00	35
1997 Splashdown	Open		45.00	45
1994 Sunday Swim	Open		35.00	35
1993 Swamp Song	Retrd.	1997	35.00	35-94
1995 Sweet Serenade	Open		35.00	35
1994 Teacher's Pet	Retrd.	1997	35.00	55-100
1996 Tin Cat	Open		35.00	35
1996 Tin Cat (brown boat)	990	1996	35.00	200
1994 Tongue And Cheek	Open		35.00	35
1997 Tony's Tabbies	Open		45.00	45
1994 Too Much of A Good Thing	Open		35.00	35
1993 Top Banana	Retrd.	1996	35.00	100-295
1996 Trumpeter's Ball	Open		45.00	45
1993 Trunk Show	Retrd.	1996	35.00	110-395
1995 Unbridled & Groomed	Open		35.00	35
1994 Unexpected Arrival	Open		35.00	35
1994 Untouchable	Retrd.	1995	35.00	300-395
1997 Whale of a Time	Open		35.00	35
1993 Who'd A Thought	Retrd.	1995	35.00	1375-2000
1995 Wise Guys	Open		35.00	35
1998 Wishful Thinking (1st Ed.)	3,000	1998	45.00	45-110
1998 Wishful Thinking (1st Ed.-Full Screw)	Retrd.	1998	45.00	110-149
1998 Wishful Thinking (2nd Ed.)	Open		45.00	45

Special Edition - P. Calvesbert

YEAR ISSUE	EDITION LIMIT	YEAR RETD.	ISSUE PRICE	*QUOTE U.S.$
1995 Primordial Soup	Open		150.00	150
1997 Scratching Post (HK Pen)	10,000		45.00	45
1997 Tabby Totem (HK Pen)	10,000		45.00	45

House of Hatten, Inc.

Amber Harvest - D. Calla

YEAR ISSUE	EDITION LIMIT	YEAR RETD.	ISSUE PRICE	*QUOTE U.S.$
1995 Elias Boy with Wild Turkey 15.5" 50550	Open		54.00	54
1995 Sarah Girl with Basket of Apples 14" 50551	Open		54.00	54
1995 Turkey 7" 50552	Open		35.00	35

American Folk Art - J. Bingham

YEAR ISSUE	EDITION LIMIT	YEAR RETD.	ISSUE PRICE	*QUOTE U.S.$
1995 Fireside Santa 36577	Retrd.	1995	210.00	210
1997 Ms. Jackie Lantern 13" 36785	Open		38.00	38
1995 Santa with Blocks 18" 36576	Retrd.	1996	180.00	180
1998 Santa with Coat of Red Stars 14" 36806	Open		70.00	70
1995 Santa with Train 20" 36575	Retrd.	1997	230.00	230
1998 Sleepy Santa with Red Reindeer 20" 36804	Open		74.00	74
1998 Sleepy Santa, green & red 15" 36807	Open		64.00	64
1995 Sleepytime Santa - Green 20" 36579	Retrd.	1996	130.00	130
1998 Snowman 18" 36808	Open		84.00	84
1995 Stars and Stripes Santa 16" 36581	Retrd.	1997	100.00	100
1995 Traditional Santa 17" 36583	Retrd.	1996	130.00	130
1995 Traditional Santa 26" 36578	Retrd.	1997	180.00	180
1995 Workshop Santa 16" 36580	Retrd.	1996	140.00	140

Angels Triumphant - D. Calla

YEAR ISSUE	EDITION LIMIT	YEAR RETD.	ISSUE PRICE	*QUOTE U.S.$
1998 Angel Cookie Wall Decoration 16"	Open		70.00	70
1998 Celestial Angel 21 1/2" 39851	Yr.Iss.		150.00	150
1998 Keeper of the Christmas 12 1/2" 39855	Open		80.00	80
1998 Peaceable Kingdom 15 1/2" 39853	Yr.Iss.		190.00	190
1998 Star Gazer Angel 7 1/2" 39859	Open		70.00	70
1998 Star Rider Angel 15" 39854	Yr.Iss.		180.00	180
1998 Star Struck Santa 18 1/2" 39852	Open		70.00	70

Belsnickle - D. Calla

YEAR ISSUE	EDITION LIMIT	YEAR RETD.	ISSUE PRICE	*QUOTE U.S.$
1995 Nick in Box 13.5" 31508	Retrd.	1997	130.00	130
1995 Santa in Red 9.5" 31514	Open		30.00	30
1995 Santa in Red 12.5" 31513	Open		36.00	36
1995 Santa in Red 15" 31512	Open		44.00	44
1995 Santa in White 9.5" 31519	Open		30.00	30
1995 Santa in White 12.5" 31518	Open		36.00	36
1995 Santa in White 15" 31517	Open		44.00	44
1995 Seated Musical Santa 31506	Retrd.	1995	130.00	130

Beyond the Garden Gate - D. Calla

YEAR ISSUE	EDITION LIMIT	YEAR RETD.	ISSUE PRICE	*QUOTE U.S.$
1994 Clover 9" 50402	Retrd.	1996	40.00	40
1994 Thistle 11.5" 50401	Open		40.00	40

Bunny Pickin's - K.A. Walker

YEAR ISSUE	EDITION LIMIT	YEAR RETD.	ISSUE PRICE	*QUOTE U.S.$
1998 Albert Bunny 6" 54801	Open		6.00	6
1998 Bitsy Girl Bunny 3 1/2" 54804	Open		4.00	4

A Christmas Alphabet - V. & S. Rawson

YEAR ISSUE	EDITION LIMIT	YEAR RETD.	ISSUE PRICE	*QUOTE U.S.$
1998 Santa 15 1/2" 33800	Open		90.00	90

Christmas Messengers - V. & S. Rawson

YEAR ISSUE	EDITION LIMIT	YEAR RETD.	ISSUE PRICE	*QUOTE U.S.$
1997 Patriotic Snowman 32756	Open		20.00	20
1998 Small Ark with Santa & Noah 4 1/4" 32850	Open		10.00	10
1997 Snowman with Raccoon 32755	Open		20.00	20
1997 Snowman with Tree 32754	Open		20.00	20

Christmas Past - N. DeCamp

YEAR ISSUE	EDITION LIMIT	YEAR RETD.	ISSUE PRICE	*QUOTE U.S.$
1994 Burgundy Santa 20" 36450	Retrd.	1994	160.00	160
1994 Green Santa 16" 36451	Retrd.	1994	130.00	130
1998 Lace Santa 13" 36851	Open		160.00	160
1995 Lace Santa 20" 36552	Retrd.	1996	170.00	170
1995 Red Seated Santa 20" 36551	Retrd.	1995	130.00	130
1995 Santa in Car 15" 36553	Retrd.	1996	200.00	200
1996 Santa on Log with Children 13" 36657	Retrd.	1997	330.00	330
1995 Santa with Children Musical 22" 36550	Retrd.	1995	300.00	300
1996 Santa with Snowman 19" 36651	Retrd.	1996	250.00	250

Christmas Traditions - D.K. Wise

YEAR ISSUE	EDITION LIMIT	YEAR RETD.	ISSUE PRICE	*QUOTE U.S.$
1997 Father Christmas with Staff 12.5" 36751	Open		66.00	66
1997 North Pole Elf 13" 36752	Retrd.	1997	53.00	53
1997 Santa with Backpack 14" 36759	Open		82.50	83

Country Christmas - P.J. Hornberger

YEAR ISSUE	EDITION LIMIT	YEAR RETD.	ISSUE PRICE	*QUOTE U.S.$
1996 "Deliver What" Santa 13 23651	Retrd.	1997	94.00	94
1996 "No Bows" Santa 14" 23652	Retrd.	1997	106.00	106
1997 Santa Riding Pig 33752	Retrd.	1997	110.00	110
1997 Santa Walking Pig 33753	Retrd.	1997	110.00	110
1997 Santa with Chicken and Sled 33751	Retrd.	1997	110.00	110

December Sky Spirit - D. Calla

YEAR ISSUE	EDITION LIMIT	YEAR RETD.	ISSUE PRICE	*QUOTE U.S.$
1991 Santa 16" 31153	Retrd.	1993	100.00	100

Easter Parade - D. Calla

YEAR ISSUE	EDITION LIMIT	YEAR RETD.	ISSUE PRICE	*QUOTE U.S.$
1997 Bunny "Jack in the Box" 10" 52701	Open		58.00	58
1997 Bunny with Carrot 9" 52702	Open		32.00	32
1997 Eggstacy Bunny 10.5" 52710	Open		40.00	40
1997 Herb Farm Bunny 9" 52709	Open		45.00	45

Enchanted Forest - D. Calla

YEAR ISSUE	EDITION LIMIT	YEAR RETD.	ISSUE PRICE	*QUOTE U.S.$
1990 Christmas Comes 10" 31079	Retrd.	1992	170.00	170
1989 Elf with Goose Basket 31953	Retrd.	1993	46.00	46
1989 Good Cheer Elf 31956	Retrd.	1996	22.00	22
1993 Jolly Santa with Bear 16" 31354	Retrd.	1995	120.00	120
1990 Large Santa Tree 9" 31095	Open		12.00	12
1988 Nick in a Box 31851	Retrd.	1991	50.00	50
1990 Reindeer 9" 31081	Retrd.	1993	28.00	28
1988 Santa with Goose 9" 31852	Retrd.	1991	42.00	42
1988 Santa with Teddy 14" 31850	Open		95.00	95
1989 Seated Santa 9" 31955	Retrd.	1995	25.00	25
1990 Sleigh 10" 31080	Retrd.	1994	85.00	85
1990 Small Santa Tree 7" 31094	Open		9.00	9
1989 St. Nick and Forest Fawn 31951	Retrd.	1992	64.00	64
1989 St. Nick and Good Cheer Elf 31950	Retrd.	1991	80.00	80
1990 St. Nick on Reindeer 11" 31082	Retrd.	1992	66.00	66
1989 St. Nick with Goose Basket 31952	Retrd.	1997	55.00	55

Father Frost - D. Calla

YEAR ISSUE	EDITION LIMIT	YEAR RETD.	ISSUE PRICE	*QUOTE U.S.$
1991 Father Frost 14" 31131	Retrd.	1994	84.00	84

Folk Art by P.J. - P.J. Hornberger

YEAR ISSUE	EDITION LIMIT	YEAR RETD.	ISSUE PRICE	*QUOTE U.S.$
1997 Bunny Gardener "It Could Happen" 56701	Retrd.	1997	56.00	56
1997 Colonel Sanders Bunny 56702	Retrd.	1997	56.00	56
1996 "Darn Rabbit" Chicken 53601	Open		40.00	40
1996 "Doin' My Part" Chicken 53604	Open		40.00	40
1996 "Good Day" Chicken 53602	Open		66.00	66
1997 "I Gotta Be Me" Chicken 56703	Open		40.00	40
1996 "Surely Not" Chicken 53603	Open		40.00	40
1997 "Texas Our Texas" Chicken 56704	Open		40.00	40

Four Seasons - D. Calla

YEAR ISSUE	EDITION LIMIT	YEAR RETD.	ISSUE PRICE	*QUOTE U.S.$
1996 Spring "Puddles" 50601	1,250		90.00	90
1996 Summer "Melons" 50602	1,250		90.00	90
1996 Fall "Cider" 50603	1,250		90.00	90
1996 Winter "Mistletoe" 50604	1,250		90.00	90

*Quotes have been rounded up to nearest dollar

From Our House to Your House - D. Calla

YEAR ISSUE	EDITION LIMIT	YEAR RETD.	ISSUE PRICE	*QUOTE U.S.$
1991 Santa with Staff 11" 31106	Retrd.	1993	57.00	57

From Out of the North - R. Leeseberg

YEAR ISSUE	EDITION LIMIT	YEAR RETD.	ISSUE PRICE	*QUOTE U.S.$
1997 Adirondack Santa with Goose, set/2 34755	Open		50.00	50
1998 American West Santa 8 1/2" 34851	Open		18.00	18
1997 Bent Over Santa 8" 34753	Open		40.00	40
1998 Celestial Santa 13" 34850	Open		24.00	24
1997 Dream Catcher 7" 34754	Open		40.00	40
1998 HO Santa 7" 34857	Open		12.00	12
1998 Joy to the World, set/2 6 1/4" 34860	Open		12.00	12
1998 Keepsake Santa 7 1/2" 34852	Open		9.00	9
1998 Moose 8 1/2" 34856	Open		15.00	15
1998 Moose Santa 7 1/2" 34855	Open		12.00	12
1997 Natureland Choir (set/8) 34771	Open		100.00	100
1998 Natureland Choir, set/5 34863	Open		15.00	15
1997 Noah's Ark, set/15 34770	Open		115.00	115
1997 Santa Riding Fish 34756	Open		66.00	66
1997 Santa Riding Rooster 5.5" 34757	Open		44.00	44
1997 Santa with Candle 7" 34758	Open		48.00	48
1997 Santa with Heart 11.25" 34751	Retrd.	1997	36.00	36
1998 Silent Night Santa 8" 34854	Open		12.00	12
1998 Snowman 8 1/2" 34853	Open		15.00	15
1997 Snowman's Bad Day with Rabbit, set/2 34772	Open		36.00	36
1997 Sunflower Santa 9" 34752	Retrd.	1997	44.00	44

Good Cheer - D. Calla

YEAR ISSUE	EDITION LIMIT	YEAR RETD.	ISSUE PRICE	*QUOTE U.S.$
1998 Aspen Snowman 7" 39808	Open		25.00	25
1998 Crested Butte Snowman 7" 39810	Open		15.00	15
1998 Jackson Hole Snowman 7" 39806	Open		50.00	50
1998 Killington Snowman 6 1/2" 39809	Open		24.00	24
1998 Noel Snowman 17 1/2" 39801	Open		100.00	100
1998 Santa and Bird Weathervane 13" 39803	Open		90.00	90
1998 The Santa Collector 13 1/2" 39800	Open		170.00	170
1998 Santa Shelf Sitter 12 1/2" 39805	Open		60.00	60
1998 Santa with Collector Sign 9" 39804	Open		60.00	60
1998 Santa with Geese 13 1/2" 39802	Open		150.00	150
1998 Snowmass Snowman 11" 39807	Open		37.00	37
1998 Steamboat Snowman 4" 39811	Open		11.00	11

Grand Finale - P. Herrick

YEAR ISSUE	EDITION LIMIT	YEAR RETD.	ISSUE PRICE	*QUOTE U.S.$
1998 Checkerboard Candlestick 10 3/4" 38813	Open		44.00	44
1998 Floral Black & White Candlestick 14" 38811	Open		56.00	56
1998 Giraffe Candlestick 19" 38814	Open		60.00	60
1998 Green & Gold Candlestick 12" 38812	Open		50.00	50
1998 Lion Candlestick 12 1/2" 38815	Open		44.00	44
1998 Monkey Candlestick 15 1/2" 38816	Open		60.00	60
1998 Tuffet 14 1/2" x 12" 38810	Open		250.00	250

Halloween - D. Calla

YEAR ISSUE	EDITION LIMIT	YEAR RETD.	ISSUE PRICE	*QUOTE U.S.$
1994 Celeste - Harvest Witch with Stars 9.5" 50451	Open		24.00	24
1992 Harvest Witch on Pumpkin 50250	Open		40.00	40
1994 Harvest Witch Pumpkin Peddler 50450	Retrd.	1997	80.00	80
1993 Katrina and Friends 14" 50351	Open		55.00	55
1993 Treat Dish 50353	Open		55.00	55
1993 Winnie Witch 8" 50352	Open		30.00	30

Halloween - D. Gann

YEAR ISSUE	EDITION LIMIT	YEAR RETD.	ISSUE PRICE	*QUOTE U.S.$
1998 Henrietta Witch 18" 55850	Open		98.00	98
1998 Samantha Witch 15" 55851	Open		86.00	86

Halloween - J. Bingham

YEAR ISSUE	EDITION LIMIT	YEAR RETD.	ISSUE PRICE	*QUOTE U.S.$
1998 Large Pumpkin Head Girl 23" 56801	Open		100.00	100
1998 Pumpkin Head Witch 24" 56800	Open		80.00	80
1998 Small Pumpkin Head Girl 14" 56802	Open		48.00	48
1998 Small Pumpkin Head Scarecrow 13" 56803	Open		40.00	40

Halloween - J. Crvich

YEAR ISSUE	EDITION LIMIT	YEAR RETD.	ISSUE PRICE	*QUOTE U.S.$
1995 Seated Ghost 51606	Open		26.00	26
1995 Witch Brew Pot 51604	Open		84.00	84

Halloween - P.J. Hornberger

YEAR ISSUE	EDITION LIMIT	YEAR RETD.	ISSUE PRICE	*QUOTE U.S.$
1997 Cat on Moon 17" 51732	Retrd.	1997	62.00	62
1997 Pumpkin with Black Cat 51731	Retrd.	1997	33.00	33
1997 Standing Witch with Cat 15.5" 51733	Retrd.	1997	80.00	80
1997 Witch Carriage 51730	Retrd.	1997	90.00	90

Halloween - R. Leeseberg

YEAR ISSUE	EDITION LIMIT	YEAR RETD.	ISSUE PRICE	*QUOTE U.S.$
1998 Guess What Witch 11" 54850	Open		15.00	15
1998 I Have Arrived Witch 6" 54852	Open		15.00	15

Halloween - V. & S. Rawson

YEAR ISSUE	EDITION LIMIT	YEAR RETD.	ISSUE PRICE	*QUOTE U.S.$
1997 Scarecrow 11" 51725	Open		44.00	44
1997 Standing Witch 13.5" 51726	Open		50.00	50
1997 Witch and Harvest Moon 10.75" 51727	Open		35.00	35

Heart Beats - D. Calla

YEAR ISSUE	EDITION LIMIT	YEAR RETD.	ISSUE PRICE	*QUOTE U.S.$
1998 Baking Santa with Candy 3 3/4" 26314	Yr.Iss.		12.00	12
1998 Caroling Angel, Santa & Snowman 26307	Yr.Iss.		17.00	17
1998 Chasing Snowflakes 5" 26303	Yr.Iss.		12.00	12
1998 Display Sign 4" 26302	Yr.Iss.		17.00	17
1998 Dreaming Bear 2 1/2" 26311	Yr.Iss.		12.00	12
1998 Giving Santa 3 1/2" 26306	Yr.Iss.		16.00	16
1998 Glad Tidings Centerpiece 10 1/2" 26300	Yr.Iss.		90.00	90
1998 Homecoming Santa 3 1/2" 26309	Yr.Iss.		16.00	16
1998 Merry Christmas Santa 4" 26315	Yr.Iss.		17.00	17
1998 Merry Making Elf 4 1/2" 26305	Yr.Iss.		12.00	12
1998 Praying Angel 3 1/2" 26304	Yr.Iss.		12.00	12
1998 Santa Centerpiece 10" 26301	Yr.Iss.		28.00	28
1998 Star Gazing Santa & Snowman 3 1/2" 26313	Yr.Iss.		12.00	12
1998 Story Telling Santa 4 1/2" 26308	Yr.Iss.		12.00	12
1998 Tree Cutting Elf 3 1/2" 26310	Yr.Iss.		12.00	12
1998 Tree Trimming 3 1/2" 26312	Yr.Iss.		12.00	12

Heirloom Angels - S. Babin

YEAR ISSUE	EDITION LIMIT	YEAR RETD.	ISSUE PRICE	*QUOTE U.S.$
1997 Angel with Burgundy/Ecru Dress 22" 35776	Open		130.00	130
1997 Angel with Green/Pink Dress 20" 35777	Open		130.00	130
1997 Angel with Off-White/Gold Dress 18" 35775	Open		130.00	130
1997 Cherub with Pink Dress 16" 35778	Open		130.00	130

Heirloom Santas - J. Tasch

YEAR ISSUE	EDITION LIMIT	YEAR RETD.	ISSUE PRICE	*QUOTE U.S.$
1993 Green Victorian Santa 26" 35301	Retrd.	1993	300.00	300
1991 Large Santa in Patchwork Coat 24" 35100	Retrd.	1992	450.00	450
1992 Red Velvet Santa 18" 35202	Retrd.	1993	130.00	130
1993 Red Victorian Santa 18" 35308	Retrd.	1993	190.00	190
1992 Santa in Burgundy Coat 18" 35201	Retrd.	1993	200.00	200
1991 Santa in Green Coat 18" 35103	Retrd.	1993	270.00	270
1991 Santa in Patchwork Coat 18" 35102	Retrd.	1992	270.00	270
1992 Santa in Patchwork Coat 24" 35200	Retrd.	1993	350.00	350
1991 Santa in Red Coat 18" 35104	Retrd.	1993	270.00	270
1994 Santa in Sleigh Musical 19" 35402	Retrd.	1994	190.00	190
1991 Santa in White Coat 18" 35101	Retrd.	1992	270.00	270
1993 Santa with Musical Trunk 19" 35302	Retrd.	1993	270.00	270
1993 White Father Christmas 24" 35300	Retrd.	1994	300.00	300
1994 Woodland Santa 17" 35403	Retrd.	1994	100.00	100

Holiday Post Santas - L. Clarkson

YEAR ISSUE	EDITION LIMIT	YEAR RETD.	ISSUE PRICE	*QUOTE U.S.$
1994 1950's American Santa 24" 36403	Retrd.	1994	190.00	190
1995 1950's Santa 25.5" 36501	Retrd.	1995	200.00	200
1994 Russian Santa 20" 36401	Retrd.	1994	170.00	170
1994 Santa and Sled 36402	Retrd.	1994	190.00	190
1995 Santa, Elf, and Sleigh 11" 36502	Retrd.	1996	100.00	100
1994 Skating Santa 17" 36404	Retrd.	1994	130.00	130

Holy Night - D. Calla

YEAR ISSUE	EDITION LIMIT	YEAR RETD.	ISSUE PRICE	*QUOTE U.S.$
1995 Holy Family, set/3 32576	Retrd.	1997	50.00	50
1995 Kings, set/3 32579	Retrd.	1996	90.00	90
1995 Shepherd and Sheep, set/3 32578	Retrd.	1997	50.00	50
1995 Stable 13" 32575	Retrd.	1997	90.00	90
1995 Stable Animals, set/3 32577	Retrd.	1997	46.00	46

Lancaster - D. Calla

YEAR ISSUE	EDITION LIMIT	YEAR RETD.	ISSUE PRICE	*QUOTE U.S.$
1996 Barn 14" 52601	Retrd.	1997	72.00	72
1996 Levi Boy 11" 52602	Retrd.	1997	42.00	42
1996 Rachel Girl 11" 52603	Retrd.	1997	42.00	42

The Magic of Christmas - V. & S. Rawson

YEAR ISSUE	EDITION LIMIT	YEAR RETD.	ISSUE PRICE	*QUOTE U.S.$
1998 Elf Holding Lightbulb 5 1/2" 32807	Open		7.00	7
1998 Elf Holding Ornament 6" 32804	Open		7.00	7
1998 Elf with Boxes 6" 32808	Open		7.00	7
1998 Elf with List 5 1/2" 32805	Open		7.00	7
1998 Elf with Presents 6 1/2" 32809	Open		7.00	7
1998 Elf with Snowman 6" 32802	Open		7.00	7
1998 Elf with Tree 5 1/2" 32803	Open		7.00	7
1998 Elf Wrapping Package 4" 32806	Open		7.00	7
1998 Santa 8" 32801	Open		20.00	20
1998 Sleigh 10 1/2" 32800	Open		110.00	110

The Magic of Spring - J. Crvich

YEAR ISSUE	EDITION LIMIT	YEAR RETD.	ISSUE PRICE	*QUOTE U.S.$
1997 Bunny Magician with Egg 15" 54701	Retrd.	1997	64.00	64

Master Gardener - D. Calla

YEAR ISSUE	EDITION LIMIT	YEAR RETD.	ISSUE PRICE	*QUOTE U.S.$
1997 Master Gardener 14" 53701	Open		84.00	84
1997 "Rain" Weather Faery 6" 53703	Open		22.00	22
1997 "Sunshine" Weather Faery 6" 53704	Open		22.00	22
1997 "Wind" Weather Faery 6"	Open		22.00	22

Merry Christmas - D. Calla

YEAR ISSUE	EDITION LIMIT	YEAR RETD.	ISSUE PRICE	*QUOTE U.S.$
1993 Santa with Girl 11" 31308	Retrd.	1995	100.00	100
1993 Santa with Heart 10" 31309	Retrd.	1995	50.00	50
1993 Snowman 9" 31313	Retrd.	1996	50.00	50

Nativity - V. & S. Rawson

YEAR ISSUE	EDITION LIMIT	YEAR RETD.	ISSUE PRICE	*QUOTE U.S.$
1996 Baby in Manger 22653	Open		7.00	7
1996 Donkey 22656	Open		9.00	9
1996 Joseph 22651	Open		18.00	18
1996 Lamb 22657	Open		5.00	5
1996 Mary 22652	Open		18.00	18
1997 Nativity Angel 32725	Open		22.00	22
1996 Shepherd with Lamb 22654	Open		20.00	20
1996 Shepherd with Staff 22655	Open		18.00	18
1997 Wise Man Kneeling 32727	Open		22.00	22
1997 Wise Man with Blue Robe 32728	Open		22.00	22
1997 Wise Man with Green Robe 32726	Open		22.00	22

Night Before Christmas - D. Calla

YEAR ISSUE	EDITION LIMIT	YEAR RETD.	ISSUE PRICE	*QUOTE U.S.$
1994 Gent in Nightshirt 12" 31408	Retrd.	1996	60.00	60
1994 Santa 22" 31403	Retrd.	1995	120.00	120
1994 Sprite on Rocking Horse 14" 31409	Retrd.	1995	90.00	90
1994 St. Nick on Chimney 16" 31406	Retrd.	1995	100.00	100

North Star - D. Calla

YEAR ISSUE	EDITION LIMIT	YEAR RETD.	ISSUE PRICE	*QUOTE U.S.$
1995 Polar Bear 16" 32507	Retrd.	1997	90.00	90
1995 St. Nick 19" 32506	Retrd.	1997	100.00	100
1995 St. Nick Riding Polar Bear 15" 32505	Retrd.	1997	140.00	140

The Nutcracker - D. Calla

YEAR ISSUE	EDITION LIMIT	YEAR RETD.	ISSUE PRICE	*QUOTE U.S.$
1993 Drosselmeir 14" 32305	Retrd.	1994	70.00	70

Nutcracker - V. & S. Rawson

YEAR ISSUE	EDITION LIMIT	YEAR RETD.	ISSUE PRICE	*QUOTE U.S.$
1998 Clara 33851	Open		10.00	10
1998 Drosselmeier 33853	Open		10.00	10
1998 Mouse King 33852	Open		10.00	10
1998 Mrs. Ginger 33854	Open		10.00	10
1998 Nutcracker 33855	Open		10.00	10
1998 Prince 33850	Open		10.00	10

Old Fashioned Toys - P. Herrick

YEAR ISSUE	EDITION LIMIT	YEAR RETD.	ISSUE PRICE	*QUOTE U.S.$
1997 Bunny Kissing Santa 33702	Open		140.00	140
1997 Bunny Tricycle with Santa 33701	Open		120.00	120
1997 Santa on Frog Tricycle 33703	Open		120.00	120

On Christmas Day - D. Calla

YEAR ISSUE	EDITION LIMIT	YEAR RETD.	ISSUE PRICE	*QUOTE U.S.$
1991 Boy 8" 32111	Retrd.	1994	29.00	29
1991 Father 12" 32108	Retrd.	1994	46.00	46
1991 Girl 8" 32110	Retrd.	1994	29.00	29
1991 Mother 11" 32109	Retrd.	1994	46.00	46

Once Upon a Christmas - D. Calla

YEAR ISSUE	EDITION LIMIT	YEAR RETD.	ISSUE PRICE	*QUOTE U.S.$
1996 Baby Bear 9" 23621	Retrd.	1997	50.00	50
1996 House 10" 23618	Retrd.	1996	84.00	84
1996 Mama Bear 11" 23620	Retrd.	1997	70.00	70
1996 Papa Bear 11" 23619	Retrd.	1997	64.00	64
1996 "Read to Me Santa" 8" 23622	Retrd.	1996	60.00	60
1996 Santa Throwing Snowball 10" 23623	Retrd.	1997	60.00	60
1996 Tweedle Dee 8.5" 23624	Retrd.	1997	34.00	34

Patchwork Heart - J. Tasch

YEAR ISSUE	EDITION LIMIT	YEAR RETD.	ISSUE PRICE	*QUOTE U.S.$
1995 Father Christmas 23" 18508	Retrd.	1995	180.00	180
1995 Workbench Musical Santa 19" 18510	Retrd.	1995	200.00	200

Patriotic - D. Calla

YEAR ISSUE	EDITION LIMIT	YEAR RETD.	ISSUE PRICE	*QUOTE U.S.$
1992 Uncle Sam 50299	Open		60.00	60

Patriotic - P.J. Hornberger

YEAR ISSUE	EDITION LIMIT	YEAR RETD.	ISSUE PRICE	*QUOTE U.S.$
1997 Uncle Sam 17.5" 50730	Open		70.00	70

Patriotic - V. & S. Rawson

YEAR ISSUE	EDITION LIMIT	YEAR RETD.	ISSUE PRICE	*QUOTE U.S.$
1997 Banner Wave Angel 8.5" 50726	Open		33.00	33
1997 Broad Stripe Angel 11" 50725	Open		33.00	33
1997 "Oh Say Can You See" Angel 8" 50727	Open		33.00	33

Peace on Earth - D. Calla

YEAR ISSUE	EDITION LIMIT	YEAR RETD.	ISSUE PRICE	*QUOTE U.S.$
1994 Angel with Lamb 16" 32401	Retrd.	1997	90.00	90
1994 Lion, Lamb, and Angel 32402	Retrd.	1997	70.00	70
1993 St. Nicholas 20" 32355	Retrd.	1997	140.00	140

Reach for the Stars - D. Calla

YEAR ISSUE	EDITION LIMIT	YEAR RETD.	ISSUE PRICE	*QUOTE U.S.$
1992 Santa 19" 31256	Open		160.00	160

Santa's Kingdom - S. Smith

YEAR ISSUE	EDITION LIMIT	YEAR RETD.	ISSUE PRICE	*QUOTE U.S.$
1998 Cat-tastrophe 9 1/2" 37850	Open		16.00	16
1998 Panda-monium 9 1/2" 37851	Open		16.00	16
1998 Santa & Penguin 3 1/4" 37853	Open		5.00	5
1998 Santa , Cat & Dog 6" 37852	Open		16.00	16
1996 Santa Fishing on Bear 37656	5,000		68.00	68
1997 Santa on Buffalo 37751	5,000		72.00	72
1996 Santa on Deer 37660	5,000		50.00	50
1996 Santa on Horse 37659	5,000		68.00	68
1996 Santa on Moose 37657	5,000		66.00	66
1997 Santa on Polar Bear 37753	5,000		77.00	77
1997 Santa on Whale 37752	5,000		72.00	72
1996 Santa with Bear 37658	5,000		50.00	50
1998 Special Delivery 6 1/4" 37854	Open		16.00	16

Santa's Legend - A. Schreck Moore

YEAR ISSUE	EDITION LIMIT	YEAR RETD.	ISSUE PRICE	*QUOTE U.S.$
1998 Santa with Chair 20" 35802	250		420.00	420
1998 Santa with Sled 22" 35801	250		500.00	500
1998 Standing Santa with Green Coat 21" 35803	250		330.00	330
1998 Standing Santa with Red Coat 22" 35800	250		430.00	430

Seasonal Gift - V. Howard

YEAR ISSUE	EDITION LIMIT	YEAR RETD.	ISSUE PRICE	*QUOTE U.S.$
1997 Bear 5.5" 35729	Open		13.00	13
1997 Bunny 5.5" 35728	Open		13.00	13
1997 Santa 5.25" 35732	Open		13.00	13
1997 Santa Candleholder 5" 35725	Open		18.00	18
1997 Scarecrow 5.5" 35730	Open		13.00	13
1997 Scarecrow Candleholder 5.5" 35727	Open		18.00	18
1997 Snowlady 5" 35733	Open		13.00	13
1997 Witch 6.25" 35731	Open		13.00	13
1997 Witch Candleholder 6" 35726	Open		18.00	18

Silent Night - S. Smith

YEAR ISSUE	EDITION LIMIT	YEAR RETD.	ISSUE PRICE	*QUOTE U.S.$
1998 Cow and Donkey, set/2 37812	Open		40.00	40
1998 Mary, Joseph, Baby & Angel, set/4 37810	Open		60.00	60
1998 Shepherd, Boy & Two Lambs, set/4 37811	Open		55.00	55
1998 Silent Night, set/10 37814	Open		150.00	150
1998 Stable 12" 37813	Open		31.00	31

FIGURINES

Simple Gifts - D. Calla

YEAR ISSUE	EDITION LIMIT	YEAR RETD.	ISSUE PRICE	*QUOTE U.S.$
1992 St. Nicholas 20" 32206	Retrd.	1994	60.00	60

Snow Meadow - D. Calla

YEAR ISSUE	EDITION LIMIT	YEAR RETD.	ISSUE PRICE	*QUOTE U.S.$
1992 Seated St. Nicholas 10" 31207	Retrd.	1995	30.00	30
1992 St. Nicholas 14" 31206	Retrd.	1996	70.00	70

Snowberries - D. Calla

YEAR ISSUE	EDITION LIMIT	YEAR RETD.	ISSUE PRICE	*QUOTE U.S.$
1990 Tall Angel 33002	Retrd.	1992	90.00	90

Snowbound - D. Calla

YEAR ISSUE	EDITION LIMIT	YEAR RETD.	ISSUE PRICE	*QUOTE U.S.$
1996 Nordic Skier 10.5" 27615	Retrd.	1997	80.00	80
1996 Ski Chalet 8" 27616	Retrd.	1997	140.00	140

SnowMa'am - D. Calla

YEAR ISSUE	EDITION LIMIT	YEAR RETD.	ISSUE PRICE	*QUOTE U.S.$
1997 SnowMa'am 14" 30752	Open		128.00	128

The Spirit of Giving - D. Calla

YEAR ISSUE	EDITION LIMIT	YEAR RETD.	ISSUE PRICE	*QUOTE U.S.$
1992 Babouschka - Russia 32253	Retrd.	1995	50.00	50
1992 Father Christmas - England 32251	Retrd.	1995	60.00	60
1992 Jule Nisse - Scandinavia 32254	Retrd.	1995	40.00	40
1992 Santa Claus - America 32255	Retrd.	1995	50.00	50
1992 St. Lucia - Sweden 32252	Retrd.	1995	30.00	30
1992 St. Nicholas - Netherlands 32250	Retrd.	1995	70.00	70

Spring - D. Calla

YEAR ISSUE	EDITION LIMIT	YEAR RETD.	ISSUE PRICE	*QUOTE U.S.$
1994 Beau Bunny 9" 50407	Retrd.	1997	25.00	25
1994 Belle Bunny 9" 50408	Retrd.	1997	25.00	25
1993 Boy Bunny 9" 50301	Open		30.00	30
1993 Girl Bunny 9" 50302	Open		30.00	30
1994 Mamma Beth Bunny 13" 50406	Retrd.	1995	50.00	50
1992 Spring Boy Bunny 13" 50201	Retrd.	1995	60.00	60
1992 Spring Girl Bunny 13" 50202	Retrd.	1995	60.00	60

Spring Harbinger - D. Calla

YEAR ISSUE	EDITION LIMIT	YEAR RETD.	ISSUE PRICE	*QUOTE U.S.$
1995 Harbinger Rabbit 20" 50521	Open		220.00	220

Ten Christmas - D. Calla

YEAR ISSUE	EDITION LIMIT	YEAR RETD.	ISSUE PRICE	*QUOTE U.S.$
1997 Santa 18" 30777	Open		190.00	190

Thanksgiving Kids - R. Morehead

YEAR ISSUE	EDITION LIMIT	YEAR RETD.	ISSUE PRICE	*QUOTE U.S.$
1997 Children Giving Thanks 6.5" 50750	Open		48.00	48
1997 Children with Basket and Squirrel 9" 50752	Open		66.00	66
1997 Children with Cornucopia 4.5" 50751	Open		54.00	54

Twelve Days of Christmas - D. Calla

YEAR ISSUE	EDITION LIMIT	YEAR RETD.	ISSUE PRICE	*QUOTE U.S.$
1990 Partridge 9" 32003	Retrd.	1993	49.00	49

Two by Two - D. Calla

YEAR ISSUE	EDITION LIMIT	YEAR RETD.	ISSUE PRICE	*QUOTE U.S.$
1994 Noah's Ark 12" 32451	Retrd.	1997	120.00	120
1994 St. Nick 12" 32452	Retrd.	1997	90.00	90

Wings of Light - D. Calla

YEAR ISSUE	EDITION LIMIT	YEAR RETD.	ISSUE PRICE	*QUOTE U.S.$
1996 Angel 14" 21655	Retrd.	1997	60.00	60
1996 Angel with Dove 9.5" 21673	Open		42.00	42
1996 Seated Santa 9" 21676	Open		26.00	26
1996 St. Nick 15" 21672	Open		84.00	84

Ye Olde Santa Maker - D. Gann

YEAR ISSUE	EDITION LIMIT	YEAR RETD.	ISSUE PRICE	*QUOTE U.S.$
1993 From Santa with Love 21" 35355	Retrd.	1993	150.00	150
1993 Goodwill to All Santa 16" 35352	Retrd.	1993	160.00	160
1993 Hanzel - The Musical Elf 12" 35359	Retrd.	1994	75.00	75
1997 Large Santa 25" 35767	Open		176.00	176
1993 Merry Ol' Santa 20" 35353	Retrd.	1994	190.00	190
1997 Musical "Merry Christmas" Santa 35766	Open		90.00	90
1995 Musical Santa in Chair 15.5" 35566	Retrd.	1995	160.00	160
1998 Nautical Santa 16" 35856	Open		90.00	90
1998 Santa Holding Mirror 16" 35852	Open		110.00	110
1997 Santa on Rocking Horse 12" 35760	Retrd.	1997	80.00	80
1996 Santa Riding Tricycle 13" 35669	Retrd.	1996	150.00	150
1995 Santa Riding Tricycle 16" 35565	Retrd.	1996	110.00	110
1998 Santa Riding Tricycle Cart 9 1/2" 35858	Open		130.00	130
1994 Santa with Angel 16" 35458	Retrd.	1994	160.00	160
1996 Santa with Angel and Bell 16.5" 35666	Retrd.	1997	76.00	76
1997 Santa with Basket 10" 35759	Retrd.	1997	57.00	57
1998 Santa with Toys 13" 35855	Open		70.00	70
1995 Seated Musical Santa 13" 35564	Open		100.00	100
1995 Seated Santa 21.5" 35556	Retrd.	1997	160.00	160
1993 Sleigh Ride Santa 16" 35350	Retrd.	1993	210.00	210
1993 Winking Santa 20" 35354	Retrd.	1993	160.00	160
1994 Ye Olde Americana Santa 17" 35450	Retrd.	1994	130.00	130
1994 Ye Olde Dutch Santa 17" 35455	Retrd.	1994	130.00	130
1994 Ye Olde German Santa 17" 35451	Retrd.	1994	130.00	130
1994 Ye Olde Russian Santa 17" 35452	Retrd.	1994	130.00	130
1994 Ye Olde Scottish Santa 17" 35454	Retrd.	1994	130.00	130
1994 Ye Olde Swedish Santa 17" 35453	Retrd.	1994	130.00	130

Hudson Creek

American West - "Where the Sun Sets" - L. Heyda

YEAR ISSUE	EDITION LIMIT	YEAR RETD.	ISSUE PRICE	*QUOTE U.S.$
1997 Matthew 18	350		295.00	295
1997 Mystic Hunter	350		195.00	195
1997 On The Horizon	350		295.00	295
1997 Sprucin' Up	350		350.00	350

Chilmark - Various

YEAR ISSUE	EDITION LIMIT	YEAR RETD.	ISSUE PRICE	*QUOTE U.S.$
1981 Budweiser Wagon - Keim/Hazen	890	1989	2000.00	3000
1986 Camelot Chess Set - P. Jackson	Retrd.	1991	2250.00	2250
1979 Carousel - R. Sylvan	950	1983	115.00	115
1980 Charge of the 7th Cavalry - B. Rodden	394	1988	600.00	950
1983 Dragon Slayer - D. LaRocca	290	1988	385.00	500
1989 The Great White Whale - A.T. McGrory	Suspd.		1050.00	1050
1994 Herald of Spring - D. LaRocca	950		295.00	295
1985 Moby Dick - J. Royce	Retrd.	1995	350.00	350-500
1979 Moses - B. Rodden	2,500	1989	140.00	235
1985 Out of Trouble - A. Petitto	9,800		245.00	245
1979 Pegasus - R. Sylvan	527	1981	95.00	175
1993 St. Nicholas - D. Liberty	Suspd.		750.00	750
1979 Unicorn - R. Sylvan	2,500	1982	115.00	550
1994 Woodland Santa - D. Liberty	Suspd.		750.00	750

Chilmark American West - D. Polland, unless otherwise noted

YEAR ISSUE	EDITION LIMIT	YEAR RETD.	ISSUE PRICE	*QUOTE U.S.$
1981 Ambushed	294	1991	2370.00	2700
1987 Apache Attack - F. Barnum	Suspd.		315.00	315-375
1982 Apache Gan Dancer	2,500		115.00	115
1987 Appeal to the Great Spirit - F. Barnum	Retrd.	1995	275.00	275-350
1982 Arapaho Drummer	2,500		115.00	115
1996 Arrow Marker - M. Boyett	Retrd.	1998	395.00	395
1989 Attack on the Iron Horse - M. Boyett	Retrd.	1998	3675.00	3675
1985 Bareback Rider	2,500		315.00	315
1985 Bear Meet - S. York	Retrd.	1992	500.00	600-800
1983 Bison's Fury - M. Boyett	Retrd.	1995	495.00	495
1982 Blood Brothers - M. Boyett	717	1991	250.00	610-800
1979 Border Rustlers	500	1989	1295.00	1500
1983 Bounty Hunter	264	1987	250.00	300-600
1976 Buffalo Hunt	2,250	N/A	300.00	1000
1976 Buffalo Hunt	2,250	1980	300.00	1625
1982 Buffalo Prayer	2,500	1989	95.00	225-400
1981 Buffalo Robe	2,500		335.00	335
1990 Buffalo Spirit	2,500	1993	110.00	185
1985 Calf Roper	2,500		395.00	395
1979 Cavalry Officer - D. LaRocca	500	1985	125.00	400-650
1974 Cheyenne	2,800	1980	200.00	3000
1987 Clash of Cultures - F. Barnum	Suspd.		385.00	385
1976 Cold Saddles, Mean Horses	2,800	1986	200.00	800
1988 Comanche Hostile	2,500		290.00	290
1982 Comanche Plains Drummer	2,500		115.00	115
1974 Counting Coup	2,800	1980	225.00	1600-2000
1987 Counting Coup - F. Barnum	Suspd.		385.00	385
1979 Cowboy - D. LaRocca	950	1984	125.00	500-750
1982 Crow Medicine Dancer	2,500		115.00	115
1974 Crow Scout	3,000	1983	250.00	1000-1700
1978 Dangerous Encounter - B. Rodden	746	1977	475.00	600-950
1989 Death Battle	2,500		335.00	335
1985 The Doctor - M. Boyett	Retrd.	1994	750.00	800-950
1981 Dog Soldier	2,500		315.00	315
1990 Eagle Dancer (deNatura)	614	1993	300.00	300
1991 Eagle Dancer (pewter)	1,800		275.00	275
1994 Enemy Territory - Sullivan	Retrd.	1998	500.00	500
1981 Enemy Tracks	2,500	1988	225.00	720
1984 Eye to Eye	2,500		500.00	500
1984 Flat Out for Red River Station - M. Boyett	2,500	1991	3000.00	3000-6000
1982 Flathead War Dancer	2,500		115.00	115
1989 Frenchie	2,500		280.00	280
1979 Getting Acquainted	950	1988	215.00	800-1100
1994 He Who Taunts the Enemy - M. Boyett	Suspd.		8900.00	8900
1988 Hightailin'	2,500		450.00	450
1982 Hopi Kachina Dancer	2,500		115.00	115
1985 Horse of A Different Color - S. York	Retrd.	1992	500.00	600-800
1982 Hostile Apache	2,500		115.00	115
1991 I Don't Do Fences	2,500		115.00	115
1979 Indian Warrior - D. LaRocca	1,186	1988	95.00	400
1989 Jedediah Smith	2,500		345.00	345
1982 Jemez Eagle Dancer	2,500	1989	95.00	450-700
1991 Kiowa Princess (deNatura)	444	1993	300.00	300
1991 Kiowa Princess (pewter)	1,200		275.00	275
1982 Last Arrow	2,500	1988	95.00	300-400
1991 Lawman	2,500		130.00	130
1983 Line Rider	2,500	1988	195.00	975-1200
1979 Mandan Hunter	5,000	1985	65.00	780-900
1988 Marauders	Retrd.	1994	850.00	850
1975 Maverick Calf	2,500	1981	250.00	1300-1700
1989 Mohawk War Party	2,500		600.00	600
1976 Monday Morning Wash	2,500	1986	200.00	1000-1300
1979 Mountain Man - D. LaRocca	764	1988	95.00	500-650
1983 The Mustanger	Retrd.	1995	425.00	425
1982 Navajo Kachina Dancer	2,500		115.00	115
1983 Now or Never	693	1991	265.00	800
1975 The Outlaws	2,500	1989	450.00	1180-1200
1976 Painting the Town	2,250	1983	300.00	1500-1700
1996 The Peace Pipe - M. Boyett	Retrd.	1998	395.00	395
1990 Pequot Wars	950	1990	395.00	800
1981 Plight of the Huntsman - M. Boyett	950	1987	495.00	850
1989 Portugee Philips	2,500		280.00	280
1985 Postal Exchange - S. York	Retrd.	1992	300.00	400-600
1990 Red River Wars	950	1990	425.00	700-850
1989 Renegade	2,500		315.00	315
1976 Rescue	2,500	1980	275.00	1200-1500
1991 Rodeo Star	2,500		90.00	90
1979 Running Battle - B. Rodden	761	1987	400.00	750-900
1990 Running Wolf (deNatura)	720	1993	350.00	350
1991 Running Wolf (pewter)	1,200		325.00	325
1982 Sioux War Chief	2,500	1989	95.00	240-480
1981 Sioux War Cry - M. Boyett	Retrd.	1998	385.00	385
1986 Stallions	2,500		315.00	315
1985 Steer Wrestling	2,500		635.00	635
1991 The Storyteller	Retrd.	1995	150.00	150
1985 Team Roping	2,500		660.00	660
1990 Tecumseh's Rebellion	950	1990	350.00	700
1991 A Test of Courage	1,200		290.00	290
1983 Too Many Aces	1,717	1993	400.00	850-1200
1981 U.S. Marshal	1,500	1986	95.00	450
1993 The Unconquered - M. Boyett	Retrd.	1998	6500.00	6500
1996 War Paint - M. Boyett	Retrd.	1998	395.00	395
1981 War Party	1,066	1991	550.00	975-1150
1981 When War Chiefs Meet	2,500	1988	300.00	800
1983 The Wild Bunch	285	1987	200.00	225-400
1982 Yakima Salmon Fisherman	2,500	1987	200.00	600-750
1991 Yellow Boy (deNatura)	460	1993	350.00	350
1991 Yellow Boy (pewter)	1,200		325.00	325

Chilmark American West Christmas Specials - D. Polland

YEAR ISSUE	EDITION LIMIT	YEAR RETD.	ISSUE PRICE	*QUOTE U.S.$
1991 Merry Christmas Neighbor	1,240	1991	395.00	750-900
1992 Merry Christmas My Love	819	1992	350.00	350-450
1993 Almost Home	520	1994	375.00	375
1994 Cowboy Christmas	427	1994	250.00	250

Chilmark American West Event Specials - D. Polland, unless otherwise noted

YEAR ISSUE	EDITION LIMIT	YEAR RETD.	ISSUE PRICE	*QUOTE U.S.$
1991 Uneasy Truce	737	1991	125.00	175-195
1992 Irons In The Fire	612	1992	125.00	150-225
1994 Bacon 'N' Beans Again?	458	1994	150.00	175-225
1994 Buffalo Skull - J. Slockbower	Yr. Iss.	1994	125.00	125
1995 Renegade Apache	Closed	1995	150.00	150

Chilmark American West Guardians of the Plains - J. Slockbower

YEAR ISSUE	EDITION LIMIT	YEAR RETD.	ISSUE PRICE	*QUOTE U.S.$
1993 Noble Elder (MetalART)	Retrd.	1998	350.00	350
1993 Noble Elder (pewter)	Retrd.	1998	275.00	275
1993 Old Storyteller (MetalART)	Suspd.		350.00	350
1993 Old Storyteller (pewter)	Suspd.		275.00	275
1993 Proud Warrior (MetalART)	Suspd.		350.00	350
1993 Proud Warrior (pewter)	Suspd.		275.00	275
1993 Valiant Leader (MetalART)	Retrd.	1998	350.00	350
1993 Valiant Leader (pewter)	Retrd.	1998	275.00	275

Chilmark American West Kindred Spirits Collection - A. McGrory

YEAR ISSUE	EDITION LIMIT	YEAR RETD.	ISSUE PRICE	*QUOTE U.S.$
1994 Brother Wolf	500	1995	500.00	500
1995 Buffalo Hide	500		750.00	750
1996 Secret Hunter	500		500.00	500

Chilmark American West Legacy of Courage - M. Boyett

YEAR ISSUE	EDITION LIMIT	YEAR RETD.	ISSUE PRICE	*QUOTE U.S.$
1983 Along the Cherokee Trace	624	1991	295.00	720
1981 Apache Signals	765	1987	175.00	550-575
1982 Arapaho Sentinel	678	1991	195.00	500
1981 Blackfoot Snow Hunter	984	1988	175.00	650
1981 Buffalo Stalker	1,034	1991	175.00	560
1983 Circling the Enemy	Retrd.	1992	295.00	395
1981 Comanche	1,553	1991	175.00	530-670
1982 Dance of the Eagles	Retrd.	1992	150.00	215-300
1983 Forest Watcher	658	1991	215.00	540
1981 Iroquois Warfare	1,477	1991	125.00	600
1982 Kiowa Scout	292	1987	195.00	525
1982 Listening For Hooves	883	1991	150.00	400
1982 Mandan Buffalo Dancer	1,494	1991	195.00	450-600
1983 Moment of Truth	1,145	1991	295.00	550-620
1982 Plains Talk-Pawnee	421	1987	195.00	625
1983 Rite of the Whitetail	Retrd.	1992	295.00	400
1982 Shoshone Eagle Catcher	2,500	1985	225.00	1600-2000
1982 The Tracker Nez Perce	686	1988	150.00	575
1981 Unconquered Seminole	1,021	1991	175.00	540
1981 Victor Cheyenne	1,299	1991	175.00	500
1983 A Warrior's Tribute	Retrd.	1992	335.00	635
1983 Winter Hunt	756	1991	295.00	400

Chilmark American West OffCanvas™ - A. T. McGrory

YEAR ISSUE	EDITION LIMIT	YEAR RETD.	ISSUE PRICE	*QUOTE U.S.$
1990 Attack	Retrd.	1998	1295.00	1295
1991 Blanket Signal	350	1993	750.00	850
1993 Buffalo Hunter (MetalART)	Retrd.	1998	295.00	295
1993 Buffalo Hunter (pewter)	Retrd.	1998	225.00	225
1991 Conjuring Back the Buffalo	950		290.00	290
1991 Dash for the Timber	950		580.00	580
1991 The Outlier	950		515.00	515
1993 Pony War Dance (MetalART)	Retrd.	1998	295.00	295
1993 Pony War Dance (pewter)	Retrd.	1998	225.00	225
1990 Smoke Signal	950	1990	345.00	550-700
1992 Trooper of the Southern Plains	Suspd.		310.00	310
1992 The Vanishing American	Suspd.		265.00	265
1990 Vigil	950	1990	345.00	500-700
1990 Warrior	950	1990	300.00	350-600

Chilmark American West Redemption Specials - D. Polland, unless otherwise noted

YEAR ISSUE	EDITION LIMIT	YEAR RETD.	ISSUE PRICE	*QUOTE U.S.$
1983 The Chief	2,459	1984	275.00	1750
1984 Unit Colors	1,394	1985	250.00	950-1500
1985 Oh Great Spirit	3,180	1986	300.00	1000-1300
1986 Eagle Catcher - M. Boyett	1,840	1987	300.00	1200-1600
1987 Surprise Encounter - F. Barnum	1,534	1988	250.00	600-800
1988 I Will Fight No More Forever (Chief Joseph)	3,404	1989	350.00	850
1989 Geronimo	1,866	1990	375.00	650-750
1990 Cochise	1,778	1991	400.00	500-600
1991 Crazy Horse	2,067	1992	295.00	600-650
1992 Strong Hearts to the Front	1,252	1993	425.00	600
1993 Sacred Ground Reclaimed	861	1994	495.00	550-650
1994 Horse Breaking	504	1995	395.00	395

*Quotes have been rounded up to nearest dollar

YEAR ISSUE	EDITION LIMIT	YEAR RETD.	ISSUE PRICE	*QUOTE U.S.$
1995 The Rainmaker - M. Boyett	Retrd.	1996	350.00	350

Chilmark American West The Great Chiefs - J. Slockbower

YEAR ISSUE	EDITION LIMIT	YEAR RETD.	ISSUE PRICE	*QUOTE U.S.$
1992 Chief Joseph	750	1992	975.00	1500-1900
1993 Crazy Horse	Retrd.	1998	975.00	975-1100
1992 Geronimo	750	1992	975.00	1300-1850
1993 Sitting Bull	750	1996	1075.00	1075-1100

Chilmark American West The Medicine Men - D. Polland

YEAR ISSUE	EDITION LIMIT	YEAR RETD.	ISSUE PRICE	*QUOTE U.S.$
1992 False Face (MetalART)	1,000		550.00	550
1992 False Face (pewter)	500	1992	375.00	375

Chilmark American West The Seekers - A. McGrory

YEAR ISSUE	EDITION LIMIT	YEAR RETD.	ISSUE PRICE	*QUOTE U.S.$
1993 Bear Vision	Suspd.		1375.00	1375
1992 Buffalo Vision	500	1993	1075.00	1075
1993 Eagle Vision	Suspd.		1250.00	1250

Chilmark American West The Warriors - D. Polland

YEAR ISSUE	EDITION LIMIT	YEAR RETD.	ISSUE PRICE	*QUOTE U.S.$
1995 Keeper of the Eastern Door (pewter)	500		375.00	375
1995 Keeper of the Eastern Door (MetalART)	1,000		500.00	500
1993 Son of the Morning Star (MetalART)	1,000		495.00	495
1993 Son of the Morning Star (pewter)	500	1993	375.00	460
1995 Soul of the Forest (pewter)	500		375.00	375
1995 Soul of the Forest (MetalART)	1,000		500.00	500
1992 Spirit of the Wolf (MetalART)	1,000	1996	500.00	500
1992 Spirit of the Wolf (pewter)	500	1993	350.00	850

Chilmark American West To The Great Spirit - T. Sullivan

YEAR ISSUE	EDITION LIMIT	YEAR RETD.	ISSUE PRICE	*QUOTE U.S.$
1993 Gray Elk	950	1998	775.00	775
1992 Shooting Star	950	1994	775.00	775
1994 Thunder Cloud	950	1998	775.00	775
1993 Two Eagles	950	1998	775.00	775

Chilmark American West Works of the Masters - Various

YEAR ISSUE	EDITION LIMIT	YEAR RETD.	ISSUE PRICE	*QUOTE U.S.$
1985 Bronco Buster (lg.) - C. Rousell	766	1989	400.00	400
1987 Bronco Buster - A.T. McGrory	2,500		225.00	225
1986 Buffalo Hunt - A. McGrory	172	1989	550.00	800
1984 Cheyenne (Remington) - C. Rousell	285	1988	400.00	600
1988 Cheyenne - A.T. McGrory	2,500		265.00	265
1987 Coming Through the Rye - A. McGrory	Retrd.	1995	750.00	750-1000
1986 End of the Trail (lg.) - A. McGrory	Retrd.	1995	450.00	495
1988 End of the Trail (mini) - A. McGrory	2,500	1992	225.00	325
1987 Mountain Man - A.T. McGrory	2,500		240.00	240-275

Chilmark Americana - L. Davis

YEAR ISSUE	EDITION LIMIT	YEAR RETD.	ISSUE PRICE	*QUOTE U.S.$
1994 City Slicker	Retrd.	1998	2500.00	2500
1994 Milkin' Time	Retrd.	1998	295.00	295
1993 Skedaddlin'	350	1995	2000.00	2000
1993 Tin Man	Retrd.	1998	2500.00	2500

Chilmark Civil War "Antietam: The Bloodiest Day" - F. Barnum

YEAR ISSUE	EDITION LIMIT	YEAR RETD.	ISSUE PRICE	*QUOTE U.S.$
1997 The Cornfield	650		395.00	395

Chilmark Civil War - F. Barnum

YEAR ISSUE	EDITION LIMIT	YEAR RETD.	ISSUE PRICE	*QUOTE U.S.$
1993 Abraham Lincoln Bust (bronze)	50	1993	2000.00	2250-2500
1996 Beefsteak Raid	650		335.00	335
1988 Brother Against Brother	2,500		265.00	265-350
1991 Dear Mother	2,500		175.00	175-185
1989 Devil's Den	2,500		280.00	280
1988 A Father's Farewell	2,500	1994	150.00	200-350
1989 Gaines Mill	Suspd.		580.00	580
1988 Johnny Shiloh	2,500	1992	100.00	175-295
1992 Kennesaw Mountain	350	1992	650.00	1500-2000
1993 Lincoln Bust (MetalART)	Retrd.	1998	1250.00	1250
1993 Lincoln Bust (pewter)	Retrd.	1998	950.00	950
1988 Nothing Left	2,500		265.00	265
1989 Old Abe	Suspd.		420.00	420
1992 Parson's Battery	500	1993	495.00	700-750
1987 Pickett's Charge	Retrd.	1994	350.00	500-595
1991 Quantrill's Raiders	Suspd.		1000.00	1000
1987 The Rescue	Retrd.	1995	275.00	450-550
1987 Saving The Colors	Retrd.	1992	350.00	500-700
1990 Spangler's Spring	2,500		235.00	235

Chilmark Civil War Cavalry Generals - F. Barnum

YEAR ISSUE	EDITION LIMIT	YEAR RETD.	ISSUE PRICE	*QUOTE U.S.$
1993 George Armstrong Custer	950	1996	375.00	375
1992 J.E.B. Stuart	950	1992	375.00	650-1500
1993 Nathan Bedford Forrest	950	1992	375.00	375-650
1994 Philip Sheridan	950	1998	375.00	375

Chilmark Civil War Christmas Specials - F. Barnum

YEAR ISSUE	EDITION LIMIT	YEAR RETD.	ISSUE PRICE	*QUOTE U.S.$
1992 Merry Christmas Yank	810	1992	350.00	450-500
1993 Silent Night	591	1993	350.00	650-700
1994 Christmas Truce	Retrd.	1994	295.00	350-600
1995 Peace on Earth	Retrd.	1995	350.00	350-475
1996 Spirit of Giving	Retrd.	1997	195.00	195

Chilmark Civil War Confederates - F. Barnum

YEAR ISSUE	EDITION LIMIT	YEAR RETD.	ISSUE PRICE	*QUOTE U.S.$
1995 The Cavalier (bronze)	75		1500.00	1500
1995 The Cavalier (pewter)	750		625.00	625
1993 The Gentleman Soldier (bronze)	75		1500.00	1500
1993 The Gentleman Soldier (pewter)	750	1995	625.00	625
1994 Old Jack (bronze)	75		1500.00	1500
1994 Old Jack (pewter)	750		625.00	625

Chilmark Civil War Event Specials - F. Barnum

YEAR ISSUE	EDITION LIMIT	YEAR RETD.	ISSUE PRICE	*QUOTE U.S.$
1991 Boots and Saddles	437	1991	95.00	850-1000
1992 140th NY Zouave	389	1992	95.00	450-500
1993 Johnny Reb	889	1993	95.00	190-325
1994 Billy Yank	Retrd.	1994	95.00	125-170
1995 Seaman, CSS Alabama	Retrd.	1995	95.00	95-110
1996 The Forager	Retrd.	1996	110.00	110-115
1997 The Farrier	Yr.Iss.	1997	95.00	95-110

Chilmark Civil War Redemption Specials - F. Barnum

YEAR ISSUE	EDITION LIMIT	YEAR RETD.	ISSUE PRICE	*QUOTE U.S.$
1989 Lee To The Rear	1,088	1990	300.00	750-850
1990 Lee And Jackson	1,040	1991	375.00	1000-1100
1991 Stonewall Jackson	1,169	1992	295.00	450-800
1992 Zouaves 1st Manassas	640	1993	375.00	475-500
1993 Letter to Sarah	Retrd.	1994	395.00	600-700
1994 Angel of Fredericksburg	Retrd.	1995	275.00	275
1995 Rebel Yell	N/A		475.00	475-500

Chilmark Civil War The Adversaries - F. Barnum

YEAR ISSUE	EDITION LIMIT	YEAR RETD.	ISSUE PRICE	*QUOTE U.S.$
1991 Robert E. Lee	950	1992	350.00	1750-2300
1992 Stonewall Jackson	950	1992	375.00	800-900
1992 Ulysses S. Grant	950	1992	350.00	800-1000
1993 Wm. Tecumseh Sherman	950	1993	375.00	700-800
1993 Set of 4		1993	1450.00	4000-4500

Chilmark Civil War The Commanders - F. Barnum

YEAR ISSUE	EDITION LIMIT	YEAR RETD.	ISSUE PRICE	*QUOTE U.S.$
1994 Grant Bust (bronze)	Suspd.		2000.00	2000
1994 Grant Bust (MetalART)	Suspd.		1000.00	1000
1994 Grant Bust (pewter)	Suspd.		750.00	750
1993 Lee Bust (bronze)	Suspd.		2000.00	2000
1993 Lee Bust (MetalART)	Suspd.		1000.00	1000
1993 Lee Bust (pewter)	Suspd.		750.00	750

Chilmark Civil War Turning Points - F. Barnum

YEAR ISSUE	EDITION LIMIT	YEAR RETD.	ISSUE PRICE	*QUOTE U.S.$
1994 Clashing Sabers	500	1995	600.00	600-1000
1993 The High Tide	500	1993	600.00	900-1000
1996 Last Resort	500		600.00	600
1995 The Swinging Gate	500	1996	600.00	600

Chilmark Wildlife - Various

YEAR ISSUE	EDITION LIMIT	YEAR RETD.	ISSUE PRICE	*QUOTE U.S.$
1980 Affirmed - M. Jovine	145	1987	850.00	1275
1980 Born Free - B. Rodden	950	1988	250.00	675
1978 Buffalo - B. Rodden	950	1986	170.00	375-400
1977 The Challenge - B. Rodden	1,600	1977	175.00	250-300
1981 Clydesdale Wheel Horse - C. Keim	2,808	1989	120.00	430
1991 Cry of Freedom - S. Knight	Retrd.	1998	395.00	395
1994 Down to the Wire - A. Petitto	950		495.00	495
1980 Duel of the Bighorns - M. Boyett	137	1987	650.00	1200
1988 Eagles Rock - C. Bronson	Retrd.	1998	3100.00	3100
1979 Elephant - D. Polland	750	1987	315.00	450-550
1992 Feeling Free - P. Sedlow	2,500		100.00	100
1981 Freedom Eagle - G. deLodzia	2,500	1983	195.00	750-900
1979 Giraffe - D. Polland	414	1981	145.00	145
1991 The Guardian - J. Mullican	950		450.00	450
1989 High and Mighty - A. McGrory	Suspd.		185.00	200
1988 The Honor and the Glory - S. Knight	2,500		345.00	345
1979 Kudu - D. Polland	204	1981	160.00	160
1980 Lead Can't Catch Him - M. Boyett	397	1987	645.00	845
1978 Paddock Walk - A. Petitto	1,277	1991	85.00	215
1980 Prairie Sovereign - M. Boyett	247	1987	550.00	800
1992 Racing the Wind - P. Sedlow	2,500		100.00	100
1979 Rhino - D. Polland	142	1981	135.00	135-550
1977 Rise and Shine - B. Rodden	1,500	1977	135.00	200
1980 Ruby-Throated Hummingbird - V. Hayton	500	1983	275.00	350
1976 Running Free - B. Rodden	2,500	1977	75.00	300
1976 Stallion - B. Rodden	2,500	1977	75.00	260
1985 Stretch Run - A. Petitto	5,000		250.00	250
1992 Tender Mercies - P. Sedlow	2,500		130.00	130
1982 Tender Persuasion - J. Mootry	155	1987	950.00	1250
1992 Untamed - P. Sedlow	2,500		100.00	100
1980 Voice of Experience - M. Boyett	174	1987	645.00	850
1985 Wild Stallion - D. Polland	179	1988	145.00	350
1987 Winged Victory - J. Mullican	Suspd.		275.00	315
1982 Wings of Liberty - M. Boyett	950	1986	625.00	1200

Chilmark World War II - D. LaRocca

YEAR ISSUE	EDITION LIMIT	YEAR RETD.	ISSUE PRICE	*QUOTE U.S.$
1991 Air Corps & the Tokyo Raid	Suspd.		350.00	350
1990 Air Corps at Hickam Field	Suspd.		200.00	210
1990 Army at Corregidor	Suspd.		315.00	325
1991 Army in North Africa	Suspd.		375.00	375
1990 Marines at Wake Island	Suspd.		200.00	210
1991 Marines In the Solomons	Suspd.		275.00	350
1990 Navy at Pearl Harbor	Suspd.		425.00	450
1991 Navy in the North Atlantic	Suspd.		375.00	375

Disney Showcase Collection - Staff

YEAR ISSUE	EDITION LIMIT	YEAR RETD.	ISSUE PRICE	*QUOTE U.S.$
1989 "Gold Edition" Hollywood Mickey	Retrd.	1990	200.00	400-750
1994 Be My Valentine	Closed	1994	65.00	75-125
1995 California or Bust! (bronze)	25	1997	2750.00	2750
1995 California or Bust! (pewter)	250	1995	1250.00	1210-1750
1994 Christmas Waltz	Closed	1994	65.00	100-200
1997 Daisy-Carousel Ride	2,500		160.00	160
1996 Donald-Carousel Ride	2,500		160.00	160
1995 The Duck (bronze)	50		1375.00	1375
1995 The Duck (MetalART))	200		650.00	650
1995 The Duck (pewter)	300		500.00	500
1989 Fantasia	Retrd.	1995	19.00	19
1996 Getting Out the Vote	Retrd.	1996	99.00	99
1995 Goofy-Carousel Ride	2,500		195.00	195
1988 Happy Birthday Mickey	Yr.Iss.	1989	60.00	150
1989 Hollywood Mickey	Suspd.	1991	165.00	200-300
1996 Hook, Line & Sinker (bronze)	75		3250.00	3250
1996 Hook, Line & Sinker (pewter)	975		1250.00	1250
1997 Just Goofy (bronze)	25		1500.00	1500
1997 Just Goofy (MetalART))	200		750.00	750
1997 Just Goofy (pewter)	300		575.00	575
1994 Lights, Camera, Action (bronze)	50		3250.00	3250
1994 Lights, Camera, Action (pewter)	500		1500.00	785-1500
1994 Mickey on Parade (bronze)	50	1994	950.00	820-1450
1994 Mickey on Parade (MetalART))	350	1994	500.00	600-900
1994 Mickey on Parade (pewter)	750	1996	375.00	259-400
1991 Mickey-Carousel Ride	2,500		150.00	160
1992 Minnie-Carousel Ride	2,500		150.00	160
1994 Mouse in a Million (bronze)	50	1994	1250.00	1375-1500
1994 Mouse in a Million (MetalART))	250	1994	650.00	303-800
1994 Mouse in a Million (pewter)	500	1994	500.00	600-900
1991 Mouse Waltz	Retrd.	1994	41.00	41
1994 Puttin' on the Ritz (bronze)	50	1994	2000.00	2200
1994 Puttin' on the Ritz (MetalART))	250		1000.00	1000
1994 Puttin' on the Ritz (pewter)	350	1997	750.00	506-750
1996 Simply Minnie (bronze)	50		1100.00	1100
1996 Simply Minnie (MetalART))	200		600.00	600
1996 Simply Minnie (pewter)	300		450.00	450
1988 Socerer's Apprentice	Retrd.	1995	25.00	25
1986 Socerer's Apprentice (lg.)	Retrd.	1995	25.00	25
1988 Socerer's Apprentice/Music Train	Retrd.	1995	28.00	28
1990 Socerer's Apprentice/No. 9 Birthday Train	Retrd.	1995	25.00	25
1990 Socerer's Apprentice/No. 9 Birthday Train-painted	Retrd.	1995	27.00	27
1988 Sweethearts	Retrd.	1993	45.00	45

Disney Showcase Collection Annual Christmas Special - Staff

YEAR ISSUE	EDITION LIMIT	YEAR RETD.	ISSUE PRICE	*QUOTE U.S.$
1993 Hanging the Stockings	Annual	1993	295.00	350-395
1994 Trimming the Tree	Annual	1994	350.00	400-425
1995 Holiday Harmony?	Annual	1995	395.00	395
1996 Christmas Tree Safari	Annual	1996	195.00	195
1997 All Wrapped Up For Christmas	Annual		175.00	175

Disney Showcase Collection Annual Santa - Staff

YEAR ISSUE	EDITION LIMIT	YEAR RETD.	ISSUE PRICE	*QUOTE U.S.$
1993 Checking it Twice	Annual	1993	195.00	195-300
1994 Just For You	Annual	1994	265.00	300-400
1995 Surprise, Santa!	Annual	1995	225.00	245
1996 Jolly Old St. Mick	Annual	1996	245.00	245
1997 Finishing Touches	Annual		195.00	195

Disney Showcase Collection Annual Special - Staff

YEAR ISSUE	EDITION LIMIT	YEAR RETD.	ISSUE PRICE	*QUOTE U.S.$
1994 Bicycle Built For Two	Retrd.	1995	195.00	225-400
1995 Riding the Rails	Retrd.	1996	295.00	295

Disney Showcase Collection Comic Capers - Staff

YEAR ISSUE	EDITION LIMIT	YEAR RETD.	ISSUE PRICE	*QUOTE U.S.$
1995 Crack the Whip (bronze)	50		2000.00	2000
1995 Crack the Whip (pewter)	500		750.00	750
1994 Foursome Follies (bronze)	50	1994	2000.00	2000
1994 Foursome Follies (pewter)	500	1994	750.00	700-1000
1994 Matched Numbrd set	500	1994	N/A	3100-3500
1994 Un-Matched Numbrd set	500	1994	N/A	2700-2900

Disney Showcase Collection Country Club - Staff

YEAR ISSUE	EDITION LIMIT	YEAR RETD.	ISSUE PRICE	*QUOTE U.S.$
1995 Mouse Trap (bronze)	75		400.00	400
1995 Mouse Trap (pewter)	950		175.00	175
1995 Perfect Form (bronze)	75		450.00	450
1995 Perfect Form (pewter)	950		195.00	195
1995 Teed Off (bronze)	75		400.00	400
1995 Teed Off (pewter)	950		175.00	175
1995 What Birdie? (bronze)	75		400.00	400
1995 What Birdie? (pewter)	950		175.00	175

Disney Showcase Collection Four Seasons Frolics - Staff

YEAR ISSUE	EDITION LIMIT	YEAR RETD.	ISSUE PRICE	*QUOTE U.S.$
1997 Beatin' The Heat	500		350.00	350

Disney Showcase Collection Generations of Mickey - Staff

YEAR ISSUE	EDITION LIMIT	YEAR RETD.	ISSUE PRICE	*QUOTE U.S.$
1987 Antique Mickey	2,500	1990	95.00	396-700
1990 The Band Concert	2,500		185.00	195
1990 The Band Concert (Painted)	500	1993	215.00	303-400
1990 Disneyland Mickey	2,500		150.00	160
1989 Mickey's Gala Premiere	2,500		150.00	160
1991 The Mouse-1935	1,200		185.00	195
1991 Plane Crazy-1928	2,500		175.00	185
1989 Sorcerer's Apprentice	2,500	1993	150.00	300-600
1989 Steamboat Willie	2,500	1993	165.00	325-425

Disney Showcase Collection Highway Highjinks - Staff

YEAR ISSUE	EDITION LIMIT	YEAR RETD.	ISSUE PRICE	*QUOTE U.S.$
1997 Coastal Cruisin' (bronze)	25		1650.00	1650
1997 Coastal Cruisin' (MetalART)	350		550.00	550
1996 Get Your Kicks (bronze)	25	1997	1650.00	1650
1996 Get Your Kicks (MetalART)	350	1996	550.00	550

Disney Showcase Collection Mickey and Friends - Staff

YEAR ISSUE	EDITION LIMIT	YEAR RETD.	ISSUE PRICE	*QUOTE U.S.$
1994 Donald (bronze)	75	1994	325.00	400
1994 Donald (pewter)	1,500		150.00	150
1994 Goofy (bronze)	75	1994	375.00	450
1994 Goofy (pewter)	1,500		175.00	175
1994 Mickey (bronze)	75	1994	325.00	400
1994 Mickey (pewter)	1,500		150.00	150
1994 Minnie (bronze)	75	1994	325.00	400
1994 Minnie (pewter)	1,500		150.00	150
1994 Pluto (bronze)	75	1994	325.00	400
1994 Pluto (pewter)	1,500		150.00	150

Disney Showcase Collection On the Road - Staff

YEAR ISSUE	EDITION LIMIT	YEAR RETD.	ISSUE PRICE	*QUOTE U.S.$
1994 Beach Bound	350	1994	350.00	800-1300
1992 Cruising	350	1992	275.00	2000-3500
1993 Sunday Drive	350	1993	325.00	1200-1800
1993 Matched Numbrd. set/3	350	1993	950.00	8000-9000
1993 Mixed & Matched Numbrd. set/3	350	1993	950.00	5000-8000

Disney Showcase Collection Sweethearts - Staff

YEAR ISSUE	EDITION LIMIT	YEAR RETD.	ISSUE PRICE	*QUOTE U.S.$
1994 Jitterbugging	500	1994	450.00	600-900
1995 Mice on Ice	500	1995	425.00	425-500
1994 Rowboat Serenade	500	1994	495.00	479-500

Disney Showcase Collection Sweethearts Too - Staff

YEAR ISSUE	EDITION LIMIT	YEAR RETD.	ISSUE PRICE	*QUOTE U.S.$
1996 First Date (bronze)	35		750.00	750

*Quotes have been rounded up to nearest dollar

FIGURINES

YEAR ISSUE	EDITION LIMIT	YEAR RETD.	ISSUE PRICE	*QUOTE U.S.$
1996 First Date (pewter)	500	1996	250.00	250
1997 Love Toons (bronze)	35		1050.00	1050
1997 Love Toons (pewter)	500		350.00	350
1996 Sippin' Soda (bronze)	35		850.00	850
1996 Sippin' Soda (pewter)	500		275.00	275

Disney Showcase Colllection The Sorcerer's Apprentice - Staff

YEAR ISSUE	EDITION LIMIT	YEAR RETD.	ISSUE PRICE	*QUOTE U.S.$
1990 The Whirlpool	Retrd.	1995	225.00	275
1990 The Dream	Retrd.	1995	225.00	215-240
1990 The Incantation	Retrd.	1995	150.00	175
1990 The Repentant Apprentice	Retrd.	1994	195.00	300-500
1990 The Sorcerer's Apprentice	Retrd.	1995	225.00	240
1990 Matched Numbrd set	Retrd.	1995	225.00	1800-2200

Disney Showcase Colllection Two Wheeling - Staff

YEAR ISSUE	EDITION LIMIT	YEAR RETD.	ISSUE PRICE	*QUOTE U.S.$
1994 Get Your Motor Runnin' (bronze)	50	1994	1200.00	1200-1300
1994 Get Your Motor Runnin' (MetalART)	950	1994	475.00	490-600
1994 Head Out on the Highway (bronze)	50	1996	1200.00	1200-1300
1994 Head Out on the Highway (MetalART)	950		475.00	475
1995 Looking For Adventure (bronze)	50		1200.00	1200
1995 Looking For Adventure (MetalART)	950		475.00	475

Hudson Pewter Figures - P.W. Baston, unless otherwise noted

YEAR ISSUE	EDITION LIMIT	YEAR RETD.	ISSUE PRICE	*QUOTE U.S.$
1972 Benjamin Franklin	Closed	1974	15.00	75-92
1969 Betsy Ross	Closed	1971	30.00	75-100
1969 Colonial Blacksmith	Closed	1971	30.00	75-100
1975 Declaration Wall Plaque	100	1975	Unkn.	500-600
1975 The Favored Scholar - P.W. Baston	6	1975	Unkn.	600-1000
1972 George Washington	Closed	1974	15.00	50-75
1969 George Washington (Cannon)	Closed	1971	35.00	100-150
1972 James Madison	Closed	1974	15.00	75-80
1972 John Adams	Closed	1974	15.00	100-175
1969 John Hancock	Closed	1971	15.00	100-125
1975 Lee's Ninth General Order	Closed	1975	Unkn.	400-500
1975 Lincoln's Gettysburg Address	Closed	1975	Unkn.	400-500
1975 Neighboring Pews	6	1975	Unkn.	600-1000
1975 Spirit of '76 - P.W. Baston	12	1975	Unkn.	750-1200
1972 Thomas Jefferson - P.W. Baston	Closed	1974	15.00	50-75
1975 Washington's Letter of Acceptance - P.W. Baston	Closed	1975	Unkn.	300-375
1975 Weighing the Baby - P.W. Baston	6	1975	Unkn.	600-1000

SebastianMiniatures Collectors Society - P.W. Baston

YEAR ISSUE	EDITION LIMIT	YEAR RETD.	ISSUE PRICE	*QUOTE U.S.$
1982 S.M.C. Society Plaque	1,530	1982	Gift	15-20
1984 S.M.C. Society Plaque	505	1984	Gift	50-75
1981 S.M.C. Society Plaque	4,957	1981	Gift	15-20
1983 S.M.C. Society Plaque	1,167	1983	Gift	30-45
1980 S.M.C. Society Plaque ('80 Charter)	11,914	1980	Gift	35-40
1984 Self Portrait	Retrd.	1994	Gift	40-45

Sebastian Miniatures Collectors Association - P.W. Baston, Jr.

YEAR ISSUE	EDITION LIMIT	YEAR RETD.	ISSUE PRICE	*QUOTE U.S.$
1995 Grace	Retrd.	1997	Gift	N/A
1996 Ezra	Retrd.	1997	Gift	N/A
1997 Rebecca	Retrd.	1997	Gift	N/A
1998 Peter	Annual		Gift	N/A

Sebastian Miniatures Member Only - P.W. Baston, Jr.

YEAR ISSUE	EDITION LIMIT	YEAR RETD.	ISSUE PRICE	*QUOTE U.S.$
1989 The Collectors	Yr.Iss.	1990	39.50	40
1992 Christopher Columbus	Yr.Iss.	1993	28.50	29-45

Sebastian Miniatures Holiday Memories-Member Only - P.W. Baston, Jr.

YEAR ISSUE	EDITION LIMIT	YEAR RETD.	ISSUE PRICE	*QUOTE U.S.$
1990 Thanksgiving Helper	Yr.Iss.	1991	39.50	29-40
1990 Leprechaun	Yr.Iss.	1991	27.50	30-35
1991 Trick or Treat	Yr.Iss.	1992	25.50	50-75
1993 Father Time	Yr.Iss.	1994	27.50	28
1993 New Year Baby	Yr.Iss.	1994	27.50	28
1994 Look What the Easter Bunny Left Me	Yr.Iss.	1995	27.50	28
1995 On Parade	Yr.Iss.		N/A	N/A

Sebastian Miniature Figurines - P.W. Baston, Jr.

YEAR ISSUE	EDITION LIMIT	YEAR RETD.	ISSUE PRICE	*QUOTE U.S.$
1991 America Salutes Desert Storm-bronze	Retrd.	1994	26.50	100
1991 America Salutes Desert Storm-painted	350	1991	49.50	100-200
1990 America's Hometown	4,750		34.00	34
1994 Boston Light	3,500		45.00	45
1994 Egg Rock Light	3,500		55.00	55
1992 Firefighter	500	1992	28.00	50-70
1991 Happy Hood Holidays	2,000	1991	32.50	95-105
1983 Harry Hood	1,000	1983	Unkn.	200-250
1992 I Know I Left It Here Somewhere	1,000		28.50	29
1985 It's Hoods (Wagon)	3,250	1985	N/A	50-75
1994 A Job Well Done	1,000		27.50	28
1993 The Lamplighter	1,000		28.00	28
1994 Nubble Light	3,500		45.00	45
1993 Pumpkin Island Light	3,500		55.00	55
1993 Soap Box Derby	500		45.00	45
1986 Statue of Liberty (AT & T)	1,000	1986	N/A	225-300
1987 White House (Gold, Oval Base)	250	1987	17.00	35-50

Sebastian Miniatures America Remembers - P.W. Baston

YEAR ISSUE	EDITION LIMIT	YEAR RETD.	ISSUE PRICE	*QUOTE U.S.$
1979 Family Sing	7,358	1979	29.50	125-150
1980 Family Picnic	16,527	1980	29.50	35-60
1981 Family Reads Aloud	21,027	1981	34.50	35-50
1982 Family Fishing	8,734	1982	34.50	35-50
1983 Family Feast	4,147	1983	37.50	150-175

Sebastian Miniatures Children At Play - P.W. Baston

YEAR ISSUE	EDITION LIMIT	YEAR RETD.	ISSUE PRICE	*QUOTE U.S.$
1979 Building Days Boy	10,000	1980	19.50	30-50
1979 Building Days Girl	10,000	1980	19.50	30-50
1981 Sailing Days Boy	10,000	1981	19.50	30-50
1981 Sailing Days Girl	10,000	1981	19.50	30-50
1982 School Days Boy	10,000	1982	19.50	30-40
1982 School Days Girl	10,000	1982	19.50	30-40
1978 Sidewalk Days Boy	10,000	1980	19.50	40-60
1978 Sidewalk Days Girl	10,000	1980	19.50	40-60
1980 Snow Days Boy	10,000	1980	19.50	30-40
1980 Snow Days Girl	10,000	1980	19.50	30-40

Sebastian Miniatures Christmas - P.W. Baston, Jr.

YEAR ISSUE	EDITION LIMIT	YEAR RETD.	ISSUE PRICE	*QUOTE U.S.$
1993 Caroling With Santa	1,000		29.00	29
1993 Harmonizing With Santa	1,000		27.00	27
1994 Victorian Christmas Skaters	1,000		32.50	33
1995 Midnight Snacks	1,000		28.50	29
1996 Victorian Christmas Santa	1,000		28.50	29

Sebastian Miniatures Firefighter Collection - P.W. Baston, Jr.

YEAR ISSUE	EDITION LIMIT	YEAR RETD.	ISSUE PRICE	*QUOTE U.S.$
1993 Firefighter No. 1	950	1995	48.00	48
1994 Firefighter No. 2	950		48.00	48
1994 Firefighter No. 3	950		48.00	48
1995 Firefighter No. 4	950		48.00	48

Sebastian Miniatures Jimmy Fund - P.W. Baston, Jr., unless otherwise noted

YEAR ISSUE	EDITION LIMIT	YEAR RETD.	ISSUE PRICE	*QUOTE U.S.$
1993 Boy With Ducks	500	1993	27.50	28
1984 Catcher - P.W. Baston	1,872	1984	24.50	35-75
1987 Football Player	1,270	1988	26.50	27
1995 Girl in Riding Outfit	500		28.00	28
1994 Girl on Bench	500	1994	28.00	28
1985 Hockey Player	1,836	1986	24.50	35-50
1988 Santa	500	1988	32.50	33
1983 Schoolboy - P.W. Baston	3,567	1983	24.50	25-35
1986 Soccer Player	1,166	1987	25.00	25

Sebastian Miniatures Private Label - P.W. Baston Jr.

YEAR ISSUE	EDITION LIMIT	YEAR RETD.	ISSUE PRICE	*QUOTE U.S.$
1993 Adams Academy w/ Steeple	75	N/A	100.00	200-225
1993 Adams Academy w/o Steeple	750	N/A	30.00	30

Sebastian Miniatures Shakespearean-Member Only - P.W. Baston, unless otherwise noted

YEAR ISSUE	EDITION LIMIT	YEAR RETD.	ISSUE PRICE	*QUOTE U.S.$
1988 Audrey	1,548	1988	22.50	35
1989 Cleopatra	Retrd.	1989	27.00	35
1987 Countess Olivia	1,893	1987	19.50	35
1985 Falstaff	3,357	1985	19.50	35
1984 Henry VIII	4,578	1984	19.50	35
1986 Juliet	2,620	1986	17.50	35
1987 Malvolio	2,093	1987	21.50	35
1989 Mark Antony	Retrd.	1989	27.00	35
1985 Mistress Ford	2,836	1985	17.50	35
1986 Romeo	2,853	1986	19.50	35
1988 Shakespeare - P.W. Baston, Jr.	Retrd.	1989	2.50	35
1988 Touchstone	1,770	1988	22.50	35
1984 Anne Boleyn	3,897	1984	17.50	35

Sebastian Miniatures Washington Irving-Member Only - P.W. Baston

YEAR ISSUE	EDITION LIMIT	YEAR RETD.	ISSUE PRICE	*QUOTE U.S.$
1980 Rip Van Winkle	12,005	1983	19.50	35
1981 Ichabod Crane	9,069	1983	19.50	35
1981 Dame Van Winkle	11,217	1983	19.50	35
1982 Brom Bones (Headless Horseman)	6,610	1983	22.50	35
1982 Katrina Van Tassel	7,367	1983	19.50	35
1983 Diedrich Knickerbocker	5,528	1983	22.50	35

Islandia International

Sonshine Promises - G. Clasby

YEAR ISSUE	EDITION LIMIT	YEAR RETD.	ISSUE PRICE	*QUOTE U.S.$
1998 A Baby Boy - A Perfect Miracle 7008B	Numbrd.		22.50	23
1998 A Baby Girl - A Perfect Miracle 7008G	Numbrd.		22.50	23
1998 Baby's First Birthday 7034	Numbrd.		19.50	20
1998 Beginnings Offer the Gift of Promise 7032	Numbrd.		21.00	21
1998 Bless This House With Joy and Love 7007	Numbrd.		22.50	23
1998 The Chorus of Life Brings us all Together 7000	15,000		39.50	40
1998 Enjoy Your Special Day 7003	Numbrd.		19.50	20
1998 Follow Your Dreams 7002	Numbrd.		19.50	20
1998 God Blesses This House But He Doesn't Clean It 7009	Numbrd.		22.50	23
1998 Golf is Not Life or Death - It's More Important 7015	Numbrd.		24.50	25
1998 Good Friends Will Lift Your Spirit 7017	Numbrd.		27.50	28
1998 Hugs Make The World a Better Place 7013	Numbrd.		22.50	23
1998 I Love You With All My Hearts 7004	Numbrd.		22.50	23
1998 Joy to You Mini Lapel Pin 9001	Open		6.00	6
1998 A Joyful Wish 7033	Numbrd.		19.50	20
1998 May Love Always be in Full Bloom 7006	Numbrd.		29.50	30
1998 Ordinary Sisters - Extraordinary Friends 7011	Numbrd.		22.00	22
1998 Remember There's a Blue Sky Behind the Blackest Cloud 7010	Numbrd.		22.50	23
1998 Shared Love is Twice The Joy 7005	Numbrd.		22.50	23
1998 Sonshine Promise Bluebird Figurine/Plaque 9000	Numbrd.		19.50	20
1998 There's an Angel Watching Over You 7001	Numbrd.		22.50	23
1998 Wash Away The Blues 7016	Numbrd.		23.50	24
1998 When Life Gives You Scraps, Make a Quilt 7012	Numbrd.		23.00	23
1998 You Are Special in my Life 7026	Numbrd.		27.50	28
1998 You Can Go Anywhere From Where You Are 7014	Numbrd.		24.00	24
1998 You're Worth The World to Me 7018	Numbrd.		21.50	22

African Wildlife - T. Swanson

YEAR ISSUE	EDITION LIMIT	YEAR RETD.	ISSUE PRICE	*QUOTE U.S.$
1998 Elephant	Numbrd.		27.50	28
1998 Giraffe	Numbrd.		27.50	28
1998 Lion	Numbrd.		27.50	28
1998 Zebra	Numbrd.		27.50	28

International Fatcats - G. Pitt

YEAR ISSUE	EDITION LIMIT	YEAR RETD.	ISSUE PRICE	*QUOTE U.S.$
1998 Canada	Numbrd.		25.00	25
1998 France	Numbrd.		25.00	25
1998 Germany	Numbrd.		25.00	25
1998 Italy	Numbrd.		25.00	25
1998 Mexico	Numbrd.		25.00	25
1998 Spain	Numbrd.		25.00	25
1998 Switzerland	Numbrd.		25.00	25
1998 USA	Numbrd.		25.00	25

North American Wildlife - T. Swanson

YEAR ISSUE	EDITION LIMIT	YEAR RETD.	ISSUE PRICE	*QUOTE U.S.$
1998 Big Horn Sheep - "Mountain Gathering"	Numbrd.		30.00	30
1998 Buffalo - "Roaming The Plains"	Numbrd.		30.00	30
1998 Gamble Quail - "Family Gathering"	Numbrd.		30.00	30
1998 Mountain Goat - "Chilly Heights"	Numbrd.		30.00	30
1998 Mule Deer - "Trouble Ahead"	Numbrd.		30.00	30
1998 Red Fox - "Prey in Sight"	Numbrd.		30.00	30
1998 Whitetail Deer - "Regal Solitude"	Numbrd.		30.00	30
1998 Wolves - "Mist Morning Hunters"	Numbrd.		30.00	30

Rocky Mountain Wildlife - T. Swanson

YEAR ISSUE	EDITION LIMIT	YEAR RETD.	ISSUE PRICE	*QUOTE U.S.$
1998 Elk - "Storm King"	Numbrd.		30.00	30
1998 Grizzly Bear - "Fishing in Still Water"	Numbrd.		30.00	30
1998 Moose - "Evening Solitude"	Numbrd.		30.00	30
1998 Mountain Lion - "Dangers Approach"	Numbrd.		30.00	30

Trevor's Farm Friends - T. Swanson

YEAR ISSUE	EDITION LIMIT	YEAR RETD.	ISSUE PRICE	*QUOTE U.S.$
1998 Catie The Cow	Numbrd.		22.50	23
1998 Gerrie The Goat	Numbrd.		22.50	23
1998 Paulie The Pig	Numbrd.		22.50	23
1998 Rollie The Rooster	Numbrd.		22.50	23

Jan Hagara Collectables

Bust Series - J. Hagara

YEAR ISSUE	EDITION LIMIT	YEAR RETD.	ISSUE PRICE	*QUOTE U.S.$
1991 David	10,000	1997	120.00	120
1990 Hannah	10,000	1997	120.00	120
1990 Jamie	10,000	1997	120.00	120
1991 Violet	10,000	1997	120.00	120

Georgetown Series - J. Hagara

YEAR ISSUE	EDITION LIMIT	YEAR RETD.	ISSUE PRICE	*QUOTE U.S.$
1997 Ben	6,000	1997	69.00	69
1997 Cassie	6,000	1997	65.00	65
1996 Cathy II	6,000	1997	65.00	65
1996 Cynthia	6,000	1997	65.00	65
1998 Enya	6,000		65.00	65
1997 Faith	6,000	1997	65.00	65
1998 Judianna	6,000		55.00	55
1998 Miss Megan	6,000		69.00	69
1996 Ricky	6,000	1997	65.00	65

Legacy Series - J. Hagara

YEAR ISSUE	EDITION LIMIT	YEAR RETD.	ISSUE PRICE	*QUOTE U.S.$
1990 Rebecca	15,000	1997	95.00	95

Make Believe - J. Hagara

YEAR ISSUE	EDITION LIMIT	YEAR RETD.	ISSUE PRICE	*QUOTE U.S.$
1998 Brianna Rose	3,000		45.00	45
1998 Butchie & Oreo	3,000		45.00	45
1997 Emily	3,000		49.00	49
1997 Jasmine	3,000		49.00	49
1997 Jimmy Chuck	3,000		49.00	49
1997 Kayla	3,000		49.00	49
1996 Leah	3,000		49.00	49
1998 Mary Lou	3,000		49.00	49
1998 Peppermint	3,000		49.00	49

Musical Series - J. Hagara

YEAR ISSUE	EDITION LIMIT	YEAR RETD.	ISSUE PRICE	*QUOTE U.S.$
1985 Allison	2-Yr.	1987	45.00	300
1985 Cara	2-Yr.	1987	45.00	45-65
1985 Heather	2-Yr.	1987	45.00	300
1994 Jenny	10,000	1997	35.00	35
1985 JoJohn	2-Yr.	1987	45.00	250
1985 Michael	2-Yr.	1987	45.00	45-75
1985 Natalie	2-Yr.	1987	45.00	45-68
1985 Rachael	2-Yr.	1987	45.00	300
1985 Shannon	2-Yr.	1987	45.00	55-125

ShelfSitter Figurine - J. Hagara

YEAR ISSUE	EDITION LIMIT	YEAR RETD.	ISSUE PRICE	*QUOTE U.S.$
1995 Adrianne	7,500	1997	55.00	55
1990 Allegra	15,000	1994	40.00	40-45
1990 Chris	15,000	1997	40.00	55-65
1991 Crystal	15,000	1994	40.00	45-65
1996 Little Sharice w/Rocker	7,500	1997	71.50	72
1990 Matthew	15,000	1994	40.00	40-50
1991 Sally	15,000	1997	40.00	40
1990 Suzy	15,000	1996	40.00	40

Signature Musical Series - J. Hagara

YEAR ISSUE	EDITION LIMIT	YEAR RETD.	ISSUE PRICE	*QUOTE U.S.$
1985 Allegra	20,000	1989	65.00	95-200
1985 Mother & Child	17,500	1989	100.00	200
1985 Wendy	17,500	1989	65.00	135-300

*Quotes have been rounded up to nearest dollar

Signature Series - J. Hagara

YEAR ISSUE	EDITION LIMIT	YEAR RETD.	ISSUE PRICE	*QUOTE U.S.$
1985 Alice & Andrew	20,000	1991	75.00	120-207
1985 Becky	20,000	1991	55.00	250
1988 Beth & Amy	10,000	1991	135.00	150-200
1992 Crista's Rabbit	800	1997	694.00	694
1985 Holly	20,000	1990	55.00	75-85
1985 In Line	10,000	1987	175.00	800-1200
1985 James	20,000	1988	55.00	75
1988 Jan & Sharice	7,500	1991	145.00	165-200
1985 Jessica	20,000	1990	55.00	75-90
1985 Julie	20,000	1990	55.00	55-75
1985 Kimmy	20,000	1990	55.00	250
1985 Linda	20,000	1988	55.00	75
1985 Mandy	20,000	1988	55.00	75
1985 Marc & Laurie	20,000	1990	55.00	250
1985 Memories	17,500	1991	75.00	300
1987 Nikki & Santa	5,000	1991	135.00	235-350
1989 Phillip's Cousins	7,500	1997	195.00	225-295
1990 Renny & Blueberry	1,200	1994	600.00	600
1992 Sophie	5,000	1995	125.00	150
1985 Storytime	17,500	1991	135.00	595
1985 Theresa	20,000	1991	55.00	135-200
1985 Todd	20,000	1990	55.00	250

Single Figurines - J. Hagara

YEAR ISSUE	EDITION LIMIT	YEAR RETD.	ISSUE PRICE	*QUOTE U.S.$
1988 Abby	15,000	1991	35.00	65
1989 Adell	15,000	1991	40.00	40
1984 Adrianne	6,000	1987	45.00	75
1984 Amanda	2-Yr.	1986	30.00	60
1986 Amy	2-Yr.	1988	30.00	85
1985 Angie & Honey	2-Yr.	1987	30.00	125
1983 Anne & The Bear	2-Yr.	1985	25.00	100-125
1989 April	15,000	1997	45.00	45-60
1986 Ashley (boy)	2-Yr.	1988	30.00	65
1994 Ashley (girl)	7,500	1997	60.00	60
1993 Baby Lee	7,500	1997	50.00	50
1991 Baby Sharice	15,000	1997	35.00	35
1983 Betsy & Jimmy	2-Yr.	1985	45.00	60-100
1990 Billy & Brenna	15,000	1992	55.00	75
1993 Blossom	7,500	1997	70.00	70-75
1984 Brian	2-Yr.	1986	30.00	50-68
1985 Brian & Cinnamon	2-Yr.	1987	30.00	250-350
1993 Brianna	7,500	1997	50.00	50
1990 Brooke	15,000	1997	42.50	43
1984 Carol	2-Yr.	1986	30.00	100-200
1987 Carrie	2-Yr.	1989	35.00	50
1990 Cathy	15,000	1997	42.50	45
1994 Chelsea	7,500	1997	90.00	90
1986 Chris	2-Yr.	1988	30.00	95-150
1984 Cristina	2-Yr.	1986	30.00	85
1991 Dacy	15,000	1994	45.00	45
1986 Daisies From Jimmy	2-Yr.	1988	45.00	125
1985 Daphanie & Unicorn	2-Yr.	1987	45.00	90-95
1992 Dee Dee	7,500	1997	50.00	50
1995 Elaina	7,500	1996	60.00	60
1984 Emily	2-Yr.	1986	30.00	65
1992 Erin	7,500	1997	70.00	70
1992 Fall (Megan)	7,500	1997	50.00	50
1987 Goldie	2-Yr.	1989	45.00	45
1987 Jeff	2-Yr.	1989	35.00	50
1994 Jennifer	7,500	1997	85.00	85
1983 Jenny & the Bye Lo	2-Yr.	1985	25.00	100-250
1983 Jody & Toy Horse	2-Yr.	1985	25.00	100
1994 Joy	7,500	1997	70.00	70
1986 Larry	2-Yr.	1988	30.00	70
1986 Laurel	2-Yr.	1988	30.00	75-85
1986 Lesley	2-Yr.	1988	30.00	58-65
1983 Lisa & Jumeau Doll	2-Yr.	1985	25.00	65-85
1994 Little Brian	7,500	1997	60.00	60
1983 Lydia & Shirley Temple	2-Yr.	1985	25.00	75-80
1991 Mary	15,000	1996	45.00	45
1988 Mary Ann & Molly	15,000	1991	50.00	85
1986 Meg	2-Yr.	1988	30.00	65
1986 Melanie & Scarlett	2-Yr.	1988	30.00	100
1984 Michelle	2-Yr.	1986	30.00	50-75
1984 Missy	2-Yr.	1986	30.00	75
1988 Nikki	15,000	1991	35.00	68-95
1986 Noel	2-Yr.	1988	30.00	100-200
1988 Paige	15,000	1991	35.00	75
1991 Paul	15,000	1994	45.00	45
1988 Sara Mae	15,000	1991	35.00	45-65
1989 Scott	15,000	1991	40.00	45
1990 Sharice	15,000	1993	42.50	43
1984 Sharice & Parry	2-Yr.	1986	50.00	55-85
1984 Spring & Lance	2-Yr.	1986	50.00	65-85
1993 Spring (Katy)	7,500	1997	60.00	60
1985 Stacy	2-Yr.	1987	30.00	75-85
1985 Stephen	2-Yr.	1987	30.00	75
1992 Summer	7,500	1997	50.00	50
1994 Tammy	7,500	1997	70.00	70
1994 Tommy	7,500	1997	70.00	70
1993 Twins	6,000	1997	75.00	75
1983 Victoria	2-Yr.	1985	25.00	75-125
1994 Winter (Aspen)	7,500	1997	60.00	60

June McKenna Collectibles, Inc.

Black Folk Art - J. McKenna

YEAR ISSUE	EDITION LIMIT	YEAR RETD.	ISSUE PRICE	*QUOTE U.S.$
1987 Aunt Bertha -3D	Closed	1991	36.00	75-125
1983 Black Boy w/Watermelon, available in 3 colors	Closed	1988	12.00	75-125
1986 Black Butler	Closed	1989	13.00	80-120
1983 Black Girl w/Watermelon, available in 3 colors	Closed	1988	12.00	75-125
1984 Black Man w/Pig, available in 3 colors	Closed	1988	13.00	100-120
1984 Black Woman w/Broom, available in 3 colors	Closed	1988	13.00	95-100
1989 Delia	Closed	1991	16.00	65-75
1992 Fishing John -3D	1,000	1997	160.00	160
1989 Jake	Closed	1991	16.00	65-75
1985 Kids in a Tub -3D	Closed	1990	30.00	110-125
1985 Kissing Cousins - sill sitter	Closed	1990	36.00	125-175
1990 Let's Play Ball -3D	Closed	1993	45.00	75-100
1987 Lil' Willie -3D	Closed	1991	36.00	75-100
1984 Mammie Cloth Doll	Closed	1988	90.00	500-590
1985 Mammie With Kids -3D	Closed	1990	90.00	175-250
1985 Mammie With Spoon	Closed	1989	13.00	100-250
1988 Netty	Closed	1991	16.00	65-75
1984 Remus Cloth Doll	Closed	1988	90.00	390-450
1988 Renty	Closed	1991	16.00	65-75
1990 Sunday's Best -3D	Closed	1993	45.00	75-100
1987 Sweet Prissy -3D	Closed	1991	36.00	75-100
1992 Sweet Sister Sue -3D	1,000	1997	160.00	160
1990 Tasha	Closed	1991	17.00	65-75
1985 Toaster Cover	Closed	1988	50.00	350
1990 Tyree	Closed	1991	17.00	65-75
1987 Uncle Jacob -3D	Closed	1991	36.00	75-100
1985 Watermelon Patch Kids	Closed	1990	24.00	100-150

Carolers - J. McKenna

YEAR ISSUE	EDITION LIMIT	YEAR RETD.	ISSUE PRICE	*QUOTE U.S.$
1985 Boy Caroler	Closed	1989	36.00	100-130
1992 Carolers, Grandparents	Closed	1994	70.00	85
1991 Carolers, Man With Girl	Closed	1994	50.00	65-85
1991 Carolers, Woman With Boy	Closed	1994	50.00	65-85
1994 Children Carolers	Closed	1997	90.00	90
1985 Girl Caroler	Closed	1989	36.00	75-100
1985 Man Caroler	Closed	1989	36.00	100-145
1985 Woman Caroler	Closed	1989	36.00	100-115

June McKenna Figurines - J. McKenna

YEAR ISSUE	EDITION LIMIT	YEAR RETD.	ISSUE PRICE	*QUOTE U.S.$
1989 16th Century Santa -3D, blue	Closed	1991	60.00	200-250
1989 16th Century Santa -3D, green	Closed	1989	60.00	350-600
1989 17th Century Santa -3D, red	Closed	1991	70.00	200-250
1993 Angel Name Plaque	Closed	1994	70.00	95-100
1983 Boy Rag Doll	Closed	1983	12.00	300-430
1985 Bride -3D	Closed	1987	25.00	200
1985 Bride w/o base -3D	Closed	1985	25.00	150-225
1993 Children Ice Skaters	Closed	1994	60.00	75
1992 Choir of Angels	Closed	1993	60.00	95-100
1992 Christmas Santa -3D	Closed	1993	60.00	100-150
1987 Country Rag Boy (sitting)	Closed	1990	40.00	100-175
1987 Country Rag Girl (sitting)	Closed	1990	40.00	155-270
1994 Decorating for Christmas -3D	Closed	1997	70.00	100-125
1985 Father Times -3D	Closed	1991	40.00	175-200
1983 Girl Rag Doll	Closed	1983	12.00	300-325
1993 A Good Night's Sleep -3D	Closed	1995	70.00	100-125
1985 Groom w/o base -3D	Closed	1985	25.00	175-235
1985 Groom-3D	Closed	1987	25.00	150-200
1989 Jolly Ole Santa -3D	Closed	1991	44.00	175-200
1992 Let It Snow	Closed	1997	70.00	85
1986 Little St. Nick -3D	Closed	1990	50.00	200-250
1986 Male Angel -3D	Closed	1986	44.00	1300-1400
1988 Mr. Santa -3D	Closed	1991	44.00	100-130
1993 Mr. Snowman	Closed	1994	40.00	65
1988 Mrs. Santa -3D	Closed	1989	50.00	150-250
1987 Name Plaque	Closed	1992	50.00	125-150
1990 Noel -3D	Closed	1992	50.00	125
1987 Patriotic Santa -3D	Closed	1989	50.00	300-350
1993 Santa and Friends -3D	Closed	1997	70.00	100-120
1993 Santa Name Plaque	Closed	1995	70.00	95-100
1993 The Snow Family	Closed	1994	40.00	65
1994 Snowman and Child	Closed	1997	70.00	85
1985 Soldier -3D	Closed	1988	40.00	205-250
1994 Star of Bethlehem-Angel	Closed	1997	40.00	40-45
1995 A Surprise For Joey -3D	Closed	1997	70.00	70
1992 Taking A Break -3D	Closed	1995	60.00	95-125
1995 Travel Plans	Closed	1997	70.00	70
1984 Tree Topper	Closed	1987	70.00	400-450

Limited Edition - J. McKenna

YEAR ISSUE	EDITION LIMIT	YEAR RETD.	ISSUE PRICE	*QUOTE U.S.$
1988 Bringing Home Christmas	4,000	1990	170.00	400-585
1987 Christmas Eve	4,000	1989	170.00	400-455
1992 Christmas Gathering	4,000	1997	220.00	300-325
1991 Coming to Town	4,000	1994	220.00	350-390
1983 Father Christmas	4,000	1986	90.00	2200-2600
1987 Kris Kringle	4,000	1990	350.00	800-900
1990 Night Before Christmas	1,500	1993	750.00	750-800
1984 Old Saint Nick	4,000	1986	100.00	850-1170
1993 The Patriot	4,000	1997	250.00	300
1988 Remembrance of Christmas Past	4,000	1992	400.00	750-800
1991 Santa's Hot Air Balloon	1,500	1993	800.00	800
1989 Santa's Wardrobe	1,500	1992	750.00	850-1000
1989 Seasons Greetings	4,000	1992	200.00	350-390
1994 St. Nicholas	4,000	1998	250.00	250
1986 Victorian	4,000	1988	150.00	780-845
1990 Wilderness	4,000	1994	200.00	300-390
1985 Woodland	4,000	1987	140.00	750-1300

Limited Edition 7" - J. McKenna

YEAR ISSUE	EDITION LIMIT	YEAR RETD.	ISSUE PRICE	*QUOTE U.S.$
1991 Christmas Bishop	7,500	1993	110.00	175-250
1993 Christmas Cheer 1st ed.	7,500	1993	120.00	245-450
1993 Christmas Cheer 2nd. ed.	7,500	1995	120.00	150-200
1990 Christmas Delight	7,500	1992	100.00	150-250
1995 Christmas Lullaby, red	7,500	1996	120.00	125-350
1988 Christmas Memories	7,500	1991	90.00	200-250
1992 Christmas Wizard	7,500	1994	110.00	150-200
1990 Ethnic Santa	7,500	1992	100.00	175-200
1988 Joyful Christmas	7,500	1991	90.00	175-250
1994 Mrs. Claus, Dancing to the Tune	7,500	1997	120.00	120-200
1989 Old Fashioned Santa	7,500	1991	100.00	150-200
1989 Santa's Bag of Surprises	7,500	1991	100.00	205-275
1994 Santa's One Man Band	7,500	1997	120.00	120-200

Limited Edition Flatback - J. McKenna

YEAR ISSUE	EDITION LIMIT	YEAR RETD.	ISSUE PRICE	*QUOTE U.S.$
1991 Bag of Stars	10,000	1993	34.00	45-75
1993 Bells of Christmas	10,000	1995	40.00	45-65
1989 Blue Christmas	10,000	1991	32.00	100
1992 Deck The Halls	10,000	1994	34.00	45-65
1991 Farewell Santa	10,000	1993	34.00	55-65
1992 Good Tidings	10,000	1994	34.00	45-65
1990 Medieval Santa	10,000	1992	34.00	65-75
1988 Mystical Santa	10,000	1991	30.00	100
1994 Not Once But Twice	10,000	1997	40.00	40-50
1990 Old Time Santa	10,000	1992	34.00	75-90
1994 Post Marked North Pole	10,000	1997	40.00	40-65
1993 Santa's Love	10,000	1995	40.00	55-65
1988 Toys of Joy	10,000	1991	30.00	70-100
1989 Victorian	10,000	1991	32.00	120-150

Nativity Set - J. McKenna

YEAR ISSUE	EDITION LIMIT	YEAR RETD.	ISSUE PRICE	*QUOTE U.S.$
1988 Nativity - 6/pc. (Mary, Joseph, Baby Jesus, Manger, Guardian Angel & creche)	Closed	1997	130.00	150
1990 Shepherds With Sheep - 2/pc.	Closed	1997	60.00	75-100
1989 Three Wise Men	Closed	1997	60.00	100-120

Personal Appearance Figurines - J. McKenna

YEAR ISSUE	EDITION LIMIT	YEAR RETD.	ISSUE PRICE	*QUOTE U.S.$
1989 Father Christmas	Closed	1993	30.00	225-250
1990 Old Saint Nick	Closed	1994	30.00	175-200
1991 Woodland	Closed	1995	35.00	85-150
1992 Victorian	Closed	1996	35.00	65-125
1993 Christmas Eve	Closed	1997	35.00	35-65
1994 Bringing Home Christmas	Closed	1998	35.00	35-65
1995 Seasons Greetings	4-Yr.		35.00	35
1996 Wilderness	4-Yr.		35.00	35
1997 Coming To town	4-Yr.		35.00	35
1998 Christmas Gathering	4-Yr.		35.00	35

Registered Edition - J. McKenna

YEAR ISSUE	EDITION LIMIT	YEAR RETD.	ISSUE PRICE	*QUOTE U.S.$
1991 Checking His List	Closed	1994	230.00	300-350
1995 Christmas Down on the Farm	Closed	1998	260.00	260
1995 Christmas Treat for All	Closed	1998	260.00	260
1986 Colonial	Closed	1990	150.00	390-450
1992 Forty Winks	Closed	1994	250.00	300
1988 Jolly Ole St. Nick	Closed	1996	170.00	350-450
1994 Say Cheese, Please	Closed	1997	250.00	250-300
1993 Tomorrow's Christmas	Closed	1995	250.00	275-300
1990 Toy Maker	Closed	1993	200.00	400
1989 Traditional	Closed	1991	180.00	228-300
1987 White Christmas	Closed	1987	170.00	1100-1225

Special Limited Edition - J. McKenna

YEAR ISSUE	EDITION LIMIT	YEAR RETD.	ISSUE PRICE	*QUOTE U.S.$
1996 All Aboard-Logging Car	Yr.Iss.	1997	250.00	250
1995 All Aboard Toy Car	Closed	1996	250.00	275
1993 Baking Cookies	2,000	1995	450.00	500
1991 Bedtime Stories	2,000	1994	500.00	500-650
1990 Christmas Dreams	4,000	1992	280.00	400-500
1990 Christmas Dreams (Hassock)	63	1990	280.00	1600-2200
1996 International Santa-German Pelznichol	Yr.Iss.	1997	100.00	100-150
1989 Last Gentle Nudge	4,000	1991	280.00	350-450
1989 Santa & His Magic Sleigh	4,000	1992	280.00	350-450
1992 Santa's Arrival	2,000	1994	300.00	350-450
1990 Santa's Reindeer	1,500	1993	400.00	400-425
1990 Up On The Rooftop	4,000	1991	280.00	400-450
1994 Welcome to the World	2,000	1995	400.00	450

Victorian Limited Edition - J. McKenna

YEAR ISSUE	EDITION LIMIT	YEAR RETD.	ISSUE PRICE	*QUOTE U.S.$
1990 Edward -3D	1,000	1991	180.00	300-600
1990 Elizabeth -3D	1,000	1991	180.00	300-600
1990 Joseph -3D	Closed	1991	50.00	100-150
1990 Victoria -3D	Closed	1991	50.00	170-175

Kurt S. Adler, Inc.

Angel Darlings - N. Bailey

YEAR ISSUE	EDITION LIMIT	YEAR RETD.	ISSUE PRICE	*QUOTE U.S.$
1996 Almost Fits H4765/1	Open		11.00	11
1996 Bottoms Up H4765/2	Open		11.00	11
1996 Buddies H4765/3	Open		11.00	11
1996 Cuddles H4765/5	Open		11.00	11
1996 Dream Builders H4765/4	Open		11.00	11
1997 For You W7951	Open		21.00	21
1996 Peek-A-Boo H4765/6	Open		11.00	11
1997 The Secret W7950	Open		19.00	19
1997 Sharing W7949	Open		21.00	21

Birthstone Bearies - H. Adler

YEAR ISSUE	EDITION LIMIT	YEAR RETD.	ISSUE PRICE	*QUOTE U.S.$
1998 Bearie w/Heart, 4 1/2" JAN Birthstone W6900/JAN	Open		12.00	12
1998 Bearie w/Heart, 4 1/2" FEB Birthstone W6900/FEB	Open		12.00	12
1998 Bearie w/Heart, 4 1/2" MAR Birthstone W6900/MAR	Open		12.00	12
1998 Bearie w/Heart, 4 1/2" APR Birthstone W6900/APR	Open		12.00	12
1998 Bearie w/Heart, 4 1/2" MAY Birthstone W6900/MAY	Open		12.00	12
1998 Bearie w/Heart, 4 1/2" JUN Birthstone W6900/JUN	Open		12.00	12
1998 Bearie w/Heart, 4 1/2" JUL Birthstone W6900/JUL	Open		12.00	12

*Quotes have been rounded up to nearest dollar

YEAR ISSUE	EDITION LIMIT	YEAR RETD.	ISSUE PRICE	*QUOTE U.S.$
1998 Bearie w/Heart, 4 1/2" AUG Birthstone W6900/AUG	Open		12.00	12
1998 Bearie w/Heart, 4 1/2" SEP Birthstone W6900/SEP	Open		12.00	12
1998 Bearie w/Heart, 4 1/2" OCT Birthstone W6900/OCT	Open		12.00	12
1998 Bearie w/Heart, 4 1/2" NOV Birthstone W6900/NOV	Open		12.00	12
1998 Bearie w/Heart, 4 1/2" DEC Birthstone W6900/DEC	Open		12.00	12

Christmas Legends - P.F. Bolinger

YEAR ISSUE	EDITION LIMIT	YEAR RETD.	ISSUE PRICE	*QUOTE U.S.$
1994 Aldwyn of the Greenwood J8196	Retrd.	1996	145.00	145
1994 Berwyn the Grand J8198	Retrd.	1996	175.00	175
1995 Bountiful J8234	Retrd.	1996	164.00	164
1994 Caradoc the Kind J8199	Open		70.00	70
1994 Florian of the Berry Bush J8199	Open		70.00	70
1994 Gustave the Gutsy J8199	Open		70.00	70
1998 Irish Santa J6623	Open		67.00	67
1998 Jolly Old St. Nick J6620	Open		50.00	50
1995 Luminatus J8241	Open		136.00	136
1998 Neptune Santa J3832	Open		60.00	60
1997 Peace Santa J6563	2,500		80.00	80
1994 Silvanus the Cheerful J8197	Retrd.	1996	165.00	165

The Fabriché™ Bear & Friends Series - KSA Design Team

YEAR ISSUE	EDITION LIMIT	YEAR RETD.	ISSUE PRICE	*QUOTE U.S.$
1992 Laughing All The Way J1567	Retrd.	1994	83.00	83
1992 Not A Creature Was Stirring W1534	Retrd.	1996	67.00	67
1993 Teddy Bear Parade W1601	Retrd.	1996	73.00	73

Fabriché™ Angel Series - K.S. Adler

YEAR ISSUE	EDITION LIMIT	YEAR RETD.	ISSUE PRICE	*QUOTE U.S.$
1992 Heavenly Messenger W1584	Retrd.	1994	41.00	41

Fabriché™ Camelot Figure Series - P. Mauk

YEAR ISSUE	EDITION LIMIT	YEAR RETD.	ISSUE PRICE	*QUOTE U.S.$
1994 King Arthur J3372	7,500	1996	110.00	110
1993 Merlin the Magician J7966	7,500	1996	120.00	120
1993 Young Arthur J7967	7,500	1996	120.00	120

Fabriché™ Holiday Figurines - KSA Design Team, unless otherwise noted

YEAR ISSUE	EDITION LIMIT	YEAR RETD.	ISSUE PRICE	*QUOTE U.S.$
1998 African American Santa, 10" W1848 - A. Epton	Open		50.00	50
1995 All Aboard For Christmas W1679	Retrd.	1996	56.00	56
1994 All Star Santa W1652	Open		56.00	56
1993 All That Jazz W1620	Retrd.	1994	67.00	67
1992 An Apron Full of Love W1582 - M. Rothenberg	Retrd.	1996	75.00	75
1995 Armchair Quarterback W1693	Retrd.	1996	90.00	90
1998 Barbeque Santa W1850 - J. Adams	Open		72.00	72
1994 Basket of Goodies W1650	Retrd.	1996	60.00	60
1998 Believe Santa ME156 - M. Engelbreit	Open		56.00	56
1992 Bringing in the Yule Log W1589 - M. Rothenberg	5,000	1996	200.00	200
1993 Bringing the Gifts W1605	Retrd.	1996	60.00	60
1992 Bundles of Joy W1578	Retrd.	1994	78.00	78
1995 Captain Claus W1680	Open		56.00	56
1994 Checking His List W1643	Retrd.	1996	60.00	65
1993 Checking It Twice W1604	Retrd.	1997	56.00	56
1998 Chef Santa W1903 - J. Adams	Open		56.00	56
1992 Christmas is in the Air W1590	Retrd.	1995	110.00	125
1997 Christmas Wish List W1773	Open		40.00	40
1995 Diet Starts Tomorrow W1691	Retrd.	1996	60.00	60
1997 Fan Mail W1804 - M. Rothenberg	Open		50.00	50
1995 Father Christmas W1687	Retrd.	1996	56.00	56
1994 Firefighting Friends W1654	Retrd.	1996	72.00	72
1997 For the Mrs. W1800 - V. Antonov	Open		42.00	42
1993 Forever Green W1607	Retrd.	1994	56.00	56
1994 Friendship W1642	Retrd.	1996	65.00	65
1997 Frosty Friends W1807	Retrd.	1997	40.00	40
1995 Gift From Heaven W1694	Retrd.	1996	60.00	60
1997 Gifts a Plenty W1775	Open		45.00	45
1992 He Did It Again J7944 - T. Rubel	Retrd.	1996	160.00	160
1993 Here Kitty W1618 - M. Rothenberg	Retrd.	1994	90.00	125
1994 Ho, Ho, Ho Santa W1632	Retrd.	1996	56.00	56
1994 Holiday Express W1636	Retrd.	1997	100.00	100
1997 Holiday on Ice W1805 - M. Rothenberg	Open		135.00	135
1992 Homeward Bound W1568	Retrd.	1996	61.00	65
1997 House Calls W1772	Open		40.00	40
1992 Hugs and Kisses W1531	Retrd.	1994	67.00	67
1992 I'm Late, I'm Late J7947 - T. Rubel	Retrd.	1995	100.00	100
1992 It's Time To Go J7943 - T. Rubel	Retrd.	1994	150.00	150
1995 Kris Kringle W1685	Retrd.	1996	55.00	55
1997 Labor of Love W1774	Open		45.00	45
1994 Mail Must Go Through W1667 - KSA/WRG	Retrd.	1996	110.00	110
1997 Making Waves W1806	Open		55.00	55
1992 Merry Kissmas W1548 - M. Rothenberg	Retrd.	1993	140.00	140
1995 Merry Memories W1735	Retrd.	1997	56.00	56
1994 Merry St. Nick W1641 - Giordano	Open		90.00	90
1995 Mrs. Santa Caroller W1690 - M. Rothenberg	Open		70.00	70
1997 My How You Have Grown W1803 - M. Rothenberg	Open		75.00	75
1995 Night Before Christmas W1692 - Wood River Gallery	Retrd.	1996	60.00	60
1994 Officer Claus W1677	Open		56.00	56
1997 One More Story W1796	Open		55.00	55
1997 Paperwork W1776	Open		56.00	56
1993 Par For The Claus W1603	Open		60.00	60
1994 Peace Santa W1631	Retrd.	1996	60.00	60
1995 Pere Noel W1686	Retrd.	1996	55.00	55
1993 Playtime For Santa W1619	Retrd.	1994	67.00	67
1997 Puppy Love W1808	Open		50.00	50
1994 Santa Calls W1678 - W. Joyce	Retrd.	1996	55.00	55
1995 Santa Caroller W1689 - M. Rothenberg	Open		70.00	70
1991 Santa Fiddler W1549 - M. Rothenberg	Retrd.	1992	100.00	100
1998 Santa in Police Car W1849	Open		45.00	45
1997 Santa on Line W1799	Open		50.00	50
1992 Santa Steals A Kiss & A Cookie W1581 - M. Rothenberg	Retrd.	1994	150.00	175
1998 Santa w/Cats & Dogs W1853 - Giordano	Open		45.00	45
1992 Santa's Cat Nap W1504 - M. Rothenberg	Retrd.	1992	98.00	110
1994 Santa's Fishtales W1640	Open		60.00	60
1992 Santa's Ice Capades W1588 - M. Rothenberg	Retrd.	1995	110.00	110
1994 Schussing Claus W1651	Retrd.	1996	78.00	78
1998 Someone Special W1917 - M. Rothenberg	Open		50.00	50
1992 St. Nicholas The Bishop W1532	Retrd.	1997	78.00	78
1998 St. Nicholas with Tree W1851	Open		50.00	50
1994 Star Gazing Santa W1656 - M. Rothenberg	Open		120.00	120
1993 Stocking Stuffer W1622	Retrd.	1994	56.00	56
1995 Strike Up The Band W1681	Retrd.	1996	55.00	55
1998 Tee For Two W1916 - M. Rothenberg	Open		95.00	95
1995 Tee Time W1734	Retrd.	1996	60.00	60
1997 Test Drive W1802	Open		45.00	45
1993 Top Brass W1630	Retrd.	1995	67.00	67
1998 Tourist Santa W1915 - V. Antonov	Open		60.00	60
1997 Up On The Roof W1783 - Giordano	Open		67.00	70
1997 What a Catch W1801	Retrd.	1997	45.00	45
1993 With All The Trimmings W1616	Open		76.00	76
1995 Woodland Santa W1731 - R. Volpi	Retrd.	1996	67.00	67

Fabriché™ Santa at Home Series - M. Rothenberg

YEAR ISSUE	EDITION LIMIT	YEAR RETD.	ISSUE PRICE	*QUOTE U.S.$
1995 Baby Burping Santa W1732	Retrd.	1996	80.00	80
1994 The Christmas Waltz 1635	Retrd.	1996	135.00	135
1995 Family Portrait W1727	Retrd.	1996	140.00	140
1993 Grandpa Santa's Piggyback Ride W1621	7,500	1996	84.00	84
1995 Santa's Horsey Ride W1728	Retrd.	1997	80.00	80
1994 Santa's New Friend W1655	Retrd.	1996	110.00	110

Fabriché™ Santa's Helpers Series - M. Rothenberg

YEAR ISSUE	EDITION LIMIT	YEAR RETD.	ISSUE PRICE	*QUOTE U.S.$
1993 Little Olde Clockmaker W1629	5,000	1996	134.00	134
1992 A Stitch in Time W1591	5,000	1997	135.00	135

Fabriché™ Smithsonian Museum Series - KSA/Smithsonian

YEAR ISSUE	EDITION LIMIT	YEAR RETD.	ISSUE PRICE	*QUOTE U.S.$
1992 Holiday Drive W1556	Retrd.	1995	155.00	155
1993 Holiday Flight W1617	Retrd.	1995	144.00	144
1992 Peace on Earth Angel Treetop W1583	Retrd.	1995	52.00	52
1992 Peace on Earth Flying Angel W1585	Retrd.	1995	49.00	49
1991 Santa On A Bicycle W1527	Retrd.	1994	150.00	150
1995 Toys For Good Boys and Girls W1696	Retrd.	1996	75.00	75

Fabriché™ Thomas Nast Figurines - KSA Design Team

YEAR ISSUE	EDITION LIMIT	YEAR RETD.	ISSUE PRICE	*QUOTE U.S.$
1992 Caught in the Act W1577	Retrd.	1993	133.00	133
1992 Christmas Sing-A-Long W1576	12,000	1996	110.00	110
1993 Dear Santa W1602	Retrd.	1993	110.00	110
1991 Hello! Little One W1552	12,000	1994	90.00	90

Gallery of Angels - KSA Design Team

YEAR ISSUE	EDITION LIMIT	YEAR RETD.	ISSUE PRICE	*QUOTE U.S.$
1994 Guardian Angel M1099	2,000	1996	150.00	150
1994 Unspoken Word M1100	2,000	1996	150.00	150

Halloween - P.F. Bolinger

YEAR ISSUE	EDITION LIMIT	YEAR RETD.	ISSUE PRICE	*QUOTE U.S.$
1996 Dr. Punkinstein HW535	Open		50.00	50
1996 Eat at Drac's HW493	Open		22.00	22
1996 Pumpkin Grumpkin HW494	Open		18.00	18
1996 Pumpkin Plumpkin HW494	Open		18.00	18
1996 Pumpkins Are Us HW534	Retrd.	1996	17.00	17

Helping Hand Santas - P.F. Bolinger

YEAR ISSUE	EDITION LIMIT	YEAR RETD.	ISSUE PRICE	*QUOTE U.S.$
1996 Harmonious J6509	Open		115.00	115
1996 Noah J6487	Open		56.00	56
1996 Uncle Sam J6488	Retrd.	1996	56.00	56

Ho Ho Ho Gang - P.F. Bolinger

YEAR ISSUE	EDITION LIMIT	YEAR RETD.	ISSUE PRICE	*QUOTE U.S.$
1997 Behavometer J6555	Open		25.00	25
1998 Born To Fish J3812	Open		22.00	22
1996 Box of Chocolate J6510	Retrd.	1997	33.00	33
1997 Boxers or Briefs J6559	Open		25.00	25
1997 Captain Noah J6550	Open		18.00	18
1998 Choo Choo Santa J3806	Open		20.00	20
1994 Christmas Goose J8201	Open		22.00	22
1996 Christmas Shopping Santa J6497	Open		22.00	22
1996 Claus-A-Lounger J6478	Retrd.	1997	33.00	33
1995 Cookie Claus J8286	Retrd.	1996	39.00	39
1995 Do Not Disturb J8233	Open		34.00	34
1996 Fire Department North Pole J6508	Open		50.00	50
1996 Fireman Santa J6476	Open		28.00	28
1997 Golf Heaven J6553	Open		25.00	25
1998 Good Luck Irish J3807	Open		14.00	14
1998 Good Tools J3814	Open		22.00	22
1994 Holy Mackerel J8201	Open		22.00	22
1998 I Clean Chimneys J3809	Open		20.00	20
1996 I Love Chocolate J6628	Open		25.00	25
1997 Java Jumpstart J6554	Open		15.00	15
1996 Joy of Cooking J6496	Open		28.00	28
1998 Joy Rider J3813	Open		23.00	23
1996 Love Santa J6493	Retrd.	1996	18.00	18
1997 Never Say Diet J6578	Retrd.	1997	15.00	15
1995 No Hair Day J8287	Retrd.	1996	50.00	50
1996 Noel Roly Poly J6489	Retrd.	1996	20.00	20
1995 North Pole (large) J8237	Retrd.	1997	56.00	56
1995 North Pole (small) J8238	Retrd.	1997	45.00	45
1997 North Pole Country Club J6557	Open		45.00	45
1996 North Pole Pro-Am J6479	Open		28.00	28
1996 On Strike For More Cookies J6506	Open		33.00	33
1996 Police Department North Pole J6507	Retrd.	1997	50.00	50
1996 Policeman Santa J6475	Open		28.00	28
1998 Psychic Santa J3810	Open		20.00	20
1998 Replace The Divots J3815	Open		22.00	22
1994 Santa Cob J8203	Retrd.	1995	28.00	28
1997 Santa With Bear J6556	Open		8.00	8
1997 Santa's Day Off J6558	Open		25.00	25
1996 Save The Reindeer J6498	Retrd.	1997	28.00	28
1997 Snowmen Are Cool J6551	Retrd.	1997	20.00	20
1996 Some Assembly Required J6477	Retrd.	1997	53.00	53
1997 Spring Sale Snowman J6549	Open		20.00	20
1994 Surprise J8201	Retrd.	1997	22.00	22
1998 Teddy Bear Santa J3816	Open		20.00	20
1998 Things Are Looking Up J3811	Open		14.00	14
1998 Tundra Runners J3808	Open		20.00	20
1998 Whoa Kitty J3805	Open		20.00	20
1994 Will He Make It? J8203	Retrd.	1995	28.00	28
1995 Will Work For Cookies J8235	Open		40.00	40
1997 Winter Fun J6552	Open		25.00	25
1995 Wishful Thinking J8239	Retrd.	1997	32.00	32

Holly Bearies - H. Adler

YEAR ISSUE	EDITION LIMIT	YEAR RETD.	ISSUE PRICE	*QUOTE U.S.$
1996 Angel Bear J7342	Retrd.	1998	14.00	15
1998 Angel Bear, 6 1/4" W6751	Open		19.00	19
1996 Angel Starcatcher (Starlight Foundation) J7222	Retrd.	1996	20.00	20
1997 Angel Starcatcher II (Starlight Foundation) W6457	Retrd.	1997	20.00	20
1998 Angel Starcatcher III (Starlight Foundation) W6912	Yr.Iss.		20.00	20
1998 Barbeque Bear, 3 1/2" W6933	Open		10.00	10
1998 Bear Angel on Cloud W6935	Open		14.00	14
1998 Bearie in Red Heart Dress, 6" W6754	Open		17.00	17
1998 Bearie in Red PJs Sitting on Box W6787	Open		19.00	19
1997 Bearies Mailing Packages, 5 1/2" W6443	Retrd.	1998	28.00	28
1997 Charlie The Fisherman, 8 1/4" W6448	Yr.Iss.	1997	33.50	34
1998 Father Christmas, 4" W6930	Open		9.00	9
1998 Holly Bearie w/Blanket & Pull Rabbit, 8" W6753	Open		28.00	28
1998 Merry Merry Holly Bearie, 4" W6930	Open		9.00	9
1996 Mother's Day Bear J7318	Retrd.	1996	15.00	16
1997 Sledding Bearies W6445	Retrd.	1998	25.00	25
1996 Teddy Tower J7221	Retrd.	1998	23.00	23
1998 Wedding Couple, 3 1/4" W6926	Open		10.00	10

Holly Bearies Calendar Bears - H. Adler

YEAR ISSUE	EDITION LIMIT	YEAR RETD.	ISSUE PRICE	*QUOTE U.S.$
1996 Fergus & Fritzi's Frosty Frolic, 3 3/4" J7215/Jan	Open		16.00	16
1996 Pinky & Victoria Are Sweeties, 3 7/8" J7215/Feb	Open		16.00	16
1996 Philo's Pot O Gold, 3 3/4" J7215/Mar	Open		16.00	16
1996 Sunshine Catching Raindrops, 3 3/4" J7215/Apr	Open		16.00	16
1996 Petunia & Nathan Plant Posies, 4" J7215/May	Open		16.00	16
1996 Thorndike & Filbert Catch Fish, 4 1/4" J7215/Jun	Open		16.00	16
1996 Clairmont, Dempsey & Pete, 4 1/8" J7215/Jul	Open		16.00	16
1996 Nicole & Nicholas Sun Bearthing, 4 7/8" J7215/Aug	Open		16.00	16
1996 Skeeter & Sigourney Start School, 4 1/4" J7215/Sep	Open		16.00	16
1996 Clara & Carnation The Kitty, 4 1/4" J7215/Oct	Open		16.00	16
1996 Thorndike All Dressed Up, 4 1/4" J7215/Nov	Open		16.00	16
1996 Grandma Gladys, 4 3/8" J7215/Dec	Open		16.00	16

Holly Dearies - H. Adler

YEAR ISSUE	EDITION LIMIT	YEAR RETD.	ISSUE PRICE	*QUOTE U.S.$
1998 Dearie Sliding on Ice (2 asst.) H5447	Open		14.00	14
1997 Santa & Reindeer (Glass Ball) J9905	Open		21.00	21
1997 Santa & Reindeer (Musical Glass Ball) J9906	Open		40.00	40
1997 Santa at the North Pole, 8" H5401	5,000		155.00	155

Inspirational - P.F. Bolinger

YEAR ISSUE	EDITION LIMIT	YEAR RETD.	ISSUE PRICE	*QUOTE U.S.$
1997 Angel with Heart J6569	Open		20.00	20
1997 Noah J6487	Retrd.	1997	56.00	56
1997 Saint Francis J6585	Open		56.00	56

Jim Henson's Muppet Nutcrackers - KSA/JHP

YEAR ISSUE	EDITION LIMIT	YEAR RETD.	ISSUE PRICE	*QUOTE U.S.$
1993 Kermit The Frog H1223	Retrd.	1995	90.00	90

*Quotes have been rounded up to nearest dollar

Nutcracker Suite - KSA Design Team

YEAR ISSUE	EDITION LIMIT	YEAR RETD.	ISSUE PRICE	*QUOTE U.S.$
1998 Clara w/Nutcracker W1904	Open		45.00	45
1998 Drosselmeir W1905	Open		45.00	45
1998 Mouse King W1907	Open		45.00	45
1998 Nutcracker Prince W1906	Open		45.00	45
1998 Sugar Plum Fairy W1918	Open		45.00	45

Old World Santa Series - J. Mostrom

YEAR ISSUE	EDITION LIMIT	YEAR RETD.	ISSUE PRICE	*QUOTE U.S.$
1992 Chelsea Garden Santa W2721	Retrd.	1994	33.50	34
1993 Good King Wenceslas W2928	3,000	1996	134.00	134
1992 Large Black Forest Santa W2717	Retrd.	1994	110.00	110
1992 Large Father Christmas W2719	Retrd.	1994	106.00	106
1993 Medieval King of Christmas W2881	3,000	1994	390.00	390
1992 Mrs. Claus W2714	5,000	1996	37.00	37
1992 Patriotic Santa W2720	3,000	1994	128.00	128
1992 Pere Noel W2723	Retrd.	1994	33.50	34
1992 Small Black Forest Santa W2712	Retrd.	1994	40.00	40
1992 Small Father Christmas W2712	Retrd.	1994	33.50	34
1992 Small Father Frost W2716	Retrd.	1994	43.00	43
1992 Small Grandfather Frost W2718	Retrd.	1994	106.00	106
1992 St. Nicholas W2713	Retrd.	1994	30.00	30
1992 Workshop Santa W2715	5,000	1997	43.00	43

Sesame Street Series - KSA/JHP

YEAR ISSUE	EDITION LIMIT	YEAR RETD.	ISSUE PRICE	*QUOTE U.S.$
1993 Big Bird Fabrich, Figurine J7928	Retrd.	1996	60.00	60
1993 Big Bird Nutcracker H1199	Retrd.	1994	60.00	60

Snow People - P.F. Bolinger

YEAR ISSUE	EDITION LIMIT	YEAR RETD.	ISSUE PRICE	*QUOTE U.S.$
1996 Coola Hula J6430	Retrd.	1996	20.00	20
1996 Snowpoke J6431	Retrd.	1997	28.00	28
1996 Snowy J6429	Retrd.	1997	28.00	28

Snowbearies - H. Adler

YEAR ISSUE	EDITION LIMIT	YEAR RETD.	ISSUE PRICE	*QUOTE U.S.$
1998 Snowbearie Couple Carrying Other Snowbearie, 3 1/4" W6878	Open		11.00	11
1998 Snowbearie Couple Dancing on Ice Block, 3 1/4" W6878	Open		11.00	11
1998 Snowbearie Couple Playing on Ice Block, 3 1/4" W6878	Open		11.00	11
1997 Snowbearie Pair Dancing & Playing Leapfrog W6451	Open		9.00	9
1997 Snowbearie Pair Dancing & Playing Leapfrog W6491	Open		9.00	9
1997 Snowbearie w/Heart, 4 1/2" W6490	Open		18.00	18
1997 Snowbearies at Play W6452	Open		5.50	6
1997 Snowbearies at Play W6492	Open		5.50	6
1997 Snowbearies Hugging, 5 1/4" W6494	Open		20.00	20
1998 Snowbearies on Sled, set/2 W6888	Open		20.00	20
1998 Snowbearies on Sled, set/3 W6887	Open		20.00	20
1998 Snowbearies on Sled, set/4 W6886	Open		21.00	21
1998 Snowbearies on Sled, set/5 W6885	Open		22.50	23
1997 White Bear w/Ribbon & Snowflake, 8 1/2" H5651	Open		10.00	10

Steinbach Camelot Smoking Figure Series - KSA/Steinbach

YEAR ISSUE	EDITION LIMIT	YEAR RETD.	ISSUE PRICE	*QUOTE U.S.$
1994 Chief Sitting Bull Smoker ES834	7,500	1998	150.00	150
1993 King Arthur ES832	7,500	1996	175.00	175-200
1992 Merlin The Magician ES830	7,500	1997	150.00	150-175
1994 Sir Lancelot Smoker ES833	7,500	1997	150.00	150-175

Steinbach Nutcracker Collectors' Club - KSA/Steinbach

YEAR ISSUE	EDITION LIMIT	YEAR RETD.	ISSUE PRICE	*QUOTE U.S.$
1995 Mini Town Crier	Retrd.	1997	Gift	50
1995 King Wenceslaus ES900	Retrd.	1997	225.00	225-500
1997 Mini Chimney Sweep	Retrd.	1998	Gift	50
1997 Marek The Royal Guardsman ES856	Retrd.	1998	225.00	225-350
1998 Mini Forester	4/99		Gift	N/A
1998 Gustav The Royal Cook ES1824	4/99		225.00	225

Steinbach Nutcracker American Inventor Series - KSA/Steinbach

YEAR ISSUE	EDITION LIMIT	YEAR RETD.	ISSUE PRICE	*QUOTE U.S.$
1993 Ben Franklin ES635	12,000	1996	225.00	240-375

Steinbach Nutcracker American Presidents Series - KSA/Steinbach

YEAR ISSUE	EDITION LIMIT	YEAR RETD.	ISSUE PRICE	*QUOTE U.S.$
1992 Abraham Lincoln ES622	12,000	1995	195.00	350-599
1992 George Washington ES623	12,000	1994	195.00	450-700
1993 Teddy Roosevelt ES644	10,000	1997	225.00	225-450
1996 Thomas Jefferson ES866	7,500	1997	260.00	260

Steinbach Nutcracker Biblical - KSA/Steinbach

YEAR ISSUE	EDITION LIMIT	YEAR RETD.	ISSUE PRICE	*QUOTE U.S.$
1998 Joseph and the Dreamcoat ES1810	7,500		255.00	255
1997 Moses ES894	10,000		250.00	250
1996 Noah ES893	10,000		260.00	260

Steinbach Nutcracker Camelot Series - KSA/Steinbach

YEAR ISSUE	EDITION LIMIT	YEAR RETD.	ISSUE PRICE	*QUOTE U.S.$
1992 King Arthur ES621	Retrd.	1993	195.00	900-1500
1991 Merlin The Magician ES610	Retrd.	1991	185.00	3000-4500
1995 Queen Guenevere ES869	10,000	1997	245.00	245-275
1994 Sir Galahad ES862	12,000	1997	225.00	325-450
1993 Sir Lancelot ES638	12,000	1997	225.00	326-450

Steinbach Nutcracker Christmas Carol Series - KSA/Steinbach

YEAR ISSUE	EDITION LIMIT	YEAR RETD.	ISSUE PRICE	*QUOTE U.S.$
1998 Bob Cratchit and Tiny Tim ES1820	7,500		265.00	265
1997 Ebenezer Scrooge ES896	7,500		250.00	275

Steinbach Nutcracker Christmas Legends Series - KSA/Steinbach

YEAR ISSUE	EDITION LIMIT	YEAR RETD.	ISSUE PRICE	*QUOTE U.S.$
1995 1930s Santa Claus ES891	7,500		245.00	245
1993 Father Christmas ES645	7,500	1996	225.00	300-750
1997 Grandfather Frost ES895	7,500		250.00	250
1998 Père Noel ES1822	7,500		250.00	250
1994 St. Nicholas, The Bishop ES865	7,500	1995	225.00	300-750

Steinbach Nutcracker Collection - KSA/Steinbach

YEAR ISSUE	EDITION LIMIT	YEAR RETD.	ISSUE PRICE	*QUOTE U.S.$
1991 Columbus ES697	Retrd.	1992	194.00	225-260
1992 Happy Santa ES601	Retrd.	1998	190.00	220
1984 Oil Sheik	Retrd.	1985	100.00	500-1000

Steinbach Nutcracker Famous Chieftains Series - KSA/Steinbach

YEAR ISSUE	EDITION LIMIT	YEAR RETD.	ISSUE PRICE	*QUOTE U.S.$
1995 Black Hawk ES889	7,500	1996	245.00	245-399
1993 Chief Sitting Bull ES637	8,500	1995	225.00	450-650
1994 Red Cloud ES864	8,500	1996	225.00	250-399

Steinbach Nutcracker Mini Series - KSA/Steinbach

YEAR ISSUE	EDITION LIMIT	YEAR RETD.	ISSUE PRICE	*QUOTE U.S.$
1998 Grandfather Frost ES343	10,000		60.00	60
1997 King Arthur ES337	15,000		50.00	50
1996 Merlin ES335	15,000		50.00	50
1997 Noah and His Ark ES339	10,000		50.00	50
1996 Robin Hood ES336	10,000		50.00	50
1998 Scrooge ES342	10,000		60.00	60
1998 Sir Lancelot ES344	10,000		60.00	60
1997 St. Nicholas ES338	15,000		50.00	50

Steinbach Nutcracker Royalty Series - KSA/Steinbach

YEAR ISSUE	EDITION LIMIT	YEAR RETD.	ISSUE PRICE	*QUOTE U.S.$
1998 King Henry ES1823	7,500		255.00	255

Steinbach Nutcracker Tales of Sherwood Forest - KSA/Steinbach

YEAR ISSUE	EDITION LIMIT	YEAR RETD.	ISSUE PRICE	*QUOTE U.S.$
1995 Friar Tuck ES890	7,500	1997	245.00	245-450
1997 King Richard the Lion-Hearted ES897	7,500		250.00	250
1992 Robin Hood ES863	7,500	1996	225.00	600-899
1996 Sherif of Nottingham ES892	7,500		260.00	275

Steinbach Nutcracker Three Musketeers - KSA/Steinbach

YEAR ISSUE	EDITION LIMIT	YEAR RETD.	ISSUE PRICE	*QUOTE U.S.$
1996 Aramis ES722	7,500	1997	130.00	130-180
1998 Athos ES1821	7,500		125.00	125

Vatican Library Collection - Vatican Library

YEAR ISSUE	EDITION LIMIT	YEAR RETD.	ISSUE PRICE	*QUOTE U.S.$
1997 Holy Family Set V29	Open		80.00	80
1997 Three Wise Men V30	Open		100.00	100

Visions Of Santa Series - KSA Design Team

YEAR ISSUE	EDITION LIMIT	YEAR RETD.	ISSUE PRICE	*QUOTE U.S.$
1992 Santa Coming Out Of Fireplace J1023	Retrd.	1993	29.00	29
1992 Santa Holding Child J826	Retrd.	1993	24.50	25
1992 Santa Spilling Bag Of Toys J1022	7,500	1994	25.50	26
1992 Santa With Little Girls On Lap J1024	7,500	1996	24.50	25
1992 Santa With Sack Holding Toy J827	7,500	1994	24.50	25
1992 Workshop Santa J825	7,500	1994	27.00	27

Zuber Nutcracker Series - KSA/Zuber

YEAR ISSUE	EDITION LIMIT	YEAR RETD.	ISSUE PRICE	*QUOTE U.S.$
1992 The Annapolis Midshipman EK7	5,000	1994	125.00	125
1992 The Bavarian EK16	5,000	1994	130.00	130
1992 Bronco Billy The Cowboy EK1	5,000	1994	125.00	125-140
1992 The Chimney Sweep EK6	5,000	1993	125.00	125
1992 The Country Singer EK19	5,000	1993	125.00	125
1992 The Fisherman EK17	5,000	1996	125.00	130-140
1994 The Gardner EK26	2,500	1996	150.00	150
1992 Gepetto, The Toymaker EK9	5,000	1994	125.00	125
1992 The Gold Prospector EK18	5,000	1994	125.00	125
1992 The Golfer EK5	5,000	1994	125.00	125-130
1993 Herr Drosselmeir Nutcracker EK21	5,000	1996	150.00	450-1029
1993 The Ice Cream Vendor EK24	5,000	1996	150.00	150
1992 The Indian EK15	5,000	1994	135.00	135
1994 Jazz Player EK25	2,500		145.00	145
1994 Kurt the Traveling Salesman EK28	2,500	1994	155.00	155
1994 Mouse King EK31	2,500		150.00	150
1993 Napoleon Bonaparte EK23	5,000	1994	150.00	150
1992 The Nor' Easter Sea Captain EK3	5,000		125.00	125
1992 Paul Bunyan The Lumberjack EK2	5,000	1993	125.00	125
1994 Peter Pan EK28	2,500		145.00	145
1992 The Pilgrim EK14	5,000	1994	125.00	125
1993 The Pizzamaker EK22	5,000		150.00	150
1994 Scuba Diver EK27	2,500		150.00	150
1994 Soccer Player EK30	2,500		145.00	145
1992 TheTyrolean EK4	5,000	1994	125.00	125
1992 The West Point Cadet With Canon EK8	5,000	1994	130.00	130

Ladie and Friends

Lizzie High® Figurines - B.&P. Wisber

YEAR ISSUE	EDITION LIMIT	YEAR RETD.	ISSUE PRICE	*QUOTE U.S.$
1997 Addie High -C202	2-Yr.		22.00	22
1997 Alice Valentine -B148	2-Yr.		22.00	22
1996 Amanda High -111	2-Yr.	1998	28.00	28
1997 Amelia High -248	2-Yr.		19.50	20
1998 Betsy Valentine -C245	2-Yr.		24.00	24
1996 Cassie Yocum -179	2-Yr.	1998	29.50	30
1998 Daphne Bowman -C235	2-Yr.		22.00	22
1996 Edward Bowman -158	2-Yr.	1998	28.00	28
1997 Edwina High -B343	2-Yr.		23.00	23
1997 Emmy Lou Valentine -B251	2-Yr.		19.50	20
1996 Grace Valentine -146	2-Yr.	1998	25.00	25
1996 Katie Bowman -178	2-Yr.	1998	28.00	28
1996 Lizzie High -100	2-Yr.	1998	26.50	27
1996 Lizzie High Sign -090	2-Yr.	1998	37.00	37
1997 Margaret Bowman -B213	2-Yr.		24.00	24
1996 Marisa Valentine -333	2-Yr.	1998	25.00	25
1997 Mary Ellen Valentine -B236	2-Yr.		21.00	21
1998 Matilda High -C393	2-Yr.		22.00	22
1996 Megan Valentine -227	2-Yr.	1998	35.00	35
1996 Minnie Valentine -336	2-Yr.	1998	29.50	30
1996 Nancy Bowman -261	2-Yr.	1998	24.00	24
1996 Natalie Valentine -284	2-Yr.	1998	28.00	28
1997 Olivia High -B205	2-Yr.		22.00	22
1997 Pauline Bowman -B228	2-Yr.		22.00	22
1997 Pearl Bowman -B303	2-Yr.		19.50	20
1997 Penny Valentine -B308	2-Yr.		23.00	23
1996 Rebecca Bowman -104	2-Yr.	1998	37.00	37
1997 Sally Bowman -B155	2-Yr.		23.00	23
1997 Santa w/Puppy -B364	2-Yr.		22.00	22
1998 Shannon Fitzpatrick -C391	2-Yr.		22.00	22
1997 Wendel Bowman -B106	2-Yr.		24.00	24

Legends

Annual Collectors Edition - C. Pardell

YEAR ISSUE	EDITION LIMIT	YEAR RETD.	ISSUE PRICE	*QUOTE U.S.$
1990 The Night Before	500	1991	990.00	1800-2535
1991 Medicine Gift of Manhood	500	1992	990.00	935-1300
1992 Spirit of the Wolf	500	1992	950.00	1073-2000
1993 Tomorrow's Warrior	500	1993	590.00	1200
1994 Guiding Hand	500	1994	590.00	875-1100
1995 Gift of the Sacred Calf	500	1995	650.00	650-900
1996 Spirit and Image	500		750.00	750

Collectors Only - Various

YEAR ISSUE	EDITION LIMIT	YEAR RETD.	ISSUE PRICE	*QUOTE U.S.$
1993 Give Us Peace - C. Pardell	1,250	1993	270.00	400-600
1994 First Born - C. Pardell	1,250	1994	350.00	400-600
1994 River Bandits - K. Cantrell	1,250	1995	350.00	425-514
1995 Sonata - K. Cantrell	1,250	1996	250.00	300-400
1995 Daydreams of Manhood - C. Pardell	2,500	1995	390.00	500
1996 Innocence Remembered - C. Pardell	Retrd.	1996	490.00	490

American Heritage - D. Edwards

YEAR ISSUE	EDITION LIMIT	YEAR RETD.	ISSUE PRICE	*QUOTE U.S.$
1987 Grizz Country (Bronze)	Retrd.	1990	350.00	350
1987 Grizz Country (Pewter)	Retrd.	1990	370.00	370-520
1987 Winter Provisions (Bronze)	Retrd.	1990	340.00	340
1987 Winter Provisions (Pewter)	Retrd.	1990	370.00	370
1987 Wrangler's Dare (Bronze)	Retrd.	1990	630.00	630
1987 Wrangler's Dare (Pewter)	Retrd.	1990	660.00	660

American Indian Dance Premier Edition - C. Pardell

YEAR ISSUE	EDITION LIMIT	YEAR RETD.	ISSUE PRICE	*QUOTE U.S.$
1996 Dancing Ground	750		2500.00	2500
1993 Drum Song	750	1995	2800.00	2000-3950
1994 Footprints of the Butterfly	750	1995	1800.00	1990
1994 Image of the Eagle	750	1997	1900.00	2100
1995 Spirit of the Mountain	750		1750.00	1850

American West Premier Edition - C. Pardell

YEAR ISSUE	EDITION LIMIT	YEAR RETD.	ISSUE PRICE	*QUOTE U.S.$
1992 American Horse	950	1995	1300.00	1300
1992 Defending the People	950		1350.00	1450
1991 First Coup	950	1993	1150.00	1170-1430
1993 Four Bears' Challenge	950	1996	990.00	1050
1994 Season of Victory	950	1997	1500.00	1580
1991 Unexpected Rescuer	950	1991	990.00	1170-1200

The Endangered Wildlife Collection - K. Cantrell

YEAR ISSUE	EDITION LIMIT	YEAR RETD.	ISSUE PRICE	*QUOTE U.S.$
1993 Big Pine Survivor	950	1998	390.00	390
1990 Forest Spirit	950	1991	290.00	1500
1991 Mountain Majesty	950	1997	350.00	390
1991 Old Tusker	950	1997	390.00	390
1992 Plains Monarch	950	1997	350.00	390
1994 Prairie Phantom	950	1997	370.00	390
1990 Savannah Prince	950	1997	290.00	290-350
1993 Silvertip	950	1997	370.00	390
1992 Songs of Autumn	950	1995	390.00	550
1992 Spirit Song	950	1992	350.00	650-700
1994 Twilight	950	1997	290.00	310
1992 Unchallenged	950	1996	350.00	390

Endangered Wildlife Eagle Series - K. Cantrell

YEAR ISSUE	EDITION LIMIT	YEAR RETD.	ISSUE PRICE	*QUOTE U.S.$
1989 Aquila Libre	2,500	1995	280.00	300-400
1993 Defiance	2,500		350.00	350
1992 Food Fight	2,500		650.00	750
1989 Outpost	2,500	1995	280.00	320-350
1989 Sentinel	2,500	1993	280.00	400-500
1993 Spiral Flight	2,500		290.00	300
1992 Sunday Brunch	2,500		550.00	650
1989 Unbounded	2,500	1994	280.00	240-400

Gallery Editions - Various

YEAR ISSUE	EDITION LIMIT	YEAR RETD.	ISSUE PRICE	*QUOTE U.S.$
1994 Center Fire - W. Whitten	350		2500.00	2600
1994 Mountain Family - D. Lemon	150	1996	7900.00	8300
1996 On Wings of Eagles - D. Lemon	250		3700.00	3700
1993 Over the Rainbow - K. Cantrell	600	1995	2900.00	3850-4000
1993 Over the Rainbow AP - K. Cantrell	Retrd.	1996	4000.00	5000
1992 Resolute - C. Pardell	250	1992	7950.00	9100-12000
1993 Visionary - C. Pardell	350		7500.00	8300
1993 The Wanderer - K. Cantrell	350		3500.00	3700
1996 Wind on Still Water - C. Pardell	350	1996	2500.00	4500

Hidden Images Collection - D. Lemon

YEAR ISSUE	EDITION LIMIT	YEAR RETD.	ISSUE PRICE	*QUOTE U.S.$
1994 In Search of Bear Rock	350	1995	1300.00	1500
1995 Sensed, But Unseen	350	1995	990.00	1200
1995 Spirit	350	1997	990.00	990

Indian Arts Collection - C. Pardell

YEAR ISSUE	EDITION LIMIT	YEAR RETD.	ISSUE PRICE	*QUOTE U.S.$
1990 Chief's Blanket	1,500	1992	350.00	600-700
1990 Indian Maiden	1,500	1997	240.00	240
1990 Indian Potter	1,500	1997	260.00	260
1990 Kachina Carver	1,500	1993	270.00	286-400
1990 Story Teller	1,500	1993	290.00	450-550

The Legacies Of The West Premier Edition - C. Pardell

YEAR ISSUE	EDITION LIMIT	YEAR RETD.	ISSUE PRICE	*QUOTE U.S.$
1991 Defiant Comanche	950	1991	1300.00	1000-2210
1993 Eminent Crow	950	1994	1500.00	1400-1755
1994 Enduring	950	1996	1250.00	1350
1992 Esteemed Warrior	950	1992	1750.00	1850-1950
1990 Mystic Vision	950	1990	990.00	1700-2080
1991 No More, Forever	950	1992	1500.00	1690-1800
1992 Rebellious	950	1996	1500.00	1600
1990 Victorious	950	1990	1275.00	1800-2200

*Quotes have been rounded up to nearest dollar

The Legendary West Collection - C. Pardell

YEAR ISSUE	EDITION LIMIT	YEAR RETD.	ISSUE PRICE	*QUOTE U.S.$
1992 Beating Bad Odds	2,500		390.00	410
1989 Bustin' A Herd Quitter	2,500		590.00	660
1993 Cliff Hanger	2,500	1996	990.00	1050
1992 Crazy Horse	2,500	1992	390.00	800-1100
1989 Eagle Dancer	2,500	1996	370.00	410
1993 Hunter's Brothers	2,500		590.00	660
1989 Johnson's Last Fight	2,500	1991	590.00	750-1200
1990 Keeper of Eagles	2,500	1997	370.00	410
1987 Pony Express (Bronze)	2,500	N/A	320.00	320-450
1989 Pony Express (Mixed Media)	2,500		390.00	410
1987 Pony Express (Pewter)	2,500	N/A	320.00	320-450
1989 Sacajawea	2,500	1995	380.00	595
1990 Shhh	2,500		390.00	410
1990 Stand of the Sash Wearer	2,500	1996	390.00	295-410
1989 Tables Turned	2,500		680.00	750
1990 Unbridled	2,500	1996	290.00	290
1991 Warning	2,500	1997	390.00	410
1989 White Feather's Vision	2,500	1991	390.00	585-1000

The Legendary West Premier Edition - C. Pardell

YEAR ISSUE	EDITION LIMIT	YEAR RETD.	ISSUE PRICE	*QUOTE U.S.$
1990 Crow Warrior	750	1990	1225.00	1235-2000
1992 The Final Charge	750	1992	1250.00	1300-1500
1989 Pursued	750	1989	750.00	2000-4000
1988 Red Cloud's Coup	750	1988	480.00	5000-5500
1989 Songs of Glory	750	1989	850.00	3500-3900
1991 Triumphant	750	1991	1150.00	2200-2600

Special Commissions - Various

YEAR ISSUE	EDITION LIMIT	YEAR RETD.	ISSUE PRICE	*QUOTE U.S.$
1988 Alpha Pair (Bronze) - C. Pardell	Retrd.	N/A	330.00	330
1988 Alpha Pair (Mixed Media) - C. Pardell	S/O	N/A	390.00	500-750
1988 Alpha Pair (Pewter) - C. Pardell	Retrd.	N/A	330.00	330
1991 American Allegiance - D. Edwards	1,250	1996	570.00	625
1995 Father-The Power Within - D. Medina	350		1500.00	1590
1990 Lakota Love Song - C. Pardell	Retrd.	1990	380.00	1950
1987 Mama's Joy (Bronze) - D. Edwards	Retrd.	N/A	200.00	200
1987 Mama's Joy (Pewter) - D. Edwards	Retrd.	N/A	250.00	250
1996 Proud Heritage - K. Cantrell	2,500		290.00	290
1995 Rapture - W. Whitten	350		1750.00	1850
1995 Scent in the Air - K. Cantrell	750		990.00	1200
1991 Symbols of Freedom - K. Cantrell	2,500		490.00	520
1987 Wild Freedom (Bronze) - D. Edwards	Retrd.	N/A	320.00	320
1987 Wild Freedom (Pewter) - D. Edwards	Retrd.	N/A	330.00	330
1992 Yellowstone Bound - K. Cantrell	600	1994	2500.00	3120-3950

Way of the Cat Collection - K. Cantrell

YEAR ISSUE	EDITION LIMIT	YEAR RETD.	ISSUE PRICE	*QUOTE U.S.$
1996 Cat's Cradle	500	1997	790.00	790
1995 Encounter	500	1995	750.00	1100-1600

Way of the Warrior Collection - C. Pardell

YEAR ISSUE	EDITION LIMIT	YEAR RETD.	ISSUE PRICE	*QUOTE U.S.$
1991 Clan Leader	1,600	1994	170.00	195-225
1991 Elder Chief	1,600	1994	170.00	225
1991 Medicine Dancer	1,600	1994	170.00	195-225
1991 Rite of Manhood	1,600	1994	170.00	189-225
1991 Seeker of Visions	1,600	1994	170.00	195-225
1991 Tribal Defender	1,600	1994	170.00	195-225

Way of the Wolf Collection - K. Cantrell

YEAR ISSUE	EDITION LIMIT	YEAR RETD.	ISSUE PRICE	*QUOTE U.S.$
1993 Courtship	500	1993	590.00	1500-2000
1995 Gossip Column	500		1250.00	1250
1994 Missed by a Hare	500	1994	700.00	850-1300
1994 Renewal	500	1994	700.00	950-1700
1995 Stink Bomb	500	1995	750.00	970

Wild Realm Premier Edition - C. Pardell

YEAR ISSUE	EDITION LIMIT	YEAR RETD.	ISSUE PRICE	*QUOTE U.S.$
1989 High Spirit	1,600	1996	870.00	1000
1991 Speed Incarnate	1,600	1996	790.00	790

Lenox, Inc.

Lenox Classics-Annual Angel - Lenox

YEAR ISSUE	EDITION LIMIT	YEAR RETD.	ISSUE PRICE	*QUOTE U.S.$
1997 Guardian of the Stars	2,500		195.00	195
1998 Guardian of Light	2,500		195.00	195

Lenox Classics-Annual Santas - Lenox

YEAR ISSUE	EDITION LIMIT	YEAR RETD.	ISSUE PRICE	*QUOTE U.S.$
1997 Santa's Joy (Santa w/Elf & Ornament)	2,500		195.00	195
1998 Santa's Journey	2,500		195.00	195

Lenox Classics-Away in a Manager - Lenox

YEAR ISSUE	EDITION LIMIT	YEAR RETD.	ISSUE PRICE	*QUOTE U.S.$
1996 Angel	Open		50.00	50
1997 Gaspar	Open		50.00	50
1997 Heralding Angel	Open		50.00	50
1996 Jesus	Open		40.00	40
1996 Joseph	Open		50.00	50
1996 Mary	Open		50.00	50

Lenox Classics-Barefoot Blessings - Lenox

YEAR ISSUE	EDITION LIMIT	YEAR RETD.	ISSUE PRICE	*QUOTE U.S.$
1997 Bedtime Prayers (Girl Praying)	Open		60.00	60
1996 Cheerful Giver (Girl w/Vegetables)	Open		60.00	60
1998 Friends Forever (Girl w/doll)	Open		60.00	60
1996 Gone Fishing (Boy w/Dog)	Open		60.00	60
1998 Graduation Princess (Girl in cap & gown)	Open		60.00	60
1997 Just Like Mommy (Girl w/Hat)	Open		60.00	60
1997 Making Friends (Girl w/Butterfly)	Open		60.00	60
1996 Morning Chores (Boy w/Cat)	Open		60.00	60
1996 Sharing Secrets (Girl w/Doll)	Open		60.00	60
1996 Spring Surprise (Girl w/Chick)	Open		60.00	60
1997 With This Kiss (Girl Bride & Boy Groom)	Open		145.00	145

Lenox Classics-China Animal Sculptures - Lenox

YEAR ISSUE	EDITION LIMIT	YEAR RETD.	ISSUE PRICE	*QUOTE U.S.$
1998 Between Sea & Sky (Ivory Dolphins)	Open		136.00	136
1998 Eagle of Freedom (Ivory Eagle)	Open		160.00	160
1998 The Majestic Elephant (Ivory Elephant)	Open		136.00	136

Lenox Classics-Crystal Cats - Lenox

YEAR ISSUE	EDITION LIMIT	YEAR RETD.	ISSUE PRICE	*QUOTE U.S.$
1997 Crystal Jaguar (Cat in Grass)	Open		160.00	175
1996 Fascination (Cat w/Butterfly)	Open		50.00	55
1998 Grace and Glamour (Crystal Cat Pair)	Open		79.00	79
1998 Hugs and Kisses (Crystal Cat Pair)	Open		79.00	79
1997 Morning Stretch (Cat Stretching)	Open		136.00	145
1996 Playtime (Cat w/Ball)	Open		50.00	55
1996 Preen & Serene (Cat Pair)	Open		76.00	79
1997 Warm & Cozy (Cat & Kitten)	Open		110.00	110

Lenox Classics-Crystal Eagles - Lenox

YEAR ISSUE	EDITION LIMIT	YEAR RETD.	ISSUE PRICE	*QUOTE U.S.$
1997 The Keeper of the Stars (Patriotic Eagle)	Open		115.00	125
1996 Soaring Majesty (Flying Eagle)	Open		195.00	195
1998 Wings of Brilliance (Eagle Taking Off)	Open		195.00	195
1996 Wings of the Sun (Eagle on Rock)	Open		195.00	195

Lenox Classics-Crystal Elephants - Lenox

YEAR ISSUE	EDITION LIMIT	YEAR RETD.	ISSUE PRICE	*QUOTE U.S.$
1998 Cotton and Candy (Elephant Pair)	Open		79.00	79
1998 Crystal Dancer	Open		136.00	136
1997 Crystal Playmate (Elephant in Grass)	Open		136.00	136
1998 Crystal Repose	Open		136.00	136
1996 Peanuts & Popcorn (Elephant Pair)	Open		76.00	79
1997 Touch of Love (Elephant Mother & Calf)	Open		195.00	195

Lenox Classics-Crystal Unicorns - Lenox

YEAR ISSUE	EDITION LIMIT	YEAR RETD.	ISSUE PRICE	*QUOTE U.S.$
1998 Unicorn	Open		136.00	136

Lenox Classics-Disney Showcase - Lenox

YEAR ISSUE	EDITION LIMIT	YEAR RETD.	ISSUE PRICE	*QUOTE U.S.$
1998 Cinderella	Open		125.00	125
1998 Dopey	Open		70.00	70
1998 Grumpy	Open		70.00	70
1998 Snow White	Open		125.00	125

Lenox Classics-Finishing Touches - Lenox

YEAR ISSUE	EDITION LIMIT	YEAR RETD.	ISSUE PRICE	*QUOTE U.S.$
1997 Checking the List (Elf w/List)	Open		70.00	70
1997 Hush Little Teddy (Elf w/Toy Bag)	Open		70.00	70
1997 Little Jingles (Elf w/Bells)	Open		70.00	70
1997 Loading the Sleigh (Elf w/Pkgs.)	Open		70.00	70
1997 Nap Time (Elf Sleeping)	Open		70.00	70
1997 Painting Stripes (Elf w/Brush)	Open		70.00	70

Lenox Classics-Inspirational - Lenox

YEAR ISSUE	EDITION LIMIT	YEAR RETD.	ISSUE PRICE	*QUOTE U.S.$
1998 Footprints (Ivory Footprints sculpt of Jesus w/Child)	Open		152.00	152

Lenox Classics-Lake & Ocean Crystal Animals - Lenox

YEAR ISSUE	EDITION LIMIT	YEAR RETD.	ISSUE PRICE	*QUOTE U.S.$
1998 Dolphin Duet (Crystal Dolphin pair)	Open		100.00	100
1996 Dolphin's Journey (Mother w/Child)	Open		76.00	100
1996 Glorious Dolphin (Dolphin Jumping Up)	Open		76.00	100
1998 Majestic Dolpin	Open		100.00	100
1996 Radiant Dolphin (Dolphin Diving Down)	Open		76.00	100
1998 Swan King (Crystal Swan on Lake)	Open		65.00	65

Lenox Classics-Little Graces - Lenox

YEAR ISSUE	EDITION LIMIT	YEAR RETD.	ISSUE PRICE	*QUOTE U.S.$
1996 Enjoyment (Cherub w/Bell)	5,000		95.00	95
1998 Faith (Cherub w/ cross & flowers)	5,000		95.00	95
1996 Guidance (Cherub w/Candle)	5,000		95.00	95
1997 Happiness (Cherub Reclining)	5,000		95.00	95
1997 Harmony (Cherub w/ Lg. Harp)	5,000		95.00	95
1996 Hope (Cherub w/Star)	5,000		95.00	95
1997 Innocence (Cherub w/Trumpet)	5,000		95.00	95
1996 Knowledge (Cherub w/Book)	5,000		95.00	95
1997 Love (Cherub w/Heart)	5,000		95.00	95
1996 Peace (Cherub w/Dove)	5,000		95.00	95
1996 Tranquility (Cherub w/Harp)	5,000		95.00	95

Lenox Classics-Victorian Ladies of Fashion - Lenox

YEAR ISSUE	EDITION LIMIT	YEAR RETD.	ISSUE PRICE	*QUOTE U.S.$
1998 Grand Voyage	Open		138.00	138
1998 Morning Promenade	Open		138.00	138
1998 Sunday Stroll	Open		138.00	138

Lenox Classics-Woodland Animals-Crystal - Lenox

YEAR ISSUE	EDITION LIMIT	YEAR RETD.	ISSUE PRICE	*QUOTE U.S.$
1997 The Keeper of the Wild (Wolf)	Open		100.00	100
1996 Lord & Lady (Wolf Pair)	Open		76.00	79
1996 Satin & Silk (Bunny Pair)	Open		76.00	79

Lladró

Lladró Collectors Society - Lladró

YEAR ISSUE	EDITION LIMIT	YEAR RETD.	ISSUE PRICE	*QUOTE U.S.$
1985 Little Pals S7600	Closed	1986	95.00	2000-3900
1985 LCS Plaque w/blue writing S7601	Closed	1985	35.00	65-125
1986 Little Traveler S7602	Closed	1987	95.00	1250-1560
1987 Spring Bouquets S7603	Closed	1988	125.00	650-1000
1988 School Days S7604	Closed	1989	125.00	475-800
1988 Flower Song S7607	Closed	1989	175.00	475-644
1989 My Buddy S7609	Closed	1990	145.00	350-600
1990 Can I Play? S7610	Closed	1991	150.00	350-495
1991 Summer Stroll S7611	Closed	1992	195.00	350-695
1991 Picture Perfect S7612	Closed	1991	350.00	380-700
1992 All Aboard S7619	Closed	1993	165.00	250-450
1992 The Voyage of Columbus LL5847	7,500	1994	1450.00	1300-1650
1993 Best Friend S7620	Closed	1994	195.00	250-375
1993 Jester's Serenade w/base LL5932	3,000	1994	1995.00	2000-2535
1994 Basket of Love S7622	Closed	1995	225.00	300-350
1994 Garden of Dreams 7634	Closed	1996	1250.00	1625-1690
1995 10 Year Society Anniversary - Ten and Growing S7635	Closed	1996	395.00	450-500
1995 Afternoon Promenade S7636	Closed	1996	240.00	275-400
1995 Now and Forever (10 year membership piece) S7642	Open		395.00	395-600
1996 Innocence In Bloom S7644	Closed	1997	250.00	275-400
1996 Where Love Begins w/base 7649	Closed	1996	895.00	1170-1300
1997 Guardian Angel 6352	Closed	1997	1300.00	1300-2000
1997 Pocket Full of Wishes 7650	Yr.Iss.	1998	360.00	360-400
1998 Dolphins at Play 01007658	Yr.Iss.		21.00	21
1998 Heaven and Earth 01001824	5,000		725.00	725
1998 It Wasn't Me! 01007672	Yr.Iss.		295.00	295

Lladró Event Figurines - Lladró

YEAR ISSUE	EDITION LIMIT	YEAR RETD.	ISSUE PRICE	*QUOTE U.S.$
1991 Garden Classic L7617G	Closed	1992	295.00	390-700
1992 Garden Song L7618G	Closed	1993	295.00	375-600
1993 Pick of the Litter L7621G	Closed	1994	350.00	350-700
1994 Little Riders L7623	Closed	1995	250.00	275-500
1995 For A Perfect Performance L7641	Closed	1995	310.00	450-500
1996 Destination Big Top L6245	Closed	1996	225.00	350-475
1997 Tailor Made (Event '97) L6489	Closed	1997	150.00	200-245
1997 Dreams of a Summer's Past (Event '97) L6401	Closed	1997	310.00	310-400

Capricho - Lladró

YEAR ISSUE	EDITION LIMIT	YEAR RETD.	ISSUE PRICE	*QUOTE U.S.$
1988 Bust w/ Black Veil & base C1538	Open		650.00	1050
1988 Small Bust w/ Veil & base C1539	Open		225.00	490
1987 Orchid Arrangement C1541	Closed	1991	500.00	1700-2100
1987 Iris Arrangement C1542	Closed	1991	500.00	1000-1500
1987 Fan C1546	Closed	1988	675.00	900-1600
1987 Fan C1546.3	Closed	1988	675.00	900-1600
1987 Iris with Vase C1551	Closed	1992	110.00	375
1987 Flowers Chest C1572	Open		550.00	1100
1987 Flat Basket with Flowers C1575	Closed	1991	450.00	750-850
1989 White Rosary C1647	Closed	1991	290.00	340-400
1989 Romantic Lady / Black Veil w/base C1666	Closed	1993	420.00	520
XX White Bust w/ Veil & base C5927	Open		550.00	1000
XX Special Museum Flower Basket C7606	Closed	1991	N/A	450-750

Crystal Sculptures - Lladró

YEAR ISSUE	EDITION LIMIT	YEAR RETD.	ISSUE PRICE	*QUOTE U.S.$
1983 Frosted Bear, Head Up L04502	Closed	1983	200.00	350
1983 Frosted Bear, Head Down L04503	Closed	1983	205.00	350
1983 Frosted Bear, Head Up L04504	Closed	1983	210.00	350
1983 Frosted Bear, Head Straight L04506	Closed	1983	200.00	350
1983 Frosted Angel w/Guitar L04507	Closed	1983	165.00	375
1983 Frosted Angel w/Cymbal L04508	Closed	1983	165.00	375
1983 Frosted Angel w/Violin L04509	Closed	1983	165.00	495
1983 Frosted Geisha, Praying L04510	Closed	1983	135.00	495
1983 Frosted Geishaw/Fan L04511	Closed	1983	135.00	375
1983 Frosted Geishaw/Flowers L04512	Closed	1983	135.00	375
1983 Clear Bear, Head Straight L04513	Closed	1983	220.00	400
1983 Clear Bear, Head Up L04514	Closed	1983	230.00	400
1983 Wedding Bell	Closed	1985	35.00	195

Disneyana Limited Edition - Lladró

YEAR ISSUE	EDITION LIMIT	YEAR RETD.	ISSUE PRICE	*QUOTE U.S.$
1992 Tinkerbell LL7518	1,500	1992	350.00	2200-3380
1993 Peter Pan LL7529	3,000	1993	400.00	750-1200
1994 Cinderella and Fairy Godmother LL7553G	2,500	1995	875.00	605-1170
1995 Sleeping Beauty Dance LL7560	1,000	1995	1280.00	1271-2340

Limited Edition - Lladró

YEAR ISSUE	EDITION LIMIT	YEAR RETD.	ISSUE PRICE	*QUOTE U.S.$
1971 Hamlet LL1144	750	1973	125.00	2800-5200
1971 Othello and Desdemona LL1145	750	1973	275.00	2500-3000
1971 Antique Auto LL1146	750	1975	1000.00	4900-6000
1971 Floral LL1184	200	1978	400.00	2200
1971 Floral LL1185	200	1974	475.00	1800
1971 Floral LL1186	200	1976	575.00	2200
1972 Eagles LL1189	750	1978	450.00	3200-4200
1972 Sea Birds with Nest LL1194	500	1975	300.00	2750
1972 Turkey Group LL1196	350	1982	325.00	1800
1972 Peace LL1202	150	1973	550.00	7500-9500
1972 Eagle Owl LL1223	750	1983	225.00	1000-1325
1972 Hansom Carriage LL1225	750	1975	1450.00	9000
1973 Buck Hunters LL1238	800	1976	400.00	3000
1973 Turtle Doves LL1240	850	1976	250.00	2300-2500
1973 The Forest LL1243	500	1976	625.00	3300
1974 Soccer Players LL1266	500	1983	1000.00	7500
1974 Man From LaMancha LL1269	1,500	1977	700.00	4200-4500
1974 Queen Elizabeth II LL1275	250	1985	3650.00	5200
1974 Judge LL1281	1,200	1978	325.00	1250-1650
1974 Partridge LL1290G	800	1974	700.00	1200-2000
1974 The Hunt LL1308	750	1984	4750.00	6900-8300
1974 Ducks at Pond LL1317	1,200	1984	4250.00	6250
1976 Impossible Dream LL1318	1,000	1983	1200.00	4500-5380
1976 Comforting Baby LL1329	750	1978	350.00	1050
1976 Mountain Country Lady LL1330	750	1983	900.00	1700
1976 My Baby LL1331	1,000	1981	275.00	900
1978 Flight of Gazelles LL1352	1,500	1984	1225.00	3100
1978 Car in Trouble LL1375	1,500	1987	3000.00	5250-6500
1978 Fearful Flight LL1377	750		7000.00	18000
1978 Henry VIII LL 1384	1,200	1993	650.00	850-1000
1981 Venus and Cupid LL1392	750	1993	1100.00	1600-2100
1982 First Date w/base LL1393	1,500		3800.00	5900
1982 Columbus LL1432G	1,200	1988	535.00	1100-1300
1983 Venetian Serenade LL1433	750	1989	2600.00	3900-5000
1985 Festival in Valencia w/base LL1457	3,000	1994	1400.00	2350
1985 Camelot LL1458	3,000	1994	950.00	1500
1985 Napoleon Planning Battle w/base LL1459	1,500	1995	825.00	1450
1985 Youthful Beauty w/base LL1461	5,000		750.00	1200
1985 Flock of Birds w/base LL1462	1,500		1060.00	1750
1985 Classic Spring LL1465	1,500	1995	620.00	1100-1300
1985 Classic Fall LL1466	1,500	1995	620.00	975-1300

*Quotes have been rounded up to nearest dollar

YEAR ISSUE	EDITION LIMIT	YEAR RETD.	ISSUE PRICE	*QUOTE U.S.$
1985 Valencian Couple on Horse LL1472	3,000		885.00	1550
1985 Coach XVIII Century w/base LL1485	500		14000.00	28000
1986 The New World w/base LL1486	4,000	1997	700.00	750-1350
1986 Fantasia w/base LL1487	5,000		1500.00	2700
1986 Floral Offering w/base LL1490	3,000		2500.00	4450
1986 Oriental Music w/base LL1491	5,000		1350.00	2445
1986 Three Sisters w/base LL1492	3,000		1850.00	3250
1986 At the Stroke of Twelve w/base LL1493	1,500	1993	4250.00	7000-8000
1986 Hawaiian Festival w/base LL1496	4,000	1997	1850.00	3200
1987 A Sunday Drive w/base LL1510	1,000		3400.00	5250
1987 Listen to Don Quixote w/base LL1520	750	1995	1800.00	2900
1987 A Happy Encounter LL1523	1,500		2900.00	4900
1988 Japanese Vase LL1536	750	1989	2600.00	3450-3650
1988 Garden Party w/base LL1578	500		5500.00	7250
1988 Blessed Lady w/base LL1579	1,000	1991	1150.00	3000
1988 Return to La Mancha w/base LL1580	500		6400.00	8350
1989 Southern Tea LL1597	1,000	1995	1775.00	2300-2900
1989 Kitakami Cruise w/base LL1605	500	1994	5800.00	7500-9000
1989 Mounted Warriors w/base LL1608	500		2850.00	3450
1989 Circus Parade w/base LL1609	1,000		5200.00	6550
1989 "Jesus the Rock" w/base LL1615	1,000	1994	1175.00	2100
1989 Hopeful Group LL1723	1,000	1993	1825.00	1825
1991 Valencian Cruise LL1731	1,000		2700.00	2950
1991 Venice Vows LL1732	1,500		3755.00	4100
1991 Liberty Eagle LL1738	1,500		1000.00	1100
1991 Heavenly Swing LL1739	1,000		1900.00	2050
1991 Columbus, Two Routes LL1740	1,000	1995	1500.00	1650
1991 Columbus Reflecting LL1741	1,000	1994	1850.00	1995
1991 Onward! LL1742	1,000	1993	2500.00	2700-2750
1991 The Prophet LL1743	300	1997	800.00	950
1991 My Only Friend LL1744	200	1991	1400.00	1700-1900
1991 Dawn LL1745	200	1993	1200.00	2550-2637
1991 Champion LL1746	300	1994	1800.00	1950
1991 Nesting Doves LL1747	300	1994	800.00	875
1991 Comforting News LL1748	300	1997	1200.00	1345
1991 Baggy Pants LL1749	300	1994	1500.00	1650
1991 Circus Show LL1750	300	1994	1400.00	1525
1991 Maggie LL1751	300	1994	900.00	990
1991 Apple Seller LL1752	300	1994	900.00	1000-1075
1991 The Student LL1753	300		1300.00	1425
1991 Tree Climbers LL1754	300	1994	1500.00	1650
1991 The Princess And The Unicorn LL1755	1,500	1994	1750.00	1950-2795
1991 Outing In Seville LL1756	500		23000.00	24500
1992 Hawaiian Ceremony LL1757	1,000		9800.00	10250
1992 Circus Time LL1758	2,500		9200.00	9650
1992 Tea In The Garden LL1759	2,000		9500.00	9750
1993 Paella Valenciano w/base LL1762	500		10000.00	10000
1993 Trusting Friends w/base LL1763	350		1200.00	1200
1993 He's My Brother w/base LL1764	350		1500.00	1500
1993 The Course of Adventure LL1765	250		1625.00	1625
1993 Ties That Bind LL1766	250		1700.00	1700
1993 Motherly Love LL1767	250		1330.00	1330
1993 Travellers' Respite w/base LL1768	250		1825.00	1825
1993 Fruitful Harvest LL1769	350		1300.00	1300
1993 Gypsy Dancers LL1770	250		2250.00	2500
1993 Country Doctor w/base LL1771	250		1475.00	1700
1993 Back To Back LL1772	350		1450.00	1450
1993 Mischevous Musician LL1773	350		975.00	1045
1993 A Treasured Moment w/base LL1774	350		950.00	965
1993 Oriental Garden w/base LL1775	750		22500.00	22500
1994 Conquered by Love w/base LL1776	2,500		2850.00	2950
1994 Farewell Of The Samurai w/base LL1777	2,500		3950.00	3950
1994 Pegasus w/base LL1778	1,500		1950.00	1950
1994 High Speed w/base LL1779	1,500	1998	3830.00	3830
1994 Indian Princess w/base LL1780	3,000		1630.00	1630
1994 Allegory of Time LL1781	5,000		1290.00	1290
1994 Circus Fanfare w/base LL1783	1,500	1998	14240.00	14240
1994 Flower Wagon w/base LL1784	3,000		3290.00	3290
1994 Cinderella's Arrival w/base LL1785	1,500		25950.00	25950
1994 Floral Figure w/base LL1788	300		2198.00	2198
1994 Natural Beauty LL1795	500		650.00	650
1994 Floral Enchantment w/base LL1796	300		2990.00	2990
1995 Enchanted Outing w/base LL1797	3,000		3950.00	3950
1995 Far Away Thoughts LL1798	1,500		3600.00	3600
1995 Immaculate Virgin w/base LL1799	2,000		2250.00	2250
1995 To the Rim w/base LL1800	1,500		2475.00	2475
1995 Vision of Peace w/base LL1803	1,500		1895.00	1895
1995 Portrait of a Family w/base LL1805	2,500		1750.00	1850
1995 A Family of Love w/base LL1806	2,500		1750.00	1850
1995 A Dream of Peace w/base LL1807	2,000	1998	1160.00	1160
1996 Noah w/base LL1809	1,200		1720.00	1720
1996 Easter Fantasy w/base LL1810	1,000		3500.00	3500
1996 Moses & The Ten Commandments w/base LL1811	1,200		1860.00	1860
1996 La Menina w/base LL1812	1,000		3850.00	3850
1997 Christmas Journey LL1813	1,000		1295.00	1295
1997 Call of the Sea LL1814	500		4250.00	4250
1997 Young Beethoven LL1815	2,500		875.00	875
1997 Venetian Carnival LL1816	1,000		3400.00	3400
1997 The Burial of Christ LL1817	1,250		5300.00	5300
1997 Spring Courtship LL1818	1,500		2350.00	2350
1998 Pope John Paul II 01001825	2,500		600.00	600
1998 On The Balcony 01001826	1,000		3000.00	3000
1970 Girl with Guitar LL2016	750	1982	325.00	1800
1970 Madonna with Child LL2018	300	1974	450.00	1750
1971 Oriental Man LL2021	500	1983	500.00	1850
1971 The Three Graces LL2028	500	1976	950.00	6000
1971 Eve at Tree LL2029	600	1976	450.00	4000
1971 Oriental Horse LL2030	350	1983	1100.00	4000

YEAR ISSUE	EDITION LIMIT	YEAR RETD.	ISSUE PRICE	*QUOTE U.S.$
1971 Lyric Muse LL2031	400	1982	750.00	3000
1971 Madonna and Child LL2043	300	1974	400.00	1500
1973 Peasant Woman LL2049	750	1977	200.00	1300
1973 Passionate Dance LL2051	500	1975	375.00	4500
1977 St. Theresa LL2061	1,200	1987	387.50	1600
1977 Concerto LL2063	1,200	1988	500.00	1235
1977 Flying Partridges LL2064	1,200	1987	1750.00	4300
1987 Christopher Columbus w/base LL2176	1,000	1995	1000.00	1350
1990 Invincible w/base LL2188	300		1100.00	1250
1993 Flight of Fancy w/base LL2243	300	1995	1400.00	1400
1993 The Awakening w/base LL2244	300		1200.00	1200
1993 Inspired Voyage w/base LL2245	1,000		4800.00	4800
1993 Days of Yore w/base LL2248	1,000		1950.00	2050
1993 Holiday Glow w/base LL2249	1,500	1998	750.00	750
1993 Autumn Glow w/base LL2250	1,500	1998	750.00	750
1993 Humble Grace w/base LL2255	2,000		2150.00	2150
1983 Dawn w/base LL3000	300	1994	325.00	550
1983 Monks w/base LL3001	300	1993	1675.00	2550
1983 Waiting w/base LL3002	125	1990	1550.00	1900
1983 Indolence LL3003	150	1993	1465.00	2100
1983 Venus in the Bath LL3005	200	1991	1175.00	1450
1987 Classic Beauty w/base LL3012	500		1300.00	1900
1987 Youthful Innocence w/base LL3013	500		1300.00	2300
1987 The Nymph w/base LL3014	250		1000.00	1450
1987 Dignity w/base LL3015	150		1400.00	1900
1988 Passion w/base LL3016	750	1998	865.00	1250
1988 Muse w/base LL3017	300	1993	650.00	875
1988 Cellist w/base LL3018	300	1993	650.00	875
1988 True Affection w/base LL3019	300	1998	750.00	1100-1155
1989 Demureness w/base LL3020	300	1993	400.00	700
1990 Daydreaming w/base LL3022	500		550.00	775
1990 After The Bath w/base LL3023	300	1991	350.00	1450
1990 Discoveries w/Base LL3024	100	1994	1500.00	1750
1991 Resting Nude LL3025	200	1993	650.00	1500
1991 Unadorned Beauty LL3026	200		1700.00	1850
1994 Ebony w/base LL3027	300		1295.00	1295
1994 Modesty w/base LL3028	300		1295.00	1295
1994 Danae LL3029	300		2880.00	3100
1995 Nude Kneeling LL3030	300		975.00	975
1982 Elk LL3501	500	1987	950.00	1200
1978 Nude with Dove LL3503	1,500	1981	250.00	700-1250
1978 The Rescue LL3504	1,500	1987	2900.00	3500-5000
1978 St. Michael w/base LL3515	1,500		2200.00	4900
1980 Turtle Dove Nest w/base LL3519	1,200	1995	3600.00	6100
1980 Turtle Dove Group w/base LL3520	750		6800.00	11900
1981 Philippine Folklore LL3522	1,500	1995	1450.00	2400
1981 Nest of Eagles w/base LL3523	300	1994	6900.00	11500
1981 Drum Beats/Watusi Queen w/base LL3524	1,500	1994	1875.00	3100
1982 Togetherness LL3527	75	1987	375.00	1100
1982 Wrestling LL3528	50	1987	950.00	1125
1982 Companionship w/base LL3529	65		1000.00	1790
1982 Anxiety w/base LL3530	125	1993	1075.00	1875
1982 Victory LL3531	90	1984	1500.00	1800
1982 Plentitude LL3532	50	1984	1000.00	1375
1982 The Observer w/base LL3533	115	1993	900.00	1700
1982 In the Distance LL3534	75	1986	525.00	1300
1982 Slave LL3535	50	1986	950.00	1200
1982 Relaxation LL3536	100	1983	525.00	1100
1982 Dreaming w/base LL3537	250	1993	475.00	1475
1982 Youth LL3538	250	1988	525.00	1000
1982 Dantiness LL3539	100	1983	1000.00	1400
1982 Pose LL3540	100	1986	1250.00	1450
1982 Tranquility LL3541	75	1983	1000.00	1400
1982 Yoga LL3542	125	1991	650.00	1000
1982 Demure LL3543	100	1986	1250.00	1700
1982 Reflections w/base LL3544	75		650.00	1050
1982 Adoration LL3545	150	1990	1050.00	1600
1982 African Woman LL3546	50	1983	1300.00	3500
1982 Reclining Nude LL3547	75	1983	650.00	975
1982 Serenity w/base LL3548	300	1993	925.00	925-1550
1982 Reposing LL3549	300	1986	425.00	575
1982 Boxer w/base LL3550	300	1993	850.00	1450
1982 Bather LL3551	300	1988	975.00	1300
1982 Blue God LL3552	1,500	1994	900.00	1575
1982 Fire Bird LL3553	1,500	1994	800.00	1350
1982 Desert People w/base LL3555	750		1680.00	3100
1982 Road to Mandalay LL3556	750	1989	1390.00	2100
1982 Jesus in Tiberias w/base LL3557	1,200		2600.00	5250
1982 The Reader LL3560	200		2650.00	2815
1993 Trail Boss LL3561M	1,500		2450.00	2595
1993 Indian Brave LL3562M	1,500		2250.00	2250
1994 Saint James The Apostle w/base LL3563	1,000		950.00	950
1994 Gentle Moment w/base LL3564	1,000		1795.00	1835
1994 At Peace w/base LL3565	1,000		1650.00	1750
1994 Indian Chief w/base LL3566	3,000		1095.00	1095
1994 Trapper w/base LL3567	3,000		950.00	950
1994 American Cowboy w/base LL3568	3,000		950.00	950
1994 A Moment's Pause w/base LL3569	3,500		1495.00	1635
1994 Ethereal Music w/base LL3570	1,000		2450.00	2500
1994 At The Helm w/base LL3571	3,500		1495.00	1495
1995 Proud Warrior w/base LL3572	3,000		995.00	995
1995 Golgotha w/base LL3773	1, 000		1650.00	1650
1996 Playing the Blues w/base LL3576	1,000		2160.00	2160
1997 Man of the Sea LL3577	1,000		1850.00	1850
1997 The Journey LL3700	500		700.00	700
1997 In Concert LL3701	350		1050.00	1050
1997 Pensive Journey LL3702	500		700.00	700
1997 Imagination LL3703	500		750.00	750
1985 Napoleon Bonaparte LL5338	5,000	1994	275.00	650
1985 Beethoven w/base LL5339	3,000	1993	760.00	1300

YEAR ISSUE	EDITION LIMIT	YEAR RETD.	ISSUE PRICE	*QUOTE U.S.$
1985 Thoroughbred Horse w/base LL5340	1,000	1993	625.00	1000
1985 I Have Found Thee, Dulcinea LL5341	750	1990	1460.00	3000
1985 Pack of Hunting Dogs w/base LL5342	3,000	1994	925.00	1200-2000
1985 Love Boat w/base LL5343	3,000	1997	825.00	1350
1986 Fox Hunt w/base LL5362	1,000		5200.00	8750
1986 Rey De Copas w/base LL5366	2,000	1993	325.00	600
1986 Rey De Oros w/base LL5367	2,000	1993	325.00	600
1986 Rey De Espadas w/base LL5368	2,000	1993	325.00	600
1986 Rey De Bastos w/base LL5369	2,000	1993	325.00	600
1986 Pastoral Scene w/base LL5386	750	1995	1100.00	2290
1987 Inspiration LL5413	500	1993	1200.00	2100
1987 Carnival Time w/base LL5423	1,000	1993	2400.00	3900
1989 "Pious" LL5541	1,000	1991	1075.00	1560-1700
1989 Freedom LL5602	1,500	1989	875.00	1100-1300
1990 A Ride In The Park LL5718	1,000	1994	3200.00	4500-4700
1991 Youth LL5800	500	1993	650.00	725
1991 Charm LL5801	500	1994	650.00	725
1991 New World Medallion LL5808	5,000	1994	200.00	225
1992 Sorrowful Mother LL5849	1,500		1750.00	925-1850
1992 Justice Eagle LL5863	1,500		1700.00	1840
1992 Maternal Joy LL5864	1,500	1998	1600.00	1700
1992 Motoring In Style LL5884	1,500	1998	3700.00	3850
1992 The Way Of The Cross LL5890	2,000		975.00	1050
1992 Presenting Credentials LL5911	1,500		19500.00	20500
1992 Young Mozart LL5915	2,500	1992	500.00	1400-1625
1993 The Blessing w/base LL5942	2,000		1345.00	1345
1993 Our Lady of Rocio w/base LL5951	2,000		3500.00	3500
1993 Where to Sir w/base LL5952	1,500		5250.00	5250
1993 Discovery Mug LL5967	1,992	1994	90.00	90
1993 Graceful Moment w/base LL6033	3,000		1475.00	1475
1993 The Hand of Justice w/base LL6035	1,000	1998	1250.00	1250
1998 Goddess of Youth 01006449	2,500		1150.00	1150
1998 Melody 01006513	2,000		870.00	870
1995 Abraham Lincoln w/base LL7554	2,500		2190.00	2190
1996 Statue of Liberty w/base LL7563	2,000		1620.00	1620
1997 George Washington LL7575	2,000		1390.00	1390

Lladró - Lladró

YEAR ISSUE	EDITION LIMIT	YEAR RETD.	ISSUE PRICE	*QUOTE U.S.$
1963 Hunting Dog 308.13	Closed	N/A	N/A	2000
1966 Poodle 325.13	Closed	N/A	N/A	2300
1970 Girl with Pigtails L357.13G	Closed	N/A	N/A	1100
1969 Shepherdess with Goats L1001G	Closed	1987	67.50	550-675
1969 Shepherdess with Goats L1001M	Closed	1987	67.50	450
1969 Girl's Head L1003G	Closed	1985	150.00	675
1969 Girl's Head L1003M	Closed	1985	150.00	800
1969 Pan with Cymbals L1006	Closed	1975	45.00	400-550
1969 Pan with Pipes L1007	Closed	1975	45.00	400-700
1969 Satyrs Group L1008G	Closed	1976	N/A	750
1969 Girl With Lamb L1010G	Closed	1993	26.00	202-225
1969 Girl With Pig L1011G	Open		13.00	95
1969 Centaur Girl L1012G	Closed	1989	45.00	400-455
1969 Centaur Girl L1012M	Closed	1989	45.00	400
1969 Centaur Boy L1013G	Closed	1989	45.00	400
1969 Centaur Boy L1013M	Closed	1989	45.00	425-455
1969 Two Women with Water Jugs L1014G	Closed	1985	85.00	550
1969 Dove L1015 G	Closed	1994	21.00	150
1969 Dove L1016 G	Closed	1995	36.00	143-190
1969 Idyl L1017G	Closed	1991	115.00	750
1969 Idyl L1017M	Closed	1991	115.00	625
1969 King Gaspar L1018M	Open		345.00	1895
1969 King Melchior L1019M	Open		345.00	1850
1969 King Baltasar L1020M	Open		345.00	1850
1969 Horse Group L1021G	Open		950.00	2380
1969 Horse Group/All White L1022M	Open		465.00	2100
1969 Flute Player L1025G	Closed	1978	73.00	750
1969 Clown with Concertina L1027G	Closed	1993	95.00	800
1969 Girl w/Heart L1028G	Closed	1970	37.50	650
1969 Boy w/Bowler L1029G	Closed	1970	37.50	550
1969 Don Quixote w/Stand L1030G	Open		225.00	1450
1969 Sancho Panza L1031G	Closed	1989	65.00	585-600
1969 Old Folks L1033G	Closed	1985	140.00	1100-1400
1969 Old Folks L1033M	Closed	1985	140.00	1500
1969 Shepherdess with Dog L1034	Closed	1989	30.00	275
1969 Girl with Geese L1035G	Closed	1995	37.50	180
1969 Girl With Geese L1035M	Closed	1992	37.50	165
1969 Horseman L1037G	Closed	1970	170.00	2500
1969 Girl with Turkeys L1038G	Closed	1978	95.00	400-550
1969 Violinist and Girl L1039G	Closed	1991	120.00	1100
1969 Violinist and Girl L1039M	Closed	1991	120.00	1000
1969 Hen L1041G	Closed	1975	13.00	350
1969 Hen L1042G	Closed	1975	13.00	350
1969 Cock L1043G	Closed	1975	13.00	350
1969 Small Hippo L1045G	Closed	1970	9.50	350-400
1969 Hunters L1048	Closed	1986	115.00	1420
1969 Del Monte (Boy) L1050	Closed	1978	65.00	N/A
1969 Girl with Duck L1052G	Open		30.00	205-250
1969 Girl with Duck L1052M	Closed	1992	30.00	190
1969 Bird L1053G	Closed	1985	13.00	100
1969 Bird L1054G	Closed	1985	14.00	135
1969 Duck L1056G	Closed	1978	19.00	275
1969 Girl with Pheasant L1055G	Closed	1978	105.00	N/A
1969 Panchito L1059	Closed	1980	28.00	N/A
1969 Bull w/Head Up L1063	Closed	1975	90.00	1100
1969 Deer L1064	Closed	1986	27.50	325
1969 Fox and Cub L1065G	Closed	1985	17.50	425
1969 Basset L1066G	Closed	1981	23.50	600
1969 Old Dog L1067G	Closed	1978	40.00	625
1969 Great Dane L1068G	Closed	1989	55.00	500
1969 Afghan (sitting) L1069G	Closed	1985	36.00	625
1969 Beagle Puppy L1070G	Closed	1991	16.50	350-390
1969 Beagle Puppy L1071G	Closed	1992	16.50	275-650
1969 Beagle Puppy L1071M	Closed	1992	16.50	250

*Quotes have been rounded up to nearest dollar

FIGURINES

YEAR ISSUE	EDITION LIMIT	YEAR RETD.	ISSUE PRICE	*QUOTE U.S.$
1969 Beagle Puppy L1072G	Closed	1991	16.50	250-390
1969 Dutch Girl L1077G	Closed	1981	57.50	363-450
1969 Herald L1078G	Closed	1971	110.00	1100
1969 Boy with Lyre L1079M	Closed	1970	20.00	500
1969 Girl with Water Can L1080M	Closed	1970	20.00	500
1969 Girl With Brush L1081G	Closed	1985	14.50	300-320
1969 Girl Manicuring L1082G	Closed	1985	14.50	320
1969 Girl With Doll L1083G	Closed	1985	14.50	300-320
1969 Girl with Mother's Shoe L1084G	Closed	1985	14.50	320
1969 Musical 19th Century L1085G	Closed	1973	180.00	2500
1969 Pregonero L1086G	Closed	1975	120.00	1500
1969 Little Green-Grocer L1087G	Closed	1981	40.00	385-450
1969 Girl Seated with Flowers L1088G	Closed	1989	45.00	750
1971 Lawyer (Face) L1089G	Closed	1973	35.00	950
1971 Girl and Gazelle L1091G	Closed	1975	225.00	1200
1971 Satyr with Snail L1092G	Closed	1975	30.00	650
1971 Satyr with Frog L1093G	Closed	1975	50.00	700
1969 Beggar L1094G	Closed	1981	65.00	650-675
1971 Girl With Hens L1103G	Closed	1981	50.00	375-455
1971 Boy With Cornet 1105G	Closed	1973	30.00	350
1971 Byzantine Head L1106G	Closed	1975	105.00	950
1971 Pups in Box L1121G	Closed	1978	33.00	1750
1971 La Tarantela L1123G	Closed	1975	550.00	2250
1971 Pelusa Clown L1125G	Closed	1978	70.00	1000-1700
1971 Clown with Violin L1126G	Closed	1978	71.00	1850
1971 Puppy Love L1127G	Closed	1997	50.00	330
1971 Dog in the Basket L1128G	Closed	1985	17.50	450
1971 Faun L1131G	Closed	1972	155.00	1500
1971 Horse L1133G	Closed	1972	115.00	900
1971 Bull L1134G	Closed	1972	130.00	1500
1971 Dog and Snail L1139G	Closed	1981	40.00	850
1971 Girl with Bonnet L1147G	Closed	1985	20.00	275
1971 Girl Shampooing L1148G	Closed	1985	20.00	310
1971 Dog's Head L1149G	Closed	1981	27.50	450
1971 Elephants (3) L1150G	Open		100.00	795
1971 Elephants (2) L1151G	Open		45.00	420
1971 Dog Playing Guitar L1152G	Closed	1978	32.50	375-550
1971 Dog Playing Guitar L1153G	Closed	1978	32.50	400-550
1971 Dog Playing Bass Fiddle L1154G	Closed	1978	36.50	400-550
1971 Dog w/Microphone L1155G	Closed	1978	35.00	400-550
1971 Dog Playing Bongos L1156	Closed	1978	32.50	400-550
1971 Seated Torero L1162G	Closed	1973	35.00	700
1971 Soldier with Gun L1164G	Closed	1978	27.50	400
1971 Soldier with Flag L1165G	Closed	1978	27.50	500
1971 Soldier with Cornet L1166G	Closed	1978	27.50	500
1971 Soldier with Drum L1167G	Closed	1978	27.50	500
1971 Kissing Doves L1169G	Open		32.00	155
1971 Kissing Doves L1169M	Closed	1992	32.00	155
1971 Kissing Doves L1170G	Closed	1988	25.00	250
1971 Girl With Flowers L1172G	Closed	1993	27.00	375
1971 Girl With Domino L1175G	Closed	1981	34.00	350
1971 Girl With Dice L1176G	Closed	1981	25.00	363
1971 Girl With Ball L1177G	Closed	1981	27.50	450
1971 Girl With Accordian L1178G	Closed	1981	34.00	400
1971 Boy With Concertina L1179G	Closed	1981	34.00	375
1971 Little Girl w/Turkeys L1180G	Closed	1981	55.00	450
1971 Platero and Marcelino L1181G	Closed	1981	50.00	238-455
1971 Girl From Manchuria L1182G	Closed	1975	60.00	750
1972 Little Girl with Cat L1187G	Closed	1989	37.00	325-400
1972 Boy Meets Girl L1188G	Closed	1989	310.00	425
1972 Eskimo L1195G	Open		30.00	135
1972 Horse Resting L1203G	Closed	1981	40.00	600
1972 Attentive Bear, brown L1204G	Closed	1989	16.00	125
1972 Good Bear, brown L1205G	Closed	1989	16.00	125
1972 Bear Seated, brown L1206G	Closed	1989	16.00	125
1972 Attentive Polar Bear, white L1207G	Open		16.00	75
1972 Bear, white L1208G	Open		16.00	75
1972 Bear, white L1209G	Open		16.00	75
1972 Round Fish L1210G	Closed	1981	35.00	625
1972 Girl With Doll L1211G	Closed	1993	72.00	352-440
1972 Woman Carrying Water L1212G	Closed	1983	100.00	475
1972 Little Jug Magno L1222.3G	Closed	1979	35.00	300
1972 Young Harlequin L1229G	Open		70.00	520
1972 Young Harlequin L1229M	Closed	1991	70.00	550
1972 Friendship L1230G	Closed	1991	68.00	475
1972 Friendship L1230M	Closed	1991	68.00	350
1972 Angel with Lute L1231G	Closed	1988	60.00	425-450
1972 Angel with Clarinet L1232G	Closed	1988	60.00	425-450
1972 Angel with Flute L1233G	Closed	1988	60.00	450-475
1972 Little Jesus of Prag L1234G	Closed	1978	70.00	725
1973 Christmas Carols L1239G	Closed	1981	125.00	750
1973 Country Flirt L1241G	Closed	1980	110.00	650
1973 Lady at Dressing Table L1242G	Closed	1978	320.00	2500-3650
1973 Fluttering Nightingale L1244G	Closed	1981	44.00	375
1973 The Cart L1245G	Closed	1981	75.00	500-650
1972 Caress and Rest L1246G	Closed	1990	50.00	320
1974 Happy Harlequin L1247M	Closed	1983	220.00	1150
1974 Sweety L1248G	Closed	1990	100.00	525
1974 The Race L1249G	Closed	1988	450.00	2250
1974 Lovers from Verona L 1250G	Closed	1990	330.00	1250
1974 Pony Ride L1251G	Closed	1979	220.00	1400
1974 Shepherd's Rest L1252G	Closed	1981	100.00	500
1974 Sad Chimney Sweep L1253G	Closed	1983	180.00	1200-1250
1974 Hamlet and Yorick L1254G	Closed	1983	325.00	1250-1275
1974 Seesaw L1255G	Closed	1993	110.00	700-847
1974 Mother with Pups L1257G	Closed	1981	50.00	650
1974 Playing Poodles L1258G	Closed	1981	47.50	800
1974 Poodle L1259G	Closed	1985	27.50	488-500
1974 Dalmatian L1260G	Closed	1981	25.00	325-350
1974 Dalmatian L1261G	Closed	1981	25.00	350
1974 Dalmatian L1262G	Closed	1981	25.00	325-350
1974 Flying Duck L1263G	Open		20.00	90
1974 Flying Duck L1264G	Open		20.00	90
1974 Flying Duck L1265G	Open		20.00	90
1974 Girl with Ducks L1267G	Closed	1993	55.00	260-300
1974 Reminiscing L1270G	Closed	1988	975.00	1375
1974 Thoughts L1272G	Open		87.50	3490
1974 Lovers in the Park L1274G	Closed	1993	450.00	1365-1400
1974 Christmas Seller L1276G	Closed	1981	120.00	700
1974 Feeding Time L1277G	Closed	1994	120.00	350
1974 Feeding Time L1277M	Closed	N/A	120.00	450
1974 Devotion L1278G	Closed	1990	140.00	475
1974 The Wind L1279M	Open		250.00	830
1974 Child's Play L1280G	Closed	1983	110.00	494-700
1974 Afghan Standing L1282G	Closed	1985	45.00	500
1974 Little Gardener L1283G	Open		250.00	785
1974 "My Flowers" L1284G	Open		200.00	550
1974 "My Goodness" L1285G	Closed	1995	190.00	307-450
1974 Flower Harvest L1286G	Open		200.00	495
1974 Picking Flowers L1287G	Open		170.00	440
1974 Aggressive Duck L1288G	Closed	1995	170.00	575
1974 Good Puppy L1289G	Closed	1985	16.60	225-250
1974 Victorian Girl on Swing L1297G	Closed	1990	520.00	1850
1974 Birds Resting L1298G	Closed	1985	235.00	975
1974 Birds in Nest L1299G	Closed	1985	120.00	750
1974 Little Bird L1301G	Closed	1983	72.50	550
1974 Blue Creeper L1302G	Closed	1985	110.00	650
1974 Bird on Cactus L1303G	Closed	1983	150.00	800
1974 Valencian Lady with Flowers L1304G	Open		200.00	625
1974 "On the Farm" L1306G	Closed	1990	130.00	325-400
1974 Ducklings L1307G	Open		47.50	150
1974 Girl with Cats L1309G	Open		120.00	310
1974 Girl with Puppies in Basket L1311G	Closed	1997	120.00	276-375
1974 Exquisite Scent L1313G	Closed	1990	201.00	650
1974 Girl From Scotland L1315G	Closed	1979	450.00	2800
1976 Collie L1316G	Closed	1981	45.00	500
1976 IBIS L1319G	Open		1550.00	2625
1977 Angel with Tamborine L1320G	Closed	1985	125.00	500
1977 Angel with Lyre L1321G	Closed	1985	125.00	450-475
1977 Angel Recital L1322G	Closed	1985	125.00	475
1977 Angel with Accordian L1323G	Closed	1985	125.00	400
1977 Angel with Violin L1324G	Closed	1985	125.00	400-500
1976 The Helmsman L1325M	Closed	1988	600.00	1220
1976 Playing Cards L1327 M, numbered series	Open		3800.00	6600
1977 Chow Time L1334G	Closed	1981	135.00	625-650
1977 Dove Group L1335G	Closed	1990	950.00	1600
1977 Girl With Watering Can L1339G	Closed	1988	325.00	550
1977 Male Jockey L1341G	Closed	1979	120.00	550
1977 Wrath of Don Quixote L1343G	Closed	1990	250.00	990
1977 Derby L1344G	Closed	1985	1125.00	2500
1978 Sacristan L1345G	Closed	1979	385.00	2200-2300
1978 Under the Willow L1346G	Closed	1990	1600.00	1950-2150
1978 Mermaid on Wave L1347G	Closed	1983	425.00	1850
1978 Pearl Mermaid L1348G	Closed	1983	225.00	1850
1978 Mermaids Playing L1349G	Closed	1983	425.00	2700-3525
1978 In the Gondola L1350G, numbered series	Open		1850.00	3250
1978 Lady with Girl L1353G	Closed	1985	175.00	575-780
1978 Girl Watering L1354G	Closed	1988	485.00	635
1978 Phyllis L1356G	Closed	1993	75.00	225
1978 Shelley L1357G	Closed	1993	75.00	225
1978 Beth L1358G	Closed	1993	75.00	225
1978 Heather L1359G	Closed	1993	75.00	225
1978 Laura L1360G	Closed	1993	75.00	225-285
1978 Julia L1361G	Closed	1993	75.00	225-285
1978 Girls in the Swing L1366G	Closed	1988	825.00	1425
1978 Playful Dogs L1367	Closed	1982	160.00	710-900
1978 Spring Birds L1368G	Closed	1990	1600.00	2500
1978 Anniversary Waltz L1372G	Open		260.00	570
1978 Chestnut Seller L1373G	Closed	1981	800.00	750-900
1978 Waiting in the Park L1374G	Closed	1993	235.00	450
1978 Watering Flowers L1376G	Closed	1990	400.00	748-1150
1978 Suzy and Her Doll L1378G	Closed	1985	215.00	600-650
1978 Debbie and Her Doll L1379G	Closed	1985	215.00	800
1978 Cathy and Her Doll L1380G	Closed	1985	215.00	650
1978 Medieval Girl L1381G	Closed	1985	11.80	400-600
1978 Medieval Boy L1382G	Closed	1985	235.00	700
1978 A Rickshaw Ride L1383G	Open		1500.00	2150
1978 Quixote on Guard L1385G	Closed	1988	350.00	775
1981 St. Joseph L1386G	Open		250.00	385
1981 Mary L1387G	Open		240.00	385
1981 Baby Jesus L1388G	Open		85.00	140
1981 Donkey L1389G	Open		95.00	215
1981 Cow L1390G	Open		95.00	215
1982 Holy Mary L1394G, numbered series	Open		1000.00	1475
1982 Full of Mischief L1395G	Closed	1998	420.00	865
1982 Appreciation L1396G	Closed	1998	420.00	584-860
1982 Second Thoughts L1397G	Closed	1998	420.00	880
1982 Reverie L1398G	Closed	1998	490.00	970
1982 Dutch Girl L1399G	Closed	1988	750.00	775
1982 Valencian Boy L1400G	Closed	1988	298.00	560
1982 Butterfly Girl L1401G	Closed	1988	210.00	550-600
1982 Butterfly Girl L1402G	Closed	1988	210.00	595
1982 Butterfly Girl L1403G	Closed	1988	210.00	550
1982 Matrimony L1404G	Closed	1998	320.00	585
1982 Illusion L1413G	Open		115.00	260
1982 Fantasy L1414G	Open		115.00	260
1982 Mirage L1415G	Open		115.00	260
1982 From My Garden L1416G	Closed	1998	140.00	315
1982 Nature's Bounty L1417G	Closed	1995	160.00	400
1982 Flower Harmony L1418G	Closed	1995	130.00	400
1982 A Barrow of Blossoms L1419G	Open		390.00	675
1982 Born Free w/base L1420G	Open		1520.00	3250
1982 Mariko w/base L1421G	Closed	1995	860.00	1300-1750
1982 Miss Valencia L1422G	Closed	1998	175.00	415
1982 King Melchior L1423G	Open		225.00	440
1982 King Gaspar L1424G	Open		265.00	475
1982 King Balthasar L1425G	Open		315.00	585
1982 Male Tennis Player L1426M	Closed	1988	200.00	400
1982 Female Tennis Player L1427M	Closed	1988	200.00	400
1982 Afternoon Tea L1428G	Open		115.00	300
1982 Afternoon Tea L1428M	Open		115.00	300
1982 Winter Wonderland w/base L1429G	Open		1025.00	2125
1982 High Society L1430G	Closed	1993	305.00	485-750
1982 The Debutante L1431G	Open		115.00	300
1982 The Debutante L1431M	Open		115.00	300
1983 Vows L1434G	Closed	1991	600.00	425
1983 Blue Moon L1435G	Closed	1988	98.00	355
1983 Moon Glow L1436G	Closed	1988	98.00	405
1983 Moon Light L1437G	Closed	1988	98.00	575
1983 Full Moon L1438G	Closed	1988	115.00	675
1983 "How Do You Do!" L1439G	Open		185.00	295
1983 Pleasantries L1440G	Closed	1991	960.00	1700-1750
1983 A Litter of Love L1441G	Open		385.00	645
1983 Kitty Confrontation L1442G	Open		155.00	285
1983 Bearly Love L1443G	Open		55.00	135
1983 Purr-Fect L1444G	Open		350.00	615
1983 Springtime in Japan L1445G	Open		965.00	1800
1983 "Here Comes the Bride" L1446G	Closed	1998	518.00	995
1983 Michiko L1447G	Open		235.00	460
1983 Yuki L1448G	Closed	1998	285.00	550
1983 Mayumi L1449G	Closed	1998	235.00	525
1983 Kiyoko L1450G	Open		235.00	550
1983 Teruko L1451G	Open		235.00	550
1983 On the Town L1452G	Closed	1993	220.00	475
1983 Golfing Couple L1453G	Open		248.00	530
1983 Flowers of the Season L1454G	Open		1460.00	2550
1983 Reflections of Hamlet L1455G	Closed	1988	1000.00	1650
1983 Cranes w/base L1456G	Open		1000.00	1950
1985 A Boy and His Pony L1460G	Closed	1988	285.00	800
1985 Carefree Angel with Flute L1463G	Closed	1988	220.00	650
1985 Carefree Angel with Lyre L1464G	Closed	1988	220.00	650-675
1985 Girl on Carousel Horse L1469G	Open		470.00	945
1985 Boy on Carousel Horse L1470G	Open		470.00	945
1985 Wishing On A Star L1475G	Closed	1988	130.00	400-520
1985 Star Light Star Bright L1476G	Closed	1988	130.00	350-400
1985 Star Gazing L1477G	Closed	1988	130.00	350-400
1985 Hawaiian Dancer/Aloha! L1478G	Open		230.00	440
1985 In a Tropical Garden L1479G	Closed	1995	230.00	440-475
1985 Aroma of the Islands L1480G	Open		260.00	480
1985 Sunning L1481G	Closed	1988	145.00	575
1985 Eve L1482	Closed	1988	145.00	700
1985 Free As a Butterfly L1483G	Closed	1988	145.00	550
1986 Lady of the East w/base L1488G	Closed	1993	625.00	1100-1250
1986 Valencian Children L1489G	Open		700.00	1225
1986 My Wedding Day L1494G	Closed	1998	800.00	1495-1550
1986 A Lady of Taste L1495G	Open		575.00	1495
1986 Don Quixote & The Windmill L1497G	Closed	1997	1100.00	2050-2100
1986 Tahitian Dancing Girls L1498G	Closed	1995	750.00	1500-1600
1986 Blessed Family L1499G	Open		200.00	395
1986 Ragamuffin L1500G	Closed	1991	125.00	400
1986 Ragamuffin L1500M	Closed	1991	125.00	300
1986 Rag Doll L1501G	Closed	1991	125.00	300
1986 Rag Doll L1501M	Closed	1991	125.00	300
1986 Forgotten L1502G	Closed	1991	125.00	300
1986 Forgotten L1502M	Closed	1991	125.00	300
1986 Neglected L1503G	Closed	1991	125.00	425
1986 Neglected L1503M	Closed	1991	125.00	325
1986 The Reception L1504G	Closed	1990	625.00	1040-1100
1986 Nature Boy L1505G	Closed	1991	100.00	300
1986 Nature Boy L1505M	Closed	1991	100.00	300
1986 A New Friend L1506G	Closed	1991	110.00	350
1986 A New Friend L1506M	Closed	1991	110.00	275
1986 Boy & His Bunny L1507G	Closed	1991	90.00	275
1986 Boy & His Bunny L1507M	Closed	1991	90.00	160-275
1986 In the Meadow L1508G	Closed	1991	100.00	325
1986 In the Meadow L1508M	Closed	1991	100.00	195-310
1986 Spring Flowers L1509G	Closed	1991	100.00	310
1986 Spring Flowers L1509M	Closed	1991	100.00	295
1987 Cafe De Paris L1511G	Closed	1995	1900.00	2950
1987 Hawaiian Beauty L1512G	Closed	1990	575.00	850-1200
1987 A Flower for My Lady L1513G	Closed	1990	1150.00	1750
1987 Gaspar 's Page L1514G	Closed	1990	275.00	500-550
1987 Melchior's Page L1515G	Closed	1990	290.00	550-650
1987 Balthasar's Page L1516G	Closed	1990	275.00	850
1987 Circus Train L1517G	Closed	1994	2900.00	4350
1987 Valencian Garden L1518G	Closed	1991	1100.00	1795
1987 Stroll in the Park L1519G	Closed	1998	1600.00	2600
1987 The Landau Carriage L1521G	Closed	1998	2500.00	3850
1987 I am Don Quixote! L1522G	Open		2600.00	3950
1987 Valencian Bouquet L1524G	Closed	1991	250.00	400
1987 Valencian Dreams L1525G	Closed	1991	240.00	400
1987 Valencian Flowers L1526G	Closed	1991	375.00	550
1987 Tenderness L1527G	Open		260.00	430
1987 I Love You Truly L1528G	Open		375.00	595
1987 Momi L1529G	Closed	1990	275.00	500-600
1987 Leilani L1530G	Closed	1990	275.00	500-600
1987 Malia L1531G	Closed	1990	275.00	500
1987 Lehua L1532G	Closed	1990	275.00	550-600
1987 Not So Fast! L1533G	Closed	1997	175.00	214-285
1988 Little Sister L1534G	Open		180.00	240
1988 Sweet Dreams L1535G	Open		150.00	240

*Quotes have been rounded up to nearest dollar

YEAR ISSUE	EDITION LIMIT	YEAR RETD.	ISSUE PRICE	*QUOTE U.S.$
1988 Stepping Out L1537G	Open		230.00	325
1988 Pink Ballet Slippers L1540	Closed	1991	275.00	500
1988 White Ballet Slippers L1540.3	Closed	1991	275.00	395
1987 Light Blue Spoon L1548G	Closed	1991	70.00	150
1987 Dark Blue Spoon L1548.1	Closed	1991	70.00	150
1987 White Spoon L1548.3	Closed	1991	70.00	150
1987 Flower Basket L1552	Closed	1991	115.00	280
1987 Small Pink Broad Brimmed Hat L1563.3M	Closed	1991	45.00	125
1987 Wild Stallions w/base L1566G	Closed	1993	1100.00	1465
1987 Running Free w/base L1567G	Open		1500.00	1600
1987 Grand Dame L1568G	Open		290.00	470
1989 Fluttering Crane L1598G	Closed	1998	115.00	123-145
1989 Nesting Crane L1599G	Closed	1998	95.00	98-115
1989 Landing Crane L1600G	Closed	1998	115.00	145
1989 Rock Nymph L1601G	Closed	1995	665.00	825-950
1989 Spring Nymph L1602G	Closed	1995	665.00	825-950
1989 Latest Addition L1606G	Open		385.00	480
1989 Flight Into Egypt w/base L1610G	Open		885.00	1150
1989 Courting Cranes L1611G	Open		565.00	695
1989 Preening Crane L1612G	Open		385.00	485
1989 Bowing Crane L1613G	Open		385.00	485
1989 Dancing Crane L1614G	Open		385.00	485
1989 Snow Queen Mask No.11 L1645G	Closed	1991	390.00	450
1989 Medieval Cross No.4 L1652G	Closed	1991	250.00	350
1989 Lavender Lady L1667M	Closed	1991	385.00	550
1989 Lacy Butterfly #1 L1673M	Closed	1991	95.00	200
1989 Beautiful Butterfly #2 L1674M	Closed	1991	100.00	195
1989 Black Butterfly #3 L1675M	Closed	1991	120.00	195
1989 Pink & White Butterfly #4 L1676M	Closed	1991	100.00	195
1989 Black & White Butterfly #5 L1677M	Closed	1991	100.00	195
1989 Large Pink Butterfly #6 L1678M	Closed	1991	100.00	175
1989 Pink & Blue Butterfly #7 L1679M	Closed	1991	80.00	150
1989 Small Pink Butterfly #8 L1680M	Closed	1991	72.50	125
1989 Blue Butterfly #9 L1681M	Closed	1991	185.00	275
1989 Pretty Butterfly #10 L1682M	Closed	1991	185.00	275
1989 Spotted Butterfly #11 L1683M	Closed	1991	175.00	260
1989 Leopard Butterfly #12 L1684M	Closed	1991	165.00	250
1989 Great Butterfly #13 L1685M	Closed	1991	150.00	225
1989 Queen Butterfly #14 L1686M	Closed	1991	125.00	200
1988 Cellist L1700M	Closed	1993	1200.00	1813
1988 Saxophone Player L1701M	Closed	1993	835.00	1840
1988 Boy at the Fair (Decorated) L1708M	Closed	1993	650.00	650
1988 Exodus L1709M	Closed	1993	875.00	875
1988 School Boy L1710M	Closed	1993	750.00	750
1988 School Girl L1711M	Closed	1993	950.00	950
1988 Nanny L1714M	Closed	1993	575.00	700
1988 On Our Way Home (decorated) L1715M	Closed	1993	2000.00	2000
1988 Harlequin with Puppy L1716M	Closed	1993	825.00	1000
1988 Harlequin with Dove L1717M	Closed	1993	900.00	1000
1988 Dress Rehearsal L1718M	Closed	1993	1150.00	1150
1989 Back From the Fair L1719M	Closed	1993	1825.00	1825
1990 Sprite w/base L1720G, numbered series	Open		1200.00	1400
1990 Leprechaun w/base L1721G, numbered series	Open		1200.00	1400
1989 Group Discussion L1722M	Closed	1993	1500.00	1500
1989 Hopeful Group L1723M	Closed	1993	1825.00	1825
1989 Belle Epoque L1724M	Closed	1993	700.00	700
1989 Young Lady with Parasol L1725M	Closed	1993	950.00	950
1989 Young Lady with Fan L1726M	Closed	1993	750.00	750
1989 Pose L1727M	Closed	1993	725.00	725
1991 Nativity L1730M	Closed	1997	725.00	725
1970 Monkey L2000M	Closed	1975	35.00	500
1970 Cat L2001G	Closed	1975	27.50	625
1970 Gothic King L2002G	Closed	1975	25.00	450
1970 Gothic Queen L2003G	Closed	1975	25.00	450
1970 Shepherdess Sleeping L2005M	Closed	1981	100.00	710
1970 Water Carrier Girl Lamp L2006M	Closed	1975	30.00	600
1970 Mounted Harlequin L2012M	Closed	1981	200	2200
1971 Girl with Dog L2013M	Closed	1975	300.00	2350
1971 Little Eagle Owl L2020M	Closed	1985	15.00	425-618
1971 Boy/Girl Eskimo L2038.3M	Closed	1994	100.00	450
1971 Aida L2039M	Closed	1979	65.00	1200
1974 Setter's Head L2045M	Closed	1981	42.50	550
1974 Magistrates L2052M	Closed	1981	135.00	950
1974 Oriental L2056M	Open		35.00	105
1974 Oriental L2057M	Open		30.00	100
1974 Thailandia L2058M	Open		650.00	1885
1974 Muskateer L2059M	Closed	1981	900.00	2000-3000
1977 Monk L2060M	Open		60.00	145
1977 Day Dream L2062M	Closed	1985	400.00	1300
1977 Chinese Farmer w/Staff L2065M	Closed	1985	340.00	1800
1977 Dogs-Bust L2067M	Closed	1979	280.00	800
1977 Thai Dancers L2069M	Open		300.00	745
1977 A New Hairdo L2070M	Open		1060.00	1525
1977 Graceful Duo L2073M	Closed	1994	775.00	1650
1977 Nuns L2075M	Open		90.00	250
1978 Lonely L2076M	Open		72.50	185
1978 Rain in Spain L2077M	Closed	1990	190.00	475-550
1978 Lola L2078M	Closed	1981	250.00	650
1978 Woman L2080M	Closed	1985	625.00	625
1978 Fisherwoman L2081M	Closed	1985	550.00	1450
1978 Carmen L2083M	Closed	1981	275.00	625
1978 Don Quixote Dreaming L2084M	Closed	1985	550.00	2100
1978 The Little Kiss L2086M	Closed	1985	180.00	500
1978 Girl in Rocking Chair L2089	Closed	1981	235.00	600
1978 Saint Francis L2090	Closed	1981	565.00	N/A
1978 Holy Virgin L2092M	Closed	1981	200.00	N/A
1978 Girl Waiting L2093M	Closed	1995	90.00	125-185
1978 Tenderness L2094M	Open		100.00	205
1978 Duck Pulling Pigtail L2095M	Closed	1998	110.00	275-295
1978 Nosy Puppy L2096M	Closed	1993	190.00	278-400
1978 Laundress and Water Carrier L2109M	Closed	1983	325.00	600
1978 Charity L2112M	Closed	1981	360.00	1200
1980 My Little Duckling L2113M	Closed	1993	240.00	295
1980 Kissing Father L2114M	Closed	1981	575.00	575
1980 Mother's Kiss L2115M	Closed	1981	575.00	700
1980 The Whaler L2121M	Closed	1988	820.00	1050
1981 Lost in Thought L2125M	Closed	1990	210.00	300
1983 Indian Chief L2127M	Closed	1988	525.00	750
1983 Venus L2128M	Open		650.00	1330
1983 Waiting for Sailor L2129M	Closed	1985	325.00	600
1983 Egyptian Cat L2130M	Closed	1985	75.00	450
1983 Mother & Son L2131M, numbered series	Closed	1998	850.00	1550
1983 Spring Sheperdess L2132M	Closed	1985	450.00	1250
1983 Autumn Sheperdess L2133M	Closed	1985	285.00	1250
1984 Nautical Watch L2134M	Closed	1988	450.00	800
1984 Mystical Joseph L2135M	Closed	1988	428.00	750
1984 The King L2136M	Closed	1988	570.00	710
1984 Fairy Ballerina L2137M	Closed	1988	500.00	1250
1984 Friar Juniper L2138M	Closed	1993	160.00	400
1984 Aztec Indian L2139M	Closed	1988	553.00	600
1984 Pepita wth Sombrero L2140M	Open		97.50	200
1984 Pedro with Jug L2141M	Open		100.00	205
1984 Sea Harvest L2142M	Closed	1990	535.00	725
1984 Aztec Dancer L2143M	Closed	1988	463.00	650
1984 Leticia L2144M	Closed	1995	100.00	225
1984 Gabriela L2145M	Closed	1994	100.00	250
1984 Desiree L2146M	Closed	1995	100.00	225
1984 Alida L2147M	Closed	1994	100.00	250
1984 Head of Congolese Woman L2148M	Closed	1988	55.00	500-700
1984 Young Madonna L2149M	Closed	1988	400.00	675
1985 A Tribute to Peace w/base L2150M	Open		470.00	930
1985 A Bird on Hand L2151M	Open		118.00	255
1985 Chinese Girl L2152M	Closed	1990	90.00	275
1985 Chinese Boy L2153	Closed	1990	90.00	275
1985 Hawaiian Flower Vendor L2154M	Open		245.00	460
1985 Arctic inter L2156M	Open		75.00	145
1985 Eskimo Girl with Cold Feet L2157M	Open		140.00	285
1985 Pensive Eskimo Girl L2158M	Open		100.00	210
1985 Pensive Eskimo Boy L2159M	Open		100.00	210
1985 Flower Vendor L2160M	Closed	1995	110.00	215
1985 Fruit Vendor L2161M	Closed	1994	120.00	230
1985 Fish Vendor L2162M	Closed	1994	110.00	205
1987 Mountain Shepherd L2163M	Open		120.00	210
1987 My Lost Lamb L2164M	Open		100.00	175
1987 Chiquita L2165M	Closed	1993	100.00	170
1987 Paco L2166M	Closed	1993	100.00	170
1987 Fernando L2167M	Closed	1993	100.00	200
1987 Julio L2168M	Closed	1993	100.00	225
1987 Repose L2169M	Open		120.00	195
1987 Spanish Dancer L2170M	Open		190.00	345
1987 Ahoy Tere L2173M	Open		190.00	325
1987 Andean Flute Player L2174M	Closed	1990	250.00	350
1988 Harvest Helpers L2178M	Open		190.00	265
1988 Sharing the Harvest L2179M	Open		190.00	265
1988 Dreams of Peace w/base L2180M	Open		880.00	1125
1988 Bathing Nymph w/base L2181M	Open		560.00	795
1988 Daydreamer w/base L2182M	Open		560.00	795
1989 Wakeup Kitty L2183M	Closed	1993	225.00	285-325
1989 Angel and Friend L2184M	Closed	1994	150.00	185
1989 Devoted Reader L2185M	Closed	1994	125.00	160
1989 The Greatest Love L2186M	Closed	1998	235.00	320
1989 Jealous Friend L2187M	Closed	1995	275.00	365-400
1990 Mother's Pride L2189M	Open		300.00	375
1990 To The Well L2190M	Open		250.00	295
1990 Forest Born L2191M	Closed	1991	230.00	336-475
1990 King Of The Forest L2192M	Closed	1992	290.00	325
1990 Heavenly Strings L2194M	Closed	1993	170.00	250
1990 Heavenly Sounds L2195M	Closed	1993	170.00	250
1990 Heavenly Solo L2196M	Closed	1993	170.00	250
1990 Heavenly Song L2197M	Closed	1993	175.00	195-250
1990 A King is Born w/base L2198M	Open		750.00	895
1990 Devoted Friends w/base L2199M	Closed	1995	700.00	895
1990 A Big Hug! L2200M	Closed	1998	250.00	310
1990 Our Daily Bread L2201M	Closed	1994	150.00	300
1990 A Helping Hand L2202M	Closed	1993	150.00	250
1990 Afternoon Chores L2203M	Closed	1994	150.00	185-250
1990 Farmyard Grace L2204M	Closed	1993	180.00	300
1990 Prayerful Stitch L2205M	Closed	1994	160.00	250
1990 Sisterly Love L2206M	Open		300.00	375
1990 What A Day! L2207M	Open		550.00	640
1990 Let's Rest L2208M	Open		550.00	665
1991 Long Dy L2209M	Open		295.00	340
1991 Lazy Day L2210M	Open		240.00	260
1991 Patrol Leader L2212M	Closed	1993	390.00	425
1991 Nature's Friend L2213M	Closed	1993	390.00	425
1991 Seaside Angel L2214M	Open		150.00	165
1991 Friends in Flight L2215M	Open		165.00	180
1991 Laundry Day L2216M	Open		350.00	400
1991 Gentle Play L2217M	Closed	1993	380.00	425
1991 Costumed Couple L2218M	Closed	1993	680.00	750
1992 Underfoot L2219M	Open		360.00	410
1992 Free Spirit L2220M	Closed	1994	235.00	245
1992 Spring Beauty L2221M	Closed	1994	285.00	295
1992 Tender Moment L2222M	Open		400.00	450
1992 New Lamb L2223M	Open		365.00	385
1992 Cherish L2224M	Open		1750.00	1850
1992 FriendlySparrow L2225M	Open		295.00	325
1992 Boy's Best Friend L2226M	Open		390.00	410
1992 Artic Allies L2227M	Open		585.00	615
1992 Snowy Sunday L2228M	Open		550.00	625
1992 Seasonal Gifts L2229M	Open		450.00	475
1992 Mary's Child L2230M	Closed	1994	525.00	550
1992 Afternoon Verse L2231M	Open		580.00	595
1992 Poor Little Bear L2232M	Open		250.00	265
1992 Guess What I Have L2233M	Open		340.00	375
1992 Playful Push L2234M	Open		850.00	875
1993 Adoring Mother L2235M	Open		405.00	440
1993 Frosty Outing L2236M	Closed	1998	375.00	410
1993 The Old Fishing Hole L2237M	Open		625.00	640
1993 Learning Together L2238M	Closed	1998	500.00	500
1993 Valencian Courtship L2239M	Open		880.00	895
1993 Winged Love L2240M	Closed	1995	285.00	310
1993 Winged Harmony L2241M	Closed	1995	285.00	310
1993 Away to School L2242M	Open		465.00	465
1993 Lion Tamer L2246M	Closed	1995	375.00	375
1993 Just Us L2247M	Closed	1995	650.00	650
1993 Noella L2251M	Open		405.00	420
1993 Waiting For Father L2252M	Open		660.00	660
1993 Noisy Friend L2253M	Open		280.00	280
1993 Step Aside L2254M	Open		280.00	280
1994 Solitude L2256M	Open		398.00	435
1994 Constant Companions L2257M	Closed	1998	575.00	625
1994 Family Love L2258M	Open		450.00	485
1994 Little Fisherman L2259M	Open		298.00	330
1994 Artic Friends L2260M	Closed	1997	345.00	380
1994 Mother and Child L2263	Closed	1998	N/A	285
1994 Little Friskies L2266	Closed	1998	N/A	260
1994 Musical Muse L2285	Closed	1998	N/A	465
1994 Barnyard Scene L2286	Closed	1998	N/A	230-270
1994 Dressing The Baby L2289	Closed	1998	N/A	325
1994 World of Fantasy L2292	Closed	1998	N/A	335
1995 Jesus and Joseph L2294M	Open		550.00	550
1995 Peaceful Rest L2295M	Open		390.00	390
1995 Life's Small Wonders L2296M	Open		370.00	370
1995 Elephants L2297M	Open		875.00	875
1995 Hindu Children L2298M	Open		450.00	450
1995 Poetic Moment L2299M	Open		465.00	465
1995 Emperor L2300M	Open		765.00	765
1995 Empress L2301M	Open		795.00	795
1995 Twilight Years L2302M	Closed	1998	385.00	385
1995 Not So Fast L2303M	Closed	1998	350.00	350
1995 Love in Bloom L2304M	Open		420.00	420
1995 Fragrant Bouquet L2305M	Open		330.00	330
1995 Hurray Now L2306M	Open		310.00	310
1995 Happy Birthday L2307M	Closed	1998	150.00	150
1995 Let's Make Up L2308M	Open		265.00	265
1995 Windblown Girl L2309M	Open		320.00	320
1995 Chit-Chat L2310M	Open		270.00	270
1995 Good Night L2311M	Open		280.00	280
1995 Goose Trying to Eat L2312M	Closed	1998	325.00	325
1995 Who's the Fairest L2313M	Open		230.00	230
1995 Breezy Afternoon L2314M	Open		220.00	220
1995 On the Green L2315M	Open		575.00	575
1995 Closing Scene L2316M	Open		560.00	560
1995 Talk to Me L2317M	Open		175.00	175
1995 Taking Time L2318M	Open		175.00	175
1995 A Lesson Shared L2319M	Closed	1998	215.00	215
1995 Cat Nap L2320M	Open		265.00	265
1995 All Tuckered Out L2321M	Open		275.00	275
1995 Naptime L2322M	Open		275.00	275
1995 Water Girl L2323M	Open		245.00	245
1995 A Basket of Fun L2324M	Open		320.00	320
1995 Spring Splendor L2325M	Open		440.00	440
1995 Physician L2326M	Closed	1998	350.00	350
1995 Sad Sax L2327M	Open		225.00	225
1995 Circus Sam L2328M	Open		225.00	225
1995 Daily Chores L2329M	Open		345.00	345
1996 The Shepherdess L2330	Open		410.00	410
1996 Little Peasant Girl (pink) L2331	Open		155.00	155
1996 Little Peasant Girl (blue) L2332	Open		155.00	155
1996 Little Peasant Girl (white) L2333	Open		155.00	155
1996 Asian Melody L2334	Open		690.00	690
1996 Young Fisherman L2335	Open		225.00	225
1996 Young Water Girl L2336	Open		315.00	315
1996 Virgin of Montserrat w/base L2337	Open		1000.00	1000
1996 Sultan's Dream L2338	Open		700.00	700
1996 The Sultan L2339	Open		480.00	480
1996 Oriental Fantasy w/bow L2340	Open		1350.00	1350
1996 Oriental Fantasy w/brooch L2341	Open		1350.00	1350
1996 Returning From the Well w/base L2342	Open		1800.00	1800
1996 Care and Tenderness w/base L2343	Open		860.00	860
1996 Oration L2344	Open		295.00	295
1996 Bedtime Story L2345	Open		360.00	360
1996 Feeding the Ducks L2346	Open		305.00	305
1996 Meditation (blue) L2347	Open		145.00	145
1996 Prayerful Moment (blue) L2348	Open		145.00	145
1996 Sleigh Ride w/base L2349	Open		1520.00	1520
1996 Pensive Clown w/base L2350	Open		680.00	680
1996 Fishing With Gramps w/base L2351	Open		1025.00	1025
1996 Under My Spell L2352	Open		225.00	225
1996 Shot on Goal w/base L2353	Open		935.00	935
1997 Waiting For Spring L2354	Open		385.00	385
1997 Gabriela L2355	Open		740.00	740
1997 Country Joy L2356	Open		310.00	310
1997 In Search of Water L2357	Open		410.00	410
1997 I'm Sleepy L2358	Open		360.00	360
1997 First Crush L2359	Open		945.00	945
1997 Hunting Butterflies L2360	Open		465.00	465
1997 Cold Weather Companions L2361	Open		380.00	380
1997 Braving The Storm L2362	Open		470.00	470

*Quotes have been rounded up to nearest dollar

FIGURINES

YEAR ISSUE	EDITION LIMIT	YEAR RETD.	ISSUE PRICE	*QUOTE U.S.$
1997 Pampered Puppy L2363	Open		345.00	345
1997 Melodies L2364	Open		590.00	590
1997 Holy Mother L2365	Open		230.00	230
1997 Bread of Life L2366	Open		230.00	230
1997 Pensive Harlequin L2367	Open		560.00	560
1997 Colombina L2368	Open		585.00	585
1997 Early Awakening 01012369	Open		595.00	595
1998 It's Magic! 01012372	Open		1045.00	1045
1998 Spring Inspiration 01012374	Open		635.00	635
1998 Emperor 01012375	Open		695.00	695
1998 Empress 01012376	Open		735.00	735
1998 Arctic Explorer 01012379	Open		550.00	550
1998 A Comforting Friend 01012380	Open		330.00	330
1998 Island Beauty 01012382	Open		180.00	180
1998 Pacific Jewel 01012383	Open		170.00	170
1998 What About Me? 01012384	Open		790.00	790
1998 Tropical Flower 01012385	Open		190.00	190
1998 Low Tide 01012386	Open		560.00	560
1998 Karina 01012387	Open		390.00	390
1998 Ready To Go 01012388	Open		350.00	350
1998 Time To Go 01012389	Open		330.00	330
1998 Loyal Companions 01012391	Open		400.00	400
1998 My Memories 01012392	Open		345.00	345
1998 A Girl in Love 01012393	Open		465.00	465
1978 Native L3502M	Open		700.00	2450
1978 Letters to Dulcinea L3509M, numbered series	Closed	1998	875.00	2175
1978 Horse Heads L3511M	Closed	1990	260.00	650
1978 Girl With Pails L3512M	Open		140.00	285
1978 A Wintry Day L3513M	Closed	1988	525.00	1100
1978 Pensive w/ base L3514M	Open		500.00	1050
1978 Jesus Christ L3516M	Closed	1988	1050.00	1500
1978 Nude with Rose w/ base L3517M	Open		225.00	780
1980 Lady Macbeth L3518M	Closed	1981	385.00	700-1200
1981 Weary w/ base L3525M	Open		360.00	685
1980 Mother's Love L3521M	Closed	1990	1000.00	1100
1982 Contemplation w/ base L3526M	Open		265.00	590
1982 Stormy Sea w/base L3554M	Open		675.00	1445
1984 Innocence w/base/green L3558M	Closed	1991	960.00	1650
1984 Innocence w/base/red L3558.3M	Closed	1987	960.00	1200
1985 Peace Offering w/base L3559M	Open		397.00	665
1969 Marketing Day L4502G	Closed	1985	40.00	400
1969 Girl with Lamb L4505G	Open		20.00	130
1969 Boy with Kid L4506M	Closed	1985	22.50	400
1969 Boy with Lambs L4509G	Closed	1981	37.50	275
1969 Girl with Parasol and Geese L4510G	Closed	1993	40.00	300-350
1969 Nude L4511M	Closed	1985	45.00	700
1969 Nude L4512G	Closed	1985	44.00	450
1969 Diana L4514G	Closed	1981	65.00	650-750
1969 Man on Horse L4515G	Closed	1985	180.00	1100
1969 Female Equestrian L4516G	Open		170.00	745
1969 Boy Student L4517G	Closed	1978	57.50	475
1969 Flamenco Dancers L4519G	Closed	1993	150.00	1200
1970 Boy With Dog L4522M	Closed	1992	25.00	170-180
1970 Boy With Dog L4522G	Closed	1998	25.00	180
1969 Girl With Slippers L4523G	Closed	1993	17.00	125
1969 Girl With Slippers L4523M	Closed	1993	17.00	125
1969 Donkey in Love L4524G	Closed	1985	15.00	375
1969 Donkey in Love L4524M	Closed	1985	15.00	350
1969 Violinist Lamp L4527G	Closed	1985	75.00	500
1969 Ballet Lamp L4528G	Closed	1985	120.00	750-850
1969 Joseph L4533G	Open		60.00	110
1969 Joseph L4533M	Open		60.00	110
1969 Mary L4534G	Open		60.00	85
1969 Mary L4534M	Open		60.00	85
1971 Baby Jesus L4535.3G	Open		60.00	70
1969 Baby Jesus L4535.3M	Open		60.00	70
1969 Angel, Chinese L4536G	Open		45.00	92
1969 Angel, Chinese L4536M	Open		45.00	92
1969 Angel, Black L4537G	Open		13.00	92
1969 Angel, Black L4537M	Open		13.00	92
1969 Angel, Praying L4538G	Open		13.00	92
1969 Angel, Praying L4538M	Open		13.00	92
1969 Angel, Thinking L4539G	Open		13.00	92
1969 Angel, Thinking L4539M	Open		13.00	92
1969 Angel with Horn L4540G	Open		13.00	92
1969 Angel with Horn L4540M	Open		13.00	92
1969 Angel Reclining L4541G	Open		13.00	92
1969 Angel Reclining L4541M	Open		13.00	92
1969 Group of Angels L4542G	Open		31.00	200
1969 Group of Angels L4542M	Open		31.00	200
1969 Troubador L4548G	Closed	1978	67.50	750
1969 Geese Group L4549G	Closed	1997	28.50	208-245
1969 Geese Group L4549M	Closed	1992	28.50	245-275
1969 Flying Dove L4550G	Open		47.50	265
1969 Turtle Dove L4550M	Closed	1992	47.50	265
1969 Ducks, Set/3 asst. L4551-3G	Open		18.00	140
1969 Shepherd w/Girl & Lamb L4554	Closed	1972	69.00	N/A
1969 Sad Harlequin L4558G	Closed	1993	110.00	650-845
1969 Ballerina L4559G	Closed	1993	110.00	500
1970 Llama Group 4561G	Closed	1970	55.00	1600
1969 Couple with Parasol L4563G	Closed	1985	180.00	900
1969 Girl with Geese L4568G	Closed	1993	45.00	358-375
1969 Girl With Turkey L4569G	Closed	1981	28.50	375
1969 Shepherd Resting L4571G	Closed	1981	60.00	475
1969 Girl with Piglets L4572G	Closed	1985	70.00	425
1969 Girl with Piglets L4572M	Closed	1985	70.00	400
1969 Mother & Child L4575G	Closed	1998	50.00	265-295
1969 New Shepherdess L4576G	Closed	1985	37.50	315
1969 New Shepherd L4577G	Closed	1983	35.00	550
1969 Mardi Gras L4580G	Closed	1975	57.50	1800
1969 Mardi Gras L4580M	Closed	1975	57.50	1800

YEAR ISSUE	EDITION LIMIT	YEAR RETD.	ISSUE PRICE	*QUOTE U.S.$
1969 Setter L4583G	Closed	1981	21.00	600
1969 Girl with Sheep L4584G	Closed	1993	27.00	170
1969 Holy Family L4585G	Open		18.00	135
1969 Holy Family L4585M	Closed	1994	18.00	135
1969 Madonna L4586G	Closed	1979	32.50	350
1969 White Cockeral L4588G	Closed	1979	17.50	300
1969 Girl with Pitcher L4590G	Closed	1981	47.50	400
1969 Girl with Cockerel L4591G	Closed	1993	20.00	275
1969 Lady with Greyhound L4594G	Closed	1981	60.00	700-850
1969 Fairy L4595G	Closed	1994	27.50	195-245
1969 Girl With Flower L4596G	Closed	1980	25.00	275
1969 Two Horses L4597	Closed	1990	240.00	1000
1969 Doctor L4602.3G	Open		33.00	220
1969 Nurse-L4603.3G	Open		35.00	220
1969 Magic L4605	Closed	1985	160.00	1100
1969 Accordian Player L4606	Closed	1978	60.00	650
1969 Cupid L4607G	Closed	1980	15.00	800
1969 Cook in Trouble L4608	Closed	1985	27.50	650-775
1969 Nuns L4611G	Open		37.50	155
1969 Nuns L4611M	Open		37.50	155
1969 Girl Singer L4612G	Closed	1979	14.00	375-450
1969 Boy With Cymbals L4613G	Closed	1979	14.00	400
1969 Boy With Guitar L4614G	Closed	1979	19.50	400
1969 Boy with Double Bass L4615G	Closed	1979	22.50	400-553
1969 Boy With Drum L4616G	Closed	1979	16.50	350
1969 Group of Musicians L4617G	Closed	1979	33.00	500
1969 Clown L4618G	Open		70.00	415
1969 Seminarist L4619G	Closed	1972	18.50	650
1969 Policeman L4620G	Closed	1972	16.00	500
1969 Sea Captain L4621G	Closed	1993	45.00	325
1969 Sea Captain L4621M	Closed	1989	42.50	300
1969 Old Man with Violin L4622G	Closed	1982	45.00	700
1969 Velazquez Bookend L4626G	Closed	1975	90.00	950
1969 Columbus Bookend L4627G	Closed	1975	90.00	950
1969 Angel with Child L4635G	Open		15.00	120
1969 Honey Peddler L4638G	Closed	1978	60.00	575
1969 Cow With Pig L4640G	Closed	1981	42.50	750
1969 Cow With Pig L4640M	Closed	1981	42.50	750
1969 Pekinese L4641G	Closed	1985	20.00	450
1969 Dog L4642	Closed	1981	22.50	390-500
1969 Skye Terrier L4643G	Closed	1985	15.00	500
1969 Pierrot w/Mandolin L4646M	Closed	1970	60.00	1950
1969 Andalucians Group L4647G	Closed	1990	412.00	1400
1969 Valencian Couple on Horseback L4648	Closed	1990	900.00	1400
1969 Madonna Head L4649G	Open		25.00	165
1969 Madonna Head L4649M	Open		25.00	165
1969 Girl with Calla Lillies L4650G	Open		16.50	155
1969 Cellist L4651G	Closed	1978	70.00	600-750
1969 Happy Travelers L4652	Closed	1978	115.00	650
1969 Orchestra Conductor L4653G	Closed	1979	95.00	950
1969 The Grandfather L4654G	Closed	1979	75.00	1200
1969 Horses L4655G	Open		110.00	760
1969 Woodcutter L4656G	Closed	1978	80.00	600
1969 Shepherdess L4660G	Closed	1993	21.00	300
1969 Countryman L4664M	Closed	1979	50.00	500
1969 Girl with Basket L4665G	Closed	1979	50.00	450
1969 Girl with Basket L4665M	Closed	1979	50.00	550
1969 Birds L4667G	Closed	1985	25.00	250
1969 Maja Head L4668G	Closed	1985	50.00	750-787
1969 Pastoral Couple L4669G	Closed	1978	100.00	850
1969 Baby Jesus L4670BG	Open		N/A	55
1969 Mary L4671G	Open		70.00	75
1969 St. Joseph L4672G	Open		70.50	90
1969 King Melchior L4673G	Open		11.00	95
1969 King Gaspar L4674G	Open		11.00	95
1969 King Balthasar L4675G	Open		11.00	95
1969 Shepherd with Lamb L4676G	Open		14.00	110
1969 Girl with Rooster L4677G	Open		14.00	90
1969 Shepherdess with Basket L4678G	Open		13.00	90
1969 Donkey L4679G	Open		11.50	100
1969 Cow L4680G	Open		12.00	90
1970 Girl with Milkpail L4682G	Closed	1991	28.00	300-375
1970 Girl with Milkpail L4682M	Closed	1991	28.00	275
1970 Hebrew Student L4684G	Closed	1985	33.00	750-975
1970 Hebrew Student L4684M	Closed	1985	33.00	620
1970 Girl's Head w/Cap L4686G	Closed	1984	25.00	750
1970 Gothic Queen L4689	Closed	1975	20.00	700
1970 Troubadour in Love L4699	Closed	1975	60.00	1000
1970 Dressmaker L4700G	Closed	1993	45.00	488-500
1970 Mother & Child L4701G	Closed	1998	45.00	295
1970 Girl Jewelry Dish L4713G	Closed	1978	30.00	550
1970 Girl Jewelry Dish L4713M	Closed	1978	30.00	550
1970 Boy Jewelry Dish L4714G	Closed	1978	30.00	600
1970 Lady Empire L4719G	Closed	1979	150.00	990
1970 Girl With Tulips L4720G	Closed	1978	65.00	600
1970 Girl With Tulips L4720M	Closed	1978	65.00	450
1970 Hamlet L4729G	Closed	1980	85.00	800
1970 Bird Watcher L4730	Closed	1985	35.00	520
1970 German Shepherd w/Pup L4731	Closed	1975	40.00	950
1971 Small Dog L4749	Closed	1985	5.50	190
1971 Romeo and Juliet L4750G	Open		150.00	1250
1971 Boy w/Dog L4755G	Closed	1978	50.00	400
1971 Doncel With Roses L4757G	Closed	1979	35.00	500
1974 Woman L4761G	Closed	1993	60.00	400-500
1971 Dentist L4762	Closed	1978	36.00	550
1971 Dentist (Reduced) L4762.3G	Closed	1985	30.00	550
1971 Obstetrician L4763G	Closed	1973	47.50	255-450
1971 Obstetrician L4763.3G	Open		40.00	255
1971 Obstetrician L4763M	Closed	1998	47.50	255
1971 Maternal Elephant L4765G	Closed	1975	50.00	700
1971 Don Quixote Vase L4770G	Closed	1975	25.00	750

YEAR ISSUE	EDITION LIMIT	YEAR RETD.	ISSUE PRICE	*QUOTE U.S.$
1971 Don Quixote Vase L4770M	Closed	1975	25.00	750
1971 Rabbit L4772G	Open		17.50	135
1971 Rabbit L4773G	Open		17.50	130
1971 Dormouse L4774	Closed	1983	30.00	375
1971 Children, Praying L4779G	Closed	1998	36.00	210
1971 Children, Praying L4779M	Closed	1992	36.00	210-225
1971 Boy with Goat L4780	Closed	1978	80.00	300-600
1972 Girl Tennis Player L4798	Closed	1981	50.00	450
1972 Japanese Woman L4799	Closed	1975	45.00	425-500
1972 Gypsy with Brother L4800G	Closed	1979	36.00	400-425
1972 The Teacher L4801G	Closed	1978	45.00	500
1972 Fisherman L4802G	Closed	1979	70.00	550-700
1972 Woman with Umbrella L4805G	Closed	1981	100.00	800
1972 Girl with Dog L4806G	Closed	1981	80.00	500
1972 Geisha L4807G	Closed	1993	190.00	500-585
1972 Wedding L4808G	Open		50.00	190
1972 Wedding L4808M	Open		50.00	190
1972 Going Fishing L4809G	Open		33.00	160
1972 Boy w/Yacht L4810G	Open		33.00	175
1972 Boy w/Yacht L4810M	Closed	N/A	33.00	225
1972 Dutch Boy L4811	Closed	1988	30.00	400
1972 Little Girl w/Goat L4812G	Closed	1988	55.00	450
1972 Girl with Calf L4813	Closed	1981	50.00	550-650
1972 Little Girl with Turkey L4814	Closed	1981	45.00	475
1972 Girl with Goose L4815G	Closed	1991	72.00	400
1972 Girl with Goose L4815M	Closed	1991	72.00	295
1972 Little Shepherd with Goat L4817M	Closed	1981	50.00	475
1972 Burro L4821G	Closed	1979	24.00	450
1974 Peruvian Girl with Baby L4822	Closed	1981	65.00	775
1974 Legionary L4823	Closed	1978	55.00	500-625
1972 Male Golfer L4824G	Open		66.00	295
1972 Veterinarian L4825	Closed	1985	48.00	475-500
1972 Rabbit's Food L4826G	Closed	1993	40.00	300-325
1972 Rabbit's Food L4826M	Closed	1993	40.00	225
1972 Caressing Calf L4827G	Closed	1981	55.00	475
1972 Cinderella L4828G	Open		47.00	245
1975 Swan L4829G	Closed	1983	16.00	400
1972 You and Me L4830G	Closed	1979	112.50	1150
1972 Romance L4831G	Closed	1981	175.00	1350-1500
1972 Chess Set Pieces L4833.3G	Closed	1985	410	2300
1972 Girl w/Lamb L4835G	Closed	1991	42.00	350
1973 Clean Up Time L4838G	Closed	1993	36.00	225-325
1973 Clean Up Time L4838M	Closed	1992	36.00	250
1973 Oriental Flower Arranger/Girl L4840G	Closed	1998	90.00	515-600
1973 Oriental Flower Arranger/Girl L4840M	Open		90.00	515
1974 Girl from Valencia L4841G	Open		35.00	235
1973 Viola Lesson L4842G	Closed	1981	66.00	375-450
1973 Donkey Ride L4843	Closed	1981	86.00	650
1973 Pharmacist L4844G	Closed	1985	70.00	1350-1650
1973 Classic Dance L4847G	Closed	1985	80.00	600
1973 Charm L4848G	Closed	1985	45.00	350
1973 Feeding The Ducks L4849G	Closed	1995	60.00	270-700
1973 Feeding The Ducks L4849M	Closed	1992	60.00	250
1973 Aesthetic Pose L4850G	Closed	1985	110.00	650
1973 Lady Golfer L4851M	Closed	1992	70.00	500
1973 Gardner in Trouble L4852	Closed	1981	65.00	550
1974 Cobbler L4853G	Closed	1985	100.00	550-600
1973 Don Quixote L4854G	Open		40.00	205
1973 Death of the Swan L4855G	Open		45.00	330
1983 Death of the Swan, white L4855.3	Closed	1987	110.00	250
1974 Waltz Time L4856G	Closed	1985	65.00	450
1974 Dog L4857G	Closed	1979	40.00	550
1974 Pleasant Encounter L4858M	Closed	1981	60.00	450
1974 Peddler L4859G	Closed	1985	180.00	750
1974 Dutch Girl L4860G	Closed	1985	45.00	363-425
1974 Horse L4861	Closed	1978	55.00	500
1974 Horse L4862	Closed	1978	55.00	500
1974 Horse L4863	Closed	1978	55.00	400
1974 Mother L4864G	Closed	1979	190.00	1100
1974 Embroiderer L4865G	Closed	1994	115.00	725
1974 Girl with Goose and Dog L4866G	Closed	1993	26.00	205
1974 Seesaw L4867G	Closed	1997	55.00	375-650
1974 Girl with Candle L4868G	Open		13.00	90
1974 Girl with Candle L4868M	Closed	1992	13.00	80
1974 Boy Kissing L4869G	Closed	1998	13.00	77-90
1974 Boy Kissing L4869M	Closed	1992	13.00	180
1974 Boy Yawning L4870G	Open		13.00	90
1974 Boy Yawning L4870M	Closed	1992	13.00	180
1974 Girl with Guitar L4871G	Open		13.00	90
1974 Girl with Guitar L4871M	Closed	1992	13.00	90
1974 Girl Stretching L4872G	Open		13.00	90
1974 Girl Stretching L4872M	Closed	1992	13.00	90
1974 Girl Kissing L4873G	Closed	1998	13.00	90
1974 Girl Kissing L4873M	Closed	1992	13.00	90
1974 Boy & Girl L4874G	Closed	1998	25.00	150
1974 Boy & Girl L4874M	Closed	1992	25.00	150
1974 The Jug Carrier L4875G	Closed	1985	40.00	300
1974 Boy Thinking L4876G	Closed	1993	20.00	170
1974 Boy Thinking L4876M	Closed	1992	20.00	120
1974 Boy with Flute L4877G	Closed	1981	60.00	450
1974 Aranjuez Little Lady L4879G	Closed	1997	48.00	325
1974 Carnival Couple L4882G	Closed	1995	60.00	300
1974 Carnival Couple L4882M	Closed	1991	60.00	375
1974 Lady w/ Young Harlequin L4883G	Closed	1975	100.00	2350
1974 Seraph's Head No.1 L4884	Closed	1985	10.00	150
1974 Seraph's Head No.2 L4885	Closed	1985	10.00	150
1974 Seraph's Head No.3 L4886	Closed	1985	10.00	150
1974 The Kiss L4888G	Closed	1983	150.00	700
1974 Spanish Policeman L4889G	Open		55.00	310
1974 Watching the Pigs L4892G	Closed	1978	160.00	1250

*Quotes ha[illegible]een rounded up to nearest dollar

YEAR ISSUE	EDITION LIMIT	YEAR RETD.	ISSUE PRICE	*QUOTE U.S.$
1976 "My Dog" L4893G	Open		85.00	235
1974 Tennis Player Boy L4894	Closed	1980	75.00	500
1974 Ducks L4895G	Open		45.00	95
1974 Ducks L4895M	Closed	1992	45.00	95
1974 Boy with Snails L4896G	Closed	1979	50.00	400
1974 Mechanic L4897G	Closed	1985	45.00	325
1974 Boy From Madrid L4898G	Closed	1998	55.00	150
1974 Boy From Madrid L4898M	Closed	1992	55.00	150
1974 Boy with Smoking Jacket L4900	Closed	1983	45.00	200
1974 Vagabond Dog L4901G	Closed	1979	25.00	300
1974 Moping Dog L4902G	Closed	1979	35.00	375
1974 Santa Claus L4904G	Closed	1978	100.00	1150
1974 Admiration/Florinda L4907G	Closed	1985	165.00	650
1974 Barrister L4908G	Closed	1985	100.00	400-595
1974 Girl With Dove L4909G	Closed	1982	70.00	450
1974 Girl With Lantern L4910G	Closed	1990	85.00	320-375
1974 Shepherd L4911G	Closed	1979	175.00	750
1974 Young Lady in Trouble L4912G	Closed	1985	110.00	450-520
1974 Lesson in the Country L4913G	Closed	1978	240.00	1250
1975 Lady with Shawl L4914G	Open		220.00	484
1975 Girl with Pigeons L4915	Closed	1990	110.00	352-400
1976 Chinese Noblewoman L4916G	Closed	1978	300.00	2000-2145
1974 Dog and Butterfly L4917G	Closed	1981	50.00	850
1974 A Girl at the Pond L4918G	Closed	1985	85.00	425
1976 Gypsy Woman L4919G	Closed	1981	165.00	1400-1820
1974 Country Lass with Dog L4920G	Closed	1995	185.00	520
1974 Country Lass with Dog L4920M	Closed	1992	185.00	495
1974 Chinese Nobleman L4921G	Closed	1978	325.00	2000-2405
1974 Windblown Girl L4922G	Open		150.00	375
1974 Lanquid Clown L4924G	Closed	1983	200.00	1500
1974 Milk For the Lamb L4926G	Closed	1980	185.00	1300
1974 Medieval Lady L4928G	Closed	1980	275.00	410
1974 Sisters L4930	Closed	1981	250.00	625
1974 Children with Fruits L4931G	Closed	1981	210.00	500
1974 Dainty Lady L4934G	Closed	1985	60.00	500
1974 "Closing Scene" L4935G	Closed	1997	180.00	520-546
1983 "Closing Scene"/white L4935.3M	Closed	1987	213.00	275
1974 Spring Breeze L4936G	Open		145.00	410
1976 Golden Wedding L4937M	Closed	1981	285.00	600
1976 Baby's Outing L4938G	Open		250.00	775
1976 Milk Maid L4939G	Closed	1981	70.00	371-400
1977 Missy L4951M	Closed	1985	300.00	850
1977 Meditation L4952M	Closed	1979	200.00	N/A
1977 Tavern Drinkers L4956G	Closed	1985	1125.00	3500
1977 Attentive Dogs L4957G	Closed	1981	350.00	1750
1977 Cherub, Puzzled L4959G	Open		40.00	125
1977 Cherub, Smiling L4960G	Open		40.00	125
1977 Cherub, Dreaming L4961G	Open		40.00	125
1977 Cherub, Wondering L4962G	Open		40.00	125
1977 Cherub, Wondering L4962M	Closed	1992	40.00	100-125
1977 Infantile Candour L4963G	Closed	1979	285.00	1250
1977 Little Red Riding Hood L4965G	Closed	1983	210.00	575
1977 Tennis Player Puppet L4966G	Closed	1985	60.00	250-800
1977 Soccer Puppet L4967G	Closed	1985	65.00	425
1977 Oympic Puppet L4968	Closed	1983	65.00	800
1977 Sheriff Puppet L4969G	Closed	1985	85.00	650-780
1977 Skier Puppet L4970G	Closed	1983	85.00	500-900
1977 Hunter Puppet L4971G	Closed	1985	95.00	968
1977 Girl with Calla Lillies sitting L4972G	Closed	1998	65.00	190
1977 Choir Lesson L4973G	Closed	1981	350.00	1500
1977 Dutch Children L4974G	Closed	1981	375.00	1150
1977 Augustina of Aragon L4976G	Closed	1979	475.00	1500-1800
1977 Harlequin Serenade L4977	Closed	1979	185.00	1250
1977 Milkmaid with Wheelbarrow L4979G	Closed	1981	220.00	950
1977 Ironing Time L4981G	Closed	1985	80.00	375
1978 Naughty Dog L4982G	Closed	1995	130.00	275-350
1978 Gossip L4984G	Closed	1985	260.00	1000
1978 Mimi L4985G	Closed	1980	110.00	650
1978 Attentive Lady L4986G	Closed	1981	635.00	2200
1978 Oriental Spring L4988G	Closed	1997	125.00	325-350
1978 Sayonara L4989G	Closed	1997	125.00	218-300
1978 Chrysanthemum L4990G	Open		125.00	310
1978 Butterfly L4991G	Open		125.00	295
1978 Dancers Resting L4992G	Closed	1983	350.00	850
1978 Gypsy Venders L4993G	Closed	1985	165.00	475
1978 Ready to Go L4996G	Closed	1981	425.00	1500-1700
1978 Don Quixote & Sancho L4998G	Closed	1983	875.00	2900
1978 Reading L5000G	Open		150.00	275
1978 Elk Family L5001G	Closed	1981	550.00	850
1978 Sunny Day L5003G	Closed	1993	193.00	425
1978 Eloise L5005G	Closed	1978	175.00	555
1978 Naughty L5006G	Open		55.00	155
1978 Bashful L5007G	Closed	1998	55.00	155
1978 Static-Girl w/Straw Hat L5008G	Open		55.00	155
1978 Curious-Girl w/Straw Hat L5009G	Open		55.00	155
1978 Prissy L5010G	Closed	1998	55.00	155
1978 Trying on a Straw Hat L5011G	Open		55.00	155
1978 Daughters L5013G	Closed	1991	425.00	900
1978 Genteel L5014G	Closed	1981	725.00	2300
1978 Painful Monkey L5018	Closed	1981	135.00	850
1978 Painful Giraffe L5019	Closed	1981	115.00	850
1978 Painful Elephant L5020	Closed	1981	85.00	800-900
1978 Painful Bear L5021	Closed	1981	75.00	800
1978 Painful Lion L5022G	Closed	1981	95.00	800
1978 Painful Kangaroo L5023G	Closed	1981	150.00	950
1978 Woman With Scarf L5024G	Closed	1985	141.00	726
1980 A Clean Sweep L5025G	Closed	1985	100.00	450
1980 Planning the Day L5026G	Closed	1985	90.00	275
1979 Flower Curtsy L5027G	Open		230.00	470
1980 Flowers in Pot L5028G	Closed	1985	325.00	575
1980 The Flower Peddler L5029G	Closed	1985	675.00	1350

YEAR ISSUE	EDITION LIMIT	YEAR RETD.	ISSUE PRICE	*QUOTE U.S.$
1980 Wildflower L5030G	Closed	1994	360.00	514-850
1979 Little Friskies L5032G	Closed	1998	108.00	220
1980 Avoiding the Goose L5033G	Closed	1993	160.00	605
1980 Goose Trying To Eat L5034G	Closed	1997	135.00	315-350
1980 Act II w/base L5035G	Open		700.00	1425
1979 Jockey with Lass L5036G	Open		950.00	2400
1980 Sleighride w/base L5037G	Closed	1997	585.00	1300
1979 Girl Bowing L5038G	Closed	1981	185.00	750
1980 Candid L5039G	Closed	1981	145.00	400
1979 Girl Walking L5040G	Closed	1981	150.00	400-1105
1980 Tulips in my Basket L5041G	Closed	1981	160.00	850
1980 Friends L5042G	Closed	1983	385.00	1000
1980 Hind and Baby Deer L5043G	Closed	1981	650.00	2600
1980 Girl with Toy Wagon L5044G	Closed	1998	115.00	221-260
1980 Belinda with Doll L5045G	Closed	1995	115.00	215
1980 Organ Grinder L5046G	Closed	1981	328.00	1650
1980 Teacher Woman L5048G	Closed	1981	115.00	625
1980 Dancer L5050G	Open		85.00	205
1980 Samson and Delilah L5051G	Closed	1981	350.00	1600
1980 At the Circus L5052G	Closed	1985	525.00	1250
1980 Festival Time L5053G	Closed	1985	250.00	375
1980 Little Senorita L5054G	Closed	1985	235.00	600
1980 Apprentice Seaman L5055G	Closed	1985	140.00	450
1980 Boy Clown with Clock L5056G	Closed	1985	290.00	850
1980 Clown with Violin L5057G	Closed	1985	270.00	850
1980 Clown with Concertina L5058G	Closed	1985	290.00	600
1980 Clown with Saxaphone L5059G	Closed	1985	320.00	700
1980 Clown with Trumpet L5060G	Closed	1985	290.00	550
1980 March Wind L5061G	Closed	1983	370.00	600
1980 Kristina L5062G	Closed	1985	225.00	400
1980 Margaretta/Dutch Girl With Braids L5063G	Closed	1985	265.00	450
1980 Gretel/Dutch Girl, Hands Akimbo L5064G	Closed	1990	255.00	425
1980 Ingrid L5065G	Closed	1990	370.00	650-726
1980 Ilsa L5066G	Closed	1990	275.00	400
1981 Halloween L5067G	Closed	1983	450.00	1400-1500
1980 Fairy Queen L5068G	Closed	1983	625.00	1600
1980 Napping L5070G	Closed	1983	240.00	850
1980 Nostalgia L5071G	Closed	1993	185.00	350-520
1980 Courtship L5072	Closed	1990	327.00	660-750
1980 Country Flowers L5073	Closed	1985	315.00	750
1980 My Hungry Brood L5074G	Closed	1998	295.00	415
1980 Little Harlequin "A" L5075G	Closed	1985	217.50	415
1980 Little Harlequin "B" L5076G	Closed	1985	185.00	415
1980 Little Harlequin "C" L5077G	Closed	1985	185.00	500
1980 Teasing the Dog L5078G	Closed	1985	300.00	600
1980 Woman Painting Vase L5079G	Closed	1985	300.00	750
1980 Boy Pottery Seller L5080G	Closed	1985	320.00	600-780
1980 Girl Pottery Seller L5081G	Closed	1985	300.00	600-650
1980 Little Flower Seller L5082G	Closed	1985	750.00	2850
1980 Dutch Mother L5083G	Closed	1983	485.00	1100
1980 A Good Book L5084G	Closed	1985	175.00	525
1980 Mother Amabilis L5086G	Closed	1983	275.00	550
1980 Roses for My Mom L5088G	Closed	1988	645.00	1150-1250
1980 Scare-Dy Cat/Playful Cat L5091G	Open		65.00	95
1980 After the Dance L5092G	Closed	1983	165.00	350-475
1980 A Dancing Partner L5093G	Closed	1983	165.00	400-500
1980 Ballet First Step L5094G	Closed	1983	165.00	363-400
1980 Ballet Bowing L5095G	Closed	1983	165.00	300-400
1989 Her Ladyship, L5097G	Closed	1991	5900.00	6700
1980 Successful Hunt L5098	Closed	1993	5200.00	5200
1982 Playful Tot L5099G	Closed	1985	58.00	275
1982 Cry Baby L5100G	Closed	1985	58.00	300
1982 Learning to Crawl L5101G	Closed	1985	58.00	300
1982 Teething L5102G	Closed	1985	58.00	300
1982 Time for a Nap L5103G	Closed	1985	58.00	275
1982 Little Ballet Girl L5105G	Closed	1985	85.00	350
1982 Natalia L5106G	Closed	1985	85.00	350
1982 Little Ballet Girl L5108G	Closed	1985	85.00	400
1982 Little Ballet Girl L5109G	Closed	1985	85.00	400
1982 Dog Sniffing L5110G	Closed	1985	50.00	625
1982 Timid Dog L5111G	Closed	1985	44.00	600
1982 Play with Me L5112G	Open		40.00	80
1982 Feed Me L5113G	Open		40.00	80
1982 Pet Me L5114G	Open		40.00	80
1982 Little Boy Bullfighter L5115G	Closed	1985	123.00	400
1982 A Victory L5116G	Closed	1985	123.00	500
1982 Proud Matador L5117G	Closed	1985	123.00	500
1982 Girl in Green Dress L5118G	Closed	1985	170.00	650
1982 Girl in Bluish Dress L5119G	Closed	1985	170.00	675
1982 Girl in Pink Dress L5120G	Closed	1985	170.00	650
1982 August Moon L5122G	Closed	1993	185.00	350
1982 My Precious Bundle L5123G	Open		150.00	245
1982 Dutch Couple with Tulips L5124G	Closed	1985	310.00	950-1150
1982 Amparo L5125G	Closed	1990	130.00	350
1982 Sewing A Trousseau L5126G	Closed	1990	185.00	425-600
1982 Marcelina L5127G	Closed	1985	255.00	275
1982 Lost Love L5128G	Closed	1988	400.00	700
1982 Jester w/base L5129G	Open		220.00	455
1982 Pensive Clown w/base L5130G	Open		250.00	475
1982 Cervantes L5132G	Closed	1988	925.00	1200
1982 Trophy with Base L5133G	Closed	1983	250.00	650
1982 Girl Soccer Player L5134G	Closed	1983	140.00	600
1982 Billy Football Player L5135G	Closed	1983	140.00	600
1982 Billy Skier L5136G	Closed	1983	140.00	800
1982 Billy Baseball Player L5137G	Closed	1983	140.00	700
1982 Billy Golfer L5138G	Closed	1983	140.00	1000
1982 A New Doll House L5139G	Closed	1983	185.00	850
1982 Feed Her Son L5140G	Closed	1991	170.00	300
1982 Balloons for Sale L5141G	Closed	1997	145.00	295
1982 Comforting Daughter L5142G	Closed	1991	195.00	375

YEAR ISSUE	EDITION LIMIT	YEAR RETD.	ISSUE PRICE	*QUOTE U.S.$
1982 Scooting L5143G	Closed	1988	575.00	1950
1982 Amy L5145G	Closed	1985	110.00	1500
1982 "E" is for Ellen L5146G	Closed	1985	110.00	1250
1982 Ivez L5147G	Closed	1985	100.00	600
1982 Olivia L5148G	Closed	1985	100.00	400
1982 Ursula L5149G	Closed	1985	100.00	400
1982 Girl's Head L5150G	Closed	1983	435.00	1300
1982 Girl's Head L5151G	Closed	1983	380.00	1400
1982 Girl's Head L5152G	Closed	1983	535.00	2000
1982 Girl's Head L5153G	Closed	1983	475.00	1350
1982 First Prize L5154G	Closed	1985	90.00	300
1982 Monks at Prayer L5155M	Open		130.00	275
1982 Susan and the Doves L5156G	Closed	1991	203.00	375
1982 Bongo Beat L5157G	Open		135.00	230
1982 A Step In Time L5158G	Open		90.00	200
1982 Harmony L5159G	Open		270.00	495
1982 Rhumba L5160G	Open		113.00	185
1982 Cycling To A Picnic L5161G	Closed	1985	2000.00	2800
1982 Mouse Girl/Mindy L5162G	Closed	1985	125.00	272-500
1982 Bunny Girl/Bunny L5163G	Closed	1985	125.00	442-450
1982 Cat Girl/Kitty L5164G	Closed	1985	125.00	450-510
1982 Sancho with Bottle L5165	Closed	1990	100.00	475
1982 Sea Fever L5166M	Closed	1993	130.00	260-306
1982 Sea Fever L5166G	Closed	1993	130.00	350
1982 Jesus L5167G	Open		130.00	265
1982 King Solomon L5168G	Closed	1985	205.00	950
1982 Abraham L5169G	Closed	1985	155.00	750
1982 Moses L5170G	Open		175.00	410
1982 Madonna with Flowers L5171G	Open		173.00	310
1982 Fish A'Plenty L5172G	Closed	1994	190.00	425
1982 Pondering L5173G	Closed	1993	300.00	700
1982 Roaring 20's L5174G	Closed	1993	173.00	425-650
1982 Flapper L5175G	Closed	1995	185.00	450
1982 Rhapsody in Blue L5176G	Closed	1985	325.00	1850
1982 Dante L5177G	Closed	1983	263.00	750
1982 Stubborn Mule L5178G	Closed	1993	250.00	500
1983 Three Pink Roses w/base L5179M	Closed	1990	70.00	300
1983 Dahlia L5180M	Closed	1990	65.00	150-250
1983 Japanese Camelia w/base L5181M	Closed	1990	60.00	100
1983 White Peony L5182M	Closed	1990	85.00	150
1983 Two Yellow Roses L5183M	Closed	1990	57.50	100
1983 White Carnation L5184M	Closed	1990	65.00	100
1983 Lactiflora Peony L5185M	Closed	1990	65.00	100
1983 Begonia L5186M	Closed	1990	67.50	100
1983 Rhododendrom L5187M	Closed	1990	67.50	190
1983 Miniature Begonia L5188M	Closed	1990	80.00	130
1983 Chrysanthemum L5189M	Closed	1990	100.00	150
1983 California Poppy L5190M	Closed	1990	97.50	190
1985 Predicting the Future L5191G	Closed	1985	135.00	450
1984 Lolita L5192G	Open		80.00	165
1984 Juanita L5193G	Open		80.00	165
1984 Roving Photographer L5194G	Closed	1985	145.00	1450
1983 Say "Cheese!" L5195G	Closed	1990	170.00	500-520
1983 "Maestro, Music Please!" L5196G	Closed	1988	135.00	575
1983 Female Physician L5197	Open		120.00	275
1984 Boy Graduate L5198G	Open		160.00	290
1984 Girl Graduate L5199G	Open		160.00	285
1984 Male Soccer Player L5200G	Closed	1988	155.00	500
1984 Special Male Soccer Player L5200.3G	Closed	1988	150.00	525
1983 Josefa Feeding Duck L5201G	Closed	1991	125.00	350
1983 Aracely with Ducks L5202G	Closed	1991	125.00	350
1984 Little Jester L5203G	Closed	1993	75.00	350
1984 Little Jester L5203M	Closed	1992	75.00	300
1983 Sharpening the Cutlery L5204	Closed	1988	210.00	975
1983 Lamplighter L5205G	Open		170.00	425
1983 Yachtsman L5206G	Closed	1994	110.00	210
1983 A Tall Yarn L5207G	Open		260.00	545
1983 Professor L5208G	Closed	1990	205.00	600-650
1983 School Marm L5209G	Closed	1990	205.00	800-950
1984 Jolie L5210G	Open		105.00	235
1984 Angela L5211G	Open		105.00	235
1984 Evita L5212G	Open		105.00	195
1984 Lawyer L5213G	Closed	1998	250.00	620
1984 Architect L5214G	Closed	1990	140.00	500
1984 Fishing with Gramps w/base L5215G	Open		410.00	895
1984 On the Lake L5216G	Closed	1988	660.00	1100
1984 Spring L5217G	Open		90.00	200
1984 Spring L5217M	Open		90.00	200
1984 Autumn L5218G	Open		90.00	200
1984 Autumn L5218M	Open		90.00	200
1984 Summer L5219G	Open		90.00	185
1984 Summer L5219M	Open		90.00	185
1984 Winter L5220G	Open		90.00	195
1984 Winter L5220M	Open		90.00	195
1984 Sweet Scent L5221G	Open		80.00	165
1984 Sweet Scent L5221M	Open		80.00	165
1984 Pretty Pickings L5222G	Open		80.00	165
1984 Pretty Pickings L5222M	Open		80.00	165
1984 Spring is Here L5223G	Open		80.00	165
1984 Spring is Here L5223M	Open		80.00	165
1984 The Quest L5224G	Open		125.00	310
1984 Male Candleholder L5226	Closed	1985	660.00	1200
1984 Playful Piglets L5228G	Open		80.00	165
1984 Storytime L5229G	Closed	1990	245.00	1100
1984 Graceful Swan L5230G	Open		35.00	95
1984 Swan with Wings Spread L5231G	Open		50.00	135
1984 Playful Kittens L5232G	Open		130.00	300
1984 Charlie the Tramp L5233G	Closed	1991	150.00	950
1984 Artistic Endeavor L5234G	Closed	1988	225.00	650
1984 Ballet Trio L5235G	Open		785.00	1675

*Quotes have been rounded up to nearest dollar

FIGURINES

YEAR ISSUE	EDITION LIMIT	YEAR RETD.	ISSUE PRICE	*QUOTE U.S.$
1984 Cat and Mouse L5236G	Open		55.00	98
1984 Cat and Mouse L5236M	Closed	1992	55.00	98
1984 School Chums L5237G	Closed	1997	225.00	485-500
1984 Eskimo Boy with Pet L5238G	Open		55.00	115
1984 Eskimo Boy with Pet L5238M	Closed	1992	55.00	95
1984 Wine Taster L5239G	Open		190.00	425
1984 Lady from Majorca L5240G	Closed	1990	120.00	395-488
1984 Best Wishes L5244G	Closed	1986	185.00	225-330
1984 A Thought for Today L5245	Closed	1986	180.00	250
1984 St. Cristobal L5246	Closed	1988	265.00	650
1984 Penguin L5247G	Closed	1988	70.00	200-250
1984 Penguin L5248G	Closed	1988	70.00	200-250
1984 Penguin L5249G	Closed	1988	70.00	200
1984 Exam Day L5250G	Closed	1994	115.00	225-260
1984 Torch Bearer L5251G	Closed	1988	100.00	500
1984 Dancing the Polka L5252G	Closed	1994	205.00	550
1984 Cadet L5253G	Closed	1984	150.00	650-700
1984 Making Paella L5254G	Closed	1993	215.00	575
1984 Spanish Soldier L5255G	Closed	1988	185.00	475-575
1984 Folk Dancing L5256G	Closed	1990	205.00	525
1984 Vase L5257.30	Closed	1988	55.00	200
1984 Vase L5258.30	Closed	1988	55.00	175
1984 Vase L5261.30	Closed	1988	70.00	150
1984 Vase L5262.30	Closed	1988	70.00	150
1984 Centerpiece-Decorated L5265M	Closed	1990	50.00	175
1985 Bust of Lady from Elche L5269M	Closed	1988	432.00	750
1985 Racing Motor Cyclist L5270G	Closed	1988	360.00	850
1985 Gazelle L5271G	Closed	1988	205.00	550
1985 Biking in the Country L5272G	Closed	1990	295.00	850
1985 Civil Guard at Attention L5273G	Closed	1988	170.00	520
1985 Wedding Day L5274G	Open		240.00	435
1985 Weary Ballerina L5275G	Closed	1995	175.00	310
1985 Weary Ballerina L5275M	Closed	1992	175.00	310
1985 Sailor Serenades His Girl L5276G	Closed	1988	315.00	950
1985 Pierrot with Puppy L5277G	Open		95.00	160
1985 Pierrot with Puppy and Ball L5278G	Open		95.00	160
1985 Pierrot with Concertina L5279G	Open		95.00	160
1985 Hiker L5280G	Closed	1988	195.00	425
1985 Nativity Scene "Haute Relief" L5281M	Closed	1988	210.00	450
1985 Over the Threshold L5282G	Open		150.00	290
1985 Socialite of the Twenties L5283G	Open		175.00	345
1985 Glorious Spring L5284G	Open		355.00	720
1985 Summer on the Farm L5285G	Open		235.00	455
1985 Fall Clean-up L5286G	Open		295.00	565
1985 Winter Frost L5287G	Open		270.00	520
1985 Mallard Duck L5288G	Closed	1994	310.00	525
1985 Little Leaguer Exercising L5289	Closed	1990	150.00	450
1985 Little Leaguer, Catcher L5290	Closed	1990	150.00	450-550
1985 Little Leaguer on Bench L5291	Closed	1990	150.00	450
1985 Love in Bloom L5292G	Open		225.00	435
1985 Mother and Child and Lamb L5299G	Closed	1988	180.00	750
1985 Medieval Courtship L5300G	Closed	1990	735.00	800
1985 Waiting to Tee Off L5301G	Open		145.00	295
1985 Antelope Drinking L5302	Closed	1988	215.00	550
1985 Playing with Ducks at the Pond L5303G	Closed	1990	425.00	875
1985 Children at Play L5304	Closed	1990	220.00	550
1985 A Visit with Granny L5305G	Closed	1993	275.00	600
1985 Young Street Musicians L5306G	Closed	1988	300.00	1650
1985 Mini Kitten L5307G	Closed	1993	35.00	100-150
1985 Mini Cat L5308G	Closed	1993	35.00	100-120
1985 Mini Cocker Spaniel Pup L5309G	Closed	1993	35.00	125
1985 Mini Cocker Spaniel L5310G	Closed	1993	35.00	125-150
1985 Mini Puppies L5311G	Closed	1990	65.00	225
1985 Mini Bison Resting L5312G	Closed	1990	50.00	150
1985 Mini Bison Attacking L5313G	Closed	1990	57.50	225
1985 Mini Deer L5314G	Closed	1990	40.00	175
1985 Mini Dromedary L5315G	Closed	1990	45.00	150
1985 Mini Giraffe L5316G	Closed	1990	50.00	225
1985 Mini Lamb L5317G	Closed	1990	30.00	200
1985 Mini Seal Family L5318G	Closed	1990	77.50	215-250
1985 Wistful Centaur Girl L5319G	Closed	1990	157.00	450
1985 Demure Centaur Girl L5320	Closed	1990	157.00	252-425
1985 Parisian Lady L5321G	Closed	1995	193.00	325
1985 Viennese Lady L5322G	Closed	1994	160.00	295
1985 Milanese Lady L5323G	Closed	1994	180.00	400
1985 English Lady L5324G	Closed	1994	225.00	475
1985 Ice Cream Vendor L5325G	Closed	1995	380.00	750
1985 The Tailor L5326G	Closed	1988	335.00	1300
1985 Nippon Lady L5327G	Open		325.00	595
1985 Lady Equestrian L5328G	Closed	1988	160.00	475
1985 Gentleman Equestrian L5329G	Closed	1988	160.00	425-525
1985 Concert Violinist L5330G	Closed	1988	220.00	400
1985 Gymnast with Ring L5331	Closed	1988	95.00	395
1985 Gymnast Balancing Ball L5332	Closed	1988	95.00	375
1985 Gymnast Exercising with Ball L5333G	Closed	1988	95.00	285-350
1985 Aerobics Push-Up L5334G	Closed	1988	110.00	295
1985 Aerobics Floor Exercies L5335G	Closed	1988	110.00	300
1985 "La Giaconda" L5337G	Closed	1988	110.00	400-500
1986 A Stitch in Time L5344G	Closed	1998	425.00	810-850
1986 A New Hat L5345G	Closed	1990	200.00	375
1986 Nature Girl L5346G	Closed	1988	450.00	775
1986 Bedtime L5347G	Open		300.00	545
1986 On The Scent L5348G	Closed	1990	47.50	300
1986 Relaxing L5349G	Closed	1990	47.50	200
1986 On Guard L5350G	Closed	1990	50.00	300
1986 Woe is Me L5351G	Closed	1990	45.00	200
1986 Hindu Children L5352G	Open		250.00	445
1986 Eskimo Riders L5353G	Open		150.00	270
1986 Eskimo Riders L5353M	Open		150.00	160
1986 A Ride in the Country L5354G	Closed	1993	225.00	425-488
1986 Consideration L5355M	Closed	1988	100.00	250
1986 Wolf Hound L5356G	Closed	1990	45.00	250
1986 Oration L5357G	Open		170.00	300
1986 Little Sculptor L5358G	Closed	1990	160.00	400
1986 El Greco L5359G	Closed	1990	300.00	650
1986 Sewing Circle L5360G	Closed	1990	600.00	1400
1986 Try This One L5361G	Closed	1998	225.00	385
1986 Still Life L5363G	Closed	1998	180.00	425-475
1986 Litter of Fun L5364G	Open		275.00	465
1986 Sunday in the Park L5365G	Closed	1997	375.00	625
1986 Can Can L5370G	Closed	1990	700.00	1400
1986 Family Roots L5371G	Open		575.00	935
1986 Lolita L5372G	Closed	1993	120.00	250
1986 Carmencita L5373G	Closed	1993	120.00	250
1986 Pepita L5374G	Closed	1993	120.00	250
1986 Teresita L5375G	Closed	1993	120.00	250
1986 This One's Mine L5376G	Closed	1995	300.00	300-520
1986 A Touch of Class L5377G	Open		475.00	795
1986 Time for Reflection L5378G	Open		425.00	745
1986 Children's Games L5379G	Closed	1991	325.00	585-750
1986 Sweet Harvest L5380G	Closed	1990	450.00	850-875
1986 Serenade L5381	Closed	1990	450.00	650
1986 Lovers Serenade L5382G	Closed	1990	350.00	850
1986 Petite Maiden L5383	Closed	1990	110.00	400
1986 Petite Pair L5384	Closed	1990	225.00	425
1986 Scarecrow & the Lady L5385G	Closed	1997	350.00	680
1986 St. Vincent L5387	Closed	1990	190.00	400
1986 Sidewalk Serenade L5388G	Closed	1988	750.00	1300
1986 Deep in Thought L5389G	Closed	1990	170.00	303-450
1986 Spanish Dancer L5390G	Closed	1990	170.00	350-450
1986 A Time to Rest L5391G	Closed	1990	170.00	375-442
1986 Balancing Act L5392G	Closed	1990	35.00	119-200
1986 Curiosity L5393G	Closed	1990	25.00	150
1986 Poor Puppy L5394G	Closed	1990	25.00	250
1986 Valencian Boy L5395G	Closed	1991	200.00	400
1986 The Puppet Painter L5396G	Open		500.00	850
1986 The Poet L5397G	Closed	1988	425.00	900
1986 At the Ball L5398G	Closed	1991	375.00	750-910
1987 Time To Rest L5399G	Closed	1993	175.00	295
1987 Time To Rest L5399M	Closed	1991	175.00	350
1987 The Wanderer L5400G	Open		150.00	245
1987 My Best Friend L5401G	Open		150.00	240
1987 Desert Tour L5402G	Closed	1990	950.00	1250
1987 The Drummer Boy L5403G	Closed	1990	225.00	400
1987 Cadet Captain L5404G	Closed	1990	175.00	360
1987 The Flag Bearer L5405G	Closed	1990	200.00	450
1987 The Bugler L5406G	Closed	1990	175.00	375
1987 At Attention L5407G	Closed	1990	175.00	325
1987 Sunday Stroll L5408G	Closed	1990	250.00	600
1987 Courting Time L5409	Closed	1990	425.00	550
1987 Pilar L5410G	Closed	1990	200.00	400
1987 Teresa L5411G	Closed	1990	225.00	375-430
1987 Isabel L5412G	Closed	1990	225.00	450
1987 Mexican Dancers L5415G	Open		800.00	1195
1987 In the Garden L5416G	Closed	1997	200.00	350
1987 Artist's Model L5417	Closed	1990	425.00	475
1987 Short Eared Owl L5418G	Closed	1990	200.00	250-280
1987 Great Gray Owl L5419G	Closed	1990	190.00	200-230
1987 Horned Owl L5420G	Closed	1990	150.00	230
1987 Barn Owl L5421G	Closed	1990	120.00	185
1987 Hawk Owl L5422G	Closed	1990	120.00	250
1987 Intermezzo L5424	Closed	1990	325.00	550
1987 Studying in the Park L5425G	Closed	1991	675.00	950
1987 Studying in the Park L5425M	Closed	1989	675.00	600
1987 One, Two, Three L5426G	Closed	1995	240.00	395
1987 Saint Nicholas L5427G	Closed	1991	425.00	700
1987 Feeding the Pigeons L5428	Closed	1990	490.00	700
1987 Happy Birthday L5429G	Open		100.00	155
1987 Music Time L5430G	Closed	1990	500.00	700
1987 Midwife L5431G	Closed	1990	175.00	650
1987 Midwife L5431M	Closed	1990	175.00	525
1987 Monkey L5432G	Closed	1990	60.00	200
1987 Kangaroo L5433G	Closed	1990	65.00	300
1987 Miniature Polar Bear L5434G	Open		65.00	115
1987 Cougar L5435G	Closed	1990	65.00	275
1987 Lion L5436G	Closed	1990	50.00	300
1987 Rhino L5437G	Closed	1990	50.00	175
1987 Elephant L5438G	Closed	1990	50.00	250
1987 The Bride L5439G	Closed	1995	250.00	488-553
1987 Poetry of Love L5442G	Open		500.00	875
1987 Sleepy Trio L5443G	Closed	1997	190.00	305
1987 Will You Marry Me? L5447G	Closed	1994	750.00	1250
1987 Naptime L5448G	Open		135.00	260
1987 Naptime L5448M	Open		135.00	260
1987 Goodnight L5449	Open		225.00	375
1987 I Hope She Does L5450G	Closed	1998	190.00	276-345
1988 Study Buddies L5451G	Open		225.00	295
1988 Masquerade Ball L5452G	Closed	1993	220.00	545
1988 Masquerade Ball L5452M	Closed	1992	220.00	350
1988 For You L5453G	Open		450.00	640
1988 For Me? L5454G	Closed	1998	290.00	395
1988 Bashful Bather L5455G	Open		150.00	190
1988 Bashful Bather L5455M	Closed	1992	150.00	180
1988 New Playmates L5456G	Open		160.00	245
1988 New Playmates L5456M	Closed	1992	160.00	190
1988 Bedtime Story L5457G	Open		275.00	355
1988 Bedtime Story L5457M	Closed	1992	275.00	330
1988 A Barrow of Fun L5460G	Open		370.00	575
1988 A Barrow of Fun L5460M	Closed	1992	370.00	450
1988 Koala Love L5461G	Closed	1993	115.00	300-320
1988 Practice Makes Perfect L5462G	Open		375.00	545
1988 Look At Me! L5465G	Open		375.00	545
1988 Look At Me! L5465M	Closed	1992	375.00	455
1988 "Chit-Chat" L5466G	Open		150.00	210
1988 "Chit-Chat" L5466M	Closed	1992	150.00	200
1988 May Flowers L5467G	Open		160.00	235
1988 May Flowers L5467M	Closed	1992	160.00	200
1988 "Who's The Fairest?" L5468G	Open		150.00	205
1988 "Who's The Fairest?" L5468M	Closed	1992	150.00	200
1988 Lambkins L5469G	Closed	1993	150.00	250
1988 Lambkins L5469M	Closed	1989	150.00	200
1988 Tea Time L5470G	Closed	1998	280.00	410
1988 Sad Sax L5471G	Open		175.00	205
1988 Circus Sam L5472G	Open		175.00	205
1988 How You've Grown! L5474G	Closed	1998	180.00	270
1988 How You've Grown! L5474M	Closed	1992	180.00	250
1988 A Lesson Shared L5475G	Closed	1998	150.00	190-215
1988 A Lesson Shared L5475M	Closed	1992	150.00	190
1988 St. Joseph L5476G	Open		210.00	270
1988 Mary L5477G	Open		130.00	165
1988 Baby Jesus L5478G	Open		55.00	75
1988 King Melchior L5479G	Open		210.00	265
1988 King Gaspar L5480G	Open		210.00	265
1988 King Balthasar L5481G	Open		210.00	265
1988 Ox L5482G	Open		125.00	175
1988 Donkey L5483G	Open		125.00	175
1988 Lost Lamb L5484G	Open		100.00	140
1988 Shepherd Boy L5485G	Open		140.00	205
1988 Debutantes L5486G	Closed	1998	490.00	528-695
1988 Debutantes L5486M	Closed	1992	490.00	655
1988 Ingenue L5487G	Open		110.00	145
1988 Ingenue L5487M	Closed	1992	110.00	150-185
1988 Sandcastles L5488G	Closed	1993	160.00	300
1988 Sandcastles L5488M	Closed	1992	160.00	200
1988 Justice L5489G	Closed	1993	675.00	950
1988 Flor Maria L5490G	Open		500.00	635
1988 Heavenly Strings L5491G	Closed	1993	140.00	250
1988 Heavenly Cellist L5492G	Closed	1993	240.00	350
1988 Angel with Lute L5493G	Closed	1993	140.00	150-175
1988 Angel with Clarinet L5494G	Closed	1993	140.00	175-250
1988 Angelic Choir L5495G	Closed	1993	300.00	550-575
1988 Recital L5496G	Open		190.00	285
1988 Dress Rehearsal L5497G	Open		290.00	420
1988 Opening Night L5498G	Open		190.00	285
1988 Pretty Ballerina L5499G	Open		190.00	285
1988 Prayerful Moment (blue) L5500G	Open		90.00	110
1988 Time to Sew (blue) L5501G	Open		90.00	110
1988 Time to Sew (white) L5501.3	Closed	1991	90.00	250
1988 Meditation (blue) L5502G	Open		90.00	110
1988 Hurry Now L5503G	Open		180.00	270
1988 Hurry Now L5503M	Closed	1992	180.00	250
1988 Silver Vase No. 20 L5531.4	Closed	1991	135.00	300
1989 Flowers for Sale L5537G	Open		1200.00	1550
1989 Puppy Dog Tails L5539G	Open		1200.00	1675
1989 An Evening Out L5540G	Closed	1991	350.00	650
1989 Melancholy w/base L5542G	Open		375.00	455
1989 "Hello, Flowers" L5543G	Closed	1993	385.00	545-845
1989 Reaching the Goal L5546G	Closed	1998	215.00	275-300
1989 Only the Beginning L5547G	Closed	1997	215.00	275
1989 Pretty Posies L5548G	Closed	1994	425.00	530-575
1989 My New Pet L5549G	Open		150.00	185
1989 Serene Moment (blue) L5550G	Closed	1993	115.00	275
1989 Serene Moment (white) L5550.3G	Closed	1991	115.00	250
1989 Serene Moment (white) L5550.3M	Closed	1991	115.00	250
1989 Call to Prayer (blue) L5551G	Closed	1993	100.00	275
1989 Call to Prayer (white) L5551.3G	Closed	1991	100.00	250
1989 Call to Prayer (white) L5551.3M	Closed	1991	100.00	250
1989 Morning Chores (blue) L5552G	Closed	1993	115.00	250
1989 Morning Chores (white) L5552G	Closed	1991	115.00	250
1989 Wild Goose Chase L5553G	Closed	1998	175.00	230
1989 Pretty and Prim L5554G	Open		215.00	270
1989 "Let's Make Up" L5555G	Open		215.00	265
1989 Wide Tulip Vase L5560G	Closed	1990	110.00	300
1989 Green Clover Vase L5561G	Closed	1991	130.00	225
1989 Sad Parting L5583G	Closed	1991	375.00	525
1989 Daddy's Girl/Father's Day L5584G	Closed	1997	315.00	425-450
1989 Fine Melody w/base L5585G	Closed	1993	225.00	325
1989 Sad Note w/base L5586G	Closed	1993	185.00	225
1989 Wedding Cake L5587G	Closed	1997	595.00	750-795
1989 Blustery Day L5588G	Closed	1993	185.00	275-325
1989 Pretty Pose L5589G	Closed	1993	185.00	230-260
1989 Spring Breeze L5590G	Closed	1993	185.00	260-275
1989 Garden Treasures L5591G	Closed	1993	185.00	195-260
1989 Male Siamese Dancer L5592G	Closed	1993	345.00	480-525
1989 Siamese Dancer L5593G	Closed	1993	345.00	420
1989 Playful Romp L5594G	Closed	1997	215.00	270
1989 Joy in a Basket L5595G	Closed	1998	215.00	230-270
1989 A Gift of Love L5596G	Open		400.00	495
1989 Summer Soiree L5597G	Open		150.00	180
1989 Bridesmaid L5598G	Open		150.00	180
1989 Coquette L5599G	Open		150.00	180
1989 The Blues w/base L5600G	Closed	1993	265.00	395
1989 "Ole" L5601G	Open		365.00	460
1989 Close To My Heart L5603G	Closed	1998	125.00	165-215
1989 Spring Token L5604G	Open		175.00	140-165
1989 Floral Treasures L5605G	Open		195.00	250
1989 Quiet Evening L5606G	Closed	1993	125.00	170-200
1989 Calling A Friend L5607G	Closed	1998	125.00	165
1989 Baby Doll L5608G	Open		150.00	180
1989 Playful Friends L5609G	Closed	1995	135.00	170
1989 Star Struck w/base L5610G	Closed	1998	335.00	420
1989 Sad Clown w/base L5611G	Closed	1998	335.00	420-475
1989 Reflecting w/base L5612G	Closed	1994	335.00	336-420

*Quotes have been rounded up to nearest dollar

YEAR ISSUE	EDITION LIMIT	YEAR RETD.	ISSUE PRICE	*QUOTE U.S.$
1989 Sealore Pipe L5613G	Closed	1993	125.00	175
1989 Startled L5614G	Closed	1991	265.00	375-425
1989 Bathing Beauty L5615G	Closed	1991	265.00	350-475
1989 Candleholder L5625G	Closed	1990	105.00	125
1989 Candleholder L5626	Closed	1990	90.00	125
1989 Lladró Vase L5631G	Closed	1990	150.00	225-395
1990 Water Dreamer Vase L5633G	Closed	1990	150.00	400
1990 Cat Nap L5640G	Open		125.00	145
1990 The King's Guard w/base L5642G	Closed	1993	950.00	1100
1990 Cathy L5643G	Open		200.00	235
1990 Susan L5644G	Open		190.00	215
1990 Elizabeth L5645G	Open		190.00	215
1990 Cindy L5646G	Open		190.00	215
1990 Sara L5647G	Open		200.00	230
1990 Courtney L5648G	Open		200.00	230
1990 Nothing To Do L5649G	Closed	1998	190.00	220
1990 Anticipation L5650G	Closed	1993	300.00	450
1990 Musical Muse L5651G	Closed	1997	375.00	440
1989 Marbella Clock L5652	Closed	1994	125.00	235
1989 Avila Clock L5653	Closed	1995	135.00	135
1990 Venetian Carnival L5658G	Closed	1993	500.00	625
1990 Barnyard Scene L5659G	Open		200.00	245
1990 Sunning In Ipanema L5660G	Closed	1993	370.00	525-600
1990 Traveling Artist L5661G	Closed	1994	250.00	290
1990 May Dance L5662G	Open		170.00	210
1990 Spring Dance L5663G	Open		170.00	210
1990 Giddy Up L5664G	Closed	1994	190.00	230
1990 Hang On! L5665G	Closed	1995	225.00	325
1990 Trino At The Beach L5666G	Closed	1995	390.00	500
1990 Valencian Harvest L5668G	Closed	1993	175.00	350-400
1990 Valencian FLowers L5669G	Closed	1993	370.00	375
1990 Valencian Beauty L5670G	Closed	1993	175.00	175-325
1990 Little Dutch Gardener L5671G	Closed	1993	400.00	475
1990 Hi There! L5672G	Closed	1997	450.00	520-550
1990 A Quiet Moment L5673G	Closed	1998	450.00	520-550
1990 A Faun And A Friend L5674G	Closed	1997	450.00	520-550
1990 Tee Time L5675G	Closed	1993	280.00	315
1990 Wandering Minstrel L5676G	Closed	1993	270.00	310
1990 Twilight Years L5677G	Closed	1998	370.00	420-500
1990 I Feel Pretty L5678G	Closed	1998	190.00	230
1990 In No Hurry L5679G	Closed	1994	550.00	640-695
1990 Traveling In Style L5680G	Closed	1994	425.00	495-550
1990 On The Road L5681G	Closed	1991	320.00	550
1990 Breezy Afternoon L5682G	Open		180.00	195
1990 Breezy Afternoon L5682M	Open		180.00	195
1990 Beautiful Burro L5683G	Closed	1993	280.00	435
1990 Barnyard Reflections L5684G	Closed	1993	460.00	650
1990 Promenade L5685G	Closed	1994	275.00	325
1990 On The Avenue L5686G	Closed	1994	275.00	350-375
1990 Afternoon Stroll L5687G	Closed	1994	275.00	350
1990 Dog's Best Friend L5688G	Open		250.00	295
1990 Can I Help? L5689G	Closed	1998	250.00	335
1990 Marshland Mates w/base L5691G	Open		950.00	1200
1990 Street Harmonies w/base L5692G	Closed	1993	3200.00	3750
1990 Circus Serenade L5694G	Closed	1994	300.00	375
1990 Concertina L5695G	Closed	1994	300.00	360
1990 Mandolin Serenade L5696G	Closed	1994	300.00	360
1990 Over The Clouds L5697G	Open		275.00	310
1990 Don't Look Down L5698G	Open		330.00	405
1990 Sitting Pretty L5699G	Open		300.00	340
1990 Southern Charm L5700G	Closed	1998	675.00	1025
1990 Just A Little Kiss L5701G	Closed	1998	320.00	375
1990 Back To School L5702G	Closed	1993	350.00	445
1990 Behave! L5703G	Closed	1994	230.00	363
1990 Swan Song L5704G	Closed	1995	350.00	410
1990 The Swan And The Princess L5705G	Closed	1994	350.00	475-495
1990 We Can't Play L5706G	Open		200.00	235
1990 After School L5707G	Closed	1993	280.00	315
1990 My First Class L5708G	Closed	1993	280.00	315
1990 Between Classes L5709G	Closed	1993	280.00	315
1990 Fantasy Friend L5710G	Closed	1993	420.00	495
1990 A Christmas Wish L5711G	Closed	1998	350.00	410
1990 Sleepy Kitten L5712G	Open		110.00	130
1990 The Snow Man L5713G	Open		300.00	350
1990 First Ballet L5714G	Open		370.00	420
1990 Mommy, it's Cold! L5715G	Closed	1994	360.00	450
1990 Land of The Giants L5716G	Closed	1994	275.00	425
1990 Rock A Bye Baby L5717G	Open		300.00	365
1990 Sharing Secrets L5720G	Closed	1998	290.00	335
1990 Once Upon A Time L5721G	Closed	1998	550.00	650-700
1990 Follow Me L5722G	Open		140.00	160
1990 Heavenly Chimes L5723G	Open		100.00	120
1990 Angelic Voice L5724G	Open		125.00	145
1990 Making A Wish L5725G	Open		125.00	145
1990 Sweep Away The Clouds L5726G	Open		125.00	145
1990 Angel Care L5727G	Open		185.00	210
1990 Heavenly Dreamer L5728G	Open		100.00	120
1991 Carousel Charm L5731G	Closed	1994	1700.00	2100
1991 Carousel Canter L5732G	Closed	1994	1700.00	1850
1991 Horticulturist L5733G	Closed	1993	450.00	495
1991 Pilgrim Couple L5734G	Closed	1993	490.00	525
1991 Big Sister L5735G	Open		650.00	685
1991 Puppet Show L5736G	Closed	1997	280.00	295-375
1991 Little Prince L5737G	Closed	1993	295.00	315
1991 Best Foot Forward L5738G	Closed	1994	280.00	305
1991 Lap Full Of Love L5739G	Closed	1995	275.00	295
1991 Alice In Wonderland L5740G	Closed	1997	440.00	440-485
1991 Dancing Class L5741G	Closed	N/A	340.00	365
1991 Bridal Portrait L5742G	Closed	1995	480.00	560-748
1991 Don't Forget Me L5743G	Open		150.00	160
1991 Bull & Donkey L5744G	Closed	1997	250.00	275-295
1991 Baby Jesus L5745G	Closed	1997	170.00	185
1991 St. Joseph L5746G	Closed	1997	350.00	375-395
1991 Mary L5747G	Closed	1997	275.00	295
1991 Shepherd Girl L5748G	Closed	1997	150.00	165
1991 Shepherd Boy L5749G	Closed	1997	225.00	245
1991 Little Lamb L5750G	Closed	1997	40.00	42
1991 Walk With Father L5751G	Closed	1994	375.00	440
1991 Little Virgin L5752G	Closed	1994	295.00	325
1991 Hold Her Still L5753G	Closed	1993	650.00	700-750
1991 Singapore Dancers L5754G	Closed	1993	950.00	1150-1195
1991 Claudette L5755G	Closed	1993	265.00	285-350
1991 Ashley L5756G	Closed	1993	265.00	300-350
1991 Beautiful Tresses L5757G	Closed	1993	725.00	875
1991 Sunday Best L5758G	Closed	1998	725.00	785
1991 Presto! L5759G	Closed	1993	275.00	295-455
1991 Interrupted Nap L5760G	Closed	1995	325.00	425-495
1991 Out For A Romp L5761G	Closed	1995	375.00	410-533
1991 Checking The Time L5762G	Closed	1995	560.00	595
1991 Musical Partners L5763G	Closed	1995	625.00	675
1991 Seeds Of Laughter L5764G	Closed	1995	525.00	600-695
1991 Hats Off To Fun L5765G	Closed	1995	475.00	510
1991 Charming Duet L5766G	Closed	1997	575.00	700
1991 First Sampler L5767G	Closed	1995	625.00	750
1991 Academy Days L5768G	Closed	1993	280.00	310
1991 Faithful Steed L5769G	Closed	1994	370.00	395
1991 Out For A Spin L5770G	Closed	1994	390.00	420
1991 The Magic Of Laughter L5771G	Closed	1997	950.00	1065
1991 Little Dreamers L5772G	Open		230.00	240
1991 Little Dreamers L5772M	Open		230.00	240
1991 Graceful Offering L5773G	Closed	1995	850.00	895-995
1991 Nature's Gifts L5774G	Closed	1994	900.00	975
1991 Gift Of Beauty L5775G	Closed	1995	850.00	900-1100
1991 Lover's Paradise L5779G	Closed	1998	2250.00	2450
1991 Walking The Fields L5780G	Closed	1993	725.00	795
1991 Not Too Close L5781G	Closed	1994	365.00	450
1991 My Chores L5782G	Closed	1995	325.00	355-400
1991 Special Delivery L5783G	Closed	1994	525.00	550-715
1991 A Cradle Of Kittens L5784G	Closed	1998	360.00	385
1991 Ocean Beauty L5785G	Open		625.00	665
1991 Story Hour L5786G	Closed	1998	550.00	625
1991 Sophisticate L5787G	Open		185.00	195
1991 Talk Of The Town L5788G	Open		185.00	195
1991 The Flirt L5789G	Open		185.00	195
1991 Carefree L5790G	Open		300.00	325
1991 Fairy Godmother L5791G	Closed	1994	375.00	403-450
1991 Reverent Moment L5792G	Closed	1994	295.00	320
1991 Precocious Ballerina L5793G	Closed	1995	575.00	625
1991 Precious Cargo L5794G	Closed	1994	460.00	550
1991 Floral Getaway L5795G	Closed	1993	625.00	745
1991 Holy Night L5796G	Closed	1994	330.00	360
1991 Come Out And Play L5797G	Closed	1994	275.00	350
1991 Milkmaid L5798G	Closed	1993	450.00	485
1991 Shall We Dance? L5799G	Closed	1993	600.00	750
1991 Elegant Promenade L5802G	Open		775.00	825
1991 Playing Tag L5804G	Closed	1993	170.00	190
1991 Tumbling L5805G	Closed	1993	130.00	175
1991 Tumbling L5805M	Closed	1992	130.00	140
1991 Tickling L5806G	Closed	1993	130.00	145
1991 Tickling L5806M	Closed	1992	130.00	145
1991 My Puppies L5807G	Closed	1993	325.00	360
1991 Musically Inclined L5810G	Closed	1993	235.00	250-300
1991 Littlest Clown L5811G	Open		225.00	240
1991 Tired Friend L5812G	Open		225.00	245
1991 Having A Ball L5813G	Open		225.00	240
1991 Curtain Call L5814G	Closed	1994	490.00	520
1991 Curtain Call L5814M	Closed	1994	490.00	520
1991 In Full Relave L5815G	Closed	1994	490.00	520
1991 In Full Relave L5815M	Closed	1994	490.00	520
1991 Prima Ballerina L5816G	Closed	1994	490.00	520
1991 Prima Ballerina L5816M	Closed	1994	490.00	520
1991 Backstage Preparation L5817G	Closed	1994	490.00	520
1991 Backstage Preparation L5817M	Closed	1994	490.00	650
1991 On Her Toes L5818G	Closed	1994	490.00	520
1991 On Her Toes L5818M	Closed	1994	490.00	520
1991 Allegory Of Liberty L5819G	Open		1950.00	2100
1991 Dance Of Love L5820G	Closed	1993	575.00	625
1991 Minstrel's Love L5821G	Closed	1993	525.00	575
1991 Little Unicorn L5826G	Closed	1998	275.00	295
1991 Little Unicorn L5826M	Closed	1998	275.00	295
1991 I've Got It L5827G	Closed	1995	170.00	180
1991 Next At Bat L5828G	Open		170.00	180
1991 Heavenly Harpist L5830	Yr.Iss.	1991	135.00	195-265
1991 Jazz Horn L5832G	Open		295.00	310
1991 Jazz Sax L5833G	Open		295.00	315
1991 Jazz Bass L5834G	Open		395.00	425
1991 I Do L5835G	Open		165.00	190
1991 Sharing Sweets L5836G	Closed	1998	220.00	245
1991 Sing With Me L5837G	Closed	1998	240.00	250
1991 On The Move L5838G	Closed	1998	340.00	395
1992 A Quiet Afternoon L5843G	Closed	1995	1050.00	1125
1992 Flirtatious Jester L5844G	Closed	1998	890.00	925
1992 Dressing The Baby L5845G	Open		295.00	295
1992 All Tuckered Out L5846G	Open		220.00	255
1992 All Tuckered Out L5846M	Open		220.00	255
1992 The Loving Family L5848G	Closed	1994	950.00	985
1992 Inspiring Muse L5850G	Closed	1994	1200.00	1250
1992 Feathered Fantasy L5851G	Closed	1997	1200.00	1250
1992 Easter Bonnets L5852G	Closed	1993	265.00	400
1992 Floral Admiration L5853G	Closed	1994	690.00	825
1992 Floral Fantasy L5854G	Closed	1995	690.00	710-895
1992 Afternoon Jaunt L5855G	Closed	1993	420.00	440
1992 Circus Concert L5856G	Closed	1997	570.00	585-600
1992 Grand Entrance L5857G	Closed	1994	265.00	275
1992 Waiting to Dance L5858G	Closed	1995	295.00	335
1992 At The Ball L5859G	Open		295.00	330
1992 Fairy Garland L5860G	Closed	1995	630.00	750
1992 Fairy Flowers L5861G	Closed	1995	630.00	655
1992 Fragrant Bouquet L5862G	Open		350.00	370
1992 Dressing For The Ballet L5865G	Closed	1995	395.00	415
1992 Final Touches L5866G	Closed	1995	395.00	415
1992 Serene Valenciana L5867G	Closed	1994	365.00	385
1992 Loving Valenciana L5868G	Closed	1995	365.00	385
1992 Fallas Queen L5869G	Closed	1995	420.00	440
1992 Olympic Torch w/Fantasy Logo L5870G	Closed	1994	165.00	145
1992 Olympic Champion w/Fantasy Logo L5871G	Closed	1994	165.00	145
1992 Olympic Pride w/Fantasy Logo L5872G	Closed	1994	165.00	495
1992 Modern Mother L5873G	Closed	1997	325.00	375-400
1992 Off We Go L5874G	Closed	1994	365.00	385
1992 Angelic Cymbalist L5876	Yr.Iss.	1992	140.00	175-195
1992 Guest Of Honor L5877G	Closed	1997	195.00	200
1992 Sister's Pride L5878G	Closed	1997	595.00	615-695
1992 Shot On Goal L5879G	Closed	1997	1100.00	1150
1992 Playful Unicorn L5880G	Open		295.00	320
1992 Playful Unicorn L5880M	Open		295.00	320
1992 Mischievous Mouse L5881G	Open		285.00	295
1992 Restful Mouse L5882G	Closed	1997	285.00	295
1992 Loving Mouse L5883G	Closed	1997	285.00	295
1992 From This Day Forward L5885G	Open		265.00	285
1992 Hippity Hop L5886G	Closed	1995	95.00	95
1992 Washing Up L5887G	Closed	1995	95.00	95
1992 That Tickles! L5888G	Closed	1995	95.00	105
1992 Snack Time L5889G	Closed	1995	95.00	105
1992 The Aviator L5891G	Closed	1998	375.00	425-450
1992 Circus Magic L5892G	Closed	1998	470.00	495
1992 Friendship In Bloom L5893G	Closed	1995	650.00	685
1992 Precious Petals L5894G	Closed	1997	395.00	415
1992 Bouquet of Blossoms L5895G	Closed	1998	295.00	295
1992 The Loaves & Fishes L5896G	Closed	1998	695.00	760
1992 Trimming The Tree L5897G	Open		900.00	925
1992 Spring Splendor L5898G	Open		440.00	450
1992 Just One More L5899G	Closed	1998	450.00	495-550
1992 Sleep Tight L5900G	Closed	1998	450.00	500-550
1992 Surprise L5901G	Open		325.00	335
1992 Easter Bunnies L5902G	Closed	1997	240.00	250
1992 Down The Aisle L5903G	Closed	1997	295.00	295
1992 Sleeping Bunny L5904G	Closed	1998	75.00	75
1992 Attentive Bunny L5905G	Open		75.00	75
1992 Preening Bunny L5906G	Closed	1998	75.00	80
1992 Sitting Bunny L5907G	Open		75.00	80
1992 Just A Little More L5908G	Closed	1998	370.00	380
1992 All Dressed Up L5909G	Closed	1998	440.00	450
1992 Making A Wish L5910G	Open		790.00	825
1992 Swans Take Flight L5912G	Open		2850.00	2950
1992 Rose Ballet L5919G	Open		210.00	215
1992 Swan Ballet L5920G	Open		210.00	215
1992 Take Your Medicine L5921G	Open		360.00	370
1990 Floral Clock L5924	Closed	1995	N/A	165
1990 Garland Quartz Clock L5926	Closed	1995	195.00	195
1992 Jazz Clarinet L5928G	Open		295.00	295
1992 Jazz Drums L5929G	Open		595.00	610
1992 Jazz Duo L5930G	Open		795.00	900
1993 The Ten Commandments w/Base L5933G	Closed	1997	930.00	930
1993 The Holy Teacher L5934G	Closed	1997	375.00	375
1993 Nutcracker Suite L5935G	Open		620.00	620
1993 Little Skipper L5936G	Closed	1997	320.00	320
1993 Riding The Waves L5941G	Closed	1998	405.00	405-425
1993 World of Fantasy L5943G	Closed	1995	295.00	295
1993 The Great Adventurer L5944G	Closed	1994	325.00	325
1993 A Mother's Way L5946G	Closed	1997	1350.00	1350-1400
1993 General Practitioner L5947G	Closed	1998	360.00	370
1993 Physician L5948G	Open		360.00	360
1993 Angel Candleholder w/Lyre L5949G	Closed	1998	295.00	315
1993 Angel Candleholder w/Tambourine L5950G	Closed	1998	295.00	315
1993 Sounds of Summer L5953G	Open		150.00	150
1993 Sounds of Winter L5954G	Open		150.00	150
1993 Sounds of Fall L5955G	Open		150.00	150
1993 Sounds of Spring L5956G	Open		150.00	150
1993 The Glass Slipper L5957G	Open		475.00	475
1993 Country Ride w/base L5958G	Open		2850.00	2875
1993 It's Your Turn L5959G	Closed	1997	365.00	365
1993 On Patrol L5960G	Closed	1998	395.00	445-475
1993 The Great Teacher w/base L5961G	Closed	1997	850.00	850
1993 Angelic Melody L5963	Yr.Iss.	1993	145.00	165-175
1993 The Great Voyage L5964G	Closed	1994	50.00	50
1993 The Clipper Ship w/base L5965M	Closed	1997	240.00	250
1993 Flowers Forever w/base L5966G	Open		4150.00	4150
1993 Honeymoon Ride w/base L5968G	Closed	1995	2750.00	2795
1993 A Special Toy L5971G	Closed	1997	815.00	815
1993 Before the Dance w/base L5972G	Open		3550.00	3550
1993 Before the Dance w/base L5972M	Open		3550.00	3550
1993 Family Outing w/base L5974G	Closed	1998	4275.00	4275
1993 Up and Away w/base L5975G	Closed	1997	2850.00	2850
1993 The Fireman L5976G	Closed	1998	395.00	465
1993 Revelation w/base (white) L5977G	Closed	1995	325.00	325
1993 Revelation w/base (black) L5978M	Closed	1995	325.00	325
1993 Revelation w/base (sand) L5979M	Closed	1995	325.00	325
1993 The Past w/base (white) L5980G	Closed	1995	325.00	325
1993 The Past w/base (black) L5981M	Closed	1995	325.00	325
1993 The Past w/base (sand) L5982M	Closed	1995	325.00	325
1993 Beauty w/base (white) L5983G	Closed	1995	325.00	325

*Quotes have been rounded up to nearest dollar

FIGURINES

YEAR ISSUE	EDITION LIMIT	YEAR RETD.	ISSUE PRICE	*QUOTE U.S.$
1993 Beauty w/base (black) L5984M	Closed	1995	325.00	325
1993 Beauty w/base (sand) L5985M	Closed	1995	325.00	325
1993 Sunday Sermon L5986G	Open		425.00	425
1993 Talk to Me L5987G	Open		145.00	175
1993 Taking Time L5988G	Open		145.00	175
1993 A Mother's Touch L5989G	Closed	1997	470.00	470
1993 Thoughtful Caress L5990G	Closed	1997	225.00	225
1993 Love Story L5991G	Open		2800.00	2800
1993 Unicorn and Friend L5993G	Open		355.00	355
1993 Unicorn and Friend L5993M	Open		355.00	355
1993 Meet My Friend L5994G	Closed	1997	695.00	695
1993 Soft Meow L5995G	Open		480.00	515
1993 Bless the Child L5996G	Closed	1994	465.00	465
1993 One More Try L5997G	Closed	1997	715.00	750-850
1993 My Dad L6001G	Closed	1995	550.00	575
1993 Down You Go L6002G	Closed	1998	815.00	815
1993 Ready To Learn L6003G	Open		650.00	650
1993 Bar Mitzvah Day L6004G	Open		395.00	430
1993 Christening Day w/base L6005G	Closed	1995	1425.00	1425
1993 Oriental Colonade w/base L6006G	Closed	1995	1875.00	1875
1993 The Goddess & Unicorn w/base L6007G	Open		1675.00	1675
1993 Joyful Event L6008G	Open		825.00	825
1993 Monday's Child (Boy) L6011G	Closed	1998	245.00	285
1993 Monday's Child (Girl) L6012G	Closed	1998	260.00	290
1993 Tuesday's Child (Boy) L6013G	Closed	1998	225.00	250
1993 Tuesday's Child (Girl) L6014G	Open		245.00	285
1993 Wednesday's Child (Boy) L6015G	Closed	1998	245.00	285-300
1993 Wednesday's Child (Girl) L6016G	Closed	1998	245.00	285-335
1993 Thursday's Child (Boy) L6017G	Closed	1998	225.00	250
1993 Thursday's Child (Girl) L6018G	Closed	1998	245.00	285
1993 Friday's Child (Boy) L6019G	Closed	1998	225.00	250
1993 Friday's Child (Girl) L6020G	Closed	1998	225.00	250
1993 Saturday's Child (Boy) L6021G	Closed	1998	245.00	285-300
1993 Saturday's Child (Girl) L6022G	Closed	1998	245.00	285
1993 Sunday's Child (Boy) L6023G	Closed	1998	225.00	250
1993 Sunday's Child (Girl) L6024G	Closed	1998	225.00	250-300
1993 Barnyard See Saw L6025G	Closed	1998	500.00	500
1993 My Turn L6026G	Closed	1998	515.00	515
1993 Hanukah Lights L6027G	Open		345.00	395
1993 Mazel Tov! L6028G	Open		380.00	395
1993 Hebrew Scholar L6029G	Closed	1997	225.00	245
1993 On The Go L6031G	Closed	1995	475.00	485-631
1993 On The Green L6032G	Open		645.00	645
1993 Monkey Business L6034G	Closed	1994	745.00	800-850
1993 Young Princess L6036G	Closed	1997	240.00	240
1994 Saint James L6084G	Closed	1998	310.00	310
1994 Angelic Harmony L6085G	Closed	1998	495.00	575
1994 Allow Me L6086G	Closed	1998	1625.00	1625
1994 Loving Care L6087G	Open		250.00	270
1994 Communion Prayer (Boy) L6088G	Open		194.00	200
1994 Communion Prayer (Girl) L6089G	Open		198.00	225
1994 Baseball Player L6090G	Closed	1998	295.00	310
1994 Basketball Player L6091G	Closed	1998	295.00	310
1994 The Prince L6092G	Closed	1998	325.00	325
1994 Songbird L6093G	Open		395.00	395
1994 The Sportsman L6096G	Closed	1998	495.00	540
1994 Sleeping Bunny With Flowers L6097G	Closed	1998	110.00	110
1994 Attentive Bunny With Flowers L6098G	Open		140.00	140
1994 Preening Bunny With Flowers L6099G	Closed	1998	140.00	140
1994 Sitting Bunny With Flowers L6100G	Open		110.00	110
1994 Follow Us L6101G	Closed	1998	198.00	215
1994 Mother's Little Helper L6102G	Open		275.00	285
1994 Beautiful Ballerina L6103G	Open		250.00	285
1994 Finishing Touches L6104	Open		240.00	250
1994 Spring Joy L6106G	Open		795.00	795
1994 Football Player L6107	Closed	1998	295.00	310
1994 Hockey Player L6108G	Open		295.00	310
1994 Meal Time L6109G	Open		495.00	525
1994 Medieval Maiden L6110G	Closed	1997	150.00	165
1994 Medieval Soldier L6111G	Closed	1997	225.00	245
1994 Medieval Lord L6112G	Closed	1997	285.00	300
1994 Medieval Lady L6113G	Closed	1997	225.00	225
1994 Medieval Princess L6114G	Closed	1997	245.00	315
1994 Medieval Prince L6115G	Closed	1997	295.00	315
1994 Medieval Majesty L6116G	Closed	1997	315.00	325
1994 Constance L6117G	Closed	1997	195.00	205
1994 Constance L6117M	Closed	1998	195.00	205
1994 Musketeer Portos L6118G	Closed	1997	220.00	230-250
1994 Musketeer Aramis L6119G	Closed	1997	275.00	295-300
1994 Musketeer Dartagnan L6120G	Closed	1997	245.00	285-300
1994 Musketeer Athos L6121G	Closed	1997	245.00	290-300
1994 A Great Adventure L6122	Closed	1998	198.00	215
1994 Out For a Stroll L6123G	Closed	1998	198.00	215
1994 Travelers Rest L6124G	Closed	1998	275.00	295
1994 Angelic Violinist L6126G	Yr.Iss.	1994	150.00	195-300
1994 Sweet Dreamers L6127G	Open		280.00	290
1994 Christmas Melodies L6128G	Closed	1998	375.00	385
1994 Little Friends L6129G	Open		225.00	235
1996 Spring Enchantment L6130G	Open		245.00	245
1994 Angel of Peace L6131G	Open		345.00	370
1994 Angel with Garland L6133G	Open		345.00	370
1994 Birthday Party L6134G	Open		395.00	455
1994 Football Star L6135	Closed	1998	295.00	295
1994 Basketball Star L6136G	Closed	1998	295.00	295
1994 Baseball Star L6137G	Closed	1998	295.00	295
1994 Globe Paperweight L6138M	Closed	1997	95.00	95
1994 Springtime Friends L6140G	Open		485.00	485
1994 Kitty Cart L6141G	Open		750.00	795
1994 Indian Pose L6142G	Closed	1998	475.00	475
1994 Indian Dancer L6143G	Closed	1998	475.00	475
1995 Caribbean Kiss L6144G	Open		340.00	340
1994 Heavenly Prayer L6145	Closed	1998	675.00	695
1994 Spring Angel L6146G	Closed	1998	250.00	265
1994 Fall Angel L6147G	Closed	1998	250.00	265
1994 Summer Angel L6148G	Closed	1998	220.00	220
1994 Winter Angel L6149G	Closed	1998	250.00	265
1994 Playing The Flute L6150G	Open		175.00	190
1994 Bearing Flowers L6151G	Open		175.00	190
1994 Flower Gazer L6152G	Open		175.00	190
1994 American Love L6153G	Open		225.00	235
1994 African Love L6154G	Open		225.00	235
1994 European Love L6155G	Open		225.00	235
1994 Asian Love L6156G	Open		225.00	235
1994 Polynesian Love L6157G	Open		225.00	235
1995 Fiesta Dancer L6163G	Open		285.00	305
1994 Wedding Bells L6164G	Open		175.00	195
1995 Pretty Cargo L6165G	Open		500.00	500
1995 Dear Santa L6166G	Open		250.00	260
1995 Delicate Bundle L6167G	Open		275.00	275
1994 The Apollo Landing L6168G	Closed	1995	450.00	450-600
1995 Seesaw Friends L6169G	Open		795.00	795
1995 Under My Spell L6170G	Open		195.00	200
1995 Magical Moment L6171G	Open		180.00	200
1995 Coming of Age L6172G	Open		345.00	345
1995 A Moment's Rest L6173G	Open		130.00	140
1995 Graceful Pose L6174G	Open		195.00	195
1995 Graceful Pose L6174M	Open		195.00	195
1995 White Swan L6175G	Open		90.00	90
1995 Communion Bell L6176G	Open		85.00	85
1995 Asian Scholar L6177G	Open		315.00	315
1995 Little Matador L6178G	Open		245.00	245
1995 Peaceful Moment L6179G	Open		385.00	385
1995 Sharia L6180G	Open		235.00	235
1995 Velisa L6181G	Open		180.00	180
1996 Wanda L6182	Open		205.00	205
1995 Preparing For The Sabbath L6183G	Open		385.00	385
1995 For a Better World L6186G	Closed	1998	575.00	575
1995 European Boy L6187G	Open		185.00	185
1995 Asian Boy L6188G	Open		225.00	225
1995 African Boy L6189G	Open		195.00	195
1995 Polynesian Boy L6190G	Open		250.00	250
1995 All American L6191G	Open		225.00	225
1995 American Indian Boy L6192G	Open		225.00	225
1995 Summer Serenade L6193G	Open		375.00	385
1995 Summer Serenade L6193M	Open		375.00	385
1996 Christmas Wishes L6194	Open		245.00	245
1995 Carnival Companions L6195G	Open		650.00	685
1995 Seaside Companions L6196G	Open		230.00	230
1995 Seaside Serenade L6197G	Open		275.00	275
1995 Soccer Practice L6198G	Open		195.00	195
1995 In The Procession L6199G	Open		250.00	250
1995 In The Procession L6199M	Open		250.00	250
1995 Bridal Bell L6200G	Open		125.00	125
1995 Cuddly Kitten L6201G	Open		270.00	270
1995 Daddy's Little Sweetheart L6202G	Open		595.00	595
1995 Grace and Beauty L6204G	Open		325.00	325
1995 Grace and Beauty L6204M	Open		325.00	325
1995 Graceful Dance L6205G	Open		340.00	340
1995 Reading the Torah L6208G	Open		535.00	535
1995 The Rabbi L6209G	Closed	1998	250.00	250
1995 Gentle Surprise L6210G	Open		125.00	125
1995 New Friend L6211G	Open		120.00	120
1995 Little Hunter L6212G	Open		115.00	115
1995 Lady Of Nice L6213G	Open		198.00	210
1995 Lady Of Nice L6213M	Open		198.00	210
1995 Leo L6214G	Closed	1998	198.00	210
1995 Virgo L6215G	Closed	1998	198.00	210
1995 Aquarius L6216G	Closed	1998	198.00	210
1995 Sagittarius L6217G	Closed	1998	198.00	210
1995 Taurus L6218G	Closed	1998	198.00	210
1995 Gemini L6219G	Closed	1998	198.00	210
1995 Libra L6220G	Closed	1998	198.00	210
1995 Aries L6221G	Closed	1998	198.00	210
1995 Capricorn L6222G	Closed	1998	198.00	210
1995 Pisces L6223G	Closed	1998	198.00	210
1995 Cancer L6224G	Closed	1998	198.00	210
1995 Scorpio L6225G	Closed	1998	198.00	210-235
1995 Snuggle Up L6226G	Open		170.00	170
1995 Trick or Treat L6227G	Closed	1998	250.00	250
1995 Special Gift L6228G	Open		265.00	265
1995 Contented Companion L6229G	Open		195.00	195
1995 Oriental Dance L6230G	Open		198.00	210
1995 Oriental Lantern L6231G	Open		198.00	210
1995 Oriental Beauty L6232G	Open		198.00	210
1995 Chef's Apprentice L6233G	Open		260.00	260
1995 Chef's Apprentice L6233M	Open		260.00	260
1995 The Great Chef L6234G	Open		195.00	195
1995 The Great Chef L6234M	Open		195.00	195
1995 Dinner is Served L6235G	Open		185.00	185
1995 Dinner is Served L6235M	Open		185.00	185
1995 Lady of Monaco L6236G	Open		250.00	260
1995 Lady of Monaco L6236M	Open		250.00	260
1995 The Young Jester-Mandolin L6237G	Closed	1998	235.00	235
1995 The Young Jester-Mandolin L6237M	Closed	1998	235.00	235
1995 The Young Jester-Trumpet L6238G	Closed	1998	235.00	235
1995 The Young Jester-Trumpet L6238M	Closed	1998	235.00	235
1995 The Young Jester-Singer L6239G	Closed	1998	235.00	235
1995 The Young Jester-Singer L6239M	Closed	1998	235.00	235
1995 Graceful Ballet L6240G	Open		795.00	815
1995 Graceful Ballet L6240M	Open		795.00	815
1995 Allegory of Spring L6241G	Open		735.00	735
1995 Allegory of Spring L6241M	Open		735.00	735
1996 Winged Companions L6242G	Open		270.00	270
1996 Winged Companions L6242M	Open		270.00	270
1996 Sweet Symphony L6243	Open		450.00	450
1996 Pumpkin Ride L6244	Open		695.00	695
1996 Sunday's Best L6246	Open		370.00	370
1995 Challenge L6247M	Closed	1997	350.00	350-375
1995 Regatta L6248G	Closed	1997	695.00	695-700
1995 Delphica w/base L6249	Open		1200.00	1200
1996 Springtime Harvest L6250	Open		760.00	760
1997 Wind of Peace L6251	Open		310.00	310
1996 Nature's Beauty w/base L6252	Open		770.00	770
1996 Making Rounds L6256	Open		295.00	295
1996 Pierrot in Preparation L6257	Open		195.00	195
1996 Pierrot in Love L6258	Open		195.00	195
1996 Pierrot Rehearsing L6259	Open		195.00	195
1996 Our Lady "Caridid Del Cobre" w/base L6268	Open		1355.00	1355
1996 Diana Goddess of the Hunt w/base L6269	Open		1550.00	1550
1996 Commencement L6270	Open		200.00	200
1996 Cap and Gown L6271	Open		200.00	200
1996 Going Forth L6272	Open		200.00	200
1996 Pharmacist L6273	Open		290.00	290
1996 Daisy L6274	Open		150.00	150
1996 Rose L6275	Open		150.00	150
1996 Iris L6276	Open		150.00	150
1996 Young Mandolin Player L6278	Open		330.00	330
1996 Flowers of Paris L6279	Open		525.00	525
1996 Paris in Bloom L6280	Open		525.00	525
1996 Coqueta L6281G	Open		435.00	435
1996 Coqueta L6281M	Open		435.00	435
1996 Medic L6282G	Open		225.00	225
1996 Medic L6282M	Open		225.00	225
1996 Temis L6283G	Open		435.00	435
1996 Temis L6283M	Open		435.00	435
1996 Quione L6284G	Open		435.00	435
1996 Quione L6284M	Open		435.00	435
1996 Dreams of Aladdin w/base L6285	Open		1440.00	1440
1996 Tennis Champion w/base L6286G	Open		350.00	350
1996 Tennis Champion w/base L6286M	Open		350.00	350
1996 Restless Dove L6287G	Open		105.00	105
1996 Restless Dove L6287M	Open		105.00	105
1996 Taking Flight L6288G	Open		150.00	150
1996 Taking Flight L6288M	Open		150.00	150
1996 Peaceful Dove L6289G	Open		105.00	105
1996 Peaceful Dove L6289M	Open		105.00	105
1996 Proud Dove L6290G	Open		105.00	105
1996 Proud Dove L6290M	Open		105.00	105
1996 Love Nest L6291G	Open		260.00	260
1996 Love Nest L6291M	Open		260.00	260
1997 Summer Egg L6293	Open		365.00	365
1998 Autumn Egg 01006294	Open		365.00	365
1996 Sweethearts L6296	Open		900.00	900
1996 Little Bear L6299	Open		285.00	285
1996 Rubber Ducky L6300	Open		285.00	285
1996 Care and Tenderness w/base L6301	Open		850.00	850
1996 Thena L6302G	Open		485.00	485
1996 Thena L6302M	Open		485.00	485
1996 Tuba Player L6303	Open		315.00	315
1996 Bass Drummer L6304	Open		400.00	400
1996 Trumpet Player L6305	Open		270.00	270
1996 Majorette L6306	Open		310.00	310
1996 Young Nurse L6307	Open		185.00	185
1996 Natural Wonder L6308	Open		220.00	220
1996 Nature's Treasures L6309	Open		220.00	220
1996 Nature's Song L6310	Open		230.00	230
1996 Cupid L6311	Open		200.00	200
1996 The Harpist L6312	Open		820.00	820
1996 Lost in Dreams L6313	Open		420.00	420
1996 Little Sailor Boy L6314	Open		225.00	225
1996 Dreaming of You L6315	Open		1280.00	1280
1996 Carnevale L6316	Open		840.00	840
1996 Making House Calls L6317	Open		260.00	260
1996 Little Distraction L6318	Open		350.00	350
1996 Beautiful Rhapsody L6319	Open		450.00	450
1996 Architect L6320	Open		330.00	330
1996 Serenading Colombina L6322	Open		415.00	415
1996 Stage Presence L6323	Open		355.00	355
1996 Princess of Peace L6324	Open		830.00	830
1996 Curtains Up L6325	Open		255.00	255
1996 Virgin of Carmen w/base L6326	Open		1270.00	1270
1996 Medieval Romance w/base L6327	Open		2250.00	2250
1996 Venice Festival w/base L6328	Open		5350.00	5350
1996 Blushing Bride L6329G	Open		370.00	370
1996 Blushing Bride L6329M	Open		370.00	370
1996 Refreshing Pause L6330	Open		170.00	170
1996 Bridal Bell L6331	Open		155.00	155
1996 Concerto L6332	Open		490.00	490
1996 Medieval Chess Set L6333	Open		2120.00	2120
1997 Little Fireman L6334	Open		185.00	185
1997 Home Sweet Home L6336	Open		85.00	85
1997 Poodle L6337	Open		150.00	150
1997 I'm Sleepy L6338	Open		360.00	360
1996 Country Sounds L6339	Open		750.00	750
1996 Sweet Country L6340	Open		750.00	750
1998 Petals of Love 01006346	Open		350.00	350
1997 Little Veterinarian L6348	Open		210.00	210
1997 Little Maestro L6349	Open		165.00	165
1997 Hunting Butterflies L6350	Open		425.00	425
1997 Tokens of Love L6351	Open		385.00	385
1997 A World of Love L6353	Open		450.00	450

*Quotes have been rounded up to nearest dollar

YEAR ISSUE	EDITION LIMIT	YEAR RETD.	ISSUE PRICE	*QUOTE U.S.$
1997 Attentive Polar Bear w/Flowers L6354	Open		100.00	100
1997 Polar Bear Resting w/Flowers L6355	Open		100.00	100
1997 Polar Bear Seated w/Flowers L6356	Open		100.00	100
1997 Kissing Doves w/Flowers L6359	Open		225.00	225
1997 St. Joseph The Carpenter L6363	Open		1050.00	1050
1997 A Dream Come True L6364	Open		550.00	550
1997 Spring Flirtation L6365	Open		395.00	395
1998 Summer Infatuation 01006366	Open		325.00	325
1997 Little Policeman L6367	Open		185.00	185
1997 Little Artist L6368	Open		175.00	175
1997 Indian Maiden L6369	Open		600.00	600
1997 Country Chores L6370	Open		260.00	260
1997 En Pointe L6371	Open		390.00	390
1997 Palace Dance L6373	Open		700.00	700
1997 Pas De Deux L6374	Open		725.00	725
1997 Pierrot's Proposal L6375	Open		1425.00	1425
1997 Light and Life L6376G	Open		220.00	220
1997 Light and Life L6376M	Open		220.00	220
1997 Unity L6377G	Open		220.00	220
1997 Unity L6377M	Open		220.00	220
1997 Beginning and End L6378G	Open		220.00	220
1997 Beginning and End L6378M	Open		220.00	220
1997 Love L6379G	Open		220.00	220
1997 Love L6379M	Open		220.00	220
1997 King Gaspar L6380	Open		75.00	75
1997 Little Roadster L6381	Open		79.00	79
1997 New Arrival L6382	Open		265.00	265
1997 The Ascension L6383	Open		775.00	775
1997 A Quiet Moment L6384	Open		270.00	270
1997 Royal Slumber L6385	Open		1390.00	1390
1997 Little Harlequin L6386	Open		79.00	79
1997 A Passionate Dance L6387	Open		890.00	890
1997 Circus Star L6388	Open		79.00	79
1997 The Bouquet L6389	Open		95.00	95
1997 The Encounter L6391	Open		150.00	150
1997 The Kiss L6392	Open		150.00	150
1997 Heavenly Flutist L6393	Open		98.00	98
1997 Through the Park L6395	Open		2350.00	2350
1997 Oriental Forest L6396	Open		565.00	565
1997 In Neptune's Waves L6397	Open		1030.00	1030
1997 Seraph w/Holly L6394	Open		79.00	79
1997 Morning Delivery L6398	Open		160.00	160
1997 Generous Gesture L6399	Open		345.00	345
1997 Daydreams L6400	Open		325.00	325
1997 Little Ballerina L6402	Open		200.00	200
1997 Breathless L6403	Open		235.00	235
1997 Sister w/Sax L6404G	Open		180.00	180
1997 Sister w/Sax L6404M	Open		180.00	180
1997 Sister Singing L6405G	Open		165.00	165
1997 Sister Singing L6405M	Open		165.00	165
1997 Sister w/Guitar L6406G	Open		200.00	200
1997 Sister w/Guitar L6406M	Open		200.00	200
1997 Sister w/Tambourine L6407G	Open		185.00	185
1997 Sister w/Tambourine L6407M	Open		185.00	185
1997 Sweet Song L6408	Open		480.00	480
1997 A Surprise Visit L6409	Open		190.00	190
1997 Would You Be Mine? L6410	Open		190.00	190
1997 Bath Time L6411	Open		195.00	195
1997 Joy of Life L6412	Open		215.00	215
1997 Spirit of Youth L6413	Open		215.00	215
1997 Hello Friend L6414	Open		235.00	235
1997 It's A Boy! L6415	Open		125.00	125
1997 It's A Girl! L6416	Open		125.00	125
1997 Unlikely Friends L6417	Open		125.00	125
1997 So Beautiful! L6418G	Open		325.00	325
1997 So Beautiful! L6418M	Open		325.00	325
1997 Arms Full of Love L6419	Open		180.00	180
1997 My Favorite Slippers L6420	Open		145.00	145
1997 Off To Bed L6421	Open		145.00	145
1997 My Chubby Kitty L6422	Open		135.00	135
1997 Precious Papoose L6423	Open		240.00	240
1997 Ceremonial Princess L6424	Open		240.00	240
1997 Female Attorney L6425	Open		300.00	300
1997 Male Attorney L6426	Open		300.00	300
1997 A Flower For You L6427	Open		320.00	320
1997 My First Step L6428	Open		165.00	165
1997 Ready To Roll L6429	Open		165.00	165
1997 Pony Ride L6430	Open		825.00	825
1997 Little Lawyer L6431	Open		210.00	210
1997 Sea of Love L6432	Open		1190.00	1190
1997 Cranes in Flight L6433	Open		1390.00	1390
1997 Pensive Harlequin L6434	Open		495.00	495
1997 Colombina L6435	Open		525.00	525
1997 The Dolphins L6436	Open		965.00	965
1997 Timid Torero L6437	Open		195.00	195
1997 Young Torero L6438	Open		240.00	240
1998 Caught In The Act 01006439	Open		260.00	260
1997 Time For Bed L6440	Open		160.00	160
1998 Spring Recital 01006452	Open		685.00	685
1998 Fountain of Love 01006458	Open		395.00	395
1998 A Prize Catch 01006466	Open		340.00	340
1998 A Father's Pride 01006467	Open		475.00	475
1998 Sounds of Peace 01006473	Open		98.00	98
1998 Sounds of Love 01006474	Open		98.00	98
1998 Happy Anniversary 01006475	Open		300.00	300
1998 A Symbol of Pride 01006476	Open		695.00	695
1998 A Perfect Day 01006480	Open		495.00	495
1998 After the Show 01006484	Open		350.00	350
1998 In Admiration 01006485	Open		370.00	370
1998 Posing For a Portrait 01006486	Open		380.00	380
1998 New Shoes 01006487	Open		150.00	150
1998 Gone Shopping 01006488	Open		150.00	150
1998 Your Special Angel 01006492	Open		92.00	92
1998 Filled With Joy 01006493	Open		92.00	92
1998 Onward and Upward 01006494	Open		170.00	170
1998 The Road To Success 01006495	Open		155.00	155
1998 A Child's Prayer 01006496	Open		89.00	89
1998 Sleepy Time 01006497	Open		89.00	89
1998 White Swan with Flowers 01006499	Open		110.00	110
1998 Jolly Santa 01006500	Open		180.00	180
1998 My Little Treasure 01006503	Open		295.00	295
1998 Daddy's Blessing 01006504	Open		340.00	340
1998 On The Farm 01006505	Open		325.00	325
1998 Guess Who? 01006506	Open		430.00	430
1998 An Unexpected Gift 01006510	Open		260.00	260
1998 A Birthday Surprise 01006511	Open		230.00	230
1998 How Skillful! 01006517	Open		390.00	390
1998 A Lovely Thought 01006518	Open		580.00	580
1998 Love's Tender Tokens 01006521	Open		895.00	895
1998 Through The Clouds 01006522	Open		440.00	440
1998 Flying High 01006523	Open		635.00	635
1998 Up And Away 01006524	Open		560.00	560
1998 Little Angel with Lyre 01006528	Open		120.00	120
1998 Little Angel with Violin 01006529	Open		120.00	120
1998 Little Angel with Tambourine 01006530	Open		120.00	120
1998 A New Life 01006531	Open		490.00	490
1998 A Christmas Song 01006532	Open		198.00	198
1998 The Christmas Caroler 01006533	Open		175.00	175
1998 The Spirit of Christmas 01006534	Open		198.00	198
1998 Cozy Companions 01006540	Open		195.00	195
1998 Bedtime Buddies 01006541	Open		195.00	195
1998 A Stroll In The Sun 01006542	Open		450.00	450
1998 On Our Way 01006544	Open		340.00	340
1998 Baby Boy Lamb 01006546	Open		105.00	105
1998 Baby Girl Lamb 01006547	Open		105.00	105
1998 Love Poems 01006548	Open		470.00	470
1998 Naptime Friends 01006549	Open		200.00	200
1998 Shhh...They're Sleeping 01006550	Open		200.00	200
1998 Pretty Posies 01006551	Open		180.00	180
1998 Pretty Pinwheel 01006552	Open		145.00	145
1998 Grandparent's Joy 01006553	Open		645.00	645
1998 Playful Poodle 01006557	Open		579.00	579
1998 Great Dane 01006558	Open		890.00	890
1998 Parading Donkey 01006573	Open		220.00	220
1998 Nightime Blessing 01006581	Open		136.00	136
1998 Bless Us All 01006582	Open		170.00	170
1998 Heaven's Lullabye 01006583	Open		186.00	186
1998 Sunday Prayer 01006584	Open		200.00	200
1998 Angelic Light Candleholder 01006586	Open		198.00	198
1998 Morning Calm 01006589	Open		130.00	130
1985 Lladró Plaque L7116	Open		17.50	18
1985 Lladró Plaque L7118	Closed	N/A	17.00	18
1992 Special Torch L7513G	Closed	1997	165.00	175-195
1992 Special Champion L7514G	Closed	1997	165.00	165-195
1992 Special Pride L7515G	Closed	1997	165.00	175-195
1993 Courage L7522G	Closed	1997	195.00	200
1994 Dr. Martin Luther King, Jr. L7528G	Open		345.00	375
1994 Doc 7533	Closed	1998	195.00	195
1995 Dopey 7534	Closed	1998	175.00	175
1995 Sneezy 7535	Closed	1998	175.00	175-225
1994 Bashful 7536	Closed	1998	175.00	175
1994 Happy 7537	Closed	1998	195.00	195-300
1994 Grumpy 7538	Closed	1998	175.00	175-250
1994 Sleepy 7539	Closed	1998	175.00	175
1994 Spike L7543G	Closed	1998	95.00	105
1994 Brutus L7544G	Closed	1998	125.00	140
1994 Rocky L7545G	Closed	1998	110.00	120
1994 Stretch L7546G	Closed	1998	125.00	140
1994 Rex L7547G	Closed	1998	125.00	140
1994 Snow White L7555G (Disney-back stamp Theme Park issue)	Closed	N/A	295.00	880
1994 Snow White L7555G	Closed	1998	295.00	295
1995 Snow White Wishing Well L7558	Closed	1998	1500.00	1500-1800
1995 16th Century Globe Paperweight L7551	Open		105.00	105
1989 Starting Forward/Lolo L7605G	Open		190.00	190
1996 By My Side L7645	Open		250.00	250
1996 Chess Board L8036	Open		145.00	145

Lladró Limited Edition Egg Series - Lladró

YEAR ISSUE	EDITION LIMIT	YEAR RETD.	ISSUE PRICE	*QUOTE U.S.$
1993 1993 Limited Edition Egg L6083M	Closed	1993	145.00	189-280
1994 1994 Limited Edition Egg L7532M	Closed	1994	150.00	150-240
1995 1995 Limited Edition Egg L7548M	Closed	1995	150.00	150-228
1996 1996 Limited Edition Egg L7550M	Closed	1996	155.00	155-175
1997 1997 Limited Edition Egg L7552M	Closed	1997	155.00	155
1998 Garden Stroll 01016590	Yr.Iss.		150.00	150

Norman Rockwell Collection - Rockwell-Inspired

YEAR ISSUE	EDITION LIMIT	YEAR RETD.	ISSUE PRICE	*QUOTE U.S.$
1982 Lladró Love Letter L1406 (RL-400G)	5,000	N/A	650.00	725-1200
1982 Summer Stock L1407 (RL-401G)	5,000	N/A	750.00	650-900
1982 Practice Makes Perfect L1408 (RL-402G)	5,000	N/A	725.00	600-800
1982 Young Love L1409 (RL-403G)	5,000	N/A	450.00	900-1350
1982 Daydreamer L1411 (RL-404G)	5,000	N/A	450.00	1400-1500
1982 Court Jester L1405 (RL-405G)	5,000	N/A	600.00	1050-1200
1982 Springtime L1410 (RL-406G)	5,000	N/A	450.00	1200-1450

Lowell Davis Farm Club

Lowell Davis Farm Club - L. Davis

YEAR ISSUE	EDITION LIMIT	YEAR RETD.	ISSUE PRICE	*QUOTE U.S.$
1985 The Bride 221001 / 20993	Yr.Iss.	1985	45.00	400-475
1987 The Party's Over 221002 / 20994	Yr.Iss.	1987	50.00	180-295
1988 Chow Time 221003 / 20995	Yr.Iss.	1988	55.00	150-199
1989 Can't Wait 221004 / 20996	Yr.Iss.	1989	75.00	125-175
1990 Pit Stop 221005 / 20997	Yr.Iss.	1990	75.00	125-189
1991 Arrival Of Stanley 221006 / 20998	Yr.Iss.	1991	100.00	100-149
1991 Don't Pick The Flowers 221007 / 21007	Yr.Iss.	1991	100.00	145-160
1992 Hog Wild	Yr.Iss.	1992	100.00	100
1992 Check's in the Mail	Yr.Iss.	1992	100.00	110-130
1993 The Survivor 25371	Yr.Iss.	1993	70.00	70
1994 Summer Days	Yr.Iss.	1994	100.00	150
1995 Dutch Treat	Yr.Iss.	1995	100.00	100
1995 Free Kittens	Yr.Iss.	1995	40.00	40
1996 Sunnyside Up	Yr.Iss.	1997	55.00	55
1997 Grandpa's Ole Tom	Yr.Iss.		80.00	70-80

Lowell Davis Farm Club Renewal Figurine - L. Davis

YEAR ISSUE	EDITION LIMIT	YEAR RETD.	ISSUE PRICE	*QUOTE U.S.$
1986 Thirsty? 892050 / 92050	Yr.Iss.	1987	Gift	30-50
1987 Cackle Berries 892051 / 92051	Yr.Iss.	1989	Gift	85
1988 Ice Cream Churn 892052 / 92052	Yr.Iss.	1990	Gift	75-85
1990 Not A Sharing Soul 892053 / 92053	Yr.Iss.	1991	Gift	50-60
1991 New Arrival 892054 / 92054	Yr.Iss.	1992	Gift	40-75
1992 Garden Toad 92055	Yr.Iss.	1993	Gift	40-75
1993 Luke 12:6 25372	Yr.Iss.	1994	Gift	40-75
1994 Feathering Her Nest	Yr.Iss.	1995	Gift	40-50
1995 After the Rain	Yr.Iss.	1996	Gift	40-50
1996 A Gift For You	Retrd.	1997	Gift	25
1997 One in the Hand 97011	6/98		Gift	N/A

Davis Cat Tales Figurines - L. Davis

YEAR ISSUE	EDITION LIMIT	YEAR RETD.	ISSUE PRICE	*QUOTE U.S.$
1982 Company's Coming 25205	Closed	1986	60.00	175-215
1982 Flew the Coop 25207	Closed	1986	60.00	125-365
1982 On the Move 25206	Closed	1986	70.00	650
1982 Right Church, Wrong Pew 25204	Closed	1986	70.00	250-325

Davis Country Christmas Figurines - L. Davis

YEAR ISSUE	EDITION LIMIT	YEAR RETD.	ISSUE PRICE	*QUOTE U.S.$
1983 Hooker at Mailbox with Presents 23550	Closed	1984	80.00	750
1984 Country Christmas 23551	Closed	1985	80.00	250-350
1985 Christmas at Fox Fire Farm 23552	Closed	1986	80.00	275
1986 Christmas at Red Oak 23553	Closed	1987	80.00	225-250
1987 Blossom's Gift 23554	Closed	1988	150.00	400-475
1988 Cutting the Family Christmas Tree 23555	Closed	1989	80.00	350
1989 Peter and the Wren 23556	Closed	1990	165.00	450
1990 Wintering Deer 23557	Closed	1991	165.00	125-200
1991 Christmas At Red Oak II 23558	Closed	1992	250.00	175-250
1992 Born on a Starry Night 23559	2,500	1993	225.00	175-225
1993 Waiting For Mr. Lowell 23606	2,500	1994	250.00	250
1994 Visions of Sugar Plums	2,500	1995	250.00	200-250
1995 Bah Humbug	2,500	1996	200.00	250

Davis Country Pride - L. Davis

YEAR ISSUE	EDITION LIMIT	YEAR RETD.	ISSUE PRICE	*QUOTE U.S.$
1981 Bustin' with Pride 25202	Closed	1985	100.00	250
1981 Duke's Mixture 25203	Closed	1985	100.00	450
1981 Plum Tuckered Out 25201	Closed	1985	100.00	950
1981 Surprise in the Cellar 25200	Closed	1985	100.00	1000

Davis Friends of Mine - L. Davis

YEAR ISSUE	EDITION LIMIT	YEAR RETD.	ISSUE PRICE	*QUOTE U.S.$
1992 Cat and Jenny Wren 23633	5,000	1993	170.00	175
1992 Cat and Jenny Wren Mini 23634	Closed	1993	35.00	40
1989 Sun Worshippers 23620	5,000	1993	120.00	135
1989 Sun Worshippers Mini 23621	5,000	1993	32.50	40
1990 Sunday Afternoon Treat 23625	5,000	1993	120.00	130
1990 Sunday Afternoon Treat Mini 23626	Closed	1993	32.50	40-50
1991 Warm Milk 23629	Closed	1993	120.00	200
1991 Warm Milk Mini 23630	5,000	1993	32.50	40

Davis Little Critters - L. Davis

YEAR ISSUE	EDITION LIMIT	YEAR RETD.	ISSUE PRICE	*QUOTE U.S.$
1992 Charivari 25707	950	1993	250.00	250
1991 Christopher Critter 25514	1,192	1993	150.00	150-175
1992 Double Yolker 25516	Yr.Iss.	1993	70.00	75
1989 Gittin' a Nibble 25294	Closed	1993	50.00	75
1991 Great American Chicken Race 25500	2,500	1993	225.00	250-300
1991 Hittin' The Sack 25510	Closed	1993	70.00	70-75
1990 Home Squeezins 25504	Closed	1993	90.00	90-100
1991 Itiskit, Itasket 25511	Closed	1993	45.00	45-50
1991 Milk Mouse 25503	2,500	1993	175.00	275-300
1992 Miss Private Time 25517	Yr.Iss.	1993	35.00	35
1990 Outing With Grandpa 25502	2,500	1993	200.00	250
1990 Private Time 25506	Closed	1993	18.00	25-35
1990 Punkin' Pig 25505	2,500	1993	250.00	250-300
1991 Punkin' Wine 25501	Closed	1993	100.00	125
1991 Toad Strangler 25509	Closed	1993	57.00	75
1991 When Coffee Never Tasted So Good (Music box) 809225	1,250	1993	800.00	800
1991 When Coffee Never Tasted So Good 25507	1,250	1993	800.00	800
1992 A Wolf in Sheep's Clothing 25518	Yr.Iss.	1993	110.00	110

Davis Pen Pals - L. Davis

YEAR ISSUE	EDITION LIMIT	YEAR RETD.	ISSUE PRICE	*QUOTE U.S.$
1993 The Old Home Place (mini) 25801	Closed	1995	25.00	25
1993 The Old Home Place 25802	1,200	1995	200.00	200

Davis Promotional Figurine - L. Davis

YEAR ISSUE	EDITION LIMIT	YEAR RETD.	ISSUE PRICE	*QUOTE U.S.$
1991 Leavin' The Rat Race 225512	Yr.Iss.	1991	80.00	150-175
1992 Hen Scratch Prom 225968	Yr.Iss.	1992	90.00	82
1993 Leapin' Lizard 225969	Yr.Iss.	1993	80.00	80
1994 Don't Forget Me 227130	Yr.Iss.	1994	70.00	70
1995 Nasty Stuff 95103	Yr.Iss.	1995	40.00	40-75

Davis RFD America - L. Davis

YEAR ISSUE	EDITION LIMIT	YEAR RETD.	ISSUE PRICE	*QUOTE U.S.$
1984 Anybody Home 25239	Closed	1987	35.00	100
1994 Attic Antics	Closed	1995	100.00	150
1982 Baby Blossom 25227	Closed	1984	40.00	325
1982 Baby Bobs 25222	Closed	1984	47.50	200-250

*Quotes have been rounded up to nearest dollar

YEAR ISSUE	EDITION LIMIT	YEAR RETD.	ISSUE PRICE	*QUOTE U.S.$
1985 Barn Cats 25257	Closed	1990	39.50	90
1993 Be My Valentine 27561	Closed	1997	35.00	40
1986 Bit Off More Than He Could Chew 25279	Closed	1992	15.00	55
1979 Blossom 25032	Closed	1983	180.00	1800
1993 Blossom 96846 (15th Anniversary)	Closed	1993	80.00	80
1982 Blossom and Calf 25326	Closed	1986	250.00	850
1995 Blossom's Best	750	1995	300.00	300-500
1987 Bottoms Up 25270	Closed	1992	80.00	105
1989 Boy's Night Out 25339	1,500	1992	190.00	250-300
1982 Brand New Day 25226	Closed	1984	23.50	50-150
1979 Broken Dreams 25035	Closed	1983	165.00	1200-1300
1993 Broken Dreams 96847 (15th Anniversary)	Closed	1993	80.00	80
1988 Brothers 25286	Closed	1990	55.00	70
1984 Catnapping Too? 25247	Closed	1991	70.00	70-150
1987 Chicken Thief 25338	Closed	1988	200.00	325-375
1983 City Slicker 25329	Closed	1990	150.00	270
1991 Cock Of The Walk 25347	2,500	1993	300.00	150-300
1986 Comfy? 25273	Closed	1997	40.00	80
1994 Companion pc. And Down the Hatch	Closed	1994	135.00	145
1994 Companion pc. Open The Lid	Closed	1994	135.00	145
1989 Coon Capers 25291	Closed	1997	67.50	90
1990 Corn Crib Mouse 25295	Closed	1993	35.00	45
1983 Counting the Days 25233	Closed	1992	40.00	60
1981 Country Boy 25213	Closed	1984	37.50	350-375
1985 Country Cousins 25266	Closed	1995	42.50	90
1982 Country Crook 25280	Closed	1984	37.50	330
1985 Country Crooner 25256	Closed	1995	25.00	50
1984 Country Kitty 25246	Closed	1987	52.00	125
1979 Country Road 25030	Closed	1983	100.00	675
1993 Country Road 96842 (15th Anniversary)	Closed	1993	65.00	65
1984 Courtin' 25220	Closed	1986	45.00	125
1980 Creek Bank Bandit 25038	Closed	1985	37.50	400
1995 Cussin' Up a Storm	Closed	1995	45.00	45
1993 Don't Open Till Christmas 27562	Closed	1997	35.00	35
1992 Don't Play With Fire 25319	Closed	1997	120.00	120
1985 Don't Play With Your Food 25258	Closed	1992	28.50	50
1981 Double Trouble 25211	Closed	1984	35.00	200-475
1981 Dry as a Bone 25216	Closed	1984	45.00	300-325
1993 Dry Hole 25374	Closed	1995	30.00	35
1987 Easy Pickins 25269	Closed	1990	45.00	85-125
1993 End of the Trail 81000A	100	1993	100.00	600
1983 Fair Weather Friend 25236	Closed	1987	25.00	85
1983 False Alarm 25237	Closed	1985	65.00	185
1989 Family Outing 25289	Closed	1995	45.00	60
1996 Farm Club Sign	Open		40.00	40
1997 Farm Club Sign	Open		40.00	40
1994 Favorite Sport 25381	Closed	1995	230.00	230
1985 Feelin' His Oats 25275	1,500	1990	150.00	300-345
1990 Finder's Keepers 25299	Closed	1997	39.50	45-75
1991 First Offense 25304	Closed	1993	70.00	80
1994 First Outing	Closed	1997	65.00	75
1988 Fleas 25272	Closed	1997	20.00	30
1980 Forbidden Fruit 25022	Closed	1985	25.00	90-150
1990 Foreplay 25300	Closed	1993	59.50	80
1979 Fowl Play 25033	Closed	1983	100.00	275-325
1993 Fowl Play 96845 (15th Anniversary)	Closed	1993	60.00	60
1992 Free Lunch 25321	Closed	1997	85.00	85
1993 The Freeloaders 95042	1,250	1995	230.00	230
1985 Furs Gonna Fly 25335	1,500	1989	145.00	200-250
1994 Get Well 96902	Closed	1997	35.00	40
1987 Glutton for Punishment 25268	Closed	1991	95.00	160
1988 Goldie and Her Peeps 25283	Closed	1991	25.00	37
1984 Gonna Pay for His Sins 25243	Closed	1989	27.50	55
1980 Good, Clean Fun 25020	Closed	1989	40.00	95-150
1984 Gossips 25248	Closed	1987	110.00	250-265
1992 The Grass is Always Greener 25367	Closed	1995	195.00	195
1991 Gun Shy 25305	Closed	1993	70.00	70
1990 Hanky Panky 25298	Closed	1993	65.00	80-145
1994 Happy Anniversary 95089	Closed	1997	35.00	40
1993 Happy Birthday My Sweet 27560	Closed	1997	35.00	35-40
1988 Happy Hour 25287	Closed	1997	57.50	80-125
1983 Happy Hunting Ground 25330	Closed	1990	160.00	235
1984 Headed Home 25240	Closed	1991	25.00	50-95
1992 Headed South 25327	Closed	1995	45.00	45
1991 Heading For The Persimmon Grove 25306	Closed	1993	80.00	80
1994 Helpin Himself	Closed	1995	65.00	75
1983 Hi Girls, The Name's Big Jack 25328	Closed	1987	200.00	300-420
1981 Hightailing It 25214	Closed	1984	50.00	150-400
1983 His Eyes Are Bigger Than His Stomach 25332	Closed	1989	235.00	350
1984 His Master's Dog 25244	Closed	1988	45.00	75-150
1994 Hittin The Trail	1,250	1995	250.00	250
1985 Hog Heaven 25336	1,500	1988	165.00	350-400
1996 Homebodies	Yr.Iss.	1996	120.00	120
1992 The Honeymoon's Over 25370	1,950	1994	300.00	300
1995 Hook, Line & Sinker 25382	Closed	1997	35.00	35
1984 Huh? 25242	Closed	1989	40.00	150-155
1993 I'm Thankful For You 27563	Closed	1997	35.00	40
1982 Idle Hours 25230	Closed	1985	37.50	150-450
1993 If You Can't Beat Em Join Em 25379	1,750	1995	250.00	250
1979 Ignorance is Bliss 25031	Closed	1983	165.00	1100
1993 Ignorance is Bliss 96843 (15th Anniversary)	Closed	1993	75.00	75
1988 In a Pickle 25284	Closed	1995	40.00	50
1980 Itching Post 25037	Closed	1988	30.00	115
1993 King of The Mountain 25380	750	1995	500.00	400-500
1991 Kissin' Cousins 25307	Closed	1993	80.00	80
1990 The Last Straw 25301	Closed	1993	125.00	165
1989 Left Overs 25290	Closed	1997	90.00	95
1983 Licking Good 25234	Closed	1985	35.00	175-225
1990 Little Black Lamb (Baba) 25297	Closed	1993	30.00	38
1990 Long Days, Cold Nights 25344	2,500	1993	175.00	190
1991 Long, Hot Summer 25343	1,950	1995	250.00	250
1985 Love at First Sight 25267	Closed	1992	70.00	115
1992 Lowell Davis Profile 25366	Closed	1997	75.00	55-75
1984 Mad As A Wet Hen 25334	Closed	1986	185.00	700-800
1987 Mail Order Bride 25263	Closed	1991	150.00	325-375
1983 Makin' Tracks 25238	Closed	1989	70.00	150-199
1988 Making a Bee Line 25274	Closed	1990	75.00	125-155
1994 Mama Can Willie Stay For Supper	1,250	1995	200.00	220
1983 Mama's Prize Leghorn 25235	Closed	1988	55.00	135
1986 Mama? 25277	Closed	1991	15.00	30-45
1989 Meeting of Sheldon 25293	Closed	1992	120.00	125
1980 Milking Time 25023	Closed	1985	20.00	240
1988 Missouri Spring 25278	Closed	1992	115.00	130
1982 Moon Raider 25325	Closed	1986	190.00	390
1995 The Morning After 10000	Closed	1995	60.00	120
1989 Mother Hen 25292	Closed	1997	37.50	50
1993 Mother's Day 95088	Closed	1997	35.00	40
1982 Moving Day 25225	Closed	1984	43.50	250-325
1992 My Favorite Chores 25362	1,500	1994	750.00	750
1980 New Day 25025	Closed	1980	20.00	165
1989 New Friend 25288	Closed	1994	45.00	60
1993 No Hunting 25375	1,000	1995	95.00	105-150
1988 No Private Time 25316	Closed	1992	200.00	300-350
1994 Not a Happy Camper	Closed	1997	75.00	75
1994 Oh Mother What is it?	1,000	1995	250.00	250
1992 OH Sheeeit . . . 25363	Closed	1995	120.00	120-150
1993 Oh Where is He Now 95041	1,250	1995	250.00	250
1984 One for the Road 25241	Closed	1988	37.50	70
1987 The Orphans 25271	Closed	1992	50.00	95
1985 Out-of-Step 25259	Closed	1989	45.00	90
1985 Ozark Belle 25264	Closed	1990	35.00	70
1992 Ozark's Vittles 25318	Closed	1997	60.00	70
1984 Pasture Pals 25245	Closed	1990	52.00	130
1993 Peep Show 25376	Closed	1997	35.00	35
1988 Perfect Ten 25282	Closed	1990	95.00	180
1990 Piggin' Out 25345	Closed	1993	190.00	250
1994 Pollywogs 25617	750	1994	750.00	750
1984 Prairie Chorus 25333	Closed	1986	135.00	1200
1996 Proud Papa 96002	Yr.Iss.	1996	250.00	250
1981 Punkin' Seeds 25219	Closed	1984	225.00	1550-1750
1994 Qu'est - Ceque C'est?	Closed	1995	200.00	220
1985 Renoir 25261	Closed	1991	45.00	85
1981 Rooted Out 25217	Closed	1989	45.00	115
1992 Safe Haven 25320	Closed	1994	95.00	95
1988 Sawin' Logs 25260	Closed	1993	85.00	105
1981 Scallawags 25221	Closed	1987	65.00	95-150
1992 School Yard Dogs 25369	Closed	1994	100.00	100
1996 See Ya There 96002	Yr.Iss.	1996	330.00	330
1990 Seein' Red (Gus w/shoes) 25296	Closed	1993	35.00	47
1992 She Lay Low 25364	Closed	1995	120.00	120
1993 Sheep Sheerin Time 25388	1,200	1995	500.00	500
1982 A Shoe to Fill 25229	Closed	1986	37.50	150-175
1979 Slim Pickins 25034	Closed	1983	165.00	750-850
1993 Slim Pickins 96846 (15th Anniversary)	Closed	1993	75.00	85
1992 Snake Doctor 25365	Closed	1995	70.00	70
1991 Sooieee 25360	1,500	1994	350.00	350
1981 Split Decision 25210	Closed	1984	45.00	195-300
1995 Sticks and Stones	Closed	1997	30.00	30
1983 Stirring Up Trouble 25331	Closed	1988	160.00	260
1980 Strawberry Patch 25021	Closed	1989	25.00	95
1982 Stray Dog 25223	Closed	1988	35.00	75
1981 Studio Mouse 25215	Closed	1984	60.00	360
1980 Sunday Afternoon 25024	Closed	1985	22.50	175-225
1993 Sweet Tooth 25373	Closed	1995	60.00	75
1982 Thinking Big 25231	Closed	1988	35.00	100
1985 Too Good to Waste on Kids 25262	Closed	1989	70.00	130
1982 Treed 25327	Closed	1988	155.00	300-320
1989 A Tribute to Hooker 25340	Closed	1992	180.00	250
1993 Trick or Treat 27565	Closed	1997	35.00	50
1990 Tricks Of The Trade 25346	Closed	1994	300.00	350-375
1987 Two in the Bush 25337	Closed	1988	150.00	300-320
1994 Two Timer	Closed	1995	95.00	95
1982 Two's Company 25224	Closed	1986	43.50	200-225
1981 Under the Weather 25212	Closed	1991	25.00	85
1995 Uninvited Caller	Closed	1995	35.00	35
1981 Up To No Good 25218	Closed	1984	200.00	850-950
1982 Waiting for His Master 25281	Closed	1986	50.00	300
1994 Warmin' Their Buns	1,250	1995	270.00	225-270
1991 Washed Ashore 25308	Closed	1993	70.00	60-70
1982 When Mama Gets Mad 25228	Closed	1986	37.50	200-350
1987 When the Cat's Away 25276	Closed	1990	40.00	60
1988 When Three Foot's a Mile 25315	Closed	1991	230.00	300
1980 Wilbur 25029	Closed	1985	100.00	550-575
1985 Will You Still Respect Me in the Morning 25265	Closed	1993	35.00	75
1988 Wintering Lamb 25317	Closed	1990	200.00	275
1988 Wishful Thinking 25285	Closed	1990	55.00	70
1983 Woman's Work 25232	Closed	1989	35.00	60-80
1989 Woodscolt 25342	Closed	1992	300.00	300
1997 You Snooze, You Lose	Open		120.00	120
1993 You're a Basket Full of Fun 27564	Open		35.00	35

Davis Route 66 - L. Davis

YEAR ISSUE	EDITION LIMIT	YEAR RETD.	ISSUE PRICE	*QUOTE U.S.$
1992 Fresh Squeezed? (w/ wooden base) 25609	350	1995	600.00	700
1992 Fresh Squeezed? 25608	2,500	1995	450.00	550
1992 Going To Grandma's 25619	Closed	1995	80.00	80
1993 Home For Christmas 25621	Closed	1995	80.00	80
1991 Just Check The Air 25600	350	1995	700.00	750
1991 Just Check The Air 25603	2,500	1995	550.00	550
1993 Kickin' Himself 25622	Closed	1995	80.00	80
1991 Little Bit Of Shade 25602	Closed	1995	100.00	100
1991 Nel's Diner 25601	350	1995	700.00	700
1991 Nel's Diner 25604	2,500	1995	550.00	550
1992 Quiet Day at Maple Grove 25618	Closed	1995	130.00	130
1992 Relief 25605	Closed	1995	80.00	80
1993 Summer Days 25607	Yr.Iss.	1995	100.00	100
1992 Welcome Mat (w/ wooden base) 25606	1,500	1995	400.00	200-400
1992 What Are Pals For? 25620	Closed	1995	100.00	100

Davis Special Edition Figurines - L. Davis

YEAR ISSUE	EDITION LIMIT	YEAR RETD.	ISSUE PRICE	*QUOTE U.S.$
1983 The Critics 23600	Closed	1986	400.00	1200-1600
1989 From A Friend To A Friend 23602	1,200	1990	750.00	1200
1985 Home from Market 23601	Closed	1988	400.00	688-1200
1992 Last Laff 23604	1,200	1994	900.00	650-900
1990 What Rat Race? 23603	1,200	1994	800.00	1025

Davis Uncle Remus - L. Davis

YEAR ISSUE	EDITION LIMIT	YEAR RETD.	ISSUE PRICE	*QUOTE U.S.$
1981 Brer Bear 25251	Closed	1984	80.00	1000-1200
1981 Brer Coyote 25255	Closed	1984	80.00	500
1981 Brer Fox 25250	Closed	1984	70.00	900-950
1981 Brer Rabbit 25252	Closed	1984	85.00	2000
1981 Brer Weasel 25254	Closed	1984	80.00	700
1981 Brer Wolf 25253	Closed	1984	85.00	500

Lucy & Me/Enesco Corporation

Christmas Lucy & Me - L. Riggs

YEAR ISSUE	EDITION LIMIT	YEAR RETD.	ISSUE PRICE	*QUOTE U.S.$
1985 Bear Holding Candle 16845	Retrd.	1989	9.00	39
1979 Bear Holding Candle E-2817	Retrd.	1983	N/A	52
1985 Bear Holding Candy Canes 16845	Retrd.	1989	9.00	27
1984 Bear Holding Doll & Lollipop E-5411	Retrd.	1989	10.00	27
1984 Bear Holding Jack in Box E-5411	Retrd.	1989	N/A	25
1984 Bear Holding Rocking Horse E-5411	Retrd.	1989	N/A	27
1985 Bear Holding Tree 16845	Retrd.	1989	9.00	25
1983 Bear Mailing Letter to Santa E-0555	Retrd.	1986	N/A	63
1983 Boy Bear Pulls Girl Bear on Sled E-0557	Retrd.	1989	15.00	30-63
1987 Boy in Blue Coat Pulling Tree in Wagon 110477	Retrd.	1989	12.00	39
1989 A Christmas Carol - Scrooge 222100	Yr.Iss.	1989	10.00	39
1987 Clown Juggler 110299	Retrd.	1989	10.00	33
1988 Couple Kissing Under the Mistletoe 510319	Retrd.	1989	15.00	31-45
1982 Dad E-5417	Retrd.	1989	9.00	N/A
1986 Dad Sleeping in Chair 105961	Retrd.	1989	10.00	39
1983 Girl Holding Teddy and Package E-0556	Retrd.	1986	N/A	25-27
1987 Girl in Nightgown Holds Stocking 110337	Retrd.	1989	N/A	30
1985 Girl Kneeling Next to Doll House 16675	Retrd.	1989	12.00	39
1987 Girl w/ Nightie and Cap 110310	Retrd.	1989	9.00	33
1989 Gnome Skiing 222062	Retrd.	1990	N/A	27
1982 Grandma E-5417	Retrd.	1989	9.00	39
1982 Grandpa E-5417	Retrd.	1989	N/A	34
1982 Mom E-5417	Retrd.	1989	N/A	N/A
1987 Mrs. Bear Strings Cranberry Garland 110957	Retrd.	1989	N/A	27
1988 Nutcracker Clara 510246	Retrd.	1989	11.00	39
1990 Red Skier 228141	Retrd.	1994	12.00	33
1985 Santa w/List of Good Girls and Boys 16640	Retrd.	1989	10.00	30-39
1987 Shoemaker Repairs Shoes 110485	Retrd.	1988	N/A	33-39
1989 Skier in Yellow & Blue Outfit 222038	Retrd.	1990	10.00	20
1986 Three Bears on a Toboggan 104981	Retrd.	N/A	20.00	57
1985 Tumbling Santa Claus (3 poses) 16039	Retrd.	1989	10.00	39-45
1987 Two Bears Dressed as Reindeer, set/2 110639	Retrd.	1990	10.00	33

Lucy & Me "Childs" - L. Riggs

YEAR ISSUE	EDITION LIMIT	YEAR RETD.	ISSUE PRICE	*QUOTE U.S.$
1986 Sunday's Child - Girl Goes to Church 107824	Retrd.	1989	11.00	40
1986 Monday's Child - Girl in Long Dress & Hat 107751	Retrd.	1989	11.00	N/A
1986 Tuesday's Child - Girl Ballerina 107778	Retrd.	1989	11.00	40
1986 Wednesday's Child - Girl w/ Handkerchief 107786	Retrd.	1989	11.00	40
1986 Thursday's Child - Girl Dressed in Hat/Coat 107794	Retrd.	1989	11.00	27
1986 Friday's Child - Bear Girl Holding Baby 107808	Retrd.	1989	11.00	40
1986 Saturday's Child - Girl as Nurse 107816	Retrd.	1989	11.00	27

Lucy & Me - L. Riggs

YEAR ISSUE	EDITION LIMIT	YEAR RETD.	ISSUE PRICE	*QUOTE U.S.$
1986 Angel Kissing 105767	Retrd.	1989	N/A	27
1985 Baby Boy Nap on Pillow 102156	Retrd.	1989	N/A	30
1988 Baby on Goose 114081	Retrd.	1988	9.50	33
1982 Baby w/Bear E-9341	Retrd.	1990	10.00	25
1987 Bear Dressed as Bunny with Carrot 111619	Retrd.	1990	11.00	39
1979 Bear in Bunny Ears w/blue Basket E-4731	Retrd.	1985	N/A	39
1985 Bear in Duck Inner Tube 101575	Retrd.	1989	8.00	45
1984 Bear in Red and White Clown Jester Suit 10170	Retrd.	1989	11.00	39
1981 Bear on Rocking Horse E-7135	Retrd.	1987	15.00	153

*Quotes have been rounded up to nearest dollar

YEAR ISSUE	EDITION LIMIT	YEAR RETD.	ISSUE PRICE	*QUOTE U.S.$
1986 Bear on Sandpile 107107	Retrd.	1989	9.50	39
1987 Bear Sitting w/honey Pot 112992	Retrd.	1989	8.00	20
1985 Bear w/Broken Leg 101621	Retrd.	1988	9.00	39
1985 Boy as Easter Egg 101370	Retrd.	1990	13.00	27
1983 Boy Bowler E-3079	Retrd.	1990	10.50	33
1979 Boy Gardener in Blue E4727	Retrd.	1985	N/A	27
1986 Boy w/Geese 106585	Retrd.	1989	9.50	39
1986 Boy w/Pail & Shovel 107107	Retrd.	1989	9.50	39
1987 Boy with Pacifier 114227	Retrd.	1991	9.50	33
1987 Canadian Bear as a Mountie 510491	Retrd.	1991	9.50	29
1990 Cavebears, Boy & Girl, set/2 228184	Retrd.	N/A	10.00	40
1985 Cookie Cutter Bear Skating 19618	Retrd.	1987	N/A	65
1989 Cow 224596	Retrd.	1992	10.00	15
1986 Dad and Son Fishing 104337	Retrd.	1989	10.00	33
1985 Dad w/Cub on Shoulders 101613	Retrd.	1991	15.00	30-39
1985 Dancing Bears in Irish Outfits 102032	Retrd.	1989	N/A	45
1986 Devil Kissing 105767	Retrd.	1989	N/A	27
1990 Elf Hammering Toy 568635	Retrd.	1992	N/A	69
1986 Family Going to Church (set/4) 106267	Retrd.	1992	11.00	65
1984 Fireman 11940	Retrd.	1989	11.00	20
1984 Four Seated Bears & Picnic Basket, set/6 12912	Retrd.	1988	N/A	123
1988 Gardener w/Cart 509353	Retrd.	1991	15.00	27
1987 Gardener w/Rake 111856	Retrd.	1990	11.00	39
1989 Gardner (w/o Flower Pot) 223659	Retrd.	1992	N/A	15
1987 German Bear w/ Bear Stein 510505	Retrd.	1991	9.50	23-33
1983 Get Well Bear E-3079	Retrd.	1990	10.50	33
1986 Girl Getting Ready For Bed 106941	Retrd.	1989	9.50	39
1984 Girl Pilgrim E-5414	Retrd.	1989	N/A	33
1987 Girl w/Coffee Pot 111635	Retrd.	1989	8.00	39
1986 Girl w/Yellow Dress w/Steno Pad 106968	Retrd.	1989	8.00	23
1987 Girl with Pacifier 114227	Retrd.	1991	9.50	27
1986 Graduate on School Books 106038	Retrd.	1991	10.00	25
1981 Hairdresser E-7137	Retrd.	1985	10.00	160
1981 Hugging Couple w/Valentine Hearts E-4729	Retrd.	1988	N/A	45-57
1987 John Hancock Bear 109681	Retrd.	1989	9.50	27
1988 Kissing Couple E-3197	Retrd.	1985	N/A	45
1989 Lamaze Couple, set/2 224537	Retrd.	N/A	20.00	45
1988 Little Red Riding Hood 510971	Retrd.	1989	N/A	30-39
1987 Mexican Bear in Sombrero Serape 510513	Retrd.	1991	9.50	33
1988 Mom w/Baby Diaper and Bag 114057	Retrd.	1988	10.00	39
1987 Mother and Child Carrying Laundry 111619	Retrd.	1989	11.00	39
1987 Party Animal 113018	Retrd.	1989	8.00	27
1986 Pilot with Plane 107018	Retrd.	1988	9.50	20-27
1985 Pregnant Mom (yellow) w/Baby Care Book (3 pc.) 101605	Retrd.	1992	12.00	27
1988 Queen of Hearts With Tarts 111791	Retrd.	1992	12.00	18
1988 Roller-skating Waitress 510602	Retrd.	1990	10.00	30-39
1979 Sailor Bear E3128	Retrd.	1989	9.00	27
1984 Sailor Bear w/Lollipop 11886	Retrd.	1988	10.50	33
1988 Sitting Bear w/Daisy 111953	Retrd.	1988	N/A	45
1984 Sitting Bear w/Heart 10715	Retrd.	1988	N/A	27
1986 Teddy Bear University 109541	Retrd.	1992	9.50	33
1982 Tennis Girl E-9342	Retrd.	1989	10.50	33
1983 Thank You Bear E-3079	Retrd.	1990	10.50	33
1982 Three Easter Bears E-9345	Retrd.	1990	N/A	75-93
1988 Turkey 510327	Retrd.	N/A	10.00	15
1985 Two Bears Playing Hearts, set/2 111538	Retrd.	1989	11.00	25-35
1986 Two Clowns Juggling Hearts 105775	Retrd.	1991	N/A	33
1979 Two Moms Hugging Cubs E-4733	Retrd.	1988	15.00	30-39
1982 Two Tumbling Bears E-8676	Retrd.	1990	10.00	45
1986 Vampire 103438	Retrd.	1989	N/A	25-33
1979 Wedding Couple E-4728	Retrd.	N/A	14.00	27
1986 Woman Holding Baby, set/2 105988	Retrd.	1988	10.00	66

Lucy & Me Alice in Wonderland - L. Riggs

YEAR ISSUE	EDITION LIMIT	YEAR RETD.	ISSUE PRICE	*QUOTE U.S.$
1988 Alice in Wonderland w/White Rabbit 510661	Retrd.	1990	35.00	123
1987 Alice in Wonderland Bear 111473	Retrd.	1989	9.00	25
1987 Mad Hatter Bear 111481	Retrd.	1989	9.00	25
1987 Tweedle-dee Bear 111503	Retrd.	1989	9.00	25
1987 Tweedle-dum Bear 111503	Retrd.	1989	9.00	25
1987 White Rabbit 111511	Retrd.	1989	9.50	25
1987 Two Bears Playing Cards 111538	Retrd.	1989	11.00	25-31
1987 March Hare 111545	Retrd.	1989	11.50	25

Lucy & Me Goldilocks - L. Riggs

YEAR ISSUE	EDITION LIMIT	YEAR RETD.	ISSUE PRICE	*QUOTE U.S.$
1986 Lucylocks Sleeping in Baby Bear's Cradle 107840	Retrd.	1989	40.00	123
1986 Lucylocks - Bear as Goldilocks 106976	Retrd.	1989	9.50	27
1986 3 Bears -Mama, Papa, Baby Table/Porridge, set/4 107034	Retrd.	1989	30.00	N/A
1986 3 Bears -Mama 107034	Retrd.	1989	30.00	27
1986 3 Bears -Papa 107034	Retrd.	1989	30.00	27
1986 3 Bears -Table 107034	Retrd.	1989	30.00	27
1986 3 Bears -Baby 107034	Retrd.	1989	30.00	27
1986 Lucylocks in Baby Bear's Chair 107875	Retrd.	1989	13.50	27
1986 Lucylocks in Mama Bear's Chair 107883	Retrd.	1989	16.50	27
1986 Lucylocks in Papa Bear's Chair 107891	Retrd.	1989	16.50	27

Maruri USA

African Safari Animals - W. Gaither

YEAR ISSUE	EDITION LIMIT	YEAR RETD.	ISSUE PRICE	*QUOTE U.S.$
1983 African Elephant	Closed	N/A	3500.00	3500
1983 Black Maned Lion	Closed	N/A	1450.00	1450
1983 Cape Buffalo	Closed	N/A	2200.00	2200
1983 Grant's Zebras, pair	500	1995	1200.00	1200
1981 Nyala	300	1995	1450.00	1450
1983 Sable	Closed	N/A	1200.00	1200
1983 Southern Greater Kudu	Closed	N/A	1800.00	1800
1983 Southern Impala	Closed	N/A	1200.00	1200
1983 Southern Leopard	Closed	1994	1450.00	1450
1983 Southern White Rhino	150		3200.00	3200

American Eagle Gallery - Maruri Studios

YEAR ISSUE	EDITION LIMIT	YEAR RETD.	ISSUE PRICE	*QUOTE U.S.$
1985 E-8501	Closed	1989	45.00	75
1985 E-8502	Open		55.00	65
1985 E-8503	Open		60.00	65
1985 E-8504	Open		65.00	75
1985 E-8505	Closed	1989	65.00	150
1985 E-8506	Open		75.00	90
1985 E-8507	Closed	1997	75.00	90
1985 E-8508	Closed	1989	75.00	85
1985 E-8509	Closed	1989	85.00	125
1985 E-8510	Open		85.00	95
1985 E-8511	Closed	1989	85.00	125
1985 E-8512	Closed	1997	295.00	325
1987 E-8721	Open		40.00	50
1987 E-8722	Open		45.00	55
1987 E-8723	Closed	1989	55.00	55
1987 E-8724	Open		175.00	195
1989 E-8931	Open		55.00	60
1989 E-8932	Open		75.00	80
1989 E-8933	Open		95.00	95
1989 E-8934	Open		135.00	140
1989 E-8935	Open		175.00	185
1989 E-8936	Open		185.00	195
1991 E-9141 Eagle Landing	Open		60.00	60
1991 E-9142 Eagle w/ Totem Pole	Closed	1997	75.00	75
1991 E-9143 Pair in Flight	Open		95.00	95
1991 E-9144 Eagle w/Salmon	Open		110.00	110
1991 E-9145 Eagle w/Snow	Closed	1997	135.00	135
1991 E-9146 Eagle w/Babies	Open		145.00	145
1995 E-9551 Eagle	Open		60.00	60
1995 E-9552 Eagle	Open		65.00	65
1995 E-9553 Eagle	Open		75.00	75
1995 E-9554 Eagle	Open		80.00	80
1995 E-9555 Eagle	Open		90.00	90
1995 E-9556 Eagle	Open		110.00	110

Americana - W. Gaither

YEAR ISSUE	EDITION LIMIT	YEAR RETD.	ISSUE PRICE	*QUOTE U.S.$
1981 Grizzley Bear and Indian	Closed	N/A	650.00	650
1982 Sioux Brave and Bison	Closed	N/A	985.00	985

Baby Animals - W. Gaither

YEAR ISSUE	EDITION LIMIT	YEAR RETD.	ISSUE PRICE	*QUOTE U.S.$
1981 African Lion Cubs	1,500	1995	195.00	195
1981 Black Bear Cubs	Closed	N/A	195.00	195
1981 Wolf Cubs	Closed	N/A	195.00	195

Birds of Prey - W. Gaither

YEAR ISSUE	EDITION LIMIT	YEAR RETD.	ISSUE PRICE	*QUOTE U.S.$
1981 Screech Owl	300		960.00	960
1981 American Bald Eagle I	Closed	N/A	165.00	585-1750
1982 American Bald Eagle II	Closed	N/A	245.00	2750
1983 American Bald Eagle III	Closed	N/A	445.00	650-1750
1984 American Bald Eagle IV	Closed	N/A	360.00	1750
1986 American Bald Eagle V	Closed	N/A	325.00	1250

Eyes Of The Night - Maruri Studios

YEAR ISSUE	EDITION LIMIT	YEAR RETD.	ISSUE PRICE	*QUOTE U.S.$
1988 Double Barn Owl O-8807	Closed	1993	125.00	130
1988 Double Snowy Owl O-8809	Closed	1993	245.00	250
1988 Single Great Horned Owl O-8803	Closed	1993	60.00	65
1988 Single Great Horned Owl O-8808	Closed	1993	145.00	150
1988 Single Screech Owl O-8801	Closed	1993	50.00	55
1988 Single Screech Owl O-8806	Closed	1993	90.00	95
1988 Single Snowy Owl O-8802	Closed	1993	50.00	55
1988 Single Snowy Owl O-8805	Closed	1993	80.00	85
1988 Single Tawny Owl O-8804	Closed	1993	60.00	65

Gentle Giants - Maruri Studios

YEAR ISSUE	EDITION LIMIT	YEAR RETD.	ISSUE PRICE	*QUOTE U.S.$
1992 Baby Elephant Sitting GG-9252	Closed	1997	65.00	65
1992 Baby Elephant Standing GG-9251	Closed	1997	50.00	50
1992 Elephant Pair GG-9255	Closed	1997	220.00	220
1992 Elephant Pair Playing GG-9253	Closed	1997	80.00	80
1992 Mother & Baby Elephant GG-9254	Closed	1997	160.00	160

Graceful Reflections - Maruri Studios

YEAR ISSUE	EDITION LIMIT	YEAR RETD.	ISSUE PRICE	*QUOTE U.S.$
1991 Mute Swan w/Baby SW-9152	Closed	1993	95.00	95
1991 Pair-Mute Swan SW-9153	Closed	1993	145.00	145
1991 Pair-Mute Swan SW-9154	Closed	1993	195.00	195
1991 Single Mute Swan SW-9151	Closed	1993	85.00	85

Horses Of The World - Maruri Studios

YEAR ISSUE	EDITION LIMIT	YEAR RETD.	ISSUE PRICE	*QUOTE U.S.$
1993 Arabian HW-9356	Closed	1995	175.00	175
1993 Camargue HW-9354	Closed	1995	150.00	150
1993 Clydesdale HW-9351	Closed	1995	145.00	145
1993 Paint Horse HW-9355	Closed	1995	160.00	160
1993 Quarter Horse HW-9353	Closed	1995	145.00	145
1993 Thoroughbred HW-9352	Closed	1995	145.00	145

Hummingbirds - Maruri Studios

YEAR ISSUE	EDITION LIMIT	YEAR RETD.	ISSUE PRICE	*QUOTE U.S.$
1995 Allen's & Babies w/Rose H-9523	Open		120.00	120
1995 Allen's w/Easter Lily H-9522	Open		95.00	95
1989 Allen's w/Hibiscus H-8906	Open		195.00	195
1989 Anna's w/Lily H-8905	Open		160.00	160
1995 Anna's w/Trumpet Creeper H-9524	Open		130.00	130
1995 Broad-Billed w/Amaryllis H-9526	Open		150.00	150
1989 Calliope w/Azalea H-8904	Open		120.00	120
1989 Ruby-Throated w/Azalea H-8911	Open		75.00	75
1989 Ruby-Throated w/Orchid H-8914	Open		150.00	150
1989 Rufous w/Trumpet Creeper H-8901	Open		70.00	75
1989 Violet-crowned w/Gentian H-8903	Open		90.00	90
1989 Violet-Crowned w/Gentian H-8913	Open		75.00	75
1995 Violet-Crowned w/Iris H-9521	Open		95.00	95
1989 White-eared w/Morning Glory H-8902	Open		85.00	85
1989 White-Eared w/Morning Glory H-8912	Open		75.00	75
1995 White-Eared w/Tulip H-9525	Open		145.00	145

Kingdom of Cats - Maruri Studios

YEAR ISSUE	EDITION LIMIT	YEAR RETD.	ISSUE PRICE	*QUOTE U.S.$
1997 Baby Cougar w/Icicles KC-9701	Open		50.00	50
1997 Bobcat w/Cactus KC-9705	Open		70.00	70
1997 Female Lions w/Cub KC-9709	Open		95.00	95
1997 Female Mountain Lion w/Cubs KC-9708	Open		90.00	90
1997 Male Lion on Rocks KC-9707	Open		85.00	85
1997 Male Tiger Jumping KC-9703	Open		60.00	60
1997 Mountain Lion on Rocks KC-9704	Open		65.00	65
1997 Mountain Lion on Trees KC-9706	Open		75.00	75
1997 Tiger Cubs Playing KC-9702	Open		55.00	55

Legendary Flowers of the Orient - Ito

YEAR ISSUE	EDITION LIMIT	YEAR RETD.	ISSUE PRICE	*QUOTE U.S.$
1985 Cherry Blossom	15,000		45.00	55
1985 Chinese Peony	15,000		45.00	55
1985 Chrysanthemum	15,000		45.00	55
1985 Iris	15,000		45.00	55
1985 Lily	15,000		45.00	55
1985 Lotus	15,000		45.00	45
1985 Orchid	15,000		45.00	55
1985 Wisteria	15,000		45.00	55

Majestic Owls of the Night - D. Littleton

YEAR ISSUE	EDITION LIMIT	YEAR RETD.	ISSUE PRICE	*QUOTE U.S.$
1988 Barred Owl	15,000		55.00	55
1987 Burrowing Owl	15,000		55.00	55
1988 Elf Owl	15,000		55.00	55

National Parks - Maruri Studios

YEAR ISSUE	EDITION LIMIT	YEAR RETD.	ISSUE PRICE	*QUOTE U.S.$
1993 Baby Bear NP-9301	Closed	1996	60.00	60
1993 Bear Family NP-9304	Closed	1996	160.00	160
1993 Buffalo NP-9306	Closed	1996	170.00	170
1993 Cougar Cubs NP-9302	Closed	1996	70.00	70
1993 Deer Family NP-9303	Closed	1996	120.00	120
1993 Eagle NP-9307	Closed	1996	180.00	180
1993 Falcon NP-9308	Closed	1996	195.00	195
1993 Howling Wolves NP-9305	Closed	1996	165.00	165

North American Game Animals - W. Gaither

YEAR ISSUE	EDITION LIMIT	YEAR RETD.	ISSUE PRICE	*QUOTE U.S.$
1984 White Tail Deer	950		285.00	285

North American Game Birds - W. Gaither

YEAR ISSUE	EDITION LIMIT	YEAR RETD.	ISSUE PRICE	*QUOTE U.S.$
1983 Bobtail Quail, female	Closed	N/A	375.00	375
1983 Bobtail Quail, male	Closed	N/A	375.00	375
1981 Canadian Geese, pair	Closed	N/A	2000.00	2000
1981 Eastern Wild Turkey	Closed	N/A	300.00	300
1982 Ruffed Grouse	Closed	N/A	1745.00	1745
1983 Wild Turkey Hen with Chicks	Closed	N/A	300.00	300

North American Songbirds - W. Gaither

YEAR ISSUE	EDITION LIMIT	YEAR RETD.	ISSUE PRICE	*QUOTE U.S.$
1982 Bluebird	Closed	N/A	95.00	95
1983 Cardinal, female	Closed	N/A	95.00	95
1982 Cardinal, male	Closed	N/A	95.00	95
1982 Carolina Wren	Closed	N/A	95.00	95
1982 Chickadee	Closed	N/A	95.00	95
1982 Mockingbird	Closed	N/A	95.00	95
1983 Robin	Closed	N/A	95.00	95

North American Waterfowl I - W. Gaither

YEAR ISSUE	EDITION LIMIT	YEAR RETD.	ISSUE PRICE	*QUOTE U.S.$
1981 Blue Winged Teal	200	1996	980.00	980
1981 Canvasback Ducks	Closed	1994	780.00	780
1981 Flying Wood Ducks	Closed	N/A	880.00	880
1981 Mallard Drake	Closed	N/A	2380.00	2380
1981 Wood Duck, decoy	950		480.00	480

North American Waterfowl II - W. Gaither

YEAR ISSUE	EDITION LIMIT	YEAR RETD.	ISSUE PRICE	*QUOTE U.S.$
1982 Bufflehead Ducks Pair	1,500		225.00	225
1982 Goldeneye Ducks Pair	Closed	N/A	225.00	225
1983 Loon	Closed	1989	245.00	245
1981 Mallard Ducks Pair	1,500		225.00	225
1982 Pintail Ducks Pair	Closed	1994	225.00	225
1982 Widgeon, female	Closed	N/A	225.00	225
1982 Widgeon, male	Closed	N/A	225.00	225

Polar Expedition - Maruri Studios

YEAR ISSUE	EDITION LIMIT	YEAR RETD.	ISSUE PRICE	*QUOTE U.S.$
1992 Arctic Fox Cubs Playing-P-9223	Open		65.00	65
1990 Baby Arctic Fox-P-9002	Open		50.00	55
1990 Baby Emperor Penguin-P-9001	Open		45.00	50
1992 Baby Harp Seal-P-9221	Open		55.00	55
1990 Baby Harp Seals-P-9005	Open		65.00	70
1992 Emperor Penguins-P-9222	Open		60.00	60
1990 Mother & Baby Emperor Penguins -P-9006	Open		80.00	85
1990 Mother & Baby Harp Seals-P-9007	Open		90.00	95
1990 Mother & Baby Polar Bears-P-9008	Open		125.00	130
1990 Polar Bear Cub Sliding-P-9003	Open		50.00	55
1990 Polar Bear Cubs Playing-P-9004	Open		60.00	65
1992 Polar Bear Family-P-9224	Open		90.00	90
1990 Polar Expedition Sign-PES-001	Open		18.00	18

Precious Panda - Maruri Studios

YEAR ISSUE	EDITION LIMIT	YEAR RETD.	ISSUE PRICE	*QUOTE U.S.$
1992 Lazy Lunch PP-9202	Open		60.00	60
1992 Mother's Cuddle-PP-9204	Open		120.00	120

*Quotes have been rounded up to nearest dollar

YEAR ISSUE	EDITION LIMIT	YEAR RETD.	ISSUE PRICE	*QUOTE U.S.$
1992 Snack Time PP-9201	Open		60.00	60
1992 Tug Of War PP-9203	Open		70.00	70

Santa's World Travels - Maruri Studios

YEAR ISSUE	EDITION LIMIT	YEAR RETD.	ISSUE PRICE	*QUOTE U.S.$
1996 Cat Nap SWT-9603	7,500		85.00	85
1996 Crossing the Tundra SWT-9605	7,500		145.00	145
1996 Desert Trip SWT-9604	7,500		95.00	95
1998 Frosty Penguins SWT-9821	7,500		60.00	60
1998 Guiding Tiger SWT-9824	7,500		95.00	95
1997 Polar Express SWT-9710	7,500		85.00	85
1998 Pouch Full of Dreams SWT-9822	7,500		70.00	70
1997 Rapid Delivery SWT-9711	7,500		85.00	85
1997 S. S. World Travels SWT-9713	5,000		175.00	175
1996 Santa's Safari SWT-9600	5,000		225.00	225
1997 A Special Gift SWT-9712	7,500		95.00	95
1998 Tea Time SWT-9823	7,500		70.00	70
1996 Trusted Friend SWT-9602	7,500		85.00	85
1996 Wild Ride SWT-9601	7,500		75.00	75

Shore Birds - W. Gaither

YEAR ISSUE	EDITION LIMIT	YEAR RETD.	ISSUE PRICE	*QUOTE U.S.$
1984 Pelican	Closed	N/A	260.00	260
1984 Sand Piper	Closed	N/A	285.00	285

Signature Collection - W. Gaither

YEAR ISSUE	EDITION LIMIT	YEAR RETD.	ISSUE PRICE	*QUOTE U.S.$
1985 American Bald Eagle	Closed	N/A	60.00	60
1985 Canada Goose	Closed	N/A	60.00	60
1985 Hawk	Closed	N/A	60.00	60
1985 Pintail Duck	Closed	N/A	60.00	60
1985 Snow Goose	Closed	N/A	60.00	60
1985 Swallow	Closed	N/A	60.00	60

Songbird Serenade - Maruri Studios

YEAR ISSUE	EDITION LIMIT	YEAR RETD.	ISSUE PRICE	*QUOTE U.S.$
1998 Black Capped Chickadee w/Daffodil SBS-9833	Open		65.00	65
1997 Blue Jay w/Oak SBS-9723	Open		70.00	70
1997 Bluebird Family w/Apple Blossom SBS-9729	Open		95.00	95
1998 Bluebird w/Poppy SBS-9836	Open		65.00	65
1997 Cardinal Family w/Rose SBS-9728	Open		90.00	90
1998 Cardinal w/Wild Grape SBS-9835	Open		65.00	65
1998 Carolina Wren w/Snow Drops SBS-9831	Open		65.00	65
1997 Cedar Waxwing Pair w/Berries SBS-9726	Open		80.00	80
1997 Chickadee Pair w/Holly & Berries SBS-9727	Open		85.00	85
1997 Goldfinch w/Violets SBS-9721	Open		65.00	65
1998 Mockingbirds w/Prarie Rose SBS-9837	Open		85.00	85
1998 Northern Baltimore Oriole w/Dogwood SBS-9834	Open		65.00	65
1998 Robin and Nest w/Hawthorn SBS-9838	Open		85.00	85
1997 Robin w/Blackberry SBS-9724	Open		70.00	70
1997 Robin w/Lily SBS-9722	Open		70.00	70
1997 Wren Pair w/Cactus SBS-9725	Open		80.00	80
1998 Yellow Warbler w/Morning Glory SBS-9832	Open		65.00	65

Songbirds Of Beauty - Maruri Studios

YEAR ISSUE	EDITION LIMIT	YEAR RETD.	ISSUE PRICE	*QUOTE U.S.$
1991 Bluebird w/ Apple Blossom SB-9105	Closed	1994	85.00	85
1991 Cardinal w/ Cherry Blossom SB-9103	Closed	1994	85.00	85
1991 Chickadee w/ Roses SB-9101	Closed	1994	85.00	85
1991 Dbl. Bluebird w/ Peach Blossom SB-9107	Closed	1994	145.00	145
1991 Dbl. Cardinal w/ Dogwood SB-9108	Closed	1994	145.00	145
1991 Goldfinch w/ Hawthorne SB-9102	Closed	1994	85.00	85
1991 Robin & Baby w/ Azalea SB-9106	Closed	1994	115.00	115
1991 Robin w/ Lilies SB-9104	Closed	1994	85.00	85

Special Commissions - W. Gaither

YEAR ISSUE	EDITION LIMIT	YEAR RETD.	ISSUE PRICE	*QUOTE U.S.$
1982 Cheetah	Closed	N/A	995.00	995-1560
1983 Orange Bengal Tiger	240		340.00	340
1981 White Bengal Tiger	240		340.00	340

Studio Collection - Maruri Studios

YEAR ISSUE	EDITION LIMIT	YEAR RETD.	ISSUE PRICE	*QUOTE U.S.$
1990 Majestic Eagles-MS-100	Closed	N/A	350.00	800
1991 Delicate Motion-MS-200	3,500	1997	325.00	325
1992 Imperial Panda-MS-300	3,500	1997	350.00	350
1993 Wild Wings-MS-400	3,500	1997	395.00	450
1994 Waltz of the Dolphins-MS-500	3,500		300.00	300
1995 "Independent Spirit" MS-600	3,500		395.00	395
1998 Fantasy in Flight MS-700	3,500		295.00	295

Stump Animals - W. Gaither

YEAR ISSUE	EDITION LIMIT	YEAR RETD.	ISSUE PRICE	*QUOTE U.S.$
1984 Bobcat	Closed	N/A	175.00	175
1984 Chipmunk	Closed	N/A	175.00	175
1984 Gray Squirrel	1,200	1995	175.00	175
1983 Owl	Closed	N/A	175.00	175
1983 Raccoon	Closed	1989	175.00	175
1982 Red Fox	Closed	N/A	175.00	175

Tribal Spirits - Maruri Studios

YEAR ISSUE	EDITION LIMIT	YEAR RETD.	ISSUE PRICE	*QUOTE U.S.$
1996 Bear Healer TS-9653	5,000		140.00	140
1996 Buffalo Hunter TS-9651	5,000		130.00	130
1996 Eagle Messenger TS-9652	5,000		140.00	140
1996 Wolf Guide TS-9654	5,000		150.00	150

Upland Birds - W. Gaither

YEAR ISSUE	EDITION LIMIT	YEAR RETD.	ISSUE PRICE	*QUOTE U.S.$
1981 Mourning Doves	Closed	N/A	780.00	780

Wings of Love Doves - Maruri Studios

YEAR ISSUE	EDITION LIMIT	YEAR RETD.	ISSUE PRICE	*QUOTE U.S.$
1987 D-8701 Single Dove w/ Forget-Me-Not	Closed	1994	45.00	55
1987 D-8702 Double Dove w/ Primrose	Open		55.00	65
1987 D-8703 Single Dove w/Buttercup	Closed	1994	65.00	70
1987 D-8704 Double Dove w/Daisy	Open		75.00	85
1987 D-8705 Single Dove w/Blue Flax	Closed	1994	95.00	95
1987 D-8706 Double Dove w/Cherry Blossom	Open		175.00	195
1990 D-9021 Double Dove w/Gentian	Open		50.00	55
1990 D-9022 Double Dove w/Azalea	Open		75.00	75
1990 D-9023 Double Dove w/Apple Blossom	Open		115.00	120
1990 D-9024 Double Dove w/Morning Glory	Closed	1997	150.00	160

Wonders of the Sea - Maruri Studios

YEAR ISSUE	EDITION LIMIT	YEAR RETD.	ISSUE PRICE	*QUOTE U.S.$
1994 Dolphin WS-9401	Open		70.00	70
1994 Great White Shark WS-9406	Open		90.00	90
1994 Green Sea Turtle WS-9405	Open		85.00	85
1994 Humpback Mother & Baby WS-9409	Open		150.00	150
1994 Manatee & Baby WS-9403	Open		75.00	75
1994 Manta Ray WS-9404	Open		80.00	80
1994 Orca Mother & Baby WS-9410	Open		150.00	150
1994 Sea Otter & Baby WS-9402	Open		75.00	75
1994 Three Dolphins WS-9408	Open		135.00	135
1994 Two Dolphins WS-9407	Open		120.00	120

Maud Humphrey Bogart/Enesco Corporation

Maud Humphrey Bogart Collectors' Club Members Only - M. Humphrey

YEAR ISSUE	EDITION LIMIT	YEAR RETD.	ISSUE PRICE	*QUOTE U.S.$
1991 Friends For Life MH911	Closed	N/A	60.00	65-100
1992 Nature's Little Helper MH921	Closed	N/A	65.00	82-95
1993 Sitting Pretty MH931	Closed	N/A	60.00	75-95

Maud Humphrey Bogart - Symbol Of Membership Figurines - M. Humphrey

YEAR ISSUE	EDITION LIMIT	YEAR RETD.	ISSUE PRICE	*QUOTE U.S.$
1991 A Flower For You H5596	Closed	N/A	Unkn.	57-65
1992 Sunday Best M0002	Closed	N/A	Unkn.	60-95
1993 Playful Companions M0003	Closed	N/A	Unkn.	65-75

Maud Humphrey Bogart - M. Humphrey

YEAR ISSUE	EDITION LIMIT	YEAR RETD.	ISSUE PRICE	*QUOTE U.S.$
1988 Tea And Gossip H1301	Retrd.	N/A	65.00	110-125
1988 Cleaning House H1303	Retrd.	N/A	60.00	88-90
1988 Susanna H1305	Retrd.	N/A	60.00	90-150
1988 Little Chickadees H1306	Retrd.	N/A	65.00	65-90
1988 The Magic Kitten H1308	Retrd.	N/A	66.00	75-80
1988 Seamstress H1309	Retrd.	N/A	66.00	74-119
1988 A Pleasure To Meet You H1310	Retrd.	N/A	65.00	90-119
1988 My First Dance H1311	Retrd.	N/A	60.00	125-130
1988 Sarah H1312	Retrd.	N/A	60.00	156-260
1988 Sealed With A Kiss H1316	Retrd.	N/A	45.00	45-70
1988 Special Friends H1317	Retrd.	N/A	66.00	75-90
1988 School Days H1318	Retrd.	N/A	42.50	43-70
1988 Gift Of Love H1319	Retrd.	N/A	65.00	60-80
1988 My 1st Birthday H1320	Retrd.	N/A	47.00	80
1990 Autumn Days H1348	24,500	N/A	45.00	45
1989 Winter Fun H1354	Retrd.	N/A	46.00	30-65
1990 School Lesson H1356	19,500	N/A	77.00	59-77
1989 Little Red Riding Hood H1381	24,500	N/A	42.50	38-43
1989 Little Bo Peep H1382	Retrd.	N/A	45.00	45-58
1991 Winter Ride 910066	Retrd.	N/A	60.00	60
1989 Springtime Gathering H1385	7,500		295.00	295
1992 Summer's Child 910252	24,500	N/A	50.00	50
1992 Stars and Stripes Forever 910201	Retrd.	N/A	75.00	113-125
1993 Playing Mama 5th Anniv. Figurine 915963	Retrd.	N/A	80.00	110-125
1993 Playing Mama Event Figurine 915963R	Retrd.	N/A	80.00	110-120

Memories of Yesterday/Enesco Corporation

Memories of Yesterday Society Figurines - M. Attwell

YEAR ISSUE	EDITION LIMIT	YEAR RETD.	ISSUE PRICE	*QUOTE U.S.$
1991 Welcome To Your New Home MY911	Yr.Iss.	1991	30.00	48
1992 I Love My Friends MY921	Yr.Iss.	1992	32.50	35
1993 Now I'm The Fairest Of Them All MY931	Yr.Iss.	1993	35.00	35
1993 A Little Love Song for You MY941	Yr.Iss.	1993	35.00	35
1994 Wot's All This Talk About Love MY942	Yr.Iss.	1994	27.50	28
1995 Sharing the Common Thread of Love MY951	Yr.Iss.	1995	100.00	100
1995 A Song For You From One That's True MY952	Yr.Iss.	1995	37.50	38
1996 You've Got My Vote MY961	Yr.Iss.	1996	40.00	40
1996 Peace, Heavenly Peace MY962	Yr.Iss.	1996	30.00	30
1997 We Take Care of One Another MY971	Yr.Iss.	1997	45.00	45
1997 You Mean the World to Me MY972	Yr.Iss.	1997	40.00	40
1998 A Little Caring Makes Everything Better MY981	Yr.Iss.		45.00	45
1998 No Worries Here MY982	Yr.Iss.		40.00	40

Memories of Yesterday Exclusive Membership Figurine - M. Attwell

YEAR ISSUE	EDITION LIMIT	YEAR RETD.	ISSUE PRICE	*QUOTE U.S.$
1991 We Belong Together S0001	Yr.Iss.	1991	Gift	37
1992 Waiting For The Sunshine S0002	Yr.Iss.	1992	Gift	35
1993 I'm The Girl For You S0003	Yr.Iss.	1993	Gift	40
1994 Blowing a Kiss to a Dear I Miss S0004	Yr.Iss.	1994	Gift	N/A
1995 Time to Celebrate S0005	Yr.Iss.	1995	Gift	N/A
1996 Forget-Me-Not! S0006	Yr.Iss.	1996	Gift	N/A
1997 Holding On To Childhood Memories S0007	Yr.Iss.	1997	Gift	N/A
1998 I'll Never Leave Your Side S0008	Yr.Iss.		Gift	N/A

Memories of Yesterday Exclusive Charter Membership Figurine - M. Attwell

YEAR ISSUE	EDITION LIMIT	YEAR RETD.	ISSUE PRICE	*QUOTE U.S.$
1992 Waiting For The Sunshine S0102	Yr.Iss.	1992	Gift	N/A
1993 I'm The Girl For You S0103	Yr.Iss.	1993	Gift	N/A
1994 Blowing a Kiss to a Dear I Miss S0104	Yr.Iss.	1994	Gift	N/A
1995 Time to Celebrate S0105	Yr.Iss.	1995	Gift	N/A
1996 Forget-Me-Not! S0106	Yr.Iss.	1996	Gift	N/A
1997 Holding On To Childhood Memories S0107	Yr.Iss.	1997	Gift	N/A
1998 I'll Never Leave Your Side S0108	Yr.Iss.		Gift	N/A

Memories of Yesterday 10th Anniversary Celebration - M. Attwell

YEAR ISSUE	EDITION LIMIT	YEAR RETD.	ISSUE PRICE	*QUOTE U.S.$
1997 Meeting Friends Along The Way Figurine 270407	Yr.Iss.	1997	85.00	85
1997 Meeting Friends Along The Way Covered Box 277746	Yr.Iss.	1997	14.00	14

Memories of Yesterday - M. Attwell

YEAR ISSUE	EDITION LIMIT	YEAR RETD.	ISSUE PRICE	*QUOTE U.S.$
1995 A Friend Like You Is Hard To Find 101176	Open		45.00	45
1995 A Helping Hand For You 101192	Retrd.	1997	40.00	40
1995 Won't You Skate With Me? 134864	5,000		35.00	35
1995 Dear Old Dear, Wish You Were Here 134872	5,000		37.50	38
1995 You're My Sunshine On A Rainy Day 137626	Retrd.	1998	37.50	38
1995 Boo-Boo's Band Set/5 137758	Open		25.00	25
1996 We're In Trouble Now! 162299	7,500		37.50	38
1998 Daddy's Little Shaver 162507	5,000		30.00	30
1996 A Basket Full of Love 162582	Open		50.00	50
1997 You're My Bouquet of Blessings 162604	5,000		30.00	30
1996 Just Longing To See You 162620	7,500		27.50	28
1996 We Are All His Children 162639	Open		30.00	30
1998 I'm A Little Lady 162655	5,000		30.00	30
1996 Just Like Daddy 162698	7,500		27.50	28
1998 This Is The Life 162817	5,000		32.50	33
1996 How Good of God To Make Us All 164135	5,000		50.00	50
1997 I Know You Can Do It 209821	5,000		35.00	35
1997 In the Hands of a Guardian Angel 209856	5,000		50.00	50
1997 There's Always a Rainbow 209864	5,000		37.50	38
1997 Bringing Gifts of Friendship To Share 209872	5,000		37.50	38
1997 Let Me Be Your Guardian Angel 279722	Open		25.00	25
1997 How 'Bout a Little Kiss 279730	Open		25.00	25
1997 Hoping To See You Soon 279706	Open		25.00	25
1997 I Pray Thee Lord My Soul To Keep 279714	Open		25.00	25
1997 Now I Lay Me Down To Sleep 279749	Open		25.00	25
1997 Time For Bed 279765	Open		25.00	25
1998 Fit For A Day 306509	5,000		30.00	30
1990 Collection Sign 513156	Closed	1993	7.00	7
1989 Blow Wind, Blow 520012	Retrd.	1997	40.00	40
1990 Hold It! You're Just Swell 520020	Suspd.		50.00	50
1990 Kiss The Place And Make It Well 520039	Suspd.		50.00	50
1989 Let's Be Nice Like We Was Before 520047	Suspd.		50.00	35-50
1991 Who Ever Told Mother To Order Twins? 520063	Open		33.50	34
1989 I'se Spoken For 520071	Retrd.	1991	30.00	30-50
1993 You Do Make Me Happy 520098	Open		27.50	28
1990 Where's Muvver? 520101	Retrd.	1994	30.00	30
1990 Here Comes The Bride And Groom God Bless 'Em! (musical) 520136	Suspd.		80.00	80
1989 Daddy, I Can Never Fill Your Shoes 520187	Retrd.	1997	30.00	30
1989 This One's For You, Dear 520195	Suspd.		50.00	50
1989 Should I . . . ? 520209	Suspd.		50.00	50
1990 Luck At Last! He Loves Me 520217	Retrd.	1992	35.00	36-58
1989 Here Comes The Bride-God Bless Her! 9" 520527	Retrd.	1990	95.00	60-95
1989 We's Happy! How's Yourself? (musical) 520616	Retrd.	1991	70.00	85-150
1989 Here Comes The Bride & Groom (musical) God Bless 'Em 520896	Open		50.00	50
1989 The Long and Short of It 522384	Retrd.	1994	32.50	33
1989 As Good As His Mother Ever Made 522392	Retrd.	1997	32.50	32-40
1989 Must Feed Them Over Christmas 522406	Retrd.	1996	38.50	39
1989 Knitting You A Warm & Cozy Winter 522414	Suspd.		37.50	38
1989 Joy To You At Christmas 522449	Retrd.	1996	45.00	45
1989 For Fido And Me (musical) 522457	Open		70.00	70
1991 Wishful Thinking 522597	Open		45.00	45
1991 Why Don't You Sing Along? 522600	Retrd.	1995	55.00	55
1995 You Brighten My Day With A Smile 522627	Retrd.	1998	30.00	30
1991 I Must Be Somebody's Darling 522635	Retrd.	1993	30.00	30
1991 Tying The Knot 522678	Retrd.	1998	60.00	60
1991 Wherever I Am, I'm Dreaming of You 522686	Suspd.		40.00	40
1993 Will You Be Mine? 522694	Retrd.	1997	30.00	30
1991 Sitting Pretty 522708	Retrd.	1993	40.00	50
1993 Here's A Little Song From Me To You (musical) 522716	Open		70.00	70
1992 A Whole Bunch of Love For You 522732	Retrd.	1996	40.00	40

*Quotes have been rounded up to nearest dollar

YEAR ISSUE	EDITION LIMIT	YEAR RETD.	ISSUE PRICE	*QUOTE U.S.$
1992 I'se Such A Good Little Girl Sometimes 522759	Suspd.		30.00	30
1992 Things Are Rather Upside Down 522775	Suspd.		30.00	30
1991 Pull Yourselves Together Girls, Waists Are In 522783	Retrd.	1997	30.00	30
1993 Bringing Good Luck To You 522791	Retrd.	1996	30.00	30
1995 I Comfort Fido And Fido Comforts Me 522813	5,000		50.00	50
1992 A Kiss From Fido 523119	Suspd.		35.00	35
1994 Bless 'Em! 523127	Retrd.	1998	35.00	35
1994 Bless 'Em! 523232	Retrd.	1998	35.00	35
1990 I'm Not As Backwards As I Looks 523240	Retrd.	1997	32.50	33
1990 I Pray The Lord My Soul To Keep 523259	Open		25.00	25
1990 He Hasn't Forgotten Me 523267	Suspd.		30.00	30
1990 Time For Bed 9" 523275	Yr.Iss.	1991	95.00	125
1991 Just Thinking 'bout You (musical) 523461	Suspd.		70.00	70
1992 Now Be A Good Dog Fido 524581	Retrd.	1997	45.00	45
1991 Them Dishes Nearly Done 524611	Suspd.		50.00	50
1995 Join Me For A Little Song 524654	5,000		37.50	38
1990 Let Me Be Your Guardian Angel 524670	Open		32.50	33
1990 A Lapful Of Luck 524689	Open		30.00	30
1990 Not A Creature Was Stirrin' 524697	Suspd.		45.00	45
1990 I'se Been Painting 524700	Suspd.		37.50	38
1992 The Future-God Bless 'Em! 524719	Retrd.	1998	37.50	38
1990 A Dash of Something With Something For the Pot 524727	Retrd.	1997	55.00	55
1991 Opening Presents Is Much Fun! 524735	Suspd.		37.50	38
1992 You'll Always Be My Hero 524743	Retrd.	1997	50.00	50
1990 Got To Get Home For The Holidays (musical) 524751	Retrd.	1994	100.00	100
1990 Hush-A-Bye Baby (musical) 524778	Retrd.	1997	80.00	80
1990 The Greatest Treasure The World Can Hold 524808	Retrd.	1997	50.00	50
1994 With A Heart That's True, I'll Wait For You 524816	Retrd.	1996	50.00	50
1990 Hoping To See You Soon 524824	Suspd.		30.00	30
1991 We All Loves A Cuddle 524832	Retrd.	1992	30.00	35
1991 He Loves Me 9" 525022	Retrd.	1992	100.00	100
1993 Now I Lay Me Down To Sleep (musical) 525413	Suspd.		65.00	65
1992 Making Something Special For You 525472	Suspd.		45.00	45
1991 I'm As Comfy As Can Be 525480	Suspd.		50.00	50
1992 I'm Hopin' You're Missing Me Too 525499	Suspd.		55.00	55
1993 The Jolly Ole Sun Will Shine Again 525502	Retrd.	1994	55.00	55
1997 May I Have This Dance? 525529	5,000		50.00	50
1991 Friendship Has No Boundaries (Special Understamp) 525545	Yr.Iss.	1991	30.00	30-50
1992 Home's A Grand Place To Get Back To (musical) 525553	Retrd.	1995	100.00	100
1991 Give It Your Best Shot 525561	Open		35.00	35
1992 I Pray the Lord My Soul To Keep (musical) 525596	Suspd.		65.00	65
1991 Could You Love Me For Myself Alone? 525618	Retrd.	1994	30.00	30
1996 Whenever I Get A Moment-I Think of You 525626	7,500		37.50	38
1992 Good Night and God Bless You In Every Way! 525634	Suspd.		50.00	50
1992 Five Years Of Memories (Five Year Anniversary Figurine) 525669	Yr.Iss.	1992	50.00	50-65
1992 Five Years Of Memories Celebrating Our Five Years 1992 525669A	Yr.Iss.	1992	N/A	N/A
1996 Loving You One Stitch At A Time 525677	5,000		50.00	50
1993 May Your Flowers Be Even Better Than The Pictures On The Packets 525685	Retrd.	1997	37.50	38
1995 Let's Sail Away Together 525707	Open		32.50	33
1993 You Won't Catch Me Being A Golf Widow 525715	Retrd.	1998	30.00	30
1995 Good Friends Are Great Gifts 525723	Open		50.00	50
1994 Taking After Mother 525731	Open		40.00	40
1994 Too Shy For Words 525758	Retrd.	1996	50.00	50
1991 Good Morning, Little Boo-Boo 525766	Retrd.	1996	40.00	40
1997 Dreams Are Sweeter With Friends 525774	5,000		37.50	38
1992 Hurry Up For the Last Train to Fairyland 525863	Suspd.		40.00	40
1992 I'se So Happy You Called 9" 526401	Yr.Iss.	1993	100.00	100
1994 Pleasant Dreams and Sweet Repose-(musical) 526592	Open		80.00	80
1998 Always Getting Stronger 526606	5,000		35.00	35
1996 Put Your Best Foot Forward 526983	5,000		50.00	50
1994 Bobbed 526991	Retrd.	1995	32.50	33
1996 Can I Keep Her, Mommy? 527025	Open		13.50	14
1992 Time For Bed 527076	Open		30.00	30
1991 S'no Use Lookin' Back Now! 527203	Yr.Iss.	1991	75.00	75
1992 Collection Sign 527300	Open		30.00	30
1993 Having A Wash And Brush Up 527424	Open		35.00	35
1994 Having a Good Ole Laugh 527432	Open		50.00	50
1993 A Bit Tied Up Just Now-But Cheerio 527467	Open		45.00	45
1992 Send All Life's Little Worries Skipping 527505	Retrd.	1997	30.00	30
1994 Don't Wait For Wishes to Come True-Go Get Them! 527645	Open		37.50	38
1993 Hullo! Did You Come By Underground? 527653	Yr.Iss.	1993	40.00	40
1993 Hullo! Did You Come By Underground? Commemorative Issue: 1913 1993 527653A	500		N/A	N/A
1993 Look Out-Something Good Is Coming Your Way! 528781	Suspd.		37.50	38
1992 Merry Christmas, Little Boo-Boo 528803	Open		37.50	38
1994 Do Be Friends With Me 529117	Open		40.00	40
1994 Good Morning From One Cheery Soul To Another 529141	Open		30.00	30
1994 May Your Birthday Be Bright And Happy 529575	Retrd.	1998	35.00	35
1996 God Bless Our Future 529583	5,000		45.00	45
1993 Strikes Me, I'm Your Match 529656	Open		27.50	28
1993 Wot's All This Talk About Love? 9" 529737	Yr.Iss.	1994	100.00	100
1994 Thank God For Fido 9" 529753	Yr.Iss.	1994	100.00	100
1994 Making the Right Connection 529907	Yr.Iss.	1994	32.50	33
1994 Still Going Strong 530344	Retrd.	1998	27.50	28
1997 Let Your Light Shine 530360	5,000		30.00	30
1993 Do You Know The Way To Fairyland? 530379	Retrd.	1996	50.00	50
1996 We'd Do Anything For You, Dear 530905	5,000		50.00	50
1994 Comforting Thoughts 531367	Retrd.	1998	32.50	33
1995 Love To You Always 602752	Open		30.00	30
1995 Wherever You Go, I'll Keep In Touch 602760	Retrd.	1996	30.00	30
1995 Love Begins With Friendship 602914	Retrd.	1997	50.00	50
1994 The Nativity Pageant 602949	Open		90.00	90
1995 May You Have A Big Smile For A Long While 602965	Open		30.00	30
1995 Love To You Today 602973	Open		30.00	30
1998 Did I Hear You Say You Like Me 602981	5,000		30.00	30
1996 You Warm My Heart 603007	7,500		35.00	35

Memories of Yesterday Charter 1988 - M. Attwell

YEAR ISSUE	EDITION LIMIT	YEAR RETD.	ISSUE PRICE	*QUOTE U.S.$
1988 Mommy, I Teared It 114480	Open		27.50	40-143
1988 Now I Lay Me Down To Sleep 114499	Open		25.00	25-65
1988 We's Happy! How's Yourself? 114502	Retrd.	1996	45.00	33-60
1988 Hang On To Your Luck! 114510	Suspd.		27.50	27-70
1988 How Do You Spell S-O-R-R-Y? 114529	Retrd.	1990	27.50	50-95
1988 What Will I Grow Up To Be? 114537	Suspd.		45.00	45
1988 Can I Keep Her Mommy? 114545	Retrd.	1995	27.50	27-70
1988 Hush! 114553	Retrd.	1990	50.00	75-125
1988 It Hurts When Fido Hurts 114561	Retrd.	1992	32.50	32-75
1988 Anyway, Fido Loves Me 114588	Suspd.		32.50	32-75
1988 If You Can't Be Good, Be Careful 114596	Retrd.	1993	55.00	55-90
1988 Welcome Santa 114960	Suspd.		50.00	50-100
1988 Special Delivery 114979	Retrd.	1991	32.50	32-70
1988 How 'bout A Little Kiss? 114987	Retrd.	1995	27.50	75-85
1988 Waiting For Santa 114995	Open		45.00	32-50
1988 Dear Santa. . . 115002	Suspd.		55.00	50-150
1988 I Hope Santa Is Home . . . 115010	Open		32.50	30-45
1988 It's The Thought That Counts 115029	Suspd.		27.50	29-75
1988 Is It Really Santa? 115347	Retrd.	1996	55.00	55-60
1988 He Knows If You've Been Bad Or Good 115355	Suspd.		45.00	45-75
1988 Now He Can Be Your Friend, Too! 115363	Suspd.		50.00	50-70
1988 We Wish You A Merry Christmas 115371 (musical)	Suspd.		75.00	75
1988 Good Morning Mr. Snowman 115401	Retrd.	1992	80.50	80-170
1988 Mommy, I Teared It, 9" 115924	Yr.Iss.	1990	95.00	140-195

Memories of Yesterday Event Item Only - M. Attwell

YEAR ISSUE	EDITION LIMIT	YEAR RETD.	ISSUE PRICE	*QUOTE U.S.$
1994 I'll Always Be Your Truly Friend 525693	Yr.Iss.	1994	30.00	30
1995 Wrapped In Love And Happiness 602930	Yr.Iss.	1995	35.00	35
1996 A Sweet Treat For You 115126	Yr.Iss.	1996	30.00	30
1997 Mommy, I Teared It 114480A	Yr.Iss.	1997	27.50	28
1998 A Circle of Friends 525030	Yr.Iss.		30.00	30

Alice in Wonderland - M. Attwell

YEAR ISSUE	EDITION LIMIT	YEAR RETD.	ISSUE PRICE	*QUOTE U.S.$
1997 Alice in Wonderland Collector Set 255254	3,000		150.00	150

Cinderella - M. Attwell

YEAR ISSUE	EDITION LIMIT	YEAR RETD.	ISSUE PRICE	*QUOTE U.S.$
1998 Cinderella Collector Set 314854	3,000		150.00	150

Comforting Thoughts - M. Attwell

YEAR ISSUE	EDITION LIMIT	YEAR RETD.	ISSUE PRICE	*QUOTE U.S.$
1997 You Make My Heart Feel Glad 209880	5,000		30.00	30

Covered Boxes - M. Attwell

YEAR ISSUE	EDITION LIMIT	YEAR RETD.	ISSUE PRICE	*QUOTE U.S.$
1998 Can I Keep Her, Mommy? 314862	Open		25.00	25
1998 Here Comes The Bride-God Bless Her 314870	Open		25.00	25
1998 May Your Birthday Be Happy And Bright 314889	Open		25.00	25
1998 Mommy, I Teared 314897	Open		25.00	25

Exclusive Heritage Dealer Figurine - M. Attwell

YEAR ISSUE	EDITION LIMIT	YEAR RETD.	ISSUE PRICE	*QUOTE U.S.$
1991 A Friendly Chat and a Cup of Tea 525510	Yr.Iss.	1991	50.00	100
1993 I'm Always Looking Out For You 527440	Yr.Iss.	1993	55.00	55
1994 Loving Each Other Is The Nicest Thing We've Got 522430	Yr.Iss.	1994	60.00	60
1995 A Little Help From Fairyland 529133	1,995	1995	55.00	55
1995 Friendship Is Meant To Be Shared 602922	Yr.Iss.	1995	50.00	50
1995 Bedtime Tales-set 153400	2,000	1996	60.00	60
1996 Tucking My Dears All Safe Away 130095	Yr.Iss.	1996	50.00	50
1996 I Do Like My Holiday Crews 522805	1,996		100.00	100
1996 Peter Pan Collector's Set 174564	1,000		150.00	150
1997 Every Stitch is Sewn With Kindness 209910	Yr.Iss.		50.00	50
1997 We're Going to Be Great Friends 525537	1,997		50.00	50

Friendship - M. Attwell

YEAR ISSUE	EDITION LIMIT	YEAR RETD.	ISSUE PRICE	*QUOTE U.S.$
1996 I'll Miss You 179183	Open		20.00	25
1996 I Love You This Much! 179191	Open		20.00	25
1996 Thinking of You 179213	Open		20.00	25
1996 You And Me 179205	Open		20.00	25

Holiday Snapshots - M. Attwell

YEAR ISSUE	EDITION LIMIT	YEAR RETD.	ISSUE PRICE	*QUOTE U.S.$
1995 I'll Help You Mommy 144673	Open		20.00	25
1995 Isn't She Pretty? 144681	Open		20.00	25
1995 I Didn't Mean To Do It 144703	Open		20.00	25
1995 Can I Open Just One? 144711	Open		20.00	25

A Loving Wish For You - M. Attwell

YEAR ISSUE	EDITION LIMIT	YEAR RETD.	ISSUE PRICE	*QUOTE U.S.$
1995 Happiness Is Our Wedding Wish 135178	Open		20.00	25
1995 A Blessed Day For You 135186	Open		20.00	25
1995 Wishing You A Bright Future 135194	Open		20.00	25
1995 An Anniversary Is Love 135208	Open		25.00	25
1995 A Birthday Wish For You 135216	Open		20.00	25
1995 Bless You, Little One 135224	Open		20.00	25
1996 You Are My Shining Star 164585	Open		20.00	25
1996 You Brighten My Days 164615	Open		20.00	25

Memories Of A Special Day - M. Attwell

YEAR ISSUE	EDITION LIMIT	YEAR RETD.	ISSUE PRICE	*QUOTE U.S.$
1994 Monday's Child... 531421	Open		35.00	35
1994 Tuesday's Child... 531448	Open		35.00	35
1994 Wednesday's Child... 531405	Open		35.00	35
1994 Thursday's Child... 531413	Open		35.00	35
1994 Friday's Child... 531391	Open		35.00	35
1994 Saturday's Child... 531383	Open		35.00	35
1994 Sunday's Child... 531480	Open		35.00	35
1994 Collector's Commemorative Edition Set of 7, Hand-numbered 528056	1,994	1994	250.00	250

Nativity - M. Attwell

YEAR ISSUE	EDITION LIMIT	YEAR RETD.	ISSUE PRICE	*QUOTE U.S.$
1994 Nativity Set of 4 602949	Open		90.00	90
1995 Innkeeper 602892	Open		27.50	28
1996 Shepherd 602906	Open		27.50	28

Once Upon A Fairy Tale™... - M. Attwell

YEAR ISSUE	EDITION LIMIT	YEAR RETD.	ISSUE PRICE	*QUOTE U.S.$
1992 Mother Goose 526428	18,000		50.00	50
1993 Mary, Mary Quite Contrary 526436	18,000		45.00	45
1993 Little Miss Muffett 526444	18,000		50.00	50
1992 Simple Simon 526452	18,000		35.00	35
1992 Mary Had A Little Lamb 526479	18,000		45.00	45
1994 Tweedle Dum & Tweedle Dee 526460	10,000		50.00	50

A Penny For Your Thoughts - M. Attwell

YEAR ISSUE	EDITION LIMIT	YEAR RETD.	ISSUE PRICE	*QUOTE U.S.$
1997 You're Nice 204722	Open		20.00	20
1997 Now Do You Love Me Or Do You Don't 204730	Open		20.00	20
1997 Roses Are Red, Violets Are Blue -Violets Are Sweet, An' So Are You 204757	Open		20.00	20

Peter Pan - M. Attwell

YEAR ISSUE	EDITION LIMIT	YEAR RETD.	ISSUE PRICE	*QUOTE U.S.$
1996 John 165441	Open		20.00	25
1996 Michael and Nana 165425	Open		25.00	30
1996 Peter Pan 164666	Open		20.00	25
1996 Wendy 164674	Open		20.00	25

Special Edition - M. Attwell

YEAR ISSUE	EDITION LIMIT	YEAR RETD.	ISSUE PRICE	*QUOTE U.S.$
1989 As Good As His Mother Ever Made 523925	Yr.Iss.	1989	32.50	44-150
1988 Mommy, I Teared It 523488	Yr.Iss.	1988	25.00	175-325
1990 A Lapful of Luck 525014	Yr.Iss.	1990	30.00	32-180
1990 Set of Three	N/A	N/A	87.50	735

When I Grow Up - M. Attwell

YEAR ISSUE	EDITION LIMIT	YEAR RETD.	ISSUE PRICE	*QUOTE U.S.$
1995 When I Grow Up, I Want To Be A Doctor 102997	Open		20.00	25
1995 When I Grow Up, I Want To Be A Mother 103195	Open		20.00	25
1995 When I Grow Up, I Want To Be A Ballerina 103209	Open		20.00	25
1995 When I Grow Up, I Want To Be A Teacher 103357	Open		20.00	25
1995 When I Grow Up, I Want To Be A Fireman 103462	Open		20.00	25
1995 When I Grow Up, I Want To Be A Nurse 103535	Open		20.00	25
1996 When I Grow Up, I Want To Be A Businessman 164623	Open		20.00	25
1996 When I Grow Up, I Want To Be A Businesswoman 164631	Open		20.00	25

Midwest of Cannon Falls

Americana Nutcracker Collection - Midwest

YEAR ISSUE	EDITION LIMIT	YEAR RETD.	ISSUE PRICE	*QUOTE U.S.$
1997 Uncle Sam 21166-3	500	1998	170.00	170

Belenes Puig Nativity Collection - J.P. Llobera

YEAR ISSUE	EDITION LIMIT	YEAR RETD.	ISSUE PRICE	*QUOTE U.S.$
1989 Angel 02087-6	Open		50.00	60
1989 Baby Jesus 02085-2	Open		62.00	62

*Quotes have been rounded up to nearest dollar

YEAR ISSUE	EDITION LIMIT	YEAR RETD.	ISSUE PRICE	*QUOTE U.S.$
1989 Donkey 02082-1	Open		26.00	26
1989 Joseph 02086-9	Open		62.00	62
1989 Mother Mary 02084-5	Open		62.00	62
1985 Nativity, set/6: Holy Family, Angel, Animals 6 3/4" 00205-6	Open		250.00	250
1989 Ox 02083-8	Open		26.00	26
1990 Resting Camel 04025-6	Open		115.00	115
1986 Sheep, set/3 00475-3	Open		28.00	28
1987 Shepherd & Angel Scene, set/7 06084-1	Open		305.00	305
1989 Shepherd Carrying Lamb 02092-0	Open		56.00	56
1989 Shepherd with Staff 02091-3	Open		56.00	56
1985 Shepherd, set/2 00458-6	Open		110.00	110
1988 Standing Camel 08792-3	Open		115.00	115
1989 Wise Man with Frankincense 02088-3	Open		66.00	66
1989 Wise Man with Frankincense on Camel 02077-7	Open		155.00	156
1989 Wise Man with Gold 02089-0	Open		66.00	66
1989 Wise Man with Gold on Camel 02075-3	Open		155.00	156
1989 Wise Man with Myrrh 02090-6	Open		66.00	66
1989 Wise Man with Myrrh on Camel 02076-0	Open		155.00	156
1985 Wise Men, set/3 00459-3	Open		185.00	185

Cooperstown Collection - Midwest

YEAR ISSUE	EDITION LIMIT	YEAR RETD.	ISSUE PRICE	*QUOTE U.S.$
1997 Chicago Cubs Baseball Player 22868-5	Retrd.	1998	180.00	180
1997 Chicago White Sox Baseball Player 22867-8	Retrd.	1998	180.00	180
1997 New York Yankees Baseball Player 22869-2	Open		180.00	180

Eddie Walker Collection - E. Walker

YEAR ISSUE	EDITION LIMIT	YEAR RETD.	ISSUE PRICE	*QUOTE U.S.$
1995 Noah's Ark Set 15155-6	2,500	1996	175.00	225-350
1997 North Pole Express Train Set 21569-2	7,500	1997	200.00	225-250
1998 Santa at Tree Farm, set/5 24941-3	7,500		200.00	200
1996 Santa in Sleigh with Reindeer 17803-4	6,000	1996	180.00	460
1998 Santa on Holiday Plane 26141-5	Yr.Iss.		55.00	55
1997 Signature Santa-1997 21919-5	Yr.Iss.	1997	50.00	50
1998 Witch on Pumpkin 24360-2	Yr.Iss.		40.00	40

Leo R. Smith III Collection - L. R. Smith

YEAR ISSUE	EDITION LIMIT	YEAR RETD.	ISSUE PRICE	*QUOTE U.S.$
1997 American Heritage Santa 21318-6	750		110.00	110
1996 Angel of the Morning 18232-1	1,000		48.00	50
1995 Angel with Lion and Lamb 13990-5	1,500	1995	125.00	126-175
1995 Circle of Nature Wreath 16120-3	500	1996	200.00	200
1991 Cossack Santa 01092-1	1,700	1993	103.00	185-200
1993 Dancing Santa 09042-8	5,000	1995	170.00	170
1992 Dreams of Night Buffalo 07999-7	1,062	1996	250.00	270-300
1991 Fisherman Santa 03311-1	4,000	1995	270.00	350-475
1993 Folk Angel 05444-4	2,095	1995	145.00	200-250
1995 Gardening Angel 16118-0	2,500	1996	130.00	175
1997 Gardening Santa 21320-9	1,000	1998	110.00	110
1994 Gift Giver Santa 12056-9	1,500	1996	180.00	180
1993 Gnome Santa on Deer 05206-8	1,463	1996	270.00	280-350
1992 Great Plains Santa 08049-8	5,000	1994	270.00	400-500
1995 Hare Leaping Over the Garden 16121-0	750	1996	100.00	100
1996 Jolly Boatman Santa 17794-5	1,500		180.00	180
1992 Leo Smith Name Plaque 07881-5	5,000		12.00	12
1995 Maize Maiden Angel 13992-9	2,500	1996	45.00	50
1991 Milkmaker 03541-2	5,000	1994	170.00	184
1992 Ms. Liberty 07866-2	5,000	1994	190.00	300
1998 Nature Santa 10" 25148-5	750		120.00	120
1998 Northwoods Santa in Canoe 7" 25147-8	1,000	1998	140.00	140
1994 Old-World Santa 12053-8	1,500	1994	75.00	200-250
1995 Orchard Santa 13989-9	1,500	1996	125.00	125
1995 Otter Wall Hanging 16122-7	750	1996	150.00	200-225
1995 Owl Lady 13988-2	1,000	1995	100.00	105-200
1991 Pilgrim Man 03313-5	5,000	1994	84.00	200
1991 Pilgrim Riding Turkey 03312-8	1,811	1994	230.00	350-500
1991 Pilgrim Woman 03315-9	5,000	1995	84.00	200
1996 Prairie Moon Market 17793-8	750		300.00	300
1993 Santa Fisherman 08979-8	1,800	1997	250.00	250-300
1998 Santa Fisherman 8" 25145-4	1,000	1998	90.00	90
1996 Santa in Red Convertible 17790-7	2,000		100.00	100
1995 Santa in Sleigh 13987-5	1,500	1996	125.00	250
1992 Santa of Peace 07328-5	5,000	1994	250.00	275-350
1997 Santa on Horse 21327-8	1,000	1997	150.00	160
1998 Santa on Moose 7" 25149-2	750	1998	150.00	150
1994 Santa Skier 12054-5	1,500	1995	190.00	195
1997 Snow King 21319-3	1,000		100.00	100
1996 Snowflake in Nature Santa 17791-4	1,500		125.00	125
1998 Snowshoe Santa 9" 25146-1	1,000		120.00	120
1994 Star of the Roundup Cowboy 11966-1	1,500	1996	100.00	100
1991 Stars and Stripes Santa 01743-2	5,000	1994	190.00	350-400
1995 Sunbringer Santa 13991-2	1,500	1996	125.00	135-185
1996 SW Bach Santa 17792-1	1,500		125.00	125
1991 Tis a Witching Time 03544-3	609	1991	140.00	1500-2000
1991 Toymaker 03540-5	5,000	1995	120.00	175-200
1997 Victorian Santa 21317-9	1,000		130.00	130
1993 Voyageur 09043-5	788	1996	170.00	170
1994 Weatherwise Angel 12055-2	1,500	1996	150.00	150-175
1995 Wee Willie Santa 13993-6	2,500	1995	50.00	50
1997 White Nite Nick 21316-2	1,000		130.00	130
1992 Woodland Brave 07867-9	1,500	1993	87.00	350-450
1991 Woodsman Santa 03310-4	5,000	1995	230.00	300-350

Ore Mountain "A Christmas Carol" Nutcrackers - Midwest

YEAR ISSUE	EDITION LIMIT	YEAR RETD.	ISSUE PRICE	*QUOTE U.S.$
1993 Bob Cratchit, 09421-1	5,000	1995	120.00	100-130
1994 Ghost of Christmas Future, 10449-1	1,500	1995	116.00	100-125
1994 Ghost of Christmas Past, 10447-7	1,500	1995	116.00	100-125
1994 Ghost of Christmas Present 12041-5	1,500	1996	116.00	100-125
1994 Marley's Ghost, 10448-4	1,500	1995	116.00	100-125
1993 Scrooge, 05522-9	2,500	1995	104.00	100-125

Ore Mountain "Nutcracker Fantasy" Nutcrackers - Midwest

YEAR ISSUE	EDITION LIMIT	YEAR RETD.	ISSUE PRICE	*QUOTE U.S.$
1995 Clara, 12801-5	5,000		125.00	137
1991 Clara, 8" 01254-3	Retrd.	1995	77.00	100
1994 Herr Drosselmeyer, 10456-9	5,000		110.00	137
1988 Herr Drosselmeyer, 14 1/2" 07506-7	Retrd.	1996	75.00	115
1993 The Mouse King, 05350-8	5,000	1997	100.00	140
1988 The Mouse King, 10" 07509-8	Retrd.	1997	60.00	85
1994 Nutcracker Prince, 11001-0	5,000		104.00	140
1988 The Prince, 12 3/4" 07507-4	Retrd.	1996	75.00	105
1988 The Toy Soldier, 11" 07508-1	Retrd.	1996	70.00	95
1995 Toy Soldier, 12804-6	5,000		125.00	125

Ore Mountain Easter Nutcrackers - Midwest

YEAR ISSUE	EDITION LIMIT	YEAR RETD.	ISSUE PRICE	*QUOTE U.S.$
1992 Bunny Painter, 06480-1	Retrd.	1993	77.00	80
1991 Bunny with Egg, 00145-5	Retrd.	1993	77.00	80
1984 March Hare, 00312-1	Retrd.	1993	77.00	80

Ore Mountain Nutcracker Collection - Midwest

YEAR ISSUE	EDITION LIMIT	YEAR RETD.	ISSUE PRICE	*QUOTE U.S.$
1995 American Country Santa, 13195-4	Retrd.	1996	165.00	170
1997 Angel w/Horn 21178-6	Retrd.	1998	250.00	250
1996 Angel with Candle 17010-6	Retrd.	1997	220.00	240
1994 Annie Oakley, 10464-4	Retrd.	1995	128.00	130
1996 Attorney 17012-0	Retrd.	1997	120.00	130
1995 August the Strong, 13185-5	Retrd.	1996	190.00	190
1997 Ballerina 21180-9	Retrd.	1998	165.00	165
1995 Barbeque Dad, 13193-0	Retrd.	1996	176.00	176
1994 Baseball Player, 10459-0	Retrd.	1995	111.00	100-120
1995 Basketball Player, 12784-1	Retrd.	1996	135.00	135
1995 Beefeater, 12797-1	Retrd.	1996	175.00	177
1998 Bell Body Snow Flake 25940-5	Open		130.00	130
1997 Bell-shaped Hunter 21172-4	Retrd.	1998	130.00	130
1997 Bell-shaped Santa 21169-4	Open		130.00	130
1994 Black Santa, 10460-6	Retrd.	1995	74.00	74
1993 Cat Witch, 09426-6	Retrd.	1995	93.00	93
1994 Cavalier, 12952-4	Retrd.	1998	80.00	110
1994 Cavalier, 12953-1	Retrd.	1998	65.00	90
1994 Cavalier, 12958-6	Open		57.00	77
1996 Chimney Sweep 17043-4	Open		120.00	130
1995 Chimney Sweep, 00326-8	Open		70.00	76
1992 Christopher Columbus, 00152-3	Retrd.	1992	80.00	80
1991 Clown, 03561-0	Retrd.	1994	115.00	118
1994 Confederate Soldier, 12837-4	Retrd.	1996	93.00	110
1996 Count Dracula 17050-2	Retrd.	1997	150.00	150
1989 Country Santa, 09326-9	Retrd.	1995	95.00	150
1996 Cow Farmer 17054-0	Retrd.	1997	120.00	145
1992 Cowboy, 00298-8	Retrd.	1995	97.00	150
1997 Doctor 21173-1	Retrd.	1998	75.00	75
1995 Downhill Santa Skier, 13197-8	Retrd.	1997	145.00	150
1996 Drummer 17044-1	Open		120.00	120
1996 East Coast Santa 17047-2	Retrd.	1997	200.00	220
1990 Elf, 04154-3	Retrd.	1993	70.00	73
1996 Emergency Medical Technician 17013-7	Retrd.	1997	140.00	140
1994 Engineer, 10454-5	Retrd.	1995	108.00	108
1992 Farmer, 01109-6	Retrd.	1994	65.00	77
1996 Female Farmer 17011-3	1,000	1997	145.00	180
1997 Fireman 21170-0	Open		75.00	75
1993 Fireman with Dog, 06592-1	Retrd.	1996	134.00	145
1997 Fisherman 21168-7	Open		165.00	165
1989 Fisherman, 09327-6	Retrd.	1995	90.00	100
1996 Frankenstein 17009-0	Retrd.	1997	170.00	190
1997 Gardener 21165-6	Retrd.	1998	160.00	160
1994 Gardening Lady, 10450-7	Retrd.	1996	104.00	112
1993 Gepetto Santa, 09417-4	Retrd.	1995	115.00	115
1989 Golfer, 09325-2	Retrd.	1994	85.00	90
1996 Guard 17046-5	Retrd.	1998	120.00	130
1995 Handyman, 12806-0	Retrd.	1996	136.00	137
1996 Harlequin Santa 17174-5	Retrd.	1998	150.00	160
1997 Hippie 21184-7	Retrd.	1998	145.00	145
1995 Hockey Player, 12783-4	Retrd.	1996	155.00	155
1995 Hunter Nutcracker 12785-8	Retrd.	1996	136.00	136
1992 Indian, 00195-0	Retrd.	1994	96.00	100
1995 Jack Frost, 12803-9	Retrd.	1997	150.00	150
1997 Jazz Musician 21177-9	Retrd.	1998	200.00	200
1995 Jolly St. Nick with Toys, 13709-3	Retrd.	1996	135.00	135
1995 King Richard the Lionhearted, 12798-8	Retrd.	1996	165.00	165
1996 King with Sceptor 17045-8	Retrd.	1998	120.00	130
1995 Law Scholar, 12789-6	Retrd.	1996	127.00	127
1996 Male Farmer 17015-1	1,000	1997	145.00	145
1990 Merlin the Magician, 04207-6	Retrd.	1995	67.00	75
1994 Miner, 10493-4	Retrd.	1995	110.00	120
1998 Ms. Liberty 25938-2	Open		200.00	200
1994 Nature Lover, 10446-0	Retrd.	1995	112.00	112
1997 Noah 21181-6	Retrd.	1998	150.00	150
1988 Nordic Santa, 08872-2	Retrd.	1995	84.00	110
1996 Northwoods Santa 17048-9	Retrd.	1997	200.00	220
1991 Nutcracker-Maker, 03601-3	Retrd.	1993	62.00	65
1995 Peddler, 12805-3	Retrd.	1996	140.00	140
1995 Pierre Le Chef, 12802-2	Retrd.	1996	147.00	147
1992 Pilgrim, 00188-2	Retrd.	1994	96.00	100
1994 Pinecone Santa, 10461-3	Retrd.	1994	92.00	92
1984 Pinocchio, 00160-8	Retrd.	1996	60.00	68
1995 Pizza Baker, 13194-7	Retrd.	1996	170.00	170
1997 Policeman 21171-7	Retrd.	1998	75.00	75
1997 Portly Carpenter 21287-5	Retrd.	1998	150.00	150
1997 Portly Chef 21163-2	Retrd.	1998	150.00	150
1998 Portly Chimney Sweep 24718-1	Open		150.00	150
1998 Portly Pirate 24436-4	Open		150.00	150
1997 Portly Santa w/Gifts 21164-9	Retrd.	1998	150.00	150
1996 Prince 17038-0	Retrd.	1998	120.00	130
1994 Prince Charming, 10457-6	Retrd.	1995	125.00	130
1994 Pumpkin Head Scarecrow, 10451-1	Retrd.	1996	127.00	140
1994 Regal Prince, 10452-1	Retrd.	1996	140.00	152
1992 Ringmaster, 00196-7	Retrd.	1993	135.00	137
1995 Riverboat Gambler, 12787-2	Retrd.	1996	137.00	140
1995 Royal Lion, 13985-1	Retrd.	1996	130.00	140
1995 Santa at Workbench, 13335-4	Retrd.	1996	130.00	140
1998 Santa in Chimney (musical) 24702-0	Open		200.00	200
1994 Santa in Nightshirt, 10462-0	Retrd.	1995	108.00	120
1996 Santa One-Man Band Musical 17051-9	Retrd.	1997	170.00	175
1988 Santa w/Tree & Toys, 07666-8	Retrd.	1993	76.00	87
1993 Santa with Animals, 09424-2	Retrd.	1994	117.00	117
1994 Santa with Basket, 10472-9	Retrd.	1996	80.00	100
1998 Santa with Rudolph 25194-2	Open		200.00	200
1992 Santa with Skis, 01305-2	Retrd.	1994	100.00	110
1990 Sea Captain, 04157-4	Retrd.	1994	86.00	95
1997 Skier 21176-2	Retrd.	1998	180.00	180
1997 Skiing Santa 21252-3	Retrd.	1998	170.00	170
1994 Snow King, 10470-5	Retrd.	1995	108.00	120
1997 Snowman 21183-0	Open		130.00	130
1994 Soccer Player, 10494-1	Retrd.	1995	97.00	107
1994 Sorcerer, 10471-2	Retrd.	1995	100.00	100
1996 Sports Fan 17173-8	Retrd.	1997	120.00	125
1994 Sultan King, 10455-2	Retrd.	1995	130.00	145
1995 Teacher, 13196-1	Retrd.	1996	165.00	165
1994 Toy Vendor, 11987-7	Retrd.	1996	124.00	145
1990 Uncle Sam, 04206-9	Retrd.	1993	50.00	62
1994 Union Soldier, 12836-7	Retrd.	1996	93.00	110
1996 Victorian Santa 17172-1	Retrd.	1998	180.00	185
1992 Victorian Santa, 00187-5	Retrd.	1994	130.00	140
1996 Western 17049-6	Retrd.	1997	250.00	250
1997 White Santa with Wreath 21175-5	Retrd.	1998	175.00	175
1993 White Santa, 09533-1	Retrd.	1995	100.00	100
1990 Windsor Club, 04160-4	Retrd.	1994	85.00	87
1990 Witch, 04159-8	Retrd.	1995	75.00	76
1990 Woodland Santa, 04191-8	Retrd.	1995	105.00	150

Porcelain Hinged Box Collection Songbird Series - Midwest

YEAR ISSUE	EDITION LIMIT	YEAR RETD.	ISSUE PRICE	*QUOTE U.S.$
1998 American Goldfinch 26929-9	5,000		19.00	19
1998 American Robin 26934-3	5,000		19.00	19
1998 Black Capped Chickadee 26931-2	5,000		19.00	19
1998 Cardinal 26932-9	5,000		19.00	19
1998 Eastern Bluebird 26933-6	5,000		19.00	19
1998 Ruby Throated Hummingbird 26930-5	5,000		19.00	19

Porcelain Hinged Box-Beatrix Potter Limited Edition Collection - Midwest

YEAR ISSUE	EDITION LIMIT	YEAR RETD.	ISSUE PRICE	*QUOTE U.S.$
1998 Benjamin Bunny 27676-1	5,000		25.00	25
1998 Jemima Puddle-duck 28289-2	5,000		25.00	25
1998 Jeremy Fischer 27674-7	5,000		25.00	25
1998 Peter Rabbit 28290-8	10,000		25.00	25
1998 Tailor of Gloucester 27675-4	5,000		25.00	25
1998 Tom Kitten 27673-0	5,000		25.00	25

Wendt and Kuhn Collection - Wendt/Kuhn

YEAR ISSUE	EDITION LIMIT	YEAR RETD.	ISSUE PRICE	*QUOTE U.S.$
1989 Angel at Piano 09403-7	Open		31.00	45
1983 Angel Brass Musicians, set/6 00470-8	Open		92.00	125
1983 Angel Conductor on Stand 00469-2	Open		21.00	28
1990 Angel Duet in Celestial Stars 04158-1	Retrd.	1994	60.00	63
1983 Angel Percussion Musicians set/6 00443-2	Open		110.00	145
1979 Angel Playing Violin 00403-6	Retrd.	1994	34.00	35
1980 Angel Pulling Wagon 00553-8	Retrd.	1995	43.00	50
1983 Angel String & Woodwind Musicians, set/6 00465-4	Open		108.00	140
1983 Angel String Musicians, set/6 00455-5	Retrd.	1995	105.00	120
1979 Angel Trio, set/3 00471-5	Open		140.00	185
1981 Angel w/Tree & Basket 01190-8	Retrd.	1993	24.00	25
1976 Angel with Sled 02940-4	Retrd.	1994	36.50	38
1981 Angels at Cradle, set/4 01193-5	Open		73.00	92
1996 Angels Bearing Gifts 17039-7	Open		120.00	130
1984 Angels Bearing Toys, set/6 00451-7	Retrd.	1995	97.00	110
1979 Bavarian Moving Van 02854-4	Open		134.00	174
1991 Birdhouse 01209-3	Retrd.	1994	22.50	23
1996 Blueberry Children 17040-3	Open		110.00	120
1991 Boy on Rocking Horse, 2 asst. 01202-4	Retrd.	1994	35.00	36
1994 Busy Elf, 3 asst. 12856-5	Open		22.00	25
1987 Child on Skis, 2 asst. 06083-4	Retrd.	1994	28.00	29
1987 Child on Sled 06085-8	Retrd.	1994	25.50	27
1994 Child with Flowers Set 12947-0	Retrd.	1996	45.00	50
1991 Display Base for Wendt und Kuhn Figures, 12 1/2 x 2" 01214-7	Open		32.00	45
1997 Flower Children Place Card Holder, set/6 22736-7	Open		150.00	150
1991 Flower Children, set/6 01213-0	Open		130.00	157
1979 Girl w/Cradle, set/2 01203-1	Retrd.	1994	37.50	40
1979 Girl w/Porridge Bowl 01198-0	Open		29.00	34
1979 Girl w/Scissors 01197-3	Open		25.00	32
1983 Girl w/Wagon 01196-6	Retrd.	1994	27.00	29
1991 Girl with Doll 01200-0	Open		31.50	37
1980 Little People Napkin Rings 6 asst. 03504-7	Open		21.00	28
1988 Lucia Parade Figures, set/3 07667-5	Retrd.	1995	75.00	80

*Quotes have been rounded up to nearest dollar

YEAR ISSUE	EDITION LIMIT	YEAR RETD.	ISSUE PRICE	*QUOTE U.S.$
1978 Madonna w/Child 01207-9	Open		120.00	153
1979 Magarita Angels, set/6 02938-1	Open		94.00	125
1983 Margarita Birthday Angels, set/3 00480-7	Retrd.	1995	44.00	53
1979 Pied Piper and Children, set/7 02843-8	Retrd.	1994	120.00	130
1981 Santa w/Angel in Sleigh 01192-8	Retrd.	1995	52.00	60
1976 Santa with Angel 00473-9	Open		50.00	55
1994 Santa with Tree 12942-5	Open		29.00	34
1994 Sun, Moon, Star Set 12943-2	Open		69.00	128
1992 Wendt und Kuhn Display Sign w/ Sitting Angel 07535-7	Retrd.	1996	20.00	23
1991 White Angel with Violin 01205-5	Retrd.	1993	25.50	27

Wendt and Kuhn Collection Music Boxes - Wendt/Kuhn

YEAR ISSUE	EDITION LIMIT	YEAR RETD.	ISSUE PRICE	*QUOTE U.S.$
1988 Angel at Pipe Organ 01929-0	Open		176.00	230
1996 Angel Musicians Music Box 17036-6	Open		260.00	270
1994 Angel Under Stars Crank Music Box 12974-6	300		150.00	190
1991 Angels & Santa Around Tree 01211-6	Open		300.00	370
1996 Children Around Tree Music Box 17037-3	Open		330.00	350
1989 Girl Rocking Cradle 09215-6	Retrd.	1994	180.00	190
1988 Rotating Angels 'Round Cradle 01911-5	Open		270.00	336

Wendt and Kuhn Figurines Candleholders - Wendt/Kuhn

YEAR ISSUE	EDITION LIMIT	YEAR RETD.	ISSUE PRICE	*QUOTE U.S.$
1988 Angel Candleholder Pair 00472-2	Open		70.00	94
1991 Angel with Friend Candleholder 01191-1	Retrd.	1994	33.30	34
1994 Angel with Sled Candleholder 12860-2	Open		35.00	44
1991 Large Angel Candleholder Pair 01201-7	Retrd.	1994	270.00	277
1996 Orchestra Stand Candleholder 17042-7	Open		130.00	145
1991 Pair of Angels Candleholder 01204-8	Retrd.	1994	30.00	32
1987 Santa Candleholder 06082-7	Retrd.	1994	53.00	54
1991 Small Angel Candleholder Pair 01195-9	Retrd.	1994	60.00	63
1991 White Angel Candleholder 01206-2	Retrd.	1994	28.00	29

Miss Martha's Collection/Enesco Corporation

Miss Martha's Collection - M. Root

YEAR ISSUE	EDITION LIMIT	YEAR RETD.	ISSUE PRICE	*QUOTE U.S.$
1993 Erin-Don't Worry Santa Won't Forget Us 307246	Retrd.	1994	55.00	110
1993 Amber-Mr. Snowman! (waterglobe) 310476	Closed	1994	50.00	100-115
1993 Kekisha-Heavenly Peace Musical 310484	Closed	1994	60.00	120
1993 Whitney-Let's Have Another Party 321559	Closed	1994	45.00	85-90
1993 Megan-My Birthday Cake! 321567	Closed	1994	60.00	115-120
1993 Doug-I'm Not Showin' Off 321575	Closed	1994	40.00	75-80
1993 Francie-Such A Precious Gift! 321583	Closed	1994	50.00	95-100
1993 Alicia-A Blessing From God 321591	Closed	1994	40.00	75-80
1993 Anita-It's For You, Mama! 321605	Closed	1994	45.00	85-90
1994 Jeffrey-Bein' A Fireman Sure Is Hot & Thirsty Work 350206	Closed	1994	40.00	80
1993 Jess-I Can Fly 350516	Retrd.	1994	45.00	90
1993 Ruth-Littlest Angel Figurine 350524	Closed	1994	40.00	80
1993 Stephen-I'll Be The Best Shepherd In The World! 350540	Closed	1994	40.00	80
1993 Jonathon-Maybe I Can Be Like Santa 350559	Closed	1994	45.00	90
1994 Charlotte-You Can Be Whatever You Dream 353191	Closed	1994	40.00	80
1992 Lillie-Christmas Dinner! 369373	Retrd.	1993	55.00	105-110
1992 Eddie-What A Nice Surprise! 369381	Retrd.	1994	50.00	95-100
1992 Kekisha-Heavenly Peace 421456	Closed	1994	40.00	75-80
1992 Angela-I Have Wings 421464	Closed	1994	45.00	90
1992 Amber-Mr. Snowman 421472	Retrd.	1993	60.00	120
1992 Mar/Jsh/Christopher-Hush Baby! It's Your B-day! Musical 431362	Closed	1994	80.00	105-160
1992 Carrie-God Bless America 440035	Closed	1994	45.00	90
1993 Hallie-Sing Praises To The Lord 443166	Retrd.	1993	60.00	120
1991 Jana-Plant With Love 443174	Closed	1994	40.00	80
1991 Hallie-Sing Praises To The Lord 443182	Closed	1994	37.50	75
1992 Belle/Maize-Not Now, Muffin 443204	Retrd.	1993	50.00	100
1991 Sammy/Leisha-Sister's First Day Of School 443190	Retrd.	1993	55.00	110
1991 Nate-Hope You Hear My Prayer, Lord 443212	Closed	1994	17.50	55
1991 Sadie-They Can't Find Us Here 443220	Retrd.	1993	45.00	90
1992 Patsy-Clean Clothes For Dolly 443239	Retrd.	1993	50.00	100
1991 Dawn-Pretty Please, Mama 443247	Closed	1994	40.00	80
1991 Tonya-Hush, Puppy Dear 443255	Closed	1994	50.00	100
1991 Jenny/Jeremiah-Birthday Biscuits, With Love... 443263	Retrd.	1993	60.00	150
1991 Suzi-Mama, Watch Me! 443271	Retrd.	1993	35.00	70
1992 Mattie-Sweet Child 443298	Retrd.	1993	30.00	60
1992 Sara Lou-Here, Lammie 443301	Retrd.	1993	50.00	100
1992 Angel Tree Topper 446521	Closed	1994	80.00	155-225
1992 Mar/Jsh/Christopher-Hush, Baby! It's Your B-day Figurine 448354	Closed	1994	55.00	110

Museum Collections, Inc.

American Family I - N. Rockwell

YEAR ISSUE	EDITION LIMIT	YEAR RETD.	ISSUE PRICE	*QUOTE U.S.$
1979 Baby's First Step	22,500		90.00	200-225
1980 Birthday Party	22,500		110.00	150
1981 Bride and Groom	22,500		110.00	125
1980 First Haircut	22,500		90.00	150
1980 First Prom	22,500		90.00	135
1980 Happy Birthday, Dear Mother	22,500		90.00	135
1980 Little Mother	22,500		110.00	125
1981 Mother's Little Helpers	22,500		110.00	135
1980 The Student	22,500		110.00	175
1980 Sweet Sixteen	22,500		90.00	125
1980 Washing Our Dog	22,500		110.00	125
1980 Wrapping Christmas Presents	22,500		90.00	125

Christmas - N. Rockwell

YEAR ISSUE	EDITION LIMIT	YEAR RETD.	ISSUE PRICE	*QUOTE U.S.$
1980 Checking His List	Yr.Iss.		65.00	110
1983 High Hopes	Yr.Iss.		95.00	175
1981 Ringing in Good Cheer	Yr.Iss.		95.00	100
1984 Space Age Santa	Yr.Iss.		65.00	100
1982 Waiting for Santa	Yr.Iss.		95.00	110

Classic - N. Rockwell

YEAR ISSUE	EDITION LIMIT	YEAR RETD.	ISSUE PRICE	*QUOTE U.S.$
1984 All Wrapped Up	Closed		65.00	100
1980 Bedtime	Closed		65.00	95-225
1984 The Big Race	Closed		65.00	90-95
1983 Bored of Education	Closed		65.00	90-95
1983 Braving the Storm	Closed		65.00	150
1980 The Cobbler	Closed		65.00	125
1982 The Country Doctor	Closed		65.00	90-95
1981 A Dollhouse for Sis	Closed		65.00	90-95
1982 Dreams in the Antique Shop	Closed		65.00	90-95
1983 A Final Touch	Closed		65.00	90-95
1980 For A Good Boy	Closed		65.00	125-225
1984 Goin' Fishin'	Closed		65.00	90-95
1983 High Stepping	Closed		65.00	90-95
1982 The Kite Maker	Closed		65.00	100
1980 Lighthouse Keeper's Daughter	Closed		65.00	125
1980 Memories	Closed		65.00	150
1981 The Music Lesson	Closed		65.00	125
1981 Music Master	Closed		65.00	125
1981 Off to School	Closed		65.00	90-95
1981 Puppy Love	Closed		65.00	90-95
1984 Saturday's Hero	Closed		65.00	90-95
1983 A Special Treat	Closed		65.00	90-95
1982 Spring Fever	Closed		65.00	90-95
1980 The Toymaker	Closed		65.00	125
1981 While The Audience Waits	Closed		65.00	100-110
1983 Winter Fun	Closed		65.00	90-95
1982 Words of Wisdom	Closed		65.00	110

Commemorative - N. Rockwell

YEAR ISSUE	EDITION LIMIT	YEAR RETD.	ISSUE PRICE	*QUOTE U.S.$
1985 Another Masterpiece by Norman Rockwell	5,000		125.00	200-250
1981 Norman Rockwell Display	5,000		125.00	200-250
1983 Norman Rockwell, America's Artist	5,000		125.00	225
1984 Outward Bound	5,000		125.00	225-250
1986 The Painter and the Pups	5,000		125.00	250
1982 Spirit of America	5,000		125.00	225

Olszewski Studios

Olszewski Studios - R. Olszewski

YEAR ISSUE	EDITION LIMIT	YEAR RETD.	ISSUE PRICE	*QUOTE U.S.$
1994 The Grand Entrance SM1	1,500	1994	225.00	325-390
1994 The Grand Entrance A/P SM1	120	1994	450.00	450-500
1994 Tinker's Treasure Chest SM2	750	1994	235.00	450-495
1994 Tinker's Treasure Chest A/P SM2	120	1994	470.00	470
1994 To Be... (included w/Treasure Chest) SM3	750	1994	Set	Set
1994 To Be... (included w/Treasure Chest) A/P SM3	120	1994	Set	Set
1994 The Little Tinker SM4	750	1995	235.00	235-295
1994 The Little Tinker A/P SM4	100	1995	470.00	470
1995 Special Treat SM5	800	1995	220.00	220
1995 Special Treat A/P SM5	100	1995	440.00	440
1995 Mocking Bird with Peach Blossoms SM6	800	1995	230.00	230
1995 Mocking Bird with Peach Blossoms A/P SM6	100	1995	460.00	460
1995 Lady With An Urn (brown dress) SM7	250	1995	235.00	275-325
1995 Lady With An Urn (brown dress) A/P SM7	36	1995	470.00	470
1995 Lady With An Urn (green dress) SM7	250	1995	235.00	250-295
1995 Lady With An Urn (green dress) A/P SM7	36	1995	470.00	470
1995 Lady With An Urn (pink dress) SM7	250	1995	235.00	250-295
1995 Lady With An Urn (pink dress) A/P SM7	36	1995	470.00	470
1995 Lady With An Urn (blue dress) SM7	250	1995	235.00	235
1995 Lady With An Urn (blue dress) A/P SM7	36	1995	470.00	470
1995 Castle of Gleaming White Porcelain SM8	750	1995	285.00	300-350
1995 Castle of Gleaming White Porcelain A/P SM8	100	1995	570.00	570
1995 ...Not to Be Lapel Pin SM10	750	1995	110.00	110
1995 ...Not to Be Lapel Pin A/P SM10	100	1995	220.00	220
1996 Spring Dance SM9	750	1996	205.00	210-225
1996 Spring Dance A/P SM9	100	1996	410.00	410
1996 Oriental Lovers SM11	750	1996	240.00	240-290
1996 Oriental Lovers A/P SM11	100	1996	480.00	480
1996 Dashing Through the Snow SM12	500	1996	480.00	480
1996 Dashing Through the Snow A/P SM12	100	1996	960.00	960
1996 The Viceroy SM13	750	1996	235.00	250-350
1996 The Viceroy A/P SM13	100	1996	470.00	470
1996 Little Red Riding Hood SM14	750	1996	235.00	235-295
1996 Little Red Riding Hood A/P SM14	100	1996	470.00	470
1996 The Departure (Sterling) SM1S	375	1996	325.00	325-395
1996 The Departure (Sterling) A/P SM1S	27	1996	650.00	650
1997 American Beauty SM15	750	1997	225.00	225
1997 American Beauty A/P SM15	100	1997	450.00	450
1997 Summer: Picking Apples SM16	750	1997	240.00	240
1997 Summer: Picking Apples A/P SM16	100	1997	480.00	480
1997 The Fox Hunt SM17	500	1997	480.00	480
1997 The Fox Hunt A/P SM17	100	1997	960.00	960
1997 Winter: Tracking the Rabbit SM18	750	1997	225.00	225
1997 Winter: Tracking the Rabbit A/P SM18	100	1997	450.00	450
1998 Dollhouse Dreams SM20	750	1997	235.00	235
1998 Dollhouse Dreams A/P SM20	100	1997	470.00	470
1997 Spring Dance with Floral Dress SM9	100	1997	275.00	300-400
1998 Autumn: Going South SM19	750	1998	230.00	230
1998 Autumn: Going South A/P SM19	100	1998	460.00	460
1998 Victorians - Mother's Pride (girl) SM21	250	1998	480.00	480
1998 Victorians - Dad's Joy (girl) SM23	250	1998	set	set
1998 Victorians - First Curl Box (girl) SM24	250	1998	set	set
1998 Victorians - Mother's Pride (girl) A/P SM21	50	1998	960.00	960
1998 Victorians - Dad's Joy (girl) A/P SM23	50	1998	set	set
1998 Victorians - First Curl Box (girl) A/P SM24	50	1998	set	set
1998 Victorians - Mother's Pride (boy) SM21	250	1998	480.00	480
1998 Victorians - Dad's Joy (boy) SM23	250	1998	set	set
1998 Victorians - First Curl Box (boy) SM24	250	1998	set	set
1998 Victorians - Mother's Pride (boy) A/P SM21	50	1998	960.00	960
1998 Victorians - Dad's Joy (boy) A/P SM23	50	1998	set	set
1998 Victorians - First Curl Box (boy) A/P SM24	50	1998	set	set
1998 Spring: Nature's Awakening SM22	750	1998	240.00	240
1998 Spring: Nature's Awakening A/P SM22	100	1998	480.00	480
1998 Cedar Waxwing SM25	750	1998	230.00	230
1998 Cedar Waxwing A/P SM25	100	1998	460.00	460
1998 Trick or Treat SM26	750	1998	235.00	235
1998 Trick or Treat A/P SM26	100	1998	470.00	470
1998 The Scholars SM27	375	1998	185.00	185
1998 The Scholars A/P SM27	37	1998	370.00	370

Original Appalachian Artworks

Extra Special - X. Roberts

YEAR ISSUE	EDITION LIMIT	YEAR RETD.	ISSUE PRICE	*QUOTE U.S.$
1985 Baby's First Step	Closed	N/A	18.00	40
1984 Bedtime Story	Closed	N/A	15.00	25
1984 Birthday Party	Closed	N/A	26.50	40-45
1984 The Building Block	Closed	N/A	8.00	12
1985 Carousel (musical)	Closed	N/A	90.00	200
1984 CPK Clubhouse	Closed	N/A	26.50	45-50
1984 Daydreams	Closed	N/A	8.00	15
1984 Deer Friends	Closed	N/A	26.50	45
1984 Discovering New Life	Closed	N/A	16.00	25
1985 The Entertainers	30,000	N/A	50.00	85-100
1984 Getting Acquainted	Closed	N/A	20.00	40
1984 I Can Do It	Closed	N/A	8.00	15
1984 Just Being Silly	Closed	N/A	8.00	15
1984 The Little Drummer	Closed	N/A	8.00	15
1985 Lovely Ladies	Closed	N/A	26.50	50-60
1984 Noel, Noel	Closed	N/A	20.00	40-45
1984 Playtime	Closed	N/A	8.00	25
1985 Rainbow Sweetheart	Closed	N/A	15.00	15
1985 Sandcastles	Closed	N/A	26.50	45-55
1984 Sharing a Soda Cream	Closed	N/A	15.00	30
1984 Sleigh Ride	Closed	N/A	18.50	30
1985 Special Delivery	25,000	N/A	50.00	100
1985 A Special Gift	Closed	N/A	15.00	35
1984 Tea For Two	Closed	N/A	16.50	30
1984 Waiting Patiently	Closed	N/A	8.00	15

Extra Special Easter Collection - X. Roberts

YEAR ISSUE	EDITION LIMIT	YEAR RETD.	ISSUE PRICE	*QUOTE U.S.$
1985 Easter Artists	Closed	N/A	40.00	50-55
1985 Findin' Easter Treats	Closed	N/A	26.50	50-55
1985 In Your Easter Bonnet	Closed	N/A	8.00	15
1985 Our Easter Bunny	Closed	N/A	8.00	15

Extra Special Valentine Collection - X. Roberts

YEAR ISSUE	EDITION LIMIT	YEAR RETD.	ISSUE PRICE	*QUOTE U.S.$
1985 Hugs and Kisses	Closed	N/A	18.00	30
1985 I Love You	Closed	N/A	14.50	30
1985 Rainbow Sweetheart	Closed	N/A	15.00	30
1985 Valentine Phone Call	Closed	N/A	14.50	30

Pemberton & Oakes

Zolan's Children - D. Zolan

YEAR ISSUE	EDITION LIMIT	YEAR RETD.	ISSUE PRICE	*QUOTE U.S.$
1982 Erik and the Dandelion	17,000	1981	48.00	48-90
1983 Sabina in the Grass	6,800	1982	48.00	48-115
1985 Tender Moment	10,000	1985	29.00	75-80
1984 Winter Angel	8,000	1984	28.00	28-150

PenDelfin

PenDelfin Family Circle Collectors' Club - J. Heap

YEAR ISSUE	EDITION LIMIT	YEAR RETD.	ISSUE PRICE	*QUOTE U.S.$
1993 Herald	Closed	1993	Gift	249-290
1993 Bosun	Closed	1993	50.00	120-200
1994 Buttons	Closed	1994	Gift	80-160
1994 Puffer	Closed	1995	85.00	205-290

*Quotes have been rounded up to nearest dollar

FIGURINES

YEAR ISSUE	EDITION LIMIT	YEAR RETD.	ISSUE PRICE	*QUOTE U.S.$
1995 Bellman	Closed	1995	Gift	100-231
1995 Georgie and the Dragon	Closed	1995	125.00	125-180
1996 Newsie	Closed	1996	Gift	60-100
1996 Delia	Closed	1996	125.00	120-245
1997 Tom	Closed	1997	Gift	60-75
1997 Woody	Closed	1997	125.00	125-165
1998 Tiny Patch	Yr.Iss.		Gift	N/A
1998 Gramps	Yr.Iss.		125.00	125

40th Anniversary Piece - PenDelfin

YEAR ISSUE	EDITION LIMIT	YEAR RETD.	ISSUE PRICE	*QUOTE U.S.$
1994 Aunt Ruby	10,000		275.00	225-400

Event Piece - J. Heap, unless otherwise noted

YEAR ISSUE	EDITION LIMIT	YEAR RETD.	ISSUE PRICE	*QUOTE U.S.$
1994 Walmsley	Retrd.	1995	75.00	185-335
1995 Runaway	Retrd.	1995	90.00	90-125
1996 Event Piece	Retrd.	1996	85.00	100-165
1997 Sylvana - D. Roberts	Retrd.	1997	85.00	75-105
1998 Event Piece	Yr.Iss.		85.00	85

Nursery Rhymes - Various

YEAR ISSUE	EDITION LIMIT	YEAR RETD.	ISSUE PRICE	*QUOTE U.S.$
1956 Little Bo Peep - J. Heap	Retrd.	1959	2.00	N/A
1956 Little Jack Horner - J. Heap	Retrd.	1959	2.00	N/A
1956 Mary Mary Quite Contrary - J. Heap	Retrd.	1959	2.00	N/A
1956 Miss Muffet - J. Heap	Retrd.	1959	2.00	N/A
1956 Tom Tom the Piper's Son - J. Heap	Retrd.	1959	2.00	N/A
1956 Wee Willie Winkie - J. Heap	Retrd.	1959	2.00	N/A

Retired Figurines - Various

YEAR ISSUE	EDITION LIMIT	YEAR RETD.	ISSUE PRICE	*QUOTE U.S.$
1985 Apple Barrel - J. Heap	Retrd.	1992	N/A	20-83
1963 Aunt Agatha - J. Heap	Retrd.	1965	N/A	1400-3000
1955 Balloon Woman - J. Heap	Retrd.	1956	1.00	990-1200
1964 Bandstand (mold 1) - J. Heap	Retrd.	1973	70.00	495
1967 The Bath Tub - J. Heap	Retrd.	1975	4.50	83-125
1955 Bell Man - J. Heap	Retrd.	1956	1.00	800-1200
1984 Blossom - D. Roberts	Retrd.	1989	35.00	85-205
1955 Bobbin Woman - J. Heap	2	1959	N/A	5000
1964 Bongo - D. Roberts	Retrd.	1987	31.00	115-150
1966 Cakestand - J. Heap	Retrd.	1972	2.00	495-595
1953 Cauldron Witch - J. Heap	Retrd.	1959	3.50	990-1250
1959 Cha Cha - J. Heap	Retrd.	1961	N/A	1485-2000
1990 Charlotte - D. Roberts	Retrd.	1992	25.00	96-205
1989 Chirpy - D. Roberts	Retrd.	1992	31.50	85-125
1985 Christmas Set - D. Roberts	2,000	1986	N/A	550-1150
1983 Clinger - J. Heap	Retrd.	1997	38.00	38
1962 Cornish Prayer (Corny) - J. Heap	Retrd.	1965	N/A	990-1200
1980 Crocker - D. Roberts	Retrd.	1989	20.00	126-150
1963 Cyril Squirrel - J. Heap	Retrd.	1965	N/A	1300-2000
1955 Daisy Duck - J. Heap	Retrd.	1958	N/A	1650-2500
1956 Desmond Duck - J. Heap	Retrd.	1958	2.50	1650-2500
1964 Dodger - J. Heap	Retrd.	1996	24.00	42-95
1955 Dungaree Father - N/A	Retrd.	1960	N/A	1240
1955 Elf - J. Heap	Retrd.	1956	1.00	990
1954 Fairy Jardiniere - N/A	Retrd.	1958	N/A	1000-3000
1953 The Fairy Shop - J. Heap	Retrd.	1958	N/A	1000-3000
1961 Father Mouse (grey) - J. Heap	Retrd.	1966	N/A	743-750
1958 Father/Mother Book Ends - N/A	Retrd.	1965	N/A	824
1955 Flying Witch - J. Heap	Retrd.	1956	1.00	825
1993 Forty Winks - D. Roberts	Retrd.	1996	57.00	60-99
1969 Gallery Pieface - J. Heap	Retrd.	1971	N/A	575
1969 The Gallery Series: Wakey, Pieface, Poppet, Robert, Dodger - J. Heap	Retrd.	1971	N/A	400-600
1961 Grand Stand (mold 1) - J. Heap	Retrd.	1969	35.00	660-775
1992 Grand Stand (mold 2)- J. Heap	Retrd.	1996	150.00	108-150
1960 Gussie - J. Heap	Retrd.	1968	N/A	436-800
1989 Honey - D. Roberts	Retrd.	1993	40.00	60-115
1988 Humphrey Go-Kart - J. Heap	Retrd.	1994	70.00	120-165
1986 Jim-Lad - D. Roberts	Retrd.	1992	22.50	205-230
1985 Jingle - D. Roberts	Retrd.	1992	11.25	125-165
1960 Kipper Tie Father - N/A	Retrd.	1970	N/A	660
1986 Little Mo - D. Roberts	Retrd.	1994	35.00	85-150
1961 Lollipop (grey) (Mouse) - J. Heap	Retrd.	1966	N/A	700-825
1960 Lucy Pocket - J. Heap	Retrd.	1967	4.20	214-300
1956 Manx Kitten - J. Heap	Retrd.	1958	2.00	33
1955 Margot - J. Heap	Retrd.	1961	2.00	248-500
1967 Maud - J. Heap	Retrd.	1970	N/A	330-400
1961 Megan - J. Heap	Retrd.	1967	3.00	495-800
1956 Midge (Replaced by Picnic Midge) - J. Heap	Retrd.	1965	2.00	400-800
1966 Milk Jug Stand - J. Heap	Retrd.	1972	2.00	500-910
1960 Model Stand - J. Heap	Retrd.	1964	4.00	400-750
1961 Mother Mouse (grey) - J. Heap	Retrd.	1966	N/A	655-800
1965 Mouse House (bronze) - J. Heap	Retrd.	1969	N/A	288-400
1965 Mouse House (stoneware) - J. Heap	Retrd.	N/A	N/A	700-990
1965 Muncher - D. Roberts	Retrd.	1983	26.00	83-200
1981 Nipper - D. Roberts	Retrd.	1989	20.50	180-200
1955 Old Adam - J. Heap	Retrd.	1956	4.00	1980
1955 Old Father (remodeled)- J. Heap	Retrd.	1970	50.	700-1000
1956 Old Mother (thin neck) - J. Heap	Retrd.	1956	6.25	410
1957 Old Mother - J. Heap	Retrd.	1978	6.25	330-400
1984 Oliver - D. Roberts	Retrd.	1995	25.00	99-120
1955 Original Father - J. Heap	Retrd.	1960	50.00	750-1450
1956 Original Robert - J. Heap	Retrd.	1967	2.50	200-500
1953 Pendle Witch (stoneware) - J. Heap	Retrd.	1957	4.00	1645-1980
1967 Phumf - J. Heap	Retrd.	1985	24.00	99-160
1955 Phynnodderee (Commissioned -Exclusive) - J. Heap	Retrd.	1956	1.00	990
1966 Picnic Basket - J. Heap	Retrd.	1968	2.00	400-495
1965 Picnic Stand - J. Heap	Retrd.	1985	62.50	132-245
1967 Picnic Table - J. Heap	Retrd.	1972	N/A	250-600
1966 Pieface - D. Roberts	Retrd.	1987	31.00	66-100
1965 Pixie Bods - J. Heap	Retrd.	1967	N/A	400
1953 Pixie House - J. Heap	Retrd.	1958	N/A	N/A
1962 Pooch - D. Roberts	Retrd.	1987	24.50	66-125
1958 Rabbit Book Ends - J. Heap	Retrd.	1965	10.00	1500-2000
1983 The Raft - J. Heap	Retrd.	1997	70.00	60-132
1954 Rhinegold Lamp - J. Heap	Retrd.	1956	21.00	N/A
1967 Robert w/lollipop - D. Roberts	Retrd.	1979	12.00	125-400
1978 Rocky (mold 2) - J. Heap	Retrd.	1997	N/A	22-50
1959 Rocky - J. Heap	Retrd.	1978	32.00	50-100
1959 Rolly - J. Heap	Retrd.	1997	17.50	22-33
1957 Romeo & Juliet - J. Heap	Retrd.	1959	11.00	N/A
1982 Rosa - J. Heap	Retrd.	1997	40.00	100-495
1960 Shiner w/black eye - J. Heap	Retrd.	1967	2.50	400-578
1981 Shrimp Stand - D. Roberts	Retrd.	1994	70.00	125-165
1985 Solo - D. Roberts	Retrd.	1993	40.00	99-125
1960 Squeezy - J. Heap	Retrd.	1970	2.50	495-695
1980 Sun Flower Plinth - N/A	Retrd.	1985	N/A	249
1957 Tammy - D. Roberts	Retrd.	1987	24.50	83-100
1987 Tennyson - D. Roberts	Retrd.	1994	35.00	80-120
1956 Timber Stand - J. Heap	Retrd.	1982	35.00	132-165
1953 Tipsy Witch - J. Heap	Retrd.	1959	3.50	N/A
1955 Toper - J. Heap	Retrd.	1956	1.00	N/A
1971 Totty - J. Heap	Retrd.	1981	21.00	125-150
1959 Uncle Soames (brown trousers) - J. Heap	Retrd.	1985	105.00	105
1959 Uncle Soames - J. Heap	Retrd.	1985	105.00	264-500
1991 Wordsworth - D. Roberts	Retrd.	1993	60.00	119-200

Polland Studios

Collector Society - D. Polland

YEAR ISSUE	EDITION LIMIT	YEAR RETD.	ISSUE PRICE	*QUOTE U.S.$
1987 I Come In Peace	Closed	1987	35.00	400-600
1987 Silent Trail	Closed	1987	300.00	1300
1987 I Come In Peace, Silent Trail -Matched Numbered Set	Closed	1987	335.00	15-1895
1988 The Hunter	Closed	1988	35.00	545
1988 Disputed Trail	Closed	1988	300.00	700-1045
1988 The Hunter, Disputed Trail-Matched Numbered Set	Closed	1988	335.00	11-1450
1989 Crazy Horse	Closed	1989	35.00	300-470
1989 Apache Birdman	Closed	1989	300.00	700-970
1989 Crazy Horse, Apache Birdman -Matched Numbered Set	Closed	1989	335.00	13-1700
1990 Chief Pontiac	Closed	1990	35.00	420
1990 Buffalo Pony	Closed	1990	300.00	600-800
1990 Chief Pontiac, Buffalo Pony-Matched Numbered Set	Closed	1990	335.00	900-1350
1991 War Drummer	Closed	1991	35.00	330
1991 The Signal	Closed	1991	350.00	730
1991 War Drummer, The Signal -Matched Numbered Set	Closed	1991	385.00	900-1150
1992 Cabinet Sign	Closed	1992	35.00	125
1992 Warrior's Farewell	Closed	1992	350.00	400
1992 Cabinet Sign, Warrior's Farewell -Matched Numbered Set	Closed	1992	385.00	465
1993 Mountain Man	Closed	1993	35.00	125
1993 Blue Bonnets & Yellow Ribbon	Closed	1993	350.00	350-400
1993 Mountain Man, Blue Bonnets & Yellow Ribbon-Matched Numbered Set	Closed	1993	385.00	385
1994 The Wedding Robe	Closed	1995	45.00	45
1994 The Courtship Race	Closed	1995	375.00	375
1994 The Wedding Robe, The Courtside Race-Matched Numbered Set	Closed	1995	385.00	420
1995 Thunder Pipe	Closed	1996	395.00	395
1995 Mystic Medicine Man	Closed	1996	Gift	N/A
1996 Two For the Price of One	Closed	1997	260.00	260
1996 Training Session	Closed	1997	Gift	N/A

Possible Dreams

Santa Claus Network® Collectors Club - Staff

YEAR ISSUE	EDITION LIMIT	YEAR RETD.	ISSUE PRICE	*QUOTE U.S.$
1992 The Gift Giver 805001	Closed	1993	Gift	40
1993 Santa's Special Friend 805050	Closed	1993	59.00	59
1993 Special Delivery 805002	Closed	1994	Gift	N/A
1994 On a Winter's Eve 805051	Closed	1994	65.00	65
1994 Jolly St. Nick 805003	Closed	1995	Gift	N/A
1995 Marionette Santa 805052	Closed	1995	50.00	50
1995 Checking His List 805004	Closed	1996	Gift	40
1996 A Tree For the Children 805054	Closed	1996	40.00	40
1996 A Cookie From Santa 805005	Closed	1996	Gift	25
1997 Santa's Rocking Horse 805055	Closed	1997	40.00	40
1997 Santa's Handiwork 805006	Closed	1997	Gift	25
1998 Cross Country Crinkle	Yr.Iss.		18.50	19
1998 Wish Upon a Star 805056	Yr.Iss.		Gift	44

African Spirit® - W. Still

YEAR ISSUE	EDITION LIMIT	YEAR RETD.	ISSUE PRICE	*QUOTE U.S.$
1997 Bororo Man 347003	Open		119.50	120
1998 Bushman and Son 347008	Open		139.60	140
1997 Fulani Woman 347004	Open		100.00	100
1997 Hausa Man 347001	Open		100.00	100
1997 Maasai Warrior 347005	Open		115.00	115
1997 Peul Woman 347002	Open		100.00	100
1998 Rendille Woman & Child 347007	Open		136.00	136

The Citizens of Londonshire® - Unknown

YEAR ISSUE	EDITION LIMIT	YEAR RETD.	ISSUE PRICE	*QUOTE U.S.$
1990 Admiral Waldo 713407	Open		65.00	68
1992 Albert 713426	Closed	1994	65.00	68
1991 Bernie 713414	Open		68.00	71
1992 Beth 713417	Open		35.00	37
1992 Christopher 713418	Open		35.00	37
1992 Countess of Hamlett 713419	Open		65.00	68
1992 David 713423	Open		37.50	39
1992 Debbie 713422	Open		37.50	39
1990 Dianne 713413	Open		33.00	35
1990 Dr. Isaac 713409	Closed	1995	65.00	68
1989 Earl of Hamlett 713400	Closed	1994	65.00	68
1992 Jean Claude 713421	Open		35.00	37
1989 Lady Ashley 713405	Open		65.00	68
1989 Lord Nicholas 713402	Open		72.00	76
1989 Lord Winston of Riverside 713403	Closed	1994	65.00	68
1994 Maggie 713428	Closed	1994	57.00	57
1990 Margaret of Foxcroft 713408	Open		65.00	68
1992 Nicole 713420	Open		35.00	37
1993 Nigel As Santa 713427	Open		53.50	56
1990 Officer Kevin 713406	Closed	1994	65.00	68
1990 Phillip 713412	Open		33.00	35
1992 Rebecca 713424	Open		35.00	37
1992 Richard 713425	Open		35.00	37
1989 Rodney 713404	Open		65.00	68
1991 Sir Red 713415	Closed	1994	72.00	76
1989 Sir Robert 713401	Open		65.00	68
1992 Tiffany Sorbet 713416	Open		65.00	68
1990 Walter 713410	Closed	1994	33.00	35
1990 Wendy 713411	Closed	1994	33.00	35

Clothtique® American Artist Collection™ - Various

YEAR ISSUE	EDITION LIMIT	YEAR RETD.	ISSUE PRICE	*QUOTE U.S.$
1996 The 12 Days of Christmas 15052 - M. Monterio	Closed	1997	48.00	50
1991 Alpine Christmas 15003 - J. Brett	Closed	1994	129.00	135
1992 An Angel's Kiss 15008 - J. Griffith	Closed	1995	85.00	125
1993 A Beacon of Light 15022 - J. Vaillancourt	Closed	1996	60.00	65
1998 Bone Appetit! 15067 - G. Benvenuti	Open		53.50	54
1993 A Brighter Day 15024 - J. St. Denis	Closed	1997	67.50	70
1994 Captain Claus 15030 - M. Monteiro	Closed	1996	77.00	77
1995 Christmas Caller 15035 - J. Vaillancourt	Open		57.50	58
1992 Christmas Company 15011 - T. Browning	Closed	1995	77.00	125
1996 Christmas Light 15055 - D. Wenzel	Closed	1997	53.50	54
1996 Christmas Stories 15054 - T. Browning	Open		63.50	64
1994 Christmas Surprise 15033 - M. Alvin	Closed	1997	88.00	88
1998 Clean Sweep 15071 - M. Humphries	Open		47.00	47
1997 Cookie Maker 15063 - T. Browning	Open		55.00	55
1995 Country Sounds 15042 - M. Monteiro	Open		74.00	74
1997 Downhill Thrills 15058 - T. Browning	Open		49.00	49
1998 Dreams Come True 15065 - T. Browning	Open		69.00	69
1998 Dress Rehearsal 15075 - L. Fletcher	Open		50.00	50
1996 Dressed For the Holidays 15050 - J. Vaillancourt	Open		27.00	27
1993 Easy Putt 15018 - T. Browning	Closed	1996	110.00	115-135
1991 Father Christmas 15007 - J. Vaillancourt	Closed	1995	59.50	75-90
1993 Father Earth 15017 - M. Monteiro	Open		77.00	80
1998 Felice Natale! 15068 - G. Benvenuti	Open		45.90	46
1995 Fresh From The Oven 15051 - M. Alvin	Closed	1997	49.00	49
1991 A Friendly Visit 15005 - T. Browning	Closed	1994	99.50	105
1997 The Fun Seekers 15064 - T. Browning	Open		48.00	48
1994 The Gentle Craftsman 15031 - J. Griffith	Closed	1996	81.00	99
1994 Gifts from the Garden 15032 - J. Griffith	Closed	1996	77.00	92
1995 Giving Thanks 15045 - M. Alvin	Open		45.50	46
1995 A Good Round 15041 - T. Browning	Closed	1997	73.00	73
1992 Heralding the Way 15014 - J. Griffith	Closed	1995	72.00	75
1993 Ice Capers 15025 - T. Browning	Closed	1996	99.50	129
1993 Just Scooting Along 15023 - J. Vaillancourt	Open		79.50	83
1997 Last Minute Prep 15060 - D. Wenzel	Open		52.50	53
1992 Lighting the Way 15012 - L. Bywaters	Closed	1996	85.00	106
1991 The Magic of Christmas 15001 - L. Bywaters	Closed	1994	132.00	139
1997 Morning Brew 15056 - J. Cleveland	Open		44.50	45
1992 Music Makers 15010 - T. Browning	Closed	1995	135.00	155
1993 Nature's Love 15016 - M. Alvin	Closed	1996	75.00	75-79
1998 New Arrival 15069 - S. Rusinko	Open		48.00	48
1995 A New Suit For Santa 15053 - T. Browning	Open		90.00	90
1997 North Country Weather 15057 - J. Cleveland	Open		40.00	40
1996 Not a Creature Was Stirring 15046 - J. Cleveland	Open		44.00	44
1992 Out of the Forest 15013 - J. Vaillancourt	Closed	1995	60.00	68
1995 Patchwork Santa 15039 - J. Cleveland	Open		67.50	68
1992 Peace on Earth 15009 - M. Alvin	Closed	1995	87.50	92
1997 Peaceable Kingdom 15061 - J. Griffith	Open		78.80	79
1991 A Peaceful Eve 15002 - L. Bywaters	Closed	1994	99.50	105
1998 Playing Through 15066 - T. Browning	Open		49.30	50
1995 Ready For Christmas 15049 - T. Browning	Closed	1997	95.00	95
1995 Refuge From The Storm15047 - M. Monterio	Closed	1997	49.00	49
1995 Riding High 15040 - L. Nillson	Closed	1997	115.00	115-125
1994 Santa and Feathered Friend 15026 - D. Wenzel	Open		84.00	84
1995 Santa and the Ark 15038 - J. Griffith	Closed	1997	71.50	75
1992 Santa in Rocking Chair 713090 - M. Monteiro	Closed	1995	85.00	100
1997 Santa on the Green 15062 - T. Browning	Open		41.00	41
1991 Santa's Cuisine 15006 - T. Browning	Closed	1994	138.00	148
1998 Santa's On A Roll 15072 - W. Still	Open		41.80	42
1998 Scandinavian Father Christmas 15078 - J. Vaillancourt	Open		40.00	40

*Quotes have been rounded up to nearest dollar

YEAR ISSUE	EDITION LIMIT	YEAR RETD.	ISSUE PRICE	*QUOTE U.S.$
1995 Southwest Santa 15043 - V. Wiseman	Closed	1996	65.00	89
1994 Spirit of Christmas Past 15036 - J. Vaillancourt	Open		79.00	79
1994 Spirit of Santa 15028 - T. Browning	Closed	1996	68.00	75
1995 The Storyteller 15029 - T. Browning	Open		76.00	76
1993 Strumming the Lute 15015 - M. Alvin	Open		79.00	83
1995 Sunflower Santa 15044 - J. Griffith	Closed	1997	75.00	75
1994 Tea Time 15034 - M. Alvin	Closed	1997	90.00	90
1994 Teddy Love 15037 - J. Griffith	Open		89.00	89
1994 A Touch of Magic 15027 - T. Browning	Open		95.00	95
1991 Traditions 15004 - T. Blackshear	Closed	1994	50.00	75
1998 Trailside Prayer 15074 - L. Fletcher	Open		59.80	60
1993 The Tree Planter 15020 - J. Griffith	Open		79.50	84
1995 Visions of Sugar Plums 15048 - J. Griffith	Closed	1997	50.00	50
1998 The Woman Behind Christmas 15073 - L. Fletcher	Open		57.70	58
1993 The Workshop 15019 - T. Browning	Closed	1995	140.00	175
1997 Yuletide Gardner 15059 - J. Griffith	Open		50.00	50
1998 Yuletide Round Up 15070 - J. Sorenson	Open		43.00	43

Clothtique® Angels-Elves

YEAR ISSUE	EDITION LIMIT	YEAR RETD.	ISSUE PRICE	*QUOTE U.S.$
1997 Irish Angel 714167	Open		29.30	30
1997 Irish Lass 713677	Open		26.80	27

Clothtique® Garfield® Collection - Staff

YEAR ISSUE	EDITION LIMIT	YEAR RETD.	ISSUE PRICE	*QUOTE U.S.$
1997 Countdown to Christmas 275003	Open		41.60	42
1996 Love Me, Love My Teddy Bear 275002	Open		51.60	52
1997 Private Stash 275004	Open		50.20	51
1996 Return to Sender 275001	Open		58.00	58

Clothtique® Limited Edition Santas - Unknown

YEAR ISSUE	EDITION LIMIT	YEAR RETD.	ISSUE PRICE	*QUOTE U.S.$
1988 Father Christmas 3001	10,000	1993	240.00	550-650
1988 Kris Kringle 3002	10,000	1992	240.00	550-650
1988 Patriotic Santa 3000	10,000	1994	240.00	550-650
1989 Traditional Santa 40's 3003	10,000	1994	240.00	550-650

Clothtique® Looney Tunes® Collection - Staff

YEAR ISSUE	EDITION LIMIT	YEAR RETD.	ISSUE PRICE	*QUOTE U.S.$
1995 Bugs Bunny's 14 Carot Santa 3402	Open		57.50	58
1996 Merry Master of Ceremonies 3404	Open		55.40	56
1996 Pepe's Christmas Serenade 3406	Open		42.80	43
1996 Selfish Elfish Daffy Duck 3405	Open		46.90	47
1995 Sylvester's Holiday High Jinks 3403	Open		65.00	65
1996 Tasmanian Rhapsody 3407	Open		47.30	48
1995 Yosemite Sam's Rootin' Tootin' Christmas 3401	Open		59.00	59

Clothtique® Santas Collection - Staff, unless otherwise noted

YEAR ISSUE	EDITION LIMIT	YEAR RETD.	ISSUE PRICE	*QUOTE U.S.$
1992 1940's Traditional Santa 713049	Closed	1994	44.00	65
1992 African American Santa 713056	Closed	1995	65.00	68
1993 African-American Santa w/ Doll 713102	Open		40.00	42
1998 Angel w/Tree Topper 713678	Open		24.00	24
1997 Autograph For a Fan 713143	Open		39.00	39
1989 Baby's First Christmas 713042	Closed	1992	42.00	46
1995 Baby's First Noel 713120	Closed	1997	62.00	65
1998 Baseball Santa 713682	Open		19.80	20
1998 Basketball Santa 713681	Open		19.80	20
1988 Carpenter Santa 713033	Closed	1992	38.00	44
1997 Celtic Sounds 713162	Open		46.00	46
1994 Christmas Cheer 713109	Closed	1997	58.00	58
1994 A Christmas Guest 713112	Closed	1997	79.00	79
1998 Christmas in the Alps 713171	Open		48.00	48
1994 Christmas is for Children 713115	Open		62.00	62
1986 Christmas Man 713027	Closed	1989	34.50	35
1998 Christmas Spruce 713172	Open		42.00	42
1987 Colonial Santa 713032	Closed	1990	38.00	40
1997 Deck The Halls 713161	Open		39.70	38
1997 Doctor Claus 713157	Open		35.00	35
1995 Down Hill Santa 713123	Open		66.50	67
1997 Down the Chimney He Came 713154	Open		42.50	43
1997 Easy Ridin' Santa 713159	Open		37.50	38
1992 Engineer Santa 713057	Closed	1995	130.00	137
1993 European Santa 713095	Closed	1996	53.00	48-69
1989 Exhausted Santa 713043	Closed	1992	60.00	65
1991 Father Christmas 713087	Closed	1993	43.00	47
1995 Finishing Touch 713121	Open		54.70	55
1993 Fireman & Child 713106	Open		55.00	58
1992 Fireman Santa 713053	Closed	1996	60.00	68
1998 Football Santa 713679	Open		19.80	20
1998 For A Special Little Girl 713179	Open		44.00	44
1996 For Someone Special 713142	Open		39.00	39
1995 Frisky Friend 713130	Closed	1997	45.50	46-50
1988 Frontier Santa 713034	Closed	1991	40.00	42
1995 Ginger Bread Baker 713135	Closed	1997	35.00	35
1998 Gloria In Cielo 713674 - G. Benvenuti	Open		33.80	34
1994 Good Tidings 713107	Closed	1996	51.00	60
1997 Grampa Claus 713146	Open		41.40	42
1990 Harlem Santa 713046	Closed	1994	46.00	55
1995 Heaven Sent 713138	Closed	1997	50.00	50-56
1998 Highland Santa 713169	Open		42.50	43
1993 His Favorite Color 713098	Closed	1996	48.00	50
1995 Ho: Ho-Hole in One 713131	Open		43.00	43
1994 Holiday Friend 713110	Open		104.00	104
1997 Holiday Gourmet 713147	Open		39.10	40
1997 Holiday Traffic 713148	Open		47.50	48
1995 Home Spun Holidays 713128	Open		49.50	50
1995 Hook Line and Santa 713129	Open		49.70	50
1998 Italian Angel Tree Topper 713673 - G. Benvenuti	Open		33.30	34
1996 Jumping Jack Santa 713139	Open		45.50	46
1991 Kris Kringle 713088	Closed	1993	43.00	46
1998 Landing Beacon 713181	Open		43.40	44
1997 Leprechaun 713153	Open		18.50	19
1993 A Long Trip 713105	Open		95.00	100
1998 Mariachi Santa 713174	Open		48.80	49
1993 May Your Wishes Come True 713096	Closed	1996	59.00	65
1993 The Modern Shopper 713103	Closed	1996	40.00	62
1995 A Modern Skier 713123	Closed	1998	59.50	60
1994 A Most Welcome Visitor 713113	Open		63.00	63
1994 Mrs. Claus 713118	Closed	1997	58.00	58
1991 Mrs. Claus in Coat 713078	Closed	1995	47.00	71
1989 Mrs. Claus w/doll 713041	Closed	1992	42.00	43
1992 Nicholas 713052	Closed	1994	57.50	60
1998 North Pole 500 713180	Open		38.80	39
1998 North Pole Party Line 713167	Open		44.90	45
1997 North Pole Polka 713163	Open		46.00	46
1997 North Pole Prescription 713164	Open		65.60	66
1998 Officer Claus 713119	Open		37.80	38
1997 On Christmas Pond 713156	Open		52.30	53
1994 Our Hero 713116	Open		62.00	62
1989 Pelze Nichol 713039	Closed	1993	40.00	47
1995 Pet Project 713134 - L. Craven	Open		37.00	37
1994 Playmates 713111	Closed	1996	104.00	104
1994 Puppy Love 713117	Closed	1997	62.00	62
1998 A Purry Friend 713168	Open		42.50	43
1995 Rooftop Santa 659006	Closed	1998	28.50	29
1988 Russian St. Nicholas 713036	Closed	1996	40.00	43
1990 Santa "Please Stop Here" 713045	Closed	1992	63.00	72
1991 Santa Decorating Christmas Tree 713079	Closed	1992	60.00	60
1991 Santa in Bed 713076	Closed	1994	76.00	139
1997 Santa O' Claus 713165	Open		41.50	175
1992 Santa on Motorbike 713054	Closed	1994	115.00	130-135
1992 Santa on Reindeer 713058	Closed	1995	75.00	83
1992 Santa on Sled 713050	Closed	1994	75.00	79
1992 Santa on Sleigh 713091	Closed	1995	79.00	83
1997 Santa Online 713151	Open		55.20	56
1991 Santa Shelf Sitter 713089	Closed	1995	55.50	60
1990 Santa w/Blue Robe 713048	Closed	1992	46.00	69
1989 Santa w/Embroidered Coat 713040	Closed	1991	43.00	43
1993 Santa w/Groceries 713099	Closed	1996	47.50	50
1997 Santa w/Nativity 713150	Open		36.00	36
1986 Santa w/Pack 713026	Closed	1989	34.50	35
1998 Santa with Tree 713183	Open		38.50	39
1997 Santa's Better Half 713155	Open		35.80	36
1998 Santa's Check Up 713175	Open		37.00	37
1998 Santa's Flying Machines 713176	Open		39.60	37
1997 Santa's Grab Bag 713158	Open		47.50	48
1998 Santa's New List 713178	Open		44.90	45
1998 Santa's Tree 713182	Open		36.40	37
1996 Shamrock Santa 713140	Open		41.50	42
1991 Siberian Santa 713077	Closed	1993	49.00	96
1990 Skiing Santa 713047	Closed	1993	62.00	65
1998 A Snack For Santa 713177	Open		37.00	37
1998 Soccer Santa 713683	Open		19.80	20
1995 Sounds of Christmas 713127	Closed	1996	57.50	58
1995 A Special Treat 713122	Open		50.50	51
1988 St. Nicholas 713035	Closed	1991	40.00	169
1995 The Stockings Were Hung 713126	Closed	1997	N/A	65
1998 Tennis Santa 713680	Open		19.80	20
1997 Test Ride 713149	Open		47.10	48
1995 Three Alarm Santa 713137	Open		42.50	43
1998 Top O' The Mornin' 713173	Open		41.50	42
1987 Traditional Deluxe Santa 713030	Closed	1990	38.00	38
1986 Traditional Santa 713028	Closed	1989	34.50	125
1989 Traditional Santa 713038	Closed	1992	42.00	43
1991 The True Spirit of Christmas 713075	Closed	1992	97.00	97
1987 Ukko 713031	Closed	1990	38.00	38
1995 Victorian Evergreen 713125	Open		49.00	49
1995 Victorian Puppeteer 713124	Closed	1997	51.50	52
1993 Victorian Santa 713097	Closed	1996	55.50	58
1998 Visitor From The North 713170	Open		39.50	40
1988 Weihnachtsman 713037	Closed	1991	40.00	43
1994 A Welcome Visit 713114	Closed	1996	62.00	65
1997 Winter Wanderer 713152	Open		56.90	57
1990 Workbench Santa 713044	Closed	1993	72.00	95
1994 Yuletide Journey 713108	Open		58.00	58

Clothtique® Saturday Evening Post J. C. Leyendecker - J. Leyendecker

YEAR ISSUE	EDITION LIMIT	YEAR RETD.	ISSUE PRICE	*QUOTE U.S.$
1991 Hugging Santa 3599	Closed	1994	129.00	150
1996 Hugging Santa 3650 (smaller re-issue)	Open		52.50	53
1992 Santa on Ladder 3598	Closed	1995	135.00	150
1996 Santa on Ladder 3651 (smaller re-issue)	Open		59.00	59
1991 Traditional Santa 3600	Closed	1992	100.00	125
1996 Traditional Santa 3652 (smaller re-issue)	Closed	1997	66.00	66

Clothtique® Saturday Evening Post Norman Rockwell - N. Rockwell

YEAR ISSUE	EDITION LIMIT	YEAR RETD.	ISSUE PRICE	*QUOTE U.S.$
1992 Balancing the Budget 3064	Open		120.00	126
1989 Christmas "Dear Santa" 3050	Closed	1992	160.00	180
1996 Christmas "Dear Santa" 3050 (smaller re-issue)	Open		70.50	71
1989 Christmas "Santa with Globe" 3051	Closed	1992	154.00	184
1996 Santa With Globe 3101 (smaller re-issue)	Open		73.00	73
1991 Doctor and Doll 3055	Closed	1995	196.00	206
1991 The Gift 3057	Closed	1996	160.00	168
1991 Gone Fishing 3054	Closed	1995	250.00	263
1997 Gone Fishing 3104 (smaller re-issue)	Open		67.70	68
1991 Gramps at the Reins 3058	Open		290.00	305
1990 Hobo 3052	Open		159.00	167
1990 Love Letters 3053	Open		172.00	180
1991 Man with Geese 3059	Open		120.00	126
1992 Marriage License 3062	Open		195.00	205
1996 Not a Creature was Stirring (smaller re-issue)	Open		44.00	44
1991 Santa Plotting His Course 3060	Open		160.00	168
1992 Santa's Helpers 3063	Closed	1994	170.00	179
1997 Santa's Helpers 3103 (smaller re-issue)	Open		64.90	65
1991 Springtime 3056	Closed	1996	130.00	137
1992 Triple Self Portrait 3061	Closed	1995	230.00	250
1997 Triple Self Portrait 3105 (smaller re-issue)	Open		65.70	66

Clothtique® Signature Series® - Stanley/Chang

YEAR ISSUE	EDITION LIMIT	YEAR RETD.	ISSUE PRICE	*QUOTE U.S.$
1995 Department Store Santa, USA/Circa 1940s 721001	Open		108.00	108
1995 Father Christmas, England/Circa 1890s 721002	Open		90.00	90
1996 St. Nicholas, Myra/Circa 1300s 721004	Open		99.00	99
1996 Kriss Kringle, USA/Circa 1840s 721005	Open		99.00	99
1998 Romanov Santa, Russia/Circa 1890s 721008	Open		83.50	84

Coca-Cola Brand Clothtique® Santas - H. Sundblom

YEAR ISSUE	EDITION LIMIT	YEAR RETD.	ISSUE PRICE	*QUOTE U.S.$
1998 Busy Man's Pause 468002	Open		49.00	49
1998 Santa's Greetings 468005	Open		46.00	46
1998 Step Up To Refreshment 468006	Open		47.00	47
1998 Thanks For the Pause That Refreshes 468003	Open		47.00	47

Crinkle Angels - Staff

YEAR ISSUE	EDITION LIMIT	YEAR RETD.	ISSUE PRICE	*QUOTE U.S.$
1996 Crinkle Angel w/Candle 659405	Open		19.80	20
1996 Crinkle Angel w/Dove 659403	Open		19.80	20
1996 Crinkle Angel w/Harp 659402	Open		19.80	20
1996 Crinkle Angel w/Lamb 659401	Open		19.80	20
1996 Crinkle Angel w/Lantern 659400	Open		19.80	20
1996 Crinkle Angel w/Mandolin 659404	Open		19.80	20

Crinkle Carousel - Staff

YEAR ISSUE	EDITION LIMIT	YEAR RETD.	ISSUE PRICE	*QUOTE U.S.$
1998 Checkmate Crinkle 659807	Open		9.00	9
1998 Crinkle Antlers 659814	Open		16.00	16
1998 Crinkle Champion 659803	Open		10.50	11
1998 Crinkle Doodle-Doo 659810	Open		15.00	15
1998 Crinkle Filly 659801	Open		16.00	16
1998 Crinkle Pony (muscial) Waterdome 659881	Open		40.00	40
1998 Crinkle Stallion (musical) Waterdome 659880	Open		40.00	40
1998 Frisky Crinkle 659806	Open		12.00	12
1998 Galloping Crinkle 659804	Open		16.00	16
1998 Happy Hog Crinkle 659808	Open		15.00	15
1998 Hippity-Hop Crinkle 659811	Open		15.00	15
1998 Honey Bear Crinkle 659809	Open		15.00	15
1998 Laughing Lion Crinkle 659812	Open		15.40	16
1998 Merry-Go Crinkle (lighted) 659860	Open		34.00	34
1998 Pachyderm Crinkle 659813	Open		16.00	16
1998 Parosol Crinkle 659805	Open		13.30	14
1998 Prancing Crinkle (muscial) 659850	Open		30.00	30
1998 Surf Rider Crinkle 659802	Open		16.00	16

Crinkle Claus - Staff

YEAR ISSUE	EDITION LIMIT	YEAR RETD.	ISSUE PRICE	*QUOTE U.S.$
1995 American Santa 657224	Open		15.50	16
1997 Appalachian Light 659030	Open		8.30	9
1995 Arctic Santa 659107	Open		15.70	16
1995 Austrian Santa 659103	Open		15.80	16
1997 Bavarian Crinkle 659029	Open		8.30	9
1998 Bavarian Om-Pah Crinkle (musical) 659605	Open		38.80	39
1997 Bedtime Story 659910	Open		31.40	32
1995 Bell Shape Santa 659008	Retrd.	1996	23.50	24
1996 Bishop of Maya 659111	Open		19.90	20
1996 Bishop of Maya Plaque 659306	Open		19.90	20
1996 Black Forest Gift Giver 659114	Open		19.90	20
1996 Black Forest Gift Giver Plaque 659302	Open		19.90	20
1997 Blarney Stone Crinkle 659125	Open		13.40	14
1998 Bottle Crinkle 659052	Open		15.90	16
1997 Brazilian Fiesta 659028	Open		8.30	9
1997 British Jubilee 659027	Open		8.30	9
1996 Buckets of Fruit for Good Girls & Boys 659903	5,000	1997	45.00	45
1997 Buckingham Crinkle 659126	Open		13.40	14
1995 Candle Stick Santa 659121	Open		15.80	16
1996 Carrying The Torch	Open		19.80	20
1996 Catch of The Day 659504	Open		19.90	20
1996 Celtic Santa 659110	Retrd.	1997	19.90	20
1996 Celtic Santa Plaque 659305	Retrd.	1997	19.90	20
1996 Choo-Choo For The Children 659904	5,000		25.00	25
1998 Christmas Expedition 659914	5,000		26.90	27
1997 Christmas King Crinkle 659123	Open		13.40	14
1997 Christmas Tree Crinkle 659036	Open		16.30	17
1995 Christmas Tree Santa 659117	Open		19.90	20
1997 Christmas Wilderness Waterdome 659603	Open		46.80	47
1998 Clickety-Clack Crinkle 659044	Open		17.20	18
1995 Crescent Moon Santa 659119	Open		19.00	19
1997 Crinkle Ark (lighted) 660301	Open		57.00	57

*Quotes have been rounded up to nearest dollar

FIGURINES

YEAR ISSUE	EDITION LIMIT	YEAR RETD.	ISSUE PRICE	*QUOTE U.S.$
1997 Crinkle Bears 660303	Open		14.90	15
1998 Crinkle Cello 659054	Open		14.80	15
1998 Crinkle Christmas Eve 659252	Open		28.50	29
1998 Crinkle Claus Cruise 659055	Open		17.20	18
1995 Crinkle Claus w/Dome-German Santa 659601	Retrd.	1998	45.00	45
1996 Crinkle Claus w/Dome-Santa/Chimney 659600	Open		45.00	45
1996 Crinkle Claus w/Dome-St. Nicholas 659602	Open		45.00	45
1998 Crinkle Cross 659053	Open		15.00	15
1998 Crinkle Elf Carpenter 659060	Open		8.50	9
1998 Crinkle Elf Chef 659059	Open		8.50	9
1998 Crinkle Elf Fireman 659062	Open		8.50	9
1998 Crinkle Elf Postman 659056	Open		8.50	9
1998 Crinkle Elf Toymaker 659058	Open		8.50	9
1998 Crinkle Elf w/Jester 659063	Open		8.50	9
1998 Crinkle Elf w/Snowman 659061	Open		8.50	9
1998 Crinkle Elf w/Teddy 659057	Open		8.50	9
1998 Crinkle Flag Bearer 659049	Open		12.40	13
1997 Crinkle Horses 660305	Open		13.30	14
1997 Crinkle Locomotive & Coal Car 660201	Open		42.00	42
1998 Crinkle Lyre 659051	Open		16.70	17
1998 Crinkle Mail Car 660202	Open		18.80	19
1997 Crinkle Noah 660302	Open		10.30	11
1997 Crinkle Reindeer 660306	Open		13.30	14
1997 Crinkle Sheep 660304	Open		10.80	11
1998 Crinkle Spirit of Giving 659253	Open		23.50	24
1998 Crinkle Uncle Sam 659045	Open		13.50	14
1996 A Crown of Antlers	Open		19.70	20
1996 Dashing Through The Snow 659902	5,000	1997	45.00	45
1998 Department Store Crinkle 659250	Open		23.50	24
1998 Ding Dong Crinkle 659046	Open		16.60	17
1996 Display Figurine-965003	Open		11.00	11
1997 Down The Chimney 659911	Open		31.10	32
1998 Dutch Treat Crinkle (musical) 659604	Open		38.80	39
1998 Emerald Isle Crinkle 659040	Open		13.40	14
1998 English Crinkle at Westminster Abbey 659355	Open		28.50	29
1995 English Santa 659100	Open		15.80	16
1996 Feeding His Forest Friends 659905	5,000	1997	27.50	28
1998 Fine Feathered Friends 659915	5,000		25.40	26
1998 Firecracker Crinkle 659047	Open		14.60	15
1997 Fjord Crinkle 659124	Open		13.40	14
1997 Flickering Crinkle 659035	Open		14.00	14
1995 Forest Santa 657225	Open		15.50	16
1995 French Santa 659108	Open		15.70	16
1998 German Crinkle at Rothenburg 659352	Open		28.50	29
1995 German Santa 659105	Open		15.80	16
1998 Grizzly Bear Helper 659912	5,000		25.90	26
1995 Hard Boiled Santa 659115	Retrd.	1997	13.70	14
1998 High Flying Crinkle 659251	Open		32.50	33
1995 High Hat Santa 657134	Open		13.40	14
1997 High Ho 659025	Open		13.20	14
1997 High Note 659023	Open		13.20	14
1997 Highland Piper 659026	Open		8.30	9
1997 Holiday Cane Crinkle 659034	Open		14.00	14
1995 Hour Glass Santa 659118	Open		15.00	15
1996 Iceland Visitor 659112	Open		19.90	20
1996 Iceland Visitor Plaque 659303	Open		19.90	20
1998 Irish Crinkle at St. Patrick's Cathedral 659354	Open		28.50	29
1995 Italian Santa 659106	Open		15.70	16
1995 Jolly St. Nick 659012	Open		15.00	15
1997 Kelly Crinkle 659132	Open		16.00	16
1997 Kelly Crinkle 659712	Open		7.80	8
1998 Kremlin Crinkle (musical) 659606	Open		38.80	39
1996 Learned Gentleman	Open		19.80	20
1998 Liberty Crinkle 659048	Open		12.40	13
1996 Lighting The Way	Open		19.80	20
1997 Lisbon Traveler 659033	Open		8.30	9
1996 Low & Behold	Open		13.90	14
1997 Madrid Crinkle 659131	Open		16.00	16
1997 Madrid Crinkle 659708	Open		7.80	8
1997 Mediterranean Treasure 659032	Open		8.30	9
1996 Merry Old England 659113	Retrd.	1997	19.90	20
1996 Merry Old England Plaque 659301	Open		19.90	20
1997 Moscow Crinkle 659128	Open		16.00	16
1997 Moscow Crinkle 659711	Open		7.80	8
1997 Munich Crinkle 659130	Open		16.00	16
1997 Munich Crinkle 659710	Open		7.80	8
1996 The Music Man	Open		19.80	20
1995 Netherlands Santa 659102	Open		15.70	16
1997 North Pole Artisan 659907	Open		30.00	30
1996 Northland Santa 659109	Open		19.90	20
1996 Northland Santa Plaque 659304	Open		19.90	20
1998 A Nutty Noel 659913	5,000		25.90	26
1998 Old Glory Crinkle 659050	Open		12.40	13
1997 Pamplona Crinkle 659122	Open		13.40	14
1997 Paris Crinkle 659709	Open		7.80	8
1995 Pine Cone Santa 657226	Retrd.	1997	15.50	16
1996 Rag/Doll Delivery 659906	5,000	1997	34.50	35
1997 Rocking Crinkle 659039	Open		17.60	18
1995 Roly Poly Santa 3.5" 657138	Retrd.	1996	12.50	17
1995 Roly Poly Santa 4" 659009	Retrd.	1996	23.00	23
1995 Rooftop Santa 659006	Retrd.	1998	28.50	29
1998 Royal Crinkle (musical) 659607	Open		38.80	39
1996 Running Down The List 659901	5,000	1997	33.00	33
1998 Russian Crinkle at St. Basil's 659353	Open		28.50	29
1995 Russian Santa 3.5" 659101	Open		15.70	16
1995 Russian Santa 4" 657228	Retrd.	1996	15.50	16
1995 Santa on Bag 657508	Retrd.	1996	15.00	15
1995 Santa Sitting Pretty 659116	Open		13.90	14
1995 Santa w/Book 659010	Retrd.	1997	13.80	14
1995 Santa w/Candy Cane 4.5" 657139	Retrd.	1996	13.00	13
1996 Santa w/Candy Cane 5" 657142	Retrd.	1996	27.00	27
1996 Santa w/Candy Cane 6.5" 657135	Retrd.	1996	17.50	18
1995 Santa w/Cane & Bag 657230	Retrd.	1996	12.00	12
1995 Santa w/Gifts 657143	Retrd.	1996	27.00	27
1995 Santa w/Lantern & Bag 657229	Retrd.	1996	15.50	16
1995 Santa w/Lantern 5" 657136	Retrd.	1996	12.50	13
1995 Santa w/Lantern 5" 657144	Retrd.	1996	27.00	27
1995 Santa w/Noah's Ark 657227	Open		15.50	16
1995 Santa w/Patchwork Bag 657232	Retrd.	1997	19.00	19
1995 Santa w/Stars 657140	Retrd.	1996	14.00	14
1995 Santa w/Teddy Bear 657231	Retrd.	1997	16.00	16
1995 Santa w/Tree 659011	Retrd.	1996	14.20	15
1995 Santa w/Wreath 657141	Retrd.	1996	16.30	17
1995 Santa's Candy Surprise	Open		27.00	27
1995 Scandinavian Santa 659104	Open		15.80	16
1998 Scottish Crinkle at Glamis 659350	Open		28.50	29
1998 Shamrock Crinkle 659041	Open		13.40	14
1997 Slavic Crinkle 659133	Open		16.00	16
1997 Slavic Crinkle 659713	Open		7.80	8
1997 Sled Filled With Joy 659908	Open		31.00	31
1995 Slimline Santa 657137	Retrd.	1996	12.00	16
1997 Something For Everyone 659909	Open		31.10	32
1997 Starburst Crinkle 659038	Open		14.20	15
1995 Tall Santa	Open		17.50	18
1998 Teddy Beefeater Crinkle 659072	Open		20.00	20
1998 Teddy Crinkle Italiano 659071	Open		20.00	20
1998 Teddy Dutch Crinkle 659070	Open		20.00	20
1998 Teddy Mc Crinkle 659076	Open		24.80	25
1998 Teddy O' Crinkle 659075	Open		24.80	25
1998 Teddy Russian Crinkle 659073	Open		20.00	20
1998 Teddy Von Crinkle 659074	Open		20.00	20
1995 Tick Tock Santa 659120	Open		15.00	15
1995 Tip Top Santa 659007	Retrd.	1996	23.50	24
1996 To The Rescue	Open		19.90	20
1997 Top of the List 659022	Open		13.20	14
1997 Top of the Tree 659024	Open		13.20	14
1997 Top Spin Crinkle 659037	Open		13.70	14
1998 US Crinkle at The Capitol 659351	Open		28.50	29
1997 Vatican Crinkle 659127	Open		13.40	14
1996 Well Rounded Santa	Open		13.70	14
1997 West Coast Beat 659031	Open		8.30	9

Crinkle Cousins - Staff

YEAR ISSUE	EDITION LIMIT	YEAR RETD.	ISSUE PRICE	*QUOTE U.S.$
1995 Crinkle Cousin w/Clock 659002	Retrd.	1997	15.50	16
1995 Crinkle Cousin w/Clown 659004	Retrd.	1997	15.50	16
1995 Crinkle Cousin w/Dolls 659003	Retrd.	1997	15.50	16
1995 Crinkle Cousin w/Lantern 659001	Retrd.	1997	15.50	16
1995 Crinkle Cousin w/Teddy 659005	Retrd.	1997	15.50	16

Crinkle Crackers - Staff

YEAR ISSUE	EDITION LIMIT	YEAR RETD.	ISSUE PRICE	*QUOTE U.S.$
1995 Admiral Crinkle Cracker 659212	Retrd.	1997	18.50	19
1995 Captain Crinkle Cracker 659211	Retrd.	1996	13.00	13
1995 Corporal Crinkle Cracker 659214	Retrd.	1996	14.60	15
1995 French Crinkle Cracker 659203	Open		22.00	22
1995 French Lieutenant Crinkle Cracker 659205	Open		13.50	14
1995 General Crinkle Cracker 659213	Retrd.	1996	15.50	16
1995 Lieutenant Crinkle Cracker 659209	Open		26.50	27
1995 Major Crinkle Cracker 659215	Open		14.50	15
1995 Private Crinkle Cracker 659210	Retrd.	1996	15.00	15
1995 Roly Poly French Crinkle Cracker 659204	Open		13.90	14
1995 Roly Poly Russian Crinkle Cracker 659207	Open		13.50	14
1995 Roly Poly Sergeant Crinkle Cracker 659216	Open		13.50	14
1995 Roly Poly U.S. Crinkle Cracker 659201	Open		13.90	14
1995 Russian Crinkle Cracker 4" 659208	Open		13.50	14
1995 Russian Crinkle Cracker 7.75" 659206	Open		29.50	30
1995 U.S. Crinkle Cracker 3.75" 659202	Open		13.50	14
1995 U.S.Crinkle Cracker 7.5" 659200	Open		29.00	29

Crinkle Professionals - Staff

YEAR ISSUE	EDITION LIMIT	YEAR RETD.	ISSUE PRICE	*QUOTE U.S.$
1996 Baseball Player 659507	Open		19.50	20
1996 Doctor 659500	Open		19.50	20
1996 Fireman 659503	Open		19.50	20
1996 Fisherman 659504	Open		19.50	20
1996 Football Player 659506	Retrd.	1997	19.50	23
1996 Golfer 659505	Open		19.50	20
1996 Hockey Player 659508	Retrd.	1997	19.50	20
1997 Lawyer 659511	Open		19.50	20
1996 Policeman 659502	Open		19.50	20
1996 Postman 659501	Open		19.50	20
1996 Soccer Player 659509	Retrd.	1997	19.50	23
1997 Teacher 659510	Open		19.50	20
1997 Tennis Player 659512	Open		19.50	20

Floristine Angels® - B. Sargent

YEAR ISSUE	EDITION LIMIT	YEAR RETD.	ISSUE PRICE	*QUOTE U.S.$
1996 Angel of Happiness 668002	Open		100.00	100
1996 An Angel's Prayer 668003	Open		98.00	98
1997 Blissful Ballet 668008	Open		72.40	73
1996 Celestial Garden 668001	Open		98.00	98
1996 Heavenly Harmony 668006	Open		100.00	100
1996 Lessons From Above 668005	Open		100.00	100
1996 My Guardian Angel 668004	Open		112.00	112
1997 My Inspiration 668007	Open		37.70	38
1997 Sacred Virgil 668009	Open		47.10	48

Ingrid's Clowns - I. White

YEAR ISSUE	EDITION LIMIT	YEAR RETD.	ISSUE PRICE	*QUOTE U.S.$
1998 Bobo 317003	Open		11.80	12
1998 Carrot Top 317004	Open		11.80	12
1998 Harley 317001	Open		11.80	12
1998 Jester 317006	Open		11.80	12
1998 Pinky 317002	Open		11.80	12
1998 Popcorn 317005	Open		11.80	12
1998 Slapstick 317007	Open		11.80	12

Spanglers Realm® - R. Spangler

YEAR ISSUE	EDITION LIMIT	YEAR RETD.	ISSUE PRICE	*QUOTE U.S.$
1997 'Twas The Night Before 191003	Open		19.90	20
1997 Bath Time 191019	Open		15.50	16
1997 Best Friends 191020	Open		18.10	19
1997 Cherish The Small Wonders of Life 191005	Open		15.00	15
1997 Chocolate Treat 191018	Open		17.30	18
1998 Christmas Cookie Express 191004	Open		27.80	28
1997 Christmas Treasures 191021	Open		18.10	19
1997 Delicious Discovery 191001	Open		35.70	36
1997 Downhill Racer 191013	Open		18.90	19
1997 Draggin' In The Morning 191009	Open		21.90	22
1998 Dragling on the Scale 191007	Open		35.60	36
1997 A Dragon's Work Is Never Done 191006	Open		19.80	20
1997 Equal Partners Stocking Holder 191150	Open		25.20	26
1997 Fishin' Chips 191017	Open		16.30	17
1997 A Flour Just For You 191016	Open		18.10	19
1997 From Dagmar, To Dewey 191015	Open		18.30	19
1997 Guardian Angel 191010	Open		15.40	16
1997 Hole In One 191014	Open		18.50	19
1997 Home Is Where The Magic Is 191101	Open		144.50	145
1998 No Smoking Sign 191002	Open		31.30	32
1997 Santa's Surprise 191008	Open		17.10	18
1998 Sleepy Time 191022	Open		18.50	19
1997 Story Time 191012	Open		21.20	22
1997 To The Rescue 191011	Open		15.90	16

The Thickets at Sweetbriar® - B. Ross

YEAR ISSUE	EDITION LIMIT	YEAR RETD.	ISSUE PRICE	*QUOTE U.S.$
1997 Amber Twinkle 350140	Open		26.80	27
1995 Angel Dear 350123	Open		32.00	32
1996 Autumn Peppergrass 350135	Open		31.00	31
1997 Berty Cosgrove 350137	Open		27.50	28
1993 The Bride-Emily Feathers 350112	Open		30.00	30
1995 Buttercup 350121	Open		32.00	32
1995 Cecily Pickwick 350125	Open		32.00	32
1998 Celeste 350146	Open		26.40	27
1998 Chip Weezley 350418	Open		10.50	11
1995 Clem Jingles 350130	Open		37.00	37
1993 Clovis Buttons 350101	Closed	1996	24.15	25
1996 Dainty Whiskers 350136	Open		30.00	30
1997 Divinity 350142	Open		27.30	28
1998 Dottie Crispin 350149	Open		26.80	27
1998 Erin Penny 350145	Open		25.50	26
1996 Goody Pringle 350134	Open		31.00	31
1993 The Groom-Oliver Doone 350111	Closed	1996	30.00	30
1997 Herman Noodles 350141	Open		27.50	28
1993 Jewel Blossom 350106	Open		36.75	37
1995 Katy Hollyberry 350124	Closed	1996	35.00	35
1997 Kitty Glitter 350143	Open		27.50	28
1995 Kris Krinkle 350414	Open		12.50	13
1994 Lady Slipper 350116	Open		20.00	20
1993 Lily Blossom 350105	Closed	1996	36.75	37
1996 Lily Blossom 350201 (musical)	Closed	1996	59.50	60
1998 Marie Periwinkle 350148	Open		25.50	26
1997 Mary Pawpins 350138	Open		26.80	27
1993 Maude Tweedy 350100	Closed	1994	26.25	27
1998 Maybelle Pudding 350144	Open		25.90	26
1996 Merry Heart 350131	Open		30.00	30
1994 Morning Dew 350113	Open		30.00	30
1993 Morning Glory 350104	Open		30.45	31
1993 Mr. Claws 350109	Closed	1996	34.00	34
1993 Mrs. Claws 350110	Closed	1996	34.00	34
1993 Orchid Beasley 350103	Closed	1996	26.25	27
1995 Parsley Divine 350129	Open		37.00	37
1996 Patience Finney 350133	Open		31.00	31
1993 Peablossom Thorndike 350102	Closed	1994	26.25	27
1995 Penny Pringle 350128	Open		32.00	32
1995 Pittypat 350122	Open		32.00	32
1994 Precious Petals 350115	Open		34.00	34
1993 Raindrop 350108	Closed	1996	47.25	48
1995 Riley Pickens 350127	Open		32.00	32
1993 Rose Blossom 350107	Open		36.75	37
1998 Samuel Goodley 350147	Open		21.00	21
1997 Smokey Longwood 350139	Open		27.50	28
1994 Sunshine 350118	Open		33.00	33
1994 Sweetie Flowers 350114	Closed	1996	33.00	33
1995 Tillie Lilly 350120	Open		32.00	32
1995 Timmy Evergreen 350126	Open		29.00	29
1996 Velvet Winterberry 350132	Open		30.00	30
1995 Violet Wiggles 350119	Open		32.00	32

Precious Art/Panton

Krystonia Collector's Club - Panton

YEAR ISSUE	EDITION LIMIT	YEAR RETD.	ISSUE PRICE	*QUOTE U.S.$
1989 Pultzr	Retrd.	1990	55.00	300-525
1989 Key	Retrd.	1990	Gift	100-135
1991 Dragons Play	Retrd.	1992	65.00	143-225
1991 Kephrens Chest	Retrd.	1992	Gift	98-200
1992 Vaaston	Retrd.	1993	65.00	185-200
1992 Lantern	Retrd.	1993	Gift	33-100
1993 Sneaking A Peak	Retrd.	1994	Gift	52-72

*Quotes have been rounded up to nearest dollar

YEAR ISSUE	EDITION LIMIT	YEAR RETD.	ISSUE PRICE	*QUOTE U.S.$
1993 Spreading His Wings	Retrd.	1994	60.00	72-135
1994 All Tuckered Out	Retrd.	1995	65.00	100-124
1994 Filler-Up	Retrd.	1995	Gift	46-70
1995 Twingnuk	Retrd.	1996	55.00	95-143
1995 Kappah Krystal	Retrd.	1996	Gift	55-104
1996 Quinzet	Yr.Iss	1997	38.00	38-68
1996 Holy Dragons	Yr.Iss	1997	65.00	65-98
1996 Frobbit	Yr.Iss	1997	Gift	40-104
1996 Glowing Mashal	Yr.Iss	1998	Gift	30-50
1997 Almost There	Yr.Iss	1998	75.00	75
1998 Cauldron	1/99		Gift	N/A
1998 The Bahl 510	5/99		55.00	55

Fair Maidens - Panton

YEAR ISSUE	EDITION LIMIT	YEAR RETD.	ISSUE PRICE	*QUOTE U.S.$
1994 Faithful Companion	1,000	1994	325.00	375-425
1995 Safe Passage	1,000	1996	350.00	350
1996 Serenity 1002	1,000		350.00	350
1998 Forever Friends	1,000		300.00	300

World of Krystonia - Panton

YEAR ISSUE	EDITION LIMIT	YEAR RETD.	ISSUE PRICE	*QUOTE U.S.$
1992 Azael - 3811	Retrd.	1995	85.00	95-105
1989 Babul - 1402	Retrd.	1995	25.00	39-45
1989 Bags-Large - 703	Retrd.	1996	12.00	12-18
1989 Bags-Small - 704	Retrd.	1996	4.00	12-18
1994 Boll - 3912	Retrd.	1994	52.00	150-299
1994 Boll - 3912R	250	1994	52.00	52-185
1989 Caught At Last! - 1107	Retrd.	1992	150.00	156-245
1991 Charcoal Cookie - 3451	Retrd.	1996	38.00	39-75
1993 Cuda Tree - 705	Retrd.	1997	35.00	35-46
1991 Culpy - 3441	Retrd.	1996	38.00	45-59
1992 Dubious Alliance - 1109	Retrd.	1995	195.00	195-260
1995 Enough Is Enough - 1114	1,500	1996	250.00	250
1992 Escublar (Classic Moment) - 1110	7,500	1997	170.00	170-208
1991 Flayla w/Fumbly - 1105	Retrd.	1995	104.00	104-125
1980 Gateway to Krystonia - 3301	Retrd.	1994	35.00	52-90
1989 Gorph In Bucket - 2801	Retrd.	1996	20.00	26-39
1989 Gorphylia - 2802	Retrd.	1996	18.00	22-35
1987 Grackene (with legs) - 1051	Retrd.	N/A	50.00	450
1987 Grackene - 1051	Retrd.	1995	50.00	50-169
1987 Graffyn on Grumblypeg Grunch-Large -1011	Retrd.	1992	52.00	110-150
1989 Graffyn on Grunch (waterglobe) - 9006	Retrd.	1992	42.00	65-85
1987 Graffyn/Grunch-Small - 1012	Retrd.	1989	45.00	108-300
1988 Grazzi - 2301	Retrd.	1998	32.00	40-85
1987 Groc - 1041	Retrd.	1995	50.00	50-65
1987 Groc-Small - 1042B	Retrd.	1987	24.00	2000-4000
1991 Groosh-Large - 3601	15,000	1997	65.00	72-98
1987 Grumblypeg Grunch - 1081	Retrd.	1992	52.00	78-125
1991 Grunch's Toothache-Large - 1082	Retrd.	1994	76.00	78-105
1989 Grunch's Toothache-Small - 1083	15,000	1998	52.00	62-78
1989 Gurneyfoot & Shadra - 1106	15,000	1998	90.00	110-117
1987 Haapf-Large - 1901	Retrd.	1991	38.00	125-350
1990 Hottlepottle - 3501	Retrd.	1997	60.00	65-85
1989 Kephren - 2702	Retrd.	1994	56.00	62-110
1988 Koozl - 2901	Retrd.	1998	36.00	46-78
1987 Krak N' Borg-Small - 3003	Retrd.	1993	60.00	117-195
1987 Krak N'Borg-Large - 3001	Retrd.	1990	240.00	500-750
1987 Krak N'Borg-Med. - 3002	Retrd.	1997	200.00	200-325
1989 Krystonia Sign - 701	Retrd.	1993	10.00	50-120
1989 Lands of Krystonia	1,500	1998	240.00	240-300
1991 Maj-Dron Migration - 1108	Retrd.	1994	145.00	155-235
1992 Mini N' Grall - 611	Retrd.	1995	27.00	29
1987 Moplos-Large - 1021	Retrd.	1991	90.00	145-280
1987 Moplos-Small - 1022	15,000	1998	80.00	80-100
1987 Mos - 1031	15,000	1998	90.00	90-140
1987 Myzer-Large - 1201	Retrd.	1991	50.00	100-180
1987 Myzer-Small - 1202	15,000	1997	40.00	48-59
1987 N' Chakk-Large - 2101	Retrd.	1995	140.00	140-228
1989 N' Grall-Small - 2203	Retrd.	1997	32.00	40-85
1992 N' Leila - 3801	Retrd.	1994	60.00	60-155
1987 N' Tormet-Small - 2602	Retrd.	1993	44.00	46-100
1989 N'Borg on Throne-Large - 1093	15,000	1997	90.00	110-293
1987 N'Borg-Large - 1092	Retrd.	1994	98.00	130-215
1991 N'Borg-Mini - 609	Retrd.	1994	29.00	29-34
1987 N'Borg-Small - 1091	Retrd.	1989	50.00	163-300
1990 N'Chaak-Mini - 607	Retrd.	1994	29.00	30-60
1988 N'Chaak-Small - 2102	15,000	1998	48.00	65-91
1988 N'Grall-Large - 2201	Retrd.	1990	108.00	195-300
1988 N'Grall-Med. - 2202	Retrd.	1994	70.00	110-390
1989 N'Tormet - 2601	15,000	1996	60.00	70-78
1990 Owhey (waterglobe) - 9004	Retrd.	1995	42.00	150-250
1987 Owhey - 1071	Retrd.	1990	32.00	100-300
1997 Ploot - 3936B	250	1997	67.00	67-100
1987 Poffles - 1401	Retrd.	1998	16.00	25-34
1996 Reamon - 3927B	250	1996	70.00	70-145
1995 Root - 3922R	250	1995	85.00	140-260
1987 Rueggan-Large - 1701	Retrd.	1989	55.00	130-300
1988 Rueggan-Med. - 1702	Retrd.	1993	48.00	66-125
1988 Rueggan-Small - 1703	Retrd.	1995	42.00	42-65
1989 Scrolls-Small - 702	Retrd.	1996	4.00	4-12
1998 Seer - 3944B	250		70.00	70
1990 Shadra - 3401	Retrd.	1994	30.00	36-98
1987 Shepf - 1151	15,000	1997	70.00	70-130
1987 Shepf-Small - 1152	Retrd.	1990	40.00	100-300
1987 Shigger - 1801	Retrd.	1998	30.00	35-98
1987 Spyke - 1061	Retrd.	1993	50.00	72-78
1989 Stoope (waterglobe) - 9003	Retrd.	1991	40.00	150-260
1987 Stoope-Large - 1103	15,000	1996	98.00	140-182
1987 Stoope-Med. - 1101	Retrd.	1990	52.00	100-300
1987 Stoope-Small - 1102	Retrd.	1995	46.00	46-85
1997 Storyteller - 1115	3,500	1998	145.00	145-155
1993 Tag - 3909R	250	1993	48.00	450
1988 Tarnhold-Large - 3201	Retrd.	1997	200.00	200-250
1988 Tarnhold-Med. - 3202	Retrd.	1992	120.00	200-260
1987 Tarnhold-Small - 3203	Retrd.	1995	60.00	60-117
1988 Tokkel - 2401	Retrd.	1995	42.00	42-62
1987 Trumph - 1501	Retrd.	1998	20.00	31-65
1989 Tulan - 2501	15,000	1996	60.00	70-96
1988 Tulan Captain-Small - 2502	Retrd.	1991	44.00	52-95
1987 Turfen-Large - 1601	Retrd.	1991	50.00	85-150
1990 Vena - 3101	15,000	1997	40.00	52-110
1996 Waldurgan - 3933	3,500	1998	195.00	195
1987 Wodema-Large - 1301	Retrd.	1990	50.00	156-325
1987 Wodema-Med. - 1302	Retrd.	1993	44.00	66-95
1987 Wodema-Small - 1303	Retrd.	1998	22.00	32-78
1990 Zygmund - 3511	Retrd.	1997	50.00	50-72

World of Krystonia-Timeless Treasures - Panton

YEAR ISSUE	EDITION LIMIT	YEAR RETD.	ISSUE PRICE	*QUOTE U.S.$
1997 Recorder	3,500		100.00	100

Precious Moments/Enesco Corporation

Precious Moments Collectors Club Welcome Gift - S. Butcher

YEAR ISSUE	EDITION LIMIT	YEAR RETD.	ISSUE PRICE	*QUOTE U.S.$
1982 But Love Goes On Forever-Plaque E-0202	Yr.Iss.	1982	N/A	70-130
1983 Let Us Call the Club to Order E-0303	Yr.Iss.	1983	21.00	60-70
1984 Join in on the Blessings E-0404	Yr.Iss.	1984	N/A	44-120
1985 Seek and Ye Shall Find E-0005	Yr.Iss.	1985	N/A	40-55
1986 Birds of a Feather Collect Together E-0006	Yr.Iss.	1986	N/A	37-50
1987 Sharing Is Universal E-0007	Yr.Iss.	1987	N/A	40-50
1988 A Growing Love E-0008	Yr.Iss.	1988	N/A	35-40
1989 Always Room For One More C-0009	Yr.Iss.	1989	N/A	31-50
1990 My Happiness C-0010	Yr.Iss.	1990	N/A	28-50
1991 Sharing the Good News Together C-0011	Yr.Iss.	1991	N/A	30-65
1992 The Club That's Out Of This World C-0012	Yr.Iss.	1992	N/A	25-50
1993 Loving, Caring, and Sharing Along the Way C-0013	Yr.Iss.	1993	N/A	33-50
1994 You Are the End of My Rainbow C-0014	Yr.Iss.	1994	N/A	28-50
1995 You're The Sweetest Cookie In The Batch C-0015	Yr.Iss.	1995	N/A	28-35
1996 You're As Pretty As A Picture C-0016	Yr.Iss.	1996	N/A	30-38
1997 A Special Toast To Precious Moments C-0017	Yr.Iss.	1997	N/A	28
1998 Focusing In On Those Precious Moments C-0018	Yr.Iss.		N/A	N/A

Precious Moments Inscribed Charter Member Renewal Gift - S. Butcher

YEAR ISSUE	EDITION LIMIT	YEAR RETD.	ISSUE PRICE	*QUOTE U.S.$
1981 But Love Goes on Forever E-0001	Yr.Iss.	1981	17.00	160-190
1982 But Love Goes on Forever-Plaque E-0102	Yr.Iss.	1982	N/A	70-125
1983 Let Us Call the Club to Order E-0103	Yr.Iss.	1983	25.00	51-75
1984 Join in on the Blessings E-0104	Yr.Iss.	1984	25.00	50-70
1985 Seek and Ye Shall Find E-0105	Yr.Iss.	1985	25.00	38-62
1986 Birds of a Feather Collect Together E-0106	Yr.Iss.	1986	25.00	38-50
1987 Sharing Is Universal E-0107	Yr.Iss.	1987	25.00	31-45
1988 A Growing Love E-0108	Yr.Iss.	1988	25.00	38-52
1989 Always Room For One More C-0109	Yr.Iss.	1989	35.00	35-45
1990 My Happiness C-0110	Yr.Iss.	1990	N/A	35-40
1991 Sharing The Good News Together C-0111	Yr.Iss.	1991	N/A	30-50
1992 The Club That's Out Of This World C-0112	Yr.Iss.	1992	N/A	40-45
1993 Loving, Caring, and Sharing Along the Way C-0113	Yr.Iss.	1993	N/A	40-45
1994 You Are the End of My Rainbow C-0114	Yr.Iss.	1994	N/A	28-35
1995 You're The Sweetest Cookie In The Batch C-0115	Yr.Iss.	1995	N/A	30-35
1996 You're As Pretty As A Picture C-0116	Yr.Iss.	1996	N/A	33-35
1997 A Special Toast To Precious Moments C-0117	Yr.Iss.	1997	N/A	25
1998 Focusing In On Those Precious Moments C-0118	Yr.Iss.		N/A	N/A

Precious Moments Special Edition Members' Only - S. Butcher

YEAR ISSUE	EDITION LIMIT	YEAR RETD.	ISSUE PRICE	*QUOTE U.S.$
1981 Hello, Lord, It's Me Again PM-811	Yr.Iss.	1981	25.00	450-495
1982 Smile, God Loves You PM-821	Yr.Iss.	1982	25.00	200-310
1983 Put on a Happy Face PM-822	Yr.Iss.	1983	25.00	200-270
1983 Dawn's Early Light PM-831	Yr.Iss.	1983	27.50	75-90
1984 God's Ray of Mercy PM-841	Yr.Iss.	1984	25.00	41-110
1984 Trust in the Lord to the Finish PM-842	Yr.Iss.	1984	25.00	65-80
1985 The Lord is My Shepherd PM-851	Yr.Iss.	1985	25.00	67-95
1985 I Love to Tell the Story PM-852	Yr.Iss.	1985	27.50	65-75
1986 Grandma's Prayer PM-861	Yr.Iss.	1986	25.00	75-95
1986 I'm Following Jesus PM-862	Yr.Iss.	1986	25.00	80-90
1987 Feed My Sheep PM-871	Yr.Iss.	1987	25.00	55-65
1987 In His Time PM-872	Yr.Iss.	1987	25.00	40-65
1987 Loving You Dear Valentine PM-873	Yr.Iss.	1987	25.00	38-45
1987 Loving You Dear Valentine PM-874	Yr.Iss.	1987	25.00	40-45
1988 God Bless You for Touching My Life PM-881	Yr.Iss.	1988	27.50	48-70
1988 You Just Can't Chuck A Good Friendship PM-882	Yr.Iss.	1988	27.50	45-50
1989 You Will Always Be My Choice PM-891	Yr.Iss.	1989	27.50	33-54
1989 Mow Power To Ya PM-892	Yr.Iss.	1989	27.50	45-60
1990 Ten Years And Still Going Strong PM-901	Yr.Iss.	1990	30.00	32-65
1990 You Are A Blessing To Me PM-902	Yr.Iss.	1990	30.00	48-60
1991 One Step At A Time PM-911	Yr.Iss.	1991	33.00	48-55
1991 Lord, Keep Me In TeePee Top Shape PM-912	Yr.Iss.	1991	33.00	49-60
1992 Only Love Can Make A Home PM-921	Yr.Iss.	1992	30.00	45-60
1992 Sowing The Seeds of Love PM-922	Yr.Iss.	1992	30.00	40-45
1993 His Little Treasure PM-931	Yr.Iss.	1993	30.00	35-52
1993 Loving PM-932	Yr.Iss.	1993	30.00	40-75
1994 Caring PM-941	Yr.Iss.	1994	35.00	40-60
1994 Sharing PM-942	Yr.Iss.	1994	35.00	35-68
1994 You Fill The Pages of My Life (figurine/book) PMB034	Yr.Iss.	1994	67.50	70-75
1995 You're One In A Million To Me PM-951	Yr.Iss.	1995	35.00	35-50
1995 Always Take Time To Pray PM-952	Yr.Iss.	1995	35.00	38-48
1996 Teach Us To Love One Another PM-961	Yr.Iss.	1996	40.00	40-50
1996 Our Club Is Soda-licious PM-962	Yr.Iss.	1996	35.00	35-40
1997 You Will Always Be A Treasure To Me PM971	Yr.Iss.	1997	50.00	50
1997 Blessed Are The Merciful PM972	Yr.Iss.	1997	40.00	40
1998 Happy Trails PM981	Yr.Iss.		50.00	50
1998 Lord Please Don't Put Me On Hold PM982	Yr.Iss.		40.00	40
1998 How Can Two Work Together Except They Agree PM983	Yr.Iss.		125.00	125

Precious Moments Club 5th Anniversary Commemorative Edition - S. Butcher

YEAR ISSUE	EDITION LIMIT	YEAR RETD.	ISSUE PRICE	*QUOTE U.S.$
1985 God Bless Our Years Together 12440	Yr.Iss.	1985	175.00	245-325

Precious Moments Club 10th Anniversary Commemorative Edition - S. Butcher

YEAR ISSUE	EDITION LIMIT	YEAR RETD.	ISSUE PRICE	*QUOTE U.S.$
1988 The Good Lord Has Blessed Us Tenfold 114022	Yr.Iss.	1988	90.00	188-260

Precious Moments Club 15th Anniversary Commemorative Edition - S. Butcher

YEAR ISSUE	EDITION LIMIT	YEAR RETD.	ISSUE PRICE	*QUOTE U.S.$
1993 15 Happy Years Together: What A Tweet 530786	Yr.Iss.	1993	100.00	100-110
1995 A Perfect Display of 15 Happy Years 127817	Yr.Iss.	1995	100.00	100-160

Precious Moments Club 20th Anniversary Commemorative Edition - S. Butcher

YEAR ISSUE	EDITION LIMIT	YEAR RETD.	ISSUE PRICE	*QUOTE U.S.$
1998 20 Years And The Vision's Still The Same 306843	Yr.Iss.		55.00	55

Precious Moments - S. Butcher

YEAR ISSUE	EDITION LIMIT	YEAR RETD.	ISSUE PRICE	*QUOTE U.S.$
1983 Sharing Our Season Together E-0501	Suspd.		50.00	135-172
1983 Jesus is the Light that Shines E-0502	Suspd.		23.00	65-70
1983 Blessings from My House to Yours E-0503	Suspd.		27.00	75-85
1983 Christmastime Is for Sharing E-0504	Retrd.	1989	37.00	50-150
1983 Surrounded with Joy E-0506	Retrd.	1987	21.00	70-95
1983 God Sent His Son E-0507	Suspd.		32.50	80-100
1983 Prepare Ye the Way of the Lord E-0508	Suspd.		75.00	100-125
1983 Bringing God's Blessing to You E-0509	Suspd.		35.00	90-105
1983 Tubby's First Christmas E-0511	Suspd.		12.00	20-55
1983 It's a Perfect Boy E-0512	Suspd.		18.50	50-68
1983 Onward Christian Soldiers E-0523	Open		24.00	38-45
1983 You Can't Run Away from God E-0525	Retrd.	1989	28.50	80-110
1983 He Upholdeth Those Who Fall E-0526	Suspd.		35.00	58-80
1987 His Eye Is On The Sparrow E-0530	Retrd.	1987	28.50	53-120
1979 Jesus Loves Me E-1372B	Retrd.	1998	7.00	22-120
1979 Jesus Loves Me E-1372G	Open		7.00	28-70
1979 Smile, God Loves You E-1373B	Retrd.	1984	7.00	35-135
1979 Jesus is the Light E-1373G	Retrd.	1988	7.00	65-125
1979 Praise the Lord Anyhow E-1374B	Retrd.	1982	8.00	85-95
1979 Make a Joyful Noise E-1374G	Open		8.00	20-55
1979 Love Lifted Me E-1375A	Retrd.	1993	11.00	70-120
1979 Prayer Changes Things E-1375B	Suspd.		11.00	100-265
1979 Love One Another E-1376	Open		10.00	40-65
1979 He Leadeth Me E-1377A	Suspd.		9.00	90-140
1979 He Careth For You E-1377B	Suspd.		9.00	90-110
1979 God Loveth a Cheerful Giver E-1378	Retrd.	1981	11.00	700-915
1979 Love is Kind E-1379A	Suspd.		8.00	95-140
1979 God Understands E-1379B	Suspd.		8.00	45-120
1979 O, How I Love Jesus E-1380B	Retrd.	1984	8.00	60-105
1979 His Burden Is Light E-1380G	Retrd.	1984	8.00	50-105
1979 Jesus is the Answer E-1381	Suspd.		11.50	112-140
1992 Jesus is the Answer E-1381R	Retrd.	1996	55.00	55-75
1979 We Have Seen His Star E-2010	Suspd.		8.00	75-85
1979 Come Let Us Adore Him E-2011	Retrd.	1981	10.00	250-315
1979 Jesus is Born E-2012	Suspd.		12.00	100
1979 Unto Us a Child is Born E-2013	Suspd.		12.00	95-135
1982 May Your Christmas Be Cozy E-2345	Suspd.		23.00	80-90
1982 May Your Christmas Be Warm E-2348	Suspd.		30.00	105-140
1983 Tell Me the Story of Jesus E-2349	Suspd.		30.00	110
1982 Dropping in for Christmas E-2350	Suspd.		18.00	65-85
1982 Holy Smokes E-2351	Retrd.	1987	27.00	94-130
1983 O Come All Ye Faithful E-2353	Retrd.	1986	27.50	70-125
1982 I'll Play My Drum for Him E-2356	Suspd.		30.00	63-110

*Quotes have been rounded up to nearest dollar

FIGURINES

YEAR ISSUE	EDITION LIMIT	YEAR RETD.	ISSUE PRICE	*QUOTE U.S.$
1982 I'll Play My Drum for Him E-2360	Open		16.00	25-35
1982 Christmas Joy from Head to Toe E-2361	Suspd.		25.00	70-85
1982 Camel Figurine E-2363	Open		20.00	33-40
1982 Goat Figurine E-2364	Suspd.		10.00	40-82
1982 The First Noel E-2365	Suspd.		16.00	50-75
1982 The First Noel E-2366	Suspd.		16.00	55
1982 Bundles of Joy E-2374	Retrd.	1993	27.50	75-125
1982 Dropping Over for Christmas E-2375	Retrd.	1991	30.00	65-110
1982 Our First Christmas Together E-2377	Suspd.		35.00	75-110
1982 3 Mini Nativity Houses & Palm Tree E-2387	Open		45.00	75
1982 Come Let Us Adore Him E-2395 (11pc. set)	Open		80.00	130-140
1980 Come Let Us Adore Him E-2800 (9 pc. set)	Open		70.00	165-175
1980 Jesus is Born E-2801	Suspd.		37.00	330-350
1980 Christmas is a Time to Share E-2802	Suspd.		20.00	78-110
1980 Crown Him Lord of All E-2803	Suspd.		20.00	90-100
1980 Peace on Earth E-2804	Suspd.		20.00	125-175
1980 Wishing You a Season Filled w/ Joy E-2805	Retrd.	1985	20.00	50-105
1984 You Have Touched So Many Hearts E-2821	Suspd.		25.00	40-50
1984 This is Your Day to Shine E-2822	Retrd.	1988	37.50	63-100
1984 To God Be the Glory E-2823	Suspd.		40.00	85-100
1984 To a Very Special Mom E-2824	Open		27.50	40-48
1984 To a Very Special Sister E-2825	Open		37.50	50-58
1984 May Your Birthday Be a Blessing E-2826	Suspd.		37.50	90-125
1984 I Get a Kick Out of You E-2827	Suspd.		50.00	165-225
1984 Precious Memories E-2828	Open		45.00	65-68
1984 I'm Sending You a White Christmas E-2829	Open		37.50	60-85
1984 God Bless the Bride E-2832	Open		35.00	50
1986 Sharing Our Joy Together E-2834	Suspd.		30.00	40-75
1984 Baby Figurines (set of 6) E-2852	Closed	N/A	15.00	125-150
1984 Boy Standing E-2852A	Suspd.		13.50	19-25
1984 Girl Standing E-2852B	Suspd.		13.50	19-22
1984 Boy & Girl Standing, set E-2852A&B	Suspd.		27.00	125
1984 Boy Sitting Up E-2852C	Suspd.		13.50	19-32
1984 Girl Sitting Clapping E-2852D	Suspd.		13.50	19-22
1984 Boy Crawling E-2852E	Suspd.		13.50	19-25
1984 Girl Laying Down E-2852F	Suspd.		13.50	19-22
1980 Blessed Are the Pure in Heart E-3104	Suspd.		9.00	20-55
1980 He Watches Over Us All E-3105	Suspd.		11.00	70-90
1980 Mother Sew Dear E-3106	Open		13.00	33-35
1980 Blessed are the Peacemakers E-3107	Retrd.	1985	13.00	53-104
1980 The Hand that Rocks the Future E-3108	Suspd.		13.00	57-63
1980 The Purr-fect Grandma E-3109	Open		13.00	33-35
1980 Loving is Sharing E-3110B	Retrd.	1993	13.00	85-125
1980 Loving is Sharing E-3110G	Open		13.00	33-85
1980 Be Not Weary In Well Doing E-3111	Retrd.	1985	14.00	50-100
1980 God's Speed E-3112	Retrd.	1983	14.00	52-110
1980 Thou Art Mine E-3113	Open		16.00	32-40
1980 The Lord Bless You and Keep You E-3114	Open		16.00	45-90
1980 But Love Goes on Forever E-3115	Open		16.50	40-113
1980 Thee I Love E-3116	Retrd.	1994	16.50	35-120
1980 Walking By Faith E-3117	Open		35.00	75-150
1980 Eggs Over Easy E-3118	Retrd.	1983	12.00	48-100
1980 It's What's Inside that Counts E-3119	Suspd.		13.00	100-125
1980 To Thee With Love E-3120	Suspd.		13.00	45-75
1981 The Lord Bless You and Keep You E-4720	Suspd.		14.00	26-35
1981 The Lord Bless You and Keep You E-4721	Open		14.00	35-125
1981 Love Cannot Break a True Friendship E-4722	Suspd.		22.50	105-175
1981 Peace Amid the Storm E-4723	Suspd.		22.50	66-90
1981 Rejoicing with You E-4724	Open		25.00	34-55
1981 Peace on Earth E-4725	Suspd.		25.00	100-120
1981 Bear Ye One Another's Burdens E-5200	Suspd.		20.00	58-130
1981 Love Lifted Me E-5201	Suspd.		25.00	80-90
1981 Thank You for Coming to My Ade E-5202	Suspd.		22.50	100-125
1981 Let Not the Sun Go Down Upon Your Wrath E-5203	Suspd.		22.50	130-155
1981 To A Special Dad E-5212	Open		20.00	35-85
1981 God is Love E-5213	Suspd.		17.00	60-125
1981 Prayer Changes Things E-5214	Suspd.		35.00	88-120
1984 May Your Christmas Be Blessed E-5376	Suspd.		37.50	60-85
1984 Love is Kind E-5377	Retrd.	1987	27.50	85-90
1984 Joy to the World E-5378	Suspd.		18.00	40-57
1984 Isn't He Precious? E-5379	Open		20.00	33
1984 A Monarch is Born E-5380	Suspd.		33.00	80-88
1984 His Name is Jesus E-5381	Suspd.		45.00	98-125
1984 For God So Loved the World E-5382	Suspd.		70.00	110-115
1984 Wishing You a Merry Christmas E-5383	Yr.Iss.	1984	17.00	18-38
1984 I'll Play My Drum for Him E-5384	Open		10.00	13-16
1984 Oh Worship the Lord (B) E-5385	Suspd.		10.00	40
1984 Oh Worship the Lord (G) E-5386	Suspd.		10.00	62-70
1981 Come Let Us Adore Him E-5619	Suspd.		10.00	32-50
1981 Donkey Figurine E-5621	Open		6.00	15-20
1981 They Followed the Star E-5624	Open		130.00	225
1981 We Three Kings E-5635	Open		40.00	75
1981 Rejoice O Earth E-5636	Open		15.00	30-80
1981 The Heavenly Light E-5637	Open		15.00	30-33
1981 Cow with Bell Figurine E-5638	Open		16.00	33-40
1981 Isn't He Wonderful (B) E-5639	Suspd.		12.00	50
1981 Isn't He Wonderful (G) E-5640	Suspd.		12.00	60-75
1981 They Followed the Star E-5641	Suspd.		75.00	190
1981 Nativity Wall (2 pc. set) E-5644	Open		60.00	120
1984 God Sends the Gift of His Love E-6613	Suspd.		22.50	70-75
1982 God is Love, Dear Valentine E-7153	Suspd.		16.00	38-68
1982 God is Love, Dear Valentine E-7154	Suspd.		16.00	30-55
1982 Thanking Him for You E-7155	Suspd.		16.00	55-80
1982 I Believe in Miracles E-7156	Suspd.		17.00	90-95
1987 I Believe In Miracles E-7156R	Retrd.	1992	22.50	65-85
1982 There is Joy in Serving Jesus E-7157	Retrd.	1986	17.00	41-80
1982 Love Beareth All Things E-7158	Open		25.00	45-75
1982 Lord Give Me Patience E-7159	Suspd.		25.00	50-55
1982 The Perfect Grandpa E-7160	Suspd.		25.00	55-95
1982 His Sheep Am I E-7161	Suspd.		25.00	70-80
1982 Love is Sharing E-7162	Suspd.		25.00	80-170
1982 God is Watching Over You E-7163	Suspd.		27.50	100-112
1982 Bless This House E-7164	Suspd.		45.00	110-185
1982 Let the Whole World Know E-7165	Suspd.		45.00	135
1983 Love is Patient E-9251	Suspd.		35.00	50-100
1983 Forgiving is Forgetting E-9252	Suspd.		37.50	70-100
1983 The End is in Sight E-9253	Suspd.		25.00	43-90
1983 Praise the Lord Anyhow E-9254	Retrd.	1994	35.00	74-110
1983 Bless You Two E-9255	Open		21.00	45-50
1983 We are God's Workmanship E-9258	Open		19.00	35-60
1983 We're In It Together E-9259	Suspd.		24.00	60-110
1983 God's Promises are Sure E-9260	Suspd.		30.00	50-65
1983 Seek Ye the Lord E-9261	Suspd.		21.00	40-45
1983 Seek Ye the Lord E-9262	Suspd.		21.00	40-50
1983 How Can Two Walk Together Except They Agree E-9263	Suspd.		35.00	160-170
1983 Press On E-9265	Open		40.00	65-70
1983 Animal Collection, Teddy Bear E-9267A	Suspd.		6.50	20
1983 Animal Collection, Dog W/ Slippers E-9267B	Suspd.		6.50	18-32
1983 Animal Collection, Bunny W/ Carrot E-9267C	Suspd.		6.50	18-20
1983 Animal Collection, Kitty With Bow E-9267D	Suspd.		6.50	16-20
1983 Animal Collection, Lamb With Bird E-9267E	Suspd.		6.50	20
1983 Animal Collection, Pig W/ Patches E-9267F	Suspd.		6.50	13-20
1983 Nobody's Perfect E-9268	Retrd.	1990	21.00	55-90
1983 Let Love Reign E-9273	Retrd.	1987	27.50	62-85
1983 Taste and See that the Lord is Good E-9274	Retrd.	1986	22.50	60-85
1983 Jesus Loves Me E-9278	Open		9.00	18-40
1983 Jesus Loves Me E-9279	Open		9.00	18-20
1983 To Some Bunny Special E-9282A	Suspd.		8.00	25-30
1983 You're Worth Your Weight In Gold E-9282B	Suspd.		8.00	15-30
1983 Especially For Ewe E-9282C	Suspd.		8.00	25-35
1983 If God Be for Us, Who Can Be Against Us E-9285	Suspd.		27.50	88-125
1983 Peace on Earth E-9287	Suspd.		37.50	150-175
1997 And A Child Shall Lead Them E-9287R	Open		50.00	50-55
1983 Sending You a Rainbow E-9288	Suspd.		22.50	95-100
1983 Trust in the Lord E-9289	Suspd.		21.00	35-85
1985 Love Covers All 12009	Suspd.		27.50	55-90
1985 Part of Me Wants to be Good 12149	Suspd.		19.00	70-90
1987 This Is The Day Which The Lord Has Made 12157	Suspd.		20.00	60-70
1985 Get into the Habit of Prayer 12203	Suspd.		19.00	40
1985 Miniature Clown 12238A	Suspd.		13.50	24-29
1985 Miniature Clown 12238B	Suspd.		13.50	29-35
1985 Miniature Clown 12238C	Suspd.		13.50	24-29
1985 Miniature Clown 12238D	Suspd.		13.50	29-35
1985 It is Better to Give than to Receive 12297	Suspd.		19.00	135-219
1985 Love Never Fails 12300	Open		25.00	40-70
1985 God Bless Our Home 12319	Retrd.	1998	40.00	52-100
1986 You Can Fly 12335	Suspd.		25.00	60-70
1985 Jesus is Coming Soon 12343	Suspd.		22.50	45-50
1985 Halo, and Merry Christmas 12351	Suspd.		40.00	150-238
1985 May Your Christmas Be Delightful 15482	Suspd.		25.00	55-60
1985 Honk if You Love Jesus 15490	Open		13.00	20-30
1985 Baby's First Christmas 15539	Yr.Iss.	1985	13.00	30-40
1985 Baby's First Christmas 15547	Yr.Iss.	1985	13.00	35
1985 God Sent His Love 15881	Yr.Iss.	1985	17.00	33-35
1986 To My Favorite Paw 100021	Suspd.		22.50	55-60
1987 To My Deer Friend 100048	Open		33.00	52-70
1986 Sending My Love 100056	Suspd.		22.50	44-80
1986 O Worship the Lord 100064	Open		24.00	34-40
1986 To My Forever Friend 100072	Open		33.00	55-70
1987 He's The Healer Of Broken Hearts 100080	Open		33.00	50-65
1987 Make Me A Blessing 100102	Retrd.	1990	35.00	80-105
1986 Lord I'm Coming Home 100110	Open		22.50	35-40
1986 Lord, Keep Me On My Toes 100129	Retrd.	1988	22.50	40-85
1986 The Joy of the Lord is My Strength 100137	Open		35.00	55-130
1986 God Bless the Day We Found You 100145	Suspd.		37.50	90
1995 God Bless the Day We Found You(Girl) 100145R	Open		60.00	60
1986 God Bless the Day We Found You 100153	Suspd.		37.50	90-96
1995 God Bless the Day We Found You(Boy) 100153R	Open		60.00	60
1986 Serving the Lord 100161	Suspd.		19.00	43-70
1986 I'm a Possibility 100188	Retrd.	1993	21.00	55-90
1987 The Spirit Is Willing But The Flesh Is Weak 100196	Retrd.	1991	19.00	35-85
1987 The Lord Giveth & the Lord Taketh Away 100226	Retrd.	1995	33.50	54-87
1986 Friends Never Drift Apart 100250	Open		35.00	60-65
1986 Help, Lord, I'm In a Spot 100269	Retrd.	1989	18.50	60-80
1986 He Cleansed My Soul 100277	Open		24.00	40-50
1986 Serving the Lord 100293	Suspd.		19.00	35-50
1987 Scent From Above 100528	Retrd.	1991	19.00	55-80
1987 I Picked A Very Special Mom 100536	Yr.Iss.	1987	40.00	70-90
1986 Brotherly Love 100544	Suspd.		37.00	65-75
1987 No Tears Past The Gate 101826	Open		40.00	70-95
1987 Smile Along The Way 101842	Retrd.	1991	30.00	109-185
1987 Lord, Help Us Keep Our Act Together 101850	Retrd.	1991	35.00	125-130
1986 O Worship the Lord 102229	Open		24.00	40
1986 Shepherd of Love 102261	Open		10.00	16-32
1986 Three Mini Animals 102296	Suspd.		13.50	25-33
1986 Wishing You a Cozy Christmas 102342	Yr.Iss.	1986	17.00	32-35
1986 Love Rescued Me 102393	Open		21.00	38-40
1986 Angel of Mercy 102482	Open		19.00	33-40
1986 Sharing our Christmas Together 102490	Suspd.		35.00	70
1987 We Are All Precious In His Sight 102903	Yr.Iss.	1987	30.00	80-85
1986 God Bless America 102938	Yr.Iss.	1986	30.00	48-85
1986 It's the Birthday of a King 102962	Suspd.		18.50	35-40
1987 I Would Be Sunk Without You 102970	Open		15.00	20-23
1987 My Love Will Never Let You Go 103497	Open		25.00	38-42
1986 I Believe in the Old Rugged Cross 103632	Open		25.00	35-44
1986 Come Let Us Adore Him 104000 (9 pc. set w/cassette)	Open		95.00	130-140
1987 With this Ring I... 104019	Open		40.00	65
1987 Love Is The Glue That Mends 104027	Suspd.		33.50	68-78
1987 Cheers To The Leader 104035	Retrd.	1997	22.50	33-60
1987 Happy Days Are Here Again 104396	Suspd.		25.00	50-60
1987 A Tub Full of Love 104817	Open		22.50	33-35
1987 Sitting Pretty 104825	Suspd.		22.50	40
1987 Have I Got News For You 105635	Suspd.		22.50	30-65
1988 Something's Missing When You're Not Around 105643	Suspd.		32.50	39-50
1987 To Tell The Tooth You're Special 105813	Suspd.		38.50	145-282
1988 Hallelujah Country 105821	Open		35.00	45-60
1987 We're Pulling For You 106151	Suspd.		40.00	65-80
1987 God Bless You Graduate 106194	Open		20.00	35
1987 Congratulations Princess 106208	Open		20.00	35
1987 Lord Help Me Make the Grade 106216	Suspd.		25.00	60-70
1988 Heaven Bless Your Togetherness 106755	Open		65.00	90
1988 Precious Memories 106763	Open		37.50	50-55
1988 Puppy Love Is From Above 106798	Retrd.	1995	45.00	65-88
1988 Happy Birthday Poppy 106836	Suspd.		27.50	45-70
1988 Sew In Love 106844	Retrd.	1997	45.00	50-60
1987 They Followed The Star 108243	Open		75.00	120-144
1987 The Greatest Gift Is A Friend 109231	Open		30.00	40-45
1988 Believe the Impossible 109487	Suspd.		35.00	55-65
1988 Happiness Divine 109584	Retrd.	1992	25.00	60-120
1987 Wishing You A Yummy Christmas 109754	Suspd.		35.00	50-60
1987 We Gather Together To Ask The Lord's Blessing 109762	Retrd.	1995	130.00	200-250
1988 Meowie Christmas 109800	Open		30.00	35-53
1987 Oh What Fun It Is To Ride 109819	Open		85.00	110-120
1988 Wishing You A Happy Easter 109886	Open		23.00	35
1988 Wishing You A Basket Full Of Blessings 109924	Open		23.00	35
1988 Sending You My Love 109967	Open		35.00	45
1988 Mommy, I Love You 109975	Open		22.50	30
1987 Love Is The Best Gift of All 110930	Yr.Iss.	1987	22.50	40-50
1988 Faith Takes The Plunge 111155	Open		27.50	35-68
1988 Tis the Season 111163	Suspd.		27.50	35-45
1987 O Come Let Us Adore Him (4 pc. 9" Nativity) 111333	Suspd.		200.00	225-250
1988 Mommy, I Love You 112143	Open		22.50	30-38
1987 A Tub Full of Love 112313	Open		22.50	33
1988 This Too Shall Pass 114014	Open		23.00	30-38
1988 Some Bunny's Sleeping 115274	Suspd.		15.00	23-30
1988 Our First Christmas Together 115290	Suspd.		50.00	70-95
1988 Time to Wish You a Merry Christmas 115339	Yr.Iss.	1988	24.00	35
1995 Love Blooms Eternal 127019 (1st in dated cross series)	Yr.Iss.	1995	35.00	35
1995 Dreams Really Do Come True 128309	Open		37.50	38

*Quotes have been rounded up to nearest dollar

YEAR	ISSUE	EDITION LIMIT	YEAR RETD.	ISSUE PRICE	*QUOTE U.S.$
1995	Another Year More Grey Hares 128686	Open		17.50	19
1995	Happy Hula Days 128694	Open		30.00	33
1995	I Give You My Love Forever True 129100	Open		70.00	70-85
1997	Love Letters in The Sand 129488	Open		35.00	35
1995	Love Makes The World Go 'Round 139475	15,000		200.00	344-450
1995	He Covers the Earth With His Beauty 142654	Yr.Iss.	1995	30.00	30-35
1995	Come Let Us Adore Him 142735-Large Nativity	Open		50.00	50-55
1995	Come Let Us Adore Him 142743-Small Nativity	Open		35.00	35
1995	Making A Trail to Bethlehem 142751	Open		30.00	30-33
1995	I'll Give Him My Heart 150088	Open		40.00	45
1995	Soot Yourself To A Merry Christmas 150096	Open		35.00	35
1995	Making Spirits Bright 150118	Open		37.50	38
1998	Even The Heavens Shall Praise Him 150312	15,000		125.00	125
1996	Standing In The Presence Of The Lord 163732 (2nd in dated cross series)	Yr.Iss.	1996	37.50	38-45
1996	Take It To The Lord In Prayer 163767	Open		30.00	30
1996	The Sun Is Always Shining Somewhere 163775	Open		37.50	38-40
1996	Sowing Seeds of Kindness 163856 (1st in Growing In God's Garden Of Love Series)	Open		37.50	38
1996	It May Be Greener, But It's Just As Hard to Cut 163899	Open		37.50	38
1996	God's Love Is Reflected In You 175277	15,000		150.00	225-250
1996	Some Plant, Some Water, But God Giveth The Increase 176958 (2nd in Growing In God's Garden Of Love Series)	Open		37.50	38
1996	Peace On Earth...Anyway 183342	Yr.Iss.	1996	32.50	33
1996	Angels On Earth-Boy Making Snow Angel 183776	Open		40.00	40
1996	Snowbunny Loves You Like I Do 183792	Open		18.50	19
1997	The Most Precious Gift of All 183814	Open		37.50	38
1996	Sing In Excelsis Deo Tree Topper 183830	Open		125.00	125
1997	You're Just Too Sweet To Be Scary 183849	Open		55.00	55
1996	Color Your World With Thanksgiving 183857	Retrd.	1998	50.00	40-50
1996	Shepard/Standing White Lamb /Sitting Black Lamb 3pc. Nativity set 183954	Open		40.00	40
1997	Shepard with Lambs 3pc. Nativity set 183962	Open		40.00	40
1996	Making a Trail to Bethlehem-Mini Nativity 184004	Open		18.50	19
1996	All Sing His Praises-Large Nativity 184012	Open		32.50	33
1996	Love Makes The World Go 'Round 184209	Yr.Iss.	1996	22.50	25-45
1997	A Bouquet From God's Garden Of Love 184268 (3rd in God's Garden of Love series)	Open		37.50	38
1997	You're A Life Saver To Me 204854	Open		35.00	35
1996	Shepherd with Sheep-Mini Nativity 2-pc. 213616	Open		22.50	23
1996	Wee Three Kings-Mini Nativity set 213624	Open		55.00	55
1997	Lead Me To Calvary 260916 (3rd in dated cross series)	Yr.Iss.		37.50	38-45
1997	Friends From The Very Beginning 261068	Open		50.00	50
1997	You Have Touched So Many Hearts 261084	Open		37.50	38
1997	Lettuce Pray 261122	Open		17.50	18
1997	Have You Any Room For Jesus 261130	Open		35.00	35
1997	Say I Do 261149	Open		35.00	55
1997	We All Have Our Bad Hair Days 261157	Open		35.00	35
1997	The Lord Is the Hope Of Our Future 261564	Open		40.00	40
1998	In God's Beautiful Garden Of Love 261629	15,000		150.00	150
1997	Happy Birthday Jesus 272523	Open		35.00	35
1997	Sharing The Light of Love 272531	Open		35.00	35
1997	I Think You're Just Divine 272558	Open		40.00	40
1997	Joy To The World 272566	Open		20.00	20
1997	Nativity Enhancement Set 4pc. 272582	Open		60.00	60
1997	I'm Dreaming Of A White Christmas 272590	Open		25.00	25
1997	Cane You Join Us For A Merry Christmas 272671	Open		30.00	30
1997	And You Shall See a Star-Large Nativity 272787	Open		32.50	33
1998	My Love Will Keep You Warm 272957	Open		37.50	38
1997	Animal Additions-Mini Nativity 3-pc. 279323	Open		30.00	30
1997	Lighted Inn-Large Nativity 283428	Open		100.00	100
1997	Mini- Nativity Wall 283436	Open		40.00	40
1997	For An Angel You're So Down To Earth-Mini Nativity 283444	Open		17.50	18
1997	Cats With Kittens Mini-Nativity 291293	Open		18.50	19
1997	Wishing Well 292753	Open		30.00	30
1998	He Shall cover You With His Wings 306935	Yr.Iss.		37.50	38
1998	For The Sweetest Tu-Lips In Town 306959	Open		30.00	30
1998	You Are Always On My Mind 306967	Open		37.50	38
1998	Missum You 306991	Open		45.00	45
1997	Charity Begins In The Heart 307009	Retrd.	1998	50.00	50
1998	Only One Life To Offer 325309	Open		37.50	38
1998	The Good Lord Will Always Uphold Us 325325	Open		50.00	50
1998	There Are Two Sides To Every Story 325368	Open		15.00	15
1998	Marvelous Grace 325503	Yr.Iss.		50.00	50
1998	Well, Blow Me Down It's Yer Birthday 325538	Open		50.00	50
1998	I'm Sending You a Merry Christmas 455601	Yr.Iss.		30.00	30
1998	Mornin' Pumpkin 455687	Open		45.00	45
1998	Praise God From Whom All Blessings Flow 455695	Open		40.00	40
1998	Praise The Lord And Dosie-Do 455733	Open		50.00	50
1998	Peas On Earth 455768	Open		32.50	33
1998	Alaska Once More, How's Yer Christmas? 455784	Open		35.00	35
1998	Wishing You A Yummy Christmas 455814	Open		30.00	30
1998	I Saw Mommy Kissing Santa Claus 455822	Open		65.00	65
1998	Time For A Holy Holiday 455849	Open		35.00	35
1998	Have A Cozy Country Christmas 455873	Open		50.00	50
1998	Friends Are Forever, Sew Bee It 455903	Open		60.00	60
1998	I Now Pronounce You Man And Wife 455938	Open		30.00	30
1998	The Light Of The World Is Jesus-Large Nativity 455954	Open		30.00	30
1998	Hang On To That Holiday Feeling-Mini Nativity 455962	Open		17.50	18
1999	My Universe Is You 487902	Open		45.00	45
1999	Believe It Or Knot I Luv You 487910	Open		35.00	35
1999	You're My Honey Bee 487929	Open		20.00	20
1999	You Can Always Count On Me 487953	Open		35.00	35
1999	What Better To Give Than Yourself 487988	Open		30.00	30
1999	Mom, You've Given Me So Much 488046	Open		35.00	35
1999	You Just Can't Replace A Good Friendship 488054	Open		35.00	35
1999	Confirmed In The Lord 488178	Open		30.00	30
1999	A Very Special Bond 488240	Open		70.00	70
1999	You Can't Take It With You 488321	Open		25.00	25
1999	Always Listen To Your Heart 488356	Open		25.00	25
1999	You Count 488372	Open		25.00	25
1999	You Always Stand Behind Me 492140	Open		50.00	50
1988	Rejoice O Earth 520268	Open		13.00	17-25
1988	Jesus the Savior Is Born 520357	Suspd.		25.00	48-68
1992	The Lord Turned My Life Around 520535	Suspd.		35.00	38-45
1991	In The Spotlight Of His Grace 520543	Suspd.		35.00	38-45
1990	Lord, Turn My Life Around 520551	Suspd.		35.00	38-45
1992	You Deserve An Ovation 520578	Open		35.00	38-45
1989	My Heart Is Exposed With Love 520624	Open		45.00	60-63
1989	A Friend Is Someone Who Cares 520632	Retrd.	1995	30.00	55-95
1989	I'm So Glad You Fluttered Into My Life 520640	Retrd.	1991	40.00	250-275
1989	Eggspecially For You 520667	Open		45.00	50-75
1989	Puppy Love 520764	Open		12.50	18-70
1989	Your Love Is So Uplifting 520675	Retrd.	1998	60.00	75
1989	Sending You Showers Of Blessings 520683	Retrd.	1992	32.50	65-100
1989	Just A LineTo Wish You A Happy Day 520721	Suspd.		65.00	75-90
1989	Friendship Hits The Spot 520748	Open		55.00	70
1989	Jesus Is The Only Way 520756	Suspd.		40.00	60-64
1989	Many Moons In Same Canoe, Blessum You 520772	Retrd.	1990	50.00	250-300
1989	Wishing You Roads Of Happiness 520780	Open		60.00	75-93
1989	Someday My Love 520799	Retrd.	1992	40.00	65-75
1989	My Days Are Blue Without You 520802	Suspd.		65.00	95-135
1989	We Need A Good Friend Through The Ruff Times 520810	Suspd.		35.00	45-60
1989	You Are My Number One 520829	Open		25.00	35-40
1989	The Lord Is Your Light To Happiness 520837	Open		50.00	65
1989	Wishing You A Perfect Choice 520845	Open		55.00	65
1989	I Belong To The Lord 520853	Suspd.		25.00	30-50
1990	Heaven Bless You 520934	Open		35.00	35-42
1993	There Is No Greater Treasure Than To Have A Friend Like You 521000	Open		30.00	30-40
1990	That's What Friends Are For 521183	Open		45.00	50-62
1997	Lord, Spare Me 521191	Open		37.50	38
1990	Hope You're Up And OnThe Trail Again 521205	Suspd.		35.00	35-62
1993	The Fruit of the Spirit is Love 521213	Yr.Iss.	1993	30.00	33
1996	Enter His Court With Thanksgiving 521221	Open		35.00	35
1991	Take Heed When You Stand 521272	Suspd.		55.00	60-90
1990	Happy Trip 521280	Suspd.		35.00	45-95
1991	Hug One Another 521299	Retrd.	1995	45.00	65-70
1990	Yield Not To Temptation 521310	Suspd.		27.50	35-52
1998	Heaven Must Have Sent You 521388	Open		60.00	60
1990	Faith Is A Victory 521396	Retrd.	1993	25.00	125-170
1990	I'll Never Stop Loving You 521418	Retrd.	1996	37.50	40-52
1991	To A Very Special Mom & Dad 521434	Suspd.		35.00	45-55
1990	Lord, Help Me Stick To My Job 521450	Retrd.	1997	30.00	35-60
1989	Tell It To Jesus 521477	Open		35.00	40
1991	There's A Light At The End Of The Tunnel 521485	Suspd.		55.00	50-90
1991	A Special Delivery 521493	Open		30.00	33
1998	Water-Melancholy Day Without You 521515	Open		35.00	35
1991	Thumb-body Loves You 521698	Suspd.		55.00	60-70
1996	My Love Blooms For You 521728	Open		50.00	50
1990	Sweep All Your Worries Away 521779	Retrd.	1996	40.00	40-125
1990	Good Friends Are Forever 521817	Open		50.00	55-68
1990	Love Is From Above 521841	Suspd.		45.00	50-55
1989	The Greatest of These Is Love 521868	Suspd.		27.50	35-57
1997	Pizza On Earth 521884	Open		55.00	55
1990	Easter's On Its Way 521892	Open		60.00	65-82
1991	Hoppy Easter Friend 521906	Open		40.00	40-63
1994	Perfect Harmony 521914	Open		55.00	55
1993	Safe In The Arms Of Jesus 521922	Open		30.00	33
1989	Wishing You A Cozy Season 521949	Suspd.		42.50	55-57
1990	High Hopes 521957	Suspd.		30.00	40-55
1991	To A Special Mum 521965	Open		30.00	35
1999	Caught Up In Sweet Thoughts Of You 521973	Open		30.00	30
1996	Marching To The Beat of Freedom's Drum 521981	Open		35.00	35
1993	To The Apple Of God's Eye 522015	Yr.Iss.	1993	32.50	35
1989	May Your Life Be Blessed With Touchdowns 522023	Open		45.00	50
1989	Thank You Lord For Everything 522031	Suspd.		55.00	80-98
1994	Now I Lay Me Down To Sleep 522058	Retrd.	1997	30.00	35-50
1991	May Your World Be Trimmed With Joy 522082	Suspd.		55.00	55-60
1990	There Shall Be Showers Of Blessings 522090	Open		60.00	70-75
1992	It's No Yolk When I Say I Love You 522104	Suspd.		60.00	65-115
1989	Don't Let the Holidays Get You Down 522112	Retrd.	1993	42.50	85-90
1989	Wishing You A Very Successful Season 522120	Open		60.00	70-82
1989	Bon Voyage! 522201	Suspd.		75.00	90-125
1989	He Is The Star Of The Morning 522252	Suspd.		55.00	65-75
1989	To Be With You Is Uplifting 522260	Retrd.	1994	20.00	35-55
1991	A Reflection Of His Love 522279	Open		50.00	50
1990	Thinking Of You Is What I Really Like To Do 522287	Suspd.		30.00	33-75
1989	Merry Christmas Deer 522317	Retrd.	1997	50.00	60
1996	Sweeter As The Years Go By 522333	Retrd.	1998	60.00	60
1989	Oh Holy Night 522546	Yr.Iss.	1989	25.00	35-38
1995	Just A Line To Say You're Special 522864	Open		50.00	50
1997	On My Way To A Perfect Day 522872	Open		45.00	45-48
1989	Isn't He Precious 522988	Suspd.		15.00	30
1990	Some Bunny's Sleeping 522996	Suspd.		12.00	18-30
1989	Jesus Is The Sweetest Name I Know 523097	Suspd.		22.50	30-50
1991	Joy On Arrival 523178	Open		50.00	55
1990	The Good Lord Always Delivers 523453	Open		27.50	30-40
1990	This Day Has Been Made In Heaven 523496	Open		30.00	35-42
1990	God Is Love Dear Valentine 523518	Open		27.50	30
1991	I Will Cherish The Old Rugged Cross 523534	Yr.Iss.	1991	27.50	35-40
1992	You Are The Type I Love 523542	Open		40.00	45
1993	The Lord Will Provide 523593	Yr.Iss.	1993	40.00	50-60
1991	Good News Is So Uplifting 523615	Open		60.00	70
1992	I'm So Glad That God Has Blessed Me With A Friend Like You 523623	Retrd.	1995	50.00	75-100
1994	I Will Always Be Thinking Of You 523631	Retrd.	1996	45.00	45-75
1990	Time Heals 523739	Open		37.50	40-50
1990	Blessings From Above 523747	Retrd.	1994	45.00	72-115
1994	Just Poppin' In To Say Halo 523755	Open		45.00	45
1991	I Can't Spell Success Without You 523763	Suspd.		40.00	60-75
1990	Once Upon A Holy Night 523836	Yr.Iss.	1990	25.00	35-40
1996	Love Never Leaves A Mother's Arms 523941	Open		40.00	40-45
1992	My Warmest Thoughts Are You 524085	Retrd.	1996	55.00	60-65
1991	Good Friends Are For Always 524123	Open		27.50	35
1994	Lord Teach Us to Pray 524158	Yr.Iss.	1994	35.00	40-45

*Quotes have been rounded up to nearest dollar

FIGURINES

YEAR ISSUE		EDITION LIMIT	YEAR RETD.	ISSUE PRICE	*QUOTE U.S.$
1991	May Your Christmas Be Merry 524166	Yr.Iss.	1991	27.50	28-38
1995	Walk In The Sonshine 524212	Open		35.00	35
1991	He Loves Me 524263	Yr.Iss.	1991	35.00	45-55
1992	Friendship Grows When You Plant A Seed 524271	Retrd.	1994	40.00	80-116
1993	May Your Every Wish Come True 524298	Open		50.00	50
1991	May Your Birthday Be A Blessing 524301	Open		30.00	35
1992	What The World Needs Now 524352	Retrd.	1997	50.00	50-55
1997	Something Precious From Above 524360	Open		50.00	50
1993	You Are Such A Purr-fect Friend 524395	Open		35.00	35-46
1991	May Only Good Things Come Your Way 524425	Open		30.00	38
1993	Sealed With A Kiss 524441	Retrd.	1996	50.00	60-100
1993	A Special Chime For Jesus 524468	Retrd.	1997	32.50	35-50
1994	God Cared Enough To Send His Best 524476	Retrd.	1996	50.00	55-68
1990	Happy Birthday Dear Jesus 524875	Suspd.		13.50	20-35
1992	It's So Uplifting To Have A Friend Like You 524905	Open		40.00	45
1990	We're Going To Miss You 524913	Open		50.00	55-65
1991	Angels We Have Heard On High 524921	Retrd.	1996	60.00	70-83
1992	Tubby's First Christmas 525278	Open		10.00	10
1991	It's A Perfect Boy 525286	Open		16.50	19-28
1993	May Your Future Be Blessed 525316	Open		35.00	35-40
1992	Ring Those Christmas Bells 525898	Retrd.	1996	95.00	100-140
1998	Let's Put The Pieces Together 525928	Open		60.00	60
1992	Going Home 525979	Open		60.00	60-94
1996	A Prince Of A Guy 526037	Open		35.00	35
1996	Pretty As A Princess 526053	Open		35.00	35-40
1998	The Pearl Of A Great Price 526061	Open		50.00	50-70
1992	I Would Be Lost Without You 526142	Open		27.50	30
1994	Friends To The Very End 526150	Retrd.	1997	40.00	45-60
1992	You Are My Happiness 526185	Yr.Iss.	1992	37.50	55-70
1994	You Suit Me to a Tee 526193	Open		35.00	35
1994	Sharing Sweet Moments Together 526487	Open		45.00	45
1996	The Lord is With You 526835	Open		27.50	28
1991	We Have Come From Afar 526959	Suspd.		17.50	25
1993	Bless-Um You 527335	Retrd.	1998	35.00	35-48
1992	You Are My Favorite Star 527378	Retrd.	1997	55.00	60-90
1992	Bring The Little Ones To Jesus 527556	Open		90.00	90-125
1992	God Bless The U.S.A. 527564	Yr.Iss.	1992	32.50	33-65
1993	Tied Up For The Holidays 527580	Suspd.		40.00	45-50
1993	Bringing You A Merry Christmas 527599	Retrd.	1995	45.00	75-85
1992	Wishing You A Ho Ho Ho 527629	Open		40.00	45
1991	You Have Touched So Many Hearts w/personalization kit 527661	Suspd.		37.50	38-45
1992	But The Greatest of These Is Love 527688	Yr.Iss.	1992	27.50	35-57
1992	Wishing You A Comfy Christmas 527750	Open		30.00	30
1993	I Only Have Arms For You 527769	Open		15.00	18-55
1992	This Land Is Our Land 527777	Yr.Iss.	1992	35.00	35-60
1994	Nativity Cart 528072	Open		16.00	19
1994	Have I Got News For You 528137	Open		16.00	19
1994	To a Very Special Sister 528633	Open		60.00	60
1993	America You're Beautiful 528862	Yr.Iss.	1993	35.00	45-65
1996	My True Love Gave To Me 529273	Open		40.00	40
1993	Ring Out The Good News 529966	Retrd.	1997	27.50	30-35
1993	Wishing You the Sweetest Christmas 530166	Yr.Iss.	1993	27.50	40-57
1994	You're As Pretty As A Christmas Tree 530425	Yr.Iss.	1994	27.50	28-45
1994	Serenity Prayer Girl 530697	Open		35.00	38-44
1994	Serenity Prayer Boy 530700	Open		35.00	38
1995	We Have Come From Afar 530913	Open		12.00	12
1995	I Only Have Ice For You 530956	Open		27.50	55
1997	Sometimes You're Next To Impossible 530964	Open		50.00	50
1998	My World's Upside Down Without You 531014	Open		15.00	15
1997	Potty Time 531022	Open		25.00	25
1998	You Are My Once In A Lifetime 531030	Open		45.00	45
1995	What The World Needs Is Love 531065	Open		45.00	45
1994	Money's Not The Only Green Thing Worth Saving 531073	Retrd.	1996	50.00	50-75
1996	What A Difference You've Made In My Life 531138	Open		50.00	50
1995	Vaya Con Dios (To Go With God) 531146	Open		32.50	35
1995	Bless Your Soul 531162	Open		25.00	28-35
1997	Who's Gonna Fill You're Shoes 531634	Open		37.50	38-60
1996	You Deserve a Halo—Thank You 531693	Retrd.	1998	55.00	55
1994	The Lord is Counting on You 531707	Open		32.50	35
1994	Sharing Our Christmas Together 531944	Open		35.00	35
1994	Dropping In For The Holidays 531952	Retrd.	1998	40.00	45
1999	Lord Speak To Me 531987	Open		45.00	45
1995	Hallelujah For The Cross 532002	Open		35.00	35
1995	Sending You Oceans Of Love 532010	Retrd.	1996	35.00	35-52
1995	I Can't Bear To Let You Go 532037	Open		50.00	50
1998	Who's Gonna Fill Your Shoes 532061	Open		37.50	38
1995	Lord Help Me To Stay On Course 532096	Open		35.00	35-57
1994	The Lord Bless You and Keep You 532118	Open		40.00	50
1994	The Lord Bless You and Keep You 532126	Open		30.00	35
1994	The Lord Bless You and Keep You 532134	Open		30.00	35
1994	Luke 2:10 11 532916	Open		35.00	38
1994	Nothing Can Dampen The Spirit of Caring 603864	Open		35.00	35
1997	May Your Christmas Be Delightful 604135	Open		40.00	40
1995	A Poppy For You 604208	Open		35.00	35-42

Anniversary Figurines - S. Butcher

YEAR ISSUE		EDITION LIMIT	YEAR RETD.	ISSUE PRICE	*QUOTE U.S.$
1984	God Blessed Our Years Together With So Much Love And Happiness E-2853	Open		35.00	50-68
1984	God Blessed Our Year Together With So Much Love And Happiness (1st) E-2854	Open		35.00	50
1984	God Blessed Our Years Together With So Much Love And Happiness (5th) E-2855	Suspd.		35.00	50
1984	God Blessed Our Years Together With So Much Love And Happiness (10th) E-2856	Suspd.		35.00	50-78
1984	God Blessed Our Years Together With So Much Love And Happiness (25th) E-2857	Open		35.00	50
1984	God Blessed Our Years Together With So Much Love And Happiness (40th) E-2859	Suspd.		35.00	50
1984	God Blessed Our Years Together With So Much Love And Happiness (50th) E-2860	Open		35.00	50
1994	I Still Do 530999	Open		30.00	30
1994	I Still Do 531006	Open		30.00	30-60

Baby Classics - S. Butcher

YEAR ISSUE		EDITION LIMIT	YEAR RETD.	ISSUE PRICE	*QUOTE U.S.$
1997	Good Friends Are Forever 272422	Open		30.00	30
1997	Make A Joyful Noice 272450	Open		30.00	30
1997	We Are God's Workmanship 272434	Open		25.00	25
1997	I Believe In Miracles 272469	Open		25.00	25
1997	God Loveth A Cheerful Giver 272477	Open		25.00	25
1997	Love Is Sharing 272493	Open		25.00	25
1997	You Have Touched So Many Hearts 272485	Open		25.00	25
1997	Love One Another 272507	Open		30.00	30
1998	Friendship Hits The Spot 306916	Open		30.00	30
1998	Loving You Dear Valentine 306932	Open		25.00	25
1998	He Cleansed My Soul 306940	Open		25.00	25

Baby's First - S. Butcher

YEAR ISSUE		EDITION LIMIT	YEAR RETD.	ISSUE PRICE	*QUOTE U.S.$
1984	Baby's First Step E-2840	Suspd.		35.00	69-110
1984	Baby's First Picture E-2841	Retrd.	1986	45.00	155-175
1985	Baby's First Haircut 12211	Suspd.		32.50	145-157
1986	Baby's First Trip 16012	Suspd.		32.50	235-275
1989	Baby's First Pet 520705	Suspd.		45.00	55-98
1990	Baby's First Meal 524077	Open		35.00	40
1992	Baby's First Word 527238	Open		24.00	25
1993	Baby's First Birthday 524069	Open		25.00	25-35

Birthday Club Figurines - S. Butcher

YEAR ISSUE		EDITION LIMIT	YEAR RETD.	ISSUE PRICE	*QUOTE U.S.$
1986	Fishing For Friends BC-861	Yr.Iss.	1986	10.00	100-145
1987	Hi Sugar BC-871	Yr.Iss.	1987	11.00	90-110
1988	Somebunny Cares BC-881	Yr.Iss.	1988	13.50	45-65
1989	Can't Bee Hive Myself Without You BC-891	Yr.Iss.	1989	13.50	45
1990	Collecting Makes Good Scents BC-901	Yr.Iss.	1990	15.00	35-45
1990	I'm Nuts Over My Collection BC-902	Yr.Iss.	1990	15.00	35-40
1991	Love Pacifies BC-911	Yr.Iss.	1991	15.00	30-40
1991	True Blue Friends BC-912	Yr.Iss.	1991	15.00	30-95
1992	Every Man's Home Is His Castle BC-921	Yr.Iss.	1992	16.50	17-30
1992	I Got You Under My Skin BC-922	Yr.Iss.	1992	16.00	16-28
1993	Put a Little Punch In Your Birthday BC-931	Yr.Iss.	1993	15.00	16-33
1993	Owl Always Be Your Friend BC-932	Yr.Iss.	1993	16.00	19-28
1994	God Bless Our Home BC-941	Yr.Iss.	1994	16.00	18-25
1994	Yer A Pel-I-Can Count On BC-942	Yr.Iss.	1994	16.00	18-30
1995	Making A Point To Say You're Special BC-951	Yr.Iss.	1995	15.00	15-17
1995	10 Wonderful Years Of Wishes BC-952	Yr.Iss.	1995	50.00	50
1996	There's A Spot In My Heart For You BC-961	Yr.Iss.	1996	15.00	25-30
1996	You're First In My Heart BC-962	Yr.Iss.	1996	15.00	15-28
1997	Hare's To The Birthday Club BC-971	Yr.Iss.	1997	16.00	16
1998	Holy Tweet BC-972	Yr.Iss.	1997	18.50	19
1998	Slide Into The Celebration BC-981	Yr.Iss.		15.00	15

Birthday Club Inscribed Charter Membership Renewal Gift - S. Butcher

YEAR ISSUE		EDITION LIMIT	YEAR RETD.	ISSUE PRICE	*QUOTE U.S.$
1987	A Smile's the Cymbal of Joy B-0102	Yr.Iss.	1987	Unkn.	70-80
1988	The Sweetest Club Around B-0103	Yr.Iss.	1988	Unkn.	50-55
1989	Have A Beary Special Birthday B-0104	Yr.Iss.	1989	Unkn.	30-50
1990	Our Club Is A Tough Act To Follow B-0105	Yr.Iss.	1990	Unkn.	35
1991	Jest To Let You Know You're Tops B-0106	Yr.Iss.	1991	Unkn.	38-40
1992	All Aboard For Birthday Club Fun B-0107	Yr.Iss.	1992	Unkn.	30-50
1993	Happiness is Belonging B-0108	Yr.Iss.	1993	Unkn.	20-35
1994	Can't Get Enough of Our Club B-0109	Yr.Iss.	1994	Unkn.	25
1995	Hoppy Birthday B-0110	Yr.Iss.	1995	Unkn.	35-40
1996	Scootin' By Just To Say Hi! B-0111	Yr.Iss.	1996	Unkn.	25
1997	The Fun Starts Here B-0112	Yr.Iss.	1997	Unkn.	23

Birthday Club Welcome Gift - S. Butcher

YEAR ISSUE		EDITION LIMIT	YEAR RETD.	ISSUE PRICE	*QUOTE U.S.$
1986	Our Club Can't Be Beat B-0001	Yr.Iss.	1986	Unkn.	70-90
1987	A Smile's The Cymbal of Joy B-0002	Yr.Iss.	1987	Unkn.	65-73
1988	The Sweetest Club Around B-0003	Yr.Iss.	1988	Unkn.	50-55
1989	Have A Beary Special Birthday B-0004	Yr.Iss.	1989	Unkn.	35-40
1990	Our Club Is A Tough Act To Follow B-0005	Yr.Iss.	1990	Unkn.	32-38
1991	Jest To Let You Know You're Tops B-0006	Yr.Iss.	1991	Unkn.	40-55
1992	All Aboard For Birthday Club Fun B-0007	Yr.Iss.	1992	Unkn.	30-40
1993	Happiness Is Belonging B-0008	Yr.Iss.	1993	Unkn.	19-35
1994	Can't Get Enough of Our Club B-0009	Yr.Iss.	1994	Unkn.	25-35
1995	Hoppy Birthday B-0010	Yr.Iss.	1995	Unkn.	25-30
1996	Scootin' By Just To Say Hi! B-0011	Yr.Iss.	1996	Unkn.	30-35
1997	The Fun Starts Here B-0012	Yr.Iss.	1997	Unkn.	Unkn.

Birthday Series - S. Butcher

YEAR ISSUE		EDITION LIMIT	YEAR RETD.	ISSUE PRICE	*QUOTE U.S.$
1988	Friends To The End 104418	Suspd.		15.00	25-60
1987	Showers Of Blessings 105945	Retrd.	1993	16.00	35-65
1987	Brighten Someone's Day 105953	Suspd.		12.50	20
1990	To My Favorite Fan 521043	Suspd.		16.00	25-35
1989	Hello World! 521175	Open		13.50	18
1993	Hope You're Over The Hump 521671	Suspd.		16.00	22-32
1990	Not A Creature Was Stirring 524484	Suspd.		17.00	22-25
1991	Can't Be Without You 524492	Open		16.00	18
1991	How Can I Ever Forget You 526924	Open		15.00	18
1992	Let's Be Friends 527270	Retrd.	1996	15.00	18-30
1992	Happy Birdie 527343	Suspd.		8.00	18-32
1993	Happy Birthday Jesus 530492	Open		20.00	20
1994	Oinky Birthday 524506	Open		13.50	15
1995	Wishing You A Happy Bear Hug 520659	Suspd.		27.50	28-30
1996	I Haven't Seen Much of You Lately 531057	Open		13.50	14
1997	From The First Time I Spotted You I Knew We'd Be Friends 260940	Open		18.50	20-55

Birthday Train Figurines - S. Butcher

YEAR ISSUE		EDITION LIMIT	YEAR RETD.	ISSUE PRICE	*QUOTE U.S.$
1988	Isn't Eight Just Great 109460	Open		18.50	23-36
1988	Wishing You Grr-eatness 109479	Open		18.50	23
1985	May Your Birthday Be Warm 15938	Open		10.00	15
1985	Happy Birthday Little Lamb 15946	Open		10.00	15
1985	Heaven Bless Your Special Day 15954	Open		11.00	18-42
1985	God Bless You On Your Birthday 15962	Open		11.00	18
1985	May Your Birthday Be Gigantic 15970	Open		12.50	20-30
1985	This Day Is Something To Roar About 15989	Open		13.50	23
1985	Keep Looking Up 15997	Open		13.50	23-42
1985	Bless The Days Of Our Youth 16004	Open		15.00	23
1991	May Your Birthday Be Mammoth 521825	Open		25.00	25
1991	Being Nine Is Just Divine 521833	Open		25.00	25-32
1999	Take Your Time It's Your Birthday 488003	Open		25.00	25

Bless Those Who Serve Their Country - S. Butcher

YEAR ISSUE		EDITION LIMIT	YEAR RETD.	ISSUE PRICE	*QUOTE U.S.$
1991	Bless Those Who Serve Their Country (Navy) 526568	Suspd.		32.50	107-175
1991	Bless Those Who Serve Their Country (Army) 526576	Suspd.		32.50	45-50
1991	Bless Those Who Serve Their Country (Air Force) 526584	Suspd.		32.50	45-70
1991	Bless Those Who Serve Their Country (Girl Soldier) 527289	Suspd.		32.50	45-50
1991	Bless Those Who Serve Their Country (Soldier) 527297	Suspd.		32.50	45-50
1991	Bless Those Who Serve Their Country (Marine) 527521	Suspd.		32.50	45-75
1995	You Will Always Be Our Hero 136271	Yr.Iss.	1995	40.00	40-90

Boys & Girls Club - S. Butcher

YEAR ISSUE		EDITION LIMIT	YEAR RETD.	ISSUE PRICE	*QUOTE U.S.$
1996	Shoot For The Stars And You'll Never Strike Out 521701	Open		60.00	60-65
1997	He Is Our Shelter From The Storm 523550	Open		75.00	75
1998	Love Is Color Blind 524204	Open		60.00	60

Bridal Party - S. Butcher

YEAR	ISSUE	EDITION LIMIT	YEAR RETD.	ISSUE PRICE	*QUOTE U.S.$
1984	Bridesmaid E-2831	Open		13.50	25-38
1985	Ringbearer E-2833	Open		11.00	18
1985	Flower Girl E-2835	Open		11.00	18
1984	Best Man E-2836	Open		13.50	25
1986	Groom E-2837	Open		13.50	25
1987	This is the Day That the Lord Hath Made E-2838	Yr.Iss.	1987	185.00	175-250
1985	Junior Bridesmaid E-2845	Open		12.50	23
1987	Bride E-2846	Open		18.00	25-28
1987	God Bless Our Family (Parents of the Groom) 100498	Open		35.00	50
1987	God Bless Our Family (Parents of the Bride) 100501	Open		35.00	50
1987	Wedding Arch 102369	Suspd.		22.50	40-65

Calendar Girl - S. Butcher

YEAR	ISSUE	EDITION LIMIT	YEAR RETD.	ISSUE PRICE	*QUOTE U.S.$
1988	January 109983	Open		37.50	45-62
1988	February 109991	Open		27.50	38
1988	March 110019	Open		27.50	38-40
1988	April 110027	Open		30.00	40-55
1988	May 110035	Open		25.00	35-150
1988	June 110043	Open		40.00	50-62
1988	July 110051	Open		35.00	45-71
1988	August 110078	Open		40.00	50-55
1988	September 110086	Open		27.50	38-52
1988	October 110094	Open		35.00	45-50
1988	November 110108	Open		32.50	38-45
1988	December 110116	Open		27.50	35-55
1997	Garnet-Color of Boldness January 335533	Open		25.00	25
1997	Amethyst-Color of Faith February 335541	Open		25.00	25
1997	Aquamarine-Color of Kindness March 335568	Open		25.00	25
1997	Diamond-Color of Purity April 335576	Open		25.00	25
1997	Emerald-Color of Patience May 335584	Open		25.00	25
1997	Pearl-Color of Love June 335592	Open		25.00	25
1997	Ruby-Color of Joy July 335606	Open		25.00	25
1997	Peridot-Color of Pride August 335614	Open		25.00	25
1997	Sapphire-Color of Confidence September 335622	Open		25.00	25
1997	Opal-Color of Happiness October 335657	Open		25.00	25
1997	Topaz-Color of Truth November 335665	Open		25.00	25
1997	Turquiose-Color of Loyalty December 335673	Open		25.00	25

Care-A-Van Tour - S. Butcher

YEAR	ISSUE	EDITION LIMIT	YEAR RETD.	ISSUE PRICE	*QUOTE U.S.$
1998	Have a Heavenly Journey 12416R	Yr.Iss.		25.00	25
1998	How Can Two Work Together Except They Agree (ornament) 456268	Yr.Iss.		25.00	25

Clown - S. Butcher

YEAR	ISSUE	EDITION LIMIT	YEAR RETD.	ISSUE PRICE	*QUOTE U.S.$
1985	I Get a Bang Out of You 12262	Retrd.	1997	30.00	45-60
1986	Lord Keep Me On the Ball 12270	Open		30.00	45-70
1985	Waddle I Do Without You 12459	Retrd.	1989	30.00	44-120
1986	The Lord Will Carry You Through 12467	Retrd.	1988	30.00	80-95

Commemorative 500th Columbus Anniversary - S. Butcher

YEAR	ISSUE	EDITION LIMIT	YEAR RETD.	ISSUE PRICE	*QUOTE U.S.$
1992	This Land Is Our Land 527386	Yr.Iss.	1992	350.00	385-425

Commemorative Easter Seal - S. Butcher

YEAR	ISSUE	EDITION LIMIT	YEAR RETD.	ISSUE PRICE	*QUOTE U.S.$
1988	Jesus Loves Me 9" fig. 104531	1,000		500.00	1400-1750
1987	He Walks With Me 107999	Yr.Iss.	1987	25.00	25-55
1988	Blessed Are They That Overcome 115479	Yr.Iss.	1988	27.50	25-40
1989	Make A Joyful Noise 9" fig. 520322	1,500		N/A	900-950
1989	His Love Will Shine On You 522376	Yr.Iss.	1989	30.00	40-55
1990	You Have Touched So Many Hearts 9" fig. 523283	2,000		500.00	700-775
1991	We Are God's Workmanship 9" fig. 523879	2,000		N/A	650-725
1990	Always In His Care 524522	Yr.Iss.	1990	30.00	32-50
1992	You Are Such A Purr-fect Friend 9" fig. 526010	2,000		N/A	600-700
1991	Sharing A Gift Of Love 527114	Yr.Iss.	1991	30.00	50-60
1992	A Universal Love 527173	Yr.Iss.	1992	32.50	85-88
1993	Gather Your Dreams 9" fig. 529680	2,000		500.00	575-625
1993	You're My Number One Friend 530026	Yr.Iss.	1993	30.00	32-40
1994	It's No Secret What God Can Do 531111	Yr.Iss.	1994	30.00	35
1994	You Are The Rose of His Creation 9" fig. 531243	2,000		N/A	500
1995	Take Time To Smell the Flowers 524387	Yr.Iss.	1995	30.00	30
1995	He's Got The Whole World In His Hands 9" fig. 526886	Yr.Iss.	1995	500.00	N/A
1996	He Loves Me 9" fig. 152277	2,000		500.00	N/A
1996	You Can Always Count on Me 526827	Yr.Iss.	1996	30.00	30
1997	Love Is Universal 9" fig. 192376	2,000		N/A	500
1997	Give Ability A Chance 192368	Yr.Iss.	1997	30.00	30-35
1998	Love Grows Here 9" fig. 272981	2,000		N/A	N/A
1998	Somebody Cares 522325	Yr.Iss.	1998	40.00	40
1999	We Are All Precious In His Sight 475068	1,500		N/A	N/A
1999	Heaven Bless You Easter Seal 456314	Yr.Iss.		35.00	35

Country Lane - S. Butcher

YEAR	ISSUE	EDITION LIMIT	YEAR RETD.	ISSUE PRICE	*QUOTE U.S.$
1999	Hogs & Kisses 261106	Open		50.00	50
1998	You're Just As Sweet As Pie 307017	Open		45.00	45
1998	Oh Taste And See That The Lord Is Good 307025	Open		55.00	55
1998	Fork Over Those Blessings 307033	Open		45.00	45
1998	Nobody Likes To Be Dumped 307041	Open		65.00	65
1998	I'll Never Tire of You 307068	Open		50.00	50
1998	Peas Pass The Carrots 307076	Open		35.00	35
1998	Bringing In The Sheaves (Musical) 307084	Yr.Iss.		90.00	90

Cruise - S. Butcher

YEAR	ISSUE	EDITION LIMIT	YEAR RETD.	ISSUE PRICE	*QUOTE U.S.$
1993	15 Year Tweet Music Together (15th Anniversary Collection Convention Medallion) 529087	Yr.Iss.	1993	Gift	N/A
1993	Friends Never Drift Apart (15th Anniversary Cruise Medallion) 529079	Yr.Iss.	1993	Gift	N/A
1995	Sailabration (15th Anniversary Collectors Club Cruise Figurine) 150061	Yr.Iss.	1995	Gift	N/A
1998	Our Future Is Looking Much Brighter (20th Anniversary Collection Cruise Figurine) 325511	Yr.Iss.	1998	Gift	N/A

Events Figurines - S. Butcher

YEAR	ISSUE	EDITION LIMIT	YEAR RETD.	ISSUE PRICE	*QUOTE U.S.$
1988	You Are My Main Event 115231	Yr.Iss.	1988	30.00	60-75
1989	Sharing Begins In The Heart 520861	Yr.Iss.	1989	25.00	50-60
1990	I'm A Precious Moments Fan 523526	Yr.Iss.	1990	25.00	45-50
1990	Good Friends Are Forever 525049	Yr.Iss.	1990	25.00	N/A
1991	You Can Always Bring A Friend 527122	Yr.Iss.	1991	27.50	55-60
1992	An Event Worth Wading For 527319	Yr.Iss.	1992	32.50	40-60
1993	An Event For All Seasons 530158	Yr.Iss.	1993	30.00	30-62
1994	Memories Are Made of This 529982	Yr.Iss.	1994	30.00	40-52
1995	Follow Your Heart 528080	Yr.Iss.	1995	30.00	35-40
1996	Hallelujah Hoedown 163864	Yr.Iss.	1996	32.50	40-60
1996	May The Sun Always Shine On You 184217	Yr.Iss.	1996	37.50	48-65
1997	We're So Hoppy You're Here 261351	Yr.Iss.	1997	32.50	33
1998	Love Is Kind 51379R	Yr.Iss.		8.00	8

Family Christmas Scene - S. Butcher

YEAR	ISSUE	EDITION LIMIT	YEAR RETD.	ISSUE PRICE	*QUOTE U.S.$
1985	May You Have the Sweetest Christmas 15776	Suspd.		17.00	35-60
1985	The Story of God's Love 15784	Suspd.		22.50	45-55
1985	Tell Me a Story 15792	Suspd.		10.00	22-40
1985	God Gave His Best 15806	Suspd.		13.00	32-50
1985	Silent Night 15814	Suspd.		37.50	75-94
1986	Sharing Our Christmas Together 102490	Suspd.		40.00	50-60
1989	Have A Beary Merry Christmas 522856	Suspd.		15.00	25-35
1990	Christmas Fireplace 524883	Suspd.		37.50	45-62

Four Seasons - S. Butcher

YEAR	ISSUE	EDITION LIMIT	YEAR RETD.	ISSUE PRICE	*QUOTE U.S.$
1985	The Voice of Spring 12068	Yr.Iss.	1985	30.00	275-320
1985	Summer's Joy 12076	Yr.Iss.	1985	30.00	100-125
1986	Autumn's Praise 12084	Yr.Iss.	1986	30.00	44-90
1986	Winter's Song 12092	Yr.Iss.	1986	30.00	96-130
1986	Set	Yr.Iss.	1986	120.00	250-550

Growing In Grace - S. Butcher

YEAR	ISSUE	EDITION LIMIT	YEAR RETD.	ISSUE PRICE	*QUOTE U.S.$
1995	Infant Angel With Newspaper 136204	Open		22.50	23-28
1995	Age 1 Baby With Cake 136190	Open		25.00	25
1995	Age 2 Girl With Blocks 136212	Open		25.00	25
1995	Age 3 Girl With Flowers 136220	Open		25.00	25
1995	Age 4 Girl With Doll 136239	Open		27.50	28
1995	Age 5 Girl With Lunch Box 136247	Open		27.50	28-33
1995	Age 6 Girl On Bicycle 136255	Open		30.00	30
1996	Age 7 Girl Dressed As Nurse 163740	Open		32.50	33
1996	Age 8 Girl Shooting Marbles 163759	Open		32.50	33
1995	Age 16 Sweet Sixteen Girl Holding Sixteen Roses 136263	Open		45.00	45-52
1996	Age 9 Girl With Charm Bracelet 183865	Open		30.00	30
1996	Age 10 Girl Bowling 183873	Open		37.50	38
1997	Age 11 Girl With Ice Cream Cone 260924	Open		37.50	38
1997	Age 12 Girl/Puppy Holding Clock 260932	Open		37.50	38
1997	Age 13 Girl/Turtle Race 272647	Open		40.00	40
1997	Age 14 Girl With Diary 272655	Open		35.00	35
1997	Age 15 Girl With List 272663	Open		40.00	40

Little Moments - S. Butcher

YEAR	ISSUE	EDITION LIMIT	YEAR RETD.	ISSUE PRICE	*QUOTE U.S.$
1996	Where Would I Be Without You 139491	Open		20.00	20
1997	You're Just Perfect In My Book 320560	Open		25.00	25
1996	All Things Grow With Love 139505	Open		20.00	20
1997	Loving Is Caring 320579	Open		20.00	20
1997	Loving Is Caring 320595	Open		20.00	20
1996	You're The Berry Best 139513	Open		20.00	20
1996	You Make The World A Sweeter Place 139521	Open		20.00	20
1996	You're Forever In My Heart 139548	Open		20.00	20
1996	Birthday Wishes With Hugs & Kisses 139556	Open		20.00	20
1997	You Have Such A Special Way Of Caring Each And Every Day 320706	Open		25.00	25
1997	What Would I Do Without You? 320714	Open		25.00	25
1996	You Make My Spirit Soar 139564	Open		20.00	20
1997	January 261203	Open		20.00	20
1997	February 261246	Open		20.00	20
1997	April 261300	Open		20.00	20
1997	March 261270	Open		20.00	20
1997	May 261211	Open		20.00	20
1997	June 261254	Open		20.00	20
1997	July 261289	Open		20.00	20
1997	August 261319	Open		20.00	20
1997	September 261238	Open		20.00	20
1997	October 261262	Open		20.00	20
1997	November 261297	Open		20.00	20
1997	December 261327	Open		20.00	20
1997	Bless Your Little Tutu 261173	Open		20.00	20
1997	You Will Always Be A Winner To Me (Boy) 272612	Open		20.00	20
1997	It's Ruff To Always Be Cheery 272639	Open		20.00	20
1997	You Set My Heart Ablaze 320625	Open		20.00	20
1997	Just The Facts...You're Terrific 320668	Open		20.00	20
1997	You Will Always Be A Winner To Me (Girl) 283460	Open		20.00	20

Little Moments Internationals - S. Butcher

YEAR	ISSUE	EDITION LIMIT	YEAR RETD.	ISSUE PRICE	*QUOTE U.S.$
1998	You Are a Dutch-ess To Me 456373	Open		20.00	20
1998	Life Is A Fiesta 456381	Open		20.00	20
1998	Don't Rome Too Far From Home 456403	Open		20.00	20
1998	You Can't Beat The Red, White And Blue 456411	Open		20.00	20
1998	Love's Russian Into My Heart 456446	Open		20.00	20
1998	Hola, Amigo 456454	Open		20.00	20
1998	Afri-can Be There For You, Then I Will Be 456462	Open		20.00	20
1998	I'd Travel The Highlands To Be With You 456470	Open		20.00	20
1998	Sure Would Love To Squeeze You 456896	Open		20.00	20
1998	You Are My Amour 456918	Open		20.00	20
1998	Our Friendship Is Always In Bloom 456926	Open		20.00	20
1998	My Love Will Stand Guard Over You 456934	Open		20.00	20

Musical Figurines - S. Butcher

YEAR	ISSUE	EDITION LIMIT	YEAR RETD.	ISSUE PRICE	*QUOTE U.S.$
1983	Sharing Our Season Together E-0519	Retrd.	1986	70.00	150-180
1983	Wee Three Kings E-0520	Suspd.		60.00	125
1983	Let Heaven And Nature Sing E-2346	Suspd.		55.00	109-150
1982	O Come All Ye Faithful E-2352	Suspd.		50.00	135-155
1982	I'll Play My Drum For Him E-2355	Suspd.		45.00	200-220
1980	Christmas Is A Time To Share E-2806	Retrd.	1984	35.00	155-175
1980	Crown Him Lord Of All E-2807	Suspd.		35.00	100-110
1980	Unto Us A Child Is Born E-2808	Suspd.		35.00	100
1980	Jesus Is Born E-2809	Suspd.		35.00	130
1980	Come Let Us Adore Him E-2810	Suspd.		45.00	115-175
1980	Peace On Earth E-4726	Suspd.		45.00	125
1981	The Hand That Rocks The Future E-5204	Open		30.00	60
1981	My Guardian Angel E-5205	Suspd.		22.50	85-90
1981	My Guardian Angel E-5206	Suspd.		22.50	85-100
1984	Wishing You A Merry Christmas E-5394	Suspd.		55.00	100-125
1981	Silent Knight E-5642	Suspd.		45.00	350
1981	Rejoice O Earth E-5645	Retrd.	1988	35.00	90-112
1982	The Lord Bless You And Keep You E-7180	Open		55.00	85-135
1982	Mother Sew Dear E-7182	Open		35.00	65
1982	The Purr-fect Grandma E-7184	Suspd.		35.00	60-110
1982	Love Is Sharing E-7185	Retrd.	1985	40.00	170-195
1982	Let the Whole World Know E-7186	Suspd.		60.00	160-170
1985	Lord Keep My Life In Tune (B) (2/set) 12165	Suspd.		50.00	125-165
1985	We Saw A Star 12408	Suspd.		50.00	75-105
1987	Lord Keep My Life In Tune (G) (2/set) 12580	Suspd.		50.00	110-350
1985	God Sent You Just In Time 15504	Retrd.	1989	60.00	88-100
1986	Heaven Bless You 100285	Suspd.		45.00	75
1986	Our 1st Christmas Together 101702	Retrd.	1992	50.00	100
1986	Let's Keep In Touch 102520	Open		85.00	90-125
1988	Peace On Earth 109746	Suspd.		120.00	150-176
1987	I'm Sending You A White Christmas 112402	Retrd.	1993	55.00	100-130
1988	You Have Touched So Many Hearts 112577	Suspd.		50.00	65
1991	Lord Keep My Life In Balance 520691	Suspd.		60.00	110
1989	The Light Of The World Is Jesus 521507	Open		65.00	70
1992	Do Not Open Till Christmas 522244	Suspd.		75.00	85-105
1992	This Day Has Been Made In Heaven 523682	Open		60.00	65
1993	Wishing You Were Here 526916	Open		100.00	100-135

*Quotes have been rounded up to nearest dollar

Rejoice in the Lord - S. Butcher

YEAR ISSUE	EDITION LIMIT	YEAR RETD.	ISSUE PRICE	*QUOTE U.S.$
1985 Lord Keep My Life In Tune 12165	Suspd.		37.50	110-160
1985 There's a Song in My Heart 12173	Suspd.		11.00	35-55
1985 Happiness is the Lord 12378	Suspd.		15.00	35-50
1985 Lord Give Me a Song 12386	Suspd.		15.00	35
1985 He is My Song 12394	Suspd.		17.50	35-55

Sammy's Circus - S. Butcher

YEAR ISSUE	EDITION LIMIT	YEAR RETD.	ISSUE PRICE	*QUOTE U.S.$
1994 Markie 528099	Suspd.		18.50	19-25
1994 Dusty 529176	Suspd.		22.50	23
1994 Katie 529184	Suspd.		17.00	17
1994 Tippy 529192	Suspd.		12.00	12-15
1994 Collin 529214	Suspd.		20.00	20
1994 Sammy 529222	Yr.Iss.	1994	20.00	20-25
1994 Circus Tent 528196 (Nite-Lite)	Suspd.		90.00	90
1995 Jordan 529168	Suspd.		20.00	20
1996 Jennifer 163708	Suspd.		20.00	20-25

Spring Catalog - S. Butcher

YEAR ISSUE	EDITION LIMIT	YEAR RETD.	ISSUE PRICE	*QUOTE U.S.$
1993 Happiness Is At Our Fingertips 529931	Yr.Iss.	1993	35.00	60-95
1994 So Glad I Picked You As A Friend 524379	Yr.Iss.	1994	40.00	50
1995 Sending My Love Your Way 528609	Yr.Iss.	1995	40.00	45-60
1996 Have I Toad You Lately I Love You 521329	Yr.Iss.	1996	30.00	45-55
1997 Happiness To The Core 261378	Yr.Iss.	1997	37.50	38
1998 Mom, You Always Make Our House A Home 325465	Yr.Iss.	1998	37.50	38

Sugartown - S. Butcher

YEAR ISSUE	EDITION LIMIT	YEAR RETD.	ISSUE PRICE	*QUOTE U.S.$
1992 Chapel 529621	Retrd.	1994	85.00	115-160
1992 Christmas Tree 528684	Retrd.	1994	15.00	25-28
1992 Grandfather 529516	Retrd.	1994	15.00	20-40
1992 Nativity 529508	Retrd.	1994	20.00	25-40
1992 Philip 529494	Retrd.	1994	17.00	20-25
1992 Aunt Ruth & Aunt Dorothy 529486	Retrd.	1994	20.00	25-44
1992 Sam Butcher 529567 (1st sign)	Yr.Iss.	1992	22.50	95-195
1993 7 pc. Sam's House Collector's Set 531774	Retrd.	1997	189.00	189-375
1993 Sam's House Night Light 529605	Retrd.	1997	80.00	85
1993 Fence 529796	Retrd.	1997	10.00	10
1993 Sammy 528668	Retrd.	1997	17.00	17-25
1993 Katy Lynne 529524	Retrd.	1997	20.00	20-30
1993 Sam Butcher 529842 (2nd sign)	Yr.Iss.	1993	22.50	50-80
1993 Dusty 529435	Retrd.	1997	17.00	17
1993 Sam's Car 529443	Retrd.	1997	22.50	23
1994 Dr. Sam Sugar 529850	Retrd.	1997	17.00	17
1994 Doctor's Office Night Light 529869	Retrd.	1997	80.00	85
1994 Sam's House 530468	Yr.Iss.	1994	17.50	18-20
1994 Jan 529826	Retrd.	1997	17.00	17-22
1994 Sugar & Her Dog House 533165	Retrd.	1997	20.00	20
1994 Stork With Baby Sam 529788	Yr.Iss.	1994	22.50	23-35
1994 Free Christmas Puppies 528064	Retrd.	1997	18.50	19-30
1994 7 pc. Doctor's Office Collectors Set 529281	Yr.Iss.	1994	189.00	190-195
1994 Leon & Evelyn Mae 529818	Retrd.	1997	20.00	20-25
1995 Sam the Conductor 150169	Yr.Iss.	1995	20.00	20-22
1995 Train Station Night Light 150150	Retrd.	1997	50.00	50-100
1995 Railroad Crossing Sign 150177	Retrd.	1997	12.00	12
1995 Tammy and Debbie 531812	Retrd.	1997	22.50	23
1995 Donny 531871	Retrd.	1997	22.50	23-25
1995 Luggage Cart With Kitten And Tag 150185	Retrd.	1997	13.00	13
1995 6 pc. Train Station Collector Set 750193	Yr.Iss.	1995	190.00	190
1996 Sugar Town Skating Sign 184020	Yr.Iss.	1996	15.00	15
1996 Skating Pond 184047	Retrd.	1997	40.00	40
1996 Mazie 184055	Retrd.	1997	18.50	23-25
1996 Cocoa 184063	Retrd.	1997	7.50	8
1996 Leroy 184071	Retrd.	1997	18.50	19
1996 Hank and Sharon 184098	Retrd.	1997	25.00	25
1996 Lighted Warming Hut 192341	Retrd.	1997	60.00	60
1997 Lighted Schoolhouse 272795	Retrd.	1997	80.00	80
1997 Chuck 272809	Retrd.	1997	22.50	23
1997 Aunt Cleo 272817	Retrd.	1997	18.50	19
1997 Aunt Bulah & Uncle Sam 272825	Retrd.	1997	22.50	23
1997 Heather 272833	Retrd.	1997	20.00	20
1997 Merry-Go-Round 272841	Retrd.	1997	20.00	20
1997 Schoolhouse Collector's Set-6-pc. 272876	Retrd.	1997	183.50	184
1997 Sugar Town Accessories 212725	Retrd.	1997	20.00	20
1997 Sugar Town Train Cargo Car 273007	Yr.Iss.	1997	27.50	28
1998 Post Office Collector's Set 456217	Yr.Iss.	1998	250.00	250

Sugartown Enhancements - S. Butcher

YEAR ISSUE	EDITION LIMIT	YEAR RETD.	ISSUE PRICE	*QUOTE U.S.$
1995 Bus Stop 150207	Retrd.	1997	8.50	9-12
1995 Fire Hydrant 150215	Retrd.	1997	5.00	5
1995 Bird Bath 150223	Retrd.	1997	8.50	9
1995 Sugartown Enhancement Pack, set/5 152269	Retrd.	1997	45.00	45
1996 Tree Night Light 184039	Retrd.	1997	45.00	45-50
1996 Flag Pole w/Kitten 184136	Retrd.	1997	15.00	15
1996 Wooden Barrel Hot Cocoa Stand 184144	Retrd.	1997	15.00	15
1996 Bonfire with Bunnies 184152	Retrd.	1997	10.00	10
1997 Bike Rack 272906	Retrd.	1997	15.00	15
1997 Garbage Can 272914	Retrd.	1997	20.00	20
1997 Enhancements 3-pc. 273015	Retrd.	1997	43.50	44
1995 Dog And Kitten On Park Bench 529540	Retrd.	1997	13.00	13-18
1994 Lamp Post 529559	Retrd.	1997	8.00	8-13
1997 Bunnies Caroling 531804	Retrd.	1997	10.00	10
1994 Mailbox 531847	Retrd.	1997	5.00	5-13
1995 Street Sign 532185	Retrd.	1997	5.00	5
1994 Village Town Hall Clock 532908	Retrd.	1997	80.00	85
1994 Curved Sidewalk 533149	Retrd.	1997	10.00	10-13
1994 Straight Sidewalk 533157	Retrd.	1997	10.00	10-13
1994 Single Tree 533173	Retrd.	1997	10.00	10-15
1994 Double Tree 533181	Retrd.	1997	10.00	10
1994 Cobble Stone Bridge 533203	Retrd.	1997	17.00	17

To Have And To Hold - S. Butcher

YEAR ISSUE	EDITION LIMIT	YEAR RETD.	ISSUE PRICE	*QUOTE U.S.$
1996 Love Vows To Always Bloom 1st Anniversary Couple With Flowers 129097	Open		70.00	70-75
1996 A Year Of Blessings-1st Anniversary Couple With Cake 163783	Open		70.00	70
1996 Each Hour Is Precious With You-5th Anniversary Couple With Clock 163791	Open		70.00	70-75
1996 Ten Years Heart To Heart-10th Anniversary Couple With Pillow 163805	Open		70.00	70
1996 A Silver Celebration To Share-25th Anniversary Couple With Silver Platter 163813	Open		70.00	70
1996 Sharing The Gift of 40 Precious Years-40th Anniversary Couple With Gift Box 163821	Open		70.00	70-75
1996 Precious Moments To Remember-50th Anniversary Couple With Photo Album 163848	Open		70.00	70

Two By Two - S. Butcher

YEAR ISSUE	EDITION LIMIT	YEAR RETD.	ISSUE PRICE	*QUOTE U.S.$
1993 Noah, Noah's Wife, & Noah's Ark (lighted) 530042	Open		125.00	125-150
1993 Sheep (mini double fig.) 530077	Open		10.00	10-25
1993 Pigs (mini double fig.) 530085	Open		12.00	12
1993 Giraffes (mini double fig.) 530115	Open		16.00	16
1993 Bunnies (mini double fig.) 530123	Open		9.00	9
1993 Elephants (mini double fig.) 530131	Open		18.00	18
1993 Eight Piece Collector's Set 530948	Open		190.00	190
1994 Llamas 531375	Open		15.00	15
1995 Congratulations You Earned Your Stripes 127809	Open		15.00	15
1996 I'd Goat Anywhere With You 163694	Open		10.00	10-15

You Are Always There For Me - S. Butcher

YEAR ISSUE	EDITION LIMIT	YEAR RETD.	ISSUE PRICE	*QUOTE U.S.$
1996 Mother Kissing Daughter's Owie 163600	Open		50.00	50-57
1996 Father Helping Son Bat 163627	Open		50.00	50
1996 Sister Consoling Sister 163635	Open		50.00	50
1997 Mother Kissing Son's Owie 163619	Open		50.00	50
1997 Father Bandaging Daughter's Doll 163597	Open		50.00	50-53

Prizm, Inc./Pipka

Pipka's Memories of Christmas Collector's Club - Pipka

YEAR ISSUE	EDITION LIMIT	YEAR RETD.	ISSUE PRICE	*QUOTE U.S.$
1998 Knock, Knock Santa Figurine 13923	Yr.Iss.		95.00	95
1998 Knock, Knock Santa Ornament 11418	Open		Gift	N/A

Pipka's Earth Angels - Pipka

YEAR ISSUE	EDITION LIMIT	YEAR RETD.	ISSUE PRICE	*QUOTE U.S.$
1996 Angel of Hearts 13801	3,400	1998	85.00	85-90
1997 Angel of Roses 13804	5,400		85.00	85
1998 Celeste-Angel of Stars 13807	5,400		90.00	90
1998 Christine-The Christmas Angel 13808	5,400		90.00	90
1996 Cottage Angel 13800	3,400	1998	85.00	85-90
1998 Elizabeth-Forget-Me-Not Angel 13809	5,400		90.00	90
1996 Gardening Angel 13802	5,400	1998	85.00	85-90
1997 Guardian Angel 13805	5,400		85.00	85
1997 Messenger Angel 13803	5,400		85.00	85
1998 Mikaela-Angel of Innocence 13810	5,400		40.00	40
1998 Samantha-The Playful Angel 13811	5,400		40.00	40
1998 Sarah-The Littlest Angel 13812	5,400		40.00	40

Pipka's Madonna Collection - Pipka

YEAR ISSUE	EDITION LIMIT	YEAR RETD.	ISSUE PRICE	*QUOTE U.S.$
1998 Queen of Roses 12000	5,400		90.00	90

Pipka's Memories of Christmas - Pipka

YEAR ISSUE	EDITION LIMIT	YEAR RETD.	ISSUE PRICE	*QUOTE U.S.$
1995 Czechoslovakian Santa 13905	3,600	1996	85.00	200-850
1995 Gingerbread Santa 13903	3,600	1996	85.00	250-500
1995 Midnight Visitor 13902	3,600	1996	85.00	500-1500
1995 Santa's Ark 13901	3,600	1997	85.00	250-500
1995 Star Catcher Santa 13904	3,600	1996	85.00	225-500
1995 Starcoat Santa 13900	3,600	1996	85.00	250-500
1995 Set of 1995 Santas (13900-13905)	Closed	N/A	510.00	1550-2000
1996 Aussie Santa & Boomer 13906	3,600	1997	85.00	110-300
1996 Good News Santa 13908	3,600	1997	85.00	125-500
1996 Storytime Santa 13909	3,600	1997	85.00	125-500
1996 Ukrainian Santa 13907	3,600	1997	85.00	125-500
1997 Norwegian/Julenisse Santa 13911	3,600	1997	90.00	250-525
1997 Polish Father Christmas 13917	3,600	1997	90.00	110-250
1997 Russian Santa 13916	3,600	1998	90.00	90-250
1997 Santa's Spotted Grey 13914	3,600	1998	90.00	90-250
1997 St. Nicholas 13912	3,600	1998	90.00	90-250
1997 Where's Rudolph? 13915	3,600	1997	90.00	110-250
1998 Father Christmas 13919	3,600	1998	95.00	95
1998 Peace Maker 13918	3,600	1998	95.00	95
1998 San Nicolas 13921	3,600	1998	95.00	95
1998 Teddy Bear Santa 13920	3,600	1998	95.00	95-1100

Pipka's Reflections of Christmas - Pipka

YEAR ISSUE	EDITION LIMIT	YEAR RETD.	ISSUE PRICE	*QUOTE U.S.$
1997 Amish Country Santa 6 1/2" 11305	9,700		40.00	40
1998 Aussie Santa & Boomer 6 1/2" 11306	9,700		40.00	40
1997 Better Watch Out Santa 6 1/2" 11304	9,700		40.00	40
1997 Czechoslovakian Santa 6 1/2" 11301	9,700		40.00	40
1998 Dear Santa 6 1/2" 11311	9,700		40.00	40
1998 Gingerbread Santa 6 1/2" 11309	9,700		40.00	40
1998 Good News Santa 6 1/2" 11307	9,700		40.00	40
1997 Midnight Visitor 6 1/2" 11300	9,700		40.00	40
1998 Norwegian Julenisse 6 1/2" 11313	9,700		40.00	40
1998 Polish Father Christmas 6 1/2" 11312	9,700		40.00	40
1997 Star Catcher Santa 6 1/2" 11303	9,700		40.00	40
1997 Starcoat Santa 6 1/2" 11302	9,700		40.00	40
1998 Storytime Santa 6 1/2" 11308	9,700		40.00	40
1998 Teddy Bear Santa 6 1/2" 11318	9,700		40.00	40
1998 Ukrainian Santa 6 1/2" 11310	9,700		40.00	40
1998 Where's Rudolph? 6 1/2" 11315	9,700		40.00	40

Pulaski Furniture, Inc.

PFC Collectors' Club

YEAR ISSUE	EDITION LIMIT	YEAR RETD.	ISSUE PRICE	*QUOTE U.S.$
1996 Jack Russell Terrier (figurine)	Closed	1997	19.95	20
1998 Rembrandt Russell - Self Pawtrait (graphic)	500		Gift	30

Reco International

Clown Figurines by John McClelland - J. McClelland

YEAR ISSUE	EDITION LIMIT	YEAR RETD.	ISSUE PRICE	*QUOTE U.S.$
1988 Mr. Cool	9,500		35.00	35
1987 Mr. Cure-All	9,500		35.00	35
1988 Mr. Heart-Throb	9,500		35.00	35
1987 Mr. Lovable	9,500		35.00	35
1988 Mr. Magic	9,500		35.00	35
1987 Mr. One-Note	9,500		35.00	35
1987 Mr. Tip	9,500		35.00	35

Faces of Love - J. McClelland

YEAR ISSUE	EDITION LIMIT	YEAR RETD.	ISSUE PRICE	*QUOTE U.S.$
1988 Cuddles	Open		29.50	33
1988 Sunshine	Open		29.50	33

Granget Crystal Sculpture - G. Granget

YEAR ISSUE	EDITION LIMIT	YEAR RETD.	ISSUE PRICE	*QUOTE U.S.$
1973 Long Earred Owl, Asio Otus	Retrd.	1974	2250.00	2250
XX Ruffed Grouse	Retrd.	1976	1000.00	1000

Laughables - J. Bergsma

YEAR ISSUE	EDITION LIMIT	YEAR RETD.	ISSUE PRICE	*QUOTE U.S.$
1997 Angel & Alex	Open		17.50	18
1997 Anna & Abigail	Open		15.00	15
1995 Annie, Geoge & Harry	Open		17.50	18
1996 Ashley	Open		13.50	14
1997 Brie & Benjamin	Open		16.50	17
1995 Cody & Spot	Open		15.00	15
1995 Daffodil & Prince	Open		13.50	14
1995 Daisy & Jeremiah	Open		15.00	15
1996 Felix & Freddie	Open		15.00	15
1997 Harry & Sally	Open		16.50	17
1997 Jenny & Jamie	Open		15.00	15
1995 Joey & Jumper	Open		15.00	15
1996 Jordan & Jessie	Open		15.00	15
1996 Leo & Lindsey	Open		17.50	18
1996 Mattie & Quackers	Open		15.00	15
1995 Merlin & Gemini	Open		15.00	15
1995 Millie & Mittens	Open		15.00	15
1996 Nicholas & Chelsea	Retrd.	1996	15.00	15
1997 Nicky	Open		15.00	15
1995 Patches and Pokey	Open		15.00	15
1995 Patty & Petunia	Open		16.50	17
1996 Peter & Polly	Open		17.50	18
1997 Rocky & Jody	Yr.Iss.		16.50	17
1996 Sammy & Mikey	Open		15.00	15
1995 Sunny	Open		13.50	14
1995 Whiskers & Willie	Open		13.50	14

Porcelains in Miniature by John McClelland - J. McClelland

YEAR ISSUE	EDITION LIMIT	YEAR RETD.	ISSUE PRICE	*QUOTE U.S.$
XX Alice	10,000		34.50	35
XX Autumn Dreams	Open		29.50	30
XX The Baker	Open		29.50	30
XX Batter Up	Retrd.	1993	29.50	30
XX Center Ice	Retrd.	1998	29.50	30
XX Cheerleader	Open		29.50	30
XX Chimney Sweep	10,000		34.50	35
XX The Clown	Open		29.50	30
XX Club Pro	Retrd.	1998	29.50	30
XX Country Lass	Open		29.50	30
XX Cowboy	Open		29.50	30
XX Cowgirl	Open		29.50	30
XX Doc	Open		29.50	30
XX Dressing Up	10,000		34.50	35
XX The Farmer	Open		29.50	30
XX Farmer's Wife	Open		29.50	30
XX The Fireman	Open		29.50	30
XX First Outing	Open		29.50	30
XX First Solo	Open		29.50	30
XX Highland Fling	7,500		34.50	35
XX John	10,000		34.50	35
XX Lawyer	Open		29.50	30
XX Love 40	Open		29.50	30
XX The Nurse	Open		29.50	30
XX The Painter	Open		29.50	30
XX The Policeman	Open		29.50	30

*Quotes have been rounded up to nearest dollar

YEAR ISSUE	EDITION LIMIT	YEAR RETD.	ISSUE PRICE	*QUOTE U.S.$
XX Quiet Moments	Open		29.50	30
XX Smooth Smailing	Open		29.50	30
XX Special Delivery	Open		29.50	30
XX Sudsie Suzie	Open		29.50	30
XX Tuck-Me-In	Open		29.50	30
XX Winter Fun	Open		29.50	30

The Reco Angel Collection - J. McClelland

YEAR ISSUE	EDITION LIMIT	YEAR RETD.	ISSUE PRICE	*QUOTE U.S.$
1986 Adoration	Open		24.00	24
1986 Devotion	Open		15.00	15
1986 Faith	Retrd.	1995	24.00	24
1986 Gloria	Retrd.	1996	12.00	12
1986 Harmony	Retrd.	1994	12.00	12
1986 Hope	Retrd.	1998	24.00	24
1986 Innocence	Retrd.	1996	12.00	12
1986 Joy	Retrd.	1994	15.00	15
1986 Love	Retrd.	1996	12.00	12
1988 Minstral	Retrd.	1995	12.00	12
1986 Peace	Retrd.	1996	24.00	24
1986 Praise	Retrd.	1996	20.00	20
1988 Reverence	Retrd.	1995	12.00	12
1986 Serenity	Retrd.	1996	24.00	24

The Reco Clown Collection - J. McClelland

YEAR ISSUE	EDITION LIMIT	YEAR RETD.	ISSUE PRICE	*QUOTE U.S.$
1985 Arabesque	Open		12.00	13
1985 Bow Jangles	Open		12.00	13
1985 Curly	Open		12.00	13
1987 Disco Dan	Open		12.00	13
1987 Domino	Open		12.00	13
1987 Happy George	Open		12.00	13
1985 Hobo	Open		12.00	13
1987 The Joker	Open		12.00	13
1987 Jolly Joe	Open		12.00	13
1987 Love	Open		12.00	13
1987 Mr. Big	Open		12.00	13
1985 The Professor	Open		12.00	13
1985 Ruffles	Open		12.00	13
1985 Sad Eyes	Open		12.00	13
1985 Scamp	Open		12.00	13
1987 Smiley	Open		12.00	13
1985 Sparkles	Open		12.00	13
1985 Top Hat	Open		12.00	13
1987 Tramp	Open		12.00	13
1987 Twinkle	Open		12.00	13
1985 Whoopie	Open		12.00	13
1985 Winkie	Retrd.	1994	12.00	13
1987 Wistful	Open		12.00	13
1987 Zany Jack	Open		12.00	13

Reco Creche Collection - J. McClelland

YEAR ISSUE	EDITION LIMIT	YEAR RETD.	ISSUE PRICE	*QUOTE U.S.$
1988 Cow	Open		15.00	15
1988 Donkey	Open		16.50	17
1987 Holy Family (3 Pieces)	Open		49.00	49
1988 King/Frankincense	Open		22.50	23
1988 King/Gold	Open		22.50	23
1988 King/Myrrh	Open		22.50	23
1987 Lamb	Open		9.50	10
1987 Shepherd-Kneeling	Open		22.50	23
1987 Shepherd-Standing	Open		22.50	23

Sandra Kuck's Treasures - S. Kuck

YEAR ISSUE	EDITION LIMIT	YEAR RETD.	ISSUE PRICE	*QUOTE U.S.$
1997 Baby Bunnies	Open		20.00	20
1997 Be Good	Open		20.00	20
1998 Bridge of Love	Open		27.50	28
1997 Christmas Morning	1,200		Gift	N/A
1997 Fishin' Buddies	Open		25.00	25
1997 For Mom	Open		20.00	20
1998 Friendship & Sharing	Open		50.00	50
1998 Gift of Love	Open		30.00	30
1998 Giving Thanks	Open		30.00	30
1998 Happy Birthday	Open		25.00	25
1998 Little Cowboy	Open		27.50	28
1997 Love and Kisses	Open		20.00	20
1998 Make Believe	Open		30.00	30
1997 Playful Kitten	Open		20.00	20
1998 Pretty Kitty	Open		30.00	30
1998 Schooldays	Open		25.00	25
1998 Sisters	Open		30.00	30
1997 Sunday Stroll	Open		20.00	20
1998 Sweet Dreams	Open		20.00	20
1997 Swing For Two	Open		25.00	25
1997 Tea With Kitty	Open		20.00	20
1997 Teacher's Pet	Open		20.00	20
1997 Teddy & Me	Open		20.00	20
1998 Thank You So Much	Open		20.00	20
1997 Victoria's Garden	Open		20.00	20
1998 Winter Fun	Open		30.00	30

River Shore

Rockwell Single Issues - N. Rockwell

YEAR ISSUE	EDITION LIMIT	YEAR RETD.	ISSUE PRICE	*QUOTE U.S.$
1982 Grandpa's Guardian	9,500	N/A	125.00	175-195
1981 Looking Out To Sea	9,500	N/A	85.00	225

Roman, Inc.

American Santas Through the Decades - Galleria Lucchese Studios

YEAR ISSUE	EDITION LIMIT	YEAR RETD.	ISSUE PRICE	*QUOTE U.S.$
1994 1800 Cloth-like Santa 7"	Closed	1995	49.50	50
1994 1800 Pencil Santa 8"	Closed	1995	29.50	30-35
1994 1810 Cloth-like Santa 7"	Closed	1995	49.50	50
1994 1810 Pencil Santa 8"	Closed	1995	29.50	30-35

Catnippers - I. Spencer

YEAR ISSUE	EDITION LIMIT	YEAR RETD.	ISSUE PRICE	*QUOTE U.S.$
1985 A Baffling Yarn	15,000	N/A	45.00	45
1985 Can't We Be Friends	15,000	N/A	45.00	45
1985 A Christmas Mourning	15,000	N/A	45.00	50
1985 Flora and Felina	15,000	N/A	45.00	50
1985 Flying Tiger-Retired	15,000	N/A	45.00	45
1985 The Paw that Refreshes	15,000	N/A	45.00	45
1985 Sandy Claws	15,000	N/A	45.00	45
1985 A Tail of Two Kitties	15,000	N/A	45.00	45

Ceramica Excelsis - Unknown

YEAR ISSUE	EDITION LIMIT	YEAR RETD.	ISSUE PRICE	*QUOTE U.S.$
1978 Assumption Madonna	5,000	N/A	56.00	56
1978 Christ Entering Jerusalem	5,000	N/A	96.00	96
1978 Christ in the Garden of Gethsemane	5,000	N/A	40.00	60
1977 Christ Knocking at the Door	5,000	N/A	60.00	60
1980 Daniel in the Lion's Den	5,000	N/A	80.00	80
1980 David	5,000	N/A	77.00	77
1978 Flight into Egypt	5,000	N/A	59.00	90
1983 Good Shepherd	5,000	N/A	49.00	49
1978 Guardian Angel with Boy	5,000	N/A	69.00	69
1978 Guardian Angel with Girl	5,000	N/A	69.00	69
1983 Holy Family	5,000	N/A	72.00	72
1978 Holy Family at Work	5,000	N/A	96.00	96
1978 Infant of Prague	5,000	N/A	37.50	60
1981 Innocence	5,000	N/A	95.00	95
1979 Jesus Speaks in Parables	5,000	N/A	90.00	90
1983 Jesus with Children	5,000	N/A	74.00	74
1981 Journey to Bethlehem	5,000	N/A	89.00	89
1983 Kneeling Santa	5,000	N/A	95.00	95
1977 Madonna and Child with Angels	5,000	N/A	60.00	60
1977 Madonna with Child	5,000	N/A	65.00	65
1979 Moses	5,000	N/A	77.00	77
1979 Noah	5,000	N/A	77.00	77
1981 Sermon on the Mount	5,000	N/A	56.00	56
1983 St. Anne	5,000	N/A	49.00	49
1977 St. Francis	5,000	N/A	60.00	60
1983 St. Francis	5,000	N/A	59.50	60
1981 Way of the Cross	5,000	N/A	59.00	59
1980 Way to Emmaus	5,000	N/A	155.00	155
1977 What Happened to Your Hand?	5,000	N/A	60.00	60

A Child's World 1st Edition - F. Hook

YEAR ISSUE	EDITION LIMIT	YEAR RETD.	ISSUE PRICE	*QUOTE U.S.$
1980 Beach Buddies, signed	15,000	N/A	29.00	600
1980 Beach Buddies, unsigned	15,000	N/A	29.00	450
1980 Helping Hands	Closed	N/A	45.00	85
1980 Kiss Me Good Night	15,000	N/A	29.00	40
1980 My Big Brother	Closed	N/A	39.00	200
1980 Nighttime Thoughts	Closed	N/A	25.00	65
1980 Sounds of the Sea	15,000	N/A	45.00	150

A Child's World 2nd Edition - F. Hook

YEAR ISSUE	EDITION LIMIT	YEAR RETD.	ISSUE PRICE	*QUOTE U.S.$
1981 All Dressed Up	15,000	N/A	36.00	70
1981 Cat Nap	15,000	N/A	42.00	125
1981 I'll Be Good	15,000	N/A	36.00	80
1981 Making Friends	15,000	N/A	42.00	46
1981 The Sea and Me	15,000	N/A	39.00	80
1981 Sunday School	15,000	N/A	39.00	70

A Child's World 3rd Edition - F. Hook

YEAR ISSUE	EDITION LIMIT	YEAR RETD.	ISSUE PRICE	*QUOTE U.S.$
1981 Bear Hug	15,000	N/A	42.00	45
1981 Pathway to Dreams	15,000	N/A	47.00	50
1981 Road to Adventure	15,000	N/A	47.00	50
1981 Sisters	15,000	N/A	64.00	75
1981 Spring Breeze	15,000	N/A	37.50	50
1981 Youth	15,000	N/A	37.50	40

A Child's World 4th Edition - F. Hook

YEAR ISSUE	EDITION LIMIT	YEAR RETD.	ISSUE PRICE	*QUOTE U.S.$
1982 All Bundled Up	15,000	N/A	37.50	40
1982 Bedtime	15,000	N/A	35.00	38
1982 Birdie	15,000	N/A	37.50	40
1982 Flower Girl	15,000	N/A	42.00	45
1982 My Dolly!	15,000	N/A	39.00	40
1982 Ring Bearer	15,000	N/A	39.00	40

A Child's World 5th Edition - F. Hook

YEAR ISSUE	EDITION LIMIT	YEAR RETD.	ISSUE PRICE	*QUOTE U.S.$
1983 Brothers	15,000	N/A	64.00	70
1983 Finish Line	15,000	N/A	39.00	42
1983 Handful of Happiness	15,000	N/A	36.00	40
1983 He Loves Me...	15,000	N/A	49.00	55
1983 Puppy's Pal	15,000	N/A	39.00	42
1983 Ring Around the Rosie	15,000	N/A	99.00	105

A Child's World 6th Edition - F. Hook

YEAR ISSUE	EDITION LIMIT	YEAR RETD.	ISSUE PRICE	*QUOTE U.S.$
1984 Can I Help?	15,000	N/A	37.50	40
1984 Future Artist	15,000	N/A	42.00	45
1984 Good Doggie	15,000	N/A	47.00	50
1984 Let's Play Catch	15,000	N/A	33.00	35
1984 Nature's Wonders	15,000	N/A	29.00	31
1984 Sand Castles	15,000	N/A	37.50	40

A Child's World 7th Edition - F. Hook

YEAR ISSUE	EDITION LIMIT	YEAR RETD.	ISSUE PRICE	*QUOTE U.S.$
1985 Art Class	15,000	N/A	99.00	105
1985 Don't Tell Anyone	15,000	N/A	49.00	50
1985 Look at Me!	15,000	N/A	42.00	45
1985 Mother's Helper	15,000	N/A	45.00	50
1985 Please Hear Me	15,000	N/A	29.00	30
1985 Yummm!	15,000	N/A	36.00	39

A Child's World 8th Edition - F. Hook

YEAR ISSUE	EDITION LIMIT	YEAR RETD.	ISSUE PRICE	*QUOTE U.S.$
1985 Chance of Showers	15,000	N/A	33.00	35
1985 Dress Rehearsal	15,000	N/A	33.00	35
1985 Engine	15,000	N/A	36.00	40
1985 Just Stopped By	15,000	N/A	36.00	40
1985 Private Ocean	15,000	N/A	29.00	31
1985 Puzzling	15,000	N/A	36.00	40

A Child's World 9th Edition - F. Hook

YEAR ISSUE	EDITION LIMIT	YEAR RETD.	ISSUE PRICE	*QUOTE U.S.$
1987 Hopscotch	15,000	N/A	67.50	70
1987 Li'l Brother	15,000	N/A	60.00	65

Classic Brides of the Century - E. Williams

YEAR ISSUE	EDITION LIMIT	YEAR RETD.	ISSUE PRICE	*QUOTE U.S.$
1989 1900-Flora	5,000	N/A	175.00	175
1989 1910-Elizabeth Grace	5,000	N/A	175.00	175
1989 1920-Mary Claire	5,000	N/A	175.00	175
1989 1930-Kathleen	5,000	N/A	175.00	175
1989 1940-Margaret	5,000	N/A	175.00	175
1989 1950-Barbara Ann	5,000	N/A	175.00	175
1989 1960-Dianne	5,000	N/A	175.00	175
1989 1970-Heather	5,000	N/A	175.00	175
1989 1980-Jennifer	5,000	N/A	175.00	175
1992 1990-Stephanie Helen	5,000	N/A	175.00	175

Divine Servant - M. Greiner Jr.

YEAR ISSUE	EDITION LIMIT	YEAR RETD.	ISSUE PRICE	*QUOTE U.S.$
1993 Divine Servant, pewter sculpture	Open		200.00	200
1993 Divine Servant, porcelain sculpture	Open		59.50	60
1993 Divine Servant, resin sculpture	Open		250.00	250

Finnians - D. Fearon

YEAR ISSUE	EDITION LIMIT	YEAR RETD.	ISSUE PRICE	*QUOTE U.S.$
1995 Aileran, the Curious	Closed	1997	35.00	35
1995 Caelon, the Lover	Closed	1997	29.50	30
1995 Enid, the Swift	Closed	1997	29.50	30
1995 Jack, the Climber	Closed	1997	29.50	30
1995 Laidech, the Songful	Closed	1997	29.50	30

Fontanini Club Members' Only - E. Simonetti

YEAR ISSUE	EDITION LIMIT	YEAR RETD.	ISSUE PRICE	*QUOTE U.S.$
1991 The Pilgrimage	Yr.Iss.	1991	24.95	25
1992 She Rescued Me	Yr.Iss.	1992	23.50	24
1993 Christmas Symphony	Yr.Iss.	1993	13.50	14
1994 Sweet Harmony	Yr.Iss.	1994	13.50	14
1995 Faith: The Fifth Angel	Yr.Iss.	1995	22.50	23

Fontanini Club Members' Only Nativity Preview - E. Simonetti

YEAR ISSUE	EDITION LIMIT	YEAR RETD.	ISSUE PRICE	*QUOTE U.S.$
1996 Mara	Yr.Iss.	1996	12.50	13
1997 Benjamin	Yr.Iss.	1997	15.00	15
1998 Hannah	Yr.Iss.	1998	15.00	15

Fontanini Club Renewal Gift - E. Simonetti

YEAR ISSUE	EDITION LIMIT	YEAR RETD.	ISSUE PRICE	*QUOTE U.S.$
1993 He Comforts Me	Yr.Iss.	1993	Gift	13
1994 I'm Heaven Bound	Yr.Iss.	1994	Gift	13
1995 Gift of Joy	Yr.Iss.	1995	Gift	13

Fontanini Club Symbol of Membership - E. Simonetti

YEAR ISSUE	EDITION LIMIT	YEAR RETD.	ISSUE PRICE	*QUOTE U.S.$
1990 I Found Him	Closed	1995	Gift	N/A
1996 Rosannah - Angel of The Roses	Yr.Iss.	1996	Gift	N/A
1997 Leah - Angel of Light	Yr.Iss.	1997	Gift	N/A
1998 Candace - The Caregiver	Yr.Iss.	1998	Gift	N/A

Fontanini Special Event Figurine - E. Simonetti

YEAR ISSUE	EDITION LIMIT	YEAR RETD.	ISSUE PRICE	*QUOTE U.S.$
1994 Susanna	Yr.Iss.	1994	12.00	12
1995 Dominica	Yr.Iss.	1995	15.00	15
1996 Sarah	Yr.Iss.	1996	15.00	15
1997 Martha	Yr.Iss.	1997	15.00	15

Fontanini Personal Tour Exclusive - E. Simonetti

YEAR ISSUE	EDITION LIMIT	YEAR RETD.	ISSUE PRICE	*QUOTE U.S.$
1990 Gideon	Closed	1995	15.00	15
1995 Luke	Closed	1998	15.00	15

Fontanini Heirloom Nativity Limited Edition Figurines - E. Simonetti

YEAR ISSUE	EDITION LIMIT	YEAR RETD.	ISSUE PRICE	*QUOTE U.S.$
1994 14 pc. Golden Edition Heirloom Nativity Set	2,500		375.00	375
1998 90th Anniversary Nativity Set, (10 pc.), includes Charis, 90th Anniversary Ltd. Ed. Angel	Yr.Iss.		300.00	300
1994 Abigail & Peter	Closed	1996	29.50	60
1992 Ariel	Closed	1992	29.50	30
1998 Celeste, Angel w/Dove	Yr.Iss.		19.50	20
1998 Charis, 90th Anniversary Angel	Yr.Iss.		29.50	30
1995 Gabriela	25,000	1995	18.00	18-30
1993 Jeshua & Adin	Closed	1996	29.50	30
1997 Judah	Closed	1997	19.50	20
1996 Raphael	Closed	1996	18.00	18-30

Fontanini Retired 5" Collection - E. Simonetti

YEAR ISSUE	EDITION LIMIT	YEAR RETD.	ISSUE PRICE	*QUOTE U.S.$
1978 3 Kings on Camels	Retrd.	1996	52.00	52
1967 Aaron	Retrd.	1993	12.50	13
1966 Baby Jesus	Retrd.	1991	5.50	12
1966 Balthazar	Retrd.	1992	5.50	12
1967 Gabriel	Retrd.	1992	5.50	12
1966 Gaspar	Retrd.	1992	5.50	12
1966 Gloria Angel	Retrd.	1979	3.00	3
1966 Joseph	Retrd.	1991	5.50	12
1967 Josiah	Retrd.	1993	5.50	12
1967 Kneeling Angel	Retrd.	1994	5.50	13
1967 Levi	Retrd.	1993	5.50	13
1966 Mary	Retrd.	1991	5.50	12
1966 Melchior	Retrd.	1992	5.50	12
1983 Micah	Retrd.	1995	5.50	14
1967 Miriam	Retrd.	1993	5.50	12
1967 Mordecai	Retrd.	1995	5.50	13
1967 Standing Angel	Retrd.	1994	5.50	13

Fontanini Retired 7.5" Collection - E. Simonetti

YEAR ISSUE	EDITION LIMIT	YEAR RETD.	ISSUE PRICE	*QUOTE U.S.$
1968 Baby Jesus	Retrd.	1993	13.00	25
1968 Balthazar	Retrd.	1994	6.00	6
1979 Daniel	Retrd.	1996	6.00	6
1979 Gabriel	Retrd.	1993	13.00	25
1968 Gaspar	Retrd.	1994	6.00	6
1968 Joseph	Retrd.	1993	13.00	25

*Quotes have been rounded up to nearest dollar

YEAR ISSUE	EDITION LIMIT	YEAR RETD.	ISSUE PRICE	*QUOTE U.S.$
1985 Judith	Retrd.	1996	6.00	6
1968 Kneeling Angel	Retrd.	1995	13.00	25
1968 Mary	Retrd.	1993	13.00	25
1968 Melchoir	Retrd.	1994	6.00	6
1979 Reuben	Retrd.	1996	6.00	6
1968 Standing Angel	Retrd.	1995	13.00	25

Frances Hook's Four Seasons - F. Hook

YEAR ISSUE	EDITION LIMIT	YEAR RETD.	ISSUE PRICE	*QUOTE U.S.$
1984 Winter	12,500		95.00	100
1985 Spring	12,500		95.00	100
1985 Summer	12,500		95.00	100
1985 Fall	12,500		95.00	100

Heartbeats - I. Spencer

YEAR ISSUE	EDITION LIMIT	YEAR RETD.	ISSUE PRICE	*QUOTE U.S.$
1986 Miracle	5,000		145.00	145
1987 Storytime	5,000		145.00	145

Hook - F. Hook

YEAR ISSUE	EDITION LIMIT	YEAR RETD.	ISSUE PRICE	*QUOTE U.S.$
1986 Carpenter Bust	Retrd.	1986	95.00	95
1986 Carpenter Bust-Heirloom Edition	Retrd.	1986	95.00	95
1987 Little Children, Come to Me	15,000	N/A	45.00	45
1987 Madonna and Child	15,000	N/A	39.50	40
1982 Sailor Mates	2,000	N/A	290.00	315
1982 Sun Shy	2,000	N/A	290.00	315

Jam Session - E. Rohn

YEAR ISSUE	EDITION LIMIT	YEAR RETD.	ISSUE PRICE	*QUOTE U.S.$
1985 Banjo Player	7,500	N/A	145.00	145
1985 Bass Player	7,500	N/A	145.00	145
1985 Clarinet Player	7,500	N/A	145.00	145
1985 Coronet Player	7,500	N/A	145.00	145
1985 Drummer	7,500	N/A	145.00	145
1985 Trombone Player	7,500	N/A	145.00	145

The Masterpiece Collection - Various

YEAR ISSUE	EDITION LIMIT	YEAR RETD.	ISSUE PRICE	*QUOTE U.S.$
1979 Adoration - F. Lippe	5,000	N/A	73.00	73
1981 The Holy Family - G. delle Notti	5,000	N/A	98.00	98
1982 Madonna of the Streets - R. Ferruzzi	5,000	N/A	65.00	65
1980 Madonna with Grapes - P. Mignard	5,000	N/A	85.00	85

The Museum Collection by Angela Tripi - A. Tripi

YEAR ISSUE	EDITION LIMIT	YEAR RETD.	ISSUE PRICE	*QUOTE U.S.$
1994 The Batter	1,000	N/A	95.00	95
1993 Be a Clown	1,000	N/A	95.00	95
1994 Blackfoot Woman with Baby	1,000	N/A	95.00	95
1990 The Caddie	1,000	N/A	135.00	135
1992 Checking It Twice	2,500	N/A	95.00	95
1990 Christopher Columbus	1,000	N/A	250.00	250
1994 Crow Warrior	1,000	N/A	195.00	195
1990 The Fiddler	1,000	N/A	175.00	176
1992 Flying Ace	1,000	N/A	95.00	95
1993 For My Next Trick	1,000	N/A	95.00	95
1992 Fore!	1,000	N/A	175.00	175
1992 The Fur Trapper	1,000	N/A	175.00	175
1991 A Gentleman's Game	1,000	N/A	175.00	175
1992 The Gift Giver	2,500	N/A	95.00	95
1994 Iroquois Warrior	1,000	N/A	95.00	95
1994 Jesus in Gethsemane	1,000	N/A	75.00	75
1993 Jesus, The Good Shepherd	1,000	N/A	95.00	95
1992 Justice for All	1,000	N/A	95.00	95
1992 Ladies' Day	1,000	N/A	175.00	175
1992 Ladies' Tee	1,000	N/A	250.00	250
1990 The Mentor	1,000	N/A	290.00	291
1993 Native American Woman-Cherokee Maiden	1,000	N/A	110.00	110
1992 Nativity Set-8 pc.	2,500	N/A	425.00	425
1994 Nurse	1,000	N/A	95.00	95
1993 One Man Band Clown	1,000	N/A	95.00	95
1992 Our Family Doctor	1,000	N/A	95.00	95
1994 The Pitcher	1,000	N/A	95.00	95
1993 Preacher of Peace	1,000	N/A	175.00	175
1992 Prince of the Plains	1,000	N/A	175.00	175
1993 Public Protector	1,000	N/A	95.00	95
1993 Rhapsody	1,000	N/A	95.00	95
1993 Right on Schedule	1,000	N/A	95.00	95
1993 Road Show	1,000	N/A	95.00	95
1995 The Runner	1,000	N/A	95.00	95
1993 Serenade	1,000	N/A	95.00	95
1995 Sioux Chief	1,000	N/A	95.00	95
1993 Sonata	1,000	N/A	95.00	95
1990 St. Francis of Assisi	1,000	N/A	175.00	175
1992 The Tannenbaum Santa	2,500	N/A	95.00	95
1992 The Tap In	1,000	N/A	175.00	175
1994 Teacher	1,000	N/A	95.00	95
1990 Tee Time at St. Andrew's	1,000	N/A	175.00	175
1992 This Way, Santa	2,500	N/A	95.00	95
1992 To Serve and Protect	1,000	N/A	150.00	150
1993 Tripi Crucifix-Large	Open		59.00	59
1993 Tripi Crucifix-Medium	Open		35.00	35
1993 Tripi Crucifix-Small	Open		27.50	28

The Richard Judson Zolan Collection - R.J. Zolan

YEAR ISSUE	EDITION LIMIT	YEAR RETD.	ISSUE PRICE	*QUOTE U.S.$
1992 Summer at the Seashore	1,200		125.00	125
1994 Terrace Dancing	1,200		175.00	175

Seraphim Classics® 12" Limited Edition Figurines - Seraphim Studios

YEAR ISSUE	EDITION LIMIT	YEAR RETD.	ISSUE PRICE	*QUOTE U.S.$
1995 Alyssa - Nature's Angel	Closed	1995	145.00	750-1385
1996 Vanessa - Heavenly Maiden	Closed	1996	150.00	150-195
1997 Chloe - Nature's Gift	Closed	1997	159.00	159-175
1997 Ariel - Heaven's Shining Star	Closed	1997	159.00	159-165
1998 Hope - Light in the Distance	12/99		175.00	175
1998 Avalon - Free Spirit	Yr.Iss.		175.00	175
1999 Annalisa - Celebrating The Millennium	2-Yr.		175.00	175

Seraphim Classics® 5th Year Anniversary Figurine - Seraphim Studios

YEAR ISSUE	EDITION LIMIT	YEAR RETD.	ISSUE PRICE	*QUOTE U.S.$
1999 Cassandra - Heavenly Beauty	Yr.Iss.		100.00	100

Seraphim Classics® 4" - Seraphim Studios

YEAR ISSUE	EDITION LIMIT	YEAR RETD.	ISSUE PRICE	*QUOTE U.S.$
1999 Celine - The Morning Star	Open		19.50	20
1995 Cymbeline - Peacemaker	Open		19.50	20
1995 Evangeline - Angel of Mercy	Open		19.50	20
1995 Felicia - Adoring Maiden	Open		19.50	20
1999 Gabriel - Celestial Messenger	Open		19.50	20
1995 Iris - Rainbow's End	Open		19.50	20
1995 Isabel - Gentle Spirit	Open		19.50	20
1995 Laurice - Wisdom's Child	Open		19.50	20
1995 Lydia - Winged Poet	Open		19.50	20
1999 Mariah - Heavenly Joy	Open		19.50	20
1995 Ophelia - Heart Seeker	Open		19.50	20
1995 Priscilla - Benevolent Guide	Open		19.50	20
1999 Rosalie - Nature's Delight	Open		19.50	20
1995 Seraphina - Heaven's Helper	Open		19.50	20
1999 Serena - Angel of Peace	Open		19.50	20

Seraphim Classics® 7" - Seraphim Studios

YEAR ISSUE	EDITION LIMIT	YEAR RETD.	ISSUE PRICE	*QUOTE U.S.$
1998 Amelia - Eternal Bloom	Yr.Iss.		65.00	65
1998 Angels' Touch - The Dedication Angel	Open		59.50	60
1998 Annabella - Announcement of Joy	Open		59.50	60
1999 Arianna - Winter's Warmth	Open		59.50	60
1999 Audra - Embraced By Love	Open		59.50	60
1996 Celine - The Morning Star	Open		55.00	55
1997 Chelsea - Summer's Delight	Open		55.00	55
1994 Cymbeline - Peacemaker	Retrd.	1997	49.50	50-65
1998 Diana - Heaven's Rose	Open		59.50	60
1994 Evangeline - Angel of Mercy	Open		49.50	55
1996 Faith - The Easter Angel	Open		55.00	55
1995 Felicia - Adoring Maiden	Retrd.	1998	49.50	55
1996 Francesca - Loving Guardian	Retrd.	1998	65.00	65
1996 Gabriel - Celestial Messenger	Open		59.50	60
1997 Grace - Born Anew	Open		55.00	55
1997 Hannah - Always Near	Open		55.00	55
1997 Harmony - Love's Guardian	Open		55.00	55
1997 Heather - Autumn Beauty	Open		55.00	55
1994 Iris - Rainbow's End	Open		49.50	55
1994 Isabel - Gentle Spirit	Open		49.50	55
1995 Laurice - Wisdom's Child	Retrd.	1997	49.50	55
1994 Lydia - Winged Poet	Retrd.	1997	49.50	50-55
1996 Mariah - Heavenly Joy	Open		59.50	60
1999 Mariah - Heavenly Joy (Musical)	Open		75.00	75
1997 Melody - Heaven's Song	Open		55.00	55
1999 Michael - Victorious	Open		59.50	60
1999 Naomi - Nurturing Spirit	Open		59.50	60
1998 Noelle - Giving Spirit	Open		59.50	60
1994 Ophelia - Heart Seeker	Retrd.	1996	49.50	50-125
1995 Priscilla - Benevolent Guide	Retrd.	1998	49.50	55
1997 Rachel - Children's Joy	Open		55.00	55
1996 Rosalie - Nature's Delight	Open		55.00	55
1997 Sabrina - Eternal Guide	Closed	1997	55.00	55
1998 Samantha - Blessed At Birth	Open		59.50	60
1995 Seraphina - Heaven's Helper	Retrd.	1996	49.50	50-144
1996 Serena - Angel of Peace	Open		65.00	65
1998 Simone - Nature's Own	Open		100.00	100
1997 Tamara - Guardian Angel	Open		65.00	65

Seraphim Classics® Angels To Watch Over Me - Seraphim Studios

YEAR ISSUE	EDITION LIMIT	YEAR RETD.	ISSUE PRICE	*QUOTE U.S.$
1996 Newborn - Girl	Open		39.50	40
1996 First Year - Girl	Open		39.50	40
1996 Second Year - Girl	Open		39.50	40
1996 Third Year - Girl	Open		39.50	40
1996 Fourth Year - Girl	Open		39.50	40
1996 Fifth Year - Girl	Open		39.50	40
1997 Sixth Year - Girl	Open		39.50	40
1997 Seventh Year - Girl	Open		39.50	40
1998 Eighth Year - Girl	Open		45.00	45
1998 Ninth Year - Girl	Open		45.00	45
1997 Newborn - Boy	Open		39.50	40
1997 First Year - Boy	Open		39.50	40
1997 Second Year - Boy	Open		39.50	40
1997 Third Year - Boy	Open		39.50	40
1997 Fourth Year - Boy	Open		39.50	40
1997 Fifth Year - Boy	Open		39.50	40
1997 Sixth Year - Boy	Open		39.50	40
1998 Seventh Year - Boy	Open		45.00	45

Seraphim Classics® Collectors Club - Seraphim Studios

YEAR ISSUE	EDITION LIMIT	YEAR RETD.	ISSUE PRICE	*QUOTE U.S.$
1997 Tess - Tender One	12/98		55.00	55
1998 Lillian - Nurturing Life	Yr.Iss.		65.00	65

Seraphim Classics® Glitterdome® - Seraphim Studios

YEAR ISSUE	EDITION LIMIT	YEAR RETD.	ISSUE PRICE	*QUOTE U.S.$
1995 Francesca - Loving Guardian	Open		50.00	50
1997 Iris - Rainbow's End	Open		50.00	50

Seraphim Classics® Heaven Sent Collection - Seraphim Studios

YEAR ISSUE	EDITION LIMIT	YEAR RETD.	ISSUE PRICE	*QUOTE U.S.$
1997 Hope Eternal	Open		37.50	38
1997 Loving Spirit	Open		37.50	38
1997 Pure At Heart	Open		37.50	38

Seraphim Classics® Heaven Sent Musicals - Seraphim Studios

YEAR ISSUE	EDITION LIMIT	YEAR RETD.	ISSUE PRICE	*QUOTE U.S.$
1997 Hope Eternal	Open		37.50	38
1997 Loving Spirit	Open		37.50	38
1998 Peaceful Embrace	Open		85.00	85
1997 Pure At Heart	Open		37.50	38

Seraphim Classics® Heavenly Guardian Musicals - Seraphim Studios

YEAR ISSUE	EDITION LIMIT	YEAR RETD.	ISSUE PRICE	*QUOTE U.S.$
1999 Heavenly Guardian - Boy	Open		49.50	50
1999 Heavenly Guardian - Girl	Open		49.50	50

Seraphim Classics® Musicals - Seraphim Studios

YEAR ISSUE	EDITION LIMIT	YEAR RETD.	ISSUE PRICE	*QUOTE U.S.$
1998 Evangeline - Angel of Mercy	Open		75.00	75
1994 Francesca - Loving Guardian	Retrd.	1998	75.00	75
1996 Iris - Rainbow's End	Open		65.00	65

Seraphim Classics® Nativity - Seraphim Studios

YEAR ISSUE	EDITION LIMIT	YEAR RETD.	ISSUE PRICE	*QUOTE U.S.$
1998 Gloria Angel	Open		59.50	60
1996 Nativity Set - 5 pc. set	Open		125.00	125
1998 Shepherds - 2 pc. Set	Open		65.00	65
1997 Three Kings - 3 pc. set	Open		125.00	125

Seraphim Classics® Special Event - Seraphim Studios

YEAR ISSUE	EDITION LIMIT	YEAR RETD.	ISSUE PRICE	*QUOTE U.S.$
1996 Dawn - Sunshine's Guardian Angel	Retrd.	1997	55.00	55-163
1997 Monica - Under Love's Wings	Yr.Iss.	1997	55.00	55
1998 Alexandra - Endless Dreams	Yr.Iss.		65.00	65

Spencer - I. Spencer

YEAR ISSUE	EDITION LIMIT	YEAR RETD.	ISSUE PRICE	*QUOTE U.S.$
1985 Flower Princess	5,000	N/A	195.00	195
1985 Moon Goddess	5,000	N/A	195.00	195

Ron Lee's World of Clowns

The Ron Lee Collector's Club Gifts - R. Lee

YEAR ISSUE	EDITION LIMIT	YEAR RETD.	ISSUE PRICE	*QUOTE U.S.$
1987 Hooping It Up CCG1	Closed	1987	Gift	145
1988 Pudge CCG2	Closed	1988	Gift	95
1989 Pals CCG3	Closed	1989	Gift	95
1990 Potsie CCG4	Closed	1990	Gift	95
1991 Hi! Ya! CCG5	Closed	1991	Gift	95
1992 Bashful Beau CCG6	Closed	1992	Gift	95
1993 Lit'l Mate CCG7	Closed	1993	Gift	95
1994 Chip Off the Old Block CCG8	Closed	1994	Gift	65
1995 Rock-A-Billy CCG9	Closed	1995	Gift	65
1996 Hey There CCG10	Closed	1996	Gift	65
1997 Thumbs Up CCG-11	Yr. Iss.		Gift	N/A

The Ron Lee Collector's Club Renewal Sculptures - R. Lee

YEAR ISSUE	EDITION LIMIT	YEAR RETD.	ISSUE PRICE	*QUOTE U.S.$
1987 Doggin' Along CC1	Yr.Iss.	1987	75.00	138
1988 Midsummer's Dream CC2	Yr.Iss.	1988	97.00	168
1989 Peek-A-Boo Charlie CC3	Yr.Iss.	1989	65.00	150
1990 Get The Message CC4	Yr.Iss.	1990	65.00	150
1991 I'm So Pretty CC5	Yr.Iss.	1991	65.00	150
1992 It's For You CC6	Yr.Iss.	1992	65.00	85-150
1993 My Son Keven CC7	Yr.Iss.	1993	70.00	150

The Classics - R. Lee

YEAR ISSUE	EDITION LIMIT	YEAR RETD.	ISSUE PRICE	*QUOTE U.S.$
1991 Huckleberry Hound HB815	2,750	1995	90.00	108
1991 Quick Draw McGraw HB805	2,750	1995	90.00	108
1991 Scooby Doo & Shaggy HB810	2,750	1995	114.00	137
1991 Yogi Bear & Boo Boo HB800	2,750	1995	95.00	114

The E.T. Collection - R. Lee

YEAR ISSUE	EDITION LIMIT	YEAR RETD.	ISSUE PRICE	*QUOTE U.S.$
1992 E.T. ET100	1,500	1995	94.00	113
1993 Flight ET115	1,500	1995	325.00	390
1993 Friends ET110	1,500	1995	125.00	150
1992 It's Mee...E.T. ET105	1,500	1995	94.00	113

The Jetsons - R. Lee

YEAR ISSUE	EDITION LIMIT	YEAR RETD.	ISSUE PRICE	*QUOTE U.S.$
1991 4 O'Clock Tea HB550	2,750	1995	203.00	244
1991 Astro: Cosmic Canine HB520	2,750	1995	275.00	330
1991 The Cosmic Couple HB510	2,750	1995	105.00	126
1991 I Rove Roo HB530	2,750	1995	105.00	127
1991 The Jetsons HB500	2,750	1995	500.00	600
1991 Scare-D-Dog HB540	2,750	1995	160.00	192

The Popeye Collection - R. Lee

YEAR ISSUE	EDITION LIMIT	YEAR RETD.	ISSUE PRICE	*QUOTE U.S.$
1992 Liberty P001	1,750	1995	184.00	184-228
1992 Men!!! P002	1,750	1995	230.00	230
1992 Oh Popeye P005	1,750	1995	230.00	230-276
1992 Par Excellence P006	1,750	1995	220.00	220
1992 Strong to The Finish P003	1,750	1995	95.00	95
1992 That's My Boy P004	1,750	1995	145.00	145-228

Premier Dealer Collection - R. Lee

YEAR ISSUE	EDITION LIMIT	YEAR RETD.	ISSUE PRICE	*QUOTE U.S.$
1992 Dream On PD002	Closed	N/A	125.00	170
1992 Framed Again PD001	Closed	N/A	110.00	140
1993 Jake-A-Juggling Balls PD008	500		85.00	90
1993 Jake-A-Juggling Clubs PD007	500		85.00	90
1993 Jake-A-Juggling Cylinder PD006	500		85.00	90
1994 Joe's Feline Friend PD009	500		105.00	105
1994 Just Big Enough PD010	500		115.00	115
1992 Moonlighting PD004	Closed	N/A	125.00	125
1992 Nest to Nothing PD003	Closed	N/A	110.00	125
1994 Off The Toe PD011	500		105.00	120
1993 Pockets PD005	500		175.00	175
1994 Storm Warning PD012	500		115.00	115
1994 Trading Places PD013	500		190.00	190

Rocky & Bullwinkle And Friends Collection - R. Lee

YEAR ISSUE	EDITION LIMIT	YEAR RETD.	ISSUE PRICE	*QUOTE U.S.$
1992 Dudley Do-Right RB610	1,750	1995	175.00	175
1992 KA-BOOM! RB620	1,750	1995	175.00	175
1992 My Hero RB615	1,750	1995	275.00	330
1992 Rocky & Bullwinkle RB600	1,750	1995	120.00	140
1992 The Swami RB605	1,750	1995	175.00	175-210

The Ron Lee Disney Collection Exclusives - R. Lee

YEAR ISSUE	EDITION LIMIT	YEAR RETD.	ISSUE PRICE	*QUOTE U.S.$
1998 70 Years Mick & Min Sweethearts MM1210	1,500		125.00	125
1993 Aladdin MM560	500	1996	550.00	550
1996 Alice In Wonderland MM840	750		295.00	295

*Quotes have been rounded up to nearest dollar

YEAR ISSUE	EDITION LIMIT	YEAR RETD.	ISSUE PRICE	*QUOTE U.S.$
1997 Ariel MM1120	5,000		47.00	47
1995 Autopia MM770	750		220.00	220
1992 Bambi MM330	2,750		195.00	195
1996 Bambi and Thumper MM990	750		130.00	130
1990 The Bandleader MM100	Closed	N/A	75.00	110
1998 Bashful MM1330	2,500		49.00	49
1992 Beauty & The Beast (shadow box) DIS100	500		1650.00	1650
1994 Beauty & The Beast MM610	800	1996	170.00	170
1996 Buzz Light Year MM960	950		135.00	135
1992 Captain Hook MM320	2,750		175.00	175
1995 The Carousel MM730	750		125.00	125
1992 Christmas '92 MM420	1,500		145.00	145
1993 Cinderella's Slipper MM510	1,750	1995	115.00	150-165
1998 Cindy's Dress MM1250	2,500		156.00	156
1996 Cruella and Pups MM1030	750		135.00	135
1997 Cruisin' MM1090	750		247.50	248
1996 A Dalmation Christmas MM970	750		98.00	98
1993 Darkwing Duck MM470	1,750		105.00	105
1991 Decorating Donald MM210	2,750		60.00	60
1992 The Dinosaurs MM370	2,750		195.00	195
1997 Disney's "5"th Anniversary MM1050	555		200.00	200
1998 Doc MM1320	2,500		49.00	49
1991 Dopey MM120	2,750	1995	80.00	135
1998 Dopey MM1310	2,500		49.00	49
1996 Dumbo & The Ringmaster MM860	750		195.00	195
1990 Dumbo MM600	2,750		110.00	110
1995 Fantasyland MM780	750		285.00	285
1992 Finishing Touch MM440	1,500		85.00	85
1993 Flying With Dumbo MM530	1,000		330.00	330
1995 Frontierland MM740	750		160.00	160
1992 Genie MM450	2,750		110.00	330
1998 Goofy Golfing MM1230	950		130.00	130
1991 Goofy MM110	2,750		115.00	115
1991 Goofy's Gift MM230	2,750		70.00	70
1998 Grumpy MM1360	2,500		49.00	49
1994 Grumpy Playing Organ MM590	800	1995	150.00	200-275
1998 Happy MM1370	2,500		49.00	49
1995 Home Improvements MM820	750		170.00	170
1996 Hunchback of Notre Dame MM910	950		185.00	185
1998 Jiminy Cricket MM1270	2,500		50.00	50
1991 Jiminy's List MM250	2,750		60.00	60
1991 Lady and the Tramp MM280	1,500	1995	295.00	295
1996 Lady and Tramp MM1010	750		150.00	150
1993 Letters to Santa MM550	1,500		170.00	170
1997 Liberty Minnie MM1130	5,000		47.00	47
1991 Lion Around MM270	2,750		140.00	140
1994 The Lion King MM640	1,750	1996	170.00	250
1992 Litt'l Sorcerer MM340	2,750		57.00	57
1992 Little Mermaid MM310	2,750		230.00	212
1997 Little Steamboat Willie MM1180	2,500		51.00	51
1992 Lumiere & Cogsworth MM350	2,750		145.00	145
1995 Main Street MM710	750		120.00	120
1995 The Matterhorn MM750	750		240.00	240
1991 Mickey & Minnie at the Piano MM180	2,750		195.00	195
1997 Mickey & Pluto's Gifts MM1110	1,000		95.00	95
1996 Mickey & The Caddie MM890	1,250		195.00	195
1997 Mickey with Flowers MM1170	2,500		51.00	51
1997 Mickey with Scissors MM1190	2,500		51.00	51
1991 Mickey's Adventure MM150	2,750		195.00	195
1997 Mickey's Broom MM1150	1,500		120.00	120
1990 Mickey's Christmas MM400	2,750		95.00	95
1991 Mickey's Delivery MM220	2,750		70.00	70
1994 Mickey, Brave Little Tailor MM570	1,750	1995	72.00	100
1997 Mickey, The King MM1160	2,500		51.00	51
1991 Minnie Mouse MM170	2,750		80.00	80
1994 Minnie, Brave Little Tailor MM580	1,750	1995	72.00	72
1992 Mrs. Potts & Chip MM360	2,750		125.00	125
1991 Mt. Mickey MM900	2,750		175.00	175
1998 New Genie MM1290	N/A		55.00	55
1998 New Sorcerer MM1220	2,500		52.00	52
1994 New Tinkerbell MM680	300	1995	99.00	99
1994 Official Conscience MM620	300	1995	65.00	65
1995 The People Mover MM760	750		190.00	190
1998 Pinocchio & Jiminy Cricket MM1280	950		115.00	115
1990 Pinocchio MM500	2,750	1995	85.00	85
1991 Pluto's Treat MM240	2,750		60.00	60
1994 Pongo & Pups MM670	800	1995	124.00	124
1995 Pooh & The Cookie Jar MM830	750		190.00	190
1996 Pooh & The Honey Pot MM870	1,250		120.00	120
1996 Pooh In The Honey Tree MM850	750		300.00	300
1996 Pooh Musical MM950	950		150.00	150
1997 Pooh with Flower MM1070	2,500		70.00	70
1997 Pooh's Honey Pot MM1100	5,000		47.00	47
1996 Pooh, Eeyore & Piglet MM880	1,250		150.00	150
1995 Reflections MM810	750	1996	99.00	99
1993 Santa's Workshop MM540	1,500		170.00	170
1998 Sir Goofy MM1260	950		80.00	80
1998 Sleepy MM1350	2,500		49.00	49
1998 Sneezy MM1340	2,500		49.00	49
1994 Snow White & Doc MM630	800		135.00	135
1990 Snow White & Grumpy MM800	2,750		140.00	140
1993 Snow White & The Seven Dwarfs (shadow box) DIS200	250		1800.00	1800
1996 Snow White's 60th Anniversary MM980	750		495.00	495
1990 The Sorcerer MM200	Closed	N/A	85.00	120
1992 Sorcerer's Apprentice MM290	2,750		125.00	125
1997 The Spaghetti Scene MM1200	950		125.00	125
1990 Steamboat Willie MM300	2,750	1995	95.00	95
1992 Stocking Stuffer MM410	1,500	1996	63.00	63
1991 The Tea Cup Ride (Disneyland Exclusive) MM260	1,250	1996	225.00	225
1996 Tigger and Eyeore MM1000	750		135.00	135
1997 Tigger and Pooh MM1060	1,500		125.00	125
1997 Tigger MM1140	5,000		47.00	47
1994 Tigger on Rabbit MM660	800	1995	110.00	110
1993 Tinker Bell MM490	1,750	1995	85.00	85
1997 Tinkerbell in Lamp MM1020	500		179.00	179
1998 Tinkerbell on Lily Pad MM1240	1,500		120.00	120
1997 Tinkerbell on Spool MM1080	5,000		47.00	47
1995 The Topiary MM720	750		145.00	145
1996 Toy Story MM930	950		197.00	197
1991 Tugboat Mickey MM160	2,750		180.00	180
1996 TV Buddies MM920	1,250		199.00	199
1991 Two Gun Mickey MM140	2,750		115.00	115
1990 Uncle Scrooge MM700	2,750		110.00	110
1993 Winnie The Pooh MM480	1,750	1996	125.00	150-200
1992 Winnie The Pooh & Tigger MM390	2,750	1995	105.00	105
1992 Wish Upon A Star MM430	1,500		80.00	80
1991 The Witch MM130	2,750		115.00	115
1992 Workin' Out MM380	2,750		95.00	95

The Ron Lee Disneyana Collection Exclusives - R. Lee

YEAR ISSUE	EDITION LIMIT	YEAR RETD.	ISSUE PRICE	*QUOTE U.S.$
1992 Big Thunder Mountain MM460	250	1995	1650.00	2360-2800
1993 Mickey's Dream MM520	250	1993	400.00	699-715
1994 MM/MN/Goofy Limo MM650	500	1994	500.00	500-1073
1995 Ear Force One MM790	500	1995	600.00	787-1300
1995 Engine Number One MM690	500	1995	650.00	726-765
1996 Heigh-ho MM940	350	1996	500.00	726-900

The Ron Lee Emmett Kelly, Sr. Collection - R. Lee

YEAR ISSUE	EDITION LIMIT	YEAR RETD.	ISSUE PRICE	*QUOTE U.S.$
1991 Emmett Kelly, Sr. Sign E208	Closed	N/A	110.00	110
1991 God Bless America EK206	Closed	N/A	130.00	250
1991 Help Yourself EK202	Closed	N/A	145.00	350
1991 Love at First Sight EK204	Closed	N/A	197.00	197-395
1991 My Protege EK207	Closed	N/A	160.00	165
1997 Playing Cello EK310	950		175.00	175
1997 Playing Piano EK305	950		175.00	175
1991 Spike's Uninvited Guest EK203	Closed	N/A	165.00	295
1997 Sweeping EK300	950		145.00	145
1991 That-A-Way EK201	Closed	N/A	125.00	135
1991 Time for a Change EK205	Closed	N/A	190.00	286-305

The Ron Lee Looney Tunes Collection - R. Lee

YEAR ISSUE	EDITION LIMIT	YEAR RETD.	ISSUE PRICE	*QUOTE U.S.$
1991 1940 Bugs Bunny LT165	Closed	N/A	85.00	120-150
1991 Bugs Bunny LT150	Closed	N/A	123.00	135-155
1991 Daffy Duck LT140	Closed	N/A	80.00	80-85
1991 Elmer Fudd LT125	Closed	N/A	87.00	102-150
1991 Foghorn Leghorn & Henry Hawk LT160	Closed	N/A	115.00	115
1991 Marvin the Martian LT170	Closed	N/A	75.00	75
1991 Michigan J. Frog LT110	Closed	N/A	115.00	115-138
1991 Mt. Yosemite LT180	850		160.00	160-300
1991 Pepe LePew & Penelope LT145	Closed	N/A	115.00	115-145
1991 Porky Pig LT115	Closed	N/A	97.00	163
1991 Sylvester & Tweety LT135	Closed	N/A	110.00	115-176
1991 Tasmanian Devil LT120	Closed	N/A	105.00	105
1991 Tweety LT155	Closed	N/A	110.00	115-139
1991 Western Daffy Duck LT105	Closed	N/A	87.00	90-132
1991 Wile E. Coyote & Roadrunner LT175	Closed	N/A	165.00	175
1991 Yosemite Sam LT130	Closed	N/A	110.00	110-142

The Ron Lee Looney Tunes Collection - R. Lee

YEAR ISSUE	EDITION LIMIT	YEAR RETD.	ISSUE PRICE	*QUOTE U.S.$
1992 Beep Beep LT220	1,500		115.00	115
1992 Ditty Up LT200	2,750		110.00	110
1992 For Better or Worse LT190	1,500		285.00	285
1992 Leopold & Giovanni LT205	1,500		225.00	225
1992 No Pain No Gain LT210	950		270.00	270
1992 Rackin' Frackin' Varmint LT225	950		260.00	260
1992 Speedy Gonzales LT185	2,750		73.00	73
1992 Van Duck LT230	950		335.00	335
1992 The Virtuosos LT235	950		350.00	350
1992 What The ...? LT195	1,500		240.00	240
1992 What's up Doc? LT215	950		270.00	403

The Ron Lee Looney Tunes Collection - R. Lee

YEAR ISSUE	EDITION LIMIT	YEAR RETD.	ISSUE PRICE	*QUOTE U.S.$
1992 Bugs Bunny w/ Horse LT245	1,500		105.00	105
1992 Cowboy Bugs LT290	1,500		70.00	70
1992 Daffy Duck w/ Horse LT275	1,500		105.00	105
1992 Elmer Fudd w/ Horse LT270	1,500		105.00	105
1992 Pepe Le Pew w/ Horse LT285	1,500		105.00	105
1992 Porky Pig w/ Horse LT260	1,500		105.00	105
1992 Sylvester w/ Horse LT250	1,500		105.00	105
1992 Tasmanian Devil w/ Horse LT255	1,500		105.00	105
1992 Wile E. Coyote w/ Horse LT280	1,500		105.00	105
1992 Yosemite Sam w/ Horse LT265	1,500		105.00	105

The Ron Lee Looney Tunes Collection - R. Lee

YEAR ISSUE	EDITION LIMIT	YEAR RETD.	ISSUE PRICE	*QUOTE U.S.$
1993 Bugs LT330	1,200		79.00	79
1993 A Christmas Carrot LT320	1,200		175.00	175
1993 The Essence of Love LT310	1,200		145.00	145
1993 Martian's Best Friend LT305	1,200		140.00	140
1993 Me Deliver LT295	1,200		110.00	110
1993 Puttin' on the Glitz LT325	1,200		79.00	79
1993 The Rookie LT315	1,200		75.00	75
1993 Yo-Ho-Ho- LT300	1,200		105.00	105

The Ron Lee Looney Tunes Collection - R. Lee

YEAR ISSUE	EDITION LIMIT	YEAR RETD.	ISSUE PRICE	*QUOTE U.S.$
1994 Bugs LT330	1,200		79.00	79
1994 A Carrot a Day LT350	1,200		85.00	85
1994 Guilty LT345	1,200		80.00	80
1994 Ma Cherie LT340	1,200		185.00	185
1994 No H20 LT355	1,200		160.00	160
1994 Puttin' on the Glitz LT325	1,200		79.00	79
1994 Smashing LT335	1,200		80.00	80
1994 Taz On Ice LT360	1,200		115.00	115

The Ron Lee Looney Tunes Collection - R. Lee

YEAR ISSUE	EDITION LIMIT	YEAR RETD.	ISSUE PRICE	*QUOTE U.S.$
1994 Bugs Pharoah LT370	500	1996	130.00	150
1994 Cleopatra's Barge LT400	500	1996	550.00	660
1994 Cruising Down the Nile LT385	500	1996	295.00	410
1994 King Bugs and Friends LT395	500	1996	480.00	550
1994 Ramases & Son LT380	500	1996	230.00	260
1994 Tweety Pharoah LT365	500	1996	110.00	140
1994 Warrior Taz LT375	500	1996	140.00	170
1994 Yosemite's Chariot LT390	500	1996	310.00	360

The Ron Lee Looney Tunes Collection - R. Lee

YEAR ISSUE	EDITION LIMIT	YEAR RETD.	ISSUE PRICE	*QUOTE U.S.$
1995 The Baron LT475	750		235.00	235
1995 Daffy Scuba Diving LT470	750		170.00	170
1995 Drive..Drive!! Putt..Putt!! LT450	750		120.00	120
1995 The Great Chase LT485	750		385.00	385
1995 Highway My Way LT460	750		280.00	280
1995 The Hustler LT465	750		397.00	397
1995 Ice Dancing LT440	750		180.00	180
1995 King Pin LT445	750		165.00	165
1995 Slam Dunk LT455	750		190.00	190
1995 Speedy Tweety LT480	750		225.00	225

The Ron Lee Looney Tunes Collection - R. Lee

YEAR ISSUE	EDITION LIMIT	YEAR RETD.	ISSUE PRICE	*QUOTE U.S.$
1996 Bugs Bunny LT490	1,500		49.00	49
1996 Daffy Duck LT520	1,500		49.00	49
1996 Daffy's New York Bistro LT575	750		350.00	350
1996 Foghorn Leghorn LT500	1,500		49.00	49
1996 Liberty Bugs LT590	750		285.00	285
1996 Marvin the Martian LT525	1,500		49.00	49
1996 Michigan J. Frog LT560	1,500		49.00	49
1996 Michigan on Broadway LT585	750		330.00	330
1996 Penelope LT555	1,500		49.00	49
1996 Pepe Le Pew LT550	1,500		49.00	49
1996 Porky Pig LT515	1,500		49.00	49
1996 Roadrunner LT545	1,500		49.00	49
1996 She-Devil LT530	1,500		49.00	49
1996 Speedy Gonzales LT505	1,500		49.00	49
1996 Sylvester LT565	1,500		49.00	49
1996 Tasmanian Devil LT495	1,500		49.00	49
1996 Taz and the Big Apple LT570	750		130.00	130
1996 Taz on Empire State LT580	750		170.00	170
1996 Tweety LT535	1,500		49.00	49
1996 Willie Coyote LT540	1,500		49.00	49
1996 Yosemite Sam LT510	1,500		49.00	49

The Ron Lee Looney Tunes Collection - R. Lee

YEAR ISSUE	EDITION LIMIT	YEAR RETD.	ISSUE PRICE	*QUOTE U.S.$
1997 The Backstroke LT640	2,500		115.00	115
1997 Down Hill LT645	2,500		157.50	158
1997 The Eighteenth Hole LT615	2,500		95.00	95
1997 I Got Me Covered LT620	2,500		80.00	80
1997 Martian Canine LT625	2,500		80.00	80
1997 Marvin LT630	2,500		125.00	125
1997 Penelope Mini #2 LT655	2,500		49.00	49
1997 Pepe Mini #2 LT650	2,500		49.00	49
1997 Pumping Iron LT610	2,500		99.00	99
1997 Senior M. J. Frog LT635	2,500		125.00	125
1997 Tornado Taz LT605	2,500		85.00	85
1997 Tweety Mini #2 LT660	2,500		49.00	49

The Wizard of Oz Collection - R. Lee

YEAR ISSUE	EDITION LIMIT	YEAR RETD.	ISSUE PRICE	*QUOTE U.S.$
1992 The Cowardly Lion WZ425	750	1996	620.00	650-675
1992 Kansas WZ400	750	1996	550.00	550-660
1992 The Munchkins WZ405	750	1996	620.00	650-675
1992 The Ruby Slippers WZ410	750	1996	620.00	620
1992 The Scarecrow WZ415	750	1996	510.00	550-650
1992 The Tin Man WZ420	750	1996	530.00	550-650

The Woody Woodpecker And Friends Collection - R. Lee

YEAR ISSUE	EDITION LIMIT	YEAR RETD.	ISSUE PRICE	*QUOTE U.S.$
1992 1940 Woody Woodpecker WL020	1,750	1996	73.00	75-89
1992 Andy and Miranda Panda WL025	1,750	1996	140.00	140
1992 Birdy for Woody WL005	1,750	1996	117.00	125-140
1992 Pals WL030	1,750	1996	179.00	179
1992 Peck of My Heart WL010	1,750	1996	370.00	495
1992 Woody Woodpecker WL015	1,750	1996	73.00	73-89

Royal Doulton

Royal Doulton International Collectors' Club - Various

YEAR ISSUE	EDITION LIMIT	YEAR RETD.	ISSUE PRICE	*QUOTE U.S.$
1980 John Doulton Jug (8 O'Clock) D6656 - E. Griffiths	Yr.Iss.	1981	70.00	95-350
1981 Sleepy Darling Figure HN2953 - P. Parsons	Yr.Iss.	1982	100.00	195-250
1982 Dog of Fo-Flambe - N/A	Yr.Iss.	1983	50.00	175
1982 Prized Possessions Figure HN2942 - R. Tabbenor	Yr.Iss.	1983	125.00	450-555
1983 Loving Cup - N/A	Yr.Iss.	1984	75.00	300-350
1983 Springtime HN3033 - A. Hughes	Yr.Iss.	1984	125.00	325-450
1984 Sir Henry Doulton Jug D6703 - E. Griffiths	Yr.Iss.	1985	50.00	200-300
1984 Pride & Joy Figure HN2945 - R. Tabbenor	Yr.Iss.	1985	125.00	350-400
1985 Top of the Hill HN2126 - P. Gee	Yr.Iss.	1986	35.00	175-300
1985 Wintertime Figure HN3060 - A. Hughes	Yr.Iss.	1986	125.00	250-450
1986 Albert Sagger Toby Jug - W. Harper	Yr.Iss.	1987	35.00	85
1986 Auctioneer Figure HN2988 - R. Tabbenor	Yr.Iss.	1987	150.00	295-500
1987 Collector Bunnykins DB54 - D. Lyttleton	Yr.Iss.	1988	40.00	650-850
1987 Summertime Figurine HN3137 - P. Parsons	Yr.Iss.	1988	140.00	225-450

*Quotes have been rounded up to nearest dollar

YEAR ISSUE	EDITION LIMIT	YEAR RETD.	ISSUE PRICE	*QUOTE U.S.$
1988 Top of the Hill Miniature Figurine HN2126 - P. Gee	Yr.Iss.	1989	95.00	125-225
1988 Beefeater Tiny Jug - R. Tabbenor	Yr.Iss.	1989	25.00	125-225
1988 Old Salt Tea Pot - N/A	Yr.Iss.	1989	135.00	200-275
1989 Geisha Flambe Figure HN3229 - P. Parsons	Yr.Iss.	1990	195.00	195
1989 Flower Sellers Children Plate - N/A	Yr.Iss.	1990	65.00	70-100
1990 Autumntime Figure HN3231 - P. Parsons	Yr.Iss.	1991	190.00	195-450
1990 Jester Mini Figure HN3335 - C.J. Noke	Yr.Iss.	1991	115.00	115
1990 Old King Cole Tiny Jug - H. Fenton	Yr.Iss.	1991	35.00	100
1991 Bunny's Bedtime Figure HN3370 - N. Pedley	9,500	1992	195.00	200-300
1991 Charles Dickens Jug D6901 - W. Harper	Yr.Iss.	1992	100.00	125
1991 L'Ambiteuse Figure (Tissot Lady) HN3359 - V. Annand	5,000	1992	295.00	300-350
1991 Christopher Columbus Jug D6911 - S. Taylor	Yr.Iss.	1992	95.00	95-125
1992 Discovery Figure HN3428 - A. Munslow	Yr.Iss.	1993	160.00	100
1992 King Edward Jug D6923 - W. Harper	Yr.Iss.	1993	250.00	295
1992 Master Potter Bunnykins DB131 - W. Platt	Yr.Iss.	1993	50.00	85
1992 Eliza Farren Prestige Figure HN3442 - N/A	Yr.Iss.	1993	335.00	250-325
1993 Barbara Figure - N/A	Yr.Iss.	1994	285.00	450-510
1993 Lord Mountbatten L/S Jug - S. Taylor	5,000	1994	225.00	225
1993 Punch & Judy Double Sided Jug - S. Taylor	2,500	1994	400.00	465
1993 Flambe Dragon HN3552 - N/A	Retrd.	1994	260.00	260
1994 Diane HN3604 - N/A	Retrd.	1995	250.00	300
1995 Le Bal HN3702 - N/A	Retrd.	1996	350.00	350
1995 George Tinworth Jug, sm. D7000 - W. Harper	Retrd.	1996	99.00	99
1995 Partners in Collecting Bunnykins DB151	Retrd.	1996	45.00	45-85
1996 Special Delivery Plate - N/A	Retrd.	1996	45.00	60-100
1996 Welcome - N/A	Retrd.	1996	80.00	80
1996 Pamela HN3756 - T. Potts	Retrd.	1996	275.00	275
1996 Mr. Pickwick Jug, sm. D7025 - M. Alcock	Retrd.	1996	138.00	150-250
1996 Winter's Day HN3769 - N. Pedley	Retrd.	1997	325.00	325-450
1996 Gifts For All plate - N. Pedley	Retrd.	1997	40.00	40
1997 Susan HN3871 - N. Pedley	Retrd.	1997	345.00	345
1997 Joy - (1997 membership gift) - N. Pedley	Retrd.	1997	85.00	85
1997 Sir Henry Doulton S/S - W. Harper	Retrd.	1997	157.50	158
1998 Janet figure HN4042 - V. Annand	Yr.Iss.		275.00	275
1998 Richard III Jug - R. Tabbenor	Yr.Iss.		275.00	275
1998 Bunnykins Builds a Snowman plate - N/A	Yr.Iss.		60.00	60

Age of Innocence - N. Pedley

YEAR ISSUE	EDITION LIMIT	YEAR RETD.	ISSUE PRICE	*QUOTE U.S.$
1991 Feeding Time HN3373	9,500	1994	245.00	300-400
1992 First Outing HN3377	9,500	1994	275.00	300-390
1991 Making Friends HN3372	9,500	1994	270.00	325-390
1991 Puppy Love HN3371	9,500	1994	270.00	300-390

Angels Of Harmony - Royal Doulton

YEAR ISSUE	EDITION LIMIT	YEAR RETD.	ISSUE PRICE	*QUOTE U.S.$
1998 Angel of Autumn	Open		80.00	80
1998 Angel of Friendship	Open		80.00	80
1998 Angel of Love	Open		80.00	80
1998 Angel of Peace	Open		80.00	80
1998 Angel of Spring	Open		80.00	80
1998 Angel of Summer	Open		80.00	80
1998 Angel of Winter	Open		80.00	80
1998 Guardian Angel	Open		80.00	80

Beatrix Potter Figures - Various

YEAR ISSUE	EDITION LIMIT	YEAR RETD.	ISSUE PRICE	*QUOTE U.S.$
1967 Amiable Guinea Pig P2061 - A. Hallam	Retrd.	1983	29.95	325-450
1992 And This Pig Had None P3319 - M. Alcock	Retrd.	1998	29.95	36
1963 Anna Maria P1851 - A. Hallam	Retrd.	1983	29.95	395-450
1971 Appley Dapply P2333 - A. Hallam	Open		29.95	36
1970 Aunt Pettitoes P2276 - A. Hallam	Retrd.	1993	29.95	65-125
1989 Babbity Bumble P2971 - W. Platt	Retrd.	1993	29.95	95-150
1992 Benjamin Ate a Lettuce Leaf P3317 - M. Alcock	Retrd.	1998	29.95	36
1948 Benjamin Bunny P1105 - A. Gredington	Open		29.95	36
1983 Benjamin Bunny Sat on a Bank P2803 - D. Lyttleton	Retrd.	1997	29.95	35-45
1975 Benjamin Bunny with Peter Rabbit P2509 - A. Musiankowski	Retrd.	1995	39.95	95
1995 Benjamin Bunny, lg. P3403 - M. Alcock	Open		65.00	75
1991 Benjamin Wakes Up P3234 - A. Hughes-Lubeck	Retrd.	1997	29.95	35
1965 Cecily Parsley P1941 - A. Gredington	Retrd.	1993	29.95	95-125
1979 Chippy Hackee P2627 - D. Lyttleton	Retrd.	1993	29.95	65-85
1991 Christmas Stocking P3257 - M. Alcock	Retrd.	1994	65.00	95-175
1985 Cottontail at Lunchtime P2878 - D. Lyttleton	Retrd.	1996	29.95	33-45
1970 Cousin Ribby P2284 - A. Hallam	Retrd.	1993	29.95	55-75
1982 Diggory Diggory Delvet P2713 - D. Lyttleton	Retrd.	1997	29.95	35
1955 Dutchess w/Pie P1355 - G. Orwell	Retrd.	1967	29.95	150-350
1995 F.W. Gent, lg. P3450 - M. Alcock	Open		65.00	73
1977 Fierce Bad Rabbit P2586 - D. Lyttleton	Retrd.	1997	29.95	35
1954 Flopsy Mopsy and Cottontail P1274 - A. Gredington	Retrd.	1997	29.95	35
1990 Foxy Reading Country News P3219 - A. Hughes-Lubeck	Retrd.	1997	49.95	58-75
1954 Foxy Whiskered Gentleman P1277 - A. Gredington	Open		29.95	36
1990 Gentleman Mouse Made a Bow P3200 - T. Chawner	Retrd.	1996	29.95	33
1976 Ginger P2559 - D. Lyttleton	Retrd.	1982	29.95	550-695
1986 Goody and Timmy Tiptoes P2957 - D. Lyttleton	Retrd.	1996	49.95	65
1961 Goody Tiptoes P1675 - A. Gredington	Retrd.	1997	29.95	45
1998 Hiding From the Cat P3766 - G. Tongue	3,500		195.00	195
1951 Hunca Munca P1198 - A. Gredington	Open		29.95	36
1992 Hunca Munca Spills the Beads P3288 - M. Alcock	Retrd.	1996	29.95	85-95
1977 Hunca Munca Sweeping P2584 - D. Lyttleton	Open		29.95	36
1990 Jemema Puddleduck-Foxy Whiskered Gentleman P3193 - T. Chawner	Open		55.00	58
1998 Jemima Puddleduck and her Ducklings P3786 - M. Alcock	Open		60.00	60
1983 Jemima Puddleduck Made a Feather Nest-P2823 - D. Lyttleton	Retrd.	1997	29.95	36
1948 Jemima Puddleduck P1092 - A. Gredington	Open		29.95	36
1993 Jemima Puddleduck, lg. P3373 - M. Alcock	Retrd.	1997	49.95	75
1988 Jeremy Fisher Digging P3090 - T. Chawner	Retrd.	1994	50.00	100-225
1995 Jeremy Fisher lg. P3372 - M. Alcock	Retrd.	1997	65.00	75
1950 Jeremy Fisher P1157 - A. Gredington	Open		29.95	36
1990 John Joiner P2965 - G. Tongue	Retrd.	1997	29.95	35-65
1954 Johnny Townmouse P1276 - A. Gredington	Retrd.	1993	29.95	75
1988 Johnny Townmouse w/Bag P3094 - T. Chawner	Retrd.	1994	50.00	250
1990 Lady Mouse Made a Curtsy P3220 - A. Hughes-Lubeck	Retrd.	1997	29.95	35-65
1950 Lady Mouse P1183 - A. Gredington	Open		29.95	36
1977 Little Black Rabbit P2585 - D. Lyttleton	Retrd.	1997	29.95	36
1987 Little Pig Robinson Spying P3031 - T. Chawner	Retrd.	1993	29.95	100-225
1991 Miss Dormouse P3251 - M. Alcock	Retrd.	1995	29.95	75-95
1978 Miss Moppet P1275 - A. Gredington	Open		32.50	36
1990 Mittens & Moppet P3197 - T. Chawner	Retrd.	1994	50.00	75-95
1989 Mother Ladybird P2966 - W. Platt	Retrd.	1996	29.95	33
1973 Mr. Alderman Ptolemy P2424 - G. Tongue	Retrd.	1997	29.95	35
1965 Mr. Benjamin Bunny P1940 - A. Gredington	Open		29.95	36
1979 Mr. Drake Puddleduck P2628 - D. Lyttleton	Open		29.95	36
1974 Mr. Jackson P2453 - A. Hallam	Retrd.	1997	29.95	36
1995 Mr. McGregor P3506 - M. Alcock	Open		42.50	45
1988 Mr. Tod P3091 - T. Chawner	Retrd.	1993	29.95	110-165
1965 Mrs. Flopsy Bunny P1942 - A. Gredington	Open		29.95	36
1997 Mrs. Rabbit and Peter P3646 - W. Platt	Open		67.50	68
1997 Mrs. Rabbit and the Four Bunnies P3672 - S. Ridge	1,997	1997	275.00	275
1992 Mrs. Rabbit Cooking P3278 - M. Alcock	Open		29.95	36
1951 Mrs. Rabbit P1200 - A. Gredington	Open		29.95	36
1976 Mrs. Rabbit with Bunnies P2543 - D. Lyttleton	Retrd.	1997	29.95	35
1995 Mrs. Rabbit, lg. P3398 - M. Alcock	Retrd.	1997	65.00	75
1951 Mrs. Ribby P1199 - A. Gredington	Open		29.95	36
1998 Mrs. Tiggy-winkle Washing P3789 - W. Platt	Open		38.00	38
1997 Mrs. Tiggywinkle, lg. P3437 - M. Alcock	Retrd.	1997	75.00	75
1948 Mrs. Tittlemouse P1103 - A. Gredington	Retrd.	1993	29.95	50-110
1992 No More Twist P3325 - M. Alcock	Retrd.	1997	29.95	35-65
1986 Old Mr. Bouncer P2956 - D. Lyttleton	Retrd.	1995	29.95	85-100
1963 Old Mr. Brown P1796 - A. Hallam	Open		29.95	36
1983 Old Mr. Pricklepin P2767 - D. Lyttleton	Retrd.	1982	29.95	95-195
1959 Old Woman Who Lived in a Shoe P1545 - C. Melbourne	Retrd.	1997	29.95	35
1983 Old Woman Who Lived in a Shoe, Knitting P2804 - D. Lyttleton	Open		29.95	36
1991 Peter & The Red Handkerchief P3242 - M. Alcock	Retrd.	1997	39.95	45
1995 Peter in Bed P3473 - M. Alcock	Open		39.95	45
1989 Peter Rabbit in the Gooseberry Net P3157 - D. Lyttleton	Retrd.	1995	39.95	60-75
1948 Peter Rabbit P1098 - A. Gredington	Open		29.95	36
1993 Peter Rabbit, lg. P3356 - M. Alcock	Retrd.	1997	65.00	75
1996 Peter with Daffodils P3597 - A. Hughes-Lubeck	Open		42.50	45
1996 Peter with Postbag P3591 - A. Hughes-Lubeck	Open		42.50	45
1996 Peter with Red Pocket Handkerchief, lg. P3592 - A. Hughes-Lubeck	Open		75.00	75
1971 Pickles P2334 - A. Hallam	Retrd.	1982	29.95	500-650
1948 Pig Robinson P1104 - A. Gredington	Open		29.95	36
1972 Pig Wig P2381 - A. Hallam	Retrd.	1982	29.95	450-500
1955 Pigling Bland P1365 - G. Orwell	Open		29.95	36
1991 Pigling Eats Porridge P3252 - M. Alcock	Retrd.	1994	50.00	50-95
1976 Poorly Peter Rabbit P2560 - D. Lyttleton	Retrd.	1997	29.95	35-45
1981 Rebeccah Puddleduck P2647 - D. Lyttleton	Open		29.95	36
1992 Ribby and the Patty Pan P3280 - M. Alcock	Retrd.	1998	29.95	36
1974 Sally Henry Penney P2452 - A. Hallam	Retrd.	1993	29.95	95-125
1948 Samuel Whiskers P1106 - A. Gredington	Retrd.	1995	29.95	95
1975 Simpkin P2508 - A. Maslankowski	Retrd.	1983	29.95	650-695
1973 Sir Isaac Newton P2425 - G. Tongue	Retrd.	1984	29.95	350-450
1948 Squirrel Nutkin P1102 - A. Gredington	Open		29.95	36
1961 Tabitha Twitchitt P1676 - A. Gredington	Retrd.	1995	29.95	45-50
1976 Tabitha Twitchitt with Miss Moppett P2544 - D. Lyttleton	Retrd.	1993	29.95	125
1949 Tailor of Gloucester P1108 - A. Gredington	Open		29.95	36
1995 Tailor of Gloucester, lg. P3449 - M. Alcock	Retrd.	1997	65.00	75
1948 Tiggy Winkle P1107 - A. Gredington	Open		29.95	36
1985 Tiggy Winkle Takes Tea P2877 - D. Lyttleton	Open		29.95	36
1948 Timmy Tiptoes P1101 - A. Gredington	Retrd.	1997	29.95	35
1949 Timmy Willie P1109 - A. Gredington	Retrd.	1993	29.95	60-195
1986 Timmy Willie Sleeping P2996 - G. Tongue	Retrd.	1996	29.95	33
1948 Tom Kitten P1100 - A. Gredington	Open		29.95	36
1995 Tom Kitten, lg. P3405 - M. Alcock	Retrd.	1997	65.00	75
1987 Tom Kittten and Butterfly P3030 - T. Chawner	Retrd.	1994	50.00	190-225
1987 Tom Thumb P2989 - W. Platt	Retrd.	1997	29.95	35-50
1955 Tommy Brock P1348 - G. Orwell	Open		29.95	36

British Sporting Heritage - V. Annand

YEAR ISSUE	EDITION LIMIT	YEAR RETD.	ISSUE PRICE	*QUOTE U.S.$
1994 Ascot HN3471	5,000	1997	475.00	475
1996 Croquet HN3470	5,000	1997	475.00	475
1993 Henley HN3367	5,000	1997	475.00	475
1995 Wimbledon HN3366	5,000	1997	475.00	475

Bunnykins - Various

YEAR ISSUE	EDITION LIMIT	YEAR RETD.	ISSUE PRICE	*QUOTE U.S.$
1995 Bathtime DB148 - M. Alcock	Retrd.	1997	40.00	42
1987 Be Prepared DB56 - D. Lyttleton	Retrd.	1995	40.00	40-65
1987 Bed Time DB55 - D. Lyttleton	Retrd.	1998	40.00	45
1995 Boy Skater DB152 - M. Alcock	Retrd.	1998	40.00	45
1991 Bride DB101 - A. Hughes	Open		40.00	45
1987 Brownie DB61 - W. Platt	Retrd.	1993	39.00	65-85
1994 Christmas Surprise DB146 - W. Platt	Open		50.00	55
1990 Cook DB85 - W. Platt	Retrd.	1994	35.00	75-85
1998 Doctor Bunnykins DB181 - M. Alcock	Open		45.00	45
1995 Easter Greetings - M. Alcock	Open		50.00	55
1996 Father Bunnykin DB154 - M. Alcock	Retrd.	1996	50.00	70-75
1988 Father, Mother, Victoria DB68 - M. Alcock	Retrd.	1995	40.00	40
1989 Fireman DB75 - M. Alcock	Open		40.00	45
1998 Fisherman - S. Ridge	Open		52.50	52
1990 Fisherman DB84 - W. Platt	Retrd.	1993	39.00	95-125
1996 Gardener DB156 - W. Platt	Retrd.	1998	40.00	45
1995 Girl Skater DB153 - M. Alcock	Retrd.	1997	40.00	42
1995 Goodnight DB157 - S. Ridge	Open		40.00	45
1991 Groom DB102 - M. Alcock	Open		40.00	45
1993 Halloween Bunnykin DB132 - M. Alcock	Retrd.	1997	50.00	53
1983 Happy Birthday DB21 - G. Tongue	Retrd.	1997	40.00	45
1988 Harry DB73 - M. Alcock	Retrd.	1993	34.00	55-95
1972 Helping Mother DB2 - A. Hallam	Retrd.	1993	34.00	75-95
1986 Home Run DB43 - D. Lyttleton	Retrd.	1993	39.00	95-150
1990 Ice Cream DB82 - W. Platt	Retrd.	1993	39.00	75
1997 Mother and Baby DB167 - S. Ridge	Open		42.00	45
1996 Mother's Day DB155 - S. Ridge	Open		42.00	45
1986 Mr. Bunnykins "At The Easter Parade" (maroon jacket) DB51 - D. Lyttleton	Yr.Iss.	1986	40.00	700-1125
1982 Mr. Bunnykins "At The Easter Parade" (red jacket) DB18 - G. Tongue	Retrd.	1993	39.00	65-125
1982 Mrs. Bunnykin "At The Easter Parade" (pink dress) DB52 - D. Lyttleton	Yr.Iss.	1986	40.00	700-1500
1982 Mrs. Bunnykins "At The Easter Parade" (blue dress) DB19 - D. Lyttleton	Retrd.	1996	40.00	65-125
1995 New Baby DB158 - G. Tongue	Open		40.00	45
1989 Nurse DB74 - M. Alcock	Open		35.00	45
1989 Paper Boy DB77 - M. Alcock	Retrd.	1993	39.00	65-85
1972 Playtime DB8 - A. Hallam	Retrd.	1993	34.00	55-75
1988 Policeman DB69 - M. Alcock	Open		40.00	45
1988 Polly DB71 - M. Alcock	Retrd.	1993	34.00	65-85
1995 Rainy Day DB147 - M. Alcock	Retrd.	1997	40.00	42-45
1997 Sailor Bunnykins DB166 - S. Ridge	Yr.Iss.	1997	52.50	55
1981 Santa Bunnykins DB17 - D. Lyttleton	Retrd.	1995	40.00	85-125
1987 School Days DB57 - D. Lyttleton	Retrd.	1994	40.00	75
1982 School Master DB60 - W. Platt	Retrd.	1995	40.00	40-65
1974 Sleepytime DB15 - A. Maslankowski	Retrd.	1993	39.00	65-75
1972 Sleigh Ride DB4 - A. Hallam	Retrd.	1997	40.00	42-85
1972 Story Time DB9 - A. Hallam	Retrd.	1997	35.00	42
1988 Susan DB70 - M. Alcock	Retrd.	1993	34.00	60-75

*Quotes have been rounded up to nearest dollar

YEAR ISSUE	EDITION LIMIT	YEAR RETD.	ISSUE PRICE	*QUOTE U.S.$
1992 Sweetheart Bunnykin DB130 - W. Platt	Retrd.	1997	40.00	42-55
1988 Tom DB72 - M. Alcock	Retrd.	1993	34.00	60-75
1986 Uncle Sam DB50 - D. Lyttleton	Open		40.00	45
1988 William DB69 - M. Alcock	Retrd.	1993	34.00	75-110

Bunnykins-Figure of the Year - M. Alcock

YEAR ISSUE	EDITION LIMIT	YEAR RETD.	ISSUE PRICE	*QUOTE U.S.$
1998 Seaside Bunnykins	Yr.Iss.		55.00	55

Character Sculptures - Various

YEAR ISSUE	EDITION LIMIT	YEAR RETD.	ISSUE PRICE	*QUOTE U.S.$
1996 Bill Sikes HN3785 - A. Dobson	Retrd.	1996	306.25	307
1996 Bowls Player HN3780 - J. Jones	Retrd.	1996	137.50	138
1993 Captain Hook - R. Tabbenor	Retrd.	1996	250.00	270-325
1995 Cyrano de Bergerac HN3751 - D. Biggs	Retrd.	1996	268.75	269
1994 D' Artagnan - R. Tabbenor	Retrd.	1996	260.00	269
1993 Dick Turpin - R. Tabbenor	Retrd.	1996	250.00	269
1995 Fagin HN3752 - A. Dobson	Retrd.	1996	268.75	269
1995 Gulliver - D. Biggs	Retrd.	1996	285.00	307
1993 Long John Silver - A. Maslankowski	Retrd.	1996	250.00	269
1996 Oliver Twist and Artful Dodger HN3786 - A. Dobson	Retrd.	1996	275.00	275
1994 Pied Piper - A. Maslankowski	Retrd.	1996	260.00	269
1993 Robin Hood - A. Maslankowski	Retrd.	1996	250.00	269
1995 Sherlock Holmes HN3639 - R. Tabbenor	Retrd.	1996	268.75	269
1996 Sir Francis Drake HN3770 - D. Biggs	Retrd.	1996	275.00	275
1995 Wizard HN3722 - A. Maslankowski	Retrd.	1996	306.25	307-330

Charity Figure of the Year - Various

YEAR ISSUE	EDITION LIMIT	YEAR RETD.	ISSUE PRICE	*QUOTE U.S.$
1998 Hope - N. Pedley	Yr.Iss.		225.00	225

Classique - Royal Doulton

YEAR ISSUE	EDITION LIMIT	YEAR RETD.	ISSUE PRICE	*QUOTE U.S.$
1998 Christina	Open		195.00	195
1998 Faye CL3984	Open		175.00	175
1998 Felicity CL3986	Open		175.00	175
1998 From This Day Forth CL3990	Open		175.00	175
1998 Helena	Open		175.00	175
1998 Isobel CL3890	Open		175.00	175
1998 Lucinda CL3983	Open		175.00	175
1998 Naomi	Open		225.00	225
1998 Vanessa CL3989	Open		175.00	175

Diamond Anniversary Tinies - Various

YEAR ISSUE	EDITION LIMIT	YEAR RETD.	ISSUE PRICE	*QUOTE U.S.$
1994 John Barleycorn - C. Noke	2,500	1994	350.00	450-500
1994 Simon The Cellarer - Noke/Fenton	2,500	1994	set	Set
1994 Dick Turpin - W. Harper	2,500	1994	set	Set
1994 Granny - W. Harper	2,500	1994	set	Set
1994 Jester - C. Noke	2,500	1994	set	Set
1994 Parson Brown - W. Harper	2,500	1994	set	Set

Femmes Fatales - P. Davies

YEAR ISSUE	EDITION LIMIT	YEAR RETD.	ISSUE PRICE	*QUOTE U.S.$
1979 Cleopatra HN2868	750	1995	750.00	1350
1984 Eve HN2466	750	1995	1250.00	1300-1500
1981 Helen of Troy HN2387	750	1993	1250.00	1400-1600
1985 Lucrezia Borgia HN2342	750	1993	1250.00	1300-1500
1982 Queen of Sheba HN2328	750	1996	1250.00	1300-1600
1983 Tz'u-Hsi HN2391	750	1996	1250.00	1300-1500

Figure of the Year - Various

YEAR ISSUE	EDITION LIMIT	YEAR RETD.	ISSUE PRICE	*QUOTE U.S.$
1991 Amy HN3316 - P. Gee	Closed	1991	195.00	650-700
1992 Mary HN3375 - P. Gee	Closed	1992	225.00	375-475
1993 Patricia HN3365 - V. Annand	Closed	1993	250.00	350-475
1994 Jennifer HN3447 - P. Gee	Closed	1994	250.00	300-375
1995 Deborah - HN3644 - N. Pedley	Closed	1995	225.00	225
1996 Belle HN3703 - V. Annand	Closed	1996	231.25	235
1997 Jessica HN3850 - N. Pedley	Closed	1997	245.00	245
1998 Rebecca HN4041 - V. Annand	Yr.Iss.		195.00	195

The Four Seasons - V. Annand

YEAR ISSUE	EDITION LIMIT	YEAR RETD.	ISSUE PRICE	*QUOTE U.S.$
1993 Springtime HN3477	Retrd.	1996	325.00	350
1994 Summertime HN3478	Retrd.	1996	325.00	350
1993 Autumntime HN3621	Retrd.	1996	325.00	350
1993 Wintertime HN3622	Retrd.	1996	325.00	350

Gainsborough Ladies - P. Gee

YEAR ISSUE	EDITION LIMIT	YEAR RETD.	ISSUE PRICE	*QUOTE U.S.$
1991 Countess of Sefton HN3010	5,000	1996	650.00	700
1991 Hon Frances Duncombe HN3009	5,000	1996	650.00	650-700
1991 Lady Sheffield HN3008	5,000	1996	650.00	650-700
1990 Mary, Countess Howe HN3007	5,000	1996	650.00	700

Great Lovers - R. Jefferson

YEAR ISSUE	EDITION LIMIT	YEAR RETD.	ISSUE PRICE	*QUOTE U.S.$
1995 Antony and Cleopatra HN3114	150	1997	5250.00	5250
1996 Lancelot and Guinevere HN3112	150	1997	5250.00	5250
1994 Robin Hood and Maid Marian HN3111	150	1997	5250.00	5250
1993 Romeo and Juliet HN3113	150	1997	5250.00	5250

Images - Various

YEAR ISSUE	EDITION LIMIT	YEAR RETD.	ISSUE PRICE	*QUOTE U.S.$
1997 Amen HN4021 - D. Tootle	Open		55.00	55
1997 Angel HN3940 - A. Maslankowski	Open		125.00	125
1997 The Ballerina HN3828 - D. Tootle	Open		95.00	95
1998 The Ballet Dancer HN4027 - D. Tootle	Open		110.00	110
1998 Ballet Lesson HN4028 - D. Tootle	Open		110.00	110
1991 Bride & Groom HN3281 - R. Tabbenor	Open		85.00	99
1991 Bridesmaid HN3280 - R. Tabbenor	Open		85.00	99
1993 Brother & Sister HN3460 - A. Hughes	Open		52.50	112
1991 Brothers HN3191 - E. Griffiths	Open		90.00	112
1981 Family HN2720 - E. Griffiths	Open		187.50	215
1988 First Love HN2747 - D. Tootle	Retrd.	1997	170.00	215
1991 First Steps HN3282 - R. Tabbenor	Open		142.00	215
1993 Gift of Freedom HN3443 - N/A	Open		90.00	112
1997 Graduation HN3942 - A. Maslankowski	Open		125.00	125
1989 Happy Anniversary HN3254 - D. Tootle	Open		187.50	215
1997 Happy Birthday HN3829 - D. Tootle	Open		95.00	95
1981 Lovers HN2762 - D. Tootle	Retrd.	1997	187.50	215
1997 The Messiah HN3952 - A. Maslankowski	Open		145.00	145
1980 Mother & Daughter HN2841 - E. Griffiths	Retrd.	1997	187.50	215
1997 Mother and Child HN3938 - A. Maslankowski	Open		125.00	125
1998 Night Watch (Owls) HN3895 - R. Tabbenor	Open		70.00	70
1993 Our First Christmas HN3452 - N/A	Retrd.	1998	185.00	215
1989 Over the Threshold HN3274 - R. Tabbenor	Retrd.	1998	187.50	215
1997 The Performance HN3827 - D. Tootle	Open		235.00	235
1983 Sisters HN3018 - P. Parson	Open		90.00	112
1987 Wedding Day HN2748 - D. Tootle	Open		187.50	215

Jody's Dreamkeepers - J. Bergsma

YEAR ISSUE	EDITION LIMIT	YEAR RETD.	ISSUE PRICE	*QUOTE U.S.$
1998 The Best Thing About Mom Is Everything	Open		20.00	20
1998 Happiness Is Made To Be Shared	Open		25.00	25
1998 Home Is Where The Heart Is	Open		30.00	30
1998 A Home Without A Dog Is Just A House	Open		15.00	15
1998 Life Is Best...Just Putting Around!	Open		20.00	20
1998 May All Our Hearts Beat As One	Open		35.00	35
1998 May Your Heart Be Filled With Simple Joys	Open		20.00	20
1998 The Memories Of Christmas	Yr.Iss.		40.00	40
1998 Never Let Go Of Your Dreams	Open		20.00	20
1998 Of All The Treasures In Life, Friendship Is The Greatest	Open		30.00	30
1998 The Purpose Of Life Is To Celebrate Living	Open		50.00	50
1998 Reach Out For The Impossible	Open		75.00	75
1998 Simple Pleasures Are The Treasures Of Life	Open		20.00	20
1998 There Are Very Few...As Special As You	Open		30.00	30
1998 To Be A Child Is To Know The Joy Of Living	Open		50.00	50
1998 We Are Always On Our Way To A Miracle	Open		20.00	20
1998 We Never Outgrow Our Need For Hugs	Open		15.00	15
1998 When I Count By Blessings, I Count You Twice	Open		20.00	20
1998 When You Need A Friend You Can Count On Me	Open		25.00	25
1998 The Work Is Hard, But The Reward Is Great	Open		15.00	15

Limited Edition Figurines - Various

YEAR ISSUE	EDITION LIMIT	YEAR RETD.	ISSUE PRICE	*QUOTE U.S.$
1992 Christopher Columbus HN3392 - A. Maslankowski	1,492	1995	1950.00	1950
1993 Duke of Wellington HN3432 - A. Maslankowski	1,500	1998	1750.00	1750
1996 Eastern Grace Flambe HN3683 - P. Parsons	2,500	1996	493.75	520
1994 Field Marshal Montgomery HN3405 - N/A	1,944	1996	1100.00	1100
1993 General Robert E. Lee HN3404 - R. Tabbenor	5,000	1995	1175.00	1175
1997 HM Queen Elizabeth, The Queen Mother HN3944 - A. Maslankowski	5,000	1998	635.00	635
1993 Lt. General Ulysses S. Grant HN3403 - R. Tabbenor	5,000	1995	1175.00	1175
1992 Napoleon at Waterloo HN3429 - A. Maslankowski	1,500	1994	1900.00	1900
1992 Samurai Warrior HN3402 - R. Tabbenor	950	1995	500.00	500
1997 Sir Henry Doulton HN3891 - R. Tabbenor	1,997		430.00	450
1997 Top o' the Hill Blue HN 3735 - L. Harradine	3,500		370.00	370
1993 Vice Admiral Lord Nelson HN3489 - A. Maslankowski	950	1996	1750.00	1750
1993 Winston S. Churchill HN3433 - A. Maslankowski	5,000		595.00	595

Myths & Maidens - R. Jefferson

YEAR ISSUE	EDITION LIMIT	YEAR RETD.	ISSUE PRICE	*QUOTE U.S.$
1986 Diana The Huntress HN2829	300	1990	2950.00	3000
1985 Europa & Bull HN2828	300	1990	2950.00	3000
1984 Juno & Peacock HN2827	300	1990	2950.00	3000
1982 Lady & Unicorn HN2825	300	1990	2500.00	2500
1983 Leda & Swan HN2826	300	1990	2950.00	3000

Old Bear And Friends - J. Hissey

YEAR ISSUE	EDITION LIMIT	YEAR RETD.	ISSUE PRICE	*QUOTE U.S.$
1998 Bramwell Brown Has a Good Idea	Open		20.00	20
1998 Don't Worry Rabbit	Open		20.00	20
1998 Long Red Scarf	Open		29.00	29
1998 Old Bear	Open		15.00	15
1998 Ruff's Price	Open		21.50	22
1998 Snowflake Biscuits	Open		29.00	29
1998 Time For A Cuddle, Hug Me Tight	Open		20.00	20
1998 Time For Bed	Open		25.00	25
1998 Waiting For Snow	Open		25.00	25
1998 Welcome Home, Old Bear	Open		21.50	22

Prestige Figures - Various

YEAR ISSUE	EDITION LIMIT	YEAR RETD.	ISSUE PRICE	*QUOTE U.S.$
1996 Charge of the Light Brigade HN3718 - A. Maslankowski	Open		17500.00	17500
1982 Columbine HN2738 - D. Tootle	Open		1250.00	1375
1982 Harlequin HN2737 - D. Tootle	Open		1250.00	1375
1964 Indian Brave HN2376 - M. Davis	500	1993	2500.00	5500
1952 Jack Point HN2080 - C.J. Noke	Open		2900.00	3400
1950 King Charles HN2084 - C.J. Noke	Open		2500.00	2500
1964 Matador and Bull HN2324 - M. Davis	Open		21500.00	25200
1952 The Moor HN2082 - C.J. Noke	Open		2500.00	3000
1964 The Palio HN2428 - M. Davis	500	1993	2500.00	6500
1952 Princess Badoura HN2081 - H. Stanton	Open		28000.00	33000
1978 St George and Dragon HN2856 - W.K. Harper	Open		13600.00	14500

Queens of Realm - P. Parsons

YEAR ISSUE	EDITION LIMIT	YEAR RETD.	ISSUE PRICE	*QUOTE U.S.$
1989 Mary, Queen of Scots HN3142	S/O	1992	550.00	850-900
1988 Queen Anne HN3141	S/O	1992	525.00	600-800
1986 Queen Elizabeth I HN3099	S/O	1992	495.00	650-1100
1987 Queen Victoria HN3125	S/O	1992	495.00	1100-1500
1987 Set of 4	S/O	1992	2065.00	3000-3450

Reynolds Collection - P. Gee

YEAR ISSUE	EDITION LIMIT	YEAR RETD.	ISSUE PRICE	*QUOTE U.S.$
1992 Countess Harrington HN3317	5,000	1995	550.00	595
1993 Countess Spencer HN3320	5,000	1995	595.00	550-595
1991 Lady Worsley HN3318	5,000	1995	550.00	595
1992 Mrs. Hugh Bonfoy HN3319	5,000	1995	550.00	595

Romance Of Literature - P. Parsons

YEAR ISSUE	EDITION LIMIT	YEAR RETD.	ISSUE PRICE	*QUOTE U.S.$
1998 Elizabeth Bennet	3,500		350.00	350
1998 Emma	3,500		375.00	375
1998 Jane Eyre	3,500		375.00	375
1998 Tess of the D'Urbervilles	3,500		350.00	350

Royal Doulton Figurines - Various

YEAR ISSUE	EDITION LIMIT	YEAR RETD.	ISSUE PRICE	*QUOTE U.S.$
1933 Beethoven HN1778 - R. Garbe	25	1935	N/A	6500
1975 The Jersey Milkmaid HN2057A - L. Harradine	Closed	1981	N/A	225
1987 Life Boatman HN2764 - W. Harper	Closed	1991	N/A	250-350
1929 Tony Weller HN1315 - L. Harradine	Open		250.00	250
1924 Tony Weller HN684 - C. Noke	Closed	1938	N/A	1800

Royalty - Various

YEAR ISSUE	EDITION LIMIT	YEAR RETD.	ISSUE PRICE	*QUOTE U.S.$
1986 Duchess Of York HN3086 - E. Griffiths	1,500	1987	495.00	650
1981 Duke Of Edinburgh HN2386 - P. Davis	750	1982	395.00	450
1982 Lady Diana Spencer HN2885 - E. Griffiths	1,500	1982	395.00	700-2000
1981 Prince Of Wales HN2883 - E. Griffiths	1,500	1982	395.00	450-650
1981 Prince Of Wales HN2884 - E. Griffiths	1,500	1982	750.00	1000
1982 Princess Of Wales HN2887 - E. Griffiths	1,500	1982	750.00	1700-2650
1997 Queen Elizabeth II & Duke of Edinburgh HN3836 - P. Parsons	750		650.00	650
1973 Queen Elizabeth II HN2502 - P. Davis	750	1975	N/A	1800
1982 Queen Elizabeth II HN2878 - E. Griffiths	2,500	1984	N/A	450-800
1992 Queen Elizabeth II, 2nd. Version HN3440 - P. Gee	3,500	1994	460.00	460
1989 Queen Elizabeth, the Queen Mother as the Duchess of York HN3230 - P. Parsons	9,500	1990	N/A	450
1990 Queen Elizabeth, the Queen Mother HN3189 - E. Griffiths	2,500	1992	N/A	450-700
1980 Queen Mother HN2882 - E. Griffiths	1,500	1983	650.00	1250

Triumphs Of The Heart - J. Griffin

YEAR ISSUE	EDITION LIMIT	YEAR RETD.	ISSUE PRICE	*QUOTE U.S.$
1998 Forever Yours	Open		150.00	150
1998 Love Conquers All	Open		150.00	150
1998 Loveswept	Open		150.00	150
1998 My Beloved	Open		150.00	150
1998 Only You	Open		150.00	150
1998 Sweet Embrace	Open		150.00	150

San Francisco Music Box Company

American Treasures Historical Reproduction Musical Carousel Collection - San Francisco Music Box Company

YEAR ISSUE	EDITION LIMIT	YEAR RETD.	ISSUE PRICE	*QUOTE U.S.$
1997 Dentzel Tiger	4,500		59.95	60
1997 Dentzel/Cernigliaro Giraffe	4,500		59.95	60
1997 Dentzel/Cernigliaro Lion	4,500		59.95	60
1997 Herschell-Spillman Hop Toad	4,500		59.95	60
1997 Looff Jumper Horse	4,500		84.95	85
1997 M.C. Illions American Beauty Horse	4,500		84.95	85
1997 Muller Eagle Horse	4,500		84.95	85
1997 PTC Armored Horse	4,500		84.95	85

Boyds Bears Musical Bearstone Figurines - G.M. Lowenthal

YEAR ISSUE	EDITION LIMIT	YEAR RETD.	ISSUE PRICE	*QUOTE U.S.$
1998 20th Anniversary Grace & Jonathon Born to Shop (1st ed.)	3,600		45.00	45
1997 Amelia's Enterprise (1st ed.)	1,512	1998	44.95	45
1997 Amelia's Enterprise (2nd ed.)	2,508		44.95	45
1995 Arthur on Trunk (1st ed.)	597	1997	39.95	69-75
1995 Arthur on Trunk (2nd ed.)	504		39.95	40
1996 Bailey & Emily (1st ed.)	779	1998	44.95	65-92
1996 Bailey & Emily (2nd ed.)	612		44.95	45
1998 Bailey Honey Bear (1st ed.)	3,600		44.95	45
1998 Bailey Honey Bear (2nd ed.)	3,000		44.95	45
1996 Bailey with Suitcase (1st ed.)	755	1998	39.95	40-75
1996 Bailey with Suitcase (2nd ed.)	600		39.95	40
1997 Bailey's Birthday (1st ed.)	3,600		44.95	45
1997 Bailey's Birthday (2nd ed.)	2,004		44.95	45
1998 Bailey's Heart Desire (1st ed.)	3,600		45.00	45
1996 Clarence Angel (1st ed.)	1,180	1998	39.95	40
1996 Clarence Angel (2nd ed.)	1,608		39.95	40
1997 The Collector (1st ed.)	3,600		49.95	50

*Quotes have been rounded up to nearest dollar

YEAR ISSUE	EDITION LIMIT	YEAR RETD.	ISSUE PRICE	*QUOTE U.S.$
1997 The Collector (2nd ed.)	4,056		49.95	50
1997 Daphne & Eloise (1st ed.)	1,512	1998	44.95	45
1997 Daphne & Eloise (2nd ed.)	2,520		44.95	45
1999 Elliot Hero Waterglobe (1st ed.)	3,600		45.00	45
1996 Emma & Bailey Tea Party Waterglobe (1st ed.)	1,162	1998	44.95	69-86
1996 Emma & Bailey Tea Party Waterglobe (2nd ed.)	304		44.95	45
1998 Grenville & Beatrice True Love Waterglobe (1st ed.)	3,600		44.95	45
1998 Grenville & Beatrice True Love Waterglobe (2nd ed.)	2,500		44.95	45
1997 Homer on Plate Waterglobe (1st ed.)	1,500		44.95	45
1997 Homer on Plate Waterglobe (2nd ed.)	3,504		44.95	45
1998 Justina Message Bearer (1st ed.)	3,600		44.95	45
1998 Justina Message Bearer (2nd ed.)	2,800		44.95	45
1998 Kringle & Co. Waterglobe (1st ed.)	3,600		45.00	45
1996 Miss Bruin & Bailey (1st ed.)	1,178	1998	44.95	45-75
1996 Miss Bruin & Bailey (2nd ed.)	1,512		44.95	45
1996 Nelville Bedtime (1st ed.)	768	1998	39.95	58-65
1996 Nelville Bedtime (2nd ed.)	504		39.95	40
1998 Neville Compubear (1st ed.)	3,600		44.95	45
1998 Neville Compubear (2nd ed.)	2,200		44.95	45
1997 The Secret (1st ed.)	3,600		49.95	50
1997 The Secret (2nd ed.)	2,016		49.95	50
1995 Ted & Teddy Waterglobe (1st ed.)	593	1997	39.95	45-86
1995 Ted & Teddy Waterglobe (2nd ed.)	N/A		39.95	40
1995 Wilson with Love Sonnets (1st ed.)	535	1997	39.95	82-88
1995 Wilson with Love Sonnets (2nd ed.)	768		39.95	40

Boyds Bears Musical Dollstone Figurines - G.M. Lowenthal

YEAR ISSUE	EDITION LIMIT	YEAR RETD.	ISSUE PRICE	*QUOTE U.S.$
1998 Wash Day (1st ed.)	3,600		45.00	45

Charming Tails Musicals - D. Griff

YEAR ISSUE	EDITION LIMIT	YEAR RETD.	ISSUE PRICE	*QUOTE U.S.$
1996 After Lunch Snooze	Closed	1996	40.00	56
1996 Getting To Know You	Closed	1996	40.00	55
1996 Spring Flowers	Closed	1996	40.00	57
1996 That's What Friends Are For	Closed	1996	40.00	55

Heart Tugs Musical Collection - M. Danko

YEAR ISSUE	EDITION LIMIT	YEAR RETD.	ISSUE PRICE	*QUOTE U.S.$
1998 20th Anniversary - "Old Friendships are the Best"	2,500		35.00	35
1998 Mother in Shoe - "Mother Means Love" (1st ed.)	3,600		35.00	35
1998 Pie Safe - "Friendship is Homemade"	6,000		49.95	50
1998 Swing - "Two Hearts Together" (1st ed.)	3,600		35.00	35
1997 Tea Time - "Forever Friends"	6,000		49.95	50
1998 Teatime - "Friends are a Joy Forever" (1st ed.)	3,600		35.00	35
1998 Toy Chest - "Sharing Begins in the Heart" (1st ed.)	3,600		50.00	50
1998 Wash Day - "Home is Where you Hang Your Heart" (1st ed.)	3,600		35.00	35

Musical Carousel Collection - M. Drdak, unless otherwise noted

YEAR ISSUE	EDITION LIMIT	YEAR RETD.	ISSUE PRICE	*QUOTE U.S.$
1998 The American Treasures™ 12-Animal Merry-Go-Round - Team	5,000		500.00	500
1998 The American Treasures™ 6-horse Carousel - Team	5,000		299.00	299
1999 Arabesque Horse, 8" - E. Kamysz	4,500		85.00	85
1998 Baroque Horse - P. Fulton	4,500		85.00	85
1998 Baroque Horse with Canopy - P. Fulton	5,000		65.00	65
1999 Florentine Horse, 8"	4,500		85.00	85
1999 Florentine Single Horse with Canopy	5,000		85.00	85
1997 Gardenia Horse with Canopy	4,000	1998	99.95	100
1998 Jewels of the Empire Jade Porcelain 6-horse Carousel	5,000		199.00	199
1997 Les Fleurs D'Amour 6-horse Carousel - Team	5,000		299.00	299
1999 Lily Double Horse with Canopy	4,000		100.00	100
1999 Lily Horse, 8"	4,500		85.00	85
1999 Lily Single Horse with Canopy	5,000		85.00	85
1998 Renaissance Horse with Canopy	5,000		85.00	85
1999 Royal Crest Double 6-horse Carousel - Team	5,000		299.00	299
1999 Royal Crest Double Horse with Canopy - Team	4,000		100.00	100
1999 Royal Crest Horse, 10" - Team	3,000		100.00	100
1997 Savannah Horse with Canopy - N. Bailey	5,000	1998	84.95	85
1998 Sultan's Dream 6-horse Carousel	5,000		299.00	299
1998 Sultan's Dream Double Horse with Canopy	4,000		100.00	100
1998 Sultan's Dream Horse, 12"	2,500		125.00	125
1998 Sultan's Dream Horse, 8"	4,500		85.00	85
1997 Venetian Rose Horse	4,500	1998	84.95	85
1997 Venetian Rose Horse with Canopy	5,000	1998	84.95	85

Musical Goose Eggs - V. Damann, unless otherwise noted

YEAR ISSUE	EDITION LIMIT	YEAR RETD.	ISSUE PRICE	*QUOTE U.S.$
1998 20th Anniversary	300		200.00	200
1998 Blue Pansies	300		165.00	165
1997 Coach	300	1998	450.00	450
1998 Coach with Crown - R. Egg	700		495.00	495
1997 Mauve Cherub	300	1998	195.00	195
1997 Purple Pansies	300	1998	160.00	160
1997 Roses	300	1998	160.00	160
1998 Silvery Blue	500		200.00	200
1997 Velvet Romance Carousel - K. Johnson	1,000	1998	240.00	240

National Geographic Musical Figurines - M. Adams, unless otherwise noted

YEAR ISSUE	EDITION LIMIT	YEAR RETD.	ISSUE PRICE	*QUOTE U.S.$
1998 African Lion Family	7,500		125.00	125
1998 Baby Chickadee	7,500		50.00	50
1998 Bald Eagle	7,500		100.00	100
1999 Dolphin	7,500		100.00	100
1998 Gray Wolf Pup	7,500		50.00	50
1998 Gray Wolves	7,500		85.00	85
1998 Lion Cub	7,500		50.00	50
1998 Mayan Jaguar - J. Kissling	7,500		90.00	90
1998 Mom & Baby Giraffe	7,500		50.00	50
1998 Mom & Baby Panda	7,500		50.00	50
1998 Mom & Baby Seal	7,500		50.00	50
1998 Mother & Baby Elephant	7,500		100.00	100
1998 Mother Zebra & Baby	7,500		100.00	100
1998 Polar Cub	7,500		50.00	50
1998 Red Eyed Tree Frog	7,500		85.00	85
1998 Scarlet Macaw	7,500		100.00	100

Seraphim Angel Musical Figurines - Seraphim Studios

YEAR ISSUE	EDITION LIMIT	YEAR RETD.	ISSUE PRICE	*QUOTE U.S.$
1997 Ariel	Open		179.95	180
1998 Avalon	Open		195.00	195
1998 Hope	Open		179.95	180
1998 Monica - 20th Anniversary Special Edition	Open		60.00	60

Teddy Hugs Musical Collection - M. Danko

YEAR ISSUE	EDITION LIMIT	YEAR RETD.	ISSUE PRICE	*QUOTE U.S.$
1998 Bears on Hall Tree - "Love is Sharing" (1st ed.)	3,600		35.00	35
1998 Carousel Ride Merry-Go-Round (1st ed.)	3,600		100.00	100
1998 Praying Bears - "Now I Lay me Down to Sleep" (1st ed.)	3,600		35.00	35
1998 Sewing Bears - "Mom's Make Memories" (1st ed.)	3,600		35.00	35
1998 Suitcase Bears - "Old Friends are the Best Friends" (1st ed.)	3,600		35.00	35
1998 Toy Hutch - "Hugs are for Sharing"	6,000		45.00	45
1998 Window Box - "Home is Where the Hugs Are" (1st ed.)	3,600		35.00	35

Sandy Dolls Inc.

Sass 'n Class by Annie Lee - A. Lee

YEAR ISSUE	EDITION LIMIT	YEAR RETD.	ISSUE PRICE	*QUOTE U.S.$
1998 5th Grade Substitute	Open		40.00	40
1998 8 1/2 Narrow	Open		40.00	40
1998 The Babysitter	Open		55.00	55
1998 Blue Monday	Open		40.00	40
1998 Blues Highway	Open		85.00	85
1998 Burn You Baby?	Open		55.00	55
1998 Daily Snooze	Open		55.00	55
1998 First Mother	Open		35.00	35
1997 Gimme Dat Gum	5,000		70.00	70
1997 Holy Ghost	5,000		40.00	40
1998 Jumping the Broom	Open		75.00	75
1998 Loving Arms	Open		35.00	35
1998 Metamorphosis	Open		60.00	60
1997 Mother Board	5,000		85.00	85
1998 Sprinklin' and Pressin'	Open		55.00	55

Sarah's Attic, Inc.

Collector's Club Promotion - Sarah's Attic

YEAR ISSUE	EDITION LIMIT	YEAR RETD.	ISSUE PRICE	*QUOTE U.S.$
1991 Diamond 3497	Closed	1992	36.00	100-150
1991 Ruby 3498	Closed	1992	42.00	98-150
1992 Christmas Love Santa 3522	Closed	1992	45.00	65
1992 Forever Frolicking Friends 3523	Closed	1992	Gift	75
1992 Love One Another 3561	Closed	1992	60.00	46-60
1992 Sharing Dreams 3562	Closed	1993	75.00	100
1992 Life Time Friends 3563	Closed	1993	75.00	125
1992 Love Starts With Children 3607	Closed	1993	Gift	75
1993 First Forever Friend Celebration 3903	Closed	1993	50.00	50
1993 Pledge of Allegiance 3749	Closed	1993	45.00	90
1993 Love Starts With Children II 3837	Closed	1994	Gift	65
1993 Gem wh. Girl w/Basket 3842	Closed	1994	33.00	150
1993 Rocky blk. Boy w/Marbles 3843	Closed	1994	25.00	65
1994 America Boy 4191	Closed	1994	25.00	25
1994 America Girl 4192	Closed	1994	25.00	25
1994 Forever Friends 4286	Closed	1994	45.00	45
1994 Saturday Night Round Up 4232	Closed	1995	Gift	25
1994 Billy Bob 4233	Closed	1995	38.00	38
1994 Jimmy Dean 4234	Closed	1995	38.00	38
1994 Sally/Jack 4235	Closed	1995	55.00	55
1994 Ellie/T.J. 4236	Closed	1995	55.00	55
1995 Flags in Heaven 4386	Closed	1995	45.00	45
1995 Friends Forever 4444	Closed	1996	60.00	60
1995 Playtime Pals 4446	Closed	1997	65.00	70
1995 Horsin' around 4445	Closed	1997	65.00	65
1996 Abigail 4543	Closed	1996	36.00	36
1996 Aretha 4542	Closed	1996	36.00	36
1997 Basket of Memories 4827	Closed	1997	35.00	35
1997 Sharing Memories 4828	Closed	1998	85.00	85
1997 Basket of Treasures 4829	Closed	1997	35.00	35
1997 Treasured Moments 4830	Closed	1998	85.00	85

Angels In The Attic - Sarah's Attic

YEAR ISSUE	EDITION LIMIT	YEAR RETD.	ISSUE PRICE	*QUOTE U.S.$
1989 Abbee-Angel-2336	Closed	1991	10.00	20
1990 Adora Girl Angel Standing 3276	4,000	1990	35.00	111-125
1994 Adora w/Harp 4137	Closed	1996	26.00	26
1991 Angel Adora With Bunny 3390	Closed	1993	50.00	65
1991 Angel Enos With Frog 3391	10,000	1993	50.00	65
1996 Angels on Assignment 4544	Closed	1996	65.00	65
1989 Ashbee-Angel 2337	Closed	1991	10.00	25
1991 Bert Angel 3416	1,000	1992	60.00	120
1990 Billi-Angel 3295	Closed	1991	18.00	22
1994 Casey Angel 4245	Closed	1996	32.00	32
1995 Christine 4420	5,000	1996	26.00	26
1990 Cindi-Angel 3296	Closed	1991	18.00	22
1989 Clyde-Angel 2329	Closed	1991	17.00	20
1992 Contentment 3500	500	1992	100.00	200
1992 Enos & Adora-Small 3671	5,000	1993	35.00	60-125
1990 Enos Boy Angel Sitting 3275	4,000	1990	33.00	100-111
1994 Enos w/Harp 4138	Closed	1996	26.00	26
1989 Floppy-Angel 2330	Closed	1990	10.00	20
1990 Flossy-Angel 3301	Closed	1991	15.00	24
1997 Flutter, pink 4896	Closed	1998	28.00	28
1997 Flutter, pink 4896	Closed	1998	28.00	28
1989 Gramps Angel 2357	Closed	1990	17.00	40
1989 Grams Angel 2356	Closed	1990	17.00	40
1992 Heavenly Caring 3661	2,500	1993	70.00	90
1992 Heavenly Giving 3663	Closed	1993	70.00	90
1992 Heavenly Loving 3664	2,500	1993	70.00	90
1993 Heavenly Peace 3833	2,500	1994	47.00	50
1992 Heavenly Sharing 3662	2,500	1993	70.00	90
1993 Heavenly Uniting 3794	2,500	1994	45.00	45
1992 Hope Angel 3659	Closed	1994	40.00	45
1990 Lena Angel 3297	Closed	1991	36.00	40
1992 Love 3501	500	1992	80.00	200
1992 Priscilla Angel 3511	5,000	1993	46.00	60
1993 Risen Christ 3931	1,994	1995	48.00	48
1989 Saint Willie Bill 2360	Closed	1991	30.00	40
1989 St. Anne 2323	Closed	1991	29.00	40
1989 St. Gabbe 2322	Closed	1991	30.00	33
1990 Trapper-Angel 3299	Closed	1991	17.00	40
1989 Wendall-Angel 2324	Closed	1991	10.00	45
1989 Wilbur-Angel 2327	Closed	1991	10.00	25
1995 Willie Bill Angel 4471	Closed	1996	34.00	34

Beary Adorables Collection - Sarah's Attic

YEAR ISSUE	EDITION LIMIT	YEAR RETD.	ISSUE PRICE	*QUOTE U.S.$
1987 Abbee Bear 2005	Closed	1989	6.00	12
1987 Alex Bear 2003	Closed	1989	10.00	12
1987 Amelia Bear 2004	Closed	1989	8.00	12
1988 Americana Bear 3047	Closed	1990	50.00	75
1992 Andy-Father Bear 3727	3,500	1994	20.00	20
1989 Angel Bear 3105	Closed	1990	24.00	25
1988 Arti Boy Bear 6319	Closed	1990	7.00	15
1987 Ashbee Bear 2006	Closed	1989	6.00	12
1990 Bailey 50's Papa Bear 3250	4,000	1991	30.00	30
1997 Beary Long Haul 4875	Closed	1998	19.50	20
1990 Belinda 50's Girl Bear 3253	4,000	1991	25.00	35
1989 Betsy Bear w/Flag 3097	Closed	1990	22.00	40
1990 Beulah 50's Mama Bear 3251	4,000	1991	30.00	30
1990 Birkey 50's Boy Bear Teddy 3252	4,000	1991	25.00	25
1988 Boy Bear Resin Candle 3070	Closed	1989	12.00	12
1992 Brandy-Baby Bear 3728	3,500	1994	14.00	14
1997 Burley 4871	Closed	1998	27.00	27
1997 Burley's Tree 4873	Closed	1998	19.50	20
1997 Burley, lg. 4870	Closed	1998	50.00	50
1997 Burley, tan w/Wings 4907	Closed	1998	45.00	45
1986 Collectible Bear 2035	Closed	1989	14.00	14
1989 Colonial Bear w/Hat 3098	Closed	1990	22.00	40
1989 Daisy Bear 3101	Closed	1990	48.00	55
1991 Dudley Bear 3355	2,500	1990	32.00	60
1988 Ghost Bear 3028	Closed	1989	9.00	25
1989 Griswald Bear 3102	Closed	1990	48.00	55
1988 Honey Ma Bear 6316	Closed	1990	16.00	20
1988 Lefty Bear in Stocking 3049	Closed	1990	70.00	70
1995 Love Heals All 4438	Closed	1997	28.00	28
1997 Love My Tree 4874	Closed	1998	19.50	20
1992 Mandy-Mother Bear 3726	3,500	1994	20.00	20
1988 Marti Girl Bear 6318	Closed	1990	12.00	20
1989 Mikey Bear 3104	Closed	1990	26.00	30
1996 Mikey II 4598	1,000	1997	60.00	60
1989 Missy Bear 3103	Closed	1990	26.00	30
1996 Missy II 4597	1,000	1997	60.00	60
1997 Reach For The Stars 4876	Closed	1998	29.00	29
1988 Rufus Pa Bear 6317	Closed	1990	15.00	20
1989 Sammy Boy Bear 3111	Closed	1990	12.00	15
1989 Sid Papa Bear 3092	Closed	1990	18.00	25
1989 Sophie Mama Bear 3093	Closed	1990	18.00	25
1989 Spice Bear Crawling 3109	Closed	1990	12.00	15
1989 Sugar Bear Sitting 3112	Closed	1990	12.00	12

Black Heritage Collection - Sarah's Attic

YEAR ISSUE	EDITION LIMIT	YEAR RETD.	ISSUE PRICE	*QUOTE U.S.$
1991 Baby Tansy blk.3388	Closed	1993	40.00	50-60
1993 Bessie Gospel Singer 3754	Closed	1996	40.00	40-50
1993 Blessed is He 3952	1,994	1994	48.00	120-150
1994 Blessed is He II 4189	2,500		66.00	75
1995 Blessed is He III 4387	4,000		60.00	60
1995 Blessed is She 4312	5,000	1997	50.00	50
1995 Book of Wisdom 4315	4,000	1997	52.00	52
1992 Booker T. Washington 3648	3,000	1993	80.00	100-150
1992 Boys Night Out 3660	2,000	1994	350.00	695-750
1993 Brewster Clapping Singer 3758	2,500	1995	27.00	27
1990 Brotherly Love 3336	5,000	1991	80.00	175
1992 Buffalo Soldier 3524	5,000	1993	80.00	125-150
1991 Caleb w/ Football 3485	6,000	1993	40.00	55
1991 Caleb w/Vegetables 3375	4,000	1991	50.00	50
1990 Caleb-Lying Down 3232	Closed	1994	23.00	35
1995 Calvin 4319	4,000	1997	28.00	28
1992 Calvin Prayer Time 3510	5,000	1993	46.00	55
1995 Charity 4318	4,000	1997	28.00	28
1993 Claudia w/Tamborine Singer 3757	2,500	1995	27.00	27
1994 Coretta Scott King 4178	Closed	1996	60.00	60
1991 Corporal Pervis 3366	8,000	1993	60.00	125

*Quotes have been rounded up to nearest dollar

YEAR ISSUE	EDITION LIMIT	YEAR RETD.	ISSUE PRICE	*QUOTE U.S.$
1996 Dear Mrs. Parks 4584	10,000	1997	70.00	70
1992 Esther w/Butter Churn 3536	Closed	1994	70.00	70
1997 Florence Nightingale 4896	Closed	1998	50.00	50
1987 Gramps 5104	Closed	1988	16.00	100
1987 Grams 5105	Closed	1988	16.00	100
1992 Granny Wynne & Olivia 3535	5,000	1994	85.00	95
1997 Harpster III 4891	Closed	1998	60.00	60
1990 Harpster w/Banjo 3257	4,000	1990	60.00	111-250
1991 Harpster w/Harmonica II 3384	8,000	1993	60.00	125
1992 Harriet Tubman 3687	3,000	1993	60.00	125-150
1991 Hattie Quilting 3483	6,000	1993	60.00	125
1990 Hattie-Knitting 3233	4,000	1990	40.00	75-100
1992 Ida B. Wells & Frederick Douglass 3642	3,000	1993	160.00	250-295
1993 Jesse Gospel Singer 3755	Closed	1996	40.00	40-50
1994 Kitty w/Microphone 4141	Closed	1996	50.00	50-75
1996 Learning 4399	3,000	1997	55.00	55
1995 Libby w/Candle 4396	4,000	1996	26.00	26
1994 Libby w/Jacks 4139	4,000	1997	26.00	26
1990 Libby w/Overalls 3259	4,000	1990	36.00	175-195
1991 Libby w/Puppy 3386	10,000	1993	50.00	100
1995 Lift Your Hearts 4413	5,000	1997	50.00	50
1995 Love 4187	Closed	1996	50.00	50
1995 Lucas w/Bear 4397	4,000	1997	26.00	26
1991 Lucas w/Dog 3387	10,000	1993	50.00	100
1990 Lucas w/Overalls 3260	4,000	1990	36.00	175
1994 Lucas w/Papers 4140	4,000	1997	26.00	26
1995 Martin Luther King Birmingham Jail 4407	Closed	1996	65.00	65
1995 Martin Luther King Wedding 4406	Closed	1996	85.00	85
1994 Martin Luther King, Jr. 4179	Closed	1996	65.00	65
1996 Mary Eliza Mahoney 4501	1,000	1996	50.00	50-75
1993 Miles Boy Angel 3752	2,500	1995	27.00	40
1993 Moriah Girl Angel 3759	2,500	1994	27.00	45
1992 Muffy-Prayer Time 3509	5,000	1993	46.00	55
1992 Music Masters 3533	1,000	1992	300.00	350-400
1992 Music Masters II 3621	1,000	1994	250.00	300-350
1994 Music Masters III 4142	Closed	1996	80.00	80-125
1993 Nat Love Cowboy (Isom Dart) 3792	2,500	1993	45.00	300-395
1991 Nighttime Pearl 3362	Closed	1993	50.00	65
1991 Nighttime Percy 3363	Closed	1993	50.00	65
1992 Nurturing with Love-3686	2,000	1993	60.00	60
1995 Old Time Tunes 4317	4,000	1997	54.00	54
1993 Otis Redding 3793	Closed	1994	70.00	300
1991 Pappy Jake & Susie Mae 3482	6,000	1993	60.00	60
1989 Pappy Jake 3100	Closed	1990	40.00	65-100
1994 Peaches-Clown 4135	4,000	1997	29.00	29
1990 Pearl-Blk. Girl Dancing 3291	5,000	1992	45.00	100
1990 Percy-Blk. Boy Dancing 3292	5,000	1993	45.00	100
1992 Porter 3525	5,000	1993	80.00	125
1991 Portia Quilting 3484	6,000	1993	40.00	40
1990 Portia Reading Book 3256	Closed	1991	30.00	45-65
1991 Portia-Victorian Dress 3373	7,000	1992	35.00	35
1990 Praise the Lord I (Preacher I) 3277	4,000	1991	55.00	150-195
1991 Praise the Lord II w/Kids 3376	5,000	1994	100.00	100
1993 Praise the Lord III 3753	2,500	1994	44.00	55-60
1995 Praise the Lord IV 4369	5,000	1997	55.00	55
1994 Pug-Clown 4136	4,000	1997	29.00	29
1989 Quilting Ladies 3099	Closed	1991	90.00	300-395
1992 Rhythm & Blues 3620	5,000	1994	80.00	80
1995 Rosa Parks 4401	Closed	1997	65.00	65
1991 Sadie & Osie Mae 3365	8,000	1993	70.00	70
1992 Sojourner Truth 3629	3,000	1993	80.00	125-150
1990 Susie Mae 3231	Closed	1994	22.00	22
1995 Tuskegee Airman W.W. II 4405	2,500	1996	60.00	60-120
1991 Uncle Reuben 3389	8,000	1993	70.00	95
1993 Vanessa Gospel Singer (Upside down book) 3756	Closed	1996	40.00	100
1990 Whoopie & Wooster 3255	4,000	1990	50.00	235-350
1991 Whoopie & Wooster II 3385	8,000	1993	70.00	111-125
1997 Whoopie III 4892	Closed	1998	45.00	45
1997 Wooster III 4893	Closed	1998	35.00	35

Cotton Tale Collection - Sarah's Attic

YEAR ISSUE	EDITION LIMIT	YEAR RETD.	ISSUE PRICE	*QUOTE U.S.$
1988 Americana Bunny 3048	Closed	1990	58.00	190
1988 Billi Rabbit 6283	Closed	1990	27.00	35
1987 Bonnie 5727	Closed	1989	30.00	125
1988 Cindi Rabbit 6282	Closed	1990	27.00	35
1987 Clyde 5728	Closed	1989	30.00	125
1989 Cookie Rabbit 3078	Closed	1990	29.00	125
1989 Crumb Rabbit 3077	Closed	1990	29.00	35-43
1989 Nana Rabbit 3080	Closed	1990	50.00	60-75
1990 Ollie Rabbit w/Vest 3239	Closed	1991	75.00	150
1989 Papa Rabbit 3079	Closed	1990	50.00	60-75
1989 Sleepy Rabbit 3088	Closed	1990	16.00	25
1991 Tabitha Victorian Rabbit 3371	Closed	1993	30.00	45
1991 Tessy Victorian Rabbit 3370	Closed	1993	20.00	35
1989 Thelma Rabbit 3084	Closed	1990	33.00	40
1989 Thomas Rabbit 3085	Closed	1990	33.00	40
1991 Toby Victorian Rabbit 3369	Closed	1993	40.00	55
1988 Wendall Mini Rabbit 6268	Closed	1990	8.00	12
1987 Wendall Rabbit 5285	Closed	1989	14.00	25
1988 Wendy Mini Rabbit 6270	Closed	1990	8.00	12
1987 Wendy Rabbit 5286	Closed	1989	15.00	25
1988 Wilbur Mini Rabbit 6269	Closed	1990	8.00	12
1987 Wilbur Rabbit 5287	Closed	1989	13.00	25
1990 Zeb Pa Rabbit w/Carrots 3217	500	1990	18.00	32
1990 Zeb Sailor Dad 3319	Closed	1992	28.00	32
1990 Zeke Boy Rabbit w/Carrots 3219	500	1990	17.00	32
1990 Zelda Ma Rabbit w/Carrots 3218	500	1990	18.00	32
1987 Zoe Girl Rabbit w/Carrots 3220	500	1990	17.00	32

Daisy Collection - Sarah's Attic

YEAR ISSUE	EDITION LIMIT	YEAR RETD.	ISSUE PRICE	*QUOTE U.S.$
1990 Bomber-Tom 3309	Closed	1993	52.00	57
1990 Jack Boy Ball & Glove 3249	Closed	1993	40.00	44
1993 Jack Boy w/Broken Arm 3970	2,000	1994	30.00	60
1990 Jewel-Julie 3310	Closed	1993	62.00	68
1989 Sally Booba 2344	Closed	1993	40.00	60
1990 Sparky-Mark 3307	Closed	1993	55.00	60
1990 Spike-Tim 3308	Closed	1993	46.00	51
1990 Stretch-Mike 3311	Closed	1993	52.00	57

Dreams of Tomorrow - Sarah's Attic

YEAR ISSUE	EDITION LIMIT	YEAR RETD.	ISSUE PRICE	*QUOTE U.S.$
1994 Annie-Nurse 4128	Closed	1996	33.00	33
1992 Annie-Teacher 3507	6,000	1993	55.00	55
1991 Benjamin w/Drums 3487	10,000	1993	46.00	55
1994 Bernie-Teacher 4132	3,000	1997	38.00	38
1992 Blossom 3502	5,000	1993	50.00	50
1994 Boyd-Basketball 4279	2,000	1997	36.00	36
1994 Boyd-Teacher 4130	3,000	1997	34.00	34
1992 Bubba-Doctor 3506	6,000	1993	60.00	66
1994 Bubba-Fireman 4229	2,000	1995	37.00	37
1994 Bubba-Football 4272	2,000	1997	36.00	36
1992 Bubba-Policeman 3685	3,000	1993	46.00	51
1992 Bud-Fireman 3668	6,000	1993	50.00	55
1994 Bud-Police (blue) 4260	Closed	1996	45.00	45
1994 Bud-Police (blue) 4260	Closed	1996	45.00	45
1994 Calvin-Bl. Golfer 4161	3,000	1997	35.00	35
1994 Calvin-Black Golfer 4161	3,000	1997	35.00	35
1994 Calvin-Soccer 4275	Closed	1996	36.00	36
1994 Champ-Soccer 4277	Closed	1996	36.00	36
1993 Champ-Wh. Boy Baseball 3776	Closed	1997	32.00	32
1991 Charity Sewing Flags 3486	10,000	1993	46.00	55
1992 Chips-Graduate 3532	6,000	1993	46.00	46
1993 Cody-Cowboy 3886	2,000	1995	30.00	30
1994 Cody-Hockey 4271	2,000	1995	38.00	38
1992 Cricket-Graduate 3531	6,000	1993	46.00	46
1992 Cupcake-Ballerina 3683	3,000	1993	46.00	46
1994 Cupcake-Dentist 4116	Closed	1996	33.00	33
1992 Cupcake-Nurse 3514	6,000	1993	46.00	46
1994 Cupcake-Soccer 4276	Closed	1996	36.00	36
1993 Dana-Wh. Waitress 3779	2,000	1994	34.00	34
1994 Dedication-Wh. Doctor 4111	3,000	1997	38.00	38
1994 Devotion-Bl. Doctor 4112	3,000	1997	33.00	33
1994 Hewett-Police (blue) 4258	2,000	1996	45.00	45
1994 Jack Boy-Graduate 3984	3,000	1997	30.00	30
1993 Jack-Boy Wh. Pharmacist 3781	Closed	1996	34.00	34
1994 Joe-Farmer w/Basket 4120	Closed	1996	33.00	33
1994 John-Farmer w/Tractor 4119	Closed	1996	36.00	36
1993 Jojo-Wh. Girl Basketball 3777	Closed	1995	32.00	32
1994 Josh-Hockey 4270	2,000	1995	38.00	38
1993 Josh-Jogger 3887	2,000	1995	25.00	25
1994 Judy-Teacher 4131	3,000	1997	38.00	38
1994 Juliana-Teacher 4129	3,000	1997	34.00	34
1992 Katie-Executive 3665	6,000	1993	46.00	46
1994 Katie-Nurse 3987	3,000	1997	33.00	33
1993 Katie-Pharmacist 3898	Closed	1996	32.00	32
1992 Madge-Farmer 3503	2,500	1993	50.00	50
1992 Marty-Farmer 3504	2,500	1993	50.00	50
1994 Moose-Football 4273	2,000	1996	36.00	36
1993 Noah-Bl. Pharmacist 3780	Closed	1996	34.00	34
1992 Noah-Executive 3508	6,000	1993	46.00	46
1992 Pansy-Ballerina 3682	3,000	1993	46.00	55
1993 Pansy-Bl. Waitress 3778	2,000	1994	40.00	40
1992 Pansy-Nurse 3505	6,000	1993	46.00	51
1993 Pansy-Pharmacist 3899	Closed	1996	32.00	32
1994 Peaches-Dentist 4113	Closed	1996	33.00	33
1994 Pug-Dentist 4114	Closed	1996	33.00	33
1993 Rachel-Photographer 3871	2,000	1995	27.00	32
1994 Sally Booba-Graduate 3983	3,000	1997	30.00	30
1992 Shelby-Executive 3666	6,000	1993	46.00	50
1994 Shelby-Nurse 4127	Closed	1996	33.00	33
1991 Skip-Building Houses 3489	10,000	1993	50.00	50
1994 Spike-Basketball 4278	2,000	1995	36.00	36
1994 Spike-Wh. Golfer 4162	3,000	1997	35.00	35
1991 Susie Painting Train 3488	10,000	1993	46.00	46
1993 Tillie-Girl Basketball 3774	Closed	1997	32.00	32
1994 Tillie-Graduate 3985	3,000	1997	30.00	30
1994 Tillie-Nurse 3989	3,000	1995	33.00	33
1993 Tillie-Photographer 3870	Closed	1996	27.00	32
1994 Tillie-Soccer 4274	Closed	1996	36.00	36
1992 Tillie-Teacher 3520	6,000	1993	50.00	50
1992 Twinkie-Doctor 3515	6,000	1993	50.00	50
1993 Twinkie-Pilot 3869	Closed	1996	27.00	35
1992 Twinkie-Policeman 3684	3,000	1993	46.00	46
1994 Twinkie-Wh. Dentist 4115	Closed	1996	33.00	33
1994 Whimpy-Doctor 3988	3,000	1997	33.00	33
1992 Whimpy-Executive 3521	6,000	1993	46.00	46
1994 Whimpy-Fireman 4230	2,000	1996	37.00	37
1993 Willie-Boy Baseball 3775	Closed	1997	32.00	32
1994 Willie-Doctor 3990	3,000	1997	33.00	33
1992 Willie-Fireman 3667	6,000	1993	46.00	50
1994 Willie-Graduate 3986	3,000	1997	30.00	30
1993 Willie-Pilot 3868	Closed	1996	27.00	27
1994 Willie-Police (blue) 4256	2,000	1996	32.00	32

Forever Ice Sculpture - Sarah's Attic

YEAR ISSUE	EDITION LIMIT	YEAR RETD.	ISSUE PRICE	*QUOTE U.S.$
1997 Beary Long Haul 4945	Closed	1998	18.00	18
1997 Burley's Tree 4947	Closed	1998	18.00	18
1996 Frozen Freddie 4864	Closed	1998	18.00	18
1997 Love My Tree 4946	Closed	1998	18.00	18
1997 Reach For The Stars 4944	Closed	1998	20.00	20

Glitterdomes - Sarah's Attic

YEAR ISSUE	EDITION LIMIT	YEAR RETD.	ISSUE PRICE	*QUOTE U.S.$
1995 Black Boy Angel S102	Closed	1998	10.00	10
1995 Black Girl Angel S101	Closed	1998	10.00	10
1995 Buffalo Soldier S407	Closed	1998	30.00	30
1995 Calvin Golfer S203	Closed	1998	25.00	25
1994 Days To Remember S403	Closed	1998	36.00	36
1995 Gospel Singers S251	Closed	1998	55.00	55
1994 Nativity S406	Closed	1998	36.00	36
1995 Quilting Ladies S502	Closed	1998	40.00	40
1994 School Days Willie/Tillie S405	Closed	1998	36.00	36
1994 Willie/Tillie Clowns S351	Closed	1998	34.00	34

Matt & Maggie - Sarah's Attic

YEAR ISSUE	EDITION LIMIT	YEAR RETD.	ISSUE PRICE	*QUOTE U.S.$
1988 Large Matt 3029	4,000	1989	48.00	58
1986 Maggie 2029	4,000	1989	14.00	28
1989 Maggie Bench Sitter 3083	Closed	1990	32.00	42
1987 Maggie on Heart 5145	Closed	1989	9.00	15
1987 Matt & Maggie w/ Bear 5730	100	1987	100.00	150
1986 Matt 2030	Closed	1989	14.00	28
1989 Matt Bench Sitter 3082	Closed	1990	32.00	42
1987 Matt on Heart 5144	Closed	1989	9.00	15
1989 Mini Maggie 2314	Closed	1989	6.00	12
1989 Mini Matt 2313	Closed	1989	6.00	12
1988 Small Sitting Maggie 5284	Closed	1989	11.50	35
1988 Small Sitting Matt 5283	Closed	1989	11.50	35
1987 Standing Maggie 2014	Closed	1989	11.00	15
1987 Standing Matt 2013	Closed	1989	11.00	15

Religious - Sarah's Attic

YEAR ISSUE	EDITION LIMIT	YEAR RETD.	ISSUE PRICE	*QUOTE U.S.$
1997 All Is Bright, pastel 4905	Closed	1998	55.00	55
1997 Feel The Spirit, purple 4973	Closed	1998	30.00	30
1997 Feel The Spirit, red 4867	Closed	1998	30.00	30
1997 Give Praise, purple 4972	Closed	1998	30.00	30
1997 Give Praise, red 4866	Closed	1998	30.00	30
1997 Holy Night, pastel 4906	Closed	1998	55.00	55
1997 Serenity Cross 4816	Closed	1998	44.00	44

Santas Of The Month-Series A - Sarah's Attic

YEAR ISSUE	EDITION LIMIT	YEAR RETD.	ISSUE PRICE	*QUOTE U.S.$
1988 January wh. Santa	Closed	1990	50.00	135-150
1988 January blk. Santa	Closed	1990	50.00	300-395
1988 February wh. Santa	Closed	1990	50.00	135-150
1988 February blk. Santa	Closed	1990	50.00	200-300
1988 March wh. Santa	Closed	1990	50.00	135-150
1988 March blk. Santa	Closed	1990	50.00	200-300
1988 April wh. Santa	Closed	1990	50.00	135-150
1988 April blk. Santa	Closed	1990	50.00	200-300
1988 May wh. Santa	Closed	1990	50.00	135-150
1988 May blk. Santa	Closed	1990	50.00	200-300
1988 June wh. Santa	Closed	1990	50.00	135-150
1988 June blk. Santa	Closed	1990	50.00	200-300
1988 July wh. Santa	Closed	1990	50.00	130-175
1988 July blk. Santa	Closed	1990	50.00	200-300
1988 August wh. Santa	Closed	1990	50.00	135-150
1988 August blk. Santa	Closed	1990	50.00	200-300
1988 September wh. Santa	Closed	1990	50.00	135-150
1988 September blk. Santa	Closed	1990	50.00	300-375
1988 October wh. Santa	Closed	1990	50.00	135-150
1988 October blk. Santa	Closed	1990	50.00	300-395
1988 November wh. Santa	Closed	1990	50.00	135-150
1988 November blk. Santa	Closed	1990	50.00	200-300
1988 December wh. Santa	Closed	1990	50.00	135-150
1988 December blk. Santa	Closed	1990	50.00	375-395
1988 Mini January wh. Santa	Closed	1990	14.00	33-35
1988 Mini January blk. Santa	Closed	1990	14.00	35-50
1988 Mini February wh. Santa	Closed	1990	14.00	33-35
1988 Mini February blk. Santa	Closed	1990	14.00	35-50
1988 Mini March wh. Santa	Closed	1990	14.00	33-35
1988 Mini March blk. Santa	Closed	1990	14.00	35
1988 Mini April wh. Santa	Closed	1990	14.00	33-35
1988 Mini April blk. Santa	Closed	1990	14.00	35
1988 Mini May wh. Santa	Closed	1990	14.00	33-35
1988 Mini May blk. Santa	Closed	1990	14.00	35
1988 Mini June wh. Santa	Closed	1990	14.00	33-35
1988 Mini June blk. Santa	Closed	1990	14.00	35
1988 Mini July wh. Santa	Closed	1990	14.00	40
1988 Mini July blk. Santa	Closed	1990	14.00	50
1988 Mini August wh. Santa	Closed	1990	14.00	33-35
1988 Mini August blk. Santa	Closed	1990	14.00	35
1988 Mini September wh. Santa	Closed	1990	14.00	33-35
1988 Mini September blk. Santa	Closed	1990	14.00	35-50
1988 Mini October wh. Santa	Closed	1990	14.00	33-35
1988 Mini October blk. Santa	Closed	1990	14.00	35-40
1988 Mini November wh. Santa	Closed	1990	14.00	33-35
1988 Mini November blk. Santa	Closed	1990	14.00	35
1988 Mini December wh. Santa	Closed	1990	14.00	33-35
1988 Mini December blk. Santa	Closed	1990	14.00	35-50

Santas Of The Month-Series B - Sarah's Attic

YEAR ISSUE	EDITION LIMIT	YEAR RETD.	ISSUE PRICE	*QUOTE U.S.$
1990 Jan. Santa Winter Fun 7135	Closed	1991	80.00	100
1990 Feb. Santa Cupids Help 7136	Closed	1991	120.00	120
1990 Mar. Santa Irish Delight 7137	Closed	1991	120.00	150
1990 Apr. Santa Spring/Joy 7138	Closed	1991	150.00	150
1990 May Santa Par For Course 7139	Closed	1991	100.00	125
1990 June Santa Graduation 7140	Closed	1991	70.00	70
1990 July Santa God Bless 7141	Closed	1991	100.00	175
1990 Aug. Santa Summers Tranquility 7142	Closed	1991	110.00	130
1990 Sept. Santa Touchdown 7143	Closed	1991	90.00	90
1990 Oct. Santa Seasons Plenty 7144	Closed	1991	120.00	120
1990 Nov. Santa Give Thanks 7145	Closed	1991	100.00	125
1990 Dec. Santa Peace 7146	Closed	1991	120.00	125
1990 Jan. Mrs. Winter Fun 7147	Closed	1991	80.00	100
1990 Feb. Mrs. Cupid's Helper 7148	Closed	1991	110.00	110
1990 March Mrs. Irish Delight7149	Closed	1991	80.00	100
1990 April Mrs. Spring Joy 7150	Closed	1991	110.00	110

*Quotes have been rounded up to nearest dollar

YEAR ISSUE	EDITION LIMIT	YEAR RETD.	ISSUE PRICE	*QUOTE U.S.$
1990 May Mrs. Par for the Course 7151	Closed	1991	80.00	100
1990 June Mrs. Graduate 7152	Closed	1991	70.00	100
1990 July Mrs. God Bless America 7153	Closed	1991	100.00	125
1990 Aug. Mrs. Summer Tranquility 7154	Closed	1991	90.00	112
1990 Sept. Mrs. Touchdown 7155	Closed	1991	90.00	100
1990 Oct. Mrs. Seasons of Plenty 7156	Closed	1991	90.00	112
1990 Nov. Mrs. Give Thanks 7157	Closed	1991	90.00	112
1990 Dec. Mrs. Peace 7158	Closed	1991	110.00	137

Sarah's Gang Collection - Sarah's Attic

YEAR ISSUE	EDITION LIMIT	YEAR RETD.	ISSUE PRICE	*QUOTE U.S.$
1989 Baby Rachel 2306	Closed	1994	20.00	30
1990 Baby Rachel-Beachtime 3248	Closed	1992	35.00	50
1988 Cupcake 4027	Closed	1994	20.00	25
1995 Cupcake 4346	Closed	1996	28.00	28
1989 Cupcake Clown 3144	Closed	1989	21.00	35
1993 Cupcake on Bench 3766	Closed	1994	28.00	28
1987 Cupcake on Heart 5140	Closed	1989	9.00	20
1987 Cupcake w/Rope 5119	Closed	1988	16.00	16
1993 Cupcake w/Snowman 3822	2,500	1994	35.00	40
1989 Cupcake-Americana 2304	Closed	1993	21.00	30
1990 Cupcake-Beachtime 3244	Closed	1992	35.00	53
1990 Cupcake-Devil 3314	Closed	1992	40.00	40
1986 Cupcake-Original 2034	Closed	1988	14.00	20-75
1989 Cupcake-Small School 2309	Closed	1990	11.00	20
1993 Cupcake-Spring 3937	1,994	1995	30.00	30
1993 Katie & Rachel in Chair 3764	Closed	1994	60.00	60
1990 Katie & Whimpy-Beachtime 3243	Closed	1992	60.00	60-75
1988 Katie 4029	Closed	1994	20.00	20
1995 Katie 4344	Closed	1996	28.00	28
1987 Katie On Heart 5141	Closed	1989	9.00	20
1992 Katie On Sled 3707	2,500	1994	35.00	35
1987 Katie Sitting 2002	Closed	1987	14.00	20
1996 Katie w/raincoat 4573	2,500	1997	40.00	40
1989 Katie-Americana 2302	Closed	1993	21.00	25
1991 Katie-Bride 3431	Closed	1994	47.00	52
1986 Katie-Original 2032	Closed	1988	14.00	20
1989 Katie-Small Sailor 2307	Closed	1990	14.00	20
1993 Katie-Spring 3935	1,994	1995	28.00	28
1991 Katie-Thanksgiving 3468	10,000	1993	32.00	32
1990 Katie-Witch 3312	Closed	1992	40.00	50
1991 Peaches-Flower Girl 3438	Closed	1994	40.00	40
1991 Percy-Minister 3440	Closed	1994	50.00	55
1996 Puddles w/umbrella 4576	Closed	1997	13.00	13
1991 Pug-Ringbearer 3439	Closed	1994	40.00	44
1995 Rachel 4348	Closed	1996	28.00	28
1993 Rachel in Snowsuit 3823	2,500	1994	25.00	25
1991 Rachel-Americana 3364	Closed	1993	30.00	30
1991 Rachel-Flower Girl 3432	Closed	1994	40.00	43
1990 Rachel-Pumpkin 3318	Closed	1992	40.00	50
1993 Rachel-Spring 3940	1,994	1995	30.00	30
1991 Rachel-Thanksgiving 3474	10,000	1993	32.00	35
1996 Sparky w/raincoat 4575	Closed	1997	15.00	15
1988 Tillie 4032	Closed	1994	20.00	25
1995 Tillie 4342	Closed	1997	28.00	28
1991 Tillie Masquerade 3412	Closed	1993	45.00	50
1987 Tillie On Heart 5150	Closed	1989	9.00	20
1992 Tillie On Log 3705	2,500	1994	35.00	35
1986 Tillie Resin Candle 2024	Closed	1987	12.00	12
1993 Tillie w/Bear 3769	Closed	1994	28.00	28
1996 Tillie w/raincoat 4574	2,500	1997	40.00	40
1989 Tillie-Americana 2301	Closed	1993	21.00	25
1990 Tillie-Beachtime 3247	Closed	1992	35.00	53
1991 Tillie-Bride 3436	Closed	1994	47.00	47
1990 Tillie-Clown 3316	Closed	1992	40.00	50
1986 Tillie-Original 2027	Closed	1988	14.00	20
1989 Tillie-Small Country 2312	Closed	1992	18.00	26
1993 Tillie-Spring 3938	1,994	1995	30.00	30
1997 Tillie-Sunday, pastel 4772	Closed	1998	75.00	75
1991 Tillie-Thanksgiving 3472	10,000	1993	32.00	32
1996 Tillie-Y 4532	2,500	1997	75.00	75
1988 Twinkie 4028	Closed	1994	20.00	20
1995 Twinkie 4347	Closed	1996	28.00	28
1989 Twinkie Clown 3145	Closed	1989	19.00	35
1987 Twinkie On Heart 5143	Closed	1989	9.00	20
1993 Twinkie w/Football 3765	Closed	1994	28.00	28
1987 Twinkie w/Pole 5107	Closed	1988	20.00	20
1993 Twinkie w/Snowballs 3821	2,500	1994	35.00	35
1989 Twinkie-Americana 2305	Closed	1993	21.00	25
1990 Twinkie-Beachtime 3245	Closed	1992	35.00	53
1990 Twinkie-Devil 3315	Closed	1992	40.00	50
1991 Twinkie-Minister 3435	Closed	1994	50.00	50
1986 Twinkie-Original 2033	Closed	1988	14.00	20
1989 Twinkie-Small School 2310	Closed	1990	11.00	20
1993 Twinkie-Spring 3936	1,994	1995	28.00	28
1991 Tyler-Ring Bearer 3433	Closed	1994	40.00	44
1988 Whimpy 4030	Closed	1994	20.00	25
1995 Whimpy 4345	Closed	1996	28.00	28
1987 Whimpy on Heart 5142	Closed	1989	9.00	20
1987 Whimpy Sitting 2001	Closed	1987	14.00	20
1992 Whimpy w/Book 3708	2,500	1994	35.00	35
1993 Whimpy w/Train 3767	Closed	1994	28.00	28
1989 Whimpy-Americana 2303	Closed	1993	21.00	25
1991 Whimpy-Groom 3430	Closed	1994	47.00	52
1986 Whimpy-Original 2031	Closed	1988	14.00	20
1990 Whimpy-Scarecrow 3313	Closed	1992	40.00	40
1989 Whimpy-Small Sailor 2308	Closed	1990	14.00	20
1993 Whimpy-Spring 3934	1,994	1995	28.00	28
1991 Whimpy-Thanksgiving 3469	10,000	1993	32.00	35
1996 Wille-Y 4533	2,500	1997	75.00	75
1988 Willie 4031	Closed	1994	20.00	25
1993 Willie Lying w/Pillow 3768	Closed	1994	28.00	28
1987 Willie On Heart 5151	Closed	1989	9.00	20
1986 Willie Resin Candle 2023	Closed	1987	12.00	12
1995 Willie w/Frog 4343	Closed	1997	28.00	28
1992 Willie w/Skates 3706	2,500	1994	35.00	35
1989 Willie-Americana 2300	Closed	1993	21.00	30
1990 Willie-Beachtime 3246	Closed	1992	35.00	53
1990 Willie-Clown 3317	Closed	1992	40.00	50
1991 Willie-Groom 3437	Closed	1994	47.00	47
1986 Willie-Original 2028	Closed	1988	14.00	20-75
1989 Willie-Small Country 2311	Closed	1992	18.00	26
1993 Willie-Spring 3939	1,994	1995	28.00	28
1997 Willie-Sunday, pastel 4773	Closed	1998	75.00	75
1991 Willie-Thanksgiving 3473	10,000	1993	32.00	32

Sarah's Neighborhood Friends - Sarah's Attic

YEAR ISSUE	EDITION LIMIT	YEAR RETD.	ISSUE PRICE	*QUOTE U.S.$
1991 Babes-Nativity Jesus 3427	Closed	1994	20.00	22
1990 Bubba w/Lantern 3268	Closed	1992	40.00	45
1991 Bubba w/Lemonade Stand 3382	Closed	1992	54.00	108
1991 Bud Nativity (Joseph) 3420	Closed	1994	34.00	36
1990 Bud w/Book 3270	Closed	1992	40.00	45
1991 Dolly Nativity (Jesus) 3418	Closed	1994	20.00	22
1993 Emily & Gideon-Small 3670	Closed	1993	40.00	75
1989 Jennifer & Max 2319	4,000	1990	57.00	85
1991 Pansy-Nativity Angel 3425	Closed	1994	30.00	32
1988 Trudy-w/Teacup 3042	Closed	1990	34.00	50
1990 Tyler Victorian Boy 3327	Closed	1992	40.00	65

Snowflake Collection - Sarah's Attic

YEAR ISSUE	EDITION LIMIT	YEAR RETD.	ISSUE PRICE	*QUOTE U.S.$
1997 Baby Snow Angel 4861	Closed	1998	17.50	18
1989 Boo Mini Snowman 3200	Closed	1993	6.00	12
1996 Chilly & Burly 4622	2,500	1998	70.00	70
1997 Chilly w/Stocking Cap 4865	Closed	1998	40.00	40
1996 Chilly/Snowflake 4482	5,000	1998	32.00	32
1995 Chilly/Snowman 4418	1,000	1998	44.00	44
1992 Christmas Love-Small 3674	5,000	1992	30.00	33
1997 Crystal Flurry 4862	Closed	1998	24.00	24
1995 Flurry & Boo 4414	1,000	1998	30.00	30
1989 Flurry 2342	Closed	1993	12.00	20
1996 Frilly/Snow Crystal 4483	5,000	1998	36.00	36
1996 Frozen Freddie 4621	2,500	1998	25.00	25
1997 Joyride Snowman 4855	Closed	1998	29.00	29
1997 Let It Snow Snowman 4857	Closed	1998	35.00	35
1997 Little Shiver Snowman 4859	Closed	1998	14.00	14
1997 Mr. Snow Jangles 4854	Closed	1998	20.00	20
1997 Mr. Winter Snowman 4858	Closed	1998	20.00	20
1990 Old Glory Snowman 3225	4,000	1992	24.00	26
1997 Snow Angel 4860	Closed	1998	40.00	40
1995 Snowy Snowman 4416	1,000	1998	30.00	30
1997 Starbright Snowman 4853	Closed	1998	20.00	20
1996 Tallman Snowman 4623	4,000	1998	25.00	25
1996 Topper/Tabby 4481	5,000	1998	32.00	32
1996 Twiggs Snowman 4624	4,000	1998	27.00	27
1997 We Love Snow 4856	Closed	1998	45.00	45
1989 Winter Frolic 3209	Closed	1992	60.00	70
1996 Woody Snowman 4625	4,000	1998	36.00	36

Sparkling Wonderland - Sarah's Attic

YEAR ISSUE	EDITION LIMIT	YEAR RETD.	ISSUE PRICE	*QUOTE U.S.$
1998 Burley w/Pastel Ribbon	Closed	1998	25.00	25

Spirit of America - Sarah's Attic

YEAR ISSUE	EDITION LIMIT	YEAR RETD.	ISSUE PRICE	*QUOTE U.S.$
1988 Betsy Ross 3024	Closed	1992	34.00	60
1991 Bright Sky Mother Indian 3345	Closed	1992	70.00	90-140
1991 Forever in Our Hearts 3413	10,000	1994	90.00	90
1991 Iron Hawk Father Indian 3344	Closed	1992	70.00	90-140
1991 Little Dove Girl Indian 3346	Closed	1992	40.00	60-85
1996 Peaches 4493	2,500	1998	26.00	26
1988 Pilgrim Boy 4009	Closed	1990	12.00	20
1988 Pilgrim Girl 4010	Closed	1990	12.00	24
1996 Proud Bear 4495	2,500	1998	10.00	10
1996 Pug 4494	2,500	1998	26.00	26
1994 Shine-Boy Indian 3980	1,000	1994	25.00	50
1994 Siyah-Girl Indian 3979	1,000	1994	25.00	50
1991 Spotted Eagle Boy Indian 3347	Closed	1992	30.00	45-85

Spirit of Christmas Collection - Sarah's Attic

YEAR ISSUE	EDITION LIMIT	YEAR RETD.	ISSUE PRICE	*QUOTE U.S.$
1995 Ahmad - Nativity 4453	Closed	1996	23.00	23
1995 Angelika - Nativity 4456	Closed	1996	25.00	25
1997 August Santa, wh. 4903	Closed	1998	50.00	50
1995 Care Basket 4424	5,000	1996	26.00	26
1995 Caring - Boy w/Globe 4423	5,000	1996	29.00	29
1995 Cherish the Children 4466	1,000	1996	70.00	70
1995 Christmas Joy 4331	Closed	1996	60.00	60
1996 Cuddles 4549	1,000	1998	60.00	60
1997 December Santa, bl. 4900	Closed	1998	50.00	50
1997 December Santa, wh. 4901	Closed	1998	50.00	50
1994 Gift of Christmas-wh. Santa 4146	Closed	1996	60.00	60
1994 Gift of Love blk. Santa 4145	Closed	1996	60.00	60
1994 Golden Memories Santa 4254	Closed	1996	70.00	70
1995 Happiness 4426	5,000	1996	34.00	34
1995 Helpfulness 4425	5,000	1996	37.00	37
1997 Homespun Santa 4849	Closed	1998	30.00	30
1995 Ishamael - Nativity 4454	Closed	1996	23.00	23
1995 Jabari - Nativity 4455	Closed	1996	23.00	23
1995 Jarrell - Nativity 4452	Closed	1996	23.00	23
1994 Jeb-Christmas 94 4155	Closed	1994	28.00	30
1995 Joah - Nativity 4451	Closed	1996	23.00	23
1997 Jolly Holly 4846	Closed	1998	29.00	29
1997 Jolly Ole Soul 4969	Closed	1998	33.00	33
1995 Joy to the World 4462	1,000	1996	64.00	64
1995 Joyfulness 4428	5,000	1996	28.00	28
1995 Kindness 4427	5,000	1996	30.00	30
1995 Lakeisha - Nativity 4450	Closed	1996	25.00	25
1993 Let The Be Peace Santa 3797	2,000	1996	70.00	70
1993 Let There Be Love Santa 3796	2,000	1996	70.00	70
1994 LOL-Christmas 4151	Closed	1994	30.00	35
1987 Long Journey 2051	Closed	1989	19.00	35
1987 Mini Santa w/Cane 5123	Closed	1990	8.00	38
1997 Mr. Christmas 4845	Closed	1998	29.00	29
1995 Mrs. Santa 4430	5,000	1996	42.00	42
1997 Old World Santa 4850	Closed	1998	34.00	34
1989 Papa Santa Sitting 3180	Closed	1990	30.00	40
1989 Papa Santa Stocking 3182	Closed	1990	50.00	60
1995 Peace on Earth 4464	1,000	1996	80.00	80
1996 Ragtime Christmas 4550	1,000	1998	60.00	60
1995 Santa 4429	Closed	1996	45.00	45
1988 Santa in Chimney 4020	4,000	1990	110.00	150
1997 Santa in Stitches 4848	Closed	1998	30.00	30
1991 Santa Tex 3392	500	1990	30.00	75
1987 Santa's Workshop 3006	Closed	1990	50.00	100
1991 Sharing Love Santa 3491	3,000	1993	120.00	140
1989 Silent Night 2343	6,000	1991	33.00	50
1995 Tillie-Caroling 4461	5,000	1996	26.00	26
1995 Willie-Caroling 4460	5,000	1996	26.00	26
1989 Woodland Santa 2345	7,500	1990	100.00	150
1997 Yule Tree 4847	Closed	1998	20.00	20

Tender Moments - Sarah's Attic

YEAR ISSUE	EDITION LIMIT	YEAR RETD.	ISSUE PRICE	*QUOTE U.S.$
1995 All Done 4395	3,000	1997	29.00	29
1993 Always & Forever Bl. Wedding 3834	4,000	1997	60.00	60
1992 Baby Boy Birth blk. 3516	Closed	1993	50.00	55
1992 Baby Boy wh. 1 3527	Closed	1993	60.00	66
1992 Baby Girl blk. 1-2 3517	Closed	1993	50.00	55
1992 Baby Girl wh. 1 3528	Closed	1993	60.00	65
1996 Betsy 4491	2,500	1997	40.00	40
1992 Blk. Baby Boy 1-2 3518	Closed	1993	50.00	50
1992 Blk. Baby Girl Birth 3526	Closed	1993	50.00	50
1995 Black Mom w/Girl Braiding 4314	Closed	1998	66.00	66
1994 Black Special Angel-Sign 4224	Closed	1997	16.00	16
1993 Bless This Child Wh. Couple 3838	2,500	1994	60.00	60
1994 Boy w/Fire Truck wh. 4-5 3960	Closed	1996	40.00	40
1994 Boy w/Hobby Horse blk. 4-5 3958	Closed	1996	33.00	33
1992 Boy wh. 2-3 3624	Closed	1993	60.00	65
1993 Catch of Love Wh. Men Fishing 3827	4,000	1995	50.00	50
1993 Days to Remember Bl. Men Fishing 3828	4,000	1995	50.00	50
1995 Family is Love 4320	4,000	1995	60.00	60
1992 Generations of Love	Closed	1994	293.00	425
1993 Gentle Touch Bl. Girls 3825	2,500	1995	40.00	40
1994 Girl on Horse blk. 4-5 3957	Closed	1996	37.00	37
1994 Girl w/Trunk wh. 4-5 3959	Closed	1996	40.00	40
1992 Girl wh. 2-3 3623	Closed	1993	60.00	66
1995 Having Fun 4322	4,000	1995	44.00	44
1993 Joy of Motherhood blk. Pregnant Woman 3791	1,000	1994	55.00	70
1993 Little Blessing blk. Couple 3839	2,500	1994	75.00	90
1995 Little Engineer 4389	3,000	1997	25.00	25
1995 Love & Hugs Girl 4255	Closed	1997	38.00	38
1993 Love of Life blk. Couple 3788	1,000	1993	70.00	75-100
1995 Lullaby 4390	3,000	1997	29.00	29
1995 Me Big Girl 4394	3,000	1997	29.00	29
1996 Misty 4539	2,000	1997	24.00	24
1993 New Beginning Wh. Pregnant Woman 3790	1,000	1994	55.00	55
1995 Precious Dreams 4391	3,000	1997	28.00	28
1993 Promise of Love Wh. Wedding 3835	4,000	1997	60.00	60
1995 Remembrance 4470	2,000	1997	100.00	100
1996 Ross 4492	2,500	1997	36.00	36
1993 Special Bl. Boy in Wheelchair 3969	Closed	1997	38.00	38
1993 Special Times Wh. Girls 3826	2,500	1995	40.00	40
1996 Summer 4538	2,000	1997	24.00	24
1995 Sweet Dreams 4388	Closed	1996	29.00	29
1994 Timeless Knowledge 4323	4,000	1995	47.00	47
1997 Too Too Cute Ballerina 4904	Closed	1998	34.00	34
1995 Treasured Moments 4321	4,000	1995	70.00	70
1993 True Love wh. Couple 3789	1,000	1994	70.00	80
1994 White Special Angel-Sign 4218	Closed	1997	16.00	16
1995 Wow! 4324	4,000	1995	36.00	36
1996 Yakky Jackie 4504	3,000	1997	32.00	32

United Hearts Collection - Sarah's Attic

YEAR ISSUE	EDITION LIMIT	YEAR RETD.	ISSUE PRICE	*QUOTE U.S.$
1992 Adora Angel-May 3632	Closed	1993	50.00	75
1991 Adora Christmas-December 3479	Closed	1992	36.00	60
1991 Barney the Great-October 3466	Closed	1992	40.00	48
1991 Bibi & Biff Clowns-October 3467	Closed	1992	35.00	42
1991 Bibi-Miss Liberty Bear-July 3457	Closed	1992	30.00	36
1991 Bubba Beach-August 3461	Closed	1992	34.00	41
1992 Carrotman-January 3619	Closed	1993	30.00	40
1991 Chilly Snowman-January 3443	Closed	1992	33.00	40
1992 Cookie-July 3638	Closed	1993	34.00	34
1991 Crumb on Stool-September 3463	Closed	1992	32.00	39
1992 Cupcake-November 3649	Closed	1993	35.00	40
1991 Cupcake-Thanksgiving 3470	Closed	1993	36.00	36
1991 Emily-Springtime May 3452	Closed	1992	53.00	60
1992 Ethan Angel-August 3641	Closed	1993	46.00	60
1991 Gideon-Springtime May 3453	Closed	1992	40.00	43
1991 Hewett w/Leprechaun-March 3448	Closed	1992	56.00	67
1991 Noah w/Pot of Gold-March 3447	Closed	1992	36.00	43
1991 Pansy Beach-August 3459	Closed	1992	34.00	41
1991 Papa Barney & Biff-July 3458	Closed	1992	64.00	76
1991 Sally Booba Graduation-June 3454	Closed	1992	45.00	50
1991 Shelby w/Shamrock-March 3446	Closed	1992	36.00	43
1991 Tillie-January 3441	Closed	1992	32.00	40
1991 Willie-January 3442	Closed	1992	32.00	40

*Quotes have been rounded up to nearest dollar

Seymour Mann, Inc.

Christmas Collection - Various

YEAR ISSUE	EDITION LIMIT	YEAR RETD.	ISSUE PRICE	*QUOTE U.S.$
1991 Reindeer Barn Lite Up House CJ-421 - Jaimy	Closed	1993	55.00	55

Doll Art™ Collection - E. Mann

YEAR ISSUE	EDITION LIMIT	YEAR RETD.	ISSUE PRICE	*QUOTE U.S.$
1996 Hope CLT-604P	25,000		30.00	30

Wizard Of Oz - 40th Anniversary - E. Mann

YEAR ISSUE	EDITION LIMIT	YEAR RETD.	ISSUE PRICE	*QUOTE U.S.$
1979 Dorothy, Scarecrow, Lion, Tinman	Closed	1981	7.50	45
1979 Dorothy, Scarecrow, Lion, Tinman, Musical	Closed	1981	12.50	75

Shenandoah Designs

Arcade Toys - N. Lindblade

YEAR ISSUE	EDITION LIMIT	YEAR RETD.	ISSUE PRICE	*QUOTE U.S.$
1996 A-Express Truck	10,000		45.95	46
1995 Aeroplane Monocoupe	10,000		45.95	46
1996 Ambulance	10,000		45.95	46
1995 Bus-Safety Coach	10,000		45.95	46
1995 Coffee Mill	10,000		49.95	50
1996 Cottage Bank	10,000		29.95	30
1995 Coupe A-Rumble Seat	10,000		49.95	50
1995 Coupe Model T	10,000		45.95	46
1995 Express Flyer Wagon	10,000		45.95	46
1996 Farm Mower	10,000		39.95	40
1995 Fire Engine Auto	10,000		55.95	56
1996 Fire Ladder Truck	10,000		45.95	46
1995 Firewagon (Horsedrawn)	10,000		69.95	70
1995 Mail Box (Special Edition)	2,500		39.95	40
1996 Motorcycle Cop	10,000		45.95	46
1996 No. 1501 Sedan	10,000		29.95	30
1996 No. 1810 Fire Engine	10,000		45.95	46
1996 Plymouth Sedan	10,000		39.95	40
1996 Prancing Horse Bank	10,000		39.95	40
1996 Rocking Chair	10,000		29.95	30
1996 Row Crop Truck	10,000		45.95	46
1995 Sedan A Tudor	10,000		45.95	46
1995 Sedan T-Fordor	10,000		45.95	46
1995 State Bank	10,000	1996	45.95	46
1995 Steamboat	10,000		49.95	50
1996 Toy Policeman Bank	10,000		45.95	46
1995 Tractor	10,000		45.95	46
1995 Truck A-Stakes Sides	10,000		45.95	46
1995 Truck T-Stake Sides	10,000		55.95	56
1996 Two-Man Racer	10,000		45.95	46
1996 Wheelbarrow with Tools	10,000		45.95	46

D. Morgans - Shenandoah Design Team

YEAR ISSUE	EDITION LIMIT	YEAR RETD.	ISSUE PRICE	*QUOTE U.S.$
1996 Father Christmas	6,000		99.95	100
1996 Magic Never Ends	6,000		99.95	100
1996 St. Nicholas	6,000		99.95	100
1996 Accessory Group, set/3	2,000		70.00	70

Flower Fairy Series I - C.M. Barker

YEAR ISSUE	EDITION LIMIT	YEAR RETD.	ISSUE PRICE	*QUOTE U.S.$
1995 Greater Celandine Fairy	Open		19.95	20
1995 Lavender Fairy	Open		19.95	20
1995 Moutain Ash Fairy	Open		19.95	20
1995 Rosehip Fairy	Open		19.95	20
1995 Wayfaring Tree Fairy	Open		19.95	20
1995 Wild Cherry Blossom Fairy	Open		19.95	20

Flower Fairy Series II - C.M. Barker

YEAR ISSUE	EDITION LIMIT	YEAR RETD.	ISSUE PRICE	*QUOTE U.S.$
1996 Blackthorn Fairy	Open		19.95	20
1996 Canterbury Bell Fairy	Open		19.95	20
1996 Fumitory Fairy	Open		19.95	20
1996 Nasturtium Fairy	Open		19.95	20
1996 Poppy Fairy	Open		19.95	20
1996 Strawberry Fairy	Open		19.95	20

Flower Fairy Series III - C.M. Barker

YEAR ISSUE	EDITION LIMIT	YEAR RETD.	ISSUE PRICE	*QUOTE U.S.$
1996 Candytuft Fairy	Open		19.95	20
1996 Christmas Tree Fairy	Open		19.95	20
1996 Columbine Fairy	Open		19.95	20
1996 Dandelion Fairy	Open		19.95	20
1996 May Fairy	Open		19.95	20
1996 White Birdweed Fairy	Open		19.95	20

Flower Fairy Series IV - C.M. Barker

YEAR ISSUE	EDITION LIMIT	YEAR RETD.	ISSUE PRICE	*QUOTE U.S.$
1997 Black Medick Boy Fairy	Open		19.95	20
1997 Black Medick Girl Fairy	Open		19.95	20
1997 Box Tree Fairy	Open		19.95	20
1997 Elm Tree Fairy	Open		19.95	20
1997 Hazelnut Fairy	Open		19.95	20
1997 Pear Blossom Fairy	Open		19.95	20

Keeper Christmas Series - Shenandoah Design Team

YEAR ISSUE	EDITION LIMIT	YEAR RETD.	ISSUE PRICE	*QUOTE U.S.$
1995 Keeper of Christmas 1995	6,000	1995	39.95	195-240
1996 Keeper of Christmas 1996	6,000	1996	39.95	150-175
1997 Keeper of Christmas 1997	6,000	1997	39.95	80
1998 Keeper of Christmas 1998	6,000		39.95	40

Keeper Klub - Shenandoah Design Team

YEAR ISSUE	EDITION LIMIT	YEAR RETD.	ISSUE PRICE	*QUOTE U.S.$
1996 Keeper of Collectors	Retrd.	1998	35.00	35-60
1996 Keeper Shelf	Retrd.	1998	Gift	N/A

Keeper Series #1 - Shenandoah Design Team

YEAR ISSUE	EDITION LIMIT	YEAR RETD.	ISSUE PRICE	*QUOTE U.S.$
1993 Keeper of The Bath	Open		34.95	35
1993 Keeper of The Bedchamber	Open		34.95	35
1993 Keeper of The Entry	Open		34.95	35
1993 Keeper of The Hearth	Open		34.95	35
1993 Keeper of The Kitchen	Retrd.	1997	34.95	50-75
1993 Keeper of The Laundry	Open		34.95	35
1993 Keeper of The Library	Retrd.	1996	34.95	40-75
1993 Keeper of The Nursery	Retrd.	1998	34.95	40

Keeper Series #2 - Shenandoah Design Team

YEAR ISSUE	EDITION LIMIT	YEAR RETD.	ISSUE PRICE	*QUOTE U.S.$
1994 Keeper of The Cowboy Spirit	Open		34.95	35
1994 Keeper of The Home Office	Open		34.95	35
1994 Keeper of The Home Workshop	Open		34.95	35
1994 Keeper of Love	Open		34.95	35
1994 Keeper of Mothers	Retrd.	1998	34.95	40
1994 Keeper of Native Americans	Retrd.	1996	34.95	80-150
1994 Keeper of The Sunroom	Open		34.95	35
1994 Keeper of The Time	Open		34.95	35

Keeper Series #3 - Shenandoah Design Team

YEAR ISSUE	EDITION LIMIT	YEAR RETD.	ISSUE PRICE	*QUOTE U.S.$
1995 Keeper of Bears	Open		34.95	35
1995 Keeper of The Catch	Open		34.95	35
1995 Keeper of Fathers	Open		34.95	35
1995 Keeper of Flight	Open		34.95	35
1995 Keeper of Rails	Open		34.95	35
1995 Keeper of Thanksgiving	Retrd.	1997	34.95	55-60

Keeper Series #4 - Shenandoah Design Team

YEAR ISSUE	EDITION LIMIT	YEAR RETD.	ISSUE PRICE	*QUOTE U.S.$
1995 Keeper of Birthdays	Open		34.95	35
1995 Keeper of Faith	Open		34.95	35
1995 Keeper of Firefighters	Open		34.95	35
1995 Keeper of The Garden	Open		34.95	35
1995 Keeper of Golfing	Open		34.95	35
1995 Keeper of Music	Open		34.95	35
1995 Keeper of The Sea	Open		34.95	35
1995 Keeper of Trails	Open		34.95	35
1995 Keeper of Woodland Animals	Open		34.95	35

Keeper Series #5 - Shenandoah Design Team

YEAR ISSUE	EDITION LIMIT	YEAR RETD.	ISSUE PRICE	*QUOTE U.S.$
1996 Keeper of The Checkered Flag	Open		34.95	35
1996 Keeper of Friendship	Open		34.95	35
1996 Keeper of Peace	Open		34.95	35
1996 Keeper of Photography	Open		34.95	35
1996 Keeper of Secrets	Open		34.95	35
1996 Keeper of Teachers	Open		34.95	35

Keeper Series #6 - Shenandoah Design Team

YEAR ISSUE	EDITION LIMIT	YEAR RETD.	ISSUE PRICE	*QUOTE U.S.$
1997 Keeper of Cats	Open		34.95	35
1997 Keeper of The Crown Jewels	6,000		39.95	40
1997 Keeper of The Galaxy	Open		34.95	35
1997 Keeper of Halloween	3,500	1997	45.00	45-49
1997 Keeper of Pubs	Open		34.95	35

Keeper Series #7 - Shenandoah Design Team

YEAR ISSUE	EDITION LIMIT	YEAR RETD.	ISSUE PRICE	*QUOTE U.S.$
1998 Keeper of Dogs	Open		34.95	35
1998 Keeper of Dolls	Open		34.95	35
1998 Keeper of Needlework	Open		34.95	35
1998 Keeper of Nurses	Open		34.95	35
1998 Keeper of Sons	Open		34.95	35

Leapers - Shenandoah Design Team

YEAR ISSUE	EDITION LIMIT	YEAR RETD.	ISSUE PRICE	*QUOTE U.S.$
1997 Kiss a Leaper	6,000		49.50	50
1997 Leap of Faith	6,000		49.50	50
1997 Leaper Went A-Courtin'	6,000		49.50	50
1997 Learn and Leap	6,000		49.50	50
1997 To Leap or Not to Leap	6,000		49.50	50
1997 To Leap...To Dream	6,000		49.50	50

Limbies - Shenandoah Design Team

YEAR ISSUE	EDITION LIMIT	YEAR RETD.	ISSUE PRICE	*QUOTE U.S.$
1997 Bruno	6,000		39.95	40
1997 First Bear	6,000		39.95	40
1997 Grace	6,000		39.95	40
1997 Guitarist	6,000		39.95	40
1997 Queen	6,000		39.95	40
1997 Zeus	6,000		49.50	50

Sports Impressions/Enesco Corporation

Collectors' Club Members Only - Various

YEAR ISSUE	EDITION LIMIT	YEAR RETD.	ISSUE PRICE	*QUOTE U.S.$
1990 The Mick-Mickey Mantle 5000-1	Yr.Iss.	N/A	75.00	40-75
1991 Rickey Henderson-Born to Run 5001-11	Yr.Iss.	N/A	49.95	50
1991 Nolan Ryan-300 Wins 5002-01	Yr.Iss.	N/A	125.00	125
1991 Willie, Mickey & Duke plate 5003-04	Yr.Iss.	N/A	39.95	50
1992 Babe Ruth 5006-11	Yr.Iss.	N/A	40.00	38-40
1992 Walter Payton 5015-01	Yr.Iss.	N/A	50.00	38-50
1993 The 1927 Yankees plate - R.Tanenbaum	Yr.Iss.	N/A	60.00	35-60

Collectors' Club Symbol of Membership - Sports Impressions

YEAR ISSUE	EDITION LIMIT	YEAR RETD.	ISSUE PRICE	*QUOTE U.S.$
1991 Mick/7 plate 5001-02	Yr.Iss.	N/A	Gift	25-50
1992 USA Basketball team plate 5008-30	Yr.Iss.	N/A	Gift	25
1993 Nolan Ryan porcelain card	Yr.Iss.	N/A	Gift	25

Baseball Superstar Figurines - Sports Impressions

YEAR ISSUE	EDITION LIMIT	YEAR RETD.	ISSUE PRICE	*QUOTE U.S.$
1988 Al Kaline	2,500	N/A	90.00	50-100
1988 Andre Dawson	2,500	N/A	90.00	50-100
1988 Bob Feller	2,500	N/A	90.00	50-100
1992 Cubs Ryne Sandberg Home (signed) 1118-23	975	1993	150.00	250
1987 Don Mattingly	Closed	N/A	90.00	225-250
1987 Don Mattingly (Franklin glove variation)	Closed	N/A	90.00	350-600
1989 Duke Snider	2,500	N/A	90.00	50-100
1994 Giants Barry Bonds (signed) 1160-46	975	1995	150.00	100-150
1992 Johnny Bench (hand signed) 1126-23	975	1994	150.00	225
1988 Jose Canseco	Closed	N/A	90.00	50-100
1987 Keith Hernandez	2,500	N/A	90.00	50-100
1989 Kirk Gibson	Closed	N/A	90.00	50-100
1991 Mark McGwire 10" (Oakland As) 1039-12	1,900	N/A	295.00	295
1987 Mickey Mantle	Closed	N/A	90.00	150-195
1996 Mickey Mantle "The Greatest Switch Hitter" (hand signed) 1228-46 - T. Treadway	975	1995	395.00	495-600
1992 Nolan Ryan Figurine/plate/stand 1134-31	500	1994	260.00	260
1990 Nolan Ryan Kings of K	Closed	N/A	125.00	89-125
1990 Nolan Ryan Mini	Closed	N/A	50.00	50
1990 Nolan Ryan Supersize	Closed	N/A	250.00	225-250
1993 Oakland A's Reggie Jackson (signed) 1048-46	975	1994	150.00	150-275
1993 Rangers Nolan Ryan (signed) 1127-46	975	1994	175.00	225-250
1994 Rangers Nolan Ryan (signed) Farewell 1161-49	975	1994	150.00	225-250
1990 Ted Williams	Closed	N/A	90.00	90-125
1994 Tom Glavine (signed) 1163-46	975	N/A	150.00	90-150
1987 Wade Boggs	Closed	N/A	90.00	50-100
1989 Will Clark	Closed	N/A	90.00	50-100
1993 Yankees Mickey Mantle (signed) 1038-46	975	1993	195.00	350

Basketball Superstar Figurines - Sports Impressions

YEAR ISSUE	EDITION LIMIT	YEAR RETD.	ISSUE PRICE	*QUOTE U.S.$
1993 Julius Erving 76ers (hand signed) 4102-46	975	1994	150.00	150-250
1995 Larry Bird (hand signed) 4086-46	975	N/A	195.00	150-250

Sunbelt Marketing Group, Inc.

Christmas Series - Sunbelt Marketing Group, Inc.

YEAR ISSUE	EDITION LIMIT	YEAR RETD.	ISSUE PRICE	*QUOTE U.S.$
1997 1931 Santa (based upon original artwork by Haddon Sundblom)	3,500		270.00	270

Decorative Series - Sunbelt Marketing Group, Inc.

YEAR ISSUE	EDITION LIMIT	YEAR RETD.	ISSUE PRICE	*QUOTE U.S.$
1998 Floral Splendor	1,000		400.00	400
1998 Twilight's Garden	1,000		400.00	400

Folk Art Series - Sunbelt Marketing Group, Inc.

YEAR ISSUE	EDITION LIMIT	YEAR RETD.	ISSUE PRICE	*QUOTE U.S.$
1998 Brazil (based upon original design/artwork by Maria de Lurdes da Silva Pereira)	1,000		300.00	300
1998 China (based upon original design by Tian Changqing and sculpting by Fan Yinghai)	1,000		350.00	350
1997 Great Britain (based upon original design/artwork by Brian Anderson)	2,500		500.00	500
1997 Morocco (based upon original design/artwork by Hassan Kdadri)	2,500		280.00	280
1997 Russia (based upon original design/artwork by Victor Yaakovlev)	2,500		500.00	500
1997 Singapore (based upon original design/artwork by Joeel Lee Kian Kong)	2,500		300.00	300
1997 U.S. Shelley (based upon original design/artwork by Mary Shelley)	2,500		160.00	160
1998 Vietnam (based upon original design/artwork by Le Huy Van)	1,000		300.00	300

Swarovski Consumer Goods Ltd.

Swarovski Crystal Memories-Annual Edition Angels

YEAR ISSUE	EDITION LIMIT	YEAR RETD.	ISSUE PRICE	*QUOTE U.S.$
1996 1996 Annual Edition Angel 9443NR960001	Retrd.	1996	75.00	105-156
1997 1997 Annual Edition Angel 9443NR970001	12/98		75.00	75-130
1998 1998 Annual Edition Angel 9443NR980001	Yr.Iss.		75.00	75

Swarovski Crystal Memories-Celebrations

YEAR ISSUE	EDITION LIMIT	YEAR RETD.	ISSUE PRICE	*QUOTE U.S.$
1995 Balloons 9460NR000067	Open		32.50	33
1996 Bells 9460NR000071	Open		32.50	33
1995 Birthday Cake 9460NR000059	Open		32.50	33
1996 Bouquet 9460NR000072	Open		40.00	40
1996 Champagne 9460NR000077	Open		32.50	33
1995 Champagne Bucket w/2 flutes 9460NR000065	Open		49.50	50
1995 Present 9460NR000066	Open		32.50	33

Swarovski Crystal Memories-Childhood Dreams

YEAR ISSUE	EDITION LIMIT	YEAR RETD.	ISSUE PRICE	*QUOTE U.S.$
1993 Baby Carriage 9460NR000024	Open		40.00	40
1997 Baby Shoes 9460NR000073	Open		25.00	25
1993 Baby's Bottle 9460NR000009	12/98		17.50	18
1998 Baby's Rattle 9460NR000086	Open		17.50	18
1998 Doll 9460NR000083	Open		49.50	50
1998 Freight Car 9460NR000082	Open		32.50	33
1993 Merry-Go-Round 9460NR000017	Open		32.50	33
1993 Pacifier 9460NR000003	Open		17.50	18
1998 Passenger Car 9460NR000081	Open		32.50	33
1996 Rocking Horse 9460NR000068	Open		40.00	40
1994 Row Boat 9460NR000034	Open		40.00	40
1997 Toy Train 9460NR000078	Open		49.50	50
1998 Tricycle 9460NR000085	Open		40.00	40

Swarovski Crystal Memories-Dedicated to Music

YEAR ISSUE	EDITION LIMIT	YEAR RETD.	ISSUE PRICE	*QUOTE U.S.$
1995 Flute 9460NR000058	Open		40.00	40
1993 Guitar 9460NR000020	Open		32.50	33
1993 Piano 9460NR000021	Open		40.00	40
1995 Saxophone 9460NR000053	Open		40.00	40
1993 Violin 9460NR000019	Open		25.00	25

Swarovski Crystal Memories-In a Class of Their Own

YEAR ISSUE	EDITION LIMIT	YEAR RETD.	ISSUE PRICE	*QUOTE U.S.$
1997 Camera 9460NR000074	Open		32.50	33

*Quotes have been rounded up to nearest dollar

YEAR ISSUE	EDITION LIMIT	YEAR RETD.	ISSUE PRICE	*QUOTE U.S.$
1993 Golf Bag 9460NR000018	Open		40.00	40
1994 Ice Skate 9460NR000051	Open		32.50	33
1994 Sailboat 9460NR000050	Open		40.00	40
1993 Ski 9460NR000029	Open		25.00	25
1994 Tennis Racket 9460NR000048	12/98		32.50	33
1994 Trophy 9460NR000052	12/98		40.00	40

Swarovski Crystal Memories-In Familiar Surroundings

YEAR ISSUE	EDITION LIMIT	YEAR RETD.	ISSUE PRICE	*QUOTE U.S.$
1994 Dinner Bell 9460NR000047	12/98		17.50	18
1996 Fruit Bowl 9460NR000069	Open		40.00	40
1994 Ice Cream Sundae 9460NR000046	12/98		25.00	25
1993 Piece of Cake 9460NR000026	Open		25.00	25
1993 Tea Set 9460NR000037	Open		49.50	50
1993 Wine Set 9460NR000038	Open		49.50	50

Swarovski Crystal Memories-Secrets

YEAR ISSUE	EDITION LIMIT	YEAR RETD.	ISSUE PRICE	*QUOTE U.S.$
1997 Beauty Case/Jewelry Box 9448NR000001	Open		85.00	85
1997 Gift/Clock 9448NR000004	Open		95.00	95
1997 Gift/Jewelry Box 9448NR000009	Open		85.00	85
1997 Globe/Clock 9448NR000008	Open		95.00	95
1997 Handbag/Clock 9448NR00002	Open		95.00	95
1997 Rose Vase/Flacon 9448NR000005	Open		65.00	65
1997 Spring Flower Vase/Flacon 9448NR000007	Open		65.00	65
1997 Suitcase/Picture Frame 9448NR000003	Open		75.00	75
1997 Tulip Vase/Flacon 9448NR000006	Open		75.00	75

Swarovski Crystal Memories-Times Past

YEAR ISSUE	EDITION LIMIT	YEAR RETD.	ISSUE PRICE	*QUOTE U.S.$
1998 Alarm Clock 9460NR000080	Open		40.00	40
1993 Coffee Mill 9460NR000001	12/98		32.50	33
1998 Film Camera 9460NR000084	Open		49.50	50
1996 Globe 9460NR000070	Open		32.50	33
1995 Gramophone 9460NR000056	Open		40.00	40
1993 Hourglass 9460NR000012	Open		25.00	25
1996 Mantel Clock 9460NR000057	Open		32.50	33
1994 Penny Farthing Bicycle 9460NR000043	12/98		32.50	33
1998 Radio 9460NR000079	Open		32.50	33
1994 Telephone 9460NR000041	Open		32.50	33
1997 Typewriter 9460NR000076	Open		40.00	40

Swarovski Crystal Memories-Your Special Treasures

YEAR ISSUE	EDITION LIMIT	YEAR RETD.	ISSUE PRICE	*QUOTE U.S.$
1993 Atomizer 9460NR000027	Open		17.50	18
1994 Diary 9460NR000055	Open		40.00	40
1993 Flower Basket 9460NR000010	Open		40.00	40
1997 Flower Pot 9460NR000075	Open		32.50	33
1993 Handbag 9460NR000013	12/98		32.50	33
1993 High-Heeled Shoe 9460NR000031	Open		32.50	33
1994 Inkwell with Quill 9460NR000060	Open		17.50	18
1993 Watering Can 9460NR000007	12/98		32.50	33

Swarovski Crystal Memories-Retired

YEAR ISSUE	EDITION LIMIT	YEAR RETD.	ISSUE PRICE	*QUOTE U.S.$
1993 Anchor 9460NR000030	Retrd.	1996	32.50	33
1993 Beer Mug 9460NR000022	Retrd.	1997	25.00	25
1993 Greek Vase 9460NR000006	Retrd.	1996	32.50	33
1993 Iron 9460NR000002	Retrd.	1996	25.00	25
1994 Kettledrum 9460NR000054	Retrd.	1997	32.50	33
1994 Knapsack 9460NR000049	Retrd.	1997	32.50	33
1993 Knitting Needles and Wool 9460NR000016	Retrd.	1996	32.50	33
1993 Lamp 9460NR000039	Retrd.	1997	25.00	25
1993 Lantern 9460NR000023	Retrd.	1997	40.00	40
1993 Salt & Pepper 9460NR000045	Retrd.	1996	25.00	25-30
1994 Spinning Wheel 9460NR000035	Retrd.	1997	40.00	40
1993 Treasure Chest 9460NR000004	Retrd.	1996	40.00	40
1993 Treasure Island 9460NR000025	Retrd.	1996	32.50	33
1993 Umbrella 9460NR000008	Retrd.	1996	32.50	33

Swarovski Selection - Various

YEAR ISSUE	EDITION LIMIT	YEAR RETD.	ISSUE PRICE	*QUOTE U.S.$
1996 Apollo Bowl 0206212 - B. Sipek	Open		650.00	650
1997 Astro Box 0210793 - A. Putman	Open		355.00	355
1996 Calix Vase 0210527 - B. Sipek	Open		650.00	650
1995 Cleo Picture Frame 0200085 - M. Zendron	Open		440.00	440
1995 Colorado Bowl 0168082 - J. Desgrippes	Open		355.00	355
1995 Curaçao Tableclock 0200086 - E. Mair	Open		440.00	440
1992 Enigma Tableclock 0168002 - L. Redl	12/98		355.00	355
1992 Euclid Caviar Bowl 0168001 - L. Redl	Open		650.00	650
1996 Gemini Vase 0206210 - B. Sipek	Open		440.00	440
1992 Helios Tableclock 0168003 - B. Sipek	Open		355.00	355
1998 Ren Candleholder 0215556 - K. Nagai	Open		525.00	525
1996 Saturn Candleholder 0206211 - B. Sipek	Open		440.00	440
1993 Shiva Box 0170301 - L. Redl	Open		440.00	440
1992 Small Vase 0167999 - J. Desgrippes	Open		650.00	650
1992 Soliflor Vase 0168000 - J. Desgrippes	Open		440.00	440
1994 Stalactite Candleholder 0182485 - A. Putman	Open		620.00	620
1994 Stalagmite Ringholder 0182484 - A. Putman	12/98		355.00	355
1992 Uranus Candleholder 0168004 - B. Sipek	12/98		385.00	385
1997 Wa Bowl 0215555 - K. Nagai	Open		850.00	850

Swarovski Selection-Retired

YEAR ISSUE	EDITION LIMIT	YEAR RETD.	ISSUE PRICE	*QUOTE U.S.$
1992 Boite meli-melo (bowl) 0168008	Retrd.	1995	210.00	185-273
1994 Buchstützen (bookends) 0168342	Retrd.	1996	385.00	360-462
1992 Cendrier (ashtray) 0168007	Retrd.	1995	190.00	228-360
1994 Coupe-papier (letter opener) 0172756	Retrd.	1997	190.00	190-225
1992 Federhalter (pen holder) 0168006	Retrd.	1995	385.00	360-500
1992 Grand Contenitore (bowl) 0167997	Retrd.	1995	620.00	1375-2188
1997 Hong Kong 0222859 - Mae Tsang	1,997	1997	1100.00	3600-5400
1993 Porte-cartes imago (card holder) 0170199	Retrd.	1995	190.00	210-228
1992 Scatola Piccola con tappo (bowl) 0167998	Retrd.	1995	515.00	515-550
1992 Schmuckdose (jewel box) 0168005	Retrd.	1995	515.00	669-685

Swarovski Collectors Society - Various

YEAR ISSUE	EDITION LIMIT	YEAR RETD.	ISSUE PRICE	*QUOTE U.S.$
1987 Togetherness-The Lovebirds - M. Schreck	Yr.Iss.	1987	150.00	3900-5000
1988 Sharing-The Woodpeckers - A. Stocker	Yr.Iss.	1988	165.00	1500-2400
1988 Mini Cactus	Yr.Iss.	1988	Gift	145-325
1989 Amour-The Turtledoves - A. Stocker	Yr.Iss.	1989	195.00	900-1500
1989 The Lovebirds, The Woodpeckers, The Turtledoves	Closed	1989	510.00	7440-7800
1989 SCS Key Chain	Yr.Iss.	1989	Gift	94-135
1990 Lead Me-The Dolphins - M. Stamey	Yr.Iss.	1990	225.00	1088-1500
1990 Mini Chaton	Yr.Iss.	1990	Gift	76-160
1991 Save Me-The Seals - M. Stamey	Yr.Iss.	1991	225.00	500-650
1991 Dolphin Brooch	Yr.Iss.	1991	75.00	139-185
1991 SCS Pin	Yr.Iss.	1991	Gift	50-135
1992 Care For Me - The Whales - M. Stamey	Yr.Iss.	1992	265.00	429-650
1992 The Dolphins, The Seals, The Whales - M. Stamey	Closed	1992	715.00	2250-2775
1992 SCS Pen	Yr.Iss.	1992	Gift	49-80
1992 5th Anniversary Edition-The Birthday Cake - G. Stamey	Yr.Iss.	1992	85.00	150-275
1993 Inspiration Africa-The Elephant - M. Zendron	Yr.Iss.	1993	325.00	1300-1900
1993 Elephant Brooch	Yr.Iss.	1993	85.00	88-150
1993 Leather Luggage Tag	Yr.Iss.	1993	Gift	50-65
1994 Inspiration Africa-The Kudu - M. Stamey	Yr.Iss.	1994	295.00	470-800
1994 Leather Double Picture Frame	Yr.Iss.	1994	Gift	55-65
1995 Inspiration Africa-The Lion - A. Stocker	Yr.Iss.	1995	325.00	450-750
1995 Centenary Swan Brooch	Yr.Iss.	1995	125.00	161-200
1995 The Elephant, The Kudu, The Lion	Closed	1995	945.00	2000-3000
1995 Miniature Crystal Swan	Yr.Iss.	1995	Gift	49-135
1996 Fabulous Creatures-The Unicorn - M. Zendron	Yr.Iss.	1996	325.00	437-850
1996 Clear Crystal Heart	Yr.Iss.	1996	Gift	52-120
1997 Fabulous Creatures-The Dragon - G. Stamey	Yr.Iss.	1997	325.00	375-700
1997 SCS 10th Anniversary Edition - The Squirrel - A. Hirzinger	Yr.Iss.	1997	140.00	135-195
1997 Blue Crystal Heart	Yr.Iss.	1997	Gift	45-125
1998 Fabulous Creatures-The Pegasus - A. Stocker	Yr.Iss.	1998	350.00	350
1998 Red Crystal Heart	Yr.Iss.	1998	Gift	70-105

Swarovski Silver Crystal-Worldwide Limited Editions - A. Stocker

YEAR ISSUE	EDITION LIMIT	YEAR RETD.	ISSUE PRICE	*QUOTE U.S.$
1995 Eagle	10,000	1995	1750.00	6800-10000
1998 Peacock	10,000	1998	1800.00	6050-7400

Swarovski Silver Crystal-Centenary Edition - A. Hirzinger

YEAR ISSUE	EDITION LIMIT	YEAR RETD.	ISSUE PRICE	*QUOTE U.S.$
1995 Centenary Swan	Yr.Iss.	1995	150.00	107-225

Swarovski Silver Crystal-Commemorative Single Issues - Team

YEAR ISSUE	EDITION LIMIT	YEAR RETD.	ISSUE PRICE	*QUOTE U.S.$
1990 Elephant, 7640NR100 (Introduced by Swarovski America as a commemorative item for Design Celebration/January '90 in Walt Disney World)	Closed	1990	125.00	1156-1500
1993 Elephant, 7640NR100001 (Introduced by Swarovski America as a commemorative item for Design Celebration/January '93 in Walt Disney World)	Closed	1993	150.00	375-680

Swarovski Silver Crystal-African Wildlife - Various

YEAR ISSUE	EDITION LIMIT	YEAR RETD.	ISSUE PRICE	*QUOTE U.S.$
1995 Baby Elephant - M. Zendron	Open		155.00	155
1994 Cheetah - M. Stamey	Open		275.00	275
1998 Chimpanzee - E. Mair	Open		125.00	125
1989 Elephant-Small - A. Stocker	Open		50.00	65
1997 Leopard - M. Stamey	Open		260.00	260
1997 Lion Cub - A. Stocker	Open		125.00	125

Swarovski Silver Crystal-Among Flowers And Foliage - C. Schneiderbauer, unless otherwise noted

YEAR ISSUE	EDITION LIMIT	YEAR RETD.	ISSUE PRICE	*QUOTE U.S.$
1994 Butterfly on Leaf	Open		75.00	85
1995 Dragonfly	Open		85.00	85
1992 Hummingbird	Open		195.00	210
1996 Snail on Vine-Leaf - E. Mair	Open		65.00	65

Swarovski Silver Crystal-Barnyard Friends - Various

YEAR ISSUE	EDITION LIMIT	YEAR RETD.	ISSUE PRICE	*QUOTE U.S.$
1993 Mother Goose - A. Stocker	Open		75.00	75
1993 Tom Gosling - A. Stocker	Open		37.50	38
1993 Dick Gosling - A. Stocker	Open		37.50	38
1993 Harry Gosling - A. Stocker	Open		37.50	38
1984 Medium Pig - M. Schreck	Open		35.00	55
1988 Mini Chicks (Set/3) - G. Stamey	Open		35.00	45
1987 Mini Hen - G. Stamey	Open		35.00	45
1982 Mini Pig - M. Schreck	Open		16.00	30
1987 Mini Rooster - G. Stamey	Open		35.00	55

Swarovski Silver Crystal-Beauties of the Lake - Various

YEAR ISSUE	EDITION LIMIT	YEAR RETD.	ISSUE PRICE	*QUOTE U.S.$
1997 Baby Carp - M. Stamey	Open		49.50	50
1994 Frog - G. Stamey	Open		49.50	50
1996 Goldfish-Mini - M. Stamey	Open		45.00	45
1989 Mallard-Giant - M. Stamey	Open		2000.00	4500
1984 Standing Drake-Mini - M. Schreck	Open		20.00	45
1987 Standing Duck-Mini - A. Stocker	Open		22.00	38
1981 Swan-Large - M. Schreck	Open		55.00	95
1995 Swan-Maxi - A. Hirzinger	Open		4500.00	4500
1981 Swan-Medium - M. Schreck	Open		44.00	85
1982 Swan-Small - M. Schreck	Open		35.00	50
1986 Swimming Duck-Mini - A. Stocker	Open		16.00	38

Swarovski Silver Crystal-Crystal Melodies - M. Zendron, unless otherwise noted

YEAR ISSUE	EDITION LIMIT	YEAR RETD.	ISSUE PRICE	*QUOTE U.S.$
1993 Grand Piano	Open		250.00	260
1992 Harp	12/98		175.00	210
1997 Saxophone	Open		125.00	125
1996 Violin - G. Stamey	Open		140.00	140

Swarovski Silver Crystal-Decorative Items For The Desk (Paperweights) - M. Schreck

YEAR ISSUE	EDITION LIMIT	YEAR RETD.	ISSUE PRICE	*QUOTE U.S.$
1990 Chaton-Giant	Open		4500.00	4500
1987 Chaton-Large	12/98		190.00	260
1987 Chaton-Small	12/98		50.00	65

Swarovski Silver Crystal-Endangered Species - Various

YEAR ISSUE	EDITION LIMIT	YEAR RETD.	ISSUE PRICE	*QUOTE U.S.$
1993 Baby Panda - A. Stocker	Open		24.50	25
1993 Mother Panda - A. Stocker	Open		120.00	125
1987 Koala-Large - A. Stocker	Open		50.00	65
1989 Mini Koala - A. Stocker	Open		35.00	45
1992 Sitting Baby Beaver - A. Stocker	Open		47.50	50
1993 Mother Kangaroo with Baby - G. Stamey	Open		95.00	95
1998 Baby Sea Lion - M. Stamey	Open		49.50	50
1998 Baby Tortoises (Set/2) - E. Mair	Open		45.00	45
1997 Tortoise - E. Mair	Open		55.00	55
1998 Tiger - M. Stamey	Open		275.00	275
1983 Turtle-Giant - M. Schreck	Open		2500.00	4500
1981 Turtle-Large - M. Schreck	12/98		48.00	75

Swarovski Silver Crystal-Exquisite Accents - Various

YEAR ISSUE	EDITION LIMIT	YEAR RETD.	ISSUE PRICE	*QUOTE U.S.$
1995 Angel - A. Stocker	Open		210.00	210
1981 Birdbath - M. Schreck	Open		150.00	210
1996 Blue Flower Jewel Box - G. Stamey	Open		210.00	210
1996 Blue Flower Picture Frame - G. Stamey	Open		260.00	260
1997 Kris Bear Picture Frame - M. Zendron	Open		95.00	95
1997 Kris Bear Table Clock - M. Zendron	Open		210.00	210
1996 The Orchid-pink - M. Stamey	Open		140.00	140
1996 The Orchid-yellow - M. Stamey	Open		140.00	140
1997 Oriental Flacon - M. Zendron	Open		185.00	185
1997 Picture Frame w/Butterfly - C. Schneiderbauer	Open		85.00	85
1997 Picture Frame w/Ladybug - E. Mair	Open		55.00	55
1997 Reindeer - A. Hirzinger	Open		185.00	185
1993 The Rose - M. Stamey	Open		150.00	155
1998 Santa Claus - M. Zendron	Open		155.00	155
1996 Sleigh - M. Zendron	Open		295.00	295
1998 Solaris Table Clock - A. Stocker	Open		375.00	375
1997 Sweet Heart - E. Mair	Open		110.00	110
1997 Sweet Heart Jewel Box - E. Mair	Open		140.00	140
1987 Table Bell-Small - M. Schreck	Open		60.00	65

Swarovski Silver Crystal-Fairy Tales - E. Mair

YEAR ISSUE	EDITION LIMIT	YEAR RETD.	ISSUE PRICE	*QUOTE U.S.$
1996 Red Riding Hood	Open		185.00	185
1996 Wolf	Open		155.00	155

Swarovski Silver Crystal-Feathered Friends - Various

YEAR ISSUE	EDITION LIMIT	YEAR RETD.	ISSUE PRICE	*QUOTE U.S.$
1996 Baby Lovebirds - A. Stocker	Open		155.00	155
1995 Dove - E. Mair	Open		55.00	55
1993 Pelican - A. Hirzinger	Open		37.50	38

Swarovski Silver Crystal-Game of Kings - M. Schreck

YEAR ISSUE	EDITION LIMIT	YEAR RETD.	ISSUE PRICE	*QUOTE U.S.$
1985 Chess Set	Open		950.00	1375

Swarovski Silver Crystal-Horses on Parade - M. Zendron

YEAR ISSUE	EDITION LIMIT	YEAR RETD.	ISSUE PRICE	*QUOTE U.S.$
1998 Arabian Stallion	Open		260.00	260
1993 White Stallion	Open		250.00	260

Swarovski Silver Crystal-In A Summer Meadow - Various

YEAR ISSUE	EDITION LIMIT	YEAR RETD.	ISSUE PRICE	*QUOTE U.S.$
1997 Bunny Rabbit - E. Mair	Open		55.00	55
1983 Butterfly-Large - Team	Open		44.00	85
1986 Butterfly-mini - Team	Open		16.00	45
1994 Field Mice (Set/3) - A. Stocker	Open		42.50	45
1991 Field Mouse - A. Stocker	Open		47.50	50
1997 Four-Leaf Clover - A. Hirzinger	Open		49.50	50
1988 Hedgehog-Medium - M. Schreck	Open		70.00	85
1988 Hedgehog-Small - M. Schreck	Open		50.00	55
1995 Ladybug - E. Mair	Open		29.50	30
1988 Mini Sitting Rabbit - A. Stocker	Open		35.00	45
1988 Mother Rabbit - A. Stocker	Open		60.00	75

Swarovski Silver Crystal-Kingdom Of Ice And Snow - Various

YEAR ISSUE	EDITION LIMIT	YEAR RETD.	ISSUE PRICE	*QUOTE U.S.$
1997 Baby Penguins (Set/3) - A. Stocker	Open		75.00	75
1996 Madame Penguin - A. Stocker	Open		85.00	85
1985 Penguin-Mini - M. Schreck	Open		16.00	38
1985 Seal-Mini - A. Stocker	Open		30.00	45
1995 Sir Penguin - A. Stocker	Open		85.00	85

*Quotes have been rounded up to nearest dollar

Swarovski Silver Crystal-Our Candleholders - Various

YEAR ISSUE	EDITION LIMIT	YEAR RETD.	ISSUE PRICE	*QUOTE U.S.$
1996 Blue Flower - G. Stamey	Open		260.00	260
1989 Star-Medium 7600NR143001 - Team	Open		200.00	260
1985 Water Lily-Large 7600NR125 - M. Schreck	Open		200.00	375
1984 Water Lily-Medium 7600NR123 - M. Schreck	Open		150.00	260
1985 Water Lily-Small 7600NR124 - M. Schreck	Open		100.00	175

Swarovski Silver Crystal-Pets' Corner - Various

YEAR ISSUE	EDITION LIMIT	YEAR RETD.	ISSUE PRICE	*QUOTE U.S.$
1990 Beagle - A. Stocker	Open		40.00	50
1993 Beagle Playing - A. Stocker	Open		49.50	50
1991 Sitting Cat - M. Stamey	Open		75.00	85
1993 Sitting Poodle - A. Stocker	Open		85.00	85
1996 St. Bernard - E. Mair	Open		95.00	95
1996 Tomcat - A. Hirzinger	Open		45.00	45

Swarovski Silver Crystal-South Sea - Various

YEAR ISSUE	EDITION LIMIT	YEAR RETD.	ISSUE PRICE	*QUOTE U.S.$
1996 Crab-Mini - M. Stamey	Open		65.00	65
1987 Blowfish-Mini - Team	Open		22.00	30
1987 Blowfish-Small - Team	Open		35.00	55
1991 Butterfly Fish - M. Stamey	12/98		150.00	175
1995 Dolphin - M. Stamey	Open		210.00	210
1987 Shell w/Pearl - M. Stamey	Open		120.00	175
1993 Sea Horse - M. Stamey	Open		85.00	85
1995 Shell - M. Stamey	Open		45.00	45
1995 Starfish - M. Stamey	Open		29.50	30
1995 Conch - M. Stamey	Open		29.50	30
1995 Maritime Trio (Shell, Starfish, Conch) - M. Stamey	Open		104.00	104
1993 Three South Sea Fish - M. Stamey	12/98		135.00	140

Swarovski Silver Crystal-Sparkling Fruit - Various

YEAR ISSUE	EDITION LIMIT	YEAR RETD.	ISSUE PRICE	*QUOTE U.S.$
1995 Grapes - Team	Open		375.00	375
1983 Pineapple-Giant /Gold - M. Schreck	Open		1750.00	3250
1982 Pineapple-Large /Gold - M. Schreck	Open		150.00	260
1987 Pineapple-Small /Gold - M. Schreck	Open		55.00	85

Swarovski Silver Crystal-When We Were Young - Various

YEAR ISSUE	EDITION LIMIT	YEAR RETD.	ISSUE PRICE	*QUOTE U.S.$
1990 Airplane - A. Stocker	Open		135.00	155
1996 Baby Carriage - G. Stamey	Open		140.00	140
1993 Kris Bear - M. Zendron	Open		75.00	75
1995 Kris Bear on Skates - M. Zendron	Open		75.00	75
1997 Kris Bear with Honey Pot - M. Zendron	Open		75.00	75
1988 Locomotive - G. Stamey	Open		150.00	155
1990 Petrol Wagon - G. Stamey	Open		75.00	95
1997 Puppet - G. Stamey	Open		125.00	125
1994 Replica Cat - Team	Open		37.50	38
1994 Replica Hedgehog - Team	Open		37.50	38
1994 Replica Mouse - Team	Open		37.50	38
1988 Wagon - G. Stamey	Open		85.00	95
1994 Rocking Horse - G. Stamey	Open		125.00	125
1994 Starter Set - Team	Open		112.50	113
1994 Sailboat - G. Stamey	Open		195.00	210
1991 Santa Maria - G. Stamey	Open		375.00	375
1998 Tank Wagon - G. Stamey	Open		95.00	95
1988 Tender - G. Stamey	Open		55.00	55
1993 Tipping Wagon - G. Stamey	Open		95.00	95
1995 Train-Mini - G. Stamey	Open		125.00	125

Swarovski Silver Crystal-Woodland Friends - Various

YEAR ISSUE	EDITION LIMIT	YEAR RETD.	ISSUE PRICE	*QUOTE U.S.$
1981 Bear-Large - M. Schreck	Open		75.00	95
1985 Bear-Mini - M. Schreck	Open		16.00	55
1987 Fox-Large - A. Stocker	Open		50.00	75
1988 Mini Sitting Fox - A. Stocker	Open		35.00	45
1989 Mushrooms - A. Stocker	12/98		35.00	45
1996 Night Owl - A. Hirzinger	Open		85.00	85
1983 Owl-Giant - M. Schreck	Open		1200.00	2000
1981 Owl-Large - M. Schreck	Open		90.00	125
1981 Owl-Mini - M. Schreck	Open		16.00	30
1995 Owlet - A. Hirzinger	Open		45.00	45
1994 Roe Deer Fawn - E. Mair	12/98		75.00	75
1985 Squirrel - M. Schreck	Open		35.00	55

Swarovski Silver Crystal-XRetired Candleholders - Various

YEAR ISSUE	EDITION LIMIT	YEAR RETD.	ISSUE PRICE	*QUOTE U.S.$
1981 Candleholder 7600NR101 - Team	Retrd.	1981	28.00	170-350
1981 Candleholder 7600NR102 - H. Koch	Retrd.	1986	40.00	134-150
1976 Candleholder 7600NR103 (European) - Team	Retrd.	1983	N/A	750-900
1986 Candleholder 7600NR103 - Team	Retrd.	1988	40.00	112-200
1986 Candleholder 7600NR104 - Team	Retrd.	1988	95.00	232-300
1981 Candleholder 7600NR106 - Team	Retrd.	1986	100.00	400-500
1981 Candleholder 7600NR107 - Team	Retrd.	1985	120.00	369-400
1976 Candleholder 7600NR108 (European) - Team	Retrd.	1987	N/A	650-850
1981 Candleholder 7600NR109 - Team	Retrd.	1985	40.00	175-194
1981 Candleholder 7600NR110 - Team	Retrd.	1986	45.00	175-198
1981 Candleholder 7600NR111 - Team	Retrd.	1985	100.00	400-660
1981 Candleholder 7600NR112 - Team	Retrd.	1985	80.00	300-350
1981 Candleholder 7600NR114 - Team	Retrd.	1985	40.00	250-407
1981 Candleholder 7600NR115 - Team	Retrd.	1986	200.00	600-700
1981 Candleholder 7600NR116 - Team	Retrd.	1985	350.00	1500-2900
1977 Candleholder 7600NR119 (European) - Team	Retrd.	1989	N/A	320-500
1986 Candleholder 7600NR122 - Team	Retrd.	1986	85.00	200-520
1985 Candleholder 7600NR127 - Team	Retrd.	1987	65.00	200-250
1985 Candleholder 7600NR128 - Team	Retrd.	1987	100.00	250-344
1985 Candleholder 7600NR129 - Team	Retrd.	1987	120.00	300-480
1981 Candleholder 7600NR130 - Team	Retrd.	1985	300.00	1750-2000
1978 Candleholder 7600NR131, set/6 (European) - Team	Retrd.	1989	N/A	550-900
1986 Candleholder 7600NR138 - Team	Retrd.	1986	160.00	500-750
1986 Candleholder 7600NR139 - Team	Retrd.	1986	140.00	750-1125
1986 Candleholder 7600NR140 - Team	Retrd.	1986	120.00	750-1063
1986 Candleholder 7600NR141 (European) - M. Schreck	Retrd.	1991	N/A	500-840
1986 Candleholder 7600NR142 (European) - M. Schreck	Retrd.	1990	N/A	280-500
1982 Candleholder-Baroque 7600NR121 - Team	Retrd.	1986	150.00	375-450
1981 Candleholder-Global-Kg. Sz. 7600NR135 - Team	Retrd.	1988	50.00	145-248
1981 Candleholder-Global-Lg. 7600NR134 - Team	Retrd.	1990	40.00	80-142
1981 Candleholder-Global-Med. (2) 7600NR133 - Team	Retrd.	1990	40.00	100-168
1981 Candleholder-Global-Sm. (4) 7600NR132 - Team	Retrd.	1989	60.00	200-275
1988 Candleholder-Neo-Classic-Lg. 7600NR144090 - A. Stocker	Retrd.	1992	220.00	275-400
1990 Candleholder-Neo-Classic-Med. 7600NR144080 - A. Stocker	Retrd.	1992	190.00	194-300
1990 Candleholder-Neo-Classic-Sm. 7600NR144070 - A. Stocker	Retrd.	1992	170.00	138-250
1985 Candleholder-Pineapple-Gold 7600NR136 - M. Schreck	Retrd.	1986	150.00	450-719
1984 Candleholder-Pineapple-Rhodium 7600NR136 - M. Schreck	Retrd.	1986	150.00	531-844
1987 Candleholder-Star-Lg. 7600NR143000 - Team	Retrd.	1996	250.00	400-450
1984 Candleholder-w/Flowers-Lg. 7600NR137 - Team	Retrd.	1990	150.00	275-350
1986 Candleholder-w/Flowers-Sm. 7600NR120 - Team	Retrd.	1987	60.00	350-420
1986 Candleholder-w/Leaves-Sm. 7600NR126 - Team	Retrd.	1987	100.00	425-560

Swarovski Silver Crystal-Retired Paperweights - Various

YEAR ISSUE	EDITION LIMIT	YEAR RETD.	ISSUE PRICE	*QUOTE U.S.$
1981 Pprwgt-Atomic-Crystal Cal 7454NR60095 - M. Schreck	Retrd.	1985	80.00	1438-1850
1981 Pprwgt-Atomic-Vitrl Med. 7454NR60087 - M. Schreck	Retrd.	1985	80.00	1875-2375
1981 Pprwgt-Barrel-Crystal Cal 7453NR60095 - M. Schreck	Retrd.	1988	80.00	381-500
1981 Pprwgt-Barrel-Vitrl Med. 7453NR60087 - M. Schreck	Retrd.	1988	80.00	375-500
1981 Pprwgt-Carousel-Crystal Cal 7451NR60095 - M. Schreck	Retrd.	1985	80.00	938-1800
1981 Pprwgt-Carousel-Vitrl Med. 7451NR60087 - M. Schreck	Retrd.	1985	80.00	1500-2000
1982 Pprwgt-Cone Crystal Cal 7452NR60095 - M. Schreck	Retrd.	1982	80.00	253-300
1982 Pprwgt-Cone Vitrl Med. 7452NR60087 - M. Schreck	Retrd.	1982	80.00	225-294
1981 Pprwgt-Egg 7458NR63069 - M. Schreck	Retrd.	1982	60.00	150-250
1987 Pprwgt-Geometric 7432NR57002 - Team	Retrd.	1990	75.00	165-300
1987 Pprwgt-Octron-Crystal Cal 7456NR41 - Team	Retrd.	1991	75.00	132-185
1988 Pprwgt-Octron-Vitrl Med. 7456NR41087 - Team	Retrd.	1991	90.00	110-185
1987 Pprwgt-One Ton 7495NR65 - Team	Retrd.	1990	75.00	125-175
1981 Pprwgt-Rd.-Berm Blue 7404NR30 - Team	Retrd.	1982	15.00	100-200
1981 Pprwgt-Rd.-Berm Blue 7404NR40 - Team	Retrd.	1981	20.00	144-175
1981 Pprwgt-Rd.-Berm Blue 7404NR50 - Team	Retrd.	1982	40.00	313-350
1981 Pprwgt-Rd.-Crystal Cal 7404NR30095/30 - Team	Retrd.	1989	15.00	85-100
1981 Pprwgt-Rd.-Crystal Cal 7404NR40095/40 - Team	Retrd.	1989	20.00	95-140
1981 Pprwgt-Rd.-Crystal Cal 7404NR50095/50 - Team	Retrd.	1989	40.00	125-200
1981 Pprwgt-Rd.-Crystal Cal 7404NR60095/60 - Team	Retrd.	1989	50.00	165-375
1981 Pprwgt-Rd.-Green 7404NR30 - Team	Retrd.	1982	15.00	100-250
1981 Pprwgt-Rd.-Green 7404NR40 - Team	Retrd.	1981	20.00	150-240
1981 Pprwgt-Rd.-Green 7404NR50 - Team	Retrd.	1982	40.00	255
1981 Pprwgt-Rd.-Sahara 7404NR30 - Team	Retrd.	1982	15.00	200-300
1981 Pprwgt-Rd.-Sahara 7404NR40 - Team	Retrd.	1981	20.00	250
1981 Pprwgt-Rd.-Sahara 7404NR50 - Team	Retrd.	1982	40.00	313-400
1981 Pprwgt-Rd.-Vitrl Med. 7404NR30087 - Team	Retrd.	1989	15.00	75-115
1981 Pprwgt-Rd.-Vitrl Med. 7404NR40087 - Team	Retrd.	1989	20.00	95-130
1981 Pprwgt-Rd.-Vitrl Med. 7404NR50087 - Team	Retrd.	1989	40.00	200-270
1981 Pprwgt-Rd.-Vitrl Med. 7404NR60087 - Team	Retrd.	1989	50.00	250-281

Swarovski Silver Crystal-Retired - Various

YEAR ISSUE	EDITION LIMIT	YEAR RETD.	ISSUE PRICE	*QUOTE U.S.$
1991 Apple 7476NR000001- M. Stamey	Retrd.	1996	175.00	200-280
1984 Apple Photo Stand-Kg. Sz. (Gold) 7504NR060G - M. Schreck	Retrd.	1988	120.00	520-688
1981 Apple Photo Stand-Kg. Sz. (Rhodium) 7504NR060R - M. Schreck	Retrd.	1988	120.00	520-750
1983 Apple Photo Stand-Lg. (Gold) 7504NR050G - M. Schreck	Retrd.	1990	80.00	240-420
1981 Apple Photo Stand-Lg. (Rhodium) 7504NR050R - M. Schreck	Retrd.	1986	80.00	250-480
1983 Apple Photo Stand-Sm. (Gold) 7504NR030G - M. Schreck	Retrd.	1990	40.00	157-219
1981 Apple Photo Stand-Sm. (Rhodium) 7504NR030R - M. Schreck	Retrd.	1986	40.00	213-294
1982 Ashtray 7461NR100 - M. Schreck	Retrd.	1990	150.00	225-363
1981 Ashtray 7501NR061 - Team	Retrd.	1981	45.00	650-1500
1983 Bear, King Size (no tail) 7637NR92 - M. Schreck	Retrd.	1987	95.00	2313-2750
1983 Bear-Giant Size 7637NR112 - M. Schreck	Retrd.	1988	125.00	1700-3750
1985 Bear-Mini 7670NR32 - M. Schreck	Retrd.	1989	16.00	207-375
1982 Bear-Sm 7637NR054000 - M. Schreck	Retrd.	1995	44.00	84-150
1992 Beaver-Baby Lying 7616NR000003 - A. Stocker	Retrd.	1995	47.50	60-90
1985 Bee (Gold) 7553NR100 - Team	Retrd.	1988	200.00	1450-2280
1985 Bee (Rhodium) 7553NR200 - Team	Retrd.	1986	200.00	1900-3600
1983 Beetle Bottle Opener (Gold) 7505NR76 - Team	Retrd.	1983	80.00	1524-2188
1981 Beetle Bottle Opener (Rhodium) 7505NR76 - Team	Retrd.	1983	80.00	1344-1650
1987 Birds' Nest 7470NR050000 - Team	Retrd.	1996	90.00	125-200
1985 Blowfish-Lg. 7644NR41 - Team	Retrd.	1991	40.00	128-219
1992 Bumblebee 7615NR000002 - C. Schneiderbauer	Retrd.	1997	85.00	94-145
1985 Butterfly (Gold) 7551NR100 - Team	Retrd.	1988	200.00	1000-2000
1985 Butterfly (Rhodium) 7551NR200 - Team	Retrd.	1986	200.00	2500-3000
1985 Butterfly-Mini 7671NR30 - Team	Retrd.	1988	16.00	200-244
1981 Cardholders-Lg., Set/4 -7403NR30095 - K. Mignon	Retrd.	1989	43.00	344-369
1981 Cardholders-Sm., Set/4-7403NR20095 - K. Mignon	Retrd.	1989	25.00	160-244
1981 Cardholders-Sm., Set/6-7403NR20095 - K. Mignon (European)	Retrd.	1989	25.00	308
1984 Cat-Lg 7634NR70 - M. Schreck	Retrd.	1991	44.00	120-180
1983 Cat-Medium 7634NR52 - M. Schreck	Retrd.	1987	38.00	500-619
1983 Cat-Mini (Retired in U.S. only) 7659NR31 - M. Schreck	Retrd.	1991	16.00	50-80
1985 Chess Set/Wooden Board 7550NR432032 - M. Schreck	Retrd.	1986	950.00	2820-3000
1981 Chicken-Mini 7651NR20 - M. Schreck	Retrd.	1988	16.00	50-95
1978 Cigarette Box 7503NR050 (European)	Retrd.	1983	N/A	2313-2344
1982 Cigarette Holder 7463NR062 - M. Schreck	Retrd.	1990	85.00	118-155
1985 Dachshund-Lg. 7641NR75 - M. Schreck	Retrd.	1991	48.00	100-160
1985 Dachshund-Mini 7672NR42 - A. Stocker	Retrd.	1988	20.00	135-210
1987 Dachshund-Mini 7672NR042000 - A. Stocker	Retrd.	1995	20.00	65-105
1982 Dinner Bell-Lg. 7467NR71 - M. Schreck	Retrd.	1991	80.00	175-219
1987 Dinner Bell-Medium 7467NR54 - M. Schreck	Retrd.	1997	80.00	95-145
1981 Dog 7635NR70 - M. Schreck	Retrd.	1990	44.00	135-150
1983 Duck-Lg. 7653NR75 - M. Schreck	Retrd.	1987	44.00	469-594
1983 Duck-Med. 7653NR55 - M. Schreck	Retrd.	1988	38.00	150-206
1981 Duck-Mini 7653NR45 - M. Schreck	Retrd.	1988	16.00	62-95
1983 Elephant-Lg. 7640NR55 - M. Schreck	Retrd.	1989	90.00	151-282
1988 Elephant-Sm. 7640NR60 - A. Stocker	Retrd.	1995	70.00	117-150
1985 Falcon Head-Lg. 7645NR100 - M. Schreck	Retrd.	1991	600.00	1400-2500
1987 Falcon Head-Sm. 7645NR45 - M. Schreck	Retrd.	1991	60.00	163-232
1988 Fox-Mini Running 7677NR055 - A. Stocker	Retrd.	1996	35.00	38-80
1985 Frog (black eyes) 7642NR48 - M. Schreck	Retrd.	1991	30.00	139-165
1983 Grapes-Lg. 7550NR30015 - Team	Retrd.	1988	250.00	1750-3000
1983 Grapes-Med. 7550NR20029 - Team	Retrd.	1995	300.00	450-556
1983 Grapes-Sm. 7550NR20015 - Team	Retrd.	1995	200.00	307-415
1982 Hedgehog-Kg. Sz. 7630NR60 - Team	Retrd.	1987	98.00	813-969
1981 Hedgehog-Lg. 7630NR50 - M. Schreck	Retrd.	1987	65.00	180-219
1988 Hedgehog-Lg. 7630NR70 - M. Schreck	Retrd.	1996	120.00	149-250
1981 Hedgehog-Med. 7630NR40 - M. Schreck	Retrd.	1987	44.00	119-213
1982 Hedgehog-Sm. 7630NR30 - Team	Retrd.	1987	38.00	450-575
1988 Hippopotamus 7626NR65 - A. Stocker	Retrd.	1992	70.00	119-150
1989 Hippopotamus-Sm. 7626NR055000 - A. Stocker	Retrd.	1995	70.00	70-120
1985 Hummingbird (Gold) 7552NR100 - Team	Retrd.	1988	200.00	1000-2280
1985 Hummingbird (Rhodium) 7552NR200 - Team	Retrd.	1986	200.00	3750-4200
1990 Kingfisher 7621NR000001 - M. Stamey	Retrd.	1992	75.00	110-240
1991 Kitten 7634NR028000 - M. Stamey	Retrd.	1995	47.50	60-115
1991 Kiwi 7617NR043000 - M. Stamey	Retrd.	1996	37.50	55-90
1977 Lighter (European) 7500NR050	Retrd.	1983	N/A	1844-3000
1982 Lighter 7462NR062 - M. Schreck	Retrd.	1990	160.00	300-350
1992 Lute 7477NR000004 - M. Zendron	Retrd.	1997	125.00	125-175
1986 Mallard 7647NR80 - M. Schreck	Retrd.	1994	80.00	138-206
1992 Mother Beaver 7616NR000001 - A. Stocker	Retrd.	1996	110.00	125-156

*Quotes have been rounded up to nearest dollar

YEAR ISSUE	EDITION LIMIT	YEAR RETD.	ISSUE PRICE	*QUOTE U.S.$
1982 Mouse-Kg. Sz. 7631NR60 - M. Schreck	Retrd.	1987	95.00	900-1500
1982 Mouse-Lg. 7631NR50 - M. Schreck	Retrd.	1987	69.00	600-1031
1981 Mouse-Med. 7631NR040000 - M. Schreck	Retrd.	1995	48.00	89-148
1981 Mouse-Mini 7655NR23 - M. Schreck	Retrd.	1988	16.00	63-110
1981 Mouse-Sm. 7631NR30 - M. Schreck	Retrd.	1991	35.00	76-140
1992 Nativity Angel 7475NR000009 - Team	Retrd.	1993	65.00	120-180
1991 Nativity Holy Family w/Arch 7475NR001 - Team	Retrd.	1993	250.00	288-480
1992 Nativity Set (European) 6475NR0000099 - Team	Retrd.	1993	N/A	813-906
1992 Nativity Shepherd 7475NR000007 - Team	Retrd.	1993	65.00	88-175
1992 Nativity Wise Men (Set/3) 7475NR200000 - Team	Retrd.	1993	175.00	185-288
1989 Old Timer Automobile 7473NR000001 - G. Stamey	Retrd.	1995	130.00	175-240
1989 Owl 7621NR000003 - M. Stamey	Retrd.	1992	70.00	140-235
1989 Owl, Parrot, Kingfisher, Toucan - M. Stamey	Retrd.	N/A	285.00	750-925
1981 Owl-Sm. 7636NR046000 - M. Schreck	Retrd.	1995	59.00	69-110
1989 Parrot 7621NR000004 - M. Stamey	Retrd.	1992	70.00	150-208
1988 Partridge 7625NR50 - A. Stocker	Retrd.	1990	85.00	120-145
1991 Pear 7476NR000002 - M. Stamey	Retrd.	1997	175.00	155-235
1984 Penguin-Lg. 7643NR085000 - M. Schreck	Retrd.	1995	44.00	110-160
1986 Picture Frame/Oval 7505NR75G - Team	Retrd.	1989	90.00	250-500
1984 Picture Frame/Square 7506NR60G - M. Schreck	Retrd.	1989	100.00	249-531
1982 Pig-Lg. 7638NR65 - M. Schreck	Retrd.	1987	50.00	261-556
1983 Pineapple/Rhodium-Giant 7507NR26002 - M. Schreck	Retrd.	1986	1750.00	3750-4000
1982 Pineapple/Rhodium-Lg. 7507NR105002 - M. Schreck	Retrd.	1986	150.00	407-625
1986 Pineapple/Rhodium-Sm. 7507NR060002 - M. Schreck	Retrd.	1986	55.00	145-160
1987 Polar Bear-Large 7649NR85 - A. Stocker	Retrd.	1997	140.00	182-225
1992 Poodle 7619NR000003 - A. Stocker	Retrd.	1997	125.00	110-180
1981 Pyramid-Lg.-Crystal Cal 7450NR50095 - M. Schreck	Retrd.	1993	90.00	200-250
1981 Pyramid-Lg.-Vitrl Med. 7450NR50087 - M. Schreck	Retrd.	1993	90.00	281-294
1987 Pyramid-Small-Crystal Cal. 7450NR40095 - M. Schreck	Retrd.	1997	100.00	109-219
1987 Pyramid-Small-Vitrail Med. 7450NR40087 - M. Schreck	Retrd.	1997	100.00	120-270
1983 Rabbit-Lg. 7652NR45 - M. Schreck	Retrd.	1988	38.00	375-425
1981 Rabbit-Mini 7652NR20 - M. Schreck	Retrd.	1988	16.00	59-115
1988 Rabbit-Mini Lying 7678NR030000 - A. Stocker	Retrd.	1995	35.00	44-80
1988 Rhinoceros-lg. (signed) 7622NR70 - A. Stocker	Retrd.	1992	70.00	135
1988 Rhinoceros-lg. 7622NR70 - A. Stocker	Retrd.	1992	70.00	124-180
1990 Rhinoceros-Sm. 7622NR060000 - A. Stocker	Retrd.	1995	70.00	82-120
1984 Salt and Pepper Shakers 7508NR068034 - Team	Retrd.	1988	80.00	275-375
1982 Schnapps Glasses, Set/3 7468NR039000 - Team (European)	Retrd.	1990	N/A	109
1982 Schnapps Glasses, Set/6 7468NR039000 - Team	Retrd.	1990	150.00	470-688
1990 Scotch Terrier 7619NR000002 - A. Stocker	Retrd.	1996	60.00	90-250
1985 Seal-Large 7646NR085000 - M. Schreck	Retrd.	1995	44.00	119-250
1990 Silver Crystal City-Cathedral 7474NR000021 - G. Stamey	Retrd.	1994	95.00	125-250
1991 Silver Crystal City-City Gates 7474NR000023 - G. Stamey	Retrd.	1994	95.00	107-175
1991 Silver Crystal City-City Tower 7474NR000022 - G. Stamey	Retrd.	1994	37.50	57-185
1990 Silver Crystal City-Houses I & II (Set/2) 7474NR100000 - G. Stamey	Retrd.	1994	75.00	90-195
1990 Silver Crystal City-Houses III & IV (Set/2) 7474NR200000 - G. Stamey	Retrd.	1994	75.00	90-150
1990 Silver Crystal City-Poplars (Set/3) 7474NR020003 - G. Stamey	Retrd.	1994	40.00	90-135
1993 Silver Crystal City-Town Hall 7474NR000027 - G. Stamey	Retrd.	1994	135.00	163-250
1986 Snail 7648NR030000 - M. Stamey	Retrd.	1995	35.00	64-90
1991 South Sea Shell 7624NR72000 - M. Stamey	Retrd.	1994	110.00	130-160
1992 Sparrow 7650NR000001 - C. Schneiderbauer	Retrd.	1997	29.50	30
1983 Sparrow-Lg. 7650NR32 - M. Schreck	Retrd.	1988	38.00	169-265
1981 Sparrow-Mini 7650NR20 - M. Schreck	Retrd.	1991	16.00	60-80
1983 Swan-Mini 7658NR27 - M. Schreck	Retrd.	1988	16.00	125-185
1981 Table Magnifyer (no chain) 7510NR01G	Retrd.	1984	70.00	1200-1800
1981 Table Magnifyer (no chain) 7510NR01R	Retrd.	1984	80.00	938-1066
1981 Table Magnifyer (with chain) 7510NR01R	Retrd.	1984	80.00	1200-1800
1989 Toucan 7621NR000002 - M. Stamey	Retrd.	1992	70.00	124-168
1982 Treasure Box (Heart/Butterfly) 7465NR52/100 - M. Schreck	Retrd.	1990	80.00	325-369
1982 Treasure Box (Heart/Flower) 7465NR52 - M. Schreck	Retrd.	1988	80.00	344-395
1982 Treasure Box (Oval/Butterfly) 7466NR063100 - M. Schreck	Retrd.	1988	80.00	369-381
1982 Treasure Box (Oval/Flower) 7466NR063000 - M. Schreck	Retrd.	1990	80.00	200-381
1982 Treasure Box (Round/Butterfly) 7464NR50/100 - M. Schreck	Retrd.	1988	80.00	195-300
1982 Treasure Box (Round/Flower) 7464NR50 - M. Schreck	Retrd.	1990	80.00	195-344
1983 Turtle-King Sz. 7632NR75 - M. Schreck	Retrd.	1988	58.00	375-656
1981 Turtle-Small 7632NR030000 - M. Schreck	Retrd.	1996	35.00	57-80
1986 Vase 7511NR70 - Team	Retrd.	1990	50.00	175-195
1989 Walrus 7620NR100000 - M. Stamey	Retrd.	1993	120.00	170-210
1987 Whale 7628NR80 - M. Stamey	Retrd.	1991	70.00	165-255

United Design Corp.

Angels Collection - D. Newburn, unless otherwise noted

YEAR ISSUE	EDITION LIMIT	YEAR RETD.	ISSUE PRICE	*QUOTE U.S.$
1993 Angel of Flight AA-032 - K. Memoli	10,000		100.00	110
1993 Angel w/ Birds AA-034	10,000	1995	75.00	75
1994 Angel w/ Book AA-058	10,000	1998	84.00	90
1994 Angel w/ Christ Child AA-061 - K. Memoli	10,000		84.00	90
1993 Angel w/ Lilies AA-033	10,000	1998	80.00	84
1993 Angel w/ Lilies, Crimson AA-040	10,000	1996	80.00	80
1992 Angel, Lamb & Critters AA-021 - S. Bradford	10,000		90.00	95
1996 Angel, Lion & Fawn AA-093 - K. Memoli	20,000		280.00	280
1992 Angel, Lion & Lamb AA-020 - K. Memoli	10,000	1994	135.00	280
1994 Angel, Roses and Bluebirds AA-054	10,000		65.00	84
1996 Angels, Roses & Doves AA-112	10,000		75.00	84
1993 Autumn Angel AA-035	10,000	1996	70.00	70
1993 Autumn Angel, Emerald AA-041	10,000	1996	70.00	70
1995 Celestial Guardian Angel AA-069 - S. Bradford	10,000	1997	120.00	120
1991 Christmas Angel AA-003 - S. Bradford	10,000	1994	125.00	125
1991 Classical Angel AA-005 - S. Bradford	10,000	1998	79.00	79
1994 Dreaming of Angels AA-060 - K. Memoli	10,000		120.00	130
1996 Dreaming of Angels, pastel AA-111 - K. Memoli	10,000		120.00	130
1994 Earth Angel AA-059 - S. Bradford	10,000	1997	84.00	84
1997 Eyes Toward Heaven AA-132 - K. Memoli	10,000		130.00	130
1991 The Gift AA-009 - S. Bradford	2,500	1991	135.00	550-665
1992 The Gift '92 AA-018 - S. Bradford	3,500	1992	140.00	325-350
1993 The Gift '93 AA-037 - S. Bradford	3,500	1993	120.00	225-235
1994 The Gift '94 AA-057	5,000	1994	140.00	175-220
1995 The Gift '95 AA-067	5,000	1995	140.00	140-180
1996 The Gift '96 AA-094	5,000	1996	140.00	140
1997 The Gift '97 AA-128 - P.J. Jonas	7,500		150.00	150
1998 The Gift '98 AA-147 - P.J. Jonas-Pendergast	5,000		150.00	150
1995 Guardian Angel, Lion & Lamb AA-083 - S. Bradford	10,000	1998	165.00	170-195
1995 Guardian Angel, Lion & Lamb, lt. AA-068 - S. Bradford	10,000		165.00	170
1994 Harvest Angel AA-063 - S. Bradford	10,000	1997	84.00	84
1991 Heavenly Shepherdess AA-008 - S. Bradford	10,000		99.00	99
1992 Joy To The World AA-016	10,000	1996	90.00	95
1995 A Little Closer to Heaven AA-081 - K. Memoli	10,000	1998	230.00	230-245
1995 A Little Closer to Heaven, lt. AA-085 - K. Memoli	10,000		230.00	230
1993 Madonna AA-031 - K. Memoli	10,000		100.00	100
1991 Messenger of Peace AA-006 - S. Bradford	10,000	1997	75.00	79
1992 Peaceful Encounter AA-017	10,000		100.00	100
1997 Rejoice AA-130 - K. Memoli	10,000		90.00	90
1997 Rejoice, silver AA-143 - K. Memoli	10,000		90.00	90
1997 Serenity AA-131 - K. Memoli	10,000		90.00	90
1997 Serenity, silver AA-144 - K. Memoli	10,000		90.00	90
1998 Spirit of Autumn AA-158 - G.G. Santiago	15,000		200.00	200
1998 Spirit of Spring AA-146 - G.G. Santiago	15,000		200.00	200
1997 Spirit of Winter AA-142 - G.G. Santiago	15,000		200.00	200
1995 Starlight Starbright AA-066	10,000	1998	70.00	80
1991 Trumpeter Angel AA-004 - S. Bradford	10,000	1997	99.00	99
1992 Winter Angel AA-019	10,000		75.00	75
1991 Winter Rose Angel AA-007 - S. Bradford	10,000	1994	65.00	65

Backyard Birds™ - Various

YEAR ISSUE	EDITION LIMIT	YEAR RETD.	ISSUE PRICE	*QUOTE U.S.$
1994 Allen's on Pink Flowers BB-044 - P.J. Jonas	Open		22.00	22
1994 Allen's on Purple Morning Glory BB-051 - P.J. Jonas	Open		22.00	22
1989 Baltimore Oriole BB-024 - S. Bradford	Retrd.	1996	19.50	22
1989 Blue Jay BB-026 - S. Bradford	Open		19.50	22
1989 Blue Jay, Baby BB-027 - S. Bradford	Retrd.	1996	15.00	15
1990 Bluebird (Upright) BB-031 - S. Bradford	Retrd.	1997	20.00	20
1988 Bluebird BB-009 - S. Bradford	Open		15.00	21
1988 Bluebird Hanging BB-017 - S. Bradford	Retrd.	1990	11.00	17
1988 Bluebird, Small BB-001 - S. Bradford	Open		10.00	11
1994 Broadbill on Blue Morning Glory BB-053 - P.J. Jonas	Open		22.00	22
1994 Broadbill on Trumpet Vine BB-043 - P.J. Jonas	Open		22.00	22
1994 Broadbill on Yellow Fuscia BB-055 - P.J. Jonas	Retrd.	1997	22.00	22
1994 Broadbill Pair on Yellow Flowers BB-048 - P.J. Jonas	Retrd.	1997	30.00	30
1988 Cardinal Hanging BB-018 - S. Bradford	Retrd.	1990	11.00	11
1988 Cardinal, Female BB-011 - S. Bradford	Open		15.00	17
1988 Cardinal, Male BB-013 - S. Bradford	Open		15.00	18
1988 Cardinal, Small BB-002 - S. Bradford	Open		10.00	11
1990 Cedar Waxwing Babies BB-033 - S. Bradford	Retrd.	1996	22.00	22
1990 Cedar Waxwing BB-032 - S. Bradford	Retrd.	1996	20.00	20
1988 Chickadee BB-010 - S. Bradford	Open		15.00	18
1988 Chickadee Hanging BB-019 - S. Bradford	Retrd.	1990	11.00	11
1988 Chickadee, Small BB-003 - S. Bradford	Open		10.00	11
1990 Evening Grosbeak BB-034 - S. Bradford	Retrd.	1996	22.00	22
1989 Goldfinch BB-028 - S. Bradford	Open		16.50	20
1989 Hoot Owl BB-025 - S. Bradford	Retrd.	1997	15.00	20
1988 Humingbird BB-012 - S. Bradford	Open		15.00	18
1988 Hummingbird Female, Small BB-005 - S. Bradford	Retrd.	1991	10.00	10
1988 Hummingbird Flying, Small BB-004 - S. Bradford	Open		10.00	11
1988 Hummingbird Sm., Hanging BB-022 - S. Bradford	Retrd.	1990	11.00	11
1988 Hummingbird, Lg., Hanging BB-023 - S. Bradford	Retrd.	1990	15.00	15
1990 Indigo Bunting BB-036 - S. Bradford	Retrd.	1996	20.00	20
1990 Indigo Bunting, Female BB-039 - S. Bradford	Retrd.	1996	20.00	20
1994 Magnificent Pair on Trumpet Vine BB-046 - P.J. Jonas	Retrd.	1997	30.00	30
1990 Nuthatch, White-throated BB-037 - S. Bradford	Retrd.	1996	20.00	20
1990 Painted Bunting BB-040 - S. Bradford	Retrd.	1996	20.00	20
1990 Painted Bunting, Female BB-041 - S. Bradford	Retrd.	1996	20.00	20
1990 Purple Finch BB-038 - S. Bradford	Retrd.	1996	20.00	20
1988 Red-winged Blackbird BB-014 - S. Bradford	Retrd.	1991	15.00	17
1988 Robin Babies BB-008 - S. Bradford	Open		15.00	19
1988 Robin Baby, Small BB-006 - S. Bradford	Open		10.00	11
1988 Robin BB-015 - S. Bradford	Open		15.00	21
1988 Robin Hanging BB-020 - S. Bradford	Retrd.	1990	11.00	11
1990 Rose Breasted Grosbeak BB-042 - S. Bradford	Retrd.	1996	20.00	20
1994 Rubythroat on Pink Fuscia BB-054 - P.J. Jonas	Retrd.	1997	22.00	22
1994 Rubythroat on Red Morning Glory BB-052 - P.J. Jonas	Open		22.00	22
1994 Rubythroat on Thistle BB-049 - P.J. Jonas	Open		16.50	17
1994 Rubythroat on Yellow Flowers BB-045 - P.J. Jonas	Retrd.	1997	22.00	22
1994 Rubythroat Pair on Pink Flowers BB-047 - P.J. Jonas	Open		30.00	30
1989 Saw-Whet Owl BB-029 - S. Bradford	Open		15.00	18
1988 Sparrow BB-016 - S. Bradford	Open		15.00	17
1988 Sparrow Hanging BB-021 - S. Bradford	Retrd.	1990	11.00	11
1988 Sparrow, Small BB-007 - S. Bradford	Retrd.	1996	10.00	11
1989 Woodpecker BB-030 - S. Bradford	Retrd.	1997	16.50	20

Easter Bunny Family™ - D. Kennicutt

YEAR ISSUE	EDITION LIMIT	YEAR RETD.	ISSUE PRICE	*QUOTE U.S.$
1994 All Hidden SEC-045	Retrd.	1996	24.50	25
1989 Auntie Bunny SEC-008	Retrd.	1992	20.00	23
1992 Auntie Bunny w/Cake SEC-033R	Retrd.	1994	20.00	22
1991 Baby in Buggy, Boy SEC-027R	Retrd.	1994	20.00	22
1991 Baby in Buggy, Girl SEC-029R	Retrd.	1994	20.00	22
1994 Babysitter SEC-049	Open		24.50	25
1994 Bath Time SEC-044	Retrd.	1997	24.50	25
1995 Bed Time SEC-057	Open		24.00	24
1992 Boy Bunny w/Large Egg SEC-034R	Retrd.	1994	20.00	22
1991 Bubba In Wheelbarrow SEC-021	Retrd.	1993	20.00	20
1990 Bubba w/Wagon SEC-016	Retrd.	1993	16.50	18
1988 Bunnies, Basket Of SEC-001	Retrd.	1991	13.00	18
1991 Bunny Boy w/Basket SEC-025	Retrd.	1993	20.00	20
1988 Bunny Boy w/Duck SEC-002	Retrd.	1991	13.00	18
1997 Bunny Express SEC-070	Open		27.00	27
1988 Bunny Girl w/Hen SEC-004	Retrd.	1991	13.00	18
1989 Bunny w/Prize Egg SEC-010	Retrd.	1993	19.50	20
1988 Bunny, Easter SEC-003	Retrd.	1991	15.00	18
1993 Christening Day SEC-040	Retrd.	1995	20.00	22
1998 Doll Buggy, 1998 SEC-071	Yr.Iss.		15.00	15
1989 Ducky w/Bonnet, Blue SEC-015	Retrd.	1992	10.00	12
1989 Ducky w/Bonnet, Pink SEC-014	Retrd.	1992	10.00	12
1996 Easter Bunny In Evening Clothes-SEC-064	Retrd.	1998	20.00	20
1992 Easter Bunny w/Back Pack SEC-030	Open		20.00	22
1990 Easter Bunny w/Crystal SEC-017	Retrd.	1995	23.00	25
1993 Easter Bunny, Chocolate Egg SEC-041	Retrd.	1996	23.00	25

YEAR ISSUE	EDITION LIMIT	YEAR RETD.	ISSUE PRICE	*QUOTE U.S.$
1995 Easter Cookies SEC-052	Open		24.00	25
1997 Easter Dress SEC-067	Open		22.00	22
1989 Easter Egg Hunt SEC-012	Retrd.	1995	16.50	22
1996 Easter Pageant - SEC-059	Open		17.00	17
1996 Easter Parade - SEC-063	Retrd.	1998	25.00	25
1998 Egg Paint Design SEC-072	Open		18.00	18
1993 Egg Roll SEC-036	Retrd.	1998	23.00	25
1991 Fancy Find SEC-028	Retrd.	1995	20.00	22
1996 First Kiss - SEC-061	Open		20.00	20
1995 First Outing SEC-054	Retrd.	1998	19.00	20
1994 First Steps SEC-048	Retrd.	1998	24.50	25
1997 Friendship, 1997 SEC-068	Yr.Iss.	1997	22.00	22
1997 The Gardener SEC-069	Open		22.00	22
1994 Gift Carrot SEC-046	Open		22.00	22
1993 Girl Bunny w/Basket SEC-039	Open		20.00	22
1992 Girl Bunny w/Large Egg SEC-035R	Retrd.	1994	20.00	22
1993 Grandma & Quilt SEC-037	Retrd.	1997	23.00	25
1992 Grandma w/ Bible SEC-031	Retrd.	1996	20.00	22
1996 Grandma's Dress Makers Form-1996-SEC-066	Yr.Iss.	1996	25.00	25
1992 Grandpa w/Carrots SEC-032R	Retrd.	1994	20.00	22
1996 Grandpa w/Sunflowers - SEC-065	Open		20.00	20
1990 Hen w/Chick SEC-018	Retrd.	1992	23.00	23
1994 Large Prize Egg SEC-047	Open		22.00	22
1989 Little Sis w/Lolly SEC-009	Retrd.	1992	14.50	18
1993 Lop Ear Dying Eggs SEC-042	Retrd.	1997	23.00	25
1996 Lop Girl w/Gift Box - SEC-060	Open		20.00	20
1991 Lop-Ear w/Crystal SEC-022	Open		23.00	25
1993 Mom Storytime SEC-043	Open		20.00	22
1996 Mom w/Chocolate Egg - SEC-062	Retrd.	1998	25.00	25
1990 Momma Making Basket SEC-019	Retrd.	1992	23.00	23
1990 Mother Goose SEC-020	Retrd.	1992	16.50	20
1991 Nest of Bunny Eggs SEC-023	Retrd.	1998	17.50	22
1995 Painting Lessons SEC-053	Retrd.	1998	19.00	20
1995 Quality Inspector SEC-055	Retrd.	1998	19.00	20
1988 Rabbit, Grandma SEC-005	Retrd.	1991	15.00	20
1988 Rabbit, Grandpa SEC-006	Retrd.	1991	15.00	20
1988 Rabbit, Momma w/Bonnet SEC-007	Retrd.	1991	15.00	20
1989 Rock-A-Bye Bunny SEC-013	Retrd.	1995	20.00	25
1993 Rocking Horse SEC-038	Retrd.	1996	20.00	22
1989 Sis & Bubba Sharing SEC-011	Retrd.	1996	22.50	25
1998 Spring Break SEC-073	Open		15.00	15
1995 Spring Flying SEC-058	Retrd.	1997	19.00	19
1995 Team Work SEC-051	Open		24.00	24
1995 Two in a Basket SEC-056	Retrd.	1997	24.00	25
1991 Victorian Auntie Bunny SEC-026	Retrd.	1993	20.00	20
1991 Victorian Momma SEC-024	Retrd.	1993	20.00	20
1994 Wheelbarrow Full SEC-050	Open		24.50	25

Easter Bunny Family™ Babies - D. Kennicutt

YEAR ISSUE	EDITION LIMIT	YEAR RETD.	ISSUE PRICE	*QUOTE U.S.$
1995 Baby in Basket SEC-815	Open		8.00	8
1994 Baby on Blanket, Naptime SEC-807	Open		6.50	7
1996 Baby w/Diaper & Bottle, Blue - SEC-825	Open		8.00	8
1996 Baby w/Diaper & Bottle, Pink - SEC-817	Open		8.00	8
1996 Baby w/Diaper & Bottle, Yellow - SEC-824	Open		8.00	8
1995 Basket of Carrots SEC-812	Open		8.00	8
1994 Boy Baby w/Blocks SEC-805	Open		6.50	7
1994 Boy w/Baseball Bat SEC-801	Open		6.50	7
1996 Boy w/Baseball Mitt - SEC-822	Open		8.00	8
1994 Boy w/Basket and Egg SEC-802	Open		6.50	7
1996 Boy w/Big Teddy - SEC-819	Open		8.00	8
1995 Boy w/Butterfly SEC-814	Open		8.00	8
1994 Boy w/Stick Horse SEC-803	Open		6.50	7
1996 Boy w/Train Engine - SEC-816	Open		8.00	8
1997 Bubble Bath SEC-828	Open		8.50	9
1998 Bunny & Birdhouse SEC-831	Open		8.50	9
1996 Dress Up Girl - SEC-821	Open		8.00	8
1996 Egg Delivery - SEC-823	Open		8.00	8
1995 Gift Egg SEC-808	Open		8.00	8
1996 Girl w/Apron Full - SEC-820	Open		8.00	8
1994 Girl w/Big Egg SEC-806	Open		6.50	7
1994 Girl w/Blanket SEC-800	Open		6.50	7
1996 Girl w/Book - SEC-818	Open		8.00	8
1994 Girl w/Toy Rabbit SEC-804	Open		6.50	7
1997 Grandpa's Boy SEC-826	Open		8.50	9
1995 Hostess SEC-810	Open		8.00	8
1995 Lop Ear & Flower Pot SEC-809	Open		8.00	8
1998 The Rocking Chair SEC-832	Open		8.50	9
1997 Soccer Player SEC-829	Open		8.50	9
1995 Spring Flowers SEC-813	Open		8.00	8
1998 Spring Showers SEC-830	Open		8.50	9
1995 Tea Party SEC-811	Open		8.00	8
1997 Thank You SEC-827	Open		8.50	9

Legend of Santa Claus™ - L. Miller, unless otherwise noted

YEAR ISSUE	EDITION LIMIT	YEAR RETD.	ISSUE PRICE	*QUOTE U.S.$
1992 Arctic Santa CF-035 - S. Bradford	7,500	1997	90.00	100-140
1988 Assembly Required CF-017	7,500	1994	79.00	130
1997 Bells of Christmas Morn CF-074 - K. Memoli	7,500		190.00	190
1997 Bells of Christmas Morn, Victorian CF-075 - K. Memoli	7,500		190.00	190
1991 Blessed Flight CF-032 - K. Memoli	7,500	1994	159.00	306-325
1996 Blessing Santa CF-066 - K. Memoli	10,000		160.00	170
1987 Checking His List CF-009	15,000	1994	75.00	120-155
1997 A Christmas Galleon CF-073 - K. Memoli	7,500		150.00	150
1989 Christmas Harmony CF-020 - S. Bradford	7,500	1992	85.00	130
1998 Christmas Sharing CF-080 - K. Memoli	10,000		150.00	150
1992 The Christmas Tree CF-038	7,500	1995	90.00	125
1993 Dear Santa CF-046 - K. Memoli	7,500	1996	170.00	225-230
1995 Dear Santa, Vict. CF-063	10,000		170.00	180
1987 Dreaming Of Santa CF-008 - S. Bradford	15,000	1988	65.00	325
1998 Drifts & Gifts CF-079 - K. Memoli	10,000		140.00	140
1992 Earth Home Santa CF-040 - S. Bradford	7,500	1997	135.00	140
1986 Elf Pair CF-005	10,000	1992	60.00	135-151
1988 Father Christmas CF-018 - S. Bradford	7,500	1993	75.00	135
1991 For Santa CF-029	7,500	1997	99.00	160
1990 Forest Friends CF-025	7,500	1993	90.00	110-125
1998 Friends of the North Santa CF-077 - J. Littlejohn	10,000		100.00	100
1995 Getting Santa Ready CF-056	10,000	1998	170.00	190
1996 High Country Santa CF-064	15,000		190.00	200
1989 Hitching Up CF-021	7,500	1993	90.00	110
1995 Into the Wind CF-061	10,000		140.00	150
1995 Into the Wind, Vict. CF-062	10,000		140.00	150
1993 Jolly St. Nick CF-045 - K. Memoli	7,500		130.00	140
1993 Jolly St. Nick, Victorian CF-050 - K. Memoli	7,500		120.00	140
1986 Kris Kringle CF-002	10,000	1991	60.00	160-170
1992 Letters to Santa CF-036	7,500	1995	125.00	185-220
1997 A Light on the Roof CF-072 - K. Memoli	7,500		160.00	160
1997 A Light on the Roof, Victorian CF-076 - K. Memoli	7,500		160.00	160
1988 Load 'Em Up CF-016 - S. Bradford	7,500	1990	79.00	350-400
1987 Loading Santa's Sleigh CF-010	15,000	1993	100.00	110-125
1992 Loads of Happiness CF-041 - K. Memoli	7,500	1996	100.00	110-135
1994 Long Stocking Dilemma, Victorian CF-055 - K. Memoli	7,500		170.00	190
1994 Longstocking Dilemma CF-052 - K. Memoli	7,500		170.00	190
1987 Mrs. Santa CF-006 - S. Bradford	15,000	1991	60.00	235
1993 The Night Before Christmas CF-043	7,500	1996	100.00	100-135
1993 Northwoods Santa CF-047 - S. Bradford	7,500	1996	100.00	100
1987 On Santa's Knee-CF007 - S. Bradford	15,000	1994	65.00	120-135
1996 Pause For a Tale CF-065	10,000		190.00	200
1996 Pause For a Tale, Victorian CF-069 - K. Memoli	10,000		190.00	200
1998 Prince of Giving CF-078 - K. Memoli	10,000		180.00	180
1998 Prince of Giving, Victorian CF-082 - K. Memoli	10,000		180.00	180
1990 Puppy Love CF-024	7,500	1994	100.00	195-220
1989 A Purr-Fect Christmas CF-019 - S. Bradford	7,500	1994	95.00	135
1991 Reindeer Walk CF-031 - K. Memoli	7,500	1997	150.00	165-175
1995 The Ride CF-057	10,000	1998	130.00	140
1986 Rooftop Santa CF-004 - S. Bradford	10,000	1991	65.00	200-225
1990 Safe Arrival CF-027 - Memoli/Jonas	7,500	1996	150.00	175
1996 Santa & Blitzen CF-067 - K. Memoli	10,000		140.00	190
1996 Santa & Blitzen, Victorian CF-070 - K. Memoli	10,000		140.00	190
1992 Santa and Comet CF-037	7,500	1995	110.00	135
1992 Santa and Mrs. Claus CF 039 - K. Memoli	7,500		150.00	160
1992 Santa and Mrs. Claus, Victorian CF-042 - K. Memoli	7,500		135.00	160
1986 Santa At Rest CF-001	10,000	1988	70.00	600
1991 Santa At Work CF-030	7,500	1995	99.00	175
1987 Santa On Horseback CF-011 - S. Bradford	15,000	1990	75.00	350-375
1994 Santa Riding Dove CF-053	7,500	1998	120.00	140-150
1986 Santa With Pups CF-003 - S. Bradford	10,000	1988	65.00	570-575
1993 Santa's Friends CF-044	7,500	1996	100.00	100
1995 Santa, Dusk & Dawn CF-060	10,000		150.00	160
1988 St. Nicholas CF-015	7,500	1992	75.00	125-135
1994 Star Santa w/ Polar Bear CF-054 - S. Bradford	7,500	1998	130.00	140
1995 Starlight Express CF-059	10,000		170.00	180
1994 The Story of Christmas CF-051 - K. Memoli	10,000	1996	180.00	250-275
1996 The Story of Christmas, Victorian CF-068 - K. Memoli	10,000		180.00	190
1998 Totem Gathering CF-081 - J. Littlejohn	10,000		120.00	120
1993 Victorian Lion & Lamb Santa CF-048 - S. Bradford	7,500	1997	100.00	100-120
1990 Victorian Santa CF-028 - S. Bradford	7,500	1992	125.00	295-325
1991 Victorian Santa w/ Teddy CF-033 - S. Bradford	7,500	1997	150.00	160
1990 Waiting For Santa CF-026 - S. Bradford	7,500	1995	100.00	250-265
1997 Wilderness Santa CF-071	10,000		300.00	300

Legend Of The Little People™ - L. Miller

YEAR ISSUE	EDITION LIMIT	YEAR RETD.	ISSUE PRICE	*QUOTE U.S.$
1989 Adventure Bound LL-002	Retrd.	1993	35.00	50
1989 Caddy's Helper LL-007	Retrd.	1993	35.00	50
1991 The Easter Bunny's Cart LL-020	Retrd.	1994	45.00	50
1991 Fire it Up LL-023	Retrd.	1994	50.00	55
1990 Fishin' Hole LL-012	Retrd.	1994	35.00	50
1989 A Friendly Toast LL-003	Retrd.	1993	35.00	50
1990 Gathering Acorns LL-014	Retrd.	1994	100.00	100
1991 Got It LL-021	Retrd.	1994	45.00	50
1990 Hedgehog In Harness LL-010	Retrd.	1994	45.00	50
1990 Husking Acorns LL-008	Retrd.	1994	60.00	65
1991 It's About Time LL-022	Retrd.	1994	55.00	60
1990 A Little Jig LL-018	Retrd.	1994	45.00	50
1990 A Look Through The Spyglass LL-015	Retrd.	1994	40.00	50
1989 Magical Discovery LL-005	Retrd.	1993	45.00	50
1990 Ministral Magic LL-017	Retrd.	1994	45.00	50
1990 A Proclamation LL-013	Retrd.	1994	45.00	55
1989 Spring Water Scrub LL-006	Retrd.	1993	35.00	50
1990 Traveling Fast LL-009	Retrd.	1994	45.00	50
1989 Treasure Hunt LL-004	Retrd.	1993	45.00	50
1991 Viking LL-019	Retrd.	1994	45.00	50
1989 Woodland Cache LL-001	Retrd.	1993	35.00	50
1990 Woodland Scout LL-011	Retrd.	1994	40.00	50
1990 Writing The Legend LL-016	Retrd.	1994	35.00	65

Lil' Doll™ - Various

YEAR ISSUE	EDITION LIMIT	YEAR RETD.	ISSUE PRICE	*QUOTE U.S.$
1992 Clara & The Nutcracker LD-017 - D. Newburn	Retrd.	1994	35.00	35
1991 The Nutcracker LD-006 - P.J. Jonas	Retrd.	1994	35.00	35

Music Makers™ - Various

YEAR ISSUE	EDITION LIMIT	YEAR RETD.	ISSUE PRICE	*QUOTE U.S.$
1991 A Christmas Gift MM-015 - D. Kennicutt	Retrd.	1993	59.00	59
1991 Crystal Angel MM-017 - D. Kennicutt	Retrd.	1993	59.00	59
1991 Dashing Through The Snow MM-013 - D. Kennicutt	Retrd.	1993	59.00	59
1989 Evening Carolers MM-005 - D. Kennicutt	Retrd.	1993	69.00	69
1989 Herald Angel MM-011 - S. Bradford	Retrd.	1993	79.00	79
1991 Nutcracker MM-024 - P.J. Jonas	Retrd.	1994	69.00	69
1991 Peace Descending MM-025 - P.J. Jonas	Retrd.	1993	69.00	69
1991 Renaissance Angel MM-028 - P.J. Jonas	Retrd.	1994	69.00	69
1989 Santa's Sleigh MM-004 - L. Miller	Retrd.	1993	69.00	69
1991 Teddy Bear Band #2 MM-023 - D. Kennicutt	Retrd.	1994	90.00	90
1989 Teddy Bear Band MM-012 - S. Bradford	Retrd.	1993	99.00	100
1989 Teddy Drummers MM-009 - D. Kennicutt	Retrd.	1993	69.00	69
1991 Teddy Soldiers MM-018 - D. Kennicutt	Retrd.	1994	69.00	84
1991 Victorian Santa MM-026 - L. Miller	Retrd.	1993	69.00	69

Party Animals™ - L. Miller, unless otherwise noted

YEAR ISSUE	EDITION LIMIT	YEAR RETD.	ISSUE PRICE	*QUOTE U.S.$
1992 Democratic Donkey ('92) - K. Memoli	Retrd.	1994	20.00	20
1984 Democratic Donkey ('84) - D. Kennicutt	Retrd.	1986	14.50	16
1986 Democratic Donkey ('86)	Retrd.	1988	14.50	15
1988 Democratic Donkey ('88)	Retrd.	1990	14.50	16
1990 Democratic Donkey ('90) - D. Kennicutt	Retrd.	1992	16.00	16
1984 GOP Elephant ('84)	Retrd.	1986	14.50	16
1986 GOP Elephant ('86)	Retrd.	1988	14.50	15
1988 GOP Elephant ('88)	Retrd.	1990	14.50	16
1990 GOP Elephant ('90) - D. Kennicutt	Retrd.	1992	16.00	16
1992 GOP Elephant ('92) - K. Memoli	Retrd.	1994	20.00	20

PenniBears™ - P.J. Jonas

YEAR ISSUE	EDITION LIMIT	YEAR RETD.	ISSUE PRICE	*QUOTE U.S.$
1992 After Every Meal PB-058	Retrd.	1994	22.00	22
1992 Apple For Teacher PB-069	Retrd.	1994	24.00	24
1989 Attic Fun PB-019	Retrd.	1992	20.00	40
1989 Baby Hugs PB-007	Retrd.	1992	20.00	35
1991 Baking Goodies PB-043	Retrd.	1993	26.00	30
1989 Bathtime Buddies PB-023	Retrd.	1992	20.00	25
1992 Batter Up PB-066	Retrd.	1994	22.00	22
1991 Bear Footin' it PB-037	Retrd.	1993	24.00	24
1992 Bear-Capade PB-073	Retrd.	1994	22.00	22
1991 Bearly Awake PB-033	Retrd.	1993	22.00	25
1989 Beautiful Bride PB-004	Retrd.	1992	20.00	35
1993 Big Chief Little Bear PB-088	Retrd.	1996	28.00	28
1989 Birthday Bear PB-018	Retrd.	1992	20.00	40
1991 Boo Hoo Bear PB-050	Retrd.	1994	22.00	22
1990 Boooo Bear PB-025	Retrd.	1993	20.00	22
1991 Bountiful Harvest PB-045	Retrd.	1994	24.00	24
1989 Bouquet Boy PB-003	Retrd.	1992	20.00	45
1989 Bouquet Girl PB-001	Retrd.	1992	20.00	45
1991 Bump-bear-Crop PB-035	Retrd.	1993	26.00	30
1991 Bunny Buddies PB-042	Retrd.	1993	22.00	25
1989 Butterfly Bear PB-005	Retrd.	1992	20.00	45-50
1990 Buttons & Bows PB-012	Retrd.	1992	20.00	45
1992 Christmas Cookies PB-075	Retrd.	1994	22.00	22
1991 Christmas Reinbear PB-046	Retrd.	1994	28.00	28
1992 Cinderella PB-056	Retrd.	1994	22.00	22
1992 Clowning Around PB-065	Retrd.	1994	22.00	22
1989 Cookie Bandit PB-006	Retrd.	1992	20.00	30
1990 Count Bearacula PB-027	Retrd.	1993	22.00	24
1991 Country Lullabye PB-036	Retrd.	1993	24.00	25
1990 Country Quilter PB-030	Retrd.	1993	22.00	30
1990 Country Spring PB-013	Retrd.	1992	20.00	45
1991 Curtain Call PB-049	Retrd.	1994	24.00	24
1992 Decorating The Wreath PB-076	Retrd.	1994	22.00	22
1989 Doctor Bear PB-008	Retrd.	1992	20.00	30
1992 Downhill Thrills PB-070	Retrd.	1994	24.00	24
1990 Dress Up Fun PB-028	Retrd.	1993	22.00	30
1992 Dust Bunny Roundup PB-062	Retrd.	1994	22.00	22
1992 First Prom PB-064	Retrd.	1994	22.00	22
1990 Garden Path PB-014	Retrd.	1992	20.00	45-50
1993 Getting 'Round On My Own PB-085	Retrd.	1996	26.00	26
1990 Giddiap Teddy PB-011	Retrd.	1992	20.00	35
1991 Goodnight Little Prince PB-041	Retrd.	1993	26.00	30
1991 Goodnight Sweet Princess PB-040	Retrd.	1993	26.00	30
1993 Gotta Try Again PB-082	Retrd.	1996	24.00	24

*Quotes have been rounded up to nearest dollar

YEAR ISSUE	EDITION LIMIT	YEAR RETD.	ISSUE PRICE	*QUOTE U.S.$
1989 Handsome Groom PB-015	Retrd.	1992	20.00	40
1993 Happy Birthday PB-084	Retrd.	1996	26.00	26
1993 A Happy Camper PB-077	Retrd.	1996	28.00	28
1991 Happy Hobo PB-051	Retrd.	1994	26.00	26
1989 Honey Bear PB-002	Retrd.	1992	20.00	45
1992 I Made It Boy PB-061	Retrd.	1994	22.00	22
1992 I Made It Girl PB-060	Retrd.	1994	22.00	22
1989 Lazy Days PB-009	Retrd.	1992	20.00	25
1992 Lil' Devil PB-071	Retrd.	1994	24.00	24
1991 Lil' Mer-teddy PB-034	Retrd.	1993	24.00	24
1992 Lil' Sis Makes Up PB-074	Retrd.	1994	22.00	22
1993 Little Bear Peep PB-083	Retrd.	1996	24.00	24
1993 Making It Better PB-087	Retrd.	1996	24.00	24
1993 May Joy Be Yours PB-080	Retrd.	1996	24.00	24
1993 My Forever Love PB-078	Retrd.	1996	28.00	28
1989 Nap Time PB-016	Retrd.	1992	20.00	25
1989 Nurse Bear PB-017	Retrd.	1992	20.00	35
1992 On Your Toes PB-068	Retrd.	1994	24.00	24
1989 Petite Mademoiselle PB-010	Retrd.	1992	20.00	40
1991 Pilgrim Provider PB-047	Retrd.	1994	32.00	32
1992 Pot O' Gold PB-059	Retrd.	1994	22.00	22
1992 Puddle Jumper PB-057	Retrd.	1994	24.00	24
1989 Puppy Bath PB-020	Retrd.	1992	20.00	25
1989 Puppy Love PB-021	Retrd.	1992	20.00	25
1993 Rest Stop PB-079	Retrd.	1996	24.00	24
1992 Sandbox Fun PB-063	Retrd.	1994	22.00	22
1990 Santa Bear-ing Gifts PB-031	Retrd.	1993	24.00	30
1993 Santa's Helper PB-081	Retrd.	1996	28.00	28
1990 Scarecrow Teddy PB-029	Retrd.	1993	24.00	25
1992 Smokey's Nephew PB-055	Retrd.	1994	22.00	22
1990 Sneaky Snowball PB-026	Retrd.	1993	20.00	25
1989 Southern Belle PB-024	Retrd.	1992	20.00	35
1992 Spanish Rose PB-053	Retrd.	1994	24.00	24
1990 Stocking Surprise PB-032	Retrd.	1993	22.00	26
1993 Summer Belle PB-086	Retrd.	1996	24.00	24
1991 Summer Sailing PB-039	Retrd.	1993	26.00	30
1991 Sweet Lil 'Sis PB-048	Retrd.	1994	22.00	22
1991 Sweetheart Bears PB-044	Retrd.	1993	28.00	30
1992 Tally Ho! PB-054	Retrd.	1994	22.00	22
1992 Touchdown PB-072	Retrd.	1994	22.00	22
1989 Tubby Teddy PB-022	Retrd.	1992	20.00	22
1991 A Wild Ride PB-052	Retrd.	1994	26.00	26
1992 Will You Be Mine? PB-067	Retrd.	1994	22.00	22
1991 Windy Day PB-038	Retrd.	1993	24.00	24

PenniBears™ Collector's Club Members Only Editions - P.J. Jonas

YEAR ISSUE	EDITION LIMIT	YEAR RETD.	ISSUE PRICE	*QUOTE U.S.$
1990 1990 First Collection PB-C90	Retrd.	1990	26.00	125
1991 1991 Collecting Makes Cents PB-C91	Retrd.	1991	26.00	150
1992 1992 Today's Pleasures, Tomorrow's Treasures PB-C92	Retrd.	1992	26.00	100
1993 1993 Chalkin Up Another Year PB-C93	Retrd.	1993	26.00	35
1994 1994 Artist's Touch-Collector's Treasure PB-C94	Retrd.	1994	26.00	26

Storytime Rhymes & Tales - H. Henriksen

YEAR ISSUE	EDITION LIMIT	YEAR RETD.	ISSUE PRICE	*QUOTE U.S.$
1991 Humpty Dumpty SL-008	Retrd.	1993	64.00	64
1991 Little Jack Horner SL-007	Retrd.	1993	50.00	50
1991 Little Miss Muffet SL-006	Retrd.	1993	64.00	64
1991 Mistress Mary SL-002	Retrd.	1993	64.00	64
1991 Mother Goose SL-001	Retrd.	1993	64.00	64
1991 Owl & Pussy Cat SL-004	Retrd.	1993	100.00	100
1991 Simple Simon SL-003	Retrd.	1993	90.00	90
1991 Three Little Pigs SL-005	Retrd.	1993	100.00	100

Teddy Angels™ - P.J. Jonas

YEAR ISSUE	EDITION LIMIT	YEAR RETD.	ISSUE PRICE	*QUOTE U.S.$
1995 Bruin & Bluebirds "Nurture nature." BA-013	Open		19.00	19
1995 Bruin Making Valentines "Holidays start within the heart." BA-012	Open		15.00	15
1995 Bruin With Harp Seal "Make your corner of the world a little warmer." BA-021	Open		15.00	15
1995 Bunny's Picnic "Make a feast of friendship." BA-007	Open		19.00	19
1995 Casey & Honey Reading "Friends are the best recipe for relaxation." BA-023	Open		15.00	15
1995 Casey Tucking Honey In "There is magic in the simplest things we do." BA-008	Open		19.00	19
1995 Cowboy Murray "Have a Doo Da Day." BA-002	Open		19.00	19
1995 Honey "Love gives our hearts wings." BA-014	Open		13.00	13
1995 Ivy & Blankie "Nothing is as comfortable as an old friend." BA-003	Open		13.00	13
1995 Ivy In Garden "Celebrate the little things." BA-009	Open		15.00	15
1995 Ivy With Locket "You're always close at heart." BA-028	Open		13.00	13
1995 Murray & Little Bit "Imagination can take you anywhere." BA-004	Open		19.00	19
1995 Murray Mending Bruin "Everybody needs a helping hand." BA-005	Open		15.00	15
1995 Murray With Angel "I believe in you, too." BA-022	Open		22.00	22
1995 Nicholas With Stars "Dreams are never too far away to catch." BA-024	Open		15.00	15
1995 Old Bear "Always remember your way home." BA-011	Open		19.00	19
1995 Old Bear & Little Bit Gardening "The well-watered garden produces a great harvest." BA-026	Open		15.00	15
1995 Old Bear & Little Bit Reading "Love to learn and learn to love." BA-006	Open		15.00	15
1995 Rufus Helps Bird "We could all use a little lift." BA-027	Open		15.00	15
1995 Sweetie "Come tell me all about it." BA-001	Open		15.00	15
1995 Sweetie With Kitty Cats "Always close-knit." BA-025	Open		15.00	15
1995 Tilli & Murray "Friendship is a bridge between hearts." BA-010	Open		15.00	15

Teddy Angels™ Christmas - P.J. Jonas

YEAR ISSUE	EDITION LIMIT	YEAR RETD.	ISSUE PRICE	*QUOTE U.S.$
1997 Angel & Sweetie BA-029	Open		22.00	22
1995 Casey "You're a bright & shining star." BA-019	Open		13.00	13
1995 Ivy "Enchantment glows in winter snows." BA-020	Open		13.00	13
1995 Sweetie & Santa Bear "Tis the season of surprises." BA-016	Open		22.00	22
1995 Tilli & Doves "A wreath is a circle of love." BA-015	Open		19.00	19

WACO Products Corp.

Melody In Motion/Collector's Society - S. Nakane, unless otherwise noted

YEAR ISSUE	EDITION LIMIT	YEAR RETD.	ISSUE PRICE	*QUOTE U.S.$
1992 Amazing Willie the One-Man Band 07152	Retrd.	1994	130.00	325-450
1992 Willie The Conductor	Retrd.	1994	Gift	40-150
1993 Charmed Bunnies	Retrd.	1993	Gift	45-50
1993 Willie The Collector 07170	Retrd.	1995	200.00	250-375
1994 Springtime	Retrd.	1994	Gift	35-50
1995 Best Friends	Retrd.	1995	Gift	35-50
1996 Willie The Entertainer 07199	Retrd.	1996	200.00	250-275
1996 '86 Santa Replica - K. Maeda	Retrd.	1997	Gift	45-50
1997 Willie on Parade/Drum 07214 - K. Maeda	Retrd.	1997	220.00	220
1997 Willie Sez - K. Maeda	Retrd.	1997	Gift	40-45
1998 Willie & Jumbo 07224 - K. Maeda	Yr.Iss.		180.00	180
1998 Purr-Fect Harmony 07307 - K. Maeda	Yr. Iss.		Gift	45

Melody In Motion - S. Nakane, unless otherwise noted

YEAR ISSUE	EDITION LIMIT	YEAR RETD.	ISSUE PRICE	*QUOTE U.S.$
1985 Willie The Trumpeter 07000	Open		90.00	175
1985 Willie The Hobo (Memories) 07001	2,500	1985	90.00	195-300
1985 Willie The Hobo (Show Me...) 07001	Retrd.	1996	90.00	275-400
1985 Willie The Whistler (Show Me...) 07002	2,500	1985	90.00	225-400
1985 Willie The Whistler (Memories) 07002	Retrd.	1998	90.00	250-300
1985 Salty 'N' Pepper 07010	Retrd.	1992	90.00	400-700
1986 The Cellist 07011	Retrd.	1995	100.00	300-400
1986 Santa Claus 1986 07012	20,000	1986	100.00	2000-3000
1986 The Guitarist 07013	Retrd.	1994	100.00	250-500
1986 The Fiddler 07014	Retrd.	1995	100.00	170-250
1987 Lamppost Willie 07051	Open		85.00	150
1987 The Organ Grinder 07053	Retrd.	1994	100.00	250-300
1987 Violin Clown 07055	Retrd.	1992	85.00	200-350
1987 Clarinet Clown 07056	Retrd.	1991	85.00	150-350
1987 Saxophone Clown 07057	Retrd.	1991	85.00	150-350
1987 Accordion Clown 07058	Retrd.	1991	85.00	175-350
1987 Santa Claus 1987 07060	16,000	1987	110.00	1600-2000
1987 Balloon Clown 07061	Open		85.00	150
1987 The Carousel (1st Edition) 07065	Retrd.	1993	190.00	225-400
1987 Madame Violin 07075	Retrd.	1991	130.00	150-400
1987 Madame Mandolin 07076	Retrd.	1994	130.00	150-500
1987 Madame Cello 07077	Retrd.	1991	130.00	150-350
1987 Madame Flute 07078	Retrd.	1992	130.00	150-400
1987 Madame Harpsichord 07080	Retrd.	1991	130.00	150-450
1987 Madame Lyre 07081	Retrd.	1994	130.00	150-300
1988 Madame Harp 07079	Retrd.	1998	130.00	150-250
1988 Spotlight Clown Cornet 07082	Retrd.	1992	120	200-250
1988 Spotlight Clown Banjo 07083	Retrd.	1992	120.00	250-350
1988 Spotlight Clown Trombone 07084	Retrd.	1992	120.00	200-350
1988 Spotlight Clown Bingo 07085	Retrd.	1996	130.00	125-200
1988 Spotlight Clown Tuba 07086	Retrd.	1992	120.00	250-300
1988 Spotlight Clown Bass 07087	Retrd.	1994	130.00	275-300
1988 Peanut Vendor 07088	Retrd.	1994	140.00	300-350
1988 Ice Cream Vendor 07089	Retrd.	1994	140.00	225-450
1988 Santa Claus 1988 07090	12,000	1988	130.00	1000-1600
1989 Clockpost Willie 07091	Open		150.00	220
1989 Santa Claus 1989 (Willie) 07092	12,000	1989	130.00	600-1000
1989 Lull'aby Willie 07093	Retrd.	1992	170.00	400-500
1989 The Grand Carousel 07094	Retrd.	1995	3000.00	4000-5000
1989 Grandfather's Clock 07096	Retrd.	1994	200.00	325-350
1990 Santa Claus 1990 07097	12,000	1990	150.00	325-950
1990 Shoemaker 07130	3,700	1993	110.00	200-350
1990 Blacksmith 07131	3,700	1993	110.00	200-350
1990 Woodchopper 07132	3,700	1993	110.00	200-350
1990 Accordion Boy 07133	4,100	1992	120.00	200-350
1990 Hunter 07134	Retrd.	1994	110.00	200-300
1990 Robin Hood 07135 - C. Johnson	2,000	1991	180.00	400-700
1990 Little John 07136 - C. Johnson	2,000	1992	180.00	300
1990 Clockpost Willie II (European) 07140	Retrd.	1990	N/A	350-450
1990 Clockpost Clown 07141	Open		220.00	220
1990 Lull' A Bye Willie II (European) 07142	Retrd.	1990	N/A	400-450
1991 The Carousel (2nd Edition) 07065	Retrd.	1995	240.00	250-350
1991 Victoria Park Carousel 07143	Open		300.00	360
1991 Hunter Timepiece 07144	Retrd.	1994	250.00	300-350
1991 Santa Claus 1991 07146	7,000	1991	150.00	400-500
1992 Wall Street Willie 07147	Open		180.00	240
1991 Willie The Fisherman 07148	Open		150.00	200
1992 King of Clowns Carousel 07149	Retrd.	1998	740.00	1000-1200
1992 Golden Mountain Clock 07150	Retrd.	1995	250.00	280-350
1992 Santa Claus 1992 07151	11,000	1992	160.00	200-250
1992 Dockside Willie 07153	Retrd.	1998	160.00	250-300
1993 Wild West Willie 07154	Retrd.	1995	175.00	200-250
1993 Alarm Clock Post 07155 (Willie European)	Retrd.	1996	240.00	300-350
1993 Lamplight Willie 07156	Retrd.	1996	220.00	210-220
1993 Madame Cello Player, glaze 07157	200	1993	170.00	300-450
1993 Madame Flute, glaze 07158	200	1993	170.00	300-450
1993 Madame Harpsichord, glaze	200	1993	170.00	300-450
1993 Madame Harp, glaze	150	1993	190.00	300-450
1993 Santa Claus 1993 Coke 07161	6,000	1993	180.00	250-475
1993 Wall Street (Japanese) 07162	Retrd.	1993	N/A	300-350
1993 Santa Claus 1993 (European) 07163	1,000	1993	N/A	375-450
1993 Willie The Golfer - Alarm 07164	Retrd.	1995	240.00	240
1993 The Artist 07165	Retrd.	1996	240.00	200-240
1993 Heartbreak Willie 07166	Open		180.00	190
1993 South of the Border 07167	Retrd.	1996	180.00	250-450
1993 When I Grow Up 07171	Retrd.	1996	200.00	200-400
1994 Low Pressure Job-Alarm 07168	Retrd.	1995	240.00	250-475
1994 Day's End-Alarm 07169	Retrd.	1996	240.00	300-350
1994 Santa '94 Coca-Cola 07174	9,000	1994	190.00	180-325
1994 Smooth Sailing 07175	Retrd.	1996	200.00	200-250
1994 Santa Claus 1994 (European) 07176	700	1994	N/A	300-400
1994 The Longest Drive 07177	Open		150.00	150
1994 Happy Birthday Willie 07178	Open		170.00	170
1994 Chattanooga Choo Choo 07179	Open		180.00	190
1994 Jackpot Willie 07180	Open		180.00	190
1994 Caroler Boy 07189	10,000	1998	172.00	180
1994 Caroler Girl 07190	10,000	1998	172.00	180
1994 Willie the Yodeler 07192	Open		158.00	160
1998 New Fiddler 07193	Open		200.00	200
1994 Willie the Golfer- Clock 07264	Open		240.00	240
1994 Day's End-Clock 07269	Retrd.	1997	240.00	240-350
1995 Campfire Cowboy 07172	Retrd.	1995	180.00	300-600
1995 Blue Danube Carousel 07173	Open		280.00	300
1995 Willie the Conductor (10th Anniversary) 07181	10,000		220.00	220
1995 Coca-Cola Norman Rockwell 07194	Open		194.00	200
1995 Santa Claus '95 07195	6,000	1995	190.00	175-250
1995 Gaslight Willie 07197	Open		190.00	190
1995 Coca Cola Polar Bear 07198	6,000		180.00	180
1995 Low Pressure Job-Clock 07268	Retrd.	1997	240.00	250-450
1995 Willie The Fireman 07271	1,500	1996	200.00	300-450
1996 The Candy Factory-I Love Lucy 07203 - Willingham/Maeda	Open		250.00	250
1996 Willie On The Road 07204 - K. Maeda	Open		180.00	180
1996 Marionette Clown 07205 - K. Maeda	Open		200.00	200
1996 Willie the Racer 07206 - K. Maeda	Open		180.00	180
1996 Willie the Organ Grinder 07207	3,000		200.00	200
1996 Santa Claus '96 07208 - K. Maeda	7,000		220.00	220
1996 Willie the Champion 07209 - K. Maeda	Open		180.00	180
1996 Willie the Photographer 07211 - K. Maeda	Open		220.00	220
1997 Willie on Parade/Trumpet 07212 - K. Maeda	Open		220.00	220
1997 Willie on Parade/Sousaphone 07213 - K. Maeda	Open		220.00	220
1997 Willie on Parade/Trombone 07215 - K. Maeda	Open		220.00	220
1997 I Love Lucy/Vitameatavegamin 07216 - K. Maeda	4,000		250.00	250
1997 Santa Claus 1997 07217 - K. Maeda	4,000	1997	220.00	220-255
1998 Wedding Couple 07220 - K. Maeda	Open		196.00	196
1998 Willie The Wanderer 07221 - K. Maeda	Open		170.00	170
1998 Santa Claus 1998 07222 - K. Maeda	4,000		220.00	220
1998 Coca Cola Santa Claus Clock 07223 - K. Maeda	3,000		250.00	250
1998 Caroler Boy II 07225	Open		190.00	190
1998 Lucy Stomping Grapes - K. Maeda	Open		250.00	250
1997 Side Street Circus/Balancing Dog 07230	Open		110.00	110
1997 Side Street Circus/Juggling 07231	Open		110.00	110
1997 Side Street Circus/Accordian 07232	Open		110.00	110
1997 Side Street Circus/Clarinet 07233	Open		110.00	110
1997 Side Street Circus/Plate Spinning 07234	Open		110.00	110

Walnut Ridge Collectibles

Cat Figurines - K. Bejma

YEAR ISSUE	EDITION LIMIT	YEAR RETD.	ISSUE PRICE	*QUOTE U.S.$
1993 Basket of Kittens 309	Open		70.00	112
1991 Calico Cat 306	Open		40.00	46
1991 Goodrich Cat 300	12/98		50.00	56
1997 Gypsy 313	Open		62.00	62
1997 Small Striped Cat 312	Open		36.00	36
1994 Tabby Cat 310	Open		50.00	56
1991 Tiny Cat 304	Open		24.00	30
1997 White Kitten 311	Open		56.00	56

Christmas Figurines - K. Bejma

YEAR ISSUE	EDITION LIMIT	YEAR RETD.	ISSUE PRICE	*QUOTE U.S.$
1996 Alpine Tree 1001	Open		24.00	26
1988 Belsnickle 102	Retrd.	1997	32.00	36

*Quotes have been rounded up to nearest dollar

YEAR ISSUE	EDITION LIMIT	YEAR RETD.	ISSUE PRICE	*QUOTE U.S.$
1988 Belsnickle 104	Retrd.	1996	48.00	48
1988 Belsnickle 105	Retrd.	1996	32.00	32
1989 Belsnickle 124	Retrd.	1996	30.00	30
1991 Belsnickle 140	Retrd.	1996	40.00	40
1994 Belsnickle 176	Retrd.	1996	28.00	32
1988 Belsnickle, mini 116	Retrd.	1997	22.00	24
1994 Belsnickle/Tree 174	Retrd.	1997	32.00	38
1994 Children on Sled 172	12/98		48.00	58
1995 Crying Snowman 189	Open		44.00	50
1994 Father Christmas 175	Retrd.	1997	28.00	32
1992 Father Christmas, lg. 161	Retrd.	1997	270.00	300
1988 Father Christmas/Apples 122	Retrd.	1996	48.00	51
1988 Father Christmas/Bag 114	Retrd.	1996	34.00	34
1993 Father Christmas/Bag 163	Retrd.	1996	38.00	42
1994 Father Christmas/Bag 166	Retrd.	1997	30.00	40
1994 Father Christmas/Bag 178	Retrd.	1996	42.00	42
1988 Father Christmas/Basket 100R	Retrd.	1996	120.00	120
1988 Father Christmas/Basket 100W	Retrd.	1996	120.00	120
1994 Father Christmas/Girl/Doll 165	12/98		52.00	62
1993 Father Christmas/Holly 164	Retrd.	1997	52.00	58
1990 Father Christmas/Toys/Switch 136	Retrd.	1996	120.00	120
1991 Gnome/Rabbit 148	Retrd.	1996	32.00	42
1990 Jolly St. Nick 135	Retrd.	1996	52.00	52
1994 Primitive Snowman 173	Open		32.00	38
1990 Rocking Santa 129	Retrd.	1996	36.00	40
1992 Santa/Horse, sm. 158	Retrd.	1997	24.00	28
1991 Santa/Walking Stick 152	Retrd.	1996	56.00	60
1996 Snow Children 1002	Open		56.00	70
1994 Snowflake Belsnickle 177	12/98		36.00	44
1994 Snowman & Boy 181	Open		34.00	38
1990 Snowman 127	Retrd.	1996	32.00	35
1996 Snowman in Forest 1003	Open		70.00	82
1993 Snowman with Scarf 162	12/98		28.00	34
1995 Snowman with Twig Arms 188	Open		32.00	38
1994 Snowman, lg. 182	Open		44.00	52
1990 Snowman, med. 131	Retrd.	1997	28.00	34
1991 Snowman, sm. 139	Retrd.	1996	22.00	28
1996 Snowman/Snowflake Scarf 1004	Open		44.00	52
1992 Snowman/Twigs 156	12/98		30.00	34
1995 Tall Tree 190	Open		28.00	34
1996 Tree 197	Open		26.00	32
1996 Tree 198	Open		22.00	26
1996 Tree 199	Open		18.00	20
1992 Tree Set 160	12/98		44.00	52
1994 Walking Santa 180	Retrd.	1996	90.00	90

Fall & Halloween Figurines - K. Bejma

YEAR ISSUE	EDITION LIMIT	YEAR RETD.	ISSUE PRICE	*QUOTE U.S.$
1996 Black Cat 410	Open		24.00	30
1997 Cat Mask, paper mache 425	Open		30.00	30
1997 Ghost on Pumpkin 423	Open		34.00	34
1996 Ghost with Pumpkin 417	Open		30.00	42
1997 Halloween Mask, paper mache 426	Retrd.	1997	32.00	32
1996 Jack-O-Lantern 414	Open		28.00	36
1996 Jack-O-Lantern Man 416	Open		40.00	46
1998 Little Cat 430	Open		30.00	30
1998 Little Witch 429	Open		30.00	30
1996 Oak Leaf, set/2 420	Open		28.00	40
1996 Owl 411	Open		22.00	28
1996 Pilgrim Set 400	Open		80.00	90
1998 Pumpkin 433	Open		44.00	44
1996 Pumpkin Kids, set/2 415	Open		56.00	62
1998 Pumpkin Man 431	Open		46.00	46
1997 Pumpkin with Black Cat 422	Open		72.00	72
1996 Pumpkin, lg. 412	Open		48.00	54
1997 Pumpkin, lg. paper mache 427	Open		36.00	36
1991 Pumpkin, set/3 404	Open		22.00	30
1997 Pumpkin, sm. paper mache 424	Retrd.	1997	32.00	32
1996 Pumpkin,sm. 413	Open		28.00	34
1996 Turkey, lg. 419	Open		44.00	50
1996 Turkey, med. 418	Open		36.00	44
1991 Turkey, sm. 401	Open		20.00	30
1998 Witch on broom, lg. 428	Open		78.00	78
1998 Witch on Gourd 432	Open		46.00	46
1997 Witch with Pumpkins 421	Open		56.00	56
1996 Witch, lg. 407	Open		68.00	82
1996 Witch, med. 408	Open		48.00	56
1996 Witch, sm. 409	Open		44.00	50

Gossamer Wings - K. Bejma

YEAR ISSUE	EDITION LIMIT	YEAR RETD.	ISSUE PRICE	*QUOTE U.S.$
1994 Addie 167	Open		40.00	46
1995 Alexandra 183	Open		54.00	64
1998 Cecelia 1011	Open		90.00	90
1997 Choirs 1010	Open		76.00	86
1996 Deborah 192	Open		50.00	64
1994 Elizabeth 170	Open		52.00	58
1997 Elysia 1005	Open		54.00	62
1997 Emma 1006	Open		50.00	58
1998 Felicia 1020	Open		76.00	76
1996 Gabriella 194	Open		64.00	74
1994 Hannah 169	Open		50.00	58
1998 Harmony 1018	Open		84.00	84
1997 Helena 1009	Open		56.00	64
1995 Julia 184	12/98		38.00	46
1996 Kathleen 193	Open		56.00	80
1995 Lucia 187	12/98		62.00	80
1995 Lydia 185	Open		58.00	70
1994 Meghan 168	Open		46.00	54
1998 Michael 1017	Open		120.00	120
1997 Noel 1008	Open		40.00	46
1996 Olivia 196	Open		56.00	62
1998 Peace 1019	Open		84.00	84
1997 Sarah 1007	Open		32.00	40
1995 Tatiana 186	12/98		58.00	66
1996 Thomas 195	Open		64.00	74
1996 Victoria 191	Open		54.00	64

Herr Belsnickle Collection - K. Bejma

YEAR ISSUE	EDITION LIMIT	YEAR RETD.	ISSUE PRICE	*QUOTE U.S.$
1993 Herr Dieter 807	Open		90.00	100
1993 Herr Franz 805	Open		90.00	100
1993 Herr Fritz 803	Open		100.00	116
1993 Herr Gottfried 806	Open		90.00	100
1994 Herr Gregor 818	Open		90.00	100
1993 Herr Gunther 809	Open		70.00	80
1993 Herr Heinrich 810	Open		60.00	68
1993 Herr Hermann 813	Open		48.00	54
1995 Herr Hobart 824	Open		68.00	68
1995 Herr Johann 820	Open		230.00	260
1993 Herr Karl 801	Open		150.00	168
1993 Herr Klaus 800	Open		180.00	200
1993 Herr Ludwig 811	Open		60.00	68
1993 Herr Nicholas 802	Open		130.00	150
1993 Herr Oskar 816	Open		44.00	50
1993 Herr Peter 815	Open		44.00	50
1993 Herr Reiner 812	Open		60.00	68
1995 Herr Roland 823	Open		64.00	64
1994 Herr Rudolph 819	Open		230.00	260
1995 Herr Rutger 822	Open		150.00	168
1995 Herr Sebastian 821	Open		70.00	80
1994 Herr Viktor 817	Open		64.00	74
1993 Herr Wilhelm 804	Open		100.00	116
1993 Herr Willi 814	Open		44.00	50
1993 Herr Wolfgang 808	Open		70.00	80

Holiday Collection - K. Bejma

YEAR ISSUE	EDITION LIMIT	YEAR RETD.	ISSUE PRICE	*QUOTE U.S.$
1997 Magnolia 1016	Open		24.00	24
1997 Snowman 1013	Open		50.00	50
1997 Snowy Tree, sm. 1015	Open		24.00	24
1997 Snowy Tree, lg. 1014	Open		26.00	26
1998 ..."Let it Snow" Snowman 1023	100		480.00	480
1998 Snow Angel 1022	Open		62.00	62
1998 Snowman with twig arms 1021	Open		74.00	74

Lamps - K. Bejma

YEAR ISSUE	EDITION LIMIT	YEAR RETD.	ISSUE PRICE	*QUOTE U.S.$
1995 Angel 510	Open		160.00	160
1988 Belsnickle, lg. 500	Open		220.00	220
1988 Belsnickle, sm. 501	Retrd.	1996	170.00	170
1993 Belsnickle, sm. 508	Open		160.00	160
1997 Bunny, lg. 512	Open		190.00	190
1990 Cat 503	Open		180.00	180
1992 Father Christmas 507	Open		280.00	280
1990 Rabbit 502	Retrd.	1996	170.00	170
1997 Santa, lg. 511	Open		220.00	220
1992 Sheep 506	Retrd.	1994	150.00	150
1994 Snowman 509	Open		280.00	280
1998 Snowman, sm 513	Open		90.00	90
1992 Spaniel 504	Retrd.	1994	170.00	170
1992 Spaniel, set 505	Retrd.	1994	330.00	330

Limited Edition Christmas Figurines - K. Bejma

YEAR ISSUE	EDITION LIMIT	YEAR RETD.	ISSUE PRICE	*QUOTE U.S.$
1993 Naughty Otto 700	Yr.Iss.	1993	70.00	70
1994 Father Christmas 701	Yr.Iss.	1994	60.00	60
1995 Sinter Klaas 702	Yr.Iss.	1995	60.00	60
1996 Snowy, Snowy Night 703	Yr.Iss.	1996	56.00	56
1997 Glad Tidings 704	Yr.Iss.	1997	60.00	60
1998 1998 Limited Edition 705	Yr.Iss.		60.00	60
1998 10th Anniversary Edition 706	Yr.Iss.		64.00	64

Limited Edition Collector's Series - K. Bejma

YEAR ISSUE	EDITION LIMIT	YEAR RETD.	ISSUE PRICE	*QUOTE U.S.$
1997 Bearing Gifts 650	500		72.00	72
1997 Bring Yuletide Cheer 657	350		250.00	250
1997 Cabbages & Violets 639	350		64.00	72
1998 Carrot Cruiser 642	750		84.00	84
1996 Christkindl 635	2,000		68.00	84
1996 Christmas Aglow 629	1,000		48.00	54
1998 Crystal Cottage 641	1,000		96.00	96
1996 Dash Away All 628	1,500		108.00	120
1995 Downhill Racer 618	2,500		48.00	60
1994 Egg Cottage 603	1,500	1997	80.00	90
1994 Egyptian Egg/Rabbits 600	1,500	1997	48.00	54
1997 Field of Flowers 636	750		56.00	62
1997 Forever Friends 638	500		52.00	60
1998 From The Chimney He Rose 659	2,500		66.00	66
1997 The Garden Gate 637	350		56.00	68
1998 Garden Party 671	2,500		54.00	54
1998 Goin' on a Ride 670	750		48.00	48
1995 Happy Christmas 622	2,000		50.00	60
1998 Hare Hansel 645	1,500		50.00	50
1995 Hareratio 613	1,500		42.00	48
1994 Hemlocks And Holly 610	750		260.00	290
1998 Hi! 668	2,000		18.00	18
1996 Hitching a Ride 625	750		44.00	58
1996 Holiday Rider 631	1,000		68.00	84
1995 Holiday Sledding 620	2,500		52.00	66
1994 Holy Night 612	750		250.00	280
1998 Humphrey 648	100		600.00	600
1998 Jack 647	750		30.00	30
1995 Jacqueline 614	1,500		48.00	54
1995 Jeffrey 615	1,500		48.00	54
1998 Jumpin' for Joy 666	1,500		24.00	24
1994 Keeping Secrets 605	3,500		52.00	64
1994 Kimbra 609	10,000		24.00	36
1996 Life is but a Dream 627	1,000		42.00	50
1994 Lite The Way 604	3,500		52.00	58
1998 Littlest Helper 660	1,500		66.00	66
1995 Magnolias in Bloom 616	1,500		90.00	110
1997 Memorable Journey 655	1,500		70.00	70
1996 A Merry Christmas Santa 100A	100		600.00	750
1998 A Merry Olde Gent 663	2,500		72.00	72
1996 A Midnight Clear 634	1,250		52.00	80
1994 Miles To Go 607	10,000		52.00	62
1997 Noel, Noel 651	750		70.00	70
1995 O' Tannenbaum 621	1,500		56.00	80
1998 Pair O' Hares 644	500		96.00	96
1995 Père Noel 619	1,500		90.00	110
1998 Pocketful of Posies 646	750		38.00	38
1994 Rabbits At Home Egg 602	1,500	1997	80.00	90
1996 Robin Tracks 624	1,000		48.00	60
1998 Rock-A-Bunny 669	1,500		20.00	20
1998 Round About Rabbit 643	1,000		60.00	60
1995 Santa Express 617	2,000		56.00	64
1997 Santa's Helper 658	500		80.00	80
1997 Scooter Claus 649	500		92.00	92
1998 Season's Greetings 664	750		160.00	160
1996 Sharing The Spirit 630	1,000		90.00	104
1998 Shedding A Tear 667	1,500		24.00	24
1994 Shhh... 606	5,000		44.00	50
1994 Silent Night 611	750		120.00	140
1997 Snowy Ride 656	2,500		108.00	108
1998 Special Delivery 661	750		104.00	104
1995 St. Nick's Visit 623	750		380.00	430
1996 The Stocking Was Hung 633	1,500		68.00	76
1994 Strolling Rabbits Egg 601	1,500	1997	80.00	90
1997 Sweet Dreams 653	750		70.00	70
1996 Sweet Messenger 632	1,500		52.00	64
1998 A Tisket, A Tasket 665	2,500		30.00	30
1997 To All A Good Night 654	500		72.00	72
1997 To Market, To Market 640	500		50.00	60
1994 Up On The Rooftop 608	5,000		56.00	62
1996 Violets for Mary 626	500		64.00	72
1997 A Walk In The Woods 652	750		56.00	56
1998 Winter Wonderland 662	1,500		76.00	76

Nativity Collection - K. Bejma

YEAR ISSUE	EDITION LIMIT	YEAR RETD.	ISSUE PRICE	*QUOTE U.S.$
1995 Elephant	Open		160.00	180
1995 Group I Stable, Joseph, Mary, Baby Jesus, Angel	Open		240.00	380
1995 Group II Wise Men, set/3	Open		180.00	220
1995 Group III Shepards and Wanderer, set/4	Open		190.00	220
1995 Group IV Farm Animals, Sheep/2, Goat, Donkey, Cow	Open		160.00	160
1995 Laying Camel	Open		170.00	190
1995 Standing Camel	Open		180.00	220

Outdoors Collection - K. Bejma

YEAR ISSUE	EDITION LIMIT	YEAR RETD.	ISSUE PRICE	*QUOTE U.S.$
1998 Acorn Birdhouse 7004	Open		64.00	64
1998 Copper Garden Angel/birdseed tray 7001C	Open		320.00	320
1998 Copper Garden Angel/flowers 7000C	Open		320.00	320
1998 Copper Praying Garden Angel 7002C	Open		320.00	320
1998 Garden Angel w/Child 7009	Open		240.00	240
1998 Garden Angel w/Roses 7008	Open		240.00	240
1998 Garden Angel w/Shell 7007	Open		240.00	240
1998 Pansy Birdhouse 7005	Open		64.00	64
1998 Rust Garden Angel/birdseed tray 7001R	Open		320.00	320
1998 Rust Garden Angel/flowers 7000R	Open		320.00	320
1998 Rust Praying Garden Angel 7002R	Open		320.00	320
1998 Sunflower Birdhouse 7006	Open		64.00	64
1998 Tabletop Angel Fountain 7003	Open		300.00	300

Spring Figurines - K. Bejma

YEAR ISSUE	EDITION LIMIT	YEAR RETD.	ISSUE PRICE	*QUOTE U.S.$
1991 Bavarian Rabbit Set 226	Open		90.00	110
1996 Bunny in Shamrocks 268	Open		52.00	60
1996 Bunny with Carrots on Base 272	12/98		48.00	55
1995 Bunny with Colored Eggs 263	Open		28.00	36
1990 Bunny/Acorns/Carrots 202	Open		32.00	36
1991 Bunny/Basket 227	Retrd.	1996	26.00	26
1993 Bunny/Cabbage 233	Open		24.00	28
1997 Cherub on Rabbit 282	Open		44.00	50
1997 Cherub, lg. 283	Open		120.00	140
1994 Chick with Egg 257	Open		48.00	56
1994 Chicks, set/3 260	Open		64.00	72
1995 Country Rabbit, lg. 265	Open		70.00	86
1996 Egg Wagon 275	Open		44.00	52
1996 Farmer Rabbit w/Carrots 270	Open		56.00	80
1992 Folksy/Rabbit 231	Open		48.00	52
1994 Hatching Chick 259	Open		20.00	36
1993 Hatching Rabbit 234	Open		34.00	42
1995 Hiking Bunny w/Egg Basket 262	12/98		28.00	36
1994 Lady Vendor Rabbit 256	Open		42.00	50
1994 Laying Sheep 245	Retrd.	1997	44.00	50
1995 Meadow Rabbit 266	Open		90.00	100
1991 Mother Rabbit/Basket 215	Retrd.	1996	48.00	48
1990 Mother Rabbit/Six Babies 200	Open		120.00	130
1990 Mother/Bowl of Eggs 207	Retrd.	1996	30.00	32
1993 Mr. Rabbit/Two Children 244	Retrd.	1996	44.00	44
1994 Professor Rabbit/Chicks 236	Retrd.	1997	30.00	44
1990 Rabbit Holding Basket 220	Retrd.	1996	50.00	54
1994 Rabbit Holding Carrot 253	Open		52.00	58
1994 Rabbit in Flower Garden 246	12/98		64.00	76
1996 Rabbit on Scooter 271	Open		44.00	50
1991 Rabbit Riding Rooster 209	Retrd.	1997	36.00	48
1996 Rabbit w/Ferns and Lillies 269	Open		120.00	140
1997 Rabbit w/Paw Up 281	Open		32.00	36
1994 Rabbit with Basket 255	12/98		52.00	60
1994 Rabbit with Vest 254	Retrd.	1997	38.00	44
1991 Rabbit/Basket Eggs 224	Open		46.00	52
1991 Rabbit/Basket/Bow 225	Retrd.	1997	46.00	52

*Quotes have been rounded up to nearest dollar

YEAR ISSUE	EDITION LIMIT	YEAR RETD.	ISSUE PRICE	*QUOTE U.S.$
1994 Rabbit/Hat/Stick 239	Retrd.	1997	28.00	36
1990 Rabbit/Holding Basket 203	Retrd.	1997	30.00	34
1990 Rabbit/Umbrella 208	Retrd.	1996	30.00	30
1994 Rabbits on See-Saw 252	12/98		44.00	50
1990 Running Rabbit 205	Open		32.00	36
1996 Shamrock Cart 273	Open		36.00	52
1990 Sitting Bunny 204	Retrd.	1996	24.00	25
1995 Sitting Bunny 261	Open		24.00	30
1990 Sitting Bunny, lg. 216	Open		68.00	72
1994 Sitting Rabbit 251	Open		36.00	42
1993 Sitting Rabbit, lg. 235	Retrd.	1997	44.00	62
1994 Squirrel on Pinecone 249	Open		40.00	46
1996 Squirrel, lg. 276	Open		48.00	54
1996 Squirrel, med. 277	Open		44.00	50
1994 Standing Chick 258	Open		24.00	28
1994 Standing Rabbit 237	Retrd.	1996	44.00	44
1990 Standing Sheep 211	Retrd.	1996	36.00	40
1997 Striped Cat, sm. 312	Open		30.00	36
1996 Tan Rabbit w/Basket on Back 267	Open		90.00	100
1990 Two Rabbits/Basket 219	Open		52.00	70
1996 Wheelbarrow Egg 274	Open		48.00	56
1994 Wheelbarrrow Rabbit 250	12/98		44.00	50
1997 White Rabbit, lg. 278	Open		36.00	44
1997 White Rabbit, med. 279	Open		30.00	34
1997 White Rabbit, sm. 280	Open		24.00	30
1995 Woodland Rabbit 264	Open		48.00	58

Valentine's Collection - K. Bejma

YEAR ISSUE	EDITION LIMIT	YEAR RETD.	ISSUE PRICE	*QUOTE U.S.$
1998 "Be Mine" Cherub 6000	Open		40.00	40
1998 Cherub Bud Vase 6001	Open		36.00	36
1998 Heart Vase w/Cherub 6002	Open		60.00	60

Walnut Ridge Everyday Collection - K. Bejma

YEAR ISSUE	EDITION LIMIT	YEAR RETD.	ISSUE PRICE	*QUOTE U.S.$
1997 Bunch of Violets 5009	Open		30.00	34
1997 Cone Topiary 5013	Open		80.00	80
1997 Fantail Rooster 5005	Open		64.00	72
1997 Flower Wall Basket 5003	Open		48.00	60
1997 Fruit Topiary, lg. 5000	Open		150.00	170
1997 Fruit Topiary, med. 5001	Open		120.00	150
1997 Fruit Topiary, sm. 5002	Open		60.00	80
1997 Hen in Basket 5006	Open		48.00	54
1997 Hen w/Shamrocks 5008	Open		36.00	40
1997 Rooster w/Shamrocks 5007	Open		36.00	40
1997 Rooster, lg. 5004	Open		120.00	140
1997 Rose Topiary 5012	Open		150.00	150
1997 Summer Flowers 5010	Open		80.00	90
1997 Victorian Vase w/Roses 5011	Open		70.00	70

Walt Disney

Walt Disney Collectors Society - Disney Studios

YEAR ISSUE	EDITION LIMIT	YEAR RETD.	ISSUE PRICE	*QUOTE U.S.$
1993 Jiminy Cricket Members Only Gift Piece (Kit)	Closed	1993	Gift	225-325
1993 Jiminy Cricket 4"	Closed	1993	Gift	160-295
1993 Brave Little Tailor 7 1/4" "I Let em' Have It!" (Animator's Choice)	Closed	1994	160.00	200-395
1994 Cheshire Cat 4 3/4"	Closed	1994	Gift	73-175
1994 Pecos Bill and Widowmaker 9 1/2"	Closed	1994	650.00	300-650
1994 Admiral Duck 6 1/4" (Animator's Choice)	Closed	1995	165.00	110-350
1995 Dumbo	Closed	1995	Gift	65-150
1995 Cruella De Vil 10 1/4" "Anita, Daahling" (Animator's Choice)	Closed	1995	250.00	300-550
1995 Dumbo Ornament "Simply Adorable"	Closed	1995	20.00	20-83
1995 Slue Foot Sue 41075	Closed	1995	695.00	400-695
1996 Winnie the Pooh "Time for something sweet" 41091	Closed	1996	Gift	55-110
1996 Winnie the Pooh Ornament "Time for something sweet" 41096	Closed	1996	25.00	25-77
1996 Princess Minnie 41095 (Animator's Choice)	Closed	1996	165.00	165-350
1996 Casey at the Bat 41107	Closed	1996	395.00	275-488
1997 Magician Mickey "On with the show" 41134	Closed	1997	Gift	50-75
1997 Magician Mickey "On with the show" Ornament 41135	Closed	1997	25.00	25-49
1997 Mickey's Debut (Steamboat Willie) (5th Anniversary) (Charter member backstamp) 41136	Yr.Iss.	1997	175.00	175-395
1997 Mickey's Debut (Steamboat Willie) (5th Anniversary) (Non-Charter member) 41255	Yr.Iss.	1997	175.00	175-345
1997 Goofy-Moving Day "Oh The World Owes Me A Livin.'" 41138 (Animator's Choice)	Yr.Iss.	1997	185.00	185
1997 Maleficent: "The Mistress of all Evil" 41177	Yr.Iss.	1997	450.00	450-550
1997 Chernabog: Night on Bald Mountain, A/P	25	1997	750.00	1350-1375
1998 Timon: "Luau!" 41197	Yr.Iss.		Gift	80
1998 Timon: "Luau!" Ornament 41262	Yr.Iss.		25.00	25
1998 Timothy Mouse: "Friendship Offering" Ornament 41179	Yr.Iss.		55.00	55
1998 Autumn Fairy: The Touch of an Autumn Fairy 41281	Yr.Iss.		495.00	495
1998 Pluto: Sticky Situation 41199 (Animator's Choice)	Yr.Iss.		150.00	150
1998 Jafar: "Oh Mighty Evil One" 41280	Yr.Iss.		395.00	395
1998 Mickey's Debut (Steamboat Willie) (5th Anniversary) (Non-Charter member) 41255	Yr.Iss.		175.00	175
1999 Lady: A Perfectly Beautiful Little Lady	Yr.Iss.		Gift	50
1999 White Rabbit Figural Ornament "No Time to Say Hello" 41373	Yr.Iss.		59.00	59
1999 Tinkerbell Pauses to Reflect 41366 (Animator's Choice)	Yr.Iss.		240.00	240

Walt Disney Classics Collection-Special Event - Disney Studios

YEAR ISSUE	EDITION LIMIT	YEAR RETD.	ISSUE PRICE	*QUOTE U.S.$
1993 Flight of Fancy 3" 41051	Closed	1994	35.00	25-95
1994 Mr. Smee 5" "Oh, dear, dear, dear."41062	Closed	1995	90.00	77-190
1994 Mr. Smee 5" 41062 (teal stamp)	Closed	1995	90.00	82-140
1995 Lucky 41080	Closed	1995	40.00	40-98
1995 Wicked Witch "Take the apple, dearie." 41084	Closed	1996	130.00	182-350
1996 Tinkerbell Ornament	Closed	1996	50.00	50-125
1996 Fairy Godmother "Bibbidi, Bobbidi, Boo" 41108	Closed	1996	125.00	119-169
1997 Evil Queen "Bring back her heart...." 41165	Closed	1997	150.00	138-245
1997 Winnie the Pooh Ornament 41176	Closed	1997	59.00	59-75
1997 Hercules and Pegasus: A gift from the Gods Ornament 41167	Closed	1997	55.00	55
1997 Blue Fairy: Making Dreams Come True 41139	Closed	1997	150.00	120-160
1998 Shere Khan: Everyone Runs From Shere Kahn 41254	Closed	1998	145.00	145-180
1998 Ursula: "We Made a Deal" 41285	11/98		165.00	165

Disney's Enchanted Places - Disney Studios

YEAR ISSUE	EDITION LIMIT	YEAR RETD.	ISSUE PRICE	*QUOTE U.S.$
1998 Alice in Wonderland: A Tea Party in Wonderland 41295	4,500		395.00	395
1997 Ariel's Secret Grotto: The Little Mermaid 41235	Open		175.00	175
1996 The Beast's Castle: Beauty & The Beast 41225	Open		245.00	245
1997 A Castle For Cinderella: Cinderella	Retrd.	1997	225.00	225-295
1997 Cruella's Car: 101 Dalmatians 41230	Retrd.	1997	165.00	165
1996 An Elegant Coach For Cinderella: Cinderella 41208	Open		265.00	265
1996 Fiddler Pig's Stick House: Three Little Pigs 41204	Open		85.00	85
1996 Fifer Pig's Straw House: Three Little Pigs 41205	Open		85.00	85
1996 Geppetto's Toy Shop: Pinocchio 41207	Open		150.00	150
1998 Geppettos Toy Creation: Pinocchio 41315	Yr.Iss.		125.00	125
1996 Grandpa's House: Peter & The Wolf 41211	Yr.Iss.	1996	125.00	125
1997 Hade's Chariot: Hercules 41246	Retrd.	1997	125.00	125-150
1996 The Jolly Roger: Peter Pan 41209	10,000		475.00	475
1997 King Louie's Temple: Jungle Book	Yr.Iss.		125.00	125
1997 Pastoral Setting: Fantasia 41232	3,000	1997	195.00	195-295
1997 Pooh Bear's House: Winnie the Pooh & The Honey Tree 41231	Open		150.00	150
1996 Practical Pig's Brick House: Three Little Pigs 41206	Open		115.00	115
1999 Rose and Table:The Enchanted Rose: Beauty & The Beast 41343	Open		100.00	100
1995 Seven Dwarf's Cottage: Snow White 41200	Open		180.00	180
1995 Seven Dwarf's Jewel Mine: Snow White 41203	Open		190.00	190
1998 Sleeping Beauty's Castle 41263	Open		225.00	225
1997 Snow White's Wishing Well: Snow White 41248	Open		160.00	160
1998 Steamboat Willie's Steamboat 41264	Open		160.00	160
1995 White Rabbit's House: Alice in Wonderland 41202	Open		175.00	175
1995 Woodcutter's Cottage: Sleeping Beauty 41201	Open		170.00	170

Disney's Enchanted Places Miniatures - Disney Studios

YEAR ISSUE	EDITION LIMIT	YEAR RETD.	ISSUE PRICE	*QUOTE U.S.$
1997 Ariel 41240	Open		50.00	50
1998 Bashful 41273	Open		50.00	50
1996 Briar Rose 41214	Open		50.00	50
1996 Captain Hook 41219	Open		50.00	50
1998 Doc 41271	Open		50.00	50
1996 Dopey 41215	Open		50.00	50
1999 Eeyore 41319	Open		50.00	50
1996 Fiddler Pig 41224	Open		50.00	50
1996 Fifer Pig 41223	Open		50.00	50
1997 Grumpy 41239	Open		50.00	50
1996 Gus 41218	Open		50.00	50
1998 Happy 41272	Open		50.00	50
1996 Jaq 41242	Open		50.00	50
1998 Jiminy Cricket 41335	Open		50.00	50
1998 Mickey Mouse 41265	Open		50.00	50
1997 Pain 41247	Retrd.	1997	50.00	50-65
1997 Panic 41250	Retrd.	1997	50.00	50-65
1996 Peter 41221	Open		50.00	50
1996 Pinocchio 41217	Open		50.00	50
1996 Practical Pig 41216	Open		50.00	50
1998 Sneezy 41318	Open		50.00	50
1996 Snow White 41212	Open		50.00	50
1998 Tigger 41274	Open		50.00	50
1997 Unicorn 41237	Open		50.00	50
1996 White Rabbit 41213	Open		50.00	50
1997 Winnie the Pooh 41238	Open		50.00	50

Disneyana - Disney Studios

YEAR ISSUE	EDITION LIMIT	YEAR RETD.	ISSUE PRICE	*QUOTE U.S.$
1996 Proud Pongo (w/backstamp)	1,200	1996	175.00	297-520
1997 Chernabog: Night on Bald Mountain	1,500	1997	750.00	1331-1800
1997 Disney Villain Ornament set/6	12,000	1997	40.00	110
1998 Snow White & Prince	1,650		750.00	750

Walt Disney Classics Collection-101 Dalmatians - Disney Studios

YEAR ISSUE	EDITION LIMIT	YEAR RETD.	ISSUE PRICE	*QUOTE U.S.$
1996 "Go get him thunder!" Two Puppies on Newspaper 41129	Open		120.00	120
1996 Lucky and Television "Come on Lucky..." 41131	Open		150.00	150
1996 Patient Perdita Perdita with Patch and Puppy 41133	Open		175.00	175
1996 Proud Pongo Pongo with Pepper and Penny 41132	Open		175.00	175
1996 Rolly "I'm hungry, Mother" 41130	Open		65.00	65
1996 Opening Title 41169	Open		29.00	29

Walt Disney Classics Collection-Aladdin - Disney Studios

YEAR ISSUE	EDITION LIMIT	YEAR RETD.	ISSUE PRICE	*QUOTE U.S.$
1998 Genie: "I'm Losing to a Rug" 41269	12,500		450.00	450

Walt Disney Classics Collection-Alice in Wonderland - Disney Studios

YEAR ISSUE	EDITION LIMIT	YEAR RETD.	ISSUE PRICE	*QUOTE U.S.$
1999 Alice: "Yes, Your Majesty" 41375	Open		145.00	145
1999 Card Player: "Playing Card" 41414	Open		120.00	120
1999 King of Hearts: "...and the King" 41419	Open		90.00	90
1999 Queen of Hearts" "Let the Game Begin!" 41413	Yr.Iss.		175.00	175
1999 Opening Title 41378	Open		29.00	29

Walt Disney Classics Collection-Bambi - Disney Studios

YEAR ISSUE	EDITION LIMIT	YEAR RETD.	ISSUE PRICE	*QUOTE U.S.$
1992 Bambi 6" "Purty Flower" 41033	Retrd.	1998	195.00	195-250
1992 Bambi & Flower 6" "He can call me a flower if he wants to" 41010	10,000	1992	298.00	335-595
1992 Field Mouse-not touching "Little April Shower" 5 3/5" 41012	Closed	1993	195.00	1200-1500
1992 Field Mouse-touching "Little April Shower" 5 3/5" 41012	Closed	1993	195.00	1089-1300
1992 Flower 3" "Oh...gosh!" 41034	Retrd.	1998	78.00	61-182
1992 Friend Owl "What's going on around here?" 8 3/5" 41011	Retrd.	1998	195.00	115-195
1992 Thumper 3" "Hee! Hee! Hee!" 41013	Retrd.	1998	55.00	55-90
1992 Thumper's Sisters "Hello, hello there!" 3 3/5" 41014	Retrd.	1998	69.00	50-80
1992 Opening Title 41015	Retrd.	1998	29.00	29-40

Walt Disney Classics Collection-Beauty & The Beast - Disney Studios

YEAR ISSUE	EDITION LIMIT	YEAR RETD.	ISSUE PRICE	*QUOTE U.S.$
1997 Lumiere: Vive L'amour! 41181	Open		115.00	115
1997 Cogsworth: Just in Time 41182	Open		120.00	120
1997 Mrs. Potts and Chip: "Good Night, Luv" 41183	Open		125.00	125
1997 Tale as Old as Time-Belle and the Beast Dancing 41156	Open		295.00	295
1997 Opening Title 41189	Open		29	29

Walt Disney Classics Collection-Canine Caddy - Disney Studios

YEAR ISSUE	EDITION LIMIT	YEAR RETD.	ISSUE PRICE	*QUOTE U.S.$
1997 Mickey Mouse: "What a swell day for a game of golf!" 41149	Open		150.00	150

Walt Disney Classics Collection-Cinderella - Disney Studios

YEAR ISSUE	EDITION LIMIT	YEAR RETD.	ISSUE PRICE	*QUOTE U.S.$
1993 A Lovely Dress For Cinderelly 41030/ wheel & clef	5,000	1993	800.00	1700-2500
1993 Birds "We'll tie a sash around it" 6 2/5" 41005	Retrd.	1994	149.00	119-250
1992 Bruno 4 2/5" "Just learn to like cats" 41002	Retrd.	1993	69.00	65-195
1992 Chalk Mouse "No time for dilly-dally" 3 2/5" 41006	Retrd.	1994	65.00	75-170
1992 Cinderella 6" "They can't stop me from dreaming" 41000	Retrd.	1992	195.00	275-695
1995 Cinderella & Prince Charming "So this is love" 41079	Open		275.00	275
1998 Cinderella & Prince Wedding Sculpture: Fairy Tale Wedding 41267	Open		195.00	195
1992 Gus "You go get some trimmin'" 3 2/5" 41007	Retrd.	1994	65.00	75-195
1992 Jaq "You go get some trimmin'" 4 1/5" 41008	Retrd.	1994	65.00	75-150
1992 Lucifer "Meany, sneaky, roos-a-fee" 2 3/5" 41001	Retrd.	1993	69.00	99-195
1992 Needle Mouse "Hey, we can do it!" 5 4/5" 41004	Retrd.	1993	69.00	75-170
1992 Sewing Book 41003	Retrd.	1994	69.00	55-150
1992 Opening Title 41009	Open		29.00	29
1992 Opening Title-Technicolor 41009	Closed	1993	29.00	22-65

Walt Disney Classics Collection-Delivery Boy - Disney Studios

YEAR ISSUE	EDITION LIMIT	YEAR RETD.	ISSUE PRICE	*QUOTE U.S.$
1992 Mickey 6" "Hey Minnie, wanna go steppin?" 41020	Retrd.	1997	125.00	105-238
1992 Minnie 6" "I'm a Jazz Baby" 41021	Retrd.	1996	125.00	125-220
1992 Pluto Dynamite Dog 3 3/5" 41022	Retrd.	1993	125.00	110-293
1992 Pluto Dynamite Dog- 1st version (raised letters) 3 3/5" 41022/ wheel	Closed	1993	125.00	270-350
1992 Opening Title 41019	Retrd.	1993	29.00	29-60

Walt Disney Classics Collection-Donald's Better Self - Disney Studios

YEAR ISSUE	EDITION LIMIT	YEAR RETD.	ISSUE PRICE	*QUOTE U.S.$
1998 Donald Duck: Donald's Decision 41296	Open		145.00	145

*Quotes have been rounded up to nearest dollar

YEAR ISSUE	EDITION LIMIT	YEAR RETD.	ISSUE PRICE	*QUOTE U.S.$
1998 Donald Duck: Little Devil 41309	Open		145.00	145
1998 Donald Duck: What An Angel 41297	Open		145.00	145
1998 Opening Title 41298	Open		29.00	29

Walt Disney Classics Collection-Double Dribble - Disney Studios

YEAR ISSUE	EDITION LIMIT	YEAR RETD.	ISSUE PRICE	*QUOTE U.S.$
1999 Goofy: Dribbling Down Court 41404	Open		175.00	175

Walt Disney Classics Collection-Dumbo - Disney Studios

YEAR ISSUE	EDITION LIMIT	YEAR RETD.	ISSUE PRICE	*QUOTE U.S.$
1997 Bundle of Joy (Dumbo and Stork) 41153	Open		125.00	125

Walt Disney Classics Collection-Fantasia - Disney Studios

YEAR ISSUE	EDITION LIMIT	YEAR RETD.	ISSUE PRICE	*QUOTE U.S.$
1993 Blue Centaurette-Beauty in Bloom 7 1/2" 41041	Retrd.	1995	195.00	105-234
1992 Broom, Bucket Brigade 5 4/5" 41017	Retrd.	1995	75.00	88-195
1992 Broom, Bucket Brigade w/water spots 5 4/5" 41017/ wheel	Retrd.	1992	75.00	180-260
1996 Ben Ali Gator 7 1/2" 41118	Open		185.00	185
1996 Hyacinth Hippo 5 1/2" 41117	Open		195.00	195
1993 Love's Little Helpers Cupids 8" 41042	Retrd.	1995	290.00	171-315
1994 Small Mushroom: Hop Low 41067	Open		35.00	35
1994 Mushroom Dancer-Medium 4 1/4" 41068	Open		50.00	50-110
1994 Mushroom Dancer-Large 4 3/4" 41058	Open		60.00	60
1993 Pink Centaurette-Romantic Reflections 7 1/2" 41040	Retrd.	1995	175.00	99-202
1992 Mickey Mouse: Mischievous Apprentice 5 1/8" 41016	Retrd.	1993	195.00	200-395
1997 Mademoiselle Upanova: Prima Ballerina 41178	Open		165.00	165
1992 Opening Title 41018	Open		29.00	29-50
1992 Opening Title-Technicolor 41018	Closed	1993	29.00	35-46

Walt Disney Classics Collection-Holiday Series - Disney Studios

YEAR ISSUE	EDITION LIMIT	YEAR RETD.	ISSUE PRICE	*QUOTE U.S.$
1995 Mickey Mouse: "Presents For My Pals" 41086	Closed	1995	150.00	132-228
1996 Pluto: Pluto Helps Decorate 41112	Closed	1996	150.00	121-160
1997 Chip 'n Dale: Little Mischief Makers 41163	Closed	1997	150.00	138-150
1997 Holiday Base 41140	Closed	1997	25.00	25
1997 Santa Candle 41172	Closed	1997	40.00	40
1998 Minnie Mouse: Caroler Minnie 41308	Yr.Iss.	1998	150.00	150

Walt Disney Classics Collection-How To Play Baseball - Disney Studios

YEAR ISSUE	EDITION LIMIT	YEAR RETD.	ISSUE PRICE	*QUOTE U.S.$
1998 Goofy Baseball: Batter Up 41266	Open		175.00	175

Walt Disney Classics Collection-Jungle Book - Disney Studios

YEAR ISSUE	EDITION LIMIT	YEAR RETD.	ISSUE PRICE	*QUOTE U.S.$
1997 King of the Swingers (King Louie) 41158	Open		175.00	175
1997 Monkeying Around (Flunky Monkey) 41159	Closed	1997	135.00	135-182
1997 Hula Baloo (Baloo) 41160	Open		185.00	185
1997 Mancub (Mowgli) 41161	Open		115.00	115
1997 Bagheera: Mowgli's Protector 41162	Open		135.00	135
1997 Opening Title 41171	Open		29.00	29

Walt Disney Classics Collection-Lady and The Tramp - Disney Studios

YEAR ISSUE	EDITION LIMIT	YEAR RETD.	ISSUE PRICE	*QUOTE U.S.$
1996 Lady: Lady in Love 4 1/2" 41089	Retrd.	1997	120.00	120-250
1996 Tramp: Tramp in Love 5 1/2" 41090	Retrd.	1996	100.00	100-180
1998 Lady and Tramp: Spaghetti Scene Base 41403	Open		75.00	75
1998 Lady and Tramp: "Bella Notte" (Matched Numbered - 3 Sculpture Set) 41284	5,000		795.00	795
1996 Opening Title 41099	Open		29.00	29-35

Walt Disney Classics Collection-Little Mermaid - Disney Studios

YEAR ISSUE	EDITION LIMIT	YEAR RETD.	ISSUE PRICE	*QUOTE U.S.$
1997 Ariel: Seahorse Surprise 41184	Open		275.00	275
1997 Ariel: Seahorse Surprise-1st version (Bandstand) 41184	Closed	1997	275.00	275-473
1997 Blackfish: Deep Sea Diva 41195	Open		95.00	95
1997 Flounder: Flounder's Fandango 41198	Open		150.00	150
1998 Fluke: The Duke of Soul 41191	Open		120.00	120
1998 Newt: Newt's Nautical Note 41193	Open		135.00	135
1998 Sebastian: Calypso Crustacean 41187	Open		130.00	130
1998 Snails: Sing-Along Snails 41196	Open		135.00	135
1997 Turtle: Twistin' Turtle 41192	Open		85.00	85
1997 Opening Title 41188	Open		29.00	29

Walt Disney Classics Collection-Main Street Electrical Parade - Disney Studios

YEAR ISSUE	EDITION LIMIT	YEAR RETD.	ISSUE PRICE	*QUOTE U.S.$
1998 Drum 41290	Open		145.00	145
1998 Lightening Bug 41291	Open		85.00	85
1998 Train 41289	Open		145.00	145

Walt Disney Classics Collection-Mickey Cuts Up - Disney Studios

YEAR ISSUE	EDITION LIMIT	YEAR RETD.	ISSUE PRICE	*QUOTE U.S.$
1999 Minnie Mouse: Minnie's Garden 41397	Open		120.00	120

Walt Disney Classics Collection-Mickey Through The Years - Disney Studios

YEAR ISSUE	EDITION LIMIT	YEAR RETD.	ISSUE PRICE	*QUOTE U.S.$
1998 Mickey Mouse (The Band Concert): From The Top 41277	Open		100.00	100
1998 Mickey Mouse (Fantasia): Summoning The Stars 41278	Open		100.00	100
1998 Mickey Mouse (Plane Crazy): How To Fly 41268	Open		100.00	100
1998 Mickey Mouse (The Prince and the Pauper): Long Live The King 41279	Open		100.00	100
1998 Bases set of 4, 41301	Yr.Iss.	1998	30.00	30

Walt Disney Classics Collection-Mickey's Birthday Party - Disney Studios

YEAR ISSUE	EDITION LIMIT	YEAR RETD.	ISSUE PRICE	*QUOTE U.S.$
1997 Mickey Mouse: "Happy Birthday" 41170	Open		95.00	95

Walt Disney Classics Collection-Mr. Duck Steps Out - Disney Studios

YEAR ISSUE	EDITION LIMIT	YEAR RETD.	ISSUE PRICE	*QUOTE U.S.$
1993 Donald & Daisy "Oh boy, what a jitterbug!" 6 3/5" 41024	5,000	1996	295.00	350-1100
1994 Donald Duck: "With love from Daisy" 6 1/4" 41060	Retrd.	1996	180.00	130-180
1993 Dewey: "I got somethin for ya" 4" 41025	Retrd.	1996	65.00	50-85
1993 Huey: Tag-Along Trouble 4" 41049	Retrd.	1996	65.00	38-78
1993 Nephew Duck-Louie 4" 41050	Retrd.	1994	65.00	50-85
1993 Opening Title 41023	Retrd.	1996	29.00	23-52

Walt Disney Classics Collection-On Ice - Disney Studios

YEAR ISSUE	EDITION LIMIT	YEAR RETD.	ISSUE PRICE	*QUOTE U.S.$
1997 Minnie Mouse: "Wheel" 41151	Open		165.00	165
1998 Mickey Mouse: "Watch Me!" 41270	Open		165.00	165
1998 Opening Title 41261	Open		29.00	29

Walt Disney Classics Collection-Peter Pan - Disney Studios

YEAR ISSUE	EDITION LIMIT	YEAR RETD.	ISSUE PRICE	*QUOTE U.S.$
1993 Captain Hook: "I've got you this time!" 8" 41044	Suspd.		275.00	198-803
1993 Crocodile: "Tick-tock, tick-tock" 6 1/4" 41054	Suspd.		315.00	200-315
1993 Peter Pan: "Nobody calls Pan a coward!" 7 1/2" 41043	Suspd.		165.00	104-225
1993 Tinkerbell: A firefly! A pixie! Amazing!" 5" 41045	12,500	1993	215.00	250-700
1993 Opening Title 41047	Suspd.		29.00	23-46

Walt Disney Classics Collection-Pinocchio - Disney Studios

YEAR ISSUE	EDITION LIMIT	YEAR RETD.	ISSUE PRICE	*QUOTE U.S.$
1996 Figaro "Say hello to Figaro" 41111	11/98		55.00	55-66
1996 Geppetto "Good-bye, Son" 41114	11/98		145.00	145-171
1996 Jiminy Cricket "Wait for me, Pinoke!" 41109	11/98		85.00	85-99
1996 Pinocchio "Good-bye Father" 41110	11/98		125.00	125-149
1996 Opening Title 41116	11/98		29.00	29-35

Walt Disney Classics Collection-Puppy Love - Disney Studios

YEAR ISSUE	EDITION LIMIT	YEAR RETD.	ISSUE PRICE	*QUOTE U.S.$
1998 Mickey Mouse: "Brought You Something" 41324	Open		135.00	135
1998 Minnie Mouse: "Oh, It's Swell!" 41325	Open		135.00	135
1998 Fifi: Flirtatious Fifi 41336	Open		95.00	95
1998 Opening Title 41326	Open		29.00	29

Walt Disney Classics Collection-Reluctant Dragon - Disney Studios

YEAR ISSUE	EDITION LIMIT	YEAR RETD.	ISSUE PRICE	*QUOTE U.S.$
1996 The Reluctant Dragon "The more the merrier" 7" 41072	7,500	1996	695.00	451-700

Walt Disney Classics Collection-Scrooge McDuck and the Money - Disney Studios

YEAR ISSUE	EDITION LIMIT	YEAR RETD.	ISSUE PRICE	*QUOTE U.S.$
1997 Money! Money! Money! Scrooge McDuck 41152	Open		175.00	175

Walt Disney Classics Collection-Simple Things - Disney Studios

YEAR ISSUE	EDITION LIMIT	YEAR RETD.	ISSUE PRICE	*QUOTE U.S.$
1999 Mickey Mouse: Something Fishy 41363	Open		150.00	150

Walt Disney Classics Collection-Sleeping Beauty - Disney Studios

YEAR ISSUE	EDITION LIMIT	YEAR RETD.	ISSUE PRICE	*QUOTE U.S.$
1997 Briar Rose: "Once upon a dream" 41157	12,500		345.00	345
1998 Aurora & Phillip: A Dance in the Clouds 41257	Open		295.00	295
1998 Fauna: A Little Bit of Both 41259	Open		100.00	100
1998 Flora: A Little Bit of Pink 41258	Open		100.00	100
1998 Merryweather: A Little Bit of Blue 41260	Open		95.00	95
1998 Opening Title 41275	Open		29.00	29

Walt Disney Classics Collection-Snow White - Disney Studios

YEAR ISSUE	EDITION LIMIT	YEAR RETD.	ISSUE PRICE	*QUOTE U.S.$
1994 Snow White: The Fairest One of All 8 1/4" 41063	Open		165.00	165-310
1995 Bashful "Aw, shucks" 5" 91069	Open		85.00	85
1995 Doc: Cheerful Leader 5 1/4" 41071	Open		95.00	95
1995 Dopey: Dopey 5" 41074	Open		95.00	95
1995 Grumpy with Pipe Organ "Humph!" 7 3/4" 41065	Open		180.00	180-198
1995 Happy "Happy, that's me!" 5 1/2" 41064	Open		125.00	125-155
1995 Sleepy "zzzzzzz" 3 1/4" 41066	Open		95.00	95
1995 Sneezy "Ah-Choo!" 4 1/2" 41073	Open		90.00	90
1995 Opening Title 41083	Open		29.00	29

Walt Disney Classics Collection-Song of the South - Disney Studios

YEAR ISSUE	EDITION LIMIT	YEAR RETD.	ISSUE PRICE	*QUOTE U.S.$
1996 Brer Bear "Duh" 7 1/2" 41112	Retrd.	1997	175.00	175-208
1996 Brer Fox 4" "I got cha, Brer Rabbit" 41101	Retrd.	1997	120.00	120-190
1996 Brer Rabbit: Born and Bred in a Briar Patch 4 3/4" 41103	Retrd.	1997	150.00	150-190
1996 Opening Title 41104	Retrd.	1997	29.00	30-50

Walt Disney Classics Collection-Symphony Hour - Disney Studios

YEAR ISSUE	EDITION LIMIT	YEAR RETD.	ISSUE PRICE	*QUOTE U.S.$
1993 Clarabelle Cow: Clarabella's Crescendo 6 4/5" 41027/ wheel	Retrd.	1993	198.00	175-250
1994 Clara Cluck: Bravo Bravissimo 41061	Retrd.	1997	185.00	150-254
1996 Donald Duck: Donald's Drum Beat 8 1/4" 41105/ hat	Retrd.	1996	225.00	225-300
1993 Goofy: Goofy's Grace Notes 6 4/5" 41026/wheel	Retrd.	1993	198.00	2700
1993 Goofy: Goofy's Grace Notes 6 4/5" 41026	Retrd.	1997	198.00	127-235
1993 Horace Horsecollar: Horace's High Notes 6 4/5" 41028	Retrd.	1997	198.00	182-250
1996 Donald Duck: Donald's Drum Beat 8 1/4" 41105	Retrd.	1997	225.00	225-300
1993 Mickey Mouse Conductor: Maestro Michael Mouse 7 3/8" 41029	Retrd.	1997	185.00	185-350
1996 Sylvester Macaroni 41106	12,500	1997	395.00	264-395
1993 Opening Title 41031	Retrd.	1997	29.00	22-46

Walt Disney Classics Collection-Three Caballeros - Disney Studios

YEAR ISSUE	EDITION LIMIT	YEAR RETD.	ISSUE PRICE	*QUOTE U.S.$
1995 Amigo Donald 7" 41076	Retrd.	1996	180.00	121-215
1995 Amigo Jose 7" 41077	Retrd.	1996	180.00	121-208
1995 Amigo Panchito 7" 41078	Retrd.	1996	180.00	140-215
1995 Opening Title 41070	Retrd.	1996	29.00	29-46

Walt Disney Classics Collection-Three Little Pigs - Disney Studios

YEAR ISSUE	EDITION LIMIT	YEAR RETD.	ISSUE PRICE	*QUOTE U.S.$
1993 Big Bad Wolf "Who's afraid of the Big Bad Wolf?" 41039 (short straight teeth/cone base) 1st version	S/O	1993	295.00	725-1000
1993 Big Bad Wolf "Who's afraid of the Big Bad Wolf?" 41039 (short straight teeth/flat base) 2nd version	S/O	1994	295.00	625-850
1993 Big Bad Wolf "Who's afraid of the Big Bad Wolf?" 41039 (long/short curved teeth) 3rd version	S/O	1994	295.00	600-975
1996 Big Bad Wolf "I'm a poor little sheep..." 41094	Open		225.00	225
1993 Fiddler Pig "Hey diddle, diddle, I play my fiddle" 4 1/2" 41038	Open		75.00	75-111
1993 Fifer Pig " I toot my flute, I don't give a hoot" 4 1/2" 41037	Open		75.00	75-111
1993 Practical Pig "Work and play don't mix" 4 1/2" 41036	Open		75.00	75-111
1993 Opening Title 41046	Open		29.00	28-46

Walt Disney Classics Collection-Touchdown Mickey - Disney Studios

YEAR ISSUE	EDITION LIMIT	YEAR RETD.	ISSUE PRICE	*QUOTE U.S.$
1998 Mickey Mouse: "Rah, Rah, Mickey!" 41252	Open		150.00	150

Walt Disney Classics Collection-Toy Story - Disney Studios

YEAR ISSUE	EDITION LIMIT	YEAR RETD.	ISSUE PRICE	*QUOTE U.S.$
1998 Buzz 41304	Open		175.00	175
1998 Woody 41305	Open		175.00	175
1998 Hamm: "It's Showtime" 41321	Open		90.00	90
1998 Bo Peep: "I Found My Moving Buddy" 41320	Open		150.00	150
1999 Rex: "I'm So Glad You're Not a Dinosaur" 41334	Yr.Iss.		140.00	140
1998 Opening Title 41306	Open		29.00	29

Walt Disney Classics Collection-Tribute Series - Disney Studios

YEAR ISSUE	EDITION LIMIT	YEAR RETD.	ISSUE PRICE	*QUOTE U.S.$
1995 Simba & Mufasa: Pals Forever 41085	Closed	1995	175.00	150-400
1996 Pocahontas "Listen With Your Heart" 6 1/2" 41098	Closed	1996	225.00	219-410
1997 Quasimodo and Esmerelda "Not a single monster line" 41143	Closed	1997	195.00	195
1998 Hercules: "From Zero To Hero" 41253	Closed	1998	250.00	250
1999 Mulan: Honorable Decision 41374	Yr.Iss.		175.00	175

Walt Disney Classics Collection-Who Framed Roger Rabbit - Disney Studios

YEAR ISSUE	EDITION LIMIT	YEAR RETD.	ISSUE PRICE	*QUOTE U.S.$
1998 Roger, Jessica: "Dear Jessica, How Do I Love Thee?" 41322	7,500		295.00	295

Walt Disney Classics Collection-Wise Little Hen - Disney Studios

YEAR ISSUE	EDITION LIMIT	YEAR RETD.	ISSUE PRICE	*QUOTE U.S.$
1997 Donald Duck: Donald's Debut (Gold Circle Dealer's Exclusive) 41175	Closed	1997	110.00	185-217

*Quotes have been rounded up to nearest dollar

FIGURINES

Wee Forest Folk

Animals - A. Petersen, unless otherwise noted

YEAR ISSUE	EDITION LIMIT	YEAR RETD.	ISSUE PRICE	*QUOTE U.S.$
1974 Baby Hippo H-2	Closed	1977	7.00	N/A
1978 Beaver Wood Cutter BV-1 - W. Petersen	Closed	1980	8.00	500
1974 Miss and Baby Hippo H-3	Closed	1977	15.00	1200
1973 Miss Ducky D-1	Closed	1977	6.00	N/A
1974 Miss Hippo H-1	Closed	1977	8.00	N/A
1977 Nutsy Squirrel SQ-1 - W. Petersen	Closed	1977	3.00	N/A
1979 Turtle Jogger TS-1	Closed	1980	4.00	N/A

Bears - A. Petersen

YEAR ISSUE	EDITION LIMIT	YEAR RETD.	ISSUE PRICE	*QUOTE U.S.$
1978 Big Lady Bear BR-4	Closed	1980	7.50	1000-3000
1977 Blueberry Bears BR-1	Closed	1982	8.75	500-700
1977 Boy Blueberry Bear BR-3	Closed	1982	4.50	300-495
1977 Girl Blueberry Bear BR-2	Closed	1982	4.25	300-495
1995 Good Pickin's BB-4	Closed	1997	64.00	87-125
1978 Traveling Bear BR-5	Closed	1980	8.00	500-750

Book / Figurine - W. Petersen

YEAR ISSUE	EDITION LIMIT	YEAR RETD.	ISSUE PRICE	*QUOTE U.S.$
1988 Tom & Eon BK-1	Suspd.	1991	45.00	325-358

Bunnies - A. Petersen, unless otherwise noted

YEAR ISSUE	EDITION LIMIT	YEAR RETD.	ISSUE PRICE	*QUOTE U.S.$
1977 Batter Bunny B-9	Closed	1982	4.50	275-500
1973 Broom Bunny B-6	Closed	1978	9.50	N/A
1972 Double Bunnies B-1	Closed	1980	4.25	N/A
1972 Housekeeping Bunny B-2	Closed	1980	4.50	N/A
1973 Market Bunny B-8	Closed	1977	9.00	N/A
1973 Muff Bunny B-7	Closed	1977	9.00	N/A
1973 The Professor B-4	Closed	1980	4.75	N/A
1980 Professor Rabbit B-11 - W. Petersen	Closed	1981	14.00	500-600
1973 Sir Rabbit B-3 - W. Petersen	Closed	1980	4.50	500-600
1973 Sunday Bunny B-5	Closed	1978	4.75	N/A
1977 Tennis Bunny BS-1	Closed	1980	3.75	500-550
1985 Tiny Easter Bunny B-12 - D. Petersen	Closed	1992	25.00	25-105
1978 Wedding Bunnies B-10 - W. Petersen	Closed	1981	12.50	1100-1500
1992 Windy Day! B-13 - D. Petersen	Closed	1998	37.00	50

Christmas Carol Series - A. Petersen

YEAR ISSUE	EDITION LIMIT	YEAR RETD.	ISSUE PRICE	*QUOTE U.S.$
1988 The Fezziwigs CC-7	Closed	1996	65.00	87-188

Cinderella Series - A. Petersen

YEAR ISSUE	EDITION LIMIT	YEAR RETD.	ISSUE PRICE	*QUOTE U.S.$
1988 Cinderella's Slipper (with Prince) C-1	Closed	1989	62.00	125-140
1989 Cinderella's Slipper C-1a	Closed	1994	32.00	94-150
1988 Cinderella's Wedding C-5	Closed	1994	62.00	135-160
1989 The Fairy Godmother C-7	Closed	1994	69.00	125-175
1988 Flower Girl C-6	Closed	1994	22.00	65-75
1988 The Flower Girls C-4	Closed	1994	42.00	85-100
1988 The Mean Stepmother C-3	Closed	1994	32.00	80-95
1988 The Ugly Stepsisters C-2	Closed	1994	62.00	115-150

Fairy Tale Series - A. Petersen

YEAR ISSUE	EDITION LIMIT	YEAR RETD.	ISSUE PRICE	*QUOTE U.S.$
1980 Red Riding Hood & Wolf FT-1	Closed	1982	29.00	1250-1600
1980 Red Riding Hood FT-2	Closed	1982	13.00	400-600

Forest Scene - W. Petersen

YEAR ISSUE	EDITION LIMIT	YEAR RETD.	ISSUE PRICE	*QUOTE U.S.$
1989 Hearts and Flowers FS-2 - W. Petersen	Closed	1998	110.00	165
1992 Love Letter FS-5	Closed	1997	98.00	145-250
1990 Mousie Comes A-Calling FS-3	Closed	1996	128.00	290-300
1988 Woodland Serenade FS-1	Closed	1995	125.00	200-325

Foxes - A. Petersen

YEAR ISSUE	EDITION LIMIT	YEAR RETD.	ISSUE PRICE	*QUOTE U.S.$
1978 Barrister Fox FX-3	Closed	1980	7.50	700-900
1977 Dandy Fox FX-2	Closed	1979	6.00	500-1200
1977 Fancy Fox FX-1	Closed	1979	4.75	350-475

Frogs - A. Petersen, unless otherwise noted

YEAR ISSUE	EDITION LIMIT	YEAR RETD.	ISSUE PRICE	*QUOTE U.S.$
1977 Frog Friends F-3 - W. Petersen	Closed	1981	5.75	450-900
1974 Frog on Rock F-2	Closed	1977	6.00	N/A
1977 Grampa Frog F-5 - W. Petersen	Closed	1981	6.00	700-1100
1974 Prince Charming F-1 - W. Petersen	Closed	1977	7.50	N/A
1978 Singing Frog F-6	Closed	1979	5.50	N/A
1977 Spring Peepers F-4	Closed	1979	3.50	N/A

Limited Edition - A. Petersen, unless otherwise noted

YEAR ISSUE	EDITION LIMIT	YEAR RETD.	ISSUE PRICE	*QUOTE U.S.$
1981 Beauty and the Beast (color variations) BB-1 - W. Petersen	Closed	1981	89.00	8000-12000
1985 Helping Hand LTD-2	Closed	1985	62.00	650-900
1984 Postmouster LTD-1 - W. Petersen	Closed	1984	46.00	750-850
1987 Statue in the Park LTD-3 - W. Petersen	Closed	1987	93.00	800-925
1988 Uncle Sammy LTD-4	Closed	1988	85.00	250-300

Mice - A. Petersen, unless otherwise noted

YEAR ISSUE	EDITION LIMIT	YEAR RETD.	ISSUE PRICE	*QUOTE U.S.$
1988 Aloha! M-158	Closed	1994	32.00	85-100
1982 Arty Mouse M-71	Closed	1991	19.00	94-125
1985 Attic Treasure M-126	Closed	1995	42.00	95-125
1977 Baby Sitter M-19	Closed	1981	5.75	350-400
1982 Baby Sitter M-66	Closed	1993	23.50	125-160
1987 Band Mice, set/3 M-153a-c - W. Petersen	Closed	1989	87.00	150-195
1981 Barrister Mouse M-57	Closed	1982	16.00	900
1987 Bat Mouse M-154	Closed	1994	25.00	70-135
1982 Beach Mousey M-76	Closed	1993	19.00	100-107
1983 Birthday Girl M-99 - W. Petersen	Closed	1997	18.50	32-95
1981 Blue Devil M-61	Closed	N/A	12.50	250-300
1982 Boy Sweetheart M-81	Closed	1982	13.50	600
1975 Bride Mouse M-9	Closed	1978	4.00	N/A
1978 Bridge Club Mouse M-20	Closed	1979	6.00	600-800
1978 Bridge Club Mouse Partner M-21	Closed	1979	6.00	450-600
1984 Campfire Mouse M-109 - W. Petersen	Closed	1986	26.00	250-450
1981 The Carolers M-63	Closed	1981	29.00	900-2000
1980 Carpenter Mouse M-49	Closed	1981	15.00	800-1300
1983 Chief Geronimouse M-107a	Closed	1995	21.00	75-135
1994 Chief Mouse-asoit M-197	Closed	1997	90.00	90-175
1978 Chief Nip-a-Way Mouse M-26	Closed	1981	7.00	1000-1200
1987 Choir Mouse M-147 - W. Petersen	Closed	1990	23.00	65-100
1979 Chris-Miss M-32	Closed	1982	9.00	300-400
1979 Chris-Mouse M-33	Closed	1982	9.00	250-350
1985 Chris-Mouse Tree M-124	Closed	1998	28.00	85
1983 Christmas Morning M-92	Closed	1987	35.00	225-250
1983 Clown Mouse M-98	Closed	1984	22.00	350-450
1986 Come & Get It! M-141	Closed	1988	34.00	157-200
1985 Come Play! M-131	Closed	1991	18.00	72-110
1989 Commencement Day M-161 - W. Petersen	Closed	1996	28.00	35-63
1980 Commo-Dormouse M-42 - W. Petersen	Closed	1981	14.00	900-1200
1978 Cowboy Mouse M-25	Closed	1981	6.00	500-1200
1983 Cupid Mouse M-94 - W. Petersen	Closed	1997	22.00	85-95
1981 Doc Mouse & Patient M-55 - W. Petersen	Closed	1981	14.00	750-950
1987 Don't Cry! M-149	Closed	1990	33.00	140-150
1986 Down the Chimney M-143	Closed	1988	48.00	200-250
1987 Drummer M-153b - W. Petersen	Closed	1989	29.00	50-75
1989 Elf Tales M-163	Closed	1995	48.00	69-169
1985 Family Portrait M-127	Closed	1987	54.00	250
1976 Fan Mouse M-10	Closed	1979	5.75	N/A
1974 Farmer Mouse M-5	Closed	1979	3.75	N/A
1983 First Christmas M-93	Closed	1986	16.00	250-295
1984 First Day of School M-112	Closed	1985	27.00	375-450
1986 First Haircut M-137 - W. Petersen	Closed	1992	58.00	134-250
1993 First Kiss! M-192	Closed	1996	65.00	125-175
1980 Fishermouse M-41	Closed	1981	16.00	750-800
1981 Flower Girl M-53	Closed	1983	15.00	375-400
1988 Forty Winks M-159 - W. Petersen	Closed	1996	36.00	65-100
1979 Gardener Mouse M-37	Closed	1981	12.00	600-800
1983 Get Well Soon! M-96	Closed	1983	15.00	600-700
1974 Good Knight Mouse M-4 - W. Petersen	Closed	1977	7.50	N/A
1981 Graduate Mouse M-58	Closed	1988	15.00	115-150
1991 Grammy-Phone M-176	Closed	1996	75.00	88-169
1992 Greta M-169b	Closed	1993	35.00	50-75
1992 Hans M-169a	Closed	1993	35.00	50-75
1990 Hans & Greta M-169	Closed	1992	64.00	100-150
1982 Happy Birthday! M-83	Closed	1997	17.50	90-95
1983 Harvest Mouse M-104 - W. Petersen	Closed	1984	23.00	400-600
1992 High on the Hog M-186	Closed	1995	52.00	110-150
1982 Holly Mouse M-87	Closed	1997	13.50	59-95
1976 June Belle M-13	Closed	1979	4.25	400-500
1977 King "Tut" Mouse TM-1	Closed	1979	4.50	1000-1200
1982 Lamplight Carolers M-86	Closed	1987	35.00	275-325
1982 Little Fire Chief M-77 - W. Petersen	Closed	1984	29.00	500-795
1982 Little Sledders M-85	Closed	1985	24.00	350-475
1982 Littlest Angel M-88	Closed	1986	15.00	125-175
1987 Littlest Witch M-156	Closed	1993	24.00	50-90
1981 Lone Caroler M-64	Closed	1981	15.50	800-1500
1993 Lord & Lady Mousebatten M-195	Closed	1995	85.00	145-175
1995 Lord Mousebatten M-195a	Closed	1996	46.00	75-100
1976 Mama Mouse with Baby M-18	Closed	1979	6.00	450-500
1987 Market Mouse M-150 - W. Petersen	Closed	1993	49.00	125
1972 Market Mouse M-1a	Closed	1978	4.25	N/A
1976 May Belle M-12	Closed	1980	4.25	350-475
1983 Merry Chris-Miss M-90	Closed	1985	17.00	219-350
1983 Merry Chris-Mouse M-91	Closed	1985	16.00	250-350
1972 Miss Mouse M-1	Closed	1978	4.25	N/A
1972 Miss Mousey M-2	Closed	1978	4.00	N/A
1972 Miss Mousey w/ Bow Hat M-2b	Closed	1979	4.25	350
1972 Miss Mousey w/ Straw Hat M-2a	Closed	1980	4.25	350-450
1973 Miss Nursey Mouse M-3	Closed	1980	4.00	400-850
1980 Miss Polly Mouse M-46	Closed	1984	23.00	475-500
1982 Miss Teach & Pupil M-73	Closed	1984	29.50	413-425
1980 Miss Teach M-45	Closed	1980	18.00	700-900
1984 Mom & Ginger Baker M-115 - W. Petersen	Closed	1998	38.00	65
1982 Moon Mouse M-78	Closed	1984	15.50	450-650
1981 Mother's Helper M-52	Closed	1983	11.00	225-350
1979 Mouse Artiste M-39	Closed	1981	12.50	350-500
1979 Mouse Ballerina M-38	Closed	1979	12.50	900-1200
1983 Mouse Call M-97 - W. Petersen	Closed	1983	24.00	500-800
1979 Mouse Duet M-29	Closed	1982	25.00	600-800
1986 Mouse on Campus M-139 - W. Petersen	Closed	1988	25.00	90-125
1979 Mouse Pianist M-30	Closed	1984	17.00	250-350
1985 Mouse Talk M-130	Closed	1993	44.00	100-125
1979 Mouse Violinist M-31	Closed	1984	9.00	250-275
1976 Mouse with Muff M-16	Closed	1977	9.00	N/A
1979 Mousey Baby M-34	Closed	1982	9.50	300-350
1981 Mousey Express M-65	Closed	1993	22.00	106-125
1983 Mousey's Cone M-100	Closed	1994	22.00	65-85
1983 Mousey's Dollhouse M-102	Closed	1985	30.00	300-475
1988 Mousey's Easter Basket M-160	Closed	N/A	32.00	110-150
1982 Mousey's Teddy M-75	Closed	1985	29.00	313-375
1983 Mousey's Tricycle M-101	Closed	1995	24.00	49
1976 Mrs. Mousey M-15	Closed	1978	4.00	N/A
1976 Mrs. Mousey w/ Hat M-15a	Closed	1979	4.25	N/A
1992 Mrs. Mousey's Studio M-184 - W. Petersen	Closed	1997	150.00	165-200
1980 Mrs. Tidy M-51	Closed	1981	19.50	500-650
1980 Mrs. Tidy and Helper M-50	Closed	1981	24.00	650-750
1976 Nightie Mouse M-14	Closed	1979	4.75	400-500
1981 Nursery Mousey M-54	Closed	1982	14.00	350-500
1982 Office Mousey M-68	Closed	1984	23.00	375-400
1983 Pack Mouse M-106 - W. Petersen	Closed	1984	19.00	400-550
1985 Pageant Shepherds M-122	Closed	1985	35.00	200-250
1985 Pageant Wiseman M-121	Closed	1985	58.00	200-275
1981 Pearl Knit Mouse M-59	Closed	1985	20.00	295-300
1992 Peekaboo! M-183 - D. Petersen	Closed	1998	52.00	95
1984 Pen Pal Mousey M-114	Closed	1985	26.00	395-450
1993 Peter Pumpkin Eater M-190	Closed	1995	98.00	108-130
1984 Peter's Pumpkin M-118	Closed	1992	19.00	70-115
1980 Photographer Mouse M-48 - W. Petersen	Closed	1981	23.00	1200
1978 Picnic Mice M-23 - W. Petersen	Closed	1979	7.25	900-1000
1985 Piggy-Back Mousey M-129 - W. Petersen	Closed	1986	28.00	350-400
1994 Pilgrim's Welcome M-198	Closed	1997	55.00	100-115
1978 Pirate Mouse M-27	Closed	1979	6.50	800-1200
1980 Pirate Mouse M-47 - W. Petersen	Closed	1981	16.00	500-700
1990 Polly's Parasol M-170	Closed	1993	39.00	73-125
1982 Poorest Angel M-89	Closed	1986	15.00	145-175
1989 Prima Ballerina M-162	Closed	1996	35.00	44
1984 Prudence Pie Maker M-119	Closed	1992	18.50	70-115
1977 Queen "Tut" Mouse TM-2	Closed	1979	4.50	1000-1200
1985 Quilting Bee M-125 - W. Petersen	Closed	1998	30.00	75
1979 Raggedy and Mouse M-36	Closed	1981	12.00	400-700
1987 The Red Wagon M-151 - W. Petersen	Closed	1991	54.00	200-250
1979 Rock-a-bye Baby Mouse M-35	Closed	1981	17.00	950
1983 Rocking Tot M-103	Closed	1990	19.00	85-150
1983 Rope 'em Mousey M-108	Closed	1984	19.00	400-500
1983 Running Doe/Little Deer M-107b	Closed	1997	35.00	50-115
1980 Santa Mouse M-43	Closed	1985	12.00	200-250
1984 Santa's Trainee M-116 - W. Petersen	Closed	1984	36.50	450-650
1982 Say "Cheese" M-72 - W. Petersen	Closed	1983	15.50	400-750
1981 School Marm Mouse M-56	Closed	1981	19.50	600-900
1987 Scooter Mouse M-152 - W. Petersen	Closed	1996	34.00	113-125
1978 Secretary Miss Pell M-22	Closed	1981	4.50	550-850
1976 Shawl Mouse M-17	Closed	1977	9.00	N/A
1987 Skeleton Mousey M-157	Closed	1993	27.00	75-93
1982 Snowmouse & Friend M-84	Closed	1985	23.50	350-400
1990 Stars & Stripes M-168	Closed	1996	34.00	40-135
1985 Strolling with Baby M-128	Closed	1997	42.00	61-90
1985 Sunday Drivers M-132 - W. Petersen	Closed	1994	58.00	293-300
1986 Sweet Dreams M-136	Closed	1992	58.00	160-225
1982 Sweethearts M-79	Closed	1982	26.00	400-600
1982 Tea for Two M-74	Closed	1984	26.00	375-425
1976 Tea Mouse M-11	Closed	1979	5.75	500-800
1984 Tidy Mouse M-113	Closed	1985	38.00	700-750
1978 Town Crier Mouse M-28	Closed	1979	10.50	900
1984 Traveling Mouse M-110	Closed	1987	28.00	350-375
1987 Trumpeter M-153a - W. Petersen	Closed	1989	29.00	50-100
1987 Tuba Player M-153c - W. Petersen	Closed	1989	29.00	50-100
1992 Tuckered Out! M-136a	Closed	1993	46.00	125-200
1975 Two Mice with Candle M-7	Closed	1979	4.50	450-550
1975 Two Tiny Mice M-8	Closed	1979	4.50	450-600
1985 Under the Chris-Mouse Tree M-123	Closed	1998	48.00	125
1986 Waltzing Matilda M-135 - W. Petersen	Closed	1993	48.00	110-135
1983 Wash Day M-105	Closed	1984	23.00	300-350
1994 We Gather Together M-199	Closed	1997	90.00	90-180
1978 Wedding Mice M-24 - W. Petersen	Closed	1981	7.50	185-500
1982 Wedding Mice M-67 - W. Petersen	Closed	1993	29.50	110-200
1980 Witch Mouse M-44	Closed	1983	12.00	200-270
1984 Witchy Boo! M-120	Closed	1995	21.00	39-90
1974 Wood Sprite M-6a	Closed	1978	4.00	N/A
1974 Wood Sprite M-6b	Closed	1978	4.00	N/A
1974 Wood Sprite M-6c	Closed	1978	4.00	N/A

Minutemice - A. Petersen, unless otherwise noted

YEAR ISSUE	EDITION LIMIT	YEAR RETD.	ISSUE PRICE	*QUOTE U.S.$
1974 Concordian On Drum with Glasses MM-4	Closed	1977	9.00	N/A
1974 Concordian Wood Base w/Hat MM-4b	Closed	1977	8.00	N/A
1974 Concordian Wood Base w/Tan Coat MM-4a	Closed	1977	7.50	N/A
1974 Little Fifer on Drum MM-5b	Closed	1977	8.00	N/A
1974 Little Fifer on Drum with Fife MM-5	Closed	1977	8.00	N/A
1974 Little Fifer on Wood Base MM-5a	Closed	1977	8.00	N/A
1974 Mouse Carrying Large Drum MM-3	Closed	1977	8.00	N/A
1974 Mouse on Drum with Black Hat MM-2	Closed	1977	9.00	N/A
1974 Mouse on Drum with Fife MM-1	Closed	1977	9.00	N/A
1974 Mouse on Drum with Fife Wood Base MM-1a	Closed	1977	9.00	N/A

Moles - A. Petersen

YEAR ISSUE	EDITION LIMIT	YEAR RETD.	ISSUE PRICE	*QUOTE U.S.$
1978 Mole Scout MO-1	Closed	1980	4.25	310-500

Mouse Sports - A. Petersen, unless otherwise noted

YEAR ISSUE	EDITION LIMIT	YEAR RETD.	ISSUE PRICE	*QUOTE U.S.$
1975 Bobsled Three MS-1	Closed	1977	12.00	N/A
1985 Fishin' Chip MS-14 - W. Petersen	Closed	1992	46.00	250-275
1981 Golfer Mouse MS-10	Closed	1984	15.50	480-500
1977 Golfer Mouse MS-7	Closed	1980	5.25	400-500
1984 Land Ho! MS-12	Closed	1987	36.50	250-325
1976 Mouse Skier MS-3	Closed	1979	4.25	350-500
1975 Skater Mouse MS-2	Closed	1980	4.50	400-800
1980 Skater Mouse MS-8	Closed	1983	16.50	400-695
1977 Skating Star Mouse MS-6	Closed	1979	3.75	250-350
1980 Skier Mouse (Early Colors) MS-9	Closed	1983	13.00	225-300
1984 Tennis Anyone? MS-13	Closed	1988	18.00	95-250
1976 Tennis Star MS-4	Closed	1978	3.75	300-750
1976 Tennis Star MS-5	Closed	1981	3.75	250-300

*Quotes have been rounded up to nearest dollar

Owls - A. Petersen, unless otherwise noted

YEAR ISSUE	EDITION LIMIT	YEAR RETD.	ISSUE PRICE	*QUOTE U.S.$
1975 Colonial Owls O-4	Closed	1977	11.50	N/A
1979 Grad Owl O-5 - W. Petersen	Closed	1979	4.25	400-600
1980 Graduate Owl (On Books) O-6 - W. Petersen	Closed	1980	12.00	550
1974 Mr. and Mrs. Owl O-1	Closed	1981	6.00	600-850
1974 Mr. Owl O-3	Closed	1981	3.25	400-500
1974 Mrs. Owl O-2	Closed	1981	3.00	400-500

Piggies - A. Petersen

YEAR ISSUE	EDITION LIMIT	YEAR RETD.	ISSUE PRICE	*QUOTE U.S.$
1978 Boy Piglet/ Picnic Piggy P-6	Closed	1981	4.00	300-400
1978 Girl Piglet/Picnic Piggy P-5	Closed	1981	4.00	300-400
1981 Holly Hog P-11	Closed	1981	25.00	600-800
1978 Jolly Tar Piggy P-3	Closed	1979	4.50	350-400
1978 Miss Piggy School Marm P-1	Closed	1979	4.50	300-600
1980 Nurse Piggy P-10	Closed	1981	15.50	300-400
1978 Picnic Piggies P-4	Closed	1981	7.75	400-600
1980 Pig O' My Heart P-9	Closed	1981	12.00	400-850
1978 Piggy Baker P-2	Closed	1981	4.50	300-350
1980 Piggy Ballerina P-7	Closed	1981	15.50	300-500
1978 Piggy Jogger PS-1	Closed	1981	4.50	700-850
1980 Piggy Policeman P-8	Closed	1981	17.50	300-800

Raccoons - A. Petersen

YEAR ISSUE	EDITION LIMIT	YEAR RETD.	ISSUE PRICE	*QUOTE U.S.$
1978 Bird Watcher Raccoon RC-3	Closed	1981	6.50	500-800
1977 Hiker Raccoon RC-2	Closed	1980	4.50	500-795
1977 Mother Raccoon RC-1	Closed	1980	4.50	400-750
1978 Raccoon Skater RCS-1	Closed	1980	4.75	400-700
1978 Raccoon Skier RCS-2	Closed	1980	6.00	600-950

Rats - A. Petersen, unless otherwise noted

YEAR ISSUE	EDITION LIMIT	YEAR RETD.	ISSUE PRICE	*QUOTE U.S.$
1975 Doc Rat R-2 - W. Petersen	Closed	1980	5.25	500-700
1975 Seedy Rat R-1	Closed	1977	5.25	N/A

Robin Hood Series - A. Petersen

YEAR ISSUE	EDITION LIMIT	YEAR RETD.	ISSUE PRICE	*QUOTE U.S.$
1990 Friar Tuck RH-3	Closed	1994	32.00	50-95
1990 Maid Marion RH-2	Closed	1994	32.00	50-88
1990 Robin Hood RH-1	Closed	1994	37.00	50-95

Single Issues - A. Petersen, unless otherwise noted

YEAR ISSUE	EDITION LIMIT	YEAR RETD.	ISSUE PRICE	*QUOTE U.S.$
1980 Cave Mice - W. Petersen	Closed	N/A	N/A	550-800
1972 Party Mouse in Plain Dress	Closed	N/A	N/A	N/A
1972 Party Mouse in Polka-Dot Dress	Closed	N/A	N/A	N/A
1972 Party Mouse in Sailor Suit	Closed	N/A	N/A	N/A
1972 Party Mouse with Bow Tie	Closed	N/A	N/A	N/A
1980 Screech Owl - W. Petersen	Closed	1982	N/A	N/A

Tiny Teddies - D. Petersen

YEAR ISSUE	EDITION LIMIT	YEAR RETD.	ISSUE PRICE	*QUOTE U.S.$
1984 Boo Bear T-3	Closed	N/A	20.00	69-150
1987 Christmas Teddy T-10	Closed	N/A	26.00	69-150
1984 Drummer Bear T-4	Closed	N/A	22.00	63-150
1986 Huggy Bear T-8	Closed	N/A	26.00	150
1984 Little Teddy T-1	Closed	1986	20.00	175-200
1989 Momma Bear T-12	Closed	N/A	27.00	95-150
1985 Ride 'em Teddy! T-6	Closed	N/A	32.00	150-200
1984 Sailor Teddy T-2	Closed	N/A	20.00	60-150
1984 Santa Bear T-5	Closed	N/A	27.00	150-200
1985 Seaside Teddy T-7	Closed	N/A	28.00	75-150
1983 Tiny Teddy TT-1	Closed	1983	16.00	700
1987 Wedding Bears T-9	Suspd.		54.00	165-200

Wind in the Willows - A. Petersen, unless otherwise noted

YEAR ISSUE	EDITION LIMIT	YEAR RETD.	ISSUE PRICE	*QUOTE U.S.$
1982 Badger WW-2	Closed	1983	18.00	375-395
1982 Mole WW-1	Closed	1983	18.00	300-350
1982 Ratty WW-4	Closed	1983	18.00	350-390
1982 Toad WW-3 - W. Petersen	Closed	1983	18.00	300-350

Willitts Designs

Ebony Visions Circle - T. Blackshear

YEAR ISSUE	EDITION LIMIT	YEAR RETD.	ISSUE PRICE	*QUOTE U.S.$
1997 A Child Shall Lead Them	Retrd.	1998	225.00	225

Carousel Classics/Carousel Memories - A. Dezendorf

YEAR ISSUE	EDITION LIMIT	YEAR RETD.	ISSUE PRICE	*QUOTE U.S.$
1998 American Musical Carousel	9,500		100.00	100
1997 Armoured Lead Horse	9,500		75.00	75
1997 Eagle-Back Stander	9,500		65.00	65
1998 English Musical Carousel	9,500		100.00	100
1998 French Musical Carousel	9,500		100.00	100
1998 German Musical Karussell	9,500		100.00	100
1997 Indian Pony Stander	9,500		75.00	75
1998 Lion with Cherub	9,500		75.00	75
1998 Middle Row Jumper w/Dog	9,500		70.00	70
1997 Outside Row Jumper w/Parrot	9,500		70.00	70
1998 Outside Row Stander w/ Scalloped Saddle	9,500		70.00	70
1997 Outside Row Stander w/Cherub	9,500		70.00	70
1997 Outside Row Stander w/Gold Mane	9,500		75.00	75
1998 Outside Row Zebra Stander	9,500		75.00	75
1997 Patriotic Outside Row Jumper	9,500		70.00	70
1997 Stander "King" Horse	9,500		70.00	70
1998 Stander w/Roached Mane	9,500		70.00	70

Ebony Visions - T. Blackshear

YEAR ISSUE	EDITION LIMIT	YEAR RETD.	ISSUE PRICE	*QUOTE U.S.$
1998 Catching The Eye	Open		235.00	235
1997 Catching The Eye (Parkwest/NALED exclusive)	1,000		225.00	225
1998 Catching The Eye A/P	50		282.00	282
1998 Catching The Eye G/P	50		305.50	306
1998 The Comforter	Open		250.00	250
1998 The Comforter A/P	50		300.00	300
1998 The ComforterG/P	50		325.00	325
1996 The Dreamer	11,500	1997	135.00	135-180
1996 The Dreamer A/P	50	1997	162.00	225
1996 The Dreamer G/P	50	1997	175.50	176
1997 Ebony Visions in Bas Relief	4,000	1998	150.00	150
1997 Ebony Visions in Bas Relief A/P	50	1998	180.00	180
1997 Ebony Visions in Bas Relief G/P	50	1998	195.00	195
1997 The Family	Open		225.00	225
1997 The Family A/P	50		270.00	270
1997 The Family G/P	50		292.50	293
1997 The Flower Girl	Open		100.00	100
1997 The Flower Girl A/P	50		120.00	120
1997 The Flower Girl G/P	50		130.00	130
1998 The Fruits of Friendship	Open		115.00	115
1998 The Fruits of Friendship A/P	50		138.00	138
1998 The Fruits of Friendship G/P	50		149.50	150
1996 The Guardian	Open		300.00	300
1996 The Guardian A/P	50		360.00	360
1996 The Guardian G/P	50		390.00	390
1997 The Heirs	Open		125.00	125
1997 The Heirs A/P	50		150.00	150
1997 The Heirs G/P	50		162.50	163
1998 Hero	Open		200.00	200
1998 Hero A/P	50		240.00	240
1998 Hero G/P	50		260.00	260
1997 Hopes & Dreams	2,500	1997	225.00	225-400
1997 Hopes & Dreams A/P	50	1997	270.00	270
1997 Hopes & Dreams G/P	50	1997	292.50	293
1998 Joyful Noise	Open		150.00	150
1998 Joyful Noise A/P	50		180.00	180
1998 Joyful Noise G/P	50		195.00	195
1997 The Kiss	Open		225.00	225
1997 The Kiss A/P	50		270.00	270
1997 The Kiss G/P	50		292.50	293
1995 The Madonna	13,325	1997	160.00	190-370
1995 The Madonna A/P	50	1997	192.00	192-230
1995 The Madonna G/P	50	1997	208.00	208
1997 Midnight	Open		250.00	250
1997 Midnight A/P	50		300.00	300
1997 Midnight G/P	50		325.00	325
1996 The Music Maker	12,375	1998	195.00	195
1996 The Music Maker A/P	50	1998	234.00	234
1996 The Music Maker G/P	50	1998	253.50	254
1998 Night in Day	Open		225.00	225
1998 Night in Day A/P	50		270.00	270
1998 Night in Day G/P	50		292.50	293
1995 The Nurturer	16,923	1998	160.00	160-320
1995 The Nurturer A/P	50	1998	192.00	192-290
1995 The Nurturer G/P	50	1998	208.00	208
1997 The Prayer	Open		150.00	150
1997 The Prayer A/P	50		180.00	180
1997 The Prayer G/P	50		195.00	195
1995 The Protector	7,900	1996	195.00	600-800
1995 The Protector A/P	50	1996	234.00	600-650
1995 The Protector G/P	50	1996	253.50	600-650
1995 Siblings	8,800	1996	120.00	300-375
1995 Siblings A/P	50	1996	144.00	275-300
1995 Siblings G/P	50	1996	156.00	156-300
1998 Sisters Fover: In Childhood	Open		140.00	140
1998 Sisters Fover: In Childhood A/P	50		168.00	168
1998 Sisters Fover: In Childhood G/P	50		182.00	182
1995 The Storyteller	2,500	1996	410.00	1500-2500
1995 The Storyteller A/P	50	1996	492.00	2900
1995 The Tender Touch	16,900	1997	185.00	340-360
1995 The Tender Touch A/P	50	1997	222.00	222
1995 The Tender Touch G/P	50	1997	240.50	241
1996 A Time To Dream	10,500	1997	120.00	120-200
1996 A Time To Dream A/P	50	1997	144.00	144
1996 A Time To Dream G/P	50	1997	156.00	156

Ebony Visions Legends Edition - T. Blackshear

YEAR ISSUE	EDITION LIMIT	YEAR RETD.	ISSUE PRICE	*QUOTE U.S.$
1998 The Madonna	550		1075.00	1075
1998 The Madonna A/P	50		1290.00	1290
1998 The Madonna G/P	50		1397.50	1398
1997 The Protector	950		1450.00	1450
1997 The Protector A/P	50		1740.00	1740
1997 The Protector G/P	50		1885.00	1885
1996 The Storyteller	650	1996	1900.00	1900-2100
1996 The Storyteller A/P	50	1996	2300.00	2300-2490
1996 The Storyteller G/P	50	1996	2470.00	2470

Just The Right Shoe - Raine

YEAR ISSUE	EDITION LIMIT	YEAR RETD.	ISSUE PRICE	*QUOTE U.S.$
1998 Afternoon Tea	Open		24.00	24
1998 Brocade Court	Open		16.00	16
1998 Deco Boot	Open		25.00	25
1998 The Empress	Open		18.00	18
1998 En Pointe	Open		17.50	18
1998 Italian Racer	Open		13.50	14
1998 Jeweled Heel Pump	Open		24.00	24
1998 Leopard Stiletto	Open		15.00	15
1998 Opera Boot	Open		25.00	25
1998 Pavé	Open		22.00	22
1998 Pearl Mule	Open		17.00	17
1998 Promenade	Open		20.00	20
1998 Ravishing Red	Open		12.00	12
1998 Rose Court	Open		15.00	15
1998 Silver Cloud	Open		14.50	15
1998 Sumptuous Quilt	Open		13.50	14
1998 Teetering Court	Open		18.00	18
1998 Tying the Knot	Open		15.00	15

MasterPeace Collection - Various

YEAR ISSUE	EDITION LIMIT	YEAR RETD.	ISSUE PRICE	*QUOTE U.S.$
1998 Forgiven - T. Blackshear	Open		200.00	200
1998 Forgiven A/P - T. Blackshear	100		240.00	240
1998 Forgiven G/P - T. Blackshear	100		260.00	260
1998 The Invitation - M. Weistling	Open		250.00	250
1998 The Invitation A/P - M. Weistling	100		300.00	300
1998 The Invitation G/P - M. Weistling	100		325.00	325
1998 Victorious Lion of Judah - M. Dudash	Open		175.00	175
1998 Victorious Lion of Judah A/P - M. Dudash	100		210.00	210
1998 Victorious Lion of Judah G/P - M. Dudash	100		227.50	228
1998 Watchers in the Night - T. Blackshear	Open		300.00	300
1998 Watchers in the Night A/P - T. Blackshear	100		360.00	360
1998 Watchers in the Night G/P - T. Blackshear	100		390.00	390

Rainbow Babies - A. Blackshear

YEAR ISSUE	EDITION LIMIT	YEAR RETD.	ISSUE PRICE	*QUOTE U.S.$
1998 Beloved	Open		31.50	32
1997 Bright Eyes	Open		27.50	28
1997 Cuddles	Open		39.50	40
1998 Lil' Blossom	Open		34.50	35
1998 Peek-A-Boo Pals	Open		47.50	48
1997 Peewee & Peeper	Open		39.50	40
1997 Pookie	Open		24.50	25
1997 Precious	Open		29.50	30
1997 Sunshine	Open		32.50	33

Woodland Winds/Christopher Radko

Woodland Winds Musicals - C. Radko

YEAR ISSUE	EDITION LIMIT	YEAR RETD.	ISSUE PRICE	*QUOTE U.S.$
1998 Blustery Bunny Sign 98-800-0	Open		35.00	35
1998 Carlton The Snowman 98-704-0	Open		60.00	60
1998 Frosty Leaf Santa 98-703-0	Open		60.00	60
1998 Is This the Way to Make Figure 8's? 98-841-0	Open		40.00	40
1998 Snow Tunes Bunny Carolers 98-802-0	Open		35.00	35
1998 Stardust Santa w/Scepter 98-804-0	Open		50.00	50
1998 Stardust Santa w/Snowflakes 98-806-0	Open		50.00	50

Woodland Winds Porcelain Figurines - C. Radko

YEAR ISSUE	EDITION LIMIT	YEAR RETD.	ISSUE PRICE	*QUOTE U.S.$
1998 All Tuckered Out 98-847-0	Open		20.00	20
1998 Carlton Snowman 98-742-0	Open		30.00	30
1998 Dashing Thru The Snow 98-852-0	Open		25.00	25
1998 Meet Our New Friend Burl 98-849-0	Open		22.00	22
1998 Santa w/Bubble Bear 98-743-0	Open		30.00	30
1998 Skiing My Way To You 98-844-0	Open		22.50	23
1998 Sled Express 98-850-0	Open		20.00	20
1998 Starburst Santa w/Flakes 98-803-0	Open		35.00	35
1998 Surrounded By Friends 98-851-0	Open		30.00	30

Woodland Winds Porcelain Lighting - C. Radko

YEAR ISSUE	EDITION LIMIT	YEAR RETD.	ISSUE PRICE	*QUOTE U.S.$
1998 Cold Hands Warm Heart 98-853-0	Open		25.00	25
1998 Snowball Snooze Candleholder 98-846-0	Open		18.00	18

Woodland Winds Snowglobes - C. Radko

YEAR ISSUE	EDITION LIMIT	YEAR RETD.	ISSUE PRICE	*QUOTE U.S.$
1998 Carlton The Snowman 98-702-0	7,500		110.00	110
1998 Frosty Leaf Santa 98-700-0	7,500		110.00	110
1998 Happy Holidays 98-701-0	7,500		110.00	110

Woodland Winds Tabletop Figurines - C. Radko

YEAR ISSUE	EDITION LIMIT	YEAR RETD.	ISSUE PRICE	*QUOTE U.S.$
1998 Carved Carlton 98-746-0	Open		40.00	40
1998 Carved Frosty Leaf Santa 98-747-0	Open		50.00	50
1998 Frosty Leaf Santa 98-744-0	5,000		125.00	125

GRAPHICS

American Artists

Fred Stone - F. Stone

YEAR ISSUE	EDITION LIMIT	YEAR RETD.	ISSUE PRICE	*QUOTE U.S.$
1979 Affirmed, Steve Cauthen Up	750	N/A	100.00	600
1988 Alysheba	950	N/A	195.00	650
1992 The American Triple Crown I, 1948-1978	1,500		325.00	325
1993 The American Triple Crown II, 1937-1946	1,500		325.00	325
1993 The American Triple Crown III, 1919-1935	1,500		225.00	225
1983 The Andalusian	750	N/A	150.00	350
1981 The Arabians	750	N/A	115.00	525
1989 Battle For The Triple Crown	950	N/A	225.00	650
1980 The Belmont-Bold Forbes	500	N/A	100.00	375
1991 Black Stallion	1,500		225.00	250
1988 Cam-Fella	950	N/A	175.00	350
1996 Cigar, canvas	250	1997	295.00	295
1996 Cigar, litho	1,200	1997	150.00	150
1981 Contentment	750	N/A	115.00	525
1982 Dance Smartly-Pat Day Up	950	N/A	225.00	325
1995 Dancers, canvas litho	350		375.00	375
1995 Dancers, print	Open		60.00	60
1983 The Duel	750	N/A	150.00	400
1985 Eternal Legacy	950	N/A	175.00	950
1980 Exceller-Bill Shoemaker	500	N/A	90.00	800
1990 Final Tribute- Secretariat	1,150	N/A	265.00	1300
1987 The First Day	950	N/A	175.00	225
1991 Forego	1,150		225.00	250
1986 Forever Friends	950	N/A	175.00	725
1985 Fred Stone Paints the Sport of Kings (Book)	750	N/A	265.00	750
1980 Genuine Risk	500	N/A	100.00	700
1991 Go For Wand-A Candle in the Wind	1,150		225.00	225
1986 Great Match Race-Ruffian & Foolish Pleasure	950	N/A	175.00	375

*Quotes have been rounded up to nearest dollar

YEAR ISSUE	EDITION LIMIT	YEAR RETD.	ISSUE PRICE	*QUOTE U.S.$
1995 Holy Bull, canvas litho	350		375.00	375
1995 Holy Bull, litho	1,150		225.00	225
1996 In Pursuit of Greatness-Cigar, canvas	250	1997	295.00	295
1996 In Pursuit of Greatness-Cigar, litho	1,500	1997	90.00	90
1981 John Henry-Bill Shoemaker Up	595	N/A	160.00	1500
1985 John Henry-McCarron Up	750	N/A	175.00	500-750
1995 Julie Krone - Colonial Affair	1,150		225.00	225
1985 Kelso	950	N/A	175.00	750
1980 The Kentucky Derby	750	N/A	100.00	650
1980 Kidnapped Mare-Franfreluche	750	N/A	115.00	575
1987 Lady's Secret	950	N/A	175.00	425
1982 Man O'War "Final Thunder"	750	N/A	175.00	2500-3100
1979 Mare and Foal	500	N/A	90.00	500
1979 The Moment After	500	N/A	90.00	350
1986 Nijinski II	950	N/A	175.00	275
1984 Northern Dancer	950	N/A	175.00	625
1982 Off and Running	750	N/A	125.00	250-350
1990 Old Warriors Shoemaker -John Henry	1,950	N/A	265.00	595
1979 One, Two, Three	500	N/A	100.00	1000
1980 The Pasture Pest	500	N/A	100.00	875
1979 Patience	1,000	N/A	90.00	1200
1989 Phar Lap	950	N/A	195.00	275
1982 The Power Horses	750	N/A	125.00	250
1997 Preakness-Silver Charm, canvas	250		295.00	295
1997 Preakness-Silver Charm, litho	1,150		195.00	195
1987 The Rivalry-Alysheba and Bet Twice	950	N/A	195.00	550
1979 The Rivals-Affirmed & Alydar	500	N/A	90.00	500
1983 Ruffian-For Only a Moment	750	N/A	175.00	1100
1983 Secretariat	950	N/A	175.00	995-1200
1989 Shoe Bald Eagle	950	N/A	195.00	675
1981 The Shoe-8,000 Wins	395	N/A	200.00	7000
1980 Spectacular Bid	500	N/A	65.00	350-400
1995 Summer Days, canvas litho	350		375.00	375
1995 Summer Days, litho	1,150		225.00	225
XX Sunday Silence	950	N/A	195.00	425
1981 The Thoroughbreds	750	N/A	115.00	425
1983 Tranquility	750	N/A	150.00	525
1984 Turning For Home	750	N/A	150.00	425
1982 The Water Trough	750	N/A	125.00	575

Anheuser-Busch, Inc.

Anheuser-Busch - H. Droog

YEAR ISSUE	EDITION LIMIT	YEAR RETD.	ISSUE PRICE	*QUOTE U.S.$
1994 Gray Wolf Mirror N4570	2,500		135.00	150

Endangered Species Fine Art Prints - B. Kemper

YEAR ISSUE	EDITION LIMIT	YEAR RETD.	ISSUE PRICE	*QUOTE U.S.$
1996 Bald Eagle Print, framed N9995	2,500	1997	159.00	135-159
1996 Bald Eagle, unframed N9995U	2,500	1997	79.00	79
1996 Cougar Print, framed N9993	2,500	1997	159.00	135-159
1996 Cougar Print, unframed N9993U	2,500	1997	79.00	79
1996 Gray Wolf Print, framed N9992	2,500	1997	159.00	135-159
1996 Gray Wolf Print, unframed N9992U	2,500	1997	79.00	79
1996 Panda Print, framed N9994	2,500	1997	159.00	135-159
1996 Panda Print, unframed N9994U	2,500	1997	79.00	79

Circle Fine Art

Rockwell - N. Rockwell

YEAR ISSUE	EDITION LIMIT	YEAR RETD.	ISSUE PRICE	*QUOTE U.S.$
XX American Family Folio	200		Unkn.	17500
XX The Artist at Work	130		Unkn.	3500
XX At the Barber	200		Unkn.	4900
XX Autumn	200		Unkn.	3500
XX Autumn/Japon	25		Unkn.	3600
XX Aviary	200		Unkn.	4200
XX Barbershop Quartet	200		Unkn.	4200
XX Baseball	200		Unkn.	3600
XX Ben Franklin's Philadelphia	200		Unkn.	3600
XX Ben's Belles	200		Unkn.	3500
XX The Big Day	200		Unkn.	3400
XX The Big Top	148		Unkn.	2800
XX Blacksmith Shop	200		Unkn.	6300
XX Bookseller	200		Unkn.	2700
XX Bookseller/Japon	25		Unkn.	2750
XX The Bridge	200		Unkn.	3100
XX Cat	200		Unkn.	3400
XX Cat/Collotype	200		Unkn.	4000
XX Cheering	200		Unkn.	3600
XX Children at Window	200		Unkn.	3600
XX Church	200		Unkn.	3400
XX Church/Collotype	200		Unkn.	4000
XX Circus	200		Unkn.	2650
XX County Agricultural Agent	200		Unkn.	3900
XX The Critic	200		Unkn.	4650
XX Day in the Life of a Boy	200		Unkn.	6200
XX Day in the Life of a Boy/Japon	25		Unkn.	6500
XX Debut	200		Unkn.	3600
XX Discovery	200		Unkn.	5900
XX Doctor and Boy	200		Unkn.	9400
XX Doctor and Doll-Signed	200		Unkn.	11900
XX Dressing Up/Ink	60		Unkn.	4400
XX Dressing Up/Pencil	200		Unkn.	3700
XX The Drunkard	200		Unkn.	3600
XX The Expected and Unexpected	200		Unkn.	3700
XX Family Tree	200		Unkn.	5900
XX Fido's House	200		Unkn.	3600
XX Football Mascot	200		Unkn.	3700
XX Four Seasons Folio	200		Unkn.	13500
XX Four Seasons Folio/Japon	25		Unkn.	14000
XX Freedom from Fear-Signed	200		Unkn.	6400
XX Freedom from Want-Signed	200		Unkn.	6400
XX Freedom of Religion-Signed	200		Unkn.	6400
XX Freedom of Speech-Signed	200		Unkn.	6400
XX Gaiety Dance Team	200		Unkn.	4300
XX Girl at Mirror-Signed	200		Unkn.	8400
XX The Golden Age	200		Unkn.	3500
XX Golden Rule-Signed	200		Unkn.	4400
XX Golf	200		Unkn.	3600
XX Gossips	200		Unkn.	5000
XX Gossips/Japon	25		Unkn.	5100
XX Grotto	200		Unkn.	3400
XX Grotto/Collotype	200		Unkn.	4000
XX High Dive	200		Unkn.	3400
XX The Homecoming	200		Unkn.	3700
XX The House	200		Unkn.	3700
XX Huck Finn Folio	200		Unkn.	35000
XX Ichabod Crane	200		Unkn.	6700
XX The Inventor	200		Unkn.	4100
XX Jerry	200		Unkn.	4700
XX Jim Got Down on His Knees	200		Unkn.	4500
XX Lincoln	200		Unkn.	11400
XX Lobsterman	200		Unkn.	5500
XX Lobsterman/Japon	25		Unkn.	5750
XX Marriage License	200		Unkn.	6900
XX Medicine	200		Unkn.	3400
XX Medicine/Color Litho	200		Unkn.	4000
XX Miss Mary Jane	200		Unkn.	4500
XX Moving Day	200		Unkn.	3900
XX Music Hath Charms	200		Unkn.	4200
XX My Hand Shook	200		Unkn.	4500
XX Out the Window	200		Unkn.	3400
XX Out the Window/ Collotype	200		Unkn.	4000
XX Outward Bound-Signed	200		Unkn.	7900
XX Poor Richard's Almanac	200		Unkn.	24000
XX Prescription	200		Unkn.	4900
XX Prescription/Japon	25		Unkn.	5000
XX The Problem We All Live With	200		Unkn.	4500
XX Puppies	200		Unkn.	3700
XX Raliegh the Dog	200		Unkn.	3900
XX Rocket Ship	200		Unkn.	3650
XX The Royal Crown	200		Unkn.	3500
XX Runaway	200		Unkn.	3800
XX Runaway/Japon	200		Unkn.	5700
XX Safe and Sound	200		Unkn.	3800
XX Saturday People	200		Unkn.	3300
XX Save Me	200		Unkn.	3600
XX Saying Grace-Signed	200		Unkn.	7400
XX School Days Folio	200		Unkn.	14000
XX Schoolhouse	200		Unkn.	4500
XX Schoolhouse/Japon	25		Unkn.	4650
XX See America First	200		Unkn.	5650
XX See America First/Japon	25		Unkn.	6100
XX Settling In	200		Unkn.	3600
XX Shuffelton's Barbershop	200		Unkn.	7400
XX Smoking	200		Unkn.	3400
XX Smoking/Collotype	200		Unkn.	4000
XX Spanking	200		Unkn.	3400
XX Spanking/ Collotype	200		Unkn.	4000
XX Spelling Bee	200		Unkn.	6500
XX Spring	200		Unkn.	3500
XX Spring Flowers	200		Unkn.	5200
XX Spring/Japon	25		Unkn.	3600
XX Study for the Doctor's Office	200		Unkn.	6000
XX Studying	200		Unkn.	3600
XX Summer	200		Unkn.	3500
XX Summer Stock	200		Unkn.	4900
XX Summer Stock/Japon	25		Unkn.	5000
XX Summer/Japon	25		Unkn.	3600
XX The Teacher	200		Unkn.	3400
XX Teacher's Pet	200		Unkn.	3600
XX The Teacher/Japon	25		Unkn.	3500
XX The Texan	200		Unkn.	3700
XX Then For Three Minutes	200		Unkn.	4500
XX Then Miss Watson	200		Unkn.	4500
XX There Warn't No Harm	200		Unkn.	4500
XX Three Farmers	200		Unkn.	3600
XX Ticketseller	200		Unkn.	4200
XX Ticketseller/Japon	25		Unkn.	4400
XX Tom Sawyer Color Suite	200		Unkn.	30000
XX Tom Sawyer Folio	200		Unkn.	26500
XX Top of the World	200		Unkn.	4200
XX Trumpeter	200		Unkn.	3900
XX Trumpeter/Japon	25		Unkn.	4100
XX Two O'Clock Feeding	200		Unkn.	3600
XX The Village Smithy	200		Unkn.	3500
XX Welcome	200		Unkn.	3500
XX Wet Paint	200		Unkn.	3800
XX When I Lit My Candle	200		Unkn.	4500
XX White Washing	200		Unkn.	3400
XX Whitewashing the Fence/Collotype	200		Unkn.	4000
XX Window Washer	200		Unkn.	4800
XX Winter	200		Unkn.	3500
XX Winter/Japon	25		Unkn.	3600
XX Ye Old Print Shoppe	200		Unkn.	3500
XX Your Eyes is Lookin'	200		Unkn.	4500

Cross Gallery, Inc.

Bandits & Bounty Hunters - P.A. Cross

YEAR ISSUE	EDITION LIMIT	YEAR RETD.	ISSUE PRICE	*QUOTE U.S.$
1994 Bounty Hunter	865		225.00	225
1998 Las Banditas, No Vacancy	754		225.00	225

The Gift - P.A. Cross

YEAR ISSUE	EDITION LIMIT	YEAR RETD.	ISSUE PRICE	*QUOTE U.S.$
1989 B' Achua Dlubh-bia Bii Noskiiyahi The Gift, Part II	S/O	1989	225.00	650
1993 The Gift, Part III	S/O	1993	225.00	350-1000

Half Breed Series - P.A. Cross

YEAR ISSUE	EDITION LIMIT	YEAR RETD.	ISSUE PRICE	*QUOTE U.S.$
1989 Ach-hua Dlubh: (Body Two), Half Breed	S/O	1989	190.00	1450
1990 Ach-hua Dlubh: (Body Two), Half Breed II	S/O	1990	225.00	800-1100
1991 Ach-hua Dlubh: (Body Two), Half Breed III	S/O	1991	225.00	850
1995 Ach-hua Dlubh: (Body Two), Half Breed IV	865		225.00	225
1998 Ach-hua Dlubh: (Body Two), Half Breed V	754		225.00	225
1999 Ijluupkaabsúum lichiilum Áakeenuuk (Riding Double)	754		225.00	225

Limited Edition Original Graphics - P.A. Cross

YEAR ISSUE	EDITION LIMIT	YEAR RETD.	ISSUE PRICE	*QUOTE U.S.$
1991 Bia-A-Hoosh (A Very Special Woman), Stone Lithograph	S/O	1991	500.00	500
1987 Caroline, Stone Lithograph	S/O	1987	300.00	600
1988 Maidenhood Hopi, Stone Lithograph	S/O	1988	950.00	1150
1990 Nighteyes I, Serigraph	S/O	1990	225.00	425
1989 The Red Capote, Serigraph	S/O	1989	750.00	1150
1989 Rosapina, Etching	74		1200.00	1200
1991 Wooltalkers, Serigraph	275		750.00	750

Limited Edition Prints - P.A. Cross

YEAR ISSUE	EDITION LIMIT	YEAR RETD.	ISSUE PRICE	*QUOTE U.S.$
1991 Ashpahdua Hagay Ashae-Gyoke (My Home & Heart Is Crow)	S/O	1991	225.00	225-350
1983 Ayla-Sah-Xuh-Xah (Pretty Colours, Many Designs)	S/O	1983	150.00	450
1990 Baape Ochia (Night Wind, Turquoise)	S/O	1990	185.00	370
1990 Biaachee-itah Bah-achbeh (Medicine Woman Scout)	S/O	1990	225.00	525
1984 Blue Beaded Hair Ties	S/O	1984	85.00	330
1991 The Blue Shawl	S/O	1991	185.00	275
1987 Caroline	S/O	1987	45.00	145
1989 Chey-ayjeh: Prey	S/O	1989	190.00	325-600
1988 Dance Apache	S/O	1988	190.00	360
1987 Dii-tah-shteh Ee-wihza-ahook (A Coat of much Value)	S/O	1987	90.00	740
1989 The Dreamer	S/O	1989	190.00	600
1987 The Elkskin Robe	S/O	1987	190.00	640
1990 Eshte	S/O	1990	185.00	200
1986 Grand Entry	S/O	1986	85.00	85
1983 Isbaaloo Eetshiileehcheek (Sorting Her Beads)	S/O	1983	150.00	1750
1990 Ishia-Kahda #1 (Quiet One)	S/O	1990	185.00	400
1988 Ma-a-luppis-she-La-dus (She is above everything, nothing can touch her)	S/O	1988	190.00	525
1984 Profile of Caroline	S/O	1984	85.00	185
1986 The Red Capote	S/O	1986	150.00	850
1987 The Red Necklace	S/O	1987	90.00	210
1989 Teesa Waits To Dance	S/O	1989	135.00	180
1984 Thick Lodge Clan Boy: Crow Indian	475		85.00	85
1987 Tina	S/O	1987	45.00	110
1985 The Water Vision	S/O	1985	150.00	325
1984 Whistling Water Clan Girl: Crow Indian	S/O	1984	85.00	85
1993 Winter Girl Bride	1,730		225.00	225
1986 Winter Morning	S/O	1986	185.00	1450
1986 The Winter Shawl	S/O	1986	150.00	1600

Miniature Line - P.A. Cross

YEAR ISSUE	EDITION LIMIT	YEAR RETD.	ISSUE PRICE	*QUOTE U.S.$
1991 BJ	S/O	1995	80.00	80
1993 Braids	447		80.00	80
1993 Daybreak	447		80.00	80
1991 The Floral Shawl	S/O	1995	80.00	80
1991 Kendra	S/O	1995	80.00	80
1993 Ponytails	447		80.00	80
1993 Sundown	447		80.00	80
1991 Watercolour Study #2 For Half Breed	S/O	1995	80.00	80

The Painted Ladies' Suite - P.A. Cross

YEAR ISSUE	EDITION LIMIT	YEAR RETD.	ISSUE PRICE	*QUOTE U.S.$
1992 Acoria (Crow; Seat of Honor)	S/O	1995	185.00	185
1992 Avisola	S/O	1995	185.00	185
1992 Dah-say (Crow; Heart)	S/O	1995	185.00	185
1992 Itza-chu (Apache; The Eagle)	S/O	1995	185.00	185
1992 Kel'hoya (Hopi; Little Sparrow Hawk)	S/O	1995	185.00	185
1992 The Painted Ladies	S/O	1992	225.00	1200
1999 Sus(h)gah-daydus(h) (Crow; Quick)	447		185.00	185
1999 Tze-go-juni (Chiricahua Apache)	447		185.00	185

Star Quilt Series - P.A. Cross

YEAR ISSUE	EDITION LIMIT	YEAR RETD.	ISSUE PRICE	*QUOTE U.S.$
1988 The Quilt Makers	S/O	1988	190.00	1200
1986 Reflections	S/O	1986	185.00	865
1985 Winter Warmth	S/O	1985	150.00	900-1215

Wolf Series - P.A. Cross

YEAR ISSUE	EDITION LIMIT	YEAR RETD.	ISSUE PRICE	*QUOTE U.S.$
1990 Agnjnaug Amaguut;Inupiag (Women With Her Wolves)	S/O	1993	325.00	350-750
1993 Ahmah-ghut, Tuhtu-loo; Eelahn-nuht Kah-auhk (Wolves and Caribou; My Furs and My Friends)	1,050		255.00	255
1989 Biagoht Eecuebeh Hehsheesh-Checah: (Red Ridinghood and Her Wolves), Gift I	S/O	1989	225.00	1500-2500

*Quotes have been rounded up to nearest dollar

YEAR ISSUE	EDITION LIMIT	YEAR RETD.	ISSUE PRICE	*QUOTE U.S.$
1997 Cheedé Bilaxpáake Áashe Áakeeshdak (Wolf People Crossing the River)	S/O	1998	225.00	225
1985 Dii-tah-shteh Bii-wik; Chedah-bah liidah (My Very Own Protective Covering; Walks w/ Wolf Woman)	S/O	1985	185.00	3275
1987 The Morning Star Gives Long Otter His Hoop Medicine Power	S/O	1987	190.00	1800-2500

Flambro Imports

Emmett Kelly Jr. Lithographs - B. Leighton-Jones

YEAR ISSUE	EDITION LIMIT	YEAR RETD.	ISSUE PRICE	*QUOTE U.S.$
1995 All Star Circus	2 Yr.		150.00	150
1994 EKJ 70th Birthday Commemorative	1,994		150.00	150
1994 I Love You	2 Yr.	1996	90.00	90
1994 Joyful Noise	2 Yr.	1996	90.00	90
1994 Picture Worth 1,000 Words	2 Yr.	1996	90.00	90

Gartlan USA

Lithograph - Various

YEAR ISSUE	EDITION LIMIT	YEAR RETD.	ISSUE PRICE	*QUOTE U.S.$
1986 George Brett-"The Swing" - J. Martin	2,000	1990	85.00	200-250
1991 Joe Montana - M. Taylor	500	1994	495.00	600-700
1989 Kareem Abdul Jabbar-The Record Setter - M. Taylor	1,989	1993	85.00	275-395
1991 Negro League 1st World Series (print) - Unknown	1,924	1993	109.00	125
1987 Roger Staubach - C. Soileau	1,979	1992	85.00	200-300

Ringo Starr - B. Forbes

YEAR ISSUE	EDITION LIMIT	YEAR RETD.	ISSUE PRICE	*QUOTE U.S.$
1998 Signed Drum Sticks & Lithograph	500		495.00	495
1998 Signed Drum Sticks & Lithograph A/P	50		595.00	595

Glynda Turley Prints

Turley - Canvas - G. Turley

YEAR ISSUE	EDITION LIMIT	YEAR RETD.	ISSUE PRICE	*QUOTE U.S.$
1996 Abundance III	350		190.00	190
1997 Abundance IV	350		190.00	190
1997 Black-eyed Susans and Blackberries	350		140.00	140
1996 Chrysanthemums and Apples	350		140.00	140
1998 Cottage Garden	350		286.00	286
1992 Courtyard II	200	1996	140.00	140
1994 Courtyard III	350		140.00	140
1988 Elegance	350		130.00	130
1991 Floral Fancy	150		130.00	130
1992 Flower Garden	350		130.00	130
1998 Garden Favorites III	350		286.00	286
1990 Garden Room	250		130.00	130
1992 The Garden Wreath II	200	1996	130.00	130
1994 The Garden Wreath III	350		140.00	140
1994 Georgia Sweet	350		140.00	140
1992 Grand Glory I	350		160.00	160
1992 Grand Glory II	350		160.00	160
1995 Grand Glory III	350		160.00	160
1995 Grand Glory IV	350		160.00	160
1997 Hand in Hand	350		160.00	160
1992 In Full Bloom	200	N/A	160.00	160
1994 In Full Bloom II	350		160.00	160
1995 In Full Bloom III	350		140.00	140
1988 Iris Basket II	350		130.00	130
1990 Iris Basket III	50	1997	130.00	130
1991 Iris Basket IV	25		130.00	130
1989 Iris Parade	350	1996	130.00	130
1997 Keeping Watch	350		214.00	214
1988 La Belle IV	25		130.00	130
1995 Little Red River	350		190.00	190
1995 Mabry In Spring	350		160.00	160
1992 Old Mill Stream	350	N/A	130.00	130
1993 Old Mill Stream II	350	1996	130.00	130
1994 Old Mill Stream III	350		190.00	190
1996 Old Mill Stream IV	350		190.00	190
1988 Once Upon A Time	200		130.00	130
1996 Pears and Roses	350		140.00	140
1989 Petals In Pink	100		190.00	190
1997 Plums and Pansies	350		140.00	140
1989 Pretty Pickings I	350		130.00	130
1989 Pretty Pickings II	300		130.00	130
1989 Pretty Pickings III	100		130.00	130
1993 Primrose Lane II	300		130.00	130
1995 Remember When	350		190.00	190
1998 Ring Around The Rosy	350		232.00	232
1991 Secret Garden	350		130.00	130
1994 Secret Garden II	350		130.00	130
1996 Secret Garden III	350		160.00	160
1991 Simply Southern	350	1996	160.00	160
1998 Southern Elegance III	350		190.00	190
1992 Southern Sunday	200		140.00	140
1995 Southern Sunday II	350		190.00	190
1993 A Southern Tradition II	350		190.00	190
1994 A Southern Tradition IV	350		190.00	190
1995 A Southern Tradition V	350		190.00	190
1998 Spring Flora III	350		190.00	190
1993 Spring's Promise II	300		130.00	130
1988 Spring's Return	350		130.00	130
1995 Summer in Victoria	350		130.00	130
1994 Summer Stroll	350	1997	160.00	160
1990 Sweet Nothings	350		130.00	130
1997 Wading at the Bridge	350		214.00	214
1996 Wreath of Spring	350		140.00	140

Turley - Print - G. Turley

YEAR ISSUE	EDITION LIMIT	YEAR RETD.	ISSUE PRICE	*QUOTE U.S.$
1996 Abundance III	7,500		73.00	73
1996 Abundance III A/P	50		109.50	110
1997 Abundance IV	3,500		73.00	73
1997 Abundance IV A/P	50		109.50	110
1995 Almost An Angel	7,500		56.00	56
1995 Almost An Angel A/P	50		84.00	84
1986 Attic Curiosity	2,000	N/A	15.00	15
1986 Attic Curiosity A/P	50	N/A	25.00	25
1997 Black-eyed Susans and Blackberries	7,500		64.00	64
1997 Black-eyed Susans and Blackberries A/P	50		96.00	96
1986 Busy Bodies I	2,000	N/A	25.00	25
1986 Busy Bodies I A/P	50	N/A	40.00	40
1986 Busy Bodies II	2,000	N/A	25.00	25
1986 Busy Bodies II A/P	50	N/A	40.00	40
1986 Callie And Company I	2,000	N/A	30.00	30
1986 Callie And Company I A/P	50	N/A	50.00	50
1987 Callie And Company II	3,000	N/A	30.00	30
1987 Callie And Company II A/P	50	N/A	50.00	50
1988 Calling On Callie	5,000	1996	30.00	30
1988 Calling On Callie A/P	50		45.00	45
1990 Childhood Memories I	3,500		30.00	30
1990 Childhood Memories I A/P	50		45.00	45
1990 Childhood Memories II	3,500		30.00	30
1990 Childhood Memories II A/P	50		45.00	45
1996 Chrysanthemums and Apples	7,500		64.00	64
1996 Chrysanthemums and Apples A/P	50		96.00	96
1988 Circle of Friends	5,000	1996	25.00	25
1988 Circle Of Friends A/P	50	N/A	40.00	40
1990 The Coming Out Party	3,500		35.00	35
1998 Cottage Garden	2,500		108.00	108
1998 Cottage Garden A/P	50		162.00	162
1991 The Courtyard I	2,500	N/A	47.00	47
1991 The Courtyard I A/P	50	N/A	70.50	71
1992 The Courtyard II	2,500	N/A	50.00	50
1992 The Courtyard II A/P	50		75.00	75
1994 The Courtyard III A/P	50		91.50	92
1990 Dear To My Heart	3,500		35.00	35
1990 Dear To My Heart A/P	50		52.50	53
1988 Elegance	5,000		30.00	30
1988 Elegance A/P	50		45.00	45
1986 A Family Affair	2,500	N/A	25.00	25
1986 A Family Affair A/P	50	N/A	40.00	40
1984 Feeding Time I	1,000	N/A	50.00	50
1984 Feeding Time I A/P	50	N/A	75.00	75
1984 Feeding Time II	1,000	N/A	25.00	25
1984 Feeding Time II A/P	50	N/A	40.00	40
1987 Fence Row Gathering I	3,000	N/A	30.00	30
1987 Fence Row Gathering I A/P	50	N/A	50.00	50
1988 Fence Row Gathering II	5,000	N/A	30.00	60-145
1988 Fence Row Gathering II A/P	50	N/A	50.00	50
1991 Floral Fancy	3,500	N/A	40.00	40
1991 Floral Fancy A/P	50		60.00	60
1992 The Flower Garden	2,500	1996	43.00	43
1992 The Flower Garden A/P	50		64.50	65
1986 Flowers And Lace	3,000	N/A	25.00	25
1986 Flowers And Lace A/P	50	N/A	40.00	40
1988 Flowers For Mommy	5,000	N/A	25.00	25
1988 Flowers For Mommy A/P	50	N/A	40.00	40
1990 Forever Roses	3,500		30.00	30
1990 Forever Roses A/P	50		45.00	45
1998 Garden Favorites III	2,500		108.00	108
1998 Garden Favorites III A/P	50		162.00	162
1987 The Garden Gate	3,000	N/A	30.00	30
1987 The Garden Gate A/P	50	N/A	50.00	50
1990 Garden Room	3,500	N/A	40.00	40
1991 The Garden Wreath I	2,500	N/A	47.00	47
1991 The Garden Wreath I A/P	50	N/A	60.00	60
1992 The Garden Wreath II	2,500	N/A	50.00	50
1992 The Garden Wreath II A/P	50	N/A	75.00	75
1994 The Garden Wreath III	5,000		61.00	61
1994 The Garden Wreath III A/P	50		91.50	92
1994 Georgia Sweet	2,500		50.00	50
1994 Georgia Sweet A/P	50		75.00	75
1995 Glynda's Garden	7,500		73.00	73
1995 Glynda's Garden A/P	50		109.50	110
1993 Grand Glory I	2,500	N/A	53.00	53
1992 Grand Glory I A/P	50		79.50	80
1993 Grand Glory II	2,500	N/A	53.00	53
1992 Grand Glory II A/P	50		79.50	80
1995 Grand Glory III	7,500		65.00	65
1995 Grand Glory III A/P	50		97.50	98
1995 Grand Glory IV	7,500		65.00	65
1995 Grand Glory IV A/P	50		97.50	98
1997 Hand in Hand	3,500		69.00	69
1997 Hand in Hand A/P	50		103.50	104
1984 Heading Home I	1,000	N/A	25.00	25
1984 Heading Home I A/P	50	N/A	40.00	40
1984 Heading Home II	1,000	N/A	25.00	25
1984 Heading Home II A/P	50	N/A	40.00	40
1984 Heading Home III	1,000	N/A	25.00	25
1984 Heading Home III A/P	50	N/A	40.00	40
1987 Heart Wreath I	3,000	N/A	25.00	25
1987 Heart Wreath I A/P	50	N/A	40.00	40
1988 Heart Wreath II	3,500	N/A	25.00	25
1988 Heart Wreath II A/P	50	N/A	40.00	40
1989 Heart Wreath III	3,500	N/A	25.00	25
1989 Heart Wreath III A/P	50	N/A	40.00	40
1987 Hollyhocks I	3,000	N/A	30.00	30
1987 Hollyhocks I A/P	50	N/A	50.00	50
1990 Hollyhocks II	3,500	N/A	25.00	25
1990 Hollyhocks II A/P	50	N/A	60.00	60
1995 Hollyhocks III	7,500		69.00	69
1995 Hollyhocks III A/P	50		103.50	104
1992 In Full Bloom I	2,500	N/A	53.00	53
1992 In Full Bloom I A/P	50	N/A	79.50	80
1994 In Full Bloom II	3,500	N/A	65.00	65
1994 In Full Bloom II A/P	50		97.50	98
1995 In Full Bloom III	7,500		64.00	64
1995 In Full Bloom III A/P	50		96.00	96
1984 In One Ear And Out The Other	950	N/A	50.00	50-165
1984 In One Ear And Out The Other A/P	50	N/A	75.00	75
1987 Iris Basket I	3,000	N/A	30.00	30
1987 Iris Basket I A/P	50	N/A	50.00	50
1988 Iris Basket II	3,500	N/A	30.00	30
1988 Iris Basket II A/P	50	N/A	50.00	50
1990 Iris Basket III	3,500	N/A	35.00	35
1990 Iris Basket III A/P	50	N/A	52.50	53
1991 Iris Basket IV	2,500		35.00	35
1991 Iris Basket IV A/P	50		52.50	53
1989 Iris Parade	3,500	1996	35.00	148
1989 Iris Parade A/P	50		52.50	53
1997 Keeping Watch	7,500		77.00	77
1997 Keeping Watch A/P	50		115.50	116
1985 La Belle I	750	N/A	25.00	25
1985 La Belle I A/P	50	N/A	40.00	40
1986 La Belle II	2,000	N/A	25.00	25
1986 La Belle II A/P	50	N/A	40.00	40
1986 La Belle III	3,500	N/A	25.00	25
1986 La Belle III A/P	50	N/A	40.00	40
1988 La Belle IV	5,000	N/A	30.00	30
1988 La Belle IV A/P	50	N/A	50.00	50
1995 Little Red River	7,500		73.00	73
1995 Little Red River A/P	50		109.50	110
1995 Mabry In Spring	7,500		65.00	65
1995 Mabry In Spring A/P	50		97.50	98
1987 Mauve Iris I	3,000	N/A	10.00	10
1987 Mauve Iris I A/P	50	N/A	25.00	25
1987 Mauve Iris II	3,000	N/A	10.00	10
1987 Mauve Iris II A/P	50	N/A	25.00	25
1983 Now I Lay Me	1,000	N/A	50.00	50
1983 Now I Lay Me A/P	50	N/A	75.00	75
1989 Old Favorites	3,500	N/A	35.00	35
1989 Old Favorites A/P	50	N/A	52.50	53
1988 Old Friends	5,000	N/A	30.00	30
1988 Old Friends A/P	50	N/A	50.00	50
1992 Old Mill Stream I	2,500	N/A	40.00	40
1992 Old Mill Stream I A/P	50		60.00	60
1993 Old Mill Stream II	2,500	N/A	43.00	43
1993 Old Mill Stream II A/P	50		64.50	65
1994 Old Mill Stream III	3,500	N/A	69.00	69
1994 Old Mill Stream III A/P	50		103.50	104
1996 Old Mill Stream IV	7,500		73.00	73
1996 Old Mill Stream IV A/P	50		109.50	110
1988 Once Upon A Time	5,000	N/A	30.00	30
1988 Once Upon A Time A/P	50		45.00	45
1988 Past Times	5,000	N/A	30.00	30
1988 Past Times A/P	50	N/A	50.00	50
1996 Pears and Roses	7,500		64.00	64
1996 Pears and Roses A/P	50		96.00	96
1988 Peeping Tom	5,000	N/A	35.00	35
1988 Peeping Tom A/P	50	N/A	55.00	55
1989 Petals In Pink	3,500	N/A	30.00	30-85
1989 Petals In Pink A/P	50	N/A	79.50	80
1987 Playing Hookie	3,000	N/A	30.00	30
1987 Playing Hookie A/P	50	N/A	50.00	50
1988 Playing Hookie Again	5,000	N/A	30.00	30
1988 Playing Hookie Again A/P	50	N/A	50.00	50
1997 Plums and Pansies	7,500		64.00	64
1997 Plums and Pansies A/P	50		96.00	96
1988 The Porch	5,000	N/A	30.00	30
1988 The Porch A/P	50	N/A	50.00	50
1989 Pretty Pickings I	3,500	N/A	30.00	130
1989 Pretty Pickings I A/P	50		45.00	45
1989 Pretty Pickings II	3,500		35.00	35
1989 Pretty Pickings II A/P	50		52.50	53
1989 Pretty Pickings III	3,500		30.00	30
1989 Pretty Pickings III A/P	50		45.00	45
1991 Primrose Lane I	3,500	N/A	40.00	40
1991 Primrose Lane I A/P	50	N/A	60.00	60
1993 Primrose Lane II	2,500	N/A	43.00	43
1993 Primrose Lane II A/P	50		64.50	65
1995 Remember When	7,500		73.00	73
1995 Remember When A/P	50		109.50	110
1998 Ring Around The Rosy	2,500		100.00	100
1998 Ring Around The Rosy A/P	50		150.00	150
1983 Sad Face Clown	950	N/A	50.00	50
1983 Sad Face Clown A/P	50	N/A	75.00	75
1991 Secret Garden I	3,500	N/A	40.00	40
1991 Secret Garden I A/P	50		60.00	60
1994 Secret Garden II A/P	50		79.50	80
1996 Secret Garden III	7,500		65.00	65
1996 Secret Garden III A/P	50		97.50	98
1991 Simply Southern	3,500	N/A	53.00	53
1991 Simply Southern A/P	50	N/A	79.50	80
1985 Snips N Snails	750	N/A	25.00	25
1985 Snips N Snails A/P	50	N/A	40.00	40
1998 Southern Elegance III	3,500		73.00	73
1998 Southern Elegance III A/P	50		109.50	110
1992 Southern Sunday I	2,500	N/A	50.00	50
1992 Southern Sunday I A/P	50		75.00	75
1995 Southern Sunday II	7,500		73.00	73
1995 Southern Sunday II A/P	50		109.50	110

*Quotes have been rounded up to nearest dollar

YEAR ISSUE	EDITION LIMIT	YEAR RETD.	ISSUE PRICE	*QUOTE U.S.$
1993 A Southern Tradition II	3,500	N/A	60.00	60
1993 A Southern Tradition II A/P	50	N/A	90.00	90
1994 A Southern Tradition IV	5,000	N/A	69.00	69
1994 A Southern Tradition IV A/P	50		103.50	104
1995 A Southern Tradition V	7,500		73.00	73
1995 A Southern Tradition V A/P	50		109.50	110
1988 A Special Time	5,000	N/A	30.00	30
1988 A Special Time A/P	50		45.00	45
1998 Spring Flora III	3,500		73.00	73
1998 Spring Flora III A/P	50		109.50	110
1993 Spring's Promise II	2,500		43.00	43
1993 Spring's Promise III A/P	50		64.50	65
1988 Spring's Return	5,000		35.00	35
1988 Spring's Return A/P	50		52.50	53
1983 Stepping Out	1,000	N/A	50.00	50
1983 Stepping Out A/P	50	N/A	75.00	75
1985 Sugar N Spice	750	N/A	25.00	25
1985 Sugar N Spice A/P	50	N/A	40.00	40
1987 A Summer Day	3,000	N/A	30.00	30
1987 A Summer Day A/P	50	N/A	50.00	50
1995 Summer In Victoria	7,500		53.00	53
1995 Summer In Victoria A/P	50		79.50	80
1994 Summer Stroll	3,500	N/A	65.00	65
1994 Summer Stroll A/P	50	1997	97.50	98
1990 Sweet Nothings	3,500		40.00	40
1990 Sweet Nothings A/P	50		60.00	60
1987 Victorian Bouquet I	3,500	N/A	25.00	25
1987 Victorian Bouquet I A/P	50	N/A	40.00	40
1989 Victorian Bouquet II	3,500	N/A	25.00	25
1997 Wading at the Bridge	7,500		77.00	77
1997 Wading at the Bridge A/P	50		115.50	116
1986 White Iris	2,000	N/A	25.00	25
1986 White Iris A/P	50	N/A	40.00	40
1987 Wild Roses I	3,000	N/A	30.00	30
1987 Wild Roses I A/P	50	N/A	50.00	50
1990 Wild Roses II	3,500		35.00	35
1990 Wild Roses II A/P	50		52.50	53
1996 Wreath of Spring	7,500		64.00	64
1996 Wreath of Spring A/P	50		96.00	96

Greenwich Workshop

Austin - C. Austin

YEAR ISSUE	EDITION LIMIT	YEAR RETD.	ISSUE PRICE	*QUOTE U.S.$
1997 Saturday Near Sunset	850		150.00	150
1996 The Storm	850		165.00	165
1996 Wheat Field	850		125.00	125

Ballantyne - Ballantyne

YEAR ISSUE	EDITION LIMIT	YEAR RETD.	ISSUE PRICE	*QUOTE U.S.$
1995 John's New Pup	850		150.00	150
1995 Kate and Her Fiddle	850		150.00	150
1996 Partners	850		150.00	150

Bama - J. Bama

YEAR ISSUE	EDITION LIMIT	YEAR RETD.	ISSUE PRICE	*QUOTE U.S.$
1993 Art of James Bama Book with Chester Medicine Crow Fathers Flag Print	2,500	N/A	345.00	345-365
1981 At a Mountain Man Wedding	1,500	N/A	145.00	145-200
1981 At Burial Gallager and Blind Bill	1,650	N/A	135.00	150
1988 Bittin' Up-Rimrock Ranch	1,250	N/A	195.00	575-635
1992 Blackfeet War Robe	1,000		195.00	195
1995 Blackfoot Ceremonial Headdress (Iris Print)	200		850.00	850
1987 Buck Norris-Crossed Sabres Ranch	1,000	N/A	195.00	700-795
1990 Buffalo Bill	1,250	N/A	210.00	165-210
1993 The Buffalo Dance	1,000		195.00	195
1991 Ceremonial Lance	1,250		225.00	225
1996 Cheyene Split Horn Headdress (Iris Print)	200		850.00	850
1994 Cheyenne Dog Soldier	1,000		225.00	225
1991 Chuck Wagon	1,000		225.00	225
1975 Chuck Wagon in the Snow	1,000	N/A	50.00	1100-1200
1992 Coming' Round the Bend	1,000		195.00	195
1978 Contemporary Sioux Indian	1,000	N/A	75.00	1325-1600
1995 A Cowboy Named Anne	1,000		185.00	185
1992 Crow Cavalry Scout	1,000		195.00	195
1977 A Crow Indian	1,000	N/A	65.00	150-165
1982 Crow Indian Dancer	1,250		150.00	150
1988 Crow Indian From Lodge Grass	1,250		225.00	225
1988 Dan-Mountain Man	1,250	N/A	195.00	165-195
1983 The Davilla Brothers-Bronc Riders	1,250		145.00	145
1983 Don Walker-Bareback Rider	1,250	N/A	85.00	175-190
1991 The Drift on Skull Creek Pass	1,500		225.00	225
1979 Heritage	1,500	N/A	75.00	235-250
1978 Indian at Crow Fair	1,500	N/A	75.00	125-150
1988 Indian Wearing War Medicine Bonnet	1,000	N/A	225.00	225
1980 Ken Blackbird	1,500	N/A	95.00	150-165
1974 Ken Hunder, Working Cowboy	1,000	N/A	55.00	600-695
1989 Little Fawn-Cree Indian Girl	1,250	N/A	195.00	165-195
1979 Little Star	1,500	N/A	80.00	995-1325
1993 Magua-"The Last of the Mohicans"	1,000		225.00	225
1993 Making Horse Medicine	1,000		225.00	225
1978 Mountain Man	1,000	N/A	75.00	265-350
1980 Mountain Man 1820-1840 Period	1,500	N/A	115.00	375-395
1979 Mountain Man and His Fox	1,500	N/A	90.00	325-350
1982 Mountain Man with Rifle	1,250	N/A	135.00	135-195
1978 A Mountain Ute	1,000	N/A	75.00	650-700
1992 Northern Cheyene Wolf Scout	1,000		195.00	195
1981 Old Arapaho Story-Teller	1,500	N/A	135.00	135-175
1980 Old Saddle in the Snow	1,500	N/A	75.00	375-525
1980 Old Sod House	1,500	N/A	80.00	375-425
1981 Oldest Living Crow Indian	1,500	N/A	135.00	150-165
1993 On the North Fork of the Shoshoni	1,000		195.00	195
1990 Paul Newman as Butch Cassidy & Video	2,000		250.00	250
1981 Portrait of a Sioux	1,500	N/A	135.00	135-150
1979 Pre-Columbian Indian with Atlatl	1,500	N/A	75.00	150-165
1991 Ready to Rendezvous	1,000		225.00	225
1995 Ready to Ride	1,000		185.00	185
1990 Ridin' the Rims	1,250	N/A	210.00	210-215
1991 Riding the High Country	1,250		225.00	225
1978 Rookie Bronc Rider	1,000	N/A	75.00	175-190
1976 Sage Grinder	1,000	N/A	65.00	995-1100
1980 Sheep Skull in Drift	1,500	N/A	75.00	150-165
1974 Shoshone Chief	1,000	N/A	65.00	1000-1200
1982 Sioux Indian with Eagle Feather	1,250	N/A	150.00	125-150
1992 Sioux Subchief	1,000		195.00	195
1994 Slim Warren, The Old Cowboy	1,000		125.00	125
1983 Southwest Indian Father & Son	1,250		145.00	145
1977 Timber Jack Joe	1,000	N/A	65.00	950-975
1988 The Volunteer	1,500		225.00	225
1996 The Warrior (Iris Print)	200		550.00	550
1987 Winter on Trout Creek	1,000	N/A	150.00	295-300
1981 Winter Trapping	1,500	N/A	150.00	525-595
1980 Young Plains Indian	1,500	N/A	125.00	1050-1500
1990 Young Sheepherder	1,500		225.00	225

Bastin - M. Bastin

YEAR ISSUE	EDITION LIMIT	YEAR RETD.	ISSUE PRICE	*QUOTE U.S.$
1997 Autumn Celebration	1,950		95.00	95
1997 Dinner Guests	2,500	1998	95.00	195-215
1997 Dinner Guests (framed)	34		277.00	277
1998 Garden Party	1,950		110.00	110

Bean - A. Bean

YEAR ISSUE	EDITION LIMIT	YEAR RETD.	ISSUE PRICE	*QUOTE U.S.$
1993 Conrad Gordon and Bean:The Fantasy	1,000		385.00	500
1997 Heavenly Reflections	850		275.00	275
1987 Helping Hands	850		150.00	150
1998 Homeward Bound	550		215.00	215
1995 Houston, We Have a Problem	1,000	1998	500.00	500
1988 How It Felt to Walk on the Moon	850	N/A	150.00	150
1992 In Flight	850	1998	385.00	385
1994 In The Beginning Apollo 25 C/S	1,000	N/A	450.00	550
1997 Reaching For the Stars (canvas)	1,500		2200.00	2200

Beecham - G. Beecham

YEAR ISSUE	EDITION LIMIT	YEAR RETD.	ISSUE PRICE	*QUOTE U.S.$
1998 Bustin' Through	750		150.00	150
1998 Tag Team	750		150.00	150

Blackshear - T. Blackshear

YEAR ISSUE	EDITION LIMIT	YEAR RETD.	ISSUE PRICE	*QUOTE U.S.$
1994 Beauty and the Beast	1,000	1998	225.00	225-350
1996 Dance of the Wind & Storm	850		195.00	195
1996 Golden Breeze	850		225.00	225
1993 Hero Frederick Douglass	746		20.00	20
1993 Hero Harriet Tubman	753		20.00	20
1993 Hero Martin Luther King, Jr.	762		20.00	20
1993 Heroes of Our Heritage Portfolio	5,000		35.00	35
1995 Intimacy	550		850.00	1200
1995 Night in Day	850		195.00	195
1994 Swansong	1,000		175.00	175

Blake - B. Blake

YEAR ISSUE	EDITION LIMIT	YEAR RETD.	ISSUE PRICE	*QUOTE U.S.$
1995 The Old Double Diamond	850		175.00	175
1994 West of the Moon	650		195.00	195

Blish - C. Blish

YEAR ISSUE	EDITION LIMIT	YEAR RETD.	ISSUE PRICE	*QUOTE U.S.$
1997 A Change in the Air w/book	950		195.00	195
1998 Father The Hour Has Come (framed)	559		95.00	95
1998 Father The Hour Has Come (gold frame)	621		150.00	150
1998 Father The Hour Has Come (unframed)	4,186		70.00	70
1997 Gathering Sea Oats	550		135.00	135
1998 He Stills the Sea (cherry frame)	Open		150.00	150
1998 He Stills the Sea (gold frame)	Open		150.00	150
1998 He Stills the Sea (unframed)	Open		110.00	110
1997 Island Church (framed)	149		95.00	95
1997 Jennifer (framed)	150		95.00	95
1997 Skywatcher (framed)	148		95.00	95
1997 The Swan (framed)	149		95.00	95
1997 Trinity (framed)	148		95.00	95
1997 Windswept Headlands (framed)	144		95.00	95

Blossom - C. Blossom

YEAR ISSUE	EDITION LIMIT	YEAR RETD.	ISSUE PRICE	*QUOTE U.S.$
1987 After the Last Drift	950		145.00	145
1984 Ah Your Majesty (poster)	N/A	N/A	45.00	45
1985 Allerton on the East River	650	N/A	145.00	145
1996 Arthur James Heading Out	850		150.00	150
1988 Black Rock	950		150.00	150
1984 December Moonrise	650	N/A	135.00	135-150
1984 December Moonrise, remarque	25	N/A	175.00	175
1990 Ebb Tide	950		175.00	175
1983 First Out	450	N/A	90.00	600-750
1983 First Out, remarque	25	N/A	190.00	800-1000
1987 Gloucester Mackeral Seiners	950		145.00	145
1998 Gold Rush Twilight	450		195.00	195
1998 Gold Rush Twilight, remarque	100		395.00	395
1989 Harbor Light	950		165.00	165
1988 Heading Home	950	N/A	150.00	250
1998 Morning Set	450		195.00	195
1985 Off Palmer Land	850		145.00	145
1995 Onshore Breeze	850		175.00	175
1992 Port of Call	850		175.00	175
1986 Potomac By Moonlight	950	N/A	145.00	145
1987 San Francisco-Eve of the Gold Rush	950		150.00	150
1992 Silhouette	850		175.00	175
1986 Southport @ Twilight	950		145.00	145
1985 Tranquil Dawn	650		95.00	95
1994 Traveling in Company	850		175.00	175
1994 Traveling in Company, Remarque	100		415.00	415
1992 Windward	950		175.00	175
1986 Winter Dawn @ Boston Wharf	850		85.00	85

Bralds - B. Bralds

YEAR ISSUE	EDITION LIMIT	YEAR RETD.	ISSUE PRICE	*QUOTE U.S.$
1997 Abyssinian	175		195.00	195
1998 American Shorthair	175		195.00	195
1995 Bag Ladies	2,500	1995	150.00	675-725
1996 Basket Cases	2,500	1996	150.00	175-225
1997 British Blue Short Hair (Nine Lives)	175		195.00	195
1996 Cabinet Meeting	2,000	1996	150.00	200-250
1996 Cheese	2,000		150.00	150
1997 Chocolate Point Siamese	175		195.00	195
1997 Cinnamon Tabby Maine Coon	175		195.00	195
1998 A Mixed Bag	2,500		125.00	125
1997 Nine Lives Suite - (Brit., Snowshoe, Persian)	1,750		150.00	150
1998 Nine Lives Suite - (Sho/Bur/Tabby)	1,750		150.00	150
1997 Nine Lives Suite - (Siamese, Abyssinian, Coon)	1,750		150.00	150
1997 Persian (Nine Lives)	175		195.00	195
1997 Siamese Twins	2,250		150.00	150
1997 Snowshoe (Nine Lives)	175		195.00	195

Bullas - W. Bullas

YEAR ISSUE	EDITION LIMIT	YEAR RETD.	ISSUE PRICE	*QUOTE U.S.$
1998 Ballet Parking	750		110.00	110
1995 The Big Game	1,500		95.00	95
1993 Billy the Pig	850		95.00	172
1997 A Chick Off The Old Block (framed)	57		125.00	125
1995 The Chimp Shot	1,000		95.00	95
1994 Clucks Unlimited	850		95.00	95
1995 The Consultant	1,000		95.00	95
1994 Court of Appeals	850	1995	95.00	275-395
1995 Dog Byte	1,000	1998	95.00	175-195
1997 Duck Tape (framed)	296		125.00	125
1994 Ductor	850		95.00	95
1997 Federal Duck Stump	1,250		95.00	95
1998 A Fool And His Bunny	950		95.00	95
1998 A Fool And His Bunny (framed)	Open		150.00	150
1995 fowl ball...	1,500		95.00	95
1994 Fridays After Five	850		95.00	95
1998 The House Swine	950		125.00	125
1995 Legal Eagles	1,000		95.00	95
1993 Mr. Harry Buns	850	N/A	95.00	95
1996 The Nerd Dogs	1,500		95.00	95
1997 No Assembly Required	99		125.00	125
1993 Our Ladies of the Front Lawn	850		95.00	95
1997 Our of the Woods (framed)	320		125.00	125
1993 The Pale Prince	850		110.00	110
1993 Sand Trap Pro	850	1998	95.00	95-195
1997 Sock Hop (framed)	211		125.00	125
1993 Some Set of Buns	850		95.00	95
1997 Supermom (framed)	100		125.00	125
1995 tennis, anyone?	1,000		95.00	95
1993 Wine-Oceros	850	1998	95.00	595
1993 You Rang, Madam?	850		95.00	114
1996 Zippo...The Fire Eater	850		95.00	95

Christensen - J. Christensen

YEAR ISSUE	EDITION LIMIT	YEAR RETD.	ISSUE PRICE	*QUOTE U.S.$
1989 The Annunciation	850	N/A	175.00	215-225
1995 Balancing Act	3,500	N/A	185.00	185-215
1996 The Bassonist	2,500		125.00	125
1996 The Believer's Etching Edition	1,000		795.00	795
1998 Benediction	950		150.00	150
1990 The Burden of the Responsible Man	850	N/A	145.00	1000-1650
1991 The Candleman	850	N/A	160.00	200-350
1993 College of Magical Knowledge	4,500	N/A	185.00	325
1993 College of Magical Knowledge, remarque	500	N/A	252.50	450-500
1996 Court of the Faeries	3,500		245.00	245
1991 Diggery Diggery Dare-Etching	75	N/A	210.00	600-1100
1994 Evening Angels	4,000	N/A	195.00	195
1994 Evening Angels w/Art Furnishings Frame	200	N/A	800.00	800
1989 Fantasies of the Sea-poster	Open		35.00	35
1995 Fishing	2,500	N/A	145.00	175-190
1993 Getting it Right	4,000	N/A	185.00	100-185
1985 The Gift For Mrs. Claus	3,500	N/A	80.00	550-600
1991 Jack Be Nimble-Etching	75	N/A	210.00	1425
1986 Jonah	850	N/A	95.00	375-395
1991 Lawrence and a Bear	850	N/A	145.00	595-800
1998 Lawyer More Than Adequately Attired	950		150.00	150
1987 Low Tech-Poster	Open		35.00	35
1991 Man in the Moon-Etching	75	N/A	210.00	650-700
1988 The Man Who Minds the Moon	850	N/A	145.00	600-650
1991 Mother Goose-Etching	75	N/A	210.00	875-1200
1987 Old Man with a Lot on His Mind	850	N/A	85.00	650-725
1986 Olde World Santa	3,500	N/A	80.00	650-695
1992 The Oldest Angel	850	N/A	125.00	1000-1225
1992 The Oldest Angel-Etching	75	N/A	210.00	1550
1991 Once Upon a Time	1,500	N/A	175.00	1100-1650
1991 Once Upon a Time, remarque	500	N/A	220.00	1550-1600
1996 One Light	1,500		125.00	125
1991 Pelican King	850	N/A	115.00	350-600
1991 Peter Peter Pumpkin Eater-Etching	75	N/A	210.00	600-1100
1995 Piscatorial Percussionist	3,000	N/A	125.00	95-125
1992 The Reponsible Woman	2,500	N/A	175.00	825-1000
1990 Rhymes & Reasons w/Booklet	Open		150.00	150

*Quotes have been rounded up to nearest dollar

YEAR ISSUE	EDITION LIMIT	YEAR RETD.	ISSUE PRICE	*QUOTE U.S.$
1990 Rhymes & Reasons w/Booklet, remarque	500	N/A	208.00	350-595
1993 The Royal Music Barque	2,750	N/A	375.00	375
1992 The Royal Processional	1,500	N/A	185.00	425-450
1992 The Royal Processional, remarque	500	N/A	252.50	475-595
1997 Santa's Other Helpers	1,950		125.00	125
1993 The Scholar	3,250	N/A	125.00	215-225
1995 Serenade For an Orange Cat	3,000	N/A	125.00	125-130
1987 The Shakespearean Poster	Open		35.00	35
1995 Sisters of the Sea	2,000	N/A	195.00	175-195
1994 Six Bird Hunters-Full Camouflage 3	4,662	N/A	165.00	165-195
1994 Sometimes the Spirit Touches w/book	3,600	N/A	195.00	195-285
1998 Superstitious w/Booket/Key	2,500		195.00	195
1998 Superstitious, remarque	200		395.00	395
1991 Three Blind Mice-Etching	75	N/A	210.00	2200-3100
1991 Three Wise Men of Gotham-Etching	75	N/A	210.00	600-1100
1991 Tweedle Dee & Tweedle Dum-Etching	75	N/A	210.00	600-1400
1994 Two Angels Discussing Botticelli	2,950	N/A	145.00	150-165
1990 Two Sisters	650	N/A	325.00	350-375
1996 The Voyage of the Basset Collector's Edition Book & The Oldest Professor	2,500		195.00	195
1987 Voyage of the Basset w/Journal	850	N/A	225.00	1100-1250
1993 Waiting for the Tide	2,250	N/A	150.00	185-200
1997 Wendall Realized He Had A Dilemma	950	1998	125.00	125
1988 The Widows Mite	850	N/A	145.00	2900-3400
1986 Your Place, or Mine?	850	N/A	125.00	225-395

Combes - S. Combes

YEAR ISSUE	EDITION LIMIT	YEAR RETD.	ISSUE PRICE	*QUOTE U.S.$
1992 African Oasis	650	N/A	375.00	795-850
1981 Alert	1,000	N/A	95.00	95
1987 The Angry One	850		95.00	95
1988 Bushwhacker	850	N/A	145.00	145
1983 Chui	275	N/A	250.00	250
1988 Confrontation	850		145.00	145
1988 The Crossing	1,250	N/A	245.00	245
1994 Disdain	850		110.00	110
1980 Facing the Wind	1,500	N/A	75.00	75-125
1993 Fearful Symmetry	850	N/A	110.00	110-215
1997 From The Shadows (canvas)	250		395.00	395
1995 Golden Silhouette	950		175.00	175
1990 The Guardian (Silverback)	1,000		185.00	185
1997 Heavy Drinkers	550		425.00	425
1992 The Hypnotist	1,250		145.00	145
1994 Indian Summer	950		175.00	175
1980 Interlude	1,500	N/A	85.00	95-115
1995 Jungle Phantom	950		175.00	175
1991 Kilimanjaro Morning	850		185.00	185
1981 Leopard Cubs	1,000	N/A	95.00	315
1992 Lookout	1,250		95.00	95
1980 Manyara Afternoon	1,500	N/A	75.00	325-425
1989 Masai-Longonot, Kenya	850		145.00	145
1992 Midday Sun (Lioness & Cubs)	850		125.00	125
1989 Mountain Gorillas	550	N/A	135.00	135-150
1995 Mountain Myth	950		175.00	175
1995 Pride	950		175.00	175
1998 Sentinels	550		125.00	125
1980 Serengeti Monarch	1,500	N/A	85.00	275
1995 Serious Intent	950		175.00	175
1995 Siberian Winter	950		175.00	175
1996 The Siberians	850		175.00	175
1988 Simba	850	1998	125.00	125
1997 Snow Pack	550		175.00	175
1995 Snow Tracker	950		175.00	175
1980 Solitary Hunter	1,500	N/A	75.00	75
1990 Standoff	850	N/A	375.00	550-695
1991 Study in Concentration	850	N/A	185.00	395
1987 Tall Shadows	850	N/A	150.00	450-825
1985 Tension at Dawn	825	N/A	145.00	900-1100
1985 Tension at Dawn, remarque	25	N/A	275.00	1150-1295
1998 There Was A Time, One of Two	250		975.00	975
1998 There Was A Time, Two of Two	250		975.00	975
1989 The Watering Hole	850		225.00	225
1986 The Wildebeest Migration	450	N/A	350.00	1500-2150

Crowley - D. Crowley

YEAR ISSUE	EDITION LIMIT	YEAR RETD.	ISSUE PRICE	*QUOTE U.S.$
1981 Afterglow	1,500		110.00	110
1992 Anna Thorne	650		160.00	160
1980 Apache in White	1,500	N/A	85.00	85-125
1979 Arizona Mountain Man	1,500	N/A	85.00	85-125
1980 Beauty and the Beast	1,500	N/A	85.00	85-135
1992 Colors of the Sunset	650		175.00	175
1979 Desert Sunset	1,500	N/A	75.00	75-125
1978 Dorena	1,000	N/A	75.00	75-115
1995 The Dreamer	650		150.00	150
1981 Eagle Feathers	1,500	N/A	95.00	95-125
1988 Ermine and Beads	550	N/A	85.00	215
1989 The Gunfighters	3,000	N/A	35.00	35
1981 The Heirloom	1,000	N/A	125.00	125
1982 Hopi Butterfly	275		350.00	350
1978 Hudson's Bay Blanket	1,000	N/A	75.00	75-125
1980 The Littlest Apache	275	N/A	325.00	325-850
1997 Morning Fire (Canvas)	650		495.00	495
1994 Plumes and Ribbons	650		160.00	160
1979 Security Blanket	1,500	N/A	65.00	65-175
1981 Shannandoah	275	N/A	325.00	275-325
1978 The Starquilt	1,000	N/A	65.00	500-525
1986 The Trapper	550		75.00	75
1997 Water in the Draw	550		160.00	160

Dawson - J. Dawson

YEAR ISSUE	EDITION LIMIT	YEAR RETD.	ISSUE PRICE	*QUOTE U.S.$
1992 The Attack (Cougars)	850		175.00	175
1993 Berry Contented	850		150.00	150
1993 Berry Contented, remarque	100		235.00	235
1994 The Face Off (Right & Left Panel)	850		150.00	150
1993 Looking Back	850		110.00	110
1993 Otter Wise	850		150.00	150
1993 Taking a Break	850	N/A	150.00	150

Doolittle - B. Doolittle

YEAR ISSUE	EDITION LIMIT	YEAR RETD.	ISSUE PRICE	*QUOTE U.S.$
1983 Art of Camouflage, signed	2,000	1983	55.00	350-395
1980 Bugged Bear	1,000	1980	85.00	3700-4000
1987 Calling the Buffalo	8,500	1987	245.00	470-695
1983 Christmas Day, Give or Take a Week	4,581	1983	80.00	1650-1716
1988 Doubled Back	15,000	1988	245.00	1000-1250
1996 Drawn From the Heart-Etching Suite	349	1996	750.00	2100-2400
1992 Eagle Heart	48,000	1992	285.00	195-285
1982 Eagle's Flight	1,500	1982	185.00	3500-3650
1983 Escape by a Hare	1,500	1983	80.00	595-695
1984 The Forest Has Eyes	8,544	1984	175.00	4500-4700
1980 Good Omen, The	1,000	1980	85.00	4600-4800
1987 Guardian Spirits	13,238	1987	295.00	695-862
1990 Hide and Seek (Composite & Video)	25,000	1990	1200.00	600-1200
1984 Let My Spirit Soar	1,500	1984	195.00	5000-6000
1997 Music in the Wind	43,500	1998	330.00	330
1979 Pintos	1,000	1979	65.00	7000-8200
1993 Prayer for the Wild Things	65,000	1993	325.00	295-350
1983 Runs With Thunder	1,500	1983	150.00	1000-1175
1983 Rushing War Eagle	1,500	1983	150.00	975-1075
1991 Sacred Circle (Print & Video)	40,192	1991	325.00	495-550
1989 Sacred Ground	69,996	1989	265.00	650-900
1987 Season of the Eagle	36,548	1987	245.00	550-700
1991 The Sentinel	35,000	1991	275.00	350-550
1981 Spirit of the Grizzly	1,500	1981	150.00	4400-4500
1995 Spirit Takes Flight	48,000	1995	225.00	225-245
1996 Three More for Breakfast	20,000	1996	245.00	245-265
1986 Two Bears of the Blackfeet	2,650	1986	225.00	725-950
1985 Two Indian Horses	12,253	1985	225.00	3000-3200
1995 Two More Indian Horses	48,000	1995	225.00	500-800
1981 Unknown Presence	1,500	1981	135.00	3200-3350
1992 Walk Softly (Chapbook)	40,192	1992	225.00	225-295
1994 When The Wind Had Wings	57,500	1994	325.00	245-325
1986 Where Silence Speaks, Doolittle The Art of Bev Doolittle	3,500	1986	650.00	2000-2200
1980 Whoo !?	1,000	1980	75.00	2000-2100
1993 Wilderness? Wilderness!	50,000	1993	65.00	65
1985 Wolves of the Crow	2,650	1985	225.00	1100-1200
1981 Woodland Encounter	1,500	1981	145.00	6500-9200

Dubowski - E. Dubowski

YEAR ISSUE	EDITION LIMIT	YEAR RETD.	ISSUE PRICE	*QUOTE U.S.$
1996 Aspen Flowers	850		145.00	145
1998 The Errand	550		125.00	125
1996 Fresh From the Garden	850		145.00	145
1998 The Readers	550		125.00	125
1997 Reflections	850		175.00	175

Entz - L. Entz

YEAR ISSUE	EDITION LIMIT	YEAR RETD.	ISSUE PRICE	*QUOTE U.S.$
1996 Apple Pie	850		150.00	150
1995 Life's a Dance	850		150.00	150
1996 New Shoes	850		150.00	150
1997 A Plot of Her Own	650		175.00	175

Ferris - K. Ferris

YEAR ISSUE	EDITION LIMIT	YEAR RETD.	ISSUE PRICE	*QUOTE U.S.$
1990 The Circus Outbound	1,000		225.00	225
1991 Farmer's Nightmare	850		185.00	185
1991 Linebacker in the Buff	1,000		225.00	225
1983 Little Willie Coming Home	1,000	N/A	145.00	1750-1850
1994 Real Trouble	1,000		195.00	195
1995 Schweinfurt Again	1,000		195.00	195
1982 Sunrise Encounter	1,000	N/A	145.00	145-195
1993 A Test of Courage	850		185.00	185
1991 Too Little, Too Late w/Video	1,000		245.00	245

Frazier - L. Frazier

YEAR ISSUE	EDITION LIMIT	YEAR RETD.	ISSUE PRICE	*QUOTE U.S.$
1998 The Concubine	750		150.00	150
1998 Constant Traveler	750		150.00	150
1998 The Nomad	Open		N/A	N/A
1997 Pay Dirt	450		425.00	425
1997 Royal Escort	450		395.00	395

Frederick - R. Frederick

YEAR ISSUE	EDITION LIMIT	YEAR RETD.	ISSUE PRICE	*QUOTE U.S.$
1990 Autumn Leaves	1,250	N/A	175.00	125-175
1996 Autumn Trail	850		195.00	195
1989 Barely Spring	1,500		165.00	165
1994 Beeline (C)	1,000		195.00	195
1987 Before the Storm (Diptych)	550	N/A	350.00	550-675
1991 Breaking the Ice	2,750	N/A	235.00	235
1997 Cascade Gold	650		175.00	175
1989 Colors of Home	1,500	N/A	165.00	295-425
1995 Drifters	850		175.00	175
1985 Early Evening Gathering	475	N/A	325.00	435-495
1992 An Early Light Breakfast	1,750	N/A	235.00	295-300
1990 Echoes of Sunset	1,750	N/A	235.00	725-775
1987 Evening Shadows (White-Tail Deer)	1,500	N/A	125.00	95-125
1992 Fast Break	2,250		235.00	235
1992 Fire and Ice (Suite of 2)	1,750		175.00	175
1984 First Moments of Gold	825	N/A	145.00	225
1984 First Moments of Gold, remarque	25	N/A	172.50	265
1984 From Timber's Edge	850	N/A	125.00	140-165
1996 Geyser Basin	850		175.00	175
1989 Gifts of the Land #2	500	N/A	150.00	150
1988 Gifts of the Land w/Wine & Wine Label	500	N/A	150.00	150
1988 Glimmer of Solitude	1,500		145.00	145
1993 Glory Days	1,750		115.00	115
1986 Great Horned Owl	1,250	N/A	115.00	135
1995 High Country Harem	1,000		185.00	185
1985 High Society	950	N/A	115.00	425
1995 Jaywalkers	850		175.00	175
1991 The Long Run	1,750	N/A	235.00	250-295
1991 The Long Run, AP	200	N/A	167.50	495
1985 Los Colores De Chiapas	950	N/A	85.00	85
1994 The Lost World	1,000		175.00	175
1985 Misty Morning Lookout	950	N/A	145.00	145
1984 Misty Morning Sentinel	850	N/A	125.00	145
1989 Monarch of the North	2,000		150.00	150
1990 Morning Surprise	1,750	N/A	165.00	165
1991 Morning Thunder	1,750	N/A	185.00	200
1988 The Nesting Call	2,500		150.00	150
1988 The Nesting Call, remarque	1,000	N/A	165.00	165
1993 New Heights	1,950		195.00	195
1987 Northern Light	1,500	N/A	165.00	165
1986 Out on a Limb	1,250	N/A	145.00	300-375
1993 Point of View	1,000		235.00	235
1992 Rain Forest Rendezvous	1,500	N/A	225.00	225
1988 Rim Walk	1,500	N/A	90.00	90
1988 Shadows of Dusk	1,500	N/A	165.00	165
1990 Silent Watch (High Desert Museum)	2,000	N/A	35.00	35
1994 Snow Pack	1,000		175.00	175
1992 Snowstorm	1,750		195.00	195
1990 Snowy Reflections (Snowy Egret)	1,500		150.00	150
1986 Sounds of Twilight	1,500	N/A	135.00	250-295
1991 Summer's Song (Triptych)	2,500		225.00	225
1993 Temple of the Jaguar	1,500		225.00	225
1988 Timber Ghost w/Mini Wine Label	3,000	N/A	150.00	150
1994 Tropic Moon	850		165.00	165
1987 Tundra Watch (Snowy Owl)	1,500	N/A	145.00	145
1994 Way of the Caribou	1,235		235.00	235
1987 Winter's Brilliance (Cardinal)	1,500	N/A	135.00	135
1986 Winter's Call	1,250	N/A	165.00	550
1986 Winter's Call Raptor, AP	100	N/A	165.00	600
1987 Woodland Crossing (Caribou)	1,500	N/A	145.00	145
1988 World of White	2,500	N/A	150.00	150

Gurney - J. Gurney

YEAR ISSUE	EDITION LIMIT	YEAR RETD.	ISSUE PRICE	*QUOTE U.S.$
1992 Birthday Pageant	2,500	N/A	60.00	60
1992 Birthday Pageant, remarque	300	N/A	275.00	295
1991 Dinosaur Boulevard	2,000	N/A	125.00	125
1991 Dinosaur Boulevard, remarque	250	N/A	196.00	425
1990 Dinosaur Parade	1,995	1995	125.00	125
1990 Dinosaur Parade, remarque	150	N/A	130.00	2500-2800
1992 Dream Canyon	N/A	N/A	125.00	125
1992 Dream Canyon, remarque	150	N/A	196.00	395
1993 The Excursion	3,500		175.00	175
1993 Garden of Hope	3,500		175.00	175
1990 Morning in Treetown	1,500	N/A	175.00	325
1993 Palace in the Clouds	3,500	N/A	175.00	175
1993 Ring Riders	2,500	N/A	175.00	175
1995 Rumble & Mist	2,500		175.00	175
1995 Santa Claus	2,000		95.00	95
1990 Seaside Romp	1,000	N/A	175.00	395
1992 Skyback Print w/Dinotopia Book	3,500	N/A	295.00	295
1994 Small Wonder	3,299	N/A	75.00	75
1994 Steep Street	3,500		95.00	95
1995 Twilight in Bonaba	3,000		195.00	195
1991 Waterfall City	3,000	N/A	125.00	125
1991 Waterfall City, remarque	250	N/A	186.00	395
1995 The World Beneath Collectors' Book w/ print	3,000		195.00	195

Gustafson - S. Gustafson

YEAR ISSUE	EDITION LIMIT	YEAR RETD.	ISSUE PRICE	*QUOTE U.S.$
1995 The Alice in Wonderland Suite	4,000		195.00	195
1994 Frog Prince	3,500	1994	125.00	150
1993 Goldilocks and the Three Bears	3,500	1993	125.00	300-400
1995 Hansel & Gretel	3,000		125.00	125
1993 Humpty Dumpty	3,500	1993	125.00	125
1995 Jack in the Beanstalk	3,500		125.00	125
1998 Little Bo Peep	950		125.00	125
1998 Little Miss Muffet	950		125.00	125
1993 Little Red Riding Hood	3,500	1993	125.00	125
1996 Old King Cole	2,750		125.00	125
1997 The Owl and the Pussycat	950		125.00	125
1994 Pat-A-Cake	4,000	1994	125.00	125
1997 Peter Peter Pumpkin Eater	950		125.00	125
1996 Puss in Boots	2,750		145.00	145
1995 Rumplestiltskin	2,750		125.00	125
1993 Snow White and the Seven Dwarfs	3,500	1993	165.00	225
1997 Tom Thumb	950	1998	125.00	125
1995 Touched by Magic	4,000		185.00	185

Hartough - L. Hartough

YEAR ISSUE	EDITION LIMIT	YEAR RETD.	ISSUE PRICE	*QUOTE U.S.$
1996 10th Hole, West Course Winged Foot	657		210.00	210
1996 11th Hole, "White Dogwood", Augusta National Golf Club	850	1998	225.00	225
1995 The 13th Hole, "Azalea"	25		225.00	225
1996 13th Hole, Augusta National	430		225.00	225
1995 14th Hole, St. Andrews	850	1995	225.00	225
1996 15th Hole, "Firethorn", Augusta National Golf Club	850		325.00	325
1996 15th Hole, Haig Point Rees Jones	226		210.00	210
1996 17th Hole Clubhouse, Royal Troon	522		165.00	165
1996 17th Hole, Royal Dornoch	86		210.00	210
1996 17th Hole, Royal St. George, 1993 Bristish Open	153		225.00	225
1997 18th Hole, 1997 Royal Troon	345		225.00	225
1997 18th Hole, Harbourtown Links	850		250.00	250

*Quotes have been rounded up to nearest dollar

YEAR ISSUE		EDITION LIMIT	YEAR RETD.	ISSUE PRICE	*QUOTE U.S.$
1996	18th Hole, Muirfield Village	780		210.00	210
1996	18th Hole, Royal Birkdale, 1991 British Open	245		210.00	210
1996	18th Hole, Royal Lytham & St. Annes Golf Club	850		225.00	225
1995	7th Hole, Pebble Beach Golf Links	850	1998	225.00	225
1996	Postage Stamp 8th Royal Troon	154		210.00	210
1996	The Ultimate 18th Eden Royal H.K.	634		210.00	210

Holm - J. Holm

YEAR ISSUE		EDITION LIMIT	YEAR RETD.	ISSUE PRICE	*QUOTE U.S.$
1998	Five Persians	550		130.00	130
1997	I Spy Summer	850		95.00	95
1998	The Sentry	550		125.00	125
1996	Slipper Thief	850		95.00	95

Howell-Sickles - D. Howell-Sickles

YEAR ISSUE		EDITION LIMIT	YEAR RETD.	ISSUE PRICE	*QUOTE U.S.$
1997	Cowgirl Rising w/And the Cowgirl Jumped Over the Moon print	1,000		245.00	245
1998	Legends	650		295.00	295

Hurley - W. Hurley

YEAR ISSUE		EDITION LIMIT	YEAR RETD.	ISSUE PRICE	*QUOTE U.S.$
1998	Late Summer Sunset	550		225.00	225
1998	The Wyoming Suite (center panel 1/3)	550		500.00	500
1998	The Wyoming Suite (left panel 2/3)	550		500.00	500
1998	The Wyoming Suite (right panel 3/3)	550		495.00	495

Johnson - J. Johnson

YEAR ISSUE		EDITION LIMIT	YEAR RETD.	ISSUE PRICE	*QUOTE U.S.$
1994	Moose River	650		175.00	175
1994	Sea Treasures	650		125.00	125
1994	Winter Thaw	650		150.00	150
1993	Wolf Creek	550	N/A	165.00	200

Kennedy - S. Kennedy

YEAR ISSUE		EDITION LIMIT	YEAR RETD.	ISSUE PRICE	*QUOTE U.S.$
1988	After Dinner Music	2,500	N/A	175.00	230
1995	Alaskan Malamute	1,000		125.00	125
1992	Aurora	2,250	N/A	195.00	195
1991	A Breed Apart	2,750	N/A	225.00	225
1992	Cabin Fever	2,250		175.00	175
1995	Cliff Dwellers	850		175.00	175
1998	Crossing Over	750		135.00	135
1997	Curious Encounter & New Generation	850		125.00	125
1988	Distant Relations	950	N/A	200.00	300
1988	Eager to Run	950	N/A	200.00	1400-1790
1990	Fish Tales	5,500	N/A	225.00	225
1997	Fishing Buddies	1,000		165.00	165
1991	In Training	3,350	N/A	165.00	295
1991	In Training, remarque	150	N/A	215.50	345
1996	Keeping Watch	850		150.00	150
1995	The Lesson	1,000		125.00	125
1996	Looking For Trouble	850		125.00	125
1993	Midnight Eyes	1,750		125.00	125
1997	Miracle Mile	750		145.00	145
1993	Never Alone	2,250		225.00	225
1993	Never Alone, remarque	250	N/A	272.50	273
1997	The New Kitten	850		125.00	125
1990	On the Edge	4,000		225.00	225
1995	On the Heights	850		175.00	175
1994	Quiet Time Companions-Samoyed	1,000	1998	125.00	125
1994	Quiet Time Companions -Siberian Husky	1,000	N/A	125.00	125
1998	Rocky Mountain Gold	550		175.00	175
1998	Samoyed Pup	1,250		95.00	95
1994	Silent Observers	1,250	N/A	165.00	165
1996	Snow Buddies	850		125.00	125
1989	Snowshoes	4,000	N/A	185.00	185
1994	Spruce and Fur	1,500		165.00	165
1995	Standing Watch	850		175.00	175
1993	The Touch	1,500		115.00	115
1989	Up a Creek	2,500	N/A	185.00	185
1997	White Christmas	750		95.00	95

Kodera - C. Kodera

YEAR ISSUE		EDITION LIMIT	YEAR RETD.	ISSUE PRICE	*QUOTE U.S.$
1986	The A Team (K10)	850		145.00	145
1995	A.M. Sortie	1,000		225.00	225
1996	Canyon Starliner	850		185.00	185
1991	Darkness Visible (Stealth)	2,671	N/A	40.00	40
1987	Fifty Years a Lady	550	N/A	150.00	450-500
1988	The Great Greenwich Balloon Race	1,000		145.00	145
1990	Green Light-Jump!	650	N/A	145.00	200
1992	Halsey's Surprise	850		95.00	95
1997	Hitting the Kwai w/Artifact	850		265.00	265
1994	Last to Fight	1,000		225.00	225
1995	Lonely Flight to Destiny	1,000	1995	347.00	895-1000
1992	Looking For Nagumo	1,000		225.00	225
1996	The Lost Squadron	850		275.00	275
1992	Memphis Belle/Dauntless Dotty	1,250		245.00	245
1990	A Moment's Peace	1,250		150.00	150
1988	Moonlight Intruders	1,000		125.00	125
1995	Only One Survived	1,000		245.00	245
1989	Springtime Flying in the Rockies	550	N/A	95.00	95
1996	Stratojet Shakedown	1,000		265.00	265
1992	Thirty Seconds Over Tokyo	1,000	N/A	275.00	275
1991	This is No Drill w/Video	1,000		225.00	225
1994	This is No Time to Lose an Engine	850		150.00	150
1994	Tiger's Bite	850		150.00	150
1987	Voyager: The Skies Yield	1,500		225.00	225

Landry - P. Landry

YEAR ISSUE		EDITION LIMIT	YEAR RETD.	ISSUE PRICE	*QUOTE U.S.$
1996	Afternoon Tea (canvas)	450	1996	495.00	495
1993	The Antique Shop	1,250	N/A	125.00	125
1992	Apple Orchard	1,250		150.00	150
1992	Aunt Martha's Country Farm	1,500	N/A	185.00	300
1996	Autumn Hayride	550		165.00	165
1995	Autumn Market	1,000		185.00	185
1987	Bluenose Country	550	N/A	115.00	175
1992	Boardwalk Promenade	1,250		175.00	175
1989	A Canadian Christmas	1,250		125.00	125
1989	Cape Cod Welcome Cameo	850	N/A	75.00	275
1990	The Captain's Garden	1,000	N/A	165.00	425
1993	Christmas at Mystic Seaport	2,000		125.00	125
1992	Christmas at the Flower Market	2,500		125.00	125
1994	Christmas Carousel Pony	2,000		125.00	125
1997	Christmas Door	850		95.00	95
1997	Christmas Door, remarque	S/O	N/A	95.00	95
1990	Christmas Treasures	2,500		165.00	165
1992	Cottage Garden	1,250	N/A	160.00	160
1995	Cottage Reflections	850		135.00	135
1998	Country Garden	850		185.00	185
1994	An English Cottage	850		150.00	150
1994	Flower Barn	1,000		175.00	175
1988	Flower Boxes	550	N/A	75.00	250
1991	Flower Market	1,500	N/A	185.00	1000
1990	Flower Wagon	1,500	N/A	165.00	165
1994	Flowers For Mary Hope	1,250		165.00	165
1997	A Gardener's Pride	950		95.00	95
1995	Harbor Garden	1,000		160.00	160
1993	Hometown Parade	1,250		165.00	165
1996	It's a Wonderful Christmas	1,250		165.00	165
1996	Joseph's Corner (canvas)	450		495.00	495
1996	Joseph's Corner, Artist Touch (canvas)	100		795.00	795
1995	Lantern Skaters	1,500		135.00	135
1990	Morning Papers	1,250	N/A	135.00	145
1994	Morning Walk	850		135.00	135
1998	Mother's Day (Watercolor Sketch)	200		180.00	180
1991	Nantucket Colors	1,500		150.00	150
1993	Paper Boy	1,500		150.00	150
1993	A Place in the Park	1,500		185.00	185
1984	Regatta	500	N/A	75.00	150
1984	Regatta, remarque	50	N/A	97.50	145
1990	Seaside Carousel	1,500	N/A	165.00	200
1988	Seaside Cottage	550	N/A	125.00	125
1986	Seaside Mist	450	N/A	85.00	200
1985	The Skaters	500		75.00	75
1985	The Skaters, remarque	50	N/A	97.50	98
1995	Spring Song	2,500		145.00	145
1997	Springtime Garden	850		185.00	185
1996	Summer Buddies	950		135.00	135
1991	Summer Concert	1,500		195.00	195
1989	Summer Garden	850	N/A	125.00	400
1997	Summer Hill	850		165.00	165
1995	Summer Mist (Fine Art Original Lithograph)	550		750.00	850
1992	Sunflowers	1,250	N/A	125.00	125
1991	The Toymaker	1,500	N/A	165.00	165
1991	Victorian Memories	1,500	N/A	150.00	150
1996	Winter Memories w/The Captain's Garden Collector's Edition Book	2,000		195.00	195

Lovell - T. Lovell

YEAR ISSUE		EDITION LIMIT	YEAR RETD.	ISSUE PRICE	*QUOTE U.S.$
1988	The Battle of the Crater	1,500	N/A	225.00	225
1988	Berdan's Sharpshooters -Gettysburg	1,500		225.00	225
1986	Blackfeet Wall	450	N/A	325.00	1195-1500
1981	Carson's Boatyard	1,000		150.00	150
1985	Chiricahua Scout	650		90.00	90
1981	The Deceiver	1,000		150.00	150
1990	Dry Goods and Molasses	1,000		225.00	225
1981	Fires Along the Oregon Trail	1,000	N/A	150.00	295
1993	The Handwarmer	1,000		225.00	225
1988	The Hunter	1,000		150.00	150
1982	Invitation to Trade	1,000	N/A	150.00	150
1989	The Lost Rag Doll	1,000		225.00	225
1988	Mr. Bodmer's Music Box	5,000		40.00	40
1975	The Mud Owl's Warning	1,000	N/A	150.00	175-250
1988	North Country Rider	2,500		95.00	95
1976	Quicksand at Horsehead	1,000		150.00	150
1976	Shotgun Toll	1,000		150.00	150
1983	Sugar in The Coffee	650	N/A	165.00	165
1987	Surrender at Appomattox	1,000	N/A	225.00	1695
1992	Target Practice	2,000		25.00	25
1976	Time of Cold-Maker	1,000		150.00	150
1989	Union Fleet Passing Vicksburg	1,500		225.00	225
1982	Walking Coyote & Buffalo Orphans	650	N/A	165.00	195-225
1982	The Wheelsoakers	1,000		150.00	150
1984	Winter Holiday	850		95.00	95
1989	Youth's Hour of Glory	1,500		175.00	175

Lyman - S. Lyman

YEAR ISSUE		EDITION LIMIT	YEAR RETD.	ISSUE PRICE	*QUOTE U.S.$
1997	Ahwahnee-The Deep Grassy Valley	1,500	1998	225.00	225-450
1990	Among The Wild Brambles	1,750	1990	185.00	600-625
1985	Autumn Gathering	850	N/A	115.00	850-1350
1996	Beach Bonfire	6,500	1996	225.00	175-225
1985	Bear & Blossoms (C)	850	N/A	75.00	600-665
1987	Canadian Autumn	1,500	1987	165.00	350-500
1995	Cathedral Snow	4,000	1996	245.00	250-265
1989	Color In The Snow (Pheasant)	1,500	N/A	165.00	350-500
1996	The Crossing	2,500	1996	195.00	185-215
1991	Dance of Cloud and Cliff	1,500	1991	225.00	375-500
1991	Dance of Water and Light	3,000	1991	225.00	225-245
1983	Early Winter In The Mountains	850	N/A	95.00	750-850
1987	An Elegant Couple (Wood Ducks)	1,000	N/A	125.00	250-350
1991	Embers at Dawn	3,500	1991	225.00	1500-1800
1983	End Of The Ridge	850	N/A	95.00	575-695
1990	Evening Light	2,500	1990	225.00	3150-3400
1995	Evening Star w/collector's edition book	9,500	1995	195.00	245-275
1993	Fire Dance	8,500	1993	235.00	540-600
1984	Free Flight	850	N/A	70.00	95-195
1987	High Creek Crossing	1,000	N/A	165.00	1350-1400
1989	High Light	1,250	1989	165.00	475-550
1986	High Trail At Sunset	1,000	N/A	125.00	700-750
1988	The Intruder	1,500	N/A	150.00	215-315
1993	Lake of the Shining Rocks	2,250	1993	235.00	400-625
1992	Lantern Light Print w/Firelight Chapbook	10,000	1993	195.00	195
1989	Last Light of Winter	1,500	1989	175.00	1050-1250
1995	Midnight Fire	8,500	1996	245.00	225-245
1994	Moon Fire	7,500	1994	245.00	575-950
1987	Moon Shadows	1,500	N/A	135.00	185-215
1998	Moonbear Listens to the Earth	1,250		175.00	175
1994	Moonlit Flight on Christmas Night	2,750	1994	165.00	195
1996	Morning Light	8,000	1996	245.00	475-550
1986	Morning Solitude	850	N/A	115.00	700-800
1990	A Mountain Campfire	1,500	1990	195.00	3100-3200
1994	New Kid on the Rock	2,250	1996	185.00	215-225
1987	New Territory (Grizzly & Cubs)	1,000	N/A	135.00	495-550
1984	Noisy Neighbors	675	N/A	95.00	1395-1450
1984	Noisy Neighbors, remarque	25	N/A	127.50	1800
1994	North Country Shores	3,000	1994	225.00	325-525
1983	The Pass	850	N/A	95.00	750-1000
1989	Quiet Rain	1,500	N/A	165.00	900-995
1988	The Raptor's Watch	1,500	N/A	150.00	600-1000
1988	Return Of The Falcon	1,500	N/A	150.00	395-500
1993	Riparian Riches	2,500	1993	235.00	215-235
1992	River of Light (Geese)	2,950	N/A	225.00	225-235
1991	Secret Watch (Lynx)	2,250	N/A	150.00	150-165
1997	Sentinel of the Grove	450		195.00	195
1990	Silent Snows	1,750	N/A	210.00	400-450
1988	Snow Hunter	1,500	N/A	135.00	295-725
1986	Snowy Throne (C)	850	N/A	85.00	575-795
1993	The Spirit of Christmas	2,750	1993	165.00	495-550
1998	Steller Autumn	1,250		225.00	225
1998	Sunrise in the Wallowas	950	1998	450.00	575-675
1996	Sunset Fire (PC)	N/A	1996	245.00	215-300
1995	Thunderbolt	7,000	N/A	235.00	550-700
1987	Twilight Snow (C)	950	N/A	85.00	450-600
1988	Uzumati: Great Bear of Yosemite	1,750	N/A	150.00	200-275
1992	Warmed by the View	8,500	1992	235.00	395-425
1992	Wilderness Welcome	8,500	N/A	235.00	900-975
1992	Wildflower Suite (Hummingbird)	2,250	N/A	175.00	225-325
1997	Winter Shadows	2,500	1997	225.00	195-225
1992	Woodland Haven	2,500	N/A	195.00	240-250

Marris - B. Marris

YEAR ISSUE		EDITION LIMIT	YEAR RETD.	ISSUE PRICE	*QUOTE U.S.$
1987	Above the Glacier	850	N/A	145.00	145
1986	Best Friends	850	N/A	85.00	235-295
1994	Big Gray's Barn and Bistro	1,000		125.00	125
1989	Bittersweet	1,000	N/A	135.00	135
1990	Bugles and Trumpets!	1,000	N/A	175.00	175
1996	Catch The Wind	850		165.00	165
1992	The Comeback	1,250		175.00	175
1991	Cops & Robbers	1,000	N/A	165.00	165
1988	Courtship	850	N/A	145.00	145
1995	Dairy Queens	1,000		125.00	125
1995	The Dartmoor Ponies	1,000		165.00	165
1987	Desperados	850	N/A	135.00	135
1996	Dog Days	1,000		165.00	165
1991	End of the Season	1,000		165.00	165
1985	The Fishing Lesson	1,000		145.00	145
1997	For the Love of Pete	950		130.00	130
1995	The Gift	1,000		125.00	125
1987	Honey Creek Whitetales	850	N/A	145.00	145
1985	Kenai Dusk	1,000	N/A	145.00	800
1994	Lady Marmalade's Bed & Breakfast	1,000		125.00	125
1996	A Little Pig with a Big Heart	1,000	1996	95.00	95
1990	Mom's Shadow	1,000		165.00	165
1994	Moonshine	1,000		95.00	95
1989	New Beginnings	1,000	N/A	175.00	375
1990	Of Myth and Magic	1,500	N/A	175.00	175
1986	Other Footsteps	950		75.00	75
1989	The Playgroud Showoff	850	N/A	165.00	165
1992	Security Blanket	1,250		175.00	175
1993	Spring Fever	1,000		165.00	165
1991	The Stillness (Grizzly & Cubs)	1,000	N/A	165.00	165
1992	Sun Bath	1,000		95.00	95
1997	Sun Splashed	750		130.00	130
1992	To Stand and Endure	1,000	N/A	195.00	275-395
1991	Under the Morning Star	1,500		175.00	175
1998	Undercover	750		145.00	145
1988	Waiting For the Freeze	1,000	N/A	125.00	125
1995	Where Best Friends Are Welcome	850	1996	95.00	195

McCarthy - F. McCarthy

YEAR ISSUE		EDITION LIMIT	YEAR RETD.	ISSUE PRICE	*QUOTE U.S.$
1996	After the Council	550		850.00	850
1996	After the Council	1,000		195.00	195
1984	After the Dust Storm	1,000	N/A	145.00	295
1982	Alert	1,000	N/A	135.00	135
1984	Along the West Fork	1,000	N/A	175.00	225
1995	Ambush at the Ancient Rocks	1,000		225.00	225
1978	Ambush, The	1,000	N/A	125.00	300
1982	Apache Scout	1,000	N/A	165.00	165
1988	Apache Trackers (C)	1,000	N/A	95.00	95
1992	The Art of Frank McCarthy	10,418	N/A	60.00	60
1982	Attack on the Wagon Train	1,400	N/A	150.00	150
1977	The Beaver Men	1,000	N/A	75.00	350
1980	Before the Charge	1,000	N/A	115.00	150
1978	Before the Norther	1,000	N/A	90.00	325

*Quotes have been rounded up to nearest dollar

YEAR ISSUE	EDITION LIMIT	YEAR RETD.	ISSUE PRICE	*QUOTE U.S.$
1990 Below The Breaking Dawn	1,250	N/A	225.00	225
1994 Beneath the Cliff (Petraglyphs)	1,500		295.00	295
1989 Big Medicine	1,000	N/A	225.00	350
1983 Blackfeet Raiders	1,000	N/A	90.00	200
1992 Breaking the Moonlit Silence	650	N/A	375.00	375
1986 The Buffalo Runners	1,000	N/A	195.00	170
1997 Buffalo Soldier Advance	1,500		225.00	225
1980 Burning the Way Station	1,000	N/A	125.00	250
1993 By the Ancient Trails They Passed	1,000	N/A	245.00	245
1989 Canyon Lands	1,250	N/A	225.00	225
1982 The Challenge	1,000	N/A	175.00	275-450
1995 Charge of the Buffalo Soldiers	1,000	1995	195.00	285
1985 Charging the Challenger	1,000	N/A	150.00	425
1991 The Chase	1,000		225.00	225
1986 Children of the Raven	1,000	N/A	185.00	550
1987 Chiricahua Raiders	1,000	N/A	165.00	225
1977 Comanche Moon	1,000	N/A	75.00	235
1992 Comanche Raider-Bronze	100		812.50	813
1986 Comanche War Trail	1,000	N/A	165.00	170
1989 The Coming Of The Iron Horse	1,500	N/A	225.00	225
1989 The Coming Of The Iron Horse (Print/Pewter Train Special Pub. Ed.)	100	N/A	1500.00	1600-2150
1981 The Coup	1,000	N/A	125.00	500
1998 The Crossing	850		185.00	185
1981 Crossing the Divide (The Old West)	1,500	N/A	850.00	450-750
1984 The Decoys	450	N/A	325.00	500
1977 Distant Thunder	1,500	N/A	75.00	500
1989 Down From The Mountains	1,500	N/A	245.00	245
1986 The Drive (C)	1,000	N/A	95.00	95-175
1977 Dust Stained Posse	1,000	N/A	75.00	650
1985 The Fireboat	1,000	N/A	175.00	175
1994 Flashes of Lighting-Thunder of Hooves	550		435.00	435
1987 Following the Herds	1,000	N/A	195.00	265-475
1980 Forbidden Land	1,000	N/A	125.00	125
1978 The Fording	1,000	N/A	75.00	250
1987 From the Rim	1,000	N/A	225.00	225
1981 Headed North	1,000	N/A	150.00	275
1992 Heading Back	1,000		225.00	225
1995 His Wealth	850		225.00	225
1990 Hoka Hey: Sioux War Cry	1,250	N/A	225.00	225
1987 The Hostile Land	1,000	N/A	225.00	235
1976 The Hostiles	1,000	N/A	75.00	475
1984 Hostiles, signed	1,000	N/A	55.00	55
1974 The Hunt	1,000	N/A	75.00	450
1988 In Pursuit of the White Buffalo	1,500	N/A	225.00	425-525
1992 In the Land of the Ancient Ones	1,250	N/A	245.00	265
1983 In The Land Of The Sparrow Hawk People	1,000	N/A	165.00	175
1987 In The Land Of The Winter Hawk	1,000	N/A	225.00	300
1978 In The Pass	1,500	N/A	90.00	265
1997 In The Shallows	1,000		185.00	185
1985 The Last Crossing	550	N/A	350.00	350
1989 The Last Stand: Little Big Horn	1,500	N/A	225.00	225
1984 Leading the Charge, signed	1,000	N/A	55.00	80
1974 Lone Sentinel	1,000	N/A	55.00	1100
1979 The Loner	1,000	N/A	75.00	225
1974 Long Column	1,000	N/A	75.00	400
1985 The Long Knives	1,000	N/A	175.00	350
1989 Los Diablos	1,250	N/A	225.00	225
1995 Medicine Man	850	1996	165.00	165
1983 Moonlit Trail	1,000	N/A	90.00	295
1992 Navajo Ponies Comanchie Warriors	1,000		225.00	225
1978 Night Crossing	1,000	N/A	75.00	200
1974 The Night They Needed a Good Ribbon Man	1,000	N/A	65.00	300
1977 An Old Time Mountain Man	1,000	N/A	65.00	200
1990 On The Old North Trail (Triptych)	650	N/A	550.00	675
1979 On the Warpath	1,000	N/A	75.00	150-175
1983 Out Of The Mist They Came	1,000	N/A	165.00	235
1990 Out Of The Windswept Ramparts	1,250	N/A	225.00	225
1976 Packing In	1,000	N/A	65.00	400
1998 Patrol at Broken Finger	750		165.00	165
1991 Pony Express	1,000		225.00	225
1979 The Prayer	1,500	N/A	90.00	450
1991 The Pursuit	650	N/A	550.00	550
1981 Race with the Hostiles	1,000	N/A	135.00	135
1987 Red Bull's War Party	1,000	N/A	165.00	165
1979 Retreat to Higher Ground	2,000	N/A	90.00	240-360
1975 Returning Raiders	1,000	N/A	75.00	300
1997 The Roar of the Falls	950		195.00	195
1980 Roar of the Norther	1,000	N/A	90.00	200
1977 Robe Signal	850	N/A	60.00	375
1988 Saber Charge	2,250	N/A	225.00	225-250
1984 The Savage Taunt	1,000	N/A	225.00	275
1985 Scouting The Long Knives	1,400	N/A	195.00	270
1993 Shadows of Warriors (3 Print Suite)	1,000		225.00	225
1994 Show of Defiance	1,000		195.00	195
1993 Sighting the Intruders	1,000		225.00	225
1978 Single File	1,000	N/A	75.00	850
1976 Sioux Warriors	650	N/A	55.00	250
1975 Smoke Was Their Ally	1,000	N/A	75.00	225
1980 Snow Moon	1,000	N/A	115.00	225
1995 Splitting the Herd	550		465.00	465
1986 Spooked	1,400	N/A	195.00	195
1981 Surrounded	1,000	N/A	150.00	350-395
1975 The Survivor	1,000	N/A	65.00	275
1980 A Time Of Decision	1,150	N/A	125.00	225
1978 To Battle	1,000	N/A	75.00	350-400
1985 The Traders	1,000	N/A	195.00	195
1996 The Trek	850		175.00	175
1980 The Trooper	1,000	N/A	90.00	165
1988 Turning The Leaders	1,500	N/A	225.00	225
1983 Under Attack	5,676	N/A	125.00	375-500
1981 Under Hostile Fire	1,000	N/A	150.00	160
1975 Waiting for the Escort	1,000	N/A	75.00	100
1976 The Warrior	650	N/A	55.00	350
1982 The Warriors	1,000	N/A	150.00	150
1984 Watching the Wagons	1,400	N/A	175.00	750
1995 The Way of the Ancient Migrations	1,250		245.00	245
1987 When Omens Turn Bad	1,000	N/A	165.00	425-500
1992 When the Land Was Theirs	1,000		225.00	225
1992 Where Ancient Ones Had Hunted	1,000	N/A	245.00	245
1992 Where Others Had Passed	1,000	N/A	245.00	245
1986 Where Tracks Will Be Lost	550	N/A	350.00	350
1982 Whirling He Raced to Meet the Challenge	1,000	N/A	175.00	400-525
1991 The Wild Ones	1,000	N/A	225.00	225
1990 Winter Trail	1,500	N/A	235.00	235
1993 With Pistols Drawn	1,000		195.00	195

Mitchell - D. Mitchell

YEAR ISSUE	EDITION LIMIT	YEAR RETD.	ISSUE PRICE	*QUOTE U.S.$
1994 Bonding Years	550		175.00	175
1993 Country Church	550		175.00	175
1997 Fort Scott Soldier	850		150.00	150
1995 Innocence	1,000		150.00	150
1995 Let Us Pray	850		175.00	175
1993 Psalms 4:1	550	N/A	195.00	195
1996 Return For Honor	850		150.00	150
1992 Rowena	550	N/A	195.00	300

Mo Da-Feng - M. Da-Feng

YEAR ISSUE	EDITION LIMIT	YEAR RETD.	ISSUE PRICE	*QUOTE U.S.$
1990 Family Boat	888		235.00	235
1993 First Journey	650		150.00	150
1989 Fishing Hut	888		235.00	235
1994 Ocean Mist	850		150.00	150

Parker, Ed. - E. Parker

YEAR ISSUE	EDITION LIMIT	YEAR RETD.	ISSUE PRICE	*QUOTE U.S.$
1996 Acadia Tea and Tennis Society	850		135.00	135
1995 The Glorious 4th	850		150.00	150
1996 St. Duffer's Golf Club	850		135.00	135
1995 A Visit From St. Nicholas	850		125.00	125
1997 Windjammer Days	850		125.00	125

Parker, Ron. - R. Parker

YEAR ISSUE	EDITION LIMIT	YEAR RETD.	ISSUE PRICE	*QUOTE U.S.$
1995 The Breakfast Club	850		125.00	125
1995 Coastal Morning	850		195.00	195
1995 Evening Solitude	850		195.00	195
1994 Forest Flight	850		195.00	195
1997 Gliding Swan	650		145.00	145
1994 Grizzlies at the Falls	850		225.00	225
1994 Morning Flight	4,000		20.00	20
1996 Summer Memories	850		125.00	125
1996 Summer Reading	850		125.00	125
1995 Tea For Two	850		125.00	125

Phillips - W. Phillips

YEAR ISSUE	EDITION LIMIT	YEAR RETD.	ISSUE PRICE	*QUOTE U.S.$
1982 Advantage Eagle	1,000	N/A	135.00	300
1992 Alone No More	850		195.00	195
1988 America on the Move	1,500	N/A	185.00	150-185
1994 Among the Columns of Thor	1,000		295.00	295
1993 And Now the Trap	850		175.00	175
1998 The Beginning of the End	1,000		365.00	365
1997 Caping the Tico	950		275.00	275
1986 Changing of the Guard	500		100.00	100
1993 Chasing the Daylight	850		185.00	185
1994 Christmas Leave When Dreams Come True	1,500	N/A	185.00	185-220
1996 Clipper at the Gate	850		185.00	185
1986 Confrontation at Beachy Head	1,000		150.00	150
1991 Dauntless Against a Rising Sun	850	N/A	195.00	195
1995 Dawn The World Forever Changed	1,000	1996	347.50	348
1995 The Dream Fulfilled	1,750		195.00	195
1997 Early Morning Visitors	1,250		195.00	195
1991 Fifty Miles Out	1,000		175.00	175
1983 The Giant Begins to Stir	1,250	N/A	185.00	1100-1400
1990 Going in Hot w/Book	1,500		250.00	250
1985 Heading For Trouble	1,000	N/A	125.00	250
1984 Hellfire Corner	1,225	N/A	185.00	600
1984 Hellfire Corner, remarque	25	N/A	225.80	800
1998 Hill Country Homecoming	1,250		195.00	195
1990 Hunter Becomes the Hunted w/video	1,500		265.00	265
1992 I Could Never Be So Lucky Again	850	N/A	295.00	750
1993 If Only in My Dreams	1,000	N/A	175.00	750
1984 Into the Teeth of the Tiger	975	N/A	135.00	925
1984 Into the Teeth of the Tiger, remarque	25	N/A	167.50	2000
1994 Into the Throne Room of God w/book "The Glory of Flight"	750	N/A	195.00	600
1991 Intruder Outbound	1,000		225.00	225
1991 Last Chance	1,000	N/A	165.00	350
1985 Lest We Forget	1,250	N/A	195.00	250
1994 Lethal Encounter	1,000		225.00	225
1996 The Lightkeepers Gift	1,000		175.00	175
1988 The Long Green Line	3,500		185.00	185
1992 The Long Ride Home (P-51D)	850	N/A	195.00	195
1991 Low Pass For the Home Folks, BP	1,000	N/A	175.00	175
1996 The Moonwatchers	1,750		185.00	185
1986 Next Time Get 'Em All	1,500	N/A	225.00	275
1989 No Empty Bunks Tonight	1,500	N/A	165.00	165
1989 No Flying Today	1,500		185.00	185
1989 Over the Top	1,000		165.00	165
1985 The Phantoms and the Wizard	850	N/A	145.00	800
1992 Ploesti: Into the Fire and Fury	850		195.00	195
1987 Range Wars	1,000		160.00	160
1996 Return of the Red Gremlin	1,000		350.00	350
1987 Shore Birds at Point Lobos	1,250	N/A	175.00	175
1989 Sierra Hotel	1,250	N/A	175.00	175
1997 Spring Fling	1,250		195.00	195
1998 The Storm Watchers	1,250		195.00	195
1995 Summer of '45	1,750	1998	195.00	990
1998 Sunset Sentinels	550		695.00	695
1987 Sunward We Climb	1,000		175.00	175
1983 Those Clouds Won't Help You Now	625	N/A	135.00	500
1983 Those Clouds Won't Help You Now, remarque	25	N/A	275.00	675
1987 Those Last Critical Moments	1,250	N/A	185.00	300
1993 Threading the Eye of the Needle	1,000		195.00	195
1996 Thunder and Lightning	850		185.00	185
1986 Thunder in the Canyon	1,000	N/A	165.00	600
1990 A Time of Eagles	1,250	1996	245.00	245
1989 Time to Head Home	1,500		165.00	165
1986 Top Cover for the Straggler	1,000	N/A	145.00	325
1983 Two Down, One to Go	3,000	N/A	15.00	15
1982 Welcome Home Yank	1,000	N/A	135.00	800
1993 When Prayers are Answered	850		245.00	245
1991 When You See Zeros, Fight Em'	1,500		245.00	245

Poskas - P. Poskas

YEAR ISSUE	EDITION LIMIT	YEAR RETD.	ISSUE PRICE	*QUOTE U.S.$
1997 Island Sea	650		175.00	175
1996 Yellow Moon Rising	850		175.00	175

Presse - H. Presse

YEAR ISSUE	EDITION LIMIT	YEAR RETD.	ISSUE PRICE	*QUOTE U.S.$
1998 Dance of the Sun	550		125.00	125
1998 Stay This Moment	550		125.00	125
1998 The Victorian	550		125.00	125

Prosek - J. Prosek

YEAR ISSUE	EDITION LIMIT	YEAR RETD.	ISSUE PRICE	*QUOTE U.S.$
1996 Alaskan Rainbow Trout	1,000		125.00	125
1996 Brook Trout	1,000		125.00	125
1997 Yellowstone Cutthroat Trout	1,000		125.00	125

Reynolds - J. Reynolds

YEAR ISSUE	EDITION LIMIT	YEAR RETD.	ISSUE PRICE	*QUOTE U.S.$
1994 Arizona Cowboys	850	N/A	195.00	245
1994 Cold Country, Hot Coffee	1,000		185.00	185
1994 The Henry	850	N/A	195.00	195
1995 Mystic of the Plains	1,000		195.00	195
1994 Quiet Place	1,000	N/A	185.00	195
1994 Spring Showers	1,000		225.00	225
1996 A Strange Sign (canvas)	550		750.00	750
1996 The Summit	950		195.00	195
1998 Swing Shift	450		495.00	495

Riddick - R. Riddick

YEAR ISSUE	EDITION LIMIT	YEAR RETD.	ISSUE PRICE	*QUOTE U.S.$
1998 Prelude to the Dance	550		185.00	185

Riley - K. Riley

YEAR ISSUE	EDITION LIMIT	YEAR RETD.	ISSUE PRICE	*QUOTE U.S.$
1997 As One (Canvas print)	550		395.00	395
1997 Ceremonial Regalia	550		495.00	495

Simpkins - J. Simpkins

YEAR ISSUE	EDITION LIMIT	YEAR RETD.	ISSUE PRICE	*QUOTE U.S.$
1994 All My Love	850		125.00	125
1993 Angels	850		225.00	225
1994 Gold Falls	1,750		195.00	195
1995 Mrs. Tenderhart	1,000		175.00	175
1995 Pavane in Gold	2,500		175.00	175
1996 Pavane von Khint	1,000		195.00	195
1994 Reverence For Life w/border & card	750	N/A	175.00	335
1994 Reverence For Life w/frame	100	N/A	600.00	600
1995 Where Love Resides (Premiere Ed.)	1,000		450.00	450
1995 Where Love Resides (Studio Ed.)	1,000		225.00	225

Smith - T. Smith

YEAR ISSUE	EDITION LIMIT	YEAR RETD.	ISSUE PRICE	*QUOTE U.S.$
1992 The Challenger	1,300		185.00	185
1995 The Refuge	1,000		245.00	245

Solberg - M. Solberg

YEAR ISSUE	EDITION LIMIT	YEAR RETD.	ISSUE PRICE	*QUOTE U.S.$
1997 Rufous and Roses	550		150.00	150

Spirin - G. Spirin

YEAR ISSUE	EDITION LIMIT	YEAR RETD.	ISSUE PRICE	*QUOTE U.S.$
1997 Carnival in Venice (Inkjet)	200		395.00	395
1997 Tournament of Honor	200		395.00	395

Terpning - H. Terpning

YEAR ISSUE	EDITION LIMIT	YEAR RETD.	ISSUE PRICE	*QUOTE U.S.$
1992 Against the Coldmaker	1,000	1992	195.00	195
1993 The Apache Fire Makers	1,000	1993	235.00	235
1993 Army Regulations	1,000		235.00	235
1997 Before the Little Big Horn	1,000		195.00	195
1987 Blackfeet Among the Aspen	1,000	1987	225.00	250
1985 Blackfeet Spectators	475	1985	350.00	1095-1200
1988 Blood Man	1,250	1988	95.00	300
1982 CA Set Pony Soldiers/Warriors	1,000	1982	200.00	450-650
1985 The Cache	1,000		175.00	175
1992 Capture of the Horse Bundle	1,250		235.00	235
1982 Chief Joseph Rides to Surrender	1,000	1982	150.00	2600-3000
1996 Color of Sun	1,000	1998	175.00	175
1986 Comanche Spoilers	1,000		195.00	195
1990 Cree Finery	1,000		225.00	225
1996 Crossing Below the Falls	1,000	1996	245.00	245
1983 Crossing Medicine Lodge Creek	1,000	1983	150.00	200-300
1994 Crow Camp, 1864	1,000	1994	235.00	235
1997 Crow Pipe Ceremony	975	1998	895.00	895
1984 Crow Pipe Holder	1,000		150.00	150
1991 Digging in at Sappa Creek MW	650	1991	375.00	375
1994 The Feast	1,850	1994	245.00	285
1992 Four Sacred Drummers	1,000	1992	225.00	225
1997 Gold Seekers to the Black Hills'	1,000	1997	245.00	245
1998 Holy Man of the Blackfoot	975	1998	895.00	895-985
1988 Hope Springs Eternal-Ghost Dance	2,250		225.00	800
1998 Horse Feathers	975		495.00	495
1994 Isdzan-Apache Woman	1,000	1994	175.00	195

*Quotes have been rounded up to nearest dollar

YEAR	ISSUE	EDITION LIMIT	YEAR RETD.	ISSUE PRICE	*QUOTE U.S.$
1991	The Last Buffalo	1,000		225.00	225
1991	Leader of Men	1,250	1991	235.00	300-500
1984	The Long Shot, signed	1,000	1984	55.00	75
1984	Medicine Man of the Cheyene	450	1984	350.00	2895-3195
1993	Medicine Pipe	1,000	1993	150.00	185
1985	One Man's Castle	1,000		150.00	150
1995	Opening the Sacred Bundle (canvas)	550	1995	850.00	1995-2295
1983	Paints	1,000	1983	140.00	200
1992	Passing Into Womanhood	650	1992	375.00	400
1987	The Ploy	1,000	1987	195.00	600-695
1992	Prairie Knights	1,000	1992	225.00	225
1996	Prairie Shade	1,000		225.00	225
1987	Preparing for the Sun Dance	1,000	1987	175.00	300-375
1988	Pride of the Cheyene	1,250		195.00	195
1993	Profile of Wisdom	1,000		175.00	175
1989	Scout's Report	1,250		225.00	225
1985	The Scouts of General Crook	1,000	1985	175.00	250-275
1988	Search For the Pass	1,000	1988	225.00	250
1982	Search For the Renegades	1,000	1982	150.00	195
1989	Shepherd of the Plains Cameo	1,250		125.00	125
1982	Shield of Her Husband	1,000	1982	150.00	600-900
1983	Shoshonis	1,250	1983	85.00	200-225
1985	The Signal	1,250	1985	90.00	400-600
1981	Sioux Flag Carrier	1,000	1981	125.00	165
1981	Small Comfort	1,000	1981	135.00	400-450
1993	Soldier Hat	1,000		235.00	235
1981	The Spectators	1,000	1981	135.00	195-295
1994	Spirit of the Rainmaker	1,500		235.00	235
1983	Staff Carrier	1,250	1983	90.00	550
1986	Status Symbols	1,000	1986	185.00	1250-1600
1981	Stones that Speak	1,000	1981	150.00	950-1200
1989	The Storyteller w/Video & Book	1,500	1989	950.00	1150
1992	The Strength of Eagles	1,250		235.00	235
1988	Sunday Best	1,250		195.00	195
1995	Talking Robe	1,250		235.00	235
1990	Telling of the Legends	1,250	1990	225.00	900-1200
1986	Thunderpipe and the Holy Man	550	1986	350.00	500-800
1997	To Capture Enemy Horses	950		225.00	225
1995	Trading Post at Chadron Creek	1,000		225.00	225
1991	Transferring the Medicine Shield	850	1991	375.00	1300-1800
1996	The Trophy (canvas)	1,000		925.00	925
1981	The Victors	1,000	1981	150.00	650-825
1985	The Warning	1,650	1985	175.00	550-750
1986	Watching the Column	1,250	1986	90.00	400
1998	The Weather Dancer Dream	1,000		225.00	225
1990	When Careless Spelled Disaster	1,000	1990	225.00	350
1987	Winter Coat	1,250	1987	95.00	175
1996	With Mother Earth	1,250		245.00	245
1984	Woman of the Sioux	1,000	1984	165.00	925-1200

Townsend - B. Townsend

YEAR	ISSUE	EDITION LIMIT	YEAR RETD.	ISSUE PRICE	*QUOTE U.S.$
1994	Autumn Hillside	1,000		175.00	175
1993	Dusk	1,250		195.00	195
1995	Gathering of the Herd	1,000		195.00	195
1993	Hailstorm Creek	1,250		195.00	195
1994	Mountain Light	1,000		195.00	195
1992	Open Ridge	1,500	N/A	225.00	225
1993	Out of the Shadows	1,500	1998	195.00	195
1996	Out of the Valley	850		185.00	185
1992	Riverbend	1,000	N/A	185.00	300

Weiss - J. Weiss

YEAR	ISSUE	EDITION LIMIT	YEAR RETD.	ISSUE PRICE	*QUOTE U.S.$
1995	All Is Well	1,250		165.00	165
1984	Basset Hound Puppies	1,000	N/A	65.00	200-300
1988	Black Labrador Head Study Cameo	1,000		90.00	90
1984	Cocker Spaniel Puppies	1,000	N/A	75.00	200-295
1992	Cuddle Time	850		95.00	95
1998	Double Trouble	1,450		95.00	95
1993	A Feeling of Warmth	1,000	N/A	165.00	475
1994	Forever Friends	1,000	1994	95.00	255
1983	Golden Retriever Puppies	1,000	N/A	65.00	900
1988	Goldens at the Shore	850	N/A	145.00	525-725
1997	Good As Gold	1,250	1998	95.00	95
1995	I Didn't Do It	1,250		125.00	125
1982	Lab Puppies	1,000	N/A	65.00	195-250
1996	New Friends	1,000	1996	125.00	195
1992	No Swimming Lessons Today	1,000	1998	140.00	140
1984	Old English Sheepdog Puppies	1,000	N/A	65.00	200-250
1993	Old Friends	1,000	1993	95.00	700-800
1986	One Morning in October	850	N/A	125.00	525-650
1985	Persian Kitten	1,000	N/A	65.00	80-95
1982	Rebel & Soda	1,000	N/A	45.00	135
1997	Storytime	850		95.00	95
1998	Three's Company	1,250		95.00	95
1991	Wake Up Call	850		165.00	165
1988	Yellow Labrador Head Study Cameo	1,000		90.00	90

Williams - B.D. Williams

YEAR	ISSUE	EDITION LIMIT	YEAR RETD.	ISSUE PRICE	*QUOTE U.S.$
1993	Avant Garde S&N	500	N/A	60.00	60
1993	Avant Garde unsigned	2,603	N/A	30.00	30

Wootton - F. Wootton

YEAR	ISSUE	EDITION LIMIT	YEAR RETD.	ISSUE PRICE	*QUOTE U.S.$
1990	Adlertag, 15 August 1940 & Video	1,500	N/A	245.00	245
1993	April Morning:France, 1918	850		245.00	245
1983	The Battle of Britain	850	N/A	150.00	300
1988	Encounter with the Red Baron	850	N/A	165.00	200
1985	Huntsmen and Hounds	650		115.00	115
1982	Knights of the Sky	850	N/A	165.00	375
1993	Last Combat of the Red Baron	850		185.00	185
1992	The Last of the First F. Wooten	850		235.00	235
1994	Peenemunde	850		245.00	245
1986	The Spitfire Legend	850	N/A	195.00	195

Wysocki - C. Wysocki

YEAR	ISSUE	EDITION LIMIT	YEAR RETD.	ISSUE PRICE	*QUOTE U.S.$
1987	'Twas the Twilight Before Christmas	7,500	N/A	95.00	150-195
1988	The Americana Bowl	3,500		295.00	295
1983	Amish Neighbors	1,000	N/A	150.00	1100-1200
1989	Another Year At Sea	2,500	N/A	175.00	450-900
1983	Applebutter Makers	1,000	N/A	135.00	1200-1350
1987	Bach's Magnificat in D Minor	2,250	N/A	150.00	800-825
1991	Beauty And The Beast	2,000	N/A	125.00	125-175
1990	Belly Warmers	2,500		150.00	195
1984	Bird House Cameo	1,000	N/A	85.00	275-295
1985	Birds of a Feather	1,250	N/A	145.00	950-1150
1989	Bostonians And Beans (PC)	6,711	N/A	225.00	625-650
1979	Butternut Farms	1,000	N/A	75.00	1350-1450
1980	Caleb's Buggy Barn	1,000	N/A	80.00	395-435
1984	Cape Cod Cold Fish Party	1,000	N/A	150.00	150-195
1986	Carnival Capers	620		200.00	200
1981	Carver Coggins	1,000	N/A	145.00	1050-1150
1989	Christmas Greeting	11,000	N/A	125.00	100-125
1982	Christmas Print, 1982	2,000	N/A	80.00	500
1984	Chumbuddies, signed	1,000		55.00	55
1985	Clammers at Hodge's Horn	1,000	N/A	150.00	1200-1250
1983	Commemorative Print, 1983	2,000	N/A	55.00	55
1983	Commemorative Print, 1984	2,000		55.00	55
1984	Commemorative Print, 1985	2,000		55.00	55
1985	Commemorative Print, 1986	2,000		55.00	55
1984	Cotton Country	1,000	N/A	150.00	350-375
1983	Country Race	1,000	N/A	150.00	235-350
1997	Cow (framed)	150		135.00	135
1986	Daddy's Coming Home	1,250	N/A	150.00	875-895
1987	Dahalia Dinalhaven Makes a Dory Deal	2,250	N/A	150.00	425-475
1986	Dancing Pheasant Farms	1,750	N/A	165.00	405-525
1980	Derby Square	1,000	N/A	90.00	1000-1100
1986	Devilbelly Bay	1,000	N/A	145.00	250-395
1986	Devilstone Harbor/An American Celebration (Print & Book)	3,500	N/A	195.00	375-400
1989	Dreamers	3,000	N/A	175.00	425-450
1992	Ethel the Gourmet	10,179	N/A	150.00	650-750
1979	Fairhaven by the Sea	1,000	N/A	75.00	700-750
1988	Feathered Critics	2,500		150.00	150
1997	Fox Hill Farms (framed)	150		135.00	135
1979	Fox Run	1,000	N/A	75.00	950-1100
1984	The Foxy Fox Outfoxes the Fox Hunters	1,500	N/A	150.00	395-425
1992	Frederick the Literate	6,500	N/A	150.00	1600-2900
1989	Fun Lovin' Silly Folks	3,000	N/A	185.00	475-495
1984	The Gang's All Here	Open		65.00	65
1984	The Gang's All Here, remarque	250		90.00	90
1992	Gay Head Light	2,500		165.00	165
1997	Hawk River Hollow (framed)	150		135.00	135
1986	Hickory Haven Canal	1,500	N/A	165.00	650-900
1988	Home Is My Sailor	2,500	N/A	150.00	150
1985	I Love America	2,000		20.00	20
1990	Jingle Bell Teddy and Friends	5,000		125.00	125
1980	Jolly Hill Farms	1,000	N/A	75.00	650-850
1997	Kitty Treat (framed)	150		135.00	135
1986	Lady Liberty's Independence Day Enterprising Immigrants	1,500	N/A	140.00	375-525
1992	Love Letter From Laramie	1,500		150.00	150
1989	The Memory Maker	2,500	1998	165.00	165-195
1985	Merrymakers Serenade	1,250	N/A	135.00	135-175
1986	Mr. Swallobark	2,000	N/A	145.00	1300-1550
1982	The Nantucket	1,000	N/A	145.00	275
1997	Nantucket Winds (framed)	150		135.00	135
1981	Olde America	1,500	N/A	125.00	450-500
1981	Page's Bake Shoppe	1,000	N/A	115.00	275-350
1997	Peppercricket Farms (framed)	150		135.00	135
1997	Pickwick Cottage (framed)	150		135.00	135
1983	Plum Island Sound, signed	1,000	N/A	55.00	675
1983	Plum Island Sound, unsigned	Open	N/A	40.00	40
1981	Prairie Wind Flowers	1,000	N/A	125.00	1375-1495
1992	Proud Little Angler	2,750	N/A	150.00	200
1994	Remington w/Book-Heartland	15,000	1998	195.00	250-300
1990	Robin Hood	2,000		165.00	165
1991	Rockland Breakwater Light	2,500	N/A	165.00	165-235
1985	Salty Witch Bay	475	N/A	350.00	2400
1991	Sea Captain's Wife Abiding	1,500	N/A	150.00	150-165
1979	Shall We?	1,000	N/A	75.00	1200-1450
1982	Sleepy Town West	1,500	N/A	150.00	600-650
1984	Storin' Up	450	N/A	325.00	700-750
1982	Sunset Hills, Texas Wildcatters	1,000	N/A	125.00	150-175
1984	Sweetheart Chessmate	1,000	N/A	95.00	1200
1983	Tea by the Sea	1,000	N/A	145.00	1000-1350
1997	Teddy Bear Express (framed)	150		135.00	135
1993	The Three Sisters of Nauset, 1880	2,500	N/A	165.00	165-195
1984	A Warm Christmas Love	3,951	N/A	80.00	200-375
1990	Wednesday Night Checkers	2,500	1998	175.00	215-295
1991	West Quoddy Head Light, Maine	2,500		165.00	165
1990	Where The Bouys Are	2,750	N/A	175.00	175-195
1991	Whistle Stop Christmas	5,000		125.00	125
1980	Yankee Wink Hollow	1,000	N/A	95.00	1000-1200
1987	Yearning For My Captain	2,000	N/A	150.00	225-325
1987	You've Been So Long at Sea, Horatio	2,500	N/A	150.00	215-295

Hadley House

Agnew - A. Agnew

YEAR	ISSUE	EDITION LIMIT	YEAR RETD.	ISSUE PRICE	*QUOTE U.S.$
1997	American Odyssey	750		125.00	125
1997	Birds of a Feather	999		50.00	50
1997	Quick Silver	999	1998	75.00	235
1997	Time Well Spent	999		150.00	150

Barnhouse - D. Barnhouse

YEAR	ISSUE	EDITION LIMIT	YEAR RETD.	ISSUE PRICE	*QUOTE U.S.$
1997	Every Boys' Dream	1,950		150.00	150
1997	A Finishing Touch	1,950		150.00	150
1997	Horsepower	1,950		150.00	150
1997	Spring Cleaning	1,950	1997	150.00	150
1997	Sunset Strip	1,950		150.00	150
1997	The Warmth of Home	1,950		150.00	150

Bogle - C. Bogle

YEAR	ISSUE	EDITION LIMIT	YEAR RETD.	ISSUE PRICE	*QUOTE U.S.$
1997	The Colors of Autumn	999	1997	75.00	75
1997	Crossing Paths	999		125.00	125
1997	A Golden Moment	999	1998	100.00	350

Bush - D. Bush

YEAR	ISSUE	EDITION LIMIT	YEAR RETD.	ISSUE PRICE	*QUOTE U.S.$
1997	Cabin Fever	1,250		125.00	125
1997	Evening Run	999	1997	125.00	125-295
1997	Legends of The Lake	1,250	1998	125.00	125
1994	Moondance	999	1995	125.00	220-315
1997	Once In a Life Time	999		125.00	125
1996	Still of the Night	1,250	1997	125.00	195-215
1997	Time Flies	1,250		125.00	125
1997	Winter Colors	Open		35.00	35

Capser - M. Capser

YEAR	ISSUE	EDITION LIMIT	YEAR RETD.	ISSUE PRICE	*QUOTE U.S.$
1997	Blossoms and Promises	999		100.00	100
1993	Briar and Brambles	999	1996	100.00	100
1992	Comes the Dawn	600		100.00	100
1994	Dashing Through the Snow	999		100.00	100
1994	Down the Lane	Open		30.00	30
1995	Enchanted Waters	999		100.00	100
1997	Grandma's Garden	999		100.00	100
1995	Grapevine Estates	999	1998	100.00	100
1997	Guiding The Sails	999	1998	100.00	100
1994	The Lifting Fog	Open		30.00	30
1995	Mariner's Point	999	1996	100.00	100
1994	Nappin'	999		100.00	100
1994	A Night's Quiet	999		100.00	100
1995	On Gentle Wings	999		100.00	100
1993	Pickets & Vines	999	1994	100.00	100
1992	Reflections	600	1993	100.00	100
1993	Rock Creek Spring	999		80.00	80
1994	September Blush	999	1996	100.00	100
1992	Silence Unbroken	600	1996	100.00	100
1993	Skyline Serenade	600	1993	100.00	100
1995	Spring Creek Fever	999	1996	100.00	100
1993	A Summer's Glow	999	1997	60.00	60
1997	Sunrise Symphony	999		100.00	100
1994	A Time For Us	999		125.00	125
1994	To Search Again	Open		30.00	30
1992	The Watch	600	1993	100.00	150-517
1994	The Way Home	Open		30.00	30
1993	Whispering Wings	1,500	1994	100.00	100
1997	Woodland Warmth	999		125.00	125

Franca - O. Franca

YEAR	ISSUE	EDITION LIMIT	YEAR RETD.	ISSUE PRICE	*QUOTE U.S.$
1988	The Apache	950	1990	70.00	175
1990	Blue Navajo	1,500	1991	125.00	319-325
1990	Blue Tranquility	999	1990	100.00	450-776
1988	Cacique	950	1990	70.00	150-216
1990	Cecy	1,500	1992	125.00	225-305
1990	Destiny	999	1990	100.00	100-345
1991	Early Morning	3,600	1994	125.00	225
1993	Evening In Taos	4,000	1994	80.00	80
1988	Feathered Hair Ties	600	1988	80.00	1198-1595
1990	Feathered Hair Ties II	999	1990	100.00	259-300
1991	The Lovers	2,400	1991	125.00	1050-1224
1991	The Model	1,500	1991	125.00	469-495
1992	Navajo Daydream	3,600	1993	175.00	425-450
1989	Navajo Fantasy	999	1989	80.00	150-302
1992	Navajo Meditating	4,000	1994	80.00	125
1992	Navajo Reflection	4,000	1992	80.00	100-225
1990	Navajo Summer	999	1988	100.00	175-345
1991	Olympia	1,500	1991	125.00	350-431
1989	Pink Navajo	999	1989	80.00	250-345
1988	The Red Shawl	600	1990	80.00	300
1991	Red Wolf	1,500	1991	125.00	125-130
1990	Santa Fe	1,500	1991	125.00	150-300
1988	Sitting Bull	950	1990	70.00	200-259
1988	Slow Bull	950	1990	70.00	200
1990	Turqoise Necklace	999	1990	100.00	200-317
1990	Wind Song	999	1990	100.00	195-345
1992	Wind Song II	4,000	1992	80.00	150-175
1989	Winter	999	1989	80.00	175
1989	Young Warrior	999	1989	80.00	450-560

Hanks - S. Hanks

YEAR	ISSUE	EDITION LIMIT	YEAR RETD.	ISSUE PRICE	*QUOTE U.S.$
1994	All Gone Awry	2,000		150.00	150
1994	All In a Row	2,000	1994	150.00	164-200
1997	Being Perfect Angels	1,500	1997	150.00	150
1995	A Captive Audience	1,500	1997	150.00	150
1995	Cat's Lair	1,500		150.00	150
1993	Catching The Sun	999	1993	150.00	495
1992	Conferring With the Sea	999	1993	125.00	495
1990	Contemplation	999	1997	100.00	150
1995	Country Comfort	999	1997	100.00	100
1995	Drip Castles	4,000		30.00	30
1991	Duet	999	1993	150.00	600
1990	Emotional Appeal	999	1998	150.00	225
1993	Gathering Thoughts	1,500	1995	150.00	345
1996	Her Side	1,500	1997	100.00	100
1992	An Innocent View	999	1992	150.00	315-450

*Quotes have been rounded up to nearest dollar

YEAR ISSUE	EDITION LIMIT	YEAR RETD.	ISSUE PRICE	*QUOTE U.S.$
1994 The Journey Is The Goal	1,500	1995	150.00	150
1995 Kali	Open		25.00	25
1996 Little Angels	999	1996	125.00	150-250
1993 Little Black Crow	1,500		150.00	150
1994 Michaela and Friends/Book	2,500		200.00	200
1997 The Music Room	1,500	1997	150.00	150
1993 The New Arrival	1,500	1995	150.00	200
1995 Pacific Sanctuary	1,500		150.00	150
1993 Peeking Out	Open		40.00	40
1993 Places I Remember	1,500		150.00	150
1990 Quiet Rapport	999	1997	150.00	300
1996 Sending Flowers	1,500	1997	150.00	180-225
1993 A Sense of Belonging	1,500	1997	150.00	150
1995 Small Miracle	1,500		125.00	125
1992 Sometimes It's the Little Things	999	1995	125.00	225
1994 Southwestern Bedroom	999	1997	150.00	180-225
1992 Stepping Stones	999	1993	150.00	295
1991 Sunday Afternoon	Open		40.00	40
1997 Sunshine Across The Sheets	1,500	1998	100.00	100
1992 Things Worth Keeping	999	1991	125.00	1100-1450
1993 The Thinkers	1,500		150.00	150
1994 Water Lilies In Bloom	750		295.00	295
1993 When Her Blue Eyes Close	999		100.00	100
1994 Where The Light Shines Brightest	1,500		150.00	150
1991 A World For Our Children	999	1992	125.00	1595

Hulings - C. Hulings

YEAR ISSUE	EDITION LIMIT	YEAR RETD.	ISSUE PRICE	*QUOTE U.S.$
1990 Ancient French Farmhouse	999		150.00	225
1989 Chechaquene-Morocco Market Square	999	1993	150.00	250
1992 Cuernavaca Flower Market	580		225.00	225
1988 Ile de la Cite-Paris	580	1990	150.00	225
1990 The Lonely Man	999	1993	150.00	150
1988 Onteniente	580	1989	150.00	425-457
1991 Place des Ternes	580	1991	195.00	700
1989 Portuguese Vegetable Woman	999	1993	85.00	216
1994 The Red Raincoat	580		225.00	225
1990 Spanish Shawl	999	1994	125.00	112-125
1993 Spring Flowers	580		225.00	225
1992 Sunday Afternoon	580		195.00	275
1988 Three Cats on a Grapevine	580	1989	65.00	225
1993 Washday In Provence	580		225.00	225

Redlin - T. Redlin

YEAR ISSUE	EDITION LIMIT	YEAR RETD.	ISSUE PRICE	*QUOTE U.S.$
1981 1981 MN Duck Stamp Print	7,800	1981	125.00	150
1982 1982 MN Trout Stamp Print	960	1982	125.00	600
1983 1983 ND Duck Stamp Print	3,438	1983	135.00	150
1984 1984 Quail Conservation	1,500	1984	135.00	135
1985 1985 MN Duck Stamp	4,385	1985	135.00	135
1985 Afternoon Glow	960	1985	150.00	1095-1475
1979 Ageing Shoreline	960	1979	40.00	395-733
1981 All Clear	960	1981	150.00	395
1994 America, America	29,500		250.00	250
1994 And Crown Thy Good w/Brotherhood	29,500		250.00	250
1977 Apple River Mallards	Retrd.	1977	10.00	100
1981 April Snow	960	1981	100.00	595-776
1989 Aroma of Fall	6,800	1989	200.00	1700
1987 Autumn Afternoon	4,800	1987	100.00	795
1993 Autumn Evening	29,500		250.00	250
1980 Autumn Run	960	1980	60.00	375
1983 Autumn Shoreline	Retrd.	1983	50.00	450-776
1997 Autumn Traditions	1,950		275.00	275
1978 Back from the Fields	720	1978	40.00	250
1985 Back to the Sanctuary	960	1986	150.00	350-475
1978 Backwater Mallards	720	1978	40.00	945
1983 Backwoods Cabin	960	1983	150.00	965
1990 Best Friends (AP)	570	1993	1000.00	1895
1982 The Birch Line	960	1982	100.00	1295-1681
1984 Bluebill Point (AP)	240	1984	300.00	785
1988 Boulder Ridge	4,800		150.00	150
1997 Bountiful Harvest	19,500		275.00	275
1980 Breaking Away	960	1980	60.00	430
1985 Breaking Cover	960	1985	150.00	400-862
1981 Broken Covey	960	1981	100.00	525-664
1985 Brousing	960	1985	150.00	895
1994 Campfire Tales	29,500		250.00	250
1988 Catching the Scent	2,400		200.00	200
1986 Changing Seasons-Autumn	960	1986	150.00	450-503
1987 Changing Seasons-Spring	960	1987	200.00	475-845
1984 Changing Seasons-Summer	960	1984	150.00	1400
1986 Changing Seasons-Winter	960	1986	200.00	600
1985 Clear View	1,500	1985	300.00	1195-1552
1980 Clearing the Rail	960	1980	60.00	850-1034
1984 Closed for the Season	960	1984	150.00	495-550
1979 Colorful Trio	960	1979	40.00	800
1991 Comforts of Home	22,900	N/A	175.00	275-300
1986 Coming Home	2,400	1986	100.00	2200-2400
1992 The Conservationists	29,500		175.00	175
1988 Country Neighbors	4,800	1988	150.00	600
1980 Country Road	960	1980	60.00	650-745
1987 Deer Crossing	2,400	1987	200.00	1195-1379
1985 Delayed Departure	1,500	1985	150.00	500-1000
1980 Drifting	960	1980	60.00	400
1987 Evening Chores (print & book)	2,400	1988	400.00	1000-1121
1985 Evening Company	960	1985	150.00	500-1300
1983 Evening Glow	960	1983	150.00	2250
1987 Evening Harvest	960	1987	200.00	1350-2155
1982 Evening Retreat (AP)	300	1982	400.00	3000
1990 Evening Solitude	9,500	1990	200.00	550-650
1983 Evening Surprise	960	1983	150.00	1000-3300
1990 Evening With Friends	19,500	1991	225.00	1500
1990 Family Traditions	Retrd.	1993	80.00	240-250
1979 Fighting a Headwind	960	1979	30.00	350
1991 Flying Free	14,500		200.00	200
1993 For Amber Waves of Grain	29,500		250.00	250
1993 For Purple Mountains Majesty	29,500		250.00	250
1995 From Sea to Shining Sea	29,500		250.00	250
1994 God Shed His Grace on Thee	29,500		250.00	250
1987 Golden Retreat (AP)	500	1986	800.00	2000
1995 Harvest Moon Ball	9,500	1995	275.00	275-350
1986 Hazy Afternoon	2,560	1986	200.00	850
1990 Heading Home	Retrd.	1993	80.00	135-200
1997 A Helping Hand	95,000		275.00	275
1983 Hidden Point	960	1983	150.00	600
1981 High Country	960	1981	100.00	600
1981 Hightailing	960	1981	75.00	350
1980 The Homestead	960	1980	60.00	640
1988 Homeward Bound	Retrd.	1993	70.00	150
1989 Homeward Bound	Retrd.	1994	80.00	250
1988 House Call	6,800	1990	175.00	1000
1991 Hunter's Haven (A/P)	1,000	N/A	175.00	1000
1989 Indian Summer	4,800	1989	200.00	725-905
1980 Intruders	960	1980	60.00	320
1982 The Landing	Retrd.	1982	30.00	80
1981 The Landmark	960	1981	100.00	400
1984 Leaving the Sanctuary	960	1984	150.00	475
1994 Lifetime Companions	29,500		250.00	250
1988 Lights of Home	9,500	1988	125.00	675-850
1979 The Loner	960	1979	40.00	300
1990 Master of the Valley	6,800		200.00	200
1988 The Master's Domain	2,400	1988	225.00	800-850
1988 Moonlight Retreat (A/P)	530	N/A	1000.00	1600
1979 Morning Chores	960	1979	40.00	1350
1984 Morning Glow	960	1984	150.00	1400-1879
1981 Morning Retreat (AP)	240	N/A	400.00	3000
1989 Morning Rounds	6,800	1992	175.00	595
1991 Morning Solitude	12,107	1991	250.00	405-600
1984 Night Harvest	960	1984	150.00	1795
1985 Night Light	1,500	1985	300.00	1195
1986 Night Mapling	960	1986	200.00	550-1500
1995 A Night on the Town	29,500		150.00	150
1980 Night Watch	2,400	1980	60.00	1000
1984 Nightflight (AP)	360	1984	600.00	2200
1982 October Evening	960	1982	100.00	1000
1989 Office Hours	6,800	1991	175.00	948
1992 Oh Beautiful for Spacious Skies	29,500		250.00	250
1978 Old Loggers Trail	720	1978	40.00	950-1200
1983 On the Alert	960	1983	125.00	400
1977 Over the Blowdown	Retrd.	1977	20.00	400-690
1978 Over the Rushes	720	1978	40.00	450
1981 Passing Through	960	1981	100.00	225
1983 Peaceful Evening	960	1983	100.00	1595
1991 Pleasures of Winter	24,500	1992	150.00	221-245
1986 Prairie Monuments	960	1986	200.00	795
1988 Prairie Morning	4,800	1988	150.00	550-603
1984 Prairie Skyline	960	1984	150.00	2328
1983 Prairie Springs	960	1983	150.00	595
1987 Prepared for the Season	Retrd.	1994	70.00	150-216
1990 Pure Contentment	9,500	1989	150.00	475-500
1978 Quiet Afternoon	720	1978	40.00	695
1988 Quiet of the Evening	4,800	1988	150.00	450-595
1982 Reflections	960	1982	100.00	600
1985 Riverside Pond	960	1985	150.00	525
1984 Rural Route	960	1984	150.00	395
1983 Rushing Rapids	960	1983	125.00	750
1980 Rusty Refuge I	960	1980	60.00	295
1981 Rusty Refuge II	960	1980	100.00	495
1984 Rusty Refuge III	960	1984	150.00	595
1985 Rusty Refuge IV	960	1985	150.00	695
1980 Secluded Pond	960	1980	60.00	295
1982 Seed Hunters	960	1982	100.00	575
1985 Sharing Season I	Retrd.	1993	60.00	150-225
1986 Sharing Season II	Retrd.	1993	60.00	225-240
1981 Sharing the Bounty	960	1981	100.00	1500
1994 Sharing the Evening	29,500		175.00	175
1987 Sharing the Solitude	2,400	1987	125.00	850-950
1986 Silent Flight	960	1986	150.00	335-400
1980 Silent Sunset	960	1980	60.00	780-1121
1984 Silent Wings Suite (set of 4)	960	1984	200.00	750
1981 Soft Shadows	960	1984	100.00	325
1989 Special Memories (AP)	570		1000.00	1000
1982 Spring Mapling	960	1982	100.00	975
1981 Spring Run-Off	1,700	1981	125.00	695-991
1980 Spring Thaw	960	1980	60.00	460
1980 Squall Line	960	1980	60.00	300
1978 Startled	720	1978	30.00	995-1336
1986 Stormy Weather	1,500	1986	200.00	550
1992 Summertime	24,900		225.00	225
1997 Sunday Morning	9,500		275.00	275
1984 Sundown	960	1984	300.00	575
1986 Sunlit Trail	960	1986	150.00	200-350
1984 Sunny Afternoon	960	1984	150.00	700
1987 That Special Time	2,400	1987	125.00	825-850
1987 Together for the Season	Open		70.00	100
1995 Total Comfort	9,500	1995	275.00	275
1986 Twilight Glow	960	1986	200.00	700-1500
1988 Wednesday Afternoon	6,800	1989	175.00	900
1990 Welcome to Paradise	14,500	1990	150.00	700-974
1985 Whistle Stop	960	1985	150.00	785
1979 Whitecaps	960	1979	40.00	445
1982 Whitewater	960	1982	100.00	400
1982 Winter Haven	500	1982	85.00	800
1977 Winter Snows	Retrd.	1977	20.00	595-690
1984 Winter Windbreak	960	1984	150.00	750
1992 Winter Wonderland	29,500	1993	150.00	250

Hamilton Collection

Mickey Mantle - R. Tanenbaum

YEAR ISSUE	EDITION LIMIT	YEAR RETD.	ISSUE PRICE	*QUOTE U.S.$
1996 An All American Legend-The Mick	Open		95.00	95

Imperial Graphics, Ltd.

Chang - L. Chang

YEAR ISSUE	EDITION LIMIT	YEAR RETD.	ISSUE PRICE	*QUOTE U.S.$
1988 Egrets with Lotus S/N	1,950		10.00	10
1988 Flamingos with Catail S/N	1,950		10.00	10

Irvine - G. Irvine

YEAR ISSUE	EDITION LIMIT	YEAR RETD.	ISSUE PRICE	*QUOTE U.S.$
1995 Pansies	Open		8.00	8
1995 Violets	Open		8.00	8

Lee - H.C. Lee

YEAR ISSUE	EDITION LIMIT	YEAR RETD.	ISSUE PRICE	*QUOTE U.S.$
1988 Blue Bird of Paradise S/N	950		35.00	35
1988 Cat & Callas S/N	1,950		30.00	30
1990 Double Red Hibiscus S/N	1,950		16.00	16
1988 Hummingbird I S/N	1,950		16.00	16
1988 Hummingbird II S/N	1,950		16.00	16
1990 Maroon & Mauve Peonies S/N	950		60.00	60
1990 Maroon & Peach Peonies S/N	950		60.00	60
1990 Maroon Peony S/N	2,950		20.00	20
1990 Peacock w/Tulip & Peony S/N	1,950		105.00	105
1990 Peonies & Butterflies S/N	2,950		40.00	40
1990 Pink Peony S/N	2,950		20.00	20
1990 Single Red Hibiscus S/N	1,950		16.00	16
1988 White Bird of Paradise S/N	950		35.00	35
1988 White Peacocks w/Peonies S/N	950		65.00	65

Liu - Angels Among Us - L. Liu

YEAR ISSUE	EDITION LIMIT	YEAR RETD.	ISSUE PRICE	*QUOTE U.S.$
1997 Angel of Light S/N	3,500		125.00	125
1997 Angel of Love S/N	3,500		80.00	80
1996 Angel with Harp S/N	5,500		40.00	40
1996 Angel with Trumpet S/N	5,500		40.00	40
1996 Guardian Angel S/N	5,500		125.00	125
1997 Urn with Irises S/N	3,500		45.00	45
1997 Urn with Tulips S/N	3,500		45.00	45

Liu - Celestial Symphony Series - L. Liu

YEAR ISSUE	EDITION LIMIT	YEAR RETD.	ISSUE PRICE	*QUOTE U.S.$
1995 Flute Interlude S/N	5,500		40.00	40
1995 French Horn Melody S/N	5,500		40.00	40
1995 Piano Sonata S/N	5,500		40.00	40
1995 Violin Concerto S/N	5,500		40.00	40

Liu - L. Liu

YEAR ISSUE	EDITION LIMIT	YEAR RETD.	ISSUE PRICE	*QUOTE U.S.$
1989 Abundance of Lilies (poster)	Closed	1993	30.00	30
1998 Abundant Blessings S/N	3,500		125.00	125
XX Afternoon Nap S/N	1,000		45.00	45
1994 Allen's Hummingbird w/Columbine S/N	3,300	1994	30.00	50
1987 Amaryllis S/N	1,950	N/A	16.00	60
1993 Anna's Hummingbird w/Fuchsia S/N	3,300	1993	30.00	30
1989 Autumn Melody S/N	1,950	1993	45.00	45
1990 Azalea Path S/N	2,500	N/A	85.00	85
1990 Azalea w/Dogwood S/N	2,500	N/A	55.00	55
1988 Baby Bluebirds S/N	1,950	N/A	16.00	30
1990 Baby Bluebirds w/Plum Tree S/N	2,500	N/A	18.00	215
1988 Baby Chickadees S/N	1,950	N/A	16.00	215
1990 Baby Chickadees w/Pine Tree S/N	2,500	N/A	18.00	18
XX Basket of Begonias S/N	2,500	N/A	40.00	40
1993 Basket of Calla Lilies S/N	3,300	1994	50.00	150
1991 Basket of Grapes & Raspberries S/N	2,500	N/A	25.00	30
1993 Basket of Hydrangi S/N	3,300	1995	50.00	60
1989 Basket of Irises & Lilacs S/N	1,950	N/A	45.00	45
1993 Basket of Magnolias S/N	3,300	1993	50.00	235
1993 Basket of Orchids S/N	3,300		50.00	50
1992 Basket of Pansies & Lilacs S/N	2,950	N/A	50.00	50
XX Basket of Pansies S/N	2,500	N/A	40.00	40
1991 Basket of Peonies S/N	2,500	N/A	40.00	40
1992 Basket of Roses & Hydrangeas S/N	2,950	N/A	50.00	50
1991 Basket of Roses S/N	2,500	N/A	40.00	40
1991 Basket of Strawberries & Grapes S/N	2,500	N/A	25.00	25
1991 Basket of Sweet Peas S/N	2,500		25.00	25
1989 Basket of Tulips & Lilacs S/N	1,950	N/A	45.00	45
1991 Basket of Wild Roses S/N	2,500	N/A	25.00	125
1991 Baskets of Primroses S/N	2,500	N/A	25.00	25
1986 Bearded Irises S/N	1,950	N/A	45.00	45
1994 Berries & Cherries S/N	3,500	1998	30.00	150
1990 Bluebirds & Dandelion S/N	2,500	N/A	40.00	40
1986 Bluebirds w/Plum Blossoms S/N	1,950	N/A	35.00	35
1988 Bluebirds w/Rhododendrons S/N	1,950		40.00	40
1990 Bouquet of Peonies S/N	2,500	N/A	50.00	50
1990 Bouquet of Poppies S/N	2,500	N/A	50.00	50
1992 Bouquet of Roses S/N	2,950	1994	20.00	20
1992 Breath of Spring S/N	2,950		135.00	135
1993 Broad-Billed HB w/Petunias S/N	3,300		30.00	30
1995 Burgundy Irises w/Foxgloves S/N	5,500		60.00	60
1995 Butterfly Garden I S/N	5,500		50.00	50
1995 Butterfly Garden II S/N	5,500		50.00	50
1994 Butterfly Kisses S/N	3,500	1998	50.00	125
1998 Butterfly Paradise S/N	3,500		80.00	80
1990 Butterfly w/Clematis S/N	2,500	1994	40.00	165-225
1990 Butterfly w/Wild Rose S/N	2,500	1993	40.00	50
1987 Calla Lily S/N	1,950		35.00	35
1994 Calliope Hummingbird w/Trumpet Vine S/N	3,300		30.00	30
1990 Cardinal & Queen Anne's Lace S/N	2,500	1994	40.00	225
XX Cat & Hummer S/N	1,000		45.00	45

YEAR ISSUE	EDITION LIMIT	YEAR RETD.	ISSUE PRICE	*QUOTE U.S.$
1989 Cherries & Summer Bouquet S/N	2,500	N/A	45.00	45
1993 Cherub Orchestra S/N	3,300	1994	80.00	195-400
1991 Cherubim w/Ivy S/N	2,500	1993	20.00	20
1988 Chickadees w/Cherry Blossoms S/N	1,950		40.00	40
1992 Conservatory S/N	2,950	1994	80.00	235-250
1987 Daylily S/N	1,950	N/A	35.00	35
1989 Daylily w/Hummingbird S/N	2,500	N/A	18.00	18
1998 The Delights of Spring S/N	3,500		80.00	80
1987 Dogwood S/N	1,950	N/A	30.00	30
1986 The Dreamer S/N	950		65.00	65
1991 Dried-Floral Bouquet S/N	2,500		25.00	25
1991 The Drying Room S/N	2,500		75.00	75
1992 Early Spring S/N	2,950	1993	85.00	85
1988 Eastern Black Swallowtail w/Milkweed S/N	1,950		45.00	45
1991 Egret's w/Queen Anne's Lace S/N	2,500	1995	60.00	60
1992 Entryway S/N	2,950		40.00	40
1997 Evening Reflections S/N	5,500		135.00	135
1993 Fairy Ballet S/N	3,300		80.00	80
1986 Fall S/N	950		35.00	35
1988 Feathered Harmony S/N	1,950	N/A	60.00	295
1991 Field of Irises S/N	2,500	1994	85.00	175
1989 First Landing S/N	1,950	N/A	16.00	25
1991 Floral Arch S/N	2,500	1996	25.00	25
1988 Floral Symphony S/N	1,950	N/A	95.00	95
1990 Forest Azalea S/N	2,500	N/A	55.00	225-250
1992 Forest Stream S/N	2,950	1995	85.00	85
1992 Fountain S/N	2,950		40.00	40
1986 Free Flight I -Rust Butterfly S/N	950		60.00	60
1986 Free Flight II -Pink Butterfly S/N	950		60.00	60
1989 Fritillaries w/ Violet S/N	2,500		18.00	18
1989 Fruit & Spring Basket S/N	1,500	N/A	45.00	225-250
1988 Garden Blossoms I S/N	1,950	N/A	35.00	35
1988 Garden Blossoms II S/N	1,950	N/A	35.00	35
1997 Garden Gate S/N	5,500		80.00	80
1991 Garden Peonies S/N	2,500	1997	60.00	60-125
1997 Garden Pleasure S/N	5,500		80.00	80
1991 Garden Poppies S/N	2,500		60.00	60
1986 Garden Poppies S/N	2,000	N/A	45.00	45
1992 Garden Seat S/N	2,950		40.00	40
1991 The Gathering S/N	2,500	N/A	75.00	75
1988 Harmonious Flight S/N	1,950		50.00	50
1994 Heavenly Tulips S/N	3,300	1994	80.00	250
1987 Herons & Irises S/N	1,950		65.00	65
1987 Hibiscus & Hummer S/N	1,950	1995	45.00	45
1988 Hummingbird & Hollyhock S/N	1,950	N/A	40.00	40
1989 Hummingbird & Floral I S/N	2,500	1994	35.00	35
1989 Hummingbird & Floral II S/N	2,500	1994	35.00	2500
1996 Hummingbird with Fuchsia S/N	5,500		50.00	50
1996 Hummingbird with Lilac S/N	5,500		50.00	50
1988 Hummingbirds & Iris S/N	1,950	N/A	40.00	40
1989 Hydrangea Bouquet S/N	2,500		30.00	30
1989 Innocents S/N	1,950		16.00	16
1993 Iris Garden II S/N	3,300	1994	105.00	425-450
1989 Iris Profusion (poster)	Closed	1995	30.00	30
1987 Iris S/N	1,950	N/A	16.00	16
1991 Irises in Bloom S/N	2,500	N/A	85.00	85
1992 Ivy & Fragrant Flowers S/N	3,300	1993	60.00	225-250
1992 Ivy & Honeysuckle S/N	3,300	1993	50.00	75
1992 Ivy & Sweetpea S/N	3,300	1994	50.00	75
1988 Kingfisher & Iris S/N	1,950		45.00	45
1986 Kingfisher S/N	950	1998	35.00	35
1995 Lilac Breezes S/N	5,500		80.00	80
1986 Lily Pond S/N	950	1998	35.00	35
1987 Lily S/N	1,950	N/A	16.00	16
1998 Magnolia Bouquet S/N	3,500		50.00	50
1995 Magnolia Path S/N	5,500		135.00	135
1987 Magnolia S/N	1,950	N/A	30.00	30
1995 Magnolias & Day Lilies S/N	5,500		80.00	80
1995 Magnolias & Hydrangeas S/N	5,500		80.00	80
1986 Mauve Veiltail S/N	950		35.00	35
1994 Mermaid Callas S/N	5,500		80.00	80
1996 Messengers of Love S/N	5,500		60.00	60
XX Misty Valley S/N	1,950		45.00	45
1990 Mixed Irises I S/N	2,500	N/A	50.00	50
1990 Mixed Irises II S/N	2,500	N/A	50.00	50
1988 Moonlight Splendor S/N	1,950	N/A	60.00	60
1987 Morning Glories & Hummer S/N	1,950	N/A	45.00	45
1989 The Morning Room S/N	2,500	N/A	95.00	325-395
1987 Motherlove S/N	1,950	N/A	45.00	265
1987 Motif Orientale S/N	1,950	N/A	95.00	95
1994 Mystic Bouquet S/N	3,300		80.00	80
1995 Nature's Retreat S/N	5,500		145.00	145
1986 Nuthatch w/Dogwood S/N	1,950	N/A	35.00	35
1992 Old Stone House S/N	2,950	1996	50.00	150
1986 Opera Lady S/N	950	N/A	95.00	95
1989 Orange Tip & Blossoms S/N	2,500		18.00	18
1989 Oriental Screen S/N	2,500	N/A	95.00	325-350
1996 Oriental Splendor S/N	5,500		145.00	145
1988 Painted Lady w/Thistle S/N	1,950		45.00	45
1988 Pair of Finches S/N	1,950	N/A	35.00	35
1992 Palladian Windows S/N	2,950	1993	80.00	80
1990 Pansies & Ivy S/N	2,500	N/A	18.00	18
1992 Pansies & Lilies of the Valley S/N	2,950	1993	20.00	20
1992 Pansies & Sweet Peas S/N	2,950	1994	20.00	20
1991 Pansies in a Basket S/N	2,500	N/A	25.00	25
1993 Pansies w/Blue Stardrift S/N	2,950	1995	25.00	25
1993 Pansies w/Daisies S/N	2,950		25.00	25
1991 Pansies w/Sweet Pea S/N	2,500	N/A	16.00	16
1991 Pansies w/Violets S/N	2,500	N/A	16.00	16
1987 Parenthood S/N	1,950	N/A	45.00	45
1992 Patio S/N	2,950		40.00	40
1993 Peach & Purple Irises S/N	3,300	1994	50.00	50
1993 Peach & Yellow Roses S/N	3,300		50.00	50
1986 Peach Veiltail S/N	950		35.00	35
1994 Peaches & Fruits S/N	3,500		30.00	30
1991 Peacock Duet-Serigraph S/N	325		550.00	550
1987 Peacock Fantasy S/N	950		65.00	65
1991 Peacock Solo-Serigraph S/N	325		550.00	550
1988 Peonies & Azaleas S/N	1,950	N/A	35.00	35
1988 Peonies & Forsythia S/N	1,950	N/A	35.00	35
1988 Peonies & Waterfall S/N	1,950	N/A	65.00	65
1993 Peonies S/N	3,300	1995	30.00	140
1990 Petunias & Ivy S/N	2,500		18.00	18
1989 Phlox w/Hummingbird S/N	2,500		18.00	18
1990 Potted Beauties S/N	2,500	1997	105.00	200-215
1996 Potted Pansies S/N	5,500		40.00	40
1996 Potted Petunias S/N	5,500		40.00	40
1996 Protectors of Peace S/N	5,500		60.00	60
1995 Purple Irises w/Foxgloves S/N	5,500		60.00	60
1991 Putti w/Column S/N	2,500		20.00	20
1990 Quiet Moment S/N	2,500	N/A	105.00	450-525
1998 Rhapsody in Yellow & Blue S/N	3,500		45.00	45
1989 Romantic Abundance S/N	1,950	N/A	95.00	95
1989 Romantic Garden (poster)	Open		35.00	35
1994 Romantic Reflection S/N	5,950	1996	145.00	265-425
1998 Romantic Reverie S/N	3,500		45.00	45
1997 Rose Arbor S/N	5,500		80.00	80
1993 Rose Bouquet w/Tassel S/N	3,300	1995	25.00	25
1994 Rose Fairies S/N	5,500	1996	80.00	195
1996 Rose Memories S/N	5,500		80.00	80
1989 Roses & Lilacs S/N	2,500		30.00	30
1992 Roses & Violets S/N	2,950	1993	20.00	20
1993 Roses in Bloom S/N	3,300	1995	105.00	105
1990 Royal Garden S/N	1,950		95.00	95
1990 Royal Retreat S/N	1,950	N/A	95.00	450
1995 Ruby Throated Hummingbird w/Hibiscus S/N	5,800		40.00	40
1993 Rufous Hummingbird w/Foxgloves S/N	3,300	1993	30.00	30
1998 Seasonal Flowers I	Open		20.00	20
1998 Seasonal Flowers II	Open		20.00	20
1998 Seasonal Flowers III	Open		20.00	20
1998 Seasonal Flowers IV	Open		20.00	20
1988 Snapdragon S/N	1,950	N/A	16.00	16
1987 Solitude S/N	1,950	N/A	60.00	295
1993 Southern Magnolia S/N	3,300	1995	30.00	30
XX Spring Blossoms I S/N	1,950		45.00	45
XX Spring Blossoms II S/N	1,950		45.00	45
1989 Spring Bouquet (poster)	Open		30.00	30
1989 Spring Bouquet (poster-signed)	Open		45.00	45
1996 Spring Bulbs S/N	5,500		50.00	50
1994 Spring Conservatory S/N	3,300		105.00	105
1986 Spring Fairy S/N	950	1998	35.00	35
1990 Spring Floral S/N	2,500	N/A	105.00	105
1995 Spring Garden S/N	5,500		125.00	125
1986 Spring S/N	950		35.00	35
XX Spring Song S/N	1,950		60.00	60
1986 Spring Tulips S/N	1,950	N/A	45.00	45
1989 Spring Tulips S/N	2,500	N/A	45.00	45
XX Stream w/Blossoms S/N	1,950		45.00	45
1992 Study for a Breath of Spring S/N	2,950		105.00	105
1996 Summer Bouquet S/N	5,500		50.00	50
1986 Summer Glads S/N	1,950	N/A	45.00	45
1988 Summer Lace w/Blue Chicory S/N	1,950	1991	45.00	45
1987 Summer Lace w/Chicadees S/N	950	N/A	65.00	170
1988 Summer Lace w/Chickadees II S/N	1,950	1991	65.00	65
1988 Summer Lace w/Daisies S/N	1,950	1991	45.00	45
1987 Summer Lace w/Dragon Fly S/N	950	N/A	45.00	45
1987 Summer Lace w/Lady Bug S/N	950	N/A	45.00	45
1989 Summer Rose S/N	2,500	N/A	45.00	45
1986 Summer S/N	950		35.00	35
1998 Sunflower Bouquet S/N	3,500		50.00	50
1987 Swans & Callas S/N	1,950	1994	65.00	65
1991 Swans w/Daylilies S/N	2,500	1993	60.00	60
1989 Swans w/Dogwood S/N	1,950	N/A	65.00	65
1995 Sweet Bounty S/N	5,500		80.00	80
1994 Sweet Delight S/N	3,500	1998	50.00	125
1988 Sweet Pea Floral S/N	1,950	N/A	16.00	16
1986 Three Little Deer S/N	950	1998	35.00	35
1987 Togetherness S/N	1,950	N/A	60.00	60
1988 Trio of Sparrows S/N	1,950	N/A	35.00	35
1993 Tulip Bouquet w/Tassel S/N	3,300	1995	25.00	30
1987 Tulips S/N	1,950	N/A	16.00	16
1993 Two Burgundy Irises S/N	3,300	1994	50.00	50
1990 Two White Irises S/N	2,500	N/A	40.00	40
1992 Victorian Pavilion S/N	2,950		50.00	50
1992 Vintage Bouquet S/N	2,950	1994	135.00	250-265
1993 Violet Crowned HB w/Morning Glories S/N	3,300	1996	30.00	30
1989 Waterfall w/Dogwood S/N	1,950		45.00	45
1989 Waterfall w/White & Pink Dogwood S/N	1,950		45.00	45
1990 White & Blue Irises S/N	2,500	N/A	40.00	40
1993 White & Burgundy Roses S/N	3,300	1995	50.00	50
1995 White Eared Hummingbird w/Hydrangea S/N	5,800		40.00	40
1991 Wild Flowers w/Single Butterfly S/N	2,500		50.00	50
1991 Wild Flowers w/Two Butterflies S/N	2,500	1998	50.00	50
1986 Winter S/N	950		35.00	35
1996 Wisteria Dreams S/N	5,500		80.00	80
1993 Woodland Path S/N	3,300	1994	135.00	325-450
1993 Woodland Steps S/N	3,300	1995	85.00	85
1993 Woodland View S/N	3,300	1995	85.00	85
1995 Wreath of Lilies S/N	5,500		55.00	55
1995 Wreath of Pansies S/N	5,500		55.00	55
1994 Wreath of Peonies S/N	3,500		55.00	55
1994 Wreath of Roses S/N	3,500	1995	55.00	225-275

Liu - The Music Room - L. Liu

YEAR ISSUE	EDITION LIMIT	YEAR RETD.	ISSUE PRICE	*QUOTE U.S.$
1994 Clarinet Ensemble S/N	5,500		115.00	115
1996 Concerto with Guitar S/N	5,500		45.00	45
1996 Concerto with Violin S/N	5,500		45.00	45
1994 Fancy Fiddle S/N	5,500	1994	80.00	180
1996 Harmonic Duet S/N	5,500		55.00	55
1994 Love Notes S/N	5,500	1994	80.00	80
1991 The Music Room I S/N	2,500	1992	135.00	2300-2400
1992 The Music Room II-Nutcracker S/N	4,500	1993	200.00	450-550
1994 The Music Room III-Composer's Retreat S/N	5,500	1994	145.00	375-475
1995 The Music Room IV -Swan Melody S/N	6,500	1997	150.00	250-265
1996 The Music Room V-Morning Serenade S/N	5,500		145.00	145
1997 The Music Room VI-Romantic Overture S/N	5,500		150.00	150
1996 Musical Trio S/N	5,500		55.00	55

Liu - Unframed Canvas Transfers - L. Liu

YEAR ISSUE	EDITION LIMIT	YEAR RETD.	ISSUE PRICE	*QUOTE U.S.$
1998 Abundant Blessings S/N	300		395.00	395
1996 Angel with Harp S/N	300		145.00	145
1996 Angel with Trumpet S/N	300		145.00	145
1993 Basket of Calla Lilies S/N	300	1995	195.00	195
1993 Basket of Magnolias S/N	300	1997	195.00	195
1998 Butterfly Paradise S/N	300		295.00	295
1993 Cherub Orchestra S/N	300	1995	295.00	400-550
1992 Conservatory S/N	300	1995	295.00	295
1998 The Delights of Spring S/N	300		295.00	295
1997 Evening Reflections S/N	300		395.00	395
1993 Fairy Ballet S/N	300		295.00	295
1994 Fancy Fiddle S/N	300		295.00	295
1997 Garden Gate S/N	300		295.00	295
1997 Garden Pleasure S/N	300		295.00	295
1996 Guardian Angel S/N	300		395.00	395
1996 Hummingbird with Fuchsia S/N	300		195.00	195
1996 Hummingbird with Lilac S/N	300		195.00	195
1993 Iris Garden II S/N	300	1995	395.00	395-475
1995 Lilac Breezes S/N	300		295.00	295
1994 Love Notes S/N	300		295.00	295
1998 Magnolia Bouquet S/N	300		195.00	195
1995 Magnolia Path S/N	300	1996	395.00	395
1994 Mermaid Callas S/N	300	1997	295.00	295-450
1995 Nature's Retreat S/N	300		395.00	395
1992 Old Stone House S/N	300		195.00	195
1996 Oriental Splendor S/N	300		395.00	395
1992 Palladian Windows S/N	300	1995	295.00	295-395
1996 Potted Pansies S/N	300		145.00	145
1996 Potted Petunias S/N	300		145.00	145
1998 Rhapsody in Yellow & Blue S/N	300		195.00	195
1994 Romantic Reflection S/N	500	1997	395.00	395-450
1998 Romantic Reverie S/N	300		195.00	195
1997 Rose Arbor S/N	300		295.00	295
1994 Rose Fairies S/N	300	1997	295.00	295
1996 Rose Memories S/N	300		295.00	295
1993 Roses in Bloom S/N	300	1995	395.00	395
1996 Spring Bulbs S/N	300		195.00	195
1994 Spring Conservatory S/N	300		395.00	395
1995 Spring Garden S/N	300		395.00	395
1996 Summer Bouquet S/N	300		195.00	195
1998 Sunflower Bouquet S/N	300		195.00	195
1995 Sweet Bounty S/N	300		295.00	295
1992 Victorian Pavillion S/N	300		195.00	195
1992 Vintage Bouquet S/N	300	1995	395.00	395
1996 Wisteria Dreams S/N	300		295.00	295
1993 Woodland Path S/N	300		495.00	495

Liu - Unframed Canvas Transfers Angels Among Us - L. Liu

YEAR ISSUE	EDITION LIMIT	YEAR RETD.	ISSUE PRICE	*QUOTE U.S.$
1997 Angel of Light S/N	300		395.00	395
1997 Angel of Love S/N	300		395.00	395

Liu - Unframed Canvas Transfers Celestial Symphony Series - L. Liu

YEAR ISSUE	EDITION LIMIT	YEAR RETD.	ISSUE PRICE	*QUOTE U.S.$
1995 Flute Interlude S/N	300		145.00	145
1995 French Horn Melody S/N	300		145.00	145
1995 Piano Sonata S/N	300		145.00	145
1995 Violin Concerto S/N	300		145.00	145

Liu - Unframed Canvas Transfers The Music Room Series - L. Liu

YEAR ISSUE	EDITION LIMIT	YEAR RETD.	ISSUE PRICE	*QUOTE U.S.$
1991 The Music Room S/N	300	1992	395.00	700-900
1992 The Music Room II-Nutcracker S/N	300	1993	395.00	600
1994 The Music Room III-Composer's Retreat S/N	300	1994	395.00	500
1995 The Music Room IV -Swan Melody S/N	300		425.00	425
1996 The Music Room V-Morning Serenade S/N	300		395.00	395
1997 The Music Room VI-Romantic Overture S/N	300		425.00	425
1997 Clarinet Ensemble S/N	300		395.00	395
1996 Harmonic Duet S/N	300		195.00	195
1996 Musical Trio S/N	300		195.00	195

McDonald - M. McDonald

YEAR ISSUE	EDITION LIMIT	YEAR RETD.	ISSUE PRICE	*QUOTE U.S.$
1988 Amaryllis Dancer S/N	1,000		55.00	55
1988 Lily Queen S/N	1,000		55.00	55

*Quotes have been rounded up to nearest dollar

Islandia International

Single Issues - S. Etem

YEAR ISSUE	EDITION LIMIT	YEAR RETD.	ISSUE PRICE	*QUOTE U.S.$
1998 Bluebird of Happiness	1,500		95.00	95
1998 The Miracle of Life	1,500		95.00	95

Lightpost Publishing

Kinkade Member's Only Collectors' Society - T. Kinkade

YEAR ISSUE	EDITION LIMIT	YEAR RETD.	ISSUE PRICE	*QUOTE U.S.$
1992 Skater's Pond	Closed	N/A	295.00	650-895
1992 Morning Lane	Closed	N/A	Gift	425-600
1994 Collector's Cottage I	Closed	1995	315.00	425-695
1994 Painter of Light Book	Closed	1995	Gift	80-100
1995 Lochavan Cottage	Closed	1995	295.00	545-675
1995 Gardens Beyond Autumn Gate-pencil sketch	Closed	1995	Gift	110-125
1996 Julianne's Cottage-Keepsake Box	Closed	1996	Gift	75-85
1996 Skater's Pond Sketch Portfolio Edition	Closed	1997	75.00	85-100
1996 Julianne's Cottage Library Print	Closed	1997	50.00	60-75
1996 Meadowood Cottage (canvas framed)	4,950	1997	375.00	650-745
1996 Meadowood Cottage (paper unframed)	950	1997	150.00	175-195
1997 Simpler Times are Better Times	Closed	1997	Gift	45-55
1997 The Village Inn Library Print	Closed	1998	65.00	75-85
1997 Collectors' Cottages Portfolio Edition	Closed	1998	175.00	250-275
1997 Home is Where the Heart Is	Closed	1998	295.00	1025-1395
1998 Let Your Light Shine	Yr.Iss.		Gift	N/A
1998 A Light In The Storm	Yr.Iss.		295.00	295
1998 Clearing Storms	3/99		49.50	50

Kinkade-Event Pieces - T. Kinkade

YEAR ISSUE	EDITION LIMIT	YEAR RETD.	ISSUE PRICE	*QUOTE U.S.$
1996 Candlelight Cottage (canvas framed)	Closed	1997	375.00	525
1996 Candlelight Cottage (canvas unframed)	Closed	1997	275.00	395-415
1996 Candlelight Cottage (paper framed)	Closed	1997	325.00	325-445
1996 Candlelight Cottage (paper unframed)	Closed	1997	150.00	150-195
1996 Lamplight Village	Closed	1997	Gift	80-125
1996 We Wish You a Merry Christmas	Closed	1997	70.00	70-125
1997 Chandler's Cottage Inspirational Print (Mother's Day Event)	Closed	1997	80.00	80-125

Kinkade-Archival Paper/Canvas-Combined Edition-Framed - T. Kinkade

YEAR ISSUE	EDITION LIMIT	YEAR RETD.	ISSUE PRICE	*QUOTE U.S.$
1989 Blue Cottage (Paper)	Retrd.	1993	125.00	225-995
1989 Blue Cottage (Canvas)	Retrd.	1993	495.00	1350-1495
1990 Moonlit Village (Paper)	Closed	1992	225.00	875-1945
1990 Moonlit Village (Canvas)	Closed	1992	595.00	2600-4495
1986 New York, 1932 (Paper)	Closed	N/A	225.00	850-2045
1986 New York, 1932 (Canvas)	Closed	N/A	595.00	2595-4495
1989 Skating in the Park (Paper) S/N	750	1994	225.00	1385-1795
1989 Skating in the Park (Canvas) S/N	750	1994	595.00	1050-3095

Kinkade-Canvas Editions-Framed - T. Kinkade

YEAR ISSUE	EDITION LIMIT	YEAR RETD.	ISSUE PRICE	*QUOTE U.S.$
1991 Afternoon Light, Dogwood A/P	98	1991	615.00	2500-3000
1991 Afternoon Light, Dogwood P/P	100	N/A	795.00	795-3000
1991 Afternoon Light, Dogwood S/N	980	N/A	515.00	1775-2500
1992 Amber Afternoon A/P	200	1992	715.00	1700-2000
1992 Amber Afternoon G/P	200	1992	765.00	1700-2150
1992 Amber Afternoon P/P	100	1992	815.00	2100-2350
1992 Amber Afternoon S/N	980	N/A	615.00	1575-1850
1994 Autumn at Ashley's Cottage A/P	395		590.00	700
1994 Autumn at Ashley's Cottage G/P	990		590.00	700
1994 Autumn at Ashley's Cottage P/P	315		640.00	750
1994 Autumn at Ashley's Cottage S/N	3,950		440.00	550
1991 The Autumn Gate A/P	200	N/A	695.00	4550-4750
1991 The Autumn Gate P/P	100	N/A	795.00	795
1991 The Autumn Gate R/E	Closed	1992	695.00	4000-5745
1991 The Autumn Gate S/N	980	N/A	595.00	4295-4445
1995 Autumn Lane A/P	295		800.00	900
1995 Autumn Lane G/P	740		750.00	900
1995 Autumn Lane P/P	240		850.00	950
1995 Autumn Lane S/N	2,950		650.00	750
1994 Beacon of Hope A/P	275	1994	765.00	1675-1845
1994 Beacon of Hope G/P	685	1994	765.00	1250-1845
1994 Beacon of Hope P/P	220	N/A	815.00	1625-1945
1994 Beacon of Hope S/N	2,750	1994	615.00	1075-1645
1996 Beginning of a Perfect Day A/P	295	1996	1240.00	1350-1450
1996 Beginning of a Perfect Day G/P	740		1240.00	1350
1996 Beginning of a Perfect Day P/P	240		1290.00	1400
1996 Beginning of a Perfect Day S/N	2,950		1090.00	1200
1996 Beginning of a Perfect Day S/P	95	N/A	3270.00	7500
1993 Beside Still Waters A/P	400	N/A	615.00	2595-3095
1993 Beside Still Waters G/P	490	N/A	665.00	2595-3095
1993 Beside Still Waters P/P	100	N/A	715.00	3295
1993 Beside Still Waters S/N	1,280	N/A	515.00	2795-3100
1995 Beside Still Waters S/P	Closed	N/A	2325.00	9500-10500
1993 Beyond Autumn Gate A/P	600	1993	915.00	3100-4595
1993 Beyond Autumn Gate G/P	500	N/A	965.00	3400-4790
1995 Beyond Autumn Gate P/P	100	N/A	1045.00	1045-5095
1993 Beyond Autumn Gate S/N	1,750	N/A	815.00	3275-4295
1995 Beyond Autumn Gate S/P	Closed	N/A	N/A	6650-11500
1997 Beyond Spring Gate A/P	345	1997	1300.00	3300-3795
1997 Beyond Spring Gate G/P	865	1997	1300.00	1300-3795
1997 Beyond Spring Gate P/P	280	1997	1350.00	3500-3995
1997 Beyond Spring Gate S/N	3,450	1997	1150.00	3100-3595
1997 Beyond Spring Gate S/P	95	1997	3450.00	3450-11500
1993 The Blessings of Autumn A/P	300	1994	715.00	1650-1995
1993 The Blessings of Autumn G/P	250	1994	765.00	1995-2245
1993 The Blessings of Autumn P/P	100	1994	815.00	815-2445
1993 The Blessings of Autumn S/N	1,250	1994	615.00	1550-1895
1994 The Blessings of Spring A/P	275	1994	665.00	700-1050
1994 The Blessings of Spring G/P	685		665.00	1050
1994 The Blessings of Spring P/P	220		715.00	1145
1994 The Blessings of Spring S/N	2,750	1994	515.00	595-895
1995 Blessings of Summer A/P	495		1015.00	1150
1995 Blessings of Summer G/P	1,240		965.00	1150
1995 Blessings of Summer P/P	400		1065.00	1200
1995 Blessings of Summer S/N	4,950		865.00	1000
1995 Blossom Bridge A/P	295		730.00	800
1995 Blossom Bridge G/P	740		680.00	800
1995 Blossom Bridge P/P	240		780.00	850
1995 Blossom Bridge S/N	2,950		580.00	650
1995 Blossom Bridge S/P	95		1740.00	3250
1992 Blossom Hill Church A/P	200	1994	715.00	1000-2195
1992 Blossom Hill Church P/P	100		815.00	2295
1992 Blossom Hill Church R/E	Closed	1993	695.00	1600-2495
1992 Blossom Hill Church S/N	980	1994	615.00	775-1995
1991 Boston A/P	50	N/A	615.00	2300-3845
1991 Boston P/P	25	N/A	715.00	715-4095
1991 Boston S/N	550	N/A	515.00	1675-3095
1997 Bridge of Faith A/P	395	1997	1300.00	2845-3200
1997 Bridge of Faith G/P	990	1997	1300.00	1300-2845
1997 Bridge of Faith P/P	320	1997	1350.00	1350-3045
1997 Bridge of Faith S/N	3,950	1997	1150.00	2050-2645
1997 Bridge of Faith S/P	95	1997	3450.00	3450-11950
1992 Broadwater Bridge A/P	200	N/A	615.00	2050-3295
1992 Broadwater Bridge G/P	200	N/A	665.00	2275-3445
1992 Broadwater Bridge P/P	100	N/A	715.00	715-3795
1992 Broadwater Bridge S/N	980	N/A	495.00	2200-3095
1995 Brookside Hideaway A/P	395	1995	695.00	835-1345
1995 Brookside Hideaway G/P	990		695.00	1295
1995 Brookside Hideaway P/P	320		745.00	1495
1995 Brookside Hideaway S/N	3,950	1996	545.00	695-1145
1991 Carmel, Delores Street and the Tuck Box Tea Room A/P	200	1992	745.00	3100-4145
1991 Carmel, Delores Street and the Tuck Box Tea Room P/P	100	1992	845.00	845-4445
1991 Carmel, Delores Street and the Tuck Box Tea Room R/P	Closed	1992	745.00	2750-4745
1991 Carmel, Delores Street and the Tuck Box Tea Room S/N	980	1992	645.00	2295-4045
1989 Carmel, Ocean Avenue A/P	50	N/A	795.00	5700-6525
1989 Carmel, Ocean Avenue P/P	25	N/A	N/A	6825
1989 Carmel, Ocean Avenue S/N	935	N/A	595.00	4550-6225
1991 Cedar Nook Cottage A/P	200	1991	315.00	315-845
1991 Cedar Nook Cottage P/P	100	1991	515.00	915-945
1991 Cedar Nook Cottage R/E	200	1991	315.00	700-1015
1991 Cedar Nook Cottage R/P	200	1991	N/A	1045
1991 Cedar Nook Cottage S/N	1,960	1991	195.00	575-695
1990 Chandler's Cottage A/P	100	N/A	N/A	4595
1990 Chandler's Cottage P/P	50	N/A	N/A	4895
1990 Chandler's Cottage S/N	550	N/A	495.00	2050-4295
1992 Christmas At the Ahwahnee A/P	200		615.00	800
1992 Christmas At the Ahwahnee G/P	200		665.00	800
1992 Christmas At the Ahwahnee P/P	100		715.00	850
1992 Christmas At the Ahwahnee S/N	980		515.00	650
1990 Christmas Cottage 1990 A/P	100	N/A	295.00	1800-2895
1990 Christmas Cottage 1990 P/P	50	N/A	N/A	3145
1990 Christmas Cottage 1990 S/N	550	N/A	N/A	1375-2595
1991 Christmas Eve A/P	200	1991	515.00	1000-2245
1991 Christmas Eve P/P	100	1991	615.00	615-2545
1991 Christmas Eve R/E	Closed	1991	495.00	1700-2595
1991 Christmas Eve R/P	200	1991	N/A	2645
1991 Christmas Eve S/N	980	N/A	415.00	950-1945
1994 Christmas Memories A/P	345	1996	695.00	800-1025
1994 Christmas Memories G/P	860		695.00	995
1994 Christmas Memories P/P	275		745.00	1095
1994 Christmas Memories S/N	3,450	1995	545.00	595-875
1994 Christmas Tree Cottage A/P	395		590.00	700
1994 Christmas Tree Cottage G/P	990		590.00	700
1994 Christmas Tree Cottage P/P	315		640.00	750
1994 Christmas Tree Cottage S/N	3,950		440.00	550
1996 A Christmas Welcome A/P	295	1996	675.00	625-700
1996 A Christmas Welcome G/P	740		675.00	700
1996 A Christmas Welcome P/P	240		725.00	750
1996 A Christmas Welcome S/N	2,950		525.00	550
1997 Clearing Storms A/P (18 x 27)	590	1998	875.00	875-1445
1997 Clearing Storms A/P (24 x 36)	590	1998	1300.00	1300-2095
1997 Clearing Storms G/P (18 x 27)	740	1998	875.00	875-1445
1997 Clearing Storms G/P (24 x 36)	740	1998	1300.00	1300-2095
1997 Clearing Storms P/P (18 x 27)	360		925.00	1295
1997 Clearing Storms P/P (24 x 36)	360		1350.00	1895
1997 Clearing Storms R/E (18 x 27)	240		2175.00	2395
1997 Clearing Storms R/E (24 x 36)	240		3450.00	3895
1997 Clearing Storms S/N (18 x 27)	2,950	1998	725.00	750-1295
1997 Clearing Storms S/N (24 x 36)	2,950	1998	1150.00	1200-1945
1997 Clearing Storms S/P (18 x 27)	120	N/A	3625.00	3625-5995
1997 Clearing Storms S/P (24 x 36)	120	N/A	5750.00	5750-8750
1997 Cobblestone Brooke A/P	495	1998	1300.00	1475-1745
1997 Cobblestone Brooke G/P	1,240	1998	1300.00	1300-1745
1997 Cobblestone Brooke P/P	400	1998	1350.00	1350-1795
1997 Cobblestone Brooke S/N	4,950	1997	1150.00	1100-1595
1997 Cobblestone Brooke S/P	95	1998	3450.00	3450-7995
1996 Cobblestone Lane A/P	295	1996	1125.00	1495-3295
1996 Cobblestone Lane G/P	740	1996	1125.00	1125-3295
1996 Cobblestone Lane P/P	240	1996	1175.00	2150-3595
1996 Cobblestone Lane S/N	2,950	1996	975.00	1700-3095
1996 Cobblestone Lane S/P	95	1996	2925.00	2925-12500
1992 Cottage-By-The-Sea A/P	200	1992	715.00	1975-2895
1992 Cottage-By-The-Sea G/P	200	N/A	765.00	2995-3045
1992 Cottage-By-The-Sea P/P	100	1992	815.00	1995-3345
1992 Cottage-By-The-Sea S/N	980	N/A	615.00	1775-2695
1992 Country Memories A/P	200	1992	515.00	1095-1345
1992 Country Memories G/P	200	1997	565.00	1300-1445
1992 Country Memories P/P	100		615.00	1450
1992 Country Memories S/N	980	1994	395.00	1145-1295
1994 Creekside Trail A/P	198		840.00	955
1994 Creekside Trail G/P	500		840.00	955
1994 Creekside Trail P/P	160		890.00	1005
1994 Creekside Trail S/N	1,984		690.00	805
1994 Days of Peace A/P	198		840.00	985
1994 Days of Peace G/P	500		840.00	1035
1994 Days of Peace P/P	160		890.00	1035
1994 Days of Peace S/N	1,984		690.00	835
1995 Deer Creek Cottage A/P	295	1996	615.00	700
1995 Deer Creek Cottage G/P	740		565.00	700
1995 Deer Creek Cottage P/P	240		665.00	750
1995 Deer Creek Cottage S/N	2,950		465.00	550
1995 Deer Creek Cottage S/P	95		1395.00	2750
1994 Dusk in the Valley A/P	198		840.00	900
1994 Dusk in the Valley G/P	500		840.00	900
1994 Dusk in the Valley P/P	160		890.00	950
1994 Dusk in the Valley S/N	1,984		690.00	750
1994 Emerald Isle Cottage A/P	275	1994	665.00	825-1045
1994 Emerald Isle Cottage G/P	685		665.00	995
1994 Emerald Isle Cottage P/P	220		715.00	1145
1994 Emerald Isle Cottage S/N	2,750	1998	515.00	650-895
1993 End of a Perfect Day I A/P	400	1994	615.00	2050-2995
1993 End of a Perfect Day I G/P	300	N/A	665.00	3195-4400
1993 End of a Perfect Day I P/P	100	N/A	715.00	715
1993 End of a Perfect Day I S/N	1,250	1994	515.00	1950-2695
1995 End of a Perfect Day I S/P	91	1996	2325	4000-8950
1994 End of a Perfect Day II A/P	275	1994	965.00	3245-3545
1994 End of a Perfect Day II G/P	685	1994	965.00	1895-3545
1994 End of a Perfect Day II P/P	220	N/A	1015.00	N/A
1994 End of a Perfect Day II S/N	2,750	1995	815.00	1895-3295
1995 End of a Perfect Day III A/P	495	1995	1145.00	1650-2195
1995 End of a Perfect Day III G/P	1,240	1998	1145.00	1245-2195
1995 End of a Perfect Day III P/P	400		1195.00	2095
1995 End of a Perfect Day III S/N	4,950	1996	995.00	1425-1995
1989 Entrance to the Manor House A/P	100	1996	595.00	1895-2195
1989 Entrance to the Manor House P/P	50	N/A	N/A	2495
1989 Entrance to the Manor House S/N	550	N/A	495.00	1695-1995
1989 Evening at Merritt's Cottage A/P	100	N/A	595.00	3500-3995
1989 Evening at Merritt's Cottage P/P	50	N/A	N/A	4195
1989 Evening at Merritt's Cottage S/N	550	N/A	495.00	3495-3995
1992 Evening at Swanbrooke Cottage Thomashire A/P	200	N/A	715.00	3600-3795
1992 Evening at Swanbrooke Cottage Thomashire G/P	200	N/A	765.00	3700-3895
1992 Evening at Swanbrooke Cottage Thomashire P/P	100	N/A	815.00	4095
1992 Evening at Swanbrooke Cottage Thomashire S/N	980	N/A	615.00	2350-3495
1992 Evening Carolers A/P	200		415.00	550
1992 Evening Carolers G/P	485		465.00	550
1992 Evening Carolers P/P	100		515.00	600
1992 Evening Carolers S/N	1,960		315.00	400
1995 Evening in the Forest A/P	495		695.00	800
1995 Evening in the Forest G/P	1,240		645.00	800
1995 Evening in the Forest P/P	400		745.00	850
1995 Evening in the Forest S/N	4,950		545.00	650
1998 Everett's Cottage A/P (16 x 20)	585		390.00	390
1998 Everett's Cottage A/P (16 x 20)	595		800.00	800
1998 Everett's Cottage A/P (20 x 24)	595		900.00	900
1998 Everett's Cottage A/P (24 x 30)	495		1150.00	1150
1998 Everett's Cottage S/N (16 x 20)	5,950		650.00	650
1998 Everett's Cottage S/N (20 x 24)	5,950		750.00	750
1998 Everett's Cottage S/N (24 x 30)	4,950		1000.00	1000
1993 Fisherman's Wharf San Francisco A/P	275	1993	1065.00	1295-2195
1993 Fisherman's Wharf San Francisco G/P	550	N/A	1115.00	1200-2195
1993 Fisherman's Wharf San Francisco P/P	230		1165.00	2295
1993 Fisherman's Wharf San Francisco S/N	2,750	1995	965.00	1050-1995
1991 Flags Over The Capitol A/P	200		715.00	900
1991 Flags Over The Capitol P/P	100		815.00	950
1991 Flags Over The Capitol R/E	Closed	N/A	695.00	1000-1345
1991 Flags Over The Capitol S/N	980		615.00	750
1994 Garden Beyond Autumn Gate S/N	Closed	1996	1025.00	2795-2895
1997 Garden of Prayer A/P (18 x 24)	990		900.00	900
1997 Garden of Prayer A/P (25 1/2 x 34)	990		1350.00	1350
1997 Garden of Prayer A/P (30 x 40)	790		2100.00	2100
1997 Garden of Prayer G/P (18 x 24)	1,750		900.00	900
1997 Garden of Prayer G/P (25 1/2 x 34)	1,750		1350.00	1350
1997 Garden of Prayer G/P (30 x 40)	1,400		2100.00	2100
1997 Garden of Prayer P/P (18 x 24)	600		950.00	950
1997 Garden of Prayer P/P (25 1/2 x 34)	600		1400.00	1400
1997 Garden of Prayer P/P (30 x 40)	480		2150.00	2150
1997 Garden of Prayer R/E (18 x 24)	400		2250.00	2250
1997 Garden of Prayer R/E (25 1/2 x 34)	400		3600.00	3600
1997 Garden of Prayer R/E (30 x 40)	320		5850.00	5850
1997 Garden of Prayer S/N (18 x 24)	4,950		750.00	750
1997 Garden of Prayer S/N (25 1/2 x 34)	4,950		1200.00	1200
1997 Garden of Prayer S/N (30 x 40)	3,950		1950.00	1950
1997 Garden of Prayer S/P (18 x 24)	200		3750.00	3750
1997 Garden of Prayer S/P (25 1/2 x 34)	200		6000.00	6000
1997 Garden of Prayer S/P (30 x 40)	160		9750.00	9750
1993 The Garden of Promise A/P	400	N/A	715.00	2795-3195
1993 The Garden of Promise G/P	300	N/A	765.00	2895-3295
1993 The Garden of Promise P/P	100	N/A	815.00	815-3495
1993 The Garden of Promise S/N	1,250	1994	615.00	2300-2895
1993 The Garden of Promise S/P	95	N/A	2800	9500-11500
1992 The Garden Party A/P	200		615.00	800
1992 The Garden Party G/P	200		665.00	800
1992 The Garden Party P/P	100		715.00	850

*Quotes have been rounded up to nearest dollar

YEAR ISSUE	EDITION LIMIT	YEAR RETD.	ISSUE PRICE	*QUOTE U.S.$
1992 The Garden Party S/N	980		515.00	650
1998 Gardens Beyond Spring Gate A/P (18 x 24)	1,190		900.00	900
1998 Gardens Beyond Spring Gate A/P (25 1/2 x 34)	1,190		1350.00	1350
1998 Gardens Beyond Spring Gate A/P (30 x 40)	1,190		2100.00	2100
1998 Gardens Beyond Spring Gate G/P (18 x 24)	2,100		900.00	900
1998 Gardens Beyond Spring Gate G/P (25 1/2 x 34)	2,100		1350.00	1350
1998 Gardens Beyond Spring Gate G/P (30 x 40)	2,100		2100.00	2100
1998 Gardens Beyond Spring Gate P/P (18 x 24)	710		950.00	950
1998 Gardens Beyond Spring Gate P/P (25 1/2 x 34)	710		1400.00	1400
1998 Gardens Beyond Spring Gate P/P (30 X40)	710		2150.00	2150
1998 Gardens Beyond Spring Gate R/E (18 x 24)	480		2250.00	2250
1998 Gardens Beyond Spring Gate R/E (25 1/2 x 34)	480		3600.00	3600
1998 Gardens Beyond Spring Gate R/E (30 X40)	480		5850.00	5850
1998 Gardens Beyond Spring Gate S/N (18 x 24)	5,950		750.00	750
1998 Gardens Beyond Spring Gate S/N (25 1/2 x 34)	5,950		1200.00	1200
1998 Gardens Beyond Spring Gate S/N (30 x 40)	5,950		1950.00	1950
1998 Gardens Beyond Spring Gate S/P (18 x 24)	240		3750.00	3750
1998 Gardens Beyond Spring Gate S/P (25 1/2 x 34)	240		6000.00	6000
1998 Gardens Beyond Spring Gate S/P (30 X40)	240		9750.00	9750
1993 Glory of Evening A/P	400	1993	365.00	900-1150
1993 Glory of Evening G/P	490	N/A	365.00	415-1200
1993 Glory of Evening P/P	100	1994	830.00	830-1300
1993 Glory of Evening S/N	1,980	1994	315.00	995-1000
1993 Glory of Evening S/P	95	1994	2000.00	2000-4000
1993 Glory of Morning A/P	400	1993	365.00	730-1150
1993 Glory of Morning G/P	490	1993	365.00	975-1700
1993 Glory of Morning P/P	100	1993	830.00	830-1300
1993 Glory of Morning S/N	1,980	1994	315.00	995-1000
1993 Glory of Morning S/P	95	1993	2000.00	2000-4000
1993 Glory of Winter A/P	300		715.00	900
1993 Glory of Winter G/P	250		715.00	900
1993 Glory of Winter P/P	175		815.00	950
1993 Glory of Winter S/N	1,250		615.00	750
1995 Golden Gate Bridge, San Francisco A/P	395	1996	1240.00	1675-2195
1995 Golden Gate Bridge, San Francisco G/P	990	N/A	1190.00	1525-2195
1995 Golden Gate Bridge, San Francisco P/P	320	1996	1290.00	1290-2395
1995 Golden Gate Bridge, San Francisco S/N	3,950	1996	1090.00	1150-1995
1995 Golden Gate Bridge, San Francisco S/P	95	1996	3270.00	4200-12500
1994 Guardian Castle A/P	475		1015.00	1150
1994 Guardian Castle G/P	1,190		1015.00	1150
1994 Guardian Castle P/P	380		1065.00	1200
1994 Guardian Castle S/N	4,750		865.00	1000
1993 Heather's Hutch A/P	400	1993	515.00	850-1245
1993 Heather's Hutch G/P	300	N/A	565.00	1295-1345
1993 Heather's Hutch P/P	100		615.00	1445
1993 Heather's Hutch S/N	1,250	N/A	415.00	695-1045
1994 Hidden Arbor A/P	375		665.00	800
1994 Hidden Arbor G/P	940		665.00	800
1994 Hidden Arbor G/P	940		665.00	800
1994 Hidden Arbor P/P	300		715.00	850
1994 Hidden Arbor S/N	3,750		515.00	650
1990 Hidden Cottage I A/P	100	N/A	595.00	2450-4795
1990 Hidden Cottage I P/P	50	N/A	N/A	5395
1990 Hidden Cottage I S/N	550	N/A	495.00	2350-4295
1993 Hidden Cottage II A/P	400	1993	615.00	1100-1445
1993 Hidden Cottage II G/P	400	1995	665.00	825-1495
1993 Hidden Cottage II P/P	100	1995	715.00	715-1695
1993 Hidden Cottage II S/N	1,480	1994	515.00	795-1245
1993 Hidden Cottage II S/P	95	1995	3250.00	3250-3950
1994 Hidden Gazebo A/P	240	1994	665.00	850-1445
1994 Hidden Gazebo G/P	600	1994	665.00	795-1445
1994 Hidden Gazebo P/P	190		715.00	1595
1994 Hidden Gazebo S/N	2,400	1994	515.00	650-1195
1996 Hollyhock House A/P	395		730.00	800
1996 Hollyhock House G/P	990		730.00	800
1996 Hollyhock House P/P	320		780.00	850
1996 Hollyhock House S/N	3,950		580.00	650
1996 Hollyhock House S/P	95		1740.00	3450
1991 Home For The Evening A/P	200	1994	315.00	925-1145
1991 Home For The Evening P/P	100	N/A	415.00	1445
1991 Home For The Evening S/N	980	N/A	215.00	675-945
1991 Home For The Holidays A/P	200	1991	715.00	2200-3895
1991 Home For The Holidays P/P	100	1991	815.00	2750-4195
1991 Home For The Holidays R/E	Closed	1991	695.00	3995-4195
1991 Home For The Holidays S/N	980	N/A	615.00	2095-3395
1992 Home is Where the Heart Is I A/P	200	N/A	715.00	2300-3295
1992 Home is Where the Heart Is I G/P	200	N/A	765.00	1800-3395
1992 Home is Where the Heart Is I P/P	100	N/A	815.00	2550-3595
1992 Home is Where the Heart Is I S/N	980	N/A	615.00	1595-2995
1996 Home is Where the Heart Is II A/P	495	1997	840.00	975-1095
1996 Home is Where the Heart Is II G/P	1,240	1997	840.00	840-1095
1996 Home is Where the Heart Is II P/P	400	1997	890.00	890-1145
1996 Home is Where the Heart Is II S/N	Closed	1997	690.00	775-950
1996 Home is Where the Heart Is II S/P	95	1997	2070.00	2070-5495
1993 Homestead House A/P	300	1996	715.00	925-1595
1993 Homestead House G/P	250	N/A	765.00	890-1695
1993 Homestead House P/P	100		815.00	1695
1993 Homestead House S/N	1,250	1996	615.00	850-1395
1995 Hometown Chapel A/P	495		1045.00	1150
1995 Hometown Chapel G/P	1,240		995.00	1150
1995 Hometown Chapel P/P	400		1095.00	1200
1995 Hometown Chapel S/N	4,950		895.00	1000
1996 Hometown Evening A/P	295	1996	1070.00	1795-2995
1996 Hometown Evening G/P	740	1996	1070.00	1795-2995
1996 Hometown Evening P/P	240	1996	1120.00	1120-3195
1996 Hometown Evening S/N	2,950	1996	920.00	1300-2695
1996 Hometown Evening S/P	95	1996	2760.00	2760-11500
1997 Hometown Lake A/P	495	1998	1125.00	1575-1995
1997 Hometown Lake G/P	1,240	1998	1125.00	1125-1995
1997 Hometown Lake P/P	400	1998	1175.00	1175-2095
1997 Hometown Lake S/N	4,950	1998	975.00	1325-1795
1997 Hometown Lake S/P	125	1998	3900.00	5350-8950
1995 Hometown Memories I A/P	495	1995	1015.00	1650-2595
1995 Hometown Memories I G/P	1,240	N/A	1015.00	1750-2595
1995 Hometown Memories I P/P	400	N/A	1065.00	1065
1995 Hometown Memories I S/N	4,950	1996	865.00	1200-2295
1996 Hyde Street and the Bay, SF A/P	395	1996	1125.00	1725-2195
1996 Hyde Street and the Bay, SF G/P	980	1996	1125.00	1125-2195
1996 Hyde Street and the Bay, SF P/P	320	1996	1175.00	1825-2295
1996 Hyde Street and the Bay, SF S/N	3,950	1996	975.00	1425-2250
1996 Hyde Street and the Bay, SF S/P	95	1996	2925.00	4500-10000
1992 Julianne's Cottage A/P	200	N/A	515.00	2795-3095
1992 Julianne's Cottage G/P	200	N/A	565.00	2995-3295
1992 Julianne's Cottage P/P	100	N/A	615.00	615-3595
1992 Julianne's Cottage S/N	980	N/A	415.00	1850-2695
1996 Lamplight Bridge A/P	295	1996	730.00	995-1295
1996 Lamplight Bridge G/P	740	N/A	730.00	775-1295
1996 Lamplight Bridge P/P	240		780.00	1345
1996 Lamplight Bridge S/N	2,950	1996	580.00	750-1095
1996 Lamplight Bridge S/P	95	1996	1740.00	3350-6450
1993 Lamplight Brooke A/P	400	1994	715.00	1550-3045
1993 Lamplight Brooke G/P	330	1994	765.00	1350-3195
1993 Lamplight Brooke P/P	230	N/A	815.00	3345
1993 Lamplight Brooke S/N	1,650	1994	615.00	1350-2745
1994 Lamplight Inn A/P	275	1994	765.00	900-1395
1994 Lamplight Inn G/P	685		765.00	1295
1994 Lamplight Inn P/P	220		815.00	1395
1994 Lamplight Inn S/N	2,750	1994	615.00	645-1195
1993 Lamplight Lane A/P	200	N/A	715.00	2650-4645
1993 Lamplight Lane G/P	200	1994	765.00	3200-4745
1995 Lamplight Lane P/P	100	N/A	815.00	815-4945
1993 Lamplight Lane S/N	980	N/A	615.00	2450-4345
1995 Lamplight Lane S/P	Closed	N/A	N/A	5200-12500
1995 Lamplight Village A/P	495	1995	800.00	1325-1595
1995 Lamplight Village G/P	1,210	N/A	800.00	1395-1595
1995 Lamplight Village P/P	400		850.00	1795
1995 Lamplight Village S/N	4,950	1995	650.00	1050-1495
1995 A Light in the Storm A/P	395	1995	800.00	1295-1345
1995 A Light in the Storm G/P	990		750.00	1245
1995 A Light in the Storm P/P	320		850.00	1345
1995 A Light in the Storm S/N	3,950	1996	650.00	1050-1195
1995 A Light in the Storm S/P	95	N/A	2070.00	3995-7500
1996 The Light of Peace A/P	345	1996	1300.00	1400-2795
1996 The Light of Peace G/P	865	1996	1300.00	2795-2850
1996 The Light of Peace P/P	280	1996	1350.00	1350-2995
1996 The Light of Peace S/N	3,450	1996	1150.00	2200-2495
1996 The Light of Peace S/P	95	1996	3450.00	3450-11500
1995 The Lights of Home S/N (8x10)	2,500	N/A	195.00	450-695
1996 Lilac Gazebo A/P	295	1997	615.00	700-1050
1996 Lilac Gazebo G/P	740		615.00	700
1996 Lilac Gazebo P/P	240		665.00	750
1996 Lilac Gazebo S/N	2,950		465.00	550
1996 Lilac Gazebo S/P	95		1395.00	2750
1998 Lingering Dusk A/P (16 x 20)	790		800.00	800
1998 Lingering Dusk A/P (20 x 24)	790		900.00	900
1998 Lingering Dusk G/P (16 x 20)	1,400		800.00	800
1998 Lingering Dusk G/P (20 X 24)	1,400		900.00	900
1998 Lingering Dusk P/P (16 x 20)	480		850.00	850
1998 Lingering Dusk P/P (20 X 24))	480		950.00	950
1998 Lingering Dusk R/E (16 x 20)	320		1950.00	1950
1998 Lingering Dusk R/E (20 X 24)	320		2250.00	2250
1998 Lingering Dusk S/N (16 x 20)	3,950		650.00	650
1998 Lingering Dusk S/N (20 x 24)	3,950		750.00	750
1998 Lingering Dusk S/P (16 x 20)	160		3250.00	3250
1998 Lingering Dusk S/P (20 X 24)	160		3750.00	3750
1991 The Lit Path A/P	200	1991	315.00	695-895
1991 The Lit Path P/P	100		415.00	895
1991 The Lit Path R/E	Closed	1991	395.00	495-1095
1991 The Lit Path S/N	1,960	1994	215.00	500-695
1995 Main Street Celebration A/P	125	1995	800.00	900
1995 Main Street Celebration P/P	400		850.00	950
1995 Main Street Celebration S/N	1,250		650.00	750
1995 Main Street Courthouse A/P	125		800.00	900
1995 Main Street Courthouse P/P	400		850.00	950
1995 Main Street Courthouse S/N	1,250		650.00	750
1995 Main Street Matinee A/P	125		800.00	900
1995 Main Street Matinee P/P	400		850.00	950
1995 Main Street Matinee S/N	1,250		650.00	750
1995 Main Street Trolley A/P	125		800.00	900
1995 Main Street Trolley P/P	400		850.00	950
1995 Main Street Trolley S/N	1,250		650.00	750
1991 McKenna's Cottage A/P	200	N/A	615.00	725-1295
1991 McKenna's Cottage P/P	100		715.00	1395
1991 McKenna's Cottage R/E	200	N/A	615.00	700-2045
1991 McKenna's Cottage S/N	980	1995	515.00	675-1045
1992 Miller's Cottage, Thomashire A/P	200	N/A	615.00	1000-2095
1992 Miller's Cottage, Thomashire G/P	200	N/A	665.00	1075-2195
1992 Miller's Cottage, Thomashire P/P	100		715.00	715
1992 Miller's Cottage, Thomashire S/N	980	1994	515.00	1350-1795
1994 Moonlight Lane I A/P	240	1995	665.00	735-800
1994 Moonlight Lane I G/P	600		665.00	800
1994 Moonlight Lane I P/P	190		715.00	850
1994 Moonlight Lane I S/N	2,400		515.00	650
1985 Moonlight on the Riverfront S/N	260	N/A	715.00	1095-2195
1992 Moonlit Sleigh Ride A/P	200	1995	415.00	850-945
1992 Moonlit Sleigh Ride G/P	200	1995	465.00	465-995
1992 Moonlit Sleigh Ride P/P	100		515.00	995
1992 Moonlit Sleigh Ride S/N	1,960	1995	315.00	550-745
1995 Morning Dogwood A/P	495		645.00	750
1995 Morning Dogwood G/P	1,240		645.00	750
1995 Morning Dogwood P/P	400		695.00	800
1995 Morning Dogwood S/N	4,950		495.00	600
1995 Morning Glory Cottage A/P	495	1997	695.00	825-895
1995 Morning Glory Cottage G/P	1,240		645.00	845
1995 Morning Glory Cottage P/P	400		745.00	895
1995 Morning Glory Cottage S/N	4,950		545.00	695
1990 Morning Light A/P	Closed	N/A	695.00	1500-2050
1998 Mountain Chapel A/P (16 x 20)	595		800.00	800
1998 Mountain Chapel A/P (24 x 30)	595		1150.00	1150
1998 Mountain Chapel A/P (32 x 40)	495		2100.00	2100
1998 Mountain Chapel S/N (16 x 20)	5,950		650.00	650
1998 Mountain Chapel S/N (24 x 30)	5,950		1000.00	1000
1998 Mountain Chapel S/N (32 x 40)	4,950		1950.00	1950
1997 A New Day Dawning A/P	395	1997	1300.00	1575-2095
1997 A New Day Dawning G/P	990	1997	1300.00	1300-2095
1997 A New Day Dawning P/P	320		1350.00	1645
1997 A New Day Dawning S/N	3,950	1998	1150.00	1350-1945
1997 A New Day Dawning S/P	95	1997	3450.00	3450-7950
1992 Olde Porterfield Gift Shoppe A/P	200	1995	615.00	875-1195
1992 Olde Porterfield Gift Shoppe G/P	200	N/A	665.00	615-1245
1992 Olde Porterfield Gift Shoppe P/P	100		715.00	1295
1992 Olde Porterfield Gift Shoppe S/N	980	1994	515.00	800-995
1991 Olde Porterfield Tea Room A/P	200	N/A	615.00	1050-2195
1991 Olde Porterfield Tea Room P/P	100	N/A	715.00	2395
1991 Olde Porterfield Tea Room R/E	Closed	1991	595.00	1500-2695
1991 Olde Porterfield Tea Room S/N	980	N/A	515.00	975-1995
1991 Open Gate, Sussex A/P	100	1994	315.00	315-925
1991 Open Gate, Sussex P/P	100	1994	415.00	415-2395
1991 Open Gate, Sussex R/E	Closed	1992	295.00	595-1175
1991 Open Gate, Sussex S/N	980	1994	215.00	495-725
1993 Paris, City of Lights A/P	600	1994	715.00	1675-3045
1993 Paris, City of Lights G/P	600	N/A	765.00	1385-3195
1993 Paris, City of Lights P/P	200	1994	815.00	815-3395
1993 Paris, City of Lights S/N	1,980	N/A	615.00	1695-2795
1993 Paris, City of Lights S/P	190	1994	3750.00	3750-10950
1994 Paris, Eiffel Tower A/P	275	1994	945.00	1150-1895
1994 Paris, Eiffel Tower G/P	685	1995	945.00	1150-1895
1994 Paris, Eiffel Tower P/P	220		995.00	1995
1994 Paris, Eiffel Tower S/N	2,750	1994	795.00	850-1595
1995 Petals of Hope A/P	395		730.00	800
1995 Petals of Hope G/P	990		680.00	800
1995 Petals of Hope P/P	320		780.00	850
1995 Petals of Hope S/N	3,950		580.00	650
1995 Petals of Hope S/P	95		1740.00	3250
1996 Pine Cove Cottage A/P	495		840.00	900
1996 Pine Cove Cottage G/P	1,240		840.00	900
1996 Pine Cove Cottage P/P	400		890.00	950
1996 Pine Cove Cottage S/N	4,950		690.00	750
1996 Pine Cove Cottage S/P	95		2070.00	3750
1994 The Power & The Majesty A/P	275		765.00	900
1994 The Power & The Majesty G/P	685		765.00	900
1994 The Power & The Majesty P/P	220		815.00	950
1994 The Power & The Majesty S/N	2,750		615.00	750
1991 Pye Corner Cottage A/P	200	N/A	315.00	425-645
1991 Pye Corner Cottage P/P	N/A		415.00	795
1991 Pye Corner Cottage R/E	Closed	N/A	295.00	395-1045
1991 Pye Corner Cottage S/N	1,960	1996	215.00	450-545
1988 Room with a View S/N	260	N/A	795.00	975-1895
1990 Rose Arbor A/P	98	N/A	595.00	1900-2295
1990 Rose Arbor S/N	935	N/A	495.00	1450-1995
1996 Rose Gate A/P	295	1996	615.00	700-1100
1996 Rose Gate G/P	740		615.00	700
1996 Rose Gate P/P	230		665.00	750
1996 Rose Gate S/N	2,950		465.00	550
1996 Rose Gate S/P	95		1395.00	2750
1994 San Francisco Market Street A/P	750		945.00	1005
1994 San Francisco Market Street G/P	1,875		945.00	1005
1994 San Francisco Market Street P/P	600		995.00	1005
1994 San Francisco Market Street S/N	7,500		795.00	855
1992 San Francisco, Nob Hill (California St.) A/P	Closed	N/A	715.00	4600-6595
1992 San Francisco, Nob Hill (California St.) G/P	200	N/A	765.00	4350-6895
1992 San Francisco, Nob Hill (California St.) P/P	100	N/A	815.00	4400-7395
1992 San Francisco, Nob Hill (California St.) S/N	980	N/A	615.00	4200-5995
1989 San Francisco, Union Square A/P	50	N/A	795.00	4900-6895
1989 San Francisco, Union Square P/P	25	N/A	N/A	7395
1989 San Francisco, Union Square S/N	935	N/A	595.00	4400-6395
1992 Silent Night A/P	200	N/A	515.00	1100-1895
1992 Silent Night G/P	200	N/A	565.00	1125-1945
1992 Silent Night P/P	100	N/A	615.00	615-2045
1992 Silent Night S/N	980	N/A	415.00	975-1645
1995 Simpler Times I A/P	345		840.00	900
1995 Simpler Times I G/P	870		790.00	900
1995 Simpler Times I P/P	280		890.00	950

*Quotes have been rounded up to nearest dollar

YEAR ISSUE	EDITION LIMIT	YEAR RETD.	ISSUE PRICE	*QUOTE U.S.$
1995 Simpler Times I S/N	3,450		690.00	750
1995 Simpler Times I S/P	95		2070.00	3750
1990 Spring At Stonegate A/P	100	N/A	515.00	895-1245
1990 Spring At Stonegate P/P	50	N/A	615.00	615-1345
1990 Spring At Stonegate S/N	550	1995	415.00	625-995
1996 Spring Gate A/P	395	1997	1240.00	1350-2295
1996 Spring Gate G/P	990	1998	1240.00	1595-2395
1996 Spring Gate P/P	320	1997	1290.00	1290-2645
1996 Spring Gate S/N	3,950	1998	1090.00	1200-2105
1996 Spring Gate S/P	95	1997	3270.00	3270-11500
1994 Spring in the Alps A/P	198		725.00	800
1994 Spring in the Alps G/P	500		725.00	800
1994 Spring in the Alps P/P	160		775.00	850
1994 Spring in the Alps S/N	1,984		575.00	650
1993 St. Nicholas Circle A/P	420	1995	715.00	1375-1795
1993 St. Nicholas Circle G/P	350	1995	765.00	900-1945
1993 St. Nicholas Circle P/P	100	1995	815.00	815-2145
1993 St. Nicholas Circle S/N	1,750	1994	615.00	900-1595
1993 St. Nicholas Circle S/P	95	1995	3750.00	3750-7500
1995 Stepping Stone Cottage A/P	295	1996	840.00	1095-1150
1995 Stepping Stone Cottage G/P	740		790.00	1055
1995 Stepping Stone Cottage P/P	240		890.00	1105
1995 Stepping Stone Cottage S/N	2,950	1996	690.00	895-945
1995 Stepping Stone Cottage S/P	95		2070.00	4524
1998 Stillwater Bridge A/P (12 x 16)	990		700.00	700
1998 Stillwater Bridge A/P (18 x 24)	790		900.00	900
1998 Stillwater Bridge G/P (12 x 16)	1,750		700.00	700
1998 Stillwater Bridge G/P (18 x 24)	1,400		900.00	900
1998 Stillwater Bridge P/P (12 x 16)	600		750.00	750
1998 Stillwater Bridge P/P (18 X 24)	480		950.00	950
1998 Stillwater Bridge R/E (12 x 16)	400		1650.00	1650
1998 Stillwater Bridge R/E (18 X 24)	320		2250.00	2250
1998 Stillwater Bridge S/N (12 x 16)	4,950		550.00	550
1998 Stillwater Bridge S/N (18 x 24)	3,950		750.00	750
1998 Stillwater Bridge S/P (12 x 16)	200		2750.00	2750
1998 Stillwater Bridge S/P (18 X 24)	160		3750.00	3750
1993 Stonehearth Hutch A/P	400	N/A	515.00	895-1375
1993 Stonehearth Hutch G/P	300	1994	565.00	895-1445
1993 Stonehearth Hutch P/P	150		615.00	1495
1993 Stonehearth Hutch S/N	1,650	N/A	415.00	795-1095
1993 Stonehearth Hutch S/P	95	N/A	2750.00	2750-3200
1993 Studio in the Garden A/P	400		515.00	795
1993 Studio in the Garden G/P	600		565.00	795
1993 Studio in the Garden P/P	100		615.00	895
1993 Studio in the Garden S/N	1,480	1996	415.00	595-695
1992 Sunday at Apple Hill A/P	200	1993	615.00	1295-1895
1992 Sunday at Apple Hill G/P	200	N/A	665.00	1750-1965
1992 Sunday at Apple Hill P/P	100	N/A	715.00	715-2195
1992 Sunday at Apple Hill S/N	980	1993	515.00	1450-1695
1996 Sunday Evening Sleigh Ride A/P	298	1996	875.00	1050-1145
1996 Sunday Evening Sleigh Ride G/P	740		875.00	1045
1996 Sunday Evening Sleigh Ride P/P	240		925.00	1095
1996 Sunday Evening Sleigh Ride S/N	2,950	1997	725.00	875-995
1996 Sunday Evening Sleigh Ride S/P	95		2175.00	4995
1993 Sunday Outing A/P	200	N/A	615.00	1795-2145
1993 Sunday Outing G/P	200	N/A	665.00	1295-2245
1993 Sunday Outing P/P	100	N/A	715.00	715-2345
1993 Sunday Outing S/N	980	N/A	515.00	1485-1945
1993 Sunday Outing S/P	95	N/A	3250.00	3250-6250
1996 Sunset on Riverbend Farm A/P	495		840.00	900
1996 Sunset on Riverbend Farm G/P	1,240		840.00	900
1996 Sunset on Riverbend Farm P/P	400		890.00	950
1996 Sunset on Riverbend Farm S/N	4,950		690.00	750
1996 Sunset on Riverbend Farm S/P	95		2070.00	3750
1992 Sweetheart Cottage I A/P	200	1992	615.00	1395-1825
1992 Sweetheart Cottage I G/P	200	N/A	665.00	1200-1875
1992 Sweetheart Cottage I P/P	100		715.00	1895
1992 Sweetheart Cottage I S/N	980	N/A	515.00	1425-1575
1993 Sweetheart Cottage II A/P	400	1993	515.00	2000-2695
1993 Sweetheart Cottage II G/P	490	N/A	665.00	1690-2695
1993 Sweetheart Cottage II P/P	100	N/A	715.00	715-2795
1993 Sweetheart Cottage II S/N	980	N/A	515.00	2025-2395
1993 Sweetheart Cottage II S/P	95	N/A	3250.00	4400-10500
1994 Sweetheart Cottage III A/P	165	1994	765.00	1275-1445
1994 Sweetheart Cottage III G/P	410		765.00	1385
1994 Sweetheart Cottage III P/P	130		815.00	1485
1994 Sweetheart Cottage III S/N	1,650	1994	615.00	750-1195
1996 Teacup Cottage A/P	295	1997	875.00	900-1095
1996 Teacup Cottage G/P	740		875.00	995
1996 Teacup Cottage P/P	240		925.00	1045
1996 Teacup Cottage S/N	2,950	1998	725.00	795-945
1997 Twilight Cottage A/P	400		N/A	850
1997 Twilight Cottage G/P	1,240		N/A	800
1997 Twilight Cottage P/P	495		775.00	800
1997 Twilight Cottage S/N	4,950		625.00	650
1997 Twilight Cottage S/P	95	1997	3250.00	3500
1997 Valley of Peace A/P	395	1997	1300.00	1450-2195
1997 Valley of Peace G/P	990	1997	1300.00	1300-2195
1997 Valley of Peace P/P	320		1350.00	1995
1997 Valley of Peace S/N	3,950	1998	1150.00	1350-1995
1997 Valley of Peace S/P	95	1997	3450.00	3450-11500
1996 Venice A/P	495		1240.00	1350
1996 Venice G/P	1,240		1240.00	1350
1996 Venice P/P	400		1290.00	1400
1996 Venice S/N	4,950		1090.00	1200
1996 Venice S/P	95		3270.00	6000
1992 Victorian Christmas I A/P	200	1992	715.00	2175-3845
1992 Victorian Christmas I G/P	200	1992	765.00	2600-3945
1992 Victorian Christmas I P/P	100	1992	815.00	4145-4550
1992 Victorian Christmas I S/N	980	1992	615.00	1950-3345
1993 Victorian Christmas II A/P	400	1994	715.00	1595-2995
1993 Victorian Christmas II G/P	300	1994	765.00	1415-3145
1993 Victorian Christmas II P/P	150	1994	815.00	815-3295
1993 Victorian Christmas II S/N	980	1994	615.00	1650-2695
1993 Victorian Christmas II S/P	95	1994	3750.00	3750-11500
1994 Victorian Christmas III A/P	395	1994	800.00	800-1245
1994 Victorian Christmas III G/P	990		800.00	1195
1994 Victorian Christmas III P/P	300		850.00	1295
1994 Victorian Christmas III S/N	3,950	1997	650.00	850-1045
1995 Victorian Christmas IV S/N	2,330	1995	650.00	650-1195
1991 Victorian Evening A/P	200	1993	N/A	1795
1991 Victorian Evening P/P	100	1993	N/A	1995
1991 Victorian Evening S/N	980	1993	495.00	895-1595
1992 Victorian Garden I A/P	200	1993	915.00	2275-3545
1992 Victorian Garden I G/P	200	1993	965.00	2150-3645
1992 Victorian Garden I P/P	100	1993	1015.00	1015-3845
1992 Victorian Garden I S/N	980	1993	815.00	2250-3145
1997 Victorian Garden II A/P	395		875.00	900
1997 Victorian Garden II G/P	990		875.00	900
1997 Victorian Garden II P/P	320		925.00	950
1997 Victorian Garden II S/N	3,950		725.00	750
1997 Victorian Garden II S/P	95	N/A	2175.00	2175-5950
1997 Village Christmas A/P (18 x 24)	990		900.00	900
1997 Village Christmas A/P (25 1/2 x 34)	390		1350.00	1350
1997 Village Christmas G/P (18 x 24)	1,240		900.00	900
1997 Village Christmas G/P (25 1/2 x 34)	490	1998	1350.00	1350
1997 Village Christmas P/P (18 x 24)	600		950.00	950
1997 Village Christmas P/P (25 1/2 x 34)	240		1400.00	1400
1997 Village Christmas R/E (18 x 24)	325		2250.00	2250
1997 Village Christmas R/E (25 1/2 x 34)	160		3600.00	3600
1997 Village Christmas S/N (18 x 24)	4,950		750.00	750
1997 Village Christmas S/N (25 1/2 x 34)	1,950		1200.00	1200
1997 Village Christmas S/P (18 x 24)	155		3750.00	3950
1997 Village Christmas S/P (25 1/2 x 34)	80	1998	6000.00	5600-10950
1993 Village Inn A/P	400	1996	615.00	860-1145
1993 Village Inn G/P	400	N/A	665.00	815-1195
1993 Village Inn P/P	100		715.00	1245
1993 Village Inn S/N	1,200	1994	515.00	625-945
1994 The Warmth of Home A/P	345		590.00	700
1994 The Warmth of Home G/P	860		590.00	700
1994 The Warmth of Home P/P	275		640.00	750
1994 The Warmth of Home S/N	3,450		440.00	550
1992 Weathervane Hutch A/P	200	1995	515.00	725-945
1992 Weathervane Hutch G/P	200	N/A	565.00	615-995
1992 Weathervane Hutch P/P	100		615.00	1095
1992 Weathervane Hutch S/N	1,960	1995	415.00	385-795
1996 Winsor Manor A/P	395		1070.00	1150
1996 Winsor Manor G/P	990		1070.00	1150
1996 Winsor Manor P/P	320		1120.00	1200
1996 Winsor Manor S/N	3,950		920.00	1000
1996 Winsor Manor S/P	95		2760.00	5000
1993 Winter's End A/P	400		715.00	900
1993 Winter's End G/P	490		765.00	900
1993 Winter's End P/P	100		815.00	950
1993 Winter's End S/N	1,450		615.00	750
1991 Woodman's Thatch A/P	200	1995	315.00	695-775
1991 Woodman's Thatch P/P	100	1995	415.00	415-875
1991 Woodman's Thatch R/E	200	N/A	295.00	695-1175
1991 Woodman's Thatch S/N	1,960	1994	215.00	355-625
1992 Yosemite A/P	200	1998	715.00	900-1245
1992 Yosemite G/P	200	1998	765.00	900-1295
1992 Yosemite P/P	100		815.00	1295
1992 Yosemite S/N	980	1997	615.00	850-1095

Kinkade-Premium Paper-Unframed - T. Kinkade

YEAR ISSUE	EDITION LIMIT	YEAR RETD.	ISSUE PRICE	*QUOTE U.S.$
1991 Afternoon Light, Dogwood A/P	98	N/A	295.00	450-1565
1991 Afternoon Light, Dogwood S/N	980	N/A	185.00	390-1065
1992 Amber Afternoon	980		225.00	270
1994 Autumn at Ashley's Cottage A/P	245		335.00	370
1994 Autumn at Ashley's Cottage S/N	2,450		185.00	220
1991 The Autumn Gate S/N	980	1994	225.00	970-1635
1995 Autumn Lane A/P	285		400.00	420
1995 Autumn Lane S/N	2,850		250.00	270
1994 Beacon of Hope A/P	275		400.00	420
1994 Beacon of Hope S/N	2,750		235.00	270
1996 Beginning of a Perfect Day A/P	285		475.00	475
1996 Beginning of a Perfect Day S/N	2,850		325.00	350
1993 Beside Still Waters S/N	980	1994	185.00	1095-1415
1993 Beyond Autumn Gate S/N	1,750	1994	285.00	625-1300
1997 Beyond Spring Gate A/P	335		475.00	500
1997 Beyond Spring Gate S/N	3,350		325.00	350
1985 Birth of a City S/N	750	N/A	150.00	250-1650
1993 The Blessings of Autumn S/N	1,250		235.00	270
1994 The Blessings of Spring A/P	275		345.00	390
1994 The Blessings of Spring S/N	2,750		195.00	240
1995 Blessings of Summer A/P	485		450.00	480
1995 Blessings of Summer S/N	4,850		300.00	330
1995 Blossom Bridge A/P	285	1996	375.00	390
1995 Blossom Bridge S/N	2,850		205.00	240
1992 Blossom Hill Church S/N	980		225.00	270
1991 Boston S/N	550	1994	175.00	525-1365
1997 Bridge of Faith A/P	385		475.00	500
1997 Bridge of Faith S/N	3,850		325.00	350
1992 Broadwater Bridge S/N	980	1994	225.00	385-995
1995 Brookside Hideaway A/P	385		355.00	390
1995 Brookside Hideaway S/N	3,850		205.00	240
1996 Candlelight Cottage S/N	Closed	1997	150.00	150-195
1991 Carmel, Delores Street and the Tuck Box Tea Room S/N	980	1994	275.00	520-1695
1989 Carmel, Ocean Avenue S/N	935	N/A	225.00	1495-2355
1990 Chandler's Cottage S/N	550	N/A	125.00	850-1365
1992 Christmas At the Ahwahnee S/N	980		175.00	240
1990 Christmas Cottage 1990 S/N	550	N/A	95.00	465-1295
1991 Christmas Eve S/N	980	1998	125.00	375-695
1994 Christmas Memories A/P	245		375.00	390
1994 Christmas Memories S/N	2,450		225.00	240
1994 Christmas Tree Cottage A/P	295		335.00	370
1994 Christmas Tree Cottage S/N	2,950		185.00	220
1996 A Christmas Welcome A/P	285		350.00	370
1996 A Christmas Welcome S/N	2,850		200.00	220
1997 Clearing Storms A/P (18 x 27)	570		420.00	420
1997 Clearing Storms A/P (24 x 36)	570		500.00	500
1997 Clearing Storms S/N (18 x 27)	2,850		270.00	270
1997 Clearing Storms S/N (24 x 36)	2,850		350.00	350
1997 Cobblestone Brooke A/P	485		475.00	500
1997 Cobblestone Brooke S/N	4,850		325.00	350
1996 Cobblestone Lane A/P	285		450.00	480
1996 Cobblestone Lane S/N	2,850		300.00	330
1992 Cottage-By-The-Sea S/N	980	N/A	250.00	495-985
1992 Country Memories S/N	980		185.00	220
1994 Creekside Trail A/P	198		400.00	420
1994 Creekside Trail S/N	1,984		250.00	270
1984 Dawson S/N	750	N/A	150.00	795-1935
1994 Days of Peace A/P	198		400.00	420
1994 Days of Peace S/N	1,984		250.00	270
1995 Deer Creek Cottage A/P	285		335.00	370
1995 Deer Creek Cottage S/N	2,850		185.00	220
1994 Dusk in the Valley A/P	198		400.00	420
1994 Dusk in the Valley S/N	1,984		250.00	270
1994 Emerald Isle Cottage A/P	275		345.00	390
1994 Emerald Isle Cottage S/N	2,750		195.00	240
1994 End of a Perfect Day I P/P	100	N/A	715.00	715
1993 End of a Perfect Day I S/N	1,250	1994	195.00	525-1165
1994 End of a Perfect Day II A/P	275		385.00	480
1994 End of a Perfect Day II P/P	220	N/A	1015.00	1015
1994 End of a Perfect Day II S/N	2,750	1996	235.00	450-515
1995 End of a Perfect Day III A/P	485		475.00	500
1994 End of a Perfect Day III P/P	400		1195.00	2095
1995 End of a Perfect Day III S/N	4,850	1998	325.00	350
1989 Entrance to the Manor House S/N	550	N/A	125.00	740-1065
1989 Evening at Merritt's Cottage S/N	550	N/A	125.00	1365-1495
1992 Evening at Swanbrooke Cottage S/N	980	1994	250.00	525-1045
1992 Evening Carolers S/N	N/A		150.00	170
1995 Evening in the Forest A/P	485		355.00	390
1995 Evening in the Forest S/N	4,850		205.00	240
1985 Evening Service S/N	Closed	N/A	90.00	495-695
1998 Everett's Cottage A/P (16 x 20)	585		390.00	390
1998 Everett's Cottage A/P (20 x 24)	585		420.00	420
1998 Everett's Cottage A/P (24 x 30)	485		480.00	480
1998 Everett's Cottage S/N (16 x 20)	5,850		240.00	240
1998 Everett's Cottage S/N (20 x 24)	5,850		270.00	270
1998 Everett's Cottage S/N (24 x 30)	4,850		330.00	330
1993 Fisherman's Wharf, San Francisco S/N	2,750		305.00	350
1991 Flags Over The Capitol S/N	980		195.00	270
1997 Garden of Prayer A/P (18 x 24)	970		420.00	420
1997 Garden of Prayer A/P (25 1/2 x 34)	970		500.00	500
1997 Garden of Prayer A/P (30 x 40)	770		650.00	650
1997 Garden of Prayer S/N (18 x 24)	4,850		270.00	270
1997 Garden of Prayer S/N (25 1/2 x 34)	4,850		350.00	350
1997 Garden of Prayer S/N (30 x 40)	3,850		500.00	500
1993 The Garden of Promise S/N	1,250	1994	235.00	450-835
1992 The Garden Party S/N	980		175.00	240
1994 Gardens Beyond Autumn Gate S/N	Closed	1996	325.00	700-825
1998 Gardens Beyond Spring Gate S/N (18 x 27)	5,850		270.00	270
1998 Gardens Beyond Spring Gate S/N (25 1/2 x 34)	5,850		350.00	350
1998 Gardens Beyond Spring Gate S/N (30 x 40)	5,850		500.00	500
1993 Glory of Winter S/N	1,250	1998	235.00	270
1995 Golden Gate Bridge, San Francisco A/P	385		475.00	500
1995 Golden Gate Bridge, San Francisco S/N	3,850		325.00	350
1994 Guardian Castle A/P	275	1996	450.00	480
1994 Guardian Castle G/P	685		450.00	480
1994 Guardian Castle S/N	2,750		300.00	330
1993 Heather's Hutch S/N	1,250		175.00	220
1994 Hidden Arbor A/P	275		375.00	390
1994 Hidden Arbor S/N	2,750	N/A	195.00	240-315
1990 Hidden Cottage I S/N	550	N/A	125.00	615-1565
1993 Hidden Cottage II S/N	1,480	1998	195.00	265
1994 Hidden Gazebo A/P	240		345.00	390
1994 Hidden Gazebo, S/N	2,400		195.00	240
1996 Hollyhock House A/P	385		355.00	390
1996 Hollyhock House S/N	3,850		205.00	240
1991 Home For The Evening S/N	980	N/A	100.00	400-495
1991 Home For The Holidays S/N	980	1994	225.00	475-1035
1992 Home is Where the Heart Is I S/N	980	1994	225.00	650-1035
1996 Home is Where the Heart Is II A/P	485	1997	400.00	435-465
1996 Home is Where the Heart Is II S/N	Closed	1997	250.00	285-315
1993 Homestead House S/N	1,250		235.00	285
1996 Hometown Evening A/P	285		450.00	480
1996 Hometown Evening S/N	2,850		300.00	330
1997 Hometown Lake A/P	485		480.00	480
1997 Hometown Lake S/N	4,850		330.00	330
1995 Hometown Memories I A/P	485		480.00	480
1995 Hometown Memories I S/N	4,850		300.00	330
1996 Hyde Street and the Bay A/P	385		450.00	480
1996 Hyde Street and the Bay S/N	3,850		300.00	330
1992 Julianne's Cottage S/N	980	N/A	185.00	550-795
1996 Lamplight Bridge A/P	285		355.00	390
1996 Lamplight Bridge S/N	2,850		205.00	240
1993 Lamplight Brook S/N	1,650	1995	235.00	395-935
1994 Lamplight Inn A/P	275		385.00	420
1994 Lamplight Inn S/N	2,750		235.00	270
1993 Lamplight Lane S/N	980	N/A	225.00	725-1435

*Quotes have been rounded up to nearest dollar

YEAR ISSUE	EDITION LIMIT	YEAR RETD.	ISSUE PRICE	*QUOTE U.S.$
1995 Lamplight Village A/P	485		400.00	420
1995 Lamplight Village S/N	4,850		250.00	270
1995 A Light in the Storm A/P	385		400.00	420
1995 A Light in the Storm S/N	3,850		250.00	270
1996 The Light of Peace A/P	335		475.00	500
1996 The Light of Peace S/N	3,350		325.00	350
1995 The Lights of Home A/P	250	1996	225.00	225-250
1996 Lilac Gazebo A/P	285		335.00	370
1996 Lilac Gazebo S/N	2,850		185.00	220
1998 Lingering Dusk A/P (16 x 20)	770		390.00	390
1998 Lingering Dusk A/P (20 x 24)	770		420.00	420
1998 Lingering Dusk S/N (16 x 20)	3,850		240.00	240
1998 Lingering Dusk S/N (20 x 24)	3,850		270.00	270
1995 Main Street Celebration A/P	195		400.00	420
1995 Main Street Celebration S/N	1,950		250.00	270
1995 Main Street Courthouse A/P	195		400.00	420
1995 Main Street Courthouse S/N	1,950		250.00	270
1995 Main Street Matinee A/P	195		400.00	420
1995 Main Street Matinee S/N	1,950		250.00	270
1995 Main Street Trolley A/P	195		400.00	420
1995 Main Street Trolley S/N	1,950		250.00	270
1991 McKenna's Cottage S/N	980		150.00	365
1992 Miller's Cottage S/N	980	1995	175.00	280-415
1994 Moonlight Lane I A/P	240		345.00	390
1994 Moonlight Lane I S/N	2,400		195.00	240
1985 Moonlight on the Riverfront S/N	260	N/A	150.00	395-1795
1995 Morning Dogwood A/P	485		345.00	370
1995 Morning Dogwood S/N	4,850		195.00	220
1995 Morning Glory Cottage A/P	485		355.00	390
1995 Morning Glory Cottage S/N	4,850		205.00	240
1998 Mountain Chapel A/P (16 x 20)	585		390.00	390
1998 Mountain Chapel A/P (24 x 30)	585		480.00	480
1998 Mountain Chapel A/P (32 x 40)	485		650.00	650
1998 Mountain Chapel S/N (16 x 20)	5,850		240.00	240
1998 Mountain Chapel S/N (24 x 30)	5,850		330.00	330
1998 Mountain Chapel S/N (32 x 40)	4,850		500.00	500
1997 A New Day Dawning A/P	385		475.00	500
1997 A New Day Dawning S/N	3,850		325.00	350
1986 New York, 6th Avenue S/N	950	N/A	150.00	1250-1685
1992 Olde Porterfield Gift Shoppe S/N	980		175.00	240
1991 Olde Porterfield Tea Room S/N	980	1998	150.00	240-765
1991 Open Gate, Sussex S/N	980		100.00	110
1993 Paris, City of Lights S/N	1,980		250.00	390
1994 Paris, Eiffel Tower A/P	275		400.00	420
1994 Paris, Eiffel Tower S/N	2,750		250.00	270
1995 Petals of Hope A/P	385		355.00	390
1995 Petals of Hope S/N	3,850		205.00	240
1996 Pine Cove Cottage A/P	485		400.00	420
1996 Pine Cove Cottage S/N	4,850		250.00	270
1984 Placerville, 1916 S/N	950	N/A	90.00	1400-3065
1994 The Power & The Majesty A/P	275		385.00	420
1994 The Power & The Majesty S/N	2,750		235.00	270
1988 Room with a View S/N	260	N/A	150.00	425-1500
1990 Rose Arbor S/N	935	1994	125.00	325-1445
1996 Rose Gate A/P	285		335.00	370
1996 Rose Gate S/N	2,850		185.00	220
1994 San Francisco Market Street A/P	750		525.00	525
1994 San Francisco Market Street S/N	7,500		375.00	375
1986 San Francisco, 1909 S/N	950	N/A	150.00	1400-2140
1992 San Francisco, Nob Hill (California St.) S/N	980	N/A	275.00	995-2635
1989 San Francisco, Union Square S/N	Closed	N/A	225.00	1895-2635
1992 Silent Night S/N	980	1994	175.00	360-445
1995 Simpler Times I A/P	335		400.00	420
1995 Simpler Times I S/N	3,895		250.00	270
1990 Spring At Stonegate S/N	550	1996	200.00	250-565
1996 Spring Gate A/P	385		475.00	500
1996 Spring Gate S/N	3,850		325.00	350
1994 Spring in the Alps A/P	198		375.00	375
1994 Spring in the Alps S/N	1,984		225.00	240
1993 St. Nicholas Circle S/N	1,750		235.00	285
1995 Stepping Stone Cottage A/P	285		400.00	420
1995 Stepping Stone Cottage S/N	2,850		250.00	270
1998 Stillwater Bridge A/P (12 x 16)	570		370.00	370
1998 Stillwater Bridge A/P (18 x 24)	770		420.00	420
1998 Stillwater Bridge S/N (12 x 16)	2,850		220.00	220
1998 Stillwater Bridge S/N (18 x 24)	3,850		270.00	270
1993 Stonehearth Hutch S/N	1,650		175.00	245
1993 Studio in the Garden S/N	980	1995	175.00	220
1992 Sunday At Apple Hill S/N	980	1994	175.00	450-495
1996 Sunday Evening Sleigh Ride A/P	285		400.00	420
1996 Sunday Evening Sleigh Ride S/N	2,850		250.00	270
1993 Sunday Outing S/N	980	1995	175.00	295-365
1996 Sunset at Riverbend Farm A/P	485		400.00	420
1996 Sunset at Riverbend Farm S/N	4,850		250.00	270
1992 Sweetheart Cottage I S/N	980	1995	150.00	365-385
1993 Sweetheart Cottage II S/N	980	1994	150.00	465-575
1993 Sweetheart Cottage III A/P	165	1995	385.00	395-420
1993 Sweetheart Cottage III S/N	1,650		235.00	270
1996 Teacup Cottage A/P	285		400.00	420
1996 Teacup Cottage S/N	2,850		250.00	270
1997 Twilight Cottage A/P	485		375.00	390
1997 Twilight Cottage S/N	3,350		225.00	240
1997 Valley of Peace A/P	385		475.00	500
1997 Valley of Peace S/N	3,850		325.00	520
1996 Venice A/P	485		475.00	500
1996 Venice S/N	4,850		325.00	350
1992 Victorian Christmas I S/N	980	N/A	235.00	925-1135
1993 Victorian Christmas II S/N	1,650	1996	235.00	335-450
1994 Victorian Christmas III A/P	295		400.00	420
1994 Victorian Christmas III S/N	2,950		250.00	270
1995 Victorian Christmas IV S/N	756	1995	250.00	295-335
1991 Victorian Evening S/N	Closed	1993	150.00	265-715
1992 Victorian Garden I S/N	980	1994	275.00	725-1300
1997 Victorian Garden II A/P	385		400.00	420
1997 Victorian Garden II S/N	3,850		250.00	270
1997 Village Christmas A/P (18 x 24)	970		420.00	420
1997 Village Christmas A/P (25 1/2 x 34)	370		500.00	500
1997 Village Christmas G/P (18 x 24)	1,240		900.00	900
1997 Village Christmas S/N (18 x 24)	4,850		270.00	270
1997 Village Christmas S/N (25 1/2 x 34)	1,850		350.00	350
1993 Village Inn S/N	1,200		195.00	240
1994 The Warmth of Home A/P	245	1996	335.00	370
1994 The Warmth of Home S/N	2,450		185.00	220
1996 Winsor Manor A/P	385		450.00	480
1996 Winsor Manor S/N	3,850		300.00	330
1993 Winter's End S/N	875		235.00	270
1992 Yosemite S/N	980	1996	225.00	270-350

Lightpost Publishing/Recollections by Lightpost

American Heroes Collection-Framed - Recollections

YEAR ISSUE	EDITION LIMIT	YEAR RETD.	ISSUE PRICE	*QUOTE U.S.$
1992 Abraham Lincoln	7,500	1997	150.00	150
1993 Babe Ruth	2,250	1996	95.00	95
1993 Ben Franklin	1,000	1997	95.00	95-125
1994 Dwight D. Eisenhower	Closed	1997	30.00	30
1994 Eternal Love (Civil War)	1,861	1997	195.00	195
1994 Franklin D. Roosevelt	Closed	1997	30.00	30
1992 George Washington	7,500	1997	150.00	150-225
1994 George Washington	Closed	1997	30.00	30
1994 John F. Kennedy	Closed	1997	30.00	30
1992 John F. Kennedy	7,500	1997	150.00	150
1992 Mark Twain	7,500	1997	150.00	150
1994 A Nation Divided	1,000	1997	150.00	150
1993 A Nation United	1,000	1997	150.00	150

Cinema Classics Collection - Recollections

YEAR ISSUE	EDITION LIMIT	YEAR RETD.	ISSUE PRICE	*QUOTE U.S.$
1993 As God As My Witness Classic Clip	Closed	1995	40.00	40
1994 Attempted Deception Classic Clip	Closed	1997	30.00	30
1994 A Chance Meeting Classic Clip	Closed	1997	30.00	30
1993 A Dream Remembered Classic Clip	Closed	1995	40.00	40
1993 The Emerald City Classic Clip	Closed	1995	40.00	40
1993 Follow the Yellow Brick Road Classic Clip	Closed	1995	40.00	40
1993 Frankly My Dear Classic Clip	Closed	1995	40.00	40
1994 The Gift Classic Clip	Closed	1997	30.00	30
1993 Gone With the Wind-Movie Ticket Classic Clip	2,000	1997	40.00	40
1994 If I Only Had a Brain Classic Clip	Closed	1997	30.00	30
1994 If I Only Had a Heart Classic Clip	Closed	1997	30.00	30
1994 If I Only Had the Nerve Classic Clip	Closed	1997	30.00	30
1993 The Kiss Classic Clip	Closed	1995	40.00	40
1993 Not A Marrying Man	12,500	1997	150.00	150
1993 Over The Rainbow	7,500	1997	150.00	150
1994 The Proposal Classic Clip	Closed	1997	30.00	30
1993 The Ruby Slippers Classic Clip	Closed	1995	40.00	40
1993 Scarlett & Her Beaux	12,500	1997	150.00	150
1994 There's No Place Like Home Classic Clip	Closed	1997	30.00	30
1993 We're Off to See the Wizard Classic Clip	Closed	1995	40.00	40
1993 You Do Waltz Divinely	12,500	1997	195.00	195
1993 You Need Kissing	12,500	1997	195.00	195

The Elvis Collection - Recollections

YEAR ISSUE	EDITION LIMIT	YEAR RETD.	ISSUE PRICE	*QUOTE U.S.$
1994 Celebrity Soldier/Regular G.I.	Closed	1997	30.00	30
1994 Dreams Remembered/Dreams Realized	Closed	1997	30.00	30
1994 Elvis the King	2,750	1997	195.00	195
1994 Elvis the Pelvis	2,750	1997	195.00	195
1994 The King/The Servant	Closed	1997	30.00	30
1994 Lavish Spender/Generous Giver	Closed	1997	30.00	30
1994 Professional Artist/Practical Joker	Closed	1997	30.00	30
1994 Public Image/Private Man	Closed	1997	30.00	30
1994 Sex Symbol/Boy Next Door	Closed	1997	30.00	30
1994 To Elvis with Love	2,750	1997	195.00	195
1994 Vulgar Showman/Serious Musician	Closed	1997	30.00	30

Gone With the Wind - Recollections

YEAR ISSUE	EDITION LIMIT	YEAR RETD.	ISSUE PRICE	*QUOTE U.S.$
1995 Final Parting Classic Clip	Closed	1997	30.00	30
1995 A Parting Kiss Classic Clip	Closed	1997	30.00	30
1995 The Red Dress Classic Clip	Closed	1997	30.00	30
1995 Sweet Revenge Classic Clip	Closed	1997	30.00	30

The Wizard of Oz - Recollections

YEAR ISSUE	EDITION LIMIT	YEAR RETD.	ISSUE PRICE	*QUOTE U.S.$
1995 Glinda the Good Witch	Closed	1997	30.00	30
1995 Toto	Closed	1997	30.00	30
1995 The Wicked Witch	Closed	1997	30.00	30
1995 The Wizard	Closed	1997	30.00	30

Marty Bell

Members Only Collectors Club - M. Bell

YEAR ISSUE	EDITION LIMIT	YEAR RETD.	ISSUE PRICE	*QUOTE U.S.$
1991 Little Thatch Twilight	Closed	1992	288.00	350-400
1991 Charter Rose, The	Closed	1992	Gift	N/A
1992 Candle At Eventide	Closed	1993	Gift	N/A
1992 Blossom Lane	Closed	1993	288.00	350
1993 Laverstoke Lodge	Closed	1994	328.00	328
1993 Chideock Gate	Closed	1994	Gift	N/A
1994 Hummingbird Hill	Closed	1995	320.00	450-495
1994 The Hummingbird	Closed	1995	Gift	N/A
1995 The Bluebird Victorian	Closed	1996	320.00	340-495
1995 The Bluebird	Closed	1996	Gift	N/A
1996 Goldfinch Garden	Closed	1997	220.00	220-275
1996 The Goldfinch	Closed	1997	Gift	N/A
1997 Wishing Well Garden	Closed	1998	180.00	180
1997 The Dove	Closed	1998	Gift	N/A
1998 Lovebirds Cottage	Yr.Iss.		190.00	190
1998 The Lovebirds	Yr.Iss.		Gift	N/A

America the Beautiful - M. Bell

YEAR ISSUE	EDITION LIMIT	YEAR RETD.	ISSUE PRICE	*QUOTE U.S.$
1993 Jones Victorian	750	1994	400.00	1300
1995 The Tuck Box Tea Room, Carmel	500	1995	456.00	1295-1495
1993 Turlock Spring	114	1995	700.00	850

Christmas - M. Bell

YEAR ISSUE	EDITION LIMIT	YEAR RETD.	ISSUE PRICE	*QUOTE U.S.$
1989 Fireside Christmas	500	1989	136.00	750
1990 Ready For Christmas	700	1990	148.00	495
1991 Christmas in Rochester	900	1991	148.00	200-300
1992 McCoy's Toy Shoppe	900	1992	148.00	350
1993 Christmas Treasures	900	1993	200.00	200
1995 Tuck Box Christmas	750	1995	250.00	450-500
1996 Sing A Song Of Christmas	750		225.00	225
1997 Bell Cottage Christmas	750		225.00	225

England - M. Bell

YEAR ISSUE	EDITION LIMIT	YEAR RETD.	ISSUE PRICE	*QUOTE U.S.$
1993 The Abbey	320	1998	400.00	424
1987 Alderton Village	500	1988	235.00	650
1988 Allington Castle Kent	646	1998	540.00	540-948
1990 Arbor Cottage	900	1990	130.00	150-250
1993 Arundel Row	282	1995	130.00	138
1981 Bibury Cottage	500	1988	280.00	800-1000
1981 Big Daddy's Shoe	700	1989	64.00	325-495
1988 The Bishop's Roses	900	1989	220.00	695
1989 Blush of Spring	1,200	1990	96.00	120-160
1988 Bodiam Twilight	900	1991	520.00	900-1100
1988 Brendon Hills Lane	860	1995	304.00	318
1992 Briarwood	217	1993	220.00	220
1993 Broadway Cottage	122	1995	330.00	350
1987 Broughton Village	900	1988	128.00	400-500
1984 Brown Eyes	312	1993	296.00	400-450
1990 Bryants Puddle Thatch	900	1990	130.00	150-295
1986 Burford Village Store	500	1988	106.00	595
1993 Byfleet	623	1998	180.00	180
1981 Castle Combe Cottage	500	1988	230.00	895
1993 The Castle Tearoom	900	1993	88.00	200
1987 The Chaplains Garden	500	1987	235.00	1100
1991 Childswickham Morning	305	1993	396.00	396
1987 Chippenham Farm	500	1988	120.00	300-900
1988 Clove Cottage	900	1988	128.00	500
1988 Clover Lane Cottage	1,800	1988	272.00	500-600
1991 Cobblestone Cottage	652	1995	374.00	404-1200
1993 Coln St. Aldwyn's	1,000	1995	730.00	1000-1295
1986 Cotswold Parish Church	500	1988	98.00	1500-2000
1988 Cotswold Twilight	900	1988	128.00	395-495
1991 Cozy Cottage	900	1991	130.00	130
1993 Craigton Cottage	371	1998	130.00	130
1982 Crossroads Cottage	S/O	1987	38.00	350-460
1992 Devon Cottage	472	1995	374.00	404
1991 Devon Roses	1,200	1991	96.00	195-500
1991 Dorset Roses	1,200	1991	96.00	250
1987 Dove Cottage Garden	900	1990	260.00	304-495
1987 Driftstone Manor	500	1988	440.00	1500-1800
1987 Ducksbridge Cottage	500	1988	400.00	2000
1987 Eashing Cottage	900	1988	120.00	200-400
1992 East Sussex Roses (Archival)	1,200	1993	96.00	96
1985 Fiddleford Cottage	500	1986	78.00	1950
1993 The Flower Box	292	1998	300.00	300
1988 Friday Street Lane	1,800	1992	280.00	600
1989 The Game Keeper's Cottage	900	1989	560.00	1850
1992 Garlands Flower Shop	900	1992	220.00	350-450
1988 Ginger Cottage	1,800	1988	320.00	650
1989 Glory Cottage	911	1993	96.00	96
1989 Goater's Cottage	900	1991	368.00	560
1990 Gomshall Flower Shop	900	1990	396.00	1500-1800
1993 Graffam House	534	1998	180.00	180
1987 Halfway Cottage	900	1988	260.00	300-500
1992 Happy Heart Cottage	636	1998	368.00	368
1992 Hollybush	1,200	1994	560.00	795
1991 Horsham Farmhouse	593	1995	180.00	200-265
1986 Housewives Choice	500	1987	98.00	750-1000
1988 Icomb Village Garden	900	1988	620.00	1300-1500
1993 Idaho Hideaway	508	1998	400.00	400-450
1988 Jasmine Thatch	900	1991	272.00	495
1989 Larkspur Cottage	900	1989	220.00	495
1985 Little Boxford	500	1987	78.00	300-900
1991 Little Bromley Lodge	1,058	1998	456.00	456-500
1991 Little Timbers	900	1992	130.00	130
1987 Little Tulip Thatch	500	1988	120.00	400-700
1990 Little Well Thatch	950	1990	130.00	150-250
1990 Longparish Cottage	900	1991	368.00	650
1990 Longstock Lane	900	1990	130.00	295
1986 Lorna Doone Cottage	500	1987	380.00	3500-4000
1990 Lower Brockhampton Manor	900	1990	640.00	1800
1988 Lullabye Cottage	900	1988	220.00	300-400
1987 May Cottage	900	1988	120.00	200-699
1988 Meadow School	816	1993	220.00	350
1985 Meadowlark Cottage	500	1987	78.00	450-699
1987 Millpond, Stockbridge, The	500	1987	120.00	1100
1992 Miss Hathaway's Garden	1,349	1998	694.00	694
1987 Morning Glory Cottage	500	1988	120.00	450-599
1988 Morning's Glow	1,800	1989	280.00	320-650
1994 Mother Hubbard's Garden	2-Yr.	1996	230.00	244
1988 Murrle Cottage	1,800	1988	320.00	650
1983 Nestlewood	500	1987	300.00	2500
1989 Northcote Lane	1,160	1993	88.00	88
1989 Old Beams Cottage	900	1990	368.00	650
1988 Old Bridge, Grasmere	453	1993	640.00	640

*Quotes have been rounded up to nearest dollar

YEAR ISSUE	EDITION LIMIT	YEAR RETD.	ISSUE PRICE	*QUOTE U.S.$
1990 Old Hertfordshire Thatch	900	1990	396.00	2000
1993 Old Mother Hubbard's Cottage	2-Yr.	1995	230.00	250
1989 Overbrook	827	1993	220.00	350
1992 Pangbourne on Thames	900	1994	304.00	675
1984 Penshurst Tea Rooms (Archival)	1,000	1988	335.00	950
1984 Penshurst Tea Rooms (Canvas)	500	1987	335.00	2995
1989 The Periwinkle Tea Rooms	1,988	1998	694.00	694
1989 Pride of Spring	1,200	1990	96.00	200-400
1988 Rodway Cottage	900	1989	694.00	700-1500
1989 Rose Bedroom, The	515	1993	388.00	388
1995 Rose Bower Cottage	500	1997	320.00	320
1990 Sanctuary	900	1992	220.00	450
1982 Sandhills Cottage	S/O	1987	38.00	38
1988 Sandy Lane Thatch	375	1993	380.00	500
1982 School Lane Cottage	S/O	1987	38.00	38
1993 Selborne Cottage	750	1995	300.00	318
1988 Shere Village Antiques	900	1988	272.00	304-699
1995 Sissinghurst Garden	88	1998	488.00	488
1991 Somerset Inn	766	1998	180.00	180
1993 Speldhurst Farms	363	1998	248.00	265
1981 Spring in the Santa Ynez	500	1991	400.00	1100
1991 Springtime at Scotney	1,200	1992	730.00	750-1500
1989 St. Martin's Ashurst	243	1993	344.00	344
1997 Staplewood	43	1998	200.00	200
1990 Summer's Garden	900	1991	78.00	400-800
1985 Summers Glow	500	1987	98.00	600-1000
1987 Sunrise Thatch	900	1988	120.00	260
1996 Sunshine Cottage	99	1998	200.00	200
1996 Sunshine Lodge	88	1998	200.00	200
1985 Surrey Garden House	500	1986	98.00	850-1499
1985 Sweet Pine Cottage	500	1987	78.00	350-1499
1988 Sweet Twilight	900	1988	220.00	350-600
1990 Sweetheart Thatch	900	1993	220.00	375-500
1991 Tea Time	900	1991	130.00	300
1994 Tea With Miss Teddy	350	1995	128.00	128
1982 Thatchcolm Cottage	S/O	1987	38.00	38
1989 The Thimble Pub	641	1993	344.00	344
1993 Tithe Barn Cottage	308	1995	368.00	398
1993 Umbrella Cottage	515	1998	176.00	176
1991 Upper Chute	900	1991	496.00	1200
1992 Valentine Cottage	526	1998	176.00	176
1987 The Vicar's Gate	500	1988	110.00	700-900
1987 Wakehurst Place	900	1988	480.00	1750
1987 Well Cottage, Sandy Lane	500	1988	440.00	650-1500
1991 Wepham Cottage	1,200	1991	396.00	1050-1200
1984 West Kington Dell	500	1988	215.00	650-800
1992 West Sussex Roses (Archival)	1,200	1993	96.00	96
1990 Weston Manor	900	1995	694.00	760
1987 White Lilac Thatch	900	1988	260.00	400-700
1992 Wild Rose Cottage	155	1993	248.00	248-422
1985 Windsong Cottage	500	1987	156.00	350-799
1986 York Garden Shop	500	1988	98.00	250-999

England-Rye - M. Bell

YEAR ISSUE	EDITION LIMIT	YEAR RETD.	ISSUE PRICE	*QUOTE U.S.$
1992 Antiques of Rye	1,100	1996	220.00	260-300
1991 Bay Tree Cottage, Rye	1,100	1992	230.00	230-520
1990 Martin's Market, Rye	962	1998	304.00	304-414
1990 The Mermaid Inn, Rye	851	1998	560.00	560-650
1993 Simon the Pieman, Rye	497	1998	240.00	240
1992 The Strand Quay, Rye	771	1998	248.00	248
1991 Swan Cottage Tea Room, Rye	933	1998	176.00	176
1991 Windward Cottage, Rye	1,100	1991	228.00	895
1991 Ye Olde Bell, Rye	542	1998	196.00	196

Gardens of the Heart - M. Bell

YEAR ISSUE	EDITION LIMIT	YEAR RETD.	ISSUE PRICE	*QUOTE U.S.$
1995 Cloister Garden	250	1996	488.00	488-695
1994 My Garden	750	1997	456.00	456

Mill Pond Press

Bateman - R. Bateman

YEAR ISSUE	EDITION LIMIT	YEAR RETD.	ISSUE PRICE	*QUOTE U.S.$
1982 Above the River-Trumpeter Swans	950	1984	200.00	850-1035
1984 Across the Sky-Snow Geese	950	1985	220.00	800-905
1980 African Amber-Lioness Pair	950	1980	175.00	475
1979 Afternoon Glow-Snowy Owl	950	1979	125.00	525-603
1990 Air, The Forest and The Watch	42,558	N/A	325.00	325-681
1984 Along the Ridge-Grizzly Bears	950	1984	200.00	700-900
1984 American Goldfinch-Winter Dress	950	1984	75.00	165-207
1979 Among the Leaves-Cottontail Rabbit	950	1980	75.00	1000
1980 Antarctic Elements	950	1980	125.00	160-216
1995 Approach-Bald Eagle	N/A		1295.00	1295
1991 Arctic Cliff-White Wolves	13,000	1991	325.00	450-750
1982 Arctic Evening-White Wolf	950	1982	185.00	1050-1700
1980 Arctic Family-Polar Bears	950	1980	150.00	1150-2200
1992 Arctic Landscape-Polar Bear	5,000	N/A	345.00	195
1992 Arctic Landscape-Polar Bear-Premier Ed.	450	1992	800.00	800
1982 Arctic Portrait-White Gyrfalcon	950	1982	175.00	325
1985 Arctic Tern Pair	950	1985	175.00	185
1981 Artist and His Dog	950	1983	150.00	550
1980 Asleep on Hemlock-Screech Owl	950	1980	125.00	575-825
1991 At the Cliff-Bobcat	12,500	1991	325.00	300-325
1992 At the Feeder-Cardinal	950	1992	125.00	200-475
1987 At the Nest-Secretary Birds	950	1987	290.00	290
1982 At the Roadside-Red-Tailed Hawk	950	1984	185.00	875
1980 Autumn Overture-Moose	950	1980	245.00	2000
1980 Awesome Land-American Elk	950	1980	245.00	2350
1989 Backlight-Mute Swan	950	1989	275.00	450
1983 Bald Eagle Portrait	950	1983	185.00	300-390
1982 Baobab Tree and Impala	950	1986	245.00	300
1980 Barn Owl in the Churchyard	950	1981	125.00	690-800
1989 Barn Swallow and Horse Collar	950	N/A	225.00	225
1982 Barn Swallows in August	950	N/A	245.00	350
1992 Beach Grass and Tree Frog	1,250		345.00	345
1985 Beaver Pond Reflections	950	1985	185.00	265
1984 Big Country, Pronghorn Antelope	950	1985	185.00	185
1986 Black Eagle	950	1986	200.00	200-250
1993 Black Jaguar-Premier Edition	450	N/A	850.00	1000
1986 Black-Tailed Deer in the Olympics	950	1986	245.00	245
1986 Blacksmith Plover	950	1986	185.00	185
1991 Bluebird and Blossoms	4,500		235.00	235
1991 Bluebird and Blossoms-Prestige Ed.	450		625.00	625
1980 Bluffing Bull-African Elephant	950	1981	135.00	1100-1450
1981 Bright Day-Atlantic Puffins	950	1985	175.00	875-1300
1989 Broad-Tailed Hummingbird Pair	950	1989	225.00	225
1980 Brown Pelican and Pilings	950	1980	165.00	1550
1979 Bull Moose	950	1979	125.00	650
1978 By the Tracks-Killdeer	950	1980	75.00	825-1025
1983 Call of the Wild-Bald Eagle	950	1983	200.00	200-250
1985 Canada Geese Family(stone lithograph)	260	1985	350.00	795-895
1985 Canada Geese Over the Escarpment	950	1985	135.00	225
1986 Canada Geese With Young	950	1986	195.00	200-265
1981 Canada Geese-Nesting	950	1981	295.00	1395-1595
1993 Cardinal and Sumac	2,510	N/A	235.00	235
1988 Cardinal and Wild Apples	12,183	1988	235.00	235
1989 Catching The Light-Barn Owl	2,000	1990	295.00	295
1988 Cattails, Fireweed and Yellowthroat	950	1988	235.00	275
1989 Centennial Farm	950	1989	295.00	295
1988 The Challenge-Bull Moose	10,671	1989	325.00	325
1980 Chapel Doors	950	1985	135.00	700-850
1986 Charging Rhino	950	1986	325.00	475-575
1982 Cheetah Profile	950	1985	245.00	365
1978 Cheetah With Cubs	950	1980	95.00	365
1988 Cherrywood with Juncos	950	1988	245.00	245
1990 Chinstrap Penguin	810	1991	150.00	150
1992 Clan of the Raven	950	1992	235.00	345-425
1981 Clear Night-Wolves	950	1981	245.00	4400-4600
1988 Colonial Garden	950	1988	245.00	400-525
1987 Continuing Generations-Spotted Owls	950	1987	525.00	475-550
1991 Cottage Lane-Red Fox	950	1991	285.00	250
1984 Cougar Portrait	950	1984	95.00	290
1979 Country Lane-Pheasants	950	1981	85.00	600
1981 Courting Pair-Whistling Swans	950	1981	245.00	275
1981 Courtship Display-Wild Turkey	950	1981	175.00	225
1980 Coyote in Winter Sage	950	1980	245.00	2250-2500
1992 Cries of Courtship-Red Crowned Cranes	950	1992	350.00	395-550
1980 Curious Glance-Red Fox	950	1980	135.00	995-1450
1986 Dark Gyrfalcon	950	1986	225.00	300
1993 Day Lilies and Dragonflies	1,250		345.00	345
1982 Dipper By the Waterfall	950	1985	165.00	485-520
1989 Dispute Over Prey	950		325.00	325
1989 Distant Danger-Raccoon	1,600	1989	225.00	225
1984 Down for a Drink-Morning Dove	950	1985	135.00	260
1978 Downy Woodpecker on Goldenrod Gall	950	1979	50.00	1000-1300
1988 Dozing Lynx	950	1988	335.00	1300-1500
1986 Driftwood Perch-Striped Swallows	950	1986	195.00	195
1983 Early Snowfall-Ruffed Grouse	950	1985	195.00	195-225
1983 Early Spring-Bluebird	950	1984	185.00	625-750
1981 Edge of the Ice-Ermine	950	1981	175.00	400
1982 Edge of the Woods-Whitetail Deer, w/Book	950	1983	745.00	925-1075
1991 Elephant Cow and Calf	950	1991	300.00	400
1986 Elephant Herd and Sandgrouse	950	1986	235.00	320
1991 Encounter in the Bush-African Lions	950	1991	295.00	345
1987 End of Season-Grizzly	950	1987	325.00	595
1991 Endangered Spaces-Grizzly	4,008	1991	325.00	325
1985 Entering the Water-Common Gulls	950	1986	195.00	195
1986 European Robin and Hydrangeas	950	1986	130.00	200-295
1989 Evening Call-Common Loon	950	1989	235.00	495-625
1980 Evening Grosbeak	950	1980	125.00	695
1983 Evening Idyll-Mute Swans	950	1984	245.00	675
1981 Evening Light-White Gyrfalcon	950	1981	245.00	775-975
1979 Evening Snowfall-American Elk	950	1980	150.00	950-1150
1987 Everglades	950	1987	360.00	360
1980 Fallen Willow-Snowy Owl	950	1980	200.00	515-600
1987 Farm Lane and Blue Jays	950	1987	225.00	300-400
1986 Fence Post and Burdock	950	1987	130.00	275
1991 Fluid Power-Orca	290		2500.00	2500
1980 Flying High-Golden Eagle	950	1980	150.00	1000
1982 Fox at the Granary	950	1985	165.00	300
1982 Frosty Morning-Blue Jay	950	1982	185.00	800-900
1982 Gallinule Family	950		135.00	135
1981 Galloping Herd-Giraffes	950	1981	175.00	950-1200
1985 Gambel's Quail Pair	950	1985	95.00	325
1982 Gentoo Penguins and Whale Bones	950	1986	205.00	550-600
1983 Ghost of the North-Great Gray Owl	950	1983	200.00	1700-3950
1982 Golden Crowned Kinglet and Rhododendron	950	1982	150.00	1800-2700
1979 Golden Eagle	950	1981	150.00	250
1985 Golden Eagle Portrait	950	1987	115.00	175
1989 Goldfinch In the Meadow	1,600	1989	150.00	250
1983 Goshawk and Ruffed Grouse	950	1984	185.00	500
1988 Grassy Bank-Great Blue Heron	950	1988	285.00	225
1981 Gray Squirrel	950	1981	180.00	685-1015
1979 Great Blue Heron	950	1980	125.00	800-1400
1987 Great Blue Heron in Flight	950	1987	295.00	295-395
1988 Great Crested Grebe	950	1988	135.00	135
1987 Great Egret Preening	950	1987	315.00	600-725
1983 Great Horned Owl in the White Pine	950	1983	225.00	450
1987 Greater Kudu Bull	950	1987	145.00	145
1993 Grizzly and Cubs	2,250	1993	335.00	400
1991 Gulls on Pilings	1,950	N/A	265.00	265
1988 Hardwood Forest-White-Tailed Buck	630	1988	300.00	1600-1950
1988 Harlequin Duck-Bull Kelp-Executive Ed.	623	1988	550.00	550
1988 Harlequin Duck-Bull Kelp-Gold Plated	950	1988	300.00	300
1980 Heron on the Rocks	950	1980	75.00	500-800
1981 High Camp at Dusk	950	1985	245.00	465-1100
1979 High Country-Stone Sheep	950	1982	125.00	600-900
1987 High Kingdom-Snow Leopard	950	1987	325.00	550-800
1990 Homage to Ahmed	290	N/A	3300.00	3500
1984 Hooded Mergansers in Winter	950	1984	210.00	400-500
1984 House Finch and Yucca	950	1984	95.00	195
1986 House Sparrow	950	1986	125.00	160-225
1987 House Sparrows and Bittersweet	950	1987	220.00	300-370
1986 Hummingbird Pair Diptych	950	1986	330.00	550-625
1987 Hurricane Lake-Wood Ducks	950	1987	135.00	200
1981 In for the Evening	950	1981	150.00	1750-2500
1994 In His Prime-Mallard	950	N/A	195.00	250-295
1984 In the Brier Patch-Cottontail	950	1985	165.00	350-400
1986 In the Grass-Lioness	950	1986	245.00	245
1985 In the Highlands-Golden Eagle	950	1985	235.00	350
1985 In the Mountains-Osprey	950	1987	95.00	200
1992 Intrusion-Mountain Gorilla	2,250	1996	325.00	325-550
1990 Ireland House	950	1990	265.00	265-295
1985 Irish Cottage and Wagtail	950	1990	175.00	200-300
1992 Junco in Winter	1,250	1992	185.00	215-280
1990 Keeper of the Land	290		3300.00	3300
1993 Kestrel and Grasshopper	1,250		335.00	335
1979 King of the Realm	950	1979	125.00	575-690
1987 King Penguins	950	1987	130.00	140-195
1981 Kingfisher and Aspen	950	1981	225.00	855-900
1980 Kingfisher in Winter	950	1981	175.00	825-1000
1980 Kittiwake Greeting	950	1980	75.00	365
1981 Last Look-Bighorn Sheep	950	1986	195.00	129-225
1987 Late Winter-Black Squirrel	950	1987	165.00	165
1981 Laughing Gull and Horseshoe Crab	950	1981	125.00	125
1982 Leopard Ambush	950	1986	245.00	395-625
1988 Leopard and Thomson Gazelle Kill	950	1988	275.00	275
1985 Leopard at Seronera	950	1985	175.00	290
1980 Leopard in a Sausage Tree	950	1980	150.00	1695-2195
1984 Lily Pads and Loon	950	1984	200.00	1250-1716
1987 Lion and Wildebeest	950	1987	265.00	265
1980 Lion at Tsavo	950	1983	150.00	350
1978 Lion Cubs	950	1981	125.00	259
1987 Lioness at Serengeti	950	1987	325.00	325
1985 Lions in the Grass	950	1985	265.00	700-825
1981 Little Blue Heron	950	1981	95.00	225
1982 Lively Pair-Chickadees	950	1982	160.00	362
1983 Loon Family	950	1983	200.00	850
1990 Lunging Heron	1,250	1990	225.00	225
1978 Majesty on the Wing-Bald Eagle	950	1979	150.00	2500-3395
1988 Mallard Family at Sunset	950	1988	235.00	235
1986 Mallard Family-Misty Marsh	950	1986	130.00	130
1986 Mallard Pair-Early Winter	41,740	1986	135.00	200
1985 Mallard Pair-Early Winter 24K Gold	950	1986	1650.00	2000
1986 Mallard Pair-Early Winter Gold Plated	7,691	1986	250.00	375
1989 Mangrove Morning-Roseate Spoonbills	2,000	1989	325.00	414
1991 Mangrove Shadow-Common Egret	1,250		285.00	285
1993 Marbled Murrelet	55	1993	1200.00	1200-1900
1986 Marginal Meadow	950	1986	220.00	220-250
1979 Master of the Herd-African Buffalo	950	1980	150.00	1895-3150
1984 May Maple-Scarlet Tanager	950	1984	175.00	625-725
1982 Meadow's Edge-Mallard	950	1982	175.00	600
1982 Merganser Family in Hiding	950	1982	200.00	575
1994 Meru Dusk-Lesser Kudu	950		135.00	135
1989 Midnight-Black Wolf	25,352	1989	325.00	1395-1983
1980 Mischief on the Prowl-Raccoon	950	1980	85.00	150-195
1980 Misty Coast-Gulls	950	1980	135.00	420
1984 Misty Lake-Osprey	950	1985	95.00	150-225
1981 Misty Morning-Loons	950	1981	150.00	1100-1300
1986 Moose at Water's Edge	950	1986	130.00	285
1990 Morning Cove-Common Loon	950	1990	165.00	185
1985 Morning Dew-Roe Deer	950	1985	175.00	175-230
1983 Morning on the Flats-Bison	950	1983	200.00	300
1984 Morning on the River-Trumpeter Swans	950	1984	185.00	320
1990 Mossy Branches-Spotted Owl	4,500	1990	300.00	475-700
1990 Mowed Meadow	950	1990	190.00	190
1986 Mule Deer in Aspen	950	1986	175.00	175
1983 Mule Deer in Winter	950	1983	200.00	275
1988 Muskoka Lake-Common Loons	2,500	1988	265.00	300-500
1989 Near Glenburnie	950		265.00	265
1983 New Season-American Robin	950	1983	200.00	325
1986 Northern Reflections-Loon Family	8,631	1986	255.00	1897-2550
1985 Old Whaling Base and Fur Seals	950	1985	195.00	300
1987 Old Willow and Mallards	950	1987	325.00	325
1980 On the Alert-Chipmunk	950	1980	60.00	350
1993 On the Brink-River Otters	1,250	1994	345.00	345-500
1985 On the Garden Wall	950	1985	115.00	300
1985 Orca Procession	950	1985	245.00	2475-4000
1981 Osprey Family	950	1981	245.00	245
1983 Osprey in the Rain	950	1983	110.00	500-600
1987 Otter Study	950	1987	235.00	360-475
1981 Pair of Skimmers	950	1981	150.00	195-220
1988 Panda's At Play (stone lithograph)	160	1988	400.00	1200-1379
1994 Path of the Panther	1,950	1997	295.00	295
1984 Peregrine and Ruddy Turnstones	950	1985	200.00	425-500

*Quotes have been rounded up to nearest dollar

GRAPHICS

YEAR ISSUE	EDITION LIMIT	YEAR RETD.	ISSUE PRICE	*QUOTE U.S.$
1985 Peregrine Falcon and White-Throated Swifts	950	1985	245.00	765-850
1987 Peregrine Falcon on the Cliff-Stone Litho	525	1988	350.00	780-1300
1983 Pheasant in Cornfield	950	1983	200.00	325
1988 Pheasants at Dusk	950	1988	325.00	550-724
1982 Pileated Woodpecker on Beech Tree	950	1982	175.00	825-900
1990 Pintails in Spring	9,651	1989	135.00	300
1982 Pioneer Memories-Magpie Pair	950	1982	175.00	175
1987 Plowed Field-Snowy Owl	950	1987	145.00	280-300
1990 Polar Bear	290	1990	3300.00	3300
1982 Polar Bear Profile	950	1982	210.00	1900-2586
1982 Polar Bears at Bafin Island	950	1982	245.00	875-1300
1990 Power Play-Rhinoceros	950	1990	320.00	320-500
1980 Prairie Evening-Short-Eared Owl	950	1983	150.00	293-325
1994 Predator Portfolio/Black Bear	950		475.00	475
1992 Predator Portfolio/Cougar	950		465.00	465
1993 Predator Portfolio/Grizzly	950		475.00	475
1993 Predator Portfolio/Polar Bear	950		485.00	485
1993 Predator Portfolio/Wolf	950		475.00	475
1994 Predator Portfolio/Wolverine	950		275.00	275
1988 Preening Pair-Canada Geese	950	1988	235.00	235
1987 Pride of Autumn-Canada Goose	15,294	1987	135.00	245-325
1986 Proud Swimmer-Snow Goose	950	1986	185.00	185
1989 Pumpkin Time	950		195.00	195
1982 Queen Anne's Lace and American Goldfinch	950	1982	150.00	700-900
1984 Ready for Flight-Peregrine Falcon	950	1984	185.00	470
1982 Ready for the Hunt-Snowy Owl	950	1982	245.00	650-770
1993 Reclining Snow Leopard	1,250		335.00	335
1988 Red Crossbills	950	1988	125.00	175
1984 Red Fox on the Prowl	950	1984	245.00	665-938
1982 Red Squirrel	950	1982	175.00	325
1986 Red Wolf	950	1986	250.00	275-395
1981 Red-Tailed Hawk by the Cliff	950	1981	245.00	425-655
1981 Red-Winged Blackbird and Rail Fence	950	1981	195.00	315
1984 Reeds	950	1984	185.00	388-415
1986 A Resting Place-Cape Buffalo	950	1986	265.00	265
1987 Rhino at Ngoro Ngoro	950	1988	325.00	171-325
1993 River Otter-North American Wilderness	350	N/A	325.00	800
1993 River Otters	290		1500.00	1500
1986 Robins at the Nest	950	1986	185.00	138-195
1987 Rocky Point-October	950	1987	195.00	420
1980 Rocky Wilderness-Cougar	950	1980	175.00	975-1600
1990 Rolling Waves-Greater Scaup	3,330	N/A	125.00	135
1993 Rose-breasted Grosbeak	290		450.00	450
1981 Rough-Legged Hawk in the Elm	950	1991	175.00	175-200
1981 Royal Family-Mute Swans	950	1981	245.00	715-950
1983 Ruby Throat and Columbine	950	1983	150.00	2000
1987 Ruddy Turnstones	950	1987	175.00	175
1994 Salt Spring Sheep	1,250		235.00	235
1981 Sarah E. with Gulls	950	1981	245.00	2500-5500
1993 Saw Whet Owl and Wild Grapes	950	N/A	185.00	185
1991 The Scolding-Chickadees & Screech Owl	12,500	1992	235.00	235
1991 Sea Otter Study	950	1991	150.00	245
1993 Shadow of the Rain Forest	9,000	1993	345.00	475-825
1981 Sheep Drop-Mountain Goats	950	1981	245.00	1900
1988 Shelter	950	1988	325.00	750-875
1992 Siberian Tiger	4,500	1992	325.00	325
1984 Smallwood	950	1985	200.00	700-925
1990 Snow Leopard	290	1990	2500.00	2200-2600
1985 Snowy Hemlock-Barred Owl	950	1985	245.00	245
1994 Snowy Nap-Tiger	950	1994	185.00	1034-1825
1994 Snowy Owl	150	N/A	265.00	600-750
1987 Snowy Owl and Milkweed	950	1987	235.00	575-845
1983 Snowy Owl on Driftwood	950	1983	245.00	650
1983 Spirits of the Forest	950	1984	170.00	2000
1986 Split Rails-Snow Buntings	950	1986	220.00	220
1980 Spring Cardinal	950	1980	125.00	512-625
1982 Spring Marsh-Pintail Pair	950	1982	200.00	302
1980 Spring Thaw-Killdeer	950	1980	85.00	121-245
1982 Still Morning-Herring Gulls	950	1982	200.00	200
1987 Stone Sheep Ram	950	1987	175.00	175
1985 Stream Bank June	950	1986	160.00	175
1984 Stretching-Canada Goose	950	1984	225.00	2300-4000
1985 Strutting-Ring-Necked Pheasant	950	1985	225.00	450-575
1985 Sudden Blizzard-Red-Tailed Hawk	950	1985	245.00	400-645
1990 Summer Morning Pasture	950	1990	175.00	175
1984 Summer Morning-Loon	950	1984	185.00	1000-1500
1986 Summertime-Polar Bears	950	1986	225.00	225
1979 Surf and Sanderlings	950	1980	65.00	1600-2000
1981 Swift Fox	950	1981	175.00	175-259
1986 Swift Fox Study	950	1986	115.00	200
1987 Sylvan Stream-Mute Swans	950	1987	125.00	175
1984 Tadpole Time	950	1985	135.00	400-500
1988 Tawny Owl In Beech	950	1988	325.00	325
1992 Tembo (African Elephant)	1,550	1992	350.00	350
1984 Tiger at Dawn	950	1984	225.00	1700-2600
1983 Tiger Portrait	950	1983	130.00	425-625
1988 Tree Swallow over Pond	950	1988	290.00	150-290
1991 Trumpeter Swan Family	290		2500.00	2500
1985 Trumpeter Swans and Aspen	950	1985	245.00	450-500
1979 Up in the Pine-Great Horned Owl	950	1981	150.00	675-795
1980 Vantage Point	950	1980	245.00	795-1121
1993 Vigilance	9,500		330.00	330
1989 Vulture And Wildebeest	550		295.00	295
1981 Watchful Repose-Black Bear	950	1981	245.00	475
1985 Weathered Branch-Bald Eagle	950	1985	115.00	300
1991 Whistling Swan-Lake Erie	1,950		325.00	375
1980 White Encounter-Polar Bear	950	1980	245.00	2950-4300
1980 White on White-Snowshoe Hare	950	1990	195.00	425
1982 White World-Dall Sheep	950	1982	200.00	600
1985 White-Breasted Nuthatch on a Beech Tree	950	1985	175.00	300
1980 White-Footed Mouse in Wintergreen	950	1980	60.00	650
1982 White-Footed Mouse on Aspen	950	1983	90.00	150-225
1992 White-Tailed Deer Through the Birches	10,000		335.00	335
1984 White-Throated Sparrow and Pussy Willow	950	1984	150.00	575-645
1991 Wide Horizon-Tundra Swans	2,862	1991	325.00	350
1991 Wide Horizon-Tundra Swans Companion	2,862		325.00	325
1986 Wildbeest	950		185.00	185
1982 Willet on the Shore	950	N/A	125.00	195-280
1979 Wily and Wary-Red Fox	950	1979	125.00	1075
1984 Window into Ontario	950	1984	265.00	1275
1983 Winter Barn	950	1984	170.00	420
1979 Winter Cardinal	950	1979	75.00	2250
1992 Winter Coat	1,250		245.00	575
1985 Winter Companion	950	1985	175.00	895
1980 Winter Elm-American Kestrel	950	1980	135.00	800-1000
1986 Winter in the Mountains-Raven	950	1987	200.00	200
1981 Winter Mist-Great Horned Owl	950	1981	245.00	500-722
1980 Winter Song-Chickadees	950	1980	95.00	550-776
1984 Winter Sunset-Moose	950	1984	245.00	1600
1992 Winter Trackers	4,500	1992	335.00	335
1981 Winter Wren	950	1981	135.00	450
1983 Winter-Lady Cardinal	950	1983	200.00	1025
1979 Winter-Snowshoe Hare	950	1980	95.00	1100-2300
1987 Wise One, The	950	1987	325.00	1800
1979 Wolf Pack in Moonlight	950	1979	95.00	1552-2150
1994 Wolf Pair in Winter	290	1994	795.00	1600
1983 Wolves on the Trail	950	1983	225.00	425-488
1985 Wood Bison Portrait	950	1985	165.00	225
1983 Woodland Drummer-Ruffed Grouse	950	1984	185.00	235
1981 Wrangler's Campsite-Gray Jay	950	1981	195.00	725
1979 Yellow-Rumped Warbler	950	1980	50.00	435
1978 Young Barn Swallow	950	1979	75.00	575-700
1983 Young Elf Owl-Old Saguaro	950	1983	95.00	325
1991 Young Giraffe	290	1997	850.00	2500
1989 Young Kittiwake	950		195.00	195
1988 Young Sandhill-Cranes	950	1988	325.00	325
1989 Young Snowy Owl	950	1990	195.00	112-195

Brenders - C. Brenders

YEAR ISSUE	EDITION LIMIT	YEAR RETD.	ISSUE PRICE	*QUOTE U.S.$
1986 The Acrobat's Meal-Red Squirrel	950	1989	65.00	475-603
1996 Amber Gaze-Snowy Owl	1,950		175.00	175
1988 Apple Harvest	950	1989	115.00	525
1989 The Apple Lover	1,500	1990	125.00	250
1987 Autumn Lady	950	1989	150.00	825-1207
1991 The Balance of Nature	1,950		225.00	225
1993 Black Sphinx	950		235.00	235
1986 Black-Capped Chickadees	950	1989	40.00	625-931
1990 Blond Beauty	1,950	1990	185.00	185
1986 Bluebirds	950	1989	40.00	150-250
1988 California Quail	950	1989	95.00	462-600
1991 Calm Before the Challenge-Moose	1,950	1991	225.00	225
1987 Close to Mom	950	1988	150.00	1095-2100
1993 Collectors Group (Butterfly Collections)	290		375.00	375
1986 Colorful Playground-Cottontails	950	1989	75.00	625-819
1989 The Companions	18,036	1989	200.00	525
1994 Dall Sheep Portrait	950		115.00	115
1989 Den Mother-Pencil Sketch	2,500	1992	135.00	135
1992 Den Mother-Wolf Family	25,000	1992	250.00	250-450
1986 Disturbed Daydreams	950	1989	95.00	425
1987 Double Trouble-Raccoons	950	1988	120.00	700-1550
1993 European Group (Butterfly Collections)	290		375.00	375
1993 Exotic Group (Butterfly Collections)	290		375.00	375
1993 Forager's Reward-Red Squirrel	1,250	1989	135.00	135
1988 Forest Sentinel-Bobcat	950	1988	135.00	425-550
1990 Full House-Fox Family	20,106	1990	235.00	450-550
1990 Ghostly Quiet-Spanish Lynx	1,950	1990	200.00	200
1986 Golden Season-Gray Squirrel	950	1987	85.00	600-700
1986 Harvest Time-Chipmunk	950	1989	65.00	216
1988 Hidden In the Pines-Immature Great Hor	950	1988	175.00	1000-1125
1988 High Adventure-Black Bear Cubs	950	1989	105.00	415-860
1988 A Hunter's Dream	950	1988	165.00	1000
1993 In Northern Hunting Grounds	1,750		375.00	375
1992 Island Shores-Snowy Egret	2,500		250.00	250
1987 Ivory-Billed Woodpecker	950	1989	95.00	775
1988 Long Distance Hunters	950	1988	175.00	895-1095
1989 Lord of the Marshes	1,250	1989	135.00	175-447
1986 Meadowlark	950	1989	40.00	170-285
1989 Merlins at the Nest	1,250	1989	165.00	235-300
1985 Mighty Intruder	950	1989	95.00	265
1987 Migration Fever-Barn Swallows	950	1989	150.00	465-776
1990 The Monarch is Alive	4,071	1990	265.00	295
1993 Mother of Pearls	5,000		275.00	275
1990 Mountain Baby-Bighorn Sheep	1,950		165.00	165-215
1987 Mysterious Visitor-Barn Owl	950	1989	150.00	325-500
1993 Narrow Escape-Chipmunk	1,750		150.00	150
1991 The Nesting Season-House Sparrow	1,950	1991	195.00	200-295
1989 Northern Cousins-Black Squirrels	950	1989	150.00	290
1984 On the Alert-Red Fox	950	1986	95.00	350-397
1990 On the Old Farm Door	1,500	1990	225.00	225
1991 One to One-Gray Wolf	10,000	1991	245.00	425-602
1992 Pathfinder-Red Fox	5,000	1992	245.00	245-300
1984 Playful Pair-Chipmunks	950	1987	60.00	628-695
1994 Power and Grace	2,500	1994	265.00	550-625
1989 The Predator's Walk	1,250	1989	150.00	175-293
1992 Red Fox Study	1,250	1992	125.00	125
1994 Riverbank Kestrel	2,500	1995	225.00	300-350
1988 Roaming the Plains-Pronghorns	950	1989	150.00	195
1986 Robins	950	1989	40.00	175-431
1993 Rocky Camp-Cougar Family	5,000	1995	275.00	275-450
1993 Rocky Camp-Cubs	950		225.00	225
1992 Rocky Kingdom-Bighorn Sheep	1,750	1997	255.00	255-300
1991 Shadows in the Grass-Young Cougars	1,950	1991	235.00	235
1990 Shoreline Quartet-White Ibis	1,950	1995	265.00	265
1984 Silent Hunter-Great Horned Owl	950	1987	95.00	450-560
1984 Silent Passage	950	1988	150.00	350-475
1990 Small Talk	1,500	1990	125.00	140
1992 Snow Leopard Portrait	1,750	1993	150.00	150-172
1990 Spring Fawn	1,500	1990	125.00	275
1990 Squirrel's Dish	1,950		110.00	110
1989 Steller's Jay	1,250	1989	135.00	150-175
1993 Summer Roses-Winter Wren	1,500	1993	250.00	595-690
1989 The Survivors-Canada Geese	1,500	1989	225.00	400
1994 Take Five-Canadian Lynx	1,500	N/A	245.00	475-500
1988 Talk on the Old Fence	950	1988	165.00	825-975
1990 A Threatened Symbol	1,950	1990	145.00	160-175
1994 Tundra Summit-Arctic Wolves	6,061	1994	265.00	300-432
1984 Waterside Encounter	950	1987	95.00	1000-1500
1987 White Elegance-Trumpeter Swans	950	1989	115.00	500
1988 Witness of a Past-Bison	950	1990	110.00	95-135
1992 Wolf Scout #1	2,500	1992	105.00	78-150
1992 Wolf Scout #2	2,500	1992	105.00	135-160
1991 Wolf Study	950	1991	125.00	75-150
1987 Yellow-Bellied Marmot	950	1989	95.00	335-595
1989 A Young Generation	1,250	1989	165.00	175-295

Calle - P. Calle

YEAR ISSUE	EDITION LIMIT	YEAR RETD.	ISSUE PRICE	*QUOTE U.S.$
1981 Almost Home	950	1981	150.00	150
1991 Almost There	950	1991	165.00	165
1989 And A Good Book For Company	950	1990	135.00	435
1993 And A Grizzly Claw Necklace	750		150.00	150
1981 And Still Miles to Go	950	1981	245.00	400
1981 Andrew At The Falls	950	1981	150.00	150
1989 The Beaver Men	950		125.00	125
1984 A Brace for the Spit	950	1985	110.00	275-300
1980 Caring for the Herd	950	1981	110.00	110
1985 The Carrying Place	950	1990	195.00	195
1984 Chance Encounter	950	1986	225.00	325
1981 Chief High Pipe (Color)	950	1981	265.00	265
1980 Chief High Pipe (Pencil)	950	1980	75.00	175
1980 Chief Joseph-Man of Peace	950	1980	135.00	165
1990 Children of Walpi	350		160.00	160
1990 The Doll Maker	950		95.00	95
1982 Emerging from the Woods	950	1987	110.00	110
1981 End of a Long Day	950	1981	150.00	225
1984 Fate of the Late Migrant	950	1985	110.00	375
1983 Free Spirits	950	1985	195.00	475
1983 Free Trapper Study	550	1985	75.00	125-300
1981 Fresh Tracks	950	1981	150.00	150
1981 Friend or Foe	950		125.00	125
1981 Friends	950	1987	150.00	150
1985 The Frontier Blacksmith	950		245.00	245
1989 The Fur Trapper	550		75.00	175
1982 Generations in the Valley	950	1987	245.00	245
1985 The Grandmother	950	1987	400.00	400
1989 The Great Moment	950		350.00	350
1992 Hunter of Geese	950		125.00	125
1993 I Call Him Friend	950		235.00	235
1983 In Search of Beaver	950	1983	225.00	600
1991 In the Beginning . . . Friends	1,250	1993	250.00	275
1987 In the Land of the Giants	950	1988	245.00	900
1990 Interrupted Journey	1,750	1991	265.00	265
1990 Interrupted Journey -Prestige Ed.	290	1991	465.00	465
1987 Into the Great Alone	950	1988	245.00	700-850
1981 Just Over the Ridge	950	1982	245.00	245
1980 Landmark Tree	950	1980	125.00	225
1991 Man of the Fur Trade	550		110.00	110
1984 Mountain Man	550	1988	95.00	225-395
1993 Mountain Man-North American Wilderness Portfolio	350		325.00	N/A
1989 The Mountain Men	300	1989	400.00	400
1989 Navajo Madonna	650		95.00	95
1988 A New Day	950		150.00	150
1981 One With The Land	950	1981	245.00	250
1992 Out of the Silence	2,500		265.00	265
1992 Out of the Silence-Prestige	290		465.00	465
1981 Pause at the Lower Falls	950	1981	110.00	250
1980 Prayer to the Great Mystery	950	1980	245.00	245
1982 Return to Camp	950	1982	245.00	500
1991 The Silenced Honkers	1,250	1993	250.00	250
1980 Sioux Chief	950	1980	85.00	140
1986 Snow Hunter	950	1988	150.00	225
1980 Something for the Pot	950	1980	175.00	1100
1990 Son of Sitting Bull	950		95.00	675
1985 Storyteller of the Mountains	950	1985	225.00	675-960
1983 Strays From the Flyway	950	1983	195.00	225
1981 Teton Friends	950	1981	150.00	225
1991 They Call Me Matthew	950		125.00	125
1992 Through the Tall Grass	950		175.00	175
1988 Trapper at Rest	550		95.00	95
1982 Two from the Flock	950	1982	245.00	500
1980 View from the Heights	950	1980	245.00	245

*Quotes have been rounded up to nearest dollar

YEAR ISSUE	EDITION LIMIT	YEAR RETD.	ISSUE PRICE	*QUOTE U.S.$
1988 Voyageurs and Waterfowl...Constant	950	1988	265.00	700-900
1980 When Snow Came Early	950	1980	85.00	250-340
1984 When Trails Cross	950	1984	245.00	750
1991 When Trails Grow Cold	2,500		265.00	265
1991 When Trails Grow Cold-Prestige Ed.	290	1991	465.00	465
1994 When Trappers Meet	750		165.00	165
1989 Where Eagles Fly	1,250	1990	265.00	350-570
1989 A Winter Feast	1,250	1989	265.00	375
1989 A Winter Feast-Prestige Ed.	290	1989	465.00	465
1981 Winter Hunter (Color)	950	1981	245.00	800
1980 Winter Hunter (Pencil)	950	1980	65.00	450
1983 A Winter Surprise	950	1984	195.00	500

Cross - T. Cross

YEAR ISSUE	EDITION LIMIT	YEAR RETD.	ISSUE PRICE	*QUOTE U.S.$
1994 April	750		55.00	55
1994 August	750		55.00	55
1993 Ever Green	750		135.00	135
1993 Flame Catcher	750	1993	185.00	185
1993 Flicker, Flash and Twirl	525		165.00	165
1994 July	750		55.00	55
1994 June	750		55.00	55
1994 March	750		55.00	55
1994 May	750		55.00	55
1992 Shell Caster	750	1993	150.00	150-391
1993 Sheperds of Magic	750	N/A	135.00	135
1993 Spellbound	750	N/A	85.00	85-115
1994 Spring Forth	750		145.00	145
1992 Star Weaver	750	1993	150.00	150
1994 Summer Musings	750		145.00	145
1993 The Summons...And Then They Are One	750	1993	195.00	195
1994 When Water Takes to Air	750		135.00	135
1993 Wind Sifter	750	1993	150.00	515

Daly - J. Daly

YEAR ISSUE	EDITION LIMIT	YEAR RETD.	ISSUE PRICE	*QUOTE U.S.$
1994 All Aboard	950		145.00	145
1990 The Big Moment	1,500		125.00	125
1991 Cat's Cradle-Prestige Ed.	950		450.00	450
1994 Catch of My Dreams	4,500		45.00	45
1994 Childhood Friends	950	1997	110.00	110
1990 Confrontation	1,500	1992	85.00	85-97
1990 Contentment	1,500	1990	95.00	275-450
1992 Dominoes	1,500		155.00	155
1992 Favorite Gift	2,500	1992	175.00	175
1987 Favorite Reader	950	1990	85.00	130-250
1986 Flying High	950	1988	50.00	525-603
1992 The Flying Horse	950		325.00	325
1993 Good Company	1,500		155.00	155
1992 Her Secret Place	1,500	1992	135.00	200-509
1991 Home Team: Zero	1,500	1998	150.00	150
1991 Homemade	1,500	1992	125.00	125
1990 Honor and Allegiance	1,500	1993	110.00	110
1990 The Ice Man	1,500	1992	125.00	135-265
1992 The Immigrant Spirit	5,000		125.00	125
1992 The Immigrant Spirit-Prestige Ed.	950		125.00	125
1989 In the Doghouse	1,500	1990	75.00	425-589
1990 It's That Time Again	1,500		120.00	120
1992 Left Out	1,500		110.00	110
1989 Let's Play Ball	1,500	1991	75.00	125-135
1990 Make Believe	1,500	1990	75.00	400-457
1994 Mud Mates	950		150.00	150
1994 My Best Friends	950	1995	85.00	365
1991 A New Beginning	5,000		125.00	125
1993 The New Citizen	5,000		125.00	125
1993 The New Citizen-Prestige Ed.	950		125.00	125
1987 Odd Man Out	950	1988	85.00	85
1988 On Thin Ice	950	1993	95.00	345-389
1991 Pillars of a Nation-Charter Ed.	20,000		175.00	175
1992 Playmates	1,500	1992	155.00	395-595
1990 Radio Daze	1,500		150.00	150
1983 Saturday Night	950	1985	85.00	1125
1990 The Scholar	1,500	N/A	110.00	112
1993 Secret Admirer	1,500		150.00	150
1994 Slugger	950		75.00	75
1982 Spring Fever	950	1988	85.00	600-759
1993 Sunday Afternoon	1,500		150.00	150
1988 Territorial Rights	950	1990	85.00	350
1989 The Thief	1,500	1990	95.00	250-379
1989 The Thorn	1,500	1990	125.00	350-688
1988 Tie Breaker	950	1990	95.00	220-293
1991 Time-Out	1,500	1993	125.00	125
1993 To All a Good Night	1,500		160.00	160
1992 Walking the Rails	1,500		175.00	175
1993 When I Grow Up	1,500		175.00	175
1994 The Wind-Up	950	1998	75.00	75-119
1988 Wiped Out	1,250	1990	125.00	500-579

Morrissey - D. Morrissey

YEAR ISSUE	EDITION LIMIT	YEAR RETD.	ISSUE PRICE	*QUOTE U.S.$
1994 The Amazing Time Elevator	950	1994	195.00	195
1993 Charting the Skies	1,250	1993	195.00	195-219
1993 Charting the Skies-Caprice Edition	550	1993	375.00	375
1993 Draft of a Dream	175	1993	250.00	195-250
1994 The Dreamer's Trunk	1,500	1997	195.00	195-276
1993 Drifting Closer	1,250		175.00	175
1994 Father Time Flying Past	450		195.00	195
1993 The Mystic Mariner	750	1993	150.00	150-175
1993 The Redd Rocket	1,250	1993	175.00	375
1994 The Redd Rocket-Pre-Flight	950	1993	110.00	110-155
1992 The Sandman's Ship of Dreams	750	1993	150.00	150-397
1994 Sighting off the Stern	950		135.00	135
1993 Sleeper Flight	1,250	1993	195.00	175-195
1993 The Telescope of Time	5,000		195.00	195

Olsen - G. Olsen

YEAR ISSUE	EDITION LIMIT	YEAR RETD.	ISSUE PRICE	*QUOTE U.S.$
1993 Airship Adventures	750		150.00	150
1993 Angels of Christmas	750	1993	135.00	135
1993 Dress Rehearseal	750	1993	165.00	2600
1993 The Fraternity Tree	750		195.00	195
1994 Little Girls Will Mothers Be	750	N/A	135.00	135
1994 Mother's Love	750	1994	165.00	165
1995 O Jerusalem	5,000	N/A	165.00	1250-2700
1994 Summerhouse	750	N/A	165.00	165

Seerey-Lester - J. Seerey-Lester

YEAR ISSUE	EDITION LIMIT	YEAR RETD.	ISSUE PRICE	*QUOTE U.S.$
1994 Abandoned	950		175.00	175
1986 Above the Treeline-Cougar	950	1986	130.00	130
1986 After the Fire-Grizzly	950	1990	95.00	95
1986 Along the Ice Floe-Polar Bears	950		200.00	200
1987 Alpenglow-Artic Wolf	950	1987	200.00	200
1987 Amboseli Child-African Elephant	950		160.00	160
1984 Among the Cattails-Canada Geese	950	1985	130.00	375
1984 Artic Procession-Willow Ptarmigan	950	1988	220.00	500-789
1990 Artic Wolf Pups	290		500.00	500
1987 Autumn Mist-Barred Owl	950	1987	160.00	160
1987 Autumn Thunder-Muskoxen	950		150.00	150
1985 Awakening Meadow-Cottontail	950		50.00	50
1992 Banyan Ambush- Black Panther	950	1992	235.00	235-300
1984 Basking-Brown Pelicans	950	1988	115.00	125
1988 Bathing-Blue Jay	950		95.00	95
1987 Bathing-Mute Swan	950	1992	175.00	275
1989 Before The Freeze-Beaver	950		165.00	165
1990 Bittersweet Winter-Cardinal	1,250	1990	150.00	175-186
1992 Black Jade	1,950	1992	275.00	350
1992 Black Magic-Panther	750	1992	195.00	225-579
1984 Breaking Cover-Black Bear	950	N/A	130.00	150-200
1987 Canyon Creek-Cougar	950	1987	195.00	435-965
1992 The Chase-Snow Leopard	950		200.00	200
1994 Child of the Outback	950		175.00	175
1985 Children of the Forest-Red Fox Kits	950	1985	110.00	325
1985 Children of the Tundra-Artic Wolf Pup	950	1985	110.00	325-395
1988 Cliff Hanger-Bobcat	950		200.00	200
1984 Close Encounter-Bobcat	950	1989	130.00	130
1988 Coastal Clique-Harbor Seals	950		160.00	160
1986 Conflict at Dawn-Heron and Osprey	950	1989	130.00	325
1983 Cool Retreat-Lynx	950	1988	85.00	125-200
1986 Cottonwood Gold-Baltimore Oriole	950		85.00	85
1985 Cougar Head Study	950		60.00	60
1989 Cougar Run	950	1989	185.00	225
1994 The Courtship	950		175.00	175
1993 Dark Encounter	3,500	N/A	200.00	200-365
1990 Dawn Majesty	1,250	1991	185.00	225-275
1987 Dawn on the Marsh-Coyote	950		200.00	200
1985 Daybreak-Moose	950		135.00	135
1991 Denali Family-Grizzly Bear	950	1991	195.00	235-550
1986 Early Arrivals-Snow Buntings	950		75.00	75
1983 Early Windfall-Gray Squirrels	950		85.00	85
1988 Edge of the Forest-Timber Wolves	950	1988	500.00	500-700
1989 Evening Duet-Snowy Egrets	1,250		185.00	185
1991 Evening Encounter-Grizzly & Wolf	1,250		185.00	185
1988 Evening Meadow-American Goldfinch	950		150.00	150
1991 Face to Face	1,250		200.00	200
1985 Fallen Birch-Chipmunk	950	1985	60.00	375-415
1985 First Light-Gray Jays	950	1985	130.00	175
1983 First Snow-Grizzly Bears	950	1984	95.00	325-395
1987 First Tracks-Cougar	950		150.00	150
1989 Fluke Sighting-Humback Whales	950	1989	185.00	185
1993 Freedom I	350		500.00	500
1993 Frozen Moonlight	2,500	1993	225.00	200-215
1985 Gathering-Gray Wolves, The	950	1987	165.00	250
1989 Gorilla	290	1989	400.00	450
1993 Grizzly Impact	950	N/A	225.00	300-385
1990 Grizzly Litho	290	1990	400.00	400-600
1989 Heavy Going-Grizzly	950	1989	175.00	240
1986 Hidden Admirer-Moose	950	1986	165.00	275
1988 Hiding Place-Saw-Whet Owl	950		95.00	95
1989 High and Mighty-Gorilla	950	1989	185.00	185
1986 High Country Champion-Grizzly	950	1986	175.00	375-465
1984 High Ground-Wolves	950	1984	130.00	225
1987 High Refuge-Red Squirrel	950		120.00	120
1984 Icy Outcrop-White Gyrfalcon	950	1986	115.00	200
1987 In Deep-Black Bear Cub	950		135.00	135
1990 In Their Presence	1,250		200.00	200
1985 Island Sanctuary-Mallards	950	1987	95.00	150-315
1986 Kenyan Family-Cheetahs	950		130.00	130
1986 Lakeside Family-Canada Geese	950		75.00	75
1988 Last Sanctuary-Florida Panther	950	1993	175.00	350
1983 Lone Fisherman-Great Blue Heron	950	1985	85.00	375
1993 Loonlight	1,500		225.00	225
1986 Low Tide-Bald Eagles	950		130.00	130
1987 Lying in Wait-Arctic Fox	950		175.00	175
1984 Lying Low-Cougar	950	1986	85.00	550
1991 Monsoon-White Tiger	950	1994	195.00	195-345
1991 Moonlight Chase-Cougar	1,250		195.00	195
1988 Moonlight Fishermen-Raccoons	950	1990	175.00	175-305
1988 Moose Hair	950	N/A	165.00	225-385
1988 Morning Display-Common Loons	3,395	1988	135.00	135
1986 Morning Forage-Ground Squirrel	950		75.00	75
1993 Morning Glory-Bald Eagle	1,250		225.00	225
1984 Morning Mist-Snowy Owl	950	1988	95.00	180-225
1990 Mountain Cradle	1,250	N/A	200.00	200
1988 Night Moves-African Elephants	950		150.00	150
1990 Night Run-Artic Wolves	1,250	1990	200.00	200-415
1993 Night Specter	1,250		195.00	195
1986 Northwoods Family-Moose	950		75.00	75
1987 Out of the Blizzard-Timber Wolves	950	1987	215.00	450-500
1992 Out of the Darkness	290		200.00	200
1987 Out of the Mist-Grizzly	950	1990	200.00	375
1991 Out on a Limb-Young Barred Owl	950		185.00	185
1991 Panda Trilogy	950	N/A	375.00	375
1993 Phantoms of the Tundra	950		235.00	235
1984 Plains Hunter-Prairie Falcon	950		95.00	95
1990 The Plunge-Northern Sea Lions	1,250		200.00	200
1986 Racing the Storm-Artic Wolves	950	1986	200.00	300
1987 Rain Watch-Belted Kingfisher	950		125.00	125
1993 The Rains-Tiger	950		225.00	225
1992 Ranthambhore Rush	950		225.00	225
1983 The Refuge-Raccoon	950	1983	85.00	275
1992 Regal Majesty	290		200.00	200
1985 Return to Winter-Pintails	950	1990	135.00	200-229
1983 River Watch-Peregrine Falcon	950		85.00	85
1988 Savana Siesta-African Lions	950		165.00	165
1990 Seasonal Greeting-Cardinal	1,250	1993	150.00	150-250
1993 Seeking Attention	950		200.00	200
1991 Sisters-Artic Wolves	1,250		185.00	185
1989 Sneak Peak	950		185.00	185
1986 Snowy Excursion-Red Squirrel	950		75.00	75
1988 Snowy Watch-Great Gray Owl	950		175.00	175
1989 Softly, Softly-White Tiger	950	1989	220.00	400-500
1991 Something Stirred (Bengal Tiger)	950		195.00	195
1988 Spanish Mist-Young Barred-Owl	950		175.00	175
1984 Spirit of the North-White Wolf	950	1986	130.00	185
1990 Spout	290		500.00	500
1989 Spring Flurry-Adelie Penguins	950		185.00	185
1986 Spring Mist-Chickadees	950	1986	105.00	1160
1990 Suitors-Wood Ducks	3,313	1989	135.00	135-160
1990 Summer Rain-Common Loons	4,500	1990	200.00	200
1990 Summer Rain-Common Loons (Prestige)	450		425.00	425
1987 Sundown Alert-Bobcat	950	N/A	150.00	195
1985 Sundown Reflections-Wood Ducks	950		85.00	85
1990 Their First Season	1,250	1990	200.00	200
1990 Togetherness	1,250		125.00	185
1986 Treading Thin Ice-Chipmunk	950		75.00	75
1988 Tundra Family-Arctic Wolves	950		200.00	200
1985 Under the Pines-Bobcat	950	1986	95.00	275-318
1989 Water Sport-Bobcat	950	1989	185.00	185-219
1990 Whitetail Spring	1,250	1990	185.00	185
1988 Winter Grazing-Bison	950		185.00	185
1986 Winter Hiding-Cottontail	950		75.00	75
1983 Winter Lookout-Cougar	950	1985	85.00	600-700
1986 Winter Perch-Cardinal	950	1986	85.00	150
1985 Winter Rendezvous-Coyotes	950	1985	140.00	140
1988 Winter Spirit-Gray Wolf	950		200.00	200
1987 Winter Vigil-Great Horned Owl	950	1990	175.00	175
1993 Wolong Whiteout	950		225.00	225
1986 The Young Explorer-Red Fox Kit	950	N/A	75.00	95
1992 Young Predator-Leopard	950		200.00	200

Smith - D. Smith

YEAR ISSUE	EDITION LIMIT	YEAR RETD.	ISSUE PRICE	*QUOTE U.S.$
1993 African Ebony-Black Leopard	1,250	1994	195.00	195
1997 Ancient Mariner	950		165.00	165
1992 Armada	950	N/A	195.00	195
1998 Brother Wolf	950	1998	125.00	249
1993 Catching the Scent-Polar Bear	950	1993	175.00	175
1994 Curious Presence-Whitetail Deer	950	1996	195.00	195-300
1991 Dawn's Early Light-Bald Eagles	950	1997	185.00	185
1993 Echo Bay-Loon Family	1,150	1993	185.00	185-400
1992 Eyes of the North	2,500	1996	225.00	225
1994 Forest Veil-Cougar	950	1994	195.00	376
1993 Guardians of the Den	1,500	N/A	195.00	195
1991 Icy Reflections-Pintails	500		250.00	250
1992 Night Moves-Cougar	950	1994	185.00	185
1994 Parting Reflections	950		185.00	185
1993 Shrouded Forest-Bald Eagle	950	N/A	150.00	650-1100
1991 Twilight's Calling-Common Loons	950	1991	175.00	250
1993 What's Bruin	1,750	1993	185.00	185-349

New Masters Publishing

Bannister - P. Bannister

YEAR ISSUE	EDITION LIMIT	YEAR RETD.	ISSUE PRICE	*QUOTE U.S.$
1982 Amaryllis	500	N/A	285.00	2000
1988 Apples and Oranges	485	N/A	265.00	650
1982 April	300	N/A	200.00	1150
1984 April Light	950	N/A	150.00	650
1987 Autumn Fields	950	N/A	150.00	300
1978 Bandstand	250	N/A	75.00	600
1992 Bed of Roses	663	N/A	265.00	525
1995 Bridesmaids	950	N/A	265.00	530
1991 Celebration	662	N/A	350.00	800
1989 Chapter One	485	N/A	265.00	1500-1700
1982 Cinderella	500	N/A	285.00	580
1991 Crossroads	485	N/A	295.00	600
1993 Crowning Glory	485	N/A	265.00	600
1992 Crystal Bowl	485	N/A	265.00	600
1989 Daydreams	485	N/A	265.00	625
1993 Deja Vu	663	N/A	265.00	1200-1400
1983 The Duchess	500	N/A	250.00	1900
1980 Dust of Autumn	200	N/A	200.00	1225
1981 Easter	300	N/A	260.00	1150
1982 Emily	500	N/A	285.00	1200
1980 Faded Glory	200	N/A	200.00	1225
1984 The Fan Window	950	N/A	195.00	600
1987 First Prize	950	N/A	115.00	275
1988 Floribunda	485	N/A	265.00	675
1994 Fountain	485	N/A	265.00	600

*Quotes have been rounded up to nearest dollar

YEAR ISSUE	EDITION LIMIT	YEAR RETD.	ISSUE PRICE	*QUOTE U.S.$
1994 From Russia With Love	950	N/A	165.00	400
1980 Gift of Happiness	200	N/A	200.00	2000
1980 Girl on the Beach	200	N/A	200.00	1400
1990 Good Friends	485	N/A	265.00	750
1988 Guinevere	485	N/A	265.00	1250-1300
1993 Into The Woods	485	N/A	265.00	500
1982 Ivy	500	N/A	285.00	750
1982 Jasmine	500	N/A	285.00	725
1981 Juliet	300	N/A	260.00	5000
1990 Lavender Hill	485	N/A	265.00	775
1992 Love Letters	485	N/A	265.00	550
1988 Love Seat	485	N/A	230.00	500
1989 Low Tide	485	N/A	265.00	650
1995 Magnolias	950	N/A	265.00	1200-1300
1982 Mail Order Brides	500	N/A	325.00	2400
1984 Make Believe	950	N/A	150.00	775
1989 March Winds	485	N/A	265.00	530
1983 Mementos	950	N/A	150.00	1450
1982 Memories	500	N/A	235.00	500
1992 Morning Mist	485	N/A	265.00	500
1981 My Special Place	300	N/A	260.00	2000
1982 Nuance	500	N/A	235.00	500
1994 Once Upon A Time	950	N/A	265.00	600
1983 Ophelia	950	N/A	150.00	700
1996 Paradise Cove	950	N/A	265.00	865
1989 Peace	485	N/A	265.00	1200
1981 Porcelain Rose	300	N/A	260.00	2000
1982 The Present	500	N/A	260.00	925
1986 Pride & Joy	950	N/A	150.00	300
1991 Pudding & Pies	950	N/A	265.00	500
1987 Quiet Corner	950	N/A	115.00	625
1989 The Quilt	485	N/A	265.00	950
1993 Rambling Rose	485	N/A	265.00	500
1981 Rehearsal	300	N/A	260.00	1900
1990 Rendezvous	485	N/A	265.00	650
1984 Scarlet Ribbons	950	N/A	150.00	325
1980 Sea Haven	300	N/A	260.00	1200
1990 Seascapes	485	N/A	265.00	550
1987 September Harvest	950	N/A	150.00	400
1980 The Silver Bell	200	N/A	200.00	2000
1990 Sisters	485	N/A	265.00	1200
1990 Songbird	485	N/A	265.00	550
1996 Southern Belle	950	N/A	265.00	850
1991 String of Pearls	485	N/A	265.00	850
1988 Summer Choices	300	N/A	250.00	850
1991 Teatime	485	N/A	295.00	700
1980 Titania	350	N/A	260.00	950
1991 Wildflowers	485	N/A	295.00	700
1983 Window Seat	950	N/A	150.00	700

Past Impressions

Limited Edition Canvas Transfers - A. Maley

YEAR ISSUE	EDITION LIMIT	YEAR RETD.	ISSUE PRICE	*QUOTE U.S.$
1990 Cafe Royale	100	N/A	665.00	665
1992 Circle of Love	250	N/A	445.00	550-850
1992 An Elegant Affair	250	N/A	595.00	1095
1992 Evening Performance	100	N/A	295.00	1050
1990 Festive Occasion	100	N/A	595.00	250-300
1990 Gracious Era	100	N/A	645.00	1500-1700
1995 The Letter	250	N/A	465.00	600
1987 Love Letter	75	N/A	445.00	1250
1994 New Years Eve	250	N/A	445.00	600-800
1994 Parisian Beauties	250	N/A	645.00	750
1993 Rags and Riches	250	N/A	445.00	550-625
1993 The Recital	250	N/A	595.00	900-1400
1990 Romantic Engagement	100	N/A	445.00	1225
1993 Sleigh Bells	250	N/A	595.00	600
1991 Summer Carousel	250	N/A	345.00	500-600
1994 Summer Elegance	250	N/A	595.00	950
1995 Summer Romance	250	N/A	465.00	575-750
1993 Visiting The Nursery	250	N/A	445.00	1400
1992 A Walk in the Park	250	N/A	595.00	650-1000
1989 Winter Impressions	100	N/A	595.00	775-1100

Limited Edition Paper Prints - A. Maley

YEAR ISSUE	EDITION LIMIT	YEAR RETD.	ISSUE PRICE	*QUOTE U.S.$
1989 Alexandra	750	1994	125.00	125
1989 Beth	750	1994	125.00	125
1988 The Boardwalk	500	N/A	250.00	395
1989 Catherine	750	1994	125.00	200
1987 Day Dreams	500	N/A	200.00	325
1989 English Rose	750	N/A	250.00	400
1990 Festive Occasion	750	N/A	250.00	500-900
1984 Glorious Summer	350	N/A	150.00	600
1989 In Harmony	750	1995	250.00	250
1988 Joys of Childhood	500	N/A	250.00	320
1987 Love Letter	450	N/A	200.00	200
1988 Opening Night	500	N/A	250.00	2000
1985 Passing Elegance	350	N/A	150.00	900
1987 The Promise	450	N/A	200.00	525
1984 Secluded Garden	350	N/A	150.00	970
1985 Secret Thoughts	350	N/A	150.00	850
1990 Summer Pastime	750	N/A	250.00	375
1986 Tell Me	450	N/A	150.00	800
1988 Tranquil Moment	500	N/A	250.00	325
1989 Victoria	750	1994	125.00	125
1988 Victorian Trio	500	N/A	250.00	325-350
1986 Winter Romance	450	N/A	150.00	1000

Pemberton & Oakes

Membership-Miniature Lithographs - D. Zolan

YEAR ISSUE	EDITION LIMIT	YEAR RETD.	ISSUE PRICE	*QUOTE U.S.$
1992 Brotherly Love	Retrd.	1992	18.00	68
1993 New Shoes	Retrd.	1993	18.00	42
1993 Country Walk	Retrd.	1993	22.00	40
1994 Enchanted Forest	Retrd.	1994	22.00	40-55

Zolan's Children-Lithographs - D. Zolan

YEAR ISSUE	EDITION LIMIT	YEAR RETD.	ISSUE PRICE	*QUOTE U.S.$
1989 Almost Home	Retrd.	1989	98.00	150-350
1991 Autumn Leaves	Retrd.	1991	98.00	115-120
1993 The Big Catch	Retrd.	1993	98.00	98-130
1989 Brotherly Love	Retrd.	1989	98.00	295
1982 By Myself	Retrd.	1982	98.00	230
1989 Christmas Prayer	Retrd.	1989	98.00	175-225
1990 Colors of Spring	Retrd.	1990	98.00	200-350
1990 Crystal's Creek	Retrd.	1990	98.00	175-225
1989 Daddy's Home	Retrd.	1989	98.00	310
1988 Day Dreamer	Retrd.	1988	35.00	130
1992 Enchanted Forest	Retrd.	1992	98.00	110-135
1982 Erik and the Dandelion	Retrd.	1982	98.00	350-400
1990 First Kiss	Retrd.	1990	98.00	229-240
1991 Flowers for Mother	Retrd.	1991	98.00	160
1993 Grandma's Garden	Retrd.	1993	98.00	100-135
1989 Grandma's Mirror	Retrd.	1989	98.00	175
1990 Laurie and the Creche	Retrd.	1990	98.00	115-165
1989 Mother's Angels	Retrd.	1989	98.00	185-295
1992 New Shoes	Retrd.	1992	98.00	150
1989 Rodeo Girl	Retrd.	1989	98.00	125-160
1984 Sabina in the Grass	Retrd.	1984	98.00	625
1988 Small Wonder	Retrd.	1988	98.00	250
1989 Snowy Adventure	Retrd.	1989	98.00	205
1991 Summer Suds	Retrd.	1991	98.00	140-175
1989 Summer's Child	Retrd.	1989	98.00	225
1986 Tender Moment	Retrd.	1986	98.00	275
1988 Tiny Treasures	Retrd.	1988	150.00	215
1987 Touching the Sky	Retrd.	1987	98.00	225-245
1988 Waiting to Play	Retrd.	1988	35.00	135
1988 Winter Angel	Retrd.	1988	98.00	230

Porterfield's

Mini Prints - R. Anders

YEAR ISSUE	EDITION LIMIT	YEAR RETD.	ISSUE PRICE	*QUOTE U.S.$
1997 Time Out	5,000		26.60	27
1997 Safe Harbor	5,000		26.60	27
1997 Digging In	5,000		26.60	27
1997 Two Bites To Go	5,000		26.60	27

Prizm, Inc./Pipka

Pipka Collectibles - Pipka

YEAR ISSUE	EDITION LIMIT	YEAR RETD.	ISSUE PRICE	*QUOTE U.S.$
1998 Knock, Knock Santa Print 10001	750	1998	180.00	180-300

Reco International

Fine Art Canvas Reproduction - J. McClelland

YEAR ISSUE	EDITION LIMIT	YEAR RETD.	ISSUE PRICE	*QUOTE U.S.$
1990 Beach Play	350		80.00	80
1991 Flower Swing	350		100.00	100
1991 Summer Conversation	350		80.00	80

Limited Edition Print - S. Kuck

YEAR ISSUE	EDITION LIMIT	YEAR RETD.	ISSUE PRICE	*QUOTE U.S.$
1986 Ashley	500	1998	85.00	150
1985 Heather	Retrd.	1987	75.00	150
1984 Jessica	Retrd.	1986	60.00	400

McClelland - J. McClelland

YEAR ISSUE	EDITION LIMIT	YEAR RETD.	ISSUE PRICE	*QUOTE U.S.$
XX I Love Tammy	500		75.00	100
XX Just for You	300		155.00	155
XX Olivia	300		175.00	175
XX Reverie	300		110.00	110
XX Sweet Dreams	300		145.00	145

Roman, Inc.

Abble Williams - A. Williams

YEAR ISSUE	EDITION LIMIT	YEAR RETD.	ISSUE PRICE	*QUOTE U.S.$
1988 Mary, Mother of the Carpenter	Closed	1995	100.00	100

The Discovery of America Miniature Art Print - I. Spencer

YEAR ISSUE	EDITION LIMIT	YEAR RETD.	ISSUE PRICE	*QUOTE U.S.$
1991 The Discovery of America	Closed	N/A	2.00	2

Divine Servant - M. Greiner, Jr.

YEAR ISSUE	EDITION LIMIT	YEAR RETD.	ISSUE PRICE	*QUOTE U.S.$
1993 Divine Servant, print of drawing	Open		35.00	35
1994 Divine Servant, print of painting	Open		95.00	95
1994 Divine Servant, print of painting w/remarque	Open		95.00	95

Fishers of Men - M. Greiner, Jr.

YEAR ISSUE	EDITION LIMIT	YEAR RETD.	ISSUE PRICE	*QUOTE U.S.$
1994 Fishers of Men 8x10	Open		10.00	10
1994 Fishers of Men 11x14	Open		20.00	20
1994 Fishers of Men 16x20	Open		35.00	35

Hook - F. Hook

YEAR ISSUE	EDITION LIMIT	YEAR RETD.	ISSUE PRICE	*QUOTE U.S.$
1982 Bouquet	Closed	1994	70.00	350
1981 The Carpenter	Closed	1981	100.00	1000
1981 The Carpenter (remarque)	Closed	1981	100.00	3000
1982 Frolicking	Closed	1994	60.00	350
1982 Gathering	Closed	1994	60.00	350-450
1982 Little Children, Come to Me	Closed	1994	50.00	500
1982 Little Children, Come to Me, remarque	50	N/A	100.00	500
1982 Posing	Closed	1987	70.00	350
1982 Poulets	Closed	1994	60.00	350
1982 Surprise	Closed	1988	50.00	350

Portraits of Love - F. Hook

YEAR ISSUE	EDITION LIMIT	YEAR RETD.	ISSUE PRICE	*QUOTE U.S.$
1988 Expectation	Closed	1991	25.00	25
1988 In Mother's Arms	Closed	1990	25.00	25
1988 My Kitty	Closed	1992	25.00	25
1988 Remember When...	Closed	1991	25.00	25
1988 Sharing	Closed	1991	25.00	25
1988 Sunkissed Afternoon	Closed	1991	25.00	25

Sarah's Attic, Inc.

Framed Prints - Sarah's Attic

YEAR ISSUE	EDITION LIMIT	YEAR RETD.	ISSUE PRICE	*QUOTE U.S.$
1997 Adora Angel 5x5, wood SA07	Closed	1998	14.00	14
1997 Angels on Earth 5x7, wood SA26	Closed	1998	15.00	15
1997 Angels on Earth 8x10, gold SA27	Closed	1998	24.00	24
1997 Chilly & Burley 5x7, wood SA21	Closed	1998	15.00	15
1997 Chilly & Burley 8x10, gold SA22	Closed	1998	24.00	24
1997 Enos Angel 5x5, wood SA06	Closed	1998	14.00	14
1997 Flutter Angel, wh. 5x5, wood SA08	Closed	1998	14.00	14
1997 Flutter Angel, wh. 5x5, wood SA09	Closed	1998	14.00	14
1997 Gingerbread 5x5, wood SA10	Closed	1998	14.00	14
1997 Katie Praying 5x5, wood SA11	Closed	1998	14.00	14
1997 Maggie Rag Doll 5x7, wood SA17	Closed	1998	15.00	15
1997 Maggie Rag Doll 8x10, gold SA18	Closed	1998	24.00	24
1997 Matt Rag Doll 5x7, wood SA19	Closed	1998	15.00	15
1997 Matt Rag Doll 8x10, gold SA20	Closed	1998	24.00	24
1997 Missy & Mikey 5x7, wood SA04	Closed	1998	15.00	15
1997 Missy & Mikey 8x10, gold SA05	Closed	1998	24.00	24
1997 Nat Rag Doll 5x7, wood SA15	Closed	1998	15.00	15
1997 Nat Rag Doll 8x10, gold SA16	Closed	1998	24.00	24
1997 Nettie Rag Doll 5x7, wood SA13	Closed	1998	15.00	15
1997 Nettie Rag Doll 8x10, gold SA14	Closed	1998	24.00	24
1997 Noah's Angel 5x7, wood SA02	Closed	1998	15.00	15
1997 Noah's Angel 8x10, gold SA03	Closed	1998	24.00	24
1997 Santa of the Woods 5x7, wood SA23	Closed	1998	15.00	15
1997 Santa of the Woods 8x10, gold SA24	Closed	1998	24.00	24
1997 Sarah's Gang 8x10, wood SA01	Closed	1998	24.00	24
1997 Tillie in Church 5x5, wood SA12	Closed	1998	14.00	14
1997 Willie & Tillie 11x14, gold SA25	Closed	1998	34.00	34

V.F. Fine Arts

Kuck - S. Kuck

YEAR ISSUE	EDITION LIMIT	YEAR RETD.	ISSUE PRICE	*QUOTE U.S.$
1994 '95 Angel Collection, S/N	750	1995	198.00	198
1995 '96 Angel Collection, S/N	750		198.00	198
1997 '98 Angel Collection	750		135.00	135
1997 '98 Angel Collection, canvas	150		330.00	330
1998 Afternoon Tea	1,250		95.00	95
1998 Afternoon Tea. Canvas	395		240.00	240
1993 Best Friend, proof	250	N/A	175.00	225
1993 Best Friends, canvas transfer	250	N/A	500.00	600
1993 Best Friends, S/N	2,500	N/A	145.00	150
1994 Best of Days, S/N	750	1994	160.00	175
1989 Bundle of Joy, S/N	1,000	1989	125.00	250
1993 Buttons & Bows, proof	95	N/A	125.00	150
1993 Buttons & Bows, S/N	950	N/A	95.00	125
1990 Chopsticks, proof	150	1991	120.00	150
1990 Chopsticks, remarque	25	1991	160.00	200
1990 Chopsticks, S/N	1,500	1990	80.00	95
1995 Christmas Magic, S/N	950		80.00	80
1987 The Daisy, proof	90	1988	40.00	175
1987 The Daisy, S/N	900	1988	30.00	125
1989 Day Dreaming, proof	90	1989	225.00	250
1989 Day Dreaming, remarque	50	1989	300.00	395
1989 Day Dreaming, S/N	900	1989	150.00	200
1994 Dear Santa, S/N	950	1994	95.00	125
1992 Duet, canvas framed	500	1994	255.00	325
1992 Duet, proof	95	N/A	175.00	200
1992 Duet, S/N	950	N/A	125.00	135
1998 Enchanted Garden	950		95.00	95
1998 Enchanted Garden, canvas	295		240.00	240
1988 First Recital, proof	25	1988	250.00	750
1988 First Recital, remarque	25	1988	400.00	1000
1988 First Recital, S/N	150	1988	200.00	500
1990 First Snow, proof	50	1990	150.00	250
1990 First Snow, remarque	25	1990	200.00	350
1990 First Snow, S/N	500	1990	95.00	150
1987 The Flower Girl, proof	90	1987	50.00	125
1987 The Flower Girl, S/N	900	1987	40.00	95
1994 Garden Memories, canvas transfer	250	N/A	500.00	500
1994 Garden Memories, S/N	2,500	N/A	145.00	175
1997 Gift From Angel	950		74.50	75
1997 Gift From Angel, AP	95		82.00	82
1997 Gift From Angel, canvas	295		119.50	120
1991 God's Gift, proof	150	N/A	150.00	175
1991 God's Gift, S/N	1,500	1993	95.00	125
1997 Golden Days	950		75.00	75
1997 Golden Days, canvas	295		120.00	120
1997 Gone Fishing	950		75.00	75
1997 Gone Fishing, canvas	495		120.00	120
1993 Good Morning, canvas	250	1993	500.00	500
1993 Good Morning, proof	50	N/A	175.00	200
1993 Good Morning, S/N	2,500	N/A	145.00	165
1997 Heavenly Whisper	950		74.50	75
1997 Heavenly Whisper, AP	95		82.00	82
1997 Heavenly Whisper, canvas	295		119.50	120
1996 Hidden Garden, canvas transfer	395		379.00	379
1996 Hidden Garden, S/N	950	1996	95.00	95
1995 Homecoming, proof	95	1995	172.50	173
1995 Homecoming, S/N	1,150	1995	125.00	125
1989 Innocence, proof	90	1989	225.00	275
1989 Innocence, remarque	50	1989	300.00	395
1989 Innocence, S/N	900	1989	150.00	220
1997 Interlude	500	1997	145.00	145
1997 Interlude, AP	50		175.00	175
1997 Interlude, canvas	200		300.00	300

*Quotes have been rounded up to nearest dollar

YEAR ISSUE	EDITION LIMIT	YEAR RETD.	ISSUE PRICE	*QUOTE U.S.$
1992 Joyous Day, canvas transfer	250	N/A	250.00	295
1992 Joyous Day, proof	120	N/A	175.00	200
1992 Joyous Day, S/N	1,200	1993	125.00	150
1997 Kate & Oliver	3,000		80.00	80
1997 Kate & Oliver, canvas	1,000		90.00	90
1997 Kitten Tails	950		75.00	75
1997 Kitten Tails, canvas	495		120.00	120
1988 The Kitten, proof	50	1988	150.00	1000
1988 The Kitten, remarque	25	1988	250.00	1200
1988 The Kitten, S/N	350	1988	120.00	1000
1990 Le Beau, proof	150	1990	120.00	225
1990 Le Beau, remarque	25	1990	160.00	275
1990 Le Beau, S/N	1,500	1990	80.00	175
1987 Le Papillion, proof	35	1990	110.00	175
1987 Le Papillion, remarque	7	1990	150.00	250
1987 Le Papillion, S/N	350	1990	90.00	150
1990 Lilly Pond, color remarque	125	1990	500.00	500
1990 Lilly Pond, proof	75	1990	200.00	200
1990 Lilly Pond, S/N	750	1990	150.00	150
1997 Lily Pond, canvas	295		135.00	135
1988 Little Ballerina, proof	25	1988	150.00	350
1988 Little Ballerina, remarque	25	1988	225.00	450
1988 Little Ballerina, S/N	150	1988	110.00	275
1987 The Loveseat, proof	90	1987	40.00	150
1987 The Loveseat, S/N	900	1987	30.00	100
1991 Memories, S/N	5,000	1991	195.00	250
1997 Merry Christmas	950		95.00	95
1997 Merry Christmas, canvas	495		240.00	240
1987 Mother's Love, proof	12	1987	225.00	1200
1987 Mother's Love, S/N	150	1987	195.00	750
1988 My Dearest, proof	50	1988	200.00	900
1988 My Dearest, remarque	25	1988	325.00	1200
1988 My Dearest, S/N	350	1988	160.00	700
1995 Night Before Christmas, S/N	1,150		95.00	95
1995 Playful Kitten	950	1995	95.00	95
1997 Precious	950		95.00	95
1997 Precious, canvas	395		265.00	265
1997 Puppy Love	950	1997	75.00	75
1997 Puppy Love, canvas	495	1997	120	120
1989 Puppy, proof	50	1989	180.00	500
1989 Puppy, remarque	50	1989	240.00	750
1989 Puppy, S/N	500	1989	120.00	400
1997 Quiet Garden	950		109.00	109
1997 Quiet Garden, AP	95		139.00	139
1997 Quiet Garden, canvas	295		249.00	249
1987 A Quiet Time, proof	90	1987	50.00	100
1987 A Quiet Time, S/N	900	1987	40.00	75
1987 The Reading Lesson, proof	90	1987	70.00	200
1987 The Reading Lesson, S/N	900	1987	60.00	150
1997 Rehearsal	950	1998	75.00	75
1997 Rehearsal, canvas	495		120.00	120
1995 Rhapsody & Lace	1,150		95.00	100
1989 Rose Garden, proof	50	1989	150.00	400
1989 Rose Garden, remarque	50	1989	200.00	500
1989 Rose Garden, S/N	500	1989	95.00	390
1986 Silhouette, proof	25	1987	90.00	250
1986 Silhouette, S/N	250	1987	80.00	200
1997 Sisters	950		75.00	75
1997 Sisters, canvas	495		120.00	120
1989 Sisters, proof	90	1989	150.00	550
1989 Sisters, remarque	50	1989	200.00	650
1989 Sisters, S/N	900	1988	95.00	300
1989 Sonatina, proof	90	1989	225.00	700
1989 Sonatina, remarque	50	1989	300.00	850
1989 Sonatina, S/N	900	1989	150.00	400
1986 Summer Reflections, proof	90	1987	70.00	300
1986 Summer Reflections, S/N	900	1987	60.00	250
1997 Take Me Home	950		125.00	125
1997 Take Me Home, canvas	295		295.00	295
1997 Tea With Kitty	950		80.00	80
1997 Tea With Kitty, canvas	295		200.00	200
1986 Tender Moments, proof	50	1986	80.00	300
1986 Tender Moments, S/N	500	1986	70.00	200
1993 Thinking of You, canvas transfer	250	1993	500.00	500
1993 Thinking of You, S/N	2,500	N/A	145.00	175
1988 Wild Flowers, proof	50	1988	175.00	300
1988 Wild Flowers, remarque	25	1988	250.00	400
1988 Wild Flowers, S/N	350	1988	160.00	250
1992 Yesterday, canvas framed	550	N/A	195.00	200
1992 Yesterday, proof	95	N/A	150.00	150
1992 Yesterday, S/N	950	N/A	95.00	95

Willitts Designs

Cooperstown Film Cels - Willitts Designs

YEAR ISSUE	EDITION LIMIT	YEAR RETD.	ISSUE PRICE	*QUOTE U.S.$
1997 Babe Ruth	Open		25.00	25
1997 Hank Aaron	Open		25.00	25
1997 Lou Gehrig	Open		25.00	25
1997 Ted Williams	Open		25.00	25

Cooperstown Lithograph w/Lighted Film Cel - Willitts Designs

YEAR ISSUE	EDITION LIMIT	YEAR RETD.	ISSUE PRICE	*QUOTE U.S.$
1997 Babe Ruth/Lou Gehrig	700		250.00	250
1997 Hank Aaron	2,500		200.00	200
1997 Jackie Robinson	2,500		200.00	200
1998 Mickey Mantle	2,500		200.00	200
1997 Ted Williams	2,500		200.00	200

Cooperstown Motion Cels - Willitts Designs

YEAR ISSUE	EDITION LIMIT	YEAR RETD.	ISSUE PRICE	*QUOTE U.S.$
1997 Babe Ruth	14,500		25.00	25
1997 Hank Aaron	14,500		25.00	25
1997 Jackie Robinson	14,500		25.00	25
1997 Lou Gehrig	14,500		25.00	25
1997 Stan Musial	14,500		25.00	25
1997 Ted Williams	14,500		25.00	25

Disney Showcase Film Cels - Willitts Designs

YEAR ISSUE	EDITION LIMIT	YEAR RETD.	ISSUE PRICE	*QUOTE U.S.$
1998 Cinderella	Open		25.00	25
1998 Memegarie	Open		25.00	25
1998 Royals	Open		25.00	25
1998 Seven Dwarfs	Open		25.00	25
1998 Snow White	Open		25.00	25
1998 Snow White Commemorative	Open		25.00	25
1998 Stepfamily	Open		25.00	25
1998 Wicked Queen	Open		25.00	25

Disney Showcase Lithograph w/Lighted Film Cel - Willitts Designs

YEAR ISSUE	EDITION LIMIT	YEAR RETD.	ISSUE PRICE	*QUOTE U.S.$
1998 Beauty & the Beast	2,500		200.00	200
1998 Cinderella	2,500		200.00	200
1998 Mickey Mouse	2,500		200.00	200
1998 Peter Pan	2,500		200.00	200
1998 Snow White	2,500		200.00	200

Disney Showcase Motion Cels - Willitts Designs

YEAR ISSUE	EDITION LIMIT	YEAR RETD.	ISSUE PRICE	*QUOTE U.S.$
1998 Cinderella	Open		25.00	25
1998 Snow White	Open		25.00	25

Ebony Visions - T. Blackshear

YEAR ISSUE	EDITION LIMIT	YEAR RETD.	ISSUE PRICE	*QUOTE U.S.$
1997 Ebony Visions-Canvas Transfer (framed)	950	1998	575.00	575
1997 Ebony Visions-Canvas Transfer A/P (framed)	100	1998	690.00	690
1997 Ebony Visions-Canvas Transfer G/P (framed)	100	1998	747.50	748
1998 Ebony Visions-Lithograph (framed)	1,950		275.00	275
1998 Ebony Visions-Lithograph A/P (framed)	50		330.00	330
1998 Ebony Visions-Lithograph G/P (framed)	50		357.00	357

MasterPeace Collection - Various

YEAR ISSUE	EDITION LIMIT	YEAR RETD.	ISSUE PRICE	*QUOTE U.S.$
1998 Forgiven - T. Blackshear	Open		40.00	40
1998 The Invitation - M. Weistling	Open		99.00	99
1998 Victorious Lion of Judah - M. Dudash	Open		99.00	99
1998 Watchers in the Night - T. Blackshear	Open		50.00	50

Titanic Film Cels - Willitts Designs

YEAR ISSUE	EDITION LIMIT	YEAR RETD.	ISSUE PRICE	*QUOTE U.S.$
1998 Jack & Rose	Open		25.00	25
1998 Jack Dawson	Open		25.00	25
1998 Titanic	Open		25.00	25

Titanic Lithograph w/Lighted Film Cel - Willitts Designs

YEAR ISSUE	EDITION LIMIT	YEAR RETD.	ISSUE PRICE	*QUOTE U.S.$
1998 Titanic	2,500		200	200

ORNAMENTS

All God's Children/Miss Martha Originals

Angel Dumpling - M. Root

YEAR ISSUE	EDITION LIMIT	YEAR RETD.	ISSUE PRICE	*QUOTE U.S.$
1993 Eric - 1570	Retrd.	1994	22.50	40-102
1994 Erica - 1578	Retrd.	1995	22.50	39-89
1996 Tia - 1587	Retrd.	1997	23.50	24-60
1997 Tori - 1592	Yr.Iss.	1997	23.00	23-46
1998 Hapi - 1601	Yr.Iss.		24.50	25

Christmas Ornaments - M. Root

YEAR ISSUE	EDITION LIMIT	YEAR RETD.	ISSUE PRICE	*QUOTE U.S.$
1987 Cameo Ornaments (set of 12) - D1912	Retrd.	1988	144.00	2000-2280
1987 Doll Ornaments (set of 24) - D1924	Retrd.	1988	336.00	3000-3936
1993 Santa with Scooty - 1571	Retrd.	1994	22.50	84-100

Anheuser-Busch, Inc.

A & Eagle Collector Ornament Series - A.-Busch, Inc.

YEAR ISSUE	EDITION LIMIT	YEAR RETD.	ISSUE PRICE	*QUOTE U.S.$
1991 Budweiser Girl-Circa 1890's N3178	Retrd.	N/A	15.00	15-20
1992 1893 Columbian Exposition N3649	Retrd.	N/A	15.00	15-20
1993 Greatest Triumph N4089	Retrd.	N/A	15.00	15-20

Christmas Ornaments - Various

YEAR ISSUE	EDITION LIMIT	YEAR RETD.	ISSUE PRICE	*QUOTE U.S.$
1992 Clydesdales 3 Mini Plate Ornament N3650 - S. Sampson	Retrd.	N/A	23.00	25
1993 Budweiser Six-Pack Mini Plate Ornament N4220 - M. Urdahl	Retrd.	1994	10.00	19-28

Annalee Mobilitee Dolls, Inc.

Ornaments - A. Thorndike

YEAR ISSUE	EDITION LIMIT	YEAR RETD.	ISSUE PRICE	*QUOTE U.S.$
1982 Elf Head (green) 7810	Closed	1986	7.00	30
1982 Elf Head (red) 7810	Closed	1986	7.00	30
1982 03" Angel on Cloud (hard) 7820	Closed	1987	13.00	50
1982 03" Angel on Cloud (soft) 7820	Closed	1987	13.00	50
1995 03" Angel Playing Instrument 7819	Closed	1997	16.00	16-25
1986 03" Baby Angel 7820	Closed	1988	12.00	50
1987 03" Baby in Basket 7816	Yr.Iss.	1987	16.00	110
1995 03" Baby in Blue PJ's 7871	Closed	1995	12.00	12-40
1995 03" Baby in Pink PJ's 7872	Closed	1995	12.00	35
1985 03" Baby in Stocking 7870	Closed	1988	13.00	50-55
1985 03" Baby in Stocking 7870	Yr.Iss.	1985	12.00	60
1993 03" Baby Jesus in Manger7881	Closed	1995	18.00	18-45
1987 03" Bear (red ribbon) 7818	Closed	1993	13.00	40
1987 03" Boy & Girl Caroller 7826, 7824	Closed	1988	28.00	75
1986 03" Clown Ornament 7945	Yr.Iss.	1986	12.00	90-100
1986 03" Drummer Boy 7935	Closed	1989	14.00	18-45
1987 03" Elf (full body) 7822	Closed	1989	14.00	14-45
1993 03" Fishing Santa 7836	Yr.Iss.	1993	25.00	25-55
1996 03" Gingerbread Boy 7829	Closed	1996	15.00	15-30
1987 03" Girl Caroller 7824	Closed	1988	14.00	40
1995 03" Honey Bear 7817	Closed	1996	14.00	30
1996 03" Just a Jester 7827	Yr.Iss.	1996	21.00	21-25
1987 03" Kid on Sled (sitting) 7812	Closed	1989	17.00	45
1987 03" Kid w/ Snowball 7814	Closed	1989	15.00	45
1987 03" Lovey Bears 7808	Closed	1990	26.00	75
1986 03" Mr & Mrs Victorian Santas 7895, 7900	Closed	1987	28.00	140
1986 03" Mr Victorian Santa 7895	Closed	1987	14.00	65
1987 03" Mrs Santa (logo print) 7838	Closed	1987	13.00	65
1986 03" Mrs Santa 7838	Closed	1986	13.00	60
1984 03" Red Heart (Be Mine) 7855	Closed	1985	4.00	30
1986 03" Skier 7930	Closed	1992	15.00	40
1984 03" Snowman 7845	Closed	1990	15.00	25
1984 03" Star 7850	Closed	1985	7.00	60
1994 03" Sun w/ Santa Hat 7876	Closed	1995	9.00	25
1997 04" When Pigs Fly 7841	Yr.Iss.	1997	17.00	17-35
1986 05" Elf w/ Stick Horse 7955	Closed	1988	19.00	60
1985 05" Gingerbread Boy 7825	Closed	1986	12.00	35
1991 05" Gingerbread Boy 7825	Closed	1995	18.00	18-30
1994 05" Old World Santa 7800	Closed	1995	24.00	30
1996 05" Old World Santa 7800	Closed	1996	24.00	30
1984 05" Rocking Deer 7840	Closed	1987	14.00	50
1986 05" Stick Horse 7960	Closed	1987	8.00	40
1985 Angel Head 7860	Closed	1986	8.00	40
1994 Annalee Crystal Ornament 7964	Closed	1994	30.00	60
1985 Clown Head 7865	Closed	1986	7.00	55
1980 Deer Head 7815	Closed	1995	11.00	15
1980 Santa Head 7805	Closed	N/A	10.00	10
1991 Snowman Head (green earmuffs) 7830	Closed	1996	13.00	20
1994 Snowman Head (large) 7831	Closed	1994	18.00	75
1994 Snowman Head (red earmuffs) 7830	Closed	1996	10.00	30

ANRI

Christmas Eve Series - L. Gaither

YEAR ISSUE	EDITION LIMIT	YEAR RETD.	ISSUE PRICE	*QUOTE U.S.$
1998 First Gift of Christmas, Mr. & Mrs. Santa	500		165.00	165

Disney Four Star Collection - Disney Studios

YEAR ISSUE	EDITION LIMIT	YEAR RETD.	ISSUE PRICE	*QUOTE U.S.$
1989 Maestro Mickey	Yr.Iss.	1989	25.00	75-95
1990 Minnie Mouse	Yr.Iss.	1990	25.00	50

Ferrandiz Message Collection - J. Ferrandiz

YEAR ISSUE	EDITION LIMIT	YEAR RETD.	ISSUE PRICE	*QUOTE U.S.$
1989 Let the Heavens Ring	1,000	1992	215.00	215
1990 Hear The Angels Sing	1,000	1992	225.00	225

Ferrandiz Woodcarvings - J. Ferrandiz

YEAR ISSUE	EDITION LIMIT	YEAR RETD.	ISSUE PRICE	*QUOTE U.S.$
1988 Heavenly Drummer	1,000	1992	175.00	225
1989 Heavenly Strings	1,000	1992	190.00	190

Sarah Kay's First Christmas - S. Kay

YEAR ISSUE	EDITION LIMIT	YEAR RETD.	ISSUE PRICE	*QUOTE U.S.$
1994 Sarah Kay's First Christmas	500		140.00	195
1995 First Xmas Stocking 57502	500		99.00	240
1996 All I Want for Xmas 57503	500		195.00	240
1997 Christmas Puppy	500		295.00	295

Armani

Christmas - G. Armani

YEAR ISSUE	EDITION LIMIT	YEAR RETD.	ISSUE PRICE	*QUOTE U.S.$
1991 Christmas Ornament 779A	Retrd.	1991	11.50	39-175
1992 Christmas Ornament 788F	Retrd.	1992	23.50	39-150
1993 Christmas Ornament 982P	Retrd.	1993	25.00	39-75
1994 Christmas Ornament 801P	Retrd.	1994	25.00	45-68
1995 Christmas Ornament-Gifts & Snow 640P	Retrd.	1995	30.00	30-39
1996 Christmas Ornament-A Sweet Christmas 355P	Retrd.	1996	30.00	30
1997 Christmas Ornament-Christmas Snow 137F	Retrd.	1997	37.50	38
1998 Christmas Ornament-Christmas Eve 123F	Yr.Iss.		35.00	35

Artists of the World

De Grazia Annual Ornaments - T. De Grazia

YEAR ISSUE	EDITION LIMIT	YEAR RETD.	ISSUE PRICE	*QUOTE U.S.$
1986 Pima Indian Drummer Boy	Yr.Iss.	1986	28.00	75-200
1987 White Dove	Yr.Iss.	1987	30.00	78-98
1988 Flower Girl	Yr.Iss.	1988	33.00	65-100
1989 Flower Boy	Yr.Iss.	1989	35.00	65-100
1990 Pink Papoose	Yr.Iss.	1990	35.00	65-100
1990 Merry Little Indian	10,000	1990	88.00	100-175
1991 Christmas Prayer (Red)	Yr.Iss.	1991	50.00	72-95
1992 Bearing Gift	Yr.Iss.	1992	55.00	78-100
1993 Lighting the Way	Yr.Iss.	1993	58.00	100
1994 Warm Wishes	Yr.Iss.	1994	65.00	70-100
1995 Little Prayer (White)	Yr.Iss.	1995	49.50	65-75
1996 Heavenly Flowers	Yr.Iss.	1995	65.00	65
1995 My Beautiful Rocking Horse	Yr.Iss.	1995	125.00	125-150
1997 Oh Holy Night	Yr.Iss	1996	67.50	75
1998 Christmas Spirit	Yr.Iss		65.00	65
1998 Little Cocopah Indian Girl	Yr.Iss		67.50	68

Bing & Grondahl

Christmas - Various

YEAR ISSUE	EDITION LIMIT	YEAR RETD.	ISSUE PRICE	*QUOTE U.S.$
1985 Christmas Eve at the Farmhouse - E. Jensen	Closed	1985	19.50	20-30

*Quotes have been rounded up to nearest dollar

YEAR ISSUE	EDITION LIMIT	YEAR RETD.	ISSUE PRICE	*QUOTE U.S.$
1986 Silent Night, Holy Night - E. Jensen	Closed	1986	19.50	30
1987 The Snowman's Christmas Eve - E. Jensen	Closed	1987	22.50	11-23
1988 In the King's Garden - E. Jensen	Closed	1988	25.00	26
1989 Christmas Anchorage - E. Jensen	Closed	1989	27.00	14-27
1990 Changing of the Guards - E. Jensen	Closed	1990	32.50	30-36
1991 Copenhagen Stock Exchange - E. Jensen	Closed	1991	34.50	30-35
1992 Christmas at the Rectory - J. Steensen	Closed	1992	36.50	30-37
1993 Father Christmas in Copenhagen - J. Nielsen	Closed	1993	36.50	18-37
1994 A Day at the Deer Park - J. Nielsen	Closed	1994	36.50	30-45
1995 The Towers of Copenhagen - J. Nielsen	Closed	1995	37.50	30-45
1996 Winter at the Old Mill - J. Nielsen	Closed	1996	37.50	30-42
1997 Country Christmas - J. Nielsen	Closed	1998	37.50	30-38
1998 Santa the Storyteller - J. Nielsen	Yr.Iss.		37.50	38

Christmas Around the World - H. Hansen

YEAR ISSUE	EDITION LIMIT	YEAR RETD.	ISSUE PRICE	*QUOTE U.S.$
1995 Santa in Greenland	Yr.Iss.	1995	25.00	25-45
1996 Santa in Orient	Yr.Iss.	1996	25.00	25-30
1997 Santa in Russia	Yr.Iss.	1997	25.00	25-27
1998 Santa in Australia	Yr.Iss.		25.00	25

Christmas In America - J. Woodson

YEAR ISSUE	EDITION LIMIT	YEAR RETD.	ISSUE PRICE	*QUOTE U.S.$
1986 Christmas Eve in Williamsburg	Closed	1986	12.50	36-75
1987 Christmas Eve at the White House	Closed	1987	15.00	25-75
1988 Christmas Eve at Rockefeller Center	Closed	1988	18.50	20-25
1989 Christmas in New England	Closed	1989	20.00	21-25
1990 Christmas Eve at the Capitol	Closed	1990	20.00	25-32
1991 Independence Hall	Closed	1991	23.50	25-30
1992 Christmas in San Francisco	Closed	1992	25.00	25-36
1993 Coming Home For Christmas	Closed	1993	25.00	25-30
1994 Christmas Eve in Alaska	Closed	1994	25.00	25-45
1995 Christmas Eve in Mississippi	Closed	1995	25.00	23-25

Santa Claus - Unknown

YEAR ISSUE	EDITION LIMIT	YEAR RETD.	ISSUE PRICE	*QUOTE U.S.$
1989 Santa's Workshop	Yr.Iss.	1989	20.00	45-60
1990 Santa's Sleigh	Yr.Iss.	1990	20.00	50-60
1991 The Journey	Yr.Iss.	1991	24.00	45-51
1992 Santa's Arrival	Yr.Iss.	1992	25.00	36-48
1993 Santa's Gifts	Yr.Iss.	1993	25.00	25-36
1994 Christmas Stories	Yr.Iss.	1994	25.00	30-36

Boyds Collection Ltd.

The Bearstone Collection ™ - G. M. Lowenthal

YEAR ISSUE	EDITION LIMIT	YEAR RETD.	ISSUE PRICE	*QUOTE U.S.$
1994 'Charity'-Angel Bear with Star 2502	Retrd.	1996	9.45	30-38
1994 'Faith'-Angel Bear with Trumpet 2500	Retrd.	1996	9.45	25-38
1994 'Hope'-Angel Bear with Wreath 2501	Retrd.	1996	9.45	27-38
1995 'Edmund'...Believe 2505	Retrd.	1997	9.45	10-32
1995 'Elliot with Tree' 2507	Retrd.	1997	9.45	10-32
1995 'Manheim' the Moose with Wreath 2506	Retrd.	1997	9.45	10-40

The Bearstone Collection ™ - G.M. Lowenthal

YEAR ISSUE	EDITION LIMIT	YEAR RETD.	ISSUE PRICE	*QUOTE U.S.$
1997 Matthew with Kip (Baby's 1st Christmas) 2508	Retrd.	1997	9.45	10

The Folkstone Collection ™ - G.M. Lowenthal

YEAR ISSUE	EDITION LIMIT	YEAR RETD.	ISSUE PRICE	*QUOTE U.S.$
1995 Father Christmas 2553	Retrd.	1997	9.45	25-28
1995 Jean Claude & Jacque...the Skiers 2561	Retrd.	1997	9.45	25-28
1995 Jingles the Snowman with Wreath 2562	Retrd.	1997	9.45	25-28
1995 Nicholai with Tree 2550	Retrd.	1997	9.45	25-28
1995 Nicholas the Giftgiver 2551	Retrd.	1997	9.45	25-28
1995 Olaf...Let it Snow 2560	Retrd.	1997	9.45	25-28
1995 Sliknick in the Chimney 2552	Retrd.	1997	9.45	25-28

Brandywine Collectibles

Custom Collection - M. Whiting

YEAR ISSUE	EDITION LIMIT	YEAR RETD.	ISSUE PRICE	*QUOTE U.S.$
1989 Lorain Lighthouse	Closed	1992	9.00	9
1994 Smithfield Clerk's Office	Closed	1995	9.00	9
1991 Smithfield VA. Courthouse	Closed	1992	9.00	9

Williamsburg Ornaments - M. Whiting

YEAR ISSUE	EDITION LIMIT	YEAR RETD.	ISSUE PRICE	*QUOTE U.S.$
1988 Apothocary	Closed	1991	9.00	9
1988 Bootmaker	Closed	1991	9.00	9
1989 Cole Shop	Closed	1991	9.00	9
1988 Finnie Quarter	Closed	1991	9.00	9
1988 Gunsmith	Closed	1991	9.00	9
1994 Gunsmith	360	1994	9.50	10
1998 Millinery Shop	Closed	1997	12.00	12
1989 Music Teacher	Closed	1991	9.00	9
1988 Nicolson Shop	Closed	1991	9.00	9
1988 Tarpley's Store	Closed	1991	9.00	9
1988 Wigmaker	Closed	1991	9.00	9
1989 Windmill	Closed	1991	9.00	9

Calico Kittens/Enesco Corporation

Calico Kittens - P. Hillman

YEAR ISSUE	EDITION LIMIT	YEAR RETD.	ISSUE PRICE	*QUOTE U.S.$
1993 Baby's First Christmas (Boy) 628204	Retrd.	1997	16.00	16
1993 Baby's First Christmas (Girl) 628255	Retrd.	1997	16.00	16
1993 Cat With Blue Hat 623814	Retrd.	1997	11.00	11
1993 Cat With Green Hat 623814	Retrd.	1997	11.00	11
1993 Cat With Red Hat 623814	Retrd.	1997	11.00	11
1994 First Christmas Together 651346	Retrd.	1997	15.00	15
1994 Joy To The World 651354	Retrd.	1997	13.50	14
1994 Peace On Earth 651354	Retrd.	1997	13.50	14

Cardew Design

Disney Tiny Ornaments - P. Cardew

YEAR ISSUE	EDITION LIMIT	YEAR RETD.	ISSUE PRICE	*QUOTE U.S.$
1997 Pooh Santa	7,500	1997	75.00	75

Carlton Cards

1988 Summit Heirloom Collection - Carlton

YEAR ISSUE	EDITION LIMIT	YEAR RETD.	ISSUE PRICE	*QUOTE U.S.$
1988 1st Christmas Together 053-047-6	Closed	1988	4.50	5
1988 Animals 053-050-6	Closed	1988	4.50	5
1988 Baby's First Christmas 053-026-3	Closed	1988	5.00	5
1988 Bundles of Joy 053-041-7	Closed	1989	11.00	11
1988 Carousel Magic 053-023-9	Closed	1988	8.00	48-58
1988 Christmas Charmer 053-038-7	Closed	1988	7.50	8
1988 Christmas Confection 053-044-1	Closed	1988	7.00	7
1988 Christmas Dreams 053-012-3	Closed	1988	12.00	12
1988 Christmas Magic 053-022-0	Closed	1988	8.00	8
1988 Christmas Wishes 053-060-3	Closed	1988	4.50	5
1988 Country Cheer 053-919-8	Closed	1988	7.50	38-45
1988 Cozy Kitten 053-053-0	Closed	1988	10.00	10
1988 Cuddly Christmas (A Good Roommate) 053-055-7	Closed	1988	6.50	60
1988 Favorite Things 053-039-5	Closed	1991	10.00	10
1988 Fluffy 053-017-4	Closed	1988	4.50	5
1988 Forever Friends 053-016-6	Closed	1989	9.50	10
1988 Friends Forever 053-032-8	Closed	1988	5.50	6
1988 Giddyap Teddy! 053-019-0	Closed	1988	9.50	10
1988 Grandma Twinkle 053-030-1	Closed	1988	N/A	N/A
1988 Happy Holly Days 053-054-9	Closed	1988	8.00	8
1988 Havin' Fun 053-037-9	Closed	1988	6.50	125-200
1988 Home, Sweet Home 053-015-8	Closed	1988	N/A	N/A
1988 Just Us 053-029-8	Closed	1988	9.50	10
1988 Kiss-Moose 053-025-5	Closed	1996	5.50	6
1988 Little One 053-027-1	Closed	1989	9.50	10
1988 Manger 053-051-4	Closed	1988	5.00	10-15
1988 Merry Christmas Grandson 053-046-8	Closed	1988	7.50	8
1988 Merry Heartwarming 053-048-4	Closed	1988	N/A	N/A
1988 O Holy Night 053-057-3	Closed	1989	9.50	10
1988 Old-Time Santa 053-040-9	Closed	1988	8.50	75
1988 Perky Penguin 053-058-1	Closed	1988	6.50	28
1988 Ring in Christmas 053-020-4	Closed	1988	6.00	6
1988 Roses 053-049-2	Closed	1988	4.50	5
1988 Song of Christmas 053-034-4	Closed	1988	4.50	5
1988 Special Delivery (dated) 053-018-2	Closed	1989	11.00	35
1988 Star of Wonder 053-024-7	Closed	1988	N/A	N/A
1988 The Sweetest Angel 053-043-3	Closed	1988	6.00	6
1988 Teacher's Treat 053-021-2	Closed	1988	5.50	6
1988 Winter Friend 053-056-5	Closed	1989	4.00	24
1988 Wonderland Waltz 053-013-1	Closed	1988	12.00	12
1988 Wood Decoy 053-036-0	Closed	1988	N/A	N/A

1989 Summit Heirloom/Carlton Baby's First Christmas - Carlton

YEAR ISSUE	EDITION LIMIT	YEAR RETD.	ISSUE PRICE	*QUOTE U.S.$
1989 Christmas Dreams 058096-1	Closed	1989	12.00	12
1989 Giddyap Teddy! 058093-7	Closed	1989	9.50	10
1989 A Gift From Heaven 058111-9	Closed	1989	8.50	9
1989 Little One 058098-8	Closed	1989	9.50	10
1989 Pa-Rum-Pa-Pum-Pum 058113-5	Closed	1989	9.50	10

1989 For Family - Carlton

YEAR ISSUE	EDITION LIMIT	YEAR RETD.	ISSUE PRICE	*QUOTE U.S.$
1989 A Daughter Is A Joy (Daughter) 058128-3	Closed	1989	5.00	5
1989 Little Frostee (Granddaughter) 058115-1	Closed	1989	8.50	9
1989 Ring In The Holidays (Grandmother) 058134-9	Closed	1989	7.50	8
1989 A Season of Fun (Grandson) 058108-9	Closed	1989	7.50	8
1989 A Sister Is A Friend (Sister) 058129-1	Closed	1989	5.00	5
1989 To A Special Mom (Mother) 058132-1	Closed	1989	7.50	8

1989 Our First Christmas Together - Carlton

YEAR ISSUE	EDITION LIMIT	YEAR RETD.	ISSUE PRICE	*QUOTE U.S.$
1989 Home, Tweet, Home 058112-7	Closed	1989	9.50	10
1989 Just Us 058091-0	Closed	1989	9.50	10
1989 Season Of Love 058126-7	Closed	1989	5.00	5
1989 Wonderland Waltz 058095-3	Closed	1989	12.00	12

1989 Special People and Moments - Carlton

YEAR ISSUE	EDITION LIMIT	YEAR RETD.	ISSUE PRICE	*QUOTE U.S.$
1989 Best Friends 058109-7	Closed	1989	9.50	10
1989 Forever Friends 053041-7	Closed	1989	9.50	10
1989 School Days (Teacher) 058125-9	Closed	1989	7.50	8

1989 Traditional - Carlton

YEAR ISSUE	EDITION LIMIT	YEAR RETD.	ISSUE PRICE	*QUOTE U.S.$
1989 Arctic Antics 058131-3	Closed	1989	5.50	6
1989 Bundles of Joy 058104-6	Closed	1989	11.00	11
1989 Christmas Charmer 058094-5	Closed	1989	6.50	7
1989 Christmas Confection 058105-4	Closed	1989	6.50	7
1989 Christmas Fantasy 058119-4	Closed	1989	5.00	5
1989 Country Christmas 058127-5	Closed	1989	5.00	5
1989 Gentle Hearts 058118-6	Closed	1989	6.50	7
1989 Golden Snowflake 058137-2	Closed	1989	5.00	5
1989 Havin' Fun 058092-9	Closed	1989	6.50	7
1989 Hello Moon! 058103-8	Closed	1989	7.50	8
1989 Here Comes Santa! 058099-6	Closed	1990	7.50	8
1989 Honey Love 058117-8	Closed	1989	6.50	7
1989 In the Workshop 058100-3	Closed	1990	11.00	11
1989 Jolly Holiday Bell 058136-4	Closed	1989	6.50	7
1989 Joy To The World 058138-0	Closed	1989	7.50	8
1989 Kiss-Moose 058107-0	Closed	1989	5.50	6
1989 A Little Shepherd 058130-5	Closed	1989	5.00	5
1989 Merrie Old Christmas 058135-6	Closed	1989	5.50	6
1989 Merry Old Santa Claus 053035-2	Closed	1992	12.00	45
1989 Perky Penguin 058121-6	Closed	1989	6.50	7
1989 Special Delivery 058090-2	Closed	1989	11.00	11

1990 Summit Heirloom/Carlton Collector's Series - Carlton

YEAR ISSUE	EDITION LIMIT	YEAR RETD.	ISSUE PRICE	*QUOTE U.S.$
1990 Christmas Express (1st) 102355-1	Closed	1990	12.00	12
1990 Christmas Go-Round (1st) 102346-2	Closed	1990	13.00	13
1990 Christmas Hello (1st) 102352-7	Closed	1990	13.00	13
1990 A Little Bit Of Christmas (1st) 102340-3	Closed	1990	10.50	11
1990 Santa's Roommate (1st) 102361-6	Closed	1990	7.50	8

1990 Baby's First Christmas - Carlton

YEAR ISSUE	EDITION LIMIT	YEAR RETD.	ISSUE PRICE	*QUOTE U.S.$
1990 Christmas Dreams (Baby Girl) 102363-2	Closed	1990	12.00	12
1990 Christmas Whirl (Granddaughter) 102378-9	Closed	1990	11.00	11
1990 A Gift From Heaven 102368-3	Closed	1990	7.50	8
1990 Little Frostee (Grandson) 102379-9	Closed	1990	8.00	8
1990 Little One 102367-5	Closed	1990	10.50	11
1990 Merry Little Christmas (Grandchild) 102380-2	Closed	1990	11.00	11
1990 Pa-Rum-Pa-Pum-Pum (Baby Boy) 102366-7	Closed	1990	9.50	10

1990 First Christmas Together - Carlton

YEAR ISSUE	EDITION LIMIT	YEAR RETD.	ISSUE PRICE	*QUOTE U.S.$
1990 Just Us 102371-3	Closed	1990	9.50	10
1990 Together Forever 102372-1	Closed	1990	11.00	11
1990 Wonderland Waltz 102370-5	Closed	1990	13.00	13

1990 For Family - Carlton

YEAR ISSUE	EDITION LIMIT	YEAR RETD.	ISSUE PRICE	*QUOTE U.S.$
1990 Friendship Is A Gift (Friend) 102377-2	Closed	1990	5.50	6
1990 A Grandmother Is Special (Grandmother) 102382-9	Closed	1990	5.50	6
1990 Home, Tweet, Home (New Home) 102374-8	Closed	1990	9.50	10
1990 Love is The Gift (Love) 102320-9	Closed	1990	7.50	8
1990 A Mother Is Love (Mother) 102381-0	Closed	1990	7.50	8
1990 Remembering Christmastime (Sister) 102384-5	Closed	1990	9.00	9
1990 Special Christmas Moments (Daughter) 102385-3	Closed	1990	8.50	9

1990 Special People and Moments - Carlton

YEAR ISSUE	EDITION LIMIT	YEAR RETD.	ISSUE PRICE	*QUOTE U.S.$
1990 Beary Christmas (Teacher) 102375-6	Closed	1990	7.50	8
1990 Best Friends (Friend) 102376-4	Closed	1990	9.50	10

1990 Traditional - Carlton

YEAR ISSUE	EDITION LIMIT	YEAR RETD.	ISSUE PRICE	*QUOTE U.S.$
1990 Bunny Love 102359-4	Closed	1991	9.50	11
1990 Checkin' It Twice 102323-4	Closed	1991	12.00	12
1990 Christmas Angel 102331-4	Closed	1990	7.50	8
1990 Christmas Blessings 102353-5	Closed	1991	8.00	8
1990 Christmas Caring 102338-1	Closed	1990	8.00	8
1990 Christmas Confection 102337-3	Closed	1990	7.00	7
1990 Christmas Flight 102329-2	Closed	1990	6.50	7
1990 Christmas Is Special 102313-6	Closed	1990	6.50	7
1990 Christmas Means Togetherness 102369-1	Closed	1990	8.50	9
1990 Christmas Memories 102347-0	Closed	1990	5.25	6
1990 A Christmas Shared 102354-3	Closed	1991	10.50	11
1990 Christmas Surprise 102312-8	Closed	1990	7.50	8
1990 Cool Yule 102310-1	Closed	1990	9.50	10-18
1990 Country Friend 102326-8	Closed	1990	7.00	7
1990 Cozy Kitten 102341-1	Closed	1990	10.50	11
1990 Crystal Thoughts 102335-7	Closed	1990	6.50	7
1990 Favorite Things 102344-6	Closed	1991	11.00	11
1990 Gentle Hearts 102330-6	Closed	1990	7.00	7
1990 Giddyap Teddy! 102364-0	Closed	1990	9.50	10
1990 Giddyap Teddy! 102365-9	Closed	1990	9.50	10
1990 Gifts 'N' Good Wishes 102345-4	Closed	1990	10.50	11
1990 Grandparents Are Always 102383-7	Closed	1990	5.25	6
1990 Heavenly Flight 102358-6	Closed	1990	7.50	8
1990 Hi-Ho Holidays 102321-7	Closed	1990	9.50	10
1990 A Holiday Hi 102360-8	Closed	1990	10.00	10
1990 Holiday Magic 102328-4	Closed	1990	6.50	7
1990 Holiday Purr-fection 102323-5	Closed	1990	6.50	7
1990 Holly Hobbie Christmas At Heart 102322-5	Closed	1990	12.00	12
1990 Home For The Holidays 1 02357-8	Closed	1990	10.50	11
1990 In The Workshop 102343-8	Closed	1990	13.00	13
1990 Merry Magic 102324-1	Closed	1990	6.00	6
1990 Not A Creature Was Stirring 102348-9	Closed	1992	13.00	13
1990 The Nutcracker 102327-6	Closed	1990	9.00	9
1990 Pandabelle 102386-1	Closed	1990	7.50	8
1990 Peace, Hope, Love 102333-0	Closed	1990	5.25	6
1990 Perky Penguin 102332-2	Closed	1990	6.50	7
1990 Rocking Horse Fun 102316-0	Closed	1990	10.50	11
1990 Sing A Song Of Christmas 102336-5	Closed	1990	6.00	6
1990 Sound Of Christmas 102317-9	Closed	1990	7.00	7
1990 A Special Gift Photo Holder 102314-4	Closed	1990	7.50	8
1990 The Stockings Were Hung 102349-7	Closed	1990	8.00	8

*Quotes have been rounded up to nearest dollar

YEAR ISSUE	EDITION LIMIT	YEAR RETD.	ISSUE PRICE	*QUOTE U.S.$
1990 Thoughts Of Christmas 102334-9	Closed	1990	5.25	6
1990 Up On The Roof Top 102309-8	Closed	1990	11.00	11
1990 Up, Up, Away 102350-0	Closed	1990	10.00	10
1990 Visions Of Sugar Plums 102351-9	Closed	1996	9.50	10
1990 Winter Filigree 102315-2	Closed	1990	6.50	7
1990 Wrapped Up In Christmas 102318-7	Closed	1990	10.00	10
1990 Ziggy 102319-5	Closed	1990	5.25	6

1991 Carlton Heirloom Collection Collector's Series - Carlton

YEAR ISSUE	EDITION LIMIT	YEAR RETD.	ISSUE PRICE	*QUOTE U.S.$
1991 Christmas Express (2nd) 114857-3	Closed	1991	14.00	14
1991 Christmas Express (Reissue-1st) 114826-5	Closed	1991	14.00	14
1991 Christmas Go-Round (2nd) 114830-3	Closed	1991	14.00	25
1991 A Little Bit Of Christmas (2nd) 114831-1	Closed	1991	11.00	11
1991 Santa's Roommate (2nd) 114828-1	Closed	1991	8.00	8
1991 There Is A Santa! (2nd) 114833-8	Closed	1991	14.00	14

1991 Baby's First Christmas - Carlton

YEAR ISSUE	EDITION LIMIT	YEAR RETD.	ISSUE PRICE	*QUOTE U.S.$
1991 Christmas Charmer 114804-4	Closed	1991	11.00	11
1991 Christmas Cutie (Granddaughter) 114811-7	Closed	1991	10.00	10
1991 Christmas Darlings (Baby Girl) 114806-0	Closed	1991	12.00	12
1991 Christmas Dreams (Baby Girl) 114807-9	Closed	1991	13.00	13
1991 A Gift From Heaven 114805-2	Closed	1991	8.00	8
1991 Holiday Hobby Horse (Grandson) 114812-5	Closed	1991	10.50	11
1991 Holiday Memories (Baby Boy) 114808-7	Closed	1991	9.50	10
1991 Little Christmas Wishes (Grandchild) 114810-9	Closed	1991	11.00	11
1991 Small Surprises (Baby Boy) 114809-5	Closed	1991	10.50	11

1991 First Christmas Together - Carlton

YEAR ISSUE	EDITION LIMIT	YEAR RETD.	ISSUE PRICE	*QUOTE U.S.$
1991 Christmas Cuddles 114817-6	Closed	1991	10.50	11
1991 Christmastime For Two 114816-8	Closed	1991	14.00	14
1991 Just Us 114813-3	Closed	1991	11.00	11
1991 Together Forever 114814-1	Closed	1991	12.00	12

1991 For Family - Carlton

YEAR ISSUE	EDITION LIMIT	YEAR RETD.	ISSUE PRICE	*QUOTE U.S.$
1991 A Christmas To Remember (Grandmother) 114822-2	Closed	1991	9.00	9
1991 Love Is All Around! (Grandparents) 114823-0	Closed	1991	11.00	11
1991 A Mother Is Love (Mother) 114819-2	Closed	1991	11.00	11
1991 Ring In the Holidays (Sister) 114821-4	Closed	1991	10.00	10
1991 A Special Gift (Daughter) 114820-6	Closed	1991	9.00	9

1991 Special People and Moments - Carlton

YEAR ISSUE	EDITION LIMIT	YEAR RETD.	ISSUE PRICE	*QUOTE U.S.$
1991 Friends At Heart (Friend) 114825-7	Closed	1991	8.00	8
1991 Happy Holidays (Teacher) 114818 4	Closed	1991	8.00	8
1991 Home For Christmas (New Home) 114884-2	Closed	1991	9.50	10
1991 Snowflake Friends (Friend) 114824-9	Closed	1991	11.00	11

1991 Traditional - Carlton

YEAR ISSUE	EDITION LIMIT	YEAR RETD.	ISSUE PRICE	*QUOTE U.S.$
1991 And Away We Go 114851-6	Closed	1992	9.00	9
1991 Bunny Love 114836-2	Closed	1992	10.00	10
1991 Catch The Christmas Spirit 114856-7	Closed	1992	8.50	9
1991 Checkin' It Twice 114844-3	Closed	1991	12.00	12
1991 A Child's Christmas 114858-3	Closed	1992	10.00	10
1991 Christmas At Heart 114838-9	Closed	1991	12.00	12
1991 Christmas Blessing 114842-7	Closed	1991	8.50	9
1991 Christmas By The Hearthful 114857-5	Closed	1991	9.00	9
1991 Christmas Caring 114852-4	Closed	1991	8.00	8
1991 Christmas Couple 114861-3	Closed	1991	13.00	13
1991 Christmas Fantasy 114872-9	Closed	1991	11.00	11
1991 Christmas Greetings 114851-6	Closed	1991	10.00	10
1991 Christmas Is In The Air 114878-8	Closed	1992	11.00	11
1991 A Christmas Shared 114841-9	Closed	1991	10.50	11
1991 Christmas Sweetie 114855-9	Closed	1991	9.50	10
1991 Christmas Wishes 114869-9	Closed	1992	14.00	14
1991 Elfkin 114870-2	Closed	1992	9.50	10
1991 Favorite Things 114837-0	Closed	1991	12.00	12
1991 Frosty Friend 114835-4	Closed	1991	8.50	9
1991 Gentle Hearts 114866-4	Closed	1991	11.00	11
1991 Happiness Is All Around! 114876-1	Closed	1992	9.00	9
1991 Happy Christmas To All 114840-0	Closed	1991	8.50	9
1991 Heavenly Flight 114853-2	Closed	1991	8.00	8
1991 Here Comes Santa! 114845-1	Closed	1991	9.00	9
1991 Holiday Beauty 114860-5	Closed	1991	9.00	9
1991 Holiday Fun 114867-2	Closed	1991	9.50	10-25
1991 Holiday Treat 114881-8	Closed	1992	10.00	10
1991 Home For The Holidays 114839-9	Closed	1991	10.50	11
1991 In The Workshop 114847-8	Closed	1991	13.00	13
1991 Little Drummer Bear 114864-8	Closed	1991	9.50	10
1991 Little Starlight 114868-0	Closed	1991	11.00	11
1991 A Little Taste Of Christmas 114862-1	Closed	1991	13.00	13
1991 The Night Before Christmas 114859-1	Closed	1991	10.00	10
1991 North Pole Parade 114874-5	Closed	1991	14.00	14
1991 Not A Creature Was Stirring 114850-8	Closed	1991	14.00	14
1991 Purr-fect Holidays 114871-0	Closed	1991	11.00	15
1991 Reindeer Games 114865-6	Closed	1991	10.00	10
1991 Rocking Horse Fun 114848-6	Closed	1991	11.00	11
1991 Sing A Song Of Christmas 114873-7	Closed	1991	12.00	12
1991 A Speciall Photo Holder 114834-6	Closed	1991	9.00	9
1991 Stocking Full Of Love 114854-0	Closed	1991	9.00	9
1991 Up On The Roof Top 114843-5	Closed	1991	11.00	11
1991 Visions Of Sugar Plums 114849-4	Closed	1992	9.50	10
1991 The Wonder Of Christmas 114875-3	Closed	1992	9.00	9

1992 Carlton Heirloom Collection Collector's Series - Carlton

YEAR ISSUE	EDITION LIMIT	YEAR RETD.	ISSUE PRICE	*QUOTE U.S.$
1992 Christmas Express Caboose (2nd) 120539-0	Closed	1993	15.00	15
1992 Christmas Express Coal Tender (3rd) 120478-5	Closed	1992	15.00	15
1992 Christmas Express Engine (1st) 120477-7	Closed	1992	15.00	15
1992 Christmas Go-Round (3rd) 120479-3	Closed	1992	14.00	12-14
1992 Christmas Sweets (1st) 120486-6	Closed	1992	11.00	25-35
1992 Ice Pals (1st) 120483-1	Closed	1992	10.00	10-30
1992 A Little Bit of Christmas (3rd) 120481-5	Closed	1992	13.00	13
1992 North Pole Parade (1st) 120482-3	Closed	1992	14.00	15
1992 Rodrick & Sam's Winter Fun (1st) 120485-8	Closed	1992	13.00	9-15
1992 Santa's Roommate (3rd) 120480-7	Closed	1992	9.00	9-12

1992 A Child's Christmas - Carlton

YEAR ISSUE	EDITION LIMIT	YEAR RETD.	ISSUE PRICE	*QUOTE U.S.$
1992 Circle of Love (Photo Frame) 120439-4	Closed	1992	11.00	11
1992 Cuddly Christmas (Child's 3rd) 120445-9	Closed	1992	10.00	10
1992 Heart Full of Christmas (Child's 4th) 120446-7	Closed	1992	10.00	10
1992 Jolly Holidays (Grandchild) 120456-4	Closed	1992	12.00	12
1992 Precious Heart (Child's 2nd) 120444-0	Closed	1992	10.00	10
1992 Sweet Season (Child's 5th) 120447-5	Closed	1992	10.00	10

1992 Baby's First Christmas - Carlton

YEAR ISSUE	EDITION LIMIT	YEAR RETD.	ISSUE PRICE	*QUOTE U.S.$
1992 Christmas Charmer 120441-6	Closed	1992	11.00	7-11
1992 Christmas Whirl (Granddaughter) 120448-3	Closed	1992	12.00	12
1992 Frosty Fun 120440-8	Closed	1992	12.00	12
1992 Giddyap, Teddy! (Baby Boy) 120443-2	Closed	1992	11.00	11
1992 Rock-A-Bye Baby (Baby Girl) 120442-4	Closed	1992	13.00	13
1992 Santa's Surprises (Grandson) 120449-1	Closed	1992	11.00	11

1992 First Christmas Together - Carlton

YEAR ISSUE	EDITION LIMIT	YEAR RETD.	ISSUE PRICE	*QUOTE U.S.$
1992 Christmas Cuddles 120461-0	Closed	1992	11.00	7-11
1992 Just Us 120460-2	Closed	1992	11.00	11
1992 Together Forever 120462-9	Closed	1992	12.00	12

1992 For Family - Carlton

YEAR ISSUE	EDITION LIMIT	YEAR RETD.	ISSUE PRICE	*QUOTE U.S.$
1992 Cherished Memories (Daughter) 120457-2	Closed	1992	11.00	11
1992 Christmas Twirl (Parents) 120455-6	Closed	1992	14.00	14
1992 Family Ties (Sister) 120459-9	Closed	1992	10.00	10
1992 Holiday Heirloom (Mother) 120450-5	Closed	1992	11.00	11
1992 Magic of Christmas (Father) 120451-3	Closed	1992	12.00	12
1992 Spirit of St. Nick (Son) 120458-0	Closed	1992	10.00	10

1992 Lasting Love - Carlton

YEAR ISSUE	EDITION LIMIT	YEAR RETD.	ISSUE PRICE	*QUOTE U.S.$
1992 Heart Full of Love (Our Christmas Together) 120463-7	Closed	1992	13.00	13
1992 The Season of Love (5 Years Together) 120464-5	Closed	1992	9.00	9
1992 A Silver Celebration (25 Years Together) 120466-1	Closed	1992	10.00	10
1992 Times to Treasure (10 Years Together) 120465-3	Closed	1992	9.00	9

1992 Special People and Moments - Carlton

YEAR ISSUE	EDITION LIMIT	YEAR RETD.	ISSUE PRICE	*QUOTE U.S.$
1992 Alpine Adventure (Friend) 120469-6	Closed	1992	11.00	7-11
1992 Christmas Warmth (Grandparents) 120452-1	Closed	1992	9.00	9
1992 Heart to Heart (Grandmother) 120454-8	Closed	1992	11.00	11
1992 Heartfelt Christmas (Friend) 120471-8	Closed	1992	10.00	10
1992 Home, Tweet Home (New Home) 120468-8	Closed	1992	10.00	10
1992 School Days (Teacher) 120472-6	Closed	1992	10.00	10

1992 Traditional - Carlton

YEAR ISSUE	EDITION LIMIT	YEAR RETD.	ISSUE PRICE	*QUOTE U.S.$
1992 Bundles of Joy 120509-9	Closed	1992	14.00	14
1992 Bunny Love 120519-6	Closed	1992	11.00	11
1992 Catch The Christmas Spirit 120522-6	Closed	1992	8.50	9
1992 A Child's Christmas (1st) 120532-3	Closed	1992	11.00	11
1992 A Child's Christmas (2nd) 120533-1	Closed	1992	11.00	11
1992 Christmas Blessing 120513-7	Closed	1992	9.50	10
1992 Christmas Couple 120511-0	Closed	1992	14.00	14
1992 Christmas Fantasy 120524-2	Closed	1992	11.00	11
1992 The Christmas Star 120527-7	Closed	1992	9.50	10
1992 Christmas Swingtime 120505-6	Closed	1992	10.00	10
1992 A Christmas to Remember 120538-2	Closed	1992	12.00	12
1992 Christmas Wishes 120516-1	Closed	1992	14.00	14
1992 Curious Cutie 120488-2	Closed	1992	11.00	11
1992 Elfkin 120497-1	Closed	1992	10.00	10
1992 Frosted Fantasy 120502-1	Closed	1992	9.00	9
1992 A Gift From The Heart 120530-7	Closed	1993	9.50	10
1992 Happiness Is All Around 120518-8	Closed	1992	9.00	9
1992 Heartwarming Holidays 120528-5	Closed	1992	9.00	9
1992 Heaven Sent 120535-8	Closed	1992	9.50	10
1992 High-Flying Holiday 120499-8	Closed	1992	11.00	11
1992 Holiday Harmony 120490-4	Closed	1992	13.00	13
1992 Holiday Helpers 120491-2	Closed	1992	13.00	15
1992 A Holiday Hi 120525-0	Closed	1992	11.00	11
1992 Holiday Treat 120523-4	Closed	1992	11.00	11
1992 Honey Bunny Christmas 120494-7	Closed	1992	12.00	12
1992 Kitty Caper 120493-9	Closed	1992	11.00	11
1992 Little Starlight 120537-4	Closed	1992	12.00	12
1992 Made With Love 120496-3	Closed	1992	15.00	15
1992 Merry Christmas to All 120506-4	Closed	1992	8.50	10
1992 Merry Marionettes 120487-4	Closed	1992	15.00	15
1992 Merry Mice Ginger 120476-9	Closed	1992	9.50	7-10
1992 Merry Mice Joy 120474-2	Closed	1992	9.50	10
1992 Merry Mice Noelle 120475-0	Closed	1992	9.50	10
1992 North Pole Putter 120473-4	Closed	1992	11.00	11
1992 Not A Creature Was Stirring 120514-5	Closed	1992	14.00	14
1992 Picture Perfect 120529-3	Closed	1992	8.50	9
1992 Polar Pals 120512-9	Closed	1992	11.00	11
1992 Pom Pom The Clown 120531-5	Closed	1992	9.50	10
1992 Purr-fect Holidays 120507-2	Closed	1992	11.00	11
1992 Ringing In Christmas 120536-6	Closed	1992	12.00	12
1992 Rocking Horse Fun 120504-8	Closed	1992	11.00	7-12
1992 Santa's Helpers 120495-5	Closed	1992	15.00	15
1992 Special Surprise 120489-0	Closed	1992	12.00	12
1992 Stocking Full of Love 120508-0	Closed	1992	9.00	9
1992 Tiny Toy Shop 120492-0	Closed	1992	15.00	15
1992 Visions of Sugar Plums 120515-3	Closed	1994	10.00	10
1992 Warmhearted Holidays 120526-9	Closed	1992	9.50	10
1992 Winter Funtime 120501-3	Closed	1992	11.00	11
1992 The Wonder of Christmas 120510-2	Closed	1992	10.00	10

1993 Carlton Heirloom Collection Collector's Series - Carlton

YEAR ISSUE	EDITION LIMIT	YEAR RETD.	ISSUE PRICE	*QUOTE U.S.$
1993 Book of Carols (1st) 126005-7	Closed	1993	13.50	14
1993 Christmas Express Caboose (2nd) 126037-5	Closed	1993	15.00	12
1993 Christmas Express Coal Tender Car (3rd) 126038-3	Closed	1993	15.00	15
1993 Christmas Express Engine (1st) 126036-7	Closed	1993	15.00	15
1993 Christmas Express Reindeer Coach (4th) 126010-3	Closed	1993	15.00	15
1993 Christmas Sweets (2nd) 126035-9	Closed	1993	12.00	15
1993 Christmas-Go-Round (4th) 126013-8	Closed	1993	14.00	7-15
1993 Ice Pals (2nd) 126006-5	Closed	1993	10.50	7-12
1993 A Little Bit of Christmas (4th) 126007-3	Closed	1993	13.00	8-13
1993 North Pole Parade (2nd) 126011-1	Closed	1993	14.00	10-15
1993 Rodrick & Sam's Winter Fun (2nd) 126008-1	Closed	1993	13.00	13-15
1993 Santa's Roommate (4th) 126039-1	Closed	1993	9.00	9
1993 Tiny Toymaker (1st) 126034-0	Closed	1993	12.50	13-16

1993 A Child's Christmas - Carlton

YEAR ISSUE	EDITION LIMIT	YEAR RETD.	ISSUE PRICE	*QUOTE U.S.$
1993 Baby Magic (Parents-To-Be) 125981-4	Closed	1993	11.00	11
1993 Beary Merry Balloon (Child's 3rd) 125971-7	Closed	1993	10.00	5-10
1993 Christmas Surprise (Child's 4th) 125972-5	Closed	1993	10.00	5-10
1993 Heavenly Love (Godchild) 125982-2	Closed	1993	9.50	10
1993 Precious Heart (Baby's 2nd) 125970-9	Closed	1993	10.00	5-10
1993 Sweet Season (Child's 5th) 125973-3	Closed	1993	10.00	5-10

1993 Baby's First Christmas - Carlton

YEAR ISSUE	EDITION LIMIT	YEAR RETD.	ISSUE PRICE	*QUOTE U.S.$
1993 Baby Kermit's Sleighride (Baby Boy) 125968-7	Closed	1993	10.50	15
1993 Baby Miss Piggy's Christmas Star (Baby Girl) 125966-0	Closed	1993	10.50	15
1993 Christmas Cutie (Granddaughter) 125974-1	Closed	1993	11.00	11
1993 Circle of Love (Child) 125963-6	Closed	1993	11.00	7-11
1993 The Holiday Star 125965-2	Closed	1993	13.00	13
1993 Merry Marcher (Grandson) 125976-8	Closed	1993	11.00	11
1993 Pop-Up Fun! 125964-4	Closed	1993	11.00	11
1993 Rock-A-Bye (Baby Girl) 125967-9	Closed	1993	14.00	14
1993 Santa's Boy (Baby Boy) 125969-5	Closed	1993	13.00	13

1993 First Christmas Together - Carlton

YEAR ISSUE	EDITION LIMIT	YEAR RETD.	ISSUE PRICE	*QUOTE U.S.$
1993 Christmas Cuddles 125995-4	Closed	1993	11.00	11
1993 Just Us 125977-0	Closed	1993	12.00	5-12
1993 Love Birds 125996-2	Closed	1993	13.00	13

1993 For Family - Carlton

YEAR ISSUE	EDITION LIMIT	YEAR RETD.	ISSUE PRICE	*QUOTE U.S.$
1993 Jumbo Wishes (Grandchild) 125977-6	Closed	1993	12.00	9-12
1993 Loving Wishes (Grandmother) 125987-3	Closed	1993	11.00	11
1993 Memories to Keep (Sister) 125985-7	Closed	1993	10.00	10

*Quotes have been rounded up to nearest dollar

YEAR ISSUE	EDITION LIMIT	YEAR RETD.	ISSUE PRICE	*QUOTE U.S.$
1993 Next Stop, North Pole (Son) 125984-9	Closed	1993	11.00	11
1993 Perfect Partners (Parents) 125980-6	Closed	1993	14.00	14
1993 Santa's Wheels (Brother) 125986-5	Closed	1993	10.00	10
1993 Stitched With Love (Mother) 125978-4	Closed	1993	12.00	12
1993 A Token of Love (Daughter) 125983-0	Closed	1993	12.00	12
1993 Trimming The Tree (Grandparents) 125988-1	Closed	1993	9.00	5-10
1993 World's Best Dad (Father) 125979-2	Closed	1993	10.50	11

1993 Lasting Love - Carlton

YEAR ISSUE	EDITION LIMIT	YEAR RETD.	ISSUE PRICE	*QUOTE U.S.$
1993 5 Yrs. Together Christmas Bell 126001-4	Closed	1993	11.00	8-11
1993 10 Yrs. Together Christmas Bell 126002-0	Closed	1993	11.00	8-11
1993 25 Yrs. Together Christmas Bell 126003-0	Closed	1993	11.00	8-11
1993 Cozy Moments 125993-8	Closed	1993	11.00	11
1993 Two Together 125994-6	Closed	1993	13.50	12-14

1993 Licensed Characters - Carlton

YEAR ISSUE	EDITION LIMIT	YEAR RETD.	ISSUE PRICE	*QUOTE U.S.$
1993 Kermit's Christmas 126032-4	Closed	1993	12.00	12
1993 Miss Piggy's Waltz 126031-6	Closed	1993	12.00	15
1993 A Muppet Christmas 126033-2	Closed	1993	6.50	7-20

1993 Lighted Ornaments - Carlton

YEAR ISSUE	EDITION LIMIT	YEAR RETD.	ISSUE PRICE	*QUOTE U.S.$
1993 Christmas Waltz 126063-4	Closed	1993	18.00	18
1993 Up on the Housetop 126061-8	Closed	1993	17.00	17
1993 Warm 'N Toasty 126054-5	Closed	1993	16.00	16

1993 Special People and Moments - Carlton

YEAR ISSUE	EDITION LIMIT	YEAR RETD.	ISSUE PRICE	*QUOTE U.S.$
1993 Festive Lace 125998-9	Closed	1993	8.50	9
1993 Frosty and Friend (Friend) 125999-7	Closed	1993	10.50	11
1993 Happy Home (From Our Home) 125991-1	Closed	1993	10.50	11
1993 Home For Christmas (New Home) 125990-3	Closed	1993	10.00	10
1993 Teacher's Pet (Teacher) 126000-6	Closed	1993	7.50	8

1993 The Merry Mice Collection - Carlton

YEAR ISSUE	EDITION LIMIT	YEAR RETD.	ISSUE PRICE	*QUOTE U.S.$
1993 Ginger 126029-4	Closed	1993	10.00	10
1993 Joy 126028-6	Closed	1993	10.00	7-10
1993 Noelle 126030-8	Closed	1993	10.00	10

1993 Traditional - Carlton

YEAR ISSUE	EDITION LIMIT	YEAR RETD.	ISSUE PRICE	*QUOTE U.S.$
1993 Airmail Delivery 126069-3	Closed	1993	12.50	13
1993 All Decked Out 126015-4	Closed	1993	12.50	13
1993 And Away We Go 126073-1	Closed	1993	12.00	12
1993 Away In A Manger 126111-8	Closed	1993	9.00	9
1993 A Beary Snowy Day 126053-7	Closed	1993	18.00	18
1993 Bundles of Joy 126086-3	Closed	1993	14.50	15
1993 Chef's Delight 126096-0	Closed	1993	11.50	12
1993 A Child's Christmas 126108-8	Closed	1993	11.00	11
1993 The Christmas Dove 126109-6	Closed	1993	10.00	10
1993 Christmas Fantasy 126094-4	Closed	1993	12.00	8-12
1993 Christmas Parade 126018-9	Closed	1993	13.00	13
1993 The Christmas Star 126098-7	Closed	1993	9.50	10
1993 A Christmas To Remember 126024-3	Closed	1993	13.00	9-13
1993 Christmas Wishes 126076-6	Closed	1993	14.00	14
1993 Curious Cutie 126070-7	Closed	1993	12.00	12
1993 December 24th Deadline 126059-6	Closed	1993	13.50	14
1993 Do Not Disturb Til Christmas 126044-8	Closed	1993	11.50	12
1993 Downhill Delight 126046-4	Closed	1993	13.00	13
1993 Father Christmas 1260106-1	Closed	1993	14.00	14
1993 Finishing Touches 126014-6	Closed	1993	13.00	13
1993 Flower Of The Season 126027-8	Closed	1993	11.50	12
1993 A Gift From the Heart 126090-1	Closed	1993	9.50	10
1993 The Gifts of Christmas 126104-5	Closed	1993	9.00	9
1993 Gingerbread Treat 126042-1	Closed	1993	10.50	11
1993 Glad Tidings 126023-5	Closed	1993	12.00	12
1993 Good Catch! 126040-5	Closed	1993	10.00	10
1993 Heart's Delight 126022-7	Closed	1993	8.00	8
1993 Heavenly Peace 136103-7	Closed	1993	11.00	11
1993 Holiday Harmony 126083-9	Closed	1993	14.00	14
1993 Holiday Helpers 126078-2	Closed	1993	14.00	14
1993 A Holiday Hi 126087-1	Closed	1993	12.00	12
1993 Holiday Treat 126089-8	Closed	1993	12.00	10-12
1993 Holiday, Ahoy! 126025-1	Closed	1993	7.50	9
1993 Holly Hippo 126101-0	Closed	1993	11.50	12
1993 Homemade Happiness 126064-2	Closed	1993	12.50	13
1993 Honeybunny Christmas 126085-5	Closed	1993	12.50	13
1993 Hooked A Good One! 126004-9	Closed	1993	11.50	12
1993 It's A Small World 126052-9	Closed	1993	16.00	16
1993 Just A Few Lines 126048-0	Closed	1993	11.00	11
1993 Kitty Caper 126081-2	Closed	1993	11.00	11
1993 Letter To Santa 126045-6	Closed	1993	12.00	12
1993 Li'l Artist 126056-1	Closed	1993	11.50	12
1993 Li'l Chimney Sweep 126100-2	Closed	1993	11.00	11
1993 Li'l Feathered Friend 126020-0	Closed	1993	8.00	9
1993 Made With Love 127072-3	Closed	1993	15.00	15
1993 Magic of the Season 126097-9	Closed	1996	11.50	12
1993 Making Music 126058-8	Closed	1993	11.50	12
1993 Merry Marionettes 126095-2	Closed	1993	15.00	10-15
1993 North Pole Putter 126082-8	Closed	1993	12.00	12
1993 On Top of The Whirl 126067-7	Closed	1993	14.50	15
1993 One Last Touch! 126051-0	Closed	1993	14.00	14
1993 Peppermint Panda 126079-0	Closed	1993	9.50	10
1993 Peppermint Waltz 126047-2	Closed	1993	11.50	12
1993 The Perfect Package 126065-0	Closed	1993	14.00	14
1993 Picture Perfect 126019-7	Closed	1993	8.50	9
1993 Polar Pals 126093-6	Closed	1993	12.50	13
1993 Pom Pom The Clown 126105-3	Closed	1993	10.00	10
1993 Pretty Bubbler 126050-2	Closed	1993	13.00	13
1993 Purr-fect Holidays 126016-2	Closed	1993	12.00	12
1993 Rocking Horse Fun 126017-0	Closed	1993	12.00	7-15
1993 Santa's Helpers 126080-4	Closed	1993	15.00	15
1993 Sewing Circle Sweetie 126102-9	Closed	1993	12.50	13
1993 Special Surprise 126084-7	Closed	1993	13.00	13
1993 Stocking Full of Love 126082-0	Closed	1993	9.00	9
1993 Swinging On A Star 126041-3	Closed	1993	10.00	10
1993 Tiny Toyshop 126071-5	Closed	1993	15.00	15
1993 Visions of Sugarplums 126075-8	Closed	1994	10.00	10
1993 Waiting For Santa 126066-9	Closed	1994	15.00	15
1993 Wake Me When It's Christmas 126049-9	Closed	1993	13.00	13
1993 Warmhearted Holidays 126099-5	Closed	1993	9.50	7-10
1993 Wee Whatnots 126062-6	Closed	1993	17.50	18
1993 Winter Funtime 126077-4	Closed	1993	11.00	11
1993 Winterland Fun 126055-3	Closed	1993	17.00	10-17
1993 Wishes On The Way 126068-5	Closed	1993	8.50	9

1994 Carlton Heirloom Collection Collector's Series - Carlton

YEAR ISSUE	EDITION LIMIT	YEAR RETD.	ISSUE PRICE	*QUOTE U.S.$
1994 Big Fun (1st) ORN001L	Closed	1994	13.50	10-14
1994 Book Of Carols (2nd) ORN004L	Closed	1994	13.50	10-14
1994 Christmas Express Caboose (2nd) ORN010L	Closed	1994	15.00	15
1994 Christmas Express Engine (1st) ORN009L	Closed	1994	15.00	15
1994 Christmas Express Reindeer (4th) ORN011L	Closed	1994	15.00	15
1994 Christmas Express Tanker (5th) ORN012L	Closed	1994	15.00	20
1994 Christmas Go-Round (5th) ORN013L	Closed	1994	15.00	12-15
1994 Christmas Sweets (3rd) ORN006L	Closed	1994	14.50	10-15
1994 Ice Pals (3rd) ORN007L	Closed	1994	12.50	10-13
1994 A Little Bit Of Christmas (5th) ORN014L	Closed	1994	13.50	12-14
1994 Rodrick & Sam's Winter Fun (3rd) ORN008L	Closed	1994	12.50	10-13
1994 Santa's Roommate (5th) ORN015L	Closed	1994	10.50	13
1994 Santa's Toy Shop (1st) ORN003L	Closed	1994	17.00	20
1994 Snug In Their Beds (1st) ORN002L	Closed	1994	16.00	12-16
1994 Tiny Toymaker (2nd) ORN005L	Closed	1994	12.50	13

1994 A Child's Christmas - Carlton

YEAR ISSUE	EDITION LIMIT	YEAR RETD.	ISSUE PRICE	*QUOTE U.S.$
1994 Baby's Second Christmas ORN027L	Closed	1994	10.50	11
1994 Child's Third Christmas ORN028L	Closed	1994	10.50	11
1994 Child's Fourth Christmas ORN029L	Closed	1994	10.50	11
1994 Circle Of Love ORN026L	Closed	1994	11.50	12
1994 Godchild ORN033L	Closed	1994	10.50	11
1994 Parents To-Be ORN032L	Closed	1994	11.50	12

1994 Baby's First Christmas - Carlton

YEAR ISSUE	EDITION LIMIT	YEAR RETD.	ISSUE PRICE	*QUOTE U.S.$
1994 Baby Boy's First Christmas ORN025L	Closed	1994	13.50	14
1994 Baby Girl's First Christmas ORN024L	Closed	1994	13.50	14
1994 Baby's First Christmas ORN022L	Closed	1994	11.50	12
1994 Baby's First Christmas ORN023L	Closed	1994	14.50	15
1994 Granddaughter's First Christmas ORN030L	Closed	1994	11.50	15
1994 Grandson's First Christmas ORN031L	Closed	1994	11.50	15

1994 First Christmas Together - Carlton

YEAR ISSUE	EDITION LIMIT	YEAR RETD.	ISSUE PRICE	*QUOTE U.S.$
1994 First Christmas Together ORN016L	Closed	1994	11.50	12
1994 First Christmas Together ORN017L	Closed	1994	18.00	18
1994 First Christmas Together ORN018L	Closed	1994	13.50	14

1994 For Family - Carlton

YEAR ISSUE	EDITION LIMIT	YEAR RETD.	ISSUE PRICE	*QUOTE U.S.$
1994 Brother ORN040L	Closed	1994	11.50	12
1994 Dad ORN035L	Closed	1994	12.50	13
1994 Daughter ORN037L	Closed	1994	12.50	13
1994 Grandmother ORN041L	Closed	1994	11.50	12
1994 Grandparents ORN042L	Closed	1994	9.50	10
1994 Mother ORN034L	Closed	1994	11.50	15
1994 Parents ORN036L	Closed	1994	14.50	15
1994 Sister ORN039L	Closed	1994	10.50	11
1994 Son ORN038L	Closed	1994	11.50	12

1994 Lasting Love - Carlton

YEAR ISSUE	EDITION LIMIT	YEAR RETD.	ISSUE PRICE	*QUOTE U.S.$
1994 Christmas By The Heartful ORN021L	Closed	1994	12.50	13
1994 Our Christmas Together ORN019L	Closed	1994	14.50	15
1994 Sweetheart ORN020L	Closed	1994	10.50	11

1994 Licensed Characters - Carlton

YEAR ISSUE	EDITION LIMIT	YEAR RETD.	ISSUE PRICE	*QUOTE U.S.$
1994 Care Bears: Tenderheart Bear ORN062L	Closed	1994	10.50	11
1994 Opus N' Bill: O' Opus Tree ORN058L	Closed	1994	12.50	15
1994 Rocky and Bullwinkle: Many Happy Returns ORN061L	Closed	1994	13.50	14-18
1994 Ziggy ORN059L	Closed	1994	12.50	10-13
1994 Ziggy ORN060L	Closed	1994	12.50	13

1994 Special People and Moments - Carlton

YEAR ISSUE	EDITION LIMIT	YEAR RETD.	ISSUE PRICE	*QUOTE U.S.$
1994 Caregiver ORN046L	Closed	1994	11.50	12
1994 Co-Worker ORN045L	Closed	1994	10.50	11
1994 Friend ORN047L	Closed	1994	9.50	10
1994 New Home ORN043L	Closed	1994	12.50	13
1994 Our House To Your House ORN044L	Closed	1994	10.50	11
1994 Sew Much Love ORN087L	Closed	1994	12.50	13
1994 Teacher ORN049L	Closed	1994	7.50	8

1994 Traditional - Carlton

YEAR ISSUE	EDITION LIMIT	YEAR RETD.	ISSUE PRICE	*QUOTE U.S.$
1994 All Decked Out ORN118L	Closed	1994	12.50	13
1994 Artistic Wishes ORN092L	Closed	1994	14.50	10-15
1994 A Basketful Of Goodies ORN077L	Closed	1994	10.50	12
1994 Bears On Parade ORN081L	Closed	1995	18.00	15-18
1994 Beary Merry Wishes ORN075L	Closed	1994	9.50	10
1994 Bunny Delight ORN112L	Closed	1994	15.00	7-15
1994 Candy-Gram ORN103L	Closed	1994	8.50	9
1994 Catch The Christmas Spirit ORN116L	Closed	1994	8.50	9
1994 Changin' For Christmas ORN109L	Closed	1994	13.50	10-14
1994 Chester's Heartfelt Holiday ORN063L	Closed	1994	10.50	11
1995 A Child's Christmas ORN135L	Closed	1994	11.50	12
1994 Christmas Bell ORN127L	Closed	1994	13.50	14
1994 Christmas Catch ORN069L	Closed	1994	11.50	12
1994 Christmas Countdown ORN089L	Closed	1995	14.50	15
1994 Christmas In The Country ORN129L	Closed	1994	8.50	9
1994 Christmas Spin ORN054L	Closed	1994	17.00	17
1994 The Christmas Star ORN076L	Closed	1994	9.50	7-10
1994 Clowning Around ORN090L	Closed	1994	13.50	14
1994 Dashing Through The Snow ORN057L	Closed	1994	16.00	12-16
1994 December 24th Deadline ORN085L	Closed	1994	13.50	14
1994 Downhill Delight ORN070L	Closed	1994	13.50	10-14
1994 Finishing Touches ORN073L	Closed	1994	12.50	13
1994 Folk Angel ORN132l	Closed	1994	7.50	8
1994 Folk Santa ORN071L	Closed	1994	13.50	14
1994 Friends Around The World ORN130L	Closed	1994	7.50	8
1994 Gift Exchange ORN078L	Closed	1994	11.50	8-12
1994 High Flying Fun ORN106L	Closed	1994	12.50	10-13
1994 High Lights ORN107L	Closed	1994	12.50	13
1994 Holiday Gardner ORN088L	Closed	1994	12.50	7
1994 Holiday Sentiment ORN128L	Closed	1994	11.50	12
1994 Holiday Swing Time ORN108L	Closed	1994	13.50	7-14
1994 Holiday Time ORN052L	Closed	1995	16.00	10-16
1994 Homemade Happiness ORN083L	Closed	1994	12.50	13
1994 Hook, Line and Singers ORN067L	Closed	1995	13.50	8-14
1994 Hoppy Holidays ORN111L	Closed	1994	13.50	14
1994 It's A Small World ORN100L	Closed	1994	16.00	18
1994 Jogging Santa ORN068L	Closed	1995	11.50	12
1994 Juggling Jester ORN050L	Closed	1994	13.50	14
1994 Jumbo Wishes ORN117L	Closed	1994	12.50	13
1994 L'il Artist ORN080L	Closed	1994	11.50	12
1994 Lion & Lamb ORN133L	Closed	1994	13.50	14
1994 Madonna Child ORN131L	Closed	1994	12.50	13
1994 Magic Of The Season ORN124L	Closed	1994	12.50	13
1994 Merry Old Santa ORN074L	Closed	1994	14.50	15
1994 Moo-ey Christmas ORN102L	Closed	1994	8.50	9
1994 Mouse With Gifts ORN086L	Closed	1994	11.50	10-12
1994 Music Box Dancers ORN053L	Closed	1994	18.00	18
1994 Nature's Friends ORN125L	Closed	1994	9.50	10
1994 Noah's Ark ORN134L	Closed	1994	13.50	15
1994 North Pole Pals ORN122L	Closed	1994	14.50	12-15
1994 Off For A Spin ORN091L	Closed	1994	14.50	15
1994 On Top Of The Whirl ORN097L	Closed	1994	14.50	15
1994 One Last Touch ORN096L	Closed	1994	14.50	15
1994 Paddling Pals ORN064L	Closed	1994	11.50	8-12
1994 Peppermint Waltz ORN119L	Closed	1994	11.50	10-12
1994 The Perfect Package ORN098L	Closed	1994	14.50	15
1994 Picture Perfect ORN126L	Closed	1994	7.50	8
1994 Playin A Holiday Tune ORN110L	Closed	1995	13.50	9-14
1994 The Polar Bear Club ORN079L	Closed	1994	13.50	10-14
1994 Pretty Bubbler ORN084L	Closed	1994	13.50	14
1994 Puffin ORN104L	Closed	1994	11.50	8-12
1994 Purr-fect Holidays ORN115L	Closed	1994	12.50	10-13
1994 Rocking Horse Fun ORN123L	Closed	1994	12.50	10-13
1994 Santa's Hotline ORN114L	Closed	1995	13.50	14
1994 Santa-In-The-Box ORN072L	Closed	1994	15.00	15
1994 Servin' Up Christmas Cheer ORN066L	Closed	1994	10.50	8-11
1994 Soccer Star ORN065L	Closed	1995	9.50	8-10
1994 St. Bernard ORN105L	Closed	1994	8.50	9
1994 Sugar Cone Castle ORN120L	Closed	1994	15.00	15
1994 Surprise! ORN049L	Closed	1994	12.50	13
1994 Sweet Season ORN082L	Closed	1994	10.50	11
1994 Swinging On A Star ORN094L	Closed	1994	10.50	11
1994 Twinkle, Twinkle Christmas Stars ORN121L	Closed	1995	13.50	15
1994 Twirling Fun ORN051L	Closed	1995	18.00	10-18
1994 Up On The Housetop ORN055L	Closed	1994	17.00	17
1994 Visions Of Sugarplums ORN095L	Closed	1994	10.50	11
1994 Waiting For Santa ORN099L	Closed	1994	15.00	15
1994 Warm 'N Toasty ORN056L	Closed	1994	16.00	12-16
1994 Wee Whatnots ORN101L	Closed	1994	17.00	17
1994 Winterland Fun (Snowdome) ORN113L	Closed	1994	17.00	12-17
1994 Yuletide News ORN093L	Closed	1994	15.00	15

1995 Carlton Heirloom Collection Collector's Series - Carlton

YEAR ISSUE	EDITION LIMIT	YEAR RETD.	ISSUE PRICE	*QUOTE U.S.$
1995 Book of Carols (3rd) ORN004M	Closed	1995	13.75	11-14
1995 Christmas Express Handcar (6th) ORN010M	Closed	1995	15.75	18
1995 Christmas Go Round (6th) ORN013M	Closed	1995	15.75	16
1995 Christmas Sweets (4th) ORN006M	Closed	1995	14.75	10-15

*Quotes have been rounded up to nearest dollar

YEAR ISSUE	EDITION LIMIT	YEAR RETD.	ISSUE PRICE	*QUOTE U.S.$
1995 Christmas Town Lane (1st) ORN011M	Closed	1995	14.75	20
1995 Holiday Garden (1st) ORN125M	Closed	1995	14.75	15-20
1995 Holiday Town (2nd) ORN003M	Closed	1995	17.75	18
1995 Ice Pals (4th) ORN007M	Closed	1995	12.75	10-13
1995 A Little Bit of Christmas (6th) ORNO14M	Closed	1995	13.75	14
1995 Pinecone Cottage (2nd) ORNO02M	Closed	1995	16.75	17
1995 Rodrick and Sam's Winter Fun (4th) ORNO08M	Closed	1995	12.75	8-13
1995 Roommate Bear (6th) ORN009M	Closed	1995	12.75	10-13
1995 Santa's Music Makers (2nd) ORN001M	Closed	1995	13.75	15
1995 Tiny Toymaker (3rd) ORN005M	Closed	1995	12.75	10-13
1995 Year By Year (1st) ORN126M	Closed	1995	12.75	13

1995 A Child's Christmas - Carlton

YEAR ISSUE	EDITION LIMIT	YEAR RETD.	ISSUE PRICE	*QUOTE U.S.$
1995 Parents To Be ORN032M	Closed	1995	11.75	12
1995 Visit With Santa Photoholder ORN132M	Closed	1995	9.75	10
1995 Baby Photoholder ORN026M	Closed	1995	9.75	7-10
1995 Baby's Second Christmas ORN027M	Closed	1995	10.75	12
1995 Child's Third Christmas ORN028M	Closed	1995	11.75	12
1995 Child's Fourth Christmas ORN029M	Closed	1995	10.75	15
1995 Godchild ORN033M	Closed	1995	10.75	12
1995 Godchild ORN071M	Closed	1995	12.75	13
1995 Godmother ORN015M	Closed	1995	11.75	12
1995 Grandaughter's First Christmas ORN030M	Closed	1995	11.75	12
1995 Grandson's First Christmas ORN031M	Closed	1995	11.75	12

1995 Baby's First Christmas - Carlton

YEAR ISSUE	EDITION LIMIT	YEAR RETD.	ISSUE PRICE	*QUOTE U.S.$
1995 Baby Boy's First Christmas ORN025M	Closed	1995	13.75	15
1995 Baby Boy's First Christmas ORN131M	Closed	1995	10.75	12
1995 Baby Girl's First Christmas ORN024M	Closed	1995	14.75	15
1995 Baby Girl's First Christmas ORN130M	Closed	1995	10.75	12
1995 Baby's First Christmas ORN022M	Closed	1995	11.75	12-20
1995 Baby's First Christmas ORN023M	Closed	1995	14.75	15

1995 Favorite Pastimes - Carlton

YEAR ISSUE	EDITION LIMIT	YEAR RETD.	ISSUE PRICE	*QUOTE U.S.$
1995 Artistic Wishes ORN092M	Closed	1995	14.75	15
1995 Christmas Kickoff ORN059M	Closed	1995	11.75	12
1995 Cyclin' Santa ORN062M	Closed	1995	14.75	15
1995 Gift Exchange ORN078M	Closed	1995	11.75	8-12
1995 Holiday Gardener ORN088M	Closed	1995	12.75	13
1995 Holiday Hoop-la ORN063M	Closed	1995	13.75	14
1995 Homerun Holiday ORN058M	Closed	1995	12.75	13
1995 Hook, Line and Singers ORN067M	Closed	1995	13.75	14
1995 Hot Doggin' Holidays ORN060M	Closed	1995	11.75	12
1995 Jogging Santa ORN068M	Closed	1995	11.75	12
1995 Just "Fore" Christmas ORN061M	Closed	1995	13.75	14
1995 Oh, Sew Merry! ORN064M	Closed	1995	13.75	10-14
1995 Servin' Up Christmas Cheer ORN066M	Closed	1995	10.75	8-11
1995 Soccer Sensation ORN065M	Closed	1995	9.75	10
1995 Ten-Pin Christmas ORN066M	Closed	1995	10.75	11

1995 First Christmas Together - Carlton

YEAR ISSUE	EDITION LIMIT	YEAR RETD.	ISSUE PRICE	*QUOTE U.S.$
1995 First Christmas Together ORN012M	Closed	1995	13.75	14
1995 First Christmas Together ORN016M	Closed	1995	11.75	12
1995 First Christmas Together ORN017M	Closed	1995	13.75	14
1995 First Christmas Together ORN018M	Closed	1995	14.75	15

1995 For Family - Carlton

YEAR ISSUE	EDITION LIMIT	YEAR RETD.	ISSUE PRICE	*QUOTE U.S.$
1995 Brother ORN040M	Closed	1995	16.75	17
1995 Dad ORN035M	Closed	1995	14.75	15
1995 Daughter ORN037M	Closed	1995	13.75	14
1995 Grandmother ORN041M	Closed	1995	10.75	11
1995 Grandparents ORN042M	Closed	1995	13.75	14
1995 Mother ORN034M	Closed	1995	14.75	15
1995 Our Family Photoholder ORN135M	Closed	1995	9.75	10
1995 Parents ORN036M	Closed	1995	15.75	16
1995 Sister ORN039M	Closed	1995	11.75	12
1995 Sister To Sister ORN133M	Closed	1995	13.75	14
1995 Son ORN038M	Closed	1995	11.75	12
1995 To Grandma Photoholder ORN134M	Closed	1995	9.75	10

1995 Lasting Love - Carlton

YEAR ISSUE	EDITION LIMIT	YEAR RETD.	ISSUE PRICE	*QUOTE U.S.$
1995 25th Wedding Anniversary ORN056M	Closed	1995	13.75	14
1995 Love at Christmas ORN021M	Closed	1995	10.75	11
1995 Our Christmas Together ORN019M	Closed	1995	11.75	12
1995 Our House To Your House ORN044M	Closed	1995	13.75	10-14
1995 Sweetheart ORN020M	Closed	1995	12.75	13

1995 Licensed Characters - Carlton

YEAR ISSUE	EDITION LIMIT	YEAR RETD.	ISSUE PRICE	*QUOTE U.S.$
1995 Care Bears: Bedtime Bear ORN107M	Closed	1995	11.75	12
1995 Elvis: Blue Christmas (1st) ORN073M	Closed	1995	25.00	125-150
1995 Hershey's Express ORN098M	Closed	1995	17.75	12-18
1995 Opus N' bill: Flashin' Through the Snow! ORN104M	Closed	1995	12.75	13
1995 Pillsbury: Poppin' Fresh Christmas ORN097M	Closed	1995	13.75	14
1995 Rocky and Bullwinkle: Merry Fishmas ORN096M	Closed	1995	15.75	16
1995 Snow Sculpturing ORN105M	Closed	1995	12.75	13-18
1995 Volkswagon: On Our Merry Way! ORN094M	Closed	1995	21.00	18-21
1995 Ziggy's Merry Tree-Some ORN095M	Closed	1995	13.75	10-14

1995 Light, Motion, Music - Carlton

YEAR ISSUE	EDITION LIMIT	YEAR RETD.	ISSUE PRICE	*QUOTE U.S.$
1995 All Around The Workshop ORN074M	Closed	1995	34.00	34
1995 A Christmas Celebration ORN084M	Closed	1995	16.75	17
1995 Christmas is Coming ORN076M	Closed	1995	32.00	30
1995 A Feeling of Christmas ORN075M	Closed	1995	34.00	34
1995 Get Your Pup-Corn Here! ORN083M	Closed	1996	21.00	16-21
1995 Greetings To You ORN070M	Closed	1995	28.00	25-28
1995 Jukebox Jingles ORN080M	Closed	1995	23.00	25
1995 Merry Matinee ORN082M	Closed	1995	21.00	18-21

1995 Special People and Moments - Carlton

YEAR ISSUE	EDITION LIMIT	YEAR RETD.	ISSUE PRICE	*QUOTE U.S.$
1995 Caregiver ORN046M	Closed	1995	8.75	9
1995 Friend ORN047M	Closed	1995	10.75	11
1995 New Home ORN043M	Closed	1995	12.75	10-13
1995 New Home ORN057M	Closed	1995	12.75	13
1995 Pet Photoholder ORN055M	Closed	1995	9.75	10
1995 Teacher ORN048M	Closed	1995	8.75	9
1995 Workplace Wishes ORN045M	Closed	1995	12.75	13

1995 Traditional - Carlton

YEAR ISSUE	EDITION LIMIT	YEAR RETD.	ISSUE PRICE	*QUOTE U.S.$
1995 Airmail Delivery ORN100M	Closed	1995	13.75	10-18
1995 Away In A Manger ORN093M	Closed	1995	11.75	12
1995 Bears on Parade ORN081M	Closed	1995	18.75	19
1995 Beary Merry Treasures ORN086M	Closed	1995	17.75	18
1995 Bunny Delight ORN112M	Closed	1995	15.75	16
1995 Changin' for Christmas ORN109M	Closed	1995	13.75	15
1995 Christmas Countdown ORN089M	Closed	1996	14.75	15
1995 Christmas Poinsettia ORN079M	Closed	1995	10.75	11
1995 Christmas Spin ORN054M	Closed	1995	17.75	18
1995 The Christmas Star ORN118M	Closed	1995	9.75	12
1995 Clowning Around ORN090M	Closed	1995	13.75	14
1995 Dancin' Prancin' Bear ORN116M	Closed	1995	8.75	9
1995 Danglin' Darlin's ORN129M	Closed	1995	13.75	14
1995 Do Not Disturb 'Til Christmas ORN049M	Closed	1995	11.75	12
1995 The Heart of Christmas ORN102M	Closed	1995	12.75	13
1995 Holiday Harmony ORN113M	Closed	1995	17.75	8-18
1995 Holiday Time ORN052M	Closed	1995	16.75	17
1995 Hoppy Holidays ORN111M	Closed	1995	13.75	14
1995 Juggling Jester ORN050M	Closed	1995	13.75	14
1995 Li'l Feathered Friend ORN117M	Closed	1995	8.75	8-17
1995 Magic of the Season ORN124M	Closed	1995	12.75	12-15
1995 Merry Meister ORN087M	Closed	1995	14.75	15-19
1995 Music Box Dancers ORN053M	Closed	1995	18.75	19
1995 North Pole Pals ORN122M	Closed	1995	14.75	8-14
1995 Off For A Spin ORN091M	Closed	1995	14.75	15
1995 Playin' A Holiday Tune ORN110M	Closed	1995	13.75	14
1995 Purr-Fect Holidays ORN115M	Closed	1995	12.75	13
1995 Rocking Horse Fun ORN123M	Closed	1995	12.75	10-13
1995 Santa's Hotline ORN114M	Closed	1995	14.75	15
1995 Santa's On His Way! ORN127M	Closed	1995	14.75	15-25
1995 Santa-In-The-Box ORN072M	Closed	1995	15.75	16
1995 A Sleighful Of Joys ORN128M	Closed	1995	15.75	16
1995 Snow Bunnies ORN103M	Closed	1995	14.75	15
1995 St. Bernard ORN119M	Closed	1995	8.75	9
1995 Stocking Full Of Fun ORN099M	Closed	1995	10.75	11
1995 Sugar Cone Castle ORN120M	Closed	1995	15.75	18
1995 Swinging Into Christmas ORN085M	Closed	1995	17.75	17-18
1995 Twinkle, Twinkle Christmas Star ORN121M	Closed	1995	13.75	14
1995 Twirling Fun ORN051M	Closed	1995	18.75	19
1995 Wake Me When It's Christmas ORN106M	Closed	1995	13.75	10-14
1995 Westward Ho Holidays ORN108M	Closed	1995	13.75	10-18
1995 The Wisemen's Journey ORN101M	Closed	1995	10.75	11

1996 Premier Event Ornaments - Carlton

YEAR ISSUE	EDITION LIMIT	YEAR RETD.	ISSUE PRICE	*QUOTE U.S.$
1996 Stirring Up Some Christmas Magic CXOR-500T	Closed	1996	9.95	10

1996 Carlton Heirloom Collection Collector's Series - Carlton

YEAR ISSUE	EDITION LIMIT	YEAR RETD.	ISSUE PRICE	*QUOTE U.S.$
1996 Book of Carols (4th) CXOR-004T	Closed	1996	17.95	15-18
1996 Christmas Go Round (7th) CXOR-011T	Closed	1996	15.95	16
1996 Christmas Sweets (5th) CXOR-005T	Closed	1996	14.95	15
1996 Christmas Town Inn (2nd) CXOR-009T	Closed	1996	14.95	15-18
1996 Holiday Garden (2nd) CXOR-010T	Closed	1996	14.95	15
1996 Holiday Town (3rd) CXOR-003T	Closed	1996	18.95	19
1996 Ice Pals (5th) CXOR-006T	Closed	1996	12.95	13
1996 Jolly Old St. Nick (1st) CXOR-015T	Closed	1996	15.95	25
1996 Joy Is In The Air (1st) CXOR-007T	Closed	1996	16.95	17
1996 Merry Mischief (1st) CXOR-012T	Closed	1996	14.95	15
1996 O Holy Night (1st) CXOR-014T	Closed	1996	17.95	18
1996 Pinecone Cottage (3rd) CXOR-002T	Closed	1996	17.95	20
1996 Santa's Music Makers (3rd) CXOR-001T	Closed	1996	13.95	18-20
1996 Wonderland Express (1st) CXOR-008T	Closed	1996	15.95	16
1996 Year By Year (2nd) CXOR-013T	Closed	1996	12.95	13

1996 A Child's Christmas - Carlton

YEAR ISSUE	EDITION LIMIT	YEAR RETD.	ISSUE PRICE	*QUOTE U.S.$
1996 Baby Photo Holder CXOR-059T	Closed	1996	9.95	10
1996 Baby's Second Christmas CXOR-036T	Closed	1996	11.95	12
1996 Child's Third Christmas CXOR-037T	Closed	1996	11.95	12
1996 Child's Fourth Christmas CXOR-038T	Closed	1996	11.95	12
1996 Godchild CXOR-039T	Closed	1996	10.95	11
1996 Godchild CXOR-040T	Closed	1996	13.95	14
1996 Little Treasures-Boy (personalized) CXOR-132T	Closed	1996	11.95	12
1996 Little Treasures-Girl (personalized) CXOR-131T	Closed	1996	11.95	12

1996 Baby's First Christmas - Carlton

YEAR ISSUE	EDITION LIMIT	YEAR RETD.	ISSUE PRICE	*QUOTE U.S.$
1996 Baby Boy's First Christmas CXOR-032T	Closed	1996	13.95	14
1996 Baby Girl's First Christmas CXOR-030T	Closed	1996	13.95	14
1996 Baby's First Christmas CXOR-028T	Closed	1996	14.95	15
1996 Baby's First Christmas CXOR-133T	Closed	1996	15.95	16
1996 Bainbridge Bear Baby Boy's First Christmas CXOR-033T	Closed	1996	11.95	12
1996 Bainbridge Bear Baby Girl's First Christmas CXOR-031T	Closed	1996	11.95	12
1996 Grandaughter's First Christmas CXOR-034T	Closed	1996	10.95	11
1996 Grandson's First Christmas CXOR-035T	Closed	1996	10.95	11

1996 Favorite Pastimes - Carlton

YEAR ISSUE	EDITION LIMIT	YEAR RETD.	ISSUE PRICE	*QUOTE U.S.$
1996 Christmas Kickoff CXOR-113T	Closed	1996	11.95	13
1996 Clubhouse Christmas CXOR-129T	Closed	1996	13.95	16
1996 Counting The Days 'Til Christmas CXOR-118T	Closed	1996	10.95	11-20
1996 Cyclin' Santa CXOR-114T	Closed	1996	14.95	15-18
1996 Goal For It! CXOR-116T	Closed	1996	12.95	13
1996 Holiday Debut CXOR-115T	Closed	1996	9.95	10-15
1996 Holiday Hoopla CXOR-119T	Closed	1996	13.95	14
1996 Homerun Holiday CXOR-112T	Closed	1996	12.95	15
1996 Ten-Pin Christmas CXOR-111T	Closed	1996	10.95	12
1996 That's The Spirit! CXOR-117T	Closed	1996	11.95	12

1996 First Christmas Together - Carlton

YEAR ISSUE	EDITION LIMIT	YEAR RETD.	ISSUE PRICE	*QUOTE U.S.$
1996 First Christmas Together CXOR-019T	Closed	1996	11.95	12
1996 First Christmas Together CXOR-020T	Closed	1996	18.95	19
1996 First Christmas Together CXOR-021T	Closed	1996	14.95	15
1996 First Christmas Together CXOR-022T	Closed	1996	12.95	13

1996 For Family - Carlton

YEAR ISSUE	EDITION LIMIT	YEAR RETD.	ISSUE PRICE	*QUOTE U.S.$
1996 Brother CXOR-049T	Closed	1996	12.95	13
1996 Dad CXOR-043T	Closed	1996	13.95	14
1996 Daughter CXOR-045T	Closed	1996	13.95	14
1996 Godmother CXOR-052T	Closed	1996	14.95	15
1996 Grandmother CXOR-050T	Closed	1996	14.95	15
1996 Grandparents CXOR-051T	Closed	1996	14.95	15
1996 Mother CXOR-042T	Closed	1996	13.95	14
1996 Our Family Photo Holder CXOR-061T	Closed	1996	9.95	10
1996 Parents CXOR-044T	Closed	1996	14.95	15
1996 Parents To Be CXOR-041T	Closed	1996	12.95	13
1996 Sister CXOR-047T	Closed	1996	13.95	14
1996 Sister To Sister CXOR-048T	Closed	1996	14.95	15
1996 Son CXOR-046T	Closed	1996	14.95	15
1996 To Grandma Photo Holder CXOR-060T	Closed	1996	9.95	10

1996 Holiday Collection-Angels - Carlton

YEAR ISSUE	EDITION LIMIT	YEAR RETD.	ISSUE PRICE	*QUOTE U.S.$
1996 Song of Hope (2nd) CXOR-097T	Closed	1996	12.95	20
1996 Song of Joy (3rd) CXOR-098T	Closed	1996	12.95	20
1996 Song of Peace (1st) CXOR-096T	Closed	1996	12.95	13-20

1996 Holiday Collection-Antique Toys - Carlton

YEAR ISSUE	EDITION LIMIT	YEAR RETD.	ISSUE PRICE	*QUOTE U.S.$
1996 Christmas Tidings (2nd) CXOR-100T	Closed	1996	13.95	18
1996 Holiday Fun (3rd) CXOR-101T	Closed	1996	13.95	18
1996 Holiday Recollections (1st) CXOR-099T	Closed	1996	13.95	20

1996 Holiday Collection-Candy Cane Buildings - Carlton

YEAR ISSUE	EDITION LIMIT	YEAR RETD.	ISSUE PRICE	*QUOTE U.S.$
1996 Candy Cane Cabin (1st) CXOR-108T	Closed	1996	13.95	15
1996 Gingerbread Farm (3rd) CXOR-110T	Closed	1996	13.95	15
1996 Sugarplum Chapel (2nd) CXOR-109T	Closed	1996	13.95	15

1996 Holiday Collection-Farm Animals - Carlton

YEAR ISSUE	EDITION LIMIT	YEAR RETD.	ISSUE PRICE	*QUOTE U.S.$
1996 Country Cow (1st) CXOR-105T	Closed	1996	11.95	15
1996 Perky Pig (3rd) CXOR-106T	Closed	1996	11.95	15
1996 Prancing Pony (3rd) CXOR-107T	Closed	1996	11.95	15

1996 Holiday Collection-Whimsical - Carlton

YEAR ISSUE	EDITION LIMIT	YEAR RETD.	ISSUE PRICE	*QUOTE U.S.$
1996 Joy (1st) CXOR-102T	Closed	1996	11.95	12
1996 Love (3rd) CXOR-104T	Closed	1996	11.95	12
1996 Merry (2nd) CXOR-103T	Closed	1996	11.95	12

1996 Lasting Love - Carlton

YEAR ISSUE	EDITION LIMIT	YEAR RETD.	ISSUE PRICE	*QUOTE U.S.$
1996 25th Wedding Anniversary CXOR-027T	Closed	1996	14.95	15
1996 Our Christmas Together CXOR-025T	Closed	1996	12.95	13

*Quotes have been rounded up to nearest dollar

YEAR ISSUE	EDITION LIMIT	YEAR RETD.	ISSUE PRICE	*QUOTE U.S.$
1996 Our Christmas Together CXOR-026T	Closed	1996	13.95	15
1996 Sweetheart CXOR-023T	Closed	1996	14.95	15
1996 Sweetheart CXOR-130T	Closed	1996	16.95	17

1996 Licensed Characters - Carlton

YEAR ISSUE	EDITION LIMIT	YEAR RETD.	ISSUE PRICE	*QUOTE U.S.$
1996 Campbell's: A Hearty Christmas CXOR-09OT	Closed	1996	17.95	20
1996 Care Bears: Tenderheart Bear CXOR-088T	Closed	1996	11.95	12
1996 Elvis: (2nd) CXOR-093T	Closed	1996	30.00	40-85
1996 Hershey's: Hugs 'N Kisses CXOR-084T	Closed	1996	15.95	20
1996 Marilyn CXOR-094T	Closed	1996	17.95	25
1996 Nickelodeon: Happy, Happy! Joy, Joy! CXOR-091T	Closed	1996	15.95	16
1996 Nickelodeon: Tommy's Christmas Adventure CXOR-092T	Closed	1996	13.95	14-20
1996 Nintendo: High Powered Holidays! CXOR-095T	Closed	1996	16.95	15-17
1996 Opus N' bill: A Brief Message CXOR-086T	Closed	1996	12.95	15
1996 Opus n' bill: Happy Holidaze! CXOR-085T	Closed	1996	15.95	16
1996 Paddington Bear: Gliding Into Christmas CXOR-089T	Closed	1996	14.95	15
1996 Play-Doh: Holiday Surprise! CXOR-08IT	Closed	1996	14.95	15-20
1996 Radio Flyer: Puppy Pals CXOR-083T	Closed	1996	14.95	17
1996 Rocky and Bullwinkle Another Magical Season CXOR-087T	Closed	1996	15.95	16
1996 Volkswagon North Pole or Bust CXOR-082T	Closed	1996	16.95	17

1996 Light, Motion, Music - Carlton

YEAR ISSUE	EDITION LIMIT	YEAR RETD.	ISSUE PRICE	*QUOTE U.S.$
1996 All Around The Workshop CXOR-074T	Closed	1996	34.00	34
1996 Christmas All Around CXOR-072T	Closed	1996	32.00	32
1996 Christmas Celebration CXOR-080T	Closed	1996	16.95	17
1996 Cozy Little Christmas CXOR-079T	Closed	1996	15.95	16
1996 Dancing 'Til Daylight CXOT-073T	Closed	1996	32.00	32
1996 Finishing Touches CXOR-071T	Closed	1996	28.00	25-28
1996 Get Your Pup-Corn Here! CXOR-078T	Closed	1996	21.00	21
1996 Greetings To You CXOR-127T	Closed	1996	28.00	28
1996 Holiday Waltz CXOR-070T	Closed	1996	34.00	34
1996 It's Showtime! CXOR-077T	Closed	1996	21.00	21
1996 Jukebox Jingles CXOR-067T	Closed	1996	23.95	24
1996 Nonstop Wishes CXOR-069T	Closed	1996	28.00	28
1996 Santa's Little Friends CXOR-068T	Closed	1996	15.95	20
1996 Up On The Housetop CXOR-066T	Closed	1996	17.95	18
1996 You're A Winner CXOR-076T	Closed	1996	16.95	17

1996 Special People and Moments - Carlton

YEAR ISSUE	EDITION LIMIT	YEAR RETD.	ISSUE PRICE	*QUOTE U.S.$
1996 Caregiver CXOR-053T	Closed	1996	10.95	11
1996 Friend CXOR-054T	Closed	1996	9.95	10
1996 Friend CXOR-055T	Closed	1996	10.95	11
1996 Merry Birthday CXOR-128T	Closed	1997	12.95	13-15
1996 New Home CXOR-016T	Closed	1996	12.95	13
1996 New Home CXOR-017T	Closed	1996	13.95	14
1996 Our House to Your House CXOR-018T	Closed	1996	13.95	14
1996 Santa's Network CXOR-058T	Closed	1996	13.95	14
1996 Teacher CXOR-056T	Closed	1996	9.95	10
1996 Teacher CXOR-057T	Closed	1996	11.95	12
1996 Tender Loving Care CXOR-064T	Closed	1996	11.95	12
1996 To The Rescue CXOR-065T	Closed	1996	12.95	13

1996 Traditional - Carlton

YEAR ISSUE	EDITION LIMIT	YEAR RETD.	ISSUE PRICE	*QUOTE U.S.$
1996 A Child's Christmas CXOR-124T	Closed	1996	13.95	14
1996 Christmas Countdown CXOR-024T	Closed	1996	14.95	15
1996 Do Not Disturd 'Til Christmas CXOR-121T	Closed	1996	11.95	12
1996 Friends Around The World CXOR-062T	Closed	1996	11.95	12
1996 High Lights CXOR-120T	Closed	1996	13.95	15
1996 A Holiday Hello CXOR-075T	Closed	1996	15.95	16
1996 Holiday Sentiment CXOR-029T	Closed	1996	11.95	12
1996 Little Cup of Dreams CXOR-135T	Closed	1996	14.95	15
1996 Magic Of The Season CXOR-123T	Closed	1996	12.95	15
1996 Noah's Ark CXOR-125T	Closed	1996	13.95	15
1996 Pet Photo Holder CXOR-063T	Closed	1996	9.95	10
1996 Purr-Fect Holidays CXOR-122T	Closed	1996	12.95	13
1996 Rocking Horse Fun CXOR-126T	Closed	1996	13.95	14
1996 Season of Giving CXOR-134T	Closed	1996	14.95	15

1997 Carlton Heirloom Collection Collector's Club - Carlton

YEAR ISSUE	EDITION LIMIT	YEAR RETD.	ISSUE PRICE	*QUOTE U.S.$
1997 Ho-Ho-Hold On! CXOR201W	Yr.Iss.	1997	Gift	N/A
1997 Heavenly Handiwork CXOR202W	Yr.Iss.	1997	14.95	15

1997 Premier Event Ornaments - Carlton

YEAR ISSUE	EDITION LIMIT	YEAR RETD.	ISSUE PRICE	*QUOTE U.S.$
1997 Carousel Dreams CXOR-174W	Yr.Iss.	1997	9.95	10

1997 Carlton Heirloom Collection Collector's Series - Carlton

YEAR ISSUE	EDITION LIMIT	YEAR RETD.	ISSUE PRICE	*QUOTE U.S.$
1997 Book of Carols (5th) CXOR-010W	Closed	1997	13.95	15
1997 Christmas Go Round (8th) CXOR-011W	Closed	1997	15.95	16
1997 Christmas Sweets (6th) CXOR-005W	Closed	1997	14.95	15
1997 Christmas Town Lane (3rd) CXOR-009W	Closed	1997	14.95	15
1997 Holiday Town (4th) CXOR-003W	Closed	1997	18.95	19
1997 Ice Pals (6th) CXOR-006W	Closed	1997	12.95	13
1997 Jolly Old St. Nick (2nd) CXOR-015W	Closed	1997	15.95	16
1997 Joy Is In The Air (2nd) CXOR-007W	Closed	1997	17.95	18
1997 Merry Mischief (2nd) CXOR-012W	Closed	1997	14.95	15
1997 Merry Mobiles (1st) CXOR-002W	Closed	1997	13.95	14
1997 O Holy Night (2nd) CXOR-014W	Closed	1997	18.95	19
1997 Santa's Music Makers (4th) CXOR-001W	Closed	1997	14.95	15
1997 Wonderland Express (1st) CXOR-008W	Closed	1997	15.95	16
1997 Wonderland Express (2nd) CXOR-004W	Closed	1997	13.95	14-35
1997 Year By Year (3rd) CXOR-013W	Closed	1997	12.95	13

1997 A Child's Christmas - Carlton

YEAR ISSUE	EDITION LIMIT	YEAR RETD.	ISSUE PRICE	*QUOTE U.S.$
1997 Baby Photo Holder CXOR-041W	Closed	1997	13.95	14
1997 Baby's Second Christmas CXOR-036W	Open		12.95	13
1997 Child's Third Christmas CXOR-037W	Open		12.95	13
1997 Child's Fourth Christmas CXOR-038W	Open		12.95	13
1997 Godchild CXOR-039W	Closed	1997	11.95	12
1997 Godchild CXOR-040W	Closed	1997	13.95	14
1997 Jumpin' Jolly Holidays-Boy CXOR-043W	Closed	1997	12.95	13
1997 Jumpin' Jolly Holidays-Girl CXOR-042W	Closed	1997	12.95	13

1997 Baby's First Christmas - Carlton

YEAR ISSUE	EDITION LIMIT	YEAR RETD.	ISSUE PRICE	*QUOTE U.S.$
1997 Baby Boy's First Christmas CXOR-032W	Closed	1997	15.95	16
1997 Baby Boy's First Christmas CXOR-033W	Open		14.95	15
1997 Baby Girl's First Christmas CXOR-030W	Closed	1997	15.95	16
1997 Baby Girl's First Christmas CXOR-031W	Open		14.95	15
1997 Baby's First Christmas CXOR-028W	Closed	1997	14.95	15
1997 Granddaughter's First Christmas CXOR-034W	Closed	1997	11.95	12
1997 Grandson's First Christmas CXOR-035W	Closed	1997	11.95	12

1997 Favorite Pastimes - Carlton

YEAR ISSUE	EDITION LIMIT	YEAR RETD.	ISSUE PRICE	*QUOTE U.S.$
1997 Dec. 26th CXOR-120W	Closed	1997	14.95	15
1997 From Heaven's Garden CXOR-121W	Closed	1997	12.95	13
1997 Fun To Spare CXOR-111W	Closed	1997	11.95	12
1997 Goal For It! CXOR-116W	Closed	1997	12.95	13
1997 Gridiron Greetings CXOR-113W	Closed	1997	12.95	13
1997 Hooked On The Holidays CXOR-114W	Closed	1997	14.95	15
1997 Hoopy Holiday CXOR-119W	Closed	1997	11.95	12
1997 Sew Very Special CXOR-118W	Closed	1997	14.95	15
1997 Star Player CXOR-112W	Closed	1997	12.95	13
1997 That's The Spirit! CXOR-117W	Closed	1997	11.95	12
1997 Twinkletoes CXOR-115W	Closed	1997	9.95	10

1997 First Christmas Together - Carlton

YEAR ISSUE	EDITION LIMIT	YEAR RETD.	ISSUE PRICE	*QUOTE U.S.$
1997 First Christmas Together CXOR-019W	Closed	1997	17.95	18
1997 First Christmas Together CXOR-020W	Closed	1997	16.95	17
1997 First Christmas Together CXOR-021W	Closed	1997	10.95	11
1997 First Christmas Together CXOR-022W	Closed	1997	13.95	14

1997 For Family - Carlton

YEAR ISSUE	EDITION LIMIT	YEAR RETD.	ISSUE PRICE	*QUOTE U.S.$
1997 Brother CXOR-053W	Closed	1997	14.95	15
1997 Dad CXOR-047W	Closed	1997	12.95	13
1997 Daughter CXOR-049W	Closed	1997	12.95	13
1997 Godmother CXOR-056W	Closed	1997	11.95	12
1997 Grandmother CXOR-054W	Closed	1997	14.95	15
1997 Grandparents CXOR-055W	Closed	1997	15.95	16
1997 Mother CXOR-046W	Closed	1997	12.95	13
1997 Our Family Photo Holder CXOR-058W	Closed	1997	9.95	10
1997 Parents CXOR-048W	Closed	1997	13.95	14
1997 Parents-To-Be CXOR-044W	Closed	1997	13.95	14
1997 Parents-To-Be CXOR-045W	Closed	1997	12.95	13
1997 Sister CXOR-051W	Closed	1997	13.95	14
1997 Sister-To-Sister CXOR-052W	Closed	1997	14.95	15
1997 Son CXOR-050W	Closed	1997	12.95	13
1997 To Grandma Photo Holder CXOR-057W	Closed	1997	12.95	13

1997 Holiday Collections-Holiday Magic - Carlton

YEAR ISSUE	EDITION LIMIT	YEAR RETD.	ISSUE PRICE	*QUOTE U.S.$
1997 Dance of the Jolly Juggler CXOR-105W	Closed	1997	13.95	14
1997 Flight of Pegasus CXOR-107W	Closed	1997	13.95	14
1997 Magic of the Snow Fairy CXOR-106W	Closed	1997	13.95	14

1997 Holiday Collections-Northland Journey - Carlton

YEAR ISSUE	EDITION LIMIT	YEAR RETD.	ISSUE PRICE	*QUOTE U.S.$
1997 Dancer CXOR-096W	Closed	1997	13.95	14
1997 Northland Santa CXOR-098W	Closed	1997	13.95	14
1997 Prancer CXOR-097W	Closed	1997	13.95	14

1997 Holiday Collections-Santas of the World - Carlton

YEAR ISSUE	EDITION LIMIT	YEAR RETD.	ISSUE PRICE	*QUOTE U.S.$
1997 England's Father Christmas CXOR-099W	Closed	1997	9.95	10
1997 Germany's Saint Nikolaus CXOR-100W	Closed	1997	9.95	10
1997 Mexico's Santa Claus CXOR-101W	Closed	1997	9.95	10

1997 Holiday Collections-Sparkling Christmas - Carlton

YEAR ISSUE	EDITION LIMIT	YEAR RETD.	ISSUE PRICE	*QUOTE U.S.$
1997 Santa Swirl CXOR-103W	Closed	1997	10.95	11
1997 Snowman Whirl CXOR-104W	Closed	1997	10.95	11
1997 Soldier Twirl CXOR-102W	Closed	1997	10.95	11

1997 Holiday Collections-Touches of Silver - Carlton

YEAR ISSUE	EDITION LIMIT	YEAR RETD.	ISSUE PRICE	*QUOTE U.S.$
1997 Silvery Bell CXOR-108W	Closed	1997	12.95	13
1997 Silvery Heart CXOR-110W	Closed	1997	12.95	13
1997 Silvery Snowflake CXOR-109W	Closed	1997	12.95	13

1997 Lasting Love - Carlton

YEAR ISSUE	EDITION LIMIT	YEAR RETD.	ISSUE PRICE	*QUOTE U.S.$
1997 Commemorative Anniversary CXOR-027W	Closed	1997	14.95	15
1997 Our Christmas Together CXOR-026W	Closed	1997	14.95	15
1997 Our Christmas Together CXOR-25W	Closed	1997	17.95	18
1997 Sweetheart CXOR-23W	Closed	1997	15.95	16
1997 Sweetheart CXOR-24W	Closed	1997	15.95	16

1997 Licensed Characters - Carlton

YEAR ISSUE	EDITION LIMIT	YEAR RETD.	ISSUE PRICE	*QUOTE U.S.$
1997 Betty Boop: Surprise! CXOR-088W	Closed	1997	22.00	22-25
1997 Campbell's: M'm M'm from the Kitchen CXOR-090W	Closed	1997	18.95	19
1997 Charlie Chaplin: Silent Star (2nd) CXOR-092W	Closed	1997	17.95	15-18
1997 Elvis: Holiday Harmony (3rd) CXOR-093W	Closed	1997	30.00	28-50
1997 Hershey's: Sweet Delivery CXOR-084W	Closed	1997	15.95	16
1997 Lassie: All Set For Santa CXOR-095W	Closed	1997	22.00	22
1997 Mustang: Classic Christmas CXOR-094W	Closed	1997	16.95	17
1997 Nancy & Sluggo: Perfect Present CXOR-083W	Closed	1997	15.95	16
1997 Nickelodeon: Havin' A Ball CXOR-091W	Closed	1997	13.95	15
1997 Opus n' bill: Chillin' Out CXOR-085W	Closed	1997	13.95	14
1997 Paddington Bear: Home For Christmas CXOR-089W	Closed	1997	14.95	15
1997 Pillsbury: Baked with Love CXOR-082W	Closed	1997	14.95	15-18
1997 Play Doh: Frosty's Best Friend CXOR-081W	Closed	1997	14.95	15
1997 Rocky & Bullwinkle: Downhill Daredevils CXOR-087W	Closed	1997	15.95	16
1997 Tom & Jerry: Come Back Here! CXOR-086W	Closed	1997	15.95	16

1997 Light, Motion, Music - Carlton

YEAR ISSUE	EDITION LIMIT	YEAR RETD.	ISSUE PRICE	*QUOTE U.S.$
1997 Baby's First Christmas CXOR-029W	Open		32.00	32
1997 The Cherub Tree (Lighted) CXOR-067W	Closed	1997	22.00	22
1997 Green Thumb Greetings (Lighted) CXOR-077W	Closed	1997	21.50	22
1997 Holiday Hits (Music) CXOR-068W	Closed	1997	24.50	25
1997 Is He Here Yet? (Lighted) CXOR-076W	Closed	1997	21.50	22
1997 Main Attraction CXOR-080W	Open		36.00	36
1997 Peanut Parade (Lighted) CXOR-075W	Closed	1997	22.00	22
1997 Piano Playmates (Music) CXOR-069W	Closed	1997	24.50	25
1997 To All A Good Night! CXOR-078W	Closed	1997	18.50	19
1997 Two By Two (Motion, Lights & Music) CXOR-073W	Open		40.00	40

1997 Little Heirloom Treasures - Carlton

YEAR ISSUE	EDITION LIMIT	YEAR RETD.	ISSUE PRICE	*QUOTE U.S.$
1997 All Creatures Great and Small CXOR-165W	Closed	1997	7.95	8
1997 Beary Good Year CXOR-142W	Closed	1997	7.95	8
1997 Beautiful Bell CXOR-151W	Closed	1997	7.95	8
1997 Brewing Up Fun CXOR-141W	Closed	1997	6.95	7
1997 Christmas Caroling CXOR-164W	Closed	1997	6.95	7
1997 Christmas in a Nutshell CXOR-160W	Closed	1997	5.95	6
1997 Christmas Messenger CXOR-167W	Closed	1997	7.95	8
1997 Frosty Frolic CXOR-150W	Closed	1997	6.95	7
1997 Furry Friend CXOR-156W	Closed	1997	6.95	7
1997 Gift Bearer CXOR-154W	Closed	1997	7.95	8
1997 Gifts of Nature CXOR-169W	Closed	1997	9.95	10
1997 Gliding By CXOR-145W	Closed	1997	7.95	8
1997 Heavenly Friends CXOR-139W	Closed	1997	7.95	8
1997 Holiday Sparkle CXOR-157W	Closed	1997	9.95	10
1997 Hope You Like It! CXOR-144W	Closed	1997	7.95	8
1997 In A Twinkling CXOR-163W	Closed	1997	8.95	9
1997 Jennifer's Wish CXOR-158W	Closed	1997	7.95	8
1997 Jump For Joy CXOR-152W	Closed	1997	7.95	8
1997 Lambkin CXOR-143W	Closed	1997	7.95	8
1997 Lighting The Way CXOR-171W	Closed	1997	7.95	8
1997 Loaded With Fun CXOR-168W	Closed	1997	9.95	10
1997 Love Token CXOR-146W	Closed	1997	7.95	8
1997 Meow-Y Christmas CXOR-140W	Closed	1997	6.95	7
1997 Mother And Child CXOR-161W	Closed	1997	5.95	6
1997 North Pole Moon and Stars CXOR-148W	Closed	1997	6.95	7
1997 The Nutcracker Prince CXOR-149W	Closed	1997	5.95	6
1997 Old-Fashioned Fun (1st) CXOR-138W	Closed	1997	9.95	10
1997 On Track For Christmas (1st) CXOR-137W	Open		9.95	10

*Quotes have been rounded up to nearest dollar

YEAR ISSUE	EDITION LIMIT	YEAR RETD.	ISSUE PRICE	*QUOTE U.S.$
1997 Partridge in a Pear Tree CXOR-170W	Closed	1997	5.95	6
1997 Stocking Stuffers CXOR-166W	Closed	1997	6.95	7
1997 Swing Time! CXOR-153W	Closed	1997	8.95	9
1997 Tiny Tailor CXOR-159W	Closed	1997	6.95	7
1997 Visit From Santa CXOR-147W	Closed	1997	7.95	8
1997 Winter Welcome CXOR-162W	Closed	1997	5.95	6
1997 Woodland Caroler CXOR-155W	Closed	1997	7.95	8

1997 Special People and Moments - Carlton

YEAR ISSUE	EDITION LIMIT	YEAR RETD.	ISSUE PRICE	*QUOTE U.S.$
1997 Caregiver CXOR-059W	Closed	1997	11.95	12
1997 Friend CXOR-060W	Closed	1997	10.95	11
1997 Friend CXOR-061W	Closed	1997	9.95	10
1997 Help's Here CXOR-066W	Closed	1997	13.95	14
1997 Love Is The Best Medicine CXOR-065W	Closed	1997	12.95	13
1997 Memo To You CXOR-064W	Closed	1997	12.95	13
1997 Merry Birthday CXOR-130W	Closed	1997	12.95	13
1997 New Home CXOR-016W	Closed	1997	14.95	15
1997 New Home CXOR-017W	Closed	1997	13.95	14
1997 Our House To Your House CXOR-018W	Closed	1997	10.95	11
1997 Teacher CXOR-062W	Closed	1997	9.95	10
1997 Teacher CXOR-063W	Closed	1997	11.95	12

1997 Traditional - Carlton

YEAR ISSUE	EDITION LIMIT	YEAR RETD.	ISSUE PRICE	*QUOTE U.S.$
1997 A Child's Christmas CXOR-125W	Closed	1997	13.95	14
1997 Christmas Goose CXOR-070W	Closed	1997	15.95	16
1997 Christmas Ties CXOR-124W	Closed	1997	13.95	14
1997 Heavenly Angel CXOR-135W	Closed	1997	14.95	15
1997 Holiday Help Wanted CXOR-122W	Closed	1997	10.95	11
1997 In The Attic CXOR-132W	Closed	1997	15.95	16
1997 The Littlest Cowpoke CXOR-133W	Closed	1997	15.95	16
1997 Memories of Christmas Photo holder CXOR-071W	Closed	1997	15.95	16
1997 north.pole.com CXOR-129W	Closed	1997	13.95	14
1997 Papa Christmas CXOR-126W	Closed	1997	14.95	15
1997 Pet Photo Holder CXOR-128W	Closed	1997	9.95	10
1997 Purr-fect Holidays CXOR-123W	Closed	1997	12.95	13
1997 Ringing in Christmas CXOR-074W	Closed	1997	14.95	15
1997 Rocking Horse Fun CXOR-127W	Closed	1997	13.95	14
1997 Simpler Times CXOR-079W	Closed	1997	22.00	22
1997 Toymakers Treasure CXOR-131W	Closed	1997	13.95	14
1997 Treasured Keepsake CXOR-134W	Closed	1997	15.95	16
1997 Treasured Toy CXOR-072W	Closed	1997	15.95	16

1998 Carlton Heirloom Collection Collector's Club - Carlton

YEAR ISSUE	EDITION LIMIT	YEAR RETD.	ISSUE PRICE	*QUOTE U.S.$
1998 McKenzie Bear CXOR-201Y	Yr.Iss.		Gift	N/A
1998 Father Christmas CXOR-202Y	Yr.Iss.		Gift	N/A
1998 Collector's Carousel CXOR-203Y	Yr.Iss.		Gift	N/A
1998 Marilyn...Glamorous in Red CXOR-204Y	Yr.Iss.		17.95	18

1998 Premier Event Ornaments - Carlton

YEAR ISSUE	EDITION LIMIT	YEAR RETD.	ISSUE PRICE	*QUOTE U.S.$
1998 Midnight Ride CXOR-173Y	Yr.Iss.		9.95	10

1998 Carlton Heirloom Collection Collectors' Series - Carlton

YEAR ISSUE	EDITION LIMIT	YEAR RETD.	ISSUE PRICE	*QUOTE U.S.$
1998 Christmas Express (3rd) CXOR-004Y	Open		15.95	16
1998 Christmas Go Round (9th) CXOR-011Y	Open		15.95	16
1998 Heaven 'N Nature (1st) CXOR-005Y	Open		15.95	16
1998 Holiday Nutcracker (1st) CXOR-001Y	Open		14.95	15
1998 Ice Pals (7th) CXOR-006Y	Open		13.95	14
1998 Joy Is In The Air (3rd) CXOR-007Y	Open		17.95	18
1998 Matchbox Memories (1st) CXOR-003Y	Open		14.95	15
1998 Merry Mischief (3rd) CXOR-012Y	Open		14.95	15
1998 Merry Mobiles (2nd) CXOR-002Y	Open		13.95	14
1998 Oh Holy Night (3rd) CXOR-014Y	Open		18.95	19
1998 Rocking Horse Fun (1st) CXOR-009Y	Open		13.95	14
1998 Star Of The Season (1st) CXOR-010Y	Open		13.95	14
1998 Toyland Wonders (1st) CXOR-080Y	Open		17.95	18
1998 Year By Year (4th) CXOR-013Y	Open		12.95	13
1998 Yesterday's Treasures (1st) CXOR-008Y	Open		13.95	14

1998 A Child's Christmas - Carlton

YEAR ISSUE	EDITION LIMIT	YEAR RETD.	ISSUE PRICE	*QUOTE U.S.$
1998 Baby's Second Christmas CXOR-035Y	Open		12.95	13
1998 Child's Christmas CXOR-040Y	Open		9.95	10
1998 Child's Fourth Christmas CXOR-037Y	Open		12.95	13
1998 Child's Third Christmas CXOR-036Y	Open		12.95	13

1998 Baby's First Christmas - Carlton

YEAR ISSUE	EDITION LIMIT	YEAR RETD.	ISSUE PRICE	*QUOTE U.S.$
1998 Baby Boy's First Christmas CXOR-031Y	Open		12.95	13
1998 Baby Boy's First Christmas CXOR-032Y	Open		12.95	13
1998 Baby Girl's First Christmas CXOR-029Y	Open		13.95	14
1998 Baby Girl's First Christmas CXOR-030Y	Open		12.95	13
1998 Baby's First Christmas CXOR-028Y	Open		13.95	14
1998 Granddaughter's First Christmas CXOR-033Y	Open		14.95	15
1998 Grandson's First Christmas CXOR-034Y	Open		14.95	15

1998 Family - Carlton

YEAR ISSUE	EDITION LIMIT	YEAR RETD.	ISSUE PRICE	*QUOTE U.S.$
1998 Brother CXOR-052Y	Open		12.95	13
1998 Dad CXOR-046Y	Open		12.95	13
1998 Daughter CXOR-048Y	Open		13.95	14
1998 Godchild CXOR-038Y	Open		12.95	13
1998 Godchild CXOR-039Y	Open		11.95	12
1998 Godmother CXOR-055Y	Open		12.95	13
1998 Grandmother CXOR-053Y	Open		12.95	13
1998 Grandparents CXOR-054Y	Open		13.95	14
1998 Mom CXOR-045Y	Open		12.95	13
1998 Our Family Photoholder CXOR-057Y	Open		9.95	10
1998 Parents CXOR-047Y	Open		15.95	16
1998 Parents-To-Be CXOR-043Y	Open		12.95	13
1998 Parents-To-Be CXOR-044Y	Open		13.95	14
1998 Sister CXOR-050Y	Open		13.95	14
1998 Sister-To-Sister CXOR-051Y	Open		12.95	13
1998 Son CXOR-049Y	Open		13.95	14
1998 To Grandma Photoholder CXOR-056Y	Open		9.95	10

1998 Favorite Pastimes - Carlton

YEAR ISSUE	EDITION LIMIT	YEAR RETD.	ISSUE PRICE	*QUOTE U.S.$
1998 Dapper Duffer CXOR-120Y	Open		14.95	15
1998 Football Folly CXOR-114Y	Open		12.95	13
1998 Grand Slam Greetings CXOR-113Y	Open		22.00	22
1998 Holiday Roller CXOR-112Y	Open		11.95	12
1998 Jennifer Ballerina CXOR-125Y	Open		10.95	11
1998 Reindeer Games CXOR-119Y	Open		11.95	12
1998 Santa's "Reel" Job CXOR-115Y	Open		14.95	15
1998 Tailor-Made Holiday CXOR-124Y	Open		11.95	12

1998 Holiday Collections-Arctic Animals - Carlton

YEAR ISSUE	EDITION LIMIT	YEAR RETD.	ISSUE PRICE	*QUOTE U.S.$
1998 Christmas Cuddles CXOR-097Y	Open		14.95	15
1998 Ready To Play CXOR-098Y	Open		14.95	15
1998 Snugglin' Season CXOR-099Y	Open		14.95	15

1998 Holiday Collections-Heavenly Holidays - Carlton

YEAR ISSUE	EDITION LIMIT	YEAR RETD.	ISSUE PRICE	*QUOTE U.S.$
1998 Gift Of Hope CXOR-101Y	Open		12.95	13
1998 Gift Of Love CXOR-102Y	Open		12.95	13
1998 Gift of Peace CXOR-100Y	Open		12.95	13

1998 Holiday Collections-Howdy Doody - Carlton

YEAR ISSUE	EDITION LIMIT	YEAR RETD.	ISSUE PRICE	*QUOTE U.S.$
1998 Buffalo Bob CXOR-111Y	Open		14.95	15
1998 Clarabell CXOR-110Y	Open		14.95	15
1998 Howdy Doody CXOR-109Y	Open		14.95	15

1998 Holiday Collections-Popeye - Carlton

YEAR ISSUE	EDITION LIMIT	YEAR RETD.	ISSUE PRICE	*QUOTE U.S.$
1998 Olive Oyl CXOR-107Y	Open		15.95	16
1998 Popeye CXOR-106Y	Open		15.95	16
1998 Wimpy CXOR-108Y	Open		15.95	16

1998 Holiday Collections-Santas of Yesteryear - Carlton

YEAR ISSUE	EDITION LIMIT	YEAR RETD.	ISSUE PRICE	*QUOTE U.S.$
1998 The Jolly Gentleman CXOR-104Y	Open		15.95	16
1998 Ol' Saint Nick CXOR-103Y	Open		15.95	16
1998 Santa and Friend CXOR-105Y	Open		15.95	16
1998 Santa and Friend CXOR-105Y	Open		15.95	16

1998 Holiday Collections-Songs of Christmas - Carlton

YEAR ISSUE	EDITION LIMIT	YEAR RETD.	ISSUE PRICE	*QUOTE U.S.$
1998 Song Of Hope CXOR-69Y	Open		12.95	13
1998 Song Of Love CXOR-70Y	Open		12.95	13
1998 Song Of Peace CXOR-71Y	Open		12.95	13

1998 Light, Motion, Music - Carlton

YEAR ISSUE	EDITION LIMIT	YEAR RETD.	ISSUE PRICE	*QUOTE U.S.$
1998 Angelic Antics CXOR-078Y	Open		22.00	22
1998 Baby's First Christmas CXOR-068Y	Open		32.00	32
1998 Down The Chimney CXOR-077Y	Open		18.95	19
1998 Greenhouse Greetings CXOR-076Y	Open		22.00	22
1998 Main Attraction CXOR-067Y	Open		36.00	36
1998 Merry Musicians CXOR-072Y	Open		25.00	25
1998 Quick As A Wink CXOR-075Y	Open		22.00	22
1998 Santa Says... CXOR-074Y	Open		22.00	22
1998 Silent Night CXOR-073Y	Open		25.00	25
1998 Two By Two CXOR-066Y	Open		40.00	40
1998 Wee Reader CXOR-079Y	Open		22.00	22

1998 Little Heirloom Treasures - Carlton

YEAR ISSUE	EDITION LIMIT	YEAR RETD.	ISSUE PRICE	*QUOTE U.S.$
1998 Angelique CXOR-162Y	Open		6.95	7
1998 Barnyard Star CXOR-172Y	Open		6.95	7
1998 Bearly Christmas (1st) CXOR-159Y	Open		9.95	10
1998 Big Top Christmas CXOR-155Y	Open		6.95	7
1998 Bradley CXOR-163Y	Open		7.95	8
1998 Candy Panda CXOR-161Y	Open		6.95	7
1998 Carousel Dreams (2nd) CXOR-140Y	Open		9.95	10
1998 Christmas Catnap CXOR-158Y	Open		7.95	8
1998 Christmas In Bloom CXOR-169Y	Open		8.95	9
1998 Christmas Kitty CXOR-141Y	Open		6.95	7
1998 Christmas Pageant CXOR-171Y	Open		7.95	8
1998 Country Kringle CXOR-144Y	Open		7.95	8
1998 Feathered Friend CXOR-160Y	Open		6.95	7
1998 A Festive Frolic CXOR-148Y	Open		7.95	8
1998 Greetings, Earthlings! CXOR-166Y	Open		9.95	10
1998 Group Hug CXOR-154Y	Open		6.95	7
1998 Holiday Birdhouse CXOR-150Y	Open		6.95	7
1998 Holiday Howdy CXOR-143Y	Open		7.95	8
1998 Holly & Berries CXOR-156Y	Open		9.95	10
1998 Holy Night CXOR-149Y	Open		8.95	9
1998 Hurray 4 Christmas! CXOR-164Y	Open		7.95	8
1998 I Spotted Santa! CXOR-165Y	Open		6.95	7
1998 Magical Snowflake CXOR-167Y	Open		9.95	10
1998 Old-Fashioned Fun (2nd) CXOR-139Y	Open		9.95	10
1998 On Track For Christmas (1st) CX OR-137Y	Open		9.95	10
1998 On Track For Christmas (2nd) CXOR-138Y	Open		9.95	10
1998 Our Snowy Friend CXOR-157Y	Open		7.95	8
1998 Partridge In Pear Tree CXOR-152Y	Open		6.95	7
1998 Patty Penguin CXOR-145Y	Open		7.95	8
1998 Sounds Like Christmas CXOR-146Y	Open		7.95	8
1998 Sugar Mill Christmas CXOR-153Y	Open		7.95	8
1998 Susie Skater CXOR-147Y	Open		7.95	8
1998 Sweet Soloist CXOR-170Y	Open		7.95	8
1998 The Sweetest Sound CXOR-151Y	Open		7.95	8
1998 Tiny Teapot CXOR-142Y	Open		8.95	9
1998 Winter Visitor CXOR-168Y	Open		8.95	9

1998 Popular Characters - Carlton

YEAR ISSUE	EDITION LIMIT	YEAR RETD.	ISSUE PRICE	*QUOTE U.S.$
1998 Campbell's: Soup's On CXOR-089Y	Open		16.95	17
1998 Curious George: Just For Kicks CXOR-118Y	Open		12.95	13
1998 Diana, Princess of Wales (1st) CXOR-015Y	Open		19.95	20
1998 Eskimo Pie: North Pole Treat CXOR-091Y	Open		14.95	15
1998 Hershey's: Tasty Trimmings CXOR-042Y	Open		15.95	16
1998 Hershey's: Yummy Yule CXOR-041Y	Open		15.95	16
1998 James Dean (3rd) CXOR-081Y	Open		15.95	16
1998 Jeep: 'Snow Stopping Us Now! CXOR-092Y	Open		16.95	17
1998 Lassie: A Letter To Santa CXOR-085Y	Open		16.95	17
1998 Marilyn Monroe (4th) CXOR-093Y	Open		17.95	18
1998 Mighty Mouse: Christmas Crusader CXOR-090Y	Open		15.95	16
1998 Nabisco: Holiday Zoo CXOR-094Y	Open		13.95	14
1998 Nickelodeon: Bestest Christmas Gift CXOR-088Y	Open		16.95	17
1998 Nintendo: Mario's Christmas Adventure CXOR-086Y	Open		15.95	16
1998 Opus n' bill: Fool For Love CXOR-082Y	Open		13.95	13
1998 Paddington Bear: One Bear Band CXOR-084Y	Open		14.95	15
1998 Pillsbury: Poppin' Up Fun CXOR-087Y	Open		16.95	17
1998 Pink Panther: Think Pink CXOR-095Y	Open		13.95	14
1998 Ren & Stimpy: Yule Really Like This! CXOR-083Y	Open		15.95	16
1998 Rugrats: Rugrat Toy Makers miniatures, set/3 (Tommy, Angelica, Chuckie) CXOR-300Y	Open		19.95	20
1998 The Simpsons: Christmas Cowabunga CXOR-116Y	Open		14.95	15
1998 Tom & Jerry: Hockey Hijinks CXOR-117Y	Open		15.95	16

1998 Special People and Moments - Carlton

YEAR ISSUE	EDITION LIMIT	YEAR RETD.	ISSUE PRICE	*QUOTE U.S.$
1998 Anniversary CXOR-027Y	Open		14.95	15
1998 Caregiver CXOR-058Y	Open		15.95	16
1998 Cup Of Holiday Cheer CXOR-063Y	Open		12.95	13
1998 First Christmas Together CXOR-019Y	Open		15.95	16
1998 First Christmas Together CXOR-020Y	Open		18.95	19
1998 First Christmas Together CXOR-021Y	Open		12.95	13
1998 First Christmas Together CXOR-022Y	Open		17.95	18
1998 Friend CXOR-059Y	Open		12.95	13
1998 Friend CxOR-060Y	Open		12.95	13
1998 Lincoln Logs: New Home CXOR-016Y	Open		15.95	16
1998 New Home CXOR-017Y	Open		13.95	14
1998 Our Christmas Together CXOR-025Y	Open		15.95	16
1998 Our Christmas Together CXOR-026Y	Open		16.95	17
1998 Our House To Your House CXOR-018Y	Open		14.95	15
1998 Spoonful Of Love CXOR-064Y	Open		12.95	13
1998 Sweetheart CXOR-023Y	Open		17.95	18
1998 Sweetheart CXOR-024Y	Open		13.95	14
1998 Teacher CXOR-061Y	Open		11.95	12
1998 Teacher CXOR-062Y	Open		13.95	14

1998 Traditional - Carlton

YEAR ISSUE	EDITION LIMIT	YEAR RETD.	ISSUE PRICE	*QUOTE U.S.$
1998 Birthday Bear! Special Celebrations CXOR-096Y	Open		13.95	14
1998 Chilly Country Gentleman CXOR-131Y	Open		13.95	14
1998 Christmas Companions CXOR-127Y	Open		10.95	11
1998 Christmas Cottontail CXOR-126Y	Open		10.95	11
1998 Come All Ye Faithful CXOR-123Y	Open		11.95	12
1998 From The Toy Shop CXOR-121Y	Open		14.95	15
1998 Good Little Girls And Boys CXOR-135Y	Open		14.95	15
1998 Miles of Smiles CXOR-130Y	Open		10.95	11
1998 Mrs. C's Special Recipe CXOR-134Y	Open		10.95	11
1998 Nature's Song CXOR-129Y	Open		12.95	13
1998 North Pole Penguin CXOR-122Y	Open		12.95	13
1998 Precious Pets CXOR-132Y	Open		9.95	10
1998 Purr-Feet Holidays CXOR-138Y	Open		12.95	13
1998 Rooftop Visitor CXOR-133Y	Open		10.95	11

*Quotes have been rounded up to nearest dollar

ORNAMENTS

YEAR ISSUE	EDITION LIMIT	YEAR RETD.	ISSUE PRICE	*QUOTE U.S.$
1998 To The Rescue CXOR-065Y	Open		12.95	13

Cast Art Industries

Bumpkins - A. & T. Fabrizio

YEAR ISSUE	EDITION LIMIT	YEAR RETD.	ISSUE PRICE	*QUOTE U.S.$
1997 Christmas Bear 01103	Closed	1998	11.00	11
1997 Christmas Duck 01095	Closed	1998	11.00	11
1997 Cool Yule 01094	Closed	1998	11.00	11
1997 Granny Green 01101	Closed	1998	11.00	11
1997 Joy 01098	Closed	1998	11.00	11
1997 Love 01097	Closed	1998	11.00	11
1997 Mrs. Claus 01093	Closed	1998	11.00	11
1997 Not Even a Mouse 01099	Closed	1998	11.00	11
1997 Peace 01096	Closed	1998	11.00	11
1997 Rudolph 01089	Closed	1998	11.00	11
1997 Santa 01092	Closed	1998	11.00	11
1997 Santa's Elf 01090	Closed	1998	11.00	11
1997 Snow Princess 01091	Closed	1998	11.00	11
1997 Sweet Treats 01102	Closed	1998	11.00	11
1997 Toy Soldier 01100	Closed	1998	11.00	11

The Cat's Meow

1986 Christmas Ornaments - F. Jones

YEAR ISSUE	EDITION LIMIT	YEAR RETD.	ISSUE PRICE	*QUOTE U.S.$
1986 Bancroft House	Retrd.	1986	4.00	40
1986 Chapel	Retrd.	1986	4.00	N/A
1986 Grayling House	Retrd.	1986	4.00	40
1986 Morton House	Retrd.	1986	4.00	N/A
1986 Rutledge House	Retrd.	1986	4.00	75
1986 School	Retrd.	1986	4.00	N/A

1988 Christmas Ornaments - F. Jones

YEAR ISSUE	EDITION LIMIT	YEAR RETD.	ISSUE PRICE	*QUOTE U.S.$
1988 Blacksmith Shop	Retrd.	1988	5.00	40-60
1988 District #17 School	Retrd.	1988	5.00	60
1988 Globe Corner Bookstore	Retrd.	1988	5.00	40-60
1988 Kennedy Birthplace	Retrd.	1988	5.00	26-75
1988 Set/4	Retrd.	1988	20.00	175-200

1995 Christmas Ornaments - F. Jones

YEAR ISSUE	EDITION LIMIT	YEAR RETD.	ISSUE PRICE	*QUOTE U.S.$
1995 Carnegie Library	Retrd.	1995	8.75	8-12
1995 Holly Hill Farmhouse	Retrd.	1995	8.75	8-12
1995 North Central School	Retrd.	1995	8.75	8-12
1995 St. James General Store	Retrd.	1995	8.75	8-12
1995 Unitarian Church	Retrd.	1995	8.75	8-12
1995 Yaquina Bay Light	Retrd.	1995	8.75	8-12

1996 Christmas Ornaments - F. Jones

YEAR ISSUE	EDITION LIMIT	YEAR RETD.	ISSUE PRICE	*QUOTE U.S.$
1996 Christ Church	Retrd.	1996	9.00	11-13
1996 Deerfield Post Office	Retrd.	1996	9.00	11-13
1996 Gimbel & Sons Country Store	Retrd.	1996	9.00	11-13
1996 Hook Windmill	Retrd.	1996	9.00	11-13
1996 Maple Manor	Retrd.	1996	9.00	11-13
1996 Parsonage	Retrd.	1996	9.00	11-13

1997 Christmas Ornaments - F. Jones

YEAR ISSUE	EDITION LIMIT	YEAR RETD.	ISSUE PRICE	*QUOTE U.S.$
1997 Christmas Church	Retrd.	1997	9.00	9-11
1997 Federal House	Retrd.	1997	9.00	9-11
1997 Garrison House	Retrd.	1997	9.00	9-11
1997 Georgian House	Retrd.	1997	9.00	9-11

1998 Christmas Ornaments - F. Jones

YEAR ISSUE	EDITION LIMIT	YEAR RETD.	ISSUE PRICE	*QUOTE U.S.$
1998 The Christmas Shop	Retrd.	1998	9.00	10
1998 The Powell House	Retrd.	1998	9.00	10
1998 The Shaw House	Retrd.	1998	9.00	10
1998 The Winthrop House	Retrd.	1998	9.00	10

1998 Dated Christmas Ornaments - F. Jones

YEAR ISSUE	EDITION LIMIT	YEAR RETD.	ISSUE PRICE	*QUOTE U.S.$
1998 Christ's Birth	Retrd.	1998	9.00	9
1998 The Snow Globe	Retrd.	1998	9.00	9

1998 Themed Christmas Ornaments - F. Jones

YEAR ISSUE	EDITION LIMIT	YEAR RETD.	ISSUE PRICE	*QUOTE U.S.$
1998 Santa Casper	Retrd.	1998	9.00	9
1998 A Wrapped House	Retrd.	1998	9.00	9

Cavanagh Group Intl.

Coca-Cola Brand Heritage Collection - Sundblom

YEAR ISSUE	EDITION LIMIT	YEAR RETD.	ISSUE PRICE	*QUOTE U.S.$
1995 Christmas Is Love (polyresin)	Closed	1997	10.00	10
1995 For Me (polyresin)	Closed	1997	10.00	10
1996 Hospitality in Your Refrigerator (porcelain & brass)	10,000		25.00	25
1997 It Will Refresh You Too (polyresin)	Open		10.00	10
1996 It Will Refresh You, Too (porcelain & brass)	10,000		25.00	25
1996 Please Pause Here (porcelain & brass)	10,000		25.00	25
1997 Ssshh! (polyresin)	Open		10.00	10
1995 Ssshhh! (polyresin)	Closed	1997	10.00	10
1997 That Extra Something (polyresin)	Open		10.00	10

Coca-Cola Brand Heritage Collection Polar Bear - CGI

YEAR ISSUE	EDITION LIMIT	YEAR RETD.	ISSUE PRICE	*QUOTE U.S.$
1997 Always Family (polyresin)	Open		10.00	10
1996 Baby's First Christmas (porcelain)	Open		12.00	12
1996 Our First Christmas (porcelain)	Open		12.00	12
1997 A Refreshing Break (polyresin)	Open		10.00	10
1996 Stocking Stuffers (porcelain)	Open		12.00	12
1997 Trimming the Tree (polyresin)	Open		10.00	10

Coca-Cola Brand Historical Building - CGI

YEAR ISSUE	EDITION LIMIT	YEAR RETD.	ISSUE PRICE	*QUOTE U.S.$
1991 1930's Service Station	Closed	1994	10.00	20-25
1991 Early Coca-Cola Bottling Company	Closed	1994	10.00	20-25
1991 Jacob's Pharmacy	Closed	1994	10.00	20-25
1991 The Pemberton House	Closed	1994	10.00	20-25

Coca-Cola Brand North Pole Bottling Works - CGI

YEAR ISSUE	EDITION LIMIT	YEAR RETD.	ISSUE PRICE	*QUOTE U.S.$
1995 Barrel of Bears	Closed	1996	9.00	9-13
1993 Blast Off	Closed	1995	9.00	15-25
1993 Delivery for Santa	Closed	1996	9.00	15
1998 Elf & Walrus	Open		9.00	9
1998 Elf on Carousel Horse	Open		9.00	9
1993 Fill 'er Up	Closed	1994	9.00	30
1995 Fountain Glass Follies	Open		9.00	9
1993 Ice Sculpting	Closed	1995	9.00	15
1993 Long Winter's Nap	Closed	1995	9.00	15
1993 North Pole Express	Closed	1994	9.00	35
1995 North Pole Flying School	Closed	1996	9.00	15
1994 Power Drive	Closed	1996	9.00	13
1996 Refreshing Surprise	Closed	1997	9.00	9
1996 Rush Delivery	Closed	1997	9.00	9
1994 Santa's Refreshment	Closed	1995	9.00	13-15
1994 Seltzer Surprise	Closed	1995	9.00	15
1993 Thirsting for Adventure	Closed	1994	9.00	20-25
1996 To: Mrs. Claus	Closed	1997	9.00	9
1994 Tops Off Refreshment	Closed	1995	9.00	13
1993 Tops On Refreshment	Closed	1995	9.00	15

Coca-Cola Brand Polar Bear - CGI

YEAR ISSUE	EDITION LIMIT	YEAR RETD.	ISSUE PRICE	*QUOTE U.S.$
1996 The Christmas Star	Open		9.00	9
1997 Double the Fun	Open		9.00	9
1997 Downhill Racers	Open		9.00	9
1994 Downhill Sledder	Closed	1996	9.00	13
1996 Hollywood	Open		9.00	9
1994 North Pole Delivery	Closed	1995	9.00	13
1995 Polar Bear in Bottle Opener	Closed	1997	9.00	9
1998 Polar Bear on Fountain Machine	Open		9.00	9
1998 Polar Bear with Coke Sled	Open		9.00	9
1994 Skating Coca-Cola Polar Bear	Closed	1995	9.00	13
1995 Snowboardin' Bear	Closed	1997	9.00	9
1994 Vending Machine Mischief	Closed	1996	9.00	9-15

Coca-Cola Brand Polar Bear Cubs - CGI

YEAR ISSUE	EDITION LIMIT	YEAR RETD.	ISSUE PRICE	*QUOTE U.S.$
1997 Baby's First Christmas	Open		8.00	8
1997 Cookies For Santa	Open		8.00	8
1997 Dreaming of a Magical Christmas	Yr.Iss.	1997	8.00	8
1997 A Refreshing Ice Cold Treat	Open		8.00	8
1998 Seal on Ball	Open		8.00	8
1998 Seal on Ice Cube	Open		8.00	8
1997 Stocking Stuffer Surprise	Yr.Iss.	1997	8.00	8
1997 Twas the Night Before Christmas	Open		8.00	8

Coca-Cola Brand Trim A Tree Collection - Sundblom

YEAR ISSUE	EDITION LIMIT	YEAR RETD.	ISSUE PRICE	*QUOTE U.S.$
1990 Away with a Tired and Thirsty Face	Closed	1993	10.00	30-35
1994 Busy Man's Pause	Closed	1995	10.00	10
1991 Christmas Is Love	Closed	1992	10.00	30
1993 Decorating the Tree	Closed	1994	10.00	20
1993 Extra Bright Refreshment	Closed	1994	10.00	15-20
1994 For Sparkling Holidays	Closed	1996	10.00	10-15
1997 Good Boys and Girls	Closed	1997	10.00	10
1992 Happy Holidays	Closed	1996	10.00	25-40
1990 Hospitality	Closed	1993	10.00	15-20
1998 Hospitality	Open		9.00	9
1995 It Will Refresh You Too	Closed	1996	10.00	13
1990 Merry Christmas and a Happy New Year	Closed	1991	10.00	40
1996 The Pause That Refreshes	Closed	1997	10.00	10
1995 Please Pause Here	Closed	1997	10.00	10
1990 Santa on Stool	Closed	1993	10.00	20
1990 Season's Greetings	Closed	1991	10.00	40
1992 Sshhh!	Closed	1993	10.00	35-75
1996 They Remembered Me	Closed	1997	10.00	10
1994 Things Go Better with Coke	Closed	1996	10.00	10
1998 Things Go Better with Coke	Open		9.00	9
1991 A Time to Share	Closed	1993	10.00	25
1993 Travel Refreshed	Closed	1995	10.00	15

Harley-Davidson - CGI

YEAR ISSUE	EDITION LIMIT	YEAR RETD.	ISSUE PRICE	*QUOTE U.S.$
1997 Adventures on the Open Road	Yr.Iss.	1997	20.00	20
1998 Elf with Special Delivery	Open		20.00	20
1997 Elves to the Rescue	Open		20.00	20
1997 King of the Road	Open		20.00	20
1998 Reindeer on Bad Boy	Open		20.00	20
1997 Three for the Road	Open		20.00	20

Humbug - T. Fraley

YEAR ISSUE	EDITION LIMIT	YEAR RETD.	ISSUE PRICE	*QUOTE U.S.$
1998 Midnight Snack	Open		15.00	15
1998 Peek-A-Boo	Open		12.00	12
1998 Ride 'em Cowboy	Open		15.00	15
1998 Sweet Tooth	Open		12.00	12
1998 To Drop or Not to Drop	Open		12.00	12
1998 A Winter's Nap	Open		12.00	12

Cherished Teddies/Enesco Corporation

Across The Seas - P. Hillman

YEAR ISSUE	EDITION LIMIT	YEAR RETD.	ISSUE PRICE	*QUOTE U.S.$
1998 American Boy 451010	Open		10.00	10
1998 Australian Boy 464120	Open		10.00	10
1998 Canadian Boy 451053	Open		10.00	10
1998 Chinese Boy 450960	Open		10.00	10
1998 Dutch Girl 450995	Open		10.00	10
1998 English Boy 451045	Open		10.00	10
1998 French Girl 450901	Open		10.00	10
1998 German Boy 451002	Open		10.00	10
1998 Indian Girl 450987	Open		10.00	10
1998 Italian Girl 464112	Open		10.00	10
1998 Japanese Girl 450936	Open		10.00	10
1998 Mexican Boy 450952	Open		10.00	10
1998 Russian Girl 450944	Open		10.00	10
1998 Scottish Girl 451029	Open		10.00	10
1998 Spanish Boy 450979	Open		10.00	10
1998 Swedish Girl 450928	Open		10.00	10

Cherished Teddies - P. Hillman

YEAR ISSUE	EDITION LIMIT	YEAR RETD.	ISSUE PRICE	*QUOTE U.S.$
1992 Angel 950777	Suspd.		12.50	44-75
1992 Bear In Stocking (dated) 950653	Yr.Iss.	1992	16.00	44-75
1992 Beth On Rocking Reindeer 950793	Suspd.		20.00	32-55
1992 Christmas Sister Bears, 3 asst. 951226	Suspd.		12.50	17-38
1993 Angel, 3 Asst. 912980	Suspd.		12.50	33-73
1993 Baby Boy (dated) 913014	Yr.Iss.	1993	12.50	20-27
1993 Baby Girl (dated) 913006	Yr.Iss.	1993	12.50	25-30
1993 Girl w/Muff (Alice) (dated) 912832	Yr.Iss.	1993	13.50	30-65
1993 Jointed Teddy Bear 914894	Suspd.		12.50	11-28
1994 Beary Christmas (dated) 617253	Yr.Iss.	1994	15.00	23-38
1994 Bundled Up For The Holidays "Our First Christmas" (dated) 617229	Yr.Iss.	1994	15.00	28-38
1994 Drummer Boy (dated) 912891	Yr.Iss.	1994	10.00	14-30
1995 Baby Angel on Cloud "Baby's First Christmas" 141240	Open		13.50	14
1995 Elf Bear W/Doll 625434	Suspd.		12.50	13-25
1995 Boy Bear Flying Cupid "Sending You My Heart" 103608	Suspd.		13.00	25-38
1995 Boy/Girl with Banner "Our First Christmas" 141259	Open		13.50	14
1995 Elf Bear W/Stuffed Reindeer 625442	Suspd.		12.50	13-25
1996 Bear w/Dangling Mittens 177768	Open		12.50	13
1995 Elf Bears/Candy Cane 651389	Suspd.		12.50	13-25
1995 Girl Bear Flying Cupid "Sending You My Heart" 103616	Suspd.		13.00	13-26
1995 Mrs Claus Xmas Holding Tray/Cookies 625426	Suspd.		12.50	13-25
1995 Teddies Santa Bear 651370	Open		12.50	13
1995 Teddy with Ice Skates (dated) 141232	Yr.Iss.	1995	12.50	15-28
1996 Toy Soldier (dated) 176052	Yr.Iss.	1996	12.50	13-20
1997 Dangling Snowflake (dated) 272175	Yr.Iss.	1997	12.50	13
1998 Bear in Picnic Basket 406627	Open		12.50	13
1998 Bear in Wagon 400793	Open		12.50	13
1998 Bear on Kitchen Hutch 406481 (Special Limited Editon)	Closed	1998	12.50	13
1998 Bear on Train 401196	Open		12.50	13
1998 Bears on Sled 406635	Open		12.50	13
1998 Gingerbread Bear 352748	Yr.Iss.		12.50	13
1998 Two Bears w/Teacup & Saucer 406473	Open		12.50	13

Christopher Radko

Christopher Radko Family of Collectors - C. Radko

YEAR ISSUE	EDITION LIMIT	YEAR RETD.	ISSUE PRICE	*QUOTE U.S.$
1993 Angels We Have Heard on High SP1	Retrd.	1993	50.00	240-540
1994 Starbuck Santa SP3	Retrd.	1994	75.00	100-228
1995 Dash Away All SP7	Retrd.	1995	34.00	50-90
1995 Purrfect Present SP8	Retrd.	1995	Gift	30-36
1996 Christmas Magic SP13	Retrd.	1996	50.00	70-75
1996 Frosty Weather SP14	Retrd.	1996	Gift	30-45
1997 Enchanted Evening SP20	Retrd.	1997	55.00	55-65
1997 Li'l Miss Angel SP21	Retrd.	1997	Gift	48
1998 Candy Castle SP36	Yr.Iss.		70.00	70
1998 Mouse Wrap SP32	Yr.Iss.		Gift	N/A

10 Year Anniversary - C. Radko

YEAR ISSUE	EDITION LIMIT	YEAR RETD.	ISSUE PRICE	*QUOTE U.S.$
1995 On Top of the World SP6	Yr.Iss.	1995	32.00	50-90

Event Only - C. Radko

YEAR ISSUE	EDITION LIMIT	YEAR RETD.	ISSUE PRICE	*QUOTE U.S.$
1993 Littlest Snowman 347S (store & C. Radko event)	Retrd.	1993	15.00	36-90
1994 Roly Poly 94125E (store & C. Radko event)	Retrd.	1994	22.00	48-90
1995 Forever Lucy 91075E (store & C. Radko event)	Retrd.	1995	32.00	48-72
1996 Poinsettia Elegance 287E (store event)	Retrd.	1996	32.00	48-50
1996 A Job Well Done SP18 (C. Radko event)	Retrd.	1996	30.00	50-59
1997 Little Golden Hood 97-261E (store event)	Retrd.	1997	39.00	39
1997 Merry Travelers SP27 (C. Radko event)	Retrd.	1997	44.00	44
1998 Elf Secrets 98-306E (store event)	Yr.Iss.		47.00	47

1986 Holiday Collection - C. Radko

YEAR ISSUE	EDITION LIMIT	YEAR RETD.	ISSUE PRICE	*QUOTE U.S.$
1986 Alpine Flowers 86-040-0	Retrd.	N/A	16.00	60-125
1986 Big Top 86-048-1	Retrd.	1988	15.00	180
1986 Deep Sea 41-1	Retrd.	N/A	N/A	55-75
1986 Emerald City 17	Retrd.	N/A	N/A	90-94
1986 Golden Alpine 86-040-1	Retrd.	N/A	N/A	48
1986 Long Icicle (red) 6	Retrd.	N/A	N/A	90-174
1986 Midas Touch 49	Retrd.	N/A	N/A	114-120
1986 Roses 86-115	Retrd.	1988	16.00	125-140
1986 Santa's Cane (pink) 5-1	Retrd.	N/A	N/A	90
1986 Siberian Sleighride 110-1	Retrd.	N/A	N/A	40-48
1986 Three Ribbon Oval 44-0	Retrd.	N/A	N/A	125-150
1986 Three Wise Swans 12	Retrd.	N/A	N/A	72

1987 Holiday Collection - C. Radko

YEAR ISSUE	EDITION LIMIT	YEAR RETD.	ISSUE PRICE	*QUOTE U.S.$
1987 Baby Balloons 87044	Retrd.	1988	6.00	75-110
1987 Celestial (red) 21-1	Retrd.	N/A	N/A	34-60
1987 Faberge Ball 34	Retrd.	N/A	N/A	48-90
1987 Grecian Column (red/gold) 520	Retrd.	N/A	N/A	125
1987 Grecian Column (silver) 520	Retrd.	N/A	N/A	125
1987 Kat Koncert 88-067	Retrd.	1994	16.00	95-140

*Quotes have been rounded up to nearest dollar

YEAR ISSUE	EDITION LIMIT	YEAR RETD.	ISSUE PRICE	*QUOTE U.S.$
1987 Memphis 18	Retrd.	N/A	15.00	100-125
1987 Neopolitan Angels 14	Retrd.	N/A	N/A	120
1987 Ruby Scarlet 10	Retrd.	N/A	N/A	36-48
1987 Serpents 38	Retrd.	N/A	N/A	30-36
1987 Twin Finial 800	Retrd.	N/A	N/A	135
1987 Victorian Lamp 63	Retrd.	N/A	N/A	90

1988 Holiday Collection - C. Radko

YEAR ISSUE	EDITION LIMIT	YEAR RETD.	ISSUE PRICE	*QUOTE U.S.$
1988 Alpine Flowers 8822	Retrd.	N/A	16.00	85-110
1988 Baby Balloon 8832	Retrd.	N/A	7.95	95-110
1988 Birdhouse 8873	Retrd.	1987	10.00	95-120
1988 Blue Rainbow 8863	Retrd.	N/A	16.00	150
1988 Buds in Bloom (pink) 8824	Retrd.	N/A	16.00	95-125
1988 Celestial (blue) 884	Retrd.	N/A	15.00	50-65
1988 Celestial 884	Retrd.	N/A	15.00	75
1988 Christmas Fanfare 8850	Retrd.	1988	15.00	72-125
1988 Circle of Santas 8811	Retrd.	N/A	16.95	90-108
1988 Cornucopia/Pear Branch 8839	Retrd.	N/A	15.00	360
1988 Crescent Moon Santa 881	Retrd.	N/A	15.00	125-140
1988 Crown Jewels 8874	Retrd.	1993	15.00	45-54
1988 Double Royal Star 8856	Retrd.	1991	23.00	114-150
1988 Exclamation Flask 8871	Retrd.	N/A	7.50	120-144
1988 Faberge Oval 883	Retrd.	N/A	15.00	75-110
1988 Gilded Leaves 8813	Retrd.	N/A	16.00	110-125
1988 Grecian Column 8842	Retrd.	1990	9.95	95
1988 Hot Air Balloon 885	Retrd.	N/A	15.00	125-150
1988 Lilac Sparkle 1814	Retrd.	N/A	15.00	140-150
1988 Merry Christmas Maiden 52	Retrd.	N/A	14.50	72
1988 Mushroom in Winter 8862	Retrd.	1993	12.00	75-135
1988 Neopolitan Angel 870141	Retrd.	1995	16.00	125-150
1988 Oz Balloon 872	Retrd.	N/A	18.00	160
1988 Ripples on Oval 8844	Retrd.	1987	6.00	75-85
1988 Royal Crest Oval 18	Retrd.	N/A	14.50	102
1988 Royal Diadem 8860	Retrd.	1987	25.00	125-135
1988 Royal Porcelain 8812	Retrd.	1991	16.00	125-180
1988 Royal Rooster 70	Retrd.	N/A	14.50	66
1988 Russian St. Nick 8823	Retrd.	N/A	15.00	125
1988 Satin Scepter 8847	Retrd.	1987	8.95	110
1988 Shiny-Brite 8843	Retrd.	N/A	5.00	36
1988 Simply Cartiere 8817	Retrd.	N/A	16.95	96-110
1988 Squiggles 889	Retrd.	N/A	15.00	100-140
1988 Stained Glass 8816	Retrd.	1990	16.00	125-175
1988 Striped Balloon 8877	Retrd.	N/A	16.95	40-96
1988 Tiger 886	Retrd.	N/A	15.00	375-500
1988 Tree on Ball 8864	Retrd.	N/A	9.00	100-144
1988 Twin Finial 8857	Retrd.	N/A	23.50	135
1988 Vienna 1900 37	Retrd.	N/A	16.00	96
1988 Zebra 886	Retrd.	N/A	15.00	125-160

1989 Holiday Collection - C. Radko

YEAR ISSUE	EDITION LIMIT	YEAR RETD.	ISSUE PRICE	*QUOTE U.S.$
1989 Alpine Flowers 9-43	Retrd.	N/A	17.00	30
1989 Baroque Angel 9-11	Retrd.	1989	17.00	125-150
1989 Carmen Miranda 9-40	Retrd.	N/A	17.00	67
1989 Charlie Chaplin (blue hat) 9-55	Retrd.	1990	8.50	30-54
1989 Circle of Santas 9-32	Retrd.	1991	17.00	95-108
1989 Clown Snake 60	Retrd.	N/A	9.00	54
1989 Clown Snake 60 (signed)	Retrd.	N/A	9.00	96
1989 Double Top 9-71	Retrd.	1989	7.00	40
1989 Drop Reflector 88	Retrd.	N/A	23.00	90
1989 Elf on Ball (matte) 9-62	Retrd.	1990	9.50	40-90
1989 Fisher Frog 9-65	Retrd.	1991	7.00	75
1989 Fleurs de Provence 30	Retrd.	N/A	17.00	96
1989 Grecian Urn 9-69	Retrd.	1989	9.00	35
1989 Harlequin Finial (tree topper) 107	Retrd.	N/A	22.00	186
1989 His Boy Elroy 9-104	Retrd.	1991	8.00	125-138
1989 The Holly 9-49	Retrd.	N/A	17.00	90
1989 Hurricane Lamp 9-67	Retrd.	1989	7.00	45
1989 The Ivy 9-47	Retrd.	N/A	16.50	120
1989 Jester 41	Retrd.	N/A	16.50	120
1989 Joey Clown (light pink) 9-58	Retrd.	1992	9.00	50-96
1989 Kim Ono 9-57	Retrd.	1990	6.50	25-50
1989 King Arthur (Lt. Blue) 9-103	Retrd.	1991	12.00	60-95
1989 Kite Face 64	Retrd.	N/A	8.50	45
1989 Lilac Sparkle 9-7	Retrd.	1989	17.00	75-125
1989 Lucky Fish 9-73	Retrd.	1989	6.50	45-55
1989 Parachute 9-68	Retrd.	1989	6.50	75-96
1989 Pastel Harlequin 22	Retrd.	N/A	17.00	66
1989 Peppermint Stripes 89	Retrd.	N/A	29.00	300
1989 Royal Rooster 9-18	Retrd.	1993	17.00	95
1989 Royal Star Tree Finial 108	Retrd.	N/A	42.00	95
1989 Seahorse 9-54	Retrd.	1992	10.00	60-90
1989 Serpent 9-72	Retrd.	N/A	7.00	30
1989 Shy Kitten 9-66	Retrd.	N/A	7.00	48-72
1989 Shy Rabbit 9-61	Retrd.	N/A	7.00	60-72
1989 Small Reflector 9-76	Retrd.	N/A	7.50	23-32
1989 Smiling Sun 9-59	Retrd.	N/A	7.00	45-78
1989 Songbirds 21	Retrd.	N/A	17.50	240
1989 Tiffany 44	Retrd.	N/A	17.00	650
1989 Vineyard 9-51	Retrd.	N/A	17.00	115
1989 Walrus 9-63	Retrd.	1990	8.00	60-106
1989 Zebra 9-10	Retrd.	1991	17.50	110

1990 Holiday Collection - C. Radko

YEAR ISSUE	EDITION LIMIT	YEAR RETD.	ISSUE PRICE	*QUOTE U.S.$
1990 Angel on Harp 46	Retrd.	1990	9.00	85
1990 Ballooning Santa 85	Retrd.	1991	20.00	175-200
1990 Bathing Baby 70	Retrd.	N/A	11.00	54-72
1990 Boy Clown on Reflector 82	Retrd.	N/A	18.00	85-125
1990 Calla Lilly 38	Retrd.	N/A	7.00	25-35
1990 Candy Trumpet Man (blue) 85-1	Retrd.	N/A	28.00	42-48
1990 Candy Trumpet Man 85-1	Retrd.	N/A	28.00	96
1990 Carmen Miranda 18	Retrd.	1991	19.00	95-125
1990 Chimney Sweep Bell 179	Retrd.	N/A	27.00	75-150
1990 Christmas Cardinals 16	Retrd.	1992	18.00	125
1990 Conch Shell 65	Retrd.	1991	9.00	48-100
1990 Crowned Prince 56	Retrd.	1990	14.00	64-96
1990 Deco Floral 29	Retrd.	N/A	19.00	110-120
1990 Dublin Pipe 40	Retrd.	1990	14.00	50
1990 Eagle Medallion 67	Retrd.	1990	9.00	40-54
1990 Early Winter 24	Retrd.	1990	10.00	40
1990 Emerald City 92	Retrd.	1990	7.50	65-94
1990 Fat Lady 35	Retrd.	N/A	7.00	35-42
1990 Father Christmas 76	Retrd.	N/A	7.00	45
1990 Frog Under Balloon 58	Retrd.	1991	14.00	60-132
1990 Frosty 62	Retrd.	N/A	14.00	36-60
1990 Golden Puppy 53	Retrd.	1990	8.00	85-95
1990 Google Eyes 44	Retrd.	1990	9.00	95-100
1990 Gypsy Queen 54	Retrd.	N/A	11.50	54
1990 Happy Gnome 77	Retrd.	1991	8.00	75
1990 Hearts & Flowers (ball) 15	Retrd.	N/A	19.00	90
1990 Heritage Santa 9075-2	Retrd.	N/A	24.00	65
1990 Holly Ball 4	Retrd.	N/A	19.00	125
1990 Honey Bear 167	Retrd.	N/A	14.00	55
1990 Jester 41	Retrd.	N/A	16.50	120
1990 Joey Clown (red striped) 55	Retrd.	N/A	14.00	85-95
1990 Kim Ono 79	Retrd.	1990	6.00	35-55
1990 King Arthur (Red) 72	Retrd.	N/A	16.00	95-110
1990 Lullaby 47	Retrd.	1990	9.00	35-60
1990 Maracca 94	Retrd.	1990	9.00	125
1990 Mediterranean Sunshine 140	Retrd.	N/A	27.00	34
1990 Mission Ball 26	Retrd.	N/A	18.00	48
1990 Mother Goose (blue bonnet/pink shawl) 52	Retrd.	N/A	10.00	20-60
1990 Nativity 36	Retrd.	1990	6.00	50
1990 Olympiad 7	Retrd.	N/A	18.00	48
1990 Peacock (on snowball) 74	Retrd.	N/A	18.00	75-100
1990 Pierre Le Berry	Retrd.	N/A	10.00	60-66
1990 Polish Folk Dance 13	Retrd.	N/A	19.00	120-150
1990 Praying Angel 37	Retrd.	N/A	5.00	75
1990 Proud Peacock 74	Retrd.	N/A	18.00	125
1990 Pudgy Clown 39	Retrd.	N/A	6.50	30-45
1990 Roly Poly Santa (Red bottom) 69	Retrd.	N/A	13.00	28-60
1990 Rose Lamp 96	Retrd.	1990	14.00	90-180
1990 Santa on Ball 80	Retrd.	1991	16.00	132-216
1990 Silent Movie (black hat) 75	Retrd.	1990	8.50	60-65
1990 Small Nautilus Shell 78	Retrd.	N/A	7.00	22
1990 Smiling Kite 63	Retrd.	1990	14.00	45-85
1990 Snowball Tree 71	Retrd.	1990	17.00	75-180
1990 Snowman on Ball 45	Retrd.	1990	14.00	75-85
1990 Southwest Indian Ball 19	Retrd.	N/A	19.00	240
1990 Spin Top 90	Retrd.	N/A	11.00	36-48
1990 Summer Parasol 88	Retrd.	N/A	7.00	156
1990 Sunburst Fish (green/yellow) 68	Retrd.	N/A	13.00	50
1990 Swami 41	Retrd.	N/A	8.00	66
1990 Tabby 42	Retrd.	N/A	7.00	30
1990 Tropical Fish 74	Retrd.	N/A	24.00	42-60
1990 Trumpet Player 83	Retrd.	N/A	18.00	100
1990 Tuxedo Penquin 57	Retrd.	1990	8.00	150-350
1990 Walrus 59	Retrd.	1990	8.50	120
1990 Yarn Fight 23	Retrd.	N/A	17.00	125-150

1991 Holiday Collection - C. Radko

YEAR ISSUE	EDITION LIMIT	YEAR RETD.	ISSUE PRICE	*QUOTE U.S.$
1991 All Weather Santa 137	Retrd.	1992	32.00	130-230
1991 Alladin 29	Retrd.	N/A	14.00	48-60
1991 Altar Boy 18	Retrd.	1992	16.00	36-66
1991 Anchor America 65	Retrd.	1992	21.50	55-72
1991 Apache 42	Retrd.	N/A	8.50	25-50
1991 Aspen 76	Retrd.	1992	20.50	60-100
1991 Aztec 141	Retrd.	1991	21.50	72-114
1991 Aztec Bird 41	Retrd.	1992	20.00	96-198
1991 Ballooning Santa 110	Retrd.	1991	23.00	150-208
1991 Barnum Clown 56	Retrd.	1991	15.00	55-95
1991 Bishop 22	Retrd.	N/A	15.00	30-54
1991 Black Forest Cone 97	Retrd.	N/A	8.00	42
1991 Blue Rainbow 136	Retrd.	1992	21.50	95-100
1991 Bowery Kid 50	Retrd.	1991	14.50	48-50
1991 Butterfly Bouquet 142	Retrd.	N/A	21.50	54
1991 By the Nile 124	Retrd.	1992	21.50	48-72
1991 Cardinal Richelieu 109	Retrd.	N/A	15.50	90
1991 Carnival (cloudy) 123	Retrd.	N/A	20.00	72
1991 Chance Encounter 104	Retrd.	1992	13.50	36-90
1991 Chief Sitting Bull 107	Retrd.	1992	16.00	90-108
1991 Chimney Santa 12	Retrd.	N/A	14.50	40
1991 Clown Drum 33	Retrd.	1991	14.00	54-60
1991 Comet 62	Retrd.	1991	9.00	60-80
1991 Cosette 16	Retrd.	1991	16.00	45-60
1991 Country Quilt 140	Retrd.	N/A	21.00	48-54
1991 Dapper Shoe 89	Retrd.	1991	10.00	42-48
1991 Dawn & Dusk 34	Retrd.	N/A	14.00	42-65
1991 Deco Floral 133	Retrd.	1991	22.00	75-125
1991 Deco Sparkle 134	Retrd.	1992	21.00	66-100
1991 Deep Sea (pale green, signed) 72	Retrd.	N/A	21.50	72
1991 Dutch Boy 27	Retrd.	1991	11.00	30-55
1991 Dutch Girl 28	Retrd.	1991	11.00	55-75
1991 Edwardian Lace 82	Retrd.	1991	21.50	125
1991 Einstein Kite 98	Retrd.	N/A	20.00	90-125
1991 Elephant on Ball (gold) 115	Retrd.	N/A	23.00	500
1991 Elephant on Ball (striped) 115	Retrd.	N/A	23.00	450-500
1991 Elf Reflector 135	Retrd.	1992	23.00	50
1991 Evening Santa 20	Retrd.	N/A	14.50	48-100
1991 Fanfare 126	Retrd.	1992	21.50	72-98
1991 Fisher Frog 44	Retrd.	1991	11.00	75
1991 Florentine 83	Retrd.	N/A	22.00	66-100
1991 Flower Child 90	Retrd.	1991	13.00	40-78
1991 Frog Under Balloon 53	Retrd.	N/A	16.00	45-75
1991 Froggy Child 26	Retrd.	N/A	9.00	25-36
1991 Fruit in Balloon 40	Retrd.	N/A	22.00	150-168
1991 Fu Manchu 11	Retrd.	N/A	15.00	75
1991 Galaxy 120	Retrd.	1991	21.50	60-72
1991 Grapefruit Tree 113	Retrd.	N/A	23.00	120-168
1991 Harvest 3	Retrd.	N/A	13.50	25-78
1991 Hatching Duck 35	Retrd.	1991	14.00	48-50
1991 Hearts & Flowers Finial 158	Retrd.	1993	53.00	150-156
1991 Her Majesty 39	Retrd.	1991	21.00	50-96
1991 Her Purse 88	Retrd.	N/A	10.00	30-66
1991 Holly Ball 156	Retrd.	N/A	22.00	60
1991 Irish Laddie 10	Retrd.	1991	12.00	65-75
1991 Jemima's Child 111	Retrd.	1991	16.00	60-100
1991 King Arthur (Blue) 95	Retrd.	N/A	18.50	55-85
1991 Lion's Head 31	Retrd.	N/A	16.00	38-45
1991 Lucy's Favorite (gold) 75-1	Retrd.	N/A	10.50	60
1991 Lucy's Favorite (signed) 75	Retrd.	N/A	10.50	72
1991 Madeleine's Puppy 25	Retrd.	N/A	11.00	45-48
1991 Madonna & Child 103	Retrd.	N/A	15.00	60-125
1991 Melon Slice 99	Retrd.	N/A	18.00	31
1991 Mother Goose 57	Retrd.	N/A	11.00	40
1991 Ms. Maus 94	Retrd.	N/A	14.00	60-150
1991 Munchkin 91	Retrd.	N/A	8.00	36
1991 Olympiad 125	Retrd.	1992	22.00	125
1991 Patrick's Bunny 24	Retrd.	N/A	11.00	30-48
1991 Peruvian 74	Retrd.	1991	21.50	60-100
1991 Pierre Le Berry 2	Retrd.	1993	14.00	125-200
1991 Pink Clown on Ball 32	Retrd.	N/A	14.00	34-60
1991 Pink Elephants 70	Retrd.	N/A	21.50	72-130
1991 Pipe Man 93	Retrd.	N/A	20.00	54-90
1991 Pipe Smoking Monkey 54	Retrd.	1991	11.00	48-75
1991 Polish Folk Art 116	Retrd.	N/A	20.50	48-75
1991 Prince on Ball (pink/blue/green) 51	Retrd.	1991	15.00	80
1991 Prince Umbrella 21	Retrd.	1991	15.00	66-100
1991 Proud Peacock 37	Retrd.	N/A	23.00	72-150
1991 Puss N Boots 23	Retrd.	N/A	11.00	36-54
1991 Rainbow Bird 92	Retrd.	1991	16.00	48-132
1991 Rainbow Trout 17	Retrd.	N/A	14.50	25
1991 Raspberry & Lime 96	Retrd.	1991	12.00	48-72
1991 Red Star 129	Retrd.	1992	21.50	72-75
1991 Royal Porcelain 71	Retrd.	N/A	21.50	72
1991 Russian Santa (coral) 112-4	Retrd.	N/A	22.00	60-75
1991 Russian Santa (white) 112	Retrd.	N/A	22.00	70-75
1991 Sally Ann 43	Retrd.	1991	8.00	36-40
1991 Santa Bootie (blue) 55	Retrd.	N/A	10.00	25-75
1991 Santa Bootie 55	Retrd.	1993	10.00	30-48
1991 Santa in Winter White (red) 112-2	Retrd.	N/A	22.00	100-200
1991 Santa in Winter White (silver) 112-1	Retrd.	N/A	22.00	50
1991 Ship To Shore 122	Retrd.	N/A	20.50	84
1991 Shirley 15	Retrd.	1991	16.00	60-75
1991 Shy Elf 1	Retrd.	1991	10.00	36-60
1991 Silver Bells (signed) 73	Retrd.	N/A	20.50	96
1991 Sleepy Time Santa 52	Retrd.	N/A	15.00	48-75
1991 Smitty 9	Retrd.	N/A	15.00	60-175
1991 Star Quilt 139	Retrd.	1991	21.50	66-75
1991 Sunburst Fish 108	Retrd.	N/A	15.00	120
1991 Sunshine 67	Retrd.	N/A	22.00	40-60
1991 Tabby 46	Retrd.	1991	8.00	30-50
1991 Talking Pipe 93	Retrd.	N/A	20.00	84
1991 Tiffany 68	Retrd.	1991	22.00	50
1991 Tiger 5	Retrd.	N/A	15.00	45-60
1991 Timepiece 30	Retrd.	N/A	8.00	42
1991 Trigger 114	Retrd.	1991	15.00	60-102
1991 Trumpet Man 100	Retrd.	1992	21.00	96
1991 Tulip Fairy 63	Retrd.	1992	16.00	30-78
1991 Vienna 1901 127	Retrd.	1992	21.50	200
1991 Villandry 87	Retrd.	1991	21.00	150-185
1991 Winking St. Nick 102	Retrd.	N/A	16.00	65-108
1991 Woodland Santa 38	Retrd.	N/A	14.00	65-84
1991 Zebra (glittered) 79	Retrd.	1991	22.00	400-500

1992 Holiday Collection - C. Radko

YEAR ISSUE	EDITION LIMIT	YEAR RETD.	ISSUE PRICE	*QUOTE U.S.$
1992 Alpine Flowers-Tiffany 162	Retrd.	1992	28.00	50-60
1992 Alpine Village 105	Retrd.	N/A	24.00	110-125
1992 Aspen 120	Retrd.	1992	26.00	50
1992 Barbie's Mom 69	Retrd.	1992	18.00	48-78
1992 Benjamin's Nutcrackers (pr.) 185	Retrd.	N/A	58.00	200-450
1992 Binkie the Clown 168	Retrd.	N/A	12.00	36-60
1992 Blue Santa 65	Retrd.	N/A	18.00	48-84
1992 Butterfly Bouquet 119	Retrd.	1992	26.50	60-125
1992 By the Nile 139	Retrd.	1992	27.00	50-75
1992 Cabaret-Tiffany (see-through) 159	Retrd.	1993	28.00	60
1992 Candy Trumpet Men (pink/blue) 98	Retrd.	N/A	27.00	48-75
1992 Candy Trumpet Men (red) w/ white glitter 98	Retrd.	1992	27.00	60-80
1992 Candy Trumpet Men (red) w/o white glitter 98	Retrd.	N/A	27.00	45
1992 Celestial 129	Retrd.	N/A	26.00	100
1992 Cheerful Sun 50	Retrd.	N/A	18.00	40
1992 Chevron 160	Retrd.	1992	28.00	40
1992 Chevron-Tiffany 160	Retrd.	N/A	28.00	98
1992 Chimney Sweep Bell 179	Retrd.	N/A	27.00	78-150
1992 Choir Boy 114	Retrd.	1992	24.00	36-50
1992 Christmas Cardinals 123	Retrd.	1992	26.00	30-60
1992 Christmas Rose 143	Retrd.	1992	25.50	45-60
1992 Circus Lady 54	Retrd.	1992	12.00	25
1992 Clown Snake 62	Retrd.	N/A	22.00	22-42
1992 Country Scene 169	Retrd.	N/A	12.00	54-90
1992 Country Star Quilt 176	Retrd.	N/A	12.00	50-100
1992 Cowboy Santa 94	Retrd.	N/A	24.00	48-100
1992 Crescent Moons 189	Retrd.	N/A	26.00	60
1992 Dawn & Dusk 96	Retrd.	N/A	19.00	36-48
1992 Delft Design 124	Retrd.	1992	26.50	170
1992 Diva 73	Retrd.	1992	17.00	36-65
1992 Dolly Madison 115	Retrd.	1992	17.00	60-85

*Quotes have been rounded up to nearest dollar

ORNAMENTS

YEAR ISSUE	EDITION LIMIT	YEAR RETD.	ISSUE PRICE	*QUOTE U.S.$
1992 Down The Chimney 191	Retrd.	N/A	16.50	36-66
1992 Downhill Racer 76	Retrd.	1992	34.00	75-140
1992 Elephant on Parade 141	Retrd.	1992	26.00	70-85
1992 Elephant Reflector 181	Retrd.	N/A	17.00	66-95
1992 Elf Reflectors 136	Retrd.	1992	28.00	48-96
1992 Eveningstar Santa 186	Retrd.	N/A	60.00	180
1992 Faberge (pink/lavender) 148	Retrd.	N/A	26.50	45-55
1992 Faith, Hope & Love 183	Retrd.	1992	12.00	30
1992 Festive Smitty	Retrd.	N/A	28.95	48-65
1992 Floral Cascade Finial 173	Retrd.	N/A	68.00	102
1992 Floral Cascade Tier Drop 175	Retrd.	1992	64.00	125-400
1992 Florentine 131	Retrd.	N/A	27.00	45-75
1992 Flutter By's 201(Set/4)	Retrd.	N/A	11.00	48-65
1992 Folk Art Set 95	Retrd.	1992	10.00	13
1992 Forest Friends 103	Retrd.	1992	14.00	20-54
1992 French Country 121	Retrd.	N/A	26.00	48-60
1992 Fruit in Balloon 83	Retrd.	N/A	28.00	60-125
1992 Gabriel's Trumpets 188	Retrd.	N/A	20.00	25
1992 Harlequin Ball 196	Retrd.	N/A	27.00	27-48
1992 Harlequin Finial (tree topper) 199	Retrd.	N/A	70.00	120-136
1992 Harlequin Tier Drop 74	Retrd.	1992	36.00	72-90
1992 Harold Lloyd Reflector 218	Retrd.	1992	70.00	200-450
1992 Her Purse 43	Retrd.	N/A	20.00	36-60
1992 Her Slipper 56	Retrd.	1992	17.00	22
1992 Holly Finial 200	Retrd.	N/A	70.00	83
1992 Honey Bear 167	Retrd.	N/A	14.00	30-55
1992 Ice Pear 241	Retrd.	N/A	20.00	48-72
1992 Ice Poppies 127	Retrd.	1992	26.00	48-60
1992 Jester Ball 151	Retrd.	N/A	25.50	66
1992 Jumbo 99	Retrd.	N/A	31.00	45-48
1992 Just Like Grandma's 164	Retrd.	N/A	10.00	25-30
1992 Kewpie 51	Retrd.	N/A	18.00	38-60
1992 King of Prussia 149	Retrd.	1992	27.00	48-100
1992 Kitty Rattle 166	Retrd.	1993	18.00	48-60
1992 Little Eskimo 38	Retrd.	N/A	14.00	30-42
1992 Little League 53	Retrd.	1992	20.00	36-65
1992 The Littlest Snowman (red hat) 67	Retrd.	N/A	14.00	36-48
1992 Littlest Snowman 67	Retrd.	N/A	14.00	36-48
1992 Locamotive Garland 216	Retrd.	N/A	60.00	75-150
1992 Majestic Reflector 187	Retrd.	N/A	70.00	120
1992 Meditteranean Sunshine 140	Retrd.	N/A	17.00	34
1992 Melon Slice 91	Retrd.	N/A	26.00	26-48
1992 Merlin Santa 75	Retrd.	N/A	32.00	48-84
1992 Merry Christmas Maiden 137	Retrd.	1992	26.00	40-48
1992 Mission Ball 153	Retrd.	N/A	27.00	27-48
1992 Mother Goose 37	Retrd.	N/A	15.00	25-48
1992 Mr. & Mrs. Claus 59	Retrd.	N/A	18.00	150-200
1992 Mushroom Elf 87	Retrd.	N/A	18.00	36-72
1992 Neopolitan Angels 152 (Set/3)	Retrd.	1992	27.00	144-300
1992 Norweigian Princess 170	Retrd.	1992	15.00	25-65
1992 Olympiad 132	Retrd.	N/A	26.00	80
1992 Palace Guard 60	Retrd.	N/A	17.00	30-54
1992 Pierre Winterberry 64	Retrd.	1993	17.00	30-75
1992 Pink Lace Ball (See Through) 158	Retrd.	1992	28.00	60-100
1992 Polar Bear 184	Retrd.	N/A	16.00	30-50
1992 Primary Colors 108	Retrd.	1992	30.00	150
1992 Quilted Hearts (Old Salem Museum) 194	Retrd.	N/A	27.50	55
1992 Rainbow Parasol 90	Retrd.	1992	30.00	60-100
1992 Royal Scepter 77	Retrd.	1992	36.00	114-120
1992 Ruby Scarlet Finial 198	Retrd.	N/A	70.00	168
1992 Russian Imperial 112	Retrd.	1992	25.00	48-75
1992 Russian Jewel Hearts 146	Retrd.	N/A	27.00	60-125
1992 Russian Star 130	Retrd.	1992	26.00	32-40
1992 Sail Away 215	Retrd.	N/A	22.00	50
1992 Santa Claus Garland 220	Retrd.	N/A	66.00	96-120
1992 Santa in Winter White 106	Retrd.	N/A	28.00	60-65
1992 Santa's Helper 78	Retrd.	N/A	17.00	36-72
1992 Scallop Shell 150	Retrd.	N/A	27.00	27-30
1992 Seafaring Santa 71	Retrd.	N/A	18.00	36-66
1992 Seahorse (pink) 92	Retrd.	1992	20.00	72-86
1992 Serpents of Paradise 97	Retrd.	N/A	13.00	30
1992 Shy Rabbit 40	Retrd.	N/A	14.00	36-72
1992 Siberian Sleigh Ride (pink) 154	Retrd.	N/A	27.00	48-150
1992 Silver Icicle 89	Retrd.	N/A	12.00	48-60
1992 Sitting Bull 93	Retrd.	1992	26.00	60-65
1992 Sleepytime Santa (pink) 81	Retrd.	N/A	18.00	60-95
1992 Sloopy Snowman 328	Retrd.	N/A	19.90	36-75
1992 Snake Prince 171	Retrd.	N/A	19.00	30-66
1992 Snowflakes 209	Retrd.	N/A	10.00	40-60
1992 Southern Colonial 142	Retrd.	N/A	27.00	48-54
1992 Sputniks 134	Retrd.	1992	25.50	84-125
1992 St. Nickcicle 107	Retrd.	N/A	26.00	36-72
1992 Star of Wonder 177	Retrd.	1992	27.00	35-50
1992 Starbursts 214	Retrd.	N/A	12.00	48-75
1992 Stardust Joey 110	Retrd.	1992	16.00	75-150
1992 Starlight Santa (powder blue) 180	Retrd.	N/A	18.00	50
1992 Sterling Silver Garland 204	Retrd.	N/A	12.00	60
1992 Talking Pipe (black stem) 104	Retrd.	N/A	26.00	110
1992 Thunderbolt 178	Retrd.	1993	60.00	222
1992 Tiffany Bright Harlequin 161	Retrd.	1992	28.00	48-114
1992 Tiffany Pastel Harlequin 163	Retrd.	N/A	28.00	48-114
1992 To Grandma's House 239	Retrd.	N/A	20.00	45-96
1992 Topiary 117	Retrd.	N/A	30.00	120-250
1992 Tropical Fish 109	Retrd.	N/A	17.00	60
1992 Tulip Fairy 57	Retrd.	1992	18.00	45
1992 Tuxedo Santa 88	Retrd.	1993	22.00	125-160
1992 Two Sided Santa Reflector 102	Retrd.	1992	28.00	48-86
1992 Umbrella Santa 182	Retrd.	N/A	60.00	120-140
1992 Victorian Santa & Angel Balloon 122	Retrd.	1992	68.00	500-600
1992 Vienna 1901 128	Retrd.	1992	27.00	150
1992 Village Carolers 172	Retrd.	N/A	17.00	30-78
1992 Virgin Mary 46	Retrd.	1992	20.00	48-60
1992 Wacko's Brother, Doofus 55	Retrd.	N/A	20.00	65
1992 Water Lilies 133	Retrd.	1992	26.00	90-100
1992 Wedding Bells 217	Retrd.	N/A	40.00	165-225
1992 Winking St. Nick 70	Retrd.	N/A	22.00	22-48
1992 Winter Kiss 82	Retrd.	N/A	18.00	48-60
1992 Winter Tree 101	Retrd.	N/A	28.00	48-84
1992 Winter Wonderland 156	Retrd.	1992	26.00	48-110
1992 Woodland Santa 111	Retrd.	N/A	20.00	55-75
1992 Ziegfeld Follies 126	Retrd.	1992	27.00	100-130

1993 Holiday Collection - C. Radko

YEAR ISSUE	EDITION LIMIT	YEAR RETD.	ISSUE PRICE	*QUOTE U.S.$
1993 1939 World's Fair 149	Retrd.	N/A	26.80	100
1993 Accordian Elf 189	Retrd.	N/A	21.00	36-65
1993 Aladdin's Lamp 237	Retrd.	N/A	20.00	54-96
1993 Allegro 179	Retrd.	N/A	26.80	48-132
1993 Alpine Village 420	Retrd.	1993	23.80	125
1993 Alpine Wings 86	Retrd.	N/A	58.00	90-108
1993 Anassazi 172	Retrd.	N/A	26.60	65-75
1993 Anchor Santa 407	Retrd.	N/A	32.00	85-126
1993 Angel Light 256	Retrd.	N/A	16.00	48
1993 Angel of Peace 132	Retrd.	1993	17.00	54-85
1993 Apache 357	Retrd.	1993	13.90	54-75
1993 Auld Lang Syne 246	Retrd.	N/A	15.00	54-78
1993 Away in a Manger 379	Retrd.	N/A	24.00	24-36
1993 Bavarian Santa 335	Retrd.	N/A	23.00	50-65
1993 Beauregard 296	Retrd.	N/A	24.00	24-42
1993 Bedtime Buddy 239	Retrd.	N/A	29.00	114-125
1993 Bell House Boy 291	Retrd.	1993	21.00	36-54
1993 Bells Are Ringing 268	Retrd.	N/A	18.00	36-50
1993 Bells-Tiffany 334	Retrd.	N/A	8.80	36
1993 Beyond the Stars 108	Retrd.	1993	18.50	54-70
1993 Bishop of Myra 327	Retrd.	1993	19.90	50
1993 Blue Top 114	Retrd.	1993	16.00	36-75
1993 Bowzer 228	Retrd.	N/A	22.80	78-125
1993 By Jiminy 285	Retrd.	N/A	16.40	25-54
1993 Calla Lilly 314	Retrd.	N/A	12.90	15-25
1993 Candied Citrus 278	Retrd.	N/A	9.00	42
1993 Candlelight 118	Retrd.	N/A	16.00	30-42
1993 Carnival Rides 303	Retrd.	N/A	18.00	65-75
1993 Cathedral Bells 343	Retrd.	N/A	8.20	54
1993 Celeste 271	Retrd.	N/A	26.00	50-100
1993 Celestial Peacock 197	Retrd.	N/A	27.90	48-84
1993 Celestial Peacock Finial 322	Retrd.	N/A	69.00	200-295
1993 Center Ring (Exclusive) 192	Retrd.	1993	30.80	48-150
1993 Centurian 224	Retrd.	1993	25.50	100-168
1993 Chimney Sweep Bell 294	Retrd.	1993	26.00	180
1993 Christmas Express (Garland) 394	Retrd.	N/A	58.00	90-120
1993 Christmas Goose 129	Retrd.	N/A	14.80	42
1993 Christmas Stars 342	Retrd.	N/A	14.00	36
1993 Church Bell 295	Retrd.	N/A	24.00	42-45
1993 Cinderella's Bluebirds 145	Retrd.	1993	25.90	54-120
1993 Circle of Santas Finial 413	Retrd.	N/A	69.00	100
1993 Circus Seal 249	Retrd.	1993	28.00	102-125
1993 Circus Star 358	Retrd.	N/A	24.00	90
1993 Class Clown 332	Retrd.	N/A	21.00	66
1993 Classic Christmas 408	Retrd.	N/A	29.00	132
1993 Cloud Nine 369	Retrd.	N/A	25.00	42-72
1993 Clowning Around 84	Retrd.	N/A	42.50	68
1993 Confucius 363	Retrd.	1993	19.00	28
1993 Cool Cat 184	Retrd.	N/A	21.00	100-150
1993 Copenhagen 166	Retrd.	1993	26.80	42-72
1993 Country Flowers 205	Retrd.	N/A	16.00	40-54
1993 Country Scene 204	Retrd.	N/A	11.90	36-48
1993 Crescent Moons Finial 397	Retrd.	N/A	69.00	69-108
1993 Crocus Blossoms 283	Retrd.	N/A	16.00	54
1993 Crowned Passion 299	Retrd.	1993	23.00	48-60
1993 Crystal Fountain 243	Retrd.	N/A	34.00	90-120
1993 Crystal Rainbow 308	Retrd.	N/A	29.90	200
1993 Dancing Harlequin 232	Retrd.	N/A	36.00	45-84
1993 Daniel Star 211	Retrd.	N/A	26.00	34-54
1993 Dawn & Dusk 318	Retrd.	N/A	18.90	19-36
1993 Deco Snowfall 147	Retrd.	1993	26.80	42-48
1993 Deer Drop 304	Retrd.	N/A	34.00	110-120
1993 Del Monte 219	Retrd.	N/A	23.50	24-54
1993 Devotion 203	Retrd.	N/A	17.00	17-30
1993 Don't Hold Your Breath 92-1	Retrd.	N/A	11.00	50
1993 Downhill Racer 195	Retrd.	1993	30.00	60-108
1993 Eggman 241	Retrd.	N/A	22.50	42-72
1993 Elf Bell 125	Retrd.	N/A	18.00	20-48
1993 Emerald Wizard 279	Retrd.	N/A	18.00	32-48
1993 Emperor's Pet 253	Retrd.	1993	22.00	90-180
1993 Enchanted Gardens 341	Retrd.	1993	5.50	13
1993 English Kitchen 234	Retrd.	1993	26.00	50-54
1993 Epiphany 421	Retrd.	N/A	29.00	48-90
1993 Eskimo Elves Garland 72	Retrd.	N/A	39.20	78
1993 Eskimo Kitty 281	Retrd.	N/A	14.50	36-60
1993 Evening Star Santa 409	Retrd.	1993	59.00	95
1993 Extravagance Garland 87	Retrd.	N/A	53.00	90
1993 Faberge Egg 257	Retrd.	N/A	17.50	42-45
1993 Fantastia 143	Retrd.	N/A	24.00	55-130
1993 Fantasy Cone 324	Retrd.	N/A	17.90	30-36
1993 Far Out Santa 138	Retrd.	N/A	39.00	60
1993 Fiesta Ball 316	Retrd.	N/A	26.40	40-85
1993 Fleurice 282	Retrd.	N/A	23.50	54
1993 Flora Dora 255	Retrd.	N/A	25.00	60-90
1993 Fly Boy 235	Retrd.	N/A	33.00	60-96
1993 Forest Bells 136	Retrd.	N/A	25.00	48-54
1993 Forest Friends 250	Retrd.	1993	28.00	40-90
1993 French Rose 152	Retrd.	1993	26.60	48-60
1993 Fruit in Balloon 115	Retrd.	N/A	27.90	80
1993 Geisha Girls 261	Retrd.	1993	11.90	25-60
1993 Georgian Santa 292	Retrd.	N/A	30.00	50-90
1993 Gerard 252	Retrd.	N/A	26.00	48-96
1993 Glory on High 116	Retrd.	N/A	17.00	84-150
1993 Gold Fish 158	Retrd.	1993	25.80	75-100
1993 Golden Crescendo Finial 381-1	Retrd.	N/A	50.00	600
1993 Goofy Fruits 367	Retrd.	N/A	14.00	66
1993 Goofy Garden (Set/4) 191	Retrd.	N/A	15.00	125-240
1993 Grandpa Bear 260	Retrd.	1993	12.80	20-36
1993 Grecian Urn 231	Retrd.	1993	23.00	50-60
1993 Guardian Angel 124	Retrd.	N/A	36.00	100-144
1993 Gypsy Girl 371	Retrd.	1993	16.00	35-42
1993 Hansel & Gretel 100	Retrd.	N/A	24.00	54
1993 Harvest 354	Retrd.	N/A	19.90	48
1993 Holiday Inn 137	Retrd.	N/A	21.00	54
1993 Holiday Sparkle 144	Retrd.	N/A	16.80	40-70
1993 Holiday Spice 422	Retrd.	1993	24.00	48-84
1993 Holly Ribbons 415	Retrd.	N/A	24.80	48-84
1993 Honey Bear 352	Retrd.	1993	13.90	55
1993 Ice Bear 284	Retrd.	N/A	17.50	30-48
1993 Ice Star Santa 405	Retrd.	1993	38.00	250-360
1993 Injun Joe 102	Retrd.	N/A	24.00	48-60
1993 It's A Small World 96	Retrd.	N/A	17.00	25-42
1993 Jack Frost (blue) 333	Retrd.	N/A	23.00	48-75
1993 Jaques Le Berry 356	Retrd.	N/A	16.90	100-175
1993 Jewel Box 213	Retrd.	N/A	12.00	12-36
1993 Joey B. Clown 135	Retrd.	N/A	26.00	60-96
1993 Jumbo Spintops 302	Retrd.	N/A	27.00	132
1993 Just Like Grandma's Lg. 200	Retrd.	N/A	7.20	25-50
1993 Just Like Grandma's Sm. 200	Retrd.	N/A	7.20	30
1993 King's Ransom 449	Retrd.	N/A	49.00	75
1993 Kissing Cousins (Pair) 245	Retrd.	N/A	30.00	156-162
1993 Kitty Rattle 374	Retrd.	1993	17.80	90
1993 Lamp Light 251	Retrd.	N/A	22.50	42-60
1993 Letter to Santa 188	Retrd.	N/A	22.00	36-65
1993 Light in the Windows 229	Retrd.	1994	24.50	30-48
1993 Little Boy Blue 361	Retrd.	N/A	25.90	60
1993 Little Doggie 180	Retrd.	1993	7.00	36-40
1993 Little Eskimo 355	Retrd.	N/A	13.90	21
1993 Little Slugger 187	Retrd.	N/A	22.00	22-36
1993 Lucky Shoe 346	Retrd.	N/A	16.00	54
1993 Majestic Reflector 312	Retrd.	1993	70.00	100
1993 Maxine 240	Retrd.	N/A	10.00	42-96
1993 Mediterranean Sunshine 156	Retrd.	N/A	26.90	75
1993 Midas Touch 162	Retrd.	N/A	27.80	68
1993 Monkey Business 126	Retrd.	N/A	14.80	54
1993 Monkey Man 97	Retrd.	1993	16.00	42-100
1993 Monterey 290	Retrd.	1993	15.00	75-100
1993 Moon Dust 128	Retrd.	N/A	15.00	78
1993 Mooning Over You 106	Retrd.	N/A	17.00	25-55
1993 Mountain Christmas 384	Retrd.	N/A	25.50	78
1993 Mr. & Mrs. Claus 121	Retrd.	1993	17.90	80-125
1993 Mushroom Elf 267	Retrd.	N/A	17.90	38
1993 Mushroom Santa 212	Retrd.	N/A	28.00	75-180
1993 Nellie (Italian ornament) 225	Retrd.	1993	27.50	132-200
1993 Nesting Stork Finial (red or gold) 380	Retrd.	N/A	50.00	150
1993 Nesting Stork Finial 380	Retrd.	N/A	50.00	228
1993 North Woods 317	Retrd.	1993	26.80	72-90
1993 Northwind 266	Retrd.	N/A	17.00	48-72
1993 Nuts & Berries (signed) 64	Retrd.	N/A	58.00	120
1993 Nuts & Berries 64	Retrd.	N/A	58.00	60-90
1993 One Small Leap 222	Retrd.	N/A	26.00	120-180
1993 Pagoda 258	Retrd.	1993	8.00	15-30
1993 Pennsylvania Dutch 146	Retrd.	1993	26.80	42-65
1993 Piggly Wiggly 101	Retrd.	N/A	11.00	42-100
1993 Pineapple Quilt 150	Retrd.	N/A	26.80	54-65
1993 Pineapple Slice 376	Retrd.	N/A	14.00	54
1993 Pinocchio 248	Retrd.	N/A	26.00	50-95
1993 Pixie Santa 186	Retrd.	N/A	16.00	30-54
1993 Plum 185	Retrd.	N/A	6.40	20
1993 Poinsetta Santa 269	Retrd.	N/A	19.80	65-76
1993 Polar Bears 112A	Retrd.	1993	15.50	16
1993 Pompadour 344	Retrd.	1993	8.80	25
1993 President Taft 92	Retrd.	N/A	15.00	60
1993 Prince Albert 263	Retrd.	N/A	23.00	48-80
1993 Purse 389	Retrd.	1993	15.60	16
1993 Quartet 392	Retrd.	1993	3.60	11
1993 Radio Monkey 104	Retrd.	N/A	16.20	48
1993 Rainbow Beads 78	Retrd.	N/A	44.00	72-96
1993 Rainbow Reflector 154	Retrd.	1993	26.60	40-96
1993 Rainbow Shark 277	Retrd.	N/A	18.00	70
1993 Rainy Day Friend 206	Retrd.	N/A	22.00	30-65
1993 Rambling Rose 148	Retrd.	N/A	16.60	42
1993 Regal Rooster 177	Retrd.	N/A	25.80	45-75
1993 Remembrance 151	Retrd.	N/A	16.60	54-72
1993 Rose Pointe Finial 323	Retrd.	1993	34.00	40
1993 Russian Santa (red) 209	Retrd.	N/A	27.90	50
1993 Sail by Starlight 339	Retrd.	1993	11.80	14-19
1993 Sailor Man 238	Retrd.	N/A	22.00	66-95
1993 Santa Baby 112	Retrd.	N/A	18.00	36-55
1993 Santa in Space 127	Retrd.	N/A	39.00	90-114
1993 Santa in Winter White 300	Retrd.	N/A	27.90	65
1993 Santa Tree 320	Retrd.	N/A	66.00	250-300
1993 Santa's Helper 329	Retrd.	N/A	16.90	40
1993 Saraband 140	Retrd.	1993	27.80	60-150
1993 Scotch Pine 167	Retrd.	N/A	26.80	48-95
1993 Serenade Pink 157	Retrd.	1993	26.80	48-60
1993 Shy Rabbit 280	Retrd.	N/A	14.00	75-90
1993 Siberian Sleigh Ride 403	Retrd.	N/A	16.80	60-78
1993 Siegfred 227	Retrd.	1996	25.00	75-90
1993 Silent Night (blue hat) 120	Retrd.	N/A	18.00	75

*Quotes have been rounded up to nearest dollar

YEAR ISSUE	EDITION LIMIT	YEAR RETD.	ISSUE PRICE	*QUOTE U.S.$
1993 Silent Night 120	Retrd.	N/A	18.00	36-75
1993 Silver Bells 52	Retrd.	N/A	27.00	90
1993 The Skating Bettinas 242	Retrd.	N/A	29.00	120-160
1993 Ski Baby 99	Retrd.	N/A	21.00	54-165
1993 Sloopy Snowman 328	Retrd.	1993	19.90	54
1993 Smitty 378	Retrd.	N/A	17.90	75-90
1993 Snow Dance 247	Retrd.	N/A	29.00	90
1993 Snowday Santa 98	Retrd.	1993	20.00	72
1993 Snowman by Candlelight 155	Retrd.	N/A	26.50	45-54
1993 Southern Colonial 171	Retrd.	N/A	26.90	85-135
1993 Special Delivery 91	Retrd.	N/A	17.00	26-36
1993 Spider & the Fly 393	Retrd.	1993	6.40	30
1993 Sporty 345	Retrd.	N/A	20.00	36-55
1993 St. Nick's Pipe 330	Retrd.	N/A	4.40	35-75
1993 St. Nickcicle 298	Retrd.	N/A	25.90	35
1993 Star Children 208	Retrd.	1993	18.00	36-60
1993 Star Fire 175	Retrd.	N/A	26.80	45-114
1993 Star Ribbons 377	Retrd.	N/A	16.00	36-102
1993 Starlight Santa 348	Retrd.	N/A	11.90	19
1993 Sterling Reindeer 21	Retrd.	N/A	113.00	540
1993 Stocking Stuffers 236	Retrd.	1993	16.00	23
1993 Sugar Shack 368	Retrd.	N/A	22.00	30-54
1993 Sunny Side Up 103	Retrd.	N/A	22.00	48-55
1993 Sweetheart 202	Retrd.	1993	16.00	48-60
1993 Talking Pipe 373	Retrd.	N/A	26.00	55
1993 Tannenbaum 273	Retrd.	N/A	24.00	24-48
1993 Tea & Sympathy 244	Retrd.	N/A	20.00	60-90
1993 Teenage Mermaid 226	Retrd.	N/A	27.50	96
1993 Texas Star 338	Retrd.	1993	7.50	8
1993 Thomas Nast Santa 217	Retrd.	N/A	23.00	30-78
1993 Tiger 90	Retrd.	N/A	23.90	24-48
1993 Time Piece 259	Retrd.	N/A	16.50	25-30
1993 Time Will Tell 349	Retrd.	N/A	22.00	30-42
1993 Tuxedo Santa 117	Retrd.	1993	21.90	125-150
1993 Tweeter 94	Retrd.	1993	3.20	20-42
1993 Twinkle Toes 233	Retrd.	N/A	28.00	60-84
1993 Twinkle Tree 254	Retrd.	N/A	15.50	28-42
1993 Twister 214	Retrd.	N/A	16.80	36-84
1993 U-Boat 353	Retrd.	1993	15.50	48
1993 V.I.P. 230	Retrd.	1993	23.00	100-200
1993 Versaille Balloon 176	Retrd.	N/A	29.00	72-90
1993 Victorian Santa Reflector 198	Retrd.	N/A	28.00	60-70
1993 Vintage 67	Retrd.	N/A	49.00	90
1993 Wacko 272	Retrd.	N/A	24.00	24-48
1993 Waddles 95	Retrd.	1993	3.80	30-65
1993 Wally 223	Retrd.	N/A	26.00	114
1993 Wings & A Prayer 123	Retrd.	N/A	12.00	66
1993 Winter Birds (cloudy) 164	Retrd.	N/A	26.80	27-42
1993 Winterbirds (pr.) 164	Retrd.	1993	26.80	100

1994 Holiday Collection - C. Radko

YEAR ISSUE	EDITION LIMIT	YEAR RETD.	ISSUE PRICE	*QUOTE U.S.$
1994 Accordion Elf 127	Retrd.	N/A	23.00	65
1994 Airplane 315	Retrd.	N/A	56.00	75-312
1994 All Wrapped Up 161	Retrd.	N/A	26.00	36-95
1994 Andy Gump 48	Retrd.	N/A	18.00	42-45
1994 Angel Bounty 208	Retrd.	N/A	44.00	44-48
1994 Angel on Board 310	Retrd.	N/A	37.00	228
1994 Angel Song 141	Retrd.	N/A	45.60	60-78
1994 Angelique 135	Retrd.	1996	33.30	36-96
1994 Autumn Tapestry 203	Retrd.	N/A	29.00	36-66
1994 Baby Booties (pink) 236	Retrd.	N/A	17.00	30-35
1994 Bag of Goodies 56	Retrd.	N/A	26.00	36-78
1994 Batter Up 397	Retrd.	N/A	13.00	25-36
1994 Berry Stripe 454	Retrd.	N/A	48.00	95
1994 Bird Bath 272	Retrd.	N/A	76.00	228
1994 Bird Brain 254	Retrd.	N/A	33.00	42-90
1994 Bloomers 354	Retrd.	N/A	18.80	48-54
1994 Blue Satin 200	Retrd.	N/A	29.00	50-78
1994 Bobo 308	Retrd.	N/A	31.00	96
1994 Bow Ties 364	Retrd.	N/A	12.00	22
1994 Brazilia 302	Retrd.	N/A	38.00	48-90
1994 Bright Heavens Above 136	Retrd.	N/A	56.00	50-108
1994 Bubbles 267	Retrd.	N/A	42.00	42-72
1994 Bubbly 258	Retrd.	1994	43.00	84
1994 Cabernet 285	Retrd.	N/A	24.00	84
1994 Candelabra 303	Retrd.	N/A	33.00	85
1994 Captain 260	Retrd.	N/A	47.20	234
1994 Carousel Willie 126	Retrd.	N/A	74.00	74-102
1994 Castanetta 321	Retrd.	N/A	37.00	102-105
1994 Celestial (blue) 408	Retrd.	N/A	28.80	29-48
1994 Checking It Twice 373	Retrd.	N/A	25.90	40-60
1994 Cheeky Santa 311	Retrd.	N/A	22.00	22-42
1994 Chianti 268	Retrd.	N/A	26.00	46-78
1994 Chic of Araby 220	Retrd.	N/A	17.00	42-65
1994 Chop Suey, set/2 329	Retrd.	N/A	34.00	168
1994 Christmas Express 437	Retrd.	N/A	72.00	72-90
1994 Christmas Harlequin 216	Retrd.	N/A	29.00	40-48
1994 Christmas in Camelot 113	Retrd.	N/A	27.00	42-85
1994 Chubbs & Slim 255	Retrd.	N/A	28.50	45-132
1994 Circus Band 92	Retrd.	1994	33.30	95
1994 Circus Delight 446	Retrd.	N/A	64.00	64-90
1994 Circus Star Balloon 201	Retrd.	N/A	29.00	60-90
1994 Classic Christmas 415	Retrd.	N/A	33.90	72-96
1994 Cool Cat 219	Retrd.	N/A	26.00	36-100
1994 Corn Husk 336	Retrd.	N/A	13.00	20-36
1994 Cow Poke 284	Retrd.	N/A	42.00	54-90
1994 Crescent Moons 195	Retrd.	N/A	29.00	40-75
1994 Crock O'Dile 297	Retrd.	N/A	33.00	48-102
1994 Crown of Thorns 222	Retrd.	N/A	26.00	42-55
1994 Crowned Peacocks 377	Retrd.	N/A	15.00	15-22
1994 Damask Rose 429	Retrd.	N/A	29.00	29-60
1994 Deep Sea 425	Retrd.	N/A	29.00	50-54
1994 Deercicle 291	Retrd.	N/A	29.00	30-96
1994 Del Monte 348	Retrd.	N/A	31.00	31-36
1994 Dolly 283	Retrd.	N/A	42.00	42-90
1994 Dutch Maiden 38	Retrd.	N/A	44.00	44-48
1994 Egg Head 166	Retrd.	N/A	19.00	35-42
1994 Einstein's Kite 375	Retrd.	N/A	29.90	45
1994 Elephant Prince 170	Retrd.	N/A	14.50	25-60
1994 English Santa 55	Retrd.	N/A	26.00	36-78
1994 Epiphany Ball 211	Retrd.	N/A	29.00	48-60
1994 Faberge Finial 417	Retrd.	N/A	78.00	78-136
1994 Fido 50	Retrd.	N/A	20.00	28-42
1994 First Snow 355	Retrd.	N/A	15.00	15-24
1994 Fleet's In 281	Retrd.	N/A	38.00	48-78
1994 Florentine 190	Retrd.	N/A	29.00	48
1994 Forest Holiday 445	Retrd.	N/A	64.00	85-150
1994 French Country 192	Retrd.	N/A	29.00	65-95
1994 French Regency Balloon 393	Retrd.	N/A	32.50	35-60
1994 French Regency Finial 388	Retrd.	N/A	78.00	156
1994 Gilded Cage 350	Retrd.	N/A	48.00	60-144
1994 Glad Tidings 430	Retrd.	N/A	44.00	114
1994 Glow Worm 275	Retrd.	N/A	32.00	78-95
1994 Golden Alpine 204	Retrd.	N/A	29.00	29-36
1994 Golden Crescendo Finial 384	Retrd.	N/A	42.00	125
1994 Grape Buzz 19	Retrd.	N/A	19.00	19-30
1994 Gretel 500	Retrd.	N/A	70.00	175
1994 H. Dumpty 46	Retrd.	N/A	19.00	19-30
1994 Hansel 501	Retrd.	N/A	70.00	175
1994 Harvest Home 414	Retrd.	N/A	28.80	54-95
1994 Harvest Moon 23	Retrd.	N/A	19.00	25-42
1994 Heavens Above 42	Retrd.	N/A	76.00	150
1994 Hieroglyph 194	Retrd.	N/A	29.00	54
1994 Holiday Sparkle 426	Retrd.	N/A	29.00	40-48
1994 Holly Heart 402	Retrd.	N/A	24.00	30
1994 Holly Jolly 399	Retrd.	N/A	40.00	54-72
1994 Holly Ribbons Finial 407	Retrd.	N/A	78.00	100
1994 Honey Belle 156	Retrd.	N/A	74.00	114-156
1994 Horse of a Different Color 309	Retrd.	N/A	28.00	60-102
1994 House Sitting Santa 240	Retrd.	N/A	26.00	30-48
1994 Ice House 98	Retrd.	N/A	14.00	23-42
1994 Ice Man Cometh 63	Retrd.	N/A	22.00	22-70
1994 Jack Clown 68	Retrd.	N/A	22.00	50
1994 Jean Claude 323	Retrd.	N/A	31.00	102
1994 Jockey Pipe 51	Retrd.	N/A	36.00	45-96
1994 Jolly Stripes 210	Retrd.	N/A	28.00	38-46
1994 Jubilee Finial 383-1	Retrd.	N/A	44.00	180
1994 Jumbo Harlequin 379	Retrd.	N/A	48.00	192
1994 Just Like Us 324	Retrd.	N/A	29.50	125
1994 Kaiser Pipe 134	Retrd.	N/A	32.00	36-60
1994 Kayo 165	Retrd.	N/A	14.00	20-42
1994 Kewpie 292	Retrd.	N/A	22.00	20-40
1994 King of Kings 18	Retrd.	N/A	22.00	75
1994 Kissing Cousins (pair) 249	Retrd.	N/A	28.00	200
1994 Kitty Tamer 331	Retrd.	N/A	65.00	195-234
1994 Kosher Dill 338	Retrd.	N/A	12.00	20
1994 Leader of the Band 94-915D (wh pants) - signed	Retrd.	1994	25.00	100-270
1994 Leader of the Band 94-915D (wh pants) - unsigned	Retrd.	1994	25.00	95-120
1994 Lemon Twist 28	Retrd.	N/A	14.00	40
1994 Letter to Santa 77	Retrd.	N/A	31.00	55-60
1994 Liberty Ball 172	Retrd.	N/A	26.00	66
1994 Liberty Bell 145	Retrd.	N/A	22.00	30-54
1994 Little Orphan 47	Retrd.	N/A	18.00	42-48
1994 Little Slugger 95	Retrd.	N/A	26.00	26-48
1994 Lola Ginabridgida 290	Retrd.	N/A	44.00	85-90
1994 The Los Angeles 155	Retrd.	N/A	26.00	46-54
1994 Madonna & Child 177	Retrd.	N/A	24.00	24-30
1994 Major Duck 327	Retrd.	N/A	58.00	198
1994 Mandolin Angel 76	Retrd.	N/A	46.00	46-66
1994 Martian Holiday 326	Retrd.	N/A	42.00	75-174
1994 Masquerade 45	Retrd.	N/A	16.00	42-48
1994 Medium Nautilus (gold) 103	Retrd.	N/A	16.00	25-50
1994 Messiah 221	Retrd.	N/A	22.00	48
1994 Metamorphisis 174	Retrd.	N/A	16.00	36-42
1994 Mexican Hat Dance 307	Retrd.	N/A	32.00	96
1994 Midnight Mass 913	Retrd.	N/A	N/A	30-60
1994 Mission Ball (tree topper) 389	Retrd.	N/A	78.00	78-136
1994 Mittens For Kittens 21	Retrd.	1994	22.00	30-42
1994 Moon Dust 133	Retrd.	N/A	18.00	30-36
1994 Moon Martian 298	Retrd.	N/A	26.00	140-144
1994 Moon Mullins 230	Retrd.	N/A	18.00	36-48
1994 Moon Ride 60	Retrd.	N/A	28.00	68
1994 Mother and Child 83	Retrd.	N/A	28.50	60-78
1994 Mountain Church 86	Retrd.	N/A	42.00	72-126
1994 Mr. Longneck 288	Retrd.	N/A	26.00	84
1994 Mr. Moto 280	Retrd.	N/A	35.60	102
1994 Mr. Smedley Drysdale 37	Retrd.	N/A	44.00	180-275
1994 My Darling 385	Retrd.	N/A	22.00	30-60
1994 My What Big Teeth	Retrd.	N/A	29.00	120-156
1994 New Year's Babe 239	Retrd.	N/A	21.00	48-66
1994 Nicky 316	Retrd.	N/A	24.00	60-65
1994 Nighty Night 299	Retrd.	N/A	36.00	90-120
1994 Oh My Stars 101	Retrd.	N/A	12.00	27-36
1994 Old Sour Puss 256	Retrd.	N/A	34.00	54-108
1994 Ollie 269	Retrd.	1996	49.50	150-288
1994 On The Run (Spoon/left side) 247	Retrd.	N/A	45.00	52-168
1994 One Small Step 314	Retrd.	N/A	58.00	174
1994 Over The Waves 261	Retrd.	N/A	38.00	48-108
1994 Owl Reflector 40	Retrd.	N/A	54.00	75-90
1994 Papa's Jamboree 427	Retrd.	N/A	29.00	30-45
1994 Partridge Pear Garland 435	Retrd.	N/A	68.00	90-95
1994 Party Hopper 274	Retrd.	N/A	37.00	75-120
1994 Party Time 902	Retrd.	N/A	24.00	24-36
1994 Peas on Earth 227	Retrd.	N/A	16.00	10-30
1994 Peking Santa 102	Retrd.	N/A	18.00	54
1994 Pickled 317	Retrd.	N/A	26.00	46-60
1994 Piggly Wiggly 169	Retrd.	N/A	14.00	40
1994 Piglet 294	Retrd.	N/A	13.00	42-45
1994 Pinecone Santa 118	Retrd.	N/A	29.50	50-100
1994 Pinocchio Gets Hitched 250	Retrd.	N/A	29.50	100-204
1994 Pixie Santa 218	Retrd.	N/A	20.00	35-50
1994 President Taft 74	Retrd.	N/A	18.00	50
1994 Pretty Bird 112	Retrd.	N/A	26.00	36-66
1994 Prince Philip 909	Retrd.	N/A	20.00	150
1994 Private Eye 163	Retrd.	N/A	18.00	35-48
1994 Quick Draw 330	Retrd.	N/A	65.00	228-300
1994 Radiant Birth 75	Retrd.	N/A	76.00	126-156
1994 Rain Dance 282	Retrd.	N/A	34.00	75
1994 Rainbow Snow 361	Retrd.	N/A	15.00	15-36
1994 Rainy Day Smile 54	Retrd.	N/A	22.00	22-30
1994 Rajah 25	Retrd.	N/A	19.00	23
1994 Razzle Dazzle 372	Retrd.	N/A	37.90	48-102
1994 Red Cap 24	Retrd.	1996	22.00	25-78
1994 Ring Master 61	Retrd.	N/A	22.00	50
1994 Ring Twice 151	Retrd.	N/A	21.00	55
1994 Ringing Red Boots 114	Retrd.	N/A	46.00	72-85
1994 Roly Poly Angel 58	Retrd.	N/A	22.00	54-84
1994 Roly Poly Clown 173	Retrd.	N/A	19.40	75
1994 Rosy Lovebirds 89	Retrd.	N/A	48.00	70-102
1994 Royale Finial 382	Retrd.	N/A	64.00	95
1994 Ruby Reflector 352	Retrd.	N/A	26.00	42-102
1994 Santa Copter 306	Retrd.	N/A	47.00	125-216
1994 Santa Hearts 461	Retrd.	N/A	66.00	96-120
1994 Santa Reflector Finial 381	Retrd.	N/A	92.00	120
1994 Santa's Helper 131	Retrd.	N/A	19.90	25-35
1994 Saturn Rings 458	Retrd.	N/A	64.00	64-72
1994 School's Out 29	Retrd.	N/A	19.00	40-48
1994 Scotch Pine Finial 419	Retrd.	N/A	78.00	78-144
1994 Season's Greetings 41	Retrd.	N/A	42.00	60-84
1994 Serenity 196	Retrd.	N/A	44.00	55-90
1994 Sex Appeal 238	Retrd.	N/A	22.00	85-90
1994 Ships Ahoy 263	Retrd.	N/A	38.00	48-85
1994 Shivers 262	Retrd.	N/A	25.00	200-250
1994 Shooting The Moon 33	Retrd.	N/A	28.00	108
1994 Siberian Bear 392	Retrd.	N/A	23.90	36-78
1994 Silent Night 129	Retrd.	N/A	27.00	55
1994 Smiley 52	Retrd.	N/A	16.00	50-78
1994 Snow Bell 237	Retrd.	N/A	13.00	42-48
1994 Snow Dancing 91	Retrd.	N/A	29.00	48-72
1994 Snowy 313	Retrd.	N/A	26.00	50
1994 Soldier Boy 142	Retrd.	N/A	19.00	66-100
1994 Spring Chick 30	Retrd.	1996	27.00	60-84
1994 Squash Man 67	Retrd.	N/A	28.00	28-70
1994 Squiggles 157	Retrd.	N/A	29.90	48-67
1994 Squirreling Away 39	Retrd.	N/A	26.00	50-54
1994 St. Nick 65	Retrd.	N/A	18.00	18-30
1994 St. Nick's Pipe 235	Retrd.	N/A	12.00	36-42
1994 Stafford Floral 205	Retrd.	N/A	29.00	29-48
1994 Starry Night 300	Retrd.	N/A	31.00	46-114
1994 Stocking Full 159	Retrd.	N/A	24.00	24-36
1994 Stocking Sam 108	Retrd.	N/A	23.00	60-72
1994 Strawberry 333	Retrd.	N/A	12.00	20-36
1994 Sugar Cone 413	Retrd.	N/A	46.50	75-144
1994 Sugar Pear 335	Retrd.	N/A	13.00	48
1994 Surf's Up 325	Retrd.	N/A	36.00	84-102
1994 Swami 128	Retrd.	N/A	18.00	25
1994 Swan Fountain 278	Retrd.	N/A	44.00	174
1994 Swan Lake 911	Retrd.	N/A	16.00	65
1994 Sweet Pear 59	Retrd.	N/A	24.00	48-84
1994 Teddy Roosevelt 232	Retrd.	N/A	22.00	75
1994 Tee Time 167	Retrd.	N/A	16.00	35
1994 Teenage Mermaid 270	Retrd.	N/A	33.00	58
1994 Terrance 53	Retrd.	N/A	16.00	42-45
1994 Time to Spare 78	Retrd.	N/A	29.00	29-60
1994 Tiny Nautilus (gold) 100	Retrd.	N/A	12.00	36-60
1994 Tiny Ted 49	Retrd.	N/A	15.00	15-20
1994 Tiny Tunes 36	Retrd.	N/A	22.00	36-78
1994 Tomba 279	Retrd.	N/A	34.00	90
1994 Top Cat 206	Retrd.	N/A	29.00	29-42
1994 Topo 318	Retrd.	N/A	33.00	42-84
1994 Tuxedo Carousel 245	Retrd.	N/A	52.00	70-90
1994 Twinkle Star 360	Retrd.	N/A	13.00	13-36
1994 Uncle Max 66	Retrd.	1994	26.00	60
1994 Valcourt 213	Retrd.	N/A	29.00	100
1994 Vaudeville Sam 57	Retrd.	N/A	18.00	30-66
1994 Waldo 17	Retrd.	N/A	22.00	45-54
1994 Wedded Bliss 94	Retrd.	N/A	88.00	195-216
1994 Wednesday 120	Retrd.	N/A	42.00	45-70
1994 What a Donkey 277	Retrd.	N/A	34.00	46-90
1994 White Nights 197	Retrd.	N/A	26.00	26-60
1994 White Tiger 223	Retrd.	N/A	25.90	36-48
1994 Wind Swept 188	Retrd.	N/A	28.80	29-48
1994 Wings and a Snail 301	Retrd.	N/A	32.00	90-125
1994 Winter Frolic 287	Retrd.	N/A	18.00	36-48
1994 Xenon 304	Retrd.	N/A	38.00	95-120
1994 Yuletide Bells 148	Retrd.	N/A	12.00	66

1995 Holiday Collection - C. Radko

YEAR ISSUE	EDITION LIMIT	YEAR RETD.	ISSUE PRICE	*QUOTE U.S.$
1995 10, 9, 8 139	Retrd.	N/A	22.00	22-36
1995 Al Pine 161	Retrd.	N/A	24.00	30
1995 Aloisius Beer 194	Retrd.	N/A	75.00	125
1995 Andrew Jacksons, pair 208	Retrd.	1995	68.00	200
1995 Another Fine Mess 160	Retrd.	N/A	16.00	72-80
1995 Aqualina 293	Retrd.	1996	26.00	48

*Quotes have been rounded up to nearest dollar

YEAR ISSUE	EDITION LIMIT	YEAR RETD.	ISSUE PRICE	*QUOTE U.S.$
1995 Autumn Oak King 23	Retrd.	N/A	28.00	28-38
1995 Bailey 283	Retrd.	N/A	46.00	100
1995 Bear Mail 38	Retrd.	1996	28.00	30-54
1995 Beezlebub 94	Retrd.	N/A	14.00	66
1995 Bishop (original coloration) 127	Retrd.	N/A	74.00	120
1995 Blue Dolphin 238	Retrd.	N/A	22.00	22-36
1995 Bordeaux 901	Retrd.	N/A	N/A	30-48
1995 Bringing Home the Bacon 204	Retrd.	N/A	26.00	34-60
1995 Buford T 63	Retrd.	N/A	14.00	30
1995 Buttons 21	Retrd.	N/A	36.00	36-84
1995 Caribbean Constable 11	Retrd.	N/A	24.00	48-55
1995 Carousel Santa 133	Retrd.	N/A	36.00	60-132
1995 Catch O' Day 93	Retrd.	N/A	13.50	20
1995 Cheeky St. Nick 274	Retrd.	N/A	32.00	32-75
1995 Christmas Cake 35	Retrd.	N/A	24.00	24-36
1995 Christmas Joy 33	Retrd.	N/A	42.00	50-78
1995 Christmas Pie 135	Retrd.	N/A	54.00	54-78
1995 Chubby Decker 3	Retrd.	N/A	36.00	40
1995 Claudette 95-017-0	Retrd.	1995	22.00	66-80
1995 Climbing Higher 146	Retrd.	N/A	26.00	30
1995 Clown Rattle 230	Retrd.	N/A	16.00	48
1995 Clown Spin 151-1	Retrd.	N/A	38.00	84
1995 Cockle Bell 175	Retrd.	N/A	38.00	50-96
1995 Creole Dancer 275	Retrd.	N/A	52.00	90
1995 Curlycue Santa 219	Retrd.	N/A	30.00	42-48
1995 David 56	Retrd.	N/A	28.00	30
1995 Della Robbia Garland 308	Retrd.	N/A	34.00	34-48
1995 Department Store Santa 131	Retrd.	N/A	36.00	36-42
1995 Dutch Dolls 136	Retrd.	N/A	22.00	36-40
1995 Eagle Eye 104	Retrd.	N/A	26.00	35
1995 Elfin 903	Retrd.	N/A	N/A	46-50
1995 Evening Owl 193	Retrd.	N/A	36.00	45
1995 Farmer Boy 108	Retrd.	N/A	28.00	42-60
1995 Flying High 8	Retrd.	N/A	22.00	50
1995 Forest Cabin 179	Retrd.	N/A	15.00	20-42
1995 French Lace 134	Retrd.	N/A	24.00	38-45
1995 Frog Lady 26	Retrd.	N/A	24.00	45-50
1995 Frosted Santa 143	Retrd.	N/A	25.00	36-66
1995 Fruit Kan Chu 267	Retrd.	1995	50.00	60
1995 Fruit Nuts 213	Retrd.	N/A	14.00	20-28
1995 Garden Girls (pair) 39	Retrd.	N/A	18.00	24-70
1995 Gay Blades 272	Retrd.	1996	46.00	55
1995 Glorianna 263	Retrd.	N/A	56.00	65
1995 Gobbles 203	Retrd.	N/A	52.00	85
1995 Grandpa Jones 144	Retrd.	N/A	22.00	45-54
1995 Gunther 233	Retrd.	N/A	32.00	32-90
1995 Gypsy Bear 908	Retrd.	N/A	N/A	30
1995 Having a Ball 126	Retrd.	N/A	26.00	36-42
1995 Heavy Load 19	Retrd.	N/A	42.00	96
1995 Helmut's Bells 28	Retrd.	N/A	18.00	35
1995 Here Boy 222	Retrd.	N/A	12.00	35
1995 High Flying 8	Retrd.	N/A	22.00	60
1995 Ho Ho Ho 78	Retrd.	N/A	18.00	18-36
1995 Holiday Star Santa 27	Retrd.	N/A	16.00	36-48
1995 Holly Santa 123	Retrd.	N/A	18.00	18-36
1995 Hooty Hoot 24	Retrd.	1996	26.00	30-42
1995 Hot Head 221	Retrd.	N/A	18.00	45
1995 Hubbard's the Name 206	Retrd.	N/A	26.00	26-55
1995 I'm Late, I'm Late 291	Retrd.	N/A	48.00	48-65
1995 Imperial Helmet 240	Retrd.	N/A	22.00	35-42
1995 Jazz Santa 196	Retrd.	N/A	28.00	45
1995 Joy To The World 42	Retrd.	N/A	68.00	70-100
1995 Jumbo Walnut 249	Retrd.	N/A	18.00	35-48
1995 Kaleidoscope Cone 25	Retrd.	N/A	44.00	66
1995 Kitty Vittles 79	Retrd.	N/A	18.00	50
1995 Laugh Til You Cry 236	Retrd.	N/A	24.00	45
1995 Lavender Light 157	Retrd.	N/A	28.00	75
1995 Lean & Lanky 95	Retrd.	N/A	23.00	30-48
1995 Little Dreamer 159	Retrd.	N/A	16.00	48
1995 Little Drummer Bear 37	Retrd.	N/A	22.00	30
1995 Little Prince 6	Retrd.	N/A	39.00	125
1995 Little Red 214	Retrd.	N/A	22.00	35-48
1995 Little Toy Maker 167	Retrd.	N/A	26.00	42-54
1995 Midnight Mass 913	Retrd.	N/A	N/A	78
1995 Miss Mamie 110	Retrd.	N/A	34.00	45
1995 My Bonnie Lass 170	Retrd.	N/A	24.00	36
1995 Neptune's Charge 113	Retrd.	N/A	36.00	90
1995 Off to Market 223	Retrd.	N/A	24.00	35-42
1995 Officer Joe 122	Retrd.	N/A	22.00	60
1995 On the Court 45	Retrd.	N/A	26.00	26-30
1995 Papa Bear Reflector 292	Retrd.	N/A	52.00	85
1995 Pecky Woodpecker 288	Retrd.	N/A	36.00	36-66
1995 Pencil Santa 232	Retrd.	N/A	18.00	36-64
1995 Penelope 197	Retrd.	N/A	26.00	36-48
1995 Percussion 255	Retrd.	N/A	50.00	100-125
1995 Pere Noel 41	Retrd.	N/A	44.00	50-78
1995 Personal Delivery 116	Retrd.	N/A	36.00	36-54
1995 Pine Tree Santa 912	Retrd.	N/A	N/A	36
1995 Pork Chop 231	Retrd.	N/A	22.00	22-40
1995 Prince of Thieves 44	Retrd.	N/A	28.00	40
1995 Quakers 261	Retrd.	1996	24.00	35
1995 Quilted Santa 187	Retrd.	N/A	68.00	68-150
1995 Rakish Charm 142	Retrd.	N/A	22.00	45
1995 Reflecto 281	Retrd.	N/A	46.00	55-60
1995 Ricky Raccoon 138	Retrd.	N/A	24.00	42
1995 Rockateer 284	Retrd.	N/A	44.00	65
1995 Round About Santa 5	Retrd.	N/A	42.00	45
1995 Rummy Tum Tum 168	Retrd.	N/A	44.00	55
1995 Santa Fantasy 20	Retrd.	N/A	44.00	95
1995 Santa Maria 286	Retrd.	N/A	64.00	140
1995 Shy Elephant 282	Retrd.	N/A	32.00	85
1995 Siamese Slippers 264	Retrd.	1995	16.00	55
1995 Sister Act-set 140	Retrd.	N/A	18.00	42-65
1995 Skater's Waltz 12	Retrd.	N/A	28.00	48-60
1995 Slim Pickins 114	Retrd.	N/A	22.00	36-42
1995 Snow Ball 100	Retrd.	N/A	28.00	48-54
1995 Snow Song 40	Retrd.	N/A	18.00	23-30
1995 Spring Arrival 82	Retrd.	N/A	44.00	65-84
1995 Springtime Sparrow 119	Retrd.	N/A	14.00	25
1995 St. Peter's Keys 298	Retrd.	N/A	8.00	18
1995 Stork Lantern 241	Retrd.	N/A	18.00	22
1995 Storytime Santa 22	Retrd.	N/A	44.00	36-50
1995 Swan Lake 911	Retrd.	N/A	36.00	50-66
1995 Sweet Madame 192	Retrd.	N/A	48.00	75-100
1995 Swinging on a Star 183	Retrd.	N/A	44.00	50
1995 Teddy's Tree 156	Retrd.	N/A	22.00	45
1995 Trick or Treat 13	Retrd.	N/A	23.00	30
1995 Turtle Bird 121	Retrd.	N/A	22.00	35-40
1995 Warm Wishes 112	Retrd.	N/A	22.00	22-36
1995 Washington's (Martha & George) 103	Retrd.	N/A	28.00	64-90
1995 Westminster Santa 189	Retrd.	N/A	24.00	48-54
1995 Wiggle Men 89	Retrd.	N/A	10.00	10-15
1995 Winter Sun 145	Retrd.	N/A	31.00	45
1995 Youthful Madonna 259	Retrd.	N/A	28.00	36-42

1996 Holiday Collection - C. Radko

YEAR ISSUE	EDITION LIMIT	YEAR RETD.	ISSUE PRICE	*QUOTE U.S.$
1996 Astro Pup 36	Retrd.	1996	32.00	30-45
1996 Baby Angel 3	Retrd.	N/A	22.00	22-30
1996 Baby Elephants 277	Retrd.	1996	18.00	30
1996 Bella D. Snowball 160	Retrd.	N/A	26.00	26-36
1996 Bottoms Up 148	Retrd.	N/A	26.00	26-36
1996 Candy Swirl 299	Retrd.	N/A	24.00	24-50
1996 Caroline 152	Retrd.	N/A	24.00	24-34
1996 Charlie Horse 4	Retrd.	N/A	20.00	20-36
1996 Christmas King 147	Retrd.	N/A	46.00	46-50
1996 Christmas Past 223	Retrd.	N/A	18.00	26-36
1996 The Clauses 159	Retrd.	N/A	26.00	26-38
1996 Crescent Kringle 40	Retrd.	N/A	36.00	67
1996 Dreamy 12	Retrd.	N/A	17.00	22-45
1996 Elfcycle 14	Retrd.	N/A	28.00	36-42
1996 Eskimo Cheer 157	Retrd.	1996	22.00	30
1996 For Clara 86	Retrd.	N/A	32.00	40-45
1996 Frosty Cardinal 215	Retrd.	N/A	32.00	32-48
1996 His Goil 67	Retrd.	N/A	40.00	50
1996 His Wizardry 255	Retrd.	N/A	22.00	25
1996 Lancer 13	Retrd.	N/A	29.00	29-36
1996 Lemon Guard 233	Retrd.	N/A	22.00	22-34
1996 Lilac Winter 50	Retrd.	1996	44.00	48
1996 Merry Matador 189	Retrd.	N/A	23.95	25
1996 Midnight Ride 169	Retrd.	1996	51.00	60-75
1996 Minuet 167	Retrd.	1996	54.00	65
1996 Monte Carlo 27	Retrd.	1996	52.00	65
1996 Ms. Peanut 42	Retrd.	1996	30.00	100
1996 Night Magic 2	Retrd.	N/A	26.00	26-36
1996 Oh Christmas Tree! 156	Retrd.	N/A	42.00	42-50
1996 Pookie 187	Retrd.	N/A	16.00	16-30
1996 Race Car Garland 1	Retrd.	N/A	66.00	66-90
1996 Ragamuffins 52	Retrd.	N/A	39.00	150
1996 Rainbow-Tiffany 302	Retrd.	N/A	26.00	26-50
1996 Reach For a Star 209	Retrd.	N/A	32.00	32-36
1996 Return Engagement 151	Retrd.	N/A	38.00	36-38
1996 Rocket Santa 38	Retrd.	N/A	48.00	48-72
1996 Rosy Cheek Santa 10	Retrd.	N/A	20.00	26-36
1996 Round Midnight 274	Retrd.	1996	30.00	40
1996 Shimmy Down 253	Retrd.	N/A	42.00	42-48
1996 Shining Armour 188	Retrd.	1996	22.00	25
1996 Sleighfull 150	Retrd.	N/A	34.00	34-42
1996 Snow Castle 139	Retrd.	1996	12.00	18
1996 Starscape Santa 143	Retrd.	N/A	44.00	36-64
1996 Strong To The Finish 66	Retrd.	N/A	48.00	50
1996 Time Flies 314	Retrd.	1996	28.00	35
1996 Topolina 288	Retrd.	1996	42.00	60
1996 Toys For All 153	Retrd.	N/A	44.00	44-48
1996 Village Santa 99	Retrd.	N/A	30.00	30-36
1996 Vintage Classics 222	Retrd.	N/A	24.00	30
1996 Winter Blossom 284	Retrd.	N/A	46.00	46-50
1996 Winter Dream 250	Retrd.	N/A	42.00	42-72
1996 Winter Wind 121	Retrd.	N/A	24.00	60
1996 Yankee Doodle Santa 251	Retrd.	N/A	34.00	34-36
1996 Yo Ho Ho 53	Retrd.	N/A	48.00	48

Aids Awareness - C. Radko

YEAR ISSUE	EDITION LIMIT	YEAR RETD.	ISSUE PRICE	*QUOTE U.S.$
1993 A Shy Rabbit's Heart 462	Retrd.	1993	15.00	50-72
1994 Frosty Cares SP5	Retrd.	1994	25.00	45-75
1995 On Wings of Hope SP10	Retrd.	1995	30.00	42-60
1996 A Winter Bear's Heart SP15	Retrd.	1996	34.00	42-50
1997 A Caring Clown 97-SP-22	Retrd.	1997	36.00	40
1998 Sugar Holiday (Elizabeth Taylor Aids Foundation) 98-SP-29	Yr.Iss.		38.00	38

Alvin And The Chipmunks - C. Radko

YEAR ISSUE	EDITION LIMIT	YEAR RETD.	ISSUE PRICE	*QUOTE U.S.$
1998 Downhill Racer 98-CHP-01	Open		26.00	26
1998 Oh Tannenbaum 98-CHP-02	Open		27.00	27
1998 Winter Fun 98-CHP-03	Open		27.00	27

Breast Cancer Research - C. Radko

YEAR ISSUE	EDITION LIMIT	YEAR RETD.	ISSUE PRICE	*QUOTE U.S.$
1998 Felina's Heart 98-SP-31	Yr.Iss.		32.00	32

Carson Pirie Scott - C. Radko

YEAR ISSUE	EDITION LIMIT	YEAR RETD.	ISSUE PRICE	*QUOTE U.S.$
1997 Carson Snowman 97-CPS-01	Retrd.	1997	44.00	44

CBS and Desilu's "I Love Lucy" - C. Radko

YEAR ISSUE	EDITION LIMIT	YEAR RETD.	ISSUE PRICE	*QUOTE U.S.$
1997 Candy Maker 97-LCY-07	Open		42.00	42
1998 Ethel and Fred Heart 98-LCY-03	Open		19.00	19
1997 Ethel's Christmas & Fred's Christmas (pair) 97-LCY-02	Open		80.00	80
1997 I Love Lucy Heart 97-LCY-08	Open		36.00	36
1997 Lucy and Ricky's Christmas 97-LCY-01	Open		45.00	45
1998 Lucy Heart 98-LCY-02	Open		19.00	19
1998 Vitametavegaimin 98-LCY-01	Open		29.00	29

Charlie Chaplain - C. Radko

YEAR ISSUE	EDITION LIMIT	YEAR RETD.	ISSUE PRICE	*QUOTE U.S.$
1997 Charlie Chaplain 97-CAR-01	Open		39.00	39

A Christmas Carol - C. Radko

YEAR ISSUE	EDITION LIMIT	YEAR RETD.	ISSUE PRICE	*QUOTE U.S.$
1998 Scrooge 98-ACC-1	10,000		62.00	62

The Christopher Radko Foundation for Children Designs - C. Radko

YEAR ISSUE	EDITION LIMIT	YEAR RETD.	ISSUE PRICE	*QUOTE U.S.$
1998 Cozykins 98-SP-28	Open		34.00	34

Disney Art Classics: Hercules - C. Radko

YEAR ISSUE	EDITION LIMIT	YEAR RETD.	ISSUE PRICE	*QUOTE U.S.$
1997 Hercules 97-DIS-79	Retrd.	1998	39.00	39
1997 Pegasus 97-DIS-91	Retrd.	1998	42.00	42

Disney Art Classics: Peter Pan - C. Radko

YEAR ISSUE	EDITION LIMIT	YEAR RETD.	ISSUE PRICE	*QUOTE U.S.$
1998 Captain Hook 98-DIS-20	Open		32.00	32
1998 The Darling Children 98-DIS-19	Open		32.00	32
1998 Peter Pan 98-DIS-18	Open		28.00	28
1998 Peter Pan Boxed Set (includes Pirate Ship 98-DIS-22) 98-DIS-44	Open		149.00	149
1998 Tinker Bell 98-DIS-21	Open		28.00	28

Disney Art Classics: Snow White & the Seven Dwarfs - C. Radko

YEAR ISSUE	EDITION LIMIT	YEAR RETD.	ISSUE PRICE	*QUOTE U.S.$
1997 Snow White 97-DIS-31	Retrd.	1998	46.00	46
1997 Bashful 97-DIS-24	Retrd.	1998	38.00	38
1997 Doc 97-DIS-28	Retrd.	1998	38.00	38
1997 Dopey 97-DIS-25	Retrd.	1998	38.00	38
1997 Grumpy 97-DIS-26	Retrd.	1998	38.00	38
1997 Happy 97-DIS-30	Retrd.	1998	38.00	38
1997 Sleepy 97-DIS-27	Retrd.	1998	38.00	38
1997 Sneezy 97-DIS-29	Retrd.	1998	38.00	38
1997 Snow White Boxed Set 98-SW-0	Retrd.	1998	390.00	575
1998 The Hag 98-DIS-13	Open		34.00	34
1998 The Queen 98-DIS-14	Open		34.00	34
1998 Snow White Boxed Set (includes Mirror, Mirror 98-DIS-16) 98-DIS-43	Open		94.00	94

Disney Art Classics: The Little Mermaid - C. Radko

YEAR ISSUE	EDITION LIMIT	YEAR RETD.	ISSUE PRICE	*QUOTE U.S.$
1997 Ariel 97-DIS-82	Retrd.	1998	42.00	42
1997 Flounder 97-DIS-84	Retrd.	1998	42.00	42
1997 Sebastian 97-DIS-85	Retrd.	1998	42.00	42
1997 Ursula 97-DIS-83	Retrd.	1998	42.00	42
1997 Ursula 97-DIS-83	Retrd.	1998	42.00	42

The Disney Catalog - C. Radko

YEAR ISSUE	EDITION LIMIT	YEAR RETD.	ISSUE PRICE	*QUOTE U.S.$
1997 4th of July Pooh 97-DIS-44	Retrd.	1997	42.00	42
1998 Chip and Dale 98-DIS-34	3,500		26.00	26
1997 Christmas Pooh 97-DIS-47	Retrd.	1997	42.00	42
1997 Easter Pooh 97-DIS-16	Retrd.	1997	50.00	50-71
1997 Halloween Pooh 97-DIS-45	Retrd.	1998	42.00	42
1998 Lady and the Tramp 98-DIS-39	3,500		30.00	30
1998 Mickey and Minnie Wedding 98-DIS-30	Open		39.00	39
1998 Pooh Snowman 98-DIS-31	Open		30.00	30
1997 Thanksgiving Pooh 97-DIS-46	Retrd.	1998	42.00	42
1997 Toy Soldier Mickey 97-DIS-77	Open		40.00	40
1997 Toy Soldier Minnie 97-DIS-78	Open		40.00	40
1997 Valentine's Day Pooh 97-DIS-15	Retrd.	1997	45.00	45-65

Disney's Mickey & Co. - C. Radko

YEAR ISSUE	EDITION LIMIT	YEAR RETD.	ISSUE PRICE	*QUOTE U.S.$
1998 Caroler Daisy Duck 98-DIS-09	Open		24.00	24
1998 Caroler Minnie Mouse 98-DIS-08	Open		24.00	24
1997 Daisy Duck 97-DIS-20	Retrd.	1997	38.00	38
1998 Daisy Duck Stocking 98-DIS-06	Open		22.00	22
1998 Donald & Daisy Block 98-DIS-11	Open		18.00	18
1998 Down the Chimney 98-DIS-23	Open		28.00	28
1997 Downhill Mickey (Starlight Exclusive) 97-DIS-42	Retrd.	1997	42.00	42
1998 Downhill Minnie 98-DIS-04	Open		26.00	26
1997 Goofy Tree 97-DIS-23	Retrd.	1997	38.00	38
1998 Happy New Year Mickey 98-DIS-01	Open		22.00	22
1998 Happy New Year Pluto 98-DIS-02	Open		22.00	22
1998 Mickey & Minnie Block 98-DIS-10	Open		18.00	18
1997 Mickey & Minnie Christmas 97-DIS-34	Retrd.	1997	42.00	42
1998 Mickey Mouse Wreath 98-DIS-03	Open		19.00	19
1998 Mickey Stocking 98-DIS-05	Open		22.00	22
1997 Mickey's Sleigh Ride (Roger's Exclusive) 97-DIS-93	Retrd.	1997	48.00	48
1997 Noel Minnie 97-DIS-21	Retrd.	1997	38.00	38
1998 Pluto & Goofy Block 98-DIS-12	Open		18.00	18
1998 Pluto Stocking 98-DIS-07	Open		22.00	22
1997 Pluto Wreath (Starlight Exclusive) 97-DIS-73	Retrd.	1997	36.00	36
1997 Pluto's Dog House 97-DIS-57	Open		39.00	39
1997 Rooftop Mickey 97-DIS-32	Open		40.00	40
1997 Three Cheers For Mickey 97-DIS-33	Open		44.00	44

Disneyana - C. Radko

YEAR ISSUE	EDITION LIMIT	YEAR RETD.	ISSUE PRICE	*QUOTE U.S.$
1997 Mistletoe Mickey & Minnie 97-DIS-65	1,500	1997	250.00	292-450
1998 My Best Pal 98-DIS-40	1,000		70.00	70

Egyptian Series - C. Radko

YEAR ISSUE	EDITION LIMIT	YEAR RETD.	ISSUE PRICE	*QUOTE U.S.$
1997 Ramses 97-EGY-1	15,000	1997	50.00	50-55
1998 Cheops 98-EGY-2	15,000		55.00	55

*Quotes have been rounded up to nearest dollar

FAO Schwarz - C. Radko

YEAR ISSUE	EDITION LIMIT	YEAR RETD.	ISSUE PRICE	*QUOTE U.S.$
1997 1920 Santa 97-FAO-03	3,000	1997	42.00	42
1998 1929 FAO Santa 98-FAO-02	3,600		38.00	38
1998 FAO Clock Tower 98-FAO-01	5,000		40.00	40
1997 Toy Block Bear 97-FAO-04	3,000	1997	52.00	52

Forest Angels - C. Radko

YEAR ISSUE	EDITION LIMIT	YEAR RETD.	ISSUE PRICE	*QUOTE U.S.$
1998 Forest Angel 98-SP-33	7,500		125.00	125

Harley-Davidson - C. Radko

YEAR ISSUE	EDITION LIMIT	YEAR RETD.	ISSUE PRICE	*QUOTE U.S.$
1998 Bar & Shield 98-HAR-03	Yr.Iss.		19.00	19
1997 Biker Boot 97-HAR-04	Open		36.00	36
1998 Fill-r-up 98-HAR-02	Open		29.00	29
1997 Free Wheeling Santa 97-HAR-01	Open		46.00	46
1998 Harley Santa 98-HAR-01	Open		32.00	32

Harold LLoyd - C. Radko

YEAR ISSUE	EDITION LIMIT	YEAR RETD.	ISSUE PRICE	*QUOTE U.S.$
1998 Holiday Reflections 98-LYD-01	Open		75.00	75

Hasbro's Monopoly - C. Radko

YEAR ISSUE	EDITION LIMIT	YEAR RETD.	ISSUE PRICE	*QUOTE U.S.$
1998 High Roller 98-MON-02	Open		26.00	26
1998 Holiday Cheer 98-MON-01	Open		26.00	26
1997 Monopoly Wreath 97-MON-04	Open		36.00	36
1997 Roadster Rich Uncle Pennybags 97-MON-03	Open		39.00	39

Hasbro's Mr. Potato Head - C. Radko

YEAR ISSUE	EDITION LIMIT	YEAR RETD.	ISSUE PRICE	*QUOTE U.S.$
1997 Mr. Potato Head 97-POT-02	Open		39.00	39
1998 Mr. Potato Head Lumberjack 98-POT-01	Open		26.00	26
1997 Mr. Potato Head Santa 97-POT-01	Open		39.00	39
1997 Mrs. Potato Head Santa 97-POT-04	Open		39.00	39
1998 Soldier Potato 98-POT-02	Open		26.00	26

Homes For The Holidays - C. Radko

YEAR ISSUE	EDITION LIMIT	YEAR RETD.	ISSUE PRICE	*QUOTE U.S.$
1997 Sugar Hill 97-HOU-1	10,000	1997	140.00	140
1998 Sugar Hill II 98-HOU-2	10,000		190.00	190

The Huntington - C. Radko

YEAR ISSUE	EDITION LIMIT	YEAR RETD.	ISSUE PRICE	*QUOTE U.S.$
1997 The Blue Boy 97-HUN-01	5,000		38.00	38
1997 Pinky 97-HUN-02	5,000		38.00	38

It's a Wonder Life - C. Radko

YEAR ISSUE	EDITION LIMIT	YEAR RETD.	ISSUE PRICE	*QUOTE U.S.$
1997 Jimmy Stewart 97-WON-01	Open		42.00	42

Jim Henson's Muppets - C. Radko

YEAR ISSUE	EDITION LIMIT	YEAR RETD.	ISSUE PRICE	*QUOTE U.S.$
1997 Bah Humbug Block 97-MPT-02	Open		38.00	38
1997 Checking It Twice 97-MPT-01	Open		39.00	39
1997 Christmas with Miss Piggy 97-MPT-06	Open		42.00	42
1997 Fozzie & Gonzo Block 97-MPT-04	Open		38.00	38
1997 Fozzie Bear Baker 97-MPT-05	Open		39.00	39
1997 Kermit and Miss Piggy Block 97-MPT-03	Open		38.00	38
1998 Kermit and Piggy Snowball 98-MPT-01	Open		30.00	30
1998 Mistletoe Miss Piggy 98-MPT-02	Open		28.00	28
1997 Muppet Totem 97-MPT-09	Open		42.00	42
1998 Nutcracker 98-MPT-03	Open		26.00	26
1997 Play It Again Santa 97-MPT-07	Open		38.00	38
1997 Wocka Wocka Christmas 97-MPT-08	Open		46.00	46

The Kennedy Center - C. Radko

YEAR ISSUE	EDITION LIMIT	YEAR RETD.	ISSUE PRICE	*QUOTE U.S.$
1997 Kennedy Center Honors 97-JFK-03	3,000		36.00	36

Laurel & Hardy - C. Radko

YEAR ISSUE	EDITION LIMIT	YEAR RETD.	ISSUE PRICE	*QUOTE U.S.$
1997 Laurel & Hardy 97-LAH-01	Open		78.00	78

Legends of the Cinema - C. Radko

YEAR ISSUE	EDITION LIMIT	YEAR RETD.	ISSUE PRICE	*QUOTE U.S.$
1997 Harold Lloyd 97-LYD-01	Open		42.00	42

Limited Edition Ornaments - C. Radko

YEAR ISSUE	EDITION LIMIT	YEAR RETD.	ISSUE PRICE	*QUOTE U.S.$
1995 And Snowy Makes Eight (set of 8) 169	15,000	1996	125.00	85-125
1996 Russian Rhapsody RUS (Set/6)	7,500	1996	150.00	150-225
1997 Yippy Yi Yo 97-SP-25	10,000	1997	70.00	70-75
1998 Cookbook Santas 98-SP-35	10,000		152.00	152
1998 Spring Maidens 98-SP-34	5,000		95.00	95
1998 Sugar Shack Extravaganza 98-SP-37	5,000		178.00	178

Lucasfilm's Star Wars - C. Radko

YEAR ISSUE	EDITION LIMIT	YEAR RETD.	ISSUE PRICE	*QUOTE U.S.$
1998 C-3PO 98-STW-03	Open		18.00	18
1998 Chewbacca 98-STW-04	Open		20.00	20
1998 Darth Vader 98-STW-01	Open		20.00	20
1998 Storm Tropper 98-STW-05	Open		20.00	20
1998 Yoda 98-STW-02	Open		18.00	18

Make-A-Wish Foundation Charity Design - C. Radko

YEAR ISSUE	EDITION LIMIT	YEAR RETD.	ISSUE PRICE	*QUOTE U.S.$
1997 Well Wishes 97-MAW-01	5,000		64.00	64

Marshall Fields - C. Radko

YEAR ISSUE	EDITION LIMIT	YEAR RETD.	ISSUE PRICE	*QUOTE U.S.$
1997 Marshall Fields Clock 97-MAR-01	Retrd.	1997	38.00	38
1998 Marshall Fields Clock 98-MAR-01	5,000		38.00	38

Matt Berry Memorial Soccer Fund - C. Radko

YEAR ISSUE	EDITION LIMIT	YEAR RETD.	ISSUE PRICE	*QUOTE U.S.$
1995 Matthew's Game 158-0	Open		12.00	12

Mattel's Barbie - C. Radko

YEAR ISSUE	EDITION LIMIT	YEAR RETD.	ISSUE PRICE	*QUOTE U.S.$
1997 Alpine Blush Barbie 97-BAR-03	Open		44.00	44
1998 Barbie Heart 98-BAR-03	Open		15.00	15
1998 Barbie Stocking 98-BAR-02	Open		19.00	19
1998 Elegant Holiday 98-BAR-01	Open		32.00	32
1997 Holiday Barbie 97-BAR-01	Open		50.00	50

Moscow Circus Series - C. Radko

YEAR ISSUE	EDITION LIMIT	YEAR RETD.	ISSUE PRICE	*QUOTE U.S.$
1997 Ivan & Misha 97-CIR-01	10,000	1997	90.00	90-110
1998 Grand Ring Master 98-CIR-02	10,000		90.00	90

Musicians Series - C. Radko

YEAR ISSUE	EDITION LIMIT	YEAR RETD.	ISSUE PRICE	*QUOTE U.S.$
1998 Hooked on Classics 98-COM-1	5,000		108.00	108

Nativity Series - C. Radko

YEAR ISSUE	EDITION LIMIT	YEAR RETD.	ISSUE PRICE	*QUOTE U.S.$
1995 Three Wise Men WM (Set/3)	15,000	1996	90.00	100-210
1996 Holy Family HF (Set/3)	15,000	1996	70.00	90-100
1997 Shepherd's Prayer, Gloria 97-NAT-3	15,000	1997	90.00	90-95

Neiman Marcus - C. Radko

YEAR ISSUE	EDITION LIMIT	YEAR RETD.	ISSUE PRICE	*QUOTE U.S.$
1997 The Original Store 97-NM-01	Retrd.	1997	48.00	48

North American Bear's Muffy Vanderbear - C. Radko

YEAR ISSUE	EDITION LIMIT	YEAR RETD.	ISSUE PRICE	*QUOTE U.S.$
1997 Portrait in Black and White 97-NAB-02	Open		38.00	38
1997 Portrait in Black and White 97-NAB-02	Open		38.00	38
1997 Seddin' and Skiddalin' 97-NAB-01	Open		38.00	38

North American Bears' Muffy Vanderbear - C. Radko

YEAR ISSUE	EDITION LIMIT	YEAR RETD.	ISSUE PRICE	*QUOTE U.S.$
1998 Muffy Candy C'angel (Roger's Garden Exclusive) 98-NAB-01	Open		29.00	29
1998 Muffy Ginger Bear 98-NAB-02	Open		29.00	29
1998 Muffy Plum Fairy 98-NAB-03	Open		29.00	29

Nutcracker Series - C. Radko

YEAR ISSUE	EDITION LIMIT	YEAR RETD.	ISSUE PRICE	*QUOTE U.S.$
1995 Nutcracker Suite I NC1 (Set/3)	15,000	1996	90.00	90-150
1996 Nutcracker Suite II NC2 (Set/3)	15,000	1997	90.00	90-150
1997 Nutcracker Suite III 97-NC3 (Set/3)	15,000	1997	90.00	90-168

Nutcracker Series II - C. Radko

YEAR ISSUE	EDITION LIMIT	YEAR RETD.	ISSUE PRICE	*QUOTE U.S.$
1998 Clara's Beaux 98-NCR-1	10,000		135.00	135

Parkwest - C. Radko

YEAR ISSUE	EDITION LIMIT	YEAR RETD.	ISSUE PRICE	*QUOTE U.S.$
1998 Special Charity Set 98-PW-SPE	Open		140.00	140

Patriots Series - C. Radko

YEAR ISSUE	EDITION LIMIT	YEAR RETD.	ISSUE PRICE	*QUOTE U.S.$
1997 LaFayette 97-PAT-1	7,500	1997	34.00	34
1998 Alexander Hamilton 98-PAT-2	7,500		40.00	40

Pediatrics Cancer Research - C. Radko

YEAR ISSUE	EDITION LIMIT	YEAR RETD.	ISSUE PRICE	*QUOTE U.S.$
1994 A Gifted Santa 70	Retrd.	1994	25.00	30-54
1995 Christmas Puppy Love SP11	Retrd.	1995	30.00	30-54
1996 Bearly Awake SP16	Retrd.	1996	34.00	36-48
1997 Kitty Cares 97-SP-23	Retrd.	1997	30.00	40
1998 Elfin Magic 98-SP-30	Yr.Iss.		32.00	32

Polish Children's Home Fund - C. Radko

YEAR ISSUE	EDITION LIMIT	YEAR RETD.	ISSUE PRICE	*QUOTE U.S.$
1997 Watch Over Me 97-SP-26	Retrd.	1997	28.00	28-35

Rosemont Special - C. Radko

YEAR ISSUE	EDITION LIMIT	YEAR RETD.	ISSUE PRICE	*QUOTE U.S.$
1997 Blue Caroline 96-1521	Retrd.	1997	26.00	26-65

Saks Fifth Avenue - C. Radko

YEAR ISSUE	EDITION LIMIT	YEAR RETD.	ISSUE PRICE	*QUOTE U.S.$
1995 Saks Santa SAK01	2,500	1997	48.00	48-150
1996 Santa Calls 95SAK02	Retrd.	1996	56.00	84-180
1997 Saks Nutcraker 97-SAK-03	5,000	1997	40.00	40
1998 Saks International Santa 98-SAK-01	3,000		36.00	36

South Bend Special - C. Radko

YEAR ISSUE	EDITION LIMIT	YEAR RETD.	ISSUE PRICE	*QUOTE U.S.$
1995 Polar Express (lilac) 95-076SB	Retrd.	1995	24.95	48-75

Special Color Variations - C. Radko

YEAR ISSUE	EDITION LIMIT	YEAR RETD.	ISSUE PRICE	*QUOTE U.S.$
1996 Snowtem Pole (Glass Pheasant) 96155G	Retrd.	1996	33.00	90-100
1996 White Dolphin (Four Seasons) 96238F	Retrd.	1996	25.00	75

Starlight and Rising Star Store Exclusives - C. Radko

YEAR ISSUE	EDITION LIMIT	YEAR RETD.	ISSUE PRICE	*QUOTE U.S.$
1998 Sterling Rider 98-SP-39	2,500		175.00	175

Starlight and Rising Star Store Exclusives/St. Nick Portrait Series - C. Radko

YEAR ISSUE	EDITION LIMIT	YEAR RETD.	ISSUE PRICE	*QUOTE U.S.$
1996 Esquire Santa 96-SP-17	750	1996	150.00	500-700
1997 Regency Santa 97-SP-24	2,500		180.00	180
1998 Moondream 98-SP-38	2,500		186.00	186

Starlight and Rising Star Store Special Colorations - C. Radko

YEAR ISSUE	EDITION LIMIT	YEAR RETD.	ISSUE PRICE	*QUOTE U.S.$
1996 Baby Bear (Christmas Dove) 322-0	N/A		30.00	30
1996 Far Away Places (Christmas Village) 321-0	N/A		40.00	40
1996 Frosty Bear (Christmas House) 326-0	N/A		30.00	30
1996 Kitty Christmas (Tuck's) 323-0	N/A		30.00	30
1996 Little St. Mick (Roger's Gardens) DIS7	N/A	1996	45.00	50-85
1996 On His Way (Geary's) 319-0	N/A		30.00	30
1996 Ruffles (Christmas Attic) 320-0	N/A		30.00	30
1996 Snow Fun (Vinny's) 324-0	N/A		30.00	30
1996 Tweedle Dee (Glass Pheasant) 325-0	N/A		40.00	40
1998 Bergdorf Star (Bergdorf Goodman) 98-BG-01	N/A		90.00	90
1998 Best of Times (Loot N Boot) 98-194-BO	N/A		42.00	42
1998 Bunny Express (FAO Schwarz) 98-378-FA	N/A		50.00	50
1998 Candy Santa (Pine Creek Collectibles) 98-301-PC	N/A		52.00	52
1998 Circle of Cheer (Four Seasons Christmas Shoppe) 98-222-F	N/A		52.00	52
1998 Derby Rocker (Bloomingdales) 98-365-BM	N/A		43.50	44
1998 Ginger Cracker (Christmas Attic) 98-162-CA	N/A		48.00	48
1998 June Buggy (Chatsworth Florist) 98-102-CF	N/A		60.00	60
1998 Lucky Laddie (Borsheim's Jewelry) 98-458-B	N/A		48.00	48
1998 Sleddin' Snowman (Carson Pirie Scott) 98-CPS-01	N/A		44.00	44
1998 Slim Traveler (Margo's Gift Shop) 98-120-M	N/A		38.00	38
1998 Snow Star (Curio Cabinet) 98-129-CC	N/A		36.00	36
1998 Spring Romance (R. Blooms) 98-321-RB	N/A		46.00	46
1998 Stuffings Full (Glass Pheasant) 98-159-GP	N/A		44.00	44
1998 Summertime Santa 98-RG-01	3,000		70.00	70
1998 Teddy Tunes (Christmas Store) 98-256-CS	N/A		42.00	42
1998 Triple Nick (Story Book Kids) 98-150-SK	N/A		36.00	36
1996 Winter Kitten (Margo's) 327-0	N/A		30.00	30
1998 Woodcut Santa (Botanicals on the Park) 98-214-BP	N/A		44.00	44

Sterling Silver Collection - C. Radko

YEAR ISSUE	EDITION LIMIT	YEAR RETD.	ISSUE PRICE	*QUOTE U.S.$
1997 Winter Spirit 97-J01-00	5,000		175.00	175
1998 Regal Reindeer 98-J02-00	5,000		150.00	150

Sunday Brunch - C. Radko

YEAR ISSUE	EDITION LIMIT	YEAR RETD.	ISSUE PRICE	*QUOTE U.S.$
1996 Hansel & Gretel and Witch HG01	7,500	1996	50.00	50-75
1997 Nibble Nibble 97-HG-02	7,500	1997	58.00	58-60

Twelve Days of Christmas - C. Radko

YEAR ISSUE	EDITION LIMIT	YEAR RETD.	ISSUE PRICE	*QUOTE U.S.$
1993 Partridge in a Pear Tree SP2	5,000	1993	35.00	600-800
1994 Two Turtle Doves SP4	10,000	1994	28.00	110-180
1995 Three French Hens SP9	10,000	1995	34.00	90-96
1995 Three French Hens (signed) SP9	Retrd.	1995	34.00	125-180
1996 Four Calling Birds SP12	10,000	1996	44.00	50-200
1997 Five Gold Rings SP19	10,000	1997	60.00	50-150
1998 Six Geese a Laying SP40	10,000		68.00	68

Universal Studios:Universal and Steven Speilberg's Lost World - C. Radko

YEAR ISSUE	EDITION LIMIT	YEAR RETD.	ISSUE PRICE	*QUOTE U.S.$
1997 Baby T-REX 97-UNI-12	Open		38.00	38
1997 Baby Trike 97-UNI-11	Open		38.00	38
1997 Stegosaurus 97-UNI-15	Open		42.00	42
1997 T-REX 97-UNI-14	Open		42.00	42

Universal Studios:Universal Monsters - C. Radko

YEAR ISSUE	EDITION LIMIT	YEAR RETD.	ISSUE PRICE	*QUOTE U.S.$
1997 Bride of Frankenstein 97-UNI-17	Open		42.00	42
1998 Creature From the Black Lagoon 98-MST-03	Open		22.00	22
1997 Dracula 97-UNI-02	Open		42.00	42
1997 Frankenstein 97-UNI-03	Open		42.00	42
1998 The Mummy 98-MST-01	Open		21.00	21
1998 Wolfman 98-MST-02	Open		22.00	22

Universal Studios:Universal's Rocky, Bullwinkle and Friends - C. Radko

YEAR ISSUE	EDITION LIMIT	YEAR RETD.	ISSUE PRICE	*QUOTE U.S.$
1998 Boris & Natasha Block 98-RAB-01	Open		19.00	19
1997 Bullwinkle's Wreath 97-UNI-09	Open		36.00	36
1997 Rocky & Bullwinkle Block 97-UNI-06	Open		38.00	38
1997 Rocky's Wreath 97-UNI-08	Open		36.00	36
1998 Sleigh Ride 98-RAB-02	Open		27.00	27
1998 Totem Trouble 98-RAB-03	Open		26.00	26

Virginia Diner Exclusive - C. Radko

YEAR ISSUE	EDITION LIMIT	YEAR RETD.	ISSUE PRICE	*QUOTE U.S.$
1998 Virginia Diner Peanut 98-VAD-01	Open		12.00	12

The Walt Disney Gallery - C. Radko

YEAR ISSUE	EDITION LIMIT	YEAR RETD.	ISSUE PRICE	*QUOTE U.S.$
1997 Bambi 97-DIS-74	5,000		44.00	44
1997 Bambi's Winter Forest (for special boxed set, 4 pc.) 96-273-DG	2,500		N/A	N/A
1997 Bambi, set/4 (signed) 97-DIS-99	1,000		180.00	180
1996 Best Friends DIS10	10,000	1996	60.00	83-138
1996 By Jiminy DIS11	7,500	1996	38.00	55-100
1996 Cruella De Vil DIS13	10,000	1996	55.00	85-110
1998 Disney's Beast 97-DIS-96	5,000		N/A	N/A
1998 Disney's Belle 97-DIS-95	5,000		N/A	N/A
1997 Eeyore 97-DIS-19	5,000		44.00	44
1997 Flower 97-DIS-75	5,000		44.00	44
1996 A Goofy Surprise DIS5	2,500	1996	38.00	38
1996 Holiday Skaters DIS8	Retrd.	1996	42.00	43-50
1997 Huey, Louie and Dewey 97-DIS-32	2,500		34.00	34
1996 Lucky DIS14	Retrd.	1996	45.00	65-100
1997 Mickey's Birthday Set, set/5 97-DIS-48	750		N/A	N/A
1995 Mickey's Tree DIS1	2,500	1995	45.00	120-275
1997 Minnie Statue of Liberty (NY City Gallery Only) 97-DIS-94	2,500		38.00	38
1996 Noel Pluto DIS3	2,500	1996	37.00	37
1997 Piglet 97-DIS-98	5,000		38.00	38
1996 Pinocchio DIS9	5,000	1996	45.00	75-100
1996 Pooh's Favorite Gift (signed) DIS2	Retrd.	1995	45.00	135-300
1995 Pooh's Favorite Gift DIS2	2,500	1995	45.00	195-250
1997 Puppy Pole 97-DIS-17	2,500		44.00	44
1996 Ready For Sea DIS4	2,500	1996	38.00	38-55
1997 Scrooge McDuck 97-DIS-97	5,000		44.00	44
1997 Snow White Set w/Apple (leather box) 97-DIS-92	500		500.00	500
1997 Thumper 97-DIS-76	5,000		44.00	44
1997 Tigger 97-DIS-18	5,000		42.00	42

*Quotes have been rounded up to nearest dollar

YEAR ISSUE	EDITION LIMIT	YEAR RETD.	ISSUE PRICE	*QUOTE U.S.$
1996 Tinker Bell DIS12	10,000	1997	55.00	65-110
1997 Winnie the Pooh 97-DIS-88	5,000		42.00	42
1996 Xmas Eve Mickey DIS06	Retrd.	1996	45.00	65-100

The Walt Disney World - C. Radko

YEAR ISSUE	EDITION LIMIT	YEAR RETD.	ISSUE PRICE	*QUOTE U.S.$
1998 Cinderella Castle 98-DIS-42	Open		39.00	39

Warner Brothers Studio Stores - C. Radko

YEAR ISSUE	EDITION LIMIT	YEAR RETD.	ISSUE PRICE	*QUOTE U.S.$
1997 Alicia Silverstone as Batgirl 97-WB-22	3,000		44.00	44
1997 Arnold Schwarznegger as Mr. Freeze 97-WB-21	3,000		44.00	44
1998 Bugs Bunny Sprite 98-WB-02	5,000		46.00	46
1998 Faberge Tweety 98-WB-01	5,000		38.00	38
1997 George Clooney as Batman 97-WB-20	3,000		44.00	44
1998 Glenda the Good Witch 98-WB-03	10,000		44.00	44
1997 Gossamer 97-WB-17	5,000		44.00	44
1998 Je t'aime Heart 98-WB-04	5,000		36.00	36
1998 K-9 (Warner Bros. Collector's Guild Exclusive) 98-WB-05	2,500		42.00	42
1996 Little Angel Tweety WB10	5,000	1996	45.00	50-120
1997 Marvin the Martian 97-WB-12	5,000		42.00	42
1995 Santa's Bugs Bunny WB1	Retrd.	1995	45.00	72-107
1997 Scooby Doo 97-WB-11	5,000		42.00	42
1998 Scooby Doo Wreath 98-WB-06	5,000		36.00	36
1996 Superman WB7	7,500	1996	48.00	70-75
1997 Sylvester & Tweety Stockings 97-WB-15	5,000		58.00	58
1996 Sylvester Sprite WB9	5,000	1996	45.00	65-75
1996 Taz & Bugs Stockings WB4	5,000	1996	65.00	65-95
1995 Taz Angel WB2	Retrd.	1995	40.00	72-90
1997 Taz Sprite WB13	5,000		46.00	46
1996 Trio Tree Topper 96-WB8	5,000	1997	78.00	240-250
1995 Tweety's Sprite WB3	Retrd.	1995	45.00	135-175
1997 Wizard of Oz Dorothy 97-WB-18	10,000		45.00	45
1998 Wizard of Oz Lion 98-WB-09	10,000		44.00	44
1997 Wizard of Oz Ruby Slippers 97-WB-19	10,000		44.00	44
1998 Wizard of Oz Scarecrow 98-WB-08	10,000		44.00	44
1997 Wizard of Oz Tin Man 97-WB-14	10,000		46.00	46

The Wubbulous World of Dr. Seuss - C. Radko

YEAR ISSUE	EDITION LIMIT	YEAR RETD.	ISSUE PRICE	*QUOTE U.S.$
1998 Cat in the Hat and Whozits 98-SUS-01	Open		26.00	26
1997 The Cat-In-The-Hat Wreath 97-SUS-03	Open		36.00	36
1997 The Grinch and Whozits 97-SUS-05	Open		44.00	44
1998 Thidwick and Whozits 98-SUS-03	Open		30.00	30

Dave Grossman Creations

Gone With the Wind Ornaments - Inspired by Film

YEAR ISSUE	EDITION LIMIT	YEAR RETD.	ISSUE PRICE	*QUOTE U.S.$
1987 Ashley - D. Geenty	Closed	N/A	15.00	45-55
1987 Rhett - D. Geenty	Closed	N/A	15.00	45-75
1987 Scarlett - D. Geenty	Closed	N/A	15.00	45-95
1987 Tara - D. Geenty	Closed	N/A	15.00	45
1988 Rhett and Scarlett - D. Geenty	Closed	N/A	20.00	40-60
1989 Mammy - D. Geenty	Closed	N/A	20.00	20-45
1990 Scarlett (Red Dress) - D. Geenty	Closed	N/A	20.00	45-55
1991 Prissy - Unknown	Closed	N/A	20.00	20-30
1992 Scarlett (Green Dress) - Unknown	Closed	N/A	20.00	20-50
1993 Rhett (White Suit) GWO-93 - Unknown	Closed	N/A	20.00	20-50
1994 Gold Plated GWO-00 - Unknown	Open		13.00	13
1994 Scarlett GWO-94 - Unknown	Closed	N/A	20.00	20
1995 The Kiss GWW-95 - Unknown	Yr.Iss.	1995	25.00	25-50
1994 Scarlett (B-B-Q Dress) GWO-94 - Unknown	Closed	1994	12.00	20-25
1996 Suellen GWO-95 - Unknown	Closed	1996	12.00	12
1996 Scarlett GWO-96 - Unknown	Closed	1996	12.00	12
1996 1996 Ornament GWW-96 - Unknown	Yr.Iss.	1996	25.00	25
1996 Set of 5 Ornaments GWOS-1 - Unknown	Yr.Iss.	1996	100.00	100
1997 Bonnie GWO-97 - Unknown	Open		12.00	12
1997 Scarlett GWW-97 - Unknown	Yr.Iss.		25.00	25

Ornaments - C. Spencer Collin

YEAR ISSUE	EDITION LIMIT	YEAR RETD.	ISSUE PRICE	*QUOTE U.S.$
1996 Cape Hatteras CSC-01	Yr.Iss.	1997	24.00	24
1997 Nubble Light CSC-O	Yr.Iss.	1997	24.00	24
1998 SF. Lightship CSC-3	Yr.Iss.		24.00	24

Rockwell Collection-Annual Rockwell Ball - Rockwell-Inspired

YEAR ISSUE	EDITION LIMIT	YEAR RETD.	ISSUE PRICE	*QUOTE U.S.$
1975 Santa with Feather Quill NRO-01	Retrd.	N/A	3.50	25-35
1976 Santa at Globe NRO-02	Retrd.	N/A	4.00	25-35
1977 Grandpa on Rocking Horse NRO-03	Retrd.	N/A	4.00	12-20
1978 Santa with Map NRO-04	Retrd.	N/A	4.50	12-20
1979 Santa at Desk with Mail Bag NRO-05	Retrd.	N/A	5.00	12-20
1980 Santa Asleep with Toys NRO-06	Retrd.	N/A	5.00	10-18
1981 Santa with Boy on Finger NRO-07	Retrd.	N/A	5.00	10
1982 Santa Face on Winter Scene NRO-08	Retrd.	N/A	5.00	10
1983 Coachman with Whip NRO-9	Retrd.	N/A	5.00	10
1984 Christmas Bounty Man NRO-10	Retrd.	N/A	5.00	10-18
1985 Old English Trio NRO-11	Retrd.	N/A	5.00	10-15
1986 Tiny Tim on Shoulder NRO-12	Retrd.	N/A	5.00	10
1987 Skating Lesson NRO-13	Retrd.	N/A	5.00	10
1988 Big Moment NRO-14	Retrd.	N/A	5.50	10
1989 Discovery NRO-15	Retrd.	N/A	6.00	10-15
1990 Bringing Home The Tree NRO-16	Retrd.	N/A	6.00	10-15
1991 Downhill Daring NRO-17	Retrd.	N/A	6.00	10-15
1992 On The Ice NRO-18	Retrd.	N/A	6.00	10
1993 Gramps NRO-19	Retrd.	N/A	6.00	10-15
1994 Triple Self Portrait-Commemorative NRO-20	Retrd.	1994	6.00	10
1994 Merry Christmas NRO-94	Retrd.	1994	6.00	7
1995 Young Love NRO-21	Retrd.	N/A	6.00	7
1996 Christmas Feast NRO-22	Retrd.	1996	6.00	7
1997 Lovers NRO-23	Yr.Iss.	1997	6.00	7-11
1998 Merrie Christmas NRO-24	Yr.Iss.		6.00	6

Rockwell Collection-Annual Rockwell Figurine Ornaments - Rockwell-Inspired

YEAR ISSUE	EDITION LIMIT	YEAR RETD.	ISSUE PRICE	*QUOTE U.S.$
1978 Caroler NRX-03	Retrd.	N/A	15.00	45
1979 Drum for Tommy NRX-24	Retrd.	N/A	20.00	30
1980 Santa's Good Boys NRX-37	Retrd.	N/A	20.00	30
1981 Letters to Santa NRX-39	Retrd.	N/A	20.00	30-50
1982 Cornettist NRX-32	Retrd.	N/A	20.00	30
1983 Fiddler NRX-83	Retrd.	N/A	20.00	30-50
1984 Christmas Bounty NRX-84	Retrd.	N/A	20.00	30
1985 Jolly Coachman NRX-85	Retrd.	N/A	20.00	30
1986 Grandpa on Rocking Horse NRX-86	Retrd.	N/A	20.00	30-50
1987 Skating Lesson NRX-87	Retrd.	N/A	20.00	30
1988 Big Moment NRX-88	Retrd.	N/A	20.00	30
1989 Discovery NRX-89	Retrd.	N/A	20.00	30-45
1990 Bringing Home The Tree NRX-90	Retrd.	N/A	20.00	40-45
1991 Downhill Daring B NRX-91	Retrd.	N/A	20.00	30-45
1992 On The Ice	Retrd.	N/A	20.00	30-40
1993 Granps NRX-93	Retrd.	N/A	24.00	30-35
1993 Marriage License First Christmas Together NRX-m1	Retrd.	N/A	30.00	30-50
1994 Merry Christmas NRX-94	Retrd.	N/A	24.00	24
1994 Triple Self-Portrait NRX-TS	Retrd.	N/A	30.00	30-50
1995 Young Love NRX-95	Retrd.	1995	24.00	50-75
1996 Christmas Feast NRX-96	Retrd.	1996	24.00	24-32
1997 Lovers NRX-97	Yr.Iss.	1997	24.00	24
1998 Tiny Tim NRX-98	Yr.Iss.		24.00	24

David Winter Cottages/Enesco Corporation

David Winter Ornaments - Various

YEAR ISSUE	EDITION LIMIT	YEAR RETD.	ISSUE PRICE	*QUOTE U.S.$
1991 Christmas Carol - D. Winter	Closed	1991	15.00	8-15
1991 Christmas in Scotland & Hogmanay - D. Winter	Closed	1991	15.00	8-15
1991 Mr. Fezziwig's Emporium - D. Winter	Closed	1991	15.00	8-15
1991 Ebenezer Scrooge's Counting House - D. Winter	Closed	1991	15.00	8-15
1992 Fairytale Castle - D. Winter	Closed	1992	15.00	8-15
1992 Fred's Home - D. Winter	Closed	1992	15.00	8-15
1992 Suffolk House - D. Winter	Closed	1992	15.00	8-15
1992 Tudor Manor - D. Winter	Closed	1992	15.00	8-15
1993 The Grange - J. Hine Studios	Closed	1993	15.00	8-15
1993 Scrooge's School - J. Hine Studios	Closed	1993	15.00	8-15
1993 Tomfool's Cottage - J. Hine Studios	Closed	1993	15.00	8-15
1993 Will-O The Wisp - J. Hine Studios	Closed	1993	15.00	8-15
1994 Old Joe's Beetling Shop - J. Hine Studios	Closed	1994	17.50	8-15
1994 Scrooge's Family Home - J. Hine Studios	Closed	1994	17.50	8-15
1994 What Cottage - J. Hine Studios	Closed	1996	17.50	8-15
1995 Buttercup Cottage - J. Hine Studios	Closed	1996	17.50	8-15
1995 The Flowershop - J. Hine Studios	Closed	1996	17.50	8-15
1995 Looking for Santa - J. Hine Studios	Closed	1996	17.50	8-15
1995 Miss Belle's Cottage - J. Hine Studios	Closed	1995	17.50	8-15
1995 Robin's Merry Mouse - J. Hine Studios	Closed	1996	17.50	8-15
1995 Porridge Pot Alley Mouse - D. Winter	Closed	1995	Gift	15-30
1995 Season's Greetings - J. Hine Studios	Closed	1996	17.50	8-15
1996 Plough Farmhouse - D. Winter	Closed	1996	17.50	8-15
1996 Tiny Tim - D. Winter	Closed	1996	17.50	8-15
1996 Stocking Mouse - D. Winter	Closed	1996	17.50	8-15
1996 Jolly Roger Mouse - D. Winter	Closed	1996	17.50	8-15
1996 Stable Mouse - D. Winter	Closed	1996	17.50	8-15

Department 56

Bisque Light-Up, Clip-on Ornaments - Department 56

YEAR ISSUE	EDITION LIMIT	YEAR RETD.	ISSUE PRICE	*QUOTE U.S.$
1986 Angelic Lite-up 8260-0	Open		4.00	6
1987 Anniversary Love Birds, (pair) w/brass ribbon 8353-4	Closed	1988	4.00	42
1986 Dessert, 6 asst. 7100-5	Closed	1987	5.00	40
1985 Humpty Dumpty 3525-4	Closed	1986	4.50	5
1990 Owl w/clip 8344-5	Closed	1994	5.00	15-18
1986 Plum Pudding 7101-3	Closed	1987	4.50	42-48
1989 Pond-Frog w/clip 8347-0	Closed	1991	5.00	36-42
1989 Pond-Snail w/clip 8347-0	Closed	1991	5.00	36-45
1988 Rabbit w/clip 8350-0	Open		4.00	4
1987 Shells, set/4 8349-6	Closed	1991	14.00	96-150
1986 Shooting Star 7106-4	Closed	1987	5.50	22-24
1985 Snowbirds, (pair) w/clip 8357-7	Open		5.00	6
1985 Snowbirds, set/6 8367-4	Closed	1988	15.00	15-21
1985 Snowbirds, set/8 8358-5	Closed	1988	20.00	20
1985 Snowmen, 3 asst. 8360-7	Closed	1988	10.50	11
1986 Teddy Bear w/clip 8262-7	Closed	1991	5.00	18-20
1986 Truffles Sampler, set/4 7102-1	Closed	1987	17.50	42
1986 Winged Snowbird 8261-9	Closed	1988	2.50	3
1989 Woodland-Field Mouse w/clip 8348-8	Closed	1991	5.00	30-36
1989 Woodland-Squirrel w/clip 8348-8	Closed	1991	5.00	36-40

CCP Ornaments-Flat - Department 56

YEAR ISSUE	EDITION LIMIT	YEAR RETD.	ISSUE PRICE	*QUOTE U.S.$
1986 Christmas Carol Houses, set/3 (6504-8)	Closed	1989	13.00	30-42
1986 • The Cottage of Bob Cratchit & Tiny Tim	Closed	1989	4.35	40
1986 • Fezziwig's Warehouse	Closed	1989	4.35	20
1986 • Scrooge and Marley Countinghouse	Closed	1989	4.35	30
1986 New England Village, set/7 (6536-6)	Closed	1989	25.00	300
1986 • Apothecary Shop	Closed	1989	3.50	18-25
1986 • Brick Town Hall	Closed	1989	3.50	50
1986 • General Store	Closed	1989	3.50	55
1986 • Livery Stable & Boot Shop	Closed	1989	3.50	18-25
1986 • Nathaniel Bingham Fabrics	Closed	1989	3.50	18-25
1986 • Red Schoolhouse	Closed	1989	3.50	40-70
1986 • Steeple Church	Closed	1989	3.50	150-225

Christmas Carol Character Ornaments-Flat - Department 56

YEAR ISSUE	EDITION LIMIT	YEAR RETD.	ISSUE PRICE	*QUOTE U.S.$
1986 Christmas Carol Characters, set/3 (6505-6)	Closed	1987	13.00	26-42
1986 • Bob Cratchit & Tiny Tim	Closed	1987	4.35	20
1986 • Poulterer	Closed	1987	4.35	20
1986 • Scrooge	Closed	1987	4.35	20-30

Christmas Carol Ornaments-Face - Department 56

YEAR ISSUE	EDITION LIMIT	YEAR RETD.	ISSUE PRICE	*QUOTE U.S.$
1988 Bob & Mrs. Crachit 5914-5	Closed	1989	18.00	18-25
1988 Scrooge's Head 5912-9	Closed	1989	12.95	13-25
1988 Tiny Tim's Head 5913-7	Closed	1989	10.00	10-25

Classic Ornament Series - Department 56

YEAR ISSUE	EDITION LIMIT	YEAR RETD.	ISSUE PRICE	*QUOTE U.S.$
1998 City Hall 98741	Open		15.00	15
1998 Craggy Cove Lighthouse 98739	Open		15.00	15
1998 Dickens' Village Church 98737	Open		15.00	15
1997 Dickens' Village Mill 98733	Open		15.00	15
1998 Dorothy's Dress Shop 98740	Open		15.00	15
1998 J. Young's Granary 98632	Open		15.00	15
1998 Nantucket 98630	Open		15.00	15
1997 North Pole Santa's Workshop 98734	Open		16.50	17
1998 The Old Curiosity Shop 98738	Open		15.00	15
1998 Santa's Lookout Tower 98742	Open		15.00	15
1998 Steepled Church 98631	Open		15.00	15

Clip On Lite-Up Ornaments - Department 56

YEAR ISSUE	EDITION LIMIT	YEAR RETD.	ISSUE PRICE	*QUOTE U.S.$
1989 Field Mouse 8348-8	Closed	1991	5.00	35
1989 Frog 8347-0	Closed	1991	5.00	60
1990 Owl 8344-5	Closed	1994	5.00	10
1989 Snail 8347-0	Closed	1991	5.00	35
1989 Squirrel 8348-8	Closed	1991	5.00	45

Dickens' Village Signature Series Ornaments - Department 56

YEAR ISSUE	EDITION LIMIT	YEAR RETD.	ISSUE PRICE	*QUOTE U.S.$
1994 Dickens Village Dedlock Arms 9872-8, (porcelain, gift boxed)	Closed	1994	12.50	8-10
1995 Sir John Falstaff 9870-1 (Charles Dickens' Signature Series)	Closed	1995	15.00	10-20
1996 The Grapes Inn 98729	Yr.Iss.	1996	15.00	10-25
1996 Crown & Cricket Inn 98730	Yr.Iss.	1996	15.00	30-38
1996 The Pied Bull Inn 98731	Yr.Iss.	1996	15.00	10-30
1997 Gad's Hill Place 98732	Yr.Iss.	1997	15.00	10-35

Home For The Holidays - Department 56

YEAR ISSUE	EDITION LIMIT	YEAR RETD.	ISSUE PRICE	*QUOTE U.S.$
1997 Ronald McDonald House ® 8961	Yr.Iss.	1997	7.50	8

Merry Makers - Department 56

YEAR ISSUE	EDITION LIMIT	YEAR RETD.	ISSUE PRICE	*QUOTE U.S.$
1994 Burgess The Bell Ringer 9368-8	Closed	1996	13.50	14-27
1993 Horatio The Hornblower 9383-1	Closed	1996	13.50	14
1993 Martin The Mandolinist 9383-1	Closed	1996	13.50	14
1993 Merry Mountain Chapel 9384-0	Closed	1996	7.50	8-15
1994 Percival/Puddingman, Leopold/ Lollipopman, 2 asst. 9396-3	Closed	1996	13.50	14
1994 Potter/Peppermint Make, Calvin/ Candy Striper, 2 asst. 9397-1	Closed	1996	13.50	14
1993 Sinclair The Singer 9383-1	Closed	1996	13.50	14-27
1995 Stanislav The Skier 93977	Closed	1996	13.50	14-22
1995 Stuart The Skater 93978	Closed	1996	13.50	14-22
1992 Tolland The Toller 9369-6	Closed	1995	11.00	11-22

Miscellaneous Ornaments - Department 56

YEAR ISSUE	EDITION LIMIT	YEAR RETD.	ISSUE PRICE	*QUOTE U.S.$
1992 Silver/Gold Ice Skate Ornament 84255	Closed	1992	2.50	20
1983 Snow Village Wood Ornaments, set/6, 5099-7	Closed	1984	30.00	N/A
1983 • Carriage House	Closed	1984	5.00	50
1983 • Centennial House	Closed	1984	5.00	100
1983 • Countryside Church	Closed	1984	5.00	125
1983 • Gabled House	Closed	1984	5.00	75
1983 • Pioneer Church	Closed	1984	5.00	75-125
1983 • Swiss Chalet	Closed	1984	5.00	75
1984 Dickens 2-sided Tin Ornaments, set/6, 6522-6	Closed	1985	12.00	440
1984 • Abel Beesley Butcher	Closed	1985	2.00	45
1984 • Bean and Son Smithy Shop	Closed	1985	2.00	45
1984 • Crowntree Inn	Closed	1985	2.00	45
1984 • Golden Swan Baker	Closed	1985	2.00	45
1984 • Green Grocer	Closed	1985	2.00	45
1984 • Jones & Co. Brush & Basket Shop	Closed	1985	2.00	45
1986 Cherub on Brass Ribbon, 8248-1	Closed	1988	8.00	72-75
1986 Teddy Bear on Brass Ribbon 8263-5	Closed	1988	7.00	72-75
1988 Balsam Bell Brass Dickens' Candlestick 6244-8	Closed	1989	3.00	15

*Quotes have been rounded up to nearest dollar

YEAR ISSUE	EDITION LIMIT	YEAR RETD.	ISSUE PRICE	*QUOTE U.S.$
1988 Christmas Carol- Bob & Mrs. Cratchit 5914-5	Closed	1989	18.00	36-45
1988 Christmas Carol- Scrooge's Head 5912-9	Closed	1989	13.00	30-35
1988 Christmas Carol- Tiny Tim's Head 5913-7	Closed	1989	10.00	25-35

Snowbabies Bootiebaby Bisque Ornaments - Department 56

YEAR ISSUE	EDITION LIMIT	YEAR RETD.	ISSUE PRICE	*QUOTE U.S.$
1997 One, Two High Button Shoe 68844	Open		12.50	13
1997 Three, Four, No Room For One More 68845	Open		12.50	13
1998 Five, Six, A Drum With Sticks 68865	Open		13.50	14
1998 Seven, Eight, Time To Skate 68886	Open		12.50	13

Snowbabies Mercury Glass Ornaments - Department 56

YEAR ISSUE	EDITION LIMIT	YEAR RETD.	ISSUE PRICE	*QUOTE U.S.$
1997 Snowbaby Atop a Glittered Green Tree 68992	Open		22.50	23
1997 Snowbaby Atop a Glittered Silver Drum 68993	Open		22.50	23
1996 Snowbaby Drummer The Night Before Christmas 68983	Open		18.00	18
1996 Snowbaby in Package The Night Before Christmas 68986	Open		18.00	18
1996 Snowbaby Jinglebaby The Night Before Christmas 68989	Open		20.00	20
1996 Snowbaby on Moon The Night Before Christmas 68988	Open		18.00	18
1996 Snowbaby on Package The Night Before Christmas 68981	Open		18.00	18
1996 Snowbaby on Snowball The Night Before Christmas 68984	Open		20.00	20
1996 Snowbaby Soldier The Night Before Christmas 68982	Open		18.00	18
1996 Snowbaby With Bell The Night Before Christmas 68987	Open		18.00	18
1996 Snowbaby With Sisal Tree The Night Before Christmas 68990	Open		20.00	20
1996 Snowbaby With Star The Night Before Christmas 68991	Open		18.00	18
1996 Snowbaby With Wreath The Night Before Christmas 68980	Open		18.00	18

Snowbabies Ornaments - Department 56

YEAR ISSUE	EDITION LIMIT	YEAR RETD.	ISSUE PRICE	*QUOTE U.S.$
1996 Baby's 1st Rattle 68828	Open		15.00	15
1994 Be My Baby 6866-7	Open		15.00	15
1998 Candle Light...Season Bright, Clip-On 68864	Open		13.50	14
1986 Crawling, Lite-Up, Clip-On, 7953-7	Closed	1992	7.00	18-46
1994 First Star Jinglebaby, 6858-6	Closed	1997	10.00	8-15
1998 Fly Me To The Moon 68885	Open		16.50	17
1998 Frosty Frolic Friends 68879 (1998 Winter Celebration Event Piece)	Open		15.00	15
1994 Gathering Stars in the Sky, 6855-1	Closed	1997	12.50	10-35
1996 Jinglebell Jinglebaby 68826	Open		11.00	11
1995 Joy 68807, set/3	Open		32.50	33
1996 Joy to the World 68829	Open		16.50	17
1994 Juggling Stars in the Sky 6867-5	Open		15.00	15
1994 Just For You Jinglebaby 6869-1	Open		11.00	11
1994 Little Drummer Jinglebaby, 6859-4	Closed	1997	11.00	8-26
1987 Mini, Winged Pair, Lite-Up, Clip-On, 7976-6	Open		9.00	12
1987 Moon Beams, 7951-0	Open		7.50	9
1991 My First Star, 6811-0	Open		7.00	8
1989 Noel, 7988-0	Open		7.50	8
1995 One Little Candle Jinglebaby 68806	Open		11.00	11
1995 Overnight Delivery, 759-5 (Event Piece)	Closed	1995	10.00	25-72
1995 Overnight Delivery, 68808	Open		10.00	10
1990 Penguin, Lite-Up, Clip-On, 7940-5	Closed	1992	5.00	20-40
1990 Polar Bear, Lite-Up, Clip-On, 7941-3	Closed	1992	5.00	14-31
1990 Rock-A-Bye Baby, 7939-1	Closed	1995	7.00	11-20
1986 Sitting, Lite-Up, Clip-On, 7952-9	Closed	1990	7.00	35-55
1992 Snowbabies Icicle With Star, 6825-0	Closed	1995	16.00	15-21
1987 Snowbaby Adrift Lite-Up, Clip-On, 7969-3	Closed	1990	8.50	109-125
1996 Snowbaby in my Stocking 68827	Open		10.00	10
1986 Snowbaby on Brass Ribbon, 7961-8	Closed	1989	8.00	150-208
1993 Sprinkling Stars in the Sky, 6848-9	Closed	1997	12.50	13
1989 Star Bright, 7990-1	Open		7.50	8
1996 Starry Pine Jinglebaby 68825	Open		11.00	11
1992 Starry, Starry Night, 6830-6	Open		12.50	13
1994 Stars in My Stocking Jinglebaby 6868-3	Open		11.00	11
1989 Surprise, 7989-8	Closed	1994	12.00	16-32
1991 Swinging On a Star, 6810-1	Open		9.50	10
1988 Twinkle Little Star, 7980-4	Closed	1990	7.00	60-94
1993 Wee...This is Fun!, 6847-0	Closed	1997	13.50	11-14
1986 Winged, Lite-Up, Clip-On, 7954-5	Closed	1990	7.00	50-58

Village Light-Up Ornaments - Department 56

YEAR ISSUE	EDITION LIMIT	YEAR RETD.	ISSUE PRICE	*QUOTE U.S.$
1987 Christmas Carol Cottages, set/3 (6513-7)	Closed	1989	17.00	78-90
1987 • The Cottage of Bob Cratchit & Tiny Tim	Closed	1989	6.00	21-38
1987 • Fezziwig's Warehouse	Closed	1989	6.00	23-34
1987 • Scrooge & Marley Countinghouse	Closed	1989	6.00	28-34
1987 Dickens' Village, set/14 (6521-8, 6520-0)	Closed	1989	84.00	361-400
1987 Dickens' Village, set/6 (6520-0)	Closed	1989	36.00	100-150
1987 • Barley Bree Farmhouse	Closed	1989	6.00	34-65
1987 • Blythe Pond Mill House	Closed	1989	6.00	43-59
1987 • Brick Abbey	Closed	1989	6.00	78-98
1987 • Chesterton Manor House	Closed	1989	6.00	34-68
1987 • Kenilworth Castle	Closed	1989	6.00	26-65
1987 • The Old Curiosity Shop	Closed	1989	6.00	58-65
1985 Dickens' Village, set/8 (6521-8)	Closed	1989	48.00	181-200
1985 • Abel Beesley Butcher	Closed	1989	6.00	26-30
1985 • Bean and Son Smithy Shop	Closed	1989	6.00	26-50
1985 • Candle Shop	Closed	1989	6.00	32-43
1985 • Crowntree Inn	Closed	1989	6.00	46-48
1985 • Dickens' Village Church	Closed	1989	6.00	39-68
1985 • Golden Swan Baker	Closed	1989	6.00	16-25
1985 • Green Grocer	Closed	1989	6.00	34-48
1985 • Jones & Co. Brush & Basket Shop	Closed	1989	6.00	40-46
1987 New England Village, set/13 (6533-1, 6534-0)	Closed	1989	78.00	700-750
1987 New England Village, set/6 (6534-0)	Closed	1989	36.00	200-275
1987 • Craggy Cove Lighthouse	Closed	1989	6.00	135-140
1987 • Jacob Adams Barn	Closed	1989	6.00	58-65
1987 • Jacob Adams Farmhouse	Closed	1989	6.00	65
1987 • Smythe Woolen Mill	Closed	1989	6.00	130-135
1987 • Timber Knoll Log Cabin	Closed	1989	6.00	100-135
1987 • Weston Train Station	Closed	1989	6.00	52-96
1986 New England Village, set/7 (6533-1)	Closed	1989	42.00	281-325
1986 • Apothecary Shop	Closed	1989	6.00	21-34
1986 • Brick Town Hall	Closed	1989	6.00	40-45
1986 • General Store	Closed	1989	6.00	46-48
1986 • Livery Stable & Boot Shop	Closed	1989	6.00	19-38
1986 • Nathaniel Bingham Fabrics	Closed	1989	6.00	39-42
1986 • Red Schoolhouse	Closed	1989	6.00	88-130
1986 • Steeple Church	Closed	1989	6.00	135-140

Duncan Royale

History Of Santa Claus - Duncan Royale

YEAR ISSUE	EDITION LIMIT	YEAR RETD.	ISSUE PRICE	*QUOTE U.S.$
1992 Santa I (set of 12)	Retrd.	1998	144.00	144
1992 Santa II (set of 12)	Retrd.	1998	144.00	144

eggspressions! inc.

Dynasty - eggspressions, unless otherwise noted

YEAR ISSUE	EDITION LIMIT	YEAR RETD.	ISSUE PRICE	*QUOTE U.S.$
1998 All Tied Up - B. Gabriella	Open		36.00	36
1998 Avanti	Open		36.00	36
1998 Belinda	Open		30.00	30
1998 Bowdatious	Open		68.00	68
1998 Catherine	Open		70.00	70
1998 Coral Cameo - B. Gabriella	Open		30.00	30
1998 Crystal Wrapped	Open		70.00	70
1998 Destiny II	Open		30.00	30
1998 Emerald Wrapped	Open		70.00	70
1998 Foil Candy	Open		60.00	60
1998 Forget Me Not	Open		64.00	64
1998 Golden Bows	Open		90.00	90
1998 Have a Heart	Open		74.00	74
1998 Hearts of Fire II	Open		30.00	30
1998 Keepsake	Open		50.00	50
1998 Marry Me II	Open		30.00	30
1998 Midnight Velvet	Open		25.00	25
1998 Natasha	Open		50.00	50
1998 Pearl Drops	Open		40.00	40
1998 Pearl Splendor - B. Gabriella	Open		36.00	36
1998 Pink Petals	Open		30.00	30
1998 Rings 'N Things	Open		50.00	50
1998 Royal Velvet	Open		25.00	25
1998 Ruby Wrapped	Open		70.00	70
1998 Sapphire Wrapped	Open		70.00	70
1998 Scalloped Satin - L. Pollard	Open		30.00	30
1998 Wedgewood Roses - B. Gabriella	Open		40.00	40

Eggsquisites - eggspressions, unless otherwise noted

YEAR ISSUE	EDITION LIMIT	YEAR RETD.	ISSUE PRICE	*QUOTE U.S.$
1998 Adoration - L. Pollard	Open		100.00	100
1998 Beaux Arts Ball - J. Neis	Open		100.00	100
1998 Candy Christmas (blue)	Open		104.00	104
1998 Candy Christmas (pink)	Open		104.00	104
1998 Delicate Dreams - J. Neis	Open		90.00	90
1998 Downhill Run	50		150.00	150
1998 Duchess - D. Botts	50		270.00	270
1998 High Society - L. Pollard	Open		120.00	120
1998 Holly Daze	Open		104.00	104
1998 Nature's Bouquet	Open		65.00	65
1998 Primrose Lady - L. Pollard	Open		130.00	130
1998 Robin's Retreat	50		110.00	110
1998 Sophisticate - L. Pollard	Open		120.00	120
1998 Spring Dream	50		120.00	120
1998 Summertime	250		144.00	144
1998 Three's Company - L. Pollard	Open		60.00	60
1998 Tiny Bubbles	250		144.00	144
1998 Topaz Crystal - C. Johnson	Open		120.00	120
1998 Victoria - L. Pollard	Open		90.00	90

Ertl Collectibles

Cat Hall of Fame - T. Epstein/J. Epstein Gage

YEAR ISSUE	EDITION LIMIT	YEAR RETD.	ISSUE PRICE	*QUOTE U.S.$
1998 Herr Drosselmeower 265	Open		14.50	15
1998 Mewria 260	Open		14.50	15
1998 Mother Ginger 266	Open		14.50	15
1998 The Nutcatter Purrince 259	Open		14.50	15
1998 Rat King 261	Open		14.50	15
1998 Sugar Plum Furry 262	Open		14.50	15

Sparrowsville - L. Davis

YEAR ISSUE	EDITION LIMIT	YEAR RETD.	ISSUE PRICE	*QUOTE U.S.$
1996 Bachelor Pad H109	Open		17.00	17
1997 Cozy Cabin 2493	Open		17.00	17
1996 The Hayloft H108	Open		17.00	17
1996 Hearthside Manor H111	Open		17.00	17
1996 Home Sweet Home H110	Open		17.00	17
1996 Leather Nest H106	Open		17.00	17
1996 Love Nest H107	Open		17.00	17
1996 The Smith's H104	Open		17.00	17
1996 Snowbirds H103	Open		17.00	17
1997 Stone Haven 2490	Open		17.00	17
1997 Winter Retreat H106	Open		17.00	17
1997 Winter Squash 2491	Open		17.00	17

Fenton Art Glass Company

Christmas Limited Edition - M. Reynolds

YEAR ISSUE	EDITION LIMIT	YEAR RETD.	ISSUE PRICE	*QUOTE U.S.$
1996 Golden Winged Angel, Hndpt. 3 1/2"	2,000	1996	27.50	28-45

Fitz & Floyd

Charming Tails Deck The Halls - D. Griff

YEAR ISSUE	EDITION LIMIT	YEAR RETD.	ISSUE PRICE	*QUOTE U.S.$
1992 Catching ZZZ's 86/785	Closed	1995	12.00	25-36
1992 Chickadees on Ball 86/787	Closed	1995	13.50	90-110
1992 Chicks with Bead Garland 86/791	Closed	1995	17.50	86-150
1992 The Drifters 86/784	Closed	1996	12.00	36-44
1992 Fresh Fruit 86/789	Closed	1995	12.00	24-75
1992 Mice/Rabbit Ball, set/2 86/788	Closed	1995	12.00	25-63
1992 Mice in Leaf Sleigh 86/786	Closed	1995	26.00	180-300
1993 Bunny & Mouse Bell 87/038	Closed	1995	10.50	81
1993 Hang in There 87/941	Closed	1996	10.00	27-47
1993 Holiday Wreath 87/939	Closed	1995	12.00	25-58
1993 Mackenzie Napping 87/940	Closed	1995	12.00	30-36
1993 Maxine Lights a Candle 87/942	Closed	1995	11.00	20-32
1993 Mouse on Snowflake (lighted) 87/037	Closed	1995	11.00	30-36
1993 Mouse w/Apple Candleholder 87/044	Closed	1995	13.00	68-88
1993 Porcelain Mouse Bell 87/036	Closed	1995	5.00	5
1994 Baby's First Christmas 87/184	Yr.Iss.	1994	12.00	27-41
1994 Binkey & Reginald on Ice 87/924	Closed	1994	10.00	40-95
1994 Friends in Flight 87/971	Closed	1994	18.00	63-130
1994 The Grape Escape (grape) 87/186	Closed	1995	18.00	25-68
1994 The Grape Escape (green) 87/186	Closed	1995	18.00	25-68
1994 High Flying Mackenzie 87/992	Closed	1997	20.00	25-50
1994 Holiday Lights 87/969	Closed	1995	10.00	36-41
1994 Horsin' Around	Closed	1996	18.00	32-45
1994 Mackenzie and Binkey's Snack (cherry & plum) 87/187	Closed	1994	12.00	50-120
1994 Mackenzie Blowing Bubbles 87/191	Closed	1994	12.00	36-75
1994 Mackenzie on Ice 87/970	Closed	1996	10.00	27-37
1994 Mackenzie's Bubble Ride 87/192	Closed	1996	13.00	42-80
1994 Mackenzie's Snowball (dated) 87/994	Yr.Iss.	1994	10.00	59-63
1994 Maxine and Mackenzie 87/185	Closed	1996	12.00	32-35
1994 Reginald's Bubble Ride 87/199	Closed	1994	12.00	40-59
1994 Apple House (lighted) 87/032	Closed	1995	13.00	59-63
1994 Pear House (lighted) 87/027	Closed	1995	13.00	63-68
1994 Mouse on Yellow Bulb (lighted) 87/045	Closed	1995	10.00	45-54
1994 Mouse Star Treetop 87/958	Closed	1995	10.00	50-55
1994 Sticky Situations 87/991	Closed	1996	16.00	36-44
1995 1995 Annual 87/306	Yr.Iss.	1995	16.00	16-25
1995 Binkey's Poinsettia 87/303	Closed	1997	12.00	12-15
1995 Christmas Cookies 87/301	Open		10.00	11
1995 Christmas Flowers 87/304	Open		12.00	13
1995 Holiday Balloon Ride 87/299	Closed	1996	16.00	16-32
1995 Mackenzie's Whirligig 87/300	Closed	1997	20.00	20-32
1995 Peppermint Party 87/314	Closed	1998	10.00	11-25
1995 Reginald in Leaves 87/302	Closed	1997	10.00	10-35
1995 Stewart at Play 87/308	Closed	1995	12.00	30-36
1995 Stewart's Winter Fun 87/307	Closed	1995	10.00	27-36
1996 1996 Annual-All Wrapped Up 87/471	Yr.Iss.	1996	12.00	12-25
1996 Baby's First Christmas 87/850	Yr.Iss.	1996	13.00	23-30
1996 Our First Christmas (dated) 86/708	Yr.Iss.	1996	18.00	20-35
1996 Christmas Stamps 87/485	Retrd.	1998	12.00	13-25
1996 Fallen Angel 87/492	Retrd.	1998	12.00	13
1996 Flights of Fancy 87/490	Retrd.	1998	12.00	13-20
1996 Frequent Flyer 87/491	Retrd.	1998	12.00	13-20
1996 Letter to Santa 87/486	Retrd.	1998	12.00	13-25
1996 Stamp Dispenser 87/483	Open		12.00	13
1996 Weeeeee! 87/493	Retrd.	1998	12.00	13-25
1997 All Lit Up (lighted) 86/660	Open		11.00	11
1997 Chauncey's First Christmas 86/710	Yr.Iss.	1997	9.00	9
1997 Mackenzie In Mitten 86/704	Open		9.00	9
1997 1997 Annual-Mackenzie's Jack in the Box 86/709	Yr.Iss.	1997	10.00	11
1997 Maxine's Angel 86/701	Open		9.00	9
1997 Our First Christmas 86/708	Yr.Iss.	1997	12.50	13
1997 A Special Delivery 86/707	Open		9.00	9
1998 Air Mail To Santa 86/652	Open		13.00	13
1998 Our First Christmas Together 86/653	Open		12.00	13
1998 Bundle of Joy - Baby's First Christmas 86/655	Open		12.00	13
1998 Heading For The Slopes 86/656	Open		13.00	13
1998 Ski Jumper 86/657	Open		13.00	13
1998 Tricycle Built From Treats 86/658	Open		13.00	13
1998 Pine Cone Predicament 86/659	Yr.Iss.		11.00	11

Charming Tails Easter Basket - D. Griff

YEAR ISSUE	EDITION LIMIT	YEAR RETD.	ISSUE PRICE	*QUOTE U.S.$
1994 Easter Parade 89/615	Closed	1996	10.00	27-35

YEAR ISSUE	EDITION LIMIT	YEAR RETD.	ISSUE PRICE	*QUOTE U.S.$
1994 Peek-a-boo 89/753	Closed	1996	12.00	25-32

Charming Tails Everyday Ornaments- D. Griff

YEAR ISSUE	EDITION LIMIT	YEAR RETD.	ISSUE PRICE	*QUOTE U.S.$
1994 Binkey in the Berry Patch 89/752	Closed	1996	12.00	32-50
1995 I'm Berry Happy 87/390	Closed	1997	15.00	16-32
1995 I'm Full 87/365	Closed	1997	15.00	16
1995 Maxine in Strawberry 89/562	Closed	1995	12.00	35-60
1993 Maxine's Butterfly Ride 89/190	Open		16.50	17
1993 Mouse on a Bee 89/191	Closed	1994	16.50	225-300
1993 Mouse on a Dragonfly 89/320	Closed	1994	16.50	225-300
1995 Picking Peppers 87/369	Closed	1996	12.00	13-35
1994 Springtime Showers 89/563	Closed	1996	10.00	25-40

Flambro Imports

Emmett Kelly Jr. Christmas Ornaments - Undis.

YEAR ISSUE	EDITION LIMIT	YEAR RETD.	ISSUE PRICE	*QUOTE U.S.$
1989 65th Birthday	Yr.Iss.	1989	24.00	150-295
1990 30 Years Of Clowning	Yr.Iss.	1990	30.00	98-160
1991 EKJ With Stocking And Toys	Yr.Iss.	1991	30.00	34-46
1992 Home For Christmas	Yr.Iss.	1992	24.00	30-75
1993 Christmas Mail	Yr.Iss.	1993	25.00	30-75
1994 '70 Birthday Commemorative	Yr.Iss.	1994	24.00	30-90
1995 20th Anniversary All Star Circus	Yr.Iss.	1995	25.00	50-70
1996 Christmas Pageant	Yr.Iss.	1996	29.00	30-75
1997 1997 Dated Ornament	Yr.Iss.	1997	30.00	30
1998 1998 Dated Ornament	Yr.Iss.		20.00	20

Little Emmett Ornaments - M. Wu

YEAR ISSUE	EDITION LIMIT	YEAR RETD.	ISSUE PRICE	*QUOTE U.S.$
1995 Little Emmett Christmas Wrap	Open		11.50	12
1995 Little Emmett Deck the Neck	Open		11.50	12
1996 Little Emmett Singing Carols	Open		13.00	13
1996 Little Emmett Your Present	Open		13.00	13
1996 Little Emmett Baby 1st Christmas	Open		13.00	13
1996 Little Emmett on Rocking Horse	Open		25.00	25

Ganz

Cottage Collectibles® Christmas Collection -Various

YEAR ISSUE	EDITION LIMIT	YEAR RETD.	ISSUE PRICE	*QUOTE U.S.$
1997 All I Want For Christmas - M. Holstad	Open		8.00	8
1997 Christmas Skate - L. Chien	Open		8.00	8
1997 Deck The Halls - T. Skorstad	Open		8.00	8
1997 Harey Situation - L. Chien	Open		8.00	8
1997 Heavenly Stars - L. Chien	Open		8.00	8
1997 Just What I Wanted - L. Chien	Open		8.00	8
1997 Li'l Angels - C. Kirby	Open		8.00	8
1997 One For You, One For Me - M. Holstad	Open		8.00	8
1997 Santa's Express - C. Kirby	Open		8.00	8
1997 Snowman - C. Rave	Open		8.00	8
1997 Surprise - T. Skorstad	Open		8.00	8
1997 'Twas The Night - M. Holstad	Open		8.00	8
1998 Christmas Kiss - L. Chien	Open		8.00	8
1998 Christmas Traditions - C. Kirby	Open		8.00	8
1998 Dashing Through The Snow - S. Coe	Open		8.00	8
1998 For Santa, With Love - C. Kirby	Open		8.00	8
1998 Honey's Song - L. Chien	Open		8.00	8
1998 A Kitty For Me - M. Holstad	Open		8.00	8
1998 My Horsy - C. Kirby	Open		8.00	8
1998 Perfect Presents - C. Tredger	Open		8.00	8
1998 Santa's Helper - M. Holstad	Open		8.00	8
1998 Stocking Stuffers - L. Chien	Open		8.00	8
1998 Treat Time - T. Skorstad	Open		8.00	8
1998 Yuletide Treasure - L. Chien	Open		8.00	8

Perfect Little Place/Christmas Collection - L. Sunarth, unless otherwise noted

YEAR ISSUE	EDITION LIMIT	YEAR RETD.	ISSUE PRICE	*QUOTE U.S.$
1995 Angel of Light - C.Thammavongsa	Retrd.	1997	12.00	12
1997 Cookies & Milk For Santa	Open		6.50	7
1997 Drummer Boy	Open		6.50	7
1997 Festive Shopping	Open		6.50	7
1997 Visions of Sugar Plums	Open		6.50	7

Gartlan USA

Jerry Garcia - S. Sun

YEAR ISSUE	EDITION LIMIT	YEAR RETD.	ISSUE PRICE	*QUOTE U.S.$
1997 Jerry Garcia	Yr.Iss.	1997	29.95	30

John Lennon - J. Lennon

YEAR ISSUE	EDITION LIMIT	YEAR RETD.	ISSUE PRICE	*QUOTE U.S.$
1997 John Lennon Christmas plate/ornament (3 1/4")	Open		16.95	17

Ringo Starr - J. Hoffman

YEAR ISSUE	EDITION LIMIT	YEAR RETD.	ISSUE PRICE	*QUOTE U.S.$
1996 Ringo Starr	Yr.Iss.	1996	19.95	20

Geo. Zoltan Lefton Company

Colonial Village Ornaments - Lefton

YEAR ISSUE	EDITION LIMIT	YEAR RETD.	ISSUE PRICE	*QUOTE U.S.$
1987 Charity Chapel	Closed	1990	6.00	18
1987 Church of the Golden Rule	Closed	1990	6.00	18
1987 Lil Red School House	Closed	1990	6.00	18
1987 Nelson House	Closed	1990	6.00	18
1987 Old Stone Church	Closed	1990	6.00	18
1987 Penny House	Closed	1990	6.00	18

GiftStar

Brian Baker's Déjà Vu Collection - B. Baker

YEAR ISSUE	EDITION LIMIT	YEAR RETD.	ISSUE PRICE	*QUOTE U.S.$
1998 Angel of the Sea 18060	Open		17.00	17
1998 Christmas Church 18030	Open		17.00	17
1998 Country Station 18010	Open		17.00	17
1998 Flower Store 18020	Open		17.00	17
1998 Looks Like Nantucket 18040	Open		17.00	17
1998 Mansard Lady 18050	Open		17.00	17
1998 Victorian Tower House 18070	Open		17.00	17

Goebel of North America

Angel Bell 3" - Goebel

YEAR ISSUE	EDITION LIMIT	YEAR RETD.	ISSUE PRICE	*QUOTE U.S.$
1994 Angel w/Clarinet - Red	Closed	1994	17.50	18
1995 Angel w/Harp - Blue	Closed	1995	17.50	18
1996 Angel w/Mandolin - Champagne	Closed	1996	18.00	18
1997 Angel w/Accordian - Rose	Closed	1997	18.00	18
1998 Angel w/Bell - Blue	Yr.Iss.		20.00	20

Angel Bells - 3 Asst. Colors - Goebel

YEAR ISSUE	EDITION LIMIT	YEAR RETD.	ISSUE PRICE	*QUOTE U.S.$
1976 Angel Bell w/Clarinet (3 colors)	Closed	1976	8.00	60
1976 Angel Bell w/Clarinet (white bisque)	Closed	1976	6.00	6-25
1977 Angel Bell w/Mandolin (3 colors)	Closed	1977	8.50	9-25
1977 Angel Bell w/Mandolin (white bisque)	Closed	1977	6.50	7-15
1978 Angel Bell w/Harp (3 colors)	Closed	1978	9.00	25
1978 Angel Bell w/Harp (white bisque)	Closed	1978	7.00	20
1979 Angel Bell w/Accordion (3 colors)	Closed	1979	9.50	10
1979 Angel Bell w/Accordion (white bisque)	Closed	1979	7.50	20
1980 Angel Bell w/Saxaphone (3 colors)	Closed	1980	10.00	25
1980 Angel Bell w/Saxaphone (white bisque)	Closed	1980	8.00	20
1981 Angel Bell w/Music (3 colors)	Closed	1981	11.00	25
1981 Angel Bell w/Music (white bisque)	Closed	1981	9.00	20
1982 Angel Bell w/French Horn (3 colors)	Closed	1982	11.75	25
1982 Angel Bell w/French Horn (white bisque)	Closed	1982	9.75	10-20
1983 Angel Bell w/Flute (3 colors)	Closed	1983	12.50	13-25
1983 Angel Bell w/Flute (white bisque)	Closed	1983	10.50	11
1984 Angel Bell w/Drum (3 colors)	Closed	1984	14.00	25
1984 Angel Bell w/Drum (white bisque)	Closed	1984	12.00	20
1985 Angel Bell w/Trumpet (3 colors)	Closed	1985	14.00	14
1985 Angel Bell w/Trumpet (white bisque)	Closed	1985	12.00	12
1986 Angel Bell w/Bells (3 colors)	Closed	1986	15.00	25
1986 Angel Bell w/Bells (white bisque)	Closed	1986	12.50	20
1987 Angel Bell w/Conductor (3 colors)	Closed	1987	16.50	17
1987 Angel Bell w/Conductor (white bisque)	Closed	1987	13.50	14
1988 Angel Bell w/Candle (3 colors)	Closed	1988	17.50	25
1988 Angel Bell w/Candle (white bisque)	Closed	1988	15.00	22
1989 Angel Bell w/Star (3 colors)	Closed	1989	20.00	20
1989 Angel Bell w/Star (white bisque)	Closed	1989	17.50	18
1990 Angel Bell w/Lantern (3 colors)	Closed	1990	22.50	25
1990 Angel Bell w/Lantern (white bisque)	Closed	1990	20.00	25
1991 Angel Bell w/Teddy (3 colors)	Closed	1991	25.00	28
1991 Angel Bell w/Teddy (white bisque)	Closed	1991	22.50	25
1992 Angel Bell w/Doll (3 colors)	Closed	1992	27.50	31
1992 Angel Bell w/Doll (white bisque)	Closed	1992	25.00	28
1993 Angel Bell w/Rocking Horse (3 colors)	Closed	1993	30.00	34
1993 Angel Bell w/Rocking Horse (white bisque)	Closed	1993	27.50	28
1994 Angel Bell w/Clown (3 colors)	Closed	1994	34.50	35-55
1994 Angel Bell w/Clown (white bisque)	Closed	1994	29.50	30
1995 Angel Bell w/Train (3 colors)	Closed	1995	37.00	37
1995 Angel Bell w/Train (white bisque)	Closed	1995	30.50	31
1996 Angel Bell w/Puppy (3 colors)	Closed	1996	40.00	40
1996 Angel Bell w/Puppy (white bisque)	Closed	1996	32.00	32
1997 Angel Bell w/Kitten (3 colors)	Closed	1997	42.50	43
1997 Angel Bell w/Kitten (white bisque)	Closed	1997	32.50	33
1998 Angel Bell w/Lamb (3 colors)	Yr.Iss.		45.00	45
1998 Angel Bell w/Lamb (white bisque)	Yr.Iss.		34.00	34

Goebel/M.I. Hummel

M.I. Hummel Annual Figurine Ornaments - M.I. Hummel

YEAR ISSUE	EDITION LIMIT	YEAR RETD.	ISSUE PRICE	*QUOTE U.S.$
1988 Flying High 452	Closed	N/A	75.00	85-104
1989 Love From Above 481	Closed	N/A	75.00	75-156
1990 Peace on Earth 484	Closed	N/A	80.00	75-155
1991 Angelic Guide 571	Closed	N/A	95.00	155-260
1992 Light Up The Night 622	Closed	N/A	100.00	75-155
1993 Herald on High 623	Closed	N/A	155.00	116-202
1997 Boy with Horse 239/B/O	Open		60.00	60
1997 Girl with Nosegay 239/A/O	Open		60.00	60
1997 Girl with Doll 239/C/O	Open		60.00	60
1997 Girl with Fir Tree 239/D/O	10,000		60.00	60

M.I. Hummel Collectibles Christmas Bell Ornaments - M.I. Hummel

YEAR ISSUE	EDITION LIMIT	YEAR RETD.	ISSUE PRICE	*QUOTE U.S.$
1989 Ride Into Christmas 775	Closed	1989	35.00	50-195
1990 Letter to Santa Claus 776	Closed	1990	37.50	38-100
1991 Hear Ye, Hear Ye 777	Closed	1991	40.00	30-100
1992 Harmony in Four Parts 778	Closed	1992	50.00	38-80
1993 Celestial Musician 779	Closed	1993	50.00	50-70
1994 Festival Harmony w/Mandolin 780	Closed	1994	50.00	38-55
1995 Festival Harmony w/Flute 781	Closed	1995	55.00	55
1996 Christmas Song 782	Closed	1996	65.00	65
1997 Thanksgiving Prayer 783	Closed	1997	68.00	68
1998 Echoes of Joy 784	Yr.Iss.		70.00	70

M.I. Hummel Collectibles Miniature Ornaments - M.I. Hummel

YEAR ISSUE	EDITION LIMIT	YEAR RETD.	ISSUE PRICE	*QUOTE U.S.$
1993 Celestial Musician 646	Closed	1993	90.00	75-115
1994 Festival Harmony w/Mandolin 647	Closed	1994	95.00	75-115
1995 Festival Harmony w/Flute 648	Closed	1995	100.00	75-115
1996 Christmas Song 645	Closed	1996	115.00	86-115
1997 Thanksgiving Prayer 642	Closed	1997	120.00	90-115
1998 Echoes of Joy 597	Yr.Iss.		120.00	120

Gorham

Annual Crystal Ornaments - Gorham

YEAR ISSUE	EDITION LIMIT	YEAR RETD.	ISSUE PRICE	*QUOTE U.S.$
1985 Crystal Ornament	Closed	1985	22.00	25
1986 Crystal Ornament	Closed	1986	25.00	25
1987 Crystal Ornament	Closed	1987	25.00	25
1988 Crystal Ornament	Closed	1988	28.00	28
1989 Crystal Ornament	Closed	1989	28.00	28
1990 Crystal Ornament	Closed	1990	30.00	30
1991 Crystal Ornament	Closed	1991	35.00	35
1992 Crystal Ornament	Closed	1992	32.50	33
1993 Crystal Ornament	Closed	1993	32.50	33

Annual Snowflake Ornaments - Gorham

YEAR ISSUE	EDITION LIMIT	YEAR RETD.	ISSUE PRICE	*QUOTE U.S.$
1970 Sterling Snowflake	Closed	1970	10.00	300-400
1971 Sterling Snowflake	Closed	1971	10.00	55-175
1972 Sterling Snowflake	Closed	1972	10.00	55-175
1973 Sterling Snowflake	Closed	1973	11.00	65-175
1974 Sterling Snowflake	Closed	1974	18.00	60-100
1975 Sterling Snowflake	Closed	1975	18.00	35-100
1976 Sterling Snowflake	Closed	1976	20.00	50-120
1977 Sterling Snowflake	Closed	1977	23.00	35-95
1978 Sterling Snowflake	Closed	1978	23.00	50-95
1979 Sterling Snowflake	Closed	1979	33.00	50-120
1980 Silverplated Snowflake	Closed	1980	15.00	130-175
1981 Sterling Snowflake	Closed	1981	50.00	175-250
1982 Sterling Snowflake	Closed	1982	38.00	60-90
1983 Sterling Snowflake	Closed	1983	45.00	70-100
1984 Sterling Snowflake	Closed	1984	45.00	65-110
1985 Sterling Snowflake	Closed	1985	45.00	70-75
1986 Sterling Snowflake	Closed	1986	45.00	50-70
1987 Sterling Snowflake	Closed	1987	50.00	50-90
1988 Sterling Snowflake	Closed	1988	50.00	60-65
1989 Sterling Snowflake	Closed	1989	50.00	60-65
1990 Sterling Snowflake	Closed	1990	50.00	60-80
1991 Sterling Snowflake	Closed	1991	55.00	50-65
1992 Sterling Snowflake	Closed	1992	50.00	50-75
1993 Sterling Snowflake	Closed	1993	50.00	60
1994 Sterling Snowflake	Closed	1994	50.00	50-70
1995 Sterling Snowflake	Closed	1995	50.00	50-65
1996 Sterling Snowflake	Closed	1995	50.00	45-55

Archive Collectible - Gorham

YEAR ISSUE	EDITION LIMIT	YEAR RETD.	ISSUE PRICE	*QUOTE U.S.$
1988 Victorian Heart	Closed	1988	50.00	60-75
1989 Victorian Wreath	Closed	1989	50.00	45-50
1990 Elizabethan Cupid	Closed	1990	60.00	45-60
1991 Baroque Angels	Closed	1991	55.00	45-55
1992 Madonna and Child	Closed	1992	50.00	45-50
1993 Angel With Mandolin	Closed	1993	50.00	45-50

Baby's First Christmas Crystal - Gorham

YEAR ISSUE	EDITION LIMIT	YEAR RETD.	ISSUE PRICE	*QUOTE U.S.$
1991 Baby's First Rocking Horse	Closed	1994	35.00	35

Greenwich Workshop

The Greenwich Workshop Collection - J. Christensen

YEAR ISSUE	EDITION LIMIT	YEAR RETD.	ISSUE PRICE	*QUOTE U.S.$
1995 The Angel's Gift	Yr.Iss.	1995	50.00	95
1996 A Gift of Light	7,500	1996	75.00	75
1997 A Gift of Music	7,500	1997	75.00	75

Hallmark Keepsake Ornaments

1973 Hallmark Keepsake Collection - Keepsake

YEAR ISSUE	EDITION LIMIT	YEAR RETD.	ISSUE PRICE	*QUOTE U.S.$
1973 Betsey Clark (1st Ed.) XHD110-2	Yr.Iss.	1973	2.50	76-113
1973 Betsey Clark XHD100-2	Yr.Iss.	1973	2.50	77-112
1973 Christmas Is Love XHD106-2	Yr.Iss.	1973	2.50	80
1973 Elves XHD103-5	Yr.Iss.	1973	2.50	75
1973 Manger Scene XHD102-2	Yr.Iss.	1973	2.50	85-125
1973 Santa with Elves XHD101-5	Yr.Iss.	1973	2.50	85

1973 Keepsake Yarn Ornaments - Keepsake

YEAR ISSUE	EDITION LIMIT	YEAR RETD.	ISSUE PRICE	*QUOTE U.S.$
1973 Angel XHD78-5	Yr.Iss.	1973	1.25	23
1973 Blue Girl XHD85-2	Yr.Iss.	1973	1.25	23
1973 Boy Caroler XHD83-2	Yr.Iss.	1973	1.25	30
1973 Choir Boy XHD80-5	Yr.Iss.	1973	1.25	28
1973 Elf XHD79-2	Yr.Iss.	1973	1.25	25
1973 Green Girl XHD84-5	Yr.Iss.	1973	1.25	21
1973 Little Girl XHD82-5	Yr.Iss.	1973	1.25	20
1973 Mr. Santa XHD74-5	Yr.Iss.	1973	1.25	25
1973 Mr. Snowman XHD76-5	Yr.Iss.	1973	1.25	25
1973 Mrs. Santa XHD75-2	Yr.Iss.	1973	1.25	23
1973 Mrs. Snowman XHD77-2	Yr.Iss.	1973	1.25	23
1973 Soldier XHD81-2	Yr.Iss.	1973	1.00	22

1974 Hallmark Keepsake Collection - Keepsake

YEAR ISSUE	EDITION LIMIT	YEAR RETD.	ISSUE PRICE	*QUOTE U.S.$
1974 Angel QX110 -1	Yr.Iss.	1974	2.50	35-75
1974 Betsey Clark (2nd Ed.) QX108-1	Yr.Iss.	1974	2.50	47-85
1974 Buttons & Bo (Set/2) QX113-1	Yr.Iss.	1974	3.50	50
1974 Charmers QX109-1	Yr.Iss.	1974	2.50	23-40
1974 Currier & Ives (Set/2) QX112-1	Yr.Iss.	1974	3.50	42-55
1974 Little Miracles (Set/4) QX115-1	Yr.Iss.	1974	4.50	55
1974 Norman Rockwell QX106-1	Yr.Iss.	1974	2.50	45-95
1974 Norman Rockwell QX111-1	Yr.Iss.	1974	2.50	85
1974 Raggedy Ann and Andy(4/set) QX114-1	Yr.Iss.	1974	4.50	75
1974 Snowgoose QX107-1	Yr.Iss.	1974	2.50	50-75

1974 Keepsake Yarn Ornaments - Keepsake

YEAR ISSUE	EDITION LIMIT	YEAR RETD.	ISSUE PRICE	*QUOTE U.S.$
1974 Angel QX103-1	Yr.Iss.	1974	1.50	28
1974 Elf QX101-1	Yr.Iss.	1974	1.50	23
1974 Mrs. Santa QX100-1	Yr.Iss.	1974	1.50	23

*Quotes have been rounded up to nearest dollar

YEAR ISSUE	EDITION LIMIT	YEAR RETD.	ISSUE PRICE	*QUOTE U.S.$
1974 Santa QX105-1	Yr.Iss.	1974	1.50	25
1974 Snowman QX104-1	Yr.Iss.	1974	1.50	23
1974 Soldier QX102-1	Yr.Iss.	1974	1.50	23

1975 Handcrafted Ornaments: Adorable - Keepsake

YEAR ISSUE	EDITION LIMIT	YEAR RETD.	ISSUE PRICE	*QUOTE U.S.$
1975 Betsey Clark QX157-1	Yr.Iss.	1975	2.50	225
1975 Drummer Boy QX161-1	Yr.Iss.	1975	2.50	225-300
1975 Mrs. Santa QX156-1	Yr.Iss.	1975	2.50	275
1975 Raggedy Andy QX160-1	Yr.Iss.	1975	2.50	375
1975 Raggedy Ann QX159-1	Yr.Iss.	1975	2.50	295
1975 Santa QX155-1	Yr.Iss.	1975	2.50	250

1975 Handcrafted Ornaments: Nostalgia - Keepsake

YEAR ISSUE	EDITION LIMIT	YEAR RETD.	ISSUE PRICE	*QUOTE U.S.$
1975 Drummer Boy QX130-1	Yr.Iss.	1975	3.50	115-175
1975 Joy QX132-1	Yr.Iss.	1975	3.50	125-150
1975 Locomotive (dated) QX127-1	Yr.Iss.	1975	3.50	125-175
1975 Peace on Earth (dated) QX131-1	Yr.Iss.	1975	3.50	100-165
1975 Rocking Horse QX128-1	Yr.Iss.	1975	3.50	125-175
1975 Santa & Sleigh QX129-1	Yr.Iss.	1975	3.50	125

1975 Keepsake Property Ornaments - Keepsake

YEAR ISSUE	EDITION LIMIT	YEAR RETD.	ISSUE PRICE	*QUOTE U.S.$
1975 Betsey Clark (3rd Ed.) QX133-1	Yr.Iss.	1975	3.00	26-45
1975 Betsey Clark (Set/2) QX167-1	Yr.Iss.	1975	3.50	25-45
1975 Betsey Clark (Set/4) QX168-1	Yr.Iss.	1975	4.50	50
1975 Betsey Clark QX163-1	Yr.Iss.	1975	2.50	40
1975 Buttons & Bo (Set/4) QX139-1	Yr.Iss.	1975	5.00	50
1975 Charmers QX135-1	Yr.Iss.	1975	3.00	31
1975 Currier & Ives (Set/2) QX137-1	Yr.Iss.	1975	4.00	40
1975 Currier & Ives (Set/2) QX164-1	Yr.Iss.	1975	2.50	35
1975 Little Miracles (Set/4) QX140-1	Yr.Iss.	1975	5.00	40
1975 Marty Links QX136-1	Yr.Iss.	1975	3.00	60
1975 Norman Rockwell QX134-1	Yr.Iss.	1975	3.00	37
1975 Norman Rockwell QX166-1	Yr.Iss.	1975	2.50	45-55
1975 Raggedy Ann and Andy(2/set) QX138-1	Yr.Iss.	1975	4.00	65
1975 Raggedy Ann QX165-1	Yr.Iss.	1975	2.50	50-65

1975 Keepsake Yarn Ornaments - Keepsake

YEAR ISSUE	EDITION LIMIT	YEAR RETD.	ISSUE PRICE	*QUOTE U.S.$
1975 Drummer Boy QX123-1	Yr.Iss.	1975	1.75	25
1975 Little Girl QX126-1	Yr.Iss.	1975	1.75	20
1975 Mrs. Santa QX125-1	Yr.Iss.	1975	1.75	22
1975 Raggedy Andy QX122-1	Yr.Iss.	1975	1.75	40
1975 Raggedy Ann QX121-1	Yr.Iss.	1975	1.75	35
1975 Santa QX124-1	Yr.Iss.	1975	1.75	22

1976 Bicentennial Commemoratives - Keepsake

YEAR ISSUE	EDITION LIMIT	YEAR RETD.	ISSUE PRICE	*QUOTE U.S.$
1976 Bicentennial '76 Commemorative QX211-1	Yr.Iss.	1976	2.50	45-60
1976 Bicentennial Charmers QX198-1	Yr.Iss.	1976	3.00	75-95
1976 Colonial Children (Set/2) 4 QX208-1	Yr.Iss.	1976	4.00	65-95

1976 Decorative Ball Ornaments - Keepsake

YEAR ISSUE	EDITION LIMIT	YEAR RETD.	ISSUE PRICE	*QUOTE U.S.$
1976 Cardinals QX205-1	Yr.Iss.	1976	2.30	45-85
1976 Chickadees QX204-1	Yr.Iss.	1976	2.30	50-65

1976 First Commemorative Ornament - Keepsake

YEAR ISSUE	EDITION LIMIT	YEAR RETD.	ISSUE PRICE	*QUOTE U.S.$
1976 Baby's First Christmas QX211-1	Yr.Iss.	1976	2.50	150

1976 Handcrafted Ornaments: Nostalgia - Keepsake

YEAR ISSUE	EDITION LIMIT	YEAR RETD.	ISSUE PRICE	*QUOTE U.S.$
1976 Drummer Boy QX130-1	Yr.Iss.	1976	3.50	160-175
1976 Locomotive QX222-1	Yr.Iss.	1976	3.50	165
1976 Peace on Earth QX223-1	Yr.Iss.	1976	3.50	95-175
1976 Rocking Horse QX128-1	Yr.Iss.	1976	3.50	165

1976 Handcrafted Ornaments: Tree Treats - Keepsake

YEAR ISSUE	EDITION LIMIT	YEAR RETD.	ISSUE PRICE	*QUOTE U.S.$
1976 Angel QX176-1	Yr.Iss.	1976	3.00	150-195
1976 Reindeer QX 178-1	Yr.Iss.	1976	3.00	115
1976 Santa QX177-1	Yr.Iss.	1976	3.00	195-225
1976 Shepherd QX175-1	Yr.Iss.	1976	3.00	115-125

1976 Handcrafted Ornaments: Twirl-Abouts - Keepsake

YEAR ISSUE	EDITION LIMIT	YEAR RETD.	ISSUE PRICE	*QUOTE U.S.$
1976 Angel QX171-1	Yr.Iss.	1976	4.50	117-132
1976 Partridge QX174-1	Yr.Iss.	1976	4.50	195
1976 Santa QX172-1	Yr.Iss.	1976	4.50	103-125
1976 Soldier QX173-1	Yr.Iss.	1976	4.50	65-95

1976 Handcrafted Ornaments: Yesteryears - Keepsake

YEAR ISSUE	EDITION LIMIT	YEAR RETD.	ISSUE PRICE	*QUOTE U.S.$
1976 Drummer Boy QX184-1	Yr.Iss.	1976	5.00	122-150
1976 Partridge QX183-1	Yr.Iss.	1976	5.00	115
1976 Santa QX182-1	Yr.Iss.	1976	5.00	165
1976 Train QX181-1	Yr.Iss.	1976	5.00	135-160

1976 Property Ornaments - Keepsake

YEAR ISSUE	EDITION LIMIT	YEAR RETD.	ISSUE PRICE	*QUOTE U.S.$
1976 Betsey Clark (4th Ed.)QX 195-1	Yr.Iss.	1976	3.00	75-100
1976 Betsey Clark (Set/3) QX218-1	Yr.Iss.	1976	4.50	45-65
1976 Betsey Clark QX210-1	Yr.Iss.	1976	2.50	38-42
1976 Charmers (Set/2) QX215-1	Yr.Iss.	1976	3.50	65-75
1976 Currier & Ives QX197-1	Yr.Iss.	1976	3.00	50
1976 Currier & Ives QX209-1	Yr.Iss.	1976	2.50	50
1976 Happy the Snowman (Set/2) QX216-1	Yr.Iss.	1976	3.50	55
1976 Marty Links (Set/2) QX207-1	Yr.Iss.	1976	4.00	45-65
1976 Norman Rockwell QX196-1	Yr.Iss.	1976	3.00	65
1976 Raggedy Ann QX212-1	Yr.Iss.	1976	2.50	65
1976 Rudolph and Santa QX213-1	Yr.Iss.	1976	2.50	75

1976 Yarn Ornaments - Keepsake

YEAR ISSUE	EDITION LIMIT	YEAR RETD.	ISSUE PRICE	*QUOTE U.S.$
1976 Caroler QX126-1	Yr.Iss.	1976	1.75	28
1976 Drummer Boy QX123-1	Yr.Iss.	1976	1.75	23
1976 Mrs. Santa QX125-1	Yr.Iss.	1976	1.75	22
1976 Raggedy Andy QX122-1	Yr.Iss.	1976	1.75	40
1976 Raggedy Ann QX121-1	Yr.Iss.	1976	1.75	35
1976 Santa QX124-1	Yr.Iss.	1976	1.75	24

1977 Christmas Expressions Collection - Keepsake

YEAR ISSUE	EDITION LIMIT	YEAR RETD.	ISSUE PRICE	*QUOTE U.S.$
1977 Bell QX154-2	Yr.Iss.	1977	3.50	35
1977 Mandolin QX157-5	Yr.Iss.	1977	3.50	65
1977 Ornaments QX155-5	Yr.Iss.	1977	3.50	65
1977 Wreath QX156-2	Yr.Iss.	1977	3.50	65

1977 Cloth Doll Ornaments - Keepsake

YEAR ISSUE	EDITION LIMIT	YEAR RETD.	ISSUE PRICE	*QUOTE U.S.$
1977 Angel QX220-2	Yr.Iss.	1977	1.75	40-50
1977 Santa QX221-5	Yr.Iss.	1977	1.75	55-80

1977 Colors of Christmas - Keepsake

YEAR ISSUE	EDITION LIMIT	YEAR RETD.	ISSUE PRICE	*QUOTE U.S.$
1977 Bell QX200-2	Yr.Iss.	1977	3.50	45
1977 Candle QX203-5	Yr.Iss.	1977	3.50	55
1977 Joy QX201-5	Yr.Iss.	1977	3.50	45
1977 Wreath QX202-2	Yr.Iss.	1977	3.50	45-55

1977 Decorative Ball Ornaments - Keepsake

YEAR ISSUE	EDITION LIMIT	YEAR RETD.	ISSUE PRICE	*QUOTE U.S.$
1977 Christmas Mouse QX134-2	Yr.Iss.	1977	3.50	65
1977 Rabbit QX139-5	Yr.Iss.	1977	2.50	95
1977 Squirrel QX138-2	Yr.Iss.	1977	2.50	95
1977 Stained Glass QX152-2	Yr.Iss.	1977	3.50	40-70

1977 Holiday Highlights - Keepsake

YEAR ISSUE	EDITION LIMIT	YEAR RETD.	ISSUE PRICE	*QUOTE U.S.$
1977 Drummer Boy QX312-2	Yr.Iss.	1977	3.50	38-65
1977 Joy QX310-2	Yr.Iss.	1977	3.50	45
1977 Peace on Earth QX311-5	Yr.Iss.	1977	3.50	65
1977 Star QX313-5	Yr.Iss.	1977	3.50	50

1977 Metal Ornaments - Keepsake

YEAR ISSUE	EDITION LIMIT	YEAR RETD.	ISSUE PRICE	*QUOTE U.S.$
1977 Snowflake Collection (Set/4) QX210-2	Yr.Iss.	1977	5.00	95

1977 Nostalgia Collection - Keepsake

YEAR ISSUE	EDITION LIMIT	YEAR RETD.	ISSUE PRICE	*QUOTE U.S.$
1977 Angel QX182-2	Yr.Iss.	1977	5.00	91-125
1977 Antique Car QX180-2	Yr.Iss.	1977	5.00	49-64
1977 Nativity QX181-5	Yr.Iss.	1977	5.00	135-140
1977 Toys QX183-5	Yr.Iss.	1977	5.00	140-155

1977 Peanuts Collection - Keepsake

YEAR ISSUE	EDITION LIMIT	YEAR RETD.	ISSUE PRICE	*QUOTE U.S.$
1977 Peanuts (Set/2) QX163-5	Yr.Iss.	1977	4.00	75
1977 Peanuts QX135-5	Yr.Iss.	1977	3.50	60
1977 Peanuts QX162-2	Yr.Iss.	1977	2.50	60

1977 Property Ornaments - Keepsake

YEAR ISSUE	EDITION LIMIT	YEAR RETD.	ISSUE PRICE	*QUOTE U.S.$
1977 Betsey Clark (5th Ed.) QX264-2	Yr.Iss.	1977	3.50	460
1977 Charmers QX153-5	Yr.Iss.	1977	3.50	65
1977 Currier & Ives QX130-2	Yr.Iss.	1977	3.50	55
1977 Disney (Set/2) QX137-5	Yr.Iss.	1977	4.00	75
1977 Disney QX133-5	Yr.Iss.	1977	3.50	45
1977 Grandma Moses QX150-2	Yr.Iss.	1977	3.50	100-175
1977 Norman Rockwell QX151-5	Yr.Iss.	1977	3.50	70

1977 The Beauty of America Collection - Keepsake

YEAR ISSUE	EDITION LIMIT	YEAR RETD.	ISSUE PRICE	*QUOTE U.S.$
1977 Desert QX159-5	Yr.Iss.	1977	2.50	25
1977 Mountains QX158-2	Yr.Iss.	1977	2.50	15
1977 Seashore QX160-2	Yr.Iss.	1977	2.50	50
1977 Wharf QX161-5	Yr.Iss.	1977	2.50	30-50

1977 Twirl-About Collection - Keepsake

YEAR ISSUE	EDITION LIMIT	YEAR RETD.	ISSUE PRICE	*QUOTE U.S.$
1977 Bellringer QX192-2	Yr.Iss.	1977	6.00	45-55
1977 Della Robia Wreath QX193-5	Yr.Iss.	1977	4.50	91-115
1977 Snowman QX190-2	Yr.Iss.	1977	4.50	60-75
1977 Weather House QX191-5	Yr.Iss.	1977	6.00	57-85

1977 Yesteryears Collection - Keepsake

YEAR ISSUE	EDITION LIMIT	YEAR RETD.	ISSUE PRICE	*QUOTE U.S.$
1977 Angel QX172-2	Yr.Iss.	1977	6.00	85
1977 House QX170-2	Yr.Iss.	1977	6.00	100-125
1977 Jack-in-the-Box QX171-5	Yr.Iss.	1977	6.00	100-125
1977 Reindeer QX173-5	Yr.Iss.	1977	6.00	106-140

1978 Colors of Christmas - Keepsake

YEAR ISSUE	EDITION LIMIT	YEAR RETD.	ISSUE PRICE	*QUOTE U.S.$
1978 Angel QX354-3	Yr.Iss.	1978	3.50	40
1978 Candle QX357-6	Yr.Iss.	1978	3.50	85
1978 Locomotive QX356-3	Yr.Iss.	1978	3.50	50
1978 Merry Christmas QX355-6	Yr.Iss.	1978	3.50	50

1978 Decorative Ball Ornaments - Keepsake

YEAR ISSUE	EDITION LIMIT	YEAR RETD.	ISSUE PRICE	*QUOTE U.S.$
1978 Drummer Boy QX252-3	Yr.Iss.	1978	3.50	35
1978 Hallmark's Antique Card Collection Design QX220-3	Yr.Iss.	1978	3.50	40
1978 Joy QX254-3	Yr.Iss.	1978	3.50	30-45
1978 Merry Christmas (Santa) QX202-3	Yr.Iss.	1978	3.50	45-55
1978 Nativity QX253-6	Yr.Iss.	1978	3.50	150
1978 The Quail QX251-6	Yr.Iss.	1978	3.50	45
1978 Yesterday's Toys QX250-3	Yr.Iss.	1978	3.50	55

1978 Handcrafted Ornaments - Keepsake

YEAR ISSUE	EDITION LIMIT	YEAR RETD.	ISSUE PRICE	*QUOTE U.S.$
1978 Angel QX139-6	Yr.Iss.	1981	4.50	85-95
1978 Angels QX150-3	Yr.Iss.	1978	8.00	345
1978 Animal Home QX149-6	Yr.Iss.	1978	6.00	141-175
1978 Calico Mouse QX137-6	Yr.Iss.	1978	4.50	95
1978 Carrousel Series (1st Ed.) QX146-3	Yr.Iss.	1978	6.00	400
1978 Dough Angel QX139-6	Yr.Iss.	1981	5.50	65-95
1978 Dove QX190-3	Yr.Iss.	1978	4.50	65-85
1978 Holly and Poinsettia Ball QX147-6	Yr.Iss.	1978	6.00	85
1978 Joy QX138-3	Yr.Iss.	1978	4.50	72-85
1978 Panorama Ball QX145-6	Yr.Iss.	1978	6.00	135
1978 Red Cardinal QX144-3	Yr.Iss.	1978	4.50	152-175
1978 Rocking Horse QX148-3	Yr.Iss.	1978	6.00	85
1978 Schneeberg Bell QX152-3	Yr.Iss.	1978	8.00	150-190
1978 Skating Raccoon QX142-3	Yr.Iss.	1978	6.00	85-95

1978 Holiday Chimes - Keepsake

YEAR ISSUE	EDITION LIMIT	YEAR RETD.	ISSUE PRICE	*QUOTE U.S.$
1978 Reindeer Chimes QX320-3	Yr.Iss.	1980	4.50	60

1978 Holiday Highlights - Keepsake

YEAR ISSUE	EDITION LIMIT	YEAR RETD.	ISSUE PRICE	*QUOTE U.S.$
1978 Dove QX310-3	Yr.Iss.	1978	3.50	125
1978 Nativity QX309-6	Yr.Iss.	1978	3.50	35-70
1978 Santa QX307-6	Yr.Iss.	1978	3.50	75
1978 Snowflake QX308-3	Yr.Iss.	1978	3.50	65

1978 Little Trimmers - Keepsake

YEAR ISSUE	EDITION LIMIT	YEAR RETD.	ISSUE PRICE	*QUOTE U.S.$
1978 Drummer Boy QX136-3	Yr.Iss.	1978	2.50	59
1978 Praying Angel QX134-3	Yr.Iss.	1978	2.50	90
1978 Santa QX135-6	Yr.Iss.	1978	2.50	59-63
1978 Set/4 - QX355-6	Yr.Iss.	1978	10.00	400-425
1978 Thimble Series (Mouse) (1st Ed.) QX133-6	Yr.Iss.	1978	2.50	265-295

1978 Peanuts Collection - Keepsake

YEAR ISSUE	EDITION LIMIT	YEAR RETD.	ISSUE PRICE	*QUOTE U.S.$
1978 Peanuts QX203-6	Yr.Iss.	1978	2.50	50
1978 Peanuts QX204-3	Yr.Iss.	1978	2.50	60
1978 Peanuts QX205-6	Yr.Iss.	1978	3.50	65
1978 Peanuts QX206-3	Yr.Iss.	1978	3.50	50

1978 Property Ornaments - Keepsake

YEAR ISSUE	EDITION LIMIT	YEAR RETD.	ISSUE PRICE	*QUOTE U.S.$
1978 Betsey Clark (6th Ed.) QX201-6	Yr.Iss.	1978	3.50	60
1978 Disney QX207-6	Yr.Iss.	1978	3.50	60-125
1978 Joan Walsh Anglund QX221-6	Yr.Iss.	1978	3.50	65
1978 Spencer Sparrow QX219-6	Yr.Iss.	1978	3.50	50

1978 Yarn Collection - Keepsake

YEAR ISSUE	EDITION LIMIT	YEAR RETD.	ISSUE PRICE	*QUOTE U.S.$
1978 Green Boy QX123-1	Yr.Iss.	1979	2.00	25
1978 Green Girl QX126-1	Yr.Iss.	1979	2.00	20
1978 Mr. Claus QX340-3	Yr.Iss.	1979	2.00	23
1978 Mrs. Claus QX125-1	Yr.Iss.	1979	2.00	22

1979 Collectible Series - Keepsake

YEAR ISSUE	EDITION LIMIT	YEAR RETD.	ISSUE PRICE	*QUOTE U.S.$
1979 Bellringer (1st Ed.) QX147-9	Yr.Iss.	1979	10.00	400
1979 Carousel (2nd Ed.) QX146-7	Yr.Iss.	1979	6.50	165-185
1979 Here Comes Santa (1st Ed.) QX155-9	Yr.Iss.	1979	9.00	425-695
1979 Snoopy and Friends QX141-9	Yr.Iss.	1979	8.00	95
1979 Thimble (2nd Ed.) QX131-9	Yr.Iss.	1980	3.00	150-175

1979 Colors of Christmas - Keepsake

YEAR ISSUE	EDITION LIMIT	YEAR RETD.	ISSUE PRICE	*QUOTE U.S.$
1979 Holiday Wreath QX353-9	Yr.Iss.	1979	3.50	35-45
1979 Partridge in a Pear Tree QX351-9	Yr.Iss.	1979	3.50	35-45
1979 Star Over Bethlehem QX352-7	Yr.Iss.	1979	3.50	75
1979 Words of Christmas QX350-7	Yr.Iss.	1979	3.50	85

1979 Decorative Ball Ornaments - Keepsake

YEAR ISSUE	EDITION LIMIT	YEAR RETD.	ISSUE PRICE	*QUOTE U.S.$
1979 Behold the Star QX255-9	Yr.Iss.	1979	3.50	40
1979 Black Angel QX207-9	Yr.Iss.	1979	3.50	25
1979 Christmas Chickadees QX204-7	Yr.Iss.	1979	3.50	30
1979 Christmas Collage QX257-9	Yr.Iss.	1979	3.50	22-37
1979 Christmas Traditions QX253-9	Yr.Iss.	1979	3.50	35
1979 The Light of Christmas QX256-7	Yr.Iss.	1979	3.50	18-30
1979 Night Before Christmas QX214-7	Yr.Iss.	1979	3.50	40

1979 Handcrafted Ornaments - Keepsake

YEAR ISSUE	EDITION LIMIT	YEAR RETD.	ISSUE PRICE	*QUOTE U.S.$
1979 Christmas Eve Surprise QX157-9	Yr.Iss.	1979	6.50	65
1979 Christmas Heart QX140-7	Yr.Iss.	1979	6.50	103-115
1979 Christmas is for Children QX135-9	Yr.Iss.	1980	5.00	83-95
1979 A Christmas Treat QX134-7	Yr.Iss.	1980	5.00	85
1979 The Downhill Run QX145-9	Yr.Iss.	1979	6.50	105-135
1979 The Drummer Boy QX143-9	Yr.Iss.	1979	8.00	90-125
1979 Holiday Scrimshaw QX152-7	Yr.Iss.	1979	4.00	225
1979 Outdoor Fun QX150-7	Yr.Iss.	1979	8.00	125-135
1979 Raccoon QX142-3	Yr.Iss.	1979	6.50	85
1979 Ready for Christmas QX133-9	Yr.Iss.	1979	6.50	95-150
1979 Santa's Here QX138-7	Yr.Iss.	1979	5.00	55-75
1979 The Skating Snowman QX139-9	Yr.Iss.	1980	5.00	65-80

1979 Holiday Chimes - Keepsake

YEAR ISSUE	EDITION LIMIT	YEAR RETD.	ISSUE PRICE	*QUOTE U.S.$
1979 Reindeer Chimes QX320-3	Yr.Iss.	1980	4.50	75
1979 Star Chimes QX137-9	Yr.Iss.	1979	4.50	75-85

1979 Holiday Highlights - Keepsake

YEAR ISSUE	EDITION LIMIT	YEAR RETD.	ISSUE PRICE	*QUOTE U.S.$
1979 Christmas Angel QX300-7	Yr.Iss.	1979	3.50	95
1979 Christmas Cheer QX303-9	Yr.Iss.	1979	3.50	95
1979 Christmas Tree QX302-7	Yr.Iss.	1979	3.50	75
1979 Love QX304-7	Yr.Iss.	1979	3.50	80-88
1979 Snowflake QX301-9	Yr.Iss.	1979	3.50	40

1979 Little Trimmer Collection - Keepsake

YEAR ISSUE	EDITION LIMIT	YEAR RETD.	ISSUE PRICE	*QUOTE U.S.$
1979 Angel Delight QX130-7	Yr.Iss.	1979	3.00	80-95
1979 A Matchless Christmas QX132-7	Yr.Iss.	1979	4.00	67-85
1979 Santa QX135-6	Yr.Iss.	1979	3.00	55
1979 Thimble Series-Mouse QX133-6	Yr.Iss.	1979	3.00	150-225

1979 Property Ornaments - Keepsake

YEAR ISSUE	EDITION LIMIT	YEAR RETD.	ISSUE PRICE	*QUOTE U.S.$
1979 Betsey Clark (7th Ed.) QX201-9	Yr.Iss.	1979	3.50	33-40
1979 Joan Walsh Anglund QX205-9	Yr.Iss.	1979	3.50	35
1979 Mary Hamilton QX254-7	Yr.Iss.	1979	3.50	14-25
1979 Peanuts (Time to Trim) QX202-7	Yr.Iss.	1979	3.50	40
1979 Spencer Sparrow QX200-7	Yr.Iss.	1979	3.50	25-40
1979 Winnie-the-Pooh QX206-7	Yr.Iss.	1979	3.50	40

1979 Sewn Trimmers - Keepsake

YEAR ISSUE	EDITION LIMIT	YEAR RETD.	ISSUE PRICE	*QUOTE U.S.$
1979 Angel Music QX343-9	Yr.Iss.	1980	2.00	20
1979 Merry Santa QX342-7	Yr.Iss.	1980	2.00	20
1979 The Rocking Horse QX340-7	Yr.Iss.	1980	2.00	23
1979 Stuffed Full Stocking QX341-9	Yr.Iss.	1980	2.00	18-25

1979 Yarn Collection - Keepsake

YEAR ISSUE	EDITION LIMIT	YEAR RETD.	ISSUE PRICE	*QUOTE U.S.$
1979 Green Boy QX123-1	Yr.Iss.	1979	2.00	20
1979 Green Girl QX126-1	Yr.Iss.	1979	2.00	18
1979 Mr. Claus QX340-3	Yr.Iss.	1979	2.00	20
1979 Mrs. Claus QX125-1	Yr.Iss.	1979	2.00	20

*Quotes have been rounded up to nearest dollar

1980 Collectible Series - Keepsake

YEAR ISSUE	EDITION LIMIT	YEAR RETD.	ISSUE PRICE	*QUOTE U.S.$
1980 The Bellringers (2nd Ed.) QX157-4	Yr.Iss.	1980	15.00	61-85
1980 Carrousel (3rd Ed.) QX141-4	Yr.Iss.	1980	7.50	140-165
1980 Frosty Friends (1st Ed.) QX137-4	Yr.Iss.	1980	6.50	625-655
1980 Here Comes Santa (2nd Ed.) QX 143-4	Yr.Iss.	1980	12.00	171-195
1980 Norman Rockwell (1st Ed.) QX306-1	Yr.Iss.	1980	6.50	158-250
1980 Snoopy & Friends (2nd Ed.) QX154-1	Yr.Iss.	1980	9.00	75-115
1980 Thimble (3rd Ed.) QX132-1	Yr.Iss.	1980	4.00	100-175

1980 Colors of Christmas - Keepsake

YEAR ISSUE	EDITION LIMIT	YEAR RETD.	ISSUE PRICE	*QUOTE U.S.$
1980 Joy QX350-1	Yr.Iss.	1980	4.00	22

1980 Decorative Ball Ornaments - Keepsake

YEAR ISSUE	EDITION LIMIT	YEAR RETD.	ISSUE PRICE	*QUOTE U.S.$
1980 Christmas Cardinals QX224-1	Yr.Iss.	1980	4.00	35
1980 Christmas Choir QX228-1	Yr.Iss.	1980	4.00	85
1980 Christmas Time QX226-1	Yr.Iss.	1980	4.00	30
1980 Happy Christmas QX222-1	Yr.Iss.	1980	4.00	30
1980 Jolly Santa QX227-4	Yr.Iss.	1980	4.00	30
1980 Nativity QX225-4	Yr.Iss.	1980	4.00	125
1980 Santa's Workshop QX223-4	Yr.Iss.	1980	4.00	15-30

1980 Frosted Images - Keepsake

YEAR ISSUE	EDITION LIMIT	YEAR RETD.	ISSUE PRICE	*QUOTE U.S.$
1980 Dove QX308-1	Yr.Iss.	1980	4.00	25-39
1980 Drummer Boy QX309-4	Yr.Iss.	1980	4.00	25
1980 Santa QX310-1	Yr.Iss.	1980	4.00	22

1980 Handcrafted Ornaments - Keepsake

YEAR ISSUE	EDITION LIMIT	YEAR RETD.	ISSUE PRICE	*QUOTE U.S.$
1980 The Animals' Christmas QX150-1	Yr.Iss.	1980	8.00	62
1980 Caroling Bear QX140-1	Yr.Iss.	1980	7.50	116-150
1980 Christmas is for Children QX135-9	Yr.Iss.	1980	5.50	95
1980 A Christmas Treat QX134-7	Yr.Iss.	1980	5.50	75
1980 A Christmas Vigil QX144-1	Yr.Iss.	1980	9.00	95-185
1980 Drummer Boy QX147-4	Yr.Iss.	1980	5.50	58-95
1980 Elfin Antics QX142-1	Yr.Iss.	1980	9.00	225
1980 A Heavenly Nap QX139-4	Yr.Iss.	1981	6.50	39-55
1980 Heavenly Sounds QX152-1	Yr.Iss.	1980	7.50	72-95
1980 Santa 1980 QX146-1	Yr.Iss.	1980	5.50	84-95
1980 Santa's Flight QX138-1	Yr.Iss.	1980	5.50	102-115
1980 Skating Snowman QX139-9	Yr.Iss.	1980	5.50	80
1980 The Snowflake Swing QX133-4	Yr.Iss.	1980	4.00	45
1980 A Spot of Christmas Cheer QX153-4	Yr.Iss.	1980	8.00	149-155

1980 Holiday Chimes - Keepsake

YEAR ISSUE	EDITION LIMIT	YEAR RETD.	ISSUE PRICE	*QUOTE U.S.$
1980 Reindeer Chimes QX320-3	Yr.Iss.	1980	5.50	25
1980 Santa Mobile QX136-1	Yr.Iss.	1981	5.50	25-50
1980 Snowflake Chimes QX165-4	Yr.Iss.	1981	5.50	35

1980 Holiday Highlights - Keepsake

YEAR ISSUE	EDITION LIMIT	YEAR RETD.	ISSUE PRICE	*QUOTE U.S.$
1980 Three Wise Men QX300-1	Yr.Iss.	1980	4.00	30
1980 Wreath QX301-4	Yr.Iss.	1980	4.00	85

1980 Little Trimmers - Keepsake

YEAR ISSUE	EDITION LIMIT	YEAR RETD.	ISSUE PRICE	*QUOTE U.S.$
1980 Christmas Owl QX131-4	Yr.Iss.	1982	4.00	30-40
1980 Christmas Teddy QX135-4	Yr.Iss.	1980	2.50	65-82
1980 Clothespin Soldier QX134-1	Yr.Iss.	1980	3.50	40
1980 Merry Redbird QX160-1	Yr.Iss.	1980	3.50	50-65
1980 Swingin' on a Star QX130-1	Yr.Iss.	1980	4.00	65-85
1980 Thimble Series-A Christmas Salute QX131-9	Yr.Iss.	1980	4.00	175

1980 Old-Fashioned Christmas Collection - Keepsake

YEAR ISSUE	EDITION LIMIT	YEAR RETD.	ISSUE PRICE	*QUOTE U.S.$
1980 In a Nutshell QX469-7	Yr.Iss.	1988	5.50	24-33

1980 Property Ornaments - Keepsake

YEAR ISSUE	EDITION LIMIT	YEAR RETD.	ISSUE PRICE	*QUOTE U.S.$
1980 Betsey Clark (8th Ed.) QX215-4	Yr.Iss.	1980	4.00	24-30
1980 Betsey Clark QX307-4	Yr.Iss.	1980	6.50	55
1980 Betsey Clark's Christmas QX194-4	Yr.Iss.	1980	7.50	14-35
1980 Disney QX218-1	Yr.Iss.	1980	4.00	30
1980 Joan Walsh Anglund QX217-4	Yr.Iss.	1980	4.00	23-25
1980 Marty Links QX221-4	Yr.Iss.	1980	4.00	11-23
1980 Mary Hamilton QX219-4	Yr.Iss.	1980	4.00	18
1980 Muppets QX220-1	Yr.Iss.	1980	4.00	40
1980 Peanuts QX216-1	Yr.Iss.	1980	4.00	40

1980 Sewn Trimmers - Keepsake

YEAR ISSUE	EDITION LIMIT	YEAR RETD.	ISSUE PRICE	*QUOTE U.S.$
1980 Angel Music QX343-9	Yr.Iss.	1980	2.00	20
1980 Merry Santa QX342-7	Yr.Iss.	1980	2.00	20
1980 The Rocking Horse QX340-7	Yr.Iss.	1980	2.00	22
1980 Stuffed Full Stocking QX341-9	Yr.Iss.	1980	2.00	25

1980 Special Editions - Keepsake

YEAR ISSUE	EDITION LIMIT	YEAR RETD.	ISSUE PRICE	*QUOTE U.S.$
1980 Checking it Twice QX158-4	Yr.Iss.	1981	20.00	175-195
1980 Heavenly Minstrel QX156-7	Yr.Iss.	1980	15.00	325

1980 Yarn Ornaments - Keepsake

YEAR ISSUE	EDITION LIMIT	YEAR RETD.	ISSUE PRICE	*QUOTE U.S.$
1980 Angel QX162-1	Yr.Iss.	1981	3.00	10
1980 Santa QX161-4	Yr.Iss.	1981	3.00	9
1980 Snowman QX163-4	Yr.Iss.	1981	3.00	9
1980 Soldier QX164-1	Yr.Iss.	1981	3.00	9

1981 Collectible Series - Keepsake

YEAR ISSUE	EDITION LIMIT	YEAR RETD.	ISSUE PRICE	*QUOTE U.S.$
1981 Bellringer (3rd Ed.) QX441-5	Yr.Iss.	1981	15.00	70-95
1981 Carrousel (4th Ed.) QX427-5	Yr.Iss.	1981	9.00	62-95
1981 Frosty Friends (2nd Ed.) QX433-5	Yr.Iss.	1981	8.00	413-495
1981 Here Comes Santa (3rd Ed.) QX438-2	Yr.Iss.	1981	13.00	205-325
1981 Norman Rockwell (2nd Ed.) QX511-5	Yr.Iss.	1981	8.50	35-50
1981 Rocking Horse (1st Ed.) QX422-2	Yr.Iss.	1981	9.00	425
1981 Snoopy and Friends (3rd Ed.) QX436-2	Yr.Iss.	1981	12.00	100-125
1981 Thimble (4th Ed.) QX413-5	Yr.Iss.	1981	4.50	150

1981 Crown Classics - Keepsake

YEAR ISSUE	EDITION LIMIT	YEAR RETD.	ISSUE PRICE	*QUOTE U.S.$
1981 Angel QX507-5	Yr.Iss.	1981	4.50	11-25
1981 Tree Photoholder QX515-5	Yr.Iss.	1981	5.50	17-30
1981 Unicorn QX516-5	Yr.Iss.	1981	8.50	15-27

1981 Decorative Ball Ornaments - Keepsake

YEAR ISSUE	EDITION LIMIT	YEAR RETD.	ISSUE PRICE	*QUOTE U.S.$
1981 Christmas 1981 QX809-5	Yr.Iss.	1981	4.50	10-25
1981 Christmas in the Forest QX813-5	Yr.Iss.	1981	4.50	145
1981 Christmas Magic QX810-2	Yr.Iss.	1981	4.50	15-25
1981 Let Us Adore Him QX811-5	Yr.Iss.	1981	4.50	28-65
1981 Merry Christmas QX814-2	Yr.Iss.	1981	4.50	13-25
1981 Santa's Coming QX812-2	Yr.Iss.	1981	4.50	12-27
1981 Santa's Surprise QX815-5	Yr.Iss.	1981	4.50	18-25
1981 Traditional (Black Santa) QX801-5	Yr.Iss.	1981	4.50	42-97

1981 Fabric Ornaments - Keepsake

YEAR ISSUE	EDITION LIMIT	YEAR RETD.	ISSUE PRICE	*QUOTE U.S.$
1981 Calico Kitty QX403-5	Yr.Iss.	1981	3.00	20
1981 Cardinal Cutie QX400-2	Yr.Iss.	1981	3.00	9-20
1981 Gingham Dog QX402-2	Yr.Iss.	1981	3.00	11-20
1981 Peppermint Mouse QX401-5	Yr.Iss.	1981	3.00	35

1981 Frosted Images - Keepsake

YEAR ISSUE	EDITION LIMIT	YEAR RETD.	ISSUE PRICE	*QUOTE U.S.$
1981 Angel QX509-5	Yr.Iss.	1981	4.00	50-65
1981 Mouse QX508-2	Yr.Iss.	1981	4.00	25
1981 Snowman QX510-2	Yr.Iss.	1981	4.00	25

1981 Hand Crafted Ornaments - Keepsake

YEAR ISSUE	EDITION LIMIT	YEAR RETD.	ISSUE PRICE	*QUOTE U.S.$
1981 Candyville Express QX418-2	Yr.Iss.	1981	7.50	83-95
1981 Checking It Twice QX158-4	Yr.Iss.	1981	23.00	195
1981 Christmas Dreams QX437-5	Yr.Iss.	1981	12.00	200-225
1981 Christmas Fantasy QX155-4	Yr.Iss.	1982	13.00	68-85
1981 Dough Angel QX139-6	Yr.Iss.	1981	5.50	80
1981 Drummer Boy QX148-1	Yr.Iss.	1981	2.50	41
1981 The Friendly Fiddler QX434-2	Yr.Iss.	1981	8.00	71-80
1981 A Heavenly Nap QX139-4	Yr.Iss.	1981	6.50	50
1981 Ice Fairy QX431-5	Yr.Iss.	1981	6.50	85-100
1981 The Ice Sculptor QX432-2	Yr.Iss.	1982	8.00	65-90
1981 Love and Joy QX425-2	Yr.Iss.	1981	9.00	75-95
1981 Mr. & Mrs. Claus QX448-5	Yr.Iss.	1981	12.00	110-135
1981 Sailing Santa QX439-5	Yr.Iss.	1981	13.00	225-290
1981 Space Santa QX430-2	Yr.Iss.	1981	6.50	67-115
1981 St. Nicholas QX446-2	Yr.Iss.	1981	5.50	40-50
1981 Star Swing QX421-5	Yr.Iss.	1981	5.50	46-60
1981 Topsy-Turvy Tunes QX429-5	Yr.Iss.	1981	7.50	68-80
1981 A Well-Stocked Stocking QX154-7	Yr.Iss.	1981	9.00	65-85

1981 Holiday Chimes - Keepsake

YEAR ISSUE	EDITION LIMIT	YEAR RETD.	ISSUE PRICE	*QUOTE U.S.$
1981 Santa Mobile QX136-1	Yr.Iss.	1981	5.50	40
1981 Snowflake Chimes QX165-4	Yr.Iss.	1981	5.50	25
1981 Snowman Chimes QX445-5	Yr.Iss.	1981	5.50	25-30

1981 Holiday Highlights - Keepsake

YEAR ISSUE	EDITION LIMIT	YEAR RETD.	ISSUE PRICE	*QUOTE U.S.$
1981 Christmas Star QX501-5	Yr.Iss.	1981	5.50	17-30
1981 Shepherd Scene QX500-2	Yr.Iss.	1981	5.50	16-27

1981 Little Trimmers - Keepsake

YEAR ISSUE	EDITION LIMIT	YEAR RETD.	ISSUE PRICE	*QUOTE U.S.$
1981 Clothespin Drummer Boy QX408-2	Yr.Iss.	1981	4.50	25-45
1981 Jolly Snowman QX407-5	Yr.Iss.	1981	3.50	37-60
1981 Perky Penguin QX409-5	Yr.Iss.	1982	3.50	42-60
1981 Puppy Love QX406-2	Yr.Iss.	1981	3.50	25-40
1981 The Stocking Mouse QX412-2	Yr.Iss.	1981	4.50	80-115

1981 Plush Animals - Keepsake

YEAR ISSUE	EDITION LIMIT	YEAR RETD.	ISSUE PRICE	*QUOTE U.S.$
1981 Christmas Teddy QX404-2	Yr.Iss.	1981	5.50	24
1981 Raccoon Tunes QX405-5	Yr.Iss.	1981	5.50	15-23

1981 Property Ornaments - Keepsake

YEAR ISSUE	EDITION LIMIT	YEAR RETD.	ISSUE PRICE	*QUOTE U.S.$
1981 Betsey Clark (9th Ed.)QX 802-2	Yr.Iss.	1981	4.50	23-35
1981 Betsey Clark Cameo QX512-2	Yr.Iss.	1981	8.50	20-30
1981 Betsey Clark QX423-5	Yr.Iss.	1981	9.00	22-32
1981 Disney QX805-5	Yr.Iss.	1981	4.50	15-30
1981 The Divine Miss Piggy QX425-5	Yr.Iss.	1982	12.00	75-95
1981 Joan Walsh Anglund QX804-2	Yr.Iss.	1981	4.50	16-30
1981 Kermit the Frog QX424-2	Yr.Iss.	1981	9.00	78-95
1981 Marty Links QX808-2	Yr.Iss.	1981	4.50	19
1981 Mary Hamilton QX806-2	Yr.Iss.	1981	4.50	10-20
1981 Muppets QX807-5	Yr.Iss.	1981	4.50	15-35
1981 Peanuts QX803-5	Yr.Iss.	1981	4.50	20-40

1982 Brass Ornaments - Keepsake

YEAR ISSUE	EDITION LIMIT	YEAR RETD.	ISSUE PRICE	*QUOTE U.S.$
1982 Brass Bell QX460-6	Yr.Iss.	1982	12.00	18-25
1982 Santa and Reindeer QX467-6	Yr.Iss.	1982	9.00	40-50
1982 Santa's Sleigh QX478-6	Yr.Iss.	1982	9.00	13-35

1982 Collectible Series - Keepsake

YEAR ISSUE	EDITION LIMIT	YEAR RETD.	ISSUE PRICE	*QUOTE U.S.$
1982 The Bellringer (4th Ed.) QX455-6	Yr.Iss.	1982	15.00	79-97
1982 Carrousel Series (5th Ed.) QX478-3	Yr.Iss.	1982	10.00	90
1982 Clothespin Soldier (1st Ed.) QX458-3	Yr.Iss.	1982	5.00	121
1982 Frosty Friends (3rd Ed.) QX452-3	Yr.Iss.	1982	8.00	270-300
1982 Here Comes Santa (4th Ed.) QX464-3	Yr.Iss.	1982	15.00	102-150
1982 Holiday Wildlife (1st Ed.) QX313-3	Yr.Iss.	1982	7.00	360-375
1982 Rocking Horse (2nd Ed.) QX 502-3	Yr.Iss.	1982	10.00	425
1982 Snoopy and Friends (4th Ed.) QX478-3	Yr.Iss.	1982	13.00	85-125
1982 Thimble (5th Ed.) QX451-3	Yr.Iss.	1982	5.00	60-75
1982 Tin Locomotive (1st Ed.) QX460-3	Yr.Iss.	1982	13.00	575-600

1982 Colors of Christmas - Keepsake

YEAR ISSUE	EDITION LIMIT	YEAR RETD.	ISSUE PRICE	*QUOTE U.S.$
1982 Nativity QX308-3	Yr.Iss.	1982	4.50	37-50
1982 Santa's Flight QX308-6	Yr.Iss.	1982	4.50	49

1982 Decorative Ball Ornaments - Keepsake

YEAR ISSUE	EDITION LIMIT	YEAR RETD.	ISSUE PRICE	*QUOTE U.S.$
1982 Christmas Angel QX220-6	Yr.Iss.	1982	4.50	10-25
1982 Currier & Ives QX201-3	Yr.Iss.	1982	4.50	10-25
1982 Santa QX221-6	Yr.Iss.	1982	4.50	12-20
1982 Season for Caring QX221-3	Yr.Iss.	1982	4.50	23

1982 Designer Keepsakes - Keepsake

YEAR ISSUE	EDITION LIMIT	YEAR RETD.	ISSUE PRICE	*QUOTE U.S.$
1982 Merry Christmas QX225-6	Yr.Iss.	1982	4.50	10-22
1982 Old Fashioned Christmas QX227-6	Yr.Iss.	1982	4.50	59
1982 Old World Angels QX226-3	Yr.Iss.	1982	4.50	7-24
1982 Patterns of Christmas QX226-6	Yr.Iss.	1982	4.50	15-22
1982 Stained Glass QX228-3	Yr.Iss.	1982	4.50	12-22
1982 Twelve Days of Christmas QX203-6	Yr.Iss.	1982	4.50	30

1982 Handcrafted Ornaments - Keepsake

YEAR ISSUE	EDITION LIMIT	YEAR RETD.	ISSUE PRICE	*QUOTE U.S.$
1982 Baroque Angel QX456-6	Yr.Iss.	1982	15.00	175
1982 Christmas Fantasy QX155-4	Yr.Iss.	1982	13.00	59
1982 Cloisonne Angel QX145-4	Yr.Iss.	1982	12.00	95
1982 Cowboy Snowman QX480-6	Yr.Iss.	1982	8.00	50
1982 Cycling Santa QX435-5	Yr.Iss.	1983	20.00	133-150
1982 Elfin Artist QX457-3	Yr.Iss.	1982	9.00	42-50
1982 Embroidered Tree QX494-6	Yr.Iss.	1982	6.50	40
1982 Ice Sculptor QX432-2	Yr.Iss.	1982	8.00	75
1982 Jogging Santa QX457-6	Yr.Iss.	1982	8.00	32-50
1982 Jolly Christmas Tree QX465-3	Yr.Iss.	1982	6.50	80
1982 Peeking Elf QX419-5	Yr.Iss.	1982	6.50	24-40
1982 Pinecone Home QX461-3	Yr.Iss.	1982	8.00	150-160
1982 Raccoon Surprises QX479-3	Yr.Iss.	1982	9.00	125-132
1982 Santa Bell QX148-7	Yr.Iss.	1982	15.00	38-60
1982 Santa's Workshop QX450-3	Yr.Iss.	1983	10.00	76-85
1982 The Spirit of Christmas QX452-6	Yr.Iss.	1982	10.00	107-125
1982 Three Kings QX307-3	Yr.Iss.	1982	8.50	17-27
1982 Tin Soldier QX483-6	Yr.Iss.	1982	6.50	30-50

1982 Holiday Chimes - Keepsake

YEAR ISSUE	EDITION LIMIT	YEAR RETD.	ISSUE PRICE	*QUOTE U.S.$
1982 Bell Chimes QX494-3	Yr.Iss.	1982	5.50	21-30
1982 Tree Chimes QX484-6	Yr.Iss.	1982	5.50	50

1982 Holiday Highlights - Keepsake

YEAR ISSUE	EDITION LIMIT	YEAR RETD.	ISSUE PRICE	*QUOTE U.S.$
1982 Angel QX309-6	Yr.Iss.	1982	5.50	16-35
1982 Christmas Magic QX311-3	Yr.Iss.	1982	5.50	22-30
1982 Christmas Sleigh QX309-3	Yr.Iss.	1982	5.50	55-75

1982 Ice Sculptures - Keepsake

YEAR ISSUE	EDITION LIMIT	YEAR RETD.	ISSUE PRICE	*QUOTE U.S.$
1982 Arctic Penguin QX300-3	Yr.Iss.	1982	4.00	8-20
1982 Snowy Seal QX300-6	Yr.Iss.	1982	4.00	13-20

1982 Little Trimmers - Keepsake

YEAR ISSUE	EDITION LIMIT	YEAR RETD.	ISSUE PRICE	*QUOTE U.S.$
1982 Christmas Kitten QX454-3	Yr.Iss.	1983	4.00	34
1982 Christmas Owl QX131-4	Yr.Iss.	1982	4.50	35
1982 Cookie Mouse QX454-6	Yr.Iss.	1982	4.50	34-49
1982 Dove Love QX462-3	Yr.Iss.	1982	4.50	32-47
1982 Jingling Teddy QX477-6	Yr.Iss.	1982	4.00	23-40
1982 Merry Moose QX415-5	Yr.Iss.	1982	5.50	38-60
1982 Musical Angel QX459-6	Yr.Iss.	1982	5.50	112-125
1982 Perky Penguin QX409-5	Yr.Iss.	1982	4.00	35

1982 Property Ornaments - Keepsake

YEAR ISSUE	EDITION LIMIT	YEAR RETD.	ISSUE PRICE	*QUOTE U.S.$
1982 Betsey Clark (10th Ed.) QX215-6	Yr.Iss.	1982	4.50	24-34
1982 Betsey Clark QX305-6	Yr.Iss.	1982	8.50	17-25
1982 Disney QX217-3	Yr.Iss.	1982	4.50	20-35
1982 The Divine Miss Piggy QX425-5	Yr.Iss.	1982	12.00	125
1982 Joan Walsh Anglund QX219-3	Yr.Iss.	1982	4.50	8-20
1982 Kermit the Frog QX495-6	Yr.Iss.	1982	11.00	62-95
1982 Mary Hamilton QX217-6	Yr.Iss.	1982	4.50	10-22
1982 Miss Piggy and Kermit QX218-3	Yr.Iss.	1982	4.50	28-40
1982 Muppets Party QX218-6	Yr.Iss.	1982	4.50	31-40
1982 Norman Rockwell (3rd Ed.) QX305-3	Yr.Iss.	1982	8.50	28
1982 Norman Rockwell QX202-3	Yr.Iss.	1982	4.50	10-28
1982 Peanuts QX200-6	Yr.Iss.	1982	4.50	20-40

1983 Collectible Series - Keepsake

YEAR ISSUE	EDITION LIMIT	YEAR RETD.	ISSUE PRICE	*QUOTE U.S.$
1983 The Bellringer (5th Ed.) QX 403-9	Yr.Iss.	1983	15.00	85-135
1983 Carrousel (6th Ed.) QX401-9	Yr.Iss.	1983	11.00	34-49
1983 Clothespin Soldier (2nd Ed.) QX402-9	Yr.Iss.	1983	5.00	34-50
1983 Frosty Friends (4th Ed.) QX400-7	Yr.Iss.	1983	8.00	215-325
1983 Here Comes Santa (5th Ed.) QX403-7	Yr.Iss.	1983	13.00	250-295
1983 Holiday Wildlife (2nd Ed.) QX309-9	Yr.Iss.	1983	7.00	68-75
1983 Porcelain Bear (1st Ed.) QX428-9	Yr.Iss.	1983	7.00	50-73
1983 Rocking Horse (3rd Ed.) QX417-7	Yr.Iss.	1983	10.00	295
1983 Snoopy and Friends (5th Ed.) QX416-9	Yr.Iss.	1983	13.00	95
1983 Thimble (6th Ed.) QX401-7	Yr.Iss.	1983	5.00	28-39
1983 Tin Locomotive (2nd Ed.) QX404-9	Yr.Iss.	1983	13.00	275-295

1983 Crown Classics - Keepsake

YEAR ISSUE	EDITION LIMIT	YEAR RETD.	ISSUE PRICE	*QUOTE U.S.$
1983 Enameled Christmas Wreath QX311-9	Yr.Iss.	1983	9.00	7-15
1983 Memories to Treasure QX303-7	Yr.Iss.	1983	7.00	30
1983 Mother and Child QX302-7	Yr.Iss.	1983	7.50	20-40

1983 Decorative Ball Ornaments - Keepsake

YEAR ISSUE	EDITION LIMIT	YEAR RETD.	ISSUE PRICE	*QUOTE U.S.$
1983 1983 QX220-9	Yr.Iss.	1983	4.50	17-30
1983 Angels QX219-7	Yr.Iss.	1983	5.00	22
1983 The Annunciation QX216-7	Yr.Iss.	1983	4.50	30
1983 Christmas Joy QX216-9	Yr.Iss.	1983	4.50	15-30
1983 Christmas Wonderland QX221-9	Yr.Iss.	1983	4.50	95-125
1983 Currier & Ives QX215-9	Yr.Iss.	1983	4.50	8-19
1983 Here Comes Santa QX217-7	Yr.Iss.	1983	4.50	38
1983 An Old Fashioned Christmas QX2217-9	Yr.Iss.	1983	4.50	29

*Quotes have been rounded up to nearest dollar

YEAR ISSUE	EDITION LIMIT	YEAR RETD.	ISSUE PRICE	*QUOTE U.S.$
1983 Oriental Butterflies QX218-7	Yr.Iss.	1983	4.50	30
1983 Season's Greeting QX219-9	Yr.Iss.	1983	4.50	10-22
1983 The Wise Men QX220-7	Yr.Iss.	1983	4.50	42-59

1983 Handcrafted Ornaments - Keepsake

YEAR ISSUE	EDITION LIMIT	YEAR RETD.	ISSUE PRICE	*QUOTE U.S.$
1983 Angel Messenger QX408-7	Yr.Iss.	1983	6.50	89-95
1983 Baroque Angels QX422-9	Yr.Iss.	1983	13.00	130
1983 Bell Wreath QX420-9	Yr.Iss.	1983	6.50	35
1983 Brass Santa QX423-9	Yr.Iss.	1983	9.00	23
1983 Caroling Owl QX411-7	Yr.Iss.	1983	4.50	25-40
1983 Christmas Kitten QX454-3	Yr.Iss.	1983	4.00	35
1983 Christmas Koala QX419-9	Yr.Iss.	1983	4.00	20-33
1983 Cycling Santa QX435-5	Yr.Iss.	1983	20.00	195
1983 Embroidered Heart QX421-7	Yr.Iss.	1983	6.50	25
1983 Embroidered Stocking QX479-6	Yr.Iss.	1983	6.50	10-22
1983 Hitchhiking Santa QX424-7	Yr.Iss.	1983	8.00	33-40
1983 Holiday Puppy QX412-7	Yr.Iss.	1983	3.50	16-30
1983 Jack Frost QX407-9	Yr.Iss.	1983	9.00	60
1983 Jolly Santa QX425-9	Yr.Iss.	1983	3.50	21-35
1983 Madonna and Child QX428-7	Yr.Iss.	1983	12.00	26-45
1983 Mailbox Kitten QX415-7	Yr.Iss.	1983	6.50	40-60
1983 Mountain Climbing Santa QX407-7	Yr.Iss.	1984	6.50	22-40
1983 Mouse in Bell QX419-7	Yr.Iss.	1983	10.00	65
1983 Mouse on Cheese QX413-7	Yr.Iss.	1983	6.50	30-50
1983 Old-Fashioned Santa QX409-9	Yr.Iss.	1983	11.00	40-65
1983 Peppermint Penguin QX408-9	Yr.Iss.	1983	6.50	29-49
1983 Porcelain Doll, Diana QX423-7	Yr.Iss.	1983	9.00	16-32
1983 Rainbow Angel QX416-7	Yr.Iss.	1983	5.50	112-125
1983 Santa's Many Faces QX311-6	Yr.Iss.	1983	6.00	30
1983 Santa's on His Way QX426-9	Yr.Iss.	1983	10.00	35
1983 Santa's Workshop QX450-3	Yr.Iss.	1983	10.00	60
1983 Scrimshaw Reindeer QX424-9	Yr.Iss.	1983	8.00	17-35
1983 Skating Rabbit QX409-7	Yr.Iss.	1983	8.00	47-55
1983 Ski Lift Santa QX418-7	Yr.Iss.	1983	8.00	50-75
1983 Skiing Fox QX420-7	Yr.Iss.	1983	8.00	30-40
1983 Sneaker Mouse QX400-9	Yr.Iss.	1983	4.50	23-40
1983 Tin Rocking Horse QX414-9	Yr.Iss.	1983	6.50	50
1983 Unicorn QX426-7	Yr.Iss.	1983	10.00	40-65

1983 Holiday Highlights - Keepsake

YEAR ISSUE	EDITION LIMIT	YEAR RETD.	ISSUE PRICE	*QUOTE U.S.$
1983 Christmas Stocking QX303-9	Yr.Iss.	1983	6.00	15-40
1983 Star of Peace QX304-7	Yr.Iss.	1983	6.00	20
1983 Time for Sharing QX307-7	Yr.Iss.	1983	6.00	40

1983 Holiday Sculptures - Keepsake

YEAR ISSUE	EDITION LIMIT	YEAR RETD.	ISSUE PRICE	*QUOTE U.S.$
1983 Heart QX307-9	Yr.Iss.	1983	4.00	50
1983 Santa QX308-7	Yr.Iss.	1983	4.00	15-17

1983 Property Ornaments - Keepsake

YEAR ISSUE	EDITION LIMIT	YEAR RETD.	ISSUE PRICE	*QUOTE U.S.$
1983 Betsey Clark (11th Ed.) QX211-9	Yr.Iss.	1983	4.50	30
1983 Betsey Clark QX404-7	Yr.Iss.	1983	6.50	35
1983 Betsey Clark QX440-1	Yr.Iss.	1983	9.00	35
1983 Disney QX212-9	Yr.Iss.	1983	4.50	45
1983 Kermit the Frog QX495-6	Yr.Iss.	1983	11.00	35
1983 Mary Hamilton QX213-7	Yr.Iss.	1983	4.50	40
1983 Miss Piggy QX405-7	Yr.Iss.	1983	13.00	225
1983 The Muppets QX214-7	Yr.Iss.	1983	4.50	40-50
1983 Norman Rockwell (4th Ed.) QX300-7	Yr.Iss.	1983	7.50	35
1983 Norman Rockwell QX215-7	Yr.Iss.	1983	4.50	50
1983 Peanuts QX212-7	Yr.Iss.	1983	4.50	22-36
1983 Shirt Tales QX214-9	Yr.Iss.	1983	4.50	25

1984 Collectible Series - Keepsake

YEAR ISSUE	EDITION LIMIT	YEAR RETD.	ISSUE PRICE	*QUOTE U.S.$
1984 Art Masterpiece (1st Ed.) QX349-4	Yr.Iss.	1984	6.50	16
1984 The Bellringer (6th & Final Ed.) QX438-4	Yr.Iss.	1984	15.00	30-45
1984 Betsey Clark (12th Ed.) QX249-4	Yr.Iss.	1984	5.00	24-34
1984 Clothespin Soldier (3rd Ed.) QX447-1	Yr.Iss.	1984	5.00	20-30
1984 Frosty Friends (5th Ed.) QX437-1	Yr.Iss.	1984	8.00	60-87
1984 Here Comes Santa (6th Ed.) QX438-4	Yr.Iss.	1984	13.00	61-90
1984 Holiday Wildlife (3rd Ed.) QX 347-4	Yr.Iss.	1984	7.25	20-30
1984 Norman Rockwell (5th Ed.) QX341-1	Yr.Iss.	1984	7.50	24-34
1984 Nostalgic Houses and Shops (1st Ed.) QX448-1	Yr.Iss.	1984	13.00	190-225
1984 Porcelain Bear (2nd Ed.) QX454-1	Yr.Iss.	1984	7.00	33-50
1984 Rocking Horse (4th Ed.) QX435-4	Yr.Iss.	1984	10.00	65-95
1984 Thimble (7th Ed.) QX430-4	Yr.Iss.	1984	5.00	40-60
1984 Tin Locomotive (3rd Ed.) QX440-4	Yr.Iss.	1984	14.00	64-79
1984 The Twelve Days of Christmas (1st Ed.) QX3484	Yr.Iss.	1984	6.00	295
1984 Wood Childhood Ornaments (1st Ed.) QX439-4	Yr.Iss.	1984	6.50	40-50

1984 Holiday Humor - Keepsake

YEAR ISSUE	EDITION LIMIT	YEAR RETD.	ISSUE PRICE	*QUOTE U.S.$
1984 Bell Ringer Squirrel QX443-1	Yr.Iss.	1984	10.00	20-40
1984 Christmas Owl QX444-1	Yr.Iss.	1984	6.00	20-33
1984 A Christmas Prayer QX246-1	Yr.Iss.	1984	4.50	10-23
1984 Flights of Fantasy QX256-4	Yr.Iss.	1984	4.50	10-20
1984 Fortune Cookie Elf QX452-4	Yr.Iss.	1984	4.50	35-40
1984 Frisbee Puppy QX444-4	Yr.Iss.	1984	5.00	40-50
1984 Marathon Santa QX456-4	Yr.Iss.	1984	8.00	39
1984 Mountain Climbing Santa QX407-7	Yr.Iss.	1984	6.50	35
1984 Musical Angel QX434-4	Yr.Iss.	1984	5.50	70
1984 Napping Mouse QX435-1	Yr.Iss.	1984	5.50	38-50
1984 Peppermint 1984 QX452-1	Yr.Iss.	1984	4.50	50
1984 Polar Bear Drummer QX430-1	Yr.Iss.	1984	4.50	30
1984 Raccoon's Christmas QX447-7	Yr.Iss.	1984	9.00	16-35
1984 Reindeer Racetrack QX254-4	Yr.Iss.	1984	4.50	10-23
1984 Roller Skating Rabbit QX457-1	Yr.Iss.	1985	5.00	18-35
1984 Santa Mouse QX433-4	Yr.Iss.	1984	4.50	45
1984 Santa Star QX450-4	Yr.Iss.	1984	5.50	33-40
1984 Snowmobile Santa QX431-4	Yr.Iss.	1984	6.50	35-40
1984 Snowshoe Penguin QX453-1	Yr.Iss.	1984	6.50	45-60
1984 Snowy Seal QX450-1	Yr.Iss.	1985	4.00	12-24
1984 Three Kittens in a Mitten QX431-1	Yr.Iss.	1985	8.00	32-50

1984 Keepsake Magic Ornaments - Keepsake

YEAR ISSUE	EDITION LIMIT	YEAR RETD.	ISSUE PRICE	*QUOTE U.S.$
1984 All Are Precious QLX704-1	Yr.Iss.	1985	8.00	13-25
1984 Brass Carrousel QLX707-1	Yr.Iss.	1984	9.00	95
1984 Christmas in the Forest QLX703-4	Yr.Iss.	1984	8.00	20
1984 City Lights QLX701-4	Yr.Iss.	1984	10.00	48
1984 Nativity QLX700-1	Yr.Iss.	1985	12.00	18-30
1984 Santa's Arrival QLX702-4	Yr.Iss.	1984	13.00	47-65
1984 Santa's Workshop QLX700-4	Yr.Iss.	1985	13.00	45-62
1984 Stained Glass QLX703-1	Yr.Iss.	1984	8.00	20
1984 Sugarplum Cottage QLX701-1	Yr.Iss.	1986	11.00	45
1984 Village Church QLX702-1	Yr.Iss.	1985	15.00	35-50

1984 Limited Edition - Keepsake

YEAR ISSUE	EDITION LIMIT	YEAR RETD.	ISSUE PRICE	*QUOTE U.S.$
1984 Classical Angel QX459-1	Yr.Iss.	1984	28.00	66-75

1984 Property Ornaments - Keepsake

YEAR ISSUE	EDITION LIMIT	YEAR RETD.	ISSUE PRICE	*QUOTE U.S.$
1984 Betsey Clark Angel QX462-4	Yr.Iss.	1984	9.00	19-35
1984 Currier & Ives QX250-1	Yr.Iss.	1984	4.50	23
1984 Disney QX250-4	Yr.Iss.	1984	4.50	23-43
1984 Katybeth QX463-1	Yr.Iss.	1984	9.00	17-33
1984 Kit QX453-4	Yr.Iss.	1984	5.50	20
1984 Muffin QX442-1	Yr.Iss.	1984	5.50	25-33
1984 The Muppets QX251-4	Yr.Iss.	1984	4.50	20-35
1984 Norman Rockwell QX251-4	Yr.Iss.	1984	4.50	35
1984 Peanuts QX252-1	Yr.Iss.	1984	4.50	20-33
1984 Shirt Tales QX252-4	Yr.Iss.	1984	4.50	8-10
1984 Snoopy and Woodstock QX439-1	Yr.Iss.	1984	7.50	95

1984 Traditional Ornaments - Keepsake

YEAR ISSUE	EDITION LIMIT	YEAR RETD.	ISSUE PRICE	*QUOTE U.S.$
1984 Alpine Elf QX452-1	Yr.Iss.	1984	6.00	32-40
1984 Amanda QX432-1	Yr.Iss.	1984	9.00	10-25
1984 Chickadee QX451-4	Yr.Iss.	1984	6.00	33-40
1984 Christmas Memories Photoholder QX300-4	Yr.Iss.	1984	6.50	25
1984 Cuckoo Clock QX455-1	Yr.Iss.	1984	10.00	45-50
1984 Gift of Music QX451-1	Yr.Iss.	1984	15.00	62-95
1984 Holiday Friendship QX445-1	Yr.Iss.	1984	13.00	20-30
1984 Holiday Jester QX437-4	Yr.Iss.	1984	11.00	20-35
1984 Holiday Starburst QX253-4	Yr.Iss.	1984	5.00	20
1984 Madonna and Child QX344-1	Yr.Iss.	1984	6.00	50
1984 Needlepoint Wreath QX459-4	Yr.Iss.	1984	6.50	10-15
1984 Nostalgic Sled QX442-4	Yr.Iss.	1984	6.00	12-30
1984 Old Fashioned Rocking Horse QX346-4	Yr.Iss.	1984	7.50	10-20
1984 Peace on Earth QX341-4	Yr.Iss.	1984	7.50	30
1984 Santa QX458-4	Yr.Iss.	1984	7.50	10-20
1984 Santa Sulky Driver QX436-1	Yr.Iss.	1984	9.00	18-20
1984 A Savior is Born QX254-1	Yr.Iss.	1984	4.50	33
1984 Twelve Days of Christmas QX415-9	Yr.Iss.	1984	15.00	100-125
1984 Uncle Sam QX449-1	Yr.Iss.	1984	6.00	42-50
1984 White Christmas QX905-1	Yr.Iss.	1984	16.00	70-95

1985 Collectible Series - Keepsake

YEAR ISSUE	EDITION LIMIT	YEAR RETD.	ISSUE PRICE	*QUOTE U.S.$
1985 Art Masterpiece (2nd Ed.) QX377-2	Yr.Iss.	1985	6.75	12
1985 Betsey Clark (13th & final Ed.) QX263-2	Yr.Iss.	1985	5.00	24-35
1985 Clothespin Soldier (4th Ed.) QX471-5	Yr.Iss.	1985	5.50	20-30
1985 Frosty Friends (6th Ed.) QX482-2	Yr.Iss.	1985	8.50	45-65
1985 Here Comes Santa (7th Ed.) QX496-5	Yr.Iss.	1985	14.00	43-63
1985 Holiday Wildlife (4th Ed.) QX376-5	Yr.Iss.	1985	7.50	20-35
1985 Miniature Creche (1st Ed.) QX482-5	Yr.Iss.	1985	8.75	30-40
1985 Norman Rockwell (6th Ed.) QX374-5	Yr.Iss.	1985	7.50	22-32
1985 Nostalgic Houses and Shops (2nd Ed.) QX497-5	Yr.Iss.	1985	13.75	93-145
1985 Porcelain Bear (3rd Ed.) QX479-2	Yr.Iss.	1985	7.50	36-60
1985 Rocking Horse (5th Ed.) QX493-2	Yr.Iss.	1985	10.75	54-80
1985 Thimble (8th Ed.) QX472-5	Yr.Iss.	1985	5.50	24-35
1985 Tin Locomotive (4th Ed.) QX497-2	Yr.Iss.	1985	14.75	55-80
1985 Twelve Days of Christmas (2nd Ed.) QX371-2	Yr.Iss.	1985	6.50	50-70
1985 Windows of the World (1st Ed.) QX490-2	Yr.Iss.	1985	9.75	82-97
1985 Wood Childhood Ornaments (2nd Ed.) QX472-2	Yr.Iss.	1985	7.00	34-50

1985 Country Christmas Collection - Keepsake

YEAR ISSUE	EDITION LIMIT	YEAR RETD.	ISSUE PRICE	*QUOTE U.S.$
1985 Country Goose QX518-5	Yr.Iss.	1985	7.75	14
1985 Old-Fashioned Doll QX519-5	Yr.Iss.	1985	15.00	40
1985 Rocking Horse Memories QX518-2	Yr.Iss.	1985	10.00	6-10
1985 Sheep at Christmas QX517-5	Yr.Iss.	1985	8.25	13-28
1985 Whirligig Santa QX519-2	Yr.Iss.	1985	13.00	12-15

1985 Heirloom Christmas Collection - Keepsake

YEAR ISSUE	EDITION LIMIT	YEAR RETD.	ISSUE PRICE	*QUOTE U.S.$
1985 Charming Angel QX512-5	Yr.Iss.	1985	9.75	6-10
1985 Keepsake Basket QX514-5	Yr.Iss.	1985	15.00	15
1985 Lacy Heart QX511-2	Yr.Iss.	1985	8.75	8-15
1985 Snowflake QX510-5	Yr.Iss.	1985	6.50	7-10
1985 Victorian Lady QX513-2	Yr.Iss.	1985	9.50	25

1985 Holiday Humor - Keepsake

YEAR ISSUE	EDITION LIMIT	YEAR RETD.	ISSUE PRICE	*QUOTE U.S.$
1985 Baker Elf QX491-2	Yr.Iss.	1985	5.75	19-29
1985 Beary Smooth Ride QX480-5	Yr.Iss.	1986	6.50	13-24
1985 Bottlecap Fun Bunnies QX481-5	Yr.Iss.	1985	7.75	33
1985 Candy Apple Mouse QX470-5	Yr.Iss.	1985	6.50	52-75
1985 Children in the Shoe QX490-5	Yr.Iss.	1985	9.50	32-50
1985 Dapper Penguin QX477-2	Yr.Iss.	1985	5.00	30
1985 Do Not Disturb Bear QX481-2	Yr.Iss.	1986	7.75	16-33
1985 Doggy in a Stocking QX474-2	Yr.Iss.	1985	5.50	25-40
1985 Engineering Mouse QX473-5	Yr.Iss.	1985	5.50	15-25
1985 Ice-Skating Owl QX476-5	Yr.Iss.	1985	5.00	15-25
1985 Kitty Mischief QX474-5	Yr.Iss.	1986	5.00	13-15
1985 Lamb in Legwarmers QX480-2	Yr.Iss.	1985	7.00	15-25
1985 Merry Mouse QX403-2	Yr.Iss.	1986	4.50	18-20
1985 Mouse Wagon QX476-2	Yr.Iss.	1985	5.75	37-60
1985 Nativity Scene QX264-5	Yr.Iss.	1985	4.75	30
1985 Night Before Christmas QX449-4	Yr.Iss.	1985	13.00	12-20
1985 Roller Skating Rabbit QX457-1	Yr.Iss.	1985	5.00	19
1985 Santa's Ski Trip QX496-2	Yr.Iss.	1985	12.00	41-60
1985 Skateboard Raccoon QX473-2	Yr.Iss.	1986	6.50	25-43
1985 Snow-Pitching Snowman QX470-2	Yr.Iss.	1986	4.50	21
1985 Snowy Seal QX450-1	Yr.Iss.	1985	4.00	16
1985 Soccer Beaver QX477-5	Yr.Iss.	1986	6.50	15-25
1985 Stardust Angel QX475-2	Yr.Iss.	1985	5.75	13-24
1985 Sun and Fun Santa QX492-2	Yr.Iss.	1985	7.75	40
1985 Swinging Angel Bell QX492-5	Yr.Iss.	1985	11.00	17-40
1985 Three Kittens in a Mitten QX431-1	Yr.Iss.	1985	8.00	35
1985 Trumpet Panda QX471-2	Yr.Iss.	1985	4.50	15-25

1985 Keepsake Magic Ornaments - Keepsake

YEAR ISSUE	EDITION LIMIT	YEAR RETD.	ISSUE PRICE	*QUOTE U.S.$
1985 All Are Precious QLX704-1	Yr.Iss.	1985	8.00	12-25
1985 Baby's First Christmas QLX700-5	Yr.Iss.	1985	17.00	30-40
1985 Chris Mouse-1st Ed.) QLX703-2	Yr.Iss.	1985	13.00	73-88
1985 Christmas Eve Visit QLX710-5	Yr.Iss.	1985	12.00	33
1985 Katybeth QLX710-2	Yr.Iss.	1985	10.75	30-43
1985 Little Red Schoolhouse QLX711-2	Yr.Iss.	1985	15.75	70-95
1985 Love Wreath QLX702-5	Yr.Iss.	1985	8.50	19-30
1985 Mr. and Mrs. Santa QLX705-2	Yr.Iss.	1986	15.00	73-90
1985 Nativity QLX700-1	Yr.Iss.	1985	12.00	18-30
1985 Santa's Workshop QLX700-4	Yr.Iss.	1985	13.00	58
1985 Season of Beauty QLX712-2	Yr.Iss.	1985	8.00	19-29
1985 Sugarplum Cottage QLX701-1	Yr.Iss.	1985	11.00	45
1985 Swiss Cheese Lane QLX706-5	Yr.Iss.	1985	13.00	34-50
1985 Village Church QLX702-1	Yr.Iss.	1985	15.00	35-50

1985 Limited Edition - Keepsake

YEAR ISSUE	EDITION LIMIT	YEAR RETD.	ISSUE PRICE	*QUOTE U.S.$
1985 Heavenly Trumpeter QX405-2	Yr.Iss.	1985	28.00	68-100

1985 Property Ornaments - Keepsake

YEAR ISSUE	EDITION LIMIT	YEAR RETD.	ISSUE PRICE	*QUOTE U.S.$
1985 Betsey Clark QX508-5	Yr.Iss.	1985	8.50	30
1985 A Disney Christmas QX271-2	Yr.Iss.	1985	4.75	30
1985 Fraggle Rock Holiday QX265-5	Yr.Iss.	1985	4.75	23
1985 Hugga Bunch QX271-5	Yr.Iss.	1985	5.00	15-30
1985 Kit the Shepherd QX484-5	Yr.Iss.	1985	5.75	24
1985 Merry Shirt Tales QX267-2	Yr.Iss.	1985	4.75	20
1985 Muffin the Angel QX483-5	Yr.Iss.	1985	5.75	24
1985 Norman Rockwell QX266-2	Yr.Iss.	1985	4.75	28
1985 Peanuts QX266-5	Yr.Iss.	1985	4.75	36
1985 Rainbow Brite and Friends QX 268-2	Yr.Iss.	1985	4.75	15-24
1985 Snoopy and Woodstock QX491-5	Yr.Iss.	1985	7.50	65

1985 Traditional Ornaments - Keepsake

YEAR ISSUE	EDITION LIMIT	YEAR RETD.	ISSUE PRICE	*QUOTE U.S.$
1985 Candle Cameo QX374-2	Yr.Iss.	1985	6.75	15
1985 Christmas Treats QX507-5	Yr.Iss.	1985	5.50	15
1985 Nostalgic Sled QX442-4	Yr.Iss.	1985	6.00	20
1985 Old-Fashioned Wreath QX373-5	Yr.Iss.	1985	7.50	25
1985 Peaceful Kingdom QX373-2	Yr.Iss.	1985	5.75	20-30
1985 Porcelain Bird QX479-5	Yr.Iss.	1985	6.50	40
1985 Santa Pipe QX494-2	Yr.Iss.	1985	9.50	10-24
1985 Sewn Photoholder QX379-5	Yr.Iss.	1985	7.00	25-35
1985 The Spirit of Santa Claus (Special Ed.) QX498-5	Yr.Iss.	1985	23.00	75-95

1986 Christmas Medley Collection - Keepsake

YEAR ISSUE	EDITION LIMIT	YEAR RETD.	ISSUE PRICE	*QUOTE U.S.$
1986 Christmas Guitar QX512-6	Yr.Iss.	1986	7.00	13-25
1986 Favorite Tin Drum QX514-3	Yr.Iss.	1986	8.50	30
1986 Festive Treble Clef QX513-3	Yr.Iss.	1986	8.75	10-28
1986 Holiday Horn QX514-6	Yr.Iss.	1986	8.00	17-33
1986 Joyful Carolers QX513-6	Yr.Iss.	1986	9.75	21-36

1986 Collectible Series - Keepsake

YEAR ISSUE	EDITION LIMIT	YEAR RETD.	ISSUE PRICE	*QUOTE U.S.$
1986 Art Masterpiece (3rd & Final Ed.) QX350-6	Yr.Iss.	1986	6.75	20-32
1986 Betsey Clark: Home for Christmas (1st Ed.) QX277-6	Yr.Iss.	1986	5.00	20-35
1986 Clothespin Soldier (5th Ed.) QX406-3	Yr.Iss.	1986	5.50	19-29
1986 Frosty Friends (7th Ed.) QX405-3	Yr.Iss.	1986	8.50	63-74
1986 Here Comes Santa (8th Ed.) QX404-3	Yr.Iss.	1986	14.00	43-65
1986 Holiday Wildlife (5th Ed.) QX321-6	Yr.Iss.	1986	7.50	20-30
1986 Miniature Creche (2nd Ed.) QX407-6	Yr.Iss.	1986	9.00	43-59
1986 Mr. and Mrs. Claus (1st Ed.) QX402-6	Yr.Iss.	1986	13.00	89-100
1986 Norman Rockwell (7th Ed.) QX321-3	Yr.Iss.	1986	7.75	20-30
1986 Nostalgic Houses and Shops (3rd Ed.) QX403-3	Yr.Iss.	1986	13.75	250-295
1986 Porcelain Bear (4th Ed.) QX405-6	Yr.Iss.	1986	7.75	27-45
1986 Reindeer Champs (1st Ed.) QX422-3	Yr.Iss.	1986	7.50	135-144
1986 Rocking Horse (6th Ed.) QX401-6	Yr.Iss.	1986	10.75	67-75
1986 Thimble (9th Ed.) QX406-6	Yr.Iss.	1986	5.75	20-30
1986 Tin Locomotive (5th Ed.) QX403-6	Yr.Iss.	1986	14.75	50-80
1986 Twelve Days of Christmas (3rd Ed.) QX378-6	Yr.Iss.	1986	6.50	34-45
1986 Windows of the World (2nd Ed.) QX408-3	Yr.Iss.	1986	10.00	40-64
1986 Wood Childhood Ornaments (3rd Ed.) QX407-3	Yr.Iss.	1986	7.50	21-33

*Quotes have been rounded up to nearest dollar

1986 Country Treasures Collection - Keepsake

YEAR ISSUE	EDITION LIMIT	YEAR RETD.	ISSUE PRICE	*QUOTE U.S.$
1986 Country Sleigh QX511-3	Yr.Iss.	1986	10.00	15-30
1986 Little Drummers QX511-6	Yr.Iss.	1986	12.50	18-35
1986 Nutcracker Santa QX512-3	Yr.Iss.	1986	10.00	25-50
1986 Remembering Christmas QX510-6	Yr.Iss.	1986	8.75	30
1986 Welcome, Christmas QX510-3	Yr.Iss.	1986	8.25	20-35

1986 Holiday Humor - Keepsake

YEAR ISSUE	EDITION LIMIT	YEAR RETD.	ISSUE PRICE	*QUOTE U.S.$
1986 Acorn Inn QX424-3	Yr.Iss.	1986	8.50	25-30
1986 Beary Smooth Ride QX480-5	Yr.Iss.	1986	6.50	20
1986 Chatty Penguin QX417-6	Yr.Iss.	1986	5.75	13-25
1986 Cookies for Santa QX414-6	Yr.Iss.	1986	4.50	17-30
1986 Do Not Disturb Bear QX481-2	Yr.Iss.	1986	7.75	15-25
1986 Happy Christmas to Owl QX418-3	Yr.Iss.	1986	6.00	15-25
1986 Heavenly Dreamer QX417-3	Yr.Iss.	1986	5.75	22-35
1986 Jolly Hiker QX483-2	Yr.Iss.	1987	5.00	16-20
1986 Kitty Mischief QX474-5	Yr.Iss.	1986	5.00	25
1986 Li'l Jingler QX419-3	Yr.Iss.	1987	6.75	22-40
1986 Merry Koala QX415-3	Yr.Iss.	1987	5.00	23
1986 Merry Mouse QX403-2	Yr.Iss.	1986	4.50	22
1986 Mouse in the Moon QX416-6	Yr.Iss.	1987	5.50	30
1986 Open Me First QX422-6	Yr.Iss.	1986	7.25	17-32
1986 Playful Possum QX425-3	Yr.Iss.	1986	11.00	33
1986 Popcorn Mouse QX421-3	Yr.Iss.	1986	6.75	45-55
1986 Puppy's Best Friend QX420-3	Yr.Iss.	1986	6.50	17-30
1986 Rah Rah Rabbit QX421-6	Yr.Iss.	1986	7.00	40
1986 Santa's Hot Tub QX426-3	Yr.Iss.	1986	12.00	55-60
1986 Skateboard Raccoon QX473-2	Yr.Iss.	1986	6.50	40
1986 Ski Tripper QX420-6	Yr.Iss.	1986	6.75	12-22
1986 Snow Buddies QX423-6	Yr.Iss.	1986	8.00	38
1986 Snow-Pitching Snowman QX470-2	Yr.Iss.	1986	4.50	23
1986 Soccer Beaver QX477-5	Yr.Iss.	1986	6.50	25
1986 Special Delivery QX415-6	Yr.Iss.	1986	5.00	17-30
1986 Tipping the Scales QX418-6	Yr.Iss.	1986	6.75	15-30
1986 Touchdown Santa QX423-3	Yr.Iss.	1986	8.00	42
1986 Treetop Trio QX424-6	Yr.Iss.	1987	11.00	17-32
1986 Walnut Shell Rider QX419-6	Yr.Iss.	1987	6.00	18-30
1986 Wynken, Blynken and Nod QX424-6	Yr.Iss.	1986	9.75	42

1986 Lighted Ornament Collection - Keepsake

YEAR ISSUE	EDITION LIMIT	YEAR RETD.	ISSUE PRICE	*QUOTE U.S.$
1986 Baby's First Christmas QLX710-3	Yr.Iss.	1986	19.50	45
1986 Chris Mouse (2nd Ed.) QLX705-6	Yr.Iss.	1986	13.00	75
1986 Christmas Classics (1st Ed.) QLX704-3	Yr.Iss.	1986	17.50	85
1986 Christmas Sleigh Ride QLX701-2	Yr.Iss.	1986	24.50	120-145
1986 First Christmas Together QLX707-3	Yr.Iss.	1986	14.00	43
1986 General Store QLX705-3	Yr.Iss.	1986	15.75	43-60
1986 Gentle Blessings QLX708-3	Yr.Iss.	1986	15.00	110-175
1986 Keep on Glowin' QLX707-6	Yr.Iss.	1987	10.00	37-50
1986 Merry Christmas Bell QLX709-3	Yr.Iss.	1986	8.50	15-25
1986 Mr. and Mrs. Santa QLX705-2	Yr.Iss.	1986	14.50	65-95
1986 Santa and Sparky (1st Ed.) QLX703-3	Yr.Iss.	1986	22.00	95
1986 Santa's On His Way QLX711-5	Yr.Iss.	1986	15.00	63-75
1986 Santa's Snack QLX706-6	Yr.Iss.	1986	10.00	40-60
1986 Sharing Friendship QLX706-3	Yr.Iss.	1986	8.50	15
1986 Sugarplum Cottage QLX701-1	Yr.Iss.	1986	11.00	45
1986 Village Express QLX707-2	Yr.Iss.	1987	24.50	120-125

1986 Limited Edition - Keepsake

YEAR ISSUE	EDITION LIMIT	YEAR RETD.	ISSUE PRICE	*QUOTE U.S.$
1986 Magical Unicorn QX429-3	Yr.Iss.	1986	27.50	80

1986 Property Ornaments - Keepsake

YEAR ISSUE	EDITION LIMIT	YEAR RETD.	ISSUE PRICE	*QUOTE U.S.$
1986 Heathcliff QX436-3	Yr.Iss.	1986	7.50	20-33
1986 Katybeth QX435-3	Yr.Iss.	1986	7.00	25
1986 Norman Rockwell QX276-3	Yr.Iss.	1986	4.75	27
1986 Paddington Bear QX435-6	Yr.Iss.	1986	6.00	31
1986 Peanuts QX276-6	Yr.Iss.	1986	4.75	30
1986 Shirt Tales Parade QX277-3	Yr.Iss.	1986	4.75	18
1986 Snoopy and Woodstock QX434-6	Yr.Iss.	1986	8.00	60
1986 The Statue of Liberty QX384-3	Yr.Iss.	1986	6.00	8-10

1986 Special Edition - Keepsake

YEAR ISSUE	EDITION LIMIT	YEAR RETD.	ISSUE PRICE	*QUOTE U.S.$
1986 Jolly St. Nick QX429-6	Yr.Iss.	1986	22.50	48-75

1986 Traditional Ornaments - Keepsake

YEAR ISSUE	EDITION LIMIT	YEAR RETD.	ISSUE PRICE	*QUOTE U.S.$
1986 Bluebird QX428-3	Yr.Iss.	1986	7.25	50-60
1986 Christmas Beauty QX322-3	Yr.Iss.	1986	6.00	10
1986 Glowing Christmas Tree QX428-6	Yr.Iss.	1986	7.00	15
1986 Heirloom Snowflake QX515-3	Yr.Iss.	1986	6.75	10-22
1986 Holiday Jingle Bell QX404-6	Yr.Iss.	1986	16.00	32-47
1986 The Magi QX272-6	Yr.Iss.	1986	4.75	23
1986 Mary Emmerling:American Country Collection QX275-2	Yr.Iss.	1986	7.95	25
1986 Memories to Cherish QX427-6	Yr.Iss.	1986	7.50	25
1986 Star Brighteners QX322-6	Yr.Iss.	1986	6.00	19

1987 Artists' Favorites - Keepsake

YEAR ISSUE	EDITION LIMIT	YEAR RETD.	ISSUE PRICE	*QUOTE U.S.$
1987 Beary Special QX455-7	Yr.Iss.	1987	4.75	16-30
1987 December Showers QX448-7	Yr.Iss.	1987	5.50	22-38
1987 Three Men in a Tub QX454-7	Yr.Iss.	1987	8.00	18-30
1987 Wee Chimney Sweep QX451-9	Yr.Iss.	1987	6.25	15-30

1987 Christmas Pizzazz Collection - Keepsake

YEAR ISSUE	EDITION LIMIT	YEAR RETD.	ISSUE PRICE	*QUOTE U.S.$
1987 Christmas Fun Puzzle QX467-9	Yr.Iss.	1987	8.00	30
1987 Doc Holiday QX467-7	Yr.Iss.	1987	8.00	43
1987 Happy Holidata QX471-7	Yr.Iss.	1988	6.50	15-30
1987 Holiday Hourglass QX470-7	Yr.Iss.	1987	8.00	25
1987 Jolly Follies QX466-9	Yr.Iss.	1987	8.50	40
1987 Mistletoad QX468-7	Yr.Iss.	1988	7.00	22-30
1987 St. Louie Nick QX453-9	Yr.Iss.	1988	7.75	16-35

1987 Collectible Series - Keepsake

YEAR ISSUE	EDITION LIMIT	YEAR RETD.	ISSUE PRICE	*QUOTE U.S.$
1987 Betsey Clark:Home for Christmas (2nd Ed.) QX272-7	Yr.Iss.	1987	5.00	17-25
1987 Clothespin Soldier (6th & Final Ed.) QX480-7	Yr.Iss.	1987	5.50	15-30
1987 Collector's Plate (1st Ed.) QX481-7	Yr.Iss.	1987	8.00	63-75
1987 Frosty Friends (8th Ed.) QX440-9	Yr.Iss.	1987	8.50	43-60
1987 Here Comes Santa (9th Ed.) QX484-7	Yr.Iss.	1987	14.00	61-95
1987 Holiday Heirloom (1st Ed./limited Ed.) QX485-7	Yr.Iss.	1987	25.00	25-48
1987 Holiday Wildlife (6th Ed.) QX371-7	Yr.Iss.	1987	7.50	17-27
1987 Miniature Creche (3rd Ed.) QX481-9	Yr.Iss.	1987	9.00	24-40
1987 Mr. and Mrs. Claus (2nd Ed.) QX483-7	Yr.Iss.	1987	13.25	45-65
1987 Norman Rockwell (8th Ed.) QX370-7	Yr.Iss.	1987	7.75	15-25
1987 Nostalgic Houses and Shops (4th Ed.) QX483-9	Yr.Iss.	1987	14.00	61-80
1987 Porcelain Bear (5th Ed.) QX442-7	Yr.Iss.	1987	7.75	23-40
1987 Reindeer Champs (2nd Ed.) QX480-9	Yr.Iss.	1987	7.50	36-51
1987 Rocking Horse (7th Ed.) QX482-9	Yr.Iss.	1987	10.75	46-80
1987 Thimble (10th Ed.) QX441-9	Yr.Iss.	1987	5.75	20-30
1987 Tin Locomotive (6th Ed.) QX484-9	Yr.Iss.	1987	14.75	46-65
1987 Twelve Days of Christmas (4th Ed.) QX370-9	Yr.Iss.	1987	6.50	27-40
1987 Windows of the World (3rd Ed.) QX482-7	Yr.Iss.	1987	10.00	20-40
1987 Wood Childhood Ornaments (4th Ed.) QX441-7	Yr.Iss.	1987	7.50	17-27

1987 Holiday Humor - Keepsake

YEAR ISSUE	EDITION LIMIT	YEAR RETD.	ISSUE PRICE	*QUOTE U.S.$
1987 Bright Christmas Dreams QX440-7	Yr.Iss.	1987	7.25	80
1987 Chocolate Chipmunk QX456-7	Yr.Iss.	1987	6.00	46-55
1987 Christmas Cuddle QX453-7	Yr.Iss.	1987	5.75	19-35
1987 Dr. Seuss:The Grinch's Christmas QX278-3	Yr.Iss.	1987	4.75	95
1987 Fudge Forever QX449-7	Yr.Iss.	1987	5.00	23-40
1987 Happy Santa QX456-9	Yr.Iss.	1987	4.75	27
1987 Hot Dogger QX471-9	Yr.Iss.	1987	6.50	21-30
1987 Icy Treat QX450-9	Yr.Iss.	1987	4.50	21-30
1987 Jack Frosting QX449-9	Yr.Iss.	1987	7.00	29-50
1987 Jammie Pies QX283-9	Yr.Iss.	1987	4.75	18
1987 Jogging Through the Snow QX457-7	Yr.Iss.	1987	7.25	22-40
1987 Jolly Hiker QX483-2	Yr.Iss.	1987	5.00	18
1987 Joy Ride QX440-7	Yr.Iss.	1987	11.50	45-75
1987 Let It Snow QX458-9	Yr.Iss.	1987	6.50	12-25
1987 Li'l Jingler QX419-3	Yr.Iss.	1987	6.75	22-36
1987 Merry Koala QX415-3	Yr.Iss.	1987	5.00	17
1987 Mouse in the Moon QX416-6	Yr.Iss.	1987	5.50	21
1987 Nature's Decorations QX273-9	Yr.Iss.	1987	4.75	35
1987 Night Before Christmas QX451-7	Yr.Iss.	1988	6.50	19-33
1987 Owliday Wish QX455-9	Yr.Iss.	1988	6.50	14-25
1987 Paddington Bear QX472-7	Yr.Iss.	1987	5.50	20-35
1987 Peanuts QX281-9	Yr.Iss.	1987	4.75	35-40
1987 Pretty Kitten QX448-9	Yr.Iss.	1987	11.00	35
1987 Raccoon Biker QX458-7	Yr.Iss.	1987	7.00	15-30
1987 Reindoggy QX452-7	Yr.Iss.	1988	5.75	20-35
1987 Santa at the Bat QX457-9	Yr.Iss.	1987	7.75	18-30
1987 Seasoned Greetings QX454-9	Yr.Iss.	1987	6.25	15-30
1987 Sleepy Santa QX450-7	Yr.Iss.	1987	6.25	35-40
1987 Snoopy and Woodstock QX472-9	Yr.Iss.	1987	7.25	50
1987 Spots 'n Stripes QX452-9	Yr.Iss.	1987	5.50	25
1987 Treetop Dreams QX459-7	Yr.Iss.	1988	6.75	15-30
1987 Treetop Trio QX425-6	Yr.Iss.	1987	11.00	25
1987 Walnut Shell Rider QX419-6	Yr.Iss.	1987	6.00	18

1987 Keepsake Collector's Club - Keepsake

YEAR ISSUE	EDITION LIMIT	YEAR RETD.	ISSUE PRICE	*QUOTE U.S.$
1987 Carousel Reindeer QXC580-7	Yr.Iss.	1987	Unkn.	55-65
1987 Wreath of Memories QXC580-9	Yr.Iss.	1988	Unkn.	48

1987 Keepsake Magic Ornaments - Keepsake

YEAR ISSUE	EDITION LIMIT	YEAR RETD.	ISSUE PRICE	*QUOTE U.S.$
1987 Angelic Messengers QLX711-3	Yr.Iss.	1987	18.75	53-60
1987 Baby's First Christmas QLX704-9	Yr.Iss.	1987	13.50	38
1987 Bright Noel QLX705-9	Yr.Iss.	1987	7.00	18-33
1987 Chris Mouse (3rd Ed.) QLX705-7	Yr.Iss.	1987	11.00	60
1987 Christmas Classics (2nd Ed.) QLX702-9	Yr.Iss.	1987	16.00	50-75
1987 Christmas Morning QLX701-3	Yr.Iss.	1988	24.50	33-50
1987 First Christmas Together QLX708-7	Yr.Iss.	1987	11.50	50
1987 Good Cheer Blimp QLX704-6	Yr.Iss.	1987	16.00	60
1987 Keeping Cozy QLX704-7	Yr.Iss.	1987	11.75	30-37
1987 Lacy Brass Snowflake QLX709-7	Yr.Iss.	1987	11.50	16-30
1987 Loving Holiday QLX701-6	Yr.Iss.	1987	22.00	38-55
1987 Memories are Forever Photoholder QLX706-7	Yr.Iss.	1987	8.50	33
1987 Meowy Christmas QLX708-9	Yr.Iss.	1987	10.00	63
1987 Santa and Sparky (2nd Ed.) QLX701-9	Yr.Iss.	1987	19.50	65-75
1987 Season for Friendship QLX706-9	Yr.Iss.	1987	8.50	20
1987 Train Station QLX703-9	Yr.Iss.	1987	12.75	50

1987 Lighted Ornament Collection - Keepsake

YEAR ISSUE	EDITION LIMIT	YEAR RETD.	ISSUE PRICE	*QUOTE U.S.$
1987 Keep on Glowin' QLX707-6	Yr.Iss.	1987	10.00	37
1987 Village Express QLX707-2	Yr.Iss.	1987	24.50	87-120

1987 Limited Edition - Keepsake

YEAR ISSUE	EDITION LIMIT	YEAR RETD.	ISSUE PRICE	*QUOTE U.S.$
1987 Christmas is Gentle QX444-9	Yr.Iss.	1987	17.50	57-85
1987 Christmas Time Mime QX442-9	Yr.Iss.	1987	27.50	46-65

1987 Old-Fashioned Christmas Collection - Keepsake

YEAR ISSUE	EDITION LIMIT	YEAR RETD.	ISSUE PRICE	*QUOTE U.S.$
1987 Country Wreath QX470-9	Yr.Iss.	1987	5.75	30
1987 Folk Art Santa QX474-9	Yr.Iss.	1987	5.25	20-35
1987 In a Nutshell QX469-7	Yr.Iss.	1988	5.50	24-35
1987 Little Whittler QX469-9	Yr.Iss.	1987	6.00	25-33
1987 Nostalgic Rocker QX468-9	Yr.Iss.	1987	6.50	26-33

1987 Special Edition - Keepsake

YEAR ISSUE	EDITION LIMIT	YEAR RETD.	ISSUE PRICE	*QUOTE U.S.$
1987 Favorite Santa QX445-7	Yr.Iss.	1987	22.50	32

1987 Traditional Ornaments - Keepsake

YEAR ISSUE	EDITION LIMIT	YEAR RETD.	ISSUE PRICE	*QUOTE U.S.$
1987 Christmas Keys QX473-9	Yr.Iss.	1987	5.75	20-33
1987 Currier & Ives: American Farm Scene QX282-9	Yr.Iss.	1987	4.75	30
1987 Goldfinch QX464-9	Yr.Iss.	1987	7.00	45-60
1987 Heavenly Harmony QX465-9	Yr.Iss.	1987	15.00	35
1987 I Remember Santa QX278-9	Yr.Iss.	1987	4.75	33
1987 Joyous Angels QX465-7	Yr.Iss.	1987	7.75	22-25
1987 Norman Rockwell:Christmas Scenes QX282-7	Yr.Iss.	1987	4.75	30
1987 Promise of Peace QX374-9	Yr.Iss.	1987	6.50	25
1987 Special Memories Photoholder QX464-7	Yr.Iss.	1987	6.75	27

1988 Artist Favorites - Keepsake

YEAR ISSUE	EDITION LIMIT	YEAR RETD.	ISSUE PRICE	*QUOTE U.S.$
1988 Baby Redbird QX410-1	Yr.Iss.	1988	5.00	19
1988 Cymbals of Christmas QX411-1	Yr.Iss.	1988	5.50	15-30
1988 Little Jack Horner QX408-1	Yr.Iss.	1988	8.00	14-28
1988 Merry-Mint Unicorn QX423-4	Yr.Iss.	1988	8.50	12-23
1988 Midnight Snack QX410-4	Yr.Iss.	1988	6.00	22
1988 Very Strawbeary QX409-1	Yr.Iss.	1988	4.75	14-23

1988 Christmas Pizzazz Collection - Keepsake

YEAR ISSUE	EDITION LIMIT	YEAR RETD.	ISSUE PRICE	*QUOTE U.S.$
1988 Happy Holidata QX471-7	Yr.Iss.	1988	6.50	15-30
1988 Mistletoad QX468-7	Yr.Iss.	1988	7.00	20-30
1988 St. Louie Nick QX453-9	Yr.Iss.	1988	7.75	15-22

1988 Collectible Series - Keepsake

YEAR ISSUE	EDITION LIMIT	YEAR RETD.	ISSUE PRICE	*QUOTE U.S.$
1988 Betsey Clark: Home for Christmas (3rd Ed.) QX271-4	Yr.Iss.	1988	5.00	18-25
1988 Collector's Plate (2nd Ed.) QX406-1	Yr.Iss.	1988	8.00	45
1988 Five Golden Rings (5th Ed.) QX371-4	Yr.Iss.	1988	6.50	18-30
1988 Frosty Friends (9th Ed.) QX403-1	Yr.Iss.	1988	8.75	45-65
1988 Here Comes Santa (10th Ed.) QX400-1	Yr.Iss.	1988	14.00	32-50
1988 Holiday Heirloom (2nd Ed.) QX406-4	Yr.Iss.	1988	25.00	24
1988 Holiday Wildlife (7th Ed.) QX371-1	Yr.Iss.	1988	7.75	18-25
1988 Mary's Angels (1st Ed.) QX407-4	Yr.Iss.	1988	5.00	49-85
1988 Miniature Creche (4th Ed.) QX403-4	Yr.Iss.	1988	8.50	20-35
1988 Mr. and Mrs. Claus (3rd Ed.) QX401-1	Yr.Iss.	1988	13.00	55
1988 Norman Rockwell (9th Ed.) QX370-4	Yr.Iss.	1988	7.75	14-23
1988 Nostalgic Houses and Shops (5th Ed.) QX401-4	Yr.Iss.	1988	14.50	42-65
1988 Porcelain Bear (6th Ed.) QX404-4	Yr.Iss.	1988	8.00	25-40
1988 Reindeer Champs (3rd Ed.) QX405-1	Yr.Iss.	1988	7.50	27-40
1988 Rocking Horse (8th Ed.) QX402-4	Yr.Iss.	1988	10.75	40-70
1988 Thimble (11th Ed.) QX405-4	Yr.Iss.	1988	5.75	17-25
1988 Tin Locomotive (7th Ed.) QX400-4	Yr.Iss.	1988	14.75	40-50
1988 Windows of the World (4th Ed.) QX402-1	Yr.Iss.	1988	10.00	22-35
1988 Wood Childhood (5th Ed.) QX404-1	Yr.Iss.	1988	7.50	15-24

1988 Hallmark Handcrafted Ornaments - Keepsake

YEAR ISSUE	EDITION LIMIT	YEAR RETD.	ISSUE PRICE	*QUOTE U.S.$
1988 Americana Drum QX488-1	Yr.Iss.	1988	7.75	17-32
1988 Arctic Tenor QX472-1	Yr.Iss.	1988	4.00	10-19
1988 Christmas Cardinal QX494-1	Yr.Iss.	1988	4.75	9-20
1988 Christmas Cuckoo QX480-1	Yr.Iss.	1988	8.00	40
1988 Christmas Memories QX372-4	Yr.Iss.	1988	6.50	25
1988 Christmas Scenes QX273-1	Yr.Iss.	1988	4.75	24
1988 Cool Juggler QX487-4	Yr.Iss.	1988	6.50	20
1988 Feliz Navidad QX416-1	Yr.Iss.	1988	6.75	20-35
1988 Filled with Fudge QX419-1	Yr.Iss.	1988	4.75	18-33
1988 Glowing Wreath QX492-1	Yr.Iss.	1988	6.00	14
1988 Go For The Gold QX417-4	Yr.Iss.	1988	8.00	16-30
1988 Goin' Cross-Country QX476-4	Yr.Iss.	1988	8.50	14-29
1988 Gone Fishing QX479-4	Yr.Iss.	1989	5.00	15-19
1988 Hoe-Hoe-Hoe QX422-1	Yr.Iss.	1988	5.00	11-20
1988 Holiday Hero QX423-1	Yr.Iss.	1988	5.00	20
1988 Jingle Bell Clown QX477-4	Yr.Iss.	1988	15.00	21-38
1988 Jolly Walrus QX473-1	Yr.Iss.	1988	4.50	30
1988 Kiss from Santa QX482-1	Yr.Iss.	1989	4.50	30
1988 Kiss the Claus QX486-1	Yr.Iss.	1988	5.00	10-19
1988 Kringle Moon QX495-1	Yr.Iss.	1988	5.00	35
1988 Kringle Portrait QX496-1	Yr.Iss.	1988	7.50	22-40
1988 Kringle Tree QX495-4	Yr.Iss.	1988	6.50	21-38
1988 Love Santa QX486-4	Yr.Iss.	1988	5.00	20
1988 Loving Bear QX493-4	Yr.Iss.	1988	4.75	10-20
1988 Nick the Kick QX422-4	Yr.Iss.	1988	5.00	25
1988 Noah's Ark QX490-4	Yr.Iss.	1988	8.50	40
1988 Old-Fashioned Church QX498-1	Yr.Iss.	1988	4.00	25
1988 Old-Fashioned School House QX497-1	Yr.Iss.	1988	4.00	23
1988 Oreo QX481-4	Yr.Iss.	1989	4.00	11-20
1988 Par for Santa QX479-1	Yr.Iss.	1988	5.00	20
1988 Party Line QX476-1	Yr.Iss.	1989	8.75	21-33
1988 Peanuts QX280-1	Yr.Iss.	1988	4.75	50
1988 Peek-a-boo Kittens QX487-1	Yr.Iss.	1989	7.50	23

*Quotes have been rounded up to nearest dollar

YEAR ISSUE	EDITION LIMIT	YEAR RETD.	ISSUE PRICE	*QUOTE U.S.$
1988 Polar Bowler QX478-4	Yr.Iss.	1989	5.00	10-20
1988 Purrfect Snuggle QX474-4	Yr.Iss.	1988	6.25	30-33
1988 Sailing! Sailing! QX491-1	Yr.Iss.	1988	8.50	27
1988 Santa Flamingo QX483-4	Yr.Iss.	1988	4.75	17-35
1988 Shiny Sleigh QX492-4	Yr.Iss.	1988	5.75	20
1988 Slipper Spaniel QX472-4	Yr.Iss.	1988	4.50	10-20
1988 Snoopy and Woodstock QX474-1	Yr.Iss.	1988	6.00	47
1988 Soft Landing QX475-1	Yr.Iss.	1988	7.00	13-25
1988 Sparkling Tree QX483-1	Yr.Iss.	1988	6.00	19
1988 Squeaky Clean QX475-4	Yr.Iss.	1988	6.75	13-25
1988 Starry Angel QX494-4	Yr.Iss.	1988	4.75	20
1988 Sweet Star QX418-4	Yr.Iss.	1988	5.00	19-33
1988 Teeny Taster QX418-1	Yr.Iss.	1989	4.75	23-30
1988 The Town Crier QX473-4	Yr.Iss.	1988	5.50	14-25
1988 Travels with Santa QX477-1	Yr.Iss.	1988	10.00	26-40
1988 Uncle Sam Nutcracker QX488-4	Yr.Iss.	1988	7.00	40
1988 Winter Fun QX478-1	Yr.Iss.	1988	8.50	17-28

1988 Hallmark Keepsake Ornament Collector's Club - Keepsake

YEAR ISSUE	EDITION LIMIT	YEAR RETD.	ISSUE PRICE	*QUOTE U.S.$
1988 Angelic Minstrel QXC408-4	Yr.Iss.	1988	27.50	39
1988 Christmas is Sharing QXC407-1	Yr.Iss.	1988	17.50	31
1988 Hold on Tight QXC570-4	Yr.Iss.	1988	Unkn.	77
1988 Holiday Heirloom (2nd Ed.) QXC406-4	Yr.Iss.	1988	25.00	24-37
1988 Our Clubhouse QXC580-4	Yr.Iss.	1988	Unkn.	33
1988 Sleighful of Dreams QC580-1	Yr.Iss.	1988	8.00	48

1988 Holiday Humor - Keepsake

YEAR ISSUE	EDITION LIMIT	YEAR RETD.	ISSUE PRICE	*QUOTE U.S.$
1988 Night Before Christmas QX451-7	Yr.Iss.	1988	6.50	33-44
1988 Owliday Wish QX455-9	Yr.Iss.	1988	6.50	14-25
1988 Reindoggy QX452-7	Yr.Iss.	1988	5.75	20-25
1988 Treetop Dreams QX459-7	Yr.Iss.	1988	6.75	15-25

1988 Keepsake Magic Ornaments - Keepsake

YEAR ISSUE	EDITION LIMIT	YEAR RETD.	ISSUE PRICE	*QUOTE U.S.$
1988 Baby's First Christmas QLX718-4	Yr.Iss.	1988	24.00	43
1988 Bearly Reaching QLX715-1	Yr.Iss.	1988	9.50	26-41
1988 Chris Mouse (4th Ed.) QLX715-4	Yr.Iss.	1988	8.75	60
1988 Christmas Classics (3rd Ed.) QLX716-1	Yr.Iss.	1988	15.00	31-45
1988 Christmas is Magic QLX717-1	Yr.Iss.	1988	12.00	35-55
1988 Christmas Morning QLX701-3	Yr.Iss.	1988	24.50	33-50
1988 Circling the Globe QLX712-4	Yr.Iss.	1988	10.50	45
1988 Country Express QLX721-1	Yr.Iss.	1988	24.50	67-75
1988 Festive Feeder QLX720-4	Yr.Iss.	1988	11.50	43-50
1988 First Christmas Together QLX702-7	Yr.Iss.	1988	12.00	21-36
1988 Heavenly Glow QLX711-4	Yr.Iss.	1988	11.75	19-30
1988 Kitty Capers QLX716-4	Yr.Iss.	1988	13.00	45
1988 Kringle's Toy Shop QLX701-7	Yr.Iss.	1988	25.00	38
1988 Last-Minute Hug QLX718-1	Yr.Iss.	1988	19.50	49
1988 Moonlit Nap QLX713-4	Yr.Iss.	1988	8.75	21-30
1988 Parade of the Toys QLX719-4	Yr.Iss.	1988	22.00	36-51
1988 Radiant Tree QLX712-1	Yr.Iss.	1988	11.75	28
1988 Santa and Sparky (3rd Ed.) QLX719-1	Yr.Iss.	1988	19.50	31-43
1988 Skater's Waltz QLX720-1	Yr.Iss.	1988	19.50	36-63
1988 Song of Christmas QLX711-1	Yr.Iss.	1988	8.50	14-30
1988 Tree of Friendship QLX710-4	Yr.Iss.	1988	8.50	25

1988 Keepsake Miniature Ornaments - Keepsake

YEAR ISSUE	EDITION LIMIT	YEAR RETD.	ISSUE PRICE	*QUOTE U.S.$
1988 Baby's First Christmas	Yr.Iss.	1988	6.00	12
1988 Brass Angel	Yr.Iss.	1988	1.50	20
1988 Brass Star	Yr.Iss.	1988	1.50	20
1988 Brass Tree	Yr.Iss.	1988	1.50	19
1988 Candy Cane Elf	Yr.Iss.	1988	3.00	20
1988 Country Wreath	Yr.Iss.	1988	4.00	12
1988 Family Home (1st Ed.)	Yr.Iss.	1988	8.50	45
1988 First Christmas Together	Yr.Iss.	1988	4.00	9-13
1988 Folk Art Lamb	Yr.Iss.	1988	2.50	14-23
1988 Folk Art Reindeer	Yr.Iss.	1988	2.50	13-20
1988 Friends Share Joy	Yr.Iss.	1988	2.00	10-16
1988 Gentle Angel	Yr.Iss.	1988	2.00	16-20
1988 Happy Santa	Yr.Iss.	1988	4.50	19
1988 Holy Family	Yr.Iss.	1988	8.50	13
1988 Jolly St. Nick	Yr.Iss.	1988	8.00	20-30
1988 Joyous Heart	Yr.Iss.	1988	3.50	20-24
1988 Kittens in Toyland (1st Ed.)	Yr.Iss.	1988	5.00	26
1988 Little Drummer Boy	Yr.Iss.	1988	4.50	20-27
1988 Love is Forever	Yr.Iss.	1988	2.00	15
1988 Mother	Yr.Iss.	1988	3.00	13
1988 Penguin Pal (1st Ed.)	Yr.Iss.	1988	3.75	27
1988 Rocking Horse (1st Ed.)	Yr.Iss.	1988	4.50	44
1988 Skater's Waltz	Yr.Iss.	1988	7.00	14-22
1988 Sneaker Mouse	Yr.Iss.	1988	4.00	14-20
1988 Snuggly Skater	Yr.Iss.	1988	4.50	27
1988 Sweet Dreams	Yr.Iss.	1988	7.00	16-23
1988 Three Little Kitties	Yr.Iss.	1988	6.00	13-19

1988 Old Fashioned Christmas Collection - Keepsake

YEAR ISSUE	EDITION LIMIT	YEAR RETD.	ISSUE PRICE	*QUOTE U.S.$
1988 In A Nutshell QX469-7	Yr.Iss.	1988	5.50	24-33

1988 Special Edition - Keepsake

YEAR ISSUE	EDITION LIMIT	YEAR RETD.	ISSUE PRICE	*QUOTE U.S.$
1988 The Wonderful Santacycle QX411-4	Yr.Iss.	1988	22.50	34-45

1989 Artists' Favorites - Keepsake

YEAR ISSUE	EDITION LIMIT	YEAR RETD.	ISSUE PRICE	*QUOTE U.S.$
1989 Baby Partridge QX452-5	Yr.Iss.	1989	6.75	10-15
1989 Bear-i-Tone QX454-2	Yr.Iss.	1989	4.75	10-20
1989 Carousel Zebra QX451-5	Yr.Iss.	1989	9.25	16-31
1989 Cherry Jubilee QX453-2	Yr.Iss.	1989	5.00	16-28
1989 Mail Call QX452-2	Yr.Iss.	1989	8.75	15-20
1989 Merry-Go-Round Unicorn QX447-2	Yr.Iss.	1989	10.75	16-25
1989 Playful Angel QX453-5	Yr.Iss.	1989	6.75	15-25

1989 Collectible Series - Keepsake

YEAR ISSUE	EDITION LIMIT	YEAR RETD.	ISSUE PRICE	*QUOTE U.S.$
1989 Betsey Clark:Home for Christmas (4th Ed.) QX230-2	Yr.Iss.	1989	5.00	29
1989 Christmas Kitty (1st Ed.) QX544-5	Yr.Iss.	1989	14.75	26-33
1989 Collector's Plate (3rd Ed.) QX461-2	Yr.Iss.	1989	8.25	21-35
1989 Crayola Crayon (1st Ed.) QX435-2	Yr.Iss.	1989	8.75	45-55
1989 Frosty Friends (10th Ed.) QX457-2	Yr.Iss.	1989	9.25	36-45
1989 The Gift Bringers (1st Ed.) QX279-5	Yr.Iss.	1989	5.00	21
1989 Hark! It's Herald (1st Ed.) QX455-5	Yr.Iss.	1989	6.75	23-30
1989 Here Comes Santa (11th Ed.) QX458-5	Yr.Iss.	1989	14.75	32-48
1989 Mary's Angels (2nd Ed.) QX454-5	Yr.Iss.	1989	5.75	95
1989 Miniature Creche (5th Ed.) QX459-2	Yr.Iss.	1989	9.25	15-25
1989 Mr. and Mrs. Claus (4th Ed.) QX457-5	Yr.Iss.	1989	13.25	33-50
1989 Nostalgic Houses and Shops (6th Ed.) QX458-2	Yr.Iss.	1989	14.25	70
1989 Porcelain Bear (7th Ed.) QX461-5	Yr.Iss.	1989	8.75	20-40
1989 Reindeer Champs (4th Ed.) QX456-2	Yr.Iss.	1989	7.75	9-25
1989 Rocking Horse (9th Ed.) QX462-2	Yr.Iss.	1989	10.75	43-70
1989 Thimble (12th Ed.) QX455-2	Yr.Iss.	1989	5.75	17-27
1989 Tin Locomotive (8th Ed.) QX460-2	Yr.Iss.	1989	14.75	32-47
1989 Twelve Days of Christmas (6th Ed.) QX381-2	Yr.Iss.	1989	6.75	20-30
1989 Windows of the World (5th Ed.) QX462-5	Yr.Iss.	1989	10.75	22-35
1989 Winter Surprise (1st Ed.) QX427-2	Yr.Iss.	1989	10.75	27-33
1989 Wood Childhood Ornaments (6th Ed.) QX459-5	Yr.Iss.	1989	7.75	15-25

1989 Hallmark Handcrafted Ornaments - Keepsake

YEAR ISSUE	EDITION LIMIT	YEAR RETD.	ISSUE PRICE	*QUOTE U.S.$
1989 Peek-a-boo Kittens QX487-1	Yr.Iss.	1989	7.50	21

1989 Hallmark Keepsake Ornament Collector's Club - Keepsake

YEAR ISSUE	EDITION LIMIT	YEAR RETD.	ISSUE PRICE	*QUOTE U.S.$
1989 Christmas is Peaceful QXC451-2	Yr.Iss.	1989	18.50	30
1989 Collect a Dream QXC428-5	Yr.Iss.	1989	9.00	43-58
1989 Holiday Heirloom (3rd Ed.) QXC460-5	Yr.Iss.	1989	25.00	30
1989 Noelle QXC448-3	Yr.Iss.	1989	19.75	50
1989 Sitting Purrty QXC581-2	Yr.Iss.	1989	Unkn.	44
1989 Visit from Santa QXC580-2	Yr.Iss.	1989	Unkn.	39

1989 Holiday Traditions - Keepsake

YEAR ISSUE	EDITION LIMIT	YEAR RETD.	ISSUE PRICE	*QUOTE U.S.$
1989 Camera Claus QX546-5	Yr.Iss.	1989	5.75	12-23
1989 A Charlie Brown Christmas QX276-5	Yr.Iss.	1989	4.75	35-40
1989 Cranberry Bunny QX426-2	Yr.Iss.	1989	5.75	11-18
1989 Deer Disguise QX426-5	Yr.Iss.	1989	5.75	17-25
1989 Feliz Navidad QX439-2	Yr.Iss.	1989	6.75	20-30
1989 The First Christmas QX547-5	Yr.Iss.	1989	7.75	14-18
1989 Gentle Fawn QX548-5	Yr.Iss.	1989	7.75	13-20
1989 George Washington Bicentennial QX386-2	Yr.Iss.	1989	6.75	9-20
1989 Gone Fishing QX479-4	Yr.Iss.	1989	5.75	17
1989 Gym Dandy QX418-5	Yr.Iss.	1989	5.75	10-20
1989 Hang in There QX430-5	Yr.Iss.	1989	5.25	25-35
1989 Here's the Pitch QX545-5	Yr.Iss.	1989	5.75	11-20
1989 Hoppy Holidays QX469-2	Yr.Iss.	1989	7.75	13-25
1989 Joyful Trio QX437-2	Yr.Iss.	1989	9.75	15-28
1989 A Kiss™ From Santa QX482-1	Yr.Iss.	1989	4.50	20
1989 Kristy Claus QX424-5	Yr.Iss.	1989	5.75	10-15
1989 Norman Rockwell QX276-2	Yr.Iss.	1989	4.75	20
1989 North Pole Jogger QX546-2	Yr.Iss.	1989	5.75	12-23
1989 Old-World Gnome QX434-5	Yr.Iss.	1989	7.75	15-30
1989 On the Links QX419-2	Yr.Iss.	1989	5.75	15-23
1989 Oreo® Chocolate Sandwich Cookies QX481-4	Yr.Iss.	1989	4.00	15
1989 Owliday Greetings QX436-5	Yr.Iss.	1989	4.00	13-23
1989 Paddington Bear QX429-2	Yr.Iss.	1989	5.75	16-27
1989 Party Line QX476-1	Yr.Iss.	1989	8.75	27
1989 Peek-a-Boo Kitties QX487-1	Yr.Iss.	1989	7.50	16-22
1989 Polar Bowler QX478-4	Yr.Iss.	1989	5.75	17
1989 Sea Santa QX415-2	Yr.Iss.	1989	5.75	13-30
1989 Snoopy and Woodstock QX433-2	Yr.Iss.	1989	6.75	22-37
1989 Snowplow Santa QX420-5	Yr.Iss.	1989	5.75	12-23
1989 Special Delivery QX432-5	Yr.Iss.	1989	5.25	12-25
1989 Spencer Sparrow, Esq. QX431-2	Yr.Iss.	1990	6.75	15-28
1989 Stocking Kitten QX456-5	Yr.Iss.	1990	6.75	13-23
1989 Sweet Memories Photoholder QX438-5	Yr.Iss.	1989	6.75	25
1989 Teeny Taster QX418-1	Yr.Iss.	1989	4.75	17

1989 Keepsake Magic Collection - Keepsake

YEAR ISSUE	EDITION LIMIT	YEAR RETD.	ISSUE PRICE	*QUOTE U.S.$
1989 Angel Melody QLX720-2	Yr.Iss.	1989	9.50	25
1989 The Animals Speak QLX723-2	Yr.Iss.	1989	13.50	78-125
1989 Baby's First Christmas QLX727-2	Yr.Iss.	1989	30.00	47-55
1989 Backstage Bear QLX721-5	Yr.Iss.	1989	13.50	27-35
1989 Busy Beaver QLX724-5	Yr.Iss.	1989	17.50	35-50
1989 Chris Mouse (5th Ed.) QLX722-5	Yr.Iss.	1989	9.50	57-63
1989 Christmas Classics (4th Ed.) QLX724-2	Yr.Iss.	1989	13.50	27-43
1989 First Christmas Together QLX734-2	Yr.Iss.	1989	17.50	33-50
1989 Forest Frolics (1st Ed.) QLX728-2	Yr.Iss.	1989	24.50	83-98
1989 Holiday Bell QLX722-2	Yr.Iss.	1989	17.50	29-35
1989 Joyous Carolers QLX729-5	Yr.Iss.	1989	30.00	47-70
1989 Kringle's Toy Shop QLX701-7	Yr.Iss.	1989	24.50	60
1989 Loving Spoonful QLX726-2	Yr.Iss.	1989	19.50	31-38
1989 Metro Express QLX727-5	Yr.Iss.	1989	28.00	71-80
1989 Moonlit Nap QLX713-4	Yr.Iss.	1989	8.75	23
1989 Rudolph the Red-Nosed Reindeer QLX725-2	Yr.Iss.	1989	19.50	51-70
1989 Spirit of St. Nick QLX728-5	Yr.Iss.	1989	24.50	75
1989 Tiny Tinker QLX717-4	Yr.Iss.	1989	19.50	50-65
1989 Unicorn Fantasy QLX723-5	Yr.Iss.	1989	9.50	17

1989 Keepsake Miniature Ornaments - Keepsake

YEAR ISSUE	EDITION LIMIT	YEAR RETD.	ISSUE PRICE	*QUOTE U.S.$
1989 Acorn Squirrel QXM568-2	Yr.Iss.	1989	4.50	9
1989 Baby's First Christmas QXM573-2	Yr.Iss.	1989	6.00	11-15
1989 Brass Partridge QXM572-5	Yr.Iss.	1989	3.00	10
1989 Brass Snowflake QXM570-2	Yr.Iss.	1989	4.50	14
1989 Bunny Hug QXM577-5	Yr.Iss.	1989	3.00	10
1989 Country Wreath QXM573-1	Yr.Iss.	1989	4.50	12
1989 Cozy Skater QXM573-5	Yr.Iss.	1989	4.50	12-15
1989 First Christmas Together QXM564-2	Yr.Iss.	1989	8.50	10
1989 Folk Art Bunny QXM569-2	Yr.Iss.	1989	4.50	9
1989 Happy Bluebird QXM566-2	Yr.Iss.	1989	4.50	10-13
1989 Holiday Deer QXM577-2	Yr.Iss.	1989	3.00	12
1989 Holy Family QXM561-1	Yr.Iss.	1989	8.50	15
1989 Kittens in Toyland (2nd Ed.) QXM561-2	Yr.Iss.	1989	4.50	15-20
1989 Kitty Cart QXM572-2	Yr.Iss.	1989	3.00	8
1989 The Kringles (1st Ed.) QXM562-2	Yr.Iss.	1989	6.00	26-33
1989 Little Soldier QXM567-5	Yr.Iss.	1989	4.50	10-24
1989 Little Star Bringer QXM562-2	Yr.Iss.	1989	6.00	15-19
1989 Load of Cheer QXM574-5	Yr.Iss.	1989	6.00	12-20
1989 Lovebirds QXM563-5	Yr.Iss.	1989	6.00	9-14
1989 Merry Seal QXM575-5	Yr.Iss.	1989	6.00	15
1989 Mother QXM564-5	Yr.Iss.	1989	6.00	9-15
1989 Noel R.R. (1st Ed.) QXM576-2	Yr.Iss.	1989	8.50	35-43
1989 Old English Village (2nd Ed.) QXM561-5	Yr.Iss.	1989	8.50	28-38
1989 Old-World Santa QXM569-5	Yr.Iss.	1989	3.00	6-10
1989 Penguin Pal (2nd Ed.) QXM560-2	Yr.Iss.	1989	4.50	16-20
1989 Pinecone Basket QXM573-4	Yr.Iss.	1989	4.50	7-10
1989 Puppy Cart QXM571-5	Yr.Iss.	1989	3.00	9-22
1989 Rejoice QXM578-2	Yr.Iss.	1989	3.00	10
1989 Rocking Horse (2nd Ed.) QXM560-5	Yr.Iss.	1989	4.50	23-30
1989 Roly-Poly Pig QXM571-2	Yr.Iss.	1989	3.00	12-18
1989 Roly-Poly Ram QXM570-5	Yr.Iss.	1989	3.00	13-18
1989 Santa's Magic Ride QXM563-2	Yr.Iss.	1989	8.50	15
1989 Santa's Roadster QXM566-5	Yr.Iss.	1989	6.00	15-20
1989 Scrimshaw Reindeer QXM568-5	Yr.Iss.	1989	4.50	10
1989 Sharing a Ride QXM576-5	Yr.Iss.	1989	8.50	15
1989 Slow Motion QXM575-2	Yr.Iss.	1989	6.00	12-17
1989 Special Friend QXM565-2	Yr.Iss.	1989	4.50	13
1989 Starlit Mouse QXM565-5	Yr.Iss.	1989	4.50	12-17
1989 Stocking Pal QXM567-2	Yr.Iss.	1989	4.50	10
1989 Strollin' Snowman QXM574-2	Yr.Iss.	1989	4.50	13-18
1989 Three Little Kitties QXM569-4	Yr.Iss.	1989	6.00	19

1989 New Attractions - Keepsake

YEAR ISSUE	EDITION LIMIT	YEAR RETD.	ISSUE PRICE	*QUOTE U.S.$
1989 Balancing Elf QX489-5	Yr.Iss.	1989	6.75	22
1989 Cactus Cowboy QX411-2	Yr.Iss.	1989	6.75	33-44
1989 Claus Construction QX488-5	Yr.Iss.	1990	7.75	19-40
1989 Cool Swing QX487-5	Yr.Iss.	1989	6.25	30-35
1989 Country Cat QX467-2	Yr.Iss.	1989	6.25	18
1989 Festive Angel QX463-5	Yr.Iss.	1989	6.75	13-27
1080 Goin' South QX410-5	Yr.Iss.	1989	4.25	18-25
1989 Graceful Swan QX464-2	Yr.Iss.	1989	6.75	20
1989 Horse Weathervane QX463-2	Yr.Iss.	1989	5.75	15
1989 Let's Play QX488-2	Yr.Iss.	1989	7.25	28
1989 Nostalgic Lamb QX466-5	Yr.Iss.	1989	6.75	10-15
1989 Nutshell Dreams QX465-5	Yr.Iss.	1989	5.75	14-23
1989 Nutshell Holiday QX465-2	Yr.Iss.	1990	5.75	17-27
1989 Nutshell Workshop QX487-2	Yr.Iss.	1989	5.75	23
1989 Peppermint Clown QX450-5	Yr.Iss.	1989	24.75	19-23
1989 Rodney Reindeer QX407-2	Yr.Iss.	1989	6.75	10-15
1989 Rooster Weathervane QX467-5	Yr.Iss.	1989	5.75	18-24
1989 Sparkling Snowflake QX547-2	Yr.Iss.	1989	7.75	23
1989 TV Break QX409-2	Yr.Iss.	1989	6.25	15-20
1989 Wiggly Snowman QX489-2	Yr.Iss.	1989	6.75	21-36

1989 Special Edition - Keepsake

YEAR ISSUE	EDITION LIMIT	YEAR RETD.	ISSUE PRICE	*QUOTE U.S.$
1989 The Ornament Express QX580-5	Yr.Iss.	1989	22.00	34-49

1990 Artists' Favorites - Keepsake

YEAR ISSUE	EDITION LIMIT	YEAR RETD.	ISSUE PRICE	*QUOTE U.S.$
1990 Angel Kitty QX4746	Yr.Iss.	1990	8.75	16-25
1990 Donder's Diner QX4823	Yr.Iss.	1990	13.75	20-23
1990 Gentle Dreamers QX4756	Yr.Iss.	1990	8.75	18-30
1990 Happy Woodcutter QX4763	Yr.Iss.	1990	9.75	18-25
1990 Mouseboat QX4753	Yr.Iss.	1990	7.75	13
1990 Welcome, Santa QX4773	Yr.Iss.	1990	11.75	30-34

1990 Collectible Series - Keepsake

YEAR ISSUE	EDITION LIMIT	YEAR RETD.	ISSUE PRICE	*QUOTE U.S.$
1990 Betsey Clark: Home for Christmas (5th Ed.) QX2033	Yr.Iss.	1990	5.00	15-25
1990 Christmas Kitty (2nd Ed.) QX4506	Yr.Iss.	1990	14.75	20-34
1990 Cinnamon Bear (8th Ed.) QX4426	Yr.Iss.	1990	8.75	30-35
1990 Cookies for Santa (4th Ed.) QX4436	Yr.Iss.	1990	8.75	25-35
1990 CRAYOLA Crayon-Bright Moving Colors (2nd Ed.) QX4586	Yr.Iss.	1990	8.75	44-50
1990 Fabulous Decade (1st Ed.) QX4466	Yr.Iss.	1990	7.75	40-45
1990 Festive Surrey (12th Ed.) QX4923	Yr.Iss.	1990	14.75	31
1990 Frosty Friends (11th Ed.) QX4396	Yr.Iss.	1990	9.75	24-38
1990 The Gift Bringers-St. Lucia (2nd Ed.) QX2803	Yr.Iss.	1990	5.00	15-25
1990 Greatest Story (1st Ed.) QX4656	Yr.Iss.	1990	12.75	26-35
1990 Hark! It's Herald (2nd Ed.) QX4463	Yr.Iss.	1990	6.75	17-28
1990 Heart of Christmas (1st Ed.) QX4726	Yr.Iss.	1990	13.75	64-80
1990 Holiday Home (7th Ed.) QX4696	Yr.Iss.	1990	14.75	80
1990 Irish (6th Ed.) QX4636	Yr.Iss.	1990	10.75	30-36

ORNAMENTS

YEAR ISSUE	EDITION LIMIT	YEAR RETD.	ISSUE PRICE	*QUOTE U.S.$
1990 Mary's Angels-Rosebud (3rd Ed.) QX4423	Yr.Iss.	1990	5.75	31-40
1990 Merry Olde Santa (1st Ed.) QX4736	Yr.Iss.	1990	14.75	65-75
1990 Popcorn Party (5th Ed.) QX4393	Yr.Iss.	1990	13.75	38-80
1990 Reindeer Champs-Comet (5th Ed.) QX4433	Yr.Iss.	1990	7.75	20-30
1990 Rocking Horse (10th Ed.) QX4646	Yr.Iss.	1990	10.75	100
1990 Seven Swans A-Swimming (7th Ed.) QX3033	Yr.Iss.	1990	6.75	20-33
1990 Winter Surprise (2nd Ed.) QX4443	Yr.Iss.	1990	10.75	19-30

1990 Holiday Traditions - Keepsake

YEAR ISSUE	EDITION LIMIT	YEAR RETD.	ISSUE PRICE	*QUOTE U.S.$
1990 Spencer Sparrow, Esq. QX431-2	Yr.Iss.	1990	6.75	15
1990 Stocking Kitten QX456-5	Yr.Iss.	1990	6.75	11-15

1990 Keepsake Collector's Club - Keepsake

YEAR ISSUE	EDITION LIMIT	YEAR RETD.	ISSUE PRICE	*QUOTE U.S.$
1990 Armful of Joy QXC445-3	Yr.Iss.	1990	8.00	41-45
1990 Christmas Limited 1975 QXC476-6	38,700	1990	19.75	95-125
1990 Club Hollow QXC445-6	Yr.Iss.	1990	Unkn.	35-40
1990 Crown Prince QXC560-3	Yr.Iss.	1990	Unkn.	16-40
1990 Dove of Peace QXC447-6	25,400	1990	24.75	49-75
1990 Sugar Plum Fairy QXC447-3	25,400	1990	27.75	50-60

1990 Keepsake Magic Ornaments - Keepsake

YEAR ISSUE	EDITION LIMIT	YEAR RETD.	ISSUE PRICE	*QUOTE U.S.$
1990 Baby's First Christmas QLX7246	Yr.Iss.	1990	28.00	49-55
1990 Beary Short Nap QLX7326	Yr.Iss.	1990	10.00	23-33
1990 Blessings of Love QLX7363	Yr.Iss.	1990	14.00	44-50
1990 Children's Express QLX7243	Yr.Iss.	1990	28.00	66-85
1990 Chris Mouse Wreath QLX7296	Yr.Iss.	1990	10.00	31-50
1990 Christmas Memories QLX7276	Yr.Iss.	1990	25.00	47
1990 Deer Crossing QLX7213	Yr.Iss.	1990	18.00	41-50
1990 Elf of the Year QLX7356	Yr.Iss.	1990	10.00	16-25
1990 Elfin Whittler QLX7265	Yr.Iss.	1990	20.00	37-55
1990 Forest Frolics QLX7236	Yr.Iss.	1990	25.00	55
1990 Holiday Flash QLX7333	Yr.Iss.	1990	18.00	28-40
1990 Hop 'N Pop Popper QLX7353	Yr.Iss.	1990	20.00	87-95
1990 Letter to Santa QLX7226	Yr.Iss.	1990	14.00	28-40
1990 The Littlest Angel QLX7303	Yr.Iss.	1990	14.00	30-50
1990 Mrs. Santa's Kitchen QLX7263	Yr.Iss.	1990	25.00	52-90
1990 Our First Christmas Together QLX7255	Yr.Iss.	1990	18.00	30-50
1990 Partridges in a Pear QLX7212	Yr.Iss.	1990	14.00	28-35
1990 Santa's Ho-Ho-Hoedown QLX7256	Yr.Iss.	1990	25.00	90
1990 Song and Dance QLX7253	Yr.Iss.	1990	20.00	59-95
1990 Starlight Angel QLX7306	Yr.Iss.	1990	14.00	27-38
1990 Starship Christmas QLX7336	Yr.Iss.	1990	18.00	36-55

1990 Keepsake Miniature Ornaments - Keepsake

YEAR ISSUE	EDITION LIMIT	YEAR RETD.	ISSUE PRICE	*QUOTE U.S.$
1990 Acorn Wreath QXM5686	Yr.Iss.	1990	6.00	9-12
1990 Air Santa QXM5656	Yr.Iss.	1990	4.50	9
1990 Baby's First Christmas QXM5703	Yr.Iss.	1990	8.50	10-20
1990 Basket Buddy QXM5696	Yr.Iss.	1990	6.00	9-12
1990 Bear Hug QXM5633	Yr.Iss.	1990	6.00	10-14
1990 Brass Bouquet 600QMX5776	Yr.Iss.	1990	6.00	7
1990 Brass Horn QXM5793	Yr.Iss.	1990	3.00	7-10
1990 Brass Peace QXM5796	Yr.Iss.	1990	3.00	7-10
1990 Brass Santa QXM5786	Yr.Iss.	1990	3.00	6
1990 Brass Year QXM5833	Yr.Iss.	1990	3.00	8
1990 Busy Carver QXM5673	Yr.Iss.	1990	4.50	10
1990 Christmas Dove QXM5636	Yr.Iss.	1990	4.50	12-15
1990 Cloisonne Poinsettia QMX5533	Yr.Iss.	1990	10.75	20
1990 Coal Car QXM5756	Yr.Iss.	1990	8.50	20-30
1990 Country Heart QXM5693	Yr.Iss.	1990	4.50	10
1990 First Christmas Together QXM5536	Yr.Iss.	1990	6.00	11
1990 Going Sledding QXM5683	Yr.Iss.	1990	4.50	11
1990 Grandchild's First Christmas QXM5723	Yr.Iss.	1990	6.00	10-12
1990 Holiday Cardinal QXM5526	Yr.Iss.	1990	3.00	10
1990 Kittens in Toyland QXM5736	Yr.Iss.	1990	4.50	16-20
1990 The Kringles (2nd Ed.) QXM5753	Yr.Iss.	1990	6.00	24-30
1990 Lion and Lamb QXM5676	Yr.Iss.	1990	4.50	7-10
1990 Loving Hearts QXM5523	Yr.Iss.	1990	3.00	8
1990 Madonna and Child QXM5643	Yr.Iss.	1990	6.00	10-12
1990 Mother QXM5716	Yr.Iss.	1990	4.50	12-18
1990 Nativity QXM5706	Yr.Iss.	1990	4.50	13-20
1990 Nature's Angels QMX5733	Yr.Iss.	1990	4.50	26-28
1990 Panda's Surprise QXM5616	Yr.Iss.	1990	4.50	11-13
1990 Penguin Pal QXM5746	Yr.Iss.	1990	4.50	14-20
1990 Perfect Fit QXM5516	Yr.Iss.	1990	4.50	9-14
1990 Puppy Love QXM5666	Yr.Iss.	1990	6.00	13-15
1990 Rocking Horse QXM5743	Yr.Iss.	1990	4.50	25
1990 Ruby Reindeer QXM5816	Yr.Iss.	1990	6.00	10-12
1990 Santa's Journey QXM5826	Yr.Iss.	1990	8.50	20-25
1990 Santa's Streetcar QXM5766	Yr.Iss.	1990	8.50	13-20
1990 School QXM5763	Yr.Iss.	1990	8.50	16-25
1990 Snow Angel QXM5773	Yr.Iss.	1990	6.00	11
1990 Special Friends QXM5726	Yr.Iss.	1990	6.00	11-13
1990 Stamp Collector QXM5623	Yr.Iss.	1990	4.50	9
1990 Stringing Along QXM5606	Yr.Iss.	1990	8.50	15-18
1990 Sweet Slumber QXM5663	Yr.Iss.	1990	4.50	10-15
1990 Teacher QXM5653	Yr.Iss.	1990	4.50	8-10
1990 Thimble Bells QXM5543	Yr.Iss.	1990	6.00	19-28
1990 Type of Joy QXM5646	Yr.Iss.	1990	4.50	7-9
1990 Warm Memories QXM5713	Yr.Iss.	1990	4.50	9-11
1990 Wee Nutcracker QXM5843	Yr.Iss.	1990	8.50	15

1990 New Attractions - Keepsake

YEAR ISSUE	EDITION LIMIT	YEAR RETD.	ISSUE PRICE	*QUOTE U.S.$
1990 Baby Unicorn QX5486	Yr.Iss.	1990	9.75	12-25
1990 Bearback Rider QX5483	Yr.Iss.	1990	9.75	17-32
1990 Beary Good Deal QX4733	Yr.Iss.	1990	6.75	11
1990 Billboard Bunny QX5196	Yr.Iss.	1990	7.75	13-24
1990 Born to Dance QX5043	Yr.Iss.	1990	7.75	15-25
1990 Chiming In QX4366	Yr.Iss.	1990	9.75	20-25
1990 Christmas Croc QX4373	Yr.Iss.	1990	7.75	13-25
1990 Christmas Partridge QX5246	Yr.Iss.	1990	7.75	13-23
1990 Claus Construction QX4885	Yr.Iss.	1990	7.75	15-20
1990 Country Angel QX5046	Yr.Iss.	1990	6.75	195
1990 Coyote Carols QX4993	Yr.Iss.	1990	8.75	17-30
1990 Cozy Goose QX4966	Yr.Iss.	1990	5.75	15
1990 Feliz Navidad QX5173	Yr.Iss.	1990	6.75	15-20
1990 Garfield QX2303	Yr.Iss.	1990	4.75	13-25
1990 Gingerbread Elf QX5033	Yr.Iss.	1990	5.75	14-20
1990 Goose Cart QX5236	Yr.Iss.	1990	7.75	15
1990 Hang in There QX4713	Yr.Iss.	1990	6.75	15-23
1990 Happy Voices QX4645	Yr.Iss.	1990	6.75	15
1990 Holiday Cardinals QX5243	Yr.Iss.	1990	7.75	23
1990 Home for the Owlidays QX5183	Yr.Iss.	1990	6.75	11-18
1990 Hot Dogger QX4976	Yr.Iss.	1990	7.75	14-20
1990 Jolly Dolphin QX4683	Yr.Iss.	1990	6.75	16-20
1990 Joy is in the Air QX5503	Yr.Iss.	1990	7.75	20-25
1990 King Klaus QX4106	Yr.Iss.	1990	7.75	13-23
1990 Kitty's Best Pal QX4716	Yr.Iss.	1990	6.75	15-25
1990 Little Drummer Boy QX5233	Yr.Iss.	1990	7.75	19-25
1990 Long Winter's Nap QX4703	Yr.Iss.	1990	6.75	15-25
1990 Lovable Dears QX5476	Yr.Iss.	1990	8.75	14-19
1990 Meow Mart QX4446	Yr.Iss.	1990	7.75	16-30
1990 Mooy Christmas QX4933	Yr.Iss.	1990	6.75	25-33
1990 Norman Rockwell Art QX2296	Yr.Iss.	1990	4.75	25
1990 Nutshell Chat QX5193	Yr.Iss.	1990	6.75	14-30
1990 Nutshell Holiday QX465-2	Yr.Iss.	1990	5.75	17-28
1990 Peanuts QX2233	Yr.Iss.	1990	4.75	15-30
1990 Pepperoni Mouse QX4973	Yr.Iss.	1990	6.75	14-23
1990 Perfect Catch QX4693	Yr.Iss.	1990	7.75	12-20
1990 Polar Jogger QX4666	Yr.Iss.	1990	5.75	9-20
1990 Polar Pair QX4626	Yr.Iss.	1990	5.75	15-30
1990 Polar Sport QX5156	Yr.Iss.	1990	7.75	12-25
1990 Polar TV QX5166	Yr.Iss.	1990	7.75	12-20
1990 Polar V.I.P. QX4663	Yr.Iss.	1990	5.75	12-20
1990 Polar Video QX4633	Yr.Iss.	1990	5.75	9-20
1990 Poolside Walrus QX4986	Yr.Iss.	1990	7.75	13-27
1990 S. Claus Taxi QX4686	Yr.Iss.	1990	11.75	25-35
1990 Santa Schnoz QX4983	Yr.Iss.	1990	6.75	40
1990 Snoopy and Woodstock QX4723	Yr.Iss.	1990	6.75	26-41
1990 Spoon Rider QX5496	Yr.Iss.	1990	9.75	14-20
1990 Stitches of Joy QX5186	Yr.Iss.	1990	7.75	25-30
1990 Stocking Kitten QX456-5	Yr.Iss.	1990	6.75	7
1990 Stocking Pals QX5493	Yr.Iss.	1990	10.75	19-25
1990 Three Little Piggies QX4996	Yr.Iss.	1990	7.75	15-30
1990 Two Peas in a Pod QX4926	Yr.Iss.	1990	4.75	25-35

1990 Special Edition - Keepsake

YEAR ISSUE	EDITION LIMIT	YEAR RETD.	ISSUE PRICE	*QUOTE U.S.$
1990 Dickens Caroler Bell -Mr. Ashbourne QX5056	Yr.Iss.	1990	21.75	35-55

1991 Artists' Favorites - Keepsake

YEAR ISSUE	EDITION LIMIT	YEAR RETD.	ISSUE PRICE	*QUOTE U.S.$
1991 Fiddlin' Around QX4387	Yr.Iss.	1991	7.75	16-20
1991 Hooked on Santa QX4109	Yr.Iss.	1991	7.75	19-25
1991 Noah's Ark QX4867	Yr.Iss.	1991	13.75	27-42
1991 Polar Circus Wagon QX4399	Yr.Iss.	1991	13.75	25-30
1991 Santa Sailor QX4389	Yr.Iss.	1991	9.75	18-27
1991 Tramp and Laddie QX4397	Yr.Iss.	1991	7.75	20-40

1991 Club Limited Editions - Keepsake

YEAR ISSUE	EDITION LIMIT	YEAR RETD.	ISSUE PRICE	*QUOTE U.S.$
1991 Galloping Into Christmas QXC4779	28,400	1991	19.75	100
1991 Secrets for Santa QXC4797	28,700	1991	23.75	48

1991 Collectible Series - Keepsake

YEAR ISSUE	EDITION LIMIT	YEAR RETD.	ISSUE PRICE	*QUOTE U.S.$
1991 1957 Corvette (1st Ed.) QX4319	Yr.Iss.	1991	12.75	175
1991 Betsey Clark: Home for Christmas (6th Ed.) QX2109	Yr.Iss.	1991	5.00	20-30
1991 Checking His List (6th Ed.) QX4339	Yr.Iss.	1991	13.75	35-49
1991 Christmas Kitty (3rd Ed.) QX4377	Yr.Iss.	1991	14.75	27
1991 CRAYOLA CRAYON-Bright Vibrant Carols (3rd Ed.) QX4219	Yr.Iss.	1991	9.75	28-65
1991 Eight Maids A-Milking (8th Ed.) QX3089	Yr.Iss.	1991	6.75	18-30
1991 Fabulous Decade (2nd Ed.) QX4119	Yr.Iss.	1991	7.75	30
1991 Fire Station (8th Ed.) QX4139	Yr.Iss.	1991	14.75	44-62
1991 Frosty Friends (12th Ed.) QX4327	Yr.Iss.	1991	9.75	30-38
1991 The Gift Bringers-Christkind (3rd Ed.) QX2117	Yr.Iss.	1991	5.00	25
1991 Greatest Story (2nd Ed.) QX4129	Yr.Iss.	1991	12.75	24
1991 Hark! It's Herald (3rd Ed.) QX4379	Yr.Iss.	1991	6.75	19-24
1991 Heart of Christmas (2nd Ed.) QX4357	Yr.Iss.	1991	13.75	27-38
1991 Heavenly Angels (1st Ed.) QX4367	Yr.Iss.	1991	7.75	30-38
1991 Let It Snow! (5th Ed.) QX4369	Yr.Iss.	1991	8.75	19-35
1991 Mary's Angels-Iris (4th Ed.) QX4279	Yr.Iss.	1991	6.75	29-55
1991 Merry Olde Santa (2nd Ed.) QX4359	Yr.Iss.	1991	14.75	85-95
1991 Peace on Earth-Italy (1st Ed.) QX5129	Yr.Iss.	1991	11.75	30-50
1991 Puppy Love (1st Ed.) QX5379	Yr.Iss.	1991	7.75	54-60
1991 Reindeer Champ-Cupid (6th Ed.) QX4347	Yr.Iss.	1991	7.75	20-31
1991 Rocking Horse (11th Ed.) QX4147	Yr.Iss.	1991	10.75	31-40
1991 Santa's Antique Car (13th Ed.) QX4349	Yr.Iss.	1991	14.75	38-45
1991 Winter Surprise (3rd Ed.) QX4277	Yr.Iss.	1991	10.75	27-35

1991 Keepsake Collector's Club - Keepsake

YEAR ISSUE	EDITION LIMIT	YEAR RETD.	ISSUE PRICE	*QUOTE U.S.$
1991 Beary Artistic QXC7259	Yr.Iss.	1991	10.00	32-40
1991 Hidden Treasure/Li'l Keeper QXC4769	Yr.Iss.	1991	15.00	36-40

1991 Keepsake Magic Ornaments - Keepsake

YEAR ISSUE	EDITION LIMIT	YEAR RETD.	ISSUE PRICE	*QUOTE U.S.$
1991 Angel of Light QLT7239	Yr.Iss.	1991	30.00	60
1991 Arctic Dome QLX7117	Yr.Iss.	1991	25.00	46-55
1991 Baby's First Christmas QLX7247	Yr.Iss.	1991	30.00	85-90
1991 Bringing Home the Tree-QLX7249	Yr.Iss.	1991	28.00	51-65
1991 Chris Mouse Mail QLX7207	Yr.Iss.	1991	10.00	25-40
1991 Elfin Engineer QLX7209	Yr.Iss.	1991	10.00	25
1991 Father Christmas QLX7147	Yr.Iss.	1991	14.00	29-40
1991 Festive Brass Church QLX7179	Yr.Iss.	1991	14.00	33
1991 Forest Frolics QLX7219	Yr.Iss.	1991	25.00	70
1991 Friendship Tree QLX7169	Yr.Iss.	1991	10.00	24
1991 Holiday Glow QLX7177	Yr.Iss.	1991	14.00	30
1991 It's A Wonderful Life QLX7237	Yr.Iss.	1991	20.00	65-75
1991 Jingle Bears QLX7323	Yr.Iss.	1991	25.00	45-58
1991 Kringles's Bumper Cars-QLX7119	Yr.Iss.	1991	25.00	47-55
1991 Mole Family Home QLX7149	Yr.Iss.	1991	20.00	37-50
1991 Our First Christmas Together QXL7137	Yr.Iss.	1991	25.00	49-60
1991 PEANUTS QLX7229	Yr.Iss.	1991	18.00	38-65
1991 Salvation Army Band QLX7273	Yr.Iss.	1991	30.00	80
1991 Santa Special QLX7167	Yr.Iss.	1992	40.00	54-80
1991 Santa's Hot Line QLX7159	Yr.Iss.	1991	18.00	33
1991 Ski Trip QLX7266	Yr.Iss.	1991	28.00	50-60
1991 Sparkling Angel QLX7157	Yr.Iss.	1991	18.00	27-38
1991 Toyland Tower QLX7129	Yr.Iss.	1991	20.00	37-45

1991 Keepsake Miniature Ornaments - Keepsake

YEAR ISSUE	EDITION LIMIT	YEAR RETD.	ISSUE PRICE	*QUOTE U.S.$
1991 All Aboard QXM5869	Yr.Iss.	1991	4.50	18
1991 Baby's First Christmas QXM5799	Yr.Iss.	1991	6.00	17-23
1991 Brass Church QXM5979	Yr.Iss.	1991	3.00	10
1991 Brass Soldier QXM5987	Yr.Iss.	1991	3.00	10
1991 Bright Boxers QXM5877	Yr.Iss.	1991	4.50	6-17
1991 Busy Bear QXM5939	Yr.Iss.	1991	4.50	13
1991 Cardinal Cameo QXM5957	Yr.Iss.	1991	6.00	18
1991 Caring Shepherd QXM5949	Yr.Iss.	1991	6.00	18
1991 Cool 'n' Sweet QXM5867	Yr.Iss.	1991	4.50	24
1991 Country Sleigh QXM5999	Yr.Iss.	1991	4.50	6-14
1991 Courier Turtle QXM5857	Yr.Iss.	1991	4.50	15
1991 Fancy Wreath QXM5917	Yr.Iss.	1991	4.50	6-14
1991 Feliz Navidad QXM5887	Yr.Iss.	1991	6.00	14
1991 Fly By QXM5859	Yr.Iss.	1991	4.50	18
1991 Friendly Fawn QXM5947	Yr.Iss.	1991	6.00	17
1991 Grandchild's First Christmas QXM5697	Yr.Iss.	1991	4.50	14
1991 Heavenly Minstrel QXM5687	Yr.Iss.	1991	9.75	21-30
1991 Holiday Snowflake QXM5997	Yr.Iss.	1991	3.00	13
1991 Inn (4th Ed.) QXM5627	Yr.Iss.	1991	8.50	22-30
1991 Key to Love QXM5689	Yr.Iss.	1991	4.50	17
1991 Kittens in Toyland (4th Ed.) QXM5639	Yr.Iss.	1991	4.50	14-20
1991 Kitty in a Mitty QXM5879	Yr.Iss.	1991	4.50	14
1991 The Kringles (3rd Ed.) QXM5647	Yr.Iss.	1991	6.00	20-25
1991 Li'l Popper QXM5897	Yr.Iss.	1991	4.50	18
1991 Love Is Born QXM5959	Yr.Iss.	1991	6.00	19
1991 Lulu & Family QXM5677	Yr.Iss.	1991	6.00	21
1991 Mom QXM5699	Yr.Iss.	1991	6.00	18
1991 N. Pole Buddy QXM5927	Yr.Iss.	1991	4.50	19
1991 Nature's Angels (2nd Ed.) QXM5657	Yr.Iss.	1991	4.50	20
1991 Noel QXM5989	Yr.Iss.	1991	3.00	13
1991 Our First Christmas Together QXM5819	Yr.Iss.	1991	6.00	18
1991 Passenger Car (3rd Ed.) QXM5649	Yr.Iss.	1991	8.50	25-50
1991 Penguin Pal (4th Ed.) QXM5629	Yr.Iss.	1991	4.50	17
1991 Ring-A-Ding Elf QXM5669	Yr.Iss.	1991	8.50	19
1991 Rocking Horse (4th Ed.) QXM5637	Yr.Iss.	1991	4.50	24-30
1991 Seaside Otter QXM5909	Yr.Iss.	1991	4.50	13
1991 Silvery Santa QXM5679	Yr.Iss.	1991	9.75	22
1991 Special Friends QXM5797	Yr.Iss.	1991	8.50	19
1991 Thimble Bells (2nd Ed.) QXM5659	Yr.Iss.	1991	6.00	10-23
1991 Tiny Tea Party (set/6) QXM5827	Yr.Iss.	1991	29.00	143-175
1991 Top Hatter QXM5889	Yr.Iss.	1991	6.00	7-17
1991 Treeland Trio QXM5899	Yr.Iss.	1991	8.50	17
1991 Upbeat Bear QXM5907	Yr.Iss.	1991	6.00	16
1991 Vision of Santa QXM5937	Yr.Iss.	1991	4.50	14
1991 Wee Toymaker QXM5967	Yr.Iss.	1991	8.50	15
1991 Woodland Babies QXM5667	Yr.Iss.	1991	6.00	12-25

1991 New Attractions - Keepsake

YEAR ISSUE	EDITION LIMIT	YEAR RETD.	ISSUE PRICE	*QUOTE U.S.$
1991 All-Star QX5329	Yr.Iss.	1991	6.75	17-23
1991 Basket Bell Players QX5377	Yr.Iss.	1991	7.75	21-28
1991 Bob Cratchit QX4997	Yr.Iss.	1991	13.75	22-35
1991 Chilly Chap QX5339	Yr.Iss.	1991	6.75	18
1991 Christmas Welcome QX5299	Yr.Iss.	1991	9.75	21
1991 Christopher Robin QX5579	Yr.Iss.	1991	9.75	40-45
1991 Cuddly Lamb QX5199	Yr.Iss.	1991	6.75	20
1991 Dinoclaus QX5277	Yr.Iss.	1991	7.75	16-23
1991 Ebenezer Scrooge QX4989	Yr.Iss.	1991	13.75	27-45
1991 Evergreen Inn QX5389	Yr.Iss.	1991	8.75	15
1991 Fanfare Bear QX5337	Yr.Iss.	1991	8.75	19
1991 Feliz Navidad QX5279	Yr.Iss.	1991	6.75	12-25
1991 Folk Art Reindeer QX5359	Yr.Iss.	1991	8.75	14-20
1991 GARFIELD QX5177	Yr.Iss.	1991	7.75	29
1991 Glee Club Bears QX4969	Yr.Iss.	1991	8.75	19
1991 Holiday Cafe QX5399	Yr.Iss.	1991	8.75	14
1991 Jolly Wolly Santa QX5419	Yr.Iss.	1991	7.75	20-30
1991 Jolly Wolly Snowman QX5427	Yr.Iss.	1991	7.75	20
1991 Jolly Wolly Soldier QX5429	Yr.Iss.	1991	7.75	20-23
1991 Joyous Memories-Photoholder QX5369	Yr.Iss.	1991	6.75	16-28
1991 Kanga and Roo QX5617	Yr.Iss.	1991	9.75	40-45
1991 Look Out Below QX4959	Yr.Iss.	1991	8.75	19

*Quotes have been rounded up to nearest dollar

YEAR ISSUE	EDITION LIMIT	YEAR RETD.	ISSUE PRICE	*QUOTE U.S.$
1991 Loving Stitches QX4987	Yr.Iss.	1991	8.75	29
1991 Mary Engelbreit QX2237	Yr.Iss.	1991	4.75	27
1991 Merry Carolers QX4799	Yr.Iss.	1991	29.75	95
1991 Mrs. Cratchit QX4999	Yr.Iss.	1991	13.75	28
1991 Night Before Christmas QX5307	Yr.Iss.	1991	9.75	21
1991 Norman Rockwell Art QX2259	Yr.Iss.	1991	5.00	30
1991 Notes of Cheer QX5357	Yr.Iss.	1991	5.75	15
1991 Nutshell Nativity QX5176	Yr.Iss.	1991	6.75	18-27
1991 Nutty Squirrel QX4833	Yr.Iss.	1991	5.75	14
1991 Old-Fashioned Sled QX4317	Yr.Iss.	1991	8.75	16
1991 On a Roll QX5347	Yr.Iss.	1991	6.75	16-22
1991 Partridge in a Pear Tree QX5297	Yr.Iss.	1991	9.75	19
1991 PEANUTS QX2257	Yr.Iss.	1991	5.00	13-25
1991 Piglet and Eeyore QX5577	Yr.Iss.	1991	9.75	45-50
1991 Plum Delightful QX4977	Yr.Iss.	1991	8.75	19
1991 Polar Classic QX5287	Yr.Iss.	1991	6.75	17-23
1991 Rabbit QX5607	Yr.Iss.	1991	9.75	25-33
1991 Santa's Studio QX5397	Yr.Iss.	1991	8.75	20
1991 Ski Lift Bunny QX5447	Yr.Iss.	1991	6.75	14-23
1991 Snoopy and Woodstock QX5197	Yr.Iss.	1991	6.75	25-35
1991 Snow Twins QX4979	Yr.Iss.	1991	8.75	20
1991 Snowy Owl QX5269	Yr.Iss.	1991	7.75	19
1991 Sweet Talk QX5367	Yr.Iss.	1991	8.75	18-25
1991 Tigger QX5609	Yr.Iss.	1991	9.75	95-105
1991 Tiny Tim QX5037	Yr.Iss.	1991	10.75	24-40
1991 Up 'N'Down Journey QX5047	Yr.Iss.	1991	9.75	28
1991 Winnie-the Pooh QX5569	Yr.Iss.	1991	9.75	50-55
1991 Yule Logger QX4967	Yr.Iss.	1991	8.75	18-27

1991 Special Edition - Keepsake

YEAR ISSUE	EDITION LIMIT	YEAR RETD.	ISSUE PRICE	*QUOTE U.S.$
1991 Dickens Caroler Bell-Mrs. Beaumont QX5039	Yr.Iss.	1991	21.75	40-50
1991 Starship Enterprise QLX7199	Yr.Iss.	1991	20.00	244-510

1992 Artists' Favorites - Keepsake

YEAR ISSUE	EDITION LIMIT	YEAR RETD.	ISSUE PRICE	*QUOTE U.S.$
1992 Elfin Marionette QX5931	Yr.Iss.	1992	11.75	22
1992 Mother Goose QX4984	Yr.Iss.	1992	13.75	18-27
1992 Polar Post QX4914	Yr.Iss.	1992	8.75	19
1992 Stocked With Joy QX5934	Yr.Iss.	1992	7.75	17-23
1992 Turtle Dreams QX4991	Yr.Iss.	1992	8.75	20-28
1992 Uncle Art's Ice Cream QX5001	Yr.Iss.	1992	8.75	22-30

1992 Collectible Series - Keepsake

YEAR ISSUE	EDITION LIMIT	YEAR RETD.	ISSUE PRICE	*QUOTE U.S.$
1992 1966 Mustang (2nd Ed.) QX4284	Yr.Iss.	1992	12.75	25-55
1992 Betsey's Country Christmas (1st Ed.) QX2104	Yr.Iss.	1992	5.00	24-30
1992 CRAYOLA CRAYON-Bright Colors (4th Ed.) QX4264	Yr.Iss.	1992	9.75	25-32
1992 Fabulous Decade (3rd Ed.) QX4244	Yr.Iss.	1992	7.75	35-40
1992 Five-and-Ten-Cent Store (9th Ed.) QX4254	Yr.Iss.	1992	14.75	28-38
1992 Frosty Friends (13th Ed.) QX4291	Yr.Iss.	1992	9.75	25-35
1992 The Gift Bringers-Kolyada (4th Ed.) QX2124	Yr.Iss.	1992	5.00	14-23
1992 Gift Exchange (7th Ed.) QX4294	Yr.Iss.	1992	14.75	30-45
1992 Greatest Story (3rd Ed.) QX4251	Yr.Iss.	1992	12.75	25
1992 Hark! It's Herald (4th Ed.) QX4464	Yr.Iss.	1992	7.75	18-25
1992 Heart of Christmas (3rd Ed.) QX4411	Yr.Iss.	1992	13.75	26-31
1992 Heavenly Angels (2nd Ed.) QX4454	Yr.Iss.	1992	7.75	19-33
1992 Kringle Tours (14th Ed.) QX4341	Yr.Iss.	1992	14.75	28-45
1992 Mary's Angels-Lily (5th Ed.) QX4274	Yr.Iss.	1992	6.75	45-50
1992 Merry Olde Santa (3rd Ed.) QX4414	Yr.Iss.	1992	14.75	34-55
1992 Nine Ladies Dancing (9th Ed.) QX3031	Yr.Iss.	1992	6.75	18-25
1992 Owliver (1st Ed.) QX4544	Yr.Iss.	1992	7.75	16-20
1992 Peace On Earth-Spain (2nd Ed.) QX5174	Yr.Iss.	1992	11.75	21
1992 Puppy Love (2nd Ed.) QX4484	Yr.Iss.	1992	7.75	41-45
1992 Reindeer Champs-Donder (7th Ed.) QX5284	Yr.Iss.	1992	8.75	26-35
1992 Rocking Horse (12th Ed.) QX4261	Yr.Iss.	1992	10.75	25-45
1992 Sweet Holiday Harmony (6th Ed.) QX4461	Yr.Iss.	1992	8.75	19-35
1992 Tobin Fraley Carousel (1st Ed.) QX4891	Yr.Iss.	1992	28.00	30-75
1992 Winter Surprise (4th Ed.) QX4271	Yr.Iss.	1992	11.75	24-33

1992 Collectors' Club - Keepsake

YEAR ISSUE	EDITION LIMIT	YEAR RETD.	ISSUE PRICE	*QUOTE U.S.$
1992 Chipmunk Parcel Service QXC5194	Yr.Iss.	1992	6.75	23
1992 Rodney Takes Flight QXC5081	Yr.Iss.	1992	9.75	23
1992 Santa's Club List QXC7291	Yr.Iss.	1992	15.00	36-40

1992 Easter Ornaments - Keepsake

YEAR ISSUE	EDITION LIMIT	YEAR RETD.	ISSUE PRICE	*QUOTE U.S.$
1992 Easter Parade (1st Ed.) 675QEO8301	Yr.Iss.	1992	6.75	30
1992 Egg in Sports (1st Ed.) 675QEO9341	Yr.Iss.	1992	6.75	20-35

1992 Limited Edition Ornaments - Keepsake

YEAR ISSUE	EDITION LIMIT	YEAR RETD.	ISSUE PRICE	*QUOTE U.S.$
1992 Christmas Treasures QXC5464	15,500	1992	22.00	123
1992 Victorian Skater (w/ base) QXC4067	14,700	1992	25.00	75

1992 Magic Ornaments - Keepsake

YEAR ISSUE	EDITION LIMIT	YEAR RETD.	ISSUE PRICE	*QUOTE U.S.$
1992 Angel Of Light QLT7239	Yr.Iss.	1992	30.00	30
1992 Baby's First Christmas QLX7281	Yr.Iss.	1992	22.00	90
1992 Chris Mouse Tales (8th Ed.) QLX7074	Yr.Iss.	1992	12.00	25-30
1992 Christmas Parade QLX7271	Yr.Iss.	1992	30.00	54-60
1992 Continental Express QLX7264	Yr.Iss.	1992	32.00	60-75
1992 The Dancing Nutcracker QLX7261	Yr.Iss.	1992	30.00	54-60
1992 Enchanted Clock QLX7274	Yr.Iss.	1992	30.00	60
1992 Feathered Friends QLX7091	Yr.Iss.	1992	14.00	28
1992 Forest Frolics (4th Ed.) QLX7254	Yr.Iss.	1992	28.00	60-65
1992 Good Sledding Ahead QLX7244	Yr.Iss.	1992	28.00	53-58
1992 Lighting the Way QLX7231	Yr.Iss.	1992	18.00	39-50
1992 Look! It's Santa QLX7094	Yr.Iss.	1992	14.00	30-50
1992 Nut Sweet Nut QLX7081	Yr.Iss.	1992	10.00	21
1992 Out First Christmas Together QLX7221	Yr.Iss.	1992	20.00	39-45
1992 PEANUTS (2nd Ed.) QLX7214	Yr.Iss.	1992	18.00	45-48
1992 Santa Special QLX7167	Yr.Iss.	1992	40.00	80
1992 Santa Sub QLX7321	Yr.Iss.	1992	18.00	34-40
1992 Santa's Answering Machine QLX7241	Yr.Iss.	1992	22.00	15-41
1992 Under Construction QLX7324	Yr.Iss.	1992	18.00	36-43
1992 Watch Owls QLX7084	Yr.Iss.	1992	12.00	24-30
1992 Yuletide Rider QLX7314	Yr.Iss.	1992	28.00	53-60

1992 Miniature Ornaments - Keepsake

YEAR ISSUE	EDITION LIMIT	YEAR RETD.	ISSUE PRICE	*QUOTE U.S.$
1992 A+ Teacher QXM5511	Yr.Iss.	1992	3.75	8
1992 Angelic Harpist QXM5524	Yr.Iss.	1992	4.50	15
1992 Baby's First Christmas QXM5494	Yr.Iss.	1992	4.50	17
1992 The Bearymores(1st Ed.) QXM5544	Yr.Iss.	1992	5.75	18-23
1992 Black-Capped Chickadee QXM5484	Yr.Iss.	1992	3.00	15
1992 Box Car (4th Ed.) Noel R.R. QXM5441	Yr.Iss.	1992	7.00	22-30
1992 Bright Stringers QXM5841	Yr.Iss.	1992	3.75	15
1992 Buck-A-Roo QXM5814	Yr.Iss.	1992	4.50	6-10
1992 Christmas Bonus QXM5811	Yr.Iss.	1992	3.00	5-9
1992 Christmas Copter QXM5844	Yr.Iss.	1992	5.75	15
1992 Church (5th Ed.) Old English V. QXM5384	Yr.Iss.	1992	7.00	22-30
1992 Coca-Cola Santa QXM5884	Yr.Iss.	1992	5.75	7-18
1992 Cool Uncle Sam QXM5561	Yr.Iss.	1992	3.00	14
1992 Cozy Kayak QXM5551	Yr.Iss.	1992	3.75	14
1992 Fast Finish QXM5301	Yr.Iss.	1992	3.75	13
1992 Feeding Time QXM5481	Yr.Iss.	1992	5.75	15
1992 Friendly Tin Soldier QXM5874	Yr.Iss.	1992	4.50	14
1992 Friends Are Tops QXM5521	Yr.Iss.	1992	4.50	9
1992 Gerbil Inc. QXM5924	Yr.Iss.	1992	3.75	11
1992 Going Places QXM5871	Yr.Iss.	1992	3.75	10
1992 Grandchild's First Christmas QXM5501	Yr.Iss.	1992	5.75	12
1992 Grandma QXM5514	Yr.Iss.	1992	4.50	5-15
1992 Harmony Trio-Set/3 QXM5471	Yr.Iss.	1992	11.75	12-21
1992 Hickory, Dickory, Dock QXM5861	Yr.Iss.	1992	3.75	13
1992 Holiday Holly QXM5364	Yr.Iss.	1992	9.75	21
1992 Holiday Splash QXM5834	Yr.Iss.	1992	5.75	13
1992 Hoop It Up QXM5831	Yr.Iss.	1992	4.50	12
1992 Inside Story QXM5881	Yr.Iss.	1992	7.25	19
1992 Kittens in Toyland (5th Ed.) QXM5391	Yr.Iss.	1992	4.50	14
1992 The Kringles (4th Ed.) QXM5381	Yr.Iss.	1992	6.00	16-23
1992 Little Town of Bethlehem QXM5864	Yr.Iss.	1992	3.00	19
1992 Minted For Santa QXM5854	Yr.Iss.	1992	3.75	15
1992 Mom QXM5504	Yr.Iss.	1992	4.50	12
1992 Nature's Angels (3rd Ed.) QXM5451	Yr.Iss.	1992	4.50	19
1992 The Night Before Christmas QXM5541	Yr.Iss.	1992	13.75	28-35
1992 Perfect Balance QXM5571	Yr.Iss.	1992	3.00	13
1992 Polar Polka QXM5534	Yr.Iss.	1992	4.50	15
1992 Puppet Show QXM5574	Yr.Iss.	1992	3.00	13
1992 Rocking Horse (5th Ed.) QXM5454	Yr.Iss.	1992	4.50	10-17
1992 Sew Sew Tiny (set/6) QXM5794	Yr.Iss.	1992	29.00	45-65
1992 Ski For Two QXM5821	Yr.Iss.	1992	4.50	15
1992 Snowshoe Bunny QXM5564	Yr.Iss.	1992	3.75	13
1992 Snug Kitty QXM5554	Yr.Iss.	1992	3.75	14
1992 Spunky Monkey QXM5921	Yr.Iss.	1992	3.00	15
1992 Thimble Bells (3rd Ed.) QXM5461	Yr.Iss.	1992	6.00	18-23
1992 Visions Of Acorns QXM5851	Yr.Iss.	1992	4.50	15
1992 Wee Three Kings QXM5531	Yr.Iss.	1992	5.75	16
1992 Woodland Babies (2nd Ed.) QXM5444	Yr.Iss.	1992	6.00	15

1992 New Attractions - Keepsake

YEAR ISSUE	EDITION LIMIT	YEAR RETD.	ISSUE PRICE	*QUOTE U.S.$
1992 Bear Bell Champ QX5071	Yr.Iss.	1992	7.75	16-30
1992 Caboose QX5321	Yr.Iss.	1992	9.75	18-25
1992 Cheerful Santa QX5154	Yr.Iss.	1992	9.75	25-28
1992 Coal Car QX5401	Yr.Iss.	1992	9.75	20
1992 Cool Fliers QX5474	Yr.Iss.	1992	10.75	20-25
1992 Deck the Hogs QX5204	Yr.Iss.	1992	8.75	23
1992 Down-Under Holiday QX5144	Yr.Iss.	1992	7.75	18-23
1992 Egg Nog Nest QX5121	Yr.Iss.	1992	7.75	14
1992 Eric the Baker QX5244	Yr.Iss.	1992	8.75	18-23
1992 Feliz Navidad QX5181	Yr.Iss.	1992	6.75	17-25
1992 Franz the Artist QX5261	Yr.Iss.	1992	8.75	19-25
1992 Freida the Animals' Friend QX5264	Yr.Iss.	1992	8.75	19-27
1992 Fun on a Big Scale QX5134	Yr.Iss.	1992	10.75	23
1992 GARFIELD QX5374	Yr.Iss.	1992	7.75	16-25
1992 Genius at Work QX5371	Yr.Iss.	1992	10.75	21
1992 Golf's a Ball QX5984	Yr.Iss.	1992	6.75	27
1992 Gone Wishin' QX5171	Yr.Iss.	1992	8.75	20
1992 Green Thumb Santa QX5101	Yr.Iss.	1992	7.75	16
1992 Hello-Ho-Ho QX5141	Yr.Iss.	1992	9.75	23
1992 Holiday Teatime QX5431	Yr.Iss.	1992	14.75	27
1992 Holiday Wishes QX5131	Yr.Iss.	1992	7.75	18
1992 Honest George QX5064	Yr.Iss.	1992	7.75	16-23
1992 Jesus Loves Me QX3024	Yr.Iss.	1992	7.75	15
1992 Locomotive QX5311	Yr.Iss.	1992	9.75	45
1992 Loving Shepherd QX5151	Yr.Iss.	1992	7.75	14
1992 Ludwig the Musician QX5281	Yr.Iss.	1992	8.75	19-23
1992 Mary Engelbreit Santa Jolly Wolly QX5224	Yr.Iss.	1992	7.75	8
1992 Max the Tailor QX5251	Yr.Iss.	1992	8.75	20
1992 Memories to Cherish QX5161	Yr.Iss.	1992	10.75	21
1992 Merry "Swiss" Mouse QX5114	Yr.Iss.	1992	7.75	15
1992 Norman Rockwell Art QX2224	Yr.Iss.	1992	5.00	16-25
1992 North Pole Fire Fighter QX5104	Yr.Iss.	1992	9.75	22
1992 Otto the Carpenter QX5254	Yr.Iss.	1992	8.75	19
1992 Owl QX5614	Yr.Iss.	1992	9.75	15-28
1992 Partridge In a Pear Tree QX5234	Yr.Iss.	1992	8.75	19
1992 PEANUTS® QX2244	Yr.Iss.	1992	5.00	19-25
1992 Please Pause Here QX5291	Yr.Iss.	1992	14.75	32
1992 Rapid Delivery QX5094	Yr.Iss.	1992	8.75	20-25
1992 Santa's Hook Shot QX5434	Yr.Iss.	1992	12.75	29
1992 Santa's Roundup QX5084	Yr.Iss.	1992	8.75	20-25
1992 A Santa-Full! QX5991	Yr.Iss.	1992	9.75	40
1992 Silver Star QX5324	Yr.Iss.	1992	28.00	54-60
1992 Skiing 'Round QX5214	Yr.Iss.	1992	8.75	19
1992 SNOOPY®and WOODSTOCK QX5954	Yr.Iss.	1992	8.75	19-25
1992 Spirit of Christmas Stress QX5231	Yr.Iss.	1992	8.75	7-10
1992 Stock Car QX5314	Yr.Iss.	1992	9.75	20
1992 Tasty Christmas QX5994	Yr.Iss.	1992	9.75	19-25
1992 Toboggan Tail QX5459	Yr.Iss.	1992	7.75	15-20
1992 Tread Bear QX5091	Yr.Iss.	1992	8.75	22

1992 Special Edition - Keepsake

YEAR ISSUE	EDITION LIMIT	YEAR RETD.	ISSUE PRICE	*QUOTE U.S.$
1992 Dickens Caroler Bell-Lord Chadwick (3rd Ed.) QX4554	Yr.Iss.	1992	21.75	45-50

1992 Special Issues - Keepsake

YEAR ISSUE	EDITION LIMIT	YEAR RETD.	ISSUE PRICE	*QUOTE U.S.$
1992 Elvis QX562-4	Yr.Iss.	1992	14.75	25-31
1992 Santa Maria QX5074	Yr.Iss.	1992	12.75	10-27
1992 Shuttlecraft Galileo 2400QLX733-1	Yr.Iss.	1992	24.00	30-55

1993 Anniversary Edition - Keepsake

YEAR ISSUE	EDITION LIMIT	YEAR RETD.	ISSUE PRICE	*QUOTE U.S.$
1993 Frosty Friends QX5682	Yr.Iss.	1993	20.00	46-50
1993 Glowing Pewter Wreath QX5302	Yr.Iss.	1993	18.75	22-30
1993 Shopping With Santa QX5675	Yr.Iss.	1993	24.00	32-45
1993 Tannenbaum's Dept. Store QX5612	Yr.Iss.	1993	26.00	25-65

1993 Artists' Favorites - Keepsake

YEAR ISSUE	EDITION LIMIT	YEAR RETD.	ISSUE PRICE	*QUOTE U.S.$
1993 Bird Watcher QX5252	Yr.Iss.	1993	9.75	19
1993 Howling Good Time QX5255	Yr.Iss.	1993	9.75	19-23
1993 On Her Toes QX5265	Yr.Iss.	1993	8.75	18-25
1993 Peek-a-Boo Tree QX5245	Yr.Iss.	1993	10.75	12-23
1993 Wake-Up Call QX5262	Yr.Iss.	1993	8.75	19

1993 Collectible Series - Keepsake

YEAR ISSUE	EDITION LIMIT	YEAR RETD.	ISSUE PRICE	*QUOTE U.S.$
1993 1956 Ford Thunderbird (3rd Ed.) QX5275	Yr.Iss.	1993	12.75	18-35
1993 Betsey's Country Christmas (2nd Ed.) QX2062	Yr.Iss.	1993	5.00	21
1993 Cozy Home (10th Ed.) QX4175	Yr.Iss.	1993	14.75	33-45
1993 CRAYOLA CRAYON-Bright Shining Castle (5th Ed.) QX4422	Yr.Iss.	1993	11.00	25-40
1993 Fabulous Decade (4th Ed.) QX4475	Yr.Iss.	1993	7.75	8-17
1993 A Fitting Moment (8th Ed.) QX4202	Yr.Iss.	1993	14.75	28-45
1993 Frosty Friends (14th Ed.) QX4142	Yr.Iss.	1993	9.75	25-40
1993 The Gift Bringers-The Magi (5th Ed.) QX2065	Yr.Iss.	1993	5.00	16-20
1993 Happy Haul-idays (15th Ed.) QX4102	Yr.Iss.	1993	14.75	27-40
1993 Heart Of Christmas (4th Ed.) QX4482	Yr.Iss.	1993	14.75	27-33
1993 Heavenly Angels (3rd Ed.) QX4945	Yr.Iss.	1993	7.75	19
1993 Humpty-Dumpty (1st Ed.) QX5282	Yr.Iss.	1993	13.75	17-35
1993 Mary's Angels-Ivy (6th Ed.) QX4282	Yr.Iss.	1993	6.75	17-35
1993 Merry Olde Santa (4th Ed.) QX4842	Yr.Iss.	1993	14.75	27-40
1993 Owliver (2nd Ed.) QX5425	Yr.Iss.	1993	7.75	16
1993 Peace On Earth-Poland (3rd Ed.) QX5242	Yr.Iss.	1993	11.75	21
1993 Peanuts (1st Ed.) QX5315	Yr.Iss.	1993	9.75	25-35
1993 Puppy Love (3rd Ed.) QX5045	Yr.Iss.	1993	7.75	30-33
1993 Reindeer Champs-Blitzen (8th Ed.) QX4331	Yr.Iss.	1993	8.75	21-35
1993 Rocking Horse (13th Ed.) QX4162	Yr.Iss.	1993	10.75	31-50
1993 Ten Lords A-Leaping (10th Ed.) QX3012	Yr.Iss.	1993	6.75	15-25
1993 Tobin Fraley Carousel (2nd Ed.) QX5502	Yr.Iss.	1993	28.00	41-56
1993 U.S. Christmas Stamps (1st Ed.) QX5292	Yr.Iss.	1993	10.75	35-43

1993 Easter Ornaments - Keepsake

YEAR ISSUE	EDITION LIMIT	YEAR RETD.	ISSUE PRICE	*QUOTE U.S.$
1993 Easter Parade (2nd Ed.) QEO8325	Yr.Iss.	1993	6.75	17
1993 Egg in Sports (2nd Ed.) QEO8332	Yr.Iss.	1993	6.75	18
1993 Springtime Bonnets (1st Ed.) QEO8322	Yr.Iss.	1993	7.75	26

1993 Keepsake Collector's Club - Keepsake

YEAR ISSUE	EDITION LIMIT	YEAR RETD.	ISSUE PRICE	*QUOTE U.S.$
1993 It's In The Mail QXC5272	Yr.Iss.	1993	10.00	10-23
1993 Trimmed With Memories QXC5432	Yr.Iss.	1993	12.00	30-38

1993 Keepsake Magic Ornaments - Keepsake

YEAR ISSUE	EDITION LIMIT	YEAR RETD.	ISSUE PRICE	*QUOTE U.S.$
1993 Baby's First Christmas QLX7365	Yr.Iss.	1993	22.00	41-50
1993 Bells Are Ringing QLX7402	Yr.Iss.	1993	28.00	65
1993 Chris Mouse Flight (9th Ed.) QLX7152	Yr.Iss.	1993	12.00	27-35
1993 Dog's Best Friend QLX7172	Yr.Iss.	1993	12.00	23
1993 Dollhouse Dreams QLX7372	Yr.Iss.	1993	22.00	35-45
1993 Forest Frolics (5th Ed.) QLX7165	Yr.Iss.	1993	25.00	48-53
1993 Home On The Range QLX7395	Yr.Iss.	1993	32.00	63-75
1993 The Lamplighter QLX7192	Yr.Iss.	1993	18.00	36-42
1993 Last-Minute Shopping QLX7385	Yr.Iss.	1993	28.00	41-60
1993 North Pole Merrython QLX7392	Yr.Iss.	1993	25.00	46-50
1993 Our First Christmas Together QLX7355	Yr.Iss.	1993	20.00	40-50
1993 PEANUTS (3rd Ed.) QLX7155	Yr.Iss.	1993	18.00	39-50
1993 Radio News Flash QLX7362	Yr.Iss.	1993	22.00	41-50

*Quotes have been rounded up to nearest dollar

YEAR ISSUE	EDITION LIMIT	YEAR RETD.	ISSUE PRICE	*QUOTE U.S.$
1993 Raiding The Fridge QLX7185	Yr.Iss.	1993	16.00	35-41
1993 Road Runner and Wile E. Coyote QLX7415	Yr.Iss.	1993	30.00	68-75
1993 Santa's Snow-Getter QLX7352	Yr.Iss.	1993	18.00	39
1993 Santa's Workshop QLX7375	Yr.Iss.	1993	28.00	60
1993 Song Of The Chimes QLX7405	Yr.Iss.	1993	25.00	50-55
1993 Winnie The Pooh QLX7422	Yr.Iss.	1993	24.00	50

1993 Limited Edition Ornaments - Keepsake

YEAR ISSUE	EDITION LIMIT	YEAR RETD.	ISSUE PRICE	*QUOTE U.S.$
1993 Gentle Tidings QXC5442	17,500	1993	25.00	50
1993 Sharing Christmas QXC5435	16,500	1993	20.00	30-43

1993 Miniature Ornaments - Keepsake

YEAR ISSUE	EDITION LIMIT	YEAR RETD.	ISSUE PRICE	*QUOTE U.S.$
1993 'Round The Mountain QXM4025	Yr.Iss.	1993	7.25	7-17
1993 Baby's First Christmas QXM5145	Yr.Iss.	1993	5.75	14
1993 The Bearymores (2nd Ed.) QXM5125	Yr.Iss.	1993	5.75	6-18
1993 Cheese Please QXM4072	Yr.Iss.	1993	3.75	9
1993 Christmas Castle QXM4085	Yr.Iss.	1993	5.75	13
1993 Cloisonne Snowflake QXM4012	Yr.Iss.	1993	9.75	20
1993 Country Fiddling QXM4062	Yr.Iss.	1993	3.75	10
1993 Crystal Angel QXM4015	Yr.Iss.	1993	9.75	40-54
1993 Ears To Pals QXM4075	Yr.Iss.	1993	3.75	9
1993 Flatbed Car (5th Ed.) QXM5105	Yr.Iss.	1993	7.00	10-18
1993 Grandma QXM5162	Yr.Iss.	1993	4.50	13
1993 I Dream Of Santa QXM4055	Yr.Iss.	1993	3.75	6-12
1993 Into The Woods QXM4045	Yr.Iss.	1993	3.75	8
1993 The Kringles (5th Ed.) QXM5135	Yr.Iss.	1993	5.75	8-14
1993 Learning To Skate QXM4122	Yr.Iss.	1993	3.00	9
1993 Lighting A Path QXM4115	Yr.Iss.	1993	3.00	9
1993 March Of The Teddy Bears (1st Ed.) QX2403	Yr.Iss.	1993	4.50	18-25
1993 Merry Mascot QXM4042	Yr.Iss.	1993	3.75	9
1993 Mom QXM5155	Yr.Iss.	1993	4.50	5-11
1993 Monkey Melody QXM4092	Yr.Iss.	1993	5.75	14
1993 Nature's Angels (4th Ed.) QXM5122	Yr.Iss.	1993	4.50	14-20
1993 The Night Before Christmas (2nd Ed.) QXM5115	Yr.Iss.	1993	4.50	15-23
1993 North Pole Fire Truck QXM4105	Yr.Iss.	1993	4.75	6-10
1993 On The Road (1st Ed.) QXM4002	Yr.Iss.	1993	5.75	10-17
1993 Pear-Shaped Tones QXM4052	Yr.Iss.	1993	3.75	5-8
1993 Pull Out A Plum QXM4095	Yr.Iss.	1993	5.75	13
1993 Refreshing Flight QXM4112	Yr.Iss.	1993	5.75	14
1993 Rocking Horse (6th Ed.) QXM5112	Yr.Iss.	1993	4.50	10-14
1993 Secret Pals QXM5172	Yr.Iss.	1993	3.75	10
1993 Snuggle Birds QXM5182	Yr.Iss.	1993	5.75	14
1993 Special Friends QXM5165	Yr.Iss.	1993	4.50	11
1993 Thimble Bells (4th Ed.) QXM5142	Yr.Iss.	1993	5.75	9-15
1993 Tiny Green Thumbs, set/6, QXM4032	Yr.Iss.	1993	29.00	38-53
1993 Toy Shop (6th Ed.) QXM5132	Yr.Iss.	1993	7.00	15-22
1993 Visions Of Sugarplums QXM4022	Yr.Iss.	1993	7.25	16
1993 Woodland Babies (3rd Ed.) QXM5102	Yr.Iss.	1993	5.75	6-15

1993 New Attractions - Keepsake

YEAR ISSUE	EDITION LIMIT	YEAR RETD.	ISSUE PRICE	*QUOTE U.S.$
1993 Beary Gifted QX5762	Yr.Iss.	1993	7.75	19
1993 Big on Gardening QX5842	Yr.Iss.	1993	9.75	19
1993 Big Roller QX5352	Yr.Iss.	1993	8.75	17
1993 Bowling For ZZZ's QX5565	Yr.Iss.	1993	7.75	19
1993 Bugs Bunny QX5412	Yr.Iss.	1993	8.75	18-22
1993 Caring Nurse QX5785	Yr.Iss.	1993	6.75	19
1993 Christmas Break QX5825	Yr.Iss.	1993	7.75	18-25
1993 Clever Cookie QX5662	Yr.Iss.	1993	7.75	16-30
1993 Curly 'n' Kingly QX5285	Yr.Iss.	1993	10.75	25
1993 Dunkin' Roo QX5575	Yr.Iss.	1993	7.75	16
1993 Eeyore QX5712	Yr.Iss.	1993	9.75	25
1993 Elmer Fudd QX5495	Yr.Iss.	1993	8.75	12-18
1993 Faithful Fire Fighter QX5782	Yr.Iss.	1993	7.75	19
1993 Feliz Navidad QX5365	Yr.Iss.	1993	9.75	16
1993 Fills the Bill QX5572	Yr.Iss.	1993	8.75	18
1993 Great Connections QX5402	Yr.Iss.	1993	10.75	24
1993 He Is Born QX5362	Yr.Iss.	1993	9.75	36
1993 High Top-Purr QX5332	Yr.Iss.	1993	8.75	25
1993 Home For Christmas QX5562	Yr.Iss.	1993	7.75	15
1993 Icicle Bicycle QX5835	Yr.Iss.	1993	9.75	19
1993 Kanga and Roo QX5672	Yr.Iss.	1993	9.75	22-25
1993 Little Drummer Boy QX5372	Yr.Iss.	1993	8.75	21-25
1993 Look For Wonder QX5685	Yr.Iss.	1993	12.75	26
1993 Lou Rankin Polar Bear QX5745	Yr.Iss.	1993	9.75	18-22
1993 Makin' Music QX5325	Yr.Iss.	1993	9.75	19
1993 Making Waves QX5775	Yr.Iss.	1993	9.75	22-25
1993 Mary Engelbreit QX2075	Yr.Iss.	1993	5.00	14-17
1993 Maxine QX5385	Yr.Iss.	1993	8.75	17-35
1993 One-Elf Marching Band QX5342	Yr.Iss.	1993	12.75	26
1993 Owl QX5695	Yr.Iss.	1993	9.75	15-20
1993 PEANUTS QX2072	Yr.Iss.	1993	5.00	14-30
1993 Peep Inside QX5322	Yr.Iss.	1993	13.75	26
1993 Perfect Match QX5772	Yr.Iss.	1993	8.75	19
1993 The Pink Panther QX5755	Yr.Iss.	1993	12.75	25
1993 Playful Pals QX5742	Yr.Iss.	1993	14.75	27-32
1993 Popping Good Times QX5392	Yr.Iss.	1993	14.75	27
1993 Porky Pig QX5652	Yr.Iss.	1993	8.75	10-20
1993 Putt-Putt Penguin QX5795	Yr.Iss.	1993	9.75	18-24
1993 Quick As A Fox QX5792	Yr.Iss.	1993	8.75	17
1993 Rabbit QX5702	Yr.Iss.	1993	9.75	15-25
1993 Ready For Fun QX5124	Yr.Iss.	1993	7.75	17
1993 Room For One More QX5382	Yr.Iss.	1993	8.75	46
1993 Silvery Noel QX5305	Yr.Iss.	1993	12.75	35
1993 Smile! It's Christmas QX5335	Yr.Iss.	1993	9.75	19
1993 Snow Bear Angel QX5355	Yr.Iss.	1993	7.75	17
1993 Snowbird QX5765	Yr.Iss.	1993	7.75	15-20
1993 Snowy Hideaway QX5312	Yr.Iss.	1993	9.75	19
1993 Star Of Wonder QX5982	Yr.Iss.	1993	6.75	32
1993 Superman QX5752	Yr.Iss.	1993	12.75	19-25
1993 The Swat Team QX5395	Yr.Iss.	1993	12.75	27
1993 Sylvester and Tweety QX5405	Yr.Iss.	1993	9.75	25-34
1993 That's Entertainment QX5345	Yr.Iss.	1993	8.75	19
1993 Tigger and Piglet QX5705	Yr.Iss.	1993	9.75	30-35
1993 Tin Airplane QX5622	Yr.Iss.	1993	7.75	20-28
1993 Tin Blimp QX5625	Yr.Iss.	1993	7.75	16-20
1993 Tin Hot Air Balloon QX5615	Yr.Iss.	1993	7.75	17-20
1993 Water Bed Snooze QX5375	Yr.Iss.	1993	9.75	10-22
1993 Winnie the Pooh QX5715	Yr.Iss.	1993	9.75	22-25

1993 Showcase Folk Art Americana - Keepsake

YEAR ISSUE	EDITION LIMIT	YEAR RETD.	ISSUE PRICE	*QUOTE U.S.$
1993 Angel in Flight QK1052	Yr.Iss.	1993	15.75	20-50
1993 Polar Bear Adventure QK1055	Yr.Iss.	1993	15.00	65
1993 Riding in the Woods QK1065	Yr.Iss.	1993	15.75	75
1993 Riding the Wind QK1045	Yr.Iss.	1993	15.75	65
1993 Santa Claus QK1072	Yr.Iss.	1993	16.75	225

1993 Showcase Holiday Enchantment - Keepsake

YEAR ISSUE	EDITION LIMIT	YEAR RETD.	ISSUE PRICE	*QUOTE U.S.$
1993 Angelic Messengers QK1032	Yr.Iss.	1993	13.75	20-40
1993 Bringing Home the Tree QK1042	Yr.Iss.	1993	13.75	20-35
1993 Journey to the Forest QK1012	Yr.Iss.	1993	13.75	20-33
1993 The Magi QK1025	Yr.Iss.	1993	13.75	20-38
1993 Visions of Sugarplums QK1005	Yr.Iss.	1993	13.75	20-35

1993 Showcase Old-World Silver - Keepsake

YEAR ISSUE	EDITION LIMIT	YEAR RETD.	ISSUE PRICE	*QUOTE U.S.$
1993 Silver Dove of Peace QK1075	Yr.Iss.	1993	24.75	35
1993 Silver Santa QK1092	Yr.Iss.	1993	24.75	35-50
1993 Silver Sleigh QK1082	Yr.Iss.	1993	24.75	32-60
1993 Silver Stars and Holly QK1085	Yr.Iss.	1993	24.75	32-35

1993 Showcase Portraits in Bisque - Keepsake

YEAR ISSUE	EDITION LIMIT	YEAR RETD.	ISSUE PRICE	*QUOTE U.S.$
1993 Christmas Feast QK1152	Yr.Iss.	1993	15.75	31
1993 Joy of Sharing QK1142	Yr.Iss.	1993	15.75	33
1993 Mistletoe Kiss QK1145	Yr.Iss.	1993	15.75	30
1993 Norman Rockwell-Filling the Stockings QK1155	Yr.Iss.	1993	15.75	35
1993 Norman Rockwell-Jolly Postman QK1142	Yr.Iss.	1993	15.75	33

1993 Special Editions - Keepsake

YEAR ISSUE	EDITION LIMIT	YEAR RETD.	ISSUE PRICE	*QUOTE U.S.$
1993 Dickens Caroler Bell-Lady Daphne (4th Ed.) QX5505	Yr.Iss.	1993	21.75	41
1993 Julianne and Teddy QX5295	Yr.Iss.	1993	21.75	35-44

1993 Special Issues - Keepsake

YEAR ISSUE	EDITION LIMIT	YEAR RETD.	ISSUE PRICE	*QUOTE U.S.$
1993 Holiday Barbie (1st Ed.) QX572-5	Yr.Iss.	1993	14.75	85-155
1993 Messages of Christmas QLX747-6	Yr.Iss.	1993	35.00	46-58
1993 Star Trek® The Next Generation QLX741-2	Yr.Iss.	1993	24.00	35-75

1994 Artists' Favorites - Keepsake

YEAR ISSUE	EDITION LIMIT	YEAR RETD.	ISSUE PRICE	*QUOTE U.S.$
1994 Cock-a-Doodle Christmas QX5396	Yr.Iss.	1994	8.95	30
1994 Happy Birthday Jesus QX5423	Yr.Iss.	1994	12.95	20-30
1994 Keep on Mowin' QX5413	Yr.Iss.	1994	8.95	15-30
1994 Kitty's Catamaran QX5416	Yr.Iss.	1994	10.95	17-24
1994 Making It Bright QX5403	Yr.Iss.	1994	8.95	14-20

1994 Collectible Series - Keepsake

YEAR ISSUE	EDITION LIMIT	YEAR RETD.	ISSUE PRICE	*QUOTE U.S.$
1994 1957 Chevy (4th Ed.) QX5422	Yr.Iss.	1994	12.95	15-22
1994 Baseball Heroes-Babe Ruth (1st Ed.) QX5323	Yr.Iss.	1994	12.95	55-66
1994 Betsey's Country Christmas (3rd Ed.) QX2403	Yr.Iss.	1994	5.00	13
1994 Cat Naps (1st Ed.) QX5313	Yr.Iss.	1994	7.95	40-45
1994 CRAYOLA CRAYON-Bright Playful Colors (6th Ed.) QX5273	Yr.Iss.	1994	10.95	22-30
1994 Fabulous Decade (5th Ed.) QX5263	Yr.Iss.	1994	7.95	23-37
1994 Frosty Friends (15th Ed.) QX5293	Yr.Iss.	1994	9.95	18-24
1994 Handwarming Present (9th Ed.) QX5283	Yr.Iss.	1994	14.95	29-40
1994 Heart of Christmas (5th Ed.) QX5266	Yr.Iss.	1994	14.95	21-30
1994 Hey Diddle Diddle (2nd Ed.) QX5213	Yr.Iss.	1994	13.95	35-46
1994 Makin' Tractor Tracks (16th Ed.) QX5296	Yr.Iss.	1994	14.95	50
1994 Mary's Angels-Jasmine (7th Ed.) QX5276	Yr.Iss.	1994	6.95	15-27
1994 Merry Olde Santa (5th Ed.) QX5256	Yr.Iss.	1994	14.95	30-38
1994 Murray Blue Champion (1st Ed.) QX5426	Yr.Iss.	1994	13.95	45-75
1994 Neighborhood Drugstore (11th Ed.) QX5286	Yr.Iss.	1994	14.95	32-40
1994 Owliver (3rd Ed.) QX5226	Yr.Iss.	1994	7.95	19
1994 PEANUTS-Lucy (2nd Ed.) QX5203	Yr.Iss.	1994	9.95	10-25
1994 Pipers Piping (11th Ed.) QX3183	Yr.Iss.	1994	6.95	16-23
1994 Puppy Love (4th Ed.) QX5253	Yr.Iss.	1994	7.95	10-25
1994 Rocking Horse (14th Ed.) QX5016	Yr.Iss.	1994	10.95	22
1994 Tobin Fraley Carousel (3rd Ed.) QX5223	Yr.Iss.	1994	28.00	56-75
1994 Xmas Stamp (2nd Ed.) QX5206	Yr.Iss.	1994	10.95	10-24
1994 Yuletide Central (1st Ed.) QX5316	Yr.Iss.	1994	18.95	33-65

1994 Easter Ornaments - Keepsake

YEAR ISSUE	EDITION LIMIT	YEAR RETD.	ISSUE PRICE	*QUOTE U.S.$
1994 Baby's First Easter QEO8153	Yr.Iss.	1994	6.75	19
1994 Carrot Trimmers QEO8226	Yr.Iss.	1994	5.00	5-20
1994 CRAYOLA CRAYON-Colorful Spring QEO8166	Yr.Iss.	1994	7.75	18-20
1994 Daughter QEO8156	Yr.Iss.	1994	5.75	6-15
1994 Divine Duet QEO8183	Yr.Iss.	1994	6.75	16
1994 Easter Art Show QEO8193	Yr.Iss.	1994	7.75	17
1994 Egg Car (1st Ed.) QEO8093	Yr.Iss.	1994	7.75	30-35
1994 Golf (3rd Ed.) QEO8133	Yr.Iss.	1994	6.75	19
1994 Horn (3rd Ed.) QEO8136	Yr.Iss.	1994	6.75	19
1994 Joyful Lamb QEO8206	Yr.Iss.	1994	5.75	15
1994 PEANUTS QEO8176	Yr.Iss.	1994	7.75	18-50
1994 Peeping Out QEO8203	Yr.Iss.	1994	6.75	15
1994 Riding a Breeze QEO8213	Yr.Iss.	1994	5.75	8-15
1994 Son QEO8163	Yr.Iss.	1994	5.75	6-15
1994 Springtime Bonnets (2nd Ed.) QEO8096	Yr.Iss.	1994	7.75	24
1994 Sunny Bunny Garden, (Set/3) QEO8146	Yr.Iss.	1994	15.00	20-29
1994 Sweet as Sugar QEO8086	Yr.Iss.	1994	8.75	10-20
1994 Sweet Easter Wishes Tender Touches QEO8196	Yr.Iss.	1994	8.75	25
1994 Treetop Cottage QEO8186	Yr.Iss.	1994	9.75	19
1994 Yummy Recipe QEO8143	Yr.Iss.	1994	7.75	8-19

1994 Keepsake Collector's Club - Keepsake

YEAR ISSUE	EDITION LIMIT	YEAR RETD.	ISSUE PRICE	*QUOTE U.S.$
1994 First Hello QXC4846	Yr.Iss.	1994	5.00	25
1994 Happy Collecting QXC4803	Yr.Iss.	1994	3.00	25-40
1994 Holiday Pursuit QXC4823	Yr.Iss.	1994	11.75	18-25
1994 Mrs. Claus' Cupboard QXC4843	Yr.Iss.	1994	55.00	135-200
1994 On Cloud Nine QXC4853	Yr.Iss.	1994	12.00	25-30
1994 Sweet Bouquet QXC4806	Yr.Iss.	1994	8.50	15-25
1994 Tilling Time QXC8256	Yr.Iss.	1994	5.00	68-75

1994 Keepsake Magic Ornaments - Keepsake

YEAR ISSUE	EDITION LIMIT	YEAR RETD.	ISSUE PRICE	*QUOTE U.S.$
1994 Away in a Manager QLX7383	Yr.Iss.	1994	16.00	36
1994 Baby's First Christmas QLX7466	Yr.Iss.	1994	20.00	39-45
1994 Candy Cane Lookout QLX7376	Yr.Iss.	1994	18.00	75
1994 Chris Mouse Jelly (10th Ed.) QLX7393	Yr.Iss.	1994	12.00	16-30
1994 Conversations With Santa QLX7426	Yr.Iss.	1994	28.00	50-57
1994 Country Showtime QLX7416	Yr.Iss.	1994	22.00	45
1994 The Eagle Has Landed QLX7486	Yr.Iss.	1994	24.00	25-45
1994 Feliz Navidad QLX7433	Yr.Iss.	1994	28.00	50-75
1994 Forest Frolics (6th Ed.) QLX7436	Yr.Iss.	1994	28.00	30-60
1994 Gingerbread Fantasy (Sp. Ed.) QLX7382	Yr.Iss.	1994	44.00	88-97
1994 Kringle Trolley QLX7413	Yr.Iss.	1994	20.00	25-45
1994 Maxine QLX7503	Yr.Iss.	1994	20.00	40-50
1994 PEANUTS (4th Ed.) QLX7406	Yr.Iss.	1994	20.00	40-45
1994 Peekaboo Pup QLX7423	Yr.Iss.	1994	20.00	43
1994 Rock Candy Miner QLX7403	Yr.Iss.	1994	20.00	36
1994 Santa's Sing-Along QLX7473	Yr.Iss.	1994	24.00	59
1994 Tobin Fraley (1st Ed.) QLX7496	Yr.Iss.	1994	32.00	68-75
1994 Very Merry Minutes QLX7443	Yr.Iss.	1994	24.00	43-48
1994 White Christmas QLX7463	Yr.Iss.	1994	28.00	54
1994 Winnie the Pooh Parade QLX7493	Yr.Iss.	1994	32.00	60-65

1994 Limited Editions - Keepsake

YEAR ISSUE	EDITION LIMIT	YEAR RETD.	ISSUE PRICE	*QUOTE U.S.$
1994 Jolly Holly Santa QXC4833	N/A	1994	22.00	40-50
1994 Majestic Deer QXC4836	N/A	1994	25.00	45-50

1994 Miniature Ornaments - Keepsake

YEAR ISSUE	EDITION LIMIT	YEAR RETD.	ISSUE PRICE	*QUOTE U.S.$
1994 Babs Bunny QXM4116	Yr.Iss.	1994	5.75	12-20
1994 Baby's First Christmas QXM4003	Yr.Iss.	1994	5.75	13
1994 Baking Tiny Treats, (Set/6) QXM4033	Yr.Iss.	1994	29.00	59-65
1994 Beary Perfect Tree QXM4076	Yr.Iss.	1994	4.75	8
1994 The Bearymores (3rd Ed.) QXM5133	Yr.Iss.	1994	5.75	7-13
1994 Buster Bunny QXM5163	Yr.Iss.	1994	5.75	6-13
1994 Centuries of Santa (1st Ed.) QXM5153	Yr.Iss.	1994	6.00	20-25
1994 Corny Elf QXM4063	Yr.Iss.	1994	4.50	6-9
1994 Cute as a Button QXM4103	Yr.Iss.	1994	3.75	15
1994 Dazzling Reindeer (Pr. Ed.) QXM4026	Yr.Iss.	1994	9.75	19
1994 Dizzy Devil QXM4133	Yr.Iss.	1994	5.75	14
1994 Friends Need Hugs QXM4016	Yr.Iss.	1994	4.50	10-14
1994 Graceful Carousel QXM4056	Yr.Iss.	1994	7.75	10-15
1994 Hamton QXM4126	Yr.Iss.	1994	5.75	6-13
1994 Hat Shop (7th Ed.) QXM5143	Yr.Iss.	1994	7.00	10-16
1994 Have a Cookie QXM5166	Yr.Iss.	1994	5.75	15
1994 Hearts A-Sail QXM4006	Yr.Iss.	1994	5.75	13
1994 Jolly Visitor QXM4053	Yr.Iss.	1994	5.75	8-12
1994 Jolly Wolly Snowman QXM4093	Yr.Iss.	1994	3.75	15
1994 Journey to Bethlehem QXM4036	Yr.Iss.	1994	5.75	8-15
1994 Just My Size QXM4086	Yr.Iss.	1994	3.75	12
1994 Love Was Born QXM4043	Yr.Iss.	1994	4.50	14
1994 March of the Teddy Bears (2nd Ed.) QXM5106	Yr.Iss.	1994	4.50	12-20
1994 Melodic Cherub QXM4066	Yr.Iss.	1994	3.75	6-10
1994 A Merry Flight QXM4073	Yr.Iss.	1994	5.75	6-13
1994 Mom QXM4013	Yr.Iss.	1994	4.50	5-14
1994 Nature's Angels (5th Ed.) QXM5126	Yr.Iss.	1994	4.50	7-12
1994 Night Before Christmas (3rd Ed.) QXM5123	Yr.Iss.	1994	4.50	10-14
1994 Noah's Ark (Sp. Ed.)) QXM4106	Yr.Iss.	1994	24.50	50-65
1994 Nutcracker Guild (1st Ed.) QXM5146	Yr.Iss.	1994	5.75	25-35
1994 On the Road (2nd Ed.) QXM5103	Yr.Iss.	1994	5.75	6-13
1994 Plucky Duck QXM4123	Yr.Iss.	1994	5.75	12-20
1994 Pour Some More QXM5156	Yr.Iss.	1994	5.75	6-12
1994 Rocking Horse (7th Ed.) QXM5116	Yr.Iss.	1994	4.50	12-18
1994 Scooting Along QXM5173	Yr.Iss.	1994	6.75	15
1994 Stock Car (6th Ed.) QXM5113	Yr.Iss.	1994	7.00	16-22
1994 Sweet Dreams QXM4096	Yr.Iss.	1994	3.00	13
1994 Tea With Teddy QXM4046	Yr.Iss.	1994	7.25	8-16

1994 New Attractions - Keepsake

YEAR ISSUE	EDITION LIMIT	YEAR RETD.	ISSUE PRICE	*QUOTE U.S.$
1994 All Pumped Up QX5923	Yr.Iss.	1994	8.95	19
1994 Angel Hare QX5896	Yr.Iss.	1994	8.95	10-18
1994 Batman QX5853	Yr.Iss.	1994	12.95	18-35

*Quotes have been rounded up to nearest dollar

YEAR ISSUE	EDITION LIMIT	YEAR RETD.	ISSUE PRICE	*QUOTE U.S.$
1994 Beatles Gift Set QX5373	Yr.Iss.	1994	48.00	65-100
1994 BEATRIX POTTER The Tale of Peter Rabbit QX2443	Yr.Iss.	1994	5.00	15-23
1994 Big Shot QX5873	Yr.Iss.	1994	7.95	18
1994 Busy Batter QX5876	Yr.Iss.	1994	7.95	16
1994 Candy Caper QX5776	Yr.Iss.	1994	8.95	12-19
1994 Caring Doctor QX5823	Yr.Iss.	1994	8.95	19
1994 Champion Teacher QX5836	Yr.Iss.	1994	6.95	16
1994 Cheers to You! QX5796	Yr.Iss.	1994	10.95	20-23
1994 Cheery Cyclists QX5786	Yr.Iss.	1994	12.95	15-27
1994 Child Care Giver QX5906	Yr.Iss.	1994	7.95	15
1994 Coach QX5933	Yr.Iss.	1994	7.95	17
1994 Colors of Joy QX5893	Yr.Iss.	1994	7.95	19
1994 Cowardly Lion QX5446	Yr.Iss.	1994	9.95	30-75
1994 Daffy Duck QX5415	Yr.Iss.	1994	8.95	16-19
1994 Daisy Days QX5986	Yr.Iss.	1994	9.95	16-25
1994 Deer Santa Mouse (2) QX5806	Yr.Iss.	1994	14.95	27
1994 Dorothy and Toto QX5433	Yr.Iss.	1994	10.95	85-95
1994 Extra-Special Delivery QX5833	Yr.Iss.	1994	7.95	17
1994 Feelin' Groovy QX5953	Yr.Iss.	1994	7.95	22
1994 A Feline of Christmas QX5816	Yr.Iss.	1994	8.95	30
1994 Feliz Navidad QX5793	Yr.Iss.	1994	8.95	12-20
1994 Follow the Sun QX5846	Yr.Iss.	1994	8.95	18
1994 Fred and Barney QX5003	Yr.Iss.	1994	14.95	18-29
1994 Friendship Sundae QX4766	Yr.Iss.	1994	10.95	23
1994 GARFIELD QX5753	Yr.Iss.	1994	12.95	18-26
1994 Gentle Nurse QX5973	Yr.Iss.	1994	6.95	18
1994 Harvest Joy QX5993	Yr.Iss.	1994	9.95	17-25
1994 Hearts in Harmony QX4406	Yr.Iss.	1994	10.95	21
1994 Helpful Shepherd QX5536	Yr.Iss.	1994	8.95	18
1994 Holiday Patrol QX5826	Yr.Iss.	1994	8.95	18
1994 Ice Show QX5946	Yr.Iss.	1994	7.95	17-20
1994 In the Pink QX5763	Yr.Iss.	1994	9.95	21-24
1994 It's a Strike QX5856	Yr.Iss.	1994	8.95	18
1994 Jingle Bell Band QX5783	Yr.Iss.	1994	10.95	20-24
1994 Joyous Song QX4473	Yr.Iss.	1994	8.95	18-25
1994 Jump-along Jackalope QX5756	Yr.Iss.	1994	8.95	17
1994 Kickin' Roo QX5916	Yr.Iss.	1994	7.95	16-20
1994 Kringle's Kayak QX5886	Yr.Iss.	1994	7.95	10-17
1994 LEGO'S QX5453	Yr.Iss.	1994	10.95	18-25
1994 Lou Rankin Seal QX5456	Yr.Iss.	1994	9.95	19
1994 Magic Carpet Ride QX5883	Yr.Iss.	1994	7.95	22-25
1994 Mary Engelbreit QX2416	Yr.Iss.	1994	5.00	14-20
1994 Merry Fishmas QX5913	Yr.Iss.	1994	8.95	16-23
1994 Mistletoe Surprise (2)QX5996	Yr.Iss.	1994	12.95	26-33
1994 Norman Rockwell QX2413	Yr.Iss.	1994	5.00	13-20
1994 Open-and-Shut Holiday QX5696	Yr.Iss.	1994	9.95	20
1994 Out of This World Teacher QX5766	Yr.Iss.	1994	7.95	19
1994 Practice Makes Perfect QX5863	Yr.Iss.	1994	7.95	17-20
1994 Red Hot Holiday QX5843	Yr.Iss.	1994	7.95	16-20
1994 Reindeer Pro QX5926	Yr.Iss.	1994	7.95	16-20
1994 Relaxing Moment QX5356	Yr.Iss.	1994	14.95	18-29
1994 Road Runner and Wile E. Coyote QX5602	Yr.Iss.	1994	12.95	15-20
1994 Scarecrow QX5436	Yr.Iss.	1994	9.95	32-75
1994 A Sharp Flat QX5773	Yr.Iss.	1994	10.95	25
1994 Speedy Gonzales QX5343	Yr.Iss.	1994	8.95	12-20
1994 Stamp of Approval QX5703	Yr.Iss.	1994	7.95	16
1994 Sweet Greeting (2) QX5803	Yr.Iss.	1994	10.95	21
1994 Tasmanian Devil QX5605	Yr.Iss.	1994	8.95	45-50
1994 Thrill a Minute QX5866	Yr.Iss.	1994	8.95	18
1994 Time of Peace QX5813	Yr.Iss.	1994	7.95	15
1994 Tin Man QX5443	Yr.Iss.	1994	9.95	38-75
1994 Tulip Time QX5983	Yr.Iss.	1994	9.95	16-25
1994 Winnie the Pooh/Tigger QX5746	Yr.Iss.	1994	12.95	35-40
1994 Yosemite Sam QX5346	Yr.Iss.	1994	8.95	12-20
1994 Yuletide Cheer QX5976	Yr.Iss.	1994	9.95	16-25

1994 Premiere Event - Keepsake

YEAR ISSUE	EDITION LIMIT	YEAR RETD.	ISSUE PRICE	*QUOTE U.S.$
1994 Eager for Christmas QX5336	Yr.Iss.	1994	15.00	28

1994 Showcase Christmas Lights - Keepsake

YEAR ISSUE	EDITION LIMIT	YEAR RETD.	ISSUE PRICE	*QUOTE U.S.$
1994 Home for the Holidays QK1123	Yr.Iss.	1994	15.75	32
1994 Moonbeams QK1116	Yr.Iss.	1994	15.75	16
1994 Mother and Child QK1126	Yr.Iss.	1994	15.75	16
1994 Peaceful Village QK1106	Yr.Iss.	1994	15.75	16

1994 Showcase Folk Art Americana Collection - Keepsake

YEAR ISSUE	EDITION LIMIT	YEAR RETD.	ISSUE PRICE	*QUOTE U.S.$
1994 Catching 40 Winks QK1183	Yr.Iss.	1994	16.75	35-38
1994 Going to Town QK1166	Yr.Iss.	1994	15.75	35
1994 Racing Through the Snow QK1173	Yr.Iss.	1994	15.75	50
1994 Rarin' to Go QK1193	Yr.Iss.	1994	15.75	35-38
1994 Roundup Time QK1176	Yr.Iss.	1994	16.75	35-43

1994 Showcase Holiday Favorites - Keepsake

YEAR ISSUE	EDITION LIMIT	YEAR RETD.	ISSUE PRICE	*QUOTE U.S.$
1994 Dapper Snowman QK1053	Yr.Iss.	1994	13.75	14
1994 Graceful Fawn QK1033	Yr.Iss.	1994	11.75	24
1994 Jolly Santa QK1046	Yr.Iss.	1994	13.75	15-28
1994 Joyful Lamb QK1036	Yr.Iss.	1994	11.75	12-24
1994 Peaceful Dove QK1043	Yr.Iss.	1994	11.75	24

1994 Showcase Old World Silver Collection - Keepsake

YEAR ISSUE	EDITION LIMIT	YEAR RETD.	ISSUE PRICE	*QUOTE U.S.$
1994 Silver Bells QK1026	Yr.Iss.	1994	24.75	40
1994 Silver Bows QK1023	Yr.Iss.	1994	24.75	40
1994 Silver Poinsettias QK1006	Yr.Iss.	1994	24.75	40
1994 Silver Snowflakes QK1016	Yr.Iss.	1994	24.75	40

1994 Special Edition - Keepsake

YEAR ISSUE	EDITION LIMIT	YEAR RETD.	ISSUE PRICE	*QUOTE U.S.$
1994 Lucinda and Teddy QX4813	Yr.Iss.	1994	21.75	30-43

1994 Special Issues - Keepsake

YEAR ISSUE	EDITION LIMIT	YEAR RETD.	ISSUE PRICE	*QUOTE U.S.$
1994 Barney QLX7506	Yr.Iss.	1994	24.00	35-45
1994 Barney QX5966	Yr.Iss.	1994	9.95	15-25
1994 Holiday Barbie™ (2nd Ed.) QX5216	Yr.Iss.	1994	14.95	30-55
1994 Klingon Bird of Prey™ QLX7386	Yr.Iss.	1994	24.00	20-45
1994 Mufasa/Simba-Lion King QX5406	Yr.Iss.	1994	14.95	15-25
1994 Nostalgic-Barbie™ (1st Ed.) QX5006	Yr.Iss.	1994	14.95	18-35
1994 Simba/Nala-Lion King (2) QX5303	Yr.Iss.	1994	12.95	18-25
1994 Simba/Sarabi/Mufasa the Lion King QLX7513	Yr.Iss.	1994	32.00	35-41
1994 Simba/Sarabi/Mufasa the Lion King QLX7513	Yr.Iss.	1994	20.00	66-81
1994 Timon/Pumbaa-Lion King QX5366	Yr.Iss.	1994	8.95	15-23

1995 Anniversary Edition - Keepsake

YEAR ISSUE	EDITION LIMIT	YEAR RETD.	ISSUE PRICE	*QUOTE U.S.$
1995 Pewter Rocking Horse QX6167	Yr.Iss.	1995	20.00	30-55

1995 Artists' Favorite - Keepsake

YEAR ISSUE	EDITION LIMIT	YEAR RETD.	ISSUE PRICE	*QUOTE U.S.$
1995 Barrel-Back Rider QX5189	Yr.Iss.	1995	9.95	25-30
1995 Our Little Blessings QX5209	Yr.Iss.	1995	12.95	26

1995 Collectible Series - Keepsake

YEAR ISSUE	EDITION LIMIT	YEAR RETD.	ISSUE PRICE	*QUOTE U.S.$
1995 1956 Ford Truck (1st Ed.) QX5527	Yr.Iss.	1995	13.95	25-35
1995 1969 Chevrolet Camaro (5th Ed.) QX5239	Yr.Iss.	1995	12.95	13-18
1995 Bright 'n' Sunny Tepee (7th Ed.) QX5247	Yr.Iss.	1995	10.95	19-35
1995 Camellia - Mary's Angels (8th Ed.) QX5149	Yr.Iss.	1995	6.95	15-20
1995 Cat Naps (2nd Ed.) QX5097	Yr.Iss.	1995	7.95	12
1995 A Celebration of Angels (1st Ed.) QX5077	Yr.Iss.	1995	12.95	25-35
1995 Christmas Eve Kiss (10th Ed.) QX5157	Yr.Iss.	1995	14.95	22-33
1995 Fabulous Decade (6th Ed.) QX5147	Yr.Iss.	1995	7.95	17-22
1995 Frosty Friends (16th Ed.) QX5169	Yr.Iss.	1995	10.95	25-33
1995 Jack and Jill (3rd Ed.) QX5099	Yr.Iss.	1995	13.95	22-35
1995 Lou Gehrig (2nd Ed.) QX5029	Yr.Iss.	1995	12.95	18-35
1995 Merry Olde Santa (6th Ed.) QX5139	Yr.Iss.	1995	14.95	29
1995 Murray® Fire Truck (2nd Ed.) QX5027	Yr.Iss.	1995	13.95	25-35
1995 The PEANUTS® Gang (3rd Ed.) QX5059	Yr.Iss.	1995	9.95	22-35
1995 Puppy Love (5th Ed.) QX5137	Yr.Iss.	1995	7.95	14-25
1995 Rocking Horse (15th Ed.) QX5167	Yr.Iss.	1995	10.95	22-35
1995 Santa's Roadster (17th Ed.) QX5179	Yr.Iss.	1995	14.95	18-30
1995 St. Nicholas (1st Ed.) QX5087	Yr.Iss.	1995	14.95	18-35
1995 Tobin Fraley Carousel (4th Ed.) QX5069	Yr.Iss.	1995	28.00	35-55
1995 Town Church (12th Ed.) QX5159	Yr.Iss.	1995	14.95	20-30
1995 Twelve Drummers Drumming (12th Ed.) QX3009	Yr.Iss.	1995	6.95	12-25
1995 U.S. Christmas Stamps (3rd Ed.) QX5067	Yr.Iss.	1995	10.95	11-25
1995 Yuletide Central (2nd Ed.) QX5079	Yr.Iss.	1995	18.95	13-30

1995 Easter Ornaments - Keepsake

YEAR ISSUE	EDITION LIMIT	YEAR RETD.	ISSUE PRICE	*QUOTE U.S.$
1995 3 Flowerpot Friends 1495QEO8229	Yr.Iss.	1995	14.95	16-28
1995 Baby's First Easter QEO8237	Yr.Iss.	1995	7.95	16-20
1995 Bugs Bunny (Looney Tunes) QEO8279	Yr.Iss.	1995	8.95	20-25
1995 Bunny w/Crayons (Crayola) QEO8249	Yr.Iss.	1995	7.95	18-25
1995 Bunny w/Seed Packets (Tender Touches) QEO8259	Yr.Iss.	1995	8.95	19-22
1995 Bunny w/Water Bucket QEO8253	Yr.Iss.	1995	6.95	10-14
1995 Collector's Plate (2nd Ed.) QEO8219	Yr.Iss.	1995	7.95	12-20
1995 Daughter Duck QEO8239	Yr.Iss.	1995	5.95	12-15
1995 Easter Beagle (Peanuts) QEO8257	Yr.Iss.	1995	7.95	15-25
1995 Easter Egg Cottages (1st Ed.) QEO8207	Yr.Iss.	1995	8.95	18-23
1995 Garden Club (1st Ed.) QEO8209	Yr.Iss.	1995	7.95	12-20
1995 Ham n Eggs QEO8277	Yr.Iss.	1995	7.95	8-16
1995 Here Comes Easter (2nd Ed.) QEO8217	Yr.Iss.	1995	7.95	12-20
1995 Lily (Religious) QEO8267	Yr.Iss.	1995	6.95	8
1995 Miniature Train QEO8269	Yr.Iss.	1995	4.95	13
1995 Son Duck QEO8247	Yr.Iss.	1995	5.95	16
1995 Springtime Barbie™ (1st Ed.) QEO8069	Yr.Iss.	1995	12.95	20-35
1995 Springtime Bonnets (3rd Ed.) QEO8227	Yr.Iss.	1995	7.95	23-45

1995 Keepsake Collector's Club - Keepsake

YEAR ISSUE	EDITION LIMIT	YEAR RETD.	ISSUE PRICE	*QUOTE U.S.$
1995 1958 Ford Edsel Citation Convertible QXC4167	Yr.Iss.	1995	12.95	45-75
1995 Brunette Debut-1959 QXC5397	Yr.Iss.	1995	14.95	35-75
1995 Christmas Eve Bake-Off QXC4049	Yr.Iss.	1995	55.00	75-170
1995 Cinderella's Stepsisters QXC4159	Yr.Iss.	1995	3.75	4
1995 Collecting Memories QXC4117	Yr.Iss.	1995	12.00	12
1995 Cool Santa QXC4457	Yr.Iss.	1995	5.75	10-12
1995 Cozy Christmas QXC4119	Yr.Iss.	1995	8.50	13-15
1995 Fishing for Fun QXC5207	Yr.Iss.	1995	10.95	15-18
1995 A Gift From Rodney QXC4129	Yr.Iss.	1995	5.00	8-10
1995 Home From the Woods QXC1059	Yr.Iss.	1995	15.95	28-65
1995 May Flower QXC8246	Yr.Iss.	1995	4.95	25-32

1995 Keepsake Magic Ornaments - Keepsake

YEAR ISSUE	EDITION LIMIT	YEAR RETD.	ISSUE PRICE	*QUOTE U.S.$
1995 Baby's First Christmas QLX7317	Yr.Iss.	1995	22.00	45
1995 Chris Mouse Tree (11th Ed.) QLX7307	Yr.Iss.	1995	12.50	27
1995 Coming to See Santa QLX7369	Yr.Iss.	1995	32.00	65
1995 Forest Frolics (7th Ed.) QLX7299	Yr.Iss.	1995	28.00	50-55
1995 Fred and Dino QLX7289	Yr.Iss.	1995	28.00	60
1995 Friends Share Fun QLX7349	Yr.Iss.	1995	16.50	38
1995 Goody Gumballs! QLX7367	Yr.Iss.	1995	12.50	33
1995 Headin' Home QLX7327	Yr.Iss.	1995	22.00	50
1995 Holiday Swim QLX7319	Yr.Iss.	1995	18.50	40
1995 Jukebox Party QLX7339	Yr.Iss.	1995	24.50	25
1995 Jumping for Joy QLX7347	Yr.Iss.	1995	28.00	60
1995 My First HOT WHEELS™ QLX7279	Yr.Iss.	1995	28.00	29-40
1995 PEANUTS® (5th Ed.) QLX7277	Yr.Iss.	1995	24.50	45-50
1995 Santa's Diner QLX7337	Yr.Iss.	1995	24.50	30
1995 Space Shuttle QLX7396	Yr.Iss.	1995	24.50	30
1995 Superman™ QLX7309	Yr.Iss.	1995	28.00	55
1995 Tobin Fraley Holiday Carousel (2nd Ed.) QLX7269	Yr.Iss.	1995	32.00	65
1995 Victorian Toy Box (Special Ed.) QLX7357	Yr.Iss.	1995	42.00	38-59
1995 Wee Little Christmas QLX7329	Yr.Iss.	1995	22.00	45
1995 Winnie the Pooh Too Much Hunny QLX7297	Yr.Iss.	1995	24.50	50

1995 Miniature Ornaments - Keepsake

YEAR ISSUE	EDITION LIMIT	YEAR RETD.	ISSUE PRICE	*QUOTE U.S.$
1995 Alice in Wonderland (1st Ed.) QXM4777	Yr.Iss.	1995	6.75	12-*25
1995 Baby's First Christmas QXM4027	Yr.Iss.	1995	4.75	14
1995 Calamity Coyote QXM4467	Yr.Iss.	1995	6.75	16
1995 Centuries of Santa (2nd Ed.) QXM4789	Yr.Iss.	1995	5.75	8-14
1995 Christmas Bells (1st Ed.) QXM4007	Yr.Iss.	1995	4.75	10-30
1995 Christmas Wishes QXM4087	Yr.Iss.	1995	3.75	5-14
1995 Cloisonne Partridge QXM4017	Yr.Iss.	1995	9.75	20
1995 Downhill Double QXM4837	Yr.Iss.	1995	4.75	13
1995 Friendship Duet QXM4019	Yr.Iss.	1995	4.75	14
1995 Furrball QXM4459	Yr.Iss.	1995	5.75	16
1995 Grandpa's Gift QXM4829	Yr.Iss.	1995	5.75	13
1995 Heavenly Praises QXM4037	Yr.Iss.	1995	5.75	13
1995 Joyful Santa QXM4089	Yr.Iss.	1995	4.75	13
1995 Little Beeper QXM4469	Yr.Iss.	1995	5.75	16
1995 March of the Teddy Bears (3rd Ed.) QXM4799	Yr.Iss.	1995	4.75	14
1995 Merry Walruses QXM4057	Yr.Iss.	1995	5.75	20-25
1995 Milk Tank Car (7th Ed.) QXM4817	Yr.Iss.	1995	6.75	20
1995 Miniature Clothespin Soldier (1st Ed.) QXM4097	Yr.Iss.	1995	3.75	20
1995 A Moustershire Christmas QXM4839	Yr.Iss.	1995	24.50	35-50
1995 Murray® "Champion" (1st Ed.) QXM4079	Yr.Iss.	1995	5.75	10-25
1995 Nature's Angels (6th Ed.) QXM4809	Yr.Iss.	1995	4.75	13-20
1995 The Night Before Christmas - (4th Ed.) QXM4807	Yr.Iss.	1995	4.75	20
1995 Nutcracker Guild (2nd Ed.) QXM4787	Yr.Iss.	1995	5.75	10-20
1995 On the Road (3rd Ed.) QXM4797	Yr.Iss.	1995	5.75	17
1995 Pebbles and Bamm-Bamm QXM4757	Yr.Iss.	1995	9.75	15
1995 Playful Penguins QXM4059	Yr.Iss.	1995	5.75	20-25
1995 Precious Creations QXM4077	Yr.Iss.	1995	9.75	20
1995 Rocking Horse (8th Ed.) QXM4827	Yr.Iss.	1995	4.75	14
1995 Santa's Little Big Top (1st Ed.) QXM4779	Yr.Iss.	1995	6.75	12-25
1995 Santa's Visit QXM4047	Yr.Iss.	1995	7.75	8-18
1995 Starlit Nativity QXM4039	Yr.Iss.	1995	7.75	20
1995 Sugarplum Dreams QXM4099	Yr.Iss.	1995	4.75	15
1995 Tiny Treasures (set of 6) QXM4009	Yr.Iss.	1995	29.00	35-56
1995 Tudor House- (8th Ed.) QXM4819	Yr.Iss.	1995	6.75	20
1995 Tunnel of Love QXM4029	Yr.Iss.	1995	4.75	13

1995 New Attractions - Keepsake

YEAR ISSUE	EDITION LIMIT	YEAR RETD.	ISSUE PRICE	*QUOTE U.S.$
1995 Acorn 500 QX5929	Yr.Iss.	1995	10.95	18
1995 Batmobile QX5739	Yr.Iss.	1995	14.95	18-28
1995 Betty and Wilma QX5417	Yr.Iss.	1995	14.95	27
1995 Bingo Bear QX5919	Yr.Iss.	1995	7.95	18
1995 Bobbin' Along QX5879	Yr.Iss.	1995	8.95	36-40
1995 Bugs Bunny QX5019	Yr.Iss.	1995	8.95	16-25
1995 Catch the Spirit QX5899	Yr.Iss.	1995	7.95	18
1995 Christmas Morning QX5997	Yr.Iss.	1995	10.95	16
1995 Colorful World QX5519	Yr.Iss.	1995	10.95	19-23
1995 Cows of Bali QX5999	Yr.Iss.	1995	8.95	18
1995 Delivering Kisses QX4107	Yr.Iss.	1995	10.95	21
1995 Dream On QX6007	Yr.Iss.	1995	10.95	21-24
1995 Dudley the Dragon QX6209	Yr.Iss.	1995	10.95	22-25
1995 Faithful Fan QX5897	Yr.Iss.	1995	8.95	19
1995 Feliz Navidad QX5869	Yr.Iss.	1995	7.95	8-18
1995 Forever Friends Bear QX5258	Yr.Iss.	1995	8.95	10-25
1995 GARFIELD QX5007	Yr.Iss.	1995	10.95	18-23
1995 Glinda, Witch of the North QX5749	Yr.Iss.	1995	13.95	20-45
1995 Gopher Fun QX5887	Yr.Iss.	1995	9.95	25
1995 Happy Wrappers QX6037	Yr.Iss.	1995	10.95	25
1995 Heaven's Gift QX6057	Yr.Iss.	1995	20.00	30-45
1995 Hockey Pup QX5917	Yr.Iss.	1995	9.95	23-28
1995 In Time With Christmas QX6049	Yr.Iss.	1995	12.95	25-30
1995 Joy to the World QX5867	Yr.Iss.	1995	8.95	20
1995 LEGO® Fireplace With Santa QX4769	Yr.Iss.	1995	10.95	23
1995 Lou Rankin Bear QX4069	Yr.Iss.	1995	9.95	20-23
1995 The Magic School Bus™ QX5849	Yr.Iss.	1995	10.95	23
1995 Mary Engelbreit QX2409	Yr.Iss.	1995	5.00	17
1995 Merry RV QX6027	Yr.Iss.	1995	12.95	30
1995 Muletide Greetings QX6009	Yr.Iss.	1995	7.95	8-18
1995 The Olympic Spirit QX3169	Yr.Iss.	1995	7.95	20
1995 On the Ice QX6047	Yr.Iss.	1995	7.95	23
1995 Perfect Balance QX5927	Yr.Iss.	1995	7.95	18
1995 PEZ® Santa QX5267	Yr.Iss.	1995	7.95	20-25
1995 Polar Coaster QX6117	Yr.Iss.	1995	8.95	30
1995 Popeye® QX5257	Yr.Iss.	1995	10.95	12-25
1995 Refreshing Gift QX4067	Yr.Iss.	1995	14.95	30
1995 Rejoice! QX5987	Yr.Iss.	1995	10.95	15-23

*Quotes have been rounded up to nearest dollar

YEAR ISSUE	EDITION LIMIT	YEAR RETD.	ISSUE PRICE	*QUOTE U.S.$
1995 Roller Whiz QX5937	Yr.Iss.	1995	7.95	20
1995 Santa in Paris QX5877	Yr.Iss.	1995	8.95	30
1995 Santa's Serenade QX6017	Yr.Iss.	1995	8.95	20
1995 Santa's Visitors QX2407	Yr.Iss.	1995	5.00	18
1995 Simba, Pumbaa and Timon QX6159	Yr.Iss.	1995	12.95	13-20
1995 Ski Hound QX5909	Yr.Iss.	1995	8.95	20
1995 Surfin' Santa QX6019	Yr.Iss.	1995	9.95	23
1995 Sylvester and Tweety QX5017	Yr.Iss.	1995	13.95	24-35
1995 Takin' a Hike QX6029	Yr.Iss.	1995	7.95	20
1995 Tennis, Anyone? QX5907	Yr.Iss.	1995	7.95	20
1995 Thomas the Tank Engine-No. 1 QX5857	Yr.Iss.	1995	9.95	19-35
1995 Three Wishes QX5979	Yr.Iss.	1995	7.95	20
1995 Vera the Mouse QX5537	Yr.Iss.	1995	8.95	19-25
1995 Waiting Up for Santa QX6106	Yr.Iss.	1995	8.95	20
1995 Water Sports QX6039	Yr.Iss.	1995	14.95	35
1995 Wheel of Fortune® QX6187	Yr.Iss.	1995	12.95	12-25
1995 Winnie the Pooh and Tigger QX5009	Yr.Iss.	1995	12.95	35-40
1995 The Winning Play QX5889	Yr.Iss.	1995	7.95	25

1995 Premiere Event - Keepsake

YEAR ISSUE	EDITION LIMIT	YEAR RETD.	ISSUE PRICE	*QUOTE U.S.$
1995 Wish List QX5859	Yr.Iss.	1995	15.00	15-30

1995 Showcase All Is Bright Collection - Keepsake

YEAR ISSUE	EDITION LIMIT	YEAR RETD.	ISSUE PRICE	*QUOTE U.S.$
1995 Angel of Light QK1159	Yr.Iss.	1995	11.95	25
1995 Gentle Lullaby QK1157	Yr.Iss.	1995	11.95	25

1995 Showcase Angel Bells Collection - Keepsake

YEAR ISSUE	EDITION LIMIT	YEAR RETD.	ISSUE PRICE	*QUOTE U.S.$
1995 Carole QK1147	Yr.Iss.	1995	12.95	25
1995 Joy QK1137	Yr.Iss.	1995	12.95	25-35
1995 Noelle QK1139	Yr.Iss.	1995	12.95	25-40

1995 Showcase Folk Art Americana Collection - Keepsake

YEAR ISSUE	EDITION LIMIT	YEAR RETD.	ISSUE PRICE	*QUOTE U.S.$
1995 Fetching the Firewood QK1057	Yr.Iss.	1995	15.95	35
1995 Fishing Party QK1039	Yr.Iss.	1995	15.95	16-35
1995 Guiding Santa QK1037	Yr.Iss.	1995	18.95	50
1995 Learning to Skate QK1047	Yr.Iss.	1995	14.95	15-38

1995 Showcase Holiday Enchantment Collection - Keepsake

YEAR ISSUE	EDITION LIMIT	YEAR RETD.	ISSUE PRICE	*QUOTE U.S.$
1995 Away in a Manger QK1097	Yr.Iss.	1995	13.95	27
1995 Following the Star QK1099	Yr.Iss.	1995	13.95	27

1995 Showcase Invitation to Tea Collection - Keepsake

YEAR ISSUE	EDITION LIMIT	YEAR RETD.	ISSUE PRICE	*QUOTE U.S.$
1995 Cozy Cottage Teapot QK1127	Yr.Iss.	1995	15.95	29
1995 European Castle Teapot QK1129	Yr.Iss.	1995	15.95	29
1995 Victorian Home Teapot QK1119	Yr.Iss.	1995	15.95	30-35

1995 Showcase Nature's Sketchbook Collection - Keepsake

YEAR ISSUE	EDITION LIMIT	YEAR RETD.	ISSUE PRICE	*QUOTE U.S.$
1995 Backyard Orchard QK1069	Yr.Iss.	1995	18.95	30
1995 Christmas Cardinal QK1077	Yr.Iss.	1995	18.95	40
1995 Raising a Family QK1067	Yr.Iss.	1995	18.95	29
1995 Violets and Butterflies QK1079	Yr.Iss.	1995	16.95	29

1995 Showcase Symbols of Christmas Collection - Keepsake

YEAR ISSUE	EDITION LIMIT	YEAR RETD.	ISSUE PRICE	*QUOTE U.S.$
1995 Jolly Santa QK1087	Yr.Iss.	1995	15.95	29
1995 Sweet Song QK1089	Yr.Iss.	1995	15.95	30

1995 Showcase Turn-of-the-Century Parade - Keepsake

YEAR ISSUE	EDITION LIMIT	YEAR RETD.	ISSUE PRICE	*QUOTE U.S.$
1995 The Fireman QK1027	Yr.Iss.	1995	16.95	40

1995 Special Edition - Keepsake

YEAR ISSUE	EDITION LIMIT	YEAR RETD.	ISSUE PRICE	*QUOTE U.S.$
1995 Beverly and Teddy QX5259	Yr.Iss.	1995	21.75	30

1995 Special Issues - Keepsake

YEAR ISSUE	EDITION LIMIT	YEAR RETD.	ISSUE PRICE	*QUOTE U.S.$
1995 Captain James T. Kirk QXI5539	Yr.Iss.	1995	13.95	35-40
1995 Captain Jean-Luc Picard QXI5737	Yr.Iss.	1995	13.95	15-35
1995 Captain John Smith and Meeko QXI6169	Yr.Iss.	1995	12.95	25
1995 Holiday Barbie™ (3rd Ed.) QXI5057	Yr.Iss.	1995	14.95	17-45
1995 Hoop Stars (1st Ed.) QXI5517	Yr.Iss.	1995	14.95	14-35
1995 Joe Montana (1st Ed.) QXI5759	Yr.Iss.	1995	14.95	25-44
1995 Percy, Flit and Meeko QXI6179	Yr.Iss.	1995	9.95	10-15
1995 Pocahontas and Captain John Smith QXI6197	Yr.Iss.	1995	14.95	22
1995 Pocahontas QXI6177	Yr.Iss.	1995	12.95	18
1995 Romulan Warbird™ QXI7267	Yr.Iss.	1995	24.00	30-40
1995 The Ships of Star Trek® QXI4109	Yr.Iss.	1995	19.95	23-40
1995 Solo in the Spotlight-Barbie™ (2nd Ed.) QXI5049	Yr.Iss.	1995	14.95	15-35

1995 Special Offer - Keepsake

YEAR ISSUE	EDITION LIMIT	YEAR RETD.	ISSUE PRICE	*QUOTE U.S.$
1995 Charlie Brown QRP4207	Yr.Iss.	1995	3.95	22-35
1995 Linus QRP4217	Yr.Iss.	1995	3.95	19-25
1995 Lucy QRP4209	Yr.Iss.	1995	3.95	17-25
1995 SNOOPY QRP4219	Yr.Iss.	1995	3.95	20-31
1995 Snow Scene QRP4227	Yr.Iss.	1995	3.95	15-25
1995 5-Pc. Set	Yr.Iss.	1995	19.95	60-75

1996 Collectible Series - Keepsake

YEAR ISSUE	EDITION LIMIT	YEAR RETD.	ISSUE PRICE	*QUOTE U.S.$
1996 1955 Chevrolet Camero (2nd Ed.) QX5241	Yr.Iss.	1996	13.95	15-29
1996 1959 Cadillac De Ville (6th Ed.) QX5384	Yr.Iss.	1996	12.95	15-30
1996 700E Hudson Steam Locomotive (1st Ed.) QX5531	Yr.Iss.	1996	18.95	45-100
1996 Bright Flying Colors (8th Ed.) QX5391	Yr.Iss.	1996	10.95	15-25
1996 Cat Naps (3rd Ed.) QX5641	Yr.Iss.	1996	7.95	12-28
1996 A Celebration of Angels (2nd Ed.) QX5634	Yr.Iss.	1996	12.95	17-30
1996 Christkind (2nd Ed.) QX5631	Yr.Iss.	1996	14.95	12-30
1996 Christy-All God's Children-Martha Holcombe (1st Ed.) QX5564	Yr.Iss.	1996	12.95	18-30
1996 Cinderella-1995 (1st Ed.) QX6311	Yr.Iss.	1996	14.95	17-45
1996 Evergreen Santa (Special Ed.) QX5714	Yr.Iss.	1996	22.00	22-40
1996 Fabulous Decade (7th Ed.) QX5661	Yr.Iss.	1996	7.95	8-18
1996 Frosty Friends (17th Ed.) QX5681	Yr.Iss.	1996	10.95	14-22
1996 Mary Had a Little Lamb (4th Ed.) QX5644	Yr.Iss.	1996	13.95	10-30
1996 Merry Olde Santa (7th Ed.) QX5654	Yr.Iss.	1996	14.95	20-30
1996 Murray Airplane (3rd Ed.) QX5364	Yr.Iss.	1996	13.95	14-35
1996 Native American Barbie™ (1st Ed.) QX5561	Yr.Iss.	1996	14.95	15-33
1996 The PEANUTS Gang (4th Ed.) QX5381	Yr.Iss.	1996	9.95	15-25
1996 Puppy Love (6th Ed.) QX5651	Yr.Iss.	1996	7.95	10-25
1996 Rocking Horse (16th Ed.) QX5674	Yr.Iss.	1996	10.95	17-35
1996 Santa's 4X4 (18th Ed.) QX5684	Yr.Iss.	1996	14.95	22-33
1996 Satchel Paige (3rd Ed.) QX5304	Yr.Iss.	1996	12.95	18-25
1996 Victorian Painted Lady (13th Ed.) QX5671	Yr.Iss.	1996	14.95	18-30
1996 Violet-Mary's Angels (9th Ed.) QX5664	Yr.Iss.	1996	6.95	12-18
1996 Yuletide Central (3rd Ed.) QX5011	Yr.Iss.	1996	18.95	25-40

1996 Keepsake Collector's Club - Keepsake

YEAR ISSUE	EDITION LIMIT	YEAR RETD.	ISSUE PRICE	*QUOTE U.S.$
1996 1937 Steelcraft Auburn by Murray® QXC4174	Yr.Iss.	1996	15.95	45-53
1996 1988 Happy Holidays® Barbie™ Doll QXC4181	Yr.Iss.	1996	14.95	50-75
1996 Airmail for Santa QXC4194	Yr.Iss.	1996	8.95	9-15
1996 Rudolph the Red-Nosed Reindeer® QXC7341	Yr.Iss.	1996	N/A	15-20
1996 Rudolph®'s Helper QXC4171	Yr.Iss.	1996	N/A	8-14
1996 Santa QXC4164	Yr.Iss.	1996	N/A	12-20
1996 Santa's Club Soda #4 QXC4191	Yr.Iss.	1996	8.50	12-17
1996 Santa's Toy Shop QXC4201	Yr.Iss.	1996	60.00	125
1996 The Wizard of Oz QXC4161	Yr.Iss.	1996	12.95	38-55

1996 Keepsake Magic Ornaments - Keepsake

YEAR ISSUE	EDITION LIMIT	YEAR RETD.	ISSUE PRICE	*QUOTE U.S.$
1996 Baby's First Christmas QLX7404	Yr.Iss.	1996	22.00	42-45
1996 Chicken Coop Chorus QLX7491	Yr.Iss.	1996	24.50	25-45
1996 Chris Mouse Inn (12th Ed.) QLX7371	Yr.Iss.	1996	14.50	20-29
1996 Father Time QLX7391	Yr.Iss.	1996	24.50	25-55
1996 Freedom 7 (1st Ed.) QLX7524	Yr.Iss.	1996	24.00	65-75
1996 THE JETSONS QLX7411	Yr.Iss.	1996	28.00	28-58
1996 Jukebox Party QLX7339	Yr.Iss.	1996	24.50	55-65
1996 Let Us Adore Him QLX7381	Yr.Iss.	1996	16.50	17-30
1996 North Pole Volunteers (Special Ed.) QLX7471	Yr.Iss.	1996	42.00	50-65
1996 Over the Rooftops QLX7374	Yr.Iss.	1996	14.50	15-30
1996 PEANUTS-Lucy and Schroeder QLX7394	Yr.Iss.	1996	18.50	20-40
1996 Pinball Wonder QLX7451	Yr.Iss.	1996	28.00	28-60
1996 Sharing a Soda QLX7424	Yr.Iss.	1996	24.50	28-49
1996 Slippery Day QLX7414	Yr.Iss.	1996	24.50	45-50
1996 STAR WARS-Millennium Falcon QLX7474	Yr.Iss.	1996	24.00	30-55
1996 The Statue of Liberty QLX7421	Yr.Iss.	1996	24.50	28-50
1996 Tobin Fraley Holiday Carousel (3rd Ed.) QLX7461	Yr.Iss.	1996	32.00	35-60
1996 Treasured Memories QLX7384	Yr.Iss.	1996	18.50	19-40
1996 Video Party QLX7431	Yr.Iss.	1996	28.00	28-55
1996 THE WIZARD OF OZ-Emerald City QLX7454	Yr.Iss.	1996	32.00	50-65

1996 Miniature Ornaments - Keepsake

YEAR ISSUE	EDITION LIMIT	YEAR RETD.	ISSUE PRICE	*QUOTE U.S.$
1996 African Elephants QXM4224	Yr.Iss.	1996	5.75	25-35
1996 Centuries of Santa (3rd Ed.) QXM4091	Yr.Iss.	1996	5.75	8-15
1996 A Child's Gifts QXM4234	Yr.Iss.	1996	6.75	13
1996 Christmas Bear QXM4241	Yr.Iss.	1996	4.75	14
1996 Christmas Bells (2nd Ed.) QXM4071	Yr.Iss.	1996	4.75	7-20
1996 Cookie Car (8th Ed.) QXM4114	Yr.Iss.	1996	6.75	10-18
1996 Cool Delivery Coca-Cola QXM4021	Yr.Iss.	1996	5.75	6-15
1996 GONE WITH THE WIND QXM4211	Yr.Iss.	1996	19.95	28-45
1996 Hattie Chapeau QXM4251	Yr.Iss.	1996	4.75	6-12
1996 Joyous Angel QXM4231	Yr.Iss.	1996	4.75	5
1996 Long Winter's Nap QXM4244	Yr.Iss.	1996	5.75	6-14
1996 Loony Tunes Lovables Baby Sylvester QXM4154	Yr.Iss.	1996	5.75	9-15
1996 Loony Tunes Lovables Baby Tweety QXM4014	Yr.Iss.	1996	5.75	24
1996 Mad Hatter (2nd Ed.) QXM4074	Yr.Iss.	1996	6.75	8-15
1996 March of the Teddy Bears (4th Ed.) QXM4094	Yr.Iss.	1996	4.75	6-12
1996 Message for Santa QXM4254	Yr.Iss.	1996	6.75	7-16
1996 Miniature Clothespin Soldier (2nd Ed.) QXM4144	Yr.Iss.	1996	4.75	8-11
1996 Murray "Fire Truck" (2nd Ed.) QXM4031	Yr.Iss.	1996	6.75	8-15
1996 Nature's Angels (7th Ed.) QXM4111	Yr.Iss.	1996	4.75	6-14
1996 The Night Before Christmas (5th Ed.) QXM4104	Yr.Iss.	1996	5.75	10-14
1996 The Nutcracker Ballet (1st Ed.) QXM4064	Yr.Iss.	1996	14.75	18-30
1996 Nutcracker Guild (3rd Ed.) QXM4084	Yr.Iss.	1996	5.75	15
1996 O Holy Night (Special Ed.) QXM4204	Yr.Iss.	1996	24.50	25-40
1996 On the Road (4th Ed.) QXM4101	Yr.Iss.	1996	5.75	7-10
1996 Peaceful Christmas QXM4214	Yr.Iss.	1996	4.75	5-13
1996 Rocking Horse (9th Ed.) QXM4121	Yr.Iss.	1996	4.75	9-18
1996 Santa's Little Big Top (2nd Ed.) QXM4081	Yr.Iss.	1996	6.75	8-15
1996 Sparkling Crystal Angel (Precious Ed.) QXM4264	Yr.Iss.	1996	9.75	15-23
1996 Tiny Christmas Helpers QXM4261	Yr.Iss.	1996	29.00	38-59
1996 A Tree for WOODSTOCK QXM4767	Yr.Iss.	1996	5.75	10-15
1996 The Vehicles of STAR WARS QXM4024	Yr.Iss.	1996	19.95	35
1996 Village Mill (9th Ed.) QXM4124	Yr.Iss.	1996	6.75	10-16
1996 Winnie the Pooh and Tigger QXM4044	Yr.Iss.	1996	9.75	15-25

1996 New Attractions - Keepsake

YEAR ISSUE	EDITION LIMIT	YEAR RETD.	ISSUE PRICE	*QUOTE U.S.$
1996 Antlers Aweigh! QX5901	Yr.Iss.	1996	9.95	10-20
1996 Apple for Teacher QX6121	Yr.Iss.	1996	7.95	8-16
1996 Bounce Pass QX6031	Yr.Iss.	1996	7.95	8-17
1996 Bowl 'em Over QX6014	Yr.Iss.	1996	7.95	16
1996 BOY SCOUTS OF AMERICA Growth of a Leader QX5541	Yr.Iss.	1996	9.95	10-20
1996 Child Care Giver QX6071	Yr.Iss.	1996	8.95	9-15
1996 Christmas Joy QX6241	Yr.Iss.	1996	14.95	15-30
1996 Christmas Snowman QX6214	Yr.Iss.	1996	9.95	10-23
1996 Come All Ye Faithful QX6244	Yr.Iss.	1996	12.95	13-30
1996 Fan-tastic Season QX5924	Yr.Iss.	1996	9.95	10-20
1996 Feliz Navidad QX6304	Yr.Iss.	1996	9.95	10-20
1996 Glad Tidings QX6231	Yr.Iss.	1996	14.95	10-15
1996 Goal Line Glory QX6001	Yr.Iss.	1996	12.95	13-28
1996 Happy Holi-doze QX5904	Yr.Iss.	1996	9.95	10-22
1996 High Style QX6064	Yr.Iss.	1996	8.95	13-20
1996 Hillside Express QX6134	Yr.Iss.	1996	12.95	13-25
1996 Holiday Haul QX6201	Yr.Iss.	1996	14.95	15-35
1996 Hurrying Downstairs QX6074	Yr.Iss.	1996	8.95	9-18
1996 I Dig Golf QX5891	Yr.Iss.	1996	10.95	11-22
1996 Jackpot Jingle QX5911	Yr.Iss.	1996	9.95	12-22
1996 Jolly Wolly Ark QX6221	Yr.Iss.	1996	12.95	13-25
1996 Kindly Shepherd QX6274	Yr.Iss.	1996	12.95	13-28
1996 Lighting the Way QX6124	Yr.Iss.	1996	12.95	13-29
1996 A Little Song and Dance QX6211	Yr.Iss.	1996	9.95	10-20
1996 Little Spooners QX5504	Yr.Iss.	1996	12.95	13-26
1996 LOONEY TUNES Foghorn Leghorn and Henery Hawk QX5444	Yr.Iss.	1996	13.95	12-30
1996 LOONEY TUNES Marvin the Martian QX5451	Yr.Iss.	1996	10.95	20-25
1996 Madonna & Child QX6324	Yr.Iss.	1996	12.95	13-27
1996 Making His Rounds QX6271	Yr.Iss.	1996	14.95	15-30
1996 Matchless Memories QX6061	Yr.Iss.	1996	9.95	10-20
1996 Maxine QX6224	Yr.Iss.	1996	9.95	19-29
1996 Merry Carpoolers QX5884	Yr.Iss.	1996	14.95	15-30
1996 Olive Oyl and Swee' Pea QX5481	Yr.Iss.	1996	10.95	10-25
1996 Peppermint Surprise QX6234	Yr.Iss.	1996	7.95	8-20
1996 Percy the Small Engine-No. 6 QX6314	Yr.Iss.	1996	9.95	12-20
1996 PEZ® Snowman QX6534	Yr.Iss.	1996	7.95	16-20
1996 Polar Cycle QX6034	Yr.Iss.	1996	12.95	13-27
1996 Prayer for Peace QX6261	Yr.Iss.	1996	7.95	8-16
1996 Precious Child QX6251	Yr.Iss.	1996	8.95	9-18
1996 Pup-Tenting QX6011	Yr.Iss.	1996	7.95	8-16
1996 Regal Cardinal QX6204	Yr.Iss.	1996	9.95	10-23
1996 Sew Sweet QX5921	Yr.Iss.	1996	8.95	10-20
1996 SPIDER-MAN QX5757	Yr.Iss.	1996	12.95	18-30
1996 Star of the Show QX6004	Yr.Iss.	1996	8.95	9-18
1996 Tamika QX6301	Yr.Iss.	1996	7.95	10-16
1996 Tender Lovin' Care QX6114	Yr.Iss.	1996	7.95	8-16
1996 This Big! QX5914	Yr.Iss.	1996	9.95	10-20
1996 Time for a Treat QX5464	Yr.Iss.	1996	11.95	10-25
1996 Tonka Mighty Dump Truck QX6321	Yr.Iss.	1996	13.95	18-35
1996 A Tree for SNOOPY QX5507	Yr.Iss.	1996	8.95	10-20
1996 Welcome Guest QX5394	Yr.Iss.	1996	14.95	15-30
1996 Welcome Him QX6264	Yr.Iss.	1996	8.95	16
1996 Winnie the Pooh and Piglet QX5454	Yr.Iss.	1996	12.95	25-30
1996 THE WIZARD OF OZ Witch of the West QX5554	Yr.Iss.	1996	13.95	20-35
1996 WONDER WOMAN QX5941	Yr.Iss.	1996	12.95	10-30
1996 Woodland Santa QX6131	Yr.Iss.	1996	12.95	10-27
1996 Yogi Bear and Boo Boo QX5521	Yr.Iss.	1996	12.95	15-30
1996 Yuletide Cheer QX6054	Yr.Iss.	1996	7.95	8-16
1996 Ziggy QX6524	Yr.Iss.	1996	9.95	15-28

1996 NFL Ornaments - Keepsake

YEAR ISSUE	EDITION LIMIT	YEAR RETD.	ISSUE PRICE	*QUOTE U.S.$
1996 Arizona Cardinals QSR6484	Yr.Iss.	1996	9.95	14
1996 Atlanta Falcons QSR6364	Yr.Iss.	1996	9.95	14
1996 Browns QSR6391	Yr.Iss.	1996	9.95	10-20
1996 Buffalo Bills QSR6371	Yr.Iss.	1996	9.95	10-20
1996 Carolina Panthers QSR6374	Yr.Iss.	1996	9.95	10-20
1996 Chicago Bears QSR6381	Yr.Iss.	1996	9.95	14
1996 Cincinnati Bengals QSR6384	Yr.Iss.	1996	9.95	14
1996 Dallas Cowboys QSR6394	Yr.Iss.	1996	9.95	14-23
1996 Denver Broncos QSR6411	Yr.Iss.	1996	9.95	14
1996 Detroit Lions QSR6414	Yr.Iss.	1996	9.95	14-20
1996 Green Bay Packers QSR6421	Yr.Iss.	1996	9.95	14-75
1996 Indianapolis Colts QSR6431	Yr.Iss.	1996	9.95	14
1996 Jacksonville Jaguars QSR6434	Yr.Iss.	1996	9.95	14-20
1996 Kansas City Chiefs QSR6361	Yr.Iss.	1996	9.95	10-20
1996 Miami Dolphins QSR6451	Yr.Iss.	1996	9.95	10
1996 Minnesota Vikings QSR6454	Yr.Iss.	1996	9.95	10-20
1996 New England Patriots QSR6461	Yr.Iss.	1996	9.95	14
1996 New Orleans Saints QSR6464	Yr.Iss.	1996	9.95	14
1996 New York Giants QSR6471	Yr.Iss.	1996	9.95	14-20
1996 New York Jets QSR6474	Yr.Iss.	1996	9.95	14-20
1996 Oakland Raiders QSR6441	Yr.Iss.	1996	9.95	10
1996 Oilers QSR6424	Yr.Iss.	1996	9.95	10-20
1996 Philadelphia Eagles QSR6481	Yr.Iss.	1996	9.95	14-20

YEAR ISSUE	EDITION LIMIT	YEAR RETD.	ISSUE PRICE	*QUOTE U.S.$
1996 Pittsburgh Steelers QSR6491	Yr.Iss.	1996	9.95	10
1996 San Diego Chargers QSR6494	Yr.Iss.	1996	9.95	14
1996 San Francisco 49ers QSR6501	Yr.Iss.	1996	9.95	14-20
1996 Seattle Seahawks QSR6504	Yr.Iss.	1996	9.95	14
1996 St.Louis Rams QSR6444	Yr.Iss.	1996	9.95	15
1996 Tampa Bay Buccaneers QSR6511	Yr.Iss.	1996	9.95	14
1996 Washington Redskins QSR6514	Yr.Iss.	1996	9.95	10-20

1996 Premiere Event - Keepsake

YEAR ISSUE	EDITION LIMIT	YEAR RETD.	ISSUE PRICE	*QUOTE U.S.$
1996 Bashful Mistletoe-Merry Minatures QFM8054	Yr.Iss.	1996	12.95	13
1996 Welcome Sign-Tender Touches QX6331	Yr.Iss.	1996	15.00	15-30

1996 Showcase Cookie Jar Friends Collection - Keepsake

YEAR ISSUE	EDITION LIMIT	YEAR RETD.	ISSUE PRICE	*QUOTE U.S.$
1996 Carmen QK1164	Yr.Iss.	1996	15.95	16
1996 Clyde QK1161	Yr.Iss.	1996	15.95	16

1996 Showcase Folk Art Americana Collection - Keepsake

YEAR ISSUE	EDITION LIMIT	YEAR RETD.	ISSUE PRICE	*QUOTE U.S.$
1996 Caroling Angel QK1134	Yr.Iss.	1996	16.95	22-35
1996 Mrs. Claus QK1204	Yr.Iss.	1996	18.95	23-35
1996 Santa's Gifts QK1124	Yr.Iss.	1996	18.95	25-55

1996 Showcase Magi Bells Collection - Keepsake

YEAR ISSUE	EDITION LIMIT	YEAR RETD.	ISSUE PRICE	*QUOTE U.S.$
1996 Balthasar (Frankincense) QK1174	Yr.Iss.	1996	13.95	14
1996 Caspar (Myrrh) QK1184	Yr.Iss.	1996	13.95	14
1996 Melchior (Gold) QK1181	Yr.Iss.	1996	13.95	14

1996 Showcase Nature's Sketchbook Collection - Keepsake

YEAR ISSUE	EDITION LIMIT	YEAR RETD.	ISSUE PRICE	*QUOTE U.S.$
1996 The Birds' Christmas Tree QK1114	Yr.Iss.	1996	18.95	19-35
1996 Christmas Bunny QK1104	Yr.Iss.	1996	18.95	19-35
1996 The Holly Basket QK1094	Yr.Iss.	1996	18.95	19-30

1996 Showcase Sacred Masterworks Collection - Keepsake

YEAR ISSUE	EDITION LIMIT	YEAR RETD.	ISSUE PRICE	*QUOTE U.S.$
1996 Madonna and Child QK1144	Yr.Iss.	1996	15.95	16
1996 Praying Madonna QK1154	Yr.Iss.	1996	15.95	16

1996 Showcase The Language of Flowers Collection - Keepsake

YEAR ISSUE	EDITION LIMIT	YEAR RETD.	ISSUE PRICE	*QUOTE U.S.$
1996 Pansy (1st Ed.) QK1171	Yr.Iss.	1996	15.95	38-65

1996 Showcase Turn-of-the-Century Parade Collection - Keepsake

YEAR ISSUE	EDITION LIMIT	YEAR RETD.	ISSUE PRICE	*QUOTE U.S.$
1996 Uncle Sam (2nd Ed.) QK1084	Yr.Iss.	1996	16.95	17-32

1996 Special Issues - Keepsake

YEAR ISSUE	EDITION LIMIT	YEAR RETD.	ISSUE PRICE	*QUOTE U.S.$
1996 101 Dalmatians-Collector's Plate QXI6544	Yr.Iss.	1996	12.95	13
1996 Featuring the Enchanted Evening-Barbie™ Doll (3rd Ed.) QXI6541	Yr.Iss.	1996	14.95	15-30
1996 Holiday Barbie™ (4th Ed.) QXI5371	Yr.Iss.	1996	14.95	13-18
1996 HUNCHBACK OF NOTRE DAME-Esmeralda and Djali QXI6351	Yr.Iss.	1996	14.95	18-30
1996 HUNCHBACK OF NOTRE DAME -Laverne, Victor and Hugo QXI6354	Yr.Iss.	1996	12.95	13-26
1996 THE HUNCHBACK OF NOTRE DAME-Quasimodo QXI6341	Yr.Iss.	1996	9.95	15-19
1996 It's A Wonderful Life™ (Anniversary Ed.) QXI6531	Yr.Iss.	1996	14.95	22-65
1996 Larry Bird-Hoop Stars (2nd Ed.) QXI5014	Yr.Iss.	1996	14.95	15-30
1996 Nolan Ryan-At the Ballpark (1st Ed.) QXI5711	Yr.Iss.	1996	14.95	20-35
1996 OLYMIC-Parade of Nations-Collector's Plate QXE5741	Yr.Iss.	1996	10.95	11
1996 OLYMPIC-Cloisonne Medallion QXE4041	Yr.Iss.	1996	9.75	10-20
1996 OLYMPIC-Invitation to the Games QXE5511	Yr.Iss.	1996	14.95	15-30
1996 OLYMPIC-IZZY-The Mascot QXE5724	Yr.Iss.	1996	9.95	10-20
1996 OLYMPIC-Lighting the Flame QXE7444	Yr.Iss.	1996	28.00	25-55
1996 OLYMPIC-Olympic Triumph QXE5731	Yr.Iss.	1996	10.95	11-22
1996 STAR TREK® THE NEXT GENERATION-Commander William T. Riker QXI5551	Yr.Iss.	1996	14.95	30-77
1996 STAR TREK®-30 Years QXI7534	Yr.Iss.	1996	45.00	60-90
1996 STAR TREK®-Mr. Spock QXI5544	Yr.Iss.	1996	14.95	30
1996 STAR TREK®-U.S.S.Voyager QXI7544	Yr.Iss.	1996	24.00	30-45
1996 Troy Aikman-Football Legends (2nd Ed.) QXI5021	Yr.Iss.	1996	14.95	25-30

1996 Spring Ornaments - Keepsake

YEAR ISSUE	EDITION LIMIT	YEAR RETD.	ISSUE PRICE	*QUOTE U.S.$
1996 Apple Blossom Lane QEO8084	Yr.Iss.	1996	8.95	17
1996 Collector's Plate QEO8221	Yr.Iss.	1996	7.95	14
1996 Daffy Duck, LOONEY TUNES QEO8154	Yr.Iss.	1996	8.95	15-17
1996 Easter Morning QEO8164	Yr.Iss.	1996	7.95	18
1996 Eggstra Special Surprise, Tender Touches QEO8161	Yr.Iss.	1996	8.95	20
1996 Garden Club QEO8091	Yr.Iss.	1996	7.95	17
1996 Here Comes Easter QEO8094	Yr.Iss.	1996	7.95	18
1996 Hippity-Hop Delivery, CRAYOLA® Crayon QEO8144	Yr.Iss.	1996	7.95	20
1996 Joyful Angels QEO8184	Yr.Iss.	1996	9.95	27-35
1996 Locomotive, Cottontail Express QEO8074	Yr.Iss.	1996	8.95	23-55
1996 Look What I Found! QEO8181	Yr.Iss.	1996	7.95	16
1996 Parade Pals, PEANUTS® QEO8151	Yr.Iss.	1996	7.95	16
1996 Peter Rabbit™ Beatrix Potter™ QEO8071	Yr.Iss.	1996	8.95	50-80
1996 Pork 'n Beans QEO8174	Yr.Iss.	1996	7.95	8-15
1996 Springtime Barbie™ QEO8081	Yr.Iss.	1996	12.95	18-28
1996 Springtime Bonnets QEO8134	Yr.Iss.	1996	7.95	28
1996 Strawberry Patch QEO8171	Yr.Iss.	1996	6.95	17
1996 Strike Up the Band! QEO8141	Yr.Iss.	1996	14.95	23

1997 Collectible Series - Keepsake

YEAR ISSUE	EDITION LIMIT	YEAR RETD.	ISSUE PRICE	*QUOTE U.S.$
1997 1950 Santa Fe F3 Diesel Locomotive (2nd Ed.) QX6145	Yr.Iss.	1997	18.95	19-35
1997 1953 GMC (3rd Ed.) QX6105	Yr.Iss.	1997	13.95	14-18
1997 1969 Hurst Oldsmobile 442 (7th Ed.) QX6102	Yr.Iss.	1997	13.95	14-18
1997 Bright Rocking Colors (8th Ed.) QX6235	Yr.Iss.	1997	12.95	13
1997 Cafe (14th Ed.) QX6245	Yr.Iss.	1997	16.95	17-22
1997 Cat Naps (4th Ed.) QX6205	Yr.Iss.	1997	8.95	9
1997 A Celebration of Angels (3rd Ed.) QX6175	Yr.Iss.	1997	13.95	14
1997 Chinese Barbie™ (2nd Ed.) QX6162	Yr.Iss.	1997	14.95	15
1997 The Claus-Mobile (19th Ed.) QX6262	Yr.Iss.	1997	14.95	15-20
1997 The Clauses on Vacation (1st Ed.) QX6112	Yr.Iss.	1997	14.95	15
1997 Daisy-Mary's Angels (10th Ed.) QX6242	Yr.Iss.	1997	7.95	8-12
1997 Fabulous Decade (8th Ed.) QX6232	Yr.Iss.	1997	7.95	8-13
1997 The Flight at Kitty Hawk (1st Ed.) QX5574	Yr.Iss.	1997	14.95	11-30
1997 Frosty Friends (18th Ed.) QX6255	Yr.Iss.	1997	10.95	11-15
1997 Jackie Robinson (4th Ed.) QX6202	Yr.Iss.	1997	12.95	13
1997 Kolyada (3rd Ed.) QX6172	Yr.Iss.	1997	14.95	10-15
1997 Little Boy Blue (5th Ed.) QX6215	Yr.Iss.	1997	13.95	14
1997 Little Red Riding Hood-1991 (2nd Ed.) QX6155	Yr.Iss.	1997	14.95	15-22
1997 Marilyn Monroe (1st Ed.) QX5704	Yr.Iss.	1997	14.95	12-30
1997 Merry Olde Santa (8th Ed.) QX6225	Yr.Iss.	1997	14.95	15-27
1997 Murray Dump Truck (4th Ed.) QX6195	Yr.Iss.	1997	13.95	14-17
1997 Nikki-All God's Children®-Martha Root (2nd Ed.) QX6142	Yr.Iss.	1997	12.95	13
1997 Puppy Love (7th Ed.) QX6222	Yr.Iss.	1997	7.95	8
1997 Scarlett O'Hara (1st Ed.) QX6125	Yr.Iss.	1997	14.95	15-30
1997 Snowshoe Rabbits in Winter-Mark Newman (1st Ed.) QX5694	Yr.Iss.	1997	12.95	20-45
1997 Yuletide Central (4th Ed.) QX5812	Yr.Iss.	1997	18.95	19

1997 Disney Ornaments - Keepsake

YEAR ISSUE	EDITION LIMIT	YEAR RETD.	ISSUE PRICE	*QUOTE U.S.$
1997 Ariel QX14072	Yr.Iss.	1997	12.95	13
1997 Bandleader Mickey (1st Ed.) QXD4022	Yr.Iss.	1997	13.95	15
1997 Cinderella (1st Ed.) QXD4045	Yr.Iss.	1997	14.95	22-30
1997 Donald's Surprising Gift (1st Ed.) QXD4025	Yr.Iss.	1997	12.95	15
1997 Esmeralda & Phoebus QXD6344	Yr.Iss.	1997	14.95	15
1997 Goofy's Ski Adventure QXD4042	Yr.Iss.	1997	12.95	13
1997 Gus & Jaq QXD4052	Yr.Iss.	1997	12.95	13
1997 Hercules QXI4005	Yr.Iss.	1997	12.95	15
1997 Honey of a Gift (Miniature) QXD4255	Yr.Iss.	1997	6.95	7
1997 Jasmine & Aladdin QXD4062	Yr.Iss.	1997	14.95	15
1997 Megara and Pegasus QXI4012	Yr.Iss.	1997	16.95	17
1997 Mickey Snow Angel QXD4035	Yr.Iss.	1997	9.95	10
1997 Mickey's Long Shot QXD6412	Yr.Iss.	1997	10.95	8-11
1997 New Pair of Skates QXD4032	Yr.Iss.	1997	13.95	14
1997 Snow White (Anniversary Ed.) QXD4055	Yr.Iss.	1997	16.95	17-20
1997 Timon & Pumbaa QXD4065	Yr.Iss.	1997	12.95	13
1997 Two Tone QXD4015	Yr.Iss.	1997	9.95	10-15
1997 Waitin' on Santa QXD6365	Yr.Iss.	1997	12.95	13
1997 Winnie the Pooh Plate QXE6835	Yr.Iss.	1997	12.95	13

1997 Keepsake Collector's Club - Keepsake

YEAR ISSUE	EDITION LIMIT	YEAR RETD.	ISSUE PRICE	*QUOTE U.S.$
1997 1937 Steelcraft Airflow by Murray® QXC5185	Yr.Iss.	1997	15.95	16
1997 1989 Happy Holidays® Barbie™ Doll QXC5162	Yr.Iss.	1997	15.95	100
1997 Away to the Window QXC5135	Yr.Iss.	1997	N/A	N/A
1997 Farmer's Market, Tender Touches QXC5182	Yr.Iss.	1997	15.00	15
1997 Happy Christmas to All! QXC5132	Yr.Iss.	1997	N/A	N/A
1997 Jolly Old Santa QXC5145	Yr.Iss.	1997	N/A	N/A
1997 Mrs. Claus (Artist on Tour) QXC5192	Yr.Iss.	1997	14.95	15
1997 Ready for Santa QXC5142	Yr.Iss.	1997	N/A	N/A
1997 Trimming Santa's Tree (Artist on Tour) QXC5175	Yr.Iss.	1997	60.00	60

1997 Keepsake Magic Ornaments - Keepsake

YEAR ISSUE	EDITION LIMIT	YEAR RETD.	ISSUE PRICE	*QUOTE U.S.$
1997 Chris Mouse Luminaria (13th Ed.) QLX7525	Yr.Iss.	1997	14.95	15
1997 Decorator Taz QLX7502	Yr.Iss.	1997	30.00	30
1997 Friendship 7 (2nd Ed.) QLX7532	Yr.Iss.	1997	24.00	24
1997 Glowing Angel QLX7435	Yr.Iss.	1997	18.95	19
1997 Holiday Serenade QLX7485	Yr.Iss.	1997	24.00	24
1997 Joy to the World QLX7512	Yr.Iss.	1997	14.95	15
1997 Lighthouse Greetings (1st Ed.) QLX7442	Yr.Iss.	1997	24.00	57-65
1997 The Lincoln Memorial QLX7522	Yr.Iss.	1997	24.00	24
1997 Madonna & Child QLX7425	Yr.Iss.	1997	19.95	20
1997 Motorcycle Chums QLX7495	Yr.Iss.	1997	24.00	24
1997 Santa's Secret Gift QLX7455	Yr.Iss.	1997	24.00	24
1997 Santa's Showboat (Special Ed.) QLX7465	Yr.Iss.	1997	42.00	50-85
1997 SNOOPY Plays Santa QLX7475	Yr.Iss.	1997	22.00	22
1997 Teapot Party QLX7482	Yr.Iss.	1997	18.95	19

1997 Miniature Ornaments - Keepsake

YEAR ISSUE	EDITION LIMIT	YEAR RETD.	ISSUE PRICE	*QUOTE U.S.$
1997 Antique Tractors (1st Ed.) QXM4185	Yr.Iss.	1997	6.95	8
1997 Candy Car (9th Ed.) QXM4175	Yr.Iss.	1997	6.95	7
1997 Casablanca, set/3 QXM4272	Yr.Iss.	1997	19.95	18-20
1997 Centuries of Santa (4th Ed.) QXM4295	Yr.Iss.	1997	5.95	6
1997 Christmas Bells (3rd Ed.) QXM4162	Yr.Iss.	1997	4.95	5
1997 Clothespin Soldier (3rd Ed.) QXM4155	Yr.Iss.	1997	4.95	5
1997 Future Star QXM4232	Yr.Iss.	1997	5.95	6
1997 Gentle Giraffes QXM4221	Yr.Iss.	1997	5.95	20
1997 He Is Born QXM4235	Yr.Iss.	1997	7.95	8
1997 Heavenly Music QXM4292	Yr.Iss.	1997	5.95	6
1997 Herr Drosselmeyer (2nd Ed.) QXM4135	Yr.Iss.	1997	5.95	6
1997 Home Sweet Home QXM4222	Yr.Iss.	1997	5.95	6
1997 Ice Cold Coca-Cola® QXM4252	Yr.Iss.	1997	6.95	7
1997 King of the Forest QXM4262	Yr.Iss.	1997	24.00	24
1997 Murray "Pursuit" Airplane (3rd Ed.) QXM4132	Yr.Iss.	1997	6.95	7
1997 Nutcracker Guild (4th Ed.) QXM4165	Yr.Iss.	1997	6.95	7
1997 On The Road (5th Ed.) QXM4172	Yr.Iss.	1997	5.95	6
1997 Our Lady of Guadalupe (Precious Ed.) QXM4275	Yr.Iss.	1997	8.95	9
1997 Peppermint Painter QXM4312	Yr.Iss.	1997	4.95	5
1997 Polar Buddies QXM4332	Yr.Iss.	1997	4.95	5
1997 Rocking Horse (10th Ed.) QXM4302	Yr.Iss.	1997	4.95	5
1997 Santa's Little Big Top (3rd Ed.) QXM4152	Yr.Iss.	1997	6.95	7
1997 Seeds of Joy QXM4242	Yr.Iss.	1997	6.95	7
1997 Sew Talented QXM4195	Yr.Iss.	1997	5.95	6
1997 Shutterbug QXM4212	Yr.Iss.	1997	5.95	6
1997 Snowboard Bunny QXM4315	Yr.Iss.	1997	4.95	5
1997 Snowflake Ballet (1st Ed.) QXM4192	Yr.Iss.	1997	5.95	6
1997 Teddy-Bear Style (1st Ed.) QXM4215	Yr.Iss.	1997	5.95	6
1997 Tiny Home Improvers,set/6 QXM4282	Yr.Iss.	1997	29.00	29
1997 Victorian Skater QXM4305	Yr.Iss.	1997	5.95	6
1997 Village Depot (10th Ed.) QXM4182	Yr.Iss.	1997	6.95	7
1997 Welcome Friends, set/4 (1st Ed.) QXM4205	Yr.Iss.	1997	6.95	7
1997 White Rabbit (3rd Ed.) QXM4142	Yr.Iss.	1997	6.95	7

1997 NBA Collection - Keepsake

YEAR ISSUE	EDITION LIMIT	YEAR RETD.	ISSUE PRICE	*QUOTE U.S.$
1997 Charlotte Hornets QSR1222	Yr.Iss.	1997	9.95	10
1997 Chicago Bulls QSR1232	Yr.Iss.	1997	9.95	10
1997 Detroit Pistons QSR1242	Yr.Iss.	1997	9.95	10
1997 Houston Rockets QSR1245	Yr.Iss.	1997	9.95	10
1997 Indiana Pacers QSR1252	Yr.Iss.	1997	9.95	10
1997 Los Angeles Lakers QSR1262	Yr.Iss.	1997	9.95	10
1997 New York Knickerbockers QSR1272	Yr.Iss.	1997	9.95	10
1997 Orlando Magic QSR1282	Yr.Iss.	1997	9.95	10
1997 Phoenix Suns QSR1292	Yr.Iss.	1997	9.95	10
1997 Seattle Supersonics QSR1295	Yr.Iss.	1997	9.95	10

1997 New Attractions - Keepsake

YEAR ISSUE	EDITION LIMIT	YEAR RETD.	ISSUE PRICE	*QUOTE U.S.$
1997 All-Round Sports Fan QX6392	Yr.Iss.	1997	8.95	9
1997 All-Weather Walker QX6415	Yr.Iss.	1997	8.95	9
1997 Angel Friend (Archive Collection) QX6762	Yr.Iss.	1997	14.95	15
1997 Biking Buddies QX6682	Yr.Iss.	1997	12.95	13
1997 Breezin' Along QX6722	Yr.Iss.	1997	8.95	9
1997 Bucket Brigade QX6382	Yr.Iss.	1997	8.95	9
1997 Catch of the Day QX6712	Yr.Iss.	1997	9.95	10
1997 Christmas Checkup QX6385	Yr.Iss.	1997	7.95	8
1997 Classic Cross QX6805	Yr.Iss.	1997	13.95	14
1997 Clever Camper QX6445	Yr.Iss.	1997	7.95	8
1997 Cycling Santa QX6425	Yr.Iss.	1997	14.95	15
1997 Downhill Run QX6705	Yr.Iss.	1997	9.95	10
1997 Elegance on Ice QX6432	Yr.Iss.	1997	9.95	10
1997 Expressly for Teacher QX6375	Yr.Iss.	1997	7.95	8
1997 Feliz Navidad QX6665	Yr.Iss.	1997	8.95	9
1997 God's Gift of Love QX6792	Yr.Iss.	1997	16.95	17
1997 Heavenly Song (Archive Collection) QX6795	Yr.Iss.	1997	12.95	13
1997 Howdy Doody (Anniversary Ed.) QX6272	Yr.Iss.	1997	12.95	13-30
1997 The Incredible Hulk QX5471	Yr.Iss.	1997	12.95	13
1997 Jingle Bell Jester QX6695	Yr.Iss.	1997	9.95	10
1997 Juggling Stars QX6595	Yr.Iss.	1997	9.95	9
1997 King Noor-First King QX6552	Yr.Iss.	1997	12.95	13
1997 Lion and Lamb QX6602	Yr.Iss.	1997	7.95	8
1997 The Lone Ranger QX6265	Yr.Iss.	1997	12.95	25-35
1997 Love to Sew QX6435	Yr.Iss.	1997	7.95	8
1997 Madonna del Rosario QX6545	Yr.Iss.	1997	12.95	13
1997 Marbles Champion QX6342	Yr.Iss.	1997	10.95	11
1997 Meadow Snowman QX6715	Yr.Iss.	1997	12.95	13
1997 Michigan J. Frog QX6332	Yr.Iss.	1997	9.95	10-20
1997 Miss Gulch QX6372	Yr.Iss.	1997	13.95	14-20
1997 Mr. Potato Head QX6335	Yr.Iss.	1997	10.95	11
1997 Nativity Tree QX6575	Yr.Iss.	1997	14.95	15
1997 The Night Before Christmas -Collector's Choice QX5721	Yr.Iss.	1997	24.00	24
1997 Playful Shepherd QX6592	Yr.Iss.	1997	9.95	10
1997 Porcelain Hinged Box QX6772	Yr.Iss.	1997	14.95	15
1997 Praise Him QX6542	Yr.Iss.	1997	8.95	9
1997 Prize Topiary QX6675	Yr.Iss.	1997	14.95	15
1997 Sailor Bear QX6765	Yr.Iss.	1997	14.95	15

*Quotes have been rounded up to nearest dollar

ORNAMENTS

YEAR ISSUE	EDITION LIMIT	YEAR RETD.	ISSUE PRICE	*QUOTE U.S.$
1997 Santa Mail QX6702	Yr.Iss.	1997	10.95	11
1997 Santa's Friend QX6685	Yr.Iss.	1997	12.95	13
1997 Santa's Magical Sleigh QX6672	Yr.Iss.	1997	24.00	24
1997 Santa's Polar Friend (Archive Collection) QX6755	Yr.Iss.	1997	16.95	17
1997 Santa's Ski Adventure QX6422	Yr.Iss.	1997	12.95	13
1997 Snow Bowling QX6395	Yr.Iss.	1997	6.95	7
1997 Snow Girl QX6562	Yr.Iss.	1997	7.95	8
1997 The Spirit of Christmas-Collector's Plate QX6585	Yr.Iss.	1997	9.95	10
1997 Stealing a Kiss QX6555	Yr.Iss.	1997	14.95	15
1997 Sweet Discovery QX6325	Yr.Iss.	1997	11.95	12
1997 Sweet Dreamer QX6732	Yr.Iss.	1997	6.95	7
1997 Swinging in the Snow QX6775	Yr.Iss.	1997	12.95	13
1997 Taking a Break QX6305	Yr.Iss.	1997	14.95	15
1997 Tomorrow's Leader QX6452	Yr.Iss.	1997	9.95	10
1997 Tonka® Mighty Front Loader QX6362	Yr.Iss.	1997	13.95	15-28
1997 What a Deal! QX6442	Yr.Iss.	1997	8.95	9

1997 NFL Ornaments - Keepsake

YEAR ISSUE	EDITION LIMIT	YEAR RETD.	ISSUE PRICE	*QUOTE U.S.$
1997 Arizona Cardinals QSR5505	Yr.Iss.	1997	9.95	10
1997 Atlanta Falcons QSR5305	Yr.Iss.	1997	9.95	10
1997 Baltimore Ravens QSR5352	Yr.Iss.	1997	9.95	10
1997 Buffalo Bills QSR5312	Yr.Iss.	1997	9.95	10
1997 Carolina Panthers QSR5315	Yr.Iss.	1997	9.95	10
1997 Chicago Bears QSR5322	Yr.Iss.	1997	9.95	10
1997 Cincinnati Bengals QSR5325	Yr.Iss.	1997	9.95	10
1997 Dallas Cowboys QSR5355	Yr.Iss.	1997	9.95	10
1997 Denver Broncos QSR5362	Yr.Iss.	1997	9.95	10
1997 Detroit Lions QSR5365	Yr.Iss.	1997	9.95	10
1997 Green Bay Packers QSR5372	Yr.Iss.	1997	9.95	10
1997 Houston Oilers QSR5375	Yr.Iss.	1997	9.95	10
1997 Indianapolis Colts QSR5411	Yr.Iss.	1997	9.95	10
1997 Jacksonville Jaquars QSR5415	Yr.Iss.	1997	9.95	10
1997 Kansas City Chiefs QSR5502	Yr.Iss.	1997	9.95	10
1997 Miami Dolphins QSR5472	Yr.Iss.	1997	9.95	10
1997 Minnesota Vikings QSR5475	Yr.Iss.	1997	9.95	10
1997 New England Patriots QSR5482	Yr.Iss.	1997	9.95	10
1997 New Orleans Saints QSR5485	Yr.Iss.	1997	9.95	10
1997 New York Giants QSR5492	Yr.Iss.	1997	9.95	10
1997 New York Jets QSR5495	Yr.Iss.	1997	9.95	10
1997 Oakland Raiders QSR5422	Yr.Iss.	1997	9.95	10
1997 Philadelphia Eagles QSR5502	Yr.Iss.	1997	9.95	10
1997 Pittsburgh Steelers QSR5512	Yr.Iss.	1997	9.95	10
1997 San Diego Chargers QSR5515	Yr.Iss.	1997	9.95	10
1997 San Francisco 49ers QSR5522	Yr.Iss.	1997	9.95	10
1997 Seattle Seahawks QSR5525	Yr.Iss.	1997	9.95	10
1997 St. Louis Rams QSR5425	Yr.Iss.	1997	9.95	10
1997 Tampa Bay Buccaneers QSR5532	Yr.Iss.	1997	9.95	10
1997 Washington Redskins QSR5535	Yr.Iss.	1997	9.95	10

1997 Premiere Event - Keepsake

YEAR ISSUE	EDITION LIMIT	YEAR RETD.	ISSUE PRICE	*QUOTE U.S.$
1997 The Perfect Tree-Tender Touches QX6572	Yr.Iss.	1997	15.00	15

1997 Showcase Folk Art Americana Collection - Keepsake

YEAR ISSUE	EDITION LIMIT	YEAR RETD.	ISSUE PRICE	*QUOTE U.S.$
1997 Leading the Way QX6782	Yr.Iss.	1997	16.95	17
1997 Santa's Merry Path QX6785	Yr.Iss.	1997	16.95	10

1997 Showcase Nature's Sketchbook Collection - Keepsake

YEAR ISSUE	EDITION LIMIT	YEAR RETD.	ISSUE PRICE	*QUOTE U.S.$
1997 Garden Bouquet QX6752	Yr.Iss.	1997	14.95	15
1997 Garden Bunnies QEO8702	Yr.Iss.	1997	14.95	15
1997 Honored Guest QX6745	Yr.Iss.	1997	14.95	15

1997 Showcase The Language of Flowers Collection - Keepsake

YEAR ISSUE	EDITION LIMIT	YEAR RETD.	ISSUE PRICE	*QUOTE U.S.$
1997 Snowdrop Angel (2nd Ed.) QX1095	Yr.Iss.	1997	15.95	16

1997 Showcase Turn-of-the-Century Parade Collection - Keepsake

YEAR ISSUE	EDITION LIMIT	YEAR RETD.	ISSUE PRICE	*QUOTE U.S.$
1997 Santa Claus (3rd Ed.) QX1215	Yr.Iss.	1997	16.95	17-20

1997 Special Issues - Keepsake

YEAR ISSUE	EDITION LIMIT	YEAR RETD.	ISSUE PRICE	*QUOTE U.S.$
1997 1997 Corvette Miniature QXI4322	Yr.Iss.	1997	6.95	7
1997 1997 Corvette QXI6455	Yr.Iss.	1997	13.95	14
1997 Ariel QXI4072	Yr.Iss.	1997	12.95	13
1997 Barbie™ And Ken Wedding Day QXI6815	Yr.Iss.	1997	35.00	35
1997 Barbie™ Wedding Day-1959-1962 (4th Ed.) QXI6812	Yr.Iss.	1997	15.95	16
1997 C-3PO & R2-D2 QXI4265	Yr.Iss.	1997	12.95	13-18
1997 Commander Data QXI6345	Yr.Iss.	1997	14.95	15
1997 Darth Vader QXI7531	Yr.Iss.	1997	24.00	30-50
1997 Dr. Leonard H. McCoy QXI6352	Yr.Iss.	1997	14.95	15
1997 Hank Aaron (2nd Ed.) QXI6152	Yr.Iss.	1997	14.95	15-20
1997 Holiday Barbie™(5th Ed.) QXI6212	Yr.Iss.	1997	15.95	16
1997 Jeff Gordon (1st Ed.) QXI6165	Yr.Iss.	1997	15.95	22-50
1997 Joe Namath (3rd Ed.) QXI6182	Yr.Iss.	1997	14.95	15-20
1997 Luke Skywalker (1st Ed.) QXI5484	Yr.Iss.	1997	13.95	22-40
1997 Magic Johnson (3rd Ed.) QXI6832	Yr.Iss.	1997	14.95	15
1997 U.S.S. Defiant QXI7481	Yr.Iss.	1997	24.00	35-40
1997 Victorian Christmas-Thomas Kinkade (1st Ed.) QXI6135	Yr.Iss.	1997	10.95	11-25
1997 The Warmth of Home QXI7545	Yr.Iss.	1997	18.95	20
1997 Wayne Gretzky (1st Ed.) QXI6275	Yr.Iss.	1997	15.95	16-22
1997 Yoda QXI6355	Yr.Iss.	1997	9.95	25-35

1997 Spring Ornaments - Keepsake

YEAR ISSUE	EDITION LIMIT	YEAR RETD.	ISSUE PRICE	*QUOTE U.S.$
1997 1935 Steelcraft Streamline Velocipede by Murray® (1st Ed.) QEO8632	Yr.Iss.	1997	12.95	20-35
1997 Apple Blossom Lane QEO8662	Yr.Iss.	1997	8.95	9
1997 Barbie™ as Rapunzel Doll (1st Ed.) QEO8635	Yr.Iss.	1997	14.95	15-30
1997 Bumper Crop, Tender Touches QEO8735	Yr.Iss.	1997	14.95	15
1997 Collector's Plate QEO8675	Yr.Iss.	1997	7.95	8
1997 Colorful Coal Car (2nd Ed.) QEO8652	Yr.Iss.	1997	8.95	9-18
1997 Digging In QEO8712	Yr.Iss.	1997	7.95	8
1997 Eggs-pert Artist QEO8695	Yr.Iss.	1997	8.95	9
1997 Garden Club QEO8665	Yr.Iss.	1997	7.95	8
1997 Gentle Guardian QEO8732	Yr.Iss.	1997	6.95	7
1997 Here Comes Easter QEO8682	Yr.Iss.	1997	7.95	8
1997 Jemima Puddle-Duck (2nd Ed.) QEO8645	Yr.Iss.	1997	8.95	12-20
1997 Joyful Angels QEO8655	Yr.Iss.	1997	10.95	11-15
1997 A Purr-fect Princess QEO8715	Yr.Iss.	1997	7.95	8
1997 Springtime Barbie™ QEO8642	Yr.Iss.	1997	12.95	15
1997 Springtime Bonnets QEO8672	Yr.Iss.	1997	7.95	8
1997 Swing-Time QEO8705	Yr.Iss.	1997	7.95	8
1997 Victorian Cross QEO8725	Yr.Iss.	1997	8.95	9

1998 25th Anniversary - Keepsake

YEAR ISSUE	EDITION LIMIT	YEAR RETD.	ISSUE PRICE	*QUOTE U.S.$
1998 Angelic Flight QXI4146	25,000		85.00	85
1998 Halls Station QX6833	Yr.Iss.		25.00	25
1998 Joyful Messenger QXI4146	Yr.Iss.		18.95	19
1998 Tin Locomotive QX6826	Yr.Iss.		25.00	25

1998 Collectible Series - Keepsake

YEAR ISSUE	EDITION LIMIT	YEAR RETD.	ISSUE PRICE	*QUOTE U.S.$
1998 1917 Curtiss JN-4D "Jenny" (2nd Ed.) QX6286	Yr.Iss.		14.95	15
1998 1937 Ford V-8 (4th Ed.) QX6263	Yr.Iss.		13.95	14
1998 1955 Murray® Tractor and Trailer (5th Ed.) QX6376	Yr.Iss.		16.95	17
1998 1970 Plymouth Hemi 'Cuda (8th Ed.) QX6256	Yr.Iss.		13.95	14
1998 Bright Sledding Colors (10th Ed.) QX6166	Yr.Iss.		12.95	13
1998 Cat Naps (5th Ed.) QX6383	Yr.Iss.		8.95	9
1998 A Celebration of Angels (4th Ed.) QX6366	Yr.Iss.		13.95	14
1998 The Clauses on Vacation (2nd Ed.) QX6276	Yr.Iss.		14.95	15
1998 Daphne-Mary's Angels (11th Ed.) QX6153	Yr.Iss.		7.95	8
1998 Fabulous Decade (9th Ed.) QX6393	Yr.Iss.		7.95	8
1998 Frosty Friends (19th Ed.) QX6226	Yr.Iss.		10.95	11
1998 Glorious Angel (1st Ed.) QX6493	Yr.Iss.		14.95	15
1998 Grocery Store (15th Ed.) QX6266	Yr.Iss.		16.95	17
1998 Joe Cool (1st Ed.) QX6453	Yr.Iss.		9.95	10
1998 Marilyn Monroe (2nd Ed.) QX6333	Yr.Iss.		14.95	15
1998 Merry Olde Santa (9th Ed.) QX6386	Yr.Iss.		15.95	16
1998 Mexican Barbie™ (3rd Ed.) QX6356	Yr.Iss.		14.95	15
1998 Mop Top Wendy (3rd Ed.) QX6353	Yr.Iss.		14.95	15
1998 Pennsylvania GG-1 Locomotive (3rd Ed.) QX6346	Yr.Iss.		18.95	19
1998 Pony Express Rider (1st Ed.) QX6323	Yr.Iss.		13.95	14
1998 A Pony for Christmas (1st Ed.) QX6316	Yr.Iss.		10.95	11
1998 Puppy Love (8th Ed.) QX6163	Yr.Iss.		7.95	8
1998 Ricky-All God's Children®-Martha Root (3rd Ed.) QX6363	Yr.Iss.		12.95	13
1998 Santa's Bumper Car (20th Ed.) QX6283	Yr.Iss.		14.95	15
1998 Scarlett O'Hara (2nd Ed.) QX6336	Yr.Iss.		14.95	15
1998 Snow Buddies (1st Ed.) QX6853	Yr.Iss.		7.95	8
1998 Timber Wolves at Play-Mark Newman (2nd Ed.) QX6273	Yr.Iss.		12.95	13
1998 A Visit From Piglet (1st Ed.) QXD4086	Yr.Iss.		13.95	14
1998 Yuletide Central (5th Ed.) QX6373	Yr.Iss.		18.95	19

1998 Collegiate Ornaments - Keepsake

YEAR ISSUE	EDITION LIMIT	YEAR RETD.	ISSUE PRICE	*QUOTE U.S.$
1998 Florida State Seminoles™ QSR2316	Yr.Iss.		9.95	10
1998 Michigan Wolverines™ QSR2323	Yr.Iss.		9.95	10
1998 North Carolina Tar Heels™ QSR2333	Yr.Iss.		9.95	10
1998 Notre Dame® Fighting Irish™ QSR2313	Yr.Iss.		9.95	10
1998 Penn State Nittany Lions™ QSR2326	Yr.Iss.		9.95	10

1998 Crown Reflections - Keepsake

YEAR ISSUE	EDITION LIMIT	YEAR RETD.	ISSUE PRICE	*QUOTE U.S.$
1998 1955 Murray® Fire Truck QBG6909	Yr.Iss.		35.00	35
1998 Festive Locomotive QBG6903	Yr.Iss.		35.00	35
1998 Frankincense QBG6896	2-Yr.		22.00	22
1998 Frosty Friends, set/2 QBG6907	Yr.Iss.		48.00	48
1998 Gold QBG6836	2-Yr.		22.00	22
1998 Myrrh QBG6893	2-Yr.		22.00	22
1998 Pink Poinsettias QBG6926	Yr.Iss.		25.00	25
1998 Red Poinsettias (1st) QBG6906	Yr.Iss.		35.00	35
1998 Sugarplum Cottage QBG6917	Yr.Iss.		35.00	35
1998 Sweet Memories, set/8 QBG6933	Yr.Iss.		45.00	45
1998 White Poinsettias QBG6923	Yr.Iss.		25.00	25

1998 Disney Ornaments - Keepsake

YEAR ISSUE	EDITION LIMIT	YEAR RETD.	ISSUE PRICE	*QUOTE U.S.$
1998 Bouncy Baby-sitter QXD4096	Yr.Iss.		12.95	13
1998 Building a Snowman QXD4133	Yr.Iss.		14.95	15
1998 Buzz Lightyear QXD4066	Yr.Iss.		14.95	15
1998 Cinderella's Coach QXD4083	Yr.Iss.		14.95	15
1998 Cruella de Vil (1st Ed.) QXD4063	Yr.Iss.		14.95	15
1998 Daydreams QXD4136	Yr.Iss.		13.95	14
1998 Donald and Daisy in Venice (1st Ed.) QXD4103	Yr.Iss.		14.95	15
1998 Flik QXD4153	Yr.Iss.		12.95	13
1998 Goofy Soccer Star QXD4123	Yr.Iss.		10.95	11
1998 Iago, Abu amd the Genie QXD4076	Yr.Iss.		12.95	13
1998 Make-Believe Boat QXD4113	Yr.Iss.		12.95	13
1998 The Mickey and Minnie Handcar QXD4116	Yr.Iss.		14.95	15
1998 Mickey's Favorite Reindeer QXD4013	Yr.Iss.		13.95	14
1998 Minnie Plays the Flute (2nd Ed.) QXD4106	Yr.Iss.		13.95	14
1998 Mulan, Mushu and Cri-Kee QXD4156	Yr.Iss.		14.95	15
1998 Princess Aurora QXD4126	Yr.Iss.		12.95	13
1998 Ready For Christmas (2nd Ed.) QXD4006	Yr.Iss.		12.95	13
1998 Runaway Toboggan QXD4003	Yr.Iss.		16.95	17
1998 Simba & Nala QXD4073	Yr.Iss.		13.95	14
1998 Tree Trimmin' Time,set/3 QXD4236	Yr.Iss.		19.95	20
1998 A Visit From Piglet QXD4086	Yr.Iss.		13.95	14
1998 Walt Disney's Snow White (2nd Ed.) QXD4056	Yr.Iss.		14.95	15
1998 Woody the Sheriff QXD4163	Yr.Iss.		14.95	15

1998 Holiday Traditions - Keepsake

YEAR ISSUE	EDITION LIMIT	YEAR RETD.	ISSUE PRICE	*QUOTE U.S.$
1998 A Child Is Born QX6176	Yr.Iss.		12.95	13
1998 A Christmas Eve Story QX6873	Yr.Iss.		13.95	14
1998 Christmas Request QX6193	Yr.Iss.		14.95	15
1998 Christmas Sleigh Ride QX6556	Yr.Iss.		12.95	13
1998 Cross of Peace QX6856	Yr.Iss.		9.95	10
1998 Cruising Into Christmas QX6196	Yr.Iss.		16.95	17
1998 Fancy Footwork QX6536	Yr.Iss.		8.95	9
1998 Feliz Navidad QX6173	Yr.Iss.		8.95	7
1998 Guardian Friend QX6543	Yr.Iss.		8.95	9
1998 Heavenly Melody (Archive Collection) QX6576	Yr.Iss.		18.95	19
1998 Holiday Decorator QX6566	Yr.Iss.		13.95	14
1998 The Holy Family, set/3 QX6523	Yr.Iss.		25.00	25
1998 Journey To Bethlehem (Collector's Choice) QX6223	Yr.Iss.		16.95	17
1998 King Kharoof-Second King QX6186	Yr.Iss.		12.95	13
1998 Madonna and Child QX6516	Yr.Iss.		12.95	13
1998 Memories of Christmas QX2406	Yr.Iss.		5.95	6
1998 Merry Chime QX6692	Yr.Iss.		9.95	10
1998 Miracle in Bethlehem QX6513	Yr.Iss.		12.95	13
1998 Mistletoe Fairy QX6216	Yr.Iss.		12.95	13
1998 Nick's Wish List QX6863	Yr.Iss.		8.95	9
1998 Night Watch QX6725	Yr.Iss.		9.95	10
1998 Our Song QX6183	Yr.Iss.		9.95	10
1998 Peekaboo Bears QX6563	Yr.Iss.		12.95	13
1998 Purr-fect Little Deer QX6526	Yr.Iss.		7.95	8
1998 Santa's Deer Friend QX6583	Yr.Iss.		24.00	24
1998 Santa's Flying Machine QX6573	Yr.Iss.		16.95	17
1998 Santa's Hidden Surprise QX6913	Yr.Iss.		14.95	15
1998 Sweet Rememberings QX6876	Yr.Iss.		8.95	9
1998 Treetop Choir QX6506	Yr.Iss.		9.95	10
1998 Warm and Cozy QX6866	Yr.Iss.		8.95	9
1998 Watchful Shepherd QX6496	Yr.Iss.		8.95	9
1998 Writing to Santa QX6533	Yr.Iss.		7.95	8

1998 Keepsake Collector's Club - Keepsake

YEAR ISSUE	EDITION LIMIT	YEAR RETD.	ISSUE PRICE	*QUOTE U.S.$
1998 1935 Steelcraft by Murray®	Yr.Iss.		N/A	N/A
1998 1990 Happy Holidays® Barbie™ Doll	Yr.Iss.		N/A	N/A
1998 Follow The Leader, set/2	Yr.Iss.		N/A	N/A
1998 Kringle Bells	Yr.Iss.		N/A	N/A
1998 Making His Way	Yr.Iss.		N/A	N/A
1998 New Christmas Friend	Yr.Iss.		N/A	N/A

1998 Keepsake Magic Ornaments - Keepsake

YEAR ISSUE	EDITION LIMIT	YEAR RETD.	ISSUE PRICE	*QUOTE U.S.$
1998 1998 Corvette® QLX7605	Yr.Iss.		24.00	24
1998 Apollo Lunar Module (3rd Ed.) QLX7543	Yr.Iss.		24.00	24
1998 Cinderella at the Ball QXD7576	Yr.Iss.		24.00	24
1998 Lighthouse Greetings (2nd Ed.) QLX7536	Yr.Iss.		24.00	24
1998 Mickey's Comet QXD7586	Yr.Iss.		24.00	24
1998 Santa's Show 'n' Tell QLX7566	Yr.Iss.		18.95	19
1998 Santa's Spin Top QLX7573	Yr.Iss.		22.00	22
1998 St. Nicholas Circle QXI7556	Yr.Iss.		18.95	19
1998 The Stone Church (1st Ed.) QLX7636	Yr.Iss.		18.95	19
1998 U.S.S. Enterprise™ NCC-1701-E QXI7633	Yr.Iss.		24.00	24
1998 The Washington Monument QLX7553	Yr.Iss.		24.00	24
1998 X-wing Starfighter™ QXI7596	Yr.Iss.		24.00	24

1998 Lifestyles & Occupations - Keepsake

YEAR ISSUE	EDITION LIMIT	YEAR RETD.	ISSUE PRICE	*QUOTE U.S.$
1998 Catch of the Season QX6786	Yr.Iss.		14.95	15
1998 Checking Santa's Files QX6806	Yr.Iss.		8.95	9
1998 Compact Skater QX6766	Yr.Iss.		9.95	10
1998 Downhill Dash QX6776	Yr.Iss.		13.95	14
1998 Future Ballerina QX6756	Yr.Iss.		7.95	8
1998 Gifted Gardener QX6736	Yr.Iss.		7.95	8
1998 Good Luck Dice QX6813	Yr.Iss.		9.95	10
1998 Holiday Camper QX6783	Yr.Iss.		12.95	13
1998 National Salute QX6293	Yr.Iss.		8.95	9
1998 North Pole Reserve QX6803	Yr.Iss.		10.95	11
1998 Polar Bowler QX6746	Yr.Iss.		7.95	8
1998 Puttin' Around QX6763	Yr.Iss.		8.95	9
1998 Rocket to Success QX6793	Yr.Iss.		8.95	9
1998 Sew Gifted QX6743	Yr.Iss.		7.95	8
1998 Spoonful of Love QX6796	Yr.Iss.		8.95	9

*Quotes have been rounded up to nearest dollar

YEAR ISSUE	EDITION LIMIT	YEAR RETD.	ISSUE PRICE	*QUOTE U.S.$
1998 Surprise Catch QX6753	Yr.Iss.		7.95	8

1998 Miniature Ornaments - Keepsake

YEAR ISSUE	EDITION LIMIT	YEAR RETD.	ISSUE PRICE	*QUOTE U.S.$
1998 1937 Steelcraft Auburn (1st Ed.) QXM4143	Yr.Iss.		6.95	7
1998 Angel Chime (Precious Ed.) QXM4283	Yr.Iss.		8.95	8
1998 Antique Tractors (2nd Ed.) QXM4166	Yr.Iss.		6.95	7
1998 Betsey's Prayer QXM4263	Yr.Iss.		4.95	5
1998 Caboose (10th Ed.) QXM4216	Yr.Iss.		6.95	7
1998 Centuries of Santa (5th Ed.) QXM4206	Yr.Iss.		5.95	6
1998 Cheshire Cat (4th Ed.) QXM4186	Yr.Iss.		6.95	7
1998 Christmas Bells (4th Ed.) QXM4196	Yr.Iss.		4.95	5
1998 Coca-Cola Time QXM4296	Yr.Iss.		6.95	7
1998 Fishy Surprise QXM4276	Yr.Iss.		6.95	7
1998 Glinda, The Good Witch™, The Wicked Witch of the West™ QXM4233	Yr.Iss.		14.95	15
1998 Holly-Jolly Jig QXM4266	Yr.Iss.		6.95	7
1998 Miniature Clothespin Soldier (4th Ed.) QXM4193	Yr.Iss.		4.95	5
1998 Murray Inc.® Dump Truck (4th Ed.) QXM4183	Yr.Iss.		6.95	7
1998 The Nativity (1st Ed.) QXM4156	Yr.Iss.		9.95	10
1998 Noel R.R. Locomotive (Anniversary Ed.)1989-1998 QXM4286	Yr.Iss.		10.95	11
1998 Nutcracker (3rd Ed.) QXM4146	Yr.Iss.		5.95	6
1998 Nutcracker Guild (5th Ed.) QXM4203	Yr.Iss.		6.95	7
1998 On the Road (6th Ed.) QXM4213	Yr.Iss.		5.95	6
1998 Peaceful Pandas QXM4253	Yr.Iss.		5.95	6
1998 Pixie Parachute QXM4256	Yr.Iss.		4.95	5
1998 Sharing Joy QXM4273	Yr.Iss.		4.95	5
1998 Singin' in the Rain™ QXM4303	Yr.Iss.		10.95	11
1998 Snowflake Ballet (2nd Ed.) QXM4173	Yr.Iss.		5.95	6
1998 SUPERMAN™ QXM4313	Yr.Iss.		10.95	11
1998 Teddy-Bear Style (2nd Ed.) QXM4176	Yr.Iss.		5.95	6
1998 Welcome Friends (2nd Ed.) QXM4153	Yr.Iss.		6.95	7
1998 Winter Fun With SNOOPY® (1st Ed.) QXM4243	Yr.Iss.		6.95	7

1998 NBA Ornaments - Keepsake

YEAR ISSUE	EDITION LIMIT	YEAR RETD.	ISSUE PRICE	*QUOTE U.S.$
1998 Charlotte Hornets QSR1033	Yr.Iss.		9.95	10
1998 Chicago Bulls QSR1036	Yr.Iss.		9.95	10
1998 Detroit Pistons QSR1043	Yr.Iss.		9.95	10
1998 Houston Rockets QSR1046	Yr.Iss.		9.95	10
1998 Indiana Pacers QSR1053	Yr.Iss.		9.95	10
1998 Los Angeles Lakers QSR1056	Yr.Iss.		9.95	10
1998 New York Knickerbockers QSR1063	Yr.Iss.		9.95	10
1998 Orlando Magic QSR1066	Yr.Iss.		9.95	10
1998 Seattle Supersonics QSR1076	Yr.Iss.		9.95	10
1998 Utah Jazz QSR1083	Yr.Iss.		9.95	10

1998 NFL Ornaments - Keepsake

YEAR ISSUE	EDITION LIMIT	YEAR RETD.	ISSUE PRICE	*QUOTE U.S.$
1998 Carolina Panthers™ QSR5026	Yr.Iss.		9.95	10
1998 Chicago Bears™ QSR5033	Yr.Iss.		9.95	10
1998 Dallas Cowboys™ QSR5046	Yr.Iss.		9.95	10
1998 Denver Broncos™ QSR5053	Yr.Iss.		9.95	10
1998 Green Bay Packers™ QSR5063	Yr.Iss.		9.95	10
1998 Kansas City Chiefs™ QSR5013	Yr.Iss.		9.95	10
1998 Miami Dolphins™ QSR5096	Yr.Iss.		9.95	10
1998 Minnesota Vikings™ QSR5126	Yr.Iss.		9.95	10
1998 New York Giants™ QSR5143	Yr.Iss.		9.95	10
1998 Oakland Raiders™ QSR5086	Yr.Iss.		9.95	10
1998 Philadelphia Eagles™ QSR5153	Yr.Iss.		9.95	10
1998 Pittsburgh Steelers™ QSR5163	Yr.Iss.		9.95	10
1998 San Francisco 49ers™ QSR5173	Yr.Iss.		9.95	10
1998 St. Louis Rams™ QSR5093	Yr.Iss.		9.95	10
1998 Washington Redskins™ QSR5186	Yr.Iss.		9.95	10

1998 Pop Culture Icons - Keepsake

YEAR ISSUE	EDITION LIMIT	YEAR RETD.	ISSUE PRICE	*QUOTE U.S.$
1998 1998 Corvette® Convertible QX6416	Yr.Iss.		13.95	14
1998 Bugs Bunny-LOONEY TUNES QX6443	Yr.Iss.		13.95	14
1998 Decorating Maxine-Style	Yr.Iss.		10.95	11
1998 Hot Wheels™ QX6436	Yr.Iss.		13.95	14
1998 Larry, Moe, and Curly-The Three Stooges™ QX6503	Yr.Iss.		27.00	27
1998 Maxine QX6446	Yr.Iss.		9.95	10
1998 Mrs. Potato Head® QX6886	Yr.Iss.		10.95	11
1998 Munchkinland™ Mayor and Cornoner QX6463	Yr.Iss.		13.95	14
1998 Superman™ QX6423	Yr.Iss.		12.95	13
1998 Sweet Treat HERSHEY'S™ QX6433	Yr.Iss.		10.95	11
1998 Tonka® Road Grader QX6483	Yr.Iss.		13.95	14

1998 Showcase Folk Art Americana Collection - Keepsake

YEAR ISSUE	EDITION LIMIT	YEAR RETD.	ISSUE PRICE	*QUOTE U.S.$
1998 Soaring With Angels QX6213	Yr.Iss.		16.95	17

1998 Showcase Nature's Sketchbook Collection - Keepsake

YEAR ISSUE	EDITION LIMIT	YEAR RETD.	ISSUE PRICE	*QUOTE U.S.$
1998 Country Home QX5172	Yr.Iss.		10.95	11

1998 Showcase The Language of Flowers Collection - Keepsake

YEAR ISSUE	EDITION LIMIT	YEAR RETD.	ISSUE PRICE	*QUOTE U.S.$
1998 Iris Angel (3rd Ed.) QX6156	Yr.Iss.		15.95	16

1998 Special Issues - Keepsake

YEAR ISSUE	EDITION LIMIT	YEAR RETD.	ISSUE PRICE	*QUOTE U.S.$
1998 Barbie™Silken Flame (5th Ed.) QXI4043	Yr.Iss.		15.95	16
1998 Boba Fett™ QXI4053	Yr.Iss.		14.95	15
1998 Captain Kathryn Janeway™ QXI4046	Yr.Iss.		14.95	15
1998 Carl Ripken Jr. (3rd) QXI4033	Yr.Iss.		14.95	15
1998 Emmitt Smith (4th) QXI4036	Yr.Iss.		14.95	15
1998 Ewoks™ QXI4223	Yr.Iss.		16.95	17
1998 Grant Hill (4th) QXI6846	Yr.Iss.		14.95	15
1998 The Grinch QXI6466	Yr.Iss.		13.95	14
1998 Holiday Barbie™(6th Ed.) QXI4023	Yr.Iss.		15.95	16
1998 Holiday Barbie™- African American (1st Ed.) QX6936	Yr.Iss.		15.95	16
1998 Joe Montana-Notre Dame QXI6843	Yr.Iss.		14.95	15
1998 Mario Lemieux (2nd) QXI6476	Yr.Iss.		15.95	16
1998 Princess Leia™ (2nd Ed.) QXI4026	Yr.Iss.		13.95	14
1998 Richard Petty (2nd) QXI4143	Yr.Iss.		15.95	16
1998 Victorian Christmas II-Thomas Kinkade (2nd Ed.) QX6343	Yr.Iss.		10.95	11

1998 Spring Ornaments - Keepsake

YEAR ISSUE	EDITION LIMIT	YEAR RETD.	ISSUE PRICE	*QUOTE U.S.$
1998 1931 Ford Model A Roadster (1st Ed.) QEO8416	Yr.Iss.		14.95	15
1998 1939 Mobo Horse (2nd Ed.) QEO8393	Yr.Iss.		12.95	13
1998 Barbie™ as Little Bo Peep Doll (2nd Ed.) QEO8373	Yr.Iss.		14.95	15
1998 Bashful Gift QEO8446	Yr.Iss.		11.95	12
1998 Benjamin Bunny™ Beatrix Potter™ (3rd Ed.) QEO8383	Yr.Iss.		8.95	9
1998 Bouquet of Memories QEO8456	Yr.Iss.		7.95	8
1998 Forever Friends QEO8423	Yr.Iss.		9.95	10
1998 Garden Club (4th Ed.)	Yr.Iss.		7.95	8
1998 The Garden of Piglet and Pooh QEO8396	Yr.Iss.		10.95	11
1998 Going Up? Charlie Brown -PEANUTS® QEO8433	Yr.Iss.		9.95	10
1998 Happy Diploma Day! QEO8476	Yr.Iss.		7.95	8
1998 Joyful Angels (3rd Ed.) QEO8386	Yr.Iss.		10.95	11
1998 Midge™-35th Anniversary QEO8413	Yr.Iss.		14.95	15
1998 Passenger Car (3rd Ed.) QEO8376	Yr.Iss.		9.95	10
1998 Practice Swing-Donald Duck QEO8396	Yr.Iss.		10.95	11
1998 Precious Baby QEO8463	Yr.Iss.		9.95	10
1998 Special Friends QEO8523	Yr.Iss.		12.95	13
1998 Star Wars™ QEO8406	Yr.Iss.		12.95	13
1998 Sweet Birthday QEO8473	Yr.Iss.		7.95	8
1998 Tigger in the Garden QEO8436	Closed	1998	9.95	10
1998 Victorian Cross QEO8453	Yr.Iss.		8.95	9
1998 Wedding Memories QEO8466	Yr.Iss.		9.95	10
1998 What's Your Name QEO8443	Yr.Iss.		7.95	8

Hamilton Collection

Christmas Angels - S. Kuck

YEAR ISSUE	EDITION LIMIT	YEAR RETD.	ISSUE PRICE	*QUOTE U.S.$
1994 Angel of Charity	Open		19.50	20
1995 Angel of Joy	Open		19.50	20
1995 Angel of Grace	Open		19.50	20
1995 Angel of Faith	Open		19.50	20
1995 Angel of Patience	Open		19.50	20
1995 Angel of Glory	Open		19.50	20
1996 Angel of Gladness	Open		19.50	20
1996 Angel of Innocence	Open		19.50	20
1996 Angel of Beauty	Open		19.50	20
1996 Angel of Purity	Open		19.50	20
1996 Angel of Charm	Open		19.50	20
1996 Angel of Kindness	Open		19.50	20

Derek Darlings - N/A

YEAR ISSUE	EDITION LIMIT	YEAR RETD.	ISSUE PRICE	*QUOTE U.S.$
1995 Jessica, Sara, Chelsea (set)	Open		29.85	30

Dreamsicles Joy of Christmas Suncatcher - N/A

YEAR ISSUE	EDITION LIMIT	YEAR RETD.	ISSUE PRICE	*QUOTE U.S.$
1997 Bearing Gifts	Open		14.95	15
1997 Open Me First	Open		14.95	15
1997 Snowflake Magic	Open		14.95	15
1997 Under The Mistletoe	Open		14.95	15

Dreamsicles Suncatchers - K. Haynes

YEAR ISSUE	EDITION LIMIT	YEAR RETD.	ISSUE PRICE	*QUOTE U.S.$
1996 Daisies and Dreamsicles	Open		19.95	20
1996 I Love You	Open		19.95	20
1996 Love Letters	Open		19.95	20
1996 Sharing Hearts	Open		19.95	20
1996 Stolen Kiss	Open		19.95	20

Little Messengers - P. Parkins

YEAR ISSUE	EDITION LIMIT	YEAR RETD.	ISSUE PRICE	*QUOTE U.S.$
1997 Ice Skater, Christmas Lights, Gingerbreadman, set/3	Open		29.90	30
1997 Shining Star, Candle, Mistletoe, set/3	Open		29.90	30
1997 Snowflake, Wreath, Choirbook, set/3	Open		29.90	30
1997 Stocking, Harp, Kitten, set/3	Open		29.90	30

Harbour Lights

Christmas Ornaments - Harbour Lights

YEAR ISSUE	EDITION LIMIT	YEAR RETD.	ISSUE PRICE	*QUOTE U.S.$
1996 Big Bay Pt. MI 7040	Closed	1996	15.00	15-30
1996 Burrows Island WA 7043	Closed	1996	15.00	15-30
1996 Holland MI 7041	Open		15.00	15
1996 Sand Island WI 7042	Closed	1996	15.00	15-30
1996 Set of 4 702	Open		60.00	60
1996 30 Mile Pt. NY 7044	Closed	1996	15.00	15-30
1996 Cape Neddick ME 7047	Open		15.00	15
1996 New London Ledge CT 7046	Open		15.00	15
1996 S.E. Block Island RI 7045	Open		15.00	15
1996 Set of 4 703	Open		60.00	60
1997 Cape Hatteras NC 7048	Open		15.00	15
1997 Saugerties NY 7049	Open		15.00	15
1997 Thomas Point MD 7050	Open		15.00	15
1997 Colchester Reef VI 7051	Open		15.00	15
1997 Set of 4 705	Open		60.00	60
1998 Montauk NY 7052	Open		15.00	15
1998 Middle Bay AL 7053	Open		15.00	15
1998 White Shoal MI 7054	Open		15.00	15
1998 Alcatraz CA 7055	Open		15.00	15
1998 Set of 4 706	Open		60.00	60

House of Hatten, Inc.

Angels Triumphant - D. Calla

YEAR ISSUE	EDITION LIMIT	YEAR RETD.	ISSUE PRICE	*QUOTE U.S.$
1998 Heavenly Flyer Angel 39856	Open		24.00	24
1998 Noel Angel 39860	Open		14.00	14
1998 Star Keeper Angel 39858	Open		60.00	60
1998 Star Rider Angel 39857	Open		25.00	25

A Christmas Alphabet - V. & S. Rawson

YEAR ISSUE	EDITION LIMIT	YEAR RETD.	ISSUE PRICE	*QUOTE U.S.$
1998 "A" Angel Block 33808	Open		8.00	8
1998 "C" Candle Block 33801	Open		8.00	8
1998 "H" Holly Elf Block 33802	Open		8.00	8
1998 "I" Ice Skates Block 33804	Open		8.00	8
1998 "M" Manger Block 33807	Open		8.00	8
1998 "R" Reindeer Block 33803	Open		8.00	8
1998 "S" Santa Block 33805	Open		8.00	8
1998 "S" Sleigh Block 33809	Open		8.00	8
1998 "T" Tree Block 33806	Open		8.00	8

Christmas Messengers - V. & S. Rawson

YEAR ISSUE	EDITION LIMIT	YEAR RETD.	ISSUE PRICE	*QUOTE U.S.$
1997 Flying Santa 32763	Open		22.00	22
1997 Noah's Ark Santa 32764	Open		26.50	27
1996 Santa on Goat 22605	Open		29.00	29
1998 Santa on Goose 32852	Open		10.00	10
1996 Santa on Hog 22612	Open		24.00	24
1998 Santa on Pull Toy 32853	Open		10.00	10
1998 Santa on Rabbit 32851	Open		10.00	10
1996 Santa on Reindeer 22601	Retrd.	1997	30.00	30
1997 Santa on Whale 32765	Retrd.	1997	26.50	27
1996 Santa Over Moon 22618	Open		28.00	28
1996 Santa with Pull Toy 22616	Open		20.00	20
1996 Santa with Toys 22614	Open		24.00	24
1998 Santa, Snowman and Sled 32854	Open		10.00	10
1998 Skating Santa 32855	Open		10.00	10

Enchanted Forest - D. Calla

YEAR ISSUE	EDITION LIMIT	YEAR RETD.	ISSUE PRICE	*QUOTE U.S.$
1991 Christmas Herald Elf 31198	Retrd.	1994	27.00	27
1988 Elf 31853	Open		15.00	15
1989 Elf with Doves 31959	Retrd.	1992	23.00	23
1989 Elf with Forest Fawn 31960	Retrd.	1996	21.00	21
1989 Elf with Lantern 31961	Retrd.	1996	19.00	19
1993 Forest Elf 31358	Retrd.	1995	19.00	19
1993 Forest Elf with Dove 31359	Retrd.	1997	21.00	21
1989 Forest Fawn, lg. 31957	Retrd.	1993	13.00	13
1989 Forest Fawn, sm. 31964	Retrd.	1996	8.00	8
1991 Girl Elf 31199	Retrd.	1994	24.00	24
1989 Mini St. Nick with Goose 31963	Open		8.00	8
1989 Mini St. Nick with Stars 31962	Open		8.00	8
1989 St. Nicholas Messenger 31954	Retrd.	1991	27.00	27

Enchanted Forest in Glass - D. Calla

YEAR ISSUE	EDITION LIMIT	YEAR RETD.	ISSUE PRICE	*QUOTE U.S.$
1998 Angel with Gold Wings 39877	Open		26.00	26
1998 Angel with White Wings 39876	Open		26.00	26
1998 Blue Santa Head 39881	Open		24.00	24
1998 Elf With Stars 39878	Open		26.00	26
1998 Green and Gold Santa Icicle 39883	Open		24.00	24
1998 Green Santa Head 39880	Open		24.00	24
1998 House 39875	Open		38.00	38
1998 Peace Santa 39879	Open		26.00	26
1998 Red and Green Santa Icicle 39884	Open		24.00	24
1998 Snowman 39882	Open		26.00	26

From Out of the North - R. Leeseberg

YEAR ISSUE	EDITION LIMIT	YEAR RETD.	ISSUE PRICE	*QUOTE U.S.$
1998 Santa and Hummingbird 34862	Open		5.00	5

Good Cheer - D. Calla

YEAR ISSUE	EDITION LIMIT	YEAR RETD.	ISSUE PRICE	*QUOTE U.S.$
1998 Eggy Santa 39814	Open		13.00	13
1998 Santa Bird Skier 39815	Open		21.00	21
1998 Santa Collector Elf 39817	Open		19.00	19
1998 St. Nick Christmas Toy 39813	Open		50.00	50
1998 Swing Home For the Holidays 39816	Open		19.00	19
1998 Telluride Snowman 39812	Open		22.00	22

Grand Finale - P. Herrick

YEAR ISSUE	EDITION LIMIT	YEAR RETD.	ISSUE PRICE	*QUOTE U.S.$
1998 Bear 38825	Open		24.00	24
1998 Bear Tassel 38835	Open		26.00	26
1998 Black and White Striped Ball 38833	Open		11.00	11
1998 Black Stocking 38802	Open		36.00	36
1998 Deer 38826	Open		24.00	24
1998 Deer Tassel 38836	Open		26.00	26
1998 Floral Striped Finial 38817	Open		24.00	24
1998 Floral Zigzag Finial 38818	Open		24.00	24
1998 Fox 38828	Open		24.00	24
1998 Fox Tassel 38838	Open		26.00	26
1998 Green and Peach Leaves Finial 38821	Open		18.00	18
1998 Green Leaves Finial 38820	Open		18.00	18
1998 Rabbit 38827	Open		24.00	24

*Quotes have been rounded up to nearest dollar

YEAR ISSUE	EDITION LIMIT	YEAR RETD.	ISSUE PRICE	*QUOTE U.S.$
1998 Rabbit Tassel 38837	Open		26.00	26
1998 Red and Gold Check Ball 38831	Open		11.00	11
1998 Red and Gold Check Finial 38819	Open		18.00	18
1998 Red and Green Swirl Ball 38832	Open		11.00	11
1998 Rose Ball 38830	Open		11.00	11
1998 Santa Head 38823	Open		20.00	20
1998 Santa Tassel 38834	Open		26.00	26
1998 Snowman 38824	Open		20.00	20
1998 Sun, Moon, Stars 38822	Open		20.00	20
1998 White Stocking 38801	Open		36.00	36

Halloween - D. Calla

YEAR ISSUE	EDITION LIMIT	YEAR RETD.	ISSUE PRICE	*QUOTE U.S.$
1993 Broomhilda 11" 50350	Open		35.00	35

Halloween - J. Crvich

YEAR ISSUE	EDITION LIMIT	YEAR RETD.	ISSUE PRICE	*QUOTE U.S.$
1996 Witch Seated on Moon 51601	Open		43.00	43

The Magic of Christmas - V. & S. Rawson

YEAR ISSUE	EDITION LIMIT	YEAR RETD.	ISSUE PRICE	*QUOTE U.S.$
1998 Elf Holding Lightbulb 32814	Open		7.00	7
1998 Elf Holding Ornament 32811	Open		7.00	7
1998 Elf with Boxes 32815	Open		7.00	7
1998 Elf with List 32812	Open		7.00	7
1998 Elf with Presents 32816	Open		7.00	7
1998 Elf Wrapping Package 32813	Open		7.00	7
1998 Seated Elf 32810	Open		7.00	7

The Nutcracker - D. Calla

YEAR ISSUE	EDITION LIMIT	YEAR RETD.	ISSUE PRICE	*QUOTE U.S.$
1993 Drosselmeir 9" 32307	Retrd.	1994	27.00	27
1993 Fritz 7" 32311	Retrd.	1994	25.00	25
1993 Marie 7" 32310	Retrd.	1994	25.00	25
1993 Mouse King 9" 32308	Retrd.	1994	27.00	27
1993 Soldier 10" 32309	Retrd.	1994	27.00	27
1993 Soldier/Owl/Candy Cane, set/3 32313	Retrd.	1994	18.00	18
1993 Stick Horse 7" 32312	Retrd.	1994	11.00	11
1993 Sugar Plum Fairy 10" 32306	Retrd.	1994	27.00	27

Peace on Earth - D. Calla

YEAR ISSUE	EDITION LIMIT	YEAR RETD.	ISSUE PRICE	*QUOTE U.S.$
1993 Doves, set/2 32356	Open		16.00	16

Snowberries - D. Calla

YEAR ISSUE	EDITION LIMIT	YEAR RETD.	ISSUE PRICE	*QUOTE U.S.$
1990 Boy Cupboard Keeper 33003	Open		29.00	29
1990 Girl Cupboard Keeper 33004	Open		29.00	29

SnowMa'am - D. Calla

YEAR ISSUE	EDITION LIMIT	YEAR RETD.	ISSUE PRICE	*QUOTE U.S.$
1997 Flutter By Flying Santa with green Coat 30754	Open		44.00	44
1997 Flutter By Santa with Star 30753	Open		44.00	44
1997 Flutter By Santa with Tree 30755	Open		44.00	44
1997 SnowMa'am on Sled 30757	Open		28.00	28
1997 Snowman Candy Cane Hanger 30756	Open		28.00	28
1997 Winged Snowman with Tree 30758	Open		28.00	28

Ten Christmas - D. Calla

YEAR ISSUE	EDITION LIMIT	YEAR RETD.	ISSUE PRICE	*QUOTE U.S.$
1997 2D Goose in Basket with Greeting 30778	Open		14.00	14
1997 Father Christmas 30781	Open		14.00	14
1997 Folk Art Santa with Hood 30779	Open		14.00	14
1997 Goose in Basket 30789	Open		9.00	9
1997 Merry Christmas Snowman 30793	Open		12.00	12
1997 North Star Bear 30795	Open		9.00	9
1997 Our House Santa 30791	Open		12.00	12
1997 Santa with Cap 30780	Open		14.00	14
1997 Simple Gifts Dove with Heart 30792	Open		7.00	7
1997 Star/Moon 30788	Open		5.50	6
1997 Ten Christmas Santa 30797	Open		8.00	8
1997 Twelve Days Partridge 30790	Open		9.00	9
1997 Two By Two Ark 30794	Open		10.00	10
1997 Wings of Light Angel 30796	Open		8.00	8

Twelve Days - V. & S. Rawson

YEAR ISSUE	EDITION LIMIT	YEAR RETD.	ISSUE PRICE	*QUOTE U.S.$
1997 Partridge on Pear 32701	Open		26.00	26
1997 Turtle Doves 32702	Open		20.00	20
1997 French Hen 32703	Open		20.00	20
1997 Calling Bird 32704	Open		20.00	20
1997 Golden Rings 32705	Open		18.00	18
1997 Goose-A-Laying 32706	Open		20.00	20
1997 Swan-A-Swimming 32707	Open		20.00	20
1997 Maid-A-Milking 32708	Open		22.00	22
1997 Lady Dancing 32711	Open		22.00	22
1997 Lord-A-Leaping 32712	Open		22.00	22
1997 Piper Piping 32710	Open		22.00	22
1997 Drummer Drumming 32709	Open		22.00	22

Twelve Days of Christmas - D. Calla

YEAR ISSUE	EDITION LIMIT	YEAR RETD.	ISSUE PRICE	*QUOTE U.S.$
1990 Partridge on Pear 32004	Open		12.00	12
1990 Turtle Doves 32005	Open		12.00	12
1990 French Hen 32006	Open		9.00	9
1990 Calling Bird 32007	Open		9.00	9
1990 Golden Rings 32008	Open		12.00	12
1990 Goose-A-Laying 32009	Open		12.00	12
1990 Swan-A-Swimming 32010	Open		13.00	13
1990 Maid-A-Milking 32011	Open		18.00	18
1990 Lady Dancing 32014	Open		18.00	18
1990 Lord-A-Leaping 32015	Open		18.00	18
1990 Piper Piping 32013	Open		18.00	18
1990 Drummer Drumming 32012	Open		18.00	18

Hudson Creek

Sebastian Christmas Ornaments - P.W. Baston Jr., unless otherwise noted

YEAR ISSUE	EDITION LIMIT	YEAR RETD.	ISSUE PRICE	*QUOTE U.S.$
1943 Madonna of the Chair - P.W. Baston	25	1943	2.00	150-200
1981 Santa Claus - P.W. Baston	5,000	1981	28.50	30
1982 Madonna of the Chair (Reissue of '43) - P.W. Baston	2,165	1982	15.00	30-45
1985 Home for the Holidays	Closed	1993	10.00	13
1986 Holiday Sleigh Ride	Closed	1993	10.00	13
1987 Santa	Closed	1993	10.00	13
1988 Decorating the Tree	Closed	1993	12.50	13
1989 Final Preparations for Christmas	Closed	1993	13.90	14
1990 Stuffing the Stockings	Closed	1993	14.00	14
1990 Christmas Rose-Red on White (Blossom Shop)	Closed	1990	22.00	25-35
1991 Merry Christmas	Closed	1993	14.50	15
1992 Final Check	Closed	1993	14.50	15
1993 Ethnic Santa	Closed	1993	12.50	25-30
1993 Caroling With Santa	Closed	1993	15.00	15
1994 Victorian Christmas Skaters	Closed	1994	17.00	17
1995 Midnight Snacks	Closed	1995	17.00	17
1996 Victorian Christmas Santa	Closed	1996	16.00	16

Islandia International

International Fatcats - G. Pitt

YEAR ISSUE	EDITION LIMIT	YEAR RETD.	ISSUE PRICE	*QUOTE U.S.$
1998 Scotland	Numbrd.		10.00	10
1998 Ireland	Numbrd.		10.00	10
1998 Great Britain	Numbrd.		10.00	10

Sonshine Promises - G. Clasby

YEAR ISSUE	EDITION LIMIT	YEAR RETD.	ISSUE PRICE	*QUOTE U.S.$
1998 Baby's First Christmas 8003	Open		12.50	13
1998 Friends Are Tied Together with Ribbons of Love 8005	Open		11.00	11
1998 A Joyful Wish - Christmas 1998 8000	Yr.Iss.		13.50	14
1998 Let Your Light Shine 8001	Open		11.00	11
1998 Love From the Heart 8007	Open		11.00	11
1998 You're an Angel to Me 8006	Open		11.00	11
1998 You're One in a Million to Me 8004	Open		11.00	11
1998 Your Friendship is a Timeless Treasure 8002	Open		11.00	11

Jan Hagara Collectables

Christmas Figural Ornaments - J. Hagara

YEAR ISSUE	EDITION LIMIT	YEAR RETD.	ISSUE PRICE	*QUOTE U.S.$
1984 Carol	2-Yr.	1986	7.00	50-60
1985 Chris	2-Yr.	1987	7.00	40-50
1986 Noel	2-Yr.	1988	10.00	40-50
1986 Jill	Yr.Iss.	1986	15.00	15-25
1987 Nikki	2-Yr.	1989	10.00	10-45
1987 Holly	Yr.Iss.	1987	15.00	18
1988 Marie	Yr.Iss.	1988	18.00	18

Non-Christmas Figural Ornaments - J. Hagara

YEAR ISSUE	EDITION LIMIT	YEAR RETD.	ISSUE PRICE	*QUOTE U.S.$
1987 Amanda	Yr.Iss.	1987	14.00	14-30
1984 Anne	2-Yr.	1986	10.00	125
1984 Betsy	2-Yr.	1986	10.00	100
1987 Brian	Yr.Iss.	1987	14.00	14-30
1988 Cara	30-day	1988	14.00	15
1987 Cristina	Yr.Iss.	1987	14.00	14-30
1988 Emily	30-day	1988	14.00	15
1993 Fall	10,000	1997	19.95	20
1984 Jenny	2-Yr.	1986	10.00	75-175
1988 Jessica	30-day	1988	14.00	15
1984 Jimmy	2-Yr.	1986	10.00	110-300
1984 Jody	2-Yr.	1986	10.00	50
1987 Laurie	Yr.Iss.	1987	14.00	14-30
1984 Lisa	2-Yr.	1986	10.00	85
1984 Lydia	2-Yr.	1986	10.00	50
1987 Marc	Yr.Iss.	1987	14.00	14-30
1988 Meg	30-day	1988	14.00	15
1988 Parry	30-day	1988	14.00	15
1988 Sharice	30-day	1988	14.00	15
1993 Spring	10,000	1997	19.95	20
1987 Stacy	Yr.Iss.	1987	14.00	14-45
1988 Stephen	30-day	1988	14.00	15
1987 Stephen	Yr.Iss.	1987	14.00	15
1993 Summer	10,000	1997	19.95	20
1984 Victoria	2-Yr.	1986	10.00	75-175
1993 Winter	10,000	1997	19.95	20

June McKenna Collectibles, Inc.

Flatback Ornaments - J. McKenna

YEAR ISSUE	EDITION LIMIT	YEAR RETD.	ISSUE PRICE	*QUOTE U.S.$
1988 1776 Santa	Closed	1991	17.00	55-75
1986 Amish Boy, blue	Closed	1989	13.00	85-100
1986 Amish Boy, pink	Closed	1986	13.00	135-200
1986 Amish Girl, blue	Closed	1989	13.00	100
1986 Amish Girl, pink	Closed	1986	13.00	300
1985 Amish Man	Closed	1989	13.00	105
1985 Amish Woman	Closed	1989	13.00	100-145
1993 Angel of Peace, white or pink	Closed	1994	30.00	50-65
1984 Angel with Horn	Closed	1988	14.00	150-175
1995 Angel with Teddy	Closed	1997	30.00	30-50
1982 Angel With Toys	Closed	1988	14.00	150-175
1995 Angel, Guiding Light, pink, green & white	Closed	1996	30.00	30-45
1983 Baby Bear in Vest, 5 colors	Closed	1988	11.00	85-115
1982 Baby Bear, Teeshirt	Closed	1984	11.00	125-175
1985 Baby Pig	Closed	1988	11.00	100-125
1983 Baby, blue trim	Closed	1988	11.00	110
1983 Baby, pink trim	Closed	1988	11.00	80-110
1991 Boy Angel, white	Closed	1992	20.00	100-125
1982 Candy Cane	Closed	1984	10.00	320-375
1993 Christmas Treat, blue	Closed	1996	30.00	50-65
1982 Colonial Man, 3 colors	Closed	1984	12.00	175
1982 Colonial Woman, 3 colors	Closed	1984	12.00	100-150
1984 Country Boy, 2 colors	Closed	1988	12.00	65-100
1984 Country Girl, 2 colors	Closed	1988	12.00	65-100
1993 Elf Bernie	Closed	1994	30.00	45-65
1995 Elf Danny	Closed	1997	30.00	45-65
1990 Elf Jeffrey	Closed	1992	17.00	50-65
1991 Elf Joey	Closed	1993	20.00	50-65
1994 Elf Ricky	Closed	1995	30.00	45-65
1992 Elf Scotty	Closed	1993	25.00	45-65
1994 Elf Tammy	Closed	1995	30.00	35-65
1988 Elizabeth, sill sitter	Closed	1989	20.00	150-175
1983 Father Bear in Suit, 3 colors	Closed	1988	12.00	100
1985 Father Pig	Closed	1988	12.00	100
1993 Final Notes	Closed	1994	30.00	55-65
1991 Girl Angel, white	Closed	1993	20.00	100-125
1983 Gloria Angel	Closed	1984	14.00	400-500
1989 Glorious Angel	Closed	1992	17.00	55-85
1983 Grandma, 4 colors	Closed	1988	12.00	80-100
1983 Grandpa, 4 colors	Closed	1988	12.00	85-100
1988 Guardian Angel	Closed	1991	16.00	40
1990 Harvest Santa	Closed	1992	17.00	65-75
1990 Ho Ho Ho	Closed	1992	17.00	65-75
1982 Kate Greenaway Boy, 3 colors	Closed	1983	12.00	155-310
1982 Kate Greenaway Girl, 3 colors	Closed	1983	12.00	125-200
1982 Mama Bear, Blue Cape	Closed	1984	12.00	100-175
1983 Mother Bear in Dress, 3 colors	Closed	1988	12.00	75-85
1985 Mother Pig	Closed	1988	12.00	100-125
1984 Mr. Claus	Closed	1988	14.00	75-100
1984 Mrs. Claus	Closed	1988	14.00	75-150
1994 Mrs. Klaus	Closed	1997	30.00	30-65
1992 Northpole News	Closed	1993	25.00	55-65
1994 Nutcracker	Closed	1995	30.00	30-45
1993 Old Lamplighter	Closed	1994	30.00	55-65
1984 Old World Santa, 3 colors	Closed	1989	14.00	185-220
1984 Old World Santa, gold	Closed	1986	14.00	275-300
1982 Papa Bear, Red Cape	Closed	1984	12.00	100-175
1992 Praying Angel	Closed	1993	25.00	30-45
1985 Primitive Santa	Closed	1989	17.00	175-230
1983 Raggedy Andy, 2 colors	Closed	1983	12.00	220-250
1983 Raggedy Ann, 2 colors	Closed	1983	12.00	300-325
1994 Ringing in Christmas	Closed	1995	30.00	45-65
1995 Santa Nutcracker	Closed	1997	30.00	30-45
1986 Santa with Bag	Closed	1989	16.00	75
1991 Santa with Banner	Closed	1992	20.00	40-65
1992 Santa with Basket	Closed	1993	25.00	40-65
1986 Santa with Bear	Closed	1991	14.00	65-75
1986 Santa with Bells, blue	Closed	1989	14.00	75
1986 Santa with Bells, green	Closed	1987	14.00	300-500
1988 Santa with Book, blue & red	Closed	1988	17.00	300-360
1991 Santa with Lights, black or white	Closed	1992	20.00	75-100
1994 Santa with Pipe	Closed	1997	30.00	30-45
1992 Santa with Sack	Closed	1993	25.00	45-65
1989 Santa with Staff	Closed	1991	17.00	65-75
1982 Santa with Toys	Closed	1988	14.00	150-210
1988 Santa with Toys	Closed	1991	17.00	100
1989 Santa with Tree	Closed	1991	17.00	45-75
1988 Santa with Wreath	Closed	1991	17.00	40-75
1995 Santa's Lil' Helper, brown	Closed	1996	30.00	63-75
1996 Santa's Lil' Helper, white	Closed	1997	30.00	30
1994 Snow Showers	Closed	1997	30.00	50
1983 St. Nick with Lantern (wooden)	Closed	1988	14.00	125-210
1995 Who's This Frosty?	Closed	1997	30.00	30-50
1989 Winking Santa	Closed	1991	17.00	75

Kirk Stieff

Colonial Williamsburg - D. Bacorn

YEAR ISSUE	EDITION LIMIT	YEAR RETD.	ISSUE PRICE	*QUOTE U.S.$
1992 Court House	Open		10.00	10
1989 Doll ornament, silverplate	Closed	N/A	22.00	30
1993 Governors Palace	Open		10.00	10
1988 Lamb, silverplate	Closed	N/A	20.00	25
1992 Prentis Store	Open		10.00	10
1987 Rocking Horse, silverplate	Closed	N/A	20.00	35
1987 Tin Drum, silverplate	Closed	N/A	20.00	28
1983 Tree Top Star, silverplate	Closed	N/A	29.50	35
1984 Unicorn, silverplate	Closed	N/A	22.00	30
1992 Wythe House	Open		10.00	10

Kirk Stieff Ornaments - Various

YEAR ISSUE	EDITION LIMIT	YEAR RETD.	ISSUE PRICE	*QUOTE U.S.$
1994 Angel with Star - J. Ferraioli	Open		8.00	8
1993 Baby's Christmas - D. Bacorn	Open		12.00	12
1993 Bell with Ribbon - D. Bacorn	Open		12.00	12
1992 Cat and Ornament - D. Bacorn	Closed	N/A	10.00	10
1993 Cat with Ribbon - D. Bacorn	Open		12.00	12
1983 Charleston Locomotive - D. Bacorn	Closed	N/A	18.00	20
1993 First Christmas Together - D. Bacorn	Closed	N/A	10.00	10
1993 French Horn - D. Bacorn	Closed	N/A	12.00	12
1992 Guardian Angel - J. Ferraioli	Closed	N/A	13.00	13
1986 Icicle, sterling silver - D. Bacorn	Closed	N/A	35.00	65-150
1994 Kitten with Tassel - J. Ferraioli	Open		12.00	12
1993 Mouse and Ornament - D. Bacorn	Closed	N/A	10.00	10
1992 Repoussé Angel - J. Ferraioli	Open		13.00	13
1992 Repoussé Wreath - J. Ferraioli	Open		13.00	13
1994 Santa with Tassel - J. Ferraioli	Open		12.00	12

*Quotes have been rounded up to nearest dollar

YEAR ISSUE	EDITION LIMIT	YEAR RETD.	ISSUE PRICE	*QUOTE U.S.$
1989 Smithsonian Carousel Horse - Kirk Stieff	Closed	N/A	50.00	50
1989 Smithsonian Carousel Seahorse - Kirk Stieff	Closed	N/A	50.00	50
1994 Teddy Bear - D. Bacorn	Open		8.00	8
1990 Toy Ship - Kirk Stieff	Closed	N/A	23.00	35
1984 Unicorn - D. Bacorn	Closed	N/A	18.00	30
1994 Unicorn - D. Bacorn	Open		8.00	8
1994 Victorian Skaters - D. Bacorn	Open		8.00	8
1994 Williamsburg Wreath - D. Bacorn	Open		15.00	15
1993 Wreath with Ribbon - D. Bacorn	Open		12.00	12

Kurt S. Adler, Inc.

Children's Hour - J. Mostrom

YEAR ISSUE	EDITION LIMIT	YEAR RETD.	ISSUE PRICE	*QUOTE U.S.$
1995 Alice in Wonderland J5751	Retrd.	1996	22.50	23
1995 Bow Peep J5753	Retrd.	1997	27.00	27
1995 Cinderella J5752	Retrd.	1996	28.00	28
1995 Little Boy Blue J5755	Retrd.	1995	18.00	18
1995 Miss Muffet J5753	Retrd.	1997	27.00	27
1995 Mother Goose J5754	Retrd.	1996	27.00	27
1995 Red Riding Hood J5751	Retrd.	1996	22.50	23

Christmas in Chelsea Collection - J. Mostrom

YEAR ISSUE	EDITION LIMIT	YEAR RETD.	ISSUE PRICE	*QUOTE U.S.$
1994 Alice, Marguerite W2973	Retrd.	1996	28.00	28
1992 Allison Sitting in Chair W2812	Retrd.	1994	25.50	26
1992 Allison W2729	Retrd.	1993	21.00	21
1992 Amanda W2709	Retrd.	1994	21.00	21
1992 Amy W2729	Retrd.	1993	21.00	21
1992 Christina W2812	Retrd.	1994	25.50	26
1992 Christopher W2709	Retrd.	1994	21.00	21
1992 Delphinium W2728	Retrd.	1997	20.00	20
1995 Edmond With Violin W3078	Retrd.	1996	32.00	32
1994 Guardian Angel With Baby W2974	Retrd.	1995	31.00	31
1992 Holly Hock W2728	Retrd.	1997	20.00	20
1992 Holly W2709	Retrd.	1994	21.00	21
1995 Jose With Violin W3078	Retrd.	1996	32.00	32
1995 Pauline With Violin W3078	Retrd.	1996	32.00	32
1992 Peony W2728	Retrd.	1997	20.00	20
1992 Rose W2728	Retrd.	1997	20.00	20

Cornhusk Mice Ornament Series - M. Rothenberg

YEAR ISSUE	EDITION LIMIT	YEAR RETD.	ISSUE PRICE	*QUOTE U.S.$
1994 3" Father Christmas W2976	Open		18.00	18
1994 9" Father Christmas W2982	Retrd.	1997	25.00	25
1995 Angel Mice W3088	Retrd.	1997	10.00	10
1995 Baby's First Mouse W3087	Open		10.00	10
1993 Ballerina Cornhusk Mice W2700	Retrd.	1994	13.50	14
1994 Clara, Prince W2948	Open		16.00	16
1994 Cowboy W2951	Retrd.	1996	18.00	18
1994 Drosselmeir Fairy, Mouse King W2949	Open		16.00	16
1994 Little Pocahontas, Indian Brave W2950	Open		18.00	18
1995 Miss Tammie Mouse W3086	Retrd.	1996	17.00	17
1995 Mr. Jamie Mouse W3086	Retrd.	1996	17.00	17
1995 Mrs. Molly Mouse W3086	Retrd.	1996	17.00	17
1993 Nutcracker Suite Fantasy Cornhusk Mice W2885	Retrd.	1994	15.50	16

Fabriché™ Ornament Series - KS. Adler, unless otherwise noted

YEAR ISSUE	EDITION LIMIT	YEAR RETD.	ISSUE PRICE	*QUOTE U.S.$
1994 All Star Santa W1665	Retrd.	1996	27.00	27
1992 An Apron Full of Love W1594 - M. Rothenberg	Retrd.	1996	27.00	27
1995 Captain Claus W1711	Open		25.00	25
1994 Checking His List W1634	Retrd.	1996	23.50	24
1992 Christmas in the Air W1593	Retrd.	1996	35.50	36
1994 Cookies For Santa W1639	Retrd.	1996	28.00	28
1994 Firefighting Friends W1668	Retrd.	1996	28.00	28
1992 Hello Little One! W1561	Retrd.	1996	22.00	22
1994 Holiday Flight W1637 - Smithsonian	Retrd.	1996	40.00	40
1993 Homeward Bound W1596	Retrd.	1996	27.00	27
1992 Hugs And Kisses W1560	Retrd.	1996	22.00	22
1993 Master Toymaker W1595	Retrd.	1996	27.00	27
1992 Merry Chrismouse W1565	Retrd.	1994	10.00	10
1992 Not a Creature Was Stirring W1563	Retrd.	1996	22.00	22
1993 Par For the Claus W1625	Retrd.	1997	27.00	27
1993 Santa With List W1510	Retrd.	1996	20.00	20
1994 Santa's Fishtales W1666	Retrd.	1997	29.00	29
1995 Strike Up The Band W1710	Retrd.	1996	25.00	25

Fabriché™ Vatican Library Collection - Vatican Library

YEAR ISSUE	EDITION LIMIT	YEAR RETD.	ISSUE PRICE	*QUOTE U.S.$
1998 Vatican Angels in Flight (2 asst.) V34/A	Open		29.00	29
1998 Vatican Angels in Flight (gold) V34/GO	Open		29.00	29

International Christmas - J. Mostrom

YEAR ISSUE	EDITION LIMIT	YEAR RETD.	ISSUE PRICE	*QUOTE U.S.$
1994 Cathy, Johnny W2945	Retrd.	1996	24.00	24
1994 Eskimo-Atom, Ukpik W2967	Retrd.	1996	28.00	28
1994 Germany-Katerina, Hans W2969	Retrd.	1996	27.00	27
1994 Native American-White Dove, Little Wolf W2970	Retrd.	1994	28.00	28
1994 Poland-Marissa, Hedwig W2965	Retrd.	1997	27.00	27
1994 Scotland-Bonnie, Douglas W2966	Retrd.	1997	27.00	27
1994 Spain-Maria, Miguel W2968	Retrd.	1997	27.00	27

Little Dickens - J. Mostrom

YEAR ISSUE	EDITION LIMIT	YEAR RETD.	ISSUE PRICE	*QUOTE U.S.$
1994 Little Bob Crachit W2961	Retrd.	1996	30.00	30
1994 Little Marley's Ghost W2964	Retrd.	1996	33.50	34
1994 Little Mrs. Crachit W2962	Retrd.	1997	27.00	27
1994 Little Scrooge in Bathrobe W2959	Retrd.	1997	30.00	30
1994 Little Scrooge in Overcoat W2960	Retrd.	1997	30.00	30
1994 Little Tiny Tim W2963	Retrd.	1997	22.50	23

Polonaise™ - KSA/Komozja, unless otherwise noted

YEAR ISSUE	EDITION LIMIT	YEAR RETD.	ISSUE PRICE	*QUOTE U.S.$
1995 Alarm Clock AP452	Retrd.	1996	25.00	25
1997 Alice Collection 4 pc set AP548	Open		150.00	150
1997 Alice Collection 5 pc set AP547	7,500	1998	175.00	175
1997 Alice in Wonderland AP692	Open		29.95	30
1994 Angel w/Bear AP396	Retrd.	1995	20.00	30-45
1996 Antique Cars boxed set AP522	Open		120.00	124
1997 Babar Elephant, 5" AP817 - Clifford Ross/Nelrana	Open		37.50	40
1994 Beer Glass AP366	Open		15.95	18
1996 Betty Boop AP624 - King Features	Open		34.95	39
1997 The Bible AP841 - Iwona Wiszniewska	Open		34.95	35
1995 Blessed Mother AP413	Retrd.	1997	19.95	25
1995 Caesar AP422	Retrd.	1998	19.95	25
1997 Calvary, Gunner, Drummer AP645	Open		29.95	30
1996 Candleholder AP450	Retrd.	1997	17.95	20
1994 Cardinal on Pine Cone AP420	Retrd.	1995	18.00	35
1995 Cat in Boot AP478 - Rothenberg	Open		29.95	30
1994 Cat w/Ball AP390	Retrd.	1995	18.00	50
1995 Cat w/Bow AP443	Open		22.50	23
1997 Charlie Brown Peanuts, 5 1/2" AP824	Open		34.95	39
1995 Christ Child AP414	Retrd.	1997	17.95	20
1997 Christmas in Poland 4pc set AP534	Open		150.00	150
1995 Christmas Tree AP461	Open		24.95	25
1996 Cinderella 4 pc boxed set AP512	Retrd.	1998	130.00	135
1996 Cinderella 6 pc boxed set AP511	7,500	1996	190.00	200-250
1996 Cinderella AP488	Retrd.	1998	27.50	28
1996 Cinderella Coach AP487	Open		34.95	35
1997 Circus Collection 5 pc set AP545	Open		180.00	180
1997 Circus Ring Master AP691	Open		34.95	35
1997 Circus Strongman AP690	Open		34.95	35
1995 Clara AP408	Open		19.95	20
1995 Clown Head 4.5" AP460	Retrd.	1997	22.50	25-30
1997 Coca Cola 3 pc AP553	Open		130.00	130
1996 Coca Cola 4 pc boxed set AP517	Retrd.	1998	135.00	135-150
1997 Coca Cola Bear 6 Pack AP803	Open		34.95	35
1996 Coca Cola Bear AP630 - Coca Cola	Open		34.95	37
1997 Coca Cola Bear Skiing AP801	Open		34.95	35
1997 Coca Cola Bear Snowmobile AP802	Open		34.95	35
1997 Coca Cola Bear Truck AP804	Open		37.50	38
1997 Coca Cola Bottle (golden) AP800	Open		34.95	35
1996 Coca Cola Bottle AP631 - Coca Cola	Open		29.95	33
1996 Coca Cola Bottle Top AP633 - Coca Cola	Open		24.95	27
1996 Coca Cola Disk AP632 - Coca Cola	Retrd.	1998	24.95	26
1996 Coca Cola Vending Machine AP634 - Coca Cola	Open		34.95	37
1996 Cossack AP604	Retrd.	1998	34.95	35
1995 Cowboy Head AP462	Open		29.95	30
1995 Creche AP458 - Stefan	Open		27.50	28
1995 Crocodile AP468	Retrd.	1996	28.00	30
1996 Dice boxed set AP509	Retrd.	1997	55.00	60
1994 Dinosaurs AP397	Retrd.	1996	22.50	24-60
1994 Dinosaurs-brown AP397	Retrd.	1995	22.50	55-60
1995 Dove on Ball AP472 - Stefan	Retrd.	1996	29.95	32
1995 Eagle AP453	Open		29.95	30
1994 Egyptian (12 pc boxed set) AP500	Retrd.	1995	214.00	360-425
1997 Egyptian 4 pc set AP515	Open		150.00	150
1996 Egyptian Cat AP351	Open		27.50	30
1996 Egyptian II boxed set AP510	Open		150.00	170
1996 Egyptian Princess AP482	Open		34.95	35
1995 Egyptian set 4 pc. boxed AP500/4	Retrd.	1997	100.00	110-120
1995 Elephant AP 464	Open		27.50	28
1997 Elmo AP843	Open		37.50	38
1996 Elves AP611/23	Open		29.95	30
1996 Emerald City AP623	Retrd.	1998	29.95	30-33
1997 English Bobbie AP814	Open		29.95	30
1997 The Evolution of Polonaise™ Kit (boxed set) AP564	Open		50.00	50
1996 Fire Engine AP605	Open		29.95	30
1995 Fish 4 pc. boxed AP506	Retrd.	1998	110.00	110-115
1997 Four Calling Birds AP828	Open		37.50	38
1996 French Hen AP626 - Stefan	Open		34.95	35
1996 Gift Boxes AP614	Open		24.95	25
1997 Gingerbread House AP664	Open		29.95	30
1994 Glass Acorn AP342	Retrd.	1995	11.00	60-150
1994 Glass Angel AP309	Retrd.	1996	18.00	20
1994 Glass Apple AP339	Retrd.	1995	11.00	15-25
1997 Glass Big Bird AP699	Open		34.95	35
1994 Glass Church AP369	Retrd.	1997	15.95	20
1997 Glass Circus Seal AP688	Open		29.95	30
1994 Glass Clown 4" AP301	Retrd.	1995	13.50	45
1994 Glass Clown 6" AP303	Retrd.	1995	22.50	40
1994 Glass Clown on Ball 6.5" AP302	Retrd.	1995	22.50	35
1997 Glass Clowns 3/asst. AP682	Open		34.95	35
1994 Glass Doll AP377	Retrd.	1995	13.50	35
1997 Glass Dr. Watson AP813	Open		29.95	30
1994 Glass Gnome AP347	Retrd.	1995	18.00	35
1997 Glass Hat Boxes AP620	Open		27.50	28
1997 Glass Holly Bear AP827	Open		29.95	30
1997 Glass Hunter AP667	Open		29.95	30
1994 Glass Knight's Helmet AP304	Retrd.	1995	18.00	22-26
1997 Glass Krakow Man AP674	Open		29.95	30
1997 Glass Mad Hatter AP696	Open		34.95	35
1994 Glass Nefertiti AP349	Retrd.	1996	24.95	40-45
1994 Glass Owl AP328	Retrd.	1998	17.50	20-48
1997 Glass Santa Head AP811	Open		22.50	23
1996 Glass Slipper AP490	Retrd.	1997	19.95	20-25
1997 Glass Snow White AP660	Open		29.95	30

YEAR ISSUE	EDITION LIMIT	YEAR RETD.	ISSUE PRICE	*QUOTE U.S.$
1997 Glass Star 3/asst. AP671	Open		19.95	20
1997 Glass Star Boy AP676	Open		34.95	35
1997 Glass Tatar Prince AP672	Open		34.95	35
1994 Glass Turkey AP326	Retrd.	1996	20.00	20
1994 Glass White Dice (original-square) AP363	Retrd.	1994	18.00	66-80
1997 Glass Wolf AP666	Open		34.95	35
1996 Glinda the Good Witch AP621	Open		34.95	35
1994 Golden Cherub Head AP372	Retrd.	1994	18.00	60-75
1994 Golden Rocking Horse AP355	Retrd.	1994	22.50	60-125
1997 Gone With The Wind 3 pc boxed set AP557	Open		150.00	150
1997 Gone With The Wind Rhett Butler AP815	Open		37.50	38
1997 Gone With The Wind Scarlett O'Hara AP805	Open		39.95	40
1997 Gone With The Wind Tara AP816	Open		37.50	38
1995 Goose w/Wreath AP475 - Stefan	Open		29.95	30
1996 Gramophone AP446	Retrd.	1996	22.50	23
1997 Grand Father Frost AP810COL	Open		50.00	50
1997 Handblown Witch, 7" AP661	Open		34.95	35
1997 Hansel & Gretel AP662	Open		29.95	30
1997 Hansel/Gretel 4 pc set AP538	Open		150.00	150
1997 Herald Rabbit AP693	Open		34.95	35
1995 Herr Drosselmeir AP465 - Rothenberg	Open		29.95	30
1995 Holy Family 3 pc. AP504	Retrd.	1997	80.00	84
1994 Holy Family AP371	Retrd.	1998	27.50	28
1996 Horus AP484	Retrd.	1998	34.95	35
1995 Humpty Dumpty AP477 - Stefan	Open		29.95	30
1995 Icicle Santa AP474 - Stefan	Retrd.	1995	25.00	40-45
1995 Indian Chief AP463	Open		29.95	30
1997 Jewelry Boxes AP637	Open		15.95	16
1997 Just Married AP829	Open		22.50	23
1996 King Balthazar AP607	Retrd.	1997	29.95	31
1996 King Neptune AP496	Open		34.95	35
1997 Krakow Castle AP670	Open		34.95	35
1996 Light Bulb AP449	Retrd.	1996	20.00	20
1996 Little Mermaid AP492	Retrd.	1997	27.50	28
1997 Little Red Riding Hood 4 pc set AP539	Yr.Iss.	1997	140.00	140-150
1997 Little Red Riding Hood 5 1/2" AP665	Open		29.95	30
1994 Locomotive AP353	Retrd.	1998	19.95	20
1995 Locomotive AP447	Open		27.50	28
1997 Lucy Peanuts AP825	Open		34.95	35
1997 Madonna Vatican Egg AP830	Open		37.50	38
1994 Madonna w/Child AP370	Retrd.	1997	22.50	23
1997 Magician's Hat AP689	Open		34.95	35
1997 Marilyn Monroe AP818	Open		37.50	38
1996 Medieval boxed set AP519	Retrd.	1998	150.00	160
1996 Medieval Dragon AP642	Open		34.95	35
1996 Medieval Knight AP641	Open		34.95	35
1996 Medieval Lady AP643	Retrd.	1998	34.95	35
1994 Merlin AP373	Retrd.	1995	20.00	30
1997 MGM Cowardly Lion AP821	Open		39.95	40
1997 MGM Dorothy AP819	Open		39.95	40
1997 MGM Scarecrow AP822	Open		39.95	40
1997 MGM Tin Man AP820	Open		39.95	40
1997 MGM Wizard of Oz 4 pc. boxed set AP555	Open		180.00	180
1995 Mickey Mouse AP392	Retrd.	1995	33.00	30-100
1995 Mickey Mouse AP392 & Minnie Mouse (pr.) AP391,set	Retrd.	1995	66.00	90-125
1995 Minnie Mouse AP391	Retrd.	1995	33.00	30-70
1994 Mouse King AP406	Open		19.95	20
1996 Mummy AP483	Open		34.95	35
1997 Napolionic Soldier AP543	Open		150.00	150
1996 Nefertiti 96 AP485	Open		29.95	30
1994 Night & Day AP307	Retrd.	1997	19.95	20
1995 Noah's Ark AP469	Open		27.50	28
1994 Nutcracker AP404	Open		19.95	20
1995 Nutcracker Suite 4 pc. boxed AP507	Open		125.00	125
1997 NY Ball 5/asst. AP677	Open		24.95	25
1994 Old Fashioned Car AP380	Open		22.50	23
1994 Parrot AP332	Retrd.	1995	15.50	40-48
1995 Partridge in a Pear Tree AP467 - Stefan	Open		34.95	35
1994 Peacock 5" AP324	Retrd.	1996	18.00	25
1994 Peacock on Ball 7.5" AP323	Retrd.	1996	28.00	28
1997 Peanuts 3 pc boxed set AP556	Open		135.00	135
1995 Peter Pan 4 pc. boxed set AP503	Retrd.	1997	125.00	105-125
1995 Peter Pan AP419	Retrd.	1998	19.95	23
1996 Pharaoh AP481	Open		34.95	35
1994 Pierrot Clown AP405	Retrd.	1995	18.00	35-40
1996 Polanaise Medieval Horse AP640	Open		34.95	35
1997 Polish Mountain Man AP675	Open		29.95	30
1995 Polonaise African-American Santa AP389/A	Retrd.	1998	22.50	28
1995 Polonaise Cardinal AP473 - Stefan	Open		29.95	30
1995 Polonaise Houses (2 asst.) AP455	Retrd.	1996	25.00	30
1995 Polonaise Santa AP389	Retrd.	1998	22.50	23
1996 Prince Charming AP489	Retrd.	1997	27.50	28
1994 Puppy (gold) AP333	Retrd.	1994	13.50	35
1994 Pyramid AP352	Open		21.95	22
1997 Queen of Hearts AP695	Open		34.95	35
1997 Raggedy Andy AP322	Open		24.95	25
1996 Raggedy Ann AP321	Open		24.95	25
1997 Raggedy Ann/Andy AP550	Open		75.00	75
1994 Rocking Horse 5" AP356	Open		22.50	23
1994 Roly-Poly Santa AP317	Open		21.95	22
1995 Roman 4 pc. boxed set AP502/4	Retrd.	1995	110.00	140-150

YEAR ISSUE	EDITION LIMIT	YEAR RETD.	ISSUE PRICE	*QUOTE U.S.$
1995 Roman 7 pc. boxed set AP502	Retrd.	1995	164.00	195
1995 Roman Centurian AP427	Retrd.	1998	19.95	23
1997 Royal Suite 4 pc set AP552	Open		140.00	140
1997 Royal Suite 4/asst. AP806	Open		29.95	30
1996 Russian 5 pc boxed set AP514	Retrd.	1998	180.00	190
1996 Russian Bishop AP603	Retrd.	1998	34.95	35
1996 Russian Woman AP602	Retrd.	1998	34.95	35
1995 Sailing Ship AP415	Open		29.95	30
1994 Saint Nick AP316	Retrd.	1998	24.95	30
1994 Santa Boot AP375	Open		19.95	20
1996 Santa Car AP367	Open		34.95	35
1994 Santa Head 4" AP315	Retrd.	1995	13.50	22-25
1994 Santa Head 4.5" AP374	Retrd.	1996	19.00	19-22
1996 Santa in Airplane AP365	Open		34.95	35
1995 Santa Moon AP454 - Stefan	Open		27.50	28
1995 Santa on Goose on Sled AP479	Open		29.95	30
1995 Santa w/Puppy AP442	Open		22.50	28
1996 Sea Horse AP494	Retrd.	1998	24.95	25
1997 Seven Dwarfs AP611	Open		29.95	30
1995 Shark AP417	Retrd.	1996	18.00	25
1997 Sherlock Holmes 3 pc set AP551	Open		125.00	125
1997 Sherlock Holmes AP812	Open		29.95	30
1997 Smithsonian Astronaut AP826	Open		34.95	35
1997 Snoopy Peanuts AP823	Open		34.95	35
1997 Snow White & 7 Dwarfs 8 pc boxed set AP558	Open		290.00	290
1994 Snowman w/Parcel AP313	Open		21.95	22
1994 Snowman w/Specs AP312	Retrd.	1995	20.00	35
1994 Soldier AP407	Retrd.	1995	15.50	175
1994 Sparrow AP329	Retrd.	1995	15.50	20
1994 Sphinx AP350	Retrd.	1995	22.50	60-65
1996 Sphinx AP480	Open		29.95	30
1994 Spinner Top AP359	Retrd.	1995	9.00	28
1996 St. Basils Cathedral AP600	Open		34.95	35
1995 St. Joseph AP412	Retrd.	1996	22.50	23
1995 Star Santa AP470 - Stefan	Open		27.50	28
1996 Star Snowman AP625 - Stefan	Open		29.95	32
1996 Sting Ray AP495	Retrd.	1996	28.00	28
1994 Swan AP325	Retrd.	1997	17.50	20
1994 Teddy Bear (gold) AP338	Retrd.	1994	13.50	25-40
1995 Telephone AP448	Retrd.	1996	25.00	25
1996 Three Kings boxed set AP516	Open		120.00	144
1994 Train Coaches AP354	Open		14.95	15
1994 Train Set (boxed) AP501	Open		100.00	100
1995 Treasure Chest AP416	Retrd.	1996	20.00	20
1994 Tropical Fish (6 asst.) AP409	Retrd.	1997	22.50	25-35
1997 Tropical Fish AP410	Open		22.50	28
1997 Tropical Fish AP554	Open		110.00	110
1994 Tropical Fish boxed set AP506	Retrd.	1997	110.00	110-125
1996 Tsar Ivan AP601	Retrd.	1998	34.95	35
1995 Turtle Doves AP471 - Stefan	Open		34.95	35
1996 Tutenkhamen #2 AP476	Open		34.95	35
1994 Tutenkhamen AP348	Retrd.	1996	28.00	30
1996 Wicked Witch AP606	Open		29.95	30
1996 Winter Boy AP615	Retrd.	1998	19.95	20
1996 Winter Girl AP615	Retrd.	1998	19.95	20
1996 Wizard in Balloon AP622	Open		34.95	35
1995 Wizard of Oz 4 pc. boxed AP505	Open		125.00	125
1995 Wizard of Oz 6 pc. boxed AP508	5,000	1995	170.00	150-250
1995 Wizard of Oz Dorothy AP434	Open		22.50	25
1996 Wizard of Oz II boxed set AP518	Open		150.00	164
1995 Wizard of Oz Lion AP433	Open		22.50	23
1995 Wizard of Oz Scarecrow AP435	Open		22.50	23
1995 Wizard of Oz Tinman AP436	Open		22.50	23
1994 Zodiac Sun AP381	Retrd.	1995	22.50	55-60

The Polonaise™ Collector's Guild - KSA/Komozja, unless otherwise noted

YEAR ISSUE	EDITION LIMIT	YEAR RETD.	ISSUE PRICE	*QUOTE U.S.$
1997 Grandfather Frost AP810/COL	12/98		Gift	50

Polonaise™ Event Signing Collection - KSA/Komozja

YEAR ISSUE	EDITION LIMIT	YEAR RETD.	ISSUE PRICE	*QUOTE U.S.$
1996 Szlachcic AP673/SIG	Yr.Iss.	1996	35.50	36
1997 Szlachcianka AP840	Yr.Iss.	1997	34.95	35
1998 Patriarch Alexis AP926/SIG	Yr.Iss.		35.95	36

Polonaise™ Vatican Library Collection - Vatican Library

YEAR ISSUE	EDITION LIMIT	YEAR RETD.	ISSUE PRICE	*QUOTE U.S.$
1996 Cherub Bust Glass AP651	Open		34.95	35
1996 Cherubum boxed set, AP 521	Open		150.00	160
1996 Dancing Cherubs on Ball AP652	Retrd.	1998	34.95	40
1996 Full Body Cherub AP 650	Open		34.95	40
1996 Garden of Mary boxed set, AP 520	Retrd.	1998	135.00	150
1996 Lily Glass AP655	Retrd.	1998	34.95	37
1996 Madonna & Child AP653	Open		34.95	37
1996 Rose Glass Pink/Ivory Rose AP654/DIV	Open		34.95	37
1996 Rose Glass Red Rose AP654/R	Open		34.95	37
1998 Vatican Angels in Flight (Gold) V34/GO	Open		29.00	29
1998 Vatican Angels in Flight (Ivory or Red) V34/A	Open		29.00	29

Royal Heritage Collection - J. Mostrom

YEAR ISSUE	EDITION LIMIT	YEAR RETD.	ISSUE PRICE	*QUOTE U.S.$
1993 Anastasia W2922	Retrd.	1994	28.00	28
1996 Angelique Angel Baby W3278	Retrd.	1996	25.00	25
1995 Benjamin J5756	Retrd.	1996	24.50	25
1995 Blythe J5756	Retrd.	1996	24.50	25
1996 Brianna Ivory W7663	Open		25.00	25
1996 Brianna Pink W7663	Open		25.00	25
1993 Caroline W2924	Retrd.	1995	25.50	26
1993 Charles W2924	Retrd.	1995	25.50	26
1993 Elizabeth W2924	Retrd.	1995	25.50	26
1996 Etoile Angel Baby W3278	Retrd.	1996	25.00	25
1996 Francis Winter Boy W3279	Retrd.	1997	28.00	28
1996 Gabrielle in Pink Coat W3276	Open		28.00	28
1996 Giselle w/Bow W3277	Retrd.	1997	28.00	28
1996 Giselle Winter Girl w/Package W3279	Retrd.	1997	28.00	28
1994 Ice Fairy, Winter Fairy W2972	Retrd.	1996	25.50	26
1993 Joella W2979	Retrd.	1993	27.00	27
1993 Kelly W2979	Retrd.	1993	27.00	27
1996 Lady Colette in Sled W3301	Retrd.	1997	32.00	32
1996 Laurielle Lady Skater W3281	Retrd.	1997	36.00	36
1996 Miniotte w/Muff W3279	Retrd.	1997	28.00	28
1996 Monique w/Hat Box W3277	Open		28.00	28
1993 Nicholas W2923	Retrd.	1996	25.50	26
1996 Nicole w/Balloon W3277	Open		28.00	28
1993 Patina W2923	Retrd.	1996	25.50	26
1996 Rene Victorian Lady W3280	Retrd.	1997	36.00	36
1993 Sasha W2923	Retrd.	1996	25.50	26
1994 Snow Princess W2971	Retrd.	1996	28.00	28

Smithsonian Museum Carousel - KSA/Smithsonian

YEAR ISSUE	EDITION LIMIT	YEAR RETD.	ISSUE PRICE	*QUOTE U.S.$
1987 Antique Bunny S3027/2	Retrd.	1992	14.50	15-22
1992 Antique Camel S3027/12	Retrd.	1996	15.00	15-22
1989 Antique Cat S3027/6	Retrd.	1995	14.50	15
1992 Antique Elephant S3027/11	Retrd.	1996	14.50	15-22
1995 Antique Frog S32027/18	Open		15.50	16
1988 Antique Giraffe S3027/4	Retrd.	1993	14.50	15
1987 Antique Goat S3027/1	Retrd.	1992	14.50	15
1991 Antique Horse S3027/10	Retrd.	1996	14.50	15-22
1993 Antique Horse S3027/14	Open		15.00	15
1988 Antique Horse S3027/3	Retrd.	1993	14.50	15
1989 Antique Lion S3027/5	Retrd.	1994	14.50	15
1994 Antique Pig S3027/16	Open		15.50	16
1994 Antique Reindeer S3027/15	Open		15.50	16
1991 Antique Rooster S3027/9	Retrd.	1994	14.50	15
1990 Antique Seahorse S3027/8	Open		14.50	15
1993 Antique Tiger S3027/13	Open		15.00	15
1990 Antique Zebra S3027/7	Retrd.	1997	14.50	15-22
1995 Armored Horse S3027/17	Open		15.50	16
1997 Graceful Horse S3027/20	Open		20.00	20
1997 Persian Cat S3027/23	Open		18.00	18
1997 Sea Monster S3027/21	Open		20.00	20
1997 Stork with Baby S3027/24	Open		18.00	18

Smithsonian Museum Fabriché™ - KSA/Smithsonian

YEAR ISSUE	EDITION LIMIT	YEAR RETD.	ISSUE PRICE	*QUOTE U.S.$
1992 Holiday Drive W1580	Retrd.	1995	38.00	38
1992 Santa On a Bicycle W1547	Retrd.	1997	31.00	31

Steinbach Ornament Series - KS. Adler

YEAR ISSUE	EDITION LIMIT	YEAR RETD.	ISSUE PRICE	*QUOTE U.S.$
1992 The King's Guards ES300	Open		27.00	27

Lenox China

Annual Ornaments - Lenox

YEAR ISSUE	EDITION LIMIT	YEAR RETD.	ISSUE PRICE	*QUOTE U.S.$
1982 1982 Ball	Yr.Iss.	1983	30.00	50-90
1983 1983 Teardrop Shape	Yr.Iss.	1984	35.00	75
1984 1984 Starburst	Yr.Iss.	1985	38.00	65
1985 1985 Bell	Yr.Iss.	1986	37.50	60
1986 1986 The Three Magi	Yr.Iss.	1987	38.50	50
1987 1987 Dickens Village	Yr.Iss.	1988	39.00	45
1988 1988 Ball	Yr.Iss.	1989	39.00	45
1989 1989 Faberge Egg	Yr.Iss.	1990	39.00	39
1990 1990 Bell	Yr.Iss.	1991	42.00	42
1991 1991 Ornament	Yr.Iss.	1992	39.00	39
1992 1992 Ball	Yr.Iss.	1993	42.00	42
1993 1993 Lantern	Yr.Iss.	1994	45.00	45
1994 1994 Star	Yr.Iss.	1995	39.00	39
1995 1995 Santa	Yr.Iss.	1996	46.50	47
1996 1996 Traditional Ball	Yr.Iss.		46.50	47

Yuletide - Lenox

YEAR ISSUE	EDITION LIMIT	YEAR RETD.	ISSUE PRICE	*QUOTE U.S.$
1994 Cat	Open		19.50	20
1995 Candle	Open		19.95	20
1996 Christmas Angel™	Open		21.00	21

Lenox, Inc.

Lenox Classics-Little Graces - Lenox

YEAR ISSUE	EDITION LIMIT	YEAR RETD.	ISSUE PRICE	*QUOTE U.S.$
1997 Little Surprise	5,000		45.00	45
1998 Little Hope (Cherub wStar)	5,000		45.00	45

Lilliput Lane Ltd./Enesco Corporation

Christmas Ornaments - Lilliput Lane

YEAR ISSUE	EDITION LIMIT	YEAR RETD.	ISSUE PRICE	*QUOTE U.S.$
1992 Mistletoe Cottage	Retrd.	1992	27.50	40-60
1993 Robin Cottage	Retrd.	1993	35.00	45
1994 Ivy House	Retrd.	1994	35.00	35-45
1995 Plum Cottage	Retrd.	1995	30.00	40
1996 Fir Tree Cottage	Retrd.	1996	30.00	30
1997 Evergreens	Retrd.	1997	30.00	30
1998 Great Expectations	Yr.Iss.		35.00	35

Ray Day/Coca Cola Country - R. Day

YEAR ISSUE	EDITION LIMIT	YEAR RETD.	ISSUE PRICE	*QUOTE U.S.$
1996 Santa's Corner	19,960		35.00	35

Lladró

Angels - Lladró

YEAR ISSUE	EDITION LIMIT	YEAR RETD.	ISSUE PRICE	*QUOTE U.S.$
1994 Joyful Offering L6125G	Yr.Iss.	1994	245.00	245-312
1995 Angel of the Stars L6132G	Yr.Iss.	1995	195.00	195-228
1996 Rejoice L6321G	Yr.Iss.		220.00	220

Annual Ornaments - Lladró

YEAR ISSUE	EDITION LIMIT	YEAR RETD.	ISSUE PRICE	*QUOTE U.S.$
1988 Christmas Ball-L1603M	Yr.Iss.	1988	60.00	60-104
1989 Christmas Ball-L5656M	Yr.Iss.	1989	65.00	34-65
1990 Christmas Ball-L5730M	Yr Iss.	1990	70.00	59-85
1991 Christmas Ball-L5829M	Yr.Iss.	1991	52.00	34-65
1992 Christmas Ball-L5914M	Yr.Iss.	1992	52.00	52-85
1993 Christmas Ball-L6009M	Yr.Iss.	1993	54.00	52-78
1994 Christmas Ball-L6105M	Yr.Iss.	1994	55.00	46-78
1995 Christmas Ball-L6207M	Yr.Iss.	1995	55.00	60-78
1996 Christmas Ball-L6298M	Yr.Iss.	1996	55.00	52-55
1997 Christmas Ball-L6442M	Yr.Iss.	1997	55.00	55
1998 Christmas Ball-01016561	Yr.Iss.		55.00	55

Miniature Ornaments - Lladró

YEAR ISSUE	EDITION LIMIT	YEAR RETD.	ISSUE PRICE	*QUOTE U.S.$
1988 Miniature Angels-L1604G, Set/3	Yr.Iss.	1988	75.00	200-300
1989 Holy Family-L5657G, Set/3	Yr.Iss.	1990	79.50	100-163
1990 Three Kings-L5729G, Set/3	Yr Iss.	1991	87.50	88-120
1991 Holy Shepherds-L5809G	Yr.Iss.	1991	97.50	108-163
1993 Nativity Trio-L6095G	Yr.Iss.	1993	115.00	165-250

Ornaments - Lladró

YEAR ISSUE	EDITION LIMIT	YEAR RETD.	ISSUE PRICE	*QUOTE U.S.$
1995 Christmas Tree L6261G	Open		75.00	75
1995 Landing Dove L6266G	Closed	1998	49.00	50
1995 Surprised Cherub L6253G	Closed	1998	120.00	120
1995 Flying Dove L6267G	Closed	1998	49.00	50
1995 Playing Cherub L6254G	Closed	1998	120.00	120
1995 Rocking Horse L6262G	Closed	1998	69.00	75
1995 Doll L6263G	Closed	1998	69.00	75
1995 Thinking Cherub L6255G	Closed	1998	120.00	120
1995 Train L6264G	Closed	1998	69.00	75
1991 Our First-1991-L5840G	Yr.Iss.	1991	50.00	50-65
1992 Snowman-L5841G	Yr.Iss.	1994	50.00	52-75
1992 Santa-L5842G	Yr.Iss.	1994	55.00	59-75
1992 Baby's First-1992-L5922G	Yr.Iss.	1992	55.00	55-65
1992 Our First-1992-L5923G	Yr.Iss.	1992	50.00	52-59
1992 Elf Ornament-L5938G	Yr.Iss.	1994	50.00	59-75
1992 Mrs. Claus-L5939G	Yr.Iss.	1994	55.00	59-75
1992 Christmas Morning-L5940G	Yr.Iss.	1992	97.50	100-200
1993 Nativity Lamb-L5969G	Yr.Iss.	1994	85.00	85-111
1993 Baby's First 1993-L6037G	Yr.Iss.	1993	57.00	57
1993 Our First-L6038G	Yr.Iss.	1993	52.00	57-75
1996 Santa's Journey-L6265	Yr.Iss.	1996	49.00	49
1996 Welcome Home-L6335	Closed	1998	85.00	85-157
1996 King Melchior-L6341	Closed	1998	75.00	75
1996 Seraph With Bells-L6342	Closed	1998	79.00	79
1996 Little Aviator-L6343	Closed	1998	79.00	79
1996 Teddy Bear-L6344	Closed	1998	67.00	67
1996 Toy Soldier-L6345	Closed	1998	90.00	90
1996 Heavenly Tenor-L6372	Closed	1998	98.00	98
1998 Seraph with Bow-01006445	Open		79.00	79
1998 Heavenly Musician-01006498	Open		98.00	98
1998 King Balthaser-01006509	Open		75.00	75
1998 Our Winter Home-01006519	Open		85.00	85
1998 Baby's First Christmas-1998 01016588	Yr.Iss.		55.00	55

Tree Topper Ornaments - Lladró

YEAR ISSUE	EDITION LIMIT	YEAR RETD.	ISSUE PRICE	*QUOTE U.S.$
1990 Angel Tree Topper-L5719G-Blue	Yr.Iss.	1990	100.00	169-185
1991 Angel Tree Topper-L5831G-Pink	Yr.Iss.	1991	115.00	117-225
1992 Angel Tree Topper-L5875G-Green	Yr.Iss.	1992	120.00	130-195
1993 Angel Tree Topper -L5962G-Lavender	Yr.Iss.	1993	125.00	143-175
1998 Message of Peace-01006587	Open		150.00	150

Lowell Davis Farm Club

Lowell Davis Country Christmas - L. Davis

YEAR ISSUE	EDITION LIMIT	YEAR RETD.	ISSUE PRICE	*QUOTE U.S.$
1983 Mailbox	Yr.Iss.	1983	17.50	75
1984 Cat in Boot	Yr.Iss.	1984	17.50	80
1985 Pig in Trough	Yr.Iss.	1985	17.50	75
1986 Church	Yr.Iss.	1986	17.50	50
1987 Blossom	Yr.Iss.	1987	19.50	36-50
1988 Wisteria	Yr.Iss.	1988	19.50	25-45
1989 Wren	Yr.Iss.	1989	19.50	45
1990 Wintering Deer	Yr.Iss.	1990	19.50	30
1991 Church at Red Oak II	Yr.Iss.	1991	25.00	25
1992 Born On A Starry Night	Yr.Iss.	1992	25.00	25
1993 Waiting for Mr. Lowell	Yr.Iss.	1993	20.00	20-25
1994 Visions of Sugarplums	Yr.Iss.	1994	25.00	25-45
1995 Bah Humbug	Yr.Iss.	1995	25.00	25-30

Lowell Davis Glass Ornaments - L. Davis

YEAR ISSUE	EDITION LIMIT	YEAR RETD.	ISSUE PRICE	*QUOTE U.S.$
1986 Christmas at Red Oak	Yr.Iss.	1986	5.00	15
1987 Blossom's Gift	Yr.Iss.	1987	5.50	15
1988 Hope Mom Likes It	Yr.Iss.	1988	5.00	15
1989 Peter and the Wren	Yr.Iss.	1989	6.50	15
1990 Wintering Deer	Yr.Iss.	1990	6.50	15
1991 Christmas at Red Oak II	Yr.Iss.	1991	7.50	15
1992 Born On A Starry Night Ball	Yr.Iss.	1992	7.50	15
1993 Waiting for Mr. Lowell	Yr.Iss.	1993	7.50	15

Margaret Furlong Designs

Annual Ornaments - M. Furlong

YEAR ISSUE	EDITION LIMIT	YEAR RETD.	ISSUE PRICE	*QUOTE U.S.$
1980 3" Trumpeter Angel	Closed	1994	12.00	150
1980 4" Trumpeter Angel	Closed	1994	21.00	150
1982 3" Star Angel	Closed	1994	12.00	150
1982 4" Star Angel	Closed	1994	21.00	150
1983 3" Holly Angel	Closed	1998	14.00	15-22
1983 4" Holly Angel	Closed	1998	23.00	25-40
1984 3" Dove Angel	Closed	1995	12.00	40-65
1984 4" Dove Angel	Closed	1995	21.00	69-100
1985 3" Wreath Angel	Open		14.00	14
1985 4" Wreath Angel	Open		23.00	23
1986 3" Heart Angel	Open		14.00	14
1986 4" Heart Angel	Open		23.00	23
1987 3" Bouquet Angel	Open		14.00	14

*Quotes have been rounded up to nearest dollar

YEAR ISSUE	EDITION LIMIT	YEAR RETD.	ISSUE PRICE	*QUOTE U.S.$
1987 4" Bouquet Angel	Open		23.00	23
1988 3" Butterfly Angel	Closed	1996	12.00	40
1988 4" Butterfly Angel	Closed	1996	21.00	65-69
1989 3" Snowflake Angel	Open		14.00	14
1989 4" Snowflake Angel	Open		23.00	23
1990 3" Christmas Tree Angel	Open		14.00	14
1990 4" Christmas Tree Angel	Open		23.00	23
1991 3" Gift Angel	Open		14.00	14
1991 4" Gift Angel	Open		23.00	23
1992 3" Noel Angel	Closed	1997	12.00	15-30
1992 4" Noel Angel	Closed	1997	21.00	25-45
1993 2" Miniature Celestial Angel	Open		12.00	12
1993 3" Cross Angel	Open		14.00	14
1993 4" Cross Angel	Open		23.00	23
1994 2" Miniature Heart Angel	Open		12.00	12
1994 3" Sun Angel	Open		14.00	14
1994 4" Sun Angel	Open		23.00	23
1995 2" Miniature Wreath Angel	Open		12.00	12
1995 3" Flower Garland Angel	Open		14.00	14
1995 4" Flower Garland Angel	Open		23.00	23
1996 2" Miniature Daisy Angel	Open		12.00	12
1996 3" Morning Glory Angel	Open		14.00	14
1997 2" Miniature Viola Angel	Open		12.00	12
1997 3" Dogwood Angel	Open		14.00	14
1997 1 1/2" Tea For Two Angel	Open		22.00	22
1998 3" Wild Rose Angel	Open		14.00	14
1998 2" Shamrock Angel	Open		12.00	12
1998 1 1/2" Gardening Friends	Open		22.00	22

Flora Angelica - M. Furlong

YEAR ISSUE	EDITION LIMIT	YEAR RETD.	ISSUE PRICE	*QUOTE U.S.$
1995 Faith Angel	10,000	1995	45.00	125
1996 Hope Angel	10,000	1996	45.00	110-116
1997 Charity Angel	10,000	1997	50.00	50-65
1998 Grace Angel	10,000		50.00	50

Gifts from God - M. Furlong

YEAR ISSUE	EDITION LIMIT	YEAR RETD.	ISSUE PRICE	*QUOTE U.S.$
1985 1985 The Charis Angel	3,000	1985	45.00	570-625
1986 1986 The Hallelujah Angel	3,000	1986	45.00	690-725
1987 1987 The Angel of Light	3,000	1987	45.00	300-800
1988 1988 The Celestial Angel	3,000	1988	45.00	300-800
1989 1989 Coronation Angel	3,000	1989	45.00	450-475

Gold Leaf Porcelain - M. Furlong

YEAR ISSUE	EDITION LIMIT	YEAR RETD.	ISSUE PRICE	*QUOTE U.S.$
1993 Catch a Falling Star 2" (gold)	Closed	1998	11.00	11
1992 Evening Star 5" (gold)	Closed	1998	16.00	16-20
1992 Morning Star 3" (gold)	Closed	1998	13.00	13-15
1996 Oak and Acorn Wreath 3" (gold)	Closed	1998	16.00	16-20
1992 A Star in the Night 2 1/2" (gold)	Closed	1998	11.00	11
1993 Sunshell 2" (gold)	Closed	1998	11.00	11
1995 Tree Top Finial 7" (gold)	Closed	1998	24.00	24

Joyeux Noel - M. Furlong

YEAR ISSUE	EDITION LIMIT	YEAR RETD.	ISSUE PRICE	*QUOTE U.S.$
1990 1990 Celebration Angel	10,000	1994	45.00	175-240
1991 1991 Thanksgiving Angel	10,000	1994	45.00	240-290
1992 1992 Joyeux Noel Angel	10,000	1994	45.00	87-105
1993 1993 Star of Bethlehem Angel	10,000	1994	45.00	175-275
1994 1994 Messiah Angel	10,000	1994	45.00	288-445

Madonna and Child - M. Furlong

YEAR ISSUE	EDITION LIMIT	YEAR RETD.	ISSUE PRICE	*QUOTE U.S.$
1996 Madonna of the Cross	20,000		80.00	80
1997 Madonna of the Flowers	20,000		80.00	80
1998 Madonna of the Heavens	20,000		80.00	80

Musical Series - M. Furlong

YEAR ISSUE	EDITION LIMIT	YEAR RETD.	ISSUE PRICE	*QUOTE U.S.$
1980 1980 The Caroler	3,000	1980	50.00	450-465
1981 1981 The Lyrist	3,000	1981	45.00	300-800
1982 1982 The Lutist	3,000	1982	45.00	300-900
1983 1983 The Concertinist	3,000	1983	45.00	230-250
1984 1984 The Herald Angel	3,000	1984	45.00	450-460

Special Edition - M. Furlong

YEAR ISSUE	EDITION LIMIT	YEAR RETD.	ISSUE PRICE	*QUOTE U.S.$
1996 4" Sunflower Angel	Yr.Iss.	1996	21.00	25-35
1997 4" Iris Angel	Yr.Iss.	1997	23.00	25-30
1998 4" Tulip Angel	Yr.Iss.		23.00	23

Victoria - M. Furlong

YEAR ISSUE	EDITION LIMIT	YEAR RETD.	ISSUE PRICE	*QUOTE U.S.$
1994 Victoria Heart	10.000	1996	24.95	24-50
1995 Victoria Lily of the Valley	30,000	1996	25.00	25-60

Memories of Yesterday/Enesco Corporation

Memories of Yesterday Society Member's Only - M. Attwell

YEAR ISSUE	EDITION LIMIT	YEAR RETD.	ISSUE PRICE	*QUOTE U.S.$
1992 With Luck And A Friend, I's In Heaven MY922	Yr.Iss.	1992	16.00	20
1993 I'm Bringing Good Luck-Wherever You Are	Yr.Iss.	1993	16.00	22

Memories of Yesterday - M. Attwell

YEAR ISSUE	EDITION LIMIT	YEAR RETD.	ISSUE PRICE	*QUOTE U.S.$
1997 Angel w/Holder 264709	Open		17.50	18
1997 Sharing Gingerbread Blessings 271721	Yr.Iss.		17.50	18
1988 Baby's First Christmas 1988 520373	Yr.Iss.	1988	13.50	40-60
1988 Special Delivery! 1988 520381	Yr.Iss.	1988	13.50	25-35
1989 Baby's First Christmas 522465	Retrd.	1996	15.00	15-20
1989 A Surprise for Santa 522473 (1989)	Yr.Iss.	1989	13.50	15-25
1989 Christmas Together 522562	Open		15.00	15-25
1995 Happy Landings (Dated 1995) 522619	Yr.Iss.	1995	16.00	16
1990 Time For Bed 524638	Yr.Iss.	1990	15.00	15-30
1990 New Moon 524646	Suspd.		15.00	15-25
1994 Just Dreaming of You 524786	Open		16.00	16
1990 Moonstruck 524794	Retrd.	1992	15.00	25
1991 Just Watchin' Over You 525421	Retrd.	1994	17.50	25
1991 Lucky Me 525448	Retrd.	1993	16.00	22
1993 Wish I Could Fly To You 525790 (dated)	Yr.Iss.	1993	16.00	16
1992 I'll Fly Along To See You Soon 525804 (1992 Dated Bisque)	Yr.Iss.	1992	16.00	16-25
1991 Star Fishin' 525820	Open		16.00	16
1991 Lucky You 525847	Retrd.	1993	16.00	16
1995 Now I Lay Me Down to Sleep 527009	Open		15.00	15
1995 I Pray the Lord My Soul to Keep 527017	Open		15.00	15
1992 Mommy, I Teared It 527041(Five Year Anniversary Limited Edition)	Yr.Iss.	1992	15.00	20
1991 S'no Use Lookin' Back Now! 527181(dated)	Yr.Iss.	1991	17.50	28
1992 Merry Christmas, Little Boo-Boo 528803	Open		37.50	38
1993 May All Your Finest Dreams Come True 528811	Open		16.00	16
1992 Star Light. Star Bright 528838	Open		16.00	16
1994 Give Yourself a Hug From Me! 529109 ('94 Dated)	Yr. Iss.	1994	17.50	18
1992 Swinging Together 580481(1992 Dated Artplas)	Yr.Iss.	1992	17.50	22
1992 Sailin' With My Friends 587575 (Artplas)	Open		25.00	25
1993 Bringing Good Wishes Your Way 592846 (Artplas)	Open		25.00	25
1994 Bout Time I Came Along to See You 592854 (Artplas)	Open		17.50	18

Event Item Only - Enesco

YEAR ISSUE	EDITION LIMIT	YEAR RETD.	ISSUE PRICE	*QUOTE U.S.$
1993 How 'Bout A Little Kiss? 527068	Closed	1993	16.50	50
1996 Hoping To See You Soon 527033	Yr.Iss.	1996	15.00	15

Friendship - Enesco

YEAR ISSUE	EDITION LIMIT	YEAR RETD.	ISSUE PRICE	*QUOTE U.S.$
1996 I Love You This Much! 185809	Open		13.50	14

Peter Pan - Enesco

YEAR ISSUE	EDITION LIMIT	YEAR RETD.	ISSUE PRICE	*QUOTE U.S.$
1996 Tinkerbell 164682	Open		17.50	20

Midwest of Cannon Falls

Eddie Walker Collection - E. Walker

YEAR ISSUE	EDITION LIMIT	YEAR RETD.	ISSUE PRICE	*QUOTE U.S.$
1997 Santa Holding Reindeer, dated 1997 22284-3	Yr.Iss.	1997	10.00	10
1998 Santa, dated 1998 25193-5	Yr.Iss.		15.00	15
1998 Mini Stocking, dated 1998 26471-3	Yr.Iss.		8.00	8

Leo R. Smith III Collection - L.R. Smith

YEAR ISSUE	EDITION LIMIT	YEAR RETD.	ISSUE PRICE	*QUOTE U.S.$
1994 Flying Woodsman Santa 11921-1	2,500	1994	35.00	200
1995 Angel of Love 16123-4	3,500	1996	32.00	40-45
1995 Angel of Peace 16199-9	3,500	1996	32.00	45-50
1995 Angel of Your Dreams 16130-2	3,500	1996	32.00	35
1995 Partridge Angel 13994-3	3,500	1996	30.00	30-35
1995 Santa on Reindeer 13780-2	3,500	1996	35.00	80-100
1996 Angel of Dependability 19218-4	Retrd.	1996	37.00	37
1996 Angel of Adventure 19219-1	Retrd.	1996	37.00	37
1996 Angel of Nurturing 19220-7	Retrd.	1996	37.00	37
1996 Angel of Generosity 19221-4	Retrd.	1996	37.00	37
1996 Angel of Knowledge 19222-1	Retrd.	1996	37.00	37
1996 Angel of Sharing 19223-8	Retrd.	1996	37.00	37
1996 Angel of Guidance 19224-5	Retrd.	1996	37.00	37
1996 Angel of Pride 19225-2	Retrd.	1996	37.00	37
1996 Angel of Heaven and Earth 18396-0	3,500		33.00	33
1996 Angel of Light 18076-1	4,000		33.00	33
1996 Angel of Music 18073-4	3,500		33.00	33
1996 Everyday Angel Ornament Stand 19554-3	Retrd.	1996	25.00	25
1996 Belsnickle Santa 18074-7	4,000	1996	39.00	39-100
1997 Santa Riding Bird 19928-2	3,000		35.00	35
1997 Stars & Stripes Santa 19929-9	3,000		35.00	35
1998 Santa with Gifts, dated 1998 25144-7	1,500		40.00	40

Wendt and Kuhn Ornaments - Wendt/Kuhn

YEAR ISSUE	EDITION LIMIT	YEAR RETD.	ISSUE PRICE	*QUOTE U.S.$
1989 Trumpeting Angel Ornament, 2 asst. 09402-0	Retrd.	1995	14.00	17
1991 Angel in Ring Ornament 01208-6	Retrd.	1995	12.00	15
1994 Angel on Moon, Star, 12 asst. 12945-6	Open		20.00	22
1990 Angel Clip-on Ornament 00729-7	Retrd.	1995	20.00	24

Miss Martha's Collection/Enesco Corporation

Miss Martha's Collection - M. Holcombe

YEAR ISSUE	EDITION LIMIT	YEAR RETD.	ISSUE PRICE	*QUOTE U.S.$
1993 Caroline - Always Someone Watching Over Me 350532	Closed	1994	25.00	50
1993 Arianna - Heavenly Sounds H/O 350567	Closed	1994	25.00	50-55
1992 Baby in Basket 369454	Closed	1994	25.00	50-75
1992 Baby In Swing 421480	Retrd.	1993	25.00	50-75
1992 Girl Holding Stocking DTD 1992 421499	Closed	1994	25.00	45-55
1992 Girl/Bell In Hand 421502	Retrd.	1993	25.00	50

Old World Christmas

Collector Club - E.M. Merck, unless otherwise noted

YEAR ISSUE	EDITION LIMIT	YEAR RETD.	ISSUE PRICE	*QUOTE U.S.$
1993 Mr. & Mrs. Claus set 1490	Retrd.	1993	Gift	125-195
1993 Glass Christmas Maidens, Set/4, 1491	Retrd.	1993	35.00	105-115
1993 Dresdener Drummer Nutcracker 7258	Retrd.	1993	110.00	230-265
1994 Santa in Moon 1492	Retrd.	1994	Gift	95-120
1994 Large Santa in Chimney 1493	Retrd.	1994	42.50	70-95
1995 Large Christmas Carousel 1587 - Inge-Glas	Retrd.	1995	79.50	95-125
1995 The Konigsee Nutcracker 7284	Retrd.	1995	125.00	260
1995 Cherub on Reflector 1545 - Inge-Glas	Retrd.	1995	Gift	45
1996 The Baroque Angel Above Reflector 1082	Yr.Iss.	1996	39.50	45-55
1996 The Saxon Santa Claus Nutcracker 7211	Yr.Iss.	1996	135.00	140-175
1996 The Victorian Christmas Stocking 1554	Yr.Iss.	1996	Gift	19-32

Angel & Female - E.M. Merck

YEAR ISSUE	EDITION LIMIT	YEAR RETD.	ISSUE PRICE	*QUOTE U.S.$
1990 Angel on Disc 1028	Retrd.	1993	11.70	16
1988 Baby in Bunting 1015	Retrd.	1990	7.70	29
1991 Baby Jesus 1036	Retrd.	1995	9.25	10
1991 Baroque Angel 1031	Retrd.	1995	12.95	13
1985 Caroling Girl 101062	Retrd.	1990	6.65	19-24
1985 Doll Head 103209	Retrd.	1989	6.40	11
1987 Girl in Grapes 1010	Retrd.	1989	8.45	32
1990 Girl in Polka Dot Dress 1030	Retrd.	1996	12.60	13
1987 Girl on Snowball with Teddy 1007	Retrd.	1995	9.25	15
1985 Girl with Flowers 101069	Retrd.	1993	7.50	19-24
1985 Gold Girl with Tree 1010306	Retrd.	1995	8.25	20
1992 Guardian Angel 1043	Retrd.	1995	8.25	15
1988 Large Blue Angel 1012	Retrd.	1994	13.40	17
1985 Light Blue Angel with Wings 101052	Retrd.	1994	9.25	20
1986 Little Red Riding Hood 1001	Retrd.	1993	9.90	16-23
1986 Mrs. Santa Claus 1003	Retrd.	1989	8.90	32
1987 Mushroom Girl 1006	Retrd.	1994	9.25	12
1986 Pink Angel with Wings 1002	Retrd.	1988	8.90	16
1990 Praying Girl 1025	Retrd.	1993	7.80	12
1985 Red Girl with Tree 1010309	Retrd.	1995	8.25	13
1985 Victorian Girl 101035	Retrd.	1989	5.30	26

Animals - E.M. Merck

YEAR ISSUE	EDITION LIMIT	YEAR RETD.	ISSUE PRICE	*QUOTE U.S.$
1993 Bear Above Reflector 1279	Retrd.	1995	33.75	40-55
1986 Bear in Crib 1203	Retrd.	1994	9.00	12-19
1993 Brilliant Butterfly 1267	Retrd.	1996	10.70	11-25
1989 Cat and the Fiddle 1221	Retrd.	1994	7.80	11
1985 Cat in Show 121103	Retrd.	1994	7.80	11-16
1991 Christmas Butterfly 1247	Retrd.	1994	7.00	9
1984 Circus Dog 121021	Retrd.	1994	9.00	12
1989 Fat Fish 1223	Retrd.	1995	5.85	12
1989 King Charles Spaniel 1222	Retrd.	1995	9.90	19
1989 Large Fish 1214	Retrd.	1993	6.70	20
1991 Large Puppy with Basket 1241	Retrd.	1993	13.25	29
1985 Large Teddy Bear 121089	Retrd.	1988	13.00	30
1985 Large Three-Sided Head 121088	Retrd.	1994	12.95	42-65
1986 Monkey 1205	Retrd.	1994	5.85	11
1991 Panda Bear 1242	Retrd.	1996	9.25	15
1985 Pink Pig 121042	Retrd.	1996	7.80	14
1990 Pink Poodle 1227	Retrd.	1994	8.80	15
1986 Playing Cat 1202	Retrd.	1994	8.80	10
1992 Proud Pug 1250	Retrd.	1996	9.25	10
1984 Puppy 121010	Retrd.	1994	7.00	12-16
1990 Sitting Black Cat 1228	Retrd.	1995	7.00	14
1986 Sitting Dog with Pipe 1206	Retrd.	1995	7.80	11
1991 Sitting Puppy 1246	Retrd.	1994	6.75	15
1985 Small Bunny 121090	Retrd.	1994	5.20	8
1986 Smiling Dog 1207	Retrd.	1994	7.80	10
1985 Snail 121041	Retrd.	1993	6.70	32
1989 Teddy Bear with Bow 1218	Retrd.	1990	6.65	17
1984 Three-Sided: Owl, Dog, Cat 121009	Retrd.	1994	8.55	13-19
1990 West Highland Terrrier 1232	Retrd.	1993	7.45	19
1989 White Kitty 1220	Retrd.	1990	7.45	10
1994 Woodland Squirrel 1291	Retrd.	1995	21.00	21

Bead Garlands - E.M. Merck

YEAR ISSUE	EDITION LIMIT	YEAR RETD.	ISSUE PRICE	*QUOTE U.S.$
1993 Angel Garland 1306	Retrd.	1993	55.00	110-120
1993 Celestial Garland 1303	Retrd.	1993	55.00	95
1996 Christmas Candy Garland 1324	Retrd.	1996	110.00	110
1993 Clown & Drum Garland 1301	Retrd.	1993	55.00	95
1993 Frog and Fish Garland 1305	Retrd.	1995	55.00	95
1993 Fruit Garland 1302	Retrd.	1993	55.00	70
1993 Pickle Garland 1304	Retrd.	1993	55.00	110
1996 Poinsettia Garland 1323	Retrd.	1996	100.00	100
1993 Santa Garland 1308	Retrd.	1995	55.00	110-135
1996 Santa/Candy Christmas Garland 1322	Retrd.	1996	110.00	110-130
1996 Shiny Gold Garland 1325	Retrd.	1996	135.00	135
1993 Teddy Bear & Heart Garland 1307	Retrd.	1993	55.00	115
1994 Woodland Christmas Garland 1311	Retrd.	1996	65.00	65

Birgit's Christmas Collection - B. Mueller-Blech

YEAR ISSUE	EDITION LIMIT	YEAR RETD.	ISSUE PRICE	*QUOTE U.S.$
1996 Guarding My Children 141	5,000	1996	65.00	65-115
1996 O' Tannenbaum 131	Retrd.	1996	35.00	35-95
1996 Old Christmas Barn 133	Retrd.	1996	50.00	50-135

Butterflies - E.M. Merck

YEAR ISSUE	EDITION LIMIT	YEAR RETD.	ISSUE PRICE	*QUOTE U.S.$
1987 Butterfly, Blue with Blue 1905	Retrd.	1991	20.95	47-54
1987 Butterfly, Gold with Gold 1906	Retrd.	1991	20.95	47-54
1987 Butterfly, Orange with Orange 1904	Retrd.	1991	20.95	47-54
1987 Butterfly, Red with Cream 1903	Retrd.	1991	20.95	47-54
1987 Butterfly, White with Blue 1902	Retrd.	1991	20.95	50
1987 Butterfly, White with Red 1901	Retrd.	1991	20.95	47-52

Churches & Houses - E.M. Merck

YEAR ISSUE	EDITION LIMIT	YEAR RETD.	ISSUE PRICE	*QUOTE U.S.$
1985 Bavarian House 201059	Retrd.	1994	8.00	19
1990 Garden House with Gnome 2011	Retrd.	1993	7.80	25
1986 Gingerbread House (A) 2001	Retrd.	1989	6.55	8-19
1986 House with Peacock 2004	Retrd.	1987	7.45	16

*Quotes have been rounded up to nearest dollar

ORNAMENTS

YEAR ISSUE	EDITION LIMIT	YEAR RETD.	ISSUE PRICE	*QUOTE U.S.$
1985 Matte Cream Church 206790-2	Retrd.	1993	6.45	11
1985 Mill 201094	Retrd.	1990	9.45	46
1986 Windmill on Form 2006	Retrd.	1988	7.45	32

Clowns & Male Figures - E.M. Merck, unless otherwise noted

YEAR ISSUE	EDITION LIMIT	YEAR RETD.	ISSUE PRICE	*QUOTE U.S.$
1984 'Shorty Clown' 241011	Retrd.	1988	5.65	20
1984 'Stop' Keystone Cop 241019	Retrd.	1989	6.65	37-47
1986 Aviator 2402	Retrd.	1994	7.80	20
1986 Baby 2405	Retrd.	1989	6.75	26
1990 Black Boy 2439	Retrd.	1995	9.00	19-24
1986 Boy Head with Stocking Cap 2411	Retrd.	1993	5.30	20
1985 Boy in Yellow Sweater 241032	Retrd.	1988	7.00	15
1995 Charlie Chaplin 2487 - Inge-Glas	Retrd.	1995	25.00	35-95
1986 Clip-on Boy Head 2416	Retrd.	1989	6.45	13
1993 Clown Above Ball 2470	Retrd.	1994	42.00	45
1986 Clown Head with Burgundy Hat 2418	Retrd.	1994	7.00	10
1984 Clown in Stocking 241006	Retrd.	1988	6.65	24
1985 Dutch Boy 243321	Retrd.	1993	7.55	22
1990 English Bobby 2442	Retrd.	1994	8.80	22-34
1986 Farm Boy 2414	Retrd.	1989	4.95	24
1985 Fat Boy with Sweater & Cap 2442265	Retrd.	1994	5.85	9
1986 Gnome Under Mushroom 2417	Retrd.	1993	7.00	16
1988 Harpo 2432	Retrd.	1991	6.20	32-37
1984 Keystone Cop 241003	Retrd.	1994	9.90	26-34
1989 Leprechaun 2435	Retrd.	1994	7.65	10
1993 Monk 2467	Retrd.	1994	7.90	10
1987 Mr. Big Nose 2426	Retrd.	1993	8.00	32-45
1995 Mr. Sci-Fi 2492 - Inge-Glas	Retrd.	1995	29.50	45
1988 Mushroom Gnome 2430	Retrd.	1989	6.20	13
1986 Pixie with Accordion 2406	Retrd.	1989	4.95	22
1984 Roly-Poly Keystone Cop 241015	Retrd.	1988	9.90	47-52
1986 Sailor Head 2404	Retrd.	1990	7.45	39-44
1986 School Boy 2415	Retrd.	1989	4.95	13
1984 Scotsman 241017	Retrd.	1988	6.20	40
1990 Scout 2440	Retrd.	1995	9.25	10
1987 Scrooge 2427	Retrd.	1995	8.55	11
1989 Small Clown Head 2436	Retrd.	1993	6.65	11
1991 Snowman in Chimney 2447	Retrd.	1996	10.50	11
1990 Snowman on Reflector 2445	Retrd.	1993	10.35	15
1985 Waiter in Tuxedo 241047	Retrd.	1989	7.00	32

Collector's Editions - E.M. Merck

YEAR ISSUE	EDITION LIMIT	YEAR RETD.	ISSUE PRICE	*QUOTE U.S.$
1994 '94 Santa/Moon on Disc 1512	Retrd.	1994	32.50	59
1992 Angel with Tinsel Wire 1522	Retrd.	1993	55.00	85
1993 Angel with Wings 1556	Retrd.	1993	12.50	80
1993 Christmas Heart 1593	Retrd.	1993	10.00	60
1995 Christmas Tree above Star Reflector 1513	2,400	1995	53.00	95
1995 Devil Bell 1599	Retrd.	1995	34.95	130-165
1992 Flying Peacock with Wings 1550	Retrd.	1995	22.50	45
1992 Flying Songbird with Wings 1551	Retrd.	1995	21.75	45
1993 Hansel and Gretal 1511	2,400	1995	45.00	110-125
1993 Heavenly Angel 1563	Retrd.	1995	20.00	36
1990 Night Before Christmas Ball 1501	500	1993	72.50	125
1992 Nutcracker Ornament 1510	Retrd.	1993	33.75	175-185
1995 Parachuting Santa 1547	Retrd.	1995	59.50	60
1993 Santa with Hot Air Balloon 1570	Retrd.	1995	38.85	39-60
1992 Santa with Tinsel Wire 1521	Retrd.	1993	55.00	80
1992 Santa's Departure 1503	500	1994	72.50	125-134
1991 Santa's Visit 1502	500	1994	72.50	100-125
1992 Snowman with Tinsel Wire 1523	Retrd.	1993	32.50	85
1995 Special Event Santa 1560	5,000	1995	15.00	42
1995 Witch 1582	Retrd.	1995	34.95	75

Easter Light Covers - E.M. Merck

YEAR ISSUE	EDITION LIMIT	YEAR RETD.	ISSUE PRICE	*QUOTE U.S.$
1988 Assorted Easter Egg 9331-1	Retrd.	1993	3.95	14
1988 Assorted Pastel Egg 9335-1	Retrd.	1994	2.95	14
1988 Bunny 9333-4	Retrd.	1994	4.20	14
1988 Bunny in Basket 9333-6	Retrd.	1994	4.20	14
1988 Chick 9333-3	Retrd.	1994	4.20	14
1988 Chick in Egg 9333-5	Retrd.	1994	4.20	14
1988 Hen in Basket 9333-1	Retrd.	1994	4.20	14
1988 Rabbit in Egg 9333-2	Retrd.	1994	4.20	14

Fruits & Vegetables - E.M. Merck

YEAR ISSUE	EDITION LIMIT	YEAR RETD.	ISSUE PRICE	*QUOTE U.S.$
1990 Cherries on Form 2825	Retrd.	1993	9.00	12
1989 Cucumber 2820	Retrd.	1989	6.65	24-33
1985 Grapes on Form 281038	Retrd.	1987	7.00	24
1985 Large Strawberry 2841432	Retrd.	1993	4.20	19-26
1990 Large Strawberry with Flower 2841	Retrd.	1993	10.50	29
1985 Mr. Apple 281071	Retrd.	1988	6.20	32-49
1984 Mr. Pear 281023	Retrd.	1993	6.75	14-19
1987 Onion 2810	Retrd.	1989	8.25	110-125
1990 Raspberry 2835	Retrd.	1993	6.20	8
1991 Strawberries/Flower on Form 2851	Retrd.	1994	8.55	10
1991 Very Large Apple 2848	Retrd.	1993	10.60	24
1991 Very Large Pear 2847	Retrd.	1993	10.60	24

Halloween Light Covers - E.M. Merck

YEAR ISSUE	EDITION LIMIT	YEAR RETD.	ISSUE PRICE	*QUOTE U.S.$
1989 Dancing Scarecrow 9241-3	Retrd.	1994	7.65	17
1987 Devil 9223-5	Retrd.	1993	3.95	24
1987 Ghost w/Pumpkin 9221-2	Retrd.	1994	3.95	12
1987 Haunted House 9223-1	Retrd.	1994	3.95	19
1987 Jack O'Lantern 9221-1	Retrd.	1993	3.95	12
1989 Man in the Moon 9241-5	Retrd.	1993	7.65	32-45
1989 Pumpkin Face 9241-2	Retrd.	1994	7.65	15
1987 Pumpkin w/Top Hat 9223-6	Retrd.	1994	3.95	15
1987 Sad Pumpkin 9221-5	Retrd.	1993	3.95	15
1987 Scarecrow 9221-3	Retrd.	1993	3.95	12
1987 Six Halloween Light Covers 9221	Retrd.	1994	25.00	56-75
1987 Six Halloween Light Covers 9223	Retrd.	1993	25.90	56-75
1987 Skull 9221-6	Retrd.	1994	3.95	18
1987 Smiling Cat 9223-2	Retrd.	1993	3.95	12
1987 Smiling Ghost 9223-4	Retrd.	1994	3.95	12
1989 Spider 9241-1	Retrd.	1994	7.65	12-16
1987 Standing Witch 9223-3	Retrd.	1994	3.95	14
1987 Witch Head 9221-4	Retrd.	1993	3.95	15
1989 Witch Head 9241-2	Retrd.	1994	7.65	15
1989 Wizard 9241-4	Retrd.	1993	7.65	29-37

Household Items - E.M. Merck

YEAR ISSUE	EDITION LIMIT	YEAR RETD.	ISSUE PRICE	*QUOTE U.S.$
1986 Black Stocking 3203	Retrd.	1993	9.45	56-75
1985 Clip-On Candle 321063	Retrd.	1995	12.95	14-19
1991 Money Bag 3206	Retrd.	1994	7.00	10
1985 Pastel Umbrella (A) 321091	Retrd.	1993	11.00	32
1986 Red Stocking 3201	Retrd.	1987	9.00	32
1991 Small Wine Barrel 3210	Retrd.	1993	6.30	15
1985 Very Large Pink Umbrella 321103	Retrd.	1986	29.50	60
1988 Wine Barrel 3204	Retrd.	1990	7.00	13

Light Covers - E.M. Merck

YEAR ISSUE	EDITION LIMIT	YEAR RETD.	ISSUE PRICE	*QUOTE U.S.$
1984 3 Men in a Tub 529007-1	Retrd.	1986	1.60	19-24
1986 Angel on Bell 529023-5	Retrd.	1991	3.95	17
1985 Apple 529011-5	Retrd.	1989	3.00	12
1986 Assorted Alphabet Blocks 529043-1	Retrd.	1991	4.50	20
1984 Assorted Animals (set of 6) 529003	Retrd.	1987	10.35	75
1986 Assorted Bells (set of 6) 529023	Retrd.	1993	22.50	75
1988 Assorted Birds 529057-1	Retrd.	1990	3.95	15
1986 Assorted Easter Eggs 529031-1	Retrd.	1993	3.00	15
1988 Assorted Fast Food 529055-1	Retrd.	1991	3.95	23-34
1984 Assorted Figurals (set of 6) 529005	Retrd.	1987	10.35	75-82
1989 Assorted Fir Cone 529209-1	Retrd.	1991	2.85	15
1993 Assorted Frosty Bell 5275	Retrd.	1993	5.65	12
1985 Assorted Fruit (set of 6) 529011	Retrd.	1989	20.00	56-75
1985 Assorted Heads (set of 6) 529009	Retrd.	1988	10.35	75
1986 Assorted Peach Roses 529045-4	Retrd.	1990	3.95	27
1986 Assorted Roses (set of 6) 529045	Retrd.	1991	22.50	48
1985 Assorted Santas (set of 6) 529015	Retrd.	1992	20.00	75
1989 Assorted Sea Shells 529301-1	Retrd.	1992	3.50	21-37
1991 Assorted Snowmen 529305-1	Retrd.	1993	5.55	19
1986 Assorted Yellow Roses 529045-2	Retrd.	1990	3.95	9-21
1985 Automobile 529019-3	Retrd.	1988	2.70	24
1985 Balloon 529019-2	Retrd.	1988	2.70	24
1984 Bear 519003-3	Retrd.	1987	2.50	19
1986 Blue Father Christmas 529047-3	Retrd.	1992	3.95	21
1993 Blue Man in the Moon 5206	Retrd.	1993	5.50	9
1986 Bunny 529033-4	Retrd.	1993	3.60	14
1986 Bunny in Basket 529033-6	Retrd.	1993	3.60	12
1985 Cable Car 529019-5	Retrd.	1988	2.70	22-30
1984 Carousel 529005-3	Retrd.	1987	2.70	22
1986 Chick 529033-3	Retrd.	1993	3.60	8
1986 Chick in Egg 529033-5	Retrd.	1993	3.60	12
1988 Christmas Carol 529053	Retrd.	1991	25.00	72
1988 Christmas Tree 529051-4	Retrd.	1992	3.95	12
1984 Church on Ball 529005-6	Retrd.	1987	2.50	12
1985 Clara-The Doll 529017-1	Retrd.	1989	2.70	12
1985 Clear Icicles (set of 6) 529205	Retrd.	1989	20.00	48
1984 Clown 529001-5	Retrd.	1986	1.60	16
1988 Clown 529051-6	Retrd.	1991	3.95	15
1985 Clown Head 529009-1	Retrd.	1988	1.60	14
1988 Cornucopia 529049-1	Retrd.	1992	3.95	14
1988 Doll 529051-2	Retrd.	1993	3.95	14
1993 Doll Head 5202	Retrd.	1993	5.65	6-14
1985 Doll Head 529009-4	Retrd.	1988	1.60	12
1988 Drum 529051-1	Retrd.	1992	3.95	19
1988 Ear of Corn 529049-6	Retrd.	1992	3.95	14
1984 Elephant 529003-4	Retrd.	1987	1.60	19
1985 Father Christmas 529009-5	Retrd.	1990	3.00	19
1986 Father Christmas Set 529047	Retrd.	1992	25.00	72-85
1984 Flower Basket 529005-1	Retrd.	1987	1.60	12
1989 Frog 529303-6	Retrd.	1993	6.45	10
1993 Frosty Acorn 5276	Retrd.	1994	5.65	8
1993 Frosty Cone 5271	Retrd.	1994	5.65	8
1993 Frosty Icicle 5272	Retrd.	1993	5.65	8
1993 Frosty Red Rose 5277	Retrd.	1993	5.65	9
1993 Frosty Snowman 5270	Retrd.	1993	5.65	9
1993 Frosty Tree 5273	Retrd.	1993	5.65	8
1984 Gnome 529001-1	Retrd.	1986	1.60	8
1985 Grapes 529011-3	Retrd.	1989	3.00	8
1986 Green Father Christmas 529047-2	Retrd.	1992	3.95	21
1984 Hedgehog 529003-5	Retrd.	1987	1.60	21-29
1986 Hen in Basket 529033-1	Retrd.	1993	3.60	8
1984 House 529005-2	Retrd.	1987	1.60	12
1988 Indian 529049-5	Retrd.	1992	3.95	19
1993 Jolly Santa Head 5201	Retrd.	1993	5.50	10
1985 King 529013-3	Retrd.	1988	2.70	12
1989 Kitten 529303-3	Retrd.	1993	6.45	10
1984 Lil' Boy Blue 529007-5	Retrd.	1986	1.60	21
1985 Lil' Rascal Head 529009-6	Retrd.	1988	1.60	21
1985 Locomotive 529019-4	Retrd.	1988	2.70	24-32
1985 Marie-The Girl 529017-3	Retrd.	1989	2.70	19
1985 Mouse King 529017-5	Retrd.	1989	2.70	16
1984 Mrs. Claus 529001-4	Retrd.	1986	1.60	20
1985 Nutcracker 529017-4	Retrd.	1989	2.70	10
1986 Nutcracker on Bell 529023-6	Retrd.	1993	3.95	17
1985 Nutcracker Suite Figures (set of 6) 529017	Retrd.	1989	19.00	75
1985 Orange 529011-6	Retrd.	1989	3.00	7
1984 Owl 529003-2	Retrd.	1987	1.60	10
1989 Panda 529303-1	Retrd.	1994	6.45	12
1985 Pastel Icicles 529207	Retrd.	1989	N/A	N/A
1984 Peacock 519003-6	Retrd.	1987	2.70	10
1993 Peacock 5203	Retrd.	1993	5.65	11
1985 Pear 529011-1	Retrd.	1989	3.00	9
1988 Pilgrim Boy 529049-3	Retrd.	1992	3.95	12
1988 Pilgrim Girl 529049-4	Retrd.	1992	3.95	12
1985 Pineapple 529011-4	Retrd.	1989	3.00	19
1985 Pink Heart 529201-3	Retrd.	1989	2.85	9
1989 Puppy 529303-4	Retrd.	1994	6.45	12
1986 Purple Father Christmas 529047-6	Retrd.	1992	3.95	22
1984 Queen of Heart 529007-3	Retrd.	1986	2.70	19
1986 Rabbit in Egg 529033-2	Retrd.	1993	3.60	9
1986 Red Father Christmas 529047-1	Retrd.	1992	3.95	23
1986 Red Father Christmas 529047-4	Retrd.	1992	3.95	23
1985 Red Heart 529201-1	Retrd.	1990	2.85	9
1985 Red Riding Hood 529009-2	Retrd.	1988	1.60	10
1986 Rocking Horse on Bell 529023-4	Retrd.	1990	3.95	19
1985 Roly-Poly Santa 529015-6	Retrd.	1989	3.00	12
1984 Santa Head 529005-4	Retrd.	1987	2.70	16
1985 Santa Head 529009-3	Retrd.	1988	3.00	10
1986 Santa on Bell 529023-3	Retrd.	1990	3.95	17
1984 Santa on Heart 529005-5	Retrd.	1987	3.00	10
1985 Santa with Tree 529015-3	Retrd.	1992	3.00	10
1985 School Bus 529019-6	Retrd.	1991	2.70	24
1985 Six Red & White Hearts 529201	Retrd.	1989	15.00	48-70
1992 Six Snowmen 529305	Retrd.	1993	29.00	75
1984 Snowman 519001-2	Retrd.	1986	2.50	10
1985 Soldier with Drum 529013-1	Retrd.	1988	2.70	19
1985 Soldier with Gun 529013-2	Retrd.	1988	2.70	15
1985 Soldiers (set of 6) 529013	Retrd.	1988	17.95	75
1989 Squirrel 529303-2	Retrd.	1994	6.45	9
1984 Standing Santa 529001-3	Retrd.	1987	3.00	12
1988 Stocking 529051-3	Retrd.	1992	3.95	10
1985 Strawberry 529011-2	Retrd.	1989	3.00	9
1993 Sugar Apple 5254	Retrd.	1993	5.50	8-10
1993 Sugar Fruit Basket 5256	Retrd.	1994	5.65	12
1993 Sugar Grapes 5252	Retrd.	1993	5.50	8-10
1993 Sugar Pear 5255	Retrd.	1993	5.50	8-12
1993 Sugar Plum 5253	Retrd.	1993	5.65	7-10
1985 Sugar Plum Fairy 529017-6	Retrd.	1989	2.70	14
1993 Sugar Strawberry 5251	Retrd.	1993	5.65	9-12
1989 Swan 529303-5	Retrd.	1994	6.45	12
1986 Teddy Bear 529023-2	Retrd.	1990	3.95	19
1988 Teddy Bear 529051-5	Retrd.	1992	3.95	19
1986 Teddy Bear with Ball 529041-5	Retrd.	1994	3.95	4-19
1986 Teddy Bear with Candy Cane 529041-1	Retrd.	1992	3.95	4-19
1986 Teddy Bear with Nightshirt 529041-4	Retrd.	1994	3.95	4-19
1986 Teddy Bear with Red Heart 529041-2	Retrd.	1992	3.95	4-19
1986 Teddy Bear with Tree 529041-3	Retrd.	1992	3.95	4-23
1986 Teddy Bear with Vest 529041-6	Retrd.	1992	3.95	4-19
1986 Teddy Bears (set of 6) 529041	Retrd.	1991	25.00	75
1988 Thanksgiving (set of 6) 529049	Retrd.	1992	25.00	79
1988 Toy (set of 6) 529051	Retrd.	1992	25.00	72-85
1985 Transportation Set 529019	Retrd.	1988	17.90	85
1986 Tree on Bell 529023-1	Retrd.	1991	3.95	16
1985 Tug Boat 529019-1	Retrd.	1988	2.70	24
1988 Turkey 529049-2	Retrd.	1992	3.95	8
1986 White Father Christmas 529047-5	Retrd.	1992	3.95	24
1985 White Heart 529201-2	Retrd.	1989	2.85	8

Porcelain Christmas - E.M. Merck

YEAR ISSUE	EDITION LIMIT	YEAR RETD.	ISSUE PRICE	*QUOTE U.S.$
1989 Angel 9435	Retrd.	1994	6.65	12
1995 Angelic Gifts 9712	Retrd.	1995	11.25	12
1988 Bear on Skates 9495	Retrd.	1988	10.00	19
1988 Bunnies on Skies 9494	Retrd.	1988	10.00	19
1987 Father Christmas (A) 9404	Retrd.	1988	11.00	13
1987 Father Christmas w/Cape 9405	Retrd.	1988	11.00	14
1987 Father Christmas w/Toys 9406	Retrd.	1988	11.00	12
1989 Hummingbird 9433	Retrd.	1994	6.65	9
1987 Lighted Angel Tree Top 9420	Retrd.	1992	29.50	37
1989 Nutcracker 9436	Retrd.	1994	6.65	12
1988 Penguin w/Gifts 9496	Retrd.	1988	10.00	19
1989 Rocking Horse 9431	Retrd.	1994	6.65	11
1987 Roly-Poly Santa 9441	Retrd.	1988	6.75	14
1987 Santa Head 9410	Retrd.	1988	6.55	12
1989 Teddy Bear 9434	Retrd.	1994	6.65	10

Santas - E.M. Merck

YEAR ISSUE	EDITION LIMIT	YEAR RETD.	ISSUE PRICE	*QUOTE U.S.$
1990 Blue Victorian St. Nick 4028	Retrd.	1993	9.95	26
1987 Burgundy Father Christmas 4013	Retrd.	1995	7.80	8-16
1987 Burgundy Santa Claus 4014	Retrd.	1994	13.95	19
1985 Father Christmas Head 403223	Retrd.	1994	7.80	10
1985 Father Christmas with Basket 403224	Retrd.	1994	7.80	10
1984 Old Father Christmas Head 401007	Retrd.	1994	7.00	10
1986 Pink Clip-On Santa 4011	Retrd.	1994	8.35	10
1984 Roly-Poly Santa 401002	Retrd.	1994	7.90	11
1987 Santa Above Ball 4018	Retrd.	1995	13.95	14
1987 Santa in Airplane 4017	Retrd.	1995	13.95	14
1986 Santa In Chimney 4005	Retrd.	1995	8.70	10-18
1985 Santa in Chimney 406912	Retrd.	1989	11.00	29
1986 Santa On Carriage 4003	Retrd.	1988	10.00	37
1986 Santa On Cone 4002	Retrd.	1993	7.90	16
1991 Victorian Father Christmas 4045	Retrd.	1996	10.00	10
1990 Victorian Scrap Santa 4043	Retrd.	1993	9.70	21

Transportation - E.M. Merck

YEAR ISSUE	EDITION LIMIT	YEAR RETD.	ISSUE PRICE	*QUOTE U.S.$
1988 Cable Car 4602	Retrd.	1989	8.45	44
1985 Cable Car 461067	Retrd.	1988	14.95	44
1985 Locomotive 461069	Retrd.	1993	7.00	24
1985 Old-Fashioned Car 463747	Retrd.	1989	6.25	40
1986 Rolls Royce 4601	Retrd.	1989	7.90	39

*Quotes have been rounded up to nearest dollar

Patricia Breen Designs

1994 Collection - P. Breen

YEAR ISSUE	EDITION LIMIT	YEAR RETD.	ISSUE PRICE	*QUOTE U.S.$
1994 Beeskep & Bee (signed) 9503-2	Retrd.	1995	28.95	50-85
1994 Beeskep & Bee 9503-2	2,000	1995	28.95	72-108
1994 Dish & Spoon (double face) 9510-11	Retrd.	1995	24.00	90-150
1994 Dish & Spoon (signed) 9510-11	Retrd.	1995	24.00	150
1994 Dish & Spoon 9510-11	2,000	1995	24.00	72-90
1994 Edwina the Victorian Girl 9407	Retrd.	1995	21.00	400-525
1994 Faberge Santa (fully glittered) 9441	2,000	1996	28.00	180-252
1994 Fiddling Cat (signed) 9509-10	Retrd.	1995	20.00	40-65
1994 Henry the Victorian Boy 9506-5	Retrd.	1995	20.00	54-96
1994 Lady Bug (red) 9501-1	Retrd.	1995	12.95	42-60
1994 Laughing Dog 9508-9	2,000	1995	20.00	36-60
1994 Magician 94-33	Retrd.	1994	24.00	560
1994 Moon & Many Stars 9517-24	Retrd.	1995	16.95	72-100
1994 Nesting Instinct (black) 9418	Retrd.	1995	20.00	90
1994 Nesting Instinct (gold) 9417-19	Retrd.	1994	15.00	150
1994 Nesting Instinct (red) 9418	Retrd.	1995	20.00	75-114
1994 Night House (glittered) 9519-B	Retrd.	1995	32.00	72-96
1994 Night House 9519-26	Retrd.	1995	32.00	55-75
1994 Queen of Hearts (gold) 9518-25	Retrd.	1995	20.00	96-108
1994 Red Square Santa 9513-16	Retrd.	1995	22.00	60-96
1994 Skydiving Santa 9522-35	2,000	1995	18.00	60-132
1994 Snow Man (signed) 9523-37	Retrd.	1995	21.00	50
1994 Spruce Goose (gold) 94-34	Retrd.	1994	25.00	500-700
1994 Spruce Goose (red) 9436	Retrd.	1994	25.00	150-480
1994 St. Petersburg Santa (gold) 9415	Retrd.	1994	20.00	108-150
1994 Summer Acorn House (signed) 9505-4	Retrd.	1995	24.95	35-95
1994 Sunflower (green) (signed) 9516-23	Retrd.	1995	16.00	105
1994 Sunflower (green) 9516-23	Retrd.	1995	16.00	24-50
1994 Valise (black) 9532-44	Retrd.	1995	30.00	120-270
1994 Valise (red) (Chapel Hill) 9532-44	Retrd.	1995	30.00	75
1994 Valise (red) (signed-St. Louis Arch) 9532-44	Retrd.	1995	30.00	90-125
1994 Valise (red) 9532-44	Retrd.	1995	30.00	65-125
1994 Versailles Balloon (red/green) 9412	Retrd.	1995	22.00	36-125
1994 Winter Acorn House 9504-3	2,000	1995	24.95	45-54
1994 Winter Wizard 9521-32	2,000	1995	32.00	42
1994 Winter Wizard (signed) 9521-32	2,000	1995	32.00	85-100
1994 Woodland Santa (bordeaux) 9515-21	Retrd.	1995	24.00	60-85
1994 Woodland Santa (cherry) 94-20	Retrd.	1995	24.00	125-150

1995 Collection - P. Breen

YEAR ISSUE	EDITION LIMIT	YEAR RETD.	ISSUE PRICE	*QUOTE U.S.$
1995 Amor Angel 9540	Retrd.	1995	24.00	55-84
1995 And The Cow Jumped Over The Moon 9507-8	Retrd.	1996	24.00	60
1995 Apple Basket (for tree) 9548	2,000	1995	14.00	24
1995 Apple Tree Boy & Basket (gold glitter ladder) 9547 & 9548	Retrd.	1995	36.00	96
1995 Apple Tree Boy & Basket (lt. green glitter) 9547 & 9548	Retrd.	1995	36.00	210
1995 Apple Tree Boy (dark green, glitter tree) 9547	Retrd.	1995	24.00	84
1995 Apple Tree Boy 9547	2,000	1995	24.00	50
1995 Bacchus w/Grapes (lg. grapes) 9553	Retrd.	1995	42.00	78-90
1995 Bacchus w/Grapes (signed) 9553	Retrd.	1995	42.00	87
1995 Bacchus w/Grapes (sm. grapes) 9553	Retrd.	1995	42.00	100-110
1995 Balloon Boy & Balloon (red) Charlecotte 9554	Retrd.	1995	30.00	200
1995 Balloon Boy & Balloon (white, signed) 9554	Retrd.	1995	30.00	120-180
1995 Balloon Boy & Balloon 9554	2,000	1995	30.00	72-90
1995 Beauteous Angel 9533	Retrd.	1995	18.95	36
1995 Beaux Artes Facade (signed) 9551	Retrd.	1995	32.00	150
1995 Beaux Artes Facade 9551	Retrd.	1995	32.00	108-150
1995 Calling Santa Phone (red/green)	Retrd.	1995	20.00	300
1995 Classic Christmas Tree	Retrd.	1995	18.95	60
1995 Elvis Cat (Christmas at the Zoo) 9509-10	24	1995	32.00	80
1995 Father Time (cobalt) 9535	Retrd.	1995	20.00	45-66
1995 Father Time (gold glitter bag) 9535	Retrd.	1995	20.00	120-125
1995 Father Time (Nordstrom) (lt. blue) 9535	Retrd.	1995	20.00	80-120
1995 French Twist 9552	2,000	1995	18.00	32
1995 French Twist on ball "Joyeux Noel" 9552	Retrd.	1995	18.00	350
1995 French Twist with spiral tail 9552	Retrd.	1995	18.00	240-250
1995 Frog Prince 9556	2,000	1996	20.00	30-42
1995 Gentleman Bug 9502	Retrd.	1995	12.00	42-48
1995 Giverny (Art Institute of Chicago)	500	1995	50.00	300
1995 Lady Bug (pink) (signed) (Christmas Shop) 9501-1	200	1995	Gift	72-96
1995 Lady Bug (yellow) 9501-1	Retrd.	1995	12.95	160
1995 Letters To My Beloved (silver) 9537-B	Retrd.	1995	12.95	50-90
1995 Lily of the Valley Egg (Art Institute of Chicago)	300	1995	50.00	150
1995 Monet Trio (Art Institute of Chicago)	Retrd.	1995	78.00	285-480
1995 Monet Trio, signed (Art Institute of Chicago)	Retrd.	1995	78.00	480-600
1995 Northward Ho Finial 9584	Retrd.	1995	70.00	420
1995 Oliver Octopus (green glittered) 9539	Retrd.	1995	30.00	155
1995 Oliver Octopus (lavender) 9539	Retrd.	1995	30.00	130-180
1995 Pharaoh's Cat (gold) 9545	Retrd.	1995	12.00	75-125
1995 Pharaoh's Cat (green glittered) 9545	Retrd.	1995	12.00	75
1995 Pharaoh's Cat (green) 9545	Retrd.	1995	12.00	18-48
1995 Rocketboy 9534	Retrd.	1995	24.95	60-84
1995 Santa Paws (gold) 9536	Retrd.	1995	28.00	90
1995 Santa Paws (lt. blue) 9536	Retrd.	1995	28.00	120-150
1995 Santa Paws (Nordstrom) 9536	Retrd.	1995	28.00	120
1995 Santa Paws 9536	Retrd.	1995	28.00	48
1995 Snow Man (Nordstrom) (lt. blue) 9523-37	Retrd.	1995	21.00	54-120
1995 Snowball Boy (Nordstrom Special)	Retrd.	1995	28.00	150
1995 Snowflake Santa (gold) (Event Piece)	Retrd.	1995	28.00	90-180
1995 St. George and The Dragon 9546 (1st of Fine Art Series)	500	1995	50.00	360-390
1995 Striped Santa (signed) 9550	Retrd.	1995	24.00	50-71
1995 Sunflower Sun (orange) 9516-23	Retrd.	1995	16.00	35
1995 Swell Starfish 9542	Retrd.	1995	16.00	48-60
1995 Versailles Balloon (blue plaid) (Nordstrom) 9511	Retrd.	1996	22.00	120
1995 Vincent's Tree 9541	2,000	1995	24.00	48-54
1995 Winter Wizard (Nordstrom) 9521	Retrd.	1995	32.00	66-83
1995 Woodland Santa (lt. blue) (Nordstrom) 9515-20/21	Retrd.	1995	24.00	90-120

1996 Collection - P. Breen

YEAR ISSUE	EDITION LIMIT	YEAR RETD.	ISSUE PRICE	*QUOTE U.S.$
1996 Alexandra's Egg (Neiman Marcus)	250	1996	34.00	65-180
1996 Angel of Peace 9601	2,000	1996	26.95	60
1996 Angel Stocking (Nordstrom) 9602	Retrd.	1996	24.00	36
1996 Angel Stocking 9602	2,000	1996	24.00	30-36
1996 Archimbaldo Santa 9603	750	1996	74.00	240-450
1996 Blow Gabriel Blow (2nd of Fine Art Series) 9604	500	1996	60.00	125-210
1996 Buddah on Ball 9605	2,000	1997	28.00	72
1996 Chocolate Box Santa (Nordstrom) 9607	Retrd.	1996	32.00	60-108
1996 Chrysalis Egg (pink) Charlecotte 9608	Retrd.	1996	36.00	45
1996 Chrysalis Egg 9608	2,000	1996	36.00	48-150
1996 Claude Monet (white) (A.I.C.) 9595	Retrd.	1996	30.00	150-200
1996 Clover Santa & Clover Medallion (Wm Andrews Exclusive), set/2	850	1996	54.00	120
1996 George's Tree 9616	2,000	1996	24.00	55-84
1996 Goldilocks 9618	2,000	1996	28.00	45
1996 Golf Bag w/Ball (gold) 6919	Retrd.	1996	34.00	60-200
1996 Grandma Josie's Fridge 9620	2,000	1996	40.00	60-96
1996 Jack Frost (lt. blue) (Nordstrom) 9628	Retrd.	1996	30.00	125
1996 Le Postal Box 9630	2,000	1996	22.00	30
1996 Le Postal Cat 9629	2,000	1996	26.00	36
1996 Letters to My Beloved (green) 9537-B	2,000	1996	36.00	66
1996 Letters to My Beloved (Nordstrom's) 9537-B	2,000	1996	36.00	48
1996 Letters to Santa (Wm. Andrews)	70	1996	38.00	96
1996 Lily of the Valley Egg (AIC Exclusive)	300	1996	50.00	126-150
1996 Little Yellow Taxi (black) 9631	2,000	1996	30.00	144-175
1996 Madonna of the Night (Gump's Exclusive)	850	1997	42.00	60
1996 Madonna of the Sun (black/white)	Retrd.	1996	36.00	60
1996 Madonna of the Sun (yellow)	Retrd.	1996	36.00	60
1996 Making His List (cobalt) 9633	Retrd.	1996	30.00	54
1996 Making His List (pearl) 9633	Retrd.	1996	30.00	48
1996 Making His List 9633	2,000	1996	30.00	48-60
1996 Marinista Santa 9529	2,000	1996	25.00	180
1996 Minsk Santa 9635	2,000	1996	28.00	100
1996 Mrs. Shaw and Veggie Basket 9636	2,000	1996	30.00	72
1996 Night Flight Santa (blue moon) (Milaeger's) 9637	Retrd.	1996	46.00	100-200
1996 Night Flight Santa 9637	2,000	1996	46.00	65-144
1996 Rock Lobster 9543	2,000	1996	22.00	60
1996 Rocket Boy 9534	2,000	1997	24.00	96
1996 Round Midnight (w/Roman numerals) 9639	Retrd.	1996	32.00	60-190
1996 Santa and Teddy (purple w/gold bag) 9642	Retrd.	1997	36.00	60
1996 Santa and Teddy (red plaid) 9642	Retrd.	1997	36.00	54
1996 Santa of the Golden Oaks (green glitter) 9641	Retrd.	1996	34.00	95-175
1996 Santa of the Golden Oaks 9641	2,000	1996	34.00	56-72
1996 Shhh Santa (red w/green bag) 9643	Retrd.	1996	28.00	60
1996 Shhh Santa (red w/green glitter bag) 9643	Retrd.	1996	28.00	60
1996 Snack for Rudolph (purple) 9644	Retrd.	1996	28.00	48
1996 Snow Cat 9526	Retrd.	1996	32.00	42
1996 Snow Family, set/4	Retrd.	1996	N/A	144
1996 Snow Woman 9524	Retrd.	1996	22.00	48-60
1996 Snowflake Santa (citrine) (Neiman Marcus) 9645	Retrd.	1996	30.00	96-114
1996 Snowflake Santa (red) 9645	Retrd.	1996	30.00	48-60
1996 Sojourning Santa (Neiman Marcus Exclusive)	Retrd.	1997	35.00	60-72
1996 Sojourning Santa (Neiman Marcus Exclusive-w/ glittered stars & dots)	Retrd.	1997	35.00	84
1996 Sojourning Santa (Savannah Breakfast Special)	Retrd.	1997	35.00	360
1996 Spiraling Santa (red) 9646	Retrd.	1996	30.00	60
1996 Spiralling Santa 9646	2,000	1996	30.00	100-200
1996 Springtime Flower 9555	2,000	1996	32.00	48
1996 St. Louis Santa (signed)	Retrd.	1996	40.00	205-216
1996 St. Ursula 9640	2,000	1996	32.00	36-48
1996 Striped Santa 9550	2,000	1996	32.00	60
1996 Summer Acorn House 9505	2,000	1996	22.00	48-60
1996 Sunflower (green) 9516-0	Retrd.	1996	26.00	66
1996 Sunflower (orange) 9516-0	Retrd.	1996	26.00	60-66
1996 Sweet Cream 9647	Retrd.	1996	32.00	36-72
1996 This Little Piggy Galleria 9649	2,000	1996	28.00	42-48
1996 This Little Piggy Went to Market 9648	2,000	1996	26.00	36
1996 Victorian Spider & Web 9650	2,000	1996	30.00	45
1996 Winter Vegetable Basket 9652	2,000	1996	16.00	25
1996 Winter Wizard (gold) (Christmas at the Zoo) 9521	36	1996	32.00	210
1996 Woodland Santa (cherry) 9515	Retrd.	1996	24.00	162
1996 Woodland Santa (pearl) (Wm. Andrews) 9515	Retrd.	1996	24.00	72-84
1996 Woodland Santa (pink) (Christmas Shop Club Member) 9515	210	1996	24.00	180-240
1996 Woodshop Santa (redl) 9653	Retrd.	1996	30.00	72

1997 Collection - P. Breen

YEAR ISSUE	EDITION LIMIT	YEAR RETD.	ISSUE PRICE	*QUOTE U.S.$
1997 Angel Nosegay 9701	Retrd.	1997	51.95	90-120
1997 Bijoux Santa (Neiman Marcus)	1,000	1997	55.00	90
1997 Blow Ye Winds 9705	2,000	1997	32.95	36
1997 Bluebell Egg (St. Louis-Neiman Marcus)	500	1997	40.00	120
1997 Bountiful Madonna9706	2,000	1997	36.95	48
1997 Calling Ann Phone (Savanah, GA Exclusive)	Retrd.	1997	N/A	60
1997 Cleopatra's Scarab (Savannah Exclusive) 9709	2,000	1997	12.95	72
1997 Cleopatra's Scarab 9709	2,000	1997	12.95	60
1997 Coastal Santa 9710	2,000	1997	39.95	84
1997 Cole Porter-Festive Stock (Champagne Bottle)	1,000	1997	50.00	60
1997 Cole Porter-Santa Steps Out	1,000	1997	37.50	72
1997 Cole Porter-Top Hat Snowman	1,000	1997	37.50	72-90
1997 Cole Porter-You Top My List	1,000	1997	N/A	N/A
1997 Cyberspace Santa (red) 9711	2,000	1997	46.00	60
1997 Escargot 9712	2,000	1997	18.95	30
1997 Esme (AIC Exclusive)	Retrd.	1997	50.00	90
1997 Lighthouse Keeper (Milaeger's Exclusive)	750	1997	N/A	120
1997 Look and You Shall Find Him 9727	2,000	1997	45.00	48
1997 Love Is In The Air (2-part) 9726	2,000	1997	56.95	72
1997 Mrs. Mouse 9730	2,000	1997	38.95	48
1997 Noel Angel (Charlecote Exclusive-gold) 9731	Retrd.	1997	34.00	114
1997 Noel Angel 9731	2,000	1997	34.00	48
1997 Phoebe (AIC Exclusive)	Retrd.	1997	50.00	90
1997 A Respite For Santa 9733	Retrd.	1997	44.95	60
1997 Ring in the New 9734	2,000	1997	39.95	48
1997 Santa Dreams of Spring 9740	2,000	1997	39.95	48
1997 Santa Hat: "Hat's Off to Santa" (Savannah-event)	Retrd.	1997	N/A	90
1997 Santa of the Mead 9742	2,000	1997	36.00	48
1997 Santa of the North (cobalt) 9743	Retrd.	1997	48.95	72
1997 Santa of the North (yellow) 9743	Retrd.	1997	48.95	48-56
1997 Smile 9744	2,000	1997	22.00	36
1997 St. Anthony (2 part) 9736	2,000	1997	44.95	60
1997 St. Appolonia 9735	2,000	1997	36.00	48
1997 St. Nicholas 9738	2,000	1997	36.00	60
1997 Sweet Dreams (Wm. Andrews Exclusive) 9747	Retrd.	1997	78.00	180
1997 Sweet Dreams 9747	Retrd.	1997	78.00	180
1997 Thimble Santa (Neiman Marcus Exclusive)	Retrd.	1997	45.00	60
1997 To My Sweet 9748	2,000	1997	38.00	48
1997 Trustee's Garden Santa (Christmas Shop Exclusive)	750	1997	35.00	90-120
1997 Venice at Dusk (St. Louis Art Museum)	Retr.	1997	N/A	60
1997 A Walk in the Woods 9651	2,000	1997	46.95	66
1997 A Walk on the Beach 9750	Retrd.	1997	52.95	90
1997 Windsor Rose Santa (Wm. Andrews Exclusive)	850	1998	40.00	72-90

1998 Collection - P. Breen

YEAR ISSUE	EDITION LIMIT	YEAR RETD.	ISSUE PRICE	*QUOTE U.S.$
1998 Patricia's Bee (Breen Breakfast Gift)	Retrd.	1998	Gift	60

Possible Dreams

Cagey Critters - B. Stebleton

YEAR ISSUE	EDITION LIMIT	YEAR RETD.	ISSUE PRICE	*QUOTE U.S.$
1998 Santa, egg shaped, wood 3 3/4" 194002	Open		5.20	6
1998 Santa, egg shaped, wood 4 3/4" 194003	Open		5.90	6
1998 Santas, bell shaped, wood, set/6 194001	Open		19.50	20

Crinkle Claus - Staff

YEAR ISSUE	EDITION LIMIT	YEAR RETD.	ISSUE PRICE	*QUOTE U.S.$
1996 Bishop of Maya-659702	Open		7.80	8
1996 Black Forest Santa-659706	Open		7.80	8
1996 Father Christmas-659703	Open		7.80	8
1996 German Santa-659701	Open		7.80	8
1996 Pere Noel Santa-659705	Open		7.80	8
1996 St. Nicholas-659704	Open		7.80	8

Garfield® Ornaments - Staff

YEAR ISSUE	EDITION LIMIT	YEAR RETD.	ISSUE PRICE	*QUOTE U.S.$
1997 Frostbite Feline 275103	Open		20.50	21
1997 Here Comes Santa Paws 275102	Open		25.50	26
1997 Wake Me When It's Christmas 275101	Open		25.50	26

Splanglers Realm® - R. Splangler

YEAR ISSUE	EDITION LIMIT	YEAR RETD.	ISSUE PRICE	*QUOTE U.S.$
1997 The Stowaway 191052	Open		8.40	9
1997 Tied To Perfection 191051	Open		9.30	10
1997 Twinkle, Twinkle, Little Dragon 191050	Open		7.90	8

*Quotes have been rounded up to nearest dollar

The Thickets at Sweetbriar® - B. Ross

YEAR ISSUE	EDITION LIMIT	YEAR RETD.	ISSUE PRICE	*QUOTE U.S.$
1995 Christmas Whiskers 350400	Closed	1996	11.50	12
1995 Jingle Bells 350407	Closed	1996	12.00	12
1996 Snuggles 350416	Open		11.70	12
1996 Nibbley-Do 350415	Open		10.50	11
1996 Twinkle Tails 350404	Closed	1996	11.50	12

Precious Moments/Enesco Corporation

Precious Moments - S. Butcher

YEAR ISSUE	EDITION LIMIT	YEAR RETD.	ISSUE PRICE	*QUOTE U.S.$
1983 Surround Us With Joy E-0513	Yr.Iss.	1983	9.00	58-72
1983 Mother Sew Dear E-0514	Open		9.00	19
1983 To A Special Dad E-0515	Suspd.		9.00	35-50
1983 The Purr-fect Grandma E-0516	Open		9.00	19-42
1983 The Perfect Grandpa E-0517	Suspd.		9.00	10-40
1983 Blessed Are The Pure In Heart E-0518	Yr.Iss.	1983	9.00	10-40
1983 O Come All Ye Faithful E-0531	Suspd.		10.00	44-70
1983 Let Heaven And Nature Sing E-0532	Retrd.	1986	9.00	10-35
1983 Tell Me The Story Of Jesus E-0533	Suspd.		9.00	45
1983 To Thee With Love E-0534	Retrd.	1989	9.00	35-62
1984 Love Is Patient E-0535	Suspd.		9.00	35-85
1984 Love Is Patient E-0536	Suspd.		9.00	55-65
1983 Jesus Is The Light That Shines E-0537	Suspd.		9.00	60-75
1982 Joy To The World E-2343	Suspd.		9.00	45-65
1982 I'll Play My Drum For Him E-2359	Yr.Iss.	1982	9.00	60-120
1982 Baby's First Christmas E-2362	Suspd.		9.00	35-40
1982 The First Noel E-2367	Suspd.		9.00	55-65
1982 The First Noel E-2368	Retrd.	1984	9.00	40-45
1982 Dropping In For Christmas E-2369	Retrd.	1986	9.00	35-40
1982 Unicorn E-2371	Retrd.	1988	10.00	45-50
1982 Baby's First Christmas E-2372	Suspd.		9.00	35-45
1982 Dropping Over For Christmas E-2376	Retrd.	1985	9.00	50
1982 Mouse With Cheese E-2381	Suspd.		9.00	100-125
1982 Our First Christmas Together E-2385	Suspd.		10.00	25-60
1982 Camel, Donkey & Cow (3 pc. set) E-2386	Suspd.		25.00	65-100
1984 Wishing You A Merry Christmas E-5387	Yr.Iss.	1984	10.00	32-100
1984 Joy To The World E-5388	Retrd.	1987	10.00	35-40
1984 Peace On Earth E-5389	Suspd.		10.00	25-35
1984 May God Bless You With A Perfect Holiday Season E-5390	Suspd.		10.00	20-26
1984 Love Is Kind E-5391	Suspd.		10.00	25-30
1984 Blessed Are The Pure In Heart E-5392	Yr.Iss.	1984	10.00	20
1981 But Love Goes On Forever E-5627	Suspd.		6.00	100-120
1981 But Love Goes On Forever E-5628	Suspd.		6.00	90-120
1981 Let The Heavens Rejoice E-5629	Yr.Iss.	1981	6.00	250-275
1981 Unto Us A Child Is Born E-5630	Suspd.		6.00	50
1981 Baby's First Christmas E-5631	Suspd.		6.00	40-60
1981 Baby's First Christmas E-5632	Suspd.		6.00	40-60
1981 Come Let Us Adore Him (4pc. set) E-5633	Suspd.		22.00	145
1981 Wee Three Kings (3pc. set) E-5634	Suspd.		19.00	100-129
1981 We Have Seen His Star E-6120	Retrd.	1984	6.00	52-75
1985 Have A Heavenly Christmas 12416	Suspd.		12.00	20-30
1985 God Sent His Love 15768	Yr.Iss.	1985	10.00	35
1985 May Your Christmas Be Happy 15822	Suspd.		10.00	35-40
1985 Happiness Is The Lord 15830	Suspd.		10.00	28-35
1985 May Your Christmas Be Delightful 15849	Suspd.		10.00	19-25
1985 Honk If You Love Jesus 15857	Suspd.		10.00	20-25
1985 Baby's First Christmas 15903	Yr.Iss.	1985	10.00	35
1985 Baby's First Christmas 15911	Yr.Iss.	1985	10.00	25-32
1986 Shepherd of Love 102288	Suspd.		10.00	25-38
1986 Wishing You A Cozy Christmas 102326	Yr.Iss.	1986	10.00	35-40
1986 Our First Christmas Together 102350	Yr.Iss.	1986	10.00	30
1986 Trust And Obey 102377	Open		10.00	19-30
1986 Love Rescued Me 102385	Open		10.00	19-23
1986 Angel Of Mercy 102407	Open		10.00	19-30
1986 It's A Perfect Boy 102415	Suspd.		10.00	26-42
1986 Lord Keep Me On My Toes 102423	Retrd.	1990	10.00	30-35
1986 Serve With A Smile 102431	Suspd.		10.00	21-25
1986 Serve With A Smile 102458	Suspd.		10.00	30-32
1986 Reindeer 102466	Yr.Iss.	1986	11.00	175-200
1986 Rocking Horse 102474	Suspd.		10.00	25-32
1986 Baby's First Christmas 102504	Yr.Iss.	1986	10.00	30-35
1986 Baby's First Christmas 102512	Yr.Iss.	1986	10.00	30-35
1987 Bear The Good News Of Christmas 104515	Yr.Iss.	1987	12.50	20
1987 Baby's First Christmas 109401	Yr.Iss.	1987	12.00	35
1987 Baby's First Christmas 109428	Yr.Iss.	1987	12.00	35
1987 Love Is The Best Gift Of All 109770	Yr.Iss.	1987	11.00	35-40
1987 I'm A Possibility 111120	Suspd.		11.00	23
1987 You Have Touched So Many Hearts 112356	Retrd.	1996	11.00	19-23
1987 Waddle I Do Without You 112364	Open		11.00	17-30
1987 I'm Sending You A White Christmas 112372	Suspd.		11.00	20
1987 He Cleansed My Soul 112380	Open		12.00	19-22
1987 Our First Christmas Together 112399	Yr.Iss.	1987	11.00	30-44
1988 To My Forever Friend 113956	Open		16.00	20-35
1988 Smile Along The Way 113964	Suspd.		15.00	29-31
1988				
God Sent You Just In Time 113972	Suspd.		13.50	30-35
1988 Rejoice O Earth 113980	Retrd.	1991	13.50	30-35
1988 Cheers To The Leader 113999	Suspd.		13.50	33
1988 My Love Will Never Let You Go 114006	Suspd.		13.50	25-30
1988 Baby's First Christmas 115282	Yr.Iss.	1988	15.00	15-25
1988 Time To Wish You A Merry Christmas 115320	Yr.Iss.	1988	13.00	35-49
1996 Owl Be Home For Christmas 128708	Yr.Iss.	1996	18.50	15-20
1995 He Covers The Earth With His Beauty 142662	Yr.Iss.	1995	17.00	17-20
1995 He Covers The Earth With His Beauty (ball) 142689	Yr.Iss.	1995	30.00	30
1995 Our First Christmas Together 142700	Yr.Iss.	1995	18.50	19
1995 Baby's First Christmas 142719	Yr.Iss.	1995	17.50	20
1995 Baby's First Christmas 142727	Yr.Iss.	1995	17.50	20
1995 Joy From Head To Mistletoe 150126	Open		18.50	19
1995 You're "A" Number One In My Book, Teacher 150142	Open		18.50	19-22
1995 Joy To The World 150320	Open		20.00	20
1996 Joy To The World 153338	Open		20.00	20
1996 Peace On Earth...Anyway (Ball) 183350	Yr.Iss.	1996	30.00	25-30
1996 Peace On Earth...Anyway 183369	Yr.Iss.	1996	18.50	19
1996 God's Precious Gift 183881	Open		20.00	20
1996 When The Skating's Ruff, Try Prayer 183903	Open		18.50	19
1996 Our First Christmas Together 183911	Yr.Iss.	1996	22.50	23-25
1996 Baby's First Christmas 183938	Yr.Iss.	1996	17.50	18-20
1996 Baby's First Christmas 183946	Yr.Iss.	1996	17.50	18
1998 In God's Beautiful Garden Of Love 261599	Open		50.00	50
1997 Cane You Join Us For A Merry Christmas 272671	Yr.Iss.	1997	18.50	19-30
1997 Cane You Join Us For A Merry Christmas 272728	Yr.Iss.	1997	18.50	19-30
1997 Our First Christmas Together 272736	Yr.Iss.	1997	20.00	20
1997 Baby's First Christmas (Girl) 272744	Yr.Iss.	1997	18.50	19
1997 Baby's First Christmas (Boy) 272752	Yr.Iss.	1997	18.50	19
1997 Slow Down For The Holidays 272760	Yr.Iss.	1997	18.50	19
1997 Puppies With Sled 272892	Open		18.50	19
1998 I'm Sending You A Merry Christmas 455628	Yr.Iss.	1998	18.50	19
1998 Our First Christmas Together 455636	Yr.Iss.	1998	25.00	25
1998 Baby's First Christmas (Girl) 455644	Yr.Iss.	1998	18.50	19
1998 Baby's First Christmas (Boy) 455652	Yr.Iss.	1998	18.50	19
1998 I'll Be Dog-ged It's That Season Again 455660	Yr.Iss.	1998	18.50	19
1998 I'm Just Nutty About The Holidays 455776	Open		17.50	18
1988 Our First Christmas Together 520233	Yr.Iss.	1988	13.00	21-25
1988 Baby's First Christmas 520241	Yr.Iss.	1988	15.00	20-25
1988 You Are My Gift Come True 520276	Yr.Iss.	1988	12.50	23
1988 Hang On For The Holly Days 520292	Yr.Iss.	1988	13.00	25-30
1992 I'm Nuts About You 520411	Yr.Iss.	1992	15.00	22-33
1995 Hippo Holy Days 520403	Yr.Iss.	1995	17.00	17-20
1991 Sno-Bunny Falls For You Like I Do 520438	Yr.Iss.	1991	15.00	23-28
1998 Happy Holi-daze 520454	Open		17.50	18
1989 Christmas is Ruff Without You 520462	Yr.Iss.	1989	13.00	25-30
1993 Slow Down & Enjoy The Holidays 520489	Yr.Iss.	1993	16.00	22
1990 Wishing You A Purr-fect Holiday 520497	Yr.Iss.	1990	15.00	23-30
1989 May All Your Christmases Be White 521302 (dated)	Suspd.		15.00	20-25
1989 Our First Christmas Together 521558	Yr.Iss.	1989	17.50	30
1990 Glide Through the Holidays 521566	Retrd.	1992	13.50	25-40
1990 Dashing Through the Snow 521574	Suspd.		15.00	23
1990 Don't Let the Holidays Get You Down 521590	Retrd.	1994	15.00	20-30
1989 Oh Holy Night 522848	Yr.Iss.	1989	13.50	25-35
1989 Make A Joyful Noise 522910	Suspd.		15.00	17-23
1989 Love One Another 522929	Open		17.50	20-25
1990 Friends Never Drift Apart 522937	Retrd.	1995	17.50	35
1991 Our First Christmas Together 522945	Yr.Iss.	1991	17.50	18-25
1989 I Believe In The Old Rugged Cross 522953	Suspd.		15.00	20
1989 Peace On Earth 523062	Yr.Iss.	1989	25.00	44-80
1989 Baby's First Christmas 523194	Yr.Iss.	1989	15.00	25
1989 Baby's First Christmas 523208	Yr.Iss.	1989	15.00	25-28
1991 Happy Trails Is Trusting Jesus 523224	Suspd.		15.00	25
1990 May Your Christmas Be A Happy Home 523704	Yr.Iss.	1990	27.50	40-52
1990 Baby's First Christmas 523798	Yr.Iss.	1990	15.00	25
1990 Baby's First Christmas 523771	Yr.Iss.	1990	15.00	25
1990 Once Upon A Holy Night 523852	Yr.Iss.	1990	15.00	20-25
1992 Good Friends Are For Always 524131	Retrd.	1996	15.00	19-22
1991 May Your Christmas Be Merry 524174	Yr.Iss.	1991	15.00	25-30
1990 Bundles of Joy 525057	Yr.Iss.	1990	15.00	30-40
1990 Our First Christmas Together 525324	Yr.Iss.	1990	17.50	20-25
1993 Lord, Keep Me On My Toes 525332	Open		15.00	19-50
1991 May Your Christmas Be Merry (on Base) 526940	Yr.Iss.	1991	30.00	35-40
1991 Baby's First Christmas (Boy) 527084	Yr.Iss.	1991	15.00	20-25
1991 Baby's First Christmas (Girl) 527092	Yr.Iss.	1991	15.00	25
1991 The Good Lord Always Delivers 527165	Suspd.		15.00	20-25
1993 Share in The Warmth of Christmas 527211	Open		15.00	15-19
1994 Onward Christmas Soldiers 527327	Open		16.00	19
1992 Baby's First Christmas 527475	Yr.Iss.	1992	15.00	20
1992 Baby's First Christmas 527483	Yr.Iss.	1992	15.00	17-22
1992 But The Greatest of These Is Love 527696	Yr.Iss.	1992	15.00	25-30
1992 But The Greatest of These Is Love 527734 (on Base)	Yr.Iss.	1992	30.00	35-44
1994 Sending You A White Christmas 528218	Open		16.00	19
1994 Bringing You A Merry Christmas 528226	Open		16.00	19
1993 It's So Uplifting to Have a Friend Like You 528846	Open		16.00	19-30
1992 Our First Christmas Together 528870	Yr.Iss.	1992	17.50	20-25
1994 Our 1st Christmas Together 529206	Yr.Iss.	1994	18.50	19-25
1993 Wishing You the Sweetest Christmas 530190	Yr.Iss.	1993	30.00	25-42
1993 Wishing You the Sweetest Christmas 530212	Yr.Iss.	1993	15.00	35
1994 Baby's First Christmas 530255	Yr.Iss.	1994	16.00	16-20
1994 Baby's First Christmas 530263	Yr.Iss.	1994	16.00	16-19
1994 You're As Pretty As A Christmas Tree 530387	Yr.Iss.	1994	30.00	25-30
1994 You're As Pretty As A Christmas Tree 530395	Yr.Iss.	1994	16.00	35-40
1993 Our First Christmas Together 530506	Yr.Iss.	1993	17.50	25
1993 Baby's First Christmas 530859	Yr.Iss.	1993	15.00	15-23
1993 Baby's First Christmas 530867	Yr.Iss.	1993	15.00	15-23
1994 You Are Always In My Heart 530972	Yr.Iss.	1994	16.00	16-20

Precious Moments Club 15th Anniversary Commemorative Edition - S. Butcher

YEAR ISSUE	EDITION LIMIT	YEAR RETD.	ISSUE PRICE	*QUOTE U.S.$
1993 15 Years Tweet Music Together 530840	Yr.Iss.	1993	15.00	19-30

Precious Moments Club 20th Anniversary Commemorative Edition - S. Butcher

YEAR ISSUE	EDITION LIMIT	YEAR RETD.	ISSUE PRICE	*QUOTE U.S.$
1998 20 Years And The Vision's Still The Same 451312	Yr.Iss.		22.50	23
1998 How Can Two Work Together Except They Agree	Yr.Iss.		25.00	25

DSR Open House Weekend Ornaments - S. Butcher

YEAR ISSUE	EDITION LIMIT	YEAR RETD.	ISSUE PRICE	*QUOTE U.S.$
1992 The Magic Starts With You 529648	Yr.Iss.	1992	16.00	23-25
1993 An Event For All Seasons 529974	Yr.Iss.	1993	15.00	19-25
1994 Take A Bow Cuz You're My Christmas Star 520470	Yr.Iss.	1994	16.00	25
1995 Merry Chrismoose 150134	Yr.Iss.	1995	17.00	22-25
1996 Wishing You a Bearie Merry Christmas 531200	Yr.Iss.	1996	17.50	20
1997 Pack Your Trunk For The Holidays 272949	Yr.Iss.	1997	20.00	20

Easter Seal Commemorative Ornaments - S. Butcher

YEAR ISSUE	EDITION LIMIT	YEAR RETD.	ISSUE PRICE	*QUOTE U.S.$
1994 It's No Secret What God Can Do 244570	Yr.Iss.	1994	6.50	7
1995 Take Time To Smell The Flowers 128899	Yr.Iss.	1995	7.50	8
1996 You Can Always Count on Me 152579	Yr.Iss.	1996	6.50	7
1997 Give Ability A Chance 192384	Yr.Iss.	1997	6.50	7
1998 Somebody Cares 272922	Yr.Iss.	1998	6.50	7
1999 Heaven Bless You 475076	Yr.Iss.		6.50	7

Special Edition Members' Only - S. Butcher

YEAR ISSUE	EDITION LIMIT	YEAR RETD.	ISSUE PRICE	*QUOTE U.S.$
1993 Loving, Caring And Sharing Along The Way PM-040 (Club Appreciation)	Yr.Iss.	1993	12.50	13-25
1994 You Are The End of My Rainbow PM-041	Yr.Iss.	1994	15.00	20-24

Sugartown - S. Butcher

YEAR ISSUE	EDITION LIMIT	YEAR RETD.	ISSUE PRICE	*QUOTE U.S.$
1993 Sugartown Chapel Ornament 530484	Yr.Iss.	1993	17.50	20-25
1994 Sam's House 530468	Yr.Iss.	1994	17.50	18-20
1995 Dr. Sugar's Office 530441	Yr.Iss.	1995	17.50	18
1996 Train Station 18a101	Yr.Iss.	1996	18.50	19

Twelve Days Of Christmas - S. Butcher

YEAR ISSUE	EDITION LIMIT	YEAR RETD.	ISSUE PRICE	*QUOTE U.S.$
1998 My True Love Gave To Me - Day 1 455989	Yr.Iss.		20.00	20
1998 We're Two' Of A Kind - Day 2 455997	Yr.Iss.		20.00	20
1998 Saying 'Oui' To Our Love - Day 3 456004	Yr.Iss.		20.00	20

*Quotes have been rounded up to nearest dollar

YEAR ISSUE	EDITION LIMIT	YEAR RETD.	ISSUE PRICE	*QUOTE U.S.$
1998 Ringing In The Season - Day 4 456012	Yr.Iss.		20.00	20

Prizm, Inc./Pipka

Pipka's Stories of Christmas - Pipka

YEAR ISSUE	EDITION LIMIT	YEAR RETD.	ISSUE PRICE	*QUOTE U.S.$
1997 Aussie Santa 11404	Open		15.00	15
1997 Czechoslovakian Santa 11401	Open		15.00	15
1998 Father Christmas 11412	Open		15.00	15
1997 Midnight Visitor 11400	Open		15.00	15
1998 Norwegian/Julenisse Santa 11407	Open		15.00	15
1998 Peace Maker 11413	Open		15.00	15
1998 Polish Father Christmas 11408	Open		15.00	15
1998 San Nicolas 11415	Open		15.00	15
1998 Santa's Spotted Grey 11411	Open		15.00	15
1998 St. Nicholas 11409	Open		15.00	15
1997 Star Catcher Santa 11403	Open		15.00	15
1997 Starcoat Santa 11402	Open		15.00	15
1998 Storytime Santa 11410	Open		15.00	15
1998 Teddy Bear Santa 11414	Open		15.00	15
1997 Ukrainian Santa 11405	Open		15.00	15
1998 Where's Rudolph? 11406	Open		15.00	15

Reed & Barton

12 Days of Christmas Sterling and Lead Crystal - Reed & Barton

YEAR ISSUE	EDITION LIMIT	YEAR RETD.	ISSUE PRICE	*QUOTE U.S.$
1988 Partridge in a Pear Tree	Yr.Iss.	1988	25.00	30
1989 Two Turtle Doves	Yr.Iss.	1989	25.00	30
1990 Three French Hens	Yr.Iss.	1990	27.50	30
1991 Four Colly birds	Yr.Iss.	1991	27.50	30
1992 Five Golden Rings	Yr.Iss.	1992	27.50	30
1993 Six Geese A Laying	Yr.Iss.	1993	27.50	30
1994 Seven Swans A 'Swimming	Yr.Iss.	1994	27.50	30
1995 Eight Maids A Milking	Yr.Iss.	1995	30.00	30
1996 Nine Ladies Dancing	Yr.Iss.	1996	30.00	30
1997 Ten Lords a-Leaping	Yr.Iss.	1997	32.50	33
1998 Eleven Pipers Piping	Yr.Iss.		32.50	33

Christmas Cross - Reed & Barton

YEAR ISSUE	EDITION LIMIT	YEAR RETD.	ISSUE PRICE	*QUOTE U.S.$
1971 Sterling Silver-1971	Closed	1971	10.00	120-300
1971 24Kt. Gold over Sterling-V1971	Closed	1971	17.50	300
1972 Sterling Silver-1972	Closed	1972	10.00	125-200
1972 24Kt. Gold over Sterling-V1972	Closed	1972	17.50	75-175
1973 Sterling Silver-1973	Closed	1973	10.00	85-100
1973 24Kt. Gold over Sterling-V1973	Closed	1973	17.50	60-85
1974 Sterling Silver-1974	Closed	1974	12.95	75-90
1974 24Kt. Gold over Sterling-V1974	Closed	1974	20.00	45-75
1975 Sterling Silver-1975	Closed	1975	12.95	35-75
1975 24Kt. Gold over Sterling-V1975	Closed	1975	20.00	50-60
1976 Sterling Silver-1976	Closed	1976	13.95	50-85
1976 24Kt. Gold over Sterling-V1976	Closed	1976	19.95	45-50
1977 Sterling Silver-1977	Closed	1977	15.00	50-65
1977 24Kt. Gold over Sterling-V1977	Closed	1977	18.50	45-50
1978 Sterling Silver-1978	Closed	1978	16.00	50-75
1978 24Kt. Gold over Sterling-V1978	Closed	1978	20.00	45-55
1979 Sterling Silver-1979	Closed	1979	20.00	60-75
1979 24Kt. Gold over Sterling-V1979	Closed	1979	24.00	32-57
1980 Sterling Silver-1980	Closed	1980	35.00	60
1980 24Kt. Gold over Sterling-V1980	Closed	1980	40.00	45-50
1981 Sterling Silver-1981	Closed	1981	35.00	45
1981 24Kt. Gold over Sterling-V1981	Closed	1981	40.00	45
1982 Sterling Silver-1982	Closed	1982	35.00	65-100
1982 24Kt. Gold over Sterling-V1982	Closed	1982	40.00	45
1983 Sterling Silver-1983	Closed	1983	35.00	50-100
1983 24Kt. Gold over Sterling-V1983	Closed	1983	40.00	40-45
1984 Sterling Silver-1984	Closed	1984	35.00	45
1984 24Kt. Gold over Sterling-V1984	Closed	1984	45.00	45
1985 Sterling Silver-1985	Closed	1985	35.00	80-90
1985 24Kt. Gold over Sterling-V1985	Closed	1985	40.00	40
1986 Sterling Silver-1986	Closed	1986	38.50	45
1986 24Kt. Gold over Sterling-V1986	Closed	1986	40.00	45
1987 Sterling Silver-1987	Closed	1987	35.00	45-80
1987 24Kt. Gold over Sterling-V1987	Closed	1987	40.00	40
1988 Sterling Silver-1988	Closed	1988	35.00	45-90
1988 24Kt. Gold over Sterling-V1988	Closed	1988	40.00	40
1989 Sterling Silver-1989	Closed	1989	35.00	45
1989 24Kt. Gold over Sterling-V1989	Closed	1989	40.00	40
1990 Sterling Silver-1990	Closed	1990	40.00	45-70
1990 24Kt. Gold over Sterling-1990	Closed	1990	45.00	45
1991 Sterling Silver-1991	Closed	1991	40.00	45-75
1991 24Kt. Gold over Sterling-1991	Closed	1991	45.00	45
1992 Sterling Silver-1992	Closed	1992	40.00	40
1992 24Kt. Gold over Sterling-1992	Closed	1992	45.00	45
1993 Sterling Silver-1993	Closed	1993	40.00	45
1993 24Kt. Gold over Sterling-1993	Closed	1993	45.00	45
1994 Sterling Silver-1994	Closed	1994	40.00	40
1994 24Kt. Gold over Sterling-1994	Closed	1994	45.00	45
1995 Sterling Silver-1995	Closed	1995	40.00	40-45
1995 24Kt. Gold over Sterling-1995	Closed	1995	45.00	45
1996 Sterling Silver-1996	Closed	1996	40.00	40
1996 Gold Vermiel-1996	Closed	1996	45.00	45
1997 Sterling Silver-1997	Closed	1997	40.00	40
1997 24Kt. Gold over Sterling-1997	Closed	1997	45.00	45
1998 Sterling Silver-1998	Yr.Iss.		40.00	40
1998 24Kt. Gold over Sterling-1998	Yr.Iss.		45.00	45

Holly Ball/Bell - Reed & Barton

YEAR ISSUE	EDITION LIMIT	YEAR RETD.	ISSUE PRICE	*QUOTE U.S.$
1976 1976 Ball	Closed	1976	14.00	40
1977 1977 Ball	Closed	1977	15.00	25-85
1978 1978 Ball	Closed	1978	15.00	25-75
1979 1979 Ball	Closed	1979	15.00	35-50
1980 1980 Bell	Closed	1980	22.50	35-50
1980 Bell, gold plate, V1980	Closed	1980	25.00	45
1981 1981 Bell	Closed	1981	22.50	30-55
1981 Bell, gold plate, V1981	Closed	1981	27.50	35
1982 1982 Bell	Closed	1982	22.50	35-70
1982 Bell, gold plate, V1982	Closed	1982	27.50	50
1983 1983 Bell	Closed	1983	23.50	45-75
1983 Bell, gold plate, V1983	Closed	1983	30.00	75
1984 1984 Bell	Closed	1984	25.00	35-80
1984 Bell, gold plate, V1984	Closed	1984	28.50	50
1985 1985 Bell	Closed	1985	25.00	80
1985 Bell, gold plate, V1985	Closed	1985	28.50	50
1986 1986 Bell	Closed	1986	25.00	75
1986 Bell, gold plate, V1986	Closed	1986	28.50	50
1987 1987 Bell	Closed	1987	27.50	70
1987 Bell, gold plate, V1987	Closed	1987	30.00	50
1988 1988 Bell	Closed	1988	27.50	40
1988 Bell, gold plate, V1988	Closed	1988	30.00	30
1989 1989 Bell	Closed	1989	27.50	55-65
1989 Bell, gold plate, V1989	Closed	1989	30.00	30
1990 Bell, gold plate, V1990	Closed	1990	30.00	30
1990 1990 Bell	Closed	1990	27.50	55-65
1991 Bell, gold plate, V1991	Closed	1991	30.00	30
1991 1991 Bell	Closed	1991	27.50	50-60
1992 Bell, gold plate, V1992	Closed	1992	30.00	30
1992 Bell, silver plate, 1992	Closed	1992	27.50	50
1993 Bell, gold plate, V1993	Closed	1993	27.50	28
1993 Bell, silver plate, 1993	Closed	1993	30.00	50
1994 Bell, gold plate, 1994	Closed	1994	30.00	30
1994 Bell, silver plate, 1994	Closed	1994	27.50	30-45
1995 Bell, gold plate, 1995	Closed	1995	30.00	30
1995 Bell, silver plate, 1995	Closed	1995	27.50	30-40
1996 Bell, gold plate, 1996	Closed	1996	35.00	35
1996 Bell, silver plate, 1996	Closed	1996	30.00	35
1997 Bell, 24Kt. gold plate, 1997	Closed	1997	35.00	35
1997 Bell, silver plate, 1997	Closed	1997	30.00	30
1998 Bell, 24Kt. gold plate, 1998	Yr.Iss.		35.00	35
1998 Bell, silver plate, 1998	Yr.Iss.		30.00	30

Roman, Inc.

Catnippers - I. Spencer

YEAR ISSUE	EDITION LIMIT	YEAR RETD.	ISSUE PRICE	*QUOTE U.S.$
1989 Bow Brummel	Closed	N/A	15.00	15
1991 Christmas Knight	Closed	N/A	15.00	15
1988 Christmas Mourning	Closed	N/A	15.00	15
1991 Faux Paw	Closed	N/A	15.00	15
1990 Felix Navidad	Closed	N/A	15.00	15
1989 Happy Holidaze	Closed	N/A	15.00	15
1991 Holly Days Are Happy Days	Closed	N/A	15.00	15
1991 Meowy Christmas	Closed	N/A	15.00	15
1991 Pawtridge in a Purr Tree	Closed	N/A	15.00	15
1988 Puss in Berries	Closed	N/A	15.00	15
1988 Ring A Ding-Ding	Closed	N/A	15.00	15
1989 Sandy Claws	Closed	N/A	15.00	15
1991 Snow Biz	Closed	N/A	15.00	15
1990 Sock It to Me Santa	Closed	N/A	15.00	15
1990 Stuck on Christmas	Closed	N/A	15.00	15

The Discovery of America - I. Spencer

YEAR ISSUE	EDITION LIMIT	YEAR RETD.	ISSUE PRICE	*QUOTE U.S.$
1991 Kitstopher Kolumbus	1,992	N/A	15.00	15
1991 Queen Kitsabella	1,992	N/A	15.00	15

Fontanini Limited Edition Ornaments - E. Simonetti

YEAR ISSUE	EDITION LIMIT	YEAR RETD.	ISSUE PRICE	*QUOTE U.S.$
1995 The Annunciation	20,000	N/A	20.00	20
1996 Journey to Bethlehem	20,000	N/A	20.00	20
1997 Gloria Angel	Yr.Iss.	1997	20.00	20-40

Millenium™ Ornament - A. Lucchesi

YEAR ISSUE	EDITION LIMIT	YEAR RETD.	ISSUE PRICE	*QUOTE U.S.$
1992 Silent Night	20,000	1992	20.00	20-40
1993 The Annunciation	20,000	1993	20.00	20
1994 Peace On Earth	20,000	1994	20.00	20-55
1995 Cause of Our Joy	20,000	1995	20.00	20
1996 Prince of Peace	30,000	1996	20.00	20
1997 Gentle Love	Yr.Iss.	1997	20.00	20

Museum Collection of Angela Tripi - A. Tripi

YEAR ISSUE	EDITION LIMIT	YEAR RETD.	ISSUE PRICE	*QUOTE U.S.$
1994 1994 Annual Angel Ornament	2,500	1994	49.50	50
1995 1995 Annual Angel Ornament	1,000	1995	49.50	50

Seraphim Classics ® Dimensional Ornaments - Seraphim Studios

YEAR ISSUE	EDITION LIMIT	YEAR RETD.	ISSUE PRICE	*QUOTE U.S.$
1999 Annalisa - Celebrating The Millennium	2-Yr.		20.00	20
1998 Noelle - Giving Spirit	Open		19.50	20

Seraphim Classics ® Faro Collection - Faro Studios

YEAR ISSUE	EDITION LIMIT	YEAR RETD.	ISSUE PRICE	*QUOTE U.S.$
1994 Rosalyn, Rarest of Heaven	20,000	1995	25.00	25-45
1995 Helena, Heaven's Herald	20,000	1996	25.00	25
1996 Flora, Flower of Heaven	20,000	1997	25.00	25
1997 Emily, Heaven's Treasure	Yr.Iss.	1997	25.00	25-35
1998 Elise - Heaven's Glory	Yr.Iss.		25.00	25

Seraphim Classics ® Heaven Sent Collection - Seraphim Studios

YEAR ISSUE	EDITION LIMIT	YEAR RETD.	ISSUE PRICE	*QUOTE U.S.$
1997 Hope Eternal	Open		30.00	30
1997 Loving Spirit	Open		30.00	30
1997 Pure At Heart	Open		30.00	30

Seraphim Classics ® Wafer Ornaments - Seraphim Studios

YEAR ISSUE	EDITION LIMIT	YEAR RETD.	ISSUE PRICE	*QUOTE U.S.$
1995 Isabel - Gentle Spirit	Open		15.00	15
1995 Iris - Rainbow's End	Open		15.00	15
1995 Lydia - Winged Poet	Retrd.	1997	15.00	15-20
1995 Cymbeline - Peacemaker	Retrd.	1997	15.00	15-20
1995 Ophelia - Heart Seeker	Retrd.	1997	15.00	15-20
1995 Evangeline - Angel of Mercy	Retrd.	1997	15.00	15-20
1996 Laurice - Wisdom's Child	Retrd.	1997	15.00	15-20
1996 Felicia - Adoring Maiden	Retrd.	1997	15.00	15-20
1996 Priscilla - Benevolent Guide	Retrd.	1997	15.00	15-20
1996 Seraphina - Heaven's Helper	Retrd.	1997	15.00	15
1997 Celine - The Morning Star	Open		15.00	15
1997 Francesca - Loving Guardian	Open		15.00	15
1997 Gabriel - Celestial Messenger	Open		15.00	15
1997 Mariah - Heavenly Joy	Open		15.00	15
1997 Rosalie - Nature's Delight	Open		15.00	15
1997 Serena - Angel of Peace	Open		15.00	15
1998 Chelsea - Summer's Delight	Open		15.00	15
1998 Melody - Heaven's Song	Open		15.00	15
1998 Harmony - Love's Guardian	Open		15.00	15
1998 Tamara - Blessed Guardian	Open		15.00	15
1998 Rachel - Children's Joy	Open		15.00	15

Vernon Wilson Signature Series - V. Wilson

YEAR ISSUE	EDITION LIMIT	YEAR RETD.	ISSUE PRICE	*QUOTE U.S.$
1995 We Three Kings	Open		34.00	34

Royal Doulton

Bunnykins - Royal Doulton, unless otherwise noted

YEAR ISSUE	EDITION LIMIT	YEAR RETD.	ISSUE PRICE	*QUOTE U.S.$
1991 Santa Bunny - D. Lyttleton	Yr.Iss.	1991	19.00	19
1992 Caroling - D. Lyttleton	Yr.Iss.	1992	19.00	19
1994 Trimming the Tree	Yr.Iss.	1994	20.00	20
1995 Fun in the Snow	Yr.Iss.	1995	20.00	20
1996 Christmas Morn	Yr.Iss.	1996	20.00	20
1997 Home for the Holidays	Yr.Iss.		20.00	20

Christmas Ornaments - Various

YEAR ISSUE	EDITION LIMIT	YEAR RETD.	ISSUE PRICE	*QUOTE U.S.$
1993 Royal Doulton-Together for Christmas - J. James	Yr.Iss.	1993	20.00	20
1993 Royal Albert-Sleighride - N/A	Yr.Iss.	1993	20.00	20
1994 Royal Doulton-Home For Christmas - J. James	Yr.Iss.	1994	20.00	20
1994 Royal Albert-Coaching Inn - N/A	Yr.Iss.	1994	20.00	20
1995 Royal Doulton-Season's Greetings - J. James	Yr.Iss.	1995	20.00	20
1995 Royal Albert-Skating Pond - N/A	Yr.Iss.	1995	20.00	20
1996 Royal Doulton-Night Before Christmas - J. James	Yr.Iss.	1996	20.00	20
1996 Royal Albert-Gathering Winter Fuel - N/A	Yr.Iss.	1996	20.00	20

Merry Wreath Ornaments - Royal Doulton

YEAR ISSUE	EDITION LIMIT	YEAR RETD.	ISSUE PRICE	*QUOTE U.S.$
1998 Angels	Open		17.50	18
1998 Candy Cane	Open		17.50	18
1998 Toyland	Open		17.50	18
1998 Winter Wonderland	Open		17.50	18

Santa Bell Ornaments - V. Heilbron

YEAR ISSUE	EDITION LIMIT	YEAR RETD.	ISSUE PRICE	*QUOTE U.S.$
1998 Father Christmas	Open		25.00	25
1998 Pere Noel	Open		25.00	25
1998 Santa Claus	Open		25.00	25
1998 St. Nicholas	Open		25.00	25

Victorian Card Ornaments - Royal Doulton

YEAR ISSUE	EDITION LIMIT	YEAR RETD.	ISSUE PRICE	*QUOTE U.S.$
1998 Joy	Open		15.00	15
1998 Merry Christmas	Open		15.00	15
1998 Noel	Open		15.00	15
1998 Peace on Earth	Open		15.00	15

Shelia's Collectibles

Amish Quilt Ornaments - S. Thompson

YEAR ISSUE	EDITION LIMIT	YEAR RETD.	ISSUE PRICE	*QUOTE U.S.$
1997 Cactus Basket AQO03	Open		16.00	16
1997 Double Irish Chain AQO05	Open		16.00	16
1997 North Carolina Lily AQO04	Open		16.00	16
1997 Pineapple AQO02	Open		16.00	16
1997 Robbing Peter to Pay Paul AQ001	Open		16.00	16
1997 Shoo-Fly AQO06	Open		16.00	16

Historical Ornament Collection - S. Thompson

YEAR ISSUE	EDITION LIMIT	YEAR RETD.	ISSUE PRICE	*QUOTE U.S.$
1995 Blue Cottage (1st ed.) OR001	Retrd.	1996	15.00	40
1996 Blue Cottage (2nd ed.) OR001	Retrd.	1997	15.00	25
1995 Cape Hatteras Light (1st ed.) OR007	Retrd.	1996	15.00	40
1996 Cape Hatteras Light (2nd ed.) OR007	Retrd.	1997	15.00	27
1995 Chestnut House (1st ed.) OR002	Retrd.	1996	15.00	20-40
1996 Chestnut House (2nd ed.) OR002	Retrd.	1997	15.00	27
1995 Drayton House (1st ed.) OR003	Retrd.	1996	15.00	31-40
1996 Drayton House (2nd ed.) OR003	Retrd.	1997	15.00	22-25
1995 East Brother Lighthouse (1st ed.) OR008	Retrd.	1996	15.00	27-40
1996 East Brother Lighthouse (2nd ed.) OR008	Retrd.	1997	15.00	27
1995 Eclectic Blue (1st ed.) OR004	Retrd.	1996	15.00	40
1996 Eclectic Blue (2nd ed.) OR004	Retrd.	1997	15.00	25
1995 Goeller House (1st ed.) OR005	Retrd.	1996	15.00	40
1996 Goeller House (2nd ed.) OR005	Retrd.	1997	15.00	25-30
1995 Point Fermin Light (1st ed.) OR009	Retrd.	1996	15.00	27-40
1996 Point Fermin Light (2nd ed.) OR009	Retrd.	1997	15.00	25
1995 Stockton Row (1st ed.) OR006	Retrd.	1996	15.00	40
1996 Stockton Row (2nd ed.) OR006	Retrd.	1997	15.00	25
1996 Artist House OR015	Open		19.00	21
1996 Capital OR018	Open		19.00	21
1996 Dragon OR010	Retrd.	1997	19.00	40
1996 E.B. Hall House OR011	Open		19.00	21
1996 Mail Pouch Barn OR016	Retrd.	1997	19.00	40
1996 Market OR013	Open		19.00	21
1996 Pink House OR020	Open		19.00	21

*Quotes have been rounded up to nearest dollar

YEAR ISSUE	EDITION LIMIT	YEAR RETD.	ISSUE PRICE	*QUOTE U.S.$
1996 Rutledge OR012	Open		19.00	21
1996 St. Philips Church OR022	Open		19.00	21
1996 Thomas Point Light OR019	Retrd.	1997	19.00	27-40
1996 Titman House OR021	Open		19.00	21
1996 Victoria OR014	Open		19.00	21
1996 White Cottage OR017	Open		19.00	21
1996 Clark House OR023	Open		19.00	21
1996 Urfer House OR024	Open		19.00	21
1996 Queen Anne OR025	Retrd.	1997	19.00	40
1996 Asendorf House OR026	Open		19.00	21
1996 Abbey II OR027	Open		19.00	21
1996 New Canal Light OR028	Open		19.00	21

Historical Ornament Collection II - S. Thompson

YEAR ISSUE	EDITION LIMIT	YEAR RETD.	ISSUE PRICE	*QUOTE U.S.$
1997 Berkeley Shore OR031	Open		21.00	21
1997 The Carlyle OR030	Open		21.00	21
1997 Hotel Webster OR029	Open		21.00	21
1997 Loew's Grand OR033	Open		21.00	21
1997 Magnolia Garden House OR034	Open		21.00	21
1997 Marlin OR032	Open		21.00	21

Nabisco Ornaments - S. Thompson

YEAR ISSUE	EDITION LIMIT	YEAR RETD.	ISSUE PRICE	*QUOTE U.S.$
1996 Animal Cracker Box, green NAB02	Open		29.00	29
1996 Animal Cracker Box, red NAB01	Open		29.00	29

Our Stars Ornament Collection - S. Thompson

YEAR ISSUE	EDITION LIMIT	YEAR RETD.	ISSUE PRICE	*QUOTE U.S.$
1996 Banta House OSR03	Retrd.	1997	23.00	27
1996 Greenman House OSR02	Retrd.	1997	23.00	25-28
1996 Riley-Cutler House OSR01	Retrd.	1997	23.00	25
1996 Weller House OSR04	Retrd.	1997	23.00	25

Swarovski Consumer Goods Ltd.

Christmas Ornaments - Swarovski

YEAR ISSUE	EDITION LIMIT	YEAR RETD.	ISSUE PRICE	*QUOTE U.S.$
1981 1981 Snowflake 7563NR35	Yr.Iss.	1981	30.00	350-420
1986 1986 Holiday Ornament 92086	Yr.Iss.	1986	N/A	250-429
1987 1987 Holiday Etching-Candle	Yr.Iss.	1987	20.00	240-360
1988 1988 Holiday Etching-Wreath	Yr.Iss.	1988	25.00	95-135
1989 1989 Holiday Etching-Dove	Yr.Iss.	1989	35.00	313-440
1990 1990 Holiday Etching-Merry Christmas	Yr.Iss.	1990	25.00	155-258
1991 1991 Holiday Ornament-Star	Yr.Iss.	1991	35.00	130-240
1992 1992 Holiday Ornament-Star	Yr.Iss.	1992	37.50	85-165
1993 1993 Holiday Ornament-Star	Yr.Iss.	1993	37.50	115-200
1994 1994 Holiday Ornament-Star	Yr.Iss.	1994	37.50	92-150
1995 1995 Holiday Ornament-Star	Yr.Iss.	1995	40.00	52-125
1996 1996 Holiday Ornament-Snowflake	Yr.Iss.	1996	45.00	45-100
1997 1997 Holiday Ornament-Star	Yr.Iss.	1997	45.00	45-85
1998 1998 Christmas Ornament - Snowflake	Yr.Iss.		49.50	50

Swarovski Crystal Memories Ornaments

YEAR ISSUE	EDITION LIMIT	YEAR RETD.	ISSUE PRICE	*QUOTE U.S.$
1996 Bells 9443NR000003	Open		45.00	45
1996 Boot 9443NR000002	Open		45.00	45
1997 Candy Cane 9443NR000008	Open		45.00	45
1998 Christmas Tree 9443NR000010	Open		45.00	45
1998 Gingerbread House 9443NR000012	Open		45.00	45
1996 Holly 9443NR000004	Open		45.00	45
1997 Icicles 9443NR000007	Open		45.00	45
1998 Locomotive 9443NR000011	Open		45.00	45
1996 Moon 9443NR000001	Open		45.00	45
1997 Pine Cone 9443NR000009	Open		45.00	45
1996 Sun 9443NR000006	Open		45.00	45
1996 Wreath 9443NR000005	Open		45.00	45

Towle Silversmiths

Christmas Angel Medallions - Towle

YEAR ISSUE	EDITION LIMIT	YEAR RETD.	ISSUE PRICE	*QUOTE U.S.$
1991 1991 Angel	Closed	1991	45.00	55-60
1992 1992 Angel	Closed	1992	45.00	50-60
1993 1993 Angel	Closed	1993	45.00	50-80
1994 1994 Angel	Closed	1994	50.00	45-50
1995 1995 Angel	Closed	1995	50.00	45-50
1996 1996 Angel	Closed	1996	50.00	45-50

Remembrance Collection - Towle

YEAR ISSUE	EDITION LIMIT	YEAR RETD.	ISSUE PRICE	*QUOTE U.S.$
1990 1990 - Old Master Snowflake	Closed	1990	40.00	45-90
1991 1991 - Old Master Snowflake	Closed	1991	40.00	45-80
1992 1992 - Old Master Snowflake	Closed	1992	40.00	45-75
1993 1993 - Old Master Snowflake	Closed	1993	40.00	45-75
1994 1994 - Old Master Snowflake	Closed	1994	50.00	45-65
1995 1995 - Old Master Snowflake	Closed	1995	50.00	45-50
1996 1996 - Old Master Snowflake	Closed	1995	50.00	45-50

Songs of Christmas Medallions - Towle

YEAR ISSUE	EDITION LIMIT	YEAR RETD.	ISSUE PRICE	*QUOTE U.S.$
1978 Silent Night Medallion	Closed	1978	35.00	45-100
1979 Deck The Halls	Closed	1979	35.00	45-100
1980 Jingle Bells	Closed	1980	53.00	45-100
1981 Hark the Hearld Angels Sing	Closed	1981	53.00	60-125
1982 O Christmas Tree	Closed	1982	35.00	60-100
1983 Silver Bells	Closed	1983	40.00	60-65
1984 Let It Snow	Closed	1984	30.00	40-45
1985 Chestnuts Roasting on Open Fire	Closed	1985	35.00	60-70
1986 It Came Upon a Midnight Clear	Closed	1986	35.00	60-70
1987 White Christmas	Closed	1987	35.00	60-100

Sterling Cross - Towle

YEAR ISSUE	EDITION LIMIT	YEAR RETD.	ISSUE PRICE	*QUOTE U.S.$
1994 Sterling Cross	Closed	1994	50.00	40-75
1995 Christmas Cross	Closed	1995	50.00	40-50
1996 1996 Cross	Closed	1996	50.00	40-50

Sterling Floral Medallions - Towle

YEAR ISSUE	EDITION LIMIT	YEAR RETD.	ISSUE PRICE	*QUOTE U.S.$
1983 Christmas Rose	Closed	1983	40.00	40
1984 Hawthorn/Glastonbury Thorn	Closed	1984	40.00	40
1985 Poinsettia	Closed	1985	35.00	40-50
1986 Laurel Bay	Closed	1986	35.00	40-45
1987 Mistletoe	Closed	1987	35.00	40-45
1988 Holly	Closed	1988	40.00	50-95
1989 Ivy	Closed	1989	35.00	50-95
1990 Christmas Cactus	Closed	1990	40.00	50-95
1991 Chrysanthemum	Closed	1991	40.00	40-55
1992 Star of Bethlehem	Closed	1992	40.00	40-50

Sterling Nativity Medallions - Towle

YEAR ISSUE	EDITION LIMIT	YEAR RETD.	ISSUE PRICE	*QUOTE U.S.$
1988 The Angel Appeared	Closed	1988	40.00	85-125
1989 The Journey	Closed	1989	40.00	60-85
1990 No Room at the Inn	Closed	1990	40.00	60-65
1991 Tidings of Joy	Closed	1991	40.00	55-60
1992 Star of Bethlehem	Closed	1992	40.00	55-60
1993 Mother and Child	Closed	1993	40.00	55-60
1994 Three Wisemen	Closed	1994	40.00	40-60
1995 Newborn King	Closed	1995	40.00	40-50

Sterling Twelve Days of Christmas Medallions - Towle

YEAR ISSUE	EDITION LIMIT	YEAR RETD.	ISSUE PRICE	*QUOTE U.S.$
1971 Partridge in A Pear Tree	Closed	1971	10.00	300-500
1972 Two Turtle Doves	Closed	1972	10.00	75-125
1973 Three French Hens	Closed	1973	10.00	40-55
1974 Four Colly Birds	Closed	1974	30.00	40-75
1975 Five Gold Rings	Closed	1975	30.00	40-45
1975 Five Gold Rings (vermeil)	Closed	1975	30.00	40-75
1976 Six Geese-a-Laying	Closed	1976	30.00	40-100
1977 Seven Swans-a-Swimming	Closed	1977	35.00	40-100
1977 Seven Swans-a-Swimming (turquoise)	Closed	1977	35.00	40-45
1978 Eight Maids-a-Milking	Closed	1978	37.00	40-45
1979 Nine Ladies Dancing	Closed	1979	37.00	40-50
1980 Ten Lords-a-Leaping	Closed	1980	76.00	40-80
1981 Eleven Pipers Piping	Closed	1981	50.00	40-50
1982 Twelve Drummers Drumming	Closed	1982	35.00	40-50

Twelve Days of Christmas - Towle

YEAR ISSUE	EDITION LIMIT	YEAR RETD.	ISSUE PRICE	*QUOTE U.S.$
1991 Partridge in A Pear Tree In A Wreath	Closed	1991	50.00	40-70
1992 Two Turtle Doves In A Wreath	Closed	1992	50.00	40-60
1993 Three French Hens In A Wreath	Closed	1993	50.00	40-50
1994 Four Colly Birds In A Wreath	Closed	1995	50.00	40-60
1996 Five Gold Rings In A Wreath	Closed	1996	50.00	40-50
1996 Six Geese A Laying In A Wreath	Closed	1996	50.00	40-50

Treasury Masterpiece Editions/Enesco Corporation

Treasury Ornaments Collectors' Club (formerly known as Enesco Treasury of Christmas Ornaments Collectors' Club) - Enesco, unless otherwise noted

YEAR ISSUE	EDITION LIMIT	YEAR RETD.	ISSUE PRICE	*QUOTE U.S.$
1993 The Treasury Card T0001 - Gilmore	Yr.Iss.	1993	Gift	20
1993 Together We Can Shoot For The Stars TR931 - Hahn	Yr.Iss.	1993	17.50	35
1993 Can't Weights For The Holidays TR932	Yr.Iss.	1993	18.50	35
1994 Seedlings Greetings TR933 - Hahn	Yr.Iss.	1994	22.50	23
1994 Spry Fry (Club) TR934	Yr.Iss.	1994	15.00	15
1995 You're the Perfect Fit T0002 - Hahn	Yr.Iss.	1995	Gift	20
1995 You're the Perfect Fit T0102 (Charter Members) - Hahn	Yr.Iss.	1995	Gift	20
1995 Things Go Better With Coke™ TR951	Yr.Iss.	1995	15.00	15
1995 Buttoning Up Our Holiday Best TR952 - Gilmore	Yr.Iss.	1995	22.50	23
1995 Holiday High-Light TR953 - Gilmore	Yr.Iss.	1995	15.00	15
1995 First Class Christmas TR954 - Gilmore	Yr.Iss.	1995	22.50	23
1996 Yo Ho Holidays T0003	Yr.Iss.	1996	Gift	20
1996 Yo Ho Holidays T0103 (Charter Members)	Yr.Iss.	1996	Gift	20
1996 Coca Cola® Choo Choo TR961	Yr.Iss.	1996	35.00	35
1996 Friends Are Tea-riffic TR962	Yr.Iss.	1996	25.00	25
1996 On Track With Coke™ TR963	Yr.Iss.	1996	25.00	25
1996 Riding High TR964 - Hahn	Yr.Iss.	1996	20.00	20
1997 Advent-ures In Ornament Collecting T0004 - Hahn	Yr.Iss.	1997	Gift	N/A
1997 Advent-ures In Ornament Collecting T0104 (Charter Members) - Hahn	Yr.Iss.	1997	Gift	N/A
1997 Coca Cola® Caboose TR971	Yr.Iss.	1997	25.00	25
1997 The Sweetest Nativity TR972 - Hahn	Yr.Iss.	1997	20.00	20

Treasury Masterpiece Editions (formerly known as Enesco Treasury of Christmas Ornaments) - Enesco, unless otherwise noted

YEAR ISSUE	EDITION LIMIT	YEAR RETD.	ISSUE PRICE	*QUOTE U.S.$
1983 Wide Open Throttle E-0242	3-Yr.	1985	12.00	35
1983 Baby's First Christmas E-0271	Yr.Iss.	1983	6.00	N/A
1983 Grandchild's First Christmas E-0272	Yr.Iss.	1983	5.00	N/A
1983 Baby's First Christmas E-0273	3-Yr.	1985	9.00	N/A
1983 Toy Drum Teddy E-0274	4-Yr.	1986	9.00	N/A
1983 Watching At The Window E-0275	3-Yr.	1985	13.00	N/A
1983 To A Special Teacher E-0276	7-Yr.	1989	5.00	15
1983 Toy Shop E-0277	7-Yr.	1989	8.00	50
1983 Merry Christmas Carousel Horse E-0278	7-Yr.	1989	9.00	20
1981 Look Out Below E-6135	2-Yr.	1982	6.00	N/A
1982 Flyin' Santa Christmas Special 1982 E-6136	Yr.Iss.	1982	9.00	75
1981 Flyin' Santa Christmas Special 1981 E-6136	Yr.Iss.	1981	9.00	N/A
1981 Sawin' Elf Helper E-6138	2-Yr.	1982	6.00	40
1981 Snow Shoe-In Santa E-6139	2-Yr.	1982	6.00	35
1981 Baby's First Christmas 1981 E-6145	Yr.Iss.	1981	6.00	N/A
1981 Our Hero E-6146	2-Yr.	1982	4.00	N/A
1981 Whoops E-6147	2-Yr.	1982	3.50	N/A
1981 Whoops, It's 1981 E-6148	Yr.Iss.	1981	7.50	75
1981 Not A Creature Was Stirring E-6149	2-Yr.	1982	4.00	25
1984 Joy To The World E-6209	2-Yr.	1985	9.00	35
1984 Letter To Santa E-6210	2-Yr.	1985	5.00	30
1984 Lucy & Me Someone Special Photo Frame E-6211	3-Yr.	1986	5.00	N/A
1984 Lucy & Me Special Friend Photo Frame E-6211	3-Yr.	1986	5.00	N/A
1984 Lucy & Me Teacher Photo Frame E-6211	3-Yr.	1986	5.00	N/A
1984 Lucy & Me Grandma Photo Frame E-6211	3-Yr.	1986	5.00	N/A
1984 Lucy & Me For Baby Photo Frame E-6211	3-Yr.	1986	5.00	N/A
1984 Lucy & Me Grandpa Photo Frame E-6211	3-Yr.	1986	5.00	N/A
1984 Baby's First Christmas 1984 E-6212 - Gilmore	Yr.Iss.	1984	10.00	30
1984 Merry Christmas Mother E-6213	3-Yr.	1986	10.00	30
1984 Baby's First Christmas 1984 E-6215	Yr.Iss.	1984	6.00	N/A
1984 Ferris Wheel Mice E-6216	2-Yr.	1985	9.00	30
1984 Cuckoo Clock E-6217	2-Yr.	1985	8.00	40
1984 Muppet Babies Baby's First Christmas E-6222 - J. Henson	Yr.Iss.	1984	10.00	45
1984 Muppet Babies Baby's First Christmas E-6223 -J. Henson	Yr.Iss.	1984	10.00	45
1984 Garfield Hark! The Herald Angel E-6224 - J. Davis	2-Yr.	1985	7.50	35
1984 Fun in Santa's Sleigh E-6225 - J. Davis	2-Yr.	1985	12.00	35
1984 Deer! Odie E-6226 -J. Davis	2-Yr.	1985	6.00	30
1984 Garfield The Snow Cat E-6227 - J. Davis	2-Yr.	1985	12.00	35
1984 Peek-A-Bear Baby's First Christmas E-6228	3-Yr.	1986	10.00	N/A
1984 Peek-A-Bear Baby's First Christmas E-6229	3-Yr.	1986	9.00	N/A
1984 Owl Be Home For Christmas E-6230	2-Yr.	1985	8.00	23
1984 Santa's Trolley E-6231	3-Yr.	1986	11.00	50
1984 Holiday Penguin E-6240	3-Yr.	1986	1.50	15-20
1984 Little Drummer E-6241	5-Yr.	1988	2.00	N/A
1984 Happy Holidays E-6248	2-Yr.	1985	2.00	5
1984 Christmas Nest E-6249	2-Yr.	1985	3.00	25
1984 Bunny's Christmas Stocking E-6251	Yr.Iss.	1984	2.00	15
1984 Santa On Ice E-6252	3-Yr.	1986	2.50	25
1984 Treasured Memories The New Sled E-6256	2-Yr.	1985	7.00	N/A
1984 Penguins On Ice E-6280	2-Yr.	1985	7.50	N/A
1984 Up On The House Top E-6281	6-Yr.	1989	9.00	N/A
1984 Grandchild's First Christmas (pink) 1984 E-6286	Yr.Iss.	1984	5.00	N/A
1984 Grandchild's First Christmas (blue) 1984 E-6286	Yr.Iss.	1984	5.00	N/A
1984 Godchild's First Christmas E-6287	3-Yr.	1986	7.00	N/A
1984 Santa In The Box E-6292	2-Yr.	1985	6.00	N/A
1984 Carousel Horse E-6913	2-Yr.	1985	1.50	N/A
1983 Arctic Charmer E-6945	2-Yr.	1984	7.00	N/A
1982 Victorian Sleigh E-6946	4-Yr.	1985	9.00	15
1983 Wing-A-Ding Angel E-6948	3-Yr.	1985	7.00	50
1982 A Saviour Is Born This Day E-6949	8-Yr.	1989	4.00	18
1982 Crescent Santa E-6950 - Gilmore	4-Yr.	1985	10.00	50
1982 Baby's First Christmas 1982 E-6952	Yr.Iss.	1982	10.00	N/A
1982 Polar Bear Fun Whoops, It's 1982 E-6953	Yr.Iss.	1982	10.00	75
1982 Holiday Skier E-6954 - J. Davis	5-Yr.	1986	7.00	N/A
1982 Toy Soldier 1982 E-6957	Yr.Iss.	1982	6.50	N/A
1982 Carousel Horses E-6958	3-Yr.	1984	8.00	20-40
1982 Dear Santa E-6959 - Gilmore	8-Yr.	1989	10.00	25
1982 Merry Christmas Grandma E-6975	3-Yr.	1984	5.00	N/A
1982 Penguin Power E-6977	2-Yr.	1983	6.00	15
1982 Bunny Winter Playground 1982 E-6978	Yr.Iss.	1982	10.00	N/A
1982 Baby's First Christmas 1982 E-6979	Yr.Iss.	1982	10.00	N/A
1983 Carousel Horses E-6980	4-Yr.	1986	8.00	N/A
1982 Grandchild's First Christmas 1982 E-6983	Yr.Iss.	1982	5.00	73
1982 Merry Christmas Teacher E-6984	4-Yr.	1985	7.00	N/A
1983 Garfield Cuts The Ice E-8771 - J. Davis	3-Yr.	1985	6.00	45
1984 A Stocking Full For 1984 E-8773 - J. Davis	Yr.Iss.	1984	6.00	N/A
1983 Stocking Full For 1983 E-8773 - J. Davis	Yr.Iss.	1983	6.00	N/A
1985 Santa Claus Balloon 55794	Yr.Iss.	1985	8.50	20
1985 Carousel Reindeer 55808	4-Yr.	1988	12.00	33
1985 Angel In Flight 55816	4-Yr.	1988	8.00	23
1985 Christmas Penguin 55824	4-Yr.	1988	7.50	43
1985 Merry Christmas Godchild 55832 - Gilmore	5-Yr.	1989	8.00	N/A
1985 Baby's First Christmas 55840	2-Yr.	1986	15.00	N/A
1985 Old Fashioned Rocking Horse 55859	2-Yr.	1986	10.00	15
1985 Child's Second Christmas 55867	5-Yr.	1989	11.00	N/A
1985 Fishing For Stars 55875	5-Yr.	1989	9.00	25

*Quotes have been rounded up to nearest dollar

YEAR ISSUE	EDITION LIMIT	YEAR RETD.	ISSUE PRICE	*QUOTE U.S.$
1985 Baby Blocks 55883	2-Yr.	1986	12.00	N/A
1985 Christmas Toy Chest 55891	5-Yr.	1989	10.00	N/A
1985 Grandchild's First Christmas 55921	5-Yr.	1989	7.00	30
1985 Joy Photo Frame 55956	Yr.Iss.	1985	6.00	N/A
1985 We Three Kings 55964	Yr.Iss.	1985	4.50	20
1985 The Night Before Christmas 55972	2-Yr.	1986	5.00	N/A
1985 Baby's First Christmas 1985 55980	Yr.Iss.	1985	6.00	N/A
1985 Baby Rattle Photo Frame 56006	2-Yr.	1986	5.00	N/A
1985 Baby's First Christmas 1985 56014 - Gilmore	Yr.Iss.	1985	10.00	N/A
1985 Christmas Plane Ride 56049 - L. Rigg	6-Yr.	1990	10.00	N/A
1985 Scottie Celebrating Christmas 56065	5-Yr.	1989	7.50	25
1985 North Pole Native 56073	2-Yr.	1986	9.00	N/A
1985 Skating Walrus 56081	2-Yr.	1986	9.00	20
1985 Ski Time 56111 - J. Davis	Yr.Iss.	1985	13.00	N/A
1985 North Pole Express 56138 - J. Davis	Yr.Iss.	1985	12.00	N/A
1985 Merry Christmas Mother 56146 - J. Davis	Yr.Iss.	1985	8.50	N/A
1985 Hoppy Christmas 56154 - J. Davis	Yr.Iss.	1985	8.50	N/A
1985 Merry Christmas Teacher 56170 - J. Davis	Yr.Iss.	1985	6.00	N/A
1985 Garfield-In-The-Box 56189 - J. Davis	Yr.Iss.	1985	6.50	25
1985 Merry Christmas Grandma 56197	Yr.Iss.	1985	7.00	N/A
1985 Christmas Lights 56200	2-Yr.	1986	8.00	N/A
1985 Victorian Doll House 56251	Yr.Iss.	1985	13.00	40
1985 Tobaoggan Ride 56286	4-Yr.	1988	6.00	15
1985 St. Nicholas Circa 1910 56359	5-Yr.	1989	6.00	15
1985 Look Out Below 56375	Yr.Iss.	1985	8.50	40
1985 Flying Santa Christmas Special 56383	2-Yr.	1986	10.00	N/A
1985 Sawin Elf Helper 56391	Yr.Iss.	1985	8.00	N/A
1985 Snow Shoe-In Santa 56405	Yr.Iss.	1985	8.00	50
1985 Our Hero 56413	Yr.Iss.	1985	5.50	N/A
1985 Not A Creature Was Stirring 56421	2-Yr.	1986	4.00	N/A
1985 Merry Christmas Teacher 56448	Yr.Iss.	1985	9.00	N/A
1985 A Stocking Full For 1985 56464 - J. Davis	Yr.Iss.	1985	6.00	25
1985 Christmas Tree Photo Frame 56871	4-Yr.	1988	10.00	N/A
1995 How...Do I Love Thee 104949	Yr.Iss.	1995	22.50	23
1995 Swishing You Sweet Greetings 105201	Yr.Iss.	1995	20.00	20
1995 Planely Delicious 109665	Yr.Iss.	1996	20.00	20
1996 Spice Up The Season 111724	Yr. Iss.	1996	20.00	20
1995 Home For The Howl-i-days 111732	Yr.Iss.	1995	20.00	20
1995 Time For Refreshment 111872	Yr.Iss.	1995	20.00	20
1995 Holiday Bike Hike 111937	Yr.Iss.	1995	20.00	20
1996 Santa's Sacks 111945 - Hahn	Yr. Iss.	1996	15.00	18
1995 Ho, Ho, Hole in One! 111953	Yr.Iss.	1995	20.00	20
1995 No Time To Spare at Christmas 111961	Yr.Iss.	1995	20.00	20
1995 Hustling Up Some Cheer 112038	Yr.Iss.	1995	20.00	20
1995 Scoring Big at Christmas 112046	Yr.Iss.	1995	20.00	20
1995 Serving Up the Best 112054	Yr.Iss.	1995	17.50	18
1995 Sea-sons Greetings, Teacher 112070 - Gilmore	Yr.Iss.	1996	17.50	18
1995 Siesta Santa 112089 - Gilmore	Yr.Iss.	1995	25.00	25
1995 We've Shared Sew Much 112097 - Gilmore	Yr.Iss.	1995	25.00	25
1995 Toys To Treasure 112119	Yr.Iss.	1995	20.00	20
1995 To Santa, Post Haste 112151 - Gilmore	Yr.Iss.	1995	15.00	15
1995 Yule Logon For Christmas Cheer 122513	Yr.Iss.	1995	20.00	20
1995 Pretty Up For The Holidays 125830 - Butcher	Yr.Iss.	1995	20.00	20
1995 You Bring The Love to Christmas 125849 - Butcher	Yr.Iss.	1995	15.00	15
1995 Happy Birthday Jesus 125857 - Butcher	Yr.Iss.	1995	15.00	15
1995 Let's Snuggle Together For Christmas 125865 - Butcher	Yr.Iss.	1995	15.00	15
1995 I'm In A Spin Over You 125873 - Butcher	Yr.Iss.	1995	15.00	15
1995 Our First Christmas Together 125881 - Butcher	Yr.Iss.	1995	22.50	23
1995 Twinkle, Twinkle Christmas Star 125903 - Butcher	Yr.Iss.	1995	17.50	18
1995 Bringing Holiday Wishes To You 125911 - Butcher	Yr.Iss.	1995	22.50	23
1995 You Pull The Strings To My Heart 125938 - Butcher	Yr.Iss.	1995	20.00	20
1995 Baby's First Christmas 125946 - Butcher	Yr.Iss.	1995	15.00	15
1995 Baby's First Christmas 125954 - Butcher	Yr.Iss.	1995	15.00	15
1995 Friends Are The Greatest Treasure 125962 - Butcher	20,000	1995	25.00	25
1995 4-Alarm Christmas 128767 - Gilmore	Yr.Iss.	1995	17.50	18
1995 Truckin'/1956 Ford F-100 Truck 128813	Yr.Iss.	1995	25.00	20-25
1995 1955 Red Ford Thunderbird 128821	19,550	1995	20.00	28
1995 57 HVN/1957 Chevy Bel Air 128848	Yr.Iss.	1995	20.00	20
1995 1965 Chevrolet Corvette Stingray 128856	Yr.Iss.	1995	20.00	20
1995 Mom's Taxi/Dodge Caravan 128872	Yr.Iss.	1995	25.00	25
1995 Choc Full of Wishes 128945	Yr.Iss.	1995	20.00	20
1995 Have a Coke and a Smile™ 128953	Yr.Iss.	1995	22.50	23
1995 Trunk Full of Treasures 128961	20,000	1995	25.00	25
1995 Make Mine a Coke™ 128988	Yr.Iss.	1995	25.00	25
1995 Dashing Through the Snow 128996	Yr.Iss.	1995	20.00	20
1995 Happy Yuleglide 129003	Yr.Iss.	1995	17.50	18
1995 Santa's Speedway 129011	Yr.Iss.	1995	20.00	20
1995 You're My Cup of Tea 129038	Yr.Iss.	1996	20.00	20
1995 Crackin' a Smile 129046	Yr.Iss.	1995	17.50	18
1995 Rx:Mas Greetings 129054	Yr.Iss.	1995	17.50	18
1996 Special Bear-Livery 129062	Yr.Iss.	1996	15.00	15
1995 Merry McMeal 129070	Yr.Iss.	1995	17.50	18
1995 Above the Crowd 129089	Yr.Iss.	1995	20.00	20
1995 Mickey at the Helm 132063	Yr.Iss.	1995	17.50	18
1995 1959 Cadillac Eldorado 132705	Yr.Iss.	1995	20.00	20
1996 Catch Of The Holiday 132888 - Hahn	Yr.Iss.	1996	20.00	20
1995 Jackpot Joy! 132896 - Hahn	Yr.Iss.	1995	17.50	18
1995 Get in the Spirit...Recycle 132918 - Hahn	Yr.Iss.	1996	17.50	18
1995 Miss Merry's Secret 132934 - Hahn	Yr.Iss.	1995	20.00	20
1995 ...Good Will Toward Men 132942 - Hahn	19,450	1995	25.00	25
1995 Friendships Bloom Through All Seasons 132950 - Hahn	Yr.Iss.	1995	22.50	23
1995 Merry Monopoly 132969	Yr.Iss.	1996	22.50	23
1995 The Night B 4 Christmas 134848 - Hahn	Yr.Iss.	1995	20.00	20
1996 A Cup Of Cheer 135070 - Gilmore	Yr.Iss.	1996	25.00	25
1995 Bubblin' With Joy 136581	Yr.Iss.	1995	15.00	15
1996 Steppin' With Minnie 136603	Yr.Iss.	1996	13.50	14
1995 Minnie's Merry Christmas 136611	Yr.Iss.	1995	20.00	20
1996 Motorcycle Mickey 136654	Yr.Iss.	1996	25.00	25
1995 Makin' Tracks With Mickey 136662	Yr.Iss.	1995	20.00	20
1995 Mickey's Airmail 136670	Yr.Iss.	1996	20.00	20
1995 Holiday Bound 136689	Yr.Iss.	1996	20.00	20
1995 Goofed-Up! 136697	Yr.Iss.	1996	20.00	20
1995 On The Ball At Christmas 136700	Yr.Iss.	1996	15.00	15
1995 Sweet on You 136719	Yr.Iss.	1995	22.50	23
1995 Nutty About Christmas 137030	Yr.Iss.	1995	22.50	23
1995 Tinkertoy Joy 137049	Yr.Iss.	1996	20.00	20
1995 Starring Roll At Christmas 137057	Yr.Iss.	1995	17.50	18
1995 A Thimble of the Season 137243 - Gilmore	Yr.Iss.	1996	22.50	23
1995 A Little Something Extra...Extra 137251	10,000	1995	25.00	25
1995 The Maze Of Our Lives 139599 - Hahn	Yr.Iss.	1995	17.50	18
1995 A Sip For Good Measure 139610	Yr.Iss.	1995	17.50	18
1995 Christmas Fishes, Dad 139629 - Hahn	Yr.Iss.	1996	17.50	18
1995 Christmas Is In The Bag 139645	Yr.Iss.	1995	17.50	18
1995 Gotta Have a Clue 139653	Yr.Iss.	1995	20.00	20
1995 Fun In Hand 139661	Yr.Iss.	1995	17.50	18
1995 Christmas Cuddle 139688	Yr.Iss.	1996	20.00	20
1995 Dreaming Of the One I Love 139696	Yr.Iss.	1996	25.00	25
1995 Sneaking a Peek 139718	Yr.Iss.	1996	22.50	23
1995 Christmas Eve Mischief 139726	Yr.Iss.	1995	17.50	18
1995 All Tucked In 139734	Yr.Iss.	1995	15.00	15
1995 Merry Christmas To Me 139742	Yr.Iss.	1995	20.00	20
1995 Looking Our Holiday Best 139750	Yr.Iss.	1995	25.00	25
1995 Christmas Vacation 142158	Yr.Iss.	1996	20.00	20
1995 Just Fore Christmas 142174	Yr.Iss.	1996	15.00	15
1995 Christmas Belle 142182	Yr.Iss.	1996	20.00	20
1995 Tail Waggin' Wishes 142190	Yr.Iss.	1995	17.50	18
1995 Holiday Ride 142204	Yr.Iss.	1995	17.50	18
1995 A Carousel For Ariel 142212	Yr.Iss.	1995	17.50	18
1995 On The Move At Christmas 142220 - Hahn	Yr.Iss.	1995	17.50	18
1995 T-Bird 146838	Yr.Iss.	1995	20.00	20
1996 Swinging On A Star 166642	Yr.Iss.	1996	20.00	20
1996 A-Joy Matie, Throw Me A Lifesavers 166677	Yr.Iss.	1996	20.00	20
1996 It's Plane To See...Coke Is It 166723	Yr.Iss.	1996	25.00	25
1996 A Century Of Good Taste 166774	Yr.Iss.	1996	25.00	25
1996 Servin' Up Joy 166847	Yr.Iss.	1996	20.00	20
1996 In-Line To Help Santa 166855	Yr.Iss.	1996	20.00	10-20
1996 I Love My Daughter 166863	Yr.Iss.	1996	9.00	9
1996 I Love Grandma 166898	Yr.Iss.	1996	9.00	9
1996 I Love Dad 166901	Yr.Iss.	1996	9.00	9
1996 I Love Mom 166928	Yr.Iss.	1996	9.00	9
1996 I Love My Godchild 166936	Yr.Iss.	1996	9.00	9
1996 Baby's 1st Christmas 166944	Yr.Iss.	1996	9.00	9
1996 A Boot Full Of Cheer 166952	Yr.Iss.	1996	20.00	20
1996 Summons For A Merry Christmas 166960	Yr.Iss.	1996	22.50	23
1996 An Appointment With Santa 166979	Yr.Iss.	1996	20.00	20
1996 Play It Again, Nick 166987	Yr.Iss.	1996	17.50	18
1996 Holiday Tinkertoy Tree 166995	Yr.Iss.	1996	17.50	18
1996 A Picture Perfect Pair 167002	Yr.Iss.	1996	25.00	25
1996 Santa's On The Line 167037	Yr.Iss.	1996	25.00	18-25
1996 Downhill Delivery 167053	Yr.Iss.	1996	25.00	25
1996 On A Roll With Diet Coke 167061	Yr.Iss.	1996	20.00	20
1996 Hold On, Santa! 167088	Yr.Iss.	1996	25.00	25
1996 There's A Friendship Brewing 167096 - Hahn	Yr.Iss.	1996	25.00	25
1996 Tails A' Waggin' 167126	Yr.Iss.	1996	20.00	20
1996 In Store For More 167134	15,000	1996	25.00	25
1996 Jeep Grand Cherokee 167215	Yr.Iss.	1996	22.50	15-23
1996 Chevy Blazer 167223	Yr.Iss.	1996	22.50	23
1996 Ford Explorer 167231	Yr.Iss.	1996	22.50	23
1996 Dodge Ram Truck 167258	Yr.Iss.	1996	22.50	23
1996 Trees To Please 168378	Yr.Iss.	1996	25.00	25
1996 Plane Crazy 168386	Yr.Iss.	1996	22.50	23
1996 I Love My Son 168432	Yr.Iss.	1996	9.00	9
1996 #1 Coach 168440	Yr.Iss.	1996	9.00	9
1996 Goin' Fishin' 168459	Yr.Iss.	1996	22.50	23
1996 Gifts From Mickey 168467	Yr.Iss.	1996	20.00	20
1996 All Fired Up For Christmas 168475	Yr.Iss.	1996	25.00	25
1996 Minnie's Mall Haul 168491	Yr.Iss.	1996	25.00	25
1996 A Magic Moment 172197	Yr.Iss.	1996	17.50	18
1996 Happy's Holiday 172200	Yr.Iss.	1996	17.50	18
1996 Sitting Pretty 172219	Yr.Iss.	1996	17.50	18
1996 Life's Sweet Choices 172634	Yr.Iss.	1996	25.00	25
1996 Holiday In Bloom 172669	Yr.Iss.	1996	25.00	25
1996 Have A Cracker Jack Christmas 172979	Yr.Iss.	1996	25.00	20
1996 Hair's The Place 173029 - Hahn	Yr.Iss.	1996	25.00	25
1996 Merry Manicure 173339 - Hahn	Yr.Iss.	1996	25.00	25
1996 100 Years...And Still On A Roll 173770	19,960	1996	17.50	18
1996 Tracking Reindeer Pause 173789 - Hahn	Yr.Iss.	1996	25.00	25
1996 Holiday Dreams Of Green 173797 - Hahn	Yr.Iss.	1996	15.00	15
1996 1965 Ford Mustang 173800	Yr.Iss.	1996	22.50	23
1996 Toyland, Joyland 173878	Yr.Iss.	1996	20.00	20
1996 Tobin's Debut Dancer 173886 - Fraley	20,000	1996	20.00	20
1996 Thou Art My Lamp, O Lord 173894 - Hahn	Yr.Iss.	1996	25.00	25
1996 'Tis The Season To Be Nutty 175234	Yr.Iss.	1996	17.50	18
1996 1956 Chevy Corvette 175269	19,560	1996	22.50	23
1996 A World Of Good Taste 175420	18,600	1996	20.00	20
1996 It's Time For Christmas 175455	Yr.Iss.	1996	25.00	25
1996 15 Years Of Hits 175463	10,000	1996	25.00	25
1996 Sew Darn Cute 176761 - Hahn	Yr.Iss.	1996	25.00	25
1996 Decked Out For Christmas 176796 - Hahn	Yr.Iss.	1996	25.00	10-25
1996 Campaign For Christmas 176818	19,960	1996	17.50	15-18
1996 Delivering Holiday Cheers 177318	Yr.Iss.	1996	25.00	25
1996 A Splash Of Cool Yule 213713	Yr.Iss.	1996	20.00	20
1997 100 Years of Soup-erb Good Taste! 265586	Yr.Iss.	1997	20.00	20
1997 Tobin's Graceful Steed 265594 - Fraley	Yr.Iss.	1997	20.00	20
1997 Movin' And Groovin' 270482	Yr.Iss.	1997	22.50	23
1997 Twist And Shout, "Have A Coke!" 277398	Yr.Iss.	1997	25.00	25
1997 Cracker Jack...The Home Run Snack 277401	Yr.Iss.	1997	25.00	25
1997 I'm So Glad I Fondue As A Friend 277428 - Hahn	Yr.Iss.	1997	20.00	20
1997 Workin' 'Round The Clock 277436	Yr.Iss.	1997	22.50	23
1997 WWW.HappyHolidays!.Com 277444	Yr.Iss.	1997	25.00	25
1997 Always Cool With Coke 277967	Yr.Iss.	1997	22.50	23
1997 The Forecast Calls For Coke 277983	Yr.Iss.	1997	20.00	20
1997 Stockin' Up For The Holidays 277991	Yr.Iss.	1997	22.50	23
1997 Home Sweet Home 278017	Yr.Iss.	1997	25.00	25
1997 Ordering Up A Merry Christmas 278068	Yr.Iss.	1997	25.00	25
1997 Best Bet's A 'Vette 278092	Yr.Iss.	1997	22.50	23
1997 Deere Santa 278106	Yr.Iss.	1997	25.00	25
1997 On Track With Santa 278114	Yr.Iss.	1997	20.00	20
1997 Prepare For Battle 278122	Yr.Iss.	1997	25.00	25
1997 Have Your Cake & Bake It, Too 278130	Yr.Iss.	1997	20.00	20
1997 G.I. Joe Loves Christmas 278149	Yr.Iss.	1997	20.00	20
1997 Primping Iron 278165 - Hahn	Yr.Iss.	1997	20.00	20
1997 On Course With Santa 278394 - Hahn	Yr.Iss.	1997	20.00	20
1997 Ice Cream Of The Crop 278408	Yr.Iss.	1997	20.00	20
1997 50 Years Of Miracles 278432	Yr.Iss.	1997	20.00	20
1997 Beep Me Up! 278440	Yr.Iss.	1997	20.00	20
1997 Bubbling With Cheer 278467 - Hahn	Yr.Iss.	1997	20.00	20
1997 Fired Up For Christmas 278491 - Hahn	Yr.Iss.	1997	22.50	23
1997 Spare Time For Christmas Fun 280291 - Hahn	Yr.Iss.	1997	25.00	25
1997 Everyone Knows It's Slinky 280992	Yr.Iss.	1997	22.50	23
1997 Cherish The Joy 281263 - Hillman	Yr.Iss.	1997	25.00	25-30
1997 Ho, Ho, Ho, A Grilling We Will Go! 281301	Yr.Iss.	1997	20.00	20
1997 Hula Hoop Holidays 281336	Yr.Iss.	1997	20.00	20
1997 Howl-A-Day Pet Shoppe 286192 - Hahn	Yr.Iss.	1997	25.00	25
1997 Heading 4-Wheel Merry Christmas 287059	Yr.Iss.	1997	22.50	23
1997 For All You Do, Merry Christmas To You 290858	Yr.Iss.	1997	25.00	25
1997 Play It Again, Santa 295256	Yr.Iss.	1997	20.00	20
1988 Making A Point 489212 - G.G. Santiago	3-Yr.	1990	10.00	N/A
1988 Mouse Upon A Pipe 489220 - G.G. Santiago	2-Yr.	1989	10.00	12
1988 North Pole Deadline 489387	3-Yr.	1990	13.50	25
1988 Christmas Pin-Up 489409	2-Yr.	1989	11.00	30
1988 Airmail For Teacher 489425 - Gilmore	3-Yr.	1990	13.50	N/A
1994 Sending You A Season's Greetings 550140 - Butcher	Yr.Iss.	1994	25.00	25
1994 Goofy Delivery 550639	Yr.Iss.	1994	22.50	23
1994 Happy Howl-idays 550647	Yr.Iss.	1994	22.50	23
1994 Christmas Crusin' 550655	Yr.Iss.	1994	22.50	23
1994 Holiday Honeys 550663	Yr.Iss.	1994	20.00	20

*Quotes have been rounded up to nearest dollar

Treasury Masterpiece Editions/Enesco Corporation to Treasury Masterpiece Editions/Enesco Corporation

YEAR ISSUE	EDITION LIMIT	YEAR RETD.	ISSUE PRICE	*QUOTE U.S.$
1994 May Your Holiday Be Brightened With Love 550698 - Butcher	Yr.Iss.	1994	15.00	15
1994 May All Your Wishes Come True 550701 - Butcher	Yr.Iss.	1994	20.00	20
1994 Baby's First Christmas 550728 - Butcher	Yr.Iss.	1994	20.00	20
1994 Baby's First Christmas 550736 - Butcher	Yr.Iss.	1994	20.00	20
1994 Our First Christmas Together 550744 - Butcher	Yr.Iss.	1994	25.00	25
1994 Drumming Up A Season Of Joy 550752 - Butcher	Yr.Iss.	1994	18.50	19
1994 Friendships Warm The Holidays 550760 - Butcher	Yr.Iss.	1994	20.00	20
1994 Dropping In For The Holidays 550779 - Butcher	Yr.Iss.	1994	20.00	20
1994 Ringing Up Holiday Wishes 550787 - Butcher	Yr.Iss.	1994	18.50	19
1994 A Child Is Born 550795 - Butcher	Yr.Iss.	1995	25.00	25
1994 Tis The Season To Go Shopping 550817 - Butcher	Yr.Iss.	1994	22.50	23
1994 The Way To A Mouse's Heart 550922	Yr.Iss.	1994	15.00	15
1994 Teed-Off Donald 550930	Yr.Iss.	1994	15.00	15
1994 Holiday Show-Stopper 550949	Yr.Iss.	1995	15.00	15
1994 Answering Christmas Wishes 551023	Yr.Iss.	1994	17.50	18
1994 Pure Christmas Pleasure 551066	Yr.Iss.	1995	20.00	20
1986 First Christmas Together 1986 551171	Yr.Iss.	1986	9.00	15-35
1986 Elf Stringing Popcorn 551198	4-Yr.	1989	10.00	20-30
1986 Christmas Scottie 551201	4-Yr.	1989	7.00	15-30
1986 Santa and Child 551236	4-Yr.	1989	13.50	25-50
1986 The Christmas Angel 551244	4-Yr.	1989	22.50	75
1986 Peace, Love, Joy Carousel Unicorn 551252 - Gilmore	4-Yr.	1989	12.00	38
1986 Have a Heavenly Holiday 551260	4-Yr.	1989	9.00	N/A
1986 Siamese Kitten 551279	4-Yr.	1989	9.00	36
1986 Old Fashioned Doll House 551287	4-Yr.	1989	15.00	N/A
1986 Holiday Fisherman 551309	3-Yr.	1988	8.00	40
1986 Antique Toy 551317	3-Yr.	1988	9.00	10
1986 Time For Christmas 551325 - Gilmore	4-Yr.	1989	13.00	N/A
1986 Christmas Calendar 551333	2-Yr.	1987	7.00	12
1994 Good Tidings, Tidings, Tidings, Tidings 551333	Yr.Iss.	1995	20.00	15-20
1986 Merry Christmas 551341 - Gilmore	3-Yr.	1988	8.00	40-50
1994 From Our House To Yours 551384 - Gilmore	Yr.Iss.	1994	25.00	25
1994 Sugar 'N' Spice For Someone Nice 551406 - Gilmore	Yr.Iss.	1994	30.00	30
1994 Picture Perfect Christmas 551465	Yr.Iss.	1994	15.00	15
1994 Toodles 551503 - Zimnicki	Yr.Iss.	1994	25.00	25
1994 A Bough For Belle! 551554	Yr.Iss.	1995	18.50	15-19
1986 The Santa Claus Shoppe Circa 1905 551562 - J. Grossman	4-Yr.	1989	8.00	15
1994 Ariel's Christmas Surprise! 551570	Yr.Iss.	1994	20.00	20
1994 Merry Little Two-Step 551589	Yr.Iss.	1995	12.50	13
1994 Sweets For My Sweetie 551600	Yr.Iss.	1994	15.00	15
1994 Friends Are The Spice of Life - 551619 - Hahn	Yr.Iss.	1995	20.00	20
1994 Cool Cruise/1964 1/2 Ford Mustang 551635	19,640	1994	20.00	20
1986 Baby Bear Sleigh 551651 - Gilmore	3-Yr.	1988	9.00	30
1994 Special Delivery 561657	Yr.Iss.	1994	20.00	20
1986 Baby's First Christmas 1986 551678 - Gilmore	Yr.Iss.	1986	10.00	20
1986 First Christmas Together 551708	3-Yr.	1988	6.00	10
1986 Baby's First Christmas 551716	3-Yr.	1988	5.50	10
1986 Baby's First Christmas 1986 551724	Yr.Iss.	1986	6.50	30
1994 A Christmas Tail 551759	Yr.Iss.	1995	20.00	20
1994 Merry Mischief- 551767	Yr.Iss.	1994	15.00	15
1994 L'il Stocking Stuffer 551791	Yr.Iss.	1994	17.50	18
1994 Once Upon A Time 551805	Yr.Iss.	1994	15.00	15
1994 Wishing Upon A Star 551813	Yr.Iss.	1994	18.50	19
1994 A Real Boy For Christmas 551821	Yr.Iss.	1995	15.00	15
1986 Peek-A-Bear Grandchild's First Christmas	Yr.Iss.	1986	6.00	23
1986 Peek-A-Bear in Stocking Present 552089	4-Yr.	1989	2.50	N/A
1986 Peek-A-Bear in Box Present 552089	4-Yr.	1989	2.50	N/A
1986 Peek-A-Bear in Shopping Bag Present 552089	4-Yr.	1989	2.50	N/A
1986 Peek-A-Bear in Cloth Bag Present 552089	4-Yr.	1989	2.50	N/A
1986 Merry Christmas (Boy) 552186 - L. Rigg	Yr.Iss.	1986	8.00	N/A
1994 Minnie's Holiday Treasure 552216	Yr.Iss.	1994	12.00	12
1994 Sweet Holidays 552259 - Butcher	Yr.Iss.	1994	12.00	12
1986 Merry Christmas (Girl) 552534 - L. Rigg	Yr.Iss.	1986	8.00	N/A
1986 Lucy & Me Christmas Tree 552542 - L. Rigg	3-Yr.	1988	7.00	25
1986 Santa's Helpers 552607	3-Yr.	1988	2.50	N/A
1986 My Special Friend 552615	3-Yr.	1988	6.00	10
1986 Christmas Wishes From Panda 552623	3-Yr.	1988	6.00	N/A
1986 Lucy & Me Ski Time 552658 - L. Rigg	2-Yr.	1987	6.50	30
1986 Merry Christmas Teacher 552666	3-Yr.	1988	6.50	N/A
1986 Country Cousins Merry Christmas, Mom (Girl on Skates) 552704	3-Yr.	1988	7.00	23
1986 Country Cousins Merry Christmas, Dad (Girl on Skates) 552704	3-Yr.	1988	7.00	23
1986 Country Cousins Merry Christmas, Mom (Boy w/Kite) 552712	4-Yr.	1989	7.00	23
1986 Country Cousins Merry Christmas, Dad (Boy w/Kite) 552712	4-Yr.	1989	7.00	25
1986 Grandmother's Little Angel 552747	4-Yr.	1989	8.00	N/A
1988 Puppy's 1st Christmas 552909	Yr.Iss.	1988	4.00	N/A
1988 Kitty's 1st Christmas 552917	Yr.Iss.	1988	4.00	25
1988 Merry Christmas Puppy 552925	Yr.Iss.	1988	3.50	N/A
1988 Merry Christmas Kitty 552933	Yr.Iss.	1988	3.50	N/A
1986 I Love My Grandparents 553263	Yr.Iss.	1986	6.00	N/A
1986 Merry Christmas Mom & Dad 553271	Yr.Iss.	1986	6.00	N/A
1986 Hollycopter 553344	4-Yr.	1989	13.50	35
1986 From Our House To Your House 553360	3-Yr.	1988	15.00	40
1986 Christmas Rattle 553379	3-Yr.	1988	8.00	35
1986 Bah, Humbug! 553387	4-Yr.	1989	9.00	N/A
1986 God Bless Us Everyone 553395	4-Yr.	1989	10.00	15
1987 Carousel Mobile 553409	3-Yr.	1989	15.00	50
1986 Holiday Train 553417	4-Yr.	1989	10.00	N/A
1986 Lighten Up! 553603 - J. Davis	5-Yr.	1990	10.00	N/A
1986 Gift Wrap Odie 553611 - J. Davis	Yr.Iss.	1986	7.00	20
1986 Merry Christmas 553646	4-Yr.	1989	8.00	N/A
1987 M.V.B. (Most Valuable Bear) Golfing 554219	2-Yr.	1988	3.00	N/A
1987 M.V.B. (Most Valuable Bear) Ice Hockey 554219	2-Yr.	1988	3.00	N/A
1987 M.V.B. (Most Valuable Bear) Skiing 554219	2-Yr.	1988	3.00	N/A
1987 M.V.B. (Most Valuable Bear) Bowling 554219	2-Yr.	1988	3.00	N/A
1988 1st Christmas Together 554537 - Gilmore	3-Yr.	1990	15.00	N/A
1988 An Eye On Christmas 554545 - Gilmore	3-Yr.	1990	22.50	60
1988 A Mouse Check 554553 - Gilmore	3-Yr.	1990	13.50	45
1988 Merry Christmas Engine 554561	2-Yr.	1989	22.50	35
1989 Sardine Express 554588 - Gilmore	2-Yr.	1990	17.50	30
1988 1st Christmas Together 1988 554596	Yr.Iss.	1988	10.00	N/A
1988 Forever Friends 554626 - Gilmore	2-Yr.	1989	12.00	27
1988 Santa's Survey 554642	2-Yr.	1989	35.00	75-100
1989 Old Town Church 554871 - Gilmore	2-Yr.	1990	17.50	20
1988 A Chipmunk Holiday 554898 - Gilmore	3-Yr.	1990	11.00	25
1988 Christmas Is Coming 554901	3-Yr.	1990	12.00	12
1988 Baby's First Christmas 1988 554928	Yr.Iss.	1988	7.50	N/A
1988 Baby's First Christmas 1988 554936 - Gilmore	Yr.Iss.	1988	10.00	25
1988 The Christmas Train 554944	3-Yr.	1990	15.00	N/A
1988 Li'l Drummer Bear 554952 - Gilmore	3-Yr.	1990	12.00	12
1987 Baby's First Christmas 555061	3-Yr.	1989	12.00	N/A
1987 Baby's First Christmas 555088	3-Yr.	1989	7.50	N/A
1987 Baby's First Christmas 555118	3-Yr.	1989	6.00	N/A
1988 Sugar Plum Bearies 555193	Yr.Iss.	1988	4.50	N/A
1987 Garfield Merry Kissmas 555215 - J. Davis	3-Yr.	1989	8.50	30
1988 Sleigh Away 555401	2-Yr.	1989	12.00	N/A
1987 Merry Christmas (Boy) 555428 - L. Rigg	Yr.Iss.	1987	8.00	N/A
1987 Merry Christmas (Girl) 555436 - L. Rigg	Yr.Iss.	1987	8.00	N/A
1987 Lucy & Me Storybook Bear 555444 - L. Rigg	3-Yr.	1989	6.50	N/A
1987 Time For Christmas 555452 - L. Rigg	3-Yr.	1989	12.00	20
1987 Lucy & Me Angel On A Cloud 555487 - L. Rigg	3-Yr.	1989	8.00	35
1987 Teddy's Stocking 555940 - Gilmore	3-Yr.	1989	10.00	N/A
1987 Kitty's Jack-In-The-Box 555959	3-Yr.	1989	11.00	30
1987 Merry Christmas Teacher 555967	3-Yr.	1989	7.50	N/A
1987 Mouse In A Mitten 555975	3-Yr.	1989	7.50	N/A
1987 Boy On A Rocking Horse 555983	3-Yr.	1989	12.00	18
1987 Peek-A-Bear Letter To Santa 555991	2-Yr.	1988	8.00	30
1987 Garfield Sugar Plum Fairy 556009 - J. Davis	3-Yr.	1989	8.50	12
1987 Garfield The Nutcracker 556017 - J. Davis	4-Yr.	1990	8.50	10-20
1987 Joy To The World Carousel Lion 556025 - Gilmore	3-Yr.	1989	12.00	25
1988 Home Sweet Home 556033 - Gilmore	2-Yr.	1989	15.00	40
1988 Baby's First Christmas 556041	3-Yr.	1990	10.00	20
1988 Little Sailor Elf 556068	2-Yr.	1989	10.00	12-20
1987 Carousel Goose 556076	3-Yr.	1989	17.00	40
1988 Night Caps Mom 556084	Yr.Iss.	1988	5.50	N/A
1988 Night Caps Dad 556084	Yr.Iss.	1988	5.50	N/A
1988 Night Caps Grandpa 556084	Yr.Iss.	1988	5.50	N/A
1988 Night Caps Grandma 556084	Yr.Iss.	1988	5.50	N/A
1988 Rocking Horse Past Joys 556157	2-Yr.	1989	10.00	20
1987 Partridge In A Pear Tree 556173 - Gilmore	3-Yr.	1989	9.00	35
1987 Skating Santa 1987 556211	Yr.Iss.	1987	13.50	75
1987 Baby's First Christmas 1987 556238 - Gilmore	Yr.Iss.	1987	10.00	25
1987 Baby's First Christmas 1987 556254	Yr.Iss.	1987	7.00	25
1988 Teddy's Suspenders 556262	3-Yr.	1990	8.50	22
1987 Baby's First Christmas (boy) 1987 556297	Yr.Iss.	1987	2.00	N/A
1987 Baby's First Christmas (girl) 1987 556297	Yr.Iss.	1987	2.00	N/A
1987 Beary Christmas Family (Grandma) 556300	2-Yr.	1988	2.00	N/A
1987 Beary Christmas Family (Grandpa) 556300	2-Yr.	1988	2.00	N/A
1987 Beary Christmas Family (Mom) 556300	2-Yr.	1988	2.00	N/A
1987 Beary Christmas Family (Dad) 556300	2-Yr.	1988	2.00	N/A
1987 Beary Christmas Family (Brother) 556300	2-Yr.	1988	2.00	N/A
1987 Beary Christmas Family (Sister)556300	2-Yr.	1988	2.00	N/A
1987 Merry Christmas Teacher (Boy) 556319	2-Yr.	1988	2.00	N/A
1987 Merry Christmas Teacher (Girl) 556319	2-Yr.	1988	2.00	N/A
1987 1st Christmas Together 1987 556335	Yr.Iss.	1987	9.00	18
1987 Katie Goes Ice Skating 556378	3-Yr.	1989	8.00	30
1987 Scooter Snowman 556386	3-Yr.	1989	8.00	30
1987 Santa's List 556394	3-Yr.	1989	7.00	23
1988 Kitty's Bed 556408	3-Yr.	1989	12.00	30
1988 Grandchild's First Christmas 556416	2-Yr.	1989	10.00	N/A
1987 Two Turtledoves 556432 - Gilmore	2-Yr.	1989	9.00	30
1987 Three French Hens 556440 - Gilmore	3-Yr.	1989	9.00	30
1988 Four Calling Birds 556459 - Gilmore	3-Yr.	1990	11.00	30
1988 Teddy Takes A Spin 556467	3-Yr.	1990	13.00	35
1987 Tiny Toy Thimble Mobile 556475	2-Yr.	1988	12.00	35
1987 Bucket O'Love (Puppy's 1st Christmas) 556491	2-Yr.	1988	2.50	N/A
1987 Bucket O'Love (Kitty's 1st Christmas) 556491	2-Yr.	1988	2.50	N/A
1987 Bucket O'Love (Christmas Kitty) 556491	2-Yr.	1988	2.50	N/A
1987 Bucket O'Love (Christmas Puppy) 556491	2-Yr.	1988	2.50	N/A
1987 Puppy Love 556505	3-Yr.	1989	6.00	N/A
1987 Peek-A-Bear My Special Friend 556513	4-Yr.	1990	6.00	30
1987 Our First Christmas Together 556548	3-Yr.	1989	13.00	20
1987 Three Little Bears 556556	3-Yr.	1989	7.50	15
1988 Lucy & Me Mailbox Bear 556564 - L. Rigg	3-Yr.	1990	3.00	N/A
1987 Twinkle Bear 556572 - Gilmore	3-Yr.	1989	8.00	N/A
1988 I'm Dreaming Of A Bright Christmas 556602	Yr.Iss.	1988	2.50	N/A
1988 Christmas Train 557196	2-Yr.	1989	10.00	N/A
1988 Dairy Christmas 557501 - M. Cook	2-Yr.	1989	10.00	30
1988 Merry Christmas (Boy) 557595 - L. Rigg	Yr.Iss.	1988	10.00	N/A
1988 Merry Christmas (Girl) 557609 - L. Rigg	Yr.Iss.	1988	10.00	N/A
1988 Toy Chest Keepsake 558206 - L. Rigg	3-Yr.	1990	12.50	30
1988 Teddy Bear Greetings 558214 - L. Rigg	3-Yr.	1990	8.00	30
1988 Jester Bear 558222 - L. Rigg	2-Yr.	1989	8.00	N/A
1988 Night-Watch Cat 558362 - J. Davis	3-Yr.	1990	13.00	35
1988 Christmas Thim-bell Mouse 558389	Yr.Iss.	1988	4.00	30
1988 Christmas Thim-bell Snowman 558389	Yr.Iss.	1988	4.00	N/A
1988 Christmas Thim-bell Bear 558389	Yr.Iss.	1988	4.00	N/A
1988 Christmas Thim-bell Santa 558389	Yr.Iss.	1988	4.00	N/A
1988 Baby's First Christmas 558397 - D. Parker	3-Yr.	1990	16.00	30
1988 Christmas Tradition 558400 - Gilmore	2-Yr.	1989	10.00	25
1988 Stocking Story 558419 - G.G. Santiago	3-Yr.	1990	10.00	23
1988 Winter Tale 558427 - G.G. Santiago	2-Yr.	1989	6.00	N/A
1988 Party Mouse 558435 - G.G. Santiago	3-Yr.	1990	12.00	30
1988 Christmas Watch 558443 - G.G. Santiago	2-Yr.	1989	11.00	32
1988 Christmas Vacation 558451 - G.G. Santiago	3-Yr.	1990	8.00	23
1988 Sweet Cherub 558478 - G.G. Santiago	3-Yr.	1990	7.00	8
1988 Time Out 558486 - G.G. Santiago	2-Yr.	1989	11.00	N/A
1988 The Ice Fairy 558516 - G.G. Santiago	3-Yr.	1990	23.00	45-55
1988 Santa Turtle 558559	2-Yr.	1989	10.00	35
1988 The Teddy Bear Ball 558567	3-Yr.	1990	10.00	25
1988 Turtle Greetings 558583	2-Yr.	1989	8.50	25
1988 Happy Howladays 558605	Yr.Iss.	1988	7.00	15
1988 Special Delivery 558699 - J. Davis	3-Yr.	1990	9.00	30
1988 Deer Garfield 558702 - J. Davis	3-Yr.	1990	12.00	30
1988 Garfield Bags O' Fun 558761 - J. Davis	Yr.Iss.	1988	3.30	N/A
1988 Gramophone Keepsake 558818	2-Yr.	1989	13.00	20
1988 North Pole Lineman 558834 - Gilmore	2-Yr.	1989	10.00	50
1988 Five Golden Rings 559121 - Gilmore	3-Yr.	1990	11.00	25
1988 Six Geese A-Laying 559148 - Gilmore	3-Yr.	1990	11.00	25
1988 Pretty Baby 559156 - R. Morehead	3-Yr.	1990	12.50	25
1988 Old Fashioned Angel 559164 - R. Morehead	3-Yr.	1990	12.50	20
1988 Two For Tea 559776 - Gilmore	3-Yr.	1990	20.00	35-40

*Quotes have been rounded up to nearest dollar

YEAR ISSUE	EDITION LIMIT	YEAR RETD.	ISSUE PRICE	*QUOTE U.S.$
1988 Merry Christmas Grandpa 560065	3-Yr.	1990	8.00	N/A
1990 Reeling In The Holidays 560405 - M. Cook	2-Yr.	1991	8.00	15
1991 Walkin' With My Baby 561029 - M. Cook	2-Yr.	1992	10.00	N/A
1989 Scrub-A-Dub Chipmunk 561037 - M. Cook	2-Yr.	1990	8.00	20
1989 Christmas Cook-Out 561045 - M. Cook	2-Yr.	1990	9.00	20
1989 Bunkie 561835 - S. Zimnicki	3-Yr.	1991	22.50	30
1989 Sparkles 561843 - S. Zimnicki	3-Yr.	1991	17.50	25-28
1992 Sparky & Buffer 561851 - S. Zimnicki	3-Yr.	1994	25.00	25
1989 Popper 561878 - S. Zimnicki	3-Yr.	1991	12.00	25
1989 Seven Swans A-Swimming 562742 - Gilmore	3-Yr.	1991	12.00	23
1989 Eight Maids A-Milking 562750 - Gilmore	3-Yr.	1991	12.00	23
1989 Nine Ladies Dancing 562769 - Gilmore	3-Yr.	1991	15.00	23
1989 Baby's First Christmas 1989 562807	Yr.Iss.	1989	8.00	20
1989 Baby's First Christmas 1989 562815 - Gilmore	Yr.Iss.	1989	10.00	N/A
1989 First Christmas Together 1989 562823	Yr.Iss.	1989	11.00	N/A
1989 Travelin' Trike 562882 - Gilmore	3-Yr.	1991	15.00	15
1989 Victorian Sleigh Ride 562890	3-Yr.	1991	22.50	23
1991 Santa Delivers Love 562904 - Gilmore	2-Yr.	1992	17.50	18
1989 Chestnut Roastin' 562912 - Gilmore	2-Yr.	1990	13.00	13
1990 Th-Ink-In' Of You 562920 - Gilmore	2-Yr.	1991	20.00	30
1989 Ye Olde Puppet Show 562939	2-Yr.	1990	17.50	34
1989 Static In The Attic 562947	2-Yr.	1990	13.00	25
1989 Mistle-Toast 1989 562963 - Gilmore	Yr.Iss.	1989	15.00	25
1989 Merry Christmas Pops 562971 - Gilmore	3-Yr.	1991	12.00	12
1990 North Pole Or Bust 562998 - Gilmore	2-Yr.	1991	25.00	25
1989 By The Light Of The Moon 563005 - Gilmore	3-Yr.	1991	12.00	24
1989 Stickin' To It 563013 - Gilmore	2-Yr.	1990	10.00	12
1989 Christmas Cookin' 563048 - Gilmore	3-Yr.	1991	22.50	25
1989 All Set For Santa 563080 -Gilmore	3-Yr.	1991	17.50	25
1990 Santa's Sweets 563196 - Gilmore	2-Yr.	1991	20.00	20
1990 Purr-Fect Pals 563218	2-Yr.	1991	8.00	8
1989 The Pause That Refreshes 563226	3-Yr.	1991	15.00	75
1989 Ho-Ho Holiday Scrooge 563234 - J. Davis	3-Yr.	1991	13.50	30
1989 God Bless Us Everyone 563242 - J. Davis	3-Yr.	1991	13.50	20
1989 Scrooge With The Spirit 563250 - J. Davis	3-Yr.	1991	13.50	30
1989 A Chains Of Pace For Odie 563269 - J. Davis	3-Yr.	1991	12.00	25
1990 Jingle Bell Rock 1990 563390 - G. Armgardt	Yr.Iss.	1990	13.50	30
1989 Joy Ridin' 563463 - J. Davis	2-Yr.	1990	15.00	30
1989 Just What I Wanted 563668 - M. Peters	3-Yr.	1991	13.50	14
1990 Pucker Up! 563676 - M. Peters	3-Yr.	1992	11.00	11
1989 What's The Bright Idea 563684 - M. Peters	3-Yr.	1991	13.50	14
1990 Fleas Navidad 563978 - M. Peters	3-Yr.	1992	13.50	25
1990 Tweet Greetings 564044 - J. Davis	2-Yr.	1991	15.00	12-20
1990 Trouble On 3 Wheels 564052 - J. Davis	3-Yr.	1992	20.00	25
1989 Mine, All Mine! 564079 - J. Davis	Yr.Iss.	1989	15.00	25
1989 Star of Stars 564389 - J. Jonik	3-Yr.	1991	9.00	15
1990 Hang Onto Your Hat 564397 - J. Jonik	3-Yr.	1992	8.00	15
1990 Fireplace Frolic 564435 - N. Teiber	2-Yr.	1991	25.00	32
1994 Merry Miss Merry 564508 - Hahn	Yr.Iss.	1994	12.00	12
1994 Santa Delivers 564567	Yr.Iss.	1994	12.00	12
1989 Hoe! Hoe! Hoe! 564761	Yr.Iss.	1989	20.00	35
1991 Double Scoop Snowmouse 564796 - M. Cook	3-Yr.	1993	13.50	14
1990 Christmas Is Magic 564826 - M. Cook	2-Yr.	1991	10.00	10
1990 Lighting Up Christmas 564834 - M. Cook	2-Yr.	1991	10.00	10
1989 Feliz Navidad! 1989 564842 - M. Cook	Yr.Iss.	1989	11.00	40
1989 Spreading Christmas Joy 564850 - M. Cook	3-Yr.	1991	10.00	10
1989 Yuletide Tree House 564915 - J. Jonik	3-Yr.	1991	20.00	20
1990 Brewing Warm Wishes 564974	2-Yr.	1991	10.00	10
1990 Yippie-I-Yuletide 564982 - Hahn	3-Yr.	1992	15.00	15
1990 Coffee Break 564990 - Hahn	3-Yr.	1992	15.00	15
1990 You're Sew Special 565008 - Hahn	Yr.Iss.	1990	20.00	35
1989 Full House Mouse 565016 - Hahn	2-Yr.	1990	13.50	75
1989 I Feel Pretty 565024 - Hahn	3-Yr.	1991	20.00	30
1990 Warmest Wishes 565032 - Hahn	3-Yr.	1992	15.00	15
1990 Baby's Christmas Feast 565040 - Hahn	3-Yr.	1992	13.50	14
1990 Bumper Car Santa 565083 - G.G. Santiago	Yr.Iss.	1990	20.00	40
1989 Special Delivery (Proof Ed.) 565091 - G.G. Santiago	Yr.Iss.	1989	12.00	15
1990 Ho! Ho! Yo-Yo! (Proof Ed.) 565105 - G.G. Santiago	Yr.Iss.	1990	12.00	15
1989 Weightin' For Santa 565148 - G.G. Santiago	3-Yr.	1991	7.50	8
1989 Holly Fairy 565199 - C.M. Baker	Yr.Iss.	1989	15.00	45
1990 The Christmas Tree Fairy 565202 - C.M. Baker	Yr.Iss.	1990	15.00	40
1989 Merry Christmas (Boy) 565210 - L. Rigg	Yr.Iss.	1989	12.00	38
1989 Top Of The Class 565237 - L. Rigg	3-Yr.	1991	11.00	11
1989 Deck The Hogs 565490 - M. Cook	2-Yr.	1990	12.00	14
1989 Pinata Ridin' 565504 - M. Cook	2-Yr.	1990	11.00	N/A
1989 Hangin' In There 1989 565598 - K. Wise	Yr.Iss.	1989	10.00	20
1990 Meow-y Christmas 1990 565601 - K. Wise	Yr.Iss.	1990	10.00	25
1990 Seaman's Greetings 566047	2-Yr.	1991	11.00	24
1990 Hang In There 566055	3-Yr.	1992	13.50	14
1990 Deck The Halls 566063	3-Yr.	1992	12.50	N/A
1991 Pedal Pushin' Santa 566071	Yr.Iss.	1991	20.00	30
1990 Merry Christmas Teacher 566098	2-Yr.	1991	11.00	11
1990 Festive Flight 566101	2-Yr.	1991	11.00	11
1993 I'm Dreaming of a White-Out Christmas 566144	2-Yr.	1994	22.50	23
1990 Santa's Suitcase 566160	3-Yr.	1992	25.00	25
1989 The Purr-Fect Fit! 566462	3-Yr.	1991	15.00	35
1990 Tumbles 1990 566519 - S. Zimnicki	Yr.Iss.	1990	16.00	25
1990 Twiddles 566551 - S. Zimnicki	3-Yr.	1992	15.00	30
1991 Snuffy 566578 - S. Zimnicki	3-Yr.	1993	17.50	18
1990 All Aboard 567671 - Gilmore	2-Yr.	1991	17.50	18
1989 Gone With The Wind 567698	Yr.Iss.	1989	13.50	30
1989 Dorothy 567760	Yr.Iss.	1989	12.00	35
1989 The Tin Man 567779	Yr.Iss.	1989	12.00	12
1989 The Cowardly Lion 567787	Yr.Iss.	1989	12.00	12
1989 The Scarecrow 567795	Yr.Iss.	1989	12.00	12
1990 Happy Holiday Readings 568104	2-Yr.	1991	8.00	8
1989 Merry Christmas (Girl) 568325 - L. Rigg	Yr.Iss.	1989	12.00	N/A
1991 Holidays Ahoy 568368	2-Yr.	1992	12.50	13
1990 Christmas Countdown 568376	3-Yr.	1992	20.00	20
1989 Clara 568406	Yr.Iss.	1989	12.50	20
1990 The Nutcracker 568414	Yr.Iss.	1990	12.50	30
1991 Clara's Prince 568422	Yr.Iss.	1991	12.50	18
1989 Santa's Little Reindear 568430	2-Yr.	1990	15.00	25
1991 Tuba Totin' Teddy 568449	3-Yr.	1993	15.00	15
1990 A Calling Home At Christmas 568457	2-Yr.	1991	15.00	15
1991 Love Is The Secret Ingredient 568562 - L. Rigg	2-Yr.	1992	15.00	15
1990 A Spoonful of Love 568570 - L. Rigg	2-Yr.	1991	10.00	10
1990 Merry Christmas (Boy) 568597 - L. Rigg	Yr.Iss.	1990	13.00	N/A
1990 Merry Christmas (Girl) 568600 - L. Rigg	Yr.Iss.	1990	13.00	N/A
1990 Bearing Holiday Wishes 568619 - L. Rigg	3-Yr.	1992	22.50	23
1992 Moonlight Swing 568627 - L. Rigg	3-Yr.	1994	15.00	15
1990 Smitch 570184 - S. Zimnicki	3-Yr.	1992	22.50	23
1992 Carver 570192 - S. Zimnicki	Yr.Iss.	1992	17.50	18
1991 Twinkle & Sprinkle 570206 - S. Zimnicki	3-Yr.	1993	22.50	23
1990 Blinkie 570214 - S. Zimnicki	3-Yr.	1992	15.00	15
1990 Have A Coke And A Smile™ 571512	3-Yr.	1992	15.00	55
1990 Fleece Navidad 571903 - M. Cook	2-Yr.	1991	13.50	25
1990 Have a Navaho-Ho-Ho 1990 571970 - M. Cook	Yr.Iss.	1990	15.00	35
1990 Cheers 1990 572411 - T. Wilson	Yr.Iss.	1990	13.50	22
1990 A Night Before Christmas 572438 - T. Wilson	2-Yr.	1991	17.50	18
1990 Merry Kissmas 572446 - T. Wilson	2-Yr.	1991	10.00	30
1992 A Rockin' GARFIELD Christmas 572527 - J. Davis	2-Yr.	1993	17.50	18
1991 Here Comes Santa Paws 572535 - J. Davis	3-Yr.	1993	20.00	20
1990 Frosty Garfield 1990 572551 - J. Davis	Yr.Iss.	1990	13.50	35
1990 Pop Goes The Odie 572578 - J. Davis	2-Yr.	1991	15.00	30
1991 Sweet Beams 572586 - J. Davis	2-Yr.	1992	13.50	14
1990 An Apple A Day 572594 - J. Davis	2-Yr.	1991	12.00	12
1990 Dear Santa 572608 - J. Davis	3-Yr.	1992	17.00	17
1991 Have A Ball This Christmas 572616 - J. Davis	Yr.Iss.	1991	15.00	15
1990 Oh Shoosh! 572624 - J. Davis	3-Yr.	1992	17.00	17
1990 Little Red Riding Cat 572632 - J. Davis	Yr.Iss.	1990	13.50	33
1991 All Decked Out 572659 - J. Davis	2-Yr.	1992	13.50	14
1990 Over The Rooftops 572721 - J. Davis	2-Yr.	1991	17.50	28-35
1990 Garfield NFL Los Angeles Rams 572764 - J. Davis	2-Yr.	1991	12.50	13
1993 Born To Shop 572942	Yr.Iss.	1993	26.50	35
1990 Garfield NFL Cincinnati Bengals 573000 - J. Davis	2-Yr.	1991	12.50	13
1990 Garfield NFL Cleveland Browns 573019 - J. Davis	2-Yr.	1991	12.50	13
1990 Garfield NFL Houston Oiliers 573027 - J. Davis	2-Yr.	1991	12.50	13
1990 Garfield NFL Pittsburg Steelers 573035 - J. Davis	2-Yr.	1991	12.50	13
1990 Garfield NFL Denver Broncos 573043 - J. Davis	2-Yr.	1991	12.50	13
1990 Garfield NFL Kansas City Chiefs 573051 - J. Davis	2-Yr.	1991	12.50	13
1990 Garfield NFL Los Angeles Raiders 573078 - J. Davis	2-Yr.	1991	12.50	13
1990 Garfield NFL San Diego Chargers 573086 - J. Davis	2-Yr.	1991	12.50	13
1990 Garfield NFL Seattle Seahawks 573094 - J. Davis	2-Yr.	1991	12.50	13
1990 Garfield NFL Buffalo Bills 573108 - J. Davis	2-Yr.	1991	12.50	13
1990 Garfield NFL Indianapolis Colts 573116 - J. Davis	2-Yr.	1991	12.50	13
1990 Garfield NFL Miami Dolphins 573124 - J. Davis	2-Yr.	1991	12.50	13
1990 Garfield NFL New England Patriots 573132 - J. Davis	2-Yr.	1991	12.50	13
1990 Garfield NFL New York Jets 573140 - J. Davis	2-Yr.	1991	12.50	13
1990 Garfield NFL Atlanta Falcons 573159 - J. Davis	2-Yr.	1991	12.50	13
1990 Garfield NFL New Orleans Saints 573167 - J. Davis	2-Yr.	1991	12.50	13
1990 Garfield NFL San Francisco 49ers 573175 - J. Davis	2-Yr.	1991	12.50	13
1990 Garfield NFL Dallas Cowboys 573183 - J. Davis	2-Yr.	1991	12.50	13
1990 Garfield NFL New York Giants 573191 - J. Davis	2-Yr.	1991	12.50	13
1990 Garfield NFL Philadelphia Eagles 573205 - J. Davis	2-Yr.	1991	12.50	13
1990 Garfield NFL Phoenix Cardinals 573213 - J. Davis	2-Yr.	1991	12.50	13
1990 Garfield NFL Washington Redskins 573221 - J. Davis	2-Yr.	1991	12.50	13
1990 Garfield NFL Chicago Bears 573248 - J. Davis	2-Yr.	1991	12.50	13
1990 Garfield NFL Detroit Lions 573256 - J. Davis	2-Yr.	1991	12.50	13
1990 Garfield NFL Green Bay Packers 573264 - J. Davis	2-Yr.	1991	12.50	13
1990 Garfield NFL Minnesota Vikings 573272 - J. Davis	2-Yr.	1991	12.50	13
1990 Garfield NFL Tampa Bay Buccaneers 573280 - J. Davis	2-Yr.	1991	12.50	13
1991 Tea For Two 573299 - Hahn	3-Yr.	1993	30.00	50
1991 Hot Stuff Santa 573523	Yr.Iss.	1991	25.00	30
1990 Merry Moustronauts 573558 - M. Cook	3-Yr.	1992	20.00	40
1991 Santa Wings It 573612 - J. Jonik	3-Yr.	1993	13.00	13
1990 All Eye Want For Christmas 573647 - Gilmore	3-Yr.	1992	27.50	32
1990 Stuck On You 573655 - Gilmore	2-Yr.	1991	12.50	13
1990 Professor Michael Bear, The One Bear Band 573663 - Gilmore	3-Yr.	1992	22.50	28
1990 A Caroling Wee Go 573671 - Gilmore	3-Yr.	1992	12.00	12
1990 Merry Mailman 573698 - Gilmore	2-Yr.	1991	15.00	30
1990 Deck The Halls 573701 - Gilmore	3-Yr.	1992	22.50	30
1992 Sundae Ride 583707	2-Yr.	1993	20.00	20
1990 You're Wheel Special 573728 - Gilmore	3-Yr.	1992	15.00	15
1991 Come Let Us Adore Him 573736 - Gilmore	2-Yr.	1992	9.00	9
1991 Moon Beam Dreams 573760 - Gilmore	3-Yr.	1993	12.00	12
1991 A Song For Santa 573779 - Gilmore	3-Yr.	1993	25.00	25
1990 Warmest Wishes 573825 - Gilmore	Yr.Iss.	1990	17.50	25
1991 Kurious Kitty 573868 - Gilmore	3-Yr.	1993	17.50	18
1990 Old Mother Mouse 573922 - Gilmore	2-Yr.	1991	17.50	20-32
1990 Railroad Repairs 573930 - Gilmore	2-Yr.	1991	12.50	25
1990 Ten Lords A-Leaping 573949 - Gilmore	3-Yr.	1992	15.00	25
1990 Eleven Drummers Drumming 573957 - Gilmore	3-Yr.	1992	15.00	25
1990 Twelve Pipers Piping 573965 - Gilmore	3-Yr.	1992	15.00	25
1990 Baby's First Christmas 1990 573973 - Gilmore	Yr.Iss.	1990	10.00	N/A
1990 Baby's First Christmas 1990 573981 - Gilmore	Yr.Iss.	1990	12.00	N/A
1991 Peter, Peter Pumpkin Eater 574015 - Gilmore	2-Yr.	1992	20.00	30
1992 The Nutcracker 574023 - Gilmore	3-Yr.	1994	25.00	25
1990 Little Jack Horner 574058 - Gilmore	2-Yr.	1991	17.50	35
1991 Mary, Mary Quite Contrary 574066 - Gilmore	2-Yr.	1992	22.50	33
1992 Humpty Dumpty 574244 - Gilmore	2-Yr.	1993	25.00	25
1991 Through The Years 574252 - Gilmore	Yr.Iss.	1991	17.50	18
1991 Holiday Wing Ding 574333	3-Yr.	1993	22.50	23
1991 North Pole Here I Come 574597	3-Yr.	1993	10.00	10
1991 Christmas Caboose 574856 - Gilmore	2-Yr.	1992	25.00	30
1990 Bubble Trouble 575038 - Hahn	3-Yr.	1992	20.00	35
1991 Merry Mother-To-Be 575046 - Hahn	3-Yr.	1993	13.50	14
1990 A Holiday 'Scent' Sation 575054 - Hahn	3-Yr.	1992	15.00	30
1990 Catch Of The Day 575070 - Hahn	3-Yr.	1992	25.00	25
1990 Don't Open 'Til Christmas 575089 - Hahn	3-Yr.	1992	17.50	18
1990 I Can't Weight 'Til Christmas 575119 - Hahn	3-Yr.	1992	16.50	30
1991 Deck The Halls 575127 - Hahn	2-Yr.	1992	15.00	25
1992 Music Mice-Tro! 575143	2-Yr.	1993	12.00	12
1990 Mouse House 575186	3-Yr.	1992	16.00	16
1991 Dream A Little Dream 575593	2-Yr.	1992	17.50	18
1991 Christmas Two-gether 575615 - L. Rigg	3-Yr.	1993	22.50	23
1992 On Target Two-Gether 575623	Yr.Iss.	1992	17.00	17
1991 Christmas Trimmings 575631	2-Yr.	1992	17.00	17

*Quotes have been rounded up to nearest dollar

ORNAMENTS

YEAR ISSUE	EDITION LIMIT	YEAR RETD.	ISSUE PRICE	*QUOTE U.S.$
1991 Gumball Wizard 575658 - Gilmore	2-Yr.	1992	13.00	13
1991 Crystal Ball Christmas 575666 - Gilmore	2-Yr.	1992	22.50	23
1990 Old King Cole 575682 - Gilmore	2-Yr.	1991	20.00	29
1991 Tom, Tom The Piper's Son 575690 - Gilmore	2-Yr.	1992	15.00	33
1992 Rock-A-Bye Baby 575704 - Gilmore	2-Yr.	1993	13.50	14
1992 Queen of Hearts 575712 - Gilmore	2-Yr.	1992	17.50	18
1993 Toy To The World 575763	2-Yr.	1994	25.00	25
1992 Tasty Tidings 575836 - L. Rigg	Yr.Iss.	1992	13.50	14
1991 Tire-d Little Bear 575852 - L. Rigg	Yr.Iss.	1991	12.50	13
1990 Baby Bear Christmas 1990 575860 - L. Rigg	Yr.Iss.	1990	12.00	28
1991 Crank Up The Carols 575887 - L. Rigg	2-Yr.	1992	17.50	18
1990 Beary Christmas 1990 576158 - L. Rigg	Yr.Iss.	1990	12.00	12
1991 Merry Christmas (Boy) 576166 - L. Rigg	Yr.Iss.	1991	13.00	13
1991 Merry Christmas (Girl) 576174 - L. Rigg	Yr.Iss.	1991	13.00	13
1991 Christmas Cutie 576182	3-Yr.	1993	13.50	14
1991 Meow Mates 576220	3-Yr.	1993	12.00	12
1991 Frosty The Snowmant 576425	3-Yr.	1993	15.00	15
1991 Ris-ski Business 576719 - T. Wilson	2-Yr.	1992	10.00	10
1991 Pinocchio 577391 - J. Davis	3-Yr.	1993	15.00	15
1990 Yuletide Ride 1990 577502 - Gilmore	Yr.Iss.	1990	13.50	50
1990 Tons of Toys 577510	Yr.Iss.	1990	13.00	30
1990 McHappy Holidays 577529	2-Yr.	1991	17.50	25
1990 Heading For Happy Holidays 577537	3-Yr.	1992	17.50	18
1990 'Twas The Night Before Christmas 577545	3-Yr.	1992	17.50	18
1990 Over One Million Holiday Wishes! 577553	Yr.Iss.	1990	17.50	30
1990 You Malt My Heart 577596	2-Yr.	1991	25.00	25
1991 All I Want For Christmas 577618	2-Yr.	1992	20.00	20
1992 Bearly Sleepy 578029 - Gilmore	Yr.Iss.	1992	17.50	18
1994 Buttons 'N' Bow Boutique 578363 - Gilmore	Yr.Iss.	1995	22.50	23
1992 Spreading Sweet Joy 580465	Yr.Iss.	1992	13.50	14
1991 Things Go Better With Coke™ 580597	3-Yr.	1993	17.00	25
1991 Christmas To Go 580600 - M. Cook	Yr.Iss.	1991	22.50	23
1991 Have A Mariachi Christmas 580619 - M. Cook	2-Yr.	1992	13.50	14
1993 Bearly Balanced 580724	Yr.Iss.	1993	15.00	15
1992 Ring My Bell 580740 - J. Davis	Yr.Iss.	1992	13.50	14
1992 4 x 4 Holiday Fun 580783 - J. Davis	2-Yr.	1993	20.00	20
1991 Christmas Is In The Air 581453	Yr.Iss.	1991	15.00	15
1991 Holiday Treats 581542	Yr.Iss.	1991	17.50	18
1991 Christmas Is My Goal 581550	2-Yr.	1992	17.50	12-18
1991 A Quarter Pounder With Cheer® 581569	3-Yr.	1993	20.00	20
1992 The Holidays Are A Hit 581577	2-Yr.	1993	17.50	18
1991 From The Same Mold 581798 - Gilmore	3-Yr.	1993	17.00	17
1991 The Glow Of Christmas 581801	2-Yr.	1992	20.00	20
1992 Tip Top Tidings 581828	2-Yr.	1993	13.00	13
1994 A Sign of Peace 581992	Yr.Iss.	1994	18.50	19
1992 Christmas Lifts The Spirits 582018	2-Yr.	1993	25.00	25
1993 Joyeux Noel 582026	2-Yr.	1994	24.50	25
1992 A Pound Of Good Cheers 582034	2-Yr.	1993	17.50	18
1994 Wishing You Well At Christmas 582050	Yr.Iss.	1994	25.00	25
1994 Ahoy Joy! 582085	Yr.Iss.	1994	20.00	20
1993 Holiday Mew-Sic 582107	2-Yr.	1994	20.00	20
1993 Santa's Magic Ride 582115	2-Yr.	1994	24.00	24
1994 Santa...Phone Home 582166	Yr.Iss.	1994	25.00	25
1993 Warm And Hearty Wishes 582344	Yr.Iss.	1993	17.50	18
1993 Cool Yule 582352	Yr.Iss.	1993	12.00	12
1994 Christmas Swishes 582379	Yr.Iss.	1994	17.50	18
1993 Have A Holly Jell-O Christmas 582387	Yr.Iss.	1993	14.50	45
1994 The Latest Scoop From Santa 582395 - Gilmore	Yr.Iss.	1994	18.50	19
1994 Chiminy Cheer 582409 - Gilmore	Yr.Iss.	1994	22.50	23
1994 Cozy Candlelight Dinner 582417 - Gilmore	Yr.Iss.	1994	25.00	25
1994 Fine Feathered Festivities 582425 - Gilmore	Yr.Iss.	1994	22.50	23
1994 Joy From Head To Hose 582433 - Gilmore	Yr.Iss.	1994	15.00	15
1993 Festive Firemen 582565 - Gilmore	2-Yr.	1994	17.00	17
1991 Lights..Camera..Kissmas! 583626 - Gilmore	Yr.Iss.	1991	15.00	35
1991 All Caught Up In Christmas 583537	2-Yr.	1992	10.00	10
1991 Sweet Steed 583634 - Gilmore	3-Yr.	1993	15.00	15
1992 Sweet as Cane Be 583642 - Gilmore	3-Yr.	1994	15.00	15
1991 Dreamin' Of A White Christmas 583669 - Gilmore	2-Yr.	1992	15.00	15
1991 Merry Millimeters 583677 - Gilmore	3-Yr.	1993	17.00	17
1991 Here's The Scoop 583693	2-Yr.	1992	13.50	20
1991 Happy Meal® On Wheels 583715	3-Yr.	1993	22.50	23
1991 Christmas Kayak 583723	2-Yr.	1992	13.50	14
1993 Light Up Your Holidays With Coke 583758	Yr.Iss.	1993	27.50	28
1992 The Cold, Crisp Taste Of Coke 583766	3-Yr.	1994	17.00	17
1991 Marilyn Monroe 583774	Yr.Iss.	1991	20.00	20
1992 Sew Christmasy 583820	3-Yr.	1994	25.00	25
1991 A Christmas Carol 583928	3-Yr.	1993	22.50	23
1991 Checking It Twice 583936	2-Yr.	1992	25.00	25
1992 Catch A Falling Star 583944 - Gilmore	2-Yr.	1993	15.00	15
1992 Swingin' Christmas 584096	2-Yr.	1993	15.00	15
1994 Yuletide Yummies 584835 - Gilmore	Yr.Iss.	1994	20.00	20
1993 Pool Hall-idays 584851	2-Yr.	1994	19.00	20
1994 Merry Christmas Tool You, Dad 584886	Yr.Iss.	1994	22.50	23
1994 Exercising Good Taste 584967	Yr.Iss.	1994	17.50	18
1994 Holiday Chew-Chew 584983 - Gilmore	Yr.Iss.	1994	22.50	23
1992 Mc Ho, Ho, Ho 585181	3-Yr.	1994	22.50	23
1991 Merry Christmas Go-Round 585203 - J. Davis	3-Yr.	1993	20.00	20
1992 Holiday On Ice 585254 - J. Davis	3-Yr.	1994	17.50	18
1991 Holiday Hideout 585270 - J. Davis	2-Yr.	1992	15.00	15
1992 Fast Track Cat 585289 - J. Davis	3-Yr.	1994	17.50	18
1992 Holiday Cat Napping 585319 - J. Davis	2-Yr.	1993	20.00	20
1993 Bah Humbug 585394 - Davis	Yr.Iss.	1993	15.00	15
1992 The Finishing Touches 585610 - T. Wilson	2-Yr.	1993	17.50	18
1992 Jolly Ol' Gent 585645 - J. Jonik	3-Yr.	1994	13.50	14
1991 Our Most Precious Gift 585726	Yr.Iss.	1991	17.50	18
1991 Christmas Cheer 585769	2-Yr.	1992	13.50	14
1993 Chimer 585777 - Zimnicki	Yr.Iss.	1993	25.00	10-25
1993 Sweet Whiskered Wishes 585807	Yr.Iss.	1993	17.00	17
1993 Grade "A" Wishes From Garfield 585823 - Davis	2-Yr.	1994	20.00	20
1992 A Child's Christmas 586358	3-Yr.	1994	25.00	25
1992 Festive Fiddlers 586501	Yr.Iss.	1992	20.00	25
1992 La Luminaria 586579 - M. Cook	2-Yr.	1993	13.50	14
1991 Fired Up For Christmas 586587 - Gilmore	2-Yr.	1992	32.50	33
1991 One Foggy Christmas Eve 586625 - Gilmore	3-Yr.	1993	30.00	30
1991 For A Purr-fect Mom 586641 - Gilmore	Yr.Iss.	1991	12.00	12
1991 For A Special Dad 586668 - Gilmore	Yr.Iss.	1991	17.50	18
1991 With Love 586676 - Gilmore	Yr.Iss.	1991	13.00	13
1991 For A Purr-fect Aunt 586692 - Gilmore	Yr.Iss.	1991	12.00	12
1991 For A Dog-Gone Great Uncle 586706 - Gilmore	Yr.Iss.	1991	12.00	12
1991 Peddling Fun 586714 - Gilmore	Yr.Iss.	1991	16.00	16
1991 Special Keepsakes 586722 - Gilmore	Yr.Iss.	1991	13.50	14
1992 Cozy Chrismas Carriage 586730 - Gilmore	2-Yr.	1993	22.50	23
1992 Small Fry's First Christmas 586749	2-Yr.	1993	17.00	17
1991 Hats Off To Christmas 586757 - Hahn	Yr.Iss.	1991	22.50	23
1992 Friendships Preserved 586765 - Hahn	Yr.Iss.	1992	22.50	23
1995 Sweet Harmony 586773 - Gilmore	Yr.Iss.	1995	17.50	18
1993 Tree For Two 586781 - Gilmore	2-Yr.	1994	17.50	18
1993 A Bright Idea 586803 - Gilmore	2-Yr.	1994	22.50	23
1992 Window Wish List 586854 - Gilmore	2-Yr.	1993	30.00	30
1992 Through The Years 586862 - Gilmore	Yr.Iss.	1992	17.50	18
1993 Baby's First Christmas 1993 586870 - Gilmore	Yr.Iss.	1993	17.50	18
1993 My Special Christmas 586900 - Gilmore	Yr.Iss.	1993	17.50	18
1991 Baby's First Christmas 1991 586935	Yr.Iss.	1991	12.50	13
1992 Baby's First Christmas 1992 586943	Yr.Iss.	1992	12.50	13
1992 Firehouse Friends 586951 - Gilmore	Yr.Iss.	1992	22.50	23
1992 Bubble Buddy 586978 - Gilmore	2-Yr	1993	13.50	14
1992 The Warmth Of The Season 586994	2-Yr.	1993	20.00	20
1993 Baby's First Christmas Dinner 587001	Yr.Iss.	1993	12.00	12
1991 Jugglin' The Holidays 587028	2-Yr.	1992	13.00	13
1991 Santa's Steed 587044	Yr.Iss.	1991	15.00	15
1991 A Decade of Treasures 587052 - Gilmore	Yr.Iss.	1991	37.50	75
1992 It's A Go For Christmas 587095 - Gilmore	2-Yr.	1993	15.00	15
1991 Mr. Mailmouse 587109 - Gilmore	2-Yr.	1992	17.00	17
1992 Post-Mouster General 587117 - Gilmore	2-Yr.	1993	20.00	20
1992 To A Deer Baby 587168	Yr.Iss.	1992	18.50	19
1991 Starry Eyed Santa 587176	2-Yr.	1992	15.00	15
1992 Moon Watch 587184	2-Yr.	1993	20.00	20
1992 Guten Cheers 587192	Yr.Iss.	1992	22.50	23
1992 Put On A Happy Face 588237	2-Yr.	1993	15.00	15
1992 Beginning To Look A Lot Like Christmas 588253	2-Yr.	1993	15.00	15
1992 A Christmas Toast 588261	2-Yr.	1993	20.00	20
1992 Merry Mistle-Toad 588288	2-Yr.	1993	15.00	15
1992 Tic-Tac-Mistle-Toe 588296	3-Yr.	1994	23.00	23
1993 A Pause For Claus 588318	2-Yr.	1994	22.50	23
1992 Heaven Sent 588423 - J. Penchoff	2-Yr.	1993	12.50	13
1992 Holiday Happenings 588555 - Gilmore	3-Yr.	1994	30.00	30
1993 Not A Creature Was Stirring... 588563 - Gilmore	2-Yr.	1994	27.50	28
1992 Seed-son's Greetings 588571 - Gilmore	3-Yr.	1994	27.00	27
1992 Santa's Midnight Snack 588598 - Gilmore	2-Yr.	1993	20.00	20
1992 Trunk Of Treasures 588636	Yr.Iss.	1992	20.00	20
1993 Terrific Toys 588644	Yr.Iss.	1993	20.00	20
1993 Christmas Dancer 588652	Yr.Iss.	1993	15.00	15
1995 Yule Tide Prancer 588660	Yr.Iss.	1995	15.00	15
1994 To The Sweetest Baby 588725 - Gilmore	Yr.Iss.	1994	18.50	19
1995 Baby's Sweet Feast 588733 - Gilmore	Yr.Iss.	1995	17.50	19
1991 Lighting The Way 588776	2-Yr.	1992	20.00	20
1991 Rudolph 588784	2-Yr.	1992	17.50	18
1992 Festive Newsflash 588792	2-Yr.	1993	17.50	18
1992 A-B-C-Son's Greetings 588806	2-Yr.	1993	16.50	17
1992 Hoppy Holidays 588814	Yr.Iss.	1992	13.50	14
1992 Fireside Friends 588830	2-Yr.	1993	20.00	20
1992 Christmas Eve-mergency 588849	2-Yr.	1993	27.00	27
1992 A Sure Sign Of Christmas 588857	2-Yr.	1993	22.50	23
1992 Holidays Give Me A Lift 588865	2-Yr.	1993	30.00	30
1992 Yule Tide Together 588903	2-Yr.	1993	20.00	20
1992 Have A Soup-er Christmas 588911	2-Yr.	1993	17.50	18
1992 Christmas Cure-Alls 588938	2-Yr.	1993	20.00	20
1993 Countin' On A Merry Christmas 588954	2-Yr.	1994	22.50	23
1994 Rockin' Ranger 588970	Yr.Iss.	1994	25.00	25
1994 Peace On Earthworm 588989	Yr.Iss.	1994	20.00	20
1993 To My Gem 589004	Yr.Iss.	1993	27.50	28
1993 Christmas Mail Call 589012	2-Yr.	1994	20.00	20
1993 Spreading Joy 589047	2-Yr.	1994	27.50	28
1993 Pitter-Patter Post Office 589055	2-Yr.	1994	20.00	20
1994 Good Things Crop Up At Christmas 589071	Yr.Iss.	1994	25.00	25
1993 Happy Haul-idays 589098	2-Yr.	1994	30.00	30
1994 Christmas Crossroads 589128	Yr.Iss.	1994	20.00	20
1993 Hot Off The Press 589292	2-Yr.	1994	27.50	28
1993 Designed With You In Mind 589306	2-Yr.	1994	16.00	16
1992 Dial 'S' For Santa 589373	2-Yr.	1993	25.00	25
1993 Seeing Is Believing 589381 - Gilmore	2-Yr.	1994	20.00	20
1992 Joy To The Whirled 589551 - Hahn	2-Yr.	1993	20.00	20
1992 Merry Make-Over 589586 - Hahn	3-Yr.	1994	20.00	20
1992 Campin' Companions 590282 - Hahn	3-Yr.	1994	20.00	20
1994 Have A Ball At Christmas 590673	Yr.Iss.	1994	15.00	15
1992 Fur-Ever Friends 590797 - Gilmore	2-Yr.	1993	13.50	14
1993 Roundin' Up Christmas Together 590800	Yr.Iss.	1993	25.00	25
1994 Have A Totem-ly Terrific Christmas 590819	Yr.Iss.	1994	30.00	30
1992 Tee-rific Holidays 590827	3-Yr.	1994	25.00	25
1992 Spinning Christmas Dreams 590908 - Hahn	3-Yr.	1994	22.50	23
1992 Christmas Trimmin' 590932	3-Yr.	1994	17.00	12-17
1993 Toasty Tidings 590940	2-Yr.	1994	20.00	20
1993 Focusing On Christmas 590983 - Gilmore	2-Yr.	1994	27.50	28
1993 Dunk The Halls 591009	2-Yr.	1994	18.50	19
1993 Mice Capades 591386 - Hahn	2-Yr.	1994	26.50	27
1993 25 Points For Christmas 591750	Yr.Iss.	1993	25.00	25
1994 Cocoa 'N' Kisses For Santa 591939	Yr.Iss.	1995	22.50	23
1994 On The Road With Coke™ 592528	Yr.Iss.	1995	25.00	25
1993 Carving Christmas Wishes 592625 - Gilmore	2-Yr.	1994	25.00	25
1995 A Well, Balanced Meal For Santa 592633	Yr.Iss.	1995	17.50	18
1994 What's Shakin' For Christmas 592668	Yr.Iss.	1994	18.50	19
1994 "A" For Santa 592676	Yr.Iss.	1994	17.50	18
1993 Celebrating With A Splash 592692	Yr.Iss.	1993	17.00	17
1994 Christmas Fly-By 592714	Yr.Iss.	1994	15.00	15
1993 Slimmin' Santa 592722	Yr.Iss.	1993	18.50	24
1993 Plane Ol' Holiday Fun 592773	Yr.Iss.	1993	27.50	28
1995 Salute 593133	Yr.Iss.	1995	22.50	23
1992 Wrappin' Up Warm Wishes 593141	Yr.Iss.	1992	17.50	18
1992 Christmas Biz 593168	2-Yr.	1993	22.50	23
1993 Smooth Move, Mom 593176	Yr.Iss.	1993	20.00	20
1993 Tool Time, Yule Time 593192	Yr.Iss.	1993	18.50	15-19
1993 Speedy 593370 - Zimnicki	2-Yr.	1994	25.00	25
1992 Holiday Take-Out 593508	Yr.Iss.	1992	17.50	18
1992 A Christmas Yarn 593516 - Gilmore	Yr.Iss.	1992	20.00	20
1993 On Your Mark, Set, Is That To Go? 593524	Yr.Iss.	1993	13.50	14
1993 Do Not Open 'Til Christmas 593737 - Hahn	2-Yr.	1994	15.00	15
1993 Greetings In Stereo 593745 - Hahn	Yr.Iss.	1993	19.50	20
1994 Santa...You're The Pops! 593761	Yr.Iss.	1994	22.50	23
1992 Treasure The Earth 593826 - Hahn	2-Yr.	1993	25.00	25
1994 Purdy Packages, Pardner! 593834	Yr.Iss.	1994	20.00	20
1994 Handle With Care 593842	Yr.Iss.	1994	20.00	20
1994 To Coin A Phrase, Merry Christmas 593877	Yr.Iss.	1994	20.00	20
1994 Featured Presentation 593885	Yr.Iss.	1994	20.00	20
1994 Christmas Fishes From Santa Paws 593893	Yr.Iss.	1994	18.50	19
1993 Tangled Up For Christmas 593974	2-Yr.	1994	14.50	15
1992 Toyful' Rudolph 593982	2-Yr.	1993	22.50	23
1992 Take A Chance On The Holidays 594075	3-Yr.	1994	20.00	20
1993 Sweet Season's Eatings 594202	Yr.Iss.	1993	22.50	23
1993 Have A Darn Good Christmas 594229 - Gilmore	2-Yr.	1994	21.00	21

*Quotes have been rounded up to nearest dollar

YEAR ISSUE		EDITION LIMIT	YEAR RETD.	ISSUE PRICE	*QUOTE U.S.$
1994	You Melt My Heart 594237 - Gilmore	Yr.Iss.	1994	15.00	15
1993	The Sweetest Ride 594253 - Gilmore	2-Yr.	1994	18.50	19
1994	Finishing First 594342 - Gilmore	Yr.Iss.	1994	20.00	20
1992	Lights..Camera..Christmas! 594369	2-Yr.	1993	20.00	20
1994	Yule Fuel 594385	Yr.Iss.	1994	20.00	20
1992	Spirited Stallion 594407	Yr.Iss.	1992	15.00	15
1993	Have A Cheery Christmas, Sister 594687	Yr.Iss.	1993	13.50	14
1993	Say Cheese 594962 - Gilmore	2-Yr.	1994	13.50	14
1993	Christmas Kicks 594989	Yr.Iss.	1993	17.50	18
1993	Time For Santa 594997 - Gilmore	2-Yr.	1994	17.50	18
1993	Holiday Orders 595004	Yr.Iss.	1993	20.00	20
1993	'Twas The Night Before Christmas 595012	Yr.Iss.	1993	22.50	23
1995	Filled To The Brim 595039 - Gilmore	Yr.Iss.	1995	25.00	25
1994	Toy Tinker Topper 595047 - Gilmore	Yr.Iss.	1994	20.00	20
1993	Sugar Chef Shoppe 595055 - Gilmore	2-Yr.	1994	23.50	24
1993	Merry Mc-Choo-Choo 595063	Yr.Iss.	1993	30.00	30
1993	Merry Christmas, Daughter 595098	Yr.Iss.	1993	20.00	20
1993	Rockin' With Santa 595195	2-Yr.	1994	13.50	14
1994	Santa Claus Is Comin' 595209	Yr.Iss.	1994	20.00	20
1993	Christmas-To-Go 595217	Yr.Iss.	1993	25.50	12-26
1994	Seasoned With Love 595268	Yr.Iss.	1994	22.50	23
1993	Sleddin' Mr. Snowman 595276	2-Yr.	1994	13.00	13
1993	A Kick Out Of Christmas 595373	2-Yr.	1994	10.00	10
1993	Friends Through Thick And Thin 595381	2-Yr.	1994	10.00	10
1993	See-Saw Sweethearts 595403	2-Yr.	1994	10.00	10
1993	Special Delivery For Santa 595411	2-Yr.	1994	10.00	10
1993	Top Marks For Teacher 595438	2-Yr.	1994	10.00	10
1993	Home Tweet Home 595446	2-Yr.	1994	10.00	10
1993	Clownin' Around 595454	2-Yr.	1994	10.00	10
1993	Heart Filled Dreams 595462	2-Yr.	1994	10.00	10
1993	Merry Christmas Baby 595470	2-Yr.	1994	10.00	10
1994	Sweet Dreams 595489	Yr.Iss.	1994	12.50	13
1994	Peace On Earth 595497	Yr.Iss.	1994	12.50	13
1994	Christmas Two-gether 595500	Yr.Iss.	1994	12.50	13
1994	Santa's L'il Helper 595519	Yr.Iss.	1994	12.50	13
1994	Expecting Joy 595527 - Hahn	Yr.Iss.	1994	12.50	13
1993	Your A Hit With Me, Brother 595535 - Hahn	Yr.Iss.	1993	10.00	10
1993	For A Sharp Uncle 595543	Yr.Iss.	1993	10.00	10
1993	Paint Your Holidays Bright 595551 - Hahn	2-Yr.	1994	10.00	10
1994	Sweet Greetings 595578	Yr.Iss.	1994	12.50	13
1994	Ring In The Holidays 595586 - Hahn	Yr.Iss.	1994	12.50	13
1994	Grandmas Are Sew Special 595594	Yr.Iss.	1994	12.50	13
1994	Holiday Catch 595608 - Hahn	Yr.Iss.	1994	12.50	13
1994	Bubblin' with Joy 595616	Yr.Iss.	1994	12.50	13
1992	A Watchful Eye 595713	Yr.Iss.	1992	15.00	15
1992	Good Catch 595721	Yr.Iss.	1992	12.50	13
1992	Squirrelin' It Away 595748 - Hahn	Yr.Iss.	1992	12.00	12
1992	Checkin' His List 595756	Yr.Iss.	1992	12.50	13
1992	Christmas Cat Nappin' 595764	Yr.Iss.	1992	12.00	12
1992	Bless Our Home 595772	Yr.Iss.	1992	12.00	12
1992	Salute the Season 595780 - Hahn	Yr.Iss.	1992	12.00	12
1992	Fired Up For Christmas 595799	Yr.Iss.	1992	12.00	12
1992	Speedin' Mr. Snowman 595802 - M. Rhyner-Nadig	Yr.Iss.	1992	12.00	12
1992	Merry Christmas Mother Earth 595810 - Hahn	Yr.Iss.	1992	11.00	11
1994	Mine, Mine, Mine 585815 - Davis	Yr.Iss.	1994	20.00	20
1992	Wear The Season With A Smile 595829	Yr.Iss.	1992	10.00	10
1992	Jesus Loves Me 595837 - Hahn	Yr.Iss.	1992	10.00	10
1994	Good Friends Are Forever 595950 - Gilmore	Yr.Iss.	1994	13.50	14
1993	Treasure The Holidays, Man! 596051	Yr.Iss.	1993	22.50	23
1993	Ariel's Under-The-Sea Tree 596078	Yr.Iss.	1993	20.00	20
1993	Here Comes Santa Claws 596086	Yr.Iss.	1993	22.50	35
1993	A Spot of Love 596094	Yr.Iss.	1993	17.50	18
1993	Hearts Aglow 596108	Yr.Iss.	1993	18.50	35
1993	Love's Sweet Dance 596116	Yr.Iss.	1993	25.00	25
1993	Holiday Wishes 596124	Yr.Iss.	1993	15.00	15
1993	Hangin Out For The Holidays 596132	Yr.Iss.	1993	15.00	35
1993	Magic Carpet Ride 596140	Yr.Iss.	1993	20.00	20
1993	Holiday Treasures 596159	Yr.Iss.	1993	18.50	35
1993	Happily Ever After 596167	Yr.Iss.	1993	22.50	23
1993	The Fairest Of Them All 596175	Yr.Iss.	1993	18.50	19
1994	Christmas Tee Time 596256	Yr.Iss.	1995	25.00	25
1994	Have a Merry Dairy Christmas 596264	Yr.Iss.	1994	22.50	23
1994	Happy Holi-date 596272 - Hahn	Yr.Iss.	1995	22.50	23
1994	O' Come All Ye Faithful 596280 - Hahn	Yr.Iss.	1994	15.00	15-75
1994	One Small Step... 596299 - Hahn	19,690	1994	25.00	45
1994	To My Favorite V.I.P. 596698	Yr.Iss.	1994	20.00	20
1993	December 25...Dear Diary 596809 - Hahn	2-Yr.	1994	10.00	10
1994	Building Memories 596876 - Hahn	Yr.Iss.	1994	25.00	25
1994	Open For Business 596906 - Hahn	Yr.Iss.	1994	17.50	18
1993	Wheel Merry Wishes 596930 - Hahn	2-Yr.	1994	15.00	15
1993	Good Grounds For Christmas 596957 - Hahn	Yr.Iss.	1993	24.50	25
1993	Ducking The Season's Rush 597597	Yr.Iss.	1993	17.50	18
1994	Twas The Nite Before Christmas 597643 - Gilmore	Yr.Iss.	1994	18.50	19
1993	Here Comes Rudolph® 597686	2-Yr.	1994	17.50	18
1993	It's Beginning To Look A Lot Like Christmas 597694	Yr.Iss.	1993	22.50	23
1993	Christmas In The Making 597716	Yr.Iss.	1993	20.00	20
1994	I Can Bear-ly Wait For A Coke™ 597724	Yr.Iss.	1995	18.50	19
1993	Mickey's Holiday Treasure 597759	Yr.Iss.	1993	12.00	12
1993	Dream Wheels/1953 Chevrolet Corvette 597856	Yr.Iss.	1993	29.50	50-75
1994	Gallant Greeting- 598313	Yr.Iss.	1994	15.00	20
1994	Merry Menage 598321	Yr.Iss.	1994	20.00	20
1993	All You Add Is Love 598429	Yr.Iss.	1993	18.50	19
1993	Goofy About Skiing 598631	Yr.Iss.	1993	22.50	23
1994	Ski-son's Greetings 599069	Yr.Iss.	1994	20.00	20
1994	Bundle Of Joy 598992	Yr.Iss.	1994	10.00	12-15
1994	Bundle Of Joy 599018	Yr.Iss.	1994	10.00	10
1994	Have A Dino-mite Christmas 599026 - Hahn	Yr.Iss.	1994	18.50	19
1994	Good Fortune To You 599034	Yr.Iss.	1994	25.00	25
1994	Building a Sew-man 599042	Yr.Iss.	1994	18.50	19
1994	Merry Memo-ries 599050	Yr.Iss.	1994	22.50	23
1994	Holiday Freezer Teaser 599085 - Gilmore	Yr.Iss.	1994	25.00	25
1994	Almost Time For Santa 599093 - Gilmore	Yr.Iss.	1994	25.00	25
1994	Santa's Secret Test Drive 599107 - Gilmore	Yr.Iss.	1994	20.00	20
1994	You're A Wheel Cool Brother 599115 - Gilmore	Yr.Iss.	1994	22.50	23
1994	Hand-Tossed Tidings 599166	Yr.Iss.	1994	17.50	18
1994	Tasty Take Off 599174	Yr.Iss.	1994	20.00	20
1994	Formula For Love 599530 - Olsen	Yr.Iss.	1994	10.00	10
1994	Santa's Ginger-bred Doe 599697 - Gilmore	Yr.Iss.	1994	15.00	15
1994	Nutcracker Sweetheart 599700	Yr.Iss.	1994	15.00	15
1994	Merry Reindeer Ride 599719	Yr.Iss.	1994	20.00	20
1994	Santa's Sing-A-Long 599727 - Gilmore	Yr.Iss.	1994	20.00	20
1994	A Holiday Opportunity 599735	Yr.Iss.	1995	20.00	20
1994	Holiday Stars 599743	Yr.Iss.	1994	20.00	20
1994	The Latest Mews From Home 653977	Yr.Iss.	1994	16.00	16
1989	Tea For Two 693758 - N. Teiber	2-Yr.	1990	12.50	30
1990	Holiday Tea Toast 694770 - N. Teiber	2-Yr.	1991	13.50	14
1991	It's Tea-lightful 694789	2-Yr.	1992	13.50	14
1989	Tea Time 694797 - N. Teiber	2-Yr.	1990	12.50	30
1989	Bottom's Up 1989 830003	Yr.Iss.	1989	11.00	32
1990	Sweetest Greetings 1990 830011 - Gilmore	Yr.Iss.	1990	10.00	27
1990	First Class Christmas 830038 - Gilmore	3-Yr.	1992	10.00	10
1989	Caught In The Act 830046 - Gilmore	3-Yr.	1991	12.50	13
1989	Readin' & Ridin' 830054 - Gilmore	3-Yr.	1991	13.50	34
1991	Beary Merry Mailman 830151 - L. Rigg	3-Yr.	1993	13.50	14
1990	Here's Looking at You! 830259 - Gilmore	2-Yr.	1991	17.50	18
1991	Stamper 830267 - S. Zimnicki	Yr.Iss.	1991	13.50	14
1991	Santa's Key Man 830461 - Gilmore	2-Yr.	1992	11.00	11
1991	Tie-dings Of Joy 830488 - Gilmore	Yr.Iss.	1991	12.00	12
1990	Have a Cool Yule 830496 - Gilmore	3-Yr.	1992	12.00	27
1990	Slots of Luck 830518 - Hahn	2-Yr.	1991	13.50	45-60
1991	Straight To Santa 830534 - J. Davis	2-Yr.	1992	13.50	14
1993	A Toast Ladled With Love 830828 - Hahn	2-Yr.	1994	15.00	15
1991	Letters To Santa 830925 - Gilmore	2-Yr.	1992	15.00	15
1991	Sneaking Santa's Snack 830933 - Gilmore	3-Yr.	1993	13.00	13
1991	Aiming For The Holidays 830941 - Gilmore	2-Yr.	1992	12.00	12
1991	Ode To Joy 830968 - Gilmore	3-Yr.	1993	10.00	10
1991	Fittin' Mittens 830976 - Gilmore	3-Yr.	1993	12.00	12
1992	Merry Kisses 831166	2-Yr.	1993	17.50	18
1992	Christmas Is In The Air 831174	2-Yr.	1993	25.00	25
1992	To The Point 831182	2-Yr.	1993	13.50	14
1992	Poppin' Hoppin' Holidays 831263 - Gilmore	Yr.Iss.	1992	25.00	25
1992	Tankful Tidings 831271 - Gilmore	2-Yr.	1993	30.00	30
1991	The Finishing Touch 831530 - Gilmore	Yr.Iss.	1991	10.00	10
1992	Ginger-Bred Greetings 831581 - Gilmore	Yr.Iss.	1992	12.00	10-12
1991	A Real Classic 831603 - Gilmore	Yr.Iss.	1991	10.00	10
1993	Delivered to The Nick In Time 831808 - Gilmore	2-Yr.	1994	13.50	14
1993	Sneaking A Peek 831840 - Gilmore	2-Yr.	1994	10.00	10
1993	Jewel Box Ballet 831859 - Hahn	2-Yr.	1994	20.00	20
1993	A Mistle-Tow 831867 - Gilmore	2-Yr.	1994	15.00	15
1991	Christmas Fills The Air 831921 - Gilmore	3-Yr.	1993	12.00	12
1992	A Gold Star For Teacher 831948 - Gilmore	3-Yr.	1994	15.00	15
1992	A Tall Order 832758 - Gilmore	3-Yr.	1994	12.00	12
1992	Candlelight Serenade 832766 - Gilmore	2-Yr.	1993	12.00	12
1992	Holiday Glow Puppet Show 832774 - Gilmore	3-Yr.	1994	15.00	15
1992	Christopher Columouse 832782 - Gilmore	Yr.Iss.	1992	12.00	12
1992	Cartin' Home Holiday Treats 832790	2-Yr.	1993	13.50	14
1992	Making Tracks To Santa 832804 - Gilmore	2-Yr.	1993	15.00	15
1992	Special Delivery 832812	2-Yr.	1993	12.00	12
1992	A Mug Full Of Love 832928 - Gilmore	Yr.Iss.	1992	13.50	14
1993	Grandma's Liddle Griddle 832936 - Gilmore	Yr.Iss.	1993	10.00	10
1992	Have A Cool Christmas 832944 - Gilmore	Yr.Iss.	1992	13.50	14
1992	Knitten' Kittens 832952 - Gilmore	Yr.Iss.	1992	17.50	18
1992	Holiday Honors 833029 - Gilmore	Yr.Iss.	1992	15.00	15
1993	To A Grade "A" Teacher 833037 - Gilmore	2-Yr.	1994	10.00	10
1992	Christmas Nite Cap 834424 - Gilmore	3-Yr.	1994	13.50	14
1993	Have A Cool Christmas 834467 - Gilmore	2-Yr.	1994	10.00	10
1993	For A Star Aunt 834556 - Gilmore	Yr.Iss.	1993	12.00	12
1994	You're A Winner Son! 834564 - Gilmore	Yr.Iss.	1994	18.50	19
1994	Especially For You 834580 - Gilmore	Yr.Iss.	1994	27.50	28
1992	North Pole Peppermint Patrol 840157 - Gilmore	2-Yr.	1993	25.00	25
1992	A Boot-iful Christmas 840165 - Gilmore	Yr.Iss.	1992	20.00	20
1994	Watching For Santa 840432	2-Yr.	1994	25.00	30
1992	Special Delivery 840440	Yr.Iss.	1992	22.50	23
1991	Deck The Halls 860573 - M. Peters	3-Yr.	1993	12.00	12
1991	Bathing Beauty 860581 - Hahn	3-Yr.	1993	13.50	35

United Design Corp.

Angels Collection-Tree Ornaments™ - P.J. Jonas, unless otherwise noted

YEAR ISSUE		EDITION LIMIT	YEAR RETD.	ISSUE PRICE	*QUOTE U.S.$
1992	Angel and Tambourine IBO-422 - S. Bradford	Retrd.	1997	20.00	20
1992	Angel and Tambourine, ivory IBO-425 - S. Bradford	Retrd.	1997	20.00	20
1993	Angel Baby w/ Bunny IBO-426 - D. Newburn	Retrd.	1996	23.00	24
1996	Angel w/Doves on Cloud IBO-472	Retrd.	1998	25.00	25
1996	Angel w/Doves on Cloud, blue IBO-473	Retrd.	1998	25.00	25
1991	Angel Waif, ivory IBO-411	Open		15.00	20
1993	Angel Waif, plum IBO-437	Retrd.	1996	20.00	20
1995	Autumn's Bounty IBO-460	Retrd.	1997	32.00	32
1995	Autumn's Bounty, light IBO-454	Retrd.	1997	32.00	32
1995	Birds of a Feather IBO-457	Retrd.	1998	27.00	27
1990	Crystal Angel IBO-401	Retrd.	1993	20.00	20
1993	Crystal Angel, emerald IBO-446	Retrd.	1997	20.00	20
1990	Crystal Angel, ivory IBO-405	Retrd.	1997	20.00	20
1991	Fra Angelico Drummer, blue IBO-414 - S. Bradford	Retrd.	1997	20.00	20
1991	Fra Angelico Drummer, ivory IBO-420 - S. Bradford	Retrd.	1997	20.00	20
1991	Girl Cupid w/Rose, ivory IBO-413 - S. Bradford	Retrd.	1997	15.00	20
1995	Heavenly Blossoms IBO-458	Retrd.	1997	27.00	27
1993	Heavenly Harmony IBO-428	Retrd.	1997	25.00	30
1993	Heavenly Harmony, crimson IBO-433	Open		22.00	30
1993	Little Angel IBO-430 - D. Newburn	Retrd.	1998	18.00	20
1993	Little Angel, crimson IBO-445 - D. Newburn	Retrd.	1996	18.00	20
1992	Mary and Dove IBO-424 - S. Bradford	Retrd.	1997	20.00	20
1994	Music and Grace IBO-448	Retrd.	1998	24.00	25
1994	Music and Grace, crimson IBO-449	Retrd.	1997	24.00	24
1994	Musical Flight IBO-450	Retrd.	1997	28.00	28
1994	Musical Flight, crimson IBO-451	Retrd.	1997	28.00	28
1991	Peace Descending, ivory IBO-412	Retrd.	1997	20.00	20
1993	Peace Descending, crimson IBO-436	Retrd.	1997	20.00	20
1993	Renaissance Angel IBO-429	Retrd.	1997	24.00	24
1993	Renaissance Angel, crimson IBO-431	Retrd.	1997	24.00	24
1990	Rose of Sharon IBO-402	Retrd.	1993	20.00	20
1993	Rose of Sharon, crimson IBO-439	Retrd.	1997	20.00	20
1990	Rose of Sharon, ivory IBO-406	Open		20.00	20
1993	Rosetti Angel, crimson IBO-434	Retrd.	1997	20.00	24
1991	Rosetti Angel, ivory IBO-410	Open		20.00	24
1995	Special Wishes IBO-456 - D. Newburn	Retrd.	1998	27.00	27
1995	Spring's Rebirth IBO-452	Open		32.00	32
1996	Spring's Rebirth, green IBO-474	Retrd.	1998	25.00	25
1992	St. Francis and Critters IBO-423 - S. Bradford	Retrd.	1997	20.00	20
1994	Star Flight IBO-447	Retrd.	1998	20.00	20
1996	Star Flight, sapphire IBO-475	Open		20.00	20
1990	Star Glory IBO-403	Retrd.	1993	15.00	15
1993	Star Glory, crimson IBO-438	Retrd.	1997	20.00	20
1990	Star Glory, ivory IBO-407	Retrd.	1997	15.00	20
1993	Stars & Lace IBO-427	Retrd.	1998	18.00	20
1993	Stars & Lace, emerald IBO-432	Retrd.	1998	18.00	20
1995	Summer's Glory IBO-453	Retrd.	1998	32.00	32
1996	Summer's Glory, green IBO-476	Open		25.00	25
1995	Tender Time IBO-459	Retrd.	1997	27.00	27
1990	Victorian Angel IBO-404	Retrd.	1993	15.00	15
1990	Victorian Angel, ivory IBO-408	Retrd.	1997	15.00	20
1993	Victorian Angel, plum IBO-435	Retrd.	1997	18.00	20
1993	Victorian Cupid, crimson IBO-440	Open		15.00	20
1991	Victorian Cupid, ivory IBO-409	Open		15.00	20
1995	Winter's Light IBO-455	Retrd.	1997	32.00	32

*Quotes have been rounded up to nearest dollar

YEAR ISSUE	EDITION LIMIT	YEAR RETD.	ISSUE PRICE	*QUOTE U.S.$
1996 Wooden Angel IBO-461 - M. Ramsey	Open		20.00	20

Teddy Angels™ - P.J. Jonas

YEAR ISSUE	EDITION LIMIT	YEAR RETD.	ISSUE PRICE	*QUOTE U.S.$
1995 Casey "You're a bright & shining star." BA-017	Open		13.00	13
1995 Ivy "Enchantment glows in winter snows." BA-018	Open		13.00	13

Wallace Silversmiths

Annual Pewter Bells - Wallace

YEAR ISSUE	EDITION LIMIT	YEAR RETD.	ISSUE PRICE	*QUOTE U.S.$
1992 Angel	Closed	1992	25.00	40
1993 Santa Holding List	Closed	1993	25.00	25
1994 Large Santa Bell	Closed	1994	25.00	25
1995 Santa Bell	Closed	1995	25.00	25
1996 Santa Bell (North Pole)	Yr.Iss.		25.00	25

Annual Silverplated Sleigh Bells - Wallace

YEAR ISSUE	EDITION LIMIT	YEAR RETD.	ISSUE PRICE	*QUOTE U.S.$
1971 1st Edition Sleigh Bell	Closed	1971	12.95	500-1200
1972 2nd Edition Sleigh Bell	Closed	1972	12.95	200-650
1973 3rd Edition Sleigh Bell	Closed	1973	12.95	170-600
1974 4th Edition Sleigh Bell	Closed	1974	13.95	110-400
1975 5th Edition Sleigh Bell	Closed	1975	13.95	100-275
1976 6th Edition Sleigh Bell	Closed	1976	13.95	100-400
1977 7th Edition Sleigh Bell	Closed	1977	14.95	50-250
1978 8th Edition Sleigh Bell	Closed	1978	14.95	50-120
1979 9th Edition Sleigh Bell	Closed	1979	15.95	50-200
1980 10th Edition Sleigh Bell	Closed	1980	18.95	50-75
1981 11th Edition Sleigh Bell	Closed	1981	18.95	50-125
1982 12th Edition Sleigh Bell	Closed	1982	19.95	50-140
1983 13th Edition Sleigh Bell	Closed	1983	19.95	50-140
1984 14th Edition Sleigh Bell	Closed	1984	21.95	50-115
1985 15th Edition Sleigh Bell	Closed	1985	21.95	50-125
1986 16th Edition Sleigh Bell	Closed	1986	21.95	50-75
1987 17th Edition Sleigh Bell	Closed	1987	21.99	50-60
1988 18th Edition Sleigh Bell	Closed	1988	21.99	50-60
1989 19th Edition Sleigh Bell	Closed	1989	24.99	30-75
1990 20th Edition Sleigh Bell	Closed	1990	25.00	30-55
1990 Special Edition Sleigh Bell, gold	Closed	1990	35.00	30-85
1991 21st Edition Sleigh Bell	Closed	1991	25.00	30-40
1992 22nd Edition Sleigh Bell	Closed	1992	25.00	30-50
1993 23rd Edition Sleigh Bell	Closed	1993	25.00	30-50
1994 24th Edition Sleigh Bell	Closed	1994	25.00	30-50
1994 Sleigh Bell, gold	Closed	1994	35.00	30-35
1995 25th Edition Sleigh Bell	Closed	1995	30.00	30
1995 Sleigh Bell, gold	Closed	1995	35.00	30-45
1996 26th Edition Sleigh Bell	Closed	1996	30.00	30-35
1996 Sleigh Bell, gold	Closed	1996	35.00	30-35

Candy Canes - Wallace

YEAR ISSUE	EDITION LIMIT	YEAR RETD.	ISSUE PRICE	*QUOTE U.S.$
1981 Peppermint	Closed	1981	8.95	100-125
1982 Wintergreen	Closed	1982	9.95	30-110
1983 Cinnamon	Closed	1983	10.95	30-75
1984 Clove	Closed	1984	10.95	30-85
1985 Dove Motif	Closed	1985	11.95	30-70
1986 Bell Motif	Closed	1986	11.95	50-135
1987 Teddy Bear Motif	Closed	1987	12.95	30-75
1988 Christmas Rose	Closed	1988	13.99	25-75
1989 Christmas Candle	Closed	1989	14.99	25-45
1990 Reindeer	Closed	1990	16.00	25-35
1991 Christmas Goose	Closed	1991	16.00	25-35
1992 Angel	Closed	1992	16.00	25-30
1993 Snowmen	Closed	1993	16.00	25-50
1994 Canes	Closed	1994	17.00	13-25
1995 Santa	Closed	1995	18.00	13-20
1996 Soldiers	Closed	1996	18.00	13-20

Cathedral Ornaments - Wallace

YEAR ISSUE	EDITION LIMIT	YEAR RETD.	ISSUE PRICE	*QUOTE U.S.$
1988 1988-1st Edition	Closed	1988	24.99	45
1989 1989-2nd Edition	Closed	1989	24.99	30
1990 1990-3rd Edition	Closed	1990	25.00	25

Grande Baroque 12 Day Series - Wallace

YEAR ISSUE	EDITION LIMIT	YEAR RETD.	ISSUE PRICE	*QUOTE U.S.$
1988 Partridge	Closed	1988	39.99	50-80
1989 Two Turtle Doves	Closed	1989	39.99	45-65
1990 Three French Hens	Closed	1990	40.00	45-75
1991 Four Colly Birds	Closed	1991	40.00	55-75
1992 Five Golden Rings	Closed	1992	40.00	45-60
1993 Six Geese-a-Laying	Closed	1993	40.00	45-60
1994 Seven Swans-a-Swimming	Closed	1994	40.00	40-50
1995 Eight Maids-a-Milking	Closed	1995	40.00	40
1996 Nine Ladies Dancing	Closed	1996	40.00	40-50

Walnut Ridge Collectibles

Gossamer Wings - K. Bejma

YEAR ISSUE	EDITION LIMIT	YEAR RETD.	ISSUE PRICE	*QUOTE U.S.$
1996 Charity Piece - Glimmer of Hope I	Yr.Iss.	1996	40.00	40
1997 Charity Piece - Glimmer of Hope II	Yr.Iss.	1997	40.00	46

Limited Edition Christmas Ornament - K. Bejma

YEAR ISSUE	EDITION LIMIT	YEAR RETD.	ISSUE PRICE	*QUOTE U.S.$
1996 Snowy, Snowy Night 703	Yr.Iss.	1996	56.00	56

Ornament Collection - K. Bejma

YEAR ISSUE	EDITION LIMIT	YEAR RETD.	ISSUE PRICE	*QUOTE U.S.$
1997 Acorn 68	Open		22.00	24
1997 Angel 84	Open		30.00	30
1994 Angel Bunny 21	Retrd.	1997	26.00	30
1995 Angel Donkey 24	Open		26.00	30
1995 Angel Elephant 23	Open		26.00	30
1996 Angel Frog 40	Open		22.00	24
1997 Angel Holding Child 52	Open		30.00	36
1993 Angel Icicle 9	Retrd.	1996	22.00	22
1994 Angel Kitty 20	Retrd.	1997	26.00	30
1998 Angel on World T-5	Open		36.00	36
1997 Angel Penguin 82	Open		30.00	30
1994 Angel Pig 22	Open		26.00	30
1996 Angel w/Star on Wand 35	Open		24.00	30
1997 Angel with 2 Children 53	Open		30.00	36
1997 Angel with Doves 51	Open		30.00	36
1994 Angels, set/3 15	Retrd.	1997	66.00	76
1995 Angels, set/3 18	Retrd.	1997	66.00	72
1998 Angels, set/3 94	Open		76.00	76
1997 Artichoke 67	Open		22.00	24
1997 Asparagus 66	Open		22.00	24
1997 Baby on Crescent Moon 50	Open		30.00	36
1993 Baby Snowman Icicle 12	Retrd.	1996	22.00	22
1996 Baby's First 33	Open		30.00	36
1998 Basket 78	Open		26.00	26
1997 Bear Angel 61	Open		26.00	30
1996 Black and White Bunny 28	Open		26.00	30
1997 Blue Father Xmas 56	Open		22.00	24
1996 Calico Cat 27	Open		26.00	32
1998 Candy Cane Santa 91	Open		36.00	36
1995 Carrot-cicle 17	Open		22.00	30
1998 Carrots, set/12 79	Open		48.00	48
1996 Cat-cicle 36	Open		22.00	28
1996 Cat-cicle w/Stocking 37	Open		22.00	26
1998 Celestial Santa 92	Open		36.00	36
1993 Cherub Icicle 8	Retrd.	1996	22.00	22
1997 Cherubs, set/3 83	Open		54.00	54
1998 Chicks, set/3 74	Open		44.00	44
1997 Chili Pepper 62	Open		22.00	24
1997 Christmas Tree 89	Open		26.00	26
1997 Corkscrew Santa 58	Open		22.00	24
1997 Corn 65	Open		22.00	24
1996 Crescent Santa 29	Open		28.00	36
1998 Dog Angel 97	Open		30.00	30
1997 Dolphin Angel 86	Open		30.00	30
1997 Eggplant 64	Open		22.00	24
1993 Father Christmas Icicle 13	Retrd.	1996	22.00	22
1994 Father Christmas, set/3 16	Retrd.	1997	66.00	80
1993 Father Snowman Icicle 10	Retrd.	1996	22.00	22
1997 Giraffe Angel 41	Open		28.00	36
1996 Golden Father Christmas 38	Open		24.00	30
1997 Golden Top Father Xmas 57	Open		22.00	24
1997 Green Pepper 63	Open		22.00	24
1997 Ice Top Santa 55	Open		24.00	26
1997 Kangaroo Angel 43	Open		26.00	30
1996 Kitty Angel 34	Open		24.00	30
1998 Lace Egg, oblong 76	Open		26.00	26
1998 Lace Egg, upright 75	Open		26.00	26
1998 Lacy Eggs, set/6 81	Open		64.00	64
1998 Lacy Hearts, set/5 77	Open		60.00	60
1993 Mother Snowman Icicle 11	Retrd.	1996	22.00	24
1994 Nutcracker 30	Retrd.	1997	22.00	24
1995 Nutcracker 31	Retrd.	1997	22.00	24
1996 Nutcracker 32	Retrd.	1997	22.00	24
1998 Ostrich Angel 99	Open		36.00	36
1997 Peach 69	Open		22.00	22
1998 Pegasus Angel 98	Open		36.00	36
1998 Pinecone with Holly 93	Open		24.00	24
1998 Pinecone, lg. T 2	Open		24.00	24
1997 Pinetree Santa 54	Open		24.00	26
1997 Polar Bear Angel 42	Open		26.00	30
1995 Reindeer 26	Open		22.00	30
1997 Reindeer Angel 88	Open		30.00	30
1997 Santa Bell 59	Open		30.00	40
1997 Santa Face, lg. 45	Open		30.00	34
1993 Santa Icicle 14	Retrd.	1996	22.00	25
1998 Santa's Heads, set/3 T-1	Open		78.00	78
1995 Snow Family, set/3 19	Retrd.	1997	66.00	80
1998 Snowbaby T-4	Open		24.00	24
1997 Snowman Face 48	Open		24.00	26
1997 Snowman Icicle/Stocking Hat 47	Open		24.00	26
1997 Snowman Icicle/Top Hat 46	Open		24.00	26
1997 Snowman with Cane 49	Open		26.00	30
1996 Snowman, set/2 39	Open		44.00	54
1998 Spiral Snowman T-3	Open		26.00	26
1997 Spring Bunnies, set/2 90	Open		60.00	60
1998 Tiger Angel 95	Open		36.00	36
1997 Tricolor Pinecones, set/3 44	Open		48.00	50
1997 Turtle Angel 60	Open		24.00	26
1998 Victorian Ball, oblong 73	Open		24.00	24
1998 Victorian Ball, round 72	Open		24.00	24
1998 Victorian Ball/1 Cherub 71	Open		28.00	28
1998 Victorian Ball/4 Cherubs 70	Open		30.00	30
1997 Whale Angel 87	Open		30.00	30
1998 Zebra Angel 96	Open		36.00	36

Walt Disney

Disney's Enchanted Castles - Disney Studios

YEAR ISSUE	EDITION LIMIT	YEAR RETD.	ISSUE PRICE	*QUOTE U.S.$
1998 A Castle for Cinderella 41293	Open		45.00	45
1998 The Beast's Castle 41294	Open		45.00	45

Disney's Enchanted Places - Disney Studios

YEAR ISSUE	EDITION LIMIT	YEAR RETD.	ISSUE PRICE	*QUOTE U.S.$
1997 Cruella's Car 41245	Open		45.00	45
1997 An Elegant Coach for Cinderella 41244	Open		45.00	45
1996 Grandpa's House from Peter & The Wolf 41222	Closed	1996	35.00	35
1997 The Jolly Roger 41243	Open		45.00	45

Mickey's Christmas Carol - Disney Studios

YEAR ISSUE	EDITION LIMIT	YEAR RETD.	ISSUE PRICE	*QUOTE U.S.$
1998 Jiminy Cricket: "Ghost of Christmas Past" 41251	Open		50.00	50
1997 Mickey Mouse: "And a Merry Christmas to you..." 41144	Open		50.00	50
1997 Minnie Mouse: Mrs. Crachit 41145	Open		50.00	50
1997 Scrooge: "Bah-humbug!" 41146	Open		50.00	50

Open House - Disney Studios

YEAR ISSUE	EDITION LIMIT	YEAR RETD.	ISSUE PRICE	*QUOTE U.S.$
1998 Simba 41256	Closed	1998	49.00	49
1998 Dumbo 41283	Closed	1998	50.00	50

Walt Disney Classics Collection-Holiday Series - Disney Studios

YEAR ISSUE	EDITION LIMIT	YEAR RETD.	ISSUE PRICE	*QUOTE U.S.$
1995 Mickey Mouse: "Presents for My Pals" 41087	Closed	1995	40.00	40-75
1996 Pluto: Pluto Helps Decorate 41113	Closed	1996	50.00	50-60
1997 Chip 'n Dale: Little Mischief Makers 41190	Closed	1997	50.00	50
1998 Minnie Mouse: Caroler Minnie 41311	Yr.Iss.	1998	50.00	50

Willitts Designs

Ebony Visions - T. Blackshear

YEAR ISSUE	EDITION LIMIT	YEAR RETD.	ISSUE PRICE	*QUOTE U.S.$
1997 Little Blue Wings	17,200	1997	28.50	50-75
1998 On Wings of Praise	Yr.Iss.	1998	29.50	30

Rainbow Babies - A. Blackshear

YEAR ISSUE	EDITION LIMIT	YEAR RETD.	ISSUE PRICE	*QUOTE U.S.$
1998 Flutterby	Open		28.50	29

Woodland Winds/Christopher Radko

Woodland Winds Glass Ornaments - C. Radko

YEAR ISSUE	EDITION LIMIT	YEAR RETD.	ISSUE PRICE	*QUOTE U.S.$
1998 Balancing Act 98-820-0	Open		47.00	47
1998 Bearly Napping 98-715-0	Open		36.00	36
1998 Blizzard Baron 98-822-0	Open		42.00	42
1998 Blizzard Santa 98-811-0	Open		45.00	45
1998 Blizzard's Tree 98-818-0	Open		39.00	39
1998 Bunny Drifter 98-714-0	Open		36.00	36
1998 Carlton The Snowman 98-712-0	Open		42.00	42
1998 Deer Friends Wreath 98-815-0	Open		39.00	39
1998 Emerald Nuts & Berries 98-717-0	Open		80.00	80
1998 Flying Squirrel 98-716-0	Open		36.00	36
1998 Frosty Leaf Santa 98-711-0	Open		47.00	47
1998 Guardian Angel 98-821-0	Open		42.00	42
1998 Maple Frost 98-489-0	Open		26.00	26
1998 Mini Maple Frost 98-148-0	Open		18.00	18
1998 Mini Oak Frost 98-164-0	Open		18.00	18
1998 Oak Frost 98-490-0	Open		26.50	27
1998 Santa's Leaf Ride 98-713-0	Open		45.00	45
1998 Scarlet Nuts & Berries 98-718-0	Open		80.00	80
1998 Snow Bunny 98-813-0	Open		45.00	45
1998 Snow Racer 98-814-0	Open		39.00	39
1998 Snow Tunes 98-812-0	Open		45.00	45
1998 Stardust Santa 98-817-0	Open		47.00	47
1998 Stardust Snowflake 98-816-0	Open		47.00	47
1998 Surrounded by Friends 98-819-0	Open		49.00	49

Woodland Winds Porcelain Ornaments - C. Radko

YEAR ISSUE	EDITION LIMIT	YEAR RETD.	ISSUE PRICE	*QUOTE U.S.$
1998 Balancing Act 98-837-0	Open		14.00	14
1998 Bearly Drifting 98-732-0	Open		12.00	12
1998 Bunny Drifter 98-733-0	Open		12.00	12
1998 Carlton The Snowman 98-729-0	Open		20.00	20
1998 Close To My Heart 98-832-0	Open		12.00	12
1998 Floating Leaf Santa 98-725-0	Open		16.00	16
1998 Frosty Leaf Santa 98-726-0	Open		22.50	23
1998 Frosty Leaf Santa 98-728-0	Open		20.00	20
1998 Frosty Leaf Santa w/Bear 98-730-0	Open		16.00	16
1998 Good Catch 98-838-0	Open		12.00	12
1998 Gotcha 98-835-0	Open		12.00	12
1998 Guardian Angel 98-836-0	Open		12.00	12
1998 High Flying 98-827-0	Open		12.00	12
1998 Jingle Bell Ride 98-833-0	Open		12.00	12
1998 Leaf Acorn Snowflake 98-736-0	Open		10.00	10
1998 Leaf Bunnies 98-731-0	Open		14.00	14
1998 Look What I Found 98-830-0	Open		14.00	14
1998 Peppermint Twist 98-829-0	Open		14.00	14
1998 Sailing The North Wind 98-831-0	Open		12.00	12
1998 Santa Leaf Ride 98-734-0	Open		16.00	16
1998 Santa w/Banner-1998 98-727-0	Yr.Iss.		20.00	20
1998 Sleeping Teddy 98-735-0	Open		12.00	12
1998 Snow Flight 98-828-0	Open		14.00	14
1998 Snowfall 98-826-0	Open		12.00	12

PLATES

American Artists

The Best of Fred Stone-Mares & Foals Series (6 1/2 ") - F. Stone

YEAR ISSUE	EDITION LIMIT	YEAR RETD.	ISSUE PRICE	*QUOTE U.S.$
1991 Patience	19,500		25.00	25-55
1992 Water Trough	19,500		25.00	25-55
1992 Pasture Pest	19,500		25.00	25-55
1992 Kidnapped Mare	19,500		25.00	25-30
1993 Contentment	19,500		25.00	25-30
1993 Arabian Mare & Foal	19,500		25.00	25-30
1994 Diamond in the Rough	19,500		25.00	25-30
1995 The First Day	19,500		25.00	25-30

Famous Fillies Series - F. Stone

YEAR ISSUE	EDITION LIMIT	YEAR RETD.	ISSUE PRICE	*QUOTE U.S.$
1987 Lady's Secret	9,500		65.00	70
1988 Ruffian	9,500		65.00	65-99
1988 Genuine Risk	9,500		65.00	68-85

*Quotes have been rounded up to nearest dollar

YEAR ISSUE	EDITION LIMIT	YEAR RETD.	ISSUE PRICE	*QUOTE U.S.$
1992 Go For The Wand	9,500		65.00	80-90

Fred Stone Classic Series - F. Stone

YEAR ISSUE	EDITION LIMIT	YEAR RETD.	ISSUE PRICE	*QUOTE U.S.$
1986 The Shoe-8,000 Wins	9,500		75.00	70-99
1986 The Eternal Legacy	9,500		75.00	95-99
1988 Forever Friends	9,500		75.00	70-85
1989 Alysheba	9,500		75.00	75

Gold Signature Series - F. Stone

YEAR ISSUE	EDITION LIMIT	YEAR RETD.	ISSUE PRICE	*QUOTE U.S.$
1990 Secretariat Final Tribute, signed	4,500		150.00	390-450
1990 Secretariat Final Tribute, unsigned	7,500		75.00	140-175
1991 Old Warriors, signed	4,500		150.00	425
1991 Old Warriors, unsigned	7,500		75.00	100

Gold Signature Series II - F. Stone

YEAR ISSUE	EDITION LIMIT	YEAR RETD.	ISSUE PRICE	*QUOTE U.S.$
1991 Northern Dancer, double signature	1,500		175.00	250-350
1991 Northern Dancer, single signature	3,000		150.00	150-199
1991 Northern Dancer, unsigned	7,500		75.00	75-99
1991 Kelso, double signature	1,500		175.00	175-325
1991 Kelso, single signature	3,000		150.00	150-199
1991 Kelso, unsigned	7,500		75.00	75-99

Gold Signature Series III - F. Stone

YEAR ISSUE	EDITION LIMIT	YEAR RETD.	ISSUE PRICE	*QUOTE U.S.$
1992 Dance Smartly-Pat Day, Up, double signature	1,500		175.00	175
1992 Dance Smartly-Pat Day, Up, single signature	3,000		150.00	150
1992 Dance Smartly-Pat Day, Up, unsigned	7,500		75.00	75
1993 American Triple Crown-1937-1946, signed	2,500		195.00	250-350
1993 American Triple Crown-1937-1946, unsigned	7,500		75.00	95-125
1993 American Triple Crown-1948-1978, signed	2,500		195.00	250-325
1993 American Triple Crown-1948-1978, unsigned	7,500		75.00	175-195
1994 American Triple Crown-1919-1935, signed	2,500		95.00	95-149
1994 American Triple Crown-1919-1935, unsigned	7,500		75.00	75-90

Gold Signature Series IV - F. Stone

YEAR ISSUE	EDITION LIMIT	YEAR RETD.	ISSUE PRICE	*QUOTE U.S.$
1995 Julie Krone - Colonial Affair	7,500		75.00	75
1995 Julie Krone - Colonial Affair, signed	2,500		150.00	150

The Horses of Fred Stone - F. Stone

YEAR ISSUE	EDITION LIMIT	YEAR RETD.	ISSUE PRICE	*QUOTE U.S.$
1982 Patience	9,500		55.00	95-125
1982 Arabian Mare and Foal	9,500		55.00	125-149
1982 Safe and Sound	9,500		55.00	75-125
1983 Contentment	9,500		55.00	125-149

Mare and Foal Series - F. Stone

YEAR ISSUE	EDITION LIMIT	YEAR RETD.	ISSUE PRICE	*QUOTE U.S.$
1986 Water Trough	12,500		49.50	149-175
1986 Tranquility	12,500		49.50	95-149
1986 Pasture Pest	12,500		49.50	125-149
1987 The Arabians	12,500		49.50	95-125

Mare and Foal Series II - F. Stone

YEAR ISSUE	EDITION LIMIT	YEAR RETD.	ISSUE PRICE	*QUOTE U.S.$
1989 The First Day	Open		35.00	35
1989 Diamond in the Rough	Retrd.		35.00	35

Racing Legends - F. Stone

YEAR ISSUE	EDITION LIMIT	YEAR RETD.	ISSUE PRICE	*QUOTE U.S.$
1989 Phar Lap	9,500		75.00	75-95
1989 Sunday Silence	9,500		75.00	75
1990 John Henry-Shoemaker	9,500		75.00	70-75

Sport of Kings Series - F. Stone

YEAR ISSUE	EDITION LIMIT	YEAR RETD.	ISSUE PRICE	*QUOTE U.S.$
1984 Man O'War	9,500		65.00	149-175
1984 Secretariat	9,500		65.00	200-249
1985 John Henry	9,500		65.00	75
1986 Seattle Slew	9,500		65.00	95-125

The Stallion Series - F. Stone

YEAR ISSUE	EDITION LIMIT	YEAR RETD.	ISSUE PRICE	*QUOTE U.S.$
1983 Black Stallion	19,500		49.50	75-199
1983 Andalusian	19,500		49.50	70-199

Anheuser-Busch, Inc.

1992 Olympic Team Series - A-Busch, Inc.

YEAR ISSUE	EDITION LIMIT	YEAR RETD.	ISSUE PRICE	*QUOTE U.S.$
1991 1992 Olympic Team Winter N3180	Retrd.	1994	35.00	20-35
1992 1992 Olympic Team Summer N3122	Retrd.	1994	35.00	20-35

Archives Plate Series - D. Langeneckert

YEAR ISSUE	EDITION LIMIT	YEAR RETD.	ISSUE PRICE	*QUOTE U.S.$
1992 1893 Columbian Exposition N3477	25-day	1996	27.50	25-35
1992 Ganymede N4004	25-day	1996	27.50	25-50
1995 Budweiser's Greatest Triumph N5195	25-day	1996	27.50	25-50
1995 Mirror of Truth N5196	25-day	1997	27.50	25-36

Civil War Series - D. Langeneckert

YEAR ISSUE	EDITION LIMIT	YEAR RETD.	ISSUE PRICE	*QUOTE U.S.$
1992 General Grant N3478	Retrd.	1994	45.00	25-45
1993 General Robert E. Lee N3590	Retrd.	1994	45.00	25-45
1993 President Abraham Lincoln N3591	Retrd.	1994	45.00	25-45

Collector Edition Series - M. Urdahl

YEAR ISSUE	EDITION LIMIT	YEAR RETD.	ISSUE PRICE	*QUOTE U.S.$
1995 "This Bud's For You" N4945	25-day		27.50	25-30

Holiday Plate Series - Various

YEAR ISSUE	EDITION LIMIT	YEAR RETD.	ISSUE PRICE	*QUOTE U.S.$
1989 Winters Day N2295 - B. Kemper	Retrd.	N/A	30.00	50-175
1990 An American Tradition N2767 - S. Sampson	Retrd.	N/A	30.00	25-75
1991 The Season's Best N3034 - S. Sampson	Retrd.	N/A	30.00	25-100
1992 A Perfect Christmas N3440 - S. Sampson	Retrd.	N/A	27.50	25-100
1993 Special Delivery N4002 - N. Koerber	Retrd.	1994	27.50	45-150
1994 Hometown Holiday N4572 - B. Kemper	Retrd.	N/A	27.50	25-75
1995 Lighting the Way Home N5215 - T. Jester	25-day	1998	27.50	28
1996 Budweiser Clydesdales N5778 - J. Raedeke	25-day		27.50	25-28
1997 Home For The Holidays N5779 - H. Droog	25-day		27.50	25-28
1998 Grant's Farm Holiday N5780 - E. Kastaris	25-day		28.00	25-28

Man's Best Friend Series - M. Urdahl

YEAR ISSUE	EDITION LIMIT	YEAR RETD.	ISSUE PRICE	*QUOTE U.S.$
1990 Buddies N2615	Retrd.	N/A	30.00	50-125
1990 Six Pack N3005	Retrd.	1992	30.00	30-125
1992 Something's Brewing N3147	Retrd.	1994	30.00	25-80
1993 Outstanding in Their Field N4003	Retrd.	1995	27.50	25-40

Anna-Perenna Porcelain

American Silhouettes Family Series - P. Buckley Moss

YEAR ISSUE	EDITION LIMIT	YEAR RETD.	ISSUE PRICE	*QUOTE U.S.$
1982 Family Outing	5,000		75.00	150-175
1982 John and Mary	5,000		75.00	125-195
1984 Homemakers Quilting	5,000		75.00	85-195
1983 Leisure Time	5,000		75.00	85

American Silhouettes Valley Series - P. Buckley Moss

YEAR ISSUE	EDITION LIMIT	YEAR RETD.	ISSUE PRICE	*QUOTE U.S.$
1982 Frosty Frolic	5,000		75.00	250
1984 Hay Ride	5,000		75.00	85
1983 Sunday Ride	5,000		75.00	85-100
1983 Market Day	5,000		75.00	120

American Silhouettes-Childrens Series - P. Buckley Moss

YEAR ISSUE	EDITION LIMIT	YEAR RETD.	ISSUE PRICE	*QUOTE U.S.$
1981 Fiddlers Two	5,000		75.00	400-500
1982 Mary With The Lambs	5,000		75.00	125-200
1983 Ring-Around-the-Rosie	5,000		75.00	200
1983 Waiting For Tom	5,000		75.00	175

Annual Christmas Plate - P. Buckley Moss

YEAR ISSUE	EDITION LIMIT	YEAR RETD.	ISSUE PRICE	*QUOTE U.S.$
1984 Noel, Noel	5,000		75.00	325-500
1985 Helping Hands	5,000		75.00	200-250
1986 Night Before Christmas	5,000		75.00	100-125
1987 Christmas Sleigh	5,000		75.00	125-275
1988 Christmas Joy	7,500		75.00	75-150
1989 Christmas Carol	7,500		80.00	125-150
1990 Christmas Eve	7,500		80.00	80-150
1991 The Snowman	7,500		80.00	80-165
1992 Christmas Warmth	7,500		85.00	85-155
1993 Joy to the World	7,500		85.00	85-155
1994 Christmas Night	5,000		85.00	85
1995 Christmas at Home	5,000		85.00	85

The Celebration Series - P. Buckley Moss

YEAR ISSUE	EDITION LIMIT	YEAR RETD.	ISSUE PRICE	*QUOTE U.S.$
1986 Wedding Joy	5,000		100.00	200-375
1987 The Christening	5,000		100.00	150-200
1988 The Anniversary	5,000		100.00	100
1990 Family Reunion	5,000		100.00	125-175

Uncle Tad's Cats - T. Krumeich

YEAR ISSUE	EDITION LIMIT	YEAR RETD.	ISSUE PRICE	*QUOTE U.S.$
1979 Oliver's Birthday	5,000		75.00	150-300
1980 Peaches & Cream	5,000		75.00	85-150
1981 Princess Aurora	5,000		80.00	80-85
1981 Walter's Window	5,000		80.00	80-175

ANRI

ANRI Father's Day - Unknown

YEAR ISSUE	EDITION LIMIT	YEAR RETD.	ISSUE PRICE	*QUOTE U.S.$
1972 Alpine Father & Children	Closed	1972	35.00	100
1973 Alpine Father & Children	Closed	1973	40.00	100-149
1974 Cliff Gazing	Closed	1974	50.00	100
1975 Sailing	Closed	1975	60.00	90

ANRI Mother's Day - Unknown

YEAR ISSUE	EDITION LIMIT	YEAR RETD.	ISSUE PRICE	*QUOTE U.S.$
1972 Alpine Mother & Children	Closed	1972	35.00	50
1973 Alpine Mother & Children	Closed	1973	40.00	50
1974 Alpine Mother & Children	Closed	1974	50.00	55
1975 Alpine Stroll	Closed	1975	60.00	65
1976 Knitting	Closed	1976	60.00	65

Christmas - J. Malfertheiner, unless otherwise noted

YEAR ISSUE	EDITION LIMIT	YEAR RETD.	ISSUE PRICE	*QUOTE U.S.$
1971 St. Jakob in Groden	6,000	1971	37.50	65
1972 Pipers at Alberobello	6,000	1972	45.00	75
1973 Alpine Horn	6,000	1973	45.00	395
1974 Young Man and Girl	6,000	1974	50.00	95
1975 Christmas in Ireland	6,000	1975	60.00	60
1976 Alpine Christmas	6,000	1976	65.00	190
1977 Legend of Heligenblut	6,000	1977	65.00	91
1978 Klockler Singers	6,000	1978	80.00	90
1979 Moss Gatherers - Unknown	6,000	1979	135.00	177
1980 Wintry Churchgoing - Unknown	6,000	1980	165.00	165
1981 Santa Claus in Tyrol - Unknown	6,000	1981	165.00	200
1982 The Star Singers - Unknown	6,000	1982	165.00	165
1983 Unto Us a Child is Born - Unknown	6,000	1983	165.00	310
1984 Yuletide in the Valley - Unknown	6,000	1984	165.00	170
1985 Good Morning, Good Cheer	6,000	1985	165.00	165
1986 A Groden Christmas	6,000	1986	165.00	200
1987 Down From the Alps	6,000	1987	195.00	250
1988 Christkindl Markt	6,000	1988	220.00	230
1989 Flight Into Egypt	6,000	1989	275.00	275
1990 Holy Night	6,000	1990	300.00	300

Disney Four Star Collection - Disney Studios

YEAR ISSUE	EDITION LIMIT	YEAR RETD.	ISSUE PRICE	*QUOTE U.S.$
1989 Mickey Mini Plate	5,000	1989	40.00	65-125
1990 Minnie Mini Plate	5,000	1990	40.00	95-125
1991 Donald Mini Plate	5,000	1991	50.00	95-175

Ferrandiz Christmas - J. Ferrandiz

YEAR ISSUE	EDITION LIMIT	YEAR RETD.	ISSUE PRICE	*QUOTE U.S.$
1972 Christ In The Manger	4,000	1972	35.00	200
1973 Christmas	4,000	1973	40.00	225-275
1974 Holy Night	4,000	1974	50.00	100
1975 Flight into Egypt	4,000	1975	60.00	95
1976 Tree of Life	4,000	1976	60.00	85
1977 Girl with Flowers	4,000	1977	65.00	185
1978 Leading the Way	4,000	1978	77.50	180
1979 The Drummer	4,000	1979	120.00	175
1980 Rejoice	4,000	1980	150.00	160
1981 Spreading the Word	4,000	1981	150.00	150
1982 The Shepherd Family	4,000	1982	150.00	150
1983 Peace Attend Thee	4,000	1983	150.00	150

Ferrandiz Mother's Day Series - J. Ferrandiz

YEAR ISSUE	EDITION LIMIT	YEAR RETD.	ISSUE PRICE	*QUOTE U.S.$
1972 Mother Sewing	3,000	1972	35.00	200
1973 Alpine Mother & Child	3,000	1973	40.00	150
1974 Mother Holding Child	3,000	1974	50.00	150
1975 Dove Girl	3,000	1975	60.00	150
1976 Mother Knitting	3,000	1976	60.00	200
1977 Alpine Stroll	3,000	1977	65.00	125
1978 The Beginning	3,000	1978	75.00	100-125
1979 All Hearts	3,000	1979	120.00	170
1980 Spring Arrivals	3,000	1980	150.00	165
1981 Harmony	3,000	1981	150.00	150
1982 With Love	3,000	1982	150.00	150

Ferrandiz Wooden Birthday Plates - J. Ferrandiz

YEAR ISSUE	EDITION LIMIT	YEAR RETD.	ISSUE PRICE	*QUOTE U.S.$
1972 Boy	Unkn.	1972	15.00	100-125
1972 Girl	Unkn.	1972	15.00	160
1973 Boy	Unkn.	1973	20.00	200
1973 Girl	Unkn.	1973	20.00	150
1974 Boy	Unkn.	1974	22.00	160
1974 Girl	Unkn.	1974	22.00	160

Ferrandiz Wooden Wedding Plates - J. Ferrandiz

YEAR ISSUE	EDITION LIMIT	YEAR RETD.	ISSUE PRICE	*QUOTE U.S.$
1972 Boy and Girl Embracing	Closed	1972	40.00	100-125
1973 Wedding Scene	Closed	1973	40.00	150
1974 Wedding	Closed	1974	48.00	150
1976 Wedding	Closed	1976	60.00	90-150
1975 Wedding	Closed	1975	60.00	150

Armstrong's

Commemorative Issues - R. Skelton

YEAR ISSUE	EDITION LIMIT	YEAR RETD.	ISSUE PRICE	*QUOTE U.S.$
1983 70 Years Young (10 1/2")	15,000		85.00	100-155
1984 Freddie the Torchbearer (8 1/2")	15,000		62.50	50-65
1994 Red & His Friends (12 1/4")	165	1994	700.00	1000-3500

Freedom Collection of Red Skelton - R. Skelton

YEAR ISSUE	EDITION LIMIT	YEAR RETD.	ISSUE PRICE	*QUOTE U.S.$
1990 The All American, (signed)	1,000	1990	195.00	400-600
1990 The All American	9,000		62.50	50-75
1991 Independence Day? (signed)	1,000	1991	195.00	250-375
1991 Independence Day?	9,000		62.50	50-65
1992 Let Freedom Ring, (signed)	1,000	1992	195.00	250-350
1992 Let Freedom Ring	9,000		62.50	50-75
1993 Freddie's Gift of Life, (signed)	1,000	1993	195.00	250-350
1993 Freddie's Gift of Life	9,000		62.50	50-60

The Golden Memories - R. Skelton

YEAR ISSUE	EDITION LIMIT	YEAR RETD.	ISSUE PRICE	*QUOTE U.S.$
1995 The Donut Dunker (signed)	1,000	1995	375.00	525-800
1996 Clem & Clementine (signed)	1,000	1996	385.00	420-600
1996 San Fernando Red (signed)	1,000	1996	385.00	375-500
1997 Jr., The Mean Widdle Kid (signed)	1,000	1997	385.00	375-500
1997 Cauliflower McPugg	1,000		295.00	295

Happy Art Series - W. Lantz

YEAR ISSUE	EDITION LIMIT	YEAR RETD.	ISSUE PRICE	*QUOTE U.S.$
1981 Woody's Triple Self-Portrait, (signed)	1,000		100.00	200
1981 Woody's Triple Self-Portrait	9,000		39.50	40
1983 Gothic Woody, (signed)	1,000	N/A	100.00	200
1983 Gothic Woody	9,000		39.50	40
1984 Blue Boy Woody, (signed)	1,000	N/A	100.00	200
1984 Blue Boy Woody	9,000	1992	39.50	40-50

The Signature Collection - R. Skelton

YEAR ISSUE	EDITION LIMIT	YEAR RETD.	ISSUE PRICE	*QUOTE U.S.$
1986 Anyone for Tennis?	9,000		62.50	75-125
1986 Anyone for Tennis? (signed)	1,000	1986	125.00	350-600
1987 Ironing the Waves	9,000		62.50	50-125
1987 Ironing the Waves (signed)	1,000	1987	125.00	200-500
1988 The Cliffhanger	9,000		62.50	65
1988 The Cliffhanger (signed)	1,000	1988	150.00	200-450
1988 Hooked on Freddie	9,000		62.50	65
1988 Hooked on Freddie (signed)	1,000	1988	175.00	250-400

Sports - Schenken

YEAR ISSUE	EDITION LIMIT	YEAR RETD.	ISSUE PRICE	*QUOTE U.S.$
1985 Pete Rose h/s (10 1/4")	1,000	N/A	100.00	200-350
1985 Pete Rose u/s (10 1/4")	10,000		45.00	75-99

Armstrong's/Crown Parian

Freddie The Freeloader - R. Skelton

YEAR ISSUE	EDITION LIMIT	YEAR RETD.	ISSUE PRICE	*QUOTE U.S.$
1979 Freddie in the Bathtub	10,000	N/A	55.00	110-450
1980 Freddie's Shack	10,000	N/A	55.00	90-325
1981 Freddie on the Green	10,000	N/A	60.00	64-250
1982 Love that Freddie	10,000	N/A	60.00	36-90

Freddie's Adventures - R. Skelton

YEAR ISSUE	EDITION LIMIT	YEAR RETD.	ISSUE PRICE	*QUOTE U.S.$
1982 Captain Freddie	15,000	N/A	60.00	26-70
1982 Bronco Freddie	15,000		62.50	24-75
1983 Sir Freddie	15,000		62.50	60-75
1984 Gertrude and Heathcliffe	15,000		62.50	84-125

*Quotes have been rounded up to nearest dollar

Armstrong's/Fairmont

Famous Clown Collection - R. Skelton

YEAR ISSUE	EDITION LIMIT	YEAR RETD.	ISSUE PRICE	*QUOTE U.S.$
1976 Freddie the Freeloader	10,000	N/A	55.00	650-1000
1977 W. C. Fields	10,000	N/A	55.00	65-200
1978 Happy	10,000	N/A	55.00	65-200
1979 The Pledge	10,000	N/A	55.00	65-200

Artaffects

Club Member Limited Edition Redemption Offerings - G. Perillo

YEAR ISSUE	EDITION LIMIT	YEAR RETD.	ISSUE PRICE	*QUOTE U.S.$
1992 The Pencil	Yr. Iss.	1992	35.00	75-150
1992 Studies in Black and White (Set/4)	Yr. Iss.	1992	75.00	100-149
1993 Watcher of the Wilderness	Yr. Iss.	1993	60.00	60

America's Indian Heritage - G. Perillo

YEAR ISSUE	EDITION LIMIT	YEAR RETD.	ISSUE PRICE	*QUOTE U.S.$
1987 Cheyenne Nation	Closed	N/A	24.50	65-75
1988 Arapaho Nation	Closed	N/A	24.50	65-75
1988 Kiowa Nation	Closed	N/A	24.50	65-75
1988 Sioux Nation	Closed	N/A	24.50	65-75
1988 Chippewa Nation	Closed	N/A	24.50	65-75
1988 Crow Nation	Closed	N/A	24.50	65-75
1988 Nez Perce Nation	Closed	N/A	24.50	65-75
1988 Blackfoot Nation	Closed	N/A	24.50	65-75

Chieftains I - G. Perillo

YEAR ISSUE	EDITION LIMIT	YEAR RETD.	ISSUE PRICE	*QUOTE U.S.$
1979 Chief Sitting Bull	7,500	N/A	65.00	275-400
1979 Chief Joseph	7,500	N/A	65.00	90-150
1980 Chief Red Cloud	7,500	N/A	65.00	114-150
1980 Chief Geronimo	7,500	N/A	65.00	74-150
1981 Chief Crazy Horse	7,500	N/A	65.00	75-200

Chieftains II - G. Perillo

YEAR ISSUE	EDITION LIMIT	YEAR RETD.	ISSUE PRICE	*QUOTE U.S.$
1983 Chief Pontiac	7,500	N/A	70.00	85-175
1983 Chief Victorio	7,500	N/A	70.00	150-175
1984 Chief Tecumseh	7,500	N/A	70.00	150-175
1984 Chief Cochise	7,500	N/A	70.00	80-175
1984 Chief Black Kettle	7,500	N/A	70.00	150-175

The Colts - G. Perillo

YEAR ISSUE	EDITION LIMIT	YEAR RETD.	ISSUE PRICE	*QUOTE U.S.$
1985 Appaloosa	5,000	N/A	40.00	40
1985 Pinto	5,000	N/A	40.00	56
1985 Arabian	5,000	N/A	40.00	56
1985 Thoroughbred	5,000	N/A	40.00	56

Council of Nations - G. Perillo

YEAR ISSUE	EDITION LIMIT	YEAR RETD.	ISSUE PRICE	*QUOTE U.S.$
1992 Strength of the Sioux	Closed	N/A	29.50	35-69
1992 Pride of the Cheyenne	Closed	N/A	29.50	35-65
1992 Dignity of the Nez Perce	Closed	N/A	29.50	35-59
1992 Courage of the Arapaho	Closed	N/A	29.50	35-55
1992 Power of the Blackfoot	Closed	N/A	29.50	26-55
1992 Nobility of the Algonquin	Closed	N/A	29.50	35-55
1992 Wisdom of the Cherokee	Closed	N/A	29.50	35-55
1992 Boldness of the Seneca	Closed	N/A	29.50	35-55

Indian Bridal - G. Perillo

YEAR ISSUE	EDITION LIMIT	YEAR RETD.	ISSUE PRICE	*QUOTE U.S.$
1990 Yellow Bird (6 1/2")	Closed	N/A	25.00	39-49
1990 Autumn Blossom (6 1/2")	Closed	N/A	25.00	39-45
1990 Misty Waters (6 1/2")	Closed	N/A	25.00	30
1990 Sunny Skies (6 1/2")	Closed	N/A	25.00	30

Indian Nations - G. Perillo

YEAR ISSUE	EDITION LIMIT	YEAR RETD.	ISSUE PRICE	*QUOTE U.S.$
1983 Blackfoot	7,500	N/A	140.00	350
1983 Cheyenne	7,500	N/A	set	Set
1983 Apache	7,500	N/A	set	Set
1983 Sioux	7,500	N/A	set	Set

March of Dimes: Our Children - G. Perillo

YEAR ISSUE	EDITION LIMIT	YEAR RETD.	ISSUE PRICE	*QUOTE U.S.$
1989 A Time to Be Born	7,500	N/A	29.00	29-75

Mother's Love - G. Perillo

YEAR ISSUE	EDITION LIMIT	YEAR RETD.	ISSUE PRICE	*QUOTE U.S.$
1988 Feelings	Yr.Iss.	1988	35.00	75-125
1989 Moonlight	Yr.Iss.	1989	35.00	65-100
1990 Pride & Joy	Yr.Iss.	1990	39.50	95-100
1991 Little Shadow	Yr.Iss.	1991	39.50	55-100

Motherhood Series - G. Perillo

YEAR ISSUE	EDITION LIMIT	YEAR RETD.	ISSUE PRICE	*QUOTE U.S.$
1983 Madre	10,000	N/A	50.00	75
1984 Madonna of the Plains	3,500	N/A	50.00	75-85
1985 Abuela	3,500	N/A	50.00	75
1986 Nap Time	3,500	N/A	50.00	75-85

Native American Christmas - G. Perillo

YEAR ISSUE	EDITION LIMIT	YEAR RETD.	ISSUE PRICE	*QUOTE U.S.$
1993 The Little Shepherd	Yr.Iss.	1993	35.00	55-65
1994 Joy to the World	Yr.Iss.	1994	45.00	45-55

Nature's Harmony - G. Perillo

YEAR ISSUE	EDITION LIMIT	YEAR RETD.	ISSUE PRICE	*QUOTE U.S.$
1982 The Peaceable Kingdom	12,500	N/A	100.00	125-299
1982 Zebra	12,500	N/A	50.00	50
1982 Bengal Tiger	12,500	N/A	50.00	60
1983 Black Panther	12,500	N/A	50.00	70
1983 Elephant	12,500	N/A	50.00	95-125

North American Wildlife - G. Perillo

YEAR ISSUE	EDITION LIMIT	YEAR RETD.	ISSUE PRICE	*QUOTE U.S.$
1989 Mustang	Closed	N/A	29.50	35-55
1989 White-Tailed Deer	Closed	N/A	29.50	30-50
1989 Mountain Lion	Closed	N/A	29.50	30-50
1990 American Bald Eagle	Closed	N/A	29.50	35-65
1990 Timber Wolf	Closed	N/A	29.50	35-55
1990 Polar Bear	Closed	N/A	29.50	30
1990 Buffalo	Closed	N/A	29.50	35-55
1990 Bighorn Sheep	Closed	N/A	29.50	30-50

Perillo Christmas - G. Perillo

YEAR ISSUE	EDITION LIMIT	YEAR RETD.	ISSUE PRICE	*QUOTE U.S.$
1987 Shining Star	Yr.Iss.	1987	29.50	70-85
1988 Silent Light	Yr.Iss.	1988	35.00	80-100
1989 Snow Flake	Yr.Iss.	1989	35.00	75-100
1990 Bundle Up	Yr.Iss.	1990	39.50	75-100
1991 Christmas Journey	Yr.Iss.	1991	39.50	50-100

Portraits of American Brides - R. Sauber

YEAR ISSUE	EDITION LIMIT	YEAR RETD.	ISSUE PRICE	*QUOTE U.S.$
1986 Caroline	Closed	N/A	29.50	45-150
1986 Jacqueline	Closed	N/A	29.50	30-95
1987 Elizabeth	Closed	N/A	29.50	60-85
1987 Emily	Closed	N/A	29.50	75-85
1987 Meredith	Closed	N/A	29.50	75
1987 Laura	Closed	N/A	29.50	45
1987 Sarah	Closed	N/A	29.50	45
1987 Rebecca	Closed	N/A	29.50	65

Pride of America's Indians - G. Perillo

YEAR ISSUE	EDITION LIMIT	YEAR RETD.	ISSUE PRICE	*QUOTE U.S.$
1986 Brave and Free	Closed	N/A	24.50	60-125
1986 Dark-Eyed Friends	Closed	N/A	24.50	65-95
1986 Noble Companions	Closed	N/A	24.50	55-95
1987 Kindred Spirits	Closed	N/A	24.50	55-95
1987 Loyal Alliance	Closed	N/A	24.50	93-125
1987 Small and Wise	Closed	N/A	24.50	55-95
1987 Winter Scouts	Closed	N/A	24.50	55-95
1987 Peaceful Comrades	Closed	N/A	24.50	75-95

The Princesses - G. Perillo

YEAR ISSUE	EDITION LIMIT	YEAR RETD.	ISSUE PRICE	*QUOTE U.S.$
1982 Lily of the Mohawks	7,500	N/A	50.00	175
1982 Pocahontas	7,500	N/A	50.00	100
1982 Minnehaha	7,500	N/A	50.00	100
1982 Sacajawea	7,500	N/A	50.00	100

Proud Young Spirits - G. Perillo

YEAR ISSUE	EDITION LIMIT	YEAR RETD.	ISSUE PRICE	*QUOTE U.S.$
1990 Protector of the Plains	Closed	N/A	29.50	75-100
1990 Watchful Eyes	Closed	N/A	29.50	55-65
1990 Freedom's Watch	Closed	N/A	29.50	45-65
1990 Woodland Scouts	Closed	N/A	29.50	35-45
1990 Fast Friends	Closed	N/A	29.50	35-45
1990 Birds of a Feather	Closed	N/A	29.50	30
1990 Prairie Pals	Closed	N/A	29.50	35-45
1990 Loyal Guardian	Closed	N/A	29.50	30

Special Issue - G. Perillo

YEAR ISSUE	EDITION LIMIT	YEAR RETD.	ISSUE PRICE	*QUOTE U.S.$
1981 Apache Boy	5,000	N/A	95.00	175-399
1983 Papoose	3,000	N/A	100.00	125
1983 Indian Style	17,500	N/A	50.00	50
1984 The Lovers	Closed	N/A	50.00	100
1984 Navajo Girl	3,500	N/A	95.00	175-250
1986 Navajo Boy	3,500	N/A	95.00	175-250

The Thoroughbreds - G. Perillo

YEAR ISSUE	EDITION LIMIT	YEAR RETD.	ISSUE PRICE	*QUOTE U.S.$
1984 Whirlaway	9,500	N/A	50.00	250-399
1984 Secretariat	9,500	N/A	50.00	350-499
1984 Man o' War	9,500	N/A	50.00	150-250
1984 Seabiscuit	9,500	N/A	50.00	150

War Ponies of the Plains - G. Perillo

YEAR ISSUE	EDITION LIMIT	YEAR RETD.	ISSUE PRICE	*QUOTE U.S.$
1992 Nightshadow	Closed	N/A	27.00	27
1992 Windcatcher	Closed	N/A	27.00	27
1992 Prairie Prancer	Closed	N/A	27.00	27
1992 Thunderfoot	Closed	N/A	27.00	27
1992 Proud Companion	Closed	N/A	27.00	27
1992 Sun Dancer	Closed	N/A	27.00	27
1992 Free Spirit	Closed	N/A	27.00	27-33
1992 Gentle Warrior	Closed	N/A	27.00	27

The Young Chieftains - G. Perillo

YEAR ISSUE	EDITION LIMIT	YEAR RETD.	ISSUE PRICE	*QUOTE U.S.$
1985 Young Sitting Bull	5,000	N/A	50.00	100-250
1985 Young Joseph	5,000	N/A	50.00	75-150
1986 Young Red Cloud	5,000	N/A	50.00	75-125
1986 Young Geronimo	5,000	N/A	50.00	75-150
1986 Young Crazy Horse	5,000	N/A	50.00	75-150

Artists of the World

Celebration Series - T. DeGrazia

YEAR ISSUE	EDITION LIMIT	YEAR RETD.	ISSUE PRICE	*QUOTE U.S.$
1993 The Lord's Candle	5,000		39.50	45-75
1993 Pinata Party	5,000		39.50	45-75
1993 Holiday Lullaby	5,000	1995	39.50	45-75
1993 Caroling	5,000	1995	39.50	45-75

Children (Signed) - T. DeGrazia

YEAR ISSUE	EDITION LIMIT	YEAR RETD.	ISSUE PRICE	*QUOTE U.S.$
1978 Los Ninos	500		100.00	1500-2200
1978 White Dove	500		100.00	450-700
1978 Flower Girl	500		100.00	450-700
1979 Flower Boy	500		100.00	450-700
1980 Little Cocopah Girl	500		100.00	299-450
1981 Beautiful Burden	500		100.00	299-450
1981 Merry Little Indian	500		100.00	299-450

Children - T. DeGrazia

YEAR ISSUE	EDITION LIMIT	YEAR RETD.	ISSUE PRICE	*QUOTE U.S.$
1976 Los Ninos	5,000		35.00	900-1100
1977 White Dove	5,000		40.00	100-200
1978 Flower Girl	9,500		45.00	43-150
1979 Flower Boy	9,500		45.00	40-150
1980 Little Cocopah	9,500		50.00	68-100
1981 Beautiful Burden	9,500		50.00	52-100
1982 Merry Little Indian	9,500		55.00	78-150
1983 Wondering	10,000		60.00	43-250
1984 Pink Papoose	10,000		65.00	32-100
1985 Sunflower Boy	10,000		65.00	150-250

Children at Play - T. DeGrazia

YEAR ISSUE	EDITION LIMIT	YEAR RETD.	ISSUE PRICE	*QUOTE U.S.$
1985 My First Horse	15,000		65.00	140-299
1986 Girl With Sewing Machine	15,000		65.00	100-275
1987 Love Me	15,000		65.00	100-250
1988 Merrily, Merrily, Merrily	15,000		65.00	100-250
1989 My First Arrow	15,000		65.00	100-250
1990 Away With My Kite	15,000		65.00	100-250

Children Mini-Plates - T. DeGrazia

YEAR ISSUE	EDITION LIMIT	YEAR RETD.	ISSUE PRICE	*QUOTE U.S.$
1980 Los Ninos	5,000		15.00	300-475
1981 White Dove	5,000		15.00	100-149
1982 Flower Girl	5,000		15.00	100-149
1982 Flower Boy	5,000		15.00	100-149
1983 Little Cocopah Indian Girl	5,000		15.00	75-149
1983 Beautiful Burden	5,000		20.00	75-149
1984 Merry Little Indian	5,000		20.00	100-149
1984 Wondering	5,000		20.00	75-149
1985 Pink Papoose	5,000		20.00	75-149
1985 Sunflower Boy	5,000		20.00	100-149

Children of the Sun - T. DeGrazia

YEAR ISSUE	EDITION LIMIT	YEAR RETD.	ISSUE PRICE	*QUOTE U.S.$
1987 Spring Blossoms	150-day		34.50	75-149
1987 My Little Pink Bird	150-day		34.50	65-149
1987 Bright Flowers of the Desert	150-day		37.90	65-149
1988 Gifts from the Sun	150-day		37.90	50-149
1988 Growing Glory	150-day		37.90	50-149
1988 The Gentle White Dove	150-day		37.90	50-149
1988 Sunflower Maiden	150-day		39.90	65-149
1989 Sun Showers	150-day		39.90	50-149

Floral Fiesta - T. DeGrazia

YEAR ISSUE	EDITION LIMIT	YEAR RETD.	ISSUE PRICE	*QUOTE U.S.$
1994 Little Flower Vendor	5,000		39.50	40-75
1994 Flowers For Mother	5,000		39.50	40-75
1995 Floral Innocence	5,000		39.50	40-75
1995 Floral Bouquet	5,000		39.50	40-75
1996 Floral Celebration	5,000		39.50	40-75
1996 Floral Fiesta	5,000		39.50	40-75

Holiday (Signed) - T. DeGrazia

YEAR ISSUE	EDITION LIMIT	YEAR RETD.	ISSUE PRICE	*QUOTE U.S.$
1976 Festival of Lights,	500		100.00	399-600
1977 Bell of Hope	500		100.00	299-450
1978 Little Madonna	500		100.00	100-450
1979 The Nativity	500		100.00	100-500
1980 Little Pima Drummer	500		100.00	100-450
1981 A Little Prayer	500		100.00	275-450
1982 Blue Boy	96		100.00	275-500

Holiday - T. DeGrazia

YEAR ISSUE	EDITION LIMIT	YEAR RETD.	ISSUE PRICE	*QUOTE U.S.$
1976 Festival of Lights	9,500		45.00	75-150
1977 Bell of Hope	9,500		45.00	38-175
1978 Little Madonna	9,500		45.00	45-75
1979 The Nativity	9,500		50.00	28-75
1980 Little Pima Drummer	9,500		50.00	42-75
1981 A Little Prayer	9,500		55.00	47-55
1982 Blue Boy	10,000		60.00	38-75
1983 Heavenly Blessings	10,000		65.00	18-75
1984 Navajo Madonna	10,000		65.00	65-250
1985 Saguaro Dance	10,000		65.00	60-250

Holiday Mini-Plates - T. DeGrazia

YEAR ISSUE	EDITION LIMIT	YEAR RETD.	ISSUE PRICE	*QUOTE U.S.$
1980 Festival of Lights	5,000		15.00	200-350
1981 Bell of Hope	5,000		15.00	75-150
1982 Little Madonna	5,000		15.00	75-150
1982 The Nativity	5,000		15.00	75-150
1983 Little Pima Drummer	5,000		15.00	25-75
1983 Little Prayer	5,000		20.00	25-75
1984 Blue Boy	5,000		20.00	25-75
1984 Heavenly Blessings	5,000		20.00	25-75
1985 Navajo Madonna	5,000		20.00	50-125
1985 Saguaro Dance	5,000		20.00	50-125

Special Release - T. DeGrazia

YEAR ISSUE	EDITION LIMIT	YEAR RETD.	ISSUE PRICE	*QUOTE U.S.$
1996 Wedding Party	5,000		49.50	50-60

Western - T. DeGrazia

YEAR ISSUE	EDITION LIMIT	YEAR RETD.	ISSUE PRICE	*QUOTE U.S.$
1986 Morning Ride	5,000		65.00	100-275
1987 Bronco	5,000		65.00	100-275
1988 Apache Scout	5,000		65.00	100-275
1989 Alone	5,000		65.00	100-275

Barbie/Enesco Corporation

Bob Mackie - Enesco

YEAR ISSUE	EDITION LIMIT	YEAR RETD.	ISSUE PRICE	*QUOTE U.S.$
1996 Queen of Hearts Barbie 157678	Open		25.00	25
1997 Goddess of the Sun 260215	7,500		35.00	35
1997 Moon Goddess 260231	7,500		35.00	35

Bob Mackie JC Penney Exclusive - Enesco

YEAR ISSUE	EDITION LIMIT	YEAR RETD.	ISSUE PRICE	*QUOTE U.S.$
1995 Queen of Hearts Barbie J1276	7,500	1995	30.00	30
1996 Goddess of the Sun J8768	7,500		30.00	30
1997 Moon Goddess 260266	5,000		30.00	30

Campus Sweetheart - Enesco

YEAR ISSUE	EDITION LIMIT	YEAR RETD.	ISSUE PRICE	*QUOTE U.S.$
1998 Campus Sweetheart, 1965 295221	7,500		30.00	30

Elite Dealer Exclusive - Enesco

YEAR ISSUE	EDITION LIMIT	YEAR RETD.	ISSUE PRICE	*QUOTE U.S.$
1997 Goddess of the Sun/Moon Goddess Set 270539	2,500		125.00	125
1997 Barbie as Dorothy/Ken as Lion/Ken as the Scarecrow/Ken as the Tin Man 284335	2,500		150.00	150

FAO Schwarz Exclusive - Enesco

YEAR ISSUE	EDITION LIMIT	YEAR RETD.	ISSUE PRICE	*QUOTE U.S.$
1994 Silver Screen Barbie 128805	3,600	1995	30.00	30

*Quotes have been rounded up to nearest dollar

YEAR ISSUE	EDITION LIMIT	YEAR RETD.	ISSUE PRICE	*QUOTE U.S.$
1995 Circus Star Barbie 150339	3,600	1995	30.00	30

Glamour - Enesco

YEAR ISSUE	EDITION LIMIT	YEAR RETD.	ISSUE PRICE	*QUOTE U.S.$
1994 35th Anniversary Barbie 655112	5,000	1994	30.00	30-99
1995 Barbie Solo In The Spotlight, 1959 114383	5,000	1995	30.00	45
1995 Barbie Enchanted Evening, 1960 175587	10,000		30.00	30
1996 Here Comes The Bride, 1966 170984	Open		30.00	30
1996 Holiday Dance, 1965 188794	10,000		30.00	30
1997 Wedding Day, 1959 260282	7,500		30.00	30

Great Eras - Enesco

YEAR ISSUE	EDITION LIMIT	YEAR RETD.	ISSUE PRICE	*QUOTE U.S.$
1996 Gibson Girl Barbie 174769	10,000		30.00	30
1996 1920's Flapper Barbie 174777	10,000		30.00	30
1997 1850's Southern Belle 174785	7,500		30.00	30
1997 Egyptian Queen 174793	7,500		30.00	30
1997 Elizabethan Queen Barbie 174815	7,500		30.00	30
1997 Medieval Lady Barbie 174807	7,500	1997	30.00	30

Happy Holidays - Enesco

YEAR ISSUE	EDITION LIMIT	YEAR RETD.	ISSUE PRICE	*QUOTE U.S.$
1994 Happy Holidays Barbie, 1994 115088	5,000	1994	30.00	75-100
1995 Happy Holidays Barbie, 1995 143154	Yr.Iss.	1995	30.00	30
1995 Happy Holidays Barbie, 1988 154180	Yr.Iss.	1995	30.00	30
1996 Happy Holidays Barbie, 1989 188859	Yr.Iss.	1996	30.00	30
1996 Happy Holidays Barbie, 1996 188816	Yr.Iss.	1996	30.00	30
1997 Happy Holidays Barbie, 1997 274259	Yr.Iss.	1997	30.00	30
1997 Happy Holidays Barbie, 1990 274232	Yr.Iss.	1997	30.00	30
1998 Happy Holidays Barbie, 1998 362751	Yr.Iss.		30.00	30
1998 Happy Holidays Barbie, 1991 362816	Yr.Iss.		30.00	30

Hollywood Legends - Enesco

YEAR ISSUE	EDITION LIMIT	YEAR RETD.	ISSUE PRICE	*QUOTE U.S.$
1996 Barbie As Scarlett O'Hara in Green Velvet 171085	10,000	1996	35.00	35
1997 Barbie As Scarlett O'Hara in Red Velvet 260169	7,500		35.00	35
1997 Barbie As Dorothy 260193	7,500		35.00	35
1997 Barbie As Dorothy/Ken as the Lion/Ken as the Scarecrow/Ken as the Tin Man 284327	5,000		35.00	35
1997 Barbie As Glinda the Good Witch 274275	7,500	1997	35.00	35

My Fair Lady - Enesco

YEAR ISSUE	EDITION LIMIT	YEAR RETD.	ISSUE PRICE	*QUOTE U.S.$
1997 Barbie As Eliza Doolittle At Ascot 270512	7,500		30.00	30
1997 Barbie As Eliza Doolittle At Embassy Ball 274291	7,500		35.00	35

Sugar Plum Fairy - Enesco

YEAR ISSUE	EDITION LIMIT	YEAR RETD.	ISSUE PRICE	*QUOTE U.S.$
1998 Sugar Plum Fairy 362832	7,500		30.00	30

Bing & Grondahl

American Christmas Heritage Collection - C. Magadini

YEAR ISSUE	EDITION LIMIT	YEAR RETD.	ISSUE PRICE	*QUOTE U.S.$
1996 The Statue of Liberty	Yr.Iss.	1996	47.50	36-48
1997 Christmas Eve at The Lincoln Memorial	Yr.Iss.	1997	47.50	48
1998 Chicago Water Tower	Yr.Iss.		34.50	35

Centennial Anniversary Commemoratives - Various

YEAR ISSUE	EDITION LIMIT	YEAR RETD.	ISSUE PRICE	*QUOTE U.S.$
1995 Centennial Plaquettes: Series of 10-5" plates featuring B&G motifs: 1895, 1905, 1919, 1927, 1932, 1945, 1954, 1967, 1974, 1982	Yr.Iss.	1995	250.00	250-300
1995 Centennial Plate: Behind the Frozen Window - F.A. Hallin	10,000	1995	39.50	40-54
1995 Centennial Platter: Towers of Copenhagen - J. Nielsen	7,500	1995	195.00	195

Centennial Collection - Various

YEAR ISSUE	EDITION LIMIT	YEAR RETD.	ISSUE PRICE	*QUOTE U.S.$
1991 Crows Enjoying Christmas - D. Jensen	Annual	1991	59.50	60
1992 Copenhagen Christmas - H. Vlugenring	Annual	1992	59.50	60-75
1993 Christmas Elf - H. Thelander	Annual	1993	59.50	63-72
1994 Christmas in Church - H. Thelander	Annual	1994	59.50	63-75
1995 Behind The Frozen Window - A. Hallin	Annual	1995	59.50	60

Children's Day Plate Series - Various

YEAR ISSUE	EDITION LIMIT	YEAR RETD.	ISSUE PRICE	*QUOTE U.S.$
1985 The Magical Tea Party - C. Roller	Annual	1985	24.50	10-25
1986 A Joyful Flight - C. Roller	Annual	1986	26.50	17-54
1986 The Little Gardeners - C. Roller	Annual	1987	29.50	51-72
1988 Wash Day - C. Roller	Annual	1988	34.50	29-45
1989 Bedtime - C. Roller	Annual	1989	37.00	46-60
1990 My Favorite Dress - S. Vestergaard	Annual	1990	37.00	37-75
1991 Fun on the Beach - S. Vestergaard	Annual	1991	45.00	57-60
1992 A Summer Day in the Meadow - S. Vestergaard	Annual	1992	45.00	50-60
1993 The Carousel - S. Vestergaard	Annual	1993	45.00	46-105
1994 The Little Fisherman - S. Vestergaard	Annual	1994	45.00	45
1995 My First Book - S. Vestergaard	Annual	1995	45.00	84-100
1996 The Little Racers - S. Vestergaard	Annual	1996	45.00	45
1997 Bath Time - S. Vestergaard	Annual	1997	45.00	45-75
1998 Little Vendors - S. Vestergaard	Annual		34.50	35

Christmas - Various

YEAR ISSUE	EDITION LIMIT	YEAR RETD.	ISSUE PRICE	*QUOTE U.S.$
1895 Behind The Frozen Window - F.A. Hallin	Annual	1895	.50	4500-6750
1896 New Moon - F.A. Hallin	Annual	1896	.50	2200-2850
1897 Sparrows - F.A. Hallin	Annual	1897	.75	975-1500
1898 Roses and Star - F. Garde	Annual	1898	.75	810-966
1899 Crows - F. Garde	Annual	1899	.75	960-1950
1900 Church Bells - F. Garde	Annual	1900	.75	950-1350
1901 Three Wise Men - S. Sabra	Annual	1901	1.00	450-600
1902 Gothic Church Interior - D. Jensen	Annual	1902	1.00	450-570
1903 Expectant Children - M. Hyldahl	Annual	1903	1.00	360-450
1904 Fredericksberg Hill - C. Olsen	Annual	1904	1.00	140-210
1905 Christmas Night - D. Jensen	Annual	1905	1.00	145-210
1906 Sleighing to Church - D. Jensen	Annual	1906	1.00	120-144
1907 Little Match Girl - E. Plockross	Annual	1907	1.00	100-150
1908 St. Petri Church - P. Jorgensen	Annual	1908	1.00	105-150
1909 Yule Tree - Aarestrup	Annual	1909	1.50	75-120
1910 The Old Organist - C. Ersgaard	Annual	1910	1.50	100-113
1911 Angels and Shepherds - H. Moltke	Annual	1911	1.50	75-96
1912 Going to Church - E. Hansen	Annual	1912	1.50	75-96
1913 Bringing Home the Tree - T. Larsen	Annual	1913	1.50	105-111
1914 Amalienborg Castle - T. Larsen	Annual	1914	1.50	80-96
1915 Dog Outside Window - D. Jensen	Annual	1915	1.50	148-165
1916 Sparrows at Christmas - P. Jorgensen	Annual	1916	1.50	90-98
1917 Christmas Boat - A. Friis	Annual	1917	1.50	104-108
1918 Fishing Boat - A. Friis	Annual	1918	1.50	90-96
1919 Outside Lighted Window - A. Friis	Annual	1919	2.00	90-99
1920 Hare in the Snow - A. Friis	Annual	1920	2.00	90-100
1921 Pigeons - A. Friis	Annual	1921	2.00	75-80
1922 Star of Bethlehem - A. Friis	Annual	1922	2.00	87-90
1923 The Ermitage - A. Friis	Annual	1923	2.00	71-90
1924 Lighthouse - A. Friis	Annual	1924	2.50	72-92
1925 Child's Christmas - A. Friis	Annual	1925	2.50	85-90
1926 Churchgoers - A. Friis	Annual	1926	2.50	81-90
1927 Skating Couple - A. Friis	Annual	1927	2.50	105-117
1928 Eskimos - A. Friis	Annual	1928	2.50	69-84
1929 Fox Outside Farm - A. Friis	Annual	1929	2.50	90-105
1930 Town Hall Square - H. Flugenring	Annual	1930	2.50	89-114
1931 Christmas Train - A. Friis	Annual	1931	2.50	96-99
1932 Life Boat - H. Flugenring	Annual	1932	2.50	75-99
1933 Korsor-Nyborg Ferry - H. Flugenring	Annual	1933	3.00	81-96
1934 Church Bell in Tower - H. Flugenring	Annual	1934	3.00	84-110
1935 Lillebelt Bridge - O. Larson	Annual	1935	3.00	75-126
1936 Royal Guard - O. Larson	Annual	1936	3.00	75-90
1937 Arrival of Christmas Guests - O. Larson	Annual	1937	3.00	90-108
1938 Lighting the Candles - I. Tjerne	Annual	1938	3.00	193-202
1939 Old Lock-Eye, The Sandman - I. Tjerne	Annual	1939	3.00	195-199
1940 Christmas Letters - O. Larson	Annual	1940	4.00	185-210
1941 Horses Enjoying Meal - O. Larson	Annual	1941	4.00	309-390
1942 Danish Farm - O. Larson	Annual	1942	4.00	225-294
1943 Ribe Cathedral - O. Larson	Annual	1943	5.00	200-225
1944 Sorgenfri Castle - O. Larson	Annual	1944	5.00	113-129
1945 The Old Water Mill - O. Larson	Annual	1945	5.00	147-276
1946 Commemoration Cross - M. Hyldahl	Annual	1946	5.00	96-105
1947 Dybbol Mill - M. Hyldahl	Annual	1947	5.00	147-236
1948 Watchman - M. Hyldahl	Annual	1948	5.50	90-105
1949 Landsoldaten - M. Hyldahl	Annual	1949	5.50	93-105
1950 Kronborg Castle - M. Hyldahl	Annual	1950	5.50	123-150
1951 Jens Bang - M. Hyldahl	Annual	1951	6.00	120-144
1952 Thorsvaldsen Museum - B. Pramvig	Annual	1952	6.00	100-120
1953 Snowman - B. Pramvig	Annual	1953	7.50	105-155
1954 Royal Boat - K. Bonfils	Annual	1954	7.00	116-120
1955 Kaulundorg Church - K. Bonfils	Annual	1955	8.00	120-146
1956 Christmas in Copenhagen - K. Bonfils	Annual	1956	8.50	150-230
1957 Christmas Candles - K. Bonfils	Annual	1957	9.00	133-195
1958 Santa Claus - K. Bonfils	Annual	1958	9.50	100-120
1959 Christmas Eve - K. Bonfils	Annual	1959	10.00	119-180
1960 Village Church - K. Bonfils	Annual	1960	10.00	125-222
1961 Winter Harmony - K. Bonfils	Annual	1961	10.50	60-100
1962 Winter Night - K. Bonfils	Annual	1962	11.00	50-90
1963 The Christmas Elf - H. Thelander	Annual	1963	11.00	69-165
1964 The Fir Tree and Hare - H. Thelander	Annual	1964	11.50	42-75
1965 Bringing Home the Tree - H. Thelander	Annual	1965	12.00	37-75
1966 Home for Christmas - H. Thelander	Annual	1966	12.00	30-60
1967 Sharing the Joy - H. Thelander	Annual	1967	13.00	20-68
1968 Christmas in Church - H. Thelander	Annual	1968	14.00	16-45
1969 Arrival of Guests - H. Thelander	Annual	1969	14.00	13-38
1970 Pheasants in Snow - H. Thelander	Annual	1970	14.50	11-20
1971 Christmas at Home - H. Thelander	Annual	1971	15.00	7-27
1972 Christmas in Greenland - H. Thelander	Annual	1972	16.50	8-27
1973 Country Christmas - H. Thelander	Annual	1973	19.50	12-45
1974 Christmas in the Village - H. Thelander	Annual	1974	22.00	21-31
1975 Old Water Mill - H. Thelander	Annual	1975	27.50	17-36
1976 Christmas Welcome - H. Thelander	Annual	1976	27.50	19-23
1977 Copenhagen Christmas - H. Thelander	Annual	1977	29.50	17-30
1978 Christmas Tale - H. Thelander	Annual	1978	32.00	30-38
1979 White Christmas - H. Thelander	Annual	1979	36.50	29-49
1980 Christmas in Woods - H. Thelander	Annual	1980	42.50	30-33
1981 Christmas Peace - H. Thelander	Annual	1981	49.50	20-27
1982 Christmas Tree - H. Thelander	Annual	1982	54.50	32-60
1983 Christmas in Old Town - H. Thelander	Annual	1983	54.50	26-55
1984 The Christmas Letter - E. Jensen	Annual	1984	54.50	40-54
1985 Christmas Eve at the Farmhouse - E. Jensen	Annual	1985	54.50	27-45
1986 Silent Night, Holy Night - E. Jensen	Annual	1986	54.50	45-57
1987 The Snowman's Christmas Eve - E. Jensen	Annual	1987	59.50	45-57
1988 In the Kings Garden - E. Jensen	Annual	1988	64.50	37-66
1989 Christmas Anchorage - E. Jensen	Annual	1989	59.50	59-75
1990 Changing of the Guards - E. Jensen	Annual	1990	64.50	70-84
1991 Copenhagen Stock Exchange - E. Jensen	Annual	1991	69.50	90-135
1992 Christmas At the Rectory - J. Steensen	Annual	1992	69.50	96-113
1993 Father Christmas in Copenhagen - J. Nielsen	Annual	1993	69.50	86-96
1994 A Day At The Deer Park - J. Nielsen	Annual	1994	72.50	72-84
1995 The Towers of Copenhagen - J. Nielsen	Annual	1995	72.50	59-105
1996 Winter at the Old Mill - J. Nielsen	Annual	1996	74.50	72-78
1997 Country Christmas - J. Nielsen	Annual	1997	69.50	70-90
1998 Santa the Storyteller - J. Nielsen	Annual		69.50	70

Christmas Around the World - H. Hansen

YEAR ISSUE	EDITION LIMIT	YEAR RETD.	ISSUE PRICE	*QUOTE U.S.$
1995 Santa in Greenland	Yr.Iss.	1995	74.50	75-100
1996 Santa in Orient	Yr.Iss.	1996	74.50	75-90
1997 Santa in Russia	Yr.Iss.	1997	74.50	70
1998 Santa in Australia	Yr.Iss.		69.50	70

Christmas In America - J. Woodson

YEAR ISSUE	EDITION LIMIT	YEAR RETD.	ISSUE PRICE	*QUOTE U.S.$
1986 Christmas Eve in Williamsburg	Annual	1986	29.50	165-170
1987 Christmas Eve at the White House	Annual	1987	34.50	35-100
1988 Christmas Eve at Rockefeller Center	Annual	1988	34.50	65-68
1989 Christmas In New England	Annual	1989	37.00	54-60
1990 Christmas Eve at the Capitol	Annual	1990	39.50	54-100
1991 Christmas Eve at Independence Hall	Annual	1991	45.00	65-90
1992 Christmas in San Francisco	Annual	1992	47.50	48-60
1993 Coming Home For Christmas	Annual	1993	47.50	36-48
1994 Christmas Eve In Alaska	Annual	1994	47.50	54-75
1995 Christmas Eve in Mississippi	Annual	1995	47.50	48

Christmas in America Anniversary Plate - J. Woodson

YEAR ISSUE	EDITION LIMIT	YEAR RETD.	ISSUE PRICE	*QUOTE U.S.$
1991 Christmas Eve in Williamsburg	Annual	1991	69.50	105
1995 The Capitol - J. Woodson	Annual	1995	74.50	75

Jubilee-5 Year Cycle - Various

YEAR ISSUE	EDITION LIMIT	YEAR RETD.	ISSUE PRICE	*QUOTE U.S.$
1915 Frozen Window - F.A. Hallin	Annual	1915	Unkn.	199-225
1920 Church Bells - F. Garde	Annual	1920	Unkn.	60-100
1925 Dog Outside Window - D. Jensen	Annual	1925	Unkn.	180-300
1930 The Old Organist - C. Ersgaard	Annual	1930	Unkn.	210-225
1935 Little Match Girl - E. Plockross	Annual	1935	Unkn.	450
1940 Three Wise Men - S. Sabra	Annual	1940	Unkn.	1800-2000
1945 Amalienborg Castle - T. Larsen	Annual	1945	Unkn.	90
1950 Eskimos - A. Friis	Annual	1950	Unkn.	90
1955 Dybbol Mill - M. Hyldahl	Annual	1955	Unkn.	210-259
1960 Kronborg Castle - M. Hyldahl	Annual	1960	25.00	90-199
1965 Chruchgoers - A. Friis	Annual	1965	25.00	25-75
1970 Amalienborg Castle - T. Larsen	Annual	1970	30.00	18-30
1975 Horses Enjoying Meal - O. Larson	Annual	1975	40.00	33-69
1980 Yule Tree - Aarestrup	Annual	1980	60.00	48-55
1985 Lifeboat at Work - H. Flugenring	Annual	1985	65.00	65-89
1990 The Royal Yacht Dannebrog - J. Bonfils	Annual	1990	95.00	85-89
1995 Centennial Platter - J. Nielsen	7,500	1995	195.00	195
1996 Lifeboat at Work (released a year late) - H. Flugenring	1,000	1996	95.00	95

Mother's Day - Various

YEAR ISSUE	EDITION LIMIT	YEAR RETD.	ISSUE PRICE	*QUOTE U.S.$
1969 Dogs and Puppies - H. Thelander	Annual	1969	9.75	396-400
1970 Bird and Chicks - H. Thelander	Annual	1970	10.00	18-30
1971 Cat and Kitten - H. Thelander	Annual	1971	11.00	9-21
1972 Mare and Foal - H. Thelander	Annual	1972	12.00	9-27
1973 Duck and Ducklings - H. Thelander	Annual	1973	13.00	18-27
1974 Bear and Cubs - H. Thelander	Annual	1974	16.50	10-30
1975 Doe and Fawns - H. Thelander	Annual	1975	19.50	9-23
1976 Swan Family - H. Thelander	Annual	1976	22.50	18-26
1977 Squirrel and Young - H. Thelander	Annual	1977	23.50	23-25
1978 Heron and Young - H. Thelander	Annual	1978	24.50	15-22
1979 Fox and Cubs - H. Thelander	Annual	1979	27.50	21-33
1980 Woodpecker and Young - H. Thelander	Annual	1980	29.50	30-60
1981 Hare and Young - H. Thelander	Annual	1981	36.50	31-37
1982 Lioness and Cubs - H. Thelander	Annual	1982	39.50	27-36
1983 Raccoon and Young - H. Thelander	Annual	1983	39.50	25-65
1984 Stork and Nestlings - H. Thelander	Annual	1984	39.50	24-65
1985 Bear and Cubs - H. Thelander	Annual	1985	39.50	32-60
1986 Elephant with Calf - H. Thelander	Annual	1986	39.50	47-54
1987 Sheep with Lambs - H. Thelander	Annual	1987	42.50	68-135
1988 Crested Plover and Young - H. Thelander	Annual	1988	47.50	87-91
1988 Lapwing Mother with Chicks - H. Thelander	Annual	1988	49.50	70-90
1989 Cow With Calf - H. Thelander	Annual	1989	49.50	54-93
1990 Hen with Chicks - L. Jensen	Annual	1990	52.50	83-120
1991 The Nanny Goat and her Two Frisky Kids - L. Jensen	Annual	1991	54.50	84-93
1992 Panda With Cubs - L. Jensen	Annual	1992	59.50	93-120
1993 St. Bernard Dog and Puppies - A. Therkelsen	Annual	1993	59.50	73-105
1994 Cat with Kittens - A. Therkelsen	Annual	1994	59.50	67-120
1995 Hedgehog with Young - A. Therkelsen	Annual	1995	59.50	58-90
1996 Koala with Young - A. Therkelsen	Annual	1996	59.50	63-90

*Quotes have been rounded up to nearest dollar

YEAR ISSUE	EDITION LIMIT	YEAR RETD.	ISSUE PRICE	*QUOTE U.S.$
1997 Goose with Gooslings - L. Didier	Annual	1997	59.50	69-90
1998 Penguin With Young - L. Didier	Annual		49.50	50

Mother's Day Jubilee-5 Year Cycle - Thelander

YEAR ISSUE	EDITION LIMIT	YEAR RETD.	ISSUE PRICE	*QUOTE U.S.$
1979 Dog & Puppies	Yr.Iss.	1979	55.00	42-75
1984 Swan Family	Yr.Iss.	1984	65.00	65-100
1989 Mare & Colt	Yr.Iss.	1989	95.00	115-150
1994 Woodpecker & Young	Yr.Iss.	1994	95.00	95

Olympic - Unknown

YEAR ISSUE	EDITION LIMIT	YEAR RETD.	ISSUE PRICE	*QUOTE U.S.$
1972 Munich, Germany	Closed	1972	20.00	15-30
1976 Montreal, Canada	Closed	1976	29.50	57-59
1980 Moscow, Russia	Closed	1980	43.00	87-89
1984 Los Angeles, USA	Closed	1984	45.00	259-359
1988 Seoul, Korea	Closed	1988	60.00	65-87
1992 Barcelona, Spain	Closed	1992	74.50	75-87

Santa Claus Collection - H. Hansen

YEAR ISSUE	EDITION LIMIT	YEAR RETD.	ISSUE PRICE	*QUOTE U.S.$
1989 Santa's Workshop	Annual	1989	59.50	113-120
1990 Santa's Sleigh	Annual	1990	59.50	90-180
1991 Santa's Journey	Annual	1991	69.50	120
1992 Santa's Arrival	Annual	1992	74.50	90
1993 Santa's Gifts	Annual	1993	74.50	75
1994 Christmas Stories	Annual	1994	74.50	75-90

Statue of Liberty - Unknown

YEAR ISSUE	EDITION LIMIT	YEAR RETD.	ISSUE PRICE	*QUOTE U.S.$
1985 Statue of Liberty	10,000	1985	60.00	75-125

The Bradford Exchange/Canada

Big League Dreams

YEAR ISSUE	EDITION LIMIT	YEAR RETD.	ISSUE PRICE	*QUOTE U.S.$
1993 Hey, Batter Batter	Closed		29.90	50
1994 The Wind Up	Closed		29.90	57
1994 Safe!!!	Closed		32.90	90
1994 A Difference of Opinion	Closed		32.90	100
1994 I Got It, I Got It!	Closed		32.90	80
1994 Victory	Closed		32.90	62

The Bradford Exchange/China

Dream of the Red Chamber

YEAR ISSUE	EDITION LIMIT	YEAR RETD.	ISSUE PRICE	*QUOTE U.S.$
1994 Pao-Choi: Precious Clasp	Closed		29.90	38
1994 Hsiang-Yun: Little Cloud	Closed		29.90	38
1994 Yuan-Chun: Beginning of Spring	Closed		29.90	38
1994 Hsi-Feng: Phoenix	Closed		29.90	46
1994 Tai-Yu: Black Jade	Closed		29.90	48
1994 Tan-Chun: Taste of Spring	Closed		29.90	30

The Bradford Exchange/Russia

The Nutcracker - N. Zaitseva

YEAR ISSUE	EDITION LIMIT	YEAR RETD.	ISSUE PRICE	*QUOTE U.S.$
1993 Marie's Magical Gift	Closed		39.87	45-47
1993 Dance of Sugar Plum Fairy	Closed		39.87	45-52
1994 Waltz of the Flowers	Closed		39.87	50-55
1994 Battle With the Mice King	Closed		39.87	48-50

Songs of Angels - Vladimirdvich

YEAR ISSUE	EDITION LIMIT	YEAR RETD.	ISSUE PRICE	*QUOTE U.S.$
1994 Heavenly Hearalds	Closed		29.87	30
1994 Divine Chorus	Closed		29.87	30
1995 Springtime Duet	Closed		32.87	33
1995 Mystical Chimes	Closed		32.87	33

The Bradford Exchange/United States

101 Dalmatians - Disney Studios

YEAR ISSUE	EDITION LIMIT	YEAR RETD.	ISSUE PRICE	*QUOTE U.S.$
1993 Watch Dogs	95-day		29.90	30
1994 A Happy Reunion	95-day		29.90	30
1994 Hello Darlings	95-day		32.90	33
1994 Sergeant Tibs Saves the Day	95-day		32.90	33
1994 Halfway Home	95-day		32.90	33
1994 True Love	95-day		32.90	33
1995 Bedtime	95-day		34.90	35
1995 A Messy Good Time	95-day		34.90	35

Aladdin - Disney Studios

YEAR ISSUE	EDITION LIMIT	YEAR RETD.	ISSUE PRICE	*QUOTE U.S.$
1993 Magic Carpet Ride	Closed		29.90	45
1993 A Friend Like Me	Closed		29.90	45
1994 Aladdin in Love	Closed		29.90	55
1994 Traveling Companions	Closed		29.90	30
1994 Make Way for Prince Ali	Closed		29.90	30
1994 Aladdin's Wish	Closed		29.90	30
1995 Bee Yourself	Closed		29.90	30
1995 Group Hug	Closed		29.90	30

Alice in Wonderland - S. Gustafson

YEAR ISSUE	EDITION LIMIT	YEAR RETD.	ISSUE PRICE	*QUOTE U.S.$
1993 The Mad Tea Party	Closed		29.90	46-79
1993 The Cheshire Cat	Closed		29.90	75-77
1994 Croquet with the Queen	Closed		29.90	75-78
1994 Advice from a Caterpillar	Closed		29.90	82-85

America's Triumph in Space - R. Schaar

YEAR ISSUE	EDITION LIMIT	YEAR RETD.	ISSUE PRICE	*QUOTE U.S.$
1993 The Eagle Has Landed	Closed		29.90	30
1993 The March Toward Destiny	Closed		29.90	30
1994 Flight of Glory	Closed		32.90	33
1994 Beyond the Bounds of Earth	Closed		32.90	33
1994 Conquering the New Frontier	Closed		32.90	33
1994 Rendezvous With Victory	Closed		34.90	35
1994 The New Explorers	Closed		34.90	35
1994 Triumphant Finale	Closed		34.90	35

Ancient Seasons - M. Silversmith

YEAR ISSUE	EDITION LIMIT	YEAR RETD.	ISSUE PRICE	*QUOTE U.S.$
1995 Edge of Night	95-day		29.90	30

Autumn Encounters - C. Fisher

YEAR ISSUE	EDITION LIMIT	YEAR RETD.	ISSUE PRICE	*QUOTE U.S.$
1995 Woodland Innocents	95-day		29.90	30

Babe Ruth Centennial - P. Heffernan

YEAR ISSUE	EDITION LIMIT	YEAR RETD.	ISSUE PRICE	*QUOTE U.S.$
1994 The 60th Homer	Closed		34.90	34-45
1995 Ruth's Pitching Debut	Closed		29.90	35-68
1995 The Final Home Run	Closed		29.90	35-79
1995 Barnstorming Days	Closed		34.90	70-82

Baskets of Love - A. Isakov

YEAR ISSUE	EDITION LIMIT	YEAR RETD.	ISSUE PRICE	*QUOTE U.S.$
1993 Andrew and Abbey	Closed		29.90	44-45
1993 Cody and Courtney	Closed		29.90	45-50
1993 Emily and Elliott	Closed		32.90	55-65
1993 Heather and Hannah	Closed		32.90	36-53
1993 Justin and Jessica	Closed		32.90	28-35
1993 Katie and Kelly	Closed		34.90	40-60
1994 Louie and Libby	Closed		34.90	58-70
1994 Sammy and Sarah	Closed		34.90	55-66

Battles of American Civil War - J. Griffin

YEAR ISSUE	EDITION LIMIT	YEAR RETD.	ISSUE PRICE	*QUOTE U.S.$
1994 Gettysburg	95-day		29.90	30
1995 Vicksburg	95-day		29.90	30

The Bunny Workshop - J. Maday

YEAR ISSUE	EDITION LIMIT	YEAR RETD.	ISSUE PRICE	*QUOTE U.S.$
1995 Make Today Eggstra Special	Closed		19.95	20

By Gone Days - L. Dubin

YEAR ISSUE	EDITION LIMIT	YEAR RETD.	ISSUE PRICE	*QUOTE U.S.$
1994 Soda Fountain	Closed		29.90	30-44
1994 Sam's Grocery Store	Closed		29.90	45-70
1995 Saturday Matinee	Closed		29.90	45-65
1995 The Corner News Stand	Closed		29.90	45
1995 Main Street Splendor	Closed		29.90	32
1995 The Barber Shop	Closed		29.90	45

Cabins of Comfort River - F. Buchwitz

YEAR ISSUE	EDITION LIMIT	YEAR RETD.	ISSUE PRICE	*QUOTE U.S.$
1995 Comfort by Camplights Fire	Closed		29.90	30

Carousel Daydreams - N/A, unless otherwise noted

YEAR ISSUE	EDITION LIMIT	YEAR RETD.	ISSUE PRICE	*QUOTE U.S.$
1994 Swept Away - Mr. Tseng	Closed		39.90	75-90
1995 When I Grow Up	Closed		39.90	195-200
1995 All Aboard	Closed		44.90	75-85
1995 Hold Onto Your Dreams	Closed		44.90	120-125
1995 Flight of Fancy	Closed		44.90	130-194
1995 Big Hopes, Bright Dreams	Closed		49.90	60
1995 Victorian Reverie	Closed		49.90	130
1995 Wishful Thinking	Closed		49.90	150
1995 Dreams of Destiny	Closed		49.90	130
1995 My Favorite Memory	Closed		49.90	100

Charles Wysocki's American Frontier - C. Wysocki

YEAR ISSUE	EDITION LIMIT	YEAR RETD.	ISSUE PRICE	*QUOTE U.S.$
1993 Timberline Jack's Trading Post	Closed		29.90	30-75
1994 Dr. Livingwell's Medicine Show	Closed		29.90	28-42
1994 Bustling Boomtown	Closed		29.90	28-48
1994 Kirbyville	Closed		29.90	30-35
1994 Hearty Homesteaders	Closed		29.90	40
1994 Oklahoma or Bust	Closed		29.90	55

Charles Wysocki's Hometown Memories - C. Wysocki

YEAR ISSUE	EDITION LIMIT	YEAR RETD.	ISSUE PRICE	*QUOTE U.S.$
1994 Small Talk at Birdie's Perch	Closed		29.90	45-60
1995 Tranquil Days/Ravenswhip Cove	Closed		29.90	36-50
1995 Summer Delights	Closed		29.90	34-52
1995 Capturing the Moment	Closed		29.90	50-90
1995 A Farewell Kiss	Closed		29.90	51
1995 Jason Sparkin the Lighthouse Keeper's Daughter	Closed		29.90	45

Charles Wysocki's Peppercricket Grove - C. Wysocki

YEAR ISSUE	EDITION LIMIT	YEAR RETD.	ISSUE PRICE	*QUOTE U.S.$
1993 Peppercricket Farms	Closed		24.90	55
1993 Gingernut Valley Inn	Closed		24.90	25
1993 Budzen's Fruits and Vegetables	Closed		24.90	25
1993 Virginia's Market	Closed		24.90	25
1993 Pumpkin Hollow Emporium	Closed		24.90	25
1993 Liberty Star Farms	95-day		24.90	25
1993 Overflow Antique Market	95-day		24.90	25
1993 Black Crow Antique Shoppe	95-day		24.90	25

Cherished Traditions - M. Lasher

YEAR ISSUE	EDITION LIMIT	YEAR RETD.	ISSUE PRICE	*QUOTE U.S.$
1995 The Wedding Ring	Closed		29.90	30

Cherubs of Innocence - Various

YEAR ISSUE	EDITION LIMIT	YEAR RETD.	ISSUE PRICE	*QUOTE U.S.$
1994 The First Kiss	Closed		29.90	30
1995 Love at Rest	Closed		29.90	30
1995 Thoughts of Love	Closed		32.90	33

Chosen Messengers - G. Running Wolf

YEAR ISSUE	EDITION LIMIT	YEAR RETD.	ISSUE PRICE	*QUOTE U.S.$
1994 The Pathfinders	Closed		29.90	22-32
1994 The Overseers	Closed		29.90	36-39
1994 The Providers	Closed		32.90	45-50
1994 The Surveyors	Closed		32.90	52-60

A Christmas Carol - L. Garrison

YEAR ISSUE	EDITION LIMIT	YEAR RETD.	ISSUE PRICE	*QUOTE U.S.$
1993 God Bless Us Everyone	Closed		29.90	60-78
1993 Ghost of Christmas Present	Closed		29.90	67-74
1994 A Merry Christmas to All	Closed		29.90	68-89
1994 A Visit From Marley's Ghost	Closed		29.90	89-95
1994 Remembering Christmas Past	Closed		29.90	54-74
1994 A Spirit's Warning	Closed		29.90	78-83
1994 The True Spirit of Christmas	Closed		29.90	79-85
1994 Merry Christmas, Bob	Closed		29.90	71-82

Christmas in the Village - R. McGinnis

YEAR ISSUE	EDITION LIMIT	YEAR RETD.	ISSUE PRICE	*QUOTE U.S.$
1995 The Village Toy Shop	Closed		29.95	27-50
1995 Little Church in the Vale	Closed		29.95	30-38
1995 The Village Confectionary	Closed		29.95	30-62
1996 The Village Inn	Closed		29.95	30-55
1996 Goodnight Dear Friends	Closed		29.95	30-55
1996 A New Fallen Snow	Closed		29.95	30-55

Christmas Memories - J. Tanton

YEAR ISSUE	EDITION LIMIT	YEAR RETD.	ISSUE PRICE	*QUOTE U.S.$
1993 A Winter's Tale	Closed		29.90	25-29
1993 Finishing Touch	Closed		29.90	43-45
1993 Welcome to Our Home	Closed		29.90	56-60
1993 A Christmas Celebration	Closed		29.90	50-57

Classic Cars - D. Everhart

YEAR ISSUE	EDITION LIMIT	YEAR RETD.	ISSUE PRICE	*QUOTE U.S.$
1993 1957 Corvette	Closed		54.00	66-68
1993 1956 Thunderbird	Closed		54.00	55-67
1994 1957 Bel Air	Closed		54.00	62-103
1994 1965 Mustang	Closed		54.00	95-100

Classic Melodies from the "Sound of Music" - M. Hampshire

YEAR ISSUE	EDITION LIMIT	YEAR RETD.	ISSUE PRICE	*QUOTE U.S.$
1995 Sing Along with Maria	Closed		29.90	48-50
1995 A Drop of Golden Sun	Closed		29.90	50-61
1995 The Von Trapp Family Singers	Closed		29.90	95-100
1995 Alpine Refuge	Closed		29.90	35

The Costuming of A Legend: Dressing Gone With The Wind - D. Klauba

YEAR ISSUE	EDITION LIMIT	YEAR RETD.	ISSUE PRICE	*QUOTE U.S.$
1993 The Red Dress	Closed		29.90	50-63
1993 The Green Drapery Dress	95-day		29.90	30
1994 The Green Sprigged Dress	95-day		29.90	55
1994 Black & White Bengaline Dress	95-day		29.90	30
1994 Widow's Weeds	95-day		29.90	25-30
1994 The Country Walking Dress	95-day		29.90	30
1994 Plaid Business Attire	95-day		29.90	30
1994 Orchid Percale Dress	95-day		29.90	30
1994 The Mourning Gown	95-day		29.90	30
1994 Final Outtake:The Green Muslin Dress	95-day		29.90	27-30

A Country Wonderland - W. Goebel

YEAR ISSUE	EDITION LIMIT	YEAR RETD.	ISSUE PRICE	*QUOTE U.S.$
1995 The Quiet Hour	Closed		29.90	30

Deer Friends at Christmas - J. Thornbrugh

YEAR ISSUE	EDITION LIMIT	YEAR RETD.	ISSUE PRICE	*QUOTE U.S.$
1994 All a Glow	Closed		29.90	38-42
1994 A Glistening Season	Closed		29.90	30-32
1994 Holiday Sparkle	Closed		29.90	30-34
1995 Woodland Splendor	Closed		29.90	35
1995 Starry Night	Closed		29.90	32-44
1995 Radiant Countryside	Closed		29.90	30

Desert Rhythms - M. Cowdery

YEAR ISSUE	EDITION LIMIT	YEAR RETD.	ISSUE PRICE	*QUOTE U.S.$
1994 Partner With A Breeze	95-day		29.90	30
1994 Wind Dancer	95-day		29.90	30
1994 Riding On Air	95-day		29.90	30

Diana: Queen of Our Hearts - J. Monti

YEAR ISSUE	EDITION LIMIT	YEAR RETD.	ISSUE PRICE	*QUOTE U.S.$
1997 The People's Princess	95-day		29.95	28

Dog Days - J. Gadamus

YEAR ISSUE	EDITION LIMIT	YEAR RETD.	ISSUE PRICE	*QUOTE U.S.$
1993 Sweet Dreams	Closed		29.90	49-65
1993 Pier Group	Closed		29.90	44-48
1993 Wagon Train	Closed		32.90	66-68
1993 First Flush	Closed		32.90	50-52
1993 Little Rascals	Closed		32.90	74-98
1993 Where'd He Go	Closed		32.90	89-99

Elvis: Young & Wild - B. Emmett

YEAR ISSUE	EDITION LIMIT	YEAR RETD.	ISSUE PRICE	*QUOTE U.S.$
1993 The King of Creole	95-day		29.90	55
1993 King of the Road	95-day		29.90	50
1994 Tough But Tender	95-day		32.90	33
1994 With Love, Elvis	95-day		32.90	33
1994 The Picture of Cool	95-day		32.90	33
1994 Kissing Elvis	95-day		34.90	35
1994 The Perfect Take	95-day		34.90	35
1994 The Rockin' Rebel	95-day		34.90	35

Faces of the Wild - D. Parker

YEAR ISSUE	EDITION LIMIT	YEAR RETD.	ISSUE PRICE	*QUOTE U.S.$
1995 The Wolf	Closed		39.90	100-150
1995 The White Wolf	Closed		39.90	150-175
1995 The Cougar	Closed		44.90	100
1995 The Bobcat	Closed		44.90	139
1995 The Bear	Closed		44.90	125
1995 The Fox	Closed		44.90	140
1995 The Bison	Closed		44.90	70
1995 The Lynx	Closed		44.90	120

Fairyland - M. Jobe

YEAR ISSUE	EDITION LIMIT	YEAR RETD.	ISSUE PRICE	*QUOTE U.S.$
1994 Trails of Starlight	95-day		29.90	30
1994 Twilight Trio	95-day		29.90	30
1994 Forest Enchantment	95-day		32.90	33
1995 Silvery Splasher	95-day		32.90	33
1995 Magical Mischief	95-day		32.90	33
1995 Farewell to the Night	95-day		34.90	35

Family Circles - R. Rust

YEAR ISSUE	EDITION LIMIT	YEAR RETD.	ISSUE PRICE	*QUOTE U.S.$
1993 Great Gray Owl Family	Closed		29.90	30
1994 Great Horned Owl Family	Closed		29.90	60
1994 Barred Owl Family	Closed		29.90	60
1994 Spotted Owl Family	Closed		29.90	60

Field Pup Follies - C. Jackson

YEAR ISSUE	EDITION LIMIT	YEAR RETD.	ISSUE PRICE	*QUOTE U.S.$
1994 Sleeping on the Job	Closed		29.90	26-38
1994 Hat Check	Closed		29.90	60-107
1994 Fowl Play	Closed		29.90	40-45
1994 Tackling Lunch	Closed		29.90	49-125

Fleeting Encounters - M. Budden

YEAR ISSUE	EDITION LIMIT	YEAR RETD.	ISSUE PRICE	*QUOTE U.S.$
1995 Autumn Retreat	95-day		29.90	30

*Quotes have been rounded up to nearest dollar

YEAR ISSUE	EDITION LIMIT	YEAR RETD.	ISSUE PRICE	*QUOTE U.S.$
Floral Frolics - G. Kurz				
1994 Spring Surprises	Closed		29.90	34-40
1994 Bee Careful	Closed		29.90	38
1995 Fuzzy Fun	Closed		32.90	49
1995 Sunny Hideout	Closed		32.90	45
Floral Greetings - L. Liu				
1994 Circle of Love	Closed		29.90	30
1994 Circle of Elegance	95-day		29.90	30
1994 Circle of Harmony	95-day		32.90	33
1994 Circle of Joy	95-day		32.90	33
1994 Circle of Romance	95-day		34.90	35
1995 Circle of Inspiration	95-day		34.90	35
Footsteps of the Brave - H. Schaare				
1993 Noble Quest	Closed		24.90	13-24
1993 At Storm's Passage	Closed		24.90	37-42
1993 With Boundless Vision	Closed		27.90	24-32
1993 Horizons of Destiny	Closed		27.90	31-40
1993 Path of His Forefathers	Closed		27.90	30-46
1993 Soulful Reflection	Closed		29.90	32-44
1993 The Reverent Trail	Closed		29.90	25-44
1994 At Journey's End	Closed		34.90	45-49
Forever Glamorous Barbie - C. Falberg				
1995 Enchanted Evening	Closed		49.90	35-44
1995 Sophisticated Lady	Closed		49.90	50
1995 Solo in the Spotlight	Closed		49.90	70
1995 Midnight Blue	Closed		49.90	65
Fracé's Kingdom of the Great Cats:Signature Collection - C. Fracé				
1994 Mystic Realm	Closed		39.90	57-74
1994 Snow Leopard	Closed		39.90	50
1994 Emperor of Siberia	Closed		39.90	72
1994 His Domain	Closed		39.90	55
1994 American Monarch	Closed		39.90	58
1995 A Radiant Moment	Closed		39.90	40
Freshwater Game Fish of North America - E. Totten				
1994 Rainbow Trout	Closed		29.90	30
1995 Largemouth Bass	Closed		29.90	30
1995 Blue Gills	Closed		32.90	33
1995 Northern Pike	Closed		32.90	33
1995 Brown Trout	Closed		32.90	33
Friendship in Bloom - L. Chang				
1994 Paws in the Posies	Closed		34.90	35
1995 Cozy Petunia Patch	Closed		34.90	35
1995 Patience & Impatience	Closed		34.90	35
Gallant Men of Civil War - J. P. Strain				
1994 Robert E. Lee	95-day		29.90	30
1995 Stonewall Jackson	95-day		29.90	30
1995 Nathan Bedford Forest	95-day		29.90	30
1995 Joshua Chamberlain	95-day		29.90	30
1995 John Hunt Morgan	95-day		29.90	30
1996 Turner Ashby	95-day		29.90	30
1996 John C. Breckenridge	95-day		29.90	30
1996 Ben Hardin Holm	95-day		29.90	30
Gardens of Innocence - D. Richardson				
1994 Hope	95-day		29.90	30
1994 Charity	95-day		29.90	30
1994 Joy	95-day		32.90	33
1994 Faith	95-day		32.90	33
1994 Grace	95-day		32.90	33
1995 Serenity	95-day		34.90	35
1995 Peace	95-day		34.90	35
1995 Patience	95-day		34.90	35
1995 Kindness	95-day		36.90	37
Getting Away From It All - D. Rust				
1995 Mountain Hideaway	95-day		29.90	30
Gone With The Wind: A Portrait in Stained Glass - M. Phalen				
1995 Scarlett Radiance	Closed		39.90	55-60
1995 Rhett's Bright Promise	Closed		39.90	55-60
1995 Ashley's Smoldering Fire	Closed		39.90	55-200
1995 Melanie Lights His World	Closed		39.90	45-120
Gone With The Wind: Musical Treasures - A. Jenks				
1994 Tara: Scarlett's True Love	95-day		29.90	30
1994 Scarlett: Belle of/12 Oaks BBQ	95-day		29.90	30
1995 Charity Bazaar	95-day		32.90	33
1995 The Proposal	95-day		32.90	33
Great Moments in Baseball - S. Gardner				
1993 Joe DiMaggio: The Streak	Closed		29.90	75
1993 Stan Musial: 5 Homer Double Header	Closed		29.90	55
1994 Bobby Thomson: Shot Heard Round the World	Closed		32.90	50
1994 Bill Mazeroski: Winning Home Run	Closed		32.90	33
1994 Don Larsen: Perfect Series Game	Closed		32.90	33
1994 J. Robinson: Saved Pennant	Closed		34.90	35
1994 Satchel Paige: Greatest Games	Closed		34.90	35
1994 Billy Martin: The Rescue Catch	Closed		34.90	35
1994 Dizzy Dean: The World Series Shutout	Closed		34.90	35
1995 Carl Hubbell: The 1934 All State	Closed		36.90	37
Great Superbowl Quarterbacks - R. Brown				
1995 Joe Montana: King of Comeback	95-day		29.90	30

YEAR ISSUE	EDITION LIMIT	YEAR RETD.	ISSUE PRICE	*QUOTE U.S.$
Guidance From Above - B. Jaxon				
1994 Prayer to the Storm	Closed		29.90	49-55
1995 Appeal to Thunder	Closed		29.90	34-50
1995 Blessing the Future	Closed		32.90	50
1995 Sharing the Wisdom	Closed		32.90	50-55
Happy Hearts - J. Daly				
1995 Contentment	Closed		29.90	30
1995 Playmates	Closed		29.90	30
1995 Childhood Friends	Closed		32.90	33
1995 Favorite Gift	Closed		32.90	33
Heart to Heart - Various				
1995 Thinking of You	Closed		29.90	30
Heaven on Earth - T. Kinkade				
1994 I Am the Light of/World	Closed		29.90	30
1995 I Am the Way	95-day		29.90	30
1995 Thy Word is a Lamp	95-day		29.90	30
1995 For Thou Art My Lamp	95-day		29.90	30
1995 In Him Was Life	95-day		29.90	30
1995 But The Path of Just	95-day		29.90	30
Heaven Sent - L. Bogle				
1994 Sweet Dreams	Closed		29.90	30
1994 Puppy Dog Tails	Closed		29.90	30
1994 Timeless Treasure	Closed		32.90	33
1995 Precious Gift	Closed		32.90	33
Heirloom Memories - A. Pech				
1994 Porcelain Treasure	Closed		29.90	70
1994 Rhythms in Lace	Closed		29.90	60-65
1994 Pink Lemonade Roses	Closed		29.90	55
1994 Victorian Romance	Closed		29.90	55-65
1994 Teatime Tulips	Closed		29.90	55-80
1994 Touch of the Irish	Closed		29.90	50-75
A Hidden Garden - T. Clausnitzer				
1993 Curious Kittens	Closed		29.90	39
1994 Through the Eyes of Blue	Closed		29.90	40
1994 Amber Gaze	Closed		29.90	30-40
1994 Fascinating Find	Closed		29.90	35-45
A Hidden World - R. Rust				
1993 Two by Night, Two by Light	Closed		29.90	30-45
1993 Two by Steam, Two in Dream	Closed		29.90	35-38
1993 Two on Sly, Two Watch Nearby	Closed		32.90	35-42
1993 Hunter Growls, Spirits Prowl	Closed		32.90	30-36
1993 In Moonglow One Drinks	Closed		32.90	40-49
1993 Sings at the Moon, Spirits Sing in Tune	Closed		34.90	48-55
1994 Two Cubs Play As Spirits Show the Way	Closed		34.90	45-55
1994 Young Ones Hold on Tight As Spirits Stay in Sight	Closed		34.90	40-55
Hideaway Lake - R. Rust				
1993 Rusty's Retreat	Closed		34.90	27-32
1993 Fishing For Dreams	Closed		34.90	38-40
1993 Sunset Cabin	Closed		34.90	34-42
1993 Echoes of Morning	Closed		34.90	50
Hunters of the Spirit - R. Docken				
1995 Provider	Closed		29.90	30
Illusions of Nature - M. Bierlinski				
1995 A Trio of Wolves	Closed		29.90	30
Immortals of the Diamond - C. Jackson				
1994 The Sultan of Swat	Closed		39.90	56-68
1994 Pride of the Yankees	Closed		39.90	45-67
1995 The Georgia Peach	Closed		39.90	52-70
1995 The Winningest Pitcher	Closed		39.90	60-78
Keepsakes of the Heart - C. Layton				
1993 Forever Friends	Closed		29.90	30-32
1993 Afternoon Tea	Closed		29.90	32-36
1993 Riding Companions	Closed		29.90	35-40
1994 Sentimental Sweethearts	Closed		29.90	38
Kindred Moments - C. Poulin				
1996 Forever Friends	95-day		29.90	30
1995 Sisters Are Blossoms	95-day		29.90	30
Kingdom of the Unicorn - M. Ferraro				
1993 The Magic Begins	Closed		29.90	30-34
1993 In Crystal Waters	Closed		29.90	41-47
1993 Chasing a Dream	Closed		29.90	60-65
1993 The Fountain of Youth	Closed		29.90	50
Legend of the White Buffalo - D. Stanley				
1995 Mystic Spirit	95-day		29.90	30
Lena Liu's Beautiful Gardens - Inspired by L. Liu				
1994 Iris Garden	Closed		34.00	65-89
1994 Peony Garden	Closed		34.00	70-84
1994 The Rose Garden	Closed		39.00	125-190
1995 Lily Garden	Closed		39.00	75
1995 Tulip Garden	Closed		39.00	75-108
1995 Orchid Garden	Closed		44.00	140
1995 The Poppy Garden	Closed		44.00	55-80
1995 Calla Lily Garden	Closed		44.00	115-155
1995 The Morning Glory Garden	Closed		44.00	100
1995 The Hibiscus Garden	Closed		47.00	70
1995 The Clematis Garden	Closed		47.00	50
1995 The Gladiola Garden	Closed		47.00	68

YEAR ISSUE	EDITION LIMIT	YEAR RETD.	ISSUE PRICE	*QUOTE U.S.$
The Life of Christ - R. Barrett				
1994 The Passion in the Garden	Closed		29.90	48-50
1994 Jesus Enters Jerusalem	Closed		29.90	50-58
1994 Jesus Calms the Waters	Closed		32.90	67
1994 Sermon on the Mount	Closed		32.90	26-50
1994 The Last Supper	Closed		32.90	66
1994 The Ascension	Closed		34.90	40-55
1994 The Resurrection	Closed		34.90	50-66
1994 The Crucifixion	Closed		34.90	40-55
The Light of the World - C. Nick				
1995 The Last Supper	Closed		29.90	30
Lincoln's Portraits of Valor - B. Maguire				
1993 The Gettysburg Address	Closed		29.90	30
1993 Emancipation Proclamation	Closed		29.90	30
1993 The Lincoln-Douglas Debates	Closed		29.90	30
1993 The Second Inaugural Address	Closed		29.90	30
The Lion King - Disney Studios				
1994 The Circle of Life	95-day		29.90	30
1995 Like Father, Like Son	95-day		29.90	30
1995 A Crunchy Feast	95-day		32.90	33
Little Bandits - C. Jagodits				
1993 Handle With Care	Closed		29.90	58
1993 All Tied Up	Closed		29.90	50-55
1993 Everything's Coming Up Daisies	Closed		32.90	43-49
1993 Out of Hand	Closed		32.90	43-57
1993 Pupsicles	Closed		32.90	55
1993 Unexpected Guests	Closed		32.90	44
Lords of Forest & Canyon - G. Beecham				
1994 Mountain Majesty	Closed		29.90	30
1995 Proud Legacy	Closed		29.90	30
1995 Golden Monarch	Closed		32.90	33
1995 Forest Emperor	Closed		32.90	33
Me & My Shadow - J. Welty				
1994 Easter Parade	Closed		29.90	40
1994 A Golden Moment	Closed		29.90	30-36
1994 Perfect Timing	Closed		29.90	40-45
1995 Giddyup	Closed		29.90	38-40
Michael Jordan: A Legend for all Time - A. Katzman				
1995 Soaring Star	Closed		79.95	225-650
1996 Rim Rocker	95-day		79.95	80
Mickey and Minnie's Through the Years - Disney Studios				
1995 Mickey's Birthday Party 1942	95-day		29.90	30-55
1995 Brave Little Tailor	95-day		29.90	30
1996 Steamboat Willie	95-day		29.90	30
1996 Mickey's Gala Premiere	95-day		32.90	33
1996 The Mickey Mouse Club	95-day		32.90	33
1996 Mickey's 65th Birthday	95-day		34.90	35
A Mother's Love - J. Anderson				
1995 Remembrance	95 days		29.90	30
Musical Tribute to Elvis the King - B. Emmett				
1994 Rockin' Blue Suede Shoes	95-day		29.90	75
1994 Hound Dog Bop	95-day		29.90	30
1995 Red, White & GI Blues	95-day		32.90	33
1995 American Dream	95-day		32.90	33
Mysterious Case of Fowl Play - H. Bond				
1994 Inspector Clawseau	Closed		29.90	39-43
1994 Glamourpuss	Closed		29.90	52-60
1994 Sophisticat	Closed		29.90	60-80
1994 Kool Cat	Closed		29.90	58-76
1994 Sneakers & High-Top	Closed		29.90	60-125
1995 Tuxedo	Closed		29.90	95-125
Mystic Guardians - S. Hill				
1993 Soul Mates	Closed		29.90	30
1993 Majestic Messenger	Closed		29.90	30
1993 Companion Spirits	Closed		32.90	33
1994 Faithful Fellowship	Closed		32.90	33
1994 Spiritual Harmony	Closed		32.90	33
1994 Royal Unity	Closed		34.90	35
Mystic Spirits - V. Crandell				
1995 Moon Shadows	95-day		29.90	30
1995 Midnight Snow	95-day		29.90	30
1995 Arctic Nights	95-day		32.90	33
Native American Legends: Chiefs of Destiny - C. Jackson				
1994 Sitting Bull	Closed		39.90	60-64
1994 Chief Joseph	Closed		39.90	50-64
1995 Red Cloud	Closed		44.90	45-58
1995 Crazy Horse	Closed		44.90	200-301
1995 Geronimo	Closed		44.90	150-175
1996 Tecumseh	Closed		44.90	160
Native Beauty - L. Bogle				
1994 The Promise	95-day		29.90	30
1994 Afterglow	95-day		29.90	30
1994 White Feather	95-day		29.90	30
1995 First glance	95-day		29.90	30
1995 Morning Star	95-day		29.90	30
1995 Quiet Time	95-day		29.90	30
1995 Warm Thoughts	95-day		29.90	30

*Quotes have been rounded up to nearest dollar

PLATES

YEAR ISSUE	EDITION LIMIT	YEAR RETD.	ISSUE PRICE	*QUOTE U.S.$
Native Visions - J. Cole				
1994 Bringers of the Storm	Closed		29.90	45-53
1994 Water Vision	Closed		29.90	44
1994 Brother to the Moon	Closed		29.90	25-30
1995 Son of the Sun	Closed		29.90	38-45
1995 Man Who Sees Far	Closed		29.90	36
1995 Listening	Closed		29.90	30
1996 The Red Shield	Closed		29.90	30
1996 Toponas	95-day		29.90	30
Nature's Little Treasures - L. Martin				
1993 Garden Whispers	Closed		29.90	48-69
1994 Wings of Grace	Closed		29.90	34-109
1994 Delicate Splendor	Closed		32.90	38-80
1994 Perfect Jewels	95-day		32.90	33
1994 Miniature Glory	95-day		32.90	33
1994 Precious Beauties	95-day		34.90	35
1994 Minute Enchantment	95-day		34.90	35
1994 Rare Perfection	95-day		34.90	35
1995 Misty Morning	95-day		36.90	37
1995 Whisper in the Wind	95-day		36.90	37
New Horizons - R. Copple				
1993 Building For a New Generation	Closed		29.90	30-33
1993 The Power of Gold	Closed		29.90	30
1994 Wings of Snowy Grandeur	Closed		32.90	33
1994 Master of the Chase	Closed		32.90	33-35
1995 Coastal Domain	Closed		32.90	33
1995 Majestic Wings	Closed		32.90	33
Nightsongs: The Loon - J. Hansel				
1994 Moonlight Echoes	Closed		29.90	62-75
1994 Evening Mist	Closed		29.90	60-68
1994 Nocturnal Glow	Closed		32.90	55-60
1994 Tranquil Reflections	Closed		32.90	58-70
1994 Peaceful Waters	Closed		32.90	65-70
1994 Silently Nestled	Closed		34.90	75-85
1994 Night Light	Closed		34.90	70-75
1995 Peaceful Homestead	Closed		34.90	65-70
1995 Silent Passage	Closed		34.90	66-70
1995 Tranquil Refuge	Closed		36.90	65-75
1995 Serene Sanctuary	Closed		36.90	42-52
1995 Moonlight Cruise	Closed		36.90	42-60
Nightwatch: The Wolf - D. Ningewance				
1994 Moonlight Serenade	Closed		29.90	30-35
1994 Midnight Guard	Closed		29.90	40-48
1994 Snowy Lookout	Closed		29.90	30-45
1994 Silent Sentries	Closed		29.90	45-50
1994 Song to the Night	Closed		29.90	30-44
1994 Winter Passage	Closed		29.90	45-47
Northern Companions - K. Weisberg				
1995 Midnight Harmony	95-day		29.90	30
Northwoods Spirit - D. Wenzel				
1994 Timeless Watch	Closed		29.90	30
1994 Woodland Retreat	Closed		29.90	30
1995 Forest Echo	95-day		29.90	30
1995 Timberland Gaze	95-day		29.90	30
1995 Evening Respite	95-day		29.90	30
Nosy Neighbors - P. Weirs				
1994 Cat Nap	Closed		29.90	30
1994 Special Delivery	95-day		29.90	30
1995 House Sitting	95-day		29.90	30
1995 Observation Deck	95-day		32.90	33
1995 Surprise Visit	95-day		32.90	33
Notorious Disney Villains - Disney Studios				
1993 The Evil Queen	Closed		29.90	46-75
1994 Maleficent	Closed		29.90	72-86
1994 Ursella	Closed		29.90	49-64
1994 Cruella De Vil	Closed		29.90	45-60
Old Fashioned Christmas with Thomas Kinkade - T. Kinkade				
1993 All Friends Are Welcome	Closed		29.90	30-55
1993 Winters Memories	Closed		29.90	30
1993 A Holiday Gathering	Closed		32.90	33
1994 Christmas Tree Cottage	Closed		32.90	33
1995 The Best Tradition	Closed		32.90	33
Panda Bear Hugs - W. Nelson				
1993 Rock-A-Bye	Closed		39.90	60
1993 Loving Advice	Closed		39.90	55-70
1993 A Playful Interlude	Closed		39.90	53-70
1993 A Taste of Life	Closed		39.90	50-70
Pathways of the Heart - J. Barnes				
1993 October Radiance	Closed		29.90	30
1993 Daybreak	Closed		29.90	30
1994 Harmony with Nature	Closed		29.90	30
1994 Distant Lights	Closed		29.90	30
1994 A Night to Remember	Closed		29.90	30
1994 Peaceful Evening	Closed		29.90	30
Peace on Earth - D. Geisness				
1993 Winter Lullaby	Closed		29.90	53-60
1994 Heavenly Slumber	Closed		29.90	45-48
1994 Sweet Embrace	Closed		32.90	40-75
1994 Woodland Dreams	Closed		32.90	45-50
1994 Snowy Silence	Closed		32.90	50
1994 Dreamy Whispers	Closed		32.90	45-48
Picked from an English Garden - W. Von Schwarzbek				
1994 Inspired by Romance	Closed		32.90	33-49
1995 Lasting Treasures	Closed		32.90	33-38
1995 Nature's Wonders	Closed		32.90	60
1995 Summer Rhapsody	Closed		32.90	55
Pinegrove's Winter Cardinals - S. Timm				
1994 Evening in Pinegrove	95-day		29.90	30
1994 Pinegrove's Sunset	95-day		29.90	30
1994 Pinegrove's Twilight	95-day		29.90	30
1994 Daybreak in Pinegrove	95-day		29.90	30
1994 Pinegrove's Morning	95-day		29.90	30
1994 Afternoon in Pinegrove	95-day		29.90	30
1994 Midnight in Pinegrove	95-day		29.90	30
1994 At Home in Pinegrove	95-day		29.90	30
Portraits of Majesty - Various				
1994 Snowy Monarch	Closed		29.90	30
1995 Reflections of Kings	Closed		29.90	30
1995 Emperor of His Realm	Closed		29.90	30
1995 Solemn Sovereign	95-day		29.90	30
Postcards from Thomas Kinkade - T. Kinkade				
1995 San Francisco	Closed		34.90	35
1995 Paris	95-day		34.90	35
1995 New York City	95-day		34.90	35
Practice Makes Perfect - L. Kaatz				
1994 What's a Mother to Do?	Closed		29.90	54
1994 The Ones That Got Away	Closed		29.90	39-60
1994 Pointed in the Wrong Direction	Closed		32.90	40-55
1994 Fishing for Compliments	Closed		32.90	34-60
1994 A Dandy Distraction	Closed		32.90	45-48
1995 More Than a Mouthful	Closed		34.90	50-60
1995 On The Right Track	Closed		34.90	34-67
1995 Missing the Point	Closed		34.90	35-40
Precious Visions - J. Grande				
1994 Brilliant Moment	95-day		29.90	30
1995 Brief Interlude	95-day		29.90	30
1995 Timeless Radiance	95-day		29.90	30
1995 Enduring Elegance	95-day		32.90	33
Promise of a Savior - Various				
1993 An Angel's Message	Closed		29.90	30
1993 Gifts to Jesus	Closed		29.90	30
1993 The Heavenly King	Closed		29.90	30
1993 Angels Were Watching	Closed		29.90	30
1993 Holy Mother and Child	Closed		29.90	30
1994 A Child is Born	Closed		29.90	30
Proud Heritage - M. Amerman				
1994 Mystic Warrior: Medicine Crow	Closed		34.90	27-30
1994 Great Chief: Sitting Bull	Closed		34.90	35
1994 Brave Leader: Geronimo	Closed		34.90	40
1995 Peaceful Defender: Chief Joseph	Closed		34.90	35
Quiet Moments - K. Daniel				
1994 Time for Tea	Closed		29.90	30
1995 A Loving Hand	95-day		29.90	30
1995 Kept with Care	95-day		29.90	30
1995 Puppy Love	95-day		29.90	30
Radiant Messengers - L. Martin				
1994 Peace	Closed		29.90	30
1994 Hope	95-day		29.90	30
1994 Beauty	95-day		29.90	30
1994 Inspiration	95-day		29.90	30
Reflections of Marilyn - C. Notarile				
1994 All That Glitters	95-day		29.90	30
1994 Shimmering Heat	95-day		29.90	30
1994 Million Dollar Star	95-day		29.90	30
1995 A Twinkle in Her Eye	95-day		29.90	30
Remembering Elvis - N. Giorgio				
1994 The King	95-day		29.90	30
1995 The Legend	95-day		29.90	30
Royal Enchantments - J. Penchoff				
1994 The Gift	Closed		39.90	66-70
1995 The Courtship	Closed		39.90	40-55
1995 The Promise	Closed		39.90	55-74
1995 The Embrace	Closed		39.90	60
Sacred Circle - K. Randle				
1993 Before the Hunt	Closed		29.90	43-45
1993 Spiritual Guardian	Closed		29.90	28-50
1993 Ghost Dance	Closed		32.90	58-64
1994 Deer Dance	Closed		32.90	62-69
1994 The Wolf Dance	Closed		32.90	44-60
1994 The Painted Horse	Closed		34.90	40-48
1994 Transformation Dance	Closed		34.90	45-50
1994 Elk Dance	Closed		34.90	55
Santa's Little Helpers - B. Higgins Bond				
1994 Stocking Stuffers	Closed		24.90	27-32
1994 Wrapping Up the Holidays	Closed		24.90	40-44
1994 Not a Creature Was Stirring	Closed		24.90	35-38
1995 Cozy Kittens	Closed		24.90	30-60
1995 Holiday Mischief	Closed		24.90	29-35
1995 Treats For Santa	Closed		24.90	29
Santa's On His Way - S. Gustafson				
1994 Checking It Twice	Closed		29.90	40-45
1994 Up, Up & Away	Closed		29.90	40-45
1995 Santa's First Stop	Closed		32.90	40-70
1995 Gifts for One and All	Closed		32.90	49-75
1995 A Warm Send-off	Closed		32.90	70
1995 Santa's Reward	Closed		34.90	60-70
Signs of Spring - J. Thornbrugh				
1994 A Family Feast	95-day		29.90	30
1995 How Fast They Grow	95-day		29.90	30
1995 Our First Home	95-day		29.90	30
1995 Awaiting New Arrivals	95-day		29.90	30
Silent Journey - D. Casey				
1994 Where Paths Cross	95-day		29.90	30
1994 On Eagle's Wings	95-day		29.90	30
1994 Seeing the Unseen	95-day		29.90	30
1995 Where the Buffalo Roam	95-day		29.90	30
1995 Unbridled Majesty	95-day		29.90	30
1995 Wisdom Seeker	95-day		29.90	30
1995 Journey of the Wild	95-day		29.90	30
Soft Elegance - R. Iverson				
1994 Priscilla in Pearls	Closed		29.90	30
1995 Tabitha on Taffeta	95-day		29.90	30
1995 Emily in Emeralds	95-day		29.90	30
1995 Alexandra in Amethysts	95-day		29.90	30
Some Beary Nice Places - J. Tanton				
1994 Welcome to the Libeary	Closed		29.90	32-35
1994 Welcome to Our Country Kitchen	Closed		29.90	27-31
1995 Bearennial Garden	Closed		32.90	36
1995 Welcome to Our Music Conserbeartory	Closed		32.90	35-46
Soul Mates - L. Bogle				
1995 The Lovers	95-day		29.90	35-46
1995 The Awakening	95-day		29.90	30
1996 The Embrace	95-day		29.90	30
1996 Warm Interlude	95-day		29.90	30
Sovereigns of the Sky - G. Dieckhoner				
1994 Spirit of Freedom	Closed		39.00	31-61
1994 Spirit of Pride	Closed		39.00	39-70
1994 Spirit of Valor	Closed		44.00	64-79
1994 Spirit of Majesty	Closed		44.00	47-65
1995 Spirit of Glory	Closed		44.00	60-75
1995 Spirit of Courage	Closed		49.00	60-75
1995 Spirit of Bravery	Closed		49.00	49
1995 Spirit of Honor	Closed		49.00	50-90
Sovereigns of the Wild - D. Grant				
1993 The Snow Queen	Closed		29.90	37
1994 Let Us Survive	Closed		29.90	36
1994 Cool Cats	Closed		29.90	49
1994 Siberian Snow Tigers	Closed		29.90	30
1994 African Evening	Closed		29.90	31-45
1994 First Outing	Closed		29.90	30-34
Superstars of Baseball - T. Sizemore				
1994 Willie "Say Hey" Mays	Closed		29.90	34-50
1995 Carl "Yaz" Yastrzemski	Closed		29.90	50-54
1995 Frank "Robby" Robinson	Closed		32.90	65
1995 Bob Gibson	Closed		32.90	45-60
1995 Harmon Killebrew	Closed		32.90	45-50
1995 Don Drysdale	Closed		34.90	58-80
1995 Al Kaline	Closed		34.90	37-65
1995 Maury Wills	Closed		34.90	44-100
Superstars of Country Music - N. Giorgio				
1993 Dolly Parton: I Will Always Love You	Closed		29.90	65
1993 Kenny Rogers: Sweet Music Man	Closed		29.90	60
1994 Barbara Mandrell	Closed		32.90	40
1994 Glen Campbell: Rhinestone Cowboy	Closed		32.90	33
Tale of Peter Rabbit & Benjamin Bunny - R. Akers				
1994 A Pocket Full of Onions	Closed		39.00	65
1994 Beside His Cousin	Closed		39.00	85-138
1995 Round that Corner	Closed		39.00	80-124
1995 Safely Home	Closed		44.00	100
1995 Mr. McGregor's Garden	Closed		44.00	70
1995 Rosemary Tea and Lavender	Closed		44.00	80
1995 Amongst the Flowerpots	Closed		44.00	100
1995 Upon the Scarecrow	Closed		44.00	105
That's What Friends Are For - A. Isakov				
1994 Friends Are Forever	Closed		29.90	48-52
1994 Friends Are Comfort	Closed		29.90	48-78
1994 Friends Are Loving	Closed		29.90	45-48
1995 Friends Are For Fun	Closed		29.90	59-85
Thomas Kinkade's Illuminated Cottages - T. Kinkade				
1994 The Flagstone Path	Closed		34.90	51-70
1995 The Garden Walk	Closed		34.90	60-125
1995 Cherry Blossom Hideaway	Closed		37.90	55-126
1995 The Lighted Gate	Closed		37.90	55-126
Thomas Kinkade's Lamplight Village - T. Kinkade				
1995 Lamplight Brooke	95-day		29.90	30
1995 Lamplight Lane	95-day		29.90	30
1995 Lamplight Inn	95-day		29.90	30
Through a Child's Eyes - K. Noles				
1994 Little Butterfly	Closed		29.90	65
1995 Woodland Rose	Closed		29.90	40
1995 Treetop Wonder	Closed		29.90	50

*Quotes have been rounded up to nearest dollar

YEAR ISSUE	EDITION LIMIT	YEAR RETD.	ISSUE PRICE	*QUOTE U.S.$
1995 Little Red Squirrel	Closed		32.90	60
1995 Water Lily	Closed		32.90	60
1995 Prairie Song	Closed		34.90	68

Thundering Waters - F. Miller

YEAR ISSUE	EDITION LIMIT	YEAR RETD.	ISSUE PRICE	*QUOTE U.S.$
1994 Niagara Falls	Closed		34.90	29-42
1994 Lower Falls, Yellowstone	Closed		34.90	61-65
1994 Bridal Veil Falls	Closed		34.90	60-64
1995 Havasu Falls	Closed		29.90	55-68

Trains of the Great West - K. Randle

YEAR ISSUE	EDITION LIMIT	YEAR RETD.	ISSUE PRICE	*QUOTE U.S.$
1993 Moonlit Journey	Closed		29.90	31-36
1993 Mountain Hideaway	Closed		29.90	45-50
1993 Early Morning Arrival	Closed		29.90	48-52
1994 The Snowy Pass	Closed		29.90	43-48

Triumph in the Air - H. Krebs

YEAR ISSUE	EDITION LIMIT	YEAR RETD.	ISSUE PRICE	*QUOTE U.S.$
1994 Checkmate!	Closed		34.90	35
1994 One Heck of a Deflection Shot	Closed		34.90	35
1994 Hunting Fever	Closed		34.90	35
1995 Struck by Thunder	Closed		34.90	35

Twilight Memories - J. Barnes

YEAR ISSUE	EDITION LIMIT	YEAR RETD.	ISSUE PRICE	*QUOTE U.S.$
1995 Winter's Twilight	95-day		29.90	30

Two's Company - S. Eide

YEAR ISSUE	EDITION LIMIT	YEAR RETD.	ISSUE PRICE	*QUOTE U.S.$
1994 Golden Harvest	Closed		29.90	100-109
1995 Brotherly Love	Closed		29.90	48-88
1995 Seeing Double	Closed		29.90	88
1995 Spring Spaniels	Closed		29.90	120

Under A Snowy Veil - C. Sams

YEAR ISSUE	EDITION LIMIT	YEAR RETD.	ISSUE PRICE	*QUOTE U.S.$
1995 Winter's Warmth	95-day		29.90	30
1995 Snow Mates	95-day		29.90	30
1995 Winter's Dawn	95-day		29.90	30
1995 First Snow	95-day		29.90	30

Untamed Spirits - P. Weirs

YEAR ISSUE	EDITION LIMIT	YEAR RETD.	ISSUE PRICE	*QUOTE U.S.$
1993 Wild Hearts	Closed		29.90	49
1994 Breakaway	Closed		29.90	50-70
1994 Forever Free	Closed		29.90	34-48
1994 Distant Thunder	Closed		29.90	42-65

Untamed Wilderness - P. Weirs

YEAR ISSUE	EDITION LIMIT	YEAR RETD.	ISSUE PRICE	*QUOTE U.S.$
1995 Unexpected Encounter	95-day		29.90	30

Vanishing Paradises - G. Dieckhoner

YEAR ISSUE	EDITION LIMIT	YEAR RETD.	ISSUE PRICE	*QUOTE U.S.$
1994 The Rainforest	Closed		29.90	40
1994 The Panda's World	Closed		29.90	60-70
1994 Splendors of India	Closed		29.90	60
1994 An African Safari	Closed		29.90	79-94

Visions from Eagle Ridge - D. Casey

YEAR ISSUE	EDITION LIMIT	YEAR RETD.	ISSUE PRICE	*QUOTE U.S.$
1995 Assembly of Pride	Closed		29.90	30

Visions of Glory - D. Cook

YEAR ISSUE	EDITION LIMIT	YEAR RETD.	ISSUE PRICE	*QUOTE U.S.$
1995 Iwo Jima	Closed		29.90	48-60
1995 Freeing of Paris	Closed		29.90	32-87

Visions of Our Lady - H. Garrido

YEAR ISSUE	EDITION LIMIT	YEAR RETD.	ISSUE PRICE	*QUOTE U.S.$
1994 Our Lady of Lourdes	Closed		29.90	30
1994 Our Lady of Medjugorje	95-day		29.90	30
1994 Our Lady of Fatima	95-day		29.90	30
1994 Our Lady of Guadeloupe	95-day		29.90	30
1994 Our Lady of Grace	95-day		29.90	30
1994 Our Lady of Mt. Carmel	95-day		29.90	30

Visions of the Sacred - D. Stanley

YEAR ISSUE	EDITION LIMIT	YEAR RETD.	ISSUE PRICE	*QUOTE U.S.$
1994 Snow Rider	95-day		29.90	30
1994 Spring's Messenger	95-day		29.90	30
1994 The Cheyenne Prophet	95-day		32.90	33
1995 Buffalo Caller	95-day		32.90	33
1995 Journey of Harmony	95-day		32.90	33

A Visit from St. Nick - C. Jackson

YEAR ISSUE	EDITION LIMIT	YEAR RETD.	ISSUE PRICE	*QUOTE U.S.$
1995 Twas the Night Before Christmas	Closed		49.00	60-65
1995 Up to the Housetop	Closed		49.00	55-60
1995 A Bundle of Toys	Closed		54.00	57-65
1995 The Stockings Were Filled	Closed		54.00	54-65
1995 Visions of Sugarplums	Closed		54.00	60-75
1995 To My Wondering Eyes	Closed		59.00	60-100
1995 A Wink of His Eye	Closed		59.00	75
1995 Happy Christmas To All	Closed		59.00	75

A Visit to Brambly Hedge - J. Barklem

YEAR ISSUE	EDITION LIMIT	YEAR RETD.	ISSUE PRICE	*QUOTE U.S.$
1994 Summer Story	Closed		39.90	49
1994 Spring Story	Closed		39.90	40-55
1994 Autumn Story	Closed		39.90	70-80
1995 Winter Story	Closed		39.90	90-95

Warm Country Moments - M.A. Lasher

YEAR ISSUE	EDITION LIMIT	YEAR RETD.	ISSUE PRICE	*QUOTE U.S.$
1994 Mabel's Sunny Retreat	95-day		29.90	30
1994 Annebelle's Simple Pleasures	95-day		29.90	30
1994 Harriet's Loving Touch	95-day		29.90	30
1994 Emily and Alice in a Jam	95-day		29.90	30
1995 Hanna's Secret Garden	95-day		29.90	30
1995 Mabel's Summer Retreat	95-day		29.90	30
1995 Harriet's Loving Touch	95-day		29.90	30
1995 Emily & Alice in a Jam	95-day		29.90	30

Welcome to the Neighborhood - B. Mock

YEAR ISSUE	EDITION LIMIT	YEAR RETD.	ISSUE PRICE	*QUOTE U.S.$
1994 Ivy Lane	Closed		29.90	62
1994 Daffodil Drive	Closed		29.90	50
1995 Lilac Lane	Closed		34.90	60
1995 Tulip Terrace	Closed		34.90	60

When All Hearts Come Home - J. Barnes

YEAR ISSUE	EDITION LIMIT	YEAR RETD.	ISSUE PRICE	*QUOTE U.S.$
1993 Oh Christmas Tree	Closed		29.90	45-57
1993 Night Before Christmas	Closed		29.90	65-79
1993 Comfort and Joy	Closed		29.90	54-75
1993 Grandpa's Farm	Closed		29.90	45-72
1993 Peace on Earth	Closed		29.90	62-75
1993 Night Departure	Closed		29.90	45-80
1993 Supper and Small Talk	Closed		29.90	43-61
1993 Christmas Wish	Closed		29.90	36-65

When Dreams Blossom - R. McGinnis

YEAR ISSUE	EDITION LIMIT	YEAR RETD.	ISSUE PRICE	*QUOTE U.S.$
1994 Dreams to Gather	95-day		29.90	30
1994 Where Friends Dream	95-day		29.90	30
1994 The Sweetest of Dreams	95-day		32.90	33
1994 Dreams of Poetry	95-day		32.90	33
1995 A Place to Dream	95-day		32.90	33
1995 Dreaming of You	95-day		32.90	33

Where Eagles Soar - F. Mittelstadt

YEAR ISSUE	EDITION LIMIT	YEAR RETD.	ISSUE PRICE	*QUOTE U.S.$
1994 On Freedom's Wing	Closed		29.90	37-42
1994 Allegiance with the Wind	Closed		29.90	30-35
1995 Pride of the Sky	Closed		29.90	45-50
1995 Windward Majesty	Closed		29.90	32-42
1995 Noble Legacy	Closed		29.90	35-42
1995 Pristine Domains	Closed		29.90	42-50
1995 Splendor in Flight	Closed		29.90	42-60
1995 Royal Ascent	Closed		29.90	30-52

Windows on a World of Song - K. Daniel

YEAR ISSUE	EDITION LIMIT	YEAR RETD.	ISSUE PRICE	*QUOTE U.S.$
1993 The Library: Cardinals	Closed		34.90	57-63
1993 The Den: Black-Capped Chickadees	Closed		34.90	36-45
1993 The Bedroom: Bluebirds	Closed		34.90	35-38
1994 The Kitchen: Goldfinches	Closed		34.90	56-62

Wings of Glory - J. Spurlock

YEAR ISSUE	EDITION LIMIT	YEAR RETD.	ISSUE PRICE	*QUOTE U.S.$
1995 Pride of America	Closed		32.90	38-42
1995 Spirit of Freedom	Closed		32.90	32-44
1996 Portrait of Liberty	Closed		32.90	42
1996 Paragon of Courage	Closed		32.90	40

Winnie the Pooh and Friends - C. Jackson

YEAR ISSUE	EDITION LIMIT	YEAR RETD.	ISSUE PRICE	*QUOTE U.S.$
1995 Time For a Little Something	Closed		39.90	375-475
1995 Bouncing's/Tiggers do Best	Closed		39.90	115-148
1995 You're a Real Friend	95-day		44.90	45
1995 Silly Old Bear	95-day		44.90	45
1995 Rumbly in my Tummy	95-day		44.90	45
1995 Many Happy Returns of the Day	95-day		49.90	50
1996 T is For Tigger	Closed		49.90	96
1996 Nobody Uncheered w/Balloons	95-day		49.90	50
1996 Do You Think It's a Woozle?	95-day		49.90	50
1996 Fine Day to Buzz with the Bees	95-day		49.90	50
1996 Pooh Sticks	95-day		49.90	50
1996 Three Cheers For Pooh	95-day		49.90	50

Winter Shadows - Various

YEAR ISSUE	EDITION LIMIT	YEAR RETD.	ISSUE PRICE	*QUOTE U.S.$
1995 Canyon Moon	Closed		29.90	30
1995 Shadows of Gray	95-day		29.90	30

Wish You Were Here - T. Kinkade

YEAR ISSUE	EDITION LIMIT	YEAR RETD.	ISSUE PRICE	*QUOTE U.S.$
1994 End of a Perfect Day	95-day		29.90	30
1994 A Quiet Evening/Riverlodge	95-day		29.90	30
1994 Soft Morning Light	95-day		29.90	30

Woodland Tranquility - G. Alexander

YEAR ISSUE	EDITION LIMIT	YEAR RETD.	ISSUE PRICE	*QUOTE U.S.$
1994 Winter's Calm	95-day		29.90	30
1995 Frosty Morn	95-day		29.90	30
1995 Crossing Boundaries	95-day		29.90	30

Woodland Wings - J. Hansel

YEAR ISSUE	EDITION LIMIT	YEAR RETD.	ISSUE PRICE	*QUOTE U.S.$
1994 Twilight Flight	Closed		34.90	38
1994 Gliding on Gilded Skies	Closed		34.90	45-80
1994 Sunset Voyage	Closed		34.90	62-68
1995 Peaceful Journey	Closed		34.90	35-60

The World Beneath the Waves - D. Terbush

YEAR ISSUE	EDITION LIMIT	YEAR RETD.	ISSUE PRICE	*QUOTE U.S.$
1995 Sea of Light	95-day		29.90	30
1995 All God's Children	95-day		29.90	30
1995 Humpback Whales	95-day		29.90	30

The World of the Eagle - J. Hansel

YEAR ISSUE	EDITION LIMIT	YEAR RETD.	ISSUE PRICE	*QUOTE U.S.$
1993 Sentinel of the Night	Closed		29.90	37-40
1994 Silent Guard	Closed		29.90	48-50
1994 Night Flyer	Closed		32.90	48-60
1995 Midnight Duty	Closed		32.90	58-81

A World of Wildlife: Celebrating Earth Day - T. Clausnitzer

YEAR ISSUE	EDITION LIMIT	YEAR RETD.	ISSUE PRICE	*QUOTE U.S.$
1995 A Delicate Balance	Closed		29.90	30

WWII: A Remembrance - J. Griffin

YEAR ISSUE	EDITION LIMIT	YEAR RETD.	ISSUE PRICE	*QUOTE U.S.$
1994 D-Day	Closed		29.90	30
1994 The Battle of Midway	Closed		29.90	30
1994 The Battle of The Bulge	Closed		32.90	33
1995 Battle of the Philippines	Closed		32.90	33
1995 Doolittle's Raid Over Tokyo	Closed		32.90	33

Cavanagh Group Intl.

Coca-Cola Brand Heritage Collection - Various

YEAR ISSUE	EDITION LIMIT	YEAR RETD.	ISSUE PRICE	*QUOTE U.S.$
1995 Boy Fishing - N. Rockwell	5,000	1997	60.00	65
1995 Good Boys and Girls - Sundblom	2,500	1995	60.00	60
1995 Hilda Clark with Roses - CGI	5,000	1997	60.00	65
1996 Travel Refreshed - Sundblom	Open		60.00	60

Cherished Teddies/Enesco Corporation

The Cherished Seasons - P. Hillman

YEAR ISSUE	EDITION LIMIT	YEAR RETD.	ISSUE PRICE	*QUOTE U.S.$
1997 Spring-"Spring Brings A Season of Beauty" 203386	Open		35.00	35
1997 Summer-"Summer Brings A Season of Warmth" 203394	Open		35.00	35
1997 Autumn-"Autumn Brings A Season of Thanksgiving" 203408	Open		35.00	35
1997 Winter "Winter Brings A Season of Joy" 203416	Open		35.00	35

Cherished Teddies - P. Hillman

YEAR ISSUE	EDITION LIMIT	YEAR RETD.	ISSUE PRICE	*QUOTE U.S.$
1997 We Bear Thanks 272426	Open		35.00	35

Christmas - P. Hillman

YEAR ISSUE	EDITION LIMIT	YEAR RETD.	ISSUE PRICE	*QUOTE U.S.$
1995 The Season of Joy Dtd 95 141550	Yr.Iss.		35.00	37-69
1996 The Season of Peace Dtd 96 176060	Yr.Iss.		35.00	28-35
1997 The Season to Believe Dtd 97 272183	Yr.Iss.		35.00	35
1998 The Season of Magic Dtd 98 352764	Yr.Iss.		35.00	35

Easter - P. Hillman

YEAR ISSUE	EDITION LIMIT	YEAR RETD.	ISSUE PRICE	*QUOTE U.S.$
1996 Some Bunny Loves You Dtd 96 156590	Yr.Iss.		35.00	35-80
1997 Springtime Happiness Dtd 97 203009	Yr.Iss.		35.00	35

Mother's Day - P. Hillman

YEAR ISSUE	EDITION LIMIT	YEAR RETD.	ISSUE PRICE	*QUOTE U.S.$
1996 A Mother's Heart is Full of Love Dtd 96 156493	Yr.Iss.		35.00	35-65
1997 Our Love Is Ever-Blooming Dtd 97 203025	Yr.Iss.		35.00	35
1998 Mom-Maker of Miracles 303046	Yr.Iss.		35.00	35

Nursery Rhymes - P. Hillman

YEAR ISSUE	EDITION LIMIT	YEAR RETD.	ISSUE PRICE	*QUOTE U.S.$
1995 Jack/Jill "Our Friendship Will Never Tumble" 114901	Open		35.00	35
1995 Mary/Lamb "I'll Always Be By Your Side" 128902	Open		35.00	35
1995 Old King Cole "You Wear Your Kindness Like a Crown" 135437	Open		35.00	35
1996 Mother Goose & Friends "Happily Ever After With Friends" 170968	Open		35.00	35
1996 Little Miss Muffet "I'm Never Afraid With You At My Side" 145033	Open		35.00	35
1996 Little Jack Horner "I'm Plum Happy You're My Friend" 151998	Open		35.00	35
1996 Wee Willie Winkie "Good Night, Sleep Tight" 170941	Open		35.00	35
1996 Little Bo Peep "Looking For A Friend Like You" 164658	Open		35.00	35

Sweet Little One - P. Hillman

YEAR ISSUE	EDITION LIMIT	YEAR RETD.	ISSUE PRICE	*QUOTE U.S.$
1997 Sweet Little One 203726	Open		35.00	35

Dave Grossman Creations

Emmett Kelly Plates - B. Leighton-Jones

YEAR ISSUE	EDITION LIMIT	YEAR RETD.	ISSUE PRICE	*QUOTE U.S.$
1986 Christmas Carol	Yr.Iss.		20.00	400
1987 Christmas Wreath	Yr.Iss.		20.00	225
1988 Christmas Dinner	Yr.Iss.		20.00	135
1989 Christmas Feast	Yr.Iss.		20.00	125
1990 Just What I Needed	Yr.Iss.		24.00	125
1991 Emmett The Snowman	Yr.Iss.		25.00	75-95
1992 Christmas Tunes	Yr.Iss.		25.00	60-75
1993 Downhill-Christmas Plate	Yr.Iss.		30.00	55-65
1994 Holiday Skater EKP-94	Yr.Iss.		30.00	50-60
1995 Christmas Tunes EKP-95	Yr.Iss.		30.00	50-65

Norman Rockwell Collection - Rockwell-Inspired

YEAR ISSUE	EDITION LIMIT	YEAR RETD.	ISSUE PRICE	*QUOTE U.S.$
1982 American Mother RGP-42	Retrd.		45.00	55
1980 Back To School RMP-80	Retrd.		24.00	24
1984 Big Moment RMP-84	Retrd.		27.00	27
1979 Butterboy RP-01	Retrd.		40.00	40
1983 Christmas Chores RXP-83	Retrd.		75.00	75
1980 Christmas Trio RXP-80	Retrd.		75.00	75
1983 Circus NRP-83	Retrd.		65.00	65
1982 Doctor and Doll NRP-82	Retrd.		65.00	95
1983 Doctor and Doll RMP-83	Retrd.		27.00	27
1983 Dreamboat RGP-83	Retrd.		24.00	30
1981 Dreams of Long Ago NRP-81	Retrd.		60.00	60
1982 Faces of Christmas RXP-82	Retrd.		75.00	75
1979 Leapfrog NRP-79	Retrd.		50.00	50
1982 Love Letter RMP-82	Retrd.		27.00	30
1980 Lovers NRP-80	Retrd.		60.00	60
1998 Marriage License NRP-ML	Open		30.00	30
1981 No Swimming RMP-81	Retrd.		25.00	25
1981 Santa's Good Boys RXP-81	Retrd.		75.00	75
1984 Tiny Tim RXP-84	Retrd.		75.00	75
1984 Visit With Rockwell NRP-84	Retrd.		65.00	65
1978 Young Doctor RDP-26	Retrd.		50.00	65

Norman Rockwell Collection-Boy Scout Plates - Rockwell-Inspired

YEAR ISSUE	EDITION LIMIT	YEAR RETD.	ISSUE PRICE	*QUOTE U.S.$
1981 Can't Wait BSP-01	Retrd.		30.00	45
1982 Guiding Hand BSP-02	Retrd.		30.00	35-65
1983 Tomorrow's Leader BSP-03	Retrd.		30.00	45-65

Norman Rockwell Collection-Huck Finn Plates - Rockwell-Inspired

YEAR ISSUE	EDITION LIMIT	YEAR RETD.	ISSUE PRICE	*QUOTE U.S.$
1979 Secret HFP-01	Retrd.		40.00	65-75
1980 ListeningHFP-02	Retrd.		40.00	65-75
1980 No Kings HFP-03	Retrd.		40.00	65-75

*Quotes have been rounded up to nearest dollar

Year Issue	Edition Limit	Year Retd.	Issue Price	*Quote U.S.$
1981 Snake Escapes HFP-04	Retrd.		40.00	65-75

Norman Rockwell Collection-Tom Sawyer Plates - Rockwell-Inspired

Year Issue	Edition Limit	Year Retd.	Issue Price	*Quote U.S.$
1975 Whitewashing the Fence TSP-01	Retrd.		26.00	50-75
1976 First Smoke TSP-02	Retrd.		26.00	50-75
1977 Take Your Medicine TSP-03	Retrd.		26.00	30-75
1978 Lost in Cave TSP-04	Retrd.		26.00	45-50

The Original Emmett Kelly Circus Collection - B. Leighton-Jones

Year Issue	Edition Limit	Year Retd.	Issue Price	*Quote U.S.$
1993 Downhill Daring	Yr.Iss.	1993	30.00	30
1994 Holiday Skater	Yr.Iss.	1994	30.00	30
1995 Merry Christmas Mr. Scrooge	Yr.Iss.	1995	30.00	30

Saturday Evening Post Collection - Rockwell-Inspired

Year Issue	Edition Limit	Year Retd.	Issue Price	*Quote U.S.$
1991 Downhill Daring BRP-91	Yr.Iss.	1991	25.00	25-55
1991 Missed BRP-101	Yr.Iss.	1991	25.00	25
1992 Choosin Up BRP-102	Yr.Iss.	1992	25.00	25-45

David Winter Cottages/Enesco Corporation

David Winter Plate Collection - M. Fisher

Year Issue	Edition Limit	Year Retd.	Issue Price	*Quote U.S.$
1991 A Christmas Carol	10,000	1993	30.00	30
1991 Cotswold Village Plate	10,000	1993	30.00	30
1992 Chichester Cross Plate	10,000	1993	30.00	34
1992 Little Mill Plate	10,000	1993	30.00	30
1992 Old Curiosity Shop	10,000	1993	30.00	30
1992 Scrooge's Counting House	10,000	1993	30.00	30
1993 Dove Cottage	10,000	1996	30.00	35
1993 Little Forge	10,000	1996	30.00	35

Delphi

The Beatles Collection - N. Giorgio

Year Issue	Edition Limit	Year Retd.	Issue Price	*Quote U.S.$
1991 The Beatles, Live In Concert	Closed		24.75	38-95
1991 Hello America	Closed		24.75	64-95
1991 A Hard Day's Night	Closed		27.75	60-85
1992 Beatles '65	Closed		27.75	65-76
1992 Help	Closed		27.75	65-100
1992 The Beatles at Shea Stadium	150-day		29.75	30-45
1992 Rubber Soul	150-day		29.75	48-70
1992 Yesterday and Today	150-day		29.75	31-50

Commemorating The King - M. Stutzman

Year Issue	Edition Limit	Year Retd.	Issue Price	*Quote U.S.$
1993 The Rock and Roll Legend	Closed		29.75	40-95
1993 Las Vegas, Live	Closed		29.75	40-85
1993 Blues and Black Leather	Closed		29.75	44-85
1993 Private Presley	Closed		29.75	35-54
1993 Golden Boy	Closed		29.75	37-45
1993 Screen Idol	Closed		29.75	32-45
1993 Outstanding Young Man	Closed		29.75	37
1993 The Tiger: Faith, Spirit & Discipline	95-day		29.75	30

Dream Machines - P. Palma

Year Issue	Edition Limit	Year Retd.	Issue Price	*Quote U.S.$
1988 '56 T-Bird	Closed		24.75	16-55
1988 '57 'Vette	Closed		24.75	14-65
1989 '58 Biarritz	Closed		27.75	20-25
1989 '56 Continental	Closed		27.75	22-25
1989 '57 Bel Air	Closed		27.75	24-37
1989 '57 Chrysler 300C	Closed		27.75	25

Elvis on the Big Screen - B. Emmett

Year Issue	Edition Limit	Year Retd.	Issue Price	*Quote U.S.$
1992 Elvis in Loving You	Closed		29.75	50-85
1992 Elvis in G.I. Blues	Closed		29.75	75-78
1992 Viva Las Vegas	Closed		32.75	95-100
1993 Elvis in Blue Hawaii	Closed		32.75	38-45
1993 Elvis in Jailhouse Rock	Closed		32.75	39-50
1993 Elvis in Spinout	Closed		34.75	30-50
1993 Elvis in Speedway	Closed		34.75	32-60
1993 Elvis in Harum Scarum	Closed		34.75	25-75

The Elvis Presley Hit Parade - N. Giorgio

Year Issue	Edition Limit	Year Retd.	Issue Price	*Quote U.S.$
1992 Heartbreak Hotel	150-day		29.75	35
1992 Blue Suede Shoes	150-day		29.75	35
1992 Hound Dog	150-day		32.75	35
1992 Blue Christmas	150-day		32.75	35
1992 Return to Sender	150-day		32.75	35
1993 Teddy Bear	150-day		34.75	35
1993 Always on My Mind	150-day		34.75	35
1993 Mystery Train	150-day		34.75	35
1993 Blue Moon of Kentucky	150-day		34.75	35
1993 Wear My Ring Around Your Neck	150-day		36.75	35
1993 Suspicious Minds	150-day		36.75	37
1993 Peace in the Valley	150-day		36.75	37

Elvis Presley: In Performance - B. Emmett

Year Issue	Edition Limit	Year Retd.	Issue Price	*Quote U.S.$
1990 '68 Comeback Special	Closed		24.75	48-95
1991 King of Las Vegas	Closed		24.75	60-85
1991 Aloha From Hawaii	Closed		27.75	64-80
1991 Back in Tupelo, 1956	Closed		27.75	63-80
1991 If I Can Dream	Closed		27.75	63-85
1991 Benefit for the USS Arizona	Closed		29.75	64-85
1991 Madison Square Garden, 1972	Closed		29.75	80-85
1991 Tampa, 1955	Closed		29.75	68-85
1991 Concert in Baton Rouge, 1974	Closed		29.75	69-85
1992 On Stage in Wichita, 1974	Closed		31.75	49-80
1992 In the Spotlight: Hawaii, '72	Closed		31.75	54-80
1992 Tour Finale: Indianapolis 1977	Closed		31.75	35-80

Elvis Presley: Looking At A Legend - B. Emmett

Year Issue	Edition Limit	Year Retd.	Issue Price	*Quote U.S.$
1988 Elvis at/Gates of Graceland	Closed		24.75	50-125
1989 Jailhouse Rock	Closed		24.75	55-70
1989 The Memphis Flash	Closed		27.75	35-95
1989 Homecoming	Closed		27.75	56-90
1990 Elvis and Gladys	Closed		27.75	38-85
1990 A Studio Session	Closed		27.75	28-80
1990 Elvis in Hollywood	Closed		29.75	44-75
1990 Elvis on His Harley	Closed		29.75	55-75
1990 Stage Door Autographs	Closed		29.75	63-75
1991 Christmas at Graceland	Closed		32.75	69-75
1991 Entering Sun Studio	Closed		32.75	50-65
1991 Going for the Black Belt	Closed		32.75	40-75
1991 His Hand in Mine	Closed		32.75	60-75
1991 Letters From Fans	Closed		32.75	61-75
1991 Closing the Deal	Closed		34.75	64-75
1992 Elvis Returns to the Stage	Closed		34.75	50-75

Fabulous Cars of the '50's - G. Angelini

Year Issue	Edition Limit	Year Retd.	Issue Price	*Quote U.S.$
1993 '57 Red Corvette	Closed		24.75	32-55
1993 '57 White T-Bird	Closed		24.75	25-72
1993 '57 Blue Belair	Closed		27.75	25-48
1993 '59 Cadillac	Closed		27.75	25-42
1994 '56 Lincoln Premier	Closed		27.75	25-39
1994 '59 Red Ford Fairlane	Closed		27.75	25-44

In the Footsteps of the King - D. Sivavec

Year Issue	Edition Limit	Year Retd.	Issue Price	*Quote U.S.$
1993 Graceland: Memphis, Tenn.	Closed		29.75	36-55
1994 Elvis' Birthplace: Tupelo, Miss	Closed		29.75	35-55
1994 Day Job: Memphis, Tenn.	Closed		32.75	32-55
1994 Flying Circle G. Ranch: Walls, Miss.	Closed		32.75	38
1994 The Lauderdale Courts	Closed		32.75	32
1994 Patriotic Soldier: Bad Nauheim, W. Germany	Closed		34.75	40

Indiana Jones - V. Gadino

Year Issue	Edition Limit	Year Retd.	Issue Price	*Quote U.S.$
1989 Indiana Jones	Closed		24.75	19-50
1989 Indiana Jones and His Dad	Closed		24.75	42-55
1990 Indiana Jones/Dr. Schneider	Closed		27.75	29-55
1990 A Family Discussion	Closed		27.75	26-55
1990 Young Indiana Jones	Closed		27.75	40-55
1991 Indiana Jones/The Holy Grail	Closed		27.75	38-55

The Magic of Marilyn - C. Notarile

Year Issue	Edition Limit	Year Retd.	Issue Price	*Quote U.S.$
1992 For Our Boys in Korea, 1954	Closed		24.75	40-75
1992 Opening Night	Closed		24.75	35-75
1993 Rising Star	Closed		27.75	44-75
1993 Stopping Traffic	Closed		27.75	69
1992 Strasberg's Student	Closed		27.75	50-66
1993 Photo Opportunity	Closed		29.75	30-50
1993 Shining Star	Closed		29.75	25-75
1993 Curtain Call	Closed		29.75	29-60

The Marilyn Monroe Collection - C. Notarile

Year Issue	Edition Limit	Year Retd.	Issue Price	*Quote U.S.$
1989 Marilyn Monroe/7 Year Itch	Closed		24.75	62-99
1990 Diamonds/Girls Best Friend	Closed		24.75	47-95
1991 Marilyn Monroe/River of No Return	Closed		27.75	60-95
1992 How to Marry a Millionaire	Closed		27.75	59-95
1992 There's No Business/Show Business	Closed		27.75	60-95
1992 Marilyn Monroe in Niagra	Closed		29.75	50-95
1992 My Heart Belongs to Daddy	Closed		29.75	60-95
1992 Marilyn Monroe as Cherie in Bus Stop	Closed		29.75	60-95
1992 Marilyn Monroe in All About Eve	Closed		29.75	60-125
1992 Marilyn Monroe in Monkey Business	Closed		31.75	40-70
1992 Marilyn Monroe in Don't Bother to Knock	Closed		31.75	40-70
1992 Marilyn Monroe in We're Not Married	Closed		31.75	48-70

Portraits of the King - D. Zwierz

Year Issue	Edition Limit	Year Retd.	Issue Price	*Quote U.S.$
1991 Love Me Tender	Closed		27.75	35-85
1991 Are You Lonesome Tonight?	Closed		27.75	70-80
1991 I'm Yours	Closed		30.75	70-85
1991 Treat Me Nice	Closed		30.75	90-97
1992 The Wonder of You	Closed		30.75	28-35
1992 You're a Heartbreaker	Closed		32.75	29-35
1992 Just Because	Closed		32.75	29-35
1992 Follow That Dream	Closed		32.75	30-34

Department 56

A Christmas Carol - R. Innocenti

Year Issue	Edition Limit	Year Retd.	Issue Price	*Quote U.S.$
1991 The Cratchit's Christmas Pudding 5706-1	18,000	1991	60.00	28-65
1992 Marley's Ghost Appears To Scrooge 5721-5	18,000	1992	60.00	39-75
1993 The Spirit of Christmas Present 5722-3	18,000	1993	60.00	38-90
1994 Visions of Christmas Past 5723-1	18,000	1994	60.00	28-90

Duncan Royale

History of Santa Claus I - S. Morton

Year Issue	Edition Limit	Year Retd.	Issue Price	*Quote U.S.$
1985 Medieval	Retrd.	1993	40.00	75
1985 Kris Kringle	Retrd.	1993	40.00	75
1985 Pioneer	10,000	1993	40.00	40
1986 Russian	Retrd.	1993	40.00	65
1986 Soda Pop	Retrd.	1993	40.00	75
1986 Civil War	10,000	1993	40.00	40
1986 Nast	Retrd.	1993	40.00	75
1987 St. Nicholas	Retrd.	1993	40.00	75
1987 Dedt Moroz	10,000	1993	40.00	45
1987 Black Peter	10,000	1993	40.00	60
1987 Victorian	Retrd.	1993	40.00	45
1987 Wassail	Retrd.	1993	40.00	45
XX Collection of 12 Plates	Retrd.	1993	480.00	480

Edna Hibel Studios

Allegro - E. Hibel

Year Issue	Edition Limit	Year Retd.	Issue Price	*Quote U.S.$
1978 Plate & Book	7,500		120.00	150

Arte Ovale - E. Hibel

Year Issue	Edition Limit	Year Retd.	Issue Price	*Quote U.S.$
1980 Takara, gold	300		1000.00	4200
1980 Takara, blanco	700		450.00	1200
1980 Takara, cobalt blue	1,000		595.00	2350
1984 Taro-kun, gold	300		1000.00	2700
1984 Taro-kun, blanco	700		450.00	825
1984 Taro-kun, cobalt blue	1,000		995.00	1050-1555

Christmas Annual - E. Hibel

Year Issue	Edition Limit	Year Retd.	Issue Price	*Quote U.S.$
1985 The Angels' Message	Yr.Iss.		45.00	300-455
1986 Gift of the Magi	Yr.Iss.		45.00	275-295
1987 Flight Into Egypt	Yr.Iss.		49.00	250-295
1988 Adoration of the Shepherds	Yr.Iss.		49.00	175
1989 Peaceful Kingdom	Yr.Iss.		49.00	165-195
1990 The Nativity	Yr.Iss.		49.00	70-170

David Series - E. Hibel

Year Issue	Edition Limit	Year Retd.	Issue Price	*Quote U.S.$
1979 Wedding of David & Bathsheba	5,000		250.00	650
1980 David, Bathsheba & Solomon	5,000		275.00	425
1982 David the King	5,000		275.00	295
1982 David the King, cobalt A/P	25		275.00	1200
1984 Bathsheba	5,000		275.00	295
1984 Bathsheba, cobalt A/P	100		275.00	1200

Edna Hibel Holiday - E. Hibel

Year Issue	Edition Limit	Year Retd.	Issue Price	*Quote U.S.$
1991 The First Holiday	Yr.Iss.		49.00	85
1991 The First Holiday, gold	1,000		99.00	150
1992 The Christmas Rose	Yr.Iss.		49.00	59-70
1992 The Christmas Rose, gold	1,000		99.00	125

Eroica - E. Hibel

Year Issue	Edition Limit	Year Retd.	Issue Price	*Quote U.S.$
1990 Compassion	10,000		49.50	65-175
1992 Darya	10,000		49.50	95-149

Famous Women & Children - E. Hibel

Year Issue	Edition Limit	Year Retd.	Issue Price	*Quote U.S.$
1980 Pharaoh's Daughter & Moses, gold	2,500		350.00	625-750
1980 Pharaoh's Daughter & Moses, cobalt blue	500		350.00	1350
1982 Cornelia & Her Jewels, gold	2,500		350.00	495-575
1982 Cornelia & Her Jewels, cobalt blue	500		350.00	350
1982 Anna & The Children of the King of Siam, gold	2,500		350.00	495-575
1982 Anna & The Children of the King of Siam, colbalt blue	500		350.00	1350
1984 Mozart & The Empress Marie Theresa, gold	2,500		350.00	395-495
1984 Mozart & The Empress Marie Theresa, cobalt blue	500		350.00	975

Flower Girl Annual - E. Hibel

Year Issue	Edition Limit	Year Retd.	Issue Price	*Quote U.S.$
1985 Lily	15,000		79.00	200-300
1986 Iris	15,000		79.00	200-300
1987 Rose	15,000		79.00	200-300
1988 Camellia	15,000		79.00	200-395
1989 Peony	15,000		79.00	250-395
1992 Wisteria	15,000		79.00	229

International Mother Love French - E. Hibel

Year Issue	Edition Limit	Year Retd.	Issue Price	*Quote U.S.$
1985 Yvette Avec Ses Enfants	5,000		125.00	225
1991 Liberte, Egalite, Fraternite	5,000		95.00	95

International Mother Love German - E. Hibel

Year Issue	Edition Limit	Year Retd.	Issue Price	*Quote U.S.$
1982 Gesa Und Kinder	5,000		195.00	195
1983 Alexandra Und Kinder	5,000		195.00	195

March of Dimes: Our Children Our Future - E. Hibel

Year Issue	Edition Limit	Year Retd.	Issue Price	*Quote U.S.$
1990 A Time To Embrace	150-day		29.00	29-59

Mother and Child - E. Hibel

Year Issue	Edition Limit	Year Retd.	Issue Price	*Quote U.S.$
1973 Colette & Child	15,000		40.00	725
1974 Sayuri & Child	15,000		40.00	425
1975 Kristina & Child	15,000		50.00	100-250
1976 Marilyn & Child	15,000		55.00	400
1977 Lucia & Child	15,000		60.00	100-200
1981 Kathleen & Child	15,000		85.00	275

Mother's Day - E. Hibel

Year Issue	Edition Limit	Year Retd.	Issue Price	*Quote U.S.$
1992 Molly & Annie	Yr.Iss.		39.00	75
1992 Molly & Annie, gold	2,500		95.00	150
1992 Molly & Annie, platinum	500		275.00	275

Mother's Day Annual - E. Hibel

Year Issue	Edition Limit	Year Retd.	Issue Price	*Quote U.S.$
1984 Abby & Lisa	Yr.Iss.		29.50	50-79
1985 Erica & Jamie	Yr.Iss.		29.50	50-125
1986 Emily & Jennifer	Yr.Iss.		29.50	300-400
1987 Catherine & Heather	Yr.Iss.		34.50	300-400
1988 Sarah & Tess	Yr.Iss.		34.90	300-400
1989 Jessica & Kate	Yr.Iss.		34.90	300-400
1990 Elizabeth, Jorday & Janie	Yr.Iss.		36.90	300-400
1991 Michele & Anna	Yr.Iss.		36.90	300-400
1992 Olivia & Hildy	Yr.Iss.		39.90	300-400

Museum Commemorative - E. Hibel

Year Issue	Edition Limit	Year Retd.	Issue Price	*Quote U.S.$
1977 Flower Girl of Provence	12,750		175.00	425
1980 Diana	3,000		350.00	395

Nobility Of Children - E. Hibel

Year Issue	Edition Limit	Year Retd.	Issue Price	*Quote U.S.$
1976 La Contessa Isabella	12,750		120.00	425

*Quotes have been rounded up to nearest dollar

YEAR ISSUE	EDITION LIMIT	YEAR RETD.	ISSUE PRICE	*QUOTE U.S.$
1977 Le Marquis Maurice Pierre	12,750		120.00	225
1978 Baronesse Johanna-Maryke Van Vollendam Tot Marken	12,750		130.00	175
1979 Chief Red Feather	12,750		140.00	200

Nordic Families - E. Hibel

YEAR ISSUE	EDITION LIMIT	YEAR RETD.	ISSUE PRICE	*QUOTE U.S.$
1987 A Tender Moment	7,500		79.00	95

Oriental Gold - E. Hibel

YEAR ISSUE	EDITION LIMIT	YEAR RETD.	ISSUE PRICE	*QUOTE U.S.$
1975 Yasuko	2,000		275.00	3000
1976 Mr. Obata	2,000		275.00	900-2100
1978 Sakura	2,000		295.00	1800
1979 Michio	2,000		325.00	595-1500

Scandinavian Mother & Child - E. Hibel

YEAR ISSUE	EDITION LIMIT	YEAR RETD.	ISSUE PRICE	*QUOTE U.S.$
1987 Pearl & Flowers	7,500		55.00	225
1989 Anemone & Violet	7,500		75.00	95
1990 Holly & Talia	7,500		75.00	85

To Life Annual - E. Hibel

YEAR ISSUE	EDITION LIMIT	YEAR RETD.	ISSUE PRICE	*QUOTE U.S.$
1986 Golden's Child	5,000		99.00	200-275
1987 Triumph! Everyone A Winner	19,500		55.00	60
1988 The Whole Earth Bloomed as a Sacred Place	15,000		85.00	85
1989 Lovers of the Summer Palace	5,000		65.00	75
1992 People of the Fields	5,000		49.00	49

Tribute To All Children - E. Hibel

YEAR ISSUE	EDITION LIMIT	YEAR RETD.	ISSUE PRICE	*QUOTE U.S.$
1984 Giselle	19,500		55.00	95-149
1984 Gerard	19,500		55.00	149-175
1985 Wendy	19,500		55.00	125-175
1986 Todd	19,500		55.00	175-195

The World I Love - E. Hibel

YEAR ISSUE	EDITION LIMIT	YEAR RETD.	ISSUE PRICE	*QUOTE U.S.$
1981 Leah's Family	17,500		85.00	150-350
1982 Kaylin	17,500		85.00	300-395
1983 Edna's Music	17,500		85.00	195-275
1983 O' Hana	17,500		85.00	195-245

Edwin M. Knowles

Aesop's Fables - M. Hampshire

YEAR ISSUE	EDITION LIMIT	YEAR RETD.	ISSUE PRICE	*QUOTE U.S.$
1988 The Goose That Laid the Golden Egg	Closed		27.90	16-30
1988 The Hare and the Tortoise	Closed		27.90	25-30
1988 The Fox and the Grapes	Closed		30.90	28-31
1989 The Lion And The Mouse	Closed		30.90	32-35
1989 The Milk Maid And Her Pail	Closed		30.90	28-30
1989 The Jay And The Peacock	Closed		30.90	30-32

American Innocents - Marsten/Mandrajji

YEAR ISSUE	EDITION LIMIT	YEAR RETD.	ISSUE PRICE	*QUOTE U.S.$
1986 Abigail in the Rose Garden	Closed		19.50	18-20
1986 Ann by the Terrace	Closed		19.50	20
1986 Ellen and John in the Parlor	Closed		19.50	13-20
1986 William on the Rocking Horse	Closed		19.50	27

The American Journey - M. Kunstler

YEAR ISSUE	EDITION LIMIT	YEAR RETD.	ISSUE PRICE	*QUOTE U.S.$
1987 Westward Ho	Closed		29.90	20-30
1988 Kitchen With a View	Closed		29.90	20-30
1988 Crossing the River	Closed		29.90	25-30
1988 Christmas at the New Cabin	Closed		29.90	22-30

Americana Holidays - D. Spaulding

YEAR ISSUE	EDITION LIMIT	YEAR RETD.	ISSUE PRICE	*QUOTE U.S.$
1978 Fourth of July	Closed		26.00	13-25
1979 Thanksgiving	Closed		26.00	10-26
1980 Easter	Closed		26.00	10-26
1981 Valentine's Day	Closed		26.00	13-26
1982 Father's Day	Closed		26.00	10-35
1983 Christmas	Closed		26.00	14-33
1984 Mother's Day	Closed		26.00	15-30

Amy Brackenbury's Cat Tales - A. Brackenbury

YEAR ISSUE	EDITION LIMIT	YEAR RETD.	ISSUE PRICE	*QUOTE U.S.$
1987 A Chance Meeting: White American Shorthairs	Closed		21.50	20-55
1987 Gone Fishing: Maine Coons	Closed		21.50	30-55
1988 Strawberries and Cream: Cream Persians	Closed		24.90	45-55
1988 Flower Bed: British Shorthairs	Closed		24.90	19-55
1988 Kittens and Mittens: Silver Tabbies	Closed		24.90	23-55
1988 All Wrapped Up: Himalayans	Closed		24.90	38-55

Annie - W. Chambers

YEAR ISSUE	EDITION LIMIT	YEAR RETD.	ISSUE PRICE	*QUOTE U.S.$
1983 Annie and Sandy	Closed		19.00	6-25
1983 Daddy Warbucks	Closed		19.00	8-10
1983 Annie and Grace	Closed		19.00	8-10
1984 Annie and the Orphans	Closed		21.00	7-35
1985 Tomorrow	Closed		21.00	7-12
1986 Annie and Miss Hannigan	Closed		21.00	7-14
1986 Annie, Lily and Rooster	Closed		24.00	10-19
1986 Grand Finale	Closed		24.00	10-17

Baby Owls of North America - J. Thornbrugh

YEAR ISSUE	EDITION LIMIT	YEAR RETD.	ISSUE PRICE	*QUOTE U.S.$
1991 Peek-A-Whoo: Screech Owls	Closed		27.90	30-35
1991 Forty Winks: Saw-Whet Owls	Closed		29.90	33-39
1991 The Tree House: Northern Pygmy Owls	Closed		30.90	38-43
1991 Three of a Kind: Great Horned Owls	Closed		30.90	30-35
1991 Out on a Limb: Great Gray Owls	Closed		30.90	32-35
1991 Beginning to Explore: Boreal Owls	Closed		32.90	44-48
1992 Three's Company: Long Eared Owls	Closed		32.90	40-44
1992 Whoo's There: Barred Owl	Closed		32.90	52-58

Backyard Harmony - J. Thornbrugh

YEAR ISSUE	EDITION LIMIT	YEAR RETD.	ISSUE PRICE	*QUOTE U.S.$
1991 The Singing Lesson	Closed		27.90	25-30
1991 Welcoming a New Day	Closed		27.90	36-45
1991 Announcing Spring	Closed		30.90	49-55
1992 The Morning Harvest	Closed		30.90	41-44
1992 Spring Time Pride	Closed		30.90	55
1992 Treetop Serenade	Closed		32.90	60
1992 At The Peep Of Day	Closed		32.90	42-45
1992 Today's Discoveries	Closed		32.90	43-45

Bambi - Disney Studios

YEAR ISSUE	EDITION LIMIT	YEAR RETD.	ISSUE PRICE	*QUOTE U.S.$
1992 Bashful Bambi	Closed		34.90	40-58
1992 Bambi's New Friends	Closed		34.90	50-92
1992 Hello Little Prince	Closed		37.90	40-64
1992 Bambi's Morning Greetings	Closed		37.90	40-48
1992 Bambi's Skating Lesson	Closed		37.90	60-67
1993 What's Up Possums?	Closed		37.90	45-54

Biblical Mothers - E. Licea

YEAR ISSUE	EDITION LIMIT	YEAR RETD.	ISSUE PRICE	*QUOTE U.S.$
1983 Bathsheba and Solomon	Closed		39.50	10-29
1984 Judgment of Solomon	Closed		39.50	10-28
1984 Pharaoh's Daughter and Moses	Closed		39.50	10-27
1985 Mary and Jesus	Closed		39.50	10-27
1985 Sarah and Isaac	Closed		44.50	10-40
1986 Rebekah, Jacob and Esau	Closed		44.50	10-35

Birds of the Seasons - S. Timm

YEAR ISSUE	EDITION LIMIT	YEAR RETD.	ISSUE PRICE	*QUOTE U.S.$
1990 Cardinals In Winter	Closed		24.90	45-55
1990 Bluebirds In Spring	Closed		24.90	40-55
1991 Nuthatches In Fall	Closed		27.90	35-55
1991 Baltimore Orioles In Summer	Closed		27.90	40-55
1991 Blue Jays In Early Fall	Closed		27.90	40-55
1991 Robins In Early Spring	Closed		27.90	35-55
1991 Cedar Waxwings in Fall	Closed		29.90	40-55
1991 Chickadees in Winter	Closed		29.90	55

Call of the Wilderness - K. Daniel

YEAR ISSUE	EDITION LIMIT	YEAR RETD.	ISSUE PRICE	*QUOTE U.S.$
1991 First Outing	Closed		29.90	30-45
1991 Howling Lesson	Closed		29.90	100-176
1991 Silent Watch	Closed		32.90	30-47
1991 Winter Travelers	Closed		32.90	30-48
1992 Ahead of the Pack	Closed		32.90	30-49
1992 Northern Spirits	Closed		34.90	40-49
1992 Twilight Friends	Closed		34.90	40-53
1992 A New Future	Closed		34.90	45-71
1992 Morning Mist	Closed		36.90	50-82
1992 The Silent One	150-day		36.90	40-56

Carousel - D. Brown

YEAR ISSUE	EDITION LIMIT	YEAR RETD.	ISSUE PRICE	*QUOTE U.S.$
1987 If I Loved You	Closed		24.90	18-39
1988 Mr. Snow	Closed		24.90	24
1988 The Carousel Waltz	Closed		24.90	10-20
1988 You'll Never Walk Alone	Closed		24.90	10-18

Casablanca - J. Griffin

YEAR ISSUE	EDITION LIMIT	YEAR RETD.	ISSUE PRICE	*QUOTE U.S.$
1990 Here's Looking At You, Kid	Closed		34.90	33-55
1990 We'll Always Have Paris	Closed		34.90	38-50
1991 We Loved Each Other Once	Closed		37.90	29-40
1991 Rick's Cafe Americain	Closed		37.90	32-40
1991 A Franc For Your Thoughts	Closed		37.90	35-50
1991 Play it Sam	Closed		37.90	42-52

Castari Grandparent - J. Castari

YEAR ISSUE	EDITION LIMIT	YEAR RETD.	ISSUE PRICE	*QUOTE U.S.$
1980 Bedtime Story	Closed		18.00	5-10
1981 The Skating Lesson	Closed		20.00	5-29
1982 The Cookie Tasting	Closed		20.00	5-25
1983 The Swinger	Closed		20.00	5-29
1984 The Skating Queen	Closed		22.00	10-25
1985 The Patriot's Parade	Closed		22.00	16-22
1986 The Home Run	Closed		22.00	14-22
1987 The Sneak Preview	Closed		22.00	12-22

China's Natural Treasures - T.C. Chiu

YEAR ISSUE	EDITION LIMIT	YEAR RETD.	ISSUE PRICE	*QUOTE U.S.$
1992 The Siberian Tiger	Closed		29.90	35-44
1992 The Snow Leopard	Closed		29.90	25-32
1992 The Giant Panda	Closed		32.90	40-49
1992 The Tibetan Brown Bear	Closed		32.90	40-44
1992 The Asian Elephant	Closed		32.90	40-65
1992 The Golden Monkey	Closed		34.90	40-53

Christmas in the City - A. Leimanis

YEAR ISSUE	EDITION LIMIT	YEAR RETD.	ISSUE PRICE	*QUOTE U.S.$
1992 A Christmas Snowfall	Closed		34.90	31-35
1992 Yuletide Celebration	Closed		34.90	52-55
1993 Holiday Cheer	Closed		34.90	60
1993 The Magic of Christmas	Closed		34.90	55-60

Cinderella - Disney Studios

YEAR ISSUE	EDITION LIMIT	YEAR RETD.	ISSUE PRICE	*QUOTE U.S.$
1988 Bibbidi, Bobbidi, Boo	Closed		29.90	45-65
1988 A Dream Is A Wish Your Heart Makes	Closed		29.90	45-85
1989 Oh Sing Sweet Nightingale	Closed		32.90	50-70
1989 A Dress For Cinderelly	Closed		32.90	60-99
1989 So This Is Love	Closed		32.90	45-80
1990 At The Stroke Of Midnight	Closed		32.90	45-72
1990 If The Shoe Fits	Closed		34.90	45-75
1990 Happily Ever After	Closed		34.90	40-75

Classic Fairy Tales - S. Gustafson

YEAR ISSUE	EDITION LIMIT	YEAR RETD.	ISSUE PRICE	*QUOTE U.S.$
1991 Goldilocks and the Three Bears	Closed		29.90	38-65
1991 Little Red Riding Hood	Closed		29.90	42-65
1991 The Three Little Pigs	Closed		32.90	36-65
1991 The Frog Prince	Closed		32.90	35-65
1992 Jack and the Beanstalk	Closed		32.90	32-65
1992 Hansel and Gretel	Closed		34.90	38-65
1992 Puss in Boots	Closed		34.90	34-65
1992 Tom Thumb	Closed		34.90	36-65

Classic Mother Goose - S. Gustafson

YEAR ISSUE	EDITION LIMIT	YEAR RETD.	ISSUE PRICE	*QUOTE U.S.$
1992 Little Miss Muffet	Closed		29.90	23-30
1992 Mary had a Little Lamb	Closed		29.90	42
1992 Mary, Mary, Quite Contrary	Closed		29.90	45-50
1992 Little Bo Peep	Closed		29.90	40-45

The Comforts of Home - H. Hollister Ingmire

YEAR ISSUE	EDITION LIMIT	YEAR RETD.	ISSUE PRICE	*QUOTE U.S.$
1992 Sleepyheads	Closed		24.90	26-34
1992 Curious Pair	Closed		24.90	25-32
1993 Mother's Retreat	Closed		27.90	28-32
1993 Welcome Friends	Closed		27.90	26-35
1993 Playtime	Closed		27.90	28-36
1993 Feline Frolic	Closed		29.90	30-35
1993 Washday Helpers	Closed		29.90	30-35
1993 A Cozy Fireside	Closed		29.90	42-50

Cozy Country Corners - H. H. Ingmire

YEAR ISSUE	EDITION LIMIT	YEAR RETD.	ISSUE PRICE	*QUOTE U.S.$
1990 Lazy Morning	Closed		24.90	35-55
1990 Warm Retreat	Closed		24.90	32-36
1991 A Sunny Spot	Closed		27.90	25-30
1991 Attic Afternoon	Closed		27.90	40-45
1991 Mirror Mischief	Closed		27.90	40-46
1991 Hide and Seek	Closed		29.90	40-45
1991 Apple Antics	Closed		29.90	62-65
1991 Table Trouble	Closed		29.90	45-50

The Disney Treasured Moments Collection - Disney Studios

YEAR ISSUE	EDITION LIMIT	YEAR RETD.	ISSUE PRICE	*QUOTE U.S.$
1992 Cinderella	Closed		29.90	30-65
1992 Snow White and the Seven Dwarves	150-day		29.90	30
1993 Alice in Wonderland	150-day		32.90	33
1993 Sleeping Beauty	150-day		32.90	33
1993 Peter Pan	150-day		32.90	33
1993 Pinocchio	150-day		34.90	35
1993 The Jungle Book	150-day		34.90	35
1994 Beauty & The Beast	150-day		34.90	35

Encyclopedia Britanica Birds of Your Garden - K. Daniel

YEAR ISSUE	EDITION LIMIT	YEAR RETD.	ISSUE PRICE	*QUOTE U.S.$
1985 Cardinal	Closed		19.50	15-25
1985 Blue Jay	Closed		19.50	15-20
1985 Oriole	Closed		22.50	15-28
1986 Chickadees	Closed		22.50	17-25
1986 Bluebird	Closed		22.50	15-20
1986 Robin	Closed		22.50	15-22
1986 Hummingbird	Closed		24.50	20-28
1987 Goldfinch	Closed		24.50	20
1987 Downy Woodpecker	Closed		24.50	20-26
1987 Cedar Waxwing	Closed		24.90	20-26

Eve Licea Christmas - E. Licea

YEAR ISSUE	EDITION LIMIT	YEAR RETD.	ISSUE PRICE	*QUOTE U.S.$
1987 The Annunciation	Closed		44.90	15-65
1988 The Nativity	Closed		44.90	15-60
1989 Adoration Of The Shepherds	Closed		49.90	15-55
1990 Journey Of The Magi	Closed		49.90	15-55
1991 Gifts Of The Magi	Closed		49.90	15-58
1992 Rest on the Flight into Egypt	Closed		49.90	15-75

Fantasia: (The Sorcerer's Apprentice) Golden Anniversary - Disney Studios

YEAR ISSUE	EDITION LIMIT	YEAR RETD.	ISSUE PRICE	*QUOTE U.S.$
1990 The Apprentice's Dream	Closed		29.90	50-95
1990 Mischievous Apprentice	Closed		29.90	50-99
1991 Dreams of Power	Closed		32.90	45-85
1991 Mickey's Magical Whirlpool	Closed		32.90	40-49
1991 Wizardry Gone Wild	Closed		32.90	40-45
1991 Mickey Makes Magic	Closed		34.90	40-63
1991 The Penitent Apprentice	Closed		34.90	40-45
1992 An Apprentice Again	Closed		34.90	40-50

Father's Love - B. Bradley

YEAR ISSUE	EDITION LIMIT	YEAR RETD.	ISSUE PRICE	*QUOTE U.S.$
1984 Open Wide	Closed		19.50	5-29
1984 Batter Up	Closed		19.50	5-29
1985 Little Shaver	Closed		19.50	5-29
1985 Swing Time	Closed		22.50	5-29

Field Puppies - L. Kaatz

YEAR ISSUE	EDITION LIMIT	YEAR RETD.	ISSUE PRICE	*QUOTE U.S.$
1987 Dog Tired-The Springer Spaniel	Closed		24.90	30-45
1987 Caught in the Act-The Golden Retriever	Closed		24.90	30-50
1988 Missing/Point/Irish Setter	Closed		27.90	30-35
1988 A Perfect Set-Labrador	Closed		27.90	30-40
1988 Fritz's Folly-German Shorthaired Pointer	Closed		27.90	25-35
1988 Shirt Tales: Cocker Spaniel	Closed		27.90	30-33
1989 Fine Feathered Friends-English Setter	Closed		29.90	25-30
1989 Command Performance/ Wiemaraner	Closed		29.90	25-30

Field Trips - L. Kaatz

YEAR ISSUE	EDITION LIMIT	YEAR RETD.	ISSUE PRICE	*QUOTE U.S.$
1990 Gone Fishing	Closed		24.90	15-25
1991 Ducking Duty	Closed		24.90	23-25
1991 Boxed In	Closed		27.90	19-28
1991 Pups 'N Boots	Closed		27.90	22-28
1991 Puppy Tales	Closed		27.90	20-28
1991 Pail Pals	Closed		29.90	25-30
1991 Chesapeake Bay Retrievers	Closed		29.90	25-30
1991 Hat Trick	Closed		29.90	20-30

First Impressions - J. Giordano

YEAR ISSUE	EDITION LIMIT	YEAR RETD.	ISSUE PRICE	*QUOTE U.S.$
1991 Taking a Gander	Closed		29.90	40
1991 Two's Company	Closed		29.90	35
1991 Fine Feathered Friends	Closed		32.90	40-42
1991 What's Up?	Closed		32.90	44
1991 All Ears	Closed		32.90	50-60

*Quotes have been rounded up to nearest dollar

YEAR ISSUE	EDITION LIMIT	YEAR RETD.	ISSUE PRICE	*QUOTE U.S.$
1992 Between Friends	Closed		32.90	34

The Four Ancient Elements - G. Lambert

YEAR ISSUE	EDITION LIMIT	YEAR RETD.	ISSUE PRICE	*QUOTE U.S.$
1984 Earth	Closed		27.50	10-49
1984 Water	Closed		27.50	10-49
1985 Air	Closed		29.50	10-49
1985 Fire	Closed		29.50	10-49

Frances Hook Legacy - F. Hook

YEAR ISSUE	EDITION LIMIT	YEAR RETD.	ISSUE PRICE	*QUOTE U.S.$
1985 Fascination	Closed		19.50	5-45
1985 Daydreaming	Closed		19.50	5-40
1986 Discovery	Closed		22.50	5-40
1986 Disappointment	Closed		22.50	5-40
1986 Wonderment	Closed		22.50	5-40
1987 Expectation	Closed		22.50	5-40

Free as the Wind - M. Budden

YEAR ISSUE	EDITION LIMIT	YEAR RETD.	ISSUE PRICE	*QUOTE U.S.$
1992 Skyward	Closed		29.90	50-55
1992 Aloft	Closed		29.90	53-55
1992 Airborne	Closed		32.90	35-50
1993 Flight	Closed		32.90	45-50
1993 Ascent	Closed		32.90	40-50
1993 Heavenward	Closed		32.90	45

Friends of the Forest - K. Daniel

YEAR ISSUE	EDITION LIMIT	YEAR RETD.	ISSUE PRICE	*QUOTE U.S.$
1987 The Rabbit	Closed		24.50	15-19
1987 The Raccoon	Closed		24.50	15-23
1987 The Squirrel	Closed		27.90	15-22
1988 The Chipmunk	Closed		27.90	15-22
1988 The Fox	Closed		27.90	15-26
1988 The Otter	Closed		27.90	15-26

Garden Secrets - B. Higgins Bond

YEAR ISSUE	EDITION LIMIT	YEAR RETD.	ISSUE PRICE	*QUOTE U.S.$
1993 Nine Lives	Closed		24.90	42-55
1993 Floral Purr-fume	Closed		24.90	53-55
1993 Bloomin' Kitties	Closed		24.90	47-55
1993 Kitty Corner	Closed		24.90	45-55
1993 Flower Fanciers	Closed		24.90	49-55
1993 Meadow Mischief	Closed		24.90	50-56
1993 Pussycat Potpourri	Closed		24.90	49-91
1993 Frisky Business	Closed		24.90	32-55

Gone with the Wind - R. Kursar

YEAR ISSUE	EDITION LIMIT	YEAR RETD.	ISSUE PRICE	*QUOTE U.S.$
1978 Scarlett	Closed		21.50	90-115
1979 Ashley	Closed		21.50	50-63
1980 Melanie	Closed		21.50	28-30
1981 Rhett	Closed		23.50	29-35
1982 Mammy Lacing Scarlett	Closed		23.50	35-85
1983 Melanie Gives Birth	Closed		23.50	41-60
1984 Scarlet's Green Dress	Closed		25.50	35-44
1985 Rhett and Bonnie	Closed		25.50	40-55
1985 Scarlett and Rhett: The Finale	Closed		29.50	40-45

Great Cats Of The Americas - L. Cable

YEAR ISSUE	EDITION LIMIT	YEAR RETD.	ISSUE PRICE	*QUOTE U.S.$
1989 The Jaguar	Closed		29.90	42-45
1989 The Cougar	Closed		29.90	42-47
1989 The Lynx	Closed		32.90	40-45
1990 The Ocelot	Closed		32.90	24-33
1990 The Bobcat	Closed		32.90	18-32
1990 The Jaguarundi	Closed		32.90	19-33
1990 The Margay	Closed		34.90	21-35
1991 The Pampas Cat	Closed		34.90	20-35

Heirlooms And Lace - C. Layton

YEAR ISSUE	EDITION LIMIT	YEAR RETD.	ISSUE PRICE	*QUOTE U.S.$
1989 Anna	Closed		34.90	38-55
1989 Victoria	Closed		34.90	45-55
1990 Tess	Closed		37.90	65-70
1990 Olivia	Closed		37.90	85-100
1991 Bridget	Closed		37.90	72-85
1991 Rebecca	Closed		37.90	55-70

Hibel Christmas - E. Hibel

YEAR ISSUE	EDITION LIMIT	YEAR RETD.	ISSUE PRICE	*QUOTE U.S.$
1985 The Angel's Message	Closed		45.00	15-75
1986 The Gifts of the Magi	Closed		45.00	15-65
1987 The Flight Into Egypt	Closed		49.00	15-55
1988 Adoration of the Shepherd	Closed		49.00	15-55
1989 Peaceful Kingdom	Closed		49.00	15-59
1990 Nativity	Closed		49.00	50-75

Home Sweet Home - R. McGinnis

YEAR ISSUE	EDITION LIMIT	YEAR RETD.	ISSUE PRICE	*QUOTE U.S.$
1989 The Victorian	Closed		39.90	25-32
1989 The Greek Revival	Closed		39.90	25-29
1989 The Georgian	Closed		39.90	25-33
1990 The Mission	Closed		39.90	25-35

It's a Dog's Life - L. Kaatz

YEAR ISSUE	EDITION LIMIT	YEAR RETD.	ISSUE PRICE	*QUOTE U.S.$
1992 We've Been Spotted	Closed		29.90	25-30
1992 Literary Labs	Closed		29.90	27
1993 Retrieving Our Dignity	Closed		32.90	33
1993 Lodging a Complaint	Closed		32.90	30-33
1993 Barreling Along	Closed		32.90	35-43
1993 Play Ball	Closed		34.90	35-55
1993 Dogs and Suds	Closed		34.90	35-55
1993 Paws for a Picnic	Closed		34.90	35

J. W. Smith Childhood Holidays - J. W. Smith

YEAR ISSUE	EDITION LIMIT	YEAR RETD.	ISSUE PRICE	*QUOTE U.S.$
1986 Easter	Closed		19.50	5-22
1986 Thanksgiving	Closed		19.50	5-22
1986 Christmas	Closed		19.50	5-22
1986 Valentine's Day	Closed		22.50	10-25
1987 Mother's Day	Closed		22.50	5-16
1987 Fourth of July	Closed		22.50	10-25

Jeanne Down's Friends I Remember - J. Down

YEAR ISSUE	EDITION LIMIT	YEAR RETD.	ISSUE PRICE	*QUOTE U.S.$
1983 Fish Story	Closed		17.50	5-29
1984 Office Hours	Closed		17.50	5-29
1985 A Coat of Paint	Closed		17.50	5-29
1985 Here Comes the Bride	Closed		19.50	5-20
1985 Fringe Benefits	Closed		19.50	5-20
1986 High Society	Closed		19.50	10-29
1986 Flower Arrangement	Closed		21.50	5-29
1986 Taste Test	Closed		21.50	5-29

Jerner's Less Traveled Road - B. Jerner

YEAR ISSUE	EDITION LIMIT	YEAR RETD.	ISSUE PRICE	*QUOTE U.S.$
1988 The Weathered Barn	Closed		29.90	16-37
1988 The Murmuring Stream	Closed		29.90	24-34
1988 The Covered Bridge	Closed		32.90	38-50
1989 Winter's Peace	Closed		32.90	31-38
1989 The Flowering Meadow	Closed		32.90	30-38
1989 The Hidden Waterfall	Closed		32.90	33-55

Jewels of the Flowers - T.C. Chiu

YEAR ISSUE	EDITION LIMIT	YEAR RETD.	ISSUE PRICE	*QUOTE U.S.$
1991 Sapphire Wings	Closed		29.90	10-35
1991 Topaz Beauties	Closed		29.90	33-40
1991 Amethyst Flight	Closed		32.90	24-35
1991 Ruby Elegance	Closed		32.90	10-35
1991 Emerald Pair	Closed		32.90	15-35
1991 Opal Splendor	Closed		34.90	15-35
1992 Pearl Luster	Closed		34.90	15-50
1992 Aquamarine Glimmer	Closed		34.90	10-35

Keepsake Rhymes - S. Gustafson

YEAR ISSUE	EDITION LIMIT	YEAR RETD.	ISSUE PRICE	*QUOTE U.S.$
1992 Humpty Dumpty	Closed		29.90	24-30
1993 Peter Pumpkin Eater	Closed		29.90	55-65
1993 Pat-a-Cake	Closed		29.90	79-105
1993 Old King Cole	Closed		29.90	75-82

The King and I - W. Chambers

YEAR ISSUE	EDITION LIMIT	YEAR RETD.	ISSUE PRICE	*QUOTE U.S.$
1984 A Puzzlement	Closed		19.50	5-10
1985 Shall We Dance?	Closed		19.50	5-16
1985 Getting to Know You	Closed		19.50	5-11
1985 We Kiss in a Shadow	Closed		19.50	5-40

Lady and the Tramp - Disney Studios

YEAR ISSUE	EDITION LIMIT	YEAR RETD.	ISSUE PRICE	*QUOTE U.S.$
1992 First Date	Closed		34.90	50-79
1992 Puppy Love	Closed		34.90	50-57
1992 Dog Pound Blues	Closed		37.90	45-49
1993 Merry Christmas To All	Closed		37.90	49-54
1993 Double Siamese Trouble	Closed		37.90	45-60
1993 Ruff House	Closed		39.90	40-50
1993 Telling Tails	Closed		39.90	45-72
1993 Moonlight Romance	Closed		39.90	40-74

Lincoln, Man of America - M. Kunstler

YEAR ISSUE	EDITION LIMIT	YEAR RETD.	ISSUE PRICE	*QUOTE U.S.$
1986 The Gettysburg Address	Closed		24.50	5-25
1987 The Inauguration	Closed		24.50	5-25
1987 The Lincoln-Douglas Debates	Closed		27.50	10-28
1987 Beginnings in New Salem	Closed		27.90	5-28
1988 The Family Man	Closed		27.90	5-24
1988 Emancipation Proclamation	Closed		27.90	5-28

The Little Mermaid - Disney Studio Artists

YEAR ISSUE	EDITION LIMIT	YEAR RETD.	ISSUE PRICE	*QUOTE U.S.$
1993 A Song From the Sea	Closed		29.90	30-42
1993 A Visit to the Surface	Closed		29.90	28-47
1993 Daddy's Girl	Closed		32.90	30-35
1993 Underwater Buddies	Closed		32.90	30-56
1994 Ariel's Treasured Collection	Closed		32.90	40-59
1994 Kiss the Girl	Closed		32.90	100-170
1994 Fireworks at First Sight	Closed		34.90	30-52
1994 Forever Love	Closed		34.90	30-73

Living with Nature-Jerner's Ducks - B. Jerner

YEAR ISSUE	EDITION LIMIT	YEAR RETD.	ISSUE PRICE	*QUOTE U.S.$
1986 The Pintail	Closed		19.50	10-25
1986 The Mallard	Closed		19.50	10-34
1987 The Wood Duck	Closed		22.50	10-40
1987 The Green-Winged Teal	Closed		22.50	10-40
1987 The Northern Shoveler	Closed		22.90	10-37
1987 The American Widgeon	Closed		22.90	10-25
1987 The Gadwall	Closed		24.90	10-32
1988 The Blue-Winged Teal	Closed		24.90	10-36

Majestic Birds of North America - D. Smith

YEAR ISSUE	EDITION LIMIT	YEAR RETD.	ISSUE PRICE	*QUOTE U.S.$
1988 The Bald Eagle	Closed		29.90	12-30
1988 Peregrine Falcon	Closed		29.90	15-30
1988 The Great Horned Owl	Closed		32.90	16-33
1989 The Red-Tailed Hawk	Closed		32.90	14-33
1989 The White Gyrfalcon	Closed		32.90	10-33
1989 The American Kestral	Closed		32.90	10-33
1990 The Osprey	Closed		34.90	10-35
1990 The Golden Eagle	Closed		34.90	10-35

Mary Poppins - M. Hampshire

YEAR ISSUE	EDITION LIMIT	YEAR RETD.	ISSUE PRICE	*QUOTE U.S.$
1989 Mary Poppins	Closed		29.90	36-55
1989 A Spoonful of Sugar	Closed		29.90	32-55
1990 A Jolly Holiday With Mary	Closed		32.90	35-40
1990 We Love To Laugh	Closed		32.90	35-40
1991 Chim Chim Cher-ee	Closed		32.90	29-75
1991 Tuppence a Bag	Closed		32.90	40-45

Mickey's Christmas Carol - Disney Studios

YEAR ISSUE	EDITION LIMIT	YEAR RETD.	ISSUE PRICE	*QUOTE U.S.$
1992 Bah Humbug!	Closed		29.90	30-50
1992 What's So Merry About Christmas?	Closed		29.90	30-36
1993 God Bless Us Every One	Closed		32.90	30-42
1993 A Christmas Surprise	Closed		32.90	35-41
1993 Yuletide Greetings	Closed		32.90	30-46
1993 Marley's Warning	Closed		34.90	35-47
1993 A Cozy Christmas	Closed		34.90	35-42
1993 A Christmas Feast	Closed		34.90	35-46

Musical Moments From the Wizard of Oz - K. Milnazik

YEAR ISSUE	EDITION LIMIT	YEAR RETD.	ISSUE PRICE	*QUOTE U.S.$
1993 Over the Rainbow	Closed		29.90	50-95
1993 We're Off to See the Wizard	Closed		29.90	50-95
1993 Munchkin Land	Closed		29.90	50-62
1994 If I Only Had a Brain	Closed		29.90	50-78
1994 Ding Dong The Witch is Dead	Closed		29.90	50-63
1993 The Lullabye League	Closed		29.90	50-92
1994 If I Were King of the Forest	Closed		29.90	50-63
1994 Merry Old Land of Oz	Closed		29.90	50-86

My Fair Lady - W. Chambers

YEAR ISSUE	EDITION LIMIT	YEAR RETD.	ISSUE PRICE	*QUOTE U.S.$
1989 Opening Day at Ascot	Closed		24.90	10-25
1989 I Could Have Danced All Night	Closed		24.90	10-35
1989 The Rain in Spain	Closed		27.90	20
1989 Show Me	Closed		27.90	18
1990 Get Me To/Church On Time	Closed		27.90	20-22
1990 I've Grown Accustomed/Face	Closed		27.90	20-35

Nature's Child - M. Jobe

YEAR ISSUE	EDITION LIMIT	YEAR RETD.	ISSUE PRICE	*QUOTE U.S.$
1990 Sharing	Closed		29.90	21-30
1990 The Lost Lamb	Closed		29.90	30
1990 Seems Like Yesterday	Closed		32.90	29-33
1990 Faithful Friends	Closed		32.90	45-49
1990 Trusted Companion	Closed		32.90	50
1991 Hand in Hand	Closed		32.90	45-50

Nature's Nursery - J. Thornbrugh

YEAR ISSUE	EDITION LIMIT	YEAR RETD.	ISSUE PRICE	*QUOTE U.S.$
1992 Testing the Waters	Closed		29.90	45-50
1993 Taking the Plunge	Closed		29.90	40-45
1993 Race Ya Mom	Closed		29.90	44-46
1993 Time to Wake Up	Closed		29.90	40-45
1993 Hide and Seek	Closed		29.90	40-45
1993 Piggyback Ride	Closed		29.90	30

Not So Long Ago - J. W. Smith

YEAR ISSUE	EDITION LIMIT	YEAR RETD.	ISSUE PRICE	*QUOTE U.S.$
1988 Story Time	Closed		24.90	18-25
1988 Wash Day for Dolly	Closed		24.90	15-25
1988 Suppertime for Kitty	Closed		24.90	26
1988 Mother's Little Helper	Closed		24.90	22-25

Oklahoma! - M. Kunstler

YEAR ISSUE	EDITION LIMIT	YEAR RETD.	ISSUE PRICE	*QUOTE U.S.$
1985 Oh, What a Beautiful Mornin'	Closed		19.50	5-9
1986 Surrey with the Fringe on Top'	Closed		19.50	10-35
1986 I Cain't Say No	Closed		19.50	12-20
1986 Oklahoma!	Closed		19.50	11-35

The Old Mill Stream - C. Tennant

YEAR ISSUE	EDITION LIMIT	YEAR RETD.	ISSUE PRICE	*QUOTE U.S.$
1991 New London Grist Mill	Closed		39.90	29-40
1991 Wayside Inn Grist Mill	Closed		39.90	34-40
1991 The Red Mill	Closed		39.90	30-40
1991 Glade Creek Grist Mill	Closed		39.90	40

Old-Fashioned Favorites - M. Weber

YEAR ISSUE	EDITION LIMIT	YEAR RETD.	ISSUE PRICE	*QUOTE U.S.$
1991 Apple Crisp	Closed		29.90	65-69
1991 Blueberry Muffins	Closed		29.90	59-68
1991 Peach Cobbler	Closed		29.90	90-98
1991 Chocolate Chip Oatmeal Cookies	Closed		29.90	145-175

Once Upon a Time - K. Pritchett

YEAR ISSUE	EDITION LIMIT	YEAR RETD.	ISSUE PRICE	*QUOTE U.S.$
1988 Little Red Riding Hood	Closed		24.90	25-35
1988 Rapunzel	Closed		24.90	20-35
1988 Three Little Pigs	Closed		27.90	20-35
1989 The Princess and the Pea	Closed		27.90	20-35
1989 Goldilocks and the Three Bears	Closed		27.90	30-35
1989 Beauty and the Beast	Closed		27.90	35-38

Pinocchio - Disney Studios

YEAR ISSUE	EDITION LIMIT	YEAR RETD.	ISSUE PRICE	*QUOTE U.S.$
1989 Gepetto Creates Pinocchio	Closed		29.90	50-95
1990 Pinocchio And The Blue Fairy	Closed		29.90	50-62
1990 It's an Actor's Life For Me	Closed		32.90	40-44
1990 I've Got No Strings On Me	Closed		32.90	35-40
1991 Pleasure Island	Closed		32.90	35-75
1991 A Real Boy	Closed		32.90	40-79

Portraits of Motherhood - W. Chambers

YEAR ISSUE	EDITION LIMIT	YEAR RETD.	ISSUE PRICE	*QUOTE U.S.$
1987 Mother's Here	Closed		29.50	10-30
1988 First Touch	Closed		29.50	10-30

Precious Little Ones - M. T. Fangel

YEAR ISSUE	EDITION LIMIT	YEAR RETD.	ISSUE PRICE	*QUOTE U.S.$
1988 Little Red Robins	Closed		29.90	13-30
1988 Little Fledglings	Closed		29.90	22-30
1988 Saturday Night Bath	Closed		29.90	27-39
1988 Peek-A-Boo	Closed		29.90	28-32

Proud Sentinels of the American West - N. Glazier

YEAR ISSUE	EDITION LIMIT	YEAR RETD.	ISSUE PRICE	*QUOTE U.S.$
1993 Youngblood	Closed		29.50	49-55
1993 Cat Nap	Closed		29.90	67-70
1993 Desert Bighorn Mormon Ridge	Closed		32.90	45-50
1993 Crown Prince	Closed		32.90	60-63

Purrfect Point of View - J. Giordano

YEAR ISSUE	EDITION LIMIT	YEAR RETD.	ISSUE PRICE	*QUOTE U.S.$
1992 Unexpected Visitors	Closed		29.90	30
1992 Wistful Morning	Closed		29.90	45-50
1992 Afternoon Catnap	Closed		29.90	50
1992 Cozy Company	Closed		29.90	35

Pussyfooting Around - C. Wilson

YEAR ISSUE	EDITION LIMIT	YEAR RETD.	ISSUE PRICE	*QUOTE U.S.$
1991 Fish Tales	Closed		24.90	19-25
1991 Teatime Tabbies	Closed		24.90	19-25
1991 Yarn Spinners	Closed		24.90	19-25
1991 Two Maestros	Closed		24.90	19-32

Romantic Age of Steam - R.B. Pierce

YEAR ISSUE	EDITION LIMIT	YEAR RETD.	ISSUE PRICE	*QUOTE U.S.$
1992 The Empire Builder	Closed		29.90	25-30
1992 The Broadway Limited	Closed		29.90	35-38

*Quotes have been rounded up to nearest dollar

YEAR ISSUE	EDITION LIMIT	YEAR RETD.	ISSUE PRICE	*QUOTE U.S.$
1992 Twentieth Century Limited	Closed		32.90	47-50
1992 The Chief	Closed		32.90	48-60
1992 The Crescent Limited	Closed		32.90	73-80
1993 The Overland Limited	Closed		34.90	50
1993 The Jupiter	Closed		34.90	55-57
1993 The Daylight	Closed		34.90	54-60

Santa's Christmas - T. Browning

YEAR ISSUE	EDITION LIMIT	YEAR RETD.	ISSUE PRICE	*QUOTE U.S.$
1991 Santa's Love	Closed		29.90	37-40
1991 Santa's Cheer	Closed		29.90	38-48
1991 Santa's Promise	Closed		32.90	62-67
1991 Santa's Gift	Closed		32.90	75-78
1992 Santa's Surprise	Closed		32.90	55-64
1992 Santa's Magic	Closed		32.90	55-57

Season For Song - M. Jobe

YEAR ISSUE	EDITION LIMIT	YEAR RETD.	ISSUE PRICE	*QUOTE U.S.$
1991 Winter Concert	Closed		34.90	40-43
1991 Snowy Symphony	Closed		34.90	41-45
1991 Frosty Chorus	Closed		34.90	52-60
1991 Silver Serenade	Closed		34.90	63-67

Season of Splendor - K. Randle

YEAR ISSUE	EDITION LIMIT	YEAR RETD.	ISSUE PRICE	*QUOTE U.S.$
1992 Autumn's Grandeur	Closed		29.90	38
1992 School Days	Closed		29.90	35-40
1992 Woodland Mill Stream	Closed		32.90	63-65
1992 Harvest Memories	Closed		32.90	50-55
1992 A Country Weekend	Closed		32.90	60
1993 Indian Summer	Closed		32.90	55-59

Shadows and Light: Winter's Wildlife - N. Glazier

YEAR ISSUE	EDITION LIMIT	YEAR RETD.	ISSUE PRICE	*QUOTE U.S.$
1993 Winter's Children	Closed		29.90	40-42
1993 Cub Scouts	Closed		29.90	50
1993 Little Snowman	Closed		29.90	45-50
1993 The Snow Cave	Closed		29.90	36-40

Singin' In The Rain - M. Skolsky

YEAR ISSUE	EDITION LIMIT	YEAR RETD.	ISSUE PRICE	*QUOTE U.S.$
1990 Singin' In The Rain	Closed		32.90	10-30
1990 Good Morning	Closed		32.90	10-30
1991 Broadway Melody	Closed		32.90	10-31
1991 We're Happy Again	Closed		32.90	10-50

Sleeping Beauty - Disney Studios

YEAR ISSUE	EDITION LIMIT	YEAR RETD.	ISSUE PRICE	*QUOTE U.S.$
1991 Once Upon A Dream	Closed		39.90	30-55
1991 Awakened by a Kiss	Closed		39.90	45-95
1991 Happy Birthday Briar Rose	Closed		42.90	35-55
1992 Together At Last	Closed		42.90	40-55

Small Blessings - C. Layton

YEAR ISSUE	EDITION LIMIT	YEAR RETD.	ISSUE PRICE	*QUOTE U.S.$
1992 Now I Lay Me Down to Sleep	Closed		29.90	30-35
1992 Bless Us O Lord For These, Thy Gifts	Closed		29.90	30-40
1992 Jesus Loves Me, This I Know	Closed		32.90	36-40
1992 This Little Light of Mine	Closed		32.90	37-55
1992 Blessed Are The Pure In Heart	Closed		32.90	37-45
1993 Bless Our Home	Closed		32.90	37

Snow White and the Seven Dwarfs - Disney Studios

YEAR ISSUE	EDITION LIMIT	YEAR RETD.	ISSUE PRICE	*QUOTE U.S.$
1991 The Dance of Snow White/Seven Dwarfs	Closed		29.90	40-50
1991 With a Smile and a Song	Closed		29.90	40-65
1991 A Special Treat	Closed		32.90	40-57
1992 A Kiss for Dopey	Closed		32.90	40-65
1992 The Poison Apple	Closed		32.90	40-75
1992 Fireside Love Story	Closed		34.90	40-55
1992 Stubborn Grumpy	Closed		34.90	35-40
1992 A Wish Come True	Closed		34.90	40-42
1993 Time To Tidy Up	Closed		34.50	40-43
1993 May I Have This Dance?	Closed		36.90	40-62
1993 A Surprise in the Clearing	Closed		36.50	50-80
1993 Happy Ending	Closed		36.90	50-85

Songs of the American Spirit - H. Bond

YEAR ISSUE	EDITION LIMIT	YEAR RETD.	ISSUE PRICE	*QUOTE U.S.$
1991 The Star Spangled Banner	Closed		29.90	30-55
1991 Battle Hymn of the Republic	Closed		29.90	45-55
1991 America the Beautiful	Closed		29.90	30-35
1991 My Country 'Tis of Thee	Closed		29.90	63-65

Sound of Music - T. Crnkovich

YEAR ISSUE	EDITION LIMIT	YEAR RETD.	ISSUE PRICE	*QUOTE U.S.$
1986 Sound of Music	Closed		19.50	8-49
1986 Do-Re-Mi	Closed		19.50	20-45
1986 My Favorite Things	Closed		22.50	15-45
1986 Laendler Waltz	Closed		22.50	22-50
1987 Edelweiss	Closed		22.50	22-45
1987 I Have Confidence	Closed		22.50	20-40
1987 Maria	Closed		24.90	22-55
1987 Climb Ev'ry Mountain	Closed		24.90	20-50

South Pacific - E. Gignilliat

YEAR ISSUE	EDITION LIMIT	YEAR RETD.	ISSUE PRICE	*QUOTE U.S.$
1987 Some Enchanted Evening	Closed		24.50	12-49
1987 Happy Talk	Closed		24.50	16-45
1987 Dites Moi	Closed		24.90	15-25
1988 Honey Bun	Closed		24.90	18-50

Stately Owls - J. Beaudoin

YEAR ISSUE	EDITION LIMIT	YEAR RETD.	ISSUE PRICE	*QUOTE U.S.$
1989 The Snowy Owl	Closed		29.90	24-38
1989 The Great Horned Owl	Closed		29.90	34-40
1990 The Barn Owl	Closed		32.90	22-33
1990 The Screech Owl	Closed		32.90	28-33
1990 The Short-Eared Owl	Closed		32.90	25-33
1990 The Barred Owl	Closed		32.90	29-33
1990 The Great Grey Owl	Closed		34.90	31-35
1991 The Saw-Whet Owl	Closed		34.90	32-35

Sundblom Santas - H. Sundblom

YEAR ISSUE	EDITION LIMIT	YEAR RETD.	ISSUE PRICE	*QUOTE U.S.$
1989 Santa By The Fire	Closed		27.90	20-30
1990 Christmas Vigil	Closed		27.90	32-35
1991 To All A Good Night	Closed		32.90	42-60
1992 Santa's on His Way	Closed		32.90	50-60

A Swan is Born - L. Roberts

YEAR ISSUE	EDITION LIMIT	YEAR RETD.	ISSUE PRICE	*QUOTE U.S.$
1987 Hopes and Dreams	Closed		24.50	25
1987 At the Barre	Closed		24.50	23-25
1987 In Position	Closed		24.50	30
1988 Just For Size	Closed		24.50	40

Sweetness and Grace - J. Welty

YEAR ISSUE	EDITION LIMIT	YEAR RETD.	ISSUE PRICE	*QUOTE U.S.$
1992 God Bless Teddy	Closed		34.90	35
1992 Sunshine and Smiles	Closed		34.90	47-50
1992 Favorite Buddy	Closed		34.90	45
1992 Sweet Dreams	Closed		34.90	58

Thomas Kinkade's Enchanted Cottages - T. Kinkade

YEAR ISSUE	EDITION LIMIT	YEAR RETD.	ISSUE PRICE	*QUOTE U.S.$
1993 Fallbrooke Cottage	Closed		29.90	30-68
1993 Julianne's Cottage	Closed		29.90	30-59
1993 Seaside Cottage	Closed		29.90	30-46
1993 Sweetheart Cottage	95-day		29.90	30
1993 Weathervane Cottage	95-day		29.90	30
1993 Rose Garden Cottage	95-day		29.90	30

Thomas Kinkade's Garden Cottages of England - T. Kinkade

YEAR ISSUE	EDITION LIMIT	YEAR RETD.	ISSUE PRICE	*QUOTE U.S.$
1991 Chandler's Cottage	Closed		27.90	40-54
1991 Cedar Nook Cottage	Closed		27.90	40-53
1991 Candlelit Cottage	Closed		30.90	40-60
1991 Open Gate Cottage	Closed		30.90	40
1991 McKenna's Cottage	Closed		30.90	40-50
1992 Woodsman's Thatch Cottage	Closed		32.90	40-50
1992 Merritt's Cottage	Closed		32.90	40-60
1992 Stonegate Cottage	Closed		32.90	40-65

Thomas Kinkade's Home for the Holidays - T. Kinkade

YEAR ISSUE	EDITION LIMIT	YEAR RETD.	ISSUE PRICE	*QUOTE U.S.$
1991 Sleigh Ride Home	Closed		29.90	40-50
1991 Home to Grandma's	Closed		29.90	40-45
1991 Home Before Christmas	Closed		32.90	40-50
1992 The Warmth of Home	Closed		32.90	40-55
1992 Homespun Holiday	Closed		32.90	40-55
1992 Hometime Yuletide	Closed		34.90	40-55
1992 Home Away From Home	Closed		34.90	45-75
1992 The Journey Home	Closed		34.90	40-60

Thomas Kinkade's Home is Where the Heart Is - T. Kinkade

YEAR ISSUE	EDITION LIMIT	YEAR RETD.	ISSUE PRICE	*QUOTE U.S.$
1992 Home Sweet Home	Closed		29.90	50-75
1992 A Warm Welcome Home	Closed		29.90	40-52
1992 A Carriage Ride Home	Closed		32.90	40-59
1993 Amber Afternoon	Closed		32.90	40-56
1993 Country Memories	Closed		32.90	50-78
1993 The Twilight Cafe	Closed		34.90	40-54
1993 Our Summer Home	Closed		34.90	40-63
1993 Hometown Hospitality	Closed		34.90	40-69

Thomas Kinkade's Thomashire - T. Kinkade

YEAR ISSUE	EDITION LIMIT	YEAR RETD.	ISSUE PRICE	*QUOTE U.S.$
1992 Olde Porterfield Tea Room	Closed		29.90	35-42
1992 Olde Thomashire Mill	Closed		29.90	40-47
1992 Swanbrook Cottage	Closed		32.90	70-94
1992 Pye Corner Cottage	Closed		32.90	40-73
1993 Blossom Hill Church	Closed		32.90	40-61
1993 Olde Garden Cottage	Closed		32.90	40-75

Thomas Kinkade's Yuletide Memories - T. Kinkade

YEAR ISSUE	EDITION LIMIT	YEAR RETD.	ISSUE PRICE	*QUOTE U.S.$
1992 The Magic of Christmas	Closed		29.90	40-69
1992 A Beacon of Faith	Closed		29.90	40-49
1993 Moonlit Sleighride	Closed		29.90	40-50
1993 Silent Night	Closed		29.90	40-65
1993 Olde Porterfield Gift Shoppe	Closed		29.90	40-55
1993 The Wonder of the Season	Closed		29.90	40-60
1993 A Winter's Walk	Closed		29.90	40-45
1993 Skater's Delight	Closed		32.90	40-55

Tom Sawyer - W. Chambers

YEAR ISSUE	EDITION LIMIT	YEAR RETD.	ISSUE PRICE	*QUOTE U.S.$
1987 Whitewashing the Fence	Closed		27.50	25-35
1987 Tom and Becky	Closed		27.90	25-35
1987 Tom Sawyer the Pirate	Closed		27.90	25-35
1988 First Pipes	Closed		27.90	23-35

Under Mother's Wing - J. Beaudoin

YEAR ISSUE	EDITION LIMIT	YEAR RETD.	ISSUE PRICE	*QUOTE U.S.$
1992 Arctic Spring: Snowy Owls	Closed		29.90	35-45
1992 Forest's Edge: Great Gray Owls	Closed		29.90	35-40
1992 Treetop Trio: Long-Eared Owls	Closed		32.90	45-50
1992 Woodland Watch: Spotted Owls	Closed		32.90	55
1992 Vast View: Saw Whet Owls	Closed		32.90	50
1992 Lofty-Limb: Great Horned Owl	Closed		34.90	50-55
1993 Perfect Perch: Barred Owls	Closed		34.90	45
1993 Happy Home: Short-Eared Owl	Closed		34.90	50

Upland Birds of North America - W. Anderson

YEAR ISSUE	EDITION LIMIT	YEAR RETD.	ISSUE PRICE	*QUOTE U.S.$
1986 The Pheasant	Closed		24.50	10-15
1986 The Grouse	Closed		24.50	11
1987 The Quail	Closed		27.50	10-14
1987 The Wild Turkey	Closed		27.50	10-19
1987 The Gray Partridge	Closed		27.50	10-17
1987 The Woodcock	Closed		27.90	10-17

Windows of Glory - J. Welty

YEAR ISSUE	EDITION LIMIT	YEAR RETD.	ISSUE PRICE	*QUOTE U.S.$
1993 King of Kings	Closed		29.90	30-54
1993 Prince of Peace	Closed		29.90	30-150
1993 The Messiah	95-day		32.90	33
1993 The Good Shepherd	95-day		32.90	33
1994 The Light of the World	95-day		32.90	33
1994 The Everlasting Father	95-day		32.90	33

Wizard of Oz - J. Auckland

YEAR ISSUE	EDITION LIMIT	YEAR RETD.	ISSUE PRICE	*QUOTE U.S.$
1977 Over the Rainbow	Closed		19.00	31-48
1978 If I Only Had a Brain	Closed		19.00	36-68
1978 If I Only Had a Heart	Closed		19.00	44-50
1978 If I Were King of the Forest	Closed		19.00	50-54
1979 Wicked Witch of the West	Closed		19.00	45-50
1979 Follow the Yellow Brick Road	Closed		19.00	45-49
1979 Wonderful Wizard of Oz	Closed		19.00	34-47
1980 The Grand Finale	Closed		24.00	45-50

Wizard of Oz: A National Treasure - R. Laslo

YEAR ISSUE	EDITION LIMIT	YEAR RETD.	ISSUE PRICE	*QUOTE U.S.$
1991 Yellow Brick Road	Closed		29.90	85-95
1992 I Haven't Got a Brain	Closed		29.90	85-90
1992 I'm a Little Rusty Yet	Closed		32.90	85-90
1992 I Even Scare Myself	Closed		32.90	85-90
1992 We're Off To See the Wizard	Closed		32.90	85-90
1992 I'll Never Get Home	Closed		34.90	85-90
1992 I'm Melting	Closed		34.90	85-90
1992 There's No Place Like Home	Closed		34.90	85-90

Yesterday's Innocents - J. Wilcox Smith

YEAR ISSUE	EDITION LIMIT	YEAR RETD.	ISSUE PRICE	*QUOTE U.S.$
1992 My First Book	Closed		29.90	44-50
1992 Time to Smell the Roses	Closed		29.90	48-55
1993 Hush, Baby's Sleeping	Closed		32.90	38
1993 Ready and Waiting	Closed		32.90	45-50

Enchantica

Retired Enchantica Collection - J. Woodward

YEAR ISSUE	EDITION LIMIT	YEAR RETD.	ISSUE PRICE	*QUOTE U.S.$
1992 Winter Dragon-Grawlfang-2200	15,000	1993	50.00	75-165
1992 Spring Dragon-Gorgoyle-2201	15,000	1993	50.00	80-165
1993 Summer Dragon-Arangast-2202	15,000	1993	50.00	75
1993 Autumn Dragon-Snarlgard-2203	15,000	1993	50.00	165

Ernst Enterprises/Porter & Price, Inc.

A Beautiful World - S. Morton

YEAR ISSUE	EDITION LIMIT	YEAR RETD.	ISSUE PRICE	*QUOTE U.S.$
1981 Tahitian Dreamer	Retrd.	1987	27.50	30
1982 Flirtation	Retrd.	1987	27.50	30
1984 Elke of Oslo	Retrd.	1987	27.50	30

Classy Cars - S. Kuhnly

YEAR ISSUE	EDITION LIMIT	YEAR RETD.	ISSUE PRICE	*QUOTE U.S.$
1982 The 26T	Retrd.	1990	24.50	40
1982 The 31A	Retrd.	1990	24.50	40
1983 The Pickup	Retrd.	1990	24.50	40
1984 Panel Van	Retrd.	1990	24.50	40-85

Commemoratives - S. Morton

YEAR ISSUE	EDITION LIMIT	YEAR RETD.	ISSUE PRICE	*QUOTE U.S.$
1981 John Lennon	Retrd.	1988	39.50	145
1982 Elvis Presley	Retrd.	1988	39.50	90-120
1982 Marilyn Monroe	Retrd.	1988	39.50	125
1983 Judy Garland	Retrd.	1988	39.50	65-120
1984 John Wayne	Retrd.	1988	39.50	110

Elvira - S. Morton

YEAR ISSUE	EDITION LIMIT	YEAR RETD.	ISSUE PRICE	*QUOTE U.S.$
1988 Night Rose	90-day		29.50	45
1988 Red Velvet	90-day		29.50	35
1988 Mistress of the Dark	90-day		29.50	35

Elvis Presley - S. Morton

YEAR ISSUE	EDITION LIMIT	YEAR RETD.	ISSUE PRICE	*QUOTE U.S.$
1987 The King	Retrd.	1991	39.50	125-195
1987 Loving You	Retrd.	1991	39.50	95-195
1987 Early Years	Retrd.	1991	39.50	110-195
1987 Tenderly	Retrd.	1991	39.50	95-195
1988 Forever Yours	Retrd.	1991	39.50	90-195
1988 Rockin in the Moonlight	Retrd.	1991	39.50	95-195
1988 Moody Blues	Retrd.	1991	39.50	90-195
1988 Elvis Presley	Retrd.	1991	39.50	90-195
1989 Elvis Presley-Special Request	Retrd.	1991	150.00	95-225

Hollywood Greats - S. Morton

YEAR ISSUE	EDITION LIMIT	YEAR RETD.	ISSUE PRICE	*QUOTE U.S.$
1981 Henry Fonda	Retrd.	1988	29.95	55
1981 John Wayne	Retrd.	1988	29.95	90-100
1981 Gary Cooper	Retrd.	1988	29.95	40-65
1982 Clark Gable	Retrd.	1988	29.95	65
1984 Alan Ladd	Retrd.	1988	29.95	60

Hollywood Walk of Fame - S. Morton

YEAR ISSUE	EDITION LIMIT	YEAR RETD.	ISSUE PRICE	*QUOTE U.S.$
1989 Jimmy Stewart	Retrd.	1992	39.50	50-125
1989 Elizabeth Taylor	Retrd.	1992	39.50	125
1989 Tom Selleck	Retrd.	1992	39.50	45
1989 Joan Collins	Retrd.	1992	39.50	125
1990 Burt Reynolds	Retrd.	1992	39.50	125
1990 Sylvester Stallone	Retrd.	1992	39.50	45

The Republic Pictures Library - S. Morton

YEAR ISSUE	EDITION LIMIT	YEAR RETD.	ISSUE PRICE	*QUOTE U.S.$
1991 Showdown With Laredo	28-day		37.50	38
1991 The Ride Home	28-day		37.50	38
1991 Attack at Tarawa	28-day		37.50	45
1991 Thoughts of Angelique	28-day		37.50	38-45
1992 War of the Wildcats	28-day		37.50	55-60
1992 The Fighting Seabees	28-day		37.50	38-50
1992 The Quiet Man	28-day		37.50	40-45
1992 Angel and the Badman	28-day		37.50	45
1993 Sands of Iwo Jima	28-day		37.50	40
1993 Flying Tigers	28-day		37.50	45-65
1993 The Tribute (12")	28-day		97.50	98
1994 The Tribute (8 1/4") AP	9,500		35.00	35

Seems Like Yesterday - R. Money

YEAR ISSUE	EDITION LIMIT	YEAR RETD.	ISSUE PRICE	*QUOTE U.S.$
1981 Stop & Smell the Roses	Retrd.	1988	24.50	59
1982 Home by Lunch	Retrd.	1988	24.50	35
1982 Lisa's Creek	Retrd.	1988	24.50	25
1983 It's Got My Name on It	Retrd.	1988	24.50	30

*Quotes have been rounded up to nearest dollar

YEAR ISSUE	EDITION LIMIT	YEAR RETD.	ISSUE PRICE	*QUOTE U.S.$
1983 My Magic Hat	Retrd.	1988	24.50	52
1984 Little Prince	Retrd.	1988	24.50	25

Star Trek - S. Morton

YEAR ISSUE	EDITION LIMIT	YEAR RETD.	ISSUE PRICE	*QUOTE U.S.$
1984 Mr. Spock	Retrd.	1989	29.50	200-295
1985 Dr. McCoy	Retrd.	1989	29.50	125-225
1985 Sulu	Retrd.	1989	29.50	100-195
1985 Scotty	Retrd.	1989	29.50	100-225
1985 Uhura	Retrd.	1989	29.50	100-225
1985 Chekov	Retrd.	1989	29.50	100-195
1985 Captain Kirk	Retrd.	1989	29.50	120-295
1985 Beam Us Down Scotty	Retrd.	1989	29.50	100-235
1985 The Enterprise	Retrd.	1989	39.50	180-295

Star Trek: Commemorative Collection - S. Morton

YEAR ISSUE	EDITION LIMIT	YEAR RETD.	ISSUE PRICE	*QUOTE U.S.$
1987 The Trouble With Tribbles	Retrd.	1989	29.50	150-225
1987 Mirror, Mirror	Retrd.	1989	29.50	150-225
1987 A Piece of the Action	Retrd.	1989	29.50	150-225
1987 The Devil in the Dark	Retrd.	1989	29.50	150-225
1987 Amok Time	Retrd.	1989	29.50	150-225
1987 The City on the Edge of Forever	Retrd.	1989	29.50	170-225
1987 Journey to Babel	Retrd.	1989	29.50	160-225
1987 The Menagerie	Retrd.	1989	29.50	175-225

Turn of The Century - R. Money

YEAR ISSUE	EDITION LIMIT	YEAR RETD.	ISSUE PRICE	*QUOTE U.S.$
1981 Riverboat Honeymoon	Retrd.	1987	35.00	20-40
1982 Children's Carousel	Retrd.	1987	35.00	20-35
1984 Flower Market	Retrd.	1987	35.00	20-35
1985 Balloon Race	Retrd.	1987	35.00	20-35

Women of the West - D. Putnam

YEAR ISSUE	EDITION LIMIT	YEAR RETD.	ISSUE PRICE	*QUOTE U.S.$
1979 Expectations	Retrd.	1986	39.50	10-40
1981 Silver Dollar Sal	Retrd.	1986	39.50	15-40
1982 School Marm	Retrd.	1986	39.50	10-40
1983 Dolly	Retrd.	1986	39.50	10-40

Fenton Art Glass Company

American Classic Series - M. Dickinson

YEAR ISSUE	EDITION LIMIT	YEAR RETD.	ISSUE PRICE	*QUOTE U.S.$
1986 Jupiter Train on Opal Satin	5,000	1986	75.00	75
1986 Studebaker-Garford Car on Opal Satin	5,000	1986	75.00	75

American Craftsman Carnival - Fenton

YEAR ISSUE	EDITION LIMIT	YEAR RETD.	ISSUE PRICE	*QUOTE U.S.$
1970 Glassmaker	Closed	1970	10.00	20-60
1971 Printer	Closed	1971	10.00	20-60
1972 Blacksmith	Closed	1972	10.00	20-60
1973 Shoemaker	Closed	1973	10.00	20-60
1974 Pioneer Cooper	Closed	1974	11.00	20-60
1975 Paul Revere (Patriot & Silversmith)	Closed	1975	12.50	20-60
1976 Gunsmith	Closed	1976	13.50	20-60
1977 Potter	Closed	1977	15.00	20-60
1978 Wheelwright	Closed	1978	15.00	20-60
1979 Cabinetmaker	Closed	1979	15.00	20-60
1980 Tanner	Closed	1980	16.50	20-60
1981 Housewright	Closed	1981	17.50	20-60

Christmas - Various

YEAR ISSUE	EDITION LIMIT	YEAR RETD.	ISSUE PRICE	*QUOTE U.S.$
1979 Nature's Christmas - K. Cunningham	Yr.Iss.	1979	35.00	35
1980 Going Home - D. Johnson	Yr.Iss.	1980	38.50	40
1981 All Is Calm - D. Johnson	Yr.Iss.	1981	42.50	43-45
1982 Country Christmas - R. Spindler	Yr.Iss.	1982	42.50	43-45
1983 Anticipation - D. Johnson	7,500	1983	45.00	45
1984 Expectation - D. Johnson	7,500	1984	50.00	50
1985 Heart's Desire - D. Johnson	7,500	1986	50.00	50
1987 Sharing The Spirit - L. Everson	Yr.Iss.	1987	50.00	50
1987 Cardinal in the Churchyard - D. Johnson	4,500	1987	39.50	40-45
1988 A Chickadee Ballet - D. Johnson	4,500	1988	39.50	40-45
1989 Downy Pecker - Chisled Song - D. Johnson	4,500	1989	39.50	40-45
1990 A Blue Bird in Snowfall - D. Johnson	4,500	1990	39.50	40-45
1990 Sleigh Ride - F. Burton	3,500	1990	45.00	45
1991 Christmas Eve - F. Burton	3,500	1991	45.00	45
1992 Family Tradition - F. Burton	3,500	1992	49.00	49
1993 Family Holiday - F. Burton	3,500	1993	49.00	49
1994 Silent Night - F. Burton	1,500	1994	65.00	65
1995 Our Home Is Blessed - F. Burton	1,500	1995	65.00	65
1996 Star of Wonder - F. Burton	1,750	1996	65.00	65
1997 The Way Home - F. Burton	1,750	1997	85.00	85
1998 The Arrival - F. Burton	2,500		75.00	75

Easter Series - Various

YEAR ISSUE	EDITION LIMIT	YEAR RETD.	ISSUE PRICE	*QUOTE U.S.$
1995 Covered Hen & Egg Opal Irid. Hndpt. - M. Reynolds	950	1995	95.00	95-120
1997 Covered Hen & Egg Opal Irid. Hndpt. - R. Spindler	950		115.00	115

Mary Gregory - M. Reynolds

YEAR ISSUE	EDITION LIMIT	YEAR RETD.	ISSUE PRICE	*QUOTE U.S.$
1994 Plate w/stand, 9"	Closed	1994	65.00	65-75
1995 Plate w/stand, 9"	Closed	1995	65.00	65-75

Flambro Imports

Emmett Kelly Jr. Plates - D. Rust, unless otherwise noted

YEAR ISSUE	EDITION LIMIT	YEAR RETD.	ISSUE PRICE	*QUOTE U.S.$
1983 Why Me? Plate I - C. Kelly	10,000	N/A	40.00	275-500
1984 Balloons For Sale Plate II - C. Kelly	10,000	N/A	40.00	215-275
1985 Big Business Plate III - C. Kelly	10,000	N/A	40.00	215-250
1986 And God Bless America IV - C. Kelly	10,000	N/A	40.00	200-250
1988 Tis the Season	10,000	N/A	50.00	120-175
1989 Looking Back- 65th Birthday	6,500	N/A	50.00	130-295
1991 Winter	10,000	1996	30.00	35-175
1992 Spring	10,000	1996	30.00	35-99
1992 Summer	10,000	1996	30.00	35-99
1992 Autumn	10,000	1996	30.00	35-85
1993 Santa's Stowaway	5,000	1996	30.00	90-100
1994 70th Birthday Commemorative	5,000	1996	30.00	90-150
1995 All Wrapped Up in Christmas	5,000	1996	30.00	65

Pocket Dragons - R. Musgrave

YEAR ISSUE	EDITION LIMIT	YEAR RETD.	ISSUE PRICE	*QUOTE U.S.$
1997 The Astronomy Lesson	1,250		35.00	35
1997 Bedtime	1,250		35.00	35

Fountainhead

As Free As The Wind - M. Fernandez

YEAR ISSUE	EDITION LIMIT	YEAR RETD.	ISSUE PRICE	*QUOTE U.S.$
1989 As Free As The Wind	Unkn.		295.00	670-775

The Wings of Freedom - M. Fernandez

YEAR ISSUE	EDITION LIMIT	YEAR RETD.	ISSUE PRICE	*QUOTE U.S.$
1985 Courtship Flight	2,500		250.00	1300-1500
1986 Wings of Freedom	2,500		250.00	1300-1500

Ganz

Cottage Collectibles® Collection - Ganz

YEAR ISSUE	EDITION LIMIT	YEAR RETD.	ISSUE PRICE	*QUOTE U.S.$
1997 All My Friends	2,400		24.00	24
1997 Celebration	2,400		24.00	24
1997 Day in the Park	2,400		24.00	24
1997 Round 'Em Up	2,400		24.00	24
1997 Tea Time	2,400		24.00	24

Gartlan USA

Club Gift - M. Taylor, unless otherwise noted

YEAR ISSUE	EDITION LIMIT	YEAR RETD.	ISSUE PRICE	*QUOTE U.S.$
1989 Pete Rose (8 1/2") - B. Forbes	Closed	1990	Gift	290-349
1990 Al Barlick (8 1/2")	Closed	1991	Gift	175-249
1991 Joe Montana (8 1/2")	Closed	1992	Gift	75-150
1992 Ken Griffey Jr. (8 1/2")	Closed	1993	Gift	69-95
1993 Gordie Howe (8 1/2")	Closed	1994	Gift	50-175
1994 Shaquille O'Neal (8 1/2")	Closed	1995	Gift	60-250
1996 Ringo Starr (8 1/2")	Closed	1996	Gift	30
1997 Jerry Garcia (8 1/8")	Yr.Iss.	1997	Gift	30
1998 John Lennon Self Portrait (8 1/4") - J. Lennon	1,000		Gift	30

Bob Cousy - M. Taylor

YEAR ISSUE	EDITION LIMIT	YEAR RETD.	ISSUE PRICE	*QUOTE U.S.$
1994 Signed Plate (10 1/4")	950	1995	175.00	100-175
1994 Plate (8 1/2")	10,000		30.00	30
1994 Plate (3 1/4")	Open		15.00	15

Brett & Bobby Hull - M. Taylor

YEAR ISSUE	EDITION LIMIT	YEAR RETD.	ISSUE PRICE	*QUOTE U.S.$
1992 Hockey's Golden Boys (10 1/4") signed by both	950	1995	250.00	150-250
1992 Hockey's Golden Boys (10 1/4") A/P, signed by both	300	1995	350.00	100-350
1992 Hockey's Golden Boys (8 1/2")	10,000		30.00	30
1992 Hockey's Golden Boys (3 1/4")	Open		15.00	15

Carl Yastrzemski - M. Taylor

YEAR ISSUE	EDITION LIMIT	YEAR RETD.	ISSUE PRICE	*QUOTE U.S.$
1993 Signed Plate (10 1/4")	950	1995	175.00	150-175
1993 Plate (8 1/2")	10,000		30.00	30
1993 Plate (3 1/4")	Open		15.00	15

Carlton Fisk - M. Taylor

YEAR ISSUE	EDITION LIMIT	YEAR RETD.	ISSUE PRICE	*QUOTE U.S.$
1993 Signed Plate (10 1/4")	950	1995	175.00	150-175
1993 Plate (8 1/2")	5,000		30.00	30
1993 Plate (3 1/4")	Open		15.00	15

Darryl Strawberry - M. Taylor

YEAR ISSUE	EDITION LIMIT	YEAR RETD.	ISSUE PRICE	*QUOTE U.S.$
1991 Signed Plate (10 1/4")	2,500	1995	150.00	50-150
1991 Plate (8 1/2")	10,000	1995	40.00	30-40
1991 Plate (3 1/4")	Retrd.	1995	15.00	15

George Brett Gold Crown Collection - J. Martin

YEAR ISSUE	EDITION LIMIT	YEAR RETD.	ISSUE PRICE	*QUOTE U.S.$
1986 George Brett "Baseball's All Star" (3 1/4")	Open		15.00	15
1986 George Brett "Baseball's All Star" (10 1/4") signed	2,000	1988	100.00	350-375
1986 George Brett "Baseball's All Star" (10 1/4"), A/P signed	24	1988	225.00	N/A

Gordie Howe - M. Taylor

YEAR ISSUE	EDITION LIMIT	YEAR RETD.	ISSUE PRICE	*QUOTE U.S.$
1993 Signed Plate (10 1/4")	2,358	1995	150.00	125-150
1993 Signed Plate (8 1/2")	10,000		30.00	30
1993 Signed Plate (3 1/4")	Open		15.00	15

Jerry Garcia - M. Taylor

YEAR ISSUE	EDITION LIMIT	YEAR RETD.	ISSUE PRICE	*QUOTE U.S.$
1997 Jerry Garcia (10 1/4")	1,995		125.00	125
1997 Jerry Garcia (10 1/4") A/P	300		225.00	225
1997 Jerry Garcia (8 1/4")	10,000		30.00	30
1997 Jerry Garcia plate/ornament (3 1/4")	Open		15.00	15

Joe Montana - M. Taylor

YEAR ISSUE	EDITION LIMIT	YEAR RETD.	ISSUE PRICE	*QUOTE U.S.$
1991 Signed Plate (10 1/4")	2,250	1991	125.00	250-389
1991 Signed Plate (10 1/4") A/P	250	1991	195.00	395-475
1991 Plate (8 1/2")	10,000	1995	30.00	30-50
1991 Plate (3 1/4")	Open		15.00	15

John Lennon - J. Lennon

YEAR ISSUE	EDITION LIMIT	YEAR RETD.	ISSUE PRICE	*QUOTE U.S.$
1997 Christmas plate (8 1/8")	10,000		30.00	30
1997 Christmas plate/ornament (3 1/4")	Open		16.95	17
1998 Borrowed Time (8 1/8")	10,000		30.00	30
1998 Borrowed Time plate/ornament (3 1/4")	Open		16.95	17
1998 Family Tree (8 1/8")	10,000		30.00	30
1998 Family Tree (3 1/4")	Open		16.95	17
1998 Imagine (8 1/8")	10,000		30.00	30
1998 Imagine (3 1/4")	Open		16.95	17
1998 Peace Brother (8 1/8")	10,000		30.00	30
1998 Peace Brother plate/ornament (3 1/4")	Open		16.95	17
1998 Self Portrait (8 1/8")	10,000		30.00	30
1998 Self Portrait plate/ornament (3 1/4")	Open		16.95	17
1998 4 plate framed ensemble, signed by Yoko Ono	950		295.00	295

John Wooden - M. Taylor

YEAR ISSUE	EDITION LIMIT	YEAR RETD.	ISSUE PRICE	*QUOTE U.S.$
1990 Signed Plate (10 1/4")	1,975	1995	150.00	150
1990 Plate (8 1/2")	10,000	1995	30.00	30
1990 Plate (3 1/4")	Retrd.	1995	15.00	15

Johnny Bench - M. Taylor

YEAR ISSUE	EDITION LIMIT	YEAR RETD.	ISSUE PRICE	*QUOTE U.S.$
1989 Signed Plate (10 1/4")	1,989	1991	100.00	125-300
1989 Plate (3 1/4")	Open		15.00	15

Kareem Abdul-Jabbar Sky-Hook Collection - M. Taylor

YEAR ISSUE	EDITION LIMIT	YEAR RETD.	ISSUE PRICE	*QUOTE U.S.$
1989 Kareem Abdul-Jabbar "Path of Glory" (10 1/4"), signed	1,989	1991	100.00	150-289
1989 Plate (3 1/4")	Closed	1993	16.00	15-30

Ken Griffey Jr. - M. Taylor

YEAR ISSUE	EDITION LIMIT	YEAR RETD.	ISSUE PRICE	*QUOTE U.S.$
1992 Signed Plate (10 1/4")	1,989	1995	150.00	100-150
1992 Plate (8 1/2")	10,000		30.00	30
1992 Plate (3 1/4")	Open		15.00	15

Kiss - M. Taylor

YEAR ISSUE	EDITION LIMIT	YEAR RETD.	ISSUE PRICE	*QUOTE U.S.$
1997 Kiss (10 1/4") signed	1,000		275.00	275
1997 Kiss (10 1/4"), A/P signed	250		495.00	495
1997 Kiss (8 1/4")	10,000		30.00	30
1997 Kiss plate/ornament (3 1/4")	Open		15.00	15

Kristi Yamaguchi - M. Taylor

YEAR ISSUE	EDITION LIMIT	YEAR RETD.	ISSUE PRICE	*QUOTE U.S.$
1993 Signed Plate (10 1/4")	950	1995	150.00	375-444
1993 Plate (8 1/2")	5,000		30.00	30
1993 Plate (3 1/4")	Open		15.00	15

Leave It To Beaver - M. Taylor

YEAR ISSUE	EDITION LIMIT	YEAR RETD.	ISSUE PRICE	*QUOTE U.S.$
1995 Jerry Mathers (10 1/4") signed	1,963		125.00	125
1995 Jerry Mathers (8 1/4")	10,000		39.95	40
1995 Jerry Mathers plate/ornament (3 1/4")	Open		14.95	15

Luis Aparicio - M. Taylor

YEAR ISSUE	EDITION LIMIT	YEAR RETD.	ISSUE PRICE	*QUOTE U.S.$
1991 Signed Plate (10 1/4")	1,984	1995	150.00	250-300
1991 Plate (8 1/2")	10,000		30.00	30
1991 Plate (3 1/4")	Open		15.00	15

Magic Johnson Gold Rim Collection - R. Winslow

YEAR ISSUE	EDITION LIMIT	YEAR RETD.	ISSUE PRICE	*QUOTE U.S.$
1987 Magic Johnson "The Magic Show" (10 1/4"), signed	1,987	1988	100.00	350-495
1987 Magic Johnson "The Magic Show" (3 1/4")	Closed	1993	14.50	15-25

Mike Schmidt "500th" Home Run Edition - C. Paluso

YEAR ISSUE	EDITION LIMIT	YEAR RETD.	ISSUE PRICE	*QUOTE U.S.$
1987 Mike Schmidt "Power at the Plate" (10 1/4"), signed	1,987	1988	100.00	325-350
1987 Mike Schmidt "Power at the Plate" (3 1/4")	Open		14.50	19
1987 Mike Schmidt A/P, signed & dated	56	1988	150.00	595

Neil Diamond - M. Taylor

YEAR ISSUE	EDITION LIMIT	YEAR RETD.	ISSUE PRICE	*QUOTE U.S.$
1998 Signed Plate (10 1/4")	1,000		225.00	225
1998 Neil Diamond (10 1/4") A/P signed	250		325.00	325
1998 Neil Diamond (8 1/8")	5,000		30.00	30
1998 Neil Diamond plate/ornament (3 1/4")	5,000		16.95	17

Pete Rose Diamond Collection - Forbes

YEAR ISSUE	EDITION LIMIT	YEAR RETD.	ISSUE PRICE	*QUOTE U.S.$
1988 Pete Rose "The Reigning Legend" (10 1/4"), signed	950	1989	195.00	250-295
1988 Pete Rose "The Reigning Legend" (10 1/4"), A/P signed	50	1989	300.00	350-395
1988 Pete Rose "The Reigning Legend"(3 1/4")	Open		14.50	15

Pete Rose Platinum Edition - T. Sizemore

YEAR ISSUE	EDITION LIMIT	YEAR RETD.	ISSUE PRICE	*QUOTE U.S.$
1985 Pete Rose "The Best of Baseball" (3 1/4")	Open		12.95	15-20
1985 Pete Rose "The Best of Baseball"(10 1/4")	4,192	1988	100.00	275

Ringo Starr - M. Taylor

YEAR ISSUE	EDITION LIMIT	YEAR RETD.	ISSUE PRICE	*QUOTE U.S.$
1996 Ringo Starr, (10 1/4") signed	1,000	1996	225.00	250-390
1996 Ringo Starr (10 1/4") A/P signed	250		400.00	400
1996 Ringo Starr (8 1/4")	10,000		29.95	30
1996 Ringo Starr plate/ornament (3 1/4")	Open		14.95	15

Rod Carew - M. Taylor

YEAR ISSUE	EDITION LIMIT	YEAR RETD.	ISSUE PRICE	*QUOTE U.S.$
1992 Signed Plate (10 1/4")	950	1995	150.00	100-150
1992 Plate (8 1/2")	10,000		30.00	30
1992 Plate (3 1/4")	Open		15.00	15

Roger Staubach Sterling Collection - C. Soileau

YEAR ISSUE	EDITION LIMIT	YEAR RETD.	ISSUE PRICE	*QUOTE U.S.$
1987 Roger Staubach (3 1/4" diameter)	Open		12.95	20
1987 Roger Staubach (10 1/4" diameter) signed	1,979	1990	100.00	300

Sam Snead - M. Taylor

YEAR ISSUE	EDITION LIMIT	YEAR RETD.	ISSUE PRICE	*QUOTE U.S.$
1994 Signed Plate (10 1/4")	950	1995	100.00	100
1994 Plate (8 1/2")	5,000		30.00	30
1994 Plate (3 1/4")	Open		15.00	15

*Quotes have been rounded up to nearest dollar

Tom Seaver - M. Taylor

YEAR ISSUE	EDITION LIMIT	YEAR RETD.	ISSUE PRICE	*QUOTE U.S.$
1993 Signed Plate (10 1/4")	1,992	1995	150.00	350-495
1993 Plate (8 1/2")	10,000		30.00	30
1993 Plate (3 1/4")	Open		15.00	15

Troy Aikman - M. Taylor

YEAR ISSUE	EDITION LIMIT	YEAR RETD.	ISSUE PRICE	*QUOTE U.S.$
1994 Signed Plate (10 1/4")	1,993	1995	225.00	250-300
1994 Plate (8 1/2")	10,000		30.00	30
1994 Plate (3 1/4")	Open		14.95	15

Wayne Gretzky - M. Taylor

YEAR ISSUE	EDITION LIMIT	YEAR RETD.	ISSUE PRICE	*QUOTE U.S.$
1989 Plate (10 1/4"), signed by Gretzky and Howe	1,851	1989	225.00	250-400
1989 Plate (10 1/4") A/P, signed by Gretzky and Howe	300	1989	300.00	400-450
1989 Plate (8 1/2")	10,000		30.00	30
1989 Plate (3 1/4")	Open		15.00	15

Whitey Ford - M. Taylor

YEAR ISSUE	EDITION LIMIT	YEAR RETD.	ISSUE PRICE	*QUOTE U.S.$
1991 Signed Plate (10 1/4")	2,360	1995	150.00	150-349
1991 Plate (8 1/2")	10,000	1995	30.00	125-175
1991 Plate (3 1/4")	Retrd.	1995	15.00	25-39

Yogi Berra - M. Taylor

YEAR ISSUE	EDITION LIMIT	YEAR RETD.	ISSUE PRICE	*QUOTE U.S.$
1991 Signed Plate (10 1/4")	2,150	1995	150.00	225-349
1991 Plate (8 1/2")	10,000		30.00	30
1991 Plate (3 1/4")	Open		15.00	15
1991 Signed Plate (10 1/4") A/P	250	1995	250.00	250

Georgetown Collection, Inc.

Children of the Great Spirit - C. Theroux

YEAR ISSUE	EDITION LIMIT	YEAR RETD.	ISSUE PRICE	*QUOTE U.S.$
1993 Buffalo Child	35-day		29.95	30
1993 Winter Baby	35-day		29.95	30

Goebel/M.I. Hummel

M.I. Hummel Annual Figural Christmas Plates - M.I. Hummel

YEAR ISSUE	EDITION LIMIT	YEAR RETD.	ISSUE PRICE	*QUOTE U.S.$
1995 Festival Harmony w/Flute 693	Closed	1995	125.00	130-163
1996 Christmas Song 692	Closed	1996	130.00	130
1997 Thanksgiving Prayer 694	Closed	1997	140.00	140
1998 Echoes of Joy 695	Yr.Iss.		145.00	145

M.I. Hummel Club Exclusive Celebration - M.I. Hummel

YEAR ISSUE	EDITION LIMIT	YEAR RETD.	ISSUE PRICE	*QUOTE U.S.$
1986 Valentine Gift (Hum 738)	Closed		90.00	85-444
1987 Valentine Joy (Hum 737)	Closed		98.00	92-444
1988 Daisies Don't Tell (Hum 736)	Closed		115.00	104-444
1989 It's Cold (Hum 735)	Closed		120.00	130-444

M.I. Hummel Collectibles Anniversary Plates - M.I. Hummel

YEAR ISSUE	EDITION LIMIT	YEAR RETD.	ISSUE PRICE	*QUOTE U.S.$
1975 Stormy Weather 280	Closed		100.00	55-295
1980 Spring Dance 281	Closed		225.00	45-245
1985 Auf Wiedersehen 282	Closed		225.00	163-364

M.I. Hummel Collectibles Annual Plates - M.I. Hummel

YEAR ISSUE	EDITION LIMIT	YEAR RETD.	ISSUE PRICE	*QUOTE U.S.$
1971 Heavenly Angel 264	Closed		25.00	400-1000
1972 Hear Ye, Hear Ye 265	Closed		30.00	44-275
1973 Globe Trotter 266	Closed		32.50	65-325
1974 Goose Girl 267	Closed		40.00	39-175
1975 Ride into Christmas 268	Closed		50.00	53-175
1976 Apple Tree Girl 269	Closed		50.00	65-155
1977 Apple Tree Boy 270	Closed		52.50	50-295
1978 Happy Pastime 271	Closed		65.00	35-175
1979 Singing Lesson 272	Closed		90.00	25-125
1980 School Girl 273	Closed		100.00	38-125
1981 Umbrella Boy 274	Closed		100.00	50-135
1982 Umbrella Girl 275	Closed		100.00	106-254
1983 The Postman 276	Closed		108.00	150-265
1984 Little Helper 277	Closed		108.00	50-195
1985 Chick Girl 278	Closed		110.00	58-215
1986 Playmates 279	Closed		125.00	95-325
1987 Feeding Time 283	Closed		135.00	275-520
1988 Little Goat Herder 284	Closed		145.00	94-225
1989 Farm Boy 285	Closed		160.00	158-275
1990 Shepherd's Boy 286	Closed		170.00	215-295
1991 Just Resting 287	Closed		196.00	130-275
1992 Wayside Harmony 288	Closed		210.00	213-500
1993 Doll Bath 289	Closed		210.00	210-349
1994 Doctor 290	Closed		225.00	195-325
1995 Come Back Soon 291	Closed		250.00	195-250
1998 Echoes of Joy 695	Yr.Iss.		145.00	145

M.I. Hummel Four Seasons - M.I. Hummel

YEAR ISSUE	EDITION LIMIT	YEAR RETD.	ISSUE PRICE	*QUOTE U.S.$
1996 Winter Melody 296	Yr.Iss.		195.00	195
1997 Springtime Serenade 297	Yr.Iss.		195.00	195
1998 Summertime Stroll 298	Yr.Iss.		195.00	195

M.I. Hummel Friends Forever - M.I. Hummel

YEAR ISSUE	EDITION LIMIT	YEAR RETD.	ISSUE PRICE	*QUOTE U.S.$
1992 Meditation 292	Closed	N/A	180.00	163-210
1993 For Father 293	Closed	N/A	195.00	163-210
1994 Sweet Greetings 294	Closed	N/A	205.00	163-210
1995 Surprise 295	Closed	N/A	210.00	210-230

M.I. Hummel Little Music Makers - M.I. Hummel

YEAR ISSUE	EDITION LIMIT	YEAR RETD.	ISSUE PRICE	*QUOTE U.S.$
1984 Little Fiddler 744	Closed		30.00	39-165
1985 Serenade 741	Closed		30.00	72-165
1986 Soloist 743	Closed		35.00	72-165
1987 Band Leader 742	Closed		40.00	125-165

M.I. Hummel The Little Homemakers - M.I. Hummel

YEAR ISSUE	EDITION LIMIT	YEAR RETD.	ISSUE PRICE	*QUOTE U.S.$
1988 Little Sweeper (Hum 745)	Closed		45.00	65-165
1989 Wash Day (Hum 746)	Closed		50.00	50-165
1990 A Stitch in Time (Hum 747)	Closed		50.00	75-125
1991 Chicken Little (Hum 747)	Closed		70.00	91-165

Gorham

(Four Seasons) A Boy and His Dog Plates - N. Rockwell

YEAR ISSUE	EDITION LIMIT	YEAR RETD.	ISSUE PRICE	*QUOTE U.S.$
1971 Boy Meets His Dog	Annual	1971	50.00	195-199
1971 Adventures Between Adventures	Annual	1971	Set	Set
1971 The Mysterious Malady	Annual	1971	Set	Set
1971 Pride of Parenthood	Annual	1971	Set	Set

(Four Seasons) A Helping Hand Plates - N. Rockwell

YEAR ISSUE	EDITION LIMIT	YEAR RETD.	ISSUE PRICE	*QUOTE U.S.$
1979 Year End Court	Annual	1979	100.00	90-200
1979 Closed for Business	Annual	1979	Set	Set
1979 Swatter's Rights	Annual	1979	Set	Set
1979 Coal Season's Coming	Annual	1979	Set	Set

(Four Seasons) Dad's Boys Plates - N. Rockwell

YEAR ISSUE	EDITION LIMIT	YEAR RETD.	ISSUE PRICE	*QUOTE U.S.$
1980 Ski Skills	Annual	1980	135.00	80-225
1980 In His Spirits	Annual	1980	Set	Set
1980 Trout Dinner	Annual	1980	Set	Set
1980 Careful Aim	Annual	1980	Set	Set

(Four Seasons) Four Ages of Love - N. Rockwell

YEAR ISSUE	EDITION LIMIT	YEAR RETD.	ISSUE PRICE	*QUOTE U.S.$
1973 Gaily Sharing Vintage Time	Annual	1973	60.00	170-195
1973 Flowers in Tender Bloom	Annual	1973	Set	Set
1973 Sweet Song So Young	Annual	1973	Set	Set
1973 Fondly We Do Remember	Annual	1973	Set	Set

(Four Seasons) Going on Sixteen Plates - N. Rockwell

YEAR ISSUE	EDITION LIMIT	YEAR RETD.	ISSUE PRICE	*QUOTE U.S.$
1977 Chilling Chore	Annual	1977	75.00	100-150
1977 Sweet Serenade	Annual	1977	Set	Set
1977 Shear Agony	Annual	1977	Set	Set
1977 Pilgrimage	Annual	1977	Set	Set

(Four Seasons) Grand Pals Four Plates - N. Rockwell

YEAR ISSUE	EDITION LIMIT	YEAR RETD.	ISSUE PRICE	*QUOTE U.S.$
1976 Snow Sculpturing	Annual	1976	70.00	119-150
1976 Soaring Spirits	Annual	1976	Set	Set
1976 Fish Finders	Annual	1976	Set	Set
1976 Ghostly Gourds	Annual	1976	Set	Set

(Four Seasons) Grandpa and Me Plates - N. Rockwell

YEAR ISSUE	EDITION LIMIT	YEAR RETD.	ISSUE PRICE	*QUOTE U.S.$
1974 Gay Blades	Annual	1974	60.00	150-175
1974 Day Dreamers	Annual	1974	Set	Set
1974 Goin' Fishing	Annual	1974	Set	Set
1974 Pensive Pals	Annual	1974	Set	Set

(Four Seasons) Life with Father Plates - N. Rockwell

YEAR ISSUE	EDITION LIMIT	YEAR RETD.	ISSUE PRICE	*QUOTE U.S.$
1982 Big Decision	Annual	1982	100.00	100-125
1982 Blasting Out	Annual	1982	Set	Set
1982 Cheering the Champs	Annual	1982	Set	Set
1982 A Tough One	Annual	1982	Set	Set

(Four Seasons) Me and My Pals Plates - N. Rockwell

YEAR ISSUE	EDITION LIMIT	YEAR RETD.	ISSUE PRICE	*QUOTE U.S.$
1975 A Lickin' Good Bath	Annual	1975	70.00	94-150
1975 Young Man's Fancy	Annual	1975	Set	Set
1975 Fisherman's Paradise	Annual	1975	Set	Set
1975 Disastrous Daring	Annual	1975	Set	Set

(Four Seasons) Old Buddies Plates - N. Rockwell

YEAR ISSUE	EDITION LIMIT	YEAR RETD.	ISSUE PRICE	*QUOTE U.S.$
1983 Shared Success	Annual	1983	115.00	115-150
1983 Endless Debate	Annual	1983	Set	Set
1983 Hasty Retreat	Annual	1983	Set	Set
1983 Final Speech	Annual	1983	Set	Set

(Four Seasons) Old Timers Plates - N. Rockwell

YEAR ISSUE	EDITION LIMIT	YEAR RETD.	ISSUE PRICE	*QUOTE U.S.$
1981 Canine Solo	Annual	1981	100.00	100-150
1981 Sweet Surprise	Annual	1981	Set	Set
1981 Lazy Days	Annual	1981	Set	Set
1981 Fancy Footwork	Annual	1981	Set	Set

(Four Seasons) Tender Years Plates - N. Rockwell

YEAR ISSUE	EDITION LIMIT	YEAR RETD.	ISSUE PRICE	*QUOTE U.S.$
1978 New Year Look	Annual	1978	100.00	125-150
1978 Spring Tonic	Annual	1978	Set	Set
1978 Cool Aid	Annual	1978	Set	Set
1978 Chilly Reception	Annual	1978	Set	Set

(Four Seasons) Young Love Plates - N. Rockwell

YEAR ISSUE	EDITION LIMIT	YEAR RETD.	ISSUE PRICE	*QUOTE U.S.$
1972 Downhill Daring	Annual	1972	60.00	180-195
1972 Beguiling Buttercup	Annual	1972	Set	Set
1972 Flying High	Annual	1972	Set	Set
1972 A Scholarly Pace	Annual	1972	Set	Set

American Artist - R. Donnelly

YEAR ISSUE	EDITION LIMIT	YEAR RETD.	ISSUE PRICE	*QUOTE U.S.$
1976 Apache Mother & Child	9,800	1980	25.00	35-56

American Landscapes - N. Rockwell

YEAR ISSUE	EDITION LIMIT	YEAR RETD.	ISSUE PRICE	*QUOTE U.S.$
1980 Summer Respite	Annual	1980	45.00	80
1981 Autumn Reflection	Annual	1981	45.00	65
1982 Winter Delight	Annual	1982	50.00	70
1983 Spring Recess	Annual	1983	60.00	75

Barrymore - Barrymore

YEAR ISSUE	EDITION LIMIT	YEAR RETD.	ISSUE PRICE	*QUOTE U.S.$
1971 Quiet Waters	15,000	1980	25.00	25
1972 San Pedro Harbor	15,000	1980	25.00	25
1972 Nantucket, Sterling	1,000	1972	100.00	100
1972 Little Boatyard, Sterling	1,000	1972	100.00	145

Bas Relief - N. Rockwell

YEAR ISSUE	EDITION LIMIT	YEAR RETD.	ISSUE PRICE	*QUOTE U.S.$
1981 Sweet Song So Young	Undis.	1984	100.00	100
1981 Beguiling Buttercup	Undis.	1984	62.50	70
1982 Flowers in Tender Bloom	Undis.	1984	100.00	100
1982 Flying High	Undis.	1984	62.50	65

Boy Scout Plates - N. Rockwell

YEAR ISSUE	EDITION LIMIT	YEAR RETD.	ISSUE PRICE	*QUOTE U.S.$
1975 Our Heritage	18,500	1980	19.50	75-80
1976 A Scout is Loyal	18,500	1990	19.50	55-75
1977 The Scoutmaster	18,500	1990	19.50	80
1977 A Good Sign	18,500	1990	19.50	50-75
1978 Pointing the Way	18,500	1990	19.50	50-75
1978 Campfire Story	18,500	1990	19.50	25-75
1980 Beyond the Easel	18,500	1990	45.00	45-75

Charles Russell - C. Russell

YEAR ISSUE	EDITION LIMIT	YEAR RETD.	ISSUE PRICE	*QUOTE U.S.$
1980 In Without Knocking	9,800	1990	38.00	65-75
1981 Bronc to Breakfast	9,800	1990	38.00	75
1982 When Ignorance is Bliss	9,800	1990	45.00	75-95
1983 Cowboy Life	9,800	1990	45.00	95-100

China Bicentennial - Gorham

YEAR ISSUE	EDITION LIMIT	YEAR RETD.	ISSUE PRICE	*QUOTE U.S.$
1972 1776 Plate	18,500	1980	17.50	35
1976 1776 Bicentennial	8,000	1980	17.50	35

Christmas - N. Rockwell

YEAR ISSUE	EDITION LIMIT	YEAR RETD.	ISSUE PRICE	*QUOTE U.S.$
1974 Tiny Tim	Annual	1974	12.50	25-40
1975 Good Deeds	Annual	1975	17.50	50
1976 Christmas Trio	Annual	1976	19.50	30
1977 Yuletide Reckoning	Annual	1977	19.50	45
1978 Planning Christmas Visit	Annual	1978	24.50	30
1979 Santa's Helpers	Annual	1979	24.50	30
1980 Letter to Santa	Annual	1980	27.50	32
1981 Santa Plans His Visit	Annual	1981	29.50	30
1982 Jolly Coachman	Annual	1982	29.50	30
1983 Christmas Dancers	Annual	1983	29.50	35
1984 Christmas Medley	17,500	1984	29.95	30
1985 Home For The Holidays	17,500	1985	29.95	30
1986 Merry Christmas Grandma	17,500	1986	29.95	65
1987 The Homecoming	17,500	1987	35.00	35-45
1988 Discovery	17,500	1988	37.50	38-45

Christmas/Children's Television Workshop - Unknown

YEAR ISSUE	EDITION LIMIT	YEAR RETD.	ISSUE PRICE	*QUOTE U.S.$
1981 Sesame Street Christmas	Annual	1981	17.50	18
1982 Sesame Street Christmas	Annual	1982	17.50	18
1983 Sesame Street Christmas	Annual	1983	19.50	20

Encounters, Survival and Celebrations - J. Clymer

YEAR ISSUE	EDITION LIMIT	YEAR RETD.	ISSUE PRICE	*QUOTE U.S.$
1982 A Fine Welcome	7,500	1983	50.00	80
1983 Winter Trail	7,500	1984	50.00	80
1983 Alouette	7,500	1984	62.50	80
1983 The Trader	7,500	1984	62.50	63
1983 Winter Camp	7,500	1984	62.50	75
1983 The Trapper Takes a Wife	7,500	1984	62.50	63

Gallery of Masters - Various

YEAR ISSUE	EDITION LIMIT	YEAR RETD.	ISSUE PRICE	*QUOTE U.S.$
1971 Man with a Gilt Helmet - Rembrandt	10,000	1975	50.00	50
1972 Self Portrait with Saskia - Rembrandt	10,000	1975	50.00	50
1973 The Honorable Mrs. Graham - Gainsborough	7,500	1975	50.00	50

Gorham Museum Doll Plates - Gorham

YEAR ISSUE	EDITION LIMIT	YEAR RETD.	ISSUE PRICE	*QUOTE U.S.$
1984 Lydia	5,000	1984	29.00	50-125
1984 Belton Bebe	5,000	1984	29.00	50-55
1984 Christmas Lady	7,500	1984	32.50	33-50
1985 Lucille	5,000	1985	29.00	35-50
1985 Jumeau	5,000	1985	29.00	35-50

Julian Ritter - J. Ritter

YEAR ISSUE	EDITION LIMIT	YEAR RETD.	ISSUE PRICE	*QUOTE U.S.$
1977 Christmas Visit	9,800	1977	24.50	29
1978 Valentine, Fluttering Heart	7,500	1978	45.00	45

Julian Ritter, Fall In Love - J. Ritter

YEAR ISSUE	EDITION LIMIT	YEAR RETD.	ISSUE PRICE	*QUOTE U.S.$
1977 Enchantment	5,000	1977	100.00	100
1977 Frolic	5,000	1977	set	Set
1977 Gutsy Gal	5,000	1977	set	Set
1977 Lonely Chill	5,000	1977	set	Set

Julian Ritter, To Love a Clown - J. Ritter

YEAR ISSUE	EDITION LIMIT	YEAR RETD.	ISSUE PRICE	*QUOTE U.S.$
1978 Awaited Reunion	5,000	1978	120.00	120
1978 Twosome Time	5,000	1978	120.00	120
1978 Showtime Beckons	5,000	1978	120.00	120
1978 Together in Memories	5,000	1978	120.00	120

Leyendecker Annual Christmas Plates - J. C. Leyendecker

YEAR ISSUE	EDITION LIMIT	YEAR RETD.	ISSUE PRICE	*QUOTE U.S.$
1988 Christmas Hug	10,000	1988	37.50	30-50

Moppet Plates-Anniversary - Unknown

YEAR ISSUE	EDITION LIMIT	YEAR RETD.	ISSUE PRICE	*QUOTE U.S.$
1976 Anniversary	20,000	1977	13.00	13

Moppet Plates-Christmas - Unknown

YEAR ISSUE	EDITION LIMIT	YEAR RETD.	ISSUE PRICE	*QUOTE U.S.$
1973 Christmas	Annual	1973	10.00	35
1974 Christmas	Annual	1974	12.00	12
1975 Christmas	Annual	1975	13.00	13
1976 Christmas	Annual	1976	13.00	15
1977 Christmas	Annual	1977	13.00	14
1978 Christmas	Annual	1978	10.00	10
1979 Christmas	Annual	1979	12.00	12
1980 Christmas	Annual	1980	12.00	12
1981 Christmas	Annual	1981	12.00	12
1982 Christmas	Annual	1982	12.00	12
1983 Christmas	Annual	1983	12.00	12

Moppet Plates-Mother's Day - Unknown

YEAR ISSUE	EDITION LIMIT	YEAR RETD.	ISSUE PRICE	*QUOTE U.S.$
1973 Mother's Day	Annual	1973	10.00	30
1974 Mother's Day	Annual	1974	12.00	20
1975 Mother's Day	Annual	1975	13.00	15
1976 Mother's Day	Annual	1976	13.00	15
1977 Mother's Day	Annual	1977	13.00	15
1978 Mother's Day	Annual	1978	10.00	10

Pastoral Symphony - B. Felder

YEAR ISSUE	EDITION LIMIT	YEAR RETD.	ISSUE PRICE	*QUOTE U.S.$
1982 When I Was a Child	7,500	1983	42.50	20-50
1982 Gather the Children	7,500	1983	42.50	20-50
1984 Sugar and Spice	7,500	1985	42.50	20-50
XX He Loves Me	7,500	1985	42.50	20-50

*Quotes have been rounded up to nearest dollar

Pewter Bicentennial - R. Pailthorpe

Year	Issue	Edition Limit	Year Retd.	Issue Price	*Quote U.S.$
1971	Burning of the Gaspee	5,000	1971	35.00	35
1972	Boston Tea Party	5,000	1972	35.00	35

Presidential - N. Rockwell

Year	Issue	Edition Limit	Year Retd.	Issue Price	*Quote U.S.$
1976	John F. Kennedy	9,800	1976	30.00	65
1976	Dwight D. Eisenhower	9,800	1976	30.00	35

Remington Western - F. Remington

Year	Issue	Edition Limit	Year Retd.	Issue Price	*Quote U.S.$
1973	A New Year on the Cimarron	Annual	1973	25.00	35-50
1973	Aiding a Comrade	Annual	1973	25.00	30-125
1973	The Flight	Annual	1973	25.00	30-95
1973	The Fight for the Water Hole	Annual	1973	25.00	30-125
1975	Old Ramond	Annual	1975	20.00	35-60
1975	A Breed	Annual	1975	20.00	35-65
1976	Cavalry Officer	5,000	1976	37.50	60-75
1976	A Trapper	5,000	1976	37.50	60-75

Silver Bicentennial - Various

Year	Issue	Edition Limit	Year Retd.	Issue Price	*Quote U.S.$
1972	1776 Plate - Gorham	500	1972	500.00	500
1972	Burning of the Gaspee - R. Pailthorpe	750	1972	500.00	500
1973	Boston Tea Party - R. Pailthorpe	750	1973	550.00	575

Single Release - F. Quagon

Year	Issue	Edition Limit	Year Retd.	Issue Price	*Quote U.S.$
1976	The Black Regiment 1778	7,500	1978	25.00	58

Single Release - N. Rockwell

Year	Issue	Edition Limit	Year Retd.	Issue Price	*Quote U.S.$
1974	Weighing In	Annual	1974	12.50	75-115
1974	The Golden Rule	Annual	1974	12.50	30-40
1975	Ben Franklin	Annual	1975	19.50	35
1976	The Marriage License	Numbrd	1985	37.50	75-95
1978	Triple Self Portrait Memorial	Annual	1978	37.50	50-95
1980	The Annual Visit	Annual	1980	32.50	50-70
1981	Day in Life of Boy	Annual	1981	50.00	50-80
1981	Day in Life of Girl	Annual	1981	50.00	50-108

Time Machine Teddies Plates - B. Port

Year	Issue	Edition Limit	Year Retd.	Issue Price	*Quote U.S.$
1986	Miss Emily, Bearing Up	5,000	1986	32.50	35-50
1987	Big Bear, The Toy Collector	5,000	1987	32.50	35-45
1988	Hunny Munny	5,000	1988	37.50	35-45

Vermeil Bicentennial - Gorham

Year	Issue	Edition Limit	Year Retd.	Issue Price	*Quote U.S.$
1972	1776 Plate	250	1972	750.00	300-800

Hackett American

Sports - Various

Year	Issue	Edition Limit	Year Retd.	Issue Price	*Quote U.S.$
1981	Reggie Jackson (Mr. Oct.) h/s - Paluso	Retrd.	N/A	100.00	695-750
1983	Steve Garvey h/s - Paluso	Retrd.	N/A	100.00	150-175
1983	Nolan Ryan h/s - Paluso	Retrd.	N/A	100.00	595-750
1983	Tom Seaver h/s - Paluso	3,272	N/A	100.00	200-300
1984	Steve Carlton h/s - Paluso	Retrd.	N/A	100.00	200-250
1985	Willie Mays h/s - Paluso	Retrd.	N/A	125.00	395
1985	Whitey Ford h/s - Paluso	Retrd.	N/A	125.00	200-250
1985	Hank Aaron h/s - Paluso	Retrd.	N/A	125.00	375-395
1985	Sandy Koufax h/s - Paluso	1,000	N/A	125.00	450
1985	H. Killebrew d/s - Paluso	Retrd.	N/A	125.00	275
1985	E. Mathews d/s - Paluso	Retrd.	N/A	125.00	275
1986	T. Seaver 300 d/s - Paluso	1,200	N/A	125.00	200-250
1986	Roger Clemens (great events) d/s - Paluso	Retrd.	N/A	125.00	595-750
1986	Reggie Jackson (great events) d/s - Paluso	Retrd.	N/A	125.00	200-250
1986	Wally Joyner (great events) d/s - Paluso	Retrd.	N/A	125.00	200-250
1986	Don Sutton d/s (great events) - Paluso	300	N/A	125.00	200-250
XX	Gary Carter d/s - Simon	Retrd.	N/A	125.00	50-150
1985	Dwight Gooden 8 1/2" u/s - Simon	Retrd.	N/A	55.00	40-55
XX	Arnold Palmer h/s - Alexander	Retrd.	N/A	125.00	200
XX	Gary Player h/s - Alexander	Retrd.	N/A	125.00	200
1983	Reggie Jackson (500 HRs) h/s - Alexander	Retrd.	N/A	125.00	200-500
1983	Reggie Jackson (500 HRs), proof - Alexander	Retrd.	N/A	250.00	1000
1986	Joe Montana d/s - Alexander	Retrd.	N/A	125.00	600

Hadley House

American Memories Series - T. Redlin

Year	Issue	Edition Limit	Year Retd.	Issue Price	*Quote U.S.$
1987	Coming Home	9,500		85.00	85
1988	Lights of Home	9,500	1994	85.00	85-150
1989	Homeward Bound	9,500	1996	85.00	85
1991	Family Traditions	9,500		85.00	85

Annual Christmas Series - T. Redlin

Year	Issue	Edition Limit	Year Retd.	Issue Price	*Quote U.S.$
1991	Heading Home	9,500	1994	65.00	225
1992	Pleasures Of Winter	19,500		65.00	125
1993	Winter Wonderland	19,500		65.00	125
1994	Almost Home	19,500		65.00	125
1995	Sharing the Evening	45-day		29.95	30

Country Doctor Collection - T. Redlin

Year	Issue	Edition Limit	Year Retd.	Issue Price	*Quote U.S.$
1995	Wednesday Afternoon	45-day		29.95	30
1995	Office Hours	45-day		29.95	30
1995	House Calls	45-day		29.95	30
1995	Morning Rounds	45-day		29.95	30

Glow Series - T. Redlin

Year	Issue	Edition Limit	Year Retd.	Issue Price	*Quote U.S.$
1985	Evening Glow	5,000	1986	55.00	250-325
1985	Morning Glow	5,000	1986	55.00	130-150
1985	Twilight Glow	5,000	1988	55.00	130-388
1988	Afternoon Glow	5,000	1989	55.00	100-129

Lovers Collection - O. Franca

Year	Issue	Edition Limit	Year Retd.	Issue Price	*Quote U.S.$
1992	Lovers	9,500	1997	50.00	50

Navajo Visions Suite - O. Franca

Year	Issue	Edition Limit	Year Retd.	Issue Price	*Quote U.S.$
1993	Navajo Fantasy	9,500		50.00	50
1993	Young Warrior	9,500		50.00	50

Navajo Woman Series - O. Franca

Year	Issue	Edition Limit	Year Retd.	Issue Price	*Quote U.S.$
1990	Feathered Hair Ties	5,000	1994	50.00	50
1991	Navajo Summer	5,000		50.00	50
1992	Turquoise Necklace	5,000		50.00	50
1993	Pink Navajo	5,000		50.00	50

Retreat Series - T. Redlin

Year	Issue	Edition Limit	Year Retd.	Issue Price	*Quote U.S.$
1987	Morning Retreat	9,500	1988	65.00	125
1987	Evening Retreat	9,500	1989	65.00	125-250
1988	Golden Retreat	9,500	1989	65.00	100-170
1989	Moonlight Retreat	9,500	1993	65.00	85

Seasons - T. Redlin

Year	Issue	Edition Limit	Year Retd.	Issue Price	*Quote U.S.$
1994	Autumn Evening	45-day		29.95	30
1995	Spring Fever	45-day		29.95	30
1995	Summertime	45-day		29.95	30
1995	Wintertime	45-day		29.95	30

That Special Time - T. Redlin

Year	Issue	Edition Limit	Year Retd.	Issue Price	*Quote U.S.$
1991	Evening Solitude	9,500	1994	65.00	95-103
1991	That Special Time	9,500	1993	65.00	95
1992	Aroma of Fall	9,500	1994	65.00	95-112
1993	Welcome To Paradise	9,500	1997	65.00	65

Tranquility - O. Franca

Year	Issue	Edition Limit	Year Retd.	Issue Price	*Quote U.S.$
1994	Blue Navajo	9,500	1997	50.00	50
1994	Blue Tranquility	9,500	1997	50.00	50
1994	Navajo Meditating	9,500		50.00	50
1995	Navajo Reflection	9,500		50.00	50

Wildlife Memories - T. Redlin

Year	Issue	Edition Limit	Year Retd.	Issue Price	*Quote U.S.$
1994	Best Friends	19,500		65.00	65
1994	Comforts of Home	19,500		65.00	65
1994	Pure Contentment	19,500		65.00	65
1994	Sharing in the Solitude	19,500		65.00	65

Windows to the Wild - T. Redlin

Year	Issue	Edition Limit	Year Retd.	Issue Price	*Quote U.S.$
1990	Master's Domain	9,500		65.00	65
1991	Winter Windbreak	9,500		65.00	65
1992	Evening Company	9,500		65.00	65
1994	Night Mapling	9,500		65.00	65

Hamilton Collection

All in a Day's Work - J. Lamb

Year	Issue	Edition Limit	Year Retd.	Issue Price	*Quote U.S.$
1994	Where's the Fire?	28-day	1994	29.50	30
1994	Lunch Break	28-day	1994	29.50	30
1994	Puppy Patrol	28-day	1994	29.50	30
1994	Decoy Delivery	28-day	1994	29.50	30
1994	Budding Artist	28-day	1994	29.50	30
1994	Garden Guards	28-day	1994	29.50	30
1994	Saddling Up	28-day	1994	29.50	30
1995	Taking the Lead	28-day	1994	29.50	30

All Star Memories - D. Spindel

Year	Issue	Edition Limit	Year Retd.	Issue Price	*Quote U.S.$
1995	The Mantle Story	28-day		35.00	35
1996	Momentos of the Mick	28-day		35.00	35
1996	Mantle Appreciation Day	28-day		35.00	35
1996	Life of a Legend	28-day		35.00	35
1996	Yankee Pride	28-day		35.00	35
1996	A World Series Tribute	28-day		35.00	35
1996	The Ultimate All Star	28-day		35.00	35
1997	Triple Crown	28-day		35.00	35

America's Greatest Sailing Ships - T. Freeman

Year	Issue	Edition Limit	Year Retd.	Issue Price	*Quote U.S.$
1988	USS Constitution	14-day	1991	29.50	27-95
1988	Great Republic	14-day	1991	29.50	27-65
1988	America	14-day	1991	29.50	27-85
1988	Charles W. Morgan	14-day	1991	29.50	27-95
1988	Eagle	14-day	1991	29.50	27-50
1988	Bonhomme Richard	14-day	1991	29.50	36-50
1988	Gertrude L. Thebaud	14-day	1991	29.50	45-50
1988	Enterprise	14-day	1991	29.50	36-50

The American Civil War - D. Prechtel

Year	Issue	Edition Limit	Year Retd.	Issue Price	*Quote U.S.$
1990	General Robert E. Lee	14-day		37.50	50-75
1990	Generals Grant and Lee At Appomattox	14-day		37.50	50
1990	General Thomas "Stonewall" Jackson	14-day		37.50	50-54
1990	Abraham Lincoln	14-day		37.50	50-60
1991	General J.E.B. Stuart	14-day		37.50	45-50
1991	General Philip Sheridan	14-day		37.50	50-60
1991	A Letter from Home	14-day		37.50	50-60
1991	Going Home	14-day		37.50	45-50
1992	Assembling The Troop	14-day		37.50	50-75
1992	Standing Watch	14-day		37.50	75-80

American Water Birds - R. Lawrence

Year	Issue	Edition Limit	Year Retd.	Issue Price	*Quote U.S.$
1988	Wood Ducks	14-day		37.50	40-54
1988	Hooded Mergansers	14-day		37.50	40-54
1988	Pintail	14-day		37.50	40-45
1988	Canada Geese	14-day		37.50	40-45
1988	American Widgeons	14-day		37.50	40-54
1988	Canvasbacks	14-day		37.50	40-54
1988	Mallard Pair	14-day		37.50	38-60
1988	Snow Geese	14-day		37.50	40-45

The American Wilderness - M. Richter

Year	Issue	Edition Limit	Year Retd.	Issue Price	*Quote U.S.$
1995	Gray Wolf	28-day		29.95	30-45
1995	Silent Watch	28-day		29.95	30
1995	Moon Song	28-day		29.95	30
1995	Silent Pursuit	28-day		29.95	30
1996	Still of the Night	28-day		29.95	30
1996	Nighttime Serenity	28-day		29.95	30
1996	Autumn Solitude	28-day		29.95	30
1996	Arctic Wolf	28-day		29.95	30-45

Andy Griffith - R. Tanenbaum

Year	Issue	Edition Limit	Year Retd.	Issue Price	*Quote U.S.$
1992	Sheriff Andy Taylor	28-day	1994	29.50	45-90
1992	A Startling Conclusion	28-day	1994	29.50	45-90
1993	Mayberry Sing-a-long	28-day	1994	29.50	45-90
1993	Aunt Bee's Kitchen	28-day	1994	29.50	45-90
1993	Surprise! Surprise!	28-day	1994	29.50	45-75
1993	An Explosive Situation	28-day	1994	29.50	45-110
1993	Meeting Aunt Bee	28-day	1994	29.50	60-75
1993	Opie's Big Catch	28-day	1994	29.50	45-75

The Angler's Prize - M. Susinno

Year	Issue	Edition Limit	Year Retd.	Issue Price	*Quote U.S.$
1991	Trophy Bass	14-day		29.50	30-80
1991	Blue Ribbon Trout	14-day		29.50	33
1991	Sun Dancers	14-day		29.50	30
1991	Freshwater Barracuda	14-day		29.50	30-36
1991	Bronzeback Fighter	14-day		29.50	30-36
1991	Autumn Beauty	14-day		29.50	30-40
1992	Old Mooneyes	14-day		29.50	30-36
1992	Silver King	14-day		29.50	33

Beauty Of Winter - N/A

Year	Issue	Edition Limit	Year Retd.	Issue Price	*Quote U.S.$
1992	Silent Night	28-day		29.50	30
1993	Moonlight Sleighride	28-day		29.50	30

The Best Of Baseball - R. Tanenbaum

Year	Issue	Edition Limit	Year Retd.	Issue Price	*Quote U.S.$
1993	The Legendary Mickey Mantle	28-day		29.50	42-55
1993	The Immortal Babe Ruth	28-day		29.50	38-45
1993	The Great Willie Mays	28-day		29.50	42-55
1993	The Unbeatable Duke Snider	28-day		29.50	25-45
1993	The Extraordinary Lou Gehrig	28-day		29.50	30-42
1993	The Phenomenal Roberto Clemente	28-day		29.50	30-42
1993	The Remarkable Johnny Bench	28-day		29.50	30-42
1993	The Incredible Nolan Ryan	28-day		29.50	30-42
1993	The Exceptional Brooks Robinson	28-day		29.50	30-42
1993	The Unforgettable Phil Rizzuto	28-day		29.50	30-42
1995	The Incomparable Reggie Jackson	28-day		29.50	30-42

Bialosky® & Friends - P./A.Bialosky

Year	Issue	Edition Limit	Year Retd.	Issue Price	*Quote U.S.$
1992	Family Addition	28-day		29.50	33
1993	Sweetheart	28-day		29.50	30-36
1993	Let's Go Fishing	28-day		29.50	30-36
1993	U.S. Mail	28-day		29.50	30-45
1993	Sleigh Ride	28-day		29.50	30
1993	Honey For Sale	28-day		29.50	30
1993	Breakfast In Bed	28-day		29.50	30-36
1993	My First Two-Wheeler	28-day		29.50	30

Big Cats of the World - D. Manning

Year	Issue	Edition Limit	Year Retd.	Issue Price	*Quote U.S.$
1989	African Shade	14-day		29.50	30-37
1989	View from Above	14-day		29.50	30
1990	On The Prowl	14-day		29.50	30
1990	Deep In The Jungle	14-day		29.50	30
1990	Spirit Of The Mountain	14-day		29.50	30
1990	Spotted Sentinel	14-day		29.50	30
1990	Above the Treetops	14-day		29.50	30
1990	Mountain Dweller	14-day		29.50	30
1992	Jungle Habitat	14-day		29.50	30
1992	Solitary Sentry	14-day		29.50	30

Bundles of Joy - B. P. Gutmann

Year	Issue	Edition Limit	Year Retd.	Issue Price	*Quote U.S.$
1988	Awakening	14-day	1991	24.50	45-125
1988	Happy Dreams	14-day	1991	24.50	52-100
1988	Tasting	14-day	1991	24.50	30-95
1988	Sweet Innocence	14-day	1991	24.50	35-85
1988	Tommy	14-day	1991	24.50	30-80
1988	A Little Bit of Heaven	14-day	1991	24.50	60-125
1988	Billy	14-day	1991	24.50	30-80
1988	Sun Kissed	14-day	1991	24.50	30-80

Butterfly Garden - P. Sweany

Year	Issue	Edition Limit	Year Retd.	Issue Price	*Quote U.S.$
1987	Spicebush Swallowtail	14-day		29.50	30-45
1987	Common Blue	14-day		29.50	30-38
1987	Orange Sulphur	14-day		29.50	30-35
1987	Monarch	14-day		29.50	30-45
1987	Tiger Swallowtail	14-day		29.50	30
1987	Crimson Patched Longwing	14-day		29.50	30-38
1988	Morning Cloak	14-day		29.50	30
1988	Red Admiral	14-day		29.50	30-38

The Call of the North - J. Tift

Year	Issue	Edition Limit	Year Retd.	Issue Price	*Quote U.S.$
1993	Winter's Dawn	28-day		29.50	30
1994	Evening Silence	28-day		29.50	30
1994	Moonlit Wilderness	28-day		29.50	30
1994	Silent Snowfall	28-day		29.50	30
1994	Snowy Watch	28-day		29.50	30
1994	Sentinels of the Summit	28-day		29.50	30
1994	Arctic Seclusion	28-day		29.50	30
1994	Forest Twilight	28-day		29.50	30
1994	Mountain Explorer	28-day		29.50	30
1994	The Cry of Winter	28-day		29.50	30

Call to Adventure - R. Cross

Year	Issue	Edition Limit	Year Retd.	Issue Price	*Quote U.S.$
1993	USS Constitution	28-day		29.50	30

*Quotes have been rounded up to nearest dollar

YEAR ISSUE	EDITION LIMIT	YEAR RETD.	ISSUE PRICE	*QUOTE U.S.$
1993 The Bounty	28-day		29.50	30
1994 Bonhomme Richard	28-day		29.50	30
1994 Old Nantucket	28-day		29.50	30
1994 Golden West	28-day		29.50	30
1994 Boston	28-day		29.50	30
1994 Hannah	28-day		29.50	30
1994 Improvement	28-day		29.50	30
1995 Anglo-American	28-day		29.50	30
1995 Challenge	28-day		29.50	30

Cameo Kittens - Q. Lemonds

YEAR ISSUE	EDITION LIMIT	YEAR RETD.	ISSUE PRICE	*QUOTE U.S.$
1993 Ginger Snap	28-day		29.50	30
1993 Cat Tails	28-day		29.50	30
1993 Lady Blue	28-day		29.50	30
1993 Tiny Heart Stealer	28-day		29.50	30-45
1993 Blossom	28-day		29.50	30
1994 Whisker Antics	28-day		29.50	30
1994 Tiger's Temptation	28-day		29.50	30
1994 Scout	28-day		29.50	30
1995 Timid Tabby	28-day		29.50	30
1995 All Wrapped Up	28-day		29.50	30

A Child's Best Friend - B. P. Gutmann

YEAR ISSUE	EDITION LIMIT	YEAR RETD.	ISSUE PRICE	*QUOTE U.S.$
1985 In Disgrace	14-day	1990	24.50	95-150
1985 The Reward	14-day	1990	24.50	65-150
1985 Who's Sleepy	14-day	1990	24.50	45-150
1985 Good Morning	14-day	1990	24.50	45-80
1985 Sympathy	14-day	1990	24.50	45-90
1985 On the Up and Up	14-day	1990	24.50	45-150
1985 Mine	14-day	1990	24.50	45-125
1985 Going to Town	14-day	1990	24.50	45-135

A Child's Christmas - J. Ferrandiz

YEAR ISSUE	EDITION LIMIT	YEAR RETD.	ISSUE PRICE	*QUOTE U.S.$
1995 Asleep in the Hay	28-day		29.95	30
1995 Merry Little Friends	28-day		29.95	30
1995 Love is Warm All Over	28-day		29.95	30
1995 Little Shepard Family	28-day		29.95	30
1995 Life's Little Blessings	28-day		29.95	30
1995 Happiness is Being Loved	28-day		29.95	30
1995 My Heart Belongs to You	28-day		29.95	30
1996 Lil' Dreamers	28-day		29.95	30

Childhood Reflections - B.P. Gutmann

YEAR ISSUE	EDITION LIMIT	YEAR RETD.	ISSUE PRICE	*QUOTE U.S.$
1991 Harmony	14-day	1990	29.50	55-99
1991 Kitty's Breakfast	14-day	1990	29.50	35-75
1991 Friendly Enemies	14-day	1990	29.50	35-80
1991 Smile, Smile, Smile	14-day	1990	29.50	35-95
1991 Lullaby	14-day	1990	29.50	35-75
1991 Oh! Oh! A Bunny	14-day	1990	29.50	35-95
1991 Little Mother	14-day	1990	29.50	35-85
1991 Thank You, God	14-day	1990	29.50	35-65

Children of the American Frontier - D. Crook

YEAR ISSUE	EDITION LIMIT	YEAR RETD.	ISSUE PRICE	*QUOTE U.S.$
1986 In Trouble Again	10-day		24.50	35-45
1986 Tubs and Suds	10-day		24.50	28-40
1986 A Lady Needs a Little Privacy	10-day		24.50	25-40
1986 The Desperadoes	10-day		24.50	28-40
1986 Riders Wanted	10-day		24.50	32-40
1987 A Cowboy's Downfall	10-day		24.50	28-40
1987 Runaway Blues	10-day		24.50	28-40
1987 A Special Patient	10-day		24.50	35-40

Civil War Generals - M. Gnatek

YEAR ISSUE	EDITION LIMIT	YEAR RETD.	ISSUE PRICE	*QUOTE U.S.$
1994 Robert E. Lee	28-day		29.50	26-35
1994 J.E.B. Stewart	28-day		29.50	35-65
1994 Joshua L. Chamberlain	28-day		29.50	30-45
1994 George Armstrong Custer	28-day		29.50	30-45
1994 Nathan Bedford Forrest	28-day		29.50	30-65
1994 James Longstreet	28-day		29.50	30-75
1995 Thomas "Stonewall" Jackson	28-day		29.50	30-45
1995 Confederate Heroes	28-day		29.50	26-36

Classic American Santas - G. Hinke

YEAR ISSUE	EDITION LIMIT	YEAR RETD.	ISSUE PRICE	*QUOTE U.S.$
1993 A Christmas Eve Visitor	28-day		29.50	30-36
1994 Up on the Rooftop	28-day		29.50	30-35
1994 Santa's Candy Kitchen	28-day		29.50	30-35
1994 A Christmas Chorus	28-day		29.50	30-35
1994 An Exciting Christmas Eve	28-day		29.50	30-35
1994 Rest Ye Merry Gentlemen	28-day		29.50	30-35
1994 Preparing the Sleigh	28-day		29.50	30-35
1994 The Reindeer's Stable	28-day		29.50	33-35
1994 He's Checking His List	28-day		29.50	30-35

Classic Corvettes - M. Lacourciere

YEAR ISSUE	EDITION LIMIT	YEAR RETD.	ISSUE PRICE	*QUOTE U.S.$
1994 1957 Corvette	28-day		29.50	30
1994 1963 Corvette	28-day		29.50	30
1994 1968 Corvette	28-day		29.50	30
1994 1986 Corvette	28-day		29.50	30
1995 1967 Corvette	28-day		29.50	30
1995 1953 Corvette	28-day		29.50	30
1995 1962 Corvette	28-day		29.50	30
1995 1990 Corvette	28-day		29.50	30

Classic Sporting Dogs - B. Christie

YEAR ISSUE	EDITION LIMIT	YEAR RETD.	ISSUE PRICE	*QUOTE U.S.$
1989 Golden Retrievers	14-day		24.50	50-70
1989 Labrador Retrievers	14-day		24.50	50-60
1989 Beagles	14-day		24.50	50-60
1989 Pointers	14-day		24.50	50-60
1989 Springer Spaniels	14-day		24.50	45-60
1990 German Short-Haired Pointers	14-day		24.50	50-60
1990 Irish Setters	14-day		24.50	40-60
1990 Brittany Spaniels	14-day		24.50	48-60

Classic TV Westerns - K. Milnazik

YEAR ISSUE	EDITION LIMIT	YEAR RETD.	ISSUE PRICE	*QUOTE U.S.$
1990 The Lone Ranger and Tonto	14-day		29.50	65-165
1990 Bonanza™	14-day		29.50	85-175
1990 Roy Rogers and Dale Evans	14-day		29.50	45-95
1991 Rawhide	14-day		29.50	45-95
1991 Wild Wild West	14-day		29.50	65-95
1991 Have Gun, Will Travel	14-day		29.50	45-95
1991 The Virginian	14-day		29.50	60-125
1991 Hopalong Cassidy	14-day		29.50	60-175

Cloak of Visions - A. Farley

YEAR ISSUE	EDITION LIMIT	YEAR RETD.	ISSUE PRICE	*QUOTE U.S.$
1994 Visions in a Full Moon	28-day		29.50	30
1994 Protector of the Child	28-day		29.50	30
1995 Spirits of the Canyon	28-day		29.50	30
1995 Freedom Soars	28-day		29.50	30
1995 Mystic Reflections	28-day		29.50	30
1995 Staff of Life	28-day		29.50	30
1995 Springtime Hunters	28-day		29.50	30
1996 Moonlit Solace	28-day		29.50	30

Comical Dalmations - Landmark

YEAR ISSUE	EDITION LIMIT	YEAR RETD.	ISSUE PRICE	*QUOTE U.S.$
1996 I Will Not Bark In Class	28-day		29.95	30-40
1996 The Master	28-day		29.95	30
1996 Spot At Play	28-day		29.95	30
1996 A Dalmation's Dream	28-day		29.95	30
1996 To The Rescue	28-day		29.95	30
1996 Maid For A Day	28-day		29.95	30
1996 Dalmation Celebration	28-day		29.95	30
1996 Concert in D-Minor	28-day		29.95	30

Coral Paradise - H. Bond

YEAR ISSUE	EDITION LIMIT	YEAR RETD.	ISSUE PRICE	*QUOTE U.S.$
1989 The Living Oasis	14-day		29.50	30-55
1990 Riches of the Coral Sea	14-day		29.50	30-40
1990 Tropical Pageantry	14-day		29.50	30-40
1990 Caribbean Spectacle	14-day		29.50	30-40
1990 Undersea Village	14-day		29.50	30-40
1990 Shimmering Reef Dwellers	14-day		29.50	30-40
1990 Mysteries of the Galapagos	14-day		29.50	30-40
1990 Forest Beneath the Sea	14-day		29.50	30-40

Cottage Puppies - K. George

YEAR ISSUE	EDITION LIMIT	YEAR RETD.	ISSUE PRICE	*QUOTE U.S.$
1993 Little Gardeners	28-day		29.50	30-35
1993 Springtime Fancy	28-day		29.50	30
1993 Endearing Innocence	28-day		29.50	30
1994 Picnic Playtime	28-day		29.50	30
1994 Lazy Afternoon	28-day		29.50	30-40
1994 Summertime Pals	28-day		29.50	30
1994 A Gardening Trio	28-day		29.50	30
1994 Taking a Break	28-day		29.50	30

Council Of Nations - G. Perillo

YEAR ISSUE	EDITION LIMIT	YEAR RETD.	ISSUE PRICE	*QUOTE U.S.$
1992 Strength of the Sioux	14-day		29.50	35-69
1992 Pride of the Cheyenne	14-day		29.50	35-65
1992 Dignity of the Nez Parce	14-day		29.50	35-59
1992 Courage of the Arapaho	14-day		29.50	35-55
1992 Power of the Blackfoot	14-day		29.50	26-55
1992 Nobility of the Algonqui	14-day		29.50	35-55
1992 Wisdom of the Cherokee	14-day		29.50	35-55
1992 Boldness of the Seneca	14-day		29.50	35-55

Country Garden Cottages - E. Dertner

YEAR ISSUE	EDITION LIMIT	YEAR RETD.	ISSUE PRICE	*QUOTE U.S.$
1992 Riverbank Cottage	28-day		29.50	30-36
1992 Sunday Outing	28-day		29.50	30
1992 Shepherd's Cottage	28-day		29.50	30
1993 Daydream Cottage	28-day		29.50	30
1993 Garden Glorious	28-day		29.50	30
1993 This Side of Heaven	28-day		29.50	30
1993 Summer Symphony	28-day		29.50	30
1993 April Cottage	28-day		29.50	30

Country Kitties - G. Gerardi

YEAR ISSUE	EDITION LIMIT	YEAR RETD.	ISSUE PRICE	*QUOTE U.S.$
1989 Mischief Makers	14-day		24.50	40-45
1989 Table Manners	14-day		24.50	36-45
1989 Attic Attack	14-day		24.50	35-45
1989 Rock and Rollers	14-day		24.50	27-45
1989 Just For the Fern of It	14-day		24.50	27-48
1989 All Washed Up	14-day		24.50	39-45
1989 Stroller Derby	14-day		24.50	35-48
1989 Captive Audience	14-day		24.50	39-45

A Country Season of Horses - J.M. Vass

YEAR ISSUE	EDITION LIMIT	YEAR RETD.	ISSUE PRICE	*QUOTE U.S.$
1990 First Day of Spring	14-day		29.50	30-55
1990 Summer Splendor	14-day		29.50	30-55
1990 A Winter's Walk	14-day		29.50	30-55
1990 Autumn Grandeur	14-day		29.50	30-55
1990 Cliffside Beauty	14-day		29.50	30-55
1990 Frosty Morning	14-day		29.50	30-55
1990 Crisp Country Morning	14-day		29.50	30-55
1990 River Retreat	14-day		29.50	30-55

A Country Summer - N. Noel

YEAR ISSUE	EDITION LIMIT	YEAR RETD.	ISSUE PRICE	*QUOTE U.S.$
1985 Butterfly Beauty	10-day		29.50	30-36
1985 The Golden Puppy	10-day		29.50	30
1986 The Rocking Chair	10-day		29.50	30-36
1986 My Bunny	10-day		29.50	30-33
1988 The Piglet	10-day		29.50	30
1988 Teammates	10-day		29.50	30

Curious Kittens - B. Harrison

YEAR ISSUE	EDITION LIMIT	YEAR RETD.	ISSUE PRICE	*QUOTE U.S.$
1990 Rainy Day Friends	14-day		29.50	30-55
1990 Keeping in Step	14-day		29.50	30-55
1991 Delightful Discovery	14-day		29.50	30-55
1991 Chance Meeting	14-day		29.50	30-55
1991 All Wound Up	14-day		29.50	30-55
1991 Making Tracks	14-day		29.50	30-55
1991 Playing Cat and Mouse	14-day		29.50	30-55
1991 A Paw's in the Action	14-day		29.50	30-55
1992 Little Scholar	14-day		29.50	30-55
1992 Cat Burglar	14-day		29.50	30-55

Dale Earnhardt - Various

YEAR ISSUE	EDITION LIMIT	YEAR RETD.	ISSUE PRICE	*QUOTE U.S.$
1996 The Intimidator - S. Bass	28-day		35.00	26-45
1996 The Man in Black - R. Tanenbaum	28-day		35.00	35-45
1996 Silver Select - S. Bass	28-day		35.00	35-45
1996 Back in Black - R. Tanenbaum	28-day		35.00	26-45
1996 Ready to Rumble - R. Tanenbaum	28-day		35.00	35-45

Daughters Of The Sun - K. Thayer

YEAR ISSUE	EDITION LIMIT	YEAR RETD.	ISSUE PRICE	*QUOTE U.S.$
1993 Sun Dancer	28-day		29.50	30-36
1993 Shining Feather	28-day		29.50	30
1993 Delighted Dancer	28-day		29.50	30
1993 Evening Dancer	28-day		29.50	30
1993 A Secret Glance	28-day		29.50	30
1993 Chippewa Charmer	28-day		29.50	30
1994 Pride of the Yakima	28-day		29.50	30
1994 Radiant Beauty	28-day		29.50	30

Dear to My Heart - J. Hagara

YEAR ISSUE	EDITION LIMIT	YEAR RETD.	ISSUE PRICE	*QUOTE U.S.$
1990 Cathy	14-day		29.50	30-50
1990 Addie	14-day		29.50	30-50
1990 Jimmy	14-day		29.50	30-65
1990 Dacy	14-day		29.50	30-50
1990 Paul	14-day		29.50	30-50
1991 Shelly	14-day		29.50	30-50
1991 Jenny	14-day		29.50	30-50
1991 Joy	14-day		29.50	30-50

Dolphin Discovery - D. Queen

YEAR ISSUE	EDITION LIMIT	YEAR RETD.	ISSUE PRICE	*QUOTE U.S.$
1995 Sunrise Reverie	28-day		29.50	30
1995 Dolphin's Paradise	28-day		29.50	30
1995 Coral Cove	28-day		29.50	30
1995 Undersea Journey	28-day		29.50	30
1995 Dolphin Canyon	28-day		29.50	30
1995 Coral Garden	28-day		29.50	30
1996 Dolphin Duo	28-day		29.50	30
1996 Underwater Tranquility	28-day		29.50	30

Dreamsicles - K. Haynes

YEAR ISSUE	EDITION LIMIT	YEAR RETD.	ISSUE PRICE	*QUOTE U.S.$
1994 The Flying Lesson	28-day		19.50	25-35
1995 By the Light of the Moon	28-day		19.50	25-29
1995 The Recital	28-day		19.50	20
1995 Heavenly Pirouettes	28-day		19.50	20
1995 Blossoms and Butterflies	28-day		19.50	20
1995 Love's Shy Glance	28-day		19.50	20
1996 Wishing Upon a Star	28-day		19.50	20
1996 Rainy Day Friends	28-day		19.50	20
1996 Starboats Ahoy!	28-day		19.50	20
1996 Teeter Tots	28-day		19.50	20
1996 Star Magic	28-day		19.50	20
1996 Heavenly Tea Party	28-day		19.50	20

Dreamsicles Christmas Annual Sculptural - K. Haynes

YEAR ISSUE	EDITION LIMIT	YEAR RETD.	ISSUE PRICE	*QUOTE U.S.$
1996 The Finishing Touches	Closed	1997	39.95	40-50

Dreamsicles Heaven Sent - N/A

YEAR ISSUE	EDITION LIMIT	YEAR RETD.	ISSUE PRICE	*QUOTE U.S.$
1996 Quiet Blessings	28-day		29.95	30
1996 A Heartfelt Embrace	28-day		29.95	30
1996 Earth's Blessings	28-day		29.95	30
1996 A Moment In Dreamland	28-day		29.95	30
1996 Sew Cuddly	28-day		29.95	30
1996 Homemade With Love	28-day		29.95	30
1996 A Sweet Treat	28-day		29.95	30
1996 Pampered And Pretty	28-day		29.95	30

Dreamsicles Home Sweet Home Sculptural - K. Haynes

YEAR ISSUE	EDITION LIMIT	YEAR RETD.	ISSUE PRICE	*QUOTE U.S.$
1997 We Love Gardening	Open		39.95	40
1998 Homemade From the Heart	Open		39.95	40
1998 Love Is the Thread of Life	Open		39.95	40

Dreamsicles Life's Little Blessings - K. Haynes

YEAR ISSUE	EDITION LIMIT	YEAR RETD.	ISSUE PRICE	*QUOTE U.S.$
1995 Happiness	28-day		29.95	30
1996 Peace	28-day		29.95	30
1996 Love	28-day		29.95	30
1996 Creativity	28-day		29.95	30
1996 Friendship	28-day		29.95	30
1996 Knowledge	28-day		29.95	30
1996 Hope	28-day		29.95	30
1996 Faith	28-day		29.95	30

Dreamsicles Love & Lace - N/A

YEAR ISSUE	EDITION LIMIT	YEAR RETD.	ISSUE PRICE	*QUOTE U.S.$
1997 Stolen Kiss	Open		19.95	20
1997 Sharing Hearts	Open		19.95	20
1997 Love Letters	Open		19.95	20
1997 I Love You	Open		19.95	20
1997 Daisies & Dreamsicles	Open		19.95	20
1997 First Love	Open		19.95	20
1997 Perfect Match	Open		19.95	20
1997 Hand In Hand	Open		19.95	20

Dreamsicles Ornamental Mini Plates - K. Haynes

YEAR ISSUE	EDITION LIMIT	YEAR RETD.	ISSUE PRICE	*QUOTE U.S.$
1996 The Flying Lesson	28-day		19.95	20
1996 By The Light of the Moon	28-day		set	set
1996 The Recital	28-day		19.95	20
1996 Heavenly Pirouettes	28-day		set	set
1997 Blossoms and Butterflies	28-day		19.95	20
1997 Love's Shy Glance	28-day		set	set
1997 Wishing on a Star	28-day		19.95	20
1997 Rainy Day Friends	28-day		set	set
1997 Starboats Ahoy	28-day		19.95	20
1997 Teeter Tots	28-day		set	set
1997 Star Magic	28-day		19.95	20
1997 A Heavenly Tea Party	28-day		set	set

*Quotes have been rounded up to nearest dollar

Dreamsicles Sculptural - N/A

YEAR ISSUE	EDITION LIMIT	YEAR RETD.	ISSUE PRICE	*QUOTE U.S.$
1995 The Flying Lesson	Open		37.50	38
1996 By The Light of the Moon	Open		37.50	38
1996 The Recital	Open		37.50	38
1996 Teeter Tots	Open		37.50	38
1996 Poetry In Motion	Open		37.50	38
1996 Rock-A-Bye Dreamsicles	Open		37.50	38
1996 The Birth Certificate	Open		37.50	38
1996 Sharing Hearts	Open		37.50	38

Dreamsicles Special Friends - K. Haynes

YEAR ISSUE	EDITION LIMIT	YEAR RETD.	ISSUE PRICE	*QUOTE U.S.$
1995 A Hug From the Heart	28-day		29.95	30
1995 Heaven's Little Helper	28-day		29.95	30
1995 Bless Us All	28-day		29.95	30
1996 Love's Gentle Touch	28-day		29.95	30
1996 The Best Gift of All	28-day		29.95	30
1996 A Heavenly Hoorah!	28-day		29.95	30
1996 A Love Like No Other	28-day		29.95	30
1996 Cuddle Up	28-day		29.95	30

Dreamsicles Special Friends Sculptural - K. Haynes

YEAR ISSUE	EDITION LIMIT	YEAR RETD.	ISSUE PRICE	*QUOTE U.S.$
1995 Heaven's Little Helper	Open		37.50	38
1996 A Hug From The Heart	Open		37.50	38
1996 Bless Us All	Open		37.50	38
1996 The Best Gift of All	Open		37.50	38
1996 A Heavenly Hoorah!	Open		37.50	38
1996 A Love Like No Other	Open		37.50	38
1997 Cuddle Up	Open		45.00	45
1997 Love's Gentle Touch	Open		45.00	45

Dreamsicles Sweethearts - K. Haynes

YEAR ISSUE	EDITION LIMIT	YEAR RETD.	ISSUE PRICE	*QUOTE U.S.$
1996 Stolen Kiss	28-day		35.00	35
1996 Sharing Hearts	28-day		35.00	35
1996 Love Letters	28-day		35.00	35
1996 I Love You	28-day		35.00	35
1996 Daisies & Dreamsicles	28-day		35.00	35
1997 First Love	28-day		35.00	35
1997 Perfect Match	28-day		35.00	35
1997 Hand in Hand	28-day		35.00	35

Drivers of Victory Lane - R. Tanenbaum

YEAR ISSUE	EDITION LIMIT	YEAR RETD.	ISSUE PRICE	*QUOTE U.S.$
1994 Bill Elliott #11	28-day		29.50	40-55
1994 Jeff Gordon #24	28-day		29.50	30-40
1994 Rusty Wallace #2	28-day		29.50	30-40
1995 Geoff Bodine #7	28-day		29.50	26-40
1995 Dale Earnhardt #3	28-day		29.50	30-40
1996 Sterling Martin #4	28-day		29.50	30-40
1996 Terry Labonte #5	28-day		29.50	26-40
1996 Ken Scharder #25	28-day		29.50	30-40
1996 Jeff Gordon #24	28-day		29.50	30-40
1996 Bill Elliott #94	28-day		29.50	40-55
1996 Rusty Wallace #2	28-day		29.50	30-40
1996 Mark Martin #6	28-day		29.50	30-40
1996 Dale Earnhardt #3	28-day		29.50	30-40

Easyriders - M. Lacourciere

YEAR ISSUE	EDITION LIMIT	YEAR RETD.	ISSUE PRICE	*QUOTE U.S.$
1995 American Classic	28-day		29.95	35-40
1995 Symbols of Freedom	28-day		29.95	30
1996 Patriot's Pride	28-day		29.95	30
1996 The Way of the West	28-day		29.95	30
1996 Revival of an Era	28-day		29.95	30
1996 Hollywood Style	28-day		29.95	30
1996 Vietnam Express	28-day		29.95	30
1996 Las Vegas	28-day		29.95	30-35
1996 Beach Cruising	28-day		29.95	30
1996 New Orleans Scene	28-day		29.95	30

Elvis Remembered - S. Morton

YEAR ISSUE	EDITION LIMIT	YEAR RETD.	ISSUE PRICE	*QUOTE U.S.$
1989 Loving You	90-day		37.50	95-195
1989 Early Years	90-day		37.50	80-195
1989 Tenderly	90-day		37.50	125-200
1989 The King	90-day		37.50	110-200
1989 Forever Yours	90-day		37.50	70-195
1989 Rockin in the Moonlight	90-day		37.50	70-195
1989 Moody Blues	90-day		37.50	70-195
1989 Elvis Presley	90-day		37.50	70-200

Enchanted Seascapes - J. Enright

YEAR ISSUE	EDITION LIMIT	YEAR RETD.	ISSUE PRICE	*QUOTE U.S.$
1993 Sanctuary of the Dolphin	28-day		29.50	30-50
1994 Rhapsody of Hope	28-day		29.50	30
1994 Oasis of the Gods	28-day		29.50	30
1994 Sphere of Life	28-day		29.50	30
1994 Edge of Time	28-day		29.50	30
1994 Sea of Light	28-day		29.50	30
1994 Lost Beneath the Blue	28-day		29.50	30
1994 Blue Paradise	28-day		29.50	30
1995 Morning Odyssey	28-day		29.50	30
1995 Paradise Cove	28-day		29.50	30

English Country Cottages - M. Bell

YEAR ISSUE	EDITION LIMIT	YEAR RETD.	ISSUE PRICE	*QUOTE U.S.$
1990 Periwinkle Tea Room	14-day		29.50	60-75
1991 Gamekeeper's Cottage	14-day		29.50	60-75
1991 Ginger Cottage	14-day		29.50	60
1991 Larkspur Cottage	14-day		29.50	45-60
1991 The Chaplain's Garden	14-day		29.50	33-60
1991 Lorna Doone Cottage	14-day		29.50	45-60
1991 Murrle Cottage	14-day		29.50	36-60
1991 Lullabye Cottage	14-day		29.50	30-60

Eternal Wishes of Good Fortune - Shuho

YEAR ISSUE	EDITION LIMIT	YEAR RETD.	ISSUE PRICE	*QUOTE U.S.$
1983 Friendship	10-day		34.95	35-50
1983 Purity and Perfection	10-day		34.95	35-50
1983 Illustrious Offspring	10-day		34.95	35-50
1983 Longevity	10-day		34.95	35-50
1983 Youth	10-day		34.95	35-50
1983 Immortality	10-day		34.95	35-50
1983 Marital Bliss	10-day		34.95	35-50
1983 Love	10-day		34.95	35-50
1983 Peace	10-day		34.95	35-50
1983 Beauty	10-day		34.95	35-50
1983 Fertility	10-day		34.95	35-50
1983 Fortitude	10-day		34.95	35-50

Exotic Tigers of Asia - K. Ottinger

YEAR ISSUE	EDITION LIMIT	YEAR RETD.	ISSUE PRICE	*QUOTE U.S.$
1995 Lord of the Rainforest	28-day		29.50	30-40
1995 Snow King	28-day		29.50	30-40
1995 Ruler of the Wetlands	28-day		29.50	30-40
1996 Majestic Vigil	28-day		29.50	30-40
1996 Keeper of the Jungle	28-day		29.50	30-40
1996 Eyes of the Jungle	28-day		29.50	30-40
1996 Sovereign Ruler	28-day		29.50	30-40
1996 Lord of the Lowlands	28-day		29.50	30-40

Familiar Spirits - D. Wright

YEAR ISSUE	EDITION LIMIT	YEAR RETD.	ISSUE PRICE	*QUOTE U.S.$
1996 Faithful Guardians	28-day		29.95	30
1996 Sharing Nature's Innocence	28-day		29.95	30
1996 Trusted Friend	28-day		29.95	30
1996 A Friendship Begins	28-day		29.95	30
1996 Winter Homage	28-day		29.95	30
1996 The Blessing	28-day		29.95	30
1996 Healing Powers	28-day		29.95	30

Farmyard Friends - J. Lamb

YEAR ISSUE	EDITION LIMIT	YEAR RETD.	ISSUE PRICE	*QUOTE U.S.$
1992 Mistaken Identity	28-day	1994	29.50	30
1992 Little Cowhands	28-day	1994	29.50	30
1993 Shreading the Evidence	28-day	1994	29.50	30
1993 Partners in Crime	28-day	1994	29.50	30
1993 Fowl Play	28-day	1994	29.50	30
1993 Follow The Leader	28-day	1994	29.50	36
1993 Pony Tales	28-day	1994	29.50	30
1993 An Apple A Day	28-day	1994	29.50	30

Favorite American Songbirds - D. O'Driscoll

YEAR ISSUE	EDITION LIMIT	YEAR RETD.	ISSUE PRICE	*QUOTE U.S.$
1989 Blue Jays of Spring	14-day		29.50	40-55
1989 Red Cardinals of Winter	14-day		29.50	40-55
1989 Robins & Apple Blossoms	14-day		29.50	40-55
1989 Goldfinches of Summer	14-day		29.50	40-55
1990 Autumn Chickadees	14-day		29.50	40-55
1990 Bluebirds and Morning Glories	14-day		29.50	40-55
1990 Tufted Titmouse and Holly	14-day		29.50	40-55
1991 Carolina Wrens of Spring	14-day		29.50	40-55

Favorite Old Testament Stories - S. Butcher

YEAR ISSUE	EDITION LIMIT	YEAR RETD.	ISSUE PRICE	*QUOTE U.S.$
1994 Jacob's Dream	28-day		35.00	35
1995 The Baby Moses	28-day		35.00	35
1995 Esther's Gift To Her People	28-day		35.00	35
1995 A Prayer For Victory	28-day		35.00	35
1995 Where You Go, I Will Go	28-day		35.00	35
1995 A Prayer Answered, A Promise Kept	28-day		35.00	35
1996 Joseph Sold Into Slavery	28-day		35.00	35
1996 Daniel In the Lion's Den	28-day		35.00	35
1996 Noah And The Ark	28-day		35.00	35

The Fierce And The Free - F. McCarthy

YEAR ISSUE	EDITION LIMIT	YEAR RETD.	ISSUE PRICE	*QUOTE U.S.$
1992 Big Medicine	28-day		29.50	30
1993 Land of the Winter Hawk	28-day		29.50	30
1993 Warrior of Savage Splendor	28-day		29.50	30
1994 War Party	28-day		29.50	30
1994 The Challenge	28-day		29.50	30
1994 Out of the Rising Mist	28-day		29.50	30
1994 The Ambush	28-day		29.50	30-35
1994 Dangerous Crossing	28-day		29.50	30

Flower Festivals of Japan - N. Hara

YEAR ISSUE	EDITION LIMIT	YEAR RETD.	ISSUE PRICE	*QUOTE U.S.$
1985 Chrysanthemum	10-day		45.00	45
1985 Hollyhock	10-day		45.00	45
1985 Plum Blossom	10-day		45.00	45
1985 Morning Glory	10-day		45.00	45
1985 Cherry Blossom	10-day		45.00	45
1985 Iris	10-day		45.00	45
1985 Lily	10-day		45.00	45
1985 Peach Blossom	10-day		45.00	45

Forging New Frontiers - J. Deneen

YEAR ISSUE	EDITION LIMIT	YEAR RETD.	ISSUE PRICE	*QUOTE U.S.$
1994 The Race is On	28-day		29.50	30
1994 Big Boy	28-day		29.50	30
1994 Cresting the Summit	28-day		29.50	30-36
1994 Spring Roundup	28-day		29.50	30
1994 Winter in the Rockies	28-day		29.50	30
1994 High Country Logging	28-day		29.50	30
1994 Confrontation	28-day		29.50	30
1994 A Welcome Sight	28-day		29.50	30

Four Seasons of the Eagle - S. Hardock

YEAR ISSUE	EDITION LIMIT	YEAR RETD.	ISSUE PRICE	*QUOTE U.S.$
1997 Winter Solstice	Open		39.95	40
1997 Spring Awakening	Open		39.95	40
1997 Summer's Glory	Open		39.95	40
1997 Autumn Bounty	Open		39.95	40

A Garden Song - M. Hanson

YEAR ISSUE	EDITION LIMIT	YEAR RETD.	ISSUE PRICE	*QUOTE U.S.$
1994 Winter's Splendor	28-day		29.50	30
1994 In Full Bloom	28-day		29.50	30
1994 Golden Glories	28-day		29.50	30
1995 Autumn's Elegance	28-day		29.50	30
1995 First Snowfall	28-day		29.50	30
1995 Robins in Spring	28-day		29.50	30
1995 Summer's Glow	28-day		29.50	30
1995 Fall's Serenade	28-day		29.50	30
1996 Sounds of Winter	28-day		29.50	30
1996 Springtime Haven	28-day		29.50	30

Gardens of the Orient - S. Suetomi

YEAR ISSUE	EDITION LIMIT	YEAR RETD.	ISSUE PRICE	*QUOTE U.S.$
1983 Flowering of Spring	10-day		19.50	20
1983 Festival of May	10-day		19.50	20
1983 Cherry Blossom Brocade	10-day		19.50	20
1983 Winter's Repose	10-day		19.50	20
1983 Garden Sanctuary	10-day		19.50	20
1983 Summer's Glory	10-day		19.50	20
1983 June's Creation	10-day		19.50	20
1983 New Year's Dawn	10-day		19.50	20
1983 Autumn Serenity	10-day		19.50	20
1983 Harvest Morning	10-day		19.50	20
1983 Tranquil Pond	10-day		19.50	20
1983 Morning Song	10-day		19.50	20

Glory of Christ - C. Micarelli

YEAR ISSUE	EDITION LIMIT	YEAR RETD.	ISSUE PRICE	*QUOTE U.S.$
1992 The Ascension	48-day		29.50	50-75
1992 Jesus Teaching	48-day		29.50	30
1993 Last Supper	48-day		29.50	30
1993 The Nativity	48-day		29.50	30
1993 The Baptism of Christ	48-day		29.50	30
1993 Jesus Heals the Sick	48-day		29.50	30
1994 Jesus Walks on Water	48-day		29.50	30
1994 Descent From the Cross	48-day		29.50	30

Glory of the Game - T. Fogarty

YEAR ISSUE	EDITION LIMIT	YEAR RETD.	ISSUE PRICE	*QUOTE U.S.$
1994 "Hank Aaron's Record-Breaking Home Run"	28-day		29.50	30
1994 "Bobby Thomson's Shot Heard 'Round the World"	28-day		29.50	30
1994 1969 Miracle Mets	28-day		29.50	30
1995 Reggie Jackson: Mr. October	28-day		29.50	30
1995 Don Larsen's Perfect World	28-day		29.50	30
1995 Babe Ruth's Called Shot	28-day		29.50	30
1995 Wille Mays: Greatest Catch	28-day		29.50	30
1995 Bill Mazeroski's Series	28-day		29.50	30
1996 Mickey Mantle's Tape Measure Home Run	28-day		29.50	30

The Golden Age of American Railroads - T. Xaras

YEAR ISSUE	EDITION LIMIT	YEAR RETD.	ISSUE PRICE	*QUOTE U.S.$
1991 The Blue Comet	14-day		29.50	65-75
1991 The Morning Local	14-day		29.50	60-75
1991 The Pennsylvania K-4	14-day		29.50	70-75
1991 Above the Canyon	14-day		29.50	65-75
1991 Portrait in Steam	14-day		29.50	60-75
1991 The Santa Fe Super Chief	14-day		29.50	75-105
1991 The Big Boy	14-day		29.50	60-75
1991 The Empire Builder	14-day		29.50	70-80
1992 An American Classic	14-day		29.50	60-75
1992 Final Destination	14-day		29.50	60-75

Golden Discoveries - L. Budge

YEAR ISSUE	EDITION LIMIT	YEAR RETD.	ISSUE PRICE	*QUOTE U.S.$
1995 Boot Bandits	28-day		29.95	30
1995 Hiding the Evidence	28-day		29.95	30
1995 Decoy Dilemma	28-day		29.95	30
1995 Fishing for Dinner	28-day		29.95	30
1996 Lunchtime Companions	28-day		29.95	30
1996 Friend or Foe?	28-day		29.95	30

Golden Puppy Portraits - P. Braun

YEAR ISSUE	EDITION LIMIT	YEAR RETD.	ISSUE PRICE	*QUOTE U.S.$
1994 Do Not Disturb!	28-day		29.50	30-35
1995 Teething Time	28-day		29.50	30-35
1995 Table Manners	28-day		29.50	30-35
1995 A Golden Bouquet	28-day		29.50	30-35
1995 Time For Bed	28-day		29.50	30-35
1995 Bathtime Blues	28-day		29.50	30-35
1996 Spinning a Yarn	28-day		29.50	30-35
1996 Partytime Puppy	28-day		29.50	30-35

Good Sports - J. Lamb

YEAR ISSUE	EDITION LIMIT	YEAR RETD.	ISSUE PRICE	*QUOTE U.S.$
1990 Wide Retriever	14-day	1994	29.50	36-40
1990 Double Play	14-day	1994	29.50	40-65
1990 Hole in One	14-day	1994	29.50	40-62
1990 The Bass Masters	14-day	1994	29.50	36-40
1990 Spotted on the Sideline	14-day	1994	29.50	36-40
1990 Slap Shot	14-day	1994	29.50	40-45
1991 Net Play	14-day	1994	29.50	34-45
1991 Bassetball	14-day	1994	29.50	36-40
1992 Boxer Rebellion	14-day	1994	29.50	33-40
1992 Great Try	14-day	1994	29.50	40

The Grateful Dead Art by Stanley Mouse - S. Mouse

YEAR ISSUE	EDITION LIMIT	YEAR RETD.	ISSUE PRICE	*QUOTE U.S.$
1997 One More Saturday Night	28-day		29.95	30
1997 The Grateful Dead Family Album	28-day		29.95	30
1998 Sunset Jester	28-day		29.95	30
1998 Lightning Rose	28-day		29.95	30
1998 Europe 81	28-day		29.95	30
1998 Timeless	28-day		29.95	30
1998 Dancing Jester	28-day		29.95	30
1998 Rose Photographer	28-day		29.95	30

Great Fighter Planes Of World War II - R. Waddey

YEAR ISSUE	EDITION LIMIT	YEAR RETD.	ISSUE PRICE	*QUOTE U.S.$
1992 Old Crow	14-day		29.50	30-35
1992 Big Hog	14-day		29.50	30-35
1992 P-47 Thunderbolt	14-day		29.50	30-35
1992 P-40 Flying Tiger	14-day		29.50	30-35
1992 F4F Wildcat	14-day		29.50	30-35
1992 P-38F Lightning	14-day		29.50	30-35
1993 F6F Hellcat	14-day		29.50	30-35
1993 P-39M Airacobra	14-day		29.50	30-35
1995 Memphis Belle	14-day		29.50	30-35
1995 The Dragon and His Tail	14-day		29.50	30-35
1995 Big Beautiful Doll	14-day		29.50	30-35

*Quotes have been rounded up to nearest dollar

YEAR ISSUE	EDITION LIMIT	YEAR RETD.	ISSUE PRICE	*QUOTE U.S.$
1995 Bats Out of Hell	14-day		29.50	30-35

Great Mammals of the Sea - Wyland

YEAR ISSUE	EDITION LIMIT	YEAR RETD.	ISSUE PRICE	*QUOTE U.S.$
1991 Orca Trio	14-day		35.00	45
1991 Hawaii Dolphins	14-day		35.00	45
1991 Orca Journey	14-day		35.00	42-45
1991 Dolphin Paradise	14-day		35.00	45
1991 Children of the Sea	14-day		35.00	45-60
1991 Kissing Dolphins	14-day		35.00	45-59
1991 Islands	14-day		35.00	45-60
1991 Orcas	14-day		35.00	45

The Greatest Show on Earth - F. Moody

YEAR ISSUE	EDITION LIMIT	YEAR RETD.	ISSUE PRICE	*QUOTE U.S.$
1981 Clowns	10-day		30.00	45
1981 Elephants	10-day		30.00	30-45
1981 Aerialists	10-day		30.00	18-45
1981 Great Parade	10-day		30.00	30-45
1981 Midway	10-day		30.00	30-45
1981 Equestrians	10-day		30.00	30-45
1982 Lion Tamer	10-day		30.00	30-45
1982 Grande Finale	10-day		30.00	30-45

Growing Up Together - P. Brooks

YEAR ISSUE	EDITION LIMIT	YEAR RETD.	ISSUE PRICE	*QUOTE U.S.$
1990 My Very Best Friends	14-day		29.50	30-36
1990 Tea for Two	14-day		29.50	30
1990 Tender Loving Care	14-day		29.50	30
1990 Picnic Pals	14-day		29.50	30
1991 Newfound Friends	14-day		29.50	30
1991 Kitten Caboodle	14-day		29.50	30
1991 Fishing Buddies	14-day		29.50	30
1991 Bedtime Blessings	14-day		29.50	30

The Historic Railways - T. Xaras

YEAR ISSUE	EDITION LIMIT	YEAR RETD.	ISSUE PRICE	*QUOTE U.S.$
1995 Harper's Ferry	28-day		29.95	30-45
1995 Horseshoe Curve	28-day		29.95	30-45
1995 Kentucky's Red River	28-day		29.95	30-45
1995 Sherman Hill Challenger	28-day		29.95	30-45
1996 New York Central's 4-6-4 Hudson	28-day		29.95	30-45
1996 Rails By The Seashore	28-day		29.95	30-45
1996 Steam in the High Sierras	28-day		29.95	30-45
1996 Evening Departure	28-day		29.95	30-45

The I Love Lucy Plate Collection - J. Kritz

YEAR ISSUE	EDITION LIMIT	YEAR RETD.	ISSUE PRICE	*QUOTE U.S.$
1989 California, Here We Come	14-day	1992	29.50	125-299
1989 It's Just Like Candy	14-day	1992	29.50	210-275
1990 The Big Squeeze	14-day	1992	29.50	150-275
1990 Eating the Evidence	14-day	1992	29.50	250-369
1990 Two of a Kind	14-day	1992	29.50	175-295
1991 Queen of the Gypsies	14-day	1992	29.50	195-300
1992 Night at the Copa	14-day	1992	29.50	150-195
1992 A Rising Problem	14-day	1992	29.50	150-195

James Dean Commemorative Issue - T. Blackshear

YEAR ISSUE	EDITION LIMIT	YEAR RETD.	ISSUE PRICE	*QUOTE U.S.$
1991 James Dean	14-day		37.50	75-195

James Dean The Legend - M. Weistling

YEAR ISSUE	EDITION LIMIT	YEAR RETD.	ISSUE PRICE	*QUOTE U.S.$
1992 Unforgotten Rebel	28-day		29.50	60-125

Japanese Floral Calendar - Shuho/Kage

YEAR ISSUE	EDITION LIMIT	YEAR RETD.	ISSUE PRICE	*QUOTE U.S.$
1981 New Year's Day	10-day		32.50	33-40
1982 Early Spring	10-day		32.50	33-40
1982 Spring	10-day		32.50	33-40
1982 Girl's Doll Day Festival	10-day		32.50	33-40
1982 Buddha's Birthday	10-day		32.50	33-40
1982 Early Summer	10-day		32.50	33-40
1982 Boy's Doll Day Festival	10-day		32.50	33-40
1982 Summer	10-day		32.50	33-40
1982 Autumn	10-day		32.50	33-40
1983 Festival of the Full Moon	10-day		32.50	33-40
1983 Late Autumn	10-day		32.50	33-40
1983 Winter	10-day		32.50	33-40

Jeff Gordon - Various

YEAR ISSUE	EDITION LIMIT	YEAR RETD.	ISSUE PRICE	*QUOTE U.S.$
1996 On The Warpath - S. Bass	28-day		35.00	35
1996 Headed to Victory Lane - R. Tanenbaum	28-day		35.00	35-45
1996 Gordon Takes the Title - S. Bass	28-day		35.00	35
1996 From Winner to Champion - R. Tanenbaum	28-day		35.00	35-45

The Jeweled Hummingbirds - J. Landenberger

YEAR ISSUE	EDITION LIMIT	YEAR RETD.	ISSUE PRICE	*QUOTE U.S.$
1989 Ruby-throated Hummingbirds	14-day		37.50	45-50
1989 Great Sapphire Wing Hummingbirds	14-day		37.50	45-50
1989 Ruby-Topaz Hummingbirds	14-day		37.50	45-50
1989 Andean Emerald Hummingbirds	14-day		37.50	45-50
1989 Garnet-throated Hummingbirds	14-day		37.50	45-50
1989 Blue-Headed Sapphire Hummingbirds	14-day		37.50	45-50
1989 Pearl Coronet Hummingbirds	14-day		37.50	45-50
1989 Amethyst-throated Sunangels	14-day		37.50	35-45

Joe Montana - Various

YEAR ISSUE	EDITION LIMIT	YEAR RETD.	ISSUE PRICE	*QUOTE U.S.$
1996 40,000 Yards - R. Tanenbaum	28-day		35.00	35-45
1996 Finding a Way to Win - A. Catalano	28-day		35.00	35-45
1996 Comeback Kid - A. Catalano	28-day		35.00	35-45
1996 Chief on the Field - Petronella	28-day		35.00	35-45

Kitten Classics - P. Cooper

YEAR ISSUE	EDITION LIMIT	YEAR RETD.	ISSUE PRICE	*QUOTE U.S.$
1985 Cat Nap	14-day		29.50	36-45
1985 Purrfect Treasure	14-day		29.50	30-45
1985 Wild Flower	14-day		29.50	30-45
1985 Birdwatcher	14-day		29.50	30-45
1985 Tiger's Fancy	14-day		29.50	33-45
1985 Country Kitty	14-day		29.50	33-45
1985 Little Rascal	14-day		29.50	30-45
1985 First Prize	14-day		29.50	30-45

Knick Knack Kitty Cat Sculptural - L. Yencho

YEAR ISSUE	EDITION LIMIT	YEAR RETD.	ISSUE PRICE	*QUOTE U.S.$
1996 Kittens in the Cupboard	Open		39.95	40
1996 Kittens in the Cushion	Open		39.95	40
1996 Kittens in the Plant	Open		39.95	40
1996 Kittens in the Yarn	Open		39.95	40

The Last Warriors - C. Ren

YEAR ISSUE	EDITION LIMIT	YEAR RETD.	ISSUE PRICE	*QUOTE U.S.$
1993 Winter of '41	28-day		29.50	30-40
1993 Morning of Reckoning	28-day		29.50	30-35
1993 Twilights Last Gleaming	28-day		29.50	30-40
1993 Lone Winter Journey	28-day		29.50	30-40
1994 Victory's Reward	28-day		29.50	30-40
1994 Solitary Hunter	28-day		29.50	30-35
1994 Solemn Reflection	28-day		29.50	30-35
1994 Confronting Danger	28-day		29.50	30-35
1995 Moment of Contemplation	28-day		29.50	30-35
1995 The Last Sunset	28-day		29.50	30-35

The Legend of Father Christmas - V. Dezerin

YEAR ISSUE	EDITION LIMIT	YEAR RETD.	ISSUE PRICE	*QUOTE U.S.$
1994 The Return of Father Christmas	28-day		29.50	30
1994 Gifts From Father Christmas	28-day		29.50	30
1994 The Feast of the Holiday	28-day		29.50	30
1995 Christmas Day Visitors	28-day		29.50	30
1995 Decorating the Tree	28-day		29.50	30
1995 The Snow Sculpture	28-day		29.50	30
1995 Skating on the Pond	28-day		29.50	30
1995 Holy Night	28-day		29.50	30

Legendary Warriors - M. Gentry

YEAR ISSUE	EDITION LIMIT	YEAR RETD.	ISSUE PRICE	*QUOTE U.S.$
1995 White Quiver and Scout	28-day		29.95	30
1995 Lakota Rendezvous	28-day		29.95	30
1995 Crazy Horse	28-day		29.95	30
1995 Sitting Bull's Vision	28-day		29.95	30
1996 Crazy Horse	28-day		29.95	30
1996 Sitting Bull's Vision	28-day		29.95	30
1996 Noble Surrender	28-day		29.95	30
1996 Sioux Thunder	28-day		29.95	30
1996 Eagle Dancer	28-day		29.95	30
1996 The Trap	28-day		29.95	30

A Lisi Martin Christmas - L. Martin

YEAR ISSUE	EDITION LIMIT	YEAR RETD.	ISSUE PRICE	*QUOTE U.S.$
1992 Santa's Littlest Reindeer	28-day		29.50	30-35
1993 Not A Creature Was Stirring	28-day		29.50	30-35
1993 Christmas Dreams	28-day		29.50	30-35
1993 The Christmas Story	28-day		29.50	30-35
1993 Trimming The Tree	28-day		29.50	30-35
1993 A Taste Of The Holidays	28-day		29.50	30-35
1993 The Night Before Christmas	28-day		29.50	30-35
1993 Christmas Watch	28-day		29.50	30-35
1995 Christmas Presence	28-day		29.50	30-35
1995 Nose to Nose	28-day		29.50	30-35

Little Fawns of the Forest - R. Manning

YEAR ISSUE	EDITION LIMIT	YEAR RETD.	ISSUE PRICE	*QUOTE U.S.$
1995 In the Morning Light	28-day		29.95	30
1995 Cool Reflections	28-day		29.95	30
1995 Nature's Lesson	28-day		29.95	30
1996 A Friendship Blossoms	28-day		29.95	30
1996 Innocent Companions	28-day		29.95	30
1996 New Life, New Day	28-day		29.95	30

Little House on the Prairie - E. Christopherson

YEAR ISSUE	EDITION LIMIT	YEAR RETD.	ISSUE PRICE	*QUOTE U.S.$
1986 Founder's Day Picnic	10-day		29.50	45-65
1986 The Woman's Harvest	10-day		29.50	30-65
1986 The Medicine Show	10-day		29.50	45-65
1986 Caroline's Eggs	10-day		29.50	30-65
1986 Mary's Gift	10-day		29.50	30-65
1986 Bell For Walnut Grove	10-day		29.50	30-65
1986 Ingalls Family Christmas	10-day		29.50	30-65
1986 Sweetheart Tree	10-day		29.50	30-65

Little Ladies - M.H. Bogart

YEAR ISSUE	EDITION LIMIT	YEAR RETD.	ISSUE PRICE	*QUOTE U.S.$
1989 Playing Bridesmaid	14-day	1991	29.50	70-75
1990 The Seamstress	14-day	1991	29.50	45-75
1990 Little Captive	14-day	1991	29.50	48-75
1990 Playing Mama	14-day	1991	29.50	40-75
1990 Susanna	14-day	1991	29.50	35-75
1990 Kitty's Bath	14-day	1991	29.50	45-75
1990 A Day in the Country	14-day	1991	29.50	40-75
1991 Sarah	14-day	1991	29.50	45-75
1991 First Party	14-day	1991	29.50	35-75
1991 The Magic Kitten	14-day	1991	29.50	35-75

The Little Rascals - Unknown

YEAR ISSUE	EDITION LIMIT	YEAR RETD.	ISSUE PRICE	*QUOTE U.S.$
1985 Three for the Show	10-day	1989	24.50	30-40
1985 My Gal	10-day	1989	24.50	25-40
1985 Skeleton Crew	10-day	1989	24.50	25-40
1985 Roughin' It	10-day	1989	24.50	25-40
1985 Spanky's Pranks	10-day	1989	24.50	25-40
1985 Butch's Challenge	10-day	1989	24.50	25-40
1985 Darla's Debut	10-day	1989	24.50	25-40
1985 Pete's Pal	10-day	1989	24.50	25-40

Little Shopkeepers - G. Gerardi

YEAR ISSUE	EDITION LIMIT	YEAR RETD.	ISSUE PRICE	*QUOTE U.S.$
1990 Sew Tired	14-day	1989	29.50	30-40
1991 Break Time	14-day	1989	29.50	30-40
1991 Purrfect Fit	14-day	1989	29.50	30-40
1991 Toying Around	14-day	1989	29.50	36-40
1991 Chain Reaction	14-day	1989	29.50	40-45
1991 Inferior Decorators	14-day	1989	29.50	36-40
1991 Tulip Tag	14-day	1989	29.50	36-40
1991 Candy Capers	14-day	1989	29.50	36-40

Lore Of The West - L. Danielle

YEAR ISSUE	EDITION LIMIT	YEAR RETD.	ISSUE PRICE	*QUOTE U.S.$
1993 A Mile In His Mocassins	28-day		29.50	30
1993 Path of Honor	28-day		29.50	30
1993 A Chief's Pride	28-day		29.50	30
1994 Pathways of the Pueblo	28-day		29.50	30
1994 In Her Seps	28-day		29.50	30
1994 Growing Up Brave	28-day		29.50	30
1994 Nomads of the Southwest	28-day		29.50	30
1994 Sacred Spirit of the Plains	28-day		29.50	30
1994 We'll Fight No More	28-day		29.50	30
1994 The End of the Trail	28-day		29.50	30

Love's Messengers - J. Grossman

YEAR ISSUE	EDITION LIMIT	YEAR RETD.	ISSUE PRICE	*QUOTE U.S.$
1995 To My Love	28-day	1994	29.50	40-45
1995 Cupid's Arrow	28-day	1994	29.50	40-45
1995 Love's Melody	28-day	1994	29.50	40-45
1995 A Token of Love	28-day	1994	29.50	40-45
1995 Harmony of Love	28-day	1994	29.50	40-45
1996 True Love's Offering	28-day	1994	29.95	40-45
1996 Love's In Bloom	28-day	1994	29.95	40-45
1996 To My Sweetheart	28-day	1994	29.95	40-45

Loving Lucy - M. Weistling

YEAR ISSUE	EDITION LIMIT	YEAR RETD.	ISSUE PRICE	*QUOTE U.S.$
1997 We're Having a Baby	28-day		29.95	30
1997 Soaking Up the Local Color	28-day		35.00	35
1997 Million Dollar Idea	28-day		35.00	35
1997 Chatter Box Ricardo	28-day		35.00	35
1997 Wanted: 'Sperinced Chicken Farmer	28-day		35.00	35

The Lucille Ball (Official) Commemorative Plate - M. Weistling

YEAR ISSUE	EDITION LIMIT	YEAR RETD.	ISSUE PRICE	*QUOTE U.S.$
1993 Lucy	28-day	1994	37.50	150-275

Lucy Meets the Stars - M. Weistling

YEAR ISSUE	EDITION LIMIT	YEAR RETD.	ISSUE PRICE	*QUOTE U.S.$
1997 L.A. at Last!	28-day		35.00	35-49
1997 Tennessee Ernie Visits	28-day		35.00	35-49
1997 Lucy Meets Harpo Marx	28-day		35.00	35-49
1997 Lucy Meets Orson Welles	28-day		35.00	35-49

Madonna And Child - Various

YEAR ISSUE	EDITION LIMIT	YEAR RETD.	ISSUE PRICE	*QUOTE U.S.$
1992 Madonna Della Sedia - R. Sanzio	28-day		37.50	38
1992 Virgin of the Rocks - L. DaVinci	28-day		37.50	38
1993 Madonna of Rosary - B. E. Murillo	28-day		37.50	38
1993 Sistine Madonna - R. Sanzio	28-day		37.50	38
1993 Virgin Adoring Christ Child - A. Correggio	28-day		37.50	38
1993 Virgin of the Grape - P. Mignard	28-day		37.50	38
1993 Madonna del Magnificat - S. Botticelli	28-day		37.50	38
1993 Madonna col Bambino - S. Botticelli	28-day		37.50	38

The Magical World of Legends & Myths - J. Shalatain

YEAR ISSUE	EDITION LIMIT	YEAR RETD.	ISSUE PRICE	*QUOTE U.S.$
1993 A Mother's Love	28-day	1994	35.00	35-55
1993 Dreams of Pegasus	28-day	1994	35.00	35-45
1994 Flight of the Pegasus	28-day	1994	35.00	35-45
1994 The Awakening	28-day	1994	35.00	35-45
1994 Once Upon a Dream	28-day	1994	35.00	35-45
1994 The Dawn of Romance	28-day	1994	35.00	35-45
1994 The Astral Unicorn	28-day	1994	35.00	35-45
1994 Flight into Paradise	28-day	1994	35.00	35
1995 Pegasus in the Stars	28-day	1994	35.00	35-45
1995 Unicorn of the Sea	28-day	1994	35.00	35

Majestic Birds of Prey - C.F. Riley

YEAR ISSUE	EDITION LIMIT	YEAR RETD.	ISSUE PRICE	*QUOTE U.S.$
1983 Golden Eagle	12,500		55.00	55-85
1983 Coopers Hawk	12,500		55.00	55-60
1983 Great Horned Owl	12,500		55.00	55-60
1983 Bald Eagle	12,500		55.00	55-60
1983 Barred Owl	12,500		55.00	55-60
1983 Sparrow Hawk	12,500		55.00	55-60
1983 Peregrine Falcon	12,500		55.00	55-60
1983 Osprey	12,500		55.00	55-60

Majesty of Flight - T. Hirata

YEAR ISSUE	EDITION LIMIT	YEAR RETD.	ISSUE PRICE	*QUOTE U.S.$
1989 The Eagle Soars	14-day		37.50	60-65
1989 Realm of the Red-Tail	14-day		37.50	40
1989 Coastal Journey	14-day		37.50	38-45
1989 Sentry of the North	14-day		37.50	38-48
1989 Commanding the Marsh	14-day		37.50	38
1990 The Vantage Point	14-day		29.50	38-45
1990 Silent Watch	14-day		29.50	48-65
1990 Fierce and Free	14-day		29.50	38-45

Man's Best Friend - L. Picken

YEAR ISSUE	EDITION LIMIT	YEAR RETD.	ISSUE PRICE	*QUOTE U.S.$
1992 Special Delivery	28-day		29.50	30
1992 Making Waves	28-day		29.50	30
1992 Good Catch	28-day		29.50	30
1993 Time For a Walk	28-day		29.50	30-45
1993 Faithful Friend	28-day		29.50	30-45
1993 Let's Play Ball	28-day		29.50	30-36
1993 Sitting Pretty	28-day		29.50	30
1993 Bedtime Story	28-day		29.50	30
1993 Trusted Companion	28-day		29.50	30

Mickey Mantle - R. Tanenbaum

YEAR ISSUE	EDITION LIMIT	YEAR RETD.	ISSUE PRICE	*QUOTE U.S.$
1996 The Mick	28-day		35.00	35-55
1996 536 Home Runs	28-day		35.00	35-55
1996 2,401 Games	28-day		35.00	35-55
1996 Switch Hitter	28-day		35.00	35-55
1996 16 Time All Star	28-day		35.00	35-55
1996 18 World Series Home Runs	28-day		35.00	35-55
1997 1956-A Crowning Year	28-day		35.00	35-55
1997 Remembering a Legendary Yankee	28-day		35.00	35-55

*Quotes have been rounded up to nearest dollar

Mike Schmidt - R. Tanenbaum

YEAR ISSUE	EDITION LIMIT	YEAR RETD.	ISSUE PRICE	*QUOTE U.S.$
1994 The Ultimate Competitor: Mike Schmidt	28-day		29.50	30
1995 A Homerun King	28-day		29.50	30
1995 An All Time, All Star	28-day		29.50	30
1995 A Career Retrospective	28-day		29.50	30

Milestones in Space - D. Dixon

YEAR ISSUE	EDITION LIMIT	YEAR RETD.	ISSUE PRICE	*QUOTE U.S.$
1994 Moon Landing	28-day		29.50	50-75
1995 Space Lab	28-day		29.50	30
1995 Maiden Flight of Columbia	28-day		29.50	30
1995 Free Walk in Space	28-day		29.50	30
1995 Lunar Rover	28-day		29.50	30
1995 Handshake in Space	28-day		29.50	30
1995 First Landing on Mars	28-day		29.50	30
1995 Voyager's Exploration	28-day		29.50	30

Mixed Company - P. Cooper

YEAR ISSUE	EDITION LIMIT	YEAR RETD.	ISSUE PRICE	*QUOTE U.S.$
1990 Two Against One	14-day		29.50	36-45
1990 A Sticky Situation	14-day		29.50	35-45
1990 What's Up	14-day		29.50	30-45
1990 All Wrapped Up	14-day		29.50	35-45
1990 Picture Perfect	14-day		29.50	30-45
1991 A Moment to Unwind	14-day		29.50	33-45
1991 Ole	14-day		29.50	33-45
1991 Picnic Prowlers	14-day		29.50	35-45

Murals From The Precious Moments Chapel - S. Butcher

YEAR ISSUE	EDITION LIMIT	YEAR RETD.	ISSUE PRICE	*QUOTE U.S.$
1995 The Pearl of Great Price	28-day		35.00	35
1995 The Good Samaritan	28-day		35.00	35
1996 The Prodigal Son	28-day		35.00	35
1996 The Good Shepherd	28-day		35.00	35

Mystic Warriors - C. Ren

YEAR ISSUE	EDITION LIMIT	YEAR RETD.	ISSUE PRICE	*QUOTE U.S.$
1992 Deliverance	28-day		29.50	30-75
1992 Mystic Warrior	28-day		29.50	30-40
1992 Sun Seeker	28-day		29.50	30-40
1992 Top Gun	28-day		29.50	30-40
1992 Man Who Walks Alone	28-day		29.50	30-40
1992 Windrider	28-day		29.50	30-40
1992 Spirit of the Plains	28-day		29.50	30-40
1993 Blue Thunder	28-day		29.50	30-40
1993 Sun Glow	28-day		29.50	30-40
1993 Peace Maker	28-day		29.50	30-40

Native American Legends - A. Biffignandi

YEAR ISSUE	EDITION LIMIT	YEAR RETD.	ISSUE PRICE	*QUOTE U.S.$
1996 Peace Pipe	28-day		29.95	30
1996 Feather-Woman	28-day		29.95	30
1996 Spirit of Serenity	28-day		29.95	30
1996 Enchanted Warrior	28-day		29.95	30
1996 Mystical Serenade	28-day		29.95	30
1996 Legend of Bridal Veil	28-day		29.95	30
1996 Seasons of Love	28-day		29.95	30
1996 A Bashful Courtship	28-day		29.95	30

Nature's Majestic Cats - M. Richter

YEAR ISSUE	EDITION LIMIT	YEAR RETD.	ISSUE PRICE	*QUOTE U.S.$
1993 Siberian Tiger	28-day		29.50	30-50
1993 Himalayan Snow Leopard	28-day		29.50	30
1993 African Lion	28-day		29.50	30
1994 Asian Clouded Leopard	28-day		29.50	30
1994 American Cougar	28-day		29.50	30
1994 East African Leopard	28-day		29.50	30
1994 African Cheetah	28-day		29.50	30
1994 Canadian Lynx	28-day		29.50	30

Nature's Nighttime Realm - G. Murray

YEAR ISSUE	EDITION LIMIT	YEAR RETD.	ISSUE PRICE	*QUOTE U.S.$
1992 Bobcat	28-day		29.50	30
1992 Cougar	28-day		29.50	30
1993 Jaguar	28-day		29.50	30
1993 White Tiger	28-day		29.50	30-40
1993 Lynx	28-day		29.50	30
1993 Lion	28-day		29.50	30
1993 Snow Leopard	28-day		29.50	30-50
1993 Cheetah	28-day		29.50	30

Nature's Quiet Moments - R. Parker

YEAR ISSUE	EDITION LIMIT	YEAR RETD.	ISSUE PRICE	*QUOTE U.S.$
1988 A Curious Pair	14-day		37.50	40-70
1988 Northern Morning	14-day		37.50	40-55
1988 Just Resting	14-day		37.50	40-50
1989 Waiting Out the Storm	14-day		37.50	38
1989 Creekside	14-day		37.50	38
1989 Autumn Foraging	14-day		37.50	38
1989 Old Man of the Mountain	14-day		37.50	38
1989 Mountain Blooms	14-day		37.50	38

Newsom Santa Takes a Break - T. Newsom

YEAR ISSUE	EDITION LIMIT	YEAR RETD.	ISSUE PRICE	*QUOTE U.S.$
1995 Santa's Last Stop	28-day		29.95	30
1996 Santa's Railroad	28-day		29.95	30
1996 A Jolly Good Catch	28-day		29.95	30
1996 Simple Pleasures	28-day		29.95	30
1996 Skating On Penguin Pond	28-day		29.95	30
1996 Santa's Sing-along	28-day		29.95	30
1996 Sledding Adventures	28-day		29.95	30
1997 Santa's Sweet Treats	28-day		29.95	30

Noble American Indian Women - D. Wright

YEAR ISSUE	EDITION LIMIT	YEAR RETD.	ISSUE PRICE	*QUOTE U.S.$
1989 Sacajawea	14-day		29.50	55-100
1990 Pocahontas	14-day		29.50	55-80
1990 Minnehaha	14-day		29.50	42-60
1990 Pine Leaf	14-day		29.50	42-60
1990 Lily of the Mohawk	14-day		29.50	40-48
1990 White Rose	14-day		29.50	40-45
1991 Lozen	14-day		29.50	40-48
1991 Falling Star	14-day		29.50	40-45

Noble Owls of America - J. Seerey-Lester

YEAR ISSUE	EDITION LIMIT	YEAR RETD.	ISSUE PRICE	*QUOTE U.S.$
1986 Morning Mist	15,000		55.00	55-60
1987 Prairie Sundown	15,000		55.00	55-60
1987 Winter Vigil	15,000		55.00	55-60
1987 Autumn Mist	15,000		75.00	60-75
1987 Dawn in the Willows	15,000		55.00	55-60
1987 Snowy Watch	15,000		60.00	60
1988 Hiding Place	15,000		55.00	55-60
1988 Waiting for Dusk	15,000		55.00	55-60

Nolan Ryan - R. Tanenbaum

YEAR ISSUE	EDITION LIMIT	YEAR RETD.	ISSUE PRICE	*QUOTE U.S.$
1994 The Strikeout Express	28-day		29.50	45-65
1994 Birth of a Legend	28-day		29.50	25-35
1994 Mr. Fastball	28-day		29.50	25-35
1994 Million-Dollar Player	28-day		29.50	25-35
1994 27 Seasons	28-day		29.50	25-35
1994 Farewell	28-day		29.50	25-35
1994 The Ryan Express	28-day		29.50	25-35

Norman Rockwell's Saturday Evening Post Baseball - N. Rockwell

YEAR ISSUE	EDITION LIMIT	YEAR RETD.	ISSUE PRICE	*QUOTE U.S.$
1992 100th Year of Baseball	Open		19.50	20
1993 The Rookie	Open		19.50	20
1993 The Dugout	Open		19.50	20
1993 Bottom of the Sixth	Open		19.50	20

North American Ducks - R. Lawrence

YEAR ISSUE	EDITION LIMIT	YEAR RETD.	ISSUE PRICE	*QUOTE U.S.$
1991 Autumn Flight	14-day		29.50	30-36
1991 The Resting Place	14-day		29.50	30
1991 Twin Flight	14-day		29.50	30
1992 Misty Morning	14-day		29.50	30
1992 Springtime Thaw	14-day		29.50	30
1992 Summer Retreat	14-day		29.50	30
1992 Overcast	14-day		29.50	30
1992 Perfect Pintails	14-day		29.50	30

North American Gamebirds - J. Killen

YEAR ISSUE	EDITION LIMIT	YEAR RETD.	ISSUE PRICE	*QUOTE U.S.$
1990 Ring-necked Pheasant	14-day		37.50	75
1990 Bobwhite Quail	14-day		37.50	80-100
1990 Ruffed Grouse	14-day		37.50	75
1990 Gambel Quail	14-day		37.50	38-42
1990 Mourning Dove	14-day		37.50	38-45
1990 Woodcock	14-day		37.50	38-45
1991 Chukar Partridge	14-day		37.50	38-45
1991 Wild Turkey	14-day		37.50	38-45

North American Waterbirds - R. Lawrence

YEAR ISSUE	EDITION LIMIT	YEAR RETD.	ISSUE PRICE	*QUOTE U.S.$
1988 Wood Ducks	14-day		37.50	45
1988 Hooded Mergansers	14-day		37.50	50
1988 Pintails	14-day		37.50	40-45
1988 Canada Geese	14-day		37.50	40-45
1989 American Widgeons	14-day		37.50	45-55
1989 Canvasbacks	14-day		37.50	45-55
1989 Mallard Pair	14-day		37.50	45-60
1989 Snow Geese	14-day		37.50	45

The Nutcracker Ballet - S. Fisher

YEAR ISSUE	EDITION LIMIT	YEAR RETD.	ISSUE PRICE	*QUOTE U.S.$
1978 Clara	28-day		19.50	36-50
1979 Godfather	28-day		19.50	15-25
1979 Sugar Plum Fairy	28-day		19.50	45-70
1979 Snow Queen and King	28-day		19.50	25-40
1980 Waltz of the Flowers	28-day		19.50	20-25
1980 Clara and the Prince	28-day		19.50	25-45

Official Honeymooner's Commemorative Plate - D. Bobnick

YEAR ISSUE	EDITION LIMIT	YEAR RETD.	ISSUE PRICE	*QUOTE U.S.$
1993 The Official Honeymooner's Commemorative Plate	28-day		37.50	200-349

The Official Honeymooners Plate Collection - D. Kilmer

YEAR ISSUE	EDITION LIMIT	YEAR RETD.	ISSUE PRICE	*QUOTE U.S.$
1987 The Honeymooners	14-day		24.50	75-270
1987 The Hucklebuck	14-day		24.50	125-250
1987 Baby, You're the Greatest	14-day		24.50	150-270
1988 The Golfer	14-day		24.50	110-290
1988 The TV Chefs	14-day		24.50	110-170
1988 Bang! Zoom!	14-day		24.50	75-150
1988 The Only Way to Travel	14-day		24.50	75-125
1988 The Honeymoon Express	14-day		24.50	72-160

On Wings of Eagles - J. Pitcher

YEAR ISSUE	EDITION LIMIT	YEAR RETD.	ISSUE PRICE	*QUOTE U.S.$
1994 "By Dawn's Early Light"	28-day		29.50	30
1994 Winter's Majestic Flight	28-day		29.50	30
1994 Over the Land of the Free	28-day		29.50	30
1994 Changing of the Guard	28-day		29.50	30
1995 Free Flight	28-day		29.50	30
1995 Morning Majesty	28-day		29.50	30
1995 Soaring Free	28-day		29.50	30
1994 Majestic Heights	28-day		29.50	30

Our Cherished Seas - S. Barlowe

YEAR ISSUE	EDITION LIMIT	YEAR RETD.	ISSUE PRICE	*QUOTE U.S.$
1992 Whale Song	48-day		37.50	38
1992 Lions of the Sea	48-day		37.50	38
1992 Flight of the Dolphins	48-day		37.50	38
1992 Palace of the Seals	48-day		37.50	38
1993 Orca Ballet	48-day		37.50	38
1993 Emporers of the Ice	48-day		37.50	38
1993 Sea Turtles	48-day		37.50	38
1993 Splendor of the Sea	48-day		37.50	38

Petals and Purrs - B. Harrison

YEAR ISSUE	EDITION LIMIT	YEAR RETD.	ISSUE PRICE	*QUOTE U.S.$
1988 Blushing Beauties	14-day		24.50	55
1988 Spring Fever	14-day		24.50	38-55
1988 Morning Glories	14-day		24.50	45-55
1988 Forget-Me-Not	14-day		24.50	36-55
1989 Golden Fancy	14-day		24.50	30-55
1989 Pink Lillies	14-day		24.50	30-55
1989 Summer Sunshine	14-day		24.50	55
1989 Siamese Summer	14-day		24.50	55

Pillars of Baseball - A. Hicks

YEAR ISSUE	EDITION LIMIT	YEAR RETD.	ISSUE PRICE	*QUOTE U.S.$
1995 Babe Ruth	28-day		29.95	30-35
1995 Lou Gehrig	28-day		29.95	30
1995 Ty Cobb	28-day		29.95	30
1996 Cy Young	28-day		29.95	30
1996 Honus Wagner	28-day		29.95	30
1996 Rogers Hornsby	28-day		29.95	30
1996 Dizzy Dean	28-day		29.95	30
1996 Christy Mathewson	28-day		29.95	30

Portraits of Childhood - T. Utz

YEAR ISSUE	EDITION LIMIT	YEAR RETD.	ISSUE PRICE	*QUOTE U.S.$
1981 Butterfly Magic	28-day		24.95	14-40
1981 Sweet Dreams	28-day		24.95	25-40
1981 Turtle Talk	28-day		24.95	36-40
1981 Friends Forever	28-day		24.95	35-40

Portraits of Jesus - W. Sallman

YEAR ISSUE	EDITION LIMIT	YEAR RETD.	ISSUE PRICE	*QUOTE U.S.$
1994 Jesus, The Good Shepherd	28-day		29.50	30
1994 Jesus in the Garden	28-day		29.50	30
1994 Jesus, Children's Friend	28-day		29.50	30
1994 The Lord's Supper	28-day		29.50	30
1994 Christ at Dawn	28-day		29.50	30
1994 Christ at Heart's Door	28-day		29.50	30
1994 Portrait of Christ	28-day		29.50	30
1994 Madonna and Christ Child	28-day		29.50	30

Portraits of the Bald Eagle - J. Pitcher

YEAR ISSUE	EDITION LIMIT	YEAR RETD.	ISSUE PRICE	*QUOTE U.S.$
1993 Ruler of the Sky	28-day		37.50	40-45
1993 In Bold Defiance	28-day		37.50	40
1993 Master Of The Summer Skies	28-day		37.50	40
1993 Spring's Sentinel	28-day		37.50	40

Portraits of the Wild - J. Meger

YEAR ISSUE	EDITION LIMIT	YEAR RETD.	ISSUE PRICE	*QUOTE U.S.$
1994 Interlude	28-day		29.50	30-35
1994 Winter Solitude	28-day		29.50	30-35
1994 Devoted Protector	28-day		29.50	30
1994 Call of Autumn	28-day		29.50	30
1994 Watchful Eyes	28-day		29.50	30
1994 Babies of Spring	28-day		29.50	30
1994 Rocky Mountain Grandeur	28-day		29.50	30
1995 Unbridled Power	28-day		29.50	30
1995 Moonlight Vigil	28-day		29.50	30
1995 Monarch of the Plains	28-day		29.50	30-35
1995 Tender Courtship	28-day		29.50	30-40

Precious Moments Bible Story - S. Butcher

YEAR ISSUE	EDITION LIMIT	YEAR RETD.	ISSUE PRICE	*QUOTE U.S.$
1990 Come Let Us Adore Him	28-day		29.50	30
1992 They Followed The Star	28-day		29.50	30
1992 The Flight Into Egypt	28-day		29.50	30
1992 The Carpenter Shop	28-day		29.50	30
1992 Jesus In The Temple	28-day		29.50	30
1992 The Crucifixion	28-day		29.50	30
1993 He Is Not Here	28-day		29.50	30

Precious Moments Classics - S. Butcher

YEAR ISSUE	EDITION LIMIT	YEAR RETD.	ISSUE PRICE	*QUOTE U.S.$
1993 God Loveth A Cheerful Giver	28-day		35.00	35
1993 Make A Joyful Noise	28-day		35.00	35
1994 Love One Another	28-day		35.00	35
1994 You Have Touched So Many Hearts	28-day		35.00	35
1994 Praise the Lord Anyhow	28-day		35.00	35
1994 I Believe in Miracles	28-day		35.00	35
1994 Good Friends Are Forever	28-day		35.00	35
1994 Jesus Loves Me	28-day		35.00	35
1995 Friendship Hits the Spot	28-day		35.00	35
1995 To My Deer Friend	28-day		35.00	35

Precious Moments of Childhood Plates - T. Utz

YEAR ISSUE	EDITION LIMIT	YEAR RETD.	ISSUE PRICE	*QUOTE U.S.$
1979 Friend in the Sky	28-day		21.50	50-70
1980 Sand in her Shoe	28-day		21.50	35-55
1980 Snow Bunny	28-day		21.50	35-55
1980 Seashells	28-day		21.50	38-55
1981 Dawn	28-day		21.50	35-55
1982 My Kitty	28-day		21.50	36-55

Precious Moments Words of Love - S. Butcher

YEAR ISSUE	EDITION LIMIT	YEAR RETD.	ISSUE PRICE	*QUOTE U.S.$
1995 Your Friendship Is Soda-licious	28-day		35.00	35
1996 Your Love Is So Uplifting	28-day		35.00	35
1996 Love Is From Above	28-day		35.00	35
1996 Love Lifted Me	28-day		35.00	35

Precious Portraits - B. P. Gutmann

YEAR ISSUE	EDITION LIMIT	YEAR RETD.	ISSUE PRICE	*QUOTE U.S.$
1987 Sunbeam	14-day	1991	24.50	30-95
1987 Mischief	14-day	1991	24.50	30-95
1987 Peach Blossom	14-day	1991	24.50	30-95
1987 Goldilocks	14-day	1991	24.50	30-95
1987 Fairy Gold	14-day	1991	24.50	30-95
1987 Bunny	14-day	1991	24.50	30-95

The Prideful Ones - C. DeHaan

YEAR ISSUE	EDITION LIMIT	YEAR RETD.	ISSUE PRICE	*QUOTE U.S.$
1994 Village Markers	28-day		29.50	30
1994 His Pride	28-day		29.50	30
1994 Appeasing the Water People	28-day		29.50	30
1994 Tribal Guardian	28-day		29.50	30
1994 Autumn Passage	28-day		29.50	30
1994 Winter Hunter	28-day		29.50	30
1994 Silent Trail Break	28-day		29.50	30
1994 Water Breaking	28-day		29.50	30
1994 Crossing at the Big Trees	28-day		29.50	30

YEAR ISSUE	EDITION LIMIT	YEAR RETD.	ISSUE PRICE	*QUOTE U.S.$
1995 Winter Songsinger	28-day		29.50	30

Princesses of the Plains - D. Wright

YEAR ISSUE	EDITION LIMIT	YEAR RETD.	ISSUE PRICE	*QUOTE U.S.$
1993 Prairie Flower	28-day		29.50	26-35
1993 Snow Princess	28-day		29.50	30-40
1993 Wild Flower	28-day		29.50	30-40
1993 Noble Beauty	28-day		29.50	35-40
1993 Winter's Rose	28-day		29.50	30-40
1993 Gentle Beauty	28-day		29.50	30-40
1994 Nature's Guardian	28-day		29.50	30-40
1994 Mountain Princess	28-day		29.50	30-40
1995 Proud Dreamer	28-day		29.50	30-40
1995 Spring Maiden	28-day		29.50	30-40

Proud Indian Families - K. Freeman

YEAR ISSUE	EDITION LIMIT	YEAR RETD.	ISSUE PRICE	*QUOTE U.S.$
1991 The Storyteller	14-day		29.50	40-45
1991 The Power of the Basket	14-day		29.50	30-36
1991 The Naming Ceremony	14-day		29.50	30
1992 Playing With Tradition	14-day		29.50	30
1992 Preparing the Berry Harvest	14-day		29.50	30
1992 Ceremonial Dress	14-day		29.50	30
1992 Sounds of the Forest	14-day		29.50	30
1992 The Marriage Ceremony	14-day		29.50	30
1993 The Jewelry Maker	14-day		29.50	30
1993 Beautiful Creations	14-day		29.50	30

Proud Innocence - J. Schmidt

YEAR ISSUE	EDITION LIMIT	YEAR RETD.	ISSUE PRICE	*QUOTE U.S.$
1994 Desert Bloom	28-day		29.50	30
1994 Little Drummer	28-day		29.50	30
1995 Young Archer	28-day		29.50	30-36
1995 Morning Child	28-day		29.50	30
1995 Wise One	28-day		29.50	30
1995 Sun Blossom	28-day		29.50	30
1995 Laughing Heart	28-day		29.50	30
1995 Gentle Flower	28-day		29.50	30

The Proud Nation - R. Swanson

YEAR ISSUE	EDITION LIMIT	YEAR RETD.	ISSUE PRICE	*QUOTE U.S.$
1989 Navajo Little One	14-day		24.50	50-75
1989 In a Big Land	14-day		24.50	35-40
1989 Out with Mama's Flock	14-day		24.50	30-40
1989 Newest Little Sheepherder	14-day		24.50	36-45
1989 Dressed Up for the Powwow	14-day		24.50	30-35
1989 Just a Few Days Old	14-day		24.50	30-35
1989 Autumn Treat	14-day		24.50	30-45
1989 Up in the Red Rocks	14-day		24.50	35-80

Puppy Playtime - J. Lamb

YEAR ISSUE	EDITION LIMIT	YEAR RETD.	ISSUE PRICE	*QUOTE U.S.$
1987 Double Take-Cocker Spaniels	14-day		24.50	65-80
1987 Catch of the Day-Golden Retrievers	14-day		24.50	45-60
1987 Cabin Fever-Black Labradors	14-day		24.50	50-60
1987 Weekend Gardener-Lhasa Apsos	14-day		24.50	30-45
1987 Getting Acquainted-Beagles	14-day		24.50	30-36
1987 Hanging Out-German Shepherd	14-day		24.50	40-45
1987 New Leash on Life-Mini Schnauzer	14-day		24.50	30-59
1987 Fun and Games-Poodle	14-day		24.50	30-65

Quiet Moments Of Childhood - D. Green

YEAR ISSUE	EDITION LIMIT	YEAR RETD.	ISSUE PRICE	*QUOTE U.S.$
1991 Elizabeth's Afternoon Tea	14-day		29.50	45
1991 Christina's Secret Garden	14-day		29.50	36
1991 Eric & Erin's Storytime	14-day		29.50	30
1992 Jessica's Tea Party	14-day		29.50	33
1992 Megan & Monique's Bakery	14-day		29.50	36
1992 Children's Day By The Sea	14-day		29.50	30
1992 Jordan's Playful Pups	14-day		29.50	33
1992 Daniel's Morning Playtime	14-day		29.50	30

The Quilted Countryside: A Signature Collection by Mel Steele - M. Steele

YEAR ISSUE	EDITION LIMIT	YEAR RETD.	ISSUE PRICE	*QUOTE U.S.$
1991 The Old Country Store	14-day		29.50	36
1991 Winter's End	14-day		29.50	36
1991 The Quilter's Cabin	14-day		29.50	45
1991 Spring Cleaning	14-day		29.50	36
1991 Summer Harvest	14-day		29.50	30
1991 The Country Merchant	14-day		29.50	36
1992 Wash Day	14-day		29.50	30
1992 The Antiques Store	14-day		29.50	33

Remembering Norma Jeane - F. Accornero

YEAR ISSUE	EDITION LIMIT	YEAR RETD.	ISSUE PRICE	*QUOTE U.S.$
1994 The Girl Next Door	28-day		29.50	48-95
1994 Her Day in the Sun	28-day		29.50	45-89
1994 A Star is Born	28-day		29.50	45-85
1994 Beauty Secrets	28-day		29.50	40-55
1995 In the Spotlight	28-day		29.50	40-50
1995 Bathing Beauty	28-day		29.50	30-40
1995 Young & Carefree	28-day		29.50	30-40
1995 Free Spirit	28-day		29.50	30-35
1995 A Country Girl at Heart	28-day		29.50	30-40
1996 Hometown Girl	28-day		29.50	30-35

The Renaissance Angels - L. Bywaters

YEAR ISSUE	EDITION LIMIT	YEAR RETD.	ISSUE PRICE	*QUOTE U.S.$
1994 Doves of Peace	28-day		29.50	30-65
1994 Angelic Innocence	28-day		29.50	36-65
1994 Joy to the World	28-day		29.50	30-65
1995 Angel of Faith	28-day		29.50	30-65
1995 The Christmas Star	28-day		29.50	30-65
1995 Trumpeter's Call	28-day		29.50	30-65
1995 Harmonious Heavens	28-day		29.50	30-65
1995 The Angels Sing	28-day		29.50	30-65

Rockwell Home of the Brave - N. Rockwell

YEAR ISSUE	EDITION LIMIT	YEAR RETD.	ISSUE PRICE	*QUOTE U.S.$
1981 Reminiscing	18,000		35.00	55
1981 Hero's Welcome	18,000		35.00	55
1981 Back to his Old Job	18,000		35.00	55
1981 War Hero	18,000		35.00	35-55
1982 Willie Gillis in Church	18,000		35.00	55
1982 War Bond	18,000		35.00	35-55
1982 Uncle Sam Takes Wings	18,000		35.00	55-75
1982 Taking Mother over the Top	18,000		35.00	35-55

Romance of the Rails - D. Tutwiler

YEAR ISSUE	EDITION LIMIT	YEAR RETD.	ISSUE PRICE	*QUOTE U.S.$
1994 Starlight Limited	28-day		29.50	30-50
1994 Portland Rose	28-day		29.50	30-50
1994 Orange Blossom Special	28-day		29.50	30-50
1994 Morning Star	28-day		29.50	30-50
1994 Crescent Limited	28-day		29.50	30-50
1994 Sunset Limited	28-day		29.50	30-50
1994 Western Star	28-day		29.50	30-50
1994 Sunrise Limited	28-day		29.50	30-50
1995 The Blue Bonnett	28-day		29.50	30-50
1995 The Pine Tree Limited	28-day		29.50	30-50

Romantic Castles of Europe - D. Sweet

YEAR ISSUE	EDITION LIMIT	YEAR RETD.	ISSUE PRICE	*QUOTE U.S.$
1990 Ludwig's Castle	19,500		55.00	55
1991 Palace of the Moors	19,500		55.00	55
1991 Swiss Isle Fortress	19,500		55.00	55-75
1991 The Legendary Castle of Leeds	19,500		55.00	55-65
1991 Davinci's Chambord	19,500		55.00	55-65
1991 Eilean Donan	19,500		55.00	55
1992 Eltz Castle	19,500		55.00	55
1992 Kylemore Abbey	19,500		55.00	55

Romantic Flights of Fancy - Q. Lemonds

YEAR ISSUE	EDITION LIMIT	YEAR RETD.	ISSUE PRICE	*QUOTE U.S.$
1994 Sunlit Waltz	28-day		29.50	30
1994 Morning Minuet	28-day		29.50	30
1994 Evening Solo	28-day		29.50	30
1994 Summer Sonata	28-day		29.50	30
1995 Twilight Tango	28-day		29.50	30
1995 Sunset Ballet	28-day		29.50	30
1995 Exotic Interlude	28-day		29.50	30-36
1995 Sunrise Samba	28-day		29.50	30

Romantic Victorian Keepsake - J. Grossman

YEAR ISSUE	EDITION LIMIT	YEAR RETD.	ISSUE PRICE	*QUOTE U.S.$
1992 Dearest Kiss	28-day		35.00	35-55
1992 First Love	28-day		35.00	35-55
1992 As Fair as a Rose	28-day		35.00	35-55
1992 Springtime Beauty	28-day		35.00	35-55
1992 Summertime Fancy	28-day		35.00	35-55
1992 Bonnie Blue Eyes	28-day		35.00	35-55
1992 Precious Friends	28-day		35.00	35-55
1994 Bonnets and Bouquets	28-day		35.00	35-55
1994 My Beloved Teddy	28-day		35.00	35-55
1994 A Sweet Romance	28-day		35.00	35-55

A Salute to Mickey Mantle - T. Fogarty

YEAR ISSUE	EDITION LIMIT	YEAR RETD.	ISSUE PRICE	*QUOTE U.S.$
1996 1961 Home Run Duel	28-day		35.00	35
1996 Power at the Plate	28-day		35.00	35
1996 Saluting a Magnificent Yankee	28-day		35.00	35
1996 Triple Crown Achievement	28-day		35.00	35
1996 1953 Grand Slam	28-day		35.00	35
1997 1963's Famous Facade Homer	28-day		35.00	35
1997 Mickey as a Rookie	28-day		35.00	35
1997 A Look Back	28-day		35.00	35

Santa Takes a Break - T. Newsom

YEAR ISSUE	EDITION LIMIT	YEAR RETD.	ISSUE PRICE	*QUOTE U.S.$
1995 Santa's Last Stop	28-day		29.95	30
1995 Santa's Railroad	28-day		29.95	30
1995 A Jolly Good Catch	28-day		29.95	30
1995 Simple Pleasures	28-day		29.95	30
1996 Skating On Penguin Pond	28-day		29.95	30
1996 Santa's Sing Along	28-day		29.95	30
1996 Sledding Adventures	28-day		29.95	30
1996 Santa's Sweet Treats	28-day		29.95	30

The Saturday Evening Post - N. Rockwell

YEAR ISSUE	EDITION LIMIT	YEAR RETD.	ISSUE PRICE	*QUOTE U.S.$
1989 The Wonders of Radio	14-day		35.00	45-50
1989 Easter Morning	14-day		35.00	60
1989 The Facts of Life	14-day		35.00	35-45
1990 The Window Washer	14-day		35.00	45
1990 First Flight	14-day		35.00	54-60
1990 Traveling Companion	14-day		35.00	35-60
1990 Jury Room	14-day		35.00	35-50
1990 Furlough	14-day		35.00	50-55

Scenes of An American Christmas - B. Perry

YEAR ISSUE	EDITION LIMIT	YEAR RETD.	ISSUE PRICE	*QUOTE U.S.$
1994 I'll Be Home for Christmas	28-day		29.50	30-35
1994 Christmas Eve Worship	28-day		29.50	30-35
1994 A Holiday Happening	28-day		29.50	30-35
1994 A Long Winter's Night	28-day		29.50	30-35
1994 The Sounds of Christmas	28-day		29.50	30-35
1994 Dear Santa	28-day		29.50	30-35
1995 An Afternoon Outing	28-day		29.50	30-35
1995 Winter Worship	28-day		29.50	30-35

Seasons of the Bald Eagle - J. Pitcher

YEAR ISSUE	EDITION LIMIT	YEAR RETD.	ISSUE PRICE	*QUOTE U.S.$
1991 Autumn in the Mountains	14-day		37.50	45-55
1991 Winter in the Valley	14-day		37.50	45-55
1991 Spring on the River	14-day		37.50	55-65
1991 Summer on the Seacoast	14-day		37.50	70-80

Sharing Life's Most Precious Memories - S. Butcher

YEAR ISSUE	EDITION LIMIT	YEAR RETD.	ISSUE PRICE	*QUOTE U.S.$
1995 Thee I Love	28-day		35.00	35
1995 The Joy of the Lord Is My Strength	28-day		35.00	35
1995 May Your Every Wish Come True	28-day		35.00	35
1996 I'm So Glad That God	28-day		35.00	35
1996 Heaven Bless You	28-day		35.00	35

Sharing the Moments - S. Butcher

YEAR ISSUE	EDITION LIMIT	YEAR RETD.	ISSUE PRICE	*QUOTE U.S.$
1995 You Have Touched So Many Hearts	28-day		35.00	35
1996 Friendship Hits The Spot	28-day		35.00	35
1996 Jesus Love Me	28-day		35.00	35

Single Issues - T. Utz

YEAR ISSUE	EDITION LIMIT	YEAR RETD.	ISSUE PRICE	*QUOTE U.S.$
1983 Princess Grace	21-day		39.50	50-79

Small Wonders of the Wild - C. Frace

YEAR ISSUE	EDITION LIMIT	YEAR RETD.	ISSUE PRICE	*QUOTE U.S.$
1989 Hideaway	14-day		29.50	45-50
1990 Young Explorers	14-day		29.50	36-50
1990 Three of a Kind	14-day		29.50	50-75
1990 Quiet Morning	14-day		29.50	36-50
1990 Eyes of Wonder	14-day		29.50	30-50
1990 Ready for Adventure	14-day		29.50	30-50
1990 Uno	14-day		29.50	30-50
1990 Exploring a New World	14-day		29.50	30-50

Space, The Final Frontier - D. Ward

YEAR ISSUE	EDITION LIMIT	YEAR RETD.	ISSUE PRICE	*QUOTE U.S.$
1996 To Boldly Go...	28-day		37.50	40-75
1996 Second Star From The Right	28-day		37.50	30-40
1996 Signs of Intelligence	28-day		37.50	30-40
1996 Preparing To Cloak	28-day		37.50	30-40
1997 Distant Worlds	28-day		37.50	38
1997 Where No One Has Gone Before	28-day		37.50	38
1997 Beyond the Neutral Zone	28-day		37.50	38
1997 We Are Borg	28-day		37.50	38
1997 Cataloging Gascous Anomalies	28-day		37.50	38
1997 Searching the Galaxy	28-day		37.50	38

Spirit of the Mustang - C. DeHaan

YEAR ISSUE	EDITION LIMIT	YEAR RETD.	ISSUE PRICE	*QUOTE U.S.$
1995 Winter's Thunder	28-day		29.95	30-35
1995 Moonlit Run	28-day		29.95	30-35
1995 Morning Reverie	28-day		29.95	30-35
1995 Autumn Respite	28-day		29.95	30-35
1996 Spring Frolic	28-day		29.95	30-35
1996 Dueling Mustangs	28-day		29.95	30-35
1996 Tranquil Waters	28-day		29.95	30-35
1996 Summer Squall	28-day		29.95	30-40

Sporting Generation - J. Lamb

YEAR ISSUE	EDITION LIMIT	YEAR RETD.	ISSUE PRICE	*QUOTE U.S.$
1991 Like Father, Like Son	14-day		29.50	45-55
1991 Golden Moments	14-day		29.50	50-55
1991 The Lookout	14-day		29.50	36-55
1992 Picking Up The Scent	14-day		29.50	36-55
1992 First Time Out	14-day		29.50	40-55
1992 Who's Tracking Who	14-day		29.50	40-55
1992 Springing Into Action	14-day		29.50	35-55
1992 Point of Interest	14-day		29.50	35-55

STAR TREK® : 25th Anniversary Commemorative - T. Blackshear

YEAR ISSUE	EDITION LIMIT	YEAR RETD.	ISSUE PRICE	*QUOTE U.S.$
1991 STAR TREK 25th Anniversary Commemorative Plate	14-day		37.50	200-349
1991 SPOCK	14-day		35.00	190-275
1991 Kirk	14-day		35.00	125-265
1992 McCoy	14-day		35.00	80-195
1992 Uhura	14-day		35.00	80-155
1992 Scotty	14-day		35.00	100-165
1993 Sulu	14-day		35.00	90-190
1993 Chekov	14-day		35.00	90-185
1994 U.S.S. Enterprise NCC-1701	14-day		35.00	90-200

STAR TREK® : 30 Years - T. Treadway

YEAR ISSUE	EDITION LIMIT	YEAR RETD.	ISSUE PRICE	*QUOTE U.S.$
1997 Captain's Tribute	28-day		37.50	38-95
1997 Second in Command	28-day		37.50	30-95
1997 Starfleet Doctors	28-day		37.50	38-89
1998 Starfleet Navigators	28-day		37.50	38-85
1998 Starfleet Security	28-day		37.50	38-99
1998 Women of Star Trek	28-day		37.50	38-95
1998 Engineers Tribute	28-day		37.50	30-89

STAR TREK® : Deep Space 9 - M. Weistling

YEAR ISSUE	EDITION LIMIT	YEAR RETD.	ISSUE PRICE	*QUOTE U.S.$
1994 Commander Benjamin Sisko	28-day		35.00	35-95
1994 Security Chief Odo	28-day		35.00	45-79
1994 Major Kira Nerys	28-day		35.00	55-125
1994 Space Station	28-day		35.00	55—275
1994 Proprietor Quark	28-day		35.00	45-85
1995 Doctor Julian Bashir	28-day		35.00	35-79
1995 Lieutenant Jadzia Dax	28-day		35.00	35-255
1995 Chief Miles O'Brien	28-day		35.00	35-75

STAR TREK® : Deep Space 9 The Episodes - D. Blair

YEAR ISSUE	EDITION LIMIT	YEAR RETD.	ISSUE PRICE	*QUOTE U.S.$
1997 The Way of the Warrior	28-day		39.95	40
1997 Emissary	28-day		39.95	40

STAR TREK® : First Contact Sculptural Plate - J. Eaves

YEAR ISSUE	EDITION LIMIT	YEAR RETD.	ISSUE PRICE	*QUOTE U.S.$
1998 Maiden Voyage	28-day		49.95	50

STAR TREK® : First Contact: A New Dimension - J. Eaves

YEAR ISSUE	EDITION LIMIT	YEAR RETD.	ISSUE PRICE	*QUOTE U.S.$
1998 U.S.S. Enterprise NCC-1701-E	28-day		55.00	55

STAR TREK® : First Contact: The Battle Begins - M. D. Ward

YEAR ISSUE	EDITION LIMIT	YEAR RETD.	ISSUE PRICE	*QUOTE U.S.$
1998 U.S.S. Defiant	28-day		39.95	40
1998 Borg Cube	28-day		39.95	40
1998 U.S.S. Enterprise NCC-1701-E	28-day		39.95	40
1998 Borg Sphere	28-day		39.95	40

STAR TREK® : First Contact: The Collective - K. Birdsong

YEAR ISSUE	EDITION LIMIT	YEAR RETD.	ISSUE PRICE	*QUOTE U.S.$
1998 Duty vs. Desire	28-day		19.95	20
1998 The Borg Are Back	28-day		19.95	20

STAR TREK® : Generations - K. Birdsong

YEAR ISSUE	EDITION LIMIT	YEAR RETD.	ISSUE PRICE	*QUOTE U.S.$
1996 The Ultimate Confrontation	28-day		35.00	55-85
1996 Kirk's Final Voyage	28-day		35.00	35-95
1996 Meeting In The Nexus	28-day		35.00	35-80
1996 Picard's Christmas In The Nexus	28-day		35.00	35-89
1996 Worf's Ceremony	28-day		35.00	35-89

*Quotes have been rounded up to nearest dollar

YEAR ISSUE	EDITION LIMIT	YEAR RETD.	ISSUE PRICE	*QUOTE U.S.$
1996 The Final Plot/Duras Sisters	28-day		35.00	35-89
1997 Stellar Cartography	28-day		35.00	35-95
1997 Act of Courage	28-day		35.00	35-89

STAR TREK® : Life of Spock - S. Stanley

YEAR ISSUE	EDITION LIMIT	YEAR RETD.	ISSUE PRICE	*QUOTE U.S.$
1997 Spock Reborn	28-day		35.00	35-99
1997 Amok Time	28-day		35.00	35-99
1997 Voyage Home	28-day		35.00	35
1997 Wrath of Khan	28-day		35.00	35
1997 Unification	28-day		35.00	35

STAR TREK® : Ships in Motion - N/A

YEAR ISSUE	EDITION LIMIT	YEAR RETD.	ISSUE PRICE	*QUOTE U.S.$
1997 Full Impulse	Open		49.95	50-75
1997 Set a Course - Warp 5	Open		49.95	50-95
1997 Warp Speed	Open		49.95	50-59
1997 Maiden Voyage	Open		49.95	50-59

STAR TREK® : Starships Mini Plates - K. Birdsong

YEAR ISSUE	EDITION LIMIT	YEAR RETD.	ISSUE PRICE	*QUOTE U.S.$
1997 U.S.S. Enterprise NCC-1701	28-day		25.90	26
1997 Klingon Battlecruiser	28-day		set	set
1997 U.S.S. Enterprise NCC-1701 D	28-day		set	set
1997 Romulan Warbird	28-day		set	set
1997 U.S.S. Enterprise NCC-1701 A	28-day		set	set
1997 Ferengei Marauder	28-day		set	set
1997 Klingon Bird of Prey	28-day		set	set
1997 Cardassian Galor Warship	28-day		set	set
1997 Triple Nacelled U.S.S. Enterprise	28-day		set	set
1997 U.S.S. Excelsior	28-day		set	set
1997 U.S.S. Defiant NX-74205	28-day		set	set
1997 U.S.S. Voyager NCC-74656	28-day		set	set

STAR TREK® : The Movies - M. Weistling

YEAR ISSUE	EDITION LIMIT	YEAR RETD.	ISSUE PRICE	*QUOTE U.S.$
1994 STAR TREK IV: The Voyage Home	28-day		35.00	65-89
1994 STAR TREK II: The Wrath of Khan	28-day		35.00	65-85
1994 STAR TREK VI: The Undiscovered Country	28-day		35.00	65-85
1995 STAR TREK III: The Search For Spock	28-day		35.00	29-89
1995 STAR TREK V: The Final Frontier	28-day		35.00	29-89
1996 Triumphant Return	28-day		35.00	65-85
1996 Destruction of the Reliant	28-day		35.00	65-89
1996 STAR TREK I: The Motion Picture	28-day		35.00	65-95

STAR TREK® : The Next Generation - T. Blackshear

YEAR ISSUE	EDITION LIMIT	YEAR RETD.	ISSUE PRICE	*QUOTE U.S.$
1993 Captain Jean-Luc Picard	28-day		35.00	70-149
1993 Commander William T. Riker	28-day		35.00	65-125
1994 Lieutenant Commander Data	28-day		35.00	70-99
1994 Lieutenant Worf	28-day		35.00	50-89
1994 Counselor Deanna Troi	28-day		35.00	50-149
1995 Dr. Beverly Crusher	28-day		35.00	35-90
1995 Lieutenant Commander Laforge	28-day		35.00	40-90
1996 Ensign W. Crusher	28-day		35.00	32-95

STAR TREK® : The Next Generation 10th Anniversary Mini Plates - N/A

YEAR ISSUE	EDITION LIMIT	YEAR RETD.	ISSUE PRICE	*QUOTE U.S.$
1997 Captain Jean-Luc Picard	28-day		25.90	30
1997 Commander William T. Riker	28-day		set	75

STAR TREK® : The Next Generation 5th Anniversary - M. Weistling

YEAR ISSUE	EDITION LIMIT	YEAR RETD.	ISSUE PRICE	*QUOTE U.S.$
1997 Guinan	28-day		35.00	55

STAR TREK® : The Next Generation Mini Plates - T. Blackshear/ K. Birdsong

YEAR ISSUE	EDITION LIMIT	YEAR RETD.	ISSUE PRICE	*QUOTE U.S.$
1997 Counselor Deanna Troi	28-day		25.50	26
1997 Dr. Beverly Crusher	28-day		set	set
1997 Lieutenant Commander Data	28-day		set	set
1997 Lieutenant Worf	28-day		set	set
1997 Best of Both Worlds	28-day		set	set
1997 Encounter at Far Point	28-day		set	set
1997 Lieutenant Commander Geordi Laforge	28-day		set	set
1997 Ensign Wesley Crusher	28-day		set	set
1997 All Good Things	28-day		set	set
1997 Yesterday's Enterprise	28-day		set	set

STAR TREK® : The Next Generation The Episodes - K. Birdsong

YEAR ISSUE	EDITION LIMIT	YEAR RETD.	ISSUE PRICE	*QUOTE U.S.$
1994 The Best of Both Worlds	28-day		35.00	50-99
1994 Encounter at Far Point	28-day		35.00	50-95
1995 Unification	28-day		35.00	50-89
1995 Yesterday's Enterprise	28-day		35.00	50-80
1995 All Good Things	28-day		35.00	50-85
1995 Descent	28-day		35.00	30-85
1996 Relics	28-day		35.00	50-79
1996 Redemption	28-day		35.00	50-79
1996 The Big Goodbye	28-day		35.00	50-85
1996 The Inner Light	28-day		35.00	50-95

STAR TREK® : The Original Episodes - J. Martin

YEAR ISSUE	EDITION LIMIT	YEAR RETD.	ISSUE PRICE	*QUOTE U.S.$
1996 The Tholian Web	28-day		35.00	75
1996 Space Seed	28-day		35.00	29-69
1996 The Menagerie	28-day		35.00	35-59
1996 City on the Edge	28-day		35.00	50
1996 Journel to Babel	28-day		35.00	35-55
1996 Trouble With Tribbles	28-day		35.00	65
1996 Where No Man Has Gone	28-day		35.00	35-55
1996 Devil in the Dark	28-day		35.00	35-75

STAR TREK® : The Power of Command - K. Birdsong

YEAR ISSUE	EDITION LIMIT	YEAR RETD.	ISSUE PRICE	*QUOTE U.S.$
1996 Captain Picard	28-day		35.00	99
1996 Admiral Kirk	28-day		35.00	99
1996 Captain Sisko	28-day		35.00	89
1996 Captain Sulu	28-day		35.00	89
1996 Janeway	28-day		35.00	99
1996 Khan	28-day		35.00	99
1996 General Chang	28-day		35.00	80
1996 Dukat	28-day		35.00	85
1997 Captain Kirk and the U.S.S. Enterprise NCC-1701	28-day		35.00	125
1997 The Borg Queen and the Borg Sphere	28-day		35.00	97

STAR TREK® : The Voyagers - K. Birdsong

YEAR ISSUE	EDITION LIMIT	YEAR RETD.	ISSUE PRICE	*QUOTE U.S.$
1994 U.S.S. Enterprise NCC-1701	28-day		35.00	50-125
1994 U.S.S. Enterprise NCC-1701-D	28-day		35.00	50-99
1994 Klingon Battlecruiser	28-day		35.00	50-89
1994 Romulan Warbird	28-day		35.00	50-95
1994 U.S.S. Enterprise NCC-1701-A	28-day		35.00	50-99
1995 Ferengi Marauder	28-day		35.00	50-99
1995 Klingon Bird of Prey	28-day		35.00	50-89
1995 Triple Nacelled U.S.S. Enterprise	28-day		35.00	50-95
1995 Cardassian Galor Warship	28-day		35.00	50-85
1995 U.S.S. Excelsior	28-day		35.00	30-90

STAR TREK® : Voyager - D. Curry

YEAR ISSUE	EDITION LIMIT	YEAR RETD.	ISSUE PRICE	*QUOTE U.S.$
1996 The Voyage Begins	28-day		35.00	50-99
1996 Bonds of Friendship	28-day		35.00	99
1996 Life Signs	28-day		35.00	89
1996 The Vidiians	28-day		35.00	95
1997 New Beginnings	28-day		35.00	89
1997 Basics	28-day		35.00	89

Star Wars 10th Anniversary Commemorative - T. Blackshear

YEAR ISSUE	EDITION LIMIT	YEAR RETD.	ISSUE PRICE	*QUOTE U.S.$
1990 Star Wars 10th Anniversary Commemorative Plates	14-day		39.50	175-200

Star Wars Heros and Villains - K. Birdsong

YEAR ISSUE	EDITION LIMIT	YEAR RETD.	ISSUE PRICE	*QUOTE U.S.$
1997 Luke Skywalker	28-day		35.00	35-49
1997 Han Solo	28-day		35.00	32-49
1997 Darth Vader	28-day		35.00	31-49
1997 Princess Leia	28-day		35.00	32-49
1997 Obi-Wan Kenobi	28-day		35.00	39
1997 Boba Fett	28-day		35.00	35

Star Wars Plate Collection - T. Blackshear

YEAR ISSUE	EDITION LIMIT	YEAR RETD.	ISSUE PRICE	*QUOTE U.S.$
1987 Hans Solo	14-day		29.50	195-295
1987 R2-D2 and Wicket	14-day		29.50	150-250
1987 Luke Skywalker and Darth Vader	14-day		29.50	190-295
1987 Princess Leia	14-day		29.50	175-225
1987 The Imperial Walkers	14-day		29.50	175-200
1987 Luke and Yoda	14-day		29.50	175-200
1988 Space Battle	14-day		29.50	200-300
1988 Crew in Cockpit	14-day		29.50	250-275

Star Wars Space Vehicles - S. Hillios

YEAR ISSUE	EDITION LIMIT	YEAR RETD.	ISSUE PRICE	*QUOTE U.S.$
1995 Millenium Falcon	28-day		35.00	35-99
1995 TIE Fighters	28-day		35.00	35-77
1995 Red Five X-Wing Fighters	28-day		35.00	35-85
1995 Imperial Shuttle	28-day		35.00	35-69
1995 STAR Destroyer	28-day		35.00	45-69
1996 Snow Speeders	28-day		35.00	40-69
1996 B-Wing Fighter	28-day		35.00	35-75
1996 The Slave I	28-day		35.00	35-80
1996 Medical Frigate	28-day		35.00	35-59
1996 Jabba's Sail Barge	28-day		35.00	35-59
1997 Y-Wing Fighter	28-day		35.00	35-59
1997 Death Star	28-day		35.00	35-59

Star Wars Trilogy - M. Weistling

YEAR ISSUE	EDITION LIMIT	YEAR RETD.	ISSUE PRICE	*QUOTE U.S.$
1993 Star Wars	28-day		37.50	150-175
1993 The Empire Strikes Back	28-day		37.50	175-225
1993 Return Of The Jedi	28-day		37.50	175-225

Starships of the Next Generation - B. Eggleton

YEAR ISSUE	EDITION LIMIT	YEAR RETD.	ISSUE PRICE	*QUOTE U.S.$
1996 Engage	28-day		39.95	85
1997 Enterprise of the Future	28-day		39.95	40-75
1997 Resistance is Futile	28-day		39.95	40-90
1997 All Good Things	28-day		39.95	40-75
1997 Klingon Defense Force	28-day		39.95	40-90
1997 Unexpected Confrontation	28-day		39.95	40-95
1997 Searching the Galaxy	28-day		39.95	40-75
1997 Shields Up	28-day		39.95	40-75
1997 Yesterday's Enterprise	28-day		39.95	40-75
1997 Earth's Last Stand	28-day		39.95	40-75

Summer Days of Childhood - T. Utz

YEAR ISSUE	EDITION LIMIT	YEAR RETD.	ISSUE PRICE	*QUOTE U.S.$
1983 Mountain Friends	10-day		29.50	30
1983 Garden Magic	10-day		29.50	30
1983 Little Beachcombers	10-day		29.50	30
1983 Blowing Bubbles	10-day		29.50	30
1983 Birthday Party	10-day		29.50	30
1983 Playing Doctor	10-day		29.50	30
1983 Stolen Kiss	10-day		29.50	30
1983 Kitty's Bathtime	10-day		29.50	30
1983 Cooling Off	10-day		29.50	30
1983 First Cucumber	10-day		29.50	30
1983 A Jumping Contest	10-day		29.50	30
1983 Balloon Carnival	10-day		29.50	30

Symphony of the Sea - R. Koni

YEAR ISSUE	EDITION LIMIT	YEAR RETD.	ISSUE PRICE	*QUOTE U.S.$
1995 Fluid Grace	28-day		29.95	30-35
1995 Dolphin's Dance	28-day		29.95	30-35
1995 Orca Ballet	28-day		29.95	30-35
1995 Moonlit Minuet	28-day		29.95	30-35
1995 Sailfish Serenade	28-day		29.95	30-35
1995 Starlit Waltz	28-day		29.95	30-35
1995 Sunset Splendor	28-day		29.95	30-35
1995 Coral Chorus	28-day		29.95	30-35

Those Delightful Dalmations - N/A

YEAR ISSUE	EDITION LIMIT	YEAR RETD.	ISSUE PRICE	*QUOTE U.S.$
1995 You Missed a Spot	28-day		29.95	25-30
1995 Here's a Good Spot	28-day		29.95	25-30
1996 The Best Spot	28-day		29.95	25-30
1996 Spotted In the Headlines	28-day		29.95	25-30
1996 A Spot In My Heart	28-day		29.95	25-30
1996 Sweet Spots	28-day		29.95	25-30
1996 Naptime Already?	28-day		29.95	25-30
1996 He's In My Spot	28-day		29.95	25-30
1996 The Serious Studying Spot	28-day		29.95	25-30
1996 Check Out My Spots	28-day		29.95	25-30

Timeless Expressions of the Orient - M. Tsang

YEAR ISSUE	EDITION LIMIT	YEAR RETD.	ISSUE PRICE	*QUOTE U.S.$
1990 Fidelity	15,000		75.00	95
1991 Femininity	15,000		75.00	75
1991 Longevity	15,000		75.00	75
1991 Beauty	15,000		55.00	55
1992 Courage	15,000		55.00	55

Treasured Days - H. Bond

YEAR ISSUE	EDITION LIMIT	YEAR RETD.	ISSUE PRICE	*QUOTE U.S.$
1987 Ashley	14-day		29.50	90-175
1987 Christopher	14-day		24.50	40-45
1987 Sara	14-day		24.50	40-45
1987 Jeremy	14-day		24.50	40-45
1987 Amanda	14-day		24.50	40-45
1988 Nicholas	14-day		24.50	40-45
1988 Lindsay	14-day		24.50	40-45
1988 Justin	14-day		24.50	40-50

A Treasury of Cherished Teddies - P. Hillman

YEAR ISSUE	EDITION LIMIT	YEAR RETD.	ISSUE PRICE	*QUOTE U.S.$
1994 Happy Holidays, Friend	28-day		29.50	30
1995 A New Year with Old Friends	28-day		29.50	30
1995 Valentines For You	28-day		29.50	30
1995 Friendship is in the Air	28-day		29.50	30
1995 Showers of Friendship	28-day		29.50	30
1996 Friendship is in Bloom	28-day		29.50	30
1996 Planting the Seeds of Friendship	28-day		29.50	30
1996 A Day in the Park	28-day		29.50	30
1996 Smooth Sailing	28-day		29.50	30
1996 School Days	28-day		29.50	30
1996 Holiday Harvest	28-day		29.50	30
1996 Thanks For Friends	28-day		29.50	30

Unbridled Spirit - C. DeHaan

YEAR ISSUE	EDITION LIMIT	YEAR RETD.	ISSUE PRICE	*QUOTE U.S.$
1992 Surf Dancer	28-day		29.50	30
1992 Winter Renegade	28-day		29.50	30
1992 Desert Shadows	28-day		29.50	30
1993 Painted Sunrise	28-day		29.50	30
1993 Desert Duel	28-day		29.50	30
1993 Midnight Run	28-day		29.50	30
1993 Moonlight Majesty	28-day		29.50	30
1993 Autumn Reverie	28-day		29.50	30
1993 Blizzard's Peril	28-day		29.50	30
1993 Sunrise Surprise	28-day		29.50	30

Under the Sea - C. Bragg

YEAR ISSUE	EDITION LIMIT	YEAR RETD.	ISSUE PRICE	*QUOTE U.S.$
1993 Tales of Tavarua	28-day		29.50	36-40
1993 Water's Edge	28-day		29.50	30-40
1994 Beauty of the Reef	28-day		29.50	36-40
1994 Rainbow Reef	28-day		29.50	36-40
1994 Orca Odyssey	28-day		29.50	30-40
1994 Rescue the Reef	28-day		29.50	36-40
1994 Underwater Dance	28-day		29.50	36-40
1994 Gentle Giants	28-day		29.50	30-40
1995 Undersea Enchantment	28-day		29.50	30-40
1995 Penguin Paradise	28-day		29.50	30-40

Undersea Visions - J. Enright

YEAR ISSUE	EDITION LIMIT	YEAR RETD.	ISSUE PRICE	*QUOTE U.S.$
1995 Secret Sanctuary	28-day		29.95	30-40
1995 Temple of Treasures	28-day		29.95	30-40
1996 Temple Beneath the Sea	28-day		29.95	30-40
1996 Lost Kingdom	28-day		29.95	30-40
1996 Mysterious Ruins	28-day		29.95	30-40
1996 Last Journey	28-day		29.95	30-40
1996 Egyptian Dreamscape	28-day		29.95	30-40
1996 Lost Galleon	28-day		29.95	30-40

Utz Mother's Day - T. Utz

YEAR ISSUE	EDITION LIMIT	YEAR RETD.	ISSUE PRICE	*QUOTE U.S.$
1983 A Gift of Love	N/A		27.50	35-38
1983 Mother's Helping Hand	N/A		27.50	28-35
1983 Mother's Angel	N/A		27.50	28-35

Vanishing Rural America - J. Harrison

YEAR ISSUE	EDITION LIMIT	YEAR RETD.	ISSUE PRICE	*QUOTE U.S.$
1991 Quiet Reflections	14-day		29.50	40-45
1991 Autumn's Passage	14-day		29.50	40-45
1991 Storefront Memories	14-day		29.50	30-40
1991 Country Path	14-day		29.50	36-40
1991 When the Circus Came To Town	14-day		29.50	36-40
1991 Covered in Fall	14-day		29.50	40-45
1991 America's Heartland	14-day		29.50	33-40
1991 Rural Delivery	14-day		29.50	33-40

Victorian Christmas Memories - J. Grossman

YEAR ISSUE	EDITION LIMIT	YEAR RETD.	ISSUE PRICE	*QUOTE U.S.$
1992 A Visit from St. Nicholas	28-day		29.50	30-35
1993 Christmas Delivery	28-day		29.50	35-40
1993 Christmas Angels	28-day		29.50	30-35
1992 With Visions of Sugar Plums	28-day		29.50	30-35
1993 Merry Olde Kris Kringle	28-day		29.50	30-35
1993 Grandfather Frost	28-day		29.50	30-35
1993 Joyous Noel	28-day		29.50	30-35
1993 Christmas Innocence	28-day		29.50	30-35
1993 Dreaming of Santa	28-day		29.50	35-40
1993 Mistletoe & Holly	28-day		29.50	30-35

*Quotes have been rounded up to nearest dollar

Victorian Playtime - M. H. Bogart

YEAR ISSUE	EDITION LIMIT	YEAR RETD.	ISSUE PRICE	*QUOTE U.S.$
1991 A Busy Day	14-day		29.50	45-65
1992 Little Masterpiece	14-day		29.50	45-65
1992 Playing Bride	14-day		29.50	65-85
1992 Waiting for a Nibble	14-day		29.50	45-65
1992 Tea and Gossip	14-day		29.50	55-65
1992 Cleaning House	14-day		29.50	45-65
1992 A Little Persuasion	14-day		29.50	45-65
1992 Peek-a-Boo	14-day		29.50	45-65

Voyages of the Starship Enterprise - K. Birdsong

YEAR ISSUE	EDITION LIMIT	YEAR RETD.	ISSUE PRICE	*QUOTE U.S.$
1997 NCC-1701-E	Closed		24.95	25-50
1997 NCC-1701-D	Closed		24.95	25-60
1997 NCC-1701-Refit	Closed		24.95	25-60
1997 NCC-1701	Closed		24.95	25-125

Warrior's Pride - C. DeHaan

YEAR ISSUE	EDITION LIMIT	YEAR RETD.	ISSUE PRICE	*QUOTE U.S.$
1994 Crow War Pony	28-day		29.50	30-35
1994 Running Free	28-day		29.50	30-35
1994 Blackfoot War Pony	28-day		29.50	30-35
1994 Southern Cheyenne	28-day		29.50	30-35
1995 Shoshoni War Ponies	28-day		29.50	30-35
1995 A Champion's Revelry	28-day		29.50	30-35
1995 Battle Colors	28-day		29.50	30-35
1995 Call of the Drums	28-day		29.50	30-35

The West of Frank McCarthy - F. McCarthy

YEAR ISSUE	EDITION LIMIT	YEAR RETD.	ISSUE PRICE	*QUOTE U.S.$
1991 Attacking the Iron Horse	14-day		37.50	50-60
1991 Attempt on the Stage	14-day		37.50	45
1991 The Prayer	14-day		37.50	45-54
1991 On the Old North Trail	14-day		37.50	45-50
1991 The Hostile Threat	14-day		37.50	45
1991 Bringing Out the Furs	14-day		37.50	45
1991 Kiowa Raider	14-day		37.50	45
1991 Headed North	14-day		37.50	39-45

Wilderness Spirits - P. Koni

YEAR ISSUE	EDITION LIMIT	YEAR RETD.	ISSUE PRICE	*QUOTE U.S.$
1994 Eyes of the Night	28-day		29.95	30
1995 Howl of Innocence	28-day		29.95	30
1995 Midnight Call	28-day		29.95	30
1995 Breaking the Silence	28-day		29.95	30
1995 Moonlight Run	28-day		29.95	30
1995 Sunset Vigil	28-day		29.95	30
1995 Sunrise Spirit	28-day		29.95	30
1996 Valley of the Wolf	28-day		29.95	30

Winged Reflections - R. Parker

YEAR ISSUE	EDITION LIMIT	YEAR RETD.	ISSUE PRICE	*QUOTE U.S.$
1989 Following Mama	14-day		37.50	38
1989 Above the Breakers	14-day		37.50	38
1989 Among the Reeds	14-day		37.50	38
1989 Freeze Up	14-day		37.50	38
1989 Wings Above the Water	14-day		37.50	38
1990 Summer Loon	14-day		29.50	30
1990 Early Spring	14-day		29.50	30
1990 At The Water's Edge	14-day		29.50	30

Winter Rails - T. Xaras

YEAR ISSUE	EDITION LIMIT	YEAR RETD.	ISSUE PRICE	*QUOTE U.S.$
1992 Winter Crossing	28-day		29.50	30-65
1993 Coal Country	28-day		29.50	30 65
1993 Daylight Run	28-day		29.50	30-65
1993 By Sea or Rail	28-day		29.50	30-65
1993 Country Crossroads	28-day		29.50	30-65
1993 Timber Line	28-day		29.50	30-65
1993 The Long Haul	28-day		29.50	30-65
1993 Darby Crossing	28-day		29.50	30-65
1995 East Broad Top	28-day		29.50	30-65
1995 Landsdowne Station	28-day		29.50	30-65

Winter Wildlife - J. Seerey-Lester

YEAR ISSUE	EDITION LIMIT	YEAR RETD.	ISSUE PRICE	*QUOTE U.S.$
1989 Close Encounters	15,000		55.00	55-60
1989 Among the Cattails	15,000		55.00	55-60
1989 The Refuge	15,000		55.00	55-60
1989 Out of the Blizzard	15,000		55.00	55-60
1989 First Snow	15,000		55.00	55-60
1989 Lying In Wait	15,000		55.00	55-60
1989 Winter Hiding	15,000		55.00	55-60
1989 Early Snow	15,000		55.00	55-60

Wizard of Oz Commemorative - T. Blackshear

YEAR ISSUE	EDITION LIMIT	YEAR RETD.	ISSUE PRICE	*QUOTE U.S.$
1988 We're Off to See the Wizard	14-day		24.50	180-250
1988 Dorothy Meets the Scarecrow	14-day		24.50	175-250
1989 The Tin Man Speaks	14-day		24.50	150-250
1989 A Glimpse of the Munchkins	14-day		24.50	140-225
1989 The Witch Casts A Spell	14-day		24.50	150-175
1989 If I Were King Of The Forest	14-day		24.50	140-225
1989 The Great and Powerful Oz	14-day		24.50	125-250
1989 There's No Place Like Home	14-day		24.50	175-240

Wizard of Oz-Fifty Years of Oz - T. Blackshear

YEAR ISSUE	EDITION LIMIT	YEAR RETD.	ISSUE PRICE	*QUOTE U.S.$
1989 Fifty Years of Oz	14-day		37.50	200-350

Wizard of Oz-Portraits From Oz - T. Blackshear

YEAR ISSUE	EDITION LIMIT	YEAR RETD.	ISSUE PRICE	*QUOTE U.S.$
1989 Dorothy	14-day		29.50	210-350
1989 Scarecrow	14-day		29.50	180-250
1989 Tin Man	14-day		29.50	180-250
1990 Cowardly Lion	14-day		29.50	160-250
1990 Glinda	14-day		29.50	160-250
1990 Wizard	14-day		29.50	180-250
1990 Wicked Witch	14-day		29.50	210-320
1990 Toto	14-day		29.50	300-350

The Wonder Of Christmas - J. McClelland

YEAR ISSUE	EDITION LIMIT	YEAR RETD.	ISSUE PRICE	*QUOTE U.S.$
1991 Santa's Secret	28-day		29.50	30
1991 My Favorite Ornament	28-day		29.50	30
1991 Waiting For Santa	28-day		29.50	30
1993 The Caroler	28-day		29.50	30

A World of Puppy Adventures - J. Ren

YEAR ISSUE	EDITION LIMIT	YEAR RETD.	ISSUE PRICE	*QUOTE U.S.$
1995 The Water's Fine	28-day		29.95	30
1996 Swimming Lessons	28-day		29.95	30
1996 Breakfast Is Served	28-day		29.95	30
1996 Laundry Tug O' War	28-day		29.95	30
1996 Did I Do That?	28-day		29.95	30
1996 DeCoy Dismay	28-day		29.95	30
1996 Puppy Picnic	28-day		29.95	30
1996 Sweet Terrors	28-day		29.95	30

The World Of Zolan - D. Zolan

YEAR ISSUE	EDITION LIMIT	YEAR RETD.	ISSUE PRICE	*QUOTE U.S.$
1992 First Kiss	28-day		29.50	55-100
1992 Morning Discovery	28-day		29.50	55-75
1993 The Little Fisherman	28-day		29.50	55-75
1993 Letter to Grandma	28-day		29.50	55-85
1993 Twilight Prayer	28-day		29.50	30-85
1993 Flowers for Mother	28-day		29.50	55-80

Year Of The Wolf - A. Agnew

YEAR ISSUE	EDITION LIMIT	YEAR RETD.	ISSUE PRICE	*QUOTE U.S.$
1993 Broken Silence	28-day		29.50	30-35
1993 Leader of the Pack	28-day		29.50	30-35
1993 Solitude	28-day		29.50	30-35
1994 Tundra Light	28-day		29.50	30-35
1994 Guardians of the High Country	28-day		29.50	30-35
1994 A Second Glance	28-day		29.50	30-35
1994 Free as the Wind	28-day		29.50	30-35
1994 Song of the Wolf	28-day		29.50	30-35
1995 Lords of the Tundra	28-day		29.50	30-35
1995 Wilderness Companions	28-day		29.50	30-35

Young Lords of The Wild - M. Richter

YEAR ISSUE	EDITION LIMIT	YEAR RETD.	ISSUE PRICE	*QUOTE U.S.$
1994 Siberian Tiger Club	28-day		29.95	30-45
1995 Snow Leopard Cub	28-day		29.95	30-45
1995 Lion Cub	28-day		29.95	30
1995 Clouded Leopard Cub	28-day		29.95	30
1995 Cougar Cub	28-day		29.95	30
1995 Leopard Cub	28-day		29.95	30
1995 Cheetah Cub	28-day		29.95	30
1996 Canadian Lynx Cub	28-day		29.95	30

Hamilton/Boehm

Award Winning Roses - Boehm

YEAR ISSUE	EDITION LIMIT	YEAR RETD.	ISSUE PRICE	*QUOTE U.S.$
1979 Peace Rose	15,000		45.00	100
1979 White Masterpiece Rose	15,000		45.00	75
1979 Tropicana Rose	15,000		45.00	63
1979 Elegance Rose	15,000		45.00	63
1979 Queen Elizabeth Rose	15,000		45.00	63
1979 Royal Highness Rose	15,000		45.00	63
1979 Angel Face Rose	15,000		45.00	63
1979 Mr. Lincoln Rose	15,000		45.00	63

Gamebirds of North America - Boehm

YEAR ISSUE	EDITION LIMIT	YEAR RETD.	ISSUE PRICE	*QUOTE U.S.$
1984 Ring-Necked Pheasant	15,000		62.50	63
1984 Bob White Quail	15,000		62.50	63
1984 American Woodcock	15,000		62.50	63
1984 California Quail	15,000		62.50	63
1984 Ruffed Grouse	15,000		62.50	63
1984 Wild Turkey	15,000		62.50	63
1984 Willow Partridge	15,000		62.50	63
1984 Prairie Grouse	15,000		62.50	63

Hummingbird Collection - Boehm

YEAR ISSUE	EDITION LIMIT	YEAR RETD.	ISSUE PRICE	*QUOTE U.S.$
1980 Calliope	15,000		62.50	80
1980 Broadbilled	15,000		62.50	63
1980 Rufous Flame Bearer	15,000		62.50	80
1980 Broadtail	15,000		62.50	63
1980 Streamertail	15,000		62.50	80
1980 Blue Throated	15,000		62.50	80
1980 Crimson Topaz	15,000		62.50	63
1980 Brazilian Ruby	15,000		62.50	80

Owl Collection - Boehm

YEAR ISSUE	EDITION LIMIT	YEAR RETD.	ISSUE PRICE	*QUOTE U.S.$
1980 Boreal Owl	15,000		45.00	95
1980 Snowy Owl	15,000		45.00	95
1980 Barn Owl	15,000		45.00	80
1980 Saw Whet Owl	15,000		45.00	75
1980 Great Horned Owl	15,000		45.00	75
1980 Screech Owl	15,000		45.00	75
1980 Short Eared Owl	15,000		45.00	75
1980 Barred Owl	15,000		45.00	75

Water Birds - Boehm

YEAR ISSUE	EDITION LIMIT	YEAR RETD.	ISSUE PRICE	*QUOTE U.S.$
1981 Canada Geese	15,000		62.50	65
1981 Wood Ducks	15,000		62.50	65
1981 Hooded Merganser	15,000		62.50	65
1981 Ross's Geese	15,000		62.50	65
1981 Common Mallard	15,000		62.50	65
1981 Canvas Back	15,000		62.50	65
1981 Green Winged Teal	15,000		62.50	65
1981 American Pintail	15,000		62.50	65

Haviland

Twelve Days of Christmas - R. Hetreau

YEAR ISSUE	EDITION LIMIT	YEAR RETD.	ISSUE PRICE	*QUOTE U.S.$
1970 Partridge	30,000		25.00	80
1971 Two Turtle Doves	30,000		25.00	30
1972 Three French Hens	30,000		27.50	30
1973 Four Calling Birds	30,000		28.50	30
1974 Five Golden Rings	30,000		30.00	30
1975 Six Geese a'laying	30,000		32.50	33
1976 Seven Swans	30,000		38.00	38
1977 Eight Maids	30,000		40.00	40
1978 Nine Ladies Dancing	30,000		45.00	45
1979 Ten Lord's a'leaping	30,000		50.00	50
1980 Eleven Pipers Piping	30,000		55.00	55
1981 Twelve Drummers	30,000		60.00	60

Haviland & Parlon

Christmas Madonnas - Various

YEAR ISSUE	EDITION LIMIT	YEAR RETD.	ISSUE PRICE	*QUOTE U.S.$
1972 By Raphael - Raphael	5,000		35.00	42
1973 By Feruzzi - Feruzzi	5,000		40.00	78
1974 By Raphael - Raphael	5,000		42.50	43
1975 By Murillo - Murillo	7,500		42.50	43
1976 By Botticelli - Botticelli	7,500		45.00	45
1977 By Bellini - Bellini	7,500		48.00	48
1978 By Lippi - Lippi	7,500		48.00	53
1979 Madonna of The Eucharist - Botticelli	7,500		49.50	112

Hudson Creek

American Expansion (Hudson Pewter) - P.W. Baston

YEAR ISSUE	EDITION LIMIT	YEAR RETD.	ISSUE PRICE	*QUOTE U.S.$
1975 Spirit of '76 (6" Plate)	4,812	1975	27.50	100-120
1975 American Independence	18,462	N/A	Unkn.	100-125
1975 American Expansion	2,250	N/A	Unkn.	50-75
1975 The American War Between the States	825	N/A	Unkn.	150-200

Sebastian Plates - P.W. Baston

YEAR ISSUE	EDITION LIMIT	YEAR RETD.	ISSUE PRICE	*QUOTE U.S.$
1978 Motif No. 1	4,878	1985	75.00	50-75
1979 Grand Canyon	2,492	1985	75.00	50-75
1980 Lone Cypress	718	1985	75.00	150-175
1980 In The Candy Store	9,098	1985	39.50	40
1981 The Doctor	7,547	1985	39.50	40
1983 Little Mother	2,710	1985	39.50	40
1984 Switching The Freight	706	1985	42.50	100-125

Hutschenreuther

The Glory of Christmas - W./C. Hallett

YEAR ISSUE	EDITION LIMIT	YEAR RETD.	ISSUE PRICE	*QUOTE U.S.$
1982 The Nativity	25,000		80.00	125
1983 The Annunciation	25,000		80.00	115
1984 The Shepherds	25,000		80.00	100
1985 The Wiseman	25,000		80.00	100

Gunther Granget - G. Granget

YEAR ISSUE	EDITION LIMIT	YEAR RETD.	ISSUE PRICE	*QUOTE U.S.$
1972 American Sparrows	5,000		50.00	75-100
1972 European Sparrows	5,000		30.00	65
1973 American Kildeer	2,250		75.00	75
1973 American Squirrel	2,500		75.00	75
1973 European Squirrel	2,500		35.00	50
1974 American Partridge	2,500		75.00	90
1975 American Rabbits	2,500		90.00	90
1976 Freedom in Flight	5,000		100.00	100
1976 Wrens	2,500		100.00	110
1976 Freedom in Flight, Gold	200		200.00	200
1977 Bears	2,500		100.00	100
1978 Foxes' Spring Journey	1,000		125.00	200

Imperial Ching-te Chen

Beauties of the Red Mansion - Z. HuiMin

YEAR ISSUE	EDITION LIMIT	YEAR RETD.	ISSUE PRICE	*QUOTE U.S.$
1986 Pao-chai	115-day		27.92	30-55
1986 Yuan-chun	115-day		27.92	30-45
1987 Hsi-feng	115-day		30.92	35-45
1987 Hsi-chun	115-day		30.92	35-45
1988 Miao-yu	115-day		30.92	35-45
1988 Ying-chun	115-day		30.92	35-45
1988 Tai-yu	115-day		32.92	35-45
1988 Li-wan	115-day		32.92	35-45
1988 Ko-Ching	115-day		32.92	35-45
1988 Hsiang-yun	115-day		34.92	35-45
1989 Tan-Chun	115-day		34.92	35-45
1989 Chiao-chieh	115-day		34.92	35-45

Blessings From a Chinese Garden - Z. Song Mao

YEAR ISSUE	EDITION LIMIT	YEAR RETD.	ISSUE PRICE	*QUOTE U.S.$
1988 The Gift of Purity	175-day		39.92	40-55
1989 The Gift of Grace	175-day		39.92	40-55
1989 The Gift of Beauty	175-day		42.92	43-55
1989 The Gift of Happiness	175-day		42.92	43-55
1990 The Gift of Truth	175-day		42.92	35-43
1990 The Gift of Joy	175-day		42.92	30-43

Flower Goddesses of China - Z. HuiMin

YEAR ISSUE	EDITION LIMIT	YEAR RETD.	ISSUE PRICE	*QUOTE U.S.$
1991 The Lotus Goddess	175-day		34.92	35-45
1991 The Chrysanthemum Goddess	175-day		34.92	35-45
1991 The Plum Blossom Goddess	175-day		37.92	38-50
1991 The Peony Goddess	175-day		37.92	38-50
1991 The Narcissus Goddess	175-day		37.92	50-62
1991 The Camellia Goddess	175-day		37.92	28-38

The Forbidden City - S. Fu

YEAR ISSUE	EDITION LIMIT	YEAR RETD.	ISSUE PRICE	*QUOTE U.S.$
1990 Pavilion of 10,000 Springs	150-day		39.92	15-40
1990 Flying Kites/Spring Day	150-day		39.92	25-40
1990 Pavilion/Floating Jade Green	150-day		42.92	25-43
1991 The Lantern Festival	150-day		42.92	20-43
1991 Nine Dragon Screen	150-day		42.92	25-43
1991 The Hall of the Cultivating Mind	150-day		42.92	30-43
1991 Dressing the Empress	150-day		45.92	33-46
1991 Pavilion of Floating Cups	150-day		45.92	32-46

*Quotes have been rounded up to nearest dollar

Garden of Satin Wings - J. Xue-Bing

YEAR ISSUE	EDITION LIMIT	YEAR RETD.	ISSUE PRICE	*QUOTE U.S.$
1992 A Morning Dream	115-day		29.92	35
1993 An Evening Mist	115-day		29.92	36
1993 A Garden Whisper	115-day		29.92	36-40
1993 An Enchanting Interlude	115-day		29.92	34-40

Legends of West Lake - J. Xue-Bing

YEAR ISSUE	EDITION LIMIT	YEAR RETD.	ISSUE PRICE	*QUOTE U.S.$
1989 Lady White	175-day		29.92	30-55
1990 Lady Silkworm	175-day		29.92	35-50
1990 Laurel Peak	175-day		29.92	17-35
1990 Rising Sun Terrace	175-day		32.92	24-33
1990 The Apricot Fairy	175-day		32.92	19-33
1990 Bright Pearl	175-day		32.92	20-33
1990 Thread of Sky	175-day		34.92	18-35
1991 Phoenix Mountain	175-day		34.92	24-35
1991 Ancestors of Tea	175-day		34.92	22-35
1991 Three Pools Mirroring/Moon	175-day		36.92	25-37
1991 Fly-In Peak	175-day		36.92	25-40
1991 The Case of the Folding Fans	175-day		36.92	40-48

Maidens of the Folding Sky - J. Xue-Bing

YEAR ISSUE	EDITION LIMIT	YEAR RETD.	ISSUE PRICE	*QUOTE U.S.$
1992 Lady Lu	175-day		29.92	35-38
1992 Mistress Yang	175-day		29.92	35-58
1992 Bride Yen Chun	175-day		32.92	50-65
1993 Parrot Maiden	175-day		32.92	70

Scenes from the Summer Palace - Z. Song Mao

YEAR ISSUE	EDITION LIMIT	YEAR RETD.	ISSUE PRICE	*QUOTE U.S.$
1988 The Marble Boat	175-day		29.92	35-45
1988 Jade Belt Bridge	175-day		29.92	35-40
1989 Hall that Dispels the Clouds	175-day		32.92	33-40
1989 The Long Promenade	175-day		32.92	39-45
1989 Garden/Harmonious Pleasure	175-day		32.92	25-33
1989 The Great Stage	175-day		32.92	33-37
1989 Seventeen Arch Bridge	175-day		34.92	19-35
1989 Boaters on Kumming Lake	175-day		34.92	20-35

International Silver

Bicentennial - M. Deoliveira

YEAR ISSUE	EDITION LIMIT	YEAR RETD.	ISSUE PRICE	*QUOTE U.S.$
1972 Signing Declaration	7,500		40.00	310
1973 Paul Revere	7,500		40.00	160
1974 Concord Bridge	7,500		40.00	115
1975 Crossing Delaware	7,500		50.00	80
1976 Valley Forge	7,500		50.00	65
1977 Surrender at Yorktown	7,500		50.00	60

Islandia International

African Wildlife - T. Swanson

YEAR ISSUE	EDITION LIMIT	YEAR RETD.	ISSUE PRICE	*QUOTE U.S.$
1997 Elephant	Numbrd.		30.00	30
1997 Lion	Numbrd.		30.00	30
1997 Giraffe	Numbrd.		30.00	30
1997 Zebra	Numbrd.		30.00	30

Celebration of Christmas - K. Dowd

YEAR ISSUE	EDITION LIMIT	YEAR RETD.	ISSUE PRICE	*QUOTE U.S.$
1997 Checking His List	Numbrd.		30.00	30
1997 Christmas Party	Numbrd.		30.00	30
1997 Harvesting Wood For Toys	Numbrd.		30.00	30
1997 The First Christmas Tree	Numbrd.		30.00	30

Coming Home - C. Hayes

YEAR ISSUE	EDITION LIMIT	YEAR RETD.	ISSUE PRICE	*QUOTE U.S.$
1997 The American Air Force	Numbrd.		30.00	30
1997 The American Army (White Male)	Numbrd.		30.00	30
1997 The American Navy	Numbrd.		30.00	30
1997 The American Marines	Numbrd.		30.00	30
1997 The American Army (African-American)	Numbrd.		30.00	30
1997 The American Army (White Female)	Numbrd.		30.00	30

Feathered Friends - S. Etem

YEAR ISSUE	EDITION LIMIT	YEAR RETD.	ISSUE PRICE	*QUOTE U.S.$
1998 Bluebird of Happiness	30-day		30.00	30
1998 Reach For Your Dreams	30-day		30.00	30

Festival of Life - W. A. Still

YEAR ISSUE	EDITION LIMIT	YEAR RETD.	ISSUE PRICE	*QUOTE U.S.$
1998 "Blessed Day" - Wedding	30-day		30.00	30
1998 "Blessed Event" - New Baby	30-day		30.00	30
1998 "Blessed Holiday" - Christmas	30-day		30.00	30

Gift of Love - S. Etem

YEAR ISSUE	EDITION LIMIT	YEAR RETD.	ISSUE PRICE	*QUOTE U.S.$
1998 The Miracle of Life	30-day		30.00	30
1998 Miracle of Friends	30-day		30.00	30

Great Bears of the World - T. Swanson

YEAR ISSUE	EDITION LIMIT	YEAR RETD.	ISSUE PRICE	*QUOTE U.S.$
1998 The Black Bear	Numbrd.		30.00	30
1998 The Grizzly Bear	Numbrd.		30.00	30
1998 The Koala Bear	Numbrd.		30.00	30
1998 The Panda Bear	Numbrd.		30.00	30
1998 The Polar Bear	Numbrd.		30.00	30

International Fatcats - G. Pitt

YEAR ISSUE	EDITION LIMIT	YEAR RETD.	ISSUE PRICE	*QUOTE U.S.$
1997 USA	Numbrd.		30.00	30
1997 Switzerland	Numbrd.		30.00	30
1997 Spain	Numbrd.		30.00	30
1997 Russia	Numbrd.		30.00	30
1997 Mexico	Numbrd.		30.00	30
1997 Japan	Numbrd.		30.00	30
1997 Italy	Numbrd.		30.00	30
1997 Israel	Numbrd.		30.00	30
1997 India	Numbrd.		30.00	30
1997 Greece	Numbrd.		30.00	30
1997 Great Britain	Numbrd.		30.00	30
1997 Germany	Numbrd.		30.00	30
1997 France	Numbrd.		30.00	30
1997 China	Numbrd.		30.00	30
1997 Canada	Numbrd.		30.00	30
1997 Australia	Numbrd.		30.00	30

North American Wildlife - T. Swanson

YEAR ISSUE	EDITION LIMIT	YEAR RETD.	ISSUE PRICE	*QUOTE U.S.$
1998 Big Horn Sheep - "Mountain Gathering"	Numbrd.		30.00	30
1998 Whitetail Deer - "Regal Solitude"	Numbrd.		30.00	30
1998 Buffalo - "Roaming The Plains"	Numbrd.		30.00	30
1998 Wolves - "Mist Morning Hunters"	Numbrd.		30.00	30
1998 Mule Deer - "Trouble Ahead"	Numbrd.		30.00	30
1998 Mountain Goat - "Chilly Heights"	Numbrd.		30.00	30
1998 Red Fox - "Prey in Sight"	Numbrd.		30.00	30
1998 Gamble Quail - "Family Gathering"	Numbrd.		30.00	30

People of Africa - W. A. Still

YEAR ISSUE	EDITION LIMIT	YEAR RETD.	ISSUE PRICE	*QUOTE U.S.$
1997 Maasai Warrior and Lion	Numbrd.		35.00	35
1997 Bororo Man and Camels	Numbrd.		35.00	35
1997 African Elephant and Bush Woman	Numbrd.		35.00	35
1997 Nigerian Woman and Giraffe	Numbrd.		35.00	35
1997 Rendille Woman and Crowned Crane	Numbrd.		35.00	35
1997 Samburu Warrior and Cheetah	Numbrd.		35.00	35
1997 Muslim Musicians and Pelicans	Numbrd.		35.00	35
1997 Peul Woman and Zebras	Numbrd.		35.00	35

Rocky Mountain Wildlife - T. Swanson

YEAR ISSUE	EDITION LIMIT	YEAR RETD.	ISSUE PRICE	*QUOTE U.S.$
1997 Elk - "Storm King"	Numbrd.		30.00	30
1997 Moose - "Evening Solitude"	Numbrd.		30.00	30
1997 Grizzly Bear - "Fishing in Still Water"	Numbrd.		30.00	30
1997 Mountain Lion - "Dangers Approach"	Numbrd.		30.00	30

Single Issue - G. Clasby

YEAR ISSUE	EDITION LIMIT	YEAR RETD.	ISSUE PRICE	*QUOTE U.S.$
1998 Snowy Day	30-day		30.00	30
1998 The Flowers of the Fields	30-day		30.00	30

Single Issue - R. Tanenbaum

YEAR ISSUE	EDITION LIMIT	YEAR RETD.	ISSUE PRICE	*QUOTE U.S.$
1997 "England's Rose" - Princess Diana	30-day	1997	30.00	30
1998 Mother Teresa	30-day		30.00	30

Single Issue - S. Etem

YEAR ISSUE	EDITION LIMIT	YEAR RETD.	ISSUE PRICE	*QUOTE U.S.$
1998 The Winner	30-day		30.00	30
1998 Second Place	30-day		30.00	30
1998 The Winner & Second Place, set	30-day		60.00	60

Single Issue - W. Christensen

YEAR ISSUE	EDITION LIMIT	YEAR RETD.	ISSUE PRICE	*QUOTE U.S.$
1997 Christmas Surprise	Numbrd.		30.00	30

Single Issue - W.A. Still

YEAR ISSUE	EDITION LIMIT	YEAR RETD.	ISSUE PRICE	*QUOTE U.S.$
1998 Vietnam Memorial	30-day		30.00	30

To Have And To Hold - R. Tanenbaum

YEAR ISSUE	EDITION LIMIT	YEAR RETD.	ISSUE PRICE	*QUOTE U.S.$
1997 The Engagement	Numbrd.		30.00	30
1997 The Bridal Shower	Numbrd.		30.00	30
1997 The Wedding Ceremony	Numbrd.		30.00	30
1997 The First Dance	Numbrd.		30.00	30
1997 The Wedding Reception	Numbrd.		30.00	30
1997 The Honeymoon	Numbrd.		30.00	30

Trevor's Farm Friends - T. Swanson

YEAR ISSUE	EDITION LIMIT	YEAR RETD.	ISSUE PRICE	*QUOTE U.S.$
1997 Paulie The Pig	Numbrd.		30.00	30
1997 Rollie The Rooster	Numbrd.		30.00	30
1997 Catie The Cow	Numbrd.		30.00	30
1997 Gerrie The Goat	Numbrd.		30.00	30

Wolves - Dusk To Dawn - T. Swanson

YEAR ISSUE	EDITION LIMIT	YEAR RETD.	ISSUE PRICE	*QUOTE U.S.$
1997 Winter Hunt	Numbrd.		30.00	30
1997 Wolves of Dawn	Numbrd.		30.00	30
1997 Distant Danger	Numbrd.		30.00	30
1997 Midnight Challenge	Numbrd.		30.00	30
1997 Close to Home	Numbrd.		30.00	30

World's Greatest - R. Tanenbaum

YEAR ISSUE	EDITION LIMIT	YEAR RETD.	ISSUE PRICE	*QUOTE U.S.$
1998 Teacher	Numbrd.		30.00	30
1998 Nurse	Numbrd.		30.00	30
1998 Attorney	Numbrd.		30.00	30
1998 Firewoman	Numbrd.		30.00	30
1998 Policewoman	Numbrd.		30.00	30
1998 Secretary	Numbrd.		30.00	30

Jan Hagara Collectables

Christmas Series - J. Hagara

YEAR ISSUE	EDITION LIMIT	YEAR RETD.	ISSUE PRICE	*QUOTE U.S.$
1983 Carol	15,000	1983	45.00	150-195
1984 Chris	15,000	1984	45.00	100-155
1985 Noel	15,000	1985	45.00	100-155
1986 Nikki	15,000	1986	45.00	100-155

Country Series - J. Hagara

YEAR ISSUE	EDITION LIMIT	YEAR RETD.	ISSUE PRICE	*QUOTE U.S.$
1984 Cristina	20,000	1986	42.50	60-150
1985 Laurel	20,000	1987	42.50	50-100
1986 Leslie	20,000	1987	42.50	45-100
1987 Mary Ann & Molly	20,000	1988	42.50	45-100

Fall in Love Again - J. Hagara

YEAR ISSUE	EDITION LIMIT	YEAR RETD.	ISSUE PRICE	*QUOTE U.S.$
1994 Tammy	7,500	1997	39.00	39

Hamilton Collection - J. Hagara

YEAR ISSUE	EDITION LIMIT	YEAR RETD.	ISSUE PRICE	*QUOTE U.S.$
1990 Cathy	14-day	1991	29.50	30-50
1990 Paul	14-day	1991	29.50	30-50
1990 Addie	14-day	1991	29.50	30-50
1990 Shelley	14-day	1991	29.50	30-50
1990 Dacy	14-day	1991	29.50	30-50
1990 Jenny	14-day	1991	29.50	30-50
1990 Jimmy	14-day	1991	29.50	30-65
1990 Joy	14-day	1991	29.50	30-50

Heart Series - J. Hagara

YEAR ISSUE	EDITION LIMIT	YEAR RETD.	ISSUE PRICE	*QUOTE U.S.$
1980 My Heart Desire (Cara)	Yr.Iss.	1981	24.50	125
1981 Hearts & Flowers	Yr.Iss.	1982	24.50	100-125
1982 Hearty Sailor	Yr.Iss.	1983	24.50	50-100
1983 Shannon's Sweetheart	Yr.Iss.	1984	24.50	70-100

Mother's Day Series - J. Hagara

YEAR ISSUE	EDITION LIMIT	YEAR RETD.	ISSUE PRICE	*QUOTE U.S.$
1979 Daisies From Mary Beth	Yr.Iss.	1980	37.50	125
1980 Daisies From Jimmy	Yr.Iss.	1981	37.50	125-150
1981 Daisies From Meg	Yr.Iss.	1982	37.50	125
1982 Daisies From Mommie	Yr.Iss.	1983	37.50	125

Romantic Designer - J. Hagara

YEAR ISSUE	EDITION LIMIT	YEAR RETD.	ISSUE PRICE	*QUOTE U.S.$
1988 Hannah 8 1/2"	5,000	1989	50.00	150-195
1988 Hannah 4 1/2"	15,000	1989	22.50	35-75
1990 Jamie 8 1/2"	5,000	1992	50.00	50-75
1991 Jamie 4 1/2"	15,000	1991	22.50	23
1991 David 8 1/2"	5,000	1993	50.00	50-75
1991 David 4 1/2"	15,000	1993	22.50	23
1991 Violet 8 1/2"	5,000	1994	50.00	50-90
1991 Violet 4 1/2"	15,000	1994	22.50	23

Yesterday's Children - J. Hagara

YEAR ISSUE	EDITION LIMIT	YEAR RETD.	ISSUE PRICE	*QUOTE U.S.$
1979 Lisa & Jumeau Doll	5,000	1980	60.00	80-200
1980 Adrianne & the Bye Lo Doll	5,000	1981	60.00	250
1981 Lydia & Shirley Temple	5,000	1982	60.00	200
1982 Melanie & Scarlett O'Hara	5,000	1983	60.00	85-185

Lalique Society of America

Annual - M. Lalique

YEAR ISSUE	EDITION LIMIT	YEAR RETD.	ISSUE PRICE	*QUOTE U.S.$
1965 Deux Oiseaux (Two Birds)	2,000		25.00	1250
1966 Rose de Songerie (Dream Rose)	5,000		25.00	75
1967 Ballet de Poisson (Fish Ballet)	5,000		25.00	95
1968 Gazelle Fantaisie (Gazelle Fantasy)	5,000		25.00	70-75
1969 Papillon (Butterfly)	5,000		30.00	50
1970 Paon (Peacock)	5,000		30.00	70
1971 Hibou (Owl)	5,000		35.00	50
1972 Coquillage (Shell)	5,000		40.00	73-75
1973 Petit Geai (Jayling)	5,000		42.50	100
1974 Sous d'Argent (Silver Pennies)	5,000		47.50	95
1975 Duo de Poisson (Fish Duet)	5,000		50.00	139
1976 Aigle (Eagle)	5,000		60.00	84-90

Lenox China

Colonial Christmas Wreath - Unknown

YEAR ISSUE	EDITION LIMIT	YEAR RETD.	ISSUE PRICE	*QUOTE U.S.$
1981 Colonial Virginia	Yr.Iss.	1982	65.00	76
1982 Massachusetts	Yr.Iss.	1983	70.00	93
1983 Maryland	Yr.Iss.	1984	70.00	185
1984 Rhode Island	Yr.Iss.	1985	70.00	82
1985 Connecticut	Yr.Iss.	1986	70.00	75
1986 New Hampshire	Yr.Iss.	1987	70.00	75
1987 Pennsylvania	Yr.Iss.	1988	70.00	75
1988 Delaware	Yr.Iss.	1989	70.00	155
1989 New York	Yr.Iss.	1990	75.00	155
1990 New Jersey	Yr.Iss.	1991	75.00	78
1991 South Carolina	Yr.Iss.	1992	75.00	75
1992 North Carolina	Yr.Iss.	1993	75.00	155
1993 Georgia	Yr.Iss.	1994	75.00	155

Lenox Collections

Boehm Birds - E. Boehm

YEAR ISSUE	EDITION LIMIT	YEAR RETD.	ISSUE PRICE	*QUOTE U.S.$
1970 Wood Thrush	Yr.Iss.	1970	35.00	91-130
1971 Goldfinch	Yr.Iss.	1971	35.00	50-70
1972 Mountain Bluebird	Yr.Iss.	1972	37.50	50-55
1973 Meadowlark	Yr.Iss.	1973	50.00	30-50
1974 Rufous Hummingbird	Yr.Iss.	1974	45.00	50-65
1975 American Redstart	Yr.Iss.	1975	50.00	35-50
1976 Cardinals	Yr.Iss.	1976	53.00	39-50
1977 Robins	Yr.Iss.	1977	55.00	31-50
1978 Mockingbirds	Yr.Iss.	1978	58.00	42-55
1979 Golden-Crowned Kinglets	Yr.Iss.	1979	65.00	80-82
1980 Black-Throated Blue Warblers	Yr.Iss.	1980	80.00	77-80
1981 Eastern Phoebes	Yr.Iss.	1981	92.50	80-95

Boehm Woodland Wildlife - E. Boehm

YEAR ISSUE	EDITION LIMIT	YEAR RETD.	ISSUE PRICE	*QUOTE U.S.$
1973 Racoons	Yr.Iss.	1973	50.00	75
1974 Red Foxes	Yr.Iss.	1974	52.50	70-75
1975 Cottontail Rabbits	Yr.Iss.	1975	58.50	60-75
1976 Eastern Chipmunks	Yr.Iss.	1976	62.50	75
1977 Beaver	Yr.Iss.	1977	67.50	75
1978 Whitetail Deer	Yr.Iss.	1978	70.00	60-75
1979 Squirrels	Yr.Iss.	1979	76.00	46-75
1980 Bobcats	Yr.Iss.	1980	82.50	83
1981 Martens	Yr.Iss.	1981	100.00	100
1982 River Otters	Yr.Iss.	1982	100.00	100

Lightpost Publishing

Kinkade-Thomas Kinkade Signature Collection - T. Kinkade

YEAR ISSUE	EDITION LIMIT	YEAR RETD.	ISSUE PRICE	*QUOTE U.S.$
1991 Chandler's Cottage	2,500		49.95	50-75
1991 Cedar Nook	2,500		49.95	40-75
1991 Sleigh Ride Home	2,500		49.95	55-75
1991 Home To Grandma's	2,500		49.95	52-75

*Quotes have been rounded up to nearest dollar

Lilliput Lane Ltd./Enesco Corporation

American Landmarks Collection - R. Day

YEAR ISSUE	EDITION LIMIT	YEAR RETD.	ISSUE PRICE	*QUOTE U.S.$
1990 Country Church	5,000	1996	35.00	35-50
1990 Riverside Chapel	5,000	1996	35.00	35-50

Ray Day/Coca Cola Country - R. Day

YEAR ISSUE	EDITION LIMIT	YEAR RETD.	ISSUE PRICE	*QUOTE U.S.$
1998 Catch of the Day (3-D)	Open		40.00	40
1998 Ice Cold Coke (3-D)	Open		40.00	40
1998 Spring Has Sprung (3-D)	Open		40.00	40
1998 When I Was Your Age... (3-D)	Open		40.00	40

Lladró

Lladró Plate Collection - Lladró

YEAR ISSUE	EDITION LIMIT	YEAR RETD.	ISSUE PRICE	*QUOTE U.S.$
1993 The Great Voyage L5964G	Closed	1995	50.00	50
1993 Looking Out L5998G	Open		38.00	38
1993 Swinging L5999G	Open		38.00	38
1993 Duck Plate L6000G	Open		38.00	38
1994 Friends L6158	Open		32.00	32
1994 Apple Picking L6159M	Open		32.00	32
1994 Turtledove L6160	Open		32.00	32
1994 Flamingo L6161M	Open		32.00	32

Lowell Davis Farm Club

Davis Cat Tales Plates. - L. Davis

YEAR ISSUE	EDITION LIMIT	YEAR RETD.	ISSUE PRICE	*QUOTE U.S.$
1982 Right Church, Wrong Pew	12,500	1986	37.50	90-150
1982 Company's Coming	12,500	1986	37.50	90-150
1982 On the Move	12,500	1986	37.50	90-150
1982 Flew the Coop	12,500	1986	37.50	90-150

Davis Christmas Plates - L. Davis

YEAR ISSUE	EDITION LIMIT	YEAR RETD.	ISSUE PRICE	*QUOTE U.S.$
1983 Hooker at Mailbox With Present 224-100	7,500	1984	45.00	130
1984 Country Christmas 224-101	7,500	1985	45.00	125
1985 Christmas at Foxfire Farm 224-102	7,500	1986	45.00	150
1986 Christmas at Red Oak 224-103	7,500	1987	45.00	100-150
1987 Blossom's Gift 224-104	7,500	1988	47.50	100
1988 Cutting the Family Christmas Tree 224-105	7,500	1989	47.50	75-100
1989 Peter and the Wren	7,500	1990	47.50	75
1990 Wintering Deer	7,500	1991	47.50	50
1991 Christmas at Red Oak II	7,500	1992	55.00	75
1992 Born On A Starry Night	7,500	1993	55.00	55
1993 Waiting For Mr. Lowell	5,000	1994	55.00	55
1994 Visions of Sugarplums	5,000	1995	55.00	55
1995 Bah Humbug	5,000		55.00	55

Davis Country Pride Plates - L. Davis

YEAR ISSUE	EDITION LIMIT	YEAR RETD.	ISSUE PRICE	*QUOTE U.S.$
1981 Surprise in the Cellar	7,500	1983	35.00	200-220
1981 Plum Tuckered Out	7,500	1983	35.00	115-150
1981 Duke's Mixture	7,500	1983	35.00	190-200
1982 Bustin' with Pride	7,500	1983	35.00	100-150

Davis Pen Pals - L. Davis

YEAR ISSUE	EDITION LIMIT	YEAR RETD.	ISSUE PRICE	*QUOTE U.S.$
1993 The Old Home Place 25800	Closed	1995	50.00	50

Davis Red Oak Sampler - L. Davis

YEAR ISSUE	EDITION LIMIT	YEAR RETD.	ISSUE PRICE	*QUOTE U.S.$
1986 General Store	5,000	1987	45.00	100-110
1987 Country Wedding	5,000	1988	45.00	125
1989 Country School	5,000	1990	45.00	110
1990 Blacksmith Shop	5,000	1991	52.50	50-110

Davis Special Edition Plates - L. Davis

YEAR ISSUE	EDITION LIMIT	YEAR RETD.	ISSUE PRICE	*QUOTE U.S.$
1983 The Critics	12,500	1985	45.00	95
1984 Good Ole Days Privy Set 2	5,000	1986	60.00	185
1986 Home From Market	7,500	1988	55.00	145

March of Dimes

Our Children, Our Future - Various

YEAR ISSUE	EDITION LIMIT	YEAR RETD.	ISSUE PRICE	*QUOTE U.S.$
1989 A Time for Peace - D. Zolan	150-day		29.00	35-75
1989 A Time To Love - S. Kuck	150-day		29.00	35-75
1989 A Time To Plant - J. McClelland	150-day		29.00	29-59
1989 A Time To Be Born - G. Perillo	150-day		29.00	29-75
1990 A Time To Embrace - E. Hibel	150-day		29.00	29-59
1990 A Time To Laugh - A. Williams	150-day		29.00	29-59

Marigold

Sport - Carreno

YEAR ISSUE	EDITION LIMIT	YEAR RETD.	ISSUE PRICE	*QUOTE U.S.$
1989 Mickey Mantle-handsigned	1,000		100.00	695
1989 Mickey Mantle-unsigned	1,000		60.00	195
1989 Joe DiMaggio-handsigned	Retrd.		100.00	1200-1400
1989 Joe DiMaggio f/s (blue sig.)	Retrd.		60.00	250
1990 Joe DiMaggio AP-handsigned	Retrd.		N/A	2000-2900

Maruri USA

Eagle Plate Series - W. Gaither

YEAR ISSUE	EDITION LIMIT	YEAR RETD.	ISSUE PRICE	*QUOTE U.S.$
1984 Free Flight	Closed	1993	150.00	150-198

Treasures of the Sky - Maruri Studios

YEAR ISSUE	EDITION LIMIT	YEAR RETD.	ISSUE PRICE	*QUOTE U.S.$
1998 Anna's w/Lily HP-9801	Open		39.95	40
1998 Allen's w/Hibiscus HP-9802	Open		39.95	40
1998 Ruby-throated w/Trumpet HP-9803	Open		39.95	40

Memories of Yesterday/Enesco Corporation

Dated Plate Series - Various

YEAR ISSUE	EDITION LIMIT	YEAR RETD.	ISSUE PRICE	*QUOTE U.S.$
1993 Look Out-Something Good Is Coming Your Way! 530298 - S. Butcher	Yr.Iss.	1993	50.00	50
1994 Pleasant Dreams and Sweet Repose 528102 - M. Atwell	Yr.Iss.	1994	50.00	50
1995 Join Me For a Little Song 134880 - M. Atwell	Yr.Iss.	1995	50.00	50

Museum Collections, Inc.

American Family I - N. Rockwell

YEAR ISSUE	EDITION LIMIT	YEAR RETD.	ISSUE PRICE	*QUOTE U.S.$
1979 Baby's First Step	9,900		28.50	48
1979 Happy Birthday Dear Mother	9,900		28.50	40-45
1979 Sweet Sixteen	9,900		28.50	35
1979 First Haircut	9,900		28.50	60
1979 First Prom	9,900		28.50	35
1979 Wrapping Christmas Presents	9,900		28.50	35
1979 The Student	9,900		28.50	35
1979 Birthday Party	9,900		28.50	35
1979 Little Mother	9,900		28.50	35
1979 Washing Our Dog	9,900		28.50	35
1979 Mother's Little Helpers	9,900		28.50	35
1979 Bride and Groom	9,900		28.50	35

American Family II - N. Rockwell

YEAR ISSUE	EDITION LIMIT	YEAR RETD.	ISSUE PRICE	*QUOTE U.S.$
1980 New Arrival	22,500		35.00	50-55
1980 Sweet Dreams	22,500		35.00	38
1980 Little Shaver	22,500		35.00	40
1980 We Missed You Daddy	22,500		35.00	38
1980 Home Run Slugger	22,500		35.00	38
1980 Giving Thanks	22,500		35.00	55
1980 Space Pioneers	22,500		35.00	35
1980 Little Salesman	22,500		35.00	38
1980 Almost Grown up	22,500		35.00	38
1980 Courageous Hero	22,500		35.00	38
1981 At the Circus	22,500		35.00	38
1981 Good Food, Good Friends	22,500		35.00	38

Christmas - N. Rockwell

YEAR ISSUE	EDITION LIMIT	YEAR RETD.	ISSUE PRICE	*QUOTE U.S.$
1979 Day After Christmas	Yr.Iss		75.00	75
1980 Checking His List	Yr.Iss		75.00	75
1981 Ringing in Good Cheer	Yr.Iss		75.00	75
1982 Waiting for Santa	Yr.Iss		75.00	75
1983 High Hopes	Yr.Iss		75.00	75
1984 Space Age Santa	Yr.Iss		55.00	55

Norman Rockwell Gallery

Norman Rockwell Centennial - Rockwell Inspired

YEAR ISSUE	EDITION LIMIT	YEAR RETD.	ISSUE PRICE	*QUOTE U.S.$
1993 The Toymaker	Closed		39.90	60-65
1993 The Cobbler	Closed		39.90	45-70

Rockwell's Christmas Legacy - Rockwell Inspired

YEAR ISSUE	EDITION LIMIT	YEAR RETD.	ISSUE PRICE	*QUOTE U.S.$
1992 Santa's Workshop	Closed		49.90	55-75
1993 Making a List	Closed		49.90	65-84
1993 While Santa Slumbers	Closed		54.90	60-85
1993 Visions of Santa	Closed		54.90	60-110

Pemberton & Oakes

Adventures of Childhood Collection - D. Zolan

YEAR ISSUE	EDITION LIMIT	YEAR RETD.	ISSUE PRICE	*QUOTE U.S.$
1989 Almost Home	Retrd.	1989	19.60	55-75
1989 Crystal's Creek	Retrd.	1989	19.60	45-75
1989 Summer Suds	Retrd.	1990	22.00	27-75
1990 Snowy Adventure	Retrd.	1990	22.00	24-85
1991 Forests & Fairy Tales	Retrd.	1991	24.40	24-95

The Best of Zolan in Miniature - D. Zolan

YEAR ISSUE	EDITION LIMIT	YEAR RETD.	ISSUE PRICE	*QUOTE U.S.$
1985 Sabina	Retrd.	1985	12.50	90-120
1986 Erik and Dandelion	Retrd.	1986	12.50	75-100
1986 Tender Moment	Retrd.	1986	12.50	85-95
1986 Touching the Sky	Retrd.	1987	12.50	49-95
1987 A Gift for Laurie	Retrd.	1987	12.50	75-100
1987 Small Wonder	Retrd.	1987	12.50	65-85

Childhood Discoveries (Miniature) - D. Zolan

YEAR ISSUE	EDITION LIMIT	YEAR RETD.	ISSUE PRICE	*QUOTE U.S.$
1990 Colors of Spring	Retrd.	1990	14.40	39-65
1990 Autumn Leaves	Retrd.	1990	14.40	29-65
1991 Enchanted Forest	Retrd.	1991	16.60	30-75
1991 Just Ducky	Retrd.	1991	16.60	32-65
1991 Rainy Day Pals	Retrd.	1991	16.60	59-65
1992 Double Trouble	Retrd.	1992	16.60	55-65
1990 First Kiss	Retrd.	1990	14.40	75-85
1993 Peppermint Kiss	Retrd.	1993	16.60	30-85
1995 Tender Hearts	Retrd.	1995	16.60	24-65

Childhood Friendship Collection - D. Zolan

YEAR ISSUE	EDITION LIMIT	YEAR RETD.	ISSUE PRICE	*QUOTE U.S.$
1986 Beach Break	Retrd.	1987	19.00	54-69
1987 Little Engineers	Retrd.	1987	19.00	66-85
1987 Tiny Treasures	Retrd.	1988	19.00	39-75
1988 Sharing Secrets	Retrd.	1988	19.00	60-85
1988 Dozens of Daisies	Retrd.	1989	19.00	39-75
1990 Country Walk	Retrd.	1989	19.00	36-75

Children and Pets - D. Zolan

YEAR ISSUE	EDITION LIMIT	YEAR RETD.	ISSUE PRICE	*QUOTE U.S.$
1984 Tender Moment	Retrd.	1984	19.00	25-95
1984 Golden Moment	Retrd.	1984	19.00	45-85
1985 Making Friends	Retrd.	1985	19.00	45-85
1985 Tender Beginning	Retrd.	1985	19.00	45-65
1986 Backyard Discovery	Retrd.	1986	19.00	39-95
1986 Waiting to Play	Retrd.	1986	19.00	45-85

Children at Christmas - D. Zolan

YEAR ISSUE	EDITION LIMIT	YEAR RETD.	ISSUE PRICE	*QUOTE U.S.$
1981 A Gift for Laurie	Retrd.	1981	48.00	75-125
1982 Christmas Prayer	Retrd.	1982	48.00	90-149
1983 Erik's Delight	Retrd.	1983	48.00	65-70
1984 Christmas Secret	Retrd.	1984	48.00	66
1985 Christmas Kitten	Retrd.	1985	48.00	50-65
1986 Laurie and the Creche	Retrd.	1986	48.00	50-80

Christmas (Miniature) - D. Zolan

YEAR ISSUE	EDITION LIMIT	YEAR RETD.	ISSUE PRICE	*QUOTE U.S.$
1993 Snowy Adventure	Retrd.	1993	16.60	30-65
1994 Candlelight Magic	Retrd.	1994	16.60	36-75
1995 Laurie and Creche	Retrd.	1995	16.60	17-75

Christmas - D. Zolan

YEAR ISSUE	EDITION LIMIT	YEAR RETD.	ISSUE PRICE	*QUOTE U.S.$
1991 Candlelight Magic	Retrd.	1991	24.80	25-95

Companion to Brotherly Love - D. Zolan

YEAR ISSUE	EDITION LIMIT	YEAR RETD.	ISSUE PRICE	*QUOTE U.S.$
1989 Sisterly Love	Retrd.		22.00	42-75

Easter (Miniature) - D. Zolan

YEAR ISSUE	EDITION LIMIT	YEAR RETD.	ISSUE PRICE	*QUOTE U.S.$
1991 Easter Morning	Retrd.		16.60	30-65

Father's Day (Miniature) - D. Zolan

YEAR ISSUE	EDITION LIMIT	YEAR RETD.	ISSUE PRICE	*QUOTE U.S.$
1994 Two of a Kind	Retrd.		16.60	45-65

Father's Day - D. Zolan

YEAR ISSUE	EDITION LIMIT	YEAR RETD.	ISSUE PRICE	*QUOTE U.S.$
1986 Daddy's Home	Retrd.		19.00	50-120

Grandparent's Day (Miniature) - D. Zolan

YEAR ISSUE	EDITION LIMIT	YEAR RETD.	ISSUE PRICE	*QUOTE U.S.$
1995 Lap of Love	Retrd.	1996	16.60	40-55

Grandparent's Day - D. Zolan

YEAR ISSUE	EDITION LIMIT	YEAR RETD.	ISSUE PRICE	*QUOTE U.S.$
1990 It's Grandma & Grandpa	Retrd.		24.40	30-75
1993 Grandpa's Fence	Retrd.		24.40	45-52

Heirloom Ovals - D. Zolan

YEAR ISSUE	EDITION LIMIT	YEAR RETD.	ISSUE PRICE	*QUOTE U.S.$
1992 My Kitty	Retrd.		18.80	36-50

March of Dimes: Our Children, Our Future - D. Zolan

YEAR ISSUE	EDITION LIMIT	YEAR RETD.	ISSUE PRICE	*QUOTE U.S.$
1989 A Time for Peace	Retrd.		29.00	35-75

Members Only Single Issue (Miniature) - D. Zolan

YEAR ISSUE	EDITION LIMIT	YEAR RETD.	ISSUE PRICE	*QUOTE U.S.$
1990 By Myself	Retrd.		14.40	58-65
1993 Summer's Child	Retrd.		16.60	44-65
1994 Little Slugger	Retrd.		16.60	52-65

Membership (Miniature) - D. Zolan

YEAR ISSUE	EDITION LIMIT	YEAR RETD.	ISSUE PRICE	*QUOTE U.S.$
1987 For You	Retrd.		12.50	130-150
1988 Making Friends	Retrd.		12.50	76-100
1989 Grandma's Garden	Retrd.		12.50	75-100
1990 A Christmas Prayer	Retrd.		14.40	59-80
1991 Golden Moment	Retrd.		15.00	50-75
1992 Brotherly Love	Retrd.		15.00	76-100
1993 New Shoes	Retrd.		16.60	42-75
1994 My Kitty	Retrd.		Gift	28-32

Mini Plates by Donald Zolan - D. Zolan

YEAR ISSUE	EDITION LIMIT	YEAR RETD.	ISSUE PRICE	*QUOTE U.S.$
1995 Golden Harvest	Retrd.		16.60	27-37
1995 My New Kitten	Retrd.	1996	16.60	37
1995 Reflections	Retrd.	1996	16.60	17
1995 Secret Friends	Retrd.	1996	16.60	17

Miniatures - D. Zolan

YEAR ISSUE	EDITION LIMIT	YEAR RETD.	ISSUE PRICE	*QUOTE U.S.$
1995 Lap of Love	Retrd.	1996	16.60	24-55

Moments To Remember (Miniature) - D. Zolan

YEAR ISSUE	EDITION LIMIT	YEAR RETD.	ISSUE PRICE	*QUOTE U.S.$
1992 Just We Two	Retrd.		16.60	54-65
1992 Almost Home	Retrd.		16.60	39-75
1993 Tiny Treasures	Retrd.		16.60	35-65
1993 Forest Friends	Retrd.		16.60	27-75

Mother's Day (Miniature) - D. Zolan

YEAR ISSUE	EDITION LIMIT	YEAR RETD.	ISSUE PRICE	*QUOTE U.S.$
1990 Flowers for Mother	Retrd.		14.40	52-65
1992 Twilight Prayer	Retrd.		16.60	45-80
1993 Jessica's Field	Retrd.		16.60	39-65
1994 One Summer Day	Retrd.		16.60	54-75
1995 Little Ballerina	Retrd.		16.60	50-75

Mother's Day - D. Zolan

YEAR ISSUE	EDITION LIMIT	YEAR RETD.	ISSUE PRICE	*QUOTE U.S.$
1988 Mother's Angels	Retrd.		19.00	75-125

Nutcracker II - Various

YEAR ISSUE	EDITION LIMIT	YEAR RETD.	ISSUE PRICE	*QUOTE U.S.$
1981 Grand Finale - S. Fisher	Retrd.		24.40	36
1982 Arabian Dancers - S. Fisher	Retrd.		24.40	68
1983 Dew Drop Fairy - S. Fisher	Retrd.		24.40	36
1984 Clara's Delight - S. Fisher	Retrd.		24.40	42-65
1985 Bedtime for Nutcracker - S. Fisher	Retrd.		24.40	45
1986 The Crowning of Clara - S. Fisher	Retrd.		24.40	36
1987 Dance of the Snowflakes - D. Zolan	Retrd.		24.40	38-75
1988 The Royal Welcome - R. Anderson	Retrd.		24.40	33
1989 The Spanish Dancer - M. Vickers	Retrd.		24.40	45-75

Plaques - D. Zolan

YEAR ISSUE	EDITION LIMIT	YEAR RETD.	ISSUE PRICE	*QUOTE U.S.$
1991 New Shoes	Retrd.		18.80	40-85
1992 Grandma's Garden	Retrd.		18.80	30-65
1992 Small Wonder	Retrd.		18.80	30-59
1992 Easter Morning	Retrd.		18.80	30-55

Plaques-Single Issues - D. Zolan

YEAR ISSUE	EDITION LIMIT	YEAR RETD.	ISSUE PRICE	*QUOTE U.S.$
1991 Flowers for Mother	Retrd.		16.80	65

Single Issue - D. Zolan

YEAR ISSUE	EDITION LIMIT	YEAR RETD.	ISSUE PRICE	*QUOTE U.S.$
1993 Winter Friends	Retrd.		18.80	45-65

Single Issue Day to Day Spode - D. Zolan

YEAR ISSUE	EDITION LIMIT	YEAR RETD.	ISSUE PRICE	*QUOTE U.S.$
1991 Daisy Days	Retrd.		48.00	50-79

*Quotes have been rounded up to nearest dollar

Single Issues (Miniature) - D. Zolan

YEAR ISSUE	EDITION LIMIT	YEAR RETD.	ISSUE PRICE	*QUOTE U.S.$
1986 Backyard Discovery	Retrd.		12.50	107
1986 Daddy's Home	Retrd.		12.50	820
1989 Sunny Surprise	Retrd.		12.50	65-75
1989 My Pumpkin	Retrd.		14.40	55-125
1991 Backyard Buddies	Retrd.		16.60	40-80
1991 The Thinker	Retrd.		16.60	40-100
1993 Quiet Time	Retrd.		16.60	66-100
1994 Little Fisherman	Retrd.		16.60	40-80

Single Issues Bone China (Miniature) - D. Zolan

YEAR ISSUE	EDITION LIMIT	YEAR RETD.	ISSUE PRICE	*QUOTE U.S.$
1992 Window of Dreams	Retrd.		18.80	65-70
1995 Little Splasher	Retrd.		16.60	30-55

Special Moments of Childhood Collection - D. Zolan

YEAR ISSUE	EDITION LIMIT	YEAR RETD.	ISSUE PRICE	*QUOTE U.S.$
1988 Brotherly Love	Retrd.		19.00	75-95
1988 Sunny Surprise	Retrd.		19.00	50-75
1989 Summer's Child	Retrd.		22.00	45-75
1990 Meadow Magic	Retrd.		22.00	36-59
1990 Cone For Two	Retrd.		24.60	30-55
1990 Rodeo Girl	Retrd.		24.60	55-65

Tenth Anniversary - D. Zolan

YEAR ISSUE	EDITION LIMIT	YEAR RETD.	ISSUE PRICE	*QUOTE U.S.$
1988 Ribbons and Roses	Retrd.		24.40	55-85

Thanksgiving (Miniature) - D. Zolan

YEAR ISSUE	EDITION LIMIT	YEAR RETD.	ISSUE PRICE	*QUOTE U.S.$
1993 I'm Thankful Too	Retrd.		16.60	40-85

Thanksgiving - D. Zolan

YEAR ISSUE	EDITION LIMIT	YEAR RETD.	ISSUE PRICE	*QUOTE U.S.$
1981 I'm Thankful Too	Retrd.		19.00	70-125

Times To Treasure Bone China (Miniature) - D. Zolan

YEAR ISSUE	EDITION LIMIT	YEAR RETD.	ISSUE PRICE	*QUOTE U.S.$
1993 Little Traveler	Retrd.		16.60	30-65
1993 Garden Swing	Retrd.		16.60	27-55
1994 Summer Garden	Retrd.		16.60	25-55
1994 September Girl	Retrd.		16.60	25-55

Wonder of Childhood - D. Zolan

YEAR ISSUE	EDITION LIMIT	YEAR RETD.	ISSUE PRICE	*QUOTE U.S.$
1982 Touching the Sky	Retrd.		19.00	39-65
1983 Spring Innocence	Retrd.		19.00	45-65
1984 Winter Angel	Retrd.		22.00	60-75
1985 Small Wonder	Retrd.		22.00	45-65
1986 Grandma's Garden	Retrd.		22.00	48-75
1987 Day Dreamer	Retrd.		22.00	36-65

Yesterday's Children (Miniature) - D. Zolan

YEAR ISSUE	EDITION LIMIT	YEAR RETD.	ISSUE PRICE	*QUOTE U.S.$
1994 Little Friends	Retrd.		16.60	40-65
1994 Seaside Treasures	Retrd.		16.60	30-65

Zolan's Children - D. Zolan

YEAR ISSUE	EDITION LIMIT	YEAR RETD.	ISSUE PRICE	*QUOTE U.S.$
1978 Erik and Dandelion	Retrd.		19.00	100-200
1979 Sabina in the Grass	Retrd.		22.00	150-250
1980 By Myself	Retrd.		24.00	55-85
1981 For You	Retrd.		24.00	40-75

Porterfield's

Rob Anders Collectors Society - R. Anders

YEAR ISSUE	EDITION LIMIT	YEAR RETD.	ISSUE PRICE	*QUOTE U.S.$
1997 Short Stories	Yr.Iss.	1997	19.00	40-45
1998 Cuddling Up	Yr.Iss.		19.00	19
1999 First Look	Yr.Iss.		19.00	19

Moments of Wonder - R. Anders

YEAR ISSUE	EDITION LIMIT	YEAR RETD.	ISSUE PRICE	*QUOTE U.S.$
1996 First Love	44-day	1996	16.60	30-65
1996 Time Out	19-day	1997	16.60	27-45
1996 Safe Harbor	19-day	1997	16.60	28-32
1996 Digging In	19-day	1997	16.60	21-35
1997 Two Bites To Go	19-day	1998	16.60	25-28
1997 Sweet Dreams	19-day	1998	16.60	17-25

Single Issues - R. Anders

YEAR ISSUE	EDITION LIMIT	YEAR RETD.	ISSUE PRICE	*QUOTE U.S.$
1997 Cookies For Daddy (Father's Day, 1997)	19-day	1998	16.60	20-40
1997 Spooky Stories (Halloween, 1997)	10-day	1998	16.60	17-26
1998 Tucked In (Mother's Day, 1998)	10-day		16.60	16
1998 A Visit to Santa (Christmas, 1998)	10-day		16.60	16

Treasures of the Heart - R. Anders

YEAR ISSUE	EDITION LIMIT	YEAR RETD.	ISSUE PRICE	*QUOTE U.S.$
1997 In Good Hands	10-day		16.60	16
1998 Bubbles Away	10-day		16.60	16
1998 Mr. Muscles	10-day		16.60	16
1998 Lazy Days	10-day		16.60	16
1998 Picture Perfect	10-day		16.60	16

Precious Moments/Enesco Corporation

Beauty of Christmas Collection - S. Butcher

YEAR ISSUE	EDITION LIMIT	YEAR RETD.	ISSUE PRICE	*QUOTE U.S.$
1994 You're as Pretty as a Christmas Tree 530409	Yr.Iss.		50.00	50
1995 He Covers the Earth With His Beauty 142670	Yr.Iss.		50.00	50
1996 Peace On Earth...Anyway 183377	Yr.Iss.		50.00	50
1997 Cane You Join Us For A Merry Christmas 272701	Yr.Iss.		50.00	50
1998 I'm Sending You a Merry Christmas 469327	Yr.Iss.		50.00	50

Christmas Blessings - S. Butcher

YEAR ISSUE	EDITION LIMIT	YEAR RETD.	ISSUE PRICE	*QUOTE U.S.$
1990 Wishing You A Yummy Christmas 523801	Yr.Iss.		50.00	50-55
1991 Blessings From Me To Thee 523860	Yr.Iss.		50.00	55-60
1992 But The Greatest of These Is Love 527742	Yr.Iss.		50.00	50
1993 Wishing You the Sweetest Christmas 530204	Yr.Iss.		50.00	50-55

Christmas Collection - S. Butcher

YEAR ISSUE	EDITION LIMIT	YEAR RETD.	ISSUE PRICE	*QUOTE U.S.$
1981 Come Let Us Adore Him E-5646	15,000		40.00	40-65
1982 Let Heaven and Nature Sing E-2347	15,000		40.00	40-45
1983 Wee Three Kings-E-0538	15,000		40.00	45-50
1984 Unto Us a Child Is Born E-5395	15,000		40.00	40-50

Christmas Love Series - S. Butcher

YEAR ISSUE	EDITION LIMIT	YEAR RETD.	ISSUE PRICE	*QUOTE U.S.$
1986 I'm Sending You a White Christmas 101834	Yr.Iss.		45.00	45-55
1987 My Peace I Give Unto Thee 102954	Yr.Iss.		45.00	45-90
1988 Merry Christmas Deer 520284	Yr.Iss.		50.00	55-65
1989 May Your Christmas Be A Happy Home 523003	Yr.Iss.		50.00	50-55

The Four Seasons Series - S. Butcher

YEAR ISSUE	EDITION LIMIT	YEAR RETD.	ISSUE PRICE	*QUOTE U.S.$
1985 The Voice of Spring 12106	Yr.Iss.		40.00	50-110
1985 Summer's Joy 12114	Yr.Iss.		40.00	50-85
1986 Autumn's Praise 12122	Yr.Iss.		40.00	53-60
1986 Winter's Song 12130	Yr.Iss.		40.00	40-58

Inspired Thoughts Series - S. Butcher

YEAR ISSUE	EDITION LIMIT	YEAR RETD.	ISSUE PRICE	*QUOTE U.S.$
1981 Love One Another E-5215	15,000		40.00	40-60
1982 Make a Joyful Noise E-7174	15,000		40.00	40-45
1983 I Believe In Miracles E-9257	15,000		40.00	40-50
1984 Love is Kind E-2847	15,000		40.00	40-50

Joy of Christmas Series - S. Butcher

YEAR ISSUE	EDITION LIMIT	YEAR RETD.	ISSUE PRICE	*QUOTE U.S.$
1982 I'll Play My Drum For Him E-2357	Yr.Iss.		40.00	40-75
1983 Christmastime is for Sharing E-0505	Yr.Iss.		40.00	40-60
1984 The Wonder of Christmas E-5396	Yr.Iss.		40.00	40-50
1985 Tell Me the Story of Jesus 15237	Yr.Iss.		40.00	40-90

Mother's Day Series - S. Butcher

YEAR ISSUE	EDITION LIMIT	YEAR RETD.	ISSUE PRICE	*QUOTE U.S.$
1981 Mother Sew Dear E-5217	15,000		40.00	40-60
1982 The Purr-fect Grandma E-7173	15,000		40.00	40-45
1983 The Hand that Rocks the Future E-9256	15,000		40.00	40
1984 Loving Thy Neighbor E-2848	15,000		40.00	40
1994 Thinking of You Is What I Really Like to Do 531766	Yr.Iss.		50.00	50
1996 Of All The Mothers I Have Known There's None As Precious As My Own 163716	Yr.Iss.		50.00	50

Open Editions - S. Butcher

YEAR ISSUE	EDITION LIMIT	YEAR RETD.	ISSUE PRICE	*QUOTE U.S.$
1982 Our First Christmas Together E-2378	Suspd.		30.00	45-55
1981 The Lord Bless You and Keep You E-5216	Suspd.		30.00	40-45
1982 Rejoicing with You E-7172	Suspd.		30.00	40
1983 Jesus Loves Me E-9275	Suspd.		30.00	40-48
1983 Jesus Loves Me E-9276	Suspd.		30.00	40-45
1994 Bring The Little Ones To Jesus 531359	Yr.Iss.		50.00	50

Precious Moments - S. Butcher

YEAR ISSUE	EDITION LIMIT	YEAR RETD.	ISSUE PRICE	*QUOTE U.S.$
1995 He Hath Made Everything Beautiful in His Time 129151	Open		50.00	50
1997 Love One Another 186406	Open		35.00	35
1997 Good Friends Are Forever 186457	Open		35.00	35

Reco International

Alan Maley's Past Impressions - A. Maley

YEAR ISSUE	EDITION LIMIT	YEAR RETD.	ISSUE PRICE	*QUOTE U.S.$
1997 Festive Occasion	95-day		29.90	30
1997 Sleigh Bells	95-day		29.90	30
1997 Summer Elegance	95-day		29.90	30
1997 The Recital	95-day		29.90	30

Amish Traditions - B. Farnsworth

YEAR ISSUE	EDITION LIMIT	YEAR RETD.	ISSUE PRICE	*QUOTE U.S.$
1994 Golden Harvest	95-day		29.50	30
1994 Family Outing	95-day		29.50	30
1994 The Quilting Bee	95-day		29.50	30
1995 Last Day of School	95-day	1998	29.50	30

Barefoot Children - S. Kuck

YEAR ISSUE	EDITION LIMIT	YEAR RETD.	ISSUE PRICE	*QUOTE U.S.$
1987 Night-Time Story	Retrd.	1994	29.50	50-54
1987 Golden Afternoon	Retrd.	1996	29.50	36-55
1988 Little Sweethearts	Retrd.	1995	29.50	40-45
1988 Carousel Magic	Retrd.	1996	29.50	56-65
1988 Under the Apple Tree	Retrd.	1995	29.50	45-55
1988 The Rehearsal	Retrd.	1995	29.50	50-65
1988 Pretty as a Picture	Retrd.	1993	29.50	70-75
1988 Grandma's Trunk	Retrd.	1993	29.50	50-65

Becky's Day - J. McClelland

YEAR ISSUE	EDITION LIMIT	YEAR RETD.	ISSUE PRICE	*QUOTE U.S.$
1985 Awakening	90-day		24.50	25
1985 Getting Dressed	Retrd.	1988	24.50	25-35
1986 Breakfast	Retrd.	1987	27.50	35-45
1986 Learning is Fun	Retrd.	1988	27.50	28
1986 Muffin Making	Retrd.	1989	27.50	28
1986 Tub Time	Retrd.	1989	27.50	33
1986 Evening Prayer	Retrd.	1990	27.50	28

Birds of the Hidden Forest - G. Ratnavira

YEAR ISSUE	EDITION LIMIT	YEAR RETD.	ISSUE PRICE	*QUOTE U.S.$
1994 Macaw Waterfall	96-day		29.50	30
1994 Paradise Valley	96-day		29.50	30
1995 Toucan Treasure	96-day		29.50	30

Bohemian Annuals - Factory Artist

YEAR ISSUE	EDITION LIMIT	YEAR RETD.	ISSUE PRICE	*QUOTE U.S.$
1974 1974	Retrd.	1975	130.00	155
1975 1975	Retrd.	1976	140.00	160
1976 1976	Retrd.	1978	150.00	160

Carnival Collection - R. Lee

YEAR ISSUE	EDITION LIMIT	YEAR RETD.	ISSUE PRICE	*QUOTE U.S.$
1998 Wheelin'	76-day		29.90	30
1998 Clown-Air	76-day		29.90	30
1998 Runaway Train	76-day		29.90	30
1998 Horsin'	76-day		29.90	30

Castles & Dreams - J. Bergsma

YEAR ISSUE	EDITION LIMIT	YEAR RETD.	ISSUE PRICE	*QUOTE U.S.$
1992 The Birth of a Dream	48-day		29.50	30
1992 Dreams Come True	48-day		29.50	30
1993 Believe In Your Dreams	48-day		29.50	30
1994 Follow Your Dreams	48-day		29.50	30

A Childhood Almanac - S. Kuck

YEAR ISSUE	EDITION LIMIT	YEAR RETD.	ISSUE PRICE	*QUOTE U.S.$
1985 Fireside Dreams-January	Retrd.	1991	29.50	40-65
1985 Be Mine-February	Retrd.	1992	29.50	35-49
1986 Winds of March-March	Retrd.	1994	29.50	54-65
1985 Easter Morning-April	Retrd.	1992	29.50	65-75
1985 For Mom-May	Retrd.	1992	29.50	35-55
1985 Just Dreaming-June	Retrd.	1992	29.50	60-65
1985 Star Spangled Sky-July	Retrd.	1995	29.50	65-69
1985 Summer Secrets-August	Retrd.	1991	29.50	35-75
1985 School Days-September	Retrd.	1991	29.50	65-75
1986 Indian Summer-October	Retrd.	1991	29.50	60-65
1986 Giving Thanks-November	Retrd.	1995	29.50	55-70
1985 Christmas Magic-December	Retrd.	1995	35.00	55-68

Children of the Sun - V. Di Fate

YEAR ISSUE	EDITION LIMIT	YEAR RETD.	ISSUE PRICE	*QUOTE U.S.$
1998 Mars The Red Planet	95-day		29.90	30
1998 The Bright Rings of Saturn	95-day		29.90	30

A Children's Christmas Pageant - S. Kuck

YEAR ISSUE	EDITION LIMIT	YEAR RETD.	ISSUE PRICE	*QUOTE U.S.$
1986 Silent Night	Retrd.	1987	32.50	75-90
1987 Hark the Herald Angels Sing	Retrd.	1988	32.50	65-69
1988 While Shepherds Watched...	Retrd.	1990	32.50	39-55
1989 We Three Kings	Yr.Iss.	N/A	32.50	55-59

The Children's Garden - J. McClelland

YEAR ISSUE	EDITION LIMIT	YEAR RETD.	ISSUE PRICE	*QUOTE U.S.$
1993 Garden Friends	Retrd.	1996	29.50	33
1993 Tea for Three	Retrd.	1996	29.50	33
1993 Puppy Love	Retrd.	1996	29.50	33

Christening Gift - S. Kuck

YEAR ISSUE	EDITION LIMIT	YEAR RETD.	ISSUE PRICE	*QUOTE U.S.$
1995 God's Gift	Open		29.90	30

The Christmas Series - J. Bergsma

YEAR ISSUE	EDITION LIMIT	YEAR RETD.	ISSUE PRICE	*QUOTE U.S.$
1990 Down The Glistening Lane	Retrd.	1996	35.00	35
1991 A Child Is Born	Retrd.	1996	35.00	35
1992 Christmas Day	Retrd.	1996	35.00	35
1993 I Wish You An Angel	Retrd.	1996	35.00	35

Christmas Wishes - J. Bergsma

YEAR ISSUE	EDITION LIMIT	YEAR RETD.	ISSUE PRICE	*QUOTE U.S.$
1994 I Wish You Love	75-day		29.50	30
1995 I Wish You Joy	75-day		29.50	30
1996 I Wish You Peace	75-day		29.50	30

Days Gone By - S. Kuck

YEAR ISSUE	EDITION LIMIT	YEAR RETD.	ISSUE PRICE	*QUOTE U.S.$
1983 Sunday Best	Retrd.	1984	29.50	65-69
1983 Amy's Magic Horse	Retrd.	1985	29.50	23-50
1984 Little Anglers	Retrd.	1985	29.50	65-69
1984 Afternoon Recital	Retrd.	1985	29.50	69-75
1984 Little Tutor	Retrd.	1985	29.50	20-55
1985 Easter at Grandma's	Retrd.	1985	29.50	45-65
1985 Morning Song	Retrd.	1986	29.50	40-45
1985 The Surrey Ride	Retrd.	1987	29.50	45-65

Dresden Christmas - Factory Artist

YEAR ISSUE	EDITION LIMIT	YEAR RETD.	ISSUE PRICE	*QUOTE U.S.$
1971 Shepherd Scene	Retrd.	1978	15.00	50
1972 Niklas Church	Retrd.	1978	15.00	25
1973 Schwanstein Church	Retrd.	1978	18.00	35
1974 Village Scene	Retrd.	1978	20.00	30
1975 Rothenburg Scene	Retrd.	1978	24.00	30
1976 Village Church	Retrd.	1978	26.00	35
1977 Old Mill	Retrd.	1978	28.00	30

Dresden Mother's Day - Factory Artist

YEAR ISSUE	EDITION LIMIT	YEAR RETD.	ISSUE PRICE	*QUOTE U.S.$
1972 Doe and Fawn	Retrd.	1979	15.00	20
1973 Mare and Colt	Retrd.	1979	16.00	25
1974 Tiger and Cub	Retrd.	1979	20.00	23
1975 Dachshunds	Retrd.	1979	24.00	28
1976 Owl and Offspring	Retrd.	1979	26.00	30
1977 Chamois	Retrd.	1979	28.00	30

Eagle of America - S. Barlowe

YEAR ISSUE	EDITION LIMIT	YEAR RETD.	ISSUE PRICE	*QUOTE U.S.$
1996 Land of The Free	96-day		29.90	30

Enchanted Gardens - S. Kuck

YEAR ISSUE	EDITION LIMIT	YEAR RETD.	ISSUE PRICE	*QUOTE U.S.$
1998 Tea For Three	95-day		32.95	33
1998 Sweetest Delights	95-day		32.95	33

The Enchanted Norfin Trolls - C. Hopkins

YEAR ISSUE	EDITION LIMIT	YEAR RETD.	ISSUE PRICE	*QUOTE U.S.$
1993 Troll Maiden	Retrd.	1996	19.50	20
1993 The Wizard Troll	Retrd.	1996	19.50	20
1993 The Troll and His Dragon	Retrd.	1996	19.50	20
1994 Troll in Shinning Armor	Retrd.	1996	19.50	20
1994 Minstrel Troll	Retrd.	1996	19.50	20
1994 If Trolls Could Fly	Retrd.	1996	19.50	20
1994 Chef le Troll	Retrd.	1996	19.50	20
1994 Queen of Trolls	Retrd.	1996	19.50	20

Everlasing Friends - S. Kuck

YEAR ISSUE	EDITION LIMIT	YEAR RETD.	ISSUE PRICE	*QUOTE U.S.$
1996 Sharing Secrets	95-day		29.95	30
1996 Sharing Dreams	95-day		29.95	30
1997 Sharing Beauty	95-day		29.95	30
1997 Sharing Love	95-day		29.95	30
1998 Sharing Harmony	95-day		29.95	30

Everyday Heroes - B. Brown

YEAR ISSUE	EDITION LIMIT	YEAR RETD.	ISSUE PRICE	*QUOTE U.S.$
1998 Out of the Blaze	95-day		29.90	30

*Quotes have been rounded up to nearest dollar

Fishtales - R. Manning

YEAR ISSUE	EDITION LIMIT	YEAR RETD.	ISSUE PRICE	*QUOTE U.S.$
1997 Rainbow River	76-day		29.90	30

The Flower Fairies Year Collection - C.M. Barker

YEAR ISSUE	EDITION LIMIT	YEAR RETD.	ISSUE PRICE	*QUOTE U.S.$
1990 The Red Clover Fairy	Retrd.	1996	29.50	35
1990 The Wild Cherry Blossom Fairy	Retrd.	1996	29.50	35
1990 The Pine Tree Fairy	Retrd.	1996	29.50	35
1990 The Rose Hip Fairy	Retrd.	1996	29.50	35

Four Seasons - J. Poluszynski

YEAR ISSUE	EDITION LIMIT	YEAR RETD.	ISSUE PRICE	*QUOTE U.S.$
1973 Spring	Retrd.	1975	50.00	75
1973 Summer	Retrd.	1975	50.00	75
1973 Fall	Retrd.	1975	50.00	75
1973 Winter	Retrd.	1975	50.00	75

Friends For Keeps - S. Kuck

YEAR ISSUE	EDITION LIMIT	YEAR RETD.	ISSUE PRICE	*QUOTE U.S.$
1996 Puppy Love	95-day		29.95	30
1996 Gone Fishing	95-day		29.95	30
1997 Golden Days	95-day		29.95	30
1997 Take Me Home	95-day		29.95	30

Furstenberg Christmas - Factory Artist

YEAR ISSUE	EDITION LIMIT	YEAR RETD.	ISSUE PRICE	*QUOTE U.S.$
1971 Rabbits	Retrd.	1977	15.00	30
1972 Snowy Village	Retrd.	1977	15.00	20
1973 Christmas Eve	Retrd.	1977	18.00	35
1974 Sparrows	Retrd.	1977	20.00	30
1975 Deer Family	Retrd.	1977	22.00	30
1976 Winter Birds	Retrd.	1977	25.00	25

Furstenberg Deluxe Christmas - E. Grossberg

YEAR ISSUE	EDITION LIMIT	YEAR RETD.	ISSUE PRICE	*QUOTE U.S.$
1971 Wise Men	Retrd.	1974	45.00	45
1972 Holy Family	Retrd.	1974	45.00	45
1973 Christmas Eve	Retrd.	1974	60.00	65

Furstenberg Easter - Factory Artist

YEAR ISSUE	EDITION LIMIT	YEAR RETD.	ISSUE PRICE	*QUOTE U.S.$
1971 Sheep	Retrd.	1973	15.00	150
1972 Chicks	Retrd.	1975	15.00	60
1973 Bunnies	Retrd.	1976	16.00	80
1974 Pussywillow	Retrd.	1976	20.00	33
1975 Easter Window	Retrd.	1977	22.00	30
1976 Flower Collecting	Retrd.	1977	25.00	25

Furstenberg Mother's Day - Factory Artist

YEAR ISSUE	EDITION LIMIT	YEAR RETD.	ISSUE PRICE	*QUOTE U.S.$
1972 Hummingbirds, Fe	Retrd.	1974	15.00	45
1973 Hedgehogs	Retrd.	1974	16.00	40
1974 Doe and Fawn	Retrd.	1974	20.00	30
1975 Swans	Retrd.	1976	22.00	23
1976 Koala Bears	Retrd.	1976	25.00	30

Furstenberg Olympic - J. Poluszynski

YEAR ISSUE	EDITION LIMIT	YEAR RETD.	ISSUE PRICE	*QUOTE U.S.$
1972 Munich	Retrd.	1972	20.00	75
1976 Montreal	Retrd.	1976	37.50	38

Games Children Play - S. Kuck

YEAR ISSUE	EDITION LIMIT	YEAR RETD.	ISSUE PRICE	*QUOTE U.S.$
1979 Me First	Retrd.	1983	45.00	50-75
1980 Forever Bubbles	Retrd.	1983	45.00	48-65
1981 Skating Pals	Retrd.	1983	45.00	48-65
1982 Join Me	10,000		45.00	45

Gardens of Beauty - D. Barlowe

YEAR ISSUE	EDITION LIMIT	YEAR RETD.	ISSUE PRICE	*QUOTE U.S.$
1988 English Country Garden	Retrd.	1996	29.50	32
1988 Dutch Country Garden	Retrd.	1996	29.50	30
1988 New England Garden	Retrd.	1996	29.50	32
1988 Japanese Garden	Retrd.	1996	29.50	30
1989 Italian Garden	Retrd.	1996	29.50	30
1989 Hawaiian Garden	Retrd.	1996	29.50	30
1989 German Country Garden	Retrd.	1996	29.50	30
1989 Mexican Garden	Retrd.	1996	29.50	30
1992 Colonial Splendor	Retrd.	1994	29.50	30

Gardens of Innocence - S. Kuck

YEAR ISSUE	EDITION LIMIT	YEAR RETD.	ISSUE PRICE	*QUOTE U.S.$
1997 Heavenly Hideaway	95-day		32.95	33
1997 Sweetly Swinging	95-day		32.95	33
1998 Gently Giving	95-day		32.95	33
1998 Precious Party	95-day		32.95	33

Generations - B. Brown

YEAR ISSUE	EDITION LIMIT	YEAR RETD.	ISSUE PRICE	*QUOTE U.S.$
1997 Passing On The Faith	95-day		29.90	30
1998 Guiding the Way	95-day		29.90	30
1998 Learning To Imagine	95-day		29.90	30

Gift of Love Mother's Day Collection - S. Kuck

YEAR ISSUE	EDITION LIMIT	YEAR RETD.	ISSUE PRICE	*QUOTE U.S.$
1993 Morning Glory	Retrd.	1994	65.00	75-85
1994 Memories From The Heart	Retrd.	1994	65.00	75-85

The Glory Of Christ - C. Micarelli

YEAR ISSUE	EDITION LIMIT	YEAR RETD.	ISSUE PRICE	*QUOTE U.S.$
1992 The Ascension	48-day		29.50	30
1993 Jesus Teaching	48-day		29.50	30
1993 The Last Supper	48-day		29.50	30
1993 The Nativity	48-day		29.50	30
1993 The Baptism Of Christ	48-day		29.50	30
1993 Jesus Heals The Sick	48-day		29.50	30
1994 Jesus Walks On Water	48-day		29.50	30
1994 Descent From The Cross	48-day		29.50	30

God's Own Country - I. Drechsler

YEAR ISSUE	EDITION LIMIT	YEAR RETD.	ISSUE PRICE	*QUOTE U.S.$
1990 Daybreak	Retrd.	1996	30.00	30
1990 Coming Home	Retrd.	1996	30.00	30
1990 Peaceful Gathering	Retrd.	1996	30.00	30
1990 Quiet Waters	Retrd.	1996	30.00	30

The Grandparent Collector's Plates - S. Kuck

YEAR ISSUE	EDITION LIMIT	YEAR RETD.	ISSUE PRICE	*QUOTE U.S.$
1981 Grandma's Cookie Jar	Yr.Iss.		37.50	38
1981 Grandpa and the Dollhouse	Yr.Iss.		37.50	38

Great Stories from the Bible - G. Katz

YEAR ISSUE	EDITION LIMIT	YEAR RETD.	ISSUE PRICE	*QUOTE U.S.$
1987 Moses in the Bulrushes	Retrd.	1994	29.50	30-45
1987 King Saul & David	Retrd.	1994	29.50	30-45
1987 Moses and the Ten Commandments	Retrd.	1994	29.50	38-45
1987 Joseph's Coat of Many Colors	Retrd.	1994	29.50	30-45
1988 Rebekah at the Well	Retrd.	1994	29.50	35-45
1988 Daniel Reads the Writing on the Wall	Retrd.	1994	29.50	45-65
1988 The Story of Ruth	Retrd.	1994	29.50	35-45
1988 King Solomon	Retrd.	1994	29.50	35-45

Guardians Of The Kingdom - J. Bergsma

YEAR ISSUE	EDITION LIMIT	YEAR RETD.	ISSUE PRICE	*QUOTE U.S.$
1990 Rainbow To Ride On	Retrd.	1993	35.00	40
1990 Special Friends Are Few	17,500		35.00	35
1990 Guardians Of The Innocent Children	17,500		35.00	35
1990 The Miracle Of Love	17,500		35.00	35
1991 The Magic Of Love	17,500		35.00	35
1991 Only With The Heart	17,500		35.00	35
1991 To Fly Without Wings	17,500		35.00	35
1991 In Faith I Am Free	17,500		35.00	35

Guiding Lights - D Hahlbohm

YEAR ISSUE	EDITION LIMIT	YEAR RETD.	ISSUE PRICE	*QUOTE U.S.$
1996 Robbins Reef	96-day		29.90	30
1996 Cape Hateras	96-day		29.90	30
1997 Cape Neddick	96-day		29.90	30
1998 Split Rock, MN	96-day		29.90	30

Haven of the Hunters - H. Roe

YEAR ISSUE	EDITION LIMIT	YEAR RETD.	ISSUE PRICE	*QUOTE U.S.$
1994 Eagle's Castle	Retrd.	1996	29.50	30
1994 Sanctuary of the Hawk	Retrd.	1996	29.50	30

Hearts And Flowers - S. Kuck

YEAR ISSUE	EDITION LIMIT	YEAR RETD.	ISSUE PRICE	*QUOTE U.S.$
1991 Patience	120-day		29.50	45
1991 Tea Party	120-day		29.50	55
1992 Cat's In The Cradle	120-day		32.50	45
1992 Carousel of Dreams	120-day		32.50	33
1992 Storybook Memories	120-day		32.50	33
1993 Delightful Bundle	120-day		34.50	35
1993 Easter Morning Visitor	120-day		34.50	35
1993 Me and My Pony	120-day		34.50	40

Heavenly Kingdom - C. Micarelli

YEAR ISSUE	EDITION LIMIT	YEAR RETD.	ISSUE PRICE	*QUOTE U.S.$
1997 The Blessed Child	95-day		29.90	30

Imaginary Gardens - S. Somerville

YEAR ISSUE	EDITION LIMIT	YEAR RETD.	ISSUE PRICE	*QUOTE U.S.$
1996 Pussywillows	76-day		29.90	30
1996 Dogwood	76-day		29.90	30
1997 Cowslip	76-day		29.90	30

In The Eye of The Storm - W. Lowe

YEAR ISSUE	EDITION LIMIT	YEAR RETD.	ISSUE PRICE	*QUOTE U.S.$
1991 First Strike	Retrd.	1996	29.50	30
1992 Night Force	Retrd.	1996	29.50	30
1992 Tracks Across The Sand	Retrd.	1996	29.50	30
1992 The Storm Has Landed	Retrd.	1996	29.50	30

J. Bergsma Mother's Day Series - J. Bergsma

YEAR ISSUE	EDITION LIMIT	YEAR RETD.	ISSUE PRICE	*QUOTE U.S.$
1990 The Beauty Of Life	Retrd.	1996	35.00	35-38
1992 Life's Blessing	Retrd.	1996	35.00	35-38
1993 My Greatest Treasures	Retrd.	1996	35.00	35-38
1994 Forever In My Heart	Retrd.	1996	35.00	35-38

Jesus And The Children - N. Mc Naulty

YEAR ISSUE	EDITION LIMIT	YEAR RETD.	ISSUE PRICE	*QUOTE U.S.$
1998 Come Unto Me	96-day		29.90	30

King's Christmas - Merli

YEAR ISSUE	EDITION LIMIT	YEAR RETD.	ISSUE PRICE	*QUOTE U.S.$
1973 Adoration	Retrd.	1974	100.00	265
1974 Madonna	Retrd.	1975	150.00	250
1975 Heavenly Choir	Retrd.	1976	160.00	235
1976 Siblings	Retrd.	1978	200.00	225

King's Flowers - A. Falchi

YEAR ISSUE	EDITION LIMIT	YEAR RETD.	ISSUE PRICE	*QUOTE U.S.$
1973 Carnation	Retrd.	1974	85.00	130
1974 Red Rose	Retrd.	1975	100.00	145
1975 Yellow Dahlia	Retrd.	1976	110.00	162
1976 Bluebells	Retrd.	1977	130.00	165
1977 Anemones	Retrd.	1979	130.00	175

King's Mother's Day - Merli

YEAR ISSUE	EDITION LIMIT	YEAR RETD.	ISSUE PRICE	*QUOTE U.S.$
1973 Dancing Girl	Retrd.	1974	100.00	225
1974 Dancing Boy	Retrd.	1975	115.00	250
1975 Motherly Love	Retrd.	1976	140.00	225
1976 Maiden	Retrd.	1978	180.00	200

Kingdom of the Great Cats - P. Jepson

YEAR ISSUE	EDITION LIMIT	YEAR RETD.	ISSUE PRICE	*QUOTE U.S.$
1995 Out of the Mist	36-day		29.50	30
1995 Summit Sanctuary	36-day		29.50	30

Kittens 'N Hats - S. Somerville

YEAR ISSUE	EDITION LIMIT	YEAR RETD.	ISSUE PRICE	*QUOTE U.S.$
1994 Opening Night	48-day		29.50	30
1994 Sitting Pretty	48-day		29.50	30
1995 Little League	48-day		29.50	30

Life's Little Celebrations - C. Tait

YEAR ISSUE	EDITION LIMIT	YEAR RETD.	ISSUE PRICE	*QUOTE U.S.$
1997 The New Baby	96-day		29.90	30
1997 An Apple For The Teacher	96-day		29.90	30
1997 School Bell	96-day		29.90	30
1997 Graduation Smile	96-day		29.90	30
1997 Celebration of Love	96-day		29.90	30
1997 I Love You	96-day		29.90	30

Little Angel Plate Collection - S. Kuck

YEAR ISSUE	EDITION LIMIT	YEAR RETD.	ISSUE PRICE	*QUOTE U.S.$
1994 Angel of Charity	95-day		29.50	30
1994 Angel of Joy	95-day		29.50	30

Little Professionals - S. Kuck

YEAR ISSUE	EDITION LIMIT	YEAR RETD.	ISSUE PRICE	*QUOTE U.S.$
1982 All is Well	Retrd.	1983	39.50	65-95
1983 Tender Loving Care	Retrd.	1985	39.50	55-70
1984 Lost and Found	Retrd.	1995	39.50	45-65
1985 Reading, Writing and...	Retrd.	1989	39.50	50-65

Little Wonders - A. Grant

YEAR ISSUE	EDITION LIMIT	YEAR RETD.	ISSUE PRICE	*QUOTE U.S.$
1998 Safely Through The Night	95-day		29.90	30
1998 First Friend	95-day		29.90	30
1998 Cherished Toys	95-day		29.90	30
1998 Tender Moments	95-day		29.90	30

Magic Companions - J. Bergsma

YEAR ISSUE	EDITION LIMIT	YEAR RETD.	ISSUE PRICE	*QUOTE U.S.$
1994 Believe in Love	48-day		29.50	30
1994 Imagine Peace	48-day		29.50	30
1995 Live in Harmony	48-day		29.50	30
1995 Trust in Magic	48-day		29.50	30

March of Dimes: Our Children, Our Future - Various

YEAR ISSUE	EDITION LIMIT	YEAR RETD.	ISSUE PRICE	*QUOTE U.S.$
1989 A Time to Love (2nd in Series) - S. Kuck	Retrd.	1993	29.00	35-75
1989 A Time to Plant (3rd in Series) - J. McClelland	150-day	1993	29.00	29-59

Marmot Christmas - Factory Artist

YEAR ISSUE	EDITION LIMIT	YEAR RETD.	ISSUE PRICE	*QUOTE U.S.$
1970 Polar Bear, Fe	Retrd.	1971	13.00	20-60
1971 Buffalo Bill	Retrd.	1972	16.00	55
1972 Boy and Grandfather	Retrd.	1973	20.00	50
1971 American Buffalo	Retrd.	1973	14.50	35
1973 Snowman	Retrd.	1974	22.00	45
1974 Dancing	Retrd.	1975	24.00	30
1975 Quail	Retrd.	1976	30.00	40
1976 Windmill	Retrd.	1978	40.00	40

Marmot Father's Day - Factory Artist

YEAR ISSUE	EDITION LIMIT	YEAR RETD.	ISSUE PRICE	*QUOTE U.S.$
1970 Stag	Retrd.	1970	12.00	40-70
1971 Horse	Retrd.	1972	12.50	40

Marmot Mother's Day - Factory Artist

YEAR ISSUE	EDITION LIMIT	YEAR RETD.	ISSUE PRICE	*QUOTE U.S.$
1972 Seal	Retrd.	1973	16.00	60
1973 Bear with Cub	Retrd.	1974	20.00	140
1974 Penguins	Retrd.	1975	24.00	50
1975 Raccoons	Retrd.	1976	30.00	45
1976 Ducks	Retrd.	1977	40.00	40

The McClelland Children's Circus Collection - J. McClelland

YEAR ISSUE	EDITION LIMIT	YEAR RETD.	ISSUE PRICE	*QUOTE U.S.$
1982 Tommy the Clown	Retrd.	N/A	29.50	35-59
1982 Katie, the Tightrope Walker	Retrd.	N/A	29.50	30-59
1983 Johnny the Strongman	Retrd.	N/A	29.50	30-55
1984 Maggie the Animal Trainer	Retrd.	N/A	29.50	30

Memories of Childhood - C. Getz

YEAR ISSUE	EDITION LIMIT	YEAR RETD.	ISSUE PRICE	*QUOTE U.S.$
1994 Teatime with Teddy	75-day		29.50	30
1995 Bases Loaded	75-day		29.50	30
1996 Mommy's Little Helper	75-day		29.50	30

Memories Of Yesterday - M. Attwell

YEAR ISSUE	EDITION LIMIT	YEAR RETD.	ISSUE PRICE	*QUOTE U.S.$
1993 Hush	Retrd.	1996	29.50	30
1993 Time For Bed	Retrd.	1996	29.50	30
1993 I'se Been Painting	Retrd.	1996	29.50	30
1993 Just Looking Pretty	Retrd.	1996	29.50	30
1994 Give it Your Best Shot	Retrd.	1996	29.50	30
1994 I Pray The Lord My Soul to Keep	Retrd.	1996	29.50	30
1994 Just Thinking About You	Retrd.	1996	29.50	30
1994 What Will I Grow Up To Be	Retrd.	1996	29.50	30

Moments At Home - S. Kuck

YEAR ISSUE	EDITION LIMIT	YEAR RETD.	ISSUE PRICE	*QUOTE U.S.$
1995 Moments of Caring	95-day		29.90	30
1995 Moments of Tenderness	95-day		29.90	30
1995 Moments of Friendship	95-day		29.90	30
1995 Moments of Sharing	95-day		29.90	30
1995 Moments of Love	95-day		29.90	30
1996 Moments of Reflection	95-day		29.90	30

Moser Christmas - Factory Artist

YEAR ISSUE	EDITION LIMIT	YEAR RETD.	ISSUE PRICE	*QUOTE U.S.$
1970 Hradcany Castle	Retrd.	1971	75.00	170
1971 Karlstein Castle	Retrd.	1972	75.00	80
1972 Old Town Hall	Retrd.	1973	85.00	85
1973 Karlovy Vary Castle	Retrd.	1974	90.00	100

Moser Mother's Day - Factory Artist

YEAR ISSUE	EDITION LIMIT	YEAR RETD.	ISSUE PRICE	*QUOTE U.S.$
1971 Peacocks	Retrd.	1971	75.00	100
1972 Butterflies	Retrd.	1972	85.00	90
1973 Squirrels	Retrd.	1973	90.00	95

Mother Goose - J. McClelland

YEAR ISSUE	EDITION LIMIT	YEAR RETD.	ISSUE PRICE	*QUOTE U.S.$
1979 Mary, Mary	Retrd.	1979	22.50	55-60
1980 Little Boy Blue	Retrd.	1980	22.50	35-39
1981 Little Miss Muffet	Yr.Iss.		24.50	25-30
1982 Little Jack Horner	Retrd.	1982	24.50	35-40
1983 Little Bo Peep	Yr.Iss.		24.50	30-38
1984 Diddle, Diddle Dumpling	Yr.Iss.		24.50	35-40
1985 Mary Had a Little Lamb	Yr.Iss.		27.50	30
1986 Jack and Jill	Retrd.	1988	27.50	35-40

Mother's Day Collection - S. Kuck

YEAR ISSUE	EDITION LIMIT	YEAR RETD.	ISSUE PRICE	*QUOTE U.S.$
1985 Once Upon a Time	Retrd.	1987	29.50	50-60
1986 Times Remembered	Yr.Iss.		29.50	45-60
1987 A Cherished Time	Yr.Iss.		29.50	45-60
1988 A Time Together	Yr.Iss.		29.50	60-70

Noble and Free - Kelly

YEAR ISSUE	EDITION LIMIT	YEAR RETD.	ISSUE PRICE	*QUOTE U.S.$
1994 Gathering Storm	95-day		29.50	30
1994 Protected Journey	95-day		29.50	30
1994 Moonlight Run	95-day		29.50	30

*Quotes have been rounded up to nearest dollar

YEAR ISSUE	EDITION LIMIT	YEAR RETD.	ISSUE PRICE	*QUOTE U.S.$
The Nutcracker Ballet - C. Micarelli				
1989 Christmas Eve Party	Retrd.	1994	35.00	35
1990 Clara And Her Prince	14-day		35.00	35
1990 The Dream Begins	14-day		35.00	35
1991 Dance of the Snow Fairies	Retrd.	1994	35.00	35
1992 The Land of Sweets	14-day		35.00	35
1992 The Sugar Plum Fairy	14-day		35.00	35
The Open Road - B. Farnsworth				
1997 Lakeside Drive	76-day		29.90	30
Oscar & Bertie's Edwardian Holiday - P.D. Jackson				
1991 Snapshot	Retrd.	1996	29.50	30
1992 Early Rise	Retrd.	1996	29.50	30
1992 All Aboard	Retrd.	1996	29.50	30
1992 Learning To Swim	Retrd.	1996	29.50	30
Our Cherished Seas - S. Barlowe				
1991 Whale Song	48-day		37.50	38
1991 Lions of the Sea	48-day		37.50	38
1991 Flight of the Dolphins	48-day		37.50	38
1992 Palace of the Seals	48-day		37.50	38
1992 Orca Ballet	48-day		37.50	38
1993 Emperors of the Ice	48-day		37.50	38
1993 Turtle Treasure	48-day		37.50	38
1993 Splendor of the Sea	48-day		37.50	38
Out of The Wild - S. Barlowe				
1996 The Pride	76-day		29.90	30
1997 Graceful Giants	76-day		29.90	30
Plate Of The Month Collection - S. Kuck				
1990 January	Retrd.	1996	25.00	28-50
1990 February	Retrd.	1996	25.00	28-50
1990 March	Retrd.	1996	25.00	28-50
1990 April	Retrd.	1996	25.00	28-50
1990 May	Retrd.	1996	25.00	28-50
1990 June	Retrd.	1996	25.00	28-50
1990 July	Retrd.	1996	25.00	28-50
1990 August	Retrd.	1996	25.00	28-50
1990 September	Retrd.	1996	25.00	28-50
1990 October	Retrd.	1996	25.00	28-50
1990 November	Retrd.	1996	25.00	28-50
1990 December	Retrd.	1996	25.00	28-50
Precious Angels - S. Kuck				
1995 Angel of Grace	95-day		29.90	30
1995 Angel of Happiness	95-day		29.90	30
1995 Angel of Hope	95-day		29.90	30
1995 Angel of Laughter	95-day		29.90	30
1995 Angel of Love	95-day		29.90	30
1995 Angel of Peace	95-day		29.90	30
1995 Angel of Sharing	95-day		29.90	30
1995 Angel of Sunshine	95-day		29.90	30
The Premier Collection - J. McClelland				
1991 Love	7,500	1996	75.00	75
Premier Collection - S. Kuck				
1991 Puppy	Retrd.	1993	95.00	125-200
1991 Kitten	Retrd.	1992	95.00	145-300
1992 La Belle	7,500	1996	95.00	95
1992 Le Beau	7,500	1996	95.00	95
Protectors of the Wild - R. Frentner				
1998 Genesis	95-day		29.90	30
Romantic Cafes Of Paris - V. Shvaiko				
1997 By The Hearth	95-day		29.90	30
Romantic Gardens - S. Kuck				
1997 Emma	95-day		35.00	35
1997 Alexandra	95-day		35.00	35
Royal Mother's Day - Factory Artist				
1970 Swan and Young	Retrd.	1971	12.00	80
1971 Doe and Fawn	Retrd.	1972	13.00	55
1972 Rabbits	Retrd.	1973	16.00	40
1973 Owl Family	Retrd.	1974	18.00	40
1974 Duck and Young	Retrd.	1975	22.00	40
1975 Lynx and Cubs	Retrd.	1976	26.00	40
1976 Woodcock and Young	Retrd.	1978	27.50	33
1977 Koala Bear	Retrd.	1978	30.00	30
Royale - Factory Artist				
1969 Apollo Moon Landing	Retrd.	1969	30.00	80
Royale Christmas - Factory Artist				
1969 Christmas Fair	Retrd.	1970	12.00	125
1970 Vigil Mass	Retrd.	1971	13.00	110
1971 Christmas Night	Retrd.	1972	16.00	50
1972 Elks	Retrd.	1973	16.00	45
1973 Christmas Down	Retrd.	1974	20.00	38
1974 Village Christmas	Retrd.	1975	22.00	60
1975 Feeding Time	Retrd.	1976	26.00	35
1976 Seaport Christmas	Retrd.	1977	27.50	30
1977 Sledding	Retrd.	1978	30.00	30
Royale Father's Day - Factory Artist				
1970 Frigate Constitution	Retrd.	1971	13.00	80
1971 Man Fishing	Retrd.	1972	13.00	35
1972 Mountaineer	Retrd.	1973	16.00	55
1973 Camping	Retrd.	1974	18.00	45
1974 Eagle	Retrd.	1975	22.00	35
1975 Regatta	Retrd.	1976	26.00	35
1976 Hunting	Retrd.	1977	27.50	33
1977 Fishing	Retrd.	1978	30.00	30
Royale Game Plates - Various				
1972 Setters - J. Poluszynski	Retrd.	1974	180.00	200
1973 Fox - J. Poluszynski	Retrd.	1975	200.00	250
1974 Osprey - W. Schiener	Retrd.	1976	250.00	250
1975 California Quail - W. Schiener	Retrd.	1976	265.00	265
Royale Germania Christmas Annual - Factory Artist				
1970 Orchid	Retrd.	1971	200.00	650
1971 Cyclamen	Retrd.	1972	200.00	325
1972 Silver Thistle	Retrd.	1973	250.00	290
1973 Tulips	Retrd.	1974	275.00	310
1974 Sunflowers	Retrd.	1975	300.00	320
1975 Snowdrops	Retrd.	1976	450.00	500
Royale Germania Crystal Mother's Day - Factory Artist				
1971 Roses	Retrd.	1971	135.00	650
1972 Elephant and Youngster	Retrd.	1972	180.00	250
1973 Koala Bear and Cub	Retrd.	1973	200.00	225
1974 Squirrels	Retrd.	1974	240.00	250
1975 Swan and Young	Retrd.	1975	350.00	360
Sandra Kuck Mothers' Day - S. Kuck				
1995 Home is Where the Heart Is	48-day		35.00	35
1996 Dear To The Heart	48-day		35.00	35
1997 Welcome Home	48-day		35.00	35
1998 Wings of Love	48-day		35.00	35
Sculpted Heirlooms - S. Kuck				
1996 Best Friends (sculpted plate)	24-mo.		29.95	30
1996 Tea Party (sculpted plate)	24-mo.		29.90	30
1996 Storybook Memories (sculpted plate)	24-mo.		29.90	30
1996 Patience (sculpted plate)	24-mo.		29.90	30
Single Issue - T. Gronland				
1997 Happiness In Heaven	95-day		29.90	30
Songs From The Garden - G. Ratnavira				
1996 Love Song	76-day		29.90	30
1996 Rhapsody In Blue	76-day		29.90	30
1997 Hummingbirds In Harmony	76-day		29.90	30
1997 Golden Melody	76-day		29.90	30
1997 Spring Serenade	76-day		29.90	30
1998 Ode To The Oriole	76-day		29.90	30
The Sophisticated Ladies Collection - A. Fazio				
1985 Felicia	21-day	1997	29.50	30-45
1985 Samantha	21-day	1994	29.50	33-45
1985 Phoebe	21-day	1994	29.50	33-45
1985 Cleo	21-day		29.50	30
1986 Cerissa	21-day	1994	29.50	33-45
1986 Natasha	21-day	1994	29.50	33-45
1986 Bianka	21-day	1994	29.50	33-45
1986 Chelsea	21-day	1994	29.50	33-45
Special Occasions by Reco - S. Kuck				
1988 The Wedding	Retrd.	1997	35.00	35-55
1989 Wedding Day (6 1/2")	Retrd.	1996	25.00	25-45
1990 The Special Day	Retrd.	1996	25.00	25
Special Occasions-Wedding - C. Micarelli				
1991 From This Day Forward (9 1/2")	Retrd.	1997	35.00	35
1991 From This Day Forward (6 1/2")	Retrd.	1996	25.00	25
1991 To Have And To Hold (9 1/2")	Open		35.00	35
1991 To Have And To Hold (6 1/2")	Retrd.	1996	25.00	25
Sugar and Spice - S. Kuck				
1993 Best Friends	95-day		29.90	30
1993 Sisters	95-day		29.90	30
1994 Little One	95-day		32.90	33
1994 Teddy Bear Tales	95-day		32.90	33
1994 Morning Prayers	95-day		32.90	33
1995 First Snow	95-day		34.90	35
1994 Garden of Sunshine	95-day		34.90	35
1995 A Special Day	95-day		34.90	35
Tidings Of Joy - S. Kuck				
1992 Peace on Earth	Retrd.	1995	35.00	49-55
1993 Rejoice	Retrd.	1996	35.00	44-55
1994 Noel	Retrd.	1995	35.00	65-100
Totems of the West - J. Bergsma				
1994 The Watchmen	96-day		29.50	30
1995 Peace At Last	96-day		29.50	30
1995 Never Alone	96-day		35.00	30
Town And Country Dogs - S. Barlowe				
1990 Fox Hunt	36-day		35.00	35
1991 The Retrieval	36-day		35.00	35
1991 Golden Fields (Golden Retriever)	36-day		35.00	35
1993 Faithful Companions (Cocker Spaniel)	36-day		35.00	35
Trains of the Orient Express - R. Johnson				
1993 The Golden Arrow-England	Retrd.	1996	29.50	30
1994 Austria	Retrd.	1996	29.50	30
1994 Bavaria	Retrd.	1996	29.50	30
1994 Rumania	Retrd.	1996	29.50	30
1994 Greece	Retrd.	1996	29.50	30
1994 Frankonia	Retrd.	1996	29.50	30
1994 Turkey	Retrd.	1996	29.50	30
1994 France	Retrd.	1996	29.50	30
Treasured Songs of Childhood - J. McClelland				
1987 Twinkle, Twinkle, Little Star	Retrd.	1990	29.50	38-49
1988 A Tisket, A Tasket	Retrd.	1991	29.50	38-45
1988 Baa, Baa, Black Sheep	Retrd.	1991	32.90	38-45
1989 Round The Mulberry Bush	150-day		32.90	33
1989 Rain, Rain Go Away	Retrd.	1993	32.90	38-50
1989 I'm A Little Teapot	Retrd.	1993	32.90	38-45
1989 Pat-A-Cake	150-day		34.90	35
1990 Hush Little Baby	150-day		34.90	35
Up, Up And Away - P. Alexander				
1996 Rally At The Grand Canyon	76-day		29.90	30
1996 Gateway To Heaven	76-day		29.90	30
1997 Boston Balloon Party	76-day		29.90	30
1998 Through The Golden Gates	76-day		29.90	30
Vanishing Animal Kingdoms - S. Barlowe				
1986 Rama the Tiger	21,500	1996	35.00	35
1986 Olepi the Buffalo	21,500	1996	35.00	35
1987 Coolibah the Koala	21,500	1996	35.00	35
1987 Ortwin the Deer	21,500	1996	35.00	35
1987 Yen-Poh the Panda	21,500	1996	35.00	35
1988 Mamakuu the Elephant	21,500	1996	35.00	35
Victorian Christmas - S. Kuck				
1995 Dear Santa	72-day		35.00	35
1996 Night Before Christmas	72-day		35.00	35
1997 Wrapped With Love	72-day		35.00	35
1998 Christmas Day Joy	72-day		35.00	35
Victorian Mother's Day - S. Kuck				
1989 Mother's Sunshine	Retrd.	1990	35.00	85-95
1990 Reflection Of Love	Retrd.	1991	35.00	90-95
1991 A Precious Time	Retrd.	1992	35.00	80-90
1992 Loving Touch	Retrd.	1993	35.00	75-90
Waterbirds - G. Ratnavira				
1998 Great Blue Herons	95-day		29.90	30
Western - E. Berke				
1974 Mountain Man	Retrd.		165.00	165
Women of the Plains - C. Corcilius				
1994 Pride of a Maiden	36-day		29.50	30
1995 No Boundaries	36-day		29.50	30
1995 Silent Companions	36-day		35.00	35
The Wonder of Christmas - J. McClelland				
1991 Santa's Secret	Retrd.	1996	29.50	30
1992 My Favorite Ornament	Retrd.	1996	29.50	30
1992 Waiting For Santa	Retrd.	1996	29.50	30
1993 Candlelight Christmas	Retrd.	1995	29.50	30-55
The World of Children - J. McClelland				
1977 Rainy Day Fun	10,000	1977	50.00	55-75
1978 When I Grow Up	15,000	1978	50.00	55-75
1979 You're Invited	15,000	1979	50.00	55-75
1980 Kittens for Sale	15,000	1980	50.00	55-85

River Shore

YEAR ISSUE	EDITION LIMIT	YEAR RETD.	ISSUE PRICE	*QUOTE U.S.$
Baby Animals - R. Brown				
1979 Akiku	20,000		50.00	50-80
1980 Roosevelt	20,000		50.00	50-90
1981 Clover	20,000		50.00	50-65
1982 Zuela	20,000		50.00	50-65
Famous Americans - Rockwell-Brown				
1976 Brown's Lincoln	9,500		40.00	40-75
1977 Rockwell's Triple Self-Portrait	9,500		45.00	45-75
1978 Peace Corps	9,500		45.00	45-75
1979 Spirit of Lindbergh	9,500		50.00	50-70
Little House on the Prairie - E. Christopherson				
1985 Founder's Day Picnic	10-day		29.50	45-100
1985 Women's Harvest	10-day		29.50	45-65
1985 Medicine Show	10-day		29.50	45-65
1985 Caroline's Eggs	10-day		29.50	45-65
1985 Mary's Gift	10-day		29.50	45-65
1985 A Bell for Walnut Grove	10-day		29.50	45-65
1985 Ingall's Family	10-day		29.50	45-65
1985 The Sweetheart Tree	10-day		29.50	45-65
Norman Rockwell Single Issue - N. Rockwell				
1979 Spring Flowers	17,000		75.00	145
1980 Looking Out to Sea	17,000		75.00	175-195
1982 Grandpa's Guardian	17,000		80.00	75-80
1982 Grandpa's Treasures	17,000		80.00	75-80
Puppy Playtime - J. Lamb				
1987 Double Take	14-day		24.50	32-35
1988 Catch of the Day	14-day		24.50	25-35
1988 Cabin Fever	14-day		24.50	25-35
1988 Weekend Gardener	14-day		24.50	25-35
1988 Getting Acquainted	14-day		24.50	25-35
1988 Hanging Out	14-day		24.50	25-35
1988 A New Leash On Life	14-day		24.50	30-35
1987 Fun and Games	14-day		24.50	30-35
Rockwell Four Freedoms - N. Rockwell				
1981 Freedom of Speech	17,000		65.00	100-149
1982 Freedom of Worship	17,000		65.00	100-125
1982 Freedom from Fear	17,000		65.00	100-200
1982 Freedom from Want	17,000		65.00	200-425

*Quotes have been rounded up to nearest dollar

Rockwell Society

Christmas - N. Rockwell

YEAR ISSUE	EDITION LIMIT	YEAR RETD.	ISSUE PRICE	*QUOTE U.S.$
1974 Scotty Gets His Tree	Yr.Iss.		24.50	75-89
1975 Angel with Black Eye	Yr.Iss.		24.50	60-65
1976 Golden Christmas	Yr.Iss.		24.50	30-55
1977 Toy Shop Window	Yr.Iss.		24.50	25-40
1978 Christmas Dream	Yr.Iss.		24.50	22-40
1979 Somebody's Up There	Yr.Iss.		24.50	25-39
1980 Scotty Plays Santa	Yr.Iss.		24.50	12-50
1981 Wrapped Up in Christmas	Yr.Iss.		25.50	17-40
1982 Christmas Courtship	Yr.Iss.		25.50	14-40
1983 Santa in the Subway	Yr.Iss.		25.50	15-40
1984 Santa in the Workshop	Yr.Iss.		27.50	18-40
1985 Grandpa Plays Santa	Yr.Iss.		27.90	16-40
1986 Dear Santy Claus	Yr.Iss.		27.90	20-40
1987 Santa's Golden Gift	Yr.Iss.		27.90	18-40
1988 Santa Claus	Yr.Iss.		29.90	20-40
1989 Jolly Old St. Nick	Yr.Iss.		29.90	20-40
1990 A Christmas Prayer	Yr.Iss.		29.90	40-50
1991 Santa's Helpers	Yr.Iss.		32.90	33-40
1992 The Christmas Surprise	Yr.Iss.		32.90	33-40
1993 The Tree Brigade	Yr.Iss.		32.90	33-65
1994 Christmas Marvel	Yr.Iss.		32.90	40-45
1995 Filling The Stockings	Yr.Iss.		32.90	45-60
1996 Christmas	Yr.Iss.		32.90	44-55

Colonials-The Rarest Rockwells - N. Rockwell

YEAR ISSUE	EDITION LIMIT	YEAR RETD.	ISSUE PRICE	*QUOTE U.S.$
1985 Unexpected Proposal	150-day		27.90	32-45
1986 Words of Comfort	150-day		27.90	10-30
1986 Light for the Winter	150-day		30.90	16-30
1987 Portrait for a Bridegroom	150-day		30.90	12-45
1987 The Journey Home	150-day		30.90	12-30
1987 Clinching the Deal	150-day		30.90	15-30
1988 Sign of the Times	150-day		32.90	30-47
1988 Ye Glutton	150-day		32.90	15-30

Coming Of Age - N. Rockwell

YEAR ISSUE	EDITION LIMIT	YEAR RETD.	ISSUE PRICE	*QUOTE U.S.$
1990 Back To School	150-day		29.90	24-45
1990 Home From Camp	150-day		29.90	37-47
1990 Her First Formal	150-day		32.90	50-65
1990 The Muscleman	150-day		32.90	33-45
1990 A New Look	150-day		32.90	30-39
1991 A Balcony Seat	150-day		32.90	20-33
1991 Men About Town	150-day		34.90	23-35
1991 Paths of Glory	150-day		34.90	25-35
1991 Doorway to the Past	150-day		34.90	23-40
1991 School's Out!	150-day		34.90	46-60

Heritage - N. Rockwell

YEAR ISSUE	EDITION LIMIT	YEAR RETD.	ISSUE PRICE	*QUOTE U.S.$
1977 Toy Maker	Yr.Iss.		14.50	50-65
1978 Cobbler	Yr.Iss.		19.50	35-50
1979 Lighthouse Keeper's Daughter	Yr.Iss.		19.50	14-35
1980 Ship Builder	Yr.Iss.		19.50	39-45
1981 Music maker	Yr.Iss.		19.50	42-55
1982 Tycoon	Yr.Iss.		19.50	35-45
1983 Painter	Yr.Iss.		19.50	35-49
1984 Storyteller	Yr.Iss.		19.50	10-30
1985 Gourmet	Yr.Iss.		19.50	10-35
1986 Professor	Yr.Iss.		22.90	12-35
1987 Shadow Artist	Yr.Iss.		22.90	35-45
1988 The Veteran	Yr.Iss.		22.90	15-35
1988 The Banjo Player	Yr.Iss.		22.90	35-55
1990 The Old Scout	Yr.Iss.		24.90	45-50
1991 The Young Scholar	Yr.Iss.		24.90	34-40
1992 The Family Doctor	Yr.Iss.		27.90	40-50
1993 The Jeweler	Yr.Iss.		27.90	28-44
1994 Halloween Frolic	Yr.Iss.		27.90	44-50
1995 The Apprentice	Yr.Iss.		29.90	39-50
1996 Master Violinist	Yr.Iss.		29.90	52-75

Innocence and Experience - N. Rockwell

YEAR ISSUE	EDITION LIMIT	YEAR RETD.	ISSUE PRICE	*QUOTE U.S.$
1991 The Sea Captain	150-day		29.90	30-35
1991 The Radio Operator	150-day		29.90	30-35
1991 The Magician	150-day		32.90	33-50
1992 The American Heroes	150-day		32.90	21-35

A Mind of Her Own - N. Rockwell

YEAR ISSUE	EDITION LIMIT	YEAR RETD.	ISSUE PRICE	*QUOTE U.S.$
1986 Sitting Pretty	150-day		24.90	14-39
1987 Serious Business	150-day		24.90	16-35
1987 Breaking the Rules	150-day		24.90	23-35
1987 Good Intentions	150-day		27.90	26-35
1988 Second Thoughts	150-day		27.90	28-30
1988 World's Away	150-day		27.90	30-39
1988 Kiss and Tell	150-day		29.90	17-35
1988 On My Honor	150-day		29.90	40

Mother's Day - N. Rockwell

YEAR ISSUE	EDITION LIMIT	YEAR RETD.	ISSUE PRICE	*QUOTE U.S.$
1976 A Mother's Love	Yr.Iss.		24.50	60-67
1977 Faith	Yr.Iss.		24.50	55-60
1978 Bedtime	Yr.Iss.		24.50	35-60
1979 Reflections	Yr.Iss.		24.50	18-25
1980 A Mother's Pride	Yr.Iss.		24.50	18-25
1981 After the Party	Yr.Iss.		24.50	15-30
1982 The Cooking Lesson	Yr.Iss.		24.50	20-40
1983 Add Two Cups and Love	Yr.Iss.		25.50	30-45
1984 Grandma's Courting Dress	Yr.Iss.		25.50	30-45
1985 Mending Time	Yr.Iss.		27.50	30-35
1986 Pantry Raid	Yr.Iss.		27.90	17-30
1987 Grandma's Surprise	Yr.Iss.		29.90	15-35
1988 My Mother	Yr.Iss.		29.90	16-32
1989 Sunday Dinner	Yr.Iss.		29.90	30-35
1990 Evening Prayers	Yr.Iss.		29.90	30-45
1991 Building Our Future	Yr.Iss.		32.90	17-35
1991 Gentle Reassurance	Yr.Iss.		32.90	30-33
1992 A Special Delivery	Yr.Iss.		32.90	18-35

Rockwell Commemorative Stamps - N. Rockwell

YEAR ISSUE	EDITION LIMIT	YEAR RETD.	ISSUE PRICE	*QUOTE U.S.$
1994 Triple Self Portrait	95-day		29.90	30-45
1994 Freedom From Want	95-day		29.90	30
1994 Freedom From Fear	95-day		29.90	30
1995 Freedom of Speech	95-day		29.90	30
1995 Freedom of Worship	95-day		29.90	30

Rockwell on Tour - N. Rockwell

YEAR ISSUE	EDITION LIMIT	YEAR RETD.	ISSUE PRICE	*QUOTE U.S.$
1983 Walking Through Merrie Englande	150-day		16.00	6-16
1983 Promenade a Paris	150-day		16.00	30
1983 When in Rome	150-day		16.00	7-16
1984 Die Walk am Rhein	150-day		16.00	7-16

Rockwell's American Dream - N. Rockwell

YEAR ISSUE	EDITION LIMIT	YEAR RETD.	ISSUE PRICE	*QUOTE U.S.$
1985 A Young Girl's Dream	150-day		19.90	13-40
1985 A Couple's Commitment	150-day		19.90	20-25
1985 A Family's Full Measure	150-day		22.90	20-30
1986 A Mother's Welcome	150-day		22.90	18-30
1986 A Young Man's Dream	150-day		22.90	25-30
1986 The Musician's Magic	150-day		22.90	20-30
1987 An Orphan's Hope	150-day		24.90	29
1987 Love's Reward	150-day		24.90	35-40

Rockwell's Golden Moments - N. Rockwell

YEAR ISSUE	EDITION LIMIT	YEAR RETD.	ISSUE PRICE	*QUOTE U.S.$
1987 Grandpa's Gift	150-day		19.90	25-35
1987 Grandma's Love	150-day		19.90	20-30
1988 End of day	150-day		22.90	30-45
1988 Best Friends	150-day		22.90	23-30
1989 Love Letters	150-day		22.90	28-40
1989 Newfound Worlds	150-day		22.90	30-45
1989 Keeping Company	150-day		24.90	30-45
1989 Evening's Repose	150-day		24.90	30-45

Rockwell's Light Campaign - N. Rockwell

YEAR ISSUE	EDITION LIMIT	YEAR RETD.	ISSUE PRICE	*QUOTE U.S.$
1983 This is the Room that Light Made	150-day		19.50	30-45
1984 Grandpa's Treasure Chest	150-day		19.50	25-45
1984 Father's Help	150-day		19.50	25-40
1984 Evening's Ease	150-day		19.50	25-45
1984 Close Harmony	150-day		21.50	15-25
1984 The Birthday Wish	150-day		21.50	14-30

Rockwell's Rediscovered Women - N. Rockwell

YEAR ISSUE	EDITION LIMIT	YEAR RETD.	ISSUE PRICE	*QUOTE U.S.$
1984 Dreaming in the Attic	100-day		19.50	35-45
1984 Waiting on the Shore	100-day		22.50	25-45
1984 Pondering on the Porch	100-day		22.50	25-45
1984 Making Believe at the Mirror	100-day		22.50	25-45
1984 Waiting at the Dance	100-day		22.50	30-45
1984 Gossiping in the Alcove	100-day		22.50	25-45
1984 Standing in the Doorway	100-day		22.50	20-45
1984 Flirting in the Parlor	100-day		22.50	25-45
1984 Working in the Kitchen	100-day		22.50	35-45
1984 Meeting on the Path	100-day		22.50	35-45
1984 Confiding in the Den	100-day		22.50	35-45
1984 Reminiscing in the Quiet	100-day		22.50	18-45
XX Complete Collection	100-day		267.00	267

Rockwell's The Ones We Love - N. Rockwell

YEAR ISSUE	EDITION LIMIT	YEAR RETD.	ISSUE PRICE	*QUOTE U.S.$
1988 Tender Loving Care	150-day		19.90	45
1989 A Time to Keep	150-day		19.90	30-45
1989 The Inventor And The Judge	150-day		22.90	18-33
1989 Ready For The World	150-day		22.90	25-30
1989 Growing Strong	150-day		22.90	25-30
1990 The Story Hour	150-day		22.90	23-35
1990 The Country Doctor	150-day		24.90	25-40
1990 Our Love of Country	150-day		24.90	25-30
1990 The Homecoming	150-day		24.90	20-30
1991 A Helping Hand	150-day		24.90	19-30

Rockwell's Treasured Memories - N. Rockwell

YEAR ISSUE	EDITION LIMIT	YEAR RETD.	ISSUE PRICE	*QUOTE U.S.$
1991 Quiet Reflections	150-day		29.90	30-35
1991 Romantic Reverie	150-day		29.90	27-30
1991 Tender Romance	150-day		32.90	20-33
1991 Evening Passage	150-day		32.90	19-33
1991 Heavenly Dreams	150-day		32.90	20-35
1991 Sentimental Shores	150-day		32.90	24-33

Roman, Inc.

Abbie Williams Collection - A. Williams

YEAR ISSUE	EDITION LIMIT	YEAR RETD.	ISSUE PRICE	*QUOTE U.S.$
1991 Legacy of Love	Closed	N/A	29.50	30
1991 Bless This Child	Closed	N/A	29.50	30

Catnippers - I. Spencer

YEAR ISSUE	EDITION LIMIT	YEAR RETD.	ISSUE PRICE	*QUOTE U.S.$
1986 Christmas Mourning	9,500	N/A	34.50	35
1992 Happy Holidaze	9,500	N/A	34.50	35

A Child's Play - F. Hook

YEAR ISSUE	EDITION LIMIT	YEAR RETD.	ISSUE PRICE	*QUOTE U.S.$
1982 Breezy Day	30-day	N/A	29.95	39
1982 Kite Flying	30-day	N/A	29.95	39
1984 Bathtub Sailor	30-day	N/A	29.95	35
1984 The First Snow	30-day	N/A	29.95	35

A Child's World - F. Hook

YEAR ISSUE	EDITION LIMIT	YEAR RETD.	ISSUE PRICE	*QUOTE U.S.$
1980 Little Children, Come to Me	15,000	N/A	45.00	49

Fontanini Annual Christmas Plate - E. Simonetti

YEAR ISSUE	EDITION LIMIT	YEAR RETD.	ISSUE PRICE	*QUOTE U.S.$
1986 A King Is Born	Yr.Iss.	1986	60.00	60
1987 O Come, Let Us Adore Him	Yr.Iss.	1987	60.00	65
1988 Adoration of the Magi	Yr.Iss.	1988	70.00	75
1989 Flight Into Egypt	Yr.Iss.	1989	75.00	85

Frances Hook Collection-Set I - F. Hook

YEAR ISSUE	EDITION LIMIT	YEAR RETD.	ISSUE PRICE	*QUOTE U.S.$
1982 I Wish, I Wish	15,000	N/A	24.95	75-85
1982 Baby Blossoms	15,000	N/A	24.95	39-45
1982 Daisy Dreamer	15,000	N/A	24.95	39-55
1982 Trees So Tall	15,000	N/A	24.95	39-55

Frances Hook Collection-Set II - F. Hook

YEAR ISSUE	EDITION LIMIT	YEAR RETD.	ISSUE PRICE	*QUOTE U.S.$
1983 Caught It Myself	15,000	N/A	24.95	25
1983 Winter Wrappings	15,000	N/A	24.95	25
1983 So Cuddly	15,000	N/A	24.95	25
1983 Can I Keep Him?	15,000	N/A	24.95	25

Frances Hook Legacy - F. Hook

YEAR ISSUE	EDITION LIMIT	YEAR RETD.	ISSUE PRICE	*QUOTE U.S.$
1985 Fascination	100-day	N/A	19.50	39-49
1985 Daydreaming	100-day	N/A	19.50	39-49
1985 Discovery	100-day	N/A	22.50	39-49
1985 Disappointment	100-day	N/A	22.50	39-49
1985 Wonderment	100-day	N/A	22.50	39-49
1985 Expectation	100-day	N/A	22.50	39-49

God Bless You Little One - A. Williams

YEAR ISSUE	EDITION LIMIT	YEAR RETD.	ISSUE PRICE	*QUOTE U.S.$
1991 Baby's First Birthday (Girl)	Closed	N/A	29.50	30-45
1991 Baby's First Birthday (Boy)	Closed	N/A	29.50	30-45
1991 Baby's First Smile	Closed	N/A	19.50	20
1991 Baby's First Word	Closed	N/A	19.50	20
1991 Baby's First Step	Closed	N/A	19.50	20
1991 Baby's First Tooth	Closed	N/A	19.50	20

The Ice Capades Clown - G. Petty

YEAR ISSUE	EDITION LIMIT	YEAR RETD.	ISSUE PRICE	*QUOTE U.S.$
1983 Presenting Freddie Trenkler	30-day	N/A	24.50	25

The Lord's Prayer - A. Williams

YEAR ISSUE	EDITION LIMIT	YEAR RETD.	ISSUE PRICE	*QUOTE U.S.$
1986 Our Father	10-day	N/A	24.50	25
1986 Thy Kingdom Come	10-day	N/A	24.50	25
1986 Give Us This Day	10-day	N/A	24.50	25
1986 Forgive Our Trespasses	10-day	N/A	24.50	25
1986 As We Forgive	10-day	N/A	24.50	25
1986 Lead Us Not	10-day	N/A	24.50	25
1986 Deliver Us From Evil	10-day	N/A	24.50	25
1986 Thine Is The Kingdom	10-day	N/A	24.50	25

The Love's Prayer - A. Williams

YEAR ISSUE	EDITION LIMIT	YEAR RETD.	ISSUE PRICE	*QUOTE U.S.$
1988 Love Is Patient and Kind	14-day	N/A	29.50	30
1988 Love Is Never Jealous or Boastful	14-day	N/A	29.50	30
1988 Love Is Never Arrogant or Rude	14-day	N/A	29.50	30
1988 Love Does Not Insist on Its Own Way	14-day	N/A	29.50	30
1988 Love Is Never Irritable or Resentful	14-day	N/A	29.50	30
1988 Love Rejoices In the Right	14-day	N/A	29.50	30
1988 Love Believes All Things	14-day	N/A	29.50	30
1988 Love Never Ends	14-day	N/A	29.50	30

The Magic of Childhood - A. Williams

YEAR ISSUE	EDITION LIMIT	YEAR RETD.	ISSUE PRICE	*QUOTE U.S.$
1985 Special Friends	10-day	N/A	24.50	25
1985 Feeding Time	10-day	N/A	24.50	25
1985 Best Buddies	10-day	N/A	24.50	35
1985 Getting Acquainted	10-day	N/A	24.50	35
1986 Last One In	10-day	N/A	24.50	35
1986 A Handful Of Love	10-day	N/A	24.50	35
1986 Look Alikes	10-day	N/A	24.50	35
1986 No Fair Peeking	10-day	N/A	24.50	35

March of Dimes: Our Children, Our Future - A. Williams

YEAR ISSUE	EDITION LIMIT	YEAR RETD.	ISSUE PRICE	*QUOTE U.S.$
1990 A Time To Laugh	150-day	N/A	29.00	29-59

The Masterpiece Collection - Various

YEAR ISSUE	EDITION LIMIT	YEAR RETD.	ISSUE PRICE	*QUOTE U.S.$
1979 Adoration - F. Lippe	5,000	N/A	65.00	65
1980 Madonna with Grapes - P. Mignard	5,000	N/A	87.50	88
1981 The Holy Family - G. Delle Notti	5,000	N/A	95.00	95
1982 Madonna of the Streets - R. Ferruzzi	5,000	N/A	85.00	85

Millenium™ Series - Various

YEAR ISSUE	EDITION LIMIT	YEAR RETD.	ISSUE PRICE	*QUOTE U.S.$
1992 Silent Night - Morcaldo/Lucchesi	2,000	1992	49.50	50-69
1993 The Annunciation - Morcaldo/Lucchesi	5,000	1993	49.50	50
1994 Peace On Earth - Morcaldo/Lucchesi	5,000	1994	49.50	50
1995 Cause of Our Joy - A. Lucchesi	7,500	1995	49.50	50
1996 Prince of Peace - A. Lucchesi	15,000	1996	49.50	50
1997 Gentle Love - A. Lucchesi	Yr.Iss.	1997	49.50	50

Precious Children - A. Williams

YEAR ISSUE	EDITION LIMIT	YEAR RETD.	ISSUE PRICE	*QUOTE U.S.$
1993 Bless Baby Brother	Closed	N/A	29.50	30
1993 Blowing Bubbles	Closed	N/A	29.50	30
1993 Don't Worry, Mother Duck	Closed	N/A	29.50	30
1993 Treetop Discovery	Closed	N/A	29.50	30
1993 The Tea Party	Closed	N/A	29.50	30
1993 Mother's Little Angel	Closed	N/A	29.50	30
1993 Picking Daisies	Closed	N/A	29.50	30
1993 Let's Say Grace	Closed	N/A	29.50	30

Pretty Girls of the Ice Capades - G. Petty

YEAR ISSUE	EDITION LIMIT	YEAR RETD.	ISSUE PRICE	*QUOTE U.S.$
1983 Ice Princess	30-day	N/A	24.50	25

Promise of a Savior - Unknown

YEAR ISSUE	EDITION LIMIT	YEAR RETD.	ISSUE PRICE	*QUOTE U.S.$
1993 An Angel's Message	95-day	N/A	29.90	30
1993 Gifts to Jesus	95-day	N/A	29.90	30
1993 The Heavenly King	95-day	N/A	29.90	30
1993 Angels Were Watching	95-day	N/A	29.90	30
1993 Holy Mother & Child	95-day	N/A	29.90	30
1993 A Child is Born	95-day	N/A	29.90	30

The Richard Judson Zolan Collection - R.J. Zolan

YEAR ISSUE	EDITION LIMIT	YEAR RETD.	ISSUE PRICE	*QUOTE U.S.$
1992 The Butterfly Net	100-day	N/A	29.50	30
1994 The Ring	100-day	N/A	29.50	30

*Quotes have been rounded up to nearest dollar

YEAR ISSUE	EDITION LIMIT	YEAR RETD.	ISSUE PRICE	*QUOTE U.S.$
1994 Terrace Dancing	100-day	N/A	29.50	30

Roman Memorial - F. Hook

YEAR ISSUE	EDITION LIMIT	YEAR RETD.	ISSUE PRICE	*QUOTE U.S.$
1984 The Carpenter	Closed	1984	100.00	135

Seraphim Classics ® Faro Collection - Faro Studios

YEAR ISSUE	EDITION LIMIT	YEAR RETD.	ISSUE PRICE	*QUOTE U.S.$
1994 Rosalyn - Rarest of Heaven	7,200	1995	65.00	65
1995 Helena - Heaven's Herald	7,200	1996	65.00	65
1996 Flora - Flower of Heaven	7,200	1997	65.00	65
1997 Emily - Heaven's Treasure	Yr.Iss.	1997	65.00	65
1998 Elise - Heaven's Glory	Yr.Iss.		65.00	65

Seraphim Classics ® Oval Plate - Seraphim Studios

YEAR ISSUE	EDITION LIMIT	YEAR RETD.	ISSUE PRICE	*QUOTE U.S.$
1996 Cymbeline - Peacemaker	2-Yr.	1998	49.95	50
1996 Isabel - Gentle Spirit	2-Yr.	1998	49.95	50
1996 Lydia - Winged Poet	2-Yr.		49.95	50
1996 Priscilla - Benevolent Guide	2-Yr.		49.95	50

Single Releases - A. Williams

YEAR ISSUE	EDITION LIMIT	YEAR RETD.	ISSUE PRICE	*QUOTE U.S.$
1987 The Christening	Open		29.50	30
1990 The Dedication	Open		29.50	30
1990 The Baptism	Open		29.50	30

The Sweetest Songs - I. Spencer

YEAR ISSUE	EDITION LIMIT	YEAR RETD.	ISSUE PRICE	*QUOTE U.S.$
1986 A Baby's Prayer	30-day	N/A	39.50	45
1986 This Little Piggie	30-day	N/A	39.50	40
1988 Long, Long Ago	30-day	N/A	39.50	40
1989 Rockabye	30-day	N/A	39.50	40

Tender Expressions - B. Sargent

YEAR ISSUE	EDITION LIMIT	YEAR RETD.	ISSUE PRICE	*QUOTE U.S.$
1992 Thoughts of You Are In My Heart	100-day	N/A	29.50	30

Rosenthal

Christmas - Unknown

YEAR ISSUE	EDITION LIMIT	YEAR RETD.	ISSUE PRICE	*QUOTE U.S.$
1910 Winter Peace	Annual		Unkn.	550
1911 Three Wise Men	Annual		Unkn.	325
1912 Stardust	Annual		Unkn.	255
1913 Christmas Lights	Annual		Unkn.	235
1914 Christmas Song	Annual		Unkn.	350
1915 Walking to Church	Annual		Unkn.	180
1916 Christmas During War	Annual		Unkn.	240
1917 Angel of Peace	Annual		Unkn.	200
1918 Peace on Earth	Annual		Unkn.	200
1919 St. Christopher with Christ Child	Annual		Unkn.	225
1920 Manger in Bethlehem	Annual		Unkn.	325
1921 Christmas in Mountains	Annual		Unkn.	200
1922 Advent Branch	Annual		Unkn.	200
1923 Children in Winter Woods	Annual		Unkn.	200
1924 Deer in the Woods	Annual		Unkn.	200
1925 Three Wise Men	Annual		Unkn.	200
1926 Christmas in Mountains	Annual		Unkn.	195
1927 Station on the Way	Annual		Unkn.	135-175
1928 Chalet Christmas	Annual		Unkn.	185
1929 Christmas in Alps	Annual		Unkn.	225
1930 Group of Deer Under Pines	Annual		Unkn.	225
1931 Path of the Magi	Annual		Unkn.	225
1932 Christ Child	Annual		Unkn.	185
1933 Thru the Night to Light	Annual		Unkn.	190
1934 Christmas Peace	Annual		Unkn.	190
1935 Christmas by the Sea	Annual		Unkn.	190
1936 Nurnberg Angel	Annual		Unkn.	175-200
1937 Berchtesgaden	Annual		Unkn.	195
1938 Christmas in the Alps	Annual		Unkn.	195
1939 Schneekoppe Mountain	Annual		Unkn.	195
1940 Marien Chruch(girl) in Danzig	Annual		Unkn.	200-225
1941 Strassburg Cathedral	Annual		Unkn.	200-225
1942 Marianburg Castle	Annual		Unkn.	300
1943 Winter Idyll	Annual		Unkn.	300
1944 Wood Scape	Annual		Unkn.	300
1945 Christmas Peace	Annual		Unkn.	400
1946 Christmas in an Alpine Valley	Annual		Unkn.	240
1947 Dillingen Madonna	Annual		Unkn.	985
1948 Message to the Shepherds	Annual		Unkn.	875
1949 The Holy Family	Annual		Unkn.	185
1950 Christmas in the Forest	Annual		Unkn.	185
1951 Star of Bethlehem	Annual		Unkn.	450
1952 Christmas in the Alps	Annual		Unkn.	195
1953 The Holy Light	Annual		Unkn.	195
1954 Christmas Eve	Annual		Unkn.	195
1955 Christmas in a Village	Annual		Unkn.	195
1956 Christmas in the Alps	Annual		Unkn.	195
1957 Christmas by the Sea	Annual		Unkn.	195
1958 Christmas Eve	Annual		Unkn.	195
1959 Midnight Mass	Annual		Unkn.	75-125
1960 Christmas in a Small Village	Annual		Unkn.	195
1961 Solitary Christmas	Annual		Unkn.	100-200
1962 Christmas Eve	Annual		Unkn.	75-150
1963 Silent Night	Annual		Unkn.	75-150
1964 Christmas Market in Nurnberg	Annual		Unkn.	225
1965 Christmas Munich	Annual		Unkn.	185
1966 Christmas in Ulm	Annual		Unkn.	275
1967 Christmas in Reginburg	Annual		Unkn.	185
1968 Christmas in Bremen	Annual		Unkn.	195
1969 Christmas in Rothenburg	Annual		Unkn.	220
1970 Christmas in Cologne	Annual		Unkn.	175
1971 Christmas in Garmisch	Annual		42.00	100
1972 Christmas in Franconia	Annual		50.00	95
1973 Lubeck-Holstein	Annual		77.00	105
1974 Christmas in Wurzburg	Annual		85.00	100

Nobility of Children - E. Hibel

YEAR ISSUE	EDITION LIMIT	YEAR RETD.	ISSUE PRICE	*QUOTE U.S.$
1976 La Contessa Isabella	12,750		120.00	120
1977 La Marquis Maurice-Pierre	12,750		120.00	120
1978 Baronesse Johanna	12,750		130.00	140
1979 Chief Red Feather	12,750		140.00	180

Oriental Gold - E. Hibel

YEAR ISSUE	EDITION LIMIT	YEAR RETD.	ISSUE PRICE	*QUOTE U.S.$
1976 Yasuko	2,000		275.00	650
1977 Mr. Obata	2,000		275.00	500
1978 Sakura	2,000		295.00	400
1979 Michio	2,000		325.00	375

Wiinblad Christmas - B. Wiinblad

YEAR ISSUE	EDITION LIMIT	YEAR RETD.	ISSUE PRICE	*QUOTE U.S.$
1971 Maria & Child	Undis.		100.00	750
1972 Caspar	Undis.		100.00	290
1973 Melchior	Undis.		125.00	335
1974 Balthazar	Undis.		125.00	300
1975 The Annunciation	Undis.		195.00	195
1976 Angel with Trumpet	Undis.		195.00	195
1977 Adoration of Shepherds	Undis.		225.00	225
1978 Angel with Harp	Undis.		275.00	295
1979 Exodus from Egypt	Undis.		310.00	310
1980 Angel with Glockenspiel	Undis.		360.00	360
1981 Christ Child Visits Temple	Undis.		375.00	375
1982 Christening of Christ	Undis.		375.00	375

Royal Copenhagen

Christmas - Various

YEAR ISSUE	EDITION LIMIT	YEAR RETD.	ISSUE PRICE	*QUOTE U.S.$
1908 Madonna and Child - C. Thomsen	Annual	1908	1.00	2760-4500
1909 Danish Landscape - S. Ussing	Annual	1909	1.00	192-240
1910 The Magi - C. Thomsen	Annual	1910	1.00	150
1911 Danish Landscape - O. Jensen	Annual	1911	1.00	144-210
1912 Christmas Tree - C. Thomsen	Annual	1912	1.00	210-225
1913 Frederik Church Spire - A. Boesen	Annual	1913	1.50	146-198
1914 Holy Spirit Church - A. Boesen	Annual	1914	1.50	165-196
1915 Danish Landscape - A. Krog	Annual	1915	1.50	125-195
1916 Shepherd at Christmas - R. Bocher	Annual	1916	1.50	122-128
1917 Our Savior Church - O. Jensen	Annual	1917	2.00	128-150
1918 Sheep and Shepherds - O. Jensen	Annual	1918	2.00	120-150
1919 In the Park - O. Jensen	Annual	1919	2.00	126-150
1920 Mary and Child Jesus - G. Rode	Annual	1920	2.00	125-150
1921 Aabenraa Marketplace - O. Jensen	Annual	1921	2.00	75-150
1922 Three Singing Angels - E. Selschau	Annual	1922	2.00	75-98
1923 Danish Landscape - O. Jensen	Annual	1923	2.00	90-95
1924 Sailing Ship - B. Olsen	Annual	1924	2.00	150-174
1925 Christianshavn - O. Jensen	Annual	1925	2.00	135-160
1926 Christianshavn Canal - R. Bocher	Annual	1926	2.00	135-162
1927 Ship's Boy at Tiller - B. Olsen	Annual	1927	2.00	135-195
1928 Vicar's Family - G. Rode	Annual	1928	2.00	110-128
1929 Grundtvig Church - O. Jensen	Annual	1929	2.00	98-128
1930 Fishing Boats - B. Olsen	Annual	1930	2.50	100-150
1931 Mother and Child - G. Rode	Annual	1931	2.50	125-150
1932 Frederiksberg Gardens - O. Jensen	Annual	1932	2.50	113-123
1933 Ferry and the Great Belt - B. Olsen	Annual	1933	2.50	188-200
1934 The Hermitage Castle - O. Jensen	Annual	1934	2.50	240-281
1935 Kronborg Castle - B. Olsen	Annual	1935	2.50	240-310
1936 Roskilde Cathedral - R. Bocher	Annual	1936	2.50	270-315
1937 Main Street Copenhagen - N. Thorsson	Annual	1937	2.50	218-306
1938 Round Church in Osterlars - H. Nielsen	Annual	1938	3.00	390-450
1939 Greenland Pack-Ice - S. Nielsen	Annual	1939	3.00	476-525
1940 The Good Shepherd - K. Lange	Annual	1940	3.00	266-630
1941 Danish Village Church - T. Kjolner	Annual	1941	3.00	300-540
1942 Bell Tower - N. Thorsson	Annual	1942	4.00	300-630
1943 Flight into Egypt - N. Thorsson	Annual	1943	4.00	626-900
1944 Danish Village Scene - V. Olson	Annual	1944	4.00	326-450
1945 A Peaceful Motif - R. Bocher	Annual	1945	4.00	475-600
1946 Zealand Village Church - N. Thorsson	Annual	1946	4.00	270-324
1947 The Good Shepherd - K. Lange	Annual	1947	4.50	200-414
1948 Nodebo Church - T. Kjolner	Annual	1948	4.50	300-336
1949 Our Lady's Cathedral - H. Hansen	Annual	1949	5.00	255-372
1950 Boeslunde Church - V. Olson	Annual	1950	5.00	200-360
1951 Christmas Angel - R. Bocher	Annual	1951	5.00	297-540
1952 Christmas in the Forest - K. Lange	Annual	1952	5.00	160-222
1953 Frederiksborg Castle - T. Kjolner	Annual	1953	6.00	195-264
1954 Amalienborg Palace - K. Lange	Annual	1954	6.00	171-210
1955 Fano Girl - K. Lange	Annual	1955	7.00	200-270
1956 Rosenborg Castle - K. Lange	Annual	1956	7.00	200-294
1957 The Good Shepherd - H. Hansen	Annual	1957	8.00	120-138
1958 Sunshine over Greenland - H. Hansen	Annual	1958	9.00	160-210
1959 Christmas Night - H. Hansen	Annual	1959	9.00	108-225
1960 The Stag - H. Hansen	Annual	1960	10.00	100-180
1961 Training Ship - K. Lange	Annual	1961	10.00	146-225
1962 The Little Mermaid - Unknown	Annual	1962	11.00	200-480
1963 Hojsager Mill - K. Lange	Annual	1963	11.00	40-90
1964 Fetching the Tree - K. Lange	Annual	1964	11.00	30-90
1965 Little Skaters - K. Lange	Annual	1965	12.00	38-75
1966 Blackbird - K. Lange	Annual	1966	12.00	24-52
1967 The Royal Oak - K. Lange	Annual	1967	13.00	20-45
1968 The Last Umiak - K. Lange	Annual	1968	13.00	16-39
1969 The Old Farmyard - K. Lange	Annual	1969	14.00	18-48
1970 Christmas Rose and Cat - K. Lange	Annual	1970	14.00	30-51
1971 Hare In Winter - K. Lange	Annual	1971	15.00	14-30
1972 In the Desert - K. Lange	Annual	1972	16.00	16-27
1973 Train Homeward Bound - K. Lange	Annual	1973	22.00	24-36
1974 Winter Twilight - K. Lange	Annual	1974	22.00	21-27
1975 Queen's Palace - K. Lange	Annual	1975	27.50	13-21
1976 Danish Watermill - S. Vestergaard	Annual	1976	27.50	36-39
1977 Immervad Bridge - K. Lange	Annual	1977	32.00	20-33
1978 Greenland Scenery - K. Lange	Annual	1978	35.00	24-36
1979 Choosing Christmas Tree - K. Lange	Annual	1979	42.50	40-121
1980 Bringing Home the Tree - K. Lange	Annual	1980	49.50	20-49
1981 Admiring Christmas Tree - K. Lange	Annual	1981	52.50	36-45
1982 Waiting for Christmas - K. Lange	Annual	1982	54.50	59-90
1983 Merry Christmas - K. Lange	Annual	1983	54.50	49-72
1984 Jingle Bells - K. Lange	Annual	1984	54.50	48-66
1985 Snowman - K. Lange	Annual	1985	54.50	99-129
1986 Christmas Vacation - K. Lange	Annual	1986	54.50	68-96
1987 Winter Birds - S. Vestergaard	Annual	1987	59.50	60-81
1988 Christmas Eve in Copenhagen - S. Vestergaard	Annual	1988	59.50	60-120
1989 The Old Skating Pond - S. Vestergaard	Annual	1989	59.50	77-117
1990 Christmas at Tivoli - S. Vestergaard	Annual	1990	64.50	164-210
1991 The Festival of Santa Lucia - S. Vestergaard	Annual	1991	69.50	100-120
1992 The Queen's Carriage - S. Vestergaard	Annual	1992	69.50	90-111
1993 Christmas Guests - S. Vestergaard	Annual	1993	69.50	150-195
1994 Christmas Shopping - S. Vestergaard	Annual	1994	72.50	75-98
1995 Christmas at the Manor House - S. Vestergaard	Annual	1995	72.50	194-240
1996 Lighting the Street Lamps - S. Vestergaard	Annual	1996	74.50	84-90
1997 Roskilde Cathedral - S. Vestergaard	Annual	1997	69.50	70-90
1998 Coming Home For Christmas - S. Vestergaard	Annual		69.50	70

Royal Doulton

All God's Children - L. DeWinne

YEAR ISSUE	EDITION LIMIT	YEAR RETD.	ISSUE PRICE	*QUOTE U.S.$
1978 A Brighter Day	10,000	1984	75.00	75-100
1980 Village Children	10,000	1984	65.00	65
1981 Noble Heritage	10,000	1984	85.00	85
1982 Buddies	10,000	1984	85.00	85
1983 My Little Brother	10,000	1984	95.00	95

American Tapestries - C.A. Brown

YEAR ISSUE	EDITION LIMIT	YEAR RETD.	ISSUE PRICE	*QUOTE U.S.$
1978 Sleigh Bells	15,000	1983	70.00	70
1979 Pumpkin Patch	15,000	1983	70.00	70
1981 General Store	10,000	1983	95.00	95
1982 Fourth of July	10,000	1983	95.00	95

Behind the Painted Mask - B. Black

YEAR ISSUE	EDITION LIMIT	YEAR RETD.	ISSUE PRICE	*QUOTE U.S.$
1982 Painted Feelings	10,000	1986	95.00	175-200
1983 Make Me Laugh	10,000	1986	95.00	175-200
1984 Minstrel Serenade	10,000	1986	95.00	175-200
1985 Pleasing Performance	10,000	1986	95.00	175-200

Celebration of Faith - J. Woods

YEAR ISSUE	EDITION LIMIT	YEAR RETD.	ISSUE PRICE	*QUOTE U.S.$
1982 Rosh Hashanah	7,500	1986	250.00	300-400
1983 Yom Kippur	7,500	1986	250.00	250
1984 Passover	7,500	1986	250.00	250
1985 Chanukah	7,500	1986	250.00	250

Character Plates - N/A

YEAR ISSUE	EDITION LIMIT	YEAR RETD.	ISSUE PRICE	*QUOTE U.S.$
1979 Old Balloon Seller	Closed	1983	100.00	120
1980 Balloon Man	Closed	1983	125.00	125
1981 Silks and Ribbons	Closed	1983	125.00	140
1982 Biddy Penny Farthing	Closed	1983	125.00	125

Charles Dickens Plates - N/A

YEAR ISSUE	EDITION LIMIT	YEAR RETD.	ISSUE PRICE	*QUOTE U.S.$
1980 Artful Dodger	Closed	1984	65.00	65
1980 Barkis	Closed	1984	80.00	80-95
1980 Cap'n Cuttle	Closed	1984	80.00	80
1980 Fagin	Closed	1984	65.00	65
1980 Fat Boy	Closed	1984	65.00	65
1980 Mr. Micawber	Closed	1984	80.00	80
1980 Mr. Pickwick	Closed	1984	80.00	80-95
1980 Old Peggoty	Closed	1984	65.00	65
1980 Poor Jo	Closed	1984	80.00	80
1980 Sairey Gamp	Closed	1984	80.00	80
1980 Sam Weller	Closed	1984	65.00	65
1980 Sergeant Buz Fuz	Closed	1984	80.00	80
1980 Tony Weller	Closed	1984	65.00	65

Childhood Christmas - N/A

YEAR ISSUE	EDITION LIMIT	YEAR RETD.	ISSUE PRICE	*QUOTE U.S.$
1983 Silent Night	Yr.Iss.	1983	35.00	75
1984 While Shepherds Watched	Yr.Iss.	1984	39.95	75
1985 Oh Little Town of Bethlehem	Yr.Iss.	1985	39.95	40
1986 We Saw 3 Ships A-Sailing	Yr.Iss.	1986	39.95	40
1987 The Holly and the Ivy	Yr.Iss.	1987	39.95	40

Children of the Pueblo - M. Jungbluth

YEAR ISSUE	EDITION LIMIT	YEAR RETD.	ISSUE PRICE	*QUOTE U.S.$
1983 Apple Flower	15,000	1985	60.00	150-195
1984 Morning Star	15,000	1985	60.00	150-195

Christmas Around the World - N/A

YEAR ISSUE	EDITION LIMIT	YEAR RETD.	ISSUE PRICE	*QUOTE U.S.$
1972 Old England	15,000	1979	35.00	35
1973 Mexico	15,000	1979	37.50	38
1974 Bulgaria	15,000	1979	37.50	38
1975 Norway	15,000	1979	45.00	45
1976 Holland	15,000	1979	50.00	50
1977 Poland	15,000	1979	50.00	50
1978 America	15,000	1979	55.00	55

Christmas Plates - Various

YEAR ISSUE	EDITION LIMIT	YEAR RETD.	ISSUE PRICE	*QUOTE U.S.$
1993 Royal Doulton-Together For Christmas - J. James	Yr.Iss.	1993	45.00	50
1993 Royal Albert-Sleighride - N/A	Yr.Iss.	1993	45.00	45
1994 Royal Doulton-Home For Christmas - J. James	Yr.Iss.	1994	45.00	45
1994 Royal Albert-Coaching Inn - N/A	Yr.Iss.	1994	45.00	45

*Quotes have been rounded up to nearest dollar

YEAR ISSUE	EDITION LIMIT	YEAR RETD.	ISSUE PRICE	*QUOTE U.S.$
1995 Royal Doulton-Season's Greetings - J. James	Yr.Iss.	1995	45.00	45
1995 Royal Albert-Skating Pond - N/A	Yr.Iss.	1995	45.00	45
1996 Royal Doulton-Night Before Christmas - J. James	Yr.Iss.	1996	45.00	45
1996 Royal Albert-Gathering Winter Fuel - N/A	Yr.Iss.	1996	45.00	45

Commedia Dell Arte - L. Neiman

YEAR ISSUE	EDITION LIMIT	YEAR RETD.	ISSUE PRICE	*QUOTE U.S.$
1974 Harlequin	15,000	1979	100.00	175-200
1975 Pierrot	15,000	1979	90.00	160-200
1977 Columbine	15,000	1979	80.00	80
1978 Punchinello	15,000	1979	75.00	75

Family Christmas Plates - N/A

YEAR ISSUE	EDITION LIMIT	YEAR RETD.	ISSUE PRICE	*QUOTE U.S.$
1991 Dad Plays Santa	Closed	1991	60.00	60

Festival Children of the World - B. Burke

YEAR ISSUE	EDITION LIMIT	YEAR RETD.	ISSUE PRICE	*QUOTE U.S.$
1983 Mariana (Balinese)	15,000	1986	65.00	65
1984 Magdalena (Mexico)	15,000	1986	65.00	65
1985 Michiko (Japanese)	15,000	1986	65.00	65

Flower Garden - H. Vidal

YEAR ISSUE	EDITION LIMIT	YEAR RETD.	ISSUE PRICE	*QUOTE U.S.$
1975 Spring Harmony	15,000	1981	80.00	80
1976 Dreaming Lotus	15,000	1981	90.00	90
1977 From the Poet's Garden	15,000	1981	75.00	75
1978 Country Bouquet	15,000	1981	75.00	75
1979 From My Mother's Garden	15,000	1981	85.00	90

The Grandest Gift - Mago

YEAR ISSUE	EDITION LIMIT	YEAR RETD.	ISSUE PRICE	*QUOTE U.S.$
1985 Reunion	10,000	1986	75.00	100-150
1985 Storytime	10,000	1986	75.00	100

Grandparents - Mago

YEAR ISSUE	EDITION LIMIT	YEAR RETD.	ISSUE PRICE	*QUOTE U.S.$
1984 Grandfather and Children	15,000	1985	95.00	200-250

I Remember America - E. Sloane

YEAR ISSUE	EDITION LIMIT	YEAR RETD.	ISSUE PRICE	*QUOTE U.S.$
1977 Pennsylvania Pastorale	15,000	1982	90.00	90
1978 Lovejoy Bridge	15,000	1982	80.00	80
1979 Four Corners	15,000	1982	75.00	75
1981 Marshland	15,000	1982	95.00	95

Jungle Fantasy - G. Novoa

YEAR ISSUE	EDITION LIMIT	YEAR RETD.	ISSUE PRICE	*QUOTE U.S.$
1979 The Ark	10,000	1984	75.00	75
1981 Compassion	10,000	1984	95.00	95
1982 Patience	10,000	1984	95.00	95
1983 Refuge	10,000	1984	95.00	95

Log of the Dashing Wave - J. Stobart

YEAR ISSUE	EDITION LIMIT	YEAR RETD.	ISSUE PRICE	*QUOTE U.S.$
1976 Sailing With the Tide	15,000	1983	115.00	115
1977 Running Free	15,000	1983	110.00	150
1978 Rounding the Horn	15,000	1983	85.00	85
1979 Hong Kong	15,000	1983	75.00	75
1981 Bora Bora	15,000	1983	95.00	95
1982 Journey's End	15,000	1983	95.00	150

Mother and Child - E. Hibel

YEAR ISSUE	EDITION LIMIT	YEAR RETD.	ISSUE PRICE	*QUOTE U.S.$
1973 Colette and Child	15,000	1982	500.00	500
1974 Sayuri and Child	15,000	1982	175.00	175
1975 Kristina and Child	15,000	1982	125.00	150-195
1976 Marilyn and Child	15,000	1982	110.00	140-195
1977 Lucia and Child	15,000	1982	90.00	90
1981 Kathleen and Child	15,000	1982	85.00	150-195

Portraits of Innocence - F. Masseria

YEAR ISSUE	EDITION LIMIT	YEAR RETD.	ISSUE PRICE	*QUOTE U.S.$
1980 Panchito	15,000	1987	65.00	200-295
1981 Adrien	15,000	1987	85.00	150-195
1982 Angelica	15,000	1987	95.00	150-195
1983 Juliana	15,000	1987	95.00	150-195
1985 Gabriella	15,000	1987	95.00	150-195
1986 Francesca	15,000	1987	95.00	195-295

Ports of Call - D. Kingman

YEAR ISSUE	EDITION LIMIT	YEAR RETD.	ISSUE PRICE	*QUOTE U.S.$
1975 San Francisco, Fisherman's Wharf	15,000	1979	90.00	90
1976 New Orleans, Royal Street	15,000	1979	80.00	80
1977 Venice, Grand Canal	15,000	1979	65.00	65
1978 Paris, Montmartre	15,000	1979	70.00	70

Reflections of China - C. Chi

YEAR ISSUE	EDITION LIMIT	YEAR RETD.	ISSUE PRICE	*QUOTE U.S.$
1976 Garden of Tranquility	15,000	1981	90.00	90
1977 Imperial Palace	15,000	1981	80.00	80
1978 Temple of Heaven	15,000	1981	75.00	75
1980 Lake of Mists	15,000	1981	85.00	85

Victorian Era Christmas - N/A

YEAR ISSUE	EDITION LIMIT	YEAR RETD.	ISSUE PRICE	*QUOTE U.S.$
1977 Winter Fun	Yr.Iss.	1977	55.00	55
1978 Christmas Day	Yr.Iss.	1978	55.00	55
1979 Christmas	Yr.Iss.	1979	25.00	25
1980 Santa's Visit	Yr.Iss.	1980	30.00	30
1981 Christmas Carolers	Yr.Iss.	1981	37.50	38
1982 Santa on Bicycle	Yr.Iss.	1982	39.95	40

Victorian Era Valentines - N/A

YEAR ISSUE	EDITION LIMIT	YEAR RETD.	ISSUE PRICE	*QUOTE U.S.$
1976 Victorian Boy and Girl	Yr.Iss.	1976	65.00	65-75
1977 My Sweetest Friend	Yr.Iss.	1977	40.00	40-65
1978 If I Loved You	Yr.Iss.	1978	40.00	40
1979 My Valentine	Yr.Iss.	1979	35.00	35
1980 Valentine	Yr.Iss.	1980	33.00	33
1981 Valentine Boy and Girl	Yr.Iss.	1981	35.00	35
1982 Angel with Mandolin	Yr.Iss.	1982	39.95	40
1985 My Valentine	Yr.Iss.	1985	39.95	40

Seymour Mann, Inc.

Connoisseur Christmas Collection™ - Bernini™

YEAR ISSUE	EDITION LIMIT	YEAR RETD.	ISSUE PRICE	*QUOTE U.S.$
1996 Cardinals CLT-310	25,000		50.00	50
1996 Chickadees CLT-300	25,000		50.00	50
1996 Doves CLT-305	25,000		50.00	50

Connoisseur Collection™ - Bernini™

YEAR ISSUE	EDITION LIMIT	YEAR RETD.	ISSUE PRICE	*QUOTE U.S.$
1997 Anna's Hummingbird CLT-440	25,000		50.00	50
1997 Blue Butterfly CLT-450	25,000		50.00	50
1995 Bluebird CLT-13	25,000	1996	50.00	50
1997 Bluebird/Lily CLT-390	25,000		50.00	50
1996 Butterfly/Lily CLT-330	25,000		50.00	50
1995 Canary CLT-10	25,000	1997	50.00	50
1995 Cardinal CLT-7	25,000	1997	50.00	50
1997 Cardinal/Dogwood CLT-405	25,000		50.00	50
1998 Costa's Hummingbird CLT-470	25,000		40.00	40
1995 Dove Duo CLT-1	25,000	1997	50.00	50
1995 Dove/Magnolia CLT-350	25,000		50.00	50
1995 Hummingbird Duo CLT-4	25,000		50.00	50
1995 Hummingbirds, Morning Glory, blue CLT-320B	25,000		50.00	50
1995 Hummingbirds, Morning Glory, pink CLT-320	25,000		50.00	50
1997 Love Doves/Roses CLT-420	25,000		50.00	50
1995 Magnolia CLT-76	25,000		50.00	50
1995 Pink Rose CLT-70	25,000		50.00	50
1995 Robin CLT-16	25,000		50.00	50
1996 Roses/Forget-Me-Not CLT-340	25,000		50.00	50
1998 Ruby Hummingbird Chicks CLT-460	25,000		40.00	40
1997 Star Gazer Lily CLT-430	25,000		50.00	60
1995 Swan Duo CLT-50	25,000		50.00	50
1997 Violet Crowned Hummingbird CLT-440B	25,000		50.00	50

Doll Art™ Collection - E. Mann

YEAR ISSUE	EDITION LIMIT	YEAR RETD.	ISSUE PRICE	*QUOTE U.S.$
1997 Hope CLT-600P	25,000		60.00	60

Sports Impressions/Enesco Corporation

Gold Edition Plates - Various

YEAR ISSUE	EDITION LIMIT	YEAR RETD.	ISSUE PRICE	*QUOTE U.S.$
XX A's Jose Canseco Gold (10 1/4") 1028-04 - J. Canseco	2,500	N/A	125.00	100-125
1990 Andre Dawson - R. Lewis	Closed	N/A	150.00	100-150
1987 Brooks Robinson F/S - R. Simon	1,000	N/A	125.00	125-150
1988 Brooks Robinson, signed - R. Simon	Closed	N/A	125.00	150-250
1987 Carl Yastrzemski, signed - R. Simon	1,500	N/A	125.00	100-150
1992 Chicago Bulls '92 World Champions - C. Hayes	Closed	N/A	150.00	150
1993 Chicago Bulls 1993 World Championship Gold (10 1/4") 4062-04 - B. Vann	1,993	1994	150.00	100-150
1987 Darryl Strawberry #1 - R. Simon	Closed	N/A	125.00	100-125
1989 Darryl Strawberry #2 - T. Fogerty	Closed	N/A	125.00	100-125
1986 Don Mattingly - B. Johnson	Closed	N/A	125.00	125-150
1991 Dream Team (1st Ten Chosen) - L. Salk	Closed	N/A	150.00	495-750
1992 Dream Team 1992 Gold (10 1/4") 5509-04 - R. Tanenbaum	1,992	1994	150.00	150-200
1992 Dream Team 1992 Platinum (8 1/2") 5507-03 - C. Hayes	7,500	1994	60.00	95
1991 Hawks Dominique Wilkins - J. Catalano	Closed	N/A	150.00	150-195
1990 Joe Montana 49ers Gold (10 1/4") 3000-04 - J. Catalano	1,990	1991	150.00	195-250
1986 Keith Hernandez - R. Simon	Closed	N/A	125.00	150-175
1991 Larry Bird - J. Catalano	Closed	N/A	150.00	195
1988 Larry Bird - R. Simon	Closed	N/A	125.00	275
1990 Living Triple Crown - R. Lewis	Closed	N/A	150.00	150
1993 Magic Johnson - T. Fogerty	Closed	N/A	150.00	150
1991 Magic Johnson Lakers Gold (10 1/4") 4007-04 - C.W. Mundy	1,991	1991	150.00	225
1992 Magic Johnson Lakers Gold (10 1/4") 4042-04 - R. Tanenbaum	1,992	1994	150.00	175
1991 Magic Johnson Lakers Platinum (8 1/2") 4007-03 - M. Petronella	5,000	1992	60.00	75
1989 Mantle Switch Hitter - J. Catalano	Closed	N/A	150.00	225-275
1992 Michael Jordan Bulls (10 1/4") 4032-04 - R. Tanenbaum	1,991	1992	150.00	225
1993 Michael Jordan Bulls Gold (10 1/4") 4046-04 - T. Fogarty	2,500	1993	150.00	150-175
1991 Michael Jordan Gold (10 1/4") 4002-04 - J. Catalano	1,991	1992	150.00	200
1991 Michael Jordan Platinum (8 1/2") 4002-03 - M. Petronella	1,991	1993	60.00	95
1995 Mickey Mantle "My Greatest Year 1956" 1229-04 - B. Vann	1,956	N/A	100.00	100-195
1991 Mickey Mantle 7 - B. Simon	Closed	N/A	150.00	150-195
1986 Mickey Mantle At Night (signed) - R. Simon	Closed	N/A	125.00	250-395
1995 Mickey Mantle double plate set, Platinum (8 1/2") 176923 - T. Treadway	2,401		75.00	75
1987 Mickey, Willie, & Duke (signed) - R. Simon	1,500	N/A	150.00	195-395
1988 Mickey, Willie, & Duke, (signed) 1041-59 - R. Simon	2,500		150.00	150
1992 NBA 1st Ten Chosen Platinum (8 1/2") (blue) 5502-03 - J. Catalano	7,500	1993	60.00	95
1992 NBA 1st Ten Chosen Platinum (8 1/2") (red) 5503-03 - C.W. Mundy	7,500	1993	60.00	95
1990 Nolan Ryan 300 Gold 1091-04 - T. Fogarty	1,990	1992	150.00	150
1990 Nolan Ryan 5,000 K's - J. Catalano	1,990		150.00	150
1995 Profiles in Courage Mickey Mantle Platinum (8 1/2") 1231-03 - M. Petronella	Open		30.00	30
1990 Rickey Henderson - R. Lewis	Closed	N/A	150.00	125-150
XX Roberto Clemente 1090-03 - R. Lewis	10,000	N/A	75.00	75
1993 Shaquille O'Neal Gold (10 1/4") 4047-04 - T. Fogarty	2,500	1994	150.00	150-195
1994 Shaquille O'Neal, Rookie of the Year - N/A	Open		100.00	100
1987 Ted Williams (signed) - R. Simon	Closed	N/A	125.00	450-495
1990 Tom Seaver - R. Lewis	Closed	N/A	150.00	150-200
1986 Wade Bogg (signed) - B. Johnson	Closed	N/A	125.00	150-175
1989 Will Clark - J. Catalano	Closed	N/A	125.00	100-150
1988 Yankee Tradition - J. Catalano	Closed	N/A	150.00	195-200

V-Palekh Art Studios

Russian Legends - Various

YEAR ISSUE	EDITION LIMIT	YEAR RETD.	ISSUE PRICE	*QUOTE U.S.$
1988 Ruslan and Ludmilla - G. Lubimov	195-day		29.87	12-30
1988 The Princess/Seven Bogatyrs - A. Kovalev	195-day		29.87	15-30
1988 The Golden Cockerel - V. Vleshko	195-day		32.87	15-33
1988 Lukomorya - R. Belousov	195-day		32.87	18-33
1989 Fisherman and the Magic Fish - N. Lopatin	195-day		32.87	15-33
1989 Tsar Saltan - G. Zhiryakova	195-day		32.87	15-33
1989 The Priest and His Servant - O. An	195-day		34.87	20-35
1990 Stone Flower - V. Bolshakova	195-day		34.87	28-35
1990 Sadko - E. Populor	195-day		34.87	30-40
1990 The Twelve Months - N. Lopatin	195-day		36.87	40-48
1990 Silver Hoof - S. Adeyanor	195-day		36.87	47-55
1990 Morozko - N. Lopatin	195-day		36.87	61-70

Villeroy & Boch

Flower Fairy - C. Barker

YEAR ISSUE	EDITION LIMIT	YEAR RETD.	ISSUE PRICE	*QUOTE U.S.$
1979 Lavender	21-day		35.00	125
1980 Sweet Pea	21-day		35.00	125
1980 Candytuft	21-day		35.00	89
1981 Heliotrope	21-day		35.00	75
1981 Blackthorn	21-day		35.00	75
1981 Appleblossom	21-day		35.00	95

Russian Fairytales Maria Morevna - B. Zvorykin

YEAR ISSUE	EDITION LIMIT	YEAR RETD.	ISSUE PRICE	*QUOTE U.S.$
1983 Maria Morevna and Tsarevich Ivan	27,500		70.00	50-70
1983 Koshchey Carries Off Maria Morevna	27,500		70.00	60-70
1983 Tsarevich Ivan and the Beautiful Castle	27,500		70.00	64-70

Russian Fairytales The Firebird - B. Zvorykin

YEAR ISSUE	EDITION LIMIT	YEAR RETD.	ISSUE PRICE	*QUOTE U.S.$
1982 In Search of the Firebird	27,500		70.00	59-100
1982 Ivan and Tsarevna on the Grey Wolf	27,500		70.00	60-90
1982 The Wedding of Tsarevna Elena the Fair	27,500		70.00	90-100

Russian Fairytales The Red Knight - B. Zvorykin

YEAR ISSUE	EDITION LIMIT	YEAR RETD.	ISSUE PRICE	*QUOTE U.S.$
1981 The Red Knight	27,500		70.00	50-80
1981 Vassilissa and Her Stepsisters	27,500		70.00	40-80
1981 Vassilissa is Presented to the Tsar	27,500		70.00	38-45

Villeroy & Boch - B. Zvorykin

YEAR ISSUE	EDITION LIMIT	YEAR RETD.	ISSUE PRICE	*QUOTE U.S.$
1980 The Snow Maiden	27,500		70.00	75-150
1980 Snegurochka at the Court of Tsar Berendei	27,500		70.00	40-80
1980 Snegurochka and Lei, the Shepherd Boy	27,500		70.00	55-90

W.S. George

Alaska: The Last Frontier - H. Lambson

YEAR ISSUE	EDITION LIMIT	YEAR RETD.	ISSUE PRICE	*QUOTE U.S.$
1991 Icy Majesty	Closed		34.50	29-40
1991 Autumn Grandeur	Closed		34.50	33-35
1992 Mountain Monarch	Closed		37.50	39
1992 Down the Trail	Closed		37.50	37-42
1992 Moonlight Lookout	Closed		37.50	57-60
1992 Graceful Passage	Closed		39.50	60
1992 Arctic Journey	Closed		39.50	50-66
1992 Summit Domain	Closed		39.50	60

Along an English Lane - M. Harvey

YEAR ISSUE	EDITION LIMIT	YEAR RETD.	ISSUE PRICE	*QUOTE U.S.$
1993 Summer's Bright Welcome	Closed		29.50	50
1993 Greeting the Day	Closed		29.50	53-60
1993 Friends and Flowers	Closed		29.50	60
1993 Cottage Around the Bend	Closed		29.50	30-55

America the Beautiful - H. Johnson

YEAR ISSUE	EDITION LIMIT	YEAR RETD.	ISSUE PRICE	*QUOTE U.S.$
1988 Yosemite Falls	Closed		34.50	26-35
1989 The Grand Canyon	Closed		34.50	21-29
1989 Yellowstone River	Closed		37.50	30-41
1989 The Great Smokey Mountains	Closed		37.50	30-45
1990 The Everglades	Closed		37.50	42-45
1990 Acadia	Closed		37.50	36-45
1990 The Grand Tetons	Closed		39.50	32-55
1990 Crater Lake	Closed		39.50	25-44

America's Pride - R. Richert

YEAR ISSUE	EDITION LIMIT	YEAR RETD.	ISSUE PRICE	*QUOTE U.S.$
1992 Misty Fjords	Closed		29.50	30-40
1992 Rugged Shores	Closed		29.50	36
1992 Mighty Summit	Closed		32.50	45
1993 Lofty Reflections	Closed		32.50	60
1993 Tranquil Waters	Closed		32.50	50
1993 Mountain Majesty	Closed		34.50	33
1993 Canyon Climb	Closed		34.50	49
1993 Golden Vista	Closed		34.50	35

*Quotes have been rounded up to nearest dollar

PLATES

Art Deco - M. McDonald

YEAR ISSUE	EDITION LIMIT	YEAR RETD.	ISSUE PRICE	*QUOTE U.S.$
1989 A Flapper With Greyhounds	Closed		39.50	42-45
1990 Tango Dancers	Closed		39.50	54-60
1990 Arriving in Style	Closed		39.50	52-55
1990 On the Town	Closed		39.50	56

Baby Cats of the Wild - C. Fracé

YEAR ISSUE	EDITION LIMIT	YEAR RETD.	ISSUE PRICE	*QUOTE U.S.$
1992 Morning Mischief	Closed		29.50	41
1993 Togetherness	Closed		29.50	42
1993 The Buddy System	Closed		32.50	50-60
1993 Nap Time	Closed		32.50	50-55

Bear Tracks - J. Seerey-Lester

YEAR ISSUE	EDITION LIMIT	YEAR RETD.	ISSUE PRICE	*QUOTE U.S.$
1992 Denali Family	Closed		29.50	35
1993 Their First Season	Closed		29.50	45
1993 High Country Champion	Closed		29.50	40-50
1993 Heavy Going	Closed		29.50	40-47
1993 Breaking Cover	Closed		29.50	60-65
1993 Along the Ice Flow	Closed		29.50	55-60

Beloved Hymns of Childhood - C. Barker

YEAR ISSUE	EDITION LIMIT	YEAR RETD.	ISSUE PRICE	*QUOTE U.S.$
1988 The Lord's My Shepherd	Closed		29.50	35-50
1988 Away In a Manger	Closed		29.50	25-35
1989 Now Thank We All Our God	Closed		32.50	29-35
1989 Love Divine	Closed		32.50	26-33
1989 I Love to Hear the Story	Closed		32.50	29-33
1989 All Glory, Laud and Honour	Closed		32.50	29-33
1990 All People on Earth Do Dwell	Closed		34.50	35-39
1990 Loving Shepherd of Thy Sheep	Closed		34.50	34-37

A Black Tie Affair: The Penguin - C. Jagodits

YEAR ISSUE	EDITION LIMIT	YEAR RETD.	ISSUE PRICE	*QUOTE U.S.$
1992 Little Explorer	Closed		29.50	40-50
1992 Penguin Parade	Closed		29.50	40-45
1992 Baby-Sitters	Closed		29.50	50-60
1993 Belly Flopping	Closed		29.50	53

Blessed Are The Children - W. Rane

YEAR ISSUE	EDITION LIMIT	YEAR RETD.	ISSUE PRICE	*QUOTE U.S.$
1990 Let the/Children Come To Me	Closed		29.50	45-55
1990 I Am the Good Shepherd	Closed		29.50	39-45
1991 Whoever Welcomes/Child	Closed		32.50	32-45
1991 Hosanna in the Highest	Closed		32.50	34-45
1991 Jesus Had Compassion on Them	Closed		32.50	45-50
1991 Blessed are the Peacemakers	Closed		34.50	45-55
1991 I am the Vine, You are the Branches	Closed		34.50	45-49
1991 Seek and You Will Find	Closed		34.50	39-45

Bonds of Love - B. Burke

YEAR ISSUE	EDITION LIMIT	YEAR RETD.	ISSUE PRICE	*QUOTE U.S.$
1989 Precious Embrace	Closed		29.50	30-55
1990 Cherished Moment	Closed		29.50	27-50
1991 Tender Caress	Closed		32.50	35-50
1992 Loving Touch	Closed		32.50	33-50
1992 Treasured Kisses	Closed		32.50	40-50
1994 Endearing Whispers	Closed		32.50	45-50

Charles Vickery's Romantic Harbors - C. Vickery

YEAR ISSUE	EDITION LIMIT	YEAR RETD.	ISSUE PRICE	*QUOTE U.S.$
1993 Advent of the Golden Bough	Closed		34.50	42
1993 Christmas Tree Schooner	Closed		34.50	60-70
1993 Prelude to the Journey	Closed		37.50	55
1993 Shimmering Light of Dusk	Closed		37.50	150-160

The Christmas Story - H. Garrido

YEAR ISSUE	EDITION LIMIT	YEAR RETD.	ISSUE PRICE	*QUOTE U.S.$
1992 Gifts of the Magi	Closed		29.50	40-45
1993 Rest on the Flight into Egypt	Closed		29.50	50
1993 Journey of the Magi	Closed		29.50	30
1993 The Nativity	Closed		29.50	49-55
1993 The Annunciation	Closed		29.50	30
1993 Adoration of the Shepherds	Closed		29.50	50

Classic Waterfowl: The Ducks Unlimited - L. Kaatz

YEAR ISSUE	EDITION LIMIT	YEAR RETD.	ISSUE PRICE	*QUOTE U.S.$
1988 Mallards at Sunrise	Closed		36.50	39-75
1988 Geese in the Autumn Fields	Closed		36.50	20-50
1989 Green Wings/Morning Marsh	Closed		39.50	19-42
1989 Canvasbacks, Breaking Away	Closed		39.50	22-40
1989 Pintails in Indian Summer	Closed		39.50	35-40
1990 Wood Ducks Taking Flight	Closed		39.50	26-42
1990 Snow Geese Against November Skies	Closed		41.50	35-45
1990 Bluebills Coming In	Closed		41.50	31-42

Columbus Discovers America: The 500th Anniversary - J. Penalva

YEAR ISSUE	EDITION LIMIT	YEAR RETD.	ISSUE PRICE	*QUOTE U.S.$
1991 Under Full Sail	Closed		29.50	30-55
1992 Ashore at Dawn	Closed		29.50	35-55
1992 Columbus Raises the Flag	Closed		32.50	30-55
1992 Bringing Together Two Cultures	Closed		32.50	39-47
1992 The Queen's Approval	Closed		32.50	25-33
1992 Treasures From The New World	Closed		32.50	50

Country Bouquets - G. Kurz

YEAR ISSUE	EDITION LIMIT	YEAR RETD.	ISSUE PRICE	*QUOTE U.S.$
1991 Morning Sunshine	Closed		29.50	45-55
1991 Summer Perfume	Closed		29.50	31
1992 Warm Welcome	Closed		32.50	50
1992 Garden's Bounty	Closed		32.50	45

Country Nostalgia - M. Harvey

YEAR ISSUE	EDITION LIMIT	YEAR RETD.	ISSUE PRICE	*QUOTE U.S.$
1989 The Spring Buggy	Closed		29.50	20-55
1989 The Apple Cider Press	Closed		29.50	20-55
1989 The Vintage Seed Planter	Closed		29.50	28-55
1989 The Old Hand Pump	Closed		32.50	46-50
1990 The Wooden Butter Churn	Closed		32.50	35-40
1990 The Dairy Cans	Closed		32.50	25-33
1990 The Forgotten Plow	Closed		34.50	28-35
1990 The Antique Spinning Wheel	Closed		34.50	29-40

Critic's Choice: Gone With The Wind - P. Jennis

YEAR ISSUE	EDITION LIMIT	YEAR RETD.	ISSUE PRICE	*QUOTE U.S.$
1991 Marry Me, Scarlett	Closed		27.50	48-75
1991 Waiting for Rhett	Closed		27.50	50-69
1991 A Declaration of Love	Closed		30.50	55-65
1991 The Paris Hat	Closed		30.50	35-75
1991 Scarlett Asks a Favor	Closed		30.50	75-85
1992 Scarlett Gets Her Way	Closed		32.50	50-75
1992 The Smitten Suitor	Closed		32.50	50-65
1992 Scarlett's Shopping Spree	Closed		32.50	50-75
1992 The Buggy Ride	Closed		32.50	35-75
1992 Scarlett Gets Down to Business	Closed		34.50	40-75
1993 Scarlett's Heart is with Tara	Closed		34.50	45-75
1993 At Cross Purposes	Closed		34.50	40-69

A Delicate Balance: Vanishing Wildlife - G. Beecham

YEAR ISSUE	EDITION LIMIT	YEAR RETD.	ISSUE PRICE	*QUOTE U.S.$
1992 Tomorrow's Hope	Closed		29.50	36
1993 Today's Future	Closed		29.50	40
1993 Present Dreams	Closed		32.50	30-35
1993 Eyes on the New Day	Closed		32.50	21-35

Dr. Zhivago - G. Bush

YEAR ISSUE	EDITION LIMIT	YEAR RETD.	ISSUE PRICE	*QUOTE U.S.$
1990 Zhivago and Lara	Closed		39.50	40-55
1991 Love Poems For Lara	Closed		39.50	40-55
1991 Zhivago Says Farewell	Closed		39.50	45-55
1991 Lara's Love	Closed		39.50	50-55

The Elegant Birds - J. Faulkner

YEAR ISSUE	EDITION LIMIT	YEAR RETD.	ISSUE PRICE	*QUOTE U.S.$
1988 The Swan	Closed		32.50	35-50
1988 Great Blue Heron	Closed		32.50	28-33
1989 Snowy Egret	Closed		32.50	21-32
1989 The Anhinga	Closed		35.50	17-36
1989 The Flamingo	Closed		35.50	27-36
1990 Sandhill and Whooping Crane	Closed		35.50	21-36

Enchanted Garden - E. Antonaccio

YEAR ISSUE	EDITION LIMIT	YEAR RETD.	ISSUE PRICE	*QUOTE U.S.$
1993 A Peaceful Retreat	Closed		24.50	40
1993 Pleasant Pathways	Closed		24.50	25-50
1993 A Place to Dream	Closed		24.50	25
1993 Tranquil Hideaway	Closed		24.50	25

Eyes of the Wild - D. Pierce

YEAR ISSUE	EDITION LIMIT	YEAR RETD.	ISSUE PRICE	*QUOTE U.S.$
1993 Eyes in the Mist	Closed		29.50	52
1993 Eyes in the Pines	Closed		29.50	30-40
1993 Eyes on the Sly	Closed		29.50	61
1993 Eyes of Gold	Closed		29.50	30-45
1993 Eyes of Silence	Closed		29.50	30-35
1993 Eyes in the Snow	Closed		29.50	30-40
1993 Eyes of Wonder	Closed		29.50	30-55
1994 Eyes of Strength	Closed		29.50	43

The Faces of Nature - J. Kramer Cole

YEAR ISSUE	EDITION LIMIT	YEAR RETD.	ISSUE PRICE	*QUOTE U.S.$
1992 Canyon of the Cat	Closed		29.50	45-50
1992 Wolf Ridge	Closed		29.50	40-45
1993 Trail of the Talisman	Closed		29.50	50-60
1993 Wolfpack of the Ancients	Closed		29.50	45-50
1993 Two Bears Camp	Closed		29.50	39
1993 Wintering With the Wapiti	Closed		29.50	32-42
1993 Within Sunrise	Closed		29.50	50-55
1993 Wambli Okiye	Closed		29.50	35-40

The Federal Duck Stamp Plate Collection - Various

YEAR ISSUE	EDITION LIMIT	YEAR RETD.	ISSUE PRICE	*QUOTE U.S.$
1990 The Lesser Scaup	Closed		27.50	28-55
1990 The Mallard	Closed		27.50	33-50
1990 The Ruddy Ducks	Closed		30.50	23-31
1990 Canvasbacks	Closed		30.50	19-31
1991 Pintails	Closed		30.50	24-29
1991 Wigeons	Closed		30.50	29
1991 Cinnamon Teal	Closed		32.50	25-33
1991 Fulvous Wistling Duck	Closed		32.50	36-44
1991 The Redheads	Closed		32.50	41-45
1991 Snow Goose	Closed		32.50	33

Feline Fancy - H. Ronner

YEAR ISSUE	EDITION LIMIT	YEAR RETD.	ISSUE PRICE	*QUOTE U.S.$
1993 Globetrotters	Closed		34.50	30-35
1993 Little Athletes	Closed		34.50	40
1993 Young Adventurers	Closed		34.50	45
1993 The Geographers	Closed		34.50	50

Field Birds of North America - D. Bush

YEAR ISSUE	EDITION LIMIT	YEAR RETD.	ISSUE PRICE	*QUOTE U.S.$
1991 Winter Colors: Ring-Necked Pheasant	Closed		39.50	42-45
1991 In Display: Ruffed Grouse	Closed		39.50	34-40
1991 Morning Light: Bobwhite Quail	Closed		42.50	41-50
1991 Misty Clearing: Wild Turkey	Closed		42.50	43-79
1992 Autumn Moment: American Woodcock	Closed		42.50	50
1992 Season's End: Willow Ptarmigan	Closed		42.50	60

Floral Fancies - C. Callog

YEAR ISSUE	EDITION LIMIT	YEAR RETD.	ISSUE PRICE	*QUOTE U.S.$
1993 Sitting Softly	Closed		34.50	45
1993 Sitting Pretty	Closed		34.50	46
1993 Sitting Sunny	Closed		34.50	35-55
1993 Sitting Pink	Closed		34.50	35-45

Flowers From Grandma's Garden - G. Kurz

YEAR ISSUE	EDITION LIMIT	YEAR RETD.	ISSUE PRICE	*QUOTE U.S.$
1990 Country Cuttings	Closed		24.50	37-50
1990 The Morning Bouquet	Closed		24.50	35-45
1991 Homespun Beauty	Closed		27.50	35-40
1991 Harvest in the Meadow	Closed		27.50	37
1991 Gardener's Delight	Closed		27.50	35-39
1991 Nature's Bounty	Closed		27.50	44-60
1991 A Country Welcome	Closed		29.50	50-55
1991 The Springtime Arrangement	Closed		29.50	50

Flowers of Your Garden - V. Morley

YEAR ISSUE	EDITION LIMIT	YEAR RETD.	ISSUE PRICE	*QUOTE U.S.$
1988 Roses	Closed		24.50	25-50
1988 Lilacs	Closed		24.50	60-85
1988 Daisies	Closed		27.50	35-39
1988 Peonies	Closed		27.50	20-39
1988 Chrysanthemums	Closed		27.50	39-49
1989 Daffodils	Closed		27.50	21-39
1989 Tulips	Closed		29.50	20-40
1989 Irises	Closed		29.50	24-39

Garden of the Lord - C. Gillies

YEAR ISSUE	EDITION LIMIT	YEAR RETD.	ISSUE PRICE	*QUOTE U.S.$
1992 Love One Another	Closed		29.50	40-45
1992 Perfect Peace	Closed		29.50	36
1992 Trust In the Lord	Closed		32.50	33
1992 The Lord's Love	Closed		32.50	33
1992 The Lord Bless You	Closed		32.50	33
1992 Ask In Prayer	Closed		34.50	35
1993 Peace Be With You	Closed		34.50	35
1993 Give Thanks To The Lord	Closed		34.50	35

Gardens of Paradise - L. Chang

YEAR ISSUE	EDITION LIMIT	YEAR RETD.	ISSUE PRICE	*QUOTE U.S.$
1992 Tranquility	Closed		29.50	37
1992 Serenity	Closed		29.50	33-40
1993 Splendor	Closed		32.50	40-64
1993 Harmony	Closed		32.50	55-66
1993 Beauty	Closed		32.50	40
1993 Elegance	Closed		32.50	50
1993 Grandeur	Closed		32.50	65
1993 Majesty	Closed		32.50	50-60

Gentle Beginnings - W. Nelson

YEAR ISSUE	EDITION LIMIT	YEAR RETD.	ISSUE PRICE	*QUOTE U.S.$
1991 Tender Loving Care	Closed		34.50	30-45
1991 A Touch of Love	Closed		34.50	45-50
1991 Under Watchful Eyes	Closed		37.50	84-89
1991 Lap of Love	Closed		37.50	55-59
1992 Happy Together	Closed		37.50	81-85
1992 First Steps	Closed		37.50	80

Glorious Songbirds - R. Cobane

YEAR ISSUE	EDITION LIMIT	YEAR RETD.	ISSUE PRICE	*QUOTE U.S.$
1991 Cardinals on a Snowy Branch	Closed		29.50	24-35
1991 Indigo Buntings and/Blossoms	Closed		29.50	20-30
1991 Chickadees Among The Lilacs	Closed		32.50	28-34
1991 Goldfinches in/Thistle	Closed		32.50	28-33
1991 Cedar Waxwing/Winter Berries	Closed		32.50	22-33
1991 Bluebirds in a Blueberry Bush	Closed		34.50	35
1991 Baltimore Orioles/Autumn Leaves	Closed		34.50	60-64
1991 Robins with Dogwood in Bloom	Closed		34.50	45-48

The Golden Age of the Clipper Ships - C. Vickery

YEAR ISSUE	EDITION LIMIT	YEAR RETD.	ISSUE PRICE	*QUOTE U.S.$
1989 The Twilight Under Full Sail	Closed		29.50	30-50
1989 The Blue Jacket at Sunset	Closed		29.50	15-30
1989 Young America, Homeward	Closed		32.50	45-50
1990 Flying Cloud	Closed		32.50	24-30
1990 Davy Crocket at Daybreak	Closed		32.50	21-35
1990 Golden Eagle Conquers Wind	Closed		32.50	31-35
1990 The Lightning in Lifting Fog	Closed		34.50	35-40
1990 Sea Witch, Mistress/Oceans	Closed		34.50	35-40

Gone With the Wind: Golden Anniversary - H. Rogers

YEAR ISSUE	EDITION LIMIT	YEAR RETD.	ISSUE PRICE	*QUOTE U.S.$
1988 Scarlett and Her Suitors	Closed		24.50	100-125
1988 The Burning of Atlanta	Closed		24.50	90-115
1988 Scarlett and Ashley After the War	Closed		27.50	60-85
1988 The Proposal	Closed		27.50	69-125
1989 Home to Tara	Closed		27.50	50-75
1989 Strolling in Atlanta	Closed		27.50	45-75
1989 A Question of Honor	Closed		29.50	60-75
1989 Scarlett's Resolve	Closed		29.50	60-85
1989 Frankly My Dear	Closed		29.50	55-60
1989 Melane and Ashley	Closed		32.50	45-65
1990 A Toast to Bonnie Blue	Closed		32.50	50-60
1990 Scarlett and Rhett's Honeymoon	Closed		32.50	60-95

Gone With the Wind: The Passions of Scarlett O'Hara - P. Jennis

YEAR ISSUE	EDITION LIMIT	YEAR RETD.	ISSUE PRICE	*QUOTE U.S.$
1992 Fiery Embrace	Closed		29.50	50
1992 Pride and Passion	Closed		29.50	50-60
1992 Dreams of Ashley	Closed		32.50	50-62
1992 The Fond Farewell	Closed		32.50	45-55
1992 The Waltz	Closed		32.50	33-65
1992 As God Is My Witness	Closed		34.50	75-85
1993 Brave Scarlett	Closed		34.50	64-79
1993 Nightmare	Closed		34.50	35-85
1993 Evening Prayers	Closed		34.50	35-45
1993 Naptime	Closed		36.50	60-65
1993 Dangerous Attraction	Closed		36.50	40-59
1994 The End of An Era	Closed		36.50	50-55

Grand Safari: Images of Africa - C. Fracé

YEAR ISSUE	EDITION LIMIT	YEAR RETD.	ISSUE PRICE	*QUOTE U.S.$
1992 A Moment's Rest	Closed		34.50	32
1992 Elephant's of Kilimanjaro	Closed		34.50	50-55
1992 Undivided Attention	Closed		37.50	42
1993 Quiet Time in Samburu	Closed		37.50	38-49
1993 Lone Hunter	Closed		37.50	38
1993 The Greater Kudo	Closed		37.50	30-38

Heart of the Wild - G. Beecham

YEAR ISSUE	EDITION LIMIT	YEAR RETD.	ISSUE PRICE	*QUOTE U.S.$
1992 A Gentle Touch	Closed		29.50	30
1992 Mother's Pride	Closed		29.50	37
1992 An Afternoon Together	Closed		32.50	46-50
1993 Quiet Time?	Closed		32.50	50

Hollywood's Glamour Girls - E. Dzenis

YEAR ISSUE	EDITION LIMIT	YEAR RETD.	ISSUE PRICE	*QUOTE U.S.$
1989 Jean Harlow-Dinner at Eight	Closed		24.50	35-55
1990 Lana Turner-Postman Ring Twice	Closed		29.50	30-50

*Quotes have been rounded up to nearest dollar

YEAR ISSUE	EDITION LIMIT	YEAR RETD.	ISSUE PRICE	*QUOTE U.S.$
1990 Carol Lombard-The Gay Bride	Closed		29.50	18-30
1990 Greta Garbo-In Grand Hotel	Closed		29.50	26-45

Hometown Memories - H.T. Becker

YEAR ISSUE	EDITION LIMIT	YEAR RETD.	ISSUE PRICE	*QUOTE U.S.$
1993 Moonlight Skaters	Closed		29.50	23-30
1993 Mountain Sleigh Ride	Closed		29.50	45
1993 Heading Home	Closed		29.50	50
1993 A Winter Ride	Closed		29.50	50

Last of Their Kind: The Endangered Species - W. Nelson

YEAR ISSUE	EDITION LIMIT	YEAR RETD.	ISSUE PRICE	*QUOTE U.S.$
1988 The Panda	Closed		27.50	55-65
1989 The Snow Leopard	Closed		27.50	35-65
1989 The Red Wolf	Closed		30.50	40-65
1989 The Asian Elephant	Closed		30.50	55-65
1990 The Slender-Horned Gazelle	Closed		30.50	17-50
1990 The Bridled Wallaby	Closed		30.50	18-50
1990 The Black-Footed Ferret	Closed		33.50	27-50
1990 The Siberian Tiger	Closed		33.50	60-65
1991 The Vicuna	Closed		33.50	39-50
1991 Przewalski's Horse	Closed		33.50	42-60

Lena Liu's Basket Bouquets - L. Liu

YEAR ISSUE	EDITION LIMIT	YEAR RETD.	ISSUE PRICE	*QUOTE U.S.$
1992 Roses	Closed		29.50	35-42
1992 Pansies	Closed		29.50	35-58
1992 Tulips and Lilacs	Closed		32.50	54-60
1992 Irises	Closed		32.50	46-60
1992 Lilies	Closed		32.50	39
1992 Parrot Tulips	Closed		32.50	49-53
1992 Peonies	Closed		32.50	45
1993 Begonias	Closed		32.50	33-70
1993 Magnolias	Closed		32.50	33-40
1993 Calla Lilies	Closed		32.50	60-65
1993 Orchids	Closed		32.50	33-58
1993 Hydrangeas	Closed		32.50	33-53

Lena Liu's Flower Fairies - L. Liu

YEAR ISSUE	EDITION LIMIT	YEAR RETD.	ISSUE PRICE	*QUOTE U.S.$
1993 Magic Makers	Closed		29.50	30-40
1993 Petal Playmates	Closed		29.50	30
1993 Delicate Dancers	Closed		32.50	33-48
1993 Mischief Masters	Closed		32.50	35
1993 Amorous Angels	Closed		32.50	33
1993 Winged Wonders	Closed		34.50	35
1993 Miniature Mermaids	Closed		34.50	35-40
1993 Fanciful Fairies	Closed		34.50	35-40

Lena Liu's Hummingbird Treasury - L. Liu

YEAR ISSUE	EDITION LIMIT	YEAR RETD.	ISSUE PRICE	*QUOTE U.S.$
1992 Ruby-Throated Hummingbird	Closed		29.50	55-65
1992 Anna's Hummingbird	Closed		29.50	64-69
1992 Violet-Crowned Hummingbird	Closed		32.50	68-90
1993 Rufous Hummingbird	Closed		32.50	68-90
1993 White-Eared Hummingbird	Closed		32.50	68-75
1993 Broad-Billed Hummingbird	Closed		34.50	30-75
1993 Calliope Hummingbird	Closed		34.50	30-68
1993 The Allen's Hummingbird	Closed		34.50	60-75

Little Angels - B. Burke

YEAR ISSUE	EDITION LIMIT	YEAR RETD.	ISSUE PRICE	*QUOTE U.S.$
1992 Angels We Have Heard on High	Closed		29.50	40-55
1992 O Tannenbaum	Closed		29.50	54-65
1993 Joy to the World	Closed		32.50	75-79
1993 Hark the Herald Angels Sing	Closed		32.50	55-65
1993 It Came Upon a Midnight Clear	Closed		32.50	33-55
1993 The First Noel	Closed		32.50	35-60

A Loving Look: Duck Families - B. Langton

YEAR ISSUE	EDITION LIMIT	YEAR RETD.	ISSUE PRICE	*QUOTE U.S.$
1990 Family Outing	Closed		34.50	19-35
1991 Sleepy Start	Closed		34.50	20-35
1991 Quiet Moment	Closed		37.50	43
1991 Safe and Sound	Closed		37.50	33-40
1991 Spring Arrivals	Closed		37.50	38
1991 The Family Tree	Closed		37.50	38-50

The Majestic Horse - P. Wildermuth

YEAR ISSUE	EDITION LIMIT	YEAR RETD.	ISSUE PRICE	*QUOTE U.S.$
1992 Classic Beauty: Thoroughbred	Closed		34.50	35
1992 American Gold: The Quarterhorse	Closed		34.50	50
1992 Regal Spirit: The Arabian	Closed		34.50	59-74
1992 Western Favorite: American Paint Horse	Closed		34.50	50-60

Melodies in the Mist - A. Sakhavarz

YEAR ISSUE	EDITION LIMIT	YEAR RETD.	ISSUE PRICE	*QUOTE U.S.$
1993 Early Morning Rain	Closed		34.50	39
1993 Among the Dewdrops	Closed		34.50	34
1993 Feeding Time	Closed		37.50	36
1994 Garden Party	Closed		37.50	38-65
1994 Unpleasant Surprise	Closed		37.50	38
1994 Spring Rain	Closed		37.50	41

Memories of a Victorian Childhood - Unknown

YEAR ISSUE	EDITION LIMIT	YEAR RETD.	ISSUE PRICE	*QUOTE U.S.$
1992 You'd Better Not Pout	Closed		29.50	30
1992 Sweet Slumber	Closed		29.50	55
1992 Through Thick and Thin	Closed		32.50	48
1992 An Armful of Treasures	Closed		32.50	57-65
1993 A Trio of Bookworms	Closed		32.50	57-60
1993 Pugnacious Playmate	Closed		32.50	55-60

Nature's Legacy - J. Sias

YEAR ISSUE	EDITION LIMIT	YEAR RETD.	ISSUE PRICE	*QUOTE U.S.$
1990 Blue Snow at Half Dome	Closed		24.50	28-35
1991 Misty Morning/Mt. McKinley	Closed		24.50	20-25
1991 Twilight Reflections on Mount Ranier	Closed		27.50	20-30
1991 Redwalls of Havasu Canyon	Closed		27.50	20-27
1991 Autumn Splendor in the Smoky Mts.	Closed		27.50	24
1991 Winter Peace in Yellowstone Park	Closed		29.50	30-35
1991 Golden Majesty/Rocky Mountains	Closed		29.50	34
1991 Radiant Sunset Over the Everglades	Closed		29.50	31-35

Nature's Lovables - C. Fracé

YEAR ISSUE	EDITION LIMIT	YEAR RETD.	ISSUE PRICE	*QUOTE U.S.$
1990 The Koala Bear	Closed		27.50	35-50
1991 New Arrival	Closed		27.50	30-50
1991 Chinese Treasure	Closed		27.50	39-50
1991 Baby Harp Seal	Closed		30.50	22-50
1991 Bobcat: Nature's Dawn	Closed		30.50	23-50
1991 Clouded Leopard	Closed		32.50	22-50
1991 Zebra Foal	Closed		32.50	32-50
1991 Bandit	Closed		32.50	43-50

Nature's Playmates - C. Fracé

YEAR ISSUE	EDITION LIMIT	YEAR RETD.	ISSUE PRICE	*QUOTE U.S.$
1991 Partners	Closed		29.50	25-33
1991 Secret Heights	Closed		29.50	25-30
1991 Recess	Closed		32.50	26-33
1991 Double Trouble	Closed		32.50	29-35
1991 Pals	Closed		32.50	26-33
1992 Curious Trio	Closed		34.50	45
1992 Playmates	Closed		34.50	33-45
1992 Surprise	Closed		34.50	26-35
1992 Peace On Ice	Closed		36.50	44-50
1992 Ambassadors	Closed		36.50	35-40

Nature's Poetry - L. Liu

YEAR ISSUE	EDITION LIMIT	YEAR RETD.	ISSUE PRICE	*QUOTE U.S.$
1989 Morning Serenade	Closed		24.50	45-55
1989 Song of Promise	Closed		24.50	30
1990 Tender Lullaby	Closed		27.50	30-35
1990 Nature's Harmony	Closed		27.50	33-40
1990 Gentle Refrain	Closed		27.50	24-35
1990 Morning Chorus	Closed		27.50	28-35
1990 Melody at Daybreak	Closed		29.50	24-30
1991 Delicate Accord	Closed		29.50	18-30
1991 Lyrical Beginnings	Closed		29.50	18-35
1991 Song of Spring	Closed		32.50	34-38
1991 Mother's Melody	Closed		32.50	24-33
1991 Cherub Chorale	Closed		32.50	35-45

On Golden Wings - W. Goebel

YEAR ISSUE	EDITION LIMIT	YEAR RETD.	ISSUE PRICE	*QUOTE U.S.$
1993 Morning Light	Closed		29.50	30-45
1993 Early Risers	Closed		29.50	46
1993 As Day Breaks	Closed		32.50	45
1993 Daylight Flight	Closed		32.50	44
1993 Winter Dawn	Closed		32.50	33
1994 First Light	Closed		34.50	50

On Gossamer Wings - L. Liu

YEAR ISSUE	EDITION LIMIT	YEAR RETD.	ISSUE PRICE	*QUOTE U.S.$
1988 Monarch Butterflies	Closed		24.50	35-50
1988 Western Tiger Swallowtails	Closed		24.50	40-50
1988 Red-Spotted Purple	Closed		27.50	35-40
1988 Malachites	Closed		27.50	20
1988 White Peacocks	Closed		27.50	25-30
1989 Eastern Tailed Blues	Closed		27.50	17-30
1989 Zebra Swallowtails	Closed		29.50	22-25
1989 Red Admirals	Closed		29.50	17-30

On the Wing - T. Humphrey

YEAR ISSUE	EDITION LIMIT	YEAR RETD.	ISSUE PRICE	*QUOTE U.S.$
1992 Winged Splendor	Closed		29.50	19-29
1992 Rising Mallard	Closed		29.50	28
1992 Glorious Ascent	Closed		32.50	33
1992 Taking Wing	Closed		32.50	37
1992 Upward Bound	Closed		32.50	37
1993 Wondrous Motion	Closed		34.50	35-40
1993 Springing Forth	Closed		34.50	55
1993 On The Wing	Closed		34.50	65

On Wings of Snow - L. Liu

YEAR ISSUE	EDITION LIMIT	YEAR RETD.	ISSUE PRICE	*QUOTE U.S.$
1991 The Swans	Closed		34.50	32-50
1991 The Doves	Closed		34.50	35-40
1991 The Peacocks	Closed		37.50	40-45
1991 The Egrets	Closed		37.50	49
1991 The Cockatoos	Closed		37.50	36-45
1992 The Herons	Closed		37.50	38

Our Woodland Friends - C. Brenders

YEAR ISSUE	EDITION LIMIT	YEAR RETD.	ISSUE PRICE	*QUOTE U.S.$
1989 Fascination	Closed		29.00	17-35
1990 Beneath the Pines	Closed		29.50	20-30
1990 High Adventure	Closed		32.50	20-33
1990 Shy Explorers	Closed		32.50	31-35
1991 Golden Season: Gray Squirrel	Closed		32.50	27-35
1991 Full House: Fox Family	Closed		32.50	33-45
1991 A Jump Into Life: Spring Fawn	Closed		34.50	33
1991 Forest Sentinel: Bobcat	Closed		34.50	22-34

Petal Pals - L. Chang

YEAR ISSUE	EDITION LIMIT	YEAR RETD.	ISSUE PRICE	*QUOTE U.S.$
1992 Garden Discovery	Closed		24.50	32
1992 Flowering Fascination	Closed		24.50	20-30
1993 Alluring Lilies	Closed		24.50	20-37
1993 Springtime Oasis	Closed		24.50	19-30
1993 Blossoming Adventure	Closed		24.50	25-40
1993 Dancing Daffodils	Closed		24.50	25-40
1993 Summer Surprise	Closed		24.50	25-32
1993 Morning Melody	Closed		24.50	20-34

Poetic Cottages - C. Valente

YEAR ISSUE	EDITION LIMIT	YEAR RETD.	ISSUE PRICE	*QUOTE U.S.$
1992 Garden Paths of Oxfordshire	Closed		29.50	35-50
1992 Twilight at Woodgreen Pond	Closed		29.50	70
1992 Stonewall Brook Blossoms	Closed		32.50	65
1992 Bedfordshire Evening Sky	Closed		32.50	46
1993 Wisteria Summer	Closed		32.50	50
1993 Wiltshire Rose Arbor	Closed		32.50	49
1993 Alderbury Gardens	Closed		32.50	56
1993 Hampshire Spring Splendor	Closed		32.50	35-59

Portraits of Christ - J. Salamanca

YEAR ISSUE	EDITION LIMIT	YEAR RETD.	ISSUE PRICE	*QUOTE U.S.$
1991 Father, Forgive Them	Closed		29.50	85-95
1991 Thy Will Be Done	Closed		29.50	50
1991 This is My Beloved Son	Closed		32.50	45
1991 Lo, I Am With You	Closed		32.50	49
1991 Become as Little Children	Closed		32.50	49-54
1992 Peace I Leave With You	Closed		34.50	45-50
1992 For God So Loved the World	Closed		34.50	42-50
1992 I Am the Way, the Truth and the Life	Closed		34.50	42-50
1992 Weep Not For Me	Closed		34.50	55-58
1992 Follow Me	Closed		34.50	60-65

Portraits of Exquisite Birds - C. Brenders

YEAR ISSUE	EDITION LIMIT	YEAR RETD.	ISSUE PRICE	*QUOTE U.S.$
1990 Backyard Treasure/Chickadee	Closed		29.50	26-30
1990 The Beautiful Bluebird	Closed		29.50	21-30
1991 Summer Gold: The Robin	Closed		32.50	24-33
1991 The Meadowlark's Song	Closed		32.50	25-33
1991 Ivory-Billed Woodpecker	Closed		32.50	29-33
1991 Red-Winged Blackbird	Closed		32.50	35

Purebred Horses of the Americas - D. Schwartz

YEAR ISSUE	EDITION LIMIT	YEAR RETD.	ISSUE PRICE	*QUOTE U.S.$
1989 The Appalosa	Closed		34.50	22-35
1989 The Tenessee Walker	Closed		34.50	34
1990 The Quarterhorse	Closed		37.50	31-37
1990 The Saddlebred	Closed		37.50	18-38
1990 The Mustang	Closed		37.50	33-38
1990 The Morgan	Closed		37.50	33-56

Rare Encounters - J. Seerey-Lester

YEAR ISSUE	EDITION LIMIT	YEAR RETD.	ISSUE PRICE	*QUOTE U.S.$
1993 Softly, Softly	Closed		29.50	35-42
1993 Black Magic	Closed		29.50	30-60
1993 Future Song	Closed		32.50	55-60
1993 High and Mighty	Closed		32.50	39-60
1993 Last Sanctuary	Closed		32.50	30-40
1993 Something Stirred	Closed		34.50	35-50

Romantic Gardens - C. Smith

YEAR ISSUE	EDITION LIMIT	YEAR RETD.	ISSUE PRICE	*QUOTE U.S.$
1989 The Woodland Garden	Closed		29.50	25-30
1989 The Plantation Garden	Closed		29.50	23-30
1990 The Cottage Garden	Closed		32.50	25-33
1990 The Colonial Garden	Closed		32.50	28-35

Scenes of Christmas Past - L. Garrison

YEAR ISSUE	EDITION LIMIT	YEAR RETD.	ISSUE PRICE	*QUOTE U.S.$
1987 Holiday Skaters	Closed		27.50	24-28
1988 Christmas Eve	Closed		27.50	26-30
1989 The Homecoming	Closed		30.50	25-36
1990 The Toy Store	Closed		30.50	18-40
1991 The Carollers	Closed		30.50	26-40
1992 Family Traditions	Closed		32.50	34-45
1993 Holiday Past	Closed		32.50	62-65
1994 A Gathering of Faith	Closed		32.50	45-50

The Secret World Of The Panda - J. Bridgett

YEAR ISSUE	EDITION LIMIT	YEAR RETD.	ISSUE PRICE	*QUOTE U.S.$
1990 A Mother's Care	Closed		27.50	30-55
1991 A Frolic in the Snow	Closed		27.50	20-30
1991 Lazy Afternoon	Closed		30.50	23-31
1991 A Day of Exploring	Closed		30.50	30
1991 A Gentle Hug	Closed		32.50	35
1991 A Bamboo Feast	Closed		32.50	65-69

Soaring Majesty - C. Fracé

YEAR ISSUE	EDITION LIMIT	YEAR RETD.	ISSUE PRICE	*QUOTE U.S.$
1991 Freedom	Closed		29.50	15-30
1991 The Northern Goshhawk	Closed		29.50	19-30
1991 Peregrine Falcon	Closed		32.50	21-33
1991 Red-Tailed Hawk	Closed		32.50	25-35
1991 The Ospray	Closed		32.50	20-33
1991 The Gyrfalcon	Closed		34.50	30-35
1991 The Golden Eagle	Closed		34.50	32-37
1992 Red-Shouldered Hawk	Closed		34.50	29-35

Sonnets in Flowers - G. Kurz

YEAR ISSUE	EDITION LIMIT	YEAR RETD.	ISSUE PRICE	*QUOTE U.S.$
1992 Sonnet of Beauty	Closed		29.50	34
1992 Sonnet of Happiness	Closed		34.50	40-62
1992 Sonnet of Love	Closed		34.50	35-55
1992 Sonnet of Peace	Closed		34.50	55

The Sound of Music: Silver Anniversary - V. Gadino

YEAR ISSUE	EDITION LIMIT	YEAR RETD.	ISSUE PRICE	*QUOTE U.S.$
1991 The Hills are Alive	Closed		29.50	30-55
1992 Let's Start at the Very Beginning	Closed		29.50	25-30
1992 Something Good	Closed		32.50	30-42
1992 Maria's Wedding Day	Closed		32.50	30-55

Spirit of Christmas - J. Sias

YEAR ISSUE	EDITION LIMIT	YEAR RETD.	ISSUE PRICE	*QUOTE U.S.$
1990 Silent Night	Closed		29.50	22-32
1991 Jingle Bells	Closed		29.50	24-30
1991 Deck The Halls	Closed		32.50	32
1991 I'll Be Home For Christmas	Closed		32.50	38-43
1991 Winter Wonderland	Closed		32.50	28-33
1991 O Christmas Tree	Closed		32.50	33-35

Spirits of the Sky - C. Fisher

YEAR ISSUE	EDITION LIMIT	YEAR RETD.	ISSUE PRICE	*QUOTE U.S.$
1992 Twilight Glow	Closed		29.50	32-40
1992 First Light	Closed		29.50	60
1992 Evening Glimmer	Closed		32.50	74
1992 Golden Dusk	Closed		32.50	35
1993 Sunset Splendor	Closed		32.50	33-45
1993 Amber Flight	Closed		34.50	42-75
1993 Winged Radiance	Closed		34.50	49
1993 Day's End	Closed		34.50	35-75

A Splash of Cats - J. Seerey-Lester

YEAR ISSUE	EDITION LIMIT	YEAR RETD.	ISSUE PRICE	*QUOTE U.S.$
1992 Moonlight Chase: Cougar	Closed		29.50	30

*Quotes have been rounded up to nearest dollar

Symphony of Shimmering Beauties - L. Liu

YEAR ISSUE	EDITION LIMIT	YEAR RETD.	ISSUE PRICE	*QUOTE U.S.$
1991 Iris Quartet	Closed		29.50	39-50
1991 Tulip Ensemble	Closed		29.50	30-45
1991 Poppy Pastorale	Closed		32.50	35-45
1991 Lily Concerto	Closed		32.50	40
1991 Peony Prelude	Closed		32.50	33-55
1991 Rose Fantasy	Closed		34.50	40-50
1991 Hibiscus Medley	Closed		34.50	34-45
1992 Dahlia Melody	Closed		34.50	35-48
1992 Hollyhock March	Closed		34.50	35
1992 Carnation Serenade	Closed		36.50	35-49
1992 Gladiolus Romance	Closed		36.50	40-55
1992 Zinnia Finale	Closed		36.50	40-50

Tis the Season - J. Sias

YEAR ISSUE	EDITION LIMIT	YEAR RETD.	ISSUE PRICE	*QUOTE U.S.$
1993 World Dressed in Snow	Closed		29.50	26-35
1993 A Time for Tradition	Closed		29.50	36
1993 We Shall Come Rejoining	Closed		29.50	40
1993 Our Family Tree	Closed		29.50	40

Tomorrow's Promise - W. Nelson

YEAR ISSUE	EDITION LIMIT	YEAR RETD.	ISSUE PRICE	*QUOTE U.S.$
1992 Curiosity: Asian Elephants	Closed		29.50	30-38
1992 Playtime Pandas	Closed		29.50	38
1992 Innocence: Rhinos	Closed		32.50	59
1992 Friskiness: Kit Foxes	Closed		32.50	39-45

Touching the Spirit - J. Kramer Cole

YEAR ISSUE	EDITION LIMIT	YEAR RETD.	ISSUE PRICE	*QUOTE U.S.$
1993 Running With the Wind	Closed		29.50	50-60
1993 Kindred Spirits	Closed		29.50	36
1993 The Marking Tree	Closed		29.50	46
1993 Wakan Tanka	Closed		29.50	40-68
1993 He Who Watches	Closed		29.50	50-65
1994 Twice Traveled Trail	Closed		29.50	41-44
1994 Keeper of the Secret	Closed		29.50	27-45
1994 Camp of the Sacred Dogs	Closed		29.50	40-55

A Treasury of Songbirds - R. Stine

YEAR ISSUE	EDITION LIMIT	YEAR RETD.	ISSUE PRICE	*QUOTE U.S.$
1992 Springtime Splendor	Closed		29.50	39-45
1992 Morning's Glory	Closed		29.50	34-45
1992 Golden Daybreak	Closed		32.50	41-51
1992 Afternoon Calm	Closed		32.50	39-45
1992 Dawn's Radiance	Closed		32.50	42-52
1993 Scarlet Sunrise	Closed		34.50	55-60
1993 Sapphire Dawn	Closed		34.50	50
1995 Alluring Daylight	Closed		34.50	65

The Vanishing Gentle Giants - A. Casay

YEAR ISSUE	EDITION LIMIT	YEAR RETD.	ISSUE PRICE	*QUOTE U.S.$
1991 Jumping For Joy	Closed		32.50	25-33
1991 Song of the Humpback	Closed		32.50	28-33
1991 Monarch of the Deep	Closed		35.50	35-40
1991 Travelers of the Sea	Closed		35.50	49-55
1991 White Whale of the North	Closed		35.50	45
1991 Unicorn of the Sea	Closed		35.50	38

The Victorian Cat - H. Bonner

YEAR ISSUE	EDITION LIMIT	YEAR RETD.	ISSUE PRICE	*QUOTE U.S.$
1990 Mischief With The Hatbox	Closed		24.50	45-55
1991 String Quartet	Closed		24.50	42
1991 Daydreams	Closed		27.50	35
1991 Frisky Felines	Closed		27.50	35-49
1991 Kittens at Play	Closed		27.50	20-40
1991 Playing in the Parlor	Closed		29.50	39-59
1991 Perfectly Poised	Closed		29.50	40-55
1992 Midday Repose	Closed		29.50	20-55

Victorian Cat Capers - Various

YEAR ISSUE	EDITION LIMIT	YEAR RETD.	ISSUE PRICE	*QUOTE U.S.$
1992 Who's the Fairest of Them All? - F. Paton	Closed		24.50	55-63
1992 Puss in Boots - Unknown	Closed		24.50	39-49
1992 My Bowl is Empty - W. Hepple	Closed		27.50	34
1992 A Curious Kitty - C. Van den Eycken	Closed		27.50	25-29
1992 Vanity Fair - C. Van den Eycken	Closed		27.50	25-29
1992 Forbidden Fruit - H. Blain	Closed		29.50	50-55
1993 The Purr-fect Pen Pal - A. Tucker	Closed		29.50	25-44
1993 The Kitten Express - L. Huber	Closed		29.50	25-49

Vieonne Morley's Romantic Roses - V. Morley

YEAR ISSUE	EDITION LIMIT	YEAR RETD.	ISSUE PRICE	*QUOTE U.S.$
1993 Victorian Beauty	Closed		29.50	40-45
1993 Old-Fashioned Grace	Closed		29.50	49
1993 Country Charm	Closed		32.50	33-42
1993 Summer Romance	Closed		32.50	33-49
1993 Pastoral Delight	Closed		32.50	33-38
1993 Springtime Elegance	Closed		34.50	35-49
1993 Vintage Splendor	Closed		34.50	45-55
1994 Heavenly Perfection	Closed		34.50	35-49

Wild Innocents - C. Fracé

YEAR ISSUE	EDITION LIMIT	YEAR RETD.	ISSUE PRICE	*QUOTE U.S.$
1993 Reflections	Closed		29.50	35
1993 Spiritual Heir	Closed		29.50	43-50
1993 Lion Cub	Closed		29.50	45
1993 Sunny Spot	Closed		29.50	46

Wild Spirits - T. Hirata

YEAR ISSUE	EDITION LIMIT	YEAR RETD.	ISSUE PRICE	*QUOTE U.S.$
1992 Solitary Watch	Closed		29.50	32
1992 Timber Ghost	Closed		29.50	50-65
1992 Mountain Magic	Closed		32.50	35
1993 Silent Guard	Closed		32.50	35-45
1993 Sly Eyes	Closed		32.50	49
1993 Mighty Presence	Closed		34.50	35-40
1993 Quiet Vigil	Closed		34.50	50-55
1993 Lone Vanguard	Closed		34.50	35

Wings of Winter - D. Rust

YEAR ISSUE	EDITION LIMIT	YEAR RETD.	ISSUE PRICE	*QUOTE U.S.$
1992 Moonlight Retreat	Closed		29.50	35-40
1993 Twilight Serenade	Closed		29.50	40
1993 Silent Sunset	Closed		29.50	36-40
1993 Night Lights	Closed		29.50	30-54
1993 Winter Haven	Closed		29.50	30-48
1993 Full Moon Companions	Closed		29.50	30-48
1993 White Night	Closed		29.50	30
1993 Winter Reflections	150-day		29.50	30

Winter's Majesty - C. Fracé

YEAR ISSUE	EDITION LIMIT	YEAR RETD.	ISSUE PRICE	*QUOTE U.S.$
1992 The Quest	Closed		34.50	35
1992 The Chase	Closed		34.50	29-35
1993 Alaskan Friend	Closed		34.50	35
1993 American Cougar	Closed		34.50	30-35
1993 On Watch	Closed		34.50	45
1993 Solitude	Closed		34.50	43

Wonders Of The Sea - R. Harm

YEAR ISSUE	EDITION LIMIT	YEAR RETD.	ISSUE PRICE	*QUOTE U.S.$
1991 Stand By Me	Closed		34.50	34-50
1991 Heart to Heart	Closed		34.50	25-35
1991 Warm Embrace	Closed		34.50	30-40
1991 A Family Affair	Closed		34.50	34

The World's Most Magnificent Cats - C. Fracé

YEAR ISSUE	EDITION LIMIT	YEAR RETD.	ISSUE PRICE	*QUOTE U.S.$
1991 Fleeting Encounter	Closed		24.50	25-59
1991 Cougar	Closed		24.50	24-46
1991 Royal Bengal	Closed		27.50	25-40
1991 Powerful Presence	Closed		27.50	42-50
1991 Jaguar	Closed		27.50	25-43
1991 The Clouded Leopard	Closed		29.50	24-50
1991 The African Leopard	Closed		29.50	22-50
1991 Mighty Warrior	Closed		29.50	55-60
1992 The Cheetah	Closed		31.50	39-45
1992 Siberian Tiger	Closed		31.50	49-55

Waterford Wedgwood USA

Bicentennial - Unknown

YEAR ISSUE	EDITION LIMIT	YEAR RETD.	ISSUE PRICE	*QUOTE U.S.$
1972 Boston Tea Party	Annual		40.00	40
1973 Paul Revere's Ride	Annual		40.00	115
1974 Battle of Concord	Annual		40.00	55
1975 Across the Delaware	Annual		40.00	105
1975 Victory at Yorktown	Annual		45.00	53
1976 Declaration Signed	Annual		45.00	45

Wedgwood Christmas - Various

YEAR ISSUE	EDITION LIMIT	YEAR RETD.	ISSUE PRICE	*QUOTE U.S.$
1969 Windsor Castle - T. Harper	Annual		25.00	95-125
1970 Trafalgar Square - T. Harper	Annual		30.00	15-35
1971 Picadilly Circus - T. Harper	Annual		30.00	19-30
1972 St. Paul's Cathedral - T. Harper	Annual		35.00	35-45
1973 Tower of London - T. Harper	Annual		40.00	60-90
1974 Houses of Parliament - T. Harper	Annual		40.00	40-45
1975 Tower Bridge - T. Harper	Annual		45.00	40-45
1976 Hampton Court - T. Harper	Annual		50.00	35-40
1977 Westminister Abbey - T. Harper	Annual		55.00	35-40
1978 Horse Guards - T. Harper	Annual		60.00	40-60
1979 Buckingham Palace - Unknown	Annual		65.00	40-65
1980 St. James Palace - Unknown	Annual		70.00	59-70
1981 Marble Arch - Unknown	Annual		75.00	75
1982 Lambeth Palace - Unknown	Annual		80.00	80-90
1983 All Souls, Langham Palace - Unknown	Annual		80.00	80
1984 Constitution Hill - Unknown	Annual		80.00	80
1985 The Tate Gallery - Unknown	Annual		80.00	80-150
1986 The Albert Memorial - Unknown	Annual		80.00	110
1987 Guildhall - Unknown	Annual		80.00	85
1988 The Observatory/Greenwich - Unknown	Annual		80.00	90
1989 Winchester Cathedral - Unknown	Annual		88.00	88

Willitts Designs

Ebony Visions - T. Blackshear

YEAR ISSUE	EDITION LIMIT	YEAR RETD.	ISSUE PRICE	*QUOTE U.S.$
1997 The Madonna	7,500		35.00	35
1997 The Protector	7,500		35.00	35
1998 The Storyteller	7,500		45.00	45

STEINS

Anheuser-Busch, Inc.

Anheuser-Busch Collectors Club - Various

YEAR ISSUE	EDITION LIMIT	YEAR RETD.	ISSUE PRICE	*QUOTE U.S.$
1995 Budweiser Clydesdales at the Bauernhof CB1 - A. Leon	Yr.Iss.	1996	Gift	150-300
1995 The Brew House Clock Tower CB2 - D. Thompson	Retrd.	1996	150.00	450-800
1996 The World's Largest Brewer CB3 - A. Leon	Yr.Iss.	1996	Gift	65-125
1996 King - A Regal Spirit CB4 - D. Thompson	Retrd.	1997	100.00	100-300
1997 Pride & Tradition CB5 - J. Turgeon	Yr.Iss.	1997	Gift	50-75
1997 The Budweiser Girls-Historical Reflections CB6 - D. Curran	Retrd.	1998	100.00	100-300
1998 Old World Heritage CB7 - J. Turgeon	Yr.Iss.		Gift	N/A
1998 Early Delivery Days CB8 - D. Curran	4/99		100.00	100

Anheuser-Busch Collectors Club-Anheuser-Busch Heritage Series - A-Busch, Inc.

YEAR ISSUE	EDITION LIMIT	YEAR RETD.	ISSUE PRICE	*QUOTE U.S.$
1998 Bevo Mill CB9	4/99		120.00	120

A & Eagle Historical Trademark Series-Giftware Edition - Various

YEAR ISSUE	EDITION LIMIT	YEAR RETD.	ISSUE PRICE	*QUOTE U.S.$
1992 A & Eagle Trademark I (1872) CS201, tin	Retrd.	1993	31.00	75-130
1993 A & Eagle Trademark I (1872) CS191, boxed	Retrd.	1993	22.00	30-95
1993 A & Eagle Trademark II (1890s) CS218, tin	Retrd.	N/A	24.00	45-80
1994 A & Eagle Trademark II (1890s) CS219, boxed	Retrd.	1994	24.00	35-75
1994 A & Eagle Trademark III (1900s) CS238, tin	20,000	1994	28.00	35-85
1995 A & Eagle Trademark III (1900s) CS240, boxed	30,000	1995	25.00	30-75
1995 A & Eagle Trademark IV (1930s) CS255, tin	20,000	1996	30.00	30-45
1996 A & Eagle Trademark IV (1930s) CS271, boxed	30,000		27.00	27

America The Beautiful Series-Collector Edition - Various

YEAR ISSUE	EDITION LIMIT	YEAR RETD.	ISSUE PRICE	*QUOTE U.S.$
1998 Grand Canyon CS334 - H. Droog	50,000		39.95	40
1997 Smoky Mountains CS297 - A-Busch, Inc.	50,000		39.95	40

American Originals Series-Collector Edition - A-Busch, Inc.

YEAR ISSUE	EDITION LIMIT	YEAR RETD.	ISSUE PRICE	*QUOTE U.S.$
1997 Black & Tan Stein CS314	5,000	1997	75.00	165-400
1997 Faust Stein CS330	5,000	1997	75.00	75-325

Anheuser-Busch Founder Series-Premier Collection - A-Busch, Inc.

YEAR ISSUE	EDITION LIMIT	YEAR RETD.	ISSUE PRICE	*QUOTE U.S.$
1993 Adophus Busch CS216	10,000	1996	180.00	110-220
1994 August A. Busch, Sr. CS229	10,000	1996	220.00	110-220
1995 Adolphus Busch III CS265	10,000		220.00	220
1996 August A. Busch, Jr. CS286	10,000		220.00	220

Animals of the Seven Continents Series-Collector Edition - J. Turgeon

YEAR ISSUE	EDITION LIMIT	YEAR RETD.	ISSUE PRICE	*QUOTE U.S.$
1997 Africa CS308	100,000		49.00	49
1998 Australia CS339	100,000		49.00	49

Archives Series-Collector Edition - D. Langeneckert

YEAR ISSUE	EDITION LIMIT	YEAR RETD.	ISSUE PRICE	*QUOTE U.S.$
1992 1893 Columbian Exposition CS169	75,000	1995	35.00	35-95
1993 Ganymede CS190	Retrd.	1995	35.00	95-200
1994 Budweiser's Greatest Triumph CS222	75,000	1996	35.00	45-75
1995 Mirror of Truth Stein CS252	75,000		35.00	35

Birds of Prey Series-Premier Edition - P. Ford

YEAR ISSUE	EDITION LIMIT	YEAR RETD.	ISSUE PRICE	*QUOTE U.S.$
1991 American Bald Eagle CS164	25,000	1995	125.00	119-200
1992 Peregrine Falcon CS183	25,000	1996	125.00	100-200
1994 Osprey CS212	Retrd.	1994	135.00	695-2200
1995 Great Horned Owl CS264	25,000	1997	137.00	109-200

Bud Label Series-Giftware Edition - A-Busch, Inc.

YEAR ISSUE	EDITION LIMIT	YEAR RETD.	ISSUE PRICE	*QUOTE U.S.$
1989 Budweiser Label CS101	Retrd.	1995	14.00	16-95
1990 Antique Label II CS127	Retrd.	1994	14.00	20-75
1991 Bottled Beer III CS136	Retrd.	1995	15.00	20-55
1995 Budweiser Label Stein CS282	Open		19.50	20

Budweiser Anglers Edition Series-Giftware Edition - D. Kueker

YEAR ISSUE	EDITION LIMIT	YEAR RETD.	ISSUE PRICE	*QUOTE U.S.$
1998 Largemouth Bass CS270	Open		24.95	25

Budweiser Classic Car Series-Collector Edition - M. Watts

YEAR ISSUE	EDITION LIMIT	YEAR RETD.	ISSUE PRICE	*QUOTE U.S.$
1998 1957 Chevrolet Bel Air CS304	50,000		49.00	49

Budweiser Military Series-Giftware Edition - M. Watts

YEAR ISSUE	EDITION LIMIT	YEAR RETD.	ISSUE PRICE	*QUOTE U.S.$
1994 Army CS224	Retrd.	1995	19.00	75-185
1994 Air Force CS228	Retrd.	1997	19.00	22-50
1995 Budweiser Salutes the Navy CS243	Retrd.	1997	19.50	22-50
1995 Marines stein CS256	Retrd.	1997	22.00	22-50
1997 Coast Guard stein CS294	Open		22.00	22

Budweiser Opera Card Series-Premier Collection - A-Busch, Inc.

YEAR ISSUE	EDITION LIMIT	YEAR RETD.	ISSUE PRICE	*QUOTE U.S.$
1997 "Martha" CS300	5,000		169.00	169
1998 "The Hugenhots" CS331	5,000		169.00	169

Budweiser Racing Series - H. Droog

YEAR ISSUE	EDITION LIMIT	YEAR RETD.	ISSUE PRICE	*QUOTE U.S.$
1993 Budweiser Racing Team CS194	Retrd.	1995	19.00	17-40
1993 Bill Elliott CS196	25,000	1995	150.00	110-155
1993 Bill Elliott, Signature Edition, CS196SE	1,500	1995	295.00	175-300

Budweiser Salutes The Fire Fighters Series-Giftware Edition - A-Busch, Inc.

YEAR ISSUE	EDITION LIMIT	YEAR RETD.	ISSUE PRICE	*QUOTE U.S.$
1997 Fire Fighter's Boot CS321	Open		32.00	32

Century In Review Series-Premier Collection - A-Busch, Inc.

YEAR ISSUE	EDITION LIMIT	YEAR RETD.	ISSUE PRICE	*QUOTE U.S.$
1997 1900-1919 Stein CS311	5,000		279.00	279
1998 1920-1939 Stein CS335	5,000		279.00	279

Civil War Series-Premier Edition - D. Langeneckert

YEAR ISSUE	EDITION LIMIT	YEAR RETD.	ISSUE PRICE	*QUOTE U.S.$
1992 General Grant CS181	25,000	1995	150.00	95-150
1993 General Robert E. Lee CS188	25,000	1995	150.00	125-175
1993 President Abraham Lincoln CS189	25,000	1995	150.00	100-150

Classic Series - A-Busch, Inc.

YEAR ISSUE	EDITION LIMIT	YEAR RETD.	ISSUE PRICE	*QUOTE U.S.$
1988 1st Edition CS93	Retrd.	N/A	34.95	149-180
1989 2nd Edition CS104	Retrd.	N/A	54.95	95-165
1990 3rd Edition CS113	Retrd.	N/A	65.00	45-149
1991 4th Edition CS130	Retrd.	1994	75.00	45-139

*Quotes have been rounded up to nearest dollar

Clydesdales Holiday Series - Various

YEAR ISSUE	EDITION LIMIT	YEAR RETD.	ISSUE PRICE	*QUOTE U.S.$
1980 1st-Budweiser Champion Clydesdales CS19 - A-Busch, Inc.	Retrd.	N/A	9.95	95-145
1981 1st-Budweiser Champion Clydesdales CS19A - A-Busch, Inc.	Retrd.	N/A	N/A	175-275
1981 2nd-Snowy Woodland CS50 - A-Busch, Inc.	Retrd.	N/A	9.95	195-275
1982 3rd-50th Anniversary CS57 - A-Busch, Inc.	Retrd.	N/A	9.95	45-95
1983 4th-Cameo Wheatland CS58 - A-Busch, Inc.	Retrd.	N/A	9.95	25-50
1984 5th-Covered Bridge CS62 - A-Busch, Inc.	Retrd.	N/A	9.95	15-30
1985 6th-Snow Capped Mountains CS63 - A-Busch, Inc.	Retrd.	N/A	9.95	10-30
1986 7th-Traditional Horses CS66 - A-Busch, Inc.	Retrd.	N/A	9.95	35-50
1987 8th-Grant's Farm Gates CS70 - A-Busch, Inc.	Retrd.	N/A	9.95	15-30
1988 9th-Cobblestone Passage CS88 - A-Busch, Inc.	Retrd.	N/A	9.95	15-30
1989 10th-Winter Evening CS89 - A-Busch, Inc.	Retrd.	N/A	12.95	15-30
1990 11th-An American Tradition, CS112, 1990 - S. Sampson	Retrd.	N/A	13.50	12-25
1990 11th-An American Tradition, CS112-SE, 1990 - S. Sampson	Retrd.	N/A	50.00	45-80
1991 12th-The Season's Best, CS133, 1991 - S. Sampson	Retrd.	N/A	14.50	10-25
1991 12th-The Season's Best, CS133-SE Signature Edition, 1991 - S. Sampson	Retrd.	N/A	50.00	45-80
1992 13th-The Perfect Christmas, CS167, 1992 - S. Sampson	Retrd.	N/A	14.50	10-20
1992 13th-The Perfect Christmas, CS167-SE Signature Edition, 1992 - S. Sampson	10,000	N/A	50.00	35-80
1993 14th-Special Delivery, CS192, 1993 - N. Koerber	Retrd.	N/A	15.00	15-40
1993 14th-Special Delivery, CS192-SE Signature Edition, 1993 - N. Koerber	10,000	N/A	60.00	95-160
1994 15th-Hometown Holiday, CS211, 1994 - B. Kemper	Retrd.	1994	14.00	15-20
1994 15th-Hometown Holiday, CS211-SE Signature Edition, 1994 - B. Kemper	10,000	1994	65.00	65-125
1995 16th-Lighting the Way Home, CS263 - T. Jester	Retrd.	1997	17.00	15-20
1995 16th-Lighting the Way Home, CS263-SE Signature Edition - T. Jester	10,000	1995	75.00	65-120
1996 17th-Budweiser Clydesdales, CS273 - J. Raedeke	Retrd.	1998	17.00	15-20
1996 17th-Budweiser Clydesdales, CS273-SE Signature Edition - J. Raedeke	10,000	1996	75.00	75-105
1997 18th-Home For The Holidays, CS313 - H. Droog	Open		19.00	19
1997 18th-Home For The Holidays, CS313-SE Signature Edition - H. Droog	20,000		75.00	75
1998 19th-Grant's Farm Holiday, CS343 - E. Kastaris	Open		19.00	19
1998 19th-Grant's Farm Holiday, CS343SE Signature Edition - E. Kastaris	15,000		75.00	75

Clydesdales Series-Giftware Edition - A-Busch, Inc.

YEAR ISSUE	EDITION LIMIT	YEAR RETD.	ISSUE PRICE	*QUOTE U.S.$
1987 World Famous Clydesdales CS74	Retrd.	N/A	9.95	25-45
1988 Mare & Foal CS90	Retrd.	N/A	11.50	40-55
1989 Parade Dress CS99	Retrd.	N/A	11.50	65-150
1991 Training Hitch CS131	Retrd.	1993	13.00	20-40
1992 Clydesdales on Parade CS161	Retrd.	1994	16.00	25-50
1994 Proud and Free CS223	Retrd.	1997	17.00	17-30
1996 Budweiser Clydesdale Hitch CS292	Open		22.50	23

Collector Edition - A-Busch, Inc., unless otherwise noted

YEAR ISSUE	EDITION LIMIT	YEAR RETD.	ISSUE PRICE	*QUOTE U.S.$
1994 Budweiser World Cup Stein CS230 - J. Tull	25,000	1994	40.00	50-100
1997 The Official 1998 Olympic Winter Games Stein CS350	12/98		50.00	50
1998 Bald Eagle Character Stein CS326	50,000		99.00	99
1998 NASCAR 50th Anniversary Stein CS360 - J. Wainright	25,000		60.00	60

Discover America Series-Collector Edition - A-Busch, Inc.

YEAR ISSUE	EDITION LIMIT	YEAR RETD.	ISSUE PRICE	*QUOTE U.S.$
1990 Nina CS107	100,000	1995	40.00	35-125
1991 Pinta CS129	100,000	1995	40.00	35-125
1992 Santa Maria CS138	100,000	1995	40.00	35-135

Endangered Species Series-Collector Edition - B. Kemper

YEAR ISSUE	EDITION LIMIT	YEAR RETD.	ISSUE PRICE	*QUOTE U.S.$
1989 Bald Eagle CS106 (First)	Retrd.	N/A	24.95	395-700
1990 Asian Tiger CS126 (Second)	Retrd.	1993	27.50	125-180
1991 African Elephant CS135 (Third)	100,000	1995	29.00	40-100
1992 Giant Panda CS173 (Fourth)	100,000	1996	29.00	40-66
1993 Grizzly CS199 (Fifth)	100,000	1996	29.50	32-66
1994 Gray Wolf Stein CS226 (Sixth)	100,000	1997	29.50	32-56
1995 Cougar Stein CS253 (Seventh)	100,000		32.00	32
1996 Gorilla Stein CS283 (Eighth)	100,000		32.00	32

Giftware Edition - A-Busch, Inc.

YEAR ISSUE	EDITION LIMIT	YEAR RETD.	ISSUE PRICE	*QUOTE U.S.$
1992 1992 Rodeo CS184	Retrd.	N/A	18.00	16-30
1993 Bud Man Character Stein CS213	Retrd.	1996	45.00	65-125
1994 "Fore!" Budweiser Golf Bag Stein CS225	Retrd.	1995	16.00	16-30
1994 "Walking Tall" Budweiser Cowboy Boot Stein CS251	Open		17.50	18
1995 "Play Ball" Baseball Mitt stein CS244	Open		18.00	18
1995 Billiards stein CS278	Open		24.00	24
1995 Bud K. Schrader N5054	Retrd.	N/A	25.00	25
1996 BUD-WEIS-ER Frog stein CS289	Open		27.95	28
1996 Indianapolis 500 N6003	Open		25.00	25
1996 "STRIKE" Bowling stein CS288	Open		24.50	25
1997 Budweiser Salutes Dad CS298	Open		19.95	20
1997 "Let Freedom Ring" CS305	Open		24.95	25
1997 Budweiser Tool Belt CS320	Open		29.95	30
1997 Budweiser Boxing Glove CS322	Open		35.00	35
1998 Budweiser Black Cowboy Boot Stein CS347	Open		20.00	20
1998 Budweiser Golf Bag II CS362	Open		24.95	25

Great Cities of Germany Series-Premier Collection - A-Busch, Inc.

YEAR ISSUE	EDITION LIMIT	YEAR RETD.	ISSUE PRICE	*QUOTE U.S.$
1997 Berlin CS328	5,000		139.00	139
1998 Munich CS346	5,000		139.00	139

Historic Budweiser Advertising-Giftware Edition - A. Busch, Inc.

YEAR ISSUE	EDITION LIMIT	YEAR RETD.	ISSUE PRICE	*QUOTE U.S.$
1998 Stein and Tin I CS359	Open		36.00	36

Historical Landmark Series - A-Busch, Inc.

YEAR ISSUE	EDITION LIMIT	YEAR RETD.	ISSUE PRICE	*QUOTE U.S.$
1986 Brew House CS67 (First)	Retrd.	N/A	19.95	25-55
1987 Stables CS73 (Second)	Retrd.	1992	19.95	20-50
1988 Grant Cabin CS83 (Third)	Retrd.	N/A	19.95	95-125
1988 Old School House CS84 (Fourth)	Retrd.	1992	19.95	25-55

Horseshoe Series - A-Busch, Inc.

YEAR ISSUE	EDITION LIMIT	YEAR RETD.	ISSUE PRICE	*QUOTE U.S.$
1986 Horseshoe CS68	Retrd.	N/A	14.95	40-55
1987 Horsehead CS76	Retrd.	N/A	16.00	35-55
1987 Horseshoe CS77	Retrd.	N/A	16.00	35-60
1987 Horsehead CS78	Retrd.	N/A	14.95	45-75
1988 Harness CS94	Retrd.	N/A	16.00	45-95

Hunter's Companion Series-Collector Edition - Various

YEAR ISSUE	EDITION LIMIT	YEAR RETD.	ISSUE PRICE	*QUOTE U.S.$
1993 Labrador Retriever CS195 - L. Freeman	50,000	1996	32.50	95-150
1994 The Setter Stein CS205 - S. Ryan	50,000	1996	32.50	35-75
1995 The Golden Retreiver Stein CS248 - S. Ryan	50,000	1998	34.00	35-40
1996 Beagle Stein CS272 - S. Ryan	50,000		35.00	35
1997 Springer Spaniel Stein CS296 - S. Ryan	50,000		35.00	35

Limited Edition Series - A-Busch, Inc.

YEAR ISSUE	EDITION LIMIT	YEAR RETD.	ISSUE PRICE	*QUOTE U.S.$
1985 Ltd. Ed. I Brewing & Fermenting CS64	Retrd.	N/A	29.95	139-200
1986 Ltd. Ed. II Aging & Cooperage CS65	Retrd.	N/A	29.95	50-110
1987 Ltd. Ed. III Transportation CS71	Retrd.	N/A	29.95	45-80
1988 Ltd. Ed. IV Taverns & Public Houses CS75	Retrd.	1994	29.95	35-60
1989 Ltd. Ed.V Festival Scene CS98	Retrd.	1994	34.95	35-60

Logo Series Steins-Giftware Edition - A-Busch, Inc.

YEAR ISSUE	EDITION LIMIT	YEAR RETD.	ISSUE PRICE	*QUOTE U.S.$
1990 Budweiser CS143	Retrd.	N/A	16.00	10-25
1990 Bud Light CS144	Retrd.	N/A	16.00	10-25
1990 Michelob CS145	Retrd.	1993	16.00	10-25
1990 Michelob Dry CS146	Retrd.	1994	16.00	10-25
1990 Busch CS147	Retrd.	N/A	16.00	10-25
1990 A&Eagle CS148	Retrd.	N/A	16.00	10-25
1990 Bud Dry CS156	Retrd.	N/A	16.00	10-25

Marine Conservation Series-Collector Edition - B. Kemper

YEAR ISSUE	EDITION LIMIT	YEAR RETD.	ISSUE PRICE	*QUOTE U.S.$
1994 Manatee Stein CS203	25,000	1997	33.50	39-65
1995 Great White Shark Stein CS247	25,000		39.50	40
1996 Dolphin Stein CS284	25,000		39.50	40

Michelob PGA Tour Series-Collector Edition - A. Leon

YEAR ISSUE	EDITION LIMIT	YEAR RETD.	ISSUE PRICE	*QUOTE U.S.$
1997 TPC at Sawgrass CS299	10,000		59.95	60
1998 TPC of Scottsdale CS329	10,000		59.95	60

Oktoberfest Series-Giftware Edition - A-Busch, Inc.

YEAR ISSUE	EDITION LIMIT	YEAR RETD.	ISSUE PRICE	*QUOTE U.S.$
1991 1991 Oktoberfest N3286	25,000	N/A	19.00	25-50
1992 1992 Oktoberfest CS185	35,000	1996	16.00	20-35
1993 1993 Oktoberfest CS202	35,000	1995	18.00	20-35
1996 1996 Oktoberfest CS291	Open		24.95	25

Olympic Centennial Collection - A-Busch, Inc.

YEAR ISSUE	EDITION LIMIT	YEAR RETD.	ISSUE PRICE	*QUOTE U.S.$
1995 1996 U.S. Olympic Team "Gymnastics" Stein CS262	10,000		85.00	85
1995 1996 U.S. Olympic Team "Track & Field" Stein CS246	10,000	1998	85.00	75-85
1995 Bud Atlanta 1996 CS249	Retrd.	N/A	17.00	17
1995 Centennial Olympic Games Giftware Stein CS266	Retrd.	1997	25.00	25-30
1995 Centennial Olympic Games Premier Edition 22" CS267	1,996	1996	500.00	995-1900
1995 Collector's Edition Official Centennial Olympics Games Stein CS259	Retrd.	1996	50.00	45-100

Olympic Team Series 1992-Collector Edition - A-Busch, Inc.

YEAR ISSUE	EDITION LIMIT	YEAR RETD.	ISSUE PRICE	*QUOTE U.S.$
1991 1992 Winter Olympic Stein CS162	25,000	N/A	85.00	50-85
1992 1992 Summer Olympic Stein CS163	Retrd.	1994	85.00	50-85
1992 1992 U.S.Olympic Stein CS168	50,000	N/A	16.00	20-60

Porcelain Heritage Series-Premier Edition - Various

YEAR ISSUE	EDITION LIMIT	YEAR RETD.	ISSUE PRICE	*QUOTE U.S.$
1990 Berninghaus CS105 - Berninghaus	Retrd.	1994	75.00	60-130
1991 After The Hunt CS155 - A-Busch, Inc.	Retrd.	1994	100.00	60-115
1992 Cherub CS182 - D. Langeneckert	25,000	1996	100.00	95-120

Post Convention Series - A-Busch, Inc.

YEAR ISSUE	EDITION LIMIT	YEAR RETD.	ISSUE PRICE	*QUOTE U.S.$
1982 1st Post Convention Olympic CS53	23,000	1982	N/A	150-200
1982 2nd Post Convention Olympic CS54	23,000	1982	N/A	150-250
1982 3rd Post Convention Olympic CS55	23,000	1982	N/A	150-250
1988 1st Post Convention Heritage CS87	25,000	1988	N/A	75-125
1988 2nd Post Convention Heritage CS102	25,000	1988	N/A	70-100
1989 3rd Post Convention Heritage CS114	25,000	1989	N/A	50-100
1990 4th Post Convention Heritage CS141	25,000	1990	N/A	50-100
1991 5th/Final Post Convention Heritage CS174	25,000	1991	N/A	40-100
1992 1st Advertising Through the Decades 1879-1912 N3989	29,000	1992	N/A	45-80
1993 2nd Advertising Through the Decades 1905-1914 N3990	31,106	1993	N/A	50-80
1994 3rd Advertising Through the Decades 1911-1915 SO85203	31,000	1994	N/A	35-80
1995 4th Advertising Through the Decades 1918-1922 SO95150	31,000	1995	N/A	35-80
1996 5th Advertising Through the Decades 1933-1938 SO95248	31,000	1996	N/A	50-80

Premier Collection - A-Busch, Inc.

YEAR ISSUE	EDITION LIMIT	YEAR RETD.	ISSUE PRICE	*QUOTE U.S.$
1997 Bud Ice Penguin CS315	10,000		199.00	199
1997 Budweiser Frog CS301	10,000		219.00	219
1997 Louie The Lizard Character CS344	25,000		99.00	99
1998 World Cup Soccer CS351	10,000		99.00	99

Sea World Series-Collector Edition - A-Busch, Inc.

YEAR ISSUE	EDITION LIMIT	YEAR RETD.	ISSUE PRICE	*QUOTE U.S.$
1992 Killer Whale CS186	25,000	1996	100.00	65-90
1992 Dolphin CS187	22,500	1996	90.00	60-150

Specialty Steins - A-Busch, Inc.

YEAR ISSUE	EDITION LIMIT	YEAR RETD.	ISSUE PRICE	*QUOTE U.S.$
1975 Bud Man CS1	Retrd.	N/A	N/A	395-590
1976 A&Eagle CS2	Retrd.	N/A	N/A	125-275
1976 A&Eagle Lidded CSL2 (Reference CS28)	Retrd.	N/A	N/A	175-350
1976 Katakombe CS3	Retrd.	N/A	N/A	225-300
1976 Katakombe Lidded CSL3	Retrd.	N/A	N/A	300-350
1976 German Tavern Scene Lidded CS4	Retrd.	N/A	N/A	55-175
1975 Senior Grande Lidded CSL4	Retrd.	N/A	N/A	700
1975 German Pilique CS5	Retrd.	N/A	N/A	375-450
1976 German Pilique Lidded CSL5	Retrd.	N/A	N/A	450-500
1976 Senior Grande CS6	Retrd.	N/A	N/A	550-600
1975 German Tavern Scene CSL6	Retrd.	N/A	N/A	150-300
1975 Miniature Bavarian CS7	Retrd.	N/A	N/A	400-600
1976 Budweiser Centennial Lidded CSL7	Retrd.	N/A	N/A	350-500
1976 U.S. Bicentennial Lidded CSL8	Retrd.	N/A	N/A	350-500
1976 Natural Light CS9	Retrd.	N/A	N/A	225-300
1976 Clydesdales Hofbrau Lidded CSL9	Retrd.	N/A	N/A	185-225
1976 Blue Delft CS11	Retrd.	N/A	N/A	1800
1976 Clydesdales CS12	Retrd.	N/A	N/A	225-325
1976 Budweiser Centennial CS13	Retrd.	N/A	N/A	250-400
1976 U.S. Bicentennial CS14	Retrd.	N/A	N/A	250-400
1976 Clydesdales Grants Farm CS15	Retrd.	N/A	N/A	135-300
1976 German Cities (6 assorted) CS16	Retrd.	N/A	N/A	1500-1700
1976 Americana CS17	Retrd.	N/A	N/A	300-400
1976 Budweiser Label CS18	Retrd.	N/A	N/A	425-595
1980 Budweiser Ladies (4 assorted) CS20	Retrd.	N/A	N/A	1400
1977 Budweiser Girl CS21	Retrd.	N/A	N/A	400-450
1976 Budweiser Centennial CS22	Retrd.	N/A	N/A	300-350
1977 A&Eagle CS24	Retrd.	N/A	N/A	450-750
1976 A&Eagle Barrel CS26	Retrd.	N/A	N/A	125-150
1976 Michelob CS27	Retrd.	N/A	N/A	150-200
1976 A&Eagle Lidded CS28 (Reference CSL2)	Retrd.	N/A	N/A	195-350
1976 Clydesdales Lidded CS29	Retrd.	N/A	N/A	200
1976 Coracao Decanter Set (7 piece) CS31	Retrd.	N/A	N/A	450-550
1976 German Wine Set (7 piece) CS32	Retrd.	N/A	N/A	550-575
1976 Clydesdales Decanter CS33	Retrd.	N/A	N/A	1250-1400
1976 Holanda Brown Decanter Set (7 piece) CS34	Retrd.	N/A	N/A	1100-1195
1976 Holanda Blue Decanter Set (7 piece) CS35	Retrd.	N/A	N/A	475-1200
1976 Canteen Decanter Set (7 piece) CS36	Retrd.	N/A	N/A	N/A
1976 St. Louis Decanter CS37	Retrd.	N/A	N/A	300
1976 St. Louis Decanter Set (7 piece) CS38	Retrd.	N/A	N/A	1100-1200
1980 Wurzburger Hofbrau CS39	Retrd.	N/A	N/A	300-350
1980 Budweiser Chicago Skyline CS40	Retrd.	N/A	N/A	95-150
1978 Busch Gardens CS41	Retrd.	N/A	N/A	175-350
1980 Oktoberfest— "The Old Country" CS42	Retrd.	N/A	N/A	175-350
1980 Natural Light Label CS43	Retrd.	N/A	N/A	250-300
1980 Busch Label CS44	Retrd.	N/A	N/A	250-300
1980 Michelob Label CS45	Retrd.	N/A	N/A	50-100
1980 Budweiser Label CS46	Retrd.	N/A	N/A	50-100
1981 Budweiser Chicagoland CS51	Retrd.	N/A	N/A	29-75
1981 Budweiser Texas CS52	Retrd.	N/A	N/A	40-65
1981 Budweiser California CS56	Retrd.	N/A	N/A	25-50
1983 Budweiser San Francisco CS59	Retrd.	N/A	N/A	150-175
1984 Budweiser 1984 Summer Olympic Games CS60	Retrd.	N/A	N/A	13-50
1983 Bud Light Baron CS61	Retrd.	N/A	N/A	35-50
1987 Santa Claus CS79	Retrd.	N/A	N/A	80-125

*Quotes have been rounded up to nearest dollar

YEAR ISSUE	EDITION LIMIT	YEAR RETD.	ISSUE PRICE	*QUOTE U.S.$
1987 King Cobra CS80	Retrd.	N/A	N/A	250-300
1987 Winter Olympic Games, Lidded CS81	Retrd.	N/A	49.95	60-75
1988 Budweiser Winter Olympic Games CS85	Retrd.	N/A	24.95	20
1988 Summer Olympic Games, Lidded CS91	Retrd.	N/A	54.95	30-75
1988 Budweiser Summer Olympic Games CS92	Retrd.	N/A	54.95	20-75
1988 Budweiser/ Field&Stream Set (4 piece) CS95	Retrd.	N/A	69.95	200-350
1989 Bud Man CS100	Retrd.	1993	29.95	75-150
1990 Baseball Cardinal Stein CS125	Retrd.	N/A	30.00	45-75
1991 Bevo Fox Stein CS160	Retrd.	1994	250.00	180-300
1992 Budweiser Racing-Elliot/Johnson N3553 - M. Watts	Retrd.	1995	19.00	25-40

Sports Action Series-Giftware Edition - J. Whitney

1997 "Play Ball" Budweiser Baseball Stein CS295	Open		29.00	29
1998 "Touchdown!" Budweiser Football Stein CS325	Open		29.00	29

Sports History Series-Giftware Edition - A-Busch, Inc.

1990 Baseball, America's Favorite Pastime CS124	100,000	1992	20.00	25-40
1990 Football, Gridiron Legacy CS128	100,000	1994	20.00	25-40
1991 Auto Racing, Chasing The Checkered Flag CS132	100,000	1995	22.00	25-30
1991 Basketball, Heroes of the Hardwood CS134	100,000	1995	22.00	20-30
1992 Golf, Par For The Course CS165	100,000	1995	22.00	25-60
1993 Hockey, Center Ice CS209	100,000	N/A	22.00	20-25

Sports Legend Series-Collector Edition - Various

1991 Babe Ruth CS142 - A-Busch	50,000	1995	85.00	50-100
1992 Jim Thorpe CS171 - M. Caito	50,000	1995	85.00	60-100
1993 Joe Louis CS206 - M. Caito	Retrd.	1994	85.00	85-150

St. Patrick's Day Series-Giftware Edition - A-Busch, Inc.

1991 1991 St. Patrick's Day CS109	Retrd.	N/A	15.00	50-85
1992 1992 St. Patrick's Day CS166	100,000	N/A	15.00	15-40
1993 1993 St. Patrick's Day CS193	Retrd.	N/A	15.30	30-70
1994 Luck O' The Irish CS210	Retrd.	1995	18.00	15-30
1995 1995 St. Patrick's Day Stein CS242	Retrd.	1995	19.00	18-25
1996 "Horseshoe" 1996 St. Patrick's Day Stein CS269	Open		19.50	20
1997 Luck O' The Longneck 1997 St. Patrick's Day Stein CS287	Open		21.95	22
1998 Erin Go Budweiser 1998 St. Patrick's Day Stein CS332	Open		22.95	23

Upland Game Birds Series-Collector Edition - P. Ford

1997 Ruffed Grouse CS316	5,000	1997	75.00	75-150
1997 Pheasant CS319	5,000	1997	75.00	75-125
1998 Turkey CS327	Retrd.	1998	75.00	75-150

Working America Series-Premier Collection - A-Busch, Inc.

1997 American Worker I CS318	10,000		209.00	209
1998 The American Worker II CS336	10,000		209.00	209

Anheuser-Busch, Inc./Collectorwerke/Meisterwerke Collection

American Heritage Collection - Gerz

1993 John F. Kennedy Stein GM4	10,000		220.00	220

Collectorwerke - Various

1993 The Dugout Stein GL1 - A-Busch, Inc.	10,000		110.00	110
1994 Winchester Stein GL2 - A-Busch, Inc.	10,000	1995	120.00	100-125
1995 "Saturday Evening Post" Christmas Stein #1 GL5 - J.C. Leyendecker	5,000		105.00	105
1996 "Saturday Evening Post" Christmas Stein #2 GL6 - A-Busch, Inc.	5,000	1997	105.00	89-105
1997 "Saturday Evening Post" Christmas Stein #3 GL13 - J.C. Leyendecker	5,000		105.00	105

Collectorwerke-Animals of the Prairie Series - N. Glazier

1997 Buffalo GL11	5,000	1997	149.00	127-175
1998 Wild Mustang GL15	5,000		149.00	149

Collectorwerke-Call of the Wild Series - J. Rideout

1996 Wolf Stein GL9	10,000		139.00	139
1997 Grizzly Stein GL12	10,000		139.00	139
1998 Mountain Lion Stein GL17	10,000		139.00	139

Meisterwerke Collection - A-Busch, Inc.

1994 Norman Rockwell-Triple Self Portrait GM6	5,000	1997	250.00	200-275
1994 Mallard Stein GM7	5,000	1996	220.00	125-200
1994 Winchester "Model 94" Centennial Stein GM10	5,000		150.00	150
1995 Giant Panda Stein GM8	3,500	1997	210.00	125-210
1995 Rosie the Riveter Stein GM9	5,000	1997	165.00	125-165
1997 Norman Rockwell-Do Unto Others GM21	7,500		189.00	189

Meisterwerke-Early Transporation Series - T. MacDonald

1997 Train Stein GM28	5,000		179.00	179
1998 Train II Stein GM29	5,000		179.00	179

Meisterwerke-First Hunt Series - P. Ford

1992 Golden Retriever GM2	10,000		150.00	150
1994 Springer Spaniel GM5	10,000		190.00	190
1995 Pointer Stein GM16	10,000	1997	190.00	140-190
1995 Labrador Stein GM17	10,000	1998	190.00	150-190

Meisterwerke-Holidays Through the Decades - A-Busch, Inc.

1996 Holidays: Decade of the 30's GM18	3,500	1997	169.00	135-169
1997 Holidays: Decade of the 40's GM23	3,500		169.00	169
1998 Holidays: Decade of the 50's GM26	3,500		169.00	169

Meisterwerke-Winchester Hunt Series - A-Busch, Inc.

1996 Pheasant Hunt Stein GM20	3,500	1997	215.00	175-225
1997 Duck Hunt Stein GM24	3,500		215.00	215

Meisterwerke-Winchester Rodeo Series - A-Busch, Inc.

1996 Rodeo Calf Roping Stein GM19	5,000		179.00	179
1997 Rodeo Bull Riding Stein GM22	5,000		179.00	179
1998 Saddle Bronc Riding Stein GM25	5,000		179.00	179

Saturday Evening Post Collection - J.C. Leyendecker

1993 Santa's Mailbag GM1	Retrd.	1993	195.00	200-250
1993 Santa's Helper GM3	7,500		200.00	200
1994 "All I Want For Christmas" GM13	5,000	N/A	220.00	150-210
1995 Fourth of July Stein GM15	5,000	1998	180.00	150-180

Cavanagh Group Intl.

Harley-Davidson - CGI

1998 The American Dream	Open		60.00	60
1998 Engineer of the Road	Open		40.00	40
1998 Evolution	15,000		150.00	150
1998 Live to Ride, Ride to Live	Yr.Iss.		90.00	90

Hamilton Collection

Mickey Mantle - R. Tanenbaum

1996 The Legendary Mickey Mantle	Open		39.95	40

The STAR TREK® Tankard Collection - T. Blackshear

1995 U.S.S. Enterprise NCC-1701	Open		49.50	50
1994 SPOCK	Open		49.50	50
1995 Kirk	Open		49.50	50
1995 McCoy	Open		49.50	50
1995 Uhura	Open		49.50	50
1995 Scotty	Open		49.50	50
1995 Sulu	Open		49.50	50
1995 Chekov	Open		49.50	50

Warriors of the Plains Tankards - G. Stewart

1995 Battle Grounds	Open		125.00	125
1992 Thundering Hooves	Open		125.00	125
1992 Warrior's Choice	Open		125.00	125
1992 Healing Spirits	Open		125.00	125

Royal Doulton

Character Jug of the Year - Various

1991 Fortune Teller D6824 - S. Taylor	Closed	1991	130.00	200-275
1992 Winston Churchill D6907 - S. Taylor	Closed	1992	195.00	225
1993 Vice-Admiral Lord Nelson D6932 - S. Taylor	Closed	1993	225.00	225
1994 Captain Hook - M. Alcock	Closed	1994	235.00	175-235
1995 Captain Bligh D6967 - S. Taylor	Closed	1995	200.00	200-275
1996 Jesse Owens, lg. D7019 - S. Taylor	Closed	1996	225.00	225-255
1997 Count Dracula, lg. D7053 - D. Biggs	Closed	1997	235.00	250
1998 Lewis Carroll - D. Biggs	Yr.Iss.		195.00	195

Character Jugs - Various

1993 Abraham Lincoln - M. Alcock	2,500	1994	190.00	225-250
1991 Airman, sm. - W. Harper	Retrd.	1996	75.00	75
1996 Albert Einstein, lg.- S. Taylor	Retrd.	1996	225.00	238
1995 Alfred Hitchcock D6987 - D. Biggs	Retrd.	1997	200.00	238
1997 Angler, sm. - D. Biggs	Open		132.50	133
1990 Angler, sm. - S. Taylor	Retrd.	1995	82.50	83
1947 Beefeater, lg. - H. Fenton	Retrd.	1996	137.50	175-200
1947 Beefeater, sm. - H. Fenton	Retrd.	1996	75.00	100-149
1998 Captain Scott - D. Biggs	Open		195.00	195
1975 Catherine of Aragon, lg. D6643 - A. Maslankowski	Retrd.	1981	N/A	115-125
1981 Catherine Parr, lg. D6664 - M. Abberley	Retrd.	1989	N/A	125-175
1995 Charles Dickens D6939 - W. Harper	2,500	1997	500.00	500
1989 Clown, lg.- S. Taylor	Retrd.	1995	205.00	300-350
1991 Columbus, lg. 6891 - S. Taylor	Retrd.	1997	137.50	138-145
1995 Cyrano de Bergerac, lg. 7004 - D. Biggs	Retrd.	1997	200.00	210
1983 D'Artagnan, lg.- S. Taylor	Retrd.	1995	150.00	150-195
1983 D'Artagnan, sm.- S. Taylor	Retrd.	1995	82.50	100-149
1995 Dennis and Gnasher, lg.- S. Ward	Open		212.50	235
1995 Deperate Dan, lg.- S. Ward	Open		212.50	235
1991 Equestrian, sm.- S. Taylor	Retrd.	1995	82.50	83
1997 General Custer, lg.- S. Taylor	Open		237.50	238
1995 George Washington - M. Alcock	2,500	1995	200.00	225
1982 George Washington, lg. - S. Taylor	Retrd.	1994	150.00	160-175
1994 Glenn Miller - M. Alcock	Retrd.	1998	270.00	335
1971 Golfer, lg. - D. Biggs	Retrd.	1995	150.00	225-249
1997 Golfer, sm. - D. Biggs	Open		132.50	133
1993 Graduate-Male, sm.- S. Taylor	Retrd.	1995	85.00	85
1986 Guardsman, lg.- S. Taylor	Open		137.50	155
1986 Gurardsman, sm.- S. Taylor	Open		75.00	85
1990 Guy Fawkes, lg. - W. Harper	Retrd.	1996	137.50	138-150
1975 Henry VIII, lg. - E. Griffiths	Open		137.50	155
1975 Henry VIII, sm. - E. Griffiths	Open		75.00	85
1991 Jockey, sm.- S. Taylor	Retrd.	1995	82.50	83
1995 Judge and Thief Toby D6988 - S. Taylor	Retrd.	1998	185.00	225
1959 Lawyer, lg. - M. Henk	Retrd.	1996	137.50	150-179
1959 Lawyer, sm. - M. Henk	Retrd.	1996	75.00	83-99
1990 Leprechaun, lg. - W. Harper	Retrd.	1996	205.00	225
1990 Leprechaun, sm. - W. Harper	Retrd.	1996	75.00	85
1986 London Bobby, lg.- S. Taylor	Open		137.50	155
1986 London Bobby, sm.- S. Taylor	Open		75.00	85
1952 Long John Silver, lg. - M. Henk	Open		137.50	155
1952 Long John Silver, sm. - M. Henk	Open		75.00	85
1965 Mad Hatter, sm. D6602 - M. Henk	Retrd.	1983	N/A	128-175
1989 March Hare, lg. D6776 - W. Harper	Retrd.	1991	N/A	198
1960 Merlin, lg. - G. Sharpe	Retrd.	1998	137.50	155
1960 Merlin, sm. - G. Sharpe	Retrd.	1998	75.00	85
1990 Modern Golfer, sm.- S. Taylor	Open		75.00	83
1961 Old Salt, lg.- G. Sharpe	Open		137.50	155
1961 Old Salt, sm.- G. Sharpe	Open		75.00	85
1955 Rip Van Winkle, lg. - M. Henk	Retrd.	1995	150.00	150-175
1955 Rip Van Winkle, sm. - M. Henk	Retrd.	1995	82.50	83-100
1991 Sailor, sm. - W. Harper	Retrd.	1996	75.00	83
1984 Santa Claus, lg. - M. Abberley	Open		137.50	155
1984 Santa Claus, sm. - M. Abberley	Open		75.00	85
1993 Shakespeare, sm. - W. Harper	Open		99.00	120
1973 The Sleuth, lg.- A. Moore	Retrd.	1996	137.50	225-249
1973 The Sleuth, sm. - A. Moore	Retrd.	1996	75.00	125-149
1991 Snooker Player, sm.- S. Taylor	Retrd.	1995	82.50	83-100
1991 Soldier, sm. - W. Harper	Retrd.	1996	75.00	83
1994 Thomas Jefferson - M. Alcock	2,500	1995	200.00	200
1991 Town Crier, lg. - S. Taylor	Retrd.	1994	170.00	170-200
1993 Winston Churchill, sm.- S. Taylor	Open		99.00	120
1990 Wizard, lg.- S. Taylor- S. Taylor	Retrd.	1996	175.00	225
1990 Wizard, sm.- S. Taylor	Open		75.00	85
1991 Yeoman of the Guard, lg. 6873 - S. Taylor	Retrd.	1997	137.50	145

Great Composers - S. Taylor

1996 Beethoven, lg. D7021	Open		225.00	250
1996 Chopin, lg. D7030	Open		225.00	250
1997 Handel, lg.	Open		237.50	238
1996 Mozart, lg. D7031	Open		225.00	250
1997 Schubert, lg. D7056	Open		225.00	250
1996 Tchaikovsky, lg. D7022	Open		225.00	250

Limited Edition Character Jugs - Various

1992 Abraham Lincoln D6936 - S. Taylor	2,500	1994	190.00	190
1994 Aladdin's Genie D6971 - D. Biggs	1,500	1994	335.00	350
1996 Angel Miniature - M. Alcock	2,500		77.50	78
1993 Clown Toby - S. Taylor	3,000	1996	175.00	175-250
1993 Elf Miniature D6942 - W. Harper	2,500	1994	55.00	75-110
1997 Explorer Tinies, set/6 - S. Taylor	2,500		495.00	495
1993 Father Christmas Toby - W. Harper	3,500	1996	125.00	125
1996 Geoffrey Chaucer, lg. - R. Tabbenor	1,500	1996	800.00	850
1995 George Washington, lg. - M. Alcock	2,500	1996	200.00	200
1990 Henry VIII - N/A	Open		150.00	150
1991 Henry VIII - W. Harper	1,991	1992	395.00	1200-1400
1991 Jester - S. Taylor	2,500	1996	125.00	135-150
1994 King & Queen of Diamonds D6969 - J. Taylor	2,500	1994	260.00	260-275
1996 King and Queen of Hearts Toby - S. Taylor	2,500	1997	275.00	275
1997 King and Queen of Spades Toby - S. Taylor	2,500		275.00	275
1997 King Arthur, lg. D7055 - R. Tabbenor	1,500		350.00	380
1992 King Charles I D6917 - W. Harper	2,500	1995	450.00	495
1994 Leprechaun Toby - S. Taylor	2,500	1996	150.00	150
1992 Mrs. Claus Miniature D6922 - S. Taylor	2,500	1994	50.00	75-100
1993 Napoleon, lg. D6941 - S. Taylor	2,000	1994	225.00	225
1994 Oliver Cromwell D6968 - W. Harper	2,500	1994	475.00	475
1996 Pharoah Flambe, lg. - R. Tabbenor	1,500	1996	500.00	500
1991 Santa Claus Miniature D6900 - M. Abberley	5,000	1993	50.00	75-100
1988 Sir Francis Drake D6805 - P. Gee	Open		N/A	100
1997 Sir Henry Doulton, lg. D7054 - W. Harper	1,997	1997	285.00	285
1992 Snake Charmer - S. Taylor	2,500		210.00	250
1994 Thomas Jefferson - S. Taylor	2,500	1996	200.00	225
1992 Town Crier D6895 - S. Taylor	2,500	1995	175.00	175
1992 William Shakespeare D6933 - W. Harper	2,500	1994	625.00	625

*Quotes have been rounded up to nearest dollar

Collectors' Information Bureau

DIRECTORY TO SECONDARY MARKET DEALERS

The CIB DIRECTORY TO SECONDARY MARKET DEALERS is designed to put you in touch with secondary market experts who are in the business of making it easier for you to buy and sell retired collectibles. Together, they have a wealth of knowledge about the field of collectibles and are eager to help you enjoy your hobby even more.

How To Use This Directory

We've organized this directory to make it easy for you to find the dealer you need. Each dealer is listed alphabetically by state. They are also listed in the INDEX TO DEALER DIRECTORY BY SPECIALTY on pages 618-619.

Locating Dealers By Their Specialty

Each dealer has been assigned a locator number in the top right-hand corner of their listing. This number will come in handy when you are looking for a dealer who is an expert in a particular line or company. For example, if you are looking for a dealer to help you buy or sell a Department 56 piece, just turn to the index and look up the Department 56 listing. The numbers you find next to the listing are the locator numbers of the dealers who specialize in Department 56. Once you've found the numbers, look over the individual dealer listings and begin contacting the dealers who most appeal to you.

Locating Dealers By State

Though most dealers are accustomed to doing business on a national basis, you may want to start by contacting dealers closer to home. That's why we've also organized the dealers by state. Within each state listing, dealers are organized in alphabetical order by business name.

Let's Get Started!

Now that you know how to use the directory, you may want to take a moment or two to turn to pages 616-617 and learn the answers to the 10 MOST FREQUENTLY ASKED QUESTIONS ABOUT BUYING AND SELLING LIMITED EDITION COLLECTIBLES. These questions have come to us from collectors like you who want to know more about buying and selling on the secondary market. We've gathered the answers from our panel of secondary market experts. Hopefully, they'll give you the background you need to make the most out of your secondary market transactions!

ABBREVIATIONS

B&G = Bing & Grondahl
Byers' = Byers' Choice
CT = Cherished Teddies
D56 or Dept. 56 = Department 56
EKJ = Emmett Kelly, Jr.
Ltd. = Limited
MO = Money Order
MOY = Memories of Yesterday
PM = Precious Moments
RC = Royal Copenhagen
WFF = Wee Forest Folk

10 MOST FREQUENTLY ASKED QUESTIONS
About Buying and Selling Limited Edition Collectibles

Q. How are prices for limited edition collectibles established on the secondary market?

A. As with most items in an open marketplace, prices are established in response to the supply of and demand for each individual item. Since limited edition pieces are, by definition, limited in the number of pieces available, demand for each piece will impact the market value of the item.

Over time, the "supply" of a particular piece may decrease, as natural disasters and home accidents result in damage or breakage. As the supply shrinks, the price may increase again.

Similarly, items that are in relatively large supply and experience small to moderate demand may see modest or low appreciation on the secondary market. Some items with broad distribution and low demand do not appreciate at all on the secondary market.

These fluctuations in the secondary market value of items are tracked by organizations like the COLLECTORS' INFORMATION BUREAU. Twice a year, the CIB surveys over 300 secondary market dealers and asks them to report back on the actual prices collectors have paid for individual pieces. This input is compiled and reported in the COLLECTIBLES PRICE GUIDE (published each May) and the COLLECTIBLES MARKET GUIDE & PRICE INDEX (published each November).

Q. What does a collector need to know if they are planning to buy or sell on the secondary market?

A. There are 4 things to consider when you begin thinking about buying or selling on the secondary market.

1.) *Know the value of the piece you want to buy or sell.* This information can be found by checking reputable price guides like the CIB's COLLECTIBLES PRICE GUIDE. Since these books list actual prices paid by collectors in recent transactions, they represent an excellent starting point for determining the market value of an item.

2.) *Understand the "terms of sale" used by the secondary market dealer that you're considering.* Individual dealers vary greatly in the services they offer the collectors and the fees they charge for these services. Some dealers buy pieces outright, while others provide a listing service or take goods on consignment. Some dealers charge as little as 10% commission, while others charge upwards of 30% to 50%. In most cases, the buyer pays the fee, however some dealers will ask the seller to pay all or part of the fee.

3.) *Be realistic about the condition of your piece.* Note any markings, mold numbers, etc. Carefully check your piece for any scratches, blemishes or cracks. If you are upfront with the dealer, you'll save yourself time and aggravation. Gather the original paperwork and box. If you don't have these materials, ask the dealer how this will affect the price of the piece you're selling. If you're looking to buy and have no intention of reselling, let the dealer know that you would accept a piece without the original paperwork. But be sure that you will not want to resell the piece later, since this will have an impact on the price you can demand.

4.) *Ask if the piece will be inspected by the dealer.* Many dealers will suggest that you write your initials or some other "code" on the bottom of the piece in pencil. By doing so, you can be sure that the piece you send in is the piece you get back should the sale fall through. Check with the dealer before putting any markings on the piece to ensure that it will not effect the value of the piece.

Q. Does a factory flaw or variation effect the selling price of a piece?

A. Usually, factory flaws are not a problem unless they are very pronounced. That's why it is extremely important to inspect each piece you buy...whether it's on the primary market (through a retailer or direct mail) or on the secondary market (at a "swap & sell" or through a dealer/exchange). And remember, everyone's definition of "perfection" is different. What one collector may find acceptable, another would reject. Variations usually do not effect the value of a piece. The exception to this rule is variations that qualify as "mistakes." Misspelling and other obvious mistakes will usually make a piece more valuable.

Q. Does the presence of an artist's signature on a piece increase its value?

A. Though the presence of a signature is not as important as it used to be, in some cases the value of a signed piece may be 15% to 25% higher than a comparable unsigned piece. Factors that impact the value of a signature include:

1.) *Age of the artist* – Artists who are reaching the end of their career may be doing fewer signings, making a signed piece more valuable to many collectors.

2.) *Accessibility of an artist* – Signatures from artists that rarely make themselves available for signings are often more coveted and therefore add to the value of a signed piece.

3.) *Buyer's preference* – More and more artists are taking to the road for personal appearances. These events give the collector the chance to share a personal experience with the artist. Some collectors prefer to buy unsigned pieces because they plan to have the artist sign the piece for them personally at an upcoming event.

Q. How important is it to save the original box?

A. Boxes are very important and the absence of an original box will often result in a lower selling price.

If you have a collectible that breaks, and you have your original box, you can buy a replacement piece without the box (since you don't need it) and usually save some money.

On a more practical note, the manufacturer designs the box to afford the best possible protection for the piece during shipment. If you and your collectible move, the original box will be your best shot at getting your collection safely to its new home.

Q. What steps should I expect to go through in buying or selling collectibles through a secondary market dealer or exchange?

A. The average secondary market transaction takes about 3 weeks to complete and will usually include the following steps:

1.) *Call the secondary market dealer/exchange and tell them about the piece you want to buy or sell.* Be specific and include the product number if possible.

2.) *If you are looking to buy a piece, the dealer will tell you if they currently have it listed (available from a seller) or in stock, and what the selling price is.* The selling price will usually include a commission or service fee for the dealer/exchange. If you are looking to sell a piece, you should be prepared to tell them your "asking price." This price is the amount of money you expect to clear after the transaction is completed, and should not include the commission. In most cases, the dealer will add the commission on top of your asking price. Keep in mind that you must pay the shipping and insurance charges necessary to get your piece to the dealer/exchange. The buyer will usually pay to have the item shipped to them from the dealer/exchange.

3.) *Once a buyer agrees to pay the price asked, the dealer contacts the seller and has the piece shipped to the dealer for inspection.* At the same time, the buyer sends his/her payment to the dealer.

4.) *After the piece is inspected by the dealer and found to be in acceptable condition, the piece is shipped to the buyer for their inspection.* Before it is shipped, most dealers will put a marking (often invisible) on the bottom of the piece. This is a safeguard to ensure that if the piece is not accepted, the same piece is returned.

5.) *The buyer usually will have a set time-period (3 to 5 days) to either accept or reject the piece.* If the piece is accepted by the buyer, the dealer pays the seller the agreed-upon asking price. If the piece is not acceptable, it is returned to the dealer who can either return it to the seller, or sell it to another buyer for the original asking price.

Q. It seems that there is a wide range of limited edition products being sold today. Has this resulted in a slow-down in secondary market trading?

A. Quite the contrary! The increased vitality of the primary market, as seen in the growing number of manufacturers and lines, has resulted in more vigorous trading on the secondary market. There are more collectors than ever before, they are younger and have more disposable income than their predecessors. In many cases, they're getting started later in a series – after the first few issues have retired – so increased demand for earlier pieces is generated. All of this fuels a very strong secondary market.

Q. Is trading or bartering an option for acquiring limited edition collectibles?

A. Trading and/or bartering is an alternative to buying and selling on the secondary market. Collectors clubs and "swap and sell" events offer the best avenue for trading or bartering, since you have the opportunity to inspect the piece and negotiate right on the spot.

Q. If you have a large collection, is it better to sell it as a "collection" or as single pieces?

A. It is very difficult to sell an entire collection unless it is comprised of all older pieces, since collectors usually have some of the pieces from the collection that they're building. Often, they are looking to supplement their own collection of later issues with some of the earlier pieces that they missed.

It's also typically quite expensive to purchase an entire collection at once, so collectors will add to a collection piece-by-piece as they can afford the investment.

You will usually receive greater value for your collection if you sell it one piece at a time, rather than trying to sell the whole collection at once to one buyer. By listing your collection as individual pieces with a secondary market dealer, you have a better chance of moving all the pieces, though it may take some time.

Q. Do club pieces increase in value faster than other collectibles?

A. Club issues tend to appreciate quickly because they are only available for one year. The first club issue may be harder to find because club membership is smaller in the beginning, making fewer pieces available and thus driving up demand.

Generally, though, club pieces are not more in demand than some very specific pieces in a line.

INDEX TO DEALER DIRECTORY BY SPECIALTY

Locating Secondary Market Dealers

Secondary market dealers have been indexed by their specialties. To find a dealer for a particular product:

1. **Use the index below to find the name of the line or manufacturer that produced the collectible(s) you're seeking.**
2. **The numbers listed after the line or manufacturer's name represent dealer locator numbers. *THESE ARE NOT PAGE NUMBERS.* Dealer locator numbers correspond to the numbers found in the upper right-hand corner of the dealer listings presented between pages 620 and 645.**
3. **Turn to the listings indicated by the dealer locator numbers and contact the dealer that you choose to work with.**
   As an example...
   A dealer specializing in Abelman Art Glass can be found by finding the dealer listing that has the number "5" in the upper-right hand corner. The dealer in this example is Crystal World, found on page 621.

Directory to Secondary Market Dealers

CAN

LAURA'S COLLECTIBLES

1

860 Memorial Ave.
Thunder Bay Ontario, Canada P7B-3Z8

Phone: (807) 343-4240
Fax: (807) 768-1362
Hours: Mon-Fri: 10-9, Sat: 10-5:30, Sun: 12-5

Laura's COLLECTIBLES

Services: Occasionally buy Barbie dolls. No consignments. Visa, MasterCard, American Express accepted. Layaway plan available. Worldwide shipping.

Secondary: Primary and secondary for Precious Moments, Cherished Teddies, Barbie, Boyds, Bradford, Gene Dolls, Ashton-Drake, Royal Doulton, Seraphim Angels, PenDelfin, Coca-Cola, Ertl Die Cast, Harley-Davidson, Fireman and Policeman Figurines, Trishia Romance, Myth & Magic, Pretty As A Picture, Lilliput Lane, David Winter, Anheuser-Busch. Also have Canadian pieces for Precious Moments, Boyds, Ty Beanies (including Precious Moments, Harley and Star Wars Beanies), etc.

Noteworthy: Laura's Collectibles carries Canadian Boyds, Precious Moments & Cherished Teddies pieces, as well as limited edition Calling Cards and Wayne Gretzky autographed Upper Deck Cards. Ask them about retired Swarovski for sale.

SECONDARY MARKET SPECIALIST CIB 1998-99

ENG

COLLECTABLES LTD.

2

18 Beach Road
Littlehampton West Sussex BN17 5HT
England

Phone: 011 44 1903 733199
Fax: 011 44 1903 733244
E-mail: 101320 3607@compuserve.com
Website: www.worldcollectorsnet.com/hblcollectables
Hours: Mon-Sat: 9:30-5:30 England Time. (From the U.S., call in the early morning or leave a message to have your call returned.)

Services: Buy/Sell/Trade. Locator service. Visa, MasterCard and checks accepted. Worldwide shipping. Layaway available.

Secondary: Current and retired David Winter, Lilliput Lane, Harmony Kingdom, Cherished Teddies, Enchantica, PenDelfin and Tudor Mint.

Noteworthy: Collectables Ltd., located on the south coast of England, was established in 1993 by owner Heather Lavender. The spacious retail shop is also a Club Redemption Center for the lines listed above. In addition to a large selection of collectibles and excellent service, Collectables Ltd.'s customers receive a quarterly newsletter which is mailed to them or can be downloaded from the store's website.

SECONDARY MARKET SPECIALIST CIB 1998-99

ENG

THE HOUSE OF CRYSTAL

3

20 Lansdowne Terrace Gosforth
Newcastle Upon Tyne NE3 1HP
England

Phone: 011 44 191-2132750
Fax: 011 44 191-2132755
Hours: Mon-Sat: 9-6

Services: Buy/Sell/Trade. Exchange and locator service. No cost, no obligation listing. Collectors may send a typed list divided into "Buy and Sell" (including prices). Quoted price is the price to the buyer. All sales handled personally. Shipping available. "Buy and Sell" lists upon request. Personal checks, Visa, and MasterCard accepted.

Secondary: Swarovski Silver Crystal (retired and current). Swarovski jewelry.

Noteworthy: The House of Crystal, specializing in Swarovski Crystal, was established in 1993 by Peter Johnson and his wife, Pen, who keep updated on Swarovski secondary market activities by attending auctions and expos worldwide. Residing in England, they are very close to the European market and often make visits to "The House of Swarovski" in Wattens, Austria.

Directory to Secondary Market Dealers

AZ **5**

CRYSTAL WORLD

2743 North Campbell Avenue
Tucson, AZ 85719-3108

Phone: (520) 326-5990
Hours: Tues-Fri: 10:30-6, Sat: 11-3

Services: Buy/sell, appraise, engrave, design and repair crystal. Brokerage fee applicable. Visa, MasterCard and checks accepted.

Secondary: Authorized Swarovski/SCS retailer, Crystal World, Austrian faceted sculptures, Abelman Art Glass limited edition clowns, Krystonia.

Noteworthy: In business for over 25 years, Crystal World specializes in cut glass, paperweights, custom engraving on wedding and anniversary gifts, corporate presentation awards and trophies expertly created. Attention Swarovski collectors: Crystal World pays your membership fee. Now you can purchase your investment collectibles with confidence. All crystal professionally inspected, evaluated and graded for mint condition by William Threm, master glass engraver. Complete crystal showroom of exquisite cut glass and art glass from around the world.
Repairs on Steuben, Baccarat, Lalique, Waterford, Swarovski, etc. Appraisal services and expert advice on future crystal investments.

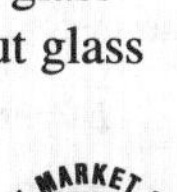

AZ **6**

BUDWEISER COLLECTIBLES
D & A INVESTMENTS

2301 Souchak Drive, Lake Havasu City, AZ 86406

Phone: (520) 453-9076
Fax: (520) 453- 9076
Hours: Mon-Fri: 9-6

Services: Buy/Sell/Trade. Buy outright one item to complete collections. Current price lists available. Visa, MasterCard, money orders and checks accepted. Shipping via UPS insured.

Secondary: Specializing in Anheuser-Busch steins, mugs, plates, figurines and other breweriana collectibles. Full line of new and retired products.

Noteworthy: D & A Investments started in breweriana collectibles in 1985. Within a few years, they became a full-time mail order business dealing with collectors throughout the world. Always willing to share their years of product knowledge, they appreciate your calls. All merchandise sold and shipped by D & A carries a full money back 30-day guarantee. Their goal is to have good product, good service and customer satisfaction.

AZ **7**

Looking For Retired Harbour Lights?

Look to America's Premier Source For Retired Harbour Lights:

LIGHTHOUSE KEEPERS
Post Office Box 4742
Scottsdale, AZ 85261-4742
602/ 451-8938
headkeeper@lighthousekeepers.com

Visit the most comprehensive source of information about Harbour Lights anywhere:
WWW.LIGHTHOUSEKEEPERS.COM

AZ **8**

Lori's COLLECTIBLES

6121 E. Broadway #134, Tucson, AZ 85711
Phone: (520) 790-6668 (Information)
Fax: (520) 790-6660
Hours: Tues-Fri: 10-6, Sat: 10-5
Closed Sun and Mon

Services: Buy outright on selected merchandise. Ship anywhere. Locator service. Will work with other dealers. Call for details.

Secondary: Lladró, M.I. Hummel, L. Davis, ANRI, D-56, Snowbabies, Snowbunnies, PM, CT, MOY, D. Winter, Lilliput Cottages, Royal Doulton (Toby & Figurines, Bunnykins, Beatrix Potter), Chilmark, Legends, Goebel minis, Plates and Wieghorst lithos, DeGrazia, Krystonia, Gnomes, M. Wideman, Fontanini, Maruri, Andrea, Seraphim, Swarovski, Disney Classics, Spencer Collin Lighthouses, sports figurines.

Noteworthy: Lori's carries a full line of collectibles, adding about two new lines per year. The store is a Redemption Center for many lines listed above and hosts several open houses during the year. A newsletter is published frequently, and interested collectors can be placed on the mailing list. Lori's offers personalized service, integrity and fair secondary market prices.

Directory to Secondary Market Dealers

AZ | 9

SÁNCHEZ COLLECTIBLES

SECONDARY MARKET SPECIALISTS IN
SWAROVSKI & LLADRÓ

Phone: (602) 395-9974 7 AM - 9 PM 7 DAYS
FAX: (602) 241-0702 24 HOURS / 7 DAYS
Email: sanchcol@primenet.com
Web Page: www.primenet.com/~sanchcol
Visits by Appointment Only

Services: BUY & SELL retired **SWAROVSKI** and **LLADRÓ.** Free locator service is available. Deal only in retired or sold-out pieces that can no longer be purchased on the primary market. Dealer and insurance replacement inquires are welcomed.NOT a Broker: Everything shipped from on-hand inventory.

Lines: SWAROVSKI and **LLADRÓ.**

Other: SANCHEZ COLLECTIBLES is owned by Charlotte Sanchez and her husband, Clark. The business is 99.9% telephone, email, and mail order and only handles retired and sold-out pieces. They specialize in the Collector's Society or 'club' pieces but offer a good selection of other pieces as well. Every Fall Charlotte edits and mails a newsletter and an updated listing of pieces and prices. This is sent FREE to all interested collectors. In addition, Charlotte and Clark participate in several collectibles shows around the country every year. A free copy of the latest product listings and show schedule is available upon request.

CA | 10

ARMIK'S Since 1984

Fine Collectables & Gallery Editions
7616 Topanga Cyn. Blvd. Canoga Park, Ca. 91304

24-HOUR 818-702-6794 FAX # 818-702-6882

A Master Showcase, Preferred, Authorized & Gold Dealer For:

- LEGENDS STUDIOS
- CHILMARK
- HOPKINS BRONZES
- MILLCREEK
- HUDSON CREEK
- GENESIS
- EBONY VISION
- BRADLEY DOLLS
- MICKEY & CO.
- DUNCAN ROYALE
- SOMERSET HOUSE
- MARTY SCULPTURE
- ENCHANTICA
- KRYSTONIA
- GREENWICH
- PERTH PEWTER
- RAWCLIFFE
- GALLO PEWTER

A Commissioned Secondary Market Dealer.

Seller receives 80% of finalized sale on all Original-Condition Products.
Ship-in and studio required reconditioning negotiated separately.

Buyer pays no commissions, receives guaranteed quality product & free shipping within the lower 48 American states;
up to 5% of purchase price paid towards shipping to all other areas.

Sellers: mail or Fax your name and address for Free Listings Documents.

Buyers: call toll free 888-4-ARMIK'S for ordering inquiries.

Buyers receive future priority listings on secondary resales.

All dealer costs of published or Internet listings are paid by Armik's Fine Collectables.
Call for Internet Address after 5-1-98

Looking for the latest news about collectibles?

ORDER YOUR SUBSCRIPTION to the *COLLECTIBLES REPORT*

Get a full year of information about new products, artists, clubs and events with the *Collectibles Report*...CIB's quarterly newsletter. Four issues are yours for only $15!

Call (847) 842-2200 today to subscribe.
Or write to: COLLECTORS' INFORMATION BUREAU
5065 SHORELINE ROAD, SUITE 200
BARRINGTON, IL 60010

CA | 12

City Lights

1202 Morena Blvd., San Diego, CA 92110
EVERYTHING SHIPS FREE

Phone: **(800) 262-5335 (619) 275-1006**
Fax: **(800) 262-5335**
Hours: **Open 7 Days**

Services: Single pieces or entire collections are bought for cash or will trade. Layaway available. Visa, MasterCard, Discover, American Express accepted. ATM.

Secondary: Department 56 (all Villages, Snowbabies, Snowbunnies, All Through The House, Winter Silhouette), Byers' Choice Carolers, Annalee, Fontanini, Cottontail Lane, Creepy Hollow, Margaret Furlong, Christopher Radko, Polonaise, Old World Christmas, Birgits Collections, Seraphim Angels, Harbour Lights, Shelia's, Possible Dreams, David Winter, Britains.

Noteworthy: City Lights is a 6,000 square foot store with award-winning permanent displays. Everything listed **ships free**. Enormous inventory of both current and retired pieces. Department 56 "Gold Key" dealer, Byers' Choice "Preferred Dealer," Annalee "Doll Society" store, Fontanini "Guild" store, Polonaise "Listed" dealer, Old World Christmas "Collector's Club" store. Knowledgeable staff and friendly efficient service.

SECONDARY MARKET SPECIALIST CIB 1998-99

Directory to Secondary Market Dealers

CA | 13

Crystal Galleria

dba **Disneyana Marketplace**

1405 Monterey Street
Alhambra, CA 91801

Phone: ***(626)308-9595***
Fax: ***(626)308-9696***
Hours: M-Sat: 10:00-7:00

Services: *Secondary market service. Large inventory of retired items in stock.* ***Listing service*** *or* ***buy outright*** *from dealers and collectors with prompt payment. Search service provided. Accepts personal checks, Visa & Mastercard. Satisfaction guaranteed.*

Lines: *Specializes in* ***Swarovski***, ***Disney Classics*** *and* ***Disneyana Convention*** *items.*

Noteworthy: *One of the dealers with the largest inventory of retired items in stock. Knowledgeable staff provides friendly and helpful service. CIB panel member.*

CA | 14

Crystal Reef

is your primary source on the secondary market for:

Pocket Dragons • Wee Forest • Swarovski Disney Classics & Disneyana • Waterford Tom Clark • Lilliput Lane • David Winter Land of Legend • Armani • Animation Art Charming Tails • Lladro • Steiff • Radko Harmony Kingdom and R. John Wright

© R. John Wright

© Walt Disney Co.

© Annette Peterson

Crystal Reef is one of the largest secondary market exchanges for retired and limited edition collectibles, offering very competitive "True" secondary market values on listed pieces. We do the work of locating and brokering your fine collectibles.
With Crystal Reef, there are no membership, subscription or listing fees, and we provide free secondary market price lists on any of the lines which we represent.

Call us today for a free secondary market price list.

Visa * Mastercard * AMEX * Check

(925) 778-8146

Visit our Web Site at www.crystal-reef.com

© RM

CA | 15

Collectibles

560 N.Moorpark Road, Suite 287, Thousand Oaks, CA 91360

Phone: (800) 266-2337 (805) 499-9222
Fax: (805) 376-5541
E-Mail: flashcoll@aol.com
Hours: Mon-Fri: 10-5, 24-Hour Answering Service

Services: Buy outright. Consignment & trades. Search service.

Secondary: Budweiser, Anheuser-Busch, Strohs, Old Style, Miller, Hamms, Pabst, Coors, steins and plates. New stein importers catalog shows over 800 steins in full color. Features traditional German steins, pewter, character, fire fighters, flasks, Rockwell, Looney Tunes, Superman and Coca-Cola.

Noteworthy: Flash Collectibles started as a part-time business in 1971. By 1973, owners Doug and Natalie Marks were totally consumed by the antiques and collectibles "bug" and opened their first store called The Antique Co. In 1984, the Marks discovered the Anheuser-Busch collectible steins. In 1986, the firm moved to their current location and changed their name to Flash Collectibles. Specializing in mail order beer steins, they offer a free brochure listing their current stock of over 1,000 beer steins. Also featured are movie stills, and an exceptionally large collection of full-color original fruit and vegetable labels.

CA | 16

THE FRAME GALLERY

305 Third Avenue
Chula Vista, CA 91910

Phone: (619) 422-1700
Fax: (619) 422-5860
Hours: Mon-Fri: 10-5:30
Sat: 10-5

Services: Specializes in searching for hard-to-find collectibles. Does not buy outright. Call for details. All major credit cards accepted.

Secondary: All collector plates. Also prints, figurines, crystal, and pewter, including Snowbabies, Perillo, Disney Classics, Kinkade, Olszewski, Enesco, Hamilton, Swarovski, M.I. Hummel, Rockwell, Kevin Francis, Mill Pond Press, Hadley House, Somerset House, and autographed celebrity photos, etc.

Noteworthy: The Frame Gallery began as a framing shop, but soon collectors began coming to the store for advice on the art of framing different collectibles. Before long, mother-daughter team Margaret and Jan introduced collectibles to their store. Today, they are a Redemption Center for Disney Classics, Kinkade, Lilliput, Krystonia, Pocket Dragons, Myth & Magic, and Hantel Miniatures. They also carry artists' works of local scenes which are of particular interest to tourists.

Directory to Secondary Market Dealers

CA | 17

THE GOLDEN SWANN

895 Lincoln Way
Auburn, CA 95603

Phone: (800) 272-7926
(530) 823-7739
Fax: (530) 823-1945
Hours: Daily: 10-5:30

Services: Buy/Sell outright. Layaway plan available. Visa, MasterCard, American Express and Discover accepted.

Secondary: Lladró, Swarovski, Armani, David Winter Cottages, M.I. Hummel, and all retired collectibles.

Noteworthy: With 25 years of business expertise, The Golden Swann has become the largest dealer in Northern California for current and retired pieces of Lladró, Swarovski, Armani, Disney Classics, Mark Hopkins, Country Artists, M.I. Hummel, Maruri, and Genesis. Free membership for all collectors clubs, call for further details. Redemption Center. CALL FOR THE BEST PRICES ON RETIRED ITEMS.

SECONDARY MARKET SPECIALIST CIB 1998-99

CA | 18

MCCURRY'S HALLMARK

1779 Tribute Road, Suite C
Sacramento, CA 95815

Phone: (800) 213-0214 (916) 567-9952
Fax: (916) 927-3469
Hours: Mon-Sat: 10-9, Sun: 11-6 (PST)

Dealers for the following: Precious Moments Century Circle Dealer (one of 41 in the U.S.), Department 56 Gold Key Dealer, Cherished Teddies Adoption Center, Boyds Gold Paw, Disney Classics and Hallmark Gold Crown Leadership store.

Secondary: Precious Moments, Department 56 (all villages and accessories).

Noteworthy: Started in 1908, McCurry's Hallmark is a family held and operated business, now in the third generation. They have two locations in major malls, one in the Sunrise Mall and the other in Arden Fair Mall. Between the two stores, there is over 7,600 square feet to serve collectors. McCurry's has the largest display of both new and retired Precious Moments in Northern California. They also have one of the most extensive and unique secondary market displays of Department 56.

CA | 19

M.S. Gallery

1304 Glen Dell Drive
San Jose, CA 95125

Phone: (408) 993-0375
24-Hour Answering Service
E-mail: MSider@aol.com
Hours: Mon-Sat: 10-5

Services: Secondary Market InSider, Buy/Sell. Ship UPS. All major credit cards accepted.

Secondary: Lladró, Precious Moments, M.I. Hummel, Jan Hagara, Armani, Swarovski, David Winter, Lilliput, Annalee, Raikes Bears, All God's Children, limited edition plates, Wee Forest Folk, Bradford Exchange, plates & dolls.
Graphics: P. Buckley Moss, Marty Bell, Donald Zolan, Penni-Ann Cross, Bannister, Sandra Kuck, Corinne Layton, Thomas Kinkade, Red Skelton.

Noteworthy: Marie Sider has been selling collectibles since 1980. She has had over 17 years of experience with both primary and secondary market sales. For all your collectible needs, call "Marie." She is anxious to serve you, **"Service is her most important product."** CIB panel member.

SECONDARY MARKET SPECIALIST CIB 1998-99

CA | 20

THE NATIONAL ARCHIVE
THOMAS KINKADE GALLERIES

550 Wave Street • Monterey, CA 93940
408-657-1550 • Fax 408-657-1559

BUY • SELL • CONSIGN

Original Oils, Remarques, Rare Sketches, Paper & Canvas Lithographs

Considered the Authoritative Source for America's foremost "Painter of Light,"™ The National Archive specializes in both Primary and Secondary art by the nation's most published artist. Over 150 original Kinkade sketches, plein air and studio paintings are available.

For dealer or wholesale inquiries, contact Lightpost Publishing at 1-800-366-3733.

Directory to Secondary Market Dealers

CA 21

Rystad's Limited Editions
since 1967

1013 Lincoln Avenue, San Jose, CA 95125

Phone: (408) 279-1960
Fax: (408) 279-1960
Hours: Tues-Sat: 10-5, Mon by Appt.

Services: Buy outright. Lists welcome.

Secondary: Red Skelton, Rockwell, Hamilton, M.I. Hummel, David Winter, Ashton-Drake, Harmony Kingdom, Noritake, Lenox, All God's Children, Bradford, Snowbabies, Disney Classics, Pooh n' Friends, Royal Copenhagen, B&G, Ebony Visions, Boyds Bears, Christmas ornaments (Radko, Adler, Dresden Dove, Midwest).

Noteworthy: Dean Rystad started in the collectibles mail order business in 1967. In 1978, Rystad opened a store, which today features over 6,000 collector plates and figurines. Rystad specializes in locating back issues of collectibles. His track record is about 98% of requests. Rystad's is a Redemption Center for most collector clubs. A new gallery was added recently to feature the artwork of Red Skelton, Thomas Kinkade, Buddy Ebsen, Sandra Kuck, Jack Terry and Donald Zolan.

SECONDARY MARKET SPECIALIST CIB 1998-99

CA 22

SUGARBUSH GIFT GALLERY

1921 W. San Marcos Blvd. #105
San Marcos, CA 92069

Phone: (800) 771-9945 (760) 599-9945
Fax: (760) 599-9945
Hours: Mon-Fri: 10-6, Sat: 10-5

Services: Primary/Secondary Market. Mail your list with asking price. Visa, MasterCard, Discover and American Express accepted. Checks and money orders also accepted. 90-day layaway plan available. Ship insured.

Secondary: Primary and Secondary for Thomas Kinkade, Dona Gelsinger, Boyds (PAW), Cherished Teddies, Charming Tails, Harbour Lights, Harmony Kingdom, Seraphim Angels, Country Artists, Wee Forest Folk, Fenton and much more.

Noteworthy: Sugarbush Gift Gallery is a primary and secondary source of marketable collectibles, with a knowledgeable and service orientated staff on hand.

SECONDARY MARKET SPECIALIST CIB 1998-99

CA 23

Swan Seekers Network

9740 Campo Road, Suite 134
Spring Valley, CA 91977 USA

Phone: (619) 462-2333
Fax: (619) 462-5517
On line: SWANSEEKERS.COM
Hours: M-Th 9:00 - 5:00 West Coast Time

SECONDARY MARKET SPECIALIST CIB 1998-99

Services: Second Market Swarovski Brokerage. We offer Swan Seekers · Newsletter, published 3 times a year and the Marketplace, (a 'For Sale' and 'Wanted to Buy' retired items list) updated and issued every 2 months ***all year round.*** We accept Master Card and Visa.

Lines: ***Exclusively Swarovski Crystal***

Noteworthy: Swan Seekers Network, established is 1989 is the *FIRST* strictly Swarovski Crystal Brokerage service. Listing your retired items for sale is ***free of charge.*** We offer UNBIASED information to any interested Swarovski collector. Keep up with what's new and what's happening. Give us a call. We may have what you're looking for. ☺

CT 24

Sue Coffee

10 Saunders Hollow Rd.
Old Lyme, CT 06371-1126

Phone: (860) 434-5641
Fax: (860) 434-2653
E-mail: SueCoffee@aol.com
Website: www.suecoffee.com
Hours: By Appointment

Dealer of **ANNALEE® DOLLS**

Services: Buy - Sell - Trade - Collect (current and retired). Locator service. Independent consultant of Annalee® Dolls. Mail order - Layaway - Checks accepted! Satisfaction guaranteed!!

Secondary: Annalee® Dolls, Breyer Horses, Peter Stone, Department 56 Snowbabies.

Noteworthy: Sue Coffee is considered an expert when it comes to Annalee® Dolls. With over 1,500 retired dolls in stock, she can fulfill almost any collector's desire. Old catalogs and collector's magazines are also available for your research needs. For her informative Annalee® list, please send $2.00 for postage. Sue Coffee is also an Annalee® Doll Society Sponsor and an Authorized Breyer Dealer through her store, Laysville Hardware.

SECONDARY MARKET SPECIALIST CIB 1998-99

Directory to Secondary Market Dealers

FL

A RETIRED COLLECTION

25

550 Harbor Cove Circle
Longboat Key, FL 34228-3544

Phone: **(800) 332-8594**
(941) 387-0102 (FL)
Fax: **(941) 383-8865**
E-mail: **LladroLady@aol.com**
Website: **http://www.lladrolady.com**
Hours: **Mail order: 8 a.m.-9 p.m. daily**
Visits by appointment

specializing in LLADRÓ a retired collection

Services: Broker service. Representing buyers and sellers. Occasionally buy outright. Dealers and insurance replacement welcome. American Express, Visa, MasterCard and Discover accepted.

Secondary: Lladró

Noteworthy: A Retired Collection, specializing in Lladró only, was established in 1992 by Janet Gale Hammer. A complimentary Newsletter/Stock & Buy List is published quarterly and available upon request. Janet maintains availabilty of almost 2,000 retired pieces on her website. Keyword "SEARCH" retrieves Lladró name, I.D. #, year issued and retired, availability, price and color photograph. She is a charter member of the Tampa Bay/Sarasota Chapter and CIB panel member. She is recognized by many as the dominant source for retired Lladró porcelain.

SECONDARY MARKET SPECIALIST CIB 1998-99

FL

THE CHRISTMAS PALACE

26

10600 N.W. 77 Ave.
Hialeah Gardens, FL 33016

Phone: **(305) 558-5352**
Fax: **(305) 558-6718**
Hours: **Mon-Sat: 10-7, Sun: 11-6** (Off Season)
Mon-Sat: 10-9, Sun: 10-7 (In Season)

Services: No consignments, buy outright. Call for details. Free shipping anywhere in the United States for orders over $50. All major credit cards accepted. No sales tax outside of Florida.

Secondary: Department 56 (Villages, Snowbabies, Snowbunnies), Swarovski, Disney Classics, Precious Moments, Armani, Boyds Bears, Ebony Visions by Willitts, Lladró, Christopher Radko.

Noteworthy: Since 1989, The Christmas Palace has become one of the top collectors' stores in the country. They are one of the largest Department 56 dealers (Gold Key status). Redemption Center for all listed lines.

FL

27

12 Castillo Drive, St. Augustine, FL 32084

Phone: **(904) 824-9898** **Fax:** **(904) 829-8555**
Website: **www.tepee.com**
Hours: **Daily: 9:30-6**

Services: Consignment, buy outright, paying cash or merchandise.

Secondary: M.I. Hummel, Chilmark, Precious Moments, Disney Classics, Department 56, David Winter, Lilliput Lane, Lowell Davis, Perillo, DeGrazia, Alexander Dolls, Cherished Teddies, Harmony Kingdom, Old World Christmas, Greenwich Workshop and more!

Noteworthy: Teepeetown, Inc., founded in 1945, operates The Christmas Shop, The Indian Shop, The Columbia Gift Shop, and the Authentic Old Drugstore. Specializing in fine gifts and collectibles, the Harris' have served the collecting market since 1945 and have been on the advisory boards of Goebel, Royal Doulton and Hudson Creek. Well versed on both the primary and secondary markets, the entire staff provides effective aftermarket assistance. The company now employs a THIRD GENERATION family member to insure credibility and ongoing support for its customers.

SECONDARY MARKET SPECIALIST CIB 1998-99

FL

28

Do You Have a Dream?

...Then Trust The Experts!

- Call for Your One-time **FREE** Newsletter
- World's Largest Disney 2ndary Market Brokerage
- Get The Inside "Scoop" Before it Happens
- Over 20,000 listings
- Your Sources for the WDCC, Convention Pieces, Animation Art, Swarovski Crystal, Dept. 56 & More!

3961 Kiawa Dr
Orlando, Fl. 32837
Ph: (407) 438-5634
FAX (407) 438-8372

Over $1 Million Traded Annually

Directory to Secondary Market Dealers

FL | 29

Donna's Collectibles Exchange

703 Endeavour Drive South
Winter Springs, FL 32708

Phone: (800) 480-5105
Fax: (407) 696-4786
Hours: Mon-Fri: 11am-8pm (EST)

Services: Secondary Market Buy & Sell listing exchange. Dealers welcome. Visa & MasterCard accepted.

Secondary: Barbies, Boyds Collection (Bearstones, Dollstones, Folkstones & Plushes), Breen Ornaments, Charming Tails, Cherished Teddies, Christopher Radko, David Winter, Department 56, Forma Vitrum, Harbour Lights, Harmony Kingdom, Kiddie Car Classics, Lefton Colonial, Lilliput Lane, Lowell Davis, Maude Humphrey, Muffy's & Raikes Bears, Snowbabies, Swarovski, Walt Disney (Classics, Convention & Videos), Wee Forest Folk & more.

Noteworthy: Donna's Collectibles Exchange is strictly a mail-order business. Subscriptions available for listing updates.

FL | 30

HEIRLOOM COLLECTIBLES

2516c McMullen Booth Rd
Clearwater, Florida 33761
1-800-929-4567
fax: 1-813-669-8052
Online: www.heirloomcollectibles.com

Lines: Lladro, Armani, Swarovski, Boyds Precious Moments, Department 56, Annalee Tom Clark Gnomes, Charming Tails, Harbor Lights, Cherished Teddies and others.

Services: All major Credit Cards Accepted. We are a retail store for all the above lines and more and also buy, sell and broker secondary items. We ship insured UPS unless other arrangements are desired. Layaways available.

Noteworthy: Established in 1993, we have built a strong reputation for quality service. Our staff is knowledgeable and helpful. The owners, Margie and Al are experienced collectors who understand the joy of finding that special something you have been searching for.

SECONDARY MARKET SPECIALIST CIB 1998-99

FL | 31

HEIRLOOMS OF TOMORROW

750 N.E. 125th Street
North Miami, FL 33161

Phone: (800) 544-2-BUY
(305) 899-0920
Fax: (305) 899-2877
Hours: Mon-Wed & Fri: 9:30-6, Thurs: 9:30-8, Sat: 9-5

Services: Commission. Collectors send a typed list divided into buy and sell.

Secondary: ANRI, Hibel, Lladró, Goebel Miniatures, David Winter, M.I. Hummel, Armani, Swarovski, Department 56, Cabbage Patch, Legends, Bradford, Krystonia, Sarah's Attic, Precious Moments, Chilmark, Disney Classics, Lilliput Lane, Lowell Davis, Caithness, Ashton-Drake dolls, Thomas Kinkade, Olszewski, Sandra Kuck, Beanie Babies.

Noteworthy: With over 16 years of experience and literally thousands of items, Heirlooms of Tomorrow is considered one of South Florida's foremost one-stop collectible shops. Family owned and operated since 1980, they have a booming mail order business. Care is taken to ensure that collectibles will arrive safely, as they are shipped worldwide.

SECONDARY MARKET SPECIALIST CIB 1998-99

FL | 32

HORN'S JEWELRY INC.

498 S.E. Kingsbay Dr.
Crystal River, FL 34429

Phone: (352) 795-5095
(800) 576-7350
Hours: Mon-Fri: 9-5 September-May
Closed: June-August

Services: Sell single or sets. Accepts cashier checks, credit cards, personal checks (allow 14 days to clear). Call for listing.

Secondary: Retired or current Disney Classics Collectibles, Swarovski Silver Crystal, M. I. Hummel figurines, bells, plates, Gnomes by Tom Clark, retired and very limited NASA Astronaut plates, cups, saucers, retired only Hallmark ornaments, plus miscellaneous collectibles and jewelry.

Noteworthy: Horn's Jewelry Inc. has been in business for 42 years. Listings sent upon request by calling or writing to the above address.

Directory to Secondary Market Dealers

FL | 33

KATHY'S HALLMARK

7709 Seminole Mall
Seminole, FL 33772

Phone: (813) 392-2459
Fax: (813) 392-2459 (call first)
Hours: Mon-Sat: 10-9, Sun: 12-5

Services: Buy and sell outright. Visa, MasterCard, American Express and Discover accepted. Ship via UPS.

Secondary: Swarovski, Collector plates, Precious Moments, Cherished Teddies, Hallmark ornaments and Kiddie Car Classics, Snowbabies, Barbie, Dreamsicles, Star Wars, and Star Trek.

Noteworthy: Kathy's Hallmark is a Redemption Center for Swarovski, Precious Moments, Cherished Teddies, Dreamsicles, and Hallmark. Many past year ornaments and some 5-piece Christmas promotion sets are available (i.e. Santa and Reindeer, Snoopy, Bearinger Bears). Call or write for specifics.

SECONDARY MARKET SPECIALIST CIB 1998-99

FL | 34

VIKING

WORLD SPECIALIST IN BING & GRONDAHL AND ROYAL COPENHAGEN COLLECTIBLES

If you want to buy or sell previous year's RC or B&G collectibles, call Viking first! We have been buying and selling RC and B&G since 1948 and have a large inventory, plus a nationwide network of sources. We buy outright, or list your RC and B&G collectibles on our active "Videx" exchange.

CALL US FOR A CURRENT PRICE LIST ON RC AND B&G COLLECTIBLES

We also carry many of the other fine collectibles you love:

Swarovski
Hummel
Bradford
Maruri
Kaiser
Wedgwood
Edna Hibel
Berlin Design

And Many Other Lines

VIKING IMPORT HOUSE, INC.
690 N. E. 13th St., Ft. Lauderdale, FL 33304
CALL US TOLL-FREE (800) 327-2297

GA | 35

THE NAUTICAL EXCHANGE

Jim and Julie Rutherford
P. O. Box 501101
Atlanta, GA 31150

Phone: (770) 754-9060
Fax: (770) 754-9411
Email: HLSG@aol.com

Services: Secondary market services, specializing completely in Harbour Lights lighthouses. Annual *Survival Guide to Harbour Lights Lighthouses* book. Quarterly informational newsletter "The Guiding Lights" about Harbour Lights, with no-cost, no-obligation listing section.

Lines: Harbour Lights lighthouses

Noteworthy: ***The Survival Guide to Harbour Lights Lighthouses*** was the original definitive information resource on Harbour Lights. It continues to expand each year, and the 1998 edition has the most complete history and analysis of Harbour Lights yet! **"The Guiding Lights"** newsletter keeps subscribers current on all breaking Harbour Lights news and secondary trends. Both are *MUSTS* for any serious Harbour Lights collector! Jim Rutherford is a quoted CIB panel member.

SECONDARY MARKET SPECIALIST CIB 1998-99

ID | 36

Donna's Place

200 Main Street
P.O. Box 520
Idaho City ID 83631

Phone: (208) 392-6000
(800) 574-8714
Fax: (208) 392-6006
E-mail: dplac2@juno.com
Website: rosemart.com/donnas-place
Hours: Seven Days a Week: 10-7

Services: Buy/Sell/Trade. Locator Service. MasterCard, Visa, American Express, Discover accepted. Worldwide shipping.

Secondary: Anheuser-Busch, Michelob, Corona, Budweiser, Bud Light steins and related collectibles. Coca-Cola products, Ertl and Spec Cast collector trucks and banks.

Noteworthy: Donna's Place has been owned and operated by Skip and Donna Myers since 1992. An avid beer stein collector for 10 years, Skip brings enthusiasm and knowledge to his collectors. His retail store carries over 4,000 steins in stock, both retail and secondary. Authorized dealer and Redemption Center for Anheuser-Busch. Skip also runs a gift shop carrying collectible dolls and other gift items. Visit their website for more information.

SECONDARY MARKET SPECIALIST CIB 1998-99

Directory to Secondary Market Dealers

ID | 37

THREE C'S GIFT GALLERY

350 N. Milwaukee - 1009
Boise, ID 83788

Phone: **(800) 847-3302**
Fax: **(208) 884-1111**
Hours: **Mon-Fri: 10-9, Sat: 10-7, Sun: 11-6**

Services: No consignments. Buy outright. Mail your list with asking price. Visa, MasterCard, Discover and American Express accepted.

Secondary: Walt Disney Classics, Thomas Kinkade, Swarovski, Looney Tunes Spotlight Collection, Chilmark, Legends, David Winter, Snowbabies, M.I. Hummel, Wee Forest Folk, Armani, Mickey Classic Enamels by Halcyon Days.

Noteworthy: Redemption Center for Walt Disney Classics, David Winter, Swarovski, Lilliput Lane, M.I. Hummel, Armani, Chilmark, Legends and Thomas Kinkade.

SECONDARY MARKET SPECIALIST CIB 1998-99

IL | 38

Andre Ammelounx

The Stein Auction Company

PO Box 136
Palatine, IL 60078

Phone: **(847) 991-5927**
Fax: **(847) 991-5947**
Hours: **Mon-Fri: 9-3 (mail order only)**

Services: They auction antique and collector's beer steins for the beginner, as well as the advanced collector. They offer five-color and black & white catalogs annually with complete descriptions. All merchandise is guaranteed.

Secondary: Steins such as Mettlach, Regimental, Anheuser-Busch, Character, including Porcelain, Glass, Stoneware, Pottery, Royal Vienna, Silver, Limited Edition and more. They also carry M.I. Hummel figurines, bells and plates.

AUTHENTIC HUMMEL FIGURINES

Andre Ammelounx carries a full line of authentic M.I. Hummel figurines. Crown through current trademarks are available at substantial savings. Rarities including International Children also available. Call or write for their free price list.

IL | 39

BRADFORD EXCHANGE

9333 N. Milwaukee Avenue
Niles, IL 60714

THE BRADFORD EXCHANGE B

Phone: **(800) 323-8078**
Hours: **Mon-Fri: 8-5**

Services: The Bradford Exchange matches buyers with sellers by phone or mail. Buyers pay a 4% commission (or $4.00 if the price of the plate is under $100). Sellers are charged a 28.5% commission. Bradford guarantees that once the Exchange notifies both parties that a match has occurred, the buyer is guaranteed delivery of a mint-condition plate at the confirmed price (less a 4% commission), and the seller is guaranteed payment of the confirmed price (less a 28.5% commission) once the plate has been certified as mint condition.

Secondary: Bradford-recommended collector's plates.

Noteworthy: Founded in 1973, The Bradford Exchange was the first entity to offer an organized secondary market for collector's plates. In 1982, Bradford's computerized Instaquote™ system went into effect, allowing the Exchange to electronically match plate buyers with plate sellers from around the country. Bradford tracks the trading activity of more than 4,000 plates eligible for trading on the U.S. Exchange, one of 11 offices around the world. Only Bradford-recommended plates may be traded on the Exchange.

SECONDARY MARKET SPECIALIST CIB 1998-99

IL | 40

C.A. Jensen

JEWELERS

709 First Street, LaSalle, IL 61301

Phone: **(815) 223-0377 (800) 499-5977**
Website: **www.cajensenjewelers.com**
Hours: **Mon-Fri: 9:30-5:30, Sat: 9:30-5**

Services: All of their many fine retired collectible lines including china, crystal and silver are new. Checks and credit cards accepted.

Secondary: Figurines: Cybis, Boehm, Royal Copenhagen, Bing & Grondahl, Lladró, M.I. Hummel, Goebel, Ispanky, Lalique, Baccarrat, Waterford, Lowell Davis, Lilliput Lane, Lenox, ANRI, and Rockwell. Dolls: Gorham musical. Ornaments: Lunt, Kirk Stieff, Wallace, as well as other sterling, wood, and crystal lines. Collector Plates: many discontinued and obscure plates in stock including B&G, Royal Copenhagen, Bradford, M.I. Hummel, and much more.

Noteworthy: C.A. Jensen Jewelers has been in business for 78 years and is second generation family owned and operated. They house a huge inventory in their 8,000 square foot warehouse and offer many fine collectible lines in their 6,500 square foot store. There are over 3,000 plates on display, of which many are discontinued. Come see for yourself!

Directory to Secondary Market Dealers

VISIT

COLLECTORS' INFORMATION BUREAU'S

WEBSITE

at

http://www.collectorsinfo.com

IL | 42

The Crystal Connection Ltd.

8510 N. Knoxville Avenue, Suite 218
Peoria • IL 61615-2034
"SWAROVSKI crystal specialist"

Phone: **(309) 692-2221 / (800) 692-0708**
Fax: **(309) 692-2221 (24 hours)**
Hours: **Mon-Fri: 4:00-9:00, Sat-Sun: 10:00-4:00 (24-hour message service)**
E-mail: **crystalconnection@worldnet.att.net**
Web: **www.crystal.org**

SECONDARY MARKET SPECIALIST CIB 1997-98

Services:
- Secondary market brokerage listing service
- Appraisal for insurance and other needs
- *Crystal News* newsletter
- Visa, MasterCard, checks & MO accepted

Lines: Swarovski crystal

Noteworthy: The Crystal Connection Ltd. is operated by Robin Yaw, the world's leading appraiser and authority on Swarovski crystal. He has appeared as a panel speaker on CIB's secondary market seminars and Swarovski's *"Ask The Experts"* shows. He also authors the *Crystal News*, a newsletter written exclusively for Swarovski collectors. Member of the Better Business Bureau (BBB) and the International Society of Appraisers (ISA).

IL | 43

EILENE'S TREASURES

P.O. Box 285
Virden, IL 62690

Phone: (217) 965-3648
Cell Phone: (217) 652-2773
Hours: 9-8 daily

Services: Buy outright. Layaways available. Fair prices. Satisfaction guaranteed.

Secondary: Precious Moments (suspended and retired figurines, bells, ornaments, plates), Memories of Yesterday figurines and ornaments, Hallmark Ornaments, Enesco Treasury Ornaments.

Noteworthy: Eilene Kruse is an expert on Precious Moments marks, purchasing many early pieces with original marks. She has expanded her business to include other Enesco lines and Hallmark ornaments. Eilene attends four to five ornament and collectible shows in the Illinois area and publishes a price list which is available upon request.

SECONDARY MARKET SPECIALIST CIB 1998-99

IL | 44

EUROPEAN IMPORTS & GIFTS

7900 N. Milwaukee Avenue
Niles, IL 60714

Phone: (800) 227-8670 (847) 967-5253
Fax: (847) 967-0133
E-mail: ei-collectibles@worldnet.att.net
Website: www.europeanimports.com
Hours: Mon-Fri: 10-8, Sat: 10-5:30, Sun: 12-5

Services: No consignments. Buy outright. Mail complete listing. Free shipping in the U.S. with purchases over $75. Visa, MasterCard, American Express and Discover accepted.

Secondary: Annalee, ANRI, Armani, Ashton-Drake, Bradford plates, Byers' Choice, Cairn Gnomes, Chilmark, Lowell Davis, Department 56, Disney Classics, Animation Art, M.I. Hummel, EKJ, Krystonia, S. Kuck, Legends, Lilliput Lane, Lladró, Memories of Yesterday, Michael's Limited, All God's Children, Precious Moments, Swarovski, WACO, Wee Forest Folk, David Winter, Madame Alexander dolls, Cherished Teddies, Radko, Ebony Visions, Dreamsicles, Harmony Kingdom, Goebel Looney Tunes, Seraphim Classics.

Noteworthy: Established in 1966, European Imports & Gifts is one of the largest dealers in the Midwest. Year-round Christmas village.

Directory to Secondary Market Dealers

IL **Gift MUSIC MINISTRY** 45

GIFT MUSIC, BOOK & COLLECTIBLES SHOPPE
420 Wallace, Chicago Heights, IL 60411

Phone: (708) 754-4387 - 24 hours
E-mail: jntschulte@rocketmail.com (want list only)
Website: www.beisecurity.com/gift (current specials)
Hours: Mon, Tues & Fri: 11-6, Wed, Thur, Sat: 10-2(CST)

Secondary: Precious Moments, Memories of Yesterday, M.I. Hummel, All God's Children, David Winter, ANRI, Tom Clark, Lladró, Cherished Teddies, Beanie Babies, Sports Impressions, Department 56, EKJ, Lilliput, Hallmark, Enesco and Carlton ornaments, Rockwell, Fontanini, Kurt S. Adler, Remington, Midwest, Swarovski, Schmid, Ron Lee, Seymour Mann, Wedgwood, Roman Seraphim Angels, Armani, Disney, CUI, Possible Dreams, Royal Doulton, Anheuser, Budweiser, Steinbach, toys, games, Bibles, plates, dolls, instruments, sheet music and books-1800s to current.

Noteworthy: Buy some outright. Worldwide locator service. In 1980, Joe and Terri Schulte began a nonprofit traveling religious music group. The store is an outgrowth of this ministry. Their desire is to bring quality religious and inspirational items into more homes, and to bring people of various cultures and backgrounds together. Besides being active on the secondary market, the store offers an appraisal service. They accept items and collections for tax donations. Visit their website above for current specials.

SECONDARY MARKET SPECIALIST CIB 1998-99

IL 46

La Galerie

1-815-899-2000

Primary & Secondary Dealer
for
Giuseppe Armani Figurines
H.Hargrove
Thomas Kinkade
Michel Delacroix
Fabienne Delacroix

219 W. State St.
Sycamore, IL 60178

IL **STONE'S HALLMARK SHOP** 47

"Specializing in Collectibles"
2508 S. Alpine, Rockford, IL 61108

Phone: (815) 399-4481 (800) 829-6406
Fax: (815) 399-0167
Hours: Mon-Fri: 9-9, Sat: 9-5:30, Sun: 11-5

Services: Locator service, layaway, Hallmark Gold Crown points with purchase. GCC, NALED, and Parade of Gifts catalog. **Web site: www.stoneshallmark.com** If you're currently not on our mailing list, please sign up through our website and receive a $10.00 store certificate.

Lines: Dept. 56, Snowbabies, Precious Moments, Charming Tails, Boyds, CT Adoption Center, Armani, **full selection of Ty Plush,** All God's Children, Dreamsicles, Warner Brothers, Seraphim Angels, Pocket Dragons, Bradford, Ashton-Drake, Mattel Barbies and much more.

Noteworthy: Stone's has been family owned and operated for over forty years. Century Circle Dealer for Enesco, Gold Paw Boyds Dealer and a Gold Key Dealer for Department 56. Redemption Center for most major collectibles. New memberships into most collector clubs are free. Call for details. In-store Department 56 club. Call for application. Some benefits include newsletter, price list, gift with purchase, and priority to limited and retired pieces. Several major artist events held each year.

SECONDARY MARKET SPECIALIST CIB 1998-99

IL 48

We have the latest.
And the greatest.

We provide the works of these artists in both primary and secondary markets.

H. Hargrove ~ Thomas Kinkade
Michel Delacroix ~ Fabienne Delacroix
& Guiseppe Armani figurines.

815/344-3390 ~ Fax:815/344-90740
27640 W. Volo Village Rd, Volo, IL 60073

Directory to Secondary Market Dealers

IN — 49

COLLECTABLES BY COIN INVESTORS

8275 Broadway Century Mall
Merrillville, IN 46410

Phone: (219) 738-2253
Fax: (219) 738-2363
Hours: Mon-Sat: 10-9, Sun: 11-5

Services: Buy outright. Layaways available. Visa, MasterCard, Discover, and AMEX accepted.

Secondary: Bradford Exchange plates, Ashton-Drake dolls, Mattel Barbies, Hawthorne houses, M.I. Hummel, and U.S. Coins.

Noteworthy: Collectables By Coin Investors has been a family owned and operated business for 16 years. As a Bradford dealer since 1990, they carry a complete line of Bradford products. They also carry Hamilton plates, Georgetown dolls, Barbies, and many other collectible doll lines. Over 1,000 plates and 300 dolls are on display. Collectables By Coin Investors is an Authorized Professional Coin Grading Dealer, offering free appraisals of coin collections.

IN — 50

GRAHAM'S CRACKERS

5981 E. 86th Street
Indianapolis, IN 46250

Phone: (800) 442-5727
(317) 842-5727
Fax: (317) 577-7777
Hours: Mon-Sat: 10-9, Sun: 12-5

Services: Buy retired pieces outright. Call for details. Host many artist appearances and special events throughout the year. Special orders are their specialty.

Secondary: Department 56 Gold Key Dealer, German Nutcrackers, Lilliput Lane, Mary Engelbreit, David Winter, Possible Dreams, Harbour Lights, Sarah's Attic, Precious Moments, Christopher Radko, Boyds Bears, Cherished Teddies, Byers' Choice, Lizzie High, M.I. Hummel, Rick Cain, Fontanini Blue Ribbon Dealer, Lang and Wise, Shelia's, Cat's Meow, North American Bear. Over 90 lines!

Noteworthy: Opened in 1986, Graham's Crackers is a Collector's Paradise, with over 20,000 square feet. They specialize in personal service, exquisite collectibles, collector clubs and seasonal merchandise for **EVERY** holiday. Interested collectors may call to have their name included on the mailing list.

IN — 51

MARKER'S HUMMELS

P.O. Box 66
603 W. South Street
Bremen, IN 46506

THE ORIGINAL "HUMMEL" FIGURES

Phone: (219) 546-3111
Hours: Mon-Sat: Best to call evenings 6-9

Services: Buy and sell outright. No consignment.

Secondary: M.I. Hummel figurines only.

Noteworthy: Marker's has been specializing in M.I. Hummel figurines for over 20 years. They stock current figurines for the beginning collector as well as Crown, Full Bee, and stylized trademarks. Marker's also maintains a stock of rare M.I. Hummel figurines which includes internationals. They have a close working relationship with Goebel because of their many trips to Germany, and the staff will be glad to answer any questions about Hummels or Goebel. Marker's recommends a visit to the Donald Stephens Museum in the O'Hare Convention Center to see some of the rare M.I. Hummel figurines they can provide for your collection.

SECONDARY MARKET SPECIALIST CIB 1998-99

IN — 52

ROSE MARIE'S

1119 Lincoln Avenue
Evansville, IN 47714
MEMBER OF BBB, NALED & GCC

Phone: (800) 637-5734 (812) 423-7557
Fax: (812) 423-7578 (call first)
Website: http://www.rosemaries.com
Hours: Mon-Sat: 10-5, Fri: 10-7
(Nov. & Dec.)
Mon-Fri: 10-7, Sat: 10-5, Sun: 12-5

Services: Buy/sell exchange. Listed price plus 10%. Accepts Visa, MasterCard, American Express and Discover plus 4%. Fully guaranteed. Dealers welcome.

Secondary: All Department 56, Disney Classics, M.I. Hummel, Armani, Swarovski and many more.

Noteworthy: Looking for a way to aid her missionary sons, Rose Marie Hillenbrand began selling religious figurines from a restored wardrobe in her living room in 1958. Today, over 39 years later, Rose Marie's specializes in assisting the collector in gift giving and in the acquisition of fine collectibles. The store services and supports over 35 collectors clubs. ***Notice to all Collector Club Members, "We pay your club dues for you."** Call for details.

SECONDARY MARKET SPECIALIST CIB 1998-99

Directory to Secondary Market Dealers

IA 53

Jerry's

NOVELTIES & COLLECTIBLES

BEER STEINS • NASCAR • APPAREL

24 Central Avenue NE
Le Mars, IA 51031

Phone: (712) 546-5060
(800) 914-9059
Fax: (712) 546-5059
E-mail: jerrys@willinet.net
Website: http://www.jerrys-collectibles.com
Hours: Mon-Fri: 9-5, Sat: 9-3

Services: Buy/Sell/Trade. Locator service available. Visa, MasterCard, American Express and Discover accepted. Worldwide shipping. Friendly and knowledgeable sales staff.

Secondary: Anheuser-Busch steins, plates & figurines, ACTION/RCCA die-cast race cars, Georgia Marketing Promotions die-cast Sprint cars, Ertl die-cast banks, ceramic steins by CUI.

Noteworthy: Jerry's Novelties & Collectibles is an authorized secondary market dealer and a Club Redemption Center for the Anheuser-Busch Collectors' Club. They specialize in older retired Anheuser-Busch steins and decanters, as well as all current issues.

IA 54

JOY'S TREASURES

108 5th Street
West Des Moines, IA 50265

Phone: (515) 279-5975
(888) 827-4319
Fax: (515) 279-5975

Services: Buy/Sell/Trade. Some consignments. Personal checks, money orders, Visa, MasterCard, Discover accepted. Items shipped UPS insured.

Secondary: Anheuser-Busch, Ertl.

Noteworthy: Joy's Treasures is owned and operated by Joy and Jerry Broman who try to locate any stein that a collector may need. They do insurance appraisals. Joy's Treasures also carries glasses, trays, signs, mirrors, banks, and coasters.

IA 55

STAMPS 'N' STUFF™

2700 University #214, West De Moines, IA 50266-1461

Phone: (515) 224-1737 (Information)
(800) 999-5964 (Orders only)
Fax: (515) 226-1651
E-mail: b.koepp@earthlink.net
Hours: Mon-Fri: 10-6, Sat: 10-4

Stamps 'n' Stuff

Services: Buy outright. Free buy or sell list on request. Major credit cards accepted. Postage and insurance paid on orders over $300 in the continental U.S.

Secondary: Department 56 (Dickens, Christmas in the City, Snow Village, Alpine, New England, Snowbabies), ANRI, M.I. Hummel, Royal Doulton figurines and character jugs, U.S. and foreign stamps and coins.

Noteworthy: In 1977, Stamps 'N' Stuff began as a stamp and coin store in Kalamazoo, MI. Owners Barbara and Jerry Koepp dabbled in antiques, handling furniture and glassware. In 1982, they moved to Des Moines, opening a store specializing in collector stamps. In 1990, they were given their first Department 56 building, and an obsession was born! They have now moved to a larger store where they can display Department 56, Royal Doulton, M.I. Hummel, ANRI and other limited edition collectibles. Already well known at National and International Stamp Exhibitions, they now attend larger collectible shows in the Midwest. They guarantee your satisfaction.

SECONDARY MARKET SPECIALIST CIB 1998-99

KS 56

Gifts & Accents

Collectibles Our Specialty

9605 Metcalf Ave. Metcalf South Mall
Overland Park, KS 66212

SECONDARY MARKET SPECIALIST CIB 1998-99

Phone: (800) 822-8856 (913) 381-8856
Fax: (913) 381-1986
Hours: Mon - Sat: 10:00 am to 9:00 pm
Sunday: Noon to 5:30 pm (Central Standard Time)

Services: Consignment. Mail your list with asking price. 30% consignment fee. Visa, Mastercard, and Discover.

Lines: Precious Moments

Noteworthy: Gifts & Accents was established in 1980. The store is known for its popular "Swap & Sell" which takes place twice every year; Eight days before Mother's day and the Saturday before Thanksgiving. Typically, a collector will find retired pieces from Precious Moments, Dept. 56, Disney, M.I. Hummel, Boyd's, Cherished Teddies, plates, dolls, cottages, ornaments, and more. Gifts & Accents is a Century Circle Retailer and a member of Gift Creations Concepts.

Directory to Secondary Market Dealers

LA **DICKENS' EXCHANGE, INC.** 57

5150 Highway 22, Suite C-9
Mandeville, LA 70471

Phone: (504) 845-1954
(888) 337-7486
Fax: (504) 845-1873
Hours: Mon-Fri: 9-5:30, Sat: 10-2

Services: 10% commission paid by purchaser on consignment listings. Exchange sells outright-no commissions. Call for details.

Secondary: Department 56: Snow Village, Dickens Village, Christmas in the City, New England, Alpine, Little Town of Bethlehem, North Pole, Cold Cast Porcelains, Snowbabies and accessories.

Noteworthy: Lynda Blankenship began as a collector of Department 56 collectibles. Eventually, this led to the publishing of ***The Dickens' Exchange***, a reliable source for Department 56 news and a thriving exchange. Today, Lynda publishes a 32-page newsletter which boasts over 12,000 subscribers! She describes her newsletter as a place for collectors to meet and share their hobby. She is also the author of "Willage Mania," a 353-page color book for Department 56 collectors, and co-author of "Display Mania."

SECONDARY MARKET SPECIALIST CIB 1998-99

MD **THE GAME FACE GALLERY** 58

P.O. Box 5820
Baltimore, MD 21282-5820

Phone: (410) 486-6210
(800) 934-1414
Hours: Mon-Fri: 9-9, Sat-Sun: 10-6

Services: Buy/Sell/Locator service. Layaway available. MasterCard, Visa, American Express accepted.

Secondary: The Art of Sport, Gartlan, Salvino, Sports Impressions.

Noteworthy: Since 1992, The Game Face Gallery has specialized in the primary and secondary market of sports and entertainment collectibles by mail order. They are an authorized dealer for the lines listed above, primarily carrying cold-cast porcelain, cold-cast resin, bisque porcelain, pewter and bronze figurines. Owner Ernest Flax brings over 30 years of sports collecting knowledge to his customers. He is also a consultant for two sports figurine companies and a top sports card company. Flax prides himself on building long-term customer relationships and fulfilling collectors' needs. Catalogs and price lists available upon request.

SECONDARY MARKET SPECIALIST CIB 1998-99

MD **TIARA** 59

GIFTS

1675 Rockville Pike
Rockville, MD 20852

Phone: (301) 468-1122
(800) 74T-IARA
Fax: (301) 468-1352
E-mail: tiaragalleries@juno.com
Website: http://www.tiaragalleries.com
Hours: Mon-Fri: 10-9, Sat: 10-6, Sun: 12-5

Services: Retail and secondary market. Layaway available. Major credit cards accepted.

Secondary: Ebony Visions, Harmony Kingdom, Armani, Lladró, Swarovski, Waterford Society, Disney Classics, David Winter, Harbour Lights and Olszewski.

Noteworthy: Family owned and operated for 40 years, Tiara Gifts is one of the finest collectible stores in America. They are a Redemption Center for most major collectible lines. Visit their website for upcoming artist appearances and open houses. National Association of Limited Edition Dealers (NALED) member.

MA **FOSTERS'** 60

100 Pleasant Street
South Weymouth, MA 02190

Phone: (800) 439-3546 (781) 337-3546
Fax: (781) 331-6277
Hours: Mon-Sat: 10-5, Sun: 12-5

Services: Consignment. Some outright buying. Call for details. Visa, MasterCard, Discover, and American Express accepted. Fosters' will ship anywhere and has a 30-day layaway plan.

Secondary: Byers' Choice Carolers only.

Noteworthy: Fosters' carries Annalee dolls, Thomas Kinkade prints, Christopher Radko ornaments, Harmony Kingdom and Harbour Lights. **They are a club Redemption Center for Cat's Meow, Christopher Radko, Lizzie High, June McKenna, Steiff and Possible Dreams.** Fosters' is a Christopher Radko Rising Star dealer and a NALED member. For over 25 years, Fosters' has been a family run business, located 15 miles south of Boston in the historical village of South Weymouth. They pride themselves on having the largest year-round display of Byers' Choice Carolers on the East coast with an in-store museum of Carolers. Fosters' is a very unique store featuring fine collectibles, country home accessories and furniture.

SECONDARY MARKET SPECIALIST CIB 1998-99

Directory to Secondary Market Dealers

MA | 61

Linda's Originals & The Yankee Craftsmen

220 Rt. 6A Brewster MA 02631
Summer (9-9 Seven Days) Winter (9-5 Seven days)
Toll Free Order Line 1-800-385-4758

Services: Buy Out Right, Consignment for Byers' Choice, Swarovski and Harbour Lights. On-Line Classified also available.

Lines: Annalee, Armani, Boyds Bears, Byers' Choice, Cats Meow, Cherished Teddies, Dept 56, Disney Classics, Harmony Kingdom, Harbour Lights, Lladro, Lizzie High, Radko, Snow Babies, Spencer Collin, Swarovski, Thomas Kinkade, Wee Forest Folk.

SECONDARY MARKET SPECIALIST CIB 1998-99

Join our Free Collectible Clubs with your First purchase.
VISIT OUR ON-LINE CATALOG
AT HTTP://WWW.MY-COLLECTIBLES.COM

MA | 62

SECONDARY MARKET SPECIALIST CIB 1998-99

Phone: 1-413-663-3643
Fax: 1-413-663-5140
Email: nece@collectiblesbroker.com
Website: http://www.collectiblesbroker.com
Or Write: 201 Pine Avenue
Clarksburg, Ma. 01247-4640
Hours: M-F 3:00-9:00 ET, Anytime Weekends

Services: Subscribers receive six newsletters a year which include listings by artist of limited editions and retired pieces. Buyers pay 15% commission, 10% on larger pieces plus shipping costs, there are no seller or listing fees.

Lines: Barbie, Boyds Bears-all kinds, Byers' Choice, Cat's Meow, Charming Tails, Cherished Teddies, Dept.56, Disney Classics, Hallmark, Harbour Lights, Harmony Kingdom, June McKenna, Lee Sievers, Lefton, Precious Moments, Shelia's, Swarovski, Tim Wolfe, Tom Clark Gnomes and many others.

Noteworthy: Established in 1992, to sell secondary market collectibles Bob Dorman developed NECE with the rules of courteous, honest, fair and confidential personal service to all buyers and sellers. Checks, Mastercard & Visa. Serving collectors and retailers - they ship pieces insured worldwide.

MI | 63

BONNIE'S HALLMARK

108 N. Mitchell Street, Cadillac, MI 49601

Phone: (800) 968-6260
(616) 775-4282
Fax: (616) 775-7499
Website: www.bonniescollectibles.com
Hours: Mon-Sat: 9-7, Sun & Holidays: 10-4

Hallmark Gold Crown

Services: Buy/sell exchange, locator service. Ship UPS. Layaways. Free gift wrapping. Major credit cards accepted.

Secondary: All God's Children, Anchor Bay, Anheuser-Busch Collection, Annalee, Boyds Collection, Charming Tails, Cherished Teddies, Department 56, Disney Classics, Enesco Treasury Ornaments, David Frykman, Hallmark Keepsake Ornaments, Harbour Lights, Harmony Kingdom, Kiddie Car Classics, Lenox Crystal Collection, Lilliput Lane, Possible Dreams, Precious Moments, Rick Cain, Sarah's Attic, Seraphim Angels, Tim Wolfe, Tom Clark Gnomes, Williraye.

Noteworthy: Gold Crown Hallmark Store. Redemption Center for All God's Children, Anheuser-Busch Collection, Annalee, Boyds Collection, Cherished Teddies, Disney Classics, Enesco Treasury Ornaments, Hallmark Keepsake Ornaments, Harbour Lights, Leaf & Acorn, Lilliput Lane, Precious Moments, Santa Claus Network, Sarah's Attic, Seraphim Angels, Snowbabies, Tom Clark Gnomes. Extensively stocked.

SECONDARY MARKET SPECIALIST CIB 1998-99

MI | 64

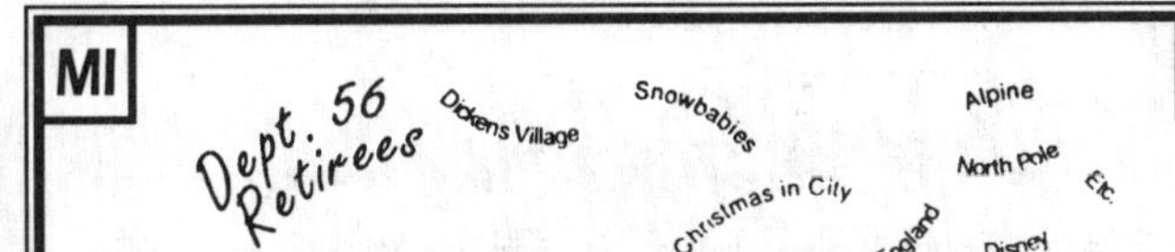

DEPARTMENT 56 RETIREES

Harry & June McGowan
6576 Balmoral Terrace, Clarkston, MI 48346

Phone: (248) 623-6664
Fax: (248) 623-6104
Website: www.dept56retirees.com
Hours: Flexible.

Services: Buy outright, "What's on our price list is in our possession" creating fast delivery. Price list always available on the Internet at www.dept56retirees.com. No added commission. Visa, MasterCard, Discover and American Express accepted. Daily UPS shipping year-round. Free shipping over $500.

Secondary: Department 56 (Dickens Village, Disney Village, Christmas in the City, New England, Alpine, North Pole and some Snow Village, Snowbabies, Snowbunnies, Merry Makers, Winter Silhouettes, All Through the House), Disney Classics.

SECONDARY MARKET SPECIALIST CIB 1998-99

Directory to Secondary Market Dealers

MI | 65

8170 Cooley Lake Road, White Lake, MI 48386

Phone: (800) 893-4494 (248) 360-4155
Fax: (248) 363-1360
E-mail: stewart@retiredfigurine.com
Website: www.retiredfigurine.com
Hours: Mon-Tues: 10-6, Wed: 10-8, Thurs-Sat: 10-6, Sun: 12-4

Services: Have large stock of items in store. Some consignments accepted. Buy outright. Exchange and locator service.

Secondary: Cherished Teddies, Disney Classics, Dreamsicles, Harmony Kingdom, Krystonia, **Lladró**, **M.I. Hummel**, PenDelfin, Precious Moments, **Royal Doulton**, **Swarovski**, **Department 56**, **Possible Dreams**, Prizm/Pipka Santas, Snowbabies, Creepy Hollow, Crinkle Claus, Beanie Babies, **Muffy Vanderbear**, Harbour Lights, Wee Forest Folk.

Noteworthy: Owners Stewart and Arlene Richardson have been dealing in collectibles for 10 years. They have an extensive background in Royal Doulton, M.I. Hummel, Precious Moments, Possible Dreams, and Department 56. In 1993, the Richardsons opened a showroom which stocks over 5,000 figurines. Visit their website at www.retiredfigurine.com.

SECONDARY MARKET SPECIALIST CIB 1998-99

MI | 66

TROY STAMP & COIN GIFTS & COLLECTIBLES

3275 Rochester Road Troy, MI 48083

Phone: (248) 528-1181
Fax: (248) 528-1565
Hours: Mon-Fri: 10-8, Sat: 10-5, Sun: 12-5

Services: Buy outright. Locator service.

Secondary: Bradford Exchange plates, Hamilton plates, Ashton-Drake dolls, Gorham dolls, Kaiser dolls, Marty Bell, Thomas Kinkade, Edna Hibel, Donald Zolan, Sandra Kuck, Masseria, Terry Redlin, Precious Moments, M.I. Hummel, Department 56 (all villages and accessories, Snowbabies, snowglobes, plates), David Winter, Lilliput Lane, Tom Clark, Emmett Kelly Jr., Krystonia, Enchantica, Randy Puckett Whales, Chilmark, Duncan Royale, Goebel Miniatures, Sarah's Attic, Lowell Davis, ANRI, Enesco Treasury ornaments, Salvino, Gartlan, Sports Impressions, Beanie Babies.

Noteworthy: Collectors may be fooled by this store's name, but, in fact, this firm carries more than 60 lines of figurines and is a Redemption Center for more than 20 collector clubs! Owners Tom and Alexa England have been in business since 1981. The firm offers a 60-day layaway plan, appraisel services, a preferred customer mailing list, and several incentive plans. Call for details.

SECONDARY MARKET SPECIALIST CIB 1998-99

MN | 67

Collectors Gallery

8306 Tamarack Village #401, Woodbury, Minnesota 55125

"The Place" for Collectibles

Phone: (800) 878-7868 or (612) 738-8351
Fax: (612) 738-6760
E-Mail: dancollect@aol.com
Web Site: http://www.collectorsgallery.com
Hours: M-F: 10-9, Sat: 9:30-6, Sun: 11-5 (Central Time)

SECONDARY MARKET SPECIALIST CIB 1998-99

Services: Competitive buyer of retired collectibles. Please send or fax list with prices desired. We accept Visa, MasterCard, Discover & Am Exp. FREE SHIPPING on all orders over $50.00.

Lines: Department 56, Lladro, Swarovski, David Winter, Armani, Boyd's Bears, JP EDITIONS, Kinkade, Forma Vitrum, Disney Classics, Loony Tunes, Harmony Kingdom, Krystonia, Snowbabies, Greenwich Workshop ... and more!

Noteworthy: Collectors Gallery, with over seventeen years experience, offers the Upper Midwest's largest selection of new and retired collectibles ... and we serve thousands of collectors from coast to coast. Our beautiful new 8,500 square foot store features a Lladro Millenium Gallery and a huge Department 56 Panorama Gallery. All major collector's clubs supported. Member GCC.

FREE Secondary Market Price Guides available on many lines. See our extensive Web Site for complete details.

MO | 68

Tra-Art, Ltd.

Your One Stop Collectibles Shop
421 West Miller Street
Jefferson City, MO 65101

Phone: (573) 635-8278
Hours: Tues-Fri: 10-6, Sat: 10-5
Phone: (573) 893-3779
(By appointment - after 7pm & weekends)

Services: Primary & secondary market. From stock or consignment. Occasionally buy outright. Layaway, Visa and MasterCard accepted. UPS insured shipping. USPS available.

Secondary: Primary and secondary market for Anheuser-Busch, Anna Perenna, Ashton-Drake, Bergsma, Bing & Grondahl, Bradford, Hadley House, Hamilton, Hibel, Knowles, Sandra Kuck, Lilliput, Moss, Old World Christmas, Possible Dreams, Pipka, Reco, Redlin, Rockwell, Roman, Shelia's, Spencer Collin, Tudor Mint, Zolan...More!

Noteworthy: Collecting since the early '70s, owners Don and Joyce Trabue have more than 25 years of experience in the collectible business. In 1980, they formed Tra-Art, Ltd. and expanded to a second location in 1993. They carry many older collectibles and have an inventory of over 9,000 collector plates. Club Redemption Center for many lines. Member of NALED. Watch for their Internet access. Personalized Service!

SECONDARY MARKET SPECIALIST CIB 1998-99

Directory to Secondary Market Dealers

MT | 69

THE SHIP'S BELL

101 E. 6th Ave.
Helena, MT 59601

Phone: **(406) 443-4470**
Fax: **(406) 442-1800**
E-mail: **AOL-ShirleyLou**
Hours: **Mon-Fri: 11-5:30, Sat: 11-4 (MTN)**

Services: Available for current and past issues. Payment in money order or certified checks get immediate shipment whereas personal checks have to clear. No outright buying.

Secondary: Bradford, Hamilton, Reco, M.I. Hummel, Ernst, Perillo, Villeroy & Boch, Christian Bell, Winston Roland, Redlin, Lowell Davis, Ashton-Drake dolls and more.

Noteworthy: Established in 1973, The Ship's Bell is an authorized Bradford and Reco dealer. A large plate gallery is featured, in addition to other collectible lines. They are secondary market specialists for the lines listed above and all other inquiries are welcome. Shirley DeWolf and her staff pride themselves on adding a personal touch as they work with each and every collector.

NJ | 70

PRESTIGE COLLECTIONS

The Mall at Short Hills, Short Hills, NJ 07078
Bridgewater Commons, Bridgewater, NJ 08807
The Westchester, White Plains, NY 10601
Garden State Plaza, Paramus, NJ 07652

Phone: **(800) 227-7979** **Fax:** **(973) 597-9408**
Hours: **Mon-Sat: 10-9:30, Sun: 11-6**

Services: Mail your list with asking price, buy outright. In-home or office shows. Layaway, gift wrapping, special orders, and delivery available. Visa, MC, Amex, Discover.

Secondary: Millenium Lladró, Armani, Swarovski, Department 56, Snowbabies, Precious Moments, Disney Classics, Lalique, Daum, Caithness, Waterford, Lenox Classics, Boehm, Lilliput, Limoges Boxes, M.I. Hummel, Michael's (Déjà Vu), Harbour Lights, Radko, Kinkade, Cherished Teddies, and much more.

Noteworthy: Established in 1977, Prestige Collections has grown to four locations in the finest regional malls in New Jersey and New York. They are a service oriented business that sells fine gifts and collectibles from $5.00-$25,000. Prestige has some of the finest selections of the best brand name collectibles. A Redemption Center for most major collectibles. Artists and collector events throughout the year. They can help you with corporate and personal shopping. JUST CALL!

NJ | 71

UNIQUE TREASURES

Olde Lafayette Village
Box 106
Lafayette, NJ 07848

Phone: **(973) 579-9190**
Fax: **(973) 827-7512**
Hours: **Mon-Sat: 10-6, Sun: 11-6**
Open Fri. Nights

Services: Buy/Sell. Sell for YOU. Appraisals on Tudor Mint. Personal checks, Visa, MasterCard, Discover and American Express accepted.

Secondary: Tudor Mint, Cow Town, Pigs Village, Little Cheesers, Lefton lighthouses, Santa's Crystal Valley. All types of steins, including Budweiser.

Noteworthy: Unique Treasures has been in the industry for over seven years. Tudor Mint Club Members receive discounts except on club and road show pieces.

NY | 72

Collectibly Yours

80 E Route 59
Spring Valley, NY 10977

Phone: **(800) 863-7227 (out of NY)**
(914) 425-9244
Hours: **Tues-Sat: 10-6, Sun. by chance.**
Holiday hours.

Services: Retail store and mail order. Visa, MasterCard, Discover accepted. NO APPRAISALS.

Secondary: Swarovski, Precious Moments, Lladró, Ebony Visions, M.I. Hummel, Wee Forest Folk, Memories of Yesterday, Cherished Teddies, All God's Children, Collector's plates, Disney Classics, Thomas Kinkade, Lowell Davis, Lilliput Lane, David Winter, Sports Impressions, Department 56 (all Villages, accessories, Snowbabies, Merry Makers). Dolls: Yolanda Bello, Annette Himstedt, Ashton-Drake, Cabbage Patch, Robin Woods, Dolls by Jerri, Gorham, Susan Wakeen, Georgetown, Hamilton, North American Bear, Virginia Turner, Wendy Lawton.

Noteworthy: Extensive selection of dolls. Department 56 Gold Key dealer, Kinkade Premier Center, NALED, GCC (Gift Creation Concepts) retailer. In collectible business since 1978.

Directory to Secondary Market Dealers

NY **Glorious Treasures Ltd.** 73

Mail: 9206 Avenue L #105; Brooklyn, N.Y. 11236
Phone: 718-241-8185 Fax: 718-241-8184

Glorious Treasures ONLINE
http://members.aol.com/GlorTreas

E-Mail: GlorTreas@aol.com
Virtually connected and on-line 24 hours a day!

Services: THE worldwide virtual dealer of beautiful and rare collectible and gift items from around the world. Item search and find. Collection and estate apprasials and sales. Items bought and traded as needed. Sales by personal check, money orders, and all major credit cards. All transactions in US funds and instruments only. Sales tax as required by law & shipping extra.

Lines: OLD & NEW: Hamilton and Bradford plates. Ashton-Drake dolls, Hummel, Disney, Schmid, Royal-Doulton, Donald Zolan, Sandra Kuck, Edna Hibel, Gregory Perillo, Francis Hook, Red Skelton, Dave Grossman, Gorham, Norman Rockwell, Anna Perenna, Lowell Davis, Bessie Pease Gutmann, ANRI, Jan Hagara, Maud Humphrey Bogart, Ted DeGrazia, Enesco, Lladro, Goebel, Olszewski and Sebastian miniatures, Emmett Kelly Jr., Fred Stone, Pat Buckley Moss, Terry Redlin, Donald Polland, John McClelland and Cabbage Patch.

Noteworthy: Established in 1977. THEMES: Star Trek, Star Wars, Beatles, Elvis Presley, Gone With The Wind, I Love Lucy, The Honeymooners, Barbie, Wizard of Oz, other popular television and movie subjects.
RELIGIOUS: Roman. Used records/tapes and memorabilia.
SPORTS: Sports Impressions, Gartlan, Scoreboard, Hackett.
BEER: Budweiser & other beer stuff. Rare stamps and coins.

SECONDARY MARKET SPECIALIST CIB 1998-99

Visit our WWW collectibles gallery!

NY 74

THE LIMITED EDITION
The Gift and Collectible Authority
2170 Sunrise Highway
Merrick, NY 11566

Phone: (800) 645-2864 (516) 623-4400
Fax: (516) 867-3701
www.thelimitededition.com
email: tle@thelimitededition
Hours: Mon-Sat: 10-6, Fri til 9 pm, Sun: 11-5

SECONDARY MARKET SPECIALIST CIB 1998-99

Services: No consignments. Buy outright. Mail your list with asking price. Visa, MasterCard, American Express, Discover.

Lines: Annalee, Cherished Teddies, Christopher Radko, Collector Plates, David Winter, Department 56 Villages, EKJ, Harmony Kingdom, Krystonia, Lladró, M.I Hummel, Precious Moments, Snowbabies, Swarovski and Walt Disney Classics Collection.

Noteworthy: Over the past 23 years, The Limited Edition has become one of the most important sources of primary and secondary market Collectibles in the country. The Limited Edition has a very knowledgeable and caring sales staff. All purchases are recorded on computer so collectors can be informed of new releases, retired items, limited editions, special offers and more. The Limited Edition is a member of GAA, BBB, NALED, & GCC.

NY 75

Main St., PO Box 201, Essex, NY 12936

Phone: (800) 898-6098 (518) 963-4347
Website: http://www.DiscoverHK.com
Hours: 10-5 (seven days per week)

Services: Retail store. Worldwide web access for 24 hr. on-line shopping and secondary market services. Flat fee for shipping and free shipping once total purchases reach $300. Personal checks, money orders, Visa, MasterCard and Amex accepted. Enjoy the personalized service your collection deserves.

Secondary: Harmony Kingdom. Queens Empress Dealer with over 400 pieces in stock.

Noteworthy: For four years, Natural Goods & Finery has been specializing in Harmony Kingdom collectibles. As a result, many loyal customers enjoy knowledge of new issues, rare and retired pieces and low numbered limited editions. They have one of the largest selections in both current and retired pieces. Call for information on joining their "Treasure Jest of the Month Club."

SECONDARY MARKET SPECIALIST CIB 1998-99

NY **Village Collectors** 76

12 Hart Place
Dix Hills, N.Y. 11746

Phone: 516-242-2457
Fax: 516-243-4607
E-Mail: dcrupi@delphi.com
Hours: M-F Days: Answering Service
Evenings: 5:30 - 10:00 EST
Weekends: 11:00 - 10:00 EST

SECONDARY MARKET SPECIALIST CIB 1998-99

Services: Offering a complete secondary market service. Including a FREE listing service, consignments, or outright buying of your Department 56 SECONDARY MARKET collectibles, UPS insured shipping, an inspection period, layaways, gift certificates, & gift wrapping. Our commission on listings or consignments is 15%, which is included in our selling price. A FREE price quote or listing is only a call away! We accept Visa, MasterCard, Discover, American Express, & checks.

Lines: All Department 56 Retired or Limited Edition collectibles. Including Villages, Snowbabies & Giftware.

Noteworthy: We started collecting D56 during Christmas of '89 and have been helping collectors find the piece of their dreams since 1992. As my husband always says "Donna collects the little white D56 sticker."
We are always willing to answer your D56 related questions.

Directory to Secondary Market Dealers

NC | **77**

CALLAHAN'S OF CALABASH

9973 Beach Drive
Calabash, NC 28467

Phone: (800) 344-3816
Fax: (910) 579-7209
Website: www.callahansgifts.com
Hours: Daily: 9am-10pm (Summer)
Daily: 9am-9pm (Winter)

Services: Price list available. Items taken on consignment with 15% commission fee added to the selling price.

Secondary: As a Department 56 "Gold Key" Dealer, Callahan's specialty is Department 56 Villages, accessories and Snowbabies. They also offer a secondary market for Wee Forest Folk and a growing Christopher Radko market.

Noteworthy: Come visit their 30,000 sq. ft. shopping extravaganza, featuring the 2,000 sq. ft. award-winning Department 56 room. In 1996, as a Rising Star Dealer, they proudly introduced their Christopher Radko Room. Gold-Wing Seraphim Angel dealer. Visit their website at www.callahansgifts.com.

SECONDARY MARKET SPECIALIST CIB 1998-99

OH | **78**

Collectible Exchange, Inc.™

Retired & Limited Edition Collectibles

Phone: (800) 752-3208
Fax: (330) 542-9644
Hours: M-F 9:00 a.m. - 8:00 p.m.
Sat: 10:00 a.m. - 4:00 p.m.

SECONDARY MARKET SPECIALIST CIB 1998-99

Services: International Secondary Market Listing Service. Serving individuals and dealers. No cost no obligation listing service. Personal check, money order, Visa, MasterCard, Discover or American Express accepted. Toll Free 800 Service.

Lines: Boyds Bears, Byers' Choice, Charming Tails, Cherished Teddies, David Winter, Department 56, Disney Classics, Dreamsicles, Emmett Kelly Jr., Forma Vitrum, Hallmark, Harbour Lights, Hummel, Jan Hagara, June McKenna, Kiddie Car Classics, Krystonia, Lefton, Lilliput, Lowell Davis, Lynn West Santas, Maud Humphrey, Memories of Yesterday, Midwest, Olszewski, Precious Moments, Shellia's, Swarovski Crystal, Wee Forest Folk and Wysocki.

Noteworthy: Started in 1989 as the first Independent Nationwide Secondary Service. Has grown to a large scale International Service trading over $2 million annually. Member of original CIB Panel. Referred by many major collectible manufactures.

OH | **79**

182 Front Street, Berea, OH 44017

Phone: (440) 826-4169 (800) 344-9299
Fax: (440) 826-0839
E-mail: yworrey@aol.com
Hours: Mon-Fri: 9-6, Sat: 10-5

Services: Buy/Sell/Trade/Appraise. MasterCard, Visa, Discover and American Express accepted.

Secondary: Royal Doulton, Department 56, M.I. Hummel, Lladró, David Winter, Lilliput Lane, Wee Forest Folk, Disney Classics, Swarovski, Precious Moments, Bing & Grondahl, Royal Copenhagen, Cherished Teddies, Harmony Kingdom, Harbour Lights, Franklin Mint Die Cast Cars, Looney Tunes Spotlight Collection, Lenox Classics, Beanie Babies.

Noteworthy: Colonial House of Collectibles has been in business for over 23 years. For the past 11 years, they have been located in an 1873 house in the southwest suburb of Cleveland. A year-round Christmas room is always on display. They are a Redemption Center for collector club pieces.

SECONDARY MARKET SPECIALIST CIB 1998-99

OH | **80**

House of Fine Gifts & Collectibles
624 Great Northern Mall
N. Olmsted, OH 44070

Phone: (440) 777-0116 (800) 777-4802
Fax: (440) 777-0116
Website: www.giftgarden.com
Hours: Mon-Sat: 10-9, Sun: 11-6

Services: Buy/Sell. No consignments. Visa, MasterCard, Discover and American Express accepted.

Secondary: Armani, ANRI, Budweiser, Disney Classics, M.I. Hummel, Swarovski, Pocket Dragons, Robert Olszewski, Animation Art, Emmett Kelly Jr., Ron Lee, Precious Moments, Cherished Teddies, Collector plates, Polonaise, Christopher Radko, Greenwich Workshop Collection, Chilmark, Legends, Krystonia, eggspressions!, Department 56, Steinbach, and Caithness paperweights.

Noteworthy: Gift Garden has been in business since 1970, serving collectors all over the country. Gift Garden showcases the best artists and creations of fine collectibles in the world. Call for further information on their artist events throughout the year. Will pay your collector club dues. Call for details on your club.

SECONDARY MARKET SPECIALIST CIB 1998-99

Directory to Secondary Market Dealers

OH 81

"a unique treasure of a gift shop"
State Route 113, Birmingham, OH 44816

Phone: (440) 965-5420
Hours: Tues-Sat: 10-6, Sun: 12-5 (except Jan/Feb)
Closed Mon (except Dec.)

Services: Specialist in Norman Rockwell figurines and plates. Occasionally buy Rockwell collections or individual pieces. No consignments. Free appraisals for insurance. Ship UPS daily. Visa and MasterCard accepted.

Secondary: Norman Rockwell figurines and plates.

Noteworthy: Little Red Gift House has become known nationwide as a major source of Norman Rockwell collectibles, both new and older pieces. In stock is a large inventory of retired, discontinued, and limited edition Rockwell figurines. Listing of in-stock Rockwell items is available upon request. Little Red Gift House also carries M.I. Hummel, Precious Moments, Disney Classics, Thomas Kinkade, Department 56, collector plates, Cherished Teddies, Sports collectibles, Ray Day, Memories of Yesterday, Seraphim Angels, Possible Dreams, Bradford, Anheuser-Busch steins, Emmett Kelly, Amish Heritage, Jan Hagara, Pretty As A Picture, and Snowbabies.

SECONDARY MARKET SPECIALIST CIB 1998-99

OH 82

MILLER'S HALLMARK & GIFT GALLERY

1322 North Barron Street, Eaton, OH 45320-1016

Phone: (937) 456-4151
Fax: (937) 456-7851
Hours: Mon-Fri: 9am-9pm,
Sat: 9-6, Sun: 12-5

Services: No consignments. Buy outright. Crystal Report and Brokerage. Collectibles Auctions: some produced on consignment. Expert appraisal services. Call for details.

Secondary: Precious Moments, M.I. Hummel, Swarovski, Department 56, Cherished Teddies, Christopher Radko, Hallmark Ornaments, Snowbabies, Boyds Bears, Dreamsicles, Cat's Meow, Swarovski Crystal Brokerage.

Noteworthy: Miller's Hallmark & Gift Gallery has grown to four stores strong, from a specialty store featuring M.I. Hummel figurines, into a full service Hallmark and collectibles Showcase Gallery. Dean A. Genth is an Associate Member of the American Society of Appraisers and has been appraising M.I. Hummel figurines for over 15 years. Private and personal appraisals are done by Mr. Genth for insurance purposes. The Miller Company and Dean A. Genth have served as counsel to many insurance companies and individuals that need expert advice on matters related to collectibles.

SECONDARY MARKET SPECIALIST CIB 1998-99

OH 83

Phone: (800) 458-6585 (419) 472-7673
Website: www.rochelles.com
Hours: Mon-Sat: 10-9, Sun: 12-6

Services: No consignments, buy outright. Mail your list with item number, description, and mold mark (if applicable), and Rochelle's will respond with an offer in writing A.S.A.P. MasterCard, Visa, Discover accepted. Lay-away plan available. Free gift wrapping. Redemption Center for most clubs.

Secondary: Precious Moments, Cherished Teddies, Boyds Bears, Harbour Lights, Department 56, Disney Classics, Swarovski, and much more.

Noteworthy: Established in 1977, Rochelle's is the best collectible store in northwest Ohio, in the area's best fashion mall. Rochelle's extensive customer list includes collectors from all 50 states. All purchases are kept in a "customer history" file so collectors can be informed when new items in their collection are available. They are a full-service collectible store, carrying most lines, and they accept advance reservations and special orders on most items. Rochelle's is a member of NALED and GCC.

SECONDARY MARKET SPECIALIST CIB 1998-99

OK 84

PICTORIAL TREASURES

SECONDARY MARKET SPECIALIST CIB 1998-99

Your Limited Edition Art Print Specialist

Current and Sold-out Prints for over 100 Artists such as Kinkade, Doolittle, Lyman, Wysocki, Moss

Pictorial Treasures is the largest secondary market Ltd. Edition Art Exchange open to both the retail dealer and private collector. "For Sale" listings always accepted. **Free price quotes** available for over **3000** art prints. All art prints are inspected and come with certificates.

Call 918 287-2668 today for friendly, reliable service.

Thomas Kinkade newsletter only $12.95 / year.
Bi-monthly articles include what's new, what's sold-out, seasonal and collector print favorites, what's hot, special events, secondary market price lists and much more.

PICTORIAL TREASURES
P.O. Box 1586
Pawhuska, OK 74056

On-line gallery
http://www.artontheweb.com
e-mail:staff@artontheweb.com

Directory to Secondary Market Dealers

OK **85**

SHIRLEY'S COLLECTIBLE EXCHANGE

1500 Ward Rd.
Ardmore, OK 73401

Phone: **(580) 226-6228**
Hours: **Daily: 9-9**

Services: Buy/Sell. Locator service.

Secondary: Mattel Barbies, Disney Classics, Swarovski, Lefton Colonial Village, M.I. Hummel, Department 56, Cherished Teddies, Boyds Bears, Precious Moments, Madame Alexander, Tom Clark, Tim Wolfe, Lee Sievers, Armani, All God's Children, Margaret Furlong, Dreamsicles, Seraphim Angels, Fontanini, and Patchville Bunnies.

Noteworthy: Shirley and Bob Fast owned and operated Shirley's Gifts Inc. for 16 years. Their store specialized in both primary and secondary market for most major collectible lines. Shirley recently retired to concentrate solely on the secondary market. Her customers can be assured that she will continue to provide that personal touch and knowledge for which she is known.

OK **86**

WINTER IMAGES

3008 Hilltop, Muskogee, OK 74403

Phone: **(918) 683-3488**
Fax: **(918) 683-2325 (24 hrs.)**
E-mail: **jeanine@netsites.net**
Hours: **Weekends and after 4pm weekdays**

Services: Secondary market exchange, listing retired pieces to buy or sell. Major credit cards accepted. If paying by check, prefer money order or certified check. Order is held for one week if paid by personal check.

Secondary: All collectible lines including: David Winter, Precious Moments, M.I. Hummel, Hallmark, Lowell Davis, Swarovski, Lladró, DeGrazia, Disney, Department 56, Lilliput Lane, Enesco, Rockwell, Lucy and Me, ANRI, Cherished Teddies, Boyds, Chilmark, Calico Kittens, Tom Clark, Armani, Chapeau Noelle, Charming Tails, Harmony Kingdom, and others.

Noteworthy: Jeanine Barrett and her children, Jamie and Kirk Brown, began their business in 1992, specializing in David Winter. The business has expanded to a secondary market exchange, helping customers buy and sell in all collectible lines. Winter Images prides itself on personalized service, including insurance appraisals.

OR **87**

CHRISTMAS TREASURES

52959 McKenzie Highway
Blue River, OR 97413

Phone: **(800) 820-8189**
Orders Only
(541) 822-3516 Information
Fax: **(541) 822-3516**
E-mail: **santa@continet.com**
Website: **http://www.christmas-treasures.com**
Hours: **Daily: 10-6 (PST)**

Services: Retail and secondary market. Credit cards accepted.

Secondary: Department 56, Byers' Choice, Old World Christmas Ornaments and Santa Lights, Christopher Radko, Roman Seraphim Angels, Duncan Royale Santas, Boyds Bears, Melody In Motion, Steinbach Nutcrackers, Christmas Reproduction Memories of Santa, Raggedy Ann and Andy cloth dolls by Applause, Possible Dreams Santas.

Noteworthy: Christmas Treasures brings you the most treasured items for gift giving and collecting. Experience the Old World charm not only during the holidays, but all through the year. Buying older retired pieces outright from the following lines: Byers' Choice, Old World Christmas Santa Lights, Steinbach Nutcrackers and Christmas Reproduction Memories of Santa. Serving customers since 1993.

PA **88**

BOB LAMSON BEER STEINS, INC.

509 N. 22nd Street
Allentown, PA 18104

Phone: **(800) 435-8611**
(610) 435-8611
Fax: **(610) 435-8188**
Hours: **Mon-Fri: 9am-9pm,**
Sat: 10-4

Services: Buy/Sell/Trade. Terms available upon request for larger purchases. Please inquire.

Secondary: Anheuser-Busch, Michelob, Budweiser, Bud Light, Coors, Strohs, Miller, steins and related collectibles with beer affiliations, i.e. neons, lights, clocks, signs, tap knobs and mirrors.

Noteworthy: Incorporated in 1990, Bob Lamson Beer Steins, Inc. is owned and operated solely by the Lamson family. The company has a retail store located in Allentown, Pennsylvania, and also ships orders to every state in the nation and to Canada. Collectors should call with any additional questions they have regarding the company. Bob Lamson Beer Steins is an Anheuser-Busch Collectors Club Redemption Center.

Directory to Secondary Market Dealers

PA **CRAYON SOUP** 89

King of Prussia Plaza, King of Prussia, PA 19406

Phone: (610) 265-0458 (800) 552-3760
Fax: (610) 265-2979
Hours: Mon-Sat: 10-9:30,
Sun: 11-6

Services: Buy outright

Secondary: All God's Children, Lladró, Department 56 (Heritage Village and accessories, Snowbabies), Lilliput Lane, EKJ, David Winter, Precious Moments, PenDelfin, Swarovski, Steinbach Nutcrackers, M.I. Hummel, Memories of Yesterday, Olszewski Miniatures, Anheuser and German Gentz steins.

Noteworthy: The formation of Crayon Soup in 1982 was a natural, considering that owners Joe and Trish Zawislack had already been collecting for 30 years! The store started in a mall kiosk, with the couple selling stickers and novelties geared toward children. Eventually, the Zawislacks entered the collectibles market. The name, Crayon Soup, was the brainchild of Trish, who formulated the name, thinking the couple would start an educational store for children. Today, the store is a Redemption Center for several collectible lines. Hummel enthusiasts will be delighted to view over 400 Hummels in stock. Crayon Soup hosts 40 collector events including artist appearances and organizes in-store collector clubs. Information on new and retired products and collectors clubs is available free of charge.

PA **Lighthouse Trading Company** 90

Worldwide Secondary Market Brokerage

112 Elio Circle, Limerick, PA 19468

Phone: (888) 409-9336 (toll free)
Fax: (610) 409-9336
On-line: www.lighthousetrading.com
Hours: Mail Order - M-F: 1:30-8:30pm (EST)

Services: Buy/Sell. Secondary/Market Service. Buys *Harbour Lights* Outright. Dealers Welcome. Visa, MasterCard, Discover Accepted.

Lines: *Harbour Lights, Harmony Kingdom, Cheryl Spencer Collin, Ebony Visions* and *Swarovski.*

Noteworthy: Lighthouse Trading Co. is the original secondary market of Harbour Lights lighthouse collectibles. We take pride in providing the best price and personalized service when buying or selling retired collectibles. Owned by Matt Rothman, a noted columnist for *Collectors Mart* magazine who writes on real estate collectibles.

Matt also writes a column on Harbour Lights collectibles for *Lighthouse Digest*.

PA **SAM'S STEINS & COLLECTIBLES** 91

2207 Lincoln Highway East RT 30
Lancaster, PA 17602

Phone: (717) 394-6404
E-mail: samssteins@msn.com
Hours: Mon-Wed & Sat: 10-6
Thurs & Fri: 10-8, Sun: 11-5
Closed Sun & Mon (Jan-Mar)

Services: Buy outright. Mail order catalog available, send two $.32 stamps.

Secondary: Specializes in beer steins (Anheuser-Busch, Miller, Coors, Strohs, Pabst, Hamm's, Yuengling, large selection of German beer steins) and brewery advertising items (steins, neons, signs, tap markers and mirrors). Authorized Anheuser-Busch Dealer. Sam also carries Cavanagh Coca-Cola Cubs, Ande Rooney porcelain signs, First Gear, ERTL, and Spec cast collector trucks and banks.

Noteworthy: Sam's Steins & Collectibles, located 1/8 mile from Dutch Wonderland, has been in business since 1967. A collector himself, owner Sam May houses one of the largest displays of beer memorabilia in the United States. Over 900 different U.S. and German steins are on display, including the stein in the Guinness Book of Records -- 4' tall which holds 8.45 gallons of beer.

PA **WORLDWIDE COLLECTIBLES AND GIFTS** 92

P.O. Box 158, 2 Lakeside Avenue
Berwyn, PA 19312-0158

Phone: (800) 222-1613 (610) 644-2442
Fax: (610) 889-9549
Hours: Mon-Sat: 10-5, order desk open 24 hrs.

Services: A 64-page mail order catalog available free, upon request. Call for specific quotes. Prompt payment on all items purchased. Prompt delivery on items ordered.

Secondary: Swarovski, Lladró, Department 56, Disney Classics, M.I. Hummel, David Winter, Duncan Royale, Steiff, collector plates, bells, collector club pieces and many others.

Noteworthy: Worldwide Collectibles is a full service company established in 1975. They deal in current and secondary market pieces and maintain a large inventory on all lines carried. The Worldwide staff is actively involved with major insurers for replacement and estimate valuation purposes. Appraisals and references are available upon request.

Directory to Secondary Market Dealers

SC | 93

1370 Broughton Street, Orangeburg, SC 29115

Phone: (803) 536-4176 (800) 822-5556 (orders only)
Fax: (803) 531-2007
Hours: Mon-Fri: 9-6, Sat: 9-5,
Sun: 1:30-5:30 (Nov. & Dec. only)

Services: Buy/Sell/Trade/Consignments. Visa, MasterCard, Discover and American Express accepted. Shipping available.

Secondary: Department 56 (Snow Village, Dickens Village, New England Village, Alpine Village, North Pole, Christmas in the City, Disney Parks Village, Snowbabies, Snowbunnies, All Through the House, Winter Silhouettes, Merry Makers), Harbour Lights, Shelia's, Keepers, Byers' Choice, and Seraphim Classics.

Noteworthy: Broughton Christmas Shoppe, in business since 1983, is a family run business, catering to their customers' collectible needs. All staff members are collectors themselves, and offer friendly, knowledgeable service. Broughton's is a Gold Key Dealer for Department 56, a Platinum Dealer for Shelia's and an Earn Your Wings Dealer for Roman, Inc.

SECONDARY MARKET SPECIALIST CIB 1998-99

TN | 94

BARBARA'S GATLINBURG SHOPS

Barbara's Elegants, The John Cody Gallery
The Gatlinburg Shop
511, 716, 963 Parkway, Gatlinburg, TN 37738

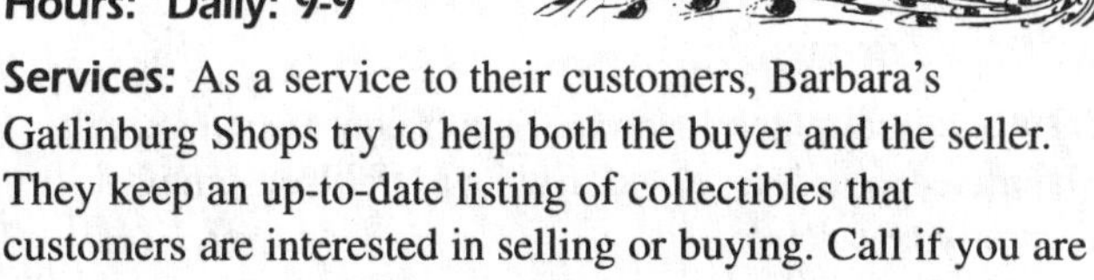

Phone: (800) 433-1132
Hours: Daily: 9-9

Services: As a service to their customers, Barbara's Gatlinburg Shops try to help both the buyer and the seller. They keep an up-to-date listing of collectibles that customers are interested in selling or buying. Call if you are interested in more information. There is no charge for the listing. A 25% commission is charged if a sale is made.

Secondary: All God's Children, Armani, Byers' Choice, Boyds Bearstone Bears, Cades Cove Cabin, Cairn Gnomes, Charming Tails, Cherished Teddies, Chilmark, Christopher Radko, Department 56, David Winter, Disney Classics, Greenwich Workshop, Harmony Kingdom, Hudson, John Cody Prints, Legends, Mark Hopkins, Mickey & Co., Sandicast, Swarovski, Wee Forest Folk, plus many more exciting lines!

Noteworthy: Barbara's started in 1977 as a small retailer. They have now grown to three shops with a large mailing list composed of customers from 49 states and several foreign countries. Barbara's ships daily, provides appraisals, and mails brochures and catalogs to customers interested in a particular line. "Our sales consultants are committed to you!"

SECONDARY MARKET SPECIALIST CIB 1998-99

TN | 95

Classic ENDEAVORS

349 Southshore Drive
Greenback, TN 37742-2301

Phone (423)856-8100
Fax (423)856-8001
Hours: M-F 11:00 - 5:00 EST

Services: Buy/Sell/Trade! No listing/membership fee. Layaways available. Accepts Visa and MasterCard - no extra fee. Quoted price includes commission - no surprises! 72 hour guarantee. Overseas shipping.

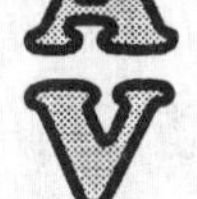

Lines: Harbour Lights, Kinkade (canvas only), Forma Vitrum, Walt Disney Classics Collection, 1990's Disneyana convention memorabilia.

Noteworthy: Established in 1993, **CLASSIC ENDEAVORS, INC.** is owned and operated by Dee Brandt. Ms. Brandt, is also free-lance writer and has had articles published in national collectibles magazines. She recently worked as a consultant on the second Greenbook Guide to the WDCC, which was published in 1996. Associate Member of NALED. Member of CIB's "Panel of Experts".

TX | 96

AMANDA'S FINE GIFTS

265 Central Park Mall
San Antonio, TX 78216-5506

Phone: (800) 441-4458
(210) 525-0412
Hours: Mon-Sat: 10-9, Sun: 12-6

Services: 10-month layaway. Consignments. Buy outright when needed. Redemption Center for Lladró, Disney, Swarovski, Armani, M.I. Hummel and Lalique Collectors Club. Appraisal service for insurance purposes.

Secondary: Lladró, Swarovski, M.I. Hummel, Ron Lee, Armani, Chilmark, Bossons, Disney.

Noteworthy: Barry Harris developed a deep appreciation for Lladró artwork, which eventually led to the purchase of Amanda's Fine Gifts in 1983. Realizing the great potential for offering Lladró artwork and information to collectors, Barry and his staff have become known as experts in the field. The largest Lladró dealer in the southwest, Amanda's has welcomed Lladró family members to the store for artist appearances. Other guests have included Don Polland, Ron Lee, Michael Boyett, M.I. Hummel representatives and Armani artists.

Directory to Secondary Market Dealers

TX | **97**

ANTIQUE HAVEN

Route 1, Box 60
Stanton, TX 79782

Phone: **(800) 299-3480 (915) 458-3480**
Fax: **(915) 458-3622**
Hours: **Mon-Sat: 9-5**

Services: Ten-month layaway. Ship freight free in U.S. Major credit cards accepted. Buy outright. Consignment. Quarterly newsletter.

Secondary: All God's Children, Miss Martha's Collection, Endearing Memories, Tom Clark Gnomes, Lee Sievers, Tim Wolfe, Cat's Meow, Daddy's Long Legs, Cherished Teddies, Fenton, Disney Classics, Lowell Davis, Maud Humphrey, Legends, Williraye, Pipka. No Beanie Babies.

Noteworthy: Antique Haven has been in existence for 29 years and is second generation owned by Vanita and Jerry Waid. The store is located 12 miles east of Midland, TX and 5 miles west of Stanton on N. Access Road off Interstate Hwy 20, mile marker 151. The Waids carry European and American antiques, glassware, candles, and many gift items and accessories in addition to specializing in the secondary market and collectibles. Antique Haven is also a Redemption Center for many collectible lines.

TX | **98**

Collectible Treasures

6850 Oakwood Trace Ct. • Houston, TX 77040 • (713) 937-0222

Specializing in the secondary market for collectibles

Primary lines carried are:

TY Beanie Babies • Boyds Bears
Cherished Teddies • Hallmark Ornaments
Harbour Lights • Harmony Kingdom
Tom Clark Gnomes

We accept personal checks, money orders, VISA and MasterCard.
Also carry listings for Department 56 and Radko Ornaments.
Will handle consignments.

Visit our web site at WWW.collectibletreasures.com
or e-mail dickens@onramp.net

VA | **99**

114 Clark Avenue, Elkton, VA 22827

Phone: **(540) 298-9234**
Hours: **Mail order: 10am-10pm (EST)**
(work from home-please keep trying)

Services: Secondary Market Dealer. Can help you fill in missing series/family ornaments, etc. Accepts Visa and MasterCard. Worldwide shipping. Buy outright when needed. Refer and sell to other dealers. Call for details.

Secondary: Hallmark Ornaments, Kiddie Car Classics, Cherished Teddies and some Barbie dolls.

Noteworthy: Memories In Motion was started by Bobbie Ann Horne in 1990 from her home in the beautiful Shenandoah Valley of Virginia. This mail order business now has clientele around the world. Bobbie Ann is a charter member of the Hallmark Ornament Collector's Club, serves as a consultant to Hallmark Stores, and donates large quantities of ornaments to local charities. She is easy to talk with and specializes in pleasing clients. Her business is a Chamber of Commerce member.

WA | **100**

23730 Bothell-Everett Hwy. Suite D
Bothell, WA 98021

Phone: **(425) 486-8199**
Fax: **(425) 486-3881**
Hours: **Mon-Sat: 10-6, Sun: 11-5**

Services: Buy/Sell/Trade. All credit cards accepted. 90-day financing and layaway. UPS shipping.

Secondary: Artworks from Thomas Kinkade, Randy Van Beek, Mary Baxter St. Clair and Stephen Shortridge. Also Coynes - David Frykman & Williraye, Prizm - Pipka Santas, Bear & Me, Nicholas Moss Pottery, Shenandoah - Keepers.

Noteworthy: Heather House was established in 1986 by Jodie Paine and her mother, Janice Atkins, and became a Thomas Kinkade dealer in 1990. Jodie keeps current on the Kinkade secondary market and is a CIB panel member.

Directory to Secondary Market Dealers

WA 101

NATALIA'S COLLECTIBLES

19949-130th NE
Woodinville, WA 98072

Phone: (425) 481-4575
Fax: (425) 487-1237
Hours: Tues-Sat: 10-6

Services: Consignments and buy outright.

Secondary: Ashton-Drake dolls, Georgetown dolls, Marie Osmond dolls, Annette Funicello bears, Ty Beanies and animals, Thomas Kinkade, Bradford, Hamilton, Reco, Royal Copenhagen, Bing & Grondahl, Winston Roland, and other limited edition plates.

Noteworthy: Natalia's Collectibles was established as a small store in a quiet garden-type surrounding in 1982. Originally dealing only in limited edition plates on the primary market, the firm soon established themselves in the secondary market for plates. Likewise, as dolls and figurines were added to the store, they assisted their clients with a secondary market outlet. As a Bradford Exchange and NALED member, Natalia's Collectibles is dedicated to friendly expert service in both the primary and secondary markets.

CIB SECONDARY MARKET SPECIALIST 1998-99

WI 102

ANDY'S VILLAGE TREES

3045 Bollenbeck St.
Cross Plains, WI 53528
(Associate Member NCC)

Phone: (608) 798-2389
E-mail: andy@andys-villagetrees.com
Website: http://www.andys-villagetrees.com

Services: Buy/Sell/Locator Service. Layaway, UPS shipping. Checks, MasterCard, Visa accepted.

Secondary: Creepy Hollow, Cannon Valley, Cottontail Lane and Department 56, including all villages, accessories and Snowbabies.

Noteworthy: Andy's Village Trees is your largest source for Creepy Hollow, Cannon Valley and Cottontail Lane. They are an authorized dealer for Lang & Wise, United Design, Ganz, Friends of a Feather, Amigos del Sol, Melly & Friends. They also carry a full line of miniature houses, amusement parks, trees and accessories for your lighted houses, farms, Halloween, Thanksgiving, Christmas, Easter and Spring/Summer displays. A 32-page catalog and colored brochures are available for $4.00.
(Associate Member of NCC)

WI 103

Hum-Haus

3555 South 27th Street, Milwaukee, WI 53221

Phone: (414) 645-HUML (4865)
Fax: (414) 645-8994
Hours: Mon-Fri: 5:30-8, Sat & Sun: 10-5

Services: Consignments. Buy outright. Layaway and shipping available.

Secondary: Exclusively M.I. Hummel figurines, plates, bells and all Hummel accessories such as calendars, books, ornaments, etc.

Noteworthy: The Hum-Haus opened June 1, 1993, as a retail store. The owners began collecting Hummels as a hobby, with one of the owners interested in Hummels since 1955. Over the years, the collection grew and grew, and as older pieces replaced newer pieces, more and more duplicate Hummels became available for sale. Collectors purchasing Hummels began asking why the owners did not have a store, and so Hum-Haus was formed. Due to a long love of M.I. Hummel collectibles, the owners hope to make the store a one-stop shopping establishment for collectors. Hum-Haus offers "full service" to collectors, locating older Hummels as well as retired or limited edition pieces, special orders, consignments and appraisals. Hum-Haus is an authorized dealer and Redemption Center for M.I. Hummel.

CIB SECONDARY MARKET SPECIALIST 1998-99

WI 104

RED CROSS GIFTS

122 Walnut Street, Spooner, WI 54801

Phone: (800) 344-9958 (715) 635-6154
Fax: (715) 635-6178
Hours: Mon-Sat: 9-5

Services: Locator service for plates, figurines, dolls, bells, and ornaments. No consignments. Layaway and major credit cards accepted.

Secondary: Department 56, Precious Moments, Cherished Teddies, Armani, Lladró, Harbour Lights, Emmett Kelly, Forma Vitrum, Seraphim Classics, Dreamsicles, Mickey & Co., Maud Humphrey, Mark Klaus, Fontanini, DeGrazia, Lucy & Me, Kitty Cucumber, Krystonia, Pocket Dragons, Enchantica. Plates: Bradford, Hamilton, Reco, Royal Copenhagen, Bing & Grondahl. Dolls: Ashton-Drake, Hamilton, Gorham, Victoria Ashlea.

Noteworthy: Over 80 years strong and in its fourth generation, Red Cross Gifts has plenty of experience to offer their collectors. The friendly and helpful staff will assist collectors in finding just what they need. They service over 70 major collectible lines with 1,700 collector plates on display. Also a Redemption Center for most collectible lines.

CIB SECONDARY MARKET SPECIALIST 1998-99

EDITORIAL INDEX